New

AMERICAN NATIONAL BIOGRAPHY

AMERICAN
NATIONAL BIOGRAPHY

Published under the auspices of the
AMERICAN COUNCIL OF LEARNED SOCIETIES

General Editors

John A. Garraty

Mark C. Carnes

VOLUME 10

OXFORD UNIVERSITY PRESS

New York   1999   Oxford

OXFORD UNIVERSITY PRESS

Oxford   New York
Athens   Auckland   Bangkok   Bogotá
Buenos Aires   Calcutta   Cape Town   Chennai
Dar es Salaam   Delhi   Florence   Hong Kong   Istanbul
Karachi   Kuala Lumpur   Madrid   Melbourne   Mexico City
Mumbai   Nairobi   Paris   São Paulo   Singapore
Taipei   Tokyo   Toronto   Warsaw
and associated companies in
Berlin   Ibadan

Published by Oxford University Press, Inc.,
198 Madison Avenue, New York, New York 10016
http://www.oup-usa.org

Oxford is a registered trademark of Oxford University Press

Funding for this publication was provided in part by
the Andrew W. Mellon Foundation, the Rockefeller Foundation,
and the National Endowment for the Humanities,
a federal agency.

Library of Congress Cataloging-in-Publication Data

American national biography / general editors, John A. Garraty, Mark C. Carnes
        p.   cm.
"Published under the auspices of the American Council of Learned Societies."
Includes bibliographical references and index.
1. United States—Biography—Dictionaries.   I. Garraty, John Arthur,
   1920–   .   II. Carnes, Mark C. (Mark Christopher), 1950–   .
   III. American Council of Learned Societies.
   CT213.A68   1998   98-20826   920.073—dc21   CIP
           ISBN 0-19-520635-5 (set)
           ISBN 0-19-512789-7 (vol. 10)

Printing (last digit): 9 8 7 6 5 4 3 2 1

Printed in the United States of America
on acid-free paper

H

— CONTINUED —

HANDERSON, Henry Ebenezer (21 Mar. 1837–23 Apr. 1918), physician and medical historian, was born near Gates Mills, Ohio, the son of Thomas Handerson and Catherine Potts, farmers. In 1839, after his father's accidental death, Henry was adopted by his uncle, Lewis Handerson, a respected pharmacist in nearby Cleveland, and his wife, Prudence Punderson. Her brother, the Reverend Ephraim Punderson, was an Episcopal missionary who frequently visited them and greatly influenced the young frail boy. In 1852 the family moved to Beersheba Springs, Tennessee, and two years later, with health improved, Handerson entered Hobart College (Episcopal) in Geneva, New York, graduating in 1858 with an A.B. in the classics. The following year he was a private tutor on a cotton plantation near Alexandria, Louisiana, and then began to study medicine in the Medical Department of the University of Louisiana (now Tulane) in New Orleans.

When the Civil War erupted, Handerson joined the Confederate army and fought in the Army of Northern Virginia until his capture in the Battle of the Wilderness in May 1864. During his year in prison at Fort Delaware and elsewhere, he organized classes among the prisoners to read Latin and Greek texts, obtaining the books with the help of his adoptive parents, who had returned to Cleveland from Tennessee during the war.

After the war, with many of his southern friends gone and Louisiana in shambles, Handerson abandoned his original idea to return to medical school there and went to New York to attend Columbia's College of Physicians and Surgeons, from which he received the M.D. in 1867 (he had also earned an M.A. from Hobart in 1866). After practicing successfully in New York City for fourteen years and serving from 1869 to 1872 as assistant surgeon of the Hospital for the Ruptured and Crippled, he experienced disaster in 1881 when his wife, Juliet Alice Root, whom he had married in 1872, died giving birth to their fourth child, and a year later his three older children all died from diphtheria. In 1885 he returned to Cleveland with his baby daughter.

While living in New York, Handerson had become interested in medical history (his commencement oration at Hobart College had been on "The Historian"). In February 1878 he read a paper on "The School of Salernum: An Historical Sketch of Mediaeval Medicine" to the Medical Society of the County of New York, which he published in 1883 as a sixty-page pamphlet. Based on detailed research and sound classical scholarship on the famous Italian medical school that flourished in the eleventh and twelfth centuries, the publication was highly praised by medical historians and established Handerson's reputation as a leading scholar in the field.

Handerson's major work was his translation of Johann Hermann Baas, *Grundriss der Geschichte der Medicin und des heilenden Standes*, which had been published in Stuttgart in 1876 and was regarded as the leading medico-historical textbook of the time. Motivated by an enthusiastic review of Baas's book in the *Virginia Medical Monthly*, which also suggested that it should be translated into English, Handerson corresponded with Baas, who sent him revisions and new material to which Handerson added extensive sections relating to British and American medicine that were not in the original work. The translation was published in New York in 1889 (reprinted in 1910) under the title *Outlines of the History of Medicine and the Medical Profession*, with Baas as author and translated, revised, and enlarged by Handerson. The copyright was in Handerson's name. Until the publication of Fielding H. Garrison's *Introduction to the History of Medicine* in 1913, the Baas-Handerson collaboration was the major source of medical history in English.

In Cleveland Handerson did not reestablish a medical practice, although he treated a few old friends in his home. A devout Episcopalian, he soon served many offices in Grace Episcopal Church, and in 1898 he wrote a history of the parish. Long interested in public health, be became professor of hygiene and sanitary science in the Medical Department of the University of Wooster (then in Cleveland) from 1894 to 1896 and from 1896 to 1907 in its successor institution, the Cleveland College of Physicians and Surgeons (the Medical Department of Ohio Wesleyan University that eventually merged with the Medical Department of Western Reserve University). He also gave lectures on medical history. He married Clara Corlett of Cleveland in 1888; they had two sons.

Handerson became involved with the Cuyahoga County Medical Society, of which he was president from 1895 to 1896, and in 1902 he was one of the founders of the Cleveland Academy of Medicine. Becoming interested in local medical history, he became aware of the need for a local medical library, since none existed in Cleveland at that time. When the Cleveland Medical Library Association was founded in 1894, Handerson was one of its creators and its president from 1896 to 1902. He immediately began to donate portions of his own substantial medical book collection. When the Allen Medical Library building was erected in 1926, eight years after Handerson's death, the heart of the building, the Henry E. Handerson Book Stacks, was named in his honor.

It is due to Handerson that much of Cleveland's early medical history has been recorded. Laboriously sifting through local society records and newspapers, Handerson published a series of articles on "Medical Cleveland in the Nineteenth Century" in the *Cleveland Medical Journal* in 1909 and a chapter on "Medical Cleveland" in Samuel P. Orth's *History of Cleveland* (1910). He also wrote twenty-seven biographical sketches for Howard A. Kelly's *Cyclopedia of American Medical Biography* (1912), which included the major physicians of the Cleveland area. Handerson's other medical writings dealt with Cleveland diseases, sanitation, and vital statistics.

Handerson's final major work was a detailed analysis of the *Compendium Medicinae* by Gilbertus Anglicus, a medieval English physician. Blinded by glaucoma in 1916, Handerson was unable to complete the proofreading before his death in Cleveland. The study was published posthumously as a 77-page monograph by the Cleveland Medical Library Association. Handerson, the cultured mentor and scholar, is remembered in Cleveland through the Handerson Medical History Society. A quiet, reclusive, and deeply religious man, he had never sought recognition in his lifetime but simply enjoyed being a scholar.

• The Allen Memorial Medical Library in Cleveland is the principal repository of Handerson biographical material and manuscripts, including lecture notes, and an oration handpenned in Greek on "The Death of Socrates." The chief source of information is his autobiography and memoirs of his experiences during the Civil War, which he wrote for his family in the 1890s. This was published with the title *Yankee in Gray, the Civil War Memoirs of Henry E. Handerson with a Selection of His Wartime Letters*, with a biographical introduction by Clyde Lottridge Cummer (1962). A biographical sketch by Samuel W. Kelley was included in the posthumous publication of Handerson's *Gilbertus Anglicus, Medicine of the Thirteenth Century* (1918). Letters to Handerson from German medical historians are reproduced in Genevieve Miller, "Henry E. Handerson's German Correspondents, Letters of Baas, Sudhoff, Oefele," *Medizinhistorisches Journal* 6 (1971): 45–52.

GENEVIEVE MILLER

HANDSOME LAKE (1735?–10 Aug. 1815), Seneca prophet, was born probably in what is now western New York State. He was the half-brother of Cornplanter and the nephew of Guyasuta. Although he served as a warrior against the Cherokees in the 1760s and aided the British during the Revolution, he does not seem to have particularly distinguished himself. Apparently during the 1790s he received the title Handsome Lake (Ganeodiyo, the name traditionally borne by one of the sachems chosen to represent the Seneca at the national Iroquois council), and in that capacity he signed the treaty of Big Tree (1797), by which the Iroquois of New York were left with eleven reservations. The name used by Handsome Lake before acquiring his title is not known. In 1799 he was living an intemperate life in Cornplanter's town on the Allegheny River in one of the Iroquois reservations.

Handsome Lake's reforms were rooted in the wretched conditions of the Iroquois communities.

Their populations had been reduced by war and disease, and their economies were faltering. As white settlement around the reservations grew, the hunting declined and the Indians became overdependent on the horticulture performed by the women and on inadequate treaty annuities. Morale was also low. The retreat of the hunting and warrior life, and with it traditional paths by which many men achieved fulfillment or prestige, created indolence and alienation. Alcoholism, violence, depression, and accusations of witchcraft were common problems.

These difficulties provoked several somewhat contradictory responses. From 1798 Quakers were at work in Cornplanter's town, not so much to proselytize as to develop the Indian economy, to intensify agriculture, and to teach stock raising, spinning, weaving, and the fencing of land. They also attacked social problems such as drunkenness. But while this program, involving the reformation of the local economy, was under way, a simultaneous nativist movement began. A Mohawk claimed that the Creator (Tarachiawagon) was displeased with the Iroquois for neglecting such ceremonies as the worship dance. This prophet was mainly influential among the Oneidas of New York and the Canadian Iroquois, but in February 1799 a Seneca in Cornplanter's town declared that he had visited hell and witnessed the torments of drunkards and other sinners. Thus, native prophets ascribed the misfortunes of the Iroquois to the anger of the Creator at the decline of traditional observances and the assimilation of undesirable white influences. Handsome Lake distilled both the Quaker and the nativist impulses for his own reforms.

Between June 1799 and February 1800 Handsome Lake experienced three visions, recorded in the contemporary Quaker diaries. According to Henry Simmons, on 15 June, Cornplanter was told that his brother was dying and found him "laying breathless for the space of half an hour, but in about two hours after he came to himself again," and related that angels had visited and instructed him. The following August the prophet "fainted or fell into a trance in which posture he remained 7 hours; his legs and arms were cold; his body warm but breathless." When he recovered, Handsome Lake claimed to have visited heaven, and after a third vision he reported a further visit of the angels. From these incidents Handsome Lake professed himself the medium of the Creator and the bringer of the Gaiwiio or Good Word.

The message was apocalyptic, declaring that unless the Indians reformed, they would suffer sickness, drought, and flood, while the sinful would be excluded from heaven. The proscribed sins were largely those already condemned by nativist preachers and the Quakers—drunkenness; the practice of witchcraft, which the Indians blamed for disease and strife; violence; the neglect of old ceremonies; and even the riotous "frolics and dancing" condemned by the Quakers. Subsequently Handsome Lake broadened his message to sanction the economic development promoted by the Quakers, but he insisted that farming should be for subsistence and that surpluses be made available to the native community rather than for commercial sale.

Not unnaturally, the Quakers and President Thomas Jefferson, whom Handsome Lake, as a member of an Iroquois land and agriculture delegation, visited in 1802, endorsed Handsome Lake's campaign, which was neither anti-American nor excessively nativist. Yet the Seneca's was not a servile doctrine. Handsome Lake recognized the need to raise the material standards of the Iroquois and to adjust to the existence of a dominant white society, and he backed economic development and peace with the United States. But he offered the Indians a religion distinct from Christianity, one that preserved native ritual and the aboriginal emphasis upon community life. Such Christian influences as it embraced were integrated into traditional Indian beliefs. For example, the notion of God and the Devil directing the forces of good and evil and competing for souls was blended into the Iroquois creation story of the good and bad twins. Handsome Lake also opposed the further sale of land to the United States. His religion facilitated Iroquois adjustment to reservation life but protected their culture and identity. It was partly for this reason that Handsome Lake's religion, while more localized than that of his contemporary, Tenskwatawa, the Shawnee prophet, enjoyed greater longevity. Handsome Lake's preaching was compatible with living alongside the European-American farming frontier; Tenskwatawa's, espousing a return to more traditional Indian ways of life, was rooted in an ultimately disappearing Indian world.

Handsome Lake's influence was strongest among the Senecas, Onondagas, and Oneidas of New York, although it spread to the Wyandots and Iroquois of the Sandusky in Ohio, whom he visited in 1806. By then Handsome Lake, the Quakers, and others had done much to reduce Iroquois drunkenness and spur economic development. Some Iroquois men were beginning to reappraise their traditional contempt for husbandry. In 1801 the prophet was briefly elevated to the unprecedented position of premier sachem of the New York Iroquois. However, he abused his power with overzealous accusations of witchcraft, and consequent executions threatened to create blood-feud conflicts. In 1801 the Senecas and Delawares of Cattaraugus were brought to the brink of hostilities on account of Handsome Lake's activities, and he divided the Senecas, denouncing his political enemy, Red Jacket, for witchcraft. After the execution of a woman in 1809, Cornplanter admitted, "I hope we shall be careful in future how we take the lives of any for witchcraft, without being sure that they were guilty." In 1803 Handsome Lake's relations with his brother had so deteriorated that the prophet had left Cornplanter's town and established a new settlement at nearby Cold Spring.

Handsome Lake died on a visit to Onondaga, but his teaching survived, reworked and codified by individual preachers, and remains a significant force in Iroquois life, offering a distinctly Indian alternative to Christianity.

• The primary sources for Handsome Lake's initial visions are printed in A. F. C. Wallace, ed., "Halliday Jackson's Journal to the Seneca Indians, 1798–1800," *Pennsylvania History* 19 (1952): 117–47, 325–49. There are interesting differences between the prophet's message as reported in the contemporary materials and the versions reworked and written after 1840. Chief among these last are the reminiscences of Blacksnake in Thomas S. Abler, ed., *Chainbreaker: The Revolutionary War Memoirs of Governor Blacksnake* (1989), and Arthur C. Parker, ed., *The Code of Handsome Lake* (1913). A. F. C. Wallace, *The Death and Rebirth of the Seneca* (1970), is the standard secondary work, but Merle H. Deardorff, "The Religion of Handsome Lake: Its Origin and Development," in *Symposium on Local Diversity in Iroquois Culture*, ed. William N. Fenton (1951), and Elisabeth Tooker, "On the Development of the Handsome Lake Religion," *Proceedings of the American Philosophical Society* 133 (1989): 35–50, are worth consulting. Attempts to fit Handsome Lake in the contemporary Indian and non-Indian revivalism are made by A. F. C. Wallace, "Handsome Lake and the Great Revival in the West," *American Quarterly* 4 (1952): 149–65, and Gregory E. Dowd, *A Spirited Resistance* (1992).

JOHN SUGDEN

HANDY, Alexander Hamilton (25 Dec. 1809–12 Sept. 1883), jurist, was born in Somerset County, Maryland, the son of George Handy and Betsy Wilson. His father was a prominent figure on Maryland's Eastern Shore and an officer in the revolutionary army. Alexander entered Washington Academy when he was only thirteen; he studied there for six years and at the age of nineteen became the deputy clerk of the court of Somerset County. His older brother George was the county clerk. He studied the law in his free time, and by 1834 he was ready to enter the bar of Maryland. The year after his bar admission he married Susan Wilson Stuart. In 1836 the couple moved to Mississippi, where he was admitted to practice before the state's high court of errors and appeals in January 1837.

Handy settled in Canton, Mississippi, and developed a successful private legal practice from 1837 to 1853, when he was elected to a seat on the high court of errors and appeals. He was elected over William Yerger, a Whig, who had made himself unpopular with his opinion in *Mississippi v. Johnson* where he had held that the bonds of the Union Bank, in which the state held a substantial interest, were a valid obligation of the state even though the bank had collapsed. Handy took his seat and held it until he resigned in October 1867 in protest over the subordination of the court to occupying federal military forces. Handy then served as associate judge until he was elected chief justice in 1864. He ran successfully for the seat in 1865 (although he was soundly beaten in some former Whig strongholds).

Handy was a Democrat throughout his life and a strong supporter of state sovereignty and the right of secession. Aside from his resignation from the court during Reconstruction, Handy's most significant political role came during the secession crisis. As one of the most prominent secessionists in the state, he was named commissioner to the state in which he was born to whip up support for secession. Despite his efforts,

Maryland's governor declined to call the legislature into session to consider cooperation with the seceding southern states. Rebuffed by the governor, Handy turned to the people of Maryland to urge their support for withdrawal from the Union. Having failed, he returned to Mississippi and the court on which he served throughout the war. Nonetheless, he was not finished with the notion of secession. Like fellow Mississippian Jefferson Davis, Handy was enamored of the theory and wrote a pamphlet on the subject in 1862 titled *Secession Considered as a Right in the States Composing the Late American Union of States, and as to the Grounds of Justification of the Southern States in Exercising the Right.*

Although Handy was deeply committed to state sovereignty, he proved to be a Confederate nationalist during the war. This was evident in a decision he wrote in *Simmons v. Miller* in late 1864. The case involved a claim by Simmons that he was wrongfully arrested by a Confederate enrolling officer; he held that even though he was otherwise subject to Confederate conscription, he was exempt because he was already in state military service. Other Confederate state judiciaries sometimes obstructed the efforts of the central government to wage war, but not the Mississippi court. Handy ruled that the war power in the Confederate congress was "for the most part exclusive . . . the ability to command the entire military force of the country" was "absolutely essential to the Government, in time of actual national war."

Handy's devotion to state sovereignty had earlier been tempered by his devotion to slavery. "The fundamental and controlling idea upon which property in slaves rests is," he wrote in a dissent in *Mitchell v. Wells* (1859), "the right of absolute disposition; and this is paramount to any question as to how, or in whose behalf, the right shall be exercised." He granted that the positive law of the state could regulate the right to dispose of slaves, and that it had in Mississippi. Slaves could not be freed in the state—but that is as far as it went. The majority held that the state could prohibit the emancipation of slaves by Mississippi owners outside the state as well as within. Handy would not cut that deeply into the master's property rights.

By 1865, of course, Handy's world, built on slavery and state sovereignty, was in ruins. What he saw was a "state of lawlessness," as he wrote in *Scott v. Billgerry* (1866), not only among the people of Mississippi, but "in the course pursued by the military officers in their mode of administering law and acting on the civil rights of the people." But those civil rights did not extend to the freedmen, in Handy's view. At the end of 1866, in a case involving James Lewis, a freedman who was hired out to a white under the Black Code of Mississippi, Handy ruled that the federal Civil Rights Act of 1866 was unconstitutional. A year later he resigned from the court, never to return.

Handy also left the state, but he returned to Mississippi in the fall of 1871 and resumed private practice in Canton until his death there. From 1867 to 1871, how-ever, he lived in Baltimore, and in 1870–1871 he taught law at the University of Maryland Law School. He declined offers to teach at the University of Mississippi Law School when he returned to the state as well as an offer to go back on the high court. Instead, he was content to enter a general legal practice and was as successful as he had been before he first went on the court two decades earlier. Handy died at a time when he was still an influential member of the state bar.

• No collection of Handy papers exists. A useful brief sketch is in Dunbar Rowland, *Courts, Judges and Lawyers of Mississippi, 1798–1935* (1935), and scattered references to Handy's work are in Meredith Lang, *Defender of the Faith: The High Court of Mississippi 1817–1875* (1977); William C. Harris, *Presidential Reconstruction in Mississippi* (1967); and Charles Fairman, *Reconstruction and Reunion 1864–1888: Part One* (1977). There is no substitute, however, for reading vols. 26 through 41 of the *Mississippi Reports* to understand the thinking of Alexander H. Handy.

THOMAS D. MORRIS

HANDY, W. C. (16 Nov. 1873–28 Mar. 1958), blues musician and composer, was born William Christopher Handy in Florence, Alabama, the son of Charles Bernard Handy, a minister, and Elizabeth Brewer. Handy was raised in an intellectual, middle-class atmosphere, as befitted a minister's son. He studied music in public school, then attended the all-black Teachers' Agricultural and Mechanical College in Huntsville. After graduation he worked as a teacher and, briefly, in an iron mill. A love of the cornet led to semiprofessional work as a musician, and by the early 1890s he was performing with a traveling minstrel troupe known as Mahara's Minstrels; by mid-decade, he was promoted to bandleader of the group. Handy married Elizabeth Virginia Price in 1898. They had five children.

It was on one of the group's tours, according to Handy, in the backwater Mississippi town of Clarksdale, that he first heard a traditional blues musician. His own training was limited to the light classics, marches, and early ragtime music of the day, but something about this performance, by guitarist Charley Patton, intrigued him. After a brief retirement from touring in 1900–1902 to return to teaching at his alma mater, he formed his first of many bands and went on the road once more. A second incident during an early band tour cemented Handy's interest in blues-based music. In 1905, while playing at a local club, the Handy band was asked if they would be willing to take a break to allow a local string band to perform. This ragged group's attempts at music making amused the more professional musicians in Handy's band until they saw the stage flooded with change thrown spontaneously by audience members and realized that the amateurs would take home more money that night than they would. Handy began collecting folk blues and writing his own orchestrations of them.

By 1905 Handy had settled in Memphis, Tennessee. He was asked in 1907 by mayoral candidate E. H. "Boss" Crump to write a campaign song to mobilize the black electorate. The song, "Mr. Crump," became a local hit and was published five years later under a new name, "The Memphis Blues." It was followed two years later by his biggest hit, "The St. Louis Blues." Both songs were actually ragtime-influenced vocal numbers with a number of sections and related to the traditional folk blues only in their use of "blue" notes (flatted thirds and sevenths) and the themes of their lyrics. Many of his verses were borrowed directly from the traditional "floating" verses long associated with folk blues, such as the opening words of "St. Louis Blues": "I hate to see that evening sun go down." In the mid-1920s early jazz vocalist Bessie Smith recorded "St. Louis Blues," making it a national hit.

In 1917 Handy moved to New York, where he formed a new band, his own music-publishing operation, and a short-lived record label. He was an important popularizer of traditional blues songs, publishing the influential *Blues: An Anthology* in 1926 (which was reprinted and revised in 1949 and again after Handy's death in 1972) and *Collection of Negro Spirituals* in 1939. Besides his work promoting the blues, he also was a champion of "Negro" composers and musicians, writing several books arguing that their musical skills equaled that of their white counterparts. In 1941 he published his autobiography, *Father of the Blues*, a not altogether reliable story of his early years as a musician.

By the late 1940s Handy's eyesight and health were failing. In the 1950s he made one recording performing his blues songs, showing himself to be a rather limited vocalist by this time of his life, and one narrative recording with his daughter performing his songs. His first wife had died in 1937; he was married again in 1954, to Irma Louise Logan. He died in New York City. His autobiography was reissued after his death. In 1979 the W. C. Handy Blues Awards were established, to recognize excellence in blues recordings.

Handy may not have "fathered" the blues, as he claimed, nor did he write true "blues" songs of the type that were performed by country blues musicians. But he did write one of the most popular songs of the twentieth century, which introduced blues tonalities and themes to popular music. His influence on stage music and jazz was profound; "St. Louis Blues" remains one of the most frequently recorded of all jazz pieces.

• Handy composed more than 150 blues, pop songs, stage songs, and spirituals. His books not mentioned above include *Negro Authors and Composers of the United States* (1935) and *Unsung Americans Sung* (1944). Eileen Southern covers Handy's life in *The Music of Black Americans: A History* (1971; repr., 1983), as does James Dickerson in *Goin' Back to Memphis: A Century of Blues, Rock 'n' Roll, and Glorious Soul* (1996). Two articles by A. Morrison appeared in *Ebony* magazine, "W. C. Handy: Broadway's Grand Old Man of Music," 9, no. 11 (1953), and "Evening Sun Goes Down," 13, no. 6 (1958).

RICHARD CARLIN

HANEY, Carol (24 Dec. 1924–10 May 1964), dancer, actress, and choreographer, was born in New Bedford, Massachusetts, the daughter of Norman Vincent Haney, a bank teller, and Ellen Christensen. She began studying dance as a child and, at the age of fifteen, started teaching dance in her own studio in New Bedford. In 1943 Haney moved to California, where she studied with Ernest Belcher and Eduardo Cansino while dancing in nightclubs and film musicals. She also studied with dancer-choreographer Jack Cole and became his dance partner and assistant around 1944. She performed with Cole's company in clubs and films and was a member of his permanent troupe of dancers at Columbia Pictures. Haney also served as assistant to director-choreographer Gene Kelly at MGM on the films *An American in Paris* (1951), *Singin' in the Rain* (1952), *Brigadoon* (1954), and *Invitation to the Dance* (1956).

In 1953 Haney danced a duet with dancer-choreographer Bob Fosse in the film *Kiss Me, Kate*. Fosse's successful choreography for this duet led to an invitation to choreograph his first Broadway musical, *The Pajama Game* (1954), in which he asked Haney to perform. Originally cast in a dancing role with only one speaking line, Haney so impressed director George Abbott with her comic ability that her part was expanded into a featured acting role. Haney won a Tony Award and two Donaldson Awards, and her performance made her an overnight sensation, described by critics as "a comic dancer of extraordinary versatility" (Brooks Atkinson, *New York Times*, 14 May 1954), "an animated cartoon [who] looks like a bowlegged gosling" (Walter Kerr, *New York Herald Tribune*, 14 May 1954), and "a tall but awkward Audrey Hepburn [with] a froggy voice, slanty eyes and an impish grin" (John A. Chapman, *New York Daily News*, 14 May 1954).

Following her Broadway success Haney was invited to appear on numerous television shows, including "Pantomime Quiz," the "Ed Sullivan Show," Edward R. Murrow's "Person to Person," the "Bob Hope Show," and the "Perry Como Show." She made guest appearances in nightclubs and performed in *The Ziegfeld Follies*, a 1956 revue that closed during out-of-town tryout performances. Haney re-created her stage role for the film version of *The Pajama Game* in 1957 and debuted as a dramatic actress in the 1959 Broadway play *A Loss of Roses*.

Haney choreographed the Broadway musicals *Flower Drum Song* (1958), *Bravo, Giovanni* (1962), *She Loves Me* (1963; London production, 1964), and *Funny Girl* (1964). She created dances for tryout performances of the 1963 Broadway musical *Jennie* but chose not to share billing with cochoreographer Matt Mattox. Haney also choreographed musicals for regional theatres and directed industrial productions (promotional musicals used as entertainment at conventions) for General Motors. She created the dances for most of the television shows in which she appeared and choreographed such specials as the *Bell Telephone Hour* (1962) and *The Broadway of Lerner and Loewe* (1962).

Haney married singer Eugene Dorian Johnston in 1945; they had no children and were divorced in 1953. In 1955 she married actor-director Larry Blyden; they had two children. Their marriage ended in divorce in 1962.

As a performer, Haney played a key role in the development of the movement styles of two of America's leading jazz dance choreographers. She was an exemplar of the Jack Cole technique, a jazz style that merged modern dance with Indian and Latin-American influences. She served as the model on whom he created much of his choreography. Haney performed a similar role in the early development of Fosse's jazz dance style. Critics have pinpointed his duet with Haney in *Kiss Me, Kate* as the first manifestation of the Fosse style and have identified the "Steam Heat" trio led by Haney in *The Pajama Game* as the first complete dance displaying Fosse's unique choreography. Dancer-actress Gwen Verdon observed that Haney possessed the unusual ability to perform any dance step she was shown: "she could look at absolutely anything and do it, she was a natural mover who, even if she had never had a lesson in her life, would still have been an extraordinary dancer" (telephone interview, 29 Dec. 1993).

As choreographic assistant to Gene Kelly, Haney contributed to the making of some of Hollywood's most important musicals. Kelly used her as a model when creating his choreography, and she then taught and coached the performers and assisted Kelly on technical and musical aspects of the dances. In addition, Haney helped to make it possible for Kelly to both choreograph and appear in his films; while Kelly danced Haney was often behind the camera, guiding him or serving as his critical "eyes." Kelly called her "invaluable."

As a choreographer, Haney contributed to the continuing development of American musical theater dance by creating dances that integrated and enhanced the dramatic fabric of the shows on which she worked, a style of choreography first introduced in the 1940s and 1950s. She received Tony Award nominations for her choreography for *Flower Drum Song, Bravo, Giovanni,* and *Funny Girl.* Haney's choreographic style developed out of her spontaneous improvisations to jazz music and is exemplified by "Satin Doll," a fluid jazz dance she created for a television appearance. The choreography is marked by contrasts: weighted lunges and walks are combined with upreaching arms or light flicks of the fingers and wrists; the fluid movements of the spine and sensual circles of the head and shoulders are punctuated with strong, accented jazz kicks or jumps; the dancer's body is shown to be strong, yet supple, and moves with a "cool" ease.

Haney suffered from diabetes and was inclined to work herself to the point of exhaustion. She sustained several injuries during her career, one of which figures prominently in a well-known show business story. Having hurt her ankle, Haney was unable to perform in *The Pajama Game* the night that Hollywood producer Hal B. Wallis came to see her. Instead, the part was performed by understudy Shirley MacLaine, to whom Wallis offered a movie contract that began her rise to stardom.

Haney died of bronchial pneumonia in New York City at age thirty-nine. Haney is remembered by colleagues for her divine sense of humor, her wit, and her imagination. Broadway director-producer Hal Prince explained that Haney invested her work with an individual quirky humor, combined with a discipline and passion that made collaborating with her a rare pleasure.

• Along with those mentioned in the text, Haney can be seen performing in the films *Invitation to the Dance* (as Schéhérazade in "Sinbad the Sailor") and *On the Town* (wearing the green dress in "A Day in New York"). The Museum of Television and Radio in New York City has tapes of her performances on "Phil Silvers' Summer in New York" (30 June 1960) and "Sunday Spectacular: The Bachelor" (15 July 1956) and houses the interview she granted Murrow on "Person to Person" (22 June 1955). Haney's choreography for NBC's variety special "The Broadway of Lerner and Loewe" can also be seen at the museum. Her choreography for "Satin Doll" was reconstructed and videotaped in performance by the American Dance Machine and is available for viewing at the Dance Collection, New York Public Library for the Performing Arts, Lincoln Center. The Dance Collection also houses films of a duet and an ensemble piece Haney choreographed for the "Bell Telephone Hour" 1962 Thanksgiving Day special. An obituary is in the *New York Times,* 12 May 1964.

LISA JO SAGOLLA

HANKS, Nancy (31 Dec. 1927–7 Jan. 1983), arts administrator and civil servant, was born in Miami Beach, Florida, the daughter of Bryan Cayce Hanks and Virginia Wooding, both farmers and entrepreneurs. Hanks received her college education at Duke University, graduating in 1947. It was there that she began her long career in public administration by working actively as a member of student government throughout her attendance and as president during her senior year. In 1951 Hanks moved to Washington, D.C., and began working as a secretary in the Office of Defense Mobilization. She worked there until 1953, when she became acquainted with Nelson Rockefeller, thus beginning a lifelong association with the Rockefeller family.

Soon after meeting him, Hanks accepted a position as Rockefeller's personal secretary. She quickly became consumed with her duties and began to work extraordinarily long hours coordinating all of the administrative tasks and activities of Rockefeller's staff. She soon displayed enormous aptitude for the demands of the position; it was undoubtedly during her work with Rockefeller that she gained the experience in administrative and personnel issues that was so crucial to her later endeavors.

Another vital experience for Hanks was accompanying Rockefeller when he traveled to Capitol Hill. She was thus exposed to the inner workings of federal legislation as well as to the lobbying and interpersonal skills needed to thrive in the Washington political theater. Hanks worked closely with Rockefeller on a number of issues and traveled with him to the 1955 presidential summit with Nikita Khrushchev in Geneva, Switzerland. These experiences gave Hanks a broad knowledge of government that covered both domestic and foreign issues.

In 1961 Hanks was diagnosed with breast cancer. In December of that year her left breast was removed. This was the first major incident in what became a series of health problems that Hanks was to contend with for the rest of her life. Two years later doctors were forced to remove her uterus as well as her left ovary because of cancer.

By 1960 Hanks had begun to work less closely with Nelson Rockefeller, but her association with that family continued. She assisted David Rockefeller, Jr., on a number of projects throughout the first half of the 1960s. Her tasks with him grew from administrative and organizational ones to ones closely connected to important research and policy issues. In 1962 she assisted David in producing the reports for the Outdoor Recreation Resources Review Commission. While with Rockefeller she also gained her first experience with arts administration when she assisted in preparing reports on private funding for the arts.

Although Hanks had no formal background in the arts, it may have been that very fact that prepared her ideally for the positions she held. Her activity in this area during the 1960s and her extensive governmental policy experience, combined with an unbiased attitude toward aesthetic issues, made her a uniquely qualified arts administrator. Hanks served as a board member of the Community Arts Council, Inc., and as president of the Associated Council for the Arts and helped to prepare the important Belmont Report, which addressed issues of funding for American museums. All of these provided Hanks with a broad background and experience with the many issues of arts funding.

On 3 September 1969 President Richard Nixon appointed Hanks to the post of chairperson of the recently created National Endowment for the Arts (NEA). Hanks soon appointed Michael Straight, a philanthropist, to the position of deputy chairman, thus creating a partnership that lasted until Hanks's resignation in 1977. Hanks quickly set herself to the task of expanding what was at that point a severely restricted NEA budget. She addressed the situation in the same tireless manner that had always characterized her work habits. By the end of her term the NEA's budget had grown exponentially, and it had become an enormous source of funding for all aspects of the creative arts in America.

Hanks was instrumental not only in expanding the NEA but also in setting the tone for its policies and in defusing controversies. One episode, regarding the novel *Fear of Flying*, is particularly illustrative of Hanks's ideological foundation. Hanks was questioned in Congress about the fact that the NEA had awarded a grant to the author Erica Jong. Senator Jesse Helms attacked the NEA's judgment in allowing public funds to be used in supporting what he and members of his constituency considered an obscene work. Hanks responded that it was not the role of the NEA to make judgments or requirements related to the content in the work of artists it supported. She steadfastly refused to make such demands on artists herself or to allow any member of the NEA to do so, thus establishing an important precedent in government funding for the arts (Straight, *An Intimate Portrait*, p. 335).

After resigning from the NEA, Hanks continued to be active in lobbying for governmental art funding. Her health, however, deteriorated, and she battled cancer for several years, eventually succumbing to it. Her funeral services, held in the Church of St. John the Divine, were attended by numerous members of the Rockefeller family, former president Nixon, and other important personalities including Helen Hayes (Straight, *An Intimate Portrait*, p. 1). Hanks's legacy is one of professionalism, untiring effort, and unwavering support for efforts to aid all aspects of American creative endeavor.

• A biography is Michael Straight, *Nancy Hanks: An Intimate Portrait, the Creation of a National Commitment to the Arts* (1988). Her work as an arts administrator is discussed in Michael Straight, *Twigs for an Eagle's Nest* (1979), and Fannie Taylor and Anthony Barnes, *The Arts at a New Frontier* (1984). See also Livingston Biddle, *Out Government and the Arts: A Perspective from the Inside* (1988).

KENNIE LUPTON

HANLEY, Sarah Eileen (7 Dec. 1883–11 Feb. 1958), artist, was born in the village of Baile Well near Easkey, County Sligo, Ireland, the daughter of Matthew Hanley and Anne Mullowney, farmers. Sarah's parents were ambitious for their children and encouraged them to pursue careers in business and the professions; most notably, Sarah's eldest brother, Dudley, was apprenticed to a haberdasher in Sligo and became lord mayor of the city in the 1920s. Two children, Marie and James, emigrated to New York City about 1900; James died in 1903, while Marie pursued a nursing career at Manhattan Hospital. Sarah joined her sister in New York in 1905 and also trained as a nurse.

In 1910 Sarah Hanley was dispatched to "Laurelton Hall," the Oyster Bay, Long Island, estate of the renowned artist Louis Comfort Tiffany, to help nurse him back to health following a kidney infection. The 62-year-old Tiffany, who had lost his second wife in 1904, took an immediate liking to Hanley and invited her to remain with him permanently. Hanley accepted his offer and became his muse, his comforter, and his constant companion for the next twenty-three years. The precise nature of Hanley's relationship to Tiffany is unknown. She may have been his mistress; his family thought so, and his daughter, Dorothy Tiffany Burlingham, records that he proposed marriage to her. Hanley reportedly turned down the offer, perhaps to avoid incurring the resentment of the Tiffany children, perhaps out of religious scruples: a devout Roman Catholic, she would have hesitated to marry outside the church. In public, however, the relationship between the artist and the model was that of father and daughter; Hanley called Tiffany by the nickname "Padre," while he addressed her with the diminutive "Patsy." Within a few years the pose probably became the reality as the aging Tiffany increasingly came to regard his protégée as a "devoted daughter."

The relationship with Hanley sparked what one critic has called "the most active and creative" period in the history of the Tiffany Studio. Tiffany designed some of his best-known works in stained glass in the years immediately following his meeting Hanley. Her role as muse is commemorated in a series of portraits painted by Tiffany; these depict Hanley reading in the garden at Laurelton Hall, painting on the beach at Miami, and majestically posed as the Madonna enthroned. Tiffany designed jewelry for Hanley and built her a house, "Laurel Hollow," on the hillside opposite Laurelton Hall. More significantly, he taught her how to paint, and over the course of the next four decades she turned this pastime into a career.

In 1918 Tiffany established the Louis Comfort Tiffany Foundation to award fellowships to gifted artists and craftspeople, enabling them to study under his supervision in the studios he had erected at Laurelton Hall. Sarah Hanley became the first director of the foundation, and she oversaw the smooth functioning of the artistic community Tiffany established. The aging artist had little patience with the avant-garde that had emerged with the New York Armory Show of 1913; by the onset of the 1920s, the distinctive Tiffany aesthetic had become passé. Tiffany was increasingly out of touch, and Hanley became his primary link with the artistic mainstream, forging friendships with influential establishment painters like Aurelio Lucioni and with the owners of the leading New York galleries.

Irish influences also shaped Hanley's development as an artist. The successful conclusion of the struggle for political independence in 1920 sparked a new enthusiasm for Irish culture among emigrants and the American public at large; Hanley herself made a late discovery of the Irish Arts and Crafts Movement, which had emerged in Dublin in the early 1900s. In particular, the Dun Emer Guild, a craft studio concentrating on the applied arts, like tapestry weaving and embroidery, and the Cuala Press, founded by Susan and Elizabeth Yeats, whetted her taste for bold patterning and strong color schemes. That the leading practitioners of the Irish Arts and Crafts Movement—Evelyn Gleeson, Katherine MacCormack, and the Yeats sisters—were women gave Hanley ready models on which to pattern her own artistic career.

In 1928 the Anderson Galleries on Park Avenue staged an exhibition of Hanley's paintings, primarily flower studies and landscapes. A number of the paintings were clearly derivative pieces, but others, like *Magnolia Branch*, marked a break from the genteel impressionism in which Tiffany had trained her. Hanley's next exhibit at the Anderson Galleries, in 1930 and 1931, reveals a dramatic shift in emphasis from light to form. Her work of this period echoes that of her contemporary, Georgia O'Keeffe, although on a lesser plane. On the whole, Hanley's vision was less bold and less radical, more acceptable to the midtown galleries in which she showed her canvases, than was that of O'Keeffe.

Tiffany died in January 1933, leaving Hanley the house at Laurel Hollow and fifty shares of stock in Tiffany and Company, the same number of shares he left to each of his daughters. Now independently wealthy, she revisited her birthplace in the summer of 1933; she never returned to Easkey again. Hanley exhibited at the Grant Gallery on East Fifty-seventh Street in November 1933 and at the Tricker Galleries in 1937. This latter show marked a turning point in her career; landscapes and cityscapes predominated over the flower paintings that formed the bulk of her earlier work. The style was increasingly geometric and primitive. A critical catalyst in this transformation may have been the Irish artist and stained-glass designer Evie Hone, whose growing fascination with abstraction and color was already evident in the works Hanley saw exhibited in Dublin during her 1933 Irish trip. The reviews of Hanley's show were positive if guarded; the *New York Times* noted that her canvases were "daringly designed" (21 Nov. 1937), and *Art Digest* termed her "a decidedly individual talent" (20 Nov. 1937).

The 1937 show marked the apex of Hanley's career, though she continued to exhibit intermittently throughout the 1940s. In 1944 she became a member of the National Arts Club, and in 1946 she was elected a fellow-for-life of the Metropolitan Museum of Art. In January 1948 Hanley participated in a landmark show titled "The Irish Academy" at the DeMotte Gallery in Manhattan; the exhibition included canvases by Lavery, Orpen, O'Connor, John Butler Yeats, and Jack Yeats. In November 1949 the DeMotte Gallery staged a retrospective of Hanley's career, including the first showing of her religious paintings. These canvases are Blakean in conception, deliberately primitive in execution; several represent attempts to present modern themes using consciously medieval techniques. The reviews were unfavorable; the *New York Sun* opined that Hanley "had erred in judgment" and that the canvases were "the perfect stage prop for a tent-performance soothsayer, but hardly the medium with which to express matters of spiritual import" (21 Oct. 1949). Hanley never exhibited her paintings again. She died at Laurel Hollow, leaving her entire estate to the Dominican Sisters of St. Mary's of the Springs. She had never married or had children. In 1985 the order sold the contents of Laurel Hollow, including some 800 paintings, vases, and objets d'art, in a major auction at the Phillips Gallery in New York. Laurel Hollow itself continues to be used as a religious retreat by the Dominican order.

Hanley carried the aesthetic ideals of Tiffany to their logical conclusion. Although his plastic works made extensive use of natural forms, Tiffany balked at turning paintings into merely aesthetic objects, continuing to regard them as "windows" onto nature. Hanley had no such qualms; stressing the patterns underlying natural objects, she transformed her canvases into exercises in pure design. Never in the avant-garde, she was nonetheless an active player on the gallery scene of the 1930s, selling her canvases for substantial prices and giving a feminist and Irish-American slant to the modern movement. Although largely forgotten in her later years, Hanley repays critical scrutiny for her collaboration with Tiffany and as an exemplar of the entry of women into American art.

• The major collection of Hanley's papers is located in the Archives of the Motherhouse of the Dominican Sisters of St. Mary's of the Springs, Columbus, Ohio. Her paintings are scattered, the largest collections remaining in the possession of Albertus Magnus College in New Haven, Conn., and the Cavanagh family in Easkey, Ireland. A catalog raisonné of Hanley's work has yet to appear. The best biographical accounts are those in the *New York Times* obituary of 13 Feb. 1958 and the note by Mary M. Walsh prefacing the Phillips Gallery auction catalog, *Sarah Hanley Collection of Tiffany and Related Items* (1985). Several authorities on Tiffany discuss Hanley, most notably Hugh F. McKean, *The "Lost" Treasures of Louis Comfort Tiffany* (1980), Robert Koch, *Louis Comfort Tiffany, Rebel in Glass*, 3d ed. (1982), and Tessa Paul, *The Art of Louis Comfort Tiffany* (1987). *Masterworks of Louis Comfort Tiffany*, the catalog for the Tiffany exhibit at the Renwick Gallery of the Smithsonian Institution (1989), contains brief but cogent observations on Tiffany's later career. Michael John Burlingham sheds valuable new light on Hanley's relationship with Tiffany in *The Last Tiffany: A Biography of Dorothy Tiffany Burlingham* (1989).

MICHAEL P. PARKER

HANLON, Ned (22 Aug. 1857–14 Apr. 1937), baseball player, manager, and executive, was born Edward Hugh Hanlon in Montville, Connecticut, the son of a house builder. Hanlon attended public school at Montville but quit in 1873 to play baseball. He played for three semiprofessional teams in Connecticut before beginning his professional career in 1876 with Providence, Rhode Island, of the New England League. From 1876 to 1879 Hanlon played for three minor league teams, including a strong Albany, New York, team that won the Eastern League championship in 1879.

In 1880 Hanlon began his major league career as an outfielder for the Cleveland team of the National League. Following an inauspicious debut in which he batted .246 and led the league in errors among outfielders, Hanlon was released, but in 1881 he signed with the Detroit Wolverines. At Detroit, Hanlon worked hard to improve his fielding and baserunning skills. Although the 5′10″, left-handed batter was an average hitter who batted above .300 only in 1885 and 1887, he became a good base runner, defensive outfielder, and team leader. As team captain, Hanlon directed the Wolverines on the playing field and helped arrange the purchase of the defunct National League Buffalo team in 1886. That transaction brought Buffalo's famous "big four" of Dan Brouthers, Hardy Richardson, Jack Rowe, and Jim White to Detroit. In 1887 Hanlon captained the team to the National League pennant and to a decisive World Series victory over the St. Louis Browns of the American Association.

When Detroit dropped out of the National League after the 1888 season, the league's Pittsburgh team purchased Hanlon's contract for $5,000. Appointed player-manager of the team late in the 1889 season, Hanlon rallied the team to a 26–18 finish. In 1890 Hanlon joined the Players League in its struggle against the owners of the two established major leagues. As player-manager of the Pittsburgh Brothers, Hanlon led his team to a sixth-place finish with a losing record. In February 1890 Hanlon married Eleanor Jane Kelly; they had five children.

After the collapse of the Players League, Hanlon rejoined the Pittsburgh team of the National League. His 1891 team finished last in the league, and a knee injury, suffered during a late-season game, effectively ended Hanlon's playing career. Although Hanlon began the 1892 season with Pittsburgh, in May he was released and permitted to join the Baltimore Orioles of the National League as player-manager. But after playing only 11 games with the Orioles, Hanlon ended his 13-year playing career, having compiled a .260 batting average in 1,267 games.

No longer an active player, Hanlon continued to manage the Orioles and in 1893 became the club's chief executive. Having saved much of his $25,000 earnings as a player and having profited from Pittsburgh real estate investments, Hanlon purchased a controlling interest in the Baltimore club. Thus, after directing the league's worst team of 1892, Hanlon was empowered to take steps to improve the team.

A shrewd judge of players, Hanlon used his contacts with minor league officials to sign four promising young players. A canny trader, Hanlon's deals with other teams landed such stars as shortstop Hugh Jennings and outfielder Joe Kelley. Such infusions helped the Orioles rise from last place in 1892 to eighth place in 1893. The next year "Foxy Ned" engineered his greatest coup when he traded two players to Brooklyn for the veteran pitcher Dan Brouthers and young outfielder Willie Keeler.

Early in 1894 Hanlon took his team to Georgia for spring training, where he drilled them in "scientific baseball" tactics such as bat control, the use of the hit-and-run play, and opportunistic baserunning. Hanlon's players soon surpassed their manager in these tactics and gained notoriety for aggressive, rowdy, and intimidating play. Subsequently Hanlon admitted to tolerating such play but insisted that he never encouraged it.

From 1894 to 1897 Hanlon's aggressive team won three consecutive league pennants (1894–1896) and two consecutive postseason Temple Cup matches (1896–1897). During these years profits from home attendance, which averaged more than 280,000 per season, augmented Hanlon's $10,000 annual salary, which was the highest of any National League manager. But when home attendance fell to 123,000 in 1898, Hanlon and co-owner Harry Von Der Horst purchased a controlling interest in the league's Brooklyn team. In this controversial "syndicate baseball" scheme, Hanlon presided over two major league teams, which enabled him to transfer star players from the Orioles to Brooklyn. As manager Hanlon led the powerful Brooklyn Superbas (later known as the Dodgers) to consecutive league championships in 1899 and 1900.

Hanlon's syndicate venture ended in 1900 when the National League cut back to eight teams by dropping Baltimore and three other clubs. From 1901 to 1905 Hanlon continued to manage the Brooklyn team, but his best effort was a second-place finish in 1902. After two losing seasons in 1904 and 1905 Hanlon, who lost controlling interest in the team to Charles Ebbets, was released. In 1906 and 1907 Hanlon managed the Cincinnati National League team to two losing seasons, after which his 19-year career as a major league manager ended. His managerial achievements included five league championships—which in the pre-1900 era is surpassed only by Harry Wright and is matched by Frank Selee of Boston and Cap Anson of Chicago—and a record of 1,313 wins and 1,164 losses. From 1893 to 1906 Hanlon was also the highest-paid manager.

Hanlon remained active in professional baseball, serving as president of the minor league Baltimore Orioles of the Eastern League from 1903 to 1909. In 1909 he sold the team to John Dunn, but he retained his ownership of the ballpark until he sold it to a developer in 1915. In 1914 Hanlon was a financial backer of the Baltimore Terrapins of the Federal League, a rival major league, but he sold his stock before the collapse of that league in 1915. From 1916 until his death in Baltimore, he served as a member of the Baltimore City Park Board, becoming head of the board in 1931.

An important figure in the rise of major league baseball, Hanlon was renowned as a manager in the 1890s. He pioneered in the so-called scientific style of play that stressed offensive and defensive tactics, and he tutored six future Hall of Fame players, including five who went on to become pennant-winning managers in the major leagues. For his achievements Hanlon was elected to the Baseball Hall of Fame in 1996.

• The National Baseball Library, Cooperstown, N.Y., has a file of newspaper clippings on Hanlon's career. A contemporary sketch of Hanlon as manager of the 1894 Baltimore Orioles is in D. Dorsey Guy, comp., *Pennant Souvenir: Baltimore Baseball Club, Season 1894* (repr. 1991). Other important sources include Dave Howell, "Ned Hanlon: The Orioles' First Great Manager," *Orioles Magazine* (1996); Mrs. John McGraw, *The Real McGraw*, ed. Arthur Mann (1953); Fred Lieb, *The Baltimore Orioles* (1955); Jerry Lansche, *Glory Fades Away* (1991); Stanley Cohn, *Dodgers, The First 100 Years* (1990); Robert Tiemann, *Dodger Classics* (1983); David Quentin Voigt, *American Baseball*, vol. 1, *From Gentleman's Sport to the Commissioner System* (1983); and Harold Seymour, *Baseball: The Early Years* (1960). Statistical records on Hanlon's career as player and manager are in John Thorn and Pete Palmer, eds., *Total Baseball*, 3d ed. (1993). An obituary is in the *Brooklyn Eagle*, 15 Apr. 1937.

DAVID Q. VOIGT

HANNA, Edward Joseph (21 July 1860–10 July 1944), third archbishop of the Archdiocese of San Francisco, was born in Rochester, New York, the son of Edward Joseph Hanna, a cooper who emigrated from Ireland in 1837, and Anne C. Clark, also from Ireland. In 1879 Hanna graduated from the Rochester Free Academy, where he was a classmate of the future Social Gospel champion, Walter Rauschenbusch. The same year he began studying to become a priest for the Diocese of Rochester, and Bishop Bernard McQuaid sent him to Rome, where he studied at the Urban College de Propaganda Fide while residing at the North American College. Hanna enjoyed a brilliant academic career, distinguishing himself in two public disputations before Pope Leo XIII—in philosophy in 1882 and in theology in 1886. His theological disputation was so impressive that the pope granted him his doctorate without further examination. Hanna had earlier been ordained a priest, on 30 May 1885, at St. John Lateran in Rome.

Following his graduation Hanna remained in Rome, tutoring students at the North American College and teaching part time at the Urban College. He was recalled to Rochester in 1887 and assigned to teach at the diocesan minor seminary, St. Andrew's. In 1893 he was appointed first professor of dogmatic theology at the newly established St. Bernard's Seminary for the Diocese of Rochester, a position he would retain until 1912. During his tenure, he pursued additional studies at the University of Cambridge in 1900 and at the University of Munich in 1906.

While a professor at the seminary, Hanna was an active member of the staff at the Rochester Cathedral parish, where he became quite popular. His fluency in Italian, developed during his time in Rome, made him an effective minister to the growing Italian immigrant community in Rochester. He established the first Sunday school for the children of Italian immigrants, and in 1910 he successfully arbitrated a conflict between Italian laborers and Rochester building contractors.

In 1907 Archbishop Patrick Riordan of San Francisco nominated Hanna to be his coadjutor archbishop with the right of succession, a nomination that was enthusiastically endorsed by Bishop McQuaid. That same year, however, Pope Pius X condemned the heresy of theological modernism, unleashing an era of widespread suspicion, and Hanna became a victim of that suspicion as a result of several articles he had written, which demonstrated too much familiarity with modern thought—"Absolution," printed in the *Catholic Encyclopedia* (1907), "The Human Knowledge of Christ," in the *New York Review* (1905–1906), and "Some Recent Books on Catholic Theology," in a Protestant journal, *The American Journal of Theology* (1906). In these articles Hanna argued that the Catholic church as an institution was located in history, not above history, and as such, Catholic doctrine had developed over time. Most objectionable, he suggested that Jesus had grown in the knowledge of his divine mission and that Jesus was limited by the culture of his day. Although he was never condemned as a modernist, Hanna was denied the appointment as coadjutor.

In 1912, as the theological controversy surrounding modernism finally subsided, Hanna was appointed auxiliary bishop of San Francisco and titular bishop of Titopolis. He was consecrated bishop in Rochester on 4 December. Not granted coadjutor status, he nonetheless succeeded Archbishop Riordan as the third archbishop of San Francisco on 1 June 1915.

During his twenty-year tenure, Hanna became one of the most beloved archbishops in the history of the church in San Francisco. His kindness and affable style won him the affection of Catholics and non-Catholics alike. Besides being pastorally adept, Hanna played a prominent role at the local, state, and national levels. In 1917 he joined with other American bishops to create the National Catholic War Council, and in 1919 he became the first chairman of the administrative board of the War Council's successor, the National Catholic Welfare Conference (NCWC), a position he retained until 1935. Hanna's position made him a national Catholic spokesman on such issues as the persecution of Catholics in Mexico, the 1922 Oregon school law, which required all children to attend public as opposed to Catholic schools, and other issues of national import. In 1931 he was awarded the American Hebrew Medal for his work in fostering better relations between Jews and Christians.

Hanna was a major civic figure in San Francisco, where he was known as one of the "Big Five," leading business and political figures prominent in public affairs during the 1920s and 1930s, when his earlier experience in labor arbitration was put to good use. From 1921 to 1923 he chaired a series of Impartial Wage Boards for the city, which established pay scales for the building trades industry. In 1934 he was appointed by President Franklin D. Roosevelt as chair of the National Longshoremen's Board, which resolved the intense labor conflict then crippling San Francisco.

Hanna served in state government as well. In 1913 he became a member of the California State Commission on Immigration and Housing, and in 1920 he was appointed chairman. During the Great Depression he served as chairman of the California State Committee on the Unemployed and of the State Emergency Committee. On a national level, he served as a member of the National Citizens' Committee on Welfare and Relief Mobilization.

Although Hanna was not noted as a great administrator, the archdiocese increased its number of parishes from 126 to 170 during his tenure. Hanna also promoted the expansion of the Catholic school system by appointing the first superintendent for Catholic schools in 1916 and by spearheading a fund-raising drive for Catholic education in the 1920s. He also established two minor seminaries, both in Mountain View: St. Joseph's College (1925), to prepare diocesan seminarians, and Maryknoll Junior Seminary (1926), for students preparing for the foreign missions.

Because of failing health, Hanna resigned as archbishop on 2 March 1935. He was succeeded by John J. Mitty, who had been appointed coadjutor three years earlier. Hanna spent his last nine years in Rome at the Villa San Francesco, where he died. His body was returned to San Francisco for burial at Holy Cross Cemetery in Colma, California.

• Hanna's papers are housed in the Archives of the Archdiocese of San Francisco in Menlo Park, Calif. Another important source is the Archives of the Sacred Congregation de Propaganda Fide in Rome. No complete biography of Hanna exists. Useful available sources are Richard Gribble, *Catholicism and the San Francisco Labor Movement, 1896–1921* (1993) and "Bishop Hanna and Labor Arbitration in San Francisco," *The Californians* 9 (Nov/Dec. 1991): 35–40; and Robert F. McNamara, "Archbishop Hanna, Rochesterian," *Rochester History* 25 (Apr. 1963): 1–24. For a series of obituaries on Hanna and for additional information on his episcopate, see "Special Supplement," *San Francisco Monitor*, 15 July 1944.

JEFFREY M. BURNS

HANNA, Marcus Alonzo (24 Sept. 1837–15 Feb. 1904), businessman, presidential campaign manager, and U.S. senator known as Mark Hanna, was born above his family's grocery store in New Lisbon, Ohio, the son of Samantha Converse, a schoolteacher, and Leonard Hanna, who practiced medicine before joining his father and brothers in the grocery business. A proposed canal to link New Lisbon to the Ohio River failed, wiping out Hanna's grandfather's investment and pushing the town into commercial decline. Hanna's father established a new wholesale grocery and shipping business in Cleveland, where he moved his family in 1852. Mark Hanna attended public schools and Western Reserve College, leaving college after getting caught in a student prank. As a traveling salesman for the family business, the gregarious Hanna proved a resourceful competitor. Elected second lieutenant in a Cleveland-based infantry in 1861, he instead became managing partner of the business following his father's illness and December 1862 death. Called to defend Washington, D.C., during the summer of 1864, he served briefly in uniform but saw no combat.

Returning to Cleveland, Hanna married Charlotte Augusta "Gussie" Rhodes, daughter of the coal and iron magnate Daniel P. Rhodes, in 1864. They had three children. Rather than join his father-in-law's business, Hanna formed an oil refinery. After fire destroyed his refinery in 1867, he became a partner in Rhodes and Company. He expanded the company from ore handling and shipping to mining, shipbuilding, railroads, and steel. Financial success permitted him to buy out his partners in 1885 and to rename the firm M. A. Hanna and Company. With the profits, he published a newspaper, the *Cleveland Herald*, bought an opera house, opened a bank, and engaged in a protracted contest with Tom L. Johnson for control of the city's street railways. He also branched into politics.

Influenced by his antislavery Quaker father, Hanna had joined the Republican party and served as secretary of the Union Young Men in 1863. In 1869 he won election to the Cleveland Board of Education. A youthful fling with liberal reform ended when Cleveland's civil service reform organization denied him membership on its executive committee. In presidential politics, Hanna campaigned for a string of Ohio Republicans, beginning with Rutherford B. Hayes in 1876. In 1880 he organized a businessmen's club for James A. Garfield and was elected to the Ohio Republican Finance Committee. In 1884 and 1888 he worked for the presidential nomination of Ohio senator John Sherman and developed a friendship with another presidential aspirant, Ohio governor Joseph B. Foraker. Each convention taught him more about the mechanics of national politics, yet most politicians continued to regard him as a novice. Hanna's genius did not emerge until he teamed with William McKinley.

In 1876, when the Massillon coal mines drastically cut wages, Hanna anticipated a strike but failed to convince other coal operators to seek arbitration. After the Ohio militia broke the strike, twenty-three strikers went on trial, charged with acts of vandalism against the mines and violence against the "scabs," or replacement workers, during the strike. The strikers' young defense attorney, McKinley, won acquittals for all but one of them, an achievement that earned him election to Congress later that year. "I became intimate with him soon after he entered Congress," Hanna later recalled, "and our friendship ripened with each succeeding year during his life" (Felt, p. 96).

Although Hanna and McKinley roomed together at the Republican convention in 1884, Hanna worked for Sherman while McKinley voted for James G. Blaine. Four years later they united behind Sherman. Hanna admired how McKinley stood firm for Sherman—preventing a stampede toward his own nomination—while Governor Foraker vacillated. Abandoning Foraker, Hanna assisted McKinley's bid to become Speaker of the House. When he lost to Thomas B. Reed, McKinley became chairman of the House Ways and Means Committee, where he sponsored the McKinley Tariff of 1890. Public reaction against the tariff's high rates helped sweep the Republican majority out of Congress, McKinley among them. With the aid of funds that Hanna raised from protectionist interests, McKinley won election as governor of Ohio in 1891.

Quietly promoting McKinley's presidential candidacy at the convention of 1892, Hanna felt certain that nothing could prevent his nomination in 1896. In the intervening years, a national economic depression restored Republican majorities in Congress and improved their likelihood of electing the next president. The depression, however, also engulfed McKinley. Having endorsed the loans of a friend who went bankrupt, the governor found himself hopelessly in debt. Hanna and other businessmen put up the money to pay McKinley's liability. Preoccupied with his own business affairs during the depression, Hanna did not actively return to politics until 1895, when he turned management of the company over to a brother and assumed control of McKinley's campaign.

McKinley entered the presidential race as the frontrunner against former House Speaker Reed, while several states offered favorite son candidates in hope of a brokered convention. From his experiences in Sherman's campaigns, Hanna identified the 200 delegates from southern states as key to the nomination. By then the South rarely elected Republicans, and local party workers had to rely on the national organization for patronage and financial support. Early in 1895 Hanna invited southern Republican leaders to his house in the winter resort of Thomasville, Georgia, to meet Governor McKinley. Convincing them that McKinley could win and that it would be in their best interest to support him, Hanna advised using any tactics necessary to field McKinley delegations. "Do it, get it done and then let the other fellow howl," attested George A. Myers, the Cleveland barber who served Hanna as a liaison with southern black delegates (Garraty, p. 15). Anticipating the formation of rival delegations, Hanna worked to ensure majority support on the Republican National Committee. After hearing challenges to 160 delegates, the national committee ruled consistently for the McKinley "regulars," and Speaker Reed's astonished campaign manager conceded that McKinley would win on the first ballot. The opposition never combined behind a single candidate but was sufficient to hamper fundraising. Hanna paid most of McKinley's preconvention expenses out of pocket.

Easterners came to the St. Louis convention determined to hammer a gold standard plank into the platform. Hanna and McKinley preferred to campaign on the tariff rather than currency, but by agreeing to the gold plank, Hanna made McKinley more palatable to the East. Only twenty-two western, prosilver delegates walked out in protest. McKinley took the nomination and Hanna became chairman of the Republican National Committee. Hanna looked forward to a vacation before the campaign started, but the Democrats upset his plans by unexpectedly nominating the dynamic young former congressman William Jennings Bryan for president. An eloquent advocate of free silver, Bryan also gained the Populist nomination.

Bryan's candidacy enhanced Hanna's fundraising abilities. Playing on fears of free silver, Hanna persuaded many business executives and bankers to contribute one-fourth of 1 percent of their capital to the Republican campaign. The unprecedented sums he collected (the Republican National Committee claimed to have collected $3.5 million; other estimates, however, ranged from $6 million to $12 million) allowed Democratic speakers to make "Hanna's moneybags" a campaign issue. Reinforcing this negative image were the widely reprinted editorial cartoons of Homer Davenport on the staff of William Randolph Hearst's New York *Journal*. Davenport drew "Dollar Mark" Hanna as a corpulent, cigar-smoking boss in a checkered suit covered with dollar signs.

Hanna spent most of his war chest in the pivotal Midwest. The McKinley headquarters in Chicago directed an "educational" campaign that produced a multitude of pamphlets in multiple languages and hired 1,400 speakers to fan out over the country. Bryan, strapped for cash, embarked on a 16,000-mile train tour to deliver more than 600 speeches. McKinley remained at home in Canton, Ohio, while Hanna organized trainloads of delegations to hear the candidate speak from his front porch. As a businessman, Hanna also valued pithy advertising slogans. He courted the labor vote by promoting McKinley as "the advance agent of prosperity" who would guarantee "a full dinner pail."

Elected president, McKinley invited Hanna to become postmaster general. "Me in the Cabinet?" Hanna scoffed. "All the newspapers would have cartoons of me selling the White House stove!" (Beer, p. 175). Instead, McKinley nominated the elderly Sherman as secretary of state and persuaded the Ohio governor to appoint Hanna to Sherman's Senate seat. McKinley advised Hanna that to win election he must show himself to the people. At sixty, Hanna had almost no experience in public speaking and at first appeared nervous and awkward. Discarding his prepared remarks, he soon developed a breezy, conversational, plain-sense style that appealed to audiences. As the muckraking journalist David Graham Phillips observed, the press had already exposed Hanna's least attractive qualities, allowing him to make favorable impressions in person. After a brutal campaign, the Ohio legislature elected Hanna by a one-vote margin to a full term in 1898. Opponents accused him of having bribed legislators for their votes, charges that the U.S. Senate dismissed for lack of evidence.

Senators awaited Hanna with apprehension, given his reputation for wanting always to be in charge. But he won their respect with his congeniality, knowledge of public affairs, and access to the White House. An unusually conspicuous freshman, he used the vice president's office in the Capitol to receive a stream of distinguished visitors. Politicians and businessmen coveted invitations to Hanna's corned beef hash breakfasts. The Washington press corps found him a reliable source of information and "an oratorical hit" at their Gridiron Club dinners. While polishing his brusk manner, Hanna retained his bite. In 1900, when the Silver Republican senator Richard Pettigrew delivered a vituperative attack, accusing him of corruption in winning his Senate seat, Hanna refuted the charges and showed himself able to hold his own on the Senate floor. Then he went to South Dakota to campaign for Pettigrew's defeat.

Primarily interested in commerce, Hanna fought unsuccessfully for federal subsidies for shipbuilding to encourage overseas trade. He initially opposed the public outcry for war to liberate Cuba on the grounds that it might stifle the business recovery, but he later worried that Democrats might embrace the slogan "free silver and free Cuba" in the next election. He felt relieved when the short, victorious Spanish-American War helped douse populist fervor in the West.

Despite ill health, Hanna chaired McKinley's reelection campaign in 1900. To fill the vice presidential vacancy, Hanna emphatically opposed nominating New York governor Theodore Roosevelt, whom he regarded as impetuous and untrustworthy. "Don't any of you realize that there's only one life between that madman and the Presidency?" he protested (Leech, p. 537). But public opinion and New York party boss Thomas C. Platt thrust Roosevelt on the ticket over Hanna's objections.

Hanna contributed most to McKinley's reelection when he averted a major coal strike in Pennsylvania by bringing the coal operators to the bargaining table. For all his business identification, he respected labor's right to bargain collectively. When George Pullman refused to negotiate with his workers in 1894, Hanna had snapped, "A man who won't meet his men halfway is a God-damn fool!" (Beer, p. 133). In 1901 Hanna became active in the National Civic Federation, where he worked with American Federation of Labor president Samuel Gompers for harmony in labor-management relations. Winning the cooperation of organized labor was a smart investment, Hanna reasoned, to make American workers less inclined toward socialism.

Six months into his second term, McKinley was assassinated and Roosevelt became president. Hanna offered the young president avuncular advice to "go slow." Although his influence had rested largely on his close friendship with McKinley, Hanna retained a hold on the party apparatus as chairman of the Republican National Committee. Publicly he supported Roosevelt's policies. He delivered such effective speeches endorsing a canal through Panama as the more practical and economical route that senators quipped about voting for the "Hannama Canal." He also backed Roosevelt's antitrust action against the Northern Securities Company, although he considered business consolidation inevitable. Hanna distrusted all economic reform, from tariff revision to business regulation, and advised Republicans to "stand pat," a term he coined from poker. Roosevelt perceived Hanna as his only formidable opponent in 1904. To the president's dismay, "Uncle Mark" resisted all entreaties to endorse his nomination. Whether he actually intended to challenge Roosevelt or not, just the possibility of his candidacy restrained Roosevelt's reform impulses.

Hanna died of typhoid fever at his hotel suite in Washington, D.C. Party workers mourned the loss of their popular chieftain, and at the national convention that summer they hung a colossal portrait of Hanna over the rostrum. During Roosevelt's second term, conservatives yearned for the "good old Hanna days," while progressives fought to reform the system that he represented. Shrewd, determined, and cynical, Hanna could also be straightforward, generous, and loyal. He was "the ideal 'Boss,'" his operatives recalled, because "he never failed a friend nor hesitated to punish an enemy" (Garraty, p. 147). Confident of his own convictions and personally honest, he showed no compunction about soliciting campaign funds from interests that benefited from government policies or that demanded commitments in return. The first modern presidential campaign manager, Hanna personified the alliance of business and politics and its consequences.

• The Hanna-McCormick Family Papers at the Library of Congress are sparse on Mark Hanna except for a series of fifty-five interviews that journalist James B. Morrow conducted with Hanna's family, friends, and business and political associates. Another small collection of Hanna's papers is at the Western Reserve Historical Society in Cleveland, Ohio, while more of his letters are scattered through the collections of his many correspondents, including John Mitchell (Catholic University), John D. Rockefeller (Rockefeller Archives Center), Thomas Platt (Yale University), and the Beer family (Yale). Hanna's family commissioned the favorable biography by Herbert Croly, *Marcus Alonzo Hanna: His Life and Work* (1912). Supplementing it are Thomas Beer, *Hanna* (1929); Thomas Edward Felt, "The Rise of Mark Hanna" (Ph.D. diss., Michigan State Univ., 1960); Marcus Alonzo Hanna, *Mark Hanna: His Book*, published after Hanna's death from articles attributed to him (1904); Solon Lauer, *Mark Hanna: A Sketch from Life* (1901); Kristie Miller, *Ruth Hanna McCormick, A Life in Politics, 1880–1944* (1992); and *Marcus A. Hanna, Memorial Addresses Delivered in the Senate and House of Representatives*, 58th Cong., 2d sess. (1904). Useful sources concerning Hanna's role in McKinley's election include Arthur Wallace Dunn, *From Harrison to Harding: A Personal Narrative, Covering a Third of a Century, 1888–1921* (1922); John A. Garraty, ed., *The Barber and the Historian: The Correspondence of George A. Myers and James Ford Rhodes, 1910–1923* (1956); Stanley L. Jones, *The Presidential Election of 1896* (1964); Margaret Leech, *In the Days of McKinley* (1959); Robert D. Marcus, *Grand Old Party: Political Structure in the Gilded Age, 1880–1896* (1971); and Michael E. McGerr, *The Decline of Popular Politics: The American North, 1865–1928* (1986). Hanna's influence as a senator is discussed in John Morton Blum, *The Republican Roosevelt* (1954; 2d ed., 1977); Lewis L. Gould, *Reform and Regulation: American Politics from Roosevelt to Wilson* (1986); Marguerite Green, *The National Civic Federation and the American Labor Movement, 1900–1925* (1956); and James Ford Rhodes, *The McKinley and Roosevelt Administrations, 1897–1909* (1922), by Hanna's brother-in-law. Obituaries are in the *New York Times* and the *Cleveland Plain Dealer*, 16–20 Feb. 1904.

DONALD A. RITCHIE

HANNAGAN, Stephen Jerome (4 Apr. 1899–5 Feb. 1953), press agent, was born in Lafayette, Indiana, the son of William John Hannagan, a patternmaker, and Johanna Gertrude Enright. At age fourteen Hannagan began working at a local newspaper, the *Lafayette Morning Journal*, and continued working there while attending high school and then Purdue University, which he left in 1919 after two years (without graduating). Moving to Indianapolis he worked briefly for another newspaper and then for an advertising agency. His newspaper experiences taught him that journalists appreciated honest and accurate sources and a good human interest story.

From those lessons Hannagan built a career as a press agent, starting in 1919 when he became director of publicity for the Indianapolis Motor Speedway and its 500-mile Memorial Day race. What he did was to focus public attention on the drivers as sports heroes rather than on the cars themselves. Following that suc-

cess he moved to New York in 1920 to work as a writer for United Press and then as a features writer and syndicated columnist for Newspaper Enterprises Association and United Features. The next year he accompanied Captain Eddie Rickenbacker, America's wartime ace fighter pilot, on a flight around the entire continent and then wrote about that adventure for popular magazines. In 1924, calling himself a "press agent," he started his own business publicizing major tourist attractions, sports events, and sports heroes. While promoting tourism for Miami Beach he employed a technique for which he became renowned—"cheesecake" photographs of bathing beauties. In 1931 he married Ruth Ellery; they had no children and divorced a few years later.

Hannagan closed his own business in 1933 to become a vice president of Lord and Thomas, the advertising agency run by Albert Lasker. One of his assignments was to combat public hostility toward the utilities magnate Samuel Insull, who had been arrested in Europe, where he had fled to evade charges of fraud. Casting his client as an aged martyr unfairly persecuted, Hannagan wrote the contrite statement that Insull read to the press when he returned to the United States. He advised Insull to delay posting bail in order to spend a short time in jail and then to live modestly while awaiting trial. Insull followed that advice and used public transportation to attend his trial. His acquittal boosted his press agent's own reputation.

Dissatisfied with Lord and Thomas's regimen after only two years, Hannagan left and again opened his own publicity agency in New York, with branches in Miami and Hollywood. Among his many large corporate clients, the Union Pacific Railroad sought help promoting an Idaho ski resort it developed. Hannagan, who had never been on skis or had any interest in outdoor recreation, focused publicity on the region's combination of abundant snow and sunshine. For "Sun Valley," the name for the resort he claimed to have suggested to board chair W. Averell Harriman, he circulated photographs, actually taken in a New York studio with cotton substituting for snow, that seemed to show skiers there wearing bathing suits or shorts. In December 1936 he attracted free press coverage for the resort by sending a train there filled with Hollywood celebrities. In 1939 he married a New York clothes model, Suzanne Brewster; childless, they divorced four years later.

As a "prince of press agents" during the 1940s and early 1950s, Hannagan provided publicity and sales promotion for a variety of corporate and other clients. When the Ford Motor Company faced criticism during World War II because it failed to meet bomber production quotas at the Willow Run factory, it hired Hannagan. By creating the image of production as a domestic battlefront, he managed to generate favorable press coverage of Ford's efforts. Hannagan generally avoided work for political candidates because he disliked election campaign compromises. Nevertheless, he did provide publicity work that helped Wendell Willkie gain the Republican presidential nomination in 1940, and four years later he performed that same role for Thomas E. Dewey when he obtained the nomination.

Flamboyant, loud, belligerent but charming, Hannagan operated in the glamorous entertainment circles of New York and Hollywood. He spent extravagantly on himself, favoring expensive clothes and entertainment, and he habitually lived in New York hotels. A celebrity in his own right, he was a friend of New York nightclub owner Sherman Billingsley and for several years after his last divorce was a companion of the movie actress Ann Sheridan. He died of a heart attack in Nairobi, Kenya, where he had gone to provide advice to Coca-Cola dealers on sales techniques. At the time he employed a staff of sixty-two, with offices in several cities. His agency subsequently was merged into Hill & Knowlton, the largest public relations firm at the time.

• Hannagan's personal papers were not placed in any repository. D. Hartwell, "Prince of Press Agents," *Collier's*, 22 Nov. 1947, provides a complimentary contemporary profile. See *Current Biography* (1944), pp. 267–69, for a list of sources. An obituary is in the *New York Times*, 6 Feb. 1953.

ALAN R. RAUCHER

HANNEGAN, Edward Allen (25 June 1807–25 Feb. 1859), U.S. senator and congressman, was born in Hamilton County, Ohio. The identities and circumstances of his parents are uncertain. Not long after his birth, his family moved to Lexington, Kentucky. Hannegan attended Transylvania University and studied law with a county clerk. In the mid-1820s he relocated to Vincennes, Indiana, but soon moved up the Wabash River to Covington, Indiana. He taught school and worked on farms in the course of establishing a legal practice that eventually thrived. In 1829 Hannegan married Margaret Chambers Duncan; the couple had one child. In 1830 the state legislature appointed him prosecuting attorney for Indiana's First Judicial District.

Capable of a perfervid eloquence, Hannegan soon entered politics. In 1831 he was elected as a Democrat to the state legislature, where he backed state funding for river improvements. He also supported chartering the State Bank of Indiana, but after being elected to the U.S. House of Representatives in 1832, he was an orthodox Jacksonian in opposing the Bank of the United States. In the early stages of the "gag rule" controversy, Hannegan, doubtlessly aware that many residents of his northern state were southern-born, declared himself opposed to congressional interference with slavery but said that he was wary, too, of intruding upon citizens' right to petition Congress. Reelected in 1834, the bibulous Indianan left Congress after the 1836 elections, at least in part because drink had gotten the better of him. He subsequently moved to La Porte County in northern Indiana, where he briefly worked in a federal land office and published a newspaper. Having sobered up, he returned to Covington and again practiced law. His 1840 bid to

return to Congress failed, but he was elected to the state house of representatives the following year.

By 1843 a rising Democratic tide in Indiana lifted Hannegan to the U.S. Senate, though just barely. He was elected by a very narrow margin, the crucial vote said to have come from a Whig legislator who owed a favor to a man who owed a favor to Hannegan. In Washington, Hannegan gave full voice to Indiana Democrats' enthusiasm for territorial expansion, an enthusiasm the party as a whole embraced in an 1844 platform calling for the "reannexation" of Texas and the "reoccupation" of the Oregon Territory, then under the joint control of the United States and Great Britain. Like other spokesmen for the Old Northwest, whose farmers were anxious that the United States secure West Coast ports as a means to developing markets in the West and Far East for their surplus crops, Hannegan emphasized the claim to Oregon. Seeming to delight in tugging the British lion's tail, he insisted that neither the prospect of war nor the lifting of restrictive British trade laws ought to keep the United States from asserting its sovereignty over the whole of the territory, which sprawled from the northern border of Spanish California to the southeastern edge of Russian Alaska. When southern Democrats suggested a willingness to see the territory divided with Britain, Hannegan, whose choleric temperament was again charged by alcohol, angrily accused them of "Punic faith." Northern Democrats had supported southerners' demand for Texas, but once the southerners' appetite for slaveholding territory had been satisfied, they seemed to shrug off the party's commitment to winning northwestern lands unsuited to slavery. Should President James K. Polk, a Tennessee Democrat, back away from the claim of a northern boundary at 54°40′, Hannegan raged in March 1846, "So long as one human eye remains to linger on the page of history, the story of his abasement will be read, sending him and his name together to an infamy so profound, a damnation so deep, that the hand of resurrection will never be able to drag him forth" (*Congressional Globe*, 29th Cong., Ist sess. [1846], p. 460). In June 1846, with thirteen other senators, Hannegan voted against Polk's treaty establishing the nation's far northwestern boundary at the forty-ninth parallel. While his bitterness demonstrated the fragility of the sectional comity that expansion had fostered among Democrats, Hannegan did remain willing to support territorial acquisitions more to the taste of his southern peers. He hesitated over the settlement with Mexico in 1848, believing that not enough of that nation's territory had been seized.

In political terms, Hannegan placed most of his eggs in the Oregon basket. He had relatively little to say about other matters of interest to his western constituents, such as the tariff and internal improvements. Over the course of several years, he equivocated with respect to the Wilmot Proviso, objecting to it as unduly provocative but later suggesting that he would obey the instructions of the legislature with respect to banning slavery in New Mexico Territory. In early 1849

Democrats in the Indiana legislature sent Governor James Whitcomb, who had been less guarded in his support of free soil, to the Senate in Hannegan's place. On the eve of leaving office, President Polk, who had earlier compared Hannegan's behavior in the Senate to that of a spoiled child, was prevailed upon to appoint Hannegan U.S. minister to Prussia. Hannegan's manner and preferred amusements, however, hardly suited him for diplomacy. His brief tenure was terminated apparently at his own request, though legend would have it that the king of Prussia insisted upon his recall after Hannegan flirted altogether too publicly with the queen. Hannegan returned to Covington in 1850.

In 1851 Hannegan lost a race for the state legislature conducted largely on local issues, but he still imagined he might secure the Democratic presidential nomination the following year. Any prospect of that vanished when he stabbed his brother-in-law to death in a drunken brawl. It was said that his mortally wounded relation forgave him before expiring, and Hannegan was never tried. After his wife died, Hannegan in 1857 moved to St. Louis, Missouri, where he practiced law, drank heavily, and apparently began using opiates. After stumbling through a stump speech, he was found dead in St. Louis of a morphine overdose the next morning.

Hannegan's term in the Senate was more colorful than constructive. However, the ire he directed at fellow Democrats over the Oregon issue served as portent of the power that territorial expansion held to disorder American politics.

• A few Hannegan letters are at the William Henry Smith Library of the Indiana Historical Society in Indianapolis. John Bartlow Martin gives a vivid account of his life in *Indiana: An Interpretation* (1947). See also William W. Woolen, *Biographical and Historical Sketches of Early Indiana* (1883), and John W. Whicker, "Edward A. Hannegan," *Indiana Magazine of History* 14 (1918): 368–75. Hannegan's place in Ind. politics is described in two articles by Roger Van Bolt, "Sectional Aspects of Expansion, 1844–1848," *Indiana Magazine of History* 48 (1952): 119–40, and "Hoosiers and the 'Eternal Agitation' 1848–1850," *Indiana Magazine of History* 48 (1952): 331–68. He is briefly noted in Morton Rosenberg and Dennis McClurg, *The Politics of Pro-Slavery Sentiment in Indiana 1816–1861* (1968). On Hannegan and the Oreg. controversy, see David Pletcher, *The Diplomacy of Annexation: Texas, Oregon, and the Mexican War* (1973); Thomas Hietala, *Manifest Design: Anxious Aggrandizement in Late Jacksonian America* (1985); Frederick Merk, *The Oregon Question: Essays in Anglo-American Diplomacy and Politics* (1967); Norman Graebner, *Empire on the Pacific: A Study in American Continental Expansion* (1955); and Allan Nevins, ed., *Polk, The Diary of a President 1845–1849* (1929).

PATRICK G. WILLIAMS

HANNEGAN, Robert Emmet (30 June 1903–6 Oct. 1949), political strategist, was born in St. Louis, Missouri, the son of John Patrick Hannegan, and Anna Holden. His father held the position of chief of detectives in the St. Louis Police Department. Hannegan graduated from Yeatman High School and St. Louis University, where he lettered in five sports and received the LL.B. with honors in 1925. He played semiprofessional baseball and coached part time for several years to supplement his income as he developed his private law practice. In 1929 he married Irma Protzmann, the daughter of a prominent St. Louis Republican councilman. They had four children.

Hannegan naturally gravitated to politics. A handsome, athletic Irish-American who stood slightly over six feet and weighed 205 pounds, Hannegan was recognized for his congenial personality, his penchant for stylish clothes, and his love for politics. He won acclaim in 1933 as the Democratic leader of the traditionally Republican Twenty-first Ward by producing the first majority for his party in many years, thereby contributing significantly to the election of Bernard F. Dickmann as mayor. He was elected chairman of the St. Louis Central Democratic Committee in 1934; after losing the chairmanship in 1935, Hannegan regained his former position in 1936. He presided over what many critics called the "Dickmann-Hannegan machine." His reputation as a political strategist increased further when he managed Dickmann's landslide reelection campaign in 1937.

In 1940 Hannegan took a major risk that propelled him to national political prominence. Despite the endorsement of Governor Lloyd Stark by the St. Louis County Democratic Central Committee for the party's U.S. Senate nomination, just two days before the 6 August primary election Hannegan endorsed incumbent Harry S. Truman. He mobilized a last-minute blitz that helped give Truman a slender 8,411-vote plurality in St. Louis County. Truman won the statewide election over Stark and another challenger by fewer than 8,000 votes. No one is certain what prompted Hannegan's switch, but it proved decisive in saving Truman's political career, a fact that was not lost on the future president.

Hannegan's reward came in January 1942, when Senator Truman persuaded President Franklin D. Roosevelt to nominate the St. Louis lawyer-politician as federal revenue collector for eastern Missouri. This nomination came shortly after Hannegan had lost much of his power in the local party structure. Not only had he engendered strong criticism for his abandonment of Governor Stark in favor of Truman, but factional disputes and Dickmann's mayoral defeat in 1941 also contributed to Hannegan's removal from the chairmanship of the St. Louis Central Democratic Committee.

It was, however, Hannegan's central role in the futile attempt to prevent the certification of Republican Forrest C. Donnell as governor following the 1940 election that had produced the most criticism. Hannegan and other state party leaders contested Donnell's apparent 3,000-vote victory. Charging vote counting irregularities, they took their case to the state assembly and eventually the Missouri Supreme Court. Their effort fizzled when the court declared Donnell the winner. Irate Republicans and most Democrats condemned what became known as "the infamous governorship steal." The St. Louis *Globe Democrat* denounced Hannegan as "the most discredited boss of a discredited party," and his political career seemed at an end. Truman, well known for his personal loyalty to friends and political allies, then came to the rescue.

Still it was not easy. The St. Louis *Post Dispatch* called his nomination to the revenue position "an affront to thousands of [Missourians]," and the outrage emanating from Missouri threatened Senate confirmation. Truman, however, refused to back down, publicly stating that, if Hannegan were not confirmed, he would block the appointment of any other nominee. Truman then called in many political debts and generated enough Senate support to secure confirmation. To the amazement of his many critics, however, Hannegan demonstrated statesmanlike qualities as revenue collector, producing major reforms in an office long identified by the ineptitude and questionable political connections of its officeholders. After an internal review concluded that Hannegan's district had been transformed into a model of efficiency and modernization free from political chicanery, in October 1943 Roosevelt named him to fill the vacancy as commissioner of internal revenue. Just three months after Hannegan assumed this important federal post, Roosevelt surprised some political observers by appointing Hannegan chairman of the Democratic National Committee.

Hannegan had thus landed in a position perfectly suited for his talents, and he immediately set about to resuscitate an outdated and undisciplined organization in preparation for the 1944 elections. Like many Democrats, Hannegan held serious reservations about retaining Vice President Henry A. Wallace on the national ticket. Hannegan's views coincided with those of other prominent Democrats, notably Bronx boss Ed Flynn, California oilman and fundraiser Edwin Pauley, Chicago mayor Edward J. Kelly, and party secretary and popular Washington lobbyist George Allen (1896–1973). They feared that Wallace's eccentricities, and especially his advanced liberal positions, could severely hurt the Democratic ticket in November. Perhaps even more important, they also had discreetly observed Roosevelt's rapidly declining health and greatly feared the prospects of a Wallace presidency.

Over a period of nearly six months Hannegan conspired with these party leaders to deny Wallace renomination. In so doing he often acted in ways that were devious and duplicitous. He nonetheless believed his cause was just. Always careful to include the names of Supreme Court Justice William O. Douglas and top presidential aide James Byrnes, among others, in his many conversations with the president and White House insiders, Hannegan also made certain that Senator Truman, by then widely recognized as one of the Senate's most effective members, received consideration. Hannegan was not determined to nominate his fellow Missourian but like others was drawn to the advantages Truman would bring to the ticket. Hannegan seemed more determined to scuttle Wallace than to secure the nomination for his friend from Independence.

Much to Hannegan's frustration, Roosevelt seemed reluctant to make a decision, frequently deflected criticisms of his vice president, and even gave the impression that the running mate question was of little import. Finally, on the evening of 11 July, at a White House dinner with a handful of top advisers, Roosevelt agreed to accept an alternative candidate and specifically named Truman and Douglas. A delighted Hannegan left this meeting with a handwritten statement signed by Roosevelt to that effect. Roosevelt continued to dissemble and sent out so many conflicting signals that several candidates, including the determined incumbent Wallace, were encouraged to seek the vice presidential nomination on the convention floor in Chicago. After an incredibly complex flurry of political maneuvering, Truman won the nomination on the second ballot. This prompted Hannegan to remark later, somewhat stretching the truth, "I was the man who kept Henry Wallace from becoming President of the United States."

Truman became president following Roosevelt's death in April 1945. In May 1945 President Truman named Hannegan to the cabinet position of postmaster general, and he served in that post until 1947. Hannegan instituted a series of reforms designed to modernize the postal service and to standardize airmail rates worldwide. Serious health problems, however, forced his retirement from politics, and he returned to his hometown to become part owner of the St. Louis Cardinals baseball team. In 1948, true to his resignation pledge that he was leaving politics forever, Hannegan played no role in Truman's dramatic reelection campaign, a fact that fueled speculation that his relationship with Truman had cooled. By this time Hannegan suffered from advanced cardiovascular disease. He sold his interest in the Cardinals and put his affairs in order, as he prepared himself for an early death. Unable to control his blood pressure and bludgeoned by a series of heart attacks, Hannegan died at his St. Louis home.

• The bulk of Hannegan's papers were destroyed, although remaining fragments are on deposit at the Harry S. Truman Library in Independence, Mo. Hannegan is widely mentioned in newspaper and magazine articles during the 1940s. Several important books touch on major aspects of his career. See especially Robert H. Ferrell, *Choosing Truman: The Democratic Convention of 1944* (1994), and David McCullough, *Truman* (1992). Also recommended are Bert Cochran, *Harry Truman and the Crisis Presidency* (1973), Margaret Truman, *Harry S. Truman* (1973), Harold F. Gosnell, *Truman's Crises: A Political Biography of Harry S. Truman* (1980), Merle Miller, *Plain Speaking: An Oral Biography of Harry S. Truman* (1974), and Robert H. Ferrell, *Harry S. Truman and the Modern American Presidency* (1983). The *New York Times*, 7 Oct. 1949, provides a detailed obituary, as do the St. Louis *Post Dispatch*, 6, 7 Oct. 1949, and the *Washington Post*, 7 Oct. 1949.

RICHARD O. DAVIES

HANSBERRY, Lorraine Vivian (19 May 1930–12 Jan. 1965), playwright, was born in Chicago, Illinois, the daughter of Carl Augustus Hansberry, a real estate agent, and Nannie Perry, a schoolteacher. Throughout her childhood, Lorraine Hansberry's home was visited by many distinguished blacks, including Paul Robeson, Duke Ellington, and her uncle, the Africanist William Leo Hansberry, who helped inspire her enthusiasm for African history. In 1938, to challenge real-estate covenants against blacks, Hansberry's father moved the family into a "white" neighborhood where a mob gathered and threw bricks, one of which nearly hit Lorraine. Two years later, after he won his case on the matter of covenants before the Supreme Court, they continued in practice. Embittered by U.S. racism, Carl Hansberry planned to relocate his family in Mexico in 1946 but died before the move.

After studying drama and stage design at the University of Wisconsin from 1948 to 1950, Hansberry went to New York and began writing for Robeson's newspaper *Freedom*. She also marched on picket lines, made speeches on street corners, and helped move furniture back into evicted tenants' apartments. In 1953 she married Robert Nemiroff, an aspiring writer and graduate student in English and history whom she had met on a picket line at New York University. They did not have children. Soon afterward, she quit full-time work at *Freedom* to concentrate on her writing, though she had to do part-time work at various jobs until the success of Nemiroff and Burt D'Lugoff's song "Cindy, Oh Cindy" in 1956 freed her to write full-time. She also studied African history under W. E. B. DuBois at the Jefferson School for Social Science.

In 1957 Hansberry read a draft of *A Raisin in the Sun* to Philip Rose, a music publisher friend who decided to produce it. Opening on Broadway in 1959, it earned the New York Drama Critic's Circle Award for best play, making Hansberry the youngest American, first woman, and first black to win the award. This play about the Youngers, a black family with differing personalities and dreams who are united in racial pride and their fight against mutual poverty, has become a classic.

Although Hansberry enjoyed her new celebrity status, she used her many interviews to speak out about the oppression of African Americans and the social changes that she deemed essential. Her private life, however, remained painful and complex. Shortly after her marriage, her lesbianism emerged, leading to conflicts with her husband and within herself, provoked by the widespread homophobia that infected even the otherwise progressive social movements she supported. At some point amid her public triumph, she and Nemiroff separated, though their mutual interests and mutual respect later reunited them.

In 1960 she wrote two screenplays of *A Raisin in the Sun* that would have creatively used the cinematic medium, but Columbia Pictures preferred a less controversial version that was closer to the original. Accepting a commission from NBC for a slavery drama to commemorate the Civil War centennial, Hansberry wrote *The Drinking Gourd*, but this too was rejected as controversial. During this busy year she began research for an opera titled *Toussaint* and a play about Mary Wollstonecraft; started writing her African play, *Les Blancs*; and began the play that evolved into *The Sign in Sidney Brustein's Window*. In 1961 the film *A Raisin in the Sun* won a special award at the Cannes Film Festival.

In 1962 she wrote her postatomic war play, *What Use Are Flowers?*, while publicly denouncing the House Un-American Activities Committee and the Cuban "missile crisis" and mobilizing support for the Student Nonviolent Coordinating Committee (SNCC). The following year, she began suffering from cancer but continued her support for SNCC and, at James Baldwin's invitation, participated in a discussion about the racial crisis with Attorney General Robert Kennedy.

During 1964 she and Nemiroff divorced, but because of her illness they only told their closest friends and saw each other daily, continuing their creative collaboration until her death. She named Nemiroff her literary executor in her will. From April to October she was in and out of the hospital for therapy but managed to deliver her "To Be Young, Gifted and Black" speech to winners of the United Negro College Fund writing contest and to participate in the Town Hall debate on "The Black Revolution and the White Backlash." In October she moved to a hotel near the site of rehearsals of *The Sign in Sidney Brustein's Window* and attended its opening night. Despite its mixed reviews, actors and supporters from various backgrounds united to keep the play running until Hansberry's death in New York City.

• The Hansberry Archives, which include unpublished plays, screenplays, essays, letters, diaries, and two drafts of an uncompleted novel, are not located in an institution. Until his death in 1991, Robert Nemiroff, as literary executor, made portions of them available to qualified scholars. Nemiroff was responsible for some of the best-known works by Hansberry that appeared after her death, including *To Be Young, Gifted and Black*, the semiautobiography that he wrote first as a drama, using excerpts from her published and unpublished works, later expanding it into a book (both versions are still in print and not to be confused with each other), and the musical *Raisin*, whose text he coauthored combining material from various drafts of *A Raisin in the Sun*. He also made small changes in the acting versions of Hansberry's plays to correct minor problems that appeared during productions. The best biographical work on Hansberry remains *To Be Young, Gifted and Black*, but chronologies and other biographical material may also be found in Steven R. Carter's critical study, *Hansberry's Drama: Commitment amid Complexity* (1991), and in Anne Cheney's *Lorraine Hansberry* (1984).

STEVEN R. CARTER

HANSBERRY, William Leo (25 Feb. 1894–17 Oct. 1965), historian of Africa, was born in Gloster, Mississippi, the son of Harriet Pauline Bailey and Eldon Hayes Hansberry, a professor at Alcorn A. & M. College in Mississippi. His father's personal library inspired him to pursue history as a career. According to

Hansberry, by the time he entered Atlanta University in 1914 he had become "something of an authority on the glory that was Greece and the grandeur that was Rome."

A second major influence on Hansberry was W. E. B. Du Bois's book, *The Negro*, published in 1916. For the first time Hansberry learned about the societies and achievements of Africans in ancient and medieval times. Unable to pursue the subject in depth at Atlanta University, he transferred to Harvard University where he studied anthropology and archaeology and received the B.A. and M.A. in 1921 and 1932. Although Harvard did not offer courses on Africa, it did have reference works on the subject, and the courses in anthropology and archaeology inspired Hansberry to commit himself to the study of the ancient heritage of Africa. He later pursued postgraduate study at the University of Chicago and Oxford University.

Upon receipt of the B.A., Hansberry announced that he would promote and facilitate the teaching of "Negro Life and History, in order to bring to the attention of teachers and students the significance of ancient African civilization." When he joined the Howard University faculty in 1922, he inaugurated the first program in African studies in the United States, and possibly the world. This program included several courses in African history and culture and a number of symposia. In 1925, for example, he organized a conference at which twenty-eight papers were read, including several by his students from Panama, Guyana, Colombia, and the United States.

During the 1920s Hansberry formulated "a plan for expanding a pioneer project in collegiate education," which included the preparation of teaching materials, publication of source books, and a program to promote interest in Africa through general publications, visual aids, and lectures. Hansberry believed that Howard University, as a predominantly and historically black institution, should undertake this initiative. He noted in letters and reports to the president and dean at Howard in 1935: "No institution is more obligated and no Negro school is in a better position to develop such a program as Howard. No institution has access to specialized libraries—the Moorland Collection [at Howard], and city repositories; nowhere else are the thought and planning put forth; no better courses exist anywhere else; there are no better trained students anywhere . . . to [enable Howard to] distinguish itself as a leader in the general cause of public enlightenment."

Hansberry knew his ideas were "at odds with prevailing notions about Africa's past." This was a period when Africa was subjected to European colonial rule justified by negative stereotypes, including the myth that "Africa had no history." Several of Hansberry's colleagues ridiculed his efforts as "professionally unsound" and "without foundation in fact," and Hansberry thus received only limited financial support from his university. He was discouraged from proceeding with an application to join an archaeological expedition to Sudan, at least partly because a trusted white adviser at the Museum of Fine Arts in Boston confessed in a letter to Hansberry on 2 February 1932 that he would "hesitate long before taking an American Negro on my staff." Finally in 1937 Hansberry received a fellowship to study at Oxford under a renowned archaeologist who conducted an expedition to Nubia, but again he was denied a place on the expedition. (That same year he married Myrtle Kelso, with whom he would have two children.) Subsequent proposals to the Rosenwald and Carnegie foundations in 1947 were also denied.

Racism was surely at work in these disappointments, but there was another factor as well. Hansberry knew more about his subject than anyone else; few nonexperts were prepared to judge his plans. As Professor Earnest A. Hooten, chairman of Harvard University's anthropology department, wrote on 17 September 1948: "I am quite confident that no present-day scholar has anything like the knowledge of this field (prehistory of Africa) that Hansberry has developed. He has been unable to take the Ph.D. degree . . . because there is no university or institution . . . that has manifested a really profound interest in this subject." Finally in 1953 Hansberry, then fifty-nine years old, received a Fulbright Research Award, which allowed him to study and conduct fieldwork in Egypt, Sudan, and Ethiopia. By this time African studies had begun to gain acceptance at U.S. universities and foundations. In fact, Howard University established its program in 1954 while Hansberry was in Africa, but even after his return to the university several of his colleagues, who remained skeptical about the objectivity of his research and the quality of African history generally, succeeded in minimizing his role in the program. But in addition to teaching at Howard, he joined the faculty part-time at the New School for Social Research in New York in 1957 to teach early African civilization.

After his retirement in 1959 as an associate professor, two internationally renowned scholars visiting the United States, Kenneth Diké of Ibadan University in Nigeria and Thomas Hodgkin of Oxford University, examined Hansberry's research and recommended that it be published. Unfortunately, Hansberry died in Chicago before he could complete that project.

Throughout his career, Hansberry gave untiringly of his time to students and took a particular interest in African students whom he believed had an obligation to return to their countries to apply their skills and an African-centered perspective of their heritage. He helped them obtain scholarships, emergency financial aid, and employment; he also helped several of them enter professional schools and corresponded with African parents regarding their children's welfare. Hansberry raised thousands of dollars for the Committee on Aid to African Students, including contributions from Liberian president W. V. S. Tubman and Ethiopian emperor Haile Selassie. During the 1950s Hansberry helped to found the African Students Association of the United States and Canada, which monitored issues and addressed problems relating to African students.

Hansberry's interest in Africa extended beyond the university. In 1927 he read a paper on African archaeology at the Fourth Pan-African Congress in New York. In 1934 he, Malaku Bayen (the first Ethiopian student at Howard University), William Steen (one of Hansberry's African-American students), and others organized the Ethiopian Research Council to promote interest in Ethiopia. When Italy invaded Ethiopia in 1934, the council served as an information center and coordinating body for contributions to the Ethiopian cause. After the defeat of the Italians in 1941, Hansberry helped to recruit African-American technicians for the Ethiopian government. The result was that several African Americans served Ethiopia with distinction as teachers, journalists, aviation pilots, and technicians.

Hansberry was a founding member of the Institute of African-American Relations, whose objective was to further understanding of Africa. Located in Washington, that organization became the African American Institute, which established Africa House, a center for African student activities; Hansberry served as chairman of the center's governing council. Among the guests hosted by Africa House were Prime Minister Sylvanus Olympio of Togo, President Sékou Touré of Guinea, and Alioune Diop, director of the International Society of African Culture.

Hansberry published a number of articles on Africa, and two volumes of his lectures and essays were published after his death. Those publications confirm Hansberry's commitment to the reinterpretation of the history of African peoples. His works foreshadowed the current controversies concerning Egyptian influence on ancient Greek culture, the need for reorientation of curricula and publications to include African peoples and their cultures, and the ultimate goal of a humane approach to the study of all peoples.

Hansberry's greatest contribution was as a teacher. Students in several African and Caribbean countries recalled him as a great teacher and mentor, and one former student wrote in 1958 that he had started a "Hansberry Club" at Queens Royal College in the West Indies. Williston H. Lofton, Hansberry's colleague at Howard University, wrote: "Along with W. E. B. Du Bois and Carter G. Woodson, Hansberry probably did more than any other scholar in these early days to advance the study of the culture and civilization of Africa." His student and the first president of Nigeria, Nnamdi Azikiwe, has written: "You [Hansberry] initiated me into the sanctuaries of anthropology and ancient African history." W. E. B. Du Bois noted in *The World and Africa*: "Mr. Hansberry, a professor at Howard University, is the one modern scholar who has tried to study the Negro in Egypt and Ethiopia."

• Hansberry's family in Washington, D.C., has his papers; the Moorland-Spingarn Research Center at Howard University holds a smaller collection under his name and that of his former student William S. Steen, who also has materials in his collection at his Washington, D.C., home.

Hansberry's publications include "Sources for the Study of Ethiopian History," *Howard University Studies in History*, vol. 2 (1930), pp. 21–41; "A Negro in Anthropology," *Opportunity* 11 (1933): 147–49; "The Social History of the Negro: A Review," *Opportunity* 1 (June 1923): 20–21; "African Studies," *Phylon* 5, no. 1 (1944): 62–67; "Imperial Ethiopia in Ancient Times," *Ethiopian Review* (Addis Ababa) 1 (Sept. 1944): 14–16; "Ethiopia in the Middle Ages," *Ethiopian Review* (Addis Ababa) 1 (Oct. 1944): 15–16; "The Historical Background of African Art," introduction to an exhibition catalog for the Howard University Gallery of Art (1953), pp. 1–5; "Africa and the Western World," *Midwest Journal* 7, no. 2 (1955): 129–55; "Indigenous African Religions," in *Africa Seen by American Negro Scholars* (1958); "Ancient Kush, Old Ethiopia and the Bilad es Sudan," *Journal of Human Relations* 8 (1960): 357–87; "Africa: The World's Richest Continent," *Freedomways* 3, no. 1 (1963): 59–77; *Africana at Nsukka* (1964); "Ethiopian Ambassadors to Latin Courts and Latin Emissaries to Prestor John," *Ethiopia Observer* 9, no. 2 (1965); "W. E. B. Du Bois's Influence on African History," *Freedomways* 5, no. 1 (1965): 73–87; "Ancient African History," in *Department of History: Howard University, 1913–1973*, ed. Michael Winston (1973). Several of Hansberry's lectures and notes appeared in Joseph E. Harris, ed., *Pillars in Ethiopian History* (1974; repr. 1981) and *Africa and Africans as Seen by Classical Writers* (1977; repr. 1981).

See also Nnamdi Azikiwe, "Eulogy on William Leo Hansberry," *Negro History Bulletin* 28 (Dec. 1965): 63; Williston H. Lofton, "William Leo Hansberry: The Man and His Mission," *Freedomways* 6, no. 2 (1966): 159–62; Raymond J. Smyke, "William Leo Hansberry: Tribute to a Heretic," *Africa Report* 10, no. 10 (1965): 28–29; James Spady, "Dr. William Leo Hansberry: The Legacy of an African Hunter," *Current Bibliography on African Affairs* 3 (Nov. 1970): 25–40; and Joseph E. Harris, "The Unveiling of a Pioneer," in *A Tribute to the Memory of Professor William Leo Hansberry* (1972), pp. 33–35, and "William Leo Hansberry: Pioneer Afro-American Africanist," *Presence Africaine*, no. 110 (1979): 167–74.

JOSEPH E. HARRIS

HANSEN, Alvin Harvey (23 Aug. 1887–6 June 1975), economist, was born in Viborg, South Dakota, the son of Niels Hansen, a farmer, and Marie Bergitta Nielsen. Education allowed Hansen to escape from the farm, but he always remained a son of Viborg even as his strict Baptist upbringing evolved into a general humanism and concern for social reform. Graduating from the nearby Yankton College in 1910 with a major in English, he enrolled in the University of Wisconsin in 1913 to study economics under Richard Ely and John R. Commons, from whom he learned to use economics to address pressing social problems.

Upon completion of the coursework for the Ph.D. in 1916, Hansen married Mabel Lewis; they had two children. He taught at Brown University while writing his doctoral dissertation, "Cycles of Prosperity and Depression." Upon completion of the dissertation in 1918 (published in 1921), he moved back west to the University of Minnesota in 1919, where he rose quickly through the ranks to full professor in 1923. Subsequently, his *Business Cycle Theory* (1927) and his introductory text *Principles of Economics* (1928, with

Frederic Garver) brought him to the attention of the wider economics profession. His *Economic Stabilization in an Unbalanced World* (1932), written with the help of a Guggenheim grant that funded travel in Europe during 1928–1929, established Hansen in the broader circle of public affairs.

The Great Depression, which spelled disaster for so many, signified opportunity for Hansen. His training had prepared him for the task of applying economics to social problems, and his new-found prominence provided a platform from which to promote the solutions that seemed to him most promising. Trusting at first in the historic dynamism of the American economy to bring recovery, he favored ameliorative programs such as unemployment insurance and the new Social Security program. He did not support the price fixing of the National Recovery Act or the monetary experimentation of Franklin D. Roosevelt's first term, but his misgivings were borne of optimism, not conservatism. Hansen's idea was to ease the pain of the depression until recovery came, as it inevitably would.

The critical turning point in Hansen's life was the renewed depression in 1937, an event that forced him to reassess his faith in the inner dynamism of the American economy. The impulse toward reassessment was all the stronger because the broad economic downturn coincided with an unexpected upturn in his own fortunes, namely an invitation to occupy the new Lucius N. Littauer Chair of Political Economy at Harvard University. Characteristically, he took advantage of his new visibility at Harvard to address the new economic troubles from an even broader standpoint. His first book at Harvard posed the question *Full Recovery or Stagnation?* (1938), and his subsequent presidential address to the American Economics Association (Dec. 1938; published in 1939) sketched the outlines of what came to be called the "secular stagnation thesis."

Hansen argued that the depression was not the trough of a particularly severe business cycle but a symptom of the exhaustion of a longer-term progressive dynamic. In his 1939 testimony to the Temporary National Economic Committee, he wrote: "In this generation we are passing over a divide which separates the great era of the growth and expansion of the nineteenth century from an era we can not as yet characterize with clarity and precision" (p. 341).

Hansen's diagnosis, it is important to emphasize, was not so much one of failure as it was one of completion. Furthermore, completion was not just an end but also an opportunity for a new beginning. Even after a decade of depression, Hansen remained optimistic, no longer about the natural dynamism of the market economy of the past but rather about the dynamic potential of the "dual economy" of the future, an economy part private and part public. He was excited about possibilities of an economy in which the government would play the new role of "investment banker."

What Hansen had in mind was not just countercyclical public spending to stabilize employment but rather major projects such as rural electrification, slum clearance, and natural resource development and conservation, all with a view to opening up new investment opportunities for the private sector and so restoring economic dynamism to the system as a whole. The interruption of World War II meant that all such plans were put on hold and were presented ultimately as part of an even larger plan for postwar reconstruction and development. For Hansen, the importance of the Bretton Woods agreement of 1944 and the Employment Act of 1946 was that they put into place the international and domestic machinery that would enable government to play the new role history demanded. His *America's Role in the World Economy* (1945) and *Economic Policy and Full Employment* (1947) made this case to a wider public.

Hansen's intellectual crisis in 1937 led him to conclude not only that the economy needed a new engine of development but also that it needed a new language or economic theory that would help make sense of the new direction. For this latter purpose, he ultimately concluded that John Maynard Keynes's *General Theory of Employment, Interest, and Money* (1936) was the right book at the right time, and he took the lead as an interpreter and advocate of the Keynesian message in his 1941 text, *Fiscal Policy and Business Cycles*, which grew out of his famous fiscal policy seminar at Harvard. Hansen's appointment as special economic adviser to Marriner Eccles at the Federal Reserve Board (1940–1945) provided a platform within the government that he used to spread the new thinking. After the war, given the successful establishment of the new institutional framework for economic management, he focused his attention more narrowly on the problem of establishing the corresponding new intellectual framework in his *Monetary Theory and Fiscal Policy* (1949), *Business Cycles and National Income* (1951), and *A Guide to Keynes* (1953).

Hansen's postwar proselytizing on behalf of his version of Keynesianism made him appear to many as simply a popularizer of Keynes, but he was much more as well, because the version he promoted was as much Hansen as it was Keynes. Hansen was not just a popularizer but also a founder of American Keynesianism. For him, economics was always about solving social problems, and if his Keynesianism had a distinct American flavor it was because the problems he was interested in solving were American problems. After retiring from active teaching in 1956, he wrote *The American Economy* (1957), *Economic Issues of the 1960s* (1960), *The Postwar American Economy: Performance and Problems* (1964), and *The Dollar and the International Monetary System* (1965).

In the dark time of depression and war, Hansen saw a bright future, and he lived to see much of that future come to pass. A child of the prairies, he brought the pioneer's optimism to Washington, D.C. He died in Alexandria, Virginia.

• Hansen's papers are in the Pusey Library at Harvard University. Scholarship on him includes William Barber, "The Career of Alvin H. Hansen in the 1920s and 1930s: A study of Intellectual Transformation," *History of Political Economy* 19, no. 2 (1987), and Perry Mehrling, *The Money Interest and the Public Interest* (1997). The latter includes a complete bibliography of Hansen's writings. Richard L. Strout, "Hansen of Harvard," *New Republic*, 29 Dec. 1941, is the best account of Hansen as he appeared in public. A useful account of Hansen by Seymour Harris, his contemporary founder of American Keynesianism, may be found in the *International Encyclopedia of the Social Sciences*, vol. 6 (1968). See also the valuable memoirs by his students and colleagues in *Quarterly Journal of Economics* 90, no. 1 (Feb. 1976).

PERRY G. MEHRLING

HANSEN, Marcus Lee (8 Dec. 1892–11 May 1938), foremost immigration historian of his era, was born in Neenah, Wisconsin, the son of Rev. Marcus Hansen, a Baptist clergyman, and Gina Lee. His father was born in Denmark and his mother in Norway; both parents emigrated in 1871 while they were still children. Hansen's father had been raised in the Lutheran state church in Denmark, then converted to the Baptist faith. Young Marcus moved frequently with his family as his father traveled to establish new churches in Wisconsin, Illinois, Iowa, Michigan, and Minnesota.

Hansen began his higher education at Central College in Pella, Iowa. He spent two years there before transferring to the University of Iowa, where he went on to receive his bachelor's degree in 1916 and his master's degree a year later. His graduate study in history was undertaken at Harvard University, where he worked under the guidance of Frederick Jackson Turner. At this time he began his studies of the Atlantic migration to North America. He received his Ph.D. in 1924. Hansen's unpublished dissertation examined the migration of continental Europeans, particularly Germans, during the mid-nineteenth century.

Hansen's first academic appointment was at Smith College, where he was an assistant professor for two years. His research took him to Europe twice in the 1920s, the first trip taking place during the summer of 1922. As a Social Science Research Council fellow, he spent the two years between 1925 and 1927 in Europe. During these visits, he spent time in Britain, France, and Central Europe. These trips were major data gathering missions, during which he made extensive use of archival holdings pertaining to emigration from Europe. By focusing attention on the European context of migration, Hansen provided compelling evidence for the centrality of economic factors in causing emigration. Upon his return in 1927, Hansen was employed by the American Council of Learned Societies for two years. His work during this period used various data sources, including the first federal census, in order to provide information to the government on the national origins of the American people in 1790. This information was used by the government to determine immigration quotas based on national origin for the restrictive immigration act passed in 1924.

Hansen returned to academe in 1928, when he was hired by the University of Illinois as an associate professor. He was promoted to full professor in 1930 and remained at that institution for the rest of his career. During his years at the university, Hansen also continued to be involved with the ACLS, working on its linguistic atlas of North America. He continued work on his major studies of the Atlantic migration to the United States, and he began a comparative study of immigration into the United States and Canada in collaboration with J. B. Brebner. He returned to Europe in 1934–1935, delivering the Commonwealth Fund Lectures at the University of London. While this trip was again research oriented, it also had a personal dimension, as Hansen made a journey to Denmark. His visit to the remote village of Snode connected him to the world of his ancestors and may have played a role in his later thinking about the future of ethnicity in America.

The major focus of his scholarship was confined to the years between the colonial era and the Civil War. His work did not deal with the great migration that began after 1880. The two books that established Hansen as a major contributor to immigration history, *The Immigrant in American History* (1940) and *The Atlantic Migration, 1607–1860* (1940), were published posthumously by Arthur Schlesinger, Sr. The latter received the 1941 Pulitzer Prize in history. J. B. Brebner finished Hansen's comparative work on Canadian and American immigration, publishing it as a coauthored work, *The Mingling of the Canadian and American Peoples* (1940). These books confirmed sociologist Nathan Glazer's assessment of Hansen as "the greatest student of American immigration." This assessment was echoed by immigration historian Moses Rischin, who characterized Hansen as "America's first transethnic historian."

Hansen conducted his work during a time when ethnicity remained a neglected topic in American historiography. He was one of a relatively small cadre of scholars who, between the world wars, devoted their scholarly energies to this topic. Among his associates in this field were Carl F. Wittke, George M. Stephenson, and Theodore C. Blegen. Hansen emerged as the most important figure to legitimize and promote the study of the role played by immigration and ethnicity throughout American history. However, it is not as clear that his work had a direct and pronounced impact on later developments in immigration history. The efflorescence of immigration and ethnic studies since the 1960s was shaped by larger developments in social history that were characterized by an attempt to utilize sociological concepts and methods in the study of history. The focus turned to the analysis of collectivities rather than individuals, and when it did so it departed from the approach advanced by Hansen.

Some scholars have found his work to be problematic for several reasons. His emphasis on push factors came at the expense of an equally detailed analysis of pull factors, and his concentration on the individual immigrant lead to a concomitant neglect of the ethnic community. He tended to pay little attention to noneconomic factors underlying migration, especially political ones. He seemed more comfortable speaking about immigrants on the farmlands of the Midwest rather than in the burgeoning cities of the East Coast. Some commentators have viewed his work as overly Eurocentric. His concern with the Atlantic migration meant that Asian and Latin American immigrants were ignored. More importantly for the particular time frame of his work, he tended to ignore that other major part of the Atlantic migration, the slave trade. Indeed, while the individual European is portrayed as an actor in history, blacks are essentially treated as a backdrop to that history.

Near the end of his life Hansen gave two speeches that dealt with the future of ethnicity in America. The first is the oft-cited "The Problem of the Third Generation Immigrant." This speech was presented to the members of the Augustana Historical Society in 1937, and while it was primarily a call for historical inquiry into the immigrant generation, Hansen formulated a way of looking at the theme of generations as a sociohistorical problem in the study of ethnicity. His formulation of "the principle of third generation interest" argues against both a straight-line assimilationist view and the cultural pluralist alternative in contending that "what the son wishes to forget, the grandson wishes to remember." Hansen seemed to dispute the claim of the former that ethnicity would inevitably erode with each succeeding generation, ultimately to vanish from American social life, while at the same time disagreeing with the latter thesis, which attributes a tenacious immutability to ethnicity. When Oscar Handlin republished this essay in 1952, it gained a wide audience and since that time has become an important starting point in considering the possible futures of ethnic identity in America. It has stimulated both theoretical development and empirical research.

Ten days after his speech at Augustana College, Hansen addressed the National Conference of Social Work with a speech entitled "Who Shall Inherit America?" Hansen went beyond the previous speech by addressing the matter of potential impacts that the multiplicity of ethnic cultures in America might have on the nation's cultural identity. Unfortunately, as the first major fruits of his career came to maturation, Hansen died of chronic nephritis in Redlands, California, where he was staying while on sabbatical leave. Having remained a bachelor, he left no immediate survivors other than his brothers and sisters.

• Hansen's papers are at the Harvard University Library. In addition to Hansen's major books cited in the text, he was the author of several articles, including "The Settlement of New England," in *Handbook of the Linguistic Geography of New England*, ed. Hans Kurath (1939). No full-length biography of Hansen has been written. Information on his life is relatively scant and can be derived from only a few sources, the most important being a memoir by his brother, C. Frederick Hansen, entitled "Marcus Lee Hansen—Historian of Migration," *Common Ground* 2 (1942): 87–94; John Christianson, "Marcus Lee Hansen Returns to His Roots," *Bridge* 10 (1987): 67–81, describes Hansen's trip to Denmark and contains letters he wrote to his family. Assessments of his work are contained in Moses Rischin, "Marcus Lee Hansen: America's First Transethnic Historian," in *Uprooted Americans*, ed. Richard Bushman et al. (1979); Alan H. Spear, "Marcus Lee Hansen and the Historiography of Immigration," *Wisconsin Magazine of History* 44 (1961): 258–68; and Carlton C. Qualey, "Marcus Lee Hansen," *Midcontinent American Studies Journal* 8 (1967): 18–25. The most thorough analysis of Hansen's third generation thesis is contained in Peter Kivisto and Dag Blanck, eds., *American Immigrants and Their Generations* (1990), a collection of essays. This volume contains a republication of "The Problem of the Third Generation Immigrant" and the only published version of "Who Shall Inherit America?" Obituaries appear in the *New York Times*, 12 May 1938, and in the *American Historical Review* 43 (1938): 976–77.

PETER KIVISTO

HANSEN, Niels Ebbesen (4 Jan. 1866–5 Oct. 1950), horticulturalist and plant explorer, was born near Ribe, Denmark, the son of Andreas Hansen, a mural designer and altar painter, and Bodil Midtgaard, who died when he was an infant. After remarrying, his father immigrated to the United States in 1872, and the following year Niels, along with his stepmother and his two sisters, joined the father in New York. Two years later the family moved to Des Moines, Iowa, where Niels attended public school, completing the first eight grades in five years. A precocious student, he finished the last two years of high school through a personal course of study with Iowa Secretary of State John A. Hull while working in his office. He graduated from Iowa Agricultural College (predecessor of Iowa State University) in 1887. After working for four years in private nurseries, he returned to the college as an assistant professor and completed the requirements for a master of science degree in botany and horticulture there in 1895.

That same year Hansen accepted appointment as professor of horticulture at South Dakota Agricultural College (later South Dakota State University) in Brookings, where he spent his entire 42-year career as a teacher and researcher. In 1898 he married Emma Elise Pammel, the youngest sister of his former mentor, Louis H. Pammel, head of the botany department at Ames, Iowa. She died in 1904 while they were expecting their third child. Three years later Hansen married her sister Dora; they had no children. The family participated in the activities of the Episcopal church and other community affairs in Brookings. Hansen loved to dance and acquired considerable expertise in Indian culture. In his later years he became an inveterate moviegoer.

Hansen's reputation as a scientist was established when he became the first plant explorer sent out by the U.S. Department of Agriculture to seek plant materials in foreign countries that could be successfully adapted to environments present in the North American environment. South Dakota's northern latitude made it desirable to develop hardy plant varieties that could withstand its harsh climatic conditions. Hansen's first trip, to Russia, came in 1894. In 1897 Secretary of Agriculture James ("Tama Jim") Wilson, who had earlier worked with Hansen when the two were together at Iowa State, sent Hansen on a ten-month excursion under the auspices of the newly created Section of Seed and Plant Introduction. In search of forage crops and other hardy plants that could flourish on the inhospitable northern plains, Hansen traveled mainly through Turkestan, Siberia, and northern China. His special interest on this trip was alfalfa. On this trip he also obtained his first examples of crested wheat grass, which ultimately became his most important plant exploration contribution. The Department of Agriculture sent him back on two more exploring trips to Europe, Asia, and Africa—for six months in 1906 and for nine months in 1908–1909. The first trip netted the famous Cossack alfalfa, along with more than 300 lots of seeds and plants for further experimentation. On the second, he obtained the seeds of two yellow-flowered alfalfas and a number of other cultivars.

Back home in Brookings, Hansen continued his teaching and his work in developing new forage crops, fruits, shrubs, and flowers. He effectively publicized his travels and discoveries through seminars, demonstrations, papers, reports, and other means. These activities also were instrumental in soliciting funds for further trips and research. The South Dakota legislature appropriated $10,000 in 1913 for another trip to Russia. This five-month foray resulted not only in plant samples but also in several Siberian fat-rumped, tailless sheep, which were used in experiments back in Brookings. It was another eleven years before the legislature sponsored him on a three-month expedition in 1924. Among the plants Hansen obtained in China this time were hardy pears. Six years later, while attending the International Horticultural and Botanical Congresses, he took the opportunity to tour several countries in western Europe. His last overseas trip came in 1934 at the invitation of the Soviet Union to attend a celebration sponsored by the Lenin Academy of Agricultural Sciences.

While establishing his reputation as a plant explorer for the U.S. government and for the state of South Dakota, Hansen discovered, experimented with, and improved hundreds of different plant cultivars in an effort to improve horticulture on the northern plains. Many of the varieties he discovered or developed were sold through seed catalogs sent out by the Gurney Nursery in Yankton, South Dakota, and by other companies. Among his contributions were the Dolgo crab apple and Anoka apple; the South Dakota plum as well as the Tecumseh, the Sapa, and the Kaga plums; bush cherries; Tartarian honeysuckle; the Siberian pea shrub, or Caragana; the Hopa Flowering crab; hedge roses; and the Manchu apricot. In addition to traveling, teaching, and directing the Agricultural Experiment Station, he published numerous horticultural bulletins and papers. He served for thirty-three years as secretary of the South Dakota Horticultural Society beginning in 1895 and then three years as president before becoming president emeritus of the organization. Hansen died in Brook-

ings. Known as the "Burbank of the Plains" (after Luther Burbank, perhaps the best-known horticulturalist in the United States), he helped transform the ecology of a major physiographic region of North America.

• The standard biography is Mrs. H. J. Taylor, *To Plant the Prairies and the Plains: The Life and Work of Niels Ebbesen Hansen* (1941). See also Arnold Nicholson, "Burbank of the Plains," *Country Gentleman*, Dec. 1940, pp. 11, 54–55; John E. Miller, "Eminent Horticulturalist: Niels Ebbesen Hansen," in *South Dakota Leaders: From Pierre Chouteau, Jr., to Oscar Howe*, ed. Herbert T. Hoover and Larry J. Zimmerman (1989).

JOHN MILLER

HANSEN, William Webster (27 May 1909–23 May 1949), physicist, was born in Fresno, California, the son of William George Hansen, a hardware merchant, and Laura Louise Gillogly. He studied for an additional year beyond graduation at Fresno Technical High School before beginning his studies as a sixteen-year-old freshman at Stanford University. Employment as an undergraduate research assistant in Stanford's physics department shifted Hansen's interests from engineering to physics. He received a bachelor's degree in 1929 and a Ph.D. in physics from Stanford in January 1933.

As an undergraduate, Hansen had learned the techniques of experimental X-ray physics, most importantly how to accelerate and manipulate streams of electrons. (X-rays are produced by the sudden halt of negatively charged particles when they collide with matter.) Stanford's physicists hoped to explore the physics of the atom by producing electrons of very high speeds and running them into targets of dense material. In response to these collisions, the target would emit an X-ray spectrum, which provided information about the structure of its constituent atoms. The work continued through Hansen's graduate training, and he emerged an accomplished experimentalist.

Hansen's thesis work, "Probabilities of K-electron Ionization of Silver by Cathode Rays," appeared in print in 1933 (*Physical Review* 43:839). His mathematical skills were sharpened during a National Research Council postdoctoral fellowship at the Massachusetts Institute of Technology and the University of Michigan, where he learned to analyze electromagnetic fields and their interactions with charged particles. Returning to Stanford as an assistant professor of physics in 1934, Hansen became a part of the department's plans to move into experimental nuclear physics.

Theoretician Felix Bloch arrived at Stanford that same year and later wrote in Hansen's National Academy of Sciences memoir that "knowing his strength, [Hansen] chose at that time the path which led him to become the applied physicist 'par excellence.'" That strength was Hansen's ability to understand the behavior of electrons as they were manipulated in laboratory equipment. The failure of more elaborate plans left Hansen free in 1936 and 1937 to pursue a low-budget scheme for accelerating electrons: a resonating chamber, fabricated of electrically conducting metal sheets, sized to speed up electrons in somewhat the same way as a bell amplifies a tone of a particular pitch. Hansen's device was called, in recognition of its rhythmic power, the "rhumbatron."

Its most important application came as part of a 1937 invention, the klystron, which could produce, detect, and amplify microwaves—that is, radar signals—as a contemporary vacuum tube did radio waves. Invented by Russell and Sigard Varian, two researchers affiliated with the Stanford physics department, developing and applying the device drew Stanford's physicists into a technological development effort, led by the department chair and with Hansen's participation. The klystron project was a group effort to produce a practical device to aid pilots' eyesight in darkness and bad weather, especially during landings and when navigating in mountainous terrain, and for aircraft detection.

The Sperry Gyroscope Company offered to sponsor klystron research at Stanford, recognizing that the new technology represented a source of potential competition to their interests in searchlights and aircraft instrumentation. Indeed, as it was developed throughout World War II, microwave radar transformed aviation. In 1937 Hansen was promoted to associate professor and the following year married Betsy Ann Ross, the daughter of a Stanford physics professor. Their only child died in infancy.

Radar work based on the klystron claimed Hansen's attention until the end of World War II. Early in 1941 Sperry moved the Stanford research group to a Long Island factory. There Hansen redoubled his efforts in microwave research and commuted to the MIT Radiation Laboratory in Cambridge, where he introduced neophyte researchers to microwave physics. He consulted for three months on the Manhattan Project, the Allied effort to build the atomic bomb. This proved to be a killing schedule for Hansen; the long hours of work and travel, and perhaps exposure to beryllium fragments during his stint on the Manhattan Project, aggravated a preexisting lung condition. Hansen was awarded the Morris N. Liebmann Prize of the Institute of Radio Engineers in 1945 for his work in microwave engineering and a Presidential Certificate of Merit in 1948 for his wartime service.

Hansen returned to Stanford in August 1945, having been promoted to full professor during his absence. He planned to use the university's accumulated klystron royalties to set up a microwave laboratory, where physicists and engineers would investigate microwave physics and its technological applications. The laboratory eventually became a division of the William W. Hansen Laboratories at Stanford. The Hansen Labs' other division, the High Energy Physics Laboratory, operated a series of klystron-powered linear electron accelerators, based on Hansen's postwar designs. Hansen also contributed to Bloch's postwar project, an investigation of the properties of the nucleus, which led to Bloch's 1952 Nobel Prize in physics

and to magnetic resonance imaging techniques for medical diagnosis.

Despite his failing health, Hansen headed a group that designed and tested model particle accelerators with the support of the Office of Naval Research. By the spring of 1947 the group had learned to build a long pipe with inside surfaces shaped so that electrical fields within the tube accelerated electrons as they passed down it. Required to file a progress report with his navy sponsors, Hansen sent four words to Washington: "We have accelerated electrons." The navy responded with funding for a 220-foot-long atom smasher. Up until he was hospitalized, Hansen continued to work on prototype accelerators, at times wearing an oxygen mask. He died in Palo Alto, California, four days before his fortieth birthday.

Hansen came of age as a physicist during a period when the discipline's most recondite aspects began to depend on increasingly complex and expensive technology, and at the same time came to promise basic knowledge that could lead to vital military and commercial technology. His work as an applied physicist, inspired by the challenges of experimental X-ray and nuclear physics, lay the instrumental groundwork for some of the basic elements of microwave technology and introduced into nuclear physics research the use of linear electron accelerators—including the two-mile long Stanford Linear Accelerator.

• Hansen's work on X-ray physics in the 1920s and 1930s is summarized in Arthur H. Compton and Samuel K. Allison, *X-Rays in Theory and Experiment* (1935). The most complete memorial, by his Stanford colleague, is Felix Bloch, "William Webster Hansen, 1909–1949," National Academy of Sciences, *Biographical Memoirs* 27 (1952): 121–37, which includes a bibliography of Hansen's twenty-nine papers and sixteen technical reports. Hansen's relationship with the Varian brothers, the invention of the klystron, and its development are described in Dorothy Varian, *The Inventor and the Pilot* (1983), and in Edward L. Ginzton, "The $100 Idea," *IEEE Spectrum* 12, no. 2 (Feb. 1975): 30–39. For Hansen's role in the rise of Stanford University and its physics program, see Stuart W. Leslie and Bruce Hevly, "Steeple Building at Stanford: Electrical Engineering, Physics, and Microwave Research," *Proceedings of the IEEE* 73 (1985): 1160–80; Leslie, "Playing the Education Game to Win: The Military and Interdisciplinary Research at Stanford," *Historical Studies in the Physical and Biological Sciences* 18 (1987): 55–88; Rebecca Lowen, "Transforming the University: Administrators, Physicists, and Industrial and Federal Patronage at Stanford, 1935–1949," *History of Education Quarterly* 31 (1991): 365–88; Peter Galison et al., "Controlling the Monster: Stanford and the Growth of Physics Research, 1935–1962," in *Big Science: The Growth of Large-Scale Research*, ed. Galison and Hevly (1992); and Leslie, *The Cold War and American Science: The Military-Industrial-Academic Complex at MIT and Stanford* (1993).

BRUCE HEVLY

HANSON, Alexander Contee (22 Oct. 1749–16 Jan. 1806), lawyer, jurist, and Federalist essayist, was born in Annapolis, Maryland, the son of John Hanson, a continental congressman and first president of the Continental Congress under the Articles of Confederation, and Jane Contee. Hanson was reared in Annapolis and educated at the College of Philadelphia. College records do not indicate that he received a degree. Upon leaving Philadelphia, Hanson returned to Annapolis, where he studied law, and was admitted to practice by the Maryland bar in 1772. By early 1776 he had pledged himself to the revolutionary effort, and in June of that year he became assistant secretary to General George Washington. Poor health, however, compelled Hanson to resign within six months. He returned to Annapolis and resumed his legal practice.

On 9 March 1778 Hanson was appointed to Maryland's general court, a position he held until 1789. On the bench he remained an ardent patriot; on one occasion he dealt so severely with Loyalists convicted of planning the escape of British prisoners of war (he sentenced them to death and dismemberment) that the Maryland legislature moved to limit the punishment courts could impose in such cases. In 1778 Hanson married Rebecca Howard. Their three children included son Alexander Contee Hanson, whose Federalist newspaper sparked the infamous Baltimore Riot of 1812, and with whom the senior Hanson is often confused.

In February 1784 Hanson published *Political Schemes and Calculations*, in which he argued for increased cooperation between states, stronger government, and the consolidation of Maryland's debts. It was the first in a series of essays that ultimately garnered him a reputation as one of the most influential figures in Maryland politics and perhaps the most articulate champion of Federalism. In March 1786 Hanson published *Considerations on the Proposed Removal of the Seat of Government*, through which he successfully challenged the efforts of Antifederalists Luther Martin, William Paca, and Samuel Chase to remove Maryland's seat of government to Baltimore.

In the years following the Revolution, scarcity of specie and general financial hardship swept across Maryland, prompting many hard-pressed debtors to petition for the emission of treasury-backed state currency (or bills of credit). In February 1787 Hanson, writing under the pseudonym "Aristides," led the fight against the issuance of paper money with his fiery tract *Remarks on the Proposed Plan for an Emission of Paper; and the Means of Effecting It*. Because bills of credit, unlike specie, were not by their nature valuable, Hanson reasoned that people could not be made to construe them as such. Paper money, he argued, benefited speculators and debtors but would ultimately destroy all confidence between private traders and between nations; thus, paper money would destroy American commerce. Only by renouncing the right to issue paper money, he concluded, could public and private confidence and credit be restored.

In April 1787 "Aristides" (Hanson) began an exchange of essays with his Antifederalist nemesis, "Publicola" (William Paca). Carried in Baltimore and Annapolis newspapers, the debate focused on the role of the individual in representative government and stemmed from assertions made in Hanson's *Emission*

of Paper. Representatives, he argued, as trustees of the citizenry, are bound to act in the interest of all. They must be permitted to legislate without interference from the general public. He wrote, "If the people shall take it upon themselves to decide nice questions of policy by a majority of their voices, they may frequently be wrought upon to choose things which will injure them the most."

In December 1787 Hanson, again under the pseudonym "Aristides," published his most memorable work. In *Remarks on the Proposed Plan of a Federal Government*, he defended the proposed Constitution with an argument similar to that offered New York newspaper readers by Alexander Hamilton, James Madison, and John Jay. "No man of sense or honesty," he contended, could deny that the future of the United States depended upon the creation of a form of government other than that provided by the Articles of Confederation. But the fear of creating a government with too much power made the people reluctant to act. Although the Constitution would greatly enhance the authority of the national government, Hanson continued, it also included an elaborate system of checks and balances to preclude the abuse of power. Furthermore, the safeguards existing within the instrument itself rendered unnecessary the addition of a bill of rights. The only powers enjoyed by the government were those expressly granted by the people, and those expressly set forth in the document. Thus, it was unnecessary to list the rights retained by the people. Moreover, he added, "the restraints laid on the state legislatures will tend to secure domestic tranquility, more than all the bills, or declarations, of rights, which human policy could devise."

Hanson continued his legal endeavors while remaining involved in political activities, and in 1787 he completed his digest of the *Laws of Maryland Made since MDCCLXIII*, often referred to as *Hanson's Laws*. In April 1788 Hanson was among those who represented Annapolis at the state convention to ratify the proposed Constitution. Later that year and again in 1792 he served as a presidential elector for Maryland. In 1789 Hanson was offered a U.S. district judgeship by George Washington but declined the appointment. On 3 October 1789 he accepted an appointment as chancellor of Maryland, a position he held until his death. Also in 1789 Hanson was appointed to prepare a digest of the testamentary laws of the state.

In 1803 Hanson returned to pamphleteering in the state political arena. Under the pseudonym "A Civil Officer of Maryland," Hanson produced *Publications Relative to the Difference of Opinion between the Governor and the Council of Maryland on Their Respective Powers*. That same year he was one of three prominent Annapolis residents commissioned by St. John's College to write a defense of that institution against accusations from those who sought its ruin.

During his lifetime, Hanson was known principally for his service on the general court and as chancellor of Maryland, and for compiling state laws. He is best remembered, though, for his work as "Aristides," shaping the course of state and national government as a strident Federalist and influential essayist. Hanson died of a stroke in Annapolis.

• Alexander Contee Hanson's principal writings are bound in a volume titled *Hanson Pamphlets*, in the rare book collection of the Maryland Historical Society. The work, which is annotated by the author, also includes Hanson's *Address of the Visitors and Governors of St. John's College, to the Senate of Maryland*. Hanson's *Remarks on the Proposed Plan of Federal Government* is reprinted in *Magazine of History* 47 (1933), and in Paul L. Ford, ed., *Pamphlets on the Constitution of the United States* (1888). The essays exchanged between Hanson and Paca, along with excerpts of other Hanson works, are reprinted in Melvin Yazawa, ed., *Representative Government and the Revolution, the Maryland Constitutional Crisis of 1787* (1975). Useful biographical sources include George A. Hanson, *Old Kent* (1876); Elihu S. Riley, *The Ancient City: A History of Annapolis in Maryland* (1887); Matthew P. Andrews et al., *Tercentenary History of Maryland* (4 vols., 1925); and G. M. Brumbaugh, *Maryland Records* (1928). The dates of Hanson's tenure on the bench are noted in Harris and McHenry, eds., *Maryland Reports*, vol. 2 (1812). Brief mention of Hanson is made throughout the *Archives of Maryland* and in *The Writings of George Washington*, vol. 5, ed. John C. Fitzpatrick (1932). Other useful sources include Edward C. Papenfuse, *In Pursuit of Profit: The Annapolis Merchants in the Era of the American Revolution, 1763–1805* (1975); Philip A. Crowl, *Maryland during and after the Revolution* (1943); and L. Marx Renzulli, Jr., *Maryland, the Federalist Years* (1972). Hanson's obituary is in the *Federal Gazette & Baltimore Daily Advertiser*, 18 Jan. 1806.

KEVIN R. CHANEY

HANSON, Alexander Contee (27 Feb. 1786–23 Apr. 1819), lawyer, newspaper editor, and U.S. representative and senator, was born in Annapolis, Maryland, the son of Alexander Contee Hanson, a jurist and legislator, and Rebecca Howard. After graduating from St. John's College in 1802, he practiced law in Annapolis, married Priscilla Dorsey, the daughter of a prominent planter, in 1805, and established his home, "Belmont," near Elkridge. The couple probably had six children, three of whom survived until adulthood. In 1808 he founded the *Federal Republican*, a Federalist newspaper in Republican-dominated Baltimore, and hired Jacob Wagner, a well-known hater of Thomas Jefferson and James Madison, as editor in chief. Hanson believed that the Republicans deliberately sought war with Great Britain. The bitter opposition to the war expressed in the *Federal Republican* resulted in threats against the paper, its editor, and proprietor.

This controversy surrounding freedom of the press not only launched Hanson's political career but pinned the nickname "mobtown" on antebellum Baltimore. It eventually led to Hanson's death at age thirty-three. On Saturday, 20 June 1812, the newspaper attacked both the war and President Madison, characterizing him as a tool of Napoleon Bonaparte. On 22 June a mob attacked the newspaper's office, tearing down walls and demolishing the press. During the next month Hanson moved his printing operations to Georgetown, District of Columbia, but rented a house in Baltimore for distribution; on Tuesday, 27

July, the paper attacked the city government for siding with the rioters. That night a mob smashed the doors and windows of the house. Armed with muskets, the beleaguered Hanson, along with twenty friends and employees, fired on the attackers, killing one man. Local militia under General John Stricker and municipal authorities headed by Republican mayor Edward Johnson then intervened, and the defenders submitted themselves to the law. For protection they were lodged in the city jail. When the mob appeared to disperse, the militia were dismissed. But that evening the mob stormed the jail, attacking and torturing some of the Federalists. Hanson was beaten into unconsciousness but escaped with help from one of the mob and resumed publication of his paper in August. However, General Henry "Light Horse Harry" Lee was crippled for life, and General James M. Lingan was murdered. When brought to trial, the mob leaders were acquitted.

Public outrage at these events resulted in Hanson being elected to the House of Representatives in the fall. In 1816 he resigned to run for Maryland's House of Delegates but was defeated. The Federalist-dominated state legislature then appointed him U.S. senator in place of Robert Goodloe Harper, who had resigned in December 1816, but ill health, stemming from his beating, caused his attendance to be sporadic until his death at Belmont.

• The Maryland Historical Society has several collections containing Hanson papers: the Hanson Family Papers; the Harper-Pennington Papers; the Robert Goodloe Harper Papers; and the Dorsey-Hanson Papers. Information about the Hanson riots may be found in *Report of the Committee of Grievances . . . on the Subject of the Recent Riots in the City of Baltimore, Together with the Depositions Taken for the Committee* (1813); *Interesting Papers Relative to the Recent Riots at Baltimore* (1812); the *Federal Republican*, June–Aug. 1812; Joseph Herman Schauinger, "Alexander Contee Hanson, Federalist Partisan," *Maryland Historical Magazine* 35 (Winter 1940): 354–88; Frank A. Cassell, "The Great Baltimore Riot of 1812," *Maryland Historical Magazine* 70 (Winter 1975): 241–59; Donald R. Hickey, "The Darker Side of Democracy: The Baltimore Riots of 1812," *Maryland Historian* 7 (1976): 1–20; Paul A. Gilje, "The Baltimore Riots of 1812 and the Breakdown of the Anglo-American Mob Tradition," *Journal of Social History* 13 (Winter 1980): 547–64; and Gilje, "'Le Menu Peuple' in America: Identifying the Mob in the Baltimore Riots of 1812," *Maryland Historical Magazine* 81 (Spring 1986): 50–66. A notice of his death appeared in the *Baltimore Patriot and Mercantile Advertiser*, 24 Apr. 1819.

GARY L. BROWNE

HANSON, Howard Harold (28 Oct. 1896–26 Feb. 1981), composer, was born in Wahoo, Nebraska, the son of Hilma Eckstrom and Hans Hanson. He was educated in the public schools of Wahoo and given lessons in piano and violoncello. At Luther College he began seriously to compose under the tutelage of A. O. Andersen, after which he briefly attended the University of Nebraska at Lincoln. He received his diploma (1914) from the Institute of Musical Art in New York, as a pupil of Percy Goetschius and James Friskin. Returning to the Midwest, he attended Northwestern University to study with Arne Oldberg and Peter Lutkin, receiving his A.B. degree in 1916.

At age nineteen Hanson began teaching at the College of the Pacific in Stockton, California, becoming dean of the Conservatory of Fine Arts in 1919. There he wrote his pageant, *California Forest Play of 1920*, for voices, dancers, and orchestra, for the Redwood Park Festival. For this composition he was awarded the first American Prix de Rome, with which he studied at the American Academy (1921–1924) in Rome.

Hanson completed his first symphony, *The Nordic*, in 1923 in Rome and his symphonic poem, *North and West*, with which he toured Europe as composer-conductor. Extending his tour to America, he led the Rochester (N.Y.) Philharmonic Orchestra in *The Nordic* (fall 1923), which so impressed President Rush Rhees of the University of Rochester and industrialist-philanthropist George Eastman that they offered him the directorship of the Eastman School of Music of the university. Immediately upon taking office in September 1924, Hanson began his twofold program of coordinating professional music training with humanistic studies and of championing the cause of American music.

In 1925 Hanson conducted the first of his many American Composers Concerts. Several years later (1931) he initiated a second series of programs for the performance of both contemporary and historic works: the Annual Festivals of American Music, which continued through 1971.

While the programs of the American Composers Concerts were more or less informal, taking place at various times of the academic year, the festivals were a series of six or seven formal concerts given during the spring term. Music was performed by the advanced students and faculty of the Eastman School and by the professional Eastman-Rochester Symphony Orchestra. American composers from many parts of the country attended the rehearsals and concerts and were available to speak to the students. By the end of the forty-year sequence of festivals, the total repertoire consisted of well over a thousand works by more than five hundred writers. A number of chosen pieces were recorded commercially and broadcast over national networks. Hanson earned the title "Protagonist of American Music."

As director of the Eastman School Hanson conducted the Symposia of Student Compositions from 1927 to 1964. Among them were early pieces by Robert Ward, Peter Mennin, Jack Beeson, Gardner Read, Emma Lou Diemer, and Mary Jeanne VanAppledorn.

Hanson also used the radio as a medium for the dissemination of music. From the 1930s through the 1950s, weekly broadcasts featured music from Eastman. Some programs followed a historical sequence ("Milestone in the History of Music") while others featured miscellaneous recitals.

As a conductor Hanson concentrated on developing vocal and instrumental ensembles within the Eastman School that were composed of performers capable of sight-reading and performing contemporary music as well as the masterpieces of the past. There were usually at least two student orchestras of symphonic proportions, the Senior Symphony or the Philharmonia being the most advanced.

In an imaginative and creative effort to adapt curricula to the demands of contemporary education, Hanson designed the doctor of musical arts (D.M.A. or A.M.D.) degree. During the 1950s new collegiate departments and schools of music were being created to accommodate the thousands of World War II veterans returning to complete their education on the G.I. Bill of Rights. Hanson saw the need for a doctorate other than the Ph.D. for aspiring collegiate teachers and administrators. The D.M.A., designed for performers and composers, demanded neither stringent foreign-language requirements nor scholarly dissertation but rather a high degree of performance and the practical application of musical training. The first Eastman D.M.A. was awarded in 1955. Although for a few years a number of educators opposed the new doctorate, by 1960 most major schools of music were offering both the D.M.A. and the Ph.D., the latter to theorists and musicologists.

In addition to his many educational activities, Hanson was able to fulfill a number of composition commissions. His most outstanding works are his seven symphonies, miscellaneous pieces for orchestra, and choral music.

His best-known work is his second symphony, the *Romantic*, commissioned for the fiftieth anniversary season of the Boston Symphony Orchestra under Serge Koussevitzky, who conducted the premiere on 28 November 1930. Popular because of its lovely themes and rich orchestration, it had great public appeal.

Hanson made sketches for his third symphony, written on commission by the Columbia Broadcasting System, in 1936. The first three movements were broadcast in September 1937, while the complete four-movement opus was aired the following March. Koussevitzky and the Boston Symphony gave the first public performance in March 1939. Closely related to the *The Nordic* in intent, this symphony is a tribute to the Swedish settlement on the Delaware, founded in 1638.

The Requiem, Hanson's fourth symphony, is dedicated to the memory of his father and was first performed by the Boston Symphony in 1943. Hanson was the conductor. More than a decade later Hanson completed his fifth symphony at Chautauqua. *Sinfonia Sacra* (1954) was written at the invitation of Eugene Ormandy, who led the first performances in February 1955. Inspired by the story of the first Easter as told in the Gospel according to St. John, the music is in a single movement. In this piece Hanson wished to invoke an atmosphere of tragedy and triumph as well as mysticism and affirmation as an essential symbol of the Christian faith.

Hanson began his sixth symphony at his summer retreat on Bold Island, off the coast of Maine, in 1967.

Commissioned for the 125th anniversary of the New York Philharmonic Orchestra, it was played at Lincoln Center under Hanson's direction in February 1968. The *Sea Symphony*, Hanson's last in his series of seven, includes a chorus to a text by Walt Whitman and was premiered at Interlochen on 7 August 1977.

Among his several miscellaneous orchestral compositions is the *Elegy (in Memory of Serge Koussevitzky)*, commissioned by the Koussevitzky Foundation for the seventy-fifth anniversary of the Boston Symphony and first led by Charles Muench on 20 January 1956. *Mosaics*, in which several short motives, related to one another, are treated in contrasting sections, was commissioned by the Cleveland Orchestra in celebration of its seventy-fifth anniversary and first played on 17 January 1958.

Hanson's *Bold Island Suite* (Cleveland Orchestra, 25 Jan. 1962) is dedicated to his uncle, Carl Magnus Eckstrom, from whom he inherited Bold Island. Among his most clearly descriptive compositions, it consists of three movements, the first of which, "Birds of the Sea," portrays the sea and echoes the cries of the gulls. The second, "Summer Seascape," commissioned by Edward Benjamin, is a sound-painting of the ocean on a bright day. The final movement, "God in Nature," was inspired by an ancient Ambrosian hymn, fragments of which are first treated in passacaglia style; eventually the hymn is cited in its entirety. The music ends with "Gloria in excelsis Deo."

Among Hanson's earliest masterpieces is *Lament for Beowulf* (1925), for full orchestra with chorus to the text translated by William Morris and A. J. Wyatt. The music, rhythmic and dramatic, has a strong archaic quality.

The composer's penchant for combining orchestra with chorus is further manifested in his *Cherubic Hymn*, to a text from the Greek liturgy of St. John Chrysostom, translated by Stephen A. Hurlbut. Its premiere on 11 May 1950 was given by the Eastman School Chorus and Symphony Orchestra to celebrate a quarter-century of the American Composers Concerts. Though intended for secular performance, much of the religious fervor and mysticism of the text pervades the work.

Hanson's only opera, *Merry Mount* (1932), to a libretto by Richard L. Stokes after Nathaniel Hawthorne, was written for the Metropolitan Opera. In three acts and six scenes, the action takes place in the Massachusetts colony where Thomas Morton set up a maypole and supervised revels to annoy the Puritans. The conflict between the forces of good and evil ends with the total, dramatic incineration of the colony. Stars such as Lawrence Tibbett, Edward Johnson, Gladys Swarthout, and Göte Ljungberg participated in the first performance at the Metropolitan Opera House on 10 February 1934. The opera continued to be staged at the Eastman Theatre in Rochester as well as at other music centers.

Hanson also produced many works for a variety of media. In general his compositions from the 1930s and 1940s are the most extensive and imaginative; during his later years he tended to be content with smaller, less structured forms. His music is characteristically rich and sensuous, with dramatic climaxes and dynamic contrasts. Although he urged his students to develop their own styles, he remained ever a neo-Romanticist.

Hanson was active in the National Association of Schools of Music since 1924, the National Committee for the Federal Music Project (1930s), and the Music Teachers National Association. He was musical adviser for the Oberlaender Trust, musical consultant to the State Department (1939), and a member of the Executive Committee of the International Music Council of UNESCO (1962). He was the founder and longtime head of the National Music Council. In 1935 he was elected to the National Institute of Arts and Letters, was a fellow of the Royal Academy of Music in Sweden, and was elected to the Hall of Fame in 1953.

Hanson married Margaret Elizabeth Nelson in 1946. They had no children. He died in Rochester, New York.

• Information on Hanson's manuscript scores can be found in R. T. Watanabe, "Howard Hanson's Manuscript Scores," *University of Rochester Library Bulletin* 5 (1950): 21, and M. Plain, comp., *Howard Hanson: A Catalog of His Manuscripts* (1993). An interview with Hanson is in D. R. Williams, *Perspectives of New Music* 20 (1981–1982): 12. "Howard Hanson," *Musical Opinion*, Feb. 1980, p. 181, contains a discography. See also B. C. Tuthill, "Howard Hanson," *Musical Quarterly* 21 (1936): 140; M. Alter, "Howard Hanson," *Modern Music* 18 (1940–1941); and Watanabe, *American Composers' Concerts and Festivals of American Music, 1925–1971* (1972).

RUTH T. WATANABE

HANSON, James Christian Meinich (13 Mar. 1864–8 Nov. 1943), librarian, was born Jens Christian Meinich Hansen at "Sørheim," a farm in the district of Nord-Aurdal, Norway, the son of Gunnerius "Gunnar" Hansen, a government official, and Eleonore Adamine Roeberg. Despite his father's position in the government, and his status as a landowner, the family, which comprised eight children, was not well off financially. When Hans Roeberg, an uncle who had emigrated to the United States, offered to educate one of his half-sister's boys, Jens, the second son, was chosen. In 1873 he was sent to Decorah, Iowa, to study at the preparatory school at Luther College. While there, he began to be called Jim, which he later formalized to James. He also Americanized his surname to Hanson. After receiving an A.B. from Luther College in 1882, he entered Concordia Theological Seminary in St. Louis but within two years realized he was not suited to the ministry. In the fall of 1884 he was appointed principal and teacher at Our Saviour's Church, a Norwegian Lutheran parochial school in Chicago, where he stayed until 1888. Concurrently he served as klokker (deacon) and as Sunday school superintendent, taught English to adult Scandinavians, and pitched for area baseball teams.

In fall 1888 Hanson began graduate study in history and political science at Cornell University, where librarian George W. Harris influenced him to choose librarianship as a career. In 1890, after financial problems forced him to drop out of graduate school, Hanson began his library career as cataloger and classifier under William Frederick Poole at the newly organized Newberry Library in Chicago. In 1892 Hanson married Sarah Nelson, with whom he would have five children. In 1893 he went to Madison as chief cataloger at the University of Wisconsin libraries, where he stayed four years. While there, in 1896, he assisted in the Venezuela-Guiana boundary investigation as a researcher. Also at Madison he modified Charles A. Cutter's multipart Expansive Classification system, changes he would put to very good use at his next position, at the Library of Congress.

When Hanson arrived in Washington, D.C., in 1897 as chief of the Catalog Division at the Library of Congress, the library's catalogs were inaccurate as well as incomplete, and the classification system was outdated. Hanson initiated a complete bibliographic reorganization that resulted in the creation of a new classification system for the library's 800,000 volumes and a new card, rather than book, catalog with a card size (three by five inches) that soon became standard in libraries worldwide. The catalog was arranged in a dictionary format (author, title, and subject interfiled in a single alphabetical sequence), an arrangement that led to major modifications incorporated into the Library of Congress subject headings. Hanson also planned and formatted the Library of Congress catalog cards for printing and for distribution. The cataloging standardization effected by these cards fundamentally changed the way in which American libraries organized their collections.

In 1910 Hanson returned to Chicago as associate director, University of Chicago libraries, where he served until 1927. He successfully reorganized the university's highly decentralized system into a more effective centralized system with better bibliographical control. In 1928 he became a professor of bibliography, classification, and cataloging in the university's newly established graduate library school.

Also in 1928 Hanson was selected as part of a commission of cataloging experts enlisted to reorganize the Vatican Library. From 1927 to 1939 Vatican Library staffers came to the United States and American experts went to Rome, all with the goal of modernizing the Vatican Library's catalogs. Hanson's group cataloged a sample portion of printed books, the Library of Congress donated a complete set of their printed cards, and the Vatican gave some books to the Library of Congress. The project, sponsored by the Carnegie Endowment for International Peace, resulted in the Vatican Library's *Norme per il Catalogo degli Stampati* (Rules for the Cataloging of Forms).

In 1931 Hanson became a consultant to the Library of Congress, and during this period he lectured for several summers at the University of Michigan and several springs (1929–1932) at Columbia University.

He retired as professor emeritus in 1934 and returned to his summer home at Sister Bay, Wisconsin. He died in Green Bay and was buried in the Lutheran cemetery at Ellison Bay, Wisconsin.

Hanson was credited with helping to shape a uniform code for library cataloging. In 1900 he chaired the American Library Association (ALA) committee established for this purpose. In 1904 the committee secured an agreement with the Library Association of Great Britain for the publication of a joint code. Hanson's diplomatic skills and his wide knowledge of both American and European library practices facilitated the agreement, published in 1908 as *Catalog Rules, Author and Title Entries* (more commonly known as the Anglo-American cataloging rules). He reviewed this work in his monumental *Comparative Study of Cataloging Rules Based on the Anglo-American Cataloging Code of 1908* (1939). Hanson also wrote articles on technical library matters, reviewed books, and contributed to the Norwegian-American press. His most frequently cited publications are "Corporate Authorship versus Title Entry" (*Library Quarterly* [Oct. 1935]) and "Organization and Reorganization of Libraries" (*Library Quarterly* [July 1942]), but his earlier article on "Rules for Corporate Entry" (*Library Journal* [1905]) also is valuable.

Hanson, who reportedly was tall and fair, had a working knowledge of sixteen languages. Noted for his integrity, he received many honors, among them appointment by the Norwegian Crown as commander of the Order of St. Olaf of the Second Class (1928). His professional memberships included the ALA, the Bibliographical Society of America, Kappa Sigma, and the Norske, Quadrangle, and University clubs.

Hanson is especially important for his work in reorganizing or reforming some of the world's largest libraries and in the national standardization of cataloging practice. As Pierce Butler noted in his obituary of Hanson in *Library Journal*, anyone who has ever used a Library of Congress card or a card prepared according to the ALA cataloging rules has benefited from Hanson's "bibliographical and administrative genius."

• The Special Collections Division, University of Chicago, has the largest collection of Hanson's papers (1900–1943); the library's archives has his correspondence and notes. Other collections are at the Norwegian-American Historical Association Archives, St. Olaf College, Northfield, Minn.; Luther College Library; and the American Library Association Archives, University of Illinois, Champaign. The Manuscript Division, Library of Congress, has material relating to Hanson's work there. See also *Papers in Honor of the Seventieth Birthday of James Christian Meinich Hanson* (1934) and the Hanson "festschrift" issue of *Library Quarterly* (Apr. 1934). A comprehensive bibliography is in Hanson's autobiography, *What Became of Jens? A Study in Americanization Based on the Reminiscences of J. C. M. Hanson, 1864–1943*, ed. Oivind M. Hovde (1974). Hanson described his early years at the Library of Congress in "The Library of Congress and Its New Catalogue," in *Essays Offered to Herbert Putnam*, ed. William W. Bishop and Andrew Keogh (1929). For additional biographical information see Edith Scott, "J. C. M. Hanson and His Contribution to Twentieth Century Cataloging" (Ph.D.

diss., Univ. of Chicago, 1970). Material on Hanson is also in *Pioneering Leaders in Librarianship*, ed. Emily M. Danton (1953); Rudolf Engelbarts, *Librarian Authors: A Biobibliography* (1981); John P. Immroth, *A Guide to the Library of Congress Classification*, 2d ed. (1971); Leo E. LaMontagne, *American Library Classification with Special Reference to the Library of Congress* (1961); and Charles H. McMullen, "The Administration of the University of Chicago Libraries, 1892–1928" (Ph.D. diss., Univ. of Chicago, 1949). Obituaries are in *Library Journal* (1 Dec. 1943) and the *New York Times*, 10 Nov. 1943. A personal tribute by J. Christian Bay is in *Library Quarterly* (Jan. 1944): 57–59.

MARTIN J. MANNING

HANSON, John, Jr. (3 Apr. 1721–15 Nov. 1783), merchant and officeholder, was born in Port Tobacco Parish, Charles County, Maryland, the son of Samuel Hanson, a planter, and Elizabeth Story. Samuel Hanson owned over 1,000 acres in Charles County and was active in politics as both a county and provincial officeholder. Little is known about John Hanson's early life. His father probably had him educated at home by a private tutor, a common practice among wealthy planters. About 1744 he married Jane Contee, daughter of Alexander Contee, a wealthy landowner and merchant. They had eight children.

By the mid-1750s, Hanson owned over 1,300 acres in Charles County. His political career began in 1750, when he was appointed sheriff of Charles County. In 1757, he was elected to the lower house of the Maryland General Assembly. Hanson soon became an expert in fiscal matters, and during the twelve years he represented Charles County in the General Assembly he served on many important committees dealing with finances.

Hanson aligned himself with the leaders of the "popular," or "country," party in the General Assembly. Maryland was a proprietary colony, the personal property of the successive Lords Baltimore. The popular party opposed any perceived expansion or abuse of the proprietor's prerogatives, arguing for a larger role for the citizens' representatives in the lower house.

The popular party likewise led the opposition to British policies when Parliament in the 1760s began to pass laws to extract more revenue from the colonies. Hanson was a leader of the opposition to the Stamp Act of 1765, and the lower house appointed him chairman of the committee that drafted instructions for the colony's delegates to the Stamp Act Congress. In 1769, by then also a merchant, he was one of forty-three Marylanders who signed the Nonimportation Resolution in opposition to the Townshend Acts of 1767.

In 1769, Hanson sold all of his land in Charles County, resigned his seat in the lower house of the General Assembly, and moved to Frederick County, apparently because it offered greater opportunity for his developing mercantile interests.

As a member of a prominent Tidewater planter family and a seasoned politician, Hanson quickly assumed a prominent role in the public life of Frederick County. He was commissioned as deputy surveyor in 1769, 1771, 1773, and 1777, as sheriff in 1771, and as county treasurer in 1775.

Hanson's experience as a popular party leader in the General Assembly enabled him to play a leading role in building opposition to British policies in Frederick County. Residents elected Hanson to several of the extralegal patriot conventions that met in 1774 and 1775, but he served in only one, concentrating instead on organizing opposition at the local level. He chaired the Frederick Town meeting in 1774 that adopted resolves opposing the Boston Port Act. The following year, Hanson signed the Association of Freemen, which declared it "necessary and justifiable to repel force by force" in opposing British policies.

By 1775, the county committees of observation had assumed control of local government throughout Maryland, and Hanson became chairman of the committee for the middle district of Frederick County. He was responsible for keeping the citizenry united and ensuring that the county could defend itself if attacked from the west. Once the revolution began, Hanson's responsibilities included overseeing the enlistment of troops and securing the necessary supplies and arms for them.

Hanson proved to be a masterful local organizer. Under his guidance, Frederick County fielded the first southern troops to join George Washington's army. Hanson often advanced his own money to cover necessary expenses, but he also used his connections with the government in Annapolis to secure money and supplies to support the war effort in Frederick County.

From 1777 on, Frederick citizens annually elected Hanson to five successive General Assembly sessions, although he attended only when local affairs would permit. When in Annapolis, he most often served on lower house committees that dealt with fiscal matters. In 1780, Hanson expressed doubt about the patriotic resolve of some of his fellow legislators, warning that "the sordid interest and private views of individuals" threatened the war effort.

In 1779, the General Assembly elected Hanson one of the state's delegates to the Continental Congress, then sitting in Philadelphia. His fellow congressmen welcomed his organizational abilities, attention to detail, and financial expertise. In a letter to his son-in-law Dr. Philip Thomas on 19 September 1780, Hanson wrote, "all our embarrassments proceed rather from the disjointed and deranged State of our finances, than the want of inclination or ability of the United States to carry on the War." He found Congress's "want of proper Exertions" to address the pressing problems "truly alarming," especially since "the Army [is] in want of everything, no money in the Treasury, and our credit exhausted."

Until the spring of 1781, the United States functioned without an official central government. The Articles of Confederation, which created a governing authority for the country, required unanimous approval by all thirteen states. Maryland precipitated a long political deadlock by refusing to join the other states in ratifying the Articles until those states with western land claims ceded them to the central government. In January 1781 the Maryland legislature, finally satisfied that the western land issue had been resolved on its terms, approved the Articles. In Philadelphia on 1 March 1781, Hanson and fellow Maryland congressional delegate Daniel Carroll formally signed the Articles on behalf of their state.

Once the Articles of Confederation were ratified, the central government specified in that document could take shape. The Articles did not provide for a separate executive department. Instead, all business of the central government was to remain under Congress. Annually, Congress was to elect from among its members a person to serve as "president of the United States in Congress Assembled." In November 1781, John Hanson was chosen as the first president of Congress under the Articles of Confederation.

Because of Hanson's title as president under the Articles, some have argued that Hanson, not George Washington, is due the honor of being known as the first president of the United States. In fact, the president under the Articles of Confederation was very different than the president later established by the Constitution.

Under the Articles, Hanson was little more than the first among equals in Congress. The duties of the position were largely ceremonial, and Hanson quickly found these aspects of the job onerous. Eight days after his election, Hanson wrote his son-in-law, "the load of Business which I have very unwillingly and very imprudently taken on me I am afraid will be more than my Constitution will be able to bear, and the form and Ceremony necessary to be observed by a president of Congress is to me Extremely irksome." Citing ill health, Hanson considered resigning "at the first opportunity," but his strong sense of duty and the fact that his resignation would have deprived Congress of the quorum necessary to elect a successor president convinced him to remain.

During his term as president, Hanson wrote letters on behalf of Congress to state governors and foreign governments, transmitted resolutions to the states, and presided over the meetings of Congress. One especially memorable event during his presidency occurred in November 1781, when Hanson welcomed General George Washington, who had come to Philadelphia to present to Congress the sword General Charles Cornwallis had surrendered at Yorktown.

When his term ended in November 1782, Hanson retired from Congress and returned to Frederick County. In failing health for more than a year, Hanson died while visiting at the home of a nephew in Oxon Hill, Prince George's County.

In 1903, a statue of John Hanson was unveiled in the statuary hall in the U.S. Capitol. Since Congress allowed each state to honor just two of its outstanding citizens, Hanson's selection was noteworthy. It has recently been argued, however, that Hanson's selection, while not entirely without merit, resulted primarily from a vigorous campaign carried out by one of his grandsons. This descendant argued that Hanson deserved to be memorialized in the U.S. Capitol because of his position as the first president of the United States.

Hanson was not, in fact, among the first rank of Maryland leaders of the revolutionary generation. Others were more brilliant, more eloquent, and more involved at the highest levels in determining the fate of the state and nation. But few men worked harder, or with greater determination, to master the myriad details required to prosecute the war effort at the local level. Furthermore, few achieved as much trust and respect from both local citizens and policymakers at the highest level. Hanson's finest achievement was not in the title bestowed upon him by Congress, but rather, like countless other local officials who contributed to the Revolution, in his success in organizing his community, raising and equipping soldiers, coping with disloyalty, contending with chronic shortages, and encouraging his neighbors when hope began to fade.

• About 100 private letters written by John Hanson are known, none dated earlier than 1775. The majority, written to Hanson's daughter, Jane, and her husband, Dr. Philip Thomas, are in the John Hanson Papers, Maryland Historical Society, Baltimore. Other Hanson letters are in the Charles Carroll of Carrollton Papers, Maryland Historical Society; and in the Ettig Collection, Simon Gratz Autograph Collection, and Richard Peters, Jr., Papers, all at the Historical Society of Pennsylvania, Philadelphia. Hanson's correspondence with Maryland officials during the early years of the war and when he represented the state in Congress are in the Maryland State Papers and Scharf Papers, Maryland State Archives, Annapolis. Hanson has been the subject of several book-length biographies, but none are adequate. Perhaps the most satisfactory is Douglas H. Thomas, *John Hanson, President of the United States in Congress Assembled, 1781–1782* (1898), written by a grandson. The best evaluation of Hanson is Ralph B. Levering, "John Hanson, Public Servant," *Maryland Historical Magazine* 71 (Summer 1976): 113–33. His family history and public career are outlined in the Hanson sketch in Edward C. Papenfuse et al., *A Biographical Dictionary of the Maryland Legislature, 1635–1789* (2 vols., 1979–1985), 1:405–6.

GREGORY A. STIVERSON

HANUS, Paul Henry (14 Mar. 1855–14 Dec. 1941), university educator, was born in Upper Silesia, Prussia, the son of Gustav Hanus, the owner of a small factory, and Ida Aust. Widowed when Paul was only six weeks old, Ida Hanus immigrated with her three children to Wisconsin and married Robert George, the owner of a fledgling mining business. The family moved as George's business opportunities demanded, and the Hanus children attended school variously in Mineral Point, Wisconsin, New York State, and Denver, Colorado. After working for three years as a pharmacist's apprentice, Hanus later attended the State Normal School at Platteville, Wisconsin. He then earned a B.S. degree from the University of Michigan in 1878. Degree in hand, Hanus returned to Denver and taught high school mathematics and science for one year before becoming an instructor in mathematics at the University of Colorado in Boulder. He left teaching briefly, during which time he opened and successfully ran a drugstore with a partner. In August 1881 he married Charlotte Hoskins, his former high school pupil. The couple had one daughter.

Gratified by his "decidedly profitable" business venture, Hanus was nonetheless eager to reembark on an academic career and returned to the University of Colorado as a professor of mathematics. He then published *An Elementary Treatise on the Theory of Determinants: A Text-Book for Colleges* (1886), one of the earliest American mathematical texts on determinants, and traveled throughout Colorado, lecturing and coordinating teacher institutes. Taking stock of his own talents, ambition, and intellectual curiosity, Hanus decided to give up his career in mathematics and focused instead on the study of schools and educational problems.

Hanus's first administrative experience came in 1886 when he was appointed principal of Denver High School, District 2. Four years later he became a professor of pedagogy at Colorado State Normal School in Greeley. Then, in 1891 Hanus accepted an offer from Harvard president Charles W. Eliot to establish a department of education of Harvard.

Arriving in Cambridge in September 1891, Hanus enthusiastically assumed his duties as an assistant professor in "the history and art of teaching" and as a member of the Division of Philosophy. He was buoyed by Eliot's encouragement, by the security of a five-year appointment, and by the cachet of overseeing one of the earliest educational departments at an endowed university. However, he soon confronted the hostility of Harvard's faculty, which he later learned had voted for the department only to block efforts to open a state institution for training secondary teachers. Reluctant to consider education intellectually equal to other subjects, the faculty withheld its approval to count education courses toward an arts degree until 1894.

Among Hanus's supporters was the philosopher-psychologist William James. Another ally was the philosopher-psychologist Josiah Royce, who advised his new colleague to adopt a psychological emphasis and to appease skeptics by acknowledging the limitations of systematic pedagogy.

Hanus, for his part, unlike many of his peers overseeing the newly established university departments of education, was not an advocate of the new experimental psychology, nor did he pursue advanced research training or earn a doctorate. Dissatisfied with the "dearth of good educational literature in English," Hanus found it necessary to draw upon his own classroom experiences and to "spin largely from [his] own substance" during his early years at Harvard. In hopes of generating interest and buttressing the department's efforts, he joined N. S. Shaler, dean of the Lawrence Scientific School, in establishing the Harvard Teachers Association, arranged practice teaching

in the local schools, and developed a cooperative arrangement with Radcliffe College for teacher training. He also joined Chicago's John Dewey and Brown University's Walter B. Jacobs in founding the National Society of College Teachers of Education in 1903. This organization's mission was to promote a closer examination of the role of academic departments of education and to encourage original contributions to the educational literature. Notwithstanding the satisfactions of these accomplishments and the security of having earned tenure and the rank of professor in 1901, Hanus still faced successive battles trying to enlarge the department's staff and specialize its offerings. Moreover, his title never formally changed, reflecting, as he put it in his autobiography, "the narrow conception of the study of education at that time."

By 1906 Hanus felt that education in its methods and aims was sufficiently distinguished from philosophy to warrant the department's independence. Although the department of education became a division within the Faculty of Arts and Sciences in 1906, it was not immediately accorded the privilege of recommending candidates for higher degrees.

If Hanus encountered persistent difficulties trying to build a department of educational research and study on a par with those at the larger and more substantially funded University of Chicago or Teachers College, Columbia University, he did become a national figure as an editor of *School Review* from 1906 to 1915 and as a leader in the National Educational Association and other professional organizations. As such, he had a prominent platform for expressing his opinion on educational issues.

Believing in the efficacy of appointed committees and voluntary associations in standardizing and reforming education, in the early 1900s Hanus drew his colleagues' attention to the "piecemeal" formulation of educational doctrine. By the decade's end Hanus and like-minded professionalizers nationwide were captivated by the principles of scientific management. Educational practice and policy, Hanus argued, needed to be based on "verifiable data." So dominant became such thinking among educators that Hanus felt confident standing before the NEA in 1913 and declaring, "We are no longer disputing whether education has a scientific basis; we are trying to find that basis." The development of a "science of education," in Hanus's estimation, rested in "exact measurement."

Hanus was particularly concerned with preparing superintendents, predominently men, who as managers of school systems would organize educational research and theory, survey the efficiency of their schools, and report to school board and community members. Like his contemporaries George Strayer at Teachers College and Charles Judd at Chicago, Hanus also became a proponent of the school survey in the 1910s and 1920s. The findings of his eleven-volume New York City Survey in 1911–1912, however, were publicly contested by Superintendent William Maxwell. For Hanus the controversy underscored the political ramifications of the uses and misuses of survey work and the need to develop further statistical methods to evaluate educational results and thereby establish professional standards. Hanus next accepted an invitation from Abraham Flexner, the secretary of the General Education Board, to conduct a survey of the Hampton Institute, which he completed from 1917 to 1920.

Concurrent with Hanus's efforts to professionalize the field of school administration were his efforts to expand and modernize the high school curriculum. During a 1904–1905 sabbatical trip to Europe, he visited Munich and was impressed by Superintendent Georg Kerschensteiner's model of vocational continuation schools, which provided workers with civic education and training for skilled trades. Hanus thereafter became an advocate of industrial education in American high schools. From his vantage point, providing an education relevant to the lives and employment opportunities of adolescents, including those who did not attend college, was a social imperative. He served as chair (1906–1909) of the Massachusetts Commission on Industrial Education, which started the first public schools for trades and agriculture, later merging with the state board of education. From 1909 to 1917 Hanus also headed the Vocational Bureau of Boston, which eventually became a bureau within Harvard's Graduate School of Education.

Hanus's final decade at Harvard, much like his early years, was marked by frustrated attempts to promote the study of education. By Eliot's retirement in 1909, support for the elective system, which had generated enrollments in education and fostered the department's transformation into a division, was dwindling. President A. Lawrence Lowell, Eliot's successor, was unsympathetic to education and other vocational studies and held little personal regard for Hanus. Lowell, in fact, appointed Henry Holmes, Hanus's former student and colleague, to assume the division's regular leadership. Slighted, Hanus nevertheless redoubled his fundraising to establish a graduate school of education. The Harvard School of Education opened in 1920, funded largely by a $500,000 contribution from the General Education Board. In naming Holmes as the School of Education's first dean, Lowell bypassed honoring Hanus for his longtime stewardship of education at Harvard. Hanus retired in 1921 and spent the remainder of his career as a consultant. He died in Cambridge.

• Paul Hanus's papers are in the Harvard University Archives. His autobiography, *Adventuring in Education* (1937), describes the formidable challenges of establishing education as a university subject and contains a personal commentary on the political controversy surrounding the 1911–1912 New York City Survey. Hanus's major writings, often compilations of previously published essays and articles, include *Educational Aims and Educational Values* (1899), *A Modern School* (1904), *Beginnings in Industrial Education and Other Educational Discussions* (1908), *School Efficiency: A Constructive Study Applied to New York City* (1913), *School Administration and School Reports* (1920), and *Opportunity and Accomplishment in Secondary Education* (1926). For a discussion of Hanus's work as a school surveyor see Raymond Callahan, *The Cult of Efficiency* (1962). The most useful evaluations of Hanus's professional contributions and the institutional constraints he encountered at Harvard are Arthur Powell, *The Uncertain Profession* (1980), and Powell, "The Education of Educators at Harvard, 1891–1920," in *Social Sciences at Harvard, 1860–1920*, ed. Paul Buck (1965). Hanus's obituary is in the *New York Times*, 15 Dec. 1941.

ANDREA WALTON

HAPGOOD, Hutchins (21 May 1869–18 Nov. 1944), journalist and author, was born in Chicago, Illinois, the son of Charles Hutchins Hapgood, a plow manufacturer, and Fanny Louise Collins Powers. Hutchins remembered his father as the first person he heard speak sympathetically of socialism and as someone who continued to regard his considerable financial success primarily as a means of supporting the social-minded cultural and intellectual development of his children, including a daughter who died during Hutchins's second year of college. His mother he remembered as an unselfish person who was always charming, sympathetic, and enthusiastic, and whose interests included literature and operatic music played on the piano and guitar.

Like his older brother, Norman, and his younger brother, William Powers, Hutchins attended Harvard, where he thrived in the intellectual atmosphere established by teachers like William James, Josiah Royce, and George Santayana. Having already spent one year at the University of Michigan, in 1892 he graduated magna cum laude after three years at Harvard and was elected to Phi Beta Kappa. He was selected to give a commencement address, which he called "The Student as Child." Following graduation, he spent two years traveling around the world and studying and socializing in Germany.

When he returned to the United States, Hapgood, thinking of an academic career, took a master of arts degree in English from Harvard and then taught briefly at the University of Chicago. But his growing curiosity about the "bohemian" art communities he had encountered in Europe, Chicago, and New York, together with the example of his brother Norman, who was working as a journalist for the *Commercial Advertiser* in New York, soon drew him to that city, where he began working for the same newspaper.

Hapgood's early interests, like those of his friend and mentor Lincoln Steffens, city editor of the *Commercial Advertiser*, were as much social and cultural as political. Much of his early writing focused on the art world of New York. But the interests that he shared with the people around him—including Steffens, Abraham Cahan, who was also writing for the *Advertiser*, and Jacob Riis, who was a friend of Steffens—were changing. Working first for the *Advertiser* and then for its successor, the *Globe and Commercial Advertiser*, he continued writing feature columns several times a week until 1923, when the *Globe and Commercial Advertiser* was purchased and then suppressed by Frank Munsey. Over those same years, he also wrote frequently for magazines and began publishing books based on his work as a journalist.

Hapgood's first important book, *The Spirit of the Ghetto* (1902), a pioneering ethnographic work, followed a minor performance called *Paul Jones* (1901) and like it grew directly out of a series of articles written for the *Advertiser*. Enhanced by the illustrations of a young, unknown man named Jacob Epstein, who knew first-hand the ghetto world of which Hapgood had written, *The Spirit of the Ghetto* became one of the classics of literary journalism in the United States. In it Hapgood employed a method he called "assisted biography," which blended sociology and biography with literary journalism to present vivid portraits of the lives and work of the new immigrants. In the process he defined the tilt of all of his best work—that of a sensitive yet probing investigator of the social, cultural, and moral fabric of his society, writing about varied, interesting, yet neglected people for educated general readers. Still regarded as Hapgood's finest achievement, *The Spirit of the Ghetto* was followed in quick succession by four other books: *The Autobiography of a Thief* (1903), which grew out of repeated interviews with an habitual thief; *The Spirit of Labor* (1907), which evolved from his effort to understand the radical spirit of the rising labor movement; *An Anarchist Woman* (1909), in which he treated radical thought and social rebels as dignified subjects; and *Types from City Streets* (1910), based on newspaper pieces about street people with names like "Jacky Doddles" and "Tough Louise."

Throughout his years as a newspaper journalist, Hapgood continued to travel frequently and widely, especially in Europe, and to live an active social life centered in New York and, later, in Provincetown. During his early years on the *Commercial Advertiser*, he met Neith Boyce, a young reporter, and in 1899 they were married. Freudian thought was already much in the news at the time, and both Hapgood and Boyce thought of themselves as members of a newly liberated generation interested in abandoning outmoded patterns and exploring new ways of relating to one another. In marrying Hapgood, Boyce kept her name and her resolve to become a writer; during the early years of their marriage, in which he published five books of literary journalism, she published four novels as well as numerous magazine stories depicting the personal lives of women in terms of their conflicts with men and outmoded, repressive mores. Over these same ten years, they had four children and tested their marriage and their personal resolve many times. But in addition to tolerating the tensions of marital life, they also managed to explore their conflicts in their letters and other writings.

Hapgood's next book, *The Story of a Lover*, written in 1914 and published anonymously in 1919, grew out of his effort to understand his and Boyce's willingness to experiment with an institution long regarded as sacred while also exploring the frustrations and pain that resulted. Having created a minor stir as well as considerable speculation about the identity of its anonymous author, the story surrounding *The Story of a Lover* became one of the many interesting tales recounted in his last and longest book—an autobiography called *A Victorian in the Modern World* (1939). In the years that followed, he and Boyce maintained their marriage and their active social life—centered at times in Paris and Italy as well as in New York and Provincetown and involving, among many others, Gertrude and Leo Stein, Bernard and Mary Berenson, John Reed, Mabel Dodge Luhan, Floyd Dell, Alfred Stieglitz, Susan Glaspell, and Eugene O'Neill. Hapgood and Boyce together epitomized the minor writers who play crucial roles in the literary and cultural life of their time. Hapgood died in Provincetown, without seeing the hoped-for end of the second great war that he had watched from a distance.

• In addition to Hapgood's autobiography mentioned above, Mabel Dodge Luhan's *Movers and Shakers* (1936) provides useful information about Hapgood and his times. Both Hapgood's autobiography mentioned above and Neith Boyce's autobiographical novel, *The Bond* (1908), are helpful in understanding them and their marriage, as is Ellen Kay Trimberger, ed., *Intimate Warriors: Portraits of a Modern Marriage, 1899–1944: Selected Writings by Neith Boyce and Hutchins Hapgood* (1991), which includes an especially valuable introduction.

DAVID MINTER

HAPGOOD, Norman (28 Mar. 1868–29 Apr. 1937), journalist, critic, and reformer, was born in Chicago, Illinois, the son of Charles Hutchins Hapgood, a farm implement manufacturer, and Fanny Louise Powers. He grew up in wealth in Alton, Illinois. In 1890 he graduated with an A.B. from Harvard University, where he was strongly influenced by Professor William James and President Charles W. Eliot. During his senior year he was editor in chief of the *Harvard Monthly*. In 1893 he received an LL.B. from Harvard Law School, but after a year with a law firm, he turned to journalism, first as a reporter for editor Finley Peter Dunne at the *Chicago Evening Post*. In 1896 he married Emilie Bigelow, daughter of Chicago banker Anson Bigelow. They had one child.

In 1897, after writing for the editorial and theatrical pages of the *Milwaukee Sentinel* and then the *New York Evening Post*, Hapgood joined Lincoln Steffens at New York's oldest daily newspaper, the *New York Commercial Advertiser*. In an effort to revive the paper's circulation, Steffens assembled a talented staff that included Hapgood, his brother Hutchins Hapgood, Hutchins's future wife Neith Boyce, Philip Littell, Abraham Cahan, Robert Dunn, and Carl Hovey. At the *Commercial Advertiser*, Hapgood was mainly a drama critic, and in his column he attacked the commercialism of the New York stage, lamented the lack of sophistication in its audience, and exposed the Syndicate, a booking monopoly that controlled the city's major theaters. Concurrently he was drama critic for the *Bookman* and published several books, including *Abraham Lincoln* (1899), *Daniel Webster* (1899), *George Washington* (1901), and the more original *The Stage in*

America, 1897–1900 (1901). His brother Hutchins remembered that Norman worked unceasingly during this period, carrying "his notebook everywhere and, with his swift shorthand, he would record everything he might conceivably use" (Hutchins Hapgood, p. 147).

In 1902 Hapgood left the *Commercial Advertiser* to travel, but he accepted an offer to become an editor of *Collier's Weekly*. Thus was launched the muckraking period of *Collier's*, during which Hapgood worked closely with editor and, from 1909, publisher Robert J. Collier to build its literary quality, circulation, respectability, and influence. During the period, even though Hapgood disapproved of sensational journalism and sought the truth between extremes, the magazine plunged into national controversies on the side of progressivism. The magazine attacked patent medicine quackery and helped to pass the Pure Food and Drug Act of 1906. In 1910 Hapgood sided with conservationist Gifford Pinchot in his famous dispute with the land development policies of William Howard Taft's secretary of the interior Richard A. Ballinger, helping to bring about Ballinger's resignation. *Collier's* waged a less successful campaign to curb the power of House of Representatives Speaker Joseph Cannon. Hapgood, Robert Collier, and Peter Collier also successfully defended themselves against a series of libel suits brought by William d'Alton Mann after *Collier's* severely criticized his scandal sheet *Town Topics* for the "'leering' quality" of its portrayal of Theodore Roosevelt's daughter Alice Roosevelt (Marcaccio, p. 90). Hapgood was very much in the maelstrom of public debate, yet while at *Collier's* he also wrote and published three books—*Theodore Roosevelt* (1905), *Everyday Ethics* (1910), and *Industry and Progress* (1911)—and edited the Harvard Classics series.

In 1912, when Robert Collier wanted the magazine to support Roosevelt for president against Taft and Woodrow Wilson, Hapgood resigned. By then he had become a strong supporter of Wilson, in part through the influence of his friend Louis D. Brandeis, who was a Wilsonian adviser. Hapgood had first met Brandeis in 1906. Through his association with Brandeis, Hapgood came to support Wilson's New Freedom and also to embrace and argue for Zionism.

In 1913 Hapgood became part owner and editor of *Harper's Weekly*, which under his editorship was strongly pro-Wilson. In that year he also entered reform politics as chair of the "Committee of 107," which campaigned successfully to elect fusion candidate John Purroy Mitchel mayor of New York City. Hapgood and his first wife divorced in 1915, and in 1916 he married Elizabeth Kempley Reynolds, a graduate of the University of Paris's École des langues orientale who was the first woman to teach Russian at Dartmouth College. They had three children. In 1916 he also ended his relationship with the failing *Harper's*. In 1919 Hapgood accepted an appointment as U.S. minister to Denmark, hoping to use this position to improve relations between the United States and the

new Bolshevik regime. But Republican opposition to his appointment was too strong for him to be confirmed by the Senate, so less than a year after his appointment he resigned.

In the 1920s and 1930s Hapgood's influence lessened but not his energy. From 1923 to 1925, after years of criticizing the yellow journalism of William Randolph Hearst, he took over *Hearst's International Magazine* and used its pages to attack the rising Ku Klux Klan and the anti-Semitism of Henry Ford's *Dearborn Independent*. In 1923 he and his wife met and befriended Konstantin Stanislavsky, the exiled cofounder of the Moscow Art Theater. Subsequently the Hapgoods championed Stanislavsky, and Elizabeth Hapgood translated and compiled various of his works, thereby helping to establish Method acting in the United States. In politics Hapgood actively worked for Robert La Follette's presidential election in 1924 and throughout the 1920s for New York governor Alfred E. Smith. In 1927 he and Henry Moskowitz wrote a campaign biography of Smith, the Democratic presidential candidate, entitled *Up from the City Streets*. In 1930 he completed his autobiography, *The Changing Years: Reminiscences of Norman Hapgood*. Soon after, he wrote *The Columbia Conserve Company and the Committee of Four* (1934) about an experiment in workers' control and profit sharing at a manufacturing plant managed by his brother William P. Hapgood. From 1936 until his death in New York City he edited the *Christian Register*.

After Al Smith lost the Democratic presidential nomination in 1932, Hapgood backed Franklin D. Roosevelt. In Roosevelt's first term he joined Brandeis and other proponents of Wilsonian progressivism who supported elements of the New Deal such as the Tennessee Valley Authority but opposed others such as the National Recovery Administration. During this period he frequently lectured on the European situation, particularly on the dangers resulting from the rise of Fascist dictator Benito Mussolini and Adolf Hitler. To some Hapgood seemed reserved, and by his own admission he lacked humor. His brother Hutchins characterized him as living "the externals of life, active, unsentimental, unreflective, clever, able, extroverted, and ambitious" (Hutchins Hapgood, p. 128). Those qualities joined to a strong work ethic and a well-defined moral center to make him a powerful Progressive influence in his time.

• A collection of Hapgood memorabilia is in the Norman and Elizabeth Reynolds Hapgood Papers at the Library of Congress. Some of his correspondence is in various manuscript collections, especially the Hutchins and Neith Boyce Hapgood Papers at Yale University, the Louis D. Brandeis Papers at the University of Louisville, and the papers of Ray Stannard Baker and William Allen White at the Library of Congress. His editorials, columns, and reviews are in the various publications for which he wrote. Hapgood's books not already mentioned are *Literary Statesmen and Others* (1897); *The Jewish Commonwealth* (1919); *The Advancing Hour* (1920); ed., *Professional Patriots* (1927); and *Why Janet Should Read Shakespeare* (1929). For the details of his life and career and estimates of his character see Hutchins Hapgood, *A Victorian in the Modern World* (1939); Lincoln Steffens, *The Autobiography of Lincoln Steffens* (1931); and Michael D. Marcaccio, *The Hapgoods: Three Earnest Brothers* (1977), which also assesses his brothers Hutchins Hapgood and William P. Hapgood. His obituary is in the *New York Times*, 30 Apr. 1937.

CHARLES HOWARD MCCORMICK

HARALSON, Jeremiah (1 Apr. 1846–1916?), congressman from Alabama, was born a slave on a plantation near Columbus in Muscogee County, Georgia. Sold twice before becoming the property of Jonathan Haralson of Selma, Alabama, a lawyer and the head of the Confederate Niter Works, the self-taught Jeremiah remained in Dallas County as a freedman following the Civil War. There he married Ellen Norwood in 1870, and his son Henry (who later attended Tuskegee Institute) was born.

Loyal to his former master, and unsure about the future of the Republican party, Haralson entered politics in 1867 as a Democrat. A gifted orator who combined humor and wit with the discussion of serious issues, he campaigned in 1868 for Democratic presidential candidate Horatio Seymour, who, he said, "represented the true principles of philanthropy and national government" (Selma *Times*, 4 Nov. 1868). When Democrats failed to attract support from newly enfranchised blacks, Haralson switched his party allegiance in 1869. He and fourteen other Republicans signed an open letter urging Selma's Benjamin Turner, a former slave, to run for Congress, and in 1870 Haralson served as chairman of the Republican district convention that nominated Turner. Campaigning across the predominantly black First District at Turner's side, he played a significant role in the election of Alabama's first black congressman.

When, in 1870, Haralson failed to receive the Republican nomination to run for a seat in the state house of representatives from Dallas County, he bolted the party and ran as an independent, winning by more than a thousand votes. Two years later he won a seat as a Republican in the state senate, where his most important achievement was the introduction of a civil rights bill. In its original form—at least as reported in the *Southern Argus* on 14 February 1873, five days before it was introduced—the bill provided blacks and whites with "equal and impartial enjoyment of any accommodation" on common carriers and in theaters, places of public amusement, hotels, cemeteries, and common schools. Persons convicted of violating the proposed statute faced a fine of $500–1,000 and a jail sentence of up to one year. By any test, it was a radical measure, although it was quickly amended to eliminate the clause pertaining to schools. The amended bill passed the senate on 4 April by a vote of 18 to 9 but failed when the legislature adjourned before the house of representatives could act.

Despite his sponsorship of civil rights legislation, Haralson faced increasing opposition within his own party. Some Republicans were suspicious of his earlier support for the Democratic party; others criticized him because some of his white supporters opposed equal rights for blacks; and still others accused him of corruption, or of entering politics for personal gain. There was probably little truth to the latter accusations, although Haralson sometimes humorously boasted of eliciting a $50 "loan" from railroad officials to support a bill prior to his ever having run for office, and he was indicted for but eventually acquitted of stealing a bale of cotton worth $100. The factionalism that developed within Alabama's Republican party pitted Haralson and former white gubernatorial candidate William Hugh Smith in one camp against black leader James Rapier, Third District congressman Charles Pelham, and U.S. senator George Spencer in another.

The factions resulted more from the fight for patronage positions (internal revenue, post office, and customs appointments) and the struggle to attract black voters than from strict ideological differences. For his part, Haralson often appealed to racial pride in his speeches, as when he told an audience that he would never look twice at a white woman unless, of course, she were rich, and when he said that he was proud to be of pure African background, in contrast to his white and mixed-blood opponents. He also appealed to racial fears, warning the audience at a convention in New Orleans, in 1872, for example, that if Grant were not elected, former slaves would be exterminated in a race war. Neither Smith nor members of the opposition faction condoned such appeals.

Haralson also became involved in the black labor union movement in Alabama during Reconstruction. At a convention in Montgomery in January 1871, he was chosen president of the newly formed Alabama Negro Labor Union, an organization seeking ways to make freedmen into landowners and provide additional money for black education. The union had little success, however.

In 1874 Haralson ran against white Liberal Republican incumbent Fredrick G. Bromberg as the regular Republican candidate for a seat in the U.S. House of Representatives from the First Congressional District. Although Bromberg enjoyed strong Democratic support, Haralson's appeal to racial pride and his support for a strongly worded civil rights bill won the day. After taking his seat in the Forty-fourth Congress on 4 March 1875, he was informed that his election was being contested. Haralson asked his former owner to write letters in his behalf to the Confederate veterans in the Democratic-controlled House, and he won the contest, but his congressional career was lackluster. Serving until 3 March 1877, he was appointed to the Committee on Public Expenditures; introduced several bills, resolutions, and petitions; and voted in favor of amnesty for former Confederates. He never rose to speak before the House, however, and none of his bills was enacted into law.

During the spring of 1876, having been selected to head the Alabama delegation at the Republican National Convention in Cincinnati, Haralson conferred with President Ulysses S. Grant at the White House about patronage appointments and possible presidential candidates. Although the Spencer faction also sent a delegation to Cincinnati, the convention seated Haralson and his followers.

With the support of Smith, Haralson launched his reelection bid during the summer of 1876 in the newly gerrymandered Fourth Congressional District, consisting of five overwhelmingly black counties (Dallas, Hale, Lowndes, Perry, and Wilcox). Former congressman James Rapier, who rented plantations in Lowndes County, also sought the nomination, and at the nominating convention Rapier won out. Outraged, Haralson ran as an independent. In the end, although the two black candidates together garnered more than 60 percent of the vote, they were defeated by white Selma sheriff Charles Shelley, the Democratic standard-bearer. Haralson contested the election, and in 1878 Congress declared him the victor, but the Forty-fifth Congress adjourned before he could be seated. The indefatigable Haralson ran for Congress again in 1878 but was "counted out" when Democratic election officials refused to accept the returns from Selma's two black wards. In 1884 a split in the Republican vote again allowed a Democrat to defeat him.

In recognition of his prominence in the Republican party, in 1879 Haralson was appointed collector of customs at the port of Baltimore by Rutherford B. Hayes. Later he found employment as a clerk in the Interior Department, and in 1882 he was appointed to a position in the Pension Bureau in Washington, D.C. He resigned the latter post in August 1884 to run for Congress in Alabama. After his defeat, he moved to Louisiana, where he engaged in farming, and then, in 1904, to Arkansas, where he served briefly as a pension agent. He returned to Selma in 1912, before moving again, first to Texas, then to Oklahoma, and finally to Colorado, where he was reportedly engaged in a mining venture when, about 1916, he was killed by a wild animal in the mountains near Denver.

An assessment of Haralson's political career is difficult because of inaccurate press coverage and the barrage of criticism he received. It seems fair to say, however, that he appealed to the black masses more successfully than either his white or black opponents, that he used the race issue effectively in his campaigns, and that he was willing to ally himself with antiblack, white Republicans such as Smith in order to win office.

• Haralson correspondence can be found in the General Records of the Department of the Treasury, Applications for Collectors of Internal Revenue, Alabama, Record Group 56, National Archives. On his life and career, see Loren Schweninger, *James T. Rapier and Reconstruction* (1978); Alston Fitts III, *Selma: Queen City of the Black Belt* (1989); and Richard Bailey, *Neither Carpetbaggers nor Scalawags: Black Officeholders during the Reconstruction of Alabama, 1867–1878* (1991).

LOREN SCHWENINGER
ALSTON FITTS III

HARASZTHY DE MOKCSA, Agoston (30 Aug. 1812–6 July 1869), pioneer and winegrower, was born in Futtak, in the county of Backsa, Hungary, the son of General Charles Haraszthy de Mokcsa and Anna Halasz. According to tradition, he was the descendant of a noble family long associated with agriculture, horticulture, viticulture, and even sericulture. After receiving a classical Greek and Latin education, as well as experience in managing the family estate, Haraszthy, at age eighteen, became a member of the imperial bodyguard of Austria-Hungary's Emperor Ferdinand. In 1834 Haraszthy married Eleanora Dödinsky, a refugee from the revolution that was crushed in Poland in 1831. The couple had three children. By 1835 he had become the private secretary to the viceroy of the palatinate of Hungary, Archduke Joseph. Haraszthy was also said to have been the hereditary lord lieutenant of his home county, a magistrate there, and an ex officio delegate to the Diet. But he became involved in the revolutionary movement sweeping Europe, and after his friend, the reformer Louis Kossuth, was arrested in 1837, Haraszthy had to retire to his estate. He apparently became persona non grata, was virtually banished, and was consequently forced to emigrate in 1840.

Settling initially in Wisconsin, Haraszthy founded a village on the Wisconsin River, naming it Széptáj (Belleview), although the name was later changed to Haraszthy, then to Westfield, and finally to Sauk City. With a partner Haraszthy built a brick store and a schoolhouse and worked to attract immigrants, most of whom were German, English, or Swiss, rather than Magyar. With the help of General Lewis Cass, Haraszthy was able to return to Hungary in order to sell his estate and bring both his parents and his own family back to his village in Wisconsin in 1842. There he opened a brickyard, developed the state's first hopyard and kiln, established a ferry across the river, and later operated a packet boat, the *Rock River*. Haraszthy also grew wheat and corn, raised livestock, and set out a vineyard, although the climate was inhospitable to wine grapes. Haraszthy founded the Emigrant Association and the Humanist Society and wrote a popular book, *Utazás Eiszakamerikábu* (Travels in North America), in 1844.

The "Colonel," as he was called to distinguish him from his father, the "General," was a brilliant conversationalist who loved parties and was a perfect host. But he was "land poor," with great holdings (heavily mortgaged) but little cash. Business problems combined with his asthma to persuade Haraszthy to make a fresh start in the more benign climate of California. Before he left Wisconsin, the legislature honored him as an outstanding citizen with a dinner in the state capital, Madison. Haraszthy was elected captain and wagon master of a train that left St. Jo, Missouri, in April 1849 and reached southern California over the Gila Trail by the year's end.

When San Diego County was formed in 1850, the self-titled "Count" Haraszthy was elected its sheriff and, shortly, was also made city marshal of the town of

San Diego. He was an effective peace officer (although he was charged with a conflict of interest in the building of the county jail), and he cleaned up the rough little port while putting down an Indian uprising of Antonio Garra in the interior. Haraszthy was also elected to the state assembly in 1852. He engaged in viticulture, and when Haraszthy found the San Diego climate too subtropical for vines he set out two vineyards near San Francisco. But the cool, foggy, and windy climate there was better for brussels sprouts and artichokes than wine grapes.

In 1857 Haraszthy, who had done some private assaying, was appointed assayer and later smelter and refiner at the branch U.S. Mint in San Francisco. He was forced to resign, however, under charges of embezzlement after an investigation by Treasury agent J. Ross Browne, only to be acquitted in 1861. Meanwhile, Haraszthy bought land near General M. G. Vallejo's proven vineyard in Sonoma, building himself a grand, white Pompeian villa, "Buena Vista," and planting 80,000 vines in one year. At Buena Vista he revolutionized the nascent wine industry by replacing the traditional but mediocre Mission grape vines with European varieties such as Zinfandel, Tokay, and Muscat of Alexandria. Zinfandel came to be the most widely planted varietal for red wine in the state. Haraszthy further violated tradition by deliberately planting his grapevines on the dry, thinly soiled hillsides of the Mayacamas Mountains rather than on rich and flat bottomland like his peers. His vintages, which won medals at the state fairs of 1858 and 1859, proved how right he was.

Haraszthy then wrote the first important California wine monograph, "Report on Grapes and Wines of California," for the 1859 *Transactions* of the California State Agricultural Society. In 1861 the governor of California appointed him to a three-man commission charged with reporting on ways to promote the improved culture of grapes in California. With the understanding that he had the legislature's blessing, Haraszthy paid his own way to Europe to survey the vineyards of France, Spain, Italy, and Germany, confident of being reimbursed for the expensive survey. He returned with notes for a Harper & Brothers book that consisted of his report in the form of a travelogue, plus an expansion of his earlier essay. The book, *Grape Culture, Wines and Wine-Making* (1862), was popular and influential. Along with his notes, Haraszthy also brought back 100,000 prime vines and cuttings of 1,400 different European varieties of *vinifera*. He also brought cuttings of choice almond, olive, fig, pomegranate, chestnut, orange, and lemon trees for propagation by grafting. The high quality of these imported species revolutionized viticulture and enhanced horticulture.

During the Civil War Haraszthy was mistakenly seen as a Confederate sympathizer by an ardently Republican legislature because he was a Democrat. Perhaps because of this, the legislators refused to reimburse him for his $10,000 European venture. Hard-pressed, he was rescued financially in 1863 when his friend, San Francisco capitalist William Ralston, joined him to incorporate the Buena Vista Vinicultural Society. The corporation did well, but Ralston was interested in the "bottom line" of quick returns and large quantities of wine, while Haraszthy insisted on the careful (slow) making of limited amounts of high-quality wine. They were soon at odds, and the financier maneuvered the vintner out of the enterprise by 1866.

Once more Haraszthy had to start all over. By 1868, with partners, he bought a sugar plantation near Corinto, Nicaragua, clearing new land and planting more canes until he had the largest plantation in the country. He then built a rum distillery and planned a sawmill to take advantage of his hacienda's natural reserves of mahogany and other rare hardwoods.

On 6 July 1869 Haraszthy suddenly vanished, and searchers traced him to a stream where he planned to put up his sawmill. Haraszthy had tied up his mule and apparently attempted to cross the arroyo by means of a large tree whose branches extended to the other side. A large limb was broken in midstream. One of the Count's sons wrote, "We must conclude that Father tried to cross the river by the tree and that, losing his balance, he fell, grasping the broken limb, and then the alligator must have drawn him down, forever."

• Most of Haraszthy's papers are in the State Historical Society of Wisconsin. Others are in the Bancroft Library at the University of California, Berkeley, including the manuscript "The Haraszthy Family." Haraszthy is also mentioned in Wisconsin and California local histories and in most accounts of the California wine industry. Details of his life are in Brian McGinty, *Haraszthy at the Mint* (1975), and Theodore Schoenman, *Father of California Wine* (1979). The latter volume is especially important because it contains a reprint of Haraszthy's seminal document *Grape Culture, Wines and Wine-Making*. An obituary is in the *San Francisco Daily Alta California*, 27 Aug. 1869.

RICHARD H. DILLON

HARBAUGH, Henry (28 Oct. 1817–28 Dec. 1867), clergyman, author, and publisher, was born near Waynesboro, Pennsylvania, the son of George Harbaugh and Anna Snyder, farmers. His early life in a rural mountain valley is reflected in his Pennsylvania Dutch poems, particularly "Das Alt Schulhaus an Der Krick" (The old schoolhouse on the creek). Confirmed at age nineteen, he wished to enter the ministry of the German Reformed church, but his father, who wanted him to continue farming, refused financial support. He trained instead as a carpenter and in 1836 went west to Ohio to earn money for his education in the thriving new towns there.

Embarking on a strenuous course of self-education, Harbaugh attended New Hagerstown Academy, Ohio, for two summers, taught school for three winters, improved his very bad English, and wrote articles for newspapers. In November 1840 he returned to Pennsylvania and entered Marshall College in Mercersburg, taking courses in the preparatory school along with college courses. Soon he added studies in the Mercersburg Seminary. By 1843 he had completed his formal education and achieved competence in standard German, while teaching Sunday school in the mountains and singing school in the town and playing an active part in student activities at the seminary.

In October 1843 Harbaugh was licensed to preach by the German Reformed church, and that December he married Louisa Goodrich, with whom he had fallen in love while working in Ohio. He was ordained in Milton, Pennsylvania, on 24 January 1844 and became pastor in Lewisburg, Pennyslvania. Along with an energetic and effective pastoral ministry, conducted in both English and German, he took a vigorous and sometimes combative position on such public issues as alcohol abuse. In 1846 he published a pamphlet, *A Word in Season; or, A Plea for Legislative Aid in Putting Down the Evils of Intemperance*, and in 1849 a sermon, "Woe to the Drunkard Maker."

A daughter was born to the Harbaughs in 1845; another child died in infancy in 1847, and shortly thereafter Louisa Harbaugh died of scarlet fever. In response to these tragedies Harbaugh wrote his first book, *The Sainted Dead* (1848). Later retitled *Heaven*, it went through fifteen editions. Two sequels dealing with life after death followed, *The Heavenly Recognition* (1851) and *The Heavenly Home* (1853). During the Civil War the three were issued in a uniform edition with deluxe binding that was boxed and sold as a gift for the bereaved. Harbaugh was remarried in November 1848 to Mary Louisa Linn of Lewisburg; they had nine children, five of whom survived infancy.

In January 1850 Harbaugh launched a magazine for youth, *The Guardian*, of which he remained the publisher until his death. In March 1850 he was called to pastor the First Reformed Church of Lancaster, Pennsylvania, where he served until 1860. Under his leadership a new church was built and liturgical worship introduced. He had an important role in the merger negotiations that eventuated in the establishment in Lancaster in 1853 of the Franklin and Marshall College. He wrote and published prolifically during the Lancaster pastorate, including *Birds of the Bible* (1854) and *The True Glory of Woman, as Portrayed in the Life of the Virgin Mary* (1858). He edited the *Journal of Michael Schlatter* (1857), a founder of the German Reformed church, and launched a multi-volume *Fathers of the German Reformed Church*, the first volume of which was published in 1857. In 1860 his *Golden Censor* appeared, a widely influential book of devotions for young people, and in the same year a book of *Poems*. He produced many hymns as well; a collection of them was published in 1861 as *Hymns and Chants* for use in Sunday schools. He served actively on the Liturgical Committee of the German Reformed church that produced a *Provisional Liturgy* in 1857 and an *Order of Worship* in 1866.

Although the Lancaster congregation thrived under his leadership, Harbaugh found himself increasingly caught in parish conflicts partly related to the transition from German to English services and to his strong position against alcohol use. In 1860 he received his D.D. from Union College and accepted a call to become pastor of St. John's church, a new English-language congregation in Lebanon, Pennsylvania. While there he was instrumental in organizing and preparing a major Tercentenary Celebration of the 1563 Heidelberg Catechism. He provided the modern German translation in the Tercentenary edition of the catechism and edited the principal publication of the celebration, the *Tercentenary Monument*.

The Synod of the German Reformed church elected Harbaugh professor of didactic and practical theology in 1863, and he moved to the Seminary at Mercersburg for the final period of his career. When Confederate raiders burned Chambersburg, the manuscript of his inaugural address on *Christological Theology* was destroyed, but he reconstructed it for publication in 1864. In addition to his classroom duties he played a major role in the founding of Mercersburg College, revived the *Reformed Church Review*, and founded the *Reformed Church Almanac*. His early death in Mercersburg was ascribed by his colleagues to the pace of his incessant activity.

From 1861 to 1866 Harbaugh published a series of Pennsylvania Dutch dialect poems in *The Guardian*, and these were collected and published as *Harbaugh's Harfe* in 1870. Over many years Harbaugh frequently contributed articles to the *Mercersburg Review*, a principal organ of the high church school in the German Reformed church that deprecated the individualistic and revivalist piety flourishing in some quarters. He emphasized a catholic view of the Christian church as an organic community of Christians of all ages and persuasions, nourished by sacramental and liturgical life and representing, even with all its divisions and failures, the incarnation of God and His presence in the life of humanity.

An active and expressive rather than a profoundly learned and creative theologian, Harbaugh always stayed close to the interests and experiences of the people. He did careful scholarly work, but his temperament was characteristically pastoral rather than academic and analytical. His best-known hymn, written in 1860, is a window into Harbaugh's defining conviction and experience that Christ is incarnate in the life of Christians:

Jesus, I live to Thee, The loveliest and the best;
My life in Thee, Thy life in me, In Thy blest love I rest.
Jesus I die to Thee, Whenever death shall come;
To die in Thee is life to me In my eternal home.

• An extensive collection of Harbaugh papers, including letters, diaries, manuscripts, and many of his publications, are located at the Evangelical and Reformed Historical Society, Lancaster Theological Seminary, Lancaster, Penn. It also includes five sets of classroom notes taken by students of his Mercersburg lectures on dogmatic theology. A collection of memorabilia and documents is at the First Reformed Church of Lancaster. Linn Harbaugh, his youngest son, published *The Life of Rev. Henry Harbaugh, D.D.*, in 1900. In addition to a narrative biography it contains two extensive sketches by friends and colleagues, a short collection of his hymns and poems, a summary bibliography of forty items, and a list of his twenty-eight contributions to the *Mercersburg Review*. A more vivid personal account is given by Elizabeth Clarke Kieffer in *Henry Harbaugh: Pennsylvania Dutchman, 1817–1867* (1945), which draws heavily on his diaries. George Warren Richards, *History of the Theological Seminary of the Reformed Church in the United States, 1825–1934* (1952), contains a short biography of Harbaugh by Kieffer. John I. Swander, *The Mercersburg Theology* (1909), has a sketch and assessment of Harbaugh.

DAVID M. STOWE

HARBEN, William Nathaniel (5 July 1858–7 Aug. 1919), novelist, was born in Dalton, Georgia, the son of Nathaniel Parks Harben and Myra Richardson, planters. His parents were prominent citizens of Dalton (which became Darley in his works), even though his father, who was fiercely outspoken in his opposition to slavery, supported the Union during the Civil War. After graduating from the local public schools, Harben was a popular man-about-town and successfully operated a general mercantile store for seven years. Here he became thoroughly acquainted with the rural types he would later describe so vividly. He then spent three years in Texas and Tennessee managing novelty shops, but he eventually returned to Dalton to write. His first short stories were published in 1888 in the *Atlanta Constitution*, where Joel Chandler Harris and Henry W. Grady encouraged him in his creative efforts. A familiar Dalton legend concerned the problems of a local white woman who had been raised as a black slave, and Harben's version of her story became his first novel, *White Marie*, in 1889. Although its literary value is questionable, the novel created a sensation throughout America. The liberal viewpoints of Harben's father are echoed in this interracial romance, leading many southerners to call Harben a traitor and to condemn the book by comparing it to Harriet Beecher Stowe's "libelous fabrications." The general reading public, however, was fascinated with the titillating tale, and *White Marie* became a national success. Thus at the age of thirty, Harben officially launched his career; he moved to New York City to join the ranks of fledgling novelists.

The decade of the 1890s was Harben's experimental period. Besides publishing many local color short stories in national magazines, he wrote six well-received novels: a religious one, *Almost Persuaded* (1891), which was so popular that Queen Victoria requested an autographed copy; a sentimental romance, *A Mute Confessor* (1892); his one foray into science fiction, *The Land of the Changing Sun* (1894), an exciting adventure into the center of the earth; and three detective novels (*From Clue to Climax*, 1896, published in *Lippincott's Monthly Magazine*; *The Caruthers Affair*, 1898; *The North Walk Mystery*, 1899), all featuring Harben's Holmesian detective, Minard Hendricks. In 1896 during one of his frequent visits to Dalton, Harben married Maybelle Chandler of Kingstree, South Carolina. The couple settled in New York City and had three children.

The turning point of Harben's career came in 1900 with *Northern Georgia Sketches*, a collection of ten of his best short stories. William Dean Howells was enthusiastic about the book and urged Harben to concentrate on writing about what he knew best: North Georgia. Howells became Harben's mentor and friend and arranged Harben's long-term association with Harper & Brothers.

Harben's early works of the twentieth century were vigorous, well constructed, and extremely popular; all were bestsellers. *The Woman Who Trusted* (1901) is a fictionalized account of Harben's own struggles as a writer in New York City. His first important regional novel was *Westerfelt* (1901), which contains some of his most fascinating secondary characters. *Abner Daniel* (1902) is Harben's most popular novel, chiefly because of the crusty title character, who is "all wool and a yard wide" and whose homespun philosophy was quoted all over America: "Old women an' old bachelors . . . are alike. The longer a man lives without a woman, the more he gits like one. I reckon that's beca'se the man 'at lives with one don't see nothin' wuth copyin' in 'er, an' vice-a-versy." Abner and his anecdotes reappear in *The Georgians* (1904), in which Uncle Ab's relentless detective work saves the lives of many residents of Darley. Another folksy, wise, but somewhat crude mountaineer is moonshiner *Pole Baker* (1905), who equals Abner in rustic wisdom: "Matrimony is like a sheet of ice, which, until you bust it, may cover pure, runnin' water or a stagnant mudhole."

One of Harben's most memorable books is *Ann Boyd* (1906), an extensive, realistic portrait of a bitter, proud woman who was wrongly accused of an indiscretion earlier in her life. The novel was adapted to the stage in 1913 and to film in 1927. Harben tackled the controversial racial issue again in his 1907 novel, *Mam' Linda* (dramatized as *The Hotheads*), admitting that his purpose was to show the injustices done to the black man in the South. As expected, such views were not popular in Harben's native land, but he courageously held his ground, as his father had done earlier; he appropriately dedicated the novel to the memory of his father. Harben's message of racial equality was so clear and precise that President Theodore Roosevelt (1858–1919) honored him by inviting him to the White House to discuss ideas suggested by the story. Harben's last novel of the decade was *Dixie Hart* (1910), a charming tale; the title heroine is a female version of Abner Daniel, a wonderfully droll, honest young woman.

Most of Harben's novels of his last ten years are not as masterful as those of the previous decade, but *Jane Dawson* (1911), a character study of another embittered hill woman, powerfully presents various religious beliefs of the mountain people. Abner Daniel and Pole Baker return in *The New Clarion* (1914) to create a pleasant book in the old Harben tradition. Abner, still "Hell's chief agent," is in prime form: "The reason I know Darwin is right about his big evolution idea is that the older I git, the more comfort I git out o' bein' like a wild animal now an' then." Finally, *The Triumph* (1917), a Civil War novel, is perhaps Harben's finest accomplishment. This carefully crafted story of a divided family contains one of Harben's strongest statements on the issue of equal rights, depicted through the beliefs of its main character, Andrew Merlin: "Every human being is entitled to an equal chance to live out his days on earth, and slave-ownin' will have to go, for you know, and I know, that yore wife's niggers hain't got the same chance in the pursuit of happiness as yore sons." *The Triumph* is a believable, moving novel.

Harben's life in New York was an agreeable one, but he made a point of visiting his southern hometown every year. He was a tall, slim, affable man who loved to regale listeners with tales of his southern friends. When he died, he was buried in his beloved Dalton. His obituary in the *New York Times* stated that "in his writings he remained faithful to the surroundings of his youth." This faithfulness is precisely what makes Harben one of the most honest and sincere interpreters of rural life in the South. Although some of his contemporary critics viewed his works as hackneyed and overly sentimental, most praised him for his straightforward realism and intrinsic knowledge of his hill people. His popularity has waned owing to the whims of literary fashion, but his works are such authentic, understanding treatments of North Georgia mountaineers that they are a worthy achievement in American literature.

• Harben left no personal papers. The only book on Harben is James K. Murphy, *Will N. Harben* (1979), a critical biography that includes primary and secondary bibliographies. William Dean Howells wrote an appreciation of Harben, "Mr. Harben's Georgia Fiction," *North American Review* (March 1910): 356–63, but the best Harben article is Robert Bush, "Will N. Harben's Northern Georgia Fiction," *Mississippi Quarterly* (Spring 1967): 103–17. An obituary is in the *New York Times*, 8 Aug. 1919.

JAMES K. MURPHY

HARBORD, James Guthrie (21 Mar. 1866–20 Aug. 1947), army officer and corporation executive, was born in Bloomington, Illinois, the son of George Washington Harbord, a farmer who had served as a cavalryman in the Union army during the Civil War, and Effie Critton Gault. When James was a child, around 1870, the family moved to Pettis County, Missouri, then in 1878 to Lyon County, Kansas. Growing up on the family farm, Harbord had an active, outdoors-oriented boyhood, but he also was an avid reader. After high school he enrolled at Kansas State Agricultural College, a land-grant institution, where military training fostered his interest in an army career. Upon graduating in 1886 with a B.S., he taught school for two years while unsuccessfully trying to obtain an appointment to the U.S. Military Academy. When this attempt failed, Harbord enlisted on 10 January 1889 as a private in Company A, Fourth U.S. Infantry.

For two years Harbord served as an enlisted man. Because of his typing skills, rare in the late nineteenth-century army, he received rapid promotions and eventually became the regimental quartermaster sergeant. On 2 August 1891, having passed the required examinations, Harbord accepted an appointment as a second lieutenant in the Fifth Cavalry. During the next decade he served mostly with his regiment on the frontier in Texas and in the Indian Territory (now Okla.). From 1893 to 1895 he also attended the Infantry and Cavalry School at Fort Leavenworth, Kansas, which provided basic instruction in military art and practical, tactical problem solving. In the Spanish-American War Harbord did not get overseas but was a quartermaster, commissary officer, and mustering officer involved with raising volunteer units in the West. Eventually he received a commission as major in the Second U.S. Volunteer Cavalry, "Torrey's Terrors," a "cowboy" unit from Wyoming similar to the more famous Spanish-American War regiment the "Rough Riders." The next year Harbord went to Cuba as a staff officer with the Tenth U.S. Cavalry.

Harbord spent the next fifteen years in increasingly responsible positions on overseas service, mostly in the Philippines. In 1899 he married Emma Yeatman Ovenshine; they had no children. Although he was promoted to the regular army rank of captain in 1901, he did not become a major until 1914. In 1903 he joined the Philippine Constabulary, the U.S.–Filipino military police formed in 1901 to perform civil and military functions throughout the islands, with the constabulary rank of colonel. Initially serving in Manila as assistant commander of the constabulary, he for ten years commanded districts in the southern islands and in central Luzon. Directing nearly continuous active operations against the Moros, Harbord earned a reputation for character, loyalty, and effectiveness. From July through December 1913 he was the acting chief of the constabulary. He returned to the United States in 1914 to command a troop of the First Cavalry in California. In 1916, during the Mexican punitive expedition, his troop served along the Mexican-Arizona border.

During World War I Harbord was an active participant in the formation of the American Expeditionary Forces (AEF). He was a student at the Army War College when Major General John J. Pershing, with whom Harbord had served on four previous occasions, selected him as chief of staff of the AEF, calling him "enormously competent." As the AEF chief of staff from May 1917 to May 1918, Harbord was Pershing's chief subordinate and principal adviser and was involved in the selection of key staff officers and commanders, the conduct of coalition strategy, and the decisions regarding tactical organization and doctrine.

Although Harbord considered serving directly under Pershing as the greatest experience of his life, his professional ambition drove him to seek a combat command. In May 1918 Pershing sent Harbord to command the Fourth Marine Brigade of the Second

Infantry Division. The brigade consisted of two regiments of marines, the marine corps' principal combat contribution to the AEF. With the regular army rank of major and the emergency rank of brigadier general, Harbord had some misgivings about commanding a brigade of marines. Even though he commanded the brigade for only two months, they were henceforth linked by the three bloody weeks of battle for control of Belleau Wood. By wresting the woods from the German defenders, the brigade helped to blunt the third major German offensive of 1918 directed toward Paris. Pershing promoted Harbord to major general and in mid-July elevated him to command of the Second Division. He led the division for only two weeks, but that period included a three-day attack (18–21 July 1918) during the Allied counteroffensive at Soissons.

On 29 July 1918 Pershing assigned Harbord to command the Services of Supply (SOS). Pershing needed a more activist commander in the SOS, in large part to derail the plan of army chief of staff Peyton C. March to establish a logistical command in France coequal with that of the AEF commander. Harbord streamlined the AEF supply organization and ensured the flow of supplies to the combat troops. Although distribution problems persisted until the armistice, Harbord prevented the massive organizational breakdown that many had expected. After the end of hostilities, he was principally concerned with the return of the AEF to the United States. In May 1919 he again became AEF chief of staff, assisting Pershing with the final demobilization of the AEF until 1 August 1919, when Pershing moved his headquarters back to Washington, D.C.

From September to November 1919 Harbord served as head of a mission to assess conditions in Armenia with the possibility of establishing a U.S. mandate there under the League of Nations. Although the mission recommended a mandate, Congress rejected the idea. When he returned to the United States, Harbord again assumed command of the now largely demobilized Second Division. In July 1921 Pershing became chief of staff of the army and selected Harbord as his executive assistant, a position that within a month became deputy chief of staff. Over the next eighteen months Harbord studied, planned, and executed a major reorganization of the War Department general staff. The result was a functional organization modeled on the general staff system developed in the AEF, which removed the general staff from administrative matters and involved it more directly in war planning. The basic structure lasted until the major reorganization during World War II.

On 29 December 1922 Harbord retired from the army. He began a business career as an executive with the Radio Corporation of America (RCA) during its years of growth and expansion. He was president until 1930 and then was chair of the board until his retirement in 1947. He also was active in civic and political affairs, serving in 1931 as president of the National Republican Club. His first wife died in 1937, and in 1938 he married Anne Lee Brown. They had no children.

In 1942 the army promoted Harbord to lieutenant general on the retired list in recognition of his wartime contributions. Harbord died in Rye, New York, and was buried in Arlington National Cemetery. An appropriate epitaph might have come from his 1916 annual efficiency report: "An officer of ability, zeal and the highest character. A true leader and self-sacrificing soldier."

• The James G. Harbord Papers in the Manuscript Division of the Library of Congress cover his entire career but particularly emphasize his World War I service. The John J. Pershing Papers at the Library of Congress also contain considerable material relating to Harbord. Harbord's official military personnel file (4929-ACP-91, RG 94) is in the National Archives, as are the records relating to his service in the American Expeditionary Forces (RG 120). His own works are *Leaves from a War Diary* (1925) and *The American Army in France, 1917–1919* (1936). The most thorough biography of Pershing, Donald Smythe, *Pershing: General of the Armies* (1986), is helpful. Harbord's role in the development of RCA is discussed in Erik Barnouw, *A Tower in Babel: A History of Broadcasting in the United States to 1933* (1966).

TIMOTHY K. NENNINGER

HARBURG, E. Y. (8 Apr. 1896–5 Mar. 1981), lyricist and librettist, known as "Yip," was born Isidore Hochberg in New York City, the son of Lewis Hochberg, a garment worker, and Mary Ricing; both parents were Jewish immigrants from Russia who settled on New York's Lower East Side. His boyhood nickname was "Yipsel," a Yiddish word meaning "squirrel." His adoption of the first name Edgar and the initials E. Y. occurred later.

Along with classmate Ira Gershwin, Harburg edited a literary column for the Townsend Harris Hall school newspaper. He also wrote songs for amateur theatricals. At the College of the City of New York, he wrote light verse for newspaper columns such as Franklin Pierce Adams's "The Conning Tower" in the *New York World* as well as for campus publications. He continued to write verse all of his life, but he always regarded poetry as what he called a "sideline."

After graduating from CCNY in 1917 with a B.S., Harburg traveled to South America, where he held various jobs in business and journalism. Returning to New York in 1920, he helped found an electrical supply business, the Consolidated Electrical Appliance Corporation, which flourished until the stock market crash of 1929. In 1923 he married Alice Richmond and at this time changed his name to Edgar Y. Harburg. They had two children and divorced in 1929. Harburg married Edelaine Roden in 1943.

Even before his business failure, Harburg, encouraged by the songwriting success of his friend Ira Gershwin, had begun writing lyrics for songs that were then interpolated into various Broadway musicals and revues. Teamed with composer Jay Gorney, Harburg had his first major success as a lyricist in 1932 with "Brother, Can You Spare a Dime?" in the revue

Americana. The lyric is bitter and sardonic, and Harburg prided himself for avoiding maudlin self-pity. He was equally adept at avoiding sentimentality in romantic lyrics, as in "April in Paris" (1932), written with composer Vernon Duke, and in "It's Only a Paper Moon" (also 1932), in collaboration with Harold Arlen.

Teamed with Arlen and colyricist Gershwin, Harburg wrote songs for the satirical revue *Life Begins at 8:40* in 1934, where one of the lyrics, "What Can You Say in a Love Song (That Hasn't Been Said Before?)," reflected Harburg's solution to the problem of writing love songs. As he explained, he tried "never to say 'I love you' head on . . . and yet to say it—to think in a curve so to speak." Like other great lyricists of his day, such as Gershwin and Lorenz Hart, Harburg not only wrote of love in witty and unsentimental terms, but he tried to integrate what he termed "pragmatic" lyrics into the dramatic context of musical shows and films.

It was difficult to achieve that aspiration in Hollywood, where Harburg migrated, along with many other songwriters in the mid-1930s, as the depression took its toll on the Broadway theater. Film producers usually wanted only what he dubbed "stop-plot" songs that had no relationship to the story of the movie but were designed purely as performance numbers to showcase the singing and dancing talents of the stars. Even when writing such songs, however, Harburg displayed his penchant for witty imagery and rhymes.

Harburg had the chance to write more "pragmatic" lyrics when he and Arlen were assigned to write all of the songs for *The Wizard of Oz* (1939). Harburg's lyrics such as "We're Off to See the Wizard" and "Ding! Dong! The Witch Is Dead" were fully integrated into the story, while "If I Only Had a Brain" provided comical but moving characterizations of the Scarecrow, the Tin Man, and the Cowardly Lion. The greatest hit from the movie, however, was a song that Harburg initially objected to writing—on the grounds that it had nothing specific to do with the plot. Only when Arlen insisted that the score needed a sumptuous ballad did Harburg write a lyric, "Over the Rainbow," for Judy Garland to sing. The song became an independent hit and won the Academy Award for best song; Harburg and Arlen also received an Oscar nomination for "Happiness Is a Thing Called Joe" from the 1943 film *Cabin in the Sky*.

During World War II Harburg returned to the Broadway stage where he wrote several successful musicals, beginning with *Bloomer Girl* in 1944, a show that celebrated the emancipation of women and blacks. In 1946 he had his greatest stage success with *Finian's Rainbow*, with composer Burton Lane. The book, by Fred Saidy and Harburg, satirized racial prejudice by having a southern senator suddenly turn black; it also made fun of an economic system that was based on burying gold in the ground at Fort Knox. Many of his lyrics made similar satiric points, such as "When the Idle Poor Become the Idle Rich," while others radiated his characteristic wit, such as "Some-

thing Sort of Grandish." Still, the songs that became independent hits were ones that bore less relation to the story and characters of the book—the winsome "How Are Things in Glocca Morra?," "When I'm Not Near the Girl I Love (I Love the Girl I'm Near)," and "Old Devil Moon," for which Harburg created vivid vernacular lyrics to Lane's sensuous melody.

In 1950 Harburg, a long-standing political liberal, found himself blacklisted in Hollywood as the result of his having joined several wartime organizations that landed on the U.S. attorney general's "subversive" list; he also was tarred in the notorious rightwing publication *Red Channels*. He asked for exoneration from executives at Metro-Goldwyn-Mayer, but at the same time he lambasted the blacklisters. His efforts went unheeded. Two years later, he still could find no songwriting assignments in motion pictures.

Unlike many other victims of the blacklist, however, Harburg could turn his energies back to Broadway. The first of his two musicals in the 1950s, *Flahooley*, opened in May 1951 but closed after only eight weeks. His second, *Jamaica*, on which he collaborated with Arlen, starred Lena Horne and was a major hit in 1957. During the next decade his musicals *The Happiest Girl in the World* (1961) and *Darling of the Day* (1968) had less than successful runs.

Harburg continued to write lyrics until his death, from a heart attack, while driving in California. Although his enduring songs may be less numerous than those of Ira Gershwin or Lorenz Hart, his work as a whole represents a highly ambitious effort to expand the thematic range and depth of the American popular song.

• Harburg's two books of verse are *Rhymes for the Irreverent* (1965) and *At This Point in Rhyme* (1976). The only biography is *Who Put the Rainbow in "The Wizard of Oz"?* (1993), an authoritative biography written by Harold Meyerson and Harburg's son, Ernie Harburg. *Creators and Disturbers* (1982), ed. Bernard Rosenberg and Ernest Goldstein, presents a short biographical profile, as does Max Wilk in *They're Playing Our Song* (1973). David Ewen in *American Songwriters* (1987) provides a biographical sketch, and Philip Furia in *The Poets of Tin Pan Alley* (1990) devotes part of a chapter to an analysis of Harburg's development as a lyricist. An obituary is in the *New York Times*, 6 Mar. 1981.

PHILIP FURIA

HARBY, Isaac (9 Nov. 1788–14 Dec. 1828), litterateur and Jewish reformer, was born in Charleston, South Carolina, the son of Solomon Harby, an auctioneer, and Rebecca Moses. Harby was educated in a private academy where he excelled in the study of Greek, Latin, and French literature. He entered the College of Charleston in 1805, but he soon left to apprentice in the law office of Langdon Cheves. Legal work did not interest him for very long, however, and he abandoned his apprenticeship in order to devote himself to intellectual and literary pursuits.

Growing up in Charleston during a period of increased intellectual interest, Harby aspired to make his living by means of his pen. Much to his disappointment, the literary promise of Charleston in the late 1790s went unrealized, and his many attempts to transform his avocational interest into vocational income yielded only frustration and failure.

Harby established a school for children known as Harby's Academy in 1810; the same year he married Rachael Mordecai; they had nine children, three of whom died in infancy. The school would ultimately become his most reliable source of income, and, with the exception of a few brief intervals, Harby depended upon his academy to support himself and his family for the rest of his life.

Harby's first editorial venture came with the publication of the short-lived literary magazine, the *Quiver*, which ran from 3 October through 23 December 1807. In 1814 he purchased a newspaper, the *Charleston Gazette and Mercantile Advertiser*, previously the *Investigator*. Changing its name to the *Southern Patriot and Commercial Advertiser*, Harby owned and edited the paper until 1817. Under Harby, the *Southern Patriot*'s politics turned decidedly pro-Republican and pro-Madison. His editorial columns covered a wide variety of topics, including foreign and domestic politics, cultural and ethical concerns, journalistic controversy, and literary criticism. From 1821 to 1823 he edited the Charleston *City Gazette and Commercial Daily Advertiser*, and, subsequently, he contributed articles to the *Charleston Mercury* and other publications.

Harby is known to have written at least three plays: *Alexander Severus* (1808?), *The Gordian Knot* (1810), and *Alberti* (1819), only the last two of which have survived. Harby's plays constitute an early example of indigenous playwriting in the United States. They exemplify a style of didactic, utilitarian drama that was in vogue during the early national period. Whereas *The Gordian Knot*'s incidental moral instruction concentrated on the essence of true religion, *Alberti* praised republicanism and political independence. These plays illustrate Harby's keen interest in the natural depiction of human nature as opposed to the exaggerated plots of the then-popular melodramatic style. Nearly 1,800 patrons reportedly crammed into the Charleston Theatre, along with President James Monroe, who was visiting the city at that time, to view a performance of Harby's *Alberti*. His dramatic criticism was also highly regarded; contemporary litterateur George Pope Morris considered it "unrivalled in this country." His many critical essays stressed a belief in the moral purpose of the theater.

Harby was also politically active. In 1822 he made an unsuccessful bid for a seat in the state legislature. A fellow Charlestonian wrote that Harby "not only exercises an influence with his co-religionists, but in no inconsiderable degree in the state where he resides." Consequently, contemporary politicians curried his favor. In 1824 he published a series of essays entitled "The Presidency" in two Charleston newspapers advocating the candidacy of Andrew Jackson and the democratic policies of republicanism.

Harby also pursued a particular interest in the "reformation of Judaism," an interest very much related to his lifelong desire to improve society through the cause of intellectual enrichment. "The great cause of IMPROVEMENT in government, in religion, in morals, in literature," Harby wrote, "is the great cause of mankind." In 1824 he was one of forty-seven petitioners requesting the board of Congregation Beth Elohim to institute liturgical reforms. First, they pointed out that most of the Jews in the city no longer understood Hebrew. Therefore they wanted to repeat in English "such parts of the Hebrew prayers as may be deemed necessary" (L. C. Moïse, p. 52–53). The petitioners also disapproved of the indecorous nature of the synagogue's traditional prayer service. In order to correct this problem, they advised the board to remove the "superfluous" elements and retain only "the most solemn portions," which should be said in a "slow, distinct, impressive tone" (L. C. Moïse, p. 54). The petitioners also sought to end the traditional practice of pledging donations during the service itself and replace it with a system of "annual subscriptions" (L. C. Moïse, p. 55). Finally, the would-be reformers sought to have the minister offer a "weekly discourse," in English, like all other ministers in the city (L. C. Moïse, p. 56).

After the petition was rejected, Harby and a dozen or so others established the Reformed Society of Israelites in 1825—the first organized expression of Jewish religious reform in North America. Harby soon became the society's most prominent intellectual, and his widely circulated *Discourse before the Reformed Society of Israelites for Promoting True Principles of Judaism according to Its Purity and Spirit*, delivered before the society in 1825, remains a compelling statement of the group's goals and aspirations: "Our desire is to yield everything to the feelings of the truly pious Israelite; to take away everything that might excite the disgust of the well-informed Israelite. . . . What the dust of antiquity may have tarnished, an enlightened reader may restore to brightness" (L. C. Moïse, pp. 101, 105). Along with David N. Carvalho and Abraham Moïse, Harby also compiled the society's first prayer service and served as the group's president in 1827.

Still hoping to advance his literary fortune, Harby moved to New York City in mid-1828, one year after the death of his wife. There he contributed regularly to the *New York Evening Post* and the *New York Mirror*, a leading literary journal. He died of acute typhoid fever in New York City. As one of the few Jews in Charleston's literary circle at that time—and certainly the most prominent Jewish member of the group—Harby made significant contributions to the world of belles lettres and the development of Jewish religious life in the South during the early national period.

• There is no single collection of Harby's papers. The American Jewish Archives houses the largest collection of Harby documents, including manuscripts of many essays. The archives of Kahal Kadosh Beth Elohim also possesses some Harby papers. Harby's library is in the possession of his great-great-great-grandson, Clifford N. Harby of Seattle, Wash. Several of Harby's plays, essays, critiques, and discourses may be found in Abraham Moïse and Henry L.

Pinckney, eds., *A Selection from the Miscellaneous Writings of the Late Isaac Harby* (1829). See *The Sabbath Service and Miscellaneous Prayers of the Reformed Society of Israelites* (1830; repr. 1974). Some of Harby's correspondence is included in Joseph Blau and Salo W. Baron, *The Jews of the United States, 1790–1840* (1964) and "Isaac Harby on Religious Equality: A Letter to Secretary of State James Monroe," *American Jewish Archives* 8 (1955): 68–72. For works on Harby, see Gary P. Zola, *Isaac Harby of Charleston: The Life of a Jewish Intellectual during the Early Republic* (1994); L. C. Moïse, *Isaac Harby* (1931); Lance J. Sussman, "Isaac Harby, Leadership, and the Liturgy of the Reformed Society of Israelites" (thesis, Hebrew Union College–Jewish Institute of Religion, 1979); Max J. Kohler, "Isaac Harby, Jewish Religious Leader and Man of Letters," *Publications of the American Jewish Historical Society* 32 (1931): 35–53; N. Bryllion Fagin, "Isaac Harby and the Early American Theatre," *American Jewish Archives* 8 (1956): 3–13; James L. Apple, "A Criticism and Critique of Isaac Harby's Plays and Essays" (thesis, Hebrew Union College–Jewish Institute of Religion, 1965); and Barnett A. Elzas, *The Jews of South Carolina* (1905). Obituaries are in the *Charleston Mercury*, 27 Dec. 1828, and the *New York Mirror*, 10 Jan. 1829.

GARY P. ZOLA

HARCOURT, Alfred (31 Jan. 1881–20 June 1954), publisher, was born in New Paltz, New York, the son of Charles M. Harcourt, a fruit farmer, and Gertrude Elting. As a child, Harcourt helped market the family's produce and developed an early love of reading. He attended New Paltz State Normal School and then Columbia University, where he received his B.A. in 1904.

That year Harcourt began his career in publishing at Henry Holt and Company, first as a salesman—an experience he later cited as the most valuable training for a publisher—and later as an editor. In 1910 he became head of the trade book department and a director of the firm. He revitalized Holt's sagging trade department, initiating more aggressive marketing strategies, traveling to England to seek out British and Continental books, and recruiting important new American authors such as philosopher John Dewey, political analyst Walter Lippmann, novelist Dorothy Canfield Fisher, and poets Louis Untermeyer, Robert Frost, and Carl Sandburg. In 1913 he helped found the Publishers' Cooperative Bureau to increase cooperation with booksellers.

Harcourt admired Henry Holt's commitment to business principles and literary quality but felt increasingly stifled by the aging publisher's conservatism. This tension erupted in a conflict over Bertrand Russell's controversial study of radical movements, *Roads to Freedom*. Harcourt obtained the rights to the book on a trip to England during the postwar winter of 1918–1919, only to find upon his return that Holt had canceled the contract. Although Holt ultimately published the book, which became a nonfiction bestseller, the incident confirmed Harcourt's fear that he would find little support at Holt for his desire to "publish books dealing with the new ideas with which the world was seething." He resigned in May 1919, taking with him some of the firm's most prominent authors.

On 29 July 1919 he founded Harcourt, Brace and Howe. His partners were Donald Brace, a Columbia classmate and head of manufacturing at Holt, and Will D. Howe, chairman of the Indiana University English department. When Howe left in 1920, the company was renamed Harcourt, Brace and Company. The interest in controversial new ideas that led to Harcourt's resignation from Holt formed the keynote of the new publishing house. The partners' decision to rely on their own small capital and investments from friends gave them the freedom to publish controversial works on politics and economics without the threat of pressure from banking interests. The firm's first major success was John Maynard Keynes's *The Economic Consequences of the Peace* (1920). Despite many warnings that such a serious book would not sell, the work received front-page reviews, and its critical and financial success firmly established the new house. It also won the attention of other British writers. In 1921 Lytton Strachey astonished British publishers by granting the American publication of *Queen Victoria* to the fledgling house, and eventually Harcourt, Brace came to handle the American rights for other members of the Bloomsbury group, including Virginia Woolf, Clive Bell, Roger Fry, and E. M. Forster.

This success continued with Sinclair Lewis's *Main Street* (1920), a novel Harcourt had been urging Lewis to write since the early days of their friendship as young publishing employees. It became the number one bestseller for the year, followed closely by another Harcourt novel, Dorothy Canfield's *The Brimming Cup*. Lewis had helped persuade Harcourt to start the business, and their close personal and editorial relationship—with Lewis taking an active role in the recruitment of new authors as well as the promotion of his own books—continued until 1931, when Lewis canceled his contracts over what he viewed as Harcourt's failure to sufficiently publicize his Nobel Prize.

In the early years of the business, Harcourt worked closely with authors and oversaw editing, selling, manufacturing, and even shipping during rush periods. As president, he increasingly delegated responsibilities after 1921 but remained the dominating spirit of the firm. He built an impressive staff, preferring to hire young men and women straight out of college, train them in his own style, and promote from within rather than bringing in established personnel from other firms. Judging from his own experience that sales was the best training for future editors and executives, Harcourt required his male textbook staff to begin their careers as salesmen. Although women employees, in contrast, began as stenographers, Harcourt, Brace was far ahead of its time in offering women more equal benefits (such as vacation time) and opportunities for advancement. An innovative arrangement with the Julia Richman High School in New York City provided an annual pool of stenographers, many of whom worked their way up to important positions. Harcourt firmly believed that editorial policy should be linked to the intellectual interests of its staff, and the freedom of employees to pursue their interests and to make suggestions to other departments made the company "peculiarly a co-operative enterprise."

Throughout the 1920s and 1930s Harcourt, Brace and Company became a leader in what publishing historian John Tebbel has called the "Golden Age" of the industry. The firm was noted for publishing fiction and nonfiction titles that were both commercially successful and of lasting importance. A strong and innovative textbook department, specializing in English and the social sciences, provided the stability that carried the firm through the Great Depression at a time when many other publishing houses were failing or being sold. Harcourt limited his fiction selection to high-quality works such as those of John Dos Passos, Ellen Glasgow, John O'Hara, Canfield, and Lewis, established nonfiction bestsellers like Giovanni Papini's *Life of Christ* (1923) and Carl Sandburg's four-volume biography of Abraham Lincoln (1926, 1929), and blurred the line between trade books and textbooks with popular works like Robert S. and Helen Merrell Lynd's *Middletown* (1929).

Harcourt's appropriation of mass advertising techniques, such as the use of billboards to advertise Lewis's *Elmer Gantry*, was tempered by a recognition of the unique status of the book as a commodity. Harcourt wrote, "Books differ so widely from each other that they can never be sold as a 'line' like soap and soft drinks" (*Some Experiences*, p. 73). Instead, he cultivated relationships with "opinion makers" such as reviewers, lecturers, librarians, and book clubs in order to appeal to a rapidly expanding market of better-educated readers. Combining high intellectual standards and an interest in controversial ideas with aggressive marketing practices, Harcourt helped shape the intellectual climate of his era by bringing important new works to the attention of a growing reading public.

Harcourt had married Susan Harreus in April 1906. In August 1923 she committed suicide after a long struggle with depression and poor health. Their son Hastings, born in 1907, later joined his father as a director of Harcourt, Brace and Company. In January 1924 Harcourt married Ellen Knowles Eayrs; they had no children. A Vassar graduate, Eayrs had been Harcourt's secretary at Holt and the first employee of Harcourt, Brace, serving initially as a stenographer, billing clerk, bookkeeper, and saleswoman and later as children's book editor and a director of the firm.

Harcourt retired as president of Harcourt, Brace in 1942 and moved to Santa Barbara, California. He remained the largest shareholder in the privately owned firm and an active member of the board of directors, spending several months each year in New York until his retirement in 1953 due to illness. He died in Santa Barbara.

• Harcourt's memoirs, *Some Experiences* (1951), provide the most comprehensive account of his career. With Roscoe Crosby Gaige he compiled an anthology of essays, *Books and Reading* (1908). His Bowker Memorial Lecture, a survey of "Publishing since 1900," appeared in the *Bulletin of the New York Public Library* 41 (Dec. 1937): 895–905. The most authoritative histories of the company and its founder are *A History of Harcourt Brace and Company* (1994) John Tebbel, *A History of Book Publishing in the United States*, vol. 3: *The Golden Age between Two Wars* (1978), and Tebbel, *Between Covers: The Rise and Transformation of Book Publishing* (1987). Harcourt's career at Holt is discussed in Charles A. Madison, *The Owl among Colophons: Henry Holt as Publisher and Editor* (1966), and Ellen D. Gilbert, *The House of Holt, 1866–1946: An Editorial History* (1993). His correspondence with Lewis is collected in Harrison Smith, ed., *From Main Street to Stockholm: Letters of Sinclair Lewis, 1919–1930* (1952). Obituaries are in the *New York Times*, 21 June 1954, and *Publishers Weekly*, 26 June 1954.

JENNIFER PARCHESKY

HARD, William (15 Sept. 1878–30 Jan. 1962), journalist, was born in Painted Post, New York, the son of Rev. Clark Pettengill Hard and Lydia E. van Someren. He spent part of his childhood in India, where his father was a Methodist missionary. Hard received a B.A. in history from Northwestern University in 1900, graduating, he wrote, "with a Phi Beta Kappa Key and no key to anything else." In 1901 he left graduate study in history to be a resident at Northwestern University Settlement House in Chicago. He was resident-in-charge for one year and wrote for and later edited the house's monthly, the *Neighbor*. While a settlement resident, Hard joined the *Chicago Tribune* as an editorial writer—"thus combining journalism and reform," he noted. Hard married Anne Nyhan Scribner in 1903. They had two children.

For more than two decades, Hard linked journalism to reform in his work. In the *New Republic* (13 Oct. 1920), he wrote of trying to promote "humane justice from the powerful to the powerless" in order to persuade people that they could bring about a "democratic and cooperative world" by "getting accustomed to performing acts of justice and kindness." His experiences as a settlement resident and his efforts to improve conditions of work and life in the city helped shape the direction of his career. One colleague, Mary McDowell of the University of Chicago Settlement, described him as "brilliant, honest, and independent—not a socialist—but a true Social Democrat" (quoted in Skocpol, p. 350). In addition to its focus on reform, Hard's work reflected his distinctive approach to journalism, which he referred to in letters to his wife as writing "entertaining articles on unentertaining but important subjects." He used language, characterization, dialogue, and description in inventive ways to write "picturesque" stories showing "human beings in action."

After leaving full-time journalism in 1905 to work for almost a year as assistant to Chicago's public works commissioner, Hard was Chicago editor for *Ridgway's* from 1906 to 1907. After it folded, he began writing for *Everybody's*. In the heyday of Progressive Era reform and muckraking, Hard wrote articles that influenced policy debate and action on such issues as child labor, industrial accidents and workmen's compensation, and women's status. One series on women was published as *The Women of Tomorrow* (1912). A *Book-man* reviewer praised Hard's "graphic and popular style" and "capacity for humanizing statistics" (June 1912).

From 1911 to 1913 Hard led the *Delineator*'s campaign for women's legal rights, writing monthly on property rights, funds for widowed mothers, and other issues. He traveled widely for the magazine, speaking, lobbying legislators, and coordinating efforts with women's groups. In 1912 a *San Francisco Bulletin* writer called him "one of the most clear-headed and vigorous of American writers in behalf of the rights and responsibilities of women." He was notably active in the campaign for mothers' pension laws and served on the New York State Commission on Relief for Widowed Mothers.

After a year as managing editor of *Everybody's*, Hard began writing monthly for *Metropolitan*. He traveled to England in 1916 to examine the British war effort for the magazine. He also became a weekly contributor to the *New Republic* in 1917, writing mostly on the U.S. war effort. One observer rated him as "perhaps the most vivid reporter the *New Republic* ever had" (Conklin, p. 556). After the war his work for the *New Republic*, *Metropolitan*, and the *Chicago Daily News* reflected reformers' concerns about postwar reaction. He noted with regret that, despite years of effort, "the world was less humane, more brutal, more savage, more willfully cruel, than ever." Hard completed a book on his friend's work in revolutionary Russia, *Raymond Robins' Own Story* (1920). Later, he joined Robins in seeking recognition for the Soviet Union. In 1920 Hard also wrote for the Federated Press, which distributed his articles to labor newspapers and campaigned for the Farmer-Labor party in the presidential campaign. After the election, he traveled in postwar Europe and in England and Ireland, writing for *Metropolitan* and the *Chicago Daily News*.

In addition to writing on national affairs for various magazines, in the 1920s Hard produced dispatches for Consolidated Press Association and other agencies. From 1923 to 1925 his "folksy but caustically analytical style" (Tobin, pp. 156–57) appeared in the pages of the *Nation*, for which he wrote the "Weekly Washington Letter" and numerous articles. One of them, "What Is Progressivism?" (9 Jan. 1924), prompted a vigorous discussion in the magazine and elsewhere. In 1928 Hard, an early supporter of Herbert Hoover, wrote *Who's Hoover?*, a campaign biography. He also began work as a commentator for the National Broadcasting Company, doing weekly programs from Washington. He remarked that he was helped "by the fact that I seldom stop talking; and, when I go to the microphone, I simply continue." He covered several international conferences and political conventions for NBC in the 1930s. During the 1936 presidential campaign, Hard made nightly broadcasts for the Republicans. *Literary Digest* noted that Republican listeners "nodded in agreement" as he "riddled this or that foible of the New Deal" (12 Sept. 1936). He worked briefly for the Republican party before resigning in

1938, stating that his "trade has been independent political journalism," so he should not have links to any parties and "be free again to treat all of their programs wholly objectively."

Hard began writing on politics, labor, and international affairs for *Reader's Digest* in 1939 and was a roving editor from 1941 until his death at his home in New Canaan, Connecticut.

For nearly sixty years, Hard made his living reporting and interpreting the important issues of his time. He earned wide respect among his contemporaries, including his many editors and publishers. *Everybody's* boasted of his "uncommon qualities as an investigator" and "gifts of clear and convincing statement, good humor, and imagination based on facts rather than on rainbows" (Dec. 1913). Hard often wrote as an advocate. "My father was a clergyman," he noted in 1932, "and I have been preaching ever since." Above all, he viewed himself as an independent, disinterested seeker of truth and justice. In an unpublished profile, Alva S. Johnston concluded that his colleague was "a real free-lance—free, and a lance at every evil he has seen." Because he was a "cause man, not an organization man," Johnston wrote, Hard was difficult to define politically. Hard labeled himself "a left-wing, pro-labor Republican." Those on opposite sides of issues labeled him as, variously, radical or reactionary. "If you just report the facts," Hard observed, "you can get any reputation from the people who don't like the facts."

• Most of Hard's papers, including letters, notes, and manuscripts, are in the Archive of Contemporary History, Twentieth Century Journalists Collection, at the University of Wyoming's American Heritage Center. Additional materials are in the Seeley G. Mudd Manuscript Library at Princeton University and in the possession of family members. Assessments of Hard and his work may be found in numerous published sources. Erman J. Ridgway, "Conversazione," *Delineator* 78 (1911): 157, offers an editor's view of one of his favorite writers. Robert S. Allen and Drew Pearson, *Washington Merry-Go-Round* (1931), presents a friendly critique of Hard in the 1920s and 1930s. Groff Conklin, ed., *The New Republic Anthology, 1915–1935* (1936), comments on his work for the journal and contains representative articles. Arthur Weinberg and Lila Weinberg, eds., *The Muckrakers* (1961), carries a brief but useful sketch of Hard, along with some of his *Everybody's* articles. Louis Filler, *The Muckrakers* (1976), mentions Hard frequently. Eugene M. Tobin, *Organize or Perish* (1986), is useful for its view of Hard's role in postwar progressivism. Theda Skocpol, *Protecting Soldiers and Mothers* (1992), tells of Hard's *Delineator* campaign. Ron Marmarelli, "William Hard as Progressive Journalist," *American Journalism* 3 (1986): 138–53, and "William Hard," in *A Sourcebook of American Literary Journalism*, ed. Thomas B. Connery (1992), examine Hard's work in the Progressive Era and his writing style. Obituaries are in the *New York Times* and *Chicago Tribune*, 1 Feb. 1962.

RONALD S. MARMARELLI

HARDEE, William Joseph (12 Oct. 1815–6 Nov. 1873), soldier, was born in Camden County, Georgia, the son of John Hardee, a wealthy planter and soldier, and Sarah Ellis. An 1838 West Point graduate, Hardee served during the removal of the Cherokees from Georgia and fought against the Seminoles in Florida before being detailed for a year's study at the French Royal Cavalry School in 1840. Before departing he married Elizabeth Dummett; they eventually had four children. Back from France, he served with the Second Dragoon Regiment in Louisiana and Texas before being captured in the opening skirmish of the Mexican War. Exchanged within a month and cleared of charges of misbehavior in the affair, he went on to fight with distinction at Vera Cruz and Molino del Rey (1847), winning two brevet promotions. Most of the next five years he spent in Texas, fighting the Commanches. In 1853 his wife died. Later that year he was assigned to produce a new tactics manual, *Rifle and Light Infantry Tactics* (1855), which became the standard guide for regimental officers down to the end of the Civil War. Assigned to the crack Second Cavalry Regiment in 1855, he was detailed the following year as West Point commandant of cadets. He resigned from the army in January 1861 because Georgia seceded.

By the following summer Hardee was a brigadier general in the Confederate army assigned to the defense of Arkansas. That fall he was transferred to Kentucky and joined the force, known later as the Army of Tennessee, with which he was to serve, with two brief interludes, for the rest of the war. Eventually he was promoted to lieutenant general. He commanded the first wave of the Confederate assault at Shiloh (6–7 Apr. 1862), and the Confederate forces engaged at Perryville (8 Oct. 1862) were under his immediate command. At Stone's River (31 Dec. 1862–2 Jan. 1863) he led the crucial left wing. Coming under the influence of General Leonidas Polk, Hardee became extremely critical of the handling of the army by its commander, General Braxton Bragg, and during 1862 and 1863 used his considerable prestige to damage Bragg's reputation in the army. Transferred to General Joseph E. Johnston's Mississippi command in July 1863, Hardee returned to the Army of Tennessee in October and took part in the battle of Missionary Ridge (25 Nov. 1863), after which he temporarily commanded the army. Offered permanent command, he declined, and the position went to Johnston.

The following year, Hardee took part in the long Confederate retreat to Atlanta. When, in July 1864, Johnston was replaced by General John B. Hood, Hardee resented being passed over and sought a transfer. After the fall of Atlanta, Hardee was given command of the defenses of coastal Georgia and the Carolinas. Unable to stop William T. Sherman's advance through the region, Hardee finally rejoined the remnants of the Army of Tennessee, now in North Carolina and again under Johnston's leadership, shortly before the end of the war.

In January 1864 Hardee wed Mary Lewis; they had one daughter. After the war he lived in Alabama, serving for a time as president of the Selma & Meridian Railroad. He died in Wytheville, Virginia, possibly of stomach cancer.

• Hardee's correspondence is contained in the following manuscript collections: the W. J. Hardee Papers, Georgia State Archives; the Felicia Shover Letters, Library of Congress; the Edmund Kirby Smith Papers, the Lewis Family Papers, and the Leonidas Polk Papers, Southern Historical Collection, University of North Carolina, Chapel Hill; the W. J. Hardee Collection, in the possession of Hardee Chambliss, Jr., Fairfax, Va.; the Clara K. Paige Papers, New York Public Library; the Dummett papers, St. Augustine Historical Society; the Hardee papers and the Charles C. Jones Papers, Duke University Library; the W. J. Hardee Letters, Historical Society of Pennsylvania; and the W. J. Hardee Papers, Henry E. Huntington Library, San Marino, Calif. Much of his official wartime correspondence has been printed in *The War of the Rebellion: A Compilation of the Official Records of the Union and Confederate Armies* (128 vols., 1880–1901).

The best available biography of Hardee is Nathaniel Cheairs Hughes, Jr., *General William J. Hardee: Old Reliable* (1965). Also of value is William Douglas Pickett, *Sketch of the Military Career of William J. Hardee, Lieutenant-General C.S.A.* (1910). See also, Steven E. Woodworth, *Jefferson Davis and His Generals: The Failure of Confederate Command in the West* (1990); Thomas L. Connelly, *Army of the Heartland* (1967) and *Autumn of Glory* (1971); and Richard M. McMurry, *John Bell Hood and the War for Southern Independence* (1982).

STEVEN E. WOODWORTH

HARDENBERGH, Henry Janeway (6 Feb. 1847–13 Mar. 1918), architect, was born in New Brunswick, New Jersey, the son of John Pool Hardenbergh, a merchant, and Frances Eliza Eddy. Descended from a family of Dutch origin, he was a great-great-grandson of the Reverend Jacob Rutsen Hardenbergh, a founder and first president of Queen's (later Rutgers) College. Around 1865, after having attended the Hasbrouck Institute in Jersey City, New Jersey, young Hardenbergh entered the New York office of Detlef Lienau, who had studied architecture first in Germany and then in the Paris atelier of Henri Labrouste. After serving with Lienau in "a true apprenticeship" (Hartmann, p. 377), he opened his own New York practice in 1871. In time, he would become a specialist in luxury hotels and apartment buildings, but first he would try his hand at producing varied building types.

Family connections favored Hardenbergh in securing his early commissions. For Rutgers College in New Brunswick, New Jersey, he designed Geological Hall (1872) and Kirkpatrick Chapel and Library (1873). He received his next commissions from Edward S. Clark, president of the Singer Sewing Machine Company, where his brother Thomas Eddy Hardenbergh held a prominent position. Clark, who had real estate interests in Cooperstown, New York, employed Hardenbergh to design three projects there: a row of three attached cottages (1875; partially extant) accompanying the Hotel Fenimore; a Turkish bath house (1876; demolished) for the grounds of Clark's summer residence, "Fernleigh"; and "Kingfisher Tower" (1876), a miniature medieval castle standing off the shore in Otsego Lake. The local Bundy brothers gave the architect his last Cooperstown project, the

"Bundy Block" (1880), a three-story commercial structure at 75–79 Main Street.

Hardenbergh's career had begun soon after the Civil War and would extend through World War I, a time span encompassing vast changes in American life. Industry and commerce flourished, cities became densely populated, and buildings grew taller with the introduction of steel-frame construction and efficient passenger elevators. In creating buildings of unprecedented height, a new breed of eclectic architects carefully studied historic styles and applied them in original ways to express symbolic meanings. Hardenbergh experimented with eclecticism in his New Brunswick and Cooperstown structures and continued to utilize it in his newer works. While he designed many types of buildings, he increasingly concentrated on urban commercial and residential architecture. In the best of his designs, he proved himself adept at forming coherent personal statements through the use of historic sources, especially various Renaissance styles.

Not surprisingly, a great many of Hardenbergh's commissions were for New York City buildings. Noteworthy among his New York office structures are the Western Union Building (1884), the John Wolfe Building (1895; demolished), and the first Whitehall Building (1903). Worthy of special mention is his elegant four-story American Fine Arts Society Building (1892), designed for a group of professional arts organizations and later the home of the Art Students League of New York.

Edward S. Clark—who had turned his attention to the development of New York City real estate—gave Hardenbergh four commissions for high-quality apartment houses, thereby introducing him to this still experimental building type. The Van Corlear (1879; demolished), occupying the western blockfront of Seventh Avenue between Fifty-fifth and Fifty-sixth streets, was particularly notable for the superior interior light provided by its spacious central courtyard. The Wyoming (1881; demolished), on the southeast corner of Fifty-fifth Street and Seventh Avenue, is not to be confused with the building that replaced it, the Wyoming (1906) designed by Rouse & Sloan. The Ontiora (1883) was built on the southwest corner of Fifty-fifth Street and Seventh Avenue. The Dakota Apartments (1884), occupying a then-remote uptown site on Central Park West between Seventy-second and Seventy-third streets, was "the largest, most substantial and most conveniently-arranged apartment house of the sort in this country," according to the *Daily Graphic* (10 Sept. 1884). Hardenbergh gave the chateauesque Dakota its domestic air by creating an irregular roof line and using light-colored building materials. He combined picturesque ornament with unadorned wall surfaces to achieve variety within an overall unity, a theme characteristic of his architecture. Clark also commissioned Hardenbergh to design two long rows of houses on the north side of Seventy-third Street to the east and west of Ninth Avenue (1879–1885; partially extant). All but one of the surviving houses stand in the easternmost row near the

Dakota. Although this row is interrupted by a twentieth-century apartment building, it still retains seventeen of its original twenty-seven houses.

Hardenbergh exerted his greatest influence on the architectural profession as a luxury hotel designer, setting precedents both aesthetically and functionally. In the mid-1890s he was becoming a specialist in the field, and a decade and a half later the *New York Architect* (Dec. 1910) declared: "It is probably not an exaggeration to say that H. J. Hardenbergh, of New York, is the best known hotel architect in America." In New York City, having first produced the Albert (1883), he went on to design five major hotels: the Waldorf (1893; demolished), Manhattan (1896; demolished), Astoria (1897; demolished), Martinique (1898; additions 1901, 1910), and Plaza (1907). He was the architect for two Washington, D.C., hotels: the Raleigh (1898; additions 1905, 1911; demolished) and New Willard (1901). In Montreal, Canada, he worked with New York architect Bradford Gilbert and the local architectural firm of Hutchison & Wood to design an addition to the Windsor (1906; converted to office use). His final hotel was Boston's Copley Plaza (1912). Despite the characteristic obsolescence of hotels, some of those designed by Hardenbergh have been carefully restored and function successfully today in their original capacity.

The Waldorf-Astoria (joined as one hotel and situated on the site now occupied by the Empire State Building), served aesthetically as a prototype. Turn-of-the-century architectural critic A. C. David remarked in the *Architectural Record* (Mar. 1905) that "the design of the contemporary American hotel must be traced in its origin to . . . the Waldorf in New York, which with its bigger brother, the Astoria, indicated the main lines of the design of a hotel 'sky-scraper.'" David commented further that this differed from commercial skyscraper design "by the use of warmer and more attractive materials, and by the treatment of the crowning member, which was converted from a cornice into a roof with dormer windows, thereby adding much to the domestic appearance of the building." It was the same "residential" formula found in the Dakota, now translated to hotels. Stylistically, Hardenbergh's later hotels no longer displayed the exuberant German Renaissance ornamentation found on the Waldorf-Astoria. Instead, they tended to exhibit chastened French Renaissance detailing such as that found on his masterpiece, the Plaza, which rises majestically above Grand Army Plaza at Fifth Avenue and West Fifty-ninth Street.

As time went on, Hardenbergh grew to understand the functional nature of the modern hotel, and in 1902 he set forth detailed new standards for its internal design. His advanced precepts included instructions for the efficient planning and placement of kitchens and bathrooms, as well as specific formulas for incorporating elevator service.

Hardenbergh was one of the founders of the American Fine Arts Society and New York's Municipal Art Society. He joined the American Institute of Architects in 1867 and was elected to fellowship in the society in 1877. A member of the Architectural League of New York, he served as its president in 1901–1902 and showed work at several of its annual exhibitions. He became an associate of the National Academy of Design in 1910.

In 1893 Hardenbergh married Emily Irene Leeds Keene; they had no children. He died in New York City.

• There appears to be no collection of Hardenbergh's papers. His article, "Hotel," setting forth functional guidelines for hotel design, can be found in Russell Sturgis, *A Dictionary of Architecture and Building* (1902). For insights into his early training, work methods, and philosophy of architecture, see Sadakichi Hartmann, "A Conversation with Henry Janeway Hardenbergh," *Architectural Record* 19 (May 1906): 376–80. For contemporary assessments of his work, see Montgomery Schuyler, "Henry Janeway Hardenbergh," *Architectural Record* 6 (Jan.–Mar. 1897): 335–75; and Richard F. Bach, "Henry Janeway Hardenbergh," *Architectural Record* 44 (July 1918): 91–93. See also Charlotte Berry Kantz, "The Public Architecture of H. J. Hardenbergh (1847–1918)" (M.A. thesis, Univ. of Delaware, 1975).

MAY N. STONE

HARDENBERGH, Jacob Rutsen (1736?–30 Oct. 1790), Dutch Reformed minister and first president of Queens College (later Rutgers University), was born in Rosendale, New York, the son of Colonel Johannes Hardenbergh, a wealthy landowner, and Maria Dubois. Hardenbergh's exact date of birth is not known, but his baptismal date is 22 February 1737. Raised in an evangelical Dutch Reformed household, Hardenbergh acquired some formal education at an academy in Kingston, New York, including enough classical language training to enable preparation for the ministry.

Hardenbergh was studying theology under John Frelinghuysen of Raritan, New Jersey, in 1754, when that minister died. Some months later, with the approval of church elders, Hardenbergh married Frelinghuysen's widow, born Dinah Van Bergh, the daughter of a wealthy Amsterdam merchant. Dinah, twelve years Hardenbergh's senior, well educated, and religiously devout, was a lifelong support to her husband, surviving him by seventeen years. She brought two children into the marriage, which produced at least two more. He continued his studies and was ordained by the Dutch Reformed Coetus in 1757, the first American minister of his church not to be educated, examined, and licensed in Holland. In May 1758 he assumed Frelinghuysen's ministry in Raritan, a post he was to hold for twenty-three years.

Hardenbergh's path into the ministry exemplified the evolving conflict among the Dutch Reformed in America. The Great Awakening had increased the number of parishioners, and the church suffered a shortage of ministers. One faction of the church wanted to train ministers and administer the denomination in the colonies, while the other favored control from Holland. The American side, led by the Reverend Theodore Frelinghuysen, Jr. (1723–1761), of Albany, sought support in Holland for a colonial church administration and college but was rebuffed. It then formed the Coetus, which ordained ministers such as Hardenbergh on its own and sought support for a Dutch college.

Hardenbergh became active in the Coetus during the early 1760s. He and others began pressuring the New Jersey legislature for a college charter, while a second attempt to persuade the home church to acquiesce in the changes sent him to Holland in 1763. The Dutch remained adamantly opposed. The American faction pushed ahead, obtaining a college charter from New Jersey in 1766. Yet the factional struggle among the colonial Dutch Reformed delayed planning and preparations. By the time a slight lessening of American conservative and Dutch church opposition occurred in 1771, allowing formal planning and site acquisition, the growing rift between the colonies and Great Britain jeopardized implementation of the plans. Fearing the English-speaking, evangelical supporters of American control of the church, the Dutch conservatives thought they stood to benefit more from English administration of the colonies, while those who desired autonomy for the church wanted the same in politics. Most conservatives became Loyalists. Coetus members were overwhelmingly patriots.

Hardenbergh embroiled himself in both the college and the political controversies. He became a leading college trustee and helped with instruction from the school's inception in 1771. From 1774 he was president pro tempore. But there was little to do. Queens College limped along through the 1770s and 1780s, disbanding on occasion during the war, often fleeing its New Brunswick home. By 1784 there were few, if any, students: there were no graduates from 1784 to 1786.

Meanwhile, the Raritan minister demonstrated ardent patriotism. He preached the patriot message from the pulpit and turned thought to action as a member of the New Jersey Provincial Assembly of 1776, the state constitutional convention, and the New Jersey Assembly for several years. For two winters George Washington's army camped within the bounds of his parish, and he entertained the general frequently. His notoriety prompted the British to burn his church in late October 1779 and to offer a £100 reward for his capture. He often fled his home to hide in the countryside, and legend has it that he slept with a loaded musket under his bed.

Perhaps worn down by the stresses of the war and the college troubles, Hardenbergh resigned his Raritan pastorate in 1781, returning to his home church in Rosendale. But love for his college and duty to his church compelled him to accept when the newly independent Dutch Reformed Church of America selected him the first formal president of Queens College and pastor of the New Brunswick Church in 1786.

Hardenbergh's challenge was to rebuild the college. At first he succeeded, arranging for new instructors, enticing students to attend, and soliciting funds from local churches that enabled him to pay the school's operating expenses. Still, the base of Dutch Reformed students and donors was small compared to those of other American denominations and Queens had to share them and the non-Dutch students with the colleges in Princeton and New York City, both more prestigious institutions. Additionally, the rift within the Dutch church still interfered with the college's operation. Nonetheless, Queen's trustees optimistically authorized construction of a new building. It was finished in 1791, but before this Hardenbergh realized that he could not sustain Queens's initial postrevolutionary growth. Knowing that the college was already in debt and that the situation would only worsen, Hardenbergh made an anguished appeal to the church synod in early October 1790. Although his effort was successful enough to allow the college to cling to life for five more years, Hardenbergh did not see them. A consumptive, the combination of his teaching and administrative duties, his ministerial obligations, and the stress of trying to keep the college afloat proved too much for him to bear. He died in New Brunswick, New Jersey. The death date of 30 October 1790 is given on the marker at Hardenbergh's grave, but Peter Stubblefield cited 2 November 1790 as the date in his *A Funeral Sermon on the Death of Rev. Jacob R. Hardenbergh* (1791) and in an article for the *New York Journal and Patriotic Advertiser*, 11 November 1790.

Jacob Hardenbergh was a capable educator and a grave, pious, well-respected minister, whom his colleagues on four occasions selected to head the church's general assembly. That he was able to keep Queens College alive during his presidency suggests that he was a talented administrator as well. But Hardenbergh's career is more important as a symbol of the Americanization of religion during the latter half of the eighteenth century. Supporting his denomination's theology, but not its culture, Hardenbergh strove throughout his career to place an American imprint on the Dutch Reformed church. In doing this, he made common cause with many other ministers and lay people representing a variety of sects and denominations for whom American nationalism was inescapable during the era of the Revolution.

• Rutgers University Library houses the Hardenbergh Family Papers, 1749–1927, which contain some sermons and other papers of Jacob Hardenbergh. A useful sketch of his life and career appears in William B. Sprague, ed., *Annals of the American Pulpit*, vol. 9 (1869; repr. 1969). Randall H. Balmer, *A Perfect Babel of Confusion: Dutch Religion and English Culture in the Middle Colonies* (1989), discusses the divisions within the Dutch Reformed church and Hardenbergh's role in them. The history of revolutionary-era Queens College is covered in the context of divisions within the Dutch church in Richard P. McCormick, *Rutgers: A Bicentennial History* (1966), more anecdotally in William H. S. Demarest, *A History of Rutgers College, 1766–1924* (1924), and in the context of early American higher education in David W. Robson, *Educating Republicans: The College in the Era of the American Revolution* (1985).

DAVID W. ROBSON

HARDEY, Mary Aloysia (8 Dec. 1809–17 June 1886), mother superior of the Society of the Sacred Heart, was born Mary Hardey in Piscataway, Maryland, the daughter of Frederick Hardey, a gentleman farmer, and Sarah Spalding. Both of her parents were descended from colonial Maryland Catholics. In 1817 the family moved to the South, and Mary grew up on the Hardey plantation in Opelousas, Louisiana. At age twelve she became one of the first pupils at the Convent of the Sacred Heart, Grand Coteau, Louisiana. In 1825, at fifteen years of age, she entered the novitiate and took the name Aloysia. She was professed in 1833. Early on her talents, obedience, and devotion to the society set her apart.

In 1833, immediately upon taking her vows, Hardey was called on to be cofounder of a convent at St. Michael's, near New Orleans. Enduring many trials, including the deaths from cholera of a number of her fellow sisters, she helped build St. Michael's into a successful school. In 1835 she was named the school's superior. There also she became acquainted with Mother Philippine Duchesne, the society's first missionary to America. Hardey was a gifted and much-loved teacher, and her organizational and administrative skills held her in good stead as she went on to found nearly thirty more convents. Bishop John Hughes of New York said of her, "She is a woman who could govern the United States" (Williams, p. 140).

Bishop John Dubois invited the Society of the Sacred Heart to open a convent in New York, and Hardey and Mother Elizabeth Galitzin from France were chosen for the task. Hardey arrived in New York in the spring of 1841, and the first of the society's many eastern foundations opened on Houston Street in the fall of that year with Hardey as its mistress general. In 1842 she attended the Seventh General Council of the society in Lyon, France, where she solidified her increasingly prominent position within the society. Stopping first in Rome, she was given an audience with Gregory XVI, from whom she received a benediction for her work in America. Of utmost significance for the young nun was the time spent with Mother Madeleine Barat, the mother general of the society, to whom she remained an obedient servant until Barat's death in 1865. Thus buoyed up, Hardey sailed for home in October 1842. New York remained the center of her work for twenty-five years.

In 1844 Hardey was appointed provincial of the American houses along the eastern seaboard. She was hesitant to accept such a position so early in her career; nevertheless, she went right to work to establish another, larger school located outside the city in Astoria, replacing the Houston Street school. In February 1847 she negotiated the purchase of property in Manhattanville, where her first act was to open a parish school even though no parish church was yet established. By 1852 the convent had more than 100 students, 12 novices, and 8 postulants. Hardey considered Manhattanville her primary home for much of her life. Before 1883 she also established foundations in Atlantic City,

Boston, Buffalo, and Philadelphia, and she opened seven convents in Canada and one in Cuba.

Hardey was tirelessly obedient to her call to found convents, enduring hardship and peril during her frequent journeys, which consisted of five voyages to Cuba and ten to Europe. Additionally, her position as provincial of the eastern houses demanded that she be constantly on the road within the United States. While the convents she founded comprise the most tangible evidence of her accomplishments, Hardey saw them as necessary for achieving her primary goal of recruiting young women to serve as devoted teachers in the service of the society.

The Civil War caused Hardey great personal anguish. Although she had made the North her home, she was raised in the South, and Manhattanville had enrolled many children from southern families. While other northern schools experienced a diminution of their southern pupils, she held her school together, sometimes taxing the school's reserves to support the children of suffering southern families. Her many other charitable acts reached beyond the boundaries of her schools. When communication was cut off with the Louisiana houses, she was instrumental in bringing aid, passing through the armies of the North and South to reach the stricken convents. Likewise, she insured assistance to Cuban homes in 1860–1870, to Chicago after its great fire, and to the South when it was ravaged by fever.

In 1871 she was appointed assistant general representing the houses of the British Empire and North America, at which time she was stationed at the mother house in Paris, France. She made official visits to the United States in 1874, 1878, and 1882. She died in Paris.

Mother Hardy entered the Society of the Sacred Heart during a pivotal time in its development. The society was only just beginning to bring its mission to the inchoate nation, and Hardey was a crucial participant in the success of that enterprise.

• For a compilation of the original documents housed in the mother house, see Marie Dufour, *Vie de la Reverende Mere Aloysia Hardey* (1890). The definitive work in English is M. A. Williams, *Second Sowing: The Life of Mary Aloysia Hardey* (1942). For a more general look at the history of the society in the United States, see L. Callan, *The Society of the Sacred Heart in North America* (1937).

CARLEEN MANDOLFO

HARDIE, James Allen (5 May 1823–14 Dec. 1876), soldier, was born in New York City, the son of Allen Wardwell Hardie, a real estate broker, and Caroline Cox. Hardie was raised in comfortable circumstances in Montrose, New York, but his father's fortunes fell dramatically in 1833. Hardie attended the Poughkeepsie Collegiate School before being appointed, at age sixteen, to the U.S. Military Academy in 1839. He graduated eleventh in the class of 1843. This class included Ulysses S. Grant, William B. Franklin (later a Civil War general), and George Deshon (later one of the founders of the Roman Catholic Paulist order).

Hardie's first commission was in the First Artillery, serving in Houlton, Maine; then, in 1845–1846, he served at the military academy as an assistant professor of geography, history, and ethics. Hardie was granted leave by Secretary of War (and former governor of New York) William L. Marcy to join the First New York Volunteers, a regiment formed by Marcy's associate Jonathan D. Stevenson to serve in the Mexican War. Hardie, a major, arrived in San Francisco with his command in March 1847 after a six-month journey around Cape Horn. Here he first met William Tecumseh Sherman; the two would become good friends. Hardie wearied of his garrison duties but was refused transfer to the scene of the fighting in Mexico. While on a recruiting mission in Oregon in 1847, according to his friend and memorialist Charles F. Benjamin, Hardie, whose father was Episcopalian and his mother of Quaker background, "became an open convert to the Roman Catholic religion, towards which he had long been tending" (Benjamin, p. 15). Before leaving San Francisco in 1849 Hardie helped raise $3,000 for the construction of St. Francis Church, the first Catholic church erected in that city.

Hardie resumed his regular army career as a first lieutenant in the Third Artillery, based at Fort Trumbull, Connecticut, until 1850, then in 1851 at the Jefferson Barracks, St. Louis, where he met and that year married Margaret Hunter; five of their eight children survived into adulthood. He became adjutant of the Third Artillery later that year, serving at Fort Adams, Rhode Island, until he became one of General John E. Wool's aides in late 1853, serving in Baltimore until 1855. Hardie returned to his regiment and served the next three years in Benica, California. In 1858 Hardie joined the expedition against the Spokane Indians and saw action at the Spokane Plain engagement (5 Sept. 1858). He was acting assistant adjutant general of the Department of Oregon in the year before the Civil War. Hardie condemned slavery as morally wrong but felt that the Constitution protected it where already established.

At the outbreak of the Civil War Hardie was first transferred to the Fifth Artillery, then became an aide to General George B. McClellan in September 1861 and acting assistant adjutant general of the Army of the Potomac. He served on McClellan's staff in the Peninsula and Antietam campaigns, was retained by General Ambrose Burnside when McClellan was removed, and was recommended for promotion to brigadier general of volunteers (he held this rank from Nov. 1862 to Jan. 1863). At the battle of Fredericksburg (13 Dec. 1862) Hardie brought Burnside's orders to Franklin, commander of the Union left, and remained with his old classmate all day to relay reports. Hardie's short dispatches back to Burnside were later publicly cited by Franklin as evidence of Franklin's innocence of wrongdoing or responsibility for the disastrous defeat. Benjamin and other biographers assert that these dispatches were accepted by both Burnside and Franklin as an accurate record of events, but there is little evidence that Burnside concurred, and at least one of the messages misled Burnside into thinking that Franklin was committing new troops to the battle in response to new orders, when Franklin's effort had basically ceased.

In January 1863 Hardie went to New York to help McClellan prepare his final military report. When General Joseph Hooker replaced Burnside he made Hardie judge advocate general of the Army of the Potomac. Hardie held this position until March, when he was promoted to major and assistant adjutant general of the army, then detailed to Edwin M. Stanton's War Department for "special duty." In this capacity he is most remembered for his part in the change of command before the battle of Gettysburg. Stanton and Lincoln feared the consequences of Hooker fighting another battle after his performance at Chancellorsville. They sent Hardie to personally give General George Meade the order to take command and convince him to accept it and to then, with Meade in tow, directly confront Hooker to ensure that he would step down. Hardie, dressed in civilian clothes and carrying a large amount of money to facilitate his movements, found Meade after some difficulty and accomplished his mission on 28 June 1863. In March 1864 Hardie was named inspector general of the army following the death of the incumbent. He was promoted in March 1865 to brevet brigadier general and then brevet major general for his war service.

Hardie and Stanton became embroiled in a public controversy in July 1865, when Hardie was accused of denying Mary Surratt visits from her Catholic priest, Jacob Walter, until Walter agreed to keep silent about her innocence in connection with Lincoln's assassination. Hardie publicly defended his actions in a newspaper denial and claimed in a private letter to Archbishop Spaulding, Walter's superior, that he was only trying to "induce discreet behavior." In fact, the promise was extracted, Spaulding was induced to pressure Walter into silence, and Surratt did not see Walter until the day before she was executed.

Hardie's postwar career consisted primarily of inspection tours and auditing claims against the War Department. He audited Kansas claims arising out of the activities of William C. Quantrill and other raiders and later the Modoc War claims. He was inspector general of the Department of the Missouri from 1869 to 1872 and helped distribute government relief supplies in Chicago after the great fire of 1871. Inspection tours took him from the Gulf of Mexico to Montana to the Southwest, where he felt he picked up his final illness, thought to be a form of malaria. Hardie died in Washington, D.C., after thirty-seven years on active duty. A career soldier, Hardie was a very well-regarded staff officer who held several important positions in the Civil War and Reconstruction period.

• The Library of Congress holds Hardie's papers, a small collection of 395 items that includes letters from William Te-

cumseh Sherman. The only biographical treatment is the short, privately printed work of Charles Frederick Benjamin, *Memoir of James Allen Hardie, Inspector-General, United States Army* (1877). Two brief articles cover two specific incidents in his life: Francis J. Weber, "The Hardie Memorandum," *Southern California Quarterly* 54, no. 4 (1972): 343–52, on Hardie's 1848 assessment of Catholicism in California; and Alfred Isacsson, "The Case of Jacob Walter," *Lincoln Herald* 89, no. 1 (1987): 21–24, on the Mary Surratt episode. An obituary is in the *New York Times*, 16 Dec. 1876.

BRIAN J. KENNY

HARDIN, Benjamin, Jr. (29 Feb. 1784–24 Sept. 1852), attorney, U.S. congressman, and Kentucky politician, was born in Westmoreland County, Pennsylvania, the son of Benjamin Hardin, Sr., and his first cousin Sarah Hardin. Hardin's father moved his family to Washington County, Kentucky, in 1788 and settled near Springfield. Hardin received his early educational training from family and tutors. He then read law under his cousin Martin D. Hardin in 1804 in Richmond, Kentucky, and in 1805 under Felix Grundy in Bardstown, Kentucky. Upon completion of his training in 1806, Hardin received a license to practice law. He established an office in Elizabethtown, Kentucky, and a partnership with Joseph Holt, the future judge advocate general under President Abraham Lincoln. In 1807 Hardin married Elizabeth Pendleton Barbour; they had three daughters and three sons. In 1808 he moved to Bardstown and established what would be his lifelong residence.

Hardin had a distinguished career as a lawyer. Like many practitioners of his time, he traveled the federal circuit representing clients in the surrounding states. He possessed a fine knowledge of the law and a strong work ethic. In 1820 Hardin represented John Green in a case brought by Richard Biddle. Biddle disputed a land title Green had possessed before the creation of the Commonwealth of Kentucky, and the quarrel raised questions regarding Kentucky's land law regarding occupying claimants' rights to the lands on which they settled. Hardin won the case in an 1821 U.S. Supreme Court decision, but Green appealed because he had no representation. The Kentucky legislature employed Henry Clay and Judge John B. Bibb to maintain the constitutionality of the disputed law. The grievance made its way through the court system before again reaching the Supreme Court in 1823. Hardin argued before the Court that the Kentucky law that Biddle employed was unconstitutional because it violated the "Compact of Virginia," which stated that all rights derived from Virginia prior to Kentucky's separation remained valid. Hardin and Green won the case. In this case, as in many he tried, Hardin gained the reputation as a quick thinker and a strong orator.

In 1810 Hardin was elected a member of the Kentucky House of Representatives, representing Nelson County. During this session he introduced and secured the passage of a bill that sought to eliminate dueling, one of the first pieces of legislation to end this ritual. He served in the house from 1810 to 1811 and from 1824 to 1825; he also served in the Kentucky Senate from 1828 until 1832. Hardin established his national reputation while serving in the U.S. House of Representatives. He represented Kentucky in Congress from 1815 to 1817, from 1819 to 1823, and from 1833 to 1837.

Hardin made his first congressional speech on 9 January 1816, arguing against a bill that would carry into effect the stipulations of the treaty of commerce with Great Britain. He maintained that the bill echoed the treaty itself and permitted Congress to transgress its powers. This speech set the tone for his future years in service, during which he opposed the policies of the Federalist party and later championed the Whig cause. Hardin's notable stands included opposition to the "national glory" policy at the end of the War of 1812, reduction of the army and navy, reduction of taxes, and opposition to rechartering the U.S. Bank in 1816. Hardin was a proponent of the "Old Court," a group of Kentuckians that opposed debtor relief and the Bank of the Commonwealth. He also presented, on 7 February 1820, a formidable speech approving the admission of Missouri as a slave state. Hardin served as a presidential elector in 1833 and 1845; in both elections he cast his vote for Henry Clay, the Whig candidate.

Hardin returned to Kentucky politics in 1844 with his support of William Owsley, a Whig and member of the Old Court, for governor of Kentucky. The two had been lifelong friends, yet Hardin offered his support only after Owsley pledged not to apply patronage to promote his own self-interest over the public welfare. Owsley rewarded Hardin's efforts with an appointment to be Kentucky secretary of state, a position Hardin held until 1847, when he resigned amid a controversy with Owsley and the Henry Clay–led faction of the Whig party.

Hardin was accused of misusing his patronage after he secured a job for the daughter of an acquaintance. The act itself was not unheard of, but Hardin's opponents used the event to undermine Owsley's confidence in him. Hardin refused either to admit guilt or to resign; this caused Owsley to order his removal on 1 September 1846. The Kentucky Court of Appeals, by writ of mandamus, compelled the state auditor to pay Hardin's salary. When the legislature returned to session, Hardin submitted a protest against the governor's appointment to fill his vacancy; a committee agreed that there was no vacancy to fill. The Kentucky Senate then voted 30–8 to confirm Hardin's proposed replacement, George B. Kinhead. With that, Hardin resigned his position. Though he was found innocent of any misdeed, the controversy surrounding the dispute irretrievably damaged Hardin's chance to become a U.S. senator. He ended his political life as a participant in the 1849–1850 state constitutional convention.

In the summer of 1852 Hardin suffered injuries in a horse-running accident, and he never recovered. He died in Bardstown, Kentucky.

• The standard biography for Hardin is Lucius P. Little, *Ben Hardin: His Times and Contemporaries, with Selections from His Speeches* (1887). A significant reference of Hardin and his role in Kentucky history is found in John Kleber, ed., *The Kentucky Encyclopedia* (1992).

RONALD BRUCE FRANKUM, JR.

HARDIN, Charles Henry (15 July 1820–29 July 1892), governor of Missouri, was born in Trimble County, Kentucky, the son of Charles Hardin and Mary Jewell, tanners. The family moved to Missouri in the fall of 1820, ultimately settling in Columbia, where his father served as the town's first postmaster. He died in 1830, and Hardin's mother successfully continued the family tanning business while raising five small children. Hardin was educated in the Columbia schools and in 1837 enrolled in Indiana University. Transferring to Miami University in Ohio, he received his B.A. in 1841 and his M.A. in 1842. While at Miami, he was one of eight founders of the national fraternity Beta Theta Pi. Following college, Hardin returned to Columbia, Missouri, where he studied law and was admitted to the bar in March 1843. He established his practice in Fulton, and he married Mary Barr Jenkins the following year.

Hardin actively engaged in politics as a Whig, being first chosen justice of the peace. He was elected circuit attorney in 1848 and sent to the Missouri House of Representatives from Callaway County in 1852 where, with the exception of the 1856–1857 session, he remained until 1860 when he was elevated to the state senate. His chief accomplishment during this service was a revision and codification of the Missouri statutes. With the demise of the Whigs, Hardin helped organize the American party in Missouri in the hope of finding a middle ground between the slavery extension platform of Missouri Democrats and that of the emerging Republican party, which called for free soil in neighboring Kansas.

In the crisis leading up to the Civil War Hardin opposed secession, favoring neutrality. In authoring the resolution that called for a convention to determine the issue of secession in 1861, he made provision for a popular referendum on any action seeking to sever federal relations. When the state legislature was deposed in July 1861, Hardin maintained its legitimacy and in October appeared at the rump session in Neosho, where he cast the lone vote in the senate against secession. He did not follow the pro-Confederate state government of Claiborne Jackson into exile but retired to a farm in Audrain County. Disfranchised and put under bond as a southern sympathizer in 1862, Hardin remained quietly on his farm until war's end. He reopened his law practice in Mexico, Missouri, in 1865.

In the postwar era Hardin joined the Democratic party in opposition to the policies of the radical Republicans, who had gained control of the state government and sought to disfranchise ex-Confederates and southern sympathizers. He returned to the state senate in 1872 as a Democrat following the overthrow of the radicals. Two years later that party nominated him for governor over the ex-Confederate general Francis M. Cockrell. Elected by a majority of 37,000, Hardin defeated William Gentry, whose "People's party" represented a coalition of the Republican party and the Grange.

Hardin inherited a state government burdened with debt from postwar expansiveness and excessive generosity to various railroad enterprises. The state was also suffering economically from the panic of 1873. Hardin preached strict economy and managed to reduce the state's debt by $632,000, thereby reestablishing the state's credit on a sound basis. Hardin had supported the calling of a new constitutional convention during the recent election. It met shortly after he took office in 1875 and, reflecting the governor's strong concern for tight fiscal management, enacted a new and stringently conservative document, which placed strong limits on governmental spending and activity. This constitution continued in effect until 1945.

Declining a second term, Hardin retired to his farm in 1877. He had long been interested in the promotion of education, and in 1873 he had established the Hardin College for Women in Mexico, Missouri. In 1889 he accepted membership on the Board of Curators of the University of Missouri but soon resigned because of failing health. He died at his farm home near Mexico.

• There is no body of Hardin papers. Hardin's wife, Mary Barr Hardin, published *Life and Writings of Gov. Charles Henry Hardin* (1896), but it is poorly arranged and uncritical. The best biographical sketch is by David H. Harris in Grace G. Avery and Floyd C. Shoemaker, eds., *Messages and Proclamations of the Governors of the State of Missouri*, vol. 5 (1924). Other sketches may be found in H. L. Conard, *Encyclopedia of the History of Missouri*, vol. 3 (1901), and in *History of Audrain County, Missouri* (1884).

WILLIAM E. PARRISH

HARDIN, Glenn Foster. *See* Hardin, Slats.

HARDIN, John (1 Oct. 1753–May 1792), soldier and scout, was born in Fauquier County, Virginia, the son of Martin Hardin, a tavern keeper and landowner, and Lydia (maiden name unknown). At about the age of twelve, Hardin moved with his parents to George's Creek in the unbroken wilderness of southwestern Pennsylvania, where he learned woodcraft and Indian ways and became such a proficient marksman that he was greatly feared by hostile natives. When he reached maturity, he married Jane Daviesse (or Davies), with whom he had six children. After their marriage the couple moved to Virginia. In early 1774 he volunteered as an ensign in Dunmore's War against the Indians. Although wounded in a battle with the Shawnee while campaigning with Captain Zachariah Morgan, he refused to be invalided out of the service.

A year later, Hardin was contemplating moving with his family to Kentucky when the revolutionary war commenced. He quickly changed his plans, recruited a company of soldiers, and joined the Continental army as a second lieutenant. Attached to General Daniel Morgan's rifle corps, he marched in 1777 with Morgan to New York and fought the British at Saratoga. He was particularly impressive as a scout, skirmisher, and marksman and won the confidence of Morgan, who entrusted him with many assignments requiring those skills. On at least one occasion, Hardin refused Morgan's proffer of a major's commission on grounds that he could better serve his country in the rank and capacity that he occupied. He also won the plaudits of General Horatio Gates, commander of the American army at Saratoga. His forte was to lure enemy officers within lethal range of his rifle and then with cool deliberation to pick them off. Later in life, he was haunted by these activities, concluding that they were hardly better than murder, and he refused to discuss them with his children. In the winter of 1777–1778 he was with Morgan at Valley Forge, foraging against British supply lines. On one notable occasion, he tomahawked one of the horses pulling an enemy wagon in order to capture the wagon for his own comrades' use. In December 1779 he resigned his commission and left the Continental army.

In 1780 Hardin received a land grant in Kentucky and in April 1786 finally effected his much-delayed move to that district. Settling his family in Nelson County, he joined his Kentucky neighbors in raiding hostile Indians north of the Ohio River. In September 1786 he accepted General George Rogers Clark's invitation to act as quartermaster with the rank of colonel in an expedition against the Indians of the Wabash River valley around Vincennes, Indiana. Three years later, he was selected to command a raiding party to interdict Indian war parties from the Wabash. In August 1789 he led a volunteer force of 220 Kentuckians against the Wea Indian towns, accomplishing little more than the murder of eight Shawnee men, women, and children who were peacefully minding their own business, and later boasted about his prowess. He accompanied General Josiah Harmar in the fall of 1790 on an expedition against the Miami Indians on the Maumee and upper Wabash rivers. Harmar's foray soon collapsed into defeat, and he only narrowly escaped a total disaster. On 19 October, while leading 180 Kentucky militiamen and regulars who had been detached from Harmar's main army, Hardin was ambushed by Indians and compelled to retreat helter-skelter back to the main camp. Thereupon Harmar and Hardin retreated and cut their losses, returning southward to the safety of Fort Washington (Cincinnati). They were court-martialed for their failure but were acquitted because the militia was blamed for their poor showing. Hardin, in fact, was adjudged to have proven himself "a brave and skillful officer."

On 24 May 1791 Hardin set out from Fort Washington with General Charles Scott on another expedition against the Indian towns near present-day Lafayette, Indiana, known as Ouiatenon. Determined to redeem his reputation after the Harmar fiasco, Hardin was pleased when on the morning of 1 June Scott detached him at the head of an advance party of sixty mounted infantrymen and a troop of horsemen to attack two small villages located some distance from the main settlements. Proceeding to his duty with alacrity, Hardin charged into one of the villages, made up of nine families, killing six Indians. The sounds of this battle carried to the second village, where the residents, mostly old men, women, and children, believed the firing was from a war party returning from a successful foray. Therefore they flocked toward Hardin's men and were captured before they could escape. Triumphantly, Hardin rejoined General Scott's main army in recently captured Ouiatenon with fifty-two captives. After the expedition's return to Kentucky, Hardin was praised by Scott for his "discernment, courage, and activity" during the campaign (Walworth, p. 236). In May 1792 Hardin was sent by General James Wilkinson under flag of truce to negotiate a peace treaty with the Miami tribes. While on his journey to the Miami villages, he was murdered by ostensibly friendly Indians in a hunting camp not far from where Fort Defiance was later built by General Anthony Wayne. While on this mission, but before his fate was known, he had been appointed a judge, as well as brigadier general of the First Brigade of Kentucky Militia, by the newly created state of Kentucky.

• Information on Hardin's role as a soldier in wars with the Indians is in the Charles Scott Papers, Margaret I. King Library, University of Kentucky. Scott's report to the secretary of war on the Ouiatenon raid is printed in the *Indianapolis Gazette*, 5 Sept. 1826. Other published sources are *American State Papers: Indian Affairs*, vol. 1 (1832), and *American State Papers: Military Affairs*, vol. 1 (1832). Some of Hardin's services in the revolutionary war are documented in James Wilkinson's unreliable *Memoirs of My Own Times*, vol. 1 (1816). A short biographical sketch is Mansfield Tracy Walworth, "Colonel John Hardin," *Historical Magazine* (Apr. 1869): 233–37. Faustina Kelly, "The Hardins in the Footsteps of the Boone Trail," *Register of the Kentucky Historical Society* 16 (1918): 27–31, provides family background. Hardin's career in the Indian wars is admirably sketched in Federal Writers Project, Works Progress Administration, *Military History of Kentucky* (1939); Richard H. Kohn, *Eagle and Sword: The Federalists and the Creation of the Military Establishment in America, 1783–1802* (1975); and, particularly, Wiley Sword, *President Washington's Indian War: The Struggle for the Old Northwest, 1790–1795* (1985). His association with Charles Scott is described in Paul David Nelson, "General Charles Scott, the Kentucky Mounted Volunteers, and the Northwest Indian Wars, 1784–1794," *Journal of the Early Republic* 6 (1986): 219–51; and Harry M. Ward, *Charles Scott and the "Spirit of '76"* (1988).

PAUL DAVID NELSON

HARDIN, John J. (6 Jan. 1810–23 Feb. 1847), soldier and politician, was born in Frankfort, Kentucky, the son of Martin D. Hardin, a politician, and Elizabeth Logan. It is not known what the middle initial, "J.," stood for, if indeed Hardin had a full middle name. He was raised in a wealthy Kentucky family. His father was a U.S. senator (1816–1817) and Kentucky's secretary of state, and his mother was the daughter of General Benjamin Logan. He graduated from Transylva-

nia University and studied law under Kentucky's chief justice John Boyle. In 1831 Hardin married Sarah Ellen Smith, with whom he would have four children.

Soon after his marriage, Hardin migrated to Jacksonville, Illinois, and quickly entered politics. Following the path of many politicians on the Jacksonian frontier, Hardin was admitted to the Illinois bar in 1831 and became a coeditor of the *Illinois Patriot*, a newspaper owned by Governor Joseph Duncan. The governor appointed Hardin a major general in the state militia during the Black Hawk War in 1831. In 1832 Democratic governor John Reynolds chose Hardin over Stephen A. Douglas to serve as state's attorney for Morgan County. By 1835 the state legislature revoked the governor's authority to appoint state's attorneys and elected Douglas to replace Hardin for the Morgan County post.

In April 1836 Hardin was elected to the state legislature. Despite helping to create the Whig party in central Illinois, he opposed the passage of a massive internal improvement program for building canals, roads, and railroads, which he viewed as fiscally irresponsible. "Popular in manners, an able lawyer, [and] a speaker of rare power," Hardin soon earned a reputation as one of Illinois's leading Whigs. He was elected again to the legislature in 1838 and 1840, and one early historian observed that no Whig in Illinois "had brighter prospects."

While in the legislature, Hardin helped pass a bill to establish an "Asylum for the Education of the Deaf and Dumb." He was also associated with other reform movements, particularly the "Yale Band," a small group of leaders promoting education. He assisted in the establishment of Illinois College, the first college in Illinois, and became one of its trustees. He also advocated temperance and asserted the state's right to regulate the sale of liquor, which resulted in Illinois's first local option law legalizing prohibition.

In October 1842 Hardin became involved in the duel between Abraham Lincoln and James A. Shields. Reporting on the event some eighteen years later, the Springfield *Illinois State Journal* (27 Apr. 1860) credited Hardin with preventing the two antagonists from fighting. According to the newspaper, Hardin "appeared on the scene, called both d——d fools, and by his arguments addressed to their common sense, and by his ridicule on the figure that they, two well grown, bearded men, were making there, each with a frog sticker in his hand, broke up the fight."

In 1843 Illinois was reapportioned into seven congressional districts. Hardin decided to seek the Whig nomination in the Seventh District and found Edward D. Baker and Lincoln contesting his nomination. In campaigning for delegates, Lincoln, realizing he had little chance for success, withdrew in favor of Baker. Hardin, nevertheless, won the nomination and was elected to Congress, defeating Democrat James A. McDougal. While in Congress, Hardin supported the Western Harbor Bill, federal aid for river and harbor improvements, and the resolution to terminate joint occupation with England of the Oregon Territory. He also declared his opposition to the annexation of Texas, calling it an "unwise, reckless, selfish, sectional and slavery-extending policy." He joined John Quincy Adams in voting against the "gag rule," which prohibited the consideration of antislavery petitions, and declared slavery "the greatest curse which has inflicted our land."

In 1844 Hardin agreed not to run again for Congress, allowing Baker to be nominated and subsequently elected. Since the Seventh Congressional District was the only district in Illinois in which the Whigs had a viable opportunity to elect a candidate, Whig leaders hailed Hardin's decision as a practical solution to prevent the party from being split apart by ambitious office-seekers.

In the fall of 1844 Governor Thomas Ford called on Hardin to help quell the mob action against the Mormons, who had settled around Nauvoo in western Illinois. Commanding a contingent of state troops, Hardin dispersed an anti-Mormon force of more than 2,000 men, who had assembled to attack Nauvoo. Civil unrest continued through 1845 and 1846, until Governor Ford again called on Hardin to restore order. Hardin helped negotiate the removal of the Mormons, who began their migration in the spring of 1846.

Hardin again decided to seek the nomination for Congress, surprising a number of Whig leaders. Lincoln, in particular, was disappointed. Hoping to sidetrack Hardin, Lincoln sought to have him nominated for governor. Hardin, however, declined, and a spirited campaign for delegates began. Lincoln argued that he, Hardin, and Baker had an agreement to "take a turn apiece." Hardin denied any such understanding, but Lincoln's campaign theme of "turn about is fair play" struck a responsive cord among Whig leaders. In January 1846 Hardin realized that Lincoln was winning the support of most of the convention delegates and proposed a direct primary election as an alternative way for choosing the party's nominee. Lincoln refused, and Hardin withdrew his candidacy in disgust, stating in an open letter to Whig voters that there never had been a bargain with Lincoln and Baker to take a turn apiece.

When war was declared with Mexico in May 1846, Hardin volunteered for service. He was commissioned a colonel of the First Regiment of Illinois Volunteers in June. Upon arriving in Texas, his regiment was ultimately put under the command of General Zachary Taylor. On 22 February 1847 Taylor's troops engaged the Mexican army at Buena Vista. At the end of the second day of the battle, Hardin was killed as his regiment held off the last Mexican charge. "We lost our best Whig man," Lincoln later wrote.

Hardin was a gifted and ambitious politician. He rose rapidly to prominence on the Illinois frontier defeating both Douglas and Lincoln in electoral contests. One Whig contemporary wrote that the "death of Hardin was not detrimental to Lincoln. Hardin had high aspirations, strong convictions and resolute purposes, and, had he survived the Mexican War, he would have added to his other elements of popularity great military renown."

• Hardin's papers are in the Chicago Historical Society. Scattered letters may be found in the David Davis Collection, Chicago Historical Society, and in *The Collected Works of Abraham Lincoln*, ed. Roy P. Basler et al. (9 vols., 1953). Important published primary sources include Joseph Gillespie, *Recollections of Early Illinois and Her Noted Men* (1880); Thomas Ford, *A History of Illinois from Its Commencement as a State in 1818 to 1847* (2 vols., 1946); Usher F. Linder, *Reminiscences of the Early Bench and Bar of Illinois* (1879); and D. W. Lusk, *Eighty Years of Illinois: Politics and Politicians, Anecdotes and Incidents, a Succinct History of the State, 1809–1859* (2 vols., 1889). Useful secondary sources include John Moses, *Illinois Historical and Statistical* (2 vols., 1889); Theodore Calvin Pease, *The Frontier State*, vol. 2 of *The Centennial History of Illinois*, ed. Clarence W. Alvord (1918; repr. 1987); Albert J. Beveridge, *Abraham Lincoln, 1809–1858* (1928); and Donald W. Riddle, *Lincoln Runs for Congress* (1948). Obsequies can be found in the Jacksonville, Ill., *Morgan Journal*, 14 July 1847.

STEPHEN L. HANSEN

HARDIN, John Wesley (26 May 1853–19 Aug. 1895), gunman, was born in Bonham, Texas, the son of James G. Hardin, a Methodist preacher, and Mary Elizabeth Dixon. He attended school in Polk and Trinity counties in East Texas, where his father also taught school and practiced law. Though he owned no slaves in 1860 and opposed secession, the elder Hardin became an ardent supporter of the Confederacy. "Wes" Hardin imbibed his family's devotion to the cause as well as his father's lessons regarding "the first law of nature—that of self preservation" (Hardin, p. 125). The Sixth Commandment and Methodist strictures regarding drinking and gambling seem to have made much less of an impression on him.

In 1868, at age fifteen, Hardin committed the first of his many homicides, shooting a Polk County freedman who had menaced him after being bested in a wrestling match. Unwilling to be tried in the Reconstruction courts for killing a black man, Hardin fled. He waylaid federal soldiers sent after him and claimed to have killed three of them. By early 1869 the fugitive had settled in Corsicana, Texas, where he taught school before hiring on as a cowboy. He became known for his marksmanship and his deep hatred of the Reconstruction regime. Hardin terrorized "impudent" freedpeople and tangled again with U.S. soldiers, killing one, according to his own account.

The identity of these early victims suggests that while Hardin has been remembered as "the most sensational gun-fighter of the gun-fighting Old West" (Nordyke, foreword), his criminal career had as much to do with the violent resistance of many conservative white southerners to the social and political consequences of emancipation and Reconstruction as with the lawlessness of a boisterous, lightly policed frontier. This postwar southern violence was particularly pronounced in Texas. Between 1865 and 1870 black Texans, Republicans, and military and civilian agents of the new order died by the score, often at the hands of nightriders or of gunmen like Hardin. To fight such violence, the Republican state government established a racially integrated police force in 1870. Its members became Hardin's chief enemies. This body included some brutal scoundrels, but it is clear that the complexion as much as the character of the state police upset Hardin. He crusaded against what he termed "Negro rule," a phantasm conjured out of black Texans' exercise—together with whites—of state authority. Sought by the police, Hardin lay low in central Texas through the beginning of 1871. He was apprehended by lawmen several times but escaped in each instance by killing his captors.

In January 1871 Hardin settled among kin in Gonzales County. He worked as a cowboy and stockman and in 1872 married Jane Bowen. Initially Hardin kept his distance from the feuding that plagued the area—though it pitted the Taylors, an extended family of unreconstructed rebels, against a faction, designated the Suttons, that included members of the Reconstruction constabulary. He hardly eschewed violence, however. In September 1871 he murdered a black state policeman and wounded another. Black citizens raised a posse to run him down, but Hardin surprised and overwhelmed the force. The next summer, while selling horses in East Texas, Hardin shot several more policemen and was wounded himself before surrendering and being returned to Gonzales to stand trial. Because many county residents either admired or feared him, Hardin quickly escaped from jail and returned home, apparently unmolested. As he later explained, "In putting down Negro rule there, I had made many friends and sympathizers" (Hardin, p. 75).

At the same time he battled Reconstruction authorities, Hardin engaged in pursuits more befitting his Wild West image. In 1871 he drove a herd of cattle up the Chisholm Trail to Abilene, Kansas, where he defied marshal James Butler "Wild Bill" Hickok's ban on carrying guns. In the course of this trip, Hardin appears to have killed ten men, including several Indians and five Mexican *vaqueros*. Other Hardin victims in these years included fellow gamblers and belligerent drunks. In every instance, Hardin claimed that he acted in self-defense. The sheer number of incidents, however, and the frequency with which his antagonists died suggest the decidedly pathological cast of Hardin's character. Contemporaries called him among the fastest and most accurate shots they had ever seen. Unfortunately for his enemies, Hardin usually aimed for the head.

By 1873 Hardin's luck, and the sympathy he enjoyed among some conservative whites, began to run out. A freshly elected Democratic legislature abolished the state police and other unpopular Reconstruction institutions, but Hardin became increasingly involved in the Sutton-Taylor feud. He helped kill a Sutton leader, former state policeman Jack Helm, and engineered the assassination of a second, William Sutton. With the installation of a Democratic governor in January 1874, Hardin's violent acts could no longer be regarded as blows against Reconstruction rule. Shortly after the William Sutton murder, Hardin started a herd of cattle north toward Kansas, stopping off in Comanche, Texas, to see his family. There, on 26 May 1874, he killed a deputy sheriff whom he said had drawn a gun behind his back. Local residents were not moved by Hardin's claims, however. He had to flee for his life, and mobs subsequently murdered his brother, four cousins, and three associates. The next time the Democratic legislature met, it offered a $4,000 reward for the "notorious murderer" Hardin.

Hardin escaped with his wife and child to Gainesville, Florida, then moved to Jacksonville, where he dealt cattle. After killing two detectives who had tracked him down, Hardin settled in southern Alabama. On 23 August 1877 Texas Rangers, having discovered his whereabouts, overpowered him on a train in Pensacola. Hardin was returned to Texas, convicted of second-degree murder, and sentenced to twenty-five years in prison for the killing in Comanche.

In prison in Huntsville, Hardin showed little remorse. Responsible, by his own count, for well over thirty deaths, he wrote his daughter that "the blood I have spilt is of that kind which can never stain" (letter, 14 July 1889 [quoted by permission of Southwest Texas State University]). After several early attempts to escape, however, he behaved well, studied law, and, ultimately, had nearly ten years shaved off his sentence. Hardin was released in February 1894 and shortly thereafter was pardoned by the state. His plans to lead a more settled life practicing law in Gonzales proved futile. His wife had died in 1892, and his three children were nearly grown. Few clients called, and he became involved in a bitter dispute with a figure from his outlaw days. After this man was elected sheriff, Hardin left Gonzales. In 1895 he married Callie Lewis in Junction, Texas, but his teenage bride left him almost immediately. Hired to handle a case in West Texas, Hardin ended up in El Paso, where he quickly resumed old habits—drinking, gambling, and gunplay. One summer night, another aging gunman, John Selman, shot him down in the Acme Saloon.

It has been difficult for those who romanticize outlaws to depict Hardin as a Robin Hood. He was not a robber or a friend to the poor. Instead—to employ historian E. J. Hobsbawm's typology of banditry—he was often pictured as an "avenger," a cruel man fighting even crueler oppressors. Attitudes toward Reconstruction have changed, however, and Americans take more seriously the dangers faced by African Americans and Republicans in postwar Texas and show more respect for the efforts of federal and state authorities to protect them. Viewed from this perspective, Hardin seems little more than a hate-filled miscreant with a penchant—and a genuine talent—for murder.

• A collection of Hardin papers, chiefly letters written and received in prison, is in Special Collections, Albert B. Alkek Library, Southwest Texas State University in San Marcos. Papers related to Hardin's pardon are in the records of the secretary of state (RG 307), Archives Division of the Texas

State Library, Austin. An autobiography, *The Life of John Wesley Hardin As Written by Himself*, uncompleted at the time of his death, was published in 1896 and has been reprinted in paperback. Certain commentators have asserted that Hardin lacked the education to have written the work himself. His prison letters, however, demonstrate that he was quite capable of having done so. The most complete biography is Lewis Nordyke's essentially sympathetic *John Wesley Hardin: Texas Gunman* (1957); unfortunately, it lacks both bibliography and notes. The motives and circumstances of Hardin's murder have been debated over the years. See Leon Metz, *John Selman, Gunfighter* (1980). Following Hardin's murder, Texas newspapers carried often unreliable accounts of his life and death. See, for instance, the *Gonzales Inquirer*, 22 Aug. 1895.

PATRICK G. WILLIAMS

HARDIN, Martin D. (21 June 1780–8 Oct. 1823), lawyer, soldier, and U.S. senator, was born near the Monongahela River in southwestern Pennsylvania, the son of John Hardin, a revolutionary war soldier and Indian fighter, and Jane Daveiss. The Hardins were a somewhat prosperous Virginia family of French Huguenots who immigrated in 1706 and settled beyond the Virginia border on the Pennsylvania frontier about 1765. In 1786 John Hardin moved the family to Nelson County in the Kentucky District (now Washington County, Ky.) along Pleasant Run, a branch of Beech Fork, near the present-day county seat of Springfield. John Hardin was murdered by Shawnee Indians in May 1792, near present-day Hardin, Ohio, while serving as a peace emissary; he became a celebrated martyr and the namesake of counties in Kentucky and Ohio.

Martin Hardin attended and studied law at Transylvania University and later read law in the Richmond, Kentucky, office of George Nicholas, then considered the leading attorney in the state. He practiced there for a time, quickly establishing a distinguished reputation. In 1804 he shared an office with a cousin, Benjamin Hardin, who later became a celebrated lawyer, orator, and congressman. The following year Hardin was elected to his first public office, representing Madison County in the state house of representatives.

In 1807 Hardin moved to Frankfort, the state capital; there he opened a law office and built upon his reputation. He was selected "reporter" by the state court of appeals, in response to a demand by the legislature that a record be kept of appellate decisions and their precedents. In 1810 he published *Reports of Cases Argued and Adjudged in the Court of Appeals of Kentucky* for 1805–1808. In January 1809 he married Elizabeth Logan, the daughter of Kentucky militia general Benjamin Logan, in Franklin County.

In April 1812, in response to the growing crisis with Great Britain, Hardin wrote a letter to revolutionary war hero Isaac Shelby, Kentucky's first governor, asking him to seek the office again. Hardin's appeal prompted a flood of support for the aging general, who was elected in August. Hardin had been elected to represent Franklin County in the state house but vacated his seat to accept a grateful Shelby's appointment as secretary of state. Meanwhile, Hardin became a major

in the First Rifle Regiment of the Kentucky militia, commanded by his brother-in-law, Colonel John Allen. Hardin participated in the battle of Frenchtown, 22 January 1813, in which Allen was killed. After his service, Hardin returned to his duties as secretary of state.

In 1816 Kentucky governor Gabriel Slaughter appointed Hardin to the U.S. Senate to fill the vacancy caused by the resignation of William T. Barry. Though serving only from 13 November 1816 to 3 March 1817, Hardin strenuously voiced his nationalist views and advocated a liberal interpretation of the Constitution that would allow for internal improvements funded by the federal government. Declining to stand for election to a full term, Hardin returned home and in 1818 was again elected to the state legislature. He was elected Speaker of the Kentucky House in 1819 and in 1820 was a presidential elector for Democrat James Monroe. He was a representative-elect when he died in Franklin County.

Hardin was remembered as a leading attorney of his time, a statesman, and a participant in the military achievements of his family. His son John J. Hardin became a congressman from Illinois (1843–1845) and a military leader. He was killed on 23 February 1847, in the battle of Buena Vista in the Mexican War.

Hardin's middle name was likely Daveiss, his mother's maiden name and the given name of at least one relative. A 15 October 1823 obituary in the *Argus of Western America* gives it as "Davis," a popular pronunciation of the Daveiss surname in Kentucky. Thomas Marshall Green, in *Historic Families of Kentucky*, argued that Hardin added the "D." to his name to distinguish himself from several other kinsmen named Martin Hardin, namesakes of his grandfather and great-great grandfather.

• Hardin's papers are at the Chicago Historical Society. The Kentucky Historical Society, Frankfort, and the University of Kentucky, Lexington, possess a few documents. The Filson Club Historical Society, Louisville, Ky., has a three-page autobiographical sketch, in addition to early nineteenth-century portraits of Hardin and his wife. Lewis Collins and Richard H. Collins, *History of Kentucky* (1874; repr. 1966), Thomas Marshall Green, *Historic Families of Kentucky* (1889; repr. 1964), and G. Glenn Clift, *Remember The Raisin!* (1961), are important sources. See also the *Kentucky Gazette* (Lexington), 18 Nov. 1816; and the *Argus of Western America* (Frankfort), 20 May 1813.

THOMAS E. STEPHENS

HARDIN, Slats (1 July 1910–6 Mar. 1975), track and field athlete, was born Glenn Foster Hardin in Derma, Calhoun County, Mississippi. While attending Greenwood High School in that community, Hardin was a good student and was considered the best three-sport athlete in the school's history. As a result he won an academic-athletic scholarship to Louisiana State University (LSU) in 1931. While still an undergraduate student, he was selected to the U.S. Olympic team in 1932 and won the silver medal in a memorable 400-meter intermediate hurdles final inside the Los

Angeles Memorial Coliseum. The winner, Robert Morton Newburgh Tisdall of Ireland, broke the world record (52.0 seconds) with a 51.7-second performance, but he knocked over the tenth and last hurdle; under the rules at that time, which were not changed until 1938, his record run was unacceptable. Hardin was thus awarded the victory with a world record 52.0 seconds. In Tisdall's autobiography *The Young Athlete*, he was so far ahead at the 200-meter mark that "I began to wonder if the rest of the field had fallen over." However, the American Olympic track coach, Dink Templeton, considered Hardin to be the next great intermediate hurdler. Templeton is quoted in Robert Pariente's track and field history as saying that "Hardin has both world-class speed over high hurdles and in the 200-meter and 400-meter sprint races. He will dominate his specialty for years to come." Templeton proved to be correct.

Hardin won four national intermediate hurdles championships between 1932 and 1936; in 1933 he was the star of his LSU team as they won the National Collegiate Athletic Association (NCAA) championship. On 17 June 1933 in Chicago's Soldier Field, Hardin won the 440-yard "flat" race in 47.1 seconds, an NCAA record, and followed with a world-record 22.9-second run over the 220-yard low hurdles. Hailed as the prototypical intermediate hurdler, possessing great sprint speed and perfect technique, he was credited with a half-mile time of 1 minute 53 seconds. He opened the 1934 season with a "440" in 46.8 seconds, then the second-best time in history; won the "440" and the low hurdles at the NCAA championships in record times for the meet (47.0 and 22.7); and set a world record of 51.8 seconds in the intermediate hurdles at the AAU championships in Milwaukee. That summer he toured in Europe; on 26 July 1934 in Stockholm, he raced in the 400-meter hurdles in 50.6 seconds—an astounding 1.4 seconds faster than the world record and a performance that remained a record for nineteen years.

In 1935 Hardin finished third in the NCAA quarter-mile (440-yard) sprint and lost the low hurdles to Jesse Owens, the quadruple-gold medalist at the following year's Olympic Games in Berlin. Hardin won the 1935 Amateur Athletic Union (AAU) national championships low hurdles in a world-record 22.4 seconds, but it was disallowed because of an "irregular timing device." He retained his form in 1936, performing brilliantly at the 400-meter intermediate hurdles in the Olympic final on 4 August before 90,000 spectators, prompting the *New York Times* journalist Arthur J. Daley to write that "Glenn Hardin slammed a victory" in the event. Hardin's brief but significant five-year career as an international hurdler complete, he retired after a successful post-Olympic relay meet against the British Empire in London. At the time of his retirement, Hardin claimed the five fastest intermediate hurdles times in the history of track and field.

Hardin married Margaret Thelma "Sis" Riddle of New Orleans in 1937. They had three children. Hardin's son Billy was an outstanding hurdler at LSU in the 1960s, made the U.S. Olympic Team in 1964, and competed in the 400-meter hurdles in Tokyo. Although Billy failed to win a medal in the event, he ran faster than his illustrious father. After retiring from the sport, Hardin worked as a salesman and then as a representative of the Louisiana state government. He died in Baton Rouge, Louisiana. Track and field experts all agree that Hardin was the first of his kind—a great sprinter who could hurdle well, rather than, as all who had preceded him, a hurdler who could run fast.

• Information on Hardin is found in Bill Mallon and Ian Buchanan, *Quest for Gold: The Encyclopedia of American Olympics* (1984); Robert Pariente, *La fabuleuse histoire de L'athletisme* (1978); David Wallechinsky, *The Complete Book of the Olympics* (1992); and F. A. M. Webster, *Great Moments in Athletics* (1947). Other books include the *American Official Report Xth Olympiad 1932* (1933), pp. 436–38; and the *British Official Report Xth Olympiad 1932* (1933), pp. 68–69. Obituaries are in the *New York Times*, 9 Mar. 1975, and the *Baton Rouge (La.) Advocate*, 7 Mar. 1975.

JOHN A. LUCAS

HARDIN, William Jefferson (1831–1890), legislator, was born in Russellville, Kentucky, the illegitimate son of a free quadroon (name unknown) and a white father. Hardin claimed that his father was the brother of Ben Hardin, a Kentucky politician and congressman, but the fact cannot be verified. Raised in a Shaker community in South Union, Kentucky, Hardin's educational and social opportunities were unusual for a person considered black in the antebellum period.

Following the completion of his own education, Hardin became a teacher for "free children of color" in Bowling Green, Kentucky, but soon left the teaching profession and traveled in the midwestern states and Canada. In 1850 he returned to Kentucky, where he married Caroline K. (maiden name unknown) and fathered one child. Sometime between his marriage and the outbreak of the Civil War, Hardin moved his family to Iowa.

Leaving his first family in Iowa, Hardin relocated in Denver, Colorado Territory, in 1863 and engaged in a number of occupations, including stock speculation, poolroom management, and barbering. During the fall of 1864 he acquired a certain local prominence in Denver and nearby mining towns by giving unpaid lectures on the contributions of noted blacks in history, especially General Toussaint L'Ouverture, a revolutionary leader in the French colony of St. Domingue (now Haiti). Because of his speaking ability and experience, Hardin became the chief spokesman for the Colorado black community when it agitated for equal suffrage in 1865.

When Congress gave Colorado leaders permission to write a state constitution in 1865, Hardin and other black leaders attended the convention as spectators and demanded equal suffrage for black men. The convention, however, chose to put the issue to a public vote at the same time that the constitution was submitted for popular approval, and black suffrage was rejected by an overwhelming majority. In response Hardin, Henry O. Wagoner, and Edward Sanderlin began a campaign to block Colorado's admission into the Union until equal suffrage was granted. They petitioned Governor Alexander Cummings to request a change in the territorial suffrage laws and to crusade against statehood until the constitution was amended to give all men the right to vote. Hardin appealed to Horace Greeley, editor of the *New York Tribune*, and to U.S. Senator Charles Sumner to oppose statehood as long as the restriction remained. Greeley paid little attention to Hardin's request, but Sumner did mention the Colorado restriction in several of his speeches on equal suffrage in the Senate.

Colorado failed to achieve statehood with its 1865 constitution and did not enter the Union until 1876. Possibly as a result of the suffrage issue that was raised, James Ashley, Radical Republican from Ohio, introduced a bill on 15 May 1866 giving black men in all territories the right to vote. The bill passed the House of Representatives but failed in the Senate during the 1866 session. Senator Benjamin Wade reintroduced the bill during the next session; it quickly passed the Senate and House, becoming law without President Andrew Johnson's signature on 31 January 1867. It was implemented for the first time during municipal elections held in Colorado in April 1867, and blacks voted without incident.

From 1867 to 1873 Hardin was an important political figure in Denver's black community and the territorial Republican party, and his ability to deliver the black vote gained him a patronage appointment as weigher at the Denver Mint. Success may have been his undoing, for by 1873 both blacks and whites in Denver turned against him. He angered blacks when he criticized their celebrations of emancipation as "disgraceful nigger frolics" and "utterly depraved and degraded" (*Rocky Mountain News*, 2 and 6 Aug. 1867). Whites and Republican politicians rebuffed Hardin in 1873, when his first wife Caroline arrived in Denver accusing him of bigamy for his recent marriage to Nellie Davidson, a white milliner, and declaring that he fled to Colorado in 1863 to avoid conscription into the Union army. Although Hardin claimed his marriage to Caroline was not legal because she was a slave and he was underage at the time, officials at the mint fired him. Threatened with legal action, he and Nellie fled to Cheyenne, Wyoming Territory.

Hardin took up barbering again in Cheyenne but did nothing to bring attention to himself until he successfully ran for the territorial legislature in 1879. He held his seat for two sessions and served on a number of legislative committees, but he did not initiate or champion any notable legislation. Even though he seems to have been well respected as a legislator, Hardin chose not to seek reelection in 1882 and for unknown reasons left Wyoming Territory. He lived for a short time in Park City, Utah, and then moved to Leadville, Colorado, where he died of natural causes.

Hardin holds the distinction of being the first black man elected to a western legislature and the only black to serve in the Wyoming territorial and state lawmaking body. His activities on behalf of black suffrage in the Reconstruction period, although confined to Colorado Territory, indicate that blacks throughout the nation sought civil equality and that the efforts made during the post–Civil War years were not confined to the eastern part of the nation alone.

• The William Jefferson Hardin File, Wyoming State Historical Library, Cheyenne, is helpful. Letters written by Hardin are found in the Charles Sumner Papers at Harvard University; the *New York Tribune*, 15 Dec. 1865; and the Denver *Rocky Mountain News*, 1865–1873, with substantial news accounts involving him appearing in Nov. 1865, during the constitutional struggle, and in July and Aug. 1873, when the scandal over his marriage and draft dodging became public. There is no biography of Hardin. A biographical sketch was printed in the *Cheyenne* (Wyo.) *Daily Sun*, 9 Nov. 1879. See also the following two articles by Eugene H. Berwanger, "William J. Hardin: Colorado Spokesman for Racial Justice, 1863–1873," *Colorado Magazine* 52 (Winter 1975): 52–65, and "Reconstruction on the Frontier: The Equal Rights Struggle in Colorado, 1865–1867," *Pacific Historical Review* 44 (Aug. 1975): 313–29.

EUGENE H. BERWANGER

HARDING, Chester (1 Sept. 1792–10 Apr. 1866), portrait painter, was born in Conway, Massachusetts, the son of Abiel Harding and Olive Smith. His father worked for a local "rye-gin" distillery and invented useless perpetual motion machines. In 1806 the family moved to Caledonia, New York, where, over the next ten years, Chester and his brothers supported the family through a variety of jobs, including tavernkeeping, peddling, and cabinetmaking. His lack of formal education later motivated Harding to provide educational opportunities for other young artists and for his own children, several of whom he sent to college.

Harding's memoir, which he called "My Egotistography," describes his first attempt at portraiture, inspired after he and his wife were painted in Pittsburgh by an itinerant artist named Nelson. His 1816 picture of Caroline Woodruff, whom Harding had married the previous year, elicited from him this reaction: "The moment I saw the likeness I became frantic with delight: it was like the discovery of a new sense."

Harding traveled to the prosperous frontier towns of Kentucky, where between 1818 and 1820 he painted nearly 100 portraits at $25 apiece. After using this money for a two-month study trip to Philadelphia, he moved further west to St. Louis, where, according to Harding, the governor of the territory, William Clark, became one of his first sitters. At Clark's request, Harding painted the only life portrait of Daniel Boone (Massachusetts Historical Society) just months before the aged pioneer's death. Harding spent the winter of 1821–1822 in Washington, D.C. In 1823 he enjoyed six months of spectacular popularity in Boston. Aware of his technical limitations, however, he determined to go abroad. On 1 August 1823 he left Boston for three years in England and Scotland.

In London, the brash young American immediately attracted enthusiastic patrons, including Augustus Frederick, the duke of Sussex and brother of King George IV, whose portrait he painted (unlocated, mezzotint by Charles Turner, London, 1825) and who sponsored him for important commissions. Harding had learned to paint by observing the work of others. In Kentucky he had absorbed the conventions of portrait painting from the work of Gilbert Stuart's pupil Matthew Harris Jouett, and in Boston Stuart's own paintings served as models. Only ten days after Harding's arrival in London, the influence of Sir Thomas Lawrence can already be seen in his portrait of Loammi Baldwin, a Boston civil engineer traveling in England (National Portrait Gallery, Washington, D.C.). The dramatic crossed-arm pose and painterly three-dimensional solidity mark a sharp improvement in Harding's developing skills. *Alexander Hamilton Douglas, 10th Duke of Hamilton*, showing the duke standing in front of a classical column (private collection), which was painted in Scotland in 1825, and the very Lawrence-like *Mrs. Thomas Grahame (Hannah Finlay)* (Glasgow Art Gallery), exhibited in 1826 at the Royal Academy, can both be directly related to paintings by Lawrence.

Back in the United States in 1826, Harding retained his new skills but quickly abandoned English painterly generalizations, reverting to strong factual immediacy. He ensured his reputation by seeking out the important figures of the day. His more than twenty portraits of Daniel Webster are based on two life sittings and two daguerreotypes (examples at Boston Athenaeum, the National Portrait Gallery, and Dartmouth College). At the 1829 Virginia constitutional convention in Richmond, he painted Presidents James Monroe (private collection) and James Madison (Washington and Lee University, Lexington, Va.; replica at the National Portrait Gallery) and other members of Virginia's establishment. In 1830 he was commissioned to paint a life-size, full-length portrait of Chief Justice John Marshall (Boston Athenaeum), one of his most accomplished works. He also painted President John Quincy Adams (Redwood Library, Newport, R.I.; Department of State, Washington, D.C.) and Charles Carroll of Carrollton, the last living signer of the Declaration of Independence (one version at the National Gallery of Art). Harding typically painted replicas of his well-known sitters' portraits and often had engravings made of them for public sale. Charles Carroll's portrait, for example, was engraved by both James Barton Longacre and Asher B. Durand.

Harding settled with his wife and ten children in Springfield, Massachusetts, in 1830, but he maintained a studio and gallery at 22 School Street in Boston, where he rented rooms to artists and provided exhibition space. He was a founder of the Boston Artists' Association (1841–1851), an effort to establish an art academy in the city. His studio became a center of Boston's artistic life.

Despite his fears that his popularity would wane once he was no longer a "backwoodsman newly caught," Harding continued to enjoy the patronage of wealthy and influential citizens of Boston and nearby cities, including Abbott and Amos Lawrence, important leaders in the early development of the New England textile industry. Especially noteworthy among his many portraits of members of the Lawrence family is a life-size seated figure of Amos Lawrence (c. 1845, National Gallery of Art; replicas at the Williams College Museum of Art and the Museum of Fine Arts, Boston).

Throughout the 1840s Harding continued to seek clients by traveling to New Orleans, Cincinnati, and St. Louis. His wife died suddenly in 1845. In 1847 he made a second trip to England. His last portrait, *General William Tecumseh Sherman* (1866, Union League Club, New York), was finished only weeks before his death, its tighter style reflecting the new popularity of photography. He died in Boston. Harding painted a number of self-portraits, including those of 1828 (National Gallery of Art), circa 1843 (Museum of Fine Arts, Boston), and 1859 (Indianapolis Museum of Art).

Through native talent, a genial personality, hard work, and a businesslike approach to art, this untrained itinerant artist catapulted to favor as one of America's most successful portrait painters in the era after Gilbert Stuart, acquiring as sitters the influential men and women of the time: presidents, congressmen, Supreme Court justices, merchants and sea captains of New England and their wives, and members of the British aristocracy. His straightforward and honest portraits provide a record of an important period of America's past, and his colorful life is a paradigm of the nineteenth-century rags-to-riches American success story.

• Harding's letters are in the Boston Athenaeum and the Boston Public Library, Department of Rare Books and Manuscripts. The primary source for Harding is his memoir, "My Egotistography," published by his daughter Margaret Eliot White as *A Sketch of Chester Harding, Artist* (1866), reprinted with his British journal and an introduction by his grandson W. P. G. Harding in 1890, and reprinted again in 1970. He also contributed an account of himself to William Dunlap's *History of the Rise and Progress of the Arts of Design in the United States* (1834; repr. 1969). Margaret White's own journal, *After Noontide* (1907), and her daughter Eliza Orne White's fictionalized account written for children, *A Little Girl of Long Ago* (1897), are both useful. See also the following works by Leah Lipton: *A Truthful Likeness: Chester Harding and His Portraits*, an exhibition catalog including a biography and catalogue raisonné (National Portrait Gallery, 1985); "Chester Harding in Great Britain," *Antiques* (June 1984), pp. 1382–90; and "Chester Harding and the Life Portrait of Daniel Boone," *American Art Journal* (Summer 1984), pp. 4–19.

LEAH LIPTON

HARDING, Florence Mabel Kling DeWolfe (15 Aug. 1860–21 Nov. 1924), first lady of the United States, was born in Marion, Ohio, the daughter of Amos

Kling, a banker, and Lousia Bouton. Florence grew up in an affluent atmosphere, attending the best school in Marion. When she demonstrated a flair for the piano, she was sent to study at the Cincinnati Conservatory of Music. At the age of nineteen, Florence eloped with Henry "Pete" DeWolfe, the ne'er-do-well son of a prominent Ohio family. The quick marriage was necessitated by Florence's pregnancy; a son was born six months later. Florence sought and was granted a divorce from DeWolfe in 1886. In 1891, she was remarried to Warren G. Harding, the publisher of the *Marion Star*.

Florence Harding assisted in running the *Star* for fourteen years. Her responsibilities included circulation, advertising, and the development of the home delivery system. She ran the paper herself during her husband's lengthy illness after their marriage. She also continually encouraged her husband's political ambitions and was pleased with his almost steady progress in Ohio politics. (Warren Harding was elected state senator in 1899, lieutenant governor in 1902, lost the Ohio gubernatorial race in 1910, and then rebounded to win election to the U.S. Senate in 1914.)

In 1920, Warren Harding secured the Republican nomination for president. While Florence Harding hoped that her husband would be successful in his campaign, she had grave misgivings about the enterprise. Just after Harding's nomination she told the *New York Times*, "I can see but one word written over the head of my husband if he is elected and that word is tragedy" ("Mrs. Harding's Foreboding," *New York Times*, 11 June 1921).

Harding played a limited yet important role in the presidential campaign. She welcomed delegations who came to visit her husband at their home in Marion and accompanied the candidate on speaking tours. On at least one occasion she served as campaign strategist. Rumors concerning Warren Harding's possible black ancestry were circulating and his advisors were planning to issue a denial. Florence Harding flatly rejected this course of action and declared that no denial would be issued by the Harding campaign. Perhaps confirming the wisdom of Florence Harding's approach, the rumor died and caused no further concern to the campaign. Warren Harding swept to victory, capturing 60.3 percent of the popular vote.

The new first lady was hard-working, conscientious, and frequently cantankerous. She was interested in the medical care of veterans and became a familiar sight at Walter Reed Hospital, where she went to visit "her boys." She and her staff handled voluminous requests from veterans regarding jobs, financial assistance, and health care. A warm and generous hostess, she opened the White House to public tours (joining many of them herself and startling tourists), entertained thousands of guests at the executive mansion, and reinstated the annual Easter egg roll down the White House lawn.

The first lady wielded uneven but definite influence on presidential decision making. There is only one confirmed instance when she might have influenced a foreign affairs decision; the thrust of her efforts was directed at domestic issues. She regularly read and edited many of her husband's speeches. She insisted that a paragraph in her husband's first message to Congress be deleted, as it seemed to commit the United States to membership in the League of Nations. (Warren Harding had vehemently opposed the league while in the Senate, and Florence Harding feared that the president would appear to be indecisive or bowing to political pressure.) On another occasion, the first lady insisted that Warren Harding refrain from suggesting a constitutional amendment limiting the president to one six-year term of office. In December 1921, the president permitted Florence Harding to choose which convicts serving sentences in federal penitentiaries should be pardoned. She was bitterly opposed to her husband's decision to pardon Eugene V. Debs, who was serving a long sentence for pacifist-related World War I activities. No source is clear regarding Harding's objections to this particular pardon; potential negative political fallout or a genuine feeling that Debs had tried to subvert the war effort might explain her strong feelings. The first lady influenced at least one decision that the president came to regret. Harding advocated the appointment of her old friend Colonel Charles R. Forbes to head the Veterans Bureau. Forbes was forced to resign from his position when it was learned that he had appropriated almost $250 million for his own use. In 1925 he was convicted of defrauding the government and was sentenced to two years in jail. Forbes was just one of a group of unscrupulous men, including Attorney General Harry Daugherty and Interior Secretary Albert Fall, who made up one of the most corrupt administrations in presidential history.

Florence Harding could be warm and affable, but she never forgot a slight or what she perceived to be rude behavior. She recorded the names of people who had not been civil to her and Warren Harding in a little red book. She disliked Vice President Calvin Coolidge and his wife and engineered the defeat of a bill that would have provided a stately home as the official residence of the vice president.

Perhaps benefiting from her years of work at the *Star*, Harding enjoyed a positive relationship with reporters. She made herself available for interviews, although she requested that she not be directly quoted. On occasion, the first lady held informal press conferences to brief the press on upcoming public events.

Harding seems to have been an early feminist. During the 1920 Republican National Convention, she told reporters that she was a suffragist. Many observers assumed that she influenced her husband's thinking on issues particularly relevant to women, including equal pay, the eight-hour workday, maternity and infancy legislation, and the creation of a federal social welfare agency. She was the author of a strongly feminist but unmailed letter regarding careers for women. During the Harding administration she accepted honorary membership in the National Women's party.

The Harding marriage was stormy, marked by frequent quarrels and unpleasantness. Warren Harding is believed to have fathered the child of a young female admirer, and he was involved in a more serious ongoing relationship with one of Florence Harding's friends. Suspicions about fidelity did little to lessen marital tensions. Those tensions dissipated considerably after Florence Harding nearly succumbed to nephritis in late fall of 1922.

In June 1923 the Hardings left on a vacation trip to Alaska that included a number of speeches in support of U.S. membership in the World Court. As they departed Washington, there were strong intimations of wrongdoing in the administration. Speculation centered on the illegal sale of government oil reserves at Teapot Dome, Wyoming, and Elk Hill, California, to private business. Members of the president's party observed that he seemed nervous and preoccupied, presumably about the unfolding scandal. On the way home, the president was taken ill and died suddenly on 2 August 1923. Florence Harding refused to permit an autopsy, and some observers suggested that she had murdered the chief executive to spare him the embarrassment of the Teapot Dome debacle. In fact, Warren Harding had been unwell for some time and probably died as a result of a cerebral hemorrhage. Suspicions regarding Florence Harding's role in the president's death grew when she burned quantities of her husband's public and private papers.

Harding returned to Marion, Ohio, where she died fifteen months later. The first presidential wife after suffrage, she enlarged the public and private roles of the first lady. Although she had no formal White House project in the modern sense, she was particularly interested in veterans. Harding allowed the press greater access than they had ever been permitted and influenced decision making. Frequently jealous and ambitious, she was nonetheless well liked by the American public and participated in some of the changes that resulted in the modern office of the first lady.

• Florence Harding's papers and letters are included with Warren Harding's papers, which are on deposit with the Ohio Historical Society, Columbus, Ohio. For a careful discussion of the Harding papers, see Kenneth W. Duckett, "The Harding Papers: How Some Were Burned," *American Heritage* 16 (Feb. 1965): 24–31, 102–109. Two secondary sources are worthy of note. Francis Russell, *The Shadow of Blooming Grove: Warren G. Harding in His Times* (1968), is outstanding. It is well documented and incisive in its analysis of the public and private Warren and Florence Harding. Andrew Sinclair, *The Available Man: The Life behind the Mask of Warren Gamaliel Harding* (1965), is a solid account of Warren Harding's political career, especially his White House tenure. Florence Harding receives critical yet fair treatment in this study as well. Harding has also been reexamined in a number of recent first lady histories: Carl S. Anthony, *First Ladies: The Saga of the Presidents' Wives and Their Power* (1990); Betty Boyd Caroli, *First Ladies* (1987); and Myra G. Gutin, *The President's Partner: The First Lady in the Twentieth Century* (1989). An obituary is in the *New York Times*, 22 Nov. 1924.

MYRA G. GUTIN

HARDING, Warren Gamaliel (2 Nov. 1865–2 Aug. 1923), twenty-ninth president of the United States, was born near Blooming Grove, Ohio, the son of George Tyron Harding, a farmer and later a physician, and Phoebe Elizabeth Dickerson. Harding attended Ohio Central College, a high school level institution in Iberia, for three years (1879–1882) and following graduation moved with his parents to Marion. After brief stints as a teacher, insurance canvasser, journalist, and printer's helper, he became in 1884 the owner-editor of the *Marion Star*, purchasing the struggling enterprise for $300. In 1891 he married Florence Kling De-Wolfe, the daughter of Marion banker Amos Kling, and with her aid turned the paper into a commercial success. The couple had no children, but Mrs. Harding had a son by her former husband.

By 1900 Harding had become one of Marion's leading and best-liked citizens. Genial, handsome, adept at small-town social life, and noted throughout central Ohio for his resonant speaking voice, he was prominent as a promoter of civic endeavors, a trustee of the Trinity Baptist Church, and a reliable fixture in the community's business and fraternal life. Editorship and community service also led naturally to politics and in Harding's case to affiliation with the conservative Old Guard wing of the state Republican party, especially with the political organization of Senator Joseph B. Foraker. His first bid for office, as a nominee for county auditor in 1892, was unsuccessful. But with Foraker's support he was elected to the state senate in 1899, served two terms there (1900–1904), and during the second term acted as floor leader for the Foraker group. His most important committee was that on municipal corporations, and the only major bill he sponsored was an amendment to the municipal code vesting greater home rule in city mayors and councils. The bill passed but was subsequently reconsidered and blocked, and in votes on specific cities Harding tended to vote with the bosses rather than the reformers. The most notable case was his support for "Boss" George B. Cox's "ripper bill" to block progressive reform in Cincinnati.

In 1903 Harding informally announced his candidacy for governor but finally agreed to accept a nomination for lieutenant-governor on a ticket headed by Myron T. Herrick. Subsequently elected, he served one term (1904–1906), during which he used his talents to preach and promote party harmony. In 1910, with disharmony mounting, he was the party's compromise nominee for governor but was easily defeated by his Democratic opponent, Judson Harmon. Two years later he made the nominating speech for President William Howard Taft at the Republican National Convention and in the campaign that followed was an outspoken critic of Theodore Roosevelt and the Progressive party.

In 1914, the first year in which U.S. senators were directly elected, Harding became a candidate for the seat vacated by Senator Theodore Burton, won the Republican nomination in a primary contest against his former sponsor, Joseph B. Foraker, and went on to defeat his Democratic opponent, Timothy Hogan. On entering the Senate, he received a number of relatively inconspicuous committee assignments, the most notable of which were commerce, claims, and territories. His committee service yielded little of note. But he did find the Senate a "very pleasant place," and he became a man of some influence in party councils. In 1916 he served as temporary chairman of the Republican convention and delivered its keynote address.

During World War I, Harding supported most of President Woodrow Wilson's war measures, including the selective service system, the espionage law, and the emergency powers vested in presidential hands. But once the war ended, he became a strong critic of Wilson's policies and was a signer of the 1919 "round robin" (a petition with signatures in a circle to conceal the order of signing) expressing disapproval of including the League of Nations covenant in the Versailles peace treaty. In 1919 he became a member of the Senate Foreign Relations Committee and subsequently supported the Lodge Reservations in the debate leading to Senate rejection of the peace treaty. Also included in his postwar record were votes in favor of women's suffrage, national prohibition, and the Esch-Cummins Act returning the railroads to private hands.

Prior to the Republican convention in 1920, most observers did not consider Harding to be a serious presidential contender. He was overshadowed by the candidacies of General Leonard Wood, Governor Frank O. Lowden of Illinois, and Senator Hiram Johnson of California, all of whom had demonstrated popular support in states that held presidential preference primaries. But in late 1919, Ohio political leader Harry M. Daugherty had opened a campaign on behalf of Harding, stressing in particular his record of party loyalty and regularity and his talents for conciliating conflicting factions. As Daugherty put it, Harding began collecting "second, third, and fourth choice votes," and once it became clear that none of the leading contenders could be nominated he emerged as the available candidate. Following an adjournment of the convention over the night of 11 June, the balloting began moving in Harding's direction, and on the tenth ballot he received the nomination. Some historians have made much of the smoke-filled room at Chicago's Blackstone Hotel where a group of Old Guard senators decided that Harding, in the words of Senator Frank Brandegee, was "the best of the second-raters" and therefore the logical man to support if the convention deadlock was to be broken. But recent accounts have minimized the importance of their decision and have stripped the story of the conspiratorial overtones once attached to it.

In the campaign of 1920, conducted mostly from his "front porch" in Marion, Harding called for a return to "normalcy" and equivocated on the League of Nations issue, urging an "association of nations" but not Wilson's League. In addition, he called for a federal budget system, a protective tariff policy, a ship subsidy, stricter immigration standards, and lower tax burdens. The result was a sweeping victory for the Republicans, not so much on any one issue but in recoil against wartime controls, postwar disturbances, and Wilsonian idealism. Harding easily defeated his Democratic opponent, James M. Cox, receiving 61 percent of the popular vote and 404 electoral votes to Cox's 127.

In constructing his cabinet, Harding found places for long-time political associates but also redeemed his campaign pledge to make use of the nation's "best minds." Among his more disastrous appointments, as evidenced by subsequent scandals, were his choices of Harry M. Daugherty for attorney general and Senator Albert B. Fall of New Mexico for secretary of the interior. Yet at the same time he appointed some of the strongest and ablest men to serve in any presidential cabinet. In the latter category were Andrew W. Mellon as secretary of the treasury, Herbert Hoover as secretary of commerce, Charles Evans Hughes as secretary of state, and Henry C. Wallace as secretary of agriculture. Appointments below the cabinet level also brought a strange admixture of private-sector talent, political mediocrity, and predatory spoilsmen into the administration, thus contributing to the combination of administrative achievement and political corruption that followed.

In the White House, the Hardings cultivated an image of being "just folks." But behind the scenes, Harding's fondness for liquor, cards, and pleasure trips persisted, and in reality most of their social contacts were with old political associates, transplanted Ohioans, and the more irresponsible elements of Washington society, especially publisher Edward B. McLean and his wife Evalyn W. McLean. None of this lent grace or dignity to the executive mansion. Nor were Harding's personal traits and habits of the kind that make for presidential greatness. To his credit he worked hard and delegated a good deal of responsibility to his abler cabinet members. But he early revealed a smallness of mind, an incapacity for judging character, and a lack of mental toughness and discipline that made him ill-suited for the tasks of presidential leadership. Policy-making tended to gravitate either to his stronger cabinet members or to congressional and interest group leaders, and Harding made little effort to arrest and reverse these trends. Instead, he continued to see himself as a "harmonizer" and at times functioned effectively in that role.

In part, this policy-making outcome reflected the conservative, probusiness, and "America first" positions with which Harding had become associated. The tariff was raised, initially through the Emergency Tariff Act of 1921 and subsequently through the Fordney-McCumber Tariff Act of 1922. Taxes were lowered, especially on high incomes and business profits. Governmental expenditures were cut and were subjected to greater control and accountability through a new Bureau of the Budget. And immigration was restricted in ways that discriminated against the "new immigration" from southern and eastern Europe. In addition,

Harding strongly championed a ship subsidy bill, but this was finally blocked in the Senate.

Beyond these generally conservative initiatives, the Harding administration made some gestures toward the progressive and managerial impulses flowing from prewar reform and wartime mobilization. It supported the Sheppard-Towner Act of 1921, providing federal subsidies for state programs of maternal and infant health care. It also urged the creation of a federal department of public welfare, the adoption of a child labor amendment, and enhanced political rights for southern blacks. In addition, and of great importance, it supported expansions of the commerce and agriculture departments intended to provide new managerial capacities operating through public-spirited groups and agencies in the private sector. In agriculture, the major agency involved in this development was the new Bureau of Agricultural Economics, and in Hoover's domain the result was new programs for the bureaus of Standards, the Census, and Foreign and Domestic Commerce. Through machinery created by a presidential conference on unemployment, Hoover took the lead in attempting to organize recovery from the recession of 1921 and secure business actions that could mitigate future cycles of boom and bust.

In dealing with farm and labor discontent, Harding was largely guided by Wallace and Hoover, but at times he vacillated toward more conservative prescriptions. While rejecting the more radical proposals of the congressional farm bloc, his administration did support and help to secure the legalization of cooperative agricultural marketing associations, the expansion of agricultural credits, and a more stringent regulation of meat-packers, stockyards, and grain exchanges. And in 1922, a year of bitter strikes in the coalfields and railway shops, federal intervention involved not only the use of court injunctions to suppress strike activity but extensive mediation efforts, the creation of a fact-finding coal commission, and the establishment of an emergency committee to control the transportation and price of available coal. In addition, Harding strongly supported Hoover's efforts to pressure the steel industry into abandoning its twelve-hour day and adopting an eight-hour one, an initiative that finally succeeded in 1923.

In foreign relations, Harding was guided by Secretary of State Hughes, with Hoover and Mellon playing important subordinate roles. The policies pursued were isolationist in the sense of rejecting membership in the League of Nations, negotiating separate peace treaties with Germany, Austria, and Hungary, and opposing any kind of "entangling alliance." But they also envisioned a significant role for the United States in world economic development, European economic reconstruction, and the creation of new peacekeeping machinery that could help maintain a stable world order. The standards established for war debt repayment and American loans and investments abroad were supposed to contribute to European reconstruction, peaceful economic development, and the containment of anticapitalist political movements as well as safeguard particular American interests. Similar developmental objectives underlay a new Latin American policy that featured the settlement of disputes with Mexico and Colombia, the intensified cultivation of Pan-American ideals and sentiments, and the substitution of economic influence for "gunboat diplomacy." And following an initial period during which the United States refused even to answer communications from the League of Nations, a policy was adopted of sending unofficial observers to League meetings and cooperating with some of its agencies and initiatives. Harding and Hughes also tried to get U.S. adherence to the World Court, but their efforts were thwarted by opposition in the Senate.

The greatest diplomatic achievement of Harding's administration, although again this was more the work of Secretary Hughes than of the president, was the complex of treaties negotiated and signed at the Washington Conference on the Limitation of Armaments and on Far Eastern and Pacific Questions meeting in the winter of 1921–1922. Through the Five Power Naval Treaty, the Four Power Treaty, and the Nine Power Treaty, the United States succeeded in slowing a naval arms race, securing the abrogation of the Anglo-Japanese alliance, and gaining international recognition for its Open Door policy in regard to China. But to do so, it agreed to provisions that in effect ceded naval control of the western Pacific to the Japanese. The treaties were supposed to lay the basis for stability and peaceful economic development in the Far East, but in operation they failed to do so.

The darker side of Harding's administration was the growth of political corruption that eventually led to highly publicized scandals involving officials in the Veterans' Bureau, the Office of the Alien Property Custodian, the Justice Department, and the Department of the Interior. Charles R. Forbes, whom Harding had appointed to head the Veterans' Bureau, was convicted of embezzling government funds and taking kickbacks on contracts for hospital construction and the sale of surplus goods. Thomas W. Miller, the alien property custodian, finally went to prison for accepting bribes intended to facilitate the return of confiscated German property to its former owners. And Attorney General Daugherty, although he avoided prison when subsequent trials ended in hung juries, was clearly guilty of violating the trust that Harding had placed in him. In the words of Senator Henry F. Ashurst, Daugherty allowed the Justice Department to become "the Department of Easy Virtue," with pardons, immunities, and bootleggers' permits for sale to those willing to pay the "Ohio gang" through the medium of Daugherty associate Jesse Smith.

The most famous of the scandals, coming in subsequent years to symbolize the corruption of the period, involved the lease of naval oil reserves located at Teapot Dome in Wyoming and Elk Hills in California. Shortly after taking office, Secretary of the Interior Fall, an avowed anticonservationist, had succeeded in having control of these reserves transferred to his department and in 1922 had leased them, secretly and without competitive bidding, to oilmen Harry F. Sinclair and Edward L. Doheny. In the subsequent investigations and trials, Fall maintained that the action was in the national interest. But he was shown to have accepted personal gifts and payments totaling more than $400,000 from the lessees, and eventually he became the first U.S. cabinet member to be convicted of a felony committed while in office. The government also won its case to cancel the oil leases on the grounds that bribery had been involved.

How much Harding knew about the corruption in his administration has remained a matter of speculation. But by early 1923 he had learned about Forbes's operations, had virtually choked a confession from him, and had then allowed him to go abroad and resign. He had also begun to learn something about what was happening in the Justice Department, especially after Jesse Smith's suicide in May 1923. And he seemed deeply troubled and worried as he made plans for a trip to Alaska that summer. Leaving Washington on 20 June with a party of sixty-five in tow, he spent most of July on his Alaskan tour and then returned to Seattle where he nearly collapsed while delivering a speech concerning Alaska's promise and needs. His doctor diagnosed the illness as a minor attack of food poisoning. But on his arrival in San Francisco, Harding went to bed with what was now diagnosed as a coronary attack followed by bronchial pneumonia. And there he suffered a cerebral hemorrhage and died.

Harding's death was followed by a spontaneous outpouring of public grief and sorrow. But as the scandals of his administration were revealed, his public reputation rapidly deflated. In the scandal-scented published accounts that followed, he became a "third-rate Babbitt" incapable of defending the republic against sinister and rapacious plunderers, and adding to the negative image were numerous revelations concerning his personal habits, moral failings, and adulterous liaisons. In 1927 his mistress, Nan Britton, published *The President's Daughter*, convincing many that Harding was the father of her illegitimate child and that their lovemaking had continued in the White House. In 1963, letters surfaced documenting his long-rumored affair with his neighbor's wife, Carrie Phillips. In Alice Longworth's *Crowded Years* (1933), he was depicted as not really a bad man, "just a slob." If remembered at all, it seemed, it would be not for his achievements but for his sordid affairs, awful prose, and slobbish behavior. H. L. Mencken, some said, had been right when he had characterized Harding as "the archetype of the Homo boobus."

Most historians have continued to regard Harding as the nation's worst president, a man not only of bad personal habits but one sadly unfitted for the office and constantly manipulated by others. Recent revisionist scholarship, however, has shown that contrary to myth Harding was a hardworking president who took his job seriously and was nobody's puppet. Revisionists also argue that he deserves considerable credit for facilitating the nation's passage through a painful transitional period, for pacifying an angry and divided

society, and for stabilizing a disintegrating executive system. And although they would concede most of his personal and intellectual weaknesses, they would balance these by noting that he was an artful practitioner of compromise, a good judge of the spirit of his times, a shrewd handler of the press, a policymaker who was more pragmatic than doctrinaire, and a man who had few illusions about himself. As president, historian Robert K. Murray has argued, Harding was "certainly the equal of a Franklin Pierce, an Andrew Johnson, a Benjamin Harrison, or even a Calvin Coolidge."

• The Harding papers are held by the Ohio Historical Society (Columbus). His public addresses are collected in Frederick E. Shortemeier, ed., *Rededicating America: Life and Recent Speeches of Warren G. Harding* (1920), and James W. Murphy, comp., *Speeches and Addresses of Warren G. Harding, President of the United States* (1923). The standard biographies, none of them fully satisfactory, are Andrew Sinclair, *The Available Man: The Life Behind the Masks of Warren G. Harding* (1965); Francis Russell, *The Shadow of Blooming Grove: Warren G. Harding and His Times* (1968); and Randolph C. Downes, *The Rise of Warren G. Harding, 1865–1920* (1970). The fullest and best account of the Harding administration is in Robert K. Murray, *The Harding Era: Warren G. Harding and His Administration* (1969), but see also Eugene P. Trani and David L. Wilson, *The Presidency of Warren G. Harding* (1977). Other works contributing to an altered understanding of the Harding period include Wesley M. Bagby, *The Road to Normalcy: The Presidential Campaign and Election of 1920* (1962); Robert K. Murray, *The Politics of Normalcy: Government Theory and Practice in the Harding-Coolidge Era* (1973); Donald L. Winters, *Henry Cantwell Wallace as Secretary of Agriculture, 1921–1924* (1970); Ellis W. Hawley, ed., *Herbert Hoover as Secretary of Commerce, 1921–1928: Studies in New Era Thought and Practice* (1974); and Eugene P. Trani, "Charles Evans Hughes: The First Good Neighbor," *Northwest Ohio Quarterly* 40 (1968): 132–62. Louis W. Potts, "Who Was Warren G. Harding?" *The Historian* 36 (August 1974): 621–45, provides a useful historiographical survey.

ELLIS W. HAWLEY

HARDING, William Proctor Gould (5 May 1864–7 Apr. 1930), banker and governor of the Federal Reserve Board, was born in Greene County, Alabama, the son of Horace Harding, a civil engineer, and Eliza Proctor Gould. After receiving both his A.B. (1880) and his A.M. (1881) from the University of Alabama, Harding became a bookkeeper in the private bank J. H. Fitts & Co. in Tuscaloosa, Alabama, in 1882. He moved to Birmingham in 1886 and worked as bookkeeper, assistant cashier, and cashier at Berney National Bank until 1896, when he became vice president of First National Bank of Birmingham. In June 1902 he was promoted to president, a position he held until 1914. As president of a large southern bank, Harding became familiar with the problems of cotton farmers, steel manufacturers, and merchants. He married Amanda Perrine Moore in Birmingham in 1895, and they had three daughters before her death in 1910.

Following advice from Colonel Edward House, President Woodrow Wilson nominated Harding to become a member of the Federal Reserve Board in 1914.

Harding helped organize and open the Federal Reserve Banks in November 1914. As a member of committees responsible for defining paper eligible for discount, setting bylaws for the board, selecting directors for four reserve banks, and transferring reserves from member banks to reserve banks, Harding played a vital role. At the same time, he became active in trying to solve a problem in marketing the cotton crop that was caused by the outbreak of war in Europe. He remained active in export problems in 1915, devising a way that a British embargo of cotton would not unduly depress its market price.

Conflict developed on the Federal Reserve Board between the "Treasury faction" (Treasury secretary William McAdoo, comptroller of the currency John Skelton Williams, and Charles Hamlin) and those who feared that the Treasury would dominate the Federal Reserve System (Adolph Miller, Frederic Delano, and Paul Warburg). In this clash Harding became the pivotal player, siding at times with each group. The dissension ended after Harding became governor of the board in August 1916, probably because his more efficient managerial style relied less on making decisions only after long debates during board meetings.

Once the United States entered World War I in 1917, Harding assisted McAdoo with meeting the borrowing needs of the Treasury and also served as managing director of the War Finance Corporation from May 1918 to early 1919. During the war, reserve bank discount rates were kept artificially low so that Liberty Loans could be floated at low interest rates. Because the Treasury relied less on taxation than on bonds and because people were encouraged to borrow from local banks in order to buy bonds, bank credit expanded and helped to fuel wartime and postwar inflation. Before the war's end, Harding's public speeches were warning of severe economic problems in the postwar period, and in 1919 he led a struggle to break away from the Treasury policy of low interest rates.

In November 1919 the reserve banks began to raise their discount rates, with the greatest advances between January and May 1920. In general, rates rose from 4.5 percent to 7 percent as the reserve system attempted to counteract widespread inflation and speculative tendencies in the economy. The policy was successful, and in the summer of 1920 a short but sharp depression began.

Distress was greatest in farming regions, in part because farmers' cost of production was extremely high in 1920 (because of inflation early in the year), and in part because the depression intensified just as crops were ready for harvest and sale. Farmers and their representatives began a sustained attack on Harding and the Federal Reserve System for the "policy of deflation." Harding defended the system by claiming that officials had only wanted to prevent further inflation, but it is clear from Harding's utterances in 1919 and early 1920 that he had believed prices and production were out of balance and that both would have to be adjusted. Harding was able to counter more successfully the farmers' claims that the reserve system had denied them credit. He demonstrated that the system had extended more credit in the fall of 1919 than ever before for the purpose of carrying crops and avoiding forced sales at artificially low prices. Farmers also criticized the system for not decreasing discount rates soon after the depression began. Harding countered that the reserve ratios of the reserve banks were near the legal minimum until mid-1921 and that to have used the board's emergency power to suspend the legal minimum would have only panicked people.

The endless vilification by farmers contributed to President Warren Harding's decision not to reappoint Harding as governor when his term expired in August 1922, even though Harding had the support of Treasury secretary Andrew Mellon and most bankers. This lack of reward for having undertaken a courageous and needed monetary policy weakened the Federal Reserve Board's ability to act decisively the next time speculation became a major factor in the economy (in the late 1920s).

After 1923 Harding served as governor of the Federal Reserve Bank of Boston. From that position he criticized the board's decision to force the Chicago reserve bank to lower its discount rate in 1927 and disagreed with the board's use of moral suasion to try to end speculation rather than using discount rates in 1929. Harding also served as an official financial adviser to Cuba (1922) and unofficially advised Hungary (1924) and Poland (1926). In 1925 he published a defense of the board, *The Formative Period of the Federal Reserve System*, which covered 1914–1922. He died in Boston; his ashes were buried in Birmingham.

Harding made an important contribution to the Federal Reserve System's development in its early years. McAdoo concluded that "Harding was the ablest man on the Board, so far as the practice and technique of domestic banking was concerned" (McAdoo, p. 279), and Mellon was upset that the president would not reappoint Harding in 1922. However, Harding's long-term influence on the system was minimal because it was the crucibles of the Great Depression and World War II that produced the modern Federal Reserve System.

• Although no collection of Harding's papers is available, some manuscript collections contain relevant materials: the papers of Carter Glass and John Skelton Williams at the University of Virginia; the papers of Woodrow Wilson, William McAdoo, Eugene Meyer, Charles Hamlin, and Adolph Miller at the Library of Congress; the Federal Reserve Board and War Finance Corporation Papers at the National Archives; and the papers of George Harrison and H. Parker Willis at Columbia University. In addition, McAdoo's autobiography, *Crowded Years* (1931), discusses Harding. Harding published one book and many articles about public policy, including "Federal Reserve on Trial," *Forum* 64 (Nov. 1920): 288–98; *The Formative Period of the Federal Reserve System* (1925); "How I Know Business Has Turned the Corner," *System* 40 (Nov. 1921): 537–41, 647; "Principles Governing the Discount Rate," *Annals of the American Academy of Political and Social Science* 99 (Jan. 1922): 183–89; and "Sectionalism in Finance," *Sewanee Review* 2 (Nov. 1893): 56–75. Many of Harding's speeches were printed by the *Federal Re-*

serve *Bulletin, Commercial and Financial Chronicle*, U.S. Government Printing Office, or Federal Reserve Banks. Harding also testified before Congress several times; the most important testimony is published in *Agricultural Inquiry: Hearing before the Joint Commission of Agricultural Inquiry under Senate Concurrent Resolution 4*, 67th Cong., 1st sess., 1921. Secondary works that deal extensively with Harding include Lester V. Chandler, *Benjamin Strong, Central Banker* (1958); S. E. Harris, *Twenty Years of Federal Reserve Policy* (1933); and Henry Parker Willis, *The Federal Reserve System* (1923). An obituary appears in the *New York Times*, 8 Apr. 1930.

SUE C. PATRICK

HARDS, Ira (24 June 1872–2 May 1938), stage actor, director, and producer, was born in Geneva, Illinois, the son of parents whose names are unknown. Hards excelled in elocution, oration, and impersonation in Geneva public schools, graduating from high school in 1887. At the University of California, Berkeley, from 1892 to 1894, the "rising star" took every course offered in the English department, "winning from one of his professors the assertion that he was the most brilliant student of English the university had ever known" (*San Francisco Bulletin*, 29 Oct. 1899). He moved to New York City to study acting, diction, stage business, drama, and Shakespeare at Frank Sargeant's American Academy of the Dramatic Arts. Upon graduating in 1895, he apprenticed with veteran actors Henry Irving and Ellen Terry at the Empire Theater in New York.

Hards used his remarkable memory and knowledge of French and Spanish to rise quickly in the ranks of Irving's stage company. Producer Charles Frohman hired Hards for a new acting company in September 1896. Hards's first assignment was as the assistant stage manager in February 1897 for William Gillette's war comedy *Secret Service*, starring Maurice Barrymore. When the stage manager resigned suddenly, Hards became the youngest stage manager in the country. His first production was on 15 May 1897 at London's Adelphi Theatre. *Secret Service* was popular in the United States and a great success abroad. However, a lack of adaptations to French culture resulted in its failure in Paris at Sara Bernhardt's Renaissance Theater.

Hards married Sargeant's star pupil, Ina Hammer, in August 1897; they had one daughter. While his wife built a reputation as a stage actress, Hards acted and directed his way toward Broadway. His success can be attributed to his determination to belie a childhood diagnosis that he would die young, his meticulous supervision of all facets of a production from stage direction to sales, his penchant for being in the right place at the right time, and his unfailing habit of taking advantage of every opportunity afforded him.

From 1899 to 1903 Hards was recognized for his stage direction and minor acting performances. He was praised for his excellent elocution by New York audiences in the title role of J. M. Barrie's *Little Minister*, starring Maude Adams, and as Mawley the Jockey with William Faversham in *Lord and Lady Algy*. Ten years of work with Frohman ended when Frohman

died in the *Lusitania* disaster. Beginning in 1906 Hards directed stock companies in Washington, Cleveland, Cincinnati, San Francisco, and Denver. He moved to Mount Vernon, New York, in 1911 and in January 1912 cofounded the city's first stock company, the Stainach-Hards Stock Company. He and his partners also commissioned the construction of the Westchester Theater in 1912. Hards directed the acting company, Steven Stainach handled the business, and their wives shared the lead roles. Hards successfully promoted the new theater by publicly vowing to produce new plays that would make Mount Vernon more famous than Los Angeles as a provider of plays for the New York market. Frank Wilcox, Helen Spring, Dorothy West, Eileen Wilson, Charles Laite, Marie Carroll, Lee Tracy, and Lew Cody were among the notables who performed with the company. Hards managed the Westchester Stock Company of Mount Vernon until 1926.

Hards had launched his career producing mainly musicals and comedies, but it was his murder mysteries that made him one of the most sought after stage directors in America. *The Thirteenth Chair* (1916), about a questionable betrothal and a murder investigation conducted through a séance, was one of the best of these "shriek-in-the-dark dramas." *The Unknown Purple* (1918) was a cross between the then popular "crook" plays and science fiction. In it an inventor's wife runs off with her lover and his latest invention and frames him for a crime he did not commit. When released from jail, he invents a device that renders him invisible, enabling him to achieve his revenge. Of the many Broadway plays that Hards directed, hits include *The Hole in the Wall* (1920); *Intimate Strangers* (1921); *Queen o' Hearts* and *Listening In* (1922); *Magnolia* (1923); *Lass o' Laughter* and *Twelve Miles Out* (1925); *Dracula* (1927); *Atlas and Eva* and *Jarnegan* (1928); *Be Your Age*, *Young Alexander*, *Scarlet Pages*, and *Cortez* (1929); *Dracula* (1931); and *The Bishop Misbehaves* (1935).

By the time Hollywood had taken notice of Hards, he was known as the director who had used every imaginable manner of murdering someone in his plays in order to effect a response from his audience. His New York production of *Dracula* (1927) with Bela Lugosi was done so convincingly that nurses reputedly had to be in attendance for every performance to help the men and women in the audience who fainted. Having directed over 300 stage plays, more than 100 of which were staged successfully in New York, Hards in April 1931 went to Hollywood to direct *Mystery by the Clock* for Paramount, in which there are three mysterious killings.

Hards's success producing murder mysteries can be attributed to his understanding that the plot of the mystery is not drawn from real life, as is the plot of a mob thriller or other realistic crime play; murder mysteries are pure entertainment designed to hold the audience in suspense, to provide a clever puzzle with which to challenge the audience, and, most of all, to provoke an affective response. Murder mysteries, he believed, should also point to a moral and contain no ethically harmful elements. Despite his success with the genre, Hards claimed he never read murder mysteries. He was known as a quiet man who read poetry and enjoyed gardening. His last assignment was as the stage director in February 1937 for the Little Theatre in Montgomery, Alabama.

Hards was a member of a number of acting and other organizations, including the Lambs in New York, the local Masonic Hiawatha Lodge, the Royal Arcarium, and the Church of the Ascension. He died at his country estate in West Norwalk, Connecticut.

• Hards's special collection at Butler Library, Rare Books and Archives, at Columbia University contains diaries, correspondence, photographs, performance programs, and scrapbooks with newspaper clippings of reviews and articles about Hards from his teenage years until his death. For information on Hards's early career, see Isaac F. Marcosson and Daniel Frohman, *Charles Frohman: Manager and Man* (1916). An obituary is in the *New York Times*, 4 May 1938.

BARBARA L. CICCARELLI

HARDWICK, Toby (31 May 1904–5 Aug. 1970), jazz alto saxophonist, was born Otto J. Hardwick in Washington, D.C. (His parents' names and occupations are unknown.) A younger neighbor of Duke Ellington, Hardwick may have worked locally as a string bassist from as early as age fourteen. He attended Dunbar High School. Ellington got Hardwick started on C-melody saxophone around 1920, and his career followed Ellington's: local jobs, many involving banjoist Elmer Snowden; two attempts to establish themselves in New York, first without Snowden in March 1923 in Wilbur Sweatman's vaudeville band and again at midyear with Snowden and his Black Sox Orchestra at Baron Wilkins's Exclusive Club; and an engagement at the Hollywood (later the Kentucky) Club, where Snowden's Washingtonians evolved into Ellington's orchestra. During the Washingtonians' years Hardwick concentrated on playing alto saxophone while doubling on violin and string bass.

As a young adult, Hardwick was unreliable, because of heavy drinking and extended romantic affairs. According to Ellington, "Lots of chicks wanted to mother him—so every now and then he'd submit! It meant he was in and out of the band rather unpredictably" (Dance, p. 58). Hardwick acquired his nickname, Toby, in Atlantic City, New Jersey, during one such absence. Nonetheless, Hardwick was the one constant element in Ellington's reed section as the orchestra grew in size in the mid-1920s. His alto saxophone led the band in ensemble passages (although evidently Harry Carney sometimes took this role after first working with the band in the summer of 1926), and Hardwick contributed solos on many of Ellington's important early recordings, playing in a sweet, pretty manner on "Immigration Blues" (1926) and "Black and Tan Fantasy" (1926 and 1927), and in a jaunty, florid style on "The Creeper" (1926) and "Jubilee Stomp" (1928). Like most professional reed players, he doubled on clarinet and other saxophones: soprano, baritone, and bass; "Birmingham Breakdown" (1927) features solos on alto and baritone saxophones. Several of these titles exist in more than one recorded version, but Hardwick's contributions do not vary appreciably from one to the next. With Ellington, he composed "Hop Head" and "Down in Our Alley Blues" (1927).

Hardwick nicknamed Joe Nanton "Tricky Sam" (because of his manual dexterity), and later in life Roy Eldridge "Little Jazz" (his physical stature), Ray Nance "Floorshow" (his flair for presentation), and Billy Strayhorn "Swee' Pea" (after the character in the Popeye comic strip). He loved to have fun, and he was curious about the world. He realized the first ambition throughout his career in music; he undertook the second in 1928. Ellington had no intention of leaving the Cotton Club, so Hardwick quit in the spring of 1928 and left for Europe, where he joined Noble Sissle's orchestra, among others.

Back in the United States the following year, he briefly joined Chick Webb's big band. According to Hardwick, he led a band full-time for three years (1930–1932), mainly at the Hot Feet Club in Greenwich Village, where Chu Berry, Garvin Bushell, and Fats Waller were among his sidemen. In 1931 at a benefit performance featuring a "battle of the bands," Hardwick's ensemble was judged to have defeated Ellington's. After the demise of the Hot Feet Club, the band continued to perform with James P. Johnson and then Count Basie as Hardwick's pianist. He then ceased band leading and rejoined Snowden at Smalls' Paradise in Harlem. Bushell, though, claims that in 1930 the bandleader was Snowden, with Hardwick playing lead alto saxophone, and that the musicians quit the Hot Feet Club as a group that same year. John Hammond recalled Hardwick in Snowden's band in 1931. Standard sources on Waller, Johnson, and Basie shed no further light on this period. In any event, Hardwick performed in Snowden's band in the movie short *Smash Yo' Baggage* (1932).

In the spring of 1932 he rejoined Ellington. As Barney Bigard explained, "Toby wasn't an improvising musician, but he played some beautiful things. He was a melody boy. He used to have all the first parts, because Johnny Hodges couldn't read so well at that time" (Dance, p. 87). By this point, Ellington's orchestra had many soloists superior to Hardwick, and his importance came in focusing the band's sound in passages for reeds and for the full ensemble. During the next fourteen years he was a soloist on only a few significant recordings, including the last phrases of "Sophisticated Lady" (1933), which he wrote in collaboration with Ellington and trombonist Lawrence Brown; "In a Sentimental Mood" (1935), at the beginning and again before the first trumpet solo; and "All Too Soon" (1940), in the opening theme intertwining Hardwick's soprano saxophone and Brown's muted trombone. In 1945 a recording session by Sonny Greer and the Duke's Men produced fine versions of "Mood Indigo" and "The Mooche" on which Hardwick figured prominently.

Tired of traveling constantly from one venue to the next, Hardwick left Ellington in May 1946 and retired from music to work on his father's tobacco farm in southern Maryland. Later he became a hotel shipping clerk. He suffered a long illness, and after the death of his wife, Gladys (details of his marriage are unknown), he died in a nursing home in Washington, D.C.

• Stanley Dance interviewed Hardwick and surveyed his career in *The World of Duke Ellington* (1970), pp. 55–62, which also includes personal stories about Hardwick. Bits of his early career are in Les Muscutt, "Discovering Elmer," *Storyville*, Apr.–May 1968, pp. 3–7; Edward Kennedy Ellington, *Music Is My Mistress* (1973), pp. 50–51; Albert McCarthy, *Big Band Jazz* (1974); Whitney Balliett, "Big Sid," *Improvising: Sixteen Jazz Musicians and Their Art* (1977), pp. 139–50, which has Hammond's comment, repr. in *American Musicians: Fifty-six Portraits in Jazz* (1986), pp. 179–87; Barney Bigard, *With Louis and the Duke: The Autobiography of a Jazz Clarinetist*, ed. Barry Martyn (1985); Garvin Bushell, *Jazz from the Beginning*, as told to Mark Tucker (1988); and Laurie Wright, *"Fats" in Fact* (1992). Rex Stewart confirms Hardwick's talent for inventing nicknames in *Jazz Masters of the Thirties* (1972), p. 103. Dick M. Bakker identifies titles featuring Hardwick's solos in *Duke Ellington on Microgroove*, vol. 1: *1923–1936* (1977). Gunther Schuller supplies musical analysis in *The Swing Era: The Development of Jazz, 1930–1945* (1989), as does Mark Tucker in *Ellington: The Early Years* (1991), the most accurate source on early biographical details. Obituaries appear in the *Washington Post*, 7 Aug. 1970, and the *New York Times*, 8 Aug. 1970.

BARRY KERNFELD

HARDY, Oliver. *See* Laurel, Stan, and Oliver Hardy.

HARE, George Emlen (4 Sept. 1808–15 Feb. 1892), Episcopal clergyman and educator, was born in Philadelphia, Pennsylvania, the son of Charles Willing Hare, a lawyer, and Ann Emlen. He was educated at Dickinson College in Carlisle, Pennsylvania, and Union College in Schenectady, New York, where Alonzo Potter, afterward the third bishop of Pennsylvania, was then a teacher. In 1827 Hare entered the General Theological Seminary in New York City, recently founded through the efforts of Bishop John Henry Hobart, and graduated in 1829. He was ordained a deacon on 20 December 1829 and a priest on 21 October 1832.

After his ordination to the diaconate Hare took charge of St. John's Church, Carlisle. On 4 June 1830 he married Elizabeth Catherine Hobart, the third daughter of Bishop Hobart; they had ten children. (One of his children, William Hobart Hare, became a bishop in the Protestant Episcopal church.) In 1834 he moved to Princeton, New Jersey, where he served as rector of Trinity Church until November 1843. Bishop Thomas March Clark of Rhode Island in his *Reminiscences* wrote of Hare's Princeton ministry, "The late Rev. Professor Hare, the father of Bishop Hare, was the first rector, and as there was no afternoon service in the seminary chapel, some of us formed the habit of attending the new church, where the simplicity of the

service and the liberal fervor of the preacher combined to impress us very favorably" (p. 30).

While at Trinity Church, Hare had the chancel of the church remodeled so that the altar was more prominent than the pulpit. Hare also restored the ancient use of the surplice. Bishop George Washington Doane of New Jersey stated, "The Rector of this Parish has discontinued the use of the gown, and uses the surplice in preaching as well as in all the services. He has done this with my approbation, and I shall be glad to see the practice adopted throughout the diocese" (quoted in Banks, p. 16). Hare was moving the parish in a High Church direction.

In 1843 Hare returned to Philadelphia and was temporarily in charge of St. James' Church, while the rector was abroad. In 1844–1845 he was assistant professor of Latin and Greek at the University of Pennsylvania. On 5 November 1844 Hare was elected rector of St. Matthew's Church in Francisville (Philadelphia) and served there until 20 January 1862, a rectorship of eighteen years. During his tenure there the communicant membership grew from 40 to 180, the Sunday school to 354 pupils and teachers. A new church to accommodate 600 persons was built; the cornerstone was laid on 26 April 1858, and the building was consecrated on 23 December 1858.

After he returned to Philadelphia, Hare devoted much of the remainder of his life to educational work. In 1846 Bishop Potter revived the Academy of the Protestant Episcopal Church in Philadelphia and named Hare its headmaster. This school was established 1 January 1785, by Bishop William White, but had languished until Potter became bishop. A new building was erected in 1849 under Hare's leadership. When Hare resigned as headmaster in 1857, Bishop Potter asked him to initiate a diocesan training school to educate young men for the ministry. From 1857 to 1862 Hare conducted this school in the academy buildings.

It was not long before the training school was to prove as inadequate to its purpose as had the former program of clerical education, wherein the student read for orders under the guidance of a priest. Gradually Hare and Potter transformed the training school into a theological seminary, and on 8 April 1862 the Philadelphia Divinity School was incorporated with Hare as dean and professor of biblical learning. "As its first professor, Dr. Hare was the living continuum from private tutoring to the training school, and from that to the Divinity School—covering a period of forty-six years" (Taylor, p. 205). The constitution of the school was adopted on 30 May 1862, and Hare was chosen dean, a position he held until 1866.

Hare was a responsible scholar but did not publish any enduring works. His first book, *Christ to Return: A Practical Exposition of the Prophecy Recorded in the 24th and 25th Chapters of the Gospel According to St. Matthew* (1840), written while he was rector of Trinity Church, Princeton, was an explanation of the line from the Apostles' Creed, " . . . from thence, He shall come to judge the quick and the dead." Hare argued that Christ will return as Lord of the world but that no one knows when that will be. Hare's last and major book was *Visions and Narratives of the Old Testament* (1889), a collection of articles he had published in various periodicals.

Hare was an able Hebrew scholar, a faithful rector, and a significant educator. He was a clear and scholarly preacher. A clerical deputy from the Diocese of Pennsylvania to numerous general conventions, Hare was a founder of a theological seminary and was fondly remembered as a great teacher. "While before his day the teacher was generally looked upon by his pupils as an enemy or a tyrant, to be evaded or circumvented, he established the relation of a teacher to his pupils as that of their trusted and best friend" (*The Churchman* 65 [27 Feb. 1892]: 258). He died in Philadelphia.

• Hare's papers have not survived. He also published two other works, *Christians and Their Offspring, a Holy People: A Sermon* (1849) and *The Misuse of the Lord's Supper at Corinth* (188?). The fullest treatment of Hare is in Franklin Spencer Edmonds, *History of St. Matthew's Church, Francisville, Philadelphia, 1822–1925* (1925), in the chapter entitled "A Great Rector and His Work." His ministry in Princeton is discussed in Alfred B. Banks, *The Records of Trinity Church, Princeton, Diocese of New Jersey, 1833–1908* (1908). Hare's work is also noted in Thomas March Clark, *Reminiscences* (1895); William Wilberforce Newton, *Yesterday with the Fathers* (1910); and in two biographical studies by Mark Anthony DeWolfe Howe, *Memoirs of the Life and Services of the Rt. Rev. Alonzo Potter, D.D., LL.D.* (1871) and *The Life and Labors of Bishop Hare: Apostle to the Sioux* (1911). His work in education is treated in Raymond R. Taylor, "A Century of the Philadelphia Divinity School, 1857–1957," *Historical Magazine of the Protestant Episcopal Church* 26 (Sept. 1957): 204–23, and John Wesley Twelves, *A History of the Diocese of Pennsylvania of the Protestant Episcopal Church in the U.S.A., 1784–1968* (1969). The most substantive obituary of Hare appeared in *The Churchman* 65 (27 Feb. 1892): 258.

DONALD S. ARMENTROUT

HARE, James Henry (3 Oct. 1856–24 June 1946), photojournalist, was born in London, England, the son of George Hare, a camera manufacturer, and Margaret Ball. He attended St. John's College in London but left school in 1871 to apprentice with his father for the next eight years. He left his father's firm in 1879 and joined another London camera-making company. Hare married Ellen Crapper on 2 August 1879; they had five children.

By the early 1880s, Hare had become a freelance photographer, and he took his first "snapshot," as such pictures were already being called, of a balloon at a London event in 1884. In 1889 he moved to Brooklyn, New York, where he lived for the rest of his life. The camera firm that employed him was sold in 1891, and the new owner cut his wages. Hare quit. During the early 1890s, he worked with Joseph Byron, who took pictures for the *Illustrated American* magazine. As magazines used more and more photographs, Hare's career prospered. He covered regattas, sporting competitions, naval cruises, and political ceremonies such as William McKinley's presidential inauguration in 1897.

In 1898 Hare's career took a new turn. His work with the *Illustrated American* ended, and he signed on with *Collier's Weekly* as war with Spain approached. "The *Maine* BLEW UP, and Jimmy BLEW IN," recalled the magazine's publisher, Robert Collier (Gould and Greffe, p. 11). Hare's coverage of the war included a clandestine visit with other reporters to a Cuban rebel camp in May 1898. He was also present when American forces stormed Spanish positions outside Santiago de Cuba on 1 July 1898. Stephen Crane and Richard Harding Davis recorded Hare's bravery under fire for their readers. Hare was becoming a journalistic celebrity.

In Cuba, Hare relied on the Kodak hand-held camera for his combat photographs. Negatives tended to "frill" in the intense heat of the Cuban jungle, and Hare learned to spray them with alcohol as they dried. Hare's insistence on being close to the action gave his pictures a realism that conveyed the nature of the Spanish-American conflict. When an American soldier said to Hare that he was a fool to be so close to the fighting voluntarily, Hare replied: "You can't get *real* pictures unless you take some risk!" (Gould and Greffe, p. 18).

Hare's photographs helped move *Collier's* toward a greater attention to world events and public issues. The photographer's career expanded during the five years that followed. He took pictures of President McKinley just before his assassination in Buffalo, New York, in September 1901, and he also covered the early months of the presidency of Theodore Roosevelt (1858–1919).

When war erupted between Russia and Japan in 1904, *Collier's* sent Hare and other newsmen to follow the fighting. The Japanese placed close restrictions on reporters but wanted the publicity that Hare's pictures could provide. He joined a Japanese army in Manchuria and recorded what the Japanese allowed him to see. As the fighting intensified, Hare was present at major engagements. With characteristic ingenuity, he found ways to get close to combat action, and his pictures supplied a vivid record of the Japanese army at the front. He took some pictures under direct shell fire.

After the Russo-Japanese war, Hare turned to civilian subjects in the United States. Aviation claimed much of his time. He captured the launching of a Wright Brothers plane at Kitty Hawk, North Carolina in 1908 that *Collier's* called "the first news photograph of a plane in flight" (Gould and Greffe, p. 70). But war remained Hare's specialty. He was in Ciudad Juarez when Francisco Madero launched the Mexican Revolution in 1911, and he returned to Mexico in April 1914 for the American intervention at Vera Cruz. Hare stayed on through the early summer and photographed Pancho Villa. As the crisis in Mexico eased and war loomed in Europe, Hare asked *Collier's* to send him to the big story that all journalists wanted to cover. The magazine decided, largely because of

Hare's advanced age, not to use his services although only a year before it had sent him to cover the war in the Balkans.

Leslie's Weekly, another pictorial news magazine, gave Hare his chance at World War I. He spent the initial months of the fighting in Great Britain and France, where reporters and photographers were closely monitored. Nonetheless, Hare did obtain good pictures in Ireland of the aftermath of the *Lusitania* sinking. Seeking more action, he went to Salonika, Greece, in 1915 but again encountered censorship and red tape. He returned to the western front in 1916 and sent back the striking images of trench warfare that the British allowed him to take.

With American entry into the war in April 1917, Hare covered the early mobilization and then eagerly accepted an invitation to accompany the Italian army on the Austrian front in March 1918. He was under artillery fire as he photographed Italian troops. Following the armistice, Hare pursued additional stories for *Leslie's*, but his active life as a photojournalist was winding down. He went on the lecture circuit in the 1920s and covered a few stories with old reporter friends. He "retired" officially in 1931. He told colleagues that he could no longer "stand the gaff" of active photographic work (Gould and Greffe, p. 149). In 1939 he was made an honorary president of the Overseas Press Club. He died in Brooklyn three months before his ninetieth birthday.

Jimmy Hare was a short man with a dapper mustache and goatee. His bravery under fire became legendary among his colleagues. The verdict of his peers was that he "never faked a picture nor ran from danger" (Gould and Greffe, p. 139). For three decades, he emphasized a photographic reportage that stressed the immediacy of the event and the accuracy of what was being recorded. He embodied the early heroic phase of photojournalism in the United States, and his combination of pictures and news stories created an effect that went beyond single-picture illustrations. In that sense, he was an important transitional figure toward the modern form of photojournalism, the joining of word-pictures and photo-essays, that emerged with *Life* magazine during the 1930s.

• Hare's photographic archive is located at the Harry Ransom Humanities Research Center at the University of Texas at Austin. Hare's personal papers have been scattered and lost. There are biographical files about Hare in the New York *Journal-American* Collection at the Ransom Center and in the *Brooklyn Eagle* Collection, Brooklyn Public Library. Some information about Hare is in the *Collier's Weekly* Memorandum Book, listed under that title, in the Library of Congress and in the William McKinley Papers, Library of Congress, Washington, D.C. For Hare's own writings, see "Photographs of the Great Hudson Railway Wreck at Garrisons, October 24," *Illustrated American* 22 (Nov. 1897): 588–89; "Our Expedition to Gomez's Camp," *Collier's Weekly*, 28 May 1908, p. 7; as editor, *A Photographic Record of the Russo-Japanese War* (1905); and "Jimmy Hare's First War Impressions," *Leslie's Weekly*, 1 Oct. 1914, p. 318. Cecil Carnes, *Jimmy Hare News Photographer: Half a Century With a Camera* (1940), is the most complete biography. Lewis L. Gould and Richard Greffe, *Photojournalist: The Career of Jimmy Hare* (1977), traces his life and reproduces more than 100 photographs. Articles on Hare include Frederick Palmer, "About 'Jimmy' Hare," *Collier's Weekly*, 25 Feb. 1905, p. 18; R. W. Ritchie, "'Jimmy' Hare," *American Magazine*, Feb. 1913, p. 31; and "James H. Hare, Greatest of War Photographers," *Leslie's Weekly*, 27 Aug. 1914, p. 193. A good obituary is in the *New York Times*, 25 June 1946.

LEWIS L. GOULD

HARE, Robert (17 Jan. 1781–15 May 1858), chemist, was born in Philadelphia, Pennsylvania, the son of Robert Hare, Sr., a prominent brewer, and Margaret Willing. After attending the Academy of the University of Pennsylvania, he attended the chemistry lectures of James Woodhouse, the leading chemist of his generation, at the University of Pennsylvania Medical School during the winters of 1798 to 1803.

Experimenting in his landlady's cellar kitchen, while seeking a method of obtaining higher temperatures than could be attained with furnaces and burning glasses, Hare in 1801 used his great mechanical skill to invent, from a keg from his father's brewery, the oxyhydrogen blowtorch (which he called the "hydrostatic blow-pipe"), the forerunner of the modern welding and metal-cutting torches. His report was published by the Chemical Society of Philadelphia (1802), of which he was corresponding secretary, and it was reprinted for European scientists in Alexander Tilloch's *Philosophical Magazine* (14 [1802]: 238, 298) and *Annales de Chimie*. Hare used his torch to fuse sizable amounts of platinum and other previously infusible materials. Hare's torch also led to a new method of illumination; by directing an oxyhydrogen flame on a block of lime (calcium oxide), Thomas Drummond obtained an intense white light used in lighthouses and in the theater (limelight). In 1839 Hare was awarded the American Academy of Arts and Sciences' Rumford Medal for his invention of almost four decades earlier.

After the winter of 1803–1804 Hare spent almost all of his time helping his father manage the brewery, leaving him little time for research. Yet even here he was able to use the mechanical skill that contributed to his success in research to devise new inventions; he constructed a tighter keg than any currently on the market, and he invented a new cock to tap casks. In his own words, "Without having become a mechanick I never could have succeeded [in my inventions]."

On Woodhouse's death in 1809 Hare attempted to leave the business world and enter the academic world by applying for the vacant professorship. He lost the election because of the opposition of the medical faculty, who opposed any candidate without a medical degree (Hare had only an honorary M.D. from Yale University, awarded to him in 1806). However, Professor Benjamin Rush persuaded the trustees to add a professorship of natural philosophy to the medical faculty, to which Hare was elected in 1810. In 1811 Hare married Harriett Clark of Providence, Rhode Island; they had six children. He resigned his position in 1812, primarily because his subject was only an elective, and medical students would not pay to attend his lectures (Hare's only remuneration).

At about this time the death of Hare's father made him completely responsible for the management of the brewery, but the economic upheaval caused by the War of 1812 ruined the firm in about 1815. Hare tried unsuccessfully to become a manufacturer of illuminating gas and then went to Providence, where he considered opening a drugstore. In early 1818 the College of William and Mary appointed him professor of natural philosophy and chemistry, but later that year he accepted the professorship of chemistry at the University of Pennsylvania Medical School, allowing him to devote himself completely to science for the first time in his life.

Hare's lectures were not brilliant but were accompanied by a large quantity and variety of vivid, large-scale demonstrations, easily visible from a distance, many of which employed apparatus of his own construction. Illustrations of these appear in his articles as well as in the following books: *A Compendium of the Course of Chemical Instruction in the Medical Department of the University of Pennsylvania* (1828, 1834, 1838, 1840) and *Engravings and Descriptions of a Great Part of Apparatus Used in the Chemical Course of the University of Pennsylvania* (2 vols., 1826). Although Hare's *Compendium* was said to be the best and most complete chemistry text written by an American to that time, it never became popular outside of the University of Pennsylvania, probably because it was too comprehensive for courses in other institutions. Hare resigned his professorship in 1847. In 1849 he donated his collection of apparatus to the Smithsonian Institution in Washington, D.C., where it remained until destroyed by fire many years later. All that now remains of his collection are a few pieces of apparatus preserved at the University of Pennsylvania. During his twenty-nine years at the country's best known medical school, Hare taught chemistry to more medical students than any other teacher of that time, and some of them became prominent chemists and scientists.

Hare was the most prodigious and versatile experimental chemist in America during his career. His interest in electricity led him to invent the calorimotor, a battery that produced powerful heating effects, which in 1819 became the model for Gaston Plante's secondary battery; the deflagrator for generating a large current (1821); and a covered electric furnace, with which he produced calcium, calcium carbide, phosphorus, and graphite from charcoal. His use of the furnace anticipated its commercial applications by a half-century. Hare was also the first to employ a mercury cathode in the electrolysis of aqueous salt solutions, and he used this method to obtain calcium amalgam, from which he isolated calcium metal, the first produced in the United States. In 1835 Michael Faraday, after constructing a voltaic trough, wrote, "On examining, however, what had been done before, I found the new trough was in all respects the same as that invented and described by Robert Hare" nearly twenty-five years earlier.

Hare was a frequent contributor to the scientific literature. He developed new methods for the isolation of a number of elements, including boron and silicon, and he synthesized ammonia from nitric oxide and hydrogen by using a platinum sponge catalyst. He invented the litrameter ("Hare's apparatus") for determining specific gravities of liquids; a hydrostatic balance (1826) similar to that created by Friedrich Mohr; a cryophorus ("palm glass," 1828); a gas density balance (1829); a method for burning metals in chlorine by shaking the powdered metal into the gas in a jar (1828); eudiometers for exploding gases (1829); and a method for using tar for lighting.

Following his retirement, Hare became interested in banking and currency reform and meteorology (he attributed tornadoes to electric currents in the air). He attempted to explain the explosion of a New York warehouse filled with potassium nitrate by carrying out experiments with potassium nitrate and organic matter. He wrote poetry and a historical novel, *Standish the Puritan* (1850), under the nom de plume "Eldred Grayson." In his later years he became involved in the spiritualism movement, invented a "spiritoscope" to prevent fraud by mediums and to communicate with the dead, and wrote pamphlets and a book on the subject, *Experimental Investigation of the Spirit Manifestations, Demonstrating the Existence of Spirits and Their Communion with Mortals* (1855). He died in Philadelphia, his belief in spiritualism unshaken.

A master experimentalist and the best American chemistry teacher of his time for advanced students, Hare was one of America's first great scientists and inventors, ranking among the major chemists of Europe in his contributions to chemical theory. However, he was less well known than many of his European contemporaries of lesser ability, probably because he did not publish in European journals and worked in the United States, which was then outside the mainstream of scientific activity. Not until specialists returned from German universities did scientists of Hare's stature appear in American chemistry, and during the nineteenth century few of them were his equal.

• The American Philosophical Society, Philadelphia, has a collection of Hare materials. The only full-length biography, Edgar Fahs Smith, *The Life of Robert Hare* (1917), gives no references to sources. In chapter 8 of Smith's *Chemistry in America: Chapters from the History of the Science in the United States* (1914), he reprints Hare's *Memoir of the Supply and Application of the Blow-Pipe* (1802), pp. 152–79, and describes with illustrations several of Hare's inventions, including the calorimotor, deflagrator, distiller, and electrolytic apparatus for preparing amalgams. Biographical articles include Wyndham D. Miles in *Great Chemists*, ed. Eduard Farber (1961), pp. 420–33, and in Miles, ed., *American Chemists and Chemical Engineers* (1976), pp. 195–96. For the history and operation of the limelight see George B. Kauffman and Kin Sing Yen, "Favorite Demonstration: Creating a Limelight in the

Laboratory," *Journal of College Science Teaching* 21 (1991): 54–56. An obituary is in the Philadelphia *Public Ledger*, 17 May 1858.

GEORGE B. KAUFFMAN

HARE, Thomas Truxtun (12 Oct. 1878–2 Feb. 1956), athlete and civic leader, was born in Philadelphia, Pennsylvania, the son of Horace Binney Hare, a distinguished attorney, and Emily Power Beale. Hare first made a name for himself in the athletic world at St. Mark's Prep School in Southborough, Massachusetts, where he starred in football, baseball, and track. Upon matriculation at the University of Pennsylvania in the fall of 1897, his exploits reached national prominence.

Refined, soft-spoken, and scholarly off the football field, Hare was characterized as a berserk iron man on it, allegedly playing every minute of every game over his four-year career. During that time Penn compiled a 47–5–2 record, winning 32 games in a row (25 during Hare's career), and held 32 opponents scoreless. Penn claimed the national college football championship with a 15–0 season in 1897; Hare's speed, strength, and versatility proved the backbone of the team. Although Hare played primarily as a lineman, Coach George Woodruff's innovative "guards back" formation allowed him to run with the ball, utilizing his speed and power. At 6′2″ and 200 pounds, Hare proved a daunting blocker and ball carrier, occasionally serving as a kicker as well. He captained the 1899 and 1900 football teams and earned All-America honors each of his four years, a feat rarely duplicated in the history of college football. Although Hare was chosen as a guard, Walter Camp, the chief selector of the All-America teams, stated that Hare's versatility would have allowed him to be honored at any position.

Hare, an all-around athlete, also competed for the Penn track team as a runner, jumper, and weight thrower in the spring. The team garnered three collegiate track championships during Hare's tenure. In 1900 he competed in the Olympic Games in Paris, France, where he won the silver medal in the initial hammer throw contest. Hare returned to the Olympics, held in St. Louis, Missouri, in 1904, to compete in the all-around championship, a ten-event spectacle that served as a forerunner to the modern decathlon. Hare finished third in the competition designed to recognize the world's greatest athlete.

Hare's versatility extended beyond the athletic field. While at Penn, he participated in drama, music, and literary activities and served as class president. Fellow students bestowed the prestigious campus honor of "spoon man" on him. After his graduation in 1901 Hare entered law school at Penn, from which he earned a degree in 1904. The following year he was engaged to Katherine Sargent Smith, a Philadelphia socialite, whom he married in 1906. The union produced two sons and two daughters.

During his early law career, Hare continued to pursue literary ventures, eventually authoring eight books for young boys. The series followed the adventures of a fictional athletic hero through his college and coaching career. By 1913 he had become a corporate attorney for the United Gas Improvement Company, a position he retained until 1943. During that time he sustained his myriad interests in both the arts and athletics. He wrote articles critical of the abuses in modern football during the 1920s; he also served on the Penn Scholarship Committee and chaired its Athletic Advisory Board in the 1930s. In 1925 he cofounded the Business Men's Art Club in Philadelphia and served as its first president, a position he filled again in 1937. The organization provided for the exhibition of local works, including Hare's own. An avid amateur sportsman, Hare played golf and tennis as a member of country clubs. He turned to trapshooting and archery after the age of forty, and he headed the United Bowmen of America.

In 1943 Hare became the managing director of the Bryn Mawr Hospital, an office held by his recently deceased brother. Retiring from the gas company to his sixty-acre farm in Radnor, Pennsylvania, he continued his hospital work as president of the institution after 1946. In 1951 Hare was honored as one of the initial selectees for the National Football Foundation's Hall of Fame. Later chosen for the Helms Athletic Foundation's College Football Hall of Fame, he was named to seventeen different all-time teams up to 1969. The Helms Foundation also designated him the player of the year for 1900. Hare died at his Radnor home.

• The University of Pennsylvania Archives contain comprehensive materials relative to Hare's life. Anecdotal information about Hare is provided in John McCallum and Charles H. Pearson, *College Football U.S.A.* (1971); John S. Bowman, ed., *Ivy League Football* (1988); Tom Perrin, *Football: A College History* (1987); William S. Jarrett, *Timetables of Sports History: The Olympic Games* (1990); and Barry J. Hugman and Peter Arnold, *The Olympic Games, Complete Track and Field Results, 1896–1988* (1988). An obituary is in the *New York Times*, 4 Feb. 1956.

GERALD R. GEMS

HARE, William Hobart (17 May 1838–23 Oct. 1909), Episcopal bishop, was born in Princeton, New Jersey, the son of George Emlen Hare, a biblical scholar and dean of the Philadelphia Divinity School, and Elizabeth Catherine Hobart, the daughter of John Henry Hobart, the third bishop of New York. Hare's father, a priest and teacher, served on the American Old Testament Committee appointed under the direction of the Convocation of Canterbury in 1870 for the revision of the authorized version of the English Bible. Hare's grandfather, John Henry Hobart, worked among the Oneida Indians in New York, and this may have influenced Hare's later vocation.

After attending the Episcopal Academy in Princeton, Hare entered the sophomore class of the University of Pennsylvania in September 1855 but never graduated. While teaching at St. Mark's Academy in Philadelphia he studied on his own for the ministry. He was ordained deacon by Samuel Bowman, suffragan bishop of Pennsylvania, on 19 June 1859, when he was just one month beyond the required age of twenty-one. Hare began his ministry as assistant at St. Luke's Church, where Mark Antony DeWolfe Howe, later first bishop of Bethlehem, was the rector, and whose daughter, Mary Amory Howe, he married on 31 October 1861. In May 1861 he had become rector of St. Paul's Church, Chestnut Hill, and on 25 May 1862 he was ordained priest by Alonzo Potter, bishop of Pennsylvania. In September 1863, hoping that a change of climate would improve his wife's failing health, he took her and their only child to Michigan and Minnesota. In Minnesota he met some Indians, and this awakened the interest that would dominate the rest of his life. Returning to the East, he resigned the rectorship of St. Paul's Church in order to take charge of St. Luke's Church in Philadelphia while his father-in-law, the rector, was absent. Mary Hare died on 7 January 1866, and in 1867 he became rector of the Church of the Ascension in Philadelphia.

In 1871 Hare was appointed secretary and general agent of the Foreign Committee of the Board of Missions and moved to New York City. In this position he served as an intermediary between the church at home and its representatives in the foreign fields of missionary work. In that same year the House of Bishops nominated him as missionary bishop of Cape Palmas and Parts Adjacent (later named Liberia), but the House of Deputies refused to elect him, wanting Hare to continue in his current position. Then, on 24 October 1871, the House of Bishops erected the Missionary District of Niobrara in Dakota Territory. "Niobrara was the name of a river running along the border between Nebraska and Dakota, and had been chosen as a convenient term in ecclesiastical nomenclature for the large tract of country of which little was known, save that it stretched northward from the river Niobrara, and was roamed over by the Poncas and different tribes of Sioux or Dakota Indians" (*Reminiscences*, p. 8). Hare was elected missionary bishop of Niobrara by the House of Bishops on 1 November 1872 and was ordained and consecrated on 9 January 1873 at St. Luke's Church, Philadelphia, by Benjamin Bosworth Smith, bishop of Kentucky and presiding bishop, assisted by Alfred Lee, bishop of Delaware, and John Williams, bishop of Connecticut. Hare was to work only among the Indians. "This action of the Church was the first and only instance of a racial episcopate," and in a sense Hare was "bishop for a race of people rather than for a particular place" (*That They May Have Life*, p. 116). On 11 October 1883 the House of Bishops voted to divide the Missionary District of Dakota into the Missionary Districts of North and South Dakota and to abolish the Missionary District of Niobrara. Hare thus became missionary bishop of South Dakota, which included white districts as well as the Indian district of Niobrara. He served in this position until his death at Atlantic City, New Jersey. He was buried beside Calvary Cathedral in Sioux Falls, South Dakota.

Hare divided his missionary district into divisions—"these divisions being ordinarily the territory connected with a United States Indian Agency"—and placed each division under an experienced presbyter who supervised the Indian ministers and catechists. He served as a general superintendent, "whose duty it was to reach the people through their pastors" (*Reminiscences*, p. 17). He also established numerous Indian boarding schools to train Indian boys to be teachers, catechists, and missionaries as well as All Saints School for girls in Sioux Falls for the daughters of his missionaries and other white girls. Hare's Indian name was "Swift Bird," and his extensive missionary and educational efforts earned him the title "Apostle to the Sioux."

• Some of Hare's papers and sermons are in the Archives of the Episcopal Church, Austin, Tex., and the South Dakota State Historical Society, Pierre. Considerable information about his work is in his reports to the *Spirit of Missions*, published by the Episcopal church. A primary source is his *Reminiscences: An Address by William Hobart Hare, Missionary Bishop of South Dakota at a Service Commemorative of the Fifteenth Anniversary of His Consecration* (1888). The major study of his life and work is M. A. DeWolfe Howe, *The Life and Labors of Bishop Hare: Apostle to the Sioux* (1911), which reproduces many of his letters. Another helpful study is Mary B. Peabody, *Swift Bird, the Indian's Bishop* (1915); Peabody was Hare's secretary for thirty-two years. Virginia Driving Hawk Sneve treats Hare in the context of the history of the diocese in *That They May Have Life: The Episcopal Church in South Dakota, 1859–1976* (1977). *A Hand-Book of the Church's Mission to the Indians, in Memory of William Hobart Hare, an Apostle to the Indians* (1914), has a lengthy chronological account of Hare's work.

DONALD S. ARMENTROUT

HARFORD, Henry (5 Apr. 1758–8 Dec. 1834), the last proprietor of Maryland, was born in London, England, the illegitimate son of Frederick Calvert, the sixth Lord Baltimore, and Hester Whalen (also known as Hester Harford) of Ireland. Harford's stepfather, Peter Prevost, raised Henry with all the advantages of the British gentry. Calvert paid Prevost a considerable sum to look after the children he had with Hester. Harford attended Richmond School near Epsom, Surrey, then attended Eton, and took a degree from Exeter College, Oxford University, in 1779.

After his father's death in 1771, Harford inherited Maryland but not his father's title. Harford seems to have paid little attention to his province. As a minor, his guardians, including his uncle Cecilius Calvert, Maryland's provincial secretary, handled his affairs. By the time he reached the age of majority, the colony had declared independence and was at war with Great Britain. In 1774 and again in 1778 his relatives challenged his proprietorship. While his paternity was commonly acknowledged, two relatives challenged his inheritance of Maryland on grounds of his illegitimacy. Robert Eden, governor of Maryland, returned to England in 1774 to pursue his wife Caroline's claims on her brother's estate. Harford's cousin Robert Browning claimed the proprietorship in English courts. Harford's legal battle with the Edens ended quickly enough as Eden chose to honor Calvert's instructions to him to recognize Harford as proprietor. Browning was eventually bought off, and a payment was made to Caroline Eden in accordance with Calvert's will. Parliament confirmed Harford's inheritance through the Estate Act of 1780. Harford garnered the bulk of Calvert's estate, totaling some £96,000.

Although the English courts had settled in his favor, Harford had far greater trouble in Maryland attempting to regain the property he lost during the War for Independence. He and former governor Eden visited the state in 1783. Harford was well received in the social circles of Annapolis. He and Eden stayed at Upton Scott's luxurious townhouse and even attended the ceremony in December 1783 at Maryland's statehouse in which George Washington resigned his commission as commander in chief.

In 1785 Harford officially petitioned the Maryland General Assembly to award him compensation for land and property confiscated under the state's laws against Loyalists. He also claimed payment for quitrents lost on land from 1771 until independence was declared. His claim totaled £327,441. Harford's petitions met mixed reactions in the assembly. In 1780 the state had issued bills of credit guaranteed by Harford's confiscated property, making legislators nervous about their redemption. The Treaty of Paris, which ended the war in 1783, was less than clear about Loyalist property claims. Harford wrote a carefully worded and respectful memorial, recognizing the "free state" and appealing to "the dictates of equity and the feelings of humanity" for relief from his financial "situation and embarrassments" (at best, a somewhat dubious description of his considerable resources). Samuel Chase supported Harford's petition in the hope of improving his chances as Maryland's agent to regain Maryland stock in the Bank of England, a process Harford had stymied the year before. Charles Carroll of Carrollton spoke well of Harford's request, a position consistent with his opposition to confiscation during the war. Although Harford's memorial was passed by the lower house in split but favorable votes, the senate unanimously rejected the claim in 1786. Harford's absence during the revolutionary period and his father's alienation of his subjects may have contributed to the rejection of his suit.

Harford returned to England, where he sought compensation from the British government. After the war, Parliament established a plan for reimbursing Loyalist losses during the Revolution. Harford and the Penn family were recognized in class eight of Loyalist losses (proprietors), a category far down the list of risks entailed by the claimants and subject to a lower rate of compensation. Harford's request for more than £400,000 was exceeded only by the Penn family's £500,000 claim. Litigation over the next thirty years resulted in payments to Harford of more than £100,000, the second largest award. During these decades of wrangling, Harford lived the life of a country gentleman. He ran for Parliament in 1781, standing for Lyme Regis. He tied in the popular vote, but his opponent, a large landowner in the region, was selected when the House of Commons decided the election.

Harford's inheritance allowed him and his first wife, Louisa Pigou, to live comfortably from their marriage in 1792 until her death in 1802. The couple had five children, one of whom died in infancy. In 1806 Harford married Esther Ryecroft; they also had five children. He died at "Down Place" near Windsor, Berkshire, and is buried in St. Michael's Churchyard in Bray, England.

Because of his youth, Harford played no role in the Revolution that cost him his province, and he was unable to provide the strong or popular leadership that might have shaped events in Maryland. He is remembered as the last proprietor of Maryland, the final vestige of the failed attempts of the lords Baltimore to transplant feudal overlordship to America. He is symbolic of the cost of loyalty to the Crown, even though his rank allowed him to live comfortably despite his losses.

• The Maryland State Archives, Special Collection SC 1178 (Biographical Files), contains research notes on Henry Harford taken from primary and secondary sources. A full-length biography is Vera F. Rollo, *Henry Harford: Last Proprietor of Maryland* (1976). Her *The Proprietorship of Maryland* (1989) is also relevant. Philip A. Crowl deals with Harford and the proprietorship in the rebellious colony and the revolutionary state in *Maryland during and after the Revolution* (1943), a volume in the series Studies in Historical and Political Science. The series also includes Bernard Steiner, *Life and Administration of Sir Robert Eden* (1898), an invaluable source on the period.

R. J. ROCKEFELLER

HARING, Clarence Henry (9 Feb. 1885–4 Sept. 1960), historian and educator, was born in Philadelphia, Pennsylvania, the son of Henry Getman Haring, a businessman, and Amelia Stoneback. He received the A.B. degree in modern languages from Harvard University in 1907, was a Rhodes scholar at Oxford University from 1907 to 1910, and studied at the University of Berlin in 1909. At Oxford, he studied with Sir Charles H. Firth and produced a book based on his major research paper, *The Buccaneers in the West Indies in the XVII Century* (1910), a study of the use of privateers by England and France against the Spanish empire. It was this research that led to Haring's lifelong interest in the Spanish empire and Latin America. He returned to Harvard as an instructor in history in 1910. In 1912 he was appointed head of the history department at Bryn Mawr. The next year he married Helen Louise Garnsey; they had two sons. In 1915 he went to Clark University. During this time Haring completed his Ph.D. at Harvard under the direction of Roger Merriman. His dissertation on Spanish colonial trade received the Wells Prize and was published as *Trade and Navigation between Spain and the Indies in the Time of the Hapsburgs* (1918). This study of imperialism and commercial expansion was based on extensive research in documents in Seville. At the time of his death it was still considered noteworthy within English language scholarship on Spanish colonial history. Haring was invited to teach at Yale in 1916 and remained there until 1923, when he was appointed Robert Woods Bliss Professor of Latin American History at Harvard, a post he held for the next thirty years. His research led him to examine Spanish colonial institutions such as government bureaucracies and the church and its social-service functions including education, health care, and charitable agencies. This approach to institutional history led to another major work, *South American Progress* (1934), on the tensions between constitutional governments and individual civil rights on the one hand, and statist authority on the other. In 1947 Haring wrote the definitive institutional history of Spanish colonialism, *The Spanish Empire in America*. This work, along with Charles Gibson's *Spain in America* (1966), was still, after several decades, considered the preeminent model of colonial institutional history. In 1953 he retired as an emeritus professor at Harvard and also took advantage of the opportunities to teach at the Naval War College (1953–1954) and the University of Puerto Rico (1955). In 1958 he published his last major book, *Empire in Brazil*, which analyzed Portuguese institutions in South America. Haring's service to the emerging discipline of Latin American studies led him to chair the Committee on Latin American Studies for the American Council of Learned Societies from 1932 to 1942 and to work on a joint committee on Latin America with the Social Science Research Council. In 1935 he organized the Bureau of Economic Research at Harvard, which produced the two-volume reference work *The Economic Literature of Latin America: A Tentative Bibliography* (1935–1936) and *The Handbook of Latin American Studies* (1936), the major research tool in the field. In 1935 he served as a delegate to the Second General Assembly of the Pan American Institute for Geography and History. He was decorated by the governments of Brazil and Venezuela for his contributions to scholarship and international goodwill.

Haring is primarily remembered as an important historian of Latin America who introduced the study of colonial institutions in South American history to American scholarship. Stanley Stein of Princeton University said of Haring that he "set high standards for the field of Latin American history," and that his work will have "enduring value." Haring died in Cambridge, Massachusetts.

• The Harvard University Library has a collection of materials relating to Haring, including an unpublished essay by S.-Y. Mak, "Biography of Prof. Haring," and papers of the Bureau of Economic Research in Latin America, which Haring supervised. Two of Haring's major works not discussed in the text are *South America Looks at the United States* (1928), which reflected his growing interest in modern Latin American republics, and *Argentina and the United States* (1941), an investigation of government institutions and world war. He contributed many articles to *Hispanic American Historical Review*, *Foreign Affairs*, *American Historical Review*, *Quarterly*

Journal of Economics, *Bulletin of the Pan American Union*, and several journals in Latin America and Spain. Obituaries are in the *New York Times*, 5 Sept. 1960; the *American Historical Review*, Jan. 1961; and *Hispanic American Historical Review*, Aug. 1961.

SALVATORE PRISCO

HARING, Keith Allen (4 May 1958–16 Feb. 1990), artist, was born in Reading, Pennsylvania, the son of Allen Haring, a foreman in the Western Electric plant, and Joan (maiden name unknown). Haring attended Kutztown High School. Dropping out of the Ivy School of Art in Pittsburgh after six months, Haring financed a cross-country trip by silkscreening T-shirts with psychedelic designs and selling them at Grateful Dead concerts along the way. After working briefly at the Arts and Crafts Center in Pittsburgh, Haring moved to New York. Haring entered the School for the Visual Arts (SVA) in the fall of 1978, studying with, among others, Keith Sonnier and Joseph Kosuth. He also met Kenny Scharf, Jean-Michel Basquiat (also known as SAMO), and John Sex (John McLaughlin), a circle of fellow artists and performers with whom he was to be professionally and personally associated.

Rising out of the art scene that was forming in the East Village, Haring became a regular contributor to the design, decor, and events at the Mudd Club and Club 57. These and other similar informal venues created an atmosphere that allowed him to experiment with a wide range of media and art forms. Poetry readings, performance art, dance, and music all combined to inspire and urge on Haring's art. By the spring of 1980 his work at Club 57 and other jobs were taking more of his time, and he left the SVA.

Haring commented that the American artist Robert Henri was one of his earliest influences: "Robert Henri had a whole lot to do with my early art education. He wrote this book called *The Art Spirit*, which was almost like a Bible to me for a while" (*Future Primeval*, p. 95). Other early influences included the French artists Pierre Alinchensky and Jean Dubbefet, as well as the cartoon art of Walt Disney, Theodore Geisel ("Dr. Seuss"), and Charles Schultz.

Early in 1980 Haring began creating a series of works that included collages of photocopied pages of books and a project of modifying Chardón Jeans advertisements in New York and pasting fake headlines (such as REAGAN SLAIN BY HERO COP and MOB FLEES AT POPE RALLY) gathered from the *New York Post* on the lampposts and walls of Manhattan. Later that year, Haring became a gallery assistant to art dealer Tony Shafrazi. Working for Shafrazi, Haring learned how to physically handle art, moving and installing artworks. He also received a disillusioning look at the behind-the-scenes politics of the New York art world: "my whole dream of what I thought the art world was going to be, was shattered" (Gruen, p. 59).

Haring began drawing on blank advertising panels in New York's subway stations in late 1980. Haring's work, done during the day in the crowded stations, was a form of performance art. It was also essentially nondestructive, limited to white chalk on black paper covering unused advertising space. Despite this, Haring was arrested by transit police on many occasions for his work. He continued his graffiti work as he became better known. At his later arrests, bystanders were treated to the incongruous scene of the apprehending transit officer asking for Haring's autograph. Haring's vocabulary of images—the small crawling baby with rays streaming from it (the "Radiant Child"), the crocodilian dog, a pointy-eared dog, flying saucers, and the faceless human form—were created at this time.

A 1981 exhibition of graffiti art at the Mudd Club organized by Haring and others brought him to the attention of collectors, and his work began to sell for high prices. In this same year, Haring met Juan Dubose, who would remain his lover-companion until early 1986, when he met Juan Rivera. Though unwilling at first to work with an art dealer, Haring soon realized that being his own dealer consumed too much of his time. Haring selected his former employer Shafrazi from a number of galleries wishing to represent him. Shafrazi gave Haring his first major solo exhibition in October 1982. The opening of the exhibition was a major event attended by celebrities of the art world. In 1983 Haring had exhibitions in the Netherlands, Italy, Japan, and the United Kingdom. He also participated in the Whitney Museum Biennial and the Bienal de São Paulo.

In the following two years Haring's career reached its peak. He painted murals at a number of sites, including the Collingwood Technical School in Melbourne, Australia, the Walker Art Center in Minneapolis, and the Children's Village orphanage in Dobbs Ferry, New York. Haring painted singer Grace Jones's body in his trademark style for a number of projects. Other work done during this time included an animated commercial for Swiss television, the set design for the ballet *Secret Pastures*, and designs for the Swatch watch company.

Haring opened the Pop Shop on Lafayette Street in New York in 1986. This adventure into consumerism saw Haring's designs gracing T-shirts, mugs, posters, and socks. Denounced by the art establishment for "cheapening" art, Haring viewed his foray into the mass marketing of art as an attempt to reach as many people as possible. Three of Haring's experiments in large-scale sculpture, begun in 1985, were placed on Dag Hammarskjöld Plaza at the United Nations headquarters in New York.

In 1987, after returning from a trip to Japan, Haring was diagnosed with Kaposi's sarcoma; he was diagnosed with Acquired Immune Deficiency Syndrome (AIDS) in late 1988. Gilbert Vazquez, whom he met in 1988, was Haring's final companion. Haring died in New York City.

Haring's artistic career lasted just over a decade, from 1979 until his death in 1990. Like Andy Warhol before him, Haring defined his life by his friends and associates. Surrounding himself with the often ephemeral figures of popular culture from the post–World War II years: the singer Madonna, writer William S. Burroughs, activist Timothy Leary, artist and singer Yoko Ono, and a plethora of rock stars, Haring became as much a mass-media personality as an artist. Like many raised in the world of pop art, Haring abandoned realism but not representation. But unlike pop art, which appropriated the images of consumerism and quotidian life, Haring's works were evocative of a more basic humanity; rather than depictions of the everyday things found in pop art, his figures were of a semiotic nature. Haring's images were those of technological and media peril, social violence, political protest, and sexuality.

• Haring's work is included in the collections of the Stedelijk Museum, Amsterdam; the Whitney Museum of American Art, New York; the Beaubourg at Centre Pompidou, Paris; and the Museum of Modern Art, Rio de Janeiro. Sculptures may be seen in the Dag Hammarskjöld Plaza Sculpture Garden (United Nations headquarters, New York City). John Gruen, *Keith Haring: The Authorized Biography* (1991), is a collection of interviews with Haring, his family, and associates. The exhibition catalog *Future Primeval* (1990) contains numerous quotes by Haring as well as comments from his associates. Haring gave an extensive and candid interview to David Sheff in *Rolling Stone*, 10 Aug. 1989, pp. 58–64, 102, before his death. An obituary is in the *New York Times*, 17 Feb. 1990.

MARTIN R. KALFATOVIC

HARIOT, Thomas. *See* Harriot, Thomas.

HARISH-CHANDRA (11 Oct. 1923–16 Oct. 1983), mathematician, was born in Kanpur, India, the son of Chandra Kishore, a civil engineer, and Satyagati Seth Chandrarani. He completed Christ Church High School in Kanpur at the age of fourteen, and after two years at an intermediate college, he entered Allahabad University. There he received his B.S. in 1941 and his M.S. in 1943. Although he was high-strung and frequently ill, he performed brilliantly on his M.S. written examination (he scored 100 percent) and attracted the attention of the well-known physicist Chandrasekhara V. Raman.

Further encouraged by another physicist, Kariamanikkam S. Krishnan, Harish-Chandra enrolled at the Indian Institute of Science at Bangalore as a research student in physics with the famed Homi J. Bhabha. There he wrote several papers on classical point-particles (two coauthored with Bhabha), on the basis of which he was accepted in 1945 by Paul Dirac as a research student at Cambridge University, where, as a student at Gonville and Caius College, he received his Ph.D. in 1947. His dissertation, "Infinite Irreducible Representations of the Lorentz Group," was directed by Dirac, and Harish-Chandra accompanied him as his assistant to the Institute for Advanced Study in Princeton, New Jersey, during the academic year 1947–1948. He remained an additional year, 1948–

1949, at the institute, before becoming a Jewett Fellow at Harvard University during 1949–1950.

The latter two years marked Harish-Chandra's shift from physics to mathematics; he was influenced by the noted algebraists Emil Artin and Claude Chevalley while at Princeton, and subsequently by the algebraic geometer Oscar Zariski at Harvard. In 1950 he joined the faculty of Columbia University, and, although he was frequently absent on various fellowships, he formally retained this position until 1963. He spent 1952–1953 at the Tata Institute in Bombay and in 1952 married Lalitha (also known as Lily) Kale, who was the daughter of old friends from his university days in Bangalore. The couple had two daughters. In 1955–1956 Harish-Chandra returned to the institute at Princeton; in 1957–1958 he was a Guggenheim Fellow in Paris; and from 1961 to 1963 he was a Sloan Fellow. Appointed a permanent member of the Institute for Advanced Study in 1963, he held the IBM–von Neumann Professorship of Mathematics from its creation in 1970 until his death.

Virtually all of Harish-Chandra's mathematical work was concerned with the theory of infinite-dimensional group representations, with particular emphasis on constructing a workable harmonic analysis on them. This focus initially arose in his doctoral research, and his early purely mathematical research dealt with Lie algebras and groups. In this area he was influenced by his association with Chevalley, and he gave new proofs and generalizations of theorems of Ado (1949) and of the Tannaka Duality Theorem (1950). He devoted the period from 1951 to 1959 primarily to the theory of semisimple Lie algebras and Lie groups, but Fourier transforms, spherical functions, and the Plancherel formula also received his attention. This work led to an interest in discrete series and then, following a decade of intense effort, to his memoirs: "Discrete Series for Semisimple Lie Groups I & II," *Acta Mathematica* 113 (1965): 241–318, and 115 (1966): 1–111. This opened the door to harmonic analysis, i.e., Eisenstein series/integrals, and automorphic forms on real reductive and p-adic groups, which was a notable achievement.

Harish-Chandra won the Cole Prize of the American Mathematical Society in 1954 for his papers on the representations of semisimple Lie algebras and groups, with his "On Some Applications of the Universal Enveloping Algebra of Semisimple Lie Algebras" (*Transactions of the American Mathematical Society* 70 [1951]: 28–96) being cited as noteworthy. He was also seriously considered for the Fields Medal of the International Congress of Mathematicians in 1958. In 1973 he was elected fellow of the Royal Society; and a fellow of both the Indian Academy of Sciences and the Indian National Science Academy in 1975. The latter academy had awarded him its Srinivasa Ramanujan Medal in 1974. He became a naturalized U.S. citizen in 1980 and a member of the National Academy of Sciences in 1981.

Harish-Chandra was one of the outstanding algebraists and analysts of his generation, in whose hands a relatively new topic in mathematics and physics was transformed into a major area of contemporary research. As the most talented mathematician to emerge from India in the second half of the twentieth century, he greatly influenced the American mathematical community. He was endowed with an analytic power and algebraic facility that was truly remarkable, permitting him to devise the novel methods he introduced in his work. In person, he was a tall, handsome man, who was somewhat reserved, but who possessed a formal courtesy that did not conceal the depth of his feelings and thought. In his early years he liked to paint and later expressed a fondness for the French Impressionists. On one occasion he commented that he regarded mathematics as an empty canvas that could be filled in *without* reference to external reality; it was the internal harmony of the subject that greatly appealed to him (Langlands, p. 202). One of his colleagues suggested that Harish-Chandra survives in his work, which faithfully mirrored his personality: intense, lofty, and uncompromising (Varadarajan, postscript to *Collected Works*).

Harish-Chandra's health, which had always been fragile, was exacerbated by an intense work schedule that demanded intense concentration and long hours. He had his first heart attack in 1969 and never fully recovered from a third attack, which occurred in 1982. Following a sixtieth birthday conference for his colleague Armand Borel (a similar conference was planned for him in April 1984), he collapsed and died while walking on the institute grounds near his home.

• There is no known archival collection of Harish-Chandra's papers. He wrote little of an autobiographical or personal nature; however, his brief essay, "My Association with Professor Dirac," in *Reminiscences about a Great Physicist: Paul Adrien Maurice Dirac*, ed. Behram N. Kursunoglu and Eugene P. Wigner (1987), offers an unusual glimpse of his expository style. His published work has been brought together in four volumes, *Collected Works*, ed. Veeraualli Varadarajan (1984), which contain detailed, expert commentaries by Nolan R. Wallach and Roger Howe on his mathematical and physical research. Biographical accounts are Varadarajan, "Harish-Chandra (1923–1983)," *Mathematical Intelligencer* 6 (1984): 9–13, 19, and Rebecca A. Herb, "Harish-Chandra and His Work," *Bulletin of the American Mathematical Society*, n.s., 1 (July 1991): 1–17. Obituaries are Robert P. Langlands, *Biographical Memoirs of Fellows of the Royal Society* 31 (1985): 199–225, and the *New York Times*, 19 Oct. 1983.

JOSEPH D. ZUND

HARJO, Chitto (1846–1909?), Creek leader also known as Crazy Snake or Wilson Jones, was born in Arbeka in Indian Territory, the son of Aharlock Harjo; his mother's identity is unknown. *Chitto* is a form of the Creek word meaning *snake*; Harjo is a common second name among the Creeks. It means recklessly brave, or one who is brave beyond discretion. The English equivalent is *crazy*, but in the sense of *passionate* rather than *insane*. Consequently, among whites Chitto Harjo was renowned as Crazy Snake and his followers were called Crazy Snakes.

Little is recorded of the first fifty years of Harjo's life, although he is known to have participated in the Civil War. A farmer by trade, his public career began in 1899 when he was selected *heneha* of Hickory Ground. A town's *heneha* was an orator designated to make speeches on behalf of the *micco* (chief), in this case Lahtah Micco. Located in what is now eastern Oklahoma, Hickory Ground had become the center of discontent among Creeks objecting to their National Council's decision in 1899 to cooperate with the Dawes Commission. Snakes looked to Hickory Ground for leadership in opposing allotment, a process initiated in 1893 with the purpose of dividing Creek tribal land into individual holdings. These Creeks contended that allotment, which had been approved by their National Council, violated the Treaty of 1832, which solemnly guaranteed land west of the Mississippi and self-government to their people.

When illness stranded Lahtah Micco in Washington, D.C., in 1900, Harjo assumed leadership of the Hickory Ground movement. Throughout the summer of 1900 he traveled from stomp dance to stomp dance to oppose *E-kun wath-ka* (allotment). By the fall, Hickory Ground Creeks had established their own government and adopted laws making transactions with whites illegal. A Snake law enforcement force punished local Creeks with fines and whippings for leasing land to whites, employing them, or participating in the allotment process. Emissaries recruited dissident Choctaws, Cherokees, and Seminoles. Afraid that the Hickory Ground crusade held the seeds of a revolutionary threat, Pleasant Porter, principal chief of the Muscogee nation, turned to the United States for help, warning federal officials that the Snakes had organized a growing intertribal movement. In January 1901 the Snakes formally announced their campaign to stop allotment in a letter to President William Mc-Kinley.

On the twenty-fifth of that month, Troop A of the Eighth U.S. Cavalry was dispatched to arrest Snake leaders and disband the movement, marking one of the last times the United States resorted to military force to resolve an Indian conflict. Ironically, even though many had expected such force would be necessary to capture Harjo, a deputy federal marshal and an interpreter arrested the Snake leader at his home without resistance several days later. Nearly 100 other Snakes were also arrested and transported to Muskogee during the following week. They appeared in federal court and pleaded guilty to charges of conspiracy, false imprisonment, and assault and battery in exchange for a suspension of fines and imprisonment. Judge John R. Thomas released them with a warning to stop their activity, but Harjo and others continued to promote gatherings at Hickory Ground to plan ways to oppose allotment. In February 1902 federal marshals again arrested Harjo, along with nine other Snake leaders, on charges of violating the terms of their release. The captured Snakes were transferred to the federal penitentiary at Leavenworth, Kansas, to complete the remainder of their two-year sentences.

The imprisonment of Harjo from March until November 1902 worked a change in Snake tactics. Rather than separate from the tribe and make militant demands, the Snakes, under Harjo's determined leadership, chose to challenge allotment and agitate other issues through established political structures. Snakes ran for Creek tribal offices, circulated petitions, retained lobbyists in Washington, and corresponded with federal officials. In 1905 Harjo traveled to Washington for a meeting with President Theodore Roosevelt. Neither man possessing the skills to make their points in the other's language, Harjo left Washington confused by Roosevelt's position regarding allotment. Snake grievances, however, prompted the U.S. Senate to launch an investigation into the final disposition of the affairs of the Five Tribes. On 23 November 1906 Chitto Harjo testified before a select Senate committee in Tulsa, eloquently petitioning for the restoration of the Treaty of 1832. His poignant plea for justice led listeners to characterize Harjo as a "warrior-statesman," "a patriot like George Washington," "a man of strong magnetism," and "the most wonderful speaker I ever heard." Dismayed by the committee's rejection of his appeal, Harjo concocted a plan to move his people to Mexico, but they refused to leave their homes.

Although some praised Harjo for his stand against allotment, most whites continued to fear him and his movement. This fear erupted into deadly violence in the early spring of 1909. Harjo and other Snakes had given sanctuary to black families after a race riot in Henryetta made it impossible for blacks to live there. Unemployed and homeless, a few men resorted to theft to feed their families. Local peace officers formed a posse and went to Hickory Ground to arrest the thieves. A shootout erupted, resulting in the deaths of an estimated fifteen men and the arrest of forty-two, including some Snakes. Harjo was at his home some twenty miles distant, but Checotah's sheriff blamed him for the battle. Four U.S. deputy marshals were sent to arrest Harjo, though neighbors testified that he had not been involved in the violence.

At sundown on 27 March the officers approached Harjo's cabin. As sentinels retreated to the cabin to alert him, the officers opened fire. The sentinels returned the gunfire, killing two of the officers. The survivors returned to Checotah, not knowing that Harjo, too, had been wounded. A large posse returned to his cabin to find he had disappeared. Frustrated by Harjo's escape, the posse looted and burned his home. Anti-Creek violence spread, leading Governor Charles N. Haskell to order the Oklahoma National Guard to Hickory Ground to restore peace and arrest Harjo. But the Snake leader evaded capture.

This disappearance has shrouded Harjo's fate in mystery. Many accounts exist, none of which can be adequately documented. A persistent story among Creeks maintained that he fled to Mexico, where he died of old age. Another story asserted that he burned to death in his cabin when the vengeful posse set it ablaze. Another account said he was hanged in Okmulgee, Oklahoma, in 1910; still another had him shot and drowned in the Canadian River. Family and friends testified, however, that Harjo died at the home of Choctaw friend Daniel Bob in the Kiamichi Mountains of southeastern Oklahoma as a result of the gunshot wound sustained in the exchange with the deputy marshals. The date has been placed as late as 1911, though the narrative recorded by Daniel Bob implied Harjo died shortly after the shooting.

Chitto Harjo's ardent opposition to allotment made him a symbol of native resistance to assimilation. His legend was furthered by his mysterious fate. The movement he led marked a significant transition in Native American history as Indians who opposed white encroachment established political structures to resist cultural and tribal change.

• Primary sources for Chitto Harjo and the Crazy Snakes include Creek National Records, Creek Enrollment Cards and Equalization Jackets, Records of the Five Civilized Tribes, and Records of the U.S. Court in Indian Territory, all housed in the Fort Worth branch of the National Archives, and the *Indian Pioneer Papers, 1860–1935* [microform collection], compiled by Grant Foreman. In addition, the Oklahoma Historical Society holds an extensive collection of newspaper accounts of Snake activity between 1900 and 1909. A scholarly analysis of Harjo and his movement is Ken McIntosh, "Chitto Harjo, the Crazy Snakes, and the Birth of Indian Political Activism in the Twentieth Century" (Ph.D. diss., Texas Christian Univ., 1993). A published biographical reference is Mel Bolster's fictionalized narrative, *Crazy Snake and the Smoked Meat Rebellion* (1976).

KEN MCINTOSH

HARKINS, Henry N. (13 July 1905–12 Aug. 1967), surgeon, was born in Missoula, Montana, the son of William Draper Harkins, a professor of chemistry, and Anne Louise Hatheway. Harkins received his early education at the elementary and high schools in Chicago. He was a Douglas Smith Fellow at the University of Chicago, graduating with a B.S. in 1925, an M.S. in 1926, and a Ph.D. in 1928. He then went on to Rush Medical College for his M.D., graduating in 1930. Harkins's surgical residency (1931–1936) was spent at the University of Chicago Clinics under Dallas Phemister, a prominent physician. He served his internship at Presbyterian Hospital from 1930 to 1931. In 1933 he went to Europe for postgraduate work at the University of Edinburgh, Scotland, and at the National Hospital, London. Obtaining a Guggenheim Memorial Fellowship in surgery, Harkins went on to study at the University of Edinburgh, the University of Ghent, the University of Uppsala, and the University of Frankfurt am Main. He married Jean Hamilton in June 1937, and they had four daughters.

Upon his return from Europe, Harkins spent four years (1939–1943) as an associate surgeon at the Henry Ford Hospital in Detroit. At Henry Ford he became interested in the surgical treatment of varicose veins and hernia, resulting in many original contributions to the medical literature. He also taught surgery at Wayne University College of Medicine during his last year at Henry Ford. In 1943 Harkins joined the Johns Hopkins University School of Medicine as associate professor of surgery and joined the university hospital as associate surgeon. Alfred Blalock, a prominent surgeon there, made a lasting impression on Harkins. In later years he combined in his practice of surgery the best of the schools of surgical thought promoted by Phemister at Chicago and by Blalock at Hopkins. During his tenure at Johns Hopkins, Harkins served as visiting surgeon in Baltimore city hospitals and spent time at Yale as a researcher and assistant professor of physiology. He also served as a consultant to the National Institutes of Health in hematology (1946–1948) and the National Research Council's Subcommittee on Shock (1943–1945), and he was a board member of the National Library of Medicine.

In 1947 Harkins accepted the chair of the Department of Surgery at the University of Washington School of Medicine in Seattle, a position he held until 1964. An effective administrator, he directed the department's research, staff, and curriculum and was instrumental in the building of Washington Hospital in Seattle. A conscientious chief surgeon of King County Hospital, Harkins doggedly pursued efforts to improve the hospital's services and attend to the needs of teachers, staff members, and interns.

Harkins also gave diligently to his community, serving as a consultant to the Veterans Administration Hospital, the Children's Orthopedic Hospital, and the U.S. Naval Hospital, among others. He was a prominent and popular representative of his profession as the Clagett Lecturer at the University of Chicago in 1942, the Phemister Lecturer at the same university in 1960, the Lee Lecturer at the University of Pennsylvania Graduate School of Medicine in 1964, the Sir Edwin Tooth Visiting Professor of Surgery at the University of Queensland in Australia in 1965, and the first Swedish Government Visiting Professor of Surgery at the University of Gothenburg in 1966. Obtaining another Guggenheim Fellowship in surgery in 1965, he traveled the world as visiting professor of surgery at universities in Adelaide and Melbourne, Australia; Singapore; Auckland and Dunedin, New Zealand; Kuala Lumpur, Malaysia; Witwatersrand, South Africa; and Uppsala, Sweden.

Harkins's scientific productivity reveals a wide variety of interests, and he published over 360 articles on surgical subjects. In his later years, the problems of the gastrointestinal tract, especially gastric physiology, peptic ulcer, and the Billroth I operation, dominated his thinking. His last articles reflect an enthusiastic inquiry into the research and clinical aspects of selective vagotomy. His published books include *The Treatment of Burns* (1942) and *The Billroth I Gastric Resection* (1954), the latter a collaborative effort with Horace Moore. He edited *Surgery: Principles and Practice* (1957; rev. eds., 1961, 1965), *Surgery of the Stomach and Duodenum* (1962; 2d ed., 1969), *Hernia* (1964), and *Geriatric Surgical Emergencies* (1963). Harkins was editor in chief of the *Quarterly Review of Surgery* (now *Current Surgery*) from 1943 until his death. He also served on the editorial boards of both the *An-*

nals of Surgery and the *Western Journal of Surgery* from 1948 on, and he was managing editor of the *Bulletin of the Johns Hopkins Hospital* from 1944 to 1947.

Harkins received the Acrel Medal from the Swedish Surgical Society in 1966 and was a founding member of the International Surgical Club, the Surgery Biology Club, and the Central Surgical Association. An active sports enthusiast and amateur photographer, he spent his spare time mainly outdoors. He died in Seattle, Washington.

Well respected by his peers and colleagues, Harkins was the epitome of the academic surgeon: a spirited teacher, investigator, and scholar and an important contributor to the practice of medicine worldwide.

• Harkins's papers are in the National Library of Medicine, Bethesda, Md. His important articles include "Mechanism of Death in Bile Peritonitis," *Proceedings of the Society for Experimental Biology and Medicine* 32 (1935): 691–93; "The Pathology of Burns," *Proceedings of the Institute of Medicine of Chicago* 12 (1938): 114; "The Prevention of Pyloric Ligation-Induced Ulcers of the Gastric Rumen of Rats by Transabdominal Vagotomy: A Prelimary Report," *Bulletin of the Johns Hopkins Hospital* 80 (1947): 174–76, which initiated a long series of important scientific presentations in the field of gastrointestinal physiology; and "Partial Gastric Vagotomy: An Experimental Study," *Gastroenterology* 32 (1957): 96–102, a presentation on modification of gastric vagotomy that had an impact on the method of performing this operative procedure. An obituary is in the *New York Times*, 13 Aug. 1967.

Lloyd M. Nyhus
Michelle E. Osborn

HARKINS, William Draper (28 Dec. 1873–7 Mar. 1951), physical chemist and nuclear scientist, was born in Titusville, Pennsylvania (where the first commercial development of the Pennsylvania natural gas fields took place), the son of Nelson Goodrich Harkins, variously described as a fruit rancher, fruit broker, and oil industry pioneer, and Sarah Eliza Draper. At the age of nineteen he moved to Escondido, California. In 1896 he matriculated at Stanford University, where he was, first, assistant (1898–1900) and, then, instructor (1900) in chemistry. After receiving his B.A. degree in 1900, he served as professor and chairman of the chemistry department at the University of Montana at Missoula (1900–1912). During this period he was president of the Missoula City Board of Health (1906–1912), chemist in charge of smelter investigations for the Anaconda Farmers' Association (1902–1910), and a consultant for the Mountain Copper Company of California (1904) and the Carnegie Institution of Washington (1911). He also pursued postgraduate work at the University of Chicago (1901, 1904) and Stanford University (1905–1906). In 1904 he married Anna Louise Hatheway, chairman of the University of Montana Department of English; they had two children. He was awarded the first Ph.D. in chemistry from Stanford on 10 June 1907.

Harkins spent the customary year abroad (1909) in Fritz Haber's Institut für Physikalische Chemie at the Technische Hochschule in Karlsruhe, Germany. During 1909–1910 he was a research associate at the Massachusetts Institute of Technology under Arthur Amos Noyes, one of the few pioneers in physical chemistry in the United States. In 1912 he accepted an appointment at the University of Chicago, where he carried out research for the rest of his life. He was assistant professor of general chemistry (1912–1914), associate professor (1914–1917), professor of physical chemistry (1917–1931), Carl William Eisendrath Professor of Chemistry (1931–1935), and Andrew MacLeish Distinguished Service Professor (1935–1939).

His first publications, supported by the Anaconda Farmers' Association, involved the polluting effects of smelter smoke from the Anaconda Copper Company on surrounding farmland. Long before the advent of the environmental movement, Harkins found that one smelter stack spewed thirty tons each of arsenic trioxide and copper per day over the surrounding twenty square miles of pastureland, raising the arsenic level to 200–500 parts per million in fall grasses and killing hundreds of cattle, horses, and sheep. The company immediately took action to reduce the pollution when Harkins demonstrated that sales of the recovered arsenic would pay for its removal from the smoke.

From 1913 to 1928 Harkins and his students were the only Americans to explore the structure of the atomic nucleus. In 1915 alone, he, together with Ernest D. Wilson, published five articles on nuclear synthesis reactions, the first of nearly eighty papers on the structure of atomic nuclei. They differentiated between chemical elements, which are mixtures of atomic species (isotopes), and isotopic species themselves. They were the first to use Einstein's famous equation $E = mc^2$ to show that an enormous amount of energy is produced in the fusion of hydrogen nuclei to produce helium. They accounted for the concomitant decrease in mass in such fusion reactions, which they called the packing effect, and they speculated that the conversion of hydrogen to helium might be the source of energy fueling the sun and stars, a process later confirmed and called nuclear fusion. They showed that the packing effect was smaller in nuclei of even atomic number than in those of odd atomic number, leading Harkins to propose that even-numbered elements are more stable, an idea later formalized in "Harkins's rules," which account for the abundance of these elements in the earth's crust and in extraterrestrial matter.

Harkins devised a new periodic system of the elements, and except for Francis W. Aston, who received the Nobel Prize for partial separation of neon isotopes, he was the first to separate isotopes, namely, those of chlorine and mercury. He also introduced the term *isobar* to designate nuclear species of the same atomic weight but different atomic numbers. In 1920 he was the first to predict the existence of a grouping of a proton and an electron, which he called a neutron in 1921. Immediately after James Chadwick's discovery of the neutron (1932), Harkins used neutrons to investigate nuclear reactions. For example, in 1933, with David M. Gans and Henry W. Newson, he used the Wilson cloud chamber to observe the neutron bombardment of fluorine to produce nitrogen-16, the first artificially produced radioactive element. Harkins also predicted the existence of heavy isotopes of hydrogen, which was confirmed in 1932 by Harold C. Urey's discovery of deuterium, for which Urey was awarded the Nobel Prize two years later.

Harkins virtually created the field of modern surface chemistry, to which the majority of his publications belong. This research originated with his postdoctoral work with Haber and Noyes (1909–1910), which preceded and led to his interest in nuclear structure. Harkins was one of the three scientists who independently proposed the theory of the orientation of molecules on surfaces (the other two were William G. Hardy and 1932 Nobel Prize laureate Irving Langmuir). He tried to make surface measurements an exact science, and he developed accurate procedures that have since become standard methods, for example, drop weight and ring methods for measuring surface tension and interfacial tension. He studied the relationship between the structure and surface properties of organic molecules. In 1920 he introduced the concepts of work of adhesion, work of cohesion, and spreading coefficient, widely used to correlate the spreading of organic materials on water or mercury. In 1937 he began an extensive, fundamental investigation of gas adsorption on solid powders. He developed the only absolute (Harkins-Jura) method for measuring the surface areas of powders, which permitted the calibration of relative methods such as the Brunauer-Emmett-Teller (BET) method. Much of the present knowledge of adsorption of oxides is based on his methods for measuring equilibrium spreading pressures of vapors or solids.

Harkins retired in 1939, but he continued his research with undiminished vigor; about one-third of his 298 publications date from his postretirement years. When the United States entered World War II, although he was not involved in the Manhattan Project, his cyclotron was turned over to this project. He also aided the war effort by working on catalysts for petroleum refining to make superior gasolines. He entered colloid chemistry, a new field for him; worked on the emulsion polymerization of rubber; and was inducted posthumously into the International Rubber Science Hall of Fame (1985). He developed new methods for measuring the formation of micelles in detergent solutions, and he determined the quantitative effect of structure, salts, hydrocarbons, and insoluble surfactants on micelle formation, work that proved useful in the search for synthetic substitutes for natural rubber. An active member of the American Chemical Society and the recipient of the ACS Chicago Section's Willard Gibbs Medal, Harkins was embittered by his failure to win the Nobel Prize. His views were generally ahead of his time, but he was often denied credit even when his ideas were experimentally confirmed. He had an abrasive personality and acquired the nickname "Priority Harkins" because of his polemical efforts to retain recognition. He died in Chicago.

One of Harkins's most striking characteristics was his failure to observe the customary boundaries between chemistry and physics, which resulted in the wide range of areas to which he made significant contributions. Although he was a chemist, he contributed greatly to nuclear physics at a time when American physicists were paying little attention to this field. A debt is owed him for many fundamental ideas of nuclear reactions and surface chemistry. He and his students developed numerous standard laboratory methods for studying and measuring surface phenomena.

• Harkins's posthumously published magnum opus, *The Physical Chemistry of Surface Films* (1952), ed. Thomas F. Young, includes a complete list of his publications and a portrait of the scientist as well as "a unified treatment of his contributions to surface chemistry, to the theory of micelles, and to the theory of emulsion polymerization." It is "the culmination of a plan cherished in the mind of its author for more than twenty years." Biographical essays include Gustav Egloff, "Fathers and Sons in Chemistry: William Draper Harkins and Henry Nelson Harkins," *Chemical and Engineering News* 22 (25 May 1944): 804–5; anon., "William Draper Harkins," *Chemical and Engineering News* 27 (18 Apr. 1949): 1146; anon., "Necrology: William D. Harkins," *Chemical and Engineering News* 29 (19 Mar. 1951): 1145; Robert S. Mulliken, "William Draper Harkins 1873–1951," *National Academy of Sciences, Biographical Memoirs* 47 (1975): 49–81; Warren C. Johnson, "William Draper Harkins," in *American Chemists and Chemical Engineers*, ed. Wyndham D. Miles (1976); and George B. Kauffman, "William Draper Harkins (1873–1951): A Controversial and Neglected American Physical Chemist," *Journal of Chemical Education* 62, no. 9 (1985): 758–61.

GEORGE B. KAUFFMAN

HARKNESS, Anna M. Richardson (25 Oct. 1837–27 Mar. 1926), philanthropist, was born in Dalton, Ohio, the daughter of James Richardson and Anna Ranck. Nothing is known of her early life or education. On 13 February 1854 she married Stephen Vanderburg Harkness, a widower nineteen years her senior with a three-year-old son. They had four children of their own, one of whom died in infancy.

Stephen Harkness, who bought and sold stock, accrued a fortune selling whiskey during the Civil War. He opened a banking house in Monroeville, Ohio, then settled on Euclid Avenue, the millionaire's row of Cleveland. In 1867 he invested his money in the oil refining business of Rockefeller, Andrews & Flagler. Renamed the Standard Oil Company, it became the largest oil producer in the world, making Stephen Harkness, a silent partner and major stockholder, a millionaire many times over. At his unexpected death in 1888, he left an estate of $150 million. In the absence of a will, the state awarded one-third to his wife and two-thirds to be divided among their four children.

Harkness moved with her children from Cleveland to New York City and devoted the rest of her life fielding inquiries for aid and distributing funds to those organizations or endeavors that were of interest to her. In keeping with her husband's generosity and philanthropic interests, Harkness, rather than reinvest untaxed earnings, close to donate monies to religious and welfare organizations. Unlike her husband, who had aided in the building of churches of all denominations, Harkness focused on the Fifth Avenue Presbyterian Church she and her daughter attended. In November 1922 she gave it $750,000, which was met by an additional $250,000 from the church, for the erection of a parish house. She also donated regularly to a New York City Christmas charity, One Hundred Neediest Cases.

Though largely unknown to the public, "few if any women have given as much to education and medicine as did Mrs. Harkness," according to the *New York Times* (28 Mar. 1926). After the death of her oldest son, Charles W. Harkness, on 1 May 1916, Harkness gave his alma mater, Yale University, the first of many large donations that at her death totaled more than $9 million. In 1917 she donated $3 million for the purpose of building the famous senior dormitories known as the Harkness Memorial Quadrangle. Yale also relied on Harkness when emergency funds were needed to replace a heating system in October 1917. When Harkness anonymously contributed $3 million in 1920 for the purpose of augmenting faculty salaries, she asked that her donation be met with $2 million by alumni, which it was.

In October 1918 Harkness established the Commonwealth Fund in New York with an initial donation of $10 million. It was dedicated at first "to do something for the welfare of mankind" and later, more particularly, for the "improvement of the mental and physical health of the American people." Since the fund was founded in the wake of World War I, the largest early grants were distributed to the United War Work Campaign and the American Committee on Armenian and Syrian Relief to help postwar sufferers in Europe and the Near East. A large donation in 1919 and in 1920 to the American Relief Administration inspired Herbert Hoover to mention the Commonwealth Fund in his *American Epic: Famine in Forty-five Nations, the Battle on the Front Line, 1914–1932*, vol. 3 (1961). The fund contributed to educational research, legal research, mental health, community health, the building of rural hospitals, and medical research and education, and it provided national and international fellowships for study in the health field. In 1922 Harkness, with her son Edward, gave New York City twenty-two acres (valued at $4 million) in upper Manhattan for the site of a new medical center for Columbia University's College of Physicians and Surgeons and the Presbyterian Hospital. Harkness added $500,000 for the building fund and an additional $250,000 for its nursing school. The same year she donated $100,000 to the endowment fund of the Union Theological Seminary.

From the time her will was executed on 23 December 1920 to her death in 1926, Harkness had distributed $29,925,000 of the $36,650,000 she had available to bequeath. Her interests may best be conveyed by the types of charitable, educational, and cultural institutions to which she donated: the Fifth Avenue Presbyterian Church; the Board of Home Missions of the Presbyterian Church in the United States of America; the Church Extension Committee of the Presbytery of New York; the Presbyterian Hospital in the City of New York; Memorial Methodist Episcopal Church of Caledonia, Ohio; Flower Hospital (now Terence Cardinal Cooke Health Care Center), New York City; Lakeside Hospital of Cleveland; Cleveland Homeopathic Hospital; the American Museum of Natural History; the Metropolitan Museum of Art; the New York Public Library; the New York Zoological Society; the Hampton Normal and Agricultural Institute of Alabama; the Charity Organization Society of the City of New York; the State Charities Aid Association of New York; and the New York Association for Improving the Condition of the Poor.

In addition to a residuary bequest to her son Edward (the executor of the will), Harkness, whose "name was synonymous with all that is gracious and good," left money for each of her employees depending on the length of his or her employment with her. She died in her Fifth Avenue home in New York City.

• For the history and descriptions of the Commonwealth Fund see Commonwealth Fund, *The Commonwealth Fund: Historical Sketch, 1918–1962* (1963); A. McGehee Harvey and Susan L. Abrams, *"For the Welfare of Mankind": The Commonwealth Fund and American Medicine* (1986); and Wilmer S. Rich, *American Foundations and Their Fields* (1955). For sketches of Stephen Harkness see J. H. Kennedy, "Stephen Vanderburg Harkness," *Magazine of Western History* 9 (Dec. 1888): 188–92; and Allan Nevins, *John D. Rockefeller: The Heroic Age of American Enterprise* (2 vols., 1940). Also see James W. Wooster, *Edward Stephen Harkness, 1874–1940* (1949). A short obituary detailing the circumstances of Harkness's husband's death is in the *New York Times*, 9 Mar. 1888. Obituaries are in the *New York Times*, 28, 29, and 30 Mar. 1926, and in the *New York Herald Tribune*, 28 Mar. 1926. See "$36,650,000 Willed by Mrs. Harkness to Charity and Public," *New York Times*, 3 Apr. 1926, for a detailed account of Harkness's will.

BARBARA L. CICCARELLI

HARKNESS, Edward Stephen (22 Jan. 1874–29 Jan. 1940), philanthropist, was born in Cleveland, Ohio, the son of Stephen Vanderberg Harkness, a businessman, and his second wife, Anna Richardson. The elder Harkness had been a silent partner in the oil refinery firm of Rockefeller, Andrews and Flagler and in 1870 became one of the six stockholders in the newly formed Standard Oil Company, a venture with meager credit and an uncertain future. As the company grew, Stephen Harkness strongly supported the leadership of John D. Rockefeller and augmented his original 1,334 shares with additional investments. When he died in 1888, the Standard Oil shares were the major asset in an estate valued in the millions.

Edward Harkness's older brother, Charles, took over the administration of the estate and the Harkness investments, one-third of which now belonged to Anna Harkness, the remainder divided equally among the four surviving children. Young Edward was sent to St. Paul's School in Concord, New Hampshire; upon graduation in 1893, he enrolled at Yale University. Not an outstanding student, he worked hard to do well and participated in sports and fraternity life. Although shy, he was popular because of his loyalty to friends and his ready sympathy for others. He received his B.A. degree in 1897 and embarked on a world tour.

Upon his return, Harkness settled in New York City and stepped into his expected role as assistant to his brother Charles and adviser to his mother. The three were very close; even after his marriage to Mary Emma Stillman in 1904, Edward visited Anna Harkness every day. Charles had maintained the family's investments in Standard Oil; the Harkness fortune grew steadily as the internal combustion engine became standard and automobile ownership increased. Anna Harkness made large donations in the early 1900s to New York civic and cultural organizations, to the Presbyterian church, to black schools and colleges, and to Yale University. She relied on the advice of both sons in these philanthropies; Edward's pattern of donations to precisely the same groups as his mother demonstrates the closeness of their collaboration.

Edward Harkness was particularly interested in the potential of scientific medicine and in fostering the relationship between medical education and research exemplified by Johns Hopkins. The Hopkins model of medical school and teaching hospital, long supported by academic physicians, was elevated to canonical status by the famous Flexner Report (1910), which harshly condemned most privately run, non-hospital-affiliated medical "diploma mills." But a medical complex like Hopkins, based on full-time faculty and well-equipped laboratories, was expensive; few schools could meet its standards without the aid of private philanthropy or government support. As early as 1910, Harkness was corresponding with Robert De Forest of the Presbyterian Hospital regarding that institution's proposed affiliation with the Columbia University College of Physicians and Surgeons, and offering a $1.3-million endowment from an "anonymous donor" conditional on the new medical center's adherence to the Hopkins model.

In 1916 Charles Harkness died, leaving much of his fortune to his younger brother. Both Edward and Anna had come to realize that they needed to take a more organized and farsighted approach to their philanthropy. They received requests for aid from organizations and individuals daily. But Edward preferred the idea of planned development of ongoing programs to random giving in response to emergency needs or personal appeals. Moreover, he had no children to carry on his plans and wanted to ensure that his estate would be dedicated to the goals he favored.

The Commonwealth Fund was the result of their deliberations. Incorporated 17 October 1918 as a nonprofit organization "to do something for the welfare of mankind," the fund was to be run by a board of five directors, selected by Edward Harkness. He himself served as president of the board; daily operations became the responsibility of the general director, first the historian Max Farrand (1919–1921) and later the educator and administrator Barry Conger Smith (1921–1947). The Harknesses provided the initial endowment of just under $10 million in stocks, augmented by a donation of $6.4 million from Anna Harkness the following year.

Edward Harkness's interests and ideas guided the development of the Commonwealth Fund. The general director and his staff reviewed proposals for presentation to the board; the staff was kept small and select, augmented by extensive use of outside consultants. Board members were chosen from among Harkness's friends and fellow Yale alumni. Malcolm P. Aldrich, who joined the fund as Harkness's assistant in 1923, only a year after he had graduated from Yale, became Edward's closest associate and confidant.

The fund's areas of emphasis included child health and child guidance, rural hospitals, mental health, medical education, and medical research. In selecting projects, Harkness and his associates emphasized prevention, research, and demonstration, seeking to fund well-defined activities that by attracting ongoing support, demonstrating impressive benefits, or laying the foundation for further work would have widespread effects. Thus the fund provided seed money and building funds for hospitals in fifteen rural communities, to be operated and maintained by the communities themselves; funded demonstration child health and guidance clinics; supported selected medical research, the results of which could be applied by other researchers and clinicians; and provided fellowships for students from Great Britain and the Commonwealth countries to study in the United States (this program later became international in scope). By 1947 the Commonwealth Fund's donations totaled more than $40 million.

The fund's major emphasis in the 1920s and 1930s was its programs in mental health, particularly child psychiatry and juvenile delinquency. Its influential series of demonstration Child Guidance Clinics, from 1922 to 1927, were succeeded in 1928 by the Institute for Child Guidance; the institute's stated function was the training of psychiatrists, psychologists, and social workers in "practical child guidance work." Also in 1928, the fund established the first of more than fifteen training fellowships in psychiatry. These programs were highly successful, but Smith and Harkness soon recognized that psychiatrists needed to be integrated into the health care system. From 1933, the Commonwealth Fund supported numerous initiatives to educate physicians in mental health, create programs linking psychiatrists with physicians, and develop standards for board certification in neuropsychiatry.

Harkness simultaneously continued his personal benefactions. In 1922 he and his mother donated twenty-two acres in upper Manhattan as the site of the new Columbia University Medical Center, which he himself had planned and endowed. The complex opened in the summer of 1928. Edward, his mother, and his wife also financed the construction of many of the buildings on the site. Other personal gifts included multiple donations to educational institutions; besides Ivy League schools, prep schools, and medical schools and hospitals, Harkness contributed to midwestern colleges, women's schools, black colleges, and schools in Scotland, Japan, and China.

At the larger universities he visited, Harkness, who valued his own college friendships deeply, was disturbed by the loss of close faculty-student associations and the restrictive economic, social, and even academic barriers that created student caste systems. As a solution, he suggested the "House Plan," the creation of small residential units where rich and poor students could live with the faculty who taught them. Yale disregarded his first proposal of this plan in 1928. Harvard, however, responded enthusiastically, and Harkness provided $13 million to set up the new Harvard "Houses." In 1930 Yale was more receptive and instituted the Quad Plan, which he also funded, including money for resident faculty salaries and aid for poorer students.

Harkness's interest in Great Britain and its people, which had prompted the Commonwealth Fund's program of British fellowships, inspired him to establish the $10-million Pilgrim Trust in 1930. The trust was run by a British board, which was allowed free rein in the use of the funds. It supported such projects as the preservation of historic sites and training for the unemployed.

Harkness's other personal benefactions, large and small, were so extensive that even he kept no complete record. A list of his contributions over $5,000 includes 1,332 separate entries totaling more than $129 million. Although he took a thoughtful, disciplined approach to philanthropy, always seeking long-term benefits rather than quick relief, he also clearly took great pleasure and personal satisfaction in using his fortune to aid others.

In 1937 Harkness asked the Commonwealth Fund's staff to investigate for him the funding of medical research in the United States, particularly for work on poliomyelitis, cancer, and chronic disease. He also requested a confidential report on eighteen research projects supported by the fund itself since 1932. After reviewing this information, he increased the fund's endowment by $5 million, designated for medical research and education, including such specific goals as research fellowships for senior investigators and grants to strengthen postgraduate teaching and the teaching of preventive medicine and psychiatry. Harkness intended the new endowment to support institutions and established researchers, in the expectation that such support would also benefit students and young physicians indirectly. The emphasis again was on establishing a foundation for ongoing progress.

Harkness in private was a modest man, warm and cheerful with his friends but rarely seeking public attention. He lived primarily in Manhattan or at "Eolia," his weekend estate on the North Shore of Long Island. He enjoyed golf and salmon fishing, loved art, and liked to read Shakespeare and Edgar Wallace. He died at his Fifth Avenue home after a brief illness. Malcolm Aldrich was named executor of his estate and various charities and succeeded him as president of the Commonwealth Fund (1940–1963), perpetuating Harkness's own philosophy into the 1960s.

• Harkness left no collection of his papers; however, the Commonwealth Fund archives, on deposit at the Rockefeller Archive Center in Pocantico Hills, N.Y., contain much information on his thinking regarding philanthropic matters, in particular his notations on copies of the General Director's Report, 1919–1940, and his contributions to the fund's annual and special reports. The major source for his life is James W. Wooster, Jr., *Edward Stephen Harkness, 1874–1940* (privately printed, 1940; Commonwealth Fund ed., 1949). A. McGehee Harvey and Susan L. Abrams, *For the Welfare of Mankind: The Commonwealth Fund and American Medicine* (1986), is an interesting history of the Commonwealth Fund that contains some material about Harkness. Representative publications on Commonwealth Fund activities under Harkness's leadership include P. R. Lee and M. R. Kenworthy, *Mental Hygiene and Social Work* (1929); C. Dinwiddie, *Child Health and the Community* (1931); New York Academy of Medicine, *Maternal Mortality in New York City: A Study of All Puerperal Deaths, 1930–32* (1933); G. S. Stevenson and G. Smith, *Child Guidance Clinics: A Quarter-Century of Development* (1934); L. A. Julianelle, *The Etiology of Trachoma* (1938); and H. L. Witmer, *Psychiatric Clinics for Children* (1940). An obituary of note is the tribute by A. Lawrence Lowell in the *Harvard Alumni Bulletin*, 9 Feb. 1940.

DANIEL M. FOX
MARCIA L. MELDRUM

HARKNESS, Georgia Elma (21 Apr. 1891–21 Aug. 1974), applied theologian, was born in Harkness, New York, the daughter of Joseph Warren Harkness and Lillie Merrill, farmers. Reared as a Methodist, she made a personal commitment to Christianity at the age of fourteen. An outstanding student, in 1908 Harkness entered on scholarship Cornell University, where she worked with the Student Volunteer Movement and was influenced by the ethos of the social gospel. She gained her B.A. in 1912 and began to teach at the high school level in Schuylerville and later in Scotia, New York. In hopes of teaching at the college level, she entered Boston University in 1918 and while there was influenced by the Boston school of personalism, a philosophical and religious system that focused on the supremacy of personality. Harkness was awarded two master's degrees in arts and in religious education in 1920 (her master's thesis, *The Church and the Immigrant*, was published in 1921). She took a Ph.D. in philosophy in 1923.

Despite the limited opportunities for women in higher teaching posts, Harkness obtained a position in 1922 at Elmira College in New York, as assistant professor of the philosophy of religion and religious education and then as a professor of philosophy from 1926 until 1937. She was awarded teaching fellowships at Harvard (1926), Yale (1928–1929), and the Union Theological Seminary (1935–1937), also writing two books during this period: *Conflicts in Religious Thought* (1929) and *John Calvin* (1931). She produced her first piece of devotional poetry, *Holy Flame*, in 1935. Harkness rapidly gained recognition as an author, lecturer, and preacher, having been ordained a local deacon in 1926. Her books and numerous articles throughout this period reflected diverse areas of interest, particularly in the history of Methodism, pacifism, systematic theology, ecumenism, and the role of women in the church. A prodigious and disciplined writer, Harkness published thirty-seven books and many articles throughout her career.

Harkness became the first female member of the American Theological Society in 1937. By this time her academic emphasis had clearly moved from philosophy to theology. At the same time her theology became Christocentric rather than personalistic, having been profoundly affected by her father's dying request in 1937 that she should "write more about Jesus Christ." Her religious standpoint, however, would always be that of an evangelical liberal. In 1937 she accepted an associate professorship in the Department of the History and Literature of Religion at Mount Holyoke College in Massachusetts. In addition to being ordained a local elder in 1938, she was offered the professorship of applied theology, a title created for her, at the Garrett Biblical Institute (later the Garrett-Evangelical Theological Seminary) in Evanston, Illinois, in 1939. This title made Harkness the first woman in the United States to be awarded a theological professorship. She also received a Scroll of Honor Award for pioneer work in religion from the General Foundation of Women's Clubs in 1941, an honor both as a woman and as a theologian.

Despite an engaging personality, Harkness was susceptible to depression and physical illness. Never having married, in 1944 she began to share a home with Verna Miller, whose friendship, combined with an increasingly spiritual approach to her own faith, eased her depression. Harkness wrote a study of the relationship between the spiritual life and depression entitled *In the Dark Night of the Soul*, which was published in 1945. In 1947, in spite of her struggle with depression, she was named by the *Christian Advocate* as one of the ten most influential living Methodists; that same year she was awarded the Abingdon-Cokesbury Award for Book Manuscripts.

Harkness was a practical theologian with a pastoral rather than abstract approach, accessible to laity. As she wrote in *Understanding the Christian Faith* (1947), which stayed in print for forty years, "It is the laymen, not the theologian in the seminary . . . who is the ultimate consumer for whom the church exists." With this, she was actively involved in the pacifist and ecumenical movements and in issues of social justice, all integral, she believed, to her work as an applied theologian. In 1937 she attended the ecumenical Life and Work Conference in Oxford, England, where she spoke of the neglect of women's talents in the church. In 1944 Harkness was elected to the Board of World Peace, serving also on the Federal Council's Commission on a Just and Durable Peace. In 1950 she was one of the Commission of Christian Scholars on the Moral Implications of Obliteration Bombing, to which she was categorically opposed. She was also a member of the Fellowship of Reconciliation from 1924 to 1951, when she withdrew her membership because she could not agree with their political tactics of tax and draft resistance.

Harkness's pacifism and social action made her the subject of Federal Bureau of Investigation surveillance in 1951. She also represented American Methodism at the first Conference of World Council of Churches in Holland (1948), Sweden (1952), and North America (1957), also serving on its Board of Social and Economic Concerns from 1952 to 1960. Harkness was entirely of the view that women should be awarded full conference membership and clergy rights, and memorably debated Karl Barth over the question of the equality of the sexes at a meeting of the World Council of Churches in 1948. Her own standing as a female theologian, combined with her views, certainly influenced the vote at the general conference in 1956 that granted these rights. She was six times the lay delegate to the General Conference of the United Methodist Church, but she herself declined full conference membership in 1956. In 1958 the Society of the Religious Heritage of America named her Churchwoman of the Year. Always prophetic in her intolerance of social inequality, she opposed the proposed merger between the Methodist church and Evangelical United Brethrens in 1968, owing to the existence of the segregated central jurisdiction of the Methodist church.

While tirelessly applying her brand of practical theology through social activism, Harkness accepted a professorship of applied theology at the Pacific School of Religion in Berkeley, California, in 1950. There she worked until she retired in 1961. Harkness was also professor of Christianity in 1956–1957 at Japan International Christian University. She remained active, both academically and pastorally, until her death in Claremont, California.

By the time of her death, Harkness was the best-known female theologian in the United States. Her standing as a theologian contributed significantly to the acceptance of women in the religious sphere, both as teachers and as ministers. A professorship of applied theology at Garrett-Evangelical Theological Seminary was named after her and is designated for women only.

• The Georgia Harkness Papers are in the archives of Garrett-Evangelical Theological Seminary, Evanston, Ill., while the Harkness Collection of manuscripts is held in the United Library, also at the seminary. Further manuscript collections exist at the Claremont School of Theology, Claremont, Calif., Cornell University, Elmira College, Mount Holyoke College, and the State University of New York at Plattsburgh. The correspondence of Harkness and Edgar Brightman is in the Brightman Collection at the Department of Special Collections of the Mugar Memorial Library of Boston University. The Harkness Family Collection is in the possession of the Overholt family, Kilmarnock, Va. For a detailed biography, see Rosemary Skinner Keller, *Georgia Harkness: For Such a Time as This* (1992), which provides a complete bibliography of Harkness's books and articles. A discussion of Harkness's theology in the context of American Methodism is given in Emory Stevens Bucke, ed., *The History of American Methodism*, vol. 3 (1964). An obituary appears in the *New York Times*, 22 Aug. 1974.

JOANNA HAWKE

HARKNESS, Mary Emma Stillman (4 July 1874–6 June 1950), philanthropist, was born in Brooklyn, New York, the daughter of Thomas Edgar Stillman, a maritime and railroad lawyer, and Charlotte Elizabeth Greenman. Little information is available about her early life, but her father earned a sufficient fortune to leave her and all of her siblings financially independent at the time of his death in 1906. In 1904, at her parents' home at 9 East 78th Street in New York City, she married Edward S. Harkness, the wealthy son of Standard Oil partner Stephen V. Harkness; they had no children. In 1908 they built a home at 1 East 75th Street, which remained her residence for the duration of her life.

Mary married into a family that believed in using its accumulated wealth for philanthropic purposes. Edward Harkness shared his mother Anna's interest in philanthropy, which culminated in her creation of the Commonwealth Fund in 1918. He expanded the Harkness family's tradition of helping to support religious and welfare organizations to include the areas of medicine and education.

Mary Stillman Harkness was an able and interested partner in her husband's philanthropy, which was estimated at more than $100 million at the time of his death in 1940. She made charitable gifts of her own in medicine, religion, and children's and women's welfare and aided educational and historical institutions in Connecticut, the home of her mother's family. Her father had established the Elizabeth Greenman Stillman Memorial at the Brooklyn Home for Aged Men, and in 1907 Mary Harkness gave the home stocks with an annual income of $7,700 to support the care of elderly couples. Records of her other gifts prior to 1918 have not survived.

Between 1918 and her death, Mary Harkness made nearly 300 contributions of $5,000 or more to twenty-two individuals and eighty-one organizations, totaling $5.7 million. The majority of these donations were made after her husband's death. Connecticut College for Women received some of her largest gifts, including $150,000 for a new dormitory in 1934 and $380,700 for a new chapel in 1938; she and her husband had contributed $3,000 toward the school's endowment in 1911. She made multiple gifts of $5,000 or more to the Presbyterian Hospital in New York City, the United Hospital Fund of New York, the Madison Avenue Presbyterian Church, the Greater New York Council of the Boy Scouts of America, the Union Settlement Association, Riverside Church, the Community Service Society of New York, the Farmers Federation Educational and Development Fund, the Marine Historical Association in Mystic, Connecticut, and the Planned Parenthood Federation of America. These and numerous other institutions and organizations received many other smaller gifts, including donations of rare and valuable books, documents, jewelry, and art work to universities, libraries, and museums.

Another aspect of Mary Harkness's philanthropy was support for sick and needy individuals, especially children. She funded research and treatment of rheumatic fever in children at two sites in rural New York, the Reed Farm near Nyack and the Martine Farm near White Plains, both under the direction of former nurse Ada Beazley. Apparently, this project began in 1906 and continued until 1941, when it was taken over by other organizations, most notably Irvington House in Irvington, New York. She also paid the costs of treating two tuberculosis patients at the Stony Wold Sanatorium in Lake Kushaqua, New York, between 1918 and 1930, when she agreed to pay the expenses of a third patient as well. In addition, beginning in 1922, she maintained a summer home for thirty to forty disadvantaged children each year at Eolia, her estate at Waterford, Connecticut, until 1943, when the grounds were converted to barracks for military use. In her will she left the property to the state of Connecticut for the care of tuberculosis patients or military servicemen and veterans.

Harkness was a member of more than forty clubs and organizations, including the American Museum of Natural History, the Colony and Cosmopolitan clubs, the Foreign Policy Association, the Women's National Republican Club, the Metropolitan Opera Guild, and the National Association of Gardeners. She was also a member of the board of managers of Presbyterian Hospital, Babies Hospital, and the Neurological Institute, honorary president of the Commonwealth Fund, and an honorary fellow of Lady Margaret Hall at Oxford College.

Harkness died at her home in New York City. In her will she left $60 million to the Commonwealth Fund and a variety of other charities.

• Biographical material on Harkness, lists of her charitable gifts, and an account book of her gifts between 1918 and about 1928 are located in the Harkness Family series in the Commonwealth Fund Records at the Rockefeller Archive Center in North Tarrytown, N.Y. A brief sketch of Mary Harkness can be found in James W. Wooster, Jr., *Edward Stephen Harkness, 1874–1940* (1949). An obituary is in the *New York Times*, 7 June 1950. Other obituaries, most notably those from the *New London* (Conn.) *Day* and *New York Herald Tribune*, are collected in the Commonwealth Fund Records.

KENNETH W. ROSE

HARKNESS, Rebekah West (17 Apr. 1915–17 June 1982), philanthropist, was born in St. Louis, Missouri, the daughter of Allen Tarwater West, a stockbroker, and Rebekah Semple. The youngest of three children, Rebekah grew up surrounded by the amenities of a prominent St. Louis family. A vivacious, headstrong teenager with a penchant for the arts, she obeyed but did not agree with her father's request that she resign from a St. Louis Opera production of *Aïda*. He considered it inappropriate behavior for a young woman of her social status to appear as a dancing girl. As an adult, she remained true to her belief that wealth and social status had no right to dictate her life. Following an unsuccessful marriage in 1938 to Dickson Pierce during her twenties, she wed New York financier and philanthropist William Hale Harkness in 1947. She dedicated herself to her husband's philanthropic endeavors, supporting the arts and composing music.

Following her second husband's death in 1954, she assumed his post as president of the William Hale Harkness Foundation. She continued his philanthropic support for medical science by allocating substantial grants, including $2 million to construct the William Hale Harkness Research Center at New York Hospital and undisclosed sums to underwrite Irving Cooper's research on Parkinson's disease and to support the Institute of Rehabilitation Medicine at the New York University Medical Center. In honor of her late husband's memory, she used his surname exclusively, regardless of a third marriage in 1961 to Benjamin Harris Kean, whom she divorced in 1965.

Her interest in composing led to studies that began in Paris with Nadia Boulanger in 1946 and continued throughout her life in New York with Frederick Werle, Stanley Hollingsworth, and Lee Hoiby. Although recognition as a composer eluded her, she derived great pleasure from her flair for composing popular songs. In 1957 the marquis de Cuevas, the founder and director of Le Grand Ballet du Marquis de Cuevas, invited her to compose a work for the Brussels World Fair in 1958. The score won little acclaim, but the experience rekindled Harkness's interest in dance. A devotee of Émile Jaques-Dalcoze's theories on the dynamics of movement, known as eurhythmics, she became intrigued with the concept of fusing classical ballet, contemporary modern, and formal ethnic dance.

Harkness wasted no time gaining recognition as a dance patron. In 1961 the Rebekah Harkness Foundation, Inc., was established to provide a nonprofit conduit for her support of American cultural endeavors and dance. In collaboration with the U.S. Department of State, funds were immediately allocated to generate international recognition of American cultural achievements by sponsoring the European and American tours of Jerome Robbins's Ballets U.S.A. company and an ethnological tour of Africa by the Pearl Primus Dance Troupe. The foundation also established a summer workshop near Harkness's estate in Watch Hill, Rhode Island, for the Robert Joffrey Ballet to create new works. Under the foundation's aegis, Joffrey's company appeared in Europe, the Far East, and Russia. In 1962 the foundation also established a summer dance festival at New York Central Park's outdoor Delacorte Theatre, free to the public, that flourished through 1972, and also in 1962 the foundation cosponsored a tour of the New York City public schools by the modern dancer Sophie Maslow's troupe.

By late 1963 funding for the Joffrey company provided by the foundation had exceeded allowable levels for a nonprofit organization not identified in the title of the receiving entity. When Joffrey was informed that the company would have to be renamed, a highly publicized power struggle ensued and the Joffrey-Harkness relationship was terminated. Regrettably, all published accounts of the estrangement, perpetuated by others as fact, reflected Joffrey's dismissal of the foundation's legal problem as a ploy by Harkness to gain artistic control of the company.

Still determined to create the first new major American ballet company in nearly twenty years, Harkness established the Harkness Ballet in 1964 under the artistic direction of George Skibine, an acclaimed choreographer and Maître de ballet of the Paris Opera Ballet from 1958 to 1961. Financial backing was provided by a combined grant of $2 million from the Rebekah Harkness and William Hale Harkness foundations.

The Harkness Ballet performed at the White House on 5 October 1964 before making its official debut in Cannes, France, on 19 February 1965. The European tour won tremendous acclaim, and Harkness received the Marquis de Cuevas Prize at the University de la Danse in Paris. She also received the Handel Award, the Bronze Medal of Appreciation from the city of New York, and a Congressional Record citation.

In 1964 Harkness purchased a five-story mansion in New York as headquarters for the company and its affiliated school, ornately renovated it, and named it the Harkness House for Ballet Arts. A successful American tour and summer rehearsals in Watch Hill preceded the company's return to the White House in 1966 to dedicate a new stage in the East Room donated by the foundation. Funding was allocated for a New York City public school tour, a modern dance season at Hunter College, and, in cooperation with the International Cultural Exchange Program, the European tours of the Alvin Ailey Dance Theatre and her own company. In 1966 Harkness was named an *officier merité culturel et artistique* by the French government.

In 1966 Harkness accepted Skibine's resignation and engaged Brian MacDonald as artistic director. The company's first New York season drew high praise for the dancers but severe criticism of the company itself. The consensus of opinion among New York critics was that company productions lacked choreographic substance and were unnecessarily lavish. Principal dancer Lawrence Rhodes replaced MacDonald in 1968 and asked Benjamin Harkarvy to join him as codirector in 1969. Under their direction, a second New York season proved more favorable. Nevertheless, Harkness dissolved the company in the midst of its 1970 European tour and turned her energies and financial support toward developing a new company originally known as the Harkness Youth Company. Numerous unsuccessful ventures followed. In 1978 Harkness redirected her foundation's philanthropic focus toward independent companies, artists, and projects representing all forms of dance.

Although her unprecedented contributions to American dance received mixed reviews during her lifetime, Rebekah West Harkness opened new horizons for dance and left an artistic legacy that continues to influence dance today through the Harkness Foundations for Dance and veterans of the original Harkness Ballet. She died in New York City.

• Biographical information is available from Theodore S. Bartwink, executive director, Harkness Foundations for Dance, New York City. The *Dance Encyclopedia*, ed. Anatole Chujoy and P. W. Manchester, rev. ed. (1978), offers valid data on Harkness and the original Harkness Ballets (pp. 441–42) and on the Rebekah Harkness Foundation (p. 381). A speech made by the Honorable Gale W. McKee of Wyoming on 29 Aug. 1966, reprinted in the *Congressional Record*, 89th Cong., indicates recognition from Congress and the Johnson administration. News, reviews, and analyses of her patronage of dance are in issues of *Dance Magazine*, beginning Feb. 1961. The obituary in the *New York Times*, 19 June 1982, contains some incorrect information. Also relevant is the obituary of William Hale Harkness in the *New York Times*, 14 Aug. 1954.

LILI COCKERILLE LIVINGSTON

HARKNESS, William (17 Dec. 1837–28 Feb. 1903), astronomer, was born in Ecclefechan, Scotland, the son of James Harkness, a Presbyterian clergyman and physician, and Jane Weild. His family immigrated to New York in 1839. During his childhood Harkness lived in New York City and Fishkill, New York, and attended private schools in the area. Harkness attended Lafayette College in Easton, Pennsylvania (1854–1855), but when his parents moved to Rochester, New York, he entered the University of Rochester, where he earned the A.B. (1858) and the A.M. (1861). He worked as a reporter for the New York legislature in 1858 and for the Pennsylvania senate in 1860, acquiring skill as a stenographer that he found useful throughout his life. Influenced by his father, he attended medical school and graduated with an M.D. from the New York Homeopathic Medical College in 1862.

In August 1862 Harkness became an aide at the U.S. Naval Observatory in Washington, D.C., the national observatory for the United States equivalent to Greenwich Observatory in England. In Civil War Washington Harkness served briefly as a surgeon at the second battle of Manassas, an experience he later repeated. In 1863 he was appointed to the Corps of Professors of Mathematics of the U.S. Navy, a position he held until his retirement in December 1899. Except for two brief periods, at sea to study terrestrial magnetism and the effect of ship's armor on the magnetic compass (1865–1866) and at the Hydrographic Office (1866–1867), his entire career was at the Naval Observatory.

Harkness's first papers were on meteors and longitude differences from Washington (both in 1867), but his first notable astronomical work came in solar eclipses, of which he observed several in his lifetime. During the total solar eclipse of 1869 Harkness discovered the "K" line in the corona of the Sun, his work displaying an interest in the astronomical applications of spectroscopy just then coming into use. The mission of the Naval Observatory, however, was in positional astronomy rather than astrophysics, and most of Harkness's career was spent in this more practical branch of the science. From 1862 to 1874 he worked as an observer on the prime vertical transit, the mural circle, and the transit circle, but ill health after 1871 limited his observing, and thereafter he turned his attention to the design of astronomical equipment and the analysis of data.

Harkness's chief work was in determining the scale of the solar system via the transit of Venus, that is, the passage of Venus across the face of the Sun, a phenomenon that occurs only about twice a century. In 1871 Harkness was appointed a member of the U.S. Transit of Venus Commission, and he designed a large part of the astronomical equipment used by the U.S. transit of Venus parties in 1874 and 1882. Harkness was in charge of one of eight U.S. transit of Venus expeditions in 1874, sailing to Hobart, Tasmania, in the ship *Swatara*. He personally devised many of the methods for measuring the photographic plates, and he himself undertook the detailed analysis. When the accuracy of the photographic method was called into question, Harkness became a champion for the continued use of the method and in his paper "On the Relative Accuracy of Different Methods of Determining the Solar Parallax" (*American Journal of Science* 22 [1881]) argued that it should be used for the 1882 transit of Venus. In this he prevailed and was given the task of analyzing all data from the American observations of the transit of Venus during that year. The difficulty of the task may be deduced from the fact that he spent about six years, with a small corps of assistants, analyzing the 1882 observations. This result was incorporated into his principal work, *The Solar Parallax and Its Related Constants*, in 1891. The entire problem of the dimensions of the planetary system was summarized in "On the Magnitude of the Solar System," his presidential address before the American Association for the Advancement of Science delivered in 1894.

Harkness was fundamentally interested in instrumentation, and in addition to papers on the transit of Venus photoheliograph (1877) and the inequalities of the pivots on a transit circle (1878), in 1879 he wrote an important paper, "On the Color Correction of Achromatic Telescopes," in which he gave the first rigorous treatment of the color correction as a function of wavelength. During the 1890s Harkness was principally involved in matters relating to the new location for the Naval Observatory, designing new instruments, repairing old ones, and setting up new observing procedures. More than any other single figure, he was responsible for the transition from the old to the new Naval Observatory. He also became involved in the controversy over civilian versus military control of the observatory. In October 1892 he was appointed chief astronomical assistant to the superintendent, and in September 1894 he was made first astronomical director of the Naval Observatory, with control over its astronomical work. While Harkness was determined to make a success of this role, a contemporary described it as "the maximum of responsibility and the minimum of power," since the naval superintendent still retained overall control. In June 1897, three months after Simon Newcomb retired as superintendent of the Nautical Almanac Office, Harkness also took on that office, until his retirement in December 1899. The burdens of these two demanding offices left Harkness in weak health. He had hoped to complete the unfinished analysis of the transit of Venus data but retired to Jersey City for rest and never was able to return to Washington. He died in Jersey City.

Harkness was a founding member of the Philosophical Society of Washington and the Cosmos Club, and he made his home in the quarters of the latter. He served as vice president of the American Association for the Advancement of Science in 1881 and 1885 and as its president in 1893. He did not become a member of the National Academy of Sciences, probably because of animosity between him and Newcomb, with whom he had personal and professional differences. He never married. Frank Bigelow, a meteorologist at the U.S. Weather Bureau who knew Harkness well, called him "a man of the highest moral principles, hating sham in science, in society and in the state, and freely expressing his appreciation of truth as he saw it."

• Four boxes of Harkness papers are located at the University of Rochester Library. Four bound volumes of his letters (1879–1896) are at the library and archives of the U.S. Naval Observatory in Washington, D.C., including an 1885 biographical statement with a list of his publications to that date. Further material related to Harkness's career can be found in the records of the U.S. Naval Observatory, Record Group 78, National Archives. Harkness's principal published works, including those on the solar parallax, are found in the appendices to the Naval Observatory volumes *Astronomical and Meteorological Observations Made during the Years . . . at the United States Naval Observatory*, beginning with observations for the year 1867. His paper "On the Color Correction of Achromatic Telescopes" appeared in the *American Journal of Science* 18 (1879): 189–96. An incomplete list of Harkness's publications is in the Royal Society *Catalogue of Scientific Papers*, vol. 7, p. 909; vol. 10, p. 142; and vol. 15, pp. 643–44. The best biographical source is Harkness's own "Biographical Memorandum," published after his death in A. N. Skinner, "William Harkness," *Science*, n.s., 17 (Apr. 1903): 601–4. An obituary is in the *New York Times*, 1 Mar. 1903.

STEVEN J. DICK

HARLAN, James (22 June 1800–18 Feb. 1863), lawyer and congressman, was born in Mercer County, Kentucky, the son of James Harlan and Sarah Caldwell, farmers. He probably attended a nearby grammar school. Harlan decided early in life that he did not wish to farm for a living and entered employment in a mercantile house in Danville, Kentucky, at age sixteen. Between 1817 and 1822 he devoted himself to commercial enterprise, but after five years he abandoned it to study law. Harlan was admitted to the Kentucky bar in 1823 and quickly acquired a reputation as an accomplished lawyer and a large law practice that he maintained throughout his life.

Harlan married Eliza Davenport on 23 December 1822. They had nine children, among them John Marshall Harlan, a future associate justice of the U.S. Supreme Court. Sometime between 1823 and 1839 Harlan's growing law practice caused him to move his family to Harrodsburg, Kentucky; he moved to the capital, Frankfort, in 1840.

Harlan's connections among Kentucky's legal and commercial fraternity carried him into Kentucky and, to a lesser extent, national politics. He was an early and ardent supporter of his fellow Kentuckian, Senator Henry Clay, leader of the American Whig party for nearly fifty years. Harlan's political views generally reflected Clay's beliefs in gradual emancipation for slaves, the need to maintain a strong federal government, and a spirit of sectional compromise.

Kentucky remained a Whig stronghold until the 1850s, and the party's predominance there was reflected in a series of public offices for Harlan. From 1829 to 1844 he served as a prosecuting attorney for the state of Kentucky. He was elected to the Twenty-fourth and Twenty-fifth congresses, serving in the House of Representatives from 1835 to 1839. During his second term in Washington, he was chairman of the House committee for investigating defalcations (embezzlement). In 1840 Harlan was appointed secretary of the Commonwealth of Kentucky by Governor Robert Perkins Letcher, serving in that post until 1844. In 1840 and 1841 he was a presidential elector on the successful Whig ticket of William Henry Harrison and John Tyler. Between 1845 and 1846 he served one term as a Whig member of the lower house of the Kentucky legislature. In 1848 Harlan was a Whig delegate at the National Anti-Democratic convention in Philadelphia, where he was the only Kentucky delegate to remain loyal to Henry Clay and to oppose the successful nomination of Zachary Taylor. In 1850 Harlan was appointed attorney general of Kentucky; twice elected, he served in that office under successive governors until 1859. During his tenure as attorney general, he was also one of the commissioners responsible for preparing Kentucky's *Code of Practice in Civil and Criminal Cases* (1854), which introduced many procedural reforms by radically simplifying common law practice.

Following the victory of the Democratic party in the gubernatorial election of 1859 and the effective end of Whig influence in Kentucky politics, Harlan spent his remaining years promoting a spirit of political compromise and the maintenance of the Union in the face of the growing sectional crisis that led to the Civil War. In the aftermath of Abraham Lincoln's victory in the 1860 presidential election, Harlan was among those Kentuckians who opposed the state's drift towards the secessionist cause under Democratic governor Beriah Magoffin. As one of the state's most prominent Union supporters, Harlan took part in the clandestine distribution during the spring and summer of 1861 of "Lincoln guns," arms purchased by the federal government, to militia units loyal to the federal cause. His Unionist efforts were recognized in 1862 with his appointment by President Lincoln as a U.S. district attorney, an office he held until his death at Frankfort, Kentucky.

Harlan's life exemplified the prominent role in politics played by eminent members of the bar. It also presented in miniature the clash of competing economic and political ideologies that divided nineteenth-century America in the antebellum period.

• Papers relating to Harlan are in the John Marshall Harlan (1833–1911) Papers, Library of Congress, Manuscript Division. Harlan's few published writings include two congressional speeches, *Remarks of Mr. Harlan, of Kentucky, on the Mississippi Contested Election, Delivered in the House of Representatives, September 28, 1837* (1837), and a *Speech of Mr. J. Harlan of Kentucky, on the Bill Appropriating Six Millions of Dollars for Prosecuting the Seminole War in Florida, and To Provide for Raising an Army to Enforce a Treaty Alleged To Have Been Made with the Cherokee Indians, Delivered in Committee of the Whole House of Representatives* (1838); and a court brief (Supreme Court of the U.S., January Term, 1837, *George H. Briscoe et al v. Bank of Kentucky*). A brief account of Harlan's early years is in David G. Farrelly, "Harlan's Formative Period: The Years before the War," *Kentucky Law Journal* 46 (1958): 367–406.

MARK WARREN BAILEY

HARLAN, James (26 Aug. 1820–5 Oct. 1899), U.S. senator and secretary of the interior, was born in Clark County, Illinois, the son of Silas Harlan and Mary Conley, farmers. The family moved to Parke County, Indiana, in 1824. Harlan graduated from Asbury (now DePauw) University in 1845, and that year he married Ann Eliza Peck. The couple had four children.

Subsequently Harlan moved to Iowa to head Iowa City College. Entering local politics as a Whig, he won a majority of votes for state superintendent of public instruction in 1847, only to be deprived of his title to the office when state authorities declared that the election was of questionable legality. He lost a second election in 1848. He then turned to law and passed the bar in 1850. In 1852 he served as a deputy surveyor of Wisconsin and Iowa, and in the following year he accepted the position of president of Mount Pleasant Collegiate Institute (now Iowa Wesleyan University). He remained there until 1855, and during his tenure he secured the support of the Methodist church for the institution.

Harlan returned to politics in 1855 as a Republican, but once more he was dogged by bad electoral luck. He was elected to the U.S. Senate by only one house of the Iowa legislature, because the state senate had adjourned. Two years later he lost his seat when the U.S. Senate concurred in a protest from the Iowa Senate asserting that his election had been illegal. This time, however, Harlan won election to the vacated seat and was reelected in 1860. He opposed statehood for Kansas under a proslavery constitution and supported the construction of a transcontinental railroad, the creation of land-grant colleges, and a homestead act, all of which would be enacted during the 1860s.

With the coming of the Civil War, Harlan became a passionate proponent of a vigorous prosecution of the war. He supported the confiscation of secessionist-owned property and pushed for the enlistment of blacks in the Union army. As chair of the Committee on Public Lands, he helped secure passage of the Homestead Act and the Pacific Railroad Act. Among the targets of his criticism was Ulysses S. Grant for his performance in the battle of Shiloh. Family relationships shaped his political future, for when Robert Todd Lincoln began to court Harlan's daughter Mary Harlan, the senator and president drew closer together. Harlan headed the Republican Congressional Committee in 1864, speaking out in defense of the Lincoln administration's censorship of Democratic papers and its arrest of opponents of the war. In part for these reasons and in part to reward prominent Methodists, Lincoln nominated Harlan as secretary of the interior on 9 March 1865. The Senate confirmed the choice that day. Washington gossips noted that the nomination came just a few days after Robert Todd Lincoln had escorted Mary Harlan, whom he later married, to the inaugural ball. Harlan took office formally on 15 May 1865, and by that time Andrew Johnson had been president for one month.

Harlan's secretaryship proved short and turbulent. Internal changes among department personnel bred resentment, while opponents later claimed that Harlan had handled public lands and railroad lands in questionable and perhaps corrupt ways. Harlan's dismissal of Walt Whitman from a department clerkship sparked criticism, and efforts to resolve tensions between the War and Interior departments over the handling of American Indian affairs proved abortive. Harlan's tenure ended because of his disagreement with Johnson over Reconstruction policy. He found unacceptable the president's refusal to stop violence against the freedpeople and his embrace of a lenient policy toward the former Confederates. When Johnson began to organize a political movement to support his policy, Harlan resigned on 27 July 1866.

Harlan was not out of a job for long. The Iowa legislature had already elected him to return to the U.S. Senate in March 1867. Although he supported Republican Reconstruction measures and the impeachment of Johnson, voting for the president's conviction in May 1868, he did not take a leading role in framing legislation. Indeed, in 1868 and 1869 he spent a good deal of his time defending himself from charges of corrupt behavior stemming from his actions as head of the Interior Department. During the Grant administration, Harlan proved to be a vigorous defender of the president, assailing critics of the administration's attempt to annex the Dominican Republic. Despite loyal service to the party, Harlan lost his bid for reelection to the Senate in 1872, as William Boyd Allison beat him out in the Republican caucus. Efforts to link him to the Crédit Mobilier scandal in 1873 made his departure a bitter one.

Returning to Iowa, Harlan was unsuccessful in another Senate bid in 1876, and in 1881 he declined a nomination for state senator. However, he remained politically active, supporting a state constitutional amendment for prohibition. Between 1882 and 1886 he served as one of three judges on the Court of *Alabama* Claims, a body formed to adjudicate several claims for the money awarded the United States as a result of the Geneva Tribunal a decade before. In 1895 and 1897 movements to make Harlan the Republican nominee for governor fell short, ending his political career. He died in Mount Pleasant, Iowa.

• The State Historical Society of Iowa holds Harlan's papers. A biography is Johnson Brigham, *James Harlan* (1913). Morton M. Rosenberg, *Iowa on the Eve of the Civil War* (1972), and Robert R. Dykstra, *Bright Radical Star: Black Freedom and White Supremacy on the Hawkeye Frontier* (1993), offer context for his political career. An obituary is in the *Iowa State Register*, 6 Oct. 1899.

BROOKS D. SIMPSON

HARLAN, John Marshall (1 June 1833–14 Oct. 1911), associate justice of the Supreme Court of the United States, was born in Boyle County, Kentucky, the son of James Harlan, a lawyer and politician, and Eliza Shannon Davenport. James Harlan, an ardent supporter of the Whig leader Henry Clay, had already named one son after his idol; on his fifth son he bestowed the name of the Whig party's patron saint, the Supreme Court's "great chief justice," John Marshall.

Shortly after John Marshall Harlan's birth, his father began a career as a Whig politician, serving two terms as a member of Congress and acting as Kentucky's attorney general and secretary of state. Like many other early American lawyers turned statesmen, he nonetheless retained his legal practice, and he was determined that all of his three surviving sons should follow him in his profession. After obtaining a classical education and an honors degree at Centre College in Danville, Kentucky, in 1850, John Marshall Harlan went to Transylvania University in Lexington to study law for two years. As was the custom in that day, he completed his legal training in a law office—his father's—and was admitted to the Kentucky bar in 1853.

The younger Harlan also followed his father into politics. In the spring of 1851, while he was still at Transylvania and not yet eighteen years old, he was offered the post of Kentucky adjutant general. Although Harlan, citing his age, demurred at the time, that autumn he was appointed to the post by the governor. The position itself demanded little responsibility and paid only $250 a year, but it gave Harlan the visibility and contacts that formed the basis of a political career. The military post also provided Harlan with the appellation "general," which was used up to the time he was appointed to the Supreme Court.

In 1854 Harlan won his first election when he was voted in as city attorney of Frankfort, Kentucky, a position to which he would be reelected in 1856. The advent of Harlan's political career, however, coincided with the death of the Whig party. Searching for an alternative, he shifted his allegiance to the emergent Know Nothings, who despite their nativism, a reaction to an influx of immigrants, nevertheless spurned the antinationalistic, secessionist sentiments associated with the Democrats. Stumping the state for Know Nothing candidates, Harlan made a number of anti-immigrant speeches that would later haunt him. As a Know Nothing he was in 1858 elected county judge of Franklin County, the only judicial post he would hold prior to his appointment to the nation's highest Court.

Although Harlan was at this time working in his father's law office and developing a few of his own clients, in the main his focus remained trained on the political arena. He would never make much money from his practice. All his life Harlan would, despite a habit of frugality, teeter on the brink of financial exigency. Early evidence of a pattern of borrowing to stay afloat is found in the circumstances of his marriage in 1856 to Malvina French Shanklin, known as Mallie. Despite a two-year, long-distance engagement, Harlan still had to borrow $500 from his father to meet the expenses of the wedding. Perhaps owing to custom or to the need to economize, after honeymooning at Mallie's parents' home in Evansville, Indiana, the couple took up residence with the elder Harlans in Frankfort, where they remained until 1861. They had six children.

In 1859 Harlan ran unsuccessfully for Congress as a member of the Opposition party. In 1860 he again changed parties, supporting Constitutional Union candidate John Bell for president. As a slaveholding member of the southern aristocracy, Harlan was attracted to the Constitutional Unionist platform, which pledged support for the Union but hostility to abolition. In 1861, in order to provide for his growing family and perhaps also to raise funds for a second congressional campaign, he moved to the thriving river port Louisville, where he hoped to develop a legal partnership with a prominent local lawyer. With the onset of civil war, he dedicated himself to the Union cause, writing antisecessionist political editorials for the Louisville *Journal* and engaging in other activities that helped prevent Kentucky from joining the Confederacy. In September 1861 Harlan formed the Tenth Kentucky Volunteers, serving as the unit's colonel and seeing action in both his home state and Tennessee. In February 1863 President Abraham Lincoln recommended to Congress that Harlan be promoted to brigadier general. Owing to his father's death the same month, however, Harlan requested that his nomination be withdrawn. Obliged now to support his father's numerous dependents as well as his own wife and children, he resigned from the Union army.

Just three weeks after his resignation, Harlan was nominated by the Union party as a candidate for attorney general of Kentucky. He won handily, and the stable income that went with the position enabled him to concentrate his efforts on maintaining his home state's allegiance to the North. Although Harlan remained steadfast in his support of the Union, he ardently opposed the Emancipation Proclamation. When it became law in 1863, the Emancipation Proclamation only applied in rebel states, and Harlan continued to be financially responsible for slaves brought into his household by his mother until the Thirteenth Amendment abolished slavery two years later. Mallie firmly opposed the institution of slavery, but in 1863 Harlan was reluctant to release his mother's slaves only to have them sold on the open market.

When the Thirteenth Amendment was proposed, Harlan opposed it, too, on grounds that it violated state sovereignty. Indeed, if he wanted to stay in office in Kentucky, he could hardly have done otherwise. In the election of 1864, Harlan and other Kentucky Unionists demonstrated their dislike of the policies of the Lincoln administration by supporting Democratic candidate George McClellan for president. Harlan soon became disenchanted, however, with this alliance with the Democrats, who were employing the strength afforded by Unionist backing to introduce former Confederates into state politics. He lost a bid for the Senate in January 1867 and was charged later that year with reorganizing the Unionists. Running in 1868 on what was then the Conservative Unionist ticket, he was defeated in his attempt to be reelected as attorney general. It would be his last race as a Unionist.

Harlan was not finished with politics, however. Leaving the Kentucky capital for Louisville, he went into partnership with a former state circuit court judge, John E. Newman, a Unionist turned Republican. Before long the law practice took on another partner, Benjamin H. Bristow, and Harlan affiliated himself with yet another party, the Republicans. Already disillusioned with the Unionists in 1868, he supported Republican candidate Ulysses S. Grant for president. After Grant's election, Harlan threw himself wholeheartedly into the campaign to establish a beachhead for the nascent party in Kentucky. Saying he would rather be right than be consistent, he now embraced the very ideas he had formerly scorned. As a tried campaigner and a skilled orator, he publicly endorsed not only the Thirteenth Amendment but also the Fourteenth, which granted black Americans full citizenship and which intended to give them the vote. Although he placed his emphasis on the Fourteenth Amendment's protection of legal, as opposed to social, equality for blacks, he also repudiated his former Know Nothing rejection of Roman Catholics and immigrants.

Harlan ran for governor on the Republican ticket in 1871 and was soundly defeated, in part because of his ideological about-face but mainly because the Democrats dominated state politics. Nonetheless, he remained a popular and influential figure in Kentucky. His efforts on behalf of the Republicans did not go unnoticed at the national level either. In 1872 there was widespread speculation that Grant would name Harlan as his running mate. Harlan was passed over at that time, but his partner, the civil rights champion Bristow, was named as secretary of the treasury.

Harlan engaged in two more abortive campaigns, an attempt to reach the U.S. Senate in 1872 and a second run for the governorship in 1875. He never again held elective office. With the Republicans apparently doomed to remain a distinct minority at the local level but still in charge of national politics, he began to see that any hope for the realization of his ambitions depended on patronage. Accordingly, he took his campaigning on behalf of Republican candidates beyond Kentucky boundaries, and he took up the cause of Bristow.

As secretary of the treasury, Bristow added to his good reputation by successfully purging his own department of graft. Grant had appointed him to the office in 1874 as a replacement for William A. Richardson, whose own involvement in a tax scandal forced his early resignation. At the time, it seemed as if Grant had appointed Bristow largely to neutralize him as a political rival. But Bristow was a standout in the largely corrupt Grant administration, and in 1876 he became a presidential contender. As leader of the Kentucky Republicans, Harlan threw his weight behind his law partner, delivering Bristow's nominating speech at the Republican National Convention in Cincinnati. When the proceedings became deadlocked, he led the Kentucky delegation over to the side of Ohio governor Rutherford B. Hayes. Hayes became the party's nominee, and once he became president, he did not forget Harlan's crucial support. As Harlan's star rose, Bristow began a campaign to denigrate him.

Following the 1876 election, charges of widespread fraud and intimidation left returns disputed in the three southern states still under Republican control, Louisiana, Florida, and South Carolina. A commission made up of five senators, five congressmen, and five Supreme Court justices—consisting of seven Republicans, seven Democrats, and one purported swing vote—was established to decide the outcome of the presidential election. After Justice David Davis, the only truly politically neutral member of the commission, unexpectedly left the Supreme Court in 1877, Justice Joseph P. Bradley, a Republican, was chosen as the commission's fifteenth man. When Hayes was declared the winner by one vote, Democratic supporters of Samuel J. Tilden cried foul. A compromise was finally reached whereby the Democrats agreed to let Hayes assume office in exchange for a Republican promise to withdraw Federal troops from the three southern states they still occupied, where they helped prop up dubiously elected Republican administrations. While the "Compromise of 1877" was promptly carried out in Florida and South Carolina, Louisiana proved a more intractable problem. Hayes set up a commission to arbitrate the conflicting claims of Republicans and Democrats. He named five commissioners, one of them Harlan. In 1893, at the request of President Benjamin Harrison, Harlan assumed a similar role when he served on the Bering Sea Arbitration Tribunal, which settled a dispute between the United States and Britain over fur seal fisheries.

Harlan acquitted himself well on the Louisiana Reconstruction Committee, and in return Hayes offered to nominate him as ambassador to England. Harlan had his eye on the vacancy left on the Supreme Court by the recent departure of Davis, who had resigned to take a seat in the U.S. Senate (and perhaps also to avoid acting as the swing vote on the 1876 electoral commission). Citing financial exigency, Harlan refused Hayes's first offer, adding, "To be entirely frank, Mr. President, I have never cared for any public position which was not in the line of my profession." Hayes, who had already made up his mind to appoint a southerner to the Court, took the hint, and on 16 October 1877 he nominated Harlan to be the next associate justice.

The battle in the Senate over Harlan's confirmation lasted six weeks, and Republican Stalwarts, suspicious of Harlan's conversion to the party, raised issues such as his early Know Nothing allegiance and his later opposition to the Civil War amendments. In the end, the Senate unanimously confirmed his appointment, and on 10 December 1877 Harlan was sworn in as the forty-fourth justice of the Supreme Court of the United States.

Harlan, who was forty-four years old when he ascended the High Court bench, cut an impressive figure. At six feet, two inches tall and something over two hundred pounds with thinning reddish blond hair and an erect bearing, he conveyed an impression of robustness that stayed with him for the nearly thirty-four years he served on the Court. He made a quick start: in one of the first cases he heard after taking his seat, *United States v. Clark* (1877), Harlan dissented from the majority's opinion that, a statute to the contrary notwithstanding, plaintiffs could enter testimony in support of their claims against the federal government. Speaking out against what he viewed as "judicial legislation," Harlan was on his way to becoming one of the Court's "great dissenters."

Until 1930 the justices customarily read their opinions from the bench, but Harlan, a seasoned orator accustomed to speaking on the stump, had a style all his own. Often he would deliver his opinions extemporaneously, without even the aid of notes. A devoted Presbyterian who taught Sunday school throughout his adult life and a lecturer at Columbian (now George Washington University) Law School from 1889 to 1911, he was prone to assume an attitude of righteous indignation, particularly in dissent. One of his most famous dissenting opinions was delivered in the controversial case of *Pollock v. Farmers' Loan & Trust Co.* (1895), in which he objected to the slim majority's overruling a federal law that imposed the nation's first peacetime income tax. Reactions to the case were emotional across the board—Harlan privately wrote that Justice Stephen J. Field acted like a "madman" throughout—but Harlan's delivery of the first of four dissenting opinions made an especially vivid impression. According to a contemporaneous New York *Tribune* report, Harlan

pounded the desk, shook his finger under the noses of the Chief Justice [Melville W. Fuller] and Mr. Justice Field, turned more than once almost eagerly upon his colleagues of the majority, and expressed his dissent from their conclusions in a tone and language more appropriate to a stump speech at a Populace barbecue than to an opinion on a question of law before the Supreme Court of the United States.

The reputation for idiosyncrasy sometimes attached to Harlan's name can, nonetheless, be traced in large measure to some of his Supreme Court brethren. The highly literate Boston Brahmin Oliver Wendell Holmes, Jr., in particular, disliked his Kentucky colleague. Holmes referred to Harlan as "the last of the tobacco-spitting judges." (It is worth noting here that tobacco chewing was a time-honored tradition of the Court, which included multiple spittoons among its furnishings well into the twentieth century.) Less condescendingly, Harlan's contemporary, Justice David J. Brewer, remarked publicly: "Mr. Justice Harlan . . . believes implicitly in the Constitution. He goes to bed every night with one hand on the Constitution and the other on the Bible, and so sleeps the sweet sleep of justice and righteousness."

The august Justice Felix Frankfurter, however, most denigrated Harlan's contributions to American jurisprudence when he remarked in *Adamson v. California* (1947), long after Harlan's death, that Harlan had been no more than "an eccentric exception" on the Court. It is hardly surprising that the conservative Frankfurter, ideologically opposed to judicial promotion of abstract principles and political outcomes, should react negatively to Harlan. Harlan tended to be a libertarian on the Court, a justice whose relatively instinctual approach to constitutional interpretation frequently put him at odds with what he saw as the majority's employment of good logic to make bad law. But he was prescient. When later Court majorities endorsed many of his dissenting views, Harlan was labeled a "premature New Dealer."

Harlan served on the Court during a time when most of his fellow justices exercised a laissez faire approach in dispensing justice. Predisposed by his early Whig orientation to endorse the priorities of the national government over states' rights, he registered the only dissenting vote in *United States v. E. C. Knight Co.* (1895), which circumscribed Congress's attempt to combat monopolies in interstate commerce by means of the Sherman Anti-Trust Act. In one of his last written opinions, *Standard Oil v. United States* (1911), Harlan sided with the majority's approval of the dissolution of one of the nation's largest monopolies while at the same time writing separately to condemn the Court's endorsement of the "rule of reason," giving federal judges, not Congress, the power to determine what constitutes an unreasonable, and unlawful, restraint of trade.

Harlan also objected to the then dominant concept of substantive due process, which in his view perverted the original intent of the Fourteenth Amendment.

As codified in the Fourteenth Amendment, due process restrains state government impositions on individual rights. Around the turn of the century, a majority of the Court consistently used this version of due process to protect property rights, such as freedom of contract, which was given the status of orthodoxy in *Lochner v. New York* (1905). Harlan dissented in *Lochner*, as he had earlier in the *Civil Rights Cases* (1883), maintaining that the Civil War amendments had been intended to protect individuals, particularly former slaves, from injustices wrought by state action and also from those rendered by private acts. As he memorably argued, the Thirteenth Amendment and its progeny were intended to outlaw not only human bondage but also "badges of slavery."

Indeed, Harlan left his most enduring mark in the field of civil rights. In his dissenting opinion in the *Civil Rights Cases*, he crafted a rationale for government control of public accommodations: because government had long regulated such private purveyors of public accommodations as hotels and railroads, their actions are really equivalent to state acts and therefore within the reach of the Civil War amendments. More than eighty years later, Congress employed a comparable doctrine in drafting the 1964 Civil Rights Act, which outlawed racial discrimination in public accommodations on grounds that it violates the Commerce Clause of Article I of the Constitution. The watershed case of *Brown v. Board of Education* (1954) overturned the notorious "separate but equal" doctrine promulgated by *Plessy v. Ferguson* (1896), in which Harlan, the lone dissenter, memorably contended that the "Constitution is colorblind, and neither knows nor tolerates classes among citizens." And Harlan's dissenting opinions in *Hurtado v. California* (1884) and *Twining v. New Jersey* (1908), in both of which he insisted that the Fourteenth Amendment rendered the due process guarantees of the Fifth Amendment applicable to state criminal procedures, have also proved to be farsighted. The "due process revolution" engendered by Justice Hugo L. Black's championship of the incorporation doctrine, making the individual protections afforded by the Bill of Rights applicable at the state as well as the federal level, was still almost a half century away.

Increasingly out of step with his colleagues, Harlan served on the Court almost until the day he died, succumbing unexpectedly to pneumonia at his home in Washington, D.C. He was one of the Court's longest serving justices, and during his tenure he participated in more than 14,000 cases and wrote 1,161 opinions. Yet by the time of his death his influence had waned. At Harlan's memorial service Attorney General George W. Wickersham recounted his lengthy record of service but added: "[Harlan] could lead but he could not follow. . . . His was not the temper of a negotiator." For the next quarter-century—a period during which a conservative, even reactionary philosophy held sway on the Court—Harlan's views were largely regarded as the product of an irascible and erratic temperament. In Charles Warren's influential *The Supreme Court in United States History* (1927), the progressive convictions Harlan expressed in the *Civil Rights Cases* were dismissed as an "interesting and vivacious dissenting opinion."

With the advent of the due process revolution in the 1940s and of the civil rights movement in the 1950s, however, Harlan's reputation was reevaluated and his opinions came to seem prophetic. But while he might have been judged a hero in the middle of the twentieth century, Harlan was a thoroughly nineteenth-century man whose instincts could just as easily lead him to strike down a statute outlawing "yellow dog" contracts prohibiting workers from joining labor unions (in *Adair v. United States* [1908]) as to uphold the rights of the downtrodden. His record, like those of most jurists, has to be seen as a mixed one. What remains most valuable about Harlan is precisely the contrariness so derided during his lifetime—his preference for being right rather than consistent.

• Harlan's papers, including letters, personal and political memorabilia, and financial and legal materials, are held by the University of Louisville and the Library of Congress. An early appraisal of these papers is in Alan F. Westin, "The First Justice Harlan: A Self-Portrait from His Private Papers," *Kentucky Law Journal* 46 (Spring 1958): 321–66. Two full-length biographical treatments of Justice Harlan are Tinsley E. Yarbrough, *Judicial Enigma: The First Justice Harlan* (1995), and Loren P. Beth, *John Marshall Harlan: The Last Whig Justice* (1992). See also Thomas Louis Owen, "The Pre-Court Career of John Marshall Harlan" (Ph.D. diss., Univ. of Louisville, 1970). Useful evaluations of Harlan's jurisprudence include Beth, "Justice Harlan and the Uses of Dissent," *American Political Science Review* 49 (Dec. 1955): 1085–1104; and Floyd B. Clark, *The Constitutional Doctrines of Justice Harlan* (1915; repr. 1969).

LISA PADDOCK

HARLAN, John Marshall (20 May 1899–29 Dec. 1971), lawyer and Supreme Court justice, was born in Chicago, Illinois, the son of John Maynard Harlan, a lawyer, and Elizabeth Palmer Flagg. He was born into a wealthy family that had achieved distinction in the law. His great-grandfather James Harlan (1800–1863) was a lawyer, and his grandfather John Marshall Harlan (1833–1911), for whom he was named, was a justice of the Supreme Court. Harlan graduated from Princeton University in 1920 and was a Rhodes scholar at Balliol College, Oxford, where he began the study of law. He received his LL.B. from New York Law School in 1924.

Harlan began his career with Root, Clark, Buckner & Howland, a large Wall Street firm that encouraged its lawyers to engage in public service. When a senior member of the firm, Emory R. Buckner, was appointed U.S. attorney for the Southern District of New York in 1925, Harlan became his assistant for a year. During this period Harlan participated in the prosecutions of former U.S. attorney general Harry M. Daugherty for official misconduct and of former alien property custodian Thomas W. Miller for fraudulent conspiracy relating to German property seized by the United States during World War I. In 1928 Harlan married Ethel Andrews, the daughter of a Yale history professor; they had one child.

Harlan was made a partner in the Root, Clark firm in 1931, and after the death of Buckner in 1941, he became its leading trial lawyer. Harlan's practice was varied: he represented the New York City Board of Higher Education in litigation that involved the appointment of Bertrand Russell to teach at City College; he handled the will of the wealthy Ella Wendel; and he represented heavyweight champion Gene Tunney against a claim that Tunney had hired the plaintiff to bring about a fight between Tunney and fellow heavyweight boxer Jack Dempsey.

During World War II Harlan commanded the Operational Analysis Section of the Eighth Air Force, composed of specialists in mathematics, physics, electronics, architecture, and law. He was awarded the United States Legion of Merit and the Croix de Guerre of Belgium and France for his advice on bombing operations.

On his return to law practice in 1945, Harlan was soon recognized as a leader of the New York bar. He participated in a large number of important matters and argued several appeals before the U.S. Supreme Court. From 1951 to 1953 he was chief counsel for the New York State Crime Commission, which Governor Thomas Dewey had appointed to investigate the infiltration of state government by organized crime. During this period he served in top positions in the Association of the Bar of the City of New York.

In January 1954 Harlan was appointed to the U.S. Court of Appeals for the Second Circuit. Less than a year later he was elevated to the Supreme Court by President Dwight Eisenhower. After a delay in the Judiciary Committee, apparently occasioned by southern dissatisfaction with the decision in *Brown v. Board of Education*, Harlan was confirmed in March 1955. He brought to his office the diligence, thoroughness, and intensity that marked his early career at the bar. He showed a willingness to take great pains with the "little" cases—the ones that never make headlines—and a commitment to understandable legal reasoning. Harlan's opinions earned him the almost universal respect of the bar, whose members looked upon him as a "lawyer's judge," aware of and responsive to the needs of practicing attorneys.

Justice Harlan is remembered most conspicuously as a leading conservative voice during the years of the Court's unparalleled liberal activism under Chief Justice Earl Warren. But Harlan also concurred in many of the liberal rulings of the Court. A true patrician, he was concerned less with results in particular controversies than with assuring that government functioned smoothly and without exciting deep-seated enmities. This philosophy was based on two overarching themes: federalism and proceduralism.

Preoccupied with keeping "'the delicate balance of federal-state relations' in good working order" and in assuring the autonomy and independence of the states, he saw federalism as a "bulwark of freedom" ("Thoughts at a Dedication"). He recognized that the founders, out of bitter experience, were suspicious of any all-powerful central authority and thus sought to diffuse power among the executive, legislative, and judicial branches. This concern was closely related to Harlan's desire to preserve the values of pluralism and local experimentation. He believed that no other political system "could have afforded so much scope to . . . a dynamic people representing such divergencies of ethnic and cultural backgrounds" and still "unif[y] them into a nation." In Harlan's jurisprudence, federalism was also a bulwark against a judiciary that would arrogate power to itself and impose its own views of government on society, thereby enervating the initiative and independence essential to a thriving democracy.

Harlan's proceduralism related not only to rules that govern trials and appeals but also to issues of justiciability that determine when the judicial power will be exercised and thus to the role of courts in American society. Harlan rejected the view that "every major social ill in this country can find its cure in some constitutional 'principle'" (*Reynolds v. Sims*, 1964). He also jealously guarded the Supreme Court's appellate authority, which he believed should be used "for the settlement of [issues] of importance to the public" and "not simply for the benefit of particular litigants" (*Sullivan v. Little Hunting Park, Inc.*, 1969). He urged judicial deference to other decision-making authorities, whether Congress, the president, or the Judicial Conference. Finally, Harlan urged deference to fact-finding by trial courts, saying that "appellate courts have no facilities for the examination of witnesses; nor in the nature of things can they have that intimate knowledge of the evidence and 'feel' of the trial scene" (*Mesarosh v. United States*, 1956).

Applying this vision of federalism and proceduralism, Justice Harlan was the leading dissenter of the Warren Court. He opposed egalitarian rulings of many kinds. He was most vehement in condemning the reapportionment decisions, first in *Baker v. Carr* (1962), in which the Court approved federal jurisdiction to decide whether state legislative districts were malapportioned, then in *Reynolds v. Sims* (1964), which established the one person–one vote rule, and in the many sequels to these rulings. Harlan also dissented from decisions that related to the right to vote, including the rulings that invalidated Virginia's poll tax and upheld Congress's power to extend the franchise to eighteen-year-olds.

Harlan especially objected to the idea that government has an obligation to eliminate economic inequalities as a way to permit everyone to exercise human rights, and he therefore dissented from cases that held that impoverished criminal defendants have a right to counsel and trial transcripts at state expense when appealing their convictions. He was also out of step with the Warren Court's transformation of criminal procedure, including the law that related to confessions and lineups, the privilege against self-incrimination, wiretapping and eavesdropping, and the admissibility of illegally obtained evidence. Relying on federalism principles, he also vigorously dissented from the *Miranda* case, which established rules for warning individuals being taken into police custody.

At the same time, Harlan, often contrary to the majority, deferred to congressional judgments that impaired civil liberties. He conceded broad authority to Congress over American citizenship; protested a softening of the immigration law that provided for deportation of an alien who had ever been a member, however nominally, of the Communist party; and opposed a constitutional right to travel abroad for persons accused of disloyalty to the United States. He rejected First Amendment claims by individuals who were held in contempt by the House Committee on Un-American Activities and were denied admission to the practice of law for refusing to answer questions concerning Communist activities.

But Harlan's conservative opinions do not provide a complete picture. Justice Potter Stewart, one of Harlan's closest colleagues, recognized this when he said, "I can assure you that a very interesting law review article could someday be written on 'The Liberal Opinions of Mr. Justice Harlan.'" There are numerous cases in which Harlan was part of the Warren Court consensus and, indeed, in which he spoke for the Court. For example, Harlan was a staunch advocate of school desegregation, and he joined every opinion that invalidated other sorts of state-enforced segregation. He concurred in *Gideon v. Wainwright* (1963), which granted a right to counsel to accused felons, and wrote the opinion in *Boddie v. Connecticut* (1971), which held that a state could not deny a divorce because a couple could not afford the judicial filing fee. In the criminal procedure area, Harlan consistently supported a strong version of the Fourth Amendment protection against unreasonable searches and seizures by federal authorities, including application of the principle to wiretapping and eavesdropping. He also supported a ruling that extended criminal due process protections to juveniles accused of delinquency.

Harlan supported free expression in many important cases. He wrote the opinion in *NAACP v. Alabama* (1958), which protected the right of individuals to join civil rights groups anonymously when exposure would entail great personal risks. He joined *New York Times Co. v. Sullivan* (1964), which first imposed limits on libel judgments against the media, and some (though not all) of the sequels to that case. He joined opinions that barred states from refusing to seat an elected legislator because of that person's critical views of the Vietnam War and from convicting a leader of the Ku Klux Klan for "seditious" speech. And he wrote for the Court to protect the right of a black man who was outraged at the shooting of a civil rights leader to criticize the country while burning the American flag.

Harlan also wrote a number of opinions, all aimed at curbing variants of McCarthyism, that nominally were decided on nonconstitutional grounds but rested on First Amendment principles. He invalidated the discharge of a federal food and drug inspector by interpreting a statute that authorized dismissals of government employees "in the interests of national security" to apply only to jobs directly concerned with internal subversion and foreign aggression (*Cole v. Young*, 1956). And in what *New York Times* columnist Anthony Lewis has described as a "masterfully subtle opinion," Harlan construed the Smith Act to permit prosecution of Communist party leaders only for speech amounting to incitement to action rather than for "abstract doctrine" (*Yates v. United States*, 1957).

Questions involving the freedom of religion also found Harlan frequently, but not invariably, protective of constitutional guarantees. He joined decisions that prohibited organized prayer in the public schools and that invalidated a requirement that state officials declare a belief in God. And while approving state loans of textbooks to church schools, he balked when tax funds were used to reimburse parochial schools for teachers' salaries, textbooks, and instructional materials. Harlan wrote a powerful concurring opinion during the Vietnam War declaring that a statute that limited conscientious objection to individuals who believed in a theistic religion "offended the Establishment Clause" because it "accords a preference to the 'religious' [and] disadvantages adherents of religions that do not worship a Supreme Being" (*Walsh v. United States*, 1968).

A final area of civil liberties, sexual privacy, is of particular importance. In 1960 a 5–4 majority refused to adjudicate, on the ground that there was no threat of prosecution, the merits of a Connecticut law that criminalized the sale of contraceptives to married couples. Harlan's emotional dissent argued extensively that Connecticut's law violated the due process clause of the Fourteenth Amendment, a position that prevailed four years later in *Griswold v. Connecticut* (1965). In economic cases Harlan often went along with the majority's support of government regulation of business, despite the fact that he was acutely aware, because of his extensive corporate clientele when he was in private practice, of the effect of government regulation on business.

The Warren era ended in mid-1969, but Harlan remained for two more terms. Possessing seniority and an unmatched professional reputation, he became the Court's leader. Thus, as Judge Henry Friendly of the Second Circuit noted, against Harlan's average of 62.6 dissenting votes per term in the period between 1963 and 1967, he cast only 24 such votes in the 1969 term and 18 in the 1970 term. Harlan now could reassert conservative themes in prevailing opinions. During this period he adhered to his longstanding opposition to expansion of the constitutional rights of poor people to public assistance by voting with the majority in the leading case that rejected welfare as an entitlement. Similarly, he prevailed in a series of criminal justice decisions, including those that denied a jury trial in juvenile delinquency proceedings and that upheld death sentences without prior judicial guidelines. In the First Amendment area, Harlan also maintained long-standing positions, but here he was more often in dissent. The most notable occasion was the *Pentagon Papers* case (1971), in which he would have permitted the prior restraint of newspaper publication of an extensive and politically embarrassing history of the Vietnam War.

But Harlan also supported some of the Court's liberal activist rulings during this period. For example, he maintained his support for school desegregation, opposed the jailing of indigents who could not pay criminal fines, and wrote a widely cited opinion that stressed the emotive content of speech in reversing the conviction of a man who wore a jacket in a courthouse saying "fuck the draft" in protest against conscription (*Cohen v. California*, 1971).

What should one conclude from the many decisions in which Justice Harlan, a conservative, supported constitutional rights in highly controversial cases? He was plainly never in step with the majority of the Warren Court, marching separately in too many instances. Though not essentially a civil libertarian, he was not insensitive to human suffering or unmoved by evidence of arbitrariness. At the core of Harlan's reaction to injustice was a deep, almost visceral, desire to keep things in balance, to resist excess in any direction. Many times he said how important it was "to keep things on an even keel," and he subtitled a major speech "Keeping the Judicial Function in Balance." Legal process theory, which had its heyday during Harlan's tenure on the Court, strongly influenced his judicial philosophy. The work of legal scholars Henry M. Hart and Albert M. Sacks emphasized the centrality of procedure in assuring judicial and legislative objectivity, as well as the importance of deferring to judgments reached by nonjudicial institutions operating within their appropriate sphere of activity. Such a philosophy was tailor-made for Harlan's cautious reformism.

Harlan, by nature a patrician traditionalist, found himself serving on a Supreme Court that for most of his years was rapidly revising and liberalizing constitutional law. In these circumstances it is not surprising that he protested the direction of the Court and the speed with which it was traveling. He did so in a remarkably forceful and principled manner. Balanced against this role, Harlan joined many significant civil liberties rulings on the Court during his tenure. His overall jurisprudence can be characterized as conservative primarily in the sense that it evinced caution, a fear of centralized authority, and a respect for process.

Harlan died in Washington, D.C., shortly after retiring because of ill health. His jurisprudential legacy remains one of the most impressive of any justice to serve on the Supreme Court.

• Harlan's papers are in the Mudd Library at Princeton University. For a personal statement of his judicial philosophy, see his "Thoughts at a Dedication: Keeping the Judicial Function in Balance," *American Bar Association Journal* 49 (1963): 943. An important source is *The Evolution of a Judicial Philosophy: Selected Opinions and Papers of Justice John M. Harlan*, ed. David L. Shapiro (1969). The only full-length biography is Tinsley E. Yarbrough, *John Marshall Harlan: Great Dissenter of the Warren Court* (1992). An impressive set of articles on Harlan, commemorating the twentieth anniversary of his retirement, is in the *New York Law School Review* 36 (1991): 1–286. Shorter articles written when he retired are in the *Harvard Law Review* 85 (1971): 369–91. See also Norman Dorsen, "The Second Mr. Justice Harlan: A Constitutional Conservative," *New York University Law Review* 44 (1969): 249; J. Harvie Wilkinson III, "Justice John Marshall Harlan and the Values of Federalism," *Virginia Law Review* 57 (1971): 1185; Nathan Lewin, "Justice Harlan: 'The Full Measure of the Man,'" *American Bar Association Journal* 58 (1972): 579; Daniel A. Farber, "Civilizing Public Discourse: An Essay on Professor Bickel, Justice Harlan, and the Enduring Significance of *Cohen v. California*," *Duke Law Journal* (1980): 283; Lewis F. Powell, Jr., "Address," *American Law Institute Proceedings: 63rd Annual Meeting* (1987): 312.

NORMAN DORSEN

HARLAN, Josiah (12 June 1799–Oct. 1871), soldier of fortune and adventurer, was born in Newlin Township, Pennsylvania, the son of Joshua Harlan, a merchant broker of Philadelphia, and Sarah Hinchman. His parents were members of the Society of Friends (Quakers), and indications are that Harlan followed in their path of independent thought though certainly not the Quaker ideal of pacifism. Almost nothing is known of his early years. The first prominent event of his career was in 1823, when he journeyed to Asia and entered the employment of the British East India Tea Company. He served as an officiating assistant surgeon in the Bengal artillery under British colonel George Pollock during the first Burmese War (1824–1826). This employment ended with the conclusion of the war, and Harlan traveled to northern India looking for other work. He had already, at the age of twenty-seven, traveled more than most Americans of his time period. He continued to expand his knowledge of the wider world in Afghanistan, which was at that time contested by Afghans, Sikhs, and the officials of the British East India Company, who feared an incursion by the forces of imperial Russia.

In 1827 Harlan came into contact with Shah Shooja-ool-Moolk, the former leader of Afghanistan who had been deposed in 1810. Harlan attached himself to the fortunes of the deposed shah, but he simultaneously offered his services to the British political assistant in Ludhiana, Martine Wade, and the leader of the Sikh nation in the Punjab, Maharajah Ranjit Singh. The British turned down Harlan's proposals, and he spent two years in the service of Shah Sooja. Harlan changed his allegiance in 1829 and became Ranjit Singh's governor of the provinces of Durpur and Jesota in the Punjab. In 1835 war broke out between Ranjit Singh and the leader of Afghanistan, Dōst Muḥammed Khān, who brought his Afghani army southward through the Khyber Pass. Desperate for a means with which to stop the invasion, Ranjit Singh sent Harlan to infiltrate the enemy's camp and to bribe his men with gold. Harlan succeeded so well that Dōst Muḥammed was forced to hastily retreat northward after seeing his army melt away from the smooth promises of Harlan and other agents.

Harlan changed sides again in October 1836. He infuriated Ranjit Singh by counterfeiting money and by refusing to treat the maharajah for an illness without being offered a large sum of money. Harlan went north and joined his fortunes to those of Dōst Muhammed, who apparently accepted the American adventurer who had blocked his invasion of 1835. In his new situation, Harlan organized and trained the army of Dōst Muhammed, whose son Muhammed Akbar Khān used Harlan's training to defeat the Sikh army of Ranjit Singh at the battle of Jamrud in 1837. Harlan continued to serve Dōst Muhammed for two more years. When the British forces moved north from India into Afghanistan in 1839, starting the first Afghan War, Harlan commanded Dōst Muhammed's forces in retreat. Nonetheless, Harlan appeared ready to switch his allegiances once again and was thwarted only by the British, who spurned his advances and insisted that the American leave Afghanistan and India at once. The British paid for his passage home to Pennsylvania.

Harlan took his time returning to the United States. He arrived in his homeland sometime in 1841 and presented his views on Afghanistan and the Afghan War to the American public in a series of newspaper interviews. In fact, his representations, which some would doubtless call his self-serving misrepresentations, of the situation in India and Afghanistan caught the attention of the American public and briefly made the Afghan War a matter of discussion in the 1842 congressional elections. Harlan subsequently wrote *A Memoir of India and Avghanistann* (1842).

In 1849 Harlan married Elizabeth Baker; the couple had one daughter. They lived near Cochranville, Chester County, Pennsylvania, where Harlan built a noteworthy estate. He was briefly involved in an attempt to import camels into the United States in 1856. When the Civil War began, Harlan raised a regiment of volunteer cavalry, Harlan's light Cavalry or the Eleventh Pennsylvania, which fought with the Army of the Potomac in several battles, notably the Peninsula campaign of 1862. Harlan retired from the army on 20 August 1862 because of ill health. Sometime after the Civil War ended, he moved to San Francisco, where he practiced medicine. He died in San Francisco.

Contemporary sources are divided in their estimates of Harlan. No doubt he was a charmer, a practical dreamer, and a would-be empire builder. He was regarded by the British as a mountebank, but it is possible that their estimation was colored by the fact that, while they were constrained by the duties of a growing imperial system, Harlan was completely independent. He was capable of gaining the affection of notable Asian leaders but remained unable to penetrate the British soldiers and officials of the East India Company. He was in some ways a man ahead of his time. One generation after his death, British audiences and readers would thrill to the stories of Rudyard Kipling regarding courageous British freebooters involved in the "Great Game," the battle for power in India and Afghanistan between Russia and Great Britain. The more restrained and dutiful servants of the British Crown in the 1830s saw Harlan as a pariah, a man without conscience or loyalty. Although there is some truth in this, he was, after all, a citizen of a country that had no interest in or connection with the far-off lands of India and Afghanistan prior to his bringing those areas to the attention of the American public in 1842. What remains most mysterious about Harlan is his original motivation: what persuaded him to go to Burma and India in the first place? Lacking a firm answer to this question, one can only say that Harlan maneuvered with skill and verve, although he brought little credit to himself in the process.

• Harlan's memoir can be supplemented by his unpublished "Personal Narrative of General Harlan's Eighteen Years' Residence in Asia," and "On the Fruits of Cabul and Vicinity," 37th Cong., 2d sess., S. Exec. Docs. 39. A condensed version of Harlan's memoir, in Frank Ross, ed., *Central Asia, Personal Narrative of General Josiah Harlan* (1939). Articles about Harlan are in the *National Gazette*, 25 Aug. 1841; the *United States Gazette*, 20 Jan. 1842; and the *Rochester Daily Advertiser*, 12 Aug. 1842. See also Louis Dupree, *Afghanistan* (1973), and C. Grey and H. Garrett, *European Adventurers of Northern India: 1785–1849* (1929). Most valuable is John H. Waller, *Beyond the Khyber Pass: The Road to British Disaster in the First Afghan War* (1990). Obituaries are in the Philadelphia *Press*, 4 Nov. 1871, and *Sunday Dispatch*, 12 Nov. 1871.

SAMUEL WILLARD CROMPTON

HARLAN, Richard (19 Sept. 1796–30 Sept. 1843), physician, anatomist, and paleontologist, was born in Philadelphia, the son of Joshua Harlan, a farmer and merchant, and Sarah Hinchman. Harlan attended schools in Philadelphia, and then entered the medical department of the University of Pennsylvania, where he studied and worked under Joseph Parrish, M.D. Before completing his studies, he served as surgeon on an East India ship (1816–1817). He returned to Philadelphia and received his medical degree in 1818. Immediately thereafter, Parrish put Harlan in charge of the dissecting room at the private medical school that Parrish had opened to provide extended training for medical school students. The study of anatomy proved to be of special interest to Harlan, and in 1824 he published *Anatomical Investigations*, which were descriptions of the brain. Harlan focused on comparative studies in anatomy, a relatively unusual approach in the United States at the time. From 1821 until 1829, Harlan lectured extensively on comparative anatomy at the Philadelphia Museum Company, an outgrowth of Charles Willson Peale's famous museum. By 1824, he had amassed what was described as an exceptional collection of specimens for the study of comparative anatomy, including human crania. He continued to collect, and by 1839, his collection numbered 275 specimens, making it one of the largest of its kind in the nation.

Harlan was deeply interested in natural history. He joined the Academy of Natural Sciences of Philadelphia in 1815. In 1823 he published the first of more than thirty papers on subjects in natural history. In 1825 his *Fauna Americana: Being a Description of the Mammiferous Animals Inhabiting North America* was published. Harlan attempted to classify living (and a few fossil) mammals in this work, assigning each a Linnaean name. Although intended to publish a second volume dealing with reptiles, his *Fauna* met with such harsh criticism, including charges of confused classification and plagiarism, that he decided not to do it. He did, however, publish "American Herpetology" in the *Journal of the Academy of Natural Sciences of Philadelphia* in 1827. He was a founding member of the Geological Society of Pennsylvania in 1832 and, as a member, worked for many years toward the establishment of a state geological survey.

Harlan's interests in natural history and comparative anatomy were combined in a lifelong fascination with fossil animals, especially reptiles. In this, he considered himself a disciple of Georges Cuvier, the French comparative anatomist, naturalist, and zoologist who used his knowledge of comparative anatomy to accurately reconstruct fossil animals. In 1833 Harlan made the first of two trips to Europe, traveling primarily in the British Isles, France, and Italy, in search of those who were interested in fossils. He was one of three Americans to attend the Third Annual Meeting of the British Association for the Advancement of Science in Cambridge, where he gave a paper on the fossil reptiles of the United States. As the result of numerous requests from Europeans for more information, Harlan compiled "Critical Notices of Various Organic Remains Hitherto Discovered in North America," which was published almost simultaneously in the *Transactions of the Geological Society of Pennsylvania* (1 [1834]: 46–112) and in the *Edinburgh New Philosophical Journal* (17 [1834]: 342–62, and 18 [1834–1835]: 28–40). In it, he recounted the known fossil mammals, reptiles, fish, and plants of the United States, citing the locality where each was found, its description, and its place in the geological series of formations. He took care to cite the individuals whose work he drew upon, often quoting them.

In addition to fossil studies, Harlan wrote several papers on living animals and on medical subjects. He compiled these, with his papers on fossils, in *Medical and Physical Researches* (1835). Included are several descriptions of new species of living animals, papers on physiological research and experimentation dealing with such diverse topics as the function of the brain in man and animals and the effect of poisons on vegetables, and several contributions in clinical medicine. His "Critical Notices" is also included, with minor revisions and additions.

In spite of his many interests, Harlan maintained a busy career as a medical practitioner and throughout the years had an extensive private practice, which, along with his teaching of anatomy, supplied his income. His institutional affiliations included the Philadelphia Dispensary, where he served as physician in 1820, and from 1822 until 1838, the Philadelphia Almshouse. In 1832 he traveled to Canada and New York as part of a committee appointed by the city of Philadelphia to study means of combatting a cholera epidemic that threatened much of the eastern United States. The committee suggested the evacuation of heavily infected areas and the establishment of cholera hospitals and emergency stations.

In January 1839 Harlan returned to Europe with the intention of making France his home for several years. Not long after arriving, he learned that his collection in comparative anatomy, which he had intended to sell, had been destroyed in a fire at a Philadelphia warehouse. Disheartened by this catastrophe, he gave up the idea of living in France and returned to the United States in the fall of 1839. He busied himself with his practice and with a translation, with notes and additions, of J. N. Gannal's *History of Embalming* (1840), in which he had become interested while in France. In December 1842 he moved to New Orleans, where he was elected vice president of the Louisiana Medico-Chirurgical Society. He intended to make the city his permanent home but died there the following year of yellow fever. He was survived by his wife, Margaret Hart Simmons Howell, a widow whom he had married in 1833 and who was, like him, a Quaker, and by their four children.

Harlan's career was a stormy one. Most of his colleagues found him unpleasant and argumentative, and many questioned his abilities as a scientist. As an American pioneer in the study of fossils, especially the reptiles, Harlan made some astute observations but committed some serious errors as well, such as identifying a whale and a fish as reptiles, which drew the denunciation of fellow scientists. But his poor relations with his peers seem to have been generated as much by his irascible nature and their dislike of him as by his errors. Harlan's work, nevertheless, called attention to a rich fossil fauna that had previously been little noticed. In addition, he worked hard to improve collections of fossils for study at learned institutions such as the Academy of Natural Sciences of Philadelphia, and he helped the European community of paleontologists become more aware of American work.

• There is no major collection of Harlan papers, but letters commonly appear in collections representing other naturalists of the period, such as John James Audubon and William Featherstonhaugh, who were among Harlan's closest friends. The best single source of information on Harlan is Whitfield J. Bell, Jr., "Richard Harlan" in the *Dictionary of Scientific Biography*, vol. 6, ed. Charles Coulston Gillespie (1972). Alpheus H. Harlan, *History and Genealogy of the Harlan Family* (1914), and Henry Simpson, *The Lives of Eminent Philadelphians, Now Deceased* (1859), provide some biographical information about Harlan, and comments about him are found in most works that deal with the period and fields in which he was active. For information on his work related to the study of fossil reptiles, see Patsy A. Gerstner, "Vertebrate Paleontology, an Early Nineteenth-Century Transatlantic Science," *Journal of the History of Biology* 3 (1970): 137–48, and "The Early Study of Fossil Reptiles in America," *Journal of Geological Education* 20 (Mar. 1972): 86–87.

PATSY A. GERSTNER

HARLAND, Henry (1 Mar. 1861–20 Dec. 1905), author and editor, was born in Brooklyn, New York, the son of Thomas Harland, a lawyer, and Irene Jones. (Harland's assertion that he was born in St. Petersburg, Russia, is false.) He attended classes at Adelphi Academy in Brooklyn from 1871 to 1872; Public School No. 35 in New York City from 1872 to 1877; and the College of the City of New York from 1877 until 1879 or perhaps 1880. He left without a degree. As early as 1876 or so, he had become interested in a movement called Ethical Culture and evidently attended classes conducted by the son of a German-born rabbi. He studied at the Harvard Divinity School from 1881 to 1882 and met several literary figures nearby (including Henry Wadsworth Longfellow's brother Samuel and Henry James, Sr., the father of William James and Henry James). Leaving with no academic credits, Harland tutored for a short while and then in 1883 went to Europe, mostly associating with writers and artists in Rome.

From 1883 to 1886 Harland clerked for Daniel G. Rollins, surrogate of New York and a friend of Harland's father. He married Aline Herminie (later Herminé) Merriam, an accomplished pianist, in 1884. The couple had no children. Soon afterward he published his first novel, using the pen name Sidney Luska. The novel was titled *As It Was Written: A Jewish Musician's Story* (1885). He managed to write it while being fully employed as a clerk by sleeping after dinner until 2:00 A.M., writing until breakfast time, and then reporting to his office. He also sold short fiction to Samuel Sidney McClure's newspaper syndicate. *As It Was Written*, which combines occultism, melodrama, and pre-Proustian involuntary memory, was so successful that Harland turned his remarkable energies exclusively to writing and published three more novels. Still written under the name Luska, they are *Mrs Peixada* (1886), with much about the law; *The Yoke of the Thorah* (1887), concerning a Jewish-Christian marriage; and *My Uncle Florimond* (1888), for juvenile readers. The title page of *My Uncle Florimond* also named Henry Harland as author on the title page, in parentheses. These works mix fantastic incidents and verisimilitude and hence reveal the contrary influences of the conservative poet-businessman Edmund Clarence Stedman, a close family friend and Harland's helpful godfather, and the more realistic William Dean Howells, who encouraged Harland steadily.

Having vacationed in Europe in 1886, Harland and his wife returned there in 1889, during which year he published *A Latin-Quarter Courtship and Other Stories*, showing a tentative advance toward realism, and *Grandison Mather; or, An Account of the Fortunes of Mr. and Mrs. Thomas Gardiner*, an autobiographical novel.

The Harlands lived briefly in Paris and established a residence in London, but they often vacationed on the Continent. At this time Harland began to suffer from bleeding, tuberculosis-infected lungs. (He was an incessant smoker.) In 1890 he cotranslated Matilde Serao's Italian novel *Fantasia*, using his own name. He continued writing sensational novels, which were rather ineffective and partly autobiographical. However, his *Mademoiselle Miss and Other Stories* (1893) was livened by more realistic European settings. By this time Harland and his wife had established a literary salon and had made friends with some of the finest creative minds in England during the tumultuous 1890s. They included Aubrey Beardsley, Edmund Gosse, Henry James, John Lane, Andrew Lang, Richard Le Gallienne, and James Abbott McNeill Whistler. In 1894 Lane established the *Yellow Book*, with fellow-founders Harland (as its brilliant literary editor) and Beardsley (as its controversial art editor). During its three short years of life, this intermittently decadent literary quarterly published the works of numerous fine contributors, notably Max Beerbohm, "Baron Corvo" (Frederick Rolfe), Gosse, James, and Lord Frederick Leighton, along with Harland and Beardsley themselves.

Soon after publishing two more collections of short stories, Harland achieved his most durable popular success with *The Cardinal's Snuff-Box* (1900). More fantastic than realistic, it concerns a well-to-do but unpopular English novelist and the English widow of an Italian duke; their idyllic romance is helped along by a cardinal who is the Englishman's uncle. The hero's conversion to Roman Catholicism is an autobiographical touch, because in 1898 Harland and his wife had become intensely serious converts themselves. The novel, quickly reissued, soon earned Harland $70,000 in royalties. Unfortunately, Harland, who earlier had written well and sympathetically of Jews, included in this novel disfiguring anti-Semitic talk (echoed also in later works).

Though ill much of the time after 1900, Harland continued to be productive. *The Lady Paramount* (1902) is about an Italian countess who thinks that an English cousin of hers is the true inheritor of her estate and seeks him out; the two happily—and unsurprisingly—get married. Despite mixed reviews, this novel also sold well. Harland and his wife returned in 1902 to the United States, where he enjoyed considerable fanfare, granted several interviews, and became a prevaricating poseur. He serialized his final novel, *My Friend Prospero*, for $10,000 in *McClure's Magazine* (June–Nov. 1903); in book form (1903) it soon became a bestseller, even though its plot and some of its characters parallel those of his two previous successes, *The Cardinal's Snuff-Box* and *The Lady Paramount*. In *My Friend Prospero*, a lowly lad turns out to be an heir to a British peerage and a lowly girl to be of Austrian nobility. Back in England in 1904, Harland worked on a novel he titled *The Royal End*. He sought more salubrious air in San Remo, Italy, and recovered enough to return to England in 1905 but suffered severe lung hemorrhages there and went back to San Remo, where he died. His widow completed *The Royal End*, which was published in 1909; it concerns a displaced American woman who tours Europe with other exiles. Harland's wife began to live her husband's fantasies, called herself Sir Henry Arnold Harland's widow Lady Harland, and eventually died in 1939 in a Long Island mental hospital. Once popular, Harland is now regarded as a witty novelist who in mid-career abandoned an impulse toward realism, perhaps out of fear of failure, and returned to sentimental romances, only to die without achieving his potential. His most memorable achievement may well be his distinguished work as an editor of the epoch-defining *Yellow Book*.

• Harland's correspondence is widely scattered. Most of his letters, however, are deposited at the Boston Public Library, Columbia University, the Berg Collection at the New York Public Library, and Westfield College of the University of London. Alice Payne Hackett lists only one of Harland's novels, *My Friend Prospero*, among scores of titles in her *60 Years of Best Sellers, 1895–1955* (1956). Karl Beckson, *Henry Harland: His Life and Work* (1978), is a comprehensive treatment of Harland and includes a full bibliography of his works and uncollected writings. Richard Le Gallienne, *The Romantic '90s* (1925), includes a thumbnail portrait of Harland during their days together in Paris. The following works contain information about Harland's friendships with Aubrey Beardsley, Max Beerbohm, John Lane, Edmund Gosse, William Dean Howells, Henry James, Edmund Clarence Stedman, and Arthur Symons: John Lane, *Aubrey Beardsley and the Yellow Book* (1903); Laura Stedman and George M. Gould, *Life and Letters of Edmund Clarence Stedman* (2 vols., 1910); *Life in Letters of William Dean Howells*, ed. Mildred Howells (2 vols., 1928); Max Beerbohm, *Letters to Reggie [Turner]*, ed. Rupert Hart-Davis (1964); *The Letters of Aubrey Beardsley*, ed. Henry Maas et al. (1970); *The Memoirs of Arthur Symons: Life and Art in the 1890s*, ed. Karl Beckson (1977); *Selected Letters of Henry James to Edmund Gosse, 1882–1915*, ed. Rayburn S. Moore (1988); and Robert L. Gale, *A Henry James Encyclopedia* (1989). Obituaries are in the *New York Times* and the *Times* (London), both 22 Dec. 1905.

ROBERT L. GALE

HARLAND, Marion. *See* Terhune, Mary Virginia Hawes.

HARLEY, Herbert Lincoln (31 Dec. 1871–12 Feb. 1951), lawyer and legal reformer, was born in Lincoln, Michigan, the son of David S. Harley, a lawyer, and Flavia Jane Phelps. Fascinated with sailing during his boyhood in Manistee, Michigan, Harley originally hoped to become a merchant marine officer. When he could not afford to move to New York State to obtain the necessary training, he enrolled at the University of Michigan Law School. After receiving an LL.B. and gaining admission to the bar in 1892, Harley returned to Manistee to practice. He did not enjoy legal work, and after someone else confessed to a crime for which one of his clients had been convicted, he concluded that he was not suited to the work.

In 1896 Harley married Blanche Hilton; their union produced one child and also facilitated his move into another profession. Blanche's father, who owned the *Manistee Daily News*, made Harley the editor and publisher, positions he held from 1900 until 1912. During this period Harley, a nominal Republican, became a devoted follower of political reformer Richard S. Childs, whose Short Ballot Organization sought to eliminate the evils of partisan politics. Among the reforms it championed was the city manager system. Prodded by Harley, Manistee embraced that form of municipal government in 1914.

The Short Ballot Organization also became the model for the American Judicature Society, which Harley founded. The AJS developed out of a movement within the legal profession to reform the administration of justice, inspired by attacks on the courts from progressive reformers who considered the judiciary unresponsive to the needs of the people. During a 1906 address to the American Bar Association, Roscoe Pound (then dean of the University of Nebraska Law School) called on his fellow attorneys to alleviate popular disaffection with the legal system by making it more efficient. Five years later Harley persuaded Charles Ruggles, a wealthy Manistee lumberman, whose experiences as a litigant had soured him on the courts, to fund an organization that would coordinate the efforts of the reform element within the bar. Financed by Ruggles, Harley toured the country in 1912, consulting with leaders of the legal profession about what he had in mind. He also dispatched a circular letter to about 250 interested individuals. He managed to persuade such prominent figures as Pound, Dean John H. Wigmore and Professor Albert M. Kales of the Northwestern University Law School, Chief Justice John B. Winslow of Wisconsin, and Chief Justice Harry Olson of the Municipal Court of Chicago to serve as trustees of the new organization, which was formally incorporated on 27 September 1913.

Between 1913 and 1925 Harley built the American Judicature Society into an effective voice for such reforms as the merit selection of judges, bar integration (the creation of lawyers' organizations to which all of the attorneys in a state are required to belong), higher standards for admission to the practice of law, the unification of all courts within each jurisdiction, and the modernization of the rules of civil procedure. AJS published a series of bulletins that explained its ideas for improving the administration of justice, and in 1917 it launched a journal, which was intended to promote the adoption of its program. Harley edited these publications and wrote most of the items that appeared in the journal.

Many of the reforms he advocated were beginning to win acceptance when Ruggles, who had lost interest in AJS, terminated his financial support in 1925. Harley's salary had already declined so far that he was managing to subsist only because Judge Olson had put him on the payroll of the Chicago Municipal Court as his assistant. He now asked readers of the *Journal* for money but could not raise enough to keep AJS afloat. Harley's first marriage ended in divorce, and in 1927 he married Helen (Ramsdell) Dempsey, who wanted to live in England. Harley resigned from AJS and sailed for Europe.

Returning in April 1928, Harley reorganized the society as an organization of dues-paying members with an expanded board of directors and a president. Former governor of New York Charles Evans Hughes served as president from 1929 to 1930, and World War I Secretary of War Newton Baker occupied the presidency from 1930 to 1937; other prominent members of the legal profession also accepted AJS offices. Almost all of them were mere figureheads, however, and contributed little more to the organization than their names. For all practical purposes, Harley was AJS. Although the society's offices were located at the Northwestern Law School, Harley, whose wife did not want to live in Chicago, ran AJS out of a home in Washington, D.C., until both he and the organization relocated to the University of Michigan Law School in 1931.

Four years later the society obtained a large grant from the Carnegie Corporation that put it back on its feet financially. Harley lived comfortably for the rest of his career, running AJS as its secretary-treasurer and propagandizing tirelessly on behalf of the reforms with which the organization had become associated. Besides editing the society's *Journal* and writing much of what appeared in its pages, he also contributed articles to a number of other publications in law and such related fields as criminology and public administration. Harley was also active in the American Bar Association (ABA), serving for a number of years as secretary of its Conference of Bar Association Delegates. In 1938 he became the sixth recipient of the ABA's prestigious American Bar Association Medal.

Although Arthur T. Vanderbilt had arranged for Harley to receive that award, the two soon became embroiled in a nasty feud. Vanderbilt, who was elected president of AJS in 1938, assumed a much more active role than had his figurehead predecessors. Harley, insecure because his health was declining, became convinced that Vanderbilt was trying to replace him with an assistant. In 1940 he fired the assistant and drove Vanderbilt, a former ABA president and champion of judicial reform, out of AJS.

During the early 1940s, Harley's eyesight and hearing faded rapidly, and he gradually turned over administration of the society's affairs to his chosen successor, Glenn R. Winters. In 1944 Winters replaced him as editor of the *Journal*, and in September 1945 Harley retired from his post as secretary-treasurer. He lived in retirement in Barton Hills, Michigan, until his death.

• Because Harley's life was the American Judicature Society, his papers and those of the society for the period that he headed it are essentially indistinguishable. They are located at the headquarters of AJS in Chicago. The most complete discussion of Harley's career is in Michal R. Belknap, *To Improve the Administration of Justice: A History of the American Judicature Society* (1992), chapters 1–4. On his early life and the launching of the society, see Belknap, "From Pound to Har-

ley: The Founding of AJS," *Judicature* 72, no. 2 (Aug.–Sept. 1988): 78–90. Also informative, although inadequately documented, is Glenn R. Winters, "Herbert Harley and the American Judicature Society," *Journal of the American Judicature Society* 30, no. 3 (Oct. 1946): 78–104. "Herbert Lincoln Harley," *Journal of the American Judicature Society* 34, no. 6 (Apr. 1951): 163–65, is a combination editorial and obituary.

MICHAL R. BELKNAP

HARLINE, Leigh (26 Mar. 1907–10 Dec. 1969), composer and songwriter, was born in Salt Lake City, Utah, the son of Carl Harline, a farmer and cobbler, and Matilda Johanna Petersen, a rugmaker. Harline was raised and educated in Salt Lake, majoring in music at the University of Utah. He studied piano and organ with J. Spencer Cornwall, conductor of the Mormon Tabernacle Choir. At the age of twenty-one Harline moved to California and worked in both Los Angeles and San Francisco composing music for radio stations in those cities. He often doubled as announcer and singer. In 1933 Harline went to work for Walt Disney and remained with the Disney studio for nine years, becoming head of the music department as well as writing music for animated shorts, Mickey Mouse cartoons, Silly Symphonies, and two full-length animated features, *Snow White and the Seven Dwarfs* and *Pinocchio*.

The Silly Symphonies, a series of animated shorts produced by Disney in the 1930s, were essentially short stories with an emphasis on music, often featuring characters other than Mickey Mouse and his assortment of pals. They generally required a more cohesive score than the sight-gag cartoons did and permitted the composer to score more symphonically. The animation director, Wilfred Jackson, who worked closely with Harline's music in an article by Ross Care for *Film Music Notebook* (1978):

To me Leigh's cartoon scores seemed . . . like a symphony by a classical composer. . . . I also believe Leigh wrote his music a little over the heads of our typical theater audience of the early and mid-30s. Leigh's music was melodic enough but it depended much more on other things than melody for its effectiveness, his counter melodies, his harmonic structure all contributed so much to the final effectiveness of his scores.

Harline's credits for the Silly Symphonies include some of the best of that series: "The Pied Piper," "The Grasshopper and the Ants," "The Wise Little Hen," "Water Babies," "Music Land," and "The Old Mill."

When Disney pioneered the first full-length animated feature in 1937, *Snow White and the Seven Dwarfs*, Harline was asked to collaborate on the score with Paul Smith. The songs were by Frank Churchill and Larry Morey. In addition to writing thematic material based on Churchill's songs throughout the picture, Harline scored most of the scenes involving the wicked queen, including the Magic Mirror sequences, the scenes in the queen's laboratory, where she devises evil potions, and the chase up the mountain by the dwarfs that resulted in the queen's death. *Snow White and the Seven Dwarfs* received an Academy Award nomination for best score.

The next Disney animated feature, *Pinocchio* (1940), is considered Harline's musical masterpiece. In addition to the dramatic scoring, Harline wrote the five songs for the picture (with lyrics by Ned Washington): "When You Wish upon a Star," "Hi-Diddle-Dee-Dee," "Little Woodenhead," "I Got No Strings," and "Give a Little Whistle." Harline received the Academy Award in 1940 for best song for "When You Wish upon a Star" and another for best score. Harline himself conducted most of the score, employing at times a fifty-piece orchestra and a chorus of forty voices.

Harline left the Disney studio in 1941 to write music on a freelance basis. He was typecast as a composer of music for comedies for several years, scoring several *Blondie* pictures for Columbia. He later drew the critics' attention with his fine scores for dramas such as *The Pride of the Yankees, China Sky, Johnny Angel, The Boy with Green Hair, Broken Lance, Ten North Frederick*, and *The Seven Faces of Dr. Lao*. In all, Harline composed the music for more than 120 feature films and 50 animated shorts.

After leaving the Disney studio, Harline was commissioned to write two concert pieces. The first was a four-movement work for Werner Janssen called *The Civic Center Suite* (1941). In 1946 the Salt Lake Centennial Committee chose Harline to create an orchestral work depicting the migration of the Mormons. The result was a three-movement composition called *Centennial Suite*. Harline returned to his hometown to conduct the Salt Lake Symphony in the premiere of the work.

Harline was married twice, first to Catherine Palmer, with whom he had two children, and then to Katherine Anne Darby. They had no children. Harline died in Long Beach, California.

Harline is best known for his film scores and was among the first to compose music for animated films in the early days of talking pictures. His lush, expressive style helped set a standard of superb musical quality at the Walt Disney studio. His hit song from Pinocchio, "When You Wish upon a Star," has become the song most identified with Walt Disney Productions, Disneyland, and the Magic Kingdom at Walt Disney World.

• Some biographical material as well as sheet music is housed in the archives of the Walt Disney Studio, Burbank, Calif. The Archives and Rare Books section of the University of Cincinnati Library holds the Leigh Harline Collection, which includes the composer's manuscript sketches, full scores, conductor's scores, and orchestral parts. A comprehensive description of Harline's work with some musical analysis appears in Ross Care, "The Film Music of Leigh Harline," *Film Music Notebook* 4, no. 1 (1978). An obituary is in the *Hollywood Reporter*, 11 Dec. 1969.

LINDA DANLY

HARLOW, Bryce (11 Aug. 1916–17 Feb. 1987), public relations official and presidential adviser, was born in Oklahoma City, Oklahoma, the son of Victor Harlow, head of Harlow Publishing Company, and Gertrude Gindling. He held part-time jobs as a youth in Oklahoma City, beginning at age eleven as an airplane mechanic at a local airport. He attended public schools and received his B.A. and M.A. in political science from the University of Oklahoma in 1936 and 1942, respectively.

In the time between his undergraduate and graduate studies, Harlow lived in Washington, D.C., serving from 1938 to 1940 as assistant librarian in the House of Representatives and from 1940 to 1941 as secretary to Democratic congressman Wesley Disney of Oklahoma, through whom he had secured the earlier patronage appointment. After receiving his master's degree, Harlow spent the rest of his career working in one capacity or another with Congress, beginning during World War II as special assistant to the chief of the army's Congressional Relations Division. He rose to the rank of lieutenant colonel before leaving the army in 1947 to become a member of the staff of the House of Representatives Armed Services Committee.

Harlow was especially effective in his various roles with Congress because he commanded respect and enjoyed friendships in both major parties. His service as a professional staff member of the House Armed Services Committee from 1947 to 1951, for example, spanned periods of both Republican and Democratic majorities in the committee, and he served as assistant to the chairman and then as chief clerk under a Democratic chairman. Powerful Democratic senator Lyndon Johnson, who had served on the Armed Services Committee while in the House, offered Harlow important positions on his staff in 1949 and again in 1953 but Harlow declined, most likely because he identified himself as a Republican.

Having returned to Oklahoma City in 1951 to serve as vice president of Harlow Publishing Company, a producer of elementary-level educational books and materials, Harlow played only a minor role in Dwight Eisenhower's 1952 presidential campaign in Oklahoma, but after Eisenhower's victory he was offered a staff position in the White House congressional liaison office by its chief, General Wilton B. Persons, with whom Harlow had served on General George C. Marshall's congressional liaison staff during World War II. Harlow accepted and served in successively more responsible positions in the White House throughout Eisenhower's two terms, ultimately bearing the title of deputy assistant to the president. Highly successful as the administration's chief congressional liaison official, Harlow was also a sometime speech writer for Eisenhower, who regarded him as uniquely capable of producing speeches that spoke clearly to the people. Consistent with his earlier service in Congress, Harlow was effective with Democrats and Republicans alike.

When Eisenhower left office in 1961, Harlow accepted another Washington-based position, as director of governmental relations for Procter and Gamble Company, a post he held until 1968, when he took leave of absence to work in Richard Nixon's presidential campaign. After Nixon won, he made Harlow his first high-level appointee, designating him as assistant to the president for legislative and congressional affairs, the same position he had held in the last years of the Eisenhower administration. Within months, Nixon raised Harlow to the cabinet-level position of counselor to the president, relieving him of operational duties with Congress (but leaving him with overall responsibility for congressional relations) and giving him responsibility for planning long-range administration strategy in domestic affairs.

Harlow was less successful in pushing Nixon's domestic agenda forward than he had been in the 1950s for Eisenhower, mostly because relations between the Democratic Congress and Nixon were so strained over the Vietnam War. Despite occasional victories, overall results were disappointing to Harlow and, after serving as a traveling strategist with Vice President Spiro Agnew in the bitterly divisive 1970 congressional campaigns, he resigned in December 1970, after serving more than the one year he had agreed to, and returned to Procter and Gamble as vice president. When Nixon's presidency began to unravel due to the early revelations of the Watergate scandal, however, he called Harlow back to the White House once again to help ward off increasing attacks from Congress. In this difficult role, Harlow did about as well as anyone could have, attempting to control the extent of political damage resulting from audits of Nixon's finances and the president's stubborn refusal to release the famous "White House tapes" to Congress. In the spring of 1974, Harlow left White House employment for the third and final time; he left on good terms, and did not criticize Nixon afterward. Harlow returned once again to Procter and Gamble. His only subsequent political roles were as a strategist in President Gerald Ford's unsuccessful 1976 campaign and as an occasional adviser on congressional strategy to President Ronald Reagan in the early 1980s. In 1981 Reagan awarded Harlow the Medal of Freedom, the highest honor a president can bestow on a civilian.

A diminutive (5′4″) and soft-spoken man of courtly manners, Harlow was known for his deep understanding of how Congress works, his quick wit, and his gentle yet persuasive touch. He was twice married. His first wife, Elizabeth Larrimore, whom he married in 1940 and with whom he had three children, died in 1982. One year later he married Sarah Jane Studebaker, with whom he lived in retirement in Harpers Ferry, West Virginia, until his death in an Arlington, Virginia, hospital.

• A substantial collection of Harlow's papers for the period 1953–1961 is available at the Dwight D. Eisenhower Presidential Library, and lesser amounts of material on his later political roles are in the Richard M. Nixon Project in Alexandria, Va., and the Gerald R. Ford Presidential Library in Ann Arbor, Mich. No biography of Harlow has yet been written, nor did he produce published memoirs. His White House activities have received attention in numerous works about the Eisenhower and Nixon presidencies, but only in passing. In addition, Harlow contributed two oral histories to the Eisenhower Oral History Project. Obituaries are in the *Washington Post* and the *New York Times*, both 18 Feb. 1987.

GARY W. REICHARD

HARLOW, Harry Frederick (31 Oct. 1905–6 Dec. 1981), comparative psychologist and primatologist, was born Harry Frederick Israel in Fairfield, Iowa, the son of Lon Israel, at times a merchandiser, inventor, and owner of a country store, and Mable Rock. He entered Reed College in 1923 but transferred after a year to Stanford University, where he earned a B.A. in 1927 (major in psychology) and a Ph.D. in 1930 (specialization in comparative psychology). In the anti-Semitic climate of the day, the name of Israel was making it difficult for Stanford faculty advisers to place him in an academic position. They recommended that he change his surname, and so in 1930, shortly before receiving his Ph.D., he legally became Harry Harlow. He accepted a faculty appointment at the University of Wisconsin that same year. Upon assuming the position, he was thwarted in conducting research using rats because the psychology department's animal laboratory had been torn down during the summer before his arrival. He therefore turned to studying primates at the local zoo and thence began his career as a primatologist. He remained at Wisconsin until his retirement in 1974, except for leaves of absence in 1939–1940 as Carnegie fellow in anthropology at Columbia University and in 1950–1952 as head of the Human Resources Research Branch of the Department of the Army. From 1974 to the time of his death he was a visiting scholar at the University of Arizona. Harlow was thrice married: to Clara Mears from 1932 until their divorce in 1946, to Margaret Kuenne from 1948 until her death in 1971, and again to his first wife, Clara, in 1972. There were two children from each of the first two marriages.

Harlow's scientific output was extensive (more than 300 publications), creative, and of a piece. Four threads stand out. First is the development of learning sets and a theoretical outgrowth, error factor theory. In this research, rhesus monkeys solved hundreds of discrimination problems, for example, selecting which of two different objects hid a food reward over a sequence of six trials. Harlow observed that in the course of the extensive practice on such problems, monkeys progressed from learning the correct item in slow trial-and-error fashion to learning it after only a single trial. Harlow inferred that the animal had acquired a general principle or cognitive strategy—what he called a learning set—and contended that it was the basis for what others had claimed was innate in chimpanzees, namely, insight. From this research came Harlow's error factor theory: discrimination learning is mediated by a single underlying process—the inhibition of all response tendencies that interfere with problem solution (for example, stimulus-perseveration errors).

A second prominent theme of Harlow's science was his emphasis on external physical stimuli as the leading incentives in prompting behavior. Partly this was the result of his work on learning sets, erroneous response tendencies in discrimination problems often being the result of responding to external stimuli. But partly it reflected his disaffection for drive reduction theory, which proposed that activity and learning are spurred by a drive to reduce biological needs. He noted that primates solve and continue to work on mechanical puzzles in the absence of any incentive save that of manipulating the puzzle itself. Unable to see what physiological needs were being satisfied in such situations, Harlow averred that the sole motivation was a curiosity-manipulative drive whose influence in no way depended on prior association with hunger, sex, or another internal drive.

The third, arguably the most original and certainly the best known, of Harlow's scientific contributions concerned the attachment of infant monkeys to their mothers, or what Harlow termed infant love. In breeding monkeys for his research, mother and offspring were separated shortly after birth, and the infants were bottle fed in their individual cages. Intrigued that they persistently picked up and clung to the gauze pads that provided a soft covering for the floor, Harlow then introduced into the cages surrogate mothers having different properties (for example, made of wire mesh, made of wood covered with rubber and then terry cloth, or providing milk from a protruding nipple). The fundamental finding was that the babies bonded far more strongly to surrogate mothers that provided contact comfort than to those that satisfied only nutritional needs. In characteristic prose, Harlow stated:

As pictures of baby monkeys clinging contentedly to soft surrogates . . . unfolded across tabloid pages throughout the world, the downfall of primary drive reduction as the predominant theory to account for the development of social attachment was assured. The cloth mother became the first female to attain fame so quickly while still retaining her virginal virtues. There is more than merely milk to human kindness. ("From Thought to Therapy," p. 539)

From infant love he moved to a fourth notable line of inquiry, the investigation of peer love in monkeys. In Harlow's view, peer interactions were of supreme importance, providing the foundation for affection for associates, the acquisition of social rules, the inhibition of aggression, and the development of sexuality and heterosexual behavior. Preventing such interactions by raising monkeys from birth without access to other monkeys—total social deprivation—produced serious adjustment problems if the period of isolation exceeded ninety days. Twelve months of such treatment created an animal that was incapable of any social interaction whatsoever. This included sexual behavior, of course, but if previously isolated females did become pregnant, they gave birth to babies that they ignored, often abused, and sometimes killed. The picture was not entirely bleak, however. Harlow also found that problems brought about by six months of total social isolation from birth could be reversed by subsequent social interactions between the animal so isolated and a younger, normally raised monkey.

Harlow's importance lay not only in his science. He was one of the most engaging speakers of his day in psychology. His articles were easily digested, and those written for a wider audience were often laced with humor, poetry, and plenty of photographs of monkeys. He was, in short, a persuasive spokesperson for the value of primate research. The primate laboratory at Wisconsin underwent substantial growth under his hand, and he was undoubtedly the reason that a Regional Primate Research Center was established at Wisconsin, an institution that he headed from 1961 to 1971. He was equally influential in the emergence of Wisconsin's psychology department as a major force in American psychology, and he was an effective graduate mentor, supervising some three dozen doctoral students, many of whom went on to successful careers in their own right. Harlow's influence was also felt through his editorship of the *Journal of Comparative and Physiological Psychology* from 1951 to 1963. Finally, he was a cofounder of the small grants program of the National Institute of Mental Health, an initiative that for many years supported numerous young investigators in their first steps along the road of productive scientific research.

Many honors came to Harry Harlow, notably, election to the National Academy of Sciences in 1951 and to the American Academy of Arts and Sciences in 1961, the Distinguished Scientific Contribution Award from the American Psychological Association in 1960, the National Medal of Science in 1967, and the Kittay Scientific Foundation Award in 1975. Most fittingly, perhaps, the University of Wisconsin named its primate laboratory in his honor in 1984. Harlow's scientific legacy is aptly captured by a statement contained in the citation accompanying his Gold Medal Award from the American Psychological Foundation in 1973: "He has enlarged the science of man through artful experimentation with monkey." He died in Tucson, Arizona.

• There is a modest collection of Harlow papers at the University of Wisconsin Archives, Madison. The following articles by Harlow provide useful introductions to important parts of his scientific research: "Learning to Think," *Scientific American* 181, no. 2 (1949): 36–39 (with M. K. Harlow); "The Nature of Love," *American Psychologist* 13 (1958): 673–85; and "From Thought to Therapy: Lessons from a Primate Laboratory," *American Scientist* 59 (1971): 538–49 (with M. K. Harlow and S. J. Suomi). A few biographical memoirs and appreciations of Harlow exist. The most extensive are Joseph B. Sidowski and Donald B. Lindsley, "Harry Frederick Harlow: October 31, 1905–December 6, 1981," in National Academy of Sciences, *Biographical Memoirs* 58 (1989): 218–57, and Stephen J. Suomi and Helen A. LeRoy, "In Memoriam: Harry F. Harlow (1905–1981)," *American Journal of Primatology* 2 (1982): 319–42. Both articles provide a complete list of Harlow's publications.

DARRYL BRUCE

HARLOW, Jean (3 Mar. 1911–7 June 1937), film actress, was born Harlean Harlow Carpenter in Kansas City, Missouri, the daughter of Mont Clair Carpenter, a dentist, and Jean Poe. Harlow attended Miss Barstow's exclusive school for girls in Kansas City from 1916 until her parents' divorce in September 1922. She and her mother subsequently moved to California, where Harlow attended the Hollywood School for Girls. Her mother's failed attempt at acting led to their return to Kansas City in the spring of 1925. Harlow attended a convent school, Notre Dame de Sion, with financial help from her maternal grandfather. Her mother, notorious for controlling Harlow, transferred her to the closer and less strict Miss Bigelow's School for Girls. When her mother moved to Chicago with salesman Marino Bello, she enrolled Harlow in the all-girls Ferry Hall of Lake Forest Academy in Illinois.

In September 1927 Harlow married Chicagoan Charles McGrew II, a business student at Lake Forest Academy boys' school and heir to a family fortune. They moved to Beverly Hills, California, in January 1928, and in the spring the seductive, ash-blond, green-eyed Harlean McGrew II was hired by Fox Studios under the stage name Jean Harlow. Harlow's first bit part was in a silent prison drama called *Honor Bound* (1928), followed by another in *Moran of the Marines* (1928). In December 1928 director Hal Roach signed her for $100 a week to star in his silent short comedies. Her first billing was for *Double Whoopee* (1929), starring Stan Laurel and Oliver Hardy, which included a legendary lingerie scene in which Harlow surprised the crew by wearing a transparent slip without the standard flesh-colored tights beneath.

Harlow was released from her contract on 2 March 1929. She picked up small roles in the melodrama *Masquerade* (1929) and *The Saturday Night Kid* (1929), featuring silent film star Clara Bow, whom she soon replaced as Hollywood's sex symbol. On 11 June 1929 she separated from her husband, and in 1931 they divorced. On 24 October 1929 Harlow signed a five-year contract with Caddo Company. She launched her career in sound movies as the British female lead who seduces airmen James Hall and Ben Lyon in Howard Hughes's World War I aviation film *Hell's Angels* (1930). Though criticized for her acting, she was identified internationally as an "antiheroine" who "sought sex without love and mocked men who equate them" (Stenn, p. 48).

Harlow's career gained momentum with the release of three films in 1931: *The Secret Six*, an underworld drama with Wallace Beery and Clark Gable produced by Metro-Goldwyn-Mayer (MGM); Universal's *The Iron Man*, a boxing film starring Lew Ayres and Robert Armstrong; and Warner Bros.' *The Public Enemy*, a gangster movie with James Cagney. Her performance in *The Public Enemy* instigated a craze for the

bell-bottom pajamas she wore in the film. With her peroxide-blond hair, green eyes, and convincingly unconscious habit of caressing herself, Harlow "was the female equivalent of the bad guys of the 1930s. . . . She was a hard-as-nails, phosphorescent tart who thought like a man and, just like a man, took what she wanted when she wanted it" (Parish and Bowers, p. 313).

Harlow made a short-lived attempt to step out of her brazen sex roles by playing a blond socialite whom the leading man marries in a comedy directed by Frank Capra and originally titled "Gallagher." However, in order to ensure the film's success, Columbia Pictures exploited Harlow's sexpot image and dubbed her the "platinum blonde." The result was a peroxide craze that flared up among the public and reached such actresses as Joan Crawford and Alice Faye. To capitalize on the public's zeal, the studio changed the name of the film to *Platinum Blonde* (1931).

Harlow's rise to stardom was confirmed by MGM's purchase of her contract in April 1932 for $30,000. MGM developed her image from a sexpot to an actress with a natural talent for comedy beginning with *Red-Headed Woman* (written by the author of *Gentlemen Prefer Blondes*, Anita Loos), followed by *Red Dust* (1932) opposite Clark Gable. In July 1932 Harlow married her professional adviser, producer and director Paul Bern, the right-hand man of Irving Thalberg, MGM's production genius. Bern was found dead on 5 September 1932 with a suicide note that hinted at impotence as a reason. The publicity Harlow received only added to the success of *Red Dust*. Harlow was paired with Gable again for Loos's *Hold Your Man* (1933) to exploit their winning combination of innocence and sexuality.

After *Bombshell* (1933), a satire about Hollywood, the Legion of Decency pressured the studio to temper Harlow's roles. Her new image involved dying her hair a soft brown for *The Girl from Missouri* (1934), in which she played a sexy gold digger who will not exchange her virtue for advancement. This image was affirmed with her role in *Wife vs. Secretary* (1936). As the secretary, she warns a wife to reconcile with her husband or risk losing him. Less than two weeks before she made her feet and hand imprints at Grauman's Chinese Theatre, Harlow married cinematographer Harold Rosson on 18 September 1933. They officially separated in May 1934 and divorced in November. Her last public suitor was actor William Powell, with whom she appeared in *Reckless* (1935).

Acclaimed for her brazen sexuality and comic wit on stage, off stage Harlow was childlike, insecure, and grateful to those who helped her. In an effort to broaden her Hollywood image, Harlow with screenwriter Carey Wilson wrote a novel, *Today Is Tonight*, about the triumph of a New York society couple over his blindness and her attraction to another man. The book was not published until 1965, the same year that Paramount released *Harlow*, a critically panned film on Harlow's life starring Carroll Baker as Harlow and Angela Lansbury as her mother. Harlow fell ill before the completion of her final film, *Saratoga* (1937), opposite

Clark Gable. She died of uremic poisoning at the Good Samaritan Hospital in Los Angeles.

• For biographical information see Irving Shulman, *Harlow: An Intimate Biography* (1964), the validity of which has been challenged; Eve Golden, *Platinum Girl: The Life and Legends of Jean Harlow* (1991); and David Stenn, *Bombshell: The Life and Death of Jean Harlow* (1993). See Jean Harlow, as told to Elinor Packer, "The Authentic Story of My Life" *New Movie Magazine*, Aug. through Oct. 1934. A chapter on Harlow appears in James Parish and Ronald L. Bowers, *MGM Stock Company: The Golden Era* (1973). For a survey of legendary female film stars see Theodore Huff, "40 Years of Feminine Glamour," *Films in Review*, Feb. 1953. Obituaries are in the *New York Times, Los Angeles Times, Los Angeles Examiner*, and *Kansas City Star*, all 8 June 1937.

BARBARA L. CICCARELLI

HARLOW, Richard Cresson (19 Oct. 1889–19 Feb. 1962), football coach and naturalist, was born in Philadelphia, Pennsylvania, the son of Louis Francis Harlow and Eugenia Pritchett. As a child he developed a lifelong fascination with birds and hoped to pursue a career in nature studies. After graduating from Episcopal Academy in Philadelphia in 1908, he enrolled at Pennsylvania State College intending to devote himself to scientific studies. When Harlow single-handedly thrashed several sophomores who had broken some birds' eggs he had collected, his classmates convinced the strapping freshman to try out for the football team. Harlow subsequently earned honors as a tackle and played baseball and track; he also won the campus light heavyweight boxing championship. He earned his B.S. in 1912 and his M.S. in zoology in 1913. After graduation he remained at Penn State as assistant football coach, boxing coach, and zoology instructor. Harlow married Lila Naivette "Nippy" Gilpin in 1914, and they had one child.

Harlow became head football coach at Penn State in 1915, leading his teams to 20 wins and eight losses. He joined the U.S. Army in 1917, serving as an infantry lieutenant. He returned to Penn State as an assistant football coach in 1918. From 1922 to 1925 Harlow was head football coach and associate professor of ornithology at Colgate University. His Colgate squads, led by All-America halfback Eddie Tryon, won 26 games, lost nine, and tied three. Following the 1925 season Harlow moved to Western Maryland College as football coach, boxing coach, and athletic director. In nine seasons at the Westminster, Maryland, school, Harlow compiled a record of 60–13–7. He led the Green Terrors to victories over prominent rivals such as Georgetown, Boston College, Temple, and the University of Maryland; undefeated seasons in 1929, 1930, and 1934; and a 27-game unbeaten streak from 1928 to 1931.

On 6 January 1935 Harlow was named head football coach at Harvard University, the first nonalumnus to hold the position. His appointment was welcomed by alumni, who believed Harvard needed an established coach to revive its sagging football fortunes, but met with skepticism by the student newspaper, which noted Harlow's gridiron victories had come at "colleges of somewhat shady character." Harlow's colorful personality, wide-ranging erudition, and manifest ability as a gridiron tactician and teacher soon won over his critics. He was honored by the American Football Coaches Association as college football's coach of the year in 1936. In 1937 Harvard defeated rivals Yale and Princeton to win its first "Big Three" championship since 1915. With the exception of the 1943 and 1944 seasons, during which he served as a lieutenant commander in the U.S. Naval Reserve, he coached the Crimson until ill health and rumors of an incipient players' revolt forced him to resign in January 1948. Harlow's 11-year coaching record at Harvard was 45 wins, 39 losses, and seven ties; his overall coaching record was 151–69–17. He was elected to the National Football Foundation and Hall of Fame in 1954 and the Helms Foundation Hall of Fame in 1956.

Throughout his coaching career Harlow remained active as a naturalist. His collection of rare birds' eggs was considered among the nation's finest, numbering 850 specimens and reportedly valued at more than $40,000. He published numerous articles in ornithology magazines and contributed data on eggs for the Smithsonian Institution's *Life Histories of North American Birds*. In 1939 Harlow was appointed curator of oology at Harvard's Museum of Comparative Zoology.

Harlow was an inventive football coach who built a creative offense based on the double-wing system pioneered by Pop Warner. His teams were noted for "mouse trap" blocking by pulling linemen and for intricate faking and ball-handling by his running backs. He is credited with developing the "shovel pass" play, which featured a quick underhand pass from the tailback to the fullback as he crashed into the line. On defense, Harlow's Harvard teams were constantly in motion, using quickness to overcome a chronic lack of size. He perfected the defensive line play technique known as "stunting" or "looping," which required his players to rush at angles rather than directly confronting their opponents. The prototypical Harlow player was Endicott "Chub" Peabody, a 185-pound guard who was the grandson and namesake of the founder of the Groton School and who later served as governor of Massachusetts. A consensus All-America pick in 1941, Peabody was nicknamed the "Babyface Assassin" because of his jarring tackles.

Harlow always maintained that tactics and strategy were secondary in building a winning football team. His Harvard players "didn't need coaching; it was a matter of psychology," he explained in the *Saturday Evening Post* (12 Oct. 1940). A successful coach, he said, "must become a man of many temperaments" who can relate to his players. He often invited players to his summer home in Pennsylvania, where they found themselves scrambling over mountain ridges in search of birds' eggs or rare ferns.

When Harlow returned from service in World War II, suffering from hypertension and restricted to a diet of rice and fruit juice, he found the psychological tricks that had worked with his prewar teams were lost on the older, more mature players of his 1946 and 1947 teams, many of whom were combat veterans. After a disappointing 4–5 campaign in 1947, several starters told Harvard's athletic director they would quit the team if Harlow returned as coach. He resigned in January 1948 and retired to his homes in Maryland and the Pocono Mountains of Pennsylvania, where he devoted himself to his birds and his gardens of rare ferns, gentians, and rhododendrons. He died in Bethesda, Maryland.

• For an example of Harlow's scientific writing, see "Notes on the Breeding Birds of Pennsylvania and New Jersey," *Auk* 35 (1918). His 1913 M.S. thesis, "The Breeding Birds of Pennsylvania," is in the Pennsylvania State University library. Assessments of Harlow's coaching career can be found in E. C. Huntington, ed., *Fifty Years of Colgate Football* (1940); Morris A. Bealle, *The History of Football at Harvard* (1948); Geoffrey H. Movius, ed., *The Second H Book of Harvard Athletics* (1964); and Joe Bertagna, *Crimson in Triumph* (1986). His Harvard career and teams were also covered in detail by the *Boston Globe* and the *Boston Herald Traveler*. For an account of his years at Western Maryland, see Walter Taylor, "A Rare Bird," in the college's alumni magazine, *Western Maryland College*, Nov. 1990. Harlow discussed his coaching philosophy in "They Didn't Need Coaching: The Coach's Story of Recent Harvard Football," *Saturday Evening Post*, 12 Oct. 1940. An obituary is in the *New York Times*, 20 Feb. 1962.

TIM ASHWELL

HARMAN, Moses (12 Oct. 1830–30 Jan. 1910), freethought and free-love journalist, was born in Pendleton County, Virginia (now West Va.), the son of Job Harman, a hardscrabble farmer and marginal land speculator, and Nancy (maiden name unknown). In pursuit of the main chance, the family relocated four times during Harman's first ten years, and consequently his formal schooling was limited to a scant few months. Through sheer perseverance, he taught himself to read and by his sixteenth year had so mastered the rudiments that he was able to hire himself out as a teacher. At age eighteen, with the assistance of his family, and with money earned by tutoring his classmates, he entered Arcadia College in Iron County, Missouri, graduating in 1851. Just before the Civil War, he spent one semester of study at the St. Louis Normal School.

Licensed to preach by the Methodist Episcopal Church, South, in 1850, Harman spent the decade preceding the Civil War as a circuit rider, schoolteacher, and farmer. Nothing in Harman's early life gave any indication of the direction of his later more illustrious and notorious career, but the Civil War proved to be a decisive turning point in his thought and life. He broke with his church over its support of slavery; he tried to enlist in the Union cavalry and then as a field nurse but was rejected both times on account of his acute lameness, the result of a childhood injury; he became an outspoken abolitionist; and he was repulsed by his firsthand observations of the depredations and atrocities committed by the Confederate guerrillas and

renegades who coursed back and forth across the border territory of Missouri.

Harman was married to Susan Scheuck in 1866; she died of postpartum complications in 1877 during the birth of their third child, who was stillborn. Although Harman's life between 1865 and 1879 was outwardly conventional—he supported his family by farming and teaching in Crawford County, Missouri—the cast of his mind was radically altered during that time by a series of tragic and unusual experiences. His wife's father, Amos, an elderly invalid, had been murdered by a band of ruthless Confederate guerrillas. His marriage had been sealed by a personal, voluntary contract that eschewed any mention of marital duty on either side. Also, by the outbreak of the Civil War, Harman had come under the influence of the Universalists, who denied the doctrine of eternal damnation. The seeds of his later character and thought—an energetic and dogged championship of the weak and powerless; a concern for the right of women to determine whether, with whom, and when they would have sexual intercourse and to control the decision for or against conception; and a rational distrust of theological cant and religious superstition—clearly were sowed in these experiences.

In 1879 Harman moved with his children to Valley Falls, Kansas, where a cousin, Noah Harman, was president of the local chapter of the National Liberal League (precursor of the American Civil Liberties Union). Moses again began to teach school and in 1880 was remarried, to Isabel Hiser; she had one child from a previous marriage. Elected local secretary of the National Liberal League, he became coeditor (with A. J. Searl) of its official organ, the *Valley Falls Liberal*, in 1880. Launched on his journalistic career, Harman became sole editor in 1881 (renaming the paper the *Kansas Liberal*) and in 1883 began to publish a journal called *Lucifer, the Light Bearer* (published between 1907 and 1910 as the *American Journal of Eugenics*).

Under Moses Harman's editorial direction, *Lucifer* emerged as the most influential free-thought, sexology, and eugenics journal of its time. Harman insisted that the periodical belonged to its readers, and he stressed that its columns were open to anyone as a communally written, liberal-reformist platform. Indeed, he allowed complete freedom of expression in its pages and did not censor the language of any communication he published. The overall philosophy of *Lucifer* was stated in its prefatory publication block: "the paper . . . stands for Light against Darkness—for Reason against Superstition—for Science against Tradition—for Investigation and Enlightenment against Credulity and Ignorance—for Liberty against Slavery—for Justice against Privilege." *Lucifer* was issued according to a unique system of dating, counting from the year 1600 (the execution date of the astronomer Giordano Bruno as a heretic) instead of from the time of Jesus. Harman's calendar coincided with the rise of a modern scientific outlook, which he called the "era of man" (abbreviated as E.M.). The date on the first issue, therefore, was E.M. 283.

Lucifer maintained a consistently radical stance on social and sexual matters, but, while Harman sympathized with the socialist position, he had little faith in political solutions and can best be described as an individualist and anarchist in the mold of Josiah Warren, Ezra Heywood, and Benjamin Tucker. Also, although he was strictly monogamous in his personal life, Harman championed sex education for children, universal use of contraception, eugenics, and the sexual liberation of women—in sum, free love, free marriage, free divorce, and free maternity. Indeed, he saw sex reform as a primary weapon against social and economic oppression and political and moral repression. "Just so long," he wrote, "as our present laws and customs in regard to Women's Rights in the Sex-Relation remain in tact [*sic*] just so long will the vast majority of children be born mental and moral imbeciles—fit for nothing else than to be ruled and exploited by the cunning, the capable, the narrowly selfish few" (*Lucifer*, 13 Apr. 1888).

A few years after Harman began publishing *Lucifer*, his sixteen-year-old daughter, Lillian, was joined to Edwin C. Walker (who was already married and the father of two children) in the kind of "autonomistic sex-relation or union" that was advocated by her father. Both partners became the first voluntary martyrs to Harman's brand of sexual liberation and served prison terms for violating a Kansas state statute outlawing cohabitation without benefit of legal marriage. Harman himself ran afoul of the draconian Comstock law enacted in 1873, which outlawed the sending of obscene materials through the mail, and conducted an ongoing legal battle for freedom of speech; consequently he was imprisoned four times (1890, 1892, 1895, and 1906), each conviction for material either written by someone else or reprinted from the more conventional press. The two most egregious cases of censorship involved the publication of the Dr. W. G. Markland letter (*Lucifer*, 18 June 1886), which asked whether sexual abuse by a husband constituted "legal rape," and the Dr. Richard V. O'Neil letter (*Lucifer*, 14 Feb. 1890), which dealt with insatiable sexual demands on wives, sex with animals, forced heterosexual oral sex, and homosexual oral sex. Of these materials, Harman declared, in his own defense, "there is nothing referred to except a free given allusion to human conduct and different members of human anatomy. I do not deem any of these obscene. All the words . . . are in Webster's dictionary" (1890). Harman emerged from Leavenworth federal prison for the last time on 1 March 1906. Although he was physically broken, his spirit was unbowed, and he resumed his journalistic career in Los Angeles, where he died a few years later.

• Most of the letters and papers of Moses Harman remain in the hands of his descendants, but a small collection is in the Labadie Collection of the University of Michigan at Ann Arbor. The bulk of Harman's writing appeared in the pages of *Lucifer, the Light Bearer* and the *American Journal of Eugenics*. Apart from his journalism, his major publications include *The Next Revolution; or, Women's Emancipation from Sex Slavery: Four Pamphlets* (1890–1891), *Love in Freedom* (1900), *Institutional Marriage* (1901), *The Right to Be Born Well* (1905), and *A Free Man's Creed: Discussion of Love in Freedom as Opposed to Institutional Marriage* (1908). Much biographical information was published intermittently in *Lucifer*, and the special memorial issue of the *American Journal of Eugenics: The Moses Harman Memorial* (Jan. 1910), edited by his daughter, Lillian, contains some useful information as well as tributes by noted intellectuals of the day, including Eugene Debs and George Bernard Shaw. Harman claimed to be working on an autobiography in 1900, and there were rumors that Lillian was editing a manuscript in 1910, but no such work was ever published. Modern biographical treatments include a short sketch by William Lemore West in the *Kansas Historical Quarterly* 37 (Spring 1971): 41–63; Hal D. Sears, *The Sex Radicals: Free Love in High Victorian America* (1977), which contains a concise biographical discussion (pp. 28–33) and presents a fine, insightful consideration of Harman's thought and influence (pp. 34–149); and William O. Reichert, *Partisans of Freedom: A Study in American Anarchism* (1976), which emphasizes the individualistic social and political implications of Harman's sexual radicalism (pp. 301–12). An obituary by his son, George, is in the *Valley Falls New Era*, 10 Feb. 1910.

LOUIS J. KERN

HARMAR, Josiah (10 Nov. 1753–20 Aug. 1813), soldier, was born in Philadelphia, Pennsylvania, and orphaned at three months of age. He was reared by a Quaker aunt and educated at a Society of Friends school. In 1775 Harmar obtained a captaincy in the First Pennsylvania Battalion and soon earned a reputation as a competent combat officer. During the American Revolution he participated in many battles, including Brandywine, Monmouth, and Stony Point, and was present at Valley Forge in the winter of 1777–1778. Harmar rose to the brevet rank of colonel and served under Generals George Washington, Anthony Wayne, Nathanael Greene and Colonel Henry Lee (1756–1818).

Harmar was one of the couriers delegated to carry notice of ratification to France after the Peace Treaty of 3 September 1783 was approved by Congress. In 1784, probably because of his close ties as personal secretary to Thomas Mifflin, the president of Congress, Harmar was named lieutenant colonel-commandant of the First United States Regiment. This was the sole regular army organization after the disbanding of the Continental army. Pennsylvania, being allotted the largest quota of troops for this regiment, was permitted to select its commander.

Although a firm disciplinarian, Harmar was strongly influenced by his urbane background. When, following his marriage to Sarah Jenkins of Philadelphia in 1784, he traveled west to assume his duties on the frontier, he brought along such refinements as elegant Windsor furniture.

After several years spent ridding the Ohio lands of illegal squatters and pursuing Indian raiding parties, Harmar was promoted to brevet brigadier general in 1787, and in 1790 he was ordered to lead an offensive against Indian "banditti" located near Miami Town (Kekongia—modern Fort Wayne, Ind.). He set out from Fort Washington (Cincinnati) in late September

1790 with a mixed force of 1,500 regulars and militia, all but about 400 of which were Kentucky and Pennsylvania militiamen.

After occupying Miami Town without significant opposition on 15 October, four days later Harmar sent a detachment to plunder a nearby Eel River village. Carelessly led by a militia colonel, this force was severely mauled by a war party under the Miami chieftain Little Turtle. Having lost more than 100 men, Harmar began his retreat to Fort Washington after razing five Indian villages. Yet on 21 October he made an impromptu decision to send a detachment commanded by Major John P. Wyllys back to Miami Town to punish any returning Indians. This 400-man party blundered into a deadly ambush of Miamis and Shawnees fighting under Little Turtle.

The resulting defeat compelled Harmar to retreat to Fort Washington in haste. Only an eclipse of the moon on the night of 22 October spared his increasingly panicky column from a devastating attack by a war party under Little Turtle and Blue Jacket. Many Indians regarded the eclipse as an evil omen and refused to pursue the white soldiers. When Harmar's column reached Fort Washington on 3 November, it was on the verge of collapse. Harmar was severely criticized by the government, and although cleared by a military court of inquiry, he was replaced by Arthur St. Clair in March 1791. Harmar resigned from the service in 1792 and served six years as adjutant general of Pennsylvania.

Following his resignation from the U.S. Army, Harmar acquired an estate on the west bank of the Schuylkill River where Gray's Ferry crossed. He resided at "The Retreat" until his death.

Despite his considerable military experience during the Revolution, Harmar was poorly suited for command in frontier warfare, where formal mass encounter and textbook methods were ineffective. Although the first commander of the U.S. Army, Harmar is remembered more for his disastrous 1790 campaign, which compelled the reorganization of the army, than for his competence as an officer in the Revolution.

• Many of Josiah Harmar's letters are at the William L. Clements Library, University of Michigan, Ann Arbor. Various correspondence is printed in U.S. Congress, *American State Papers*, Indian Affairs, vol. 1, Military Affairs, vol. 1 (1832–1861); and William H. Smith, ed., *The St. Clair Papers* (1882). See also Ebenezer Denny, *A Military Journal Kept by Major E. Denny, 1781–1795* (1860); Howard H. Peckham, "Josiah Harmar and His Indian Expedition," *Ohio State Archaeological and Historical Quarterly* 50, no. 3 (June-Sept. 1946): 227–41; and John Parker Huber, "General Josiah Harmar's Command: Military Policy in the Old Northwest" (Ph.D. diss., Univ. of Michigan, 1964). Also useful are William H. Guthman, *March to Massacre: A History of the First Seven Years of the U.S. Army, 1784–1791* (1975), and Wiley Sword, *President Washington's Indian War, the Struggle for the Old Northwest, 1790–1795* (1985).

WILEY SWORD

HARMON, Daniel Williams (19 Feb. 1778–23 Apr. 1843), fur trader and diarist, was born in Bennington, Vermont, the son of Daniel Harmon and Lucretia Dewey, innkeepers, whose roots in New England reached back more than a century and a half. Harmon's parents were pious stalwarts of the Congregational church. During the revolutionary war, his father fought with the victorious Americans at the Battle of Bennington. Later, the family moved to Vergennes. What turned Harmon north into British territory is uncertain, but tales of Canadian travelers, parental restrictions, and wanderlust probably helped. In 1799 or early 1800 he journeyed to Montreal and entered the fur trade with the North West Company. Leaving Lachine (Montreal Island) for the West on 29 April 1800, he began a remarkable diary of life in the North American wilderness.

Harmon's journal was no mere business ledger, as were so many journals of the day; rather, it was an intensely personal memoir of his encounters with the elements, the natives, friends, and ultimately his own inner self. The abiding appeal of these encounters derives from their extraordinary nature. The native broths of buffalo dung and cariboo dung must have shocked the "civilized" palate of New Englanders. So too the claim that the seventy souls at Fort Alexandria (near Fort Pelly, Saskatchewan) devoured 450 pounds of meat a day.

Sharp contrasts marked Harmon's account of this untamed world. On the one hand, fishermen heaved from the cold lakes of New Caledonia (British Columbia) ten- or twelve-foot sturgeons, four or five feet around the middle, weighing 400 to 600 pounds. On the other hand, starvation was ever nigh. When it struck in the deep of winter, the grim remedy often enough was cannibalism. According to Harmon's account, one bad winter a native woman ate of no less than fourteen friends and relatives.

Despite several threats on his life, Harmon, nicknamed "Big Knife," lived in relative peace with the natives—until his memorable thrashing of Carrier chief Kwah with a square yardstick. Kwah had exasperated Harmon by insisting on credit for one whom Harmon considered "worthless," but the real issue was whether Kwah could dictate policy to Harmon. The dispute was amicably settled a few days later at a feast of boiled beaver. The penitent chief declared that he was now Big Knife's "wife," for as Harmon treated him, so Kwah treated his four wives. A sensitive observer, Harmon was ever mindful of the plight of native women. Widows among the Carriers became slaves to the relatives of their dead husbands. During the cremation of one Sikani husband, his two surviving wives were nearly consumed with him. In fits of jealousy, males might disfigure their partners so that they would no longer appear beautiful to others. Chastisement with clubs and axes was common. Not surprisingly, many women, but few men, resorted to suicide.

Harmon's judgment of the indigenous cultures was mixed. He lauded the generosity and hospitality of the natives, and he allowed that, in copying the whites' fondness for luxuries and liquor, the Indians hardly improved themselves. But the commonness of murder and its treatment as less than a sin troubled him. He was guided, sometimes racked, by his inner surety of the moral supremacy of his own Christian ethic. Frequently, Harmon despaired. Ever reflective, with recurrent bouts of regret and reformation, he contemplated his "too often dejected spirits," his "polluted heart." He lamented his own heedlessness and carelessness, and he longed for the embrace of his Maker.

When first offered an Indian maiden in marriage, he was sorely tempted, for as he understated, "I had no dislike of her." In the end, his puritan head triumphed, and he accepted the consolations of self-denial. "Thanks be to God," said he, "if I have not been brought into a snare laid no doubt by the Devil himself." More than three years later, he finally accepted a female companion "as it is customary"—a terse remark befitting the accommodations the wilderness usually exacted. Lizette Duval, a woman of mixed blood, became his partner, and their relationship was tender and lasting. Together, they had at least a dozen children, perhaps fourteen. George, born in 1807, was likely Harmon's favorite. At just three and a half years of age, the stripling was sent to an uncle in Vermont to experience the refinements of civilization. He arrived well but shortly grew sick and died. His untimely end devastated Harmon.

Over two decades, Harmon lived in five different trading districts, from Lake Superior almost to the Pacific. He sojourned at Fort Alexandria, South Branch House (near Batoche, Saskatchewan), Fort Dunvegan on the Peace River, Fort St. James on Stuart Lake in present-day British Columbia, and at other camps. In 1810 he crossed the Great Divide to help organize the trade in New Caledonia. Harmon witnessed the struggle for control of the fur traffic between his own Nor'westers and both the XY Company and the Hudson's Bay Company. Blood flowed, but generally the conversation-starved Harmon was more inclined to visit rivals than to vanquish them.

After nearly fourteen years with Lizette, who was later baptized Elizabeth, Harmon prepared to depart the wilderness. Normally this meant leaving a country wife behind. "I consider that I am under a moral obligation," Harmon wrote after much thought, "not to dissolve the connexion, if she is willing to continue it. We have wept together over the early departure of several children, and especially over the death of a beloved son. We have children still living, who are equally dear to us both. How could I spend my days in the civilized world, and leave my beloved children in the wilderness?" The family left intact in summer 1819, and Elizabeth and Daniel were formally wed. That winter they spent in Vermont.

Harmon soon returned to the West, briefly. He retired in summer 1821, a chief trader of the Hudson's Bay Company, which that year absorbed the old North West Company. Always a small cog in the larger fur trade, Harmon is remembered for his long service and, especially, for his diary, one of the era's richest legacies. Later, Daniel and his brother Calvin helped found the town of Coventry in northern Vermont. Six more children were born there, including, in 1838, Abby Maria, who preserved the manuscript of her father's diary. Likely in straitened circumstances, the family migrated again to Canada, but tragedy overtook them. A few months on, in spring 1843, smallpox struck. Harmon succumbed in Sault-au-Recollet, leaving a paltry estate worth less than £100.

• Harmon's original diary is lost, but the manuscript copy of it is at the State University of Iowa in Iowa City, and a photostat is at the National Archives of Canada in Ottawa. It was published as *A Journal of Voyages and Travels in the Interior of North America, between the 47th and 58th Degrees of North Latitude, Extending from Montreal Nearly to the Pacific Ocean, a Distance of About 5,000 Miles, Including an Account of the Principal Occurrences during a Residence of Nineteen Years in Different Parts of the Country* in 1820; the book was reprinted in 1903, 1904, and 1911. These early versions replicated the original heavy editing of the Reverend Daniel Haskel. In 1957 W. Kaye Lamb, dominion archivist of the Public Archives of Canada, prepared a new edition, following the text of Harmon's manuscript copy and adding in brackets important supplements in Haskel's version. Lamb's edition is called *Sixteen Years in the Indian Country: The Journal of Daniel Williams Harmon 1800–1816.* It includes diary entries to 1819 and a full introduction. John Spargo, *Two Bennington-Born Explorers and Makers of Modern Canada* (1950), includes brief but valuable biographies of Daniel Harmon and Simon Fraser. Walter O'Meara's search for Harmon in Vermont appeared in his "Adventures in Local History," *Minnesota History* 31 (Mar. 1950): 1–10. O'Meara then wrote a fictional, historical romance of Daniel and Elizabeth, *The Grand Portage* (1951).

DAVID C. JONES

HARMON, Judson (3 Feb. 1846–22 Feb. 1927), attorney general of the United States and governor of Ohio, was born in Newtown, Ohio, the son of Benjamin Franklin Harmon, a Baptist minister, and Julia Bronson, a former teacher. During the Civil War, Harmon, at age seventeen, joined the Cincinnati Home Guard and briefly participated in the pursuit of John Hunt Morgan's raiders as they cut across southwestern Ohio in July 1863. He was among the 50,000 mourners who filed past Abraham Lincoln's casket at the capitol rotunda in Columbus, Ohio. Harmon worked his way through Denison University, graduating in 1866, and the Cincinnati Law School, graduating in 1869. In 1869 he began to practice law in Cincinnati. In 1870 he married Olivia Scobey; they had three daughters.

Harmon attended the Liberal Republican Convention in 1872 as a delegate for Horace Greeley. Switching to the Democratic party, Harmon was elected judge of the common pleas court in 1876 and of the superior court in 1878. He resigned his judgeship in 1887 and developed a firm specializing in railroad law.

As a leading Ohio Democrat, Harmon became an adviser to President Grover Cleveland on patronage questions. When Attorney General Richard P. Olney became secretary of state, Cleveland appointed Harmon as Olney's replacement in the Justice Department. Serving from June 1895 to March 1897, Harmon prosecuted four important antitrust cases, including *United States v. Trans-Missouri Freight Association* (1897), in which the Supreme Court first applied the Sherman Anti-Trust Act to railroads. That decision became the legal foundation for the more famous Northern Securities case (1904).

After returning to Cincinnati, Harmon served as the receiver for several bankrupt railroads, including the Cincinnati, Hamilton, and Dayton and its subsidiary lines, the Toledo Railway, and the Pere Marquette Railroad, which extended into Canada. In 1905, after being purchased by J. Pierpont Morgan, the Cincinnati, Hamilton, and Dayton consolidation went into bankruptcy. Harmon maintained administrative control of the bankrupt railroads until after he was elected governor. Harmon received national headlines in 1905, when as special counsel investigating an alleged violation of a federal injunction by the Atchison, Topeka & Santa Fe Railroad, he urged that both the corporation and the responsible company officers be indicted for contempt. Overruled by President Theodore Roosevelt, Harmon resigned his position and in his letter of resignation asserted that "Guilt is always personal. So long as officials can hide behind their corporations no remedy can be effective."

In the early twentieth century the Ohio Democratic party was caught up in a struggle between the forces emphasizing social justice and those promoting business efficiency in government. In 1908 Harmon emerged as the gubernatorial candidate of the business wing of the party. Nominated over the opposition of Cleveland's reform mayor, Tom Johnson, Harmon was elected in the face of extensive Republican victories throughout Ohio and the nation. Reelected in 1910 with more than a 100,000-vote margin over Republican Warren Gamaliel Harding, Harmon's coattails helped elect Democratic party majorities in both houses of the legislature.

An advocate of economy, efficiency, and order in government, Harmon viewed his efforts in these areas as his most important achievements as governor. During his two terms, he rooted out corruption in the handling of state funds, instituted new accounting procedures to keep track of revenue and expenditures, centralized the management of the Ohio penal system and the welfare program, and successfully promoted a voluntary, state-run, no fault workmen's compensation program. In 1910 he called out the National Guard during a Columbus, Ohio, streetcar strike. He suspended the mayor of Newark, Ohio, and the Licking County sheriff after a saloon keeper was shot in a temperance riot and the alleged murderer was lynched in the courthouse square.

During Harmon's second administration, the legislature, with Harmon's support, placed a 1 percent ceiling on property taxes and established a tax commission to eliminate discrimination by politically appointed assessors. In 1912, when Ohio convened a constitutional convention to revise the state constitution, Harmon addressed the delegates and strongly criticized proposals to adopt the initiative and referendum and the calls for governmental activism on social issues.

As one who could win in Ohio, Harmon emerged as the choice of old line Democrats for the party's presidential nomination in 1912. He entered several presidential primaries, coming in third behind Champ Clark and Woodrow Wilson. He won in Ohio, but the Ohio delegation at the Baltimore convention split, with Newton D. Baker leading a group of Wilson supporters. William Jennings Bryan referred to Harmon as "the prince of reactionaries," while Wilson remarked, "Harmon hasn't had a new political thought since Cleveland's administration." No Harmon boom developed at the convention, and Wilson's nomination marked the end of Harmon's approach to politics in the Democratic party.

In January 1913 Harmon's term as governor ended. He returned to Cincinnati to practice law and to teach at the law school of the University of Cincinnati. He became an elder statesman in Ohio Democratic party politics. After the Republican victory in the 1924 presidential election, Harmon wrote that the Democratic party "never recovered from the effects of Bryan's three candidacies and I fear that in our time it never will." Harmon died in Cincinnati.

• Harmon's official papers from his tenure as governor of Ohio are at the Ohio Historical Society in Columbus, Ohio. The Cincinnati Historical Society also has a collection of his personal papers relating to his service as governor, his personal life, and his effort to secure the presidential nomination in 1912. RG 60, the general records of the Department of Justice, is located in the National Archives at College Park, Md. Walter P. Griffin, "Judson Harmon" (M.A. thesis, Univ. of Cincinnati, 1965), discusses Harmon as attorney general and governor of Ohio. Hoyt Landon Warner, *Progressivism in Ohio: 1897–1917* (1964), is the most detailed account of Harmon's governorship. An obituary is in the *Cincinnati Enquirer*, 23 Feb. 1927.

JAMES CEBULA

HARMON, Tom (28 Sept. 1919–15 Mar. 1990), football player and sportscaster, was born Thomas Dudley Harmon in Rensselaer, Indiana, the son of Louis A. Harmon, a steel mill policeman, and Rose Marie Guinn. Harmon grew up in Gary, Indiana, where, under the coaching of Doug Kerr at Horace Mann High School, he earned fourteen varsity letters in four sports, started three years for the football team, was the leading national interscholastic football scorer with 150 points in a season, and won state track and field championships. Coach Kerr steered Harmon toward the University of Michigan, where Kerr had played, and where he took the high school's backfield each spring for a clinic.

When Harmon arrived at Michigan in 1937, he could run, pass, and kick with equal skill. He stood 6' and weighed close to 200 pounds. As a single-wing tailback in the explosive Michigan offensive system developed by Fritz Crisler, he became one of the nation's most publicized college players. Sportswriters dubbed him the "Gary Ghost," a reference to Red Grange, the "Galloping Ghost," who had starred at the University of Illinois. Harmon broke all the Western Conference records set by Grange and led the nation in scoring in 1939 and 1940. He was the first college player to win consecutive national scoring titles, and his career scoring mark at Michigan stood for forty-two years.

Harmon was a memorable "big-game" player who produced stunning performances. In his final game against Ohio State, he rushed for 139 yards, completed 11 of 22 passes for 151 yards, ran for two touchdowns, passed for two, kicked four extra points, averaged 50 yards per punt, and on defense intercepted three passes and returned one for a touchdown. In the 1939 game against undefeated Iowa, he scored all 27 points for the Wolverines, including the touchdown return of a 95-yard pass interception.

As a two-way player, Harmon helped bring Michigan back to national prominence, although none of the three teams he played on won a conference championship and were ranked in the Associated Press top ten national rankings only once, placing third in 1940. During his college career he scored 237 points on 33 touchdowns (breaking Grange's record of 31), ran for 2,134 yards in 398 attempts (a 5.4-yard average), and passed for 1,304 yards and 16 touchdowns with 101 completions in 233 passes (a respectable mark for his era). He was an All-America selection in 1939 and 1940, and in his senior year he won the Heisman Trophy, the Maxwell Award, and the Walter Camp trophy and was named Associated Press Athlete of the Year. Fielding H. Yost, Michigan's coach from 1901 through 1925 and athletic director during Harmon's career, called him the best player at the school since Willie Heston, a two-time All-America in 1903 and 1904.

In 1941 Harmon was drafted by the Chicago Bears of the National Football League, but he chose to play for the New York Americans of the rival five-team American Football League, coached by Benny Friedman, an All-America at Michigan in 1925 and 1926. Harmon's play in the 1941 season was limited to one professional game because of an injury. He also worked for radio station WJR in Detroit as a sports announcer, broadcasting Michigan games with Harry Wismer. He starred as himself in a Hollywood film, *Harmon of Michigan* (1941).

In November 1941 Harmon enlisted in the U.S. Army Air Corps and was called to service several months later. He became a P-38 fighter pilot and saw duty in North Africa and in China under General Claire Chennault. He survived a crash of his bomber in South America, and his fighter plane was shot down over China. An autobiographical book, *Pilots Also Pray*, was published in 1944. For his wartime exploits he was awarded a Purple Heart and a Silver Star. On 26 August 1944 he married Elyse Knox, an actress whom he met in Hollywood. They had three children.

Harmon joined the NFL in 1946 and played two seasons with the Los Angeles Rams. His five years away from football and wartime injuries to his legs hindered his performance, but he rushed for 542 yards on 107 carries and caught 15 passes for 288 yards, scoring six touchdowns during two seasons. His no-cut contract of $25,000 a year made him the league's highest-paid player.

Harmon retired as a player after the 1947 season and began his 41-year career as a sportscaster in the Los Angeles area, eventually becoming nationally known in that role. He first worked in television for KTLA in Los Angeles; then from 1949 to 1961 he was sports director for the CBS Pacific Radio Network. In 1961 he joined ABC Radio and hosted a nightly sports program heard nationwide. In 1974 he became sports director of Hughes Television Network. At ease before microphone and camera and knowledgeable about his subject, he communicated his love of the college and professional game.

Harmon retired from sportscasting in 1988. He died in Westwood, California. During his lifetime he was honored by induction into the National Football Foundation Hall of Fame, the College Football Hall of Fame, the Michigan Sports Hall of Fame, and the University of Michigan's Hall of Honor. His number 98 jersey was permanently retired.

• Harmon's papers and personal memorabilia are located at the American Heritage Center of the University of Wyoming. For the Michigan football program of 22 Oct. 1955, Harmon wrote an autobiographical article, "This I Remember." His career at Michigan is documented in Allison Danzig's *The History of American Football: Its Great Teams, Players, and Coaches* (1956), John D. McCallum's *Big Ten Football since 1895* (1976), Will Perry's *The Wolverines: A Story of Michigan Football* (1974), and Kenneth L. Wilson and Jerry Brondfield's *The Big Ten* (1967). Harmon was the subject of numerous magazine pieces, the most notable of which are Ed Fitzgerald, "Tom Harmon of Michigan," *Sport*, Dec. 1956, and Cameron Shipp, "The Truth about Tommy Harmon," *Sport*, Dec. 1946. Harmon is the subject of chapters in Al Hirshberg's *Glory Runners* (1968), Dave Newhouse's *Heismen, After the Glory* (1985), and Robert H. Shoemaker's *Famous Football Players* (1953). Worthwhile obituary articles include those by Thomas Rogers in the *New York Times* and George Puscas in the *Detroit Free Press*, both 17 Mar. 1990.

DOUGLAS A. NOVERR

HARNETT, Cornelius, Jr. (20 Apr. 1723?–28 Apr. 1781), politician and Revolutionary leader, was born in eastern North Carolina, probably in Chowan County, the son of Cornelius Harnett, a merchant, and Elizabeth (maiden name unknown). As a provincial leader of resistance against British policies from 1765 to 1776, Cornelius Harnett, Jr., had few equals. He also did yeoman service for the American cause as a dependable delegate to the Continental Congress. This merchant and distiller of rum has been called the "Pride of the Cape Fear" and the "Samuel Adams of North Carolina."

The Harnett family moved to Brunswick Town on the Cape Fear River during 1726. In 1750 Cornelius, Jr., moved to Wilmington, North Carolina, which remained his home until his death. There he became a justice of the peace, and by 1754 he represented the borough of Wilmington in the North Carolina General Assembly. In 1765 he stepped forward to lead the North Carolina Sons of Liberty in their opposition to the Stamp Act.

During the protests against the Stamp Act, Harnett led a mob of about 600 men to Brunswick Town where they confronted Governor William Tryon and forced public officials there not to issue "stamped paper." Henceforth Harnett was in the forefront of the resistance in North Carolina. Subsequently he served as chairman of the Wilmington Council of Safety, delegate to the second through fifth provincial congresses, and president of the Provincial Council of Safety. Under the new state constitution of 1776, he was elected president of the seven-member Council of State, established to assist the governor in determining policy. As a delegate to the provincial congresses, Harnett served on numerous committees, including the committee that produced the state constitution of 1776. Moreover, he was chairman of the committee that produced the famous Halifax Resolves of 12 April 1776—resolutions authorizing North Carolina's congressional delegates to approve a declaration of independence.

In May 1777 the first General Assembly of the new state elected him to the Continental Congress. As a member of that body for three and a half years, he received appointments to many committees, and he sat on the important Treasury Board. Never vocal in debate or flashy in carrying out his responsibilities, he served with quiet distinction. His most significant contribution as a congressional delegate was the strong support he gave the Articles of Confederation. While Harnett urged North Carolina leaders to approve the articles, Thomas Burke, another North Carolina delegate, called the proposed union "a chymerical Project" and actively sought to postpone ratification until the war was over. Partly because of Harnett's intervention, Burke's obstructionist tactics delayed North Carolina's approval for only a few months.

Harnett left Congress in December 1779, never to return. When the British took Wilmington in 1781, he fell into Tory hands and died while he was a prisoner on parole.

Unfortunately, little is known of Harnett's personal life. He married Mary Holt, and they apparently had no children. They lived at Maynard (later called Hilton), north of Wilmington, and had a second plantation called "Poplar Grove" on Topsail Sound. Mary died in 1792. Harnett was well educated, and he ranked high in the masonic order. Although a deist, he served for many years as a vestryman of St. James Parish in Wilmington. While in Congress he sorely missed his beloved Wilmington and berated life in Philadelphia, but he vowed to endure any hardship for his country. Above all else, Harnett was an American patriot.

• Letters from Harnett are in the Cornelius Harnett Papers at the Southern Historical Collection, University of North Carolina at Chapel Hill, and in the Governors Papers and Secretary of State Papers (Provincial Convention and Congresses, 1774–1776) at the North Carolina State Archives in Raleigh; in Edmund C. Burnett, ed., *Letters of Members of the Continental Congress* (8 vols., 1921–1936); Walter Clark, ed., *The State Records of North Carolina* vols. 11–26 (1895–1914); William L. Saunders, ed., *The Colonial Records of North Carolina* vols. 1–10 (1886–1890); and Paul H. Smith and others, ed., *Letters of Delegates to Congress, 1774–1789,* (16 vols., 1976–1991). See also Donald R. Lennon, "Cornelius Harnett, Jr.," in *Dictionary of North Carolina Biography*, vol. 3 (1988); David T. Morgan and William J. Schmidt, *North Carolinians in the Continental Congress* (1976); and Morgan, "Cornelius Harnett: Revolutionary Leader and Delegate to the Continental Congress," *North Carolina Historical Review* 49 (Summer 1972): 229–41.

DAVID T. MORGAN

HARNETT, William Michael (10 Aug. 1848–29 Oct. 1892), painter, was born in Clonakilty, County Cork, Ireland, the son of William Harnett, a shoemaker, and Honora (Hannah) Holland, a seamstress. Around 1849 the family immigrated to Philadelphia, undoubtedly on account of famine conditions in their homeland. His father's death by drowning in the early 1860s ended Harnett's conventional schooling. He was obliged to help support his mother and four siblings, at first selling newspapers and later working as an errand boy. In 1865 Harnett became an engraver, a profession he pursued for the next ten years. He initially worked with steel, copper, and wood and later became skilled in designing and executing patterns in silver.

Harnett's practice as an engraver provided a steady income, yet he quickly developed higher artistic ambitions. In 1866 he enrolled in classes at the Pennsylvania Academy of the Fine Arts, where he began a standard course of academic training, drawing from casts of antique sculpture.

Harnett continued his studies at the Pennsylvania Academy until 1869, when he relocated to New York. In the early 1870s he worked for the firm of Wood & Hughes, engraving monograms and table patterns. He also held a position at Tiffany & Company. Like many artists, Harnett had a full-time job during the day and pursued artistic training in the evenings. His goal in New York, as he later stated, was "to study in the National Academy of Design, and take advantage of the free art school in the Cooper Institute" (*New York News*, c. 1889–1890). Records indicate that Harnett did enroll at the Cooper Union for the Advancement of Science and Art, where he was a "subscriber" in 1870–1871.

Harnett had a more sustained relationship with the National Academy of Design, studying there between 1872 and 1876 under the tutelage of Lemuel Wilmarth. Two presentation drawings in charcoal dated 1873, *Borghese Warrior* (Museum of American Art at the Pennsylvania Academy of the Fine Arts) and *Venus de Milo* (Yale University Art Gallery), attest to Harnett's mastery of the academic practice of drawing from works of classical antiquity.

Harnett's first tentative efforts in oil date from 1874. He focused on simple items in works such as *Paint*

Tube and Grapes (Chase Manhattan Bank, N.A.) and *Study of a Pipe and Other Objects* (Fine Arts Museums of San Francisco). Each work indicates a developing command of the formal properties of light, shade, and color. Harnett's initial experience with painting fueled his determination to become an artist: "I devoted more than half my day and my evenings to my art studies, only working at my trade enough to supply me with money for clothes, food, shelter, paints and canvas" (*New York News*). In 1875 Harnett began to exhibit his paintings. That spring *Fruit* (unlocated) was displayed at the National Academy of Design, the institution at which he showed his paintings most frequently. That year he "moved wholly into painting." Although he continued to design and produce silver objects as friendship tokens, he never again worked as a professional engraver.

In 1875 Harnett had a brief and unpleasant apprenticeship to the portraitist Thomas Jensen. From then on he was devoted to still-life themes, rarely venturing to complete figural subjects. For the first two years of his career, he most frequently depicted readily available fruit arranged on marble tabletops—for example, *A Wooden Basket of Catawba Grapes* (1876; Charles and Emma Frye Art Museum, Seattle). Gradually Harnett introduced other types of inanimate articles into his compositions, attaining his mature style and subject matter by 1877. He drew on a familiar repertoire of objects—mugs, pipes, inkwells, letters, coinage, books—that were arranged and rearranged in simple, pleasing compositions. The "mug-and-pipe" paintings became his means of livelihood and offered him the security to experiment with more daring themes and formal arrangements. *The Banker's Table* (1877; Metropolitan Museum of Art), with its assemblage of currency and well-worn books, is one such example of a "portrait of things."

The combination of the artist's precise brushwork and his use of everyday items, depicted to scale, produced paintings so illusionistic in effect that Harnett immediately achieved and sustained a stream of patrons, many of whom were upper-middle-class drygoods merchants. Art critics and other painters were less admiring of Harnett's trompe l'oeil (fool-the-eye) efforts. Still-life painting, especially that imitative in nature, held the lowest position in the traditional ranking of artistic subject matter of the time. Nevertheless, Harnett exhibited widely, often in unconventional places, such as department stores, factories, and restaurants. He earned a consistent income from his paintings: their prices rose steadily as his reputation spread and the compositions became more ambitious.

Harnett returned to Philadelphia in 1876, the same year that the great Centennial Exhibition took place there. He contributed a fruit composition to the art display and also observed the vast and impressive array of contemporary foreign paintings. Efforts such as *Mortality and Immortality* (1876; Wichita Art Museum) and *Music and Literature* (1878; Albright-Knox Art Gallery, Buffalo) confirm that Harnett was looking to older European models, particularly Dutch still lifes, for thematic and stylistic inspiration. He established a studio on Locust Street and resumed his association with the Pennsylvania Academy, enrolling in life classes that autumn. Presumably during this time Harnett made the acquaintance of a fellow academy student, John Frederick Peto, who became a close friend and collegial competitor in still-life subjects. In 1879 both artists completed their first rack paintings—vertical arrangements of letters, notes, and calling cards, secured in grids of cloth tape. Harnett's *Artist's Letter Rack* (Metropolitan Museum of Art), the first of his two such efforts, is a compilation of memorabilia pertaining to the Philadelphia hide and wood firm, C. C. Pierson and Sons. This painting and *Still Life with Letter to Thomas B. Clarke* (1879; Addison Gallery of American Art, Phillips Academy, Andover, Mass.) are two of the few compositions that Harnett tailored specifically to patrons, generally preferring not to "paint to order."

With earnings from the sale of his paintings, Harnett "was able to indulge in the one cherished dream of [his] life": to travel and study in Europe. In 1880 he arrived in London, where he set up a studio and remained several months. He then worked exclusively for a wealthy patron in Frankfurt, an arrangement that lasted for six months. Harnett then went to Munich, which, along with Paris, was a locus for art students. His early encounters there were disappointing: in October 1881 he was rejected for admission to the prestigious Munich Academy. Instead, he visited studios and museums, for, as he explained, "I wanted to do such work as the other young artists were doing, and I wanted to follow instructions of older painters. . . . After making repeated trials I became discouraged and went back to my own original way of working." His "original way" proved highly successful. In Munich he enjoyed international patronage and continued to exhibit his paintings widely, including at an international exposition at the Munich Glaspalast in 1883. He also immersed himself in the cultural life of the city and became an artist member of the Kunstverein, participating in the group's weekly shows.

The style and themes of Harnett's paintings underwent a noticeable transition during his years abroad. He experimented with a miniaturistic approach, executing smaller-than-life compositions, some only four by six inches. These paintings suggest the stylistic influence of two well-known European contemporaries, Jean-Louis-Ernest Meissonier and Camilla Friedländer. On the other hand, Harnett also produced large, often cluttered compositions, using as his models old bric-a-brac that he collected avidly. As he explained in the *New York News* interview, "As a rule, new things do not paint well. . . . I want my models to have the mellowing effect of age." *A Study Table* (1882; Munson-Williams-Proctor Institute Museum of Art, Utica, N.Y.) was one of his most imposing paintings to date, depicting treasured books, sheet music, and other collectibles that appeared repeatedly in later works. Harnett's painting style also changed; most noticeable is the darkened palette, a response to Dutch and Flemish Old Masters and modern Germans and Austrians.

The crowning achievement of Harnett's European years, and perhaps of his career, is the masterful series *After the Hunt* (Huntington Library, Art Collections and Botanical Gardens, San Marino, Calif.; Columbus Museum of Art, Ohio; Butler Institute of American Art, Youngstown, Ohio; and Fine Arts Museums of San Francisco). Completed between 1883 and 1885, the four paintings depict arrangements of hunting gear and dead game suspended on wooden doors. The last and most complex of the group, the San Francisco version, assured Harnett's contemporary fame. After it triumphed in the Paris Salon of 1885, the painting was purchased by the New York restaurateur Theodore Stewart, who installed it in his Warren Street establishment. Viewers flocked to the canvas, many suspending belief that the illusionistic objects were only painted. Popular response to the painting became legendary among journalists and the subject of scorn among highbrow art critics.

Harnett was in Paris and London during 1885 but returned to the United States the following year. He settled in New York and further developed the theme of the single, everyday object hanging against a wooden backdrop; compositions depict dead game, horseshoes, pipes, and currency. His most celebrated effort in this genre is *The Old Violin* (1886; National Gallery of Art, Washington, D.C.). This painting was exhibited in midwestern industrial expositions in Minneapolis and Cincinnati, where it won the admiration of crowds who were "uncertain as to how much is painting and how much reality." *The Old Violin* was the basis for chromolithographs (1887) by the F. Tuchfarber Company of Cincinnati, the only Harnett composition to be translated into the print medium.

The Old Violin is one of several ambitious compositions of the late 1880s that have music as a central theme. Harnett was an amateur musician who played the flute, and his love for melody was frequently expressed in paint. A well-worn flute and violin make repeated appearances, from tabletop arrangements such as *Ease* (1887; Amon Carter Museum) to vertical paintings, including *Still Life—Violin and Music* (1888; Metropolitan Museum of Art). Sheet music, almost always legible, ranges in theme from tragic operas to Irish tunes.

As Harnett reached the crest of his career, his health began to fail, and his output declined. Between 1889 and his death he completed only ten paintings. Harnett had rheumatism, debilitating to an artist whose style relied on tightly rendered brushwork.

While Harnett's production faltered, the technical quality of his late work showed no sign of his illness. Several late works have been read as autobiographical statements acknowledging his waning powers and suggest that the artist indeed viewed his paintings as more than just satisfying artistic arrangements. Regardless of symbolic or personal content, *The Old Cupboard Door* (1889; City Art Galleries, Sheffield, England) and his final effort, *Old Models* (1892; Museum of Fine Arts, Boston), reveal Harnett at the height of his ability, for which he assembled his favorite models on wooden doors and narrow ledges in the foreground.

In 1888 and 1889 Harnett sought relief—to no avail—for his rheumatism in hospitals and at well-known spas, in the summer of 1889 abroad at Carlsbad, and in the fall of 1892 at Hot Springs, Arkansas. His condition worsened, and he died in New York City, ultimately of kidney failure. He had never married or had children. Although his career lasted just seventeen years, Harnett popularized the use of inanimate objects as still-life models and worked in an illusionistic style that inspired his reputation as the leading exemplar of the American school of trompe l'oeil painting.

• Harnett's only published interview, "Painted Like Real Things: The Man Whose Pictures Are a Wonder and a Puzzle," is in an article from an undated issue of *New York News*, probably 1889 or 1890. It is partially reprinted in the first modern scholarly treatment of the artist, Alfred Frankenstein, *After the Hunt: William Harnett and Other American Still Life Painters* (1953; rev. ed., 1969). Frankenstein's papers at the Archives of American Art, Smithsonian Institution, Washington, D.C., contain the results of invaluable and indefatigable research on Harnett, including extensive correspondence and photo files. The Downtown Gallery Papers, Archives of American Art, are also a critical source of archival information on the revitalization of Harnett's reputation during the mid-twentieth century. William H. Gerdts, *Painters of the Humble Truth: Masterpieces of American Still Life, 1801–1939* (1981), places Harnett in the context of late nineteenth-century still-life painting and traces his role in the emergence of an American trompe l'oeil school of artists. The most authoritative assessment of Harnett is Doreen Bolger et al., *William M. Harnett* (1992), containing twenty-two scholarly essays, a chronology, an exhibition listing, and an extensive bibliography.

THAYER TOLLES

HARNEY, Benjamin Robertson (6 Mar. 1871–1 Mar. 1938), pioneer ragtime pianist, vocalist, and composer, was born in or near Louisville, Kentucky, the son of Benjamin Mills, a captain in the Civil War, and Margaret Draffen. Both parents were from distinguished Kentucky families. The 1880 census lists as living at the home of John Draffen near Frankfort, Kentucky, Margaret, age forty-two (divorced), and Draffen's grandson, Ben Harney, age nine. Harney's whereabouts and activities for the next nine years remain obscure. That he spent some of those years in Louisville is indicated by a statement by his Louisville publisher, who wrote that Harney was "raised on Madison Street here in Louisville in a neighborhood of good families."

On 1 July 1890, Harney enlisted in a unit of the Kentucky State Guard that was stationed in the coal and iron boom town of Middlesborough (now Middlesboro), Kentucky. (The town, then still under construction, received its name in 1890.) Years later Harney would be described in the local paper as being one of the town's "original boomers." He worked by day at the post office, but since only six years later he achieved success and fame in New York City playing and singing a black-styled music, he must have spent his nights at the local saloons listening to black singers and instrumentalists, as well as singing and playing himself. Of Middlesborough's population of about 5,000, more than 1,000 were black.

In December 1890 Harney's father joined him in Middlesborough to work as a civil engineer. Then, in June, Harney and his wife were mentioned in the local paper as attending an outing with a group of young people. Though not named, it may be presumed that his wife was Jessie Boyce. Nothing is known of her early life (no records of her birth or marriage to Harney have been found), but within a few years she was singing and dancing with Harney in minstrel shows, and some years later she began to perform, both with Harney and independently, using the name Jessie J. Haynes.

In May 1891 Harney was arrested and fined for fighting on Main Street in Middlesborough. In July he participated with eleven other citizens, including the chief of police and the jailer, in the lynching of a white man. On 27 August the State Guard went off to summer camp near Frankfort, but on the same day Harney was indicted for the lynching, put under guard, and later returned to Middlesborough. The trial, set for early 1892, was postponed; in the summer the charges were dropped because of a lack of evidence. Meanwhile, the town's economic boom had ended. British capital, which had subsidized the construction of Middlesborough, had dried up in late 1890. The U.S. stock market crash of 1893 was the final straw, and the town's four banks closed their doors. By June, when Harney, Jessie, and his father had returned to Louisville, he had already been mustered out of the guard.

Harney found work for a time performing at a saloon and dancehall on the southwest corner of Eighth and Liberty (then Green) streets. His ragtime song "You've Been a Good Old Wagon . . ." was published in Louisville in 1895. To this song was appended a syncopated, 56-measure piano solo entitled "Dance." The term *ragtime* had not yet come into use, but if E. A. Phelps's "Darkies' Patrol" (1892) is to be considered the first piano rag, as has been suggested by Edward A. Berlin, then Harney's selection appears to be the second.

By 1895 Harney and his wife were performing in traveling minstrel shows, and he had written another ragtime song, "Mr. Johnson Turn Me Loose," which was plagiarized and published in 1896 in Evansville, Indiana. Harney filed suit, won, and then sold the copyright to M. Witmark and Sons of New York, who republished it and "You've Been a Good Old Wagon . . ." the same year. On the strength of the songs' popularity, Harney appeared in February 1896 at Keith's Union Square Theater in New York City, where he was an overnight sensation.

For the next twenty-six years Harney continued to tour and perform. His ragtime playing was later compared to the piano style of Thomas "Fats" Waller. That he probably received formal piano instruction in his pre-Middlesborough days is suggested by his facility at the piano and the fact that he was the first pianist to "rag the classics." *Ben Harney's Ragtime Instructor*, published in 1897 by Sol Bloom of Chicago, attempted to teach the musical student how to play any tune in ragtime; also, though Harney composed no piano pieces per se, he did write more than a score of successful songs. He made three world tours. A heart attack suffered in 1923 ended his career, and as jazz replaced ragtime Harney was soon forgotten. By 1930 he was living with his wife in poverty in a black section of Philadelphia, where he died. Jessie Harney died by her own hand a few years later.

Harney's popularity as a pioneering ragtime pianist and composer of ragtime songs opened a commercial market that made it easier for later ragtime composers, such as Scott Joplin, to be published and ragtime pianists, such as Mike Bernard, to achieve success. Although Harney's popularity declined after 1900, his place in the history of American popular music as the first composer of ragtime songs and the first commercially successful performer of piano ragtime is assured.

• For copies of various news clippings, together with letters, including those of Ann Brown Metheny of Middlesborough, who discovered the Harney-Middlesborough connection, see the Harney file in the library of the Kentucky Historical Society in Frankfort. Harney's death certificate is on record at the Pennsylvania Department of Health in Philadelphia. For a discussion of Harney's place in ragtime, see Rudi Blesh and Harriet Janis, *They All Played Ragtime*, 4th ed. (1971), and Edward A. Berlin, *Ragtime: A Musical and Cultural History* (1980). Other sources are William H. Tallmadge, "Ben Harney: White? Black? Mulatto?" *Sonneck Society Newsletter* (Fall 1979), and the obituary in *Variety*, 9 Mar. 1938.

WILLIAM H. TALLMADGE

HARNEY, William Selby (22 Aug. 1800–9 May 1889), soldier, was born in Haysborough, Tennessee, the son of Thomas Harney, a merchant and surveyor, and Margaret Hudson. Harney was first home educated and later received advanced schooling at Cumberland College. He began his U.S. Army career in 1818 when he was commissioned second lieutenant. Harney was an ambitious, daring, and impulsive officer, traits that would both help and hinder his military career.

Because Harney served his country during an era of rapid expansion, it was inevitable that most of his military assignments were on the frontier. In 1825 he accompanied General Henry Atkinson and Indian agent Benjamin O'Fallon to the upper Missouri River on an expedition with the objective of signing treaties and increasing American influence among the tribal nations. He fought in the battle of Bad Axe against Black Hawk in 1832 and defended American action by claiming that the Sauk and Fox tribes had broken the treaty and had to be punished. In 1833 he married Mary Mullanphy; they had three children.

The Second Seminole War brought Harney to Florida in 1837. To fight the war, Congress created the Second Dragoons. Harney, a Tennessee Democrat, sought a position in the new unit and appealed to President Andrew Jackson, who made him the second ranking officer. As a dragoon, he was bold and daring, and he left the Florida war with a reputation as an Indian fighter and with honors for gallant and meritorious service.

In June 1846, as the nation moved toward war with Mexico, Harney became colonel and commander of the Second Dragoons. When hostilities began, the headstrong commander conducted an unauthorized expedition into Mexico from Texas, and General Winfield Scott ordered Harney to surrender most of his command to a subordinate. Harney subsequently defied Scott by retaking command. Scott then ordered a court-martial, which convicted Harney of disobedience and ordered him to apologize to Scott. After the trial, however, Harney retaliated by using political channels to obtain a reprimand against Scott from Secretary of War W. L. Marcy.

Harney served with distinction during the march to Mexico City. He captured Cerro Gordo, a hill overlooking the road to Mexico City, and turned Mexican guns on the retreating enemy. During the siege of Mexico City, he busied himself by guarding prisoners and hanging American deserters.

Harney spent the next decade in the American West. He studied plains tribes while on inspection duty in Texas, then commanded the Sioux expedition of 1855 to punish the Upper Brulé for ongoing depredations against Americans. In September 1855, at the battle of Blue Water, Nebraska, his troops routed Little Wound's Brulé village, enhancing Harney's reputation as an Indian fighter. From western Nebraska he marched overland to Fort Pierre, trying to draw the Lakota into battle. Based on his Great Plains experiences, Harney recommended mobile mounted units instead of permanent posts. He also wanted the Department of the Interior to return American Indian affairs to the army, as the former could not control hostilities.

Harney was promoted to brigadier general in 1858 and assumed command of the Department of Oregon. He created an international incident when he ordered troops onto San Juan Island "for the better protection" of American citizens from both Indian and British forces. Without authorization, this anti-British expansionist move recklessly violated the joint occupation agreement and pushed American and British forces to the brink of war. To prevent further embarrassment, his superiors removed Harney from Oregon.

Harney assumed command of the Department of the West in May 1861 and returned to St. Louis, where secessionists and Unionists were fighting for Missouri. Harney, a border state Unionist, capitulated to General Sterling Price's states' rights tactic whereby Harney agreed to not attack state forces if they did not attack Federal forces. Harney was removed from command for making this agreement and never received another command because of his southern sympathies. This was the low point in his career. He retired in 1863 and in 1865 was breveted major general.

After the war, President Andrew Johnson appointed Harney to the 1865 peace commission to the southern plains tribes, and two years later he became a member of the Peace Commission of 1867. Emerging as a statesman negotiating peace between the United States and plains tribes, Harney's last official act was to establish in 1868 three agencies for the western Sioux on the Missouri River; these agencies, which served as supply posts and symbols of American control, inaugurated the reservation era for these tribes.

Harney was estranged from his wife when she moved to France in 1853 to seek medical care for their son, but military life, Harney's temper, and his fiscal irresponsibility also contributed to the rift. Mary died in 1860. Harney spent the last twenty years of his life in retirement living in Missouri, Mississippi, and Florida. In 1884 he married Mary St. Cyr. He died in Orlando, Florida.

Because of his strong will and boldness, Harney was an effective officer under combat situations. As a result, he emerged as one of the nation's finest Indian fighters. On the other hand, these same qualities led Harney into some embarrassing situations, such as the San Juan affair and the Missouri crisis, in which tact and diplomacy should have been used. His shortcomings notwithstanding, Harney's career exemplified the antebellum politics that characterized the army officer corps.

• Letters from Harney are found in several manuscript collections and depositories. The National Archives contains most of the material relating to Harney in his official capacity as an American soldier. Records of the Adjutant General's Office, 1783–1917, Record Group 94, hold correspondence by and pertaining to Harney. Records of the U.S. Army Continental Commands, 1821–1920, Record Group 393, contain official correspondence from Harney's western campaigns and commands. The best biography is George Rollie Adams, "General William Selby Harney: Frontier Soldier, 1880–1898" (Ph.D. diss., Univ. of Arizona, 1983); for a short discussion of his career, see Richmond L. Clow, "William S. Harney," in *Soldiers West: Biographies from the Military Frontier*, ed. Paul Hutton (1987). For a discussion of Harney as commander, see Clow, "General William Harney on the Northern Plains," *South Dakota History* 16, no. 3 (1986): 229–48; and William Hill Lecheminant, "A Crisis Averted? General Harney and the Change of the Utah Expedition," *Utah Historical Quarterly* 51, no. 1 (1983): 30–45. An obituary is in the *New York Times*, 10 May 1889.

RICHMOND L. CLOW

HARNWELL, Gaylord Probasco (29 Sept. 1903–17 Apr. 1982), physicist and university president, was born in Evanston, Illinois, the son of Frederick William Harnwell, a lawyer, and Anna Jane Wilcox, a playwright. The family later moved to Frederick, Maryland, where Harnwell attended public schools. At his parents' urging, he then attended Haverford College, where he received a B.S. in physics in 1924. Receiving a Cope Fellowship from Haverford, he studied for a year with the distinguished physicist Ernest Rutherford at the Cavendish Laboratory in Cambridge, England, where the scientists were carrying out early studies of bombarding elements with alpha particles into disintegration. Harnwell entered Princeton University in 1925 for graduate work. There he developed a series of instruments for use in gaseous electronics and received an M.A. in 1926 and a Ph.D. in physics in 1927. Also in 1927 he married Mary Louise Rowland; they had four children, one of whom died in childhood.

On a fellowship from the National Research Council, Harnwell conducted research at the California Institute of Technology in 1927–1928 and continued it the next year at Princeton University. In 1929 he became assistant professor of physics at Princeton and in 1936 advanced to associate professor. With John J. Livingood he wrote *Experimental Atomic Physics* (1933). His textbook *Principles of Electricity and Electromagnetism* (1938) was widely used in upper-level physics curricula.

In 1938 Harnwell became professor of physics at the University of Pennsylvania and simultaneously chair of its physics department and director of its Randal Morgan Laboratory of Physics. From 1941 to 1953 he was editor of *Review of Scientific Instruments*, published by the American Institute of Physics.

On leave of absence from the University of Pennsylvania from 1942 to 1946, Harnwell was director of the University of California Division of War Research at the U.S. Navy Radio and Sound Laboratory in San Diego, California, whose wartime mission was to find means of detecting submarines. Concentrating primarily on underwater sound, the researchers carried out major scientific advances in sonar and related equipment. At the conclusion of the work in 1946 Harnwell wrote, "There have been physicists, engineers, psychologists, artists, writers, draftsmen, illustrators, and many other technically trained personnel, as well as people with little or no previous technical training. In some instances housewives and high school students joined to help us in our phase of the war effort. . . . We have frequently been gratified by very welcome acknowledgments from the Navy of the value of our work" (final report of University of California Division of War Research, 1946). Harnwell was awarded a Medal of Merit in 1947 by the navy for his contributions.

On his return to the University of Pennsylvania, Harnwell increased the number of faculty and improved the facilities of the physics department. Under his direction, the physics laboratory obtained a two million-electron-volt atom-smashing betatron in 1948, and he led the effort to obtain a new building for physics, mathematics, and astronomy. His own researches were on collisions of the second kind in rare gases, in mass spectroscopy, and in nuclear physics. In addition to his appointment in physics, he was professor of radiological physics in the graduate school of medicine. He served as editorial director of *Physics Today* from 1951 to 1953.

In 1953 Harnwell was appointed president of the University of Pennsylvania, a position he held until his retirement in 1970. Under his leadership the faculty and the teaching facilities of the University of Pennsylvania increased greatly. He emphasized graduate programs, vastly enlarged the research activities, and encouraged education for women. In spite of his former involvement with wartime research, Harnwell ended the university's involvement with classified research during the late 1960s, when college students at many locations were objecting to the role of the United States in Vietnam. At that time he arranged meetings of the university trustees with students and faculty to air differences. He concerned himself with the relationship of the university to its surrounding community, and he participated in resolving civic and labor problems in Philadelphia. Colleagues noted that as president he "was good at delegating responsibility, yet never delegated the power of ultimate decision. . . . He made decisions with alacrity and moved on to the next problem" (Mann et al., p. 94). His biographer Jonathan E. Rhoads described him as "relaxed and efficient, gracious yet driving, conservative yet enterprising . . . with a very genuine sense of humor" (p. 407).

Harnwell continued to teach an undergraduate course in physics throughout his tenure at the University of Pennsylvania. With William E. Stephens he published *Atomic Physics* in 1955, and with George Legge he published *Physics: Matter, Energy and the Universe* in 1967. Both of these textbooks were widely adopted.

Harnwell's service on a number of committees for the federal government included chairmanships of the Ordnance Committee of the Research and Development Board of the Department of Defense (1951–1953) and of the Committee on Undersea Warfare of the National Research Council (1950–1955), on which he continued as a member for some years.

From 1958 to 1960 Harnwell was a member of the executive committee of the American Council on Education. He was the first chair of the Council of Presidents of Universities Research Association in 1965 and 1966, and he was chair of the board of trustees of the Carnegie Foundation for the Advancement of Teaching in 1968 and 1969. He received the Navy Distinguished Public Service Award in 1958, and he was awarded more than thirty honorary doctorates. He served on the board of several companies, including that of the Pennsylvania Railroad Company and its successors for many years.

Harnwell toured universities in the Soviet Union in 1958 and summarized his trip in *Russian Diary* (1960). He advised the shah of Iran on establishing a university in Shiraz along the lines of ones in the United States. This resulted in the founding of Pahlavi University. Following his trip, he wrote *Education Voyaging in Iran* (1962). Harnwell died in Haverford, Pennsylvania.

• Harnwell's archival records are at the University of Pennsylvania. A biographical sketch by Jonathan E. Rhoads is in American Philosophical Society, *Yearbook* (1983), pp. 403–7. Obituaries are in the *New York Times*, 19 Apr. 1982, and by Alfred K. Mann et al. in *Physics Today* 35 (1982): 92 and 94.

ELIZABETH NOBLE SHOR

HARPER, Fletcher (31 Jan. 1806–29 May 1877), publisher, was born in Newtown, Long Island, New York, the son of Joseph Harper and Elizabeth Kolyer. Joseph Harper, born in England, was a farmer, carpenter, and storekeeper; his wife was a Dutch burgher's daughter. His parents, who were wise and loving, pious and strict, taught him and his three brothers, James, John, and (Joseph) Wesley, the values of hard work, careful study, honesty, sobriety, and family loyalty. Circuit Methodist preachers, who often stayed overnight at the Harper home, also strongly influenced the brothers.

When Fletcher was ten years old, his parents rented their farm and moved to New York City to supervise their energetic sons. By this time, Fletcher's brother James had served an apprenticeship to a printer and was a journeyman printer, John was a printer's apprentice, and Wesley was a printer's devil. Fletcher went to a school on Roosevelt Street, where he was taught by Alexander T. Stewart, later the city's leading dry-goods merchant. In 1817 James and John formed their own printing firm, called J. and J. Harper, Printers, and that summer hired Fletcher as their copy boy. In 1823 Wesley became a partner in the firm. After serving an apprenticeship, Fletcher was made a partner in 1825. That same year he married Jane Freelove Lyon, who was then seventeen years old and with whom he eventually had two children.

In 1825 the honest, ambitious, hard-working brothers decided to become publishers instead of merely printers. Recognizing their different talents, they divided their responsibilities: James became pressroom supervisor; John, purchasing and production manager and bookkeeper; Wesley, proofreader and company correspondent; and Fletcher, chief editor and general executive officer. Not until 1833 was the company name changed to Harper & Brothers. Until about 1859 each of the four brothers, by then all husbands and fathers, took whatever sums of money from the profits of the firm he needed for personal expenses.

It seemed evident to friends, authors, business associates, and rivals that Fletcher was the most able brother. He was an energetic administrator and a fine judge of literary merit, and he was persuasive and witty. In 1828 he contracted with Edward Bulwer-Lytton to publish the American edition of his novel *Pelham* and soon followed this pioneering success by being the first in America to publish many works by Charles Dickens, George Eliot, William Makepeace Thackeray, and other British authors—often pirated, in the absence of any international copyright law (until 1891). However, the Harpers often bought proof sheets from British authors, published from them, and thus outsmarted rival American "pirates." By the time John Harper died in 1875, he as financial officer had paid British authors nearly $250,000 for proof sheets. At this time, British authors published by the Harpers also included all three Brontë sisters, Thomas Carlyle, Wilkie Collins, Charles Darwin, Thomas Hardy, Thomas Babington Macaulay, Anthony Trollope, and Queen Victoria. American authors published by the Harpers included William Cullen Bryant, Washington Irving, Henry Wadsworth Longfellow, William Gilmore Simms, and John L. Stephens.

Fletcher was astute. He had much to do with the decision to issue several series. The most successful were Harper's Family Library, their most famous nonfiction series, which started in 1830 with six books and grew to 187 titles by 1845; the Harper's Library of Select Novels, from 1830 to 1834 growing to thirty-six volumes before being discontinued; the Boys' and Girls' Library, growing from 1831 to twenty-two works and ending in 1840; and Harper's Classical Library, which started in 1831, included thirty-seven titles, and was discontinued in 1847. When Fletcher learned in 1839 that every large school district in New York state would be required by law to have a library, he went to the state superintendent of schools in Albany, obtained a contract to publish the District School Library, and from 1841 to 1846 supplied thousands of the 295-volume sets throughout the state. A less admirable professional arrangement was Fletcher's paying Richard Henry Dana, Jr., $250 for rights to *Two Years before the Mast*, publishing it in 1840, and making $50,000 on it.

When James Harper established *Harper's New Monthly Magazine* in 1850, Fletcher was its managing editor; Fletcher later suggested *Harper's Weekly* (1857) and regularly selected the contents of both journals. He made the *Weekly* an internationally respected family newspaper. He helped draw up partnership papers for the four brothers in 1860. Coverage in the *Weekly* of the Civil War was unparalleled in quality. Fletcher hired the artist Winslow Homer to provide front-line illustrations. The firm also published books about the war, including the multivolume *Harper's Pictorial History of the Great Rebellion* (1862–1868) and *Battle Pieces and Aspects of the War* (1866) by Herman Melville, one of their most controversial authors ever since Fletcher had accepted *Omoo* sight unseen in 1846. Fletcher established *Harper's Bazar* (1867) and habitually selected its contents. Two of his most competent associates and closest friends were author George William Curtis (a writer for the *Monthly Magazine* from 1853) and cartoonist Thomas Nast (who joined Harper & Brothers in 1862 as an illustrator). Curtis wrote *Weekly* reformist editorials beginning in 1863. Nast's political cartoons, beginning in 1869, helped destroy the infamous Tweed ring. William Marcy Tweed, the ringleader, threatened in 1871 to cancel the schoolbook contract that the Harpers enjoyed, but Fletcher defied him, *Weekly* circulation doubled, and Tweed was soon indicted, convicted, and ruined.

Fletcher Harper became head of the firm when James Harper died in 1869. After Fletcher's death in New York City, five Harper sons managed the firm. Eventually Fletcher's favorite grandson, J. Henry Harper, headed it. The firm encountered financial difficulties in the late 1890s, reorganized, downsized in the 1920s, did well in the 1930s and 1940s, and began a series of mergers in 1962.

• Harper's relatively few personal papers are scattered, with several being in the Butler Library at Columbia University. John Tebbel, *A History of Book Publishing in the United States* (4 vols., 1972–1981), and Lewis A. Coser et al., *Books: The Culture and Commerce of Publishing* (1982), place the firm in historical perspective. Eugene Exman, *The Brothers Harper: A Unique Publishing Partnership and Its Impact upon the Cultural Life of America from 1817 to 1853* (1965), is the definitive biography of the Harper brothers. Exman, *The House of Harper: One Hundred and Fifty Years of Publishing* (1967), is the standard history of the publishing firm. Exman's two books rely on but supersede *The House of Harper* (1912) and *I Remember* (1934) by J. Henry Harper, Fletcher Harper's grandson. Albert Bigelow Paine, *Th. Nast: His Period and His Pictures* (1904), includes comments on Harper's friendship with Thomas Nast. Frank Luther Mott, *A History of American Magazines, 1850–1865* (1957), pp. 383–405, 469–87, devotes separate chapters to the establishment and development of *Harper's New Monthly Magazine* and *Harper's Weekly*. Allan Nevins, *The Price of Survival* (1967), praises "the House of Harper" for 150 years of publishing excellence. A laudatory obituary of Fletcher Harper was published by the *New York Times*, 30 May 1877.

ROBERT L. GALE

HARPER, Frances Ellen Watkins (1825–20 Feb. 1911), political activist and author, was born in Baltimore, Maryland, the only child of free parents. She was orphaned at an early age and raised by an aunt. She attended a school for free blacks, which was run by her uncle, the Reverend William Watkins. Her formal education ended at age thirteen. Harper became a nursemaid and found additional employment as a seamstress, needlecraft teacher, and traveling abolitionist lecturer. She also lectured in support of woman suffrage. She later became a schoolteacher in Ohio and Pennsylvania.

In 1860 she married Fenton Harper; they had one child, who died in 1909. After her husband's death in 1864, she returned to the lecture circuit, promoting black education and Sunday school teaching. She also served as superintendent of colored work in the Women's Christian Temperance Union and often made speeches on its behalf, pointing out the evils of strong drink and the need for higher standards of morality. Continuing her feminist pursuits after the abolition of slavery, Harper spoke at the Women's Rights convention in 1866 and the Equal Rights Association in 1869. Although she more strongly advocated black male suffrage at that time, she continued to stress the need for women's right to vote. She was a founder of the National Association of Colored Women in the 1890s and served as a vice president until her death.

Harper is best known for her ten volumes of poetry and her novels. Her first book of poetry, *Poems of Miscellaneous Subjects*, was published in 1854. It sold 10,000 copies in five years, was reprinted frequently, and was her biggest commercial success. Her novel, *Iola Leroy; or, Shadows Uplifted* (1892), is considered the first book on the subject of Reconstruction written by an African American. She was the first black woman to publish a short story, "The Two Offers," which appeared in the *Anglo-African* in 1859. Her other works include *Moses: A Story of the Nile* (1869) and *Sketches of Southern Life* (1872). She was also a frequent contributor to *Godey's Lady's Book* and other periodicals.

Harper's poetry and prose were political. Her works tackled the issue of slavery and the cruelty endured by slave women. The final two lines of one of her more popular poems, "Bury Me in a Free Land," poignantly expresses the desire of slaves: "All that my yearning spirit craves / Is bury me not in a land of slaves." The "Slave Auction" addressed the issue of children being sold away from their mothers:

> And mothers stood with streaming eyes
> And saw their dear children sold
> Unheeded rise their bitter cries,
> While tyrants bartered them for gold.

Feminism was often the theme of Harper's works. The poem "Deliverance" (from *Sketches of a Southern Life*) is concerned with the response of women to men who abused the privilege of voting:

> Day after day did Milly Green
> Just follow after Joe
> And told him if he voted wrong
> To take his rags and go.

In the poem "A Double Standard," Harper condemns the gender gap: "And what is wrong in woman's life / In man's cannot be right." Harper's feminist themes are also present in her short stories and novels. Her short story, "The Two Offers," examines the role of women in society, exploring sentimental notions of love and marriage and the use of the term "old maid." She notes that men who never marry have no term designating their status. The story takes issue with many Victorian views and attitudes. Harper's novel *Iola Leroy* is a political and socially conscious work. It is the story of a young octoroon woman who escapes slavery and locates the family from whom she had been separated. She refuses to pass as white and asserts her independence by declaring that she was "going to join the great rank of bread-winners." She focuses her energy on uplifting the race. Thus, in this novel, Harper again emphasizes her themes of feminism and civil rights.

Harper's skills as an elocutionist helped promote the sale of her books. Critics, however, have said her work lacked technique and that her poems were best when kept short and simple. For example, *Iola Leroy* has been criticized for being too similar to William Wells Brown's *Clotel* and for not being well written. Literary critics have acknowledged the value of the novel but do not rank it as first-rate literature. Harper died in Philadelphia. Her residence, the Harper House at 1006 Bainbridge Street, has been declared a National Historic Landmark.

• An extensive biography of Harper can be found in the *Dictionary of American Negro Biography* (1982). Shorter sketches of her life are in Henry A. Ploski and James Williams, comps. and eds., *The Negro Almanac: A Reference Work on the African American* (1989), and Marianna W. Davis, ed.,

Contributions of Black Women to America, vol. 1 (1982). Hugo Gloster, *Negro Voices in American Fiction* (1948), and Linda Riggins, "The Works of Frances E. W. Harper," *Black World* (1972), are very useful sources. Gerda Lerner, *Black Women in White America: A Documentary History* (1972), has excerpts from Harper's speeches and poems and a short biographical sketch. Hallie Quinn Brown, *Homespun Heroines* (1926) is an excellent early account of Harper's life.

MAMIE E. LOCKE

HARPER, Ida Husted (18 Feb. 1851–14 Mar. 1931), suffragist and journalist, was born in Fairfield, Indiana, the daughter of John Husted, a saddler, and Cassandra Stoddard. When Ida was ten years old the Harpers moved to Muncie, Indiana, seeking a better school system. She graduated from the local high school and then entered Indiana University as a sophomore in 1868. A year later she withdrew from college to become a high school principal in Peru, Indiana.

In 1871 she married Thomas Winans Harper, a lawyer, and went to live with him in Terre Haute, Indiana. The couple had one child. Harper's new husband was an ally of Eugene V. Debs in the local Democratic party, and he served for nineteen years as chief counsel of Debs's union, the Brotherhood of Locomotive Firemen (BLF). During these years Harper began writing for the *Terre Haute Saturday Evening Mail* and various Indianapolis papers under a male pseudonym. Though her husband disapproved, she earned money for her journalism, and for twelve years she wrote a weekly column for the *Evening Mail*, first under a pseudonym and later under her own name. She also contributed to the BLF publication edited by Debs, *Locomotive Fireman's Magazine*, becoming editor of its "Woman's Department" in 1884. At the same time Harper became increasingly active in the woman suffrage movement; starting in 1887 she served as secretary of the Indiana suffrage society.

Harper was divorced in 1890 and almost immediately took a position as editor in chief of the *Terre Haute Daily News*. But after three months she left this job to move to Indianapolis, where her daughter was in school. She continued her work for *Locomotive Firemen's Magazine* and also began contributing political articles to the *Indianapolis News*. Three years later, when her daughter entered Stanford University in California, Harper moved there too, resigning her position with the BLF publication though she continued to write for the *News* for many years.

Harper enrolled at Stanford at the same time as her daughter, but she never received a degree. Instead she began dedicating most of her time to the woman suffrage movement. During the drive for a California suffrage amendment in 1896, she was chosen by the head of the National American Woman Suffrage Association (NAWSA), Susan B. Anthony, to organize the campaign's press relations. Besides producing reams of written material, maintaining contact with 250 California newspapers, and establishing a network of volunteers around the state, Harper was soon helping Anthony with her writing. Anthony said, "The moment I give the idea—the point—she formulates it into a good sentence—while I should have to haggle over it half an hour."

The California amendment went down to defeat, but in 1897 Anthony asked Harper's help in writing her memoirs. Moving to her subject's home in Rochester, New York, Harper spent two years distilling Anthony's rough notes and a vast collection of letters and documents into a multivolume biography—a task so daunting that both women referred to the project as "the bog." The outcome was Harper's *Life of Susan B. Anthony*, two volumes of which were published in 1898; the third appeared in 1908, soon after Anthony's death. Although this work is not as lively as Harper's journalistic writing, it is a painstaking and useful contribution to suffrage literature.

From 1901 to 1902 Harper helped Anthony prepare the fourth volume of the *History of Woman Suffrage* (1902), which brought the story of the movement up to 1900. She also accompanied Anthony when she lectured and attended conventions, both in the United States and abroad. After traveling to London in 1899 as a delegate to the International Council of Women, Harper began attending nearly all of the council's European meetings, as well as those of the International Suffrage Alliance. She chaired the council's press committee for three years (1899–1902) and wrote articles for the *International Suffrage News*, published in Europe. She also remained active at home, editing a woman's column in the *New York Sunday Sun* (1899–1903). Besides discussing suffrage her outspoken columns criticized "the usual gush over 'wifehood and motherhood,'" questioned whether there was anything holy about unlimited childbearing, and scolded wives who dedicated themselves to drunken husbands.

As chair of NAWSA's National Press Bureau in New York City, starting in 1910, Harper not only kept sixteen local papers supplied with information but also broke new ground in developing a market for suffrage articles in magazines and the syndicated press. She edited a woman's page in *Harper's Bazaar* (1909–1913) and published articles and letters in city newspapers from Boston to Chicago. Although she preferred writing, she also lectured on suffrage around the country and testified before numerous congressional committees.

Like many suffragists of her class and time, Harper accommodated herself to and perhaps even shared certain social and racial prejudices. At a time of growing concern about the influence of immigrants in the electorate, she suggested that women's suffrage could help offset "the great conglomerate of voters that we have in this country." She also preferred the federal campaign to the state-by-state approach, explaining that a ratification drive would have the advantage of limiting the debate to "the selected men in each state"—the legislature—rather than having to appeal to the whole electorate. And in 1918 she actively discouraged an organization of 6,000 black women from joining NAWSA, arguing that their participation might turn southern congressmen against the drive for suffrage. On the other hand, she did encourage the movement to reach beyond its middle-class base to working women.

In 1916 Harper moved to Washington to head the Leslie Bureau of Suffrage Education, which coordinated national publicity in the final push for a constitutional amendment. Only in 1918 when victory was near did she take her final job with the movement: the preparation of the fifth and sixth volumes of *History of Woman Suffrage* (1922), which gave a detailed description of state and national activities between 1900 and 1920, culminating in the passage of the Nineteenth Amendment. Harper remained in Washington, becoming active in the American Association of University Women and making her home at the organization's headquarters. She died in Washington.

In 1915 Debs praised Harper for "having a great part in a great work." The career of advocate-journalist was not common for women of her time, but the combination of energy, humor, and dedication that she brought to her career made a unique and distinctive contribution to the suffrage movement and to the larger field of women's rights.

• There are several scrapbooks of Harper's writings in the Library of Congress, and a few of her letters are in the Indiana State Library, Indianapolis, and at the Huntington Library, San Marino, Calif. Regarding her career, see volumes 4 and 5 of the *History of Woman Suffrage* (1902, 1922), which she edited; Alma Lutz, *Susan B. Anthony: Rebel, Crusader, Humanist* (1960); Marjorie Spruill Wheeler, ed., *One Woman, One Vote: Rediscovering the Woman Suffrage Movement* (1995); Aileen S. Kraditor, *The Ideas of the Woman Suffrage Movement, 1890–1920* (1965); Mari Jo Buhle and Paul Buhle, "Introduction" to *The Concise History of Woman Suffrage: Selections from the Classic Work of Stanton, Anthony, Gage, and Harper* (1918); Elinor Rice Hays, *Morning Star: A Biography of Lucy Stone* (1961); Ray Ginger, *The Bending Cross: A Biography of Eugene V. Debs* (1949); and *Letters of Eugene V. Debs*, vols. 1 and 2, ed. J. Robert Constantine (1990). An obituary is in the *New York Times*, 17 Mar. 1931.

SANDRA OPDYCKE

HARPER, James (13 Apr. 1795–27 Mar. 1869), publisher, was born in Newtown, Long Island, New York, the oldest son of Joseph Harper, a farmer, carpenter, and storekeeper, and Elizabeth Kollyer, a Dutch burgher's daughter. Joseph and Elizabeth Harper taught James and his three brothers, John, Wesley, and Fletcher, the values of hard work, careful study, honesty, sobriety, and family loyalty. Circuit Methodist preachers, who often stayed overnight at the Harper home, strongly influenced the brothers.

James Harper read assiduously from his earliest years, was particularly impressed by the *Autobiography* of Benjamin Franklin, and is said to have desired to become a printer because of Franklin's success in that profession. When James was sixteen years old, he was apprenticed to a Methodist friend of the Harper family who was the senior partner in a New York City printing firm. James's example led to his brother John's becoming a printer's apprentice in 1812. Their example

caused their brother Wesley to become a printer's devil in 1816. During that same year, their parents rented their farm and moved to the city with Fletcher to supervise the older boys' activities.

In March 1817 James and John formed their own printing firm, J. & J. Harper, Printers, on Dover Street. Doing only job printing at first, they received a boost in July when Evert Duyckinck, the Manhattan bookseller and publisher, placed an order with them to print 2,000 copies of a translation of Seneca's *Morals*—with the name Harper on the title page. That same summer, James and John employed Wesley and Fletcher as copy boys. In 1818 they showed proofs of John Locke's *An Essay Concerning Human Understanding* to several booksellers and put the name of each bookseller on the title page of copies he ordered in advance of printing. In 1820 they began pirating Sir Walter Scott's popular novels, printing and binding one volume in twenty-one hours after receiving a copy from a packet from London. Such pirating was legal in the absence of any international copyright law (until 1891). In 1823 James married Maria Arcularius, the daughter of an alderman-merchant. So with James and John, who had married in 1820, in homes of their own, their industrious parents began to provide room and board for the apprentices of J. & J. Harper. In 1823 Wesley became a partner, as did Fletcher two years later.

In 1825 James and his brothers decided to be publishers rather than merely printers. They bought stereotyping equipment, produced excellent book plates, gained a reputation for reliability and professional excellence, and added to it over the years—moving to Fulton Street, then to Pearl Street, and finally to 82 Cliff Street. Long aware that they were loyal to each other but that their talents differed, they divided their responsibilities. James put himself in charge of the printing plant. John became purchasing manager, production manager, and bookkeeper; Wesley was proofreader, company correspondent, and in charge of the family's charitable obligations; and Fletcher became chief editor and general executive officer. By 1830 the firm was the biggest book publisher in the United States. In 1833 James installed steam presses, and the company name changed to Harper & Brothers. If any brother were asked who was the "Harper," he would answer that any one of them was Mr. Harper and the other three were his brothers. James went abroad on business in 1835–1836 and 1837. It was his resolve that kept the company afloat after the panics of 1837 and 1857.

In 1844 James Harper was elected mayor of New York City on an American Republican party—i.e., Nativist—ticket, against Democratic and Whig rivals. Once in his City Hall office, four blocks from his publishing business, he instituted many reforms: he hired and retained employees on the basis of ability, not country of birth, religion, or friends in high places; modernized the police system; reduced animal traffic on the streets; made garbage collecting and street sweeping more efficient; reduced grog-shop hours;

and enforced honesty among hackmen. The election in 1844 of James Polk, the Democratic candidate for president, assured that James Harper, who reluctantly ran for reelection, was a one-term, one-year mayor.

Under James's leadership, the firm weathered many storms and became arguably the greatest publishing firm in the world. In the late 1840s three of his most successful ventures were *Harper's Illuminated and New Pictorial Bible* (1846, the finest example of book publishing in the United States to that date), a three-volume *Shakespeare* (1847, edited by Gulian C. Verplanck), and a revision of Jedidiah Morse's *Geography Made Easy* (1847). The most successful of several American women writers published by the Harpers in the 1840s were the popular Catharine Maria Sedgwick and the indefatigable Lydia Sigourney. New nonfiction male writers at this time included J. Ross Browne and George Ticknor. Meanwhile, James's wife, Maria, with whom he had had one child, died in 1847. A year later, James married Augusta Thorne, with whom he had three children. By 1850 the firm was one of the three largest in the world (and perhaps the largest). By the early 1850s Harper production—with forty-one presses—rose to twenty-five books a minute, ten hours a day, six days a week, partly by electrotyping. Annual income reached $2 million. In 1853 the firm issued 4.5 million copies of books, pamphlets, and magazines. The most significant novel James Harper and his brothers published was Herman Melville's *Moby-Dick* in 1851.

At 1:00 P.M., on Saturday, 10 December 1853, tragedy struck the firm. Fire broke out and destroyed ten Harper buildings and their contents, including binding equipment, the engine room and boiler, presses, stamping dies, books and printed sheets, plates, woodcuts, supplies of paper, manuscripts, and account books. The loss was estimated at $1,115,000, but no lives were lost, and some plates in vaults survived. That same day, the Harper brothers vowed to rebuild. They bought twenty new presses and negotiated with owners of forty-two presses in New York and elsewhere to reprint their books within weeks, and they reorganized and rebuilt. They were able to list in their 1855 catalog more than a thousand old and new titles. Until about 1859 each of the four brothers, by then all married and with children, took whatever money from firm profits he needed for personal expenses.

In spring 1869 James Harper and his daughter were driving down Fifth Avenue near Central Park when their carriage pole broke, the horses bolted, and he was thrown to the street and fatally injured. Wesley died of heart trouble in 1870, and John lost interest in the company and died in 1875. Fletcher was in charge until his death in 1877, after which five Harper sons inherited the firm.

• Harper's personal papers are widely scattered, but many are at the New-York Historical Society in New York City, and some are at the Historical Society of Pennsylvania in Philadelphia. John Tebbel, *A History of Book Publishing in the United States* (4 vols., 1972–1981), and Lewis A. Coser et al., *Books: The Culture and Commerce of Publishing* (1982), place the firm in a wide historical perspective. Eugene Exman's *The Brothers Harper: A Unique Publishing Partnership and Its Impact upon the Cultural Life of America from 1817 to 1853* (1965) is the definitive biography of the Harper brothers. *The House of Harper: One Hundred and Fifty Years of Publishing* (1967), also by Exman, is the standard history of the publishing firm. Exman's two books rely on but supersede *The House of Harper* (1912) and *I Remember* (1934), by J. Henry Harper, James Harper's grandnephew. Frank Luther Mott, *A History of American Magazines, 1850–1865* (1957), devotes separate chapters to the establishment and development of *Harper's New Monthly Magazine* and *Harper's Weekly*. In *The Price of Survival* (1967), Allan Nevins reviews the 150-year life of the firm. A laudatory obituary of James Harper is in the *New York Times*, 29 Mar. 1869.

ROBERT L. GALE

HARPER, Robert Goodloe (Jan. 1765–14 Jan. 1825), U.S. representative and senator, was born near Fredericksburg, Virginia, the son of Jesse Harper and Diana Goodloe. About 1769 he moved with his parents to Granville County, North Carolina, where his father worked as a cabinetmaker. Harper received his early education at home and at a local grammar school. His education was interrupted when he joined a volunteer corps of cavalry at age fifteen and served in the revolutionary army in the Carolinas. The war experience embued in Harper a fascination for the military that continued throughout his life. After the war, Harper made a surveying tour through Kentucky and Tennessee in 1783 and very early developed an interest in the potential of the American West.

Harper graduated from the College of New Jersey (now Princeton University) in 1785 and relocated to Charleston, South Carolina, because he considered the opportunities to be greater there. In Charleston, Harper studied law, teaching school to finance his education, and was admitted to the bar in 1786. He soon moved again, this time to the Ninety-Six District, in a section of the South Carolina up-country named for a revolutionary war fort, and commenced practice in the town of Cambridge. In 1789 he returned to Charleston and plunged into the law and land speculation, working as attorney-representative for one of the Yazoo land companies in which Wade Hampton (1751?–1835) was involved. His speculative activities entangled Harper in large debts that required years to pay off.

In the early 1790s South Carolina was caught up in one of the state's periodic reappointment struggles. Harper seized the opportunity: returning to Ninety-Six in 1794, he threw himself into the struggle to gain better representation for South Carolina's up-country and successfully stood for election to the district's U.S. congressional seat in the Fourth Congress. After a brief disillusioning flirtation with pro-French Charleston republicanism, he moved to the Federalist side. Harper and his western constituents were attracted to the proactive nationalism of the Federal party. Had he lived long enough, Harper would have made a good southern Whig. At the same time he was elected to fill out the unexpired term of a congressman from another district in the Third Congress and to the state house of representatives, where he served several months during 1794. Under state election laws of the time one could stand for office in any district where one owned property. He was reelected to the Fifth and Sixth Congresses, representing the Ninety-Six District, and served from February 1795 to March 1801.

Harper rose to a position of considerable influence and importance within the House Federalist caucus: he worked hard at representing his district, taking great interest in western land policy, relations with the American Indians, the regularization of land surveys, and internal improvements designed to more effectively link the West to the established states. His career to this point reveals some of the differences between the northern and southern "wings" of the Federalist party. Southerners saw the West as an asset, while northern Federalists saw only Democratic-Republican voters and liabilities. On western issues Harper voted with the emerging Jeffersonian Republicans more often than with his northern colleagues.

Harper served as chairman of the Committee on Ways and Means in the Fifth and Sixth Congresses; was one of the managers appointed by the House of Representatives in 1798 to conduct the intensely partisan impeachment proceedings against Senator William Blount from Tennessee; and became one of the party's most knowledgeable and effective pamphleteers on foreign policy matters. His earlier southern Federalist progressive political views, with regard to the development of the West and the uses of federal power for internal improvements in transportation and commerce, began to give way to xenophobia and nativism of the most strident variety during the French crisis of 1798–1799. He became one of the leaders of the movement to save the country from succumbing to French domination, infection by revolutionary radicalism, French-inspired internal division and subversion, and the loss of political and social stability due to the waves of new immigrants arriving daily.

The evidence suggests that Harper should be credited with the rallying cry "Millions for defense, but not one cent for tribute." He clearly played a major role in shaping the alien and sedition legislation of the late 1790s and the High Federalist attempt to suppress dissent generally and the emerging Jeffersonian Republican party specifically.

Harper's greatest fear and perhaps most fundamental motivation for this turn to the right was a morbid and pervasive fear of insurrection among the slave population in the South. The refugees from Santo Domingo (now Dominican Republic) only reinforced his fear of racial conflagration inspired by French agents. This paranoia remained with Harper, and he was to have a leadership role in the creation of the American Colonization Society in 1816, whose goal was the resettlement outside the United States of the growing number of free African Americans. There is no evidence that he envisioned a day when slavery would no longer exist.

Sensing Thomas Jefferson's victory in 1800, Harper chose not to stand for reelection and quit South Carolina, moving to Baltimore, where he had developed law and political connections through John Adams's (1735–1826) secretary of war James McHenry (1753–1816). With McHenry's entrée, and even more as the result of his marriage in 1801 to Catherine Carroll (with whom he had four children), daughter of Charles Carroll (1736–1832) of Carrollton, Harper rose to a position of political and professional leadership in Baltimore, practicing in both state and federal courts, including the U.S. Supreme Court, for a quarter of a century. He was instrumental in keeping the Federalist party alive, serving as an elder statesman until his death.

Harper served in the War of 1812, even while opposing the conflict as the wrong war with the wrong enemy, attaining the rank of major general in the defense of Baltimore in 1814. He was involved in organizing one of Baltimore's major commercial innovations of the antebellum period, a forerunner of later corporations, the Baltimore Exchange Company, in 1815 and was a member of the first board of directors. General Harper, as he preferred to be addressed, served in the state senate of Maryland and was elected from Maryland to the U.S. Senate for the term beginning 4 March 1815. Harper served from February 1816 until December 1816, when, because of business concerns and frustrated with the Republican-dominated upper house, he resigned. After an unsuccessful candidacy for the vice presidential spot on the Federalist ticket in the election of 1816, Harper traveled extensively in Europe in 1819 and 1820. His last major public act was a prominent part in the ceremonies on the occasion of the Marquis de Lafayette's visit to Baltimore in 1824. Harper died in Baltimore.

• Harper's papers and related collections are in the Maryland Historical Society in Baltimore. Additional Maryland-era material can be found in the Maryland Hall of Records, Annapolis. The South Carolina Archives at Columbia contain most of the surviving materials related to Harper's early career. A small Harper collection is contained in the South Caroliniana Collection at the University of South Carolina. The Library of Congress houses some Harper manuscripts as well as those of both South Carolina and Maryland contemporaries. Finally, the John Rutledge, Jr., Papers, Southern Historical Collection of the University of North Carolina, also contain Harper material. Charles W. Sommerville, "Robert Goodloe Harper" (Ph.D. diss., Johns Hopkins Univ., 1899), and Joseph W. Cox, *Champion of Southern Federalism: Robert Goodloe Harper of South Carolina* (1972), are the two primary biographies. Lisle A. Rose, *Prologue to Democracy: The Federalists in the South, 1789–1800* (1968), and George C. Rogers, *The Evolution of a Federalist: William Loughton Smith of Charleston, 1758–1812* (1962), afford genuine insight into both southern federalism and Harper's political career. For the Federalists after 1800, see David H. Fischer, *The Revolution of American Conservatism; The Federalist Party in the Era of Jeffersonian Democracy* (1965).

JOSEPH W. COX

HARPER, William (17 Jan. 1790–10 Oct. 1847), jurist and U.S. senator, was born on the island of Antigua, the son of the Reverend John Harper, a Methodist missionary, and Henrietta Hawes. The elder Harper moved his ministry to Boston in 1794, then to Charleston, South Carolina, in 1799, and finally to Columbia, South Carolina, in 1802. Following the death of their mother in 1795, William and his younger brother, John Wesley, were sent to school in Baltimore for three years. After rejoining their father in South Carolina, the boys attended Mount Bethel Academy and, later, the Jefferson Monticello Seminary under the Reverend James Rogers's strict eye. When South Carolina College opened its doors in 1805, both young Harpers joined the entering student body. After graduating with distinction in 1808, William took charge of Cambridge Academy in the Edgefield District and, while there, studied medicine for a time before reading law under Abram Dozier. Admitted to the Columbia bar, he embarked on a practice that eventually fixed him among the most prominent South Carolinians of the time.

Militia service in the War of 1812 interrupted Harper's legal career. After being discharged as a sergeant in 1815, he married Catherine Coalter, daughter of Judge David Coalter of Columbia, and resumed practice there until leaving South Carolina in the fall of 1818. They had at least three children, including two lost to yellow fever in 1833. Lured in part by the chance for William's swift political advancement, the Harpers followed Judge Coalter to the Missouri Territory. Within a year Harper received a prized appointment as chancellor and was elected to the same office after Missouri attained statehood. In 1821 he served as a member of the Missouri constitutional convention.

His reputation growing, Harper resigned the judgeship in 1823 and returned home to South Carolina, where a position as reporter of the state supreme court lay waiting. A published volume of *Reports* (1825), invaluable as a record of court precedents, was the accomplishment of his two-year tenure.

Following the death of John Gaillard in February 1826, Governor Richard Manning chose Harper, a Democrat, to fill the vacated U.S. Senate seat from 28 March until 7 December of that year, when the legislature elected Gaillard's successor. While discreetly independent from quarreling South Carolina factions, Harper identified in principle with states' rights Democrats, hostile to the ideas of consolidated central government and federal support of state projects. Along with Senator Robert Y. Hayne, he opposed a land grant to Illinois for a canal between the Illinois River and Lake Michigan and voted against a bill to maintain the Cumberland Road.

Opportunities in state politics abounded for Harper after his move to Charleston in 1826. Blending smoothly among the Lowcountry elite, he served in the state house of representatives and won the Speakership in 1828. Only months later he was elected chancellor of the state, replacing Waddy Thompson, and served there until elected one of three judges on the South Carolina Court of Appeals in 1830. In these years, Harper's intense antinationalist convictions grew more focused, and so did his contempt for northern critics of slavery. He condemned protective tariffs, advocated nullification theory, and in an article for the *Southern Review*, deplored the "vehement invectives" of abolitionists. Such ardent views masked a mild personality. A contemporary of Harper described him as "patient, learned, courteous, and acute." His powers of memory, forensic gifts, and skill in listening impressed people around him. To relax he wrote poetry. An "imperturbable calmness of temper" suited him better for the bench than for the storms of lawmaking. Reticent in mixed company, he warmed among close friends and opened volubly on subjects of interest to him. After the legislature abolished the Court of Appeals in 1834, Harper again became chancellor in 1835 and served in that office until his death.

In Harper's mind, service on the state's highest court required no withdrawal from political controversies, especially the nullification question. He thought protective tariffs violated the federal Constitution and threatened the security of South Carolina. For other reasons—the panic of 1819, the 1822 discovery of Denmark Vesey's slave insurrection plot in Charleston, and the mounting force of abolitionist attacks—the state looked vulnerable as never before. Harper represented South Carolina at the Philadelphia antitariff convention of 1831. As a delegate to the state convention that defied the tariffs of 1828 and 1832, he wrote the famous Ordinance of Nullification, adopted in November 1832.

The chancellor's political thought relied heavily on the "compact theory" espoused by John C. Calhoun. In an 1830 speech, given in Columbia and published two years later as *The Remedy by State Interposition*, Harper declared "the sovereign power of the state has the right . . . to arrest the operation, within its own limits, of a law which it shall judge to be unconstitutional." According to theory, state interposition could be overridden only by three-fourths of the Union or by a federal constitutional convention. The states, not the U.S. Supreme Court, stood as "authority of the last resort" on the meaning of the Constitution. Harper saw nullification as a middle road "between disunion and consolidation." The intention, he announced in 1832, was not to make but "to prevent a revolution" by preserving state autonomy.

Harper's dissenting opinion in the famous 1834 test oath case (*State ex Relatione Ed. McCready v. B. F. Hunt*) highlighted the ideological rift between nullifiers and Unionists in South Carolina. The Ordinance of Nullification included a clause requiring civil and military officials to pledge support of state interposition. After repeal of the ordinance in March 1833, the legislature replaced the old oath with a simpler pledge of "faithful and true allegiance" to the state. Harper's colleagues on the Court of Appeals, John Belton O'Neall and David Johnson, both Unionists, struck down the revised oath as a violation of civil liberties protected under the state constitution. Harper, by contrast, found no difficulty in having South Carolinians swear primary allegiance to their state—over and above competing loyalties.

From the mid-1830s on, Harper turned to more contemplative pursuits, including the intellectual defense of slavery. His 1838 *Memoir on Slavery*, presented first as a lecture before the South Carolina Society for the Advancement of Learning, placed him among the likes of Thomas Dew, William Gilmore Simms, and James Henry Hammond as a premier proslavery writer. Though conceding that slavery might be an evil—a necessary one—the chancellor joined other slavery apologists in repudiating the natural rights doctrines of Thomas Jefferson's day. The *Memoir* drew heavily on British and West Indian arguments. Slaveholding, Harper declared, was "compatible with freedom, stability, and long duration of civil government."

The final literary effort of Harper's life was his published memoir of Chancellor Henry W. De Saussure in 1841. The following year his health failed after a trip to Mammoth Cave, Kentucky, to comfort his only remaining son, Wesley, who was dying from consumption. After several years of physical decline, Harper died at his plantation in Fairfield District, near Columbia, where he had moved in 1833.

• Harper's private papers are widely scattered. His *Memoir on Slavery*, first published in 1838, is collected with essays by Dew, Hammond, and Simms in *The Pro-Slavery Argument* (1852). E. N. Elliot, ed., *Cotton Is King and Proslavery Arguments* (1860), contains Harper's essay "Slavery in the Light of Social Ethics." Secondary sources that cover Harper's defense of slavery include Drew G. Faust, *A Sacred Circle: The Dilemma of the Intellectual in the Old South, 1840–1860* (1977); John McCardell, *The Idea of a Southern Nation: Southern Nationalists and Southern Nationalism, 1830–1860* (1979); and Larry E. Tise, *Proslavery: A History of the Defense of Slavery in America, 1701–1840* (1987). On Harper's role in the tariff crisis, see William W. Freehling, *Prelude to Civil War: The Nullification Controversy in South Carolina, 1816–1836* (1965). Obituaries are in the Charleston *Courier*, 15 Oct. 1847, and the Columbia *South Carolinian*, 19 and 29 Oct. 1847.

JOHN R. VAN ATTA

HARPER, William Rainey (24 July 1856–10 Jan. 1906), first president of the University of Chicago and pioneering biblical scholar, was born in New Concord, Ohio, the son of Samuel Harper and Ellen Elizabeth Rainey, general store owners. Raised "down the hill" from Muskingum College, Harper entered the Presbyterian college's preparatory school at age eight. Six years later, at his graduation from the college, he astounded the audience by delivering the salutatorian's address in Hebrew. The address, which, impressive, must be judged in the context of a frontier, antebellum college education that had few standards, was the first indicator of a proficiency at Semitic languages that would soon carry Harper to prominence. With a B.A. in hand at the age of fourteen, Harper spent three years at home clerking in his parents' store

and studying languages. Before he left home to study at Yale College he had already taught his first introduction to Hebrew course.

Harper arrived at Yale in 1873, just at the time the college was becoming a modern university. He completed his Ph.D. in two years, working primarily with William Dwight Whitney, who, as first president of the American Philological Association, was the nation's premier linguist. Having studied in Germany, Whitney had carried back to the United States a new kind of specialized inductive linguistic study, which Harper set out to pursue on his own.

Not yet twenty years old, Harper returned to New Concord in 1875 to marry Ella Paul, the daughter of Muskingum College's president; they had four children. That same year Harper became principal of Masonic College in Macon, Tennessee, where he taught Latin and mathematics. A year later he became tutor of ancient languages at Denison University in Granville, Ohio. Hired by Denison to teach Greek, Harper also taught Hebrew in an extracurricular class, which soon counted several faculty members among its students. His classroom prowess soon became apparent. He stayed in Granville for two and a half years, long enough to become a convert to the Baptist denomination, and in January 1879 became instructor of Hebrew at the Baptist Union Theological Seminary in Morgan Park, Illinois, then a suburb of Chicago.

The 22-year-old scholar quickly took the institution by storm. Within two years Harper's energies and successes as a teacher spilled beyond the confines of the seminary curriculum, and Harper's "Hebrew movement" began to extend across the nation. Summer schools for Hebrew studies began in 1881; within two years he was offering his Hebrew program in New York at Lake Chautauqua, which at that time was the nation's leading popular educational institution and which would eventually be called the Chautauque Institution. Harper had already in 1880 created a correspondence school, which allowed students to study Hebrew through the mail. An academic entrepreneur, Harper created the *Hebrew Student*, his first journal, in 1882. His first books, *Elements of Hebrew* (1882) and *Hebrew Vocabularies* (1882), appeared during these productive early Chicago years.

To support his fledgling enterprise, Harper founded a joint stock company that sold shares at $100 each, a harbinger of his later accomplishments as a fundraiser. In addition to teaching, running his correspondence and summer schools, editing his journal, and writing books, Harper somehow found time to complete a bachelor of divinity degree at the seminary and play a number of roles at Morgan Park Baptist Church, including that of Sunday school superintendent.

Harper's energy, educational leadership abilities, and institution-building skills quickly brought him to the attention of others. Bishop John Heyl Vincent, the founder of the Chautauqua Institution, recruited Harper to join his efforts to provide educational opportunities to those who could not afford the conventional four-year undergraduate type of education. In 1883 Harper taught his first class at the summer institute, which by then also featured a home reading plan called the Chautauqua Literary and Scientific Circle, a School of Languages, and a School of Theology. The mesh between Harper's native energy and creativity and Bishop Vincent's expansive vision for a type of popular evangelical education was catalytic. By 1887 Harper had become the principal of the College of Liberal Arts, where he reorganized the school's curriculum and added new courses. By the time the University of Chicago opened in 1892 Harper had become the principal of the entire Chautauqua System of Education, a program which, unlike any other in the nation, featured such national leaders as Washington Gladden, Woodrow Wilson, Booker T. Washington, Theodore Roosevelt, and Frances Willard among its teachers, lecturers, and preachers.

The Chautauqua years widened Harper's understanding of his own vocation. No longer merely a Hebrew expert (although he did create an entire series of schools of sacred literature during his association with Chautauqua), Harper had become one of the leading educational administrators of his day and had come into contact with leaders in the world of American religion, politics, and higher education. At Chautauqua Harper was also the beneficiary of Vincent's expansive vision for higher education and his many programmatic innovations, which were sources for many of the ideas—such as the quarter system and the university extension program—that would be prominent features in Harper's design for the University of Chicago.

In 1886 Yale offered Harper positions in the Semitic languages field of the Graduate Department and at the university's Divinity School. Harper accepted and spent a summer moving his sprawling Hebrew enterprise to New Haven, Connecticut, where a three-story building was needed to house it. Characteristically, he lost little time in making his presence felt at Yale. Teaching Hebrew, Arabic, Assyrian, and Aramaic, he built a department around four of his protégés. The first department he directed was Semitic Studies, and his protégés, one of whom was his brother Robert Harper, studied and taught in various specialized fields, such as Ethiopic and Babylonian studies. In 1890 he became Woolsey Professor of Biblical Literature and University Professor of Semitic Languages. President Timothy Dwight was so impressed by Harper's abilities as a teacher that he encouraged him to teach regular undergraduate courses on various English Bible topics. Dwight also began to speak of Harper as a possible future president of the university.

At the height of Harper's influence at Yale and Chautauqua, colleagues from his Morgan Park days, especially Thomas Wakefield Goodspeed, joined forces with oil magnate and philanthropist John D. Rockefeller to present Harper with an offer he could not refuse—the presidency of the new University of Chicago. Harper's role in the emergence of the university began before he took office. At the time that he considered moving to Yale, his Morgan Park colleagues had

offered him the presidency of the "old" University of Chicago. Founded in 1857, the institution was virtually moribund, and Harper opted for the greener academic pastures of New Haven. The idea, however, that Chicago needed a university and that the Baptists had a special role to play in creating it did not die. Goodspeed and Frederick T. Gates worked relentlessly to build support in Chicago for the idea and also cultivated Rockefeller, a fellow Baptist and the first American billionaire, as the lead donor for the undertaking. Rockefeller had had opportunity to hear Harper lecture at Vassar College, and he began to enter into conversations with Harper and the Chicagoans about the possibility of a new university.

When Harper was offered the presidency in September 1890, the university did not actually exist. He did not accept the offer until it became clear that the Chicago Baptists would commit to more than another denominational college, that in fact they would strive to build a new and complete American university. When Rockefeller, after a period of vacillation about the size of his commitment, added $1 million to his original pledge of $600,000 for the new institution, Harper accepted.

During the interim between the offer and his acceptance in 1891, Harper sketched his vision for the new university and waited as key Baptists, including Rockefeller, weighed heresy charges that had suddenly been placed against him by Augustus H. Strong, a Baptist clergyman who had dreams of a Baptist university in New York City. Key Baptists, like Goodspeed and Gates, backed Harper so strongly that Rockefeller decided to commit his money to the Chicago plan. Once Rockefeller opted for Chicago and Harper, the controversy quieted and resulted in eventual hatchet burying between Harper and Strong. The charges point to Harper's key, and at times controversial, role as one of the mediators of modern biblical criticism into American life.

Unlike most of the new generation of biblical scholars who were challenging conventional literal readings of the Bible, Harper was not German-trained. His exposure to the fires of the *Neuhumanismus* of Continental scholarship came through contact with mediators like Whitney at Yale and through his own reading. *Neuhumanismus* was a major cultural movement in German universities during the nineteenth century that shaped a new view of the world based on historical and linguistic studies of the classical period of antiquity. In the 1880s and 1890s Harper became an ever-more outspoken advocate for insights from the higher criticism developed by Julius Wellhausen, Franz Delitzsch, and other leading German scholars. As editor of the *Hebrew Student*, which in turn became the *Old Testament Student*, then the *Old and New Testament Student*, and finally in 1893 the more popular *Biblical World*, and the scholarly *Hebraica*, which he created in 1884, Harper cautiously introduced readers to critical scholarship and encouraged American interpreters to "make haste, slowly" with the new knowledge. Championing what he called "reverent criticism," Harper embraced modern historical consciousness but did not accept its rationalistic presuppositions, which tended to explain away divine participation in human events. Instead, Harper advocated a view that found God at work in history as it evolved toward the higher life. While his liberal and theistically progressive reading of biblical history ultimately proved unsatisfactory to radical historicists and fundamentalists alike, Harper's mediating position provided an attractive harbor for many.

Distinctive about Harper's response to the new criticism was his ability to blend stances toward the Scriptures that increasingly came to be polarized between traditionalists and modernists. Even after becoming president of the University of Chicago, Harper saw himself first as a missionary for a new way of reading the Scriptures, one which welcomed discoveries about other religions as well as those about Judaism and Christianity. A steady stream of his own articles; late night and early morning work as editor of his journals; leadership of the American Institute of Sacred Literature; and publication of a commentary on *Amos and Hosea* (1905) in the International Critical Commentary Series, were all signs of the centrality of biblical scholarship in his life.

Harper is now remembered chiefly for his role in creating one of the nation's preeminent research universities. Few recall him as biblical scholar or as a leader of popular education movements. Yet his plans for the University of Chicago reveal how central those two concerns were for his new institution. His fifteen years as president can be viewed as a realization of plans that he sketched in six *Official Bulletins* (1891– 1892) published before the university opened. Close reading of them and of Harper's biography reveal several distinctive features. First, Harper did not, like so many of his contemporaries, attempt to copy the German university paradigm. Rather, as Lawrence Veysey put it in *The Emergence of the American University* (1965), he blended and reconciled several competing university models. More precisely, Harper took elements from his Chautauqua experience, features from the revolutionary plan that guided the creation of Johns Hopkins University in 1876, and dimensions of his own Hebrew movement to create something quite different. Several of his most important innovations reveal his eclecticism and his abilities as an institutional architect. The quarter system, which created a new academic calendar; classification of courses as majors and minors; university extension programs; and the first university press in America (the University of Chicago Press, which began publishing work in 1891) were all results of his own distinctive educational and professional background.

Harper proposed and sought to create a configuration of institutions centered around the university. Affiliated colleges and academies were to prepare students for the higher work of university research. He raided faculties of other institutions, courted donors, established new degree programs (even proposing at one point an LL.D. degree for academic specialization

beyond the Ph.D.), and created departments at a breathtaking pace, moving his university quickly to the forefront of research-centered institutions. But unlike other nineteenth-century champions of research, he also attempted to create new systems of popular education that could make learning publicly available and useful. At one point Harper proposed creating a national system of university education, with a capstone national institution in Washington, D.C.

Harper's efforts reached beyond the world of the university. He developed a specialized Sunday school curriculum at Hyde Park Baptist Church, which became a prototype for national Sunday school reform in keeping with new biblical scholarship; he advocated reform of Chicago's public schools as a member of a special citywide commission; and he attempted to bring seminaries into the modern era with numerous proposals for reform. At the center of all his efforts was a conviction that his new kind of critical biblical scholarship could provide a public, religious basis that could integrate the increasingly pluralistic and specialized world of higher learning.

Before reaching his fiftieth birthday Harper died of cancer in Chicago. As his disease progressed he struggled to place his young university on a secure economic footing at the same time that he rushed to finish his commentary on Amos and Hosea (his largest single work of biblical scholarship), two other books on prophetic and priestly elements in the Old Testament, and *Religion and the Higher Life* (1904) and *The Trend in Higher Education* (1905), two collections of essays that demonstrate the wider educational vision that lay behind his specific efforts at the university. In essence he attempted to conduct a critical reformation of the nation's reading of its sacred Christian book, the Bible, and to institutionalize a top to bottom reconfiguration of its educational life.

Harper's frantic pace and institutional creativity often became the target of critics and satirists. Robert Welch Herrick, for example, joined Harper's faculty in 1893 and experienced such profound disillusionment that he published a roman à clef, *Chimes*, thirty-three years later, long after Harper's death. His novel targeted Harper as a "grotesque" figure, a "big Barnum" directing an educational system that took on all the worst aspects of the "factory process." Novelist Upton Sinclair and economist Thorstein Veblen (also an early faculty member at Chicago) added their book-length dissents, in each case situating Chicago's story in the context of a tragic transformation of higher education by "captains of erudition" like Harper, who used the wealth and institutional systems of the "plutocracy" to build their new institutions.

To be sure, Harper gave the satirists rich material. His daily appointment books regularly listed dozens of "things to do" ranging from securing funding for an observatory to writing a letter to a parent grieving over a student's death. The university he built grew at such a rapid rate that it threatened to exhaust the resources and patience of its funders. Some Chicago faculty members viewed Harper as an autocrat and questioned his commitment to academic freedom. But Harper persevered, believing that his new university had a messianic role to play. By struggling with the age's great problems, he felt that his school could lead America, and through it the world, to the next stage in humanity's quest for the higher life. His energy and progressive faith now seem almost quaint relics of a more optimistic age. But in his own time, Harper had changed the religious and educational landscape of the nation.

• Harper's personal papers, complete collections of his journals, and the papers that relate to his years as president of the University of Chicago are in the Joseph Regenstein Library of the University of Chicago. Harper's views on a wide range of biblical topics are available only in articles and editorials in his journals, especially the *Biblical World*. The best accounts of his role in the founding of the University of Chicago are Thomas Wakefield Goodspeed, *A History of the University of Chicago: The First Quarter Century* (1916; reissued in 1966), and Richard J. Storr, *Harper's University: The Beginnings* (1966). Goodspeed, *William Rainey Harper: First President of the University of Chicago* (1928), is the most complete biographical treatment to date. The interconnections between Harper's efforts as biblical scholar and university builder and the vision behind them are explored in James P. Wind, *The Bible and the University: The Messianic Vision of William Rainey Harper* (1987). Laurence R. Veysey, *The Emergence of the American University* (1965), and George M. Marsden, *The Soul of the American University* (1994), place Harper's presidential years in larger, if differing, interpretive contexts. For critical assessments of Harper's presidential years, see Robert Herrick, *Chimes* (1926); Upton Sinclair, *The Goose-Step: A Study of American Education* (1923); and Thorstein Veblen, *The Higher Learning in America: A Memorandum on the Conduct of Universities by Businessmen* (1957).

JAMES P. WIND

HARPUR, Robert (25 Jan. 1731–15 Apr. 1825), college professor and government official, was born in Ballybay, County Monaghan, Ireland, the son of Andrew Harpur and Elizabeth Creighton, immigrants from Scotland. Raised a devout Presbyterian, Harpur graduated from Glasgow University. He intended to enter the ministry but found that he lacked the necessary oratorical skills. Harpur taught grammar school for several years in Newry, Ireland.

Arriving in September 1761 in New York City, Harpur was immediately hired as a professor of mathematics and natural philosophy at King's College (now Columbia University), which occupied a single building on the "King's Farm" near Trinity Church. Harpur was one of the three professors at the Anglican school, which seldom had more than thirty students. In 1762 he received an M.A. from King's College and in the same year was appointed the school's first librarian. President Samuel Johnson had found it difficult to acquire a competent new faculty member, and he happily wrote to the Archbishop of Canterbury in January 1762 stating that "we have already been providentially provided for with an ingenious young gentleman, one Mr. Harpur, bred at Glasgow, who does very well in teaching mathematics and experimental philosophy."

In 1763 Harpur involved himself in real estate speculation, arranging with the New York government to settle eighty-seven persons from northern Ireland in an area close to Lake George. The settlers, however, did not like the quality of the lands and soon moved away to more fertile territory. It is not known whether Harpur was further involved in trying to realize his scheme.

At King's College Harpur assisted his two colleagues in teaching Latin, Greek, rhetoric, and logic in addition to his specialties. Probably because of his belief in strict discipline, Harpur became decidedly unpopular with some of his students. In May 1765 one person, probably a student, complained that Harpur had insufficient knowledge and lacked "a proper way of communicating his Ideas." He argued further that, because of Harpur, New Yorkers were reluctant to send their sons to King's College. In 1766 a cartoon was posted depicting Harpur as "Patrick Pagan," wearing academic robes and arranging an abortion for "Miss Myng," who says, "Your spruce beer has made me pregnant." Although supported by President Myles Cooper and his colleagues against such outrageous slanders, Harpur resigned from the faculty in 1767. He stayed on as a tutor in a private capacity; among his private pupils were John Jay and Alexander Hamilton.

In 1773 Harpur married Elizabeth Crygier; they had three children. After her death he married Myra Lackey in 1789; they had three children before her death in 1806.

With the coming of the Revolution, Harpur was the only person on the college's staff to join the rebel cause. King's College closed in April 1776, and its building was used as a hospital during the war. Harpur moved to Esopus (now Kingston), where a British raiding party burned his library and papers. Harpur served in the New York Provincial Congresses of 1776–1777 and in the interim Council of Safety, which conducted government until the state constitution of 1777 could take effect. He was a member of the New York General Assembly as a delegate from New York City and County, 1777–1784.

From 1778 to 1781 Harpur was one of the state commissioners charged with detecting and defeating conspiracies. His duties were largely confined to Dutchess County and involved prosecuting loyalists as well as robbers, counterfeiters, and murderers. During late 1776 and early 1777 Harpur was a member of the Committee of Arrangement, which confirmed ranks of Continental army officers from New York, reporting to the Congressional Board of War. In 1781 he also served as a clerk to the Council of Appointments, and from 1780 to 1795 he was a deputy secretary of state under Governor George Clinton.

Classes resumed at the college, now renamed Columbia, in 1784. The state had taken control and intended to make the college part of the University of the State of New York. Harpur was one of the regents of the college, serving also as secretary to this board. In April 1787 the legislature returned the corporate charter to Columbia; as long as it assumed a secular character the college would function as a private institution. Harpur and most of the former regents now sat on the college's new board of twenty-nine trustees; he held this position until 1795.

As deputy secretary of state Harpur acted as secretary of the state's Land Board, which was established in 1784. He is credited (although proof is lacking) as being the "godfather of the christened west," the one who supplied the classical names for the townships created from military bounty lands in central New York. Harpur was a member of the "Boston Company" of sixty persons who bought from Massachusetts 230,400 acres along the Susquehanna River in New York for 12.5 cents per acre. Massachusetts had retained this claim when it surrendered to the Confederation Congress the rest of its western claims. Harpur, as a proprietor in the company, patented 15,360 acres for himself in present Broome County. Harpursville was named for him. Keeping farmland for himself, he distributed the rest of the lands to settlers. In 1795 Harpur and his family moved to Broome County. He never returned to public life and lived quietly on his farm until his death. A contemporary of Harpur, Betsy Andrews, recalled that "though a man of the most indomitable will, he was possessed of a feeling heart, the poor always found a friend in him, every living thing was looked upon as worthy of his attention and care."

• Harpur's Columbia (King's College) years are fully documented at Columbia University, with materials including college papers, minutes of the governors of King's College (1770–1781), and various items in the Columbiana collection. The New York State Library has an account book of Harper, in manuscript, and "Notes furnished by Julia C. Andrews, of Nineveh, Broome County, New York, on the Life of Robert Harpur and Family" (n.d.). Harpur's prewar public career may be traced in *Journals of the Provincial Congress, Provincial Convention, Committee of Safety and Council of Safety of the State of New York* (2 vols., 1842), and as a state official (post-1776) in *Public Papers of George Clinton*, ed. Hugh Hastings, vols. 1–8 (1899–1904). David C. Humphrey, *From King's College to Columbia, 1746–1800* (1976), presents a thorough, scholarly treatment of the college in its formative years. Useful also are Herbert and Carol Schneider, eds., *Samuel Johnson, President of King's College: His Career and Writings*, vols. 1 and 4 (1929), and *A History of Columbia University, 1754–1904* (1904); and Elizabeth P. McCaughey, *From Loyalist to Founding Father: The Political Odyssey of William Samuel Johnson* (1980). Harpur's tenure as a regent of Columbia College is related in Daniel J. Pratt, ed., *Annals of Public Education in the State of New York, Proceedings of the Twelfth Anniversary of the University Convocation of the State of New York . . . 1875* (1876). Harpur's later land connections are treated in H. P. Smith, *History of Broome County* (1885), and Charles Marr, "Origin of the Classical Place Names of Central New York," *Quarterly Journal of the New York State Historical Association* 7 (1926): 155–67.

HARRY M. WARD

HARRAH, William Fisk (2 Sept. 1911–30 June 1978), casino owner and automobile collector, was born in South Pasadena, California, the son of John Garrett Harrah, a lawyer and businessman, and Amanda Fisk. Harrah attended Chapman College in 1931 and studied mechanical engineering at the University of California at Los Angeles in 1932. He was an undistinguished student and was once caught cheating on a chemistry examination. When his family encountered financial problems during the Great Depression, Harrah dropped out of college. His family moved to Venice, California, where his father served a term as mayor. In 1932 Harrah's father opened an establishment featuring the circle game, a variation of bingo in which some skill was required in shooting balls into a hopper. The circle game was akin to gambling, putting the operation at the edge of the law. William began as an employee but soon purchased the operation from his father for $500. Since gambling was illegal in Venice, the game was periodically closed when authorities chose to enforce the law strictly. In 1937 Hannah moved with his father to the more hospitable gambling environment of Reno, Nevada, and opened a bingo parlor.

Harrah's first bingo parlor closed in two months, but several months later he opened another parlor that was successful. In 1946 Harrah opened Reno's first full-fledged casino, Harrah's Club. Rather than catering to the high roller, Harrah assiduously cultivated the middle-class player. His casino was noted for its cleanliness and friendly atmosphere, and he pursued an aggressive advertising campaign. Harrah was an excellent businessman. Deeply interested in the habits and psychology of his customers, he commissioned several studies by the Stanford Research Institute. Harrah also became known for hiring expensive, famous entertainers. Partly to head off any attempts at federal regulation, Harrah advocated strong state control of gambling and helped bring about Nevada's 1955 decision to create a state Gaming Control Board. A paternalistic employer, Harrah vehemently opposed unions and worked for passage of a right-to-work law in Nevada.

In 1952 Harrah incorporated his operation. Three years later, he opened a new casino at Lake Tahoe, considered a bold move at the time since the area was known only as a modest winter ski resort. Harrah devised a scheme to bring his patrons by bus from California to Lake Tahoe, and the operation was spectacularly successful. Harrah's went public in 1971 and eventually was traded on the New York Stock Exchange, but Harrah retained an 83 percent controlling interest in the corporation.

Apart from his casino business, Harrah had a wide-ranging interest in automobiles. He liked to drive cars fast, sometimes recklessly, and once broke his neck in an accident. He owned four automobile dealerships in Nevada and Idaho and held the Ferrari dealership for the entire western United States. He occasionally had cars custom made for his personal use; one of his favorites was a Jeep Wagoneer with a Ferrari engine. Even more than driving or selling cars, Harrah loved collecting them.

Harrah's automobile collection started in 1948 with purchases of a 1911 Maxwell and a 1911 Ford. From then on, the collection grew prodigiously. In 1962 he opened a museum, putting 1,400 of his cars on display at the Harrah Automobile Collection, just outside Reno in Sparks, Nevada. The largest display of automobiles in the world, Harrah's collection included many exquisitely restored vintage cars, but he also insisted that it include every car his family had ever owned and an example of every Ford ever produced. A research library, considered the finest of its kind, was established in 1955, consisting of restoration manuals and technical data on thousands of automobiles produced over the course of automotive history. The collection was valued between $40 and $50 million when it was sold at auction in 1985.

Harrah shunned publicity and refused to give interviews. He was married seven times to six different women. He first married Thelma Batchelor, from Venice, in 1937. The marriage ended in divorce in 1948. He next married Mayme Kandis "Scherry" Lucille Teague Fagg in August 1948. They were divorced in April 1952, remarried in December 1954, and divorced again in March 1969. During their second marriage, they adopted two sons. A few months after his divorce, Harrah married the singer Bobbie Gentry (of "Ode to Billy Joe" fame), but they divorced four months later. He married Mary May Burger in August 1970; they divorced a little over a year later, in October 1971. Harrah then married Roxana Darlene Carlson in October 1972, but again the marriage lasted barely a year, and they divorced in November 1973. In June 1974 he married Verna Rae Harrison, who survived him.

Harrah underwent a successful operation for an aortal aneurysm in 1972. In 1978 he traveled to Rochester, Minnesota, for a similar operation but died after the surgery. At the time of his death, Harrah's had yet to expand to the lucrative market of Las Vegas. He left an estate valued at around $150 million, including a lodge in Idaho and a 162-acre spread, "Rancharrah," near Reno, but the bulk of his estate consisted of stock in the publicly traded Harrah's casinos.

• A statement by Harrah titled "My Recollections of the Hotel-Casino Industry, and as an Auto Collecting Enthusiast" is in the Oral History Collection at the University of Nevada, Reno. See also Leon Mandel, *William Fisk Harrah: The Life and Times of a Gambling Magnate* (1982); Keith Monroe, "The New Gambling King and the Social Scientists," *Harper's*, Jan. 1962; Kathleen Wiegner, "The Last Harrah," *Forbes*, 16 Oct. 1978; and Celia Scully, "Harrah's Automobile Collection," *Travel Incorporating Holiday*, Nov. 1977. An obituary is in the *New York Times*, 2 July 1978.

WILLIAM J. HAUSMAN

HARRAR, Jacob George (2 Dec. 1906–18 Apr. 1982), plant pathologist, educator, and foundation officer, was born in Painesville, Ohio, the son of Ellwood Scott Harrar, an electrical engineer, and Lucetta E. Sterner, a schoolteacher. Encouraged to develop a wide range of interests in his youth, Harrar became an avid naturalist, developed skill in musical performance, and was active in interscholastic sports, fishing, and hunting. He entered Oberlin College in 1923 at age sixteen and enrolled in the premedical curriculum, completing it in five years. At Oberlin, professor Frederick Glover recognized and promoted Harrar's interest in botany. After graduation Harrar took a teaching fellowship at Iowa State University, where he received an M.S. in plant pathology in 1929. He was then recruited to head the department of biology in the College of Agriculture at the University of Puerto Rico, where he learned to speak Spanish. In 1930 he married Georgetta Steese, a musician whom he had met at Oberlin; they had two children.

Harrar left Puerto Rico in 1933 to begin doctoral studies at the University of Minnesota under Elvin Stakman, a leading American plant pathologist. Harrar spent some of 1934–1935 in Liberia as a Firestone Fellow studying the diseases of the rubber tree, and he received his Ph.D. in plant pathology in 1935. He then accepted a position as assistant professor in the biology department at Virginia Polytechnic Institute.

In 1940 Harrar moved to Washington State University to head the Department of Plant Pathology and to serve as state plant pathologist. There he had the opportunity to do more research and less teaching. After just three years, however, he moved to a new position with the Rockefeller Foundation, joining an institution and a program that absorbed the rest of his working life.

In 1941–1942 the Rockefeller Foundation had investigated the possibility of a major philanthropic investment in Mexico and had decided that an attempt to improve the agricultural sector held the best promise for a contribution to the life of that nation. The foundation offered Stakman the opportunity to head up the Mexican program, but Stakman declined and instead recommended Harrar, whom he described as perhaps the only outstanding American plant pathologist who spoke Spanish. After completing his commitment to Washington State and undergoing orientation at the New York office of the foundation, Harrar moved to Mexico in March 1943.

The foundation gave Harrar considerable flexibility in developing an approach to the improvement of Mexican agriculture. Through Harrar's assiduous development of contacts within the Mexican Department of Agriculture, a bureaucratic entity, the Office of Special Studies, was established solely to give Mexican sanction to the foundation's enterprise. Harrar was designated a sub-chief of the department and head of the Office of Special Studies. He obtained office space and the site for an experimental farm at the National School of Agriculture in Chapingo near Mexico City. Over the next few years Harrar molded a few American agricultural scientists (including visiting consultants such as Stakman, Richard Bradfield, Paul C. Mangelsdorf, and Edwin J. Wellhausen) and several dozen Mexican agronomists, engineers, and technicians into a team that initiated what has become known as the "Green Revolution."

The Green Revolution was predicated on the development of hybrid varieties of corn and wheat (the primary market crops of Mexican agriculture) that were highly productive, disease-resistant, and adapted to the varied soil and climatic conditions in Mexico. To initiate this work Harrar's team collected hundreds of varieties of corn and wheat grown in Mexico, observed how productive and how disease- and insect-resistant they were in various settings, and then grew thousands of hybrids of the most promising varieties. They also assessed the milling and baking qualities of the harvested grains.

By 1944 Harrar had begun to distribute seed to farmers for testing and now tackled a range of practical problems, such as proper fertilizing practices, irrigation and crop rotation, adoption of mechanized farming techniques, application of insecticides and fungicides, and seed storage. Other needs included the development of programs to encourage farmers to adopt the new hybrids and associated technologies and the diffusion of accurate information. By 1950 the Mexican agricultural program had distributed several promising hybrids, and within a few years Mexico stopped importing grain, even though its population was expanding. The continuity of the program was guaranteed in part by Harrar's strategy of training Mexicans in advanced agricultural science: over 700 served in the Office of Special Studies, and subsequently many received fellowships to study in the United States or abroad.

The Mexican program under Harrar's leadership constituted the beginning of the Green Revolution, which has had a major effect on virtually every area in the world with developed agriculture. Harrar personally helped to establish hybridization programs throughout Latin America in the 1950s, instituted a program of support for agricultural research in India in 1956, and in 1961 was instrumental in founding the International Rice Research Institute in the Philippines.

Harrar moved to the Rockefeller Foundation's headquarters in New York in 1952 to assume the position of deputy director for agriculture. In 1955 he became director of that division, and in 1959 he was appointed vice president of the foundation. When Dean Rusk left the presidency of the foundation in 1961 to become U.S. secretary of state, Harrar became acting president and was elected president in 1962. He served until mandatory retirement in 1972.

During Harrar's presidency the Rockefeller Foundation continued a strong agricultural program. He worked with the Ford Foundation and host nations to support a global network of research centers (the Consultative Group on International Agricultural Research) that focused on developing more productive varieties of the world's primary food crops. Under Harrar the foundation also continued international programs of grants to the humanities and arts, medical science, and education. Harrar supported the establishment of new grant programs in population control, equal opportunity for minorities, and environmental protection.

At Rockefeller, Harrar became a leading promoter of international development through agricultural reform. He argued that if developing nations vigorously applied the methods and lessons of the Green Revolution they were sure to improve their food supply, better the health of their people, and acquire new wealth through trade in surplus crops. According to Harrar, "The future economic growth of many of the less well-developed nations of the world will depend precisely upon the rapidity with which their citizens can be trained for the multiplicity of responsibilities related to agricultural production, distribution, marketing, and utilization and attendant problems" (*Science*, 10 Mar. 1961).

Harrar had no systematic response to critics of the first two decades of the Green Revolution, who argued that a major effect of the new crops and technologies was to create a new class of wealthy landowners, while providing little benefit to small landowners and tenant farmers who did not have the resources to invest in the new system.

In 1969 Harrar testified before the Ways and Means Committee of the U.S. House of Representatives regarding a plan to tax and regulate foundations. In that and other forums he was a vigorous defender of organized philanthropy as a vital segment of American society.

After his retirement from the Rockefeller Foundation Harrar was a leader in creating the Rockefeller Archive Center, which provided scholars access to the records of the Rockefeller family, the foundation, and several other philanthropic institutions. Harrar served on the boards of several nonprofit organizations and businesses, such as the Overseas Development Council, the Near East Foundation, the Nutrition Foundation, Campbell Soup, Merck, and Viacom, and he remained an advocate for science and agriculture until his death in Scarsdale, New York.

• Harrar's career as one of the chief architects of the Green Revolution was characterized by organizational skill serving his conviction that scientific research could conquer world hunger. Harrar's personal papers and documentation of his long association with the Rockefeller Foundation are in the Rockefeller Archive Center, North Tarrytown, N.Y. The Oberlin College archives holds items relating to his college career. A collection of Harrar's addresses and essays was published as *Strategy toward the Conquest of Hunger* (1967). Elvin C. Stakman et al. described the early years of the Green Revolution sympathetically in *Campaigns against Hunger* (1967). Deborah Fitzgerald, "Exporting American Agriculture: The Rockefeller Foundation in Mexico, 1943–53," *Social Studies of Science* 16, no. 3 (1986): 457–83, offers a more critical view. An obituary is in the *New York Times*, 20 Apr. 1982.

DARWIN H. STAPLETON

HARRIDGE, William (16 Oct. 1883–9 Apr. 1971), baseball executive, was born in Chicago, the son of English parents (names unknown) who had come to the United

States probably in the 1870s. His father had no special trade and worked as a laborer. After graduating from high school, Harridge took a job with the Wabash Railroad as an office boy. At night he attended business college to learn bookkeeping, typing, and stenography. The railroad promoted him to the passenger ticket department where he soon was put in charge of booking transportation for theatrical companies and sports organizations. These included major league baseball's American League, all of whose travel was arranged through the Wabash by league secretary Robert McRoy. In 1911 Harridge married Maude Hunter of Decatur, Illinois. They had one child.

Harridge did his booking job so well that when McRoy left in 1911, he recommended Harridge as his successor to league president Ban Johnson. "I was scared to death when I reported for work," Harridge recalled. "I never had seen a professional baseball game. What made it worse for me was that McRoy had promised to stay for a couple of weeks to show me the ropes and then ran out on me the very first day."

Harridge quickly mastered his duties and justified his $50 a week salary, a raise from $90 a month with the railroad. Johnson taught him how baseball operated, and Harridge repaid his mentor with a fierce loyalty. "Ban was a forceful, aggressive leader and a brilliant organizer. He, more than anyone else, made baseball the National Game," Harridge asserted.

Harridge's devotion was put to the test, however, in February 1927, when the American League club owners, upset with Johnson's erratic behavior and frequent tirades against baseball commissioner Kenesaw Mountain Landis, asked Johnson to retire. Johnson brusquely refused and took out his anger on Harridge, whom the owners had elected acting league secretary. Johnson locked Harridge out of the league office and did not resign until November 1927. One day later, the owners elected Ernest Barnard of Cleveland as president and confirmed Harridge as secretary.

In March 1931 Barnard died unexpectedly, and the task of administering the league devolved to Harridge. Two months later, the club owners, at the instigation of Charles Comiskey of the Chicago White Sox, elected Harridge president. Harridge later insisted that the job as he inherited it was not especially difficult. "Outside of assigning umpires and ruling on occasional player disturbances on the field, there was little to do." The new president received his baptism by fire just a year after taking office. Carl Reynolds of the Washington Senators slid hard into New York Yankees' catcher Bill Dickey in a July 1932 game, and Dickey reacted by punching Reynolds and breaking his jaw. Baseball observers wondered whether Harridge would summon the courage to punish a player on the league's dominant team. Harridge acted quickly, fining Dickey $1,000 and suspending him for a month in the heat of a pennant race.

In 1933 Harridge played a leading role in creating baseball's All-Star game. Arch Ward, sports editor of the *Chicago Tribune*, had conceived the idea of the game as a special event during the Chicago World's Fair. Harridge convinced American League owners to accept the proposal on a one-time basis. But the game proved so popular that it quickly became an annual part of baseball's schedule. Harridge viewed the All-Star game as one way for the American League to assert its supremacy over the National League. He came to regard the 1941 game, won by Ted Williams of the Boston Red Sox with a three-run home run in the ninth inning, as his greatest baseball thrill.

Harridge used his power cautiously and often deferred to the league's owners in matters of policy. Nevertheless, he meted out discipline sternly against players, managers, and umpires alike. Even before the Dickey-Reynolds altercation, he settled a fight pitting Chicago manager Lew Fonseca and three of his players against umpire George Moriarty by fining all four White Sox and both fining and suspending Moriarty for goading the others into the fray. One player, Jimmy Dykes, who later managed several teams, felt the wrath of Harridge justice thirty-seven times. "I always respected Dykes," said Harridge. "He never carried grudges. He'd always say after paying a fine or finishing a suspension, 'Well, Will, we're starting from scratch again.' And he meant it."

Harridge supported progressive changes in baseball such as night games, but only if they did not contradict his own rather solemn view of how the sport should be conducted. In 1945 he fired umpire Ernest Stewart after determining that Stewart was trying to unionize his colleagues. In 1951 he chastised St. Louis Browns' owner Bill Veeck for signing Eddie Gaedel, a midget, to a contract and inserting him into a game for one plate appearance. "Actually, we never approved the contract," he said. "It was in our safe unsigned. We never would have approved it on the grounds the midget just wasn't qualified."

American League owners reelected Harridge to office three times, culminating in a ten-year term starting in 1956. But Harridge stepped down just two years later. He was seventy-five and in good health but anxious to retire before being asked to do so. The league created a new position for him, chairman of the board, which he occupied until his death in Evanston, Illinois. One year later, he was inducted into the Baseball Hall of Fame.

• Clipping files on Harridge are at the National Baseball Library, Cooperstown, N.Y., and the *Sporting News* offices in St. Louis. For some general background, see Lee Allen, *The American League Story* (1965), and Eugene Murdock, *Ban Johnson* (1982). Obituaries appear in the *New York Times*, 10 Apr. 1971, and the *Sporting News*, 24 Apr. 1971.

STEVEN P. GIETSCHIER

HARRIGAN, Ned (26 Oct. 1844–6 June 1911), playwright and actor, was born on the Lower East Side of New York City, the son of William Harrigan, a sea captain and ship caulker, and Helen Rogers. Ned Harrigan, born Edward, left public school at fourteen, served a while as printer's devil, and then apprentice ship caulker until he was eighteen. As a boy he learned much of minstrel stage business and old songs from his mother, who also taught him to play the banjo. And he saw minstrel shows, burlesques, Irish farces, and especially F. S. Chanfrau's revivals of Benjamin A. Baker's plays about Mose, the firefighter. The Mose works served as forerunners of Harrigan's Mulligan plays.

In early 1867 Harrigan traveled to San Francisco where he found work as a caulker. At the suggestion of friends he applied to a local melodeon (a variety hall featuring singing, dancing, acrobatics, minstrelsy, and drama, which was attached to saloons and gambling rooms), the Olympic, as an Irish comic singer. He was accepted, and he gained experience both singing and acting in extravaganzas. He joined Lotta Crabtree in duets at Gilbert's and the Bella Union, learning many tricks of the stage from her. He became a minstrel show end man at the Bella Union for two years. His first partner was Alex O'Brien; the second was Sam Rickey, with whom he played a duo act (*The Mulcahey Twins*) at the Pacific Melodeon.

Harrigan, Rickey, and Otto Burbank, calling themselves the California Comedians, traveled across the country; when they arrived in New York City, they were booked at the Globe (728 Broadway) and opened 21 November 1870; ten years later the Globe became Harrigan and Hart's Theatre Comique. Harrigan and Rickey played for two weeks in their own sketches and two in G. L. Stouts's *A Morning with Judge Dowling*. Harrigan returned alone to Chicago in 1871; while there he met Tony Hart (born Anthony Cannon; Hart's training had also been with a minstrel company), and for the next fourteen years their names, Harrigan and Hart, were tied together. The new partners tried out their act, *The Little Fraud*, at the Winter Garden in Chicago and again tried out the act in Boston, at the Howard Athenaeum, in mid-April 1871. They next moved on to New York, where they met David Braham, the orchestra leader at the Comique. In 1872 Harrigan wrote the words and Braham the music to "The Mulligan Guard," the first of over 200 songs the two created together:

> We shouldered arms and marched and marched away,
> From Baxter Street we marched to Avenue A.
> With drums and fifes how sweetly they did play,
> As we marched, marched, marched in the Mulligan
>   Guard.

The song achieved incredible popularity—in England, the Coldstream Guards marched to it; it was popular, in French translation, in Paris; and Rudyard Kipling used it in *Kim*. Harrigan wrote songs, sketches, and comic patter for minstrel routines. But he soon abandoned minstrel writing and shifted to New York scenes and characters; he wrote forty sketches for the first three years he and Hart performed at the Theatre Comique. In May 1873 he wrote a ten-minute sketch, "The Mulligan Guard," a satire on the pseudomilitary target companies manned by immigrants excluded from the regular militia. Harrigan's Mulligan Guard was, at first, a marching troop of two with a young

black target bearer. The nonsense and horseplay of this sketch became Harrigan trademarks.

The Harrigan and Hart troupe grew in reputation and numbers as they traveled all over the country: thirty-seven actors, musicians, and marching boys. Harrigan ultimately presided over four theaters in New York, the last of which he owned (its name changed from the Theatre Comique to the Harrigan and then to the Garrick, where it served as the first home of the Theatre Guild). He married Braham's daughter Annie in 1876, and of their six children who survived childhood, three stayed in the theater.

Harrigan's sketches grew into full-length plays, and over twenty of them ran for more than 100 performances each on Broadway (considered long runs in those days). His plays might feature up to seventy roles and involve more than 100 costumes—three hours of entertainment at prices that ran from twenty-five cents to one dollar. Braham, leading an orchestra of twelve, was always in the pit. In three years, from 1879 to 1881, Harrigan wrote seven Mulligan plays, beginning with *The Mulligan Guard Ball* and ending with *The Mulligans' Silver Wedding*, though some others dealt with the Mulligans except in title (for example, *Cordelia's Aspirations* [1883]). All starred himself and Hart, each taking several roles.

Harrigan wrote primarily of the slums—newsboys, toughs, sailors, prostitutes—of first- or second-generation Irish and German and Italian immigrants, and he featured blacks as well. The authenticity of his characters was complemented by songs and by what Harrigan referred to as "knockdown and slambang." In *The Mulligan Guard Ball*, for example, while Dan Mulligan's son is eloping with Gustavus Lochmuller's daughter in a dance hall, the Harp and Shamrock, and while the Mulligan Guards are dancing, the black regiment, the Skidmore Guard, is dancing on the floor above. The floor collapses, and the entire Skidmore Guard crashes down to the dance floor below. Various recognizable New York types (Lochmuller, for example, is a German butcher) made Harrigan's plays popular with audiences and critics alike. Some of Harrigan's early sketches were performed abroad in variety halls, but none of his full-length plays was ever exported.

Hart left Harrigan in 1885, but Harrigan continued to write for his company (plus a book, *The Mulligans*, in 1901). Of the forty-two plays he wrote, thirty-three reached the stage. All of his plays had thin plots, but all featured singing and dancing, an important development from the minstrel show and a step leading to the musicals of George M. Cohan. Harrigan presented recognizable locales on the Lower East Side and recognizable local types. William Dean Howells (in *Harper's*, July 1886) said of Harrigan, "In his own province we think he cannot be surpassed" and compared him to Goldoni; other critics compared him to Charles Dickens, Aristophanes, William Hogarth, and Honoré de Balzac. And Cohan, whose song about Harrigan ("H-A-double-R-I-G-A-N spells Harrigan") was featured in his *Fifty Miles from Boston* (1907) and whose works represented the next big step in the development of the American musical, admitted that Harrigan was the inspiration for his own work in the theater.

Ned Harrigan's last public appearance was on 16 March 1910 as guest of honor at a Friends of Ireland dinner. He died the following year at his home in New York.

• Harrigan papers are deposited in the University of Wyoming Library. Many libraries contain Harrigan material: the New York Public Library, for example, lists thirteen songsters (lyrics not put to music) plus sketches and a farce; most of the play scripts are in the Manuscript and Archive Division; and the Theatre Collection of the Library and Museum of the Performing Arts has scrapbooks, clippings, letters, and programs. Other repositories in New York include the Museum of the City of New York, the Players Club, and the New-York Historical Society. Other libraries with Harrigan material include the Library of Congress, the Boston Public Library, and the Theatre Collection of the Harvard Library. The Indiana University Library has about 150 pieces of Harrigan-Braham sheet music. Moody's biography has an extensive bibliography listing books, articles, and unpublished materials relating to Harrigan. A comprehensive biography of Edward Harrigan is Richard Moody, *Ned Harrigan: From Corlear's Hook to Herald Square* (1980); also useful is E. J. Kahn, J., *The Merry Partners: The Age and Stage of Harrigan and Hart* (1955).

JULIAN MATES

HARRIMAN, Daisy (21 July 1870–31 Aug. 1967), political activist and diplomat, was born Florence Jaffray Hurst in New York City, the daughter of Francis William Jones Hurst, the head of a steamship company, and Caroline Elise Jaffray. Daisy, as she was always called, was three years old when her mother died. She grew up in the home of her grandfather Edward S. Jaffray, whose connections to British and American politicians inaugurated Daisy's political education. Her formal education was private and scanty. She married Jefferson Borden Harriman, a New York banker, in 1889; they had one daughter.

Daisy Harriman, having a "notion that a woman should be able to do something in the workaday world," was appointed to her first political post in 1906 as manager of the New York State Reformatory for Women at Bedford, serving until 1918. In addition Harriman worked for improvements in children's health and welfare, particularly to provide pure, subsidized milk and to fight tuberculosis. Her husband's disapproval of women staying alone in hotels inspired her to found the Colony Club, New York's first women's social club, which opened in 1907 with Harriman as president, a position she held until 1916. She met Woodrow Wilson at that time, when, as president of Princeton University, he was invited to the opening.

Through the club Harriman became involved in political activities. She helped to create a women's welfare committee in the National Civic Federation to lobby for better conditions for working women in stores, hotels, and factories. Through the NCF, Harriman toured cotton mills in the South to inspect child labor conditions and in 1911 wrote articles for *Harper's Weekly* about her findings ("the first money I had ever earned"). This earning power became not merely a source of pride but a necessity after her husband died in 1914.

Harriman, like many reform-minded women at this time, became active in electoral politics. In 1912 she chaired the Women's National Wilson and Marshall Association (later the Women's Division of the Democratic National Committee) and in 1913 campaigned for John Mitchel as mayor of New York City. In 1913 Wilson recognized her support by appointing her to the Federal Industrial Relations Commission, created during the Taft administration to investigate the overall causes of industrial unrest. Harriman was the first woman appointed to a federal commission. Although supportive of labor generally, she took exception to the committee's final report, which was strongly prolabor, and contributed to a dissenting report more sympathetic to the "technical problems of production."

During World War I, Samuel Gompers named her chairperson of the Committee of Women in Industry of the advisory committee of the Council of National Defense, and she reported on safeguards for women in the munitions mills. She also organized the Red Cross Motor Corps and served in France as assistant director of transportation in 1918. She was a delegate to the Inter-Allied Women's Council to consult with Peace Conference committees on matters of interest to women and children and a vigorous advocate of woman suffrage.

Harriman published a book of memoirs, *From Pinafores to Politics*, in 1923. She worked throughout the 1920s to consolidate gains made by women and to rally the Democratic party during a period of Republican supremacy. As chairperson of the campaign committee of the Consumers League she fought the Equal Rights Amendment as a threat to protective legislation for women. She also worked for the League of Nations and the outlawry of war. In 1922 she cofounded the Women's National Democratic Club, serving as president 1923–1926, 1929–1931, and 1947–1949. From 1924 to 1936 she was Democratic committeewoman from Washington, D.C. Harriman's celebrated Sunday night suppers provided a forum for Democrats to meet the most stimulating of the capital's intelligentsia and were notable not only for the quality of conversation but also for the equal representation of women and men.

Harriman, as a delegate to the 1932 Democratic convention, favored Wilson's secretary of war, Newton D. Baker, a stance that rankled Franklin Roosevelt for four long years. She continued to network with New Deal adherents, most importantly, Frances Perkins, at her "tea cup chancellery," and campaigned for FDR in 1936. She even defended his controversial court-packing proposals and in 1937 was rewarded with an appointment as minister to Norway, the second woman head of a diplomatic mission (Ruth Bryan Owen Rohde had served in Denmark from 1933 to 1936).

Roosevelt had wanted a quiet post for Harriman, then a 67-year-old grandmother, but the war made Norway a crisis center. In November 1939 an American freighter, *City of Flint*, was seized by a German crew and brought to the Norwegian port of Bergen in violation of the laws of neutrality. Harriman located the ship before journalists did and negotiated with the German naval attaché to ensure that the *City of Flint* could sail for the United States.

When the Germans invaded Norway in April 1940, Harriman's was the first official report. She followed the government of King Haakon as it fled through the countryside; her military attaché was killed by shrapnel. She withdrew to Sweden and oversaw the evacuation of more than 800 Americans fleeing the region as well as Crown Princess Martha of Norway and her children. The party, including Harriman, sailed from Petsamo, Finland, in August.

Also in 1940 Harriman again campaigned for Roosevelt and served as vice chairman of the White Committee to Defend America by Aiding the Allies. In 1941 she published an account of her assignment to Norway, *Mission to the North*. After the war she continued her political salon, rivaled only by that of Alice Roosevelt Longworth, and campaigned for home rule in the District of Columbia, leading a protest march in 1955 at the age of eighty-four. In 1942 she received the Great Cross of St. Olav, the highest honor of Norway, and in 1963 President John F. Kennedy awarded her the first Citation for Distinguished Service. She died in Washington.

Daisy Harriman broke new ground for women in many different venues, from the Colony Club to industrial commissions, political campaigns, and the American embassy in Norway. Always she demonstrated the qualities that made her a successful diplomat: an interest in social problems, a balanced point of view, and access to people in power. Unafraid to try new things, it was said that her only fear throughout her long life was boredom.

• The Florence Jaffray Harriman Papers in the Library of Congress consist primarily of correspondence from 1937 to 1941, when she served as U.S. minister to Norway, and from 1940 to 1950, when she was active in organizations advocating international peace. Official reports are in the U.S. Department of State, *Foreign Relations of the United States, 1940*, vol. 1 (1955). *The Reminiscences of Florence J. Harriman* (1950) are in the Oral History Collection, Columbia University. Other articles include those in *Time*, 12 Apr. 1937, p. 21, and the *Independent Woman*, May 1937, p. 131, Sept. 1938, pp. 277–78, and May 1940, p. 128. An obituary is in the *New York Times*, 1 Sept. 1967.

KRISTIE MILLER

HARRIMAN, Edward Henry (20 Feb. 1848–9 Sept. 1909), railroad leader, was born in the Episcopal rectory at Hempstead, Long Island, New York, the son of Orlando Harriman, an Episcopal minister, and Cornelia Neilson. With church support provided for clergy-

men's sons, Harriman and his three brothers attended Trinity School in New York City. In 1860 Harriman won the top prize for scholarship at Trinity.

Wall Street expansion in the Civil War attracted young Harriman, pulling him from school in 1861. Starting as an office boy he advanced to messenger-clerk, working the street market, and by 1868 or 1869 he became the managing clerk for D. C. Hayes Company. In the summer of 1870 Harriman, with a loan from an uncle, bought a seat on the New York Stock Exchange. His friend James B. Livingston joined him in the mid-1870s and their firm became E. H. Harriman & Company.

Harriman was a successful stock market investor and became a dominant figure on Wall Street. Finance wizard Bernard Baruch wrote of Harriman that "he was the man I did my best to emulate when I first entered Wall Street" and that Harriman seemed "to be the epitome of all that was dashing."

Harriman was instrumental in the opening of the Tompkins Square Boys' Club in New York. He belonged to the Seventh Regiment of the National Guard, was a director of the Traveler's Club, and belonged to both the Union and Racquet clubs.

In the late 1870s Harriman met Mary Williamson Averell, whose father, William J. Averell, was the leading banker of Ogdensburg, New York, and president of the Ogdensburg & Lake Champlain Railroad Company. Married in 1879, over the next sixteen years six children were born to the couple.

In 1880 Harriman entered the railroad world as a director on the board of his father-in-law's railroad, turning his attention to the railroad as a business and investment vehicle. In 1881 Harriman and several partners bought a controlling interest in the 34-mile-long Lake Ontario Southern, reorganized in 1882 as the Sodus Bay & Southern. In October 1883 Harriman became the sole owner of the railroad.

Harriman offered the road for sale to both the Pennsylvania and the New York Central in the spring of 1884. He exploited the strategic location of his road and the competition between the giants. The New York Central took an option on the road until noon on 1 July; the Pennsylvania also expressed interest in purchasing it. When the New York Central desired to extend its option, Harriman was conveniently absent from his office, and the road was sold to the Pennsylvania. This first excursion into railroad finance proved profitable for Harriman, and his basic principles of railroading were developed at this time. A railroad's physical condition and equipment must be excellent and well maintained, he believed, and location and strategic position were valuable assets.

The combined influence of the Boissevain Brothers firm and Stuyvesant Fish, a prominent director and vice president of the Illinois Central, led to Harriman's election as an Illinois Central director in 1883. Harriman became closely associated with Fish in the management of the road, serving as chairman of the finance committee of the board of directors and for a couple of years as vice president. Harriman retired from the firm of E. H. Harriman & Company in 1885 to devote himself to railroads. Harriman and Fish installed a highly centralized management structure for the Illinois Central in 1888 that Harriman would use in his later railroads.

In 1885 Harriman bought the 7,863-acre Parrott estate in the Ramapo Highlands at auction; it was situated about forty-five miles north of Jersey City and ten miles west of the Hudson River. By 1905 the estate was almost thirty square miles; construction began that same year on the Harriman mansion. The estate became the Harrimans' permanent summer home, and it was named "Arden," after Mrs. Parrott's family.

Harriman's major business achievement was the reorganization and rebuilding of the Union Pacific Railroad. After its 1893 bankruptcy, the reorganization effort was put in the hands of Jacob Schiff of Kuhn, Loeb & Company. Schiff's efforts failed because of Harriman's opposition. Harriman's original idea was to unite the Illinois Central and the Union Pacific. Using Illinois Central credit, Harriman could get the funds for reorganization cheaper than Schiff could. He finally agreed to a plan of Schiff's that made him a director of the reorganized company and a member of its executive committee. Harriman assumed those posts in December 1897. Just short of the age of fifty Harriman began the great works of his railroading career. On 1 December 1898 he became chairman of the board of directors of the Union Pacific and chairman of its executive committee.

The reorganization plan of the Union Pacific reduced fixed charges, settled the construction debt to the federal government, and laid the foundation for Harriman's control of the Union Pacific and later the Southern Pacific.

In the summer of 1898 Harriman took his two older daughters and several Union Pacific officials for a daylight examination of the Union Pacific line from the Missouri River to the Pacific. A telegram from Portland asked the board of directors for $25 million for improvements and equipment. By 1904 more than $50 million had been invested in rebuilding and new equipment. The average capacity of the company's freight cars increased from twenty to thirty-four tons between 1898 and 1907. The average Union Pacific locomotive weighed thirty-seven tons in 1898 and sixty-eight tons in 1909. Harriman insisted on adequate maintenance to keep the road in first-class condition. The Union Pacific was a great operational success under Harriman, providing a handsome investment return.

Harriman took his family along with scientists, photographers, and artists to Alaska in the summer of 1899. The Alaska expedition produced a substantial volume of scientific accomplishments.

In 1899 Harriman and some associates acquired the Chicago & Alton, spending about $25 million on betterments. Because of a substantial increase in nominal capitalization and a rise in fixed payment, Harriman's control of the railroad has been severely criticized, especially by his greatest critic, Professor William Z.

Ripley of Harvard. In fact, Harriman's improvements were reflected in increased profitability of the railroad and a rise in both passenger and freight productivity greater than the national average. Rather than being worthless, as critics charged, Chicago & Alton common varied from 57⅞ to 74¾ and preferred from 70 to 78½ on the New York Stock Exchange in 1909. Harriman's management of the railroad improved it rather than looting it, as critics had charged.

In the spring of 1899 Harriman joined the New York reorganization committee of the Kansas City, Pittsburgh & Gulf Railroad. Significant improvements and equipment additions were made. Gross earnings rose from $4.1 million to $6.6 million, and passenger and freight productivity rose faster than the national average. With a new board of directors in 1905, Harriman disposed of his interest and left the railroad.

Also in 1899 Harriman offered to purchase the Burlington on behalf of the Union Pacific for $140 per share in cash. Charles E. Perkins, president of the Burlington, held out for $200 per share. Harriman then formed a syndicate with Schiff, James Stillman of National City Bank, and George J. Gould, a major railroad man and speculator, to purchase Burlington stock. James Hill, president of the Great Northern, entered (along with Northern Pacific interests) into negotiations with Perkins and capitulated to Perkins's price. Harriman then decided to purchase a majority interest in the Northern Pacific, which would give him half-interest in the Burlington. The price of Northern Pacific stock rose in the market, alerting Hill to the Harriman attack. Hill cabled J. P. Morgan in Italy for permission to purchase Northern Pacific common. A Harriman order to purchase the last Northern Pacific common needed for control was not filled, and the price of Northern Pacific shot up when the Morgan purchasers entered the market, creating a panic.

Rather than costly litigation, Hill suggested a compromise. Harriman and some of his associates were placed on the Burlington and Northern Pacific boards. The Northern Securities Company became a holding company for the stocks of the Great Northern, Northern Pacific, and Burlington. In 1904 the Supreme Court on a five-to-four vote found the Northern Securities Company guilty of monopoly and ordered divestiture of Great Northern and Northern Pacific stock. Against Harriman's wishes the stock was distributed pro rata, but with a rising stock market the Union Pacific earned a profit of about $70 million.

The Central Pacific Railroad between Sacramento and Ogden, which was the western end of the Union Pacific Railroad, presented an obstacle to the increased efficiency Harriman sought with reconstruction of the Union Pacific. His efforts to buy it were rebuffed, but the death of Collis Huntington, the last of the four men who built the Central Pacific as the western half of the first transcontinental, in 1900 allowed him to achieve his goal by purchasing control of the Southern Pacific. By mid-1901 the Union Pacific owned 45.5 percent of the outstanding Southern Pacific shares.

Over three years, $22 million was spent on reconstruction of the Central Pacific. Another $30 million was spent on betterments for the Southern Pacific and an additional $41 million for new equipment. Profitability of the Southern Pacific increased under Harriman, and its passenger and freight productivity far outpaced both the pre-Harriman record and the national averages. But the Interstate Commerce Commission (ICC) attacked Harriman's control of the Southern Pacific. The government eventually won a judgment in the Supreme Court. The Union Pacific was forced to divest itself of its Southern Pacific stock in May 1913.

Because of a curiosity to see the Orient and his vision of an around-the-world transportation line, Harriman traveled to Japan in 1905. Harriman's all-world plan failed in part because of Japanese reaction to President Theodore Roosevelt's role in negotiations to end the war with Russia. Opposition by Baron Komura to American influence was the final blow to Harriman's plans.

President Roosevelt reneged on a promise to Harriman with regard to Harriman's fundraising in 1904, and thus Harriman refused to aid in Republican party fundraising for the 1906 campaign. This resulted in a break between the two men. One result of the bitter breakup was Roosevelt's letter to James Sherman, chairman of the Republican Congressional Committee, characterizing Harriman as an "undesirable citizen." Roosevelt's animus also led to an ICC investigation of the Harriman lines focusing on the Chicago & Alton. Nothing came of this investigation.

Floods on the Colorado River in 1905 created a large new lake in the Salton Sink of California. In 1906 the inflow continued. The battle against the Colorado River flood fell to the Southern Pacific, under the leadership of Harriman, which spent about $3 million containing the river. Also in 1906 Harriman raced to San Francisco after the great earthquake, and he and the Southern Pacific assisted in recovery efforts.

In part because of misuse of Illinois Central monies, Stuyvesant Fish had come under attack by the company's directors starting in 1903. In 1906 matters came to a head with the election of Henry W. De Forest to the board of directors over Fish's opposition. When James T. Harahan was elected president over Fish, Fish felt he had been betrayed by Harriman and pushed unsuccessfully for the next year and a half for an investigation of Harriman's management of the Illinois Central. On 3 March 1908 Fish was defeated for reelection as a director, ending his more than three decades with the railroad.

In the spring of 1908 receivership for the Erie Railroad Company appeared inevitable; $5.5 million was needed. At a meeting in J. P. Morgan's library, Harriman offered to put up half the money if the others would put up the remainder. They refused, and Harriman put up the entire amount, which he borrowed from the National City Bank. With Harriman's action

the stock market rallied strongly. Harriman was hailed by the financial community and the general public.

During the summer of 1909 Harriman went to Europe seriously ill. He returned to his mansion at Arden, where he died the day before his thirtieth wedding anniversary, probably from cancer of the stomach.

• There are a great many books with information on Edward Henry Harriman. The place to start is the fine biography by George Kennan, *Edward Henry Harriman: A Biography* (1922). Kennan also wrote several other books that bear on parts of Harriman's life and career. These include *The Chicago & Alton Case: A Misunderstood Transaction* (1916), *Misrepresentation in Railroad Affairs* (1916), *E. H. Harriman's Far Eastern Plans* (1917), and *The Salton Sea: An Account of Harriman's Fight with the Colorado River* (1917). A fine short biography is in Jonathan Hughes, *The Vital Few* (1966). Another major biography is H. J. Eckenrode and Pocohontas Wight Edmunds, *E. H. Harriman: The Little Giant of Wall Street* (1933; repr. 1981). Friends wrote short biographies. These include Otto H. Kahn, *Edward Henry Harriman* (1911) and *Of Many Things* (1926); John Muir, *Edward Henry Harriman* (1912); and Robert A. Lovett, *Forty Years After: An Appreciation of the Genius of Edward Henry Harriman* (1949). Aspects of Harriman's Illinois Central career are included in Carlton J. Corliss, *Main Line America: The Story of the Illinois Central* (1950). Details of the Southern Pacific years can be found in Stuart Daggett, *Chapters on the History of the Southern Pacific* (1922), and in Neill C. Wilson and Frank J. Taylor, *Southern Pacific: The Roaring Story of a Fighting Railroad* (1952). Union Pacific period information is included in Nelson Trottman, *History of the Union Pacific* (1923). Two books by John Moody contain information on Harriman, *The Masters of Capital* (1919) and *The Railroad Builders* (1920). Three excellent articles are Carl Snyder, "Harriman: Colossus of Roads," *Review of Reviews* 35 (Jan. 1907): 37–48; Thomas Warner Mitchell, "The Growth of the Union Pacific and Its Financial Operations," *Quarterly Journal of Economics* (Aug. 1907): 569–612; and Samuel Morse Felton, "He Never Commanded—Yet He Never Forgot Good Work," *System* (Mar. 1923). An interesting book detailing Harriman's Alaska trip is William H. Goetzmann and Kay Sloan, *Looking Far North* (1982). Interesting insights on Harriman the man are in Bernard Baruch, *Baruch: My Own Story* (1911; repr. 1957).

The critic William Z. Ripley is heard from in *Railroads: Finance and Organization* (1920). Also see Lloyd J. Mercer, *E. H. Harriman: Master Railroader* (1985).

LLOYD J. MERCER

HARRIMAN, Job (15 June 1861–25 Oct. 1925), Socialist and utopian colonist, was born in Clinton County, Indiana, the son of Newton Springer Harriman and Elizabeth Miller, farmers. At the age of eighteen Harriman traveled to Irvington, Indiana (a suburb of Indianapolis), where he enrolled in Northwest Christian University and began religious studies. After graduation he served for three years as a minister in the Disciples of Christ church, but a growing interest in secular matters drew him away from organized religion, and at twenty-three he left the church. In 1883 Harriman headed west to Colorado Springs. He enrolled in Colorado College, where he studied philosophy but after one year returned to Indiana unsure about his future.

In 1886 Harriman moved to San Francisco where his concerns turned increasingly toward social issues. He observed on the West Coast contradictions between progress and poverty. Doubts arose about the capitalist system and the feasibility of free enterprise. Harriman saw in the nationalist movement a chance to serve humankind. Edward Bellamy's idea of a cooperative equality had both a religious and agrarian identification that made sense to a transplanted Indiana farmer. Gradually, however, he moved to the more rigid and doctrinaire tenets of Daniel De leon and the Socialist Labor Party (SLP). In 1894 he married fellow Socialist Theodora Gray Harriman. Their only children, boy and girl twins, were born the next year, but only the boy survived.

Harriman's oratorical skills together with his political dexterity quickly made him a rising figure in the SLP, and in 1898 he became the party's candidate for governor of California. In the midst of the campaign Harriman resumed his earlier study of the law and after reading for many months was admitted to the Bar. Internecine struggles within the SLP finally drove Harriman to the Social Democratic Party (SDP), where his finely honed political proficiency and growing popularity made him an instant leader. In 1900 he became Eugene Debs's running mate for vice president of the United States. As a result of his activities in the SLP and SDP Harriman became by the middle of the first decade of the twentieth century one of the most provocative and influential Socialists in the American West. He decided early in his career that the future of socialism lay in extending its base to include organized labor. The Harriman policy in California was one "of boring from within" the trade union movement and turning it into a political force committed to socialism. For a few years the policy proved successful.

Harriman also became known as an attorney who would take on unpopular labor or civil rights cases. Of particular note was his defense in 1907 of the famous Mexican anarchist, Ricardo Flores Magon, and particularly his defense with Clarence Darrow of the McNamara brothers who were accused in the 1910 bombing of the *Los Angeles Times*. Of even greater importance was Harriman's spirited socialist campaign for mayor of Los Angeles in 1911. Having forged an effective labor/socialist alliance, Harriman challenged the status quo candidates at the polls and ran a vigorous campaign. He almost carried off a socialist victory, but his involvement with the McNamaras and an all-out opposition from the city's newspapers ended the campaign quest. The *Los Angeles Times* and its publisher Harrison Grey Otis led the attacks on Harriman with a continuous barrage of hostile editorials. The Merchants and Manufacturers Association painted a picture of economic collapse if Harriman won. When the final votes were counted Harriman had lost but not before frightening the status quo half to death. A second attempt at the mayor's post in 1913 was also unsuccessful. Harriman grew disillusioned with the electoral process and attempted to find new means to secure his objectives. Seeking in microcosm the kind of cooperative alliance dedicated to socialist principles that had escaped him in urban society, Harriman moved away from practical politics.

Returning to his farming roots, the land and the economic base it represented, he led a hegira in 1914 to the desert terrain northeast of Los Angeles, where he established the most successful utopian colony in the history of the American West. Called Llano del Rio, it took as its motto "The Gateway to Freedom through Co-operative Action." At its height in 1916 the colony contained almost 1,000 members. For a time the utopia flourished, replete with dairy animals, wheatfields, fruit orchards, a Montessori school, print shops, vegetable gardens, a tent city, adobe buildings, and a commissary. By 1917, however, water shortages and internal feuding led to the colony's demise. There had always been water limitations at Llano, but hostility from neighbors suspicious of any socialist endeavor led to costly legal battles over water rights. Even more threatening were disputes among colonists over leadership roles, food shortages, adverse weather conditions, living arrangements, and interpersonal relationships. As Harriman put it during one period of despair, "we'll never be able to make a good colony until we change human nature."

Harriman's dream was for the evolution of a socialist America, and he saw the Llano experiment as furthering that goal. His dream was thwarted not only by lack of water but by forms of human frailty that ranged from greed to laziness to lust for power. The common bond that was supposed to provide the mortar for the colony was a theoretical belief in the concept of socialism that proved unequal to the practical hardships of hewing an agriculture community out of an inhospitable desert. In addition, the bond and discipline of religion, common to many colonies, was missing at Llano.

In 1918, at Harriman's urging, more than 100 loyal colonists left California by train and moved to a location near Leesville, Louisiana, which they named New Llano. The colony struggled on for almost twenty more years before it collapsed in 1937. Plagued most of his life by lung problems, Harriman did not follow the colonists to New Llano, though he did visit the site on several occasions. Instead, he remained in California engaged in extended litigation over the breakup of the California experiment. Harriman continued to dabble in socialist affairs, but his influence waned, and his concerns were largely ignored. The last years of his life were beset with ill health and frustration over the failure of his utopian dream. He died of consumption complications in a Sierre Madre, California, sanitarium.

Job Harriman influenced American life as a socialist Leader, an exponent of organized labor, a trial lawyer in defense of those whose civil rights were in peril, and as founder of the Llano Colony, which, though short-lived, played an important role in the history of utopian experimentation.

• Material on both the socialist and Llano Colony periods in Harriman's life can be found in the Job Harriman Collection at the Henry E. Huntington Library, San Marino, Calif. Standard death certificate for Harriman is at the Bureau of Vital Statistics, County Recorder, Los Angeles, filed 29 Oct. 1925. A starting point for anyone interested in the Llano Colony is Robert V. Hine, *California's Utopian Colonies* (1966). See also Knox Mellon, "Job Harriman and Llano del Rio: The Chimerical Quest for a Secular Utopia," *Communal Societies* 5 (1985): 194–206. The best account of Harriman's early life is contained in Knox Mellon, Jr., "Job Harriman: The Early and Middle Years, 1861–1925" (Ph.D. diss., Claremont Graduate School, 1972). An excellent account of Harriman's role in the mayoralty campaign of 1911 is contained in Alexander Irvine, *Revolution in Los Angeles* (1912).

KNOX MELLON, JR.

HARRIMAN, Mary Williamson Averell (22 July 1851–7 Nov. 1932), philanthropist, was born in New York City, the daughter of William John Averell, a noted businessman, and Mary Laurence Williamson. During Mary's childhood the family resided in Ogdensburg, New York, where William Averell's business affiliations included banking and the presidency of the Ogdensburg and Lake Champlain Railroad. A very religious and civic-minded individual, he served as a vestryman for the Episcopal church and as an elected Democratic alderman.

Mary attended finishing school in New York City for a short period, but most of her formative years were spent performing charity work. Her dedication caused her pastor to remark that her "services . . . to the ignorant, the distressed and the poor" were valuable assets to the community, and he lamented losing her services when she married Wall Street financier Edward Henry Harriman in 1879 and moved to New York City, where the couple—Republicans and staunch Episcopalians—raised six children. Edward Harriman shared his wife's benevolent attitude, having founded, three years before their marriage, the first club for underprivileged boys in the United States.

Intrigued by his father-in-law's railroading ventures, Edward Harriman followed in his footsteps and thereby amassed an empire as well as a fortune. Until her husband's death in 1909, Mary Harriman devoted herself to their children and to the family's extended household. (The Harrimans' far-flung properties included a camp on Upper Klamath Lake in Oregon, a ranch on the Snake River in Idaho, and "Arden," their estate in New York State.) Mary was not a disinterested housewife, however. A great believer in efficiency, she kept abreast of her husband's business ventures and even acquired a broad knowledge of railroads. Thus when Edward died, she was named executor of his nearly $70 million estate. A highly organized person, she managed his financial and railroad empire until her sons came of age and then dedicated herself to advancing charitable causes.

The large inheritance prompted many to write to Harriman, telling her of their desperate situations and pleading for money. Unsure of how to evaluate these myriad requests, she commissioned William H. Allen of the Bureau of Municipal Research (BMR) to evaluate the needs expressed in the letters and to determine the most effective ways of providing help. Allen's conclusions were published in *Modern Philanthropy: A Study of Efficient Appealing and Giving* (1912). Critical of waste and duplication, the book sought to eliminate indiscriminate gift giving by urging donors to support only those organizations that distributed monies efficiently. In the book's foreword Harriman stressed the importance of equal opportunity for all and of individual involvement in the general welfare of the community.

Another concern for Harriman was the government's handling of the problems related to health issues and hospital care. In 1911 she began annual donations to the BMR for "scientific research" to determine which methods maximized governmental techniques to raise the efficiency of operations. Very capable of determining the value of a proposal, Harriman also took a special interest in Allen's plan to establish a BMR-affiliated school that would train specialists for research related to government services. Harriman raised funds for and actively participated in the founding and activities of the Training School for Public Service. Established in 1911, the facility was the first school designed specifically for training in public administration. She served as a trustee on the BMR board from 1914 until its reorganization in 1921, when it became known as the National Institute of Public Administration, whereupon she served on the institute's board until her death.

In the years immediately preceding and following World War I, Harriman supported organizations and causes that were closest to her and to the memory of her late husband. Her interest in eugenics led Harriman to establish in 1910 the Eugenics Records Office on Long Island to study heredity and its relationship to mental illness. Other endowments went to the American National Red Cross, the Trudeau Tuberculosis Sanatorium, the New York Academy of Medicine for a Committee on Public Health, and the Harriman Research Laboratory for the study of physiological chemistry. She also established the Harriman Fund for Orthopaedics at the Yale School of Medicine. Her service positions included membership on the Women's Advisory Committee of the National War Council (1917–1919) and the National Committee on Volunteer Service (1922–1928) and a seat on the board of visitors of Letchworth Village, a state institution for retarded children (1913–1932). Beginning in 1913, as an incentive for railroads to operate competently and in an attempt to reduce rail accidents, the Harriman Memorial Medal was awarded annually to the railroad with the best safety record. Through the donation of $1 million and 10,000 acres of timberland, much of her Arden estate was converted into Harriman State Park.

After the war Harriman focused on the arts, assisting young artists by commissioning paintings or sculptures. She helped launch many careers, such as that of sculptor Malvina Hoffman, whose studio was provided by Harriman. She also enabled young musicians to receive the experience they needed to play with professional orchestras by founding in 1920 the American Orchestral Society. Because of her contributions in the area of music, the National Institute of Social Sciences awarded her its gold medal in 1925. Harriman died at a New York City hospital following surgery for an intestinal tumor.

Many of Harriman's contributions remained private, as she never sought acknowledgment or recognition and preferred action to words. Her philosophies of life were simple, and her genuine concerns took priority. She retained a belief that people needed to rely on one another and that sharing brought happiness in one's lifetime. Secure in her own life, Harriman contributed to the opening of new avenues in public service.

• Biographical information can be obtained in Persia Campbell, *Mary Williamson Harriman* (1960). See also Board of Visitors of Letchworth Village, *Annual Report* (1933); Edward H. Lewinski-Corwin and E. V. Cunningham, *Thirty Years in Community Service, 1911–41* (1942); Mark H. Haller, *Eugenics* (1963); Malvina Hoffman, *Yesterday Is Tomorrow: A Personal History* (1965); Roy Lubove, *The Professional Altruist: The Emergence of Social Work as Career 1880–1930* (1965); and Rudy Abramson, *Spanning the Century: The Life of W. Averell Harriman; 1891–1986* (1992). Obituaries are in the *New York Times* and the *New York Herald Tribune*, both 8 and 9 Nov. 1932.

MARILYN ELIZABETH PERRY

HARRIMAN, W. Averell (15 Nov. 1891–26 July 1986), businessman and government official, was born William Averell Harriman in New York City, the son of the railroad organizer Edward H. Harriman and Mary Averell. He spent his early years in New York and on the family estate of Arden in the nearby Ramapo Mountains. He was educated at Groton and Yale. Harriman did poorly in preparatory studies, which brought admonishment from his father, and it is possible that his stammer, which he carried throughout his long life, resulted from this experience. At Yale he did better academically, and excelled socially.

After college Harriman prepared to move up the ladder of his father's Union Pacific Railroad and spent two years in Omaha studying railroading from the laying of track on up. In 1915 he was called back to New York to become a junior vice president. Railroading did not, however, hold his attention. When the United States entered World War I in 1917 he espied a way to follow in the footsteps of his father, who had taken an interest in ships in the years before he died, by going into shipbuilding. He presided over construction of a vast shipyard at Chester, Pennsylvania, for his Merchant's Shipbuilding Corporation which, like all government-financed yards, was just beginning to turn out ships by the time of the armistice in 1918. After the war the world shortage of ships continued, and Harriman created the United American Lines, one of the largest merchant fleets in the world. He arranged a joint service with the German-owned Hamburg-American Line. Not yet thirty, he was hailed as "Harriman II" and "the Steamship King." When the glut of ships, merchant and passenger, became evident in 1926, he abandoned the shipping business.

Turning next to European investments, Harriman became involved with the Georgian Manganese Company, which exploited manganese deposits in Soviet Georgia. He entered the business in 1925 without personally examining the mines, an error that his father would never have made. He concluded a contract with the Soviet government that permitted him to exploit only lesser deposits and again lost out: the Soviets took over a rich preserve in the neighborhood and a German firm picked up the remnants of the Harriman company. Other European efforts during the 1920s, notably an attempt to electrify vast areas of Poland, also failed.

Returning to Union Pacific, Harriman was elected chairman of the board in 1932 and sponsored the first streamliner trains in the hope of rejuvenating the road's declining passenger traffic. Pulled by diesel engines, the trains made the run from Chicago to the West Coast in record time, with luxurious accommodations, reasonably priced meals, and conductors replaced by stewardesses in imitation of increasingly attractive airline travel. The experiment was only a modest success. If Harriman and the Union Pacific board had instead concentrated on reconstructing its freight operations, they would have positioned the road far better for the freight-carrying requirements of World War II and for the competition with trucks that followed.

With his brother Roland, Harriman meanwhile established an investment firm, which in 1931 combined with Brown Brothers to create Brown Brothers Harriman. Although in its initial years the partnership did not do well, it eventually proved profitable. Until the beginning of the administration of President Franklin D. Roosevelt in 1933, Harriman had not enjoyed success in his work, in spite of his efforts in the fields that had occupied his father.

In 1915 he married Kitty Lanier Lawrance; they had two daughters. After their divorce in 1929, he married Marie Norton Whitney in 1930. Upon his second wife's death in 1970, he married Pamela Digby Churchill Hayward in 1971. From his second and third marriages there were no children. An excellent sportsman, he took up polo and became a member of the American team in 1928 with a handicap of eight (out of a possible ranking of ten). When his interest in polo waned he turned to croquet and eventually was listed in the Croquet Hall of Fame. Early in the 1930s, seeking a way to advance business for the Union Pacific, he created the Sun Valley resort in Ketchum, Idaho, and took up skiing.

At the beginning of the Roosevelt administration, Harriman's interest began to turn from business to politics. He sensed that power in the country had passed from Wall Street to Washington. His political interests focused on the Democratic party. During his attempt to mine manganese in the Soviet Union he had tangled with Secretary of Commerce Herbert Hoover, which may have been the reason that he voted in 1928 for the Democratic presidential candidate. In 1932 he voted for Roosevelt, whose Hudson Valley family he knew. The result was a post in the National Recovery Administration, which he owed partly to his friendship with its administrator, Brigadier General Hugh Johnson. After Johnson's dismissal by the president, Harriman ran the NRA until the Supreme Court declared it unconstitutional in 1935. Thereafter, Harriman served the administration only as chairman of the business advisory council for the department of commerce from 1937 to 1939.

With the coming of war in Europe and increasing evidence that the United States would be involved, Harriman unabashedly sought a post in Washington or abroad. Early in 1941 he joined the Office of Production Management. Then came a major assignment. With passage of the lend-lease legislation in March, the administration undertook to support the nation's allies with massive war materials, a program that eventually totaled approximately $50 billion. At the outset it was necessary to send a special presidential representative to Britain, and Harriman flew to London first as minister, then, after August, as ambassador. He soon was intimate with Prime Minister Winston Churchill and often joined him at his country place on weekends. The "defense expediter," as President Roosevelt designated Harriman, bypassed the American ambassador in London, John G. Winant, the State Department, and the American military to communicate directly with the president, often through his close friend Harry Hopkins, who at that time lived in the White House.

When the Soviet Union entered the war, Harriman extended his operations to Russian lend-lease. He recommended the removal of the American ambassador in Moscow, Laurence Steinhardt, whom the president replaced with Admiral William H. Standley. When Harriman bypassed Standley, the latter quit and was replaced by Harriman, who served in Moscow from 1943 to 1946. His access to the president, however, no longer obtained when Hopkins became ill in 1944, and Harriman had to communicate with Washington through the State Department. Although he was present at the Big Three conferences at Teheran, Yalta, and Potsdam, he was no longer a major figure.

Harriman served conspicuously in postwar foreign relations during the administrations of Presidents Harry S. Truman, John F. Kennedy, and Lyndon B. Johnson. The businessman-turned-public servant played many roles but was disappointed when the post that he dearly wished for, secretary of state, went in 1949 to his Yale friend, Dean Acheson. At the beginning of the Kennedy administration he again hoped for the secretaryship, which to his chagrin went once more to a younger man, Dean Rusk.

After serving briefly as ambassador to Great Britain in 1946, Harriman replaced Secretary of Commerce Henry A. Wallace when the latter resigned in September of that year. He remained in the Truman cabinet until 1948, when an opportunity arose with passage through Congress of the first appropriation for the Marshall Plan. He became the number-two man in the Economic Cooperation Administration, balancing the Republican administrator of the plan, Paul G. Hoffman. Upon virtual completion of the plan in 1950, he returned to Washington as a special assistant to the president during the outbreak and initial course of the Korean War. From 1951 to 1953 he served as director of the Mutual Security Administration, supervising rearmament of America's allies in Europe. In these positions his work varied in importance. At the department of commerce he presided over a vast bureaucracy that largely ran itself, but the position gave him the opportunity to participate in cabinet meetings, which in the Truman administration (unlike the Roosevelt administration) were important affairs. In the ECA, Harriman's talents as a troubleshooter were much in evidence; division of the Marshall Plan's $13.3 billion among the nations of western Europe called for the highest qualities of diplomacy. The months as special presidential assistant were an interlude, after which in the MSA he dispensed billions in military assistance as well as the final appropriations of the Marshall Plan and the Truman administration's 1949 Point IV program of technical assistance to developing countries.

During the administration of Dwight D. Eisenhower, Harriman turned his energies to political office. He sought the Democratic presidential nomination in 1952 and 1956, but was defeated by Governor Adlai E. Stevenson II of Illinois. Running for governor of New York in 1954, he was elected by a slim margin of 11,000 votes out of 5 million. The governorship constituted the apogee of his political career. He enjoyed Albany, and for the rest of his life insisted upon being known as "Governor Harriman." Privately he described himself as "the guv." In attempting to manage the state's deteriorating finances, he instituted an austerity program, which was understandably unpopular. To that program he added his own ineptitude as a politician, giving miserable speeches and displaying little judgment on matters politic. He persuaded his Republican friend, Nelson Rockefeller, to head up an attempt to revise the state's archaic constitution, which overrepresented upstate and rural areas at the expense of New York City. Rockefeller used the public attention that this appointment brought him to defeat the man who had appointed him. Harriman lost his bid for a second term to Rockefeller in 1958 by a half million votes, at a time when the Democratic party was displaying a national resurgence.

In 1961 Harriman became part of the Kennedy administration by taking on the posts of ambassador-at-large, assistant secretary of state for Far Eastern affairs, and undersecretary of state for political affairs, which made him available for tasks that did not interest Secretary of State Rusk. These appointments led to a series of international missions that took him all over the world. He enjoyed them, as he loved to travel. Among other tasks, he took up the problem of civil war in Laos, which the Kennedy administration considered its largest international problem until the Cuban missile crisis of 1962. Here he was in his element, willing to negotiate patiently and, when necessary, badger the factional leaders into achieving peace, which he appeared to have attained by the time the negotiation came to an end (although critics later claimed that he only had made Laotian territory available as a highway for men and supplies passing from North to South Vietnam). In 1963 Harriman negotiated and signed the limited test-ban treaty, a momentary triumph during a decade of tense Soviet-American relations. He continued as undersecretary for political affairs in the Johnson administration and in 1965 resumed the post of ambassador-at-large. In this role he began negotiations for peace in Vietnam, which were concluded by the subsequent administration of Richard M. Nixon.

The advent of the Nixon presidency brought Harriman's nearly thirty-year diplomatic and political career to an end. He continued his interest in foreign policy and, as a private citizen, journeyed to many places, including the Soviet Union, where he talked with leading figures in Moscow. Undertaking to write his memoirs, he resorted to several assistants, but, except for a book about his World War II work in Britain and Russia, which was written in collaboration with the journalist Elie Abel, he did not approve of their work. Gradually, as age limited his activities, he slowed down. Increasing deafness made conversation difficult, and his eyesight nearly failed. In his last years he suffered from bone cancer. He died in Westchester County, New York.

Harriman's life spanned the century from President Benjamin Harrison (1833–1901) to Ronald Reagan, two vastly different eras. His movement from business to politics, particularly international affairs, well-reflected the basic power change of his time. His strengths as a negotiator and envoy did not lie in personal relations. Having started at the top, he disliked dealing with people below. This fact was evident in business dealings and government assignments, in which he always sought out the source of authority. If he had to deal with lower levels, he did his best to retrace quickly his steps to the top. In diplomacy he fared best as the protégé of Hopkins in 1941–1943, and as an administrator of the Marshall Plan and Mutual Security Administration, when his forceful personality made an impression. In his occasional forays into domestic politics he invariably proved inept.

• Harriman's papers are in the Library of Congress. They include a remarkable series of memoranda by one of Harriman's literary assistants, Mark L. Chadwin, which were compiled from interviews with Harriman and other individuals. The National Archives contains major files of documents that concern his offices and posts. His memoir is W. Averell Harriman and Elie Abel, *Special Envoy to Churchill and Stalin: 1941–1946* (1975). The only biography, Rudy Abramson, *Spanning the Century: The Life of W. Averell Harriman,* *1891–1986* (1992), is based in part on interviews with its subject and friends and acquaintances. Harriman wrote *Peace with Russia?* (1959) and *America and Russia in a Changing World: A Half Century of Personal Observation* (1971). An obituary is in the *New York Times,* 27 July 1986.

ROBERT H. FERRELL

HARRINGTON, John Lyle (7 Dec. 1868–20 May 1942), civil engineer, was born in Lawrence, Kansas, the son of Robert Charles Harrington and Angeline Virginia Henry. Living and working on the family farm near De Soto, a community about fifteen miles east of Lawrence, Harrington had an early education that was erratic, not untypical of Kansas farm boys in those days. So intense was his desire for self-improvement, however, that he was admitted to the University of Kansas, having passed the entry exams with only four years of primary and secondary education. He graduated with degrees in the arts and sciences and civil engineering in 1895.

From 1895 to 1907 Harrington prepared for the independent practice of consulting engineer by apprenticing with a number of notable bridge-fabricating companies that were upgrading the bridges of U.S. railroads and building new vehicular bridges that linked the country's burgeoning metropolitan centers. He held these various positions with the Elmira Bridge Company of Elmira, New York; the Pencoyd Iron Works of Philadelphia; Keystone Bridge and Carnegie Steel of Pittsburgh; Cambria Steel of Johnstown, Pennsylvania; the Bucyrus Company in South Milwaukee; the Northwestern Elevated Railroad of Chicago; the Berlin Iron Bridge Company of East Berlin, Connecticut; the Baltimore & Ohio Railroad in Baltimore; the C. W. Hunt Company of New York; and with the Locomotive & Machine Company of Montreal, a subsidiary of American Locomotive. He married Daisy June Orton in 1899; they had one son. He also continued his education, receiving a B.S. (1906) and an M.S. (1908) from McGill University in Montreal and a doctor of engineering degree (1930) from the Case School of Applied Science in Cleveland, Ohio.

Now thoroughly experienced in every aspect of bridge building, Harrington entered into a partnership with another famous bridge engineer at the turn of the century—John Alexander Low Waddell. From 1907 to 1914 Waddell & Harrington pioneered moveable bridges in the United States, especially the vertical lift type. This proved to be Harrington's most outstanding contribution to engineering. Harrington, who had gained considerable experience in mechanical engineering during his four-year stint (1901–1904) with the C. W. Hunt Company, and Waddell were issued several of the key patents for various mechanical devices required for the operation of moveable bridges. Two of the most notable bridges Harrington designed were double-deck rail and highway bridges over the Missouri River in Kansas City and over the Willamette River in Portland, Oregon. The only two of this type ever constructed in the United States, they were equipped with several options for opening. In both, the lower deck could be raised without affecting the flow of traffic on the upper. On the Willamette River Bridge both decks could be raised simultaneously to allow for a high-masted ship to pass. This interesting movement was accomplished by the trusses being designed so that they could telescope into each other. In 1914 Harrington established the firm of Harrington, Howard & Ash, and after 1928, Harrington & Cortelyou. In all, seventy-four vertical bridges were built by Harrington's firms.

Harrington finished his engineering career in the service of his country. Called to Washington, D.C., by President Herbert Hoover, Harrington was appointed a member of the Engineers Advisory Board of the Reconstruction Finance Corporation established to ease the country out of the depression of 1929–1933. From 1932 to 1934 he was responsible for the review and approval of loans for new construction projects, mostly public works that provided jobs for unemployed workers. His board reviewed more than 700 applications for projects ranging from a few thousand to over 100 million dollars. Loans were made to approximately one third of the applicants, and all but one made a profit, enabling the government to eventually recover all its loans.

Although he was a civil engineer by training and a member of the American Society of Civil Engineers, Harrington's expertise in mechanical equipment related to moveable bridges qualified him for membership in the sister organization, the American Society of Mechanical Engineers, of which he served as vice president (1920–1922) and president (1923). He also held memberships and associations with a number of other professional, honorary, and social organizations. Harrington, who died in Kansas City, was characterized by his peers as a forceful individual, with high energy, an active mind, and a remarkable memory, and as influential in developing both the character and the careers of his employees. He was an effective speaker and writer but published little, leaving only his considerable engineering works as testimony to his abilities.

• The key source of information on Harrington is in *Transactions of the American Society of Civil Engineers* 107 (1942): 1768–72. The memoir was prepared by his former business partner Frank M. Cortelyou and several other engineering associates. An obituary is in the *New York Times*, 21 May 1942.

ERIC DELONY

HARRINGTON, John Peabody (29 Apr. 1884–21 Oct. 1961), linguist and ethnologist, was born in Waltham, Massachusetts, the son of Elliott A. Harrington, a lawyer, and Mary L. Peabody, a teacher. The Harringtons moved to Santa Barbara, California, when John was two years old. As a high school student, Harrington exhibited a talent for languages, particularly German. He completed a B.A. in classical and modern languages at Stanford University in 1905, after only

two and one-half years, and took graduate courses at the universities of Leipzig and later Berlin in anthropology and languages, with an emphasis on phonetics.

While an undergraduate at Stanford, Harrington had also taken some summer courses at Berkeley, studying with the dean of California anthropologists Alfred L. Kroeber. Fifty-one years later Harrington remarked to Kroeber, "If I had had any sense, I would have taken a doctor's degree under you years ago. You are directly responsible for my coming into anthropology."

In the fall of 1906 Harrington returned to California to teach high school German and Russian in Santa Ana, devoting his summers to studying the Mojave and Yuman (Quechan) languages. Between 1909 and 1911 he lectured on Native American languages at the University of Colorado and the University of Washington. In 1910 he published articles on Tiwa and Tewa language groups of the Southwest in the *American Anthropologist* (12 [1910]), in addition to a short paper detailing his discovery of a genetic relationship between Kiowa and Tanoan. In 1911 he began a long association with Edgar L. Hewett and the School of American Archaeology (now School of American Research) in Santa Fe, doing archaeological, ethnographic, and linguistic fieldwork.

In 1910 Frederick Webb Hodge, chief of the Bureau of American Ethnology (BAE), asked the renowned Franz Boas if he might consider Harrington for work on the *Handbook of American Indian Languages*. Hodge asked Boas for his opinion regarding the young linguist and received a rather unfavorable reply. Hodge was apparently referring to Boas's reservations about Harrington when he wrote, "I am rather inclined to interpret the vagaries which you mentioned as those of a genius." The Smithsonian Institution hired Harrington in 1915, and his early BAE years seemed to reflect Hodge's estimation. Harrington published *Ethnozoology of the Tewa Indians* with Junius Henderson in 1914; *Ethnogeography of the Tewa Indians*, a 600-page annual report, in 1916; and the bulletin *Ethnobotany of the Tewa Indians*, coauthored with Barbara Freire-Marreco and W. W. Robbins, also in 1916.

Harrington married Carobeth Tucker, a twenty-year-old summer-school student in 1916. Their only child, Awonawilona, was born in 1917 while he was away in the field. In a letter to Hodge, Harrington wrote that his daughter's name in Zuni was "something like God, meaning trail holder, the equivalent to the Taos soul holder."

Harrington's research for the BAE in the early years was concerned principally with California Indian languages, such as the Chumashan languages, in addition to Chemehuevi and Yokuts. He later gathered data from the last surviving speakers of the Salinan, Esselen, and Costanoan language families as well as Chimariko.

Chumashan was a lifelong interest of Harrington's. He began a survey of the languages and dialects in 1912, eventually collecting data from native Californians who spoke a variety of Chumashan languages, including Inezeño, Barbareño, Juaneño, Obispeño, and Purismeño. In *Encounter with an Angry God*, an account of their brief marriage, which ended in divorce in 1923, Harrington's ex-wife, Carobeth Laird, wrote, "Even then he was in the grip of his grand obsession, his compulsion to record all that could be recovered of the remnants of the cultures, and most especially of the languages, of the Indians of Southern California" (p. 3). "Chumashan," Harrington noted in a letter to Hodge in 1917, encompassed a "large and very important culture area which is right at the present moment in the last gasp." He continued to collect and "rehear" material on Chumashan languages and culture throughout his career. Even in the last year of his life he was interviewing members of the Yee family, descendents of one of his first Barbareño Chumash informants.

Harrington considered California to be his private preserve, and he adopted a field methodology that was at once highly productive and intensely secretive. In 1921 he laid out his plans to Jesse Walter Fewkes for the collection of native place names for the whole of southern California. Chauffeuring "the oldest and best Indian informants" through their native lands, Harrington felt he could work with each of them "in rapid succession . . . [stopping] for closer inspection of village sites" where he would record and measure features "with a view to future excavation." An added advantage of having the consultants on location was that they could identify plants and animals, provide their names and uses as well as native terms for minerals and geological formations, for example. "Best of all, [being there] brings an atmosphere of the past which helps [the informant] call to mind the myths, folklore, and all kinds of superstition and early history of his people."

Harrington's greatest fear was the last surviving native speakers would die before he could record their language. His second greatest fear was that another anthropologist would record them first. As a result, he spent all his time and money on fieldwork, furtively and anonymously searching out and recording last survivors. As he scoured the greater part of California, he diligently kept his whereabouts unknown. From the late 1920s until his retirement, the location of Harrington's fieldwork was a closely guarded secret except to his boss, Matthew Stirling, and later the BAE secretary, Jessie Shaw.

In 1928 Harrington published *Exploration of the Burton Mound*, BAE Forty-fourth Annual Report. The archaeological excavations in Santa Barbara were part of a joint project with the Heye Foundation in New York. In the same year the BAE published his *Vocabulary of the Kiowa Language* (Bulletin 84) and *Picuris Children's Stories* with Helen H. Roberts. In 1932 Harrington published another monumental study, *Tobacco among the Karuk of California*. Filled with ethnographic data, this work has become a classic.

While the rescue of California Indian languages was Harrington's principal pursuit, he often made forays into other linguistic fields. During the early 1920s he worked with William Gates, the founder of the Maya Society, to record a Quiche Maya speaker from Guatemala. Gates arranged for Harrington to be given the position of associate in the Department of Middle American Research at Tulane in 1924. Harrington was interested in studying Nahuatl, Maya, and Quechua, the languages of America's high cultures, throughout his career.

Harrington worked with Robert Young and others in the mid-1930s to create an alphabetic system for writing Navajo. They successfully developed an orthography that became the standard method. The Bureau of Indian Affairs used the alphabet in a series of children's books titled *The Little Herder*.

Occasionally Harrington's fascination with language led even farther afield. In 1935 he became intensely interested in the trial of Bruno Hauptman (the man accused in the Lindbergh kidnapping). In correspondence with Harold G. Hoffman, the New Jersey governor who stayed Hauptman's execution, Harrington expressed his belief that the structure of Hauptman's speech made it impossible for him to have composed the ransom letter. Hauptman, he believed, was either innocent or had an accomplice. "In a case of broken English like this, there is a surer key to authorship than through handwriting," Harrington wrote to the defense lawyer.

At the beginning of World War II Harrington worked as a consultant on BAE's *Handbook of South American Indians*. He continued his work on Quechua and became convinced that he had discovered that some South American languages belonged to the supposed Hokan linguistic family of North America. This belief, which was controversial and remains so, would have extended a single language family over two continents, relating a large number of languages. With the war effort in full swing, Smithsonian employees were required to do "war work," which meant Harrington had to forgo fieldwork. His talents were put to use translating letters sent to his office via the Censorship Bureau. Toward the end of the war he was commended for his work with nearly sixty languages, including several American Indian ones. Despite the burden of war translations, however, Harrington managed to publish articles in 1944 and 1945 on diverse languages such as Chilcotin, Russian, Quechua, Hopi, Aymara, Witoto, Tlinkit, Yunka, and Navajo.

Harrington retired from the BAE the day after his seventieth birthday, and he was given the status of research associate on the following day. He returned to his native California to complete his Chumash work. There his colleagues continued to send him "linguistic" inquiries for quite some time.

Harrington's bibliography contains more than 125 titles, but this represents only a fraction of his life's work. His early discoveries of the relationships between such languages as Kiowan and Tanoan, as well as his Navajo alphabet, are lasting achievements. Harrington perceived early in his career, and demonstrated through his fieldwork and publications, that the collection of linguistic, ethnographic, and ethnohistoric data could eventually enhance the insights provided by archaeology. In addition, he understood that collaboration with botanists, geologists, and biologists would broaden the anthropologist's understanding of native classification systems.

Harrington's obsession with rescuing dying languages allowed little time to interpret, generalize, theorize, or publish. In a review of *Ethnogeography of the Tewa Indians*, Harrington's first major publication, Kroeber worried that Harrington might defer synthesis and theory until he felt his field utility was over. "It should hardly be necessary to recall that no one but the author can ever extract the full value of the author's own observations." Almost none of Harrington's work among the Chumash was ever published during his lifetime, but at least a dozen books on Chumash language and culture have appeared using his field notes. His greatest contribution was the exceedingly careful, phonetically accurate record of numerous Indian languages and culture, now housed in the Smithsonian's National Anthropological Archives, which he amassed over his lifetime. This extraordinary collection, encompassing more than a million manuscript pages and hundreds of sound recordings, provides a unique and important source for scholars and for the descendants of the Indian people whose knowledge he recorded. Harrington died in Santa Barbara.

• The majority of John Peabody Harrington's field notes and correspondence is housed in the National Anthropological Archives, Smithsonian Institution, Washington, D.C., and is available through Kraus International Publications. Also see Elaine L. Mills, *Guides to the Field Notes: The Papers of John Peabody Harrington in the Smithsonian Institution, 1907–1957*; volumes one through eight (1981–1989) detail the entire collection as arranged for microfilm, and Harrington's correspondence is described in volume nine (1979). Other correspondence from the period can be found in the records of the Bureau of American Ethnology, particularly from F. W. Hodge and Matthew Stirling. A number of biographical sketches have been written about Harrington, including Stirling's recollections of his career in an obituary that appeared in *American Anthropologist* 65 (1963): 370–81, and Carobeth Laird's *Encounter with an Angry God: Recollections of My Life with John Peabody Harrington* (1975). Numerous shorter pieces are available, including Jane MacLaren Walsh's monograph, *John Peabody Harrington: The Man and His California Indian Field Notes* (1976), and Victor Golla, "John P. Harrington and His Legacy," in an issue of *Anthropological Linguistics* 33, no. 4 (Winter 1991): 337–49, dedicated to Harrington's life and work.

JANE WALSH

HARRINGTON, Mark Walrod (18 Aug. 1848–9 Oct. 1926), meteorologist and astronomer, was born in Sycamore, Illinois, the son of James Harrington, a physician, and Charlotte Walrod. He grew up on an Illinois farm, attended Northwestern University, and then entered the University of Michigan, from which he received bachelor's and master's degrees in 1868 and 1871, respectively. He traveled in the summer of 1871 to Alaska, where he worked as an astronomer's assistant for the U.S. Coast and Geodetic Survey. Employed at the University of Michigan's museum until 1876, he became assistant curator and was also an assistant professor who taught mathematics and several sciences. In 1876–1877 he studied in Leipzig, Germany. He then went to Peking, China, where he taught astronomy in the Foreign Office's Cadet School. Developing an illness, he moved in 1878 to Louisiana State University, where he was a professor in 1878–1879. In 1879 he obtained a post as astronomy professor and observatory director at the University of Michigan, where he remained for twelve years. In 1884 he started the *American Meteorological Journal*, which he edited until 1892.

At that time, the U.S. weather service was run by the military's Signal Service (also called Signal Corps). To meet the needs of farmers, some members of Congress pushed to place weather forecasters under the civilian control of the U.S. Department of Agriculture, which had been elevated to Cabinet status. On 1 July 1891 the civilian U.S. Weather Bureau officially opened, "charged with the forecasting of weather, the issue of storm warnings, the display of weather and flood signals for the benefit of agriculture, . . . the taking of such meteorological observations as may be necessary to establish and record the climatic conditions of the United States," and similar tasks (Whitnah, p. 60).

The agriculture secretary, Jeremiah M. Rusk, selected Harrington as the bureau's first civilian chief. Harrington took over an agency that, as of 1892, had a budget nearing $900,000 and 172 weather stations. Its far-flung employees telegraphed daily observations to the Washington headquarters, which issued 36-hour forecasts twice a day.

Harrington placed major emphasis on climate studies. Under his leadership, data on rain and snow patterns were published in one book. In 1892 he launched a Division of Climatology and Hygiene, a reflection of the then-common belief in a close correlation between weather and health. He also pushed to use more automated instruments for recording weather phenomena and tried to improve severe-storm warnings. In the summer of 1892, for instance, the bureau conducted a study of thunderstorms in which observers sent postcards describing the storms and related meteorological measurements to Washington. One of Harrington's prouder moments came in early 1895, when the Weather Bureau telegraphed to Florida a correct 24-hour warning of a cold wave.

In "The value of Weather Forecasts to Agriculture and Inland Commerce" (*Review of Reviews* 12 [1895]: 303–5), Harrington observed that meteorology needed "some Galileo, Kepler, Copernicus and Newton if we are to lift the art of weather forecasting from its present ptolemaic stage into the stage of true theory as they lifted astronomy." He acknowledged that a "true and complete theory of local storms, might not be completed for a century." But "three competent physicists, left to pursue their investigations for ten years without disquiet and given proper encouragement and assistance, would probably be able to so improve our art of weather forecasting as to satisfy all ordinary requirements." Weather research needed financial support from the U.S. government, partly because "meteorology is a general terrestrial science, and, like geology, is too great for private resources." By fiscal year 1894 Harrington's budget had risen to $951,000. But a nationwide depression led to substantial cuts.

Although, personally, Harrington was "a man of rare conversational gifts, an interesting personality, genial at all times," as an admirer would recall many years later (*Science* [4 Dec. 1908]: 792), his relations with politicians were strained during the later stages of his career. In 1893 Harrington feuded with President Grover Cleveland's secretary of agriculture, J. Sterling Morton, who investigated alleged questionable practices and management within the Weather Bureau. Harrington wrote Cleveland that the charges were "a willful and malicious falsification of the testimony taken in the case" (Whitnah, p. 76). In mid-1893 Morton announced that the investigation had exonerated Harrington. However, Morton continued to pressure the Weather Bureau to cut costs and quarreled with a pioneering U.S. meteorologist, Cleveland Abbe. Harrington defended Abbe. Morton appealed to the president, who fired Harrington. The 3 July 1895 *New York Tribune* lamented the news: "Cleveland wields his axe and Professor Harrington's official head falls. Partisan politics and science come into collision."

Soon afterward, Harrington was offered a job as president of the University of Washington in Seattle. One of his backers was David Starr Jordan, the president of Stanford University, who joked of Harrington: "Perhaps [he] has had enough of political forecasting" (Gates, p. 58). As president, however, Harrington lacked charisma and leadership skills. He battled with the state legislature over appropriations, including his high salary. Some faculty members and members of the board of regents doubted his competence and dedication to duty. He resigned in March 1897.

That December in New York, Harrington wrote a friend in Seattle and hinted at personal difficulties: "As to myself—but why expand on that theme—I am still trying to solve the unsolvable" (Gates, p. 64). In September 1898 he became section director of the Weather Bureau's office in San Juan, Puerto Rico. There he failed in his managerial duties. Early the next year, he moved to the bureau's New York City office. He retired three months later. Soon after, he departed home for a dinner, and was not seen again for almost a decade.

In June 1907 he showed up at a police station in Newark, New Jersey, asking for shelter. He was unable to state his name. He was placed in a mental institution under the name "John Doe, eighth." The next year his wife Rose Smith Harrington and his son discovered him there. During his absence, it appeared, he had retraced some of the steps in his early career, but in less elegant ways: He had traveled as far as China, worked on a Louisiana sugar plantation, and labored at a lumber camp in the northwestern United States. After 1908 his mental condition improved, but never enough for him to be released from the asylum, where he died.

Despite his troubles as a scientific and academic administrator, Harrington guided the civilian U.S. Weather Bureau through its first years, spurred the emerging science of climatology, and foresaw the modern age of greatly improved weather forecasts.

• Harrington wrote the Weather Bureau's first bulletin, *Notes on the Climate and Meteorology of Death Valley, California* (1892). He also wrote articles for popular magazines. His book *About the Weather* appeared in 1899. Donald R. Whitnah, *A History of the United States Weather Bureau* (1965), depicts Harrington's work and political battles at that agency. His presidency of the University of Washington is described in Charles M. Gates, *The First Century at the University of Washington, 1861–1961* (1961). The 4 Dec. 1908 issue of *Science* magazine reprints a letter, originally published in the *Boston Transcript*, that commented on Harrington's career, personality, and institutionalization for mental illness. The *New York Times* (8 Jan. 1909) describes how Harrington's wife and son discovered him in the asylum.

KEAY DAVIDSON

HARRINGTON, Michael (24 Feb. 1928–31 July 1989), writer and socialist political leader, was born in St. Louis, Missouri, the son of Edward Michael Harrington, a lawyer, and Catherine Fitzgibbon, a teacher. He grew up in a middle-class Catholic family, attended parochial schools, and graduated from Holy Cross College in 1947, after which he attended Yale Law School for one year, then enrolled at the University of Chicago, where he received a master's degree in English literature in 1949.

Back home in St. Louis that same year, Harrington took a temporary job as a social worker, hoping to earn enough money to go to New York to write poetry. On his job, "one rainy day in 1949," he recounted in *The Long-Distance Runner* (1988): "I went into a decayed, beautiful house, near the Mississippi River, which stank of stopped-up toilets, dead rats, and human misery. . . . An hour or so later . . . it dawned on me that I should spend the rest of my life putting an end to that house and all that it symbolized."

In 1951, while he was living in New York where he had moved to pursue his goal of becoming a poet, Harrington joined the Catholic Worker movement, led by Dorothy Day. Taking a voluntary vow of poverty, he lived in the Catholic Worker commune and worked among the alcoholics and homeless in the Bowery. The lively political discourse within the Catholic Worker community spurred him to explore radical political philosophies, and in 1952 he became a Marxist.

Harrington quickly became a leader, first of the Young Socialist League, and then of the Socialist party, the party of Eugene Victor Debs and, later, Norman Thomas. As an activist, Harrington attended and spoke at party meetings, organized demonstrations against the Korean War, and edited the party journal, *New America*. Along with other party activists, he became involved in the civil rights movement, primarily working in Harlem. In 1960 he was a chief organizer of the demonstrations in Los Angeles outside the Democratic party convention, demanding (and winning) the adoption of a strong civil rights plank in the party's platform.

In 1962 Harrington gained celebrity with the publication of *The Other America*, a journalistic indictment of the persistence of poverty amid the nation's growing wealth. Arguing that poverty was systemic to American capitalism and virtually hidden from the eyes of the majority, the book's heartrending portraits of poverty in Appalachia, in the southern Black Belt, and among the elderly in the nation's cities captured the American imagination. Shortly before his death, President John F. Kennedy read the book and asked aides to develop a strategy for a campaign against poverty. The War on Poverty was a major initiative of the Lyndon B. Johnson administration. Harrington served as a consultant to Johnson's War on Poverty, which greatly expanded the Aid to Families with Dependent Children and Social Security Disabilities programs, developed Food Stamp and Head Start programs, and funded hundreds of community action agencies before President Richard Nixon began to cut it back in the 1970s.

In the early 1960s, when the New Left began to emerge, Harrington, then executive director of the democratic socialist League for Industrial Democracy, attempted to play a bridging role between the new campus insurgents and the old socialist movement, but he failed; after the founders of Students for a Democratic Society (SDS) did not fully accept his arguments that the organization's statement of principles should include an explicit condemnation of communism and not include one condemning American liberalism, he attacked SDS publicly, for which he later apologized. Nevertheless, the renown he had won for his incisive critique of American capitalism and his oratorical skills and passion made him a popular antiwar speaker on college campuses during the later sixties and early seventies.

In 1963 he married Stephanie Gervis, a journalist. They had two children.

During the 1960's, Harrington and the Socialist party he led advocated a new political strategy. Abandoning the independent political campaigns that his predecessors Debs and Thomas had used as a means to introduce radical ideas into American political discourse, he argued that the socialist party should work to realign the Democratic party by encouraging its conservative southern wing to go over to the Republicans, while attracting liberal Republicans to the Democrats. In a realigned party system, he argued in *Toward a Democratic Left* (1968), socialists could work on "the left wing of the possible" to advocate reforms that not only would improve people's lives but change the structure of the system to make it more egalitarian and democratic.

Harrington's leadership of the Socialist party foundered over the Vietnam war. Most of the party's executive committee, still bearing the scars of their battles with the Communist party, supported the war as necessary to halt the advance of global communism; Harrington, an equally ardent anti-Communist, wholeheartedly opposed the war as an extension of colonialism in Indochina. Between 1968 and 1973, his relationship with party officials became increasingly strained; finally, in 1973, he asked a small group of supporters to help him establish the Democratic Socialist Organizing Committee (DSOC). Having decided as a result of his experience in the Socialist party that he could not be the spokesman for an organization unless he was intimately involved in its decision making, he became DSOC's organizational leader as well as its public face. He chaired local and national executive meetings, edited the party publication, the *Newsletter of the Democratic Left*, and spoke at chapter meetings throughout the nation.

A DSOC initiative, the Democratic Agenda, played a leading role in coalescing labor, liberal, civil rights, and feminist forces within the Democratic party in the mid-1970s, enhancing DSOC's reputation on the left. By 1982 the DSOC had enlisted 3,000 members, mainly from college campuses, the old socialist movement, and progressive trade unions, especially the United Auto Workers, the International Association of Machinists, and the American Federation of State, County, and Municipal Employees. In that year, the DSOC agreed to merge with the New American Movement, another democratic socialist organization that had its origins in the New Left. As co-chair of the merged Democratic Socialists of America, Harrington played an active role in the Socialist International, where he worked closely with such leaders of European mass socialist parties as Olaf Palme of Sweden's Labor party and Willy Brandt of West Germany's Social Democratic party.

During the time he led the American socialist movement, Harrington became a prolific political theorist, writing more than a dozen books after *The Other America*. In such works as *Socialism* (1972), *The Twilight of Capitalism* (1976), and *The Next Left* (1986), and in the pages of *Dissent* magazine, he tried to rescue Marxism from the dogmatism and authoritarianism that he believed distorted Marx's legacy; at the same time, he sought to demonstrate Marxism's power to illuminate the dynamics of rapidly changing capitalist societies. In Harrington's hands, Marxism became both a democratic tradition and a rigorous method of political and economic analysis.

In 1972, in part because the birth of his children necessitated that he earn a steady income, Harrington obtained his first job outside the political movement, as a professor of political science at Queens College of the City University of New York. In 1988 he became Distinguished Professor of Political Science there. But, in a sense, he had been a teacher his entire adult life, as a scholar and polemicist, as a party spokesman, as a lecturer at hundreds of movement "internal education" meetings, as a campus orator, and as a guest speaker at innumerable union meetings and conventions. As a teacher, his effectiveness sprang not only from his erudition and polemical sharpness, but from his moral passion and personal gentleness.

In the last three years of his life, as he battled the cancer that eventually caused his death, Harrington wrote speeches for the Reverend Jesse Jackson's presidential campaign in 1988 and completed *The Long-Distance Runner* and *Socialism: Past and Future* (1989). In these final two works, he reaffirmed his commitment to democratic social change, arguing that the collapse of communism and the globalization of capitalism made it more necessary than ever to find ways to democratize the increasingly bureaucratic, collective institutions that dominate modern life. He died in Larchmont, New York.

• Harrington's papers, along with those of the DSOC, are in the Tamiment Library of New York University. Papers of the Socialist party, which he chaired until 1972, are at the Duke University Library. The most extensive accounts of his life are in his three autobiographical works, *Fragments of the Century* (1973), *Taking Sides: The Education of a Militant Mind* (1985), and *The Long-Distance Runner*. Maurice Isserman treats portions of Harrington's career in *If I Had a Hammer: The Death of the Old Left and the Birth of the New Left* (1987). Loren J. Okroi analyzes Harrington's economic ideas in his book *Galbraith, Harrington, Heilbroner: Economics and Dissent in an Age of Optimism* (1988). Harrington wrote nineteen books. Other than those books cited in the text, his most influential were *The Accidental Century* (1965), *The Vast Majority* (1977), *Decade of Decision* (1980), *The Politics at God's Funeral* (1983), and *The New American Poverty* (1984). An obituary is in the *New York Times*, 1 Aug. 1989.

DAVID BENSMAN

HARRINGTON, Thomas Francis (10 June 1866–19 Jan. 1919), physician and public health educator, was born in Lowell, Massachusetts, the son of Thomas Harrington and Mary Callaghan. In October 1885, following graduation from Lowell High School, he matriculated at the Harvard Medical School, enrolling at a time when the college degree was not yet a requirement for admission. He graduated in the class of 1888 and continued his medical education for another year in Europe, at the Rotunda Hospital in Dublin and at the Children's Hospital in London, and in Paris and Vienna. Late in 1889 he established a medical practice in his native Lowell, focusing on internal medicine, including pediatrics and gynecology. Harrington held appointments as visiting physician to St. John's Hospital for fifteen years and as consulting physician for three years afterward. In 1891 he married Mary I. Dempsey of Lowell, with whom he had three sons.

From the beginning of practice, Harrington displayed a progressive and active spirit that won him recognition in medical circles in Lowell and beyond. In 1894 he was made examining surgeon of the U.S. Pension Board, a position he held for fifteen years; and from 1895 to 1898 he served as chairman of the Lowell Board of Health, with special interest in the health of schoolchildren. He enlarged the idea of a floating hospital as a means of providing fresh air and sunshine to sick children, and he introduced the wetting down of

streets in congested districts during hot summer months, an idea that was soon adopted elsewhere. He also served as medical superintendent of day nurseries in Lowell.

A variety of articles grew out of Harrington's public health work. Among them, "The Child and the Public Health Curriculum" (1906), was a well-reasoned and forceful argument for correcting many of the pathological conditions that originated or existed in the schoolroom and for improving the physical and mental growth of children. Sometimes referred to in the literature as his "growth paper," it brought Harrington to the attention of educators as well as physicians, and it influenced events that followed.

Early in 1907 the Boston School Committee voted to create a Department of School Hygiene, the first department of its kind in the country, and the search for a competent physician to head it resulted in the unanimous selection of Harrington. For the next eight years he served as director of school hygiene in the Boston public schools. In 1908 he incorporated into the annual report of the superintendent of schools an eighty-page summary of health matters in school. Taking the position that the promotion of health and the cultivation of physical faculties form the foundation of medicine, Harrington reviewed the history and status of physical training in school, school athletics, playgrounds, sanitation, medical inspection, and related topics, making recommendations to improve them. And in 1909 his department issued a *Manual for Public School Playgrounds*.

In 1910 Harrington issued two more important publications: an article, "Medical Supervision versus Medical Inspection in Public Schools," and a pamphlet published by the Health Education League of Boston, *Observance of Health Day in Schools*. The latter called for one day each year to be set aside for promoting sanitary affairs in schools. In 1910 Harrington attended the International School Hygiene Conference in Paris and was appointed physician in chief of Saint Elizabeths Hospital, then on East Brookline Street in Boston. In 1911 he was chosen as a U.S. delegate to the Seventh International Congress of Medicine, held in London, and also in Brussels and later at London in 1913. Also during this period Harrington was elected president of the Boston Playground Association, and he served as examiner for the Civil Service Commission and as a director of St. Vincent's Orphan Asylum in Boston.

In May 1915 Harrington was selected to be deputy health commissioner of the State Board of Labor and Statistics from a list of more than forty candidates and afterward issued industrial safety bulletins relating to the protection of eyes and the prevention of accidents in industry (1916) and regulations for the prevention of anthrax (1918). He also continued to serve as a public health advocate and to promote the health of children. In 1913, when Harvard combined with the Massachusetts Institute of Technology to form a School for Health Officers, the forerunner of the Harvard School of Public Health, Harrington began giving three lectures in the curriculum on the organization and administration of school hygiene programs. He especially outlined the role of the physician, nurse, and teacher in running school clinics and teaching physiology, personal hygiene, and athletics to pupils. These lectures continued through 1917.

Harrington had a taste for history, holding membership in the Lowell Historical Society and the Boston Medical Library. In 1903 he read before the Johns Hopkins Historical Club a paper on "Dr. Samuel Fuller, of the *Mayflower* (1620), the Pioneer Physician," which was published in the *Johns Hopkins Hospital Bulletin* (Oct. 1903) and still remains definitive on the life of the first qualified physician to immigrate to America. And in 1906, coincidental with the relocation of the Harvard Medical School to its new Longwood campus in 1905, a three-volume work, *The Harvard Medical School, a History, Narrative and Documentary, 1782–1905*, compiled by Harrington and edited by his medical school classmate James Gregory Mumford, was published. Growing out of his activity on behalf of the Harvard Medical Alumni Association, the work is replete with documentary information, but its length, discursiveness, and lack of an index make it unwieldy and difficult to use. Nonetheless, it remains the most detailed source on the school and, because of the biographical register of students it contains, will never completely go out of use. Harrington was honored by the Massachusetts Medical Society in 1908, being chosen its annual orator and delivering a historical and philosophical talk on "The Sanctity of Medicine."

When World War I broke out, Harrington was appointed with the rank of captain to the medical staff of the new State Guard, afterward advancing to major. For four months during the 1918 influenza epidemic he took charge of a U.S. Marine Hospital in Brookline, his work at this difficult time being recognized by his promotion to the rank of lieutenant colonel in the State Guard. His promising career and likelihood of further advancement were abruptly cut short in late 1918, when he contracted a case of ptomaine poisoning, to which he succumbed in mid-January after an illness of five weeks.

• A brief overview of Harrington's life is in the *Dictionary of American Medical Biography*. His obituary appears in several journals, including the *Journal of the American Medical Association*, 1 Feb. 1919, and the *Boston Medical and Surgical Journal*, 13 Feb. 1919. Newspaper obituaries for Harrington are in the *Boston Transcript* and *Boston Herald*, both 20 Jan. 1919.

RICHARD J. WOLFE

HARRIOT, Thomas (1560–2 July 1621), scientist, linguist, and author of the first English book on North America, was born in Oxford (city or county), England; his parentage is unknown. As an undergraduate he entered St. Mary's Hall (attached to Oriel College, Oxford) in 1576, matriculated in the University of Oxford in 1557, and graduated B.A. in 1580. He never married.

Harriot worked for some time in London, perfecting his applied mathematical skills, and entered the service of Walter Ralegh (knighted 1585) in 1582 or 1583, his task being to instruct leaders and navigators in the craft of mathematical navigation. He thus had a part in planning the Roanoke voyages of 1584–1587, while he also began carrying out astronomical observations from the roof of Durham House in the Strand, where Ralegh lived. He studied cartography and began to learn the Algonquian language of what is now North Carolina from the two Native Americans brought to England by Ralegh's men in the autumn of 1584. He accompanied the expedition under Sir Richard Grenville that planted the first English colony on Roanoke Island in 1585. With the painter John White, he was given the task of collecting all the information he could about the environment and, in particular, about the indigenous people. For ten months the two studied and recorded in words and pictures all they could assimilate, greatly facilitated by Harriot's expertise in the local language (into which he could even translate from the Bible). Together, they carried on the first survey of the greater part of the area between Pamlico Sound and Chesapeake Bay, creating the first accurate map of any part of North America.

Harriot's contributions on the local culture were especially valuable in relation to language, agriculture, tribal organization, and religion. Many of his notes were lost when leaving Roanoke Island in June 1586, though more of White's drawings survived, including the scaled-down version of their map. He also retained much on the physical as well as human resources of the area, fauna, flora, minerals, and potential building materials. He was influential in advocating settlement in the Chesapeake Bay area when Roanoke Island was abandoned. His phonetic system for reading the Algonquian language was one fruit of his studies. He continued to advise Ralegh on the Guiana expedition of 1595 and even on a minor expedition in 1602, but in 1592 he entered the service of the eighth earl of Northumberland, who sponsored him for the rest of his life and was to give him a salary and a residence on his estate at Sion.

Ralegh's fall and imprisonment, followed by Northumberland's in 1605, left Harriot under something of a cloud. He retired from contacts with the aristocracy, though he maintained them with fellow scientists (he had a reputation for atheism on account of his skeptical philosophical attitude). He helped Ralegh and Northumberland while they were imprisoned in the Tower of London with books, and with their elementary chemical experiments, but he devoted himself to mathematics, astronomy, and the study of humanist writings. He was using a telescope at Sion almost at the same time as Galileo, making the first accurate map of the moon, identifying sunspots, and examining the moons of Jupiter. His main task was the exploration of spherical geometry and of algebra, in both areas making discoveries that anticipated much later work. He did not always pursue his analyses of many such problems long enough to reach finite conclusions, and he was not always correct, but the body of his work (some 9,000 worksheets and drafts survive) has only gradually been analyzed, elucidated, and evaluated in the late twentieth century.

Harriot's lasting contribution to North American studies was a short book, *A Briefe and True Report of the New Found Land of Virginia*, written in 1587 and published the following year in support of further proposed expeditions under Ralegh's auspices. His associate, John White, had saved his drawings of Native Americans and their ways of life, together with much of the fauna and a little of the flora of the area surveyed in 1585. Theodor de Bry obtained copies of Harriot's work and of a group of White's Native-American drawings and published them at Frankfurt in 1590 in four languages as the first volume of his *America* ("Grand Voyages"). Harriot added some notes to the drawings. This publication gave Harriot's American work a European currency that lasted for more than a century.

Harriot's last years were hampered by the rodent ulcer that eventually killed him, but he was able to organize some of his work into what he saw as publishable form. He desired in his will in 1621 that his friend Nathaniel Torporley, together with his fellow-pensioner Walter Warner, publish his completed mathematical papers. They took until 1631 to get his *Artis Analyticae Praxis* into print, described by Jon V. Pepper as "an important but incomplete account of his algebraic work and numerical analysis" (*British Journal of Historical Science* 19 [1986]: 12–15). Some papers appear to have been lost, but most of them remained in the possession of the Northumberland family and are now divided between the British Library and Petworth House, Sussex. They remained virtually unknown until the nineteenth century and have been studied systematically, though still far from completely, only since Rosalind Tanner formed the annual Harriot Seminar in 1969 and founded an annual Harriot Lecture at Oriel College, Oxford.

Harriot achieved so much through the patronage of Sir Walter Ralegh and his close friend the eighth earl of Northumberland. He aided them both, both before and after their long confinement in the Tower of London, and was continued on a generous salary, a house, and even the lease of land by Northumberland, who, however, emerged from imprisonment only a short time after Harriot's death in St. Christopher Parish, London.

• David B. Quinn, *The Roanoke Voyages*, vol. 1 (1955), pp. 104–5, contains an edited version of Harriot's *A Briefe and True Report*. John W. Shirley, *Thomas Harriot, a Biography* (1983), remains the standard biography. The same author's *A Source Book for the Study of Thomas Harriot* (1981) presents a generous selection of published material on Harriot to 1980. He also edited *Thomas Harriot: Renaissance Scientist* (1974). Other modern studies are Quinn, *Thomas Harriot and the Problem of America* (1992), and Hilary Gatti, *The Natural Philosophy of Thomas Harriot* (1993). Worth consulting are *The Harrioteer* (1994) and the Occasional Papers of the Durham Thomas Harriot Seminar, especially no. 8 in the series, Vivian Salmon, "Thomas Harriot and the English Origins of Algonkian Linguistics."

DAVID B. QUINN

HARRIS, Abram Lincoln, Jr. (17 Jan. 1899–16 Nov. 1963), economist, author, and educator, was born in Richmond, Virginia, the son of Abram Lincoln Harris, a butcher, and Mary Elizabeth Lee, both descendants of slaves freed before the Civil War. After completing his secondary education in the public schools of Richmond, Harris enrolled at Virginia Union University, where he earned a Bachelor of Science degree in 1922. In 1924 he received a Master of Arts degree from the University of Pittsburgh.

Harris then joined the faculty of West Virginia Collegiate Institute (later West Virginia State College), where he taught economics. He remained there until 1925, at which time he began a short stint as executive secretary of the Urban League in Minneapolis. Also in that year, Harris married Callie Ellen McGuinn; they had no children and divorced in 1955. After his year with the Urban League, he went to work as a researcher for Columbia University's Department of Banking in 1926. Harris then embarked on a relationship with Howard University that would continue until 1945, beginning in 1927 as an assistant professor. He briefly left Howard, obtaining a Ph.D. in political economy from Columbia in 1930 on a Social Science Research Council Fellowship, but returned that same year to serve as chairman of the university's economics department. In 1936 he achieved full professor status.

Harris had earned his Ph.D. with a dissertation titled "The Black Worker," which dealt with the difficulties blacks had in reaching social and economic equality within the U.S. labor force. Along with coauthor Sterling D. Spero, Harris published the work under the title *The Black Worker—The Negro and the Labor Movement* (1931; repr. 1968), and wrote in the preface that the book was intended as a study of "the relation of the dominant section of the working class to the segregated, circumscribed, and restricted Negro minority" (p. vii). The authors were not particularly optimistic about their findings and seemed to sense a troublesome future for working blacks. They made it clear, again in the preface, that they considered their text to be "neither a good will tract on race relations nor an attempt to offer a program for the solution of a vexing problem" (p. vii). The book was highly critical of most American trade unions and also of the dominant black leadership of the day. Harris and Spero lamented the ways in which the black worker had lost his place as "an industrial labor reserve" in order to become "a regular element in the labor force of every basic industry."

In 1934, in addition to his teaching duties, Harris served on the Consumers Advocacy Board of the National Recovery Administration. He also continued his research and writing. Following the success of *The*

Black Worker, Harris produced The Negro as Capitalist (1936), in which he continued a critical analysis of the various reform programs under discussion for improving the conditions of blacks in the work force. One such program called for a consumer boycott of white businesses operating in the black community. The rallying cry of this strategy was "Don't Buy Where You Can't Work." Harris dismissed the idea of a boycott, contending that most white stores were merely family-run operations that employed no outside help; therefore, any economic pressure would likely cause more harm than good. "What would be more natural than a retaliatory movement of whites demanding that Negroes be employed only by those white capitalists whose income is mainly derived from Negro patronage?" he wrote. "Nationalism, whether racial or otherwise, has never found, nor has it ever sought, validity in sheer economics."

A related reform program looked to the development of black business enterprise. Harris rejected this strategy as well, arguing that black capitalism was a bad idea because black businesses were, for the most part, too small in comparison to white businesses and, thus, could not compete efficiently. Harris also disapproved of the economic program put forth earlier in the century by black leader Booker T. Washington. He felt that Washington's plan, which involved an increase in industrial training for blacks, was futile in a developing economy where independent small businessmen were to have smaller roles and where white trade unions regulated the opportunities for jobs. Harris instead supported a reform program in which both black and white workers united together to form a stronger labor movement meant to achieve practical goals. He believed that only under this program were the interests of whites—as well as blacks—furthered, and he felt that only when the interests of white labor were advanced would the white trade union leadership be persuaded to act in a manner beneficial to the black worker.

In 1946 Harris accepted a position at the University of Chicago, where he taught economics and philosophy. Having been interested in the subject of economic philosophy throughout his career, he performed a series of studies in which he analyzed the methods of economic reform espoused by such philosophers as Karl Marx, Werner Sombart, Thorstein Veblen, and John R. Commons. Harris went on to write numerous articles in which he ultimately denounced their proposals and instead came to adopt the philosophies of English economist John Stuart Mill. In 1958 Harris published Economics and Social Reform, in which he wrote, "Progress consists not primarily in material improvement but in moral-aesthetic cultivation. . . . [I]nnovations and social reform must . . . be effected within a framework of common moral principles, loyalties and political obligations. . . . [Mill's] philosophy upholds the ideal of a kind of classless society, that is, one in which all divisions except those of taste, interest, and ability are nonexistent."

Harris was working on a book dealing with Mill's philosophy in more depth at the time of his death in Chicago. He was survived by his second wife, the former Phedorah Prescott, whom he had wed in 1962.

• In addition to the books mentioned in the text, Harris authored numerous articles on the subject of economics, the last of which was "John Stuart Mill," Canadian Journal of Economics and Political Science 30, no. 2 (May 1964): 185–202. See also William Darity, Jr., and Julian Ellison, "Abram Harris, Jr.: The Economics of Race and Social Reform," History of Political Economy 22, no. 4 (1990): 611–27. Obituaries are in the New York Times and the Chicago Tribune, 17 Nov. 1963.

FRANCESCO L. NEPA

HARRIS, Benjamin (fl. 1673–1716), publisher, writer, and first American journalist, was born in Great Britain, of unknown parents. Harris married a woman named either Sarah or Ruth and had at least one son. Harris's turbulent career as a sensationalistic and incautious, yet successful, publisher began in London in 1673 when he began to produce religious books and pamphlets, many attacking Catholics. In 1679 Harris, an ardent Anabaptist, joined Titus Oates in publicizing the "Popish Plot" and worked with other Whigs, including the earl of Shaftesbury, in trying to exclude the Catholic brother of King Charles II (later James II) from succeeding him. Charles resisted these moves, dissolving Parliament and arresting Shaftesbury in 1681; Oates was arrested when James gained the Crown in 1685. Harris, after publishing the pamphlet Appeal from the Country to the City in 1679, was convicted of sedition, sentenced to the pillory, and ordered to pay a fine he could not afford. Released from prison, Harris resumed his anti-Catholic diatribes, which continued even after James became king.

From 1679 to 1681, Harris also published Domestick Intelligence: Or News both from City and Country, a paper that displayed an early use of local news (as opposed to news from abroad, which was most newspapers' staple well into the nineteenth century). Disasters, including fires and murders, were reported, revealing Harris's penchant for covering local sensations. One story reported a man found hanging "by the Arms in a Wood . . . with his Head and Hands cut off, and his Bowels pulled out" (Stephens, p. 2), and another told of "a Popish Priest . . . who . . . had occasion to make use of his Ladies Chamber maid" (Stephens, p. 184).

Facing increasing pressure from the government, Harris moved to Boston in 1686. There he started the London Coffee House, one of the first in the city, which admitted both men and women, a rare practice at the time. In addition to coffee, the shop provided Bostonians with the latest foreign newspapers and books, and it placed Harris in Boston's most important circles. Harris also resumed his own publishing with The New-England Primer, the leading textbook in America well into the next century, and the very successful Tulley's Almanach. He then set out to publish a newspaper.

The result was *Publick Occurrences Both Foreign and Domestick*, America's first newspaper. The date on its first page is 25 September 1690, printed by "R. Pierce for Benjamin Harris, at the London-Coffee-House." A little paper, slightly smaller than the modern 8½-by-11 letter size, *Publick Occurrences* had three pages of text, leaving the fourth and final page blank for people to add their own handwritten news before passing the paper on to others. Harris planned more issues, to be "furnished once a moneth (or if any Glut of Occurrences happen, oftener." The first American news story was thoroughly indigenous. It begins, "The Christianized *Indians* in some parts of *Plimouth*, have newly appointed a day of Thanksgiving to God for his Mercy in supplying their extream and pinching Necessities under their late want of Corn, & for His giving them now a . . . very *Comfortable Harvest*. Their Example may be worth Mentioning."

In some ways, *Publick Occurrences* reads more like a modern newspaper than the stodgier colonial papers that came later. First, unlike most of the later American newspapers, *Publick Occurrences* focused on local news. A suicide in Watertown, local epidemics, including a "Smallpox Disaster," and fires in Boston were among the items. Second, Harris appealed to his readers' more prurient interests: the suicide was described as found hanging "with his feet near touching the ground." The alleged crimes of Native Americans received special attention and were explicitly rendered. The third reason that Harris's newspaper seems modern is its reliance on gossip and unflattering reports, even at the expense of the civic authorities.

Two items in particular raised the ire of the colonial authorities. The first was a report that some American Indians who were aligned with the British had committed atrocities against their French captives and the conclusion that England had relied too much on the "assistance of those miserable Salvages [*sic*]." The second alluded to a rumor that the king of France was in trouble with his son because "if reports be true, that the *Father used to lie with the Sons Wife*." Within a week, the governor and council of Massachusetts colony issued a statement declaring that the paper had been published "Without the least Privity or Countenance of Authority. . . . that therein is contained Reflections of a very high nature: As also sundry doubtful and uncertain Reports," and they declared their "high Resentment and Disallowance of said Pamphlet." Finally, they reiterated the ban on printing without license, which Harris did not possess. Benjamin Harris's first issue was also his last.

Although the censorship of *Publick Occurrences* has long been viewed by historians as a battle between Puritan sensibilities and a licentious press, more recent scholarship (Sloan, for example) has shown that two clergymen, Increase Mather and Cotton Mather, supported Harris and that the council included people of differing political and religious positions. Not all supported the censorship, and those who did may have had conflicting reasons. Some members of the council, for example, may have shared Harris's dislike of the

French king but may have resisted Harris's stridence. Others may have been against the principle of printing without a license. Yet another faction may have wanted to disgrace the Mathers. After the single issue of *Publick Occurrences*, it was fourteen years before the next newspaper got underway in the colonies; John Campbell's Boston *News-Letter*, in 1704, was the first American newspaper to last beyond its first issue.

From 1690 to 1695 Harris continued to run his coffeehouse and to publish books, and he joined another printer, John Allen, in a partnership. He received an official assignment to print *The Acts and Laws of Massachusetts* in 1692. But Harris missed London and in 1695 returned to start a series of short-lived newspapers before publishing the London *Post* from 1699 to 1706. From his printing shop and store he sold his paper, books, almanacs, and dubious patent medicines. The location and date of his death are unknown.

The course of journalism history, as outlined by Walter Lippmann and others, was a journey from a press controlled by government and party to a partisan, and then nonpartisan, popular press. With *Publick Occurrences*, Harris tried to publish a nongovernmental, nonparty-based, popular paper at a time before this practice was viable. Journalists in the early eighteenth century generally enjoyed government support, often through sinecures and postmaster positions. Their newspapers were drier and stodgier than *Publick Occurrences*, and they often shunned local and sensational news. Thus the modern, popular press in some ways relates more closely to *Publick Occurrences* than it does to the papers that followed it.

• Harris's life in America and his newspaper are detailed in Victor H. Paltsists, "New Light on 'Publick Occurrences': America's First Newspaper," American Antiquarian Society, *Proceedings*, vol. 59 (1949), pp. 75–88. Another important article is William David Sloan, "Chaos Polemics, and America's First Newspaper," *Journalism Quarterly* 70 (1993): 666–81. For a facsimile of the paper, beyond the first page printed in many textbooks, see Samuel Abbott Green, *Ten Fac-simile Reproductions Relating to Old Boston and Neighborhood* (1901), pp. 1–4. Sidney Kobre tries, with mixed success, to place Harris and his paper in a social and cultural context in *The Development of American Journalism* (1969) and in "The First American Newspaper: A Product of Environment," *Journalism Quarterly* 17 (1940): 335–45. A few journalism history textbooks examine Harris's life, including events before and after his coming to America, Mitchell Stephens, *A History of News: From the Drum to the Satellite* (1988); F. L. Mott, *American Journalism: A History, 1690–1960* (1962); and Edwin Emery and Michael Emery, *The Press and America*, 6th ed. (1988). Isaiah Thomas, *The History of Printing in America* (1810, repr. 1970), and Worthington C. Ford, *Boston Book Market 1679–1700* (1917) and "Benjamin Harris," Massachusetts Historical Society, *Proceedings*, vol. 57 (1924), pp. 34–68, are useful despite their age. A discussion of journalism history can be found in Walter Lippmann, "Two Revolutions in the American Press," *Yale Review* 20 (1931): 433–41.

DAVID T. Z. MINDICH

HARRIS, Bucky (8 Nov. 1896–8 Nov. 1977), baseball player and manager, was born Stanley Raymond Harris in Port Jervis, New York, the son of Thomas Harris, a coal miner, and Katherine Rupp. In 1901 the family moved to Pittstown, Pennsylvania, where at age 13 Harris worked full-time as a breaker boy and later became an assistant weighmaster at the Butler colliery. Despite his diminutive size at the time, the 14-year-old Harris played semiprofessional baseball with men. A right-handed batting infielder, he played with the Scranton team against the New York Yankees in a 1915 exhibition game in which his performance won him a tryout with the Detroit Tigers. Hugh Jennings, the Detroit manager, recommended him to the Muskegon, Ohio, team of the Central League the following spring. After an inauspicious start with Muskegon, the improving Harris, who now stood at 5′9½″, played at Reading, Pennsylvania, in the New York State League in 1917 and with Buffalo of the International League in 1918. Following his solid performance with Buffalo in 1919, three major league clubs sought to purchase his contract. Harris elected to join the Washington Senators, whose manager and part-owner, Clark Griffith, had seen him collect six hits in a game despite playing with a broken finger. When Griffith purchased Harris's contract for $4,500, it marked the beginning of their lifelong friendship.

Over the next four seasons Harris established himself as the Senators' second baseman. An average hitter, Harris was brilliant defensively; in 1922 he set a then-major league record for the most putouts (479) by a second baseman in one season. His aggressive style of play prompted Griffith to appoint him team captain in 1923 and playing manager the next year, making him at 27 the youngest manager in the major leagues. In 1924 Harris led the Senators to their first pennant in a close race with the dominant New York Yankees. In the World Series in which the Senators defeated the favored New York Giants, he batted .333 with two home runs; he also set four fielding records for a seven-game Series at second base with 54 chances and 54 putouts (including eight in one game) and by taking part in eight double plays. The Series grossed over $1 million in receipts, made a national celebrity of the "boy manager," as sportswriters had dubbed him, and at the time the dramatic seven-game contest was widely regarded as the greatest yet played. In the aftermath, Griffith rewarded Harris with a three-year contract at $30,000 a year.

In 1925 Harris, who batted safely in 24 consecutive games, managed the Senators to a second pennant, but the team lost the World Series to the Pittsburgh Pirates in seven games. The following year Harris married Elizabeth Sutherland, a daughter of the U.S. senator from West Virginia. The couple had three children but were divorced in 1950.

Harris's five years as player-manager of the Senators ended in 1928, the year that his full-time on-field career ended. In 13 seasons he batted .274 and fielded .965. He left Washington to manage the Detroit Tigers; his five seasons there (1929–1933) produced only one team finish above .500. Although urged to stay on, he said: "I feel that if a manager cannot deliver in five years, he should resign." After one year as manager of the Boston Red Sox, he rejoined his mentor Griffith with the Senators. His second try at managing the Senators (1935–1942) produced only one winning season, and after the 1942 team finished in seventh place, Griffith reluctantly released him. The following year Harris briefly managed the Philadelphia Phillies, whose controversial owner, William Cox, precipitated a near-mutiny among the players when he fired the popular manager in mid-season.

In 1944 and 1945 Harris served as team manager and general manager at Buffalo of the International League, and in 1946 he worked in a liaison capacity for the New York Yankees. Then, in a surprising reversal of fortune, he returned to the major leagues as manager of the Yankees. He led New York to a pennant and a World Series victory over the Brooklyn Dodgers in 1947, his second and last world championship; for that reason the *Sporting News* voted him manager of the year. But after the 1948 Yankees finished third in a hotly contested race, he was fired by general manager George Weiss.

After a season managing San Diego in the Pacific Coast League in 1949, he was summoned by Griffith for a third stint as manager of the Senators. His five years there (1950–1954) produced one winner and one .500 club. Released in 1954, he managed the Detroit Tigers for a second time; his teams had winning seasons in 1955 and 1956.

Harris's 29-year odyssey as an itinerant major league manager ended in 1956. One of the longest-serving managers in the game's history, he led five different teams and was widely respected for his ability to get maximum performances from sometimes limited talent. Although his teams finished in the second division 20 times, Harris piloted three American League pennant and two World Series winners. Among major league managers, he ranks third with his 2,157 victories, but his 2,218 losses rank second. Harris served as assistant to the general manager of the Boston Red Sox from late 1956 through 1960, and from 1962 through 1971 he was a scout with the Chicago White Sox and the Washington Senators. Elected to the Baseball Hall of Fame in 1975, he died at Bethesda, Maryland, survived by two sons and a daughter from his first marriage and by his second wife, Cecelia Desmond, whom he married in 1950.

• A ghostwritten autobiography, Stanley Raymond "Bucky" Harris, *Playing the Game: From Mine Boy to Manager* (1925), covers Harris's early years. For his terms with the Senators, see Shirley Povich, *The Washington Senators* (1954), and Morris A. Beale, *The Washington Senators* (1947). For his stints at Detroit and Philadelphia, see Frederick G. Lieb, *The Detroit Tigers* (1946), and Lieb and Stan Baumgartner, *The Philadelphia Phillies* (1953). Harvey Frommer, *New York City Baseball* (1980), covers his time with the Yankees. Books comparing Harris with other managers include Charles B. Cleveland, *The Great Baseball Managers* (1950), and Donald G. Honig, *The Man in the Dugout* (1977). The National Baseball Library in Cooperstown, N.Y., has a newspaper clipping file on his career. An obituary is in the *New York Times*, 10 Nov. 1977.

DAVID QUENTIN VOIGT

HARRIS, Chapin Aaron (6 May 1806–29 Sept. 1860), a founder of American dentistry, was born at Pompey, Onondaga County, New York, the son of John Harris and Elizabeth Brundage. At eighteen years of age he began the study of medicine, surgery, and dentistry with his brother John at Madison, Lake County, Ohio. In 1826 he married Lucinda Hawley, with whom he would have nine children. Harris progressed rapidly in his apprenticeship and by 1827 was made a partner. However, during that year he moved to Canfield, Ohio, where he started the practice of medicine. The following year he changed his practice from medicine to dentistry. As was the custom of many practitioners of dentistry, for many years he was an itinerant, traveling and treating patients throughout the South. He practiced for a time in Greenfield, Ohio, but moved to Bloomfield in 1828 and settled in Fredericksburg, Virginia, where he practiced dentistry full time until 1835. Having received a license to practice dentistry from the Medical and Chirurgical Faculty of Maryland in 1833 no doubt influenced him to move to Baltimore permanently.

A lover of art and literature, Harris corresponded with many eminent literary men both in the United States and abroad. A diligent reader and collector, he was known to have the finest library in Baltimore. He enriched the literature of dentistry with his prodigious output of scientific articles in the periodic literature. A few examples are "Treatise on the Teeth and Gums" (*Maryland Medical and Surgical Journal* [1841]), "Ulcerated Gums and Exfoliating of Aleola from Defective Nutrition in Children" (*Maryland Medical and Surgical Journal* [1840]), and "Relative Importance of Chemistry as a Branch of Medical Education" (*Baltimore Medical and Surgical Journal* [1841]). His most influential book was *The Dental Art: A Practical Treatise on Dental Surgery* (1839), which was reedited with added material incorporated by several authors under the title *Principles and Practice of Dental Surgery*; it appeared in thirteen editions in the next seventy-four years as a standard work. Another landmark publication was *A Dictionary of Dental Science: Bibliography, Biography and Medical Terminology* (1839); the first of its kind, it went through six editions.

Harris's activities on behalf of the advancement of dentistry are legendary. He was a cofounder of the first dental school in the world, Baltimore College of Dental Surgery (1840), and cofounder of the first dental journal in the world, the *American Journal of Dental Science* (1849), serving as its editor for more than twenty years. He translated many French articles and published them in the journal. He firmly believed in the establishment of dentistry as a profession based on the concept that dentistry was both an art and a science. As dean and professor of operative dentistry and prosthetic dentistry at the dental school, he created order and system from the fund of existing knowledge and organized and systematized the teaching of dental surgery. He was also responsible for organizing the first national dental society, the American Society of Dental Surgeons (1840), serving as its first president.

He was awarded the doctor of dental surgery degree from this society, which laid the foundation for a scientific body of professionals by granting a dental degree, publishing a journal devoted to dentistry, and conducting meetings during which dentists presented papers on the scientific aspects of dentistry.

Having passed the examination of the Maryland State Medical Examination, Harris was awarded the M.D. in 1833. He also was awarded two honorary degrees. To Harris belongs the credit for placing dental education, literature, and organization on a firm and permanent basis. He has been characterized as "a tower of strength" in the field of scientific dentistry. According to T. A. Heatwole, "It is difficult to estimate the influence which his literary efforts exerted, but there is no doubt as to their tremendous and far-reaching value." Harris died in Baltimore.

• For biographical overviews consult John M'Calla, "Chapin A. Harris, A.M., M.D., D.D.S.," *Pennsylvania Journal of Dental Science* 1: 5; (unsigned), "Unveiling of the Chapin A. Harris Memorial," *Dental Cosmos* 19: 190; M. L. Thorpe and Charles R. E. Koch, *History of Dental Surgery*, vol. 3 (1909); James A. Taylor, *A History of Dentistry* (1922); E. F. Cordell, ed., *Medical Annals of Maryland, 1799–1899* (1903); C. G. Burrett Lennard, "Professor Harris," *International Dental Journal* 3: 920; and Gardner P. H. Foley, *Hall of Fame* (brochure) (1976). For Harris's professional accomplishments see Milton A. Asbell, *Dentistry—A Historical Perspective* (1987), and "Chapin A. Harris and Horace H. Hayden: An Historical Review," *Bulletin of the History of Dentistry* 17: 27; also Van Broadus Dalton, *The Genesis of Dental Education in the United States* (1946). Obituaries are in the *Journal of the American Dental Society* (Oct. 1860) and *Dental Cosmos* (Dec. 1860).

MILTON B. ASBELL

HARRIS, Charles Kassell (1 May 1865 or 1867–22 Dec. 1930), songwriter and publisher, was born in Poughkeepsie, New York, the son of Jacob Harris, a tailor, and Rachel Kassell. Harris's date of birth is uncertain; his obituary in the *New York Times* gives the 1865 date, whereas the American Society of Composers, Authors and Publishers (ASCAP), of which he was a charter member, lists it as 1867. The synagogue records for the period of his birth have been lost, and birth records for Duchess County begin in 1882. Little is known about Harris's youth. During his childhood the family moved to East Saginaw, Michigan, and then to Milwaukee, Wisconsin. His father supported the family of ten children with income from a general store and tailor shop and by purchasing skins from the Indians.

Harris learned to play the banjo and by his late teens was writing songs with titles like "If I Were the Chief of Police" and "Bake That Matzoth Pie," which he performed at amateur entertainments. He rented an office and advertised "Songs Written to Order." In the 1880s, eager to prove himself, Harris wrote a song (with words supplied by a friend) to be used in the musical show *The Skating Rink*, in which the touring comedian Nat C. Goodwin was appearing. Goodwin liked "Since Maggie Learned to Skate" and added the song to the show.

In 1892, at the request of a friend who needed a new song for an amateur minstrel show, Harris wrote "After the Ball." At a dance he attended the previous night, Harris had watched a couple break their engagement, the man leaving with another woman. Harris found a phrase running through his head—"Many a heart is aching after the ball"—and he wrote the song in an hour. At this same dance Harris met his future wife, Cora Lerhberg, with whom he later had two children.

As Milwaukee correspondent for the *New York Dramatic News*, Harris interviewed James Aldrich Libby, the star baritone of Charles Hoyt's *A Trip to Chinatown*, and talked him into trying out "After the Ball." Though the show's composer, Percy Gaunt, had a contract to supply all the musical numbers, star singers like Libby were a law unto themselves, and "After the Ball" was interpolated. The song made a sensation, with the audience demanding six encores of the chorus at the first performance. Libby continued to sing "After the Ball" on the rest of the tour throughout the East, and orders began to pour in for a song not yet in print. The actress May Irwin obtained a copy of the song and orchestration, and at her first performance in New York, the song again caused a tremendous sensation. Harris received an order dated 1 April from the Oliver Ditson Company for 75,000 copies of "After the Ball." Assuming an April Fool's joke, he threw it away. A wire ten days later convinced him the offer was genuine, and after having the copies printed up and mailed, he received a check for $14,250. John Philip Sousa complained to Harris that playing "After the Ball" again and again at the 1893 Chicago World's Fair had "tired him out."

In 1897 Harris wrote another hit song, "Break the News to Mother," which became popular during the Spanish-American War and was revived during the First World War. His 1901 success, "Hello, Central, Give Me Heaven," was inspired by a newspaper story about a widower whose little daughter tried to call her dead mother over the telephone.

With the enormous profits he earned on sales of "After the Ball," Harris was able to open a New York branch of his Milwaukee publishing company. In addition to publishing songs by himself and others, he offered the book and music to several of the shows produced by Joe Weber and Lew Fields. In 1910, at the suggestion of the producer David Belasco, Harris wrote movie scenarios based on some of his songs; *After the Ball* and *When It Strikes Home* were two he turned into photoplays. That same year his story *The Barker*, written for Lew Fields, was made into a picture distributed by the Essanay, Selig and Vitagraph Company.

Harris claimed to be the first publisher to use a singer's picture on the cover of a song. He also claimed to have started the practice of showing slides during the performance of a song to depict scenes from the story and to flash the words so the audience could sing along. He staged the slides for his own songs, chose their background locations, and directed the actors in their poses. The operatic and concert diva Adelina Patti commissioned Harris to write "The Last Farewell" for her final tour of the United States in 1903, and she sang it at all her engagements. Mae West, just beginning her career in vaudeville, promoted songs for Harris around 1912.

In 1903 Harris had discovered that his songs "Hello, Central, Give Me Heaven" and "Always in the Way" (1903) were selling thousands of records daily, from which he received no royalties. Since the law at that time covered only sheet music sales, a composer received nothing from the sale or license of a piece of recorded music. Joining with Herbert, Sousa, and Reginald De Koven, Harris fought for the passage of the copyright bill; he even met personally with Theodore Roosevelt (1858–1919), who supplied him with letters of support to the congressmen involved. The copyright bill was passed in 1909. The American Society of Composers, Authors and Publishers was founded in 1914, and Harris served as a member of its board of directors from 1921 until his death at his New York home in 1930.

Harris is important in the history of American popular song because he wrote songs that reflected the desires of his audience and the particular tastes of his time. The slightly stilted, formal phrases he used suited a country still finding its voice in the midst of enormous cultural and artistic ferment. As styles in dress and attitude changed and became more open and exuberant, Harris's sentiments and the way he expressed them came to seem old-fashioned and quaint. Song titles like "Just Behind the Times" (1896) and "Songs of Yesterday" (1916) seem to indicate that Harris was aware of the changes. He was a man of great energy and dedication in the promotion of popular music—as songwriter, performer, and publisher. His realization that a popular song could be "promoted," just like any other product, helped bring the genteel business of music publishing roaring into the twentieth century.

• The fullest picture of Harris is given in his autobiography, *After the Ball: Forty Years of Melody* (1926). In his memoir, *They All Sang: From Tony Pastor to Rudy Vallee* (1935), music publisher Edward B. Marks mentions Harris's contributions both as songwriter and publisher and pictures in vivid detail the musical life of their times. Charles Hamm's *Yesterdays: Popular Songs in America* (1979) contains an excellent synopsis of Harris's life and career, complete with an evaluation of his place in popular music. Jerome Kern included "After the Ball" in the vaudeville sequence of the musical comedy *Show Boat* in 1927. A 1974 recording by mezzo-soprano Joan Morris and pianist William Bolcom, *After the Ball: A Treasury of Turn-of-the-Century Popular Songs* (Nonesuch Records), contains a sampling of Harris's songs; it was a popular and critical success. An obituary is in the *New York Times*, 23 Dec. 1930.

JOAN MORRIS

HARRIS, Corra (17 Mar. 1869–9 Feb. 1935), novelist and critic, was born Corra May White, the daughter of Tinsley Rucker White, a planter, and Mary Elizabeth

Matthews, in Elbert County, Georgia. She was educated at home, at the Elberton Female Academy, and at the Old Salem School in Banks County, Georgia. At the latter institution she met Lundy Howard Harris, a brilliant but troubled Methodist clergyman who served as pastor for a rural Georgia circuit. Married in 1887, they had three children, only one of whom survived to adulthood.

Corra Harris's next twelve years were devoted to her family, which moved to Oxford, Georgia, in 1889, when Lundy accepted the chair in Greek at Emory College. Her literary career began in 1899, when a nervous collapse forced her husband to give up his professorship and his ministry. Almost instinctively she turned to writing for a much-needed income. An editorial in the *Independent* (published in New York) denouncing lynching drew from her a reply defending the practice of lynching in particular and southern racial views in general, which aroused wide interest. At the invitation of the editors, she became a regular contributor to the *Independent*, writing numerous articles, book reviews, and editorials.

In Harris's view, the beginning of the twentieth century was a barren time for southern literature. In a series of essays and reviews that appeared in the *Independent* and the *Critic* (published in New York) she argued that southern literature was in a state of decline because too many southern authors were characterized by extreme defensiveness, devotion to the glories of the Old South, and worship at the patriotic tomb of the Old South. Her outspoken critical commentary on the literary achievements of her native region was certainly not typical of turn-of-the-century southerners.

Nursed back to health by Corra, Lundy took a position in 1903 with the Methodist board of education in Nashville, Tennessee. Harris's first book and first work of fiction, *The Jessica Letters*, written with Paul Elmer More, formerly literary editor of the *Independent*, appeared the following year. But real literary success came with her novel *The Circuit Rider's Wife*, which drew on her experiences as a minister's wife in the Georgia hills and criticized the Methodist church for the stressful conditions under which rural preachers had to work. Published first as a serial in the *Saturday Evening Post* and then in book form in 1910, this became her best-known work, displaying her characteristically ironic wit. The same year, Lundy slipped again into melancholia and committed suicide. When her daughter Faith married several months after Lundy's death, Harris left Nashville, living in hotels until she built a house in the Georgia mountains near Cartersville in 1914.

The Circuit Rider's Wife was followed by thirteen more novels during the next sixteen years. All of Harris's fiction is basically didactic: the shortcomings of Methodism are exposed in the circuit rider series; the backwardness of an entire town in *The Recording Angel* (1912); and small-town political corruption in *The Co-Citizens* (1915). The remaining novels address the problems of marriage. Four of them depict the ways in which a strong-minded, modern young woman makes

a successful marriage, while the other four explore the various ways in which a worthy wife deals with a weak or unfaithful husband. Harris's readership found her novels enjoyable and edifying. Given their popularity, the *Saturday Evening Post* continued to serialize them into the 1920s.

Literary success brought Harris opportunities to travel. In 1911 the *Saturday Evening Post* sent her to Europe, where she wrote a series of essays on women in various countries. Three years later, as World War I began, Harris returned to Europe for the *Post* to report on conditions there. Following a stay in New York in 1914, Harris penned her negative impressions of the city for the *Independent*.

Harris suffered through another period of personal loss when her daughter died in 1919. Professional disappointment followed as she lived to see her fiction pass out of fashion. In 1927 reviewers savaged *The Happy Pilgrimage*, her record of a trip to California. That same year Harris suffered a heart attack. She spent her remaining years at her mountain retreat, writing little except for a triweekly column that appeared in the *Atlanta Journal*. She died in Atlanta.

• Most of Corra Harris's papers are in the University of Georgia Library. Other works by Harris include *Eve's Second Husband* (1911); *In Search of a Husband* (1913); *Justice* (1915); *A Circuit Rider's Widow* (1916); *Making Her His Wife* (1918); *From Sunup to Sundown*, with Faith Harris Leech (1919); *Happily Married* (1920); *My Son* (1921); *The Eyes of Love* (1922); *A Daughter of Adam* (1923); *The House of Helen* (1923); *My Book and Heart* (1924); *As a Woman Thinks* (1925); and *Flapper Ann* (1926). The standard biography is John E. Talmadge, *Corra Harris: Lady of Purpose* (1968). On Harris's literary criticism, see L. Moody Simms, Jr., "Corra Harris on Patriotic Literary Criticism in the Post–Civil War South," *Mississippi Quarterly* 25 (Fall 1972): 459–66, "Corra Harris on Southern and Northern Fiction," *Mississippi Quarterly* 27 (Fall 1974): 475–81, "Corra Harris on the Decline of Southern Writing," *Southern Studies* 18 (Summer 1979): 247–50, and "Corra Harris, William Peterfield Trent, and Southern Writing," *Mississippi Quarterly* 32 (Fall 1979): 641–50.

L. MOODY SIMMS, JR.

HARRIS, E. Victor (10 June 1905–23 Feb. 1978), Negro League baseball player, coach, and manager, was born Elander Victor Harris in Pensacola, Florida, the son of William Harris and Frances Calloway. Harris attended elementary school in the South, until his family moved to Pittsburgh, Pennsylvania, in 1914. In 1922 he graduated from Schenley High School and in 1923 signed a professional baseball contract with the Cleveland Tate Stars. He played briefly with the Cleveland Browns and the Chicago American Giants of the Negro National League (NNL) before returning to Pittsburgh in 1925 as a member of the Homestead Grays, a team owned and managed by Cumberland Posey, Pittsburgh's most successful black businessman of the time. Harris spent 22 of the next 24 years in the Grays organization.

Having grown to 5'10" and 164 pounds, Harris batted left-handed and threw right-handed. A skillful outfielder and a lifetime .314 hitter, he was best known as an aggressive baserunner who would not hesitate to spike an opposing infielder. In his early playing days he was noted for a hot temper. Infielders on his own team asked him to be less aggressive so that they would not bear the brunt of opposing players' retaliation, and umpire Jimmy Ahern once filed an assault charge against Harris. The charge was later dropped, and Harris matured; however, one of his temper tantrums proved fateful. A barnstorming club, the Grays lacked a permanent home stadium. In a 1930 game at Pittsburgh's Forbes Field, Posey used portable lights for an experiment in night baseball. The Grays' catcher was injured in the first game of a doubleheader, and Harris refused to catch the second, convinced that he would not be able to see under the lights. Posey turned to an 18-year-old rookie, Josh Gibson, who would become one of the greatest players in the Negro Leagues, and with whom Harris would have a sometimes stormy relationship.

A salary dispute after the 1933 season led Harris to accept the overtures of Gus Greenlee, who owned the Pittsburgh Crawfords of the NNL, the Grays' crosstown rivals. Harris played left field and batted .360 that season on a team that featured Gibson, Judy Johnson, Oscar Charleston, and Satchel Paige. When Posey allowed the Grays to join the NNL, Harris rejoined the club as player-manager for the 1935 season. Like many fine players in the Jim Crow era, Harris often found work hard to come by in the off-season. In 1935 he managed the Newark Eagles in a series of exhibition matches in Puerto Rico. Harris returned to the Grays for the start of the 1936 season; that year he married Dorothy Smith, and they would have one daughter and one son. The next season Harris's team captured the first of nine straight NNL crowns. The next year Harris enjoyed one of his best seasons as a player. He hit .380 and was selected to hit leadoff in the annual East-West All-Star game, the most prestigious event in black baseball; Harris played or managed in nine of these games. (A world series was not always held, on account of barnstorming schedules. In any event, the proliferation of rival Negro leagues made a world series title dubious.) The 1938 Grays—sporting talent such as Gibson, Buck Leonard, Sam Bankhead, and Edsell Walker—won more than 80 percent of its games and is thought by some to be the greatest team in Negro League history. In 1939 the Grays repeated their mastery of the NNL, and Harris played with a team of Negro League stars on an exhibition tour of Cuba in the off-season.

As a manager Harris displayed a different temperament from what he exhibited as a youthful player. He was known for being quiet and demanding, and he was a strict disciplinarian. When Gibson returned to the Grays from a two-year stint in the Mexican League (1940–1941), Harris did not hesitate to pull him from the lineup because of Gibson's drinking problem. Cool Papa Bell complained that Harris put him in the outfield every day in 1945, even though Bell suffered from arthritis. But Harris got results. The Grays'

string of pennants did not end until 1946, though Harris did not manage the 1943 and 1944 teams, having taken time off to work in a defense plant. He continued to play in the outfield as well as manage and was selected to play in East-West games in 1942, 1943, and 1947. His 1948 Grays team again won the pennant, after which they quit the NNL and became once again an independent barnstorming team (they disbanded a short time later).

By then change was in the air, as Jackie Robinson had broken professional baseball's color barrier in 1947 when he joined the Brooklyn Dodgers. As major league teams began to raid black talent, attendance at Negro League games sagged and marginally profitable teams folded. Harris spent 1949 as a coach for the Baltimore Elite Giants. In 1950, his last year in organized baseball, Harris managed the Birmingham Black Barons, whose star outfielder, Willie Mays, would sign with the New York Giants.

Most Negro League teams collapsed after 1950, and the 45-year-old Harris was forced to seek other employment to support his family. Although he doubtless possessed managerial ability and led the Santurce team of the Puerto Rican Winter League from 1947 to 1950, major league baseball remained riddled with racism and prejudice. No African American would manage in the major leagues until 1975. Harris eventually drifted to Pacioma, California, where he was a head custodian for the Castiac Union Schools. He died in Mission Hills, California.

• For more information see the E. Victor Harris folder in the National Baseball Library, Cooperstown, N.Y. Other useful sources include Microsoft Corporation's computer software *Complete Baseball* (1994); Robert Petterson, *Only the Ball Was White* (1970); Vic Harris with John Holway, "Vic Harris Managed Homestead Grays," *Dawn Magazine*, 8 March 1975; Holway, *Voices from the Great Black Baseball Leagues* (1975); and James Riley, *The All-Time All-Stars of Black Baseball* (1983).

ROBERT E. WEIR

HARRIS, Frank (14 Feb. 1856–26 Aug. 1931), journalist and writer, was born James Thomas Harris in Galway, Ireland, the son of Thomas Vernon Harris, a customs shipmaster, and Anne Thomas. He was raised in a nonconformist family of Pembrokeshire stock, and in his early years the family moved about within Ireland. He was educated in Britain and at age fifteen, having finished school, he used a cash prize to buy a steerage ticket to the United States. He moved from New York to Illinois and Texas doing odd jobs, including, he always claimed, a stint as a cowboy, finally settling for a time in Kansas. This, and much else of his life, would be elaborated on in his sensational and infamous autobiography, and would become the basis for some of his fiction. The facts of his life often conflicted with his elaborate fantasies. He began studying for a degree at the University of Kansas, Lawrence, and though various accounts of his career in Lawrence exist, it is certain that he was admitted to the bar there in 1875.

Harris spent the next few years traveling, teaching, and studying in England, France, and Germany. In 1878 he married Florence Ruth Adams, whom he had met while he was employed as a teacher of French at Brighton College, England, and the pair settled in Germany. She died the following year. By 1882 Harris had moved to London, where he found work as a journalist on the *Spectator*. By 1883 he had become the editor of the *Evening News*, a Conservative paper. At this point he really began to make a name as both a journalist and a London figure, and over the next few years he mixed in London society and talked about himself and his projects, always his favorite of subjects. He was famed as an individualistic conversationalist. His editorial technique was equally idiosyncratic, for he thought of his younger self as an ideal reader, and worked accordingly. He claimed that "I went back in my life and when I edited it [the *Evening News*] as a boy of fourteen I began to succeed; my obsessions were then kissing and fighting: when I got one or the other or both of those interests into every column, the circulation of the paper increased steadily." Harris boosted circulation by sensationalizing the paper and in the process carefully developed a personality cult around himself. He was a small, swarthy man with a formidable moustache and swagger and wore heels to increase his stature. He was egocentric, emotional, and loud, and he loved to dramatize. His youthful obsessions never really altered, and he was well known for his verbal sparring and his boasts of sexual conquests.

In 1887 Harris married Emily Mary Clayton, a wealthy widow; theirs was an unhappy union that did little to inhibit his sexual adventurism. The couple had no children, though Harris had several illegitimate children at different points in his life. In the same year he became editor of the *Fortnightly Review*, a position he continued in until 1894. Harris used his wide social and literary connections to great effect, and the journal included contributions from significant writers, some of whom became famous through its pages. in 1891 he started to write fiction, and in June 1891 "A Modern Idyll," a story about an affair between a Baptist minister and a deacon's wife, appeared in the *Fortnightly Review* to a mixed reception due to its controversial subject matter. The journal's publishers, Chapman and Hall, asked Harris not to submit any more of his stories. His uneasy relationship with his publishers continued until 1894, when an article by Charles Mulato on the anarchists Henry and Ravachol apparently so incensed Frederick Chapman that he fired Harris.

In the same year Harris made two further substantial changes to his life. He left his wife, and he purchased the *Saturday Review*, which he also edited. He flourished in his new role, employing a collection of talent that made the *Saturday Review* justifiably famous and demonstrating his own remarkable talents as an editor. This period was the highlight of his career. In 1895 his *Elder Conklin and Other Stories*, a collection of realist local color tales of the American West, was published. They had their basis in his experiences

in the United States and were generally well received. In 1898, when Harris sold the *Saturday Review*, among the reasons he gave for his move were ill health, a desire for more money, and a wish to write more fiction. He hoped in this way to leave a more permanent mark on the world. By this time Harris had certainly met Nellie O'Hara, with whom he was to continue a relationship until the end of his life. In 1900 *Montes the Matador and Other Stories* appeared, but Harris had not devoted himself to writing fiction full time. He became involved in many moneymaking schemes, and over the next few years he purchased and edited a number of journals, including the *Candid Friend*, the *Motorist and Traveler*, and *Vanity Fair*. He spent September to November 1907 on a moneymaking tour of what he called, in one of his periodic moments of hostility toward the United States, "that awful America," travelling 15,000 miles in forty days ("forty days in the wilderness"). In 1908 his first novel, *The Bomb*, was published, "a sort of confession of faith—the first reasoned defense of anarchy which has ever been seen in print," as he described it. In 1909 *The Man Shakespeare* appeared. After a brief spell of editing yet another magazine, *Health and Home*, Harris bought and began to edit *Modern Society* in 1913; but the next year he was sent to prison for contempt of court after commenting on a divorce case in the journal. After his release he wrote in a letter, "I am very nearly dead."

In 1914 Harris left Europe for the United States, which he had revisited briefly in 1911 both to make money and to see whether taking American citizenship would make it easier for him to obtain a divorce. He moved about a great deal and was often separated from Nellie O'Hara, to whom he wrote frequent and impassioned letters. His hostility to British imperialism, and to the class and judicial systems of Britain, never well disguised, emerged very publicly. He began to take an aggressively pro-German stance in the autumn of 1914. He collected a series of polemical articles he had written for the *New York Sun* and published them early in 1915 as *England or Germany?* His anti-British posturing caused fury in Britain, and he was widely attacked there. The United States became something of a refuge for him. In 1916 his *Oscar Wilde: His Life and Confessions* was published. That October Harris was made editor of the American magazine *Pearson's*. In 1921 Harris and O'Hara both became naturalized American citizens, though Harris was already tiring of his adopted country. He sold the magazine in 1922 and left what he now referred to as the "Benighted States" for Nice, where O'Hara was living. In that year the first volume of his autobiography, *My Life and Loves*, was privately printed. Several other volumes appeared later. The work scandalized many of his contemporaries because of its candid sexual detail, and it caused him considerable problems with the censors owing in part to its being illustrated with photographs of naked women. His last collection of stories, *Undream'd of Shores*, appeared in 1924. In 1927, after the death of Emily Clayton, Harris finally married O'Hara. He died in Nice.

Harris is generally remembered as being a self-promoting and vulgar man of great talent and energy but with dubious taste. With his distinctive looks, raffish clothes, and habitual pursuit of women he cut a curious and disreputable dash across the 1890s, the time of his greatest fame or notoriety. He spent most of his later life reliving past glories, traveling between the United States and Europe and pursuing ways of raising large sums of money. He had a complex relationship to the United States and would both champion and denigrate it, yet he spent a significant part of his life there, and would often pose as an Irish-American by birth. His most impressive journalistic achievement was his editorship of the *Saturday Review*. Though he wrote a significant amount of fiction, the writing Harris is best remembered for is his autobiography.

• A significant collection of manuscripts and correspondence is held in the Humanities Research Center at the University of Texas at Austin; archival materials are also located at the Berg Collection in the New York Public Library and at the British Library. Biographies of Harris include Elmer Gertz and A. I. Tobin, *Frank Harris* (1931); Hugh Kingsmill, *Frank Harris* (1932); Vincent Brome, *Frank Harris* (1959); Robert B. Pearsall, *Frank Harris* (1970); and Philippa Pullar, *Frank Harris* (1975). For a hostile account of Harris see Kate Stephens, *The Lies and Libels of Frank Harris* (1929). See also Stanley Weintraub, ed., *The Playwright and the Pirate: Bernard Shaw and Frank Harris, a Correspondence* (1982). Obituaries are in the London *Times*, and the *New York Times*, 27 Aug. 1931.

BRIDGET BENNETT

HARRIS, George Washington (20 Mar. 1814–11 Dec. 1869), humorist, was born in Allegheny City, Pennsylvania, the son of George Harris and Mary Glover Bell. What happened to his parents is not known, but at the age of five he was taken by his much-older half-brother, Samuel Bell, and his wife to Knoxville, Tennessee, a sleepy frontier settlement that in the following decades grew into a thriving town on the Tennessee River.

Harris had little formal education, but as an apprentice in Samuel Bell's prosperous metalworking shop, he learned metallurgy and mechanics. Inspired by the visit of the first steamboat to Knoxville in 1826, he built a miniature of his own and, with much fanfare, put it on public exhibition on the village pond. At the age of nineteen he became captain of the steamboat *Knoxville*. The boat, rechristened *Indian Chief*, was used in the forced removal of the Cherokees in 1838 during which, according to tradition, Harris exercised his prerogative as captain to countermand orders given by General Winfield Scott, the supervisor of the infamous "Trail of Tears."

In the meantime, in 1835, Harris married Mary Emeline Nance. Perhaps in deference to his wife and growing family, which eventually numbered five children, Harris left the river to take up farming in 1839. They settled in relative affluence on a 375-acre farm in nearby Blount County with three slaves, a white servant girl, and Harris's personal library of seventy-six

books. Harris's attempt at farming failed, but he was able to save enough capital from that venture to open his own metalworking shop in Knoxville early in 1843.

As early as 1839, perhaps as part of his attempt to live the life of a Southern gentleman farmer, Harris contributed original unsigned pieces to the Democratic Knoxville *Argus and Commercial Herald*. In 1843 as "Mr. Free," he began a series of letters for William T. Porter's New York *Spirit of the Times*, describing aspects of East Tennessee mountain life. Finally, as "Sugartail," in "The Knob Dance" (1845), Harris achieved the quality of mountain dialect, the fresh imagery, and the sarcastic humor that would characterize the best of his future writings. At this time Harris indicated that he had plans for a book entitled *Smokey Mountain Panther*, but it never materialized.

In 1854, modeling his main character after a chain bearer he had recently encountered while surveying in southeastern Tennessee, Harris wrote "Sut Lovengood's Daddy 'Acting Horse'"—the first of over thirty Sut stories. (He later changed the *e* to *i* in Lovengood.) Sut, he wrote, was "a queer looking, long legged, short bodied, small headed, white haired, hog eyed funny sort of genius" (*Yarns* [1867], p. 19) whose main adversary was authoritarianism whether it came from home (father), state (sheriff, judge), or church (preacher, deacon). Through outrageous, often cruel, practical jokery, Sut sought to destroy the elevated position these figures enjoyed in their mountain society. In contrast, Harris himself was small in stature, dignified, even formal, a family man who brooked no dissent from the Presbyterian regimen of religious observances. Between this man and his literary creation, Sut Lovingood, there is a strange dichotomy.

Harris's family always seems to have lived just enough beyond their means to keep him under pressure to earn more money. In 1849 he became superintendent of the Holston Glass Works; in 1854 he again briefly captained a steamboat on the Tennessee, but later that year he supervised a major surveying project in lower eastern Tennessee. After the mid-1850s he got into Knoxville politics, serving as postmaster for a few months in 1857. An unwavering Democrat, Harris found himself at painful odds with his half-brother, a leading Unionist Whig, during the political strife preceding the Civil War.

In 1859 the Harrises moved to Nashville, where he worked for the Nashville and Chattanooga Railroad until 1862, when the fear of Union troops turned the family into nomads trying to stay out of harm's way in Alabama, Georgia, and Tennessee for the remainder of the war. In 1866, readjusting in the drastically changed postwar South, Harris went to work for the Wills Valley Railroad in northern Alabama. His wife's death in 1867 cast a pall over his newfound prospects, but with revived hopes, in 1869 he married Jane E. Pride, a young widow. Two months later, returning from Lynchburg, Virginia, where he had gone on railroad business, he became ill and was taken unconscious from the train in Knoxville. He died that night, having uttered only the mystifying word "Poisoned!"

At times, before and after the Civil War, Harris used the persona of Sut to launch satirical attacks on his own political foes, but when he selected the stories for the Dick & Fitzgerald publishing company's edition of *Yarns* (1867), he wisely chose only those genuinely evocative of mountain life. In 1869 he was planning a second volume, *High Times and Hard Times*, but the manuscript that he showed to a printer in Lynchburg shortly before his death has never been located.

Applauded by Mark Twain, *Yarns* continued through the years to find a small reading public willing to decipher the dialect and appreciate the coarse imagery and rough humor. William Faulkner, Irvin S. Cobb, and Stark Young were among the notable fans of this volume. Edmund Wilson was not: he created a scholarly tempest when he described it as "by far the most repellent book of any real literary merit in American literature" (*New Yorker*, 7 May 1955, p. 138). From the original plates, *Yarns* remained in print until 1960, by which time the growing interest in American culture had carried the folk humor of the old Southwest—Harris being a major example—into the historical mainstream of American humor.

• For Harris's life, see Donald Day, "The Life of George Washington Harris," *Tennessee Historical Quarterly* 7 (1947): 3–38. The earliest significant scholarly appreciations of Harris's writings were Walter Blair, *Native American Humor* (1937), and F. O. Matthiessen, *American Renaissance* (1941). In the 1960s Harris scholarship flourished through the efforts of Milton Rickels, whose critical volume, *George Washington Harris* (1965), is easily the best single study of Harris; M. Thomas Inge, who published frequently and well on the subject; and the Sut Society and its publication *The Lovingood Papers* (1962–1965), which republished hitherto unknown newspaper sketches by Harris and assorted related materials. Ben Harris McClary, "George Washington Harris's 'Special Vision': His *Yarns* as Historical Casebook," in *No Fairer Land: Studies in Southern Literature before 1900 in Honor of Richard Beale Davis*, ed. J. Lasley Dameron and James W. Mathews (1986), reviews the history of *Yarns* and Harris scholarship.

BEN HARRIS McCLARY

HARRIS, Isham Green (10 Feb. 1818–8 July 1897), governor of Tennessee and U.S. senator, was born in Franklin County, Tennessee, the son of Isham Green Harris, a minister and cotton farmer, and Lucy Davidson. In 1832, after studying for three years at Carrick Academy, Harris moved to Paris, located in Henry County in northwest Tennessee, and obtained a job as a store clerk. Although he demonstrated some talent as a merchant, eventually he decided to pursue a legal career. After a short stint in Mississippi, Harris returned to Tennessee with enough money to study law full time. In 1841 he passed the bar and began what became a prosperous legal practice. He also purchased a farm in Henry County, and by 1849 he owned nearly 300 acres and at least seven slaves and had become one of the most prominent members of Henry County society. In 1843 he married Martha Travis, with whom he had eight children.

In 1847 Harris was elected to the Tennessee Senate, where he quickly established himself as a vigorous defender of states' rights. In 1849 he was elected to the U.S. Congress. He served there until 1853, when he retired to practice law in Memphis. In August 1855 he was appointed associate justice of the Tennessee Supreme Court. With Governor Andrew Johnson's ambitions having been turned toward the U.S. Senate, Harris secured the 1857 Democratic nomination for governor without opposition and won in the general election. Most of his first term was spent dealing with problems caused by the panic of 1857, and in 1859 he easily won reelection.

Tennessee secessionists looked to Harris for leadership after Abraham Lincoln was elected president in 1860. On 7 January 1861 Harris addressed a meeting of the legislature, and in this speech he reiterated his well-known states' rights sentiments and condemned Republican efforts to oppress the South. At his behest, the legislature called for a convention to consider secession, but on 9 February Tennessee voters rejected their call. In April, however, after Lincoln issued his call for troops following the attack against Fort Sumter, Harris indignantly refused to comply and called the state legislature back into session. The legislature, at Harris's urging, passed a resolution of secession and made provisions for military preparations. Despite heavy opposition from the mountainous regions of East Tennessee, a statewide referendum endorsed the secession resolution on 8 June 1861—a full month after the Tennessee legislature had voted to join the Confederacy and to place state troops under the authority of the administration of Confederate president Jefferson Davis.

Although he managed to raise more than 100,000 troops and to oversee their organization, Harris initially placed them under the command of the inept, but politically well-connected, Gideon Pillow. The arrival of Leonidas Polk in June somewhat relieved the situation, but only after Albert Sidney Johnston assumed command in September did military affairs in Tennessee truly receive firm, professional leadership. Although he was feverishly engaged in efforts to place Tennessee on a wartime footing, Harris managed to win overwhelming reelection as governor that fall.

In addition to overseeing the organization of Tennessee's military resources, Harris also took measures to deal with staunchly pro-Union East Tennessee. He initially attempted to conciliate the East Tennesseans by directing Felix Zollicofer, the commander in the area, to avoid any measures that might alienate the local population. But after a Unionist uprising in November 1861, Harris abandoned conciliation and ordered the arrest of Unionist leaders. Confusion in Unionist ranks prevented the emergence of a well-organized, anti-Harris political faction, and this had the effect of facilitating Harris's efforts in the region.

During the summer of 1861 Pillow and Harris, counting on the continued neutrality of Kentucky to protect Tennessee's northern border, overly concentrated their efforts on protecting the Mississippi River at the expense of defending the state's other large rivers. The surrender of Forts Henry and Donelson in February 1862 opened the Tennessee and Cumberland rivers to Federal gunboats and shattered the Confederate line protecting Tennessee. In March Harris joined the principal western Confederate army at Corinth, Mississippi. He served as an aide on the staffs of Albert Sidney Johnston, Braxton Bragg, Joseph E. Johnston, and John B. Hood and in so doing participated in virtually every major campaign conducted by the Army of Tennessee. All the time Harris attempted to maintain a semblance of governmental structure, going so far as to oversee a vote that chose Robert L. Caruthers as his successor in August 1863. Yet, because the Confederate army was forced from the state before Caruthers could be sworn into office, Harris officially remained governor until the end of the war.

Tennessee's Reconstruction legislature proclaimed Harris guilty of treason in April 1865 and issued a $5,000 reward for his capture. Harris fled to Mexico and eventually was elected mayor of a settlement of Confederate exiles. The community disbanded, however, after the French regime of Maximilian was overthrown, and Harris fled to Britain. In October 1867 the Tennessee legislature repealed the bounty on Harris, and the former governor returned home.

On his return Harris formed a legal partnership with Pillow in Memphis. It was successful, and in 1877 he returned to politics, winning election to the U.S. Senate. During his long tenure in the Senate, Harris aligned himself with the agrarian wing of the Democratic party. He actively championed paper money and the free coinage of silver and, in keeping with his antebellum views on states' rights, sought to limit the power of the federal government. He also fought against protective tariffs and played a key role in killing the "Force Bill" proposed by Henry Cabot Lodge to control obvious voting fraud in the South. Harris remained active in the Senate until 1897. By the summer of that year ill health confined him to his bed in Washington, D.C., where he died.

Throughout his long political career, Harris maintained a commitment to the agrarian ideology that had dominated the political culture of his West Tennessee boyhood. It was during his tenure as Tennessee's wartime governor, however, that Harris made his greatest mark on American history. Yet despite his effectiveness in mobilizing Tennessee for war, he was unable to overcome the strategic problem of defending territory in which several large navigable rivers provided convenient routes of invasion.

• Collections of Harris's papers are located at the Manuscript Division, Library of Congress, and in the Tennessee State Library and Archives in Nashville. The best full-length study of Harris's life and career is George W. Watters, "Isham Green Harris: Civil War Governor and Senator from Tennessee, 1818–1897" (Ph.D. diss., Florida State Univ., 1977). Harris figures prominently in all studies of the Civil War in Tennessee. Standard works on this topic include the following by Thomas L. Connelly: *Army of the Heartland: The Army of the Tennessee, 1861–1862* (1967), *Autumn of Glory: The Army of the Tennessee, 1862–1865* (1971), and *Civil War Tennessee* (1979). See also Robert Tracy McKenzie, *One South or Many? Plantation Belt and Upcountry in Civil War–era Tennessee* (1994), and Stephen V. Ash, *Middle Tennessee Society Transformed, 1860–1870* (1988). Obituaries are in the Memphis *Commercial Appeal* and the *Nashville American*, both 9 July 1897.

ETHAN S. RAFUSE

HARRIS, James Arthur (29 Sept. 1880–24 Apr. 1930), botanist and biometrician, was born in Plantsville, Ohio, the son of Jordan Thomas Harris, a farmer and day laborer, and Ida Ellen Lambert. Early in his childhood he moved with his family to western Nebraska; a few years later the family resettled in Lawrence, Kansas. Harris was compelled to support himself from the age of thirteen. One of his major concerns was his education, for which he managed to pay with his earnings alone. By 1901 he completed undergraduate studies in biology at the University of Kansas. As an undergraduate he was assigned a research problem of determining whether the gonads of the dimorphous crayfishes of the region showed characteristic differences; his successful work resulted in the publication of four systematic papers on crayfish. Immediately after graduating, Harris taught botany at the University of Kansas summer school; a year later he was appointed as assistant in the Missouri Botanical Garden. There he worked under William Trelease on the incorporation of new specimens into the herbarium. This experience and Trelease's encouragement led Harris to pursue postgraduate studies in botany. In 1902 he received his M.A. from the University of Kansas, submitting a thesis titled "Pollination in the Genus *Solanum*." A year later he completed the requirements for his Ph.D. in botany from Washington University in St. Louis; his dissertation was "Dehiscence of Anthers by Apical Pores."

From 1903 to 1907 Harris served as librarian at the Missouri Botanical Garden and taught botany at Washington University. In addition to these responsibilities he engaged in independent research. The intriguing problems he tackled were related to the nature and origin of variation of species, the survival of variants, and similar problems in organic evolution. In 1904 Hugo De Vries, one of the biologists credited with the rediscovery of the Mendelian laws, visited St. Louis, and Harris became acquainted with him. Their exchange of ideas and inspiration resulted in a series of papers by Harris on the application of the new mutation theory to the problems of organic evolution.

Mutation theory was not the only area in which De Vries influenced Harris. De Vries advocated the adoption of statistical analysis and correlational studies in biology. Harris led studies in both areas for many years, especially after 1907, when he became botanical investigator with the Station for Experimental Evolution of the Carnegie Institution of Washington at Cold Spring Harbor, a post he held until 1924. During his years at Carnegie he organized research projects and conducted series of experiments to study variation, correlation, and inheritance. Harris became known for his large-scale studies. The annual reports of the Institution show that he was engaged simultaneously on several projects, including studies of variation in wild plants, vegetable teratology, selective elimination, plant fertility and fecundity, and variations, correlation, and inheritance of quantitative characters in garden beans.

Harris appreciated the significance of quantitative studies of biological problems, and even in his early botanical research he had attempted to employ statistical analysis. Convinced of the need to put biology on a more exact basis, he continued his education in statistics by studying biometry in Karl Pearson's laboratory at University College, London, during the winters of 1908–1909 and 1909–1910. His interaction with Pearson's pioneering work in biometry played a formative role in his scientific development. Harris returned to the United States a strong advocate of biometry. He began his contribution to its establishment and recognition in biological circles by publishing a series of papers in which he recommended statistical methods for use in biological studies. Among his major contributions were the solution of the problem of measuring the correlation between a variable and the deviation of a dependent variable from its proportionate value; the simplification of the coefficient of correlation; and the solution of agricultural problems using biometric methods. The significance of Harris's campaign was great, in view of the indifference or even hostility of biologists to biometry and biometrical subjects in the first two decades of the twentieth century. In recognition for his work in biometry Harris in 1921 was awarded the Weldon Medal and Weldon Memorial Prize by Oxford University.

In 1924 Harris left the Carnegie Institution to become professor of botany and head of the department of botany at the University of Minnesota. He accepted the appointment on the condition that he could include courses in biometry in the departmental curriculum. Within a short time he had instituted three courses in biometry. Along with his teaching, Harris continued research he had started at Carnegie on the physicochemical properties of plant saps in relation to their taxonomic affinities, to geographical distribution, and to various ecological factors. Most of these studies were done in the deserts and alkali lands of Arizona and Utah during the period 1925–1929. In 1926 Harris served as president of the American Society of Naturalists, and from 1928 to 1930 he was a member-at-large of the Division of Biology and Agriculture of the National Research Council.

Harris was an influential scientific figure in the United States during the first three decades of the century. Most notable is the fact that he was a pioneer in several fields. Although he began in botany with his research on mutation and correlation, he soon moved on to the new field of biometry, which he helped to establish in the United States. For Harris, being on the frontier was a part of the identity shaped in his early childhood migrations westward.

Harris married Emma Lay in 1910; they had four sons. He died in St. Paul, Minnesota, after an operation following a case of acute appendicitis.

• Some of Harris's correspondence and records from his University of Minnesota years are at the department of botany there. Photographs, biographical information, and obituaries are in his biographical folder in the University of Minnesota Archives. The most important source for his life and scientific work is Carl Otto Rosendahl et al., eds., *J. Arthur Harris: Botanist and Biometrician* (1936), reviewed by H. Reed, in *Science* 83 (1936): 598–99, and by G. Steward in *Ecology* 18 (1937): 295–98. Of Harris's more than 300 publications, one very significant in biometry is James Arthur Harris and Francis Gano Benedict, *A Biometric Study of Basal Metabolism in Man* (1919). For his perspectives on science see also his "Frontiers," *Scientific Monthly* 30 (1930): 29–32. Obituaries are in the *New York Times*, 27 Apr. 1930; the *Minneapolis Tribune*, 25 Apr. 1930; and *Science*, 9 and 23 May 1930.

EFFY VAYENA

HARRIS, Jed (25 Feb. 1900–15 Nov. 1979), Broadway theatrical producer and director, was born Jacob Hirsch Horowitz in Lemburg, Austria, the son of Meyer Horowitz and Esther (maiden name unknown). Before his first birthday, the family emigrated to Newark, New Jersey, where his father began a retail/wholesale business selling cheeses, grains, and vegetables. Upon being graduated from a local high school in June 1917, Jacob entered Yale University, only to be ostracized for being poor and Jewish. After three years he dropped out, disgusted with this treatment and generally disinclined to study anyway.

In 1923, after a year's adventure in Europe and a voyage home as a ship stowaway, Horowitz got a job with a show business trade paper. The position led to his becoming a theatrical press agent. By the time he was twenty-five he had married his college sweetheart, Anita Green; had changed his name to Jed Harris; and was involved with two Broadway plays, helping raise production money. He then seized upon a script that a young director named George Abbott had submitted to him—a script that he believed would make his fortune. The play was *Broadway*, co-written by Abbott and Philip Dunning. Harris urged that it be presented with the speed of a farce and the rhythm of a musical. This conception was a complete break with the formal and ornate dramatic style of the period; it reflected the up-to-the-minute mood of the Jazz Age, the era of Prohibition.

Starring Lee Tracy (with James Cagney his understudy), *Broadway* opened at the Broadhurst Theater in New York on 16 September 1926; it was a sensation. The premiere was followed by successful productions throughout the world. More important historically, this play introduced the kind of smart, crackling entertainment that for decades to come characterized all Broadway theater. Over the next fifteen months, the suddenly wealthy Harris produced three consecutive hits: Ann Bridgers's *Coquette* (1927), starring Helen Hayes; *The Royal Family* (1927), by Edna Ferber and George S. Kaufman; and the Ben Hecht and Charles

MacArthur melodrama *The Front Page* (1928). At the time, Harris was earning $40,000 a week, and he appeared on the cover of *Time* magazine. He was considered one of America's golden young successes, ranked with George Gershwin and Charles Lindbergh.

Harris was bored with his marriage and unfaithful to his wife (with whom he had had no children), but she refused his pleas for a divorce. He had affairs with many of the actresses he met, most notably Judith Anderson and Ruth Gordon. When Gordon became pregnant in 1929 and refused an abortion, Harris, fearful of a scandal, took her to Paris to have their child. Although his wife finally granted him a divorce in 1929, he and Gordon never married.

When the New York stock market crashed in October 1929, Harris lost nearly all of his fortune and returned to the theater, from which only months earlier he had grandiosely announced his retirement. Although he was never able to repeat the astonishing success of his first four shows, his reputation persisted. He was known as "The Meteor" and "Wonder Boy"; Moss Hart later wrote in his autobiography, *Act One* (1959): "Every aspiring playwright's prayer in those days [was] 'Please, God, let Jed Harris do my play!'"

In 1930 Harris ventured into the realm of directing, audaciously beginning with a production of Chekhov's *Uncle Vanya* that starred Ruth Gordon. Although the play was not successful, within three years he had developed a superb talent for staging. For the 1933–1934 season he brought Laurence Olivier to New York and directed him in Mordant Shairp's strikingly mysterious *The Green Bay Tree*. (Olivier found Harris so malicious as to later base a characterization of Shakespeare's evil Richard III on him.) That same season he presented Katharine Hepburn in *The Lake*, by Dorothy Mussingham and Murray MacDonald. But whether his shows were praised (*The Green Bay Tree*) or panned (*The Lake*), they proved equally unsuccessful financially. In the years that followed, Harris fared no better with boulevard comedies and melodramas.

Thus, as quickly as Harris had found his golden touch, he lost it. Flop was followed by failure and then disaster. He grew more interested in the personal side of his life and developed a sinister reputation. People feared him as a perverse manipulator of private lives. His hooded eyes, scowling expression, malevolent whisper, and dominating presence became the stuff of legend. Various victims wrote thinly disguised books about him, including Hecht's *A Jew in Love* (1928) and Frederic Wakeman's *The Saxon Charm* (1947).

In 1938 Harris came upon Thornton Wilder's *Our Town*. Producing and directing it himself, he launched a pre-Broadway trial run in Boston. The play nearly closed there because of the public's icy response to the lack of scenery and its poetic, philosophical manner. But when Harris opened it on Broadway in 1938, *Our Town* immediately became a tremendous success, winning that year's Pulitzer Prize and becoming an instant classic.

Nevertheless, the show proved to be Harris's undoing. During the Boston run, he took up with Rosamond Pinchot, an aspiring actress and the niece of the governor of Pennsylvania. She fell in love with him so absolutely that she left her husband and children to work for him as a production assistant. When he publicly rejected her, Pinchot's suicide became front-page news across the country. The theater world seemed to agree that Harris was responsible for Pinchot's suicide. He never fully recovered, professionally or personally, and the next forty years were a downhill slide.

Harris produced a series of disasters, plays that were either mediocre or made mediocre by his own revisions. In 1940 he married the actress Louise Platt after a stormy courtship; by the time their daughter was born the following year, they were already divorced. Harris did achieve occasional professional success, including his direction of Ruth and Augustus Goetz's *The Heiress*, a 1947 dramatization of the Henry James novel *Washington Square*. His direction six years later of *The Crucible*, Arthur Miller's first play after *Death of a Salesman*, should have been another golden opportunity. By this time, however, Harris was consumed by self-destruction, and his staging of the play was disastrous.

By this time, too, the commercial New York stage had changed. The days of the entrepreneurial producer were over. Broadway, whose very style and energy Harris had helped create with the play *Broadway*, had changed. Theaters had become too expensive for an individual producer to finance, thereby dooming the solitary producer. Directing styles had changed as well, and Harris's notions of farce, melodrama, and pageant seemed creaky to contemporary audiences.

Retiring from the theater and moving to the South, Harris was largely forgotten, and he lived his last decades relying on handouts. When he was finally nominated for Broadway's hall of fame two years after his death in New York, it was almost as an afterthought, even though he was, in many ways, the man who had invented Broadway.

• Harris wrote two reminiscences: *Watchman, What of the Night?* (1963) and *A Dance on a High Wire* (1980). There are five videotaped PBS interviews with Harris that Dick Cavett conducted in 1979 for Daphne Productions. Works that are presumably based on him include S. N. Behrman's 1930 play *Meteor*. Lengthy passages from Harris are contained in Noël Coward, *Present Indicative* (1937). An obituary is in the *New York Times*, 16 Nov. 1979.

MARTIN GOTTFRIED

HARRIS, Joel Chandler (9 Dec. 1848–3 July 1908), journalist and author, was born near Eatonton, Georgia, the son of Mary Harris. His father was apparently a young itinerant Irish day laborer who lived with Harris's mother until the child was born and then deserted her. The Harrises moved to a cottage on the Andrew Reid plantation, where the boy was exposed to the major components of mid-nineteenth-century Georgia society—poor white farmers; the social and economic upper-class, plantation-owning elite; and black slaves. At this time Harris began thinking about becoming a writer. Recalling his early life in *Lippin-*

cott's Magazine (1886), he wrote, "My desire to write . . . grew out of hearing my mother read *The Vicar of Wakefield*. I was too young to appreciate the story, but there was something in the humor of that remarkable little book that struck my fancy, and I straight away fell into composing little tales."

Harris attended a coeducational private school, Kate Davidson's Academy, and then the all-male Hillsbrough Academy. Nevertheless, he also suffered from what he considered a series of physical disabilities. He was short, had red hair, and suffered from a pronounced stammer. These perceived inadequacies, coupled with his early knowledge of his illegitimacy, resulted in lifelong shyness.

In March 1862 Harris answered an advertisement in the *Countryman*, a newspaper edited by Joseph Addison Turner. Harris moved to Turner's plantation to become an apprentice printer. During his four years there, in his free time he visited the slave cabins, where he heard the inhabitants telling folktales; hunted fur-bearing animals; and joined Turner on fox hunts. Occasionally Harris inserted some of his own paragraphs into columns of the journal. Through the *Countryman*, Turner tried to change the southern notion that literature was a form of self-indulgence by providing a place where authors could publish pieces representative of the South thematically and stylistically. When he discovered that his "printer's double" had writing ambitions, Turner opened his 6,000-volume library to Harris and tutored him in the art of writing. The purity of Harris's later style, together with his use of the materials found around him in his everyday life, were tied directly to Turner's influence.

The *Countryman* ceased in May 1866, so Harris returned to Eatonton. He carried with him, however, the memories of the raconteurs that he had heard in the slaves' quarters. A proficient typesetter, Harris next worked on the daily *Macon Telegraph* newspaper. Besides typesetting, he reviewed books and magazines and composed humorous "puffs" about local merchants. One of the magazines that he reviewed was the *Crescent Monthly*, published in New Orleans by William Evelyn. Like Turner, Evelyn devoted his magazine to "literature, art, science, and society." He wanted to demonstrate the importance of southern writing in American literature. In October 1866 Harris became Evelyn's private secretary. Although he published two poems in the *New Orleans Times*, Harris did not feel comfortable in New Orleans, and he returned to Georgia to take a position with the *Monroe Advertiser*, a weekly newspaper in Forsyth. For three years he set type, prepared forms, printed the newspaper, and mailed it. He also wrote humorous paragraphs about Georgia life and characters and a series of sketches about fox hunting.

Unfortunately he suffered from a "morbidly sensitive" nature, an "*absolute horror* of strangers," and "awkwardness and clumsiness." Readers of his tales, naturally, had no knowledge of these matters, and he gained a considerable reputation in area newspapers for his efforts. As a result, in 1870 he was invited to become the associate editor of the *Savannah Morning News*, a major Georgia paper. The founder-editor of the *News* was William Tappan Thompson, the creator of the "Major Jones" stories so important in the development of southwestern local color. Harris wrote a daily column, "State Affairs" (later changed to "Affairs of Georgia"), that contained humorous comments on personalities and current events. The entries were typical of the time. Comic relief was Harris's contribution to the creation of a "New South" of self-confidence and optimism appreciated by his contemporaries, such as the editor of a Georgia paper who wrote, "What shall we say of the bright, sparkling, vivacious, inimitable Harris? There is no failing in his spirit of wit and humor, playful raillery and pungent sarcasm. As a terse and an incisive paragraphist, he is unequaled in the South. . . . Harris is a genius."

About this time Harris met Esther "Essie" LaRose, the seventeen-year-old daughter of a steamboat owner who was staying in the Florida House in Savannah where Harris lived. The couple married in 1873 and had nine children, three of whom died in childhood. Harris's happy marriage and strong family life provided him with a solidity that he had lacked. For years he had suffered black moods of depression; these disappeared.

Savannah was paralyzed by yellow fever in August 1876, and Harris and his family fled to Atlanta. He became allied with the *Atlanta Constitution*, edited by Evan Howell and Henry Grady. Howell and Grady were involved in the New South movement, and they welcomed Harris as an associate editor. The move was Harris's last major change of address. As he had in Savannah, Harris wrote a column of humorous paragraphs, this one titled "Roundabout in Georgia." Sam Small, a staff writer who wrote dialect sketches featuring Old Si, an old-time Atlanta black, for the *Constitution*, resigned, and Harris composed the first of his Uncle Remus stories. "Markham's Ball," in which he detailed old Uncle Ben's humorous comments about a party celebrating a political victory, and "Jeem's Rober'son's Last Illness," a sketch about an old black man and a black youth waiting in the Union Station for the younger man's train to depart, were published in the 26 October 1876 edition of the newspaper. Shortly after "Jeem's Rober'son's" was published, Harris's "politics and provisions" appeared. In it one of the black characters is called "Remus." In November and December 1876 six additional Uncle Remus stories appeared. Within four years Harris had enough sketches about the old man whom he called Uncle Remus that he could collect them in *Uncle Remus: His Songs and His Sayings* (1880). The volume sold 7,500 copies in the first month of publication and 10,000 copies within four months; critics in the United States and England responded positively. In 1878 the *Constitution* serialized Harris's novel *The Romance of Rockvill*. This effort was not as successful, and Harris returned to writing about Uncle Remus.

Harris's first serious attempt to re-create a folktale was "The Story of Mr. Rabbit and Mr. Fox as Told by

Uncle Remus," published on the *Constitution*'s 20 July 1879 editorial page under the heading "Negro Folklore." His most popular folktale, about Brer Rabbit and the Tar Baby, appeared four months later. Over the next twenty-seven years, 180 Uncle Remus stories were published in ten books. Uncle Remus had two incarnations: an old black man who lived in Atlanta and who was bitter about his poverty and wistful about having left the country, and an old black man who told folktales featuring humanized animals to an inquisitive white boy.

In 1882 Harris traveled to New Orleans to meet with Mark Twain and George W. Cable. While there, Harris "deeply disappointed" a number of children when, due to shyness, he would not recite his Uncle Remus tales; Twain read them for him. *Nights with Uncle Remus* was published in 1883, and *Mingo and Other Sketches in Black and White* followed in 1884. Harris found that his work on the *Constitution* allowed him little time for his literary career, however, and it was three years before his fourth volume, *Free Joe and Other Georgian Sketches*, appeared. The pressure of work combined with illness slowed Harris further, though *Daddy Jake the Runaway and Short Stories Told After Dark* was published in 1889. Surprisingly, during the 1890s Harris wrote and edited fourteen books, including *Balaam and His Master* in 1891. He tried to kill off Uncle Remus in his introduction to *Uncle Remus and His Friends* (1892) because he was afraid that the public was losing interest in the character, but the old man was brought back later.

A series of six volumes of old plantation stories written for children appeared between 1894 and 1903. In 1895, for the fifteenth anniversary of the publication of *Uncle Remus: His Songs and His Sayings*, a new edition was published, illustrated with 112 drawings by Arthur B. Frost. In 1896 *Sister Jane: Her Friends and Acquaintances* was published and quickly sold 3,000 copies, though reviews were mixed. *Tales of the Homefolks in Peace and War* and *The Chronicles of Aunt Minervy Ann* followed in 1898 and 1899. In 1899 the *Saturday Evening Post* began a series about Civil War blockade-running and spy adventures, collected as *On the Wing of Occasions* in 1900. In "The Kidnapping of President Lincoln," Harris created Billy Sanders, a middle-class Georgian who served as the author's persona regarding current events, political issues, and politicians. That year Harris resigned from the *Constitution*.

Harris was ill during much of 1902–1903, yet he managed to publish the last of his old plantation books in 1903 and *Little Union Scout* (1904), a novel about the Civil War adventures of Harry Herndon and his black companion, "Whistling Jim." *The Tar Baby and Other Rhymes of Uncle Remus* also was published in 1904 and *Told by Uncle Remus: New Stories of the Old Plantation* in 1905. In the latter, the white boy to whom Uncle Remus told stories was replaced by Miss Sally's grandson. *Uncle Remus and Brer Rabbit* (1907) and *Uncle Remus and the Little Boy* (1910) completed the Uncle Remus series. The final venture of Harris's publishing career was as editor of *Uncle Remus's Maga-*

zine (the initial issue appeared in June 1907). Harris died of euremic poisoning in Atlanta.

As a symbol of the nation's appreciation of Harris's writing, in a speech in Atlanta in October 1905 President Theodore Roosevelt said, "Presidents may come and presidents may go, but Uncle Remus stays put. Georgia has done a great many things for the Union, but she has never done more than when she gave Joel Chandler Harris to American literature." Among Harris's contemporaries in literary criticism, William Malone Baskervill's opinion is typical: "Mr. Harris's skill in narrative is well-nigh perfect, and the conversation, in which his books abound, is carried on with absolute naturalness and fidelity to life" (*Southern Writers: Biographical and Critical Studies* [1987]). Ten years after Harris's death, H. E. Harman noted, "As a story teller [Harris] had few equals" and "Through all of his writing runs a golden thread of poetry."

With his ability to replicate dialectical patterns of blacks and his recording of folk tradition, Harris contributed to the local color movement and created characters and stories influential and popular not only in his own time but worldwide today. A self-described "transcriber" of "geniune folklore tales," Harris inadvertently stimulated scholarly debate about folktale origins. J. W. Powell claimed that some of the Uncle Remus tales originated with North American Indians. In 1879 H. H. Smith disputed this: "One thing is certain. The animal stories told by the negroes of our Southern States and in Brazil were brought by them from Africa." Harris agreed, and research by Denise Paulma, Bernard Wolfe, and others has demonstrated that "the tar baby and the rabbit" and other tales were clearly African in origin. The fact that the Uncle Remus tales are still in print and have been translated into at least twenty-seven foreign languages is evidence that Harris was an important American humorist who borrowed from traditions around him and made the material his own.

• The primary collection of Harris materials is at the Joel Chandler Harris Memorial Collection at Emory University in Atlanta, which contains more than 6,000 pages of letters, manuscripts, and other material. The text of five letters between Twain and Harris, along with critical commentary, is found in Thomas H. English, *Mark Twain to Uncle Remus: 1881–1885* (1953). A 1918 biography by Julia Collier Harris, Harris's daughter, *The Life and Letters of Joel Chandler Harris*, is an interesting and thorough account notable for her personal asides. Also in 1918 Robert Lemuel Wiggins published *The Life of Joel Chandler Harris, from Obscurity in Boyhood to Fame in Early Manhood*. Paul M. Cousins, *Joel Chandler Harris: A Biography* (1968), focuses on the author's youth, regional background, and time as a printer, along with his positive philosophy. A standard bibliography is R. Bruce Bickley, Jr., *Joel Chandler Harris: A Reference Guide* (1978). Additional bibliographic information is in the Cousins and Harris biographies; Stella Brewer Brookes, *Joel Chandler Harris: Folklorist* (1950); and Louis D. Rubin, *A Bibliographical Guide to the Study of Southern Literature* (1969). Besides Brookes's study, book-length examinations include Alvin P. Harlow, *Joel Chandler Harris: Plantation Storyteller* (1941); Julia Collier Harris, *Joel Chandler Harris: Editor and Essayist*

(1931); and Bickley, *Joel Chandler Harris* (1978). Obituaries are in the *New York Times* and the *Atlanta Journal*, 4 July 1908.

STEVEN H. GALE

HARRIS, Johana (31 Dec. 1912–5 June 1995), pianist, composer, and teacher, was born Beula Aleta Duffey in Ottawa, Ontario, Canada, the daughter of Claude Duffey, a grocery supplier, and Laura Coughlan. Before she was two, Harris climbed up on the parlor piano stool to play music she had heard the Royal Canadian Mounties Band play on Parliament Hill for the changing of the guard. Her mother, afflicted by familial deafness, couldn't hear her playing exactly what the band had played, but she noticed the enchanted spectators watching her dance on the bandstand; consequently, she arranged Harris's debut at the age of four as a professional dancer.

But Harris begged for piano study, beginning private lessons when she was six. Her teacher soon took her to Henry Puddicombe's Canadian Conservatory, and she became his protégée, also studying French, arithmetic, and English at a small girls' academy. Her first public concert, at age nine, combined adult piano repertoire with her own compositions. Critics compared her to a young Mozart in the maturity of her performances and the freshness of her original works. At age eleven she toured in concerts throughout eastern Canada, having graduated from the conservatory in a class of twenty-year-olds.

Known as "Ottawa's Child Pianiste," Harris soon developed her talents in a wider world, and Puddicombe persuaded her mother to take her to Ernest Hutcheson in New York City for further study. When Hutcheson became the first dean of the Juilliard Graduate School (there was no undergraduate program), Harris auditioned for admission and was awarded a full scholarship with highest praise. At age fourteen, she was the youngest graduate student ever, and in composition classes with Ruben Goldmark (Aaron Copland's teacher) it was she who sight-read all the student works.

Beginning in 1928 Harris won annual scholarships for Juilliard's summer festivals in Chautauqua, New York. She was a concerto soloist there, coached Juilliard student ensembles, and played chamber music concerts with world-class instrumentalists. Hutcheson made Harris his Juilliard assistant three years later, in which role she taught piano students much older than herself. She was his piano partner in 200 national network Sunday night radio broadcasts of two-piano programs, and she appeared as a soloist with major symphony orchestras. Graduating from Juilliard in 1932, Harris became a secondary faculty member.

During Juilliard's 1935 summer session, Harris was assigned to play Bach's Forty-eight Preludes and Fugues for keyboard, illustrating lectures by budding composer Roy Harris. He was the age of her father and married to his third wife, but he became enchanted by the "Belle of Juilliard." She, in turn, was proud to be chosen as his fourth wife, becoming the muse for this pioneer of American music. To accommodate Roy's numerology system, which honored Johann Sebastian Bach, Beula Duffey became Johana Harris at their midnight marriage on 10 October 1936 in Union, Oregon. They had five children.

From the beginning of their marriage, Harris was expected to sit with her husband each morning as he composed. She could "hear" what he wrote and suggest other musical possibilities. Her greatest gift was as an improviser, and her pitch-perfect ear, flawless memory, and natural technique assisted him in composing Roy Harris's Third Symphony—which *Time* quoted Boston Symphony Orchestra conductor Serge Koussevitzky as calling "the first truly great symphonic work to be written in America" (8 Apr. 1940). Thereafter he called for piano parts in nearly all of his compositions, even the symphonies; and, pressed by deadlines, he left keyboard parts open, knowing that Harris could improvise in his style by listening to what other musicians were playing—an approach common to jazz ensembles.

Harris was an unusually active recitalist, often giving three or four different programs in a week. She memorized most music in the first reading. Besides presenting world premieres of fifty-seven of her husband's works, she premiered Walter Piston's Concertino for Piano and Orchestra and Alberto Ginastera's Piano Sonata No. 1 and played North American premieres of piano concertos by Rodolfo Halffter and Blas Galindo. Another feature of Harris's piano programs were improvisations that she created on the spot; most notably, in 1963 she replaced a previously scheduled program at what was then Stockton (Calif.) College with a thirty-minute musical recollection of President John F. Kennedy.

An RCA Red Seal artist, Harris recorded the world premiere of the Bach-Busoni Chaconne in D Minor, featured at New York's 1939 World's Fair, and AS-CAP recorded and released her world premiere performance of the Ginastera Piano Sonata (1952). She made more than 100 recordings, including all of her husband's solo, orchestral, choral, and chamber works with piano, most of Beethoven's solo piano and chamber compositions, and fifty-one discs of Irish and American folk songs sung to her own accompaniments for broadcast by the Office of War Information to soldiers during World War II. At age seventy-five she recorded her entire solo repertoire—178 pieces—during fifty-six consecutive evenings. A major rock 'n 'roll studio gave her free studio time, and in 1988 MCA released two recordings, *Johana Harris: A Living Legacy, Music of J. S. Bach* and *Johana Harris: A Living Legacy, Music of Debussy.*

Harris taught piano technique and literature in numerous academic settings, including Juilliard, Lebanon Valley College, Westminster Choir School, Henry Street Settlement, Williams College, Cornell University, Colorado College, Utah State Agricultural College, George Peabody College for Teachers, Western Kentucky State Teachers College, University of the South, Pennsylvania College for Women, Royal Conservatory of Music (University of Toronto), Indiana University, Universidad Interamericana de Puerto Rico, California Institute of the Arts, University of the Pacific (Stockton), Loyola Marymount University, Mt. St. Mary's College, and UCLA. Her legions of piano pupils included Peter Schickele (a.k.a. P. D. Q. Bach), John Browning, Robert Evett, and composer-pianist Jake Heggie whom she married in 1982, three years after Roy Harris had died. In 1986 UCLA named Harris as its first distinguished lecturer from the music faculty. She taught and performed there until fourteen months before her death in Los Angeles.

Research reveals that Harris composed in her husband's name. She was the surrogate composer, to varying degrees, of seventy-one compositions attributed to Roy Harris as he became progressively disabled after 1950 by undiagnosed manic-depressive disease. Harris anonymously completed compositional commitments in her husband's name until his death.

• Archival material on Harris is accessible in the Library of Congress, the New York Library of Performing Arts, and the Roy Harris Collection at California State University (Los Angeles). A comprehensive biography by Louise Spizizen was published by the University of Illinois Press in 1999. For an abbreviated but detailed account of Harris's early life and her unique participation in compositions attributed to Roy Harris, see Louise Spizizen, "Johana and Roy Harris: Marrying a *Real* Composer," *Musical Quarterly* 77, no. 4, (1993): 579–606. Extensive analysis of the history of her husband's works, documenting her input into seventy-one of his compositions, is in Dan Stehman, *Roy Harris: A Bio-Bibliography* (1991). The liner notes on MCA's 1988 CD *Johana Harris: A Living Legacy, Music of J. S. Bach* give a brief but comprehensive view of her life. During Harris's tenure in the early 1940s as the keyboard editor for Mills Music, Inc., an edition of Bach Organ Preludes was published (1946), "transcribed for piano by Johana and Roy Harris," but these minimal transcriptions bear little resemblance to her performances and/or recordings of them. She was also a consultant on piano accompaniments for Follett Publishing Company's *Music 'round the Clock* folk-song series: two books and fifteen recordings created for elementary school use (1954–1961). Obituaries are in the *New York Times*, 15 June 1995, and *The Times* (London), 4 July 1995.

LOUISE SPIZIZEN

HARRIS, John (1726–30 July 1791), ferryman, Indian trader, and founder of Harrisburg, Pennsylvania, was born in Paxton, Pennsylvania, the son of John Harris, a trader and brewer, and Esther Say. Harris, often designated "the founder" to distinguish him from his father, apparently had little formal education, although he was literate. Harris's father arrived in Philadelphia from England in the early eighteenth century with very little in the way of financial resources. He worked for a time as a laborer, but through a friendship with Philadelphia's first mayor, Edward Shippen, he became a prominent figure. By 1718 he had established an American Indian trading post on the banks of the Susquehanna River at an Indian village near the mouth of Paxton Creek, then deep into the colonial frontier. When he died in 1748, his son John

Harris inherited 710 acres on the east bank of the river and an additional 210 acres on the west side. In 1749 Harris married Elizabeth McClure, with whom he had three surviving children. Following Elizabeth's death, Harris in 1764 married Mary Reed. They had three children who survived to adulthood.

With the property left to him by his father, Harris continued the already successful trading business, which consisted of houses, barns, and cleared fields. He sold a variety of supplies, such as sugar, salt, tobacco, butter, beef, turkey, venison, and alcohol, especially rum, along with blankets and ammunition. The success of the Harris post was in no small measure due to geography. As one of the most ideal places to cross the Susquehanna River en route to the Ohio country, the Harris plantation was located on one of the principal routes west. Among the nearby Native American peoples were the Shawnee, the Delaware, and the most mighty of all, the Six Nations of the Iroquois Confederacy. Indian agents such as Conrad Weiser and George Croghan were visitors to the Paxton post. Gifts of goods from the proprietors of Pennsylvania to the various Indian tribes for the purpose of maintaining good relations were at times sent to Harris for delivery. Harris corresponded often with Richard Peters, secretary of the Province of Pennsylvania, regarding matters of provincial–Native American diplomacy.

In February 1753 the Penn family granted Harris the exclusive ferry rights for a mile and a quarter on both sides of the crossing. The importance of Harris Ferry, as Paxton became known, increased even more with the contest between England and France over the Ohio country, specifically the forks of the Ohio River at present-day Pittsburgh.

In May 1754 Tanacharison, the important Seneca chief known by the English as "the Half-King," warned George Washington of an approaching French force while Washington was leading a body of Virginians seeking control of the Ohio country for the British Crown. The ensuing "Jumonville affair" was arguably the start of the French and Indian War. In October 1754 Half-King died while on a visit to Harris Ferry. Harris wrote to Peters that he buried Half-King and took his family and entourage under his care, but "I hae been at Expenses for their Provisions and his Funeral; my account I shall send down which I hope you'll be pleas'd to lay before the Assembly." In December the province paid Harris the sum of fifteen shillings, four pence for the services he had provided to their valuable native allies.

The defeat of Washington at Great Meadows in July 1754 and the battle of the Monongahela the following year put posts such as Harris's in the front lines of the ensuing Indian raids on the frontier. Harris built a stockade around his home and cut loopholes for defense. In letters to the Pennsylvania government, he often pleaded for aid in the form of weapons and men, citing the numerous raids by French and Indians in the region. The expedition against Fort Duquesne led by Brigadier General John Forbes in 1758 passed through Harris Ferry and utilized its supply storage capacity.

In 1766 Harris displayed his wealth with the construction of a stone house facing the ferry landing and his father's grave site. The building was modified later and in the nineteenth century served as the home of Pennsylvania senator and secretary of war Simon Cameron.

According to his grandson George Washington Harris, John Harris was reluctant to rush to the side of rebellion in the growing rift between the colonies and England. However, once Harris decided to aid the patriot cause, he offered material aid to the Pennsylvania Committee of Safety. He took the Oath of Allegiance and Fidelity in 1778 as required by an act of the Pennsylvania General Assembly of 13 June 1777. Harris vigorously impounded goods of suspected Tories passing by his strategic riverfront property. In one particular case, the Committee of Safety urged him to be less vehement in taking possession of a shipment of salt, a commodity much in demand at the time, a request that Harris refused. Patriot victims of the frontier was came to the Harris property to seek refuge, among them a large number of the survivors of the 1778 Wyoming massacre in the upper Susquehanna Valley.

Following the Revolution, Harris in 1784 proposed to the Pennsylvania General Assembly a plan for laying out a town, Harrisburg, on his property. He contributed lots for a jail and a court house plus an additional four acres. A successful move by the Pennsylvania Supreme Court to rename the town Louisbourg in honor of Louis XVI was never accepted by Harris. The town's founder lived to see the name restored to Harrisburg on 16 May 1791. He died there two months later. A man of considerable wealth, Harris left the ferry rights to the Commonwealth of Pennsylvania.

• For primary sources on Harris see the Harris-Fisher Family Papers, microfilm 4007, Pennsylvania State Archives, William Penn Museum. A transcribed copy of Harris's will is in the John Harris, Jr., Scrapbook at the Dauphin County Historical Society in Harrisburg, Pa., located behind the Harris mansion. Harris's letters to and from the provincial government are in the Colonial Records of Pennsylvania, Pennsylvania State Archives. The best index to the series was compiled by Mary Maples Dunn in 1992. Letters from Harris during the American Revolution are in the Pennsylvania Archives, First Series. Some correspondence between Harris and Colonel Henry Bouquet, a leader in the Forbes expedition of 1758 and the relief of Fort Pitt during Pontiac's Rebellion, is in *The Papers of Henry Bouquet*, ed. S. K. Stevens et al. (1951). Secondary works include *A Chronicle of the Harris and McIntosh Families* (1980); Kyle Weaver, "John Harris Jr., Founder of Harrisburg," *Cumberland County History*, no. 1 (Summer 1990); *Commemorative Biographical Encyclopedia of Dauphin County, Pennsylvania, Containing Sketches of Prominent and Representative Citizens, and Many of the Early Scotch-Irish and German Settlers* (1896); and George H. Morgan, *Annals, Comprising Memoirs, Incidents and Statistics of Harrisburg from the Period of Its First Settlement* (1858).

DAVID EDWARD MICHLOVITZ

HARRIS, John Howard (24 Apr. 1847–4 Apr. 1925), educator and university president, was born in Buffington, Indiana County, Pennsylvania, the son of Reese Harris and Isabel Coleman, both of whom were farmers. Harris showed an early interest in teaching, securing his first job in Mechanicsburg, Pennsylvania, when he was fifteen. The Civil War soon intervened, and he served one year with the Second Battalion, Pennsylvania Volunteers before returning to teaching. When Abraham Lincoln called for more troops in 1864 Harris volunteered again and served in the last battles of the war, including Petersburg and Richmond, with the 206th Pennsylvania Volunteers.

After his discharge in 1865, Harris enrolled at the University of Lewisburg (now Bucknell University). Following his graduation in 1869, Harris was appointed principal of a new Baptist academy in Factoryville, near Scranton, founded as part of the Baptists' attempt to strengthen their secondary schools in Pennsylvania. Harris taught the first class of sixteen in the basement of the local Baptist church; when he left twenty years later, Keystone Academy had over 200 students and occupied three buildings. Ordained in 1872, Harris also served as the pastor of the Factoryville Baptist Church from 1881 to 1889. Harris married Mary Mace in 1872. After her death, he married Lucy A. Bailey; they had nine children.

In 1889 Harris's alma mater, the recently renamed Bucknell University, called Harris to be its fourth president. The former University of Lewisburg had been the product of a uniquely American blend of denominationalism and local boosterism. During the 1840s, the Philadelphia Baptist Association had been called on to oversee the creation of a Baptist institution of higher education for Pennsylvania. When it failed to do so the tiny Northumberland Baptist Association of Lewisburg, a village on the Susquehanna River in the middle of Pennsylvania, seized the opportunity. With the help of local leaders from other denominations, the association members successfully founded the University of Lewisburg in 1846. The graduate and professional departments implied in the title "University" never materialized, but the founders developed an academy, a "Female Institute," and a modest college.

In 1881 the college had been rescued from internal disputes and potential fiscal collapse by a wealthy Philadelphia Baptist, William Bucknell. Taking control of the university, Bucknell and other Philadelphians financed a successful restructuring that featured a modest, traditional program. When Harris succeeded David Jayne Hill as president in 1889, the recently renamed Bucknell University consisted of eight faculty members and seventy-one students.

The new president vigorously pursued God and mammon. On the one hand he enforced rules of student conduct and religious services that President Hill had relaxed. On the other hand he was determined to raise enrollment and the endowment. He turned to the trustees for donations, but since most were clergy or educators, they did not have the means to finance his ambitions. Harris resolved, consequently, that future members of the board would be wealthy businessmen and professionals. By 1908 Harris could boast that the board consisted mainly of businessmen, mostly drawn from the elite of small Pennsylvania towns. During the period that Harris was reconstituting the board, the university was assisted by John D. Rockefeller, who in 1888 had begun funding Baptist colleges and universities through the American Baptist Education Society (ABES). Harris procured three grants from the ABES to underwrite an expansion of the school. Rockefeller and the ABES thus enabled Harris, and likewise other Baptist educators, to promote expansion while maintaining the traditional vision of a denominational college. At the same time, Harris participated in the Northumberland Baptist Association and preached to Baptists across the state, often temporarily filling vacant pulpits.

The convenient convergence of denominationalism and expansionism ended in 1902, when Rockefeller created the General Education Board to administer his educational philanthropy, an organization that did not confer special privileges on Baptists. The ABES collapsed, leaving denominational fundraising in disarray. The Northern Baptist Convention was unable to create a replacement source of funding.

Fortunately for Harris, Rockefeller's benevolence had already underwritten the initial phases of expansion. Harris obtained some further grants, including $30,000 for a library from Andrew Carnegie in 1904 and another Rockefeller grant through the General Education Board in 1911. In addition, growing alumni loyalty and affluence increasingly provided a substitute for funding from denominational sources and nonalumni Baptist trustees. When an early fund drive for a gymnasium stalled, Harris declared that "nearly all the alumni were ministers who were unable to do much." He rectified the situation by recruiting children of businessmen and lawyers, championing alumni representation on the board of trustees, and encouraging the formation of alumni clubs. Athletics further boosted alumni pride, especially after Christy Mathewson (class of 1902) became a major league baseball star.

President Harris's campaign to create an affluent board of trustees and alumni body led to further growth of the university. During his tenure from 1889 to 1919, college enrollment increased from seventy-one to over 700, the endowment grew from $200,000 to $800,000, and the campus was transformed by the construction of new facilities.

To increase the student body, Harris vigorously recruited throughout Pennsylvania and New Jersey, and he added programs in engineering, medicine, law, education, and home economics to the traditional liberal arts curriculum. Although he recruited large numbers of non-Baptist students, the university continued to be governed by Baptists; over 80 percent of the board of trustees and most of the faculty were members of that denomination.

Harris built the faculty largely by recruiting his own students and sending them to graduate school for training. The result was an inbred faculty, consisting predominately of Bucknell alumni, that he ruled with a firm hand. Throughout his presidency Harris continued to carry a heavy teaching load, including an ethics course required for every senior.

By the time of his retirement in 1919, Harris had transformed a small, rural college into the sixth largest institution of higher education in Pennsylvania. He combined the piety characteristic of a traditional denominational president with the entrepreneurial administrative policies usually associated with a new breed of college president. Harris died in Scranton, Pennsylvania.

• A small number of Harris's papers are held at the Bucknell University Archives, and a few materials are at the American Baptist Historical Society, Rochester, N.Y. Mary B. Harris, ed., *Thirty Years as President of Bucknell University with Baccalaureate and Other Addresses* (1926), contains a biographical sketch and many of his speeches. Two of his former students and faculty members, John W. Rice and Lewis E. Theiss, wrote reminiscences of the Harris years that are in the Bucknell University Archives. Two excellent histories of Bucknell cover the Harris presidency very well: Lewis E. Theiss, *Centennial History of Bucknell University, 1846–1946* (1946), is very thorough; and J. Orin Oliphant, *The Rise of Bucknell University* (1965), is an outstanding college history that places Harris within a thoughtful historical context. Obituaries are in the *Watchman-Examiner* 13 (30 Apr. 1925), and *The Baptist* 6 (25 Apr. 1925).

W. BRUCE LESLIE

HARRIS, Little Benny (23 Apr. 1919–11 Feb. 1975), jazz musician and composer, was born Benjamin Michel Harris in New York. Details about his parents are unknown, although an unconfirmed report claimed that his father was a Panamanian Indian named Cholmondeley, not Harris. At the age of twelve Harris began playing French horn and E-flat mellophone in a band sponsored by the *New York Daily Mirror*. After taking up trumpet, he toured with a band in Pennsylvania at age fifteen, but he was fired for paying too much attention to girls. Harris described himself as a tough kid who boxed professionally.

In 1937 he met Dizzy Gillespie, who two years later found him a job in Tiny Bradshaw's big band. Around that time Harris got to know Charlie Parker, who at some point lived at Harris's family home, and he subsequently made Gillespie aware of Parker's fine recordings of 1941–1942 with Jay McShann's band. After playing in Earl Hines's big band from early 1941 until June of that year, Harris joined alto saxophonist Pete Brown's sextet at Kelly's Stable in New York, and he then played with Benny Carter's small group and big band. Early in 1943 he rejoined Hines, whose band by then included Gillespie and Parker.

Compared to his famous friends, Harris was a lesser light in the development of the bebop style during informal sessions at Minton's Playhouse and Monroe's Uptown House in Harlem. According to Al Tinney, the pianist at Monroe's, Harris was obsessed with the song "How High the Moon"; from this obsession came a bop theme, "Ornithology" (based on "How High the Moon"), which Harris and Parker probably wrote in collaboration.

Harris left Hines in August 1943 to work with Don Redman's big band and then quickly returned to Hines, but his lip muscles were not strong enough to keep up with the rigorous playing schedule, and this stay was another brief one. In 1944 he played alongside Thelonious Monk in Coleman Hawkins's group at the Yacht Club on 52d Street, played and recorded in Boyd Raeburn's orchestra, and in December recorded a few titles with a group led by pianist Clyde Hart. These recordings include Harris's bop theme "Little Benny" (based on "I Got Rhythm"), which was later retitled "Crazeology" in a version by Parker, "Bud's Bubble" in a version by Bud Powell, and "King Kong" on a reissue of Hart's session. Early in 1945 Harris played in Oscar Pettiford's bop group at the Spotlite in New York. He began a brief period with John Kirby's swing sextet in June, and with Don Byas in November he made three more recordings as a soloist: "How High the Moon," "Donby," and "Byas-a-Drink." "Donby," based on "Perdido," begins with a thematic pattern composed by Harris and subsequently heard on many renditions of "Perdido" and alternate melody lines based on its chord changes. At year's end he played at Manhattan's Three Deuces with alto saxophonist Johnny Bothwell.

Little is known of Harris after this time. He performed at an all-star bop session in 1948, played in Gillespie's big band in 1950, and worked with Parker in 1952. He traveled to Sacramento, California, and in 1961 to San Francisco, where he expressed bitterness over having been deprived of composer royalties that he now recognized were his due. He died in San Francisco.

Jazz entrepreneur Monte Kay and writer Max Harrison support an assessment of Harris by saxophonist Budd Johnson: "his thoughts were always ahead of his chops; he knew more than he could play." Critic Jim Burns offers a more skeptical view, arguing that Harris scarcely deserves credit for unrealized thought and that his significance rests solely on his composing a few well-known themes. His recordings as a soloist support this view: Harris was no more than a competent player, with a pleasant tone, a modest and clean sense of melody, and a gentle sense of swing. He shared with Parker a fondness for inserting quotations form diverse melodies into his solos, but he did so crudely compared with Parker's genius.

• Leonard Feather, *Inside Bebop* (1949), gives an early assessment of Harris's contributions. Informative interviews with Harris are by Dick Hadlock, "Benny Harris and the Coming of Modern Jazz," *Metronome*, Oct. 1961, pp. 18–20; and Robert Reisner, *Bird: The Legend of Charlie Parker* (1975), pp. 106–9. These in turn serve as sources for surveys by Jim Burns, "Trumpeter, Where Are You Sounding Now?" *Jazz Journal*, July 1963, p. 23; Jean Wagner, "Le mort vivant," *Jazz Magazine*, May 1964, pp. 40–41; and Burns, "The Legendary Who?" *Jazz and Blues*, Nov. 1972, pp. 12–13. Arnold Shaw gathers references to Harris's mid-1940s work in New York in *The Street That Never Slept* (1971; repr. as *52nd Street: The Street of Jazz* [1977]). Tinney's recollection appears in James Patrick, "Al Tinney, Monroe's Uptown House, and the Emergence of Modern Jazz in Harlem," *Annual Review of Jazz Studies* 2 (1983): 164.

BARRY KERNFELD

HARRIS, Mary Belle (19 Aug. 1874–22 Feb. 1957), prison administrator, was born in Factoryville, Pennsylvania, the daughter of John Howard Harris, a Baptist minister, and Mary Elizabeth Mace, who died when Mary Belle was six years old. First educated at the Keystone Academy, Mary Belle graduated from Bucknell University, where her father had become president in 1889. In 1893 she received a music degree from Bucknell; she earned an A.B. in 1894 and an A.M. in Latin and classics in 1895. She next enrolled at the University of Chicago, where she obtained a Ph.D. in Sanskrit and Indo-European Comparative Philology in 1900.

Over the next ten years Harris taught Latin at schools in Chicago and Baltimore. While in Chicago she served as director of the boys' club at Hull-House, the settlement house founded by Jane Addams; she also continued in music with the publication of some of her compositions. In Baltimore her interest in archaeology and numismatics led her to enroll in courses at Johns Hopkins University. In 1912 she traveled to the American Classical School in Rome, where she served as a teacher-chaperone. The trip afforded Harris the opportunity to study Roman coins both in Italy and at Berlin's Kaiser Friedrich Museum.

When Harris returned to the United States in 1914, she was approached by Katharine Bement Davis, a classmate and New York City's commissioner of corrections. Davis asked Harris to be a temporary superintendent of women and deputy warden at the Workhouse, a short-term women's prison, on Blackwell Island. Although Harris had no previous experience with prison work, she accepted.

After arriving at the Workhouse, Harris often felt "utter discouragement and a paralyzing hopelessness" when she witnessed the deplorable conditions, but she felt confident that she could improve the inmates' environment. During her first year approximately 7,000 women entered the Workhouse. The daily population averaged 700 women, who lived in 150 cells. Although the female prisoners were serving sentences of six months or less for alcoholism, prostitution, and drugs, they were kept in their cells and did not have the recreational facilities available at other prisons. Because Harris felt confinement was unhealthy, she ordered an outdoor area fenced to provide a place where the inmates could have at least an hour of daily exercise. She remodeled the dining room, gave the inmates access to a library, and allowed them to play cards or knit in their cells. Most important, Harris stressed trust between personnel and inmates, fostering better relations and lessening tensions. After three and a half years, Harris's position was terminated when a new mayor took office following the defeat of the reform candidate.

In 1918 Harris's career in penal reform continued when she became superintendent of the New Jersey State Reformatory. Commonly called Clinton Farms, the "anti-institutional" facility had no characteristics of a prison or a reformatory. Because of its small staff Harris found it necessary to institute a system of self-government among the inmates. The inmates lived in cottages, each of which ran independently of the others with its own "commission government." The cooperation and self-discipline Harris found at Clinton provided a pattern that she sought to instill in the institutions that she headed in later years.

In the fall of 1918 Harris took a seven-month leave of absence from her duties at Clinton Farms to become an assistant director of the Section on Reformatories and Detention Houses with the War Department's Commission on Training Camp Activities. She traveled through the southeastern states to set up detention camps and health facilities, while periodically returning to Clinton. In May 1919 she became superintendent of the State Home for Girls in Trenton, New Jersey. An institution in disrepair, the home housed juvenile girls who were notorious for escaping. Harris reduced the escapes by developing a sense of community, and she introduced programs such as music appreciation, which had been successful at the Workhouse. The self-government Harris established grew rapidly.

Harris tendered her resignation from the home to become the executive secretary in charge of organizing activities for the International Policewoman's Association at the beginning of 1925. Her position was short lived, though, because legislation was passed to build a much-needed women's prison, and Harris was named its first superintendent. Construction began in March 1925 on the Federal Industrial Institution for Women in Alderson, West Virginia. Although the first inmates did not arrive for two years and the institution was not opened officially until November 1928, Harris spent the two-year interim planning a very different prison community.

Alderson had no walls or guards in towers. Small, self-governed cottages in two quadrangles replaced cell blocks. Recreation, religious practice, and education were stressed. Harris felt that each female prisoner should be treated as an individual and should be allowed to reach the full potential of her resources. She devised systems of scientific classification to give women the right job training for their return to society, although most training was done in domestic science areas. The inmates were interviewed and screened by professionals, including the resident physician, a psychologist, the head teacher, and the warders of the cottages. This "classification committee" helped each inmate function to the best of her ability. Parole was earned through a system of good conduct and attendance at classes for reintegration into society. In a 1919 paper Harris explained that if inmates were prepared for the outside world, they

would be returned to society "trained in self-control, cognizant of the meaning of law in their lives and in society, conversant with the problems confronting the country, and well-grounded in the fundamental principles of cooperative living" (Lekkerkerker, p. 438). Harris earned praise for establishing a well-run prison.

Harris never married. She retired from Alderson in 1941 and returned to Pennsylvania, where she served on the state Board of Parole. She held the position until 1943 and moved to Lewisburg, Pennsylvania, where she maintained an active lifestyle as a lecturer, writer, and trustee of both Bucknell University and the First Baptist Church. She died in Lewisburg.

In the true spirit of the reform era into which she was born, Mary Belle Harris never faltered in her belief in the "basic goodness" of every person. She thought that if a person reached that inner goodness and touched it, change would evolve. To Harris the change came by breaking down large groups of inmates into smaller ones and stressing individuality, cleanliness, and harmonious surroundings; she also believed in allowing inmates a chance to practice self-government. Women, she felt, must also gain independence and become self-sufficient without the aid of men. A capable administrator, Harris achieved success in her goals as she tore down the walls and opened up prison surroundings to allow women a more ample opportunity to improve their lives.

• Mary Belle Harris's papers are in the Archives and Bertrand Library of Bucknell University. Her personnel file is at the National Personnel Records Center in St. Louis, Mo. Harris's life and career are best described in her book, *I Knew Them in Prison* (1936). Among other works published by Harris are her doctoral thesis, *Kalidasa, Poet of Nature* (1936); *The Pathway of Mattie Howard to and from Prison: True Story of the Regeneration of an Ex-convict and Gangster Woman* (1937); and "I Suppose I Was Stupid," *Survey*, 15 Nov. 1928, pp. 235–37. Other sources that offer details of her career are Eugenia C. Lekkerkerker, *Reformatories for Women in the United States* (1931); Ruth Bryan Owen Rohde, "Uncle Sam's Finishing School," *Rotarian*, June 1942, pp. 31–34; Estelle B. Freedman, *Their Sisters' Keepers: Women's Prison Reform in America, 1830–1930* (1981); Dorothy M. Brown, *Setting a Course: American Women in the 1920s* (1987); and Lois Stiles Edgerley, ed., *Women's Words, Women's Stories* (1994).

MARILYN ELIZABETH PERRY

HARRIS, Merriman Colbert (9 July 1846–8 May 1921), Methodist missionary bishop, was born in Beallsville, Ohio, the son of Colbert Harris, a farmer and schoolteacher, and Elizabeth Crupper. Under the influence of a teacher, Robert L. Morris, and his minister, James M. Thoburn, who later became a missionary to India, Harris determined to enter the Methodist ministry and seek the mission field. The Civil War interrupted his preparation, and he enlisted in the Twelfth Ohio Volunteer Cavalry, serving from 1863 until 1865. He served with Philip H. Sheridan in Tennessee and William T. Sherman on the march through Georgia. After the war he entered theological school, first at

Harlem Springs, in the state of Washington, and later at Scio, Ohio. His meager savings depleted, he taught school for two years at Fairview, Ohio, before joining the Pittsburgh Conference of the Methodist Episcopal church in 1869. The conference appointed him to a pastorate in Urichsville, Ohio, where he served for two years before entering Allegheny College in Meadville, Pennsylvania. He received his A.B. degree in 1873 and on 23 October of that year married Flora Lydia Best of Meadville; the couple did not have children.

Harris received immediate appointment to the new Methodist mission field in Japan and set out for the northern port of Hakodate. His church grew rapidly, and he and his wife founded the Caroline Wright School for Girls, which offered a western-style education to young women, who traditionally had not received such training in Japan. During the same period he represented the United States government as vice consul, from 29 October 1875, and as consul, from 3 January 1877 until 1879, when his success in Hakodate led to his promotion to presiding elder and transfer to Tokyo. His consular work was largely clerical but afforded him the opportunity to meet and win the respect of Japanese government officials. His work in the larger mission field enjoyed noteworthy success until his wife fell ill and he was transferred to San Francisco, where he served as superintendent of the Methodist Episcopal mission to Japan from 1886 to 1904. In this capacity he supervised the creation of missions in the Pacific Rim and in Hawaii. These he organized into the Pacific Japanese Mission. In 1904, in recognition of the size of this new mission field and his success in creating it, Harris was elected to the episcopacy and assigned as bishop of Japan and Korea. He served with distinction in this role until he asked to be relieved in 1916. Thereafter he retained the title of bishop emeritus and lived in Japan until his death.

In addition to his ecclesiastical success, Harris remained popular with his Japanese hosts. He influenced a generation of rising educational and political leaders in Japan, even baptizing the "Sapporo Band," the first graduating class of the new agricultural university at Sapporo. These leaders, in turn, helped to counteract the traditional tension between nationalism and Christianity in Japan. He received three decorations from the Japanese government; the most important was the order of the Sacred Treasure, which was presented to him by the emperor. At his retirement the Japanese foreign minister, Viscount Kaneko, said, "If all Americans dealt with us as openheartedly as Dr. Harris does, and if we revered Americans as we revere Dr. Harris, friendship between Japan and America would remain unchanged forever" (*Outlook*, 28 June 1916, p. 455).

Much of Harris's success can be attributed to his appreciation for the literature and culture of Japan and the other Pacific Rim countries. He became a student and translator of Japanese literature, publishing a volume of *Japanese Proverbs* (1908). Harris also pub-

lished a book, *One Hundred Years of Missions, Christianity in Japan* (1908), and numerous shorter articles for church publications. Flora Harris, also a noted translator of Japanese literature and a poet in her own right, died in 1909; he married her cousin Elizabeth Best ten years later. Harris died at the home presented to him by the Japanese government in the Methodist compound in Aoyama and was buried there.

Harris went to Japan at a time when traditional Japanese nationalism regarded the West, and especially Christianity, with great suspicion and hostility. His interest in and affection for Japanese culture, his support of educational institutions, and his more sensitive and accepting approach to Christian evangelism all contributed to the developing rapprochement of Japan with the West.

• Harris's papers are in the archives of the Methodist church in Japan. His career was detailed after his death in *The Methodist Yearbook* (1922) and other lesser denominational publications in that year. The most complete assessment of his significance can be found in William C. Barclay, *History of Methodist Missions*, vol. 3 (1957). Obituaries are in the *New York Times*, 9 and 12 May 1921, and the *Japan Times*, 11 and 12 May 1921.

MICHAEL R. McCoy

HARRIS, Miriam Coles (7 July 1834–23 Jan. 1925), novelist, was born the daughter of Julia Anne Weeks and Butler Coles on Dosoris, an island in Long Island Sound owned by the Coles family. She attended St. Mary's Hall, a boarding school in New Jersey (the basis for her children's novel, *Louie's Last Term at St. Mary's* [1871]), and Miss Canda's school for girls in New York City.

Unlike many of her contemporaries, Coles did not begin her career with an apprenticeship of poetry and short prose for periodicals. J. C. Derby reported that Coles's uncle E. A. Weeks brought Coles's manuscript for her first novel, *Rutledge*, to him and offered to underwrite its publication after Harper's turned the book down. Derby was impressed enough to take on the book without subsidy, and, at Coles's insistence, it was published anonymously in 1860. The popular press raised many questions about the identity of the author, which undoubtedly helped sales of the book.

In *Woman's Fiction*, Nina Baym identified *Rutledge* as both "the first fully developed American example . . . [of] the so-called 'gothic romance',", and as a book whose popularity marked readers' turning away from the female bildungsroman that had dominated much of women's reading and writing at mid-century. The novel rejects many of the conventions of the woman's novel that Baym identified. *Rutledge*'s heroine disregards for the most part the intellectual, spiritual, and emotional growth so central to the lives of other heroines. The unnamed narrator expresses on several occasions a keen awareness of the critical standards of her day and ironically acknowledges how her own story of secret love, murder, hidden rooms, and mysteries of all sorts might be read. In an early chapter she finds herself reading "a third-rate novel of the highly wrought order, into whose pages characters, incidents, scenes, were crowded in such bewildering profusion, that one's appreciative powers were fagged out and exhausted, before the first chapter was accomplished. . . . The wearying tide of adjectives and interjections stunned my senses" (p.116). This might remind the reader of the book in hand, whose first twenty pages have included a train wreck, the heroine's entrance into a mysterious household, and a darkly handsome possible hero.

Later, the heroine quotes a passage from *Uncle Tom's Cabin*, noting that on the whole it is a "strange story," and dismisses Eva's "unnatural angelhood" (p. 267). The heroine's skeptical view of the world around her includes commentary on other aspects of middle-class culture: she decries the discomfort of rail travel, vividly portrays a charity ball, and describes an aborted attempt at home theatricals (very popular at the time) thus: "It appeared at dinner, that the theatricals were given up, owing, principally, I could not but suspect, to the want of harmony that has characterized all the attempts at private theatricals that I have ever witnessed, no one, under any circumstances, having been known to be pleased with the role assigned to him or her, and all manner of discontent prevailing on all sides" (p. 343). After many travails, the young heroine and her much older true love are united. Although critical commentary on the novel and its protagonist was not and has not been positive (in 1860 the *Athenaeum* (London) condemned "the self-conceit and arrogance of the heroine"; a feminist critic of the 1990s called the narrator/heroine a masochist), the novel's ordinary readers responded enthusiastically to this book and to Harris's later tales.

Having developed for herself a successful American version of the gothic, Harris used it again and again, often choosing first-person narrators. Generally a relationship with a "bad" or unsuitable match delays true love, but all ends happily. Although even contemporary critics found her habit of sprinkling bits of French into her narrative an annoying affectation, the novels were steadily reprinted, some in London as well as in the United States, into the first decades of the twentieth century. Her "southern" novel, *The Sutherlands* (1862), benefited from the intense interest in that genre before the Civil War and continued to be popular afterward, going through at least eleven editions by 1871. A year later, *Frank Warrington* appeared.

Coles married lawyer Sydney S. Harris in 1864. After her marriage she sometimes published under the name "Mrs. Sydney Harris" but more frequently used "Miriam Coles Harris," with most editions adding "by the author of *Rutledge*" to the title page. *St. Philip's* was published the year after her marriage, but then came a break in her writing, while the couple's two children, a son and a daughter, were born and grew up. A collection of children's stories, *Roundhearts and Other Stories*, appeared in 1867, and her previous work remained in print, but no new novel was published until 1871, when Scribner's brought out *Richard Vandermarck*, another story of a young girl who for most of the novel does not recognize her true love, instead finding herself attracted to an inappropriate, but more romantic, man. In *Phoebe* (1884), Barry Crittenden seduces and impregnates the heroine during a three-week vacation in her hometown and only marries her on the insistence of his mother. It was a "not altogether pleasant theme," in the opinion of the *Boston Literary World*, but "a vivid and powerful story" and one that ends happily, although, the review concluded, "another example of the superior woman sacrificed to the inferior man" (9 Aug. 1884).

It seems likely that she was raised as an Episcopalian, and Derby called her a "devout adherent" of that faith. However, at some point, perhaps in the 1890s (Wallace Rice noted her sympathy for Catholicism in his 1898 review of her travel book *A Corner of Spain*), she converted to Roman Catholicism. Harris's last novel, *The Tents of Wickedness*, was described by the *Nation* (24 Oct. 1907) as "a spirited (not to say acrimonious) attack upon New York society, divorce, and the Episcopal Church," and the *Catholic World* (Dec. 1907) praised the convert author for treating "in an able way a theme of the utmost practical importance today." After the death of her husband in 1892, Harris moved to Europe where she lived until her death in Pau, France.

• No collection of Harris's papers or manuscripts is available. J. C. Derby devotes a few pages to Harris in his *Fifty Years among Authors, Books, and Publishers* (1884), and there is a brief profile in the *Boston Literary World*, 9 Aug. 1884; most compendiums of women writers and nineteenth-century popular writers contain brief references. Critical attention to her work has been slight, with Frank Luther Mott, *Golden Multitudes* (1947), drawing his comments primarily from Derby, and Nina Baym, *Woman's Fiction*, 2d ed. (1993), discussing Harris primarily in terms of her difference from the "scribbling women" that Baym celebrates.

JOANN E. CASTAGNA

HARRIS, Patricia Roberts (31 May 1924–23 Mar. 1985), cabinet member and ambassador, was born in Mattoon, Illinois, the daughter of Bert Fitzgerald Roberts, a Pullman car waiter, and Hildren Brodie Johnson, a schoolteacher. After graduating from a Chicago high school, she entered Howard University, from which she was graduated, summa cum laude, with an A.B. in 1945. In 1943, while a student at Howard, she joined the nascent civil rights movement and participated in a sit-in to desegregate a cafeteria lunch counter in Washington, D.C. Roberts did graduate work at the University of Chicago. In 1946, while attending graduate school, she was also program director of the local YWCA. In 1949 she returned to Washington, D.C., where she pursued further graduate study at the American University until 1950. From 1949 to 1953 she served as an assistant director in the Civil Rights Agency of the American Council on Human Rights. Married in 1955 to attorney William B. Harris, who encouraged her to enter law school (the marriage was childless), she earned a J.D. degree at the George Washington University Law Center in

1960. Recognized early in her youth as an outstanding and diligent student, Harris graduated first out of ninety-four in her class.

In 1960 Harris moved to the Department of Justice, where she worked for a year as a trial attorney in the Appeals and Research Section of the Criminal Division. She left the Justice Department in order to become a member of the faculty of Howard University Law School, eventually reaching the rank of associate professor. It was that position she left in 1965, when President Lyndon B. Johnson named her U.S. ambassador to Luxembourg. Senate confirmation made her the first African-American woman to serve in an ambassadorial post. After leaving the diplomatic corps in 1967, Harris returned to Howard University as a full professor, serving until 1969, when, as a result of student and faculty conflicts, she resigned to enter private practice. She remained active in the civil rights movement and served on the executive board of the NAACP Legal Defense Fund from 1967 to 1977.

Having served in professional and voluntary positions at the national and local levels to promote adequate and safe housing and shelter for the poor, including chair of the Housing Committee of the Washington Urban League (1956–1960), vice president of the Brookland Civic Association (1962–1965), and member of the board of directors of the American Council on Human Rights, Harris was nominated by President Jimmy Carter in 1977 to become secretary of the Department of Housing and Urban Development (HUD). During her Senate confirmation hearing before the Committee on Banking, Housing, and Urban Affairs, on 10 January 1977, she challenged Senator William Proxmire's suggestion that she might not be attuned to the problems of the poor. Harris responded:

Senator, I am one of them, You do not seem to understand who I am. I'm a black woman, the daughter of a dining car waiter. I'm a black woman who even eight years ago could not buy a house in some parts of the District of Columbia. Senator, to say I'm not by and of and for the people is to show a lack of understanding of who I am and where I came from.

Once confirmed by the Senate, Harris brought control and order to the department that had been criticized for ineffective, inefficient, and inconsistent management. Although some characterized her as having an abrasive manner, Harris proved to be hardworking and focused, determined to address the problems of the poor. She brought with her experience in providing minorities improved access to better housing, a higher standard of living, and greater economic opportunities. In particular she directed an effort to prevent discrimination against women who applied for mortgage loans.

When President Carter reshuffled his cabinet in the summer of 1979, Harris left HUD and was named secretary of Health, Education, and Welfare (HEW). Soon after she was confirmed by the Senate, HEW became the Department of Health and Human Servic-

es, which Harris directed until the end of the Carter administration.

Harris returned to the practice of law in Washington, D.C., in 1981. The following year she ran for mayor of the District of Columbia but lost the race to Marion S. Barry, Jr., having failed to convince voters that the city needed an administrator rather than a politician. In the end, however, her identification as a member of the middle class contributed to her defeat.

Harris was a member of numerous organizations, including Phi Beta Kappa, and was the recipient of many awards and honorary degrees, and the author of a large number of articles and publications. She was recognized as a skilled, competent, and effective leader in both the public and the private arena. She died of cancer in Washington, D.C.

• Harris's published writings include "Law and Moral Issues," *Journal of Religious Thought* (1964), "To Fill the Gap," *Many Shades of Black*, ed. Stanton L. Wormley and Lewis H. Fenderson (1969), and "Problems and Solutions in Achieving Equality for Women," in *Women in Higher Education*, ed. W. Todd Furniss and Patricia Albjerg Graham (1974). Biographical information on Harris is scant. The publications of the Senate hearings include some biographical and educational information and list the honors and awards she received, her membership in organizations, and her publications. See U.S. Congress, Senate, Committee on Banking, Housing, and Urban Affairs, *Nomination of Patricia Roberts Harris*, 95th Cong., 1st sess., 10 Jan. 1977; and U.S. Congress, Senate, Committee on Finance, *Nomination of Patricia Harris*, 96th Cong., 1st sess., 25 and 26 July 1979. Also see Homer L. Calkin, *Women in the Department of State: Their Role in American Foreign Affairs* (1978). An obituary is in the *New York Times*, 23 Mar. 1985.

JUDITH R. JOHNSON

HARRIS, Paul Percy (19 Apr. 1868–27 Jan. 1947), attorney and founder of Rotary International, was born in Racine, Wisconsin, the son of George Harris and Cornelia Bryan. The family had moved from Wallingford, Vermont, to Racine, where Harris's father established a pharmacy. However, because of free-spending habits and poor business acumen, the business failed and the family of four was broken up. Three-year-old Paul and his younger brother Cecil were sent to live with paternal grandparents Howard and Pamela Rustin Harris in Wallingford in July 1871. Paul would call this his home, as it was where he spent most of his youth. Several attempts to reunite him with his parents and five siblings failed, leading Paul Harris to become lonelier and more withdrawn. The last attempted reunion lasted three years, ending once again as a result of a business failure that forced his father from the pharmacy business. Harris returned to his grandparents while his siblings, including Cecil, remained with their parents. Harris's relationship with his immediate family was never close although he remained very close to his grandparents.

Harris had great difficulty in school. He was known as a prankster and constantly sought the attention of others. After he was asked to leave Wallingford High School, he was sent to live with an uncle and aunt in

Rutland, Vermont, in order to attend school there. When this did not work out, he entered the Black River Academy but was expelled after one year for his unruly behavior. He was then sent to the Vermont Academy, a military school, and did well enough to graduate and enroll at the University of Vermont in 1885. However, he was expelled from the university in 1887 for violating school rules. In fact, Harris had been protecting a friend's indiscretion, and later, in 1919, when the real culprit admitted his guilt, Harris was awarded the Ph.B. degree from the university retroactive to 1899. In the fall of 1887 he began attending Princeton University but left after one year because of his grandfather's death and his lack of a financial trust. He returned to Wallingford and found work as an office boy for a local marble company. He and his grandmother decided that he should study the law so he took a job in a family friend's law office in Des Moines, Iowa, in September 1889. The following year he enrolled in law school in Iowa City and in the summer of 1891 graduated with his law degree.

Harris decided not to take up his profession immediately. He chose instead to spend five years as a wanderer to better understand the world and his place in it and to test his inner strength and his will to survive. From Iowa he went west through the mountains to San Francisco, where he worked for a short time as a reporter for the *Chronicle*. In a cycle repeated over the next five years, he worked just long enough to get a stake that enabled him to move on to another adventure. He hiked through the Sierra Nevada, sometimes with little or no food or shelter. He took a succession of jobs, from raisin packer in Fresno to teacher in Los Angeles, all the while exploring the natural environments of the unspoiled California wilderness. After jobs with newspapers in Denver, a short stint as a cowboy, and a year-long job as a traveling marble salesman in Florida, Harris signed on as a cattle handler on a stock ship bound for Britain. Although he remembered it as one of his worst experiences, when he returned to the United States he signed on as a subforeman on another cattle ship and went to England again in late summer 1893. When he returned to the United States he ventured to Chicago for the World's Columbian Exposition and then traveled south to New Orleans, where he picked and packed oranges. He quit this job after it began to adversely affect his health and then returned to the marble sales job, this time traveling throughout the Caribbean and Europe. His wanderlust ended in February 1896, when his law career began in Chicago.

Harris's new life in the big city was rife with problems. It was difficult finding clients, and even though he entered into partnerships with several other lawyers, who also came from small towns, and joined as many Chicago clubs as possible, he remained lonely and felt alienated. Like many migrants from the small towns to the cities of the late nineteenth century, Harris had few close friends and felt isolated. It was during this time that he began to wonder why the small-town attitude of working together for fellowship and service could not be reproduced in the city. He hoped to effect "the transfer of the simple, uncluttered . . . helpfulness of village life, to the vaster social milieu of the city" (Walsh, p. 79).

On 23 February 1905 three other men from small towns, Sylvester Schiete, Hiram Shorey, and Gustavus Loehr, joined Harris to form the first Rotary in Chicago. They agreed to open the club to one representative from each profession or trade and to require that they do business with one another. In this way Rotary would aid in the expansion of business and also bring businessmen together to help eliminate much of the alienation they felt. The name came from the fact that initially the meetings rotated to each member's office. Rotary expanded rapidly over the next twenty years, largely as a result of Harris's and Rotary secretary Chesley R. Perry's active recruitment. Membership in the organization became a status symbol, due to its exclusivity, and did much to promote business growth, fellowship, and service to society. In an era when American society was coming to define itself more and more along the lines of the middle class, Rotary was instrumental in empowering and helping to outline the new ideals. Urban life and the demands of a capital economy placed pressure on members of the middle class to define themselves by their occupations, residences, material possessions, and service clubs. Rotary, the first to aid in this definitional process, helped spawn a host of other middle-class men's and women's fellowship and service organizations such as Sertoma (1912), Kiwanis (1915), Lions (1917), Altrussa (1917), Optimist (1919), National Federation of Professional Women's Clubs (1919), Civitan (1920), and Pilot (1921). Harris was instrumental also in founding the group's journal, *The Rotarian* (1911), for which he wrote regularly over the next thirty years.

In 1910 Harris married Jean Thomas of Edinburgh, Scotland. Because of declining health, he stepped down from active involvement after his term as president (1907–1912) but was made president emeritus for life by the national Rotary in 1912. Continuing to travel and serve as an ambassador of Rotary, he witnessed its expansion to more than a quarter million members worldwide. He received the Silver Buffalo Award from the Boy Scouts of America in 1934, the French Legion of Honor in 1937, and the Rotary's highest honor, the Chicago Merit Award, in 1946. Harris died in Chicago and was buried near his home in Morgan Park, Illinois.

• Harris wrote numerous articles for *The Rotarian*, and many of them were collected and published after his death as *My Road to Rotary: The Story of a Boy, a Vermont Community, and Rotary* (1948). His early autobiography, published by Rotary International, is *The Founder of Rotary: Paul Percy Harris* (1928). Both romanticize his childhood and his early difficulties. James P. Walsh, *The First Rotarian: The Life and Times of Paul Percy Harris, Founder of Rotary* (1979), a full study of Harris and the Rotary, is taken largely from these books. An early work, Charles F. Marden, *Rotary and Its Brothers: An Analysis and Interpretation of the Men's Service Club* (1935), covers the impact and influence of the Rotary on men's clubs and is similar to Charles W. Ferguson's overview, *Fifty Million Brothers: A Panorama of American Lodges and Clubs* (1937). For studies placing the rise of Rotary in context, see Robert H. Wiebe, *The Search for Order, 1877–1920* (1967); T. J. Jackson Lears, *No Place of Grace: Antimodernism and the Transformation of American Culture* (1981); Raymond Mohl, *The New City: Urban America in the Industrial Age, 1860–1920* (1985); and David W. Noble, *The Progressive Mind, 1890–1917* (1973). An obituary is in the *New York Times*, 28 Jan. 1947.

KENNETH J. BINDAS

HARRIS, Roy (12 Feb. 1898–1 Oct. 1979), composer, was born Leroy Ellsworth Harris in Chandler, Oklahoma, the son of Elmer Ellsworth Harris, a farmer of Irish and Scottish descent, and Laura Broddle, who was from Wales. Born on Abraham Lincoln's birthday, in Lincoln County, Harris always strongly identified with the president. In 1903 his family moved to farmland in the San Gabriel Valley of California. Leroy graduated from high school in 1916. During adolescence, he helped his father on the farm and later briefly farmed his own land. He then worked as a truck driver for a dairy firm. It was around this time that he shortened his name to Roy. During World War I he served as a private in the army training corps at Berkeley, California.

His mother gave Harris early piano lessons, and he also took up the clarinet. As he grew up he listened to recordings, attended concerts when he could, and studied music in a somewhat desultory fashion. Though never earning a formal degree, Harris attended the University of California in Berkeley (about 1919) and in Los Angeles (about 1921). Crucial to his decision to become a composer were his informal musical studies under Arthur Farwell, a noted advocate for a distinctively American-sounding music, in 1924 and 1925. Farwell introduced him to Walt Whitman's writings, which later inspired several of Harris's compositions. Although he also learned from other musicians, Harris remained mostly self-taught. His lack of thorough formal training enhanced his original turn of mind but also sometimes produced faulty technique.

An *Andante* for orchestra (1925) brought Harris his first acclaim. During a trip east (first to Rochester, then to New York City) in 1926 to attend its first performance, Harris met Aaron Copland, who urged him to study with Nadia Boulanger in Paris. This he did, from 1926 to 1929, aided financially by Alma Wertheim and two Guggenheim Fellowships. While abroad, he completed a Concerto for Piano, Clarinet, and String Quartet (1927). Its Paris premiere strengthened his reputation as an up-and-coming composer. The Piano Sonata dating from this time already reveals Harris's style in all its cragginess and crudeness. It features singular modal-scale constructions, wide-ranging melodic lines, contrapuntal treatment of thematic material, and dissonant harmonies resulting from the simultaneous sounding of two or more different chords.

Boulanger's teaching proved uncongenial and ended when a fall injured Harris's spine and forced him to return to America. At last, with the *Symphony 1933*, given its first performance by Serge Koussevitzky and the Boston Symphony Orchestra, Harris took his place as one of America's handful of outstanding composers. Koussevitzky considered this work "the first truly tragic symphony by an American."

By the early thirties, Harris had already been married and divorced three times—to Charlotte Schwartz (whom he married in 1922 and with whom he had a daughter prior to their divorce in 1924), Sylvia Feningston (married in 1926), and Hilda Hemingway (married in 1931), respectively. While teaching at the Juilliard School, in New York City, he met Beula Duffey, a Canadian pianist, whom he married in 1936. He persuaded her to change her given name to Johana, in honor of Johann Sebastian Bach. They had five children together.

A succession of teaching positions at various institutions gave Harris a livelihood, two of the last being at the University of California at Los Angeles (1961–1971) and California State University at Los Angeles (1971–1976). Among his students were William Schuman and Peter Schickele. During World War II he served as director of the Music Section in the Office of War Information.

Roy Harris had strong opinions about music. Among the contemporary European composers he disliked were Igor Stravinsky and Arnold Schoenberg, whom he criticized as rejecters of tradition; among those he approved were Sergei Prokofiev and Ralph Vaughan Williams. He was devoted to the music of Beethoven, Bach, and the Renaissance composers. American folksong from Anglo-Celtic sources and Protestant hymnody were springboards for his own melodic lines. These last are often lengthy, generated by an initial idea out of which grows phrase after phrase. One of the longest thematic statements, almost 120 measures, is in his Fifth Symphony. He rejected atonality. He also frequently used ancient church modes, sometimes simultaneously employing two different modes based on the same tonic. Textures tend to the contrapuntal, and structures to the preclassical—passacaglia, canon, fugue, chorale, and variation. Bichordal harmonies abound, as do asymmetrical rhythms. Harris's orchestration remains functional, repudiates instrumental color for its own sake, and features the instrumental choirs in organ-stop fashion. Open spacing and intervals of the fourth and fifth help produce the western-outdoors impressions for which his music is noted. He often created unexpected accents and sudden contrasts. A favorite expressive procedure was to write reflectively or sorrowfully and then contrast the result with sounds of heroic exuberance. Harris insisted that his music was emotional rather than intellectual and, however tragic, ultimately affirmative in its message.

Harris wrote rapidly, hardly pausing for self-criticism. Indeed, he always struck others as egocentric and incapable of judging any of his works as less than a masterpiece. At times his melody may sound nondistinctive, his harmony clumsy. Sections and movements may end abruptly; structures may sprawl. Yet even the flawed pieces have their moments—perhaps some measures where texture turns gorgeous, a passage when melodic-harmonic combinations sound fresh and sophisticated, a stretch of profoundly moving meditation, or an ear-catching outburst of angular melody and rugged asymmetrical rhythm.

Although a prolific composer in most genres, Harris wrote hardly any dramatic or stage music. One film score for *One-tenth of a Nation* (1941) and three ballets—*From This Earth* (1941), *Namesake* (1942), and *What So Proudly We Hail* (1942)—constitute most of it. On the other hand, he produced an abundance of chamber, orchestral, and choral works. The best-known of the chamber pieces are the Quintet for Piano and Strings (1936) and the Third String Quartet (1937). The Quintet contains three organically linked movements: Passacaglia, Cadenza, and Fugue. The Quartet consists of four preludes and fugues. Of the thirteen numbered symphonies, the Third (1939) is the most outstanding. It is considered the finest work that Harris ever composed. Although it was constructed in one movement, the composition has five sections: Tragic, Lyric, Pastoral, Fugue-Dramatic, Dramatic-Tragic. This symphony and *When Johnny Comes Marching Home*, an American overture (1934), based on the song melody that Patrick Gilmore wrote in 1863 (under the pen name Louis Lambert), have received numerous performances.

Compositions based on American themes appeared in abundance, beginning with the *American Portrait* of 1929. The *Folksong Symphony*, Harris's Fourth Symphony (1940, revised 1942), for chorus and orchestra, has proved popular. It contains five choral and two instrumental sections. The first choral section employs the tune "When Johnny Comes Marching Home"; the second, "The Dying Cowboy" and "As I Walked Out in the Streets of Laredo"; the third, the "Mountaineer Love Song"; the fourth, "De Trumpet Sounds It in My Soul"; and the fifth, "The Gal I Left Behind Me." Other important Americanist works are the Sixth Symphony, *Gettysburg* (1944); the Eighth Symphony, *San Francisco* (1962); the Tenth Symphony, *Abraham Lincoln* (1965), for speaker, chorus, and orchestra; and the Thirteenth Symphony, *Bicentennial* (1976), for chorus and orchestra. The Ninth Symphony (1962), which expresses the Constitution of the United States, contains a Prelude ("We the people . . . "), a Chorale ("to form a more perfect union . . . "), and Contrapuntal Structures ("promote the general welfare"). Harris also relates these movements to three short passages from Walt Whitman. Other works of considerable merit include the solo cantatas *Abraham Lincoln Walks at Midnight* (1953) and *Give Me the Splendid Silent Sun* (1955, revised 1956) and the song setting of Carl Sandburg's poem "Fog" (1945). Finally, Harris composed a great deal of functional music intended for use by amateurs and students.

Abundant honors came Harris's way, including the Award of Merit from the National Association of Composers and Conductors, in 1940; the Award of the National Committee for Music Appreciation, in 1940, for the *Folksong Symphony*; the Coolidge Medal, in 1942; election to the National Institute of Arts and Letters, in 1944 (and to the American Academy of Arts and Letters, in 1979); and appointment as Honorary Composer Laureate of the State of California, in 1975. Several universities granted him an honorary doctorate of music.

During the fifties, sixties, and seventies, influential members of the music world came to reject musical Americanism. As first atonality, then highly experimental music came to the fore, Harris's reputation suffered an eclipse. His artistic point of view was attacked, and his compositions were disdained. However, the eighties and nineties saw a renewed appreciation of his contributions to American musical literature.

For most of his life Harris was constantly on the move, teaching in at least twelve institutions in various states, with California, and particularly Los Angeles, being his place of residence for the last twenty or so years of his life. It was here that he died, a few months after falling in his studio and fracturing his pelvis.

• The Roy Harris Archive at California State University, Los Angeles, holds the largest collection of his music manuscripts, scores, letters, interviews, memorabilia, and recordings as well as microfilm copies of the Harris material in the Library of Congress. Some papers and scores are also located at the Louisville Academy of Music and in the Haverlin Collection/BMI Archives and the Moldenhauer Archives. A fine study of Harris's life and music is Dan Stehman, *Roy Harris: An American Musical Pioneer* (1984). Stehman has also issued a complementary *Roy Harris, A Bio-Bibliography* (1991). Dan Stehman and L. Chesley Gibbs, "The Roy Harris Revival," published in two parts in the *American Record Guide* for May and June 1979, provides a new assessment of the composer at the time of his death. Some informative articles are Nicolas Slonimsky, "Roy Harris," *Musical Quarterly* 33 (1947); Robert Evett, "The Harmonic Idiom of Roy Harris," *Modern Music* 23 (Spring 1946); Walter Piston, "Roy Harris," *Modern Music* 11 (1–2, 1934); and Arthur Farwell, "Roy Harris" *Musical Quarterly* 18 (1932).

NICHOLAS E. TAWA

HARRIS, Sam Henry (3 Feb. 1872–3 July 1941), theatrical producer, was born in New York City, the son of Max (sometimes called Marks) Harris, a tailor, and Lena (or Sara) Lippman. Leaving the New York public schools at the age of eleven, he ran errands, hawked towels and newspapers, served as a printer's devil, and organized holiday entertainments. Harris owned race horses, but in 1895, after watching four of his horses finish fourth, fifth, sixth, and seventh in a seven-horse race, he gave up the turf. He also managed prize fighters, and in 1900 featherweight champion Terry McGovern starred for Harris in a national burlesque tour of *The Bowery After Dark*. In 1902 Harris joined theatrical producers Patrick H. Sullivan and Albert H. Woods to present thrillers such as *The Fatal Wedding*, with child actress Mary Pickford.

In 1904 Harris was introduced to all-around theater man George M. Cohan, and after playing in a theatrical club's baseball game on Staten Island, the two formed a seventeen-year partnership that resulted in fifty plays. *Little Johnny Jones* (1904) was the first of Harris's thirty-two Broadway musicals. An intuitive gambler in many fields ("If you didn't have the money, borrow it. If borrowing didn't work, gambling might"), Harris frequently broke new ground with his shows. Cohan's music, lyrics and libretto, carved from the American vernacular, helped to create a uniquely American type of musical comedy.

Cohan and Harris presented all of Cohan's major successes, including *Forty-Five Minutes from Broadway* (1905), which introduced the great clown Victor Moore; and Elmer Rice's earliest Melodrama *On Trial* (1914). They also introduced the classic actor John Barrymore and the swashbuckling Douglas Fairbanks. Not as successful was one of the six 1908–1909 Cohan-Harris shows, *The Cohan and Harris Minstrels*, which lost $250,000 and proved that minstrelsy was dead. The Actor's Equity strike in 1919 was particularly stressful for Cohan, who sided with management, and his partnership with Harris was mysteriously dissolved by mutual agreement in 1920. When Cohan subsequently formed his own company, Harris gave him an office in the Harris building.

Over the next twenty-one years Harris produced 110 shows and enjoyed, as a writer for the *New York Times* remarked, a "phenomenal percentage of successes." In 1920 he began a long association with composer Irving Berlin. Having convinced Berlin by his own example that the way to artistic independence was through owning one's own theater, Harris had the Music Box built for Berlin. The theater was designed by C. Howard Crane particularly for the comfort of performers. The first *Music Box Revue* (1921) prompted Alexander Woollcott to write of the partners, "They have built them a playhouse in West Forty-fifth Street that is a thing of beauty in itself." The Music Box (which cost $1 million, a sum Harris regarded as essentially good publicity) quickly became the "home of hits," especially the smart modern revues composed by Berlin. It remained a Broadway jewel until the advent of the huge, high-tech musicals of the 1980s.

Harris became known as an authors' producer. According to humorist Robert Benchley, Harris changed his life by placing his monologue "The Treasurer's Report" in the second *Music Box Revue*. The first Harris-produced play to win a Pulitzer Prize was Owen Davis's *Icebound* (1923). That same year Harris backed F. Scott Fitzgerald's absurdist, Ring Lardneresque farce *The Vegetable*, but the play never left Atlantic City. (He was luckier with Lardner and George S. Kaufman's 1929 satirical comedy *June Moon*.)

Harris's "marvelous bonhomie with theater people," an ability to calm the most enraged, appears to have failed only once. The Four Marx Brothers had sold themselves to Harris in an uproarious office audition, and Harris talked Kaufman into collaborating on a show for them (the original librettist had quit in terror of the muscular Zeppo, and Harris had put out a call for a large writer who could wrestle). The show, called *The Coconuts* (1925), was threatened by a stagehands' revolt against the comics' time-consuming antics. Trying to mediate, Harris walked into the brothers' dressing room only to emerge moments later, stripped naked.

In 1930 Kaufman collaborated with newcomer Moss Hart to write the comedy *Once in a Lifetime*. According to Hart, it was Harris's intuitive response to the "noisy" last act—"Except for those two minutes at the beginning of the first act there isn't another spot where two people sit down and talk quietly to each other . . . it tires an audience out"—that resulted in the final rewrite, which guaranteed the show's success. But Harris was usually laconic. Concerning *Of Thee I Sing*, a satire by Ira and George Gershwin, Kaufman, and Morrie Ryskind that opened in December 1931 (the first musical to win a Pulitzer Prize), Harris said only, "It's interesting."

In 1933 Harris helped to form Marx Brothers, Inc. which was supposed to make films. In 1935 he and producer Max Gordon joined Metro-Goldwyn-Mayer in a deal that resulted in the production of the play and film of Cole Porter's *Jubilee*, which completed 169 performances, was a moderately successful film, and is now best known for Porter's "Begin the Beguine." Harris received the Pennsylvania Athletic Club's medal for distinguished service as "America's greatest living theatrical manager." In 1937 Harris produced *I'd Rather Be Right*, with music by Richard Rodgers and starring Cohan as Franklin Delano Roosevelt (whom Cohan detested). The production ran for 290 performances—mainly because of Cohan—and was the first show to portray a sitting president. Also in 1937 Kaufman and Hart won a Pulitzer for *You Can't Take It with You* (Harris sold the film rights for a record sum). Harris's production of John Steinbeck's *Of Mice and Men* (1938) was voted the New York Drama Critics' best play.

Some of Harris's failures were the inevitable fate of a peripatetic producer. *Of Thee I Sing* had helped to close the Harris-Berlin revue *Face the Music* in 1932. A year later the Harris-Berlin revue *As Thousands Cheer* easily outpointed *Let 'em Eat Cake*, the Harris-Gershwins sequel to *Of Thee I Sing*. Other 1930s stage hits produced by Harris include the melodrama *Stage Door*, the chiller *Night Must Fall*, and the drama *Dinner at Eight*; all three were sold to Hollywood. The role of Sam Harris was written into the 1938 film *Alexander's Ragtime Band* and the 1943 Cohan film biography, *Yankee Doodle Dandy*. Harris's production of Kaufman and Hart's *The Man Who Came to Dinner* was still running at the time of Harris's death in New York City. So was the Kurt Weill–Ira Gershwin–Moss Hart *Lady in the Dark*, the first musical with a psychiatric theme.

In 1908 Harris had married actress Alice Nolan. She died in 1930, and in 1939 he had married Kathleen Watson. There were no children from either marriage. A man who completely understood the theater of his time, Harris—whose word was his bond—deserved the title of Broadway's "last aristocrat."

• The most rounded portraits of Harris are in Moss Hart, *Act One* (1957); Lawrence Bergreen, *As Thousands Cheer: The Life of Irving Berlin* (1990); and Ward Morehouse, *George M. Cohan: Prince of the American Theatre* (1943). Also helpful are Cohan, *Twenty Years on Broadway* (1924); Howard Teichmann, *George S. Kaufman* (1973); Joe Adamson, *Groucho, Harpo, Chico and Sometimes Zeppo* (1973); and Harpo Marx with Rowland Barber, *Harpo Speaks!* (1961). A good obituary is in the *New York Times*, 4 July 1941.

JAMES ROSS MOORE

HARRIS, Samuel (14 June 1814–25 June 1899), theologian and educator, was born in East Machias, Maine, the son of Josiah Harris, a merchant and clerk of the court, and Lucy Talbot. At age fifteen Harris entered Bowdoin College, where he acquired a lifelong love of language and literature under the tutelage of Henry Wadsworth Longfellow. After graduating in 1833, Harris served for a year as principal at the Limerick (Maine) Academy and the next year at his childhood school, the Washington Academy, in East Machias. He attended Andover Theological Seminary from 1835 to 1838, after which he returned to serve another three years as principal at Washington Academy (1838–1841). In 1839 Harris married Deborah Robbins Dickinson, a fellow Washington Academy graduate. The Harrises adopted one daughter.

Harris began his ordained ministry in 1841 at the Congregational church in Conway, Massachusetts. In 1851 he was called to the South Congregational Church of Pittsfield, Massachusetts. Harris left the pastorate to become professor of systematic theology at Bangor Seminary in 1855. In 1867 he was installed as president of Bowdoin College, a position he held for four years until accepting an appointment as Dwight Professor of Systematic Theology at Yale in 1871. He continued to preach almost every week while serving his academic posts.

Harris defies classification as a theologian. From his earliest days in the pastorate he published reviews, sermons, and addresses on political and social issues, especially support for temperance and opposition to slavery. While sharing such concerns with nineteenth-century liberals he also retained a more conservative strain in his thinking, especially concerning the person of Christ, the primacy of revelation, and the new methods of biblical criticism, about which he felt apprehensive. Shortly after Harris's death, one critic suggested that Harris could best be understood as one who "formed the transition from the New England to later theologies," but belonged to neither.

Harris's wife died in 1876 before his major theological works were published, and in 1877 he married Mary Sherman Skinner Fitch. Six years later he published *The Philosophical Basis of Theism* (1883), his best-known and most influential work. Harris's theology not only stressed reason as the basis of faith but emphasized the necessity of a philosophical basis for theology. Harris defined God as Absolute Reason and then argued that reason was what distinguished personal beings, that is, human beings, from impersonal beings. Reason enabled people to work from their experience to understand and know God, since "the universe in its deepest significance and reality is the expression of the archetypal thoughts of the Absolute Reason." The fundamental insight to which this logic pointed was that the existence of personality in human beings had to be an expression of a divine archetype, thereby confirming the existence of a personal God. Harris's other theological writings, *The Self-Revelation of God* (1887), a volume of doctrinal theology, and *God the Creator and Lord of All* (1896), the first two volumes of a systematic theology, continued his emphasis on reason as the ground of faith. Reason was the means by which human beings made sense of the preeminently important experience of revelation. The revelations of God in Christ, nature, and humanity were not deposits of doctrine or truth, but rather the actions of God in history from which doctrine, by means of reason, could then be deduced.

Harris's emphasis on reason also led to a concerted effort to reconcile theology and science. Just as science was concerned with harmonizing the laws of the universe, Harris argued that theism was the doctrine that the universe was an all-inclusive rational system grounded in reason. Science could exist only if laws and principles were everywhere the same, and if this was so, it meant they were in accordance with Absolute Reason. Thus, he argued that "it is impossible that the true science of facts and laws of the universe can be in conflict with the true science of the God of the universe." Theology merely explained the highest source of the facts and laws that science observed and described.

In accordance with his social ethics, Harris's theology stressed the value and worth of individuals. He emphasized the similarity between God and humanity by characterizing humanity as rational, self-determining, and capable of exercising love—a divine-human correlation most clearly revealed in Christ. Central to Harris's understanding of humanity was free will, defined as "the capacity of choosing in the light of reason." The essential choice was making either God and others, or the self, "the supreme object of trust and service." Sin was equated with rejecting God and others for self. This doctrine of free will also contributed to Harris's understanding of progress. While he shared in the optimism of the late nineteenth century, his vision focused not on technical or industrial advancement, but, as the title of his first book suggested, *The Kingdom of Christ on Earth* (1874). While the divine promise of such a kingdom was enough to assure its eventual existence, Harris's manuscript "God Our Savior" stressed that, in practical terms, the kingdom would be brought about by the gradual efforts of free agents applying their reason to God's continuing revelation: "God's action is designed progressively to bring all persons in their reciprocal relations and interactions, and all human society in its political constitution, laws and institutions and in the administration of government, and all international relations and actions, into conformity with this law of love."

Although Harris's career included work as a pastor and administrator, his colleagues at Yale believed that, as an "introverted, brooding meditative man" who often seemed aloof and distant, he was best suited to be a theological teacher and writer. Except for his work as a guest preacher, Harris dedicated virtually all of his time and energy to his teaching and writing. In recognition of this commitment, Harris was named professor emeritus upon his retirement from Yale in 1895. He continued writing and was working on the second part of his systematic theology, preliminarily titled "God Our Savior," when he died in Litchfield, Connecticut.

• Harris's papers, including a draft of "God Our Savior," the second part of his systematic theology, are in the Samuel Harris Papers, Special Collections, Yale Divinity School Library. Prior to publishing his philosophical and theological works, Harris published frequently in the *New Englander* and *Bibliotheca Sacra*. Other early notable publications include "Zaccheus; or, The Scriptural Plan of Benevolence," in *Systematic Beneficence: Premium Essays* (1850); and the pamphlets *Pernicious Fiction; or, The Tendencies and Results of Indiscriminate Novel Reading* (1853) and *Christ's Prayer for the Death of His Redeemed*, published as *A Gift for Mourners* (1861). A biography is Frederick William Whittaker, *Samuel Harris, American Theologian* (1982). See also Lewis O. Brastow, *A Memorial Address Commemorative of the Life and Services of Samuel Harris* (1899). An obituary is in the *New Haven Evening Register*, 26 June 1899.

JAMES B. BENNETT

HARRIS, Seale (13 Mar. 1870–16 Mar. 1957), physician and medical writer and editor, was born in Cedartown, Georgia, the son of Charles Hooks Harris, a medical doctor, and Margaret Ann Monk. Harris received his early education in Cedartown and nearby Marietta, Georgia. During these years he often drove his father's horse and buggy to the homes of patients, where the majority of his father's practice occurred. At age nineteen he was rodman on a team of engineers surveying in South Carolina for what became the Seaboard Air Line Railroad Co. During this time Seale received a letter from his brother James, who along with two other brothers offered to lend him money to attend the University of Georgia and then to obtain a medical degree from the Columbia University College of Physicians and Surgeons in New York City. He finished his two years at Georgia but was frightened away from New York by a cholera scare. He entered the University of Virginia medical school in 1892, living there in a room previously occupied by Edgar Allan Poe. He received the M.D. in June 1894, and in the early fall of that year he entered practice in Union Springs, Alabama. Joining the county medical society, he was elected reporter almost immediately, secretary

in 1896, and later served as president (1900–1902) and county health officer (1898–1905). In 1897 Harris married Stella Rainer, with whom he had two children. He moved to Baltimore, Maryland, in January 1906 for postgraduate study in medicine and gastrointestinal diseases, after which he studied in Vienna, Austria, and elsewhere in Europe.

Late in 1906 Harris moved to Mobile, Alabama, to become professor and chair of medicine in the independent Medical College of Alabama and chief of medicine at the Mobile General Hospital, which in 1907 officially became part of the University of Alabama. In October 1915 he moved to Birmingham, Alabama, then a booming industrial steel city, and his practice prospered until 1917, when he entered the Medical Reserve Corps of the U.S. Army under General William C. Gorgas. There he edited a book, *War Medicine* (n.d.), published in Paris. He served in Europe from May 1918 to March 1919 and was part of President Woodrow Wilson's party to Italy in January 1919. Harris was a member of the Research Committee of the American Expeditionary Forces to France and investigated food and nutritional diseases in Italy, Austria, and Germany, after which he was promoted to lieutenant colonel and was cited by General John J. Pershing "for conspicuous and meritorious service in France." On President Wilson's steamship *George Washington*, returning from France, Harris came to know a number of interesting people, including the assistant secretary of the navy, Franklin D. Roosevelt. He next was assigned to the surgeon general's office in Washington, D.C., under a General Ireland, where he wrote the chapters on gastrointestinal diseases for *The Medical History of the World War* (c. 1918). Upon leaving active service in 1919, he was promoted to full colonel in the Medical Reserve Corps.

Returning to Birmingham in 1919, Harris purchased a large, two-story brick home and established his office there with a nursing home on the second floor. Soon he opened another nursing home nearby, and in 1923–1924 a fifty-bed hospital, the Gorgas Hotel Hospital. The hospital failed in the depression of the 1930s, and Harris lost everything, becoming deep in debt. The Baptist church rented the hospital in 1930 and purchased it in 1934; it thus became an important foundation of the Baptist Health System, a major health care provider in the southeastern United States at the close of the twentieth century, with more than 10,000 employees, a hospital system with 2,700 beds, and 60 satellite clinics.

Harris was a member of many associations, including the American College of Physicians, the American Gastroenterological Association, the American Diabetes Association, and the American Medical Association. But none was more important to him than the Southern Medical Association, founded in 1906 in Chattanooga. He was secretary-treasurer from 1910 to 1921 and president in 1921–1922. In 1910 he purchased the *Southern Medical Journal of Nashville* and, consolidating it with the *Gulf States Journal of Medicine and Surgery* (formerly the *Mobile Medical and Sur-*

gical Journal), continued its publication as the *Southern Medical Journal*, the journal of the Southern Medical Association. He sold the journal in 1921 to the Southern Medical Association for $55,000 to help raise money for the Gorgas Hotel Hospital. On 6 June 1921 he received a certificate of appreciation from the American Medical Editors Association. In 1939 he served as president of the Medical Association of the State of Alabama.

Harris is probably best known for his discovery of hyperinsulism. Having traveled to the Toronto General Hospital in March 1923 as a guest of Frederick Banting, he later observed in his own patients symptoms reminiscent of the hypoglycemia due to excessive doses of exogenous insulin he had seen there. He demonstrated the hypoglycemia in his patients and published his findings in 1924. The Southern Medical Association awarded its research medal to him at its Cincinnati meeting in 1949, and in 1958 an award was designated the Seale Harris Medal for "important research accomplishment in the broad field of metabolism, endocrinology, nutrition, or for research which contributes to a better understanding of the chemical changes occurring in disease."

Harris published with his son, Seale Harris, Jr., *Clinical Pellagra* (1941) and *Banting's Miracle* (1946); he also wrote *Woman's Surgeon: The Life Story of J. Marion Sims* (1950). *Banting's Miracle* was published in Swedish and Dutch as well as English. In 1949 he was awarded the Distinguished Service Medal of the American Medical Association, and in 1950 the University of Virginia Alumni Association voted him a member of the Thomas Jefferson Society of Patriarchs. Camp Seale Harris, a camp for diabetic children, was founded by Dr. Samuel Eichold of Mobile in 1947. It operated during most of the twentieth century for two weeks every summer, during which children ages eight to fourteen and dieticians, nurses, and physicians learn how to care optimally for the disease in children.

Harris, despite—or perhaps because of—his many accomplishments, never accumulated much money and died in the Birmingham Veterans Administration Hospital. However, his work continued through Camp Seale Harris, the *Southern Medical Journal*, and the excellent Seale Harris Clinic, which may be dated from either 1945, when he constructed a separate building for it, or 1922, when he actually established the clinic. Through his work, hyperinsulinism became a recognized clinical entity.

• A more complete biography of Harris is available in E. B. Carmichael, "Seale Harris—Physician-Scientist-Author," *Journal of the Medical Association of the State of Alabama* 33 (1964): 189–95. Harris's article "Hyperinsulinism and Dysinsulinism" appeared in the *Journal of the American Medical Association* 83 (1924): 729–33. Obituaries are in the *New York Times*, 17 Mar. 1957, and the *Journal of the American Medical Association* 163 (1957): 1376–77.

JAMES A. PITTMAN, JR.

HARRIS, Seymour Edwin (8 Sept. 1897–27 Oct. 1974), economist, educator, and author, was born in New York City, the son of Henry Harris and Augusta Kulick. After graduating from high school, Harris entered Harvard University, from which he earned his B.A. in 1920. For the next two years, he taught at Princeton University, then he returned to Harvard in 1922 as a graduate student and an instructor in economics. In 1923 he married Ruth Black; they had no children. He received his Ph.D. in 1926, and his doctoral dissertation won him the David A. Wells Prize for 1927. In that same year, he advanced from instructor to lecturer within the Harvard faculty.

Harris wrote his first book, *The Assignats*, a study of finance during the French Revolution, in 1930. Although he would publish six other books in the next dozen years, his early works met with mixed critical success. Reviewers often maintained that the value of the content of the books was lost through sloppy organization and technical language incomprehensible to lay people. A review of his 1941 effort, *The Economics of Social Security*, is typical: the reviewer in the May 1942 issue of *Annals of the American Academy of Political and Social Science* praised Harris's analysis of the impact of the U.S. Social Security program on national productivity but lamented that "a large part will hardly be understood by readers not adequately trained in mathematics."

Despite such lukewarm notices, Harris's career as an academic began to flourish. By 1933 he had risen to the position of assistant professor, and by 1936 he was named an associate professor with tenure. During this time, he became a prominent member of a group of economists at Harvard—also including John Kenneth Galbraith, Alvin Hansen, and Paul A. Samuelson—who applied the theories of British monetary expert John Maynard Keynes to the problems of the American economy. Harris and his colleagues injected nontraditional ideas into the business-oriented, aristocratic Harvard economics department, advocating as part of the so-called Keynesian revolution increased government spending and lower taxes as a remedy for economic depression.

After the onset of World War II, Harris lent his expertise in economic matters to both the war effort abroad and the preparation for peace at home. In 1942 he served as a member of the Board of Economic Warfare, and in 1942–1943 he worked for the Office of Price Administration. The following year he joined the secretary of state's committee on postwar commercial policy.

In 1945, while helping President Franklin D. Roosevelt with the country's transition back to economic health, Harris became a full professor in the economics department at Harvard. He also continued his prolific output as an author, writing as well as editing several books in the late 1940s. Among them was *National Debt and the New Economics* (1947), an optimistic study of the nation's capacity for taxation and debt, which clashed with the views of many economists who predicted that another depression was imminent.

During the Republican administration of Dwight D. Eisenhower, Harris's role in the government became much more limited. He settled in as the chairman of Harvard's economics department in 1955 but continued to take notice of the economic policies issuing from the White House. Harris disagreed with Eisenhower's strong focus on balancing the budget, stating in a letter to the *New York Times* on 3 April 1957 that "[t]he Eisenhower Administration has gone in too much for economy and not enough for needed government services. . . . The size of the budget is not so serious as it seems to many."

Harris had attempted to defeat the policies of Eisenhower by joining the team of Democrat Adlai Stevenson as an economic adviser in Stevenson's campaign against Eisenhower in 1956. The effort was ultimately unsuccessful as Eisenhower won reelection, but Harris's fortunes were reversed four years later when he served as an economic adviser in John F. Kennedy's victorious presidential campaign. Under President Kennedy, Harris was named as the chairman of a panel of economic consultants that met with Secretary of the Treasury Douglas Dillon on a weekly basis. Reportedly, Kennedy had later planned to name Harris to the Federal Reserve Board, hoping to add a more liberal influence to the generally conservative board; but Kennedy was assassinated before the plan could be put into effect.

In *Economics of the Kennedy Years and a Look Ahead* (1964), Harris credited Kennedy for the period of economic recovery from 1961 to 1964. He mentioned that the president had initial reservations about Keynesian economics, unsure about the idea of lowering taxes to avert a recession, but he finally overcame his fears. "It was a long struggle," Harris wrote, but "by 1963 he had clearly become a convert." Harris continued: "The major credit for this remarkable recovery and for the increasing acceptance of modern economics belongs to President Kennedy. He had become the most literate of Presidents in his understanding of economics."

In 1963 Harris left Harvard to accept a position as the chairman of the economics department at the University of California at La Jolla. Additionally, he became one of the chief economic consultants to President Lyndon B. Johnson, necessitating frequent flights from California to Washington, D.C. After the death of his first wife, Harris married Dorothy Marshall in 1968; they had no children.

Although Harris could never quite shake the allegations that his published efforts suffered from carelessness—in a review of Harris's book on the Kennedy years, professor Robert Lekachman accused the narrative of being unclear and poorly organized and the statistics undigested—his reputation as a practical economist is difficult to question. In reviewing *The Economics of the Political Parties* (1962) for the *New York Times*, Sidney Hyman wrote that Harris "does not spend his time in theorizing about a perfect economic world where crabs will walk straight, moles will see and elephants will fly. He is a committed political

economist, at grips with the problems of the here and the now as they present themselves in the context of concrete cases and controversies." Harris died in San Diego.

• Harris's other published books include *Monetary Problems of the British Empire* (1931); *Twenty Years of Federal Reserve Policy* (1933); *The Economics of the Recovery Program* (1934); *Exchange Depreciation* (1936); *Economics of Social Security* (1941); *Economics of American Defense* (1941); *Economics of America at War* (1943); *Price and Related Controls* (1945); *Inflation and the American Economy* (1945); *Stabilization Subsidies* (1948); *Foreign Economic Policy for the United States* (1948); *The European Recovery Program* (1948); *How Shall We Pay for Education?* (1948); *The Market for College Graduates* (1949); *Economics of Mobilization and Inflation* (1951); *The Economics of New England* (1952); *John Maynard Keynes* (1955); *Inflation and Anti-Inflationary Policies of American States* (1956); *Interregional and International Economics* (1957); *Higher Education in the United States* (1960); *American Economic History* (1961); *More Resources for Education* (1961); *Higher Education* (1962); *Economic Aspects of Higher Education* (1964); *The Economics of American Medicine* (1964); *Challenge and Change in American Education* (1965); *Economics of Harvard* (1970); and *The Economics of Health Care* (1975). An obituary is in the *New York Times*, 29 Oct. 1974.

FRANCESCO L. NEPA

HARRIS, Thaddeus Mason (7 July 1768–3 Apr. 1842), minister, was born in Charlestown, Massachusetts, the son of William Harris, a schoolteacher, and Rebekah Mason. His early life was marked by poverty and hardship. When he was about seven the family fled their Charlestown home with only what they could carry, his parents fearing what might happen if war began with England. Later that fear was justified when the British, during the battle of Bunker Hill, burned the town to the ground. His father began anew in the country town of Sterling, about fifty miles northwest of Boston, where he taught school until he joined the American army. Within three years he was dead from a fever, and his wife was left alone to bring up their children.

Harris's mother coped as best she could. Harris was sent to work at several nearby farms, where he picked up what schooling was available. Eventually his mother placed him in Boylston with Dr. Ebenezer Morse. Harris did manual labor while Morse trained him, along with Morse's son, for entrance to Harvard. However, Harris's mother, now remarried, did not approve of this plan and arranged for him to learn a trade. An accident on the job cut short that career, so he ended up working for his grandfather Mason, the clerk of the Courts of Session for Middlesex County.

In his spare time Harris studied at the Cambridge school of the Reverend Samuel Kendal. This time when he was ready for college his mother gave her approval. Still extremely poor, he worked his way through Harvard waiting on tables in the Commons and in 1787 earned his long sought-after goal, the A.B.

The year before an event had occurred that influenced the direction of his life. Quite by chance he found a gold ring bearing the inscription "God speed thee, friend." He understood this as a message of encouragement from God, and it led him to become a church member. To earn money after college he taught school in Worcester for a year and then returned to Harvard to prepare for ministry, graduating in 1790 but receiving no degree for his work. For the next few years he served as the college's librarian (1791–1793). In 1789 the Cambridge Association approved him to preach, which he did until 1793, when the Dorchester church called him as their minister. He remained there until his retirement in 1836. Two years after the call to Dorchester, in 1795, Harris married Mary Dix. They had eight children, the oldest of whom, Thaddeus William Harris, was also to serve as librarian of Harvard College.

A few years before his retirement Harris gave two discourses on the religious history of the Dorchester church. What he wrote in Memorials of the First Church in Dorchester (1830) about his call perfectly expresses the style of his entire ministry.

On the 8th of July, 1793, the Church voted to give me an invitation to become their Pastor, and, on the 15th following, the town concurred in the election. Upon receiving these votes, I deemed it proper to resign my office in the University at Cambridge, and take up my residence here that I might give the people an opportunity of being intimately acquainted with me, before I gave my answer. I went to live, in succession, in various parts of the town, for the purpose of visiting familiarly all the families; and when sufficient experience had been obtained to confirm or change the proposition which had been made to me, on the Lord's Day, September 8th, my answer of acceptance was given, and on the 23rd of October following, I was solemnly ordained.

During Harris's pastorate the church became Unitarian. Harris himself, however, was little involved in theological disputes. His main interest was the proper care of his people, and as his friend Samuel Osgood observed, he had "the tenderest sympathy with all who were in distress." Indeed his own temperament was frail and sensitive, and he was known to openly break into tears while preaching.

In addition to his parochial duties, Harris was active in the community. He continued his interest in the Harvard Library and was an overseer of the college for years. He was also interested in the library of the Massachusetts Historical Society and served as its librarian for the last five years of his life. He held membership in a number of other organizations, including the American Academy of Arts and Sciences, the American Peace Society, the Humane Society, the Congregational Charitable Society, and the Society for Propagating the Gospel among the Indians.

Scholarly endeavors had a special attraction for Harris. When he was teaching in Worcester he was offered the position of secretary to George Washington. He accepted but then came down with smallpox and so lost the opportunity. Later he helped Jared Sparks edit Washington's papers. Harris's illness and the need for rest resulted in several books, including *Journal of a Tour into the Territory Northwest of the Alleghany Mountains* (1805) and *Biographical Memorials of James Oglethorpe* (1841). One of his most useful works was *The Natural History of the Bible* (1820), an encyclopedic listing of the animals, birds, fishes, flowers, and trees mentioned in the Bible. Besides these projects, he found time to edit the *Massachusetts Magazine* (1795–1796), issue the *Constitutions of the Ancient and Honorable Fraternity of Free and Accepted Masons* (1792, 1798) as well as other related Masonic items, and compose verse.

Harris's life was a continuation of the intellectual standards and concerns established in New England by the Puritans. His career reflected their commitment to religion, education, scholarship, and community. Yet his life was also a reflection of that American spirit that lies behind the novels of Horatio Alger, Jr. Through struggle and persistence he overcame economic hardship to achieve the social status that enabled him to play a constructive leadership role in the society of his times. His colleague, Nathaniel Hall, was able to justly say that he "filled a large and important place in the community," for which the community "honored him, early and late, with its confidence." He died in Boston.

• The Harvard University archives has an extensive collection of Harris's manuscripts; further material is held by the Cambridge Historical Society. A memorial by Nathanial L. Frothingham, *Massachusetts Historical Society Collections*, 4th ser. (1854): 130–55, is informative. See also William B. Sprague, *Annals of the American Unitarian Pulpit* (1865), pp. 215–22, and William Ware, *American Unitarian Biography*, vol. 1 (1850), pp. 259–70.

ALAN SEABURG

HARRIS, Thaddeus William (12 Nov. 1795–16 Jan. 1856), librarian and entomologist, was born in Dorchester, Massachusetts, the son of Unitarian clergyman Thaddeus Mason Harris and Mary Dix. He graduated from Harvard College in 1815 and in 1820 received the M.D. degree from Harvard Medical School. During the years 1820–1831 Harris practiced medicine, first in Milton (with the older physician Amos Holbrook) and later in Dorchester, Massachusetts. In 1824 he married Catherine Holbrook, a daughter of his mentor. Of the twelve children born to the couple, two predeceased their father.

Harris gave up the practice of medicine and was appointed librarian of Harvard University in 1831, a post he held for the remainder of his life. During his tenure the library collection grew from 30,000 to 65,000 volumes. In his annual report in 1840, Harris requested permission to undertake what he called a slip catalogue for the library. The alphabetical author catalog that followed was one of the earliest card catalogs in an American library, though used for official rather than readers' use. Initially, it was prepared by pasting slips on cards but later by writing on the cards directly.

Gore Hall, the first building at the university devoted exclusively to housing the library, opened in 1841.

Although credited with an effective and conscientious approach to his work as librarian, Harris's primary interests were his scientific studies. The direction if not the origins of these interests were influenced through his friendship with William Dandridge Peck, professor of natural history at Harvard. Harris's first publication (1823) was on the salt marsh caterpillar and the damage it caused to hay. He was an original member of the Massachusetts Horticultural Society, and from the year of its founding in 1829 until his death he held the title of professor of entomology. He lectured on natural history at Harvard College from 1837 to 1842 and had his sights on a permanent teaching position. When a new professorship of natural history was instituted at Harvard, Harris was in position to achieve his aim. But the needs of the university's botanical garden and perhaps Harris's overspecialization in one branch of zoology brought disappointment; in 1842 the Fisher professorship went to botanist Asa Gray.

Through methods of study and note-taking that were reflected also in his library cataloging innovations, Harris had exerted what must have been enormous personal effort to master the work of European entomologists and to compile and organize data for his own use. He contributed a list of insects to the 1833 state geological and natural history report by Edward Hitchcock (1793–1864), which Harris designated as the first attempt at a tolerably complete inventory of the insects of any region of the United States. In 1839 he began publication of a catalog of his collection (assembled chiefly during the years of his medical practice) with a paper in the *American Journal of Science*. By 1842 Harris was able to claim the best entomological collection in the country and one that included specimens from all insect orders. Inclination and circumstances, however, took his entomological interests and achievements in a direction other than descriptive and systematic work.

Many of Harris's papers, in fact, appeared in the agricultural press, notably in the *New England Farmer*. While engaged in the development and description of his collection and in the study especially of the lepidoptera (moths), Harris was appointed in 1837 to prepare a report on insects for the Massachusetts Commission on the Zoological and Botanical Survey. The report appeared in 1841, and the next year he had it privately reprinted as *A Treatise on Some of the Insects of New England, Which Are Injurious to Vegetation* (1842). A second edition appeared in 1852, and a posthumous third, illustrated edition was issued in 1862. Harris's reputation rests largely on this work, and through its influence he is credited with founding practical or economic entomology, emphasizing the control of insect pests, in the United States. At the end of the century it still was considered an essential manual for entomologists of the Northeast. Arranged by insect orders and presented in a clear and largely nontechnical language, the *Treatise* drew upon the au-

thor's solid grounding in the life stages of insects, knowledge which he valued and which distinguished him, for example, from Thomas Say, the other important founder of American entomology whose works were largely descriptive. Although not an agriculturalist, Harris promoted the idea that familiarity with life histories would assist farmers in the control of insects. Such knowledge involved familiarity with the form and activities of insects at different life stages and allowed intervention that included procedures such as hand picking, application of washes, and poisoned baits. Harris is noted as the first government-paid entomologist, but this distinction rests on the small fee he received for his 1841 state report. Asa Fitch's appointment as New York state entomologist in 1854 is the more meaningful precedent. Harris and Fitch were correspondents from the mid-1840s, and Fitch visited him in Cambridge. Comparisons of the careers of the two early economic entomologists in America suggest that Fitch was more personally involved with agriculture and with field work than was Harris.

After the appearance of his *Treatise*, Harris was frequently consulted for advice by farmers, but increasing duties in the library prevented a resumption of his former level of involvement in entomological studies. During his later years he engaged also in historical and genealogical efforts as well as botanical investigations on pumpkins and squashes (the Cucurbitaceae). He died in Cambridge, Massachusetts.

Harris was a member of the American Academy of Arts and Sciences and was active in the Boston Society of Natural History, serving as a curator from 1835 to 1848 (1838–1848 in charge of insects). His own collection was purchased by the society after his death; it contained nearly 10,000 specimens and half that number of species. Louis Agassiz described Harris as the greatest entomologist in the world, but the nature of his long-term influence is indicated by the fact that his profile was on the cover of the *Journal of Economic Entomology* from 1917–1953.

• Harris's entomological correspondence and related papers, as well as his insect collection, are in the Museum of Comparative Zoology at Harvard; his records as librarian are in the Harvard University Archives. In addition to his *Treatise*, his publications include "Upon the Natural History of the Salt-Marsh Caterpillar," *Massachusetts Agricultural Repository and Journal* 7, no. 4 (1823): 322–31; "Insects," in Edward Hitchcock, *Report on the Geology, Mineralogy, Botany and Zoology of Massachusetts* (1833); and "Descriptive Catalogue of the Northern American Insects Belonging to the Linnaean Genus Sphinx in the Cabinet of the Author," *American Journal of Science* 36 (July 1839): 282–320. The basic source on Harris's life and work is Samuel H. Scudder, ed., *Entomological Correspondence of Thaddeus William Harris* (1869), which includes Thomas Wentworth Higginson's "Memoir," a bibliography of Harris's works, and reprints of some of his articles. For a supplement to the bibliography see *Proceedings of the Boston Society of Natural History* 21 (1881): 150–2. Also useful are an account by Harris's son, Edward D. Harris, "Memoir," *Proceedings of the Massachusetts Historical Society* 19 (1881–1882): 313–22; Augustus Radcliffe Grote, "The Rise of Practical Entomology in America," *20th Annual Re-*

port of the *Entomological Society of Ontario 1889* (1890): 75–82; and Arnold Mallis, *American Entomologists* (1971), particularly pages 25–33.

CLARK A. ELLIOTT

HARRIS, Thomas Lake (15 May 1823–23 Mar. 1906), poet, writer, and founder of a religious community, was born in Fenny Stratford, England, the son of Thomas Harris, a grocer and auctioneer, and Annie Lake. When he was five, his parents emigrated to America, settling in Utica, New York. The death of his mother and his father's remarriage, along with his aversion to the Calvinistic Baptist faith of his parents, occasioned Harris's early departure from home. He sought a more liberal worldview in Universalism, receiving an informal theological education and financial help from Universalist ministers in Utica. By 1844 he had his first "settlement" at a church in the Mohawk Valley and was contributing poetry to Universalist newspapers. He married Mary Van Arnum in 1845; they had two children before her death in 1850.

In 1847 Harris came under the influence of spiritualists: first the medium Andrew Jackson Davis, with whom he became disillusioned for personal and religious reasons; and then Samuel B. Brittan, who encouraged him to develop his powers as poet and medium. Through Davis, Harris also encountered the ideas of the eighteenth-century Swedish spiritualist Emanuel Swedenborg and was drawn to his claims of angelic revelation that would form the basis of a spiritual science.

For ten years Harris was involved in spiritualist activities. From 1850 to 1853 he participated in the Mountain Cove community in Virginia and served as one of the mediums through whose revelations the community was governed. When Mountain Cove collapsed, he traveled and lectured on spiritualism and in 1854 published his first long poem, *An Epic of the Starry Heaven*, in which he articulated what was to be a lifelong theme: the relationship between divine love and human sexual union. Similar poems followed, probably the products of trance: *A Lyric of the Morning Land* (1854) and *A Lyric of the Golden Age* (1856). In 1855 Harris married Emily Isabella Waters of New Orleans but professed that he lived a celibate life with her until her death in 1885.

By 1857 Harris had left spiritualism behind and was serving a Swedenborgian church in New York City. He founded the *Herald of Light* (1857–1861), a Swedenborgian periodical, and published the first volume of *The Arcana of Christianity* (1858), followed by two other volumes in 1859 and 1867 (part of vol. 2 was not published until 1878). In 1859 he accepted an invitation to preach in England, but his more mystical Swedenborgianism was not well received. Nonetheless, on this trip he made a famous convert, Laurence Oliphant, British diplomat, writer, and member of Parliament, who with his mother (and later his wife) joined Harris's community. Their economically and psychologically complex relationship, one of the most

publicized of Harris's career, persisted until an acrimonious break in 1881.

On his return to the United States in 1861, Harris moved away from formal ties with Swedenborgianism and established a community, the Brotherhood of the New Life, first in Wassaic, New York, then in Amenia, and finally in Brocton, where Harris called the community "Salem-on-Erie." The community, which included various kinds of Protestants, a Quaker, several Shakers, and twenty Japanese Christians, operated a winery, a restaurant, and a general store. There were no Catholics, "this being one faith Harris could not tolerate" (Schneider and Lawton, p. 150). Members were under Harris's authority and subscribed to his teachings, but the community was not religious in the traditional sense: there was no prescribed creed, nor was there official observance of the Sabbath.

Harris continued to develop his own particular teachings based on concepts that had emerged early in his thought. Two of the most prominent, open breathing and spiritual counterparts, point to his inclination to literalize or materialize spiritual concepts. Open breathing, a fundamental practice of the community, was based on Harris's elaborate teachings about the need to attune respiration to the Divine Breath and his conviction that the Divine Spirit breathed directly into those who were sufficiently developed spiritually. Harris connected the efficacy of the practice not only to individual well-being, but to broad historical patterns and the potential to bind human society together. The doctrine of spiritual counterparts, with its Swedenborgian underpinnings, emerged from Harris's conviction that each person's spiritual affinity resided in the celestial realms but must be sought through the body of a person of the opposite sex (almost never the earthly spouse). This teaching generated criticism and much speculation as to how literally the search for the counterpart was to be taken, particularly since Harris claimed to live a celibate life and discouraged sexual relationships in the community. Harris's own counterpart, the Lily Queen, was referred to constantly in his writings and in daily discourse.

In 1875 Harris and many members of the community moved to Santa Rosa, California, where they established Fountain Grove. After the move the ever-present apocalyptic theme became more pronounced in Harris's writing, such as in *A Voice from Heaven* (1879) and *The Holy City and the Light Therein* (1880). Harris looked upon Fountain Grove as an "arch-natural" community that would persist after a cataclysmic crisis brought about a new life and the disappearance of "inferior races." In 1881, at the time of the rupture with Oliphant, the Fountain Grove members also broke with those who had remained at the Brocton community. Over the next decade there was increasing criticism of the community, in large part from Swedenborgians, and in 1892 Harris and Jane Lee Waring, whom he married that same year (she had been a member of the community from its earliest years) moved to New York City. In 1890 he had sold his remaining interest in Fountain Grove and deeded the land to a community member, Kanaye Nagasawa. Harris continued to write poetry and was attended by a small group of followers until his death in New York City.

Harris's personal eccentricities and his preoccupation with celestial sexuality attracted the attention and the censure of his contemporaries, including many from whom he had derived inspiration for his own teachings. For example, Emma Hardinge Brittan, a spiritualist and historian of the movement, spoke favorably of Harris's talents as a medium while he was a spiritualist but presented a negative view of his "pretensions" in conjunction with the Mountain Cove community (E. H. Brittan, pp. 207–17). In his movement from Calvinism through Universalism, spiritualism, and Swedenborgianism to his own worldview, and in the formation of his several communities, Harris demonstrated one particular but not atypical path through the social and religious history of nineteenth-century America. Harris grappled with pressing issues about the nature of religion and religious authority, family, sexuality, gender roles, and community. In many respects his place is on the far boundaries of religious and social thought, but his primary biographers have acknowledged "something elemental and genuine beneath all the make-believe, something earnest beneath the adventures" (Schneider and Lawton, p. xiii).

• Some of Harris's papers are in the Library of Congress. In addition to the works cited above, some of the more prominent of Harris's writings include *Hymns of Spiritual Devotion for the Christian New Age* (2 vols., 1861), *The Wisdom of the Adepts, Esoteric Science in Human History* (1884), *Star-Flowers: A Poem of the Woman's Mystery* (1886–1887), *God's Breath in Man and in Humane Society* (1884), and *The Brotherhood of the New Life: Its Fact, Law, Method and Purpose* (1891). Emma Hardinge Brittan, *Modern American Spiritualism: Twenty Years' Record* (1870; repr. 1970), includes a description of Harris and the Mountain Cove community by a contemporary and fellow spiritualist. Herbert W. Schneider and George Lawton, *A Prophet and a Pilgrim: Being the Incredible History of Thomas Lake Harris and Laurence Oliphant; Their Sexual Mysticisms and Utopian Communities Amply Documented to Confound the Skeptic* (1942), offers the most complete academic study of Harris, including also the life of Laurence Oliphant and his relationship to Harris, as well as a lengthy bibliography of Harris's writings (and Oliphant's) and a more general bibliography. Schneider and Lawton refer to papers made available to them in San Diego and Fountain Grove by members of Harris's communities who were alive at the time they did their research (c. 1940).

MARY FARRELL BEDNAROWSKI

HARRIS, Vic. *See* Harris, E. Victor.

HARRIS, William (1610–1681), Rhode Island land proprietor and expansionist, was born in England. Practically nothing is known about his parents and early life, although Roger Williams disparagingly called him an "impudent morris dancer from Kent."

In February 1631 Harris and his brother Thomas arrived in New England aboard the same ship that carried Williams. By 1635 Harris and Williams were both residing in Salem, and it is possible that Harris came under the sway of the young Separatist preacher. After Williams was banished from Massachusetts Bay in 1636, Harris followed him to Narragansett Bay and became one of the six original proprietors of Providence. By 1638 the number of Providence Proprietors had increased to thirteen, and in that year Harris and the other twelve granted themselves exclusive shares in a section of land called Pawtuxet, which had been included in the original gift of lands given to Roger Williams by the Narragansett Indians. Located to the south of the main Providence settlement, Pawtuxet was the place where Harris established his permanent residence. In 1640 he and several other Providence men signed an agreement called the Combination, which set the boundaries between Providence and Pawtuxet and spelled out the details of town government.

Harris was a difficult man; pugnacious, crusty, and aloof, he repelled most people with whom he came in contact. Williams said that Harris was forced to live apart from the other Providence settlers because he was so disagreeable, but it is just as likely that Harris's exile was self-imposed. He was a well-read student of the law, not in any professional way, but as a talented amateur who knew how to buttress his political arguments with legal precedents and citations. He frequently cited law cases in his writings, and the inventory of his estate reveals that he owned, among other legal treatises, editions of Lord Coke's *Commentary upon Littleton*, *The Complete Clerk*, and *The Touchstone of Wills*. His formalistic approach to government and land practices belied his often conveniently anarchistic attitudes and opportunistic tendencies toward politics and religion.

Despite their early close associations, Harris and Williams could not abide one another. The real trouble began in 1657 when Williams accused Harris of high treason against the colony. Williams was reacting to one of Harris's antiauthoritarian writings that called for "no lords, no masters" and that, according to Williams, argued against "all governments and governors (of what rank soever), all lords and masters, against all laws and lawmaking assemblies, against all courts, all punishments, prisons, rates, and all records." It is difficult to know, however, if his arguments were truly as "horrid" as Williams claimed them to be, for this particular treatise by Harris has never been found. Despite Williams's fiery indictment of Harris, the colony court could not reach a verdict. As a result of the impasse, the case documents were sent to England, but the ship carrying the papers was lost at sea.

More fundamental to the differences between Harris and Williams was their dispute over the Providence and Pawtuxet lands. Harris, it appears, worked for several years to develop his scheme for extending the boundaries of Providence beyond their original limits. Based on his reading of the land evidences Williams had prepared after receiving the gift of land from the

American Indians, Harris maintained that the Indian chieftains had given the Providence settlers the right to graze their livestock as far inland as they wanted. This right, said Harris, amounted to a grant of land far more extensive than the Providence territory that had been specified as lying between the Blackstone and the Pawtuxet rivers.

In particular, Harris sought an extension westward of the boundaries of Pawtuxet, the section of Providence that had been granted in exclusive shares to the thirteen Providence Proprietors, but his land schemes soon also got him into difficulties with the Warwick settlers, who had themselves acquired from the Indians a tract of land that was located immediately south of the Pawtuxet section. Williams thought of the Pawtuxet land as consisting of a few square miles; Harris contended that it extended twenty miles to the west, just like the original Providence section, and that it followed the south branch of the Pawtuxet River into lands claimed by the settlers of Warwick. In the spring of 1657 Harris began to acquire confirmation deeds from relatives of the Narragansett chieftains; he acquired more of these deeds in 1659 as well.

Williams was outraged by Harris's bold ploy. The contest over the extension of boundaries, which went on for decades, divided the citizens of Providence into warring political factions, alienated the Narragansett Indians from the colony's white settlers, and kept Williams and Harris at odds with one another for the rest of their lives. In 1667, as the storm of controversy spread to the colony government, Harris was dismissed as an assistant from the Rhode Island Assembly. As a result of this rebuke, Harris decided to appeal his case—and his bid for the extension of the boundaries—directly to the king, and in 1675 he traveled to England for that purpose. The Privy Council, responding to Harris's petition, issued a royal order in August 1675 for a court of commissioners to be convened in New England to adjudicate Harris's case.

The deliberations of the commissioners were delayed by King Philip's War, a cataclysmic conflict between the white settlers and Indians of southern New England that ended in the late summer of 1676. Harris was a keen observer of the bloody encounters between the American Indians and the English that occurred during the war, and he wrote two detailed reports for officials in England. One of his sons was killed during an Indian raid on Pawtuxet in January 1676. Harris stayed in Providence with Roger Williams and several other men to defend the town when it was attacked on 29 March 1676.

The king's special commission finally met in November 1677. After hearing evidence and considering several petitions from Harris, Williams, and their respective supporters, the court of commissioners ultimately ruled in Harris's favor: he was awarded monetary damages and Providence was ordered to run the dividing line between the town and the Pawtuxet lands according to the extended boundaries.

Despite this victory, the town of Providence refused to obey the court's order, and the upheaval over land again produced political turmoil in the community.

The court of commissioners met again in 1678, but they were still unable to obtain satisfactory results from Harris's opponents. Finally in the spring of 1679, Harris returned to England to plead his case once more; after getting a confirmation of the court's verdict from the Committee for Plantations, he sailed back to New England in September. Realizing that his opponents steadfastly refused to obey all the various orders that had been granted in his favor and having decided in 1672 to back Connecticut in its boundary and jurisdictional dispute with Rhode Island, Harris agreed to serve as a Connecticut agent and again sailed for England in December 1679. By embracing the Connecticut cause, Harris was probably looking for a powerful ally to assist him in his own personal land crusade, but the facts behind his alliance with Connecticut are hazy and the documents reveal few hints about Harris's motivation or Connecticut's expectations. It is likely that Harris sided with Connecticut only out of expediency and not out of any permanent shift in loyalty.

Harris's mission to England, however, was undone by an unanticipated event. En route across the Atlantic, his ship was attacked by Algerian pirates and he was taken captive and held for ransom. Eventually Connecticut contributed a portion of the ransom money, and Harris's wife, Susannah (maiden name and date of marriage unknown), acquired the rest through loans. Harris was released by the Algerians in the summer of 1681 and found passage to London, but he died there three days after his arrival in late November. The Pawtuxet land controversy was not resolved until 1712, long after Harris and Williams had passed from the scene, when a royal edict successfully put an end to the dispute.

Harris served several terms in the colony government as an assistant and a deputy and in the town government as a moderator, although his periods of public service were sporadic; at the very least, his participation in government seemed to indicate some fundamental change of heart in his antiauthoritarian opinions. He and his wife had five children. Harris was an industrious man, who was said to be very wealthy. But much was said about him, including the absolutely bitter and vindictive testimony of Roger Williams, that cannot be substantiated. All in all, one suspects that Harris was somewhat less villainous than Williams, his other enemies, and several generations of historians have assumed.

• Most of Harris's surviving papers, including many that have never been published, are among several different collections of the Rhode Island Historical Society: the William Harris Papers, Moses Brown Papers, and Austin collection (contained in the Quaker Archives). Another important source of Harris documents is the collection of Rhode Island Manuscripts at the John Hay Library, Brown University. A good number of Harris manuscripts have been published: "Notes on William Harris," comp. Wilfred H. Munro, Rhode Island Historical Society, *Publications* 1 (1893): 214–29; "Harris Papers," ed. Clarence Brigham, Rhode Island Historical Society, *Collections* 10 (1902); *Some William Harris Memoranda* (n.d.); *A Rhode Islander Reports on King Philip's*

War: The Second William Harris Letter of August, 1676, ed. Douglas Edward Leach (1963). Many enlightening Harris documents have also been printed throughout the various volumes of Horatio Rogers, George M. Carpenter, and Edward Field, eds., *The Early Records of the Town of Providence* (21 vols., 1892–1951), and in Howard M. Chapin, ed., *Documentary History of Rhode Island* (2 vols., 1916). There is no adequate biography of Harris. The significant events in his life may be pieced together from the relevant documents and annotations published in *The Correspondence of Roger Williams*, ed. Glenn W. LaFantasie (2 vols., 1988).

GLENN W. LAFANTASIE

HARRIS, William Alexander (29 Oct. 1841–20 Dec. 1909), stockman, U.S. senator, and U.S. congressman, was born in Loudoun County, Virginia, the son of William Alexander Harris, a lawyer, congressman, diplomat, and journalist, and Frances Murray. He attended school in Luray, Page County, Virginia, and then enrolled at Columbian College (now George Washington University) in Washington, D.C., from which he graduated in 1859. He spent the next few months in Nicaragua preparing a preliminary survey for a projected interocean canal before entering Virginia Military Institute, graduating early, in 1861, so he and his classmates could join the Confederate army.

Harris's military service is a conundrum. He entered the army as a second lieutenant training Confederate recruits but soon became assistant adjutant general in the brigade of General Cadmus M. Wilcox, Army of Northern Virginia. He was later an ordnance officer on the staffs of Generals Daniel H. Hill and Robert E. Rodes. Although later known in Kansas as "Colonel Harris," his highest rank was that of captain. There is no information relevant to his military service after the battle of Gettysburg, July 1863. He may have deserted or been captured. In 1863 he married Mary A. Lionberger; they had six children. In 1865 he was employed in Kansas as a civil engineer on the Eastern Division, Union Pacific Railway.

In 1868 Harris became an agent involved in selling the Delaware Indian Reservation and other lands. Around this time he also began farming and raising stock near Linwood, Kansas, about fifteen miles southwest of Kansas City. By the late 1870s he was recognized as one of the nation's premier breeders of Scottish Shorthorn cattle. He secured a fine income, enabling him to dabble in politics.

Like his father before him, Harris was a Democrat but allied himself with the Granger and Farmers' Alliance movements. When the People's party of Kansas was founded in 1890, he joined it. He had held local office as a Democrat, and once he became a Populist, he acted as a major spokesman for fusion of the two parties. Although Populists believed that, in nominating candidates, the office should seek the man, the politically ambitious Harris sought the office. He was mentioned as a replacement for Republican senator John J. Ingalls, but the People's party controlled the state legislature and instead elected William A. Peffer in 1891. In 1892 Harris was a fusionist candidate for the Populist nomination in the First Congressional

District but was defeated by a middle-of-the-road (antifusionist), Union army veteran, Fred J. Close. A few months later, at the state convention in Wichita, where fusionists prevailed, Harris was nominated as Kansas's congressman at large, and he was elected.

As a member of the House, Harris served on the Committee on the Pacific Railroads and made repayment of debts they owed to the U.S. government his major concern. The Union Pacific portion of that obligation, which was due in 1893, became his primary interest in the Fifty-third Congress. Irritated by the financial maneuvering of railroad investors, he suggested that the government force the roads into default and assume ownership and operation of them. Unlike those who wrote the Populist platform of 1892, he was not a genuine advocate of state ownership of railroads, but he did favor making telegraph communications an exclusive function of the postal service.

Harris's first major speech was in support of "free silver," asking that it be remonetized under circumstances prior to 1873. He voted against the Democrats' repeal of the Sherman Silver Purchase Act, maintaining that while it was imperfect it was better than nothing, and he opposed Secretary of the Treasury John G. Carlisle's efforts to issue bonds to build up the nation's dwindling gold reserve. He later voted against the Gold Standard Act of 1900.

Harris was dissatisfied with the upward revision by Senate Democrats of the Wilson-Gorman Tariff of 1893 but voted for it because of the income tax provision. He then joined other low tariff men to support a series of "pop-gun" tariffs designed to free list coal, iron ore, barbed-wire fence, and sugar. He voted for a House bill to define and tax market futures, a bill to establish a uniform system of bankruptcy, and a resolution that would have amended the Constitution by providing for the direct election of senators. On the biggest foreign policy issue of the day, he backed a resolution that recommended Queen Liliuokalani not be returned to the Hawaiian throne but that henceforth the United States should stay out of the islands' affairs. He then refrained from voting for a resolution condemning American intervention in the Hawaiian revolution of 1893, and he championed a big navy.

Harris failed of reelection in 1894, when a united Republican party in Kansas cleverly discredited Populism and fusion. After his first wife's death in 1894, he married Cora M. Mackey that year. Returning to Linwood, he resumed stock raising but remained interested in politics. He coveted the Populist nomination for governor in 1896, but when it went to John Leedy, Harris settled for a seat in the Kansas State Senate, which Populists controlled. When the legislature voted for a U.S. senator to replace Peffer, they chose Harris, who despite his election continued as a leader of the state senate, where he chaired the Railroad Committee. He was largely responsible for the railroad bill that Governor Leedy vetoed in 1897. As first entered, it increased the power of the Kansas Railroad Commission and established maximum freight rates. Harris opposed legislatively determined rates, arguing that they would cause endless litigation and that the commission was better able to fix rates. At a caucus of Populist and Democratic senators, he was able to kill the part of the bill that mandated legislative rate making, thus causing Leedy's veto.

During his six years in the U.S. Senate, Harris served on the Committee on Civil Service and Retrenchment, the Committee on Pacific Railroads, the Select Committee on the Construction of the Nicaragua Canal, and the Committee on the Interocean Canal. For a freshman senator, he spoke frequently on the floor and entered a variety of bills. His legislative offerings were rarely reported out of the committees to which they were assigned. He tried to strengthen the Interstate Commerce Commission, reduce postage on letters sent by the blind, promote the eight-hour day, give Civil War veterans preferences in civil service appointments, and strengthen the Sherman Anti-Trust Act. He wished to change the electoral system by providing for the direct election of senators, establishing four-year terms for members of the House of Representatives, and allowing for a single six-year term for the president. He opposed the Dingley Tariff of 1897. The most important local bill he filed assigned the Fort Hays Military Reservation to the state of Kansas for educational purposes, and subsequently some of the land was used to found Fort Hays State University.

Harris spoke and voted for all measures associated with the Spanish-American War and the Treaty of Paris, 1899, saying: "God hates a coward, and a nation timid, halting, and hesitating in its foreign policy is a sight despised of God and men. A just war promotes and preserves all that is highest and best in national life" (*Congressional Record*, 55th Cong., 2d sess., p. 3547).

Harris had no chance for reelection to the Senate in January 1903, because Republicans had recaptured their historic hold on Kansas politics and government. Although he kept his Linwood property, he spent most of his time in Chicago, where for several years he worked for the Shorthorn Breeders Association and the National Livestock Association. When Democrats nominated him for governor in 1906, Republicans charged that he was not an eligible candidate because he was not a Kansan. Nevertheless, he ran a strong race against the GOP incumbent, Edward W. Hoch. Harris lost by only 2,123 votes.

Harris is best remembered as the last Populist senator, but by the end of his term he had become a supporter of the Progressive reform movement and an admirer of Theodore Roosevelt. In early 1909 Governor William R. Stubbs, a Progressive Republican, appointed Harris to the Board of Regents of the Kansas State Agricultural College (now Kansas State University), but before he could become active, Harris suffered a mild heart attack in August. Four months later, while attending the International Livestock Exposition, he had a second attack and died at the home of his sister-in-law in Chicago.

• A few letters, newspaper clippings, and miscellaneous items related to Harris are at the library of the Kansas State Historical Society, Topeka. Information about his youth and military service is in Clyde Leon Fitch, "William A. Harris of Kansas: His Economic Interests" (M.S. thesis, Kansas City Teachers College, 1967); the National Archives Microfilms, Southwest Region, Fort Worth, Tex., Roll M-382, "Index to Virginia Confederate Soldiers"; and *The War of the Rebellion: A Compilation of the official Records of the Union and Confederate Armies*, ser. 1, vol. II, nos. 1 and 2, and vols. 21, 27, 51 (128 vols., 1880–1901). Information about his congressional and senatorial careers is in the *Congressional Record*, 53d Cong., 1893–1895, 55th–57th Congs., 1897–1903. For his Kans. political involvements see Peter H. Argersinger, *Populism and Politics: William Alfred Peffer and the People's Party* (1974); O. Gene Clanton, *Kansas Populism: Ideas and Men* (1969); Walter T. K. Nugent, *The Tolerant Populists: Kansas Populism and Nativism* (1963); and the *Topeka State Journal*, 1–12 Nov. 1906. Obituaries are in the *New York Times*, the *Topeka Daily Capital*, and the *Topeka State Journal*, 21 Dec. 1909.

ROBERT S. LA FORTE

HARRIS, William Torrey (10 Sept. 1835–5 Nov. 1909), philosopher and educator, was born in North Killingly, Connecticut, the son of William Harris and Zilpah Torrey, farmers. Recognized for his intellectual ability at a young age, Harris attended several preparatory schools prior to entering Yale College in 1854. After only two years of study Harris left Yale and moved to St. Louis in the summer of 1857 to seek an income in teaching shorthand. Even in his youth Harris made strong impressions on acquaintances, not only through his intellectual ability but through his force of character and ability to lead. "Harris was a zealous missionary by nature, as well as a born teacher" (Snider, p. 10).

In St. Louis Harris's life took several turns. In 1858 he began teaching in the St. Louis public school system at Franklin Grammar School and married his childhood friend Sarah Tully Bugbee of Providence, Rhode Island. They had four children, two of whom died in childhood. Harris rose steadily in the school system. In 1859 he was appointed principal of Clay School, and in 1867 he became assistant superintendent of schools with an aim toward rebuilding the postwar system.

During this same period Harris began his philosophical career. A firm believer in phrenology in his youth, Harris gradually turned to philosophy proper, guided in part by the influence of several informal tutors such as Bronson Alcott and Henry C. Brokmeyer. His reading led him to the work of Kant and Hegel, and it was under the influence of Hegel's thinking that he produced most of his own philosophical writing. In a letter to Sarah in 1857 he described himself aptly: "I am an eclectic in philosophy. . . . If anything I lean towards idealism in my tenets" (quoted in Leidecker, p. 84). In 1866 Harris helped found the St. Louis Philosophical Society, which included Brokmeyer, George Holmes Howison, and Denton Snider. Harris, officially secretary of the society, used his organizational ability to give it prominence. In conjunction with his work with the society, in 1867 he began the *Journal of Speculative Philosophy*, the first philosophical journal of importance in the United States. In it Harris, as editor, not only introduced Hegel to the American intellectual scene but published early work by Charles S. Peirce, William James, Josiah Royce, and John Dewey. The journal survived until 1893 and was revived at Pennsylvania State University in 1987.

Harris became the tenth superintendent of the St. Louis schools in 1868; in this capacity he began to make his mark on American educational practice. Under his leadership the first public school kindergarten was established, music became a central feature of the school curriculum, and the system gained a national reputation for its excellence. Although Harris decided to relinquish his position as superintendent in 1880, his career in education continued.

He returned to New England, settling in Concord, Massachusetts, where he worked with Alcott and F. B. Sanborn in organizing and maintaining the Concord Summer School of Philosophy from 1880 to 1888. From 1882 to 1885 he also served as superintendent of Concord's small school system. During this transitional period Harris continued to study and write about both philosophy and literature; in particular he maintained his focus on Hegel but gave attention as well to Shakespeare, Goethe, and Dante. Then, on 12 September 1889 he began work in his most influential position when he became the fourth U.S. commissioner of education, a post he held until 1906.

Harris's tenure as commissioner was marked by a conservative temper that oversaw a gradual development of new educational practices. He initiated examinations of how to regularize degrees in medicine and dentistry, argued for the importance of coeducation, urged a system of kindergartens, and tried to bring educational breadth to "training" programs in agriculture and trades. Philosophy continued to inform his thinking concerning educational policy, as is exemplified in two of the books that he published in his later years, *Hegel's Logic: A Book on the Genesis of the Categories of the Mind* (1890) and *Psychologic Foundations of Education: An Attempt to Show the Genesis of the Higher Faculties of the Mind* (1898). The texts, though neither is stylishly presented nor highly original, reveal Harris's lifelong concern to integrate the individual's energies with the development of the community. As an educator, Harris enjoyed a wide popularity in the United States, and his work was noted by European educators as well. His influence—like his character—was neither radical nor flashy but sustained and deep. His biographer well captures the sense of this influence: "Harris was not a teacher of the young merely, he was a teacher of teachers who could imbue them with a sense of the dignity of their profession and inspire belief in the ideals of education and thus . . . through compelling loyalty to a cause, help them in achieving the supreme thing in life" (Leidecker, p. 479).

Harris's working career ended in 1906 when he was awarded an honorary pension by the Carnegie Foundation for the Advancement of Teaching. This allowed him to spend his final years working on a variety of projects in philosophy and education, among which was finishing his work as editor in chief of the 1910 edition of *Webster's New International Dictionary*. Some of these projects were left unfinished when Harris died in his wife's home town of Providence.

Harris's life's accomplishments, including his nearly 500 publications, exemplified well both the self-reliant spirit of New England Transcendentalism and the systematic idealism of the St. Louis Hegelian movement that he helped to initiate. Although his philosophical work was often of good quality, it is now for the most part overlooked. He is remembered primarily as the editor of the journal that made Hegel available to Americans and that introduced the work of the classical American philosophers. Likewise, his work in education had its most lasting effect through the habits and practices that emerged under his guidance; by and large his philosophy of education has been recognized for its importance to its time and place but has had no lasting influence on U.S. educational policy.

• Harris's papers are located in several places including the Missouri Historical Society, St. Louis; the headquarters of the National Education Society, Washington, D.C.; and the Concord Public Library, Mass. See also William H. Goetzmann, *The American Hegelians* (1973); Kurt F. Leidecker, *Yankee Teacher: The Life of William Torrey Harris* (1946); Henry A. Pochmann, *New England Transcendentalism and St. Louis Hegelianism* (1948); and Denton J. Snider, *The St. Louis Movement in Philosophy, Literature, Education, Psychology with Chapters of Autobiography* (1920). A memorial is in the *Journal of Proceedings and Addresses of the National Educational Association* (1910).

DOUGLAS R. ANDERSON

HARRISON, Alexander (17 Jan. 1853–13 Oct. 1930), painter, was born Thomas Alexander Harrison in Philadelphia, Pennsylvania, the son of Apollos Wolcott Harrison, a civil engineer and merchant, and Margaret Belden. He attended private schools in the Germantown section of Philadelphia, and then he went to work briefly for his father. Soon afterward he entered the studio of the Philadelphia artist George Pettit, intending to become a painter. But within a month or two, he left Pettit's tutelage for a four-year stint with the U.S. Coast Survey. He did surveying in New England, Florida, and on the Pacific coast before determining again to be a painter. Once he had made that decision he enrolled at the School of Design in San Francisco, then at the Pennsylvania Academy of the Fine Arts. By mid-1879 he was studying in Paris at the École des Beaux-Arts with Jean-Léon Gérôme.

Paris was Harrison's home for the rest of his life, although he did return to the United States occasionally. He exhibited at the Paris Salons of 1880 and 1881, but his first real success there came in 1882 with the submission of *Castles in Spain*, now part of the collection of the Metropolitan Museum of Art in New York. The painting, which showed a boy daydreaming on the seashore, "attracted universal attention and sold on the opening day." Other paintings he created over the course of the next few years, among them *Twilight* (1884, Saint Louis Art Museum), *The Wave* (1885, Pennsylvania Academy of Fine Arts), and *In Arcadia* (c. 1886, Musee d'Orsay, Paris), earned him a reputation as the leading American painter then living in France. *The Wave*, for instance, earned an honorable mention at the Paris Salon of 1885 and a Temple silver medal at the Pennsylvania Academy in 1887; and the leading critic Charles Caffin, in his *Story of American Painting* (1907), wrote of the painting: "For the first time the true colouring of the blue water, curling over a smooth, sandy shore, had been searched into and recorded; the light that glinted on its crest, lay on the shining curve of the swell, or nestled in the hollow of the trough—each aspect had been rendered in its true relation. And the result of this truthful rendering of the passage of light over the wave was to increase the suggestion of the latter's movement. The picture was a beautiful lesson in colour, light, and movement." *In Arcadia* caused considerable debate when it was exhibited at the Universal Exposition in Paris in 1889 and at the Pennsylvania Academy in 1891 because of the almost photographically rendered nudity of the figures lounging in the woodland setting. However, it was given a place of honor at the 1893 World's Columbian Exposition in Chicago in 1893, and it was purchased by the French government in 1905 for the Luxembourg Museum. It was largely on the strength of *In Arcadia* that the French government awarded Harrison the Legion of Honor and offered him the post of officer of public instruction, a position he held until his death.

As time passed Harrison's style changed from a fairly literal one, with careful underdrawing and smooth brushwork, to a looser, more impressionistic, or "tonal," style (his earlier style has been defined as "naturalism" or straightforward "realism"). But whatever style he worked in, his efforts were well received on both sides of the Atlantic, as can be deduced from the host of awards and honors he garnered during his career. When the Salon of the Champs de Mars was created in 1890, for example, with Ernest Meissonier as its president, Harrison was asked to be a juror. He was also a member of the jury at the Paris Exposition of 1900. He was made an associate member of the National Academy of Design in New York in 1898 and a full member in 1901. He was invited to join most of the leading artists' organizations of the day, among them the Society of American Artists, the Secessionists of Berlin and Munich, the Royal Institute of Painters in Oil Colours of London, and the Century Association of New York. His works won him medals not only in Paris and Philadelphia, but also in Berlin, Brussels, Dresden, Munich, and elsewhere. He never married, but he spent much of his time in the company of his brother Birge Harrison, an equally well-known painter of the period. He died in his studio in Paris. After his death Alexander Harrison was forgotten quickly by Americans, who in the nationalistic 1930s saw his work as too derivative of French ideas and styles. In the 1980s, however, American scholars rediscovered him, and he has been cast as a leader of the late nineteenth-century movement now called "naturalism."

• Archival materials by and about Harrison can be found at the Pennsylvania Academy of the Fine Arts in Philadelphia and at the Archives of American Art, at the Smithsonian Institution. Informative early articles include Charles Francis Browne, "Alexander Harrison—Painter," *Brush and Pencil* 4 (1899): 132–44; Charles Louis Borgmeyer, "Alexander Harrison," *Fine Arts Journal* 29 (1913): 514–44; and "A Twin Exhibition—Alexander and Birge Harrison at the Albright Art Gallery," *Academy Notes* 8 (1913): 152–73. The painter was almost forgotten from the time of his death until the 1980s and 1990s, when he was re-evaluated as a leading naturalist in such books as David Sellin, *Americans in Brittany and Normandy, 1860–1910* (1982); Annette Blaugrund et al., *Paris 1889: American Artists at the Universal Exposition* (1989); Lois Marie Fink, *American Art at the Nineteenth-Century Paris Salons* (1990); and Gabriel P. Weisberg, *Beyond Impressionism: The Naturalist Impulse* (1992). An obituary is in the *New York Times*, 14 Oct. 1930, and in *Art Digest*, 15 Oct. 1930.

MARK W. SULLIVAN

HARRISON, Benjamin (1726?–24 Apr. 1791), Virginia planter, legislator, governor, and signer of the Declaration of Independence, was born at the family seat, "Berkeley," Charles City County, Virginia, the son of Benjamin Harrison and Anne Carter, daughter of Robert "King" Carter, one of the largest landowners in the colony. The Harrisons were among the early settlers in Virginia, and Benjamin "the Signer" was the fifth of that name in a direct line of descent. His father and grandfather had been prominent in the affairs of colonial government. His son, William Henry Harrison, and great grandson, Benjamin Harrison (1833–1901), would become presidents of the United States.

At the time of his father's death in 1745, Benjamin Harrison was a student at the College of William and Mary. He left without graduating and assumed management of his father's estate, which included the "Berkeley" plantation and extensive lands across the James River in Surry County. Shortly thereafter he married Elizabeth Bassett, scion of another prominent Virginia family. They had many children, but only seven survived infancy: three sons and four daughters.

Harrison was elected to the Virginia House of Burgesses in 1749 and was reelected annually until 1774 when the Virginia Convention sent him to the First Continental Congress. His wealth, pedigree, and collegiality quickly won him admission to the leadership elite, which included Peyton Randolph, Harrison's brother-in-law, Robert Carter Nicholas, a nephew of Harrison's wife, and John Robinson, who doubled as both treasurer of the colony and Speaker of the House of Burgesses. After Speaker Robinson's death in 1766, it was learned that in his capacity as treasurer Robinson had loaned parcels of Virginia paper money to favored friends. The money had been issued to finance the French and Indian War and was subsequently retired by the assembly. The scandal rocked the assembly and opened the path for new and more radical leaders such as Patrick Henry and Richard Henry Lee. Among the beneficiaries of Robinson's largesse was Benjamin Harrison, whose political career was not damaged by the scandal.

With this background it is not surprising that Harrison approached the Revolution cautiously. He opposed Patrick Henry's inflammatory resolutions denouncing the Stamp Act, and four years later, in 1769, he refused to sign the "Association" that aligned Virginia with northern merchants in a refusal to import British goods. He was nevertheless able to trim his sails as the storm of Revolution approached. In 1773 he served on Virginia's committee of correspondence, which worked with other colonies to map out the program of resistance, and in 1774 he was placed on Virginia's delegation to the First Continental Congress.

The Virginia delegation to the First Continental Congress was led by radicals Patrick Henry and Richard Henry Lee. The Convention that named the delegation probably regarded Harrison as a balance, a representative of the colony's elderly, conservative elite. The impression he conveyed to fellow members of Congress was that of a complacent country gentleman, corpulent and lazy. John Adams (1735–1826), a man of exacting standards, was initially thrilled when Harrison told him that he regarded the Congress as so important he would have gone to Philadelphia on foot if necessary. However, after watching Harrison at work, Adams concluded that he was "an indolent, luxurious, heavy gentleman, of no use in Congress or committee, but a great embarrassment to both." In the course of the session during the autumn of 1774, Harrison opposed a motion by Richard Henry Lee recommending that the colonies arm themselves, saying "It will only tend to irritate, whereas Our Business is to reconcile." In the Virginia Convention in the spring of 1775, he opposed a similar measure initiated by Patrick Henry for the arming of Virginia.

Nevertheless, when the Revolution broke out Harrison swam with the tide. In November 1775 he was named chair of a committee to correspond "with our friends in Great Britain, Ireland and other parts of the world," Congress's first venture into foreign affairs. The following year Harrison's committee sent Silas Deane and Benjamin Franklin (1706–1790) to France as its diplomatic agents. His prestige in the House was such that he consistently was placed in the chair when Congress went into committee of the whole to debate the question of independence in June 1776. As committee chair, he had the honor of reporting the approved Declaration of Independence to the Congress on the Fourth of July. Afterward he affixed his name to it, along with the other members of the Virginia delegation. He served in Congress until 1777 and then took a seat in Virginia's newly constituted House of Delegates. He served as Speaker from 1778 until 1781 and then as governor from 1781 to 1784. In 1781, when Banastre Tarleton, General Charles Cornwallis's hard-riding lieutenant, descended on Charlottesville in an effort to capture the Virginia legislature, Speaker Harrison fled across the Blue Ridge Mountains with Patrick Henry and John Tyler, encountering difficulties that have long enriched Virginia folklore.

Just as he was slow in coming to terms with the Revolution, Harrison only belatedly perceived the need to reform the government after the war. James Madison, leading efforts to reform the Virginia legal system, to abolish the connection between church and state, and to strengthen the central government by amending or replacing the Articles of Confederation, looked to Harrison for help but received none. As governor, Harrison stood by helplessly in 1782 when the assembly revoked its previous approval of an amendment that would have given Congress the power to levy taxes. As a member of the House of Delegates from 1785 to 1787, Harrison opposed amendments to the Articles of Confederation that would have conferred greater power on Congress and resisted the bill initially drafted by Thomas Jefferson to reform the Virginia law code.

Harrison opposed giving added powers to the central government because he feared the government would be dominated by northern merchants. As governor in the early 1780s he had sponsored a state navigation act that would have given Virginia merchants a monopoly of Virginia's trade. When he saw a copy of the Constitution, drafted by the Federal Convention at Philadelphia in 1787, he predicted that under the new federal government "the States south of the Potomac will be little more than appendages to those to the northward of it." Elected to the Virginia ratifying convention (from Surry County where he had lands but no residence), Harrison joined Patrick Henry and George Mason (1725–1792) in opposing the Constitution. The Antifederalists lost that fight, but they controlled Virginia politics for the next few years. In 1788 Harrison was elected to a final term as governor with the support of the Antifederalists in the assembly. He died in his home on the James River, not knowing whether the new federal government could be made to work and what its effect would be on the future of Virginia.

• The only biography of Benjamin Harrison is the sketch by John Sanderson in *Biographies of the Signers of the Declaration of Independence* vol. 8 (1827). W. G. Stanard, "Harrison of James River," *Virginia Magazine of History and Biography*, vols. 31–33 (1922–1925), has a genealogical account of the Harrison family and includes part of Sanderson's biography. Recent studies that discuss Harrison's role in the Revolution and Confederation periods are: Norman K. Risjord, *Chesapeake Politics, 1781–1800* (1978); George F. Willison, *Patrick Henry and His World* (1969); and Henry Mayer, *A Son of Thunder: Patrick Henry and the American Republic* (1986).

NORMAN K. RISJORD

HARRISON, Benjamin (20 Aug. 1833–13 Mar. 1901), twenty-third president of the United States, was born in North Bend, Ohio, the son of John Scott Harrison and Elizabeth Irwin, farmers. Harrison graduated from Miami University in 1852. The following year he married Caroline Scott; they had two children. After studying law for two years, in 1854 Harrison moved to Indianapolis to begin a legal practice. He enthusiastically supported the new Republican party and soon launched his own political career. The Republicans recognized an attractive candidate in Harrison, whose great-grandfather, another Benjamin Harrison, had signed the Declaration of Independence, and whose grandfather, the legendary general William Henry Harrison, "Old Tippecanoe," had served briefly as the ninth president of the United States. Harrison moved up the political ladder from city attorney to secretary of the Republican State Committee to reporter for the Indiana Supreme Court between 1857 and 1862.

Harrison then served with distinction in the Civil War. He organized the Seventieth Indiana Regiment in July 1862 and within a month was promoted from second lieutenant to colonel. The regiment was stationed in Kentucky and Tennessee through 1863, then moved to Georgia in 1864 to join the command of General William Tecumseh Sherman in the campaign to capture Atlanta. Harrison demonstrated his leadership abilities in the clashes at Resaca and New Hope Church in May, and he was put in command of the First Brigade for the final drive toward Atlanta. When Confederate forces then launched a desperate attack at Peach Tree Creek, just two miles from Atlanta, on 20 July, Harrison led the Union forces that beat back the attack, thereby securing his reputation. He received a promotion to the rank of brigadier general in February 1865.

After the war Harrison returned to Indiana. Because of his formidable combination of family name and outstanding war record, Republican leaders continually urged him to run for a seat in the House of Representatives or for governor. When he tried and failed to win the nomination for governor in 1872, Harrison learned a lesson in the intricacies of Indiana politics. He refused to be a candidate for the gubernatorial nomination in 1876. Allegations of misconduct forced the Republican nominee to withdraw from the race on 2 August, however, and the party leaders nominated Harrison two days later. Harrison had only two months to campaign, and he lost by 5,000 votes. But there was widespread agreement that he had run a very strong race and had served the party well. Republican leaders outside of Indiana began to consider Harrison's potential. He had taken the first step along the path that would lead to the White House.

Over the next five years Harrison emerged as an important figure on the national political scene. The death of Senator Oliver P. Morton in 1877 had allowed him to take over as leader of the Republican party in Indiana. Indiana was one of four "swing" states—along with Connecticut, New Jersey, and New York—that could be carried by either party in late nineteenth-century presidential elections. President Rutherford B. Hayes had acknowledged Harrison's service to the party in Indiana and had provided the opportunity for Harrison to develop his reputation outside of Indiana. Hayes considered Harrison for a cabinet position but instead appointed him to the Mississippi River Commission in 1879.

Harrison chaired the Indiana delegation to the Republican National Convention of 1880 and strengthened his ties to the "Plumed Knight," Senator James G. Blaine of Maine. Blaine had lost the presidential nomination to Hayes in 1876. When Hayes chose not to seek a second term, one faction of the party—the Stalwarts—hoped to nominate Ulysses S. Grant for an unprecedented third term as president. An opposing faction—the Half Breeds—rallied behind Blaine. As the two sides deadlocked through ballot after ballot, Harrison steadfastly supported Blaine. Finally, when Blaine withdrew in favor of Representative James A. Garfield, Harrison delivered Indiana's votes to Garfield on the thirty-fifth ballot.

Garfield's victory in the presidential election presented Harrison with an opportunity to enter the cabinet, but the Indiana legislature elected Harrison to the Senate in 1881. From that point on he had as much claim to a possible presidential nomination as did any other Republican, with the exception of Blaine. Blaine, who had served briefly as secretary of state in 1881, finally did win the nomination at the Republican National Convention of 1884. As it turned out, the possible nomination of Harrison had been prevented by a clash in the Indiana delegation between Harrison forces and those supporting Walter Q. Gresham, a reformer who had waged a continuing struggle with Harrison for control of the party in Indiana. Ironically, a bitter rival had spared Harrison from what might have been a damaging contest with Blaine.

Blaine lost the presidential election to Democrat Grover Cleveland in a very close contest, and the "Blaine Legion" of his followers assumed that he would be willing to run again in 1888. Meanwhile, Louis T. Michener, leader of the Harrison forces in Indiana, and the influential Philadelphia banker Wharton Barker formed an effective national organization to build support for Harrison. They had two goals: to make sure that Gresham could not prevent the Indiana delegation from nominating Harrison and to convince delegates from other states that even though the Democrats had taken control of the Indiana legislature and had denied Harrison a second term in the Senate in 1887, he represented an attractive alternative should Blaine refuse the nomination. Everything began to fall into place when Blaine insisted that he did not wish to run again and advised his followers to support Harrison.

Though Harrison trailed four other candidates on the first ballot at the Republican National Convention of 1888, the backing of Blaine and the move to Harrison on the fourth ballot by most of New York's seventy-two delegates provided the momentum that led to the presidential nomination on the eighth ballot. The delegates then chose New York banker Levi Morton, a former congressman and former minister to France, as Harrison's running mate.

President Cleveland had defined the major issue in the election of 1888 when he devoted his entire Annual

Message of 1887 to a call for tariff reform. Harrison responded with what was recognized as a very effective campaign in defense of the protective tariff, delivering some ninety speeches from his "front porch" in Indianapolis. At the same time, Blaine campaigned enthusiastically for the Harrison-Morton ticket. Harrison carried the two most important "swing" states, New York and Indiana, and received 233 electoral votes to 168 for Cleveland, even though Cleveland, with a huge percentage of the popular vote in states throughout the solidly Democratic South of the post-Reconstruction era, led Harrison by about 100,000 votes in the nationwide total.

Harrison served as president during the four years preceding the depression of 1893. He has been criticized for contributing to the collapse of the nation's economy by accepting the agenda of the "Billion Dollar" Congress of 1890, which produced controversial legislation on monetary policy and tariff rates. The Sherman Silver Purchase Act assured silver producers that the federal government would purchase 4.5 million ounces of silver a month, a guarantee perceived as a threat to the gold standard. The McKinley Tariff raised import duties to a record high level, and Democrats lashed out at the legislation as the cause of higher prices. Even if the two laws did not create the conditions that brought about a crisis in the economy, they led the list of issues that contributed to landslide victories for the Democrats in the congressional election of 1890 and in the presidential election of 1892.

In control of both the executive and legislative branches of the federal government for the first time in fifteen years, Republicans had steamrollered the Democratic opposition in the House of Representatives and in the Senate. Speaker of the House Thomas B. Reed had eliminated use of the "silent" or "disappearing" quorum to block legislation. When Democrats called for a quorum and refused to answer to their names, "Czar" Reed ruled that they were "present," making it possible for Republicans to pass any legislation on a party line vote. Even more dramatic developments had changed the character of the Senate. When six new states (Idaho, Montana, North Dakota, South Dakota, Washington, and Wyoming) entered the Union in 1889–1890, they produced twelve new Republican members of the Senate who formed the "silver" bloc, along with their Republican colleagues from Colorado, Kansas, Nebraska, and Nevada. Thus, some twenty senators from the West could often block legislation unless they received support for silver producers in return.

If Republicans had chosen to interpret their narrow victory in 1888 as a mandate for "activism," they had ignored an erosion of support for the party in the Midwest, which seemed to signal voter discontent with Republican activism on social issues. For example, Republicans, many of them native-born middle- and upper-class Protestants, had crusaded for a ban on the Sunday sale of alcoholic beverages, against the wishes of working-class voters, many of them German and Irish Catholic immigrants. Some Republicans had

called for a complete prohibition on the sale of alcoholic beverages. At the same time Republicans had demanded that only the English language be used for instruction in all schools, a stand that alienated Americans of German origin throughout the Midwest. Both Iowa and Ohio elected Democratic governors in 1889, losses that presaged hard times ahead for Republicans.

In 1890 the party lost some eighty seats in the House of Representatives and lost control to the Democrats. The election seemed to be a referendum on Harrison's leadership, particularly because he had tried to reverse the tide with a campaign tour of almost 3,000 miles across the Midwest. Many Republicans, including some of the most powerful figures in the party, began to see Harrison as a "lame duck" who could not possibly lead them to victory in the presidential election of 1892. Three state bosses—Thomas C. Platt of New York, Senator Matthew Quay of Pennsylvania, the national chairman of the party, and James S. Clarkson of Iowa, the party's national vice chairman—created an extremely awkward situation for Harrison by convincing Blaine, serving once again as secretary of state, to be a candidate for the nomination at the Republican National Convention of 1892.

Ironically, Harrison and Blaine had agreed on the objectives of the new, more aggressive foreign policy that they began developing in the early 1890s and that would culminate in the creation of an American Empire, stretching from Puerto Rico in the Caribbean to Hawaii and the Philippines in the Pacific, in the aftermath of the Spanish-American War of 1898. Traditionally, historians had assumed that Blaine, who had launched several important initiatives during his nine months as secretary of state in 1881, once again had taken charge of foreign policy in the Harrison administration. Actually, as Blaine struggled with deteriorating health and devastating personal problems, Harrison became the driving force behind his administration's foreign policy. Harrison vigorously pursued three related objectives: construction of a modern navy, control of a Central American canal, and acquisition of naval bases in the Caribbean and in the Pacific.

Harrison provided unqualified support for Secretary of the Navy Benjamin F. Tracy, who in 1890 convinced the Congress to approve construction of the first three American battleships. The United States had delayed building a modern navy of steel warships until 1883. Through the 1880s Congress had continued to emphasize the defensive character of the navy. The new battleships—the *Indiana*, the *Massachusetts*, and the *Oregon*—advanced naval construction by a generation. Designated "coastline" battleships to appease those in Congress who opposed building a navy that could be used for offensive purposes, the three warships of more than 10,000 tons displacement had the potential to do more than merely defend American territory. Finally, in 1892, Harrison and Tracy persuaded Congress to vote the funds for construction of the *Iowa*, the first seagoing battleship of 11,400 tons displacement. The president and his secretary of the navy did not try to disguise their belief that the United States should become a legitimate naval power.

Harrison and Blaine failed to convince Congress to guarantee the bonds of the private company that had hoped to build a canal across Nicaragua, and they also failed to obtain the first American naval base in the Caribbean—in Haiti. These failures, however, along with some important firsts, established the foundation for what the United States would accomplish before the end of the decade. In 1889 the Harrison administration accepted the first protectorate for the United States, working with Germany and Great Britain to share control over Samoa in the distant Pacific. Blaine presided over the first modern Pan-American Conference, held in Washington between October 1889 and April 1890. Finally, Harrison attempted to annex Hawaii in February 1893, after a coup organized by American residents had overthrown the monarchy. But being a lame duck, he had no chance of accomplishing that goal.

Harrison had won a second nomination on the first ballot at the Republican National Convention of 1892. It had not been easy. Blaine, who resigned just days before the opening of the convention, had allowed the bosses to use his name, and he received 182 votes. Another 182 delegates supported Governor William McKinley of Ohio. The combined votes for Blaine and McKinley indicated the depth of the opposition to Harrison, who seemed reluctant to accept another nomination, particularly because of his wife's serious illness. Caroline Harrison died in the midst of the campaign, on 25 October, and Harrison lost all interest in the race.

Grover Cleveland, the Democratic candidate for president for the third straight time, capitalized on continuing opposition to the McKinley Tariff and on the threat to Democrats of the so-called "Force Bill," a failed attempt by Republicans in Congress to protect the voting rights of African Americans in the South. Even the emergence of a third national party, the People's party, or Populists, which drew almost all of its support from discontented farmers in the states of the Great Plains, did not diminish the scope of Cleveland's victory in 1892. The Democrats carried all four swing states and, for the first time since the Civil War, Illinois and Wisconsin as well. The voters returned Grover Cleveland to office by an electoral count of 277 to 145.

Harrison returned to Indianapolis to practice law for clients who wished to retain the services of a former president and who could afford his fees. In 1894, one year after the death of railroad magnate Leland Stanford, who had served with Harrison in the Senate, Harrison accepted a generous honorarium and agreed to honor the memory of Stanford with a series of lectures at Stanford University. In 1896 he married a much younger woman, Mary Lord Dimmick, the widowed niece of Caroline Harrison. They had one child. Harrison then agreed, for a very large fee, to represent the government of Venezuela in a lingering boundary dispute with British Guiana. He went to Europe for

the first time in 1899 to take part in the arbitration of the case. Harrison died in Indianapolis.

Historians consistently have rated Harrison at the low end of the "average" presidents of the United States. Typically described as reserved and self-contained, perhaps he was unsuited for the political arena of the late nineteenth century. But he was the president who appointed Theodore Roosevelt to his first national office, as civil service commissioner, and whose administration produced the Sherman Antitrust Act, the most important legislation of its kind in the nation's history. He deserves recognition as one of those devout, honest, sober leaders of the generation that founded the Republican party and as one who tried to keep the nation on an even keel through the turbulent years of the Gilded Age.

• Harrison's papers are in the Manuscripts Division, Library of Congress. Albert T. Volwiler, with exclusive access to the Harrison papers and continuing financial support from Mary Harrison and several other influential individuals in Indianapolis, worked on an authorized biography between 1926 and 1940 but did not complete the project. Volwiler did, however, make an important contribution to the limited body of literature on Harrison, editing *The Correspondence between Benjamin Harrison and James G. Blaine, 1882–1893* (1940). The Reverend Harry J. Sievers produced a three-volume biography of Harrison. In *Benjamin Harrison, Hoosier Warrior, 1833–1865* (1952) and *Benjamin Harrison, Hoosier Statesman: From the Civil War to the White House, 1865–1888* (1959), Sievers provides a detailed account of Harrison's life before he became president. He does not provide the same detail in the final volume, *Benjamin Harrison, Hoosier President: The White House and After* (1968). Homer Socolofsky and Allan Spetter, *The Presidency of Benjamin Harrison* (1987), is the only recent book-length treatment of any aspect of Harrison's career.

ALLAN BURTON SPETTER

HARRISON, Caroline Lavinia Scott (1 Oct. 1832–25 Oct. 1892), first wife of Benjamin Harrison (1833–1901), the twenty-third president of the United States, was born in Oxford, Ohio, the daughter of John Witherspoon Scott, an ordained Presbyterian minister and college professor, and Mary Potts Neal. She attended the Oxford Female Institute, a school her father had helped found, and she briefly taught piano there (1851–1852). In 1853 she married Benjamin Harrison, whom she had met while he was attending Miami University, and the next year she moved with him to Indianapolis, Indiana, where he practiced law. Although he was a grandson of the ninth president of the United States, Benjamin Harrison earned little the first years of their marriage, and acquaintances commented on how cheerfully his wife accepted her reduced circumstances. Records of the First Presbyterian Church in Indianapolis (where the Harrisons were members) referred to her "artistic tastes" and "charming vitality." She gave birth to two children before her husband's law practice was well established. A third child died at birth.

After Benjamin Harrison volunteered to serve in the Civil War in 1862, his wife visited him in Kentucky and became active in several U.S. organizations centered on the war effort, including the U.S. Sanitary Commission. At the conclusion of the war he resumed his law practice and rose quickly in the ranks of the Indiana Republican party. During his term in the U.S. Senate (1881–1887), Caroline Harrison accompanied him to the nation's capital, where the family lived in a rented suite, and she devoted time to several of Washington's charitable organizations, including the City Orphan Asylum.

As first lady (1889–1892) Harrison exemplified domesticity. One report singled her out as the "best housekeeper the White House has ever known," although her mother once pointed out that she had never shown interest in such matters. She did oversee the installation of electricity in the White House (1891) and arrange for the cleaning and modernization of the kitchens, but her plan for an elaborate enlargement of the Executive Mansion failed. Several of her predecessors had complained about the cramped living quarters on the second floor of the White House. The problem of space was a pressing one for the Harrisons because they had a large extended family living with them, including their son and daughter with their respective spouses and children and the first lady's father, sister, and a widowed young niece. Rather than move her family elsewhere, Harrison planned a drastic enlargement of the existing White House. Working with architect Frederick D. Owen, she developed a plan for a huge, horseshoe-shaped building with two new wings, one to serve as a museum for the nation's treasures and the other as office space for the president's staff. Congress, however, balked at providing funds for the addition, reportedly because of dissatisfaction with one of the president's appointments, and the Harrisons had to make do with a general cleanup and reorganization of the existing space.

As first lady, Harrison is remembered for her artistic interests. She painted china, often surprising a friend or an admiring fan with a piece she had decorated. In selecting a new dining service for the Executive Mansion, she chose a nationalistic motif (very much in style at the time) but one that was more restrained than those chosen by some of her predecessors. Rather than turn to a professional artist, she herself designed a pattern that featured a delicate border of corn and goldenrod surrounding forty-eight stars and the seal of the United States.

Emphasizing patriotic themes and American workmanship in her private life as well as in her purchases for the president's house, she enthusiastically sought out her country's products. With reluctance she agreed to have the presidential china made in France when American samples were judged inferior. In an attempt to enhance the historical significance of the Executive Mansion, she began to collect presidential china, including remnants of sets of dishes used by previous presidents and their families. When the Daughters of the American Revolution formed in 1890, she consented to serve as that group's first president general.

Evidence suggests that Harrison had considerable interest in politics, even though the society in which she lived did not encourage women to follow such an interest. Most of her early letters have not survived, but the extant ones contain extensive references to political matters. She also lent her prestige to a group of Baltimore women who were raising funds to help open the Johns Hopkins University Medical School: their assistance was offered on the condition that women candidates be admitted.

Harrison became ill in early 1892, and in an attempt to recuperate she chose not to take the usual family vacation at Cape May, New Jersey, in order to go to Loon Lake, a vacation area of the Adirondacks. The mountain air did little for her tuberculosis, and she returned to Washington, D.C., where she died in October, the second president's wife to succumb in the Executive Mansion. She was buried in the Crown Hill Cemetery in Indianapolis.

• Caroline Harrison's papers, including many letters from her husband to her and a few from her to him, are included in the Benjamin Harrison Presidential Papers, Manuscript Division, Library of Congress. No full biography of her exists, but she is the subject of a very laudatory 27-page pamphlet: Harriet McIntire Foster, "Mrs. Benjamin Harrison: First President General of the National Society of the DAR" (1908). Her husband's biographers refer to her role in his life and career: Harry J. Sievers, *Benjamin Harrison* (3 vols., 1952–1968), and Homer Socolofsky and Allan B. Spetter, *The Presidency of Benjamin Harrison* (1987). For her role in the founding of the Johns Hopkins Hospital and School of Medicine, see Alan M. Chesney, *The Johns Hopkins Hospital and School of Medicine*, vol. 1 (1943), pp. 193–201.

BETTY BOYD CAROLI

HARRISON, Carter Henry (15 Feb. 1825–28 Oct. 1893), mayor of Chicago, was born in Fayette County, Kentucky, the son of Carter Henry Harrison, a plantation owner, and Caroline Evalind Russell. Harrison was born in a log cabin, but this did not imply poverty or deprivation, simply the newness of his family estate in the bluegrass region of Kentucky. He came from a family that traced its lineage back to the 1630s in colonial Virginia, and he was distantly related to two American presidents, William Henry Harrison and Benjamin Harrison (1833–1901). Though called Carter Henry Harrison I in Chicago to distinguish him from his son Carter Henry Harrison, Jr. (1860–1953), who also became mayor, he was actually the third of his line to carry the name.

His father died when Harrison was only four months old, so he was educated at home by his mother until about age fifteen, when a private tutor prepared him for college. He graduated from Yale in 1845, returned to Kentucky to operate his plantation, took a law degree at Transylvania College in Lexington, and was admitted to the bar in 1855. He married Sophonisba Preston the same year, and they determined to leave Kentucky and make their lives elsewhere.

After visiting St. Louis and Galena, the couple settled in Chicago, sold their Kentucky property, and invested the proceeds in city real estate. "A buyer rather than a seller," Harrison invested for the long term, and therefore the growth of his adopted city also meant the growth of his personal capital. He became an outspoken city booster who wedded his fortunes to the growth of this brash, boisterous boom town. He unblushingly called Chicago "his bride."

Harrison's family had been Whigs in Kentucky, but he became a Unionist Democrat, supporting Stephen A. Douglas, just before the Civil War. He entered politics relatively late in life, at age forty-five, when the leading citizens of Chicago put together an emergency slate to reconstruct the city after the devastating Chicago fire of 1871. He was elected to one term as county commissioner on this "Fire Proof Ticket" in 1871, then ran unsuccessfully for Congress in 1872. He subsequently gained election to Congress as a Democrat in 1874 and 1876, championing transportation improvements for Illinois and delivering patriotic oratory at the 1876 Centennial Exposition in Philadelphia.

In September 1876 Harrison's wife died in Germany, where she had been journeying for her health. Returning to Chicago with his four surviving children (six others had died in childhood), Harrison ran successfully for mayor in 1879 and was elected to four consecutive two-year terms. Readily identified by the black felt slouch hat that he wore, he crisscrossed the city's dusty streets on his white mare, often at a full gallop. He held court for the public daily in city hall and applied business methods to the administration of his office, restoring the city's credit by a policy of retrenchment during his first term.

The city's first full-time professional politician, Harrison built a personal following of loyal retainers, but it would be inaccurate to call this a political machine. Chicago politics was too fragmented for any one man to control. No organization like the Tammany Hall machine in New York or the Richard J. Daley machine later in Chicago dominated the scene. Chicago politics was a bipartisan jungle of rival bosses and factions. Harrison earned his support through a combination of personal charisma and businesslike administration. He balanced different ethnic and economic groups and many rival leaders and factions in an uneasy coalition.

Though Harrison was a Protestant by upbringing, he was no Puritan. Holding broad-minded views on gambling, liquor, and prostitution, he never attempted to enforce Sunday closing ordinances or any other blue laws that the city council might pass. A rip-roaring stump speaker, able to discourse off-the-cuff for hours and utter a convincing phrase or two in nearly every European language, he appealed forcefully to immigrant voters. Throughout his mayoral years, he combined the support of the business classes with the working masses, though the press, the Protestant pulpit, and the evangelical middle class usually opposed him.

During his second term as mayor, in 1881 Harrison married Marguerite Stearns, whom he had met on a European vacation. They had no children. During his third term, he ran unsuccessfully for governor of Illinois. His wife's ill health prompted him to retire after his fourth term, but Marguerite Harrison died shortly after he left office in 1887, leaving him a widower for the second time. He spent the next eighteen months on a round-the-world tour.

Harrison was defeated in the 1891 mayoralty race but earned one more term as mayor in 1893. He served as host to the world at the Columbian Exposition, which ran in Chicago throughout 1893. His enthusiastic city boosterism suited the mood of the World's Fair perfectly. On Saturday, 28 October 1893, in the waning days of the fair, he greeted the mayors of cities from all over the United States with a final soaring speech: "This is a city that was a morass when I came into the world sixty-eight and one-half years ago. . . . What is it now? The second city of America." That evening, when he returned to his home on the West Side of the city, Harrison was shot to death by a disappointed office seeker, Patrick Eugene Prendergast. His assassination shocked the city and led to the passage of Chicago's first civil service ordinance.

Since Harrison served for five terms as Chicago mayor and his son also served five terms, the forty years from the Chicago fire to the outbreak of the First World War may be termed the age of Harrison in Chicago politics. Harrison presided over a transitional period in city politics, combining the personal touch of a small-town notable with the ethnic appeals and backroom deals of the professional politician. His attraction of the Catholic and Jewish immigrant masses into the Democratic party laid the foundation for the later Democratic machine in Chicago.

A panel of forty scholars polled in 1987 by historians Paul M. Green and Melvin G. Holli ranked Harrison second only to Daley as the best mayor Chicago had ever had. Harrison's biographer, Claudius O. Johnson, called him "an honest man who was at the same time a good politician and a good administrator." An ethnic newspaper, the *Skandinaven*, summed up his political style perfectly, "His career was a series of dramatic incidents enveloped in a haze of festivities."

• No collection of Harrison papers has survived. A brief sketch of his life was published along with the "Proceedings of a Memorial Meeting of the City Council of the City of Chicago," 16 Nov. 1893. Two indifferent biographies are Willis John Abbot, *Carter Henry Harrison: A Memoir* (1895), and Claudius O. Johnson, *Carter Henry Harrison I: Political Leader* (1928). A poll of scholars ranking Chicago mayors can be found in Paul M. Green and Melvin G. Holli, eds., *The Mayors: The Chicago Political Tradition* (1987). That volume does not include an article about Carter Harrison I, but the chapter by Edward R. Kantowicz on Carter Harrison, Jr., does contain a few pages summarizing the father's career.

EDWARD R. KANTOWICZ

HARRISON, Carter Henry, Jr. (23 Apr. 1860–25 Dec. 1953), five-time mayor of Chicago, was born in Chicago, Illinois, the son of Carter Henry Harrison, Sr., who also served five terms as mayor, and Sophonisba Preston. Harrison grew up on the western outskirts of the city, in a district heavily populated by Kentucky natives like his father. Educated first in Chicago public schools, he attended a German Gymnasium from 1873 to 1876 while his mother visited Europe for a rest cure. After his mother's death in 1876, he returned to Chicago, where the public school authorities refused to recognize his foreign courses. He enrolled instead at the Catholic prep school St. Ignatius College and received the equivalent of his high school and undergraduate schooling, graduating in 1881. He earned a law degree from Yale University in 1883.

The young Harrison of Chicago resembled in many ways the young Theodore Roosevelt of New York, his close contemporary in age. Both men idolized their wealthy, handsome fathers; both traveled extensively in Europe and attended the best schools. Their independently wealthy status enabled them each to devote time to "finding himself." While Roosevelt headed west in the 1880s to punch cows and write history, Harrison spent that decade writing poetry and practicing journalism under the pseudonym Cecil H. Harcourt. The future president was a Republican and the Chicagoan a Democrat, and Harrison lacked Roosevelt's boundless energy and bellicose temperament. Yet both men were well-bred patricians who plunged willingly into the hurly-burly of politics. Had Harrison later gained the Democratic presidential nomination, which he sought in 1904, he would have opposed the Republican president Theodore Roosevelt.

Although his presidential ambitions were to be thwarted, Harrison's background suited him perfectly for Chicago politics. A Protestant by birth, educated in Germany, at Irish-Catholic St. Ignatius, and at WASPY Yale, he was nearly a balanced ticket all by himself. His wife, Edith Ogden (whom he married in 1888), was a southern Catholic from New Orleans, who raised the two Harrison children as Catholics. This multiethnic background, plus the memory of his popular father, who had been assassinated in 1893 by a disappointed office seeker, gave Harrison many advantages when he ran for mayor himself. In 1897 he won election to the first of four consecutive two-year terms, becoming the first native Chicagoan elected mayor. In 1905 he retired to California for a time; he then returned to serve Chicago's first four-year mayoral term from 1911 to 1915.

Throughout his career, Harrison practiced the politics of balance, juggling the support of diverse and seemingly incompatible groups. He counted heavily on Catholic and Jewish immigrants, whose loyalty had been won by his father, but he also earned a significant number of votes from middle-class Protestants who appreciated his honest and businesslike approach to administration. Yet his most consistent support came from the unsavory political bosses "Bathhouse" John Coughlin and Michael "Hinky Dink" Kenna, who controlled the brothels, saloons, and flophouses of the downtown First Ward.

Harrison was, in his fashion, a progressive reformer, though many of his contemporaries did not consider him so. He avoided moral reform causes, such as Prohibition, that would alienate both the immigrants and the saloonkeeper politicians. Although his father had been murdered by a spoilsman, Harrison did not push civil service reform because he relied too heavily on political patronage himself. He did, however, adopt consistent and courageous reform positions on many of the economic issues facing the city. In particular, he insisted that utility and transportation companies that had been granted franchises to operate in Chicago pay a fair share of their profits as compensation to the city government.

Harrison earned his reputation as a reformer primarily for his firm and successful opposition to the streetcar companies controlled by Charles Tyson Yerkes. In 1897, the year Harrison was first elected mayor, Yerkes tried to bribe the state legislature into granting him a fifty-year franchise for the streetcar lines on the west and north sides of the city, with minimal compensation to the city government. Harrison raced to the state capital in Springfield with reform aldermen and lobbied enough legislative votes to defeat the bill. Yerkes then changed tactics and obtained another bill authorizing city councils to grant fifty-year franchises. The political struggle thus shifted to the Chicago City Council. In December 1898 Harrison's allies, including the notorious Kenna and Coughlin, voted down Yerkes's fifty-year franchise.

Harrison pursued a consistent transportation policy for the city. He demanded that streetcar companies improve the speed, safety, and comfort of their service; pay adequate compensation to the city for their franchises; and grant the city an option to purchase and operate the streetcar lines as a municipal system at some future date. He also hoped to build a subway system for the city. He did not attain any of these objectives during his terms of office, but a comprehensive settlement between the city and the streetcar companies was passed in 1907, largely along the lines Harrison had proposed. A subway was built much later in the 1940s.

After his short retirement, Harrison entered the city's first mayoral primary in 1911, winning the Democratic nomination, then defeating another reform candidate, political science professor Charles E. Merriam, for the first four-year term. Scandals in the First Ward eventually forced Harrison to denounce his unsavory allies, Kenna and Coughlin. The opposition of the Irish political bosses finally brought his career to a close with a defeat in the 1915 Democratic primary.

Though he lived nearly forty more years in Chicago, where he also died, he never ran for elective office again. He wrote not one but two autobiographies, evening old scores and telling his side of the political story. He was appointed U.S. Customs collector for the port of Chicago by Franklin D. Roosevelt in the 1930s.

Harrison was neither a flamboyant speaker like his father nor a crusading zealot like so many other progressives. In fact, he combined some of the qualities of both boss and reformer, thus blurring his image and making him hard to define. The most frequent criticism of his administration was his failure to lead the city vigorously enough. A harmonizer and unifier, Harrison practiced the politics of balance, which, in a rapidly growing, ethnically divided, and politically factionalized city, represented no easy task. He himself provided his best epitaph: "I have always been a little in advance of public opinion in Chicago. It is true I have not been so far ahead the people could not see me."

• There is a small collection of Harrison papers at the Newberry Library in Chicago. Unfortunately, Harrison himself "sanitized" his correspondence before donating it to the library. Of his two autobiographies, *Stormy Years* (1935) and *Growing Up with Chicago* (1944), the former is the more interesting and valuable source. Edward R. Kantowicz is the author of a chapter on Harrison in *The Mayors: The Chicago Political Tradition*, ed. Paul M. Green and Melvin G. Holli (1987), and a chapter on Harrison's ethnic politics in Kantowicz, *Polish-American Politics in Chicago* (1972).

EDWARD R. KANTOWICZ

HARRISON, Constance Cary (25 Apr. 1843–21 Nov. 1920), writer, was born in Lexington, Kentucky, the daughter of Archibald Cary, a lawyer and newspaper editor, and Monimia Fairfax. Her forebears included many distinguished Americans. Her paternal grandfather was Wilson Jefferson Cary, nephew of Thomas Jefferson, and her paternal grandmother, Virginia Randolph Cary, was the author of novels, essays, and poems. Her maternal grandfather, Thomas Fairfax, was ninth Lord Fairfax, baron of Cameron in the Scottish peerage, though he never claimed the title. Constance Cary's distinguished ancestry shaped her life— making her at home in society in Virginia, in New York City, and in Europe—and her work. Her first signed contribution to a national magazine, "A Little Centennial Lady," published in *Scribner's Monthly Magazine* in July 1876, tells the story of Sally Fairfax, the younger sister of Constance's grandfather, Thomas Fairfax. Sally Fairfax died young, but at her last ball General George Washington danced with her and devoted "himself to her especially." Constance wrote other historical pieces drawing upon family diaries and records, and she also used her knowledge of her aristocratic Virginian past in her fiction.

When Constance Cary was born, her father was studying law at Transylvania University; later, the family lived in Cumberland, Maryland, where Archibald Cary edited the *Cumberland Citizen*. After his death in 1854, Constance's mother took her three children home to the Fairfax family estate, "Vaucluse," outside Alexandria, Virginia. There Constance was educated, first by a French governess and then sent to the boarding school of Hubert Pierre Lefebvre in Richmond. When Vaucluse was threatened by Union troops in 1861, Constance fled to Richmond, where her mother joined her in 1862. They nursed soldiers and suffered the privations and rigors of wartime Richmond, but Constance was able to participate in the social life of the city, mingling with well-known figures of the Confederacy—Robert E. Lee, Jefferson

Davis, and others. Auburn-haired Constance was one of three Cary cousins, the other two Jennie and Hetty Cary. Early in the war these three cousins made the first Confederate flags; Constance's flag traveled with General Earl Van Dorn. Mary Chesnut makes frequent mention of the Cary cousins, calling Constance "witty" and noting her "classically perfect" profile.

Constance Cary began her long writing career in Richmond with a romantic love story, "A Summer Idyll," published serially in the *Southern Illustrated News* in November and December 1862. She continued to publish for that periodical during the war under the pen name "Refugitta," and she contributed as well to the *Magnolia: A Southern Home Journal*. She fell in love with Burton Norvell Harrison during the war years. An 1859 Yale graduate, Harrison was selected to be Jefferson Davis's private secretary. He served in that position until 1865 when he was arrested in Georgia along with Davis and then imprisoned at Fort Delaware for nine months.

After the war, Constance and her mother spent a year in France, where she studied music and French. They returned home in 1867, and Constance was married to Burton Harrison on 26 November at the New York home of her uncle, Gouverneur Morris. The Harrisons lived in New York City, where he was a successful lawyer, and she was active in New York society, participating in charitable activities and the literary life of the city. The Harrisons were the parents of three sons and a daughter who died in infancy. Constance traveled widely—to England, France, Italy, Russia, Spain, Greece, Egypt, Morocco, and other countries. After her husband's death in 1904, she moved to Washington, D.C., where she died.

Along with family and social life, Constance Cary Harrison was a prolific author. She published numerous novels and books of short fiction as well as magazine articles, plays, folk tales, fairy tales, children's stories, a conduct book for debutantes, and a book of home decoration. She translated and adapted French plays. In her autobiography, *Recollections Grave and Gay* (1911), she referred to her writing casually as "professional ink splashing" that brought her pleasure, but her correspondence, her diaries, and the quantity of her work show that she was a disciplined and serious writer.

Her work is all but forgotten now with the exception of the autobiography, published when she was sixty-eight, which includes a detailed account of her experiences in wartime Richmond. More idealized than Mary Chesnut's account, it contains, nevertheless, moving accounts of such events as Jefferson Davis's inauguration, Stonewall Jackson's death, Hetty Cary's marriage to General John Pegram in St. Paul's Church and then his funeral three weeks later in the same church.

Her fiction is, in general, about two subjects—the idealized life of the old South, Virginia specifically, and the manners of New Yorkers in the Gilded Age, frequently as they came in contact with Europeans.

Two novels published in 1890 illustrate her subjects. *Flower de Hundred*, a plantation novel, depicts an Edenic life in the South before the Civil War with the last great ball before that way of life is replaced by the hellishness of the war. In *The Anglomaniacs* Harrison treats the manners of New Yorkers satirically as she tells the story of spirited young Lily Floyd-Curtis, whose mother is so determined to bring about a marriage between her daughter and Lord Melrose that she offers the titled Englishman $4 million to marry Lily.

In all of her fiction Harrison was superb in depicting setting, whether a plantation in Virginia, an ocean liner, or places in England, Spain, or Morocco. She was also adept in writing dialogue, including dialect. Those two qualities she shares with other local-color writers. But she was never able to construct believable plots based on the needs of her characters. She drew instead on formulaic, romantic plots with farfetched, frequently Gothic, elements. Her characters lack depth and are depicted with attention to surface appearance. She knew well only her own class and was unable to treat believably the great conflicts of her time. Her work is of the genre of Thomas Nelson Page and lacks the irony, depth, and realism of Ellen Glasgow, who dealt with Virginian materials a generation after Harrison.

In both her autobiography and *Flower de Hundred*, for example, Harrison expresses her opposition to slavery and to war. Her fictional depictions of slaves, however, are stereotypical and lack any awareness of slaves as individual human beings. Even as she satirized materialistic New Yorkers striving to gain respectability by marrying titled Europeans, she treated the material as surface comedy without the insight of Edith Wharton or Henry James (1843–1916).

Constance Cary Harrison was a serious writer who produced a large body of work. She was, in a sense, an artistic prisoner of her class and of her time who remained committed to the values of her genteel and aristocratic past.

• Relevant papers, including the typed manuscript of "About It and About," the autobiography of Harrison's son, Francis Burton Harrison, are found in the Alderman Library, University of Virginia. The Burton Norvell Harrison Family Papers in the Library of Congress Manuscript Collection include papers of Mrs. Harrison. Selected other books by Constance Cary Harrison not mentioned in the text are: *The Story of Helen Troy* (1881), *Woman's Handiwork in Modern Homes* (1881), *The Old-Fashioned Fairy Book* (1884), *Folk and Fairy Tales* (1885), *Bar Harbor Days* (1887), *Belhaven Tales; Crow's Nest; Una and King David* (1892), *An Edelweiss of the Sierras; Golden-rod, and Other Tales* (1892), *A Daughter of the South, and Shorter Stories* (1892), *Sweet Bells Out of Tune* (1893), *A Bachelor Maid* (1894), *An Errant Wooing* (1895), *A Son of the Old Dominion* (1897), *Good Americans* (1898), *The Well-Bred Girl in Society* (1898), *The Carcellini Emerald, with Other Tales* (1899), *A Triple Entanglement* (1899), *A Princess of the Hills* (1901), *The Carlyles* (1905), and *The Count and the Congressman* (1908). Dorothy Scura, "Homage to Constance Cary Harrison," *Southern Humanities Review*, Bicentennial Issue (1976): 35–46, connects Harrison and her fiction to the Civil War and the American centennial. Sherrolyn Maxwell, "Constance Cary Harrison: American Woman of Letters, 1843–1920," (Ph.D. diss., Univ. of North Carolina, 1977), is the fullest available treatment of Harrison's life and fiction. See also Edna Hartness, "Plantation Life in Virginia as Revealed in Mrs. Burton Harrison's Fiction" (M.A. thesis, Duke Univ., 1939). An obituary is in the *Richmond News Leader*, 23 Nov. 1920.

DOROTHY M. SCURA

HARRISON, Dutch (29 Mar. 1910–19 June 1982), professional golfer, was born Ernest Joseph Harrison in Conway, Arkansas, the son of David Harrison, a plantation overseer, and Tessia (maiden name unknown).

As a small child Harrison worked on the plantation at various chores. When his father took employment as a police officer in Little Rock, the family moved to a farm about fifty yards from the third hole of Little Rock Country Club. At age twelve Harrison began caddying at the club and at fifteen began to play regularly. Naturally left-handed, he became a right-handed player at the instruction of the club professional, Herman "Hack" Hackbarth. He won the Arkansas Amateur Championship in 1929 and turned professional in 1930.

Initially Harrison played primarily in tournaments in Texas, barely subsisting on his meager winnings. Often he rode railroad freight cars to sites of play. With the aid of businessmen in Little Rock, he began playing on the Professional Golfers Association (PGA) Tour in 1935. Giving him connections with the businessmen was Emma Plunkett, a secretary for a law firm in which the governor of Arkansas had an interest. She and Harrison married in 1937. He won four minor tournaments that year and captured his first championship on the tour, the Texas Open, in 1939. For nine of the next ten years Harrison finished among the top ten money winners on the tour. He also gained notoriety at the U.S. Open in 1940 when he and Ed "Porky" Oliver were disqualified for starting play before their assigned tee time.

During World War II Harrison served in the U.S. Army Air Corps. With the air corps providing him leaves and transportation, he played in numerous exhibitions and many tour events. After his discharge in 1945 he returned to the tour and won the Hawaiian Open in 1947, the Canadian Open in 1949, and the Western Open in 1953. Although never claiming a major championship, he won the Vardon Trophy in 1954 for the lowest average score per round, 70.41, in tournament play; at that time he was the oldest man ever to win the trophy. Altogether he captured 14 PGA titles and played on the U.S. Ryder Cup team three times. Playing on the senior tour in the 1960s, he won five National Senior opens. In 1962 he was elected to the PGA Hall of Fame.

Harrison possessed a fluid swing marked by a "beautiful natural rhythm." He was particularly good in iron play, often making "brilliant" approach shots to the flag. He was not long off the tee, concentrating on keeping his ball in the fairway. Nonetheless, when necessary he was able to hit a long ball by lengthening the arc of his swing.

Harrison was a colorful man who made friends with people from all walks of life. His biographer Beach Leighton called him the "Will Rogers of the Fairway." He played in numerous pro-amateur tournaments, frequently with figures from the world of entertainment as his partners. He was especially popular with galleries, always engaging them in witty repartee as he chewed on a cigar. His language was an important element in his self-definition. His nickname came, he explained, "from my habit of twistin' word an' confusin' pals. They'd understand 'bout every third word." He always had a story on the "tip of his tongue" told in an Arkansas drawl, a "cornpone" style of the Old South. He addressed everyone as "Mistuh" or "Missus." Bob Broeg, sports editor of the *St. Louis Post-Dispatch*, once called him the "Satchel Paige of the knickers set." At the Seminole Open in 1940, paired with the duke of Windsor, he introduced himself in a familiar way: "Dukie, ol' boy, it's nice to meet you. I'm the Dutch of Arkansas." When the duke hit a good shot, Harrison slapped him on the back and said "Atta boy, Dukie." He was notorious in a picaresque way as a hustler, setting up a "pigeon" as an easy mark on a nassau, in which players wager an equal amount of money on the front nine, the back nine, and the entire round. What money he won betting on golf was usually lost betting on the horses.

Constantly traveling to tour events and pro-amateur tournaments in the United States and tournaments in the Far East and Europe, Harrison ineluctably became known as the "Arkansas Traveler." He was also in motion as a club professional, taking positions at clubs in Pennsylvania, Illinois, Oklahoma, and Missouri. His journeys in golf fashioned much of his personal life. After his first marriage ended in divorce in 1950, he married Thelma Akana, territorial senator from Hawaii, that same year; he had met her in 1949 on his way to the Luzon to play in the Philippine World Open Championship. She died in 1972. That year he met Shirley Perlstein Rubin on a flight to the Las Vegas National Senior Open; they were married in 1973 and remained together until his death in St. Louis. He had no children from any of his marriages.

Harrison played on the tour in two decades when, despite the increasing size of purses, public interest in golf slackened, a result, in part, of Bobby Jones's retirement and the Great Depression, and did not revive until the emergence of Arnold Palmer and television broadcasts of golf events. In his day, the dispassionate "precisionists"—Ben Hogan and Byron Nelson, for example—dominated the game; but Harrison, with his rollicking ways, helped sustain its human dimension. Akin to Dizzy Dean in baseball, he gave professional golf a flamboyant touch.

• The PGA Tour at Sawgrass, Fla., has records relating to Harrison on the tour. Brief but not very useful entries on Harrison are in several golf and sports encyclopedias. Beach Leighton, a good friend of Harrison, published a biography, *Mr. Dutch: The Arkansas Traveler* (1991). Though reverential, eulogistic, and curiously omissive at important points, it provides a wealth of anecdotal detail. For an explanation of the status of golf in the nation during the period, see Benjamin G. Rader, *American Sports: From the Age of Folk Games to the Age of Spectators* (1983). Dave Dorr wrote a lengthy column effectively summarizing his life as a golfer and his personality in the *St. Louis Post-Dispatch*, 20 June 1982. An obituary is in the *New York Times*, 20 June 1982.

CARL M. BECKER

HARRISON, Elizabeth (1 Sept. 1849–31 Oct. 1927), kindergarten educator, was born in Athens, Kentucky, the daughter of Isaac Webb Harrison, a dry goods merchant, and Elizabeth Thompson Harrison. When she was seven years old, the family moved to Davenport, Iowa, where she attended school, finishing high school first in her class.

In 1879 she moved to Chicago, where she enrolled in the kindergarten training classes of Alice Putnam, a leader in the kindergarten movement in the city, and in 1882 studied with Susan Blow, who, along with William T. Harris, had made St. Louis a center for the study and promotion of kindergartens. In 1883 she went to New York to study with Maria Kraus-Boelte. Putnam, Blow, and Kraus-Boelte were all well-known followers of Friedrich Froebel, and Harrison carried to the teachers and mothers she soon began to train the Froebel-inspired message of the importance of bringing forth the inherent spiritual and moral nature of young children.

Returning to Chicago as a kindergarten teacher, Harrison invited mothers to classes on early childhood education. One of the mothers, Rumah Avilla Crouse, the wife of a prosperous dentist, became an indispensable ally. Together they founded in 1887 the Chicago Kindergarten Training School with Harrison serving as the romantic, impassioned leader able to inspire others to support the cause of early education, while Crouse did the organizing and made contact with influential members of the community. Over the next twenty-five years the school's program was gradually expanded to a three-year course of liberal studies, a much longer and more demanding program than that of most kindergarten training schools. In 1930 the school became the National College of Education and in 1990 National-Louis University.

As her school for teachers grew, Harrison continued her work with mothers, believing (in the tradition of Froebel) that the training of mothers in a "clearer understanding of how to cultivate the better emotions of their children" was a key to the improvement both of the status of women and of society as a whole. In 1894 Harrison and Crouse organized the first of several national conferences of mothers, which led to the founding in 1897 of the National Congress of Mothers, later the National Congress of Parents and Teachers, or PTA.

An active member for thirty years of the International Kindergarten Union, Harrison came to serve as a bridge for that organization between the Child Study movement, which, beginning in the 1890s, sought understanding of children in the framework of Darwinism through systematic observation, and the older Froebelians, who held to the romantic view of childhood and to the specific activities Froebel prescribed for children. Harrison was much sought after as a lecturer and spoke at meetings of the National Education Association as well as to women's clubs and gatherings of teachers. In 1890 she published her lectures as *A Study of Child Nature*, a compendium of constructive advice for parents and teachers, which appeared in eight languages and fifty-two editions.

She died in San Antonio, Texas.

Elizabeth Harrison was a compelling teacher. One of her students wrote that studying with her was "akin to 'getting religion.'" Mary McDowell, commissioner of public welfare in Chicago, said, "I never had anything that took a deeper hold of me than this philosophy of Froebel's as Elizabeth Harrison taught it." Her message was that the kindergarten was the setting where children could be led through play to a sense of self in a context of responsibility to others and to an understanding of the interrelatedness of humanity with God and nature. Beyond her personal impact on students and readers, she was an institution-builder. Harrison's philosophy of a liberal education for teachers of young children, as embodied in her school, had an enduring influence on early childhood education.

• The papers of Elizabeth Harrison are in the archives of the National-Louis University in Evanston, Ill. Her autobiography is *Sketches Along Life's Road* (1930). An informative chapter on her life by Agnes Snyder appears in *Dauntless Women in Childhood Education, 1856–1931*, ed. Margaret Rasmussen (1972). See also Janet Messenger, *The Story of National College of Education, 1886–1986*, written for the centennial of the college; Edna Dean Baker, *An Adventure in Higher Education* (1956); and the biography by Robert L. McCaul in *Notable American Women* (1971). The context for Harrison's work is described in Michael Shapiro, *Child's Garden: The Kindergarten Movement from Froebel to Dewey* (1983). No bibliography of Harrison's many books and extensive writings in periodicals exists. In addition to her autobiography and her collected lectures, she published a number of books of fiction for children, including *In Storyland* (1985), *Christmas-tide* (1902), *The Stone Cutter* (1906), *The Legend of the Christ Child* (1916), and books about children for parents and teachers, including *The Kindergarten Building Gifts* (1903), *Some Silent Teachers* (1903), *Misunderstood Children* (1910), *When Children Err* (1917), *Two Children of the Foothills* (1922), and *The Unseen Side of Child Life* (1922). After her death her most popular stories were collected in *In the Story World: Best Legends for Boys and Girls* (1931).

NANCY S. GREEN

HARRISON, Francis Burton (18 Dec. 1873–21 Nov. 1957), politician, was born in New York City, the son of Burton Norvell Harrison, an attorney and private secretary to Jefferson Davis, and Constance Cary, a noted author. Harrison attended the Cutler School in New York City. He graduated from Yale University in 1895 and from New York Law School in 1897. He was admitted to the New York bar in 1898. After the out-

break of the Spanish-American War in April 1898 he, like many other young men of his class, enlisted as a private in Troop A of the New York Volunteer Cavalry. He quickly was promoted to the rank of captain and served as assistant adjutant general with the unit that trained at Camp Alger and saw action at Coamo and Santa Isabel, Puerto Rico.

After his demobilization from the army in December 1898, Harrison became active in Democratic party politics in New York. He served as a member of the U.S. House of Representatives from New York's Thirteenth District for the 1903–1905 term and ran unsuccessfully for lieutenant governor of New York in 1904. Harrison represented New York's Sixteenth District in the U.S. House from 1906 to 1912. During his tenure in Congress, Harrison served on the Ways and Means and Foreign Affairs committees. In 1914 he sponsored the landmark Harrison Narcotics Act that required physicians to account for their distribution of addictive drugs. Throughout his political career he opposed the Republican administrations' so-called Dollar Diplomacy.

Harrison's attitude toward American expansion mirrored that of his party in the matter of the Philippines. An important plank in the Democratic platform of 1912 called for Philippine independence as soon as the islands were capable of self-government. Acting to implement that plank, newly elected president Woodrow Wilson in 1913 appointed Harrison as governor-general of the Philippines and directed him to guide the preparation of that country for independence swiftly.

Harrison's goal was the Filipinization of all levels of government so that the country might, in reality, be self-governing even before a formal declaration of independence. Of primary importance were fundamental changes in the legislative structure and economy of the islands. Until 1913 the Philippines had been governed by a bicameral legislature. The assembly, the lower house, was popularly elected while the Philippine Commission, which was appointed by the president of the United States, served as the upper house. Harrison immediately moved to place a Filipino majority on the commission, thus putting both houses under local control. He then quietly, and informally, subordinated his role as governor-general to the wishes of the legislative branch.

Harrison also forged ahead with the Filipinization of the civil service and administrative departments. Between 1913 and 1921 the number of Americans in the Philippine civil service fell by more than 430 percent, while the number of Filipinos in all levels of government more than doubled to 13,200. These institutional changes were further legitimized when, in 1916, the U.S. Congress replaced the Organic Act of 1902 with the Jones Act, legislation promising Philippine independence as soon as a stable government was established. It also abolished the Philippine Commission, establishing in its stead a popularly elected senate, and granted the legislature authority to reorganize the government. The only presidential appointees remaining were the governor-general and vice governor.

In addition to administrative reforms, Harrison supervised and tried to stimulate the growth of the Philippine infrastructure and economy. He encouraged state-owned and -operated railroads, banks, and mines and supported industrial development. Under Harrison the length of paved roads doubled, school enrollments grew by nearly a half million pupils, public works projects flourished, agricultural production doubled, and government revenues quadrupled.

After his resignation in 1921, Harrison recommended that his successor be a Filipino. However the Warren G. Harding administration, contending that the scope and speed of his reforms had led to a deterioration of government efficiency and public services, ignored his recommendation. Many of Harrison's policies were reversed by subsequent Republican administrations.

Between 1921 and 1941 Harrison divided his time among his homes in Tangier, France, Scotland, and the Philippines. He became a trusted adviser to Presidents Manuel Quezon, Sergio Osmena, and Manuel Roxas of the Philippines, and in 1936 the Philippine commonwealth made Harrison an honorary citizen. Harrison served as an adviser to Quezon's government-in-exile during World War II. He acted as U.S. commissioner of claims in the Philippines in 1946–1949 and was an adviser to the first three presidents of the independent Republic of the Philippines, established in 1946. He was an avid hunter and fisherman and a member of the Yale, Knickerbocker, Union, Manhattan, Democratic, Racquet and Tennis, and University clubs of New York.

Harrison was married in 1900 to Mary Crocker, with whom he had two children before her death in 1905. In 1907 he married Mabel Judson Cox; they had three children before divorcing in 1919. That same year he wed Salena Elizabeth Wrentmore, with whom he had three children. They divorced in 1927, and Harrison married Margaret Wrentmore, his third wife's sister, and they had one child. After their divorce, he married Doria Lee in 1934; they had one child and were divorced. Harrison's sixth and final marriage was to Maria Teresa Lorrucea in 1949. Harrison died in Flemington, New Jersey.

• The Francis B. Harrison Papers are part of the Harrison Family Collection at the Library of Congress. The University of Virginia, Charlottesville, has a copy of his unpublished memoirs. For Harrison's defense of his policy in the Philippines, see his *Corner-Stone of Philippine Independence* (1922). His other writings consist mainly of family history, including *Aris sonis focisque: Being a Memoir of an American Family . . .* (1910), *The Burton Chronicles of Colonial Virginia* (1933), *Archibald Cary of Carysbrook, Virginia* (1942), and *A Selection of the Letters of Fairfax Harrison* (1944). See also Michael P. Onorato, ed., *Origins of the Philippine Republic: Extracts from the Diaries and Records of Francis Burton Harrison* (1974). On Harrison's career in the Philippines, see Napoleon J. Casambre, "Francis Burton Harrison: His Administration in the Philippines, 1913–1921" (Ph.D. diss., Stanford Univ., 1968); Onorato, "Governor General Francis Burton Harrison and His Administration in the Philippines: A Re-Appraisal," *Philippine Studies* 18 (1970); and Peter W. Stanley, *A Nation in the Making: The Philippines and the United States, 1899–1921* (1974). Also useful is Andrew J. Bacevich, *Diplomat in Khaki: Major General Frank Ross McCoy and American Foreign Policy, 1898–1949* (1989).

ANNE CIPRIANO VENZON

HARRISON, Gabriel (25 Mar. 1818–15 Dec. 1902), actor, daguerreotypist, and prose writer, was born in Philadelphia, Pennsylvania, the son of Charles Harrison, an engraver, and Elizabeth Foster. In 1824 the family moved to Manhattan. The house became a meeting place for artists of the time, and there young Harrison met painters John Trumbull and J. J. Audubon, singer Maria Malibran, and writer N. P. Willis. Around 1830 Harrison was befriended by an elderly neighbor, Aaron Burr, who taught him elocution.

It was probably early in 1838 that Harrison married Sarah Stephenson, since the first of at least six children (two of whom died in infancy) was born in November of that year. By 1843 he had opened a general store at Broadway and Prince in Manhattan. One customer was Edgar Allan Poe, with whom he remained lifelong friends.

The bulk of Harrison's professional career lay in the arts. In 1832 he had met émigré actor and playwright John Howard Payne and had seen Edwin Forrest at the Park Theatre in New York City. Inspired by these two men, Harrison joined the American Histrionic Society in 1835 and acted in its productions. In 1838 H. J. Wallack saw Harrison play Rolla in R. B. Sheridan's *Pizarro* and brought him to the National Theatre in New York City for his professional debut in the role of Othello. Harrison was an actor of the Forrest school, in which forceful elocution was prized. His signature role was Julian St. Pierre in Sheridan Knowles's play *The Wife*, but he also performed many of the century's standards, including Damon, Carwin, and William Tell. Once he moved to Brooklyn in 1848, the remainder of his acting career—into the 1870s—was primarily in amateur productions.

As a playwright, he had little impact. In 1836 he wrote a play called *The Author*, which was performed at the American Histrionic Association of New York City. His 1866 *Melanthia* was written for aging actress Matilda Heron, to provide her with a noble matron role. The only extant play is his version of Nathaniel Hawthorne's *The Scarlet Letter*, published in 1876; two years later he played Chillingworth to his daughter Viola's Hester.

Harrison's great success came in photography. He began training in 1844 as a daguerreotype operator in the Broadway studio of John Plumbe. Working with Plumbe's chief operator, William Butler, Harrison began winning prizes for his work as early as 1845. Like most operators, he took portraits, but he began to branch out into more "artistic" styles and specialized in allegorical pictures. The height of this phase occurred during the years 1849 through 1851, while he was working for Martin M. Lawrence, one of the most skillful of New York daguerreotypists. Harrison's daguerreotype *Past, Present, and Future*, modeled after a miniature by Edward Malbone, won a top prize for Lawrence at the Crystal Palace exhibition in London in 1851. Another prize winner was *The Infant Saviour Bearing the Cross* (c. 1850).

Harrison's most creative writing occurred when he began contributing to H. H. Snelling's *Photographic Art Journal* in 1851. Producing essays, technical descriptions of daguerreotype procedures, "gossip," opinion, and romantic hybrid texts—part essay, part dream-vision-allegory—Harrison sought to promulgate photography as an art, not just a technique. These writings offer an insight into a creative figure whose sentimental style would soon go out of fashion but whose forward-looking ideas would influence later generations of photographic artists. In "Lights and Shadows of Daguerrean Life, No. 2" (1851), the photographer-narrator pursues a sprite who represents both nature's light and the artistic ideal: "I take the picture from the camera. Great heaven! as I live, I have daguerreotyped fair Helia in the natural colors! This is indeed the perfection of my art!" A contemporary nickname, the "Poet Daguerrean," seems as justified for Harrison the writer as for Harrison the picture taker.

Harrison opened his own studio at 283 Fulton Street in Brooklyn in 1852. It was here in 1854 that he took his most famous daguerreotypes, those of his friend and Brooklyn neighbor, Walt Whitman. An engraving of one (not extant) appears as the frontispiece of Whitman's 1855 *Leaves of Grass*. Another is called *The Christ Likeness* (now at New York Public Library). Whitman may have met Harrison as early as 1846, when the then-journalist wrote about the wonders of Plumbe's portrait gallery. The two men moved in the same political circles, and both were elected as delegates from Brooklyn to various Free Soil conventions in 1848. As late as 1888 Whitman still remembered Harrison as a friend.

Harrison pursued many arts, but none gave him the renown of his photography. As a self-taught painter, he executed landscapes, naval scenes, and theatrical pictures but earned little money or fame for this work. After closing his photography studio in 1859, Harrison managed theaters, including the Adelphi in Troy, New York. Returning to Brooklyn in 1861, he launched the city's first real theater, the Park, in September 1863, for which he designed the first-ever sunken footlights. His management was initially a success, but the cost of mounting operas and his own declining health nearly ruined him. Harrison resigned in 1864.

Thereafter, Harrison pursued a quieter though still busy life. In 1865 he joined a committee that founded the Brooklyn Academy of Design. Harrison promoted free art lessons for Brooklyn youth in the belief that art and mass culture were compatible. He also engineered the erection of a bust of Payne in Prospect Park in 1873 and published a biography of the dramatist that would inspire W. W. Corcoran to bring Payne's body from Tunis, Tunisia, to the United States. At age seventy-one Harrison published his last book, a biography of his longtime friend Forrest.

His last years were spent leading troupes of amateur performers in Brooklyn and giving elocution and acting lessons. His last known public performance, a reading, was in 1893. Harrison died at the home of a daughter in Brooklyn. He was eulogized as a pioneer of the fine and performing arts in Brooklyn. He also deserves acknowledgment as a creative photographer and writer who was one of the first to understand the artistic possibilities of the camera.

• The largest collections of Harrison's daguerreotypes are at Eastman House in Rochester, N.Y., and the Gilman Paper Co. His chief books include *The Life and Writing of John Howard Payne* (1875), a revised edition, *John Howard Payne . . . His Life and Writings* (1885; repr. 1969), and *Edwin Forrest, the Actor and the Man* (1889). He also wrote "The Progress of the Drama, Opera, Music and Art in Brooklyn," in *The Civil . . . History . . . of the County of Kings*, ed. H. R. Stiles (1884). Many of Harrison's essays and short prose pieces are in the *Photographic Art Journal* and its successor, *Photographic and Fine Art Journal*.

The best modern articles are Grant B. Romer, "The Poetic Daguerrean," *Image* 22 (Sept. 1979): 8–18; and Robert P. Rushmore, "Gabriel Harrison: Artist, Writer, and 'Father of the Drama' in Brooklyn," *Journal of Long Island History* 18 (1982): 30–44. Biographies include S. J. Burr, "Gabriel Harrison and the Daguerrean Art," *Photographic Art Journal* 1 (Mar. 1851): 169–77; and Virginia Chandler, "Gabriel Harrison," in *The Civil . . . History . . . of the County of Kings*, ed. Stiles (1884).

Recent commentaries focus on his photography. See Richard Rudisill, *Mirror Image: The Influence of the Daguerreotype on American Society* (1971); Alan Trachtenberg, *Reading American Photographs: Images as History, Mathew Brady to Walker Evans* (1989); Ed Folsom, *Walt Whitman's Native Representations* (1994); and John Wood, *The Scenic Daguerreotype: Romanticism and Early Photography* (1995). Obituaries are in the *Brooklyn Daily Eagle*, 15 Dec. 1902, and the *New York Times*, 16 Dec. 1902.

JEFFREY H. RICHARDS

HARRISON, Henry Sydnor (12 Feb. 1880–14 July 1930), journalist and novelist, was born in Sewanee, Tennessee, the son of Caskie Harrison, a professor of Greek and Latin at the University of the South, and Margaret Coleman Sydnor. Both the paternal and maternal sides of Harrison's family related him to the Virginia aristocracy, a connection of great value to him in his popular novels involving themes of class conflict and cultural change.

In 1885 Harrison's father founded the Brooklyn, New York, Latin School. He taught his own son there and evidently imbued him with an intense classical training apparent in the mature syntax and style of his son's later novels. After Henry Sydnor Harrison received his B.A. in 1900 from Columbia University, he taught for his father for two years at the Brooklyn school. After his father's death, Margaret Harrison, Henry Sydnor, and his brother and sister took up residency in Richmond, Virginia.

Joseph Bryan, the owner of the *Richmond Times-Dispatch*, hired Harrison in 1902 to write paragraph fillers for the newspaper. Harrison's humor—restrained and classical in nature—made him an immediate success with his Edwardian audience. From fillers Harrison expanded to a small but successful column, "Rhymes for the Day." By 1908 he was appointed chief editorial writer for the *Times-Dispatch*, a post he resigned in January 1910 in order to pursue a career in fiction writing. He spent the rest of his life living in New York City, with occasional trips to Virginia and Europe.

It is primarily as a novelist and social critic that Harrison is remembered today. From the training, knowledge, and experiences of his patrician background and obvious liberal humanitarian disposition, Harrison was able to capture the mood, the ambience, and the personal and political privacies of a southern civilization and social structure on the verge of dramatic change. As a distinctly "southern" writer, he captured in his best work (*Queed* and *V. V.'s Eyes*, for example) the spirit of the *kulturroman*, which he evidently knew and admired, to a degree reminiscent of George Washington Cable, the Louisiana local-color writer. In Harrison's fictional world, agrarianism and capitalism, chivalry and democracy, sociology and church, and business and family are so often at odds that his novels achieve a psychological tension, at times hopeless and deterministic and nearly always melodramatic in the manner of Charles Dickens.

Harrison's first novel, *Captivating Mary Carstairs*, was published in 1910 under the pen name of "Henry Second." Completed as early as 1908 but then twice rewritten, the pseudonymously issued novel was not to undercut *Queed*, which was already scheduled for publication and evidently considered the more important of the two works.

Critical reception of *Queed* was largely favorable, the novel being reviewed in major periodicals such as the *Athenaeum*, *ALA Booklist*, *Current Literature*, *Bookman*, and the *New York Times*. What early critics objected to was true of all Harrison fiction. His "sermons" often intruded on his storytelling. His liberal humanitarian instincts and social engineering distracted readers from the main story line. His causes, such as child labor laws, taxed the reader's imagination. An autobiographical novel concerning newspaper life, power, and privilege, the dramatic intensity of *Queed* is owed to Harrison's ability to capture the intimidation implicit in change to the southern provincial mind. Sharlee, the heroine of the novel, tells the idealistic journalist Queed, who is a satirical version of the author himself, "'You are standing here directly between two civilizations. . . . On one side there is the old slaveholding aristocracy; on the other the finest Democracy in the world'" (pp. 158, 159).

Early reviewers of *V. V.'s Eyes* (1913) were charmed by the largely "convincing" portrait of V. Vivian, the hero, an idealist-reformer, a youthful physician sharply critical of the tobacco industry for its exploitation of labor. In its economic determinism, *V. V.'s Eyes* provides along the way such a realistic portrayal of the callowness of some members of the moneyed bourgeoisie in the South that the *Bookman* described Carlisle Heth's mother as a "vulgar, selfish, and designing mother" (p. 455). Unusual for a southern male writer in the period, Harrison is strongly feminist in the novel when he creates his portrait of Carlisle Heth: "'I'd like,' she said, hesitatingly, 'to have *one* man I meet—see me in some other light than as a candidate for matrimony'" (p. 448). Hence, Harrison presents the revolt against chivalry, a phenomenon that was part of the southern feminist movement.

Angela's Business (1915) studies the progress of feminism of the day in its creation of Charles King Garrott, writer, reformer, and anthropologist, who learns through experience, not books, the difference between biological and purely social sexual distinctions. Mary Wing, a working professional woman in the novel, becomes Harrison's ideal modern woman in contrast to Angela Flower, who symbolizes the traditional social conformity of southern women.

By 1919, his best fiction behind him and having served in World War I, Harrison published *When I Come Back*, a tribute to his brother, who was killed in the Argonne. The eulogy was based on letters from his brother and was filled with the angst shared by many readers of the day. Reviewers praised the biographical memorial for its maturity of style and purpose.

A feminist novel truly ahead of its time, *Saint Teresa* (1922) is the story of Teresa DeSilver, Wall Street executive, who wrests control of her steel company from the manager of the corporation, Dean Masury. In a clash of ideologies at the outbreak of World War I, DeSilver refuses to make munitions in order to make greater profits. Although the *Times Literary Supplement* gave the novel a very positive review, most American reviewers saw it as slipping in quality.

In a surprisingly Jamesian manner, unlike fellow southern writers of the day, Harrison turned to the American abroad theme in *Andrew Bride of Paris* (1925), where an American expatriate who disdains American culture meets a Europeanized American girl. In the ensuing conflict of values and wills, the "American" woman emerges the stronger.

On 10 July 1930 Harrison underwent emergency surgery for gallstones and appendicitis in Atlantic City, New Jersey, where he was vacationing. He died four days later as a result of complications following that surgery. *The Good Hope* (1931), his last novel, was all but ignored, perhaps because of its posthumous publication. Harrison never married.

Harrison's novels have fallen into critical obscurity over the past sixty years. His real gift to posterity is as a chronicler of change within the American South, for he depicts with both sensitivity and discernment the extent to which the old order would change and yield to the new. Whether depicting tobacco magnates, newspaper powers, or steel company reformers, Harrison remains the unique measure of his own civilization with his interests in the rights of females and children and a rich appreciation of the largely positive traditions that often, ironically, created the very social problems he so deplored.

• Harrison's papers are found in various collections, the main collection being at Duke University, Durham, N.C. William K. Bottorf has a brief discussion of Harrison's life and work in Louis D. Rubin, Jr., ed., *A Bibliographical Guide to the Study of Southern Literature* (1969), and a slightly fuller biographical treatment in Rubin, ed., *Southern Writers: A Biographical Dictionary* (1979). The most sensitive discussion of Harrison as a Richmond personality is Edgar E. MacDonald, "Henry Sydnor Harrison: A Centennial Appreciation," *Richmond Quarterly* 3 (Summer 1980): 13–20. James Southall Wilson, "Henry Sydnor Harrison," *Library of Southern Literature*, supp. (1923): 285–89, although limited, is helpful. Obituaries are in the Richmond *News Leader* and the *New York Times*, both 15 July 1930.

GEORGE C. LONGEST

HARRISON, Hubert Henry (27 Apr. 1883–17 Dec. 1927), black intellectual and radical political activist, was born in Concordia, St. Croix, Danish West Indies (now U.S. Virgin Islands), the son of William Adolphus Harrison and Cecilia Elizabeth Haines. Little is known of his father. His mother had at least three other children and, in 1889, married a laborer. Harrison received a primary education in St. Croix. In September 1900, after his mother died, he immigrated to New York City, where he worked low-paying jobs, attended evening high school, did some writing, editing, and lecturing, and read voraciously. In 1907 he obtained postal employment and moved to Harlem. The following year he taught at the White Rose Home, where he was deeply influenced by social worker Frances Reynolds Keyser, a future founder of the National Association for the Advancement of Colored People (NAACP). In 1909 he married Irene Louise Horton, with whom he had five children.

Between 1901 and 1908 Harrison broke "from orthodox and institutional Christianity" and became an "Agnostic." His new worldview placed humanity at the center and emphasized rationalism and modern science. He also participated in black intellectual circles, particularly church lyceums, where forthright criticism and debate were the norm and where his racial awareness was stimulated by scholars such as bibliophile Arthur Schomburg and journalist John E. Bruce. History, free thought, and social and literary criticism appealed to him, as did the protest philosophy of W. E. B. Du Bois over the more "subservient" one of Booker T. Washington. Readings in economics and single taxism and a favorable view of the Socialist party's position on women drew him toward socialism. Then in 1911, after writing letters critical of Washington in the *New York Sun*, he lost his postal job through the efforts of Washington's associates and turned to Socialist party work.

From 1911 to 1914 Harrison was the leading black in the Socialist party of New York, where he insisted on the centrality of the race question to U.S. socialism; served as a prominent party lecturer, writer, campaigner, organizer, instructor, and theoretician; brief-ly edited the socialist monthly the *Masses*; and was elected as a delegate to one state and two city conventions. His series on "The Negro and Socialism" (*New York Call*, 1911) and on "Socialism and the Negro" (*International Socialist Review*, 1912) advocated that Socialists champion the cause of the Negro as a revolutionary doctrine, develop a special appeal to Negroes, and affirm their duty to oppose race prejudice. He also initiated the Colored Socialist Club (CSC), a pioneering effort by U.S. socialists at organizing blacks. After the party withdrew support for the CSC, and after racist pronouncements by some Socialist party leaders during debate on Asian immigration, he concluded that Socialist leaders put the white "Race First and class after."

Harrison believed "the crucial test of Socialism's sincerity" was "the Negro," and he was attracted to the egalitarian practices and direct action principles of the Industrial Workers of the World (IWW). He defended the IWW and spoke at the 1913 Paterson Silk Strike with Elizabeth Gurley Flynn and "Big Bill" Haywood. Although he was a renowned socialist orator, and was described by author Henry Miller (1891–1980) as without peer on a soapbox, Socialist party leaders moved to restrict his speaking.

Undaunted, Harrison left the Socialist party in 1914 and over the next few years established the tradition of street corner oratory in Harlem. He first developed his own "Radical Lecture Forum," which included citywide indoor and outdoor talks on free thought, evolution, literature, religion, birth control, and the racial aspects of World War I. Then, after teaching at the Modern School, writing theater reviews, and selling books, he started the "Harlem People's Forum," at which he urged blacks to emphasize "Race First."

In 1917, as war raged abroad, along with race riots, lynchings, and discrimination at home, Harrison founded the Liberty League and *The Voice*, the first organization and newspaper of the militant "New Negro" movement. He explained that the league was called into being by "the need for a more radical policy than that of the NAACP" (*Voice*, 7 Nov. 1917) and that the "New Negro" movement represented "a breaking away of the Negro masses from the grip of the old-time leaders" (*Voice*, 4 July 1917). Harrison stressed that the new black leadership would emerge from the masses and would not be chosen by whites (as in the era of Washington's leadership), nor be based in the "Talented Tenth of the Negro race" (as advocated by Du Bois). The league's program was directed to the "common people" and emphasized internationalism, political independence, and class and race consciousness. *The Voice* called for a "race first" approach, full equality, federal antilynching legislation, labor organizing, support of socialist and anti-imperialist causes, and armed self-defense in the face of racist attacks.

Harrison was a major influence on a generation of class and race radicals, from socialist A. Philip Randolph to Marcus Garvey. The Liberty League developed the core progressive ideas, basic program, and leaders utilized by Garvey, and Harrison claimed that, from the league, "Garvey appropriated every feature that was worthwhile in his movement." Over the next few years Garvey would build what Harrison described as the largest mass movement of blacks "since slavery was abolished"—a movement that grew, according to Harrison, as it emphasized "racialism, race consciousness, racial solidarity—the ideas first taught by the Liberty League and *The Voice*."

The Voice stopped publishing in November 1917, and Harrison next organized hotel and restaurant workers for the American Federation of Labor. He also rejoined, and then left, the Socialist party and chaired the Colored National Liberty Congress that petitioned the U.S. Congress for federal antilynching legislation and articulated militant wartime demands for equality. In July 1918 he resurrected *The Voice* with influential editorials critical of Du Bois, who had urged blacks to "Close Ranks" behind the wartime program of President Woodrow Wilson. Harrison's attempts to make *The Voice* a national paper and bring it into the South failed in 1919. Later that year he edited the *New Negro*, "an organ of the international consciousness of the darker races."

In January 1920 Harrison became principal editor of the *Negro World*, the newspaper of Garvey's Universal Negro Improvement Association (UNIA). He reshaped the entire paper and developed it into the preeminent radical, race-conscious, political, and literary publication of the era. As editor, writer, and occasional speaker, Harrison served as a major radical influence on the Garvey movement. By the August 1920 UNIA convention Harrison grew critical of Garvey, who he felt had shifted focus "from Negro Self-Help to Invasion of Africa," evaded the lynching question, put out "false and misleading advertisements," and "lie[d] to the people magniloquently." Though he continued to write columns and book reviews for the *Negro World* into 1922, he was no longer principal editor, and he publicly criticized and worked against Garvey while attempting to build a Liberty party, to revive the Liberty League, and to challenge the growing Ku Klux Klan.

Harrison obtained U.S. citizenship in 1922 and over the next four years became a featured lecturer for the New York City Board of Education, where Yale-educated NAACP leader William Pickens described him as "a plain black man who can speak more easily, effectively, and interestingly on a greater variety of subjects than any other man I have ever met in the great universities." In 1924 he founded the International Colored Unity League (ICUL), which stressed that "as long as the outer situation remains what it is," blacks in "sheer self-defense" would have to develop "race-conscious" so as to "furnish a background for our aspiration" and "proof of our equal human possibilities." The ICUL called for a broad-based unity—a unity of action, not thought, and a separate state in the South for blacks. He also helped develop the Division of Negro Literature, History, and Prints of the New York Public Library, organized for the American Negro Labor Congress, did publicity work for the Urban League, taught on "Problems of Race" at the Workers School, was involved in the Lafayette Theatre strike, and lectured and wrote widely. His 1927 effort to develop the *Voice of the Negro* as the newspaper of the ICUL lasted several months. Harrison died in New York City after an appendicitis attack. His wife and five young children were left virtually penniless.

Harrison, "The Father of Harlem Radicalism," was a leading black socialist, the founder and leading force of the militant "New Negro" movement, and the man who laid the basis for, and radically influenced, the Garvey movement. During a heyday of black radicalism he was the most class conscious of the race radicals and the most race conscious of the class radicals. He critically and candidly challenged the ruling classes, racists, organized religion, politicians, civil rights and race leaders, Socialists, and Communists. During his life, though well respected by many, Harrison was often slighted. In death, his memory was much neglected, not least by "leaders" who had felt the sting of his criticism. He was, however, a political and cultural figure of great influence who contributed seminal work on the interrelation of race and class consciousness and whose book and theater reviews drew praise from leading intellectuals of the day. Historian J. A. Rogers stressed that "No one worked more seriously and indefatigably to enlighten his fellow-men; none of the Aframerican leaders of his time had a saner and more effective program—but others, unquestionably his inferiors, received the recognition that was his due."

• Harrison's papers are in private possession. His two books, *The Negro and Nation* (1917) and *When Africa Awakes: The "Inside Story" of the Stirrings and Strivings of the New Negro in the Western World* (1920), contain editorials and articles. There are scattered issues of *The Voice* (1917–1919), the *New Negro* (1919), and the *Negro World* (1920) and a complete set of the *Embryo of the Voice of the Negro* and the *Voice of the Negro* (1927). Biographical sketches of Harrison by those who knew him include "Hubert Harrison: Intellectual Giant and Free-Lance Educator," in *World's Great Men of Color*, vol. 2, ed. Joel A. Rogers (1947), pp. 611–19; Richard B. Moore, "Harrison, Hubert Henry," in *Dictionary of American Negro Biography*, ed. Rayford W. Logan and Michael R. Winston (1982), pp. 292–93; and a pamphlet by John G. Jackson, *Hubert Henry Harrison: The Black Socrates* (1987). Good portraits are provided by Portia James, "Hubert H. Harrison and the New Negro Movement," *Western Journal of Black Studies* 13, no. 2 (1989): 82–91, and Wilford D. Samuels, "Hubert H. Harrison and 'The New Negro Manhood Movement,'" *Afro-Americans in New York Life and History* 5 (Jan. 1981): 29–41. Very useful are the chapter "Local New York, the Colored Socialist Club, Hubert H. Harrison, and W. E. B. Du Bois," in *American Socialism and Black Americans: From the Age of Jackson to World War II*, ed. Philip S. Foner (1977), pp. 202–19, and "Hubert Henry Harrison," in *The Marcus Garvey and Universal Negro Improvement Association Papers*, vol. 1, ed. Robert A. Hill (1983), pp. 210–11. The most in-depth treatment of Harrison's early years is Jeffrey B. Perry, "Hubert Henry Harrison 'The Father of Harlem Radicalism': The Early Years—1883 through the Founding of the Liberty League and *The Voice* in 1917" (Ph.D. diss., Columbia Univ., 1986), which includes a lengthy bibliography.

JEFFREY B. PERRY

HARRISON, John Pollard (5 June 1796–2 Sept. 1849), physician and medical educator, was born in Louisville, Jefferson County, Kentucky, the son of Major John Harrison and Mary Ann Johnson. After completing his early schooling, Harrison apprenticed himself, possibly as early as 1811, to local physician John Croghan, who had recently returned to Louisville to practice after completing one year of medical lectures at the University of Pennsylvania. In the fall of 1817 Harrison enrolled in the Medical Department of the University of Pennsylvania, Philadelphia, and also became the private pupil of Dr. Nathaniel Chapman. The following year he became a student of Dr. William Potts Dewees. After attending two years at the University of Pennsylvania, he submitted a thesis titled "Analogies of Plants and Animals" and was awarded his M.D. in March 1819. Returning to Louisville, he announced the opening of his practice in the *Louisville Public Advertiser* in mid-June 1819. In 1820 he married Mary T. Warner; they had six children.

A fever epidemic, associated with a high rate of mortality, during each summer and fall of 1821 and 1822, would give rise to Harrison's teaching career. Today we know that "fever epidemic"—also called intermittent or remittent bilious fever—was most probably Vivax Malaria. Therapeutic excesses of phlebotomy, emetics, and mercurial cathartics (calomel) undoubtedly contributed to its high mortality rate. Peruvian Bark (quinine source) was seldom used. An account of the epidemic, presented as a medical thesis at Transylvania University Medical Department (Lexington, Ky.) in 1823 by one of Harrison's private pupils, Samuel L. Metcalfe, was followed by Harrison's own account, published in Chapman's *The Philadelphia Journal of Medical and Physical Sciences* (1824).

Hospitalized patients were extremely important to the medical teachers of the community; seeing a sick patient and reviewing the findings of inspection, palpation, and history with the preceptor was much more effective in teaching clinical skills than simply reading about them in a book. When the Louisville Marine (City) Hospital was ready to receive patients in 1823, Harrison was one of two attending physicians appointed to minister to its patients. By 1824 the local medical community consisted of about twenty-five M.D.s; that same year Harrison presented his own appraisal of the local fever epidemics of 1821 and 1822 to the Louisville Society for the Promotion of Medical Knowledge.

Having accumulated a medical library of several hundred volumes by 1827, Harrison inserted in Louisville's two newspapers that summer an advertisement offering medical tuition. In this lengthy ad, Harrison offered the use of his "well furnished medical library of the best modern works . . . and the liberty of attending the clinical teachings in the Louisville Hospital." He clearly outlined a weekly program of two formal lectures (Wednesdays and Saturdays) and four days of discussions of selected hospital cases. The course was to begin in mid-March and last sixteen weeks, for a total of thirty-two lectures. He also offered opportunities for students to witness "post-morten [*sic*] inquest," as well as, "in winter, [anatomy] to be prosecuted on the recent subject" (*Louisville Public Advertiser*, 28 Feb. 1827). As advertised, Harrison had access to hospital facilities for teaching interested students, and in March 1827, for the first time in Kentucky, clinical lectures in medicine were presented at the public hospital.

In 1833 the first charter for the Louisville Medical Institute was obtained, with Harrison named one of the incorporators, but under the original charter as well as several revisions a functional faculty could not be assembled, and Harrison left Louisville (1834) for Philadelphia in search of another appointment. He subsequently obtained the chair of materia medica and therapeutics at the Cincinnati Medical College in Cincinnati, Ohio (1835). When the school suspended operation in 1839, he established a private practice in Cincinnati. In 1841 he was appointed professor of materia medica and therapeutics in the Medical College of Ohio, a chair he occupied until his death, except for two sessions from 1847 to 1849, when he was professor of theory and practice of medicine.

While at the Medical College of Ohio, Harrison published his *The Elements of Materia Medica and Therapeutics* (2 vols., 1844–1845), establishing himself, like his mentor, Nathaniel Chapman, as a "solidist." Solidists claimed that some mysterious force they called "sympathy" accounted for the effects of medicine on the patient. Such spurious doctrines of the eighteenth century were no longer tenable following François Magendie's 1821 observations that active principles of crude drugs injected intravenously were carried by the circulating blood throughout the body. Harrison's solidist philosophy had made his textbook outmoded before it was published. Samuel D. Gross, who had served for three years (1835–1839) with Harrison on the faculty of the Medical Department of Cincinnati College, commented in his *Autobiography* (2 vols., 1887), that Harrison "wrote a work on Materia Medica and Therapeutics which fell as he might have supposed it would, stillborn from the press." A later biographer, Henry E. Handerson, in 1920 noted that Harrison "published his great work on The Elements of Materia Medica," but failed to indicate whether this "great" refers only to its size.

Although Harrison published more than eighteen papers and addresses, mostly in western medical publications, and a collection of four essays in book form (*Essays and Lectures on Medical Subjects* [1835]), both Gross and Physician Otto Juettner characterized him as "an imitator," and "never original." His editorial abilities appear not to have been compromised by this deficiency for he was on the editorial board of several medical journals in Louisville and Cincinnati.

Harrison was one of those pioneers in medical education who, with others, took the initial steps in Louisville to institutionalize the educational process, albeit a proprietary system, and transformed medical education from apprentice-training to lecture courses and clinical lectures in hospitals. He practiced medicine and cared for patients in homes and hospitals, but in addition, devoted much of his professional life to the education of students of medicine, including apprentices, private pupils, his peers, and himself. He gained a reputation as a lecturer, writer, and medical editor and showed considerable leadership ability locally in Louisville and Cincinnati as well as on the state (Ohio) and national levels. Active in the medical convention of Ohio, he became its president in 1843 and was vice president of the American Medical Association in 1849 at the time of his death. He died in Cincinnati.

• Some of Harrison's published papers are in the Medical Library of the University of Cincinnati. Evidence of his early efforts at medical education appear in *The Louisville Public Advertiser*, 28 Feb. 1827. A partial list of his publications appears as an advertisement in *The Index-Catalogue of the Library of the Surgeon General's Office* (1880–1932). His correspondence has been lost. No formal biography has been published, but his obituary in the *Western Lancet* (Cincinnati), vol. 10 (1849), contains some biographical information.
EUGENE H. CONNER

HARRISON, Mary Scott Lord Dimmick (30 Apr. 1858–5 Jan. 1948), second wife of Benjamin Harrison (1833–1901), the twenty-third president of the United States, was born in Honesdale, Pennsylvania, the daughter of Russell Farnham Lord, chief engineer and general manager of the Delaware and Hudson Canal Company, and Elizabeth Scott, whose younger sister, Caroline, had married Benjamin Harrison in 1853. In 1881, after having attended Mrs. Moffat's School in Princeton, New Jersey, and Elmira College (1875–1876), Mary Scott Lord married Walter Dimmick, a young lawyer whose father had served as attorney general of Pennsylvania. Three months later the bridegroom died of typhoid fever, and Mary Dimmick was left a widow at age twenty-three. When her uncle, Benjamin Harrison, won election to the presidency in November 1888, Mary Lord Dimmick was traveling in Europe, but she wrote several letters inquiring about his cabinet choices. Mary's mother, also widowed by the time of the election, was invited by her sister, Caroline Harrison, to stay at the White House and assist the first lady. On her return from Europe, Mary Lord Dimmick also joined the extended family of the president. Large families often accompanied nineteenth-century presidents to the White House, and the Harrison household included the first lady's father and the Harrisons' two adult children with their respective spouses and children.

Caroline Harrison thus had the assistance of several female relatives, including Mary Dimmick, and she depended on her niece to act as her social secretary at a time when no professional staff was provided for the distaff side of the White House. When Caroline Harrison became ill with tuberculosis in 1892, Mary Dimmick helped nurse her, traveling with her to the Adi-

rondacks for rest and recuperation and then returning with her to the White House where she died in October 1892.

After Benjamin Harrison lost his bid for reelection in 1892, he returned to live in Indianapolis. In December 1895 he announced that he would marry Mary Lord Dimmick. More than three years had elapsed since his wife's death, and most of his political colleagues approved of his decision to remarry; but his son and daughter were bitterly opposed. They did not attend the ceremony and were not reconciled with their father before his death. The marriage of Mary Dimmick and Benjamin Harrison took place in St. Thomas's Protestant Episcopal Church in New York City on 6 April 1896 in the presence of thirty-six guests (most of them former cabinet members and other high-ranking political figures). The Harrisons returned to live in Indianapolis and the following year had a child.

In 1901 Benjamin Harrison died, and his widow was left in a rather unusual situation. Although the widow of a president, she had never actually served as first lady and, as a result, was often excluded from the list of honors customarily accorded presidents' widows. In 1909 she received the franking privilege routinely granted to every president's widow since Martha Washington, but Congress did not authorize a pension for her until 1936. When President William Howard Taft and his wife invited both Frances Cleveland and Mary Harrison to a White House dinner in 1913, the former was given a place of honor while the latter was generally ignored.

Much of the nearly half-century that Mary Harrison survived her husband was devoted to preserving his memory and enhancing his reputation. A volume of his speeches and articles, published the year of his death, lists him as author but carries the additional notation: "Compiled by Mary Lord Harrison." The introduction to the Library of Congress collection of Benjamin Harrison papers credits her by noting that the story of the papers is "largely that of Mrs. Harrison's search for a biographer." She selected several different historians in turn, but each had to withdraw from the project because of poor health or other circumstances that made the task impossible. Reluctant to have her husband's papers opened to the public until the biographer had finished using them, she retained control over access of the papers until 1945, nearly forty-four years after Benjamin Harrison's death.

Mary Harrison maintained a strong interest in politics until her death. She served for twenty-five years as treasurer of the Republican Committee of One Hundred, a women's organization founded to stimulate interest in political problems, and she attended her party's national conventions until 1940. In her one substantial break with the Republican party she chose to support Alfred E. Smith in 1928 because of the Republican party's stand on prohibition. When Herbert Hoover was elected president in 1928, she reiterated her view in a letter to him saying that prohibition was constitutionally and theoretically wrong.

After 1913 she made her home in New York City but spent considerable time in Europe. She died at her home in New York City but was buried in Indianapolis in the same cemetery where Benjamin Harrison and his first wife are buried.

• The Library of Congress collection of Benjamin Harrison's papers includes several letters that Mary Harrison wrote to him as well as her correspondence with other persons at the time of his death. Her correspondence with Albert Volwiler, one of the prospective biographers of Benjamin Harrison, is in the Albert Volwiler Papers at the Lilly Library, Indiana University. Because she married an ex-president and did not serve as first lady, she has never been the subject of a full-length biography and has been largely ignored by her husband's biographers. Her marriage to Harrison received front-page coverage in major New York newspapers, including the *New York Times* and the *New York Tribune*, both 7 Apr. 1896. For references to her political activities see the *New York Times*, 15 Feb. 1922 and 12 May 1940. An obituary is in the *New York Times*, 6 Jan. 1948.

BETTY BOYD CAROLI

HARRISON, Pat (29 Aug. 1881–22 June 1941), U.S. senator and congressman, was born Byron Patton Harrison in Crystal Springs, Mississippi, the son of Robert Adams Harrison, a small merchant, and Myra Anna Patton. When Harrison was six his father died, leaving his mother to support the four children by keeping boarders. After two years at what is now Louisiana State University (1899–1891), Harrison became a public school teacher and principal and studied law at night. He began a legal practice in Leakesville, Mississippi, in 1902. In 1905 he married Mary Edwina McInnis; of their five children, three survived to adulthood.

Harrison entered politics in 1906 and won two terms as district attorney for the Second Judicial District of Mississippi. He subsequently moved to Gulfport where he maintained a home until his death. It was during his successful campaign for Congress in 1910 that his name was shortened to "Pat." The new congressman's future depended not as much on how well he served his agrarian, solidly Democratic district as it did on his ability to survive the factionalism and personal animosity that characterized Mississippi politics. During his four terms in the House of Representatives (1911–1919), Harrison became a protégé of Mississippi senator John Sharp Williams and an ardent supporter of President Woodrow Wilson's program for national preparedness and the League of Nations. Such allegiances provoked an ugly break with Mississippi senator James K. Vardaman, whose Senate seat Harrison won in a raucous campaign in 1918. Harrison pitched his campaign on the issues of Vardaman's pacifism and inclusion by Wilson as one of the obstructionist "little group of wilful men." During the 1920s, as a minority party senator, Harrison gained a reputation as an effective gadfly and zestful opponent of Republican tariff and fiscal policies, and he won a ranking position on the Committee on Finance. He handily defeated one opponent in 1924 and ran unopposed in 1930. His sharp wit and repartee served him well in his political campaigns and on the Senate floor throughout his life.

With the Democratic ascension in 1933, Pat Harrison became chairman of the powerful Finance Committee, which handled many crucial New Deal measures. President Franklin D. Roosevelt relied on Harrison to effect passage of his administration's keystone measure, the National Industrial Recovery Act. Enactment of the Social Security Act of 1935 and its 1939 amendments, the Reciprocal Trade Agreements Acts of 1934 and 1940, and fourteen separate revenue acts were all due to Harrison's influence and tactics. Among the revenue bills, the "wealth tax" of 1935 and the undistributed profits tax of 1936 were difficult to pass but set new precedents in Democratic tax policy. Never the author of any major legislation, Harrison was the broker for the ideas of others. Through artful compromise and "horse-trading," Harrison was a master in the conference committee, where he could cajole opponents to retreat from unachievable demands. Congressional longevity, masterful parliamentary skills, and a pleasing personality combined to make Harrison a power in the Senate and reputedly its most popular member. A Republican adversary once characterized him as "square, approachable, and intensely human"; he was never known to renege on a pledge. In 1939 Washington correspondents named him the most influential of all senators.

Harrison was devoted to President Roosevelt, and grateful for New Deal aid to Mississippi, until the two men broke over tax philosophy. Convinced that taxes should be levied for revenue only and not for income redistribution or other social purposes, Harrison opposed the undistributed profits feature of the 1936 measure and a continuation of excessive taxation on capital gains in 1938. The Roosevelt-Harrison accord on tax legislation was always tenuous, with Harrison resisting the president's move toward "share-the-wealth" measures. *Fortune* magazine once called Harrison a "New Deal wheelhorse suspicious of his load." After the president gave his support to Alben W. Barkley for majority leader in 1937, a position Harrison lost by one vote, the senator became less loyal to Roosevelt and lost enthusiasm for the New Deal, particularly as it turned to increased deficit financing and social engineering. Harrison's liberalism, like that of many of his southern colleagues, was pragmatic, based on economic exigencies, and fell far short of embracing any social reforms that would threaten prevailing race relations in the South. As a mainstay of the increasingly conservative coalition of southern senators, he opposed wages and hours legislation in 1938 and joined filibusters against antilynching and anti–poll tax bills.

It was clear by 1938 that Harrison and Roosevelt were estranged, but the need to finance national defense and to grant aid to Britain after 1939 brought Harrison back into the fold. With Roosevelt, he held to tenets of internationalism and the defense of democracies, opinions traceable to old Wilsonian principles still popular in the South. His final success as Finance Committee chairman was the passage in 1941 of the Lend-Lease bill that Roosevelt directed to Harrison's committee rather than the Foreign Relations Committee because of the Mississippian's legislative expertise. Harrison was already debilitated by the colon cancer that took his life in Washington six months after he had been named president pro tempore of the Senate.

• Most of Harrison's personal papers were disposed of after his death, but a small collection of his correspondence and public records is in the University of Mississippi Library; some duplications and additional materials are in the Mitchell Memorial Library, Mississippi State University. The most useful sources are the Official File and the President's Personal File of the Roosevelt papers (Franklin D. Roosevelt Library, Hyde Park, N.Y.). Also see Martha H. Swain, *Pat Harrison: The New Deal Years* (1978). Indispensable to understanding Harrison is James T. Patterson, *Congressional Conservatism and the New Deal: The Growth of the Conservative Coalition in Congress, 1933–1939* (1967). An obituary is in the *New York Times*, 23 June 1941.

MARTHA H. SWAIN

HARRISON, Peter (14 June 1716–30 Apr. 1775), architect, was born in York, England, the son of Elizabeth Dennyson and Thomas Harrison, Jr. His father's occupation is not known. Peter spent his early years in England, where he was raised a Quaker, but he was lured to America and became Episcopalian. The Episcopal (or Anglican) Church and its parishioners better suited the image Harrison would create for himself. He was very close to his eldest brother, Joseph, and followed him both to America and into the profession of ship's captain. He spent most of his life in Newport, Rhode Island, where he first located around 1740.

Designing country houses was one of the genteel accomplishments of the English gentry. Harrison was very aware of the building being undertaken in the neo-Palladian style and was familiar with Richard, Lord Burlington, William Kent, and other gentleman/architects. He was also privy to their libraries containing volumes on architecture, including Kent's *Designs of Inigo Jones*, James Gibbs's *Book of Architecture*, and Edward Hoppus's *Andrea Palladio's Architecture*. At the time of Harrison's death, his library contained approximately thirty volumes on architecture that he had used freely in designing New England buildings.

The upward mobility Harrison sought was not a possibility in England but was attainable in America where class divisions were not as rigid and where property was easier to acquire. Harrison's religious conversion, his business acumen, his keen observation, and his marriage to Elizabeth (Betty) Pelham all enabled him to become an English colonial gentleman. Pelham, a twenty year old "spinster" when she fell in love with Harrison, was also the mistress of Leamington Farm and heiress of an estate valued at £20,000. In opposition to her family's wishes, the couple married in 1746; they would have four children. As a symbol of their social station, the young Harrisons had their portraits painted by John Smibert, c. 1756.

Harrison's interest in design was expressed as early as 1746 when he is known to have drawn plans for Louisburg, Cape Breton Island; he also served on a committee that drafted plans to build Fort George on Goat Island. Although this project extended to 1755, it was never carried out. It was not long after that he supervised the fitting and launching of the three-masted, square-rigged ship, the *Leathley*. These projects, and his design for the Beavertail Lighthouse (1853) in Jamestown, Rhode Island, were related to his career as a ship's captain. His later works were more in line with his position as a merchant, and the related status he achieved as a colonial gentleman.

Harrison's design of the imposing Redwood Library in Newport (1748–1750) clearly indicates his newly established position in life. When the committee met to contemplate a gift of £500 for the erection of a library, his brother Joseph was placed on the committee to collect additional funds. He no doubt used the influence he had to suggest Peter as a possible designer—the younger Harrison was abroad but quickly sent sketches home based on architectural books he had seen in the libraries of the gentlemen/architects he knew in England. Harrison lifted the classic temple portico he used on the library from Hoppus's book on Palladio, the engraved plate on page 185. It was this building that established Harrison as a gentleman/architect, and he became known throughout New England. He received neither pound nor shilling for his trouble, and historians are unsure whether he was even invited to the dedication of Redwood Library.

His next commission came from the Anglicans of King's Chapel, Boston (1749–1758). Harrison was familiar with a number of gentlemen on the committee to erect the new church and was no doubt honored that he was chosen to submit a plan. Again he consulted the pattern books; he used Gibbs's design for Marylebone Chapel. King's Chapel was completed without the spire that Harrison planned; it was the first church in America to be built of stone.

Harrison's succeeding design was for a Jewish temple in his adopted hometown of Newport. The Jews there enjoyed the religious freedom that Roger Williams established in founding the colony. In spite of the supposed liberal atmosphere of Rhode Island, after the structure was built, it was referred to locally as the "Synagogue of Satan." The temple was officially named Touro Synagogue (1759–1763), in honor of its rabbi, Isaac Touro, who arrived in the New World fresh from studies in Amsterdam. The project provided Harrison with problems that arose from his unfamiliarity with Jewish ritual and the lack of a prototype in America. Harrison collaborated with Touro, referred to pattern books, and relied on the interior arrangement of the Portuguese Synagogue in London, completed in 1701. He consulted William Kent's *Designs of Inigo Jones* for the problems related to the interior architectural treatment. There the plate of Whitehall Palace provided a model with its two storied galleried hall. The twelve columns that Harrison designed represent the twelve tribes of ancient Israel; the columns are Ionic on the first story and Corinthian above. According to Wayne Craven, the very plain exterior was executed deliberately because "the Jewish community did not want to flaunt their wealth or incur envy" (p. 81). But some believe the elegant interior is a colonial masterpiece. During the summer of 1790 George Washington addressed the Touro congregation extolling the virtues of freedom of religion that the newly adopted constitution embraced.

During the early autumn of 1759 a committee was formed in the college town of Cambridge, Massachusetts, to investigate the construction of a new church. It was natural that they looked to Newport and Harrison for the design as many of them worshiped at King's Chapel and were familiar with Harrison's work. The result of the joint endeavor stands today as Christ Church (1760). The only pay the gentleman/architect ever received for his labor came from the gentlemen of the building committee, who awarded Harrison a stipend of £45.

Harrison's final effort was the Brick Market in Newport (1761–1772). Perhaps the building most dependent on English models, he used the plate of Inigo Jones's Somerset House in Colen Campbell's *Vitruvius Britannicus*. Some of the domestic buildings Harrison is known to have had a hand in designing or those that have been attributed to him include: the Matthew Cozzens house in Middletown, Rhode Island; the Nichols-Wanton-Hunter House, Vernon House, Francis Malbone House, and Peter Buliod House, all in Newport; the Shirley-Eustis House in Roxbury, Massachusetts; and Governor John Wentworth's mansion in Wolfeborough, New Hampshire. He built a small summer house for Abraham Redwood that has been moved to the Redwood Library property. In 1766 Harrison left Newport to become the customs collector in New Haven, where he died of apoplexy. Twentieth century writers referred to Harrison as America's first architect. It was not his intention to become a professional architect, nor did he. He belongs to a type known as gentlemen/amateur/architects.

• The major biographical source on Harrison is Carl Bridenbaugh, *Peter Harrison: First American Architect* (1949). A more recent biography is Lamia Doumato, *Peter Harrison: Colonial Architect* (1986). A number of articles have been written concerning his life and/or specific buildings he designed. Bridenbaugh updated his book with "Peter Harrison, Addendum," *Journal of the Society of Architectural Historians* 18 (Dec. 1959): 158–59. Others include Wayne Craven, *American Art: History and Culture* (1994); William Wade Cordingly, "Shirley Place, Roxbury, Massachusetts, and its Builder, governor William Shirley," *Old-Time New England* 12 (1921): 51–63; Antoinette F. Downing and Vincent J. Scully, Jr., *The Architectural Heritage of Newport, Rhode Island, 1640–1915*, 2d ed., rev. (1952) 1967. Lee M. Friedman, "The Newport Synagogue," *Old-Time New England* 36 (1946): 49–57; Norman Morrison Isham, "The Brick Market," *Bulletin of the Society for the Preservation of New England Antiquities* 6, no. 2 (1916): 3–11, 20–23; Sidney Fiske Kimball, "The Colonial Amateurs and Their Models: Peter Harrison," *Architecture* 53, no. 6 (1926): 155–60, and 54, no. 1 (1926): 185–90, 209; George C. Mason, *Annals of Redwood Library and Athenaeum* (1891); Nancy Halverson Schless, "Peter Harrison, The Touro Synagogue and the Wren City Church," *Journal of the Society of Architectural Historians* 30 (Oct. 1971): 242; Esther I. Schwartz, "Touro Synagogue Restored, 1827–29." *Journal of the Society of Architectural Historians* 17, no. 2 (1958): 23–26. *Touro Synagogue of Congregation Jeshuat Israel*, Society of Friends of Touro Synagogue National Historic Shrine, 1948.

MARIANNE BERGER WOODS

HARRISON, Richard Berry (28 Sept. 1864–14 Mar. 1935), African-American actor, was born in London, Ontario, Canada, the son of Thomas L. Harrison and Ysobel Benton, fugitive slaves who escaped from the United States via the underground railroad. As a boy, Harrison augmented the family income by selling papers outside the local theater, where he first saw professional actors perform. Following his father's death and the family's move to Detroit, Michigan, Harrison helped support his five younger siblings by working as a bellhop and porter. With the assistance of Chambless Hull, a theater manager, Harrison was admitted to the Detroit Training School of Dramatic Art, graduating in 1887. Prevented from working in the legitimate theater by racial discrimination, Harrison made his first appearance in 1891 as a dramatic reader, touring the United States and Canada with a repertoire that included *Macbeth, Julius Caesar, The Merchant of Venice*, and *Damon and Pythias*, as well as the poems of Poe, Burns, Byron, Longfellow, Tennyson, Hugo, and Shakespeare.

In 1893, while preparing a program for the Chicago Exposition, he met the African-American poet Paul Laurence Dunbar. The two became good friends, touring the country to promote Dunbar's book, *Oak and Ivory*. It was while reading Dunbar's poetry that Harrison gained experience with the dialectical speech that he would use later in his career. In late 1900 Dunbar wrote two plays for Harrison, *Robert Herrick* and *Winter Roses*. He also served as Harrison's best man when he married Gertrude Janet Washington in 1895; the couple had a daughter, Marian Ysobel, and a son, whom they named after the poet.

Near the turn of the century Harrison went into railroad service as a Pullman-car porter and waiter, becoming a superintendent of mail for the Santa Fe Railroad in Los Angeles. It was there that he was hired by L. E. Behymer as a reader for the Behymer Lyceum Bureau (later the Great Western Bureau). Harrison had a long career touring his one-man show, giving readings and lectures at tents, churches, schools, social functions, and celebrations throughout Canada, the southern United States, and Mexico. During World War I, Harrison was involved with work for various African-American church schools, including fundraising and teaching courses in elocution. He established summer courses in New York for young black men and women as part of his work with the Greater New York Federation of Churches. In 1922, after having taught at Branch Normal in Arkansas, Flipper-Key College in Oklahoma, and the Haines Institute in Augusta, Georgia, Harrison convinced J. B. Dudley, the president of North Carolina A & T in Greensboro, North Carolina, to establish a summer drama school for teachers. As the chair of dramatics for seven years, Harrison helped the enrollment of the program grow from seventeen to over 200 students.

During the winter months, Harrison continued his work as a lecturer, educator, and reader, making his headquarters in New York City. In 1923 he appeared at the Lafayette Theatre as the leading role in *Pa Williams' Gal*, a commercially unsuccessful play by actor Frank Wilson. Harrison was the solo reader for a backer's audition of Garland Anderson's play, *Appearances*, at the Waldorf Astoria Grand Ballroom in 1925 and may have appeared in a revue along with Paul Robeson, Will Mercer Cook, and Carl White.

In 1929 Harrison received a call from a casting agent at the Immense Thespians, Inc., in Harlem, one week before rehearsals for Marc Connelly's *The Green Pastures* were to begin. Although he was offered the role of the Lord immediately, Harrison, a deeply religious man, hesitated before accepting the immense responsibility of playing God on stage. His fears of committing a sacrilegious act were calmed by Episcopal bishop Herbert Shipman, and Harrison accepted the task of performing a black God for a nearly all-white audience. Having little experience with performing as a cast member in a fully mounted professional production, Harrison worked throughout the five-week rehearsal period with acting coach Danton Walker.

The resulting production, which opened on 26 February 1930, was one that New York audiences immediately recognized, in Brooks Atkinson's words, as having "ethereal beauty." No small amount of this praise was due to Harrison's appearance as "De Lawd." Although Harrison's name did not join the title of the play on the marquee until five years later, Heywood Broun attested to the debt that was owed him: "You can run along Broadway night after night, sprinting from show to show, and see no better rounded and complete performance than that given by Richard Harrison." Following a long run in New York, Harrison set out on four consecutive national tours of the play, creating a steady stream of admirers. While on tour, Harrison was frequently sought by church groups, social organizations, schools, and literary societies to give readings and lectures, a responsibility he accepted with grace and humility.

On 22 March 1930 Harrison was presented with the Spingarn Medal, awarded annually by the president of the NAACP to an American citizen of African descent for the most distinguished achievement of the year in any honorable field of human endeavor. The *New York Herald Tribune* capsulized the singular accomplishment of Richard Harrison: "To give this recognition to Mr. Harrison seems peculiarly appropriate. . . . It is peculiarly fitting that this triumph should come to a man who worked for so many unrecognized decades as dramatic reader and entertainer, interpreting to the mass of his own people the finest things in English literature. In his sixty-seventh year he receives this recognition for a role which caps a lifetime of service."

While on tour, Harrison was given the keys to the cities of Chicago and London, Ontario, by their respective mayors. The tours were not entirely without difficulty, however. In many of the cities in which the all-black company performed, Jim Crow laws made it impossible for them to attain any but third-class accommodations. The most publicized controversy occurred in Washington, D.C., where *The Green Pastures* was scheduled to open at the segregated National Theatre. Harrison received pressure to boycott the performance by influential members of politics, literature, and scholarship and by organizations such as the NAACP. Refusing to make his art an instrument of politics, Harrison performed as scheduled, despite threats of physical violence against him and the cast. Soon after the show returned to New York City in 1935, Harrison became ill, "plumb tuckered out," and suddenly died. Thousands paid their respects at a service in New York before his body was returned to his family in Chicago for burial.

Throughout his life, Harrison had suffered professionally because of his race. Unable to gain employment in any of the legitimate theaters, he supported his family and his art by working in menial jobs and maintaining the grueling schedule of performing his one-man show. He dedicated himself to the betterment of his race by the establishment of elocution and speech programs across the southern states. It was his goal to establish a college of dramatic arts for black actors and to further the visible contributions of black artists to the theater. Despite his own struggles to succeed as an actor, and his subsequently enormous success in his only starring professional role, Harrison remained a gentle and humble man, unimpressed with his own success and dedicated to creating a better future for those who followed.

• Harrison's papers are located in the Richard B. Harrison Collection in the F. D. Bluford Library at North Carolina A & T State University, Greensboro. The Billy Rose Theatre Collection at the New York Public Library for the Performing Arts, Lincoln Center, also maintains a clipping file with reviews and photos of *The Green Pastures* and Harrison's performance, as well as a scrapbook. The most complete documentation can be found in Walter C. Daniel, *"De Lawd": Richard B. Harrison and "The Green Pastures"* (1986). Other informative articles are Olyve L. Jeter, "'De Lawd' on Broadway," *Crisis* (Apr. 1931), and Andrea J. Nouryeh, "When the Lord Was a Black Man: A Fresh Look at the Life of Richard Berry Harrison," *Black American Literature Forum* (Winter 1982). Obituaries are in the *New York World Telegram* and the *New York Evening Post*, both 14 Mar. 1935, and the *New York Times*, the *New York Herald*, the *New York American*, and the *New York Sun*, all 15 Mar. 1935.

SUSAN F. CLARK

HARRISON, Ross Granville (13 Jan. 1870–30 Sept. 1959), biologist, was born in Germantown, Pennsylvania, the son of Samuel Harrison, a mechanical engineer, and Catherine Barrington Diggs. Harrison's family moved from Germantown to Baltimore during his childhood, and he prepared at local schools to enter the Johns Hopkins University in 1886. Declaring his interest in medicine at that time, he completed his A.B. at age nineteen and continued on to graduate school in biology at Johns Hopkins, finishing his Ph.D. there in 1894. Along the way he established close lifelong friendships with fellow students such as Edwin Grant Conklin and Thomas Hunt Morgan as well as developed a lifelong love for hiking trips and began the research interest in experimental embryology that occupied his entire career. Harrison pursued his medical interests through biology—for, as he said, medicine was essentially applied biology—and through his studies for an M.D. in Germany.

This was an exciting time in biology at Johns Hopkins, where students studied morphology with William Keith Brooks and physiology with Henry Newell Martin. Those interested in morphological problems such as anatomy or embryology also spent summers in fieldwork, either through the Chesapeake Zoological Laboratory in Jamaica, Bermuda, or in North Carolina, or at the United States Fish Commission in Woods Hole, Massachusetts. Harrison spent 1890 in Woods Hole and 1892 with Brooks's group in Jamaica. Although he did not pursue his study of marine organisms, Harrison clearly found the experiences at these research stations valuable and was pleased to serve on the board of trustees at the Marine Biological Laboratory in Woods Hole from 1908 to 1940.

In 1892–1893 Harrison went to Europe, as many scientists did throughout the nineteenth century. He settled in Bonn, where he continued with Moritz Nussbaum the study of teleost fin development that he had begun at Hopkins and where, in 1899, he received his M.D. Immediately after completing his Ph.D., Harrison spent the year 1894–1895 as lecturer in morphology at Bryn Mawr College, replacing Morgan while Morgan visited Europe to study frog development. Harrison returned to Bonn for 1895–1896 and married Ida Lange in Altoona, Germany, in 1896. That year he returned to Hopkins as an instructor (1896–1897), then associate (1897–1899), and then associate professor of anatomy (1899–1907) in the medical school. He and his wife also began their family of five children during the Hopkins period. During this period, Harrison also began his study of the nervous system, focusing on how nerves develop in the peripheral nervous system to make functional connections.

Though he was comfortable at Hopkins, Harrison moved in 1907 to Yale, where he became Bronson Professor of Comparative Anatomy and in 1912 chair of the zoology department. Previously the sciences had resided in the Sheffield Scientific School rather than at Yale College, but Harrison's appointment was at the university level with membership in the college, Sheffield, and the graduate school and eventually the medical school. He was promised a new university laboratory building, but the Osborn Memorial Laboratory was not finally occupied until 1913. With his move to

Yale, Harrison began his administrative career at the same time that his research career also reached a peak. Though he was tempted by an offer to return to Hopkins in 1914 to replace Franklin Paine Mall as head of the anatomy department, Harrison remained at Yale for the rest of his career. He served there as chairman of zoology (1912–1938), director of the Osborn Zoological Laboratory (1918–1938), Sterling Professor of Biology (1927–1938), and professor emeritus after 1938.

As Harrison moved to Yale, he also published the results of his nerve development studies. Three different explanations had been offered for how nerve fibers develop to make their functional connections: Either preexisting protoplasmic bridges guide the fibers, the protoplasmic bridge or plasmoderm outgrowth theory; or the cells that form the nerve sheath arise first and serve as a chain to guide the nerve fiber, the cell-chain theory; or the fiber develops by protoplasmic outgrowth, the outgrowth theory. Harrison believed that if he could get the fibers to grow into foreign material without any bridges or sheath cells, he would have supported the outgrowth theory. As an experimental embryologist, he turned to laboratory experiments to provide the appropriate conditions and produced a successful tissue culture. Using frog lymph, he got frog nerve fibers to grow out into the surrounding medium under controlled experimental conditions. While his publications of 1907–1910 detailed this work and its role as evidence for the outgrowth theory, the work also showed for the first time that tissues can be cultured outside the living body—a discovery with obvious and immediate medical implications. He chose not to develop the practical applications himself but encouraged others to do so and to develop improved culture techniques.

Although in 1917 a majority of the Nobel Prize committee supported the choice of Harrison for this work, as Harrison's chief biographer, J. S. Nicholas, has explained, no award was made because of the war. Harrison was again considered in 1933, but the age of his work and its "rather limited value" kept it from receiving a prize—a conclusion which Nicholas found ridiculous, since "Never has a *method* of as *limited value* (v. supra) been used so much" (1961, p. 148). In fact, the importance of tissue culture and its application for medicine and biological research was considered one of Harrison's major accomplishments and contributed to his receiving a number of other prizes and honorary degrees, including the John Scott Medal and Premium of the City of Philadelphia in 1925 and the John J. Carty Medal of the National Academy of Sciences in 1947.

Throughout his career Harrison explored various problems of embryonic development, including issues of symmetry and polarity, asking how the three body axes (anteroposterior, mediolateral, and dorsoventral) are established. While his contemporaries worried about the nature and cause of "organization" in the embryo, Harrison asked about the nature and causes of symmetry. By transplanting pieces of tissue, such as the limb bud, which normally gives rise to a limb with a certain pigmentation, onto a host body with different pigmentation, he examined the relative contributions of central and peripheral tissue. This technique, called heteroplastic grafting, revealed, for example, that the limb grows at its own rate rather than that of the host. Other parts, such as parts of the eye, respond to directions from the host, while others depend on interactions between host and grafted material.

With the salamander, Harrison showed in 1921 that a disk of mesoderm produces the limb. When he grafted this disk onto the "wrong" side of the body, it developed a reversed limb, so a left disk produced a left limb on the body's right side. If he inverted the disk, however, it developed a "proper" right limb. Similar experiments with other parts through the 1920s led Harrison to conclude that the anteroposterior axis is determined very early while the body remains unfixed and more nearly what Hans Driesch had called a "harmonious equipotential system" until later. He tried to discover what it is that effects the determination of axes, and he thought there must be some structural, particulate basis. But experiments with X-ray crystallography did not produce any results, and the underlying cause remained unknown.

In addition to his own substantial research contributions (presented in more than eighty professional papers and invited lectures at the Harvey Society, Harvard, the Royal Society of London, St. John's College, Cambridge, and Yale), Harrison played important leadership roles. He served as managing editor of the *Journal of Experimental Zoology* from 1904 to 1946 and on boards for other major journals, including the *Proceedings of the National Academy of Sciences* from 1915 to 1916 and from 1921 to 1946. He served on various supervisory boards and held presidencies of numerous professional societies, including the American Society of Anatomists, 1912–1914; chair of section F for the American Association for the Advancement of Science, 1936; American Society of Naturalists, 1913; American Society of Zoologists, 1924; Anatomische Gesellschaft, 1934–1935; Beaumont Medical Club, 1933; Society for the Study of Development and Growth, 1946–1947; and the Sixth Pacific Science Congress, 1939. Perhaps his most important administrative role involved his chairmanship of the National Research Council during World War II from 1938 to 1946, where he worked to rationalize the distribution of penicillin and other medical procurement issues. (The place of death has not been ascertained, but it is assumed that Harrison died in New Haven.)

In all capacities, Harrison retained a sense of control and reason that Jane Oppenheimer has characterized as "his dispassionate temperament and his calm judiciousness." Even though he was very reserved and even shy, Harrison's students held him in awe as the rather intimidating but inspiring "chief." Former students and colleagues reported that he never managed to keep up with his paperwork or clean his desk, but he always had time for a visitor or to show appreciation for excellent work by others. As Nicholas enthused about Harrison, "It is seldom that one man can attain

such true greatness. Every major effort was constructive and conspicuously successful. His contribution to biological thought is equivalent to that of Einstein or Planck in other branches of science" (1960, p. 412).

• Harrison's papers, cataloged and described by his longtime assistant, Sally Wilens, are in Manuscripts and Archives, Yale University. J. S. Nicholas, "Ross Granville Harrison, 1870–1959," National Academy of Sciences, *Biographical Memoirs* (1961): 132–62, is a major biography and contains a complete bibliography of Harrison's publications. Jane Oppenheimer in *Dictionary of Scientific Biography* and "Ross Harrison's Contributions to Experimental Embryology," *Bulletin of the History of Medicine* (1967) 40: 525–43, provide the best assessments of his research. See also Nicholas's entry in the *Yale Journal of Biology and Medicine* 32 (1960): 407–12.

JANE MAIENSCHEIN

HARRISON, Tinsley Randolph (18 Mar. 1900–4 Aug. 1978), physician, was born in Talladega, Alabama, the son of William Groce Harrison, a physician, and Louisa Marcia Bondurant. Harrison received his primary and secondary educations in Alabama before entering the University of Michigan at age sixteen. His grades there were sufficient to qualify him to use his fourth year of college as his first year of medical school. He then transferred to Johns Hopkins Medical School on the encouragement of his father, who had become a friend of Sir William Osler, the first chief of medicine at Johns Hopkins and probably the most famous physician in America at that time. While a medical student there, Harrison befriended Alfred Blalock, later chief of surgery at Johns Hopkins and originator in the 1940s of the first "blue baby" operations for congenital heart disease

Following two years of training as house officer at Harvard University's Peter Bent Brigham Hospital, Harrison returned to Johns Hopkins for his senior assistant residency in 1924–1925. When the new Vanderbilt Medical School and Hospital opened in Nashville, Tennessee, in 1925, the first chief resident in medicine was Harrison, and the first chief resident in surgery was Blalock. They both remained there until 1941, when Blalock became chairman of surgery at Johns Hopkins, and Harrison became the first chairman of medicine at the new Bowman Gray School of Medicine in Winston Salem, North Carolina, named after the second great Carolina tobacco magnate, the first having been James Duke. Harrison remained at Bowman Gray for three years, departing in 1944 to take the positions of dean of medicine and chairman of the Department of Medicine at the new Southwestern Medical School, being established at that time in Dallas, Texas.

During his time at Southwestern, Harrison conceived and brought to fruition his textbook *Principles of Internal Medicine* (1950), the achievement for which he became best known. Reaching its fourteenth edition in 1996 and published in twelve languages, it is probably the largest selling textbook of medicine in history. Similar texts, such as the *Cecil Textbook of*

Medicine or the textbook by Sir William Osler, had been organized according to disease categories, but Harrison introduced an organization by symptom categories, since the patient presents the physician with symptoms rather than a ready-made diagnosis. The latter two-thirds of Harrison's textbook—some 2,000 large pages of fine print—contains the traditional disease-oriented descriptions. Harrison himself generally used the book in reference to specific individual patients under the care of medical students or residents. They would read and report on a sign or a symptom of that patient, or the patient's disease, to the group for discussion.

In 1950 Harrison moved yet again, this time to take the positions of dean and chairman of medicine at the new medical school of the University of Alabama in Birmingham (now University of Alabama at Birmingham School of Medicine), where he shepherded his textbook through its second and third editions as editor in chief. He then retired to become one of the work's five general editors through 1965. He ceased active participation in preparation of the book after that, apparently dispirited by the death in 1964 of his lifelong close friend Blalock.

Harrison always claimed to be "just a general doctor" and would never permit the establishment of subspecialty divisions in his departments of medicine. He said, "If you want to take a special interest in blood, or the heart, or the endocrine or GI system, that's fine. But we are not going to have any hematologists, or cardiologists, or endocrinologists, or gastroenterologists, or any other 'ologists here—who are subspecialist nondoctors!" (Pittman, audiotape interview, 1974). Despite this, virtually all of Harrison's publications and academic recognitions were as a cardiologist. His book *Failure of the Circulation* (1935) was a classic according to cardiologists, as was the completely revised second edition in 1938. He was president of the American Heart Association in 1948, when it was evolving from a quiet academic group for exchange of scientific information into one of the nation's largest and most influential fundraising and lobbying organizations. Also in 1948 he was a founding member of the National Advisory Council for the National Heart Institute at the National Institutes of Health of Bethesda, Maryland. A former Harrison pupil T. Joseph Reeves, wrote *Principles and Problems of Ischemic Heart Disease* (1968) with Harrison. Virtually all of his more than 250 scientific papers, chapters, books, and lay articles concerned cardiac physiology or diseases.

Although he was intensely dedicated to laboratory and clinical research, having served as president of the American Society for Clinical Investigation in 1939, Harrison was most dedicated to his patients and his students. In teaching, he felt that a teacher's stimulation of the student's desire to learn was the primary sine qua non, and that this was as much "a matter of the heart as of the mind." In other words, without an enthusiastic and intense desire to learn on the student's part, all the knowledge, expertise, and pontifications of the teacher would be wasted. In response to

Harrison's dedication to them, his students remained devoted to him throughout their lives, particularly in medical matters.

In 1924, while a house officer at the Brigham Hospital Harrison had married nurse Elizabeth Woodward; they had five children. Together the couple observed and discussed the changes in nursing over the years. Late in life he became as outspoken a critic of the way some of these changes were affecting nursing and those previously known as "the allied health professions"—the increasing bureaucracy, separation from bedside care, and feminist causes that seemed to be taking precedence over dedication to the care of patients; and the increasingly militant independence of the nursing profession and nurses' assumption of activities previously the province of physicians—as he was of political attempts to garner professional turf from physicians. He was also critical of the large amounts of money physicians began earning in the 1960s.

Harrison reserved his severest and most vocal criticism, however, for the mindless and excessive use of high technology by physicians as a substitute for thoughtful examination of the patient and reliance on simpler and non-invasive techniques. He was not opposed to the technology itself, only the thoughtless and unwarranted use of it. When terminal illness befell him, he refused hospitalization until enticed for "just a few hours to see the new instrument for visualizing the myocardial infarct" (Harrison to James A. Pittman, Jr., 30 Dec. 1977; McCallum Archives, UAB). He remained lucid, though in shock, and insisted on going home. He died quietly in Birmingham, in his own bed with his family around him.

• The Charles A. McCallum Archives, University of Alabama at Birmingham, holds a collection of Harrison's personal papers as well as an audiotape interview that James A. Pittman, Jr., conducted with Harrison in 1974. Biographical sources include Samuel S. Riven, "Teacher Without Peer: Tinsley Harrison," in his *Worthy Lives: Medical Men and Women at Vanderbilt in the 1930s* (1993), chap. 5; J. D. Wilson, *Harrison's Principles of Internal Medicine 1950–1987* (1987). See also W. P. Longmire, Jr., *Alfred Blalock—His Life and Times* (1992), and W. B. Fye, *American Cardiology. The History of a Specialty and Its College* (1996). An obituary is "Tinsley Randolph Harrison, 1900–1978," in *Transactions of the Association of American Physicians* 92 (1979): 30.

JAMES A. PITTMAN, JR.

HARRISON, Wallace Kirkman (28 Sept. 1895–2 Dec. 1981), architect, was born in Worcester, Massachusetts, the only son of James Harrison, an iron foundry superintendent, and Rachel Kirkman, whose mill-working family had emigrated from England to the United States in the 1870s. From early childhood, Harrison was motivated by a burning ambition to better himself. Forced to leave school and earn his own living at age fourteen, Harrison first worked for A. O. W. Norcross, a well-known construction company. This experience stimulated his interest in architecture and led to a stint as a draftsman with the local firm of Frost & Chamberlain (1913–1916). At the same time he undertook a grueling schedule of regular attendance at Worcester Polytechnic night school, which he continued until his late twenties. Dissatisfied with the limited scope of his responsibilities at Frost & Chamberlain, Harrison sought work with a larger office in New York City. He was hired in 1916 by Mc-Kim, Mead & White, pre-eminent architects of the time.

During the First World War, Harrison served overseas as an ensign in the U.S. Navy. In 1920 he studied briefly at the École des Beaux-Arts in Paris, where he met Robert Perry Rodgers, a direct descendent of the naval hero, Oliver Hazard Perry. Rodgers became friendly with Harrison, whom he introduced to his wealthy, well-born friends.

Harrison returned to New York City, where he worked as a draftsman for several firms and studied with Harvey Wiley Corbett, a successful architect, with whom he maintained a relationship after completing his studies. In 1922 he won a Rotch Traveling Scholarship that allowed him to visit Europe and the Near East.

Back in New York in the fall of 1923, thanks to Rodgers, the tall, blond, and handsome Harrison became an habitué of some of the city's most socially prominent homes. In 1926 he married Ellen Milton, a sister-in-law of Abby Rockefeller. The couple had one daughter.

In 1927 Harrison joined in partnership with Corbett, and in 1929 Corbett, Harrison & MacMurray became one of three architectural firms that participated in the design and building of Rockefeller Center (1933). It was this commission that brought Harrison and Nelson Rockefeller together in what became a lifelong friendship. Harrison subsequently received commissions for some of New York City's most important buildings. In 1935 Harrison formed a new partnership with André Fouilhoux, and in 1939 their firm contributed the Trylon and Perisphere theme buildings to New York City's World's Fair. Max Abramovitz joined Harrison & Fouilhoux in 1941; four years later, the firm was renamed Harrison & Abramovitz and continued in business until 1976.

During the Second World War Harrison worked with Nelson Rockefeller as cultural director of the office of Inter-American Affairs, for which Rockefeller served as bureau coordinator. In Washington, Harrison established his credentials as a man of exquisite probity and unusual diplomatic skills. Thanks in large part to this reputation, in addition to his architectural skills, in 1947 Harrison was named director of planning for the United Nations headquarters in New York City (1953). At a time when American corporate architecture was at its peak, Harrison & Abramovitz was one of the premiere firms engaged in that work. One of Harrison's strengths lay in the development of new technologies: the thirty-nine floor UN Secretariat (1950) was essential to the evolution of the glazed curtain-wall skyscraper; his Alcoa Building in Pittsburgh

(1953) was the first aluminum skyscraper; the monolithic concrete units he developed for Nelson Rockefeller's International Basic Economy Corporation low-cost housing (c. 1947) contributed to the knowledge of on-site mass production in concrete.

In the late 1950s, working with his old friends Arthur A. Houghton, Jr., president of Steuben, and Robert Moses, the powerful city parks commissioner, Harrison played a major role in the creation of Lincoln Center for the Performing Arts, for which he designed the Metropolitan Opera House (1966). Before the Opera House was completed, Nelson Rockefeller, then governor of New York State, asked Harrison to design and build Albany's South Mall (1971), which, after completion, was renamed Nelson A. Rockefeller Plaza.

In 1956 *Time* magazine rated Harrison equal to Frank Lloyd Wright, Le Corbusier, and other modern masters. He was respected by other architects as well. By the time he had completed the Albany mall, he had been vilified for the cold monumentality of what many perceived as an already outdated modern style. Lincoln Center and the Rockefeller Center expansion to Sixth Avenue (1974) met with adverse criticism for the same reasons.

Harrison's talent for organizing large-scale projects was undeniable. His design talents, however, appeared to be strongest in smaller-scale endeavors. His Rockefeller Apartment House in New York City (1936); the private houses he built for Nelson Rockefeller at Pocantico Hills, New York (1939), and on Mt. Desert Island, Maine (1941); the First Presbyterian Church in Stamford, Connecticut (1958); and the Hall of Science (which, much later, became the Museum of Science and Technology) built for the 1964 World's Fair in Flushing, New York, exemplify Harrison's personal combination of modern and expressionist sensibilities. He worked until a few weeks before his death in New York City.

• Harrison's papers are at the Avery Library, Columbia University, New York City. There are also transcripts of ten interviews with Harrison conducted by R. Daum between 11 March and 4 November 1978 at the Oral History Research office at Columbia University. The only book-length biography is by Victoria Newhouse, *Wallace K. Harrison, Architect* (1989); articles on Harrison's different buildings are cited in the notes to the biography. A three-part profile by Herbert Warren Wind, "Architect," was published in the *New Yorker*, 20 and 27 Nov. and 4 Dec. 1954.

VICTORIA NEWHOUSE

HARRISON, William Henry (9 Feb. 1773–4 Apr. 1841), ninth president of the United States, was born at "Berkeley," his family's plantation on the James River in Virginia, the son of Benjamin Harrison, a prominent revolutionary statesman, and Elizabeth Bassett. Harrison's father was at various times Virginia's governor, a member of each of the Continental Congresses (where he chaired the committee charged with reporting a declaration of independence), Speaker of the Virginia House of Burgesses, and an Anti-Federalist delegate to the Richmond Convention of 1788, besides being related by blood or marriage to virtually all the leading Virginia families. He was also fabulously wealthy, so his father's economic, social, and political legacy stood young William Henry—the youngest of seven children—in good stead.

William may have been sent to a grammar school near Berkeley in his childhood; he certainly attended Hampden-Sidney College beginning in 1787, though he departed without graduating. He joined his older brother in Richmond for medical study in 1790, then headed to Philadelphia for medical study under the famous Dr. Benjamin Rush. When word of his father's death arrived, William Henry acted on his unhappiness with medicine: he left Philadelphia with a commission in the U.S. Infantry.

Harrison was posted to the Old Northwest, where tensions with the Indians ran high and the British had not yielded the forts they were obliged to surrender under the Treaty of Paris. Harrison received a lieutenancy and in 1792 served temporarily as a company commander—a position normally allocated to a captain. In the campaign of the Battle of Fallen Timbers in 1794, Harrison distinguished himself as an aide-decamp to General Anthony Wayne. He married Anna Symmes, the daughter of Judge John Cleves Symmes of North Bend, in November 1795. They eventually had ten children. Harrison soon was appointed commander of Fort Washington; it thus came as no surprise that in May 1797 he was promoted to the rank of captain. Finding garrison duty tedious, Harrison resigned from the army effective 1 June 1798.

Harrison next applied for the position of secretary of the Northwest Territory, and he asked his friend Robert Goodloe Harper, chairman of the House Committee on Ways and Means, for assistance. Harrison's commission was dated 6 July 1798. On 3 October 1799 the territory's first legislature elected Harrison to be its delegate to the U.S. Congress by a vote of 11 to 10.

While in Congress Harrison was made chairman of a committee for the revision of the public lands laws. This committee reported the Land Act of 1800, which facilitated the sale of public lands in the Northwest Territory. In addition, Harrison instigated the division of the Northwest Territory into the two territories of Indiana (which then included present-day Illinois, Michigan, and Wisconsin) and Ohio. On 12 May 1800 Harrison was appointed governor of Indiana by President John Adams. Holding virtually all non-judicial powers in Indiana, Harrison served there for four three-year terms.

When he had first gone to the Northwest Territory, Harrison had invested in a distilling business. The second time, with a huge salary, he speculated in land and engaged in farming. His close ties to the people of Vincennes, the territorial capital, may account for his successful opposition to efforts to relocate the government's seat. Among his ties to the town was his trusteeship at Vincennes University. Although legislative power in the territory was transferred to a legislative body in 1805, the governor retained an absolute veto and power to appoint all territorial officers. Harrison's manifold duties and great power naturally attracted opponents' sniping (including some whispers about his connection to Aaron Burr, some of whose fugitive followers he did shelter), but no corrupt misfeasance was ever proven.

Harrison also favored the introduction of slavery into the territory. He briefly had been a member of an abolition society in 1791, but he believed that Indiana's residents favored slavery, which the Northwest Ordinance of 1787 had purported to ban in the territory. In 1802 Harrison called a convention on the question, and the convention petitioned Congress to allow suspension of the prohibition. Congress did not act on it. In response, Harrison pushed legislation in 1803 allowing slavery under another name. In 1810 the legislature repealed the statute, and Harrison did not object.

Besides a tolerance for slaveholding, Harrison maintained other personality traits of the Virginia aristocracy. He was prone to keep Virginians around him in his Indiana days. In addition, Harrison's table reputedly was always accessible to strangers, travelers, and neighborhood people. As in the Virginia Tidewater of his youth, so in his adulthood, the Harrison home was a social center. Harrison was said by one sometime visitor to his house to be easygoing and affable, and he apparently did not put on airs.

While he was governor, Harrison was also Superintendent of Indian affairs for the territory. Following the directions of Presidents Thomas Jefferson and James Madison, Harrison did his best to acquire all the Indians' land. Jefferson wanted him to loan money to the Indians, then collect by seizing their land; Harrison did precisely that, earning himself a reputation as a land grabber. However, he also attempted to comply with the chiefs' requests that he impede the traffic in liquor between the whites and the Indians and that he better regulate the whites who traded with their peoples. Harrison thought more emphasis should have been put on maintaining friendly relations with the Indians, saying of the War of 1812 that more might have been achieved by placating the Indians than had been by waging war on Great Britain.

The War of 1812 gave Harrison a way out of a deteriorating personal political situation. He thought the British were behind the uprising of the Shawnee leader Tecumseh and his brother, the "prophet" Elskwatawa. The climactic confrontation was precipitated by Harrison's decision to survey the section of land purchased by the government from the Indians in the 1809 Treaty of Fort Wayne. Tecumseh's attempt to intimidate Harrison into conceding the justice of the Indians' claims failed, and a series of murders and raids by the Indians heightened tensions. Finally, when Tecumseh told Harrison he would be leaving the area for a few weeks, Harrison gathered a force of 1,000 men, including Indiana militia, Kentucky volunteers, and a regiment of regulars, for an advance into Tecumseh's territory.

Having arranged a peace parley, Harrison encamped at Tippecanoe Creek; to his surprise, his men were set upon by an enemy force of about 400 Indians just as he was rousing them from sleep on 7 November 1810, the scheduled day of the parley. The Americans narrowly won the two-hour battle of Tippecanoe (although they suffered very heavy casualties—far heavier than did the Indians), and Tecumseh's main village was destroyed that day. The battle of Tippecanoe was first reported as an American defeat, and it did not yield peace. Soon, Tecumseh and his brother were rallying more Indians for war. Their quarrel with the United States would be subsumed by the War of 1812.

In response to their widespread depredations, and in hopes of burnishing his damaged military reputation, Harrison resolved to initiate new offensive operations. President Madison, however, disapproved. Though Harrison was not on the initial list of generals appointed to fight the War of 1812, his old congressional mentor Henry Clay interceded with Secretary of State James Monroe on Harrison's behalf. When that gambit apparently had failed, Clay had Harrison made a brevet major general of Kentucky militia. Within days Harrison learned that he had been appointed brigadier general in the regular army and charged with the defense of the Indiana and Illinois frontier, and so he simultaneously held military office under the governments of Kentucky, the United States, and—as governor—Indiana. Unsure about which of his duties to fulfill, Harrison had his problem solved for him when Madison made him commander of the United States' northwestern army and charged him with retaking Detroit (which had fallen to the British in August 1812) and invading Upper Canada.

Harrison's first attempt to recoup Detroit was a costly failure; it was also ill-conceived, for Detroit would have been of little use to the Americans without control of Lake Erie, which lay firmly in Britain's grasp. Recognizing the futility of an endeavor he had already undertaken, Harrison awaited Secretary of War Monroe's decision to bring it to a halt; he did not want to accept the responsibility. Harrison's strategic grasp, exposed as weak by the conception of his campaign in the winter of 1812, was proven so again by his failure to reinforce defeated units quickly and to isolate small enemy detachments when the opportunity presented itself.

On 2 March 1813, again probably at Clay's instance but consistently with the nation's high estimate of Harrison's military capacities, Harrison was promoted to major general and made commander of the Eighth Military District, which comprised Ohio, Kentucky, Michigan, Missouri, Indiana, and Illinois. When, as he had done in the Detroit campaign, Harrison divided his force in the face of the enemy, one detachment was isolated by the British and forced to surrender on 4 May 1813. The greater part of Harrison's 1,500 Kentuckians were lost. Fortunately for the Americans, the tenuousness of his supply lines led the cautious British commander to retrace his steps northward.

In 1813 Harrison's plan to invade Canada was preempted by the second British invasion of Ohio. Commodore Oliver Hazard Perry's victory over the British fleet on Lake Erie made the British position in Michigan untenable, and Harrison retook Detroit on 29 September. On 15 October 1813 Harrison's force caught the retreating British at the Thames River and won a smashing victory over poorly-armed, badly-outnumbered opposition. Tecumseh was killed on the field, and virtually all of his British allies were either killed or captured.

Harrison had broken both the British and the Indian resistance in the Northwest. He was a national hero, feted throughout the country. The idea of taking Canada had been thoroughly abandoned, however; with the Northwest at peace, Harrison, the commander of the army in that region, displayed little initiative. He retired in 1814 and turned his attention to straightening out his finances and defending his reputation for fiscal probity (since, thanks to his political opponents in the Northwest, his fiscal stewardship was under attack in Congress). In 1818 Congress voted Harrison a gold medal for his wartime service.

From 1816 to 1828 Harrison served in Congress and in the Ohio Senate. His chief concern in his two-term tenure as a congressman from Ohio (1816–1819) was provision for the widows and orphans of soldiers, and he tried unsuccessfully to win approval of a more robust federal oversight and patronage of the state militias. Though he chaired the Committee on the Organization of the Militia in his second term, his efforts came to naught. Harrison endorsed Clay's policy of supporting the South American insurgencies, and he took the South's position on slavery in the new states.

As a senator in Ohio from 1819 to 1821, Harrison—who had once been a director of the Cincinnati branch of the United States Bank—took a firmly anti-bank tack, saying he had always been opposed to all banks. Political vicissitudes outweighed ideological consistency in Harrison's mind. He also chaired the committee that reported the bill initiating the Ohio "Canal Era." Yet, his position on slavery extension offended his constituents, and not only did he fail in races for the U.S. Senate in 1821 and for governor in 1820 (receiving no votes in his own county), but his district declined to reelect him. In 1822 he lost a race for the U.S. House of Representatives, and in 1824 Monroe rejected his pleas for appointment to the ambassadorship in Mexico City.

In the 1824 presidential campaign Harrison worked for Clay in Ohio. Clay won Ohio's electoral votes, and in 1825 the legislature chose Harrison to be U.S. senator from Ohio. Although he was chairman of the Committee on Military Affairs, his three-year service in the Senate was undistinguished. In 1828 he failed to attain nomination as President John Quincy Adams's running mate, and he then accepted appointment as ambassador to Colombia.

In Bogotá Harrison soon became convinced that Bolívar wanted to make himself monarch. When he was asked to mediate between Colombia and Peru, he was

convinced the true design was to further the Colombian president's ambitions. Harrison, as a Clay man,
was recalled when President Andrew Jackson instituted the infamous "spoils system." In parting, Harrison
wrote Bolívar, urging him to emulate Washington and
forego the opportunity to take a crown. After he had
left his office, Harrison was charged with fomenting
revolution and was expelled from the country on 19
October 1829, but Bolívar soon forswore monarchical
pretensions.

The period between Harrison's return to the United
States in 1830 and his election to the presidency in
1840 was a fallow one. In the 1836 presidential season,
Harrison was put forward by politicians in a few
northern states, and he drew seventy-three electoral
votes—a very good showing for a sectional candidate.
In 1840 he was chosen by the Whig national convention over Clay to face Democrat Martin Van Buren,
the incumbent president, whose party's candidates
around the country had fared poorly ever since the
Crash of 1837. Daniel Webster's support threw the
convention behind Harrison, and John Tyler of Virginia was chosen as Harrison's running mate. Apparently, Harrison's most important qualifications were
his fame and fellow Whigs' impressions of him as plia-
ble, loyal, and—in keeping with the Whig ideology
that had grown up in response to Andrew Jackson's
assertive presidency—willing to defer to Congress.
The Whig campaign of 1840, in which Benjamin Harrison's son was portrayed as the occupant of a log cabin and a man of the people, is remembered derisively
by historians (as it was derided by Democrats at the
time) as the "Log Cabin and Hard Cider" campaign.
"Tippecanoe and Tyler, Too" (the slogan that converted a controversial battle into a rousing victory in
American popular memory) is supposed to have
swayed a drunken electorate. In fact, as Henry Clay
lamented, it was a Whig election cycle, and virtually
anyone nominated as a Whig would probably have defeated Van Buren. Harrison did so, 234 electoral votes
to 60.

Harrison chose Webster to be secretary of state, and
soon he had alienated Clay for life. Advised by Clay to
call Congress into a special session, Harrison told Clay
that the Kentuckian's advice must take a back seat to
that of others, and that he should not visit the White
House in the foreseeable future. Stunned at this rebuke, Clay resolved to dominate the administration
from his seat in the Senate, setting the stage for his later impasse with Tyler. Harrison served as president
for one month, during which he did call Congress into
special session to enact the Whigs' active-government
program. Before that could happen, Harrison died of
pneumonia in Washington, D.C.

William Henry Harrison's significance is not great.
His tenure as president was truncated, and his career
in federal political office was a relatively undistinguished one. His record as a territorial governor was
solid, but its social basis—the dominance of "the Virginians" in the Old Northwest—did not survive him.
As for his military career, one can safely say that his
record in that field was less incompetent than those of
most of the major military and civilian leaders responsible for the United States' rashly-launched, poorly-
conceived, and ineptly-run War of 1812. Harrison's
death left the office of the presidency to an opponent of
his party's program, with the result that the election of
1840 was, in retrospect, a great Whig debacle. Where
President Harrison likely would have overseen the enactment of all of Henry Clay's nationalizing measures,
President Tyler vetoed them.

• Nearly all of Harrison's personal papers were destroyed
when the "Old Log Cabin" at North Bend, Ohio, burned
down in 1858. Most of those that remain can be found in the
Library of Congress. Dorothy B. Goebel, *William Henry
Harrison: A Political Biography* (1926), pp. 383–88, lists Harrison materials found elsewhere.

Any treatment of Harrison's life must begin with David A.
Durfee's bibliography, *William Henry Harrison, 1773–1841:
John Tyler, 1790–1862* (1970), which focuses on Harrison's
attitude toward and preparation for the presidency. The biographies of Harrison are all very old. Besides Goebel's, they
include Freeman Cleaves's *Old Tippecanoe: William Henry
Harrison and His Times* (1939) and James A. Green's *William
Henry Harrison: His Life and Times* (1941). The campaign of
1840 and Harrison's month as president are chronicled in
Norma Peterson, *The Presidencies of William Henry Harrison
and John Tyler* (1989), which includes a useful bibliographical essay. His tenure as Indiana governor is the topic of *Governors' Messages and Letters, Indiana Historical Collections*,
vols. 2 and 9 (1922), and of "William Henry Harrison's Administration of Indiana Territory," *Indiana Historical Society
Publications*, vol. 4, no. 3 (1907). Harrison's self-justificatory
pamphlet regarding the Colombian imbroglio is *Remarks of
General William Henry Harrison, Late Envoy Extraordinary
and Minister Plenipotentiary of the United States to the Republic
of Colombia, on Certain Charges Made against Him by That
Government . . .* (1830).

K. R. CONSTANTINE GUTZMAN

HARRISS, Robert Preston (19 Aug. 1902–26 Sept.
1989), journalist, was born in Fayetteville, North Carolina, the son of Frank McCullough Harriss, a wholesale grocery clerk, and Hattie Anderson. He was educated in the public schools of Fayetteville and at Duke
University (called Trinity College when he entered),
where he received an A.B. degree in 1926 and was
elected to Phi Beta Kappa. He earned his way through
college as director of the campus news bureau. His
most valuable service in this position came in December 1924, when he acted as liaison between college officials and journalists clamoring for news regarding
the change in name of Trinity College to Duke University. The change had been falsely reported as a condition imposed by James Buchanan Duke, heir to a tobacco fortune, of his $6 million gift to the school.

While in college, Harriss began publishing poems,
essays, and stories in professional magazines under the
signature R. P. Harriss. In his senior year he edited
The Archive, a literary magazine in which he successfully combined undergraduate and professional writing, a combination that brought him praise from national critics.

After his graduation Harriss worked for the *Evening Sun* in Baltimore as a reporter, but he also wrote book reviews and drama criticism. He left the *Evening Sun* in 1929 to work on the Paris edition of the *New York Herald Tribune* (later called the *International Herald Tribune*), which was read by thousands of Americans traveling or living in Europe. In Paris Harriss attended courses at the Sorbonne and studied art in the École d'Art Animalier. In 1934 he came back to the United States to visit his ailing father in Fayetteville. Before returning to Paris he stopped in Baltimore to see his friends Gerald W. Johnson and H. L. Mencken and was offered an editorial position on the *Evening Sun*, which he promptly accepted. He soon rose to the position of associate editor. He wrote editorials, columns, and special feature articles, including the first article in an American newspaper on the atomic bomb, which the *Sun* published on 12 September 1939. It was based on information in a scientific magazine published at Cambridge University. This was before the classified Manhattan Project had begun in the United States and six years before the bombs were dropped on Hiroshima and Nagasaki in Japan.

In 1936 Harriss published *The Foxes*, a novel that chronicled the lives of a family of foxes through the four seasons and shared how they survived in a fox-hunting country. The book is remarkable for the author's encyclopedic knowledge of the fauna, flora, weather, topography, and way of life on the plantation, which Harriss had observed or heard about in his youth, when he hunted and fished with his father. *The Foxes* became a bestseller, an alternate selection of the Book-of-the-Month Club, and the winner of the British Book Society Award for 1937. Critics praised it as nature writing at its best. Several of Harriss's short stories, poems, and essays were also reprinted in anthologies.

On 21 June 1937 Harriss married Margery Orem Willis, a prominent educator, socialite, and civic leader in Baltimore. After serving as departmental head and assistant principal in two high schools, she taught at Goucher College and Loyola College and was twice invited to serve on the Baltimore Board of Education. The Harrisses purchased from Whitaker Chambers a house in Charles Village, where their daughter was born. In 1951 they moved to Guilford, in the northern part of Baltimore.

In 1946 Harriss left the *Evening Sun* to become editor and co-owner of *Gardens, Houses, and People*, a magazine that became widely read in affluent suburbs of the Chesapeake region. This publication was financially successful, but after ten years Harriss tired of the editorial routine and resigned to become art critic and drama editor of the *News American*. After the Hearst organization sold this paper in 1986, Harriss joined the editorial staff of the Baltimore *Sun* and finished his distinguished career as one of the *Sun*'s most popular columnists.

Harriss was also a very courageous man. He wrote his last column for the *Sun* three days before his painful death from bone cancer, and it met his usual high standard. At the time of his death, all the Baltimore and New York newspapers carried obituaries. His colleague Albert Sehlstedt, Jr., said in his memorial tribute:

Mr. Harriss was one of the last surviving links to a talented coterie of *Evening Sun* editorialists and columnists who were at their journalistic peak in the Roaring '20s and the Depression '30s. . . . They brought a breezy, libertarian and sometimes irreverent style to their writing, often infuriating Maryland Puritans and delighting editors across the country who frequently reprinted their commentaries.

Another colleague, Neil A. Grauer, wrote:

He may have been the last true boulevardier in Baltimore. Sophisticated, witty, elegant, always dapperly attired and at ease in art galleries, symphony halls, theatres, museums, or salons; a connoisseur of food, wine, whiskey; a watcher of birds, rider to hounds, cultivator of roses; a keen observer of life who wrote about it with style and observed it all.

• A vast collection of Harriss's columns, travel essays, and related materials is contained in the manuscript collections at Duke University, including an unpublished autobiography, "Not All Magnolia." In addition to his novel *The Foxes*, a short story appeared in John Towner Frederick, ed., *Present-Day Stories* (1941). Obituaries are in the *Evening Sun*, 27 Sept. 1989, and the *Fayetteville Observer*, 28 Sept. 1989. A memorial tribute followed in the Baltimore *Sun*, 1 Oct. 1989.

GAY WILSON ALLEN

HARROD, James (1742–July 1793), frontiersman and soldier, was born at Big Cove (in present-day Bedford County), Pennsylvania, the son of John Harrod and Sarah Moore, pioneer farmers. Harrod's father, an immigrant from England, was killed by Indians in 1754. Harrod himself had no schooling and was barely literate, although in his youth he learned woodcraft. In 1755 the family narrowly escaped from a Delaware Indian raid. The sixteen-year-old Harrod served as a private in the campaign of 1758 against Fort Duquesne led by General John Forbes. From 1760 to 1764 Harrod farmed along with his mother and brothers. He was a ranger in Captain John Piper's company, which fought in Colonel Henry Bouquet's army versus the Indians at the battle of Bushy Run in August 1763. Harrod began going into the wilderness as a long hunter and trapper, and by 1767 he and his brothers Samuel and William had traversed westward to the French settlements on the Mississippi River in the Illinois country. The Harrod brothers brought their cargoes of furs to New Orleans. They hunted and trapped in central Kentucky and Tennessee and also down the Allegheny Ridge into North Carolina. In 1772 the Harrods settled on Ten Mile Creek, a tributary of the Monongahela River, near Pittsburgh.

In 1773 Harrod accompanied a Virginia surveying team down the Ohio and assisted in laying out a town at the falls (Louisville). In the spring of the next year, Harrod led a party of forty-one prospective farmers by canoes down the Ohio River and ninety miles up the

Kentucky River. Six miles west of the Kentucky River in June 1774 the Harrod group began building cabins for what would become Harrodstown (later Harrodsburg), the first settlement in Kentucky. On 8 July Daniel Boone appeared to warn the Harrod party of an outbreak of war with the Ohio Valley Indians. Harrod and his followers fled eastward to find refuge in the Holston River settlements. Harrod raised a company of twenty-two men, serving as their captain, for Colonel William Christian's regiment. These troops headed to the Ohio River to join Governor Lord Dunmore's Virginia militia army. Harrod saw no action, just missing the battle of Point Pleasant of 10 October 1774 by a few hours. The spring of 1775 found Harrod and most of his original party of settlers back at Harrodsburg finishing the cabin building. A few of the group broke off to start a settlement, Boiling Springs Station, in the Dick's River valley.

Richard Henderson and other members of the Transylvania Company soon arrived, laying claim to most of Kentucky on the basis of a treaty with the Cherokee Indians. Henderson wanted to organize the "Colony of Transylvania." Realizing that he had to make an accommodation with settlers already in Kentucky, Henderson called for a meeting of representatives from the four Kentucky settlements—Boonesborough, Harrodsburg, St. Asaph's, and Logan's. From 23 to 25 May this first assembly west of the Alleghenies met, with Harrod one of the eighteen delegates. A form of government and basic laws were agreed upon. Harrod and other original settlers were unhappy with the Transylvania arrangement, preferring to be under the distant administration of Virginia. They also resented Henderson and the Transylvania proprietors preempting for themselves lands at the falls of the Ohio and the high land prices and quitrents. In June 1776 George Rogers Clark called a convention of settlers, which repudiated the role of the Transylvania Company and petitioned Virginia to make Kentucky a county of that colony. With the creation of Kentucky County in December 1776, Harrod was made a captain of militia and a justice of the peace.

During the revolutionary war Harrod played an important role in defense preparations and in warding off Indian attacks on Harrodsburg. In January 1777, amidst Indian hostiles, he and thirty men boldly brought to Harrodsburg 500 pounds of powder sent by Virginia, which George Rogers Clark had been forced to bury near Limestone (Maysville) Kentucky. From October to December 1778 Harrod was on an expedition to secure salt from Kaskaskia on the Mississippi.

In February 1778 Harrod married Ann McDaniel, a 22-year-old widow who after her husband was killed by Indians in 1775 had been living with her father, Samuel Coburn. One child was born of the union, who, it was recognized even by Harrod, had been fathered by Harrod's farm manager; despite the embarrassment and his wife's continued flirtations with other men, Harrod was a loving husband and parent. His only stepson, James McDaniel, Jr., was captured and burned at the stake by Indians. In 1779 the Harrods moved to Boiling Springs, where James Harrod built the first frame house in Kentucky.

Harrod served in the Kentucky invasions against the Indians of the Ohio country. He went as a captain in John Bowman's expedition of 1779. With Clark, he fought at the battle of Piqua on 8 August 1780. He was in the Clark expedition of 1782, and on the expedition of 1786 led by Benjamin Logan, Harrod was credited with the capture of the Shawnee chief Moluntha.

In 1779 voters of Kentucky County sent Harrod to the Virginia House of Delegates. In the legislature Harrod voted for improvement of the Wilderness Road and the Virginia Land Act of 1779, which recognized preemption rights above all other claims for settlers residing in Kentucky before 1 January 1778, thus making Harrod a beneficiary. Under the law a preemptioner could obtain 400 acres near a town for free and an adjoining 1,000 acres at the cost of 10 shillings per 100 acres. Harrod was generous in allowing newcomers to stay on his estate while making their own arrangements. For Lincoln County, one of the three new jurisdictions created from Kentucky County in 1781, Harrod served on the grand jury. In December 1784 Harrod served in the Danville convention of representatives from each militia company; he opposed a special real-estate tax and an immediate break with Virginia, though he favored eventual statehood for Kentucky. Harrod was named one of the trustees for Harrodsburg when it was incorporated in 1785.

Looking after his 20,100-acre estate, Harrod lived quietly as a model citizen, though drinking heavily and once being indicted for bootlegging. For a while his home was open for a chapel and also a school. Harrod was involved, as were other Kentuckians, in many land suits, and one may have been the cause of his death. A disgruntled litigant surnamed Bridges in the summer of 1793 lured Harrod into the woods in search of the legendary Swift's Silver Mine. Harrod did not return, and his wife and others were certain but could not prove that Bridges had murdered Harrod. Harrod had made his mark as an explorer and pioneer. Brave, keen of judgment, and good-natured, he won the highest respect among the early settlers of Kentucky.

• Information on Harrod is in the Lyman C. Draper Collections, State Historical Society of Wisconsin: the Pittsburgh and Northwest Virginia, William Harrod, George Rogers Clark, and Kentucky papers. Most of Harrod's papers were destroyed in a fire at his house in the early 1800s, but a few can be found in the Kentucky Papers of the Draper Collections. A full biography is Kathryn H. Mason, *James Harrod of Kentucky* (1951). George M. Chinn, *Kentucky: Settlement and Statehood, 1750–1800* (1975), contains an in-depth appraisal of Harrod's career. Also see Lewis Collins, rev. by Richard H. Collins, *History of Kentucky* (2 vols., 1874), and Archibald Henderson, *The Conquest of the Old Southwest* (1920). William S. Lester, *The Transylvania Colony* (1935), notes the rivalry between the proprietors and the settlers. For Harrod's war experience, see Reuben G. Thwaites and Louise P. Kellogg, eds., *Documentary History of Dunmore's War 1774* (1905), Alexander Withers, *Chronicles of Border Warfare* (1895), and Charles G. Talbert, *Benjamin Logan: Kentucky*

Frontiersman (1962). For the Boone and Clark connection, see John M. Faragher, *Daniel Boone: The Life and Legend of an American Pioneer* (1992), and Temple Bodley, *George Rogers Clark: His Life and Public Services* (1926).

HARRY M. WARD

HARRON, Marion Janet (3 Sept. 1903–26 Sept. 1972), judge, was born in San Francisco, California, the daughter of Charles M. Harron and Minnie Jane Little. In the 1906 earthquake she escaped across the bay with her parents, who lost their home and possessions. Harron attended the University of California at Berkeley on scholarships, graduating Phi Beta Kappa in 1924 in economics. Her mentor was Jessica Peixotto, the first woman full professor of economics at Berkeley. While supporting herself as a teaching fellow and as an auditor for the state Industrial Welfare Commission, she attended Boalt Hall, worked on the law review, and earned her J.D. in 1926 with a thesis on Justice Louis Brandeis's dissenting opinions. At Boalt she joined Phi Delta Delta, a women's legal fraternity that provided her with a national network of women lawyers.

Harron was admitted to the California bar in 1926, but her interest in labor relations took her to New York City to direct a survey of the state's labor laws for the National Industrial Conference Board. In 1927 she joined the legal defense team for city rapid transit workers who defied an injunction preventing their unionizing. Also in 1927 she became an associate in a private law firm and developed a new specialty in tax law. A year later she accepted an invitation to the Institute for the Study of Law at Johns Hopkins University and prepared the 1928–1929 volume of *Current Research in Law*.

Returning to New York City in 1929, Harron joined the office of legal counsel of Manufacturers Trust Company and handled estates, bank liquidations, and corporate reorganizations during the depression. She volunteered her professional skills to the National Consumers League and produced a compilation of the state minimum wage laws for women, which was used in the League's amici briefs defending state protective laws against constitutional challenges. At the inception of the New Deal in 1933, she accepted an appointment as attorney, later assistant counsel, at the National Recovery Administration (NRA), where she drafted codes for the textile and food industries. With the demise of NRA she transferred in 1935 to the Resettlement Administration and returned to Berkeley as property custodian for the western region to handle the liquidation of corporations. She also began her own practice in California to develop her litigation skills.

In 1936 President Franklin Roosevelt appointed Harron to a twelve-year term on the board of tax appeals, an Article One court, renamed the Tax Court of the United States in 1942. She replaced the Republican incumbent, Annabel Matthews, whose reappointment to the "woman's seat" was strongly recommended by the board chairman. The general practice was to retain competent judges regardless of party, but FDR was under pressure from Eleanor Roosevelt and Molly Dewson at the Women's Division of the Democratic National Committee (DNC) to find positions for Democratic women activists. Harron's name was on the list, prepared by the general counsel of the Treasury department, of women lawyers with tax expertise who were qualified and available. California politicians and professional women supported her candidacy.

The court's geographical jurisdiction was national, so Harron held court in major cities across the country. She traveled by train and plane under difficult conditions during the war, living in hotels, holding night hearings, and adjusting to the mores of the local tax bars. Her cross-country plane trips in the 1940s took eighteen hours. She wrote that her workload was heavy, "grimy and tiring," relieved only by socializing with local tax lawyers.

Harron developed a reputation for fairness to the taxpayer and for mastery of the complicated and changing tax laws. In one of her important cases, *Trimble v. Commissioner* (1945), her opinion against the government rested on such competent legal analysis that the IRS gave up its plan to appeal its loss.

In 1942 Harron came close to nomination to the federal district bench in southern California. She survived the scrutiny of the attorney general and the White House staff, but Ed Flynn, DNC chair, intervened in favor of a California state judge, whose selection was favored by the party's financial backers. Harron and her women activist supporters were not large contributors.

Harron wanted to resign from the tax court and return to the West Coast and the stimulation of private practice after losing the Article Three judgeship. However, California law firms found the idea of a female partner unpalatable. In 1948 the secretary of the treasury and the DNC recommended her reappointment, but the Senate delayed consideration of her nomination in expectation of a Republican victory. Harry Truman gave her an interim appointment during the campaign period, then renewed her nomination after his reelection. Harron faced a protracted Senate committee hearing and was not confirmed until August 1949.

Her major opposition during the Senate Finance Committee hearings came from the Section of Taxation of the American Bar Association (ABA). The section, which had authority from the ABA to make four recommendations to the president for each vacancy on the tax court, refused to recommend Harron. After her nomination, the section asked for and received from the ABA authority to oppose nominees. It surveyed its membership of approximately 905 (which included only three or four women) and received fifty-seven responses in her favor, 104 in opposition, and 113 with no preference; a large majority did not return the questionnaire. On the basis of this response, section members testified against her, claiming that Harron lacked judicial temperament and was arrogant, rude, dictatorial, and critical of counsel appearing in her court. In her defense, the chief counsel of the Bureau of Internal Revenue testified: "I think men do not like to be criticized by women, and I think that is the real gravamen of her offense." Her 1935 law clerk, Carolyn Agger, testified that "as one of the relatively few women of the tax bar, it has always been a matter of profound gratification to see another woman doing . . . a very good job on the bench." An important element in her eventual success was the compilation and presentation to the Senate committee of her outstanding record between 1936 and 1947. Only 3 percent of her decisions had been reversed or remanded, the best record of the sixteen judges.

Harron gave primary credit for her confirmation to India Edwards, director of the women's division at DNC. She also had the strong backing of Congresswoman Helen Gahagan Douglas, Judge Dorothy Kenyon, national committeewoman Emma Guffey Miller, and the American Association of University Women, the National Woman's party, and women's bar associations. Congresswoman Mary Norton made a personal visit to the president to convince him not to withdraw her name and also did "a little missionary work with a few Senators."

Harron was a member of an informal national network of prominent women professionals and politicians. In Washington she belonged to a cluster of political women around Eleanor Roosevelt who worked in the DNC women's division or held high patronage positions and regularly met at the Women's National Democratic Club. The club served the same functions for female Democratics as the male politicians' social clubs that excluded women. Harron supported the Democratic party discreetly, attending the 1944 national convention and reporting to her friend Lorena Hickok enthusiastically on the equal rights and equal pay provisions in the platform.

She was also part of a small circle of women judges, serving between the 1930s and 1960s, who met at national conventions of the National Association of Women Lawyers and the ABA. Wherever she was assigned to trial duty, she contacted and encouraged the local party and law women and in turn received support from older judges, including Florence Allen of the federal Sixth Circuit. Harron shared Allen's concern for world peace and served as director of the Women's Action Committee for Lasting Peace in 1945. When assigned to cases in New York City, Harron attended meetings of a group working on plans for creation of the United Nations.

During the war years she had an intimate relationship with Hickok. Harron often visited the White House, where Hickok lived in guest quarters, and vacationed with her on Long Island. She was always invited to the joint birthday party for Hickok and Norton that Eleanor Roosevelt hosted for almost twenty years at Hyde Park. Harron was a hiker, horseback rider, and enthusiastic gardener, but her social and personal life was always subordinate to her work.

Harron retired from the tax court at the end of her second term in 1960. Eisenhower replaced Harron

with her longtime associate, Irene Feagin Scott. Due to the court's heavy caseload Harron was immediately recalled as a senior judge and continued to try cases for the next ten years. Harron never married. She lived with her mother, who made heavy demands on her attention, until the latter's death only one year before her own in Washington, two years after deciding her last case.

Harron was a workaholic, determined to perform to the highest professional standards. A plaintiff's lawyer in Detroit wrote in 1948: "That Judge Harron should have succeeded so admirably in a field so carefully scrutinized, so long regarded as an exclusively male province, is the best possible evidence of her really great ability." A San Francisco attorney wrote: "Personally, I would rather appear before her than any one of the other Judges." Although a few women had broken the barrier on courts with domestic or general jurisdictions, she was the first to show her ability in a technical, specialized, and complex legal field.

• The course of Harron's first nomination can be followed through the memos in Official Files 143 and 208h in the Franklin Delano Roosevelt Papers at the Roosevelt Presidential Library, Hyde Park, N.Y. These files contain the blue document of her nomination to federal district court torn in half. Personal information comes from letters written to Lorena Hickok, found in the Eleanor Roosevelt Collection, Lorena Hickok Papers (Boxes 9, 13, 14, 16, 17), at the Roosevelt Presidential Library, and from one chapter in Doris Faber, *The Life of Lorena Hickok* (1980). Harron delivered speeches on many occasions to women's groups; see "Judge Marion Harron Suggests Tax Field to Women Lawyers," *New York Herald Tribune*, 8 May 1934. Her renomination can be traced through memos and letters in Official File 41-F, Box 222, Papers of Harry S. Truman and General Correspondence: Harron, Papers of India Edwards in the Truman Presidential Library. The renomination hearings are reported in U.S. Congress, Senate, Committee on Finance, *Nomination of Judge Marion J. Harron* (14, 19 Apr.; 12, 13 May; 23 June 1949). Brief biographies appear in *Current Biography 1949* and in the memorial proceedings published in *U.S. Tax Court Reports* 58, pp. v–vii (1972). An obituary is in the *Washington Post*, 29 Sept. 1972.

BEVERLY B. COOK

HARSHBERGER, John William (1 Jan. 1869–27 Apr. 1929), botanist, was born in Philadelphia, Pennsylvania, the son of Abram Harshberger, a physician, and Jane Harris Walk. He attended Philadelphia public schools and graduated from Central High School in 1888 with a bachelor of arts degree. An aunt of his, who was a teacher, introduced him to botany through excursions in the city and in the country north of Philadelphia and provided him with a small herbarium. One result of this early introduction was a published paper—"A Few Pennsylvania Forestry Statistics" in *Forest Leaves* (37 [Mar.–Apr. 1889]). In 1888 Harshberger entered the University of Pennsylvania on a city scholarship and graduated with a bachelor of science degree in 1892. He had combined studies for the bachelor's degree with courses required for a doctorate, so he was able to graduate with a Ph.D. in 1893. His thesis was titled "Maize—A Botanical and Economic Study" and was published in the university's *Contributions from the Botanical Laboratory*.

Harshberger's first teaching experience had been in 1890 as assistant instructor in botany at Harvard University, where he had been studying trees and shrubs at the Arnold Arboretum, but it was at the University of Pennsylvania that he spent his life's work. His first appointment there was as an instructor in botany, biology, and zoology in 1893. He became a lecturer in the Department of Philosophy (or Graduate School) in 1896, assistant professor of botany in 1907, and professor of botany in 1911. He also taught astronomy, chemistry, and physics for three years (1892–1895) at the Rittenhouse Academy in Philadelphia. During his summers away from the University of Pennsylvania, Harshberger taught nature studies at the Pocono Pines Summer School (1903–1908); from 1913 to 1922 he was professor in charge of ecology at the Marine Biological Laboratory on Long Island, New York, and also directed botanical studies at the Maria Mitchell Association, Nantucket Island, Massachusetts, in the summers of 1914 and 1915. In 1907, the year that he became an assistant professor, he married Helen B. Cole, with whom he had two children.

Harshberger's interests were various and wide-ranging, and his numerous publications bear witness to this. His biographer Francis W. Pennell wrote, "Few have published more extensively, or on more sides of botanical science." The list included in his autobiography has 320 titles of books and articles, the most numerous being in ecology. Other subjects to which he devoted his research and writing were phytogeography, history of botany, biography, morphology, plant genetics, ethno-botany, economic botany, trees and forestry, botanical nomenclature and terminology, mycology, and wild flower preservation and conservation. His library of more than 2,500 bound volumes and 10,000 pamphlets also reflected the latitude of his intellectual curiosity. He was, in addition, an enthusiastic photographer, especially of flora that would be useful for his students' work, and he possessed a large collection of photographs in bound volumes along with lantern slides and plant specimens.

One of his early studies was of the history of botany in his own region, and the result was the book *The Botanists of Philadelphia and Their Work* (1899). It includes a hundred biographical sketches and describes the development of botanical science from the eighteenth century to the last decades of the nineteenth. His next major publication was *Student's Herbarium for Descriptive and Geographic Purposes* (1901).

Harshberger's paramount interest was in the field of phytogeography, and he gathered extensive data from Mexico, the West Indies, and the United States in preparation for his most impressive accomplishment, *Phytogeographic Survey of North America*, published, in English, in 1911 as volume thirteen of the German series *Die Vegetation der Erde* (ed. A. Engler and O. Drude). This was an ambitious work in which the author sought to describe all of the phytogeographic regions of the continent, detailing the geologic background for each, and portraying the present forms of plant life, by species, for all regions. Because of the great amount of data involved, the work grew to more than 700 pages. One of the most important goals of the book was to explain the origin and dispersal of floras as they were found growing together in their "societies" or "associations." This method of grouping component species was European in its origin, and Harshberger was one of the first American botanists to utilize it. In later writings, such as *The Vegetation of South Florida* (1914) and *The Vegetation of the New Jersey Pine-Barrens* (1916), he continued to emphasize the geographic side of plant study.

Another area of interest for him was in mycology, resulting in the publication of *A Text-Book of Mycology and Plant Pathology* (1917). Other publications were *Textbook of Pastoral and Agricultural Botany, for the Study of the Injurious and Useful Plants of Country and Farm* (1920) and, in a lighter vein, "The Old Gardens of Pennsylvania," published in the *Garden Magazine* (32 [1920–1921] and 33 [1921]).

In addition to his university teaching and research, Harshberger was an active participant in many organizations and projects away from the campus. He was a member of more than twenty-five scientific or conservation societies and served as president and vice president of the Ecological Society of America; president of the Anthropological Society of Philadelphia, of the Philadelphia Society of Natural History, and of the Pennsylvania Chapter of Sigma Xi; and vice president of the national Wild Flower Preservation Society. He was an outspoken advocate for the conservation of resources and the preservation of natural conditions and served for a number of years on the council of the Pennsylvania Forestry Association. He was the first president of the Pennsylvania Wild Flower Preservation Society.

Harshberger's botanical interests were worldwide, as shown by his extensive travels. He traveled in 1896 to Mexico; to Europe in 1898, 1907, and 1923; in 1901 to the West Indies; Alaska in 1926; South America in 1927; and northern Africa in 1928. In 1929, the year of his death, he was planning a trip to Australia and New Zealand. He always reported on his travels to the Philadelphia Botanical Club, and one member said, "We have always known that we could ask him freely to share with us the store of botanical experience that he had gathered." He was held in high esteem by both his colleagues and his students, and his contributions to the study of botany in the United States in both the nineteenth and twentieth centuries were of major importance. Harshberger died in Philadelphia.

• *The Life and Work of John W. Harshberger, Ph.D.* (1928), an autobiography, contains a bibliography as well as an interesting account of his ancestry. A useful biographical sketch is in H. B. Humphrey, *Makers of North American Botany* (1961). Further references may be found in F. Stafleu, *Taxonomic Literature*, vol. 2 (1979): 59–60. Obituary notices include G. E. Nichols in *Ecology* 11 (1930): 443–44, and Francis W. Pennell in *Bartonia* 11 (1929): 51–55. The latter contains a selected bibliography.

ROBERT F. ERICKSON

HART, Albert Bushnell (1 July 1854–16 June 1943), historian, was born in Clarksville, Pennsylvania, the son of Albert Gaillard Hart, a physician, and Mary Crosby Hornell. Hart, who grew up and went to school during the Civil War and Reconstruction, viewed the historic events of the period through the eyes of his father, an abolitionist during the antebellum era and a volunteer surgeon in an Ohio regiment during the war. As an adult, Hart often spoke of his antislavery, pro-Union background and how it had helped shape his sense of civic morality and his basic understanding of the nation's history.

Hart graduated from West High School in Cleveland (where his family had moved in 1864) in 1871. He then worked as a bookkeeper for five years before applying in 1876 to Harvard College, where he was somewhat older than most of his college classmates and one of the few to have attended public high school.

Hart's academic record at Harvard distinguished him further. He graduated second in his class with honors in history and English composition, and he was chosen by his classmates (among them Theodore Roosevelt, with whom he developed a lifelong friendship) to deliver the traditional "Ivy Oration" at commencement exercises in 1880. Awarded a scholarship to study modern constitutional history at Harvard's newly instituted Graduate Department of Arts and Sciences (1872), he did so for one year before traveling to Germany, where he earned a doctorate in history at the University of Freiburg in 1883. His dissertation, "The Coercive Powers of the Government of the United States," was supervised by Hermann von Holst.

On returning to the United States in August 1883, Hart was appointed an instructor of American history by Harvard's influential, young president Charles W. Eliot, one of the country's leading advocates of educational reform. Many of the reforms that Eliot advanced during his administration (1869–1909) contributed directly to an emerging culture of professionalism in American life. Whereas classical studies had traditionally dominated school and college curricula, Eliot, and many others, thought students would be better prepared to participate in an increasingly urban, industrial society if greater emphasis were placed on "modern" disciplines and on professional subjects. Hart's most significant accomplishments as a historian are best understood in this context of educational and professional reform.

Hart remarked late in life that he counted himself "fortunate in having . . . steered into a profession where the opportunities were great and trained men were few" (*Secretary's Report* [1930], p. 38). The comment describes fairly accurately the state of the field at the outset of his career. Historical scholarship throughout most of the eighteenth and nineteenth centuries had largely been an avocation of patrician gentlemen, and the study of history in schools and colleges had generally been accorded only minor curriculum status. In 1884, for example, the year the American Historical Association (AHA) was founded, there were only about twenty full-time history professors and thirty graduate-level history students in the entire country.

Hart played a leading role in reforming this situation. He contributed in many ways, especially during the first twenty-five years of his career, to the development of a new spirit of professionalism among historians and to the expansion of history education in schools and colleges throughout the country. He shared a conviction with other historians of his generation that history should be more "scientific" in its methodology and outlook. This notion had long been a historiographic ideal in Germany, where many reform-minded American historians had been trained. But it was Charles Darwin, more than Leopold von Ranke, who influenced Hart's conception of scientific history. In Darwin's theories of change and continuity in the natural universe Hart saw great potential for fruitful study of similar phenomena in the social universe.

Accordingly, Hart urged his colleagues and his students throughout his career to adopt research methods that were analogous to those Darwin had used so successfully. In his 1909 presidential address to the AHA, for example, he specifically cited Darwin in calling for "a genuinely scientific school of history, which shall remorselessly examine the sources . . . critically balance evidence . . . [and] dispassionately and moderately set forth results" (*American Historical Review* [1910], p. 232). But Hart did not think such a scientific approach provided a sufficient condition for historical generalization. He cautioned that facts, no matter how rigorously established, were meaningful only as interpreted by a historian, and he further argued that "history is not simply a condensation of facts, . . . [but] a transmutation of the lifeless lead of the annals into the shining gold of the historian" (p. 246). Key to this intellectual alchemy, he insisted, is the historian's sense of judgment, insight, empathy, and proportion. Hart believed, therefore, that history had much to gain by adopting methods of modern scientific inquiry, but also that "there is no great history . . . or, for that matter, scientific discovery" without sound, analytical judgment (pp. 250–51).

As a teacher, Hart sought to develop a pedagogy that was consistent with his understanding of the nature of history. Rather than rely on rote recitation, the most common form of history instruction at the time, he endeavored to put students in a position to exercise their judgment about historical issues and questions. He explained this approach to teaching in some of his earliest writings, "Methods of Teaching American History" (1885) and "History in High and Preparatory Schools" (1887), and in detailed syllabi that he prepared for his students. Eventually, these syllabi became the basis for the famous *Harvard Guide to American History* (1896) that he edited with Edward

Channing. (Hart, Channing, and Frederick Jackson Turner edited a second edition of the *Guide* in 1912.)

Hart's ideas about teaching probably had their greatest impact at the secondary school level. He was the only person to serve on both the National Education Association's Committee of Ten and the AHA's Committee of Seven, whose final reports, the *Report of the Committee on Secondary School Studies* (1893) and *The Study of History in Schools* (1899), respectively, drew a parallel between the habits of mind that history education provided and those that citizens needed in order to participate intelligently in society's decision-making processes. In doing so, these historic committees helped define the rationale that has supported history's place as a core component of the secondary school curriculum throughout the twentieth century.

Hart contributed further to the promotion of history education in schools by writing and editing textbooks and other instructional materials, which included the four-volume textbook series he edited, *Essentials in History* (first published in 1905), and his innovative series of source readers, *American History Told by Contemporaries* (1897–1929).

As a scholar, Hart's record is more remarkable for its size than its originality. His published works number more than 900 articles and about 100 books edited or authored, but many works involve a synthesis of other people's ideas, often for popular audiences. His real genius as a scholar was, as he once said, in "forming groups of allied [researchers] in cooperative historical enterprises" (*Secretary's Report* [1930], p. 38). Two such projects are particularly noteworthy: his work as editor of the first *American Nation* series (1904–1907) and his role in founding the *American Historical Review*. The former, a 26-volume history of the United States, is widely regarded as an enduring monument to the country's first generation of professional historians, and the latter, founded in 1895 and affiliated with the AHA in 1898, is the country's oldest and most prestigious journal of historical scholarship.

Hart served on the editorial board of the *Review* from its founding until his election as president of the AHA in 1909. Thereafter, however, his leadership role in history and history education began to wane. He became increasingly interested in political science and served as the first chair of Harvard's newly instituted Department of Government and as president of the American Political Science Association in 1912. His influence in this new discipline, however, was never as great as it had been in history. In the 1910s he also became increasingly involved in political and personal activities, which drew him further from history and from academe in general. In 1912 he served as a Roosevelt delegate to the Republican and Bull Moose party conventions, and he supported Roosevelt for president again in 1916. During the fifteen or so years before his retirement in 1926, he also traveled a great deal, often volunteering to speak to Harvard alumni groups around the country and using sabbaticals and other opportunities for extended trips abroad.

Hart's post-retirement years, especially after 1935, were a time of decline. His wife, Mary Hurd Putnam, whom he married in 1889, died in 1924, and his adopted twin sons moved away, leaving him alone and increasingly unhappy. He died in Belmont, Massachusetts.

By every measure, history and history education grew dramatically over the sixty-year course of Hart's career. Few historians of his generation were more instrumental in advancing this development. He helped to define new and more rigorous intellectual standards for historical scholarship, to institute formal means for historians to review and disseminate recent research in the field, and to fashion educational policies and programs to promote historical knowledge more generally in society. In sum, he helped to establish a profession essentially nonexistent at the start of his career.

• Hart's papers are in the Harvard University Archives and in Harvard's Houghton Library. Additional papers, especially relevant to his service on the Committee of Ten, are in Charles W. Eliot's papers in the Harvard University Archives. Interesting first-person accounts of his career are included in the *Secretary's Reports* of the Harvard Class of 1880 in the Harvard University Archives. For analyses of his career, see Carol F. Baird, "Albert Bushnell Hart: The Rise of the Professional Historian" in *Social Sciences at Harvard, 1820–1920*, ed. Paul Buck (1965); Lester Cappon, "Channing and Hart: Partners in Bibliography," *New England Quarterly* 24 (1956): 318–40; Samuel Eliot Morison, "A Memoir and Estimate of Albert Bushnell Hart," *Massachusetts Historical Society Proceedings* 77 (1966): 28–52; and Michael Whelan, "Albert Bushnell Hart and the Origins of Social Studies Education," *Theory and Research in Social Education* 22 (Fall 1994): 423–40.

MICHAEL WHELAN

HART, Edwin Bret (25 Dec. 1874–12 Mar. 1953), biochemist and nutritionist, was born near Sandusky, Ohio, the son of William Hart and Mary Hess, farmers. Hart developed an interest in the natural sciences at Sandusky High School. In 1892 he entered the University of Michigan and became an assistant to the chemist E. D. Campbell, who had lost his eyesight in a laboratory explosion. Hart's duties included reading to Campbell and taking him places by tandem bicycle. In 1897 he received a B.S. in chemistry and had his research published as coauthor with Campbell. He then became an assistant chemist at the New York Agricultural Experiment Station in Geneva, New York, performing routine food analyses for a year before being given the opportunity to work with Lucius Van Slyke on animal nutrition and dairy chemistry. In 1900 he took a two-year leave of absence to study for a Ph.D. with the protein chemist Albrecht Kossel at the University of Marburg in Germany. Kossel moved to Heidelberg in 1901, and Hart went with him. Heidelberg, however, would not accept the academic credits earned at Marburg. Unable to finish the degree requirements before returning to New York, Hart never obtained a Ph.D. From 1902 to 1906 he developed an outstanding reputation as a dairy chemist. In 1903 he married Ann Virginia De Mille, an actress and relative of Cecil B. De Mille; they had one child.

In 1906 the University of Wisconsin offered Hart the positions of department chairman and professor of agricultural chemistry. He gained a university-wide reputation as one of the outstanding teachers on campus. He combined stimulating expositions with a vigorous and challenging questioning of students; many declared his classes to be the best they had at Wisconsin. His best-known student was Conrad Elvehjem (Ph.D., 1927), his successor as chairman and future president of the university. As chairman Hart led the department during the time it achieved renown for its nutritional research and also managed its transformation in 1938 into a department of biochemistry. In honor of his role in establishing a department of prestige, in 1972 the university created the Edwin Bret Hart Professorship of Biochemistry.

Almost all of Hart's research was a collaborative effort, beginning with Van Slyke in New York and then at Wisconsin with Elmer McCollum, Harry Steenbock, and Elvehjem. With Van Slyke he made substantial contributions to dairy chemistry, especially on the proteins and enzymes in milk. In 1903 Hart and W. H. Andrews differentiated between bound (organic) and free (inorganic) phosphorus and established the presence and importance of phosphorus in various foods. At Wisconsin Hart continued this study with McCollum, demonstrating in 1909 that all of the phosphorus required by animals was available from the free phosphorus. This discovery led to the recognition of phosphorylation, the addition of phosphorus by covalent bonding to organic substances during metabolism.

Hart organized the single-grain feeding experiment of 1907–1911, which opened a new era in vitamin and mineral research. Scientists believed that foods were nothing but protein, carbohydrate, and fat, and that a proper balance of these met the nutritional needs of animals. Stephen Babcock, Hart's predecessor as professor of agricultural chemistry, wondered if the kind of food contributed to the nutritional value and in 1901 initiated a single-grain dietary experiment with cows from the university dairy herd. When the cows became ill, the experiment was terminated. Soon after coming to Wisconsin, Hart revived the experiment with his new appointees, McCollum, Steenbock, and George Humphrey. Sixteen cows were divided into four groups and each group was fed either a corn, oat, wheat, or mixed grain diet. The study proved that a balanced ration of protein, carbohydrate, and fat was insufficient in terms of growth rate, appearance, vigor, and ability to give birth to healthy calves. They raised the possibility that additional nutrients may be needed and called for new experimental approaches to nutrition.

The new approach came from McCollum who developed the first white rat colony in the United States for nutritional research. Using the rats as laboratory animals in carefully controlled experiments, he dis-

covered in 1914 "fat soluble A" and in 1915 "water soluble B." Hart collaborated with McCollum in the isolation and differentiation of the two new nutrients. After the departure of McCollum from Wisconsin in 1917, Hart pursued vitamin research with Steenbock and from the mid-1920s with Elvehjem as well. Steenbock and Hart demonstrated in 1919 the relation between vitamin A and the carotene in foods. Their study in the 1920s of leg deformity in chicks produced from the indoor feeding of hens revealed that the problem was caused by lack of vitamin D. They showed that the vitamin was needed for the absorption of calcium into the bones and that the vitamin D content of milk and other foods could be greatly increased by ultraviolet light radiation, findings that led to the prevention of rickets.

From 1923 Hart collaborated with Steenbock and Elvehjem in a comprehensive study of iron nutrition. By 1928 they proved that iron could not be utilized in the building of hemoglobin unless a small amount of copper was present. This discovery led Hart to basic aspects of the mechanism by which copper functions in cells and to a better understanding of anemia. Hart then studied the functional role of manganese, molybdenum, zinc, boron, and other trace elements in animals. In 1928 he determined the physiological effect of fluorine and its toxicity at various levels in the body. Among his last public acts was his congressional testimony in 1952 when fluoridation of drinking water was being advocated to prevent dental caries. He emphasized the need for more extensive studies before reaching any conclusions regarding possible benefits and dangers. In 1942 he revealed that iodine was essential in preventing goiter and advocated the use of iodized salt as a preventive measure in the diet of children. In 1945 with Elvehjem he studied the function of cobalt in the prevention of anemia. They also published many papers on all of the B vitamins, their role in nutrition, and the effects of their deficiency. In 1938 they demonstrated the curative effect of niacin on pellagra, which like rickets was an ailment afflicting millions of Americans.

Hart continued his research after his retirement in 1944, walking daily from his Madison home to his office, including the day he died. He belonged to the American Society of Biochemists, among other professional organizations, and he was elected to the National Academy of Sciences in 1944. He had great personal charm and was a brilliant conversationalist. He loved sports, attending both the indoor and outdoor athletic events at the university. For twenty-five years he spent summers at a cottage on Green Bay, where he sailed, swam, and played tennis. He also loved to travel, making several Christmas trips to Central and South America and to Hawaii.

Hart's career at the University of Wisconsin coincided with the discovery of vitamins and minerals as essential to animal and human health, and he played a key role in Wisconsin's contribution to both the basic science and public health aspects of nutrition.

• Hart's correspondence and other unpublished material are in the University of Wisconsin Archives. Conrad Elvehjem wrote the biography for the National Academy of Sciences, *Biographical Memoirs* 28 (1954): 117–61, with a bibliography of Hart's publications. A five-article tribute written by former students, "The Life and Accomplishments of Edwin Bret Hart," *Food Technology* 9 (Jan. 1955): 1–13, includes personal reminiscences and a survey of his contributions to animal and human nutrition and to food technology. Ellery Harvey gives a good, concise account of Hart at the time of his retirement in *Chemical and Engineering News* 22 (25 Mar. 1944): 435, 451. An obituary is in the *New York Times*, 13 Mar. 1953.

ALBERT B. COSTA

HART, James D. (18 Apr. 1911–23 July 1990), author, editor and college and library administrator, was born James David Hart in San Francisco, California, the son of Julien Hart, the owner of a silk company, and Helen Neustadter. He grew up in San Francisco, where his mother died when he was ten. He received his degrees in English: an A.B. from Stanford University in 1932, and an M.A. (1933) and Ph.D. (1936) from Harvard University. Before moving back to his native state, Hart taught at Amherst College in Massachusetts for one semester. He then became an instructor of English at the University of California at Berkeley from 1936 to 1941; he later became assistant professor (1941–1947), associate professor (1947–1951), and finally professor, a position he held for thirty-nine years. Hart served as department chairman twice, from 1955 to 1957 and 1965 to 1969 and as vice chancellor of the university from 1957 to 1960.

Known by his colleagues as a scholar, Hart is probably most accurately described as a literary historian because he devoted much of his time to collecting, ordering, and systemizing information. As one of his colleagues observed, "He was more of an informer than an interpreter. He amassed immense amounts of information, making it easily available" to historians, as well as students. His best-known work of this type is the *Oxford Companion to American Literature*, a standard reference for literature students, first published in 1941. This volume was one of the first major reference books on American literature; even more remarkable is that all of the information was culled and arranged by a single person, not a staff of editors.

Hart's specialty as a gatherer/organizer of information reflects his personal life: he kept records and chronicles all of his life, including a record of every book he read and the date finished. He collected books, art, people, and places, as can be seen in the list of works he wrote, published, and edited. Hart had a lifelong interest in fine printing. He started his own printing company, Hart Press, around 1940, and he printed Christmas booklets for over forty years. Hart also wrote books on fine printing and printers.

Other works by Hart include *The Popular Book: A History of America's Literary Taste* (1950) and *America's Literature*, with Clarence Gohdes (1955). He was the editor of *My First Publication: Eleven California Authors Describe Their Earliest Appearances in Print* (1961), Robert Louis Stevenson's *From Scotland to Silverado* (1966); Frank Norris's *A Novelist in the Making: A Collection of Student Themes and the Novels "Blix" and "Vandover and the Brute"* (1970); *New Englanders in Nova Albion: Some Nineteenth-Century Views of California* (1976); and *A Companion to California* (1978). He contributed to *American Heritage* and *American Literature* and was on the editorial board of the latter from 1952 to 1955 and again from 1964 to 1967.

In addition to his work in the English department, Hart also played a very active role in the expansion of Berkeley's Bancroft Library, where he was acting director from 1961 to 1962 and director from 1969 until his death. While a member of the English department, he initiated the collection of manuscripts of California authors, such as Frank Norris, Gertrude Atherton, and Jack London. As director, he expanded this collection to include letters of Hart Crane, Ambrose Bierce, and J. Ross Browne, whose correspondence to his wife provides a firsthand description of the pioneer development of California, a resource of significant value for studying the inception of the West.

As director, Hart made substantial changes to the holdings at the Bancroft library. He added the manuscripts of important contemporary British and American authors, such as Sean O'Faolain, Joan Didion, John Mortimer, Maxine Hong Kingston, and Tom Stoppard. He transferred to the library the Department of Rare Books and Special Collections, which included more than 300 volumes of incunabula; the Mark Twain Collection of more than 400 literary manuscripts, thousands of letters, and forty-five diaries and notebooks; and the university archives. He brought in source materials for the History of Science and Technology Collection and organized the Social Protest Ephemera Collection, which included pamphlets, posters, leaflets, and other records of right- and left-wing groups of the 1960s. In addition, Hart traveled to Mexico and El Salvador to visit libraries, museums, archives, universities, booksellers, and private collectors to maintain Bancroft's dominance as a research center for Mexico and Central America. He acquired an archive of Manila Galleon Trade from the 1770s to the 1820s—a collection full of information on shipping arrangements and cargoes as well as the correspondence of a sixteenth-century Guatemalan man to his uncle in Spain, which described life among the Indians in the highlands.

Hart's contributions to the Bancroft Library go beyond merely increasing its holdings. In the midst of a recession, he was able to expand the library's holdings and facilities, notably the construction of the Edward H. Heller Reading Room, funded almost entirely with private money raised in great part by himself. When Hart became the director of the library, the total endowment was $140,000; at the time of his death, it had grown to $8,450,000. In addition, Hart brought Bancroft into the computer age: the old catalog was converted to a computer system and on-line cataloguing was introduced.

During his library administration, Hart remained an active member in his profession. He was visiting professor at Harvard University in 1964 and a visiting Phi Beta Kappa scholar at several universities from 1980 to 1981. Earlier he had also been a visiting professor at the University of Uppsala, in Sweden. He was a fellow of the American Academy of Arts and Sciences and of the American Antiquarian Society. From 1970 to 1978 Hart was a trustee of Mills College, in Oakland, California, a position he assumed again in 1979 and held until 1986; from 1973 to 1976 he served as president of the board.

Hart married Ruth Arnstein in 1938. They had two children, Carol Hart Field and Peter Hart, both of whom helped Hart in his revisions of the *Oxford Companion to American Literature*. His wife died in 1977, and he later married Constance Crowley Bowles.

Hart's name will always be synonymous with the *Oxford Companion to American Literature*, particularly because it continues to be a valuable reference book for American literature. His service to the University of California at Berkeley has been recognized by the university's endowing in his name a chair for the director of the Bancroft Library. Although they came from different eras and held different notions of scholarship, former students and colleagues spoke of him with great respect as a scholar and an administrator. Although Hart preferred to keep quiet about his accolades and achievements, they will long be remembered because of his contributions to reference materials and the holdings of the Bancroft Library.

• Hart's collected papers can be found at the Bancroft Library. Other works by Hart include *Richard Henry Dana* (1935), *Melville and Dana* (1937), *An Original Leaf from the First Edition of Alexander Barclay's English Translation of Sebastian Brant's Ship of Fools* (1938), *A Note on Sherman Kent's "Russian Christmas before the Mast"* (1942), *A Puritan Bookshelf* (1948), *An Eyewitness of Eight Months before the Mast* (1950), *Interchanges from America's Literature* (1956), *Fine Printing in California* (1960), *American Images of Spanish California* (1960), *The Significance of the Library* (1962), *Fine Printers of the San Francisco Bay Area* (1969), *A Tribute to Edwin Grabhorn and the Grabhorn Press* (1969), *Influences on California Printing* (1970), *John Steinbeck, His Language: An Introduction* (1970), *The Scholar and the Book Collector* (1971), *E & RG: The Grabhorn Brothers* (1978), *Rare Book Stores in San Francisco* (1984). An obituary is in the *New York Times*, 24 July 1990.

MICHELLE M. PAGNI

HART, James Morgan (2 Nov. 1839–18 Apr. 1916), educator, translator, and writer, was born in Princeton, New Jersey, the son of John Seely Hart and Amelia Caroline Morford. After spending his childhood in Pennsylvania, he attended the College of New Jersey (now Princeton), graduating with an A.B. in 1860 and an A.M. in 1863. He also studied abroad in Geneva, Göttingen, and Berlin; he received the degree of Juris Utriusque Doctor (doctor of civil and canon law) from the University of Göttingen in 1864. Hart practiced law in New York City for several years and became an

assistant professor of modern languages at Cornell (1868–1872), where he taught southern European languages. He published a number of translations, the most important being his version of Franz Dingelstedt's *The Amazon* (1868) and *Cavé on Colour* (1869), as well as editions of other works that included selections from Goethe, Schiller, and De Quincey.

Hart returned to Europe to study English and German philology and was a special correspondent in Vienna for the New York *World* in 1873. In 1874, back in New York, he published a translation of Auguste Laugel's *England, Political and Social*, as well as his own *German Universities: A Narrative of Personal Experience*, which became a standard work for American graduate students seeking a degree abroad. Hart also wrote a number of book reviews, many of which were printed in the *Nation*. Between 1876 and 1890 Hart was chair of modern languages and English literature at the University of Cincinnati; he then returned to Cornell as professor of rhetoric and English philology between 1890 and 1907, when he retired. He was elected the fifth president of the Modern Language Association of America (MLA) in 1895, having served on the MLA Executive Council and as vice president.

In 1894 Hart began writing English composition textbooks. *The Handbook of English Composition* appeared in 1895, *The Essentials of Prose Composition* in 1902, and other works at various times. One of the first American college composition textbooks, Hart's *Essentials*, was based on his earlier *Handbook* and lectures on writing given to freshmen at Cornell. The book is a substantial and interesting contribution to the pedagogy of writing, providing practical assistance to beginning writers in composing sentences, paragraphs, and larger compositions. Hart used numerous examples from works of professional writers, selected from both earlier literature and writings of his own time. In placing an emphasis on models written by experts, Hart was on solid pedagogical ground.

In Hart's time, close professional, even personal, associations between high school teachers and college professors were common; Hart recognized the necessity of strengthening and building on these connections. Indeed, in his MLA presidential address, "English as a Living Language," Hart proposed a model English curriculum extending from grammar school through college, a model that, if adopted, would demand close cooperation between schools and colleges. He further suggested that for both secondary and higher education, English reading and writing be put at the center of the curriculum. Admission to college would depend on "the ability to state one's knowledge in clear and proper English" because such ability is "the one universally recognized badge of scholarship." But Hart insisted that the same kind of training be given to students not going to college "because such training is the vital and informing spirit of all education." Hart used his position at Cornell and his influence in the MLA to campaign for improvement in the teaching of English; he was especially active in the New York schools, attending meetings of teachers, preparing teacher-training courses, and writing.

One of Hart's major complaints about the teaching of English was that "both school and college seem to be resting under the comfortable delusion that good writing is a matter which concerns the English department alone. Is not correct writing the business of everybody? Ought not every teacher to be a teacher of clear and coherent expression?" Further, Hart recommended that in English courses, students begin with instruction in description and narration: "Strangely enough, the greater part of the little school writing that is now taught is expository. The young are called upon to *discuss* things before they have been trained to *see* them. From this it results that they learn neither to see nor to discuss. Their writing is aimless and immethodical."

Hart's personal life was marked by the respect and admiration of his students and colleagues. He was married briefly (date unknown) to a Miss Wadsworth of New York; she died shortly after their marriage. In 1883 he married Clara Doherty of Cincinnati; they had no children. Hart was honored on his seventieth birthday by a Festschrift edited by Clark Sutherland Northup and others. He lived in Ithaca, New York, until 1914, when he moved for his health to Washington, D.C., where he died.

• The Division of Rare and Manuscript Collections, Cornell University Library, has a collection of Hart's personal and professional correspondence. See also Hart's *Syllabus of Anglo-Saxon Literature* (1881), *International Exhibitions: Paris, Philadelphia, Vienna*, coauthored with Charles Gindriez (1878), and *The Development of Standard English in Outline* (1907). Biographical information may be found in W. T. Hewett, ed., *Cornell University: A History* (1905), and in C. S. Northup, ed., *Addresses at the Presentation of the Memorial Tablet to J. M. Hart in Sage Chapel, June 3, 1917* (Cornell Univ. Official Pubs., 8D, July 1917).

RICHARD E. MEZO

HART, Joel Tanner (11 Feb. 1810–2 Mar. 1877), sculptor, was born on a farm in Clark County, Kentucky, the son of Josiah Hart, a surveyor, hunter, and farmer, and Judith Tanner. He grew up in rural Clark County, where he received only about three years of elementary education. Despite this lack of formal education, he became an avid reader and took advantage of the library of local architect Philip B. Winn, who owned books on architecture and sculpture. Following his mother's death in 1825, he moved with his brothers to nearby Bourbon County, Kentucky, in search of employment. There he met Samuel Houston, who was a stonemason, painter, and carpenter as well as a man of some erudition. Like Winn, Houston owned a small library that Hart used, and it was probably Houston who taught Hart the rudiments of stone carving.

During the late 1820s and early 1830s Hart worked in Kentucky as a stonemason, designing and building fences, chimneys, springhouses, steps, fireplaces, and foundations in Bourbon, Clark, and Nicholas counties. He supplemented his income by teaching English

and rhetoric. At this time he began to produce his first rather crude works of art—a low relief carving of three cherubs and several watercolors and drawings (all now at the Kentucky Historical Society, Frankfort), for example—and to set his sights on higher career goals.

Around 1835 he moved to Lexington, Kentucky, which at the time was the social and cultural center of the state. There he carved tombstones in a marble yard operated by Patrick Doyle. His abilities attracted the attention of the journalist and abolitionist Cassius Marcellus Clay, who persuaded Hart to try his hand at more complicated forms of sculpting. Hart's first effort was to carve a portrait bust of Clay, which he did with some success. The finished product (Margaret I. King Library, University of Kentucky, Lexington) impressed the Cincinnati sculptor Shobal V. Clevenger. Clevenger gave Hart advice, and, realizing how much they had in common, the two artists returned to Cincinnati together. Hart may have stayed there for as long as a year, studying and carving reliefs for Clevenger, who rewarded him with his first set of professional tools.

In 1837 Hart established a studio in Lexington for the production of portrait busts; in order to improve his skills as an artist, he began studying anatomy at nearby Transylvania College. Late the following year a committee of Lexington citizens commissioned him to produce a bust of Andrew Jackson. Hart traveled to the former president's home, the "Hermitage," outside Nashville, Tennessee, to model the work from life. Jackson and the committee members were pleased with the results (Kentucky Historical Society). The bust was exhibited in Cincinnati and Lexington, and Hart's fame began to rise, at least locally. Over the next several years he produced a substantial number of portrait busts of prominent Kentuckians. The best known of these was of Henry Clay (plaster casts at Kentucky Historical Society and Maryland Historical Society, Baltimore) whose bust Hart first modeled in the early 1840s. Among his other works from this period were portraits of Benjamin Winslow Dudley, professor of anatomy and surgery at Transylvania College in Lexington (1839, private collection, Lexington); and the Reverend Alexander Campbell, who was in Lexington for a well-publicized debate on Christian baptism in 1843 (casts at Louisville Free Public Library and Bethany College, W.Va.). Later in the decade Hart modeled the busts of Kentuckians James Taylor (1847, Kentucky Historical Society), Robert Wickliffe (c. 1847–1848, Speed Museum, Louisville, Ky.), and John J. Crittenden (1849, Kentucky Historical Society).

Hart had hopes for a wider fame and fortune. He decided to make a promotional tour of the major cities of the eastern United States, starting in Richmond, Virginia, where the newly formed Ladies Clay Association was preparing to award a major commission for a statue of their hero, Henry Clay. Hart departed Lexington in late August 1845 and arrived in Richmond about two weeks later. His meeting with the Clay committee was successful, and he was awarded the coveted commission for the statue. After visiting Washington, Philadelphia, and New York, where he exhibited examples of his work and made important connections with other artists such as Asher B. Durand, Thomas Sully, and James Reid Lambdin, he returned to Kentucky to begin work on the statue for Richmond.

At Clay's home, "Ashland," outside Lexington, Hart made a new model of the statesman's head as well as a small clay model of his entire figure. The artist knew that the only way he could satisfactorily complete the commission was to go to Italy, where he could find quality marble and workmen who were adept at carving it. He departed Lexington in September 1849 and, after visiting Paris, Naples, and Rome, arrived in Florence in November. Work on the statue of Clay was delayed when the ship on which the model was being transported sank, only the first of many delays for the project. Once established in Florence, Hart was easily distracted by other projects. Soon after his arrival in Italy he began working on a pointing device, used for the enlargement and reproduction of sculpture, which he eventually patented and for which he achieved some notoriety. He became an active participant in the Anglo-American expatriate community in Florence, which included leading neoclassic sculptors Hiram Powers, Chauncey Ives, Randolph Rogers, and William Henry Rinehart. As the decade progressed, Hart's studio in the Piazza della Indipendenza joined those of other artists as a mandatory stopping place for many foreign visitors, some of whom ordered portrait busts from him. These included Mrs. Cornelius Vanderbilt I (1854, unlocated), the actress Genevieve Ward (1855, Royal Shakespeare Theatre, Stratford-on-Avon, England), and former president Millard Fillmore (1856, Buffalo and Erie County [N.Y.] Historical Society). In 1853 Hart received a commission for his first ideal work, an allegorical bust he called *Il Penserosa* (Margaret I. King Library).

Meanwhile, work on the statue of Clay was progressing, though far behind schedule. To delay matters further, Hart received a commission from the city of New Orleans for a bronze replica of the work. The prospect of this new project made Hart insecure about his technical abilities, and late in 1856 he went to London to study and to seek further commissions. During the fifteen months he spent in that city, he received commissions for at least twelve busts, including an order from Charles Dickens for a portrait of Dr. Southwood Smith, the British sanitary reformer (1856, National Portrait Gallery, London).

With the help of his nephew Robert Hart, who had come to Florence from his home in Missouri to learn to be a sculptor, the elder Hart finally finished the clay and plaster models of his statue of Henry Clay in July 1858. Shortly thereafter a bronze version was cast in Munich and shipped to New Orleans, and the marble for Richmond was completed in Florence and shipped to the United States early in 1859. The long delay in completing the Richmond version caused ill feeling between the Ladies Clay Association and Hart; therefore, the sculptor decided not to go to Virginia for the unveiling of the sculpture, scheduled for 12 April 1860, the anniversary of Clay's birth. Instead Hart made his first and last return trip to the United States to attend the inauguration of the bronze cast in New Orleans, which occurred on the same day as the unveiling in Richmond. After brief visits to Lexington and Washington, D.C., Hart sailed again for Italy.

The Civil War years were difficult for Hart and other American artists; commissions were rare, and the Americans on whom Hart depended for these were less likely to make the Grand Tour, which would bring them to his studio. The one bright spot during this period was an order from the city of Louisville for yet another replica of the statue of Clay. This version, in marble, was unveiled in the Jefferson County courthouse in Louisville in 1867.

The money Hart received from the Louisville commission allowed him to pursue a more artistically expressive idea, one he had been contemplating for many years. This was a classicizing, life-size sculpture eventually called *Woman Triumphant*. It depicted an idealized nude female figure, not unlike the traditional image of Venus, holding an arrow above her head and out of reach of a Cupid-like child at her feet. Hart spent the final decade of his life working on this sculpture; *Morning Glory*, an ideal figure of a little girl; and several portrait commissions. Shortly after he completed the model for *Woman Triumphant*, he fell ill with "stone in the bladder." Hart, who never married, died in Florence.

Hart was buried in the English Cemetery in Florence, but the Kentucky legislature appropriated funds to have his remains brought back to the state of his birth. On 18 June 1887 he was reinterred with appropriate ceremonies in the state cemetery in Frankfort.

In the early 1880s a group of women from Lexington formed the Hart Memorial Association to raise money to purchase *Woman Triumphant*. The marble sculpture, which was carved from Hart's model under the supervision of sculptor George Saul, was shipped to Lexington and erected in the rotunda of the Fayette County courthouse. Sadly, it was destroyed when the building burned in May 1897.

The attention given to Hart by the citizens of his native state—in their transferral of his body to Kentucky and in their concern over his chef d'oeuvre, *The Woman Triumphant*—is evidence of the effect he had on the art and culture of at least one region of the United States. At the same time and against great odds, he became a significant member of the second generation of American neoclassic sculptors and survived in the competitive atmosphere of Florence's expatriate community.

• Following his death Hart's papers entered the collection of his friend, Kentucky antiquarian and bibliophile Reuben Durrett. Some years later they were purchased from Durrett's estate by the University of Chicago's Joseph Regenstein Library, where they remain. The collection contains the first drafts of hundreds of letters Hart sent, the originals of those he received, and his diary for the years 1845–1849. Other notable repositories of Hart material are the Margaret I. King

Library, University of Kentucky, Lexington; the Filson Club, Louisville, Ky.; and Transylvania Library, Transylvania University, Lexington. The first published biography of Hart was a brief work by Carrie Williams Berry, undated but probably published privately in Lexington in the 1880s. The events surrounding the completion of *Woman Triumphant* led to the publication of Issa Desha Breckinridge and Mary Desha, *"The Work Shall Praise the Master": A Memorial to Joel T. Hart* (1884). Samuel W. Price devoted a lengthy chapter to Hart in his *The Old Masters of the Bluegrass* (1902). See also J. Winston Coleman, *Joel T. Hart, Kentucky Sculptor* (1962). Of more recent date are two articles by David B. Dearinger, "Joel Tanner Hart: Kentucky's Neo-Classic Sculptor," *Kentucky Review* 8 (Spring 1988): 3–32, and "The Diary of Joel Tanner Hart," *Filson Club History Quarterly* 64 (Jan. 1990): 5–31. An interesting account of events following Hart's death is given in Clifford Amyx, "Joel T. Hart's Executors: George Saul and Edward Silsbee," *Filson Club History Quarterly* 65 (Oct. 1991): 474–85.

DAVID B. DEARINGER

HART, John (1714–11 May 1779), signer of the Declaration of Independence, was born in Hopewell Township, Hunterdon County, New Jersey, to Edward and Martha Hart, Presbyterians from Newtown, Long Island, who began farming there about 1699. Raised in comfortable circumstances, Hart purchased an estate of 193 acres in 1739, when he married Deborah Scudder, with whom he had thirteen children. By 1775 Hart was Hopewell's largest landholder; he possessed at least 611 acres, owned three slaves, bred racing horses, and operated grain and fulling mills.

The son and son-in-law of justices of the peace, John Hart first sat as a justice on the county court in 1755. He entered the assembly in 1761 and won reelection five consecutive times, serving until 1771. Though often appointed to the exclusive committee that drafted the assembly's addresses to the governor, he rarely chaired committees on important legislation and had only modest impact on the lower house during these years.

Hart narrowly lost his assembly seat in 1772 and did not reenter the legislature until after independence. His position as judge of common pleas, held since 1768, maintained his prestige, however, and rising colonial dissatisfaction with parliamentary laws allowed him to strengthen his reputation as a firm opponent of unconstitutional laws. Having consistently and conspicuously objected to parliamentary taxation since 1765, Hart took a leading role in organizing Hunterdon County's Committee of Correspondence in July 1774 and its Committee of Safety in September 1775.

From 1774 to 1776 Hart attended every session of New Jersey's extralegal Provincial Congress. He played a prominent role at the 1775 session by drafting a financial plan to fund the newly organized congressional militia, writing an ordinance to compel payment of extralegal taxes to support it, and disbursing money from the treasury. On 28 October 1775 he was named to the Committee of Safety, which coordinated financial and defensive affairs between sessions of the Provincial Congress. He took office as vice president of the New Jersey Congress on 15 June 1776.

The Provincial Congress appointed him a delegate to the Continental Congress on 22 June 1776. He took his seat at Philadelphia on 1 July and voted for independence the next day. Shortly after signing the Declaration of Independence on 2 August he left the Continental Congress to participate in New Jersey's forthcoming state elections. Hart never again held national office.

On 13 August 1776, Hart was elected to the legislature's lower chamber. Meeting in late August, New Jersey's assembly unanimously chose him as the first Speaker of the House under the state's revolutionary constitution. From then until 2 December Hart presided over the assembly six days each week as it struggled to send money and troops to the beleaguered Continental army. During this critical period, Hart absented himself from the speaker's chair only once, in order to be at his wife's bedside when she died on 8 October.

The Continental army's retreat in December 1776 left New Jersey's Whigs virtually defenseless against advancing British forces. Hart found himself in particular danger, since a reward was offered for his capture and his home lay close to British garrisons at Trenton and Princeton. After burying his valuables, driving his livestock into the woods, and hiding his youngest children with relatives, the sixty-three-year-old signer abandoned his farm in late December; he fled into the wilderness for a few days, until Washington's victories at Trenton and Princeton permitted him to return home. During his absence, however, his estate had been damaged by enemy foragers, and again in mid-January British troops almost plundered the flour stored at his mills before being repulsed by local militia.

On 18 March 1777 Hart became a member of New Jersey's Council of Safety—an executive committee given virtually unrestricted military and judicial powers to prosecute the war—and served as its treasurer. Reelected as Speaker of the state assembly in 1777 and 1778, he continued in that position until 9 November 1778, when he was confined to bed with painful urinary disorders. John Hart died following a protracted illness at his home in Hopewell Township.

• Few of the signer's personal papers survive aside from the John Hart Manuscripts at the New Jersey Historical Society in Newark. Sources concerning Hart's revolutionary career are in State of New Jersey, *Minutes of the Provincial Congress and the Council of Safety of the State of New Jersey, 1774–1776* (1879) and *Minutes of the Council of Safety of the State of New Jersey, 1777–1778* (1872). The only full-scale biography is Cleon E. Hammond, *John Hart: The Biography of a Signer of the Declaration of Independence* (1977).

THOMAS L. PURVIS

HART, Joseph Kinmont (16 Feb. 1876–10 Mar. 1949), educator, editor, and writer, was born in Thorncreek Township, Whitley County, near Columbia City, Indiana, the son of David N. Hart and Lucy Kinmont, farmers. Hart's early religious upbringing as a member of a small, closely knit Protestant community contributed to his later writings emphasizing community influences in education.

Hart attended Franklin College, a small, Baptist-affiliated college in Franklin, Indiana. A call to military service in the Spanish-American War in 1898 interrupted his studies, but he returned to complete an A.B. in 1900. At the age of twenty-four Hart set off for graduate study at the University of Chicago. There his interaction with the large cosmopolitan city of Chicago, as well as the newly established graduate programs at the University of Chicago, proved to be a formative experience that set the tone and direction for his later work as social theorist and educator. Hart studied with several influential scholars who broke new ground in the social sciences. James Tufts and George Herbert Mead in philosophy, James Rowland Angell in experimental psychology, Charles Richmond Henderson and William I. Thomas in sociology, and especially John Dewey's educational writings and direction of the university's laboratory school, all guided Hart in a broadly interdisciplinary approach to educational theory. During the years 1903 through 1905 Hart left Chicago for schoolteaching assignments in rural Illinois and Iowa. He married Lulu Calvert in 1903. Hart resumed his studies at the university in 1906 as a university fellow, completing work for the Ph.D. in 1909.

Hart's college teaching career began with his appointment as professor of philosophy and psychology at Baker University in Baldwin, Kansas, in 1909. The following year Hart accepted a position as assistant professor of education at the University of Washington in Seattle. Although Hart's work with pedagogy and the training of teachers proved to be an unqualified success, his controversial public speaking activities, both on and off campus, created dissension among colleagues and administrators. His eloquent speeches tended to stir emotions and make enemies because of his provocative approach to ethical, religious, and political topics. In July 1915 Washington's president, Henry Suzzulo, dismissed Hart from the university, precipitating one of the early AAUP (American Association of University Professors) academic freedom investigations and hearings. Hart spent the following year teaching in a county school near Seabeck, Washington, a small, rural community along the Puget Sound. At this time Hart completed his first substantial book of educational history and theory, *Democracy in Education: A Social Interpretation of the History of Education* (1918). It displayed Hart's broad grasp of educational theory with a skillfully written, progressive slant on contemporary educational problems.

William T. Foster, president of Reed College in Portland, Oregon, offered Hart a provisional teaching position in the education department in the fall of 1916. Foster, the first president of Reed, innovated a remarkable program there that grew to become a national model of liberal undergraduate education noted for its academic rigor, close relationships between dedicated faculty and students, community outreach, and the conspicuous absence of intercollegiate athletics. Foster recognized Hart's talent and promise as an exciting young teacher and scholar, one who inspired his students toward progressive ideals. In 1919, during U.S. involvement in World War I, Hart left the college for work in the War Camp Community Service, serving as a trainer of volunteer counselors and social workers. At this time Hart composed a book of sociological analysis, *Community Organization* (1920), based on his experiences in the field.

Hart's movement toward the burgeoning area of human social welfare and the training of social workers led him to accept a position as associate editor for the *Survey*, a social welfare, reform-oriented periodical published in New York City. Beginning in October 1920 Hart's expressive journalistic writing and editorial work for the *Survey* (a weekly until 1922, when it became a bimonthly publication) allowed him wide latitude for the advocacy of educational and social reform. He reported on educational and community issues on the local and national levels, and he excelled as an articulate voice calling out for progressive reform. In 1921 Hart became a lecturer at the New School for Social Research, giving courses on various facets of progressive education and theory. There he formed close ties with James Harvey Robinson, one of the founders and early theorists of the school.

Through his writings and lectures in the 1920s, Hart assumed a leadership role in the new and rising adult education movement. Following a trip to Denmark in 1925, Hart advanced the Danish Folk School as a practical model for an intimate, community-based education. During 1924–1925 Hart contributed articles and helped edit two influential special issues of the *Survey Graphic*: "Giant Power" (1 Mar. 1924) and "Regional Planning" (1 May 1925). These efforts allied him with the Regional Planning Association of America (RPAA), a group of farsighted intellectuals, including Lewis Mumford, Charles Stein, and Benton MacKaye, that advocated a more humane organization for cities and regions. Two books derived from his *Survey* writings, *Adult Education* (1927) and *Light from the North* (1927), provided Hart with wide exposure as an influential, potent educational writer and critic. He also demonstrated his closeness to the educational philosophy of John Dewey with a third book, *Inside Experience: A Naturalistic Philosophy of Life and the Modern World* (1927). A broadly philosophical but nontechnical work, it was Hart's interpretive explication of Dewey's seminal book *Experience and Nature* (1925).

Hart returned to academe in the fall of 1927 when he accepted a teaching position in the education department at the University of Wisconsin. He became a prime mover in the university's newly established Milwaukee Extension Center, an innovative educational outreach program. With the publication of *A Social Interpretation of Education* (1929), Hart reached the peak of his influence and stature as a nationally known educational theorist and critic. He moved to Nashville, Tennessee, in 1930 to head the newly created Department of Education at Vanderbilt University.

By the spring of 1934, however, Hart again found himself in the center of a storm of controversy, and Vanderbilt's chancellor, James Kirkland, arbitrarily dismissed him from the faculty. Many on Campus viewed Hart as the provocateur of an editorial attack published in the student newspaper harshly critical of the staid and tradition-bound Vanderbilt faculty and administration. Also, Hart's iconoclastic outspokenness tended to isolate and alienate him from colleagues and administrators. As at Washington, Reed College, and Wisconsin, a similar pattern held true at Vanderbilt as well. Another AAUP investigation ensued but did not further Hart's cause.

After his fall from grace at Vanderbilt, Hart reluctantly returned to New York, where he found employment as a part-time instructor at Teachers College, Columbia University. There he associated with the "social reconstructionists," a group of leftist educators and theorists centered at Teachers College in the 1930s. Hart served as contributing editor and wrote several pieces for their journal, the *Social Frontier*. Hart retired from Teachers College in 1940. He had married Frances Stuyvesent Uhrig, his second wife, in 1929. It is not known how his first marriage ended. He had no children and died in Hudson, New York.

• Collections of Hart materials are in the University Archives of the University of Washington, Seattle; in the Survey Papers, part of the Social Welfare History Archive at the University of Minnesota, Minneapolis–St. Paul; and in the University Archives of Vanderbilt University, Nashville, Tenn. Additional published works by Hart include *Educational Resources of Village and Rural Communities* (1913); *The Discovery of Intelligence* (1924); *Prophet of a Nameless God* (1927); as editor, *Creative Moments in Education: A Documentary Interpretation of the History of Education* (1931); *Education for an Age of Power: The TVA Poses a Problem* (1935); *Mind in Transition: Patterns, Conflicts, and Changes in the Evolution of the Mind* (1938); and *Education in the Humane Community* (published posthumously in 1951 by the John Dewey Society). The most complete biographical treatment of Hart is Kenneth J. Potts, "Joseph Kinmont Hart: Educator for the Humane Community" (M.A. thesis, Vanderbilt Univ., 1995). Harold W. Stubblefield, *Toward a History of Adult Education in America: The Search for a Unifying Principle* (1988), evaluates Hart's life in terms of his adult education writings. Other secondary treatments include Neil Betten and Michael Austin, *The Roots of Community Organizing, 1917–1939* (1990), and James M. Wallace, *Liberal Journalism and American Education, 1914–41* (1991). An obituary is in the *New York Times*, 12 Mar. 1949.

KENNETH J. POTTS

HART, Lorenz (2 May 1895–22 Nov. 1943), Broadway lyricist, was born Lorenz Milton Hart in New York City, the son of Max Hart, a business entrepreneur, and Frieda Isenberg. Equally important to his future professional life were his education at the Columbia Grammar School from 1911 to 1914 and the summer dramatic productions at the Weingart Institute in the Catskills in 1908–1909 and at Camp Paradox in the Adirondack Mountains from 1910 to 1913, in which Hart took part as an actor. In 1914 he matriculated at Columbia University's School of Journalism, where he wrote skits and lyrics and appeared as a female impersonator in all-male varsity shows in 1915 and 1916. In 1916 Hart adapted and translated songs from the operetta *Die Tolle Dolly*, and in 1917 he copyrighted his own lyrics for the operetta *Hello Central*. After leaving Columbia in 1917 without a degree, Hart served for three summers from 1918 to 1920 as a dramatics counselor at Brant Lake Camp in the Adirondacks.

Probably in late 1918 and certainly by 1919, Hart was introduced by a mutual friend to an aspiring sixteen-year-old songwriter, Richard Rodgers, who was looking for a lyricist. In an often-quoted remark, Rodgers remembers in his autobiography that he "left Hart's house having acquired in one afternoon a career, a partner, a best friend, and a source of permanent irritation." In 1919 Hart directed Rodgers's second amateur show, *Up Stage and Down*, and by 1920 the team of Rodgers and Hart had begun their twenty-four years of exclusive collaboration that produced nine amateur productions, including the Columbia University varsity shows of 1920, 1921, and 1923, and three shows at the Institute of Musical Art (later Juilliard), where from 1921 to 1923 Rodgers took classes in ear training and music theory and studied composition with Percy Goetschius.

Shortly after Rodgers and Hart became a team in 1919, their song "Any Old Place with You" was interpolated in a Broadway show, and more of their songs appeared in *Poor Little Ritz Girl* the following year. Otherwise, Rodgers and Hart's professional credits before 1925 were sparse and disappointing. Their first solo Broadway venture, *The Melody Man* in 1924, proved an unsuccessful collaborative debut with Herbert Fields, their principal librettist from 1923 to 1928. During these difficult years Hart also worked as an adapter and translator for United Plays; among his uncredited work was an English translation of Ferenc Molnar's *Liliom*, the source of Rodgers and Hammerstein's second hit musical, *Carousel*.

Success arrived belatedly in 1925, when Rodgers and Hart were asked to contribute songs in a fundraising effort sponsored by the Theatre Guild. The production, called *The Garrick Gaieties*, was an intimate revue that parodied popular Broadway plays and performers well known to Broadway audiences of the time. Rodgers and Hart received much of the credit for the success of this limited-run engagement, which was expanded to include 211 performances. One song from the revue, "Manhattan," originally composed for the unproduced *Winkle Town* in 1922, became Rodgers and Hart's first hit. Later in 1925, their first book musical, *Dearest Enemy* (with Fields), launched a succession of popular, well-received musicals full of perennial song favorites, including *Peggy-Ann* in 1926 ("Where's That Rainbow?"), *A Connecticut Yankee* in 1927 ("My Heart Stood Still" and "Thou Swell"), *Present Arms* in 1928 ("You Took Advantage of Me"), and *Ever Green* in 1930 ("Dancing on the Ceiling").

At this stage in his career, Hart earned much acclaim for his clever settings of Rodgers's memorable songs that characteristically exhibit triple rhymes and other verbal pyrotechnics. Even less successful works dating from these productive years, such as *Spring Is Here* (1929) and *Simple Simon* (1930), yielded such lasting popular songs as "With a Song in My Heart" and "Ten Cents a Dance."

During the early years of the depression, from 1931 to 1935, Rodgers and Hart left Broadway for Hollywood. The team produced three memorable and innovative movie musicals during this period: *Love Me Tonight* and *The Phantom President* in 1932 and *Hallelujah, I'm a Bum* in 1933. Rodgers and Hart also produced numerous songs for popular film stars like Bing Crosby and the spoof of love that became a hit "Blue Moon" (1934). *Love Me Tonight*, directed by Rouben Mamoulian and featuring Maurice Chevalier and Jeanette MacDonald singing "Isn't It Romantic?" and "Lover," is widely considered one of Hollywood's finest movie musicals. In 1934 Hart contributed singable and idiomatic English lyrics to the successful film musical version of Franz Lehár's Viennese hit of 1905, *The Merry Widow*. In addition to their movie musicals, a dozen of Rodgers and Hart's Broadway shows were made into film musicals between 1930 and 1962.

The return of Rodgers and Hart to Broadway in 1935 inaugurated a final flowering of their most distinguished and revivable shows, each graced by one or more hits. Especially noteworthy are *Jumbo* (1935), with "The Most Beautiful Girl in the World" and "My Romance"; *On Your Toes* (1936), with "It's Got to Be Love," "There's a Small Hotel," and "Glad to Be Unhappy"; *Babes in Arms* (1937), with "My Funny Valentine," "Johnny One Note," "The Lady Is a Tramp," and "Where or When"; *I'd Rather Be Right* (1937), with "Have You Met Miss Jones?"; *The Boys from Syracuse* (1938), with "Falling in Love with Love" and "This Can't Be Love"; and *Pal Joey* (1940), which featured "Bewitched, Bothered, and Bewildered" and "I Could Write a Book." Hart himself collaborated with Rodgers on the librettos to *On Your Toes* (one of the first musicals to integrate dance into the dramatic fabric), *Babes in Arms*, and *I Married an Angel*. The realistic *Pal Joey*, which was based on John O'Hara's series of *New Yorker* short stories in letter form and treated such unsavory themes as adultery and blackmail, is generally considered a masterpiece of Broadway realism combined with superbly crafted and well-integrated lyrics and music; it remains one of the earliest pure (if not unadulterated) musical comedies in the Broadway canon.

By the time Rodgers and Hart collaborated on their final musical in 1942, *By Jupiter* (at 427 performances, the longest-running musical of their twenty-six before the revival of *Pal Joey* in 1952), the lovable but unreliable Hart had become increasingly incapacitated by alcoholism and neuroses about his physical appearance (he was barely five feet tall and possessed a large, balding head) as well as his difficulty accepting his homosexuality. Having lost much of his will to work, he did not collaborate with Rodgers on a new property, *Oklahoma!*, a task taken up by Oscar Hammerstein II. In 1943 Hart managed to complete several new lyrics for a revival of *A Connecticut Yankee*, including his brilliant final song, "To Keep My Love Alive." The death in April 1943 of his mother, with whom Hart lived for most of his adult life, contributed further to disregard for his own health, which led to a short but fatal bout of pneumonia. He died in New York City.

Although Hart was capable of both simplicity and sentimentality, as in "My Heart Stood Still," he is best remembered for his technical virtuosity, wit, and good-natured misanthropy that treated love as a sickness, as in "It's Got to Be Love" ("It couldn't be tonsilitis") from *On Your Toes*. Along with Cole Porter, Ira Gershwin, and Hammerstein, the witty, swell, and grand Lorenz Hart (to paraphrase from "Thou Swell") is universally recognized as one of the three or four major Broadway lyricists of his generation.

• The major repository of Hart's lyrics and other materials for his shows with Rodgers is the Rodgers and Hammerstein Theatre Library in New York City. Scripts and lyrics for many Hart shows are located in the New York Public Library, and holograph manuscripts of numerous Rodgers and Hart songs are housed in the music division of the Library of Congress. Seventy-three Rodgers and Hart songs are collected in *Rodgers & Hart: A Musical Anthology* (1984). The most comprehensive primary source for Hart's lyrics is *The Complete Lyrics of Lorenz Hart*, ed. Dorothy Hart and Robert Kimball (1986). The most complete assemblage of factual information on Hart's amateur and professional collaborations with Rodgers (including production histories, casts, act-by-act song rosters, plot summaries, and excerpts from reviews) is Stanley Green, ed., *Rodgers and Hammerstein Fact Book* (1980). The most substantial biographical profile of Hart was written by his sister-in-law, Dorothy Hart, *Thou Swell, Thou Witty: The Life and Lyrics of Lorenz Hart* (1976). Additional worthwhile biographical material is contained in Samuel Marx and Jan Clayton, *Rodgers & Hart* (1976); Richard Rodgers, *Musical Stages* (1975); David Ewen, *Richard Rodgers* (1957); Frederick Nolan, *Lorenz Hart: A Poet on Broadway* (1994); and William G. Hyland, *Richard Rodgers* (1998). See also Geoffrey Block, *Enchanted Evenings: The Broadway Musical from "Show Boat" to Sondheim* (1997). For an insightful discussion of Hart's lyrics see Philip Furia, *The Poets of Tin Pan Alley* (1990). An obituary is in the *New York Times*, 23 Nov. 1943.

GEOFFREY BLOCK

HART, Moss (24 Oct. 1904–20 Dec. 1961), playwright and stage director, was born in New York City, the son of Barnet Hart, a tobacconist, and Lillian Solomon. Hart claimed that he "grew up in an atmosphere of unrelieved poverty with . . . the grim smell of actual want always at the end of my nose." As a teenager, he worked as an office boy for the theatrical road producer Augustus Pitou in Manhattan. Under a pseudonym, in 1923 Hart wrote a play called, variously, *The Hold-Up Man* or *The Beloved Bandit*, which Pitou produced in Chicago, where it failed. Hart became a summertime social director at hotels in the Catskills (where, by the end of the 1920s, he said he was "the most highly paid, most eagerly sought-after social director of the Borscht Circuit"); he then started directing at small theaters in New York and New Jersey.

As a young writer Hart was particularly fond of the popular comedies co-written by George S. Kaufman and Marc Connelly. These inspired him to try his hand at a similar genre. By 1929 the first talking pictures were being produced, the introduction of sound revolutionizing the film industry. Hart wrote a comedy about a trio of vaudevillians who "go Hollywood" to make their fortunes. He sent the play, *Once in a Lifetime*, to Broadway producer Jed Harris, who in turn sent it to Kaufman. This proved to be a cruel joke, as Harris and Kaufman had a long-running feud. However, the play was also read and admired by another producer, Sam H. Harris (no relation to Jed Harris), who was a colleague of Kaufman's. Harris encouraged Kaufman to collaborate with the 25-year-old Hart on bringing *Once in a Lifetime* to the stage.

After two harrowing out-of-town tryouts, the show opened in New York in September 1930 to a delighted audience. In an uncharacteristic curtain speech, Kaufman (who directed and played a supporting part) said, "I would like the audience to know that eighty percent of this play is Moss Hart."

Hart's fortunes were made. He collaborated with Irving Berlin on two well-received revues, *Face the Music* (1932) and *As Thousands Cheer* (1933), as well as adapting the book of a Viennese operetta, *The Great Waltz* (1934). But Hart had more ambitious projects in mind. Having seen Noël Coward's *Cavalcade*, an epic history of a British family, he was determined to create a comparable spectacle on American themes. Collaborating with Kaufman for a second time, he wrote *Merrily We Roll Along* in 1934, a huge play that traced the fall and rise of a Broadway playwright through the century by telling his story in reverse chronological order. The project was unsuccessful.

That play's failure was made up for by the team's next effort in 1936. (Hart had spent the season in between collaborating with Cole Porter on *Jubilee*, a satire of British royalty.) *You Can't Take It with You* was not only Kaufman and Hart's greatest financial bonanza; it remains one of the more popular and specifically American theater pieces. A couple—the young man from a wealthy Wall Street family, the young woman from an anarchically unconventional family—fall in love despite the culture clash between the clans. The play ran for 837 performances and won a Pulitzer Prize for its authors.

After writing the book for a provocative musical portrait of President Franklin D. Roosevelt in *I'd Rather Be Right* (1937), with a score by Richard Rodgers and Lorenz Hart, Kaufman and Hart turned to two more grandiose projects, both doomed to repeat the history of *Merrily We Roll Along*. *The Fabulous Invalid* (1938), an encyclopedic cavalcade of the American theater, and *The American Way* (1939), an epic story of immigration, both failed to find favor with the audience. However, the team bounced back in the same year by using the idiosyncrasies of critic Alexander Woollcott, a friend, as the basis for a play about an egomaniacal celebrity and raconteur who invades the domain of a quiet Midwestern family. *The Man Who Came to Dinner* was a great popular success on stage and screen. Hart played a supporting character (based on Noël Coward) in summer stock and eventually played the lead, Sheridan Whiteside, on a USO tour during World War II.

After their final collaboration, *George Washington Slept Here* (1940), Hart left Kaufman amicably, with great admiration for his partner's work, but, more insistently, with a need to write his own material. Considerable discussion has occurred over which parts of the plays are Kaufman's and which are Hart's. No concrete documentation exists to unravel this riddle, and the riddle itself is somewhat irrelevant since the collaboration was meticulous and comprehensive. Certainly Hart's love of spectacle inspired the three large-scale plays, but he also brought to Kaufman an appreciable, if sentimental, humanity. The romantic scenes in their plays, which Kaufman notoriously despised writing, are both romantic and funny, especially in *You Can't Take It with You*, to an extent not found elsewhere in Kaufman's work. Kaufman described Hart as his favorite collaborator.

For Hart, some of his greatest achievements lay ahead. Among them was the 1941 musical *Lady in the Dark*, written and directed by Hart, with a score by Kurt Weill and Ira Gershwin. Hart had been suffering from depression and insomnia for years and turned to psychoanalysis to address his problems. Whatever else it provided, psychoanalysis gave him the angle for this groundbreaking musical. A famous magazine editor, played by Gertrude Lawrence, is wracked by indecision. When she sees an analyst, her dreams come to life in the form of musical extravaganzas; only by connecting with a musical refrain from her past does she find the secret to happiness. The panache of execution on all its levels made the show a hit.

Hart achieved a second success on his own with *Winged Victory* (1943), a tribute to the U.S. Army Air Corps. Film rights for the play, which Hart directed, sold for $1 million, a sum he donated to the air corps.

In 1946 Hart married the actress and singer Kitty Carlisle; they had two children.

During this period of his career, Hart's fame sent him in three directions: as a Broadway director, he had successes with the light comedies *Junior Miss* (1941), *Dear Ruth* (1944), and *Anniversary Waltz* (1954) as well as the Irving Berlin musical *Miss Liberty* (1949); as a screenwriter, he wrote *Gentleman's Agreement* (1947), *Hans Christian Andersen* (1952), the Judy Garland vehicle *A Star Is Born* (1954), and *Prince of Players* (1955); and as a playwright, Hart's three plays in the 1940s and 1950s, which he also directed, were a varied group: *Christopher Blake* (1946), a serious and unsuccessful treatment of a child coping with his parents' divorce; *Light Up the Sky* (1948), a return to the frenetic comic mode he excelled in during his partnership with Kaufman; and *The Climate of Eden* (1952), about a missionary and his family in British Guiana.

Hart's next task as a director of the musical *My Fair Lady* (1956) provided a success he could not have prepared for. The librettist/lyricist Alan Jay Lerner and composer Frederick Loewe managed to be faithful to George Bernard Shaw's *Pygmalion* while releasing their own elegant lyricism. Hart worked carefully with the team, helping to hone the book, shape the performances of Rex Harrison and Julie Andrews in the leading parts, and generally apply his considerable taste to the task of balancing the intellectual and entertainment values of the piece. *My Fair Lady* became one of the greatest successes in musical theater history. It brought Hart the Tony Award and the New York Drama Critics' Award for best director, and the show was equally well received in London in 1958.

Hart worked with Lerner and Loewe a second time, on *Camelot*, a musical version of T. H. White's book about King Arthur and the Knights of the Round Table, *The Once and Future King*. This time the project was more unwieldy, and during its tryout in Toronto, Hart suffered a heart attack. Lerner took over the direction and in 1960 brought the musical to Broadway, where it received mixed to good reviews. Hart recovered after the opening and returned to the show to make substantial changes. Between word of mouth and exposure on television, the musical became a hit. In between the musicals Hart wrote a memoir of his early years up until the success of *Once in a Lifetime*. Published in 1959, *Act One* stayed on the *New York Times*'s bestseller list for forty-one weeks and remains one of the better books on the American theater.

Hart was known for his largesse toward friends and colleagues and for his lavish ways, prompting Edna Ferber's comment that "Moss Hart is monogrammed in the most improbable places." Ferber went on to praise him thus: "Limited to five adjectives in describing his character, one would probably say: gentle, kind, witty, generous, companionable." After the experience with *Camelot*, Hart and his wife moved to Palm Springs, California, in 1961. He had begun work on what he called a "drawing room comedy" there when he died of heart failure.

Hart was a major figure in the world of Broadway for three decades, during which his manner, style, and taste came to epitomize the glamour and sophistication that Broadway represented. Although he was less successful as a solo playwright than as a collaborator with Kaufman, his contributions as a director, especially on musicals, helped mature an important American art form. *Act One* remains one of the great, inspiring memoirs of the American theater, with its almost storybook transposition of the Horatio Alger myth to the world of the theater.

• Hart's personal papers are located at the Wisconsin Center for Film and Theater Research, Madison. In 1941 Random House published *Six Plays by Kaufman and Hart*, which has long been out of print. Although no full-scale biography of Hart has appeared, accounts of him can be found in almost every biography or memoir of his collaborators. The best of those books are Alan Jay Lerner's *The Street Where I Live* (1978) and Kitty Carlisle Hart's *Kitty* (1987). An obituary is in the *New York Times*, 21 Dec. 1961.

LAURENCE MASLON

HART, Nancy (c. 1735–c. 1830), revolutionary war heroine, was born Ann Morgan, in Pennsylvania or North Carolina, the daughter of Thomas Morgan and Rebecca Alexander. Nothing is known of her childhood except that she grew up in North Carolina. Portrayed as "unlearned" in most accounts, she probably received little education. She married Benjamin Hart, a Virginia-born North Carolinian, with whom she had eight children. In the early 1770s the Harts migrated to Georgia and settled in the upcountry area that became Elbert County. There her revolutionary exploits took place. Like many uneducated eighteenth-century women who left no personal writings, the real Nancy Hart is an elusive figure, making it difficult to separate fact from myth. The early information of her deeds was oral tradition, with the earliest extant written accounts dating to the 1840s. She does not appear in the earliest Georgia histories, and even modern Georgia scholars have dealt with her in qualified terms.

The core story about Nancy Hart that has survived in several versions involves her capture of several Tories during the American Revolution. The first extant printed story appeared in Elizabeth Fries Ellet's *The Women of the American Revolution* (1848), the source for which, so Ellet claimed in an article in *Godey's Lady's Book and Lady's American Magazine*, was a "gentleman resident of Georgia." According to this account, Tories from the Augusta area, after murdering a Whig colonel in August 1780, infiltrated the upcountry bent on further action. A detachment of five went to the Harts' home to determine whether Nancy had helped a Whig escape from his Loyalist pursuers. Nancy audaciously confirmed the rumor, angering the Tories, who ordered her to prepare a meal for them. One of the intruders shot her only turkey and forced her to cook it. With the Tory party loosened by liquor, Hart served their meal and while they feasted began to slip their guns though the chinking in the pine cabin. Her daughter Sukey meanwhile went to the spring to blow the signal for the men to come immediately. As Hart attempted to remove the third of the five guns, she was caught. The Tories jumped to their feet, and Hart raised the weapon, swearing to kill the first man to approach her. She made good on the promise, and one Tory fell dead. She immediately seized another musket ready to fire again. At this point Sukey returned and picked up the final gun, reporting that the men were on their way. In a final attempt to escape, the men rushed Hart, and a second Tory was shot. Hart held the remaining Tories at gunpoint until Benjamin and the neighbors arrived. The men wanted to shoot the Tories on the spot, but Nancy insisted that shooting "was too good for them." Instead she oversaw their hanging.

Ellet's version captured the imagination of George White, whose *Statistics of the State of Georgia* (1849) carried it verbatim. By the time he published his *Historical Collections of Georgia* in 1854, White had done some investigation into Nancy Hart's legend and added several stories. According to White, his information came from oral interviews with those acquainted with Hart and from notes furnished by the Reverend Snead, a relative of the Hart family. White also had a letter from the Harts' grandnephew, Missouri senator Thomas Hart Benton (1782–1858), and an account originally appearing in the *Yorkville Pioneer* in South Carolina. Historian E. Merton Coulter believed that this was the same account later writers read in an 1825 Milledgeville *Southern Recorder* article, probably the first public story of her exploits.

According to this account, Hart was a tall, muscular woman and an excellent hunter, with antlers lining the walls of her cabin. The Tories appeared at her door demanding a meal. Her considerable culinary skills produced a meal that made the soldiers leave their guns while sitting down to feast. At that point, ". . . the dauntless Nancy seized one of the guns, cocked it, and with blazing oath declared she would blow out the brains of the first mortal that offered to rise, or taste a mouthful!" She then sent her son to inform the Whigs that she was holding "six base Tories." In this story the intimidated Loyalists offered no resistance.

White also offered several other stories. The Reverend Snead, who said "Aunt Nancy" was six feet tall and well built, told of Hart splashing boiling soap through a chimney crevice into the face of a spying Tory, whom she then took prisoner. An elderly woman in Elbert County told White several additional adventures. In one, Hart made a raft of logs tied with grapevine, crossed the Savannah River to spy on Tories in South Carolina, and returned with needed information for the Whigs. The truth of these stories will never be known, but as historian Coulter said ". . . if Aunt Nancy Hart were half what tradition had made of her, she was largely responsible for the rescue of all upper Georgia from the Tories."

Various records tell the Hart story after the Revolution. In 1790 and 1791 the Harts advertised two tracts of land for sale and subsequently moved to the southern Georgia coast, where Benjamin acquired fifty acres of land and by 1794 owned fifteen slaves. Benjamin Hart served there as a justice of the peace and later a justice of the inferior court. The couple advertised their fifty acres for sale in November 1801, and Benjamin Hart died in 1802. Nancy Hart then lived with her son John in Athens, Georgia, where references to both appear in numerous documents. Several years later Hart moved with her son and his family to Henderson County, Kentucky, where John died in 1821 and she survived until perhaps the end of the decade.

The commemoration of the real and legendary Nancy Hart began in 1853, when the Georgia legislature created a new county out of a portion of Elbert, naming it in honor of "dauntless Nancy of revolutionary memory." In 1931 Congress erected a monument in her honor in Hart County. The Daughters of the American Revolution later placed a monument on her supposed grave there. But the Nancy Hart story belongs to Georgia, where the American Revolution was a civil war between Whigs and Tories and Hart was representative of those upcountry folks who fought for independence.

• In 1855 an additional undocumented story about a scuffle between Nancy Hart and a Nancy Wilder appeared in George R. Gilmer, *Sketches of Some of the First Settlers of Upper Georgia, of the Cherokees, and the Author.* More recently the legends of Nancy Hart were presented at face value in Zell Miller, *Great Georgians* (1983). The facts of Nancy Hart's life can be pieced together in records from various Georgia counties, including Wilkes, Glynn, Clarke, and Elbert. The best account of the building of the legend is E. Merton Coulter, "Nancy Hart: Georgia Heroine of the Revolution: The Story of the Growth of a Tradition," *Georgia Historical Quarterly* 39 (1955): 118–51, which argues that the 1825 Milledgeville *Southern Recorder* article probably reflected the resurgence of interest in the American Revolution that accompanied the marquis de Lafayette's visit in that year.

LEE ANN CALDWELL

HART, Oliver (5 July 1723–31 Dec. 1795), Baptist minister, was born in Warminster, Bucks County, Pennsylvania, the son of John Hart and Eleanor Crispin. Raised in a small, rural township in Pennsylvania, he received a formal but basic English education. Hart, however, was diligent in his private studies, and he obtained an advanced understanding of the English language as well as a deep knowledge and love for theology. As a result of Hart's studies, he developed an extensive library used by the ministerial students whom he later instructed.

Early in his life Hart worked as a carpenter and became an active member of the Philadelphia Baptist Association, the first such association in America. He married Sarah (maiden name unknown) in 1747. In September 1749 it came to the attention of the brethren of the association that South Carolina was without a Baptist minister. Because of his personal diligence and devout faith, Hart was chosen to become the primary minister of the Baptist church in Charleston, South Carolina. He was ordained minister on 18 October 1749, and he left for Charleston on 13 November 1749, leaving behind his wife and infant son.

Hart arrived in Charleston on 2 December, and his work began immediately. The minister whom Hart replaced had actually died almost two years earlier, and the Reverend Isaac Chandler, the only other Baptist minister in South Carolina, was buried on the day Hart arrived. Hart wasted no time in his work, and within three months he had persuaded another minister to join him in South Carolina. Six months later the most significant event in Hart's ministry occurred, the founding of the Charleston Baptist Association in October 1751. The establishment of this association led to the spread of the Baptist ministry in the southern United States. It was through the association that Hart and others whom he ordained were able to minister throughout Georgia, North Carolina, South Carolina, and Virginia. A unified force of southern Baptist churches was essential in order to appear more respectable to the provincial governments at a time when religious freedom was still precarious.

In July 1752 Hart's wife, his son, Seth, and newborn daughter arrived in Charleston. In September of that year a hurricane destroyed their home, and in October Seth died. These events devastated Hart but only seemed to strengthen his resolve. After rebuilding his home, Hart continued to expand his ministry. In October 1754, with the ordination of Samuel Stillman, Hart had succeeded in providing for a permanent Baptist presence in Charleston. Stillman was a native of Charleston, and his ordination established a connection with the community that created the foundation of Hart's mission. Hart, Stillman, and the Charleston Baptist Association developed educational programs for the Charleston area in accordance with Baptist theology.

Hart continued to expand his work as far north as Rhode Island. He became so well respected that in 1769, on a visit to Rhode Island College (later Brown University), Hart received an honorary master's degree. In 1772 Hart met with Morgan Edwards, who was compiling a history of the American Baptists. Edwards assisted Hart in revising a disciplinary code for Baptist ministers that standardized the acceptable levels of behavior expected of ministers.

In October 1772 Hart's wife died giving birth to their eighth child. (Hart later married Anne "Nancy" Sealy Grimball.) Hart seems to have channeled the grief over the loss of his wife into a renewed zeal for his ministry. He recruited more preachers, and in 1774 he met Richard Furman, who became a disciple of Hart's and after Hart's death, feverishly continued his work. Late in 1775 the British threatened to take Charleston, and Hart moved to Euhaw, South Carolina, where he stayed until 1779. During his years in Euhaw Hart was asked by colonial patriots to sway the backcountry of South Carolina that was populated with British sympathizers toward their own cause. Hart's success in keeping the peace and quelling possible uprising led to his recognition by the Committee of Safety as a great patriot of the American Revolution.

After his service to the American cause, Hart moved back to Charleston. There he refocused his attention to spreading his ministry, primarily in the local countryside but also in urban areas such as Baltimore and New York City. However, in 1780 the British again advanced on Charleston, forcing many to evacuate the city, As a result, Hart accepted an invitation to be minister in Hopewell, New Jersey, and moved there in December of that year. In 1788 Hart attempted an arduous yet unsuccessful journey back to South Carolina. He met with too many hardships and was forced to return to Hopewell, never to visit Charleston again. Gradually, Hart's age and health began restricting his ministry, and in 1795 he settled in Hopewell, where he died.

Through the continued efforts of men such as Robert Furman, many of Hart's goals were achieved. These included his most important objective—the unification of the southern Baptist congregations. Furman completed Hart's dream in 1800, with the union of the Association (Regular) churches and the Separa-

tist churches throughout South Carolina. Other organizations would soon follow, leading to a truly national Baptist Association.

• A comprehensive work on Hart's life is Loulie Latimer Owens, *Oliver Hart 1723–1795* (1966). For further insight into his life and career see Leah Townsend, *South Carolina Baptists, 1670–1805* (1935); and M. Jean Heriot, *Blessed Assurance: Beliefs, Actions, and the Experience of Salvation in a Carolina Baptist Church* (1994). Other references include Owens, *Saints of Clay: The Shaping of South Carolina Baptists* (1971); and Thomas Sharp Griffiths, *A History of Baptists in New Jersey* (1821).

ELLEN T. BASTIO

HART, Tony (25 July 1855–4 Nov. 1891), actor and singer, was born Anthony Cannon in Worcester, Massachusetts, the son of Anthony Cannon and Mary Sweeney, both of whom had emigrated from Ireland. He put on amateur performances as a child, but a pattern of delinquency began with disruptions at school and culminated in the near murder of a rival during a performance; his parents placed him in the Lyman School (a state reformatory at Westborough, outside Worcester) in 1865. He escaped several months later and traveled to Boston, where he supported himself as a singer, a bootblack, and a newsboy, and then to Providence, where he sang and danced in saloons and was dubbed Master Antonio by a saloon keeper. He joined a touring circus, and then Billy Arlington's Minstrels; in 1870, at age fifteen, he joined Madame Rentz's Female Minstrels. Dressed as a little girl, he evoked tears with a sentimental song, "Put Me in My Little Bed."

After leaving Madame Rentz's company, Cannon went to Chicago in 1871, where he met Edward Harrigan (while both were having their shoes shined). Harrigan was twenty-six at the time, and Hart was sixteen. They agreed to tour as a team, and they worked together for the next fourteen years. Cannon changed his name to Tony Hart, and he and Harrigan traveled together initially as the Nonpareils. They began their careers together at the Howard Athenaeum in Boston in April 1871, where their act was enormously popular. It was called "The Little Fraud," and it featured character songs and comic dancing, with each man singing, dancing, and clowning. Within two years they commanded top vaudeville salaries. Their first major road tour, with a company of thirty-seven performers, lasted from August 1875 to June 1876 and covered a good part of the East and South.

Now established as "Harrigan and Hart," the team rented the Theatre Comique in Manhattan in 1876 and stayed there for nine years, performing in musical sketches, minstrel routines, and one-act plays, all written by Harrigan; Hart was especially noted for his female impersonations. After theater owner Tony Pastor (nicknamed the "father of modern American vaudeville") advised them in 1875 to weave some of their musical sketches into a unified production, they started to feature longer plays, about one-hour in length. All of their works had plots with singing and dancing, and as they dropped the variety acts, their plays began to bridge the gap between vaudeville and the legitimate theater.

While all of the plays and song lyrics were written by Harrigan, and all the music composed by David Braham (Harrigan's father-in-law), it was the performing team of Harrigan and Hart that achieved national prominence. In 1872 Harrigan and Braham's song "The Mulligan Guard" achieved enormous popularity; it was a satire on the pseudomilitary target companies (processions of men with a boy at the end carrying a target bearing the name of the company) manned by those immigrants who were not permitted in the regular militia. The next step was a ten-minute sketch featuring a marching troop of two (Harrigan and Hart), with a young, black target-bearer. As these brief sketches developed into hour-long and then full-length plays, Harrigan and Hart turned the Comique into a new kind of theater: customers saw both a full-length play and variety acts on the same stage, in the same evening, all for one price. Eventually, Harrigan wrote seven Mulligan plays, each starring Hart and himself, each man taking several parts: Harrigan always performed Dan Mulligan, and Hart acted his son Tommy, as well as Rebecca Allup, a boisterous black woman.

In the dozens of plays Harrigan wrote, Hart became noted for his versatility—he sang and danced well and played an amazing range of roles of both sexes, frequently in the same play. Some of his parts included a cockney servant in *The Major*; Dick, the rat, in *Old Lavender*; the Widow Nolan in *Squatter Sovereignty*; and, after he left Harrigan, an Italian, a Hebrew, an Irishwoman, and a Chinaman in *Toy Pistols*.

Hart married Gertrude Granville in London in 1882. She was four years older than he, had been married twice before, and had performed with P. T. Barnum's circus when she was nineteen. They adopted a thirteen-year-old, the orphaned son of a fellow actor named Billy Gray. They lived in a brownstone on Forty-sixth Street, just east of Park Avenue. Hart met his wife when she performed with the company, but partly because she tended to pull him away from the company and partly because she did not get along with either Braham's wife or Harrigan's, a certain amount of friction developed between Hart and Harrigan. Hart broke off the partnership, and Harrigan and Hart appeared together for the last time in 1885 (though this performance was after their breakup, they felt it important to fulfill a last contractual commitment). Hart then toured with several plays, all failures. Syphilis gradually took over his body and mind (Harrigan had felt Hart needed a rest, and others had noted a lisp in his performances), and he was forced to leave the stage in 1887. A testimonial benefit for him raised $14,000, but by 1888 he had become unmanageable, and he was committed to the Worcester insane asylum. His wife died in 1890, and he, hopelessly paralyzed and demented, died in the asylum.

Despite the rowdy comedy of Harrigan and Hart's plays, there was a realistic strain in all their work. William Dean Howells wrote in *Harper's* in July 1886 that the comedies realized "the actual life of the city . . . part of the great tendency toward the faithful representation of life which is now animating fiction." They roamed the streets of New York collecting scenes and characters and costumes. Harrigan said, "In the old days, Tony and I spent more time hunting for costumes than anything else." The *New York Times* obituary said Hart was "a really clever actor . . . and his versatility was not the least quality that won and held the attention of the public." Nat C. Goodwin (a well-known comedian and friend of Hart) said of him, "He sang like a nightingale, danced like a fairy, and acted like a master comedian."

Harrigan and Hart brought to the stage a variety of realistic character types and helped to shape the American musical into a cohesive whole. While Hart wrote none of the material that he performed, it was acknowledged by all that his varied abilities on stage helped make Harrigan's plays popular. When Tony Hart died, a large pillow of flowers on his coffin from Harrigan spelled out "Partner."

• A *New York Times* obituary of 5 Nov. 1891 provides most of the basic facts about Tony Hart's life. E. J. Kahn, Jr., had access to much primary material (through Hart's nephew, Anthony Hart Athy, and through Athy's family), and he includes it in *The Merry Partners: The Age and Stage of Harrigan and Hart* (1955). Any work dealing with Edward Harrigan must, perforce, include extensive material on Hart, and the best and most complete of these is Richard Moody's *Ned Harrigan: From Corlear's Hook to Herald Square* (1980). The significance of Harrigan and Hart to the musical stage is best conveyed by Gerald Bordman, *American Musical Comedy: From Adonis to Dreamgirls* (1982).

JULIAN MATES

HART, William Surrey (6 Dec. 1870–24 June 1946), actor and film director, was born in Newburgh, New York, the second son of Nicholas Hart, an itinerant English mill mechanic, and Roseanna McCauley. Like many actors, Hart tried to make himself younger and may have been born as early as 1862. He grew up in Minnesota, South Dakota, Kansas, and Iowa during the last days of the Wild West. As a child he played with Sioux boys, spoke Lakota, and was one of the rare movie cowboys who had worked on cattle ranches.

Hart began his theatrical career in 1889 in New York City, achieving success as a touring Shakespearean actor and in *Ben Hur* on Broadway. By 1900 his roles in *The Squaw Man, Dead or Alive, The Virginian* and *Trail of the Lonesome Pine* gave him a reputation as an actor who could convincingly portray western characters. His athletic physique and six-foot frame made him an impressive figure on stage. In 1913 the veteran actor moved to California to make *The Bargain* (1914), his first movie for his friend Thomas H. Ince. This commercial success was followed by more than thirty popular cowboy movies. His roles in *Hell's Hinges* (1916) and *The Narrow Trail* (1917) established Hart as the classic cowboy star—tall, laconic, brave, chivalrous, and noble—whether playing the outlaw or the hero.

In 1917 Hart followed the shrewd and successful Ince to the Famous Players-Lasky Company, later known as Paramount Studio. Jesse Lasky made Hart a producer, director, and screenwriter as well as a leading man. Although best remembered as a cowboy star, Hart took pains to make each film as realistic as possible, he was concerned with accurate production values and even performed his own stunts. This preference for plot and character over action and insistence on stark authenticity is most apparent in westerns such as *The Return of Draw Egan* (1916), *The Toll Gate* (1920), *Travelin' On* (1922), and *Wild Bill Hickok* (1923). Drawing on the techniques of D. W. Griffith, Hart's movies fused careful camera work and understated performances with his frontier themes. Unlike some stage actors working in silent movies, Hart took himself quite seriously, and he was unforgiving when Buster Keaton burlesqued him in a deadpan comedy, *The Frozen North* (1922). By 1922 Adolph Zukor was paying Hart $200,000 per picture to keep him with the studio.

Often the harsh landscape portrayed in his films seemed to overwhelm Hart and the actors he directed. In the midst of this natural world, his complex characters were moral but tempted by drink or vices. Evil men and a corrupt government threatened the westerners intent on civilizing the frontier. Although these movies were critical and box-office successes, by 1925 younger cowboy stars like Tom Mix and scripts with more vivid action were beginning to overshadow Hart's somber symbolism.

In private life Hart was unassuming and quiet. He avoided Hollywood social life and was somewhat puritanical, although he often proposed to his leading ladies. In 1921 he married one of them, Winifred Westover, and they had a son, William S. Hart, Jr., but soon separated and divorced in 1927. Thereafter Hart lived with his sister Mary and (after breaking with Ince) earned a movie star's salary that he invested prudently and spent quietly on his own philanthropies.

Like many cowboys, Hart was very fond of his movie horse, a pinto called Fritz. He tried repeatedly to buy the pony, but the studio refused. Finally, Hart appeared in one movie without a salary in exchange for the horse, which brought the price of the talented animal to $40,000. Thereafter he insisted that his horse receive screen credits.

Hart sued United Artists for poor distribution of his last film, *Tumbleweeds* (1925). He won $278,000 in damages, but his age, distaste for the studio system, and this lawsuit ended his movie career. Hart retired to his California ranch and wrote his autobiography, *My Life East and West* (1929). Nonetheless, he remained a popular movie star in the 1930s and his silent pictures were still shown in smaller theaters. In 1939 Hart added a poignant introduction to the reissue of his classic silent movie *Tumbleweeds*, which may be his best film and is remembered for its spectacular Oklahoma land rush scenes. He continued his close identi-

fication with the Wild West, even serving as a pallbearer at Wyatt Earp's funeral on 16 January 1929 in Los Angeles. He was painted by both Charles Russell and James Montgomery Flagg, whose art he collected along with other western Americana.

In addition to screenplays that attempted to recapture the vanishing frontier that he remembered from childhood, Hart also wrote western novels and short stories, including *The Golden West Boys* (1920); *A Lighter of Flames* (1923); *Hoofbeats* (1933), *The Law on Horseback* (1935), and *All Points West* (1940).

Hart is best remembered as the first western movie star, and a top box-office leading man in silent movies from 1914 to 1925. The "Two Gun Man" was famous for his commanding, manly portrait as the good badman. The western hero, popularized in Owen Wister's bestseller, *The Virginian* (1902), and embellished by Theodore Roosevelt and Frederic Remington, was personified by Hart on the silver screen. To a great extent these performances created the western movie genre whose conventional romantic narratives were fixed in a mythical late nineteenth-century frontier where anarchy and civilization threatened both villains and heroes, and the gun, the horse and the saloon were essential icons. During the moral passion of World War I, his movies helped to define the American national character. When Hart died in Los Angeles, he bequeathed his Horseshoe Ranch in Newhall, California, to Los Angeles County as a park and museum. Later a local school district, high school, and a city park were named in his memory.

• Hart's papers are at the Seaver Center for Western History Research in Santa Clarita, Calif. For additional information, see William K. Everson, *A Pictorial History of the Western Film* (1969); William S. Hart, *My Life East and West* (1994); Diane Kaisar Koszarski, *The Complete Films of William S. Hart* (1980); and Archie P. McDonald, ed., *Shooting Stars: Heroes and Heroines of Western Film* (1987). An obituary is in the *New York Times*, 25 June 1946.

PETER C. HOLLORAN

HARTE, Bret (25 Aug. 1836–5 May 1902), writer, was born Francis Brett Harte in Albany, New York, the child of Henry Harte, a teacher, and Elizabeth Ostrander. His heritage was a mixture of Dutch, English, Huguenot, and Jewish; his father was Roman Catholic, his mother Episcopalian. Frank, as he came to be called, spent much time indoors reading because of poor health. His formal schooling was minimal. After having been an instructor at the Albany Female Academy, his father turned to accepting seasonal teaching jobs, and the family became increasingly nomadic, finally settling in either 1844 or 1845 in Brooklyn, where Henry Harte died. Harte grew up reading Emerson, Irving, Tennyson, Poe, Byron, and Dickens, in addition to the Bible and *Pilgrim's Progress*. In 1853, his mother became engaged to marry Colonel Andrew Williams, and they moved to Oakland, California.

Little is known and much has been conjectured about Harte's first three years in California. Possibly he taught school in La Grange in the Sierras, did some mining, and met several of the colorful models for his later stories. We do know that he arrived in the northern California seacoast town of Union (now called Arcata) during the summer of 1857. Here he became a printer's devil and editorial assistant on the newly founded weekly newspaper, the *Northern Californian*. Soon he became a regular contributor and sometime editor of the newspaper. But he was forced to leave this outpost of civilization on short notice. He had been left in charge of the *Northern Californian* at the time of the Mad River Indian massacre (sometimes referred to as the Gunther's Island massacre) in 1860. A group of drunken townsmen from Union murdered numerous Indians, mostly women and children. In a scathing editorial, Harte condemned these men as "worse than common murderers." He was run out of town, lucky to escape with his life.

Harte went to San Francisco, where he began writing for a much better newspaper, the *Golden Era*. He produced a long series of satiric "Bohemian" papers on subjects as diverse as "Sensation Plays," "Restaurants," "The Sacramento Fair," and "Female Gymnastics." With such fiction as "A Night at Wingdam" and "The Work at Red Mountain" (later entitled "M'liss"), Harte was beginning to find himself as a writer. From the *Golden Era* he moved in 1864 to the *Californian*, serving as co-editor of the paper and later as author of the parodies titled "Condensed Novels."

During the 1860s Bret Harte, as he now called himself, was a much-admired guest at the social functions of Jessie Benton Frémont, perhaps the area's leading art patron. He became a parishioner at the Unitarian church of Thomas Starr King, who became a father figure to him, criticizing his poetry, teaching him much about philosophy and life. King also enlisted Harte's help in working for abolitionist causes during the Civil War. At about this time, Harte was also informing East Coast readers about happenings in northern California through letters to the *Springfield Republican* and *Christian Register*. In 1862 he married Anna Griswold, who sang contralto in the Unitarian choir. Both families thought the match an unfortunate one—Anna was older, her musical career was well established, and the groom's salary was small. The years proved their relatives to be right. Before the end of the decade, Harte had two small sons along with a frustrated and unhappy wife. The couple had a total of four children.

As editor of *Outcroppings: An Anthology of California Verse* (1865), Harte was involved in a literary *cause célèbre* over his exclusion of several recognized, if antiquated, local poets. He had also become well known by 1868 for such writings as "Neighborhoods I Have Moved From" (an essay) and "To the Pliocene Skull" (a poem). Now called Bret Harte, he was named in this same year editor in chief of the *Overland Monthly*, California's first quality literary journal. Harte wrote for the *Overland* a monthly column called "Etc.," book reviews, poems, and stories, including "The Luck of Roaring Camp," which took realism in American letters a significant step forward. He also accepted Henry

George's (1839–1897) famous radical criticism of progress and land development, "What the Railroad Will Bring Us."

Harte's writing proved to be more varied than substantial. He wrote many topical poems, two series of burlesques on recent novels, a number of first-rate book reviews, essays of literary criticism, as well as plays and novels. He is, of course, most famous for his parabolic short stories, such as "The Luck of Roaring Camp," but his literary accomplishments were clearly multidimensional. Harte was also the leader of a large and diverse literary movement in San Francisco, which included Mark Twain, Ambrose Bierce, Charles Warren Stoddard, and Ina Coolbrith. Harte's *Overland* stories and poems about the California mining camps made his name a household word. At thirty-two he won a $10,000 contract from the James T. Fields Publishing Company as a reward for being the most exciting young writer in America. But in 1871 Harte and his family left for Boston, never to see California again.

In Boston, Harte became intimate with Ralph Waldo Emerson, James Russell Lowell, and Henry Wadsworth Longfellow. He was courted as a celebrity, as the conquering western voice with a far-reaching future. But his success was brief. His social life eclipsed his writing career. Because he failed to meet the terms of that lucrative contract by not writing enough stories and poems, it was not renewed. As his debts accumulated, he turned to lecturing. With bill collectors in the wings, he gave profitable lectures in Boston and New York, but his financial difficulties were not solved. Despite his initial success, the word began to spread that Bret Harte was not a very entertaining lecturer. His last tour ended in a near nervous breakdown. He then turned to a new literary venture: writing a novel. He continued to be saddled with debts and attendant scandals, but the huge advance for the promised novel *Gabriel Conroy* eased for a while the financial and emotional strain. The novel, finally completed in 1876, was a commercial disappointment except in Germany, where it went through several editions. Harte would have been stunned and probably none too pleased to learn that James Joyce would name the lead character Gabriel Conroy in his most famous short story, "The Dead."

Once again Harte had failed to achieve financial security; so he turned to drama, a lifelong interest. Enlisting the help of Stuart Robson, Dion Boucicault, and other luminaries of the theater, he spent much time rewriting into a play the successful story "Two Men of Sandy Bar." This project proved another financial and artistic failure, and as a last hope Harte collaborated with Mark Twain on a play—the "swag," as Twain put it, to be divided on an equal basis. By this time, of course, the two authors' fortunes had been reversed. The old mentor was down at the heels, and his protégé was now a literary success and married to a coal heiress, with whom he shared the most splendid house in Hartford, Connecticut. Their play, *Ah Sin*, was not only a failure, but the issue that broke up a warm and loyal friendship. Scandals about Harte's dilatory writing habits, excessive drinking, and debts appeared in newspapers. The end of the road came when Harte edited a new magazine, the *Capitol*, which folded before publishing its first issue.

The low point of Bret Harte's life came in 1877. He had failed miserably at several literary ventures, his health was starting to deteriorate, and his relationship with Anna was severely strained. Rescue came from an unexpected quarter. Friends convinced newly inaugurated President Rutherford B. Hayes to appoint Harte commercial agent in Krefeld, Germany. But the income from the position was too slight to enable Anna and the family to go with him. Harte began a new period of life—on his own, but constantly fighting to find enough money to support himself and his distant family. He returned to writing fiction modeled on his earlier successes, and the new stories sold well, especially in England. As the years wore on, he sold stories to magazines of decreasing sophistication and collected them in separately issued volumes. (From 1880 until his death, Harte published a volume of short fiction almost yearly.) He traveled a good deal on the Continent. In 1880, however, he was transferred to a new consular post in Glasgow, a city he grew to detest for its foggy climate and industrial pollution; he spent as little time there as possible. With the inauguration of Democrat Grover Cleveland in 1885, Harte was relieved of consular duties and went to live in London at the invitation of Mme. Marguerite Suzanne Van de Velde and her family. He lived out the rest of his days in a kind of velvet-lined prison, what his biographer George Stewart calls "Grub Street De-Luxe." He continued producing nostalgic stories about a long-gone California as the literary world was turning to the realism of Henry James (1843–1916) and William Dean Howells, the naturalism of Stephen Crane and Frank Norris, and always the humor of Mark Twain.

Harte enjoyed the company of many colorful personages of *fin de siècle* London, including James Anthony Froude and Richard Monckton Milnes, Lord Houghton. He became the literary adviser and confidant to several women, among them Florence Henniker, collaborator with Thomas Hardy, and prototype of Sue Bridehead in *Jude the Obscure*. Anna arrived in London in 1898 but declined to live with her husband, spurring more stories about Harte and women. But the spiritual depression caused by his unfulfilled artistry and life in these final years was a sad contrast to the Spanish grandees, miners in red flannel shirts, and blushing maidens who rode on the green, picturesque landscape of Harte's later romances. Ill for years with throat cancer, Harte died at the Van de Velde home near Camberley, England.

• Harte manuscripts are spread out all over North America. The best collections are at Bancroft Library, University of California, Berkeley, and the Huntington Library in San Marino, Calif. *The Writings of Bret Harte* (20 vols.) is the standard collection of Harte's work; the twentieth volume originally appeared as Charles M. Kozlay, ed., *Sorties and Poems and Other Uncollected Writings of Bret Harte* (1914). Linda Diz Barnett, *Bret Harte: A Reference Guide* (1980), is a thorough bibliography of writings by and about Harte. The definitive critical biography is George R. Stewart, *Bret Harte: Argonaut and Exile* (1931). Margaret Duckett, *Mark Twain and Bret Harte* (1964), is a stimulating and provocative analysis. Patrick D. Morrow, *Bret Harte, Literary Critic* (1979), is an intellectual reading of his critical and creative writing. Franklin Walker, *San Francisco's Literary Frontier* (1939), is the most complete literary history of early San Francisco.

PATRICK D. MORROW

HARTECK, Paul (20 July 1902–21 Jan. 1985), chemist, was born Paul Gabriel Karl Joseph Maria Harteck in Vienna, Austria, the son of Josef Harteck, a civil servant, and Gabriele Schattenfroh. The boy was sent to an excellent school in Vienna, the Schotten Gymnasium, run by the Benedictines. He entered the University of Vienna in 1921, where he followed the normal course in chemistry but completed all the requirements within two years. He then went to the University of Berlin, where he attended the lectures on theoretical physics by Max Planck and on applied mathematics by Richard von Mises, receiving the Ph.D. in physical chemistry in 1926 under the direction of Max Bodenstein with a dissertation on the photochemical formation and reactions of chlorine hexoxide and phosgene.

From 1926 to 1928 Harteck was an assistant to Arnold Eucken at the Technische Hochschule, Breslau. From 1928 to 1933 he worked under Fritz Haber at the Kaiser Wilhelm Institut für Physikalische Chemie, Berlin-Dahlem. In 1929 Karl-Friedrich Bonhöffer and Harteck published their method of converting ortho to parahydrogen and described the properties of the latter. This experimental work was an important triumph for the new quantum theory, which had predicted the existence of these hitherto unknown forms of hydrogen. Subsequently Harteck reported the conversion of ortho and para forms of deuterium and of tritium, in 1934 and 1964, respectively. During his stay at the Kaiser Wilhelm Institut, Harteck worked on gas kinetics, photochemical reactions, and isotope separations. At Haber's Institute, Harteck collaborated with Bonhöffer and Ladislaus Farkas and had the opportunity to form friendships with people such as nuclear physicist Leo Szilard and physical chemist turned scientific epistemologist Michael Polanyi.

In 1932 Harteck applied to the Rockefeller Foundation for a stipend to study at the Cavendish Laboratory, Cambridge, England, under the guidance of Lord Rutherford. His application, which was backed by a strong recommendation from Haber and by an impressive list of thirty-four scientific publications, was approved. He stayed at Cambridge only a little more than a year, yet within that time he collaborated with Mark L. E. Oliphant and Rutherford on an important experimental investigation, the bombardment of the compound $(ND_4)_2SO_4$ with deuterons (the D + D reaction), producing tritium, $_1H^3$, and hydrogen, $_1H^1$ (as well as neutrons and $_2He^3$).

$$_1D^2 + {}_1D^2 = [_2He^4] = {}_1H^1 + {}_1H^3$$

From the range of the tracks of particles in the cloud chamber (14.3 cm for H^1 and 1.6 cm for H^3) it was possible to deduce the mass of this new artificially produced isotope of hydrogen $H^3 = 3.0151 \pm 0.0001$. The research was directed by Rutherford, the equipment was built by Oliphant, and the deuterium-containing chemicals were made by Harteck from a concentrated supply of heavy water that he had prepared as his first task at the Cavendish. A stable salt of deuterium that would have negligible vapor pressure in a vacuum and that would not be subject to surface exchanges was required for the experiments: From his heavy water, Harteck made heavy ammonium chloride, heavy ammonium sulfate, and heavy ammonium chloride covered with a film of heavy orthophosphoric acid. Ultimately, the experiments were successful because of the happy choice of salts; a choice that really depended on Harteck's knowledge of the properties of materials. Neither of his collaborators was a chemist.

Harteck left Cambridge in 1934 to accept the chair of physical chemistry, recently vacated by Otto Stern, at the University of Hamburg. The appointment of a young man of thirty-two to this post testifies to the reputation that he had already acquired. During World War II Harteck was one of the main actors in the German effort to harness nuclear power. He originated some of its significant processes such as the enrichment of the uranium isotope by means of the gas ultracentrifuge, the catalytic production of heavy water, and the lattice arrangement of uranium in a pile. Harteck suspected that carbon would be a better moderator than heavy water, but the difficulty and expense of purifying graphite in wartime Germany was an insuperable obstacle. He suggested using solid carbon dioxide (dry ice), which can be readily obtained in the required purity, and actually commenced, independently of everyone else, to design such a reactor. His effort was never fully completed owing to the insufficient availability of uranium. Jeremy Bernstein wrote: "It is clear to me that if Harteck had been able to build his reactor in 1940, . . . the Army, in my opinion, would have taken over and pushed the project" (Bernstein, p. 367).

Harteck continued his researches in the postwar years. During this time, in 1947, he married Marcella Maria Piccino-Hay; they had three children. In 1948 he became rector of the University of Hamburg and remained at that post until 1950. During these years at Hamburg, both before and after the war, his work included the production and reactions of atomic oxygen and the discovery of tritium in the earth's atmosphere.

In 1951 Harteck emigrated to the United States in order to provide a safer haven for his family than Hamburg appeared to be at that time; he subsequently became a U.S. citizen in 1957. In 1953 He was appointed Distinguished Research Professor of Physical Chemistry at the Rensselaer Polytechnic Institute of Troy, New York. Within a few years of his arrival he had formed an active research group of young collaborators. He broached a new and basic field of research in the investigation of the chemistry and photochemistry of the earth's upper atmosphere, which he soon extended to include planetary atmospheres. With his colleague W. Groth, Harteck promoted the concept of a large reaction vessel in which chemical reactions occurring in the upper atmosphere of the earth might be simulated. A spherical vessel seven meters in diameter was constructed in Groth's Institute at the University of Bonn, Germany. It could be operated at the low pressures and high pumping velocities required for such experiments.

By means of the iodine photochemical lamp of his invention, Harteck enriched the C^{13} isotope of carbon in the product C_3O_2, in which the C^{13} appears as the central carbon atom. Perhaps motivated by his early association with Haber, nitrogen reactions and the fixation of nitrogen for the commercial production of fertilizer continued to interest him. He incorporated enriched U^{235} into very fine glass fibers (glass wool), which he irradiated with neutrons in the Brookhaven reactor. In this way, most of the energy of fission (200 million electron volts per fission) was transferred into the gas phase (an air-type mixture) around the fibers, to produce oxides of nitrogen.

Harteck retired from Rensselaer in 1982 and passed his remaining years at Santa Barbara, California, where he died.

Harteck received the Jean Servais Stas medal in 1957 and was elected an honorary member of the Société Chimique de Belgique. He received the Wilhelm Exner Medal of Vienna in 1961, "for outstanding and many-sided work in physical chemistry." He shared the Alfred Krupp von Bohlen and Halbach Foundation prize of West Germany in 1977 for his work on the gas ultracentrifuge and received the Grand Decoration of Honor of Austria in 1978.

• Harteck's papers, including a list of his published books and articles, are preserved at the R.P.I. Archives, Troy, N.Y. His work on the German atomic project during the war years is discussed in David Irving, *The Virus House* (1967), where he is singled out as the driving force behind that effort. The confinement of ten leading German atomic scientists, which included Harteck, at Farm Hall, England, and the secret recording of their conversations is published in Jeremy Bernstein, ed., *Hitler's Uranium Club* (1996). An obituary is in the *New York Times*, 24 Jan. 1985.

SYDNEY ROSS

HARTFORD, George Huntington (5 Sept. 1833–29 Aug. 1917), cofounder of the Great Atlantic and Pacific Tea Company (A&P) grocery store chain, was born in Augusta, Maine, the son of J. Brackett Hartford, a farmer and merchant, and Martha Soren. His schooling was sparse, and he never pursued higher education. His Roman Catholic parents were active in the small fledgling Catholic community in southwest Maine and helped to purchase a former Unitarian church building for the first Catholic church in Augusta, St. Mary's.

At age eighteen Hartford sailed to Boston, Massachusetts, where his mother had relatives, and took a job as a clerk in a dry-goods store. Around 1858 he went to New York City, where he met George F. Gilman, a leather merchant who advised him to go to St. Louis, Missouri. Arriving in St. Louis, Hartford set up a leather shop and secured commissions for Gilman. In 1860 he returned to New York to clerk for Gilman, who was diversifying his interest in leather goods and had decided to go into the tea-importing business. Gilman's father owned a fleet of ships that were involved in overseas trade; with the use of these ships, Gilman could greatly facilitate his new venture. Gilman and Hartford realized that by importing directly from China, without going through middlemen, they could sell tea in New York more cheaply than other merchants—for thirty cents a pound rather than at the going rate of one dollar a pound.

In 1862 Hartford married Josephine Ludlum; they had five children. The following year Hartford and Gilman informally became partners and named their new business the Great American Tea Company. Their first store was located in Lower Manhattan, on Vesey Street. Unlike the reserved and modest Hartford, Gilman had a flair for the theatrical and the ostentatious. He decorated the store, and the others that followed, in a flamboyant Oriental motif, using red, black, and gold colors. The store was a success from the start, and by 1865 Hartford and Gilman had twenty-five other stores. Diversifying their product line, they began offering goods such as coffee, spices, and soap. They also used extensive advertising and various other promotional efforts, including premiums, and they offered credit and mail-ordering.

Seeing the success of the Hartford and Gilman operation, other entrepeneurs started their own tea stores, even using the same name or one similar to it, of Hartford and Gilman's company. Consequently, in 1869 they started calling their company the Great Atlantic and Pacific Tea Company (A&P). In the meantime Hartford developed a new product, Thea Nectar, which he described as a "tea product." Thea Nectar was made from damaged tea, which Hartford could purchase very cheaply because there was a lot of it, and it was otherwise always discarded. His new product, a black tea with a green tea taste, became an extremely successful and popular product, selling at a price well below that of the specialty tea.

Hartford and Gilman opened stores in Baltimore, Boston, Buffalo, Cleveland, Milwaukee, New Haven, St. Louis, and St. Paul, among other places. By 1878 there were over seventy A&P stores in the eastern United States. That year Gilman retired from the company and turned over the management to Hartford. Sales continued to increase, based on Hartford's strategy of maintaining low cost and high volume. Also in 1878 Hartford was elected mayor of Orange, New Jersey, where he and his family had moved a few years earlier; he would serve twelve one-year terms. In 1880 he opened A&P's 100th store, and by the turn of the century there were nearly 200 stores.

In the early 1880s, finding his mayoral duties more time-consuming than expected, Hartford brought two of his sons into the business, George Ludlum and John Augustine; they were later joined by a third son, Edward, who became A&P's corporate secretary. In 1901 Gilman died without leaving a will; moreover, he had never established a formal legal partnership with Hartford. Their amicable business relationship was based on trust, respect, and honesty, and their only contract was in the form of a handshake. At the time of Gilman's death, A&P sold $5.5 million worth of goods annually. Although Gilman had no children, he had several nieces and nephews who as heirs filed suit.

The following year Hartford worked out an agreement with Gilman's relatives. He then organized A&P as a corporation in the state of New Jersey, which had more favorable laws concerning corporations than the state of New York. His new corporation had a capital stock valued at $2.1 million, although the court had found that A&P's real property was worth about $1 million. He put most of the stock in a preferred issue—$1.4 million—giving $1.25 million to Gilman's heirs. The remaining preferred and common stock he kept for himself, but he had virtually absolute control of the company; over time he gained control of the preferred stock as well.

In the following years Hartford gave his sons increasing authority and responsibility in the company. His son John, after much discussion, convinced him to expand the company by opening so-called economy stores. John was convinced that the company could reap larger profits through this new type of store, which had no frills and sold groceries as cheaply as possible on a cash-and-carry basis, with no deliveries, no credit, and no premiums. In 1912 A&P opened an economy store next to its conventional store in Jersey City; it did so well that the regular store was closed within six months. Within a year A&P opened its 500th store. By the end of 1919 there were over 4,200 stores throughout the country, and by 1930 there were nearly 16,000 stores.

In 1913 A&P started selling products under its own name, finding that it could undersell name products like Cream of Wheat, which had recently won a suit preventing A&P from selling Cream of Wheat at wholesale prices. In 1916 Hartford turned the company over to his sons. Because A&P was a family-owned business, he had maintained a benevolent, even paternalistic, posture toward his employees. This had been possible before the huge expansion of the company after 1912, but became more and more difficult thereafter. Under Hartford it was policy that no one was ever fired from A&P except for dishonesty or violence; moreover, promotion in the company was from within. He even instituted a kind of pension plan known as the "retired payroll" and encouraged his employees to buy company stock—all without pressure from the union movement.

Hartford's diligence and business acumen enabled him to build a solid company. Although it was not the first chain store in the United States, A&P became one of the longest lasting as well as best known. He died in Spring Lake, New Jersey, leaving an estate of $125 million. Although one of the wealthiest individuals in the country, the press took very little notice of his death, reflecting his modest, ordinary unassuming personality.

• Information on Hartford's role in cofounding A&P is in two articles by R. J. Bullock in the *Harvard Business Review*: "The Early History of the Great Atlantic and Pacific Tea Company," Apr. 1933; and "A History of the Great Atlantic and Pacific Tea Company," Oct. 1933. For a history of the chain store, tracing its origin to China before the birth of Christ, see John P. Nichols, *The Chain Store Tells Its Story* (1940). Another interesting study is Godrey M. Lebhar, *Chain Stores in America 1859–1959* (1963). See also M. A. Adelman, *A&P: A Study in Price-Cost Behavior and Public Policy* (1959), and Milton Moscowitz et al., *Everybody's Business* (1980). An obituary is in the *New York Times*, 30 Aug. 1917.

GEOFFREY GNEUHS

HARTFORD, George Ludlum (7 Nov. 1864–23 Sept. 1957), and **John Augustine Hartford** (10 Feb. 1872–20 Sept. 1951), chain store executives, were born, respectively, in Brooklyn, New York, and Orange, New Jersey, the sons of George Huntington Hartford, a partner with George F. Gilman in a tea store in New York, and Josephine Ludlum. Begun in 1859, Hartford and Gilman's tea store had become by 1869 a chain known as the Great Atlantic and Pacific Tea Company (A&P). The brothers worked in their father's store part-time and during the summers until they turned sixteen, when each left school to work full-time in the business. In 1901 Gilman died, and the Hartfords purchased complete ownership of the firm, which then numbered about 200 stores. The senior George Hartford wanted to expand the firm and increase the variety of goods sold. John Hartford supported even greater expansion, although his brother George opposed it. The stores gradually began to offer credit and delivery services.

By 1912 John became convinced that credit and delivery were the wrong way to go, even though the firm was adding stores and increasing profits. He opened an economy store in Jersey City, New Jersey, next to the regular A&P store. This new store had plain fixtures, did not offer credit or delivery, but sold groceries at lower prices. It soon put the regular store out of business. The A&P then began opening hundreds of new stores on the economy-store model. Eventually there were thousands.

By 1915 the father had turned over much of the control of the business to his sons. He died in 1917, and in 1920 the brothers formalized their roles: John became president and was responsible for the stores and business operations, and George handled finances. George, who was reclusive, had married Josephine Plume Burnett Logan in 1903; they had one child. After their marriage he avoided publicity and resided quietly in New Jersey. John, who was at ease with people, enjoyed visiting the individual stores. He was pa-

ternalistic toward his workers and opposed unionization. He often tested products himself. A fastidious dresser, he wore tailor-made clothes, favoring a gray suit with a red flower in the lapel. In 1893 he had married Pauline Corwin, whom he divorced in 1923. He married Francis Bolger soon after but was divorced again in 1924. He remarried his first wife in 1925; they had no children.

The A&P grew quite large during the 1920s, with more than 15,000 grocery stores by 1927. It epitomized the notion of the chain store and was the symbol of the threat of big business to small independent grocers. "Mr. George," as George Hartford was known, anticipated the 1929 crash and in 1927 put all the stores on one-year leases, thus helping to control costs during the depression. But the stores were small, old, and often in the wrong locations as urban patterns changed. More and more they faced opposition from independent supermarkets with larger and better-located units offering lower prices. Because of its relative inefficiency, A&P was forced to raise prices during this period. Although slow to change, the depression forced A&P to respond to its competition, and by 1937 John Hartford had switched A&P to a supermarket operation. He closed numerous smaller stores and opened larger new ones in locations better suited to the use of the automobile. By 1939 the number of units was reduced to 9,200. But while the number of units decreased, sales and profits increased as a result of improved efficiency and economies of scale.

During the 1930s chain stores, particularly grocery chains, became the subject of sustained opposition from independent merchants, who claimed that chains engaged in unfair competition. Antichain measures, usually in the form of taxes, were passed in many states. By the late 1930s U.S. representative Wright Patman of Texas had introduced a national chain store tax in Congress. A&P and the Hartfords were the chief targets of this measure. It failed to pass, however, and interest in the antichain movement declined with the coming of World War II. After the war, chain store taxes were largely repealed as the chain supermarket became increasingly popular. A&P also became involved at this time in antitrust litigation. In 1946 it was convicted of violating antitrust laws, and the Hartfords (and other A&P executives) had to pay small fines.

By the mid-1950s A&P had become the nation's largest food chain. When John Hartford died in New York City, his estate (A&P stock) was left to the John A. Hartford Foundation, which he had established in 1929 to support applied medical and biomedical research. George Hartford, who was chairman of the board of A&P at the time of his death in Montclair, New Jersey, left much of his wealth to the foundation.

• For additional information see J. C. Furnas, "Mr. George and Mr. John," *Saturday Evening Post*, 31 Dec. 1938, and M. A. Adelman, *A&P: A Study in Price-Cost Behavior and Public Policy* (1959). Obituaries are in the *New York Times*, 21 Sept. 1951 and 25 Sept. 1957.

CARL RYANT

HARTLEY, Fred Allan, Jr. (22 Feb. 1902–11 May 1969), U.S. congressman, was born in Harrison, Hudson County, New Jersey, the son of Fred Allan Hartley, a produce merchant and realtor, and Frances Alice Hartley (they were not related). He attended the public schools of Harrison and Kearny, and then Rutgers Prep and Rutgers University until age seventeen. He married Hazel Lorraine Roemer in 1921; they had three children.

Hartley early became politically active, serving on the Kearny Library Commission, as municipal fire commissioner, and two terms as chairman of his Republican County Committee. In 1928 he won election to the U.S. House of Representatives and, at age twenty-six, was the youngest congressman elected that year. Although he served in Congress for twenty years, he ultimately listed his occupations as farmer and lecturer.

As a congressman, Hartley was an isolationist who opposed lend-lease and amendments to the neutrality acts in the late 1930s. He was credited with obtaining an Office of Price Administration (OPA) ruling in 1943 allowing additional gasoline rations for vacationers taking annual trips to summer resorts. He opposed OPA and formed an anti-OPA coalition of Democrats and Republicans.

Hartley left no mark in Congress, however, until after the 1946 election and the organization of a Republican-controlled Congress. In 1947 he became chairman of the Labor and Education Committee, on which he had served since coming to Congress, and at age forty-four was the youngest committee chairman at that time. He had voted for the pro–American Federation of Labor amendments to the Wagner Act in 1935 and during World War II became known as anti-union for his votes for an anti-strike bill and a portal-to-portal pay bill. The Congress of Industrial Organizations especially opposed his political views. Early in 1947 he introduced the Hartley bill in Congress, which some observers argued was even more anti-union than the views of the National Association of Manufacturers.

Strikes and labor unrest in the post–World War II period produced a public and congressional reaction against labor leaders. The Republican leadership chose Senator Robert A. Taft and Hartley in the House to carry out their party's 1946 campaign pledge to curtail the power of organized labor. They believed that the Wagner Act of 1935 had been erroneously interpreted by the National Labor Relations Board to allow labor leaders too much control over labor-management relations and that the intent of the Wagner Act—balance between industrial and union power—should be restored.

Hartley's strategy was to add several extremely antilabor provisions to his proposal, such as a ban on industry-wide bargaining, so that when his and the Senate's bill reached the conference committee, he would have something to trade. He could sacrifice some of his most radical provisions and still come out of conference with a strong measure. Events developed as he predicted; the committee deleted several of his harsh-

est provisions. He was pleased that the press helped his strategy succeed by assuring readers that the Labor-management Relations Bill, which eventually emerged from conference, was not nearly as harsh as Hartley's original measure.

President Harry S. Truman studied the Taft-Hartley Bill and, against the advice of many of his advisers, decided to veto it. Although he recognized it as a good law, Truman knew that Congress would likely override his veto and that he could, thereby, have his cake and eat it too. His veto would win the support of organized labor for his presidential campaign in 1948, and he would still have the Taft-Hartley injunctive powers, which he used in industrial conflicts over the next few years. As expected, both houses of Congress overrode his veto in June 1947 by 4-to-1 majorities. Anti-union southern Democrats in great numbers joined the Republicans to pass what union leaders immediately dubbed the "slave labor law." Truman had acquired a major political issue for the 1948 campaign.

The Taft-Hartley Act, which amended the Wagner Act, sought to make the NLRB an impartial referee of labor-management relations by denying unions the right to employ a series of unfair-labor practices. The act forbade the closed shop; allowed the union shop if workers petitioned and approved it by majority vote; and, in Section 14(b), permitted states to pass so-called "right to work" laws that banned compulsory union membership. It also required union officials to sign anticommunist affidavits, prohibited government employees from striking, and forbade the use of union funds for political purposes. The most famous feature of the Taft-Hartley Act provided for eighty-day "cooling off" injunctions where strikes that threatened to create a national emergency were involved.

This law was Hartley's only major claim to fame. Declining to run for reelection in 1948, he wrote a book explaining his law that same year and retired to his cattle farm near Frenchtown, New Jersey. He also became active as a business and legislative consultant and went on the lecture tour for several years to defend his controversial law and to promote "right to work" laws. In 1954 the conservative Hartley broke with the liberal wing of his party when New Jersey Republicans chose Clifford Case to run for the Senate. Hartley staged an unsuccessful write-in campaign against the liberal Case. He died in Linwood, New Jersey.

• The location of Hartley's papers is unknown. Hartley's *Our New National Labor Policy: The Taft-Hartley Act and the Next Steps* (1948) exaggerates his role in the passage of the law. R. Alton Lee, *Truman and Taft-Hartley* (1966), is a political history of the labor policy. An obituary is in the *New York Times*, 12 May 1969.

R. ALTON LEE

HARTLEY, Marsden (4 Jan. 1877–2 Sept. 1943), artist, essayist, and poet, was born Edmund Hartley in Lewiston, Maine, the son of Thomas Hartley, a spinner in a cotton mill, and Eliza Jane Horbury. His childhood was marred by the death of his mother in 1885, at which time her eight children were separated. Hartley remained with his father and an older married sister, Elizabeth, in Auburn, Maine, until 1889, when his father remarried Martha Marsden, an Englishwoman, and moved with her to Cleveland, Ohio. (In 1908 Hartley dropped his first name and decided to call himself Marsden, his stepmother's maiden name, which he had adopted in 1906.) Left behind with Elizabeth, Hartley dropped out of school at fifteen and worked in a shoe factory. In 1893 he moved to Cleveland, where he joined his family and took a job as an office boy in a marble quarry.

At the quarry, Hartley met John Semon, a local painter, with whom he began to study. He subsequently took sketching classes. His talent won him tuition at the Cleveland School of Art, where Nina Waldeck, a drawing teacher, introduced him to Ralph Waldo Emerson's *Essays*. A wealthy school trustee offered him a five-year stipend that enabled him to study in New York City. In the fall of 1889 he enrolled in the New York School of Art, studying with F. Luis Mora and Frank Vincent Dumond and attending the Saturday critiques by William Merritt Chase. That first year he also attended critiques by Kenyon Cox at the Art Students League, but he switched the following autumn to the National Academy of Design, where he spent the next four years. Hartley left New York each summer to return to Maine, where he developed a strong interest in landscape painting, especially of mountains.

By the time his stipend ended in 1904, Hartley had also begun to write poetry. He supported himself by working part time as an extra with Proctor's Theater Company of New York, with which he toured during 1905–1906. Around this time, he became acquainted with Horace Traubel, who had been a close friend of Walt Whitman, whose influence Hartley felt in his search for transcendental meaning and in the poet's celebration of nature and of individual freedom. When he returned to Lewiston in the autumn of 1906, hoping to paint and to earn his living by teaching art, he shifted from the academic realist style that he had practiced at the National Academy to postimpressionism.

By the spring of 1907 Hartley, in desperate need of work, found employment at Green Acre, a utopian community in Eliot, Maine, where he did odd jobs and developed a deeper interest in mysticism. At the end of the summer, Mrs. Ole Bull gave him a show of his work in her home there, from which he earned ninety dollars in sales. That winter in Boston, his work attracted the attention of artist and critic Philip Leslie Hale and of collector and art writer Desmond Fitzgerald. With the latter's help, Hartley went during the summer of 1908 to North Lovell, Maine, where he painted landscapes influenced by postimpressionism.

Ever on the move, Hartley met artists Maurice and Charles Prendergast in Boston in early 1909. With their encouragement and letters of introduction to Robert Henri and William Glackens, he returned to New York City, where he showed his work to a number of artists in Glackens's studio. That April poet Shaemas O'Sheel introduced him to Alfred Stieglitz, who the next month gave Hartley his first one-man show in New York at his gallery 291. The vanguard critic Sadakichi Hartmann wrote a favorable review in *Camera Work*, praising Hartley's color and calling his style "up-to-date impressionism." Hartley also met the dealer N. E. Montross, who offered him a stipend and introduced him to the work of Albert Pinkham Ryder. Enthusiastic, Hartley met the older artist and then began painting a series of dark landscapes influenced by him.

Now a member of the circle of 291, Hartley discovered the European avant-garde, especially Cézanne, Matisse, and Picasso. He participated in group shows and had his second one-man show (featuring still lifes) there in February 1912. That spring, with the proceeds from sales and with contributions from patrons, Hartley sailed to Europe, settling first in Paris, where his American friend Lee Simonson rented him his first studio and introduced him to Gertrude Stein, who became a supporter of his work. Hartley's interest in the Parisian vanguard was soon supplemented by his discovery of the art and ideas of the Russian expatriate Wassily Kandinsky through the artist's books, especially *Der Blaue Reiter*, an almanac he coedited with Franz Marc. Corresponding to his own fascination with mystical ideas, the almanac motivated Hartley to explore "primitive" art, which he sought out in the ethnographic collections of the Trocadero Museum. His initial response was to include some Native American objects in his still-life paintings.

Hartley soon shifted to abstractions that included references to musical composition and to mystical symbols. He called these canvases "subliminal or cosmic cubism." At the time he felt the influence of reading that, among other authors, included Henri Bergson and William James. Motivated by these texts as well as by friendships with German sculptor Arnold Rönnebeck and his cousin Karl von Freyburg, a handsome Prussian officer whom he met in Paris, Hartley was drawn to visit Germany in 1913. On his return to Paris, he met Kandinsky and his companion, the German artist Gabriele Münter, in Munich. Impressed with Kandinsky and with Germany, Hartley sensed exhibition opportunities for himself in Munich and wrote ecstatically to Stieglitz that he had found his place "in the art circles of Europe."

Returning to Germany that spring, Hartley visited Marc in Sindelsdorf and arranged with the Galerie Goltz in Munich to show some of his paintings informally to a group of artists associated with *Der Blaue Reiter*. Encouraged, Hartley settled in Berlin, where military pageantry stimulated new content in his painting. That fall he showed five abstractions in Berlin in the First Germany Autumn Salon. Sales failed to materialize, and Hartley was forced to appeal to Stieglitz and Stein for help. At Stieglitz's insistence, Hartley returned to New York to have a show that opened at 291 in January 1914. The catalog included a foreword by Stein.

In the spring Hartley returned to Berlin. Political and aesthetic currents coalesced in Hartley's new pictures, which where boldly colored, abstract, and emblematic; they represent some of his best work (*Indian Composition*, Vassar College Art Museum, Poughkeepsie, N.Y.). He devoted one series to Native American themes that reflect his interest in non-Western art reproduced in the almanac *Der Blaue Reiter* and shown in the collections of the Berlin ethnographic museum as well as his response to nationalistic currents at home and abroad. He also became interested in German folk art. A few weeks after the start of World War I, Karl von Freyburg was killed in action on 7 October 1914. His death inspired *Portrait of a German Officer* (Metropolitan Museum of Art, New York), one of a series of abstract memorial pictures the disconsolate Hartley painted in memory of his friend. After a major one-person exhibition at the Münchner Graphik-Verlag in Berlin in October 1915, Hartley sailed for New York in December.

Back in the United States, Hartley's reputation continued to grow. For the summer of 1916 his peripatetic nature took him to the art colony in Provincetown, Massachusetts, where he painted pale abstractions with geometric forms referring to sailboats. For two months there that fall, he shared a house with artist Charles Demuth. For the winter he traveled to Bermuda, where he was joined briefly by Demuth and produced stylized still lifes. For the summer of 1917 Hartley returned to Maine. At Hamilton Easter Field's art colony in Ogunquit, he experimented with painting on the back of glass. Popular in American folk art, this technique had been practiced by Kandinsky and other artists in the circle of *Der Blaue Reiter* who had also collected Bavarian folk examples.

Hartley's talent for writing was evident in 1918, when he published six of his poems in the magazine *Poetry* and essays in the *Dial*, the *Little Review*, and elsewhere. In June he traveled to New Mexico, where he worked first in Taos and then in Santa Fe. He painted still lifes that depicted the characteristic Mexican-American *santos* and wrote essays defending Native American culture, which he praised for its "very aristocratic notion of religion" and "superb gift for stylistic expression." Attracted to the rugged, open landscape along the Rio Grande, he worked first in pastels, then in oil paints. In November he left for New York, but he continued to paint southwestern landscapes based on pastels.

Hartley became the first secretary of the Société Anonyme, Inc., which was founded by Katherine Dreier, Marcel Duchamp, Man Ray, and others associated with New York dada. The summer of 1920 found him painting still lifes in Gloucester, Massachusetts. The following spring he auctioned off 117 of his works at the Anderson Galleries in order to finance a return to Europe. His collection of essays *Adventures in the Arts: Informal Chapters on Painters, Vaudeville, and Poets* was published in 1921.

After a stay in Paris in July, Hartley visited the American sculptor John Storrs in Orléans and then settled in Berlin and painted still lifes. He began making lithographs in September 1922, but by the spring of 1923 he had begun a series of paintings he called *New Mexico Recollections*. That summer, when his *Twenty-five Poems* was published, he produced a number of pastel drawings of nudes, his first figures for many years. He returned to New York in February 1924 for just three months to arrange for a syndicate to finance his living expenses in Europe over the next four years. After painting in Paris, he moved in August 1925 to Vence, in the south of France, where he produced landscapes of the Italian Alps and a series of still lifes. Recalling his early enthusiasm for Cézanne, Hartley moved to Aix-en-Provence in the autumn of 1926, and he too began to draw and paint Mont Sainte-Victoire, a development that pleased neither Stieglitz nor critics who favored American subject matter in art.

A show at the Arts Club of Chicago in the winter of 1928 occasioned Hartley's return to the United States for a seven-month stay. That summer he spent two months in Conway, New Hampshire, and two weeks in Georgetown, Maine, where he stayed with sculptor Gaston Lachaise and his wife Isabel and saw their mutual friends photographer Paul Strand and his wife Rebecca, an artist. Hartley was not yet ready to return to Maine, but he already appreciated the significance of making "vital contact with my native soil."

Critics were not enthusiastic about Hartley's January 1929 show at Stieglitz's Intimate Gallery. Over the next several years he suffered discouragement and painted irregularly. The award of a yearlong Guggenheim grant stipulating that he had to work outside of the country prompted him to leave in March 1932 for Mexico, where he was in touch with Hart Crane shortly before the poet's suicide, which Hartley memorialized in his painting *Eight Bells' Folly, Memorial for Hart Crane* (Frederick R. Weisman Museum, University of Minnesota, Minneapolis). In April 1933 Hartley sailed from Veracruz for Germany, settling in Garmisch-Partenkirchen. He produced a series of drawings, paintings, and lithographs (*Garmisch-Partenkirchen*, Milwaukee Art Museum) of the landscape, returning to New York in mid-February 1934, never again to visit Germany.

After a brief stay painting in Bermuda in 1935, Hartley traveled to Nova Scotia, where he lived with the Mason family in Eastern Points. After returning in December 1935 to New York City, he was employed by the Works Project Administration; he then returned to live with the Masons. The tragic drowning death of the Masons' two fishermen sons, whom Hartley adored, resulted initially in some somber seascapes and later in some expressionist memorial portraits, most notably two versions of the *Fisherman's Last Supper*, the first begun after he moved to Vinalhaven, an island off the Maine coast, in the summer of 1938 (both in private collections). That spring he had his first exhibition at the Hudson D. Walker Gallery in New York.

With the exception of brief periods in New York, Hartley spent his last five years painting in Maine: figure paintings featuring sunbathers, lobstermen, and religious themes, still lifes of flowers, dead birds, and fish, and landscapes, including a series of Mount Katahdin (National Gallery of Art) in northern Maine, which he visited for eight days in October 1939. He published two more collections of poems, *Androscoggin* (1940) and *Sea Burial* (1941).

Homosexuality emerges as an important theme in many of Hartley's late works, when he was less concerned with concealing it than he had been in his earlier, more private memorial to von Freyburg. His remembrance of Crane is overt, even more so than his paintings recalling the drowned fishermen. All of Hartley's tribute paintings concern the death of male subjects whom he idolized. Other late figure compositions also suggest his sexual preference: the heroic athletes, lifeguards, and male bathers and the all-male pietà, *Christ Held by Half-Naked Men*.

Hartley died in Ellsworth, Maine. Obituaries proclaimed him "a visionary painter" and "a noted artist," and the Museum of Modern Art scheduled a memorial retrospective a year later. Appreciation for his art has grown with greater understanding of the symbolic content of his work and its rich significance.

• The most comprehensive collection of Hartley's work is the Lone and Hudson Walker Collection in the Frederick R. Weisman Museum at the University of Minnesota in Minneapolis. The largest collection of Hartley's papers is located in the Collection of American Literature at the Beinecke Rare Book and Manuscript Library at Yale University, including his letters to Alfred Stieglitz, Gertrude Stein, and others. Other important collections are at Bates College, Lewiston, Maine, and at the Archives of American Art of the Smithsonian Institution. A biography is Townsend Ludington, *Marsden Hartley: The Biography of an American Artist* (1992). *The Collected Poems of Marsden Hartley, 1904–1943* (1987) and his essays *On Art* (1982) have been collected by Gail R. Scott, whose monograph, *Marsden Hartley* (1988), is also useful. See also Barbara Haskell, *Marsden Hartley* (1980); Gail Levin, *Marsden Hartley in Bavaria* (1989), and "Marsden Hartley's 'America': Between Native American and German Folk Art," *American Art Review* (Winter 1992): 122–25, 170–72; Levin et al., *Theme and Improvisation: Kandinsky and the American Avant-garde, 1912–1950* (1992); Levin, "Photography's 'Appeal' to Marsden Hartley," *Yale University Library Gazette* 68 (Oct. 1993): 12–42; Jeanne Hokin, *Pinnacles & Pyramids: The Art of Marsden Hartley* (1993); and Jonathan Weinberg, *Speaking for Vice: Homosexuality in the Art of Charles Demuth, Marsden Hartley, and the First American Avant-garde* (1993).

GAIL LEVIN

HARTLINE, Haldan Keffer (22 Dec. 1903–18 Mar. 1983), biophysicist, was born in Bloomsburg, Pennsylvania, the son of Daniel Schollenberger Hartline, a teacher in the natural sciences at Bloomsburg State Normal School, and Harriet Franklin Keffer, a teacher of English at the normal school. Hartline referred to his father as his "first and best teacher." The love of nature that his father instilled in him strongly influenced his choice of experimental research in biology as a lifelong career. In 1920 Hartline spent the summer studying comparative anatomy at the marine laboratory in Cold Spring Harbor, Long Island. That fall he entered Lafayette College. Hartline spent the summer of 1923 at the marine laboratory at Woods Hole, Massachusetts, where the eminent biologist Jacques Loeb introduced him to quantitative experimental biology. In 1923 Hartline graduated from Lafayette and entered the Johns Hopkins University School of Medicine, from which he received an M.D. in 1927. Hartline never practiced medicine and instead devoted his life to research.

Hartline continued his studies in physiology at Johns Hopkins for two years as a National Research Council Fellow, but his strong interest in mathematics and physics led him to accept a scholarship in 1929 from the Eldridge Reeves Johnson Foundation to study in Germany. There he studied under two eminent physicists, Arnold Sommerfeld at Munich and Werner Heisenberg at Leipzig. Hartline soon found that he lacked the necessary mathematical background for this advanced work, and, somewhat disappointed and uncertain about his future, he returned in 1931 to the United States.

Detlev W. Bronk, who was then head of the Johnson Foundation, became a lifelong friend and patron of Hartline. A biophysicist, Bronk recognized Hartline's extraordinary abilities in the application of the techniques of physics to the study of biology. In 1931 Bronk appointed him Fellow in medical physics at the foundation, where Hartline remained until 1949, except for a brief move in 1940, with Bronk, to Cornell University Medical College. There they felt constrained by a lack of academic and scientific freedom, and both returned to the foundation in 1941. In 1949 Bronk became president of the Johns Hopkins University and appointed Hartline the first professor of biophysics and chairman of the university's new Department of Biophysics. In 1953 Hartline followed Bronk to the Rockefeller Institute for Medical Research and in 1965 became professor of biophysics at the recently renamed Rockefeller University. In 1972, not long after Bronk's death, Hartline was named Detlev W. Bronk Professor at Rockefeller, a post he held until his retirement in 1974.

Bronk, along with E. D. Adrian, had pioneered in the study of how single nerve fibers conduct impulses. Hartline's basic research followed their lead and focused on how the retina of the eye processes visual information and transmits that information to the brain via the optic nerve. In the first of his four greatest achievements, which were all "firsts" in their respective fields, he and Clarence H. Graham recorded in 1932 the electrical activity of single nerve fibers dissected from the optic nerve of the compound eye of an invertebrate, the horseshoe crab. They found that the information conducted from the eye to the brain by these fibers is encoded in a series of discrete, essentially identical nerve impulses that vary in frequency rather than in amplitude with variations in the light on the eye. They deduced that the optic nerve is an FM (frequency-modulated) rather than an AM (amplitude-modulated) system.

In 1940 Hartline found that in a vertebrate (frog) visual system a given optic nerve fiber may respond to light falling anywhere within an extensive region of the retina because many photoreceptors are connected by convergent neural pathways to that fiber. Hartline called this region the fiber's receptive field. Different fibers may have different types of fields. Some respond with a steady discharge of impulses as long as the light is on. Others respond only when the light is turned on and again when it is turned off. Some, surprisingly, respond only when the light is turned off. (Many other types of receptive fields have since been found.) Thus, different optic nerve fibers, with their different receptive fields, respond simultaneously—in parallel—to different aspects of the pattern of light and shade on the retina.

In 1952 Hartline recorded, along with Henry G. Wagner and Edward F. MacNichol, electrical potentials within the cell bodies of the retinal neurons that give rise to the optic nerve fibers. These potentials are the generators of the nerve impulses propagated by the nerve fibers. They found that the amplitude of a generator potential varies with the intensity of the light and that the frequency of the resulting discharge of optic nerve impulses is proportional to the amplitude of the generator potential. Thus a local AM signal in the retina is converted into an FM signal more suitable for transmission, along the optic nerve, over the long distance from the eye to the brain.

In 1949 Hartline published his discovery of lateral inhibition—a form of negative feedback—in the retina, in which excitatory activity in one region of the retina diminishes (inhibits) excitatory activity in neighboring regions. Lateral inhibition serves to enhance contrast and sharpen edges in retinal images. In 1957 Hartline and Floyd Ratliff, an associate at the Rockefeller Institute for Medical Research, mathematically modeled the integration, or summation, of these opposed excitatory and inhibitory influences and were able to predict almost exactly the pattern of neural activity resulting from any pattern of light on the retina.

Hartline had little interest in the administration of science and none at all in its politics. With Bronk's protection from such distractions, he was able to spend most of his time doing laboratory research. It was considered both a privilege and an honor to work in Hartline's laboratory, and over the years he collaborated with investigators from all over the world, many of whom became distinguished in the field and made significant contributions of their own, including Tsuneo Tomita, Charles F. Stevens, Robert B. Barlow, Jr., and Robert M. Shapley.

Hartline received many honors and awards for his contributions to science. While still in medical school he received the William H. Howell Award in physiology. In the 1940s experimental and physiological psychologists were among the first to recognize the importance of his work to the understanding of human visual perception, and the Society of Experimental Psychologists awarded him the Howard Crosby Warren Medal in 1948. That same year he was elected to the National Academy of Sciences. He was elected to the American Philosophical Society in 1962, received Case Institute of Technology's Albert A. Michelson Award in 1964, and became a foreign member of the Royal Society (London) in 1966. In 1967 he won the Nobel Prize in Physiology or Medicine jointly with Ragnar Granit of Karolinska Institute and George Wald of Harvard University "for their discoveries concerning the primary physiological and chemical visual processes in the eye." In 1969 he received the Lighthouse Award for Distinguished Service and in 1980 was elected an honorary member of the Optical Society of America.

In 1936 Hartline had married Elizabeth Kraus, an instructor in comparative psychology at Bryn Mawr College; they had three children. The family lived near Hydes, Maryland, and had a summer home just north of Bar Harbor, Maine. While at Rockefeller, Hartline kept an apartment in New York City and returned home for long weekends and holidays with family.

Despite Hartline's slight stature and rather frail appearance, he was an active outdoorsman. As a young mountain climber, he had some first ascents to his credit in the Wyoming Rockies. For a time, to the alarm of his friends, he piloted his own open-cockpit plane around the country. Later in his life he enjoyed sailing, which he engaged in with Bronk in Maine and with Granit in the Baltic. In his seventies he took a rafting trip with his wife down the Colorado River through the rapids in the Grand Canyon. He died at the Fallston General Hospital near his home in Maryland.

For more than a half-century Hartline conducted biophysical research on vision and the retina. He elucidated numerous fundamental principles of retinal physiology, laying the foundations for the present-day study of the neurophysiology of vision. Although Hartline was awarded the highest of all honors in science for his discoveries, he remained modest and unassuming in character and was actually somewhat embarrassed by fame and public acclaim.

• A collection of Hartline's most important papers is reprinted in Floyd Ratliff, ed., *Studies on Excitation and Inhibition in the Retina* (1974). Detailed biographical sketches include John E. Dowling and Floyd Ratliff, "Nobel Prize, Three Named for Medicine, Physiology Award," *Science* 158 (1967): 468–73; Ragnar Granit and Floyd Ratliff, "Haldan Keffer Hartline, 1903–1983," *Biographical Memoirs of Fellows of the Royal Society* 31 (1985): 262–92; Floyd Ratliff, "Haldan Keffer Hartline (1903–1983)," American Philosophical Society *Year Book* (1984): 111–20; and Ratliff, "Haldan Keffer Hartline, 1903–1983," National Academy of Sciences, *Biographical Memoirs* 59 (1990): 196–213.

FLOYD RATLIFF

HARTMAN, Samuel Brubaker (1 Apr. 1830–30 Jan. 1918), physician and proprietary medicine manufacturer, was born near Harrisburg, Pennsylvania, the son of Christian Hartman and Nancy Brubaker, farmers and immigrants from Switzerland. His father died when Hartman was six months old, and the boy had a peripatetic youth. Speaking only German until the age of fourteen, Hartman learned woodchopping from an uncle, then carpentry while living with a brother in Medway, Ohio. At twenty he taught school for a year in Pennsylvania, then toured the countryside selling German-English Bibles.

Having studied medicine for a term in 1852 at Farmers' College near Cincinnati, Hartman undertook a two-year apprenticeship with a Medway physician, then six months of medical study at Cleveland Medical College, the medical department of Western Reserve College. He began practice in Vandalia, Ohio, and moved in 1855 to Tippecanoe City. In 1856 he began to attend lectures at Jefferson Medical College in Philadelphia, from which he received an M.D. the next year. For twelve years Hartman practiced in Millersville, Pennsylvania, near his boyhood home. In 1860 he married Sallie Ann Martzall of Lancaster; the couple had two children.

In 1870 Hartman, who had lost his savings because of unwise investments, launched a twenty-year career as itinerant physician and surgeon, moving from city to city across the land treating patients recruited by advertising. He specialized in ear and eye afflictions, chronic catarrh (inflammation of the respiratory tract), and orthopedics, especially club feet. His average annual income he estimated at $50,000.

Hartman's favorite prescription was a so-called "neutralizing mixture" for the treatment of catarrh that he had begun to use in Millersville and for which he later coined the name "Pe-Ru-Na," a term that had no meaning but was easy to remember. Variant sources ascribe the medication's origin to a formula from a treatise by the eclectic physician Wooster Beach and to an "Herb Bitters" made by a Pennsylvania distiller, Benjamin Mishler. Hartman, who continually modified the ingredients, complained that pharmacists could not fill the prescription properly. So in 1877 he began manufacturing the medicine in a small plant in Osborn, Ohio, managed by a brother. In 1883 a larger factory was built in Columbus. In 1890 Hartman settled in that city, devoting much of his time to the manufacture and promotion of Pe-Ru-Na, for which he received a trademark in 1895. Hartman marketed two other proprietaries, Man-A-Lin, a laxative, in 1877, and La-Cu-Pi-A, a blood purifier, in 1879.

For some years in Columbus, Hartman also practiced with a corps of other physicians in an elaborate Surgical Hotel, a cross between a hospital and a hotel, that he had built in 1890 and then expanded and renamed the Hartman Sanitarium. In 1902 he added an adjunct, the Hartman Hotel. Through the 1890s a stream of pamphlets sought to attract patients to its various divisions for the treatment of diseases of the eyes, ears, spine, joints, and feet; for diseases peculiar to women and to men; and for eradicating the narcotic, liquor, and tobacco habits. Hydrotherapy, electro-

therapy, and mechanical massage were among the therapeutic modes employed.

Although Pe-Ru-Na was promoted to cure only catarrh, the millions of brochures and almanacs Hartman issued and his extensive newspaper advertising defined catarrh as encompassing all ailments known to humanity. Hartman's promotional efforts owed much to his second in command, Frederick W. Schumacher, a genius at innovative advertising, who married Hartman's daughter Maribel. By the new century Pe-Ru-Na was the most widely advertised—at a million dollars a year—and the bestselling proprietary medicine in the nation. Babies were named for it. Agents recruited testimonials and obtained pictures from humble citizens who were paid a quarter for each letter they answered from inquirers about the product's merits. Fees were paid to local dignitaries and to national celebrities to praise the prowess of Pe-Ru-Na. These included former Union and Confederate generals, Spanish-American War admirals, such stage stars as Julia Marlowe, and fifty members of the national Senate and House of Representatives. "Indeed," chided a skeptical member, "Peruna seems to be the favorite Congressional drink."

In the muckraking of patent medicine at the start of the new century, Pe-Ru-Na became a prime target. Journalist Samuel Hopkins Adams termed it "the most conspicuous of all medical frauds." It was condemned for promising to ward off yellow fever during the major 1905 epidemic in the South as well as for redefining all dread diseases as catarrh. Pe-Ru-Na was denied status as a medicine by the American Medical Association and deemed just a secret liquor with its 27 to 30 percent alcohol content and flavoring from cubebs, an aromatic stimulant from the fruit of a vine. The "Peruna jag," a slight intoxication from drinking the nostrum, became so common a phenomenon, especially in areas dry by Prohibition laws, that druggists had trouble keeping it in stock. Hartman privately defended Pe-Ru-Na but publicly retreated from his advertising claims, adopting the therapeutic nihilism popular among leading physicians at the time. He denied that most drugs, with the possible exception of quinine for malaria, would cure disease. But he held that the slight stimulation of Pe-Ru-Na, bolstered by the impact of testimonials on the patient's mind, would produce good results.

Government policy sided with Pe-Ru-Na's critics. In 1905 the Office of Indian Affairs banned Pe-Ru-Na from reservations. That same year the Internal Revenue Service decreed that, inasmuch as Hartman's nostrum was not truly a medicine, all retailers who sold it must possess a liquor license. The next year the Food and Drugs Act required that the amount of alcohol in proprietaries must be stated on the label. Henceforth, drinkers of Pe-Ru-Na could not keep a secret from themselves. To bring a reversal of the IRS ruling, Hartman, without public announcement, added the medicinal ingredients buckthorn and senna, strong cathartics. Throughout the nation, heavy users suffered badly, and sales of Pe-Ru-Na fell sharply. In 1916

Hartman began remarketing his original formula, alcohol and all, under a new name that echoed an old message, Ka-Tar-No, acknowledging that it must be sold by outlets with a liquor license.

In spite of his setbacks, Hartman continued to be deemed the wealthiest man in Columbus. He spent much time during his declining years on his elegant 5,000-acre establishment south of Columbus, which was stocked with fancy breeds of cattle, horses, and poultry. He died in his apartment in the Hartman Hotel. Pe-Ru-Na as a product outlasted its originator by many years, being sold in 1926 to a Chicago concern, although, while slightly revived by radio advertising, it never regained its lost luster.

• The archives of the American Medical Association contain numerous documents concerning Hartman and Pe-Ru-Na, and the Smithsonian Institution archives have an interchange of letters between the Pe-Ru-Na Company and a user of the nostrum. Among numerous promotional pamphlets issued by Hartman, especially revealing are *The Ills of Life* and *Lectures on Chronic Catarrh*, both published in many editions. Other pamphlets issued through the 1890s are listed in the *Index-Catalogue of the Surgeon-General's Library*, 2d ser., vol. 6 (1901). At the peak the company published 45 million pamphlets a year. Accounts of Hartman's career appear in Samuel Hopkins Adams, *The Great American Fraud* (1906), from his *Collier's* series of 1905–1906; American Medical Association, *Miscellaneous Nostrums* (1923); Robert Gunning, "The Hypocrite's Highball," *American Mercury* (Dec. 1942), 722–29; Stewart H. Holbrook, *The Golden Age of Quackery* (1959); Jean Kahler, "The Fabulous Empire of Peruna," a seven-part series in *Columbus Dispatch Magazine*, 10 Sept. through 22 Oct. 1961; Henry W. Holcombe, *Patent Medicine Tax Stamps* (1979); and James Harvey Young, "Pe-Ru-Na: A Catarrh Cure from Columbus," *Timeline* 12 (Nov.–Dec. 1995), 2–17. Obituaries are in the *Columbus Citizen*, the *Ohio State Journal*, and the *New York Times*, 31 Jan. 1918. Richard J. Hopkins supplied items from *Columbus Vignettes*, 1966–1969, and other useful material.

JAMES HARVEY YOUNG

HARTMANN, George Wilfred (29 Mar. 1904–11 June 1955), psychologist and pacifist, was born in Union Hill, New Jersey, the son of Herman Carl Hartmann, a roofer and tinsmith, and Veronica Ruff. As a scholarship student at Columbia University (A.B. 1924), Hartmann excelled in German (his major), history, and psychology. Shifting to psychology for its greater opportunities and social utility, he combined graduate study at Columbia (A.M. 1925; Ph.D. 1928) with instructorships there and at Dartmouth College. As a student he met his wife, Esther Leah Norton; they had two children. From 1928 to 1935 he served as a professor of psychology at Pennsylvania State College. In 1935 he returned to New York as a postdoctoral fellow and then became a professor of educational psychology at Teachers College (1936–1949).

As a young psychologist, Hartmann applied theories of learning and personality to practical problems ranging from fashion preferences to the performance of college football teams. Most of these he approached from the perspective of Gestalt psychology, which he studied in Berlin and Leipzig (1930–1931). In the mid-1930s Hartmann became known for his innovative studies of political attitudes, inspired by a personal commitment to socialism and progressive education. While he was a Socialist party candidate for U.S. Congress in 1934, Hartmann polled rural voters and found them agreeing with socialist reforms if they were dissociated from the party name. A year later, while running for state supreme court, he tested the effects of two different campaign leaflets on voters in Allentown. Validating the approach of his friend Norman Thomas, Hartmann found that an emotional, personalized message elicited more votes than did the dispassionate, impersonal appeals of the Socialist Old Guard. Although his party's decline in popularity thwarted further research, Hartmann persevered as a candidate. Moving to New York, he ran for lieutenant governor (1938) and mayor of New York City (1941).

At Teachers College Hartmann was a leader of the progressive education movement, editing *Social Frontier* from 1937 to 1939, and he was president of the university's chapter of the Teachers Union. A virulent anticommunist, he resigned from the union in 1939 to protest his inability to gain influence at the city and national levels. As a friendly witness before Martin Dies's Committee on Un-American Activities, he accused communists of blocking his efforts by factionalist maneuvering. Simultaneously he founded the Jane Addams Peace School, a short-lived, pacifist-socialist evening school for anticommunists.

In 1939 Hartmann served as chairman of the Society for the Psychological Study of Social Issues, founded by leftist psychologists wanting to help shape social policy. In his chairman's address, he advocated scientific research to establish a hierarchy of social values and urged his colleagues to "cease apologizing . . . for their desire to establish a World State" free of poverty, war, and ugliness. Sincere experts were so valuable, he suggested, that perhaps "the deep convictions of ten percent ought to prevail against the feeble views of the opposing ninety percent" (*Journal of Social Psychology* 10 [1939]: 563–75).

In 1942–1943 Hartmann took a leave from Teachers College, which he extended when wartime enrollments declined. With the help of Gordon Allport he became research supervisor of the Cambridge-Somerville Youth Study and a visiting lecturer at Harvard University. A leader of the War Resisters League and other pacifist organizations, Hartmann agreed to his employers' request that he keep silent on the war for a year. The following summer he helped found and became director of Peace Now, a popular front of opponents of the war, pacifist and nonpacifist alike, that campaigned for an immediate, negotiated peace. Politically naive, Hartmann denied the significance of anti-Semitism and nativism within the group and thought its investigation by the Dies Committee would help win public support. Instead, the group was denounced as seditious by Dies, the national media, and groups across the political spectrum. In response, Hartmann sued his critics, including Walter Winchell and *Life* magazine, whose issue of 17 January 1944 had superimposed the caption "U.S. Indicts Fascists" over Hartmann's photograph. Isolated, he confided that he felt compelled to continue by a "strange sense of duty . . . and the inability to forget the cries of wounded humanity all over the globe." In March 1944 he moved the group's office—which had been burglarized with the help of the FBI—to his basement in Cambridge and planned to launch a national political party. In May Columbia and Harvard announced the termination of his appointments, and Hartmann was hospitalized for severe depression.

With the assistance of the American Association of University Professors, Hartmann won reinstatement at Columbia in late 1945, and through a subsequent lawsuit he obtained his lost year's salary. In 1949 he moved from Teachers College to the psychology department at Roosevelt University and soon became its chairman. Typical of his postwar writing was "The Psychology of American Socialism" in the influential *Socialism and American Life*, ed. Donald Drew Egbert and Stow Parsons (2 vols., 1952). There he described socialists as motivated by a gestalt desire for closure, preferring comprehensive civic reforms to the anarchy of traditional politics. Praising the Socialist administrations in Milwaukee, Wisconsin, and Bridgeport, Connecticut, he suggested that voters there were of a higher moral type, unlikely to experience a change in their political gestalt and return to a nonsocialist perspective.

In 1954 his older daughter was stricken by a debilitating illness while she was a medical resident; at the same time, Hartmann was despairing over his own career. Suffering a recurrence of his earlier depression, he committed suicide at his home in Flossmoor, Illinois.

Within psychology, Hartmann is memorable as a pioneer in the study of political behavior, the author of the influential text *Gestalt Psychology* (1935), and for his influence on a generation of students at Teachers College. In pacifist and socialist circles he was prized as a powerful orator with a commanding presence, broad intellect, and uncompromising moral stance.

• Hartmann left no personal papers, but significant correspondence is in the Gordon W. Allport Papers at Harvard University, the Socialist Party of America Papers at Duke University, and the Anna Melissa Graves Papers at Swarthmore College. Also useful are the papers of the Peace Now movement, which are divided between the New York Public Library and Swarthmore College (in the Dorothy Hutchinson Papers). See also Hartmann's approximately 1,800-page FBI file for documentary and wiretap evidence of Communist party and FBI involvement in the sabotage of Peace Now. Hartmann's works include *Industrial Conflict: A Psychological Interpretation* (1939), a collection co-edited with Theodore Newcomb; *Educational Psychology* (1941); and *Socialism Versus Communism: An Ethical and Psychological Contrast*, co-authored with Roger Payne (1953). His "Frustration Phenomena in the Social and Political Sphere," *Psychological Review* 48 (1941): 362–63, is a semi-autobiographical analysis of the emotional costs of failed election campaigns. On Hartmann's work in the Society for the Psychological Study of So-

cial Issues, see the articles by Benjamin Harris et al. in "Fifty Years of the Psychology of Social Issues," *Journal of Social Issues* 42 (1986).

BENJAMIN HARRIS

HARTMANN, Sadakichi (8 Nov. 1867?–21 Nov. 1944), art critic, was born Carl Sadakichi Hartmann in Nagasaki, Japan, the son of Carl Herman Oscar Hartmann, a German government official and businessman, and a Japanese woman, Osada. His mother died within several months of his birth, and Sadakichi was sent to live with relatives in Germany. His formal education ended at fourteen when he ran away from military school. Hartmann's father responded by sending him to the United States to live with a family in Philadelphia, but he struck out on his own within a year. Hartmann schooled himself and cultivated relationships with local art and literary figures, including Thomas Eakins and Walt Whitman. Whitman shared his philosophy with the young man and became an important mentor to him.

In 1885 Hartmann continued his cultural education by traveling to Germany, where he spent eight months apprenticing at a theater in Munich and visiting artists' studios. After one more trip abroad, Hartmann settled in Boston and began freelance writing and lecturing on art and other cultural subjects. Following a third European tour, Hartmann moved to New York in 1889. He spent the next three years socializing with writers and artists and writing his own poetry, plays, and essays. In 1891 he suffered a severe bout of depression and attempted suicide. He was hospitalized and later that year married his nurse, Elizabeth Blanche Walsh.

In 1892 publisher S. S. McClure sent a rejuvenated Hartmann to Paris as a roving correspondent. He immersed himself in French art and literature, spending time with poet Stéphane Mallarmé and his circle of symbolist friends. He met painters Claude Monet and expatriate American James A. M. Whistler, among others. Hartmann returned to the United States in 1893 and began planning his own journal. The first issue of the *Art Critic* included a detailed program for developing a "national art," one of Hartmann's passions, and an introduction to French symbolist art and poetry. Among the 750 subscribers were many important art figures, including William Merritt Chase, Albert Bierstadt, Albert Pinkham Ryder, Augustus St. Gaudens, George Inness, Robert Henri, and Frank Furness. Even with this support, the magazine went bankrupt after only three issues. Its demise was due largely to Hartmann's arrest and personal financial collapse after publishing his own symbolist work, an erotic free-verse play about the life of Christ that included nude scenes and an orgy.

Even after this disaster, Hartmann remained interested in symbolism. He went on to write symbolist-inspired poetry and a number of other dramas about religious figures. In 1902 he staged the first of several "perfume concerts," during which floral scents were circulated while the audience listened to a travelogue.

Though these creative endeavors were intriguing, if not of enduring literary value, Hartmann's early association with the French symbolists found lasting and significant expression in his critical advocacy of a "suggestive" American style of art, as practiced by such painters as Whistler, Thomas Dewing, Childe Hassam, and John Twachtman.

Hartmann spent the mid-1890s developing his artistic theories, writing, and lecturing on art and the theater. In 1897 he published four issues of another periodical, *Art News*. The following year, in the widely circulated journal *Musical America*, Hartmann articulated the difference between the modern critic's enterprise and traditional writing about art: "It is the art critic's duty to enter an artist's individuality, to discover his intentions—intentions of which the artist himself is perhaps unconscious—to judge how far he has realized them, and then to determine what place he occupies in the development of national and cosmopolitan art." Hartmann applied this approach not only to painting and sculpture but also to photography. Alfred Stieglitz invited him to join the staff of his journal, *Camera Notes*, in 1898. As one of the first writers to address photography as a form of visual expression, Hartmann played an important role in broadening the medium beyond its traditional documentary role. He appreciated the accessibility of photography and understood it as key in the development of modernism.

In 1902 Hartmann published *A History of American Art*, largely a compilation of earlier articles, and, disturbingly, with passages apparently plagiarized from an earlier historian's writings. In this work, Hartmann attempted to define American art. Of the so-called "Old School," he claimed that the works of Winslow Homer and Thomas Eakins best embodied a frank and vigorous native art. Among those representing the "New School" of distinctly American artists, Hartmann included Chase and Dewing. Ryder defied categorization by representing the "old" in technique and the "new" in conception. Though some of its assessments are dated or simply inaccurate, the work stands as an important survey of contemporary American art anchored in a historical context. Hartmann also published critical surveys of modern American sculpture (1902) and Japanese art (1904).

Hartmann continued to write on photography and in 1903 began contributing to Stieglitz's new Photo-Secessionist journal, *Camera Work*. Feeling his independence as a critic threatened and uncomfortable with Stieglitz's authoritarianism, Hartmann left *Camera Work* in 1904 and began writing about the Salon Club photographers, a group led by Curtis Bell. By 1908, though, Hartmann and Stieglitz were once again on cordial terms and Hartmann resumed writing for *Camera Work*. In the meantime, Hartmann had begun a series of cross-country lecture tours that lasted until 1910. During these years he also assisted the Carnegie Institute in choosing American drawings for its collection, published a few issues of another art journal, *The Stylus*, wrote several books on composition, and produced thoughtful criticism on a number of young art-

ists, including Marsden Hartley, George Luks, Edward Steichen, and Max Weber. His insightful and well-crafted monograph on Whistler was published in 1910. It was during this productive period that Hartmann's eccentricity manifested itself in the form of a gentlemanly alter ego. He signed much of his writing on photography at this time as "Sidney Allan," and he often appeared as "Allan" when lecturing. Unlike the rough, abrasive Hartmann, "Allan" was genteel and refined and never bothered friends and acquaintances with requests for financial assistance.

In 1911 Hartmann withdrew from the New York City art world, though he continued writing, including an important article on cubism. The chronology and circumstances are unclear, but Hartmann's marriage to Elizabeth Walsh, with whom he had five children, was over by 1911. His health was poor, and he moved to the Roycrofters' colony in East Aurora, New York, seeking relief from severe asthma. He met artist Lillian Bonham, who became his common-law wife and bore him seven children. The family lived nomadically, marginally supported by Hartmann's lecturing and writing, until 1923, when they settled in southern California. Hartmann became involved with the movie industry, lecturing frequently at Rudolf Schindler's studio, writing a "Hollywood" gossip column for a British journal, and appearing in a Douglas Fairbanks, Jr., film, *The Thief of Baghdad*. Hartmann's eccentric reputation was bolstered by wild nights of dancing, drinking, and socializing with the likes of W. C. Fields, John Barrymore, and John Decker.

In a final attempt to control his asthma, Hartmann moved in 1938 to the desert near Palm Springs, where he spent the rest of his life in a small cabin, writing poetry and corresponding with such writers as Ezra Pound, Booth Tarkington, and George Santayana. This rural existence did not, however, bring him peace. His health and finances continued to be precarious, and because of his Japanese ancestry the family was hounded during World War II. In 1944 Hartmann made a last transcontinental journey to visit a daughter in St. Petersburg, Florida, where he died.

Though his later writing was generally unremarkable, at the peak of his career Hartmann addressed all major, and many minor, artists active during the two decades bracketing the turn of the century. His aggressive promotion of a native art, his early analyses of modernism, and his perceptive writing on photography have guaranteed him a place in the history of American art and criticism.

• The University of California, Riverside, holds an important collection of Hartmann's papers. The university's English department published *The Sadakichi Hartmann Newsletter* for several years, beginning in 1969. The most important resource is *Sadakichi Hartmann: Critical Modernist* (1991), a collection of Hartmann's writings on art edited and introduced by Jane Calhoun Weaver. In *Buddha, Confucius, Christ: Three Prophetic Plays* (1971), Harry Lawton and George Knox collect several of Hartmann's plays. For Hartmann on photography, see Lawton and Knox, *The Valiant Knights of Daguerre: Selected Critical Essays on Photography and Profiles of Photographic Pioneers* (1978). See also Gene Fowler's account of Hartmann's later years in *Minutes of the Last Meeting* (1954). Harry Lawton's series of articles in the *Riverside (Calif.) Daily Press*, Aug. 1954, provides some balance to and corrects certain inaccuracies in Fowler's account.

MARJORIE A. WALTER

HARTNESS, James (3 Sept. 1861–2 Feb. 1934), inventor, business leader, and governor, was born on a farm near Schenectady, New York, the son of John Williams Hartness, a mechanic, and Ursilla Jackson. In 1863 the family moved to Cleveland, Ohio, where Hartness's formal education ended after elementary school. The Hartness family lived a comfortable life in Cleveland, as Hartness's mother doted on her three surviving sons while his father succeeded as a foreman and then superintendent.

At the age of thirteen Hartness began eight years of apprenticeship in three Cleveland machine shops. In 1882 he left his family and his job as a highly skilled toolmaker to accept a position as a foreman in Winsted, Connecticut. For the next seven years, Hartness was employed in a number of machine shops in Connecticut and Pennsylvania. During this period he established himself as an innovator as well as a shop foreman by patenting nine inventions. In 1885 he married Lena Sanford Pond; they had two children.

While migrating among various companies, Hartness conceptualized a new form of lathe that would handle long pieces of stock and accommodate multiple tools. He was unsuccessful in selling his idea to a number of companies before being offered employment at Jones and Lamson Machine Company in Springfield, Vermont. When Hartness began there as superintendent in early 1889, Jones and Lamson was struggling to maintain a viable business. Company directors encouraged Hartness to pursue development of his radical new design, the flat turret lathe. While fleshing out that design and building a prototype, Hartness also reduced the Jones and Lamson product line and restored business profitability. When the flat turret lathe was finally introduced to the market in 1893, it was an instant success and was responsible for the emergence of Jones and Lamson as a major supplier of machine tools. Two years later Hartness was appointed general manager of Jones and Lamson.

The success of the flat turret lathe depended not only on Hartness's basic concept, but also on a number of other Hartness patents, notably a continuous feed mechanism for long bar stocks. These patents secured for Jones and Lamson substantial licensing income from other firms that adopted Hartness's ideas. In 1900 Hartness became president of Jones and Lamson but continued to invent as well as administer. In 1903 he patented the cross-sliding head lathe, which was Jones and Lamson's first radical departure from the flat turret concept and became an equally important part of their product line.

As Hartness's reputation in machine tool design grew, he became more active as a member, and then as a leader, in the American Society of Mechanical Engineers (ASME). His benevolent management style at Jones and Lamson served as a model during a period of industrial strife as management emphasized operational efficiency and major industries were unionized. Hartness's book *The Human Factor in Works Management* garnered widespread approval. In 1914 Hartness was recognized for his technical and business leadership by election to the ASME presidency.

Appointed chairman of the Vermont Board of Education in 1915, Hartness's public leadership role soon broadened. After the United States entered World War I, he served as Vermont's federal food administrator. This was followed by war-related appointments to the Inter-Allied Aircraft Standardization Commission (Hartness was one of the earliest licensed amateur pilots) and to the National Screw Thread Commission. Hartness chaired several screw thread subcommissions, including one on gages and methods of test.

It was while serving on the latter that Hartness crystallized his invention of the optical comparator. He employed Russell W. Porter, a friend of long standing through their mutual interest in astronomy, as a freelance inventor and product-development draftsman to develop the optical comparator. The comparator was first patented in 1921, then greatly improved and repatented with Porter in 1929. The importance of the optical comparator to Jones and Lamson soon matched that of the flat turret and cross-sliding head lathes.

His taste for public service whetted by his war-time experience, Hartness in 1920 decided to run for governor of Vermont. His successful campaign for the Republican primary, tantamount to election in Vermont at that time, was later characterized as a model for an independent attack on an entrenched political machine. Limited by tradition to one term, Hartness's two years as governor were turbulent. His appointments based on technical competence rather than political patronage earned him the enmity of machine politicians. Although normally reserved and somewhat reticent about public contacts, Hartness relished the confrontations of Vermont political life and thoroughly enjoyed his two-year term as governor. Still, he was disappointed not to have achieved more in those two years.

Late-life recognition of Hartness included an honorary LL.D. from the University of Vermont (1921) and his election as president of the American Engineering Council (1924–1925). In later years, Hartness renewed his interest in mechanical devices, securing fifteen new patents in his last decade. This brought his lifetime total to 119 patents, of which only four were shared with copatentees. Hartness's interest in astronomy expressed itself in many ways, including the design of unique, accurate sundials. He sponsored a telescope-making club, led by Porter, that later stimulated a nationwide movement. He enjoyed observing the night skies with his patented all-weather Hartness Turret Telescope. He died in Springfield, Vermont.

In his brilliant career as an inventor and business and political leader, Hartness not only made the very most of his opportunities, he actively afforded others the same opportunities, as evidenced by at least three other major Springfield machine tool companies that were spawned by inventor/businessmen who left Jones and Lamson, with Hartness's encouragement and support, to establish their own successful companies. His generous encouragement of others to make maximum use of their own faculties and his service to his industry, city, state, and nation in the process place Hartness among the great business leaders of his generation.

• Most of Hartness's papers are in the Bailey-Howe Library of the University of Vermont, the exception being his gubernatorial records, which are located in the Vermont secretary of state's archives. Other than patents, Hartness's publishing was limited to a few technical articles and three books. Jones and Lamson published Hartness's first book privately, *Evolution of the Machine Shop* (1905). His popular book *The Human Factor in Works Management* (1912) went through three editions and was translated into several languages. Hartness summarized views he had expressed earlier in *Industrial Progress* (1920), a small book that was privately published. A full-length biography by Joseph Wickham Roe, *James Hartness: A Representative of the Machine Age at Its Best* (1937), was commissioned and published by ASME as one of a series of biographies of important figures in mechanical engineering. Roe includes a useful list of 119 Hartness patents by date and patent number as well as title. Hartness is a key figure in Wayne G. Borehl, Jr., *Precision Valley: The Machine Tool Companies of Vermont* (1959), which is valuable in the context it offers for Hartness's achievements. Several other books about figures in Springfield history include important references to Hartness and his contributions and provide insight into his character in the process, for example, Berton C. Willard's biography, *Russell W. Porter: Arctic Explorer, Artist, Telescope Maker* (1976), and Oscar Seth Marshall's autobiography, *Journeyman Machinist en Route to the Stars: Stellafane to Palomar* (1979). An interesting description of the Hartness gubernatorial campaign is John A. Neuenschwander, "An Engineer for Governor: James Hartness in 1920," *Vermont History* 38, no. 2 (Spring 1970): 139–49.

THOMAS R. WILLIAMS

HARTNETT, Gabby (20 Dec. 1900–20 Dec. 1972), baseball player, was born Charles Lee Hartnett in Woonsocket, Rhode Island, the son of Frederick William Hartnett, a laborer, and Ellen Tucker. He was the oldest of 14 children. The family moved to Millville, Massachusetts, soon after his birth. Hartnett learned baseball from his father and had the skills to play for industrial and semiprofessional teams while still a teenager.

After a brief enrollment at Dean Academy in Franklin, Massachusetts, Hartnett returned to Millville to play industrial league baseball. A catcher like his father, young Dowdy, as he was called at the time, soon attracted the attention of John McGraw, manager of the New York Giants. McGraw sent a scout, former major leaguer Jesse Burkett, to observe the youngster, but Burkett reported that Hartnett's hands were too small to make him a prospect.

Hartnett took a job with the American Steel and Wire Company in Worcester, Massachusetts, in order to play on its team in 1921. While there, he practiced with the Worcester Boosters of the Eastern League, tried out, and won a job as the team's second-string catcher. He played fairly well, but he was still surprised to learn at the end of the season that his contract had been sold to the Chicago Cubs.

Hartnett joined the Cubs in 1922 at their spring training camp on Catalina Island, California. On the train from Chicago, he acquired the nickname "Gabby" for his studied reticence in the presence of several veteran players. He made the team as a reserve, but on opening day he started and caught Grover Cleveland Alexander. His first major league hit came in the next game against the Cincinnati Reds' Dolf Luque. For the season, Hartnett hit only .194 in 31 games. A broken thumb in June sidelined him for nearly two months and limited him to 72 at bats.

Hartnett played in the major leagues for 20 years, all but the last one with the Cubs. He spent his final year as a player-coach with the Giants. Over two decades he became known as one of the best catchers ever. He compiled a .297 career batting average, hit 236 home runs, and drove in 1,179 runs. His best season was 1930 when he hit .339 with 37 homers and 122 runs batted in. In 1935 he won the National League's Most Valuable Player award for hitting .344 and leading the Cubs during a 21-game winning streak that brought them the pennant.

Hartnett married Martha Henrietta Marshall in 1929. They had two children.

The Cubs finished first four times during Hartnett's career but failed to capture even one World Series. They lost to the Philadelphia Athletics in 1929, the New York Yankees in 1932 and 1938, and the Detroit Tigers in 1935. Hartnett hit .300 in the 1932 and 1935 Series, but his two home runs came in games the Cubs lost.

Hartnett was behind the plate in the 1932 World Series for one of the legendary events in baseball history when Babe Ruth hit his "called shot" home run. Accounts of this event are contradictory. Hartnett denied that Ruth had predicted his homer, saying that Ruth had raised a finger to indicate that he needed only one pitch to get a hit.

Hartnett also caught for the National League team in the first five All-Star games starting in 1933. In the 1934 game, he was catching when pitcher Carl Hubbell struck out five future Hall of Fame members in succession.

In July 1938, with the Cubs in third place, Chicago owner Philip Wrigley appointed Hartnett manager. Slowly the team climbed in the standings. On 28 September Hartnett hit the famous "homer in the gloaming," a ninth-inning home run in the gathering darkness against the Pittsburgh Pirates. The victory vaulted the Cubs into the league lead and carried them on to the pennant.

The Cubs of 1939 and 1940 were less successful, and Hartnett was fired. After a 1941 season with the Giants, he played and managed in the minor leagues for five years and then retired. He made a brief return to baseball in the mid-1960s with the Kansas City Athletics but devoted most of his time to operating a bowling alley and recreation center in Chicago. Elected to the Hall of Fame in 1955, he died in Park Ridge, Illinois.

• The only biography of Hartnett is James M. Murphy, *The Gabby Hartnett Story: From a Mill Town to Cooperstown* (1983). See also Bob Broeg, "Hartnett: Baseball's Perfect Catcher," *Sporting News*, 5 Sept. 1970, and "Gabby Hartnett" in Marty Appel and Burt Goldblatt, *Baseball's Best: The Hall of Fame Gallery* (1977). An obituary is in the *Sporting News*, 6 Jan. 1973.

STEVEN P. GIETSCHIER

HARTRANFT, John Frederick (16 Dec. 1830–17 Oct. 1889), Civil War officer and politician, was born near Pottstown, Pennsylvania, the child of Samuel E. Hartranft, a local landowner, and Lydia Bucher, both of German ancestry. He graduated from Union College in 1853 with a degree in civil engineering. About the same time as his marriage to Sallie Sebring (with whom he had one son and two daughters) in 1854, Hartranft changed his life's vocation to law and politics.

Hartranft was elected deputy sheriff of Montgomery County in 1854, a position he held until 1860, and he identified himself as a Republican when the new party was formed. Admitted to the bar in 1860, he scarcely had a chance to practice his profession. Already a colonel in the Pennsylvania militia, he and the troops under his command were mustered into federal service when the Civil War erupted in April 1861. As a result of Hartranft's heroism at Spotsylvania and Petersburg, he earned battlefield promotions first to brigadier general (1864) and then to major general (1865).

In common with many other military heroes of the Civil War, Hartranft returned home to reenter politics as a Republican. In 1865 he won election as auditor general of Pennsylvania on the Republican ticket and was reelected to the same office in 1868. Elected governor in 1872, he served two terms during especially difficult times. The heady economic expansion of the Civil War and immediate postwar years burst during the great depression of 1873–1877. Hard times, falling wages, and rising unemployment led to numerous conflicts between workers and employers. In no state was industrial conflict more common and severe than in Pennsylvania, one of the nation's leading industrial centers. As governor, Hartranft found himself involved in one violent strike after another. During a struggle between railroad workers and their bosses in Susquehanna, Pennsylvania in 1874, he sent state militia to the scene of the conflict to, in his words, "Suppress the riot, disperse the rioters, and afford security and protection to the owners of property in its lawful use." The state troops played a major role in breaking the strike.

The following year Hartranft found his political reputation soiled by association with the Molly Maguires, a group of Irish immigrant workers alleged to belong to a secret society that practiced terrorism in the anthracite district. During the trials of several Irish-American miners and Mollies charged with murder and other acts of violence, opponents of the governor falsely accused him of leniency toward the defendants in order to gain Irish votes for the Republicans. Although Hartranft wooed Irish voters with some success, he allowed the convicted Mollies to go to their deaths on the gallows.

In 1877, the year of several of the most violent strikes in American history, Hartranft again used the state militia to curb "rioting" among railroad workers in Pittsburgh and miners in the anthracite district. When state troops proved unable to quell disturbances effectively, he asked President Hayes to send federal troops, who promptly suppressed the strikes by railroad workers and coal miners.

Hartranft's experiences with labor conflicts between 1873 and 1877 convinced him that compulsory arbitration should replace strikes; that state militias had to be reorganized to serve more effectively; and that employers should have the right to hire private police to protect their property. As governor, he also implemented the revised state constitution of 1873; tightened public regulation of banking; assisted in the arrangements for the centennial exposition of 1876; and reorganized the state militia as part of the national guard.

After leaving the governor's office, he served as commander of the Pennsylvania militia, a position he held with the title of major general until his death. As a reward for his services to the party, Republican leaders appointed him postmaster at Philadelphia (1879) and collector of the port of Philadelphia (1881–1885). He died in Norristown, Pennsylvania.

• No biography, autobiography, or scholarly history of Hartranft now exists. His official papers as governor are located in the Pennsylvania state archives. Several of his personal letters are in the library of the Pennsylvania Historical Society. His role in the labor conflicts of the 1870s can best be traced in the following books: Herbert Gutman, *Work, Culture, and Society in Industrializing America* (1976); Wayne G. Broehl, Jr., *The Molly Maguires* (1964); Robert V. Bruce, *1877: Year of Violence* (1959); and Philip S. Foner, *The Great Labor Uprising of 1877* (1977). For his record as governor, see Frank B. Evans, *Pennsylvania Politics, 1872–1877: A Study in Political Leadership* (1966).

MELVYN DUBOFSKY

HARTSHORNE, Henry (16 Mar. 1823–10 Feb. 1897), physician, medical teacher, and writer, was born in Philadelphia, Pennsylvania, the son of Joseph Hartshorne, a physician, and Anna Bonsall, the daughter of a prominent Quaker. He graduated from the Haverford School (later Haverford College) with an A.B. degree in 1839; in 1860 he was awarded an A.M. degree from the same school. Encouraged by his father to study medicine, he enrolled in the medical school of the University of Pennsylvania and graduated with an M.D. degree in 1845.

In 1846 Hartshorne was appointed resident physician at the Pennsylvania Hospital. The same year, he married Mary E. Brown of Philadelphia; they had two children. When Hartshorne completed his residency, he began private practice in Philadelphia. From 1853 to 1858 he was also professor at the Institute of Medicine at the Philadelphia College of Medicine. When the school was incorporated into the Pennsylvania Medical College in 1859, he was appointed to the chair of the department of the practice of medicine. In 1856 he became an attending physician and clinical lecturer at the Philadelphia Hospital; that same year he received the annual award of the American Medical Association for an essay titled "Arterial Circulation." He served as attending and consulting physician at the Magdalen Asylum, Episcopal Hospital (1860–1862), and Woman's Hospital of Philadelphia (1865–1876). In 1857–1858 he gave a series of ten lectures, "The Natural History of Man," at the Franklin Institute.

The overworked Hartshorne and his wife took a year's vacation in Europe. After his return he volunteered his services in Columbia, Pennsylvania, during an outbreak of cholera in 1854; he had previously assisted during an 1849 cholera epidemic in Philadelphia. His practical experience gave him a better understanding of the nature of cholera, on which he published a book in 1866. In 1860 he withdrew from private practice to devote himself to medical education and literature.

Hartshorne often held teaching positions at several institutions simultaneously. In 1862, after the Pennsylvania Medical School closed, he was appointed professor of anatomy and physiology at the Central High School in Philadelphia, serving until 1868. From 1863 to 1868 he taught physiology and hygiene at the Pennsylvania College of Dental Surgery. During the Civil War he volunteered to treat soldiers in Philadelphia hospitals. He also tended the sick and wounded on the battlefield at Gettysburg.

In 1865 Hartshorne was named a lecturer on hygiene in an endowed auxiliary faculty of the University of Pennsylvania Medical School, and the next year he was appointed the first professor of hygiene at the university. He had no formal training in hygiene or the sanitary sciences; his interest evolved from his teaching of physiology, which examined the body as a machine, and hygiene as a means of keeping that machine running well. His experiences as a delegate to the first and second Quarantine and Sanitary Conventions in 1857 and 1858 and his intense study habits compensated for his lack of training. He believed that with the proper sanitary measures, most zymotic diseases (those infectious and contagious diseases caused by pathogenic microorganisms) could be prevented.

Hartshorne was a firm and outspoken advocate of the right of women to take an equal role in medicine, and he sought their admission to national, state, and local medical societies. In 1869 Hartshorne and Charles H. Thomas accepted positions at the Women's Medical College of Pennsylvania; their presence gave the college's prestige a much-needed boost. He was professor of hygiene, physiology and children's diseases there (1869–1876). In an address to the graduating class in 1872, he asked the women graduates to forgive the members of the Philadelphia medical fraternity for their prejudice against women physicians. In 1883 the first woman physician was accepted into the County Medical Society.

Other teaching positions were at Haverford College (professor of science and philosophy, physiology and hygiene, and biblical literature, 1868–1876), and at Girard College (physiology and natural history, 1872). In 1876 Hartshorne moved to Union Springs, New York, to become president of Howland Collegiate School for Young Women. In 1878 he returned to Philadelphia to open a school for women.

Hartshorne was an active member of medical, scientific, religious and literary societies. Important among these were the Academy of Natural Sciences, the American Association for the Advancement of Science, and the American Philosophical Society; he was also a fellow of the College of Physicians of Philadelphia. In 1872 he attended the first meeting of the American Public Health Association and was elected vice president in 1875–1876. He contributed to medical, public health, scientific, philosophical, and religious journals; wrote and edited medical books; edited the *Friends Review*; and wrote varied literary works, including *Woman's Witchcraft; or, The Curse of Coquetry*, a romantic novel written under the pseudonym Corinne L'Estrange, and three volumes of verse.

Throughout his life Hartshorne had a close attachment to the Society of Friends (Quakers). In 1891 he visited Japan, and on his return he agreed to go back as a missionary for the Society. He returned to Japan in 1895 and became active in the campaign to prohibit the opium trade in Formosa Taiwan; he wrote religious pamphlets and articles, met with Japanese physicians, became interested in establishing a hospital for the mentally ill, and participated in other philanthropic and religious activities. He died in Tokyo.

• Hartshorne's more important works include *Glycerine and Its Uses* (1865); *Facts and Conclusions upon Cholera*; *On Cholera* (1866); *Essentials of the Principles and Practice of Medicine* (1867); *Guide to the Medicine Chest*; *Conspectus of the Medical Sciences for Students* (1869); *Our Homes*, a health primer (1880); and *Household Manual of Hygiene and Domestic Medicine*. He contributed important articles to *Johnson's New Illustrated Cyclopedia* (1872–1873); John Russell Reynolds, *Systems of Medicine*, American ed., Hartshorne (1880); and William Pepper, *Standard System of Medicine* (1885). He also edited Thomas Watson, *Practice of Medicine* (1870). Biographical works on Hartshorne include James Darrach, "A Biographical Sketch of Henry Hartshorne, M.D., LL.D.," *Transactions of the College of Physicals of Philadelphia* 19 (1897): lxv–lxxvii, and the entry by H. W. Kelly and W. L. Burrage in *American Medical Biography* (1920), pp. 499–500. He is also discussed in Sam Alewitz, *Filthy Dirty: A Social History of Unsanitary Philadelphia in the Late Nineteenth Century* (1989); George W. Corner, *Two Centuries of Medicine: A History of the School of Medicine, University of Pennsylvania* (1965); Burton A. Konkle, *Standard History of the Medical*

Profession of Philadelphia, ed. Frederick P. Henry (1977); and Wilson G. Smillie, *Public Health: Its Promise for the Future* (1955).

SAM ALEWITZ

HARTWICK, John Christopher (6 Jan. 1714–17 July 1796), Lutheran pastor, was born in Molschleben, Duchy of Saxe-Gotha (later part of Germany), the son of Andrew Hartwick. His mother's name is not known. Hartwick studied at the University of Halle, having matriculated there in 1739. In response to a call from several New York congregations directed through a London pastor, the Lutheran Ministerium of Hamburg, Germany, recruited him for service in America. He was ordained in London in November 1745.

Arriving in New York in March or April 1746, Hartwick took charge of a parish in the central Hudson River valley, eventually consisting of five congregations. He soon incurred the wrath of the dominant Lutheran pastor in New York, William C. Berkenmeyer, by spending about nine weeks in Philadelphia visiting two pastors, Henry Melchior Muhlenberg and Peter Brunnholtz, both of whom had strong Halle connections, and by then returning to Pennsylvania in 1747 and 1748.

In 1749 Berkenmeyer, who had little sympathy with Halle pastors and their pietistic beliefs, published several pamphlets accusing Hartwick of Moravian sympathies. The following year he called a meeting of New York Lutheran pastors in one of Hartwick's congregations, hoping to bring about his dismissal. It did not, but several months later Muhlenberg recommended that Hartwick spend six months in Pennsylvania helping with pastoral work there, while one of Muhlenberg's ministerial students served the Rhinebeck parish. Hartwick was in Pennsylvania until May 1751, when he returned to New York. Finally resigning his parish in 1757, he never again accepted a pastoral call.

For most of his long career in America, Hartwick was closely associated with those Pennsylvania pastors who had Halle connections. While in Pennsylvania in 1748, he helped organize a ministerium, or synod, designed to bring Halle pastors and their congregations into a closer working relationship. At a time when properly trained pastors were in short supply, Muhlenberg and his associates could have placed Hartwick in some of the most desirable parishes in Pennsylvania. But when Hartwick did accept an invitation, he made it clear that he was only a visiting pastor and soon moved on. This was true in Reading, Pennsylvania (1757–1758); Hackensack, New Jersey (1759); Frederick, Maryland (1762, 1768–1769); and Baltimore, Maryland (about 1764 and again about 1772). When Muhlenberg moved into Philadelphia in 1761, the understanding was that Hartwick would serve his two country congregations for an indefinite time. Tiring of the task, he left after less than five months. During the years 1763–1764 he pushed his friendship with the Philadelphia pastors close to the breaking point by preaching independently of them, even if only briefly, at two places in the city.

Beginning about 1770 it becomes more difficult to trace Hartwick's movements. During this decade he spent considerable time in Virginia. While attending the 1773 ministerium meeting in Philadelphia, he stated that he had recently been in Albany, New York, and could report on the needs of the few Lutherans there. In the spring of 1774 he was called to a Lutheran congregation in Waldoboro, Maine. He apparently paid a visit and then, true to form, declined the call. In a 1778 letter to Halle, Muhlenberg reported that Hartwick "continues his office as a voluntary traveling preacher from one province to another" (*Documentary History*, p. 155).

Between 1780 and Muhlenberg's death in 1787 Hartwick often appeared in Pennsylvania, uninvited, intent on an extended and increasingly unwelcome stay with members of Muhlenberg's family. He was in New York after the British evacuated early in 1784, hoping to persuade those Lutherans who had not left with their loyalist pastor to remain in the city and in their church. Afterward he visited vacant congregations in what was then Albany County.

In 1750, four years after Hartwick arrived in America, the Mohawk Indians deeded him a large tract southwest of Otsego Lake between Schoharie and Cherry Valley. Apparently only then did he learn that one needed a government license before a legal purchase from the Indians could be made. He secured a license (1752) and a survey of 21,500 acres (1754). In April 1761 a patent deed was issued to Hartwick and ten other persons, most of whom were members of St. Michael's Lutheran Church in Philadelphia. Although he tried from time to time to derive an income from the tract, as late as 1791, when William Cooper, the founder of Cooperstown, New York, purchased the mortgage, which Hartwick had given thirty years earlier and never repaid, it still had only a few settlers. This may have been because of social regulations that Hartwick sought to impose on purchasers. Once he gained effective control of the land, Cooper quickly leased most of it, promising Hartwick a share of the net income, but Hartwick died before realizing more than a small return.

As an ordained German Lutheran pastor, Hartwick possessed a genuine religious and social commitment as well as a command of the English language. In 1751 he wrote a preface for an edition of John Arndt's famous pietistic tract, *Wahres Christenthum*, which Benjamin Franklin published. About this time, using an interpreter, he was preaching to Mohawk Indians. In a 1756 letter to Sir William Johnson, recently named superintendent of the affairs of the six Indian nations, he urged the government to secure the long frontiers by sending settlers into them, furnished at its expense with cattle and farming implements, and defended by strategically placed forts. He even offered to travel to England to "promote the scheme, with all my might" (*Memorial Volume*, pp. 124–27). Eight years later in Philadelphia, he wrote an essay opposing the death penalty in cases of theft, as a violation of divine law, and tried unsuccessfully to have it published. In 1764 the *Philadelphia Staatsbote* carried his letter calling attention to the deplorable conditions experienced by many recent German immigrants. Muhlenberg credited Hartwick's effort with being a major factor in bringing about the organization of the German Society of Pennsylvania a month later. During the Revolution, Hartwick's support helped Elizabeth Graeme Ferguson, a leading social and cultural figure in Philadelphia, secure an act in 1781 restoring the inherited property she had lost after her husband, a British supporter, was declared a traitor in 1778.

There was another side to Hartwick. His thoughtlessness permitted him to preach excessively long sermons, dress slovenly, and be rude to women (he never married). He did not hesitate to tell acquaintances that he detested the details of parish work, important as he knew them to be. He resented being in a place where compensation depended in large part on lay evaluation of a pastor's performance. At times he was not above claiming that he possessed the authority of a Lutheran superintendent, an office most Lutherans were pleased they had left behind in Europe. To the end of his life he cherished the goal of a community in which his religious and political views would provide the guide for all.

Although Hartwick participated in the first meeting of the Pennsylvania ministerium in 1748 and attended many meetings thereafter, the last one being in 1785, he was not listed among the members enumerated in the text of the first constitution, which that body adopted in 1778, and was not asked to sign the document in 1781. He was never a member of the ministerium founded in the state of New York in 1786.

While on his way from New York City to Albany, where he then lived, Hartwick died unexpectedly at Clermont, the estate of the Robert R. Livingston family, in the area of his only parish.

Hartwick's will was a complex and confusing document, to which he attached at least four codicils. After making several bequests, he directed that all of his remaining assets be used to establish a town to be called New Jerusalem, as well as an institution to prepare missionaries "to red or black heathens" and also to train Lutheran pastors. Instruction of theological candidates began in New York City in 1797. After a building was completed in Hartwick, New York, in 1815 and a charter secured in 1816, Hartwick Seminary offered instruction at several levels for more than a century. The theological department moved to New York City in 1930 and closed ten years later. The rest of the institution moved to Oneonta, New York, in 1928 and became Hartwick College.

• Some manuscript sources, dealing mostly with Hartwick's last years and with the settling of his estate, are in the Stevens-German Library, Hartwick College, Oneonta, N.Y., and the Abdel Ross Wentz Library, Lutheran Theological Seminary, Gettysburg, Penn. Primary sources with information on recruiting Hartwick for service in America and on his New York parish ministry are available in *Lutheran Church in New York and New Jersey, 1722–1760 . . .* , trans. Simon Hart and Harry J. Kreider (1962); *Protocol of the Lutheran Church in New York City, 1702–1750 . . .* , trans. Hart and Kreider (1958); and *The Albany Protocol . . .* , trans. Hart and Sibrandina Geertruid Hart-Runeman (1971). Harry Julius Kreider, *Lutheranism in Colonial New York* (1942), is a secondary account using some of these sources that places Hartwick's New York ministry in perspective. There are more than one hundred references to Hartwick, extending over some forty years, in *The Journals of Henry Melchior Muhlenberg*, trans. Theodore G. Tappert and John W. Doberstein (3 vols., 1942–1958). Evidence of Hartwick's participation in the Pennsylvania ministerium is available in the *Documentary History of the Evangelical Lutheran Ministerium of Pennsylvania and Adjacent States . . .* (1898). The *Memorial Volume of the Semi-Centennial Anniversary of Hartwick Seminary, . . .* (1867) reprints many important documents relating to Hartwick, beginning with the Indian deed of 1750 and including his last will and testament, probated in 1796. Alan Taylor, in *William Cooper's Town: Power and Persuasion on the Frontier of the Early American Republic* (1995), discusses what happened to Hartwick's patented land during the last few years of his life.

CHARLES H. GLATFELTER

HARTZELL, Joseph Crane (1 June 1842–6 Sept. 1928), Methodist pastor, administrator, and missionary bishop, was born in Moline, Illinois, the son of Michael Bash Hartzell, a farmer and cabinetmaker, and Nancy Worman Stauffer. Hartzell was the fourth of thirteen children born to devout Methodists whose ancestors had emigrated from Germany to Pennsylvania in the early eighteenth century. In 1835 Hartzell's parents moved to Illinois, and he grew up in a log cabin where Methodist worship services and class meetings were regularly held. Nurtured in a spiritual environment that included much religious instruction at home and inspired by his parents' example of Christian faith, Hartzell at the age of sixteen had a conversion experience and felt a strong call to the ministry. His father, pastor, and district superintendent all urged him to become licensed as a Methodist preacher immediately, but Hartzell was convinced he could minister more effectively if he first gained more education. After completing high school, he worked for the next seven years at manual labor, supply preaching, and teaching mathematics and Latin to put himself through both Illinois Wesleyan (B.A., 1868) and Garrett Biblical Institute (B.D., 1868), where he graduated as valedictorian. In 1864 he saved the lives of four members of the crew of a lumber schooner that had wrecked in Lake Michigan by courageously swimming to them through frigid water with a lifeline. That same year Hartzell tried to enlist in the Union army but was denied because the quota for the local unit was full.

After his graduation from seminary, he served as a Methodist minister in Pekin, Illinois. In 1869 he married Jennie Culver of Chicago. Having been deeply moved by the reports at the Methodist General Conference sessions in Chicago in 1868 of the conditions among blacks in the South during Reconstruction, he accepted a call in 1870 as the pastor of the Ames Methodist Church in New Orleans. For the next forty-six years he worked valiantly on three continents in an effort to improve relationships between blacks and whites. While urging his parishioners in New Orleans to be loyal to the federal government, Hartzell was very critical of the political activities of carpetbaggers. Although sharply disagreeing with many southerners about racial and political issues, his personal warmth, sensitivity to their views, and respect for many of their characteristics enabled him to develop many close friendships. Despite threats to his life and contracting yellow fever and cholera, which killed two of his five children, Hartzell carried on a very successful ministry. In 1873 he was appointed the presiding Methodist elder of the New Orleans district. In this capacity he established and oversaw schools and orphanages and a hospital for African Americans and in 1873 founded a weekly newspaper, the *Southwestern Christian Advocate*, to promote Methodist work among blacks in the South.

His interest in improving economic, political, educational, and religious conditions for blacks led Hartzell to work from 1882 until 1896 for the Methodist Freedmen's Aid and Southern Education Society, headquartered in Cincinnati, first as assistant corresponding secretary and then as corresponding secretary. Through this position and his passionate advocacy of assistance for the South as a delegate to Methodist General Conferences from 1876 to 1896, Hartzell helped to inspire Methodists to build forty schools and colleges and many churches to serve both races in this region.

These experiences prepared Hartzell for the new challenge he accepted in 1896 when he was consecrated as the Methodist missionary bishop for Africa. For many years Methodist missions in Africa had been suffering from both neglect and disorganization. An able administrator and a shrewd publicist, Hartzell traveled 1.3 million miles by ocean steamer, rowboat, train, stagecoach, and cart and on the backs of donkeys and oxen and on foot during the next twenty years to investigate, oversee, and promote Methodist work in Africa. His work led him to meet and negotiate with many political leaders. The bishop enjoyed cordial relations with five American presidents, and he convinced Theodore Roosevelt and William Taft to speak at conferences to raise funds for African missions. Acting as a special representative for Liberia in 1898, Hartzell helped to persuade the United States and Great Britain to establish a joint protectorate over Liberia. The same year the bishop inspired Cecil Rhodes, the British governor of South Africa, to donate 13,000 acres of land in eastern Rhodesia for an industrial and agricultural mission station. Personal conferences with Premier Georges Clemenceau of France and the king of Portugal led to the establishment of missions in French North Africa, Angola, and Inhambane (a seaport in Mozambique). Audiences with these and other leaders of European nations led to correction of abuses and greater religious freedom in African colonies under their control. Hartzell worked

to develop indigenous leaders of African churches, recruited many American blacks to serve as missionaries in Africa, and convinced his denomination to evangelize the Muslims living in North Africa. His inveterate optimism and strong desire to gain support for his missions led the bishop sometimes to exaggerate the success of Methodist stations in Africa. Nevertheless, Hartzell's frequent travels throughout North America, Europe, and Africa, combined with his winsome personality and public relations skills, produced a much larger budget (from an average of $2,500 a year for the twenty years before 1896 to an average of $50,000 a year for the twenty years after 1896) and greatly expanded Methodist missions in Africa (from one primary center to six).

After his retirement in 1916, Hartzell continued through speaking and writing to further the cause of Methodist missions in Africa. Near the end of his life, the bishop declared that he was especially thankful for four things: his dramatic conversion and unmistakable call to the ministry, good health, traveling mercies, and membership in a denomination with a world vision and a commitment to racial equality (*Christian Advocate*, Sept. 1928). Governed by that vision and commitment, Hartzell played an important role in promoting the advancement of blacks in both the United States and Africa. Having survived the perils of disease, racial hatred, and extensive travel, Hartzell died three months after he was assaulted by robbers in his home at Blue Ash, Ohio.

• Hartzell's personal papers are at the Methodist Collection of Drew University. Hartzell wrote several tracts to advance his denomination's efforts to assist blacks, including *Education in the South* (n.d.), *The Negro Exodus* (1879), and *Methodism and the Negro in the United States* (1894), as well as many tracts to promote the work of Methodist missionaries in Africa, including *The Open Door in Africa* (1903), *Four Years of Progress in Africa* (1904), *Forward Movements in Africa* (1908), *The African Diamond Jubilee* (1909), *The African Mission of the Methodist Episcopal Church* (1909), *Diamond Investments in America* (1909), *Women's Work in Africa* (1909), and *The Call of Moslem Children*, with Samuel Zwemer (1913). The two best sources on his life and career are "The Man with the Life-Line," *Christian Advocate*, 13 Sept. 1928, pp. 1099–1101, and Wilson S. Naylor, "Bishop Joseph Crane Hartzell, 1842–1928," *Methodist Review* 113 (Jan. 1930): 99–108. J. Tremayne Copplestone, *History of Methodist Missions*, vol. 4: *Twentieth-century Perspectives* (1973), describes his work as a missionary bishop in Africa in considerable detail. See also *Minutes of the Annual Conferences of the Methodist Episcopal Church* (1870–1896); *Journals of the General Conferences of the Methodist Episcopal Church* (1896–1916); *Annual Reports, Freedmen's Aid and Southern Education Society* (1870–1896); and the *Southwestern Christian Advocate*, 7 July 1898, 18 Mar. 1920, 28 June 1923, and his obituary on 13 Sept. 1928.

GARY SCOTT SMITH

HARVARD, John (Nov. 1607–14 Sept. 1638), Puritan minister and benefactor of Harvard College, was born in St. Saviour's Parish, Southwark, England, the son of Robert Harvard, a butcher, and Katherine Rogers, the daughter of a cattle dealer and alderman in Stratford-upon-Avon. Few details of John Harvard's early life are known. His father and four of his siblings died in the plague of 1625, leaving John the eldest surviving son. His mother remarried, but her second husband, a prosperous cooper named John Elletson, died within five months, and his estate further enhanced the family's resources.

From the size of his eventual inheritance, it is clear that John Harvard's parents were successful middle-class artisans who amassed enough money to send John to university and maintain him comfortably there. In December 1627 John Harvard entered Emmanuel College, Cambridge, noted for its Puritan sympathies, where he remained for seven years, receiving his A.B. in 1631 and his A.M. in 1635. Although trained for the ministry, there is no record of Harvard's ordination or connection to any particular parish church in England. In July 1635 his mother died, leaving John and his brother Thomas in possession of the family's considerable resources. John married Anne Sadler, the sister of a college classmate, in 1636; they had no children. His brother Thomas died before 5 May 1637, and John inherited part of his estate as well.

With most of his family ties now severed, John Harvard began making plans to leave England, and in the summer of 1637 he joined the Puritan migration to New England. In August 1637 he was admitted as an inhabitant of Charlestown, Massachusetts, where he and his wife joined the Puritan church. In November 1637 he became a freeman, enjoying full political rights and privileges within the colony. As a wealthy citizen, Harvard received extensive lands in the town's division of property and built a house that stood for several generations. He became the teaching elder of the Charlestown church, where he served as colleague to Zechariah Symmes.

Less than a year after his admission to the Charlestown church, John Harvard died in Charlestown of "a consumption," probably tuberculosis. There was no will but before he died, John Harvard's noncupative will promised half his estate and his eclectic library of theological and secular writings, totalling roughly 400 volumes, to the new college that the Massachusetts General Court had founded in Cambridge. The value of his gift was thought to be somewhere between £400 and £800, and was later recorded as £779 17s. 2d. by the college treasurer. In 1936 Harvard's tercentennial historian, Samuel Eliot Morison, could discover no more than £375 3s. actually received by the college. The money was used to construct the building originally called Harvard College, which in later incarnations has become Harvard Hall. The amount of Harvard's gift was indeterminate probably because the estate consisted largely of real estate in London, and the process of converting these assets to ready cash was difficult and uncertain. Nevertheless, Harvard's gift far exceeded any given the college by other contemporary benefactors, and the Massachusetts General Court voted on 13 March 1639 to name the college after him. In January 1764 a fire in Old Harvard Hall

(built in 1677 to replace the original college building) destroyed all save one volume of the library of John Harvard, but the memory of his original donation was preserved in a catalogue of the college library.

There are remarkably few references in existing sources that give any indication of John Harvard's character or personality. None of his sermons, writings, or papers have survived. In describing the founding of the college, the Cambridge minister Thomas Shepard asserted that John Harvard "was a scholar and pious in his life and enlarged toward the country and the good of it in life and death." An early, anonymous description of the college, *New England's First Fruits* (1643), called him "a godly gentleman and a lover of learning." Beyond that, very little can be said about him. However, in the late nineteenth and early twentieth centuries a persistent fantasy among Harvard graduates and anglophiles attempted to link John Harvard to William Shakespeare. Henry C. Shelley's *John Harvard and His Times* (1907) argued that Harvard's parents must have been introduced to each other by Shakespeare, while Alfred Rodway's *The Sword of Harvaard* (1912) tried to prove through heraldry and etymology that Shakespeare and John Harvard were both descended from a sixth-century Danish invader of England. A connection between Shakespeare and John Harvard is not utterly implausible; Harvard's mother did come from Stratford-upon-Avon and Robert Harvard's butcher shop was located in Southwark in the vicinity of the Globe Theatre. But the desire to link John Harvard to Shakespeare seems to stem from the obscurity surrounding the lives of these two household names and from the embarrassment that many liberal-minded descendants of New England's founders felt about the Puritan origins of their leading educational institution. For these authors, John Harvard's obscurity was perhaps his greatest legacy. It allowed them to associate the origins of their alma mater with the humane genius, wit, worldliness, and liberality of Shakespeare and thereby soften their perception of Harvard College's Puritan founders as narrow, intolerant theocrats. In reality, John Harvard was an obscure but not atypical victim of the disease epidemics that wiped out families in early modern Europe and America. The fortunes that passed through his hands helped to sustain a tiny college through its first years and almost by accident linked John Harvard's name to an institution that became a great university.

• The most thorough and reliable treatment of John Harvard's life, including a discussion of the contents of his library, can be found in Samuel Eliot Morison, *The Founding of Harvard College* (1935). Henry C. Shelley's fanciful *John Harvard and His Times* (1907) is the only book-length treatment. Brief references to John Harvard can be found in reprints of several seventeenth-century works, including Thomas Shepard, *God's Plot, the Paradoxes of Puritan Piety, Being the Autobiography and Journal of Thomas Shepard* (1972), Edward Johnson, *Johnson's Wonder-Working Providence, 1628–1651* (1912), Cotton Mather, *Magnalia Christi Americana* (1820), and *The Diary of Samuel Sewall* (1973).

Evidence of John Harvard's genealogy was first uncovered in Henry F. Waters, "John Harvard and His Ancestry," *New England Historical and Genealogical Register* (July 1885): 265–84 (Oct. 1886): 362–80. A complete description of John Harvard's library is in *Publications of the Colonial Society of Massachusetts* 21 (1920): 190–230.

MARK A. PETERSON

HARVEY, Beatrix Loughran (30 June 1900–7 Dec. 1975), figure skater and coach, was born in New York City, the daughter of Thomas Loughran, a wealthy real estate broker, and Marguerite Foley. A well-versed individual, Beatrix graduated from the Friends Seminary and Parsons School of Design before entering a career in figure skating. Her first American championship came in the ladies' junior singles division in 1921, and she earned second place in the ladies' senior singles event the following two years.

Harvey earned her first Olympic figure-skating medal at the 1924 winter Games in Chamonix, France, winning the silver medal as runner-up to champion Herma Planck-Szabo. Later that year she became the first American skater to enter the World Championships, held in Oslo, Norway. There, Harvey won the bronze medal for her performance. Her career really started to bloom in 1925, however, when she won the first of three consecutive American championships (1925 through 1927) and two North American ladies' singles titles in 1925 and 1927. At the 1928 Olympics in St. Moritz, Switzerland, Harvey won her second Olympic medal, earning the bronze behind the immortal Norwegian figure skater Sonja Henie and silver medalist Fritzi Burger of Austria. Harvey retired from singles skating following the St. Moritz Games and focused on paris skating.

She had earlier excelled as an accomplished pairs skater with Raymond Harvey, whom she later married. They skated to a gold medal in the national ladies' junior pairs competition in 1926 and finished second in the senior portion of the event the following year. Her most successful pairs skating, however, came with another partner, Sherwin C. Badger, a former U.S. and North American skating champion. They placed fourth in the 1928 St. Moritz Olympics and fifth at the World Championships that same year. Harvey and Badger won three consecutive U.S. Pairs Championship titles from 1930 to 1932. At the 1932 Olympic games in Lake Placid, New York, Harvey teamed with Badger to earn a silver medal, nearly defeating the defending champions, Andrée Joly and Pierre Brunet. Following a third-place finish at the 1932 World Championships, Harvey retired from amateur skating as the only American figure skater to have won medals (two silvers and a bronze) in three different Olympic Games. She also captured eight national titles in both singles and pairs competitions during her twelve-year amateur career.

Following her Olympic success, Harvey starred in many ice carnivals and shows in New York City. Her most prominent appearances came in presentations of the Skating Club of New York at Madison Square Garden in New York City. Harvey was also an incredibly versatile athlete. She paired with Edward M. Howland to win the 1922 national waltzing title, became an accomplished skier, and won prizes in both golf and diving, holding a 1-handicap in golf. She did not completely fade out of the skating picture, however. Harvey coached her niece, Audrey Peppe Rappé, who became an internationally known skater and competed on two U.S. Olympic teams in 1936 and 1940.

In 1940 she married Raymond Harvey, who had become a wealthy manufacturer. Following her career on the ice, she began a life of travel, golf, and even learned to fly airplanes solo in her spare time. Following her death in Long Beach, New York, she was elected to the U.S. Figure Skating Association Hall of Fame in 1977.

• Much of the information about Beatrix Harvey came from interviews with USFSA research associate Diane Krieder on 11 Jan. 1984 and with Harvey's niece, Audrey Peppe Rappé, 25 June 1984. See also "Beatrix Loughran," *Skating*, Jan. 1976; "Beatrix Loughran," *Skating*, Dec. 1977; Bill Mallon and Ian Buchanan, *Quest for Gold: The Encyclopedia of American Olympians* (1984); and David Wallechinsky, *The Complete Book of the Olympics* (1988).

KURT R. ZIMMERMAN
SHARON KAY STOLL

HARVEY, Coin (16 Aug. 1851–11 Feb. 1936), economic reformer, lawyer, and real estate investor, was born William Hope Harvey in Buffalo, West Virginia, the son of Robert Trigg Harvey and Anna Maria Hope, farmers. After two years at a local academy, he entered Marshall College in nearby Huntington but remained there only a few months. He then began to study law on his own while supporting himself by teaching school. After being admitted to the West Virginia bar, he practiced law, first in Barboursville (1870–1874), then with his brother in Huntington for two years, then in Cleveland, Ohio. He married Anna R. Halliday in 1876; they had four children. In 1879 they moved to Chicago and two years later to Gallipolis, Ohio, where Harvey served as attorney for several wholesale firms.

In 1884 Harvey went west to Colorado. He invested in several mines near Ouray and served for three years as superintendent of the Silver Bell mine there. When falling silver prices brought hard times, he speculated in real estate in Pueblo, in Denver, and in Ogden, Utah. During the depression of 1893 Harvey moved his family back to Chicago. By this time he had become convinced that national prosperity would be restored if the nation returned to using silver currency as well as gold. Silver had been demonetarized in 1873, a change in policy that many silverites believed had been sneaked through Congress under the influence of capitalists in New York and London. Harvey was certain that bringing back "the money of the people" would revive the economy by expanding the money supply and thus making credit easier to obtain. (Coining silver would also, of course, benefit those with an interest in silver mining.) In 1893 he was hired as a publicist by the pro-silver American Bimetallic League.

To disseminate his views, Harvey established the Coin Publishing Company. After a brief try at publishing a weekly, *Coin*, he began issuing four paperback books per year under the title Coin's Financial Series. The third in the series became Harvey's best-known work: *Coin's Financial School* (1894). The book consists of a series of fictional lectures presented at the Chicago Art Institute by the eponymous hero, a young entrepreneur, to an audience of city leaders that includes real magnates like Philip Armour and Marshall Field. After frequent questions from the floor, also presented in the text, these notables are converted to Coin's view that coining silver will save the nation's economy. The book became wildly popular; sales estimates range from 650,000 to more than a million. If not all readers mastered every detail of Harvey's analysis, they responded to his vivid description of the economic troubles they faced, his attribution of their problems to schemers in high places, and his persuasive formula for bringing back prosperity. The text was also enlivened by H. L. Goodall's vigorous drawings. One historian compares the book's impact to that of *Uncle Tom's Cabin*.

Between 1894 and 1896 Harvey published many more free-silver tracts written by himself and others; among these was his *Tale of Two Nations* (1894), which described a plot between a pair of British and American plutocrats to ruin the United States by tricking Congress into ending the coinage of silver. The other publications took a similar line, blending praise for the beneficent effects of inflation with accusations of a conspiracy to maintain the gold standard. Established economists and journalists often sought to refute Harvey's theories—one article was titled "Coin's Financial Fool"—but for many of his readers these attacks only seemed to confirm the existence of an anti-silver conspiracy among the powerful.

Harvey emerged on the public scene just as the new Populist party, with its critique of eastern capital and deflationary monetary policies, was attracting growing support in the South and West. There was tension among the Populist, however, between those advocating more sweeping social reform and those focusing primarily on the silver issue. In this division, Harvey took the more conservative side, supporting the silver wing in various local party conventions in 1894 and helping to organize a secret free-silver group in 1895. The silver wing prevailed, and when William Jennings Bryan was nominated for president by both the Democrats and the Populists in 1896 Bryan campaigned on a platform of free silver. His defeat in the national election spelled the end of Populism and of free silver as a significant political movement. Harvey continued to promote monetary reform, however. In tracts such as *Coin on Money, Trusts and Imperialism* (1899), *The Remedy* (1915), and *Common Sense; or, The Clot on the Brain of the Body Politic* (1920), he attacked a growing assortment of economic arrangements, including rent, interest, profit, and taxes.

In 1900 Harvey moved to Monte Ne in the Ozarks of northwestern Arkansas, where he tried to develop an elaborate resort. He started building a short-line railroad, a bank, a hotel, and a mercantile company, but none was entirely successful. In 1929 he divorced his first wife and married his longtime secretary, May Ellston Leake. They had no children. He also began constructing a huge pyramid in which were to be preserved items that would explain to future generations the downfall of his civilization. Among the objects deposited was his own work, *The Book* (1930), summarizing most of his earlier reform proposals. Harvey organized a tiny political party (first called the Liberty party and later the Prosperity party), which nominated him for president in 1932. He also participated in the widespread agitation against America's adherence to the gold standard. President Franklin Roosevelt abandoned the gold standard in 1933, but Harvey still found Roosevelt's policies wanting; in 1935 he directed his final sally at the president's methods of purchasing gold and silver. He died in Monte Ne and was buried near his unfinished pyramid.

Harvey's vision of a monolithic conspiracy to prevent the coinage of silver was far from accurate, and many of his later reform proposals were quite unrealistic, but he was right in one of his major points, that the steady contraction of the currency during the decades after the Civil War favored creditors over debtors. His vivid writing on this subject helped shape public debate during the 1890s and led thousands of Americans to consider for the first time the effect of monetary policy on their daily lives.

• Harvey wrote many tracts besides those cited above; among the better-known ones are *Coin's Financial School Up to Date* (1895), *Patriots of America* (1895), and *Paul's School of Statesmanship* (1924). The best biographical sketch appears in Richard Hofstadter's introduction to the Harvard University Press edition of *Coin's Financial School* (1963), pp. 1–80. Further discussion of his role in the free-silver debates of the 1890s appears in Stanley L. Jones, *The Presidential Election of 1896* (1964); Matthew Josephson, *The Politicos, 1865–96* (1938); and Lawrence Goodwyn, *The Populist Moment: A Short History of the Agrarian Revolt in America* (1978). Joseph Reeve, *Monetary Reform Movements: A Survey of Recent Plans and Panaceas* (1943), also describes some of Harvey's post-1896 experiences. An obituary appears in the *New York Herald Tribune*, 12 Feb. 1936.

SANDRA OPDYCKE

HARVEY, Edmund Newton (25 Nov. 1887–21 July 1959), physiologist, was born in Germantown, Pennsylvania, the son of William Harvey, a businessman and manufacturer, and Althea Ann Newton. As a boy Harvey attended the Germantown Academy, where despite the little attention given to science he developed a keen interest in natural history. In 1905 he entered the University of Pennsylvania and began intensive study in science. His interest was diverted to the systematic study of biology, and to extend his knowledge he spent a great deal of time at the Academy of Natural Sciences in Philadelphia. During his undergraduate years Harvey traveled extensively, collecting many biological specimens. He spent one summer collecting in Europe with the botanist J. M. MacFarlan, two other summers in British Columbia, and the summer of his senior year at the Tortugas Laboratory of the Carnegie Institute of Washington. Harvey received his B.S. from Pennsylvania in 1909 and that fall enrolled as a graduate student in zoology at Columbia University. His doctoral thesis, based on work carried out at the Tortugas Laboratory, Woods Hole, and Columbia, was "Studies on the Permeability of Cells." He received his Ph.D. from Columbia in 1911. He obtained an appointment as instructor in biology at Princeton University in 1911, and in 1919 he became a full professor, holding this position until 1933, when he was named Henry Fairfield Osborn Research Professor. Harvey's wide knowledge of physiology and biology helped make him a stimulating teacher.

A turning point in Harvey's work occurred in 1913 while he was on a trip to the Great Barrier Reef in Australia. There he developed an interest in animal luminescence. Studies of this energy-requiring phenomenon claimed a large proportion of his research time for the remainder of his life. Harvey published numerous papers on the chemistry and physics of bioluminescence, on the various organisms that produced light, and on the ecological and evolutionary significance of this phenomenon. The extensive information he gathered on luminescence was summarized in a 700-page monograph published by the American Philosophical Society as volume 44 of its *Memoirs*, titled *A History of Luminescence from the Earliest Times until 1900* (1957). Harvey's interest was not confined to luminescence, however; he did important work in other areas such as cell permeability, the ecological effects of ultrasound, the effects of centrifugal force on cells, electroencephalography, bubble formation in tissue, and wound ballistics. In all these areas he was an explorer and pioneer.

Harvey was instrumental in founding the *Journal of Cellular and Comparative Physiology*, which he edited from 1931 to 1939. Throughout his scientific career he also maintained a close association with the marine biological laboratories at Woods Hole, Massachusetts.

In 1916 Harvey married Ethel Nicholson Browne, who had received her Ph.D. from Columbia in 1913 and had shared laboratory facilities with Harvey at Woods Hole and Princeton for a number of years. They had two sons. Harvey's homes on Cleveland Place in Princeton and on Penzance Point at Woods Hole were throughout his career places where colleagues and students enjoyed congeniality and good conversation. Harvey died suddenly at Woods Hole.

• Harvey's papers from 1913 to 1959 are at the American Philosophical Society, Philadelphia. Two biographical sketches are Frank H. Johnson, "Edmund Newton Harvey, November 25, 1887–July 21, 1959," National Academy of Sciences, *Biographical Memoirs* 39 (1967): 193–266; and El-

mer Grimshaw Butler, "Edmund Newton Harvey (1887–1959)," *Year Book of the American Philosophical Society* (1960): 126–30.

DAVID Y. COOPER

HARVEY, Ethel Nicholson Browne (14 Dec. 1885–2 Sept. 1965), biologist, was born in Baltimore, Maryland, the daughter of Jennie R. Nicholson and Bennet Bernard Browne, an obstetrician-gynecologist and founder of the Woman's Medical College of Baltimore. After attending the Bryn Mawr School (1895–1902), Ethel earned an A.B. in 1906 from the Women's College of Baltimore (later Goucher College), where she majored in both Latin and biology. Immediately following college graduation, Ethel spent the first of many summers at the Marine Biological Laboratory (MBL) in Woods Hole, Massachusetts. She began graduate study in biology at Columbia University, from which she received an M.A. in 1907 and a Ph.D. in 1913 for work done under the direction of E. B. Wilson on the cytology of developing spermatozoa in insects. At Columbia, she was supported by a Goucher College fellowship (1906–1907) and a fellowship from the Society for Promotion of University Education of Women (1911–1912), as well as teaching positions as instructor in science at the Bennett School, Millbrook, New York (1908–1911), and as assistant in biology at Princeton University (1912–1913). Following the award of the Ph.D., she held positions as instructor in biology at the Dana Hall School, Wellesley, Massachusetts (1913–1914), as Sarah Berliner Fellow at the University of California Hopkins Marine Station (1914–1915), and as assistant in histology at the Cornell Medical College (1915–1916).

In March 1916 Ethel Browne married Edmund Newton Harvey, at that time an assistant professor of biology at Princeton University. Although Harvey had two children (born in 1916 and 1922), her continuous record of scientific publications gives clear evidence of her determination to maintain a career as a research scientist along with the demands of marriage and motherhood. Her first paper (1909), published while she was still a graduate student, demonstrated that specific tissue grafted from the hypostome (mouth area) could induce formation of a second individual in the coelenterate *Hydra*. Although Harvey received little recognition for this work at the time, Gairdner Moment later noted in a 1956 address during Harvey's receipt of an honorary degree from Goucher that "outstanding among her achievements must be rated Mrs. Harvey's early work on animal grafting, which opened up the way for the discovery of the 'Organizer Principle' in animal development" (for which Hans Spemann received the Nobel Prize in 1924). H. M. Lenhoff (1991) further suggests that the signed and dated reprint from Harvey in Spemann's reprint collection (as well as notes on the reprint) are indicative that Spemann was well aware of Harvey's work and, in fact, quite likely used it as a model for his experiments with amphibians.

Harvey is best known for her work on the embryology of sea urchins, which began in 1927 with studies on the effect of oxygen deprivation on sea urchin eggs. Most of her subsequent work examined the early development of fertilized or parthenogenetically activated eggs and egg fragments. In a series of published papers in the 1930s and 1940s, Harvey documented the complexity and importance of the egg cytoplasm. This was long before there was any understanding of the role of preformed stable messenger RNA stored in the cytoplasm in providing a template for early embryonic proteins. This work was of considerable popular interest, and an article in *Life* magazine (13 Sept. 1937) featured Harvey and her work on sea urchins. In addition, her years of laboratory experiments led her to develop a number of methods for manipulating and culturing sea urchin embryos, eggs, and egg fragments that became standard procedures for other workers in the field. Her work with sea urchins culminated in the publication of *The American Arbacia and Other Sea Urchins* (1956). This book was an instant "classic" because of its scholarship and breadth—covering as it did the natural history, distribution, behavior, normal embryology, and experimental analysis of development. It is a formidable reference, continues to be cited widely, and will doubtless remain the primary source of information prior to 1955.

In spite of her outstanding academic credentials and approximately eighty scientific articles and books, Harvey, like other women scientists of the time, received essentially none of the recognition from the scientific community given men for comparable work. Although she was hired to teach part-time at New York University (1928–1931), she was never offered a paid full-time faculty position at a research university—a position that would have included a laboratory of her own and the opportunity to train her own graduate students. However, like many other scientist husbands, Newton Harvey helped facilitate many of the connections that made his wife's work possible. She was given office space in E. G. Conklin's laboratory in the zoology department at Princeton, an informal arrangement that was a courtesy to her husband. Princeton also paid for the Harveys' lab space at the MBL where Ethel did most of her experimental work, using the space at Princeton primarily for writing. Newton, by contrast, did his experimental work at Princeton and wrote during the summers at the MBL. In 1932 Princeton gave Ethel Harvey the title of research biologist (which carried no salary) and then largely ignored her. According to John T. Bonner, a longtime member of the Princeton zoology faculty, "The most shocking thing to me was how little the University would have to do with her. . . . Ethel never had a graduate student. Such a thought would have never entered anyone's mind. . . . I think Princeton offered Ethel almost nothing. She partially carried the day because of her own determination and independence" (personal communication, 30 June 1991).

At the Marine Biological Laboratory in Woods Hole, by contrast, Harvey became a presence early in her career. In 1909, while still a graduate student, she was elected to membership in the MBL Corporation; in 1944 she was the third woman to deliver a prestigious Friday Night Lecture at the MBL; and in 1950 she became the second woman elected to the MBL board of trustees. Throughout their nearly fifty summers of attendance, Ethel and Newton presided over what was considered the "Harvey Table" in the MBL cafeteria, where during dinner each night they interacted with and entertained internationally renowned biologists and scientific colleagues. Harvey died in Falmouth, Massachusetts, six years after her husband's death. As historians of science begin to carefully assess the work of underrecognized early women scientists, it is likely that the work of Ethel Browne Harvey will continue to appreciate with time.

• Ethel Browne Harvey's published papers along with a typed list of these papers (incomplete for the last few years) are in the library at the Marine Biological Laboratory. Other unpublished material includes alumni records from Goucher College, the address by Gairdner Moment at Goucher for Harvey's honorary degree, and a biographical checklist on Ethel Browne Harvey in the files of *Notable American Women* at Radcliffe College. Many of her papers are listed in the bibliography of *The American Arbacia and Other Sea Urchins*. See also E. G. Butler, "Ethel Browne Harvey," *Biological Bulletin* 133 (1967): 9–11; M. J. Hogue, "The Contribution of Goucher Women to the Biological Sciences," *Goucher Quarterly* 29 (Summer 1951): 16–17; G. Kass-Simon's "Biology Is Destiny," in *Women of Science*, ed. G. Kass-Simon and P. Farnes (1990); and H. M. Lenhoff, "Ethel Browne, Hans Spemann, and the Discovery of the Organizer Phenomenon," *Biological Bulletin* 181 (1991): 72–80. See C. Fulton and A. O. Klein, "Messengers for Early Sea Urchin Development," in *Explorations in Developmental Biology* (1976) for the connection of Harvey's work with later work on messenger RNA. For further reference to Ethel Harvey see also Frank H. Johnson, "Edmund Newton Harvey, 1887–1959," National Academy of Sciences, *Biographical Memoirs* 39 (1967): 192–266, and Aurin M. Chase, "Edmund Newton Harvey," *Biological Bulletin* 119 (1960): 9–10. An obituary is in the *New York Times*, 3 Sept. 1965.

PATRICIA STOCKING BROWN

HARVEY, Fred (27 June 1835–Feb. 1901), caterer, hotelier, and restaurateur, was born Frederick Henry Harvey in London, England, the son of English-Scottish parents, whose names are unknown. Harvey emigrated from Liverpool, arriving in New York City in 1850. He immediately found employment at the Smith and McNewill Café earning two dollars a week as a busboy and pot scrubber. In the early 1850s he traveled by coastal packet to New Orleans, where he worked in restaurants and survived a bout with yellow fever. In the mid-1850s he traveled by stern-wheeler up the Mississippi to St. Louis. There he became involved in a jewelry business and a clothing store. His early training, however, sparked his desire to have his own restaurant. He became a U.S. citizen in 1858, and a year later he married Barbara Sarah Mattas; they had six children.

While in St. Louis Harvey opened a café; although it was successful, a bout with typhoid fever and the outbreak of the Civil War disrupted his business. The restaurant closed when Harvey's partner, sympathetic to the South, left with their money and enlisted in the Confederate army. Harvey then worked at another café and also on packet boats on the Mississippi River.

In 1862 Postmaster William A. Davis hired Harvey as one of the first postal clerks to sort mail in a specially designed post office rail car on the Hannibal and St. Joseph Railroad, based in St. Joseph, Missouri. Approximately a year later, Harvey became the railroad's freight agent. In 1867 he invested in a cattle ranch, and the following year he invested in a hotel in Ellsworth, Kansas.

The Hannibal and St. Joseph Railroad was acquired by the Chicago, Burlington and Quincy Railroad, and by 1876 Harvey had become its general western freight agent. Shortly thereafter he was transferred to Leavenworth, Kansas, which became his permanent residence.

While riding on the system's trains throughout the Midwest, Harvey discovered how deplorable the food service was for travelers. Believing he could improve conditions, Harvey, in partnership with Jeff Rice, built three eating houses along the route of the Kansas-Pacific Railroad in 1873. Although quite successful, by 1876 Harvey's partnership with Rice had dissolved over disputes regarding operating standards. During this time, Harvey also had a part-time job soliciting advertisements for the *Leavenworth Conservative*.

Harvey's vision of a catering system that offered wholesome food with exceptional service in sanitary railside eating houses, linked and supplied by the railroad, would soon dramatically shift the paradigm of railway food service. Since the Chicago, Burlington and Quincy Railroad was not interested in his food-service concept, Harvey approached his friend Charles Morse, the superintendent of the Atchison, Topeka and Santa Fe Railroad, in 1876. Although eating facilities existed in some of the railroad's passenger stations, the food quality was bad and the service was poor. After a deal sealed with a gentlemen's handshake, Harvey opened a ten-seat lunch counter on the second floor of the Topeka depot in the spring of 1876. As the first passenger, freight, and general office building of the Santa Fe, it was known thereafter as the Topeka Harvey House.

According to the agreement, Harvey operated eating houses for passengers along the Santa Fe railway, paying no rent. Morse and the railroad also agreed to transport his personnel and supplies without cost. All profits went to Harvey.

In 1876 Harvey purchased a hotel in Florence, Kansas, which was the site of an important rail terminal. Here he transformed the poorly managed, vermin-infested third-class hotel into the first Harvey House that offered sleeping accommodations and dining room service for rail travelers. He paid Konrad Allgaier, the head chef from Potter Palmer's Hotel in Chicago, $5,000 per year to prepare European cuisine for travelers of the Santa Fe railway. The food was so extraordinary that commercial travelers, or "drummers," soon began to arrange their schedules so they could arrive when dinner was served at the Florence Harvey House.

A unique symbiotic relationship developed between Harvey and the Santa Fe. Ridership on the Santa Fe, which had been dangerously low before Harvey arrived, increased as services in his eating houses, dining cars, hotels, and resorts expanded. As a result of his friendship with F. Willis Rice, the Chicago editor and publisher of the *National Hotel Reporter* and founder of the Hotel Men's Mutual Benefit Association in 1879, Harvey met America's leading hotel managers. From them Harvey sought advice on hotel management, restaurant operations, advertising, promotion, and negotiating. This knowledge, together with his own natural creative genius and his aggressive spirit, contributed to his success.

In 1881 Harvey established his office in Topeka, Kansas. In 1882, the same year he resigned from the CB and Q, Harvey established the company's general office in the Union Depot in Kansas City.

Perhaps Harvey's greatest contribution came in 1883, when he first hired women to serve as waitresses at his Santa Fe railroad eating houses. During one of his frequent surprise inspections to a Harvey House in Raton, New Mexico, he fired the entire staff of waiters because of their rude conduct toward his customers; he immediately replaced them with inexperienced but respectable young women, whom he soon found to be reliable, hardworking, and dedicated. As a result of their success, he advertised in newspapers and magazines throughout the East and Midwest for intelligent, attractive, single women between the ages of eighteen and thirty to come and work for the Harvey hotel/restaurant chain in the territory of the American Southwest.

Interviewing offices were opened in both Chicago and Kansas City. The screening process for these "Harvey Girls" was rigid: if accepted, they agreed not to marry until at least one year of service was fulfilled. They lived in Harvey dormitories that were managed by a senior Harvey Girl who enforced the rules regarding curfews and chaperoned courting parlors and uniforms, enhancing the Harvey Girls' image of wholesomeness. Not surprisingly, by 1900 5,000 Harvey Girls were said to have married and settled in the West. American humorist Will Rogers once remarked that Harvey "kept the West in food and wives."

In 1889 the Atchison, Topeka and Santa Fe Railroad granted Harvey the exclusive right to operate all of its eating houses and hotel facilities on their system west of the Missouri River. At the time of his death, Harvey's hospitality empire controlled forty-seven restaurants, fifteen hotels (creating the first interstate restaurant and hotel chains), thirty railroad dining cars, and several elegant resorts along the Atchison, Topeka and Santa Fe Railroad in the southwestern United States. By this time he also managed the food service on the San Francisco Bay ferry system.

Harvey was one of the first entrepreneurs to build a food-service company emphasizing managerial efficiency and effective operational standards regarding the quality of food, service, and cleanliness. Never abandoning his vision of the "maintenance of standard regardless of cost," Harvey won loyal customers who helped him transform his company into one of the largest and most scientifically managed businesses in the world. Considered one of the "great caterers of the world," he developed a system of management and inspection that created not only a successful business but also safer, more comfortable, and more enjoyable rail travel on the Santa Fe.

• A biography of Harvey is Donald Duke, *Fred Harvey: Civilizer of the American Southwest* (1995). Books with information on Harvey include Keith L. Bryant, Jr., *History of the Atchison, Topeka and Santa Fe Railway* (1974); George H. Foster and Peter C. Weiglin, *The Harvey House Cookbook* (1992); and Lesley Poling-Kempes, *The Harvey Girls: Women Who Opened the West* (1989). Articles include Carla Kelly, "No More Beans: The Restaurants That Won the West," *American History Illustrated* 16 (Oct. 1981): 42–47; James A. Cox, "How Good Food and Harvey 'Skirts' Won the West," *Smithsonian* 18, no. 6 (Sept. 1987): 130–39; Lucius Beebe, "Purveyor to the West," *American Heritage* 18, no. 2 (Feb. 1967): 28–31, 99–102; "How Fame Has Been Won for the Harvey Service by Devotion to a Business Principle," *Santa Fe Magazine* 10, no. 3 (Feb. 1916): 31–47; and John Willy, "Personalities in the Hotel Business," *Hotel Monthly* 51, no. 606 (Aug. 1943): 21–25, 48. See also Stephen B. Shiring, "American Hotelkeepers and Higher Learning: An Early Era of This Emerging Profession," (Ph.D. diss., Univ. of Pittsburgh, 1995). An obituary is in the *Hotel Monthly* 9, no. 96 (Mar. 1901): 25.

STEPHEN B. SHIRING

HARVEY, George Brinton McClellan (16 Feb. 1864–20 Aug. 1928), editor, publisher, and diplomat, was born in Peacham, Vermont, the son of Duncan Harvey, a country store merchant, and Margaret Varnum. George Harvey did not attend college, but he did complete a traditional college preparatory curriculum at the local grammar school. Several faculty served as his first mentors and references and assisted in his placement to a position on the *Springfield Republican*. Harvey made strategic career moves to Chicago and to New York City, and at the age of twenty-six he became managing editor of the *New York World* and a favorite protégé of Joseph Pulitzer. He also invested successfully in electric railways. In October 1887 he married Alma Arabella Parker; they had one daughter.

Harvey's public career closely interwove magazine and newspaper journalism, book publishing, and national politics. In 1899, when he purchased the *North American Review* to serve as publisher and editor, he was fully aware that he now owned and directed the most distinguished periodical in the United States. From its inception in 1815, the *North American Review* was the principal national journal in arts, letters, and politics, and it was a forum for serious commentary on social issues. Harvey followed a distinguished series of editors that included John Adams and Henry Adams.

His editorship of the *Review* paved the way for his selection as president of the distinguished publishing house of Harper and Brothers. His biographer, Willis Fletcher Johnson, takes great pains to demonstrate that the venerable publishing house was not indebted to J. P. Morgan and that Harvey's financial reorganization of the company served to insure the continuing independence of Harper and Brothers from New York City bankers. From 1901 to 1913 Harvey edited *Harper's Weekly*.

Harvey's role as publisher and editor placed him in the public limelight. As a lagniappe, he enjoyed entertaining and providing public recognition for writers, such as William Dean Howells and Mark Twain. Although Harvey published most major writers, including Henry James, Howells, and Twain, he favored popular writers such as H. G. Wells and Owen Wister over Joseph Conrad. As a publicist, in the custom of the day, he invited over four hundred guests to celebrations in honor of a given writer at major New York clubs such as Delmonico's. These flourishes among influential and wealthy members of New York society gave Harvey a forum to comment on many issues and soon led him to engage in political kingmaking.

As a staunch Democrat, Harvey was most interested in the public career possibilities of the president of Princeton University, Woodrow Wilson. To that end, he encouraged Wilson to stand for the New Jersey governorship, and following that success, Harvey urged Wilson to seek the Democratic nomination in the 1912 presidential race. For his service in New Jersey politics, Harvey was called "Colonel," but not for any military accomplishment. Harvey was a conservative who believed that the protection and support of big business by government was in the best interest of the nation at large. He turned against Wilson, when he realized that Wilson opposed political machines and threatened the "Money Trust" in typical progressive reformer fashion.

After Wilson's election, the turmoil of international politics severed Wilson and Harvey's friendship, and their public compatibility, too, was strained. Harvey's political and economic views left little room for pragmatic approaches or steps to reform. He came to believe that Wilson was no genuine neutral and, most importantly, that Wilson would not protect the future fortunes of big business. Harvey and his friend Henry Clay Frick were shocked that the Sherman Act could be used to break up trusts. They preferred to use antitrust legislation against labor organizations.

Harvey once advised Wilson to think earnestly about requirements for world peace when the Great War would finally end. Wilson's thoughts moved in the direction of a World Court, an image that became anathema to Harvey. After Wilson left office, Harvey cast his lot with the national Republican leadership, and he once again identified the next president of the United States, Warren Gamaliel Harding. Harding rewarded Harvey with the plum of ambassadorial appointments, plenipotentiary to the Court of St. James's. Harvey's friends had frequently commented that Wilson betrayed Harvey when he overlooked him for the ambassadorship to Britain. Harvey was no statesman, however. He embarrassed the secretary of state and President Harding by his antics during his period of service. Soon after Harding's death in office, Harvey in 1923 resigned from the ambassadorship. He returned to Washington and worked as editor of the *Washington Post* for one year. He left Washington for Allenhurst, New Jersey, in 1925. He lived there until he moved to Dublin, New Hampshire, in July 1928. He spent his remaining years writing a biography of Frick, which was published just before Harvey's death in Dublin. Throughout his career, Harvey's contributions to journalism were intensely personal. He was not reluctant to offer his opinions on the commonweal. Moreover, his views on the major issues of his time often were self-serving. He was a publicist who occasionally succumbed to rabble rousing in his periodicals in his attacks against Wilson and the League of Nations. He successfully secured Henry Clay Frick's financial support in the campaign to defeat the League of Nations, and he was an avid supporter of political machines that worked for the advancement of business interests.

• For Harvey's own view, see "The Magazines in Journalism," *Harper's Weekly*, 19 Mar. 1910, p. 8. A biography of Harvey by a personal friend and colleague is Willis Fletcher Johnson, *George Harvey, "A Passionate Patriot"* (1929). On Harvey's role in politics, see especially Arthur S. Link, *Wilson: The Road to the White House* (1947); Link, *Wilson: The New Freedom* (1956); and Thomas A. Bailey, *Woodrow Wilson and the Great Betrayal* (1945). For Harvey's significant contributions to the U.S. publishing industry, see Frank Luther Mott, *A History of American Magazines*, vol. 2 (1957); John Tebbel, *A History of Book Publishing in the United States*, vol. 2, *The Expansion of an Industry, 1865–1919* (1975); and Tebbel and Mary Ellen Zuckerman, *The Magazine in America, 1741–1990* (1991). An obituary is in the *New York Times*, 21 Aug. 1928, with a feature article on 26 Aug. 1928.

SALME HARJU STEINBERG

HASBROUCK, Lydia Sayer (20 Dec. 1827–24 Aug. 1910), dress reformer and editor, was born in Warwick, New York, the daughter of Benjamin Sayer, a farmer and distiller, and Rebecca Forshee, a farmer. Lydia grew up in comfortable surroundings as the farm prospered and the family grew in social prominence. The spirited and daring Lydia developed into a skilled horsewoman who had a penchant for reading. Her desire for a superior education led her to leave the Warwick district school and enter Miss Galatian's Select School. She then attended high school and Central College in Elmira, New York.

In 1849 Lydia Sayer traded dresses, heavy petticoats, and tight-fitting corsets for more comfortable attire in the new "bloomer" costume, a knee-length skirt over trousers. When her application to Seward Seminary was turned down because it considered her apparel improper, Sayer was outraged. From that moment on she became an activist for women's rights,

speaking out for dress reform and temperance. In 1853 she served as a delegate to the Whole World's Temperance Convention in New York. She continued to wear bloomers throughout her lifetime.

Following the convention, Sayer's interest in the latest reforms broadened to include water-cure therapy. She attended the Hygeio-Therapeutic College in New York City for three months to study hydropathic medicine. She then practiced medicine for a year in Washington, D.C., and was frequently seen in outlying towns lecturing on the health consequences of women's fashions and the benefits of dress reform. She also contributed to a number of newspapers on the subject. Critics of her "immodest" clothes hardened her resolve.

In 1856 she accepted an invitation by John Whitbeck Hasbrouck, editor and publisher of the *Whig Press*, to come to Middletown, New York, to lecture. After Sayer arrived, Hasbrouck established *Sibyl*, a "review of the tastes, errors, and fashions of society," and placed Sayer in charge as editor. The periodical championed dress reform, proclaiming that unconfining clothing was at the core of women's struggle for equality and good health. Featured on the top of *Sibyl* was an illustration of a woman wearing pantaloons and a smock.

When Sayer and Hasbrouck married shortly after *Sibyl* made its first appearance, she wore white satin bloomers and a white silk tunic. In her specially prepared wedding vows she promised to "walk equally . . . through life" without "renouncing my individuality in yielding unto you the true wife's love and duty." The couple had three children. They lived in an octagonal stone house called "Sibyl Ridge."

After 1861 the eight-page biweekly *Sibyl* was published monthly. Throughout its duration the periodical remained primarily concerned with dress reform. Hasbrouck's contention in every issue was that as long as women dressed in confining fashions they were reduced to "helplessness." She urged women to rise up in an American Revolution of their own, overthrowing the fashions of London and Paris for the new dress that would free them. She was not necessarily partial to bloomers but recommended that women wear whatever gave them freedom and individuality. The periodical interspersed tips on diets, benefits of baths and fresh air, and the avoidance of tobacco.

Offering a highly personal account of her own life and the freedoms she enjoyed through dress reform, Hasbrouck encouraged her subscribers to correspond with "Sister Lydia" about their own experiences. A list of women who had braved ridicule to wear bloomers appeared in the publication. She also published articles and advertised books written by advocates of free love and communitarian living.

In 1859 Hasbrouck refused to pay taxes because she had been denied the right to vote. The tax collector then confiscated a pair of her bloomers, advertising their sale for payment of taxes. She counterattacked in *Sibyl* by running an editorial condemning the tax collector as a "vulgar sneak," and he dropped the advertisement. In 1863 she declined to pay a road tax and was required to work for several days alongside a road-work crew to compensate for her flouting of the law.

From 1861 to 1863 Hasbrouck opened her home to the public as a health spa, which she named the Sibyl Ridge Hygienic Retreat. She equipped the establishment with baths, electromagnetic equipment, and hot-air furnaces, but she failed to reach a large enough clientele to sustain it. She published the yearly activities of the National Dress Reform Association and served as its president in 1863–1864. But dress reform and *Sibyl* had begun to lose momentum with the outbreak of the Civil War, which directed women's attention to other concerns. Unable to sustain itself financially, the publication's last issue appeared in June 1864. Hasbrouck then helped her husband edit his paper until it was sold in 1868.

Hasbrouck's commitment to dress reform led her to target those persons less zealous than herself. When such notable women's rights advocates as Lucy Stone and others stopped wearing their bloomers, she criticized them as "traitors" to the cause and cowards for not standing up for their rights. She also claimed that other women had already begun wearing bloomers before Amelia Bloomer and that she therefore was not the originator of the dress reform movement.

Following the passage of a New York State law in 1880 that allowed women to vote for and hold school board offices, Hasbrouck was elected as the first woman to serve on the Middletown school board. In 1881 she and her husband began a newspaper called *Liberal Sentinel*, which advocated equal rights for both men and women. Hasbrouck also denounced formalized religion, choosing a more personalized belief in nature and science. While she continued to work for reforms, her interests in the 1880s veered toward real estate development. She died in Middletown, New York.

Restrictive dress led the strong-minded Lydia Sayer Hasbrouck to a career in reform. *Sibyl* became her platform for advocating women's rights, and it allowed other women a forum as well. Unrelenting in her drive for women's liberty, she stood by her demands for sex equality in education, in medicine, and in politics. A true reformer, Hasbrouck adamantly held to her course even when she stood alone.

• Lydia Sayer Hasbrouck left no papers. Her ideas are best expressed in issues of *Sibyl*. See also Edward Manning Ruttenber and L. H. Clark, *History of Orange County, New York* (1881); Bertha-Monica Sterns, "Reform Periodicals and Female Reformers," *American Historical Review* 37 (July 1932): 678–99; William Leach, *True Love and Perfect Union: The Feminist Reform of Sex and Society* (1980); and Lynn Sherr and Jurate Kazickas, *Susan B. Anthony Slept Here: A Guide to American Women's Landmarks* (1994). An obituary is in the *New York Herald*, 26 Aug. 1910.

MARILYN ELIZABETH PERRY

HASCALL, Milo Smith (5 Aug. 1829–30 Aug. 1904), soldier and businessman, was born in Le Roy, New York, the son of Amasa Hascall and Phoebe Ann Smith, farmers. Milo Smith Hascall spent most of his

youth on his parents' farm in New York but eventually moved while still a boy to Goshen, Indiana, where his three brothers lived. In Goshen he taught school and worked in his brother's store before receiving an appoinment to attend the U.S. Military Academy at West Point, New York. Hascall attended West Point from 1848 until he graduated in 1852, ranking fourteenth out of forty-three cadets. He found his first assignment to the peacetime U.S. Army at Fort Adams, Rhode Island, distasteful and boring, resigned his commission in September 1853, and returned to civilian life in Indiana.

In 1854, using the engineering skills he had acquired at West Point, Hascall won a contract to build part of the Michigan Southern and Northern Indiana Railroad. He subsequently established a successful law practice in Goshen and was a county prosecuting attorney as well. In 1855 he married Julia Emeline Swift; they had no children.

Upon the outbreak of the Civil War in 1861, Hascall immediately enlisted as a private with a ninety-day militia regiment from Indiana. He spent most of his time as aide-de-camp involved in organizing, equipping, and training the mass of volunteers that rushed forward to serve after the fall of Fort Sumter. On 12 June 1861 the governor of Indiana appointed him colonel of the three-year Seventeenth Indiana Volunteer Infantry Regiment.

After several minor skirmishes in Kentucky, he was appointed to command a brigade with the Army of the Ohio, then under General Don Carlos Buell. While assigned to the divisional command of fellow Indianan General Thomas Wood, Hascall's brigade participated in February 1862 in the capture of Nashville, the first Confederate state capital to fall to the Union army. For services at Nashville and minor actions at the battle of Shiloh, he was appointed to the rank of brigadier general of volunteers on 25 April 1862.

From October 1862 to the spring of 1863 Hascall participated in the Army of the Cumberland's campaign under General William S. Rosecrans to drive the Confederate armies out of Tennessee. On 31 December 1862 Braxton Bragg's Army of Tennessee launched a surprise attack on Rosecrans's army at Stones River. In some of the hardest fighting of the war, Hascall rallied his troops, took command of the division after Wood was wounded, and held out against repeated Confederate assaults. After the battle, which generated the highest casualty rate of the war, Hascall was assigned the task of collecting stragglers and sorting out the wounded and dead of the campaign.

In August 1863 Hascall was assigned to command a division in the Army of the Cumberland at the battles of Chickamauga, Missionary Ridge, and the defense of Knoxville. In preparation for the invasion of Georgia and the Atlanta campaign, he was assigned the command of a brigade in the XXIII Corps under John M. Schofield, with whom he enjoyed excellent relations. In May 1864, Schofield made him division commander, following the battle of Resaca. On 2 June 1864

Hascall led the attempt to outflank the Confederate left at Allatoona Creek. The attempt failed but forced the Confederate retreat to Kennesaw Mountain. On 22 June 1864 his division repulsed General John B. Hood's assault at Kolb's Farm. On 8 July 1864 his division crossed the Chattahoochee River, triggering the Confederate withdrawal to Atlanta. In September his troops destroyed sections of the Macon and Western Railroad just prior to the fall of Atlanta. Hascall's performance was solid throughout the highly fluid fighting, but despite the active support of Schofield, he was not chosen for promotion to major general after Atlanta fell. Discouraged at this lack of recognition, Hascall resigned from his command on 27 October 1864 and returned to civilian life in Indiana. He was only thirty-five years old at the time.

After the war Hascall enjoyed a long and unusually prosperous career in banking and real estate, first in his home of Goshen, Indiana, and later in Chicago. His first wife died in 1883, and in 1886 he married Rose Miller; they had no children. In 1890 he moved to Chicago and participated with considerable success in the real estate boom that followed the Great Chicago Fire. He died at his home in Oak Park, Illinois.

Hascall's career during and after the war typified that of many of the young Union generals who rose to command in the western theater of the war. He was energetic, bold, and effective in battle and a competent administrator as well, but he was also extremely sensitive about his rank among his peers, as his resignation after Atlanta in 1864 demonstrated. The reputation and connections that he made during the war served him well for the rest of his life, and he died a wealthy man in no little part because the Civil War imparted to him confidence in the future of the nation and his own abilities.

• A short biographical article covering Hascall's Civil War career is in Ezra J. Warner, *Generals in Blue: Lives of the Union Commanders* (1964). Hascall appears as a minor character throughout Albert Castel's *Decision in the West: The Atlanta Campaign of 1864* (1992), the best recent study of that campaign. See also John Marszalak, *Sherman: A Soldier's Passion for Order* (1992). His obituary is in the *Chicago Tribune*, 31 Aug. 1904.

JAMES K. HOGUE

HASENCLEVER, Peter (24 Nov. 1716–15 June 1793), industrialist, was born in Remscheid, Germany, the son of Luther Hasenclever, an iron works proprietor, and Klara Moll. After attending school Hasenclever was, at age fourteen, apprenticed to a cutler and thereafter received some instruction in the iron works of his father. At seventeen he was sent for six months to Liège, Belgium, to learn French. During the following years he traveled widely in France, Germany, and Russia, even though his father's fortunes were in decline. After 1742 he struck up a connection with a relative active in the textile commerce in Burtscheid near Aix-la-Chapelle. His main role in this relationship was to secure business orders. Later journeys led him several times to Spain, notably Cadiz, and to Portugal,

where in 1745 in Lisbon he married the daughter of a British sea captain, Katherine Wilds, with whom he subsequently had a daughter. On the basis of his commercial successes he decided in 1755 to found his own trading firm. He even entered into negotiations with Frederick II (the Great), king of Prussia, with a view to improving linen manufacturing in the Prussian province of Silesia. As a result, he was able to establish his brother Franz in Landeshut, Silesia, as a textile manufacturer. However, his own interests, along with concern for the health of his wife, caused him in 1758 to move to England, where he settled down at Putney near London and became a British subject.

Continuously successful in his enterprises, Hasenclever resolved to try his hand at some business ventures in North America. In 1763 he went into partnership with two British merchants, Andrew Seton and Charles Crofts, in order to take up the overseas production of iron, potash, hemp, and flax. The following year he journeyed to America, where in the colonies of New York and New Jersey he went on a buying spree. He purchased iron works, woodlots, iron mines, and potash production facilities, as well as lands on which to raise hemp and flax. His cousin Franz Kaspar Hasenclever brought from Germany miners, charcoal burners, blacksmiths, and carpenters—with their families a total of 535 people. By his own account, Hasenclever in 1765 owned 122 horses, 214 teams of oxen, 51 cows, and 53 iron mines, as well as numerous houses, sheds, stables, smelters, mills of various kinds, and other holdings. His activities initially showed much promise: in 1765 he shipped his first iron bars to England, where they were pronounced to be of good quality. But difficulties quickly arose. The German workers, incited by their American colleagues, asked for wage increases, and severe winter weather in 1765 and 1766 destroyed earth works built to stabilize the water supply. Most disconcerting was Hasenclever's discovery, when he returned to London in December 1766, that his business partners had bankrupted the firm. As a consequence, he had to cover the losses from his own fortune as best he could. When in midsummer 1767 he returned to America to salvage his enterprises there, he found that during his absence incompetence, neglect, and even dishonesty had caused additional damage. Still further trouble loomed. Bills of exchange, which he used to pay for various expenses, were returned from London with costs. Ultimately he had to surrender all holdings, even those that were his personal possessions, to the creditors. Suspecting fraud, he decided to return to Britain to shed light on the entire affair. By way of Charleston, South Carolina, where he interested himself in rice, tobacco, and indigo production, he arrived in London in mid-1769, only to discover that his former partners Seton and Croft had used their connections to unload the remaining debts of the firm on him personally.

There ensued a rather discouraging period, during which Hasenclever was deprived of the right to engage in any gainful occupation pending a satisfactory solution to his firm's financial problems. He complained about the dishonesty of his business partners, notably in a letter to the lord chancellor dated 4 April 1771 and in a lengthy brief to king and Parliament in the spring of 1773. Having despaired of winning justice soon, though, he decided to go back to Germany. Leaving his wife behind, he arrived in Silesia in the fall of 1773, where he settled down in Landeshut. By engaging in various commercial activities, he was able to sustain himself in adequate, if modest, fashion until his death there. In 1787 he had the satisfaction of being pronounced free of his debts in Great Britain. However, it was only six months following his death that two of his British persecutors were forced to pay a considerable sum to a firm to which he had transferred his claim.

While many details of the tribulations resulting from his American ventures are known only from Hasenclever's own accounts, there is little doubt that he was the victim of various malevolent intrigues. Whether or not he was an innocent victim is open to debate. Enterprising and inventive, assiduous and honest, he was willing to take risks from which good judgment might have held him back. Although he had done well enough during his early years, especially in Spain and his final stay of almost two decades in Silesia, the great adventure of his life was the American undertaking. Almost visionary in his pursuits, he not only failed to gain a solid grasp of the technical, logistical, political, and commercial exigencies of the enterprise, but apparently also misinterpreted the intentions of his backers in London. Although his endeavors thus did not bear immediate fruit, he is entitled to some enduring fame. He can claim credit for having at least attempted to become one of the early pioneers of industrialization in North America.

• There does not seem to exist any collection of personal papers of Hasenclever. The most important source on his American undertakings is his petition to king and Parliament, *The Remarkable Case of Peter Hasenclever, Merchant: Formerly One of the Proprietors of the Iron Works, Potash Manufactory, &c, Established, and Successfully Carried on under His Direction, in the Provinces of New York and New Jersey, in North America, 'till November 1766. [Etc.]* (1773). The story of Hasenclever's life was first put together by Christian Gottlieb Glauber, who published three articles in *Schlesische Provinzialblätter* 18 (June–Dec. 1793): 291–319; 373–402; 473–95. These articles were also published in combined form as *Peter Hasenclever* (1794). All subsequent biographical publications are apparently based on this source. The most extensive modern biography is Adolf Hasenclever, *Peter Hasenclever aus Remscheid-Ehringhausen: Ein deutscher Kaufmann des 18. Jahrhunderts: Seine Biographie, Briefe und Denkschriften* (1922); as its title implies, this publication also contains various letters, briefs, and memoranda written by Hasenclever or his correspondents.

UDO SAUTTER

HASKELL, Ella Louise Knowles (31 July 1860–27 Jan. 1911), lawyer and suffragist, was born in Northwood Ridge, New Hampshire, the daughter of Louisa Bigelow and David Knowles, farmers. After graduating from Northwood Seminary (1875) and Plymouth State Normal College (1876), she taught school for four years to save money for further study. Manifesting ambition and persistence, she contested her society's conventions of gender and attended Bates College in Lewiston, Maine. Few women had previously attended the school, but she edited a college magazine and won prizes in debating and oratory before graduating with high honors in 1884. Knowles then moved to Manchester, New Hampshire, where she studied law in the office of Henry E. Burnham, later a U.S. senator.

Knowles fell ill in 1887, and her physician, fearing the onset of tuberculosis, advised her to move west to a drier climate. She taught rhetoric and elocution at Western Normal College in Iowa for a year and then in 1888 settled in Helena, Montana. After teaching for a year at Central School, she was offered the job of principal at the West Side School. Instead of accepting the appointment, she chose to pursue her improbable dream of becoming an attorney, returning to the study of law, this time in the office of Joseph W. Kinsley. She also participated in a network of native New Englanders living in Montana, serving for a time as secretary of the New England Society for the Helena area. This network assisted her in entering the legal profession.

Had Ella Knowles succeeded in becoming an attorney in New Hampshire, she might have been the first woman to do so. Instead, Marilla Ricker managed the feat in New Hampshire in 1890, and Knowles became the first in Montana. First, however, the Montana statute governing admission to the bar had to be changed. In February 1889 Montana's last territorial legislature enacted a bill permitting qualified people to practice law "without regard to sex" (Montana, *Laws* [1889], p. 101). In typical fashion for the time, debate hinged on whether women should stay at home and remain free of "the sights and scenes of courtrooms, where the demoralizing and degrading trials and tribulations of mankind were ever in progress," as Charles Middleton argued, or, rather, as Samuel Murray urged, the "presence of women in Court would do much to purify the atmosphere." On 24 December 1889 Knowles passed her bar examination, with one of her examiners, Cornelius Hedges, commenting, "She beat all that I have ever examined." For the first few years, she had her law office in the Masonic Building. She worked for a time with her mentor Kinsley in the firm of Kinsley and Knowles, but she subsequently practiced on her own.

In 1892 the Populist party nominated her to run for state attorney general against Henri J. Haskell, a native of Maine and a Republican seeking reelection. As fellow lawyers in Helena and fellow members of the New England Society there, he and she had no doubt known each other for some time. Upon request, Haskell supplied an opinion that, though she could not vote, she could run for the office. After a vigorous campaign—she spoke throughout the state and was dubbed the "Portia of the People's Party"—she finished third behind Haskell and his Democratic challenger, Edward C. Day, though her 11,465 votes surpassed the 7,794 for the Populist candidate for governor, Will Kennedy. A few months later, Haskell appointed her assistant attorney general. In that capacity she went to Washington, D.C., and convinced Interior Secretary Hoke Smith to award the state $200,000 worth of contested school lands near Great Falls. Haskell was a widower; in 1895, before his second term ended, they married, and after his term ended they moved to his home town, Glendive. Not long after, their marriage dissolved; they had no children.

Ella Knowles Haskell returned to Helena, the state capital. There she practiced law and was active in the suffrage movement. She belonged to the Helena Business Women's Suffrage Club from its inception in 1896 and was chosen that year to serve as president of the Montana Equal Suffrage Association. Another woman with aspirations to enter the legal profession, Adelaide Staves, studied law with her in 1899–1900. While the Populist party remained vibrant in Montana, Haskell remained active in it. In 1896 she was a delegate to the state and national party conventions. She served on the national committee for four years, and she traveled and spoke in support of William Jennings Bryan, the Populist and Democratic candidate for the presidency in 1896 and the Democratic nominee in 1900.

Helena lost a quarter of its population in the 1890s, and by 1902 she had moved her office south to Butte, a burgeoning city and a center of the state's mining industry with a thriving labor movement and a supportive atmosphere for political feminism. She remained active as a lawyer—she was admitted to practice law before the U.S. Supreme Court—and continued to promote women's rights. She also invested shrewdly in mining properties. She was a delegate to the International Mining Congress in Milwaukee in 1900, and she was elected a member of its executive committee. In addition, she served as regent with the Daughters of the American Revolution. In 1910 she made a trip around the world.

Ella Knowles Haskell died in Butte of a throat infection. She had embodied her generation's feminist quest for higher education, professional opportunity, and political rights.

• The Montana Historical Society in Helena has several collections with materials about Haskell; the Ella Knowles Haskell vertical file contains a number of newspaper clippings, including a feature on her from the *New Hampshire Sunday News*, 21 July 1957. An early sketch of her appeared in *Progressive Men of the State of Montana* (1902). The fullest treatment of her life and career is Richard B. Roeder, "Crossing the Gender Line: Ella L. Knowles, Montana's First Woman Lawyer," *Montana: The Magazine of Western History* 32 (Summer 1982): 64–75. Paula Petrick, *No Step Backwards: Women and Family on the Rocky Mountain Mining Frontier, Helena, Montana, 1865–1900* (1987), discusses her activities in the suffrage movement. An obituary is in the *Anaconda Standard*, 28 Jan. 1911.

PETER WALLENSTEIN

HASKELL, Franklin Aretas (13 July 1828–3 June 1864), soldier, was born at "East Hill" in the town of Tunbridge, Vermont, the son of Aretas Haskell and Anna Folsom, farmers. Frank's early life was typical for a New England farm boy, plowing in the spring, tending to the livestock in the summer, and harvesting in the fall. After the harvest he attended a "select school" (for superior students) for a month or so, then a district school in the winter. He passed his life in this routine until age seventeen, when he became a local schoolmaster, which his older brother, Harrison Haskell, recalled was "the almost inevitable fate of all New England boys, of any promise." After three years of teaching in the winter and working on the family farm the rest of the year, Frank moved to Columbus, Wisconsin, to join Harrison, who had established a law practice there. Frank obtained the position of town clerk. One month later he was named superintendent of schools of the then still highly rural community. In 1850 he returned east to attend Dartmouth College. Haskell described the rigorous academic regime of his first year as "exceedingly laborious," but he received an excellent education and learned valuable leadership skills. Edwin D. Sanborn, a distinguished professor of Latin at the university, apprized Haskell: he "ranked well as a scholar—ambitious as Lucifer and possibly mischievous and irregular."

Haskell graduated in 1854 and in the fall returned to Wisconsin, where he settled in Madison. He stood six feet tall and was erect and steady in bearing. In 1856 he was admitted to the bar and embarked on a successful legal practice. He joined the Governor's Guard, a local militia company to which many of the leading young men of Madison belonged, entering as a corporal. Two years later he was elected first lieutenant. He made a brief foray into politics, when he ran for mayor on the Republican ticket in 1859 and was soundly trounced.

When war broke out in 1861, Haskell accepted a commission as first lieutenant and adjutant of the Sixth Wisconsin Infantry. Rufus R. Dawes, who later rose to command the regiment, recalled that Haskell "exercised at that time a marked influence upon the progress of the regiment in soldierly knowledge and quality. . . . Haskell had been born with every quality that goes to make a model soldier." In May 1862 Haskell was selected as an aide-de-camp by General John Gibbon, his brigade commander, but Haskell believed he was worthy of higher rank and attempted to use his political connections to win a field grade rank in the Sixth Wisconsin. His efforts failed, and he lost an election for major to Dawes by one vote. He vented his frustrations in a letter to his family: "You ask me what my chances of promotion are. I answer, they are nothing. If I could myself win some great battle, alone, and then could blow in the papers, and pay some news papers to blow for me, and then was besides a d——d politician, I suppose I could be promoted."

Haskell participated in some of the bloodiest fighting in the eastern theater between August and September 1862, at Brawner Farm, Second Manassas, South

Mountain, and Antietam. During this fighting Gibbon's brigade earned the nickname the "Iron Brigade." His success with the brigade earned Gibbon promotion to division command, and Haskell accompanied him, winning increased responsibility but still no higher rank. He saw further service during the Fredericksburg and Chancellorsville campaigns. His greatest moment, however, came in 1863 at Gettysburg, where Gibbon commanded the Second Division of the Second Army Corps. The division participated in fierce fighting on 2 July. On 3 July it held the center of the Union line and received the brunt of the Pickett-Pettigrew charge. When Gibbon and other key officers were wounded, Haskell, who remained mounted during the bloody combat, provided conspicuous leadership and direction. Gibbon wrote later of Haskell's performance that day, "I have always thought that to him more than to any one man, are we indebted for the repulse of Lee's assault." Second Corps commander Winfield S. Hancock also singled out Haskell for praise in his battle report.

Haskell would earn more lasting fame as a result of an essay on the battle that he began immediately after the engagement. The finished document was 138 pages in length. Some speculate that Haskell composed his paper for publication in a Wisconsin newspaper, but the candid nature of his narrative argues against this. More likely he intended it to be an accurate record of the greatest battle of the war to date, for his own and his family's benefit, written while the event was still fresh in his mind. In 1881 his brother Harvey Haskell edited the essay and privately published it. Since then Haskell's narrative has been reprinted many times, even finding its way into the Harvard Classics series.

Haskell's outstanding performance at Gettysburg finally earned him promotion in February 1864 to colonel of the Thirty-sixth Wisconsin Infantry. On 3 June he led his regiment forward in the forlorn Union assault at Cold Harbor and was shot in the head. He died three hours later. Hearing of Haskell's death, Gibbon remarked: "My God! I have lost my best friend, and one of the best soldiers in the Army of the Potomac has fallen."

His early death prevented Haskell from realizing his true potential as a soldier and as an individual. (He never married.) His performance at Gettysburg offered strong evidence that his career would have been a promising one.

• Haskell's personal papers are held by the Wisconsin State Historical Society in Madison. Frank L. Byrne and Andrew T. Weaver, eds., *Haskell of Gettysburg: His Life and Civil War Papers* (1970), contains a good sketch of his prewar life, but the meat of the book consists of his Civil War correspondence. His long essay on the battle of Gettysburg is also included. Glen Lafantasie provides an insightful assessment of Haskell in the extensive foreword to *Gettysburg: Lieutenant Frank Haskell, U.S.A., and Colonel William C. Oates, C.S.A.* (1992), which also includes Haskell's Gettysburg essay. For the official praise Haskell received after the battle of Gettysburg, see US War Department, *The War of the Rebellion: A*

Compilation of the Official Records of the Union and Confederate Armies, vol. 27, pt. 1 (128 vols., 1880–1901). Haskell's account of the battle was challenged by the veterans of Alexander Webb's brigade in a rare pamphlet, *The Battle of Gettysburg: How General Meade Turned the Army of the Potomac Over to Lieutenant Haskell* (1910). John Gibbon, *Personal Recollections of the Civil War* (1994), contains invaluable information on Haskell from his commander's perspective. For additional information see Rufus Dawes, *Service with the Sixth Wisconsin Volunteers* (1984), and Alan Nolan, *The Iron Brigade* (1983). An obituary is in the *Portage* (Wis.) *State Register*, 18 June 1864.

D. SCOTT HARTWIG

HASKINS, Charles Homer (21 Dec. 1870–14 May 1937), historian and educator, was born in Meadville, Pennsylvania, the son of George Washington Haskins, a teacher and college registrar, and Rachel McClintock. As a youth Haskins received a thorough classical education from his father and attended Allegheny College. He then transferred to the Johns Hopkins University, where he received the B.A. in 1887 and the Ph.D. (under the auspices of the Herbert Baxter Adams Seminar) in history in 1890 at age nineteen. His academic advancement was swift and sure. After serving as an instructor at Johns Hopkins in 1889, he moved to the University of Wisconsin, where he served first as instructor and assistant professor (1890–1891), and then as professor of European history from 1892 to 1902. In 1902 he moved to Harvard University, where he remained for the rest of his academic career, serving as professor until 1912, Gurney Professor of History and Political Science until 1928, and Henry Charles Lea Professor of Medieval History until 1931, when he retired as a professor emeritus. For more than half of these years, from 1908 to 1924, he also served as dean of the Harvard Graduate School of Arts and Sciences.

Haskins's related academic activities and the honors and distinctions he was accorded were as numerous as they were imposing. He helped found the American Council of Learned Societies and served as its chair from 1920 to 1926. He was president of the American Historical Association in 1922 and of the Mediaeval Academy of America (founded 1925) in 1926–1927. He was a fellow of the American Academy of Arts and Sciences and of the American Philosophical Society, and was a corresponding member or fellow of the British Academy, the Royal Historical Society of the United Kingdom, and the Société des Antiquaires of France and of Normandy. His renown earned him no less than nine honorary doctoral degrees from institutions in five countries.

Special honors were awarded by the governments of France (Officer of the Legion of Honor) and of Belgium (Commander of the Order of the Crown) in recognition of Haskins's single, and singular, foray into the world outside the academy. He served as an aide to President Woodrow Wilson at the Paris Peace Conference following World War I. Haskins headed up or served on advisory commissions dealing with issues concerning Belgium, Alsace-Lorraine, and the Saar.

After his return to academic life he coauthored, with Robert Howard Lord, *Some Problems of the Peace Conference* (1920) recounting his experiences and his outlook. In the book Haskins defended the commission's work as an equitable solution to the problems of Franco-German relations and echoed Wilson's positions that continued American involvement and a vigorous League of Nations were vital for a lasting European peace.

Haskins shaped and dominated the academic study of medieval history in the United States in the early decades of the twentieth century. He published extensively in two discrete but related fields, the history of the Normans and the cultural history of the Mediterranean world. His two earliest, and highly influential, books stemmed from his training in the Hopkins tradition of the study of institutions, *The Normans in European History* (1915) and *Norman Institutions* (1918). The latter contains still-standard analyses of aspects of judicial administration and of feudal custom in Norman lands, while the former, intended for a more general audience of students and the public at large, sought to place Norman enterprise in the wider context of the rapidly changing world of Europe as a whole in the eleventh and twelfth centuries.

The Normans of Haskins's studies had gravitated not only to England and the British Isles, but also to the south, where in Sicily they encountered and were blended into the traditions of Latin Catholic, Byzantine Orthodox, and Muslim Arabic cultures. Haskins's own scholarship reflected a similar odyssey. His greatest productivity came in the 1920s, when in quick succession he published four seminal books, *The Rise of Universities* (1923), *Studies in the History of Medieval Science* (1924), *The Renaissance of the Twelfth Century* (1927), and *Studies in Medieval Culture* (1929). His priorities were to trace the dissemination of Greek and Arabic scientific and philosophical texts in the Latin West and to record the professionalization of learning in the schools and universities of Italy and France.

Consciously or not, Haskins chose as his subjects for investigation those very processes of the development of scholarship and of specialized learned elites in twelfth century Europe that he both exemplified and stimulated in American higher education during his lifetime. Like so many other scholars of his generation and background, he was both familiar and comfortable with the classically modeled essay, and his *Studies* are not so much extended monographs as they are series of tightly structured essays integrated by a largeness of vision and command of an overall conceptual context. The other two books in this group of four, *The Rise of Universities* and *The Renaissance of the Twelfth Century*, were less technical and were intended to reach a wider, general audience, an objective that was amply realized. They became, in fact, widely adopted texts for college courses in medieval civilization and retained their popularity into the 1960s. Even if no longer frequently assigned, these books still hold honored places in the bibliographies of the standard medieval and Western civilization textbooks of the 1980s and beyond.

Perhaps the greatest, and certainly the most famous, of Haskins's books was *The Renaissance of the Twelfth Century*. The title, which is so familiar as to amount to a kind of cliche, was deliberately, and provocatively, chosen. Haskins challenged the then-current Burckhardtian orthodoxy that "Renaissance" was a postmedieval, indeed antimedieval, phenomenon beginning in fifteenth-century Italy and spread to the rest of Europe in the sixteenth century. His thesis, vigorously argued and amply illustrated, was that a knowledge of the pre-Christian classics, the rise of systematic humanistic learning, and the creativity exemplified in literature and in art, were as characteristic, *mutatis mutandis*, of the twelfth century as of the later period. This one book caused some incautious medievalists to deny the existence of, or to misrepresent the nature of, the later Italian Renaissance; but at least this one book, more than any other, politely but firmly denuded the terms "medieval" and "the Middle Ages" of their pejorative connotations in general educated parlance.

As dean, Haskins was instrumental in developing Harvard's eminence and national influence in graduate training. The production of a scrupulously researched and publishable dissertation became the norm for entry into an academic career in the arts and sciences. Disciplinary autonomy and professionalism also were goals that Haskins exemplified by his personal dedication to the growth of the American Historical Association and its series of annual reports. As teacher and scholar he had the rare distinction of achieving eminence in multiple fields. His long tenure as dean did not detract from, but rather coincided with, his most active publishing period. He was able to devote more attention to graduate students after leaving the deanship, and he trained an entire generation of specialists in English medieval history, the history of the papacy, Byzantine history, and the history of the classical tradition in the Middle Ages. They in turn honored him with a festschrift in 1929.

Poor health forced Haskins's retirement at age sixty in 1931 and made it impossible for him to maintain his scholarly activities thereafter. He wished only to remain in Cambridge, where he died. In 1912 he had married Clare Allen; they had three children, one of whom, George Lee, became a distinguished scholar of the origins and development of the medieval English Parliament.

Despite his early retirement Haskins's accomplishments both as a scholar and an administrator were daunting. Along with historians George Sarton and Lynn Thorndike, he helped to establish the history of medieval science as a legitimate and significant field, and he introduced more than one generation of younger American medievalists to the mysteries and delights of research in French provincial and local archives. Haskins was as much at home with the paleographical and textual difficulties of Norman charters as with the conceptual obscurities of Latin translations of Arabic treatises on natural philosophy. If many of his own books are now more honored than read, it is because his interpretations have been incorporated as standard components of our understanding and portrayal of medieval society, or because more recent research has advanced our knowledge beyond his findings on the very bases of questions he asked and lines of inquiry he opened.

Another testimony to Haskins's stature and legacy was the creation in the 1980s of the American-based Charles Homer Haskins Society, a large and active international community of scholars specializing in Viking, Anglo-Norman, and Angevin studies. The society holds an annual conference in Houston, Texas, and publishes both a newsletter and an annual volume of articles, the *Haskins Society Journal*. Haskins doubtless could not have asked for a more fitting memorial to his place in the development of humanistic teaching and scholarship in American higher education in the twentieth century.

• Some of Haskins's personal letters are in the National Archives, Washington, D.C., and in the George L. Burr Papers in the Archives of Cornell University. A full bibliography of his books, articles, and reviews was compiled by George W. Robinson and is contained in the festschrift volume, *Anniversary Essays in Medieval History by Students of Charles Homer Haskins*, ed. Charles Taylor (1929), pp. 389–98. Haskins's career at Harvard is discussed in Samuel Eliot Morison, ed., *The Development of Harvard University 1869–1929* (1930). Theodore Mommsen provided an appreciation of Haskins, as a "Prefatory Note" (pp. v–ix) to the Cornell paperback edition of *The Rise of Universities* (1957). Obituaries are in the *New York Times*, 15 May 1937; the *American Historical Review* 42, no. 4 (July 1937): 856–58; the *English Historical Review* 52 (1937): 649–56; and *Speculum* (the journal of the Medieval Academy of America) 14 (1939): 414.

MICHAEL ALTSCHUL

HASKINS, Thomas (7 Nov. 1760–29 June 1816), American Methodist preacher, was born near Preston, Caroline County, Maryland, the son of Joseph Haskins, a sea captain, and Sarah Ennalls. He apparently graduated from William and Mary College, and then read law with Gustavus Scott, of Cambridge, Maryland, and later with Richard Bassett of Dover, Delaware. The preaching of Freeborn Garrettson, a Methodist itinerant, led to his conversion and in August 1780 Judge Thomas White, a prominent Methodist of Kent County, recommended Haskins to Francis Asbury, the acknowledged leader of American Methodism. That year Haskins became a traveling preacher on the Baltimore circuit. Three years later the Methodist conference appointed him to the Chester circuit, which included Philadelphia, Pennsylvania, and all preaching places westward to the Susquehanna River. During 1784–1785 he served respectively the Somerset and Talbot circuits in Maryland. In 1785 he married Martha Potts; she died in 1797. They had one daughter. Due to the strain on his health, he located in

Philadelphia in 1786 and affiliated with St. George's Methodist Church, entering the wholesale grocery business with Colonel Caleb North.

In 1784 at the Christmas Conference in Baltimore, Francis Asbury, Thomas Coke, Richard Whatcoat, and Thomas Vasey, acting on instructions from John Wesley, organized the Methodist Episcopal church. Haskins, one of the youngest delegates and a few of his colleagues, let it be known that they thought the older leaders were moving too fast. In his diary, Haskins, while expressing respect for Wesley, questioned his understanding of the political, civil, and religious affairs in America. "I fear *haste will make waste* if we don't take care," he wrote on 24 December 1784. He believed the whole matter should be laid before the next conference in June for consideration. In the meantime, delegates could be selected and sent to the General Convention of the Protestant Episcopal church when it convened in Philadelphia. His worry was that Methodists who had frequently professed themselves "dutiful Sons of the Episcopal Church" would be criticized for separating too hastily from the Church of England. His hope was that a way would be found to continue a union with "our Mother Church."

For fifteen years Haskins served as a local preacher at St. George's, under the direction of the appointed elder. During this period he drew up the original charter for the church and served as trustee, treasurer, and secretary. Before John Dickins opened the first Methodist Book Room in St. George's church in 1789, Haskins undoubtedly participated in the decision of the trustees to lend funds for the enterprise. He served as a member of the first Book Committee of the denomination, prepared its first report, and presented it to the General Conference in 1792. At Asbury's direction, he drafted the Articles Of Association, which converted the Preacher's Fund, created by the Christmas Conference, into the Chartered Fund. The former fund had been designed to assist superannuated preachers, their widows, and orphans, but was found to be inadequate. The Chartered Fund was structured to serve the needs of a more comprehensive constituency. In 1796 Asbury called upon Haskins to transcribe Aubrey's journal, which was published in 1821. In 1799 Haskins married Elizabeth Richards; they had three daughters.

In 1801 a dispute in St. George's Church produced a fracture within Methodism in Philadelphia and led to Haskins's departure from the congregation. The problem seems to have involved disagreements over repairs to the building. Some eighty male members petitioned Asbury to remove the presiding elder, Joseph Everett, from the charge. This effort failed and over fifty members withdrew, including Haskins and Caleb North. The separating group rented part of George Whitefield's old academy on Fourth Street and organized a new society, which became Union Methodist Episcopal Church. In 1811 some of the members of Union Church, Haskins being one of them, allegedly to accommodate a few wealthy Methodists in Philadelphia, built a church on Tenth Street between Chestnut and

Market streets and named it St. Stephen's Church. This enterprise did not succeed and the church was eventually sold to the Episcopalians who renamed it St. Thomas's.

Haskins remained a loyal Methodist in spite of his occasional dissent from the centralized authority of the leaders of early American Methodism. His thoughtful concern for his denomination's debt to the Church of England mark him as a man of respectful and judicious temperament. He died in Philadelphia. Reports indicated that he was buried in Union Methodist Episcopal Church graveyard and also in New York City, and that his first wife was buried in St. George's graveyard. But Haskins, his two wives, and his daughters Sarah and Elizabeth are now interred in the United Methodist Historical Site No. 223, Pleasant Mills, New Jersey.

• The essential works on Haskins are Joseph S. Ames, "Genealogies Of Four Families Of Dorchester County: Harrison, Haskins, Caile, Loockerman," *Maryland Historical Magazine* 11 (1916): 76–79; Elmer E. Clark et al., eds., *Journal and Letters of Francis Asbury* (3 vols., 1958); Charles M. Dupuy, *A Genealogical History of the Dupuy Family* (1910); and Thomas Haskins Mss Diaries, Library of Congress, Washington, D.C. See also Nolan B. Harmon, ed., *The Encyclopedia of World Methodism* (2 vols., 1974); John Lednum, *A History of the Rise of Methodism in America* (1859); and Francis H. Tees et al., *Pioneering In Penn's Woods* (1937).

FREDERICK V. MILLS, SR.

HASSAM, Childe (17 Oct. 1859–27 Aug. 1935), painter, illustrator, and graphic artist, was born Frederick Childe Hassam in Dorchester, Massachusetts, the son of Frederick Fitch Hassam, an antiques dealer and cutlery merchant, and Rose Delia Hawthorne. The family name was a derivation of the original Puritan name Horsham.

After completing studies at the Cotton Mather School, Hassam attended Dorchester High School but withdrew during his second year in 1876 and went to work. This was most likely a result of the family's loss of their modest fortune four years previously when his father's business went up in flames during the great fire of Boston in 1872. Hassam's first job, which lasted only three weeks, was in the accounting department of Little, Brown and Company, publishers. As a child, Hassam had shown some skill with watercolors. When a supervisor at Little, Brown saw Hassam's drawing ability and his lack of ability with numbers, he suggested that Hassam follow a career in art. In 1876 Hassam was apprenticed to wood engraver George E. Johnston from whom he learned all aspects of engraving, from the most menial tasks to designing. Hassam's talent for drawing facilitated his rapid rise to staff artist. His 1876 design for the masthead of the *Marblehead Messenger* was still being used by the paper fifty years later.

Hassam worked for Johnston until 1881 when he established his own studio in Boston. During this period he also worked as a freelance illustrator for *Harper's*, *The Century*, and *Scribner's* as well as for juvenile periodicals such as *Babyland* and *Saint Nicholas*. He took lessons in drawing and painting in the evenings at the Boston Art Club and received private painting lessons from Ignaz Marcel Gaugengigl and from William Rimmer, a self-taught painter, sculptor, master of anatomical drawing, and sometime doctor of medicine, at Boston's Lowell Institute. At this time Hassam's principal work was in watercolor, and he once said, "I learned to paint in Boston before I ever went to France." His first solo exhibition, held at Williams & Everett Gallery in Boston in 1882 included about fifty watercolors; many were derived from a stay on Nantucket and were paintings of the beach, boats, old cottages, and the sea. Hassam also taught painting part-time; one of his students was Celia Laighton Thaxter, a poet and patron of the arts, who would become a close friend. According to Hassam, it was Thaxter who persuaded him to drop his Christian name Frederick by pointing out that a man in search of fame should capitalize on the memorable quality of a name like Childe.

Hassam's first of several trips to Europe was in 1883 with his friend and fellow illustrator Edmund Henry Garrett. They started in Scotland, touring and visiting museums, and then went to England, where Hassam was particularly impressed by the watercolors and drawings of J. M. W. Turner. Continuing on to France, Italy, the Netherlands, Switzerland, and Spain, Hassam painted at every stop, as well as on shipboard. Sixty-seven of these watercolors formed the basis of his second solo exhibition at the Williams & Everett Gallery in 1884.

When Hassam returned to Boston, he continued both his freelance work and his studies. In February 1884 he married his sweetheart of long standing, Kathleen Maude Doane; the couple had no children. The newlyweds moved into Boston, to Columbus Avenue, and Hassam began painting a series of views of the city. He was particularly fond of scenes of rainy days and nights as evidenced in *Columbus Avenue, Rainy Day* (1885) and *Rainy Day, Boston* (1885), both characterized by the movement and vitality of carriages and pedestrians. One of his best-known cityscapes is *Boston Common at Twilight* (1885–1886). To Hassam, the cityscape represented a challenge to the academic tradition by portraying a modern theme, relevant to contemporary life.

In 1886 Hassam returned to Paris to study, specifically to acquire experience in the type of "rigorous figure drawing" taught in the French academic system. He attended the Académie Julian, working under the direction of academic painters Jules-Joseph Lefebvre and Gustave Boulanger. He realized, however, that the mechanical stiffness stressed by his instructors was not for him, and he remarked about French academic training, "It is nonsense. It crushes all originality out of the growing men" (quoted in Hiesinger, p. 32). From the outset he worked independently of Julian's program, following his own "method." His first major painting completed in Paris was *Cab Station, Rue Bonaparte* (1887), which was accepted for exhibition at the 1887 Paris Salon, "a triumph that any American painter in Paris might envy" (quoted in Hiesinger, p. 35).

Hassam's greatest pleasure was wandering the streets of Paris in search of subjects for his paintings. This he did with increasing frequency, and by spring 1888 he had stopped going to the Académie Julian and was working entirely on his own. His output of paintings increased dramatically, and his style reflected his growing affinity to the French impressionists. His work continued to show his interest in city life from the public parks and famous landmarks to the cab drivers and other people of Paris. During the summer months, he left the city for Villiers-le-Bel, where he created a series of garden paintings featuring women, including *Geraniums* (1888) with his wife as a model.

After the Hassams returned to the United States in 1889, they relocated to New York City. In 1890 Hassam helped found the New York Water Color Club and was its first president (1890–1896). As had happened in Paris, the new surroundings inspired Hassam to a burst of activity; many of his most important New York compositions were created in his first few years in the city. *Fifth Avenue in Winter* (1890), painted from the window of his apartment and depicting people and carriages, was one of his personal favorites. Contemporaries remarked on his "uncanny sensitivity to the nuances of place" that allowed him to capture the distinct flavor of any locale, whether city or small town.

Although he wintered in New York City, Hassam's summers were spent in country and seaside locations. He often visited Appledore Island, just off the coast of New Hampshire. There he would spend time with his friend Celia Thaxter. His ultimate tribute to the woman who was his friend and spiritual mentor and had predicted his future greatness in her sonnets was *The Room of Flowers* (1894), a view of Thaxter's salon with a female figure, painted just before her death. Hassam also spent summers at Cos Cob and Old Lyme, both in Connecticut. Just as Monet, studying the effect of light, painted several versions of the cathedral at Rouen, Hassam painted his series of the old Congregational Church at Old Lyme.

Hassam's first major one-man show in New York was at the American Art Galleries in 1896. The show was a two-night sale and included 205 paintings in oil, watercolor, and pastel from every phase of his career. However, it was not a success; critics felt that he had carried impressionism too far and that his vision had degenerated. Excellent paintings went for $30 to $50, barely the price of the frames. The disappointed Hassam returned to Italy for the winter and then traveled to Paris and England, returning to New York in 1897.

Hassam and his friends and fellow painters John Twachtman and J. Alden Weir had become interested in impressionism. Hassam identified art with modern, urbanized society, and his enthusiasm for dynamism and change was shared by impressionist painters in France and America. In December 1897 Hassam and nine other impressionist painters, including Twacht-man and Weir, seceded from the Society of American Artists to form a new exhibition society known as The Ten American Painters. Their action resulted from continuing conflict between the society's conservative artists and the impressionist camp. The first exhibition mounted by The Ten was at the Durand-Ruel Gallery in New York on 30 March 1898. Of the forty-five works in the show, seven were by Hassam. Most of these were from his recent European trip and were described by critics as "quite incomprehensible" and "queer," or "too experimental to be taken seriously" (Hiesinger, p. 116).

Unlike many of his colleagues who depended on teaching or commissioned portrait work, Hassam supported himself entirely from the sale of his works. He was thus constantly preoccupied with the business of exhibiting and selling his pictures. He also did a number of book illustrations, including the water-color pictures for William Dean Howells's *Venetian Life* (1892) and for *An Island Garden* (1894) by Celia Thaxter.

In 1910 Hassam returned to Paris. During this stay he painted *July Fourteenth, Rue Daunou* (1910) from the balcony of his hotel. A depiction of the Bastille Day celebration, it was full of flags and movement and can be seen as a forerunner of his World War I flag paintings. These paintings were done between 1916 and 1919 and were inspired by the Preparedness Day Parade down Fifth Avenue on 13 May 1916. The series included more than twenty-five paintings; the most famous was *Allies Day, May 1917* (1917), commemorating the "historic scene" when the flags of Great Britain and of France were first hung with the Stars and Stripes. Hassam considered the flag paintings among his greatest achievements.

In 1915 Hassam became interested in printmaking, particularly etching. His prints were highly acclaimed, and he noted, "I began my career in the graphic arts, and I am ending it in the graphic arts" (quoted in Hoopes, p. 18). A 1933 catalog of Hassam's work records 376 etchings and drypoints. In 1920 he purchased an early eighteenth-century farmhouse in East Hampton, New York. He stayed there from May to October, giving up his other summer retreats. During the winter he returned to New York City. He died in East Hampton.

His will is a commentary on Hassam the man and an expression of his confidence in the future of American art. He bequeathed all his remaining oil paintings, watercolors, and pastels (more than four hundred works) to the American Academy of Arts and Letters, to be sold to establish the Hassam Fund, named in his wife's honor, not his own. The income was to be used to buy pictures from living American and Canadian artists for museums in the United States and Canada. An important American impressionist, Hassam used color and light to paint the cities, towns, and people of his own time, creating a visual history of America.

• Hassam's papers are housed in New York City at the American Academy and Institute of Arts and Letters. Books that include biographical material and color prints are Adeline Adams, *Childe Hassam* (1938); Donelson F. Hoopes, *Childe Hassam* (1979); Ilene Susan Fort, *The Flag Paintings of Childe Hassam* (1988); David Park Curry, *Childe Hassam: An Island Garden Revisited* (1990); and Ilene Susan Fort, *Childe Hassam's New York* (1933). Ulrich W. Hiesinger, *Childe Hassam, American Impressionist* (1994), includes primary source documents. Periodical articles are Grant Reynard, "The Prints of Childe Hassam, 1859–1935," *American Artist*, Nov. 1960, and David G. Lowe, "The Banner Years," *American Heritage*, June 1969. See also Kenna Simmons, "Banner Years," *Horizon*, May 1988; "Hassam and the American Garden," *Antiques*, Apr. 1990; and Stephen May, "An Island Garden, a Poet's Passion, a Painter's Muse," *Smithsonian*, Dec. 1990. An obituary is in the *New York Times*, 28 Aug. 1935.

MARCIA B. DINNEEN

HASSELQUIST, Tuve Nilsson (2 Mar. 1816–4 Feb. 1891), Lutheran pastor, educator, and church leader, was born in Hasslaröd, Ousby Parish, Sweden, the son of Nils Tufvasson and Lissa Svensdotter, farmers. Graduating from Lund University in Sweden in 1835, he was ordained a Lutheran pastor in 1839 and served several parishes in Sweden.

In response to a letter from a Swedish pastor in America, in 1852 Hasselquist led an emigrant party to America, settling in Galesburg, Illinois, where he became pastor to a Lutheran congregation. Although he originally intended only a temporary stay, he eventually settled permanently in the United States. He married Eva Helena Cervin in May 1852; they had four children.

Hasselquist was strongly influenced by pietist, reforming ideas and was an outspoken critic of what he saw as the flaws of the Church of Sweden. Early in his career he was attracted to the free-church position, where congregations would consist of true Christians rather than all citizens, and his ministerial style was much less formal than that common in the Church of Sweden. However, in conflict with other denominations in America, even with some branches of American Lutheranism, Hasselquist moved to a more conservative Lutheran position, although not a position as formal as that of the Church of Sweden.

When Hasselquist arrived in America in 1852, he and other Swedish-American Lutheran pastors joined a regional synod affiliated with the General Synod, an American Lutheran denomination. Hasselquist found the Lutheranism of the General Synod to be questionable, however, and in 1860 the Swedish pastors broke away to found the Augustana Synod, which would become the principal Lutheran denomination for Swedes in America. He served the Augustana Synod as its first president, from 1860 to 1870. As one of the founders of the synod, and one of its leading members, he put his own indelible stamp on the early history of that institution.

In 1863 Hasselquist accepted a call to serve as president and professor of theology at Augustana Theological Seminary, which was then located in Paxton, Illinois, a position he held until his death. The seminary was a small and struggling institution, and it took all of Hasselquist's efforts to keep it alive. In 1864 a preparatory department was added to the seminary, which was the beginning of Augustana College, although the first college class did not graduate until 1877. The location at Paxton proved unsatisfactory, and in 1875 the college and seminary were moved permanently to Rock Island, Illinois. Hasselquist was the guiding force of this institution for nearly thirty years and was greatly responsible for its growth and development.

For many years Hasselquist edited church publications, beginning with his founding of the paper *Hemlandet* in Galesburg in 1855, which became *Augustana*, the official publication of the Augustana Synod. He remained as editor of *Augustana* until 1889. From the beginning, he and the Augustana Synod faced conflicts with other Swedish-American denominations, especially with the Swedish Baptists and Swedish Methodists. In his position as editor and writer he evidenced a strong Lutheran position and a sharp opposition to non-Lutheran denominations. The periodicals also mirrored Hasselquist's other strong commitments, among them the Republican party and the Union in the Civil War, the abolition of slavery, and temperance. As an editor and as a protagonist he could be rather sharp, although contemporaries suggested that this was not generally indicative of his usual personality.

Hasselquist stood strongly for the centralization of power within the synod. In his long conflict with the free-church movement in the Swedish-American community he came to the position that the church was more than just the sum of its individual congregations. Beginning in the 1870s, within the Augustana Synod there were many who sought to move power from the synod itself, to local conferences, congregations, and institutions. Hasselquist advocated a strong and powerful central synod with one educational institution, Augustana College and Seminary, and one synodical publication, *Augustana*. Although perhaps his control of these institutions was partially responsible for his stand, it can also be said that his position was based on ideology as much as interest. A twenty-year struggle over this issue within the synod ended in 1890, with the central power of the synod mostly reaffirmed. But in this process he made a number of enemies, and the last years of his life were spent defending his position as president of Augustana College and Seminary. He died in Rock Island, Illinois.

Hasselquist was one of the dominant personalities within the Augustana Synod in the nineteenth century and a major figure in the Swedish-American community. As a church leader, editor, and college president, he was one of the chief architects of the Augustana Synod and a principal influence within the immigrant religious community.

• Hasselquist's papers are in the Archives of Augustana College, Rock Island, Ill., where the papers of other of the synod's early leaders are also maintained. Hasselquist wrote several books and pamphlets, but most important for his biography are the articles and editorials he wrote for *Hemlandet* and *Augustana* from 1855 to 1889. Eric Norelius, *T. N. Hasselquist: Lefnadsteckning* (n.d.), is a biography by a contemporary, with whom Hasselquist did not always agree. Oscar Fritiof Ander, *T. N. Hasselquist: The Career and Influence of a Swedish-American Clergyman, Journalist, and Educator* (1931), is a detailed examination of Hasselquist's public career but less useful as a biography. For a general history of the Augustana Synod, see G. Everett Arden, *Augustana Heritage* (1963). On Augustana College, see Conrad Bergendoff, *Augustana . . . A Profession of Faith* (1969).

MARK GRANQUIST

HASSLER, Ferdinand Rudolph (7 Oct. 1770–20 Nov. 1843), geodesist and mathematician, was born in Aarau, Switzerland, the son of Jakob Hassler, a prosperous watch manufacturer and a member of the town council. His mother's name is unknown. Hassler received his early schooling in Aarau and at the age of sixteen went to work in the state archives department in Bern. His father felt that this experience would prepare him for a career in the civil service and the law, but he found himself drawn to mathematical studies and land surveying (geodesy) and studied mathematics and geodesy with Johann Georg Tralles, a German professor of mathematics and physics. Tralles's method of surveying, known as triangulation, made Swiss mapmaking more accurate, and Hassler became an accomplished surveyor.

With the support of his father, Hassler traveled to Paris and Germany to purchase instruments and books and to attend the lectures of scientists such as Joseph-Jérôme Le Français de La Lande, Jean-Charles Borda, Jean-Baptiste Joseph Delambre, Antoine-Laurent Lavoisier, Franz Xaver von Zach, and Johann Gottlieb Friedrich von Bohnenberger. He impressed them with his ability with mathematical instruments, but the French invasion of German-speaking territories in 1798 made it difficult for him to continue geodetic work. After fruitless efforts to find employment, Hassler decided to emigrate to America. He married Marianne Gaillard in 1798, and they eventually had nine children. In 1805 he took his growing family, his servants, his books and equipment, and more than one hundred laborers to America, to establish a Swiss colony in South Carolina. When they arrived in Philadelphia, Hassler discovered that the company that had backed the venture was insolvent, and he had no means of support.

Hassler's reputation among some of Philadelphia's leading men of science helped him out of his difficulties. While waiting for financial assistance from his father, he sold his instruments and much of his library through contacts he made at the American Philosophical Society, where he regularly attended meetings. Impressed by this energetic Swiss surveyor and mathematician, the society elected him a member in 1807. With the strong recommendation of members of the society like Robert Patterson, director of the U.S. Mint, Hassler was appointed to head a survey of the Atlantic coast of the United States after Congress passed a bill authorizing such an undertaking.

Growing political instability and the troubled situation in Europe forced Hassler to delay his work on the coast survey. In the meantime, he served at the U.S. Military Academy at West Point as an acting professor of mathematics (1807–1809). He had to leave this position, however, because civilians could not be regularly employed at the academy, and he then became professor of natural philosophy and mathematics at Union College in Schenectady, New York. In 1811 Hassler was given the title of scientific ambassador to London and Paris; supported by a salary comparable to that of a foreign minister, he traveled freely in Europe, purchasing instruments and other materials needed for the survey. His return home was delayed until 1815 because of war in Europe and the United States.

Hassler was formally approved as superintendent of the U.S. Coast Survey in 1816. He began work in New York harbor and often worked in severe weather so that he could extend the surveying season and collect the most accurate data. However, he neglected to make friends in the political arena, and his desire to uphold the highest scientific standards in conducting the survey often interfered with the demands of powerful congressmen who wanted to see maps of the coastal regions produced as rapidly as possible. In 1818, in spite of his personal sacrifices and his attention to scientific detail, Congress changed the survey's charter, stipulating that only military officers could direct the project; since Hassler was a civilian, he had to resign.

For the next fourteen years (1818–1832) the U.S. Coast Survey foundered under military appointees. During much of this period Hassler farmed in upstate New York. Briefly, he was called on to arbitrate a northeastern boundary dispute with Canada, and he served a short stint as gauger in the New York Custom House. While out of government service, he remained in contact with the leading figures in the field of geodesy and practical mathematics in Europe, and he continued to correspond with Thomas Jefferson and James Madison. When the political climate changed, he returned as superintendent of the Bureau of Weights and Measures (1830), a department he had helped to organize. In 1832 Congress reactivated the 1807 charter that had created the U.S. Coast Survey, and Hassler resumed his duties as superintendent of the survey under the Treasury Department.

Although no longer young and in declining health, Hassler reinvigorated the survey, insisting that the work should be conducted as a scientific investigation and not as an exercise in mapmaking. He reintroduced triangulation, a method enabling the observer to calculate the position of a given point from the location of two other points miles apart. He was also successful in designing new instruments that made the task of surveying easier and more accurate. For example, he replaced the spherical reflectors he had originally recommended in 1807 with truncated cones of tin that were easier to operate and cheaper to produce. Although he resisted interference from government officials and opponents in Congress more successfully than before, his lack of tact and his insistence that scientists should be properly paid, embroiled him in continual strife and eventually sapped his strength. Hassler continued to work until his health gave out; he died in Philadelphia.

Hassler brought scientific rigor and many innovations of European geodesy to American surveying. He developed new instruments and adapted others to meet the unique conditions in America, broadening the scope of the U.S. Coast Survey to include terrestrial magnetism and tides. He long argued in favor of standard weights and measures to correct the disparity that existed in different custom houses, and he used the instruments and the standard weights and measures he brought with him from abroad. His commitment to scientific precision served as a model for later projects.

• Hassler's letters are in the Gordon Lester Ford Collection of the New York Public Library, the Dreer Collection of Autographs in the Library of the Historical Society of Philadelphia, and the Archives of the American Philosophical Society Library. His papers are in the Coast and Geodetic Survey and National Bureau of Standards records in the U.S. Archives in Washington, D.C., and documents relating to his work on the coast survey and weights and measures are in the *Niles Weekly Register*, vols. 40, 43–44, and 52, and the *Niles National Register*, vols. 54, 56–57, 59–63, 65, and 71. His published work includes *A Popular Exposition of the System of the Universe* (1828) and *Elements of Analytic Trigonometry, Plane and Spherical* (1826). Biographical references include Florian Cajori, *The Chequered Career of Ferdinand Rudolph Hassler, First Superintendent of the United States Coast Survey* (1929); A. Hunter Dupree, *Science in the Federal Government* (1986); Arthur H. Frazier, *United States Standards of Weights and Measures: Their Creation and Creators* (1978); Nathan Reingold, "Research Possibilities in the U.S. Coast and Geodetic Survey Records," *Archives internationales d'histoire des sciences* 11 (1958): 337–46; Gustavus Adolphus Weber, *The Bureau of Standards, Its History, Activities and Organization* (1925); Weber, *The Coast and Geodetic Survey: Its History, Activities and Organization* (1923); and Emil Zchokke, *Translation from the German of the Memoirs of Ferdinand Rudolph Hassler, with Supplementary Documents* (1882).

JOEL S. SCHWARTZ

HASTIE, William Henry (17 Nov. 1904–14 Apr. 1976), civil rights attorney, law school professor, and federal judge, was born in Knoxville, Tennessee, the son of Roberta Childs, a teacher, and William Henry Hastie, a clerk in the U.S. Pension Office (now the Veterans Administration). He was a superb student and athlete. His father's transfer to Washington, D.C., in 1916 permitted Hastie to attend the nation's best black secondary school, the Paul Lawrence Dunbar High School, from which he graduated as valedictorian in 1921. He attended Amherst College, where he majored in mathematics and graduated in 1925, valedictorian, Phi Beta Kappa, and magna cum laude. After teaching for two years in Bordentown, New Jersey, he studied law at Harvard University, where one instructor adopted the custom of saying after asking a ques-

tion of the class, "Mr. Hastie, give them the answer" (Ware, p. 30). He worked on the *Law Review* and earned an LL.B. in 1930.

Hastie returned to Washington, D.C., in 1930, passed the bar exam, and began his legal career as a practitioner and an educator. He joined the firm of Charles Hamilton Houston and Houston's father, William L. Houston, which then became Houston, Houston, and Hastie. He also joined the law faculty at Howard University, where his first students included Thurgood Marshall and Oliver Hill. He took a year away to study again at Harvard, where he shared an apartment with his friend Robert C. Weaver and earned his S.J.D. in 1933. He returned to Howard, where, when he was working in Washington, he taught until 1946. At the same time he became active in civil rights. For him the two were one. His students researched current civil rights cases, participated in rehearsals of arguments on those cases, and attended the Supreme Court to watch Hastie and other civil rights giants argue cases. In 1935 he married Alma Syphax; they had no children before they divorced. In 1943 he married Beryl Lockwood; they had two children.

Hastie believed that, in the pursuit of justice, people should "struggle as best they know how to change things that seem immutable" (Ware, p. 147). In 1933, he was a founding member in Washington, D.C., of the New Negro Alliance, part of the "don't buy where you can't work" movement of the 1930s. He took a case in which a local court issued injunctions against African Americans picketing at chainstore outlets that, though operating in black areas, hired only white clerks. He argued the case in trial court and in federal appeals court but lost both attempts. He was unavailable to argue the case before the Supreme Court, which, convinced by the arguments Hastie and other attorneys had mounted, ruled in *New Negro Alliance v. Sanitary Grocery Co.* (1938) that the Norris-LaGuardia Act barred injunctions against peaceful labor-related picketing.

A champion of equal opportunity and racial integration, Hastie worked with the National Association for the Advancement of Colored People (NAACP) on major civil rights cases elsewhere, among them the 1933 *Hocutt* case in North Carolina, in which a black applicant unsuccessfully challenged the white-only admissions policy of the University of North Carolina. He also participated in cases that sought equalization of teachers' salaries, including the 1939 *Mills* case in Maryland and the 1940 *Alston* case in Virginia, both of which the NAACP won. With Marshall he argued cases before the Supreme Court that secured victories against the white Democratic primary in *Smith v. Allwright* (1944) and against segregated interstate transportation in *Morgan v. Virginia* (1946). In 1945 he presided at a conference in Chicago on segregated housing that the NAACP called to plan litigation against the constitutionality of restrictive covenants.

A series of appointments with the federal government began in November 1933, when Interior Secretary Harold L. Ickes recruited Hastie as assistant solicitor. In that capacity Hastie helped draft the Organic Act of 1936 for the Virgin Islands, which established a fully elective legislature and broadened the electorate to include residents regardless of their property, income, or gender. Hastie, like Weaver, was an early member of what became known as President Franklin D. Roosevelt's "black cabinet." His performance at the Interior Department led to his appointment in March 1937 to a four-year term as district judge in the Virgin Islands, the first black federal judge in U.S. history. He resigned from his judgeship in early 1939 to become dean of the Howard Law School. He took leave of the deanship in June 1940 to become civilian aide to Secretary of War Henry L. Stimson, in charge of handling matters of race in the military. In 1942 President Roosevelt also named Hastie a member of the Caribbean Advisory Committee, to advise the Anglo-American Caribbean Commission, established to foster the wartime social and economic cooperation of British and U.S. possessions in the Caribbean. Though Hastie's work in the War Department earned him the title "father of the black air force" (Ware, p. 133), he resigned his position there in early 1943 in frustration over his limited effectiveness in curtailing racial segregation and discrimination in the military. For his efforts and his resignation over what he called the Army Air Force's "reactionary policies and discriminatory practices," he won the NAACP's Spingarn Award in 1943.

Hastie resumed his work at Howard University, and he presided at a rally in 1944 for a permanent Fair Employment Practices Committee. In 1946 President Harry S. Truman nominated him for the governorship of the Virgin Islands. The only African American who had previously served as governor of any U.S. jurisdiction was P. B. S. Pinchback, who served for a month as acting governor of Louisiana after being elected to the state senate during Reconstruction. Hastie had a rough time dealing effectively with public affairs in the islands, but he tried to enhance Virgin Islanders' self-government. He fostered a civil rights law that prohibited discrimination on the basis of race or color.

In 1948 Hastie briefly returned to the mainland, where he campaigned effectively in black communities in support of President Truman's reelection bid. In 1949 Truman appointed him to the U.S. Court of Appeals for the Third Circuit. Hastie took his seat as a recess appointment in December 1949, the first black federal judge with life tenure. Confirmed in 1950, he served as appeals judge until 1968, then as chief judge until he retired in 1971, and as senior judge thereafter. He wrote the decisions in more than 400 cases. He was considered for a Supreme Court appointment as early as 1954 and as late as 1967, when President Lyndon Johnson nominated Hastie's former student Marshall instead.

A member of the Board of Directors of the NAACP Legal Defense and Educational Fund from 1941 to 1968, Hastie continued to give public lectures on civil rights. He also served on the Boards of Trustees of Amherst College and Temple University. Cool and suave, committed yet dignified, Hastie died in Norristown, Pennsylvania. He excelled as a law school professor and dean, as a civil rights attorney and leader, and as a pioneer black officeholder in the federal government.

• The William H. Hastie Papers at the Law School Library, Harvard University, are available on microfilm. The Beck Cultural Exchange Center in Knoxville, Tenn., has a collection of Hastie's papers, books, and memorabilia and maintains a permanent Hastie exhibit. Other materials are at Howard University and in the NAACP Papers at the Library of Congress. Hastie's publications include "Judicial Method in Due Process Inquiry," in *Government under Law*, ed. Arthur E. Sutherland (1956); "Toward an Equalitarian Legal Order, 1930–1950," *Annals of the American Academy of Political and Social Science* 407 (May 1973): 18–31; and "Affirmative Action in Vindicating Civil Rights," *University of Illinois Law Journal* 14 (1975). The major works on Hastie are Gilbert Ware, *William Hastie: Grace under Pressure* (1984), which covers his childhood, his education, and his public life through his confirmation as a federal appeals judge in 1950; Jonathan J. Rusch, "William Henry Hastie and the Vindication of Civil Rights," *Howard Law Review* 21 (1978): 749–820; and Phillip McGuire, *He, Too, Spoke for Democracy: Judge Hastie, World War II, and the Black Soldier* (1988). Memorials are in the *Federal Reporter* (535 F.2d 1–10 [1976]); the *Crisis* 83 (Oct. 1976): 267–70; and the *University of Pennsylvania Law Review* 125 (Nov. 1976): 1–13. Obituaries are in the *New York Times* and the *Washington Post*, 15 Apr. 1976.

PETER WALLENSTEIN

HASTINGS, Albert Baird (20 Nov. 1895–24 Sept. 1987), biochemist, was born in Dayton, Kentucky, the son of Otis Luther Hastings, a salesman, and Elizabeth Baird. When Hastings was six his family moved to Indianapolis, Indiana, where he attended public schools. In high school he enjoyed Greek and Latin and considered becoming a classics teacher, but he then decided that engineering would make a good practical career and enrolled at the University of Michigan in chemical engineering in 1913. He changed his major to chemistry after taking a second-year physical chemistry course and being offered the job of assistant in the laboratory course in that subject. He was also given a small laboratory of his own, which he made his "home by day and much of the night for most of the next two years" (Hastings, 1970, p. 2).

Although he did not receive his baccalaureate degree until June 1917, Hastings began graduate studies in physical chemistry at Michigan in January of that year. When the United States entered World War I, he tried to enlist but was rejected for being underweight. Hastings was offered a job as assistant sanitary chemist in the U.S. Public Health Service in the fall of 1917. His duties were to determine whether fatigue in workers was caused by acidosis, a matter of concern to the war effort. At first he was assigned to the Ford Motor Company to test the urine of workers engaged in different levels of physical activity, but he soon argued that it would be more productive to investigate the problem in laboratory animals, using blood samples. He was transferred to the Department of Physiology at Columbia University, where he undertook laboratory studies on the effect of prolonged exercise on animals.

When the war ended Hastings stayed on at Columbia as a graduate student in physiology, working under Ernest Scott. On 31 May 1918 he married Margaret Johnson; they had one son. Hastings continued in the employment of the Public Health Service during his graduate studies, and it was anticipated that after completing his doctorate he would develop the program in physiology at the Service's Hygienic Laboratory (forerunner of the National Institutes of Health). Instead, he accepted the position of first assistant to Donald D. Van Slyke at the hospital of the Rockefeller Institute in New York on obtaining his Ph.D. in 1921.

Hastings spent the next five years at the Rockefeller Institute. He was a key participant in the studies of Van Slyke's group on gas and electrolyte equilibria in blood, including the acid-base balance. In this period he also initiated his investigation of the physicochemical basis for bone deposition. His collaboration with clinicians at the hospital made a lasting impression on Hastings, and he remained interested in the application of biochemistry to clinical problems throughout his career. Along with Van Slyke, he was one of the pioneers of clinical biochemistry in the United States.

In 1926 Hastings accepted a professorship in the Department of Physiological Chemistry at the University of Chicago. He continued to pursue research interests initiated at the Rockefeller Institute as well as embarking on new paths. Hastings and his colleagues demonstrated that the response of the body to a disturbance in the acid-base balance is an effort to maintain normal carbon dioxide tension as well as hydrogen ion concentration. They helped to clarify the equilibrium involving the deposition and dissolution of calcium salts in bone. The Hastings group also calculated the mass and electrolyte composition of the extracellular and intracellular phases of normal muscles, and they studied the effects of experimentally-produced edema, dehydration, acidosis, and alkalosis on these parameters.

Hastings moved to Harvard University Medical School in 1935 as Hamilton Kuhn Professor and head of the Department of Biological Chemistry. He built a strong department which was widely recognized for its excellence. His teaching and administrative duties at Harvard, coupled with substantial professional service activities outside the university, prevented him from spending extended periods of time in the laboratory. Under his direction, however, graduate students and postdoctoral fellows in his laboratory carried out an active research program. Among the most important work of this group were studies of intermediary metabolism using radioactive isotopes, then a new research tool. For example, they discovered in experiments with rats that carbon dioxide is incorporated into liver glycogen, a previously unsuspected use of carbon dioxide by mammals.

During World War II Hastings served on the Committee on Medical Research, established to mobilize civilian biomedical research resources for the solution of medical problems important to the war effort. For more than four years Hastings spent several days a week in Washington, D.C., at meetings of the committee. In 1944 he went on a special mission to Moscow to exchange information with the Russians on medical subjects such as penicillin. Hastings was awarded the President's Medal for Merit in 1948 for his service on the Medical Research Committee.

After the war Hastings became a member of four of the councils established by the National Institutes of Health to help administer its newly-established extramural grants program. He was also asked to serve on numerous editorial and advisory boards of institutions and publications. Hastings was an active member of many professional societies, including the American Association for the Advancement of Science (vice president, 1965), the American Society of Biological Chemists (treasurer, 1936–1940; vice president, 1943–1944; and president, 1945–1947), and the Society for Experimental Biology and Medicine (vice president, 1943–1945; president, 1945–1947). He was elected to the National Academy of Sciences in 1937.

Hastings took early retirement from Harvard in 1959 in order to give up his administrative duties and return to full-time laboratory research, now at the Scripps Clinic and Research Foundation in La Jolla, California. Among his most significant contributions from this period was his discovery of the effect of carbon dioxide concentration on carbohydrate and lipid metabolism. In 1966 he retired from Scripps and joined the staff of the Department of Neurosciences of the University of California, San Diego. His active laboratory career was over, but Hastings served in a consulting role and did occasional teaching. He died in La Jolla.

• The extensive personal papers of Hastings are housed at the National Library of Medicine, along with the transcript of an oral history interview with him conducted by Peter Olch in 1969. Hastings's autobiography, *Crossing Boundaries: Biological, Disciplinary, Human. A Biochemist Pioneers for Medicine* (1989), edited by Halvor N. Christensen from the Olch interview, supplemented for the post-1969 period by another interview conducted in 1975 and by records and recollections provided by Hastings. See also Hastings's autobiographical article, "A Biochemist's Anabasis," *Annual Review of Biochemistry* 39 (1970): 1–24. The best biography is Christensen's obituary in National Academy of Sciences, *Biographical Memoirs* 63 (1994): 173–216, which includes a selected bibliography. Also of value, especially for a more personal view, is Chester S. Keefer, "A. Baird Hastings: The Man—the Scientist—the Cosmopolite," *Federation Proceedings* 25 (1966): 822–26.

JOHN PARASCANDOLA

HASTINGS, Serranus Clinton (22 Nov. 1814–18 Feb. 1893), jurist, politician, educational philanthropist, and real estate magnate, was born near Watertown, Jefferson County, New York, the son of Robert Collins Hastings, a farmer, and Patience Brayton, who was from an early settler family in western New York. Robert Hastings, a Bostonian, saw action in the War of 1812 as a militia officer during the several attacks on the U.S. Naval Station at Sackets Harbor on Lake Ontario. Serranus attended Gouverneur Academy for six years, taught by graduates of the Hamilton Literary and Theological Institution in a strenuously moral classicism acceptable to Baptist tenets. He instituted that learning, aged twenty, as principal of the Norwich Academy, Chenango, New York. Within a year, however, he began the westward trek that brought him first to Lawrenceburg, southeastern Indiana, in 1835, to study law with two prominent lawyers there, meanwhile editing the *Indiana Sentinel* and vigorously supporting Martin Van Buren for president. He set off again in late 1836, pausing just long enough in Terre Haute to be called to the bar by the circuit court before settling in Muscatine, Iowa, in 1837.

Successful practice at the growing Iowa bar enabled Hastings in 1845 to marry Azalea Brodt, nine years his junior, an immigrant from Ohio; they would have eight children, the first three born in Muscatine. Oscar T. Shuck noted that Hastings was "a man of large stature, capable of great physical endurance, shrewd, energetic, alert in mind and body, simple in tastes and habits, peculiarly adapted to the border, and was not to be found wanting in the ebb and flow of frontier life" (*History of the Bench and Bar*, p. 455). Justice of the peace, major in the territorial militia, and renowned advocate, he was elected to the new territorial legislature in 1838 as a Democrat (a lifelong allegiance) and served in one or the other of its houses until 1846. With Iowa's admission as a state that year he was elected one of its two members of Congress, sitting with fellow Democrat Stephen A. Douglas and freshman Whig opponent Abraham Lincoln, both from Illinois. On completing his single term, he was appointed chief justice of the Iowa Supreme Court in 1848. He would not make his mark there.

The next year Hastings joined the Gold Rush by wagon train, leaving his family behind (they did not join him in California until 1851). Avoiding the diggings, he opened a law office and a loan company at Sutter's Fort, in the first three days taking in $20,000 on deposit, which he then lent on good security at 10 percent interest per month to miners in need of a grubstake. Within six months he settled in Benicia and on 20 December 1849 was chosen by the legislature as the new state's first chief justice of the supreme court. The salary was better than in Iowa; the term was two years; and the office opened future possibilities. In the next two years, in concert with (and sometimes in dissent from) his two associates, Henry A. Lyons and Nathaniel Bennett, Hastings made his contribution to jurisprudence. During five terms, March 1850 to June 1851, the court was compelled to establish the rule of law, both substantive and procedural, in a jurisdiction where there had been little formal law (and what there was a compound of custom and the Civil Law) and negligible legal record. In the "instant society," sud-

denly dominated by a hoard of immigrants and their frenetic commerce, realty was critical. Confused Mexican *alcalde* (mayoral) land grants that were badly recorded seemed to Hastings the principal barrier to the establishment of civil order and the encouragement of economic development. Faced with a chaos that would take state and federal courts, legislature and Congress, a generation to untangle, the first California Supreme Court astutely used a dictionary of Spanish law, Joaquin Escriche y Martin's *Diccionario Razonado de Legislación Civil, Penal, Commercial, y Forense* (probably the 1842 Mexico City edition), in order to follow Mexican-Spanish law in giving almost summary judgment of possession until at some future time title could be settled. In his opinions, Hastings demonstrated distaste for fictions, overly fine procedural technicalities, and any legal device that might perpetuate clouded title. He was also well disposed to the regulatory power of the state in a raw society, even against claims of property right, as he showed in his separate majority opinion in a public nuisance case involving encroachments on the San Francisco waterfront, *Gunter et al. v. Geary et al.* (1851).

Leaving the bench in straitened circumstances, Hastings won election to a two-year term as attorney general (1852–1854), which enabled him to recoup his finances by private practice as well as to advance his agenda for California development. Afterward he practiced law for only a couple of more years, having begun a full-time career in banking and land acquisition that made him a multimillionaire by the 1870s. Unostentatious, he built no mansion on Nob Hill, but resided in a hotel. Among his large tracts of agricultural and vine lands in the counties north of San Francisco he set up a summer residence and permanent domicile in Napa. He made generous settlements and trusts for his children.

Following the sudden death of his wife in the south of France during a European tour in 1876, a grieving Hastings found a philanthropy appropriate to his calling. In 1878 he gave $100,000 to the state for the creation of "the law department of the University of California," under terms for its endowment with a separate board of directors, the college to be named for the founder-benefactor. It was the first law school west of Des Moines. At the university's 1878 commencement, Hastings announced that the college was "intended to supply a substitute for the Inns of Court, the historic Inner Temple, a temple of the law, which shall extend its arms and draw within its portals all who shall be worthy to worship at its shrine, resulting in the coronation of its votaries, as a reward for application, industry, and merit" (*Address*, 1878). This was a perfect reflection of the man and his aspirations. Like so many of his frontier contemporaries, Hastings was a "Blackstone barrister" with no formal legal education. He was determined to create a postgraduate institution with a rigorous three-year curriculum producing not only jurists but cultivated citizens knowledgeable in the law. With Hastings as titular dean and the eminent New York University lawyer John Norton Pomeroy as professor, the first class enrolled that fall. Within a year, Hastings and his appointed board fell out over the admission of women and integration with the University of California and its regents (both of which Hastings favored), and he and Pomeroy split over the course of study. By 1886 Hastings had lost every battle with the board and was no longer a part of his institution.

After this deeply wounding defeat, Hastings abandoned San Francisco for residence elsewhere, latterly in Napa County, while retaining ties to the city. His consolations in his old age were religion and remarriage. He was converted to Roman Catholicism by the magnetic Dominican archbishop of San Francisco, Joseph Alemany. In 1885 he married a much younger woman, Lillian Knust. It was not an easy relationship: they divorced five years later, only to be reconciled and remarried shortly before his death. He died in San Francisco.

Hastings College of the Law proved permanent. So too did the work of the first California Supreme Court in providing both the direction for all subsequent adjudication in critical areas and the foundation for California's total codification a generation later. Such permanency marks Hastings as the quintessential juristic pioneer of the Golden State.

• There does not appear to be any major collection of Hastings papers. Some correspondence and reports as attorney general are in California State Archives, Sacramento (cat. nos. GP1:236, Dr 575, and Dr 4718). His work as chief justice of the California Supreme Court is found in the first volume of *California Reports* (San Francisco, 1851) reported by his associate, Nathaniel Bennett. *Address of S. C. Hastings* (San Francisco, 1878) and *Annual Address . . . August 1879*, by S. Clinton Hastings (San Francisco, 1879) reveal his philanthropic intentions. Insight into his land acquisitions is provided by C. Kasch, "The Yokayo Rancheria," *California Historical Quarterly* 26 (1947): 209–15; *People v. S. C. Hastings, John Currey and the Tract* (1868) and by the defendants' brief in Bancroft Library, UC–Berkeley (cat. no. 868.M5.M2). Hastings is noticed in Oscar T. Shuck, *History of the Bench and Bar in California* (1901), pp. 454–56. He is most fully treated in Thomas G. Barnes, *Hastings College of the Law: The First Century* (1978), chaps. 1 and 2.

THOMAS G. BARNES

HASTINGS, Thomas (11 Mar. 1860–22 Oct. 1929), architect, was born in New York City, the son of Thomas Samuel Hastings, a prominent clergyman, and Fanny de Groot, whose ancestors were of Dutch and Huguenot descent. Hastings was raised in New York, where his father was pastor of the West Presbyterian Church and the president of the Union Theological Seminary. Hastings's paternal grandfather, also named Thomas Hastings, was a distinguished composer of sacred music, his most famous song being "Rock of Ages." His maternal grandfather, Henry de Groot, was a merchant and writer on law. The family's commitment to scholarship may have influenced Thomas Hastings's academic approach to the discipline and practice of architecture, but according to his biographer David Gray, Hastings was compelled neither to "accept the tenets of his father's faith nor join any church" (p. 16).

Considered to be a sensitive and nervous child, Hastings received his early education from his father. Later he attended private school in preparation for college, but at age seventeen he abandoned it to enter the offices of Herter Brothers, New York cabinetmakers and decorators. There Charles Atwood, chief designer in the architectural department, and G. Howard Walker, director of construction, served as Hastings's mentors. Working for Herter Brothers Hastings designed one of the rooms at the Seventh Regiment Armory in New York City. In 1880 Hastings traveled to Paris to study at the École des Beaux-Arts. He entered the second class and joined the conservative atelier of Jules André. In 1882 he entered the first class and achieved success in the architectural competition early the following year.

Hastings returned to New York City, and in October 1883 he entered the firm of McKim, Mead & White. There he became reacquainted with John M. Carrère, who had also been at the École in the early 1880s. In 1885 they entered into partnership. Hastings was in charge of design, Carrère of the office management, production of working drawings, and client relations. Architect and critic H. Van Buren Magonigle described their partnership: "Hastings was as helpless as a shedder crab when anything practical was in question, and although Carrère was a thoroughly trained designer and for years by his sensible and penetrating criticism kept Hastings within bounds, he found himself forced . . . to handle the practical and business aspects of the practice" (p. 563).

A commission for a luxury resort hotel in St. Augustine, Florida, launched the careers of Carrère and Hastings. Henry M. Flagler, the Florida developer and a parishioner and friend of the Reverend Hastings, selected the firm to design the Ponce de Leon Hotel (1885–1888). Reflecting the scale and planning of an École *projet*, the design of the Ponce de Leon Hotel displayed an eclectic fusion of Renaissance, Spanish, and Moorish styles. Its progressive construction methods employed concrete with an aggregate of a local shell and coral stone called coquina. The success of this hotel prompted Flagler to commission other buildings in St. Augustine: the Alcazar Hotel (1887–1888), Grace Methodist Church (1887), and the Flagler Presbyterian Church (1889–1900). In 1900 Hastings married Helen B. Benedict of Greenwich, Connecticut. They had no children.

A charter member of the Society of Beaux-Arts Architects, Hastings promoted both the influence of the French School in America and a national style of architecture founded on its theory and design. In an attempt to check the proliferation of revival styles—Greek, Gothic, Romanesque, Queen Anne—that had dominated nineteenth-century architecture, Hastings advanced the cause of Renaissance classicism, also known as "modern Renaissance." Hastings considered the revival styles to be defective because they encouraged an architecture of imitation and "archaeology" and were anachronistic to "modern life" in the nineteenth century and the ideals of progress, order, and science.

Along with prominent Beaux-Arts practitioners such as Ernest Flagg, Whitney and Lloyd Warren, William Boring and Edward Tilton, and Samuel B. P. Trowbridge, Hastings was committed to infusing "architectural" rather than "archaeological" objectives into architectural education in the United States. Only the Renaissance, Hastings maintained, had produced a style that had survived and evolved for four centuries. "With the revival of learning . . . with the birth of modern science and literature . . . with this modern world there was evolved what we should now recognize as the modern architecture, the Renaissance" ("The Relations of Life to Style in Architecture," p. 960). But Hastings also advanced a particularly determinist view of style. "The laws of natural selection and of the survival of the fittest," he argued in the same article, "have shaped the history of architectural style just as truly as they have the different successive forms of life" (p. 959). By retrieving the lost thread of Renaissance architecture, Hastings hoped to direct its evolution toward a national style appropriate to modern times. Nonetheless, in posing this theory of architecture in the 1890s Hastings still did not resolve its central conflict: the objective to be both Renaissance and modern.

The firm of Carrère & Hastings was known for its prominent commissions and for the wide range of its work. As the firm's principal designer, Hastings consulted building type and program to determine the *parti* of a given project. Committed to the evolution of modern Renaissance ideals, he employed a wide range of styles associated with academic classicism: Spanish Renaissance for the Ponce de Leon Hotel; Italian Renaissance for the Jefferson Hotel in Richmond, Virginia (1893–1894); French Renaissance for the H. T. Sloane House at 9 East Seventy-second Street, New York City (1894–1896, now Lycée Français de New York) and for the Henry Clay Frick House on Fifth Avenue at Seventieth Street, New York City (1912–1914); Georgian Federal for the Elihu Root House, New York City (1903); and a Beaux-Arts interpretation of the colonial revival for City Hall in Portland, Maine (1909–1912, in association with John Calvin Stevens).

In 1897 Carrère & Hastings won the competition for the New York Public Library. Architectural historians regard the library as the summit of the firm's professional achievement not only because it represented their most important commission, but also because John Carrère was killed in an automobile accident only months before its dedication in 1911. Carrère & Hastings employed a restrained French classicism (similar to Claude Perrault's east facade of the Louvre) for the library's monumental stone entrance on Fifth Avenue. This contrasted with the tall banks of metal and glass openings on its Bryant Park elevation (designed with Theodore E. Blake). The library demonstrated Hastings's use of academic classicism for the ceremonial function of the formal entrance and structural rationalism for the Bryant Park facade to serve the utilitarian needs of lighting the stack spaces within.

Among the firm's most critically acclaimed commercial buildings was the Blair Building in New York City (1902–1903, demolished). In his writings Hastings proposed principles governing high buildings in the city. In an article of 1894, "High Buildings and Good Architecture," he advocated "rational limitations for all buildings constructed solely for revenue," proposed that their design "be solved in an artistic way," and employed the term "curtain-wall" (p. 67). An advocate of building and zoning laws that would assist rather than hinder the architect, Hastings called for the use of "exposed iron in a partly decorative way to indicate the constructive members which are concealed of necessity, for fireproof reasons" and "to treat these iron and steel constructions with curtain-walls, by honestly showing the iron or steel on the facade, with a filling-in of terra-cotta, brick or faience" (p. 67). For the fifteen-story Blair Building, Hastings applied the late Beaux-Arts method of designing a rational envelope for an American skyscraper that would not simulate solid stone construction but would denote its skeletal steel structure instead. Through a thin veneer of masonry combined with shafts of metal and glass for the central tiers, the exterior of the Blair Building expressed its interior.

Among the firm's other important works are the Mail & Express Building on Broadway, New York City (1891, demolished); the Giraud Foster House, Lenox, Massachusetts (1896–1898); the C. Ledyard Blair estate, "Blairsden," in Peapack, New Jersey (1898–1903); the bridge and pylons and fountains for the Pan American Exposition, Buffalo, New York (1901); the H. M. Flagler house, "Whitehall," Palm Beach, Florida (1901–1903); Woolsey Hall, Yale University (1901–1903); Staten Island Ferry Terminals, New York City (1901–1904); a campus plan and buildings for Cornell University (1902); Manhattan Bridge and Approaches, New York City (1904–1911); the Senate Office Building and the House of Representatives Office Building, Washington, D.C. (1905–1909); and the Alfred I. du Pont House, Wilmington, Delaware (1909).

After Carrère's death in 1911 Hastings joined with a number of collaborators, including Beaux-Arts architect Benjamin Wistar Morris for the Cunard Building at 25 Broadway, New York City (1919–1921); the New York firm of Shreve, Lamb, and Blake for the Standard Oil Building at 26 Broadway (1921–1924); New York commercial architect Emery Roth for the Ritz Tower on Park Avenue and Fifty-seventh Street (1925); and British architect C. H. Reilly for the Devonshire Apartments in London, England (1925–1926). One of the most successful Beaux-Arts architectural firms in the United States, Carrère & Hastings designed more than 600 buildings.

Thomas Hastings died at the Nassau Hospital, Mineola, Long Island, following an operation for appendicitis. Like Charles Follen McKim, the Warren brothers, Boring, Tilton, and Trowbridge, Hastings belonged to a second generation of architects (after Richard Morris Hunt and Henry Hobson Richardson) who trained in Paris at the École des Beaux-Arts and promoted French theory and design on their return to the United States. An articulate writer, Hastings advanced the cause of Beaux-Arts architecture in America. An accomplished practitioner, Hastings designed some of the country's most elegant and sophisticated Beaux-Arts buildings. During the two decades before the First World War Hastings helped to lead the profession of architecture toward its first maturity.

• The most extensive collection of Carrère & Hastings papers, including architectural drawings, is at the Avery Architectural and Fine Arts Library at Columbia University. The New York Public Library contains forty-four volumes of Hastings's "Scrapbooks of Architecture." Hastings's notable architectural writings include "The Relations of Life to Style in Architecture," *Harper's New Monthly Magazine*, May 1894, pp. 957–62; "High Buildings and Good Architecture," *American Architect and Building News* 46 (Nov. 1894): 67–68; "Architecture and Modern Life," *Harper's New Monthly Magazine*, May 1897, pp. 402–8; and "The Influence of the École des Beaux-Arts upon American Architecture," *Architectural Record*, "The Beaux-Arts Number" (1901): 66–90. The standard biography is David Gray, *Thomas Hastings, Architect* (1933). The most comprehensive analysis of the partnership and the firm's work (including a list of works) is Curtis Channing Blake, "The Architecture of Carrère and Hastings" (Ph.D. diss., Columbia Univ., 1976). See also "The Work of Messrs. Carrère & Hastings," *Architectural Record* 27 (1910): 1–120; and H. Van Buren Magonigle, "A Half Century of Architecture," pts. 6 and 7, *Pencil Points* 15 (1934): 465–66, 563–65. On individual buildings, see H. W. Desmond, "A Beaux-Arts Skyscraper—The Blair Building, New York City," *Architectural Record* 14 (1903): 436–43; and Henry Hope Reed, *The New York Public Library, Its Architecture and Decoration* (1986). An obituary is in the *New York Times*, 23 Oct. 1929.

MARDGES BACON

HASTINGS, William Wirt (31 Dec. 1866–8 Apr. 1938), congressman, was born in Benton County, Arkansas, the son of Yell Hastings, a Confederate soldier and farmer, and Louisa Stover. Three years after Hastings's birth, his family moved to the Delaware District of the Cherokee Nation, Indian Territory (now Delaware County, Okla.), where they purchased the old Benjamin Franklin Thompson farm on Beattie's Prairie. The youth attended the Beattie's Prairie Public School of the Cherokee Nation before earning his B.S. in 1884 from the Cherokee Male Seminary at Tahlequah. From 1884 to 1886 he taught in a Cherokee public school. He then studied law at Vanderbilt University in Nashville, Tennessee, graduating in 1889. He was admitted to the bar that same year. Hastings returned to the Cherokee Nation and formed a law partnership with E. C. Boudinot and William P. Thompson that lasted until the federal government abolished the courts of the Cherokee Nation in 1898.

Settling in Tahlequah, Hastings practiced law and, from 1891 to 1893, held the principalship of the Cher-

okee Orphan Asylum. From 1890 to 1891 he was tribal superintendent of education, and from 1891 to 1895 he was attorney general for the Cherokee Nation. He was also appointed to represent the Cherokee Nation in Washington, D.C., and served as the national attorney for the Cherokee tribe from 1907 to 1914. In 1896 he married Lulu Starr; they had three children.

Hastings's interest in politics quickly broadened. In 1892 he was chair of the first Indian Territory Democratic Convention. When the western half of the Indian Territory opened to white settlement, the Native Americans in 1905 met in convention to organize the separate state of Sequoyah. Hastings helped to write the constitution, which Congress rejected. In 1907 Oklahoma and the Indian Territory were combined and admitted to the Union, becoming the nation's forty-sixth state.

In 1912 Hastings was a delegate to the Oklahoma Democratic State Convention and to the Democratic National Convention in Baltimore, which nominated New Jersey governor Woodrow Wilson, whom Hastings supported, for the presidency. In 1914 Hastings was elected to the U.S. House of Representatives, where he served until 1921. He chaired the Committee on Expenditures in the Department of the Interior in the Sixty-fifth Congress. Unsuccessful in his bid for reelection in the Republican landslide of 1920, he recaptured his seat in 1922 and remained in the House until 1935.

Hastings distinguished himself as a capable legislator. For many years he was an important and active member of the Committee on Indian Affairs, where his background served him well. He was considered an authority on tribes in Oklahoma and the nation, and many in Congress turned to him for advice on Native American legislation. In 1925 his House Committee on Indian Affairs published a report regarding the administration of Native American affairs and the lives of Native Americans in Oklahoma. Hastings also served on the House Appropriations Committee.

In 1934 Congress passed the Indian Reorganization or Wheeler-Howard Act. Known as the "Indian New Deal," the act pledged to return to Native Americans all lands within reservation boundaries that remained unsold to whites. It also authorized an annual $2 million fund to purchase lands for tribes, individuals, and conservation programs. Under the act, tribes could organize for such purposes as economic development and limited self-government. Hastings and his Oklahoma House colleagues worked together to oppose the application of this law to their state, claiming that Native Americans in Oklahoma did not require protection. Aided by the Oklahoma press, Hastings succeeded through legislation in excluding Native Americans in Oklahoma from the main provisions of the act.

In 1934 Hastings chose not to seek reelection, preferring to resume his extensive law practice in Tahlequah and to pursue his banking and agricultural activities. In January 1936 he returned briefly to public life when President Franklin D. Roosevelt commissioned him chief of the Cherokees for one day to sign various legal papers. Hastings died in Muskogee, Oklahoma.

Hastings was a Native American who rose to a position of leadership among his people and gained national recognition. He championed federal protection of Native American property and promoted Native American day schools and formal education. He encouraged Native Americans to integrate fully into American society and not to accept a state of inferiority. Respected by both Native Americans and white citizens, Hastings was a forceful spokesman and firm advocate for the rights of his people.

• Hastings left no personal papers. His letters are scattered in the manuscript collections of his contemporaries, including some in the Woodrow Wilson Papers in the Manuscripts Division of the Library of Congress. His speeches are in the *Congressional Record* from 1915 to 1921 and from 1923 to 1935. Additional information on his career is in Angie Debo, *And Still the Waters Run* (1940); Harry F. O'Beirne and E. S. O'Beirne, *The Indian Territory: Its Chiefs, Legislators, and Leading Men* (1892); *Biographical Dictionary of Indians of the Americas* (2 vols., 1983); Luther B. Hill, *A History of the State of Oklahoma* (2 vols., 1908); Amos Maxwell, *The Sequoyah Constitutional Convention* (1953); Emmet Starr, *History of the Cherokee Indians and Their Legends and Folk Lore* (1921); and William P. Thompson, "W. W. Hastings," *Chronicles of Oklahoma* 18 (1938): 269–70. Obituaries are in the *New York Times*, 9 Apr. 1938, and the Oklahoma City *Daily Oklahoman*, 10 Apr. 1938.

LEONARD SCHLUP

HATATHLI, Ned (11 Oct. 1923–16 Oct. 1973), Navajo leader and educator, was born in Coalmine Mesa, Arizona, on the Navajo reservation. His parents' names are not available, but they probably herded sheep and farmed. Hatathli was one of ten children, and he was reared in a traditional Navajo family of this time. Hatathli grew up near the western Navajo settlement of Tuba City, Arizona. In common with most Navajo children of this period, he helped herd the livestock of his parents and extended family and probably imagined himself living a life comparable to that of his older relatives. Unlike many children of this time, however, he was encouraged by one of those relatives to go to school. The heavy-handed assimilation of Bureau of Indian Affairs schools—denying the use of the Navajo language and discouraging other dimensions of the people's culture—had reduced enrollment. Even though Hatathli began his education at a boarding school, he came of age in the 1930s, when changing BIA philosophies fostered a greater degree of cultural pluralism, including more appreciation for Indian languages and arts. Hatathli eventually attended Haskell Institute, a prominent bureau school in Lawrence, Kansas, and then served in the U.S. Navy before returning home to northern Arizona. In the town of Flagstaff, bordering the Navajo reservation, he attended and graduated from Arizona State Teachers College, known today as Northern Arizona University.

In 1940 the Navajo tribe had established an arts and craft guild, prompted by the encouragement of the national Indian arts and crafts board, established during the days of the Indian New Deal. The guild was run initially by a young anthropologist, John Adair, who had come to Navajo country to learn more about silversmithing and who later wrote an authoritative account on the subject. Adair trained Hatathli to take his place. When the Navajo tribe made the guild into an official tribal enterprise, with full support and recognition from the tribal government, Hatathli served as a key force in the operation's crucial first years in the Navajo capital of Window Rock, Arizona. Hatathli helped encourage more effective marketing of Navajo weaving and silversmithing and pushed for continuing improvement in the rugs and silver work.

He assumed his next post in 1955 as an elected member of the Navajo Tribal Council. A young man by the political standards of the community, Hatathli gained election from his home community because of his obvious skills in English and Navajo and his dedication to the well-being of the tribe. Although elected to serve that community, Hatathli quickly emerged as a leader with concerns for the entire Navajo nation, particularly in the area of economic development. Federal funds through the recently passed Navajo-Hopi Rehabilitation Act of 1950 allowed for the building of needed roads, school construction, and other improvements. Based on his earlier experience with another tribal enterprise, Hatathli was among those who advocated using this approach to take advantage of the considerable timber resources of the Navajos. The Tribal Council voted to establish the Navajo Forest Products Industries and in 1960 a new management board was appointed to take over operation of the tribal sawmill and to expand into new aspects of the lumber industry. Hatathli was one of eight people chosen for the board.

In the 1960s Hatathli's attention turned to education. He played a vital role in the establishment and development of the Rough Rock Demonstration School. As the treasurer of the school, Hatathli offered his voice toward the growing efforts by Navajos to take control of their own education. At the time of the founding of Rough Rock School in 1966, many children still attended BIA schools or mission schools. A growing number went to public schools, but those institutions were governed by school boards dominated by non-Indians who rarely had much interest in Navajo history and culture. Rough Rock was a contract school—a newly constructed campus that the BIA agreed to contract to the community. In this isolated locale, more than thirty miles from the town of Chinle, Arizona, Rough Rock took advantage of community interest and the commitment of three prominent Navajos from outside the community (Guy Gorman, Ned Hatathli, and Allen Yazzie). The three men formed a corporation, Demonstration in Navajo Education (or DINE, the acronym standing for the word the Navajos call themselves in their own language), and contracted with the federal government for the local school board in order to obtain the facility.

Two years later, the Navajo tribe established its own college, Navajo Community College. Hatathli was a natural choice to help in its initial development. Sharing the campus of the BIA boarding high school in Many Farms, Arizona, while a permanent campus was being built in Tsaile, Arizona, the college tried to incorporate the study of Navajo language, history, and culture as a central feature of its curriculum. As executive vice president, Hatathli supported such initiatives. Robert Roessel, a non-Navajo married to a Navajo, served as the college's first president but, as he had at Rough Rock, quickly stepped aside so a member of the tribe could assume the top administrative position. Hatathli became president in 1969 and remained in this capacity until his death in Many Farms from an accidental gunshot wound. During his tenure as president he continued to speak to the college's importance as an example of Indian control over Indian education. In a statement for the 1970–1971 college catalog, he said that Navajo Community College's "view of education is derived from the realities of Indian life. Its course of instruction opens the world of ideas and opportunities to Indians. Most importantly, the policy direction and guidance for the College is Navajo Indian because the members of the Board of Regents are selected by the Navajo Tribal Government and people." He concluded, "We can join forces for economic and social betterment of all Indian people through education of our own choosing." In 1993 Navajo Community College celebrated its twenty-fifth anniversary, as hundreds of students were enrolled at its main campuses in Tsaile, Arizona, and Shiprock, New Mexico, as well as in centers in other sites, including Tuba City and Ganado, Arizona, and Crownpoint, New Mexico. The more than two dozen colleges on Indian reservations serve the needs of local communities and offer hope and opportunity otherwise unavailable to their students. Together with Navajo Community College they exemplify Ned Hatathli's commitment to Indian self-determination.

• Information about Ned Hatathli may be found in Frederick J. Dockstadter, *Great North American Indians* (1977); "The Indian Achievement Award of the Indian Council Fire," published by the Indian Council Fire of Chicago (1982); Peter Iverson, *The Navajo Nation* (1981); Laura Gilpin, *The Enduring Navaho* (1968); and issues of the *Navajo Times*, the newspaper of the Navajo nation.

PETER IVERSON

HATCH, Alfrederick Smith (24 July 1829–13 May 1904), financier, was born in Norwich, Vermont, the son of Horace Hatch, a physician, and Mary Smith. He received a "fair education" (his own description) and at the age of twenty was advised to go to sea to "relieve an asthmatic affection of the lungs." He traveled to New York, where he signed on board *The New World* as a seaman under Captain Ebenezer Knight. In 1849 and 1850 Hatch made two round-trip voyages on the New York–Liverpool route. His experiences are narrated in lively detail in his unpublished autobiographical memoir titled "Sailor Jack" (c. 1890).

Soon after Hatch's return to the United States in 1850, he began to work as a bookkeeper at the City Bank in New Haven, Connecticut. In 1854 he married Theodosia Ruggles; they had eleven children.

In 1856 Hatch moved to Jersey City, New Jersey, to become cashier of the recently founded Bank of Jersey City. In Jersey City he actively supported the abolitionist cause through his membership in a Congregationalist church, the Tabernacle, and as an organizer of the New England Society of Jersey City.

On 12 March 1862 Hatch entered into partnership with Harvey Fisk to found the banking firm of Fisk & Hatch, located at 38 Wall Street in Manhattan with capital of $15,000 borrowed from family members and friends, including L. E. Chittenden, the register of the U.S. Treasury. On 9 May 1864 the firm moved to larger quarters at 5 Nassau Street. Over a period of three years the business generated profits of more than $400,000, half of which was paid to the investors. At this point, Fisk & Hatch reorganized the firm, with themselves as sole equal partners, using their own capital of $250,000.

The primary business of Fisk & Hatch during the Civil War years was dealing in U.S. government bonds, which were an essential source of financing for the war effort. In addition to their youth and energy, the partners brought to the task an ardent belief in the Union cause. At a time when many banking firms were reluctant to take responsibility for government bond issues, Fisk & Hatch sold hundreds of millions of dollars' worth of bonds. Salmon P. Chase, secretary of the treasury under President Abraham Lincoln, had appointed Jay Cooke as a special agent for the sale of bonds; Cooke in turn appointed Fisk & Hatch, among others, as subagents for New York and New England. Chase referred to Hatch as "one in ten thousand fitted for leadership" and praised his "clear head" and "courageous candor." At one point, some southern sympathizers notified Fisk and Hatch that if they did not stop their activity, "their lives would be in danger." In response, the partners decorated their offices with bunting, inside and out, and sold bonds with even greater determination, using every means available including extensive advertising campaigns.

Toward the end of the war, Fisk & Hatch began to deal extensively in bonds of the Union Pacific and Central Pacific railroads, which were completed in 1869. Fisk & Hatch also became fiscal agent for the Chesapeake & Ohio Railroad, led by Collis P. Huntington and others. However, the firm suffered in the panic of 1873—known as the "Jay Cooke panic" because it had been precipitated by the failure of the Northern Pacific Railroad, which Cooke had been financing. In the wake of this collapse, Fisk & Hatch in 1873 suspended payments; however, they were able to pay off their debts, and after a three-month period of suspension of payments, they reopened their doors. But their business continued on a considerably smaller scale. In 1879 they began to make up lost ground by marketing a new refunding issue of U.S. government bonds. The firm continued in this line of business into the early 1880s. Hatch was elected president from 1883 to 1884 of the New York Stock Exchange, of which he had long been a member.

In May 1884 another financial crisis erupted, following the failures of several banks, including Ulysses S. Grant's firm, Grant & Ward. Fisk and Hatch were again compelled to suspend payment and to find means to satisfy their creditors. They achieved this goal but nevertheless decided to liquidate the firm, and in March 1885 the partnership was dissolved. In its place two new firms were founded: Harvey Fisk & Sons and A. S. Hatch & Company. Hatch's firm soon closed, and he devoted the rest of his life to philanthropic activity at such institutions as the Howard Mission and Home for Little Wanderers (an orphanage and children's aid society founded in 1864) and the Jerry McAuley Water-Street Mission (established in 1872 with the assistance of Hatch, who had long been a temperance advocate and had taken a keen interest in social rehabilitation).

Hatch died at Tarrytown, New York, where, from 1880 to 1888 he had lived in a massive, medieval-style crenelated stone villa designed by Alexander Jackson Davis and known as "The Castle" (originally called "Ericstan," 1855). Hatch had earlier lived in Manhattan in a townhouse at 49 Park Avenue, where the parlor filled with the entire family—fifteen figures in all—was depicted by Eastman Johnson in a painting titled *The Hatch Family* (1870).

In the course of Hatch's more than three decades as a banker, he faced several crises during the turbulent post–Civil War period. However, he was always able to repay his debts and to retain the confidence of important customers, such as the Astors, the Vanderbilts, members of Standard Oil, Hetty Green, Peter Cooper, and William R. Travers. He maintained cordial relations with fellow bankers, especially J. P. Morgan; he also had important relations with European banks such as L. Speyer-Ellisen & Company of Frankfurt am Main. Hatch's most notable achievement, which brought him nationwide fame, was his major fundraising for the Union during the Civil War—work that he accomplished at considerable financial and personal risk and with energy, courage, and dedication.

• A collection of material relating to Hatch is in the archives of the New York Stock Exchange, and documents referring to him are in the archives of the Jerry McAuley Mission; see also the extensively illustrated book (with interesting details about Hatch) by Arthur Bonner, *Jerry McAuley and His Mission* (1967; rev. ed., 1990). A copy of Hatch's "Sailor Jack" is in the Francis J. Sypher Collection at the Rare Book and Manuscript Library of Columbia University. Numerous sources of information about him exist, especially in newspaper articles, including a fiftieth wedding anniversary article, with extensive biographical and genealogical information, that appeared in the *Tarrytown Argus*, 7 May 1904, and an information-filled local history article (illustrated) by William

H. Richardson, "New England's Part in Making Jersey City," in the (Jersey City) *Jersey Journal*, 1 Aug. 1916. Generations of Hatch family financial figures are profiled in Henry Alloway, "Of Wall Street's Hall-Mark Names," *Wall Street Journal*, 16 May 1930, reprinted as "Name of A. S. Hatch Has High Place in Wall St. Hall of Fame," in the *Greenwich (Conn.) Press*, 19 June 1930. The family portrait by Eastman Johnson is in the Metropolitan Museum of Art in New York City. See also the valuable, authoritative article by Harvey E. Fisk, "Fisk & Hatch, Bankers and Dealers in Government Securities 1862–1885," *Journal of Economic and Business History* 2, no. 4 (Aug. 1930): 706–22. On Hatch's historic house in Tarrytown, see John Zukowsky and Robbe Pierce Stimson, *Hudson River Villas* (1986). *The National Union Catalogue, Pre-1956 Imprints*, lists under the heading "Fisk firm" numerous financial brochures published by the firm. On Harvey Fisk, see *Letters of Harvey Fisk, with an Introductory Memoir*, ed. Harvey Edward Fisk (his son), with a genealogical sketch (1896). An obituary is in the *New York Times*, 14 May 1904.

F. J. SYPHER

HATCH, Carl Atwood (27 Nov. 1889–15 Sept. 1963), U.S. senator, was born in Kirwan, Kansas, the son of Harley Atwood Hatch and Esther Shannon Ryan, Kansas pioneers. The family moved in 1900 to Eldorado, Oklahoma, a booming railroad town, where his father ran a country store. After finishing high school, Hatch worked for the weekly *Eldorado Courier*, which he and a friend later purchased. Deciding to study law, he went to Cumberland University at Lebanon, Tennessee. After graduation in 1912 he was admitted to the bar. In September 1913 he married Winifred Ruth Caviness; they had two children.

In 1916 he moved to Clovis, New Mexico, to further his law practice. A Democrat, between 1917 and 1919 he served as assistant state attorney general, and then as collector of internal revenue for the district of New Mexico, as a state district judge, a post to which he was elected in 1924, as chairman of the Democratic State Central Committee (1930), and as a presidential elector (1932). On 10 October 1933 Governor A. W. Hockenhull appointed him to the U.S. Senate to fill a vacancy caused by the resignation of Sam G. Bratton. In November 1934 Hatch was elected to serve the remainder of Bratton's term. He was elected again in 1936 and 1942, but did not seek reelection in 1948. President Harry S. Truman then appointed him a federal district judge in New Mexico, a post he filled until pulmonary emphysema led him to retire in May 1963.

Hatch was best known nationally for his efforts to improve the status of partisan politics. The Hatch Acts of 1939 and 1940 regulated campaign contributions and political expenditures. The first barred all but top-level federal officials from political activity and prohibited, among other things, solicitation of funds from federal employees. The second extended these provisions to state and local employees whose salaries were derived in part from federal funds. An additional amendment limited the annual expenditure of the national committee of any party to $3 million and individual contributions to $5,000. The laws proved to be full of loopholes and often ignored. In 1946 Hatch said they were a failure and should be abandoned. In their place he called for full publicity of campaign expenditures.

As a senator, Hatch, an ardent New Dealer, was active in the interests of agriculture, conservation, and labor legislation, advocating compulsory arbitration in key industries. He was a staunch defender of trade reciprocity, and after World War II he was a leading spokesman for legislation pertaining to the preservation of peace. In 1943 he co-sponsored a Senate resolution calling for a United Nations organization.

Possessed of a pleasing personality and reluctant to question a colleague's motives or to hurt his feelings, he was at times called "Smiling Carl." Hatch was a Methodist, a 32nd degree Mason, a Noble of the Order of the Mystic Shrine, and a member of the Knights Templar. When the Senate and later the district court were not in session, he attended to his ranch and grain farm near Clovis. Hatch died in Albuquerque.

• There is no known collection of Hatch's papers. The Carl Albert Center at the University of Oklahoma has three volumes which contain a history of legislation introduced by Hatch while in the Senate. There are Hatch letters in collections at both the Franklin D. Roosevelt and Harry S. Truman Presidential Libraries. See also David Porter, "Senator Carl Hatch and the Hatch Act of 1939," *New Mexico Historical Review* 48 (1973): 151–61. Eulogies and obituary notices can be found in the *Congressional Record*: 88th Congress, 1st Session, pp. 1701–02, 17347, 17824–25, and in the Appendix volume for this session, p. A5881.

RICHARD LOWITT

HATCH, Edward (23 Dec. 1832–11 Apr. 1889), soldier, was born in Bangor, Maine, the son of Nathaniel Hatch and Mary Elizabeth Scott. In his early youth he served as a merchant seaman. In 1855 he moved to Muscatine, Iowa, where he engaged in the lumber business. With the outbreak of the Civil War, Hatch enlisted in the Second Iowa Cavalry and on 12 August 1861 was appointed as a company captain. Rising rapidly in rank, on 13 June 1862 he was promoted to colonel commanding the regiment.

Hatch earned a reputation for clear judgment and cold courage in combat actions along the Mississippi-Tennessee border. In April 1863 the Second Iowa formed part of Colonel Benjamin Grierson's brigade that launched a large-scale raid through the heart of Mississippi to divert Confederate attention from General Ulysses S. Grant's operations south of Vicksburg. The raid succeeded beyond expectations, and no small part of that success was attributable to Hatch and his command. Ordered by Grierson to move eastward and attack stations along the Mobile and Ohio Railroad so as to disguise Grierson's true intentions, Hatch reached the railroad and then fought a skillful and destructive withdrawal to the safety of Union lines at La Grange, Tennessee. Important to Hatch's future, his friend Grierson was promoted to brigadier general as a result of the raid.

Hatch led small-scale operations against Confederate raiders into Tennessee during the later months of 1863, and on 3 December, while engaged in an action near Moscow, he was shot through the lungs. The wound was first thought to be fatal, but he recovered and recuperated as commander of the St. Louis M Missouri cavalry depot.

On his return to active duty in the spring of 1864, Hatch was promoted to brigadier general not only on his past record but also on a strong recommendation from General Grierson. Hatch was assigned command of a division in the Cavalry Corps in Tennessee under Major General James H. Wilson. After the battles of Franklin (30 Nov. 1864) and Nashville (15–16 Dec. 1864), Hatch received high praise from Wilson for outstanding leadership of his division. Hatch closed out his Civil War career at the rank of major general of volunteers.

Remaining in the army, in July 1866 Hatch was appointed colonel of the Ninth Cavalry, an all-black regiment with white officers. He organized his new command at Greenville, Louisiana, in the fall and spring of 1866–1867 and in May was ordered to Texas. By midsummer of 1867 Hatch had established headquarters at Fort Stockton, and he began the work of trying to bring peace and order to hundreds of miles of frontier, where conditions bordered on anarchy. For eight years Hatch and his troopers strove to accomplish this formidable task and did achieve modest success. In September 1875 the Ninth was transferred to the District of New Mexico.

If Hatch expected some relief from his trying service in Texas, he was doomed to disappointment. New Mexico Territory presented daunting challenges to any military commander. Hatch was confronted with serious civil strife, notably the El Paso Salt War in the winter of 1877 and the Lincoln County War in the summer of 1878. In the former, quarrels over the use of salt deposits near El Paso led to rioting and bloodshed. Texas officials asked for federal assistance, and Hatch marched to the scene with three battalions of his regiment. In a matter of hours he had dispersed the rioters and restored peace and order. In Lincoln County the overzealous and partisan lieutenant colonel of the Ninth, N. A. M. Dudley, intervened in the conflict and brought strong criticism to the regiment. Hatch's efforts to relieve Dudley came to naught because Dudley had powerful friends in Washington, D.C.

By all odds, however, the most formidable challenge faced by Hatch was the seemingly interminable Apache wars, which reached a peak in 1879–1880 with the outbreak of the Victorio War. In August 1879 Victorio and his Warm Springs Apaches broke from their reservation at Fort Stanton and launched a yearlong nightmare for the Ninth. Despite near continuous skirmishes, ambushes, and pursuits, Hatch was unable to bring Victorio to bay and was the object of bitter criticism in the New Mexico press.

In 1881 the Ninth was ordered to stations in Kansas and Indian Territory, with headquarters at Fort Riley,

Kansas. The move was supposed to give the regiment a rest after years of arduous duty, but Hatch was soon involved in removing aggressive "Boomers" who entered Indian Territory illegally, trying to settle there. Though temporarily successful, it proved to be a thankless and unpopular task.

Hatch died at Fort Robinson, Nebraska, from injuries incurred when the carriage in which he was riding overturned. He was an outstanding leader of cavalry during the Civil War, but his long career on the western frontier was characterized more by frustration and lack of accomplishment. In large measure, however, the persistent prejudice that dogged him and his black troopers denied him recognition for his devotion to duty and tireless efforts to solve the problems that confronted him.

• There is no biography of Hatch and little in the way of collections of papers or private correspondence. One must rely almost entirely on official records to piece together his long military career. Some useful information can be found in a small file on Hatch in the Iowa State Historical Society, Iowa City. Of some use also is Clarence C. Buel and Robert U. Johnson, eds., *Battles and Leaders of the Civil War*, vols. 3 and 4 (repr. 1983). For Hatch's role in Grierson's raid see D. Alexander Brown, *Grierson's Raid* (1954). Hatch's western career is detailed in William H. Leckie, *The Buffalo Soldiers* (1967).

WILLIAM H. LECKIE

HATCH, William Henry (11 Sept. 1833–23 Dec. 1896), congressman and agricultural reformer, was born near Georgetown in Scott County, Kentucky, the son of Reverend William Hatch, a Campbellite minister, and Mary Adams. Educated in the public schools of Lexington, Hatch studied law for a year in Richmond, Kentucky, before securing admission to the bar in September 1854. He began his legal practice in Harrodsburg, Kentucky, but shortly thereafter he joined the stream of migration from Kentucky to Missouri and settled in Hannibal, where he practiced law and became active in politics as a Democrat. In 1855 he married Jennie L. Smith; they had one child before Jennie died in 1858. In 1861 he married Thetis Clay Hawkins; they had one child.

Hatch won election in 1858 as circuit attorney for the Sixteenth Judicial District and was reelected in 1860. In the presidential election of 1860 he supported the Constitutional Union ticket, although his sentiments clearly lay with the cause of "southern rights." By 1862, when Hatch could not meet the requirements of the Missouri loyalty oath, he was removed from office. Notwithstanding his father's New England antecedents (his father was a native of Exeter, N.H., and a graduate of Bowdoin College), Hatch left Missouri to join the Confederate army.

In December 1862 Hatch was commissioned captain and appointed assistant adjutant general in the Confederate army, eventually rising in rank to lieutenant colonel. In March 1863 he was assigned as assistant commissioner of prisoner exchanges under Colonel Robert Ould and served in this capacity at Richmond, Virginia, until the close of the war. Although prisoner exchanges had nearly emptied war prisons by the fall of 1862, they ended abruptly in the wake of the Emancipation Proclamation and the federal decision to enroll black troops. The Confederate government refused to recognize black soldiers or their white officers as prisoners of war and, instead, ordered them delivered to state authorities for punishment under the laws of slavery. Abraham Lincoln responded by halting prisoner exchanges. There matters stood from early 1863 until October 1864 when the Union and Confederate secretaries of the navy agreed to a prisoner exchange that included blacks as well as whites. During the winter of 1864–1865 Confederate exchanges of wounded and sick prisoners included both blacks and whites. Finally, in January 1865, when the Confederate government prepared to enlist black soldiers in the southern cause, it authorized Hatch's commission to include all prisoners in its procedures. The Federal government quickly accepted the new proposal, and in February and March 1865 the exchange of prisoners approached a thousand men a day.

Hatch returned to Hannibal after the war but found himself, like other former Confederates and Confederate sympathizers, barred from voting or holding political office. Known as "Colonel" Hatch by his Missouri supporters, he saw his political fortunes revive in the early 1870s, when Democrats in Missouri joined forces with Liberal Republicans to defeat the state's Radical Republicans. Hatch was a leading contender for (but did not receive) the Democratic party's nomination for governor in 1872. In 1878, however, he won election to the U.S. House of Representatives from Missouri's First District and held office for eight consecutive terms (1879–1895).

As a congressman and chairman of the House Committee on Agriculture, Hatch became widely known as a proponent of federal support for agricultural experiment stations, federal inspection of food products, and the elevation of the Department of Agriculture to cabinet rank in the executive branch of government. He took leading roles in the creation of the Bureau of Animal Industry (1884); in securing the passage of the first Oleomargarine Act (1886), requiring federal inspection; and in securing the passage of the Meat Inspection Act of 1890.

His most important legislative achievement came with the passage of the Hatch Act (1887), which provided $15,000 a year from public land sales to each state and territory for support of agricultural experiment stations. The federal money went to land-grant colleges except where state laws had created independent experiment station systems. For the rest of the century, the experiment stations became the principal source of information for the various bureaus, divisions, and sections of the Department of Agriculture, and they also received federal appropriations to study irrigation, nutrition, and a host of other agricultural subjects. The World's Columbian Exposition held in

Chicago in 1893 presented the first display of the work of the stations.

Hatch had expected to be named secretary of the Department of Agriculture when it achieved cabinet status in 1889. President Grover Cleveland's decision to pass over the congressman in selecting the first secretary of agriculture and Hatch's failed bid for Speaker of the House marked the beginning of a rapid decline in power.

Hatch's declining political fortune coincided with his growing reputation as a Populist-leaning Democrat. Of particular significance in this regard was his support for legislation designed to curb speculation in agricultural commodities. These legislative efforts all met with failure, but they brought aspects of the Populist crusade to the floor of Congress. In February 1888, for example, Hatch introduced "a Bill to prohibit fictitious and gambling transactions on the price of articles produced by American Farm Industries." Hatch intended to prohibit financial transactions not based on the actual delivery of agricultural goods and thereby to make illegal the trade in agricultural goods for future delivery. Specifically, he hoped to stop the speculative practice of "selling short." His proposed legislation became known as the Anti-Option Bill, and it attracted the sustained opposition of grain merchants and commodity traders, including the St. Louis Merchants' Exchange Commission, which kept close watch on the bill into the spring of 1894. Hatch believed that selling short depressed agricultural markets and hurt farmers. Hatch lost his congressional seat to a Republican in 1894 and retired to his 150-acre family farm near Hannibal, where he died.

• The William H. Hatch Papers and the Clarence Cannon Papers, Western Historical Manuscripts Collection of the University of Missouri, and the George Washington Atherton Papers, Pennsylvania State University Libraries, contain some letters written by Hatch as well as miscellaneous materials relating to the Hatch Act.

Hatch's Anti-Option Bill is analyzed in Chas. F. Orthwein to Hon. Wm. H. Hatch, copy of letter, 10 May 1888, and Merchants' Exchange of St. Louis to the Honorable Senators and Representatives of the State of Missouri, copy of letter, 9 Apr. 1895, St. Louis Merchants' Exchange Commission Collection, Missouri Historical Society, St. Louis. Two printed speeches expressed Hatch's Populist leanings: *The Farmer's Movement . . .* (1891) and *Free Coinage of Both Gold and Silver . . .* (n.d.).

For Hatch's ancestry and early life see Walter Williams, ed., *A History of Northeast Missouri* (1913), pp. 2077–79. The Civil War prisoner exchange cartel is treated in James M. McPherson, *Ordeal by Fire: The Civil War and Reconstruction*, 2d ed. (1992), pp. 451–56. On the Hatch Act as agricultural reform see Fred A. Shannon, *The Farmer's Last Frontier: Agriculture, 1860–1897* (1945), pp. 280–81; and Roger Williams, *The Origins of Federal Support for Higher Education: George W. Atherton and the Land-Grant College Movement* (1991), pp. 87–122.

LOUIS GERTEIS

HATCHER, Robert Anthony (6 Feb. 1868–1 Apr. 1944), pharmacologist, was born in New Madrid, Missouri, the son of Richard Hardaway Hatcher, an attor-

ney, and Harriet Hinton Marr. The family had lost much in the Civil War, so Robert was raised in the home of his uncle Robert Marr, a prominent judge. He developed an interest in pharmacy and attended the Philadelphia College of Pharmacy, where he received his graduate in pharmacy degree in 1889. After spending five years working in a pharmacy in New Orleans, Hatcher enrolled in the Tulane University Medical School, where he obtained his M.D. in 1898. In 1899 he accepted a position teaching materia medica at the Cleveland School of Pharmacy.

At the turn of the twentieth century, the traditional didactic subject of materia medica was beginning to be transformed in the United States into modern experimental pharmacology. Materia medica emphasized the natural history, appearance, constituents, and traditional therapeutic uses of crude drugs, whereas the science of pharmacology was based on the development of an understanding of the physiological action of drugs, largely through animal experimentation. Modern pharmacology was established as an independent discipline in Europe in the nineteenth century. John Jacob Abel, the founder of American pharmacology, had brought the new science from Europe to the United States in 1890, when he was appointed to the faculty of the University of Michigan.

When Hatcher accepted a position as a demonstrator in pharmacology at the Western Reserve University School of Medicine in 1900, he came under the influence of another important founder of American pharmacology, Torald Sollmann. He worked with Sollmann for four years, becoming well versed in the methods of experimental pharmacology. Together, they authored *A Textbook of Materia Medica* (1904).

In 1904 Hatcher was appointed instructor in materia medica and therapeutics at the Cornell University Medical College in New York. In that same year he married May Quinn Burton; they had one child. Upon the retirement of the professor of materia medica and therapeutics in 1908, Hatcher was made professor and head of the department, which was renamed pharmacology and materia medica in recognition of the new science of experimental pharmacology that Hatcher espoused. In 1921 the term "materia medica" was finally dropped from the name of the department.

As a research scientist, Hatcher is best known for his investigations on digitalis. His studies on the bioassay, absorption, elimination, and mechanism of action of crude and purified preparations of digitalis helped make possible the safe and routine use of this drug in heart disease. In this connection, his role in the development of the Hatcher-Brody cat unit of digitalis leaf (the dose per kilogram of body weight required to arrest the heart of a decerebrated cat) was especially important in establishing an accurate, safe, and effective dosage of the drug.

Hatcher's other major research contribution involved the study of emesis (vomiting). Although a common symptom of many diseases, the process of emesis had attracted little attention from scientists. Hatcher's research helped to elucidate the complex paths of the vomiting reflex arc, the location and nature of the vomiting center, and the mechanism of action of drugs that stimulate emesis.

Hatcher also played a significant role in the promotion of clinical pharmacology, involving research on the effects of drugs on humans, as a field in the United States. His influence in this area was exerted especially through his students, upon whom he impressed the importance of studying the action of drugs, including their distribution and elimination, in humans. For Hatcher, the ultimate goal of experimental pharmacology was to provide a rational basis for drug therapy. One of his most important students, Harry Gold, was important in the design of modern clinical testing for drugs and has sometimes been referred to as the "father of clinical pharmacology." Other noted students of Hatcher include Cary Eggleston, an important contributor to knowledge on the clinical pharmacology of cardiac drugs; Janet Travell, the first woman to serve as personal physician to a president (John F. Kennedy); and Soma Weiss, a pioneer in the use of radioactive tracers in biomedicine.

Hatcher's commitment to improving drug therapy was also reflected in his long service on the Council of Pharmacy and Chemistry of the American Medical Association (AMA), which had been created in 1905 to investigate the composition and standing of proprietary medicines. The council made recommendations, for example, as to whether certain proprietary medicines deserved the patronage of physicians and pharmacists, and whether the AMA's journal should accept advertising for these products. Hatcher was an active member of the council from its establishment until 1943. For many years he was also one of the editors of its publication, *Useful Drugs*. Hatcher also served as chairman of the AMA's section on pharmacology and therapeutics in 1915–1916. In 1934 he was elected president of the American Society for Pharmacology and Therapeutics, an organization he had helped found in 1908.

Hatcher was a dedicated teacher who encouraged student participation in the classroom and the laboratory. He was a devout Presbyterian and showed little interest in social activities. His work consumed much of his life, and his chief recreation was reading history, biography, science, and the classics. He was politically conservative but rejected prejudice, judging individuals on merit and employing a staff of diverse origins.

During the last years of his life, Hatcher's activities were limited by heart disease, which ultimately resulted in his death at his home in Flushing, New York. His principal significance in American science was as one of the founders of the field of experimental pharmacology in the United States, through his contributions to drug research, training of future pharmacologists, and service to professional organizations.

• Biographical articles on Hatcher include Harry Gold, "Robert Anthony Hatcher (1868–1944)," *Journal of Clinical Pharmacology and New Drugs* 11 (1971): 245–48, and Theodore Koppanyi, "Robert Anthony Hatcher (1868–1944)," *Science* 99 (1944): 420–21. See also Martin Kaufman et al., eds., *Dictionary of American Medical Biography*, vol. 1 (1984), p. 334. For his contributions to the Council on Pharmacy and Chemistry of the AMA, see the statement by the council in the *Journal of the American Medical Association* 125 (1944): 911. An obituary is in the *New York Times*, 2 Apr. 1944.

JOHN PARASCANDOLA

HATCHER, William Eldridge (25 July 1834–24 Aug. 1912), minister, editor, and author, was born in Bedford County, Virginia, near the Peaks of Otter, the son of Henry Hatcher and Mary Latham, farmers. His mother was a close relative of General Nathanael Greene, principal foe of British general Cornwallis in Georgia and South Carolina campaigns of the revolutionary war. She died on William's fourth birthday. Henry Hatcher's family in America extended back to seventeenth-century Virginia, where another William Hatcher had served in the Virginia House of Burgesses.

Young William attended several local schools in the Bedford area, finishing this stage of his education at age seventeen. In 1854, after teaching school for three years, he entered Richmond College (later the University of Richmond), from which he was graduated in 1858 with the bachelor of arts degree. While in college he led a religious revival that resulted in the conversion of many students. With two other students he also founded the Philologian Literary Society. Having been converted earlier at the Mt. Hermon Baptist Church in Bedford County and baptized in Otter Creek, he was ordained into the ministry at Mt. Hermon in the summer of 1857 while still a student at Richmond College.

Immediately upon graduation from college, Hatcher was called to pastor the Baptist church in Manchester, Virginia. During his nine-year pastorate, in 1864, he married Oranie Virginia Snead, with whom he would have nine children. In 1868, after serving for a year at the Franklin Square Baptist Church in Baltimore, Hatcher returned to his native state to become pastor of the First Baptist Church in Petersburg. After a seven-year ministry there, in 1875 he assumed his final pastorate at the Grace Street Baptist Church in Richmond, where he remained until 1901. Under his leadership the church built two new facilities, greatly increased its membership, sent out ten new ministers, and established four new churches.

In the pulpit Hatcher was "a man of commanding presence and great versatility." Called the "Great Baptist Commoner," he was a gifted preacher who appealed to the masses. His special appeal to so many people through his sermons appears to have been due to his reasoned, conversational style that did not depend on emotional outbursts. His warm personality contributed both to his popularity as an inspirational speaker and to his reputation as a gifted leader of boys. Hatcher's theology was consistent with historical, conservative Baptist beliefs, including the sovereignty of God, the deity of Jesus Christ, personal sin, and the necessity of individual salvation.

Hatcher maintained a variety of activities during his pastoral career. Along with being acclaimed "the greatest platform master of his time in Virginia," he held the top position in the Baptist denomination in Virginia. In addition to being one of the most powerful influences in the Southern Baptist Convention, he also was highly regarded as a speaker at Baptist meetings in the North. Although undoubtedly among the elite within Baptist circles, he maintained a common touch, helping weaker and more needy churches raise money to pay debts or build new edifices.

The high regard in which Hatcher was held by his peers is indicated by his many elected positions of leadership. He served on the board of trustees of Richmond College for forty-two years, from 1870 until his death; from 1897 to 1908 he was board president. The enlarging of the college and the relocation of its campus to its present site were accomplished largely under his influence. As president of the education board of the Baptist General Association of Virginia from 1875 to 1901, he worked to provide financial assistance to ministerial students of the state who were attending Richmond College or the Southern Baptist Theological Seminary. He was a trustee of the Seminary as well as president of the board of trustees of the Woman's College of Richmond from 1892 to 1893. He also served as president of the board of trustees of the Virginia Baptist Orphanage. After resigning the pastorate of Grace Street Baptist Church in 1901, he founded the Fork Union Academy (later the Fork Union Military Academy) and served for some time as president of its board of trustees.

Hatcher's leadership among Southern Baptists was established also through his editing and writing. From 1882 to 1885 he was junior editor of the *Religious Herald* and in his later years was a regular contributor to this paper. For many years he was editor of the *Baltimore Baptist* and the *Baptist Argus* and wrote for the *Baptist World*. He was the author of *Sketch of the Life and Writings of A. B. Brown* (1886), *Life of J. B. Jeter* (1887), *The Pastor and the Sunday School* (1902), *John Jasper* (1908), and his autobiography, *Along the Trail of the Friendly Years* (1910).

Hatcher died at the home he kept in his later years, "Careby Hall," at Fork Union, Virginia. Following funeral services at Fork Union Academy and at Grace Street Baptist Church, he was buried at Hollywood Cemetery in Richmond.

• Minutes of the Baptist General Association of Virginia and other accounts of Hatcher's denominational leadership are available through the Virginia Baptist Historical Society at the University of Richmond. Probably the most informative look at his life is *Wm. E. Hatcher* (1915), written by his son Eldridge B. Hatcher, a Baptist minister. Additional information about his life is available in M. D. Ackerley and L. E. J. Parker, *"Our Kin": The Geneals. of Some of the Early Families who Made History in the Founding and Development of Bedford County, Va.* (1930). Issues of the *Religious Herald* and the *Richmond Times-Dispatch* from the period 1858 to 1912 contain accounts of Hatcher's activities and travels.

ROBERT R. MATHISEN

HATFIELD, Devil Anse. *See* Hatfield, William Anderson.

HATFIELD, Edwin Francis (9 Jan. 1807–22 Sept. 1883), Presbyterian pastor, writer, hymnologist, and national church official, was born in Elizabethtown, New Jersey, the son of Oliver S. Hatfield and Jane Mann. Young Hatfield made his public profession of faith on 25 March 1827 at New York City's Central Presbyterian Church. He graduated from Middlebury College in 1829. He studied theology at Andover Theological Seminary from 1829 to 1831, and on 6 October 1831 the Third Presbytery of New York licensed him to preach. Hatfield served as assistant to Barnabas Kind in Rockaway, New Jersey, from October 1831 to February 1832, and assisted Asa R. Hillyer in Orange, New Jersey, from March to September 1832. The Third Presbytery of New York ordained Hatfield on 14 May 1832, and he served as pastor of the Second Presbyterian Church in St. Louis, Missouri, from October 1832 to February 1835. In July 1835 he became the second pastor of New York's Seventh Presbyterian Church; he was formally installed on 2 March 1836 and served there until February 1856. During his 21-year tenure he became known as a "preacher of deep spiritual earnestness and power," and more than 2,200 new members joined his congregation. He was released from duties at Seventh Church on 4 February 1856 and installed 13 February as pastor of New York City's North Presbyterian Church, where he served until poor health forced his early retirement in October 1863.

Hatfield married Mary E. Taylor on 27 April 1837. They had two sons and three daughters.

Hatfield had an active career as an advocate for New York's Union Theological Seminary. A member of the seminary's board of directors for thirty-seven years, from 1846 until his death, he served as the board's recorder from 1864 to 1874. He emerged from retirement in 1864 to become a financial agent for the seminary and helped to raise $150,000 in the next year. He helped to raise an additional $300,000 from 1870 to 1872. In 1876 he prepared the *General Catalogue of Union Theological Seminary in the City of New York 1836–1876* and published it, together with his account of the seminary's first fifty years, *The Early Annals of the Union Theological Seminary in the City of New York* (1876). After his death Hatfield's children donated his 6,000-volume library to the seminary.

Concurrent with his pastoral work, Hatfield wrote and published several books. To help Presbyterian pastors fight the growing menace of universalism, he explained the movement's history and theological deficiencies in a series of seventeen articles, first published in the *New York Evangelist* and later revised and collected as *Universalism As It Is; or, Text Book of Modern Universalism in America* (1841). His *A Memoir of Elihu W. Baldwin, D.D.* (1843) recounted the life of the minister who preceded him as pastor of New York's Seventh Presbyterian Church. After the missionary James McGregor Bertram visited New York City in 1851, Hatfield told his story in *St. Helena and the Cape of Good Hope* (1852). Hatfield's ancestors were among the 1665 founders of Elizabeth, New Jersey, and after two years of research, he published the *History of Eliz-*

abeth, New Jersey: Including the Early History of Union County (1868). Several of his pamphlets were published in the Presbyterian Tract series, and many of his sermons were reprinted.

Hatfield was also a respected hymnologist. His pocket-sized abolitionist hymnal *Freedom's Lyre; or, Psalms, Hymns, and Sacred Songs, for the Slave and His Friends* (1840), undertaken, as his prefaces states, "at the request of the Executive Committee American Anti-Slavery Society," contained 291 freely edited or adapted hymns, psalms, and doxologies, including twenty-four original works by Hatfield. His monumental *The Church Hymn Book for the Worship of God* (1872), including ten of his own compositions among its 1,416 hymns, was one of the first hymnals to provide thoroughly researched annotations on the authorship and dates of the original texts and tunes. A year later, an abridged version with tunes was published as *The Chapel Hymn Book, with Tunes; for the Worship of God* (1873). The use of his hymnal and its abridged version rivaled that of the hymnals authorized by the general assembly of the Presbyterian church. Hatfield's *The Poets of the Church: A Series of Biographical Sketches of Hymn Writers* (1884) was edited and published posthumously by his son, J. B. Taylor Hatfield. Several decades later, the hymnologist Louis F. Benson hailed Hatfield as one of the earliest hymnologists of the Presbyterian church (*The English Hymn: Its Development and Use in Worship* [1915]).

Hatfield was best known, however, as an administrator and statesman of the Presbyterian church. He served as a stated clerk at regional and national levels of the denomination, assuming responsibility for minutes, records, and correspondence. He was elected stated clerk of the Third Presbytery of New York in October 1838 and served as the second stated clerk of the general assembly of the Presbyterian church (New School) from 23 May 1846, until its 1870 merger with the Presbyterian church (Old School). In 1847 Hatfield joined Presbyterians Robert Baird, Lyman Beecher, and others, to found the American Alliance, a short-lived ecumenical coalition adopting the abolitionist constitution of the Evangelical Alliance established in London in 1846. In 1849 he was instrumental in persuading the New School denomination to abandon its brief experiment with triennial general assemblies and return to annual assemblies. In 1866 he helped to reestablish an American chapter of the Evangelical Alliance. As the New School and Old School denominations began merger discussions in 1866, Hatfield became secretary of the Joint Committee on Reunion. He briefly acted as secretary of the Presbyterian Committee of Home Missions from May to October 1868, when he became secretary of the committee's Freedmen's Department. When the New School and Old School denominations merged in 1870, Hatfield was unanimously elected as the reunited church's stated clerk; he assumed the additional duties of the denomination's treasurer in 1871. That same year he was appointed to a committee to prepare a Presbyterian hymnal, but he resigned to publish his own hymnal. In 1875 he served on an unsuccessful delegation to improve relations with the (southern) Presbyterian church in the United States, and the general assembly named him as a founding delegate to the 1877 meeting of the Presbyterian Alliance in Edinburgh. When the general assembly met in Saratoga in May 1883, Hatfield was elected as moderator; he died a few months later at his home in Summit, New Jersey. That same year the Seventh Presbyterian Church purchased a building on Ridge Street adjacent to their church and converted it to a men's hotel, renamed "Hatfield House" in honor of their former pastor.

• The Presbyterian Historical Society in Philadelphia contains some of Hatfield's papers and correspondence, and the New York Genealogical and Biographical Society has his research notes. Papers concerning Hatfield and the Third Presbytery of New York are in the Evert Jansen Wendell Collection, Houghton Library, Harvard University. Biographical sketches are in *Presbyterian Reunion: A Memorial Volume, 1837–1871* (1871); Samuel Willoughby Duffield, *English Hymns: Their Authors and History*, 3d ed. (1888); and John Julian, *A Dictionary of Hymnology* (1891; rev. ed., 1907, repr. 1957). Hatfield is discussed in Jon Michael Spencer, "Moral Abolitionism in an Antislavery Hymnal," *Reformed Liturgy and Music* (Summer 1987): 148–51; Philip D. Jordan, "The Evangelical Alliance and American Presbyterians, 1867–1873," *Journal of Presbyterian History* 51 (Fall 1973): 309–26; and Philip D. Jordan, *The Evangelical Alliance for the United States of America, 1847–1900: Ecumenism, Identity, and the Religion of the Republic* (1982). Hatfield's work is chronicled in the official records of the Presbyterian church, including the *Minutes of the Presbyterian Church in the U.S.A. General Assembly [New School]*, vols. 1–15 (1839–1869); the *Minutes of the Presbyterian Church in the U.S.A. General Assembly*, n.s., vols. 1–13 (1871–1884); and William E. Moore, *The Presbyterian Digest of 1886* (1886). An obituary is in the *New York Times*, 23 Sept. 1883.

DAVID B. McCARTHY

HATFIELD, Henry Drury (15 Sept. 1875–23 Oct. 1962), physician and politician, was born at Mate Creek, Logan County, West Virginia, the son of Elias "Good 'Lias" Hatfield, a farmer and landowner, and Elizabeth Chafin. He was the nephew of feudist William Anderson "Devil Anse" Hatfield. Henry Hatfield graduated from Franklin College in New Athens, Ohio, in 1890. Subsequently he received two M.D. degrees, the first from the University of Louisville in 1893 and the second from New York University in 1904. In 1895 he married South Carolina "Caroline" Bronson; they had one child, a daughter, Hazel, who married steel magnate Benjamin F. Fairless.

The dearth of hospitals in southern West Virginia and the sufferings of injured coal miners led Hatfield into medicine and inspired his political career. He began nearly seventy years of medical practice in 1893 in Eckman, where he often had to ride on horseback to treat patients in remote hollows. He was a Norfolk and Western Railroad surgeon from 1895 to 1913, serving also as Mingo County health officer from 1895 to 1900. He helped to set up three hospitals in the southern

West Virginia coal fields. The first was Miners Hospital at Welch, where he was chief surgeon and director from 1900 to 1910 and continued as chief surgeon to 1912.

Hatfield, a lifelong Republican, entered politics with service on the McDowell County Court (1906–1912). His political star rose quickly, lifted by respect for his profession and the magnetism of the Hatfield name. He was in the state senate from 1908 until 1912, when he overcame sectional Republican factionalism, the challenge of Theodore Roosevelt's Progressive party, and Democrat Woodrow Wilson's victory in the presidential race to win the West Virginia governorship.

Hatfield's first crisis in office was the Cabin Creek–Paint Creek coal "mine war." For over a year the United Mine Workers of America (UMWA) had battled operators to organize the Kanawha field. Outgoing governor William E. Glasscock had twice declared martial law. The day after his inauguration in March 1913, Hatfield journeyed through the industrial battleground treating the sick, including incarcerated labor organizer Mary Harris "Mother" Jones, whom he sent to a hospital. Gradually, he withdrew the National Guard and reversed court-martial convictions of most strikers. In April he imposed the "Hatfield Contract" to end the strike. This compromise required operators to grant the miners some concessions, including a vague "right to organize," but it brought only temporary labor peace for it did not compel owners to recognize the UMWA.

Although Hatfield's use of the spoils system and ballot box stuffing was traditional, he was one of a new generation of Mountain State leaders who sought to regain control of the state's government and resources from absentee corporate owners. His political program reflected progressivism. In February 1913, before his inauguration, the legislature passed the state's first workmen's compensation law, which the governor-elect had campaigned for and had helped to draft when he was in the state senate and which he claimed as his administration's greatest achievement. Other acts were designed to punish political corruption, limit corporate power and influence, restore competition among railroads, curb the notorious deputy sheriff–mine guard system, enforce Prohibition, and grant woman suffrage. By 1915 opposition stymied Hatfield's reforms. He could not deliver promised gas and coal severance taxes, tougher mine inspections, old-age pensions, or free surgical treatment for indigent children. Critical legislators found him too "strong, domineering and vindictive." Conservative opponents labeled him a Socialist even though his suppression of actual Socialist publications belied their claim. For his part, Hatfield maintained that his purpose as governor was to protect individuals from monopolistic power in whatever form.

In 1917 Hatfield retired from the governorship after a single term as the law required and spent World War I as an army surgeon. After the war he returned to private medical practice in Huntington, West Virginia.

In 1928 he reentered politics and defeated Democrat Matthew Mansfield Neely for the U.S. Senate. In Washington he soon emerged, in deference to West Virginia coal jobs and profits, as an economic protectionist. Early in the Great Depression he loyally supported beleaguered President Herbert Hoover, blaming European economic difficulties for America's Great Crash in 1929. After Franklin D. Roosevelt succeeded Hoover in 1933, Hatfield strenuously opposed the centralizing tendencies of the New Deal. He called the Agricultural Adjustment Act a "red collectivist effort" and the National Industrial Recovery Act a "communistic conspiracy." He claimed the latter would harm the Constitution, hurt consumers by creating wage-profit escalation, and place labor under national control. Even the National Recovery Administration (NRA) emblem, the blue eagle, he said, was "as much a symbol of tyranny as the hammer and sickle of Russia." His opposition to the NRA cost him the political support of labor leaders John L. Lewis of the UMWA and William Green (1870–1952) of the American Federation of Labor (AFL) for Senate reelection in 1934 and was a factor in his defeat by upstart Democrat Rush Dew Holt. His loss underscored West Virginia Republicans' disunity in the face of an emergent Democratic majority. Never again would he run for public office.

For the next twenty-eight years, Hatfield practiced medicine, operated a farm, and was influential in West Virginia GOP circles. In this era of liberal Democratic ascendancy, his political views were in the minority. He had denounced nazism and Japanese aggression in Asia in the early 1930s and was always a fervent anti-Communist, but more than that he was an isolationist who feared foreign entanglements, especially after World War II. In speeches and letters he opposed growing American overseas military and economic involvement, a policy he laid at the door of the Democrats and Republicans such as Wendell Willkie, Arthur Vandenberg, and Thomas E. Dewey, who he thought had led their party astray. How far astray was evident in 1952 when, over his strenuous objections, West Virginia Republicans nominated his old enemy Holt for governor. Hatfield died in Huntington.

Hatfield is remembered as an outstanding physician, a key architect of the Republican party in West Virginia and the upper South, a progressive turned out of office with the GOP during the Great Depression, and a Cold Warrior thereafter.

• Hatfield's papers, including political and medical correspondence, draft speeches, and newspaper clippings, are at West Virginia University. He wrote little, but some of his communications as governor were published: *Excerpts from Messages . . .* (1915), *Governor Hatfield's Special Message on Virginia Debt and Master Littlefield's Report* (1915), and *First Biennial Message . . .* (1915). A profile of his political career is Carolyn Karr, "A Political Biography of Henry Hatfield," *West Virginia History* 28 (Oct. 1966): 35–63 and 28 (Jan. 1967): 137–70. His early career and governorship are detailed in Neil Shaw Penn, "Henry D. Hatfield and Reform Politics: A Study of West Virginia Politics from 1908 to 1917" (Ph.D.

diss., Emory Univ., 1973). John A. Williams interprets Hatfield's political role in *West Virginia and the Captains of Industry* (1976) and *West Virginia: A Bicentennial History* (1976). Among journalistic brief biographies is John C. Morgan, *West Virginia Governors* (1960). Outstanding for its scholarly analysis of the Hatfield-McCoy feud is Altina L. Waller, *Feud: Hatfields, McCoys and Social Change in Appalachia, 1860–1900* (1988). Obituaries are in the *Charleston Gazette* and the *New York Times*, 24 Oct. 1962.

CHARLES H. MCCORMICK

HATFIELD, William Anderson (9 Sept. 1839–6 Jan. 1921), feudist, landowner, and logger, was born on Mate Creek in the hills of the Tug Valley in present-day West Virginia, the son of Ephraim "Big Eaf" Hatfield, a farmer and landowner, and Nancy Vance. Illiterate and uneducated, Hatfield spent his childhood hunting and farming on his father's property, some of the best land in the Tug Valley. His wilderness prowess earned Hatfield the nickname Devil Anse, his mother claiming that he was not afraid of even the devil. (Other legendary accounts claim his nickname was not acquired until late in the feud.) Before enlisting in the Confederate army as a private in 1861, he married Levicy Chafin. Together they produced thirteen children, all living to maturity.

Hatfield deserted the Confederacy in late 1863 and formed the Logan Wildcats, a local militia consisting of relatives and friends (even McCoys). Established for community protection against isolated Union and Confederate fighting and general lawlessness, the militia was responsible for the death of former Union soldier Harmon McCoy, the brother of Randolph "Old Ranel" McCoy, the other principal feudist. Harmon's killing apparently did not incite retaliatory violence.

The years succeeding the war were initially difficult for Hatfield. The only son not to receive a parcel of land from his father, he struggled for economic survival and social status. Land in the Tug Valley decided that status. Using his brothers' lands, Hatfield established a logging company in 1869 that became the family business and not only sustained the entire extended family but made him a wealthy and important man.

The true beginning of the Hatfield-McCoy feud is difficult to pinpoint. In 1878 Ranel McCoy accused Floyd Hatfield, a cousin of Anse, of stealing one of Ranel's pigs. With a jury evenly divided between Hatfields and McCoys, Floyd was found not guilty. Incensed, Ranel accepted the verdict and sought no retaliation. Two years later, in 1880 during a local election, often a community social event, flirtatious Johnse, Anse's son, and Rose Anna, Ranel's daughter, became infatuated and fell in love. Fearful of her father's reaction, Rose Anna fled to the Hatfield home and remained for six months. Hardly a Romeo and Juliet story as the press would later portray the liaison, their romance was short lived. While hospitable, Anse had no intention of allowing the pair to marry, nor was Johnse particularly interested in marriage. A probably pregnant Rose left the Hatfield household and many years later died of melancholy.

The incident that incited violence was another election-day gathering at the Blackberry polling place in Pike County, Kentucky, on 7 August 1882. Drunkenness and tempers caused a simple argument over minor debts between Tolbert McCoy, Ranel's son, and Elias Hatfield, a cousin, to escalate into a fight and the fatal wounding of Ellison Hatfield, Anse's brother. Without question of guilt, three McCoy sons were arrested and transported to the Pike County jail. During their transport, Anse and a posse captured the prisoners, executing them several days later, after Ellison's death. Indictments were issued but never served against Anse and the other members of the posse.

Following Ellison's murder, violent hostilities between the families temporarily ceased. In the 1880s Anse appeared in court for a series of legal problems that included moonshining and various contractual violations. The timbering industry by which he earned a prosperous living became a corporate business, with land speculators dealing with large logging organizations. Ranel McCoy was less content over the succeeding years, insisting that the authorities serve the warrants for his sons' killers. Finding an ally in Kentucky lawyer Perry Cline, who had lost land to Anse Hatfield in an earlier legal battle, McCoy convinced Cline to persuade Kentucky's governor to issue extradition papers for Hatfield and his posse. When West Virginia refused to honor Kentucky's request, Hatfield's extradition became both a political and a state sovereignty issue. On 1 January 1888 Hatfield called a family council. Cap, his son, decided to raid the McCoy homestead and "eliminate" the evidence against the Hatfields. Anse did not participate in or probably approve of the brutal battle of Grapevine Creek that resulted in the deaths of two of Ranel's children and his wife's severe beating. Nine Hatfields and their supporters were arrested and tried for the murders. Sensationalized in the northern press, the trial resulted in life sentences for all the participants except Ellison Mounts, who received the death penalty. Constructing a fortress to hide from bounty hunters, Hatfield retired with his family to Island Creek, north of Logan, West Virginia.

Hatfield lived out his days at his Island Creek home. Plagued by debts and other legal financial difficulties, he was forced to sell some land below market value even though mining and railroad interests made his property valuable. Unreligious most of his life, he was converted and baptized in the Primitive Baptist Church in 1911. He died, in his own bed, of pneumonia. Hundreds of mourners attended his funeral. His family erected a life-size statue of Italian marble on his grave.

The Hatfield and McCoy feud consisted more of legend than of fact. Many feuds in Kentucky and West Virginia were bloodier and lengthier. Division was not along family lines, as McCoys and Hatfields had intermarried for years. The feud was not a result of Civil War loyalties, as both families were Confederates. The Hatfield and McCoy feud was a result of individuals caught in a changing and dying culture. Oral agreements were no longer upheld in courts that relied on codified law, not community mores. Social status formerly achieved through land ownership was replaced by the large, outside corporate interests of mining and the railroads. Portrayed as obstructors of progress, the Hatfields and McCoys symbolized the evils and backwardness of Appalachian culture.

• Little of the information concerning the feud appears in official sources. There are no family papers, but several accounts were published by family members many years after the feud. Newspaper stories of the era are sensationalized and generally inaccurate. The most commonly cited family account is Truda McCoy, *The McCoys: Their Story as Told to the Author by Eye Witnesses and Descendants* (1976). One of Randolph McCoy's nephews wrote *Squirrel Huntin' Sam McCoy, His Memoir and Family Tree*, ed. Hobart McCoy and Orville McCoy (1979). For the Hatfield view, see G. Elliot Hatfield, *The Hatfields* (1974; 1988). The best factual and most detailed account of the feud is Otis K. Rice, *The Hatfields and the McCoys* (1978). For analysis of the feud relation to the culture, economy, and other feuds, see Altina L. Waller, *Feud: Hatfields, McCoys, and Social Change in Appalachia, 1860–1900* (1988), and John Pearce, ed., *Days of Darkness: Feuds of Eastern Kentucky* (1994). An obituary appears in the *New York Times*, 8 Jan. 1921.

JENNY PRESNELL

HATHAWAY, Henry (13 Mar. 1898–11 Feb. 1985), film director, was born Henri Leopold de Fiennes in Sacramento, California, the son of Rhoady de Fiennes, a theatrical manager, and Jean Hathaway, an actress and singer. The family later took the name of Hathaway. Hathaway's early childhood was spent in San Francisco. In about 1910, the family moved to southern California when Hathaway's mother signed up as a performer with the American Film Company. Hathaway and his sister played child roles in American Film Company productions, which were mostly short, one-reel (ten-minute) westerns shot outdoors near the Mexican border. In 1912 Hathaway and his family left American Film to freelance for the Ince, Universal, and Christie motion picture companies. Hathaway's formal education was scant. In 1915 he quit school altogether and went to work as a property man at Universal Pictures.

After spending 1917 to 1919 as a gunnery soldier with the U.S. Army, Hathaway returned to the motion picture industry. He became an assistant to directors Josef Von Sternberg and Victor Fleming at Paramount Pictures. "I mostly learned from them how to handle people. I would take a script home and think, now what would I tell these people to do to make the scene, how would I start it, where would be the climax. . . . And I'd make up my mind and I'd make a lot of notes, and then I'd see what they did. Entirely different! But you learn," Hathaway said (*Focus on Film*, p. 12). Hathaway assisted Von Sternberg with such films as *The Last Command* (1928) with Emil Jannings and William Powell, *Thunderbolt* (1929) with George Bancroft and Fay Wray, *Morocco* (1930) with Marlene Dietrich and Gary Cooper, and *Shanghai Express*

(1932) with Dietrich and Warner Oland. Hathaway helped Fleming direct *The Way of All Flesh* (1927) with Emil Jannings, *The Virginian* (1929) with Gary Cooper, and other westerns. Hathaway was also befriended by urbane producer Paul Bern, who advised him to make up for his lack of formal education by reading for two hours each day, a practice Hathaway maintained for many years. At Bern's recommendation, Hathaway spent nine months in India, gathering material for a documentary about pilgrimages, but the project was never made. In 1933 Hathaway married Blanca (Blanche) Estrella Gonzales with whom he had a son.

Hathaway's debut as a director was *Heritage of the Desert* (1932), the first of eight low-budget westerns that he made from 1932 to 1934, all but one starring Randolph Scott. The well-received *The Lives of a Bengal Lancer* (1935), starring Gary Cooper and Franchot Tone, moved Hathaway into the ranks of major directors and is a prime example of the male-oriented action pictures for which he is best known. Although the film was not intended as a realistic look at India and only a small amount of footage actually shot in India was woven into the picture, Hathaway's firsthand knowledge of the country landed him the assignment. Showing the versatility that also became a Hathaway trademark, he reteamed with Cooper on *Peter Ibbetson* (1935), a romantic fantasy based on the popular 1891 novel by George Du Maurier. Indifferently received by mainstream audiences and critics at the time of its release, the film earned praise from "surrealists" such as writer André Breton and filmmaker Luis Buñuel for its dream sequences, which were photographed by Charles Lang. Cooper also appeared in Hathaway's *Now and Forever* (1934), a lackluster comedy with Carole Lombard and Shirley Temple; *Souls at Sea* (1937), a shipwreck drama costarring George Raft; and *The Real Glory* (1939), the story of American soldiers in the Philippines also featuring Broderick Crawford and David Niven. Other Hathaway films of the 1930s are *The Trail of the Lonesome Pine* (1936), a tale of a mountain family feud starring Fred MacMurray, Sylvia Sydney, and Henry Fonda (the first Technicolor film shot on location); *Go West, Young Man* (1936), a Mae West comedy; and *Spawn of the North* (1938), a drama of the Alaskan fishing industry with George Raft and Henry Fonda.

Moving from Paramount to 20th Century–Fox Pictures in 1940, Hathaway directed *Johnny Apollo* (1940), a gangster story, and *Brigham Young, Frontiersman* (1940), a historical western, both starring Tyrone Power. He then made several "semi-documentary" suspense thrillers based on real-life espionage and crime incidents. These films, which were photographed on location where the events actually took place, include *The House on 92nd Street* (1945), about a Federal Bureau of Investigation infiltration of a Nazi spy ring with Lloyd Nolan and Signe Hasso; *13 Rue Madeleine* (1946), starring James Cagney as an OSS officer attempting to locate a German missile site in occupied France; *Call Northside 777* (1948), starring

James Stewart as a Chicago newspaper reporter who investigates what he believes to be an unjust murder conviction; and *Fourteen Hours* (1951), the story of a suicidal man (Richard Basehart) poised on a Manhattan building ledge and the various onlookers (including Grace Kelly in her screen debut) who gather to watch.

Some critics considered the burly, gray-haired Hathaway to be a directorial visionary (the equal of John Ford and Howard Hawks), whose unpretentious style caused him to be underestimated. Other critics relegated him to the top ranks of "B" level directors—a clever, efficient craftsman who gave the studio bosses what they wanted. Critic Andrew Sarris, while acknowledging the amiability and unpretentiousness of Hathaway's work, ranked it well below that of Ford and Hawks, directors with whom he was often compared. Hathaway believed that there were only so many basic plotlines and that creative direction and good performances could bring freshness to familiar material. He uncomplainingly accepted the scripts assigned to him but was fussy about the casting of actors. Although he was a salty-tongued and somewhat tyrannical presence on a movie set, Hathaway earned a reputation as a director who showcased performers, especially males, to their best advantage. He was a favorite of John Wayne, whose association with Hathaway began with *The Shepherd of the Hills* (1941), the story of a young man who discovers that the long-lost father whom he has vowed to kill (vengeance is a frequent theme in Hathaway's films) is a kindly Ozark mountaineer beloved by his community. Hathaway's other films with Wayne are *Legend of the Lost* (1957) with Sophia Loren, *North to Alaska* (1960) with Stewart Granger and Ernie Kovacs, *Circus World* (1964) with Rita Hayworth, *The Sons of Katie Elder* (1965) with Dean Martin, and *True Grit* (1969), for which Wayne won an Academy Award as aging, one-eyed marshal Rooster Cogburn who helps a young girl track down her father's killer. As film historian John Kobal points out, "Hathaway made more films with John Wayne than anybody else except John Ford; and while Ford won his Oscar for directing Wayne, Wayne won his for being directed by Hathaway" (p. 610).

The versatile Hathaway's other notable films include *Home in Indiana* (1944) with Walter Brennan and Jeanne Crain; *Kiss of Death* (1947), a "film noir" in which Richard Widmark made his celebrated screen debut as a giggling psychopath who pushes a wheelchair-bound old woman down the stairs; *Down to the Sea in Ships* (1949) with Widmark and Lionel Barrymore; *The Black Robe* (1950) with Tyrone Power and Orson Welles; *Niagara* (1953) with Joseph Cotten and Marilyn Monroe; *Prince Valiant* (1954) with James Mason and Robert Wagner; *From Hell to Texas* (1958) with Don Murray; *Nevada Smith* (1966) with Steve McQueen; *Five Card Stud* (1968) with Dean Martin and Robert Mitchum; and *Raid on Rommel* (1971) with Richard Burton. Hathaway also directed "The Clarion Call" story in *O. Henry's Full House* (1952) and "The Rivers," "The Plains," and "The Outlaws" epi-

sodes in the box-office smash *How the West Was Won* (1962), and he did uncredited work on *Airport* (1970). His last film was *Hang-Up* (1974), a poorly received thriller about drug trafficking. Hathaway died in Los Angeles.

• The personal papers of Hathaway are at the American Film Institute, Los Angeles. *World Film Directors*, vol. 1, *1890–1945* (1987), offers a detailed essay on Hathaway's life and career. An interview with Hathaway is in John Kobal, *People Will Talk* (1985). *Focus on Film*, no. 7 (1971): 11–27, offers an interview with Hathaway and an analysis of his films. See also Jean-Pierre Coursodon, *American Directors*, vol. 1 (1983), and Andrew Sarris, *The American Cinema: Directors and Directions, 1929–1968* (1968). An obituary is in the *New York Times*, 13 Feb. 1985.

MARY C. KALFATOVIC

HATHAWAY, Starke Rosecrans (22 Aug. 1903–4 July 1984), clinical psychologist, was born in Central Lake, Michigan, the son of Martin Walter Hathaway and Bertha Belle Rosecrans. Hathaway grew up in and around Marysville, Ohio, and as a boy, liked to tinker with electronic equipment. He enrolled in electrical engineering at Ohio University but changed his major to psychology and mathematics in his junior year. Interested in the physiological aspects of psychology, Hathaway set up a campus workshop where he developed several pieces of psychological apparatus. One of these was a vacuum-tube psychogalvanometer, a device Hathaway claimed was a forerunner to lie-detectors utilizing the galvanic skin reflex.

Hathaway obtained his master's degree in psychology from Ohio State University in 1928. That same year he married Virginia Riddle; they had no children. Hathaway accepted a lecturing position in psychology in 1930 at the University of Minnesota, a notable center for behavioristic experimentation and applied psychology. He continued to study neurophysiology and in 1932 gained a Ph.D. from the University of Minnesota with the thesis "An Action Potential Study of Neuromuscular Relations."

Soon after arriving at Minnesota, Hathaway initiated an ex officio course in clinical psychology. He taught under the auspices of the medical school and emphasized neuropsychiatric aspects of psychology and quantitative methods. Hathaway's supervision of graduate students in 1938 represented the formal beginnings of a fully fledged clinical program. Eccentric in style and eclectic in intellect, Hathaway spelled out his ideas with a deliberate minimum of cohesion and resisted requests to systematize his theories. Instead, he encouraged his students to develop practical clinical techniques based on their own experience.

In 1937 Hathaway and neuropsychiatrist J. Charnley McKinley began work on a new test for psychiatric diagnosis. Hathaway and McKinley "wanted to condense those long psychiatric interviews, which were very expensive for the patient" (Hathaway, in Colligan et al., p. iv). They managed to solicit Works Progress Administration funds for the project in 1938 by emphasizing the test's potential to standardize psychiatric classification and distinguish physical illness from "psychoneurotic" malingering. The introduction of radical psychiatric treatments, such as shock therapy and psychosurgery, required new methods of evaluating patient suitability and therapeutic efficacy. This need provided an additional stimulus for the project.

Hathaway and McKinley drafted over 500 item statements for the test, which became known as the Minnesota Multiphasic Personality Inventory. Nine clinical scales were derived from these items by contrasting the item response frequencies of "normal" groups with those groups with a specific psychiatric diagnosis—an unusual procedure characteristic of Hathaway's pragmatic, empirical approach to test construction. Hathaway also authored a major innovation by constructing three validity indices for the test designed to guard against "faking." Early versions of the MMPI were administered on a trial basis in the armed forces toward the end of the war, thus introducing the test to many psychiatrists and psychologists.

Hathaway had envisaged the MMPI as a straightforward diagnostic gauge. However, attempts to corroborate psychiatric diagnoses with the new test were only moderately successful. With clinical psychologists less concerned with psychiatric diagnosis, alternative interpretive strategies were needed to match the professional priorities of postwar clinical practice and the performance characteristics of the MMPI. The original goal of psychiatric classification was largely shelved. Instead, Hathaway and his colleagues reinterpreted the test as a measure of *psychological* character types.

In the 1950s, 1960s, and 1970s other researchers introduced general user guides, specific subscales, and automated interpretative services that enhanced the MMPI's versatility and efficiency. However, critics argued that the MMPI was psychometrically flawed and a better indicator of the respondent's desire to agree or to present favorably than it was a measure of personality. Hathaway and colleagues also had to defend the MMPI's use against invasion of privacy charges sparked by the odd and inquisitive nature of the original item set. The test survived these attacks to become the most researched and used personality test in the world, and was carefully updated in the mid-1980s. Hathaway always maintained an active though non-proprietary interest in the MMPI's development. Much of his later work focused on adolescent problems, particularly the identification of juvenile delinquency.

Throughout his career, Hathaway worked hard to consolidate clinical psychology at Minnesota and raise the national profile of the profession. Hathaway was director of the Clinical Psychology Division in the Minnesota's medical school from 1951 until his retirement in 1970. He was a participant at the landmark 1949 Boulder Conference, which devised the scientist-practitioner model that dominated postwar clinical training in the United States. He was also the American Psychological Association's Clinical Division president in 1963 and a member of the APA Board of Pro-

fessional Affairs during the early 1960s. Hathaway received numerous honors, among them two APA awards for his contribution to personality testing and clinical psychology in 1959 and 1977. He was well versed in cross-cultural psychiatry; he taught in various colleges in Latin America and studied Aztec culture. Hathaway died at his home in Minneapolis.

Hathaway's quiet manner and distaste for self-promotion tended to obscure his achievements as a teacher and therapist. Yet he managed to inspire a generation of influential, Minnesota-trained psychologists, such as Paul Meehl and Harrison Gough. He remained open to new ideas and willing to share his own. An unconventional researcher who "broke every rule of scientific method," Hathaway made a lasting impact on clinical psychology as the man who devised the MMPI.

• Hathaway's personal papers are in the University of Minnesota Archives, Minneapolis. He destroyed most of his scientific work, including data used in the construction of the MMPI. Hathaway's "A Comparative Study of Psychogalvanic and Association Time Measures," *Journal of Applied Psychology* 13 (1929): 632–46, and "A Pendulum Chronoscope," *Journal of General Psychology* 4 (1930): 423–42, exemplify Hathaway's early research in physiological psychology. For Hathaway's latter-day thoughts on the development of the MMPI see his "Foreword" in Robert C. Colligan et al., *The MMPI: A Contemporary Normative Study* (1983). See also Hathaway, "The MMPI: Professional Use by Professional People," *American Psychologist* 19 (1964): 204–10. For an autobiographical account of his life and a selected publications list, see his "Through Psychology My Way," in *The Psychologists: Autobiographies of Distinguished Living Psychologists*, ed. T. S. Krawiec (1978), vol. 3, pp. 105–23. See also Harrison G. Gough, "Along the Way: Recollections of Some Major Contributors to Personality Assessment," *Journal of Personality Assessment* 53 (1988): 5–29; William Schofield, "In Memoriam: Starke R. Hathaway (1903–1984)," *Minnesota Psychologist* (Fall 1984): 13; and Hathaway, "Bibliographic Sketch," July 1963, Hathaway papers B H284, University of Minnesota Archives. Hathaway references for the MMPI can be culled from textbooks and manuals, especially W. Grant Dahlstrom et al., *An MMPI Handbook*, vols. 1 and 2 (1972 and 1975), and from Hathaway's work on reinterpreting the MMPI in terms of personality profile types, in Hathaway and Paul E. Meehl, *An Atlas for the Clinical Use of the MMPI* (1951); and his studies of adolescents, in Hathaway and E. D. Monachesi, *Analysing and Predicting Juvenile Delinquency with the MMPI* (1953).

RODERICK BUCHANAN

HATHORNE, William (c. 1607–Apr. 1681), developer of Salem, Massachusetts, and progenitor of the Ha(w)thorne family in America, was born in Bray, Berkshire, England, the son of William Hathorne, a yeoman, and Sarah (full name unknown). Little is known of his early years except that he received more education than was usual for one of his family's standing and grew up in relatively comfortable surroundings. As a young man of eighteen or nineteen, he was converted to Puritanism and, soon after, announced that he intended to migrate to New England. His close friend Richard Davenport, betrothed to Hathorne's sister Elizabeth Hathorne, left for America in 1628 with the understanding that William and his sister would soon follow. When the Hathornes reached New England is unclear. Probably they arrived after 1630 and no later than the fall of 1633.

Their destination was Naumkeag, soon to be renamed Salem. Hathorne then moved to Dorchester, where he took the oath as a freeman in May 1634. By the end of the year he had been named a deputy to the General Court and elected as a selectman. About that time he married Ann Smith; they had seven children.

Before the end of 1636 the Hathorne family returned to Salem, where in addition to a house lot, William was granted 200 acres in an area soon to be known as Salem Village. He immediately transferred his allegiance to the Salem Church from which Roger Williams had recently been banished by the deputies, a vote in which Hathorne had concurred. The Hathornes lived on their farm for approximately four years and then moved to the center of town, where William could better carry out his duties as a magistrate.

Hathorne developed a reputation as a strict disciplinarian. Any breach of the law brought his full wrath on the defendant. His unswerving harshness brought him into direct conflict with John Winthrop (1588–1649), who sought to have him dismissed from the General Court for a brief period of time. Their clash arose over Hathorne's insistence on seeking severe punishments for such crimes as swearing and lying and over his openly questioning Winthrop's efforts to control the General Court. They seemed to have settled their differences, for by 1643 the two men were members of a committee to establish an intercolonial defense organization. Hathorne was one of the first delegates to be chosen by Massachusetts to serve on the New England Confederation, a consortium of New England colonies that planned and organized for mutual defense against Indian attacks, and he would continue as a representative for some twenty years. Hathorne, riding the crest of popularity, was then named as the first Speaker of the deputies when they became a separate body from the General Court in 1644.

While building a comfortable fortune as a farmer, merchant, warehouse owner, and overseas trader, Hathorne served as an assistant magistrate for Essex County until 1655 and subsequently as its chief magistrate. He rose in rank in the train band (the local militia) from lieutenant to major.

As one of the magistrates of Massachusetts, Hathorne wielded enormous influence in law, government, and church affairs. He threw his support behind efforts to create conformity in church doctrine and strict adherence to nonseparatism in the church. It has been suggested that Hathorne's meteoric rise resulted from his arrival in Salem at a time when two conflicting groups of Puritans, emanating from East and West Anglia, were vying for control of congressional affairs. Hathorne, regarded as somewhat of a neutral—not having come from those regions—and respected for his speaking ability, could mediate the differences. In

the process he built a solid political base for his own career.

Hathorne is also closely associated with pursuing the Quakers, who appeared in Salem and sought to openly proselytize among the Puritan congregants. Hathorne, who as early as the 1640s had demonstrated a dislike for anyone who sought to disturb the church covenants, passed judgment on Mary Oliver, who continually questioned exclusivity of church membership and criticized those who supported strict adherence. Of Hathorne, Oliver exclaimed, "I do hope to live and tear his flesh in pieces, and all such as he." For this she was sentenced to the stocks.

When Quakers began to regularly appear in Massachusetts and particularly in Salem in the 1650s, Hathorne awaited them with the full fury of the law. He was ruthless in punishing avowed Quakers as well as those who sought to help them. Whippings or hours spent in the stocks with a piece of split wood over their tongues were "lenient" punishments. As a member of the General Court, Hathorne participated in votes leading to banishments and to four executions. Nonetheless, owing to a shift in Crown policy and the rise of a new generation of inhabitants more tolerant of religious distinctions, by the time of Hathorne's death Quakers were openly active in Salem.

When Governor John Endecott left Salem and moved to Boston in 1655, Hathorne became Salem's leading citizen. He constantly sought to make Salem at least equal in importance to Boston if it could not surpass that port community. He used his connections in church, government, and legislative circles to obtain Salem's advancement. In doing so, he enhanced his own mercantile and political positions. One historian has described Hathorne as an "ingenious coalition builder who appealed carefully to the varied interests that made up the town and colony." Lawrence S. Mayo, in *John Endecott: A Biography* (1936), notes that Hathorne "was an assertive, belligerent hustler, who enjoyed politics and made the most of every opportunity for his own advancement in that field."

Hathorne continued to sit as an assistant and as a magistrate into 1680 although severely hobbled by physical ailments and old age; his political enemies derogatorily categorized him as "a white-hat limping rogue." By 1681 he was confined to bed in his farmhouse about a mile outside Salem, where he died. Hathorne's great-great-great-grandson Nathaniel Hawthorne would modify the family name and bring a luster to it.

• Official records mentioning Hathorne's activities are in Nathaniel B. Shurtleff, ed., *Records of the Governor and Company of the Massachusetts Bay in New England* (5 vols., 1853–1854; repr. 1968), and *Salem Town Records*, vol. 1 (1868) and vols. 2 and 3 (1913 and 1934). The most complete commentary on Hathorne's career may be found in Vernon Loggins, *The Hawthornes* (1951; repr. 1968). Since Hathorne was so closely associated with Salem's development, that phase of his activities may be found in Richard P. Gildrie, *Salem, Massachusetts, 1626–1683: A Covenant Community* (1975). The relationship between church, state, and the business world is in Stephen Foster, *The Long Argument: English Puritanism and the Shaping of New England Culture, 1570–1700* (1991). Hathorne and the Quakers may be followed in Carla Gardina Pestana, "The Quaker Executions as Myth and History," *Journal of American History* 80, no. 2 (Sept. 1993): 441–69, and *Quakers and Baptists in Colonial Massachusetts* (1991).

JACOB JUDD

HATTON, Ann Julia Kemble (29 Apr. 1764–26 Dec. 1838), novelist and poet, was the daughter of Roger Kemble, a theater company owner, and Sarah Ward. The location of her birth is unknown. Her eldest sister, named Sarah after their mother, came to be known in the theater as "the incomparable Siddons." At age eleven Ann (also spelled "Anne") wrote a play that was performed by her father's company at Brecon in Wales, but possibly because of lameness and a squint, she was discouraged by her family from further theatrical pursuits and apprenticed to a costume maker. Then in one eventful year, 1783, Ann Kemble married an actor named Curtis, who proved to be a bigamist (it is unknown when, or if, they divorced); lectured at London quack doctor James Graham's Temple of Hymen "on chastity and other delicate subjects"; published her first volume of poems; and placed in all the London newspapers notices calling for "Donations in Favour of Mrs. Curtis," badly in need of aid because her siblings "*Messrs. Kemble* and Mrs. *Siddons*, whom she has repeatedly solicited for relief, . . . have flatly refused her."

In 1789 Ann Curtis attempted (or pretended to attempt) suicide in Westminster Abbey and was later accidentally shot in a brothel, which led to newspaper speculation about her way of life. In 1792, married to William Hatton, a maker of musical instruments, she moved to New York, where she had success as a songwriter and librettist for two productions staged in the John Street Theater. The first was a slight piece, *Needs Must; or, The Ballad Singers*, which received a single performance in 1793. The second, far more important, was *Tammany; or, The Indian Chief: A Serious Opera*, produced in 1794; it was performed several times in New York, Boston, and Philadelphia as well. In 1795, reduced to two acts, it played as *America Discovered; or, Tammany, the Indian Chief*. Members of the Tammany Society, a patriotic organization founded during the American Revolution with chapters in principal cities, were predominantly Republican in sentiment and packed the house at performances, which became focal points for Republican-Federalist confrontation. Capitalizing on her status as "poetess to the Tammany Society," Ann Hatton offered a program of readings "from the most select authors" at "Tammanial Hall" in September 1794. She also printed and sold the songs from *Tammany*—solos, duets, choruses, and a full operatic finale.

In 1800 the Hattons were back in Great Britain, operating a hotel in Swansea. Widowed in 1806, Ann Hatton entered her most productive literary phase a few years later. As "Anne of Swansea" she published between 1810 and 1831 one volume of poetry and thirteen works of fiction, variously designated novel, romance, or tale, all exploiting familiar topics, themes, and character types. The fiction appeared through the Minerva Press of William Lane and his successor, Andrew King Newman, who renamed the firm in 1820 and continued with substantially the same authors, more than half of them women, whose works were stocked by the circulating library belonging to the publishers.

Hatton lived out her years and died in Swansea, her meager income augmented by a stipend of £20 annually granted by Sarah Siddons on the condition that she live at least 150 miles from London, a bequest of £20 annually from her father, and a legacy of £60 annually left by her brother John Philip Kemble, the eminent actor, in his will. There is some evidence as well that she was never completely repudiated by the Kemble family despite her embarrassing behavior, for example, her letter publicly denying assertions of neglect that were made in a newspaper account of the shooting accident.

• Ann Hatton's manuscripts, concerned with family history and planned literary projects, are in the Folger Shakespeare Library. Hatton's published works include *Poems on Miscellaneous Subjects* (1783), *The Songs of T-a-m-m-a-n-y; or, The Indian Chief* (1794), *Cambrian Pictures; or, Every One Has Errors* (1810?), *Poetic Trifles* (1811), *Conviction; or, She Is Innocent! A Novel* (1814), *Secret Avengers; or, The Rock of Glotzden: A Romance* (1815), *Gonzalo de Baldivia; or, A Widow's Vow: A Romantic Legend* (1817), *Secrets in Every Mansion; or, The Surgeon's Memorandum Book* (1818), *Lovers and Friends; or, Modern Attachments: A Novel* (1821), *Guilty or Not Guilty; or, A Lesson for Husbands: A Tale* (1822), *Uncle Peregrine's Heiress: A Novel* (1828), and *Gerald Fitzgerald: An Irish Tale* (1831). For the New York period and the importance of *Tammany*, see William Dunlap, *A History of the American Theatre* (1832), Walter J. Meserve, *An Emerging Entertainment: The Drama of the American People to 1828* (1977), and George C. D. Odell, *Annals of the New York Stage*, vol. 1 (1927). For the novels see Dorothy Blakey, *The Minerva Press, 1790–1820* (1939). See also Herschel Baker, *John Philip Kemble: The Actor in His Theatre* (1942), Yvonne Ffrench, *Mrs. Siddons: Tragic Actress* (1954), Mrs. A. Kennard, *Mrs. Siddons* (1893), and Mrs. Clement Parsons, *The Incomparable Siddons* (1909; repr. 1969).

VINCENT FREIMARCK

HATTON, Fanny Cottinet Locke (6 Mar. 1869–27 Nov. 1939), playwright, was born in Chicago, Illinois, the daughter of the Reverend James de Witt Clinton Locke and Adela Gleim Douthitt. For fifty years her father was rector of Grace Episcopal Church, whose parishioners were among the social elite of Chicago. Hatton was educated at Waterman Hall in Waterbury, Connecticut. In the late 1880s she went to Germany, lived in the home of American novelist Blanche Willis Howard, and studied at the Von Priese School in Stuttgart, where she frequently attended the theater. Travels in France interspersed her education, which continued in Berlin under the outstanding German tragedienne Marie Seebach, who encouraged Hatton's interest in writing. In 1889, as Fanny Locke, Hatton published travel articles in the *Chicago Tribune*.

Married to John Kenneth MacKenzie in 1890, she was familiarly known in Chicago social circles as "Mrs. Jack." Three children, one of whom died in infancy, were born to the marriage. Over the years, eight or ten of her one-act plays were given amateur performances at charity benefits in Chicago and near her summer home in Michigan. One of her comedies, *The Snowman*, was professionally performed in vaudeville by John Mitchell, a nephew of Charles Hoyt. Hatton's first husband, a mining engineer, was killed by Yaqui Indians in Mexico in 1905, causing an international scandal and the execution of sixteen Indians in reprisal.

It was at the theater that the charming widow met her second husband, Frederic Hatton, drama critic for the *Chicago Evening Post*. They married in 1909, and she soon began collaborating on his play reviews. The couple had no children. The signature "F. Hatton" served for both, as their judgments and writing styles proved indistinguishably similar. After July 1914 they wrote reviews and feature articles for the *Chicago Herald* and signed themselves "The Hattons." In 1920–1921 they were co-critics for the *Chicago Tribune*.

The Hattons launched their joint career as playwrights with *Years of Discretion*, a comedy of middle-aged love in an upper-class setting, produced by David Belasco and starring Effie Shannon. Chicago audiences gave the clever material an ecstatic reception in the play's initial run at the Powers Theatre (opening on 19 Nov. 1912). It went on to open in New York (25 Dec. 1912) at the Belasco Theatre, winning further accolades and a 190-performance run. *Years of Discretion* established the characteristic "happy Hatton" style: sparkling—sometimes risqué—repartee in a light, sophisticated vein that contrasted smartly with the hackneyed melodramas and farces that had been Broadway's standard fare. The Hattons themselves were a "debonair couple," according to Charles W. Collins, "Fred with his quiet affability as a writer and man, Fanny with her vivacity and sprightly conversation."

The Great Lover (1915), produced by George M. Cohan and Sam Harris, starred Leo Ditrichstein (who also shared authorship credit with the Hattons) as the philandering star of a metropolitan opera. One of the Hattons' most successful comedies, it ran 245 performances at the Longacre Theatre, was revived on Broadway in 1932, and was made into a 1931 movie. *Upstairs and Down* (1916) clearly demonstrates the Hattons' role in ushering in the spirit of the Roaring Twenties. Set at a Long Island weekend house party, the satiric exposé of the idle rich and their equally lusty servants introduced a "baby vampire" character who was later called the prototype of the flapper. With *Lombardi, Ltd.* (1917), the Hattons incorporated their characteristic "patter of racy and spicy lines" into an Italian dressmaker's studio setting, which provided ample opportunity for satirizing the vanity of society women and showing models "in an undress that would

make one sit up at the Winter Garden" (*New York Times*, 26 Sept. 1917); the 1927 revival again starred Leo Carriollo. *The Indestructible Wife* found fun in the figure of "the restless woman of indomitable energy, who in her frantic attempts to be always doing something, bores and exhausts her friends, relatives, and servants" (*Theatre*, Mar. 1918). *The Walk-offs* combined wit, vulgarity, and titillating subjects such as "divorce, cocktails, and cigarettes for women" (*New York Evening World*, 18 Sept. 1918). Other successful comedies from "the pioneers of polite indecorum in the Drama" (Hammond) included *The Checkerboard* (1920), *We Girls* (1921), *Treat 'em Rough* (1926), and *Synthetic Sin* (1927). Their later plays were mostly adaptations of foreign originals. By the mid-1920s however, they had moved to Hollywood, where they wrote the subtitles for approximately 125 silent films and later worked on screenplays for Universal Pictures, Metro-Goldwyn-Mayer, Warner Brothers, Paramount, and First National. They also wrote many short stories and articles.

Nothing is known of her life after the 1920s. Fanny Hatton died at the home of her son Dr. Locke MacKenzie in New York City.

• The Billy Rose Theatre Collection at the Lincoln Center Library for the Performing Arts houses the Hatton scrapbooks and clippings files. Sources of biographical data on Fanny Hatton include Charles W. Collins, "When Belasco Accepts Your Play: The Experience of the Hattons," *Green Book Album* (Feb. 1913): 222–34, and obituaries in the *New York Times* and *New York Herald Tribune*, both 28 Nov. 1939. Other useful articles are Keene Sumner, "The Happy Hattons and Their Creed," *American Magazine*, Oct. 1918, pp. 36–37, 60–71; [anon.], "*Years of Discretion*—A Play of Cupid at Fifty," *Current Opinion*, Feb. 1913, pp. 116–20; and A. P., "Novelties in a Novel Play," *Theatre Magazine*, Apr. 1913, pp. 119–20. Percy Hammond's assessment of the Hattons' contribution to the theater appears in the *New York Herald Tribune*, 24 Sept. 1932.

FELICIA HARDISON LONDRÉ

HAUGE, Gabriel Sylfest (7 Mar. 1914–24 July 1981), economist, White House aide, and banker, was born in Hawley, Minnesota, the son of Soren Gabrielson Hauge, a Lutheran minister, and Anna B. Thompson. Hauge lived in the small town of Hawley until he enrolled in Concordia College at Moorhead, Minnesota, in 1931. Active in clubs as well as the student newspaper and radio station, he was elected class president each of his first three years. As a senior, he was student body president and class valedictorian.

After receiving his A.B. in 1935, Hauge remained at Concordia for a year as assistant dean of men and coach of forensics. In 1936 he enrolled at Harvard University, where he earned a master's degree in economics in 1938. He taught economics at Harvard for two years before accepting a similar position at Princeton. Joining the navy early in World War II, he served in the Pacific and rose to the rank of lieutenant commander. He then returned to Harvard, where in 1947 he finished his doctoral dissertation on "Banking Aspects of Treasury Borrowing during World War II."

Encouraged by one of his professors at Harvard, in 1947 Hauge accepted a position as chief of research, under Elliott V. Bell, at the New York State Banking Commission. Hauge remained with the commission until 1950, although during the 1948 presidential campaign he took time out to serve as an economic adviser to the Republican nominee, New York governor Thomas Dewey. When Bell subsequently moved to McGraw-Hill Publishing, Hauge followed and served from August 1950 to December 1952 as an editor of *Business Week*. He married Helen Landsdowne Resor in 1948; they had seven children.

Hauge's connection with Dwight D. Eisenhower began in late 1951, when he became a member of the eastern-based and moderate Republican exploratory group, "Citizens for Eisenhower." The following June, he joined Eisenhower's staff as research director but soon became a key speech writer because of his ability to frame issues in the plain language that the candidate preferred. After the election, he was appointed to the White House staff as Eisenhower's "personal economic adviser" and occasional speech writer. He continued in this capacity until he left the White House staff in late 1958.

As an economic adviser, Hauge was an advocate of what he called "dynamic conservatism." Unlike the more traditional Republican, the dynamic conservative acknowledged that the federal government should play a role in dampening inflation and stimulating growth to avoid depressions. Such federal intervention, however, was to be done cautiously, and always constrained by the recognition that the government should "reinforce rather than replace" the marketplace. More specifically, a dynamic conservative was, according to Hauge, "not much taken with the idea that government price fixing, wage control, rationing, production planning and materials allocation can do the job better than the free market system—except, of course, in time of war" (Eisenhower, p. 488).

Hauge's views placed him on the liberal end of the spectrum within the Eisenhower administration in debates over economic policy. Most significantly, he frequently sided with Arthur Burns, chief of the Council of Economic Advisers, in largely successful efforts to combat Secretary of the Treasury George Humphrey's rigid insistence on balanced budgets. In addition, he encouraged Eisenhower's belief that the interstate highway system could be used as a means of "leveling out peaks and valleys" in the nation's economy, but he agreed with conservatives that federal operation of the Hell's Canyon Dam was unwarranted interference with the private sector. Although Eisenhower praised his "highly valuable advice" and regarded his aide as presidential timber, Hauge's efforts to sway his boss were not always successful. Indeed, the president rejected a Hauge/Burns aid-to-depressed areas program in 1955 and in 1958 sided with Secretary of the Treasury Robert Anderson in rejecting Hauge's proposal for a tax cut as an emergency antirecession measure.

Hauge left government service in 1958 to join the Manufacturers Trust Company as chair of its finance committee. After Manufacturers Trust merged with Hanover Bank in 1961, he became vice chairman of the board, then president in 1963, and board chairman from 1971 until his retirement in 1979. During this period, he led the successful legal fight to defend the Manufacturers-Hanover merger against antitrust prosecution and presided over the bank's tremendous growth.

While working for Manufacturers Hanover, Hauge frequently spoke out on such favorite topics as the need for free trade and a restrained monetary policy. During the 1960s he warned the Democratic administrations of John F. Kennedy and Lyndon B. Johnson against excessive tinkering with the economy, and later he enthusiastically endorsed President Richard M. Nixon's efforts to enhance trade with the communist bloc, even to the point of having his bank open a branch in Rumania. Hauge also retained the Washington contacts to be expected of someone with his background and his status as head of the nation's fourth largest bank. A strong candidate for several posts within the Nixon administration, Hauge nonetheless announced that he preferred to remain with Manufacturers Hanover. The Ford administration included him among the private economists called to Washington to advise on economic policy, and President Jimmy Carter consulted with him prior to nominating Paul Volcker to head the Federal Reserve Board. He died on Manhattan Island in New York.

Hauge played a significant role in articulating and defending Eisenhower's more liberal economic impulses against some of the more conservative voices within the administration. As an influential White House aide, he promoted a moderate policy that accepted limited government intervention to avoid dramatic swings in the economy, while at the same time displaying an enduring faith in the free market as the key to the nation's economic growth and political freedom.

• The Columbia Oral History Project contains a 1967 interview with Hauge, and the Dwight David Eisenhower Presidential Library has a small collection of his papers (1952–1958). No biography of Hauge has been published. Dwight D. Eisenhower, *Mandate for Change* (1963), contains useful material on the president's evaluation of Hauge as well as a discussion of Hauge's economic views. See also Herbert Parmet, *Eisenhower and the American Crusades* (1972), and Stephen Ambrose, *Eisenhower: The President* (1984). Iwan Morgan, *Eisenhower versus the Spenders* (1990), is very helpful in placing Hauge in the context of the administration's economic policy debates. For his White House and later years, the *New York Times* articles at the time of his resignation (16 July 1958) and death (25 July 1981) are most helpful.

KENNETH M. JONES

HAUGEN, Gilbert Nelson (21 Apr. 1859–18 July 1933), farm politician and businessman, was born in Rock County, Wisconsin, the son of Niels Haugen and Kari Nielsdatter, farmers. Haugen's parents came to the United States from Norway in 1846. When Gilbert was only a year old, his father died, but the family remained in Rock County. At age fourteen he followed the grain harvest into the Norwegian settlements of northern Iowa. There his contacts grew into business and educational arrangements, acquisition of land, lifelong associations, and a political career.

While engaged in horse trading during the mid-1870s, Haugen spent his winter months at Decorah (Iowa) Institute. He then completed his formal education at Janesville (Wis.) Business College in 1877, bought a farm near Kensett, Iowa, and established farm service businesses in Kensett. At twenty-one he was elected justice of the peace, and in 1885 he married a sprightly school teacher, Bertha Elise Evenson (known as Elise).

Elected county treasurer in 1887, Haugen moved to Northwood, the county seat. Twice reelected as treasurer, he also acquired a failing bank and successfully reorganized it. In 1892 tragedy struck when Elise died following the birth of their second child. Haugen never remarried.

In 1893 Haugen was elected to the lower house of the Iowa General Assembly, where he subsequently served two terms but was defeated in the nomination process for a third in 1897. Republican leaders saw his potential for drawing the Scandinavian vote in Iowa's Fourth Congressional District, consisting of two tiers of counties below the Minnesota border from Worth County in the west to the Mississippi in the east. In an 1898 district convention that went to 366 ballots, Haugen won the Republican nomination for Congress and defeated his Democratic opponent that fall. Subsequently, he mastered political forces in the bucolic Fourth District so successfully that the electorate kept him in Congress for seventeen successive terms. His maiden speech in the House came in support of a bill to prohibit the coloration of oleomargarine. Iowa then led all states in the production of butter; according to Haugen, dairy farmers and creameries deserved protection from "fraud and deception."

The rise of progressivism in Iowa, and later nationally, caught Haugen off guard, and his response was to try to hold ground at the center of the Republican party. In 1907–1908 Scandinavian supporters urged him to declare for the governorship or a seat in the U.S. Senate, but he concluded that this would draw him into the progressive/standpat fray. His ambition notwithstanding, he stepped back from such ideological feuds and ran his Fourth District campaigns as independently as possible from party machinery. In time, however, people (including Iowa senator Jonathan P. Dolliver and trusted political adviser James Albert Smith of Osage), circumstances (such as the rule of "Czar" Joseph G. Cannon in the House), and his own inclination nudged Haugen into insurgency and progressivism. In 1910 he stood with the insurgents to break Cannon's power, and subsequently he supported much of the progressive legislation of Woodrow Wilson's first term. Historian Gilbert Fite

has correctly labeled Haugen a "pragmatic progressive."

As did other midwestern progressives, Haugen opposed American entry into World War I. During the war he also challenged the policies of "food dictator" Herbert C. Hoover, which, he concluded, required farmers to make greater sacrifices than businesspeople.

In 1919 Haugen assumed the chairmanship of the House Agriculture Committee and used this position for the next twelve years to influence American farm policy. Proud of his role in the repeal of the Daylight Savings Act in 1919 and the passage of the Packers and Stockyard Act of 1921, he conducted lengthy hearings on the postwar "farm problem." Haugen urged farmers to organize and work collectively through national political institutions, just as industrialists and laborers had done, but he believed that his role in government required him to hear impartially a full spectrum of ideas. As did many of his generation, Haugen rejected production control as a means of stabilizing farm prices. The solution he settled upon was a two-price system for specified commodities—a pegged domestic price, based on the farmer's buying power during the prosperous years 1906 to 1915, and a lower world market price. Farmers who produced eligible commodities would pay a pro rata "equalization fee" and receive compensation between the domestic and world price as determined by a Federal Farm Marketing Board. Haugen never tired of explaining that the benefits to farmers would resemble those that manufacturers received from protective tariffs.

Complex McNary-Haugen bills containing the above features passed both houses of Congress in 1927 and 1928. Voting for these bills (and related ones that did not clear both houses) disrupted traditional regional and party alignments. McNary-Haugenism drew strong support from the agricultural Midwest and Far West, broke up the "solid South," and repulsed urbanites, particularly in the East and Northeast. Among the staunchest supporters and opponents of the concept were members of both political parties. Republican Calvin Coolidge vetoed the 1927 bill, calling it unconstitutional and without benefit to the farmer; he also vetoed the 1928 version as "the very essence of price fixing." Hoover likewise condemned McNary-Haugenism, preferring cooperative marketing as his approach to farm relief.

Haugen continued to embrace "Mary Haugen," as cartoonists labeled the concept, after the sponsor in the Senate, fellow Republican Charles McNary of Oregon, gave up. Defeated in the 1932 Roosevelt landslide, Haugen died four months later in Northwood. His thirty-four years in the House established a record (since broken) for continuous service. A week after the funeral, Franklin D. Roosevelt presented his New Deal farm policy, and an Illinois editor speculated that Haugen's old farm relief colleagues, several of them now New Dealers, "must have chuckled up their sleeves at the progress of events." The same editor credited Haugen with "building a foundation for an ordered agriculture." An old line progressive, Haugen saw no problem in using the powers of government to benefit citizens, including farmers. There is no evidence that he changed his mind about crop and livestock reduction schemes; in his value system, the farmer's duty was to produce.

Internationalists regarded the "dumping abroad" aspect of the McNary-Haugen Bills as a flaw that could cause serious problems with other nations—a legitimate criticism that Haugen did not answer satisfactorily. Haugen strained his party loyalty to the limit in futile attempts to pass a McNary-Haugen bill over the veto of a Republican president. In his analysis, failure to deal with the farm problem of the 1920s led to disaster for the nation's economy. Prolonged agricultural depression and attempts to alleviate it generated frustration and acrimony. Through it all, Haugen maintained his composure. His credibility within and beyond the agricultural community was due, in large part, to his presence and bearing. The genial, white-haired, grandfatherly Iowan, a master of statistics, convinced audiences that government intervention in agriculture need not lead to bolshevism. Particularly in the Midwest, many farm families idolized Haugen for his dedication to the farmer's cause.

• The Haugen papers, consisting of 189 boxes of correspondence, speeches, business papers, photographs, and records, are at the State Historical Society of Iowa in Iowa City. Peter T. Harstad and Bonnie Lindemann have used this collection and other sources to prepare a full-length biography, *Gilbert N. Haugen: Norwegian-American Farm Politician* (1992). See also Gilbert C. Fite, "Gilbert N. Haugen: Pragmatic Progressive," in *Three Progressives from Iowa*, ed. John N. Schacht (1980); and John D. Black, "The McNary-Haugen Movement," *American Economic Review* 18 (Sept. 1928): 406–27. Obituaries are in the *Des Moines Register* and the *New York Times*, both 19 July 1933.

PETER T. HARSTAD

HAUGHTON, Billy (2 Nov. 1923–15 July 1986), harness driver and horse trainer, was born William Robert Haughton in Gloversville, New York, the son of William F. Haughton, a silk mill proprietor, and Edith Greene. Haughton's interest in horses and harness driving began early. He was five when his father bought him a pony with a standard basket cart. Some years later, mimicking the harness drivers at a nearby track, the boy converted the cart into a makeshift sulky. His father rewarded him by purchasing a standard sulky for him.

During his teenage years Haughton groomed horses at the Fonda, New York, fairgrounds. He got his first racing experience there, riding a thoroughbred. He continued to work as a groom until he enrolled at the Cobbleskill (New York) Agricultural College, where he earned an associate's degree in animal husbandry in 1946. At college he worked part time for Billy Muckle, a standardbred trainer. Largely through Muckle's influence he gravitated toward harness racing, winning his first race in 1942 with one of his employer's horses. During World War II Haughton volunteered for the U.S. Army, but he was rejected because of a riding injury.

Haughton went to Saratoga Springs where he found employment as a stable operator in 1947. The following year he began training and racing at Roosevelt Raceway in Westbury, New York, and he moved his operation there in 1949. He married Dorothy Bischoff in November 1951; they had five children.

In 1963 Haughton moved his winter quarters from South Carolina to Florida and built one of the largest and most successful stables in the country. Often more than a hundred horses were on hand at the same time. Horsemen and trainers criticized his stable as too large and unwieldy, but Haughton's record was his best retort, for his horses won nearly every major harness stakes race from the late 1940s to the mid-1980s.

As a driver, Haughton compiled a superlative record. He made his way to the top by age thirty, leading all harness drivers in both victories and earnings in 1954. He won the Hambletonian, harness racing's most prestigious event, four times, beginning in 1974. He drove Green Speed, the 1977 Harness Horse of the Year, to victory there, and in 1980 he brought Burgomeister to the winner's circle. The 1980 victory was especially gratifying because Haughton's son, Peter, killed earlier that year in an auto accident, had trained the horse. He captured the Little Brown Jug at Delaware, Ohio, five times. Rum Customer won the race in 1968 and then swept pacing's triple crown with victories in the Cane Futurity at Yonkers, New York, and the Messenger Stakes at Roosevelt Raceway. In terms of money won, Haughton was the leading driver nationally twelve times: consecutively from 1952 through 1959, and in 1963, 1965, 1967, and 1968.

Haughton's training techniques, a departure from the traditional methods of breaking horses rapidly for the track, proved to be highly effective. Ignoring adverse criticism, he instructed his trainers to bring yearlings along very slowly, jogging them twice daily for weeks before preparing them for racing. His best results came with Nihilator, the Little Brown Jug winner and 1985 Horse of the Year. Nihilator for a time held records for the fastest race mile and highest earnings among standardbreds.

Haughton was active off the track in harness associations. He served as a district director of the U.S. Trotting Association from 1955 until his death. He also served as president of standardbred owners' associations in New York and Florida. His advice on training, published in harness-racing journals, and his contributions to chapters on yearling selection and race driving in *The Care and Training of the Trotter and Pacer* (1968) are valuable resources for owners and drivers.

Haughton's career and his contributions to harness racing were capped by his 1968 election to the Living Hall of Fame at the Trotting Horse Museum, Goshen, New York, harness racing's highest honor. Among his other awards were the Harness Writers Association's Proximity Achievement Award in 1958 for outstanding service to the sport and the association's "Good Guy" Award in 1975.

Haughton's death resulting from a three-horse accident at Yonkers Raceway in 1986 stunned the harness-racing world. During his career, Haughton won 4,910 races with purses totaling more than $40 million; he ranked fourth among all-time harness-racing victors and fifth among money-winners. After Haughton's death, Del Miller, a fellow hall of famer and driver-trainer, described him as "the most complete horseman that the sport had. He meant every bit as much to harness racing as Arnold Palmer means to golf or Babe Ruth meant to baseball."

• A harness racing publication, *Hoof Beats*, published several useful articles about Haughton: Jim Harrison, "That Haughton Boy," Jan. 1954, pp. 26–31; Mary Louise McGregor, "Billy Haughton Training Techniques," Mar. 1964, pp. 32–33, 66–73; and "William R. Haughton" (an obituary), Aug. 1986, pp. 13, 156. An obituary also appears in the *New York Times*, 16 July 1986.

J. THOMAS JABLE

HAUGHTON, Percy Duncan (11 July 1876–27 Oct. 1924), college football coach and baseball executive, was born on Staten Island, New York, the son of Malcolm Graeme Haughton and Mary Nesbit Lawrence. Haughton grew up in Brookline, Massachusetts, and attended Groton School, where he captained the football team and played baseball. Entering Harvard University in 1895, he continued to play baseball, serving as team captain his senior year. He also played varsity football for three years, as tackle and fullback. Recognized as one of the great punters in football history, Haughton after his junior year was accorded second-team All-America status by Walter Camp. Following graduation in 1899, he coached football at Cornell University for two years, compiling a 16–5 won-lost record and achieving recognition by beating Princeton University twice. Haughton returned to the Boston area, where he entered a banking firm; in 1910 he joined a stock brokerage firm. In 1911 he married a widow, Gwendolen Whistler Howell, the grandniece of the painter James McNeill Whistler. They had one daughter.

On his return to the Boston area, Haughton had acted as a nonpaid assistant coach for Harvard's football teams until in 1908 he was asked to become head coach. Since 1876 Harvard had beaten Yale University only three times in twenty-six games, and Harvard had not scored at all against Yale in the past six years. In his first season as head coach, Haughton ended the string of Yale's shutouts. He coached at Harvard through 1916, and during his tenure Harvard won 5, lost 2, and tied 2 against Yale, won 5 of 6 against Princeton, and compiled a 71–7–5 record, including a 33-game unbeaten streak.

Not employed by the college, Haughton was highly paid through an alumni fund. For the decade preceding U.S. entry into World War I, Harvard's team under his guidance was a dominant competitor in college

football. He was an innovative coach, who used ball-handling deception, popularized the trap play, and was one of the first coaches to deploy a five-man defensive line with linebackers shifting positions behind the scrimmage line. When he became part owner and president of the Boston Braves baseball team in 1916, Haughton stayed on for one more season as football coach at Harvard. In 1917, after the United States entered World War I, he resigned from the Braves to serve in the army. He was a major in the chemical warfare service, fighting in France in the Tryon Sector and the Meuse-Argonne offensive.

Following the war, Haughton reentered the investment business, but in 1923, since the position he sought as athletic director at Harvard was not forthcoming, he accepted an offer to coach the Columbia University football team. In the middle of his second season at Columbia, after having compiled an 8–5–1 record, he died unexpectedly of angina pectoris.

Haughton was known for his severe and highly organized practices. He wrote of football as "a miniature war game played under somewhat more civilized rules of conduct." Later, describing his coaching methods, he said: "I am a strict disciplinarian and my football squad is going to be like an army." His teams were well drilled in fundamentals, and they played with a marked team spirit. His combined coaching record was 95 wins, 17 losses, and 6 ties, a .831 winning record. In 1951 he was elected to the National Football Foundation Hall of Fame. He was also national squash racquets champion in 1906 and a doubles champion in 1913.

• Materials related to Haughton, including sketches in the *Harvard College Class of 1899*, are in the Harvard University Archives. Haughton's views on football can be found in his book *Football and How to Watch It* (1922; rev. ed., 1924). Biographical sketches are in *Harvard Graduates' Magazine*, Mar. 1925; Edwin Pope, *Football's Greatest Coaches* (1955); and Ronald L. Mendell and Timothy B. Phares, *Who's Who in Football* (1974). See also Thomas G. Bergin, *The Game: The Harvard-Yale Football Rivalry, 1875–1983* (1984); John A. Blanchard, ed., *The H Book of Harvard Athletics, 1852–1922* (1923); Morris A. Bealle, *The History of Harvard Football, 1874–1948* (1948); Tom Perrin, *Football: A College History* (1987); Donald G. Herring, Sr., *Forty Years of Football* (1940); Tim Cohane, *Gridiron Grenadiers* (1948); Allison Danzig, *The History of American Football: Its Great Teams, Players, and Coaches* (1956); and Alexander M. Weyand, *American Football: Its History and Development* (1926). Obituaries are in the *New York Times*, 28 Oct. 1924, and *Literary Digest*, 15 Nov. 1924.

RONALD A. SMITH

HAUPT, Alma Cecilia (19 Mar. 1893–15 Mar. 1956), public health nursing leader, was born in St. Paul, Minnesota, the daughter of Charles Edgar Haupt, an Episcopal minister, and Alexandra Dougan. As the young sister of four brothers, Haupt described her childhood as a "tomboy existence tempered with exposure to the cultural and religious life" of her prominent St. Paul family. After completion of secondary education at West High School in St. Paul, she entered the

Liberal Arts College at the University of Minnesota in 1911 and graduated four years later with a bachelor's degree in physical education. After working for a year as a playground instructor in St. Paul and a social worker in Minneapolis, Haupt searched for a career that would provide her with mobility and, consequently, enrolled in the University of Minnesota School of Nursing. Upon graduation in 1919, she accepted a nursing position with the Minneapolis Visiting Nurse Association (MVNA), and within three years she became its nursing superintendent (1922–1924). Years later, Haupt recalled that the MVNA tasks of supervising home care and establishing a public health course for university nursing students were instrumental in directing her lifelong commitment to nursing's critical role in the public's health.

In 1924 Haupt was appointed by the Commonwealth Fund to become associate director of its child welfare demonstration project in Vienna, Austria. Haupt worked with the Commonwealth Fund project, which operated between 1923 and 1929, to demonstrate the effectiveness of public health nurses in improving both the mortality rates and the health of mothers, infants and children. Accompanied to Europe by her artist brother Theodore, she worked to restore the war-torn country's public health system. In recognition of her assistance in reshaping the country's health care, she received the Gold Cross of Austria. After returning to the United States in 1927, she was named associate director of the Commonwealth Fund's Division of Rural Hospitals and was asked to demonstrate that well-educated nurses were necessary for improvement of the country's rural health standards.

In 1929 Haupt's concern with the health of Americans motivated her to accept the position of assistant director of the National Organization for Public Health Nursing (NOPHN). She remained a leader within the NOPHN for six years, assuming the acting director position when Katharine Tucker, its well-known director, became ill. Through the inclusion of school, tuberculosis, communicable disease, and maternity nursing into the Civil Works Administration's projects, Haupt effectively advocated for more nursing care to the poor and more jobs for unemployed nurses. Moreover, after a six-week tour of six southern states, she boldly urged the improvement of the status of black nurses. Convinced of the power of the written word, she published more than twenty articles appealing for the interaction of education, health values, and financial resources to support the critical mission of public health nursing. Haupt advocated nursing reforms designed to improve the education of public health nurses while also increasing their responsibilities. Fighting for the "right" of nurses to administer injections, to complete urinalyses, and to take blood pressures, Haupt maintained that nurses, not physicians, should control the practice of public health nursing and that nurses were skilled in monitoring patient care.

In early 1935, Haupt, who had become a well-established national leader, was invited by Fred Ecker, president of the Metropolitan Life Insurance Company, to become director of the company's Visiting Nurse Service. As a pioneer in providing home care to industrial insurance policyholders, Metropolitan Life Insurance Company assumed that "public health is purchasable" (Marquis James, *The Metropolitan Life: A Study of Business Growth* [1947]). Organized in 1909 by Lee Frankel, Metropolitan's Welfare Division housed ten bureaus that provided educational programs, health pamphlets, and research demonstration projects to its forty million policyholders. In addition, the division's Visiting Nurse Service provided 4.8 million home visits (1931) to sick Metropolitan policyholders throughout the nation. Metropolitan executives believed that visiting nurses promoted health and saved the company millions of dollars in death benefits. But, by the late 1930s, changing disease patterns, higher overhead expenses, increased utilization of hospitals, and lower productivity of nurses had begun to increase the cost of a nursing visit, while the volume of visits declined.

Pragmatic, outspoken, and ferociously dedicated to the public's health, Haupt believed that she could halt the inverse relationship between cost of services and volume of visits, while participating in "a national health council which had the programs, the leadership, and the finances to do effective health care" (*Quarterly Bulletin*, 1951). Thus, in October 1935 she accepted the directorship of the Metropolitan Life Insurance Company's Visiting Nurse Service in New York City.

A hard-driving businesswoman, Haupt worked to increase productivity and lower the cost of home nursing visits throughout the United States and Canada. Believing that education would increase efficiency, she initiated teaching and practice centers for staff nurses, provided nurses with a six-week course on the "Nurse and the Family," statistically analyzed records kept by nurses, and, impressed by the industrial model of management, added layers of supervisors and educators to ensure the efficiency of nurses. World War II interrupted her work when, in 1942, Metropolitan granted her a leave of absence to serve as a consultant to the nursing subcommittee of the Office of Defense Health and Welfare Services in Washington, D.C. She coordinated the wartime nursing activities of twelve government agencies, including the American Red Cross, the National Nursing Council for War Service, and the War Manpower Commission. After returning to Metropolitan in 1943, she remained concerned with the production of qualified public health nurses and served as a consultant to the national committees until the close of the war. Forever convinced that the nation's health depended on the efficacy of public health nursing, Haupt and Canadian Metropolitan nurse Alice Girard attended the Fiftieth International Council of Nurses Convention in Stockholm, Sweden, in 1949 to deliver a paper on the effectiveness of home health care in the United States.

Despite Haupt's diligent endeavors, the rising cost and declining volume of home visits remained a critical issue for the Metropolitan Visiting Nurse Service. By April 1950, the nursing service was caring for only 1 percent of policyholders. Arguing that the future of health care would rest with government programs and prepaid hospital insurance, Metropolitan executives decided to close the Visiting Nurse Service. Haupt was devastated by the abrupt decision but agreed to remain with the company to close the service. On 1 January 1953 the Metropolitan Life Insurance Company Visiting Nurse Service closed, and Haupt retired.

Although impaired by severe hypertension and arthritis, Haupt remained a champion of public health nursing after her retirement to California. She never married. At the time of her death in San Francisco, she had completed a manuscript for a textbook of public health nursing administration.

A well-known figure in the history of American nursing, Haupt is remembered for her administrative and leadership contributions to public health and visiting nursing, home care, and the education of public health nurses.

• Haupt's papers are located in the Metropolitan Life Insurance Company Archives, New York City; the University of Minnesota Library, Minneapolis; and the University of Minnesota School of Nursing Records. A listing of Haupt's published works can be found in the *Nursing Studies Index*, ed. Susan Reverby (1963; repr. 1984), pp. 849, 923. Haupt's works include "The Function of the Public Health Nurse in the Mental Hygiene Movement," *Public Health Nursing* 14 (Nov. 1922): 563–67; "The First Congress of Nurses of Middle and East European Red Cross," *Public Health Nursing* 17 (July 1925): 384; "Meeting the Need of the Small and Rural Hospital," *American Journal of Nursing* 29 (Jan. 1929): 42–46; "Nursing Councils: An Aid to Understanding Nursing," *Public Health Nursing* 32 (Apr. 1932): 410–14; "A Pioneer in Negro Nursing," *American Journal of Nursing* 35 (Sept. 1935): 857–59; "Organization of Nursing in Defense," *American Journal of Nursing* 41 (Dec. 1941): 1415–16; and "Forty Years of Teamwork in Public Health Nursing," *American Journal of Nursing* 53 (Jan. 1953): 81–4. Haupt is discussed in Diane Hamilton, "The History of Metropolitan Life Insurance Company, 1909–1953," (Ph.D. diss., Univ. of Virginia, 1987). Obituaries are in the *New York Times*, 17 Mar. 1956, and the *American Journal of Nursing* 56 (June 1956): 564.

DIANA HAMILTON

HAUPT, Herman (26 Mar. 1817–14 Dec. 1905), railway engineer, inventor, author, and administrator, was born in Philadelphia, Pennsylvania, the son of Jacob Haupt, a businessman of modest attainments, and Anna Margaretta Wiall, proprietress of a small dry goods store. Herman attended several private schools in Philadelphia, but in 1827 his father, suffering from poor health, gave up the grocery store he then owned and moved to Woodville, New Jersey. Jacob Haupt died the next year, leaving his widow in straitened circumstances; Herman, the eldest of six children, was only eleven years of age. Two years later Herman Haupt's congressman, John B. Sterigere, offered to help the boy gain admission to the U.S. Military Academy at West Point. He received a presidential appointment in 1830, but his entry was deferred for a year because of his youth. Unhappy with the strict upbringing he had received from his father, he was very uncertain about subjecting himself to the hard discipline of the academy, but his mother prevailed.

Haupt graduated thirty-first in his class of fifty-six men in 1835, after which he became a brevet 2d lieutenant of infantry. His military career was short; he resigned at the end of September 1835 and worked briefly as a draftsman and transitman for several Pennsylvania railroads. In January 1836, at only nineteen years of age, he was appointed an assistant engineer for a railroad running from Gettysburg to Hagerstown, Maryland.

In 1838 Haupt married Ann Cecilia Keller of Gettysburg. Their first home, Oakridge, was built on several acres of land on Seminary Ridge, west of the town, near where Haupt would support Union troops twenty-five years later. The couple had eleven children, eight of whom lived to adulthood. One son, Lewis, was himself a graduate of West Point and later a professor of civil engineering at the University of Pennsylvania.

In 1840 Haupt helped construct the York and Wrightsville Railroad in Pennsylvania. In so doing he discovered that no American railway engineer had previously assessed the strength of railway trusses in bridge construction. He therefore completed some technical experiments, and he was later recognized as having devised a means of "representing strains of geometrical solids; deflections by parabolic areas; and the variable pressures at various parts of beams by the corresponding ordinates of plane curves" (Lord, p. 24). He continued with this work and in 1841 published an anonymous booklet, *Hints on Bridge Construction*. Ten years later a revised and expanded version, *The General Theory of Bridge Construction*, appeared under his authorship. This pioneering study became a respected text in the field.

Haupt was an unpaid instructor in civil engineering and architecture at Pennsylvania College in Gettysburg from 1837 to 1839. He was granted an honorary M.A. by the college in lieu of salary in the latter year. He also operated a private school in Gettysburg from 1837 to 1845, which was then taken over by the college. For two years (1845–1847) Haupt served as a half-time professor of mathematics at Pennsylvania College while operating the Female Seminary of Gettysburg.

In 1847 Haupt joined the Pennsylvania Railroad as assistant to the chief engineer. When the first division of that line was completed in 1849, he became its superintendent. Within a few years he had become general superintendent of the company, in charge of construction, passenger, and freight operations. Much of Haupt's time was spent in controversies with the state canal commission, which owned the main line the company had to use until its own network had been completed. Haupt also battled the Pennsylvania trustees over a variety of issues and finally resigned late in

1852. He accepted the post of chief engineer for the Southern Railroad of Mississippi, but six months later a reconstituted Pennsylvania Railroad board asked him to return. While working with the Pennsylvania, he demonstrated that the company could make money by encouraging the development of local industries along its right of way. Haupt was sometimes abrupt and less than tactful with his superiors, and ill feelings frequently resulted. During his final year with the Pennsylvania, Haupt was elected to the line's board to represent the city of Philadelphia's interests in the company.

In 1856 Haupt accepted a new post as chief engineer and contractor for the Troy and Greenfield Railroad and Hoosac Tunnel in Massachusetts. This association, which continued on and off for nearly thirty years, would prove the most frustrating, costly, and vexatious venture of his life. Haupt invested heavily in the company, in which he held a controlling interest for some time. Although he was able to resolve the many technical challenges that arose, Haupt's progress was continually undercut by executives of the rival Western Railway Company and their political allies in the Massachusetts state government. In addition, he had to deal with a byzantine series of organizational and fiscal complications, resulting in frequent interruptions in construction. The financial panic of 1857 nearly drove Haupt out of business. Owing to disagreements with state officials about his handling of the contract, state authorities held up reimbursement of several hundred thousand dollars he had spent on wages, supplies, and equipment. In the spring of 1862 state authorities terminated his railroad construction contract and took control of the incomplete line pending an investigation.

With the coming of the Civil War in 1861, Haupt sought the newly created post of assistant secretary of war, for which an experienced railway man was needed. As a member of the West Point Board of Visitors, however, he had earlier antagonized Secretary of War Simon Cameron when the latter proposed a weakening of standards at West Point, and the job went to another man. In April 1862, however, Edwin M. Stanton, Cameron's successor, asked Haupt to come to Washington. Stanton recognized that civilian railroad men were better prepared to construct and maintain railroads than the military engineers, who had more experience with field fortifications and coastal defenses. Haupt was initially appointed to the post of aide-de-camp to Major General Irvin McDowell with the nominal rank of colonel, even though he had accepted with the understanding that he might work in civilian clothes. He declined any salary, asking only that his expenses be paid.

For nearly seventeen months, until September 1863, Haupt designed, built, and repaired critically important railway lines and bridges. President Abraham Lincoln inspected one bridge project Haupt had completed and characterized it as "the most remarkable structure that human eyes ever rested upon. That man Haupt has built a bridge across Potomac Creek,

about 400 feet long and nearly 100 feet high, over which loaded trains are running every hour, and upon my word . . . there is nothing in it but bean poles and corn stalks" (Lord, p. 77). Haupt had to cope with conflicting lines of authority, appealing to the War Department when more senior officers attempted to take over his lines for the movement of their own troops and equipment. At no time, despite Haupt's strong urging, was any one individual given overall authority over military railroads. Historians have generally agreed that he coped brilliantly with most logistical challenges, moving troops to the front, wounded to the rear, and equipment to where it was most needed with efficiency and dispatch. Haupt's unflagging efforts to assist Major General John Pope during the latter's withdrawal from the battle of Second Bull Run (Second Manassas) in August and September 1862 won him a promotion to brigadier general of volunteers. He never formally accepted his new commission, however, because he wanted to be free to cope with the ongoing railroad imbroglio in Massachusetts. He designated himself as chief of construction and transportation, U.S. Military Railroads, although his authority never extended beyond ground held by the Army of the Potomac.

At odd moments between his railroad duties with the Union army and return trips to Massachusetts to attempt some resolution of his continuing difficulties there, Haupt turned his mind to the possible solution of other military needs. These included ideas about coastal defenses and the propulsion of boats by water jets for the Union navy. He also developed a torpedo for destroying railroads and bridges, endorsed and utilized a subordinate's effective portable track-wrecking device, and proposed new methods of destroying locomotives and rolling stock. He also put forward proposals for a more effective military intelligence system. Save for the track-wrecking project, few of his ideas were adopted. Some of his suggestions for change and reform got him into difficulties with Stanton and with Secretaries Salmon P. Chase of the Treasury Department and Gideon Welles of the navy. Haupt was particularly caustic toward Welles. Early in 1863 he found time to draft another book, this one an instructional text, *Military Bridges: With Suggestions of New Expedients and Constructions for Crossing Streams and Chasms*, which was published in 1864.

Haupt anticipated and met most of the army's demanding logistical requirements before and during the battle of Gettysburg. Within a three-day period at the beginning of July 1863, for example, his work crews had reconstructed nineteen destroyed bridges between Hanover and Harrisburg, Pennsylvania. For the balance of his time with the army, his people were engaged primarily in guarding existing railway lines.

In September 1863 Haupt's military work came to an abrupt end when Massachusetts governor John Andrews, who had opposed Haupt on the Troy and Greenfield matter, pressed Stanton to insist that Haupt formally accept his brigadier general's commission. Andrews, a staunch administration supporter, reasoned that with Haupt in uniform, his military obligations would prevent him from returning to Massachusetts to press his claims for financial restitution against the state. Stanton insisted that Haupt sign his commission, which Haupt declined to do, and Stanton angrily relieved him of all responsibilities with the army. When the final report of military railroad operations was submitted by Haupt's successor after the war, Haupt's name was not mentioned, an unfortunate omission.

Haupt's long disputes with the state of Massachusetts were not resolved for twenty years. In 1868 his construction firm was awarded $53,000—Haupt had claimed nearly $400,000—for losses and expenses while building the Troy and Greenfield Railroad. Haupt received less than $22,000; the remainder went to former partners and retired old debts. Not until 1884 did the state agree to pay Haupt and his former partners $150,000, or eight cents on the dollar, for the shares they held in the railroad company. All told, Haupt's personal loss in the Troy and Greenfield Railroad exceeded $400,000.

Haupt attempted a number of other business ventures between 1863 and his death, most with little or only short-term success. He began a farm in Virginia and later tried creating a resort in a remote western part of that state. He developed an effective rock drill, but turned the project over to a son, who could not market it effectively. In many joint enterprises with others, he was saddled with partners less than straightforward in their financial dealings with him, which got him into financial difficulties. From late 1872 until the end of 1875 he was superintendent of the Richmond and Danville Railroad, a subsidiary of the Pennsylvania Railroad, but he was discharged after the Pennsylvania pulled out of the project.

In 1878 Haupt was named superintendent of the Tide Water Pipe Company, which successfully built an oil pipeline between Coryville and Williamsport, Pennsylvania. Following a rate war with the competing Standard Oil Company, however, Tide Water was obliged to enter an oil traffic pool in 1880, which gave it less than 20 percent of the business in the state. Named general manager of the Northern Pacific Railroad in 1881, Haupt completed construction two years later, despite formidable obstacles. A successful company union he formed was still operating well into the twentieth century. Operating costs were too high to satisfy investors, however, and Haupt resigned. His efforts to complete the Dakota and Great Southern Railroad foundered, owing to poor financial conditions following the panic of 1883.

Haupt invested time and money on the use of compressed air in urban transportation systems and in the National White Cross Milk Company, which was engaged in the manufacture of condensed and powdered milk. For years, the stock in this firm had little value, but when it was taken over by the Borden Company after Haupt's death, it earned income for his heirs until the patents expired in 1930. Books and articles published by Haupt during his later years reflected the wide range of his interests. They included: *Tunneling by Machinery* (1867); *Herman's Wooing: A Parody on Hiawatha* (1881); *Street Railway Motors* (1893); *Compressed Air and Electricity for City, Suburban, and Rapid Transit Service* (1895); *The Presidential Election of 1900 and Its Probable Consequences* (1901); and *Reminiscences of General Herman Haupt* (1901).

Haupt's financial position was often precarious, and his last ten years were spent living on borrowed money. At the age of eighty-seven he suffered a heart attack following an unproductive meeting with the owners of the National White Cross Milk Company in New York; he died on a train returning to his home in Washington.

• The bulk of Haupt's papers are in the archives of the Yale University Library. Smaller collections are in the National Archives and at the Minnesota Historical Society. A complete biography is James A. Ward, *That Man Haupt* (1973). Francis A. Lord, *Lincoln's Railroad Man: Herman Haupt* (1969), focuses on Haupt's Civil War career. See also sketches of Haupt in Ezra J. Warner, *Generals in Blue* (1964), and Roger J. Spiller et al., eds., *Dictionary of American Military Biography* (1984). Haupt's work is also discussed in George E. Turner, *Victory Rode the Rails: The Strategic Place of the Railroads in the Civil War* (1953), Thomas Weber, *The Northern Railroads in the Civil War* (1952), and Bruce Catton, *Mr. Lincoln's Army* (1951). See also Richard Snow, "American Characters: Herman Haupt," *American Heritage* (Feb.–Mar. 1985); George H. Burgess and Miles C. Kennedy, *Centennial History of the Pennsylvania Railroad Company, 1846–1946* (1949); and William Henry Haupt, *The Haupt Family in America* (1924).

KEIR B. STERLING

HAUPT, Paul (25 Nov. 1858–15 Dec. 1926), Assyriologist and biblical scholar, was born in Görlitz, Germany, the son of Carl Gottlieb Haupt, a police officer, and Elise Hülse. He dropped his two original first names, Hermann Hugo, early in life. Graduating from the Gymnasium Augustum in Görlitz, he prepared for a career in music, but after entering the University of Leipzig, he concentrated in Semitic languages. He received his Ph.D. in 1878, under Friedrich Delitzsch; his dissertation was published in 1879 as *Sumerische Studien*. In the same year he published his first major study, "Die Sumerischen Familiengesetze," a pioneering study in Sumerian philology. He was appointed Privatdocent at the University of Göttingen (1880) and commenced a series of publications on Sumerian dialectology and Akkadian phonology and morphology that were both original and important for later studies by others. His work in Sumerian abandoned the fantastic speculations of his predecessors on the relationship of Sumerian to other languages and treated it as a language to be studied in its own right according to rigorous linguistic standards.

In 1882 Haupt's *Akkadische und Sumerische Keilschrifttexte (Assyriologische Bibliothek* 1) appeared. This published in clear, accurate copies a considerable body of Sumerian lexical, dialectal, and bilingual religious texts and was a contribution of outstanding importance to Assyriology. It was followed in 1891 by his

Das Babylonische Nimrodepos (*Assyriologische Biblio-thek* 2), which presented the fragments then known of the Akkadian Epic of Gilgamesh. This remained the basic text publication of the epic for forty years.

In 1883 Haupt was appointed professor at Göttin-gen and in the same year the first professor of Semitic languages at Johns Hopkins University, though he was only twenty-four years old; for the next six years he held these posts concurrently. In 1884 Haupt mar-ried Margaret Giede; she died two months later. In 1886 he married her sister, Minna Giede; they had four children.

After 1889 Haupt's sole position was at Johns Hop-kins as W. W. Spence Professor. He made annual trips to Germany until the outbreak of the First World War. Together with Delitzsch he founded a periodi-cal, *Beiträge zur Assyriologie und vergleichende Sprach-wissenschaft* (ten volumes through 1927). So substan-tial were Haupt's contributions to Akkadian grammar, morphology, and phonetics that Delitzsch dedicated his *Assyrische Grammatik* (1889) to his former pupil. Haupt also collaborated with William Rainey Harper for some years in editing the American journal *He-braica*.

Under the influence of the biblical scholar Paul de Lagarde, Haupt turned his energies to biblical studies after 1890, seeking to reform American biblical schol-arship along the lines of German Semitic philology, with a particular emphasis on biblical Hebrew poetry and metrics. He published a commentary on the Song of Songs (*The Book of Canticles*, 1902; *Biblical Love-Ditties*, 1902), which drew attention to its love lyrics and explicit sensuality. This was followed by a rapid series of studies of the Hebrew Bible based on his as-sumption that the poetry had a rigid metrical scheme often altered by later editors; Haupt therefore permit-ted himself extensive emendation of the received text to fit his notions of its meter and poetics. Among his major works were *Koheleth* (1905), *The Book of Ecclesi-astes* (1905), *Purim* (1906), *The Book of Nahum* (1907), *Biblische Liebeslieder* (1907), *Jonah's Whale* (1907), *The Book of Esther* (1908), *The Aryan Ancestry of Jesus* (1909), *The Burning Bush and the Origins of Judaism* (1910), *The Book of Micah* (1910), *Ancient Protest Against Curse on Eve* (1911), *Yolgotha* (1920), and *To-bit's Blindness and Sara's Hysteria* (1921); in addition he was the author of over four hundred articles and essays on various subjects of biblical and Semitic phi-lology. But his critical judgment did not match his philological gifts, and despite occasional brilliant in-sights, his biblical scholarship had little long-term ef-fect.

Haupt's most ambitious enterprise was the *Sacred Books of the Old Testament* (1893–1904). This was a major statement of the "Documentary Hypothesis," according to which the Hebrew Bible was compiled and edited from several different written sources that could be identified and reconstructed. Haupt and his coworkers undertook to publish a version of the He-brew Bible with these documents as they reconstruct-ed them printed in different colors within a running text; this work is referred to as the "Polychrome Bi-ble." Sixteen volumes were printed of Hebrew text, thanks to a generous subvention, but only six in the English version before it was abandoned by its pub-lisher on financial grounds. Although various leading biblical scholars edited the Hebrew text, Haupt con-tributed notes and comments throughout each volume on the most diverse subjects.

Under Haupt's leadership, Johns Hopkins became one of America's most active centers for the study of Semitic languages and literatures. He was a gifted and demanding teacher, whose best-known student was William F. Albright, who was to become a dominating figure in American biblical scholarship and Haupt's successor at Johns Hopkins.

Haupt was associated with the Smithsonian Muse-um in various curatorial capacities from 1888 until his death. He was a member of the International Congress of Orientalists, the Society of Biblical Literature (pres-ident, 1905–1906), the American Oriental Society (president, 1913–1914), the Johns Hopkins Philologi-cal Association (president, 1915–1916), the Society of Oriental Research, the Vorderasiatische Gesellschaft, the American Philosophical Society, and Phi Beta Kappa. He died in Baltimore.

Haupt's substantial accomplishments in Assyriolo-gy and Semitics were overshadowed by his subsequent biblical publications, which were of far less impor-tance. His career marks a turning point in the develop-ment of American Semitic and biblical studies. Whereas previously promising American Semitists had been obliged to travel to Germany to complete their studies, Haupt created a program at Johns Hop-kins that in effect transplanted the Leipzig philological tradition to the United States and so contributed sig-nificantly to raising the standards of American Semitic philology. He was also important in creating an Amer-ican biblical and Semitic discipline at home in a pro-fessional, secular, university academic department rather than in a theological seminary, as had been the case for much of the nineteenth century.

• Haupt's papers and correspondence are in the archives of the Johns Hopkins University. A bibliography of his publica-tions through 1926 appears in *Oriental Studies Published in Commemoration of the Fortieth Anniversary (1883–1923) of Paul Haupt as Director of the Oriental Seminary of the Johns Hopkins University*, under the editorial direction of C. Adler and A. Ember (1926), which contains an essay by William F. Al-bright, "Professor Haupt as Scholar and Teacher" (pp. xxi–xxii). Personal and family data are in *Neue Deutsche Biogra-phie*, 8:102–3. Obituaries and appreciations include W. F. Albright, *Beiträge zur Assyriologie*, vol. 10, no. 2 (1927): xiii–xxii; Cyrus Adler, *Journal of the American Oriental Society* 47 (1927): 1–2; H. Zimmern, *Zeitschrift für Assyriologie* 37 (1927): 295–6; and the *Baltimore Sun*, 16 Dec. 1926.

BENJAMIN R. FOSTER

HAUPTMANN, Bruno Richard (26 Nov. 1899–3 Apr. 1936), convicted kidnapper and murderer, was born in Kamenz, Saxony, Germany, the son of Herman Hauptmann, a stone mason, and Paulina (maiden name unknown). As the youngest of five children, Richard, as he was called, grew up pampered and spoiled by his mother and older siblings. At the age of fourteen, he quit school and began an apprenticeship to a master carpenter; he quickly grew to love carpentry and to become expert at it. In 1918 he was drafted into the German army and suffered two minor wounds during his service as a machine gunner. In early 1919, hungry and out of work, Hauptmann and a friend burglarized three houses in his home region. They were arrested and sentenced to five years in jail. Released after four years, Hauptmann again burglarized houses and businesses, for which he served another year in jail. After escaping, he tried twice unsuccessfully to stow away on German ships bound for the United States. On his third try, he stowed away on an American liner and landed in Hoboken, New Jersey, in the spring of 1924.

Hauptmann easily blended into the vast immigrant community in New York City. As a skilled carpenter, he found steady work and managed to save more than $1,000 a year. He met a German immigrant named Anna Schoeffler with whom he fell in love; they were married in 1925. For the next six years, they accumulated considerable savings through their frugal lifestyle. They put money in the bank and bought a car, and Richard began to invest in the stock market. He also entered into a fur trading business with Isidor Fisch, another German. By early 1932 Hauptmann had obtained a good job as a carpenter at the Majestic Arms apartments, and Anna had begun working at a bakery. By all accounts, the Hauptmanns, now living in a rented apartment in the Bronx, enjoyed a happily married life, one that would be enhanced by the birth of their only child, Manfred, in 1933.

On the evening of 1 March 1932, the eighteen-month-old son of Charles and Anne Lindbergh was kidnapped from their home in Hopewell, New Jersey. Because of Lindbergh's international fame as an aviator, the crime made headlines all over the world. The publicity, however, prevented Lindbergh from communicating directly with the kidnappers, who had identified themselves as at least two people through their use of the plural "we" in the original ransom note they had left in the baby's bedroom. On 10 March 72-year-old, eccentric John Condon, whom the kidnappers had contacted, was assigned to serve as Lindbergh's intermediary with them. On 2 April Condon handed over $50,000 in ransom money, much of it in gold notes. The child, however, was not returned, and on 12 May the badly decomposed body of a male baby was found in a wooded area about six miles from the Lindbergh estate. Lindbergh and Betty Gow, the baby's nurse, positively identified the corpse as that of his son.

For nearly two and a half years, the authorities made no progress in the Lindbergh kidnapping case, but on 16 September 1934 a gold note from the ransom was turned in as payment at a gas station in the Bronx. The note was traced to Bruno Richard Hauptmann, who was arrested on 19 September. Six days later, he was indicted for extortion. On 19 October Hauptmann was extradited to New Jersey to stand trial on the much more serious charges of murder and kidnapping. The heavily publicized trial took place in the Flemington, New Jersey, courthouse from 2 January to 13 February 1935. Personally led by the state's attorney general, David Wilentz, the prosecution successfully convinced the jury of Hauptmann's guilt on first-degree murder charges, and he was sentenced to die in the electric chair. Various appeals through the New Jersey court system and to Governor Harold Hoffman delayed the execution. But after his appeals were exhausted, Hauptmann was electrocuted at the state penitentiary in Trenton on 3 April 1936, maintaining his innocence to the end.

The question of Hauptmann's complicity in the Lindbergh kidnapping remains the subject of considerable controversy. The prosecution's case against Hauptmann rested on several categories of evidence. First, nearly $14,000 in gold notes from the ransom was found carefully hidden in Hauptmann's garage. Second, Arthur Koehler, a wood expert, testified that the wood from a board in Hauptmann's attic matched the wood on one of the side rails of a ladder used by the kidnapper to reach the baby's second-floor bedroom. Third, handwriting experts testified that all ransom notes and other communications with Lindbergh through Condon were written by Hauptmann. Fourth, Condon testified that the kidnapper with whom he had twice met and talked was Hauptmann. Fifth, Lindbergh testified that the voice that called out to Condon outside the cemetery where the ransom was paid was Hauptmann's. Finally, witnesses placed Hauptmann in the vicinity of the Lindbergh estate on the day of the crime.

Although Hauptmann's defense at the trial proved incompetent, research later uncovered some evidence pointing to Hauptmann's possible innocence of the charges of murder and kidnapping. Nevertheless, his possession of such a large sum of the ransom money clearly implicates him in the crime of extortion. Whether Hauptmann actually kidnapped and murdered the Lindbergh baby, however, has not been proven or refuted by the available evidence. Koehler's testimony about the match between a ladder rail and a floorboard from Hauptmann's attic assumed an imaginary "gap" in the floorboard that he failed to substantiate. The original ransom note found in the baby's bedroom had several distinctive differences in writing style, spelling, and cursive handwriting from the subsequent notes. To arrive at their conclusion, the handwriting experts compared only a very small number of the words and letters on the notes with Hauptmann's handwriting. Of the witnesses who testified against Hauptmann, one was legally blind, and another agreed to testify only after receiving payment in advance. Although both Lindbergh and Gow identified the corpse as that of his son, no scientifically credible evidence was produced to positively identify the skeletal remains as that of the Lindbergh baby.

As the man convicted and executed for the kidnapping and murder of the Lindbergh baby, Bruno Richard Hauptmann became one of the most famous criminals in American history. The inordinate amount of publicity given to the case, much of it sensational and irresponsible, led to Hauptmann's conviction in the minds of many Americans before the trial began. Actions by the authorities strongly militated against his chances of acquittal. For example, testimony given at evidentiary hearings in the Bronx was suppressed; thus at the trial neither Condon's initial refusal to identify Hauptmann as the kidnapper with whom he met nor Lindbergh's failure to detect Hauptmann's voice was brought up. More than 100,000 pages of New York and New Jersey police and FBI documents concerning the case were also suppressed. And the authorities were not rigorous in respecting Hauptmann's rights as the accused in a case involving a capital offense. Under severe press criticism for failing to solve the mystery, law enforcement officials reversed themselves once they had Hauptmann in custody. Rather than hold to their original assumption that a gang had perpetrated the crime, they attributed the entire kidnapping to him. From the available evidence, it appears certain that Hauptmann engaged in the plot to extort money from the Lindberghs, and it seems quite likely that others were involved as well.

• Among the numerous works on the Lindbergh kidnapping, those worth reading are John F. Condon, *Jafsie Tells All* (1936); Sidney B. Whipple, *The Lindbergh Crime* (1935); George Waller, *Kidnap* (1961); Anthony Scaduto, *Scapegoat* (1976); and Ludovic Kennedy, *The Airman and the Carpenter: The Lindbergh Kidnapping and the Framing of Richard Hauptmann* (1985). The first three strongly support the prosecution's case against Hauptmann, while the last two strongly endorse Hauptmann's claim of innocence.

MICHAEL L. KURTZ

HAUROWITZ, Felix Michael (1 Mar. 1896–2 Dec. 1987), biochemist, was born in Prague, the capital of the Austro-Hungarian province of Bohemia (later Czechoslovakia and now the Czech Republic), the son of Rudolf Haurowitz and Emilie Russ. The success of his family in the textile business provided him with an early education at home from private teachers. He then attended a Catholic school run by a German religious order, where, for eight years, he received a classical education emphasizing Latin and Greek. His education continued at a Prague Gymnasium, where he was able to study mathematics but little chemistry. Throughout his years at the Catholic school and the Prague Gymnasium, his private education continued, and he was able to expand his linguistic abilities from Czech and German to English, French, and Italian, skills he would make excellent use of in his future peripatetic life. After his graduation from the Gymnasium he attended a textile school to prepare himself for the family business.

Following the start of World War I Haurowitz was drafted into the Austrian army and trained to be an artillery battalion commander at an officer's school in Hungary. His active military service took place at the Tyrrollean front in southwest Austria, where he had sufficient free time to read chemical textbooks to prepare himself for medical school. In the spring of 1918 he was given permission to enroll in the medical school of the German University in Prague. He did well in his courses and also served as a volunteer assistant in the Department of Physiological Chemistry, where he began his research career (his first paper, published in 1920, was on fats in the gonads of a jellyfish). While he was a medical student he also had the chance to study for a semester at the University of Würzburg in Bavaria and to meet protein chemists who encouraged his interest in the important blood component hemoglobin. In 1922 Haurowitz received his M.D. from the German University in Prague, followed by a Doctor of Science degree in 1923.

Throughout the 1920s and 1930s, he continued to be associated with his doctoral institution, first as assistant in its medical chemical laboratory, then as docent in medical chemistry (1925–1930), finally as supervisor of the medical chemical institute. During the 1930s, he advanced from assistant to associate professor in the medical school. He married Gina Perutz in June 1925; they had two children. Through this marriage he became friendly with Max Perutz, the Austrian-born English biochemist who would later win a Nobel Prize for his work on the molecular structure of blood components.

In the 1920s Haurowitz continued the scientific research on hemoglobin that he had begun as a medical student. This iron-containing respiratory protein in red blood cells consists of about 6 percent heme (the deep red, nonprotein, ferrous part) and 94 percent globin (the colorless protein part). Working with horse hemoglobin, because it was easily crystallized, Haurowitz and a co-worker showed in 1929 that heme is linked to globin through its iron atom. By reacting heme with acetic acid and sodium chloride, Haurowitz formed hemin, the reddish-brown crystalline chloride of heme (the laboratory test for the presence of blood), and in the 1930s he compared hemin with various porphyrin complexes (porphyrin is a nitrogen-containing organic compound occurring widely in living things and providing the foundation structure for hemoglobin, chlorophyll, and other important biological substances). He studied the optical and magnetic properties of these complexes and discovered that, unlike such metal-porphyrins as chlorophyll (with its magnesium-porphyrin complex), hemin's iron-porphyrin complex actually catalyzed hydrogen peroxide's decomposition into water and oxygen. In 1935 he succeeded in crystallizing complexes of hydrogen peroxide and methemoglobin, a brownish-red crystalline compound formed when hemoglobin combines with such toxic agents as carbon monoxide. In the late 1930s, he observed in a microscope the striking change that takes place when crystalline horse hemoglobin combines with oxygen. During the summer of 1937, on a visit to Gina and Felix Haurowitz in Prague, Max Perutz also witnessed this crystal conversion of hexagonal deoxyhemoglobin plates into elongated oxyhemoglobin prisms (Perutz has stated that this experience stimulated him to study how combination with oxygen modified the protein part of hemoglobin).

In 1930 Haurowitz was able to prepare crystals of human hemoglobin by slowly freezing an aqueous solution of hemoglobin and removing the ice crystals. However, his most important discovery was that a human fetus contains a different kind of hemoglobin from an adult. In 1930 he found spectrophotometric evidence indicating the presence of two different hemoglobins in the umbilical blood of a newborn child. In 1935 he discovered that, in red blood cells, the fetal hemoglobin's affinity for oxygen was higher than that of the adult hemoglobin's, and he even succeeded in separating the two hemoglobins from each other and in crystallizing the fetal hemoglobin. Haurowitz's discovery of fetal hemoglobin was the first proof of the existence of more than one hemoglobin in humans (more than 150 different human hemoglobins were later discovered).

Karl Landsteiner, an Austrian-American medical researcher, who had discovered blood groups (for which he would receive the 1930 Nobel Prize in Physiology or Medicine), had published extensively on immunological specificity, the ability of cells to manufacture antibodies against antigenic substances that they had never before experienced. In 1929 Haurowitz, who had closely followed Landsteiner's papers, wanted to provide immunological specificity with a secure chemical basis. Working with the virologist Friedrich Breinl, he started an experimental program designed to probe the nature and formation of antibodies. Antibodies of the immune system are globulins; they make up 45 percent of the total serum protein of blood. Globulins are proteins, widely distributed in plants and animals, that are insoluble in pure water and soluble in diluted salt solutions. He and Breinl already knew that the globulin fraction of immune serum had antibody properties, but did this mean that antibodies are globulins? To answer this question, Haurowitz isolated and analyzed various antigen-antibody precipitates, discovering that the globulin bound to antigen increased when the determinant groups per antigen increased. Indeed, a prerequisite for antigenicity seemed to be the polarity and rigidity of the determinant groups of the injected antigen. By the early 1930s, Haurowitz believed that antibodies were indeed globulins, and he theorized that the stunning specificity of serological reactions resulted from the antibody and antigen having mutually complementary combining regions. This came to be called the template theory of antibody formation, since antibodies are molded by direct contact with their antigens, just as a template serves as a guide in making an accurate pattern of some object.

Critics pointed out a crucial defect in the Breinl-Haurowitz theory of antibody formation: their template determined only the linear sequence of amino acids and did not provide direct information for the antibody's three-dimensional structure. Linus Pauling, the distinguished American physical chemist, built on Haurowitz's idea that an antibody assumes a shape that fits snugly around an incoming antigen. Since Pauling wanted a theory that made chemical sense, he devised a detailed explanation for antibody specificity based on his proposal that the antibody has two combining sites, with the specificity of the antibody's fusion with antigen resulting from the antigen's influence on the final folding of the polypeptide chain.

As the political situation deteriorated in Europe in the late 1930s, cooperation among scientists suffered, and some scientists fled to the United States. In 1939 Haurowitz emigrated to Turkey, where he became professor of biological chemistry at the University of Istanbul and head of the Department of Medical and Biological Chemistry. While there he learned Turkish quickly and was soon lecturing and publishing papers in Turkish. His textbook on biochemistry in Turkish was so successful that it passed through several editions. Once World War II began, many immunologists became part of the war effort, since producing vaccines for the military was a necessity (much information on immune phenomena was a helpful by-product). During the war, Haurowitz's and Pauling's idea of molecular complementariness as the basis of the specificity of serological reactions became an accepted theory, but it had serious problems. For example, their theory had no way to account for tolerance of self molecules, those that the immune system of an individual living thing recognizes as belonging to itself alone. If antibodies form simply through shaping themselves by contact with antigens, then why wouldn't antibodies form by wrapping themselves around self molecules, just as they do around foreign (non-self) molecules? Another shortcoming of the template theory was its inability to provide a satisfactory explanation of immunological memory. From the earliest days of immunology, scientists had observed that exposure to an antigen resulted in a heightened state of responsiveness in the exposed organism. The first time a given antigen enters an organism, the antibody response is sluggish, but subsequent exposure to the same antigen results in a speedy appearance of an antibody. Haurowitz was able to respond to some of these challenges to the template theory. For example, in 1942 he defused the objection that the antigen's determinant group would be incorporated into the antibody molecule by showing that antibodies directed against antigens containing arsenic, phosphorus, or iodine in their determinant groups were free of these elements.

By the time World War II ended, immunologists had established their discipline's practical importance and generated enough data to challenge biochemists such as Haurowitz to assemble these facts into a theoretical framework. Such a theory needed to explain not only how the immune response occurs when foreign antigenic material enters an organism but also why there is no response to an organism's own constituents. From 1948 on, Haurowitz pursued these issues in the United States, where he had moved that year to become a professor in the Department of Chemistry at Indiana University. He continued to emphasize immunochemistry in his research in Bloomington, but his teaching covered a wide range of topics. For example, his course on proteins and nucleic acid, much of which was later published, revealed that he was still committed to the template theory of antibody formation and that he also believed that protein is the genetic material. Protein chemists such as Haurowitz were slow to accept the implications of Oswald T. Avery's experiments in 1944 that he felt proved that deoxyribonucleic acid (DNA) was the information-carrying molecule. Haurowitz argued that proteins duplicate themselves through a like-with-like attraction between amino acids of the template polypeptide chain and free amino acids. Nucleic acid's role was to serve as a stretcher holding the template chain in an extended configuration. James Watson, who attended Haurowitz's course, later became convinced that nucleic acid, not protein, is the genetic material, and he, with Francis Crick, discovered the double-helical, three-dimensional structure of DNA. Indeed, it was not until 1961, when Crick and his co-workers demonstrated the unidirectional reading of DNA's triplet nucleotide code that Haurowitz finally accepted DNA as the hereditary substance.

Not only the protein theory of the gene came under attack in the 1950s; the template theory of antibody formation was also a target, mainly of biologists. A number of biologists, but especially Frank Macfarlane Burnet, took issue with the template theory, chiefly on the grounds that it failed to explain many biological phenomena of immunity, including memory and tolerance. Building on the natural selection theory of antibody formation proposed by the immunologist Niels K. Jerne, Burnet proposed a model in which the combining site of the specific antibody is completely determined before it ever encounters antigen. Through his studies Jerne had become convinced that the ten million trillion antibody molecules in human blood represented a sufficiently large number of potential locks for any conceivable antigenic key. Unlike Jerne, Burnet asserted that the antigen does not select individual antibody molecule per se for reproduction but somehow selects individual antibody-forming *cells* capable of making one and only one antibody. When such a cell encounters an antigen, it is stimulated to start production of antibody and to divide, giving rise to clonal progeny, all capable of making the same antibody. The ideas Burnet advanced in his 1957 paper, "A Modification of Jerne's Theory of Antibody Production Using the Concept of Clonal Selection," were destined to dominate immunology, to the detriment of Haurowitz's and Pauling's template theory.

When experiments showed that the specificity of the combining site is inherent in the amino-acid sequence of the antibody and that antibody-producing cells can synthesize large amounts of antibody in the absence of antigen, the central idea of the clonal selection theory seemed securely established. New discoveries in molecular biology made after Watson and Crick's discovery of the double helix validated that the configuration of proteins is determined entirely by their amino-acid sequence, which is in turn dictated entirely by the DNA sequence encoding them, in other words, by their genes. If, in response to multifarious antigenic challenges, an animal produces millions of different antibodies in a lifetime, then animals must come equipped with the genes necessary to make these antibodies. Despite the growing evidence in support of the new clonal selection theory, Haurowitz, like Pauling, continued to argue for the template theory.

Haurowitz continued to be interested in the mechanism of antibody formation for the rest of his life. It formed a significant part of what he considered his best book, *Chemistry and Biology of Proteins*, first published in 1950, with a second edition (with a new title) in 1963. He published reviews of antibody formation in *Nature* in 1966 and in *Physiological Reviews* in 1965, and he proposed a new theory of the mechanism of antibody formation in 1968. He synthesized much of his thinking on this subject in *Immunochemistry and Biosynthesis of Antibodies*, which was also published in 1968. At a historic conference at Cold Spring Harbor, Long Island, New York, in 1967, Haurowitz stated that template theories now seemed less attractive to him than in previous years. The reason for his long resistance to selection theories was the difficulty he had in believing that animals could carry the enormous amount of information necessary to code for every antibody needed to neutralize even greater numbers of natural and artificial antigens. However, the trillions of lymphocytes in human blood and the billions of nucleotides in cell nuclei convinced him that the potential existed for coding gigantic amounts of protein information, including the information for making many different antibody molecules.

Haurowitz was recognized with awards and honors celebrating his many discoveries related to hemoglobin and his template theory of immunology. In 1956 he was elected to the Leopoldina Academy of Sciences in Germany. In 1960, in Frankfurt, Germany, he received the Paul Ehrlich Prize and Gold Medal for his work in immunochemistry. In 1970 he was made a member of the American Academy of Arts and Sciences. In 1972 he was elected an honorary member of the French Société de Chimie Biologique and in 1973 of the Société Immunologique. He was chairman of the Division of Biological Chemistry of the American Chemical Society in 1962–1963, and he was elected to the National Academy of Sciences in 1975. He died in Bloomington, Indiana.

• Correspondence between Haurowitz and Linus Pauling can be found in the Ava Helen and Linus Pauling Papers at Oregon State University. Haurowitz's "Protein Heterogeneity: Its History, Its Bases, and Its Limits," *Annals of the New York Academy of Sciences,* vol. 325: *The Origins of Modern Biochemistry: A Retrospect on Proteins* (1979): 37–50, contains some autobiographical reflections on his work. Haurowitz discusses his own work in his books: *Chemistry and Biology of Proteins* (1950; 2d ed., *Chemistry and Function of Proteins* [1963]) and *Immunochemistry and the Biosynthesis of Antibodies* (1968). Many of Haurowitz's scientific publications are listed in Johann Christian Poggendorff, *Biographisch-Literarisches Handwörterbuch der Exakten Naturwissenschaften, Band VIIa, Teil 2: F-K* (1958), pp. 399–401. The most extensive biographical article is by Frank E. Putnam, "Felix Haurowitz, March 1, 1896–December 2, 1987," National Academy of Sciences, *Biographical Memoirs* 64 (1994), pp. 134–63. A shorter biographical article is in the *McGraw-Hill Modern Scientists and Engineers*, vol. 2 (1980). Some biographical material about Haurowitz is in Robert Olby, *The Path to the Double Helix* (1974), and in Arthur M. Silverstein, *A History of Immunology* (1989), which also includes a discussion of the "instruction template concept of antibody formation" of Breinl and Haurowitz. Further assessment of Haurowitz's achievements can be found in David Pressman and Allan L. Grossberg, *The Structural Basis of Antibody Specificity* (1968).

ROBERT J. PARADOWSKI

HAUSER, Gayelord (17 May 1895–26 Dec. 1984), nutritionist and author, was born Helmut Eugene Benjamin Gellert Hauser in Tübingen, Württemburg (now in unified Germany), the son of Christian Hauser, a schoolmaster, and Agate Rothe. He had his name legally changed to Bengamin (or Benjamin) Gayelord Hauser in 1923. In 1911 Hauser, then only sixteen, came to the United States from Germany to join his elder brother, Otto Robert Hauser, the pastor of a church in Milwaukee, Wisconsin. Unfortunately, very soon thereafter, the young Hauser was stricken with tuberculosis of the hip; after several operations, doctors declared his case hopeless.

Determined to find a cure, Hauser sought (as written in his unpublished memoirs) the advice of a naturopath, Dr. Benedict Lust. Noel F. Busch (*Saturday Evening Post*, 11 Aug. 1951) attributes the beginning of young Hauser's recovery to Lust's prescription of "long warm baths, clay packs and herb teas." Hauser also experimented with a form of osteopathy known as naprapathy. His symptoms grew less virulent. Encouraged by the initial results, in 1922 Hauser followed Lust's suggestion of visiting Switzerland to discover what natural "food science" (*Nahrungswissenschaft*)—at the time a new and burgeoning field—could do to improve his health. He met a monk, Brother Maier, who put him on a strict diet of salads, fruit juices, vegetable broths, and herbs. Within a few weeks, the diet had achieved what must have seemed a miracle: his hip abscess was permanently cured.

Infused with renewed vigor, Hauser was determined to learn more about "the power of food." His medical pilgrimage began with Vienna, where he devoured Baron Clemens von Pirquet's caloric theory. He proceeded to Zurich, where "Dr. Bircher-Benner and his two sons with their ideas on sunlit foods were teaching people how to eat their way back to health" (*Diet Does It*). His travels also brought him to Dresden, where he met a food chemist, Dr. Ragnar Berg; and Copenhagen, where he met Dr. Mikkel Hindhede, who advocated undereating in preference to overeating as a maxim of health.

Fortified with his newly acquired knowledge, as well as his health, Hauser returned to Chicago (where he had his name changed) to set up a small office at 116 Michigan Boulevard (*Saturday Evening Post*, 11 Aug. 1951). He toured the Midwest proclaiming the efficacy of his five "wonder foods" rich in vitamin B—yogurt, brewer's yeast, powdered skim milk, wheat germ, and blackstrap molasses—as daily staples. In the late 1920s Hauser became a partner in a Milwaukee firm called Modern Food Products, which specialized in a herb laxative, "Swiss Kriss." "Hauser broth," a health food that he created, was later marketed by the same company.

Hauser was not a doctor of medicine, which often led to controversy. He was sharply criticized by the medical establishment, particularly for his outspoken opposition to the traditional American diet of potatoes and meat. He was even arrested in Florida for lecturing, on the grounds that he was practicing medicine without a license. Worse, in 1951, the Food and Drug Administration confiscated copies of *Look Younger, Live Longer*, claiming that the book was being used to promote the false claim that blackstrap molasses is a panacea.

Nevertheless, Hauser persisted at and succeeded in becoming an authority on nutrition. He earned degrees in naprapathy from the Chicago College of Naprapathy in 1921; in naturopathy from the American School of Naturopathy in New York City in 1922; and in chiropractic from the American School of Chiropractic in 1923. Also in 1923 he received a degree in Immutable Naturopathy from the Naturopathic Health School in Chicago. Yet the degrees in which he displayed the most pride were the honorary doctorate he was awarded by the University of Philotechnique in Brussels, Belgium, in 1932, an honorary B.S. from the American University in Los Angeles in 1942, and another honorary doctorate from the Argentina School of Nutrition in Buenos Aires in 1954. He also became the adviser on nutrition of the Republic of Argentina in 1954. Furthermore, in 1972 he was named one of the makers of the twentieth century by the *Sunday Times*, London; in 1977, a statue was erected in his honor in Kyoto, Japan.

Yet perhaps his success as a health food advocate stemmed less from his accrued professional degrees and honors, and more from his success at converting Hollywood to his health maxims. In 1927 he moved to Hollywood, where his "natty good looks and brash, exuberant approach" (*Annual Obituary*, 1984) and his promise of youth and beauty devoid of the inconveniences of surgery, drugs, or starvation resulted in a huge following. Among his devotees was Adele Astaire, who later, as Lady Cavendish, became his most effective promoter in notable circles in London and Paris. Paulette Goddard, Marlene Dietrich, Greta Garbo, Gloria Swanson, Queen Alexandra of Yugoslavia, Baron Philippe de Rothschild, and the Duchess of Windsor were among those who flocked to him.

A prolific writer and tireless promoter, Hauser wrote eight health manuals from 1930 to 1936, among which were *Harmonized Food Selection, with the Famous Hauser Body-Building System* (1930); *Dictionary of Foods*, with Dr. Ragnar Berg (1932); and *Eat and Grow Beautiful* (1936). In the following years, he also wrote nine books, among which the most popular was *Look Younger; Live Longer* (1950), which was serialized in Hearst newspapers, condensed in *Reader's Digest*, and translated into twelve languages—the French edition was introduced by the Duchess of Windsor. Among his other popular books were *Be Happier, Be Healthier* (1952) and *Gaylord Hauser's New Treasury of Secrets* (rev. ed., 1974). His books were eventually translated into twenty-seven languages.

Hauser died in Hollywood, California, as a result of complications from pneumonia. His legacy was his pioneering work in food science, and his own long life and good health, to many people, seemed to prove his theories. Controversial as Hauser's methods of promotion may have been, scientific researches conducted in the 1970s validated many of his theories, paving the way for later notions of diet and health.

• Other health manuals Hauser wrote that were not presented in the text are *Food Selection and Health with the Famous Hauser Eliminative Feeding System* (1931), *Types and Temperaments: A Key to Foods* (1931), *Child Feeding: Written for Mothers* (1932); *Keener Vision without Glasses* (1932); and *Here's How to Be Healthy* (1934). Some of Hauser's other published books are *Better Eyes without Glasses* (1938); *Diet Does It* (1944); *The Gaylord Hauser Cook-book* (1949); *Gaylord Hauser's Treasury of Secrets* (1951); *New Guide to Intelligent Reducing* (1955); and *Mirror, Mirror on the Wall* (1961). Obituaries and other sources on Hauser may be found in the *Los Angeles Times*, 28 Dec. 1984; the *Washington Post*, 29 Dec. 1984; the *Fort Lauderdale Sun-Sentinel* 30 Dec. 1984; and *Newsweek*, 7 Jan. 1985.

CAROLINE JOAN S. PICART

HAVEMEYER, Louisine Waldron (28 July 1855–6 Jan. 1929), collector, patron, and suffragist, was born Louisine Waldron Elder in New York City, the daughter of George William Elder, a merchant, and Mathilda Adelaide Waldron. In 1874 Louisine accompanied her sisters and recently widowed mother to Europe. She and her sister Adaline resided in Paris at the fashionable Del Sartre rooming house favored by women art students. Emily Sartain, an art student from Philadelphia, befriended the Elder sisters, and in June she introduced Louisine to another American artist, Mary Cassatt. Louisine was enchanted by Cassatt's knowledge and love of art, and a lifelong friendship ensued. Their friendship and professional association became one of the most significant collecting alliances between a nineteenth-century patron and an artist. Cassatt became both mentor and guide, encouraging Louisine's life of collecting from her first purchase of paintings by Edgar Degas and Claude Monet in 1875. Louisine was singular among women collectors and patrons in both her support of Cassatt's artistic career and her own role in the popularization of contemporary art, especially that of the impressionists and the American expatriate painter James Abbott

McNeill Whistler, through her patronage, exhibition loans, and her bequest to the Metropolitan Museum of Art.

Louisine's marriage to Henry Osborne Havemeyer in 1883 resulted in the formation of one of America's most important private art collections. During the early years of their marriage, Louisine Havemeyer devoted herself to their three children and the building of their homes designed by Samuel Colman and Louis Comfort Tiffany in New York City and in Greenwich. In August 1889 Henry and their children met Cassatt in Paris. As her husband's artistic tastes shifted from Japanese porcelains and Chinese textiles to Old Masters and impressionist paintings, Havemeyer enlisted Cassatt as their art broker assisting in both the purchase and commissioning of works.

Following her husband's death in December 1907 Havemeyer continued her art collection with her daughter Electra's assistance. Between 1910 and 1911 she reentered the art world and extended her horizons with public support of the woman suffrage movement. Her mother had both an interest in the women's rights movement and friendships with the pioneers of the movement. Havemeyer had attended boarding school with the granddaughter of Lucretia Mott, a contemporary of Elizabeth Cady Stanton and Susan B. Anthony. She had been further encouraged by her husband and by Cassatt, who shared an interest in the education and suffrage of women. As a model of the "new woman"—educated, cosmopolitan, independent, and motivated—Havemeyer aided in the establishment of the National Women's Party and offered financial assistance through exhibition loans from her extensive art collections beginning in 1912. With Cassatt as collaborator, she organized the exhibition for woman suffrage at Knoedler Galleries in April 1915. Her goals were to show great works of art for the public's edification and to garner support, both moral and financial, for the suffrage cause. Then a reticent public speaker, Havemeyer spoke about the art of Degas and Cassatt at the private benefit preview. The three-week exhibition, *Masterpieces by Old and Modern Painters*, netted more than $1,000. That same year she campaigned for woman suffrage throughout New York, averaging seven daily speeches on her ten-day June tour with special displays of the "Torch of Liberty." Following the theft of the symbolic torch Havemeyer commissioned a battery-powered miniature model of the *Mayflower*, known as the "Ship of State," which quickly became the symbol of the suffrage movement. Despite their best efforts, woman suffrage was defeated in the November 1915 New York state referendum.

Beginning in 1916 Havemeyer served on the advisory council of the National Women's Party and spoke nationwide on behalf of the enfranchisement of women. On the eve of the Senate vote on the Susan B. Anthony amendment in February 1919, she joined an invited group of one hundred women in Washington, D.C., at a public demonstration at which she and thirty-eight other women were arrested for incinerating an effigy of President Woodrow Wilson. After one night in jail the 64-year-old grandmother and society matron boarded the "prison special" with other suffragists. This cross-country train trip lasted twenty-nine days, with Havemeyer serving as lead-off speaker at each stop. In May and June the House and Senate each passed the woman suffrage amendment, and Havemeyer initiated travel to garner support for the necessary ratification votes. She campaigned tirelessly and even joined the picket line at the Republican National Convention in June 1920. The Nineteenth Amendment became law with the ratification by the Tennessee legislature on 26 August 1920. Havemeyer presented the "Ship of State" and other memorabilia for a permanent exhibition on the woman suffrage movement to the Smithsonian Institution.

Havemeyer continued her art patronage throughout her political years, and she also expanded her cultural activities with talks and publications on contemporary art. She wrote her memoirs and a series of articles on the woman suffrage movement. Havemeyer was awarded the Cross of the Knight of the Legion of Honor in 1922 for her efforts on behalf of French art and culture, and she was promoted to officer in 1928. She was also honored by the National Women's Party in 1923 and elected a benefactor of the Metropolitan Museum of Art in 1924. Her friendship with Cassatt ruptured in 1923, but they reconciled before Cassatt's death in 1926. Havemeyer devoted her last years to cataloging her extensive art collection and to organizing its eventual dispersal to her children and the Metropolitan Museum of Art. Havemeyer died in New York City.

• Primary sources about Havemeyer's life and work are her own writings, *Sixteen to Sixty: Memoirs of a Collector* (1961); a series of articles in *Scribner's Magazine*, "The Suffrage Torch: Memories of a Militant," May 1922, pp. 528–39, "The Prison Special: Memories of a Militant," June 1922, pp. 661–76, and "The Freer Museum of Oriental Art, with Personal Recollections of the Donor," May 1923, pp. 529–40. See also her "Mary Cassatt," *Pennsylvania Museum Bulletin* (May 1927): 377–82, and "Notes to Her Children," a typescript in the Metropolitan Museum of Art Archives. Major secondary sources are three by Frances Weitzenhoffer, "The Creation of the Havemeyer Collection, 1875–1900," (Ph.D. diss., City Univ. of New York, 1982); "The Earliest American Collectors of Monet," *Aspects of Monet: A Symposium on the Artist's Life and Times* (1986), pp. 73–92; and *The Havemeyers: Impressionism Comes to America* (1986). The exhibition catalog *Splendid Legacy: The Havemeyer Collection* (1993) includes detailed chronologies of Havemeyer's life and an extensive bibliography. For the relationship between Havemeyer and Mary Cassatt, consult the work of Adelyn Dohme Breeskin, *Mary Cassatt: A Catalogue Raisonné of the Graphic Work* (1979) and *Mary Cassatt: A Catalogue Raisonné of the Oils, Pastels, Watercolors, and Drawings* (1970). See also Alicia Faxon, "Painter and Patron: Collaboration of Mary Cassatt and Louisine Havemeyer," *Women's Art Journal* (Fall 1982–Winter 1983): 15–20; Nancy Mowll Mathews, ed., *Cassatt and Her Circle* (1984); and Kathleen D. McCarthy, *Women's Culture* (1991). For Havemeyer's role in the woman suffrage movement, consult "Exhibition for Suffrage Cause," *New York Times Magazine*, 4 Apr. 1915; "Loan Exhibition in Aid of Suffrage," *Sun*, 6 Apr. 1915; Christine A. Lunardini, *From Equal Suffrage to Equal Rights* (1986); "Notable Exhibition of Old and Modern Painters for Benefit of Woman Suffrage Cause," *World*, 4 Apr. 1915; and "Suffrage Art Show Nets $1,100 in a Day," *World*, 7 Apr. 1915.

DIANE APOSTOLOS-CAPPADONA

HAVEMEYER, William Frederick (12 Feb. 1804–30 Nov. 1874), politician, was born in New York City, the son of William Havemeyer, a German immigrant sugar refiner and merchant. No information about his mother is available. After graduating from Columbia College in 1823, Havemeyer briefly studied law before entering his father's business. In 1828 he married Sarah Agnes Craig; they had ten children. A few months after his father's death in 1828, Havemeyer combined his father's firm with one owned by his cousin, Frederick Christian Havemeyer. The new business thrived and Havemeyer retired in 1842. From that point, he devoted his life to a variety of interests, including banking, governmental reform, and politics.

Havemeyer was affiliated with the Martin Van Buren wing of the New York Democratic party. In the spring of 1844 a sweep of New York City municipal elections by nativists, who favored extending the naturalization period to twenty-one years and called for Bible reading in the schools, set the stage for Havemeyer's entry into electoral politics. After President James K. Polk passed over Havemeyer for the position of collector of the Port of New York, Tammany Hall selected Havemeyer to challenge Native American mayor James Harper in the April 1845 elections. The election was a rout of the Native Americans, who failed to carry a single ward, and Havemeyer easily defeated Harper and a Whig candidate. As would be the case for all his administrations, Havemeyer's first mayoral term was marked by disputes with the Common Council over patronage and reform. The Tammany-controlled council ignored his calls for a new city charter that would limit the council's powers and give the mayor a veto. The mayor was more successful in creating a new municipal police force, though he failed in his effort to make the force a more nonpartisan unit by naming a Whig as chief. He urged federal and state involvement to improve health and sanitary conditions on immigrant ships and in May 1847 was appointed the first head of the New York Board of Commissioners of Emigration. He addressed street and sanitation problems and launched a highly publicized campaign to bring the notorious abortionist Madame Restell (Ann Trow Lohman) to trial.

Havemeyer refused renomination in March 1846. As the Van Buren wing of the party became more openly antislavery after 1844, Havemeyer followed his political friends into the Barnburner faction. Led by Van Buren and Silas Wright, the Barnburners, or the liberal/radical wing of the New York Democracy, were hostile to banks, enlargement of the state's canal system, and extension of slavery into the free territories. The split in the New York Democracy opened the way for the election of a Whig mayor in 1847. The next year, at a sharply divided Tammany nominating convention marred by fistfights, Havemeyer emerged again as his party's nominee for mayor. In April 1848 he defeated his Whig opponent by 920 votes. During his term, the mayor joined other Barnburners in bolting the Democratic party to support former president Van Buren, the Free Soil party nominee, in the 1848 presidential election.

Havemeyer's second administration followed a pattern similar to his first, with calls for reform often stalling in the Tammany-controlled council. He enjoyed some successes, police force reforms, ordinances to enforce garbage collection, and paving and lighting the streets. He also gained from the Common Council and state legislature more money for the city's public school system and, again demonstrating his nonpartisan approach to administration, named Whig Horace Greeley as commissioner of the common schools. In April 1849 city voters approved a Havemeyer-backed city charter that gave the mayor more power (though not a veto), but he declined renomination that month.

Out of office, Havemeyer became a trustee of the Astor Public Library and president of two banking institutions. His ten-year retirement from active politics ended in 1859, when Tammany turned to him as its best hope for defeating the renegade former mayor Fernando Wood, who broke with the Wigwam (Tammany Hall) and launched his own organization. In a race that also featured Republican and Whig nominees, Havemeyer finished second to Wood by about 1,400 votes. During the Civil War, Havemeyer supported the Union cause. In August 1863 he wrote to Abraham Lincoln, warning of a repeat of the July draft riots if changes were not made in the local conscription process.

Havemeyer's final term as mayor resulted from his involvement in successful efforts to bring down the political machine of William Marcy "Boss" Tweed. In April 1871 Havemeyer presided over a mass meeting called to protest the corruption in city hall, and that fall he headed the Committee of Seventy, a group of prominent men seeking exposure and ouster of the Tweed Ring. Havemeyer and his friend and associate, Samuel J. Tilden, chair of the state Democratic party, played key roles in two crucial actions. First, Havemeyer persuaded the incumbent city comptroller to appoint the Committee of Seventy's choice, Andrew H. Green, as deputy comptroller, thereby giving the reformers access to the city's books. Next, he and Tilden obtained a court order allowing the committee to inspect the personal bank accounts of Tweed and his associates. The findings, which revealed that the members of Tweed Ring were siphoning city monies into their personal accounts, doomed them. Although Havemeyer had successfully participated in organizing a reform Democratic ticket that smashed Tammany in the 1871 state legislative elections, he was nominated the next year for mayor by the Republican party. In the election, he easily defeated two Democratic candidates.

Havemeyer's third term was marked by fights with the Republican-controlled council over patronage. Eventually, on 8 July 1874, the council asked the governor of New York to remove the mayor from office in the wake of a police scandal. Though Havemeyer survived, he had lost nearly all of his supporters. He did gain some reforms to the city charter that strengthened the mayor's office; however, he was regularly attacked by Republicans over his tendency to appoint Democrats and by Tammany Democrats still resentful of his actions against Tweed.

In November 1874 Havemeyer was sued by the Tammany boss, John Kelly, for libel. However, before the case ended Havemeyer suffered a fatal heart attack at his desk. In some ways, Havemeyer can be seen as an early version of the good-government reformer of the late nineteenth and early twentieth centuries, committed to efficient, businesslike management of government regardless of party affiliation.

• The best secondary source for information on Havemeyer is Howard B. Furer, *William Frederick Havemeyer: A Political Biography* (1965). Family information is in John Craig Havemeyer, *Life, Letters and Addresses of John Craig Havemeyer* (1914); "William F. Havemeyer," *In Memoriam* (1881); and Henry O. Havemeyer, *Biographical Record of the Havemeyer Family, 1600–1954* (1944). A close look at Havemeyer's first efforts to reform the New York City Charter is Ira M. Leonard, "The Politics of Charter Revision in New York City, 1845–1847," *New-York Historical Society Quarterly* 62 (Jan. 1978): 43–70. An obituary is in the *New York Times*, 1 Dec. 1874.

ROBERT D. SAMPSON

HAVEN, Emily Bradley Neal (13 Sept. 1827–23 Aug. 1863), author and editor, was born in Hudson, New York, the daughter of George Bradley and Sarah Brown. George Bradley descended from a long line of sea captains, but a prolonged invalidism destroyed any hopes of a seafaring career. Presumably he supported his family on a pension, inheritance, or savings, but the record is not clear. George Bradley died on Emily's third birthday. His death left the family in some distress, resulting in Emily's being adopted, when she was six years old, by her mother's brother, the Reverend J. Newton Brown, and his wife. The couple had no children of their own but had already adopted another little girl, Louise, of whom Emily became very fond. Brown was minister of the Baptist church in Exeter, New Hampshire. In 1835 Emily became seriously ill, perhaps with scarlet fever. In addition to being physically painful, the illness affected her eyesight, making her nearly blind. Attending school, which she enjoyed, became impossible, and the little girl was confined of necessity to darkened rooms for several months. During this time Emily consigned to memory whatever her uncle and aunt read to her, and she and Louise made up stories and poems.

This lesson in patience and the exercise of imagination by virtue of adversity proved invaluable for the child's well-being as well as for the life and career that she would build for herself. The illness also imposed on Emily a stoic reserve, noticed by others as a standoffish personality, that "increased the privacy of her inner life, and led her to say frequently that she passed two childhoods equally real, one that all knew of, and another that no one suspected" (Richards, p. 24).

In 1838 Emily returned to Hudson, New York, and to her mother, who had remarried. She returned to New Hampshire a few years later to continue her education at the young ladies' school in New Hampton, which her elder sister had also attended. While still in Hudson, though, Emily began writing the diary that she continued to keep until the end of her life. A short story she later wrote, titled "Keeping a Journal," tells of her first efforts in journal writing.

Throughout her teenage years Emily continued to suffer bouts of blindness and accompanying pain. She seems to have regarded this as some failing within herself, seeking surcease through religious faith and yet reproaching herself for her discontent. In her journal she wrote,

I have never known positive happiness. My sorrow is all regret, my joy is hope. I live only in the past and future. Often my heart is full of love—love to all around me, even to those whom I treat with apparent coldness and indifference. I cannot let those I love, know it by outward signs, still less by words. Few understand me. I do not understand myself, I think. (Richards, p. 32)

Shortly after the preceding entry, she wrote,

Of all my wild and ambitious dreams, I have never dared commit one to paper; but to-day I am too full of them to repress the thoughts which are crowding upon me. I sometimes feel that I am not born for a common destiny, that I have talents which might elevate me above those with whom I now associate. . . . But hundreds have had these same thoughts and feelings. . . . Henceforth, ambition, be thou my angel! (Richards, pp. 33–34)

Emily's adolescent determination held. Though tormented by what she saw as her intellectual vanity, she refused to deny what she felt was her talent. She read widely, deeply, and eclectically. She submitted essays, poems, and sketches to her school's literary society and publication, and she showed a cool wit and skill at parody and satire, evidenced at school in a "travesty" of the Fourth Book of the *Aeneid*. Because of her recurring blindness, she had developed a phenomenal memory and was able to recall whole passages from only one reading or hearing.

In the early 1840s Emily started submitting her work to magazines and journals, including the story "The First Declaration," which she sent to *Neal's Saturday Gazette* under the pseudonym Alice Gordon Lee. The *Gazette*'s editor, Joseph C. Neal, was quite taken with the story, published it, and began a regular correspondence with its author. Neal critiqued "Alice's" writings, warning her against too much indulgence in sarcasm and bitter irony. Under Neal's tutelage, Haven redirected her literary style in a more compassionate and charitable direction. In his letters, Neal also told Emily how much her name—Alice Gordon Lee—appealed to him, because it sounded Scottish and his mother was a Scot. Upon learning her real name from a subscriber, Neal wrote to her praising her ruse and asking if he might continue to call her "Alice." In September 1846 Neal visited her in Hudson and shortly thereafter proposed marriage, and in December she married him and moved to Philadelphia.

Emily joined Joseph in his magazine work, assisting him with his editorial responsibilities and, as "Clara Cushman," writing a regular column (her popularity with the *Gazette*'s readers having already been established as "Alice Lee"). She and her husband also enjoyed the swirl of literary society in Philadelphia at the time. But Emily and Joseph's happiness together was short-lived. Joseph, who was more than twice Emily's age, died suddenly in July 1847, barely seven months after their wedding. Emily was a young widow responsible for a business in which her husband had been a partner. The business was probably what kept her from succumbing to grief (although it spilled out in her journal writings of the time), for she threw herself into her work as an editor, with a special interest in the juvenile department. Her column for children, "The Bird's Nest," was written under the pseudonym "Cousin Alice."

Emily Neal's religious temperament helped her to deal with sorrow as well as with her vanities. Her faith manifested itself further when, in 1849, she was confirmed into the Episcopal church. Also in 1849 the General Protestant Episcopal Sunday School Union published *Helen Morton's Trial*, the first in her series of books for Sunday schools. *Helen Morton's Trial* was the story of a child's temporary blindness.

Her stories for both children and adults contained moral and ethical lessons that gained Emily her fame and which her readers praised and came to expect from her. She never deviated from that charge except once, in 1850. *The Gossips of Rivertown, with Sketches in Prose and Verse* embraced all that her late husband had warned her away from: sarcasm, irony, wit, and cool, sharp observation. It was the only work she ever regretted publishing, yet to modern readers it may be the saving grace of an oeuvre seemingly weighted down with moral uplift. Even in those works, though, there is a pragmatism that makes the sentiment and idealism manageable. The existence of *The Gossips of Rivertown*, however, is evidence of the complexity of the person and the writer Emily was.

By 1850 Emily was an unquestioned success as a popular writer and publishing regularly. In January 1853 she married Samuel L. Haven, a New York stockbroker whom she had met in 1848. Their first son was born the following October, and in the spring of 1854 the family moved to Mamaroneck, New York. The next four years saw the birth of three more children and a nearby move to James Fenimore Cooper's former home "Closet Hall"; the Havens renamed it "The Willows." Haven's children and husband kept her busy and happy. She and her husband also traveled to California, the Southwest, and the Caribbean. Haven was something of an international celebrity, her Sunday school books having made her popular and well known wherever there was an Episcopal congregation. She also continued to be professionally prolific, publishing more books and magazine sketches, including an introduction to *The Widow Bedott Papers*, a collection of stories by another writer, Miriam Berry (later Mrs. Frances Whicher), who wrote pseudonomously as Widow Bedott and whom Haven's husband Joseph Neal had supported and published in the *Gazette*. Haven also became involved in emancipation efforts (her interest and ire had been piqued during a visit to St. Croix) and vigorously supported the Union forces when the Civil War broke out.

For several years Haven's bouts with blindness had been intermittent and fairly manageable. But her constitution had never been robust, and four pregnancies had weakened it further. By late 1862 it was clear she had tuberculosis; she was also pregnant with her fifth child. On 21 July 1863 she gave birth to a daughter. One month later Emily Bradley Neal Haven died at home in The Willows. She was thirty-five years old.

The number of people who attended her funeral in Rye, New York, was testament to how much she was loved and admired. Her gravestone bears simply her name and age and the inscription she chose: "Bear ye one another's burdens, and so fulfil the law of Christ" (Richards, p. 375).

Afflicted with severe health problems and possessed of an ambitious and sometimes acerbic mien, Haven was still able to write, act, and profess Christian charity and optimism throughout her life. She maintained successfully a difficult balance, not only with the two sides of her nature, but also with the demands of being a much-loved professional writer—a professional woman writer—and a much-loved wife and mother. Her family and her public greatly mourned her passing. While her name has not survived as a literary figure of note, she was valued in her time and had a profound effect on many people. The cloying titles and the rosy outlook and gentle beneficence advocated in most of her works were desired by the reading public. Haven gave them some common sense too.

What Haven wrote about Mrs. Whicher, alias the Widow Bedott, could apply equally well to her own self:

A modest, humble-hearted Christian woman . . . she remained until her pen was laid aside for the last time, and she passed to a home where all doubt and misunderstanding are denied an entrance . . . How she looked, spoke, and moved . . . we can recall but a fragment[:]

> "Hands and feet
>   Of respectable size,
> *Mud-colored* hair,
>   And dubious eyes." (pp. xiv–xv)

Contrary to her own assessment, Haven did understand herself. Her few extant journal entries show the struggles, the victories, and the life of the mind and body that she had to set down and sort through before she could write her other words. Those articulate journals, wherever they are now, are Haven's true and lasting literary legacy.

• Emily Bradley Neal Haven, under the pseudonym of "Cousin Alice" as well as her own name, wrote several highly popular children's books and adult fiction, including *No Such Word as Fail* (1852), *Patient Waiting No Loss* (1853), *"All's Not Gold That Glitters"; or, The Young Californian* (1853), *Contentment Better Than Wealth* (1853), *Out of Debt, Out of Danger* (1856), *The Coopers; or, Getting Under Way* (1858), *The Pet Bird, and Other Stories*, by Cousin Alice (c. 1863), and *The Good Report* and *Home Studies*, a collection of her tales (both published posthumously in 1867 and 1869, respectively). Before her marriage to Joseph Neal in 1846, she had published poems and sketches under the name "Alice G. Lee" in *Neal's Saturday Gazette* and in *Lady's Literary Museum*. Selections of her poetry appear in *The Female Poets of America* (1851), published when she was still Emily Neal. The fullest account of Haven's life is Cornelia H. B. Richards [Mrs. Manners], *Cousin Alice: A Memoir of Alice B. Haven* (1865), which reprints substantial excerpts from Haven's journal. Obituaries and tributes from *Arthur's Home Magazine*, the *New York World*, and Chicago's *Christian Times* are reproduced in Richards, *Cousin Alice*. *Godey's Ladies Book* published a lengthy tribute to her in their Jan. 1864 issue.

E. D. LLOYD-KIMBREL

HAVEN, Gilbert (19 Sept. 1821–3 Jan. 1880), Methodist bishop, editor, and abolitionist, was born in Malden, Massachusetts, the son of "Squire" Gilbert Haven, a bookkeeper and clerk, and Hannah Burrill. Young Gilbert attended local schools and then Wesleyan Academy in Wilbraham, Massachusetts, for two terms in 1839. After he worked in Boston in clothing and carpet businesses, he did another term at Wilbraham to prepare for entering Wesleyan University in 1842.

Graduating in 1846, Haven was a teacher and then the principal at Amenia Seminary in upstate New York for five years. Before resigning to enter the ministry of the New England annual Conference of the Methodist Episcopal (ME) Church, he preached his first abolitionist sermon in November 1850, attacking the Fugitive Slave Law. In the spring of 1851 he began a decade in Methodist pastorates in Massachusetts. In 1851 he married former Amenia student Mary Ingraham. The couple, who eventually had two children, moved every two years—from Northampton to Wilbraham to Westfield to Roxbury and to Cambridge. In the last pastorate, Mary died in childbirth in 1860.

Schooled by his father, who first voted for the Liberty party in 1842, to champion the abolitionist movement, Haven preached antislavery and racial equality from his pulpits throughout the 1850s. Some of his sermons attacking slavery in the South and "caste" in the North were printed locally, but only his eulogy for John Brown reached a wider audience. Not a member of any national antislavery organization, he joined the small Church Antislavery Society formed in 1859 to promote Christian abolitionism. He continued to be active in it throughout the Civil War. His long-standing conviction was that Christian churches ought to be reform societies, especially promoting human rights and the ideal of a multiracial society. He fervently hoped that the Republican party would join such a reform crusade.

On 19 April 1861 Haven's father, by then a magistrate, swore him into military service as chaplain of the Eighth Massachusetts Regiment. That role took him South for his first direct encounter with slavery. His attacks in the Methodist press on the compromises with slavery made in the border conferences of his denomination provoked opposition from Maryland and northern Virginia. Deciding not to reenlist after his three months' service ended, Haven returned to the family home in Malden, where his parents cared for his children, William and Mary. After a short assignment at a Methodist congregation in Newark, New Jersey, and still grieving his wife's death, he went abroad in April 1862 for ten months of travel through Great Britain, Europe, Egypt, and the Holy Land. His trip was the subject of his first book, *The Pilgrim's Wallet*, in 1866.

Throughout the trip, he wrote for Methodist journals and a religious weekly, the *New York Independent*, to advocate emancipation. Upon his return, his father died and Haven moved to live with his mother. Resuming a pastoral ministry in Boston for the next two and a half years, he enhanced his reputation as the foremost Methodist proponent for ending slavery and racial discrimination. In 1864 his denomination took an unequivocal stand to outlaw slaveholding members and ministers. Celebrating that success, Haven next wanted to influence ME policy on missions to the former slaves and to southern whites sympathetic to the Union cause. He advocated a racially inclusive standard for postwar Methodism by giving clergy status to black preachers in the North and by ministering to Methodists of both races together in southern missions. To test him, Bishop Edward R. Ames in June 1865 ordered Haven to go to Mississippi as a missionary to "colored people." When he failed to get an unqualified affirmation of his equal rights principles from Ames, and after the ME missionary board adopted policies of racial separation in its southern program, Haven refused his appointment and returned to Malden to recuperate from stress that turned into a collapse lasting more than a year. During that time he did not preach, and he even refrained from his favorite avocation, writing for the religious press. By the following March, his old passions reemerged when he became editor of the oldest Methodist weekly in New England, *Zion's Herald*. His debut was an article on the first page, titled "No Caste in the Church of God."

Until he was elected to the episcopacy in May 1872, editor Haven promoted lay representation and women preachers. He backed the civil rights and voting rights constitutional amendments of congressional Republicans as essential to national political reformation. He praised the success of southern racial integration in state politics and education. He promoted woman suffrage, temperance, coeducational schools, cooperation of labor and capital, a more just policy toward Native Americans, and even the legal recognition of Christianity in the U.S. Constitution. He attacked lotteries and capital punishment, and he deplored trends in the theater, liberal divorce laws, and urban conditions for new immigrants.

In 1872, given his social radicalism, Haven's selection as bishop and his assignment to Atlanta for his base were a surprise. Like other Methodist bishops, he presided over annual conferences all across the country and in mission fields such as Mexico and Liberia. His first tour in 1873–1874 took him throughout the South, where he ordained black and white pastors in the same services and broke down the color line in seating and at the communion table. His practices provoked not only ridicule and disdain from the separate Methodist Episcopal Church, South, but also opposition from white members and ministers in his own northern-based denomination, which at its 1876 General Conference imposed racial separation on its regional annual conferences. That move was anathema to Haven, and he protested before going to West Africa as a presiding bishop for the missionary conferences. There he contracted malaria, and his health declined.

Before the election of 1876, Bishop Haven had endorsed a third term for President U. S. Grant because he believed that protection of black citizenship would cease without a strong executive. The results of the compromise of 1877, therefore, deeply offended him. He sought unsuccessfully to resurrect the movement for racial justice not only in the South but throughout the nation. He praised Charles Sumner's Civil Rights Bill and eulogized the senator when he died in 1875. In the *Independent* the same year, he wrote to challenge white supremacy, "The word for America to-day is not Abolition, but Amalgamation." The black exodus to the West in 1879 confirmed his fear—first expressed eight years earlier when supporting Sojourner Truth's petition for homestead lands for former slaves—that without federal protection they would have to leave South.

Both his church and the Republican party marginalized Haven, who died in Malden. Not compromising his convictions, he went to his grave most appreciated by African Americans who kept his memory alive in naming schools, church buildings, a library, and even their own children after him. One black Methodist, Marshall W. Taylor from Kentucky, put it in 1880, "He is the nation's dead, the church's dead; but much more is he our dead" (Daniels, p. 214).

• Some of Haven's papers are scattered in more than twenty manuscript collections listed in William B. Gravely, *Gilbert Haven, Methodist Abolitionist* (1973). Haven coauthored (with Thomas Russell) the biography of Edward Taylor, Herman Melville's model for Father Mapple in *Moby Dick*, titled *Father Taylor, the Sailor Preacher* (1871). Of his foreign missionary trips he wrote *Our Next-Door Neighbor: A Winter in Mexico* (1875) and "America in Africa," *North American Review* 125 (1877): 145–58 and 517–28. A biography based on manuscripts no longer extant is George Prentice, *The Life of Gilbert Haven* (1883). A briefer biography, with eulogies, tributes, and a selected anthology of his writings is W. H. Daniels, ed., *Memorials of Gilbert Haven* (1880). Haven's abolitionist speeches between 1850 and 1868 were published as *National Sermons* (1869; repr. 1969). His son, William, edited and published some of his nonpolitical sermons as *Christus Consolator* (1893). Spiritualists published *Heavenly Messengers* (1890) to claim that Haven communicated through a medium from beyond the grave. An obituary is in the *New York Times*, 5 Jan. 1880.

WILLIAM B. GRAVELY

HAVERLY, Jack H. (30 June 1837–28 Sept. 1901), minstrel showman, was born Christopher Heverly in Boiling Springs (later known as Axemann), Pennsylvania, the son of Christopher Heverly, whose occupation is unknown, and Eliza Steel. After schooling in Axemann, Heverly moved to Bellefonte, Pennsylvania, in 1854 as a tailor's apprentice. A dispute with the tailor led to a thirty-day jail sentence for Heverly, who soon left for Ohio. Many of the details of his next few years are obscure, though he apparently performed a number of jobs, including "baggage smasher" on the railroads. By 1864 he was well settled in Toledo and opened his first variety theater. A printer's misspelling of his name on a batch of huge colored posters—one of many trademarks of his later work—was more cheaply left uncorrected and Heverly became Haverly. He had married Sara Hechsinger, one-half of the singing Duval Sisters, probably by 1864. She died in 1867 in Toledo, and he married her sister Eliza Hechsinger that same year. He had no children.

Although Haverly eventually acquired enough theaters to be acknowledged as the originator of the theatrical chain, it was another 1864 venture that began his ascent to fame. On 1 August the first Haverly's Minstrel troupe began a one-month tour of Michigan. Later in the year Haverly joined his troupe with Cool Burgess's, performing in Toronto, Canada. For the next several years, in keeping with America's boom-and-bust Gilded Age, Haverly formed and dissolved various minstrel partnerships throughout the Midwest. Between 1870 and 1873 he managed Cal Wagner's Minstrels; in Kansas City in 1873 he again formed Haverly's Minstrels.

Minstrelsy had already wandered from the classic three-part format of Edwin P. Christy. Haverly eventually expanded it to its historical limits in satisfying his P. T. Barnum–like ambition, "To astonish and satisfy the most exacting amusement seeker in the world." As theatrical historian Robert Toll wrote, variety, drama, opera, and equestrian shows "had all increased and enlarged their dimensions until their attractive qualities appeared unlimited."

By the 1870s there were black minstrels as well as whites in blackface makeup, and in 1876 Haverly set up a "colored" troupe with Tom Maguire in Nevada. In 1878 he went into partnership with Charles Callender to run the Georgia Colored Minstrels. With a show bigger than most, Haverly and Callender introduced religious music and attracted an African-American audience. Laying the groundwork for generations of show-business stereotypes of African Americans, Haverly advertised his company as "The darky as he is at home, darky life in the cornfield, canebrake, barnyard, and on the levee and flatboat."

As Haverly's shows and reputation grew, so did the tales of his debacles—eventually he was supposed to have lost as many as seven fortunes. By 1877 he was reportedly $104,000 in debt. Still, Haverly bought out Callender and increased the size of the company enormously. In 1879 the first of many songbooks attributed to him, *Haverly's Genuine Georgia Colored Minstrel Songster*, was published.

Meanwhile in 1878 Haverly had organized his most famous company, which would invent a new theatrical form, bridging the gap between old-style minstrelsy and the enlarged, highly organized form of variety that became known as vaudeville. Haverly simply threw everything that proved popular into his shows and spent enough on them so that the customers could see the money. He quadrupled the standard number of performers and advertised them thus: "Forty—Count 'Em—40—Forty—Haverly's United Mastodon Minstrels!" Haverly was superstitious about forty, recalling wanderings in the wilderness and Noah's flood. As for Mastodons, this was the era when herds of circus elephants were stampeding the customers into the big tops.

When Haverly's Mastodon Minstrels came to town, they came in with a drum corps and a brass band, wearing silk hats, frock coats, and lavender trousers, marching two abreast through the town. Charles Frohman, Haverly's treasurer (later a major theatrical producer), marched with them, carrying a three-foot iron money safe. In the "humbug" style of the era, it was probably empty, but the display created awe anyway. Everything was vast and tasteful. In a single program could be found a scene showing a "Turkish Barbaric Palace in Silver and Gold" as well as a baseball sketch, a tableaux of the dying athlete, and a parody of Barnum: "Pea Tea Bar Nones Kolossal Cirkuss, Museum, Menagerie and Kaynes' Kicadrome Kavalkade." By 1879 the Mastodons were offering serious, if Marx Brothersish, parodies of Gilbert and Sullivan.

Using a barrage of publicity, including what minstrel historian Harry Reynolds called "Haverly's gorgeous lithographed posters, about 30 by 40 inches," the Mastodons conquered Britain in 1880, displaying two rows of vocalists, two of instrumentalists, and an enormous drummer. There were sixteen corner men and eight each of Bones and Tambourine. The Mastodons toured to Germany, where arrest was threatened for impersonating Negroes. An all–African American Mastodon troupe repeated the company's success in 1881.

The high point of Haverly's career proved to be 1881; he owned three theaters in New York, and one each in Brooklyn, Chicago, and San Francisco, and he ran the largest black and white minstrel troupes. There were two opera companies, two sporting organizations, two mining companies, an agency in London, and a great many ventures in the stock market. A slight, grey-eyed man with a drooping mustache, Haverly gained the reputation of an expert poker player.

Using the advice of his friend John Cudahy, the packing-house magnate, he apparently tried unsuccessfully to corner the market on pork. "Haverly" shoes, neckties, and hats became fashion hits.

Haverly was able to boast of his entertainment empire that "The most select society in every large city in America visits periodically." He insisted, "I've got only one method . . . to find out what the people want and then give them that thing . . . There's no use trying to force the public into a theater."

In response to the "refined" minstrelsy of Sam Haynes's Touring British Minstrels in 1881, Haverly mounted a "colossal Japanese show," hailing from "the court theatre of his Imperial Majesty, the Mikado of Japan." In 1883 Haverly acquired the San Francisco Minstrels, New York's last resident minstrel company, dating to 1865.

The Mastodons returned to Britain in 1884. A heat wave and the competition from Callender's new troupe turned the venture into a nightmare, and in August Haverly was back in New York, his latest fortune gone. He continued to run minstrel troupes until 1898.

By 1901 Haverly was running a small museum in Brooklyn. The last three years of his life were spent trying to build another fortune by gold-mining. Haverly died in Salt Lake City.

• The Harvard Theater Collection, Cambridge, Mass., specializing in minstrelsy, contains a number of references to Haverly. Haverly's various songbooks can be found in the British Library, London. Hugh Manchester, *Colonel Jack Haverly* (1976), a monograph by an author from Bellefonte, Penn., corrects many inaccuracies in earlier biographical sketches and includes data not to be found elsewhere. The Bellefonte Bicentennial Celebration (1976) honored Haverly. Highly useful books include Robert C. Toll, *The Minstrel Show in Nineteenth Century America* (1974) and *On With the Show: The First Century of Show Business in America* (1976), as well as Harry Reynolds, *Minstrel Memories: The Story of Burnt Cork Minstrelsy in Great Britain* (1928), and Carl Wittke, *Tambo and Bones* (1934). An obituary is in the *Salt Lake City Deseret Evening News*, 30 Sept. 1901.

JAMES ROSS MOORE

HAVILAND, John (15 Dec. 1792–28 Mar. 1852), architect, was born at "Gundenham Manor" near Taunton, Somerset, in southwestern England, the son of James Haviland, an Anglican minister and "small squire," and Ann Cobley. After schooling in his native county, Haviland began his architectural training as a pupil in the office of James Elmes in London—a connection probably made through Elmes's friendship with painter Benjamin Robert Haydon, son of Haviland's maternal aunt. Accounts differ, but according to a revealing biographical draft by William Parker Foulke from 1852, Haviland worked under Elmes for "about seven years," roughly 1807 through 1813. One building, the Chapel of Saint John the Evangelist in Chichester (1812–1813), whose construction Haviland supervised during a time when Elmes was ill, exhibits elements of the British modernity to which Haviland would have

been exposed and which would remain a strong current throughout his career, as would Elmes's inclination toward writing about architecture and his interest in prison design.

The Foulke account notes that Haviland "was 6 months in the latter part of his studentship, with *Nash*" (i.e., John Nash, planner of Regent Street and Regent's Park), but he soon turned to prospects further afield. Another maternal aunt had married Count Nikolai Semenovich Mordvinov, a Russian naval minister, and early in 1815, before the battle of Waterloo and the revival of building in England, Haviland went to St. Petersburg with an expectation of employment with the Imperial Corps of Engineers. Mordvinov was an anglophilic liberal as well as an intimate friend of English penal reformer John Howard, who had died at his side in southern Russia in 1790. Through this uncle Haviland was exposed to firsthand recollections of Howard, even designing a monument to his memory in 1815. This may have spurred a special sympathy in Haviland for prison work; Howard's example certainly spurred the efforts of Pennsylvanian penal reformers that were later to be so critical in Haviland's career. Russia did not suit him, he found, and Haviland soon learned of more attractive prospects in the United States touted by Philadelphia-born George von Sonntag, a general in the Russian army and admiral in the Russian navy, and by future U.S. president John Quincy Adams, then American minister to Russia.

Haviland, in his mid-twenties, arrived in Philadelphia in September 1816 to find a city on the eve of architectural transformation after the hiatus of the War of 1812. He would enjoy the patronage of institutions and governments recasting themselves in vivid, large-scale imagery at the heart and on the edges of the city. Alongside William Strickland, he reaped the newly won confidence of clients prepared to rely on professional architects as image makers conversant with modern new revival styles and as technicians with competence in monumental masonry construction and new structural, heating, and plumbing systems. Among Haviland's principal commissions of this sort were the First Presbyterian Church (1820–1822; demolished), the Eastern State Penitentiary (1821–1837), St. Andrew's P. E. Church (1822–1824), the Pennsylvania Institution for the Deaf and Dumb (1824–1826), the Franklin Institute (1825–1826), and the House of Refuge (1828; demolished), all in or near Philadelphia. Most of these bore the imprint of monumental classical languages, Roman or Greek, rather severely rendered, but Haviland also indulged other styles, as in the castellated Gothic of the penitentiary, the recreational Labyrinth Garden (1828) with its Chinese pagoda (demolished), or the Egyptian forms he favored on several buildings of the 1830s, such as courthouse and jail complexes in New York City ("The Tombs," 1835–1838; demolished) and in Newark, New Jersey (1836; demolished) and the Pennsylvania Fire Insurance Company (1838).

Haviland's many domestic commissions quickly spread from Philadelphia to Massachusetts, Virginia, and Ohio and ranged from mansions and villas to unified townhouse rows. Haviland was also responsible for a number of commercial commissions, including theaters, banks, hotels, and the landmark arcades—combining a number of small shops arrayed along the sides of a roofed, top-lit promenade—that he designed for downtown sites in Philadelphia (1825–1828) and New York City (1826–1827), both demolished.

Other landmark contributions were in the realms of pedagogy, publishing, and professionalism. Shortly after his arrival in Philadelphia, he established a private drawing academy with a fellow immigrant from England, painter Hugh Bridport, and together they prepared a three-volume compendium titled *The Builder's Assistant . . . for the Use of Carpenters and Others* (1818–1821). Their school closed in 1822, but from 1824 through 1826 he and Bridport taught architectural drawing and ornamental drawing, respectively, to ambitious young "mechanics" at the newly founded Franklin Institute. Another publication was an 1833 reissue of Owen Biddle's 1805 *Young Carpenter's Assistant*, to which Haviland added some text and plates. In 1836 Haviland was one of the founders of the short-lived national professional organization the American Institution of Architects, forerunner to the American Institute of Architects founded two decades later.

Despite these achievements, Haviland's career encountered a serious challenge with the failures of the Labyrinth Garden and the arcades, in which he held financial interest. Impending bankruptcy led him to cover debts with funds allocated for construction of his design for the U.S. Naval Hospital at Norfolk, Virginia (1826–1833). The diversion was discovered, and the resulting scandal effectively foreclosed future federal patronage, a rich vein of commissions for his peers. Still, Haviland managed to overcome this in his last two decades because of a reputation for innovation and expertise in penal design that was founded on his penitentiaries, particularly that at Philadelphia and another built at Trenton for the state of New Jersey (1833–1836), both of which attracted worldwide notice and a steady stream of visitation and emulation. These facilities were designed as vehicles of the "Pennsylvania system," in which inmates were kept separate day and night, with work, sleep, and even exercise taking place in individual cells or in their adjoining yards, as opposed to New York's "Auburn system" with its congregate workplaces. (The two approaches illustrated a major point of public debate at the time.) Haviland continued to fine tune his scheme for strict separation, with cellblocks radiating from an observational hub, separate but (for the time) sizable individual cells with yards, and advanced service systems. He maintained a reputation for expertise that was the basis of much of his later work. He provided designs for rebuilding Pennsylvania's Western State Penitentiary (1833) and for new penitentiaries in Missouri (1833–1836), Rhode Island (1834–c. 1837), and Arkansas (1838) as well as for Pennsylvania county prisons at Pittsburgh (1834), Harrisburg (1840), Reading (1846–1848), and Lancaster (1848–1851). He also designed Pennsylvania's State Insane Asylum at Harrisburg (1848–1851).

After his sudden death in Philadelphia, Haviland was recalled as a man of "singular modesty of deportment and of speech, . . . frank and amiable in his intercourse, and liberal in the instruction of those who sought his advice." He had married Mary von Sonntag Wells, the widowed sister of the Russian general, shortly after his arrival in Philadelphia, and his household soon grew to include two sons in addition to two stepsons. Haviland was depicted by John Neagle in a portrait from 1828 (Metropolitan Museum of Art) amid attributes of his profession and the instrument of his greatest renown, Eastern State Penitentiary, represented by a plan and perspective. He is remembered today as one of the more mercurial eclectics of the 1820s and 1830s, one less bound by Greek revival orthodoxies than many of his peers, and as a pioneer in penitentiary design at a point when it was a critical social concern and a topical focus in architecture.

• Haviland's manuscript journals dating from his most active years of practice are held in Special Collections, Van Pelt Library, University of Pennsylvania. Other Haviland documents and architectural drawings are scattered among several repositories, including the Historical Society of Pennsylvania, the Athenaeum of Philadelphia, and the American Philosophical Society Library. Very informative are obituary drafts at the latter by William Parker Foulke, one dated 14 Apr. 1852, among the W. P. Foulke Papers; the final version appeared in the *Pennsylvania Journal of Prison Discipline* 7 (July 1852). Renewed interest in Haviland led in the late twentieth century to numerous articles and two dissertations: Norman B. Johnston, "The Development of Radial Prisons: A Case Study in Cultural Diffusion" (Ph.D. diss., Univ. of Pennsylvania, 1958), and Matthew E. Baigell, "John Haviland" (Ph.D. diss., Univ. of Pennsylvania, 1965). See also Agnes Addison Gilchrist, "John Haviland before 1816," *Journal of the Society of Architectural Historians* 20 (1961): 136–37; Johnston, "John Haviland, Jailor to the World," *Journal of the Society of Architectural Historians* 23 (1964): 101–5; and Baigell, "John Haviland in Philadelphia, 1818–1826," *Journal of the Society of Architectural Historians* 25 (1966): 197–208, and "John Haviland in Pottsville," *Journal of the Society of Architectural Historians* 26 (1967): 306–9. For more recent assessments see John C. Poppeliers in James C. Massey, *Two Centuries of Philadelphia Architectural Drawings* (1964), pp. 24–34; Richard Webster in Philadelphia Museum of Art, *Three Centuries of American Art* (1976), pp. 57–58; and Jeffrey A. Cohen in James F. O'Gorman et al., *Drawing toward Building: Philadelphia Architectural Graphics, 1732–1986* (1986), pp. 71–72. The Haviland building to attract the greatest amount of historiographic attention has always been Eastern State Penitentiary, which was the subject of a detailed, three-volume Historic Structures Report in 1994.

JEFFREY A. COHEN

HAVILAND, Laura Smith (20 Dec. 1808–20 Apr. 1898), abolitionist and evangelist, was born in Leeds County, Ontario, Canada, the daughter of Daniel Smith and Sene Blancher, farmers. She grew up in western New York State in a community of the Society of Friends and received several years of education in a Quaker school. In 1825 she married Charles Haviland,

Jr.; they had eight children. In 1829 the young couple moved to Michigan Territory, where they joined her parents and siblings in establishing farms in the valley of the River Raisin (near present-day Adrian, Mich.) and living pious lives in a tightly knit extended family.

In 1834 Haviland joined with Elizabeth Chandler to form the Logan Female Anti-Slavery Society, but the interdenominational character of the meetings and the activist aims of the society drew criticism from orthodox members of the Quaker meeting. The Society of Friends had long condemned the practice of slavery (Quaker settlements such as Raisin actually harbored free blacks and escaped slaves), but "worldly" political agitation was seen as inappropriate. By 1837 the Havilands and Smiths had resigned from the Society of Friends, citing specifically the doctrinal primacy of Scripture and the abolition of slavery as points at issue. Haviland as a child had been drawn to the Methodist revivalist emphasis on spiritual renewal; when the Wesleyan Methodists branched off from the older organization in 1841 in support of unqualified abolitionism, she and her family formally joined that church.

In 1837 the Havilands founded the Raisin Institute, a school open to both sexes and all races and with a curriculum influenced by Ohio's Oberlin College. The school, which always had a few black students, became influential in abolitionist thinking, particularly since it was the first institution in Michigan to prepare teachers.

In 1845 Haviland's husband, infant daughter, parents, closest sister, and many others of the community died suddenly from erysipelas, an epidemic disease that she herself barely survived. Prophetic dreams, Scripture readings, and the timely appearance of a fugitive slave at her door convinced her that God now called her to greater action. She soon had opportunities to conceal local blacks from southern slave catchers and help them pass through Detroit to Canada, seeking "the protection of the British lion from the merciless talons of the freedom-shrieking American eagle" (*A Woman's Life-Work*, 1887 ed., p. 53). Passage of the Fugitive Slave Law in 1850 raised the stakes for abolitionists and slave catchers. Entrusting her farm and younger children to her grown children and the Raisin Institute to its trustees, Haviland began a peripatetic life. For over a decade she moved through the cities of Michigan and Ohio, ministering to the souls and bodies of blacks. She often earned her keep as a sick nurse, guiding her white patients to Christian salvation while at the same time teaching in schools for black children. In Cincinnati she worked with Levi and Catherine Coffin in the Underground Railroad, preparing food and mending clothes with the women and conducting escapees from "station to station" with the abolitionist men. Unlike most who sheltered fleeing slaves from the "biped bloodhounds" of that era, she was publicly vocal in her denunciations of slavery as an evil no true Christian could allow to exist. She made several trips into slave states in order to rescue illegally held free blacks (not always with success).

In 1863, armed with letters from Michigan political leaders, a railroad pass, and fifteen dollars, Haviland went south with a load of medical supplies to offer "tender nursing" to wounded Union soldiers. She traveled down the Mississippi River, bringing blankets and religious instruction to the freedmen who sought refuge behind Union lines, inspecting military hospitals and prisons, and exposing injustice and cruelty—usually by complaining immediately to the highest military commander in the area. From 1864 to 1866 she was a paid agent of the Michigan Freedmen's Aid Commission, working especially with destitute refugees in Kansas, "seeing unfaithful officers dismissed, prisoners released, and the suffering and dying relieved." In 1867 she investigated relief work in the middle South on behalf of the American Missionary Association. Ill health then prevented her effort to revive the Raisin Institute as an orphan asylum, but she lobbied successfully for the founding in 1871 of a State Public School for Dependent and Neglected Children in Grand Rapids, Michigan, where she worked as a nurse and seamstress for two years.

In 1879 and 1882 Haviland, having rejoined the Friends in 1872, returned to Kansas in association with the Quaker reformer Elizabeth L. Comstock and played a role in founding welfare institutions for black migrants there. A Quaker village in that state was named Haviland in her honor. She also continued to teach Methodist beliefs. In 1881 she published her memoirs, *A Woman's Life-Work*, which contained eyewitness accounts of cruelty to blacks both during and after slavery. In old age she inveighed against the moral slavery of alcohol and supported woman suffrage as a means to temperance legislation. She died in Grand Rapids. Her several funeral services brought an outpouring of public acclaim, and a statue of her holding her memoirs was erected in Adrian, Michigan, by popular subscription.

Although Haviland remains an admired figure in Michigan history, she has not received great national attention. Her public role did not conform to contemporary expectations of female domesticity, nor did her life easily fit the categories of later historical study; her chosen church had no official role for women as religious leaders, while her efforts in helping to free slaves generally fell outside the organizational patterns favored by the leadership of the Underground Railroad and its subsequent chroniclers.

• Haviland's papers are in the Bentley Historical Library of the University of Michigan and the Lenawee County Historical Museum in Adrian, Mich. Later editions of *A Woman's Life-Work* (eds., 1881–1902) contain informative testimonials regarding the veracity of her accounts. Mildred E. Danforth, *A Quaker Pioneer* (1961), is a popular biography with some additional information on her family. Anthony P. Glesner, "Laura Haviland: Neglected Heroine of the Underground Railroad," *Michigan Historical Review* 21, no. 1 (Spring 1995): 19–48, concerns historiography. See also Elizabeth E. Grammer, "A Pen in His Hand" (Ph.D. diss., Univ. of Virginia, 1995), for analysis of her memoirs in the context of other female itinerant evangelists of the nineteenth century. An obituary is in the *Grand Rapids Democrat*, 21 Apr. 1898.

EFFIE K. AMBLER

HAWES, Elizabeth (16 Dec. 1903–6 Sept. 1971), fashion designer and social critic, was born in Ridgewood, New Jersey, the daughter of John Hawes, a railroad executive, and Henrietta Houston, a community activist. Hawes learned to sew as a child and even as an adolescent sold dresses to family friends and a store in Pennsylvania. Hawes majored in economics at Vassar College, graduating in 1925. She sailed for Paris, where she spent several years learning various aspects of haute couture. She worked at a copy house and was hired by an American dressmaking firm to secretly sketch designer fashions. She subsequently worked in the Paris offices of Macy's and Lord & Taylor and designed clothes for Nicole Groult. Hawes also reported on Paris fashion for American newspapers and the *New Yorker*.

Hawes's experience in France led her to conclude that American fashion must become independent of Paris, then the arbiter of fashion. American working women and housewives, she observed, led more active lives than the leisured upper-class Parisian consumers of haute couture. She returned to the United States in 1928 to open her own shop in Manhattan. In 1930 she married sculptor Ralph Jester, who influenced her architectural, body-conscious designs. She also credited modern art and dance as inspirations for color, shape, and movement in her designs. She and Jester divorced in 1935; they had no children.

In 1931 Hawes became the first American to show a collection in Paris—on the Fourth of July, which she considered a publicity stunt to promote American design; in 1935 she was the first American to have a fashion show in the Soviet Union since 1917. A populist, Hawes believed that everyone should have beautiful clothes and that the future belonged to mass-market rather than custom-made clothing. Nevertheless, most of her own designing was for a custom-made clientele. Her own forays into mass-market manufacturing in the 1930s left her frustrated with the systemic obstacles to good mass-market designing. Among those she cited were cut-throat competition, shoddy workmanship, the poor fit of mass-produced clothes, and the arbitrary changes in fashion to sell more clothing.

Hawes's fashion ideas can be found in the autobiographical *Fashion Is Spinach* (1938); *Men Can Take It* (1939), on men's clothing; *Why Is a Dress?* (1942); and *It's Still Spinach* (1954). The whimsically vegetarian titles refer to the famous *New Yorker* cartoon of a child rejecting her greens: "I say it's spinach—and I say to hell with it." So, too, did Hawes reject ephemeral fashion in favor of the more enduring concept of style. When she reported fashion news for the *New Yorker*, she used the pen name "Parasite," for she believed "fashion is a parasite on style." Picking up on political events in the late 1930s, Hawes likened fashion to a dictator. She urged the buying public to be neither

sheep nor snobs when it came to fashion. Conversely, she advocated that designers use psychology, sociology, anthropology, and economics to anticipate fashion trends consistent with changing lifestyles. In addition to a utilitarian approach to clothes (clothes should be comfortable, clothes should have pockets), Hawes believed clothing should be expressive. Pleasure, amusement, sensuality, and sexuality all had a role in her sense of design. By the time she wrote the even more iconoclastic *It's Still Spinach*, Hawes was playing with ideas of cross dressing for men and women and nudity for children. In a futurist chapter, "How Will You Dress in 1960?," Hawes contrasted a dystopian and regimented society that required protective clothing from the threat of atomic war with a free and individualistic society in which people dress for personal pleasure.

In 1937 Hawes married film and theater director Joseph Losey, and they had a son in 1938. Hawes closed her own design business in 1940, turning her attention to journalism and social commentary. She wrote on clothing, food, beauty, housing, and education for the New York newspaper *PM*. Among her causes was publicly funded child care for working women, and she developed a keen interest in early childhood education. Hawes was a leader in the New York Committee for the Care of Young Children in Wartime, whose efforts prompted Mayor Fiorello La Guardia to voice his famous remark, "The worst mother is better than the best nursery school."

In 1943 Hawes described her brief experience working as a grinder on the nightshift at Wright Aeronautical in *Why Women Cry; or, Wenches with Wrenches*, a sympathetic account of exhausted female defense workers trying to care for their homes and families during wartime. A self-avowed feminist, Hawes believed the role of the isolated housewife was obsolete and that it stunted the human development of women. A proponent of all forms of collective action, Hawes envisioned public housing projects that would include cooperative kitchens and nurseries. She later lampooned society's rules for feminine behavior that she had culled from women's magazines, film, and radio in her satiric *Anything but Love* (1948).

After divorcing Losey in 1944, Hawes went to work for the International Education Department of the United Automobile Workers (UAW) to help organize women workers. In *Hurry Up Please Its Time* (1946), Hawes criticized the failure of union leaders to address the problems of women workers. Her book also described internecine battles and Red-baiting within the UAW as well as what she viewed as the opportunistic leadership of Walter Reuther.

A year spent on St. Croix in 1947 yielded the fictionalized account *But Say It Politely* (1951). In 1948, and again in the early 1950s, Hawes made attempted comebacks in the world of fashion but was unable to establish successful business ventures. After living in California for almost two decades, she returned to New York City in the late 1960s. She died in her residence at the Chelsea Hotel.

In *It's Still Spinach* Hawes sanguinely predicted, "I do honestly believe the triumph of the female mind over fashion is not too far off." Her own importance as a pioneer and innovator on the American fashion scene was acknowledged in 1967 by the Fashion Institute of Technology in a retrospective show of her designs. Hawes once put her far-flung career as a dress designer and social activist into perspective by quoting with pleasure a friend who said she was not sure if Hawes was a good dress designer, but she made an excellent rabble-rouser.

• The Random House Papers in the Rare Book and Manuscript Library at Columbia University contain Hawes's correspondence regarding *Fashion Is Spinach* and *Men Can Take It*. In addition to the works cited above, she wrote a book for teenagers, *Good Grooming* (1942). Her clothing can be found in the collections of the Brooklyn Museum, the Fashion Institute of Technology, and the Costume Institute of the Metropolitan Museum of Art. An obituary appears in the *New York Times*, 7 Sept. 1971.

CHRISTINE KLEINEGGER

HAWES, Harriet Ann Boyd (11 Oct. 1871–31 Mar. 1945), archaeologist and nurse, was born in Boston, Massachusetts, the daughter of Alexander Boyd, a manufacturer of fire-fighting equipment, and Harriet Fay Wheeler. She lost her mother before her first birthday and was raised by her father and four older brothers. She studied Latin, Greek, and economics at Smith College from 1888 to 1892. Not yet considered old enough to study nursing, an early and lifelong avocation, she taught classics at boarding and finishing schools until her father died in 1896.

Deciding to attend the American School of Classical Studies at Athens in order to teach at college, Harriet Boyd sailed to Greece and attended Wilhelm Doerpfeld's lectures on the Acropolis. When Greeks were mobilizing against Turks in Crete and northern Greece in 1897, she attended some nursing classes before volunteering for nursing duty in Thessaly. With the aid of experienced Greek nurses, she learned to clean and dress wounds and to run a series of impromptu hospitals around Volos as the outnumbered Greek soldiers were retreating south. She also served at Lamia, where she witnessed fighting, and in the far west near the Epirot front.

Boyd went to serve the Red Cross again briefly in Tampa, Florida, during the Spanish-American War before accepting a fellowship from the Archaeological Institute of America (AIA) to return to Greece in 1898. There she was honored for her war service and frequently received by Queen Olga. After accepting another fellowship for 1899–1900, she proposed to use some of this money to look for tombs at Corinth, where the American School had begun digging in 1896. As she later wrote, "the regular School excavations gave occupation to the men students of the school but did not afford enough material for the women also." While the director of the American School did not approve of her proposal to dig at Corinth, she did receive encouragement from Heinrich Schliemann's widow; Arthur Evans, who was about to begin excavating at Knossos; and David Hogarth, the director of the British School, on her proposal to dig on the island of Crete, recently independent from Turkey. She set out in April 1900 with Jean Patten, an old school friend, and an Epirot rebel and his mother, who served as cook and chaperone.

After visiting Evans's excavations at Knossos as the throne was being uncovered, Boyd and Patten traveled by mule east to the isthmus, which Boyd decided should have had early trading settlements. Hiring local workers and disinclined to delegate, she dealt with them directly without a foreman. In a few weeks of careful excavations, including the admirably early use of sieving the excavated soil, she cleared several rooms of a Geometric settlement on a peak near Kavousi and some Geometric tholos tombs. On her return home, her report earned her an M.A. from Smith College, where she was hired to teach modern Greek, archaeology, and epigraphy as "instructress."

With the financial support of the American Exploration Society of Philadelphia, Boyd returned to Crete in 1901, and, after being shown Gournia by a local collector of antiquities, she and her amazed workmen uncovered houses, a shrine, and much of the "palace" from the field beneath their feet. Giving her workers a taste of ancient democracy, she divided them into a senate of older, more experienced workers and an assembly of younger ones, with both having to agree on a proposed coffee shop and their method of pay. Back in the United States, she addressed ten local chapters of the AIA on the results of her dig, the first woman to be invited to do so, a fact that elicited comment from newspapers.

Boyd uncovered most of the rest of the site in 1903, and for her final campaign in 1904 she was joined by Richard Seager and Edith Hall, two archaeology students who would go on to excavate many more sites in eastern Crete over the next decade. Apart from discovering and excavating the first and most extensively uncovered Minoan town, Boyd's greatest archaeological achievement was her pioneering effort to classify Cretan pottery into a sequence of use. For this purpose she sent workmen to excavate briefly at Vasiliki, a nearby site with pottery from earlier periods. She also looked for burials from all periods to connect the pottery sequences into a continuous whole and define the periods ceramically. Since by now she had excavated more Cretan sites than any other excavator up to this time, she was uniquely qualified for this task. The Cretan government allowed her to export nearly three hundred vases and thousands of sherds, the first such export, which now forms the collection at the University of Pennsylvania Museum, the largest outside Crete and Evans's collection at Oxford.

During one final season in Crete to analyze the finds, she met, and in 1906 married, Charles Henry Hawes, a Cambridge anthropologist, with whom she had two children. In a 1908 newspaper contest for the most creative solution to a murder mystery, "When the Mummy Moves," Harriet Boyd Hawes won first prize over nearly 13,000 other contestants. Her book, *Gournia, Vasiliki and Other Prehistoric Sites on the Isthmus of Hierapetra, Crete* (1908), was the earliest final publication of a Cretan excavation to appear; moreover, keen to produce color plates for American museums of the objects that could not leave Crete, she financed part of the cost of the oversized book with her prize money. In 1909 she and her husband published *Crete the Forerunner of Greece* to reach a broader audience. In 1910 she was awarded the first honorary doctor of humanities ever conferred by Smith College.

In 1915 in the Adriatic war zone Hawes organized an international effort to feed thousands of starving Serbian soldiers fleeing to Corfu. In 1917 she organized the creation, funding, and equipping of a group of Smith College volunteer women to serve as a relief unit in France bringing food, animals, and housing to devastated regions near Amiens within earshot of enemy fire. She helped to organize and run a Young Men's Christian Association canteen for soldiers for six months before serving as a Red Cross nurse during the last German advance in 1918.

From 1920 until her retirement in 1936 Hawes was a lecturer on ancient art at Wellesley College while her husband was associate curator at the Boston Museum of Fine Arts. A remarkable example of her determination and courage was her visit to Prague during the German takeover of the Sudetenland in October 1938; she traveled by herself in the company of three different mobilizing armies, witnessed Hitler addressing his troops in the newly occupied territory, was briefly detained twice by the occupying forces for intemperate comments, and walked twelve miles to cross the border into what remained of Czechoslovakia. After witnessing Nazi actions in Czechoslovakia and Austria for two months she returned home to Washington, D.C., where she had a private meeting with Eleanor Roosevelt. After nursing her ailing husband until his death in 1943, she died in Washington.

Harriet Boyd Hawes was recognized for her courageous and wide-ranging nursing services although she was never trained as a nurse. She not only led the first American excavations in Crete, but she was also the first woman anywhere to have directed both the excavation and publication of a site. She found the sites and the sequence of pottery styles that made Evans's ceramic chronology system possible. Were it not for her initiative, it seems likely that Seager and Hall would not have been active in Crete, many sites would have remained undiscovered and unexcavated, and there would have been no American archaeological presence in Crete.

• Harriet Boyd Hawes's excavation notebooks are in the University of Pennsylvania Museum, and her personal papers are at Smith College. Extracts of the first two, and only, chapters of her unpublished memoirs are in "Memoirs of a Pioneer Excavator in Crete," *Archaeology* 18 (1965): 94–101, 268–76. The biography by her daughter Mary Allsebrook, *Born to Rebel* (1992), is based on the memoirs. Recently discovered excavation notebooks, some of which are in Vasso Fotou, *New Light on Gournia* (1993), have helped to put Hawes's archaeo-logical work into historical perspective. Brief summaries of Hawes's career can be found in Alden Murray's "Harriet Boyd Hawes," in *A Land Called Crete: Minoan and Mycenaean Art*, a Smith College Museum of Art exhibition catalog (1967), and P. W. Lehmann's "Harriet Boyd Hawes: Introductory Remarks," in *A Land Called Crete: A Symposium* (1967). An obituary appears in the *American Journal of Archaeology* 49, no. 3 (July–Sept. 1945): 359.

D. J. I. BEGG

HAWKINS, Benjamin (15 Aug. 1754–6 June 1816), U.S. senator and Indian agent, was born in Bute, later Warren County, North Carolina, the son of Philomen Hawkins, a planter and land speculator, and Delia Martin. Family wealth enabled the young Hawkins to attend the College of New Jersey (later Princeton), class of 1777, but the approaching British army cut short his senior year. Fluent in French, he briefly served on General George Washington's staff as a civilian interpreter, but by the end of 1778 he was back in North Carolina as a trade commissioner and member of the legislature. In 1781 Hawkins won election to Congress, where he remained until 1784; he served again in 1786–1787.

Hawkins sat on Congress's Committee on Indian Affairs, which sought to win peace in the West by negotiating treaties with the Indian tribes. In 1785, as Congress moved to put this policy into effect, it appointed Hawkins to chair a five-man commission to meet with the southern tribes. Talks with the Creeks collapsed, but negotiations conducted over the next six months at Hopewell with the Cherokees, Choctaws, and Chickasaws achieved Congress's aims of making peace. Hawkins emerged with a reputation as a skilled practitioner of Indian diplomacy.

For the rest of the decade Hawkins, a Federalist, divided his time between congressional sessions in Philadelphia and North Carolina where, like many delegates to Congress, he expressed his frustration with the Articles of Confederation as a frame of government by supporting the Constitution. He did not attend North Carolina's first ratification convention, which rejected the Constitution, but he was active at the second convention in November 1789, which approved it. Shortly thereafter the North Carolina legislature elected Hawkins to one of its seats in the U.S. Senate. Hawkins's term in the Senate was undistinguished, and he chose not to stand for reelection. The administration drew on his experience with southern Indians, however, by enlisting his advice during the negotiations with the Creeks in 1790 that resulted in the Treaty of New York.

In 1795, as Hawkins's term expired, President Washington appointed him to head a commission to attempt to ease tensions between the Creeks and Georgia over disputed land claims. The talks, held at Colerain on the St. Marys River, opened in late spring 1796 and fulfilled Washington's hope that the Creeks would cooperate in surveying the newly established boundary between the United States and Spanish Florida. More important, Hawkins and his colleagues rejected Georgia's claim to lands purchased in the 1780s without congressional authorization. The Georgia legislature had already sold the lands in question as part of what became known as the Yazoo Frauds, and the position taken by Hawkins at Colerain that Georgia's claim was invalid marked an important step in the growing federal-state controversy in the South over the land claims and political rights of Indian tribes.

Later in 1796 Washington offered and Hawkins accepted an appointment in the federal Indian affairs bureaucracy. Though theoretically responsible for the entire South, as his title principal temporary agent for Indian affairs south of the Ohio River indicates, Hawkins was always mainly involved with the Creeks. He literally lived among them, moving from town to town and staying in people's homes. Soon after he arrived, he asked a friend to send him a "housekeeper." Lavinia Downs became mother to Hawkins's seven children and, in 1812, his wife. In 1803, following an administrative reorganization in which Hawkins's appointment was changed to principal agent for the Creeks, he and his family settled down at a permanent agency on the Flint River in central Georgia. The agency compound of five miles square included the agency offices, residences, shops, and a plantation staffed by Hawkins's slaves (who numbered seventy-two at the time of his death), which the agent used as an experimental, instructional, and productive facility. Under Hawkins's direction, the agency plantation became the model for Creek emulation.

As Indian agent, Hawkins represented the federal government to the tribes assigned to him. His principal duties included administering federal Indian policy, reporting on local events, and influencing tribal actions. Federal Indian policy changed over time but the Adams, Jefferson, and Madison administrations shared basic principles. One was that peaceful relations between Native Americans and European Americans were preferable to violent conflict. Part of Hawkins's job was therefore to keep the peace, largely by enforcing the many congressional trade and intercourse acts, which regulated trade, recognized tribal land claims, guaranteed boundaries against encroachment, and recognized tribal sovereignty and political autonomy. At the same time, however, the United States responded to the wishes of its citizens and the interests of many states by also seeking cessions of tribal land. In pursuit of this policy, Hawkins and other agents tried to convince tribal leaders to agree to sell land to the United States. The government used many arguments and techniques to produce Indian signatures on land treaties, but the heart of Washington's approach, continued by his Federalist and Republican successors into the early nineteenth century, was the so-called civilization policy. At its most basic level, to "civilize" Indians meant to transform them culturally and ideologically into European Americans. The assumption was that if they became God-fearing, market-oriented, independent small family farmers they would willingly sell most of their tribal lands for money to invest in their farms and to buy goods. Many, including Hawkins, were also committed to "civilizing" the Indians because they sincerely believed that the European-American way of life was far preferable to the Indian way.

Along with everyone else involved in the efforts to "civilize" Indians, Hawkins believed that native people had to make fundamental and interrelated cultural changes. One was to depend on farming for a livelihood; another was to rearrange their gender roles so that the men, not the women, owned and tilled the soil. In pursuit of these goals, Hawkins encouraged Creek men to grow cotton and trained the women to use spinning wheels and looms. He introduced plows and other implements as well as a wide variety of new crops. Furthermore, Hawkins restructured Creek government by dividing the nation into electoral districts and providing for the election of delegates to the national council, which was to meet regularly and hear his annual state-of-the-nation address. He encouraged the council to assert powers over the semiautonomous towns, to enact laws to enforce its authority, and to develop an American political consciousness.

In some ways Hawkins was a success as an Indian agent. He was a fair, honest, efficient, likeable man, and he won the trust and respect of many Creeks, some of whom accepted his economic and social messages, became planters, entered the regional markets, sent their children to schools, and generally became, as Hawkins would have described them, civilized. His political and governmental innovations, though never achieving the sweeping change he desired, nevertheless formed an important marker on the path toward centralized state making begun in the 1780s under the guidance of Alexander McGillivray and culminating in 1867 with the establishment of constitutional government. Ultimately, however, most Creeks rejected the more fundamental changes Hawkins demanded.

The last years of Hawkins's life and career were filled with turmoil, controversy, and failure. Largely in response to Hawkins's civilization program, the Creeks experienced a cultural crisis during his tenure that climaxed in a movement of religious revitalization and civil war. Beginning with a series of bitter confrontations and stimulated by Shawnee chief Tecumseh's visit in 1811, the Creek civil war became entangled with the War of 1812. Invaded and ravaged by American armies under the direction of Andrew Jackson, in 1814 the Creeks succumbed to a peace treaty that cost them a massive tract of rich land in present Alabama. Events had swept completely out of Hawkins's hands and he lost his influence over both the Creeks and U.S. policy toward them. After the war, suffering from recurrent ill health as well as professional frustration, he resigned. Hawkins died in office, at the Creek Agency on the Flint River, during the search for his successor.

• Hawkins's manuscripts can be found in Record Group 75, Records of the Bureau of Indian Affairs, National Archives, Washington, D.C.; the Georgia Historical Society, Savannah; the Georgia Department of Archives and History, Atlanta; and Independence National Historical Park, Philadelphia, Pa. Many of Hawkins's writings have been published. His fascinating *Sketch of the Creek Country in the Years 1798 and 1799* first appeared as vol. 1, pt. 1 of the *Collections* of the Georgia Historical Society (1848) and have been reprinted (1974). The Georgia Historical Society also printed *Letters of Benjamin Hawkins* as vol. 10 of its *Collections* (1918). A more comprehensive collection that includes letters, reports, and documents housed in over a dozen archives is C. G. Grant, ed., *Letters, Journals and Writings of Benjamin Hawkins* (2 vols., 1980). Merritt B. Pound, *Benjamin Hawkins, Indian Agent* (1951), remains the standard biography, but it should be supplemented with Florette Henri, *The Southern Indians and Benjamin Hawkins* (1986). The best account of Creek history in Hawkins's period is Joel Martin, *Sacred Revolt* (1991).

MICHAEL D. GREEN

HAWKINS, Coleman (21 Nov. 1904–19 May 1969), jazz tenor saxophonist, was born Coleman Randolph Hawkins in St. Joseph, Missouri, the son of William Hawkins, an electrical worker, and Cordelia Coleman, a schoolteacher and organist. Hawkins began to study piano at age five and the cello at seven; he then eagerly took up the C-melody saxophone he received for his ninth birthday. Even before entering high school in Chicago, he was playing professionally at school dances. Recognizing his talent, his parents sent him to the all-black Industrial and Educational Institute in Topeka, Kansas, his mother insisting that he take only his cello with him. During vacations, however, Hawkins played both cello and C-melody saxophone in Kansas City theater orchestras, where blues singer Mamie Smith heard him in 1921.

Smith hired Hawkins to tour with her Jazz Hounds, and he traveled and recorded with the group until June 1923, when he moved to New York City. There he played with a variety of groups and in numerous jam sessions. In August 1923 he recorded "Dicty Blues" with a Fletcher Henderson group, and in early 1924 Henderson hired him for his new band. Although Hawkins doubled on both clarinet and bass saxophone for Henderson, he increasingly concentrated on the tenor and soon developed a style that revolutionized saxophone playing. At first he employed the technique that was all but universal among saxophonists at the time, slapping his tongue against the reed and producing sharp, staccato notes. Gradually, though, he adopted a more legato style. He was also influenced by trumpeter Louis Armstrong during Armstrong's brief stay with the Henderson band and by the complex harmonic improvisations of the young pianist Art Tatum, whom he heard in 1926.

By 1927 Hawkins was the band's featured soloist and was playing only tenor sax. His solo on "The Stampede" (1926) is a dramatic example of his growth, displaying a full, smooth tone and rhythmic assurance. Hawkins also played with other small groups during the late twenties and early thirties; his solo on "One Hour" (1929) with the Mound City Blue Blowers, for instance, showcases his rich tone and powerful emotionalism. He made several outstanding recordings with the trumpeter Henry "Red" Allen, including the classic "It's the Talk of the Town" (1933). By now the master of his instrument, Hawkins had fully developed his harmonic approach to improvisation, a marked contrast to the more melodic, scalar approach of tenor saxophonist Lester Young and others. Hawkins thought about the implications of each chord as it came, adding notes or changing them to create sweeping melodic lines. By then he was a jazz celebrity, but success began to take its toll on his personal life when he and his wife, Gertrude (they had married in 1923), separated.

Hawkins left Henderson in 1933 and arranged a deal with the English impressario Jack Hylton to tour England. He initially planned to take only a six-month leave, but he remained overseas until 1939, traveling and performing constantly. Noteworthy recordings include 1935 sessions with a Dutch group known as the Ramblers and a 1937 Paris session with Benny Carter on alto saxophone and trumpet and the Belgian guitarist Django Reinhardt.

When Hawkins returned to New York City in July 1939, his fans greeted him ecstatically. He initially planned to form his own big band, but musicians of his caliber were more interested in leading their own groups than in joining his. So he put together a small group to play at Kelly's Stable, then on West 51st Street. On 11 October, only six days after opening there, he cut four sides at a recording date for RCA Victor. Almost as an afterthought, and with no rehearsal, he concluded the session with one of the most celebrated and influential performances in jazz history, "Body and Soul."

Hawkins had already experimented a number of times with three- and four-minute ballad improvisations, and he recorded two side-long solos in London accompanied only by pianist Stanley Black. Although he often spoke of the spur-of-the-moment nature of his choice, it could not have been a complete surprise, since he had been playing an extended late-night version of "Body and Soul" at Kelly's. Now, in one sixty-four bar improvisation with only minimal rhythm accompaniment, he created a solo that composer-critic Gunther Schuller describes as "a melodic/harmonic journey through a musical landscape without any fault lines." He flirts with the original melody for the first few bars, then quickly moves away, developing his own related harmonic ideas and gradually raising the pitch and intensifying the rhythm and dynamics with each extended group of phrases. By the final bars his initially warm, vibratoless sound becomes almost strident, intensified by a wide, pulsing vibrato. The recorded performance was a bestseller, and it has since become the ultimate touchstone of great tenor playing.

Hawkins did tour with his own big band in early 1940, but he lacked the showmanship essential to such a venture and the group folded. In May 1940 he cut a series of recordings for the Commodore label with a group called the Chocolate Dandies that included three of the best swing players of the era—trumpeter Roy Eldridge, drummer Sid Catlett, and Benny Carter. A few months later he met the young Delores Sheridan in Chicago, and they were married in October 1941. Hawkins moved back to New York in early 1942 to spend more time with his family, which grew to include three children by the end of the decade. Among his recording highlights during the middle 1940s were three sessions for Signature records and the legendary 1944 Keynote recordings. He also began a long and satisfying relationship with Norman Granz's Jazz at the Philharmonic tours.

Unlike other swing players, Hawkins warmly embraced the modernist bop movement. In February 1944 he led a band that included Dizzy Gillespie on trumpet and Max Roach on drums in the first bop recordings; later that year he included pianist Theolonius Monk on a recording session. Throughout his life Hawkins offered younger players encouragement and advice, often talking with them on the phone for hours and inviting them to his apartment to listen to and examine his extensive collection of classical records, books, and scores. At the same time he continued to strongly influence swing-oriented contemporaries like Ben Webster, Don Byas, Herschel Evans, Budd Johnson, and many others.

By 1947 the club scene on 52nd Street was dying, and Hawkins left for a series of engagements in Paris, returning to Europe again in 1949. The artistic highlight of this period was his recorded solo improvisation "Picasso," a revolutionary venture for the time. He continued to record extensively during the 1950s and to perform continuously in Europe and the United States, and he initiated a performance relationship with Roy Eldridge that was to last, off and on, for the next fifteen years. Two of their best albums together were *The Big Challenge* and a collection of emotionally powerful ballads, *The High and Mighty Hawk*. Once again, though, the demands of his career affected Hawkins's personal life. In 1958 he and his second wife separated, and the sense of order and balance that had come to characterize his life seemed to dissipate.

For a few years his career hardly missed a beat. He appeared on the television programs "The Sound of Jazz" (1957) and "After Hours" (1961), toured South America in 1961, played a series of dates with Eldridge at the Museum of Modern Art, and recorded several landmark albums, including a 1962 session with Duke Ellington and the classic *Further Definitions* (1961), a small band effort led by Benny Carter and featuring four leading saxophonists. Hawkins also maintained a home base at the Club Metropole, often playing there with Eldridge. Although dismayed by the appearance of free jazz—the first modernist movement he could not understand or enjoy—he did record with some of the more traditionally grounded modernists such as Sonny Rollins and John Coltrane, both of whom were profoundly influenced by Hawkins's playing.

A fear of aging had always possessed Hawkins, and it seemed to overcome him in the early 1960s. He steadily withdrew, eating less and drinking more; he was fired from several jobs because he could not get along with other players or because of his drinking. He lost a frightening amount of weight, and by early 1966 his physical appearance, once a source of great personal pride, began to deteriorate. In February 1967 he collapsed while playing in Toronto, but he refused to be hospitalized and returned two nights later to complete the engagement. He embarked on a thirteen-week tour of Canadian and American cities, but he often played poorly. He collapsed again on stage in Oakland, California, on 30 June and was never healthy again. For the most part he remained in his New York apartment, his children and second wife visiting and trying to care for him. When writer-producer Dan Morgenstern met him at the Chicago airport in April 1969, he was stunned by the saxophonist's emaciated appearance; Hawkins collapsed there while waiting for a car. He performed a moving version of "Yesterdays" for a TV show, but it was all he could manage. The pianist at the session, Barry Harris, took Hawkins back to New York, and when Hawkins failed to show up for a rehearsal Harris asked that an apartment house security guard check on him. Hawkins was found crawling across the floor of his apartment, dragging his horn. He was taken to Wickersham Hospital where he died.

Hawkins brought the tenor saxophone into the mainstream of jazz and popular music, and he helped pioneer a then-modernist approach to improvisation, based on chords rather than melody. He profoundly influenced tenor saxophonists of his own generation, served as a mentor to the bop movement, and was a model and inspiration to some of the most important later players, particularly Sonny Rollins and John Coltrane. His musical presence could be overwhelming, and listening to his recordings can be a moving experience. More than most of his jazz contemporaries, finally, Hawkins was a man of the world, driven by a deep sense of intellectual curiosity. He listened to music of every kind, and he loved Bach most of all, especially Bach's mastery of improvising on a theme. "It's just music-adventure," he once noted. "That's what music is, adventure."

• Hawkins has been the subject of intense critical scrutiny. The best full-length biography, which also contains excellent musical analysis, is John Chilton, *Song of the Hawk* (1990). Also see Albert McCarthy, *Coleman Hawkins* (1963), and B. James, *Coleman Hawkins* (1984). The best brief introduction to Hawkins's career and music is Gunther Schuller, *The Swing Era: The Development of Jazz, 1930–1945* (1989). In addition, the following works offer outstanding assessments: John McDonough, *Coleman Hawkins* (1979); Frank Tirro, *Jazz: A History*, 2d ed. (1993); Martin Williams, *The Jazz Tradition*, rev. ed. (1983); James Lincoln Collier, *The Making of Jazz: A Comprehensive History* (1978); and Stanley Dance, *The World of Swing* (1974). The best of his early work on records is covered by Max Harrison, Charles Fox, and Eric Thacker, *The Essential Jazz Records*, vol. 1 (1984). An obituary is in the *New York Times*, 20 May 1969.

RONALD P. DUFOUR

HAWKINS, Erick (23 Apr. 1909–23 Nov. 1994), dancer and choreographer, was born Frederick Hawkins in Trinidad, Colorado, the only son of an inventor. During his childhood he moved briefly to Pomona, California, and then to Kansas City, Missouri, where he completed his schooling in public schools. Receiving a scholarship to Harvard College from the local alumni association, he matriculated in 1926 and graduated four years later with a major in ancient Greek language and civilization.

In New York City during a college break, Hawkins had seen a performance of the German modern dancer Harald Kreutzberg, in which dance, music, and visual design were equal partners. Hawkins credits this experience for his decision to study with Kreutzberg for two months in Austria. In 1934 he relocated to New York City and began dance training at the School of American Ballet, founded by choreographers George Balanchine and Lincoln Kirstein. He performed for Balanchine's American Ballet Company from 1935 to 1937, and in 1936 he began to dance for Ballet Caravan, a company formed by Kirstein to emphasize ballets on American themes. In 1937 Ballet Caravan gave Hawkins his first choreographic opportunity, with the premiere of *Show Piece* (score by Robert McBride), which critic Edwin Denby commended for its "good-humored inventiveness" (Denby, p. 193).

Company residencies at Bennington College's summer dance program brought Hawkins into contact with the modern dancer Martha Graham. In 1938 Graham featured him as a guest artist in her new work *American Document*. He officially joined the Martha Graham Dance Company in 1939, where he partnered with Graham for thirteen years. Hawkins originated many principal roles in her works, including the Husbandman in *Appalachian Spring* (1944) and Oedipus in *Night Journey* (1947). Hawkins's other contributions to the company included fundraising and choreography. He choreographed a piece about the American abolitionist *John Brown* (1947), which featured a poem by Robert Richman and a set design by Isamu Noguchi. He revived the piece twenty years later for his own company. Graham's company also premiered his *Stephen Acrobat* (1949), a dance for two men with set by Noguchi. Graham and Hawkins married in 1948; they had no children and were divorced in 1954.

During this period a dance injury motivated Hawkins to begin to theorize and develop a safer approach to dancer training, which he termed "free-flow" and "self-sensing." He also began to challenge the prevailing aesthetics of modern dance and ballet. Reading widely in philosophy, especially Zen Buddhism, Hawkins rejected the idea of narrative dance, instead looking for "pure movement" that would embody the "suchness" or essence of a thing rather than a literal representation. He also disclaimed the trend toward overtly personal or angst-ridden modern dance. In 1941 he gave a solo recital of his experiments (one of which was a coyote dance, early evidence of his interest in nature and animals as his dance subjects). Reviewers felt these lacked dynamics or were not fully developed, although his use of music was thought interesting (Denby, p. 289). Hawkins committed himself to live music accompaniment to make the dance

performance fully immediate, and he believed the music and design should be integrated equally with the dance.

In 1951 Hawkins split from the Martha Graham Dance Company to devote himself to his own choreography and technique. In Lucia Dlugoszewski, a musician and composer, he found a lifelong artistic and personal partner, with their first collaborative work being *Opening of the (eye)*. Hawkins choreographed his pieces, after which Dlugoszewski composed music—often percussion on original instruments and sometimes chamber music—in response to the choreographed movement and rhythm. Sculptor Ralph Dorazio and artist Ralph Lee worked closely with Hawkins on set designs, costumes, and masks. In 1957 the Erick Hawkins Dance Company was officially formed. His 1960 work *Eight Clear Places* was typical of his compositions during this period: an eight-part piece for Hawkins and a woman dancer that explored movement metaphors for different nature images—cloud, pine tree, and snow, for example. For *Eight Clear Places*, Dorazio designed the set and created 101 original percussion instruments for Dlugoszewski's score.

In the 1960s Hawkins's troupe appeared frequently at Hunter College in New York City and continued an extended touring schedule of college campuses in North America. Among the works that attracted critical attention and remained in his repertory were *Here and Now with Watchers* (1957), a seventy-minute duet in eight sections; *Geography of Noon* (1964), in which the choreography threaded the four dancers around Dlugoszewski as she played a percussion accompaniment; *Lords of Persia* (1965), which transformed the game of polo into an elegant ritual; and *Black Lake* (1969), eight impressions of the night sky. Hawkins's solo *Naked Leopard* (1965) deviated from his usual process by using a preexisting musical work: a cello sonata by Zoltán Kodály. Recurrent lateral entrances and exits characterized the circus-like *Tightrope*, which premiered in 1968 at the Brooklyn Academy of Music.

Hawkins, with Lucia—whom he had secretly married in the early 1960s (they had no children)—and company, led lecture demonstrations and summer residency programs at numerous colleges. Many of his new works received their first public screening on college campuses, including *Running on a Hanging Bridge* and *Dawn Dazzled Door* (both 1972) at Oakland University and *Plains Daybreak* (1978) at the University of Cincinnati. As Hawkins refined his aesthetic, his work reflected his new thoughts. Countering what he regarded as puritanical attitudes toward the body, even in dance, Hawkins celebrated sensuality in *Of Love* (1971) at the ANTA Theater in New York City. Among painted hanging panels designed by Helen Frankenthaler, the four couples danced attired in G-strings.

The mid-1970s saw Hawkins turning to American themes for choreographic inspiration. *Hurrah!* (1975) celebrated a turn-of-the-century courtship on the occasion of the Fourth of July. The witty depiction of George Washington in *Parson Weems and the Cherry Tree, Etc.* responded humorously to the fabricated myth about the cherry tree that Weems inserted into a late edition of his biography of the first president. Virgil Thomson, whose music Hawkins used for *Hurrah!*, wrote a score corresponding to Hawkins's scenario and time-length specifications. Hawkins's childhood exposure to Native-American culture in the Southwest resurfaced in *Plains Daybreak*. With a seven-instrument score by Alan Hovhaness and partial head masks by Ralph Lee, the dance of eight animals was a ritual celebration of the creation of the world. In 1979 *Dance Magazine* honored Hawkins with its annual award.

In 1986 Hawkins created *Ahab*, a dance based on the tale of Moby Dick with a style reminiscent of Japanese Noh drama. His *God the Reveller* (1987), with a score by Hovhaness and diaphanous Greek chitons by Dorazio, ventured into a more dynamic sphere of dancing, an experiment that Hawkins described as celebrating the "unleashedness" Dionysian side of dance and life (Mazo, p. 48). *New Moon* (1989) returned to nature imagery, with Dorazio's spare wire sculptural setting suggestive of a tent and Lou Harrison's score. Navaho and Apache myths inspired his 1991 *Killer of Enemies*. Another venture into abstract movement, *Intensities of Space and Wind* (1991), choreographed in opposition to the score by Katsuhisa Hattori and Meisho Tosha, scattered figures in space; it evoked a baffled critical response. His last piece, *Each Time You Carry Me This Way*, premiered at the Joyce Theater in 1993.

On 14 October 1994 Hawkins received the National Medal of Arts from President Clinton. He died of cancer at Lenox Hill Hospital in New York City. At the time of his death, Hawkins's company and school intended to continue his work. Throughout his career, reviewers continued to be mystified by his aesthetic, grappling with the studied inexplicitness of his compositions and often confusing the feeling of ease in his work with a lack of precision in his technique. But with continued exposure, especially through lecture demonstrations on college campuses nationwide, Hawkins reached an accepting audience and accrued a following for his choreography and his training. In particular, four aspects of his career are especially significant: his attempt to divorce the art of dance and movement from storytelling and literal representation; his development of a technique that extends the length of a dancer's professional performance life; his published and videotaped discourses on dance aesthetics and philosophy; and his refusal to balleticize modern dance.

• The Dance Collection at the New York Public Library for the Performing Arts, Lincoln Center, holds an extensive group of newspaper clippings and audiovisual materials about Hawkins and his dance company. Hawkins's essays on aesthetics are published in his *The Body Is a Clear Place* (1992); *The Dance Experience: Readings in Dance Appreciation*, ed. Myron Howard Nadel and Constance Nadel (1978); and *Modern Dance: Seven Statements of Belief*, ed. Selma

Jeanne Cohen (1966). One of his company dancers describes aspects of his dance technique in Beverly Brown, "Training to Dance with Erick Hawkins," *Dance Scope* (Fall–Winter 1971–1972): 7–30. One of Hawkins's residency programs is described in Mark Woodworth, "Sensing Nature's Flow, Hawkins Teaches up a Storm—Showers of Dance-Poems!" *Dance Magazine*, Oct. 1972, pp. 24–29. Ralph Dorazio, "To See What Is before Us," *Dance Magazine*, Sept. 1962, pp. 41–43, describes the artist-choreographer-composer collaboration. Collections of articles are available in Richard Lorber, ed., *Erick Hawkins: Theory and Training* (1979), and *Seven Essays on the Dance of Erick Hawkins* (1982). Other significant articles include: Joseph H. Mazo, "Zen and the Art of Dance Making: Here and Now with Hawkins," *Dance Magazine*, Feb. 1992, pp. 46–48; Norma McLain Stoop, "The Greek Dreams and American Vigor of Erick Hawkins," *Dance Magazine*, May 1978, pp. 88–91; and Parker Tyler, "Erick Hawkins: American Life Stylist," *Dance Magazine*, Mar. 1971, pp. 44–49. Excerpts of several interviews form the basis of the chapter on Hawkins in Elinor Rogosin, *The Dance Makers: Conversations with American Choreographers* (1980). Several reviews of Hawkins's early performances are included in Edwin Denby, *Looking at the Dance* (1968). Kathleen Verity Shorr, "Dancing the Miao-yu: Asian Influences in the Dance Arts of Merce Cunningham and Erick Hawkins" (Ph.D. diss., Univ. of Arizona, 1984), and Sheryl S. Popkin, "The Influence of Eastern Thought in the Dance of Erick Hawkins" (Ed.D. diss., Temple Univ., 1978), treat Hawkins's Asian influence. Julia L. Keefer, "Erick Hawkins, Modern Dancer: History, Theory, Technique and Performance" (Ph.D. diss., New York Univ., 1979), provides details of his early career. An obituary is in the *New York Times*, 24 Nov. 1994.

LIBBY SMIGEL

HAWKINS, Hawkshaw (22 Dec. 1921–5 Mar. 1963), country musician, was born Harold Franklin Hawkins in Huntingdon, West Virginia, the son of Alex Hawkins, a foreman for the Kerr Glass Company. (His mother's name is unknown.) Harold was given the nickname "Hawkshaw" at an early age. His major interests as a boy were horses, hunting, and fishing. At age thirteen he traded some rabbits he had caught for a homemade guitar and taught himself how to play it. Hawkins's first radio appearance is thought to have been on WCMI in Ashland, Kentucky, when he was sixteen. In the late 1930s he won a talent contest on WSAZ, Huntingdon, and was hired to perform regularly on the station. He formed a duet with singer and instrumentalist Clarence Jack called Hawkshaw and Sherlock.

Hawkins and his partner were popular in the tristate area of West Virginia, Kentucky, and Ohio. His only other occupations appear to have been that of cab driver (c. 1941) and nursery worker. Hawkins and Jack left Huntingdon in 1941 and traveled with a western tent show as far as Lawrence, Massachusetts, where they spent the summer performing in the parks and on WLAW. From Massachusetts, Hawkins and Jack went to Baltimore to work in the shipyards. In November 1943 Hawkins entered the army, receiving engineering training with the 197th Engineering Maintenance Company near Paris, Texas. While he was there Hawkins got a sponsorship on KPLT and played locally. Later Hawkins served in France and participated in the Battle of the Bulge, winning four battle stars during fifteen months of combat duty. He also served in the Philippines.

After his discharge, Hawkins pursued a career as a solo act. He joined the "Hayloft Frolic" at WKST, in New Castle, Pennsylvania. Then, in 1946, he signed with King Records, the Cincinnati-based independent label. That same year he moved to WWVA, Wheeling, West Virginia. At King Records, Hawkins often covered other artists' work (for example, he recorded cover versions of Hank Williams's "Pan American," Lefty Frizzell's "I Love You a Thousand Ways," and Pee Wee King's "Slow Poke"). He became a popular attraction at WWVA's Saturday night "Jamboree," which was broadcast on 50,000 watts and had a listenership across the eastern United States and Canada. Hawkins assembled his own band for touring purposes in January 1948. Later in 1948 he briefly quit WWVA to join WFIL and its television affiliate, WFIL-TV, in Philadelphia, but he returned to WWVA and assembled another band led by guitarist Billy Grammer, who later had a major pop and country hit with "Gotta Travel On." Hawkins headlined the 1 January 1953 show in Canton, Ohio, at which Hank Williams was supposed to have been the star attraction (Williams died en route to the show). Immediately after the show, his management was taken over by Clyde Perdue, who had been Williams's manager in Shreveport.

In May 1953 Hawkins moved from King Records to RCA Victor Records, and in July of the following year, he moved from the WWVA "Jamboree" to the "Ozark Jubilee," which was networked nationally over ABC radio and subsequently on ABC-TV. In the spring of 1955 Hawkins moved on yet again, to the Grand Ole Opry in Nashville. In Hawkins's case, his visual appeal was greater than his appeal on records. He fronted a wild west show with a trained horse act, and music was only one part of his package. Hawkins was a tall (six feet, four inches), gregarious performer, and despite the fact that his record sales tailed off during the 1950s, he remained an excellent draw on the road.

Hawkins had married Reva Barbour in 1941, but the marriage ended in divorce. Starting in 1955, Hawkins was sent out on Grand Ole Opry package shows with Capitol recording artist Jean Shepard, and on 26 November 1960 they were married onstage at the Forum in Wichita, Kansas. The couple had two children.

In 1959 Hawkins signed with Columbia Records, hoping to reinvigorate his recording career. He signed at a time when saga songs such as those recorded by Johnny Horton and Marty Robbins were becoming popular, and Hawkins attempted several songs in the same vein. The first, a vocal version of the fiddle tune "Soldier's Joy," was a minor pop and country hit in the fall of 1959. That, however, was the only success that Hawkins saw during his two-year affiliation with Columbia, and in 1962 he returned to King Records. During a session in September 1962 he recorded "Lonesome 7-7203," a song written by Justin Tubb, the oldest son of Ernest Tubb. It had originally been pitched to Jean Shepard, but her version for Capitol went unreleased. Hawkins's King recording entered the country charts on 2 March.

On 3 March Hawkins played a benefit in Kansas City for the family of disc jockey "Cactus" Jack Call, who had died in January. Among those who participated were Patsy Cline, Billy Walker, George Jones, Cowboy Copas, and Hawkins. After the show, Hawkins, Cline, and Copas elected to fly back to Nashville in a private four-seater plane piloted by Copas's son-in-law, Randy Hughes. The plane crashed near Camden, Tennessee, killing all of the occupants. Hawkins's recording of "Lonesome 7-7203" became his biggest hit, posthumously peaking at number one in May 1963.

Hawkins was a journeyman country singer. His style was not especially distinctive, and with the exception of the posthumous success of "Lonesome 7-7203," he was not especially successful. His appeal was rooted in his live show, where his natural gregariousness and outgoing personality won him a loyal following.

• There is no extended biography of Hawkins, but there are a few extended articles. These include Eduard K. Moench, "The Hawk of West Virginia," *Hillbilly*, Sept. 1979, p. 3, and "Meet Hawkshaw Hawkins," *Country Western Jamboree*, Nov. 1956, p. 11. *King Record Review* (the house publication of King Records), Sept. 1947, and a questionnaire filled out by Hawkins in Dec. 1947 (in the King Records Archives) contain basic biographical information. The most extensive writing about Hawkins is in the booklet by Otto Kitsinger that accompanies *Hawk* (Bear Family Records BCD 15539; 1991).

COLIN ESCOTT

HAWKS, Howard (30 May 1896–26 Dec. 1977), film director, was born Howard Winchester Hawks in Goshen, Indiana, the son of Frank Hawks, a hotel company executive, and Helen Howard. When Howard was two, the family moved to Neenah, Wisconsin, and then, eight years later, to Pasadena, California. Hawks attended a series of elite schools: Throop Polytechnic Institute, Phillips Exeter Academy, and Cornell University, graduating with a mechanical engineering degree conferred in absentia in 1918. During World War I he served in the U.S. Army as a flight instructor. After the war he raced cars and flew airplanes, directed one-reel comedies, and produced independent feature films. In 1923, with the encouragement of his future brother-in-law Irving Thalberg, Hawks hired on as a production editor in the story department at Famous Players–Lasky (Paramount); in 1924 Hawks took a similar position, under Thalberg, at Metro-Goldwyn-Mayer. By 1925 Hawks had signed a contract to direct films for William Fox, and he continued the practice of periodically switching studios and making his own quietly maverick movies—notable among them *The Big Sleep* (1946) and *Red River* (1948)—until his last film, *Rio Lobo* (1970).

Despite his long tenure as one of the most bankable practitioners of America's least publicity-shy profession, Hawks maintained a curious anonymity. Few biographical sketches, for example, are more elaborate than the one above regarding his early years; add that Hawks worked in the Famous Players–Lasky props department during his summer vacations in 1916 and 1917 and that he directed Mary Pickford in *The Little Princess* (1917) when the regular director was too drunk to work and you have almost the whole picture. Hawks had longstanding personal and professional relationships with some culturally high-profile friends, most notably Ernest Hemingway and William C. Faulkner (Faulkner and Hawks collaborated, for example, on the 1944 Humphrey Bogart/Lauren Bacall version of Hemingway's *To Have and Have Not*); many well-educated Americans are still likely to think of Hawks as a bit player in the William Faulkner story, Faulkner's Hollywood meal ticket, if they think about Hawks at all. So what most needs accounting for in the Howard Hawks story is the fact that Hawks suddenly became supremely visible after decades of cultural "invisibility." Though he was not listed in *Who's Who* until 1971, Hawks is nearly synonymous with "Hollywood" among contemporary film scholars.

There are two ways of understanding this shift of historical focus, each keying on Hawks's relationship to Hollywood's repertoire of genres. The first portrays Hawks as the consummate Hollywood professional, an "entertainer" unconcerned with abstract ideas or aesthetic theories; his art "has affinities, in its unselfconsciousness, its tendency to deal directly with basic human needs, its spontaneous-intuitive freshness, with folk-song." The emphasis of this view falls on the unobtrusive "functional" qualities of Hawks's style. During the years in which most of his films were made—that is, before television—the tendency was to see each Hawks movie as instancing an already well-developed Hollywood genre. Thus, Hawks's first sound film, *The Dawn Patrol* (1930), seemed indebted to William Wellman's *Wings* (1927) and Lewis Milestone's *All Quiet on the Western Front* (1930); the Howard Hughes–produced *Scarface* (1932) seemed an energetically amplified rat-a-tat echo of Mervyn LeRoy's *Little Caesar* (1930) and Wellman's *The Public Enemy* (1931)—despite the fact that Hawks began filming *Scarface* in 1930; and the screwball Cary Grant/Katharine Hepburn comedy *Bringing Up Baby* (1938) seemed an obvious variation on sexual and emotional themes elaborated in Frank Capra's *It Happened One Night* (1934) and Leo McCarey's *The Awful Truth* (1937). Indeed, Hawks himself described his 1959 masterpiece *Rio Bravo* as a sardonic cinematic rejoinder to Fred Zinnemann's "adult" or "message" western, *High Noon* (1952).

Perhaps because Hawks, by contrast with his tinseltown peers, was so personally guarded, and because his visual style typically avoided obtrusive or unmotivated camera movements or commentative montage sequences, it was difficult at the time to see *past* the genre to the auteur in the background. However, the post–World War II development of archival film preservation and exhibition, combined with the rise of television, made it (literally) possible to see Hawks's films in series, in which case genre components tend to fade in interest while the idiosyncratic continuities that bind all the various genre threads into an oeuvre are foregrounded, for example, the constant interplay of comedy and adventure elements regardless of genre, the emphasis on vocation and companionship, sexually loaded if laconic "three-cushion" dialogue that conceals yet reveals depths of feeling and intellect, etc. Indeed, the return of Hawks, though anticipated in the early 1950s by French cineasts like François Truffaut and Jacques Rivette, can be clearly dated from a retrospective showing of his films, organized by Peter Bogdanovich to coincide with the 1962 release of *Hatari!*, at the Museum of Modern Art. Bogdanovich's *The Cinema of Howard Hawks* (1962) was published to accompany the series.

Construing Hawks as an intuitive artistic "primitive" is not to write him off as uninteresting. Rather, he can be seen, like other "folk" artists, as "unconsciously" involved with underlying cultural contradictions, the more disturbing implications of which are avoided, by Hawks no less than his audiences, by saying "it's only entertainment." Yet from the beginning of his career—say, *Fig Leaves* (1926), his earliest surviving feature—Hawks's films took up questions of sex and gender roles, of sexual equity and difference, of social power and mythology. Role reversal is a dominant theme throughout his career, most emphatically when Cary Grant briefly becomes a WAC in *I Was a Male War Bride* (1949), more subtly when Angie Dickinson's Feathers stands shotgun guard to protect John Wayne's Sheriff Chance in *Rio Bravo*. That so many Hawks films are deeply and wittily comic—*Fig Leaves* features a farcical working-class husband (Adam) whose fashion-conscious wife (Eve) takes an outside job at the devilish urging of her slinky next-door neighbor—permits at least some viewers to overlook the underlying seriousness of the questions they confront (as, for instance, who works and who doesn't and why).

How serious an artist Hawks himself was is subject to considerable dispute. French critics, for example, were describing Hawks as a self-consciously "modernist" artist well in advance of their American colleagues. Truffaut, in 1953, declared the surrealistically garish Marilyn Monroe/Jane Russell *Gentlemen Prefer Blondes* an "intellectual film"; Jacques Rivette, in 1955, cited Mack Sennett, Hawks, and George Cukor as evidence that the "American cinema is more modern, in a certain sense, than American literature"; while Henri Langlois of the Cinémathèque Française, on the basis of the 1962 Museum of Modern Art retrospective, was moved to declare: "The modern man—that's Hawks completely."

As William Rothman points out, in his later years Hawks worked hard (perhaps too hard) to disclaim intellectual pretensions. Yet a systematic and analytical self-consciousness is in evidence all across the Hawksian canon. Partly this involves an almost Joycean taste for elaborately sustained verbal-visual tropes or puns; Cary Grant is always searching his pockets for a match in *Only Angels Have Wings* (1939)—cigarettes are lit, exchanged, and wordlessly lingered over throughout Hawks's oeuvre—yet he repeatedly declares himself averse to fire (he never gets "burned in the same place twice"), a contradiction that reveals sexual vulnerability in the very act of denying it (he would "never ask a woman for anything"). As Rothman demonstrates, this (often sexual) interplay of word and image allows for a constant allegorical subtext just beneath the more accessible genre surface.

This ironic doubleness in Hawks finally renders most of his films virtual studies of authorship and interpretation. Many of his characters *are* authors or dramatists in one way or another—John Barrymore's theatrical producer in *Twentieth Century*, the reporters in *His Girl Friday*, the professors in *Ball of Fire*—and nearly all of his films place crucial emphasis on the art of observation, on looking. In their appreciation of each other ("you're good, awful good"), Hawksian characters model the role Hawks invites his audience to play. In retrospect, indeed, the engagement with genre that rendered Hawks invisible for so long must finally be understood as a systematic lifelong exploration of the language of cinema. Because Hawks was "good, awful good," his films could be appreciated on their genre merits alone. But the real center of gravity was less the action depicted on film—be it race car driving or deep-sea fishing—than the action of the filmmaker and his appreciative viewers who moved together through the Hollywood lexicon, seeing how many different ways one could find of saying nearly the same thing, of telling nearly the same story. By the end of his career—in the *Rio Bravo*, *El Dorado* (1966), *Rio Lobo* western trilogy—this theme and variation procedure was readily apparent. But this unending investigation of the possibilities of cinema remains for many the most significant element of the Hawksian legacy. Indeed, his deconstructive investigations of film genre go hand in hand with his meditations on questions of sexual and social power, as if exploring the visual language of contemporary American culture amounted to an "underground" critique of that culture.

The "invisibility" of Howard Hawks was ironically confirmed in 1975 when he (finally, belatedly) received a special Oscar for lifetime achievement. Prior to that, his closest encounters with the Academy Awards were his nomination as best director for *Sergeant York* (1941) and the Oscar for best original story awarded to John Monk Saunders for *The Dawn Patrol*, a story Hawks claimed he wrote himself and paid Saunders to "put his name on."

Hawks was married three times (another "theme and variation" story). In 1928 he married Athole Shearer Ward (Norma Shearer's sister), whose son by a previous marriage he adopted; they had two children of their own. In 1941, a year after divorcing his first wife, he married Nancy Raye Gross, whom he divorced in 1949 and with whom he had one child. His last marriage, in 1953, was to Dee Hartford, with whom he also had one child; they divorced in 1963. Hawks died at his home in Palm Springs, California.

• The private papers of Howard Hawks are in the Harold B. Lee Library at Brigham Young University. Joseph McBride, *Hawks on Hawks* (1982), is a compendium of interviews with the director. Bibliographies on Hawks are appended to a number of critical works on his films: Jean Gili, *Howard Hawks* (1971); Joseph McBride, *Focus on Howard Hawks* (1972); Gerald Mast, *Howard Hawks, Storyteller* (1982); Leland A. Poague, *Howard Hawks* (1982). Other important critical works include Robin Wood, *Howard Hawks* (1968, 1981); John Belton, *Howard Hawks, Frank Borzage, Edgar G. Ulmer* (1974), vol. 3 of *The Hollywood Professionals*, ed. Kingsley Canham; Bruce Kawin, *Faulkner and Film* (1977); Stanley Cavell, *Pursuits of Happiness* (1982); Clark Branson, *Howard Hawks: A Jungian Study* (1987); James Harvey, *Romantic Comedy in Hollywood from Lubitsch to Sturges* (1987); William Rothman, *The "I" of the Camera* (1988); Ed Sikov, *Screwball* (1989) and *Laughing Hysterically* (1994); Jim Hillier and Peter Wollen, *Howard Hawks: American Artist* (1996); David Thomson, *The Big Sleep* (1997); and Todd McCarthy, *Howard Hawks: The Grey Fox of Hollywood* (1997). An obituary appears in the *New York Times*, 28 Dec. 1977.

LELAND POAGUE

HAWLEY, Gideon (5 Nov. 1727–3 Oct. 1807), missionary to the Indians, was born in the part of Stratford, Connecticut, that later became Bridgeport, the son of Gideon Hawley, a malt maker, and Anna Bennett. Gideon's mother died after his birth. Following his father's death when Gideon was three, he was taken in by a nineteen-year-old married woman who had just lost her first child. Her husband, however, died three years later, leaving her with her two children and pregnant and thus unable to take care of Gideon. He was sent to his oldest, recently married brother but ran away, back to the only mother he knew. He then lived mainly with her father, until he died nine years later. Gideon, then fifteen, was taken in again by his oldest brother, who boarded him for three years. He entered Yale, was ranked high in his class, and graduated in 1749.

Hawley was licensed to preach by the Congregational church in May 1750 and later entered the mission service of the Society for Propagating the Gospel among the Indians of North America (the New England Company). In February 1752 Jonathan Edwards, missionary to the Indians in Stockbridge, hired Hawley to teach the Iroquois there. Besides teaching, Hawley studied their language, but he was not happy because of the quarrels between two white cliques in Stockbridge, which placed the supporters of Ephraim Williams and Jonathan Edwards at odds. Hawley began to lose his pupils due to the factional bickering, and a mysterious fire in early 1753 destroyed the boarding school, where he lived, consuming all of his possessions.

Hawley became convinced that the best way to Christianize the Indians was to deal with them in their native environment, instead of organizing them into an English township. With permission from the commissioners of the New England Company, he established in June a mission among the Six Nations on the Susquehanna River at Oghwaga, near the modern Binghamton, New York, where he remained for more than two years and made substantial headway. He was ordained in July 1754. In addition to his regular activities, Hawley served as interpreter, playing crucial roles in various diplomatic councils, including the one at Sir William Johnson's castle. Hawley considered this period the most fruitful part of his missionary career. The French and Indian War, however, forced him to leave the mission in January 1756. After the campaign against Crown Point, in which he joined as chaplain to Colonel Richard Gridley's regiment, from July to October, he tried to resume his mission, but a severe winter and smallpox among the natives prevented him.

In 1757 the commissioners of the New England Company sent Hawley to visit and report on the Indians in Plymouth, Massachusetts. The Mashpees, who for some time had been without an English minister, liked Hawley so much that they petitioned that he be made permanent minister. The commissioners and the Harvard Corporation approved it. Hawley was dismayed by the Mashpees' loss of independence, symbolized by the English clothing they wore, and he saw them as unlike the Indians he had worked among until then. Nevertheless, Hawley, who was formally installed in April 1758 with a salary of £80 a year, devoted the rest of his long life to the Mashpees. He married Lucy Fessenden, second daughter of Reverend Benjamin Fessenden of Sandwich, in 1759. Their growing family relied on her substantial dowry. They had five children, one of whom died in infancy. In 1763 he asked Harvard for an M.A., which was granted.

Hawley was a staunch defender of the Indians, although he avoided controversy. He adhered to traditional tribal landownership and opposed giving individual Indians the fee simple title, which would enable them to sell their lands to covetous whites and would lead to the destruction of the Indian community. He also protested against Indians being fined for minor offenses, for such fines would force them to sell their cattle and indenture their boys, and insisted on corporal punishment instead.

During the American Revolution, Hawley was determined to stay with the Mashpees to protect them. His congregation raised an 18s. contribution to the Bostonians suffering under the Port Bill. Overall, however, Hawley chose not to become involved in the political issues of the Revolution, which led to difficulties at times with the patriots. The funds of the New England Company and the Harvard Indian mission were quickly exhausted. His wife died in December 1777, leaving a family of four children. Within ten months he had married Elizabeth Burchard, one year his senior, who was a widow twice previously and had a large estate.

In 1789 Hawley succeeded in having Mashpee as a "district" (a town without representation in the General Court) abolished. Since its incorporation in 1763, he had opposed the idea because the district status might be used "as the means of oppression and greater injustice." A board of overseers replaced the district government. Until 1795 Hawley was its treasurer and the only resident overseer, thus holding the substantial responsibility for the Mashpee government.

Hawley opposed mixing whites and Indians. In Stockbridge several English families lived on the reservation with the goal of civilizing the Indians by example. He argued that this had caused the natives to leave, while the number of Indians in Mashpee had increased because no whites were admitted into the village. He also insisted that the natives learn English, the only language in which he preached. In the Mashpee church, all offices were filled by natives. The front pews were only for Indians as well; white visitors sat in the back, and their children were not allowed to attend the Mashpee schools. Hawley believed that the way to civilize Indians was to train them in agricultural skills, rather than to teach them Latin and Greek.

After Hawley's second wife died in August 1797, two of his children took care of him. The death in 1800 of his youngest and favorite son, James, was a devastating blow. James, who attended Harvard on a Mashpee missionary scholarship, was just starting his ministerial life. Hawley lived thriftily: he allowed himself "three quarts of good wine a week to drink and give away" and considered "wine and water and a crust" a good part of his living. He died at Mashpee surrounded by the Native Americans who had treated him with attention, affection, and respect. Because of his ceaseless dedication and hard work to keep it intact, the Indian village of Mashpee survived, in contrast to the one in Stockbridge, which disintegrated.

• Hawley's "Journals and Letters, 1753–1805" (bound in four volumes) are in the Library of the American Congregational Association, Boston. His works include "Biographical and Topographical Anecdotes Respecting Sandwich and Marshpee, Jan. 1794," in Massachusetts Historical Society *Collections*, vol. 3 (1794), pp. 188–93; "A Letter . . . Containing an Account of His Services among the Indians of Massachusetts and New York, and a Narrative of His Journey to Onohoghgwage, July 31, 1794," *Collections*, vol. 4 (1795), pp. 50–67; his autobiographical letters, addressed to the Reverend Belknap, in *Collections*, 6th ser., vol. 4 (1891), pp. 617–19, and 627–30; and Hawley to Sir William Johnson, a letter written at the desire of the Delaware Indians, in *An Account of Conferences Held and Treaties Made between Johnson and the Indian Nations in 1755 and 1756* (1756), pp. 10–14. Major secondary works on Hawley include Franklin B. Dexter, *Biographical Sketches of the Graduates of Yale College*, vol. 2 (1896); Clifford K. Shipton, *Sibley's Harvard Graduates: Biographical Sketches of Those Who Attended Harvard College*, vol. 12, 1746–1750 (1962); and William B. Sprague, *Annals of the American Pulpit*, vol. 1 (1857).

YASUHIDE KAWASHIMA

HAWLEY, James Henry (17 Jan. 1847–3 Aug. 1929), attorney and governor, was born in Dubuque, Iowa, the son of Thomas Hawley and Ann Carr. Hailing from Brooklyn and Cooperstown, New York, they had an English, Irish, and Dutch ancestry that included veterans of the Revolution and the War of 1812. At the time of Hawley's mother's death in 1849, his father joined a California gold rush party prior to settling in Texas; left behind, Jim grew up as part of his Uncle James Carr's family, attending school in Dubuque until 1861.

Unlike his father, who became a Confederate army veteran, Hawley left Dubuque on a troop ship as a volunteer for Union military service. His enlistment terminated quickly, though, because he was only fourteen years old. As an alternative, he joined Carr on a fast trip to California that July and August. Reaching their destination via Panama, they soon went on to participate in a new Idaho gold rush. Arriving in a fabulous camp at Florence too late in 1862 to acquire any really rich claims, they mined and worked in other profitable ventures. Hawley worked in a butcher shop when he could not mine and came out $500 ahead—a modest fortune in those days for a still-growing lad. In any event, he experienced an unforgettable season of adventure in a truly wild west bonanza district, complete with bandits, outlaws, and shootings.

New Boise Basin gold discoveries in 1862 attracted Carr and Hawley to Placerville a year later. Although that area offered much greater gold resources than they had found in Florence, Hawley preferred to join Milton Kelly—a pioneer Idaho legislator and supreme court justice—in a local newspaper distribution enterprise. Kelly later encouraged him to pursue a legal career, to which Hawley brought an exceptionally diverse background of unusual youthful experiences.

After Hawley became a successful prospector at age seventeen in 1864, his profits from mining in several Idaho districts enabled him to continue his education. Returning to San Francisco that October, he completed his studies at age twenty in 1867. He pursued an academic program in science at City College, and he also (as was customary for attorneys in those days) studied law with the Sharpstein and Hastings firm.

Meanwhile, Hawley got into another wild adventure with two of his San Francisco pals, whom he joined in a sea voyage to China. After landing there they borrowed a local gunboat in a decidedly belated effort to help a defeated revolutionary army overthrow China's emperor. As a result of their dangerous move, they wound up as captives, sentenced to beheading—a fate they escaped only when British consular authorities secured their release. Having seen enough of China, Hawley sailed back to San Francisco as a member of a clipper ship crew. Determined to resume mining and to embark on a legal career, he returned to Boise Basin early in 1869 and discovered new lode properties that produced rich surface gold.

Within a year of his return to Idaho, Hawley embarked on a notable political and legal career. Two years after becoming old enough to vote, he won election as a Democratic member of Idaho's legislature in 1870. Hawley had to participate in some wild political battles (typical of that era) that reflected his youthful talent for getting embroiled in strange escapades.

These included outlandish accusations that Hawley got Idaho's chief justice transferred to Washington Territory—an accomplishment for which he declined to accept credit. Yet during his legislative service in Boise, Hawley managed to qualify to practice law on 14 Feb. 1871. He went on to hold a variety of elective and appointive offices before becoming U.S. attorney for Idaho in 1885. He retained that office, which no other Democrat had held, until 1889. His success as a northern Democrat in a Confederate secessionist territory required considerable political skill.

Hawley became Idaho's Democratic congressional candidate in 1888, but he confronted a hopeless situation. For a decade after 1884, Idaho Mormons were forbidden by law to vote. That restriction deprived Hawley of about a third of his total strength. No Idaho candidate who opposed disfranchising all Mormons could win election in territorial or statewide voting during that era, so for a decade Hawley retired from government service, except for temporary appointments as special counsel. During that time, his personal law practice flourished, bringing him widespread recognition.

Effective participation in major conflicts that afflicted late nineteenth-century Idaho—primarily mine labor and sheep and cattle wars—contributed to Hawley's reputation. During an era of mining strife (1892–1899), he arranged for the organization of miners' unions into a regional Western Federation of Miners while successfully defending those unions from criminal prosecution. When violent clashes continued in 1899, however, Hawley helped convict a union official of conspiracy to dynamite mine property.

Meanwhile, he entered an extended criminal litigation in 1897 that grew out of a long skirmish between cattlemen and sheep herders. Hawley displayed exceptional skill in that conflict. Prominent cattle interests had employed J. L. Davis, known as Diamondfield Jack, to frighten sheep herders away from traditional range land. Davis had cultivated such a reputation as a gunman that Hawley could not successfully defend his wild but innocent client during a jury trial. After Davis was convicted in an 1896 shootout, Hawley persuaded two cattlemen who had actually participated in that incident to confess. Then he got them acquitted on grounds of self-defense. But he had no way of getting a new hearing for Diamondfield Jack, aside from a belated pardon from the governor and the secretary of state in 1902 following a sensational series of temporary reprieves that brought Hawley a great deal of publicity by that time. The pardon enabled Davis to flee to safety in Nevada, where he soon became a millionaire miner.

After a term as mayor of Boise (1903–1905), Hawley accepted primary responsibility as special prosecutor for a still more notable criminal case. After former Idaho governor Frank Steunenberg was assassinated in a bombing, William D. Haywood—a nationally prominent miners' union official—was charged with conspiracy in the crime. Haywood's case inspired massive demonstrations of support in places as distant as San

Francisco, Chicago, Boston, and New York. Harry Orchard, Steunenberg's confessed assassin, attempted to implicate Haywood and other union officials as co-conspirators, but Hawley's prosecution of them collapsed in court in 1907 when Pinkerton detectives could not supply corroborating evidence essential for a conviction.

Hawley went on to handle other significant legal cases, including some involving problems the lumber companies had in obtaining timberlands for their industry. He also engaged in a variety of business enterprises, which were interrupted when he was elected governor in 1910. In his biennial legislative message early in 1911, he called for much-needed tax reform and for a convention to correct numerous "defects, omissions, contradictions, and absurdities of our state constitution." His administration featured a number of major progressive reforms: provisions for initiative, referendum, and recall; nonpartisan election of judges; a unified state board of education to handle all public schools, colleges, and universities; tax reform; and initiation of Idaho's state parks system.

Hawley's marriage to Mary Bullock in 1875 resulted in seven children, most of whom became prominent in state affairs. All four of his sons became attorneys, carrying on a family tradition that had an important impact on both political parties. Hawley remained active in civic and state historical agency operations in his later years. He died in Boise.

• Hawley's law office and gubernatorial files constitute major Idaho State Historical Society collections. He also served as editor for the four-volume *History of Idaho* (1920) that contributes important information. John F. MacLane, *A Sagebrush Lawyer* (1953), is by one of his legal associates. Two volumes by David H. Grover, *Debaters and Dynamiters: The Story of the Haywood Trial* (1964) and *Diamondfield Jack: A Study in Frontier Justice* (1968), are important sources. A noteworthy obituary is Fremont Wood, "James H. Hawley," *Twelfth Biennial Report of the Board of Trustees of the State Historical Society of Idaho* (1930), pp. 112–18.

MERLE WELLS

HAWLEY, Joseph (8 Oct. 1723–10 Mar. 1788), legislator and revolutionary leader, was born in Northampton, Massachusetts, the son of Joseph Hawley, a trader and cattle drover, and Rebekah Stoddard. He was educated in Northampton and at Yale College (1739–1742), following in the footsteps of his cousin, Jonathan Edwards. Perhaps influenced by Edwards, he briefly studied theology and then served as chaplain to one of the Massachusetts regiments at Louisbourg in 1745. He abandoned this occupation as his religious beliefs shifted. Adhering to the Arminian tenets and liberal practices of his grandfather, Solomon Stoddard, he reacted against Edwards's strict, Calvinist preaching and played a leading role, later regretted, in forcing Edwards from the Northampton church. He subsequently studied law with Phineas Lyman of Suffield and began practicing in Hampshire County in 1749. While his clients included Boston merchants, most were his small-propertied neighbors from the Connecticut Valley. He became a justice of the peace in the 1750s and a barrister, able to plead before the Superior Court, in the early 1760s. He married Mercy Lyman in 1752; they had one adopted child.

Hawley's public life began with election to the Northampton board of selectmen in 1747. He continued to hold town positions for thirty years. First elected to the Massachusetts General Court in 1751, he represented Northampton irregularly in the early 1750s, clashing with Israel Williams, a fellow representative from the Connecticut Valley and a leading defender of the royal prerogative. Hawley was not reelected until 1766 when the purported Stamp Act supporters were swept from office; thereafter, he served continuously until prevented by illness in 1777. As described by Thomas Hutchinson and other royal officials, he became one of the key revolutionary leaders, ranking with Samuel Adams and James Otis. Peter Oliver in his *Origin & Progress of the American Rebellion* claimed that Otis and Hawley "had, both of them, great Interest with, & Sway over the Country Members" (p. 49). His rise to fame followed his defense of Seth Warren, an anti–Stamp Act rioter, in a case that went to the Superior Court of Massachusetts, and in which the chief justice, Thomas Hutchinson, ordered the jury to find the defendant guilty. Unhappy with the verdict on principle, Hawley took the unprecedented step of attacking the court publicly in a series of letters published in the *Boston-Evening Post* (Jan.–July 1767), claiming that without stamps, law had collapsed temporarily in Massachusetts, and that people had found themselves in a state of nature that had forced them to take the law into their own hands. The court subsequently disbarred him temporarily in punishment, but his career as critic of royal authority continued, exemplified by his leadership in legislating a general pardon of those involved in the Stamp Act riots.

Hawley worked actively and more consistently than any other Massachusetts revolutionary leader for internal social reforms, including notably the freedom from religious taxes for Baptists and other minority denominations. With the suspension of the Massachusetts legislature in 1774, Hawley declined election to the Continental Congress but wrote for the delegates a masterful brief entitled "Broken Hints," a quite comprehensive analysis of all of the major issues which came before the First Congress. "It is now or never, that we must assert our liberty," he wrote; "Fight we must finally, unless Britain retreats" (Adams, vol. 9, p. 641). Meanwhile, he became one of the most active participants in the Massachusetts Provincial Congress (1774–1775), which met following the suspension of royal government, serving on important committees, studying finance and the manufacture of gun powder, organizing the militia, and urging general preparation for war. Eager to precipitate hostilities, he called on Massachusetts to resume operation of its charter government, with the Council assuming the duties of governor, believing that this defiance of royal authority would force Britain into open warfare with the colonies.

After Hawley read Thomas Paine's *Common Sense* in February 1776, he pressed his friends in Congress to catch up with the ordinary people of western Massachusetts, who by then eagerly sought independence. He also urged the taking of Quebec and the establishment of "a firm and well digested Confederation," in which Congress must be supreme in regulating currency (*Publications of the Colonial Society of Massachusetts*, vol. 34, p. 401). While he never served in Congress and declined its appointment of him as Indian commissioner for the northern department, he was probably more influential than any other person in advising the Massachusetts delegates.

In the period before and just after the Declaration of Independence when key figures like John Adams and Samuel Adams, John Hancock, Thomas Cushing, and Robert Treat Paine were in Philadelphia, Hawley was generally acknowledged as the Popular party leader in the revived Massachusetts General Court. The political challenges he faced within the new state were many. To avoid a split between east and west, he attempted to steer a middle course, supporting the executive power of the upper house or Council (an eastern position), but then reacting angrily to its continuation of patronage and other political methods of the old Court party (a principal concern of western reformers). When the Popular party itself began to break apart under the strain of personal conflicts and divergent views of policy, Hawley alone seems to have retained the respect and friendship of the rivals. Perhaps from the pressure of events in the year 1776, he suffered a nervous collapse, at the time called melancholia. He declined to run for office in 1777 and never again returned to the legislature, although he remained active in his county and continued to write critically about state politics.

By 1780 Hawley's views of the Revolution had consolidated around the demands of his western rural neighbors for a more democratized system. Insisting that government reflect the Declaration of Independence's principle that all men are born free and equal, he denounced slavery, called for universal manhood suffrage, and insisted on freedom of religion. He attacked the proposed Massachusetts constitution, largely the work of his one-time friend John Adams, as the work of an unrepresentative rump convention and as "an unadvised, unconsulted, undiscussed, indigested, tautological, ragged, inconsistent, and in some parts unmeaning, not to say futile plan" (*Smith College Studies*). Yet, after the constitution was adopted, he urged its acceptance, and when harsh economic circumstances drove his western neighbors to stage conventions and organize protests, he preached caution and moderation. At the same time, he urged legislators to recognize the growing discontent in western Massachusetts and prophetically warned that it could lead to rebellion. He died in Northampton.

While some contemporaries considered Hawley inconsistent, and attributed this to his mental illness, his chosen role seems to have followed a rational and explainable pattern. He was both an idealist and a practical politician. He knew that his western constituents and neighbors were determined to have reform, and when opportunities arose to articulate their ideals, he did so. But he was also a lawyer who believed in the rule of law, and an experienced politician who recognized the contrary political currents flowing in other parts of the state. He thus sought as best he could to bring these discordant pieces together. Hawley was a political broker, in a word, yet one whose practical understanding of politics was harnessed to firmly held principles. Among all of the revolutionary leaders of Massachusetts, Hawley stands out as the most clearly committed social and political reformer, in many ways a man ahead of his time.

• Hawley's papers can be found in the New York Public Library, where he is also prominently mentioned in the Samuel Adams Papers; the Massachusetts Historical Society; and among the Judd manuscripts, Forbes Library, Northampton, Mass. Important Hawley letters have been published in Paul H. Smith, ed., *Letters of Delegates to Congress, 1774–1789*, vols. 1–6 (1976–1980); *American Historical Review* 36 (1931): 776–77; and *Publications of the Colonial Society of Massachusetts* 34 (1940): 399–403. Hawley's "Broken Hints" (1774) is in *The Works of John Adams*, ed. Charles Francis Adams, vol. 9 (1854), pp. 641–43; and his "Protest to the Constitutional Convention of 1780," is in *Smith College Studies in History* no. 3 (1917): 31–52. The principal biography is Ernest Francis Brown, *Joseph Hawley, Colonial Radical* (1931). Hawley's law career is treated in the same author's "The Law Career of Major Joseph Hawley," *New England Quarterly* 4 (1931): 482–508. A Tory view of Hawley's revolutionary role is well developed in Douglass Adair and John A. Schutz, eds., *Peter Oliver's Origin & Progress of the American Rebellion* (1961). Hawley's political career is placed in context by Lee Nathaniel Newcomer, *The Embattled Farmers* (1953); Robert Taylor, *Western Massachusetts in the Revolution* (1954); and Stephen E. Patterson, *Political Parties in Revolutionary Massachusetts* (1973).

STEPHEN E. PATTERSON

HAWLEY, Joseph Roswell (31 Oct. 1826–18 Mar. 1905), soldier, editor, and politician, was born in Stewartsville, North Carolina, the son of Francis Hawley, a Baptist minister, and Mary McLeod. Hawley's father wrote and spoke widely against the sins of affluence and slavery, and when the boy was eleven, his family moved to his father's native state, Connecticut. Young Hawley was educated there and in New York. In 1847 he graduated from Hamilton College, and during the early 1850s he taught school and embarked on a law career.

Caught up in the antislavery crusade, Hawley was a delegate to the 1852 national convention of the Free Soil party, and he founded an abolitionist newspaper. In 1856 he helped organize the Republican party in Connecticut and stumped the state for its first presidential candidate, John C. Frémont. Hawley gave up the profession of law in 1857 to edit the state Republican party organ, the *Hartford Evening Press*. In 1855 he married Harriet Foote; their union, which produced no children, lasted until Harriet's death in 1886.

The bombardment of Fort Sumter in April 1861 ushered in what Hawley called a "holy war." Reportedly he was the first citizen of Hartford to enlist in the Union ranks. He helped recruit the First Connecticut Volunteers, in which he was commissioned captain. At First Bull Run (First Manassas), 21 July, he won praise for adroit leadership that helped him become lieutenant colonel of the Seventh Connecticut. In November he led that regiment during a part of the Port Royal expedition, and on 11 April 1862 his troops helped force the surrender of Fort Pulaski outside Savannah, Georgia.

Promoted to colonel on 20 June 1862, Hawley served with distinction in 1863 at Secessionville and Pocotaligo (near Charleston), South Carolina, and early the following year at Olustee (Ocean Pond), Florida. In May 1864, at the outset of Ulysses S. Grant's Overland campaign, Hawley's brigade, part of Brigadier General Alfred H. Terry's division, was sent to the Virginia front. During the subsequent operations against Richmond and Petersburg, the brigade served in Major General Benjamin F. Butler's Army of the James. Throughout the campaign Hawley's energy never flagged. He wrote his wife, "I *never* felt so willing to fight," despite being "stooped every day, like an old man, with rheumatism." For his able leadership, which came to the attention of Grant, Butler, and Abraham Lincoln, Hawley on 13 September 1964 was appointed a brigadier general of volunteers.

In October Hawley led a division of African-American troops in fighting outside Richmond. The following month he had direct command of troops sent to New York City to prevent rumors of election day violence from becoming reality. Back in Virginia in mid-November 1864, he led Terry's division when Terry was sent south to capture Fort Fisher. In late February 1865 Hawley rejoined his superior in North Carolina, serving as Terry's chief of staff. By the war's end he was in Wilmington, North Carolina, commanding a military district. In July he accompanied Terry to Richmond, where he helped oversee the occupation command known as the Department of Virginia.

Mustered out of the army in January 1866 as a brevet major general of volunteers, Hawley allied himself with the Radical Republicans, although in some political matters he demonstrated a conservative outlook. That fall, having become well known among the state's voters and active in veterans' affairs, he was elected governor of Connecticut by a narrow margin over Democrat James E. English. During his year in office he was caught in a battle between the state's railroad and shipping interests. He was also hurt by the political effects of a statewide recession and gained unfavorable publicity by criticizing unemployed laborers who organized marches to publicize their plight and pressure state officials for relief.

Defeated for reelection by English in 1867, Hawley renewed his career in journalism, merging his newspaper with the *Hartford Courant* and becoming its editor. He also resumed his speaking engagements in behalf of Republican causes. As chairman of the party's national convention in 1868, he supported Grant and denounced the trend toward paying government bonds in depreciated currency. At the party conventions of 1872 and 1876, he was secretary of the Resolutions Committee. From 1872 to 1877 he served as president of the U.S. Centennial Commission. One historian observed that, thanks to Hawley's supervision, "on the day specified, buildings and grounds were in complete readiness for the reception of objects to be exhibited, a feat that had not been accomplished at any previous exhibition."

In 1872 Hawley was appointed, as a Republican, to fill a sudden vacancy in the House of Representatives; later that year he was elected to a full term. Turned out of office in 1874, he returned to the House five years later. In 1881 he entered the U.S. Senate, where he advocated sound currency, civil service reform, and a strong military. As a member of the Military Affairs Committee and a Select Committee on Naval Affairs, he strove to reorganize and reform the army, to provide the navy with more modern warships, and to upgrade the nation's coastal defenses. During the Spanish-American War of 1898 he sponsored a bill that added two artillery regiments to the regular service. In 1887 he married Edith Horner; they had two daughters. Declining renomination in 1904, he died in Washington, D.C., two weeks after completing his fourth term in the Senate.

Although he was an able journalist, a gifted orator, and a talented party organizer, Hawley failed to win prominence as governor, congressman, or senator. His major contributions as a lawmaker were to strengthen the regular army and to help shape the nascent Civil Service Commission. He left a larger mark as a regimental, brigade, and division leader during the Civil War. His devotion to duty and his fearlessness under fire won the respect of his troops, but his impulsiveness and hypercritical nature involved him in feuds with several superiors. Antagonists included West Pointers, such as Henry W. Benham and Quincy A. Gillmore, as well as political generals, including Butler, whom Hawley threatened to beat up on at least two occasions.

• The Library of Congress houses more than 13,000 pieces of Hawley's personal correspondence and the papers of Lincoln's secretary of the navy, Gideon Welles, which include numerous letters from Hawley. Another body of papers, mainly relating to Hawley's Senate career, reposes in the Connecticut Historical Society, Hartford. Also useful are the memoirs of Lieutenant Ferdinand Davis in the University of Michigan's Bentley Historical Library. Selections from his Civil War correspondence are included in Albert D. Putnam, ed., *Major General Joseph R. Hawley, Soldier and Editor (1826–1905)* (1964). Hawley's battle and campaign reports are in *The War of the Rebellion: A Compilation of the Official Records of the Union and Confederate Armies* (128 vols., 1880–1901), and his postwar account of the battle of Olustee is in Robert U. Johnson and Clarence C. Buel, eds., *Battles and Leaders of the Civil War*, vol. 4 (4 vols., 1887–1888). Biographical works include Elias S. Hawley, *The Hawley Record* (1890); John Allan Nicolson, "New England Idealism in the Civil War: The Military Career of Joseph Roswell Hawley"

(Ph.D. diss., Claremont College, 1970); *Biographical Encyclopedia of Connecticut and Rhode Island of the Nineteenth Century* (1881); *Representative Men of Connecticut, 1861–1894* (1894); and Frederick Calvin Norton, *The Governors of Connecticut* (1905). Glimpses of Hawley as regimental and brigade leader are in Stephen Walkley, comp., *History of the Seventh Connecticut Volunteer Infantry* (1905), and Vaughn D. Bornet, ed., "A Connecticut Yankee after Olustee," *Florida Historical Quarterly* 27 (1949): 385–403. For details of Hawley's political and military careers, see also Forrest Morgan, ed., *Connecticut as a Colony and as a State . . .* (4 vols., 1904). A lengthy obituary is in the *Hartford Courant*, 18 Mar. 1905.

EDWARD G. LONGACRE

HAWORTH, Leland John (11 July 1904–5 Mar. 1979), physicist, administrator, and government official, was born in Flint, Michigan, the son of Paul Leland Haworth and Martha Ackerman. He grew up on a large fruit farm in West Newton, Indiana, near Indianapolis, where his father was a professor of history at both Indiana University and Butler University. In 1921 Haworth graduated from West Newton High School, where he played on the baseball team.

In 1921 Haworth entered Indiana University and majored in physics. He played on the varsity baseball and tennis teams and graduated with a bachelor's degree in physics in 1925. A year later he earned a master's degree in physics from Indiana University. From 1926 to 1928 Haworth taught physics at the Arsenal Technical High School in Indianapolis, and during the summer of 1927 he performed technical work for the Indianapolis Power and Light Company. In 1927 he also married Barbara Mottier; they would have two children. Haworth entered the University of Wisconsin as a doctoral student in physics in the autumn of 1928. Appointed as an instructor in the physics department in 1930, he graduated with a doctorate in 1931. Haworth continued to teach until 1937 at the University of Wisconsin, where he studied solid-state physics, particularly the surface structure of metals; in 1934 he switched to nuclear physics.

In 1937 Haworth received the Lalor Fellowship in physical chemistry at the Massachusetts Institute of Technology (MIT). After a year of research at MIT he became a research associate in physics at the University of Illinois. In 1939 the University of Illinois promoted him to assistant professor. At Illinois Haworth developed one of the first real-time methods for the direct determination of slow neutron velocities. His experiments determined the mean life of neutrons in water, hydrogen capture cross-section, and the velocity dependence of the absorption of slow neutrons by boron. In 1941 Haworth obtained a leave of absence from Illinois to join the staff of the Radiation Laboratory of MIT. He started work as a components development engineer in microwave radar and, in 1942, became a group leader. In 1943 Haworth became the head of the receiver components division and a member of the laboratory's Steering Committee. He remained in that position until 1946, when he returned to the University of Illinois. In 1944, while Haworth was working at MIT, Illinois promoted him to a full professor in the physics department.

In April 1947 Haworth became a consultant to the Brookhaven National Laboratory, and in August 1947 he became the assistant director in charge of special projects. An outgrowth of the Manhattan Project, which produced the nuclear weapons that ended World War II, the Brookhaven National Laboratory was the first laboratory entirely dedicated to examining the peaceful uses of nuclear energy. As assistant director, Haworth participated in the planning and construction of Brookhaven's graphite research nuclear reactor, which became operational in August 1950. He also assisted in the development of an accelerator, the 3-GeV Cosmotron, which was then the world's largest particle accelerator, capable of accelerating heavy particles of matter to 500,000,000 volts. In July 1948, after Phillip M. Morse announced his resignation as the director of Brookhaven to resume his professorship at MIT, Haworth became acting director of the laboratory, in October beginning a thirteen-year tenure as the laboratory's director. From 1951 to 1960 Haworth also served as the vice president of Associated Universities, Inc., the consortium of research institutions contracted by the Atomic Energy Commission to operate Brookhaven. In 1960 he became the consortium's president, holding that post until 1961. Haworth, who participated on many advisory panels to government agencies, served as the president of the American Nuclear Society from 1957 to 1958.

In 1961 President John F. Kennedy appointed Haworth to the Atomic Energy Commission, where he became involved in matters of national security, civilian energy development, and support for basic research. He called for restraint in the development of nuclear weapons and advocated a test ban that could be readily monitored. Haworth's efforts led to the Limited Test Ban Treaty that prohibited testing in the atmosphere and underwater. His analytical approach, rigorous logical presentations, and other contributions to the Atomic Energy Commission's Report to the President on Civilian Nuclear Power in 1962 gave that major planning document substance and credibility. Following the death of his first wife in 1961, Haworth married Irene Benik, secretary to Kennedy's science advisor, in 1963; they had no children. Also in 1963 Kennedy appointed Haworth director of the National Science Foundation (NSF). He came to the organization at a time that witnessed an expansion of federal support for basic scientific research. Haworth guided the development of high-quality institutions across the nation, pioneered the NSF's efforts to link fundamental science to applied science and technology, and brought the social sciences into the fold of the NSF. He resigned from the NSF in 1969 and returned to Associated Universities as a special assistant to the president. Following his retirement in 1977, Haworth continued as a consultant to the president of Associated Universities and to the director of the Brookhaven National Laboratory. He died in Port Jefferson, New York.

Haworth, like many other American physicists during the middle twentieth century, significantly benefited from the Manhattan Project, which produced history's first nuclear weapons during World War II. Although he did not participate directly in that project, his work on slow boron neutron absorption contributed to later nuclear reactor technologies. Haworth made his contribution to nuclear energy, not through weapons development but through the peaceful applications developed at the Brookhaven National Laboratory. Under his leadership, Brookhaven became the leading laboratory for the study of nuclear medicine, subatomic structure, and high energy physics. He demonstrated his commitment to the peaceful uses of nuclear energy as a member of the Atomic Energy Commission, in which he promoted the development of nuclear power and adoption of the nuclear test ban treaty in 1963. As the head of the National Science Foundation, Haworth encouraged federal financial support of the basic sciences as the primary avenue to technological innovation.

• Some of Haworth's correspondence is in the files of the National Science Foundation at the National Archives and Records Administration, College Park, Md. The archives of the Brookhaven National Laboratory contain papers dealing with Haworth's tenure as director. The American Institute of Physics Library has papers of Philip Morse and Leland Haworth, 1946–1961. The archives at the University of Illinois include papers of Francis Wheeler Loomis, which refer to Haworth's MIT work. For the history of the role of the U.S. government in the promotion of science, in which Haworth played a significant role after World War II, see A. Hunter Dupree, *Science in the Federal Government: A History of Policies and Activities* (1986). The history of American physics, to which Haworth made major contributions, is told in Daniel J. Kevles, *The Physicists: The History of Scientific Community in Modern America* (1979). Obituaries are in the *New York Times*, 6 Mar. 1979; the *Oak Ridge Associated Universities Newsletter*, Fall 1978–Winter 1979; and *Physics Today*, July 1979.

ADAM R. HORNBUCKLE

HAWTHORNE, Charles Webster (8 Jan. 1872–29 Nov. 1930), painter, was born in Lodi, Illinois, the son of Joseph Jackson Hawthorne, a ship captain, and Cornelia Jane Smith. He spent his childhood in Richmond, Maine, and graduated from Richmond High School. At the age of eighteen Hawthorne moved to New York, earning his living during the day and undertaking art studies in the evenings. He was first employed as a dockhand and later in a stained glass factory—perhaps J. and R. Lamb—where he eventually was involved in the design and production of windows. In 1893 he enrolled in courses at the Art Students League under the tutelage of Frank Vincent Du Mond, and during the following two years he worked with George de Forest Brush and H. Siddons Mowbray. Hawthorne's contact with William Merritt Chase had far greater consequences. Although Chase taught at the league, Hawthorne did not study with him until the summer of 1896, when he enrolled in Chase's school at Shinnecock, Long Island. The fol-

lowing October Hawthorne assisted him in the founding and management of Chase's School of Art in New York. During the summer of 1897 he acted as the secretary and treasurer of the Shinnecock Summer School of Art. At that time Hawthorne also met Ethel Marion Campbell, the corresponding secretary at the Shinnecock school, to whom he was married in 1903. They had one child.

In June 1898 Hawthorne traveled to Holland. His letters indicate a profound attraction to the simple lifestyle of Zandvoort's inhabitants, a quality that was echoed later in his canvases of the fishermen and families of Provincetown, Massachusetts. Hawthorne also studied the works of the Old Masters, finding a particular kinship with the virtuoso brushwork of Frans Hals. Following his return to New York in the autumn of 1898 he rented a studio at the Holbein, located at 146 West Fifty-fifth Street. There he exhibited twenty-eight "Hollandische Pictures," which *Brush and Pencil* critic Frederick Benjamin approvingly described as "still-life studies of quaint Dutch ewers and tankards, stretches of hot sunny beach, and a few genres of old folks . . . painted at the poor house" (Aug. 1899).

Bolstered by his teaching experience at Shinnecock and the lessons he conducted in New York City on his return, in 1899 Hawthorne established his own summer school in Provincetown. He directed the small fishing village's first formal art school and taught there every year until his death, except for two summers (1907 and 1929) when he was abroad. By 1903 Hawthorne had constructed his summer residence atop Miller Hill; he later built a barnlike adjacent studio. According to a 1903 brochure for the thriving school, the new setting was "only two minutes walk from the harbor . . . situated in the midst of most interesting material. Old sand-roads and bayberry bush furnish ever present backgrounds." Hawthorne firmly ensconced himself as a popular local presence and was active in the establishment of several organizations, including the Provincetown Art Association (founded 1914) and the Beachcombers Club (founded 1916), an informal alliance of artists.

Like his mentor, Chase, Hawthorne advocated plein-air painting, so the majority of classes were held outdoors. Each week Hawthorne conducted a demonstration in which he completed on-the-spot studies. His teaching principles are codified in a published collection of students' lecture notes assembled by his wife in 1938. Hawthorne set as a primary goal for his students a mastery of the rudiments of painting, stressing *how* rather than what to paint. He urged them to reduce the composition to pure shapes and to consider "the mechanics of putting one spot of color next to another." He suggested that stimuli for painting could be found anywhere. "One of the greatest things in the world is to train ourselves to see beauty in the commonplace," he advised. "Anything under the sun is beautiful if you have the vision—it is the seeing of the thing that makes it so."

Hawthorne reiterated and demonstrated his teaching principles in his own paintings, which often depict the town's inhabitants, the New England and immigrant Portuguese fishermen and their families. *Cleaning Fish* (1899; town of Provincetown) was one of Hawthorne's first large-scale canvases portraying laborers from the local fishing industry, while *The Family* (1911; Albright-Knox Art Gallery) reveals the domestic side of the fisherman's existence.

Most of Hawthorne's likenesses are inner-directed, revealing the sitters' personalities as well as physical features. Their introspective quality derives from the artist's admiration of Italian (particularly Venetian) sixteenth-century masters whose works he studied during a 1906 trip to Italy. Two of his most esteemed canvases, *Three Women of Provincetown* (c. 1921; Mead Art Museum, Amherst College, Mass.) and *The Selectmen of Provincetown* (1921; Art Institute of Chicago), demonstrate how Hawthorne translated lessons he learned abroad into character studies of individuality and local pride. Writing for *International Studio* in 1905, Sadakichi Hartmann championed Hawthorne's work as the essence of nationalistic expression, selecting him as an exemplar of an American artist "whose work smacks of the native soil, as does the poetry of Whitman, our greatest poet, largely because he was a true expression of his country and his time."

Hawthorne was also a consistent presence in the New York art world. From 1897 to 1906 he exhibited with the Society of American Artists. Beginning in 1901 he consistently submitted works to the annuals of the National Academy of Design. His first one-artist show was held at the Clausen Galleries in 1902. Hawthorne often spent the winters in New York, especially after 1919, when he bought a house at 280 West Fourth Street. He taught at the leading art schools, including the National Academy of Design, the Art Students League, and the New York School of Art. In spite of his teaching commitments, Hawthorne and his wife traveled widely, especially during the winters. In the winter of 1910–1911 they visited Bermuda and then spent the following three winters in Paris. Later travels to Florida, Texas, Mexico, and Europe presented the opportunity to experiment in watercolor and to produce confident, freely finished renderings of landscapes and architecture. In 1925 and 1928 Hawthorne had solo showings of his watercolors at the Macbeth and the Babcock galleries, respectively.

Hawthorne's career was marked by consistent acclaim for both his teaching and his painting. He was the recipient of numerous awards, including the first Hallgarten Prize at the National Academy of Design in 1904, and was elected an associate there in 1908 and an academician in 1911. He won silver medals at the Argentine International Exposition in 1910 and at the Panama-Pacific International Exposition of 1915. His reputation extended beyond national boundaries: he was named a full member of the Société Nationale des Beaux-Arts in Paris in 1914. Hawthorne was active in many art-related organizations, including the National Society of Portrait Painters, the American Water Color

Society, and the Lotos, Century, and Salmagundi clubs, among others. During his lifetime his paintings entered the collections of major American museums, including *The Trousseau* (c. 1911; Metropolitan Museum of Art) and *Fisherman's Daughter* (c. 1912; Corcoran Gallery of Art). He died in Baltimore of heart disease.

• The papers of Charles Webster and Marion Campbell Hawthorne are located at the Archives of American Art, Smithsonian Institution, Washington, D.C. *Hawthorne on Painting: From Students' Notes Collected by Mrs. Charles W. Hawthorne* (1938; rev. ed., 1960) explicates the artist's teaching philosophies. Elizabeth McCausland, *Charles W. Hawthorne: An American Figure Painter* (1947), the first monograph on the artist, is still highly useful. Two exhibition catalogs with informative essays and numerous illustrations are *Hawthorne Retrospective* (Chrysler Art Museum, Provincetown, Mass.; 1961) and *The Paintings of Charles W. Hawthorne* (University of Connecticut Museum of Art, Storrs; 1968). Janet Altic Flint, *Charles W. Hawthorne: The Late Watercolors* (1983), provides concise biographical material and explores a little-known aspect of Hawthorne's career. An obituary is in the *New York Times*, 30 Nov. 1930.

THAYER TOLLES

HAWTHORNE, Edward William (30 Nov. 1921–7 Oct. 1986), physician, physiologist, and educator, was born near Port Gibson, Mississippi, the son of Edward William Hawthorne, a minister, and Charlotte Bernice Killian, a teacher. As a child, Hawthorne endured a bout with polio at the age of seven and the untimely death of his father. After graduating from Dunbar High School in Washington, D.C., he entered Fisk University and later transferred to Howard University, where he earned a B.S. in biology (1941) and an M.D. (1946). As an intern at Freedmen's Hospital in 1946–1947, he developed an interest in cardiac research. He went on to earn an M.S. (1949) and Ph.D. (1951), both in physiology, at the University of Illinois, Chicago. In 1948 he married Eula Roberts; they had five children.

Hawthorne's appointment in 1951 to the faculty of Howard University marked the beginning of a lifelong career in teaching, research, and administration. At Howard, he helped to devise a graduate-level program in physiology at the master's and, ultimately, doctoral levels. He was instrumental in building a cardiovascular research laboratory and in establishing a core research unit—the Cardiovascular Renal Research Group—that attracted and trained many African-American cardiovascular physiologists. He headed the physiology department for eleven years (1958–1969) and also served as assistant dean from 1962 to 1967 and associate dean from 1967 to 1970 of the College of Medicine. In 1969 he became chairman of the newly constituted department of physiology and biophysics, a position that he relinquished in 1974 to serve as dean of the Graduate School of Arts and Sciences.

Hawthorne once referred to his research as "a personal vendetta against ignorance" (according to an obituary in a Howard University publication, *Cap-*

stone, 14 Oct. 1986). This commitment remained intact despite the lingering effects of childhood polio, which confined him to a wheelchair by the mid-1970s. An acknowledged leader in the field of cardiovascular-renal physiology, he pioneered the use of electronically instrumented techniques to record heart function in conscious, non-tranquilized animals. One of his research projects, "Movements of the Mitral Valve," was supported by the National Institutes of Health and involved a collaboration between Howard University and Tuskegee Institute during the 1960s and 1970s. In this project, which was codirected by Hawthorne and Walter C. Bowie, professor of physiology and pharmacology at Tuskegee, the scientists attached instruments to the hearts of horses to measure mitral valve movements, changes in heart size and shape, and rates of blood flow in the coronary vessels. Such measurements would have been difficult if not impossible to take in smaller, more commonly used laboratory animals because of the size of the measuring instruments involved. With heart surgery in humans having evolved to the point where diseased valves could be replaced, Hawthorne and his colleagues aimed to advance knowledge about the relationship of valve closure to the tension of connecting cords, the shortening of the papillary muscles, and the pressure of blood inside the heart chambers.

Using a mathematical model, Hawthorne developed an innovative theoretical framework for heart research. His findings demonstrated subtle changes in the size and shape of the left ventricle, as well as functionally related modulations in aortic pressure, during the contraction and expansion phases of the cardiac cycle. On this basis, he proposed the nonprolate ellipsoid as a geometric analogue for the shape of the left ventricle. This and other pioneering research on ventricular and peripheral vascular function brought him widespread recognition.

A fellow of the American College of Cardiology (elected 1969), Hawthorne was active in national and state associations concerned with cardiac care and research. The NIH and other federal agencies frequently called on his expertise as a consultant and adviser. His participation in the American Heart Association included terms as vice president (1969–1972) and as a member of the Task Force on Heart Association Responsibilities in Poverty Areas. He was a member of the research committee (1963–1967) and of the board of directors (1966–1971) of the Washington (D.C.) Heart Association. He had numerous other professional affiliations and was active in a number of predominantly black medical and scientific associations, including the John A. Andrew Clinical Society (president, 1965–1966), Alpha Omega Alpha, Alpha Phi Alpha, and the Association of Former Interns and Residents of Freedmen's Hospital (executive secretary, 1957–1969; president, 1971–1972). He also served on the editorial board of the *Journal of Medical Education* from 1969 to 1972. In 1980 he was elected to membership in the Institute of Medicine of the National Academy of Sciences. A symposium on myocardial hyper-

trophy, sponsored in part by the National Aeronautics and Space Administration, was held in his honor at the Heart House Auditorium, American College of Cardiology, in 1984. Hawthorne died in Washington, D.C.

• Clippings, obituary notices, and other materials on Hawthorne's life and career are at Howard University, in the Health Sciences Library and in the Moorland Room, Moorland-Spingarn Research Center. For examples of Hawthorne's cardiac research, see "Dynamic Geometry of the Left Ventricle," *American Journal of Cardiology* 18 (Oct. 1966): 566–73; "Instantaneous Changes of Left Ventricular Volume in Anesthetized Horses," *American Journal of Veterinary Research*, with W. C. Bowie et al., 32 (Oct. 1971): 1533–42; and "Development of a Heart-lung Machine Used during Open-heart Surgical Operation in Horses and Calves," *American Journal of Veterinary Research*, with W. C. Bowie et al., 35 (Apr. 1974): 597–605. See also his review article, "Heart," in *Annual Review of Physiology*, ed. Victor E. Hall et al. (1965), pp. 351–94. Obituaries are in the *Washington Times*, 9 Oct. 1986, and in Howard University Medical Alumni Association *MedicAnnales* 38 (Nov. 1986): 33–34.

KENNETH R. MANNING

HAWTHORNE, Julian (22 June 1846–21 July 1934), author, editor, and journalist, was born in Boston, Massachusetts, the only son and middle child of Nathaniel Hawthorne and Sophia Peabody. Nathaniel Hawthorne was America's preeminent novelist, and Julian grew up at the center of American literate culture. From 1853 to 1860 Hawthorne lived first in Liverpool, where his father was consul, then in Italy. Until his family resettled The Wayside of Concord, his education came from his parents and tutors. He entered Frank Sanborn's Transcendental coeducational academy in 1860. Matriculating at Harvard in 1863, he attended irregularly until 1866, emotionally and financially shaken by his father's death in 1864.

Counseled by former president Franklin Pierce, Hawthorne took civil engineering at Cambridge's Lawrence Scientific School, then at Dresden's Realschule (1869–1870), where he moved with his mother and sisters. He followed May Albertina "Minnie" Amelung back to New York, where he worked as a city hydrographic engineer. They were married in 1870.

After Hawthorne's mother died in 1871, Robert Carter, who had similarly encouraged Hawthorne's father, urged him to publish under his famous name. His first novel, *Bressant*, serialized in *Appleton's* (1873), features a Faustian hero attracted to two sisters (one spiritual, one fleshy) who threaten to be his half-sisters, only to prove unrelated after the incestuous tension has been exploited. Hawthorne's next novel, *Idolatry* (1874), is an ambitious moral allegory of men invoking historic myths to make themselves God. Egyptian and Scandinavian lore transplanted to the Hudson River distanced the narrative enough to allow Hawthorne to linger on sensuality and (again) incest, which disgusted contemporaries but now seem only slightly ahead of cultural obsession. A later novel, *Dust* (1883), reemploys a hero torn between two ladies but displaces the incest to a father who makes a libertine of his adopted child.

Hawthorne published more than twenty-five novels, including five detective novels about Inspector Byrnes, and over fifty short stories. His best works, such as *Archibald Malmaison* (1879) or the story "The Laughing Mill," look back to Washington Irving's "Rip Van Winkle" and forward to Luigi Pirandello's *Enrico IV*, presenting a man displaced from time who tries to reenter his world. Nathaniel Hawthorne also was severed from history when his father's death left him with small share in the New England his ancestors had shaped. Yet the author of *The Scarlet Letter* recovered that history and made his fiction a vital part of it. Julian lived surrounded by historical men and women who became myths; he never grew large enough to fit.

His work has been called "Swedenborgian Gothic" by his biographer Maurice Bassan, yet Hawthorne insists on revealing the artificiality of his gothic machinery even as he remains hostile to "realism." His consistent preoccupations are moral earnestness, natural versus rural or village simplicity, and a fascination for illicit passion with an incestuous shadow (including *Beatrix Randolph* [1883], *The Professor's Sister* [1888], and *The Golden Fleece* [1892]). Distrust of American democracy emerges in *Love—or a Name* (1885) and *A Fool of Nature* (1896). His works freely ransack his father's notebooks and stories for characters, situations, and themes.

Residence in Dresden and Twickenham, England (1875), inspired his travel narrative, *Saxon Studies* (1876), which Dresdeners and Henry James found vulgar and mean spirited. Hawthorne quarreled publicly with his sister Rose's husband, George Lathrop, from 1872 to 1881 and spurred Lathrop's writing about and editing of his father's work. The quarrel ended at the death of Rose's son. In 1882 Hawthorne settled on a Long Island farm, where he wrote to support his wife and seven of nine children (two had died). He became a national fixture and a member of the American Copywrite League, the Author's Club, and the Kinsmen (including Thomas Aldrich, Mark Twain, and William Dean Howells), but he never achieved artistic acclaim. His sixteen novels from the 1880s were received as popular sellers and failed promises. In 1893 he moved to Jamaica, writing *A Fool of Nature* under the name of Judith Hollinshed, ironically winning the $10,000 prize of the New York *Herald*.

Hawthorne was best in writing about the lives of New Englanders. *Nathaniel Hawthorne and His Wife* (1884) is a staple of Nathaniel Hawthorne biography, notable for its extensive focus on Sophia. *Hawthorne and His Circle* (1903) reveals that Julian Hawthorne felt that living in his father's world was both a blessing and a lifelong burden. He also edited popular anthologies, including *American Literature* (1891), critical essays on American authors; *Hawthorne's History of the United States: From the Landing of Columbus to the Signing of the Peace Protocol with Spain* (1898, frequently reissued); the ten-volume *Literature of All Nations and All Ages* (1897); the twenty-volume *Masterpieces of the World's Literature* (1898); and the 61-volume *World's Great Classics* (1899). He edited Collier's *The Works of Nathaniel Hawthorne* in 1900 and two series of detective stories for the *Review of Reviews* (1908–1909).

Journalism brought an effective end to Hawthorne's fiction. He covered the Indian famine for *Cosmopolitan* in 1897 and the Spanish-American War for the New York *Journal* in 1898. He wrote for the Philadelphia *North American* and as a sports reporter in New York. The years from 1901 onward include Hawthorne's utopian socialist journalism written under the tutelage of California millionaire Henry Gaylord Wilshire, the "Socialist Barnum."

Hawthorne disgraced his family name by writing prospectuses, hortatory tales about the glory of investing (such as *The Secret of Solomon* and *Ishmael in Search of an Oasis*), and hundreds of personal appeals for fraudulent mining shares from which he, William Morton, Josiah Quincy, and Albert Freeman grossed over $3.5 million and never paid a dollar. Hawthorne and Morton served a year at the Atlanta penitentiary in 1913 for mail fraud. His response to jail was an incoherent, self-righteous attack on imprisonment and society, *The Subterranean Brotherhood* (1914).

Hawthorne moved to California in 1915, leaving Minnie back east. He attempted screenplays and wrote for the *Pasadena Star-News* (1923–1934). From 1906 onward Hawthorne consorted with Edith Garrigues, whom he married a month after Minnie's death in 1925. They had no children together. She published his *Memoirs* (1938), a retrospective filled with mellowed pleasure at the figures of his youth. He died in San Francisco.

• Large collections of Hawthorne papers are available at the University of California, Berkeley; Berg Collection of the New York Public Library; Henry Huntington Library in San Marino, Calif.; and Yale University. Consult Maurice Bassan, *Hawthorne's Son: The Life and Literary Career of Julian Hawthorne* (1970), for more detail.

HENRY RUSSELL

HAWTHORNE, Nathaniel (4 July 1804–19 May 1864), author, was born in Salem, Massachusetts, the son of Nathaniel Hathorne, a ship's captain, and Elizabeth Manning; both were descended from seventeenth-century English settlers. In 1808 Hawthorne's father died of yellow fever in Surinam. His mother then took her son and his two sisters to live with her parents and eight unmarried siblings in the Mannings' house on nearby Herbert Street. The stagecoach line her father had founded supported them all comfortably if not lavishly, and when Richard Manning died in 1813, his son Robert succeeded him as head of the family business and caretaker of his nephew and nieces.

That same year, when Hawthorne was nine, a ball-playing accident left him lame for fourteen months. Released from regular schooling, he immersed himself in the family's books, among them *The Faerie Queene*,

Pilgrim's Progress, and even *The Newgate Calendar*. But the real Eden of his youth was a lakeside wilderness in Raymond, Maine, where the Mannings owned property. Between 1816 and 1819 Hawthorne lived there with his mother and sisters, free to swim, fish, and hunt. That idyll ended when his Uncle Robert summoned him back to Salem to prepare for college. Resenting his dependence on the Mannings and homesick for Raymond, he devoured Gothic romances and Sir Walter Scott. His part-time clerking in the family's stagecoach office made him conclude that "No Man can be a Poet & a Book-Keeper at the same time." The problem would recur.

From 1821 to 1825 Hawthorne attended Bowdoin College in Brunswick, Maine. He was "negligent of college rules and the Procrustean details of academic life," as he later declared, "rather choosing to nurse my own fancies than to dig into Greek roots and be numbered among the learned Thebans." He graduated eighteenth in a class of thirty-eight. Three of his classmates would become lifelong friends: his most intimate Bowdoin companion Horatio Bridge (who would help arrange publication of his first book), Henry Wadsworth Longfellow (who would review it), and Franklin Pierce (who would become president of the United States and appoint Hawthorne consul to Liverpool).

Even before entering college, Hawthorne had rejected the three professions most graduates entered—the ministry, medicine, and law. "What do you think of my becoming an Author, and relying for support upon my pen?" he asked his mother at age seventeen, whimsically musing how proud she would be "to see my works praised." After graduating from Bowdoin, he returned to Herbert Street to pursue that ambition, settling in for what he later summed up as "twelve lonely years."

If Hawthorne exaggerated his problems in his letters and his early tales about melancholy writer-dreamers, they were real enough. Most of the books on American bookshelves then were imported from England or pirated, and most magazine fiction was low paid and published anonymously. Washington Irving was one of the few American writers who had attained literary recognition and a reasonable income. But in Hawthorne's view, an even more formidable obstacle to becoming an author was separation from the "main current of life." As he told Longfellow in 1837, he had only "thin air to concoct my stories of and it is not easy to give a lifelike semblance to such shadowy stuff." The complaint would recur.

Yet even during his "lonely years," he never wholly confined himself to his "chamber under the eaves." If his social life was not then (or ever) lively, he enjoyed dances and card games. He also intently scrutinized the world during his long walks in and beyond Salem and during his long summer excursions in and beyond New England (sometimes accompanying his Uncle Sam on horse-buying trips for the Mannings' stagecoach lines and at one point traveling along the Erie Canal to Niagara Falls). As still another source of story

materials, he read through hundreds of the volumes in the Salem Athenaeum, including numerous chronicles of New England's Puritan past. Meanwhile he kept journals where he recorded "characteristics" and "remarkables" of what he had seen and what he had read, interspersed with ideas and images that piqued his imagination.

In 1828—soon after adding a *w* to his family name—Hawthorne made his first concerted bid for literary recognition. Though he had almost no money, he financed the publication of a slender, unsigned Gothic romance drawn from his college experience, titled *Fanshawe*. A few reviewers offered mild praise, but Hawthorne's painful awareness of the book's shortcomings made him pledge his friend Bridge and his sister Elizabeth to secrecy. To the end of his life, he never acknowledged authorship of *Fanshawe*.

Three other planned volumes fared worse. Because no one would publish it "unless at the writer's risk," Hawthorne burned his first linked collection, "Seven Tales of My Native Land." When he found no one to publish two other planned volumes, "Provincial Tales" and "The Story Teller," he more sensibly allowed their tales separate publication. He would be paid about a dollar a page. In 1830 his work began appearing anonymously in newspapers, magazines, and literary annuals. Within six years, five of his stories were published in his hometown newspaper the *Salem Gazette*, twenty-eight in Samuel Goodrich's Christmas giftbook *The Token*, and over a dozen in the *New-England Magazine* and other regional monthlies.

In January 1836 Hawthorne's determination to support himself by his pen made him agree to edit the *American Magazine of Useful and Entertaining Knowledge* for a promised annual salary of $500. Leaving his "owl's nest" for a room in Boston, he produced all the text for six successive issues (using his sister Elizabeth as his assistant). Though the publisher went bankrupt, and Hawthorne received only $20 for his work, Samuel Goodrich then paid him $100 for his first children's book, *Peter Parley's Universal History, on the Basis of Geography*.

In 1837 Hawthorne's status as "the obscurest man of letters in America" ended when *Twice-told Tales* was published with his name on the cover (after his friend Bridge secretly guaranteed the publisher against loss). The eighteen tales Hawthorne selected from the dozens already in print were clearly calculated to display his range and to win literary recognition. Genial sketches of everyday life, such as "Little Annie's Ramble" and the even more popular "A Rill from the Town-Pump," appealed especially to his women readers, as did the celebration of marital love that Longfellow liked best, "The Great Carbuncle." But Hawthorne also included speculative sketches such as "Wakefield" and disturbing stories about the Puritan past such as "The Minister's Black Veil" and "The Gentle Boy." Readers who had admired those stories before now learned Hawthorne's name, and he could anticipate widening his readership and opening "an intercourse with the world." Pragmatically, he sent a presentation copy of *Twice-told Tales* to his Bowdoin classmate Longfellow, who was by then a distinguished poet. Almost immediately Longfellow produced an essay for the influential *North American Review* that lauded Hawthorne's poetic imagination, his style, and his use of New England materials, comparing him to Irving and hailing him as a new star in the American literary firmament. Other critics followed suit, and from then on Hawthorne's name was marketable.

Twice-told Tales also resulted in Hawthorne's introduction to Sophia Peabody, the frail amateur artist he would marry five years later. Her sister Elizabeth Peabody was so enthusiastic about her fellow Salemite's "genius" that she invited him to call; he and Sophia soon fell in love, and they became secretly engaged a year later. But Sophia's invalidism was a serious impediment to their marriage, as were Hawthorne's possessive mother and sisters and his own limited income.

To increase his earnings, Hawthorne accepted his first political appointment: in January 1839 he became a measurer of salt and coal in the Boston Custom House at an annual salary of $1,500. Before long, he was complaining that his routine duties dulled his imagination (as he would complain during his next two political appointments). But he felt up to writing children's books, and when Longfellow showed no interest in collaborating on a book of fairy tales, Hawthorne produced a collection of historical sketches titled *Grandfather's Chair*, then two others that Elizabeth Peabody would also publish— *Famous Old People* and *Liberty Tree*. Though he rarely saw his "sweetest Dove" while he was living in Boston, Hawthorne sent her copious letters assuring her that only their love made him fully alive.

Hawthorne left the custom house in November 1840, a few months before his two-year term was up. Then, in April 1841 he invested $1,000 of his hardearned savings in Brook Farm, a community of utopian idealists near Boston committed to both manual and intellectual labor, hoping that there he could resume serious writing and prepare a home for himself and Sophia. But strenuous farm work left him too exhausted to write anything but letters and journal entries, and he left in the fall. His third novel, *The Blithedale Romance*, would anatomize that venture.

He then published a two-volume edition of *Twice-told Tales*, adding twenty-one tales to the original eighteen, and seven months later began an idyll that would last over three years. On 9 July 1842 Nathaniel Hawthorne married Sophia Amelia Peabody and moved into the "Old Manse" in Concord, Massachusetts, a house built by one of Ralph Waldo Emerson's ancestors. Though none of his family attended the wedding and though Sophia's mother regretted losing her "sweetest confidante" and worried about her daughter's health, the newlyweds regarded themselves as a new Adam and Eve as they took possession of their new home. There the groom planted a garden, iceskated with Emerson, rowed with Thoreau, conversed with Bronson Alcott and Margaret Fuller, took long walks with Sophia, and produced stories in a study Sophia lovingly decorated (where Emerson had earlier written *Nature*). Hawthorne would publish twenty manuscripts while living at the Old Manse, including major stories such as "The Birth-mark" and "Rappaccini's Daughter" (which portray obsessed and coldhearted men who destroy the innocent women who love and trust them). In those stories and others, including "The Artist of the Beautiful," "Drowne's Wooden Image," "Egotism; or, the Bosom-Serpent," and "The New Adam and Eve," as in his courtship letters to Sophia and in earlier stories such as "The Maypole of Merry Mount," Hawthorne celebrated love as crucial to self-completion.

But he had trouble paying his bills. Editors paid little at best and often delayed or defaulted on their payments, and Hawthorne could not recover his Brook Farm investment or money he had loaned friends. His financial problems intensified when Una was born in March 1844, and that fall he and Sophia briefly returned to their parents' homes. Yet he never stopped working. He edited Bridge's *Journal of an African Cruiser* and arranged for its publication; he wrote *Biographical Stories for Children*; and the distinguished editor Evert Duyckinck persuaded him to assemble a new volume of his own short fiction. Then, in October 1845 the owner of the Old Manse declared he needed the house for his own family, and the Hawthornes were "driven out of Paradise."

Again Hawthorne's recourse was a political appointment, and friends in the Democratic party secured him a lucrative post. He became surveyor of the Salem Custom House in April 1846. Relieved of immediate financial worries, he nonetheless felt "my doom was on me . . . as if Salem were for me the inevitable centre of the Universe." That June, his son Julian was born, and *Mosses from an Old Manse* was published, a collection of nearly two dozen tales and sketches preceded by a genially nostalgic essay titled "The Old Manse." Most were recent: in addition to profound stories such as "Rappaccini's Daughter," "The Birth-mark," and "The Artist of the Beautiful," the volume included lighter pieces such as "Buds and Bird Voices" and the Bunyanesque dream-vision satirizing moral complacency called "The Celestial Rail-road." Hawthorne also reprinted two stories with dense historical settings written years before and now ranked among his best, "Young Goodman Brown" and "Roger Malvin's Burial," and an early tale about a melancholy writerdreamer titled "Passages from a Relinquished Work." The book "met with good acceptance," and Hawthorne's literary reputation was higher than ever.

Yet his routine duties stifled his imagination. During his three years in the Custom House, he completed only two stories, "Ethan Brand" and "Main Street." But his salary enabled him to rent a house large enough to accommodate his mother and sisters, and when the victorious Whigs fired him in June 1849, Hawthorne struggled for reinstatement on the grounds that he was apolitical. Despite wide support from distinguished politicians and sympathetic treatment in the national press, local "political bloodhounds" insisted on his ouster. Then, in July Hawthorne's mother died. In September, still frustrated by his dismissal and anguished by her death, he began writing his novel *The Scarlet Letter*.

That November James T. Fields—the junior partner in Ticknor, Reed, and Fields, Boston's most eminent publishing firm—entered Hawthorne's professional and personal life. He called on Hawthorne in Salem, returned to Boston with an unfinished manuscript, and soon began advertising "a new volume by Hawthorne." At that point Hawthorne planned to lighten his dark tale of adultery with a group of "old-time legends" that presumably included "Ethan Brand," but Fields soon dissuaded him. Hawthorne then wrote the long autobiographical introduction called "The Custom-House" and completed his novel. *The Scarlet Letter* appeared in March 1850, a story of a proud adulteress sentenced by her stern Puritan judges to wear a scarlet *A* on her breast, the hypocritical minister who was her lover, her beautiful, unruly child, and her revenge-obsessed husband. Despite Salemites' complaints of being maligned in the introduction and some critics' objections to the novel's "scandalous" subject, it was immediately hailed as a work of genius and America's first major novel. Its sales were brisk.

This first novel, Hawthorne's masterpiece, is an indictment of Puritan America but also of his own society. Its introductory essay, "The Custom-House," purportedly a straightforward account of his experience as surveyor, attacks officials who connived in his dismissal while vindicating himself. Like the novel's heroine, Hester Prynne, Hawthorne confronts a self-righteous society with self-assured dignity.

In this introduction—as in the introductions to his next three novels—Hawthorne also defined himself as a romancer (as distinguished from a reality-bound novelist), whose creative imagination required "a neutral territory, somewhere between the real world and fairy-land, where the Actual and the Imaginary may meet, and each imbue itself with the nature of the other." Implicitly he was explaining his repeated use of dream, reverie, and transformed vision in his fiction, as when at the midpoint of *The Scarlet Letter* Dimmesdale perceives a meteor as an immense scarlet letter that signifies his guilt. An even stronger connection between the introduction and the novel is signaled by Hawthorne's admission that he felt haunted by two paternal ancestors: William Hathorne, "who came so early, with his Bible and his sword" and became a "bitter persecutor" of Quakers, and William's son John, a judge in Salem's notorious witchcraft trials, men with "all the Puritanic traits, both good and evil." Though he imagined the contempt they would feel for a mere "writer of story-books," *The Scarlet Letter* amply proves that "strong traits of their nature have intertwined themselves with mine." Hawthorne's tightly plotted, densely symbolic, and psychologically probing story of concealed and revealed sin in seventeenth-century Boston is his most serious work of moral and cultural history. In his day as in ours, readers struggle to understand its main characters in the context of a repressive society. Arguably, Hawthorne's greatest achievement is his heroine Hester Prynne.

Leaving Salem forever in the spring of 1850, Hawthorne moved his family to a small house in Lenox, Massachusetts, and soon wrote his second novel, *The House of the Seven Gables*, centering on a Salem family burdened by, but finally extricating themselves from, ancestral guilt. In this most novelistic of his romances, Hawthorne dealt with mid-nineteenth-century social change but also with older themes: the persistence of the past in public and personal life and the healing power of love. His sprawling narrative is at once a sentimental domestic drama and a Gothic romance set in a haunted house (primarily though not exclusively based on his cousin Susan Ingersoll's house). The occupants' problems originated with Colonel Pyncheon (based on John Hathorne), who had been cursed by a victim of the Salem witchcraft frenzy. Through the colonel's villainous descendant Judge Pyncheon, Hawthorne avenged himself on his chief political opponent and also on his controlling Uncle Robert Manning, and through his plucky heroine who bore Sophia's nickname "Phoebe," he paid tribute to his wife. Though some critics faulted its happy ending, many ranked *The House of the Seven Gables* above *The Scarlet Letter*, and Hawthorne himself claimed that its sunniness was more characteristic of his own disposition than his first novel's gloom.

While living at Lenox, Hawthorne also completed his last collection of short fiction, *The Snow-Image*, which included his most recent work—"Ethan Brand," "Main-street," "The Great Stone Face," and the title story—as well as eleven earlier stories including one now ranked among his best, "My Kinsman, Major Molineux." If this collection was not as popular as its predecessors, its range was as wide, and it was well received.

To support his growing family (his third child, Rose, was born in May 1851), Hawthorne also produced a volume of Greek myths titled *A Wonder-Book for Girls and Boys*, which recast the protagonists as children. In addition, he gathered four earlier children's books into a single volume titled *True Stories from History and Biography*, and he prepared a new preface for a third edition of *Twice-told Tales*.

Hawthorne's Lenox residency was also the period of his intimacy with Herman Melville, a writer fifteen years his junior who was then living in nearby Pittsfield, Massachusetts, and who soon proved to be Hawthorne's Ideal Reader. Soon after they met in August 1850, Melville anonymously published an enthusiastic review of *Mosses from an Old Manse*, praising Hawthorne's "power of blackness" and his stories that probed "the very axis of reality." In the process he defined his own literary ambitions, and when *Moby-Dick* was published in November 1851, it was dedicated to Hawthorne, with "admiration for his genius." That same month the Hawthornes moved from Lenox to West Newton and then to Concord; though the men's friendship continued through letters and a few visits (Melville called on Hawthorne in Concord and four years later in England), their close relationship ended.

While living in the West Newton house of his brother-in-law Horace Mann, Hawthorne speedily completed his third novel, *The Blithedale Romance*, somewhat ingenuously claiming in his preface that he used his Brook Farm experience only as "a theatre, a little removed from the highway of ordinary travel, where the creatures of his brain may play their phantasmagorical antics, without exposing them to too close a comparison with the actual events of real lives." Critics have nevertheless pursued such connections, tracing particular passages back to entries in Hawthorne's notebooks and identifying the dream-haunted first person narrator Coverdale as Hawthorne's most self-mocking fictive self—a minor poet who becomes vicariously involved in other people's lives. Coverdale's story of a failed utopia presents the would-be reformer Hollingsworth and the two sisters who loved him, though Coverdale cannot understand his own attraction to all three. Both the passionate Zenobia and the submissive Priscilla emerge as objects of men's but also women's fears and desires; especially through Zenobia (partly based on Margaret Fuller), Hawthorne examined women's subjection to their culture and their own sexual needs. The novel won serious attention and high praise, though many critics found fault with Hawthorne's unreliable narrator.

In February 1852 Hawthorne bought a house in Concord that he called the "Wayside," the only house he ever owned. That June the Hawthornes moved in, though their initial occupancy would last little more than a year. That same month, Franklin Pierce was nominated for the presidency, and Hawthorne agreed to write his campaign biography, though grief at his sister Louisa's sudden death delayed its completion. Hawthorne's reward after Pierce's election in November was a lucrative four-year post as consul to Liverpool; in July 1853—shortly before the publication of *Tanglewood Tales*, a second volume of Greek myths retold for children—the Hawthorne family sailed for England. They would remain abroad for seven years.

During the next four years, Hawthorne not only performed routine consular duties with remarkable conscientiousness but made speeches at civic banquets, loaned money to destitute Americans, intervened on behalf of mistreated American seamen, lobbied to change inequitable maritime laws, and offered advice about America's political and commercial relationships with England. But (predictably) his creative imagination was stultified. Throughout his stay in what he called "Our Old Home," Hawthorne enjoyed visiting historical sites, cathedrals, and museums, and he developed a few close friendships. Except for his detailed notebook entries, letters, and official reports, he wrote nothing.

When he left the consulship in 1857, he had saved enough money for an extended stay in Italy, meaning to see the greatest art of the western world and so fulfill Sophia's lifelong dream while furthering the children's education and refining his own taste. In Rome and Florence, the Hawthornes became part of a large expatriate community that included the American sculptors Hiram Powers, William Wetmore Storey, Louisa Lander, and Harriet Hosmer. Meantime, in his notebooks, Hawthorne carefully recorded all his visits to celebrated paintings, statues, and buildings, noting their "characteristics" and "remarkables," monitoring his "receptive faculty," and exulting in each epiphanic moment when he was "surprised into admiration." His sensitivity to the interrelationship of creator, creation, and spectator as well as his intimacy with art and artists would generate his last completed novel, *The Marble Faun*. After writing almost ninety pages of a Gothic romance based on an English legend, "The Ancestral Footstep," Hawthorne put them aside to begin drafting *The Marble Faun*. But in November 1858 all the Hawthornes' lives were darkened when Una was stricken with malaria, an illness that lasted for six months and from whose effects she never fully recovered.

The Hawthornes returned to England the following June, and on Fields's advice Hawthorne remained there to complete *The Marble Faun* and then secure the English copyright. The novel was published during the winter of 1860 and won critical acclaim on both sides of the Atlantic. As in *The Blithedale Romance*, Hawthorne followed the permutations and variations of intimacy among two couples, this time two Americans (the sculptor Kenyon and the copyist Hilda) and two Italians (the painter Miriam and the count Donatello). Some reviewers disparaged the narrative as a fictionalized guidebook to Italy; some resisted Donatello's transformation from an embodied Faun to a guilt-ridden sinner; and some complained about the indeterminacy of Hawthorne's ending. Yet from the start, reviewers praised Hawthorne's skill, his psychological probings of his four major characters, his development of the "international novel" (pitting moral Americans against guilt-stained Europeans), his inquiries into the nature of art, and his incorporation of perplexing moral questions about original sin, the fortunate fall, and the ongoing struggle between good and evil.

In June 1860 Hawthorne returned to Concord and tried to resume his career as a romancer. In the tower study he added to the Wayside, modeled after the tower of the villa he had rented in Florence (and incorporated into *The Marble Faun*), he struggled to draft one moralized Gothic romance after another—"Dr. Grimshawe's Secret," "Septimius Felton," and "The Dolliver Romance." But each draft became overloaded with symbols and plot devices, and he repeatedly interrupted his narratives with self-critical expostulations. He brought none to completion. Distraught by the prospect and then the actuality of Civil War, he thought slavery was evil and hoped for Union victory, yet he had always been skeptical of radical change and felt "no kindred to nor leaning towards the Abolitionists." Except for the eyewitness report "Chiefly about

War Matters" (which included a long description of Lincoln), during his last years Hawthorne published only a series of sketches drawn from his English notebooks (collected as *Our Old Home*) and the beginning of *The Dolliver Romance*—all in the *Atlantic Monthly*, the prestigious periodical owned by Ticknor and Fields and edited by Fields. Though Hawthorne's primary motive was supporting his family, his vibrant sketches of English people and places delighted American readers (as did English critics' outrage at his caricature of the beefy English dowager).

During his last six months Hawthorne's health swiftly deteriorated, though no one could pinpoint a precise cause. On 12 May 1864 he left Boston with his friend Franklin Pierce for a leisurely trip through New Hampshire, which even the devoted Sophia only faintly believed would restore him to health. He died in his sleep in Plymouth, New Hampshire, and four days later he was buried in Concord's Sleepy Hollow Cemetery, with Longfellow, Emerson, and Fields among his mourners.

For more than a century, despite changes in perspective and methodology, the verdict on Hawthorne's stature has remained virtually constant. For Henry James, Hawthorne was a great imaginative writer who was limited by the thinness of American culture and sometimes trapped into allegory; early twentieth-century critics saw him as a dreamer of dreamlike fiction and the heir of Puritan gloom; mid-century "new critics" stressed the organic unity of his fiction and analyzed recurring symbols, character types, and themes; and psychoanalytic critics have theorized about Hawthorne's psychological problems and his characters' mental states.

More recently, reader response theorists have explored the ways Hawthorne's texts "create" his readers; semioticians have examined signifiers such as the embroidered scarlet letter on Hester Prynne's breast; and deconstructionists have read his texts as hieroglyphs that resist final interpretation. New historians move beyond questions of how he used history to ask how the social construction of gender and family constellations shaped him and how marketplace values affected his career. Hawthorne's literary theory and rhetorical performance meanwhile continue to engage critics who approach him not only as a consummate craftsman but also as a self-aware writer who concealed even while revealing himself through his narrators and his characters, as in the fictionalized autobiography of "The Custom-House" and in the novel it informs.

Feminists in particular say that through sympathetic characters such as Beatrice Rappaccini and Hester Prynne, Hawthorne indicted patriarchal society by showing how it victimizes women. Yet many also note his uneasiness about women's sexuality and his conflicted attitudes toward independent women (including his friend Margaret Fuller, historical figures such as Anne Hutchinson, and his own "dark" heroines Hester, Zenobia, and Miriam). Most of those critics quote Hawthorne's resentful 1855 remark to his publisher Ticknor about the "damned mob of scribbling women" whose novels sold far better than his, interpreting it as a blanket condemnation of women writers without noting Hawthorne's gender-free praise of "genuine" writing.

Yet everyone agrees that close textual analysis of Hawthorne's subtle prose style has been abetted by the Centenary volumes and that biographical study of the writer has been aided by definitive editions of his letters and notebooks. Whatever their disagreements, most of his critics and biographers continue to regard Hawthorne as his distinguished contemporaries Fields and Melville did—as a shrewd and large-minded writer who read widely and pondered deeply about the human condition and about American identity from Puritan times to his own. Though afflicted by self-doubt and constrained by a materialistic society that did not adequately reward serious artists, he created texts whose power, profundity, and artistry command our attention.

Major writers from Hawthorne's day to our own have paid him the compliment of serious critical appraisal and implicitly acknowledged him as a strong precursor within their own fiction—among them Herman Melville, Henry James, Rebecca Harding Davis, Sarah Orne Jewett, William Dean Howells, William Faulkner, Eudora Welty, Flannery O'Connor, Joyce Carol Oates, and Jorge Luis Borges. The particularly strong influence of *The Scarlet Letter* has also been manifested through its numerous adaptations, as operas, plays, films, and a television miniseries.

Hawthorne's structured irresolutions require all his readers to become collaborators who examine his characters and their behavior, attentive to the narrator's tone of voice and developments of plot, theme, and imagery. Hawthorne requires his readers to probe beneath surface appearances, and he permits no simplistic judgments. Characters are not simply good or bad but mixed, and we evaluate them in terms of their interfusion of mind, heart, and imagination, and what they nurture or destroy. Thus Hawthorne encourages readers to condemn Dimmesdale's self-protective hypocrisy while admiring Hester's loving loyalty and moral growth.

Readers quickly recognize many of Hawthorne's recurrent images: light and dark, masks and veils, shadows and mirrors, the moonlight of imagination, the fire of passion, the cave of the heart, the labyrinthine path of confusion. But interpretation of his work is never simple. Thus the scarlet letter is a badge of shame that Hester's embroidery transforms into an emblem of triumph signifying not only *adulteress* but proud defiance and artistic assertion, while its color suggests hellfire but also life-giving blood and sexual passion.

Hawthorne's recurrent themes include the interpenetration of past and present; the antagonism between the individual and society; the dangers of isolation; the importance of self-knowledge; the "fortunate fall," or lost innocence as the price of mature awareness; and the impossibility of earthly perfection.

Those themes are usually veiled and layered, as in "Young Goodman Brown" (about a journey into evil undertaken by a "good man" whose imagination has been distorted by the stern morality of his Puritan society) and in "My Kinsman, Major Molineux" (about a youth on the verge of adulthood and America on the verge of revolution). Confronting Hawthorne's art of ironic multiplicity expands a reader's imagination. By writing about his own society and its antecedents, he wrote about ours.

• Major collections of Hawthorne's papers and related manuscripts are at the Hawthorne-Longfellow Library at Bowdoin College, the Essex Institute of Salem, Mass., the Boston Athenaeum, the Boston Public Library, the Berg Collection of the New York Public Library, the Pierpont Morgan Library in New York City, the Houghton Library at Harvard University, the Bancroft Library of the University of California at Berkeley, and the Beinecke Rare Book and Manuscript Library of Yale University.

The definitive edition of Hawthorne's works is *The Centenary Edition of the Works of Nathaniel Hawthorne*, a projected 26-volume edition that began in 1962. The prior "standard" edition was *The Complete Works of Nathaniel Hawthorne* (12 vols., 1883)—the "Riverside Edition." The Library of America has issued Hawthorne's *Tales and Sketches* in a single comprehensive volume (1982) and his completed novels in another (1983).

Useful secondary studies include Nina Baym, *The Shape of Hawthorne's Career* (1976); Sacvan Bercovitch, *The Office of the Scarlet Letter* (1991); Richard H. Brodhead, *The School of Hawthorne* (1987); Michael Colacurcio, *The Province of Piety* (1984); Frederick Crews, *The Sins of the Fathers: Hawthorne's Psychological Themes* (1966); Gloria Erlich, *Family Themes and Hawthorne's Fiction: The Tenacious Web* (1984); Rita K. Gollin, *Nathaniel Hawthorne and the Truth of Dreams* (1979); T. Walter Herbert, *Dearest Beloved: The Hawthornes and the Making of the Middle Class Family* (1993); James R. Mellow, *Nathaniel Hawthorne in His Times* (1980); Edwin H. Miller, *Salem Is My Dwelling Place: A Life of Nathaniel Hawthorne* (1991); and Arlin Turner, *Nathaniel Hawthorne: A Biography* (1980).

RITA K. GOLLIN

HAWTHORNE, Sophia Peabody (21 Sept. 1809–26 Feb. 1871), artist and wife of Nathaniel Hawthorne, was born Sophia Amelia Peabody in Salem, Massachusetts, the daughter of Dr. Nathaniel Peabody, a dentist, and Elizabeth Palmer Peabody, a teacher. The family resided in Salem during most of Sophia's childhood and adolescence, though they lived briefly in Lancaster, Massachusetts, during which time her mother ran a school. As the youngest daughter whose health was often precarious, Sophia became the object of her mother's overprotective ministrations, against which she periodically rebelled. In 1824 Sophia began to study drawing with one of her aunts; by 1830, when the family moved to Boston, she had become an accomplished copyist and enjoyed the opportunities Boston provided for meeting artists and other art students.

Though she continued to progress in her development as a painter, Sophia suffered from headaches that often left her incapacitated. In December 1833 she

sailed to Cuba to rest and recuperate in the company of her sister Mary who was to serve as a governess and teacher in a plantation household. During her stay, Sophia wrote lengthy letters home, filled with her observations on the life and landscape that surrounded her. These letters were collected by her family and bound under the title "Cuba Journal"; they provide significant insights into Sophia's artistic temperament and vision. The sisters returned to Salem in 1835 and shortly after their return Sophia again experienced debilitating headaches that left her exhausted. Seeking relief, Sophia consulted a mesmerist, who tried to cure her through hypnosis. The treatment did not succeed, but it marked the beginning of Sophia's lifelong interest in alternative medicine, including homeopathy. During this period, Sophia also assisted Bronson Alcott, with whom her sister Elizabeth ran a school in Boston, by recording material for what would become his controversial volume *Conversations with Children on the Gospels*. When the sisters returned to Salem in 1837, Elizabeth initiated contact with the Hawthornes who were neighbors, but it was Sophia who attracted Nathaniel Hawthorne's interest. She was impressed by him and his work, drawing an illustration for his story "The Gentle Boy" that later appeared in a special printing. Sophia continued to interact with members of the Transcendentalist circle, attending Margaret Fuller's "conversations" in the Peabody bookstore in Boston, founded and owned by her sister Elizabeth. She also supported Hawthorne's decision to invest and participate in the Transcendentalist experiment at Brook Farm.

Sophia Peabody married Nathaniel Hawthorne on 9 July 1842 in Boston, and the couple resided at the Old Manse in Concord, Massachusetts, owned by Ralph Waldo Emerson. Though their financial resources were few, the newlywed couple was happy at the Manse. In addition to its being a productive period for Nathaniel's writing, the first years of their marriage brought Sophia contentment as the couple kept a joint journal and decorated the house with Sophia's paintings and painted furniture. Their first child, Una, was born in March 1844. With the demands placed upon her as wife and mother, Sophia found little time to continue painting and seemed pleased to fulfill the domestic role upheld for women by the "cult of true womanhood." Financial difficulties plagued the couple, and they left the Manse, returning briefly to Hawthorne's family home in Salem, where Nathaniel had secured a position in the Custom House, before they settled in Boston in 1846. In June 1846, their son Julian was born. In the fall of 1847 the family again returned to Salem, where they remained until 1850, when they moved to a cottage in Lenox, Massachusetts. The Hawthornes lived in Lenox through the spring of 1851, and their last child, Rose, was born there in May of that year. The family lived for a short time in West Newton, Massachusetts, moving once again to Concord in 1852 when they purchased the Wayside, previously the home of Bronson Alcott. Through these years as her husband's career flourished, Sophia embraced the role of supportive spouse and most appreciative audience.

After a short stay in Concord, the Hawthornes moved to Liverpool, England, where in 1853 Nathaniel assumed the post of U.S. consul, a position awarded by an appreciative President Franklin Pierce, whose campaign biography Hawthorne had authored. The family remained in England through 1857, embarking on a tour of Italy in 1858. Sophia found Rome a source of inspiration, both for its landscapes, familiar from her work as a copyist, and its galleries, in which she viewed the paintings of the masters she had heard discussed years earlier. In Florence she became acquainted with Elizabeth Barrett Browning, who shared Sophia's interest in spiritualism, and with the circle of American artists and sculptors. This period in Italy began as a rewarding one for Sophia but changed markedly when Una contracted malaria and lay perilously ill in the spring of 1859. Though her daughter recovered, Sophia was shaken by the severity of the illness, and she began to treat her daughters in the same overprotective manner that she had endured in her youth. The family returned to England that summer and the following year took up residence once again at the Wayside.

In Concord, Sophia resumed her role as supporter of her husband's career, often accompanying him to the Boston home of Nathaniel's publisher James T. Fields and his wife. Both of Sophia's sisters also lived in Concord at this time, but Sophia's conservative political and social views caused strained relations with them. After the outbreak of the Civil War, Nathaniel began to suffer depression and found himself unable to bring writing projects to completion, and soon his physical health declined. Sophia found there was little she could do to help. She encouraged Nathaniel to take a trip with Franklin Pierce, hoping that a change of scene would restore him, but Nathaniel died on 19 May 1864 while in Plymouth, New Hampshire.

Her husband's death caused Sophia to focus her attention more intensely on her children. She also discovered that her financial situation was not as secure as she had assumed, that the problem of limited resources that marked her early years of marriage would also affect her widowhood. Disagreements over accounts erupted with Fields, and though he published *Passages from the American Notebooks* (1868) and other of Nathaniel's writings edited by Sophia, her friendship with James and Annie Fields disintegrated. By the end of the decade, Sophia decided that she could live more economically abroad; she lived first in Dresden in what was to become Germany, then settled with her daughters in London in November 1870. She died there the following spring and was buried in Kensal Green.

• Sophia Hawthorne's papers are in the Berg Collection of the New York Public Library and in the Boston Public Library. Louise Hall Tharp's *The Peabody Sisters of Salem* (1950) is an important biographical source; the recollections provided by Julian Hawthorne in *Nathaniel Hawthorne and His Wife*, 2 vols. (1884), provide more personal appraisals. Biographical information can also be found in the many studies of Nathaniel Hawthorne, including Edwin H. Miller's *Salem Is My Dwelling Place* (1991) and James R. Mellow's *Nathaniel Hawthorne in His Times* (1980). See also Patricia Dunlavy Valenti, "Sophia Peabody Hawthorne: A Study of Artistic Influence," *Studies in the American Renaissance* (1990): 1–21, and Julie M. Norko, "Hawthorne's Love Letters: The Threshold World of Sophia Peabody," *American Transcendentalist Quarterly* 7 (1993): 127–39.

MELISSA MCFARLAND PENNELL

HAY, George (15 Dec. 1765–21 Sept. 1830), lawyer and political writer, was born in Williamsburg, Virginia, the son of Anthony Hay, a cabinetmaker, and Elizabeth Davenport. The early death of his father deprived Hay of a college education. As a teenager, he moved to Albemarle County, where he read law under the direction of Edmund Randolph and possibly with additional guidance from Thomas Jefferson. After securing his license, Hay by 1787 established a legal practice in the thriving commercial town of Petersburg. He married Rebecca Brodnax in 1789, and the couple had two children.

One of the leading advocates at the Petersburg bar, Hay gradually turned to Jeffersonian politics. He appeared before numerous public meetings, introducing resolutions against the Jay Treaty at Petersburg in 1795 and offering Dinwiddie County's resolutions against the Alien and Sedition Acts in 1798. The endeavor that captured the attention of Republican party leaders, however, was his publication in 1799, under the pseudonym "Hortensius," of *An Essay on the Liberty of the Press*. First printed in the Philadelphia *Aurora* and then as a pamphlet, the essay ranked as the first Republican publication in America to enunciate modern libertarian doctrines based on the constitutional guarantees of freedom of expression (Leonard W. Levy, *Freedom of the Press from Zenger to Jefferson* [1966], p. 186).

Hay actively campaigned on behalf of Jefferson in the presidential election of 1800. As a member of the Republican Party Correspondence Committee for Dinwiddie County, he drafted a pamphlet titled *A Vindication of the General Ticket Law* (1800), defending legislative approval of an act requiring voters to choose a slate of presidential electors rather than individual electors, an action that in effect diluted Federalist party strength in western Virginia.

After Jefferson's triumph, Hay relocated to Richmond, not only to place himself at the center of Virginia politics but also to practice law in the state's superior courts. In Richmond he became a strong partisan of James Monroe, who appointed him to a number of minor offices, including a post on the Board of Inspectors of the State Penitentiary. When Hay failed to win election to the general assembly in 1802, Monroe successfully championed his nomination for a seat on the Governor's Council.

In the wake of Hay's outspoken support for the principles of freedom of the press, Monroe urged him to defend James Thomson Callender, a contentious Scottish immigrant political writer whose pamphlet, *The Prospect before Us*, both advocated Jefferson's election and launched an unbridled verbal attack on the administration of John Adams (1735–1826). Enraged Federalists jailed the author in early 1800 for seditious libel. Representing Callender in the federal circuit court at Richmond, Hay saw his defense, based on the unconstitutionality of the Sedition Law, thwarted at every turn by the antics of Supreme Court Justice Samuel Chase. Hay and his associates, William Wirt (1772–1834) and Philip N. Nicholas, finally stormed out of the courtroom in protest. Chase's mishandling of defense counsel ultimately led to impeachment proceedings against him. Ironically, Callender would later turn on Hay, Jefferson, and other former Republican associates. Tensions between Callender and Hay led to a heated war of words in Richmond newspapers, culminating in a physical confrontation and the issuance by Hay of a new *Essay on the Liberty of the Press* (1803), arguing a difference between official and personal defamation.

This high visibility, some of it distasteful to Hay, convinced Jefferson in 1803 to appoint the Richmond lawyer as U.S. district attorney for Virginia. As such, Hay prosecuted Aaron Burr (1756–1836) for treason in 1807 and in the process defended the principle of executive privilege advanced by the president. In 1810 he represented the former president in the so-called Batture Case (*Livingston v. Jefferson*), concerning the federal government's right to alluvial land created by action of the Mississippi River. Edward Livingston of New Orleans, who owned the adjacent land, sued the former president for having barred Livingston from the batture. Although Hay felt the case could be won on its legal merits, he thwarted Livingston's suit by successfully challenging the jurisdiction of the federal court in Richmond.

Hay's political fortunes soured temporarily when he supported Monroe rather than James Madison (1751–1836) for the Republican presidential nomination in 1808 and lost his standing among the local Republican leadership (known as the Richmond Junto). Hay's wife died in March 1807, and a year later he married Monroe's daughter, Elizabeth Kortright. The couple had one child. Monroe gave the family his plantation "Ashfield" in nearby Henrico County in 1809. Thereafter, Hay served as Monroe's closest political adviser, spending much of his time in Washington when the latter served as secretary of state and president. He managed Monroe's presidential campaigns in Virginia in 1816 and 1820 and regained his former ranking within the state Republican party.

While engaged in national politics, Hay continued his political writing. A strong supporter of the War of 1812, he published *A Treatise on Expatriation* (1814), defending the rights of emigrants to renounce their former allegiance. Hay also contributed to a literary series compiled by his old friend Wirt called *The Rainbow*, publishing an essay on "Truth and Eloquence" and assailing the practice of dueling (1804–1805).

In January 1816 Hay resigned as federal district attorney to run successfully for a seat in the Virginia House of Delegates. The following session he was selected to complete the term of William G. Poindexter in the state senate, and the next year he secured election to his own four-year term. While a member of the assembly, he vainly sought to repeal state laws forbidding usury and took a prominent role in enacting a charter for the University of Virginia. He also wrote a strong series of articles for the Richmond *Enquirer*, signed "An American," criticizing the Missouri Compromise (1819–1820). Later, he found himself at odds with Monroe on this issue.

During Monroe's second presidential term, Hay moved his family to "Oak Hill" in Loudoun County, Monroe's northern Virginia estate, and spent long periods in Washington. He solicited a number of political appointments, but Monroe preferred not to show favor to a member of his family. Republicans nominated Hay for governor of Virginia in December 1822, but James Pleasants defeated him. He continued to publish political tracts in Virginia and District of Columbia newspapers and began work on an American constitutional law commentary, which he never completed.

While in Washington, Hay associated with John Quincy Adams, often serving as Monroe's messenger when the president sought the secretary of state's political advice. Although Adams questioned Hay's friendship and actually suspected him of Jacksonian sentiments, he nominated Hay federal judge of the Eastern District of Virginia in 1825 and gave Hay's son, Charles, the post of chief clerk of the Navy Department. After a confirmation process made difficult by Monroe's old political antagonists, among them William Branch Giles, Hay actually spent little time on the circuit bench with his Supreme Court colleague, John Marshall. Ill health hindered his performance. On a return trip to Oak Hill from a visit to the Virginia springs, Hay died in Albemarle County.

A man of dignified appearance and manner, Hay was sometimes pompous and vindictive. He did not have a forgiving nature and at times vigorously sought revenge on political opponents. Aspiring to political fame, he never gained the recognition he craved; but he did cherish his accomplishments as a Jeffersonian pamphleteer. Late in life, reviewing his long string of political writings, he stated, "Upon the whole I believe I may confidently affirm that I have been not only a faithful but a vigilant Centinel, over the constitution, and the rights and interests of the people" (Hay to Tazewell, 8 Feb. 1826).

• Numerous Hay letters may be found at the Library of Congress; the Maryland Historical Society, Baltimore; the New York Public Library; the University of Virginia Library; the James Monroe Law Office and Museum, Fredericksburg, Va.; and the Virginia Historical Society, Richmond. Correspondence with Littleton Waller Tazewell in the Library of Virginia, Richmond, includes Hay's own list of political writings submitted during his 1825 confirmation hearings. Leonard W. Levy reprinted both of Hay's early libertarian tracts in *Two Essays on the Liberty of the Press* (1970). He comments on these essays in *Emergence of a Free Press* (1985) and *Jefferson & Civil Liberties: The Darker Side* (1963). On Hay's relationship with Monroe, see Harry Ammon, *James Monroe: The Quest for National Identity* (1971), and Charles Francis Adams, ed., *Memoirs of John Quincy Adams* (12 vols., 1874–1877), especially vols. 4, 5, 6, and 8. On the Callender case, see Michael Durey, *"With the Hammer of Truth": James Thomson Callender and America's Early National Heroes* (1990), and Steven H. Hockman, "On the Liberty of the Press in Virginia: From Essay to Bludgeon, 1798–1803," *Virginia Magazine of History and Biography* 84 (Oct. 1976): 431–45. Edward Dumbauld covers the Batture case in *Thomas Jefferson and the Law* (1978), and for Hay's role in the Burr trial, see Dumas Malone, *Jefferson the President, Second Term, 1805–1808* (1974). For Hay's contributions to *The Rainbow* series, see especially Jay B. Hubbell, "William Wirt and the Familiar Essay in Virginia," *William and Mary Quarterly*, 2d ser., 23 (1943): 136–52. The sketches of Hay in the *Dictionary of American Biography* and in A. M. Dobie, "Federal District Judges in Virginia before the Civil War," *Federal Rules Decisions* 12 (1952): 461–64, suffer from serious inaccuracies. Obituaries are in the *Richmond Commercial Compiler*, 29 Sept. 1830, and the *Political Arena* (Fredericksburg, Va.), 28 Sept. 1830.

E. LEE SHEPARD

HAY, George Dewey (9 Nov. 1895–8 May 1968), radio announcer, writer, and country music promoter, was born in Attica, Indiana, the son of George Hay, a jeweler and merchant, and Bertha Dewey. Growing up amid the cornfields of rural Indiana, Hay absorbed the Norman Rockwell–like midwestern values that tended to romanticize the past and the bucolic, small-town life. He was a gifted writer and began his career as a journalist in 1919, working for the Memphis *Commercial Appeal*. One of his first assignments was the city court beat, where he turned the routine exchanges between the judge and those charged with petty crimes into a popular humorous column called "Howdy, Judge." Its success won Hay the nickname "Solemn Old Judge," even though he was in his twenties and had no special legal training. (These columns were so popular that in 1925 Hay published a collection of them in book form, *Howdy, Judge*, which he sold by mail.) In 1923 the Memphis newspaper started its own radio station—one of the first in the South—called WMC, and Hay, because of his smooth voice, was assigned to be the announcer.

Hay, who continued to use "The Solemn Old Judge" as his radio name, soon found that he had a flair for radio work and created a number of attention-getting gimmicks. He chanted the station's call letters, scripted his shows, and blew an imitation steamboat whistle (dubbed "Hushpickney") to announce the start of a new evening's show. His popularity grew so fast that in 1924 he was hired by the giant Sears Roebuck and Company in Chicago to work on their new station WLS (which stood for "World's Largest Store"). There his popularity continued, and WLS artists who made phonograph records asked him to introduce them on their records just as he did on the air. He also began announcing for a new music variety show called "The National Barn Dance" and was surprised at its popularity; it featured fiddlers, banjo players, and square-dance bands but came from the heart of downtown Chicago.

By late 1925 Hay had established a national reputation and had won the *Radio Digest* voters' award as the most popular radio announcer in the country. In September of that year he was invited to attend the grand opening of another new radio station, WSM in Nashville, Tennessee. He came and was impressed with the style with which the WSM owners, the National Life and Accident Insurance Company, were running their operation. They were also impressed with him, and a month later they offered him the job of station manager. He took it and came to Nashville with a number of ideas. One was to recreate a program of barn-dance music similar to that at WLS, except in a setting where such music was commonplace. In fact, he found that such performers, including Dr. Humphrey Bate and singer Uncle Dave Macon, were already appearing irregularly on WSM.

In November 1925 Hay, on the spur of the moment, invited Uncle Jimmy Thompson, a 78-year-old fiddler from nearby Laguardo, Tennessee, to come up one night and play a few fiddle tunes. Thompson played far into the night, and Hay was deluged by phone calls and telegrams asking for more. He was by now convinced that the idea for a new barn dance would work and began planning one. The station's owners, as well as many of the older gentry of Nashville, were not enthusiastic about such music on their new station; they preferred light opera, religious lectures, and brass bands. But by coincidence, the newspapers that winter were full of stories about a series of old-fashioned fiddling contests being sponsored by Henry Ford—who saw old-time fiddling as an antidote to the jazz and Roaring Twenties immorality that he believed was sweeping the country. (Uncle Jimmy Thompson himself had been one of the finalists in the Ford contests.) All this attention played right into the hands of Hay, who was a master publicist and knew how to capitalize on a trend. By December 1925 he was planting stories about how WSM was planning to broadcast "an hour or two" of old-time tunes every Saturday night.

First called simply the "WSM Barn Dance," the new radio show caught on, and during 1926 Hay lined up about twenty local string bands and singers who agreed to perform regularly for the modest fee of five dollars. Hay kept up a steady stream of press releases in which he trumpeted the values of this "folk music" and attached colorful names to his bands. Dr. Bate's Augmented String Orchestra became Dr. Humphrey Bate and His Possum Hunters; Paul Warmack's String Band became Paul Warmack's Gully Jumpers. Some musicians resented being stereotyped in this way and were especially incensed when Hay posed them at feed stores and in hog pens for publicity photos. But the mail continued to roll in, and by 1930 some of the bands were so popular that they were able to tour theaters as far away as Iowa. One night in May 1927 Hay renamed the program the Grand Ole Opry after he found himself following an NBC network feed featuring Grand Opera.

Yet Hay soon became a victim of the program's success. Though he was its figurehead, its announcer, its publicist, and its master of ceremonies, he began to lose power in the 1930s. The station owners, who had found out they could use the show to sell life insurance, began to bring in a series of professional managers who took over many of Hay's duties. In the late 1930s Hay suffered a nervous breakdown, which kept him off the show for a year or so, and during part of this time he worked on a pioneer fan magazine called *Rural Radio*. However, by the fall of 1939 he had returned and played key roles in two events that catapulted the Opry into the national spotlight. One was the short-lived but important movement of part of the show onto the national NBC network in October 1939, guaranteeing it a national audience; the second was the 1940 Hollywood film *Grand Ole Opry*, which featured Roy Acuff, Macon, and Hay himself.

Throughout the 1940s Hay announced on the radio show and toured with Opry troupes around the country. Again, though, his health interfered, and in October 1947 at a special concert in Washington, D.C., he became ill and made one of his last appearances with a real Opry show troupe. In 1945 he wrote and privately published a fascinating book, *A Story of the Grand Ole Opry*, and in the early 1950s he became the editor of an important early country music newspaper, *Pickin' and Singin' News*. He appeared on a TV series of Opry performances done by Bill Gannaway productions in 1955 (which are still available today), and in the 1960s he had two different syndicated radio shows on which he reminisced about the Opry. By the end of the 1950s, disgruntled at the new management and the direction of his Opry, he left Nashville and settled in Virginia Beach, Virginia, where he died. At the time of his death he was divorced from his wife, Lena Jamison, with whom he had two daughters.

Hay's role in the founding of one of America's longest running radio shows and one of its most venerable musical institutions has been sadly neglected. His faith in folk and country music, romantic though it was, was strong, and it helped create an image of the Opry and of country music that still endures.

• Relevant materials on Hay are in the Grand Ole Opry Collection at the Jean and Alexander Heard Special Collections Library at Vanderbilt University in Nashville, Tenn. See also Charles K. Wolfe, *Grand Ole Opry: The Early Years, 1925–1935* (1975). An obituary is in the *New York Times*, 10 May 1968.

CHARLES K. WOLFE

HAY, John Milton (12 Oct. 1838–1 July 1905), diplomat and author, was born in Salem, Indiana, the son of Charles Hay, a physician, and Helen Leonard, a schoolteacher. The family lived in modest circumstances in Salem and then in Warsaw, Illinois. Hay attended Illinois State University (later Concordia College) in Springfield from 1852 to 1855. In 1855 he transferred to Brown University and graduated in 1858 with an M.A., although in fact the degree was more equivalent to a bachelor's degree.

Hay did not find academic life at Brown stimulating but was attracted to the literary circles of Providence and found it difficult to return to the Illinois prairie, where he read law with an uncle in Springfield and was admitted to the bar in 1860. He took a small part in the presidential campaign of Abraham Lincoln and went to Washington as one of Lincoln's personal secretaries. Technically he was a Pension Office clerk. In 1864 he was commissioned as a major and assistant adjutant general in the volunteers. In 1865 he was promoted to colonel, although he never served actively in the military, being deputed to the Executive Mansion. He left Washington in May 1865 following Lincoln's assassination but retained his military commission until 1867. Initially unimpressed with Lincoln, by 1863 Hay had come to consider him the indispensable leader. Lincoln influenced Hay's social and political thought significantly.

Following the Civil War, Hay secured minor diplomatic posts in Europe, serving as secretary of the American legation at Paris (1865–1866), secretary and chargé d'affaires ad interim at Vienna (1867–1868), and secretary at Madrid (1869–1870). He conducted no serious diplomatic work and devoted his time to becoming acquainted with European culture. His democratic beliefs also matured in these years, and he developed a loathing for European autocracy. In *Castilian Days* (1871) and several poems, Hay praised such romantic democrats as the Spanish Republican Emilio Castelar and even defended the radical Paris Commune.

In 1870–1871 Hay achieved fame as a poet, many of his pieces dealing with life on the Mississippi and the frontier. Most appeared in *Harper's Weekly*. His first collection, *Pike County Ballads and Other Pieces* (1871), thrust him to national prominence. His writing was often compared with that of Mark Twain, with whom he became a lifelong friend. Several of the poems celebrated political and social democracy.

In 1870 Whitelaw Reid hired Hay as an editorial writer for the New York *Tribune*, a position he held until 1875. Hay's years in New York served to introduce him to the nation's literary elite.

In 1874 Hay married Clara Louise Stone, daughter of Cleveland investor and railroad magnate Amasa Stone. They had four children. Already economically comfortable from a handsome salary and royalties, Hay gained instant wealth from the marriage. In 1875 he moved to Cleveland. Thereafter, until 1897 when he was appointed American ambassador to Great Britain, Hay held only one official position: from November 1878 to 1881 he was assistant secretary of state, resigning shortly after President James A. Garfield's assassination. He wrote, with John G. Nicolay, his ten-volume *History* of Lincoln, which was serialized in *Century* magazine from 1886 to 1890, was first published as a complete set in 1894, and remains important. In addition, he spent his time managing investments, editing the *Tribune* for six months in 1881 while Reid was away on his honeymoon, working for Republican political candidates, and taking extended trips to Europe, particularly to England.

During these years Hay's social views underwent an important transformation. His pronouncedly democratic, even radical, views receded, and Hay became more and more conservative. The crucial cause was the Great Railway Strike of 1877, which affected Stone's (and Hay's) personal investments. Hay found the strike frightening. In 1883 he responded with an anonymous novel, *The Bread-winners: A Social Study*, which strongly attacked the labor unions that had struck the railroads. The book, which was widely reviewed, was the first fictional defense of the new industrialism of the Gilded Age, almost a mirror image of such famous reform novels as Edward Bellamy's *Looking Backward* (1888), Frank Norris's *The Octopus* (1901), and Upton Sinclair's *The Jungle* (1906). The novel also revealed a certain disdain for uncultivated, nouveaux riches businessmen, but its primary message was that the upper class, whether cultured aristocrats or crass business leaders, should join forces to resist labor leaders and the unwashed masses (particularly Irish immigrants), who challenged those "old-fashioned decencies" (like good manners, hard work, and deference to one's social betters) that Hay increasingly held dear (Hay, *Bread-winners*, p. 109).

Now Hay identified even more closely with the Republican party; increasingly he saw the Democrats as the source of all evil tendencies in American history. *The Bread-winner*'s villain was Andrew Jackson Offitt, a name indicating Hay's contempt for social and perhaps political democracy. Each election year the Republicans benefited from Hay's purse as well as from his literary talents.

Hay had an extraordinary talent for attracting and keeping friends. "Make all good men your well-wishers," he poeticized, "and then, in the years' steady sifting, / Some of them turn into friends. Friends are / the sunshine of life" (Hay, *Complete Poetical Works* [1917], p. 185). Hay counted people of many sorts among his friends and acquaintances, including journalists, politicians, and businessmen. He was "much liked by all grades of people in Washington," observed the poet Walt Whitman (Horace Traubel, ed., *With Walt Whitman in Camden* [1959], vol. 4, p. 43). He thrived on social relationships with literary men and women and cultivated friendships with everyone who was anyone in American literary circles. He was close to Twain, William Dean Howells, Bret Harte, Henry James (1843–1916), and John La Farge (1835–1910), for example.

Hay's closest friends were in a private circle called the Five of Hearts, consisting of John and Clara Hay, Henry B. Adams and Marian "Clover" Adams, and Clarence King. King was a geologist and writer, who led a life of mystery and adventure envied by the more conventional Hay. It was the brilliant and eccentric Henry Adams with whom Hay was closest, despite their disagreements on several issues. When Hay

moved to Washington, D.C., in 1886, he and Adams built adjoining houses. After Hay died, Adams made him the hero of his work, *The Education of Henry Adams* (1918).

Hay also established many friendships with prominent literary people and men of affairs in England. He fell in love with England, with its culture, manners, orderliness, and perhaps also its sharper class distinctions. Hay also believed increasingly in Anglo-Saxon domination as a principle for maintaining peace and order in the world, a view shared by many of his British friends.

Hay's familiarity with England gave rise to rumors by the late 1880s that President Benjamin Harrison (1833–1901) would name him ambassador to the Court of St. James's. Harrison demurred, and Hay had to await the election of William McKinley in 1896. There is no question that Hay wanted the appointment. He contributed substantial funds to the McKinley campaign and also to a fund to help McKinley pay some private debts. During the campaign he visited the candidate in Canton, Ohio, and also contributed a campaign speech, "The Platform of Anarchy," which in highly colored language compared the Democratic and Populist candidate William Jennings Bryan and his supporters to "burglars and incendiaries." He then helped McKinley move Reid out of the running for the ambassadorship (a particularly difficult assignment that tested the very limits of Hay's ability to remain friends with Reid) and was elated when, in February 1897, McKinley asked him to go to London.

The nearly seventeen months that Hay spent in London were the happiest of his life. His reputation as a man of letters and his many British friendships gave him immediate entrée into the highest British circles. More fundamental to his diplomatic successes, Hay arrived in London at a time when the British government had decided to forge closer ties with the United States. Hay, a thoroughgoing Anglophile, wanted nothing more than to reciprocate. He was a key player in bringing about the "great rapprochement" that paved the way for the generally close ties between the two countries in the twentieth century. Henry Adams caught Hay's contribution perfectly. "In the long list of famous American Ministers in London," he wrote, "none could have given the work quite the completeness, the harmony, the perfect ease of Hay" (Adams, *The Education of Henry Adams*, p. 363).

At first, however, much to Hay's irritation, he was not entrusted to conduct negotiations on important matters. Instead McKinley dispatched former secretary of state John W. Foster to handle discussions about a long-standing and dangerous dispute between the United States and Canada over hunting seals in the Bering Sea, while Colorado senator Edward O. Wolcott (because his state's interest in the silver question) represented the United States in currency negotiations. Furthermore, as a sop to Reid, the president asked the editor to represent him at Queen Victoria's Diamond Jubilee. Hay acknowledged Wolcott's competence but feared that Foster would behave tactlessly and botch the negotiations over the seals. In the end an agreement was not reached until 1911, and Hay blamed Foster's bad manners as well as a contentious American press determined to attack England at every opportunity.

If at first Hay had to make way for special representatives, caring for Anglo-American relations during the Spanish-American War of 1898 fell entirely to him. His views about a possible war with Spain are obscure. He was not among those urging a bellicose policy on McKinley, and he admired the president's courage in standing against the storm of popular opinion that demanded war. Even after the *Maine* was destroyed, Hay exhibited no sense of urgency. Vacationing in Egypt at the time, the ambassador did not cut short his holiday, causing some to complain. Theodore Roosevelt (1858–1919), for example, wrote privately that he could not "understand how John Hay was willing to be away from England at this time" (Elting Morison, ed., *Letters of Theodore Roosevelt*, vol. 1 [1951], p. 797).

On the other hand, Hay did not oppose war and sent the State Department many reports from British newspapers that detailed horrendous conditions in Cuba. Many Britons called for American intervention to restore order and even to annex the island. Most important of all, Hay saw that a war with Spain had the potential to improve Anglo-American relations significantly. Once war was declared he used his skills to encourage subtle British support for the United States; among other instances, the British allowed Filipino resistance leader Emilio Aguinaldo to return from Hong Kong to the Philippines to fight the Spanish. In his arguments, Hay emphasized the advantages of a world ruled by Anglo-Saxon benevolence.

With the Spanish-American War in progress and the United States on the verge of a greatly expanded international role, McKinley needed a knowledgeable and experienced person to replace the aging and reputedly senile John Sherman (1823–1900) as secretary of state. In August 1898 he turned to Hay. The prospects of leaving England depressed Hay, and he considered declining the offer. In the end his sense of duty won out, but he was not happy. "All the fun of my life ended on the platform at Euston," he wrote to his wife shortly after his return (Dennett, *John Hay*, p. 196).

By the time Hay arrived in Washington, the "splendid little war," as Hay put it in one of his most remembered expressions, was over, but peace negotiations had not begun. The most important unsettled question was whether the United States should demand that Spain cede the Philippine Islands.

Hay was not an early advocate of imperial expansion. Although he may have approved of efforts in the 1860s to annex Santo Domingo (now Dominican Republic), his democratic idealism of the early years militated against imperialism. In 1884 he penned a poem urging the United States not to take Hawaii, but when in 1893 Grover Cleveland decided to reject Harri-

son's treaty of annexation, Hay strongly criticized the action.

As for the Philippines, like most Americans Hay had given little thought to the archipelago prior to May 1898. He soon came to favor retention of a coaling station, and during the summer his fears of German ambitions in the Pacific drove him toward annexation. In addition, the British wanted the United States to annex the islands, and Hay was aware of possible commercial advantages that might flow from annexation. The president's thought evolved in a manner very similar to Hay's, and in late October he demanded the cession of the entire archipelago.

When the Philippine-American War began in February 1899, Hay supported military efforts to defeat the Filipino resistance. He portrayed the Filipino leaders as venal and incompetent and in the spring of 1899 rejected advice that, since the United States had achieved major military victories in the initial encounters, it ought to make conciliatory gestures to bring about a settlement. American authority, he stated, would be established by military means. Hay defended America's imperial course against a chorus of bitter, sometimes personal, attacks from anti-imperialists. Some of the critics were his close friends, including Andrew Carnegie, Henry Adams, Twain, and Howells.

Acquisition of the Philippines heightened American interest in China. Fears that China might be divided among the European powers and Japan led Hay to issue the famous Open Door notes in 1899. The notes urged the powers to avoid discrimination against other countries within their spheres of influence and was implicitly hostile to the very idea of spheres. The next year, when Chinese traditionalists (Boxers) rose in revolt to challenge Western influence, the powers, including the United States, sent troops to relieve the besieged Western legations in Peking (Beijing). Fearing that this action might lead the powers finally to divide China, Hay sent another Open Door note that committed the United States to the maintenance of China's "territorial and administrative entity," thus challenging the spheres directly. Although Hay announced that all of the powers had accepted the American position, in fact none of the powers accepted it without reservations or exceptions. Hay knew that a successful policy required available force, and in one of his few disagreements with the president, he opposed withdrawing American troops from China.

Given the limited tools that he possessed, Hay's attempt to restrain the powers in China was probably the most he could have done, but whether it was the Open Door policy that preserved China is questionable. More likely the rivalries among the powers prevented a full-scale division. The Open Door notes also demonstrated Western contempt for China, which was not even informed of the policy in advance. Nevertheless, Hay's China policy was immensely popular in the United States and was an important political success for the McKinley administration.

Hay sought unsuccessfully to align his China policy with that of Great Britain but took the British point of view in South Africa, where in 1899 the Boer War broke out between Britain and Afrikaners. Although the American public sympathized with the Boer rebellion, Hay stood steadfast against it. He inhibited Boer efforts to acquire material and political support in the United States, fired American consuls who sympathized with the Boers, and appointed his own son, Adelbert Stone Hay, as consul at Pretoria.

In the western hemisphere, Hay was able to bring Britain and the United States closer by working to remove points of disagreement. The disputed boundary between Alaska and Canada was the most difficult to resolve. Originally a matter of small concern, the discovery of gold in the region made a specific delineation important.

Hay, primarily interested in forging strong Anglo-American ties, was willing to compromise. When an Anglo-American Joint High Commission proved unable to resolve the boundary issue, Hay wanted to submit it to binding arbitration but the Senate resisted, and the Canadians were intransigent. He then suggested leasing a strip of land that would allow the Canadians railroad access to the sea, a major Canadian objective. The Senate was strongly opposed, however, and the best Hay could do for the moment was to negotiate a modus vivendi with Britain that established temporary demarcation lines in crucial areas.

Another issue involved the Clayton-Bulwer Treaty of 1850, which provided that any canal across the Central American isthmus be jointly owned and operated by Britain and the United States. Many Americans wanted any canal to be American-controlled. After the modus vivendi on the Alaska boundary was reached in October 1899, the British accepted a new isthmian treaty negotiated by Hay and the British ambassador in Washington, Lord Pauncefote. However, jingoist Americans, including New York governor Theodore Roosevelt, felt that the treaty was insufficiently nationalistic and forced Hay to renegotiate it. After further British concessions, the Hay-Pauncefote Treaty was finally approved in December 1901. The British gave up their rights to mutual control of a canal.

Meanwhile, Hay sought to resolve the Alaska issue in an amicable way but by then Theodore Roosevelt, who thought the American position was unassailable, was president. Under great pressure, in 1903 the British accepted the essence of the American claim after a quasi arbitration. It was further evidence of the British determination to conciliate the United States, but Hay felt a settlement could have been reached with much better grace.

Although Hay thought Roosevelt too pugnacious on the boundary question, generally the two men got along well, as the acquisition of the Panama Canal Zone demonstrated. Freed by the Hay-Pauncefote Treaty of external restraints, Hay negotiated a treaty with Colombia (Panama then being a province of that country) for a canal zone. When Colombian legislators rejected the treaty, Hay preferred to investigate an alternative route through Nicaragua but offered no objection when Roosevelt decided to intervene directly in Panama. When in November 1903 Panamanians rose in revolt against Colombia, Hay supported Roosevelt's intervention and quickly negotiated an American-controlled canal zone with Panama.

With the completion of the canal treaty, Hay's creative days as secretary of state were over. He suffered increasingly from poor health, and Roosevelt more often controlled foreign policy directly. Hay, however, left a record of solid diplomatic achievements. He forged closer Anglo-American ties, presided over the acquisition of an overseas empire in the Pacific, issued the Open Door notes, and expanded American influence in Latin America. He died at Lake Sunapee, New Hampshire.

• The two major collections of Hay papers are at Brown University and the Library of Congress. Substantial numbers of Hay letters are available in other collections, including the Wadsworth Family Papers, the Whitelaw Reid Papers, the Henry White Papers, and the Joseph Choate Papers, all in the Library of Congress. For descriptions of these and other collections of Hay's letters, see the bibliographical essays in Kenton Clymer, *John Hay: The Gentleman as Diplomat* (1975), and Patricia O'Toole, *The Five of Hearts: An Intimate Portrait of Henry Adams and His Friends, 1880–1918* (1990). Hay's diplomatic correspondence is available at the National Archives.

There is no complete published edition of Hay's letters and diaries. Shortly after Hay's death Clara Hay and Henry Adams published an unreliable edition, *Letters of John Hay and Extracts from His Diary* (1908). More reliable, but limited in scope, are Tyler Dennett, ed., *Lincoln and the Civil War in the Diaries and Letters of John Hay* (1939); George Montiero, *Henry James and John Hay: The Record of a Friendship* (1965); and George Monteiro and Brenda Murphy, eds., *John Hay–Howells Letters: The Correspondence of John Milton Hay and William Dean Howells 1861–1905* (1980). William R. Thayer, *The Life and Letters of John Hay* (1915), also reproduces many Hay letters. A nearly complete bibliography of Hay's own writings by William Easton Louttit, Jr., is appended to the most complete biography available, Dennett, *John Hay: From Poetry to Politics* (1933).

There are several other good biographies. Howard I. Kushner and Anne Hummel Sherrill, *John Hay: The Union of Poetry and Politics* (1977), emphasizes the importance of Lincoln. A critical analysis of Hay's social thought and diplomacy is Clymer, *John Hay* (1975). The best account of Hay's life among the Five of Hearts is O'Toole, *The Five of Hearts* (1990). For Hay's relationship with Henry Adams one should not overlook Harold Dean Cater, ed., *Henry Adams and His Friends: A Collection of His Unpublished Letters* (1947). Other noteworthy accounts of Hay include Robert L. Gale, *John Hay* (1978); Lorenzo Sears, *John Hay: Author, Statesman* (1914); Alfred L. P. Dennis, "John Hay," in *The American Secretaries of State and Their Diplomacy*, ed. Samuel F. Bemis (1928); and Foster R. Dulles, "John Hay," in *An Uncertain Tradition: American Secretaries of State in the Twentieth Century*, ed. Norman Graebner (1961). Important analyses of *The Bread-winners* include Frederic Cople Jaher, "Industrialism and the American Aristocracy: A Social Study of John Hay and His Novel, *The Bread-winners*," *Journal of the*

Illinois State Historical Society 65 (Spring 1972): 69–93, and Charles Vandersee's introduction to *The Bread-winners* (1973). An obituary is in the *New York Times*, 2 July 1905.
KENTON J. CLYMER

HAY, Mary Garrett (20 Aug. 1857–29 Aug. 1928), suffragist and reformer, was born in Charlestown, Indiana, the daughter of Andrew Jennings Hay, a prosperous physician, and Rebecca Garrett. Hay was close to her father, a committed Republican, and got her first taste of politics as a young girl, attending meetings with him and helping him host political gatherings at their home. After attending Western College for Women in Oxford, Ohio (1873–1874), she returned home. She participated in a number of reform groups and women's clubs but soon began giving most of her time to the Woman's Christian Temperance Union (WCTU). After a brief period as secretary-treasurer of its local branch, she served for seven years as treasurer of the state organization. By 1885 Hay was running a small department in the national office.

During this period the WCTU was changing from a crusade against alcohol to a much broader movement embracing a wide range of reforms, including woman suffrage. Like many temperance workers of her day, Hay became active in the suffrage movement, serving first in the local association and then assuming state office.

During these years Hay began working with Carrie Chapman Catt, who with the help of a few volunteers was organizing suffrage campaigns in a number of states. Hay became Catt's trusted aide, traveling thousands of miles every year, making speeches, raising money, and helping to establish local suffrage clubs. In 1894 she set up mass meetings in each of New York State's sixty counties, trying unsuccessfully to get woman suffrage included in the state constitution. When Catt's group was officially designated the Organizing Committee of the National American Woman Suffrage Association (NAWSA) in 1895, Hay moved to New York City to establish the committee headquarters. In addition to serving as committee secretary, she continued her cross-country travels. West Virginia suffragists had been told by one representative from NAWSA that their state would be impossible to organize; a few months later Hay appeared on the scene, and within two weeks she had set up a state organization as well as a network of local clubs. She and Catt traveled tirelessly; in 1899 alone the two women covered 13,000 miles, giving fifty-one speeches in twenty states.

When Catt succeeded Susan B. Anthony as NAWSA president in 1900, she dissolved the Organizing Committee, despite Hay's strong objections. Many observers believed that Catt was pressed to make this decision by leaders within the organization who found Hay abrasive and were reluctant to see her inherit the leadership of the powerful committee. Nevertheless, Hay remained Catt's closest adviser and lived with her after Catt was widowed in 1905. Hay continued her organizing and fundraising activities and assisted Catt

with NAWSA's 1909–1910 drive for a constitutional amendment, gathering more than 400,000 signatures on petitions to Congress.

By 1910 NAWSA had organized hundreds of campaigns across the country, yet women still had the vote in only a few states. Hay continued her efforts, heading both the New York Equal Suffrage League (1910–1918) and the Woman Suffrage Party of Greater New York (1912–1918). She also joined reformers and unionists in organizing the Women's Peace Parade soon after World War I started in Europe in 1914, an action that broke new ground in bringing women of all classes together to make their own statement about a matter of international concern.

Hay's years of organizing stood her in good stead when New York State scheduled a referendum on woman suffrage in 1915. As head of the campaign in the Greater New York district, she organized an avalanche of dinner parties, mass meetings, conferences, concerts, neighborhood block parties, hilltop bonfires, and parades. Her volunteers covered the city, distributing nearly three million leaflets and galvanizing attention with their "days" devoted to canvassing particular occupations—barbers, bankers, subway excavators, dockworkers, firemen, and streetsweepers. The referendum was defeated, but after another all-out drive in 1917, Hay won enough votes in the city to offset the negative outcome upstate, and New York became the first state east of the Mississippi to grant women the vote.

Hay met with failure when she organized a group of New York City women's groups in 1918 to urge the inclusion of women in the U.S. delegation to the Versailles peace conference. The same year, however, she became the first president of the New York City League of Women Voters; she was also appointed to the executive committee of the state Republican party and was chosen to head the platform committee at its state convention that year. In addition, she served for two years as member (1918–1920) and then president (1919–1920) of the Republican Women's National Executive Committee. Meanwhile, she took a leading role in the campaign for a constitutional amendment to give all American women the vote, first serving as "steer" among Republican legislators until the bill passed Congress in 1919, and then spearheading the ratification effort in a number of Republican-dominated states.

Hay resigned from the city League of Women Voters in 1923, following many disagreements with the state organization. After helping Catt organize three annual peace conferences in Washington (1926–1928), she returned to the temperance movement, campaigning for the enforcement of prohibition. At the time of her death in New Rochelle, New York, she was serving as chair of the Women's Committee for Law Enforcement.

In the course of her long career Hay was associated with many of the most important reform efforts of her day, but she made her most historic contribution to the suffrage movement, which she served as an indefatigable speaker, organizer, and fundraiser, as Catt's lieutenant, and as the principal architect of the suffrage victory in New York State. Hay dedicated her energy, her imagination, and half the years of her life to this cause—not simply the ballot, but the larger reform it symbolized, the vision of women organizing themselves to win their rightful place in American society.

• A small collection of Hay's papers is in the Schlesinger Library, Radcliffe College. Other materials are in the papers of Maud Wood Park, Leonore O'Reilly, Harriet Burton Laidlaw, and Carrie Chapman Catt, all at Radcliffe, and in those of Catt, NAWSA, and the Leslie Woman Suffrage Commission held at the Library of Congress. A scrapbook on her work is in the Manuscript Division of the New York Public Library. Her years with Catt are documented in Mary Grey Peck, *Carrie Chapman Catt* (1944), and Jacqueline Von Voris, *Carrie Chapman Catt* (1987). See also Aileen S. Kraditor, *The Ideas of the Woman Suffrage Movement, 1890–1920* (1965); Marjorie Spruill Wheeler, ed., *One Woman, One Vote: Rediscovering the Woman Suffrage Movement* (1995); Alma Lutz, *Susan B. Anthony: Rebel, Crusader, Humanist* (1960); C. Roland Marchand, *The American Peace Movement and Social Reform, 1898–1918* (1972); and Susan B. Anthony and Ida Houston Harper, eds., *History of Woman Suffrage*, vol. 4 (1902) and vol. 5 (1922). Her obituary is in the *New York Times*, 31 Aug. 1928.

SANDRA OPDYCKE

HAYAKAWA, S. I. (18 July 1906–27 Feb. 1992), semanticist and politician, was born Samuel Ichiye Hayakawa in Vancouver, British Columbia, Canada, the son of Ichora Hayakawa, a Japanese immigrant to Canada who ran an import-export business, and Tora Isono. Hayakawa went to high school in Winnipeg, Manitoba, and graduated with a B.A. from the University of Manitoba in 1927. He went to Montreal and studied for his master's degree in English literature at McGill University. To support himself during these student days, he drove a taxicab in Montreal and worked as a department store clerk.

Following his studies in Montreal, Hayakawa went to the University of Wisconsin on a fellowship; he earned his Ph.D. in 1935. In 1937 he married Margedant Peters, a former student; the couple had three children. Hayakawa found a dearth of opportunities for teaching at first; as an Asian-Canadian, he was barred from many jobs. Therefore, he taught in the continuing education division at the University of Wisconsin (1936–1939) before he landed his first true academic job: teaching at Armour Institute of Technology (later renamed the Illinois Institute of Technology) in Chicago. While teaching there, Hayakawa also wrote for the *Chicago Defender*, a newspaper for African Americans.

Hayakawa broke into the forefront of his academic field with the publication of *Language in Action* (1941). In this, the first popular work written in the area of semantics, Hayakawa popularized many of the ideas of Polish scholar Alfred Korzybski, notably the concept that words are not identical with reality; that they can, at best, approximate reality. In his rendition of Korzybski's idea, Hayakawa was probably influenced by watching how words and symbols were being used by totalitarian rulers in Europe (such as Hitler, Stalin, and Mussolini) during the 1930s. *Language in Action* became a bestseller, a college textbook, and the surest means of identifying Hayakawa.

Hayakawa taught at the Illinois Institute of Technology (1939–1947) and then lectured in semantics at the University of Chicago (1950–1955). During World War II he, as a Canadian immigrant, was spared the possibility of being interned in a camp for Japanese Americans. He did not receive his U.S. citizenship until 1954. In 1955 he accepted a teaching position at San Francisco State College in California.

Hayakawa developed a reputation as a maverick while teaching in California. In the early 1960s he appeared to sympathize with some of the aims of the student activists who championed free speech and the expansion of the college curriculum, but he became more conservative during the decade. By the time he took over as the acting president of San Francisco State College (28 Nov. 1968), Hayakawa had become convinced that the student movement had gotten out of hand.

A two-month student strike had driven out his predecessor, Robert R. Smith. Hayakawa insisted on order on the campus, asserting that "We have a standing obligation to the 17,500 or more students—white, black, yellow, red and brown—who are not on strike and have every right to expect continuation of their education." Hayakawa was as good as his word; he summoned more than 600 police officers from San Francisco. On 2 December 1968 he made national headlines when he mounted a protester's truck carrying a loudspeaker; Hayakawa ripped the wires out of the sound system and marched back to his office through a crowd of hostile, but temporarily cowed, student protesters. The newspaper photograph made Hayakawa into a temporary hero; members of the older generation in the United States generally applauded his action, and California governor Ronald Reagan and San Francisco mayor Joseph Alioto gave strong support to Hayakawa. The student strike ended in March 1969 with some concessions made by the administration, including a black studies department created with an eleven-member faculty.

Hayakawa served as acting president until 9 July 1969 and then president (July 1969–Aug. 1973). One day after he resigned the position, he changed his political affiliation from Democrat to Republican. In 1976 he ran for the post of U.S. senator, challenging incumbent Democrat John Tunney. The election was hotly contested. The seventy-year-old Hayakawa came across as jaunty and cool and won a close race. Coming as it did on the heels of Watergate and the Nixon presidency, Hayakawa's election was celebrated by Republicans throughout the country, who had little else to cheer about in November 1976.

Hayakawa became known as a conservative maverick in the Senate. He advocated reducing the entry minimum wage level for teenagers, and he opposed school busing. In a move that demonstrated his independence from his California constituency, he tried to outlaw federal subsidies to colleges and universities that had affirmative action programs. Although he was motivated by personal experience and had the courage of his convictions, Hayakawa proved to be ineffective as a senator. Some colleagues called him "Sleepin' Sam" in reference to his occasional dozing off during committee sessions (it was not generally known that he suffered from narcolepsy).

Hayakawa chose not to run for reelection in 1982. He served as special adviser to the U.S. secretary of state for East Asia and Pacific Affairs (1983–1990), and he led a movement to establish English as the official language of the country. He died in Greenbrae, California.

Hayakawa's life and career cannot be summarized with dispatch. An ambitious and self-made man, the son of Japanese immigrants, he came to dislike the notion of the 1960s youth that merit (as well as law and order) could be bypassed in the creation of a new society. A moderate, perhaps even a liberal, in his early and middle years, Hayakawa became a maverick conservative in reaction to the events of the 1960s. As a result of his actions during the strike of 1968–1969, he stood as a potent symbol of law and order on college campuses. For all of his success, however, one might well ponder whether Hayakawa had remained true to his earlier principles: had he manipulated words and symbols in the manner he had so accurately ascribed to the fascist and communist leaders of the 1930s? In any event, the image of the diminutive college president, wearing a tam-o'-shanter, pulling the wires out of the sound system, endured in the memory of Americans when they recalled the stress and tumult on college campuses during the 1960s.

• Hayakawa's writings serve as the best documentary record for the scholar to follow. *Language in Action* (1941) was followed by many other works, notably *Language, Meaning and Maturity* (1954) and *Our Language and Our World* (1959). See also Dikran Karagueuzian, *Blow It Up! The Black Student Revolt at San Francisco State College and the Emergence of Dr. Hayakawa* (1971), and numerous articles in *Time* and *Newsweek*, especially "Semantics in San Francisco," *Time*, 6 Dec. 1968, p. 83, and "Word Power in Action," *Time*, 13 Dec. 1968, p. 52. An obituary is in the *New York Times*, 28 Feb. 1992.

SAMUEL WILLARD CROMPTON

HAYDEN, Carl Trumbull (2 Oct. 1877–25 Jan. 1972), U.S. representative and senator, was born in Hayden's Ferry (now Tempe), Arizona, the son of Charles Trumbull Hayden, a mill owner, and Sallie Davis. He was raised in Hayden's Ferry, a town founded by his father in the arid Salt River valley. Hayden graduated from Tempe Normal School in 1896 and entered Stanford University later that year. He failed to complete his degree at Stanford, returning home in 1900 to help his ailing father run the business.

Hayden was elected to his first political office, the Tempe Town Council, in 1902. In 1903 he organized a National Guard unit in Tempe. He was already rising in state Democratic politics, and one year later the party chose him to be a delegate to the 1904 Democratic National Convention in St. Louis. In 1907 he successfully won election as sheriff of Maricopa County and served for five years. As sheriff, Hayden and the sheriff's office became involved in the *Hurley v. Abbott* case, an early Arizona water dispute that yielded the so-called Kent Decree, upholding the doctrine of prior appropriation in Arizona. In 1908 Hayden married Nan Downing, a schoolteacher. They had no children.

In 1912, the same year that Arizona gained statehood, Hayden decided to run for election to the U.S. House of Representatives. He won the election and became Arizona's first and, for several years, only representative. Hayden remained in the House until 1926 and served on several committees important to his western state, including Indian Affairs, Irrigation and Arid Lands (later Irrigation and Reclamation), Public Lands, and Water Power. The young congressman quickly established himself as an important figure in reclamation and water issues, which remained the central focus of his entire political career.

In the House Hayden was a key sponsor of the 1919 Grand Canyon National Park Act. His mother, who died in 1907, was a suffragette and inculcated in him support for the right of women to vote. Consequently, in 1913 Hayden introduced a joint resolution proposing a woman suffrage amendment. The resolution failed in committee but anticipated the Nineteenth Amendment by several years. He also supported organized labor. When in 1917 mine owners and vigilantes deported more than 1,000 copper miners who were union members from the town of Bisbee, Arizona, to the New Mexico desert, Hayden denounced the move, parting company with Arizona's two senators, Mark Smith and Henry Ashurst. His effort to introduce legislation to halt such deportations in the future gained him support among Arizona's labor movement.

In 1927 Hayden moved into the Senate, where he served until 1968. In his first term he was chosen to sit on the Appropriations Committee, eventually becoming its chairman in 1955. During his tenure in the Senate, he also served on the Mines and Mining, Territories and Insular Affairs, Printing (which oversaw the Government Printing Office), Post Office and Post Roads, and Rules and Administration committees.

In 1928 the freshman Hayden joined his senior Arizona colleague Ashurst to successfully filibuster the Swing-Johnson bill. The proposed bill called for construction of a hydroelectric dam on the Colorado River (now Hoover Dam) in Boulder Canyon and a canal to deliver water to California's Imperial Valley. Hayden opposed the bill, claiming that it would hurt future development in Arizona by reducing that state's access to Colorado River water. Hayden and Ashurst ended their filibuster in the second session after forcing an amendment to the measure that limited California's Colorado River water allotment to 4.4 million acre-feet.

In 1947 Hayden, along with fellow senator Ernest McFarland, introduced legislation that became the capstone of his career, the Central Arizona Project (CAP), an extensive aqueduct system to bring Colorado River water to the arid regions of central and southern Arizona, including the cities of Tucson and Phoenix. California lawmakers strongly opposed the plan, and the original bill did not make it past committee. Hayden criticized California legislators for blocking the measure, noting the disparity of federal funding between the two states. In fact, despite early opposition to the Boulder Canyon project, Hayden had supported many water development projects in neighboring California, including the extensive Central Valley Project. "Each one of these reclamation projects in California is a good investment," Hayden declared, "and nobody in Arizona begrudges this development over there." For Hayden, the CAP was a simple matter of fairness.

In 1949 Hayden reintroduced the CAP legislation, which passed the Senate despite the continued opposition of California's legislators. The bill stalled in the House, however, after the Interior and Insular Affairs Committee halted hearings pending a judicial clarification of water rights on the lower Colorado River. Arizona officials opposed the move, and the matter went before the Supreme Court in 1952, ultimately yielding the 1963 *Arizona v. California* decision, a major victory for Arizona's claims on the Colorado River. In view of the favorable decision, Hayden reintroduced the CAP bill on the same day the Supreme Court handed down its decision. He relied on his position on the powerful Appropriations Committee to push through the bill by threatening to stall projects in other states. After twenty years, he finally achieved congressional approval of the legislation in 1968.

Hayden's primary preoccupation during his Senate career revolved around western water issues, but he also concerned himself with transportation, specifically road and highway construction. Along with chairman of the House Committee on Roads, Wilburn Cartwright of Oklahoma, Hayden cosponsored the 1934 Hayden-Cartwright Act (Federal Aid Highway Act of 1934). The act allocated funds for state highway planning and construction on a matching basis and required that state taxes on motor vehicles be used solely to fund road and highway construction. This legislation provided the framework for the much more extensive Federal Highway Act of 1956, which Hayden helped to draft, and with some modifications, it is still the basis for federal-state highway construction.

A party stalwart in the Senate, Hayden supported most of the policies of the Franklin D. Roosevelt, Harry Truman, John Kennedy, and Lyndon B. Johnson administrations. He identified with the conservative southern wing of the Democratic party, particularly in the area of civil rights. In 1948 he voted against eliminating poll taxes, a significant barrier to African-American voting. He also repeatedly refused to help end filibusters, a favorite tactic of anti–civil rights forces in the Senate. Hayden did, however, support the 1964 Civil Rights Act and the 1965 Voting Rights Act. He was considered friendly to labor, generally voting in favor of prolabor legislation and against measures, such as the Taft-Hartley Act, to restrict the power of unions.

In recognition for his long service, in 1957 Hayden was named dean of the Senate and also served for many years as president pro tempore of that body. In 1961 he celebrated fifty years of service in Congress, for which he was honored in his home state by President Kennedy and Vice President Johnson, among numerous other dignitaries. That same year his wife died. Hayden retired in 1968 and returned home to Arizona. He spent his final years in Tempe, working on histories of Arizona's pioneers. He died in Mesa, Arizona.

Although Hayden made only a handful of speeches on the floor of the Senate during his tenure, he wielded extensive power. From his position as chairman of the Appropriations Committee, he had influence over which projects received funding, and he was not above using this power to secure projects in his own state, most notably the CAP. His real influence was less coercive than that. Hayden had a keen appreciation for how the legislative process worked, and during his decades in Congress under numerous administrations, he built longstanding relationships with fellow politicians.

• Hayden's papers are at the Hayden Library, Arizona State University, Tempe. For an uncritical overview of his career see Ross R. Rice, *Carl Hayden: Builder of the American West* (1994). For Hayden's role in the Central Arizona Project see Rich Johnson, *The Central Arizona Project, 1918–1968* (1977). For his early involvement in water issues see Jack August, "Carl Hayden, Arizona, and the Politics of Water Development in the Southwest, 1923–1928," *Pacific Historical Review* 58 (May 1989): 195–216. On his early political career see August, "'A Sterling Young Democrat': Carl Hayden's Road to Congress, 1900–1912," *Journal of Arizona History* 28 (Autumn 1987): 217–42. A lengthy obituary is in the *Arizona Republic*, 26 Jan. 1972.

SCOTT C. ZEMAN

HAYDEN, Ferdinand Vandeveer (7 Sept. 1828?–22 Dec. 1887), geologist and naturalist, was probably born in Westfield, Massachusetts, the son of Asa Hayden and Melinda Hawley. No reliable record of his birth survives, and because no record of his parents' marriage exists, it is possible he was born out of wedlock. In his early years Hayden lived in poverty and humiliation. His family migrated from place to place in Massachusetts and New York as his father attempted to earn a living, perhaps as a doctor. Hayden's father was in jail on at least two occasions. An alcoholic, he embarrassed his entire family until he died in 1857. Hayden and his younger sister and brother grew up trying to avoid him. Melinda Hayden left Asa and went to live in Rochester, New York, around 1838. Before she remarried in 1841, Ferdinand was sent to live with a paternal aunt on her farm in Ohio, where he enjoyed a settled family life for the next five years. Later in his life, Hayden disguised the sordid facts of his upbringing behind an agreeable mythology, which he invented for his colleagues and first biographers.

At Oberlin College (1845–1850) Hayden discovered a passion for natural history. In also embracing poetry and literature he showed the broad intellectual capacity that became his hallmark. At Oberlin Hayden also found a powerful attraction for the opposite sex, which he indulged over the next twenty years, sometimes carelessly, until his marriage in 1871 to Emma Woodruff, the daughter of a prominent Philadelphia merchant. The couple had no children.

Following his graduation from Oberlin, Hayden taught in several district schools of Ohio while trying to find a way of earning a living as a naturalist—not an easy thing to do at the time. Probably through Professor George Allen of Oberlin he met the renowned naturalist Jared Potter Kirtland, who in turn introduced him to John Strong Newberry, a recent graduate of medical school and a budding geologist. From December 1851 to the spring of 1853 Hayden studied medicine with Kirtland at the Cleveland Medical School and with Newberry as an apprentice. Newberry introduced him to James Hall, the formidable paleontologist of the New York geological survey. In the company of Fielding Bradford Meek, Hall sent Hayden on his first major expedition during the summer of 1853, as a fossil collector to the White River Bad Lands of Dakota (then in Nebraska Territory).

Between 1853 and 1860 Hayden explored western territories that are now parts of Kansas, Nebraska, North and South Dakota, Montana, Idaho, Utah, Wyoming, and Colorado. Displaying energy and ingenuity, he gained patronage for his expeditions from the American Fur Company, the Smithsonian Institution, and the Corps of Topographical Engineers as well as from several individual sponsors. By the outbreak of the Civil War, Hayden had established a reputation as the most versatile collector of natural history specimens in the United States and the country's foremost exploring geologist. In collaboration with Meek he outlined for the first time the geologic structure of the entire upper Missouri Basin. Their joint publications raised fundamental questions of methodology and challenged many assumptions of European geologists. They were early leaders in pointing out the uniqueness of American geology.

A brilliant field geologist, Hayden learned to integrate from numerous unconnected outcrops an accurate sense of the structure and extent of geological formations, many of which he discovered and named. He made numerous pioneering observations on the uplift and erosion of the Rocky Mountains, though he never synthesized his major insights in a particular work; they are scattered throughout his 140 publications. His *Geology and Natural History of the Upper Missouri* (1862) best epitomizes his style as a collector and naturalist. That book also provides unintended confirmation for Charles Darwin's ideas on evolution—unintended, because Hayden wrote it before he read Darwin's *Origin of Species* (1859).

During the Civil War Hayden served as a volunteer surgeon and later as a medical administrator. After the war he became a popular lecturer on geology in the Auxiliary Department of Medicine at the University of Pennsylvania (1865–1872). Working for the Department of the Interior from 1867 through 1878, Hayden directed an ambitious series of geologic and natural history surveys, whose scope and purpose he himself largely determined. Hayden encouraged the federal government to increase substantially its funding of his Geological and Geographical Survey of the Territories, which attracted more attention and talent than any other scientific institution during the postwar years. His survey's most influential publication was the *Atlas of Colorado* (1877 and 1881), a classic compilation of geology, topography, and landscape delineation.

Hayden solicited numerous monographic studies from a variety of naturalists, which he then published through his survey (see Schmeckebier). His patronage encouraged important works by scores of specialists, especially Meek, Joseph Leidy, Edward Drinker Cope, Leo Lesquereux, Cyrus Thomas, Samuel Hubbard Scudder, Thomas C. Porter, John Merle Coulter, Elliott Coues, Alpheus Spring Packard, Joel Asaph Allen, Charles Abiathar White, and Albert Charles Peale. By distributing numerous photographs and reports, especially of Colorado and the Yellowstone region of Wyoming, Hayden profoundly influenced the way Americans saw and understood the West. He was ahead of his colleagues in recognizing and promoting the scenic values of western topography. A genuine enthusiast of science, Hayden wanted laymen to appreciate both the erudite monographs and the more appealing annual reports of his survey. In these ways he pioneered the popularization of science.

Hayden possessed great ability, but his ruthless ambition, impatience, and combative style earned him widespread enmity. The creation of the U.S. Geological Survey in 1879 gave his leading rivals (John Wesley Powell and Clarence King) and his strongest enemies (Newberry and Othniel Charles Marsh) an opportunity to unseat him from his preponderant position in exploratory science. Hayden gained a sinecure under the new geological survey, enabling him to live in Philadelphia and return to his broad studies of natural history. For four seasons between 1883 and 1886 he undertook more fieldwork, but declining health forced him to retire from the survey at the end of 1886. He died—of syphilis—less than a year later in Philadelphia.

Although Hayden was an influential naturalist, an innovative geologist, and a masterful entrepreneur for science, his place in history has been obscured since his own days by conflicting views of him. From his explorations of the Yellowstone region, beginning in 1871, he gained a reputation as the popularizer of natural wonders and scenery. Nonetheless his colleagues elected him to the National Academy of Sciences (in 1873), as well as to the leading scientific bodies in the United States and Europe, because of the important research he engendered. Both views of him persist in the historical literature, which has been unduly influenced by the hostile views of his opponents.

• There are two sources for the collected letters and papers of Ferdinand Hayden, the Western Reserve Historical Society in Cleveland (for the years 1846–1853) and Letters of the Hayden Survey, in Record Group 57 at the National Archives (for the period after 1853). Letters Hayden wrote are scattered in numerous places, but the major collections are the several collections of S. F. Baird Papers and the Fielding Bradford Meek Papers at the Smithsonian Institution Archives; the James Hall Papers at the New York State Library and the New York State Archives in Albany; the Joseph Leidy Papers at the Academy of Natural Sciences of Philadelphia; and the George Engelmann Papers at the Missouri Botanical Gardens. The George P. Merrill Collection at the Library of Congress contains many Hayden letters. Laurence F. Schmeckebier, *Catalogue and Index of the Publications of the Hayden, King, Powell and Wheeler Surveys* (1904), is the indispensable guide to his survey's many publications.

Mike Foster, *Strange Genius: The Life of Ferdinand Vandeveer Hayden* (1994), the only critical study of Hayden's life and career to date, appraises his published works and reviews the historiography on him. Richard A. Bartlett gives prominent attention to Hayden in *Great Surveys of the American West* (1962), as does William H. Goetzmann, *Exploration and Empire: The Explorer and the Scientist in the Winning of the American West* (1966). Older but still valuable perspectives on Hayden are in G. P. Merrill, *The First One Hundred Years of American Geology* (1924), and Charles R. Keyes, "Last of the Geological Pioneers: Ferdinand Vandiveer Hayden," *Pan American Geologist* 41 (Mar. 1924): 80–96.

Articles that draw attention to particular periods or aspects of Hayden's career are Clifford M. Nelson and F. M. Fryxell, "The Ante-Bellum Collaboration of Meek and Hayden in Stratigraphy," in *Two Hundred Years of Geology in America*, ed. Cecil J. Schneer (1979), pp. 187–200; Nelson et al., "Ferdinand Vandeveer Hayden: The U.S. Geological Survey Years, 1879–1886," *Proceedings of the American Philosophical Society* 125 (June 1981): 238–43; and two by Foster, "Ferdinand Vandeveer Hayden as Naturalist," *American Zoologist* 26 (1986): 343–49, and "The Permian Controversy of 1858: An Affair of the Heart," *Proceedings of the American Philosophical Society* 133 (Sept. 1989): 370–90.

MIKE F. FOSTER

HAYDEN, Lewis (1811–7 Apr. 1889), abolitionist, was born in Lexington, Kentucky, the son of slave parents whose names are not known. Separated from his family by the slave trade at age ten, he was eventually owned by five different masters. The first, a Presbyterian clergyman, traded him for a pair of horses. The second, a clock peddler, took Hayden along on his travels throughout the state, exposing him to the variety of forms that the "peculiar institution" could take. About 1830 he married Harriet Bell, also a slave. They had three children; one died in infancy, another was sold away, and a third remained with the couple. Hayden's third owner, in the early 1840s, whipped him often. These experiences stirred his passionate personal hatred for bondage. Hayden secretly learned to read and write, using the Bible and old newspapers as study materials. By 1842, when he belonged to Thomas Grant and Lewis Baxter of Lexington, he began to

contemplate an escape. Because his last owners hired him out to work in a local hotel, he had greater freedom than most slaves, which made it easier to flee. In September 1844 Lewis, Harriet, and their remaining son were spirited away to Ohio and then on to Canada West (now Ontario), by local teachers and Underground Railroad agents Calvin Fairbanks and Delia Webster.

Following their flight to freedom, the Haydens lived for six months among other refugees in the village of Amherstburg, Canada West. Haunted by memories of those still in bondage, they resettled in the small but thriving African-American community in Detroit. This heightened their risk of recapture but placed them at the center of a major base of operations of the Underground Railroad. Hayden immersed himself in efforts to build community institutions; he organized a school and church and toured New England during the fall and winter of 1845–1846 to raise funds for the struggling congregation. Finding Boston a larger vehicle for his antislavery efforts, he relocated his family there by July 1846. He then traveled for nearly a year as a lecturing agent of the American Anti-Slavery Society, carrying the abolitionist message to dozens of towns in New York, New Jersey, and southern New England. In 1848 he opened a clothing store on Cambridge Street in Boston that soon developed into a thriving business. Hayden was, by 1855, "probably the wealthiest black in Boston" (Runyon, p. 121).

After the passage of the Fugitive Slave Act of 1850, Hayden worked tirelessly to fight its enforcement. He lectured fellow Bostonians on the need for "united and persevering resistance to th[e] ungodly anti-republican law." As a member of the executive board of the Boston Vigilance Committee, which was created to aid and protect fugitive slaves in the city, he often functioned as a liaison between local white and black activists, including members of the Twelfth Baptist Church, to which he belonged. He personally fed and housed hundreds of runaways and used his clothing store to outfit many more. "His Beacon Hill residence," noted one scholar, "was the main Boston depot on the Underground Railroad, harboring at least a quarter of all the fugitives who passed through the city" (Runyon, pp. 140–41). On one occasion, Harriet Beecher Stowe visited the Hayden home and found thirteen escaped slaves on the premises. Protecting refugees from bondage often became a public matter. Hayden openly resisted the law in the case of William and Ellen Craft (1850), the rescue of Shadrach Minkins from federal custody (1851), and the attempted rescues of Thomas Sims (1851) and Anthony Burns (1854). In the Craft case, he stacked kegs of gunpowder in his basement and threatened to ignite it if slave catchers attempted to enter the house to capture the couple. He was arrested but not convicted for his prominent role in the Minkins and Burns incidents. In 1855 his testimony before the Massachusetts legislature helped prompt the passage of a strong personal liberty law to protect fugitive slaves in the state.

The panic of 1857 brought financial reverses and forced Hayden to move his clothing business into a smaller store, which was soon destroyed by a fire. In the midst of this personal crisis, he continued his anti-slavery radicalism. He hosted John Brown during several visits to Boston between 1857 and 1859, was privy to his insurrection plans, and even raised funds for the effort. Hayden was appointed to the office of messenger to the Massachusetts secretary of state in July 1858. This provided some financial comfort and offered a vantage point from which to influence key officials in the state government. After the administration of President Abraham Lincoln sanctioned the enlistment of African-American troops in the middle of the Civil War, Hayden successfully lobbied Governor John A. Andrew to organize the Massachusetts Fifty-fourth Colored Infantry Regiment, the first black unit in the North. He then raised volunteers for the regiment and two other black units in Canada West and the northern United States.

When the war ended Hayden found new outlets for his energies. He focused much of his attention on the Masonic movement among African Americans. Named grand master of the Prince Hall Lodge in Boston and deputy grand master of the National Grand Lodge, he traveled through Virginia and the Carolinas in 1865 to organize new lodges among the former slaves. After returning to Boston, he delivered dozens of lectures and penned several pamphlets attacking racial discrimination among the Masons and defending the legitimacy of black Masonic lodges, including *Caste among Masons* (1866), *Grand Lodge Jurisdictional Claims; or, War of Races* (1868), and *Masonry among Colored Men in Massachusetts* (1871). Active in Republican party politics, Hayden was elected in 1873 to the Massachusetts Senate. In the 1880s he successfully campaigned for the erection of a monument in Boston to Crispus Attucks, a black hero of the American Revolution. In their later years Lewis and Harriet Hayden contributed much of their personal wealth to local cultural institutions, including the Massachusetts Historical Society and the Boston Museum of Fine Arts. They posthumously donated $5,000 to establish a scholarship for black students at Harvard and particularly for those at the Harvard Medical School. After his death in Boston, abolitionists and prominent African Americans lionized Hayden as one of the heroes of the antislavery struggle.

• Autobiographical fragments by Hayden on his almost thirty-five years in slavery can be found in Harriet Beecher Stowe, *A Key to Uncle Tom's Cabin* (1853). Other Hayden documents, including dozens of letters and speeches relevant to his work as an abolitionist, are available in the microfilm edition of the *Black Abolitionist Papers*, ed. C. Peter Ripley and George Carter (1981). A brief biography of Hayden is in Ripley et al., eds., *The Black Abolitionist Papers*, vol. 4 (1992). Stanley J. Robboy and Anita W. Robboy, "Lewis Hayden: From Fugitive Slave to Statesman," *New England Quarterly* 46 (1973): 591–613, is a longer and very useful sketch. Also informative are James O. Horton and Lois E. Horton, *Black Bostonians: Family Life and Community Struggle in the Antebellum North* (1979), George A. Levesque, *Black Boston: African-American Life and Culture in Urban America, 1750–1860* (1994), and Randolph P. Runyon, *Delia Webster and the Underground Railroad* (1996).

ROY E. FINKENBINE

HAYDEN, Mother Bridget (26 Aug. 1814–23 Jan. 1890), Roman Catholic missionary nun and educator, was born Margaret Hayden in Kilkenny, Ireland, the daughter of Thomas Hayden and Bridget Hart. She and her family emigrated to the United States around 1820, settling in Perryville, Missouri, where her Father worked as a wheelwright. She attended schools at the Barrens near Perryville and at Cape Girardeau, Missouri. Both schools were run by the Sisters of Loretto at the Foot of the Cross, a congregation of Catholic women religious of chiefly American origin. After two of her sisters joined the congregation, Hayden followed their example in 1841, taking the religious name of Sister Mary Bridget. She received her early training at Ste. Genevieve, Missouri, and at the congregation's mother house in Loretto, Kentucky.

The Lorettines had been founded in 1812 by Charles Nerinckx, a Belgian priest, and Mary Rhodes, a Maryland schoolteacher, to provide elementary education for frontier children in Kentucky. But growing demands for their services quickly led them to extend their activities into the trans-Mississippi frontier. Hayden played an important role in that expansion. In 1847 the congregation received an invitation from John Schoenmakers, recently appointed Jesuit superior of Osage Mission (later St. Paul, Kans.), to take up missionary work in southeastern Kansas. Schoenmakers, who ran the mission's industrial school for Native-American boys, sought sisters to teach the girls. Hayden volunteered for the work, along with Mother Concordia Henning and Sisters Mary Petronella Van Prater and Vincentia Gale. Arriving at the mission on 10 October 1847, the Lorettines immediately opened a school. In 1859 Sister Bridget succeeded Mother Henning as mother superior of the Loretto convent and academy. Typical of most government-funded frontier schools of the day, the mission school promoted the assimilation of Native-American and métis girls through instruction in English grammar, reading, writing, arithmetic, drawing, geography, and Christian doctrine. To prepare the students for their future roles as homemakers, the sisters taught them domestic skills, such as sewing, cooking, gardening, and laundry work. Through their contact with the children, the sisters, like their Jesuit co-workers, hoped to influence the tribe as a whole by converting them to a sedentary life and to Christianity. Although that plan was undermined by the Civil War and its aftermath, the school prospered under Mother Bridget's direction, enrolling about 100 Osage girls by the eve of hostilities. In addition to her other responsibilities, she nursed travelers who became sick. Her skill in treating the various diseases that ravaged the tribe led the Osage to call her "Medicine Woman."

During the Civil War the Osage Mission suffered numerous setbacks. Many parents withdrew their children from the school when the struggle began. Located on the borderline between belligerents, the mission was subject to threats and raids by both Confederate and Union guerrillas. Father Schoenmakers, who outraged southern sympathizers in the region by urging the Osage to support the Union, was forced to flee the mission during the conflict.

In 1863 Mother Bridget left Kansas to become superior of St. Vincent's Academy at Cape Girardeau, Missouri. It was a difficult assignment that tested her administrative abilities because local anti-Catholics opposed the sisters and their school. In 1865 Missouri passed a law prohibiting from teaching or preaching anyone who would not take a loyalty oath to the state constitution, which forbade rendering any assistance to former secessionists. Unwilling to accept such a constraint on their ministry, Hayden and her sisters were on at least one occasion threatened with imprisonment for refusing to take the oath. In 1867 she returned as superior to the Osage Mission at a time of great transformation. Harassed by both Confederate and Union sympathizers during the Civil War, the Osages had encountered new difficulties in 1865 when the region's growing white population began to compel many of the tribe to abandon their Kansas homeland and relocate to Indian Territory (now Oklahoma).

The departure of most of the Osage marked the end of the mission. As homesteaders poured into the ceded lands of the natives, the number of white students in the Lorettines' school increased, while Native-American attendance steadily declined. Hayden's reaction to this development is not recorded, but she continued to support Indian students by sending those with special talents to other U.S. academies for advanced training in art and music. In 1870 the school for Indian girls became St. Ann's Academy, its student body composed primarily of children of white settlers. By 1890 the school enrolled only twenty-eight Osage girls. Flood, drought, and disease frequently threatened the academy. "We are just living and keeping out of debt, still hoping for better times," Mother Bridget wrote in 1877. However, the school eventually became one of the principal educational institutions in southeastern Kansas, attracting students from as far away as Missouri and Texas. Sometimes enrolling as many as 300 girls, its curriculum included languages, mathematics, history, the sciences, music, and painting. Under Mother Bridget's direction, new buildings were added to the institution. She died in St. Paul at the academy on the eve of its twentieth anniversary. Five years after her death, the school was destroyed by fire, and the Loretto sisters departed.

During her life, much of Hayden's reputation rested on the fact that she manifested personal qualities admired by her pioneer contemporaries—perseverance in adversity, generosity to the needy and underprivileged, administrative skill, and physical courage. "Mother Bridget was tall, of generous proportions, with a heart as large as herself," declared Margaret Bray McCall, a pupil at St. Ann's in 1870. "No one ever appealed to her in vain for assistance, counsel, or comfort," especially the Native-American girls, whom she preferred because they seemed in greater need of her assistance. A Jesuit co-worker, missionary Paul M. Ponziglione, praised her as an "enterprising, intelligent and devout lady" who endured "an untold amount of labor and suffering, which she might well have avoided." A participant in Kansas's evolution from an Indian frontier to a state, this pioneer educator and religious leader was for more than forty years one of the region's most influential women.

• A few letters of Mother Bridget, obituaries, and other manuscript materials about her are preserved in the archives of the motherhouse of the Sisters of Loretto in Nerinx (Loretto), Ky. Biographical information is found in Mary Paul Fitzgerald, *Beacon on the Plains* (1939); William W. Graves, *Life and Times of Mother Bridget Hayden* (1938) and *Life and Letters of Fathers Ponziglione, Schoenmakers and Other Early Jesuits at Osage Mission; Sketch of St. Francis' Church; Life of Mother Bridget* (1916); Sister Mary Lilliana Owens, "The History of the Sisters of Loretto in the Trans-Mississippi West" (Ph.D. diss., St. Louis Univ., 1935) and *Loretto on the Old Frontier* (1965). See also Peter Beckman, *The Catholic Church on the Kansas Frontier, 1850–1877* (1943); Mary Ewens, *The Role of the Nun in Nineteenth Century America* (1978); Gilbert J. Garraghan, *The Jesuits of the Middle United States* (3 vols., 1938); Barbara Misner, *'Highly Respectable and Accomplished Ladies:' Catholic Women Religious in America, 1790–1850* (1988); and Paul Ponziglione, "Osage Mission during the Civil War," *St. Louis Catholic Historical Review* 4 (1922): 219–29.

GERALD MCKEVITT

HAYDEN, Robert Earl (4 Aug. 1913–25 Feb. 1980), poet and teacher, was born Asa Bundy Sheffey in Detroit, Michigan, the son of Asa Sheffey, a steel-mill worker, and Gladys Ruth Finn. Early in his childhood, his parents separated and he was given to neighbors William and Sue Ellen Hayden, who also were black, and who reared and renamed him. Hayden grew up in a poor, racially mixed neighborhood. Extremely nearsighted, unathletic, and introverted, he spent much of his youth indoors reading and writing. When he was eighteen, he published his first poem. Hayden attended Detroit City College from 1932 to 1936; worked for the Federal Writers' Project of the Works Progress Administration (WPA) from 1936 to 1938; published his first volume of poetry, *Heart-Shape in the Dust*, in 1940; and, studying with W. H. Auden, completed an M.A. in English at the University of Michigan in 1944. In 1946 he began teaching English at Fisk University in Nashville, Tennessee.

During his twenty-three years at Fisk, he published four volumes of poetry: *The Lion and the Archer* (with Myron O'Higgins, 1948), *Figure of Time* (1955), *A Ballad of Remembrance* (1962), and *Selected Poems* (1966). These were years of demanding college teaching and creative isolation, but they were brightened by a Rosenwald Fellowship in 1947; a Ford Foundation grant to write in Mexico in 1954–1955; and the Grand Prize for Poetry in English at the First World Festival of Negro Arts in Dakar, Senegal, in 1966. At a writers' conference at Fisk, also in 1966, Hayden was attacked by younger blacks for a lack of racial militance in his poetry. Hayden's position, however, first articulated in 1948, was that he did not wish to be confined to racial themes or judged by ethnocentric standards. His philosophy of poetry was that it must not be limited by the individual or ethnic identity of the poet. Although inescapably rooted in these elements, poetry must rise to an order of creation that is broadly human and universally effective. He said, "I always wanted to be a Negro, or a black, poet . . . the same way Yeats is an Irish poet." He was trying, like Yeats, to join the myths, folk culture, and common humanity of his race with his special, transcendent powers of imagination. Hayden's Baha'i faith, which he adopted in the 1940s, and which emphasized the oneness of all peoples and the spiritual value of art, also helped sustain him as a poet. In the late 1970s he said, "today when so often one gets the feeling that everything is going downhill, that we're really on the brink of the abyss and what good is anything, I find myself sustained in my attempts to be a poet . . . because I have the assurance of my faith that this is of spiritual value and it is a way of performing some kind of service."

In 1969 Hayden joined the Department of English of the University of Michigan at Ann Arbor, where he taught until his death. During these years, he published *Words in the Mourning Time* (1970), *The Night-Blooming Cereus* (1973), *Angle of Ascent: New and Selected Poems* (1975), and *American Journal* (1978, rev. ed., 1982). He was elected to the American Academy of Poets in 1975 and appointed consultant in poetry to the Library of Congress in 1976–1978, the first African American to be selected.

Shifting from a romantic and proletarian approach in *Heart-Shape in the Dust* to an interest in rich language and baroque effects in *The Lion and the Archer*, Hayden's mature work did not appear until *A Ballad of Remembrance*. *Ballad* presents the first well-rounded picture of Hayden's protean subjects and styles as well as his devotion to craft. *Selected Poems* extends this impression and is followed by *Words in the Mourning Time*, which responds to the national experience of war, assassination, and racial militance in the late 1960s. Hayden's next volumes—*The Night-Blooming Cereus*, the eight new poems in *Angle of Ascent*, and *American Journal*—reveal an aging poet yielding to his aesthetic nature and his love of art and beauty for their own sake.

An obsessive wordsmith and experimenter in forms, Hayden searched for words and formal patterns that were cleansed of the egocentric and that gave his subjects their most objective aspect. Believing that expert craft was central, he rejected spontaneous expression in favor of precise realism, scrupulous attention to tone, and carefully wrought verbal mosaics. In Hayden's poetry, realism and romanticism interact, the former deriving significantly from his interest in black history and folk experience, the latter from his desire to explore subjective reality and to make poetry yield aesthetic pleasure. As Wilburn Williams, Jr., has observed, "spiritual enlightenment in his poetry is never the reward of evasion of material fact. The realities of the imagination and the actualities of history are bound together in an intimate symbiotic alliance that makes neither thinkable without the other." Some of the major themes of Hayden's poetry are the tension between the tragic nature of life and the richness of the imagination, the past in the present, art as a form of spiritual redemption, and the nurturing power of early life and folk memories. His favorite subjects include the spirit of places, folk characters, his childhood neighborhood, and African-American history.

In the debate about the purpose of art, Hayden's stance, closer to the aesthete than the propagandist, has exposed him to criticism. Yet the coalescence in Hayden's poetry of African-American material with a sophisticated modernism represents a singular achievement in the history of American poetry. His poetry about black culture and history, moreover, reveals the deepest of commitments to his own racial group as well as to humanity as a whole.

Hayden was married in 1940 to Erma Morris, with whom he had one child. He died in Ann Arbor.

• Since Hayden's death, editions of his *Collected Prose* (1984) and *Collected Poems* (1985), both edited by Frederick Glaysher, have been published. The prose volume contains four invaluable interviews with Hayden. Another excellent source based on interview material is Dennis Joseph Gendron, "Robert Hayden: A View of His Life and Development as a Poet" (Ph.D. diss., Univ. of North Carolina at Chapel Hill, 1975). For a summary of biographical information and a critical overview of Hayden's poetry, see Robert M. Greenberg, "Robert Hayden," in *American Writers: A Collection of Literary Biographies*, suppl. 2, ed. A. Walton Litz (1981), or a shortened, updated version in *African American Writers*, ed. Valerie Smith and A. Walton Litz (1991). See also John Hatcher, *From the Auroral Darkness: The Life and Poetry of Robert Hayden* (1984); Pontheolla T. Williams, *Robert Hayden: A Critical Analysis of His Poetry* (1987), with a foreword by Blyden Jackson; Charles T. Davis, "Robert Hayden's Use of History," in *Modern Black Poets: A Collection of Critical Essays*, ed. Donald B. Gibson (1973); Michael S. Harper, "Angle of Ascent," *New York Times Book Review*, 22 Feb. 1976; and Wilburn Williams, Jr., "Covenant of Timelessness and Time: Symbolism and History in Robert Hayden's *Angle of Ascent*," *Massachusetts Review* 18 (Winter 1977): 731–49. For a bibliography of secondary sources, see Nicholas Xavier, "Robert Hayden," *Bulletin of Bibliography* 42 (1985).

ROBERT M. GREENBERG

HAYDEN, Scott (31 Mar. 1882–16 Sept. 1915), ragtime pianist and composer, was born in Sedalia, Missouri, the son of Marion Hayden and Julia (maiden name unknown). Born in the birthplace of famed ragtime pianist Scott Joplin, Hayden began composing ragtime works as a student at Lincoln High School, influenced by a schoolmate, Arthur Marshall, who was another nascent ragtime pianist; both Marshall and Hayden would become devoted pupils of Joplin's. Joplin and Hayden became a composing pair when Joplin began to court Hayden's widowed sister-in-law, Belle, about the turn of the century. After Joplin's marriage to Belle, Hayden and his wife, Nora Wright, followed the Joplins to St. Louis, sharing a home with them from about 1901 to 1905. At that time, with the death of his wife in childbirth, Hayden moved to Chicago, married Jeanette Wilkens, and became an elevator operator.

Hayden and Joplin collaborated on four published rags, all presumably written during the duo's shared time in St. Louis. "Sunflower Slow Drag" (published by John Stark in 1901) is said to have been written while Joplin was courting Belle Hayden; its third theme is credited to Joplin, with the balance purportedly written by Hayden. At the time, it was second in popularity only to Joplin's own "Maple Leaf Rag," and it is believed to be the first rag recorded on a piano roll (Aeolian 8479). Hayden's sections are designed to show off his pianistic skills, whereas Joplin's are more varied in texture, moving through a wider range of keys, and shows more sophisticated writing.

"Something Doing" (Val A. Reis Music Co.) from 1903 is their second masterpiece. It is one of the most melodic of the early rags, with the first three sections probably Hayden's and Joplin most likely responsible for the fourth section since it features a style of syncopation that was common in Joplin's other works of this time.

The duo's other two collaborations, "Felicity Rag" and "Kismet Rag," were published by Stark in 1911 and 1913, respectively, and were probably "trunk pieces" (earlier pieces, pulled from a trunk) that either the publisher or Joplin discovered and had printed. "Felicity" again probably features a trio section by Joplin, whereas "Kismet" seems to be derived from floating ideas found in other common folk rags of the time. Hayden died of pulmonary tuberculosis.

• Hayden's life and career is documented in Rudi Blesch and Harriet Janis's classic, *They All Played Ragtime*, 4th ed. (1971), as well as in Dave Jasen and Trebor Jay Tichenor's *Rags and Ragtime: A Musical History* (1978). Edward A. Berlin also discusses Hayden in *King of Ragtime: Scott Joplin and His Era* (1994). See also David A. Jasen, *Recorded Ragtime, 1897–1958* (1973).

RICHARD CARLIN

HAYDEN, Sophia Gregoria (17 Oct. 1868–3 Feb. 1953), architect, was born in Santiago, Chile, the daughter of George Henry Hayden, a dentist; her mother (full name unknown) was of Spanish descent. In 1874 Sophia Hayden went to live with her grandparents in Jamaica Plain, a suburb of Boston. After graduating from West Roxbury High School in 1886, she immediately entered the Massachusetts Institute of Technology and became the first woman to enroll in the architecture program directed by Eugène Létang, who had been trained at the École des Beaux-Arts in Paris. This program concentrated on the planning and rendering of monumental buildings but also offered courses in architectural history and structural engineering. Hayden's thesis project, which employed a

neoclassical style, was titled "A Design for a Museum of Fine Arts." She received the bachelor of architecture degree with honors in 1890, becoming the first woman to complete Létang's four-year architecture course. After graduation, she taught mechanical drawing at the Elliot School in Jamaica Plain but declared her intention to practice architecture.

In 1891, at the age of twenty-two, Hayden responded to an announcement called "An Unusual Opportunity for Women Architects" and was ultimately commissioned to design the Woman's Building for the World's Columbian Exposition in Chicago. The Board of Lady Managers, headed by Bertha Honoré Palmer, sought to select a designer for the Woman's Building by holding a competition confined to women contestants with professional training or experience. The winner was to be awarded $1,000. The Woman's Building, like its predecessor at the 1876 Centennial Exposition in Philadelphia, had to accommodate a wide range of exhibition and meeting spaces for the display of "woman's progress and development, and her increased usefulness in the arts, sciences, manufactures, and industries of the world." According to the competition announcement, specific details would be left to "the ingenuity of the architect," but the maximum dimensions of the building and its budget were fixed; the structure was to be monumental in scale yet substantially smaller than the other main buildings of the fair. Thirteen architects submitted drawings to the competition, though Louise Blanchard Bethune, one of the most prominent woman practitioners at the time, refused to enter, citing the insufficient resources devoted to the building and the unfair and inadequate pay of its female architect. Working at home, Hayden prepared the initial drawings for the Woman's Building in an Italian Renaissance style consistent with the overall "classical" tone of the fair but also (in Hayden's words) "more delicate and refined," in keeping with its scale. In choosing this scheme, Bertha Palmer praised "that harmony of grouping and gracefulness of detail which indicated the architectural scholar."

Hayden traveled to Chicago to prepare the working drawings for the building and to supervise its construction; over the next year she was repeatedly pressured by the Board of Managers and the Board of Construction to make changes in the final form of the structure and its decoration and to hurry the completion of the building, all with little pay beyond her competition prize. She attended the informal dedication of the Woman's Building in October 1892 but did not attend the official opening of the fair the following May. Seizing on reports of a "mental collapse," an editorial in the *American Architect and Building News* suggested that Hayden's apparent breakdown provided "a much more telling argument against the wisdom of women entering this especial profession than anything else could." Minerva Parker Nichols, a Philadelphia architect whose competition entry was given an honorable mention, countered this argument with an essay in the same journal. Nichols declared that it was Hayden's inexperience rather than her sex that caused the difficulty. "It is not fair," she wrote, "because one woman makes a doubtful success, to draw conclusions from her example. It is time to put aside prejudice and sentimentalism, and judge women's work by their ability."

Very little is known about Hayden's career after the provisional triumph of the Woman's Building, which, like most other structures at the fair, was a temporary building constructed largely of plaster. With the exception of a proposed memorial building for American women's clubs in 1894, there is no evidence of further architectural work by her.

In 1900 Hayden married William Blackstone Bennett, an artist with a ten-year-old daughter, but was widowed thirteen years later. For the rest of her life, she lived in Winthrop, Massachusetts, where she was listed as an artist in city directories until 1939.

• The manuscript of Sophia Hayden's report to the Board of Lady Managers and other documents concerning the World's Columbian Exposition in Chicago are housed at the Chicago Historical Society. A description of the Woman's Building by Hayden is in Rand McNally & Company, *A Week at the Fair* (1893). The most complete biographical sources are Madeleine B. Stern, *We the Women: Career Firsts of Nineteenth-Century America* (1963), and Judith Paine, "Sophia Hayden and the Woman's Building Competition," in *Women in American Architecture: A Historic and Contemporary Perspective,* ed. Susana Torre (1977). For a detailed history of the Woman's Building, see Jeanne Madeline Weimann, *The Fair Women* (1981). A brief architectural analysis of Hayden's design is in Gwendolyn Wright, "On the Fringe of the Profession: Women in American Architecture," in *The Architect: Chapters in the History of the Profession,* ed. Spiro Kostof (1977). For adverse commentary on Hayden's performance and her design, see "Letter from Chicago," *American Architect and Building News* 38 (Nov. 1892): 134; for Minerva Parker Nichols's reply, see "A Woman on the Woman's Building," *American Architect and Building News* 38 (Dec. 1892): 170. Additional bibliographic sources on Hayden are noted in Lamia Doumato, *Architecture and Women* (1988).

LISA B. REITZES

HAYDEN, Sterling (26 Mar. 1916–23 May 1986), actor, was born Sterling Relyea Walter in Montclair, New Jersey, the son of George Walter, a newspaper advertising salesman, and Frances Simonson, a pianist. Hayden described his home and early life as "a nice house in a nice part of a nice town . . . the parents were nice too." When he was nine years old his father died, and four years later his mother married James Watson Hayden, an unsuccessful businessman who gave Sterling his surname but not much else. The new family moved up and down the East Coast in search of business deals and rich relatives. Hayden attended a number of schools but none for long; James Hayden generally disregarded tuition, as well as hotel bills and outstanding loans. In 1931 the family spent a year on an island in Maine's Boothbay Harbor, where Hayden discovered the sea.

When he was sixteen Hayden dropped out of school and went to work as an ordinary seaman. At twenty he was first mate on legendary seaman Irving Johnson's first world cruise. By the age of twenty-two he was captain of the *Florence C. Robinson,* which he sailed to Tahiti. His plans to run a shipping business sank along with his first ship—a schooner originally built for Kaiser Wilhelm. Needing money, Hayden let a friend send his picture and newspaper clippings detailing his nautical feats to a Hollywood agent. Within months Paramount Pictures gave him a screen test and a seven-year contract.

After his debut in *Virginia* (1941), Hayden was quickly reteamed with leading lady Madeleine Carroll in *Bahama Passage* (1941). He and Carroll shared an interest in the impending war in Europe, as well as a disdain for their work. "She feels the same as I do about Hollywood. It is, we agree, a place to be used, a means to an end, nothing more."

In 1942 Hayden and Carroll were married. They had no children. World War II soon took the couple away from Hollywood and from each other. Carroll, whose sister had been killed in the bombing of London, spent the balance of the war working with the Red Cross and at the orphanage she had created at her French chateau. Hayden, who had wanted to be a war correspondent, signed on with the Marines and then transferred to the Office of Strategic Services. The spy organization sent Hayden to Yugoslavia, where he ran guns and ammunition to Josip Broz Tito's rebel troops. Using the code name "John Hamilton," he also served in Albania, Italy, and Germany.

After the war ended, Hayden returned to the United States with a silver star and the rank of captain. In 1946, inspired by the Yugoslavian partisans he had aided during the war, he joined the Communist party, but he dropped out after six months. "I was the only person to buy a yacht and join the Communist party in the same week," he later said.

That same year Hayden and Carroll divorced, and in 1947 he married actress Betty Ann De Noon, with whom he had four children. Hayden supported his growing family with performances in such films as *Blaze of Noon* (1947) and *El Paso* (1949).

In 1950 John Huston cast Hayden in *The Asphalt Jungle.* Hayden played Dix Hanley, a horse-loving thug who supplies the muscle in a high-stakes jewel robbery gone wrong. Called "an electrifying picture of the whole vicious circle of a crime" by critic Bosley Crowther, *The Asphalt Jungle* quickly gained classic status and boosted the careers of much of its cast, which included Louis Calhern and Marilyn Monroe. Hayden's performance was roundly applauded, and one critic termed it "spectacularly controlled and powerful." The next year Hayden was called to testify before the House Un-American Activities Committee, which was investigating Communist activities in Hollywood. He came across as an eager witness, proclaiming that joining the party was the "stupidest thing [he had] ever done" and that the many others like him should come forward and tell their own stories. In addition, he named names, among them screenwriter Robert Lees. Hayden later regretted his "stoolie show," writing, "I was a real daddy longlegs of a worm."

In the next decade Hayden completed more than thirty movies, mostly B westerns and crime films, "made back to back," he wrote, "in an effort to cash in fast on my new status as a sanitary culture hero." Films such as *Suddenly* (1954), in which he took on bad guy Frank Sinatra, the cult western *Johnny Guitar* (1954), and Stanley Kubrick's *The Killing* (1956) brought him good reviews and helped finance the purchase and renovation of a schooner, the *Wanderer*. In 1955 he and his wife divorced, and Hayden received custody of their children.

In 1959 Hayden was offered a role in the film *A Summer Place*, which later became a major hit, but he turned it down in favor of an ambitious personal project. He planned to take the *Wanderer*, complete with a full crew and his children, around the world and to make a documentary film about the trek. The plans were temporarily halted by Hayden's ex-wife, who persuaded Superior Court judge Emil Gumpert to issue a court order forbidding Hayden from taking the children on the voyage, citing an inexperienced crew and the *Wanderer*'s questionable seaworthiness.

The *Wanderer* set sail from Sausalito, California, in January 1959, in defiance of the court order. When the journey ended ten months later in Tahiti, Hayden returned to the United States without money or a film but a bigger celebrity than ever. He retained custody of his children and received a suspended sentence from Judge Gumpert, who said, "The court is not blind to forces which control human behavior under emotionally charged circumstances." In 1960 Hayden married again, to Catherine Denise McConnell, and they had two sons.

Hayden spent much of the late 1950s and early 1960s acting in numerous television dramas, including a number of "Playhouse 90" productions. In 1963 he wrote his autobiography, *Wanderer*, which he described as "the struggle of a tortured individual to be himself in a society which is hostile to breaking away from the herd." The book was well received, and its success led Hayden to write a novel, *Voyage: A Novel of 1896* (1976), which became a Book of the Month Club main selection. Walter Clemons of *Newsweek* called Hayden "a storyteller of unaffected energy and verve" (27 Dec. 1976).

In 1964 Hayden created the mad general Jack D. Ripper in Stanley Kubrick's *Dr. Strangelove*. Other memorable performances were in *The Godfather* (1972), as the corrupt police captain who is gunned down in the middle of a pasta feed, and as John Brown in the television film *The Blue and the Gray* (1982). His own favorite performance was as an alcoholic novelist in Robert Altman's *The Long Goodbye* (1973). He attributed the performance to the "prodigious powers of pot." In 1981 he was arrested in Canada for possession of hashish but was released without punishment.

In 1983 Hayden was the subject of a documentary, *Pharos of Chaos*, in which he discussed his HUAC testimony, his Hollywood career, his exploits at sea, and his dependence on alcohol. Called "an unhappy spectacle" by *New York Times* film critic Janet Maslin, the film was described by Hayden himself as "a record of exactly what alcoholism is." In 1982 he had quit drinking.

In later years Hayden and his family split their time between Sausalito, Wilton, Connecticut, and a 100-foot barge in France. Hayden acted when he felt like it. "I work maybe once a year," he said, "and often I'll take jobs because they offer good locations." He died in Sausalito.

• Hayden provided fairly comprehensive documentation of both his personal and professional life in *Wanderer* (1963). Articles detailing his testimony before HUAC are in the *New York Times* and the *San Francisco Chronicle*, both 11 Apr. 1951. For information on his *Wanderer* voyage, see *Life*, 14 Dec. 1959. See also Walter Clemon's interview and review of *Voyage*, *Newsweek*, 27 Dec. 1976. Obituaries are in the *Washington Post*, *Los Angeles Times*, and *New York Times*, all 24 May 1986.

DIANA MOORE

HAYES, Alfred (17 Apr. 1911–15 Aug. 1985), reporter and author, was born in London, England, the son of Michael Hayes, a Jewish barber, and Rachel Topper. When Hayes was two years old, the family emigrated to New York City. After attending classes at the City College of New York (now the City University of New York), Hayes became a crime reporter for the *New York American* and the *Daily Mirror* from 1932 to 1935. A proponent of labor unions, he wrote the poem "I Dreamed I Saw Joe Hill Again," which was published in the *New Masses* (18 Sept. 1934), celebrating the famous Industrial Workers of the World leader executed in Utah in 1915. The poem gained worldwide popularity after it was set to music in 1936 by singer Earl Robinson. Hayes came to dislike the poem because of its simplistic form and excessive notoriety. In 1938 he adapted Erskine Caldwell's novel *Journeyman* for Broadway and two years later wrote the lyrics for the Broadway musical *'Tis of Thee*. In 1940–1941 he was a movie critic for the weekly *Friday* and also provided patter for radio variety shows.

In 1943 Hayes joined the U.S. Army and was assigned to a special services unit, serving in Italy. He published his first book of poetry, *The Big Time*, in 1944. Poems in it, some having previously appeared in *Esquire*, the *New Yorker*, and *Poetry*, deal with miserable urbanites in bars, dance halls, and movie houses. The tone is ironic, the form loose. While in Italy, he wrote *Paisan*, his first screenplay. After he revised it, with the help of other writers, it became Roberto Rossellini's 1949 film of the same name. Released in 1945 from military service, Hayes returned to New York and published his first novel, *All Thy Conquests* (1946). Cast in recently liberated Rome, it is based on a real-life incident concerning a petty Fascist thug who becomes a functionary for German soldiers, only to be grabbed by vengeful Italians and lynched. American soldiers are graphically depicted as irresponsible, homesick, and hungry for women.

Hayes went to Hollywood as a Warner Brothers script writer for about a year and then returned to New York to write two more novels. *Shadow of Heaven* (1947) is about a burned-out American labor organizer disillusioned with unionism, love, and life itself. *The Girl on the Via Flaminia* (1949), Hayes's most popular novel, followed. In it a lonely, naive American soldier finds a hungry, bitter teenage girl in Rome, a city ravaged during World War II. He rents an apartment and makes use of her sexually. To prevent her being jailed for prostitution, the young couple would have to prove that they are married; but they cannot. The novel, a kind of parable of conqueror and vanquished, was highly praised, one reviewer even comparing its clipped style to that of Ernest Hemingway. Between these two novels Hayes wrote the lyrics for a musical show titled *Jewish Holiday Dances* (1948). He dramatized *The Girl on the Via Flaminia* for the New York stage in 1954. A movie version, titled *Act of Love*, appeared in 1954, with the setting shifted to Paris. An Italian translation of the novel was published in 1954, a German one in 1956.

Hayes returned to Hollywood and Warner Brothers, and he soon wrote for Metro-Goldwin-Mayer, RKO, and Twentieth Century-Fox as well. In the nearly two decades following, he adapted two plays and eight novels for the screen, occasionally in cooperation with other writers. His credits include *Clash by Night* (adapted in 1952 from Clifford Odets's play), *Human Desire* (from Émile Zola's *La Bête humaine*, 1954), *These Thousand Hills* (from A. B. Guthrie, Jr.'s novel, 1959), and *In Enemy Country* (from Sy Barnett's novel, 1969). In 1960 Hayes bought a house in Encino, California. In a 1980 interview, he described his Hollywood work as nonsensical and dull—but a job.

In the meantime, Hayes had been publishing what he regarded as more significant and representative writing. His *Welcome to the Castle* (1950) is a tiny collection of poems, mostly about "the grim and comic castle of my middle age." Two more novels followed. *In Love* (1953) concerns a middle-aged artist who releases his girlfriend to a millionaire with a way of life more to her liking. Reviewers praised the clever stream-of-consciousness technique employed in it. *My Face for the World to See* (1958) is the taut account of a New York screen writer in Hollywood, his ambitious starlet girlfriend, and his soon-to-reappear wife. Hayes gathered three novellas into *The Temptation of Don Volpi* (1960). The main story concerns a saintly priest and his carnal passion. The second details the legal problems of witnesses to a southern lynching. The third presents a mother whose child's death causes her to ponder the meaning of life. In *The End of Me* (1968), yet another novel, a middle-aged Californian moves to New York to help his nephew, only to be treated cruelly by the lad and his vicious girlfriend. By this time Hayes seems to have lost confidence in his undeniable talent as a sardonic observer and a curt recorder of the tawdrier aspects of life in the United States. His last collection of poems, *Just before the Divorce* (1968), is quite slim and is mostly in prosy free verse. In the title piece a man thinks of his wife's malice, mulls over the terms of their approaching settlement, evidently rapes and kills her, then "hangs her perfect breasts from the attic rafter." Reviewers have compared Hayes to Robert Browning for drama and to Robinson Jeffers for wild plotting. *The Stockbroker, the Bitter Young Man, and the Beautiful Girl* (1973), Hayes's last novel, is something of a compressed reprise of *The End of Me* and tells about an honest little fellow who tries to win a girlfriend only to lose her, his dignity, and his hope. Hayes said that he sought to make this work funny but could not. It was published only in England, where he was always more popular than in the United States—which he explained on the grounds that the English have higher critical standards and are better able to recognize quality.

During his last years Hayes became slightly bitter because of his lack of success and steady productivity but mostly philosophical about life in general. He deplored the drift of most movies away from what he called any connection to literature. He dismissed virtually all fiction of the 1970s and 1980s. He wrote for television, including about thirty episodes of the popular *Mannix* series, which ran from 1967 to 1975. He did such easy work, he said, simply for pay. He continued to write poems but only for his own amusement; he admitted that he no longer had any professional ambition. He died in a Sherman Oaks, California, hospital, near his home in Encino; he was survived by his wife Marietta (maiden name unknown) and their three children.

• Hayes's 1980 interview, with Judith Spiegelman, is reported in *Contemporary Authors*, vol. 106 (1982), pp. 232–34. His writings merit brief consideration in Granville Hicks, *Proletarian Literature in the United States* (1935); John W. Aldridge, *After the Lost Generation: A Critical Study of the Writers of Two Wars* (1951); and Harry R. Warfel, *American Novelists of Today* (1951). Hayes's two war novels are summarized in Desmond Taylor and Philip E. Hager, *The Novels of World War II: An Annotated Bibliography* (1993). Lori Elaine Tàylor, "Joe Hill Incorporated: We Own Our Past," in *Songs about Work: Essays in Occupational Culture*, ed. Archie Green (1993), pp. 223–36, traces the history of Hayes's "Joe Hill" poem and the song it inspired. Obituaries are in the *New York Times*, 15 Aug. 1985, and the *Hollywood Reporter*, 22 Aug. 1985.

ROBERT L. GALE

HAYES, Augustus Allen (28 Feb. 1806–21 June 1882), chemist, was born in Windsor, Vermont, the son of Thomas Allen Hayes, a prosperous merchant, and Sophia West. In 1820 Hayes entered Captain Alden Partridge's newly founded American Literary, Scientific, and Military Academy in Norwich, Vermont, where he studied the practical and military sciences, and from which he graduated in 1823. In 1824 he enrolled as a first-year student at Dartmouth's medical school, where he learned chemistry from James Freeman Dana and assisted in the demonstrations that Dana performed during his chemical lectures. In 1827–1828, Hayes served as assistant chemist to Benjamin

Hale, the professor of chemistry, mineralogy, and legal medicine who had replaced Dana at Dartmouth. Hayes did not, however, earn a medical degree and was never licensed to practice medicine.

In 1828 Hayes moved to Boston, Massachusetts, where until 1847 he directed the chemical laboratory at the Roxbury Color and Chemical Company, a manufacturer of textile dyes. In 1848–1849 he briefly worked in the chemistry department at the Middlesex Company, a large textile mill in Lowell founded by Samuel Lawrence. By 1850 he had returned to Boston, where he received certification for the reliability of the assays he performed for individuals and companies as a state assayer of ores and metals, an appointment he held until his death. In 1836 he married Henrietta Dana of Marblehead, Massachusetts; they had three children.

Along with his former teacher's brother, Samuel Luther Dana, who was also a distant relative of his wife's, Hayes became one of New England's premier industrial and consulting chemists—a pioneer in the application of chemical analysis to mining, minerals, and fuels; to dyeing, bleaching, and other processes in the textile industry; to the heavy chemical, iron, and steel industries; and to municipal water supplies and public health. Nearly all of Hayes's ninety published papers or reports concern the practical application of chemistry in various economic or public health contexts. This number of publications ranks Hayes among the most prolific American chemists of his generation; their breadth reveals that Hayes worked in nearly every area of mid-nineteenth-century applied chemistry.

Hayes's earliest papers applied chemistry to industrial settings. In research published in 1828 by his teacher, J. F. Dana, Hayes tried without success to separate coloring agents for use as textile dyes from the blood root *Sanguinaria*; he did, however, identify a new vegetable alkali as the source of color in the plant. In the 1830s Hayes worked with S. L. Dana to determine the arrangements of large industrial boilers by which coal could be burned most efficiently. They also developed techniques to measure the relative energy content of coals, methods subsequently employed by the U.S. Navy Department in a massive study of American and foreign coals that it commissioned in 1843. In 1848 Hayes proposed a new method for manufacturing pure sulphuric acid. In the 1850s he examined for the Revere Copper Company the efficacy of copper sheathing to protect ships from the corrosive action of sea water. After laboratory tests and monitoring of sheathing on vessels in service, Hayes offered only a negative conclusion: neither silver nor zinc alloyed with copper improves the longevity of ships' sheathing. In 1856 he studied the internal structural changes that cause metals to become brittle under gentle percussive actions such as trains rolling over rails. In the same year, Hayes published one of the first chemical analyses of the Bessemer process for manufacturing steel. He also monitored for manufacturers the purity or safety of chemical products such as illu-

minating gas, kerosene oils, chloroform and chloric ether, and pharmaceuticals. Hayes's name frequently appeared in advertisements "certifying" the reliability of products.

Hayes's work in public health began in 1830, when he determined the mineral content of spring water from Saratoga Springs, New York. With S. L. Dana, he studied the corrosive action of water on metal pipes and concluded that lead pipes contaminate drinking water. In the late 1840s, as Boston completed a new aqueduct to deliver water to the city from Lake Cochituate, Hayes and Dana mounted a vigorous public campaign to prohibit the use of lead pipes in the city; yet they were unable to refute the experiments and public health data from other cities that Harvard chemist Eben N. Horsford and local officials had marshaled in defense of lead pipes. In 1859–1860, as the city of Charlestown sought a new water supply, Hayes invented a means to measure the purity of water in ponds or rivers as a function of depth. He showed that a copper wire, suspended vertically in waters of slightly different composition, would become electrically polarized and display electrolytic action. Sulphuric compounds in the water would blacken the wire, enabling Hayes to measure the relative amounts of sea water or sewage at different depths. Hayes was also well known as an expert in forensic chemistry. He reported a peculiar case of immunity from arsenic poisoning, discussed how to detect poisons in the bodies of victims, and warned of the dangers of small traces of metallic salts in wines and spirits. With Augustus A. Gould, a leading Boston physician, he studied the composition of urine of a diabetic and claimed to confirm the efficacy of "Dr. Champlin's bran cakes" as a treatment for this disease. Although not much involved in agricultural chemistry, Hayes did explore the use of sulphurous acid gas to check the spread of potato rot.

Many of Hayes's published papers report the results of his chemical assays of various commodities for various clients. In them he analyzed the recoverable iron, gold, manganese, borate, and cobalt content in ore samples; nitrates in South American minerals; gum and wax obtained from various plants; the weathering capacities of marble quarried in New England; the composition of heat-resistant clays for making firebricks; the viability of sorghum grasses grown in the United States as a source for sugar; and the composition of various types of guano. With prominent geologists such as Charles T. Jackson and Henry D. Rogers, Hayes determined the composition and energy content of bituminous and anthracite coals mined across North America. Hayes also assayed many mineral specimens for the authors of standard mineralogical treatises, such as James D. Dana and Francis Alger. In most of these cases, Hayes employed standard techniques of inorganic chemical analysis and did not seek to relate his work to chemical theory.

Only occasionally did Hayes offer theoretical speculations about the formation of guano, coal, or various minerals, the crystallization of liquids, or the organization of chromium compounds. In 1832 he discovered two new chlorine compounds, which European chemists such as J. J. Berzelius praised for their theoretical significance. And, in 1844 Hayes declared a sample of hydrous borate of lime from Peru to be a new mineral species, which Alger named Hayesine but which J. D. Dana later showed to be Ulexite, a species more correctly analyzed in 1849 by a German chemist. Yet despite these theoretical contributions, Hayes's work as a whole epitomized the applied, non-university-based chemistry that prevailed in America before 1870.

Hayes belonged to the Boston Society of Natural History from 1834 to 1874 and was active in the Thursday Club, a men's club founded by the Harvard surgeon John C. Warren in 1846 to promote social and scientific conversation among Boston's elite. The American Academy of Arts and Sciences elected Hayes a fellow in 1838. After spending 1867–1868 in Europe, Hayes suffered a debilitating disease and spent the final thirteen years of his life as an invalid. He died in Brookline, Massachusetts.

• Hayes's papers have not been found. In 1882 he donated more than 300 volumes on chemistry and geology from his personal library to Dartmouth College. Some of Hayes's correspondence is in the Eben N. Horsford Papers at Rensselaer Polytechnic Institute, and in the Dana Family Papers and the Silliman Family Papers at Yale University. For partial bibliographies of Hayes's published works, see the *Royal Society Catalogue of Scientific Papers*, vols. 3, 7, and 10, and the *National Union Catalogue, Pre-1956 Imprints*, vol. 236, pp. 393–94. Hayes's works also include *Report of the Consulting Physicians of the City of Boston in Relation to the Action of Cochituate Water upon Mineral Substances* (1848); with Henry D. Rogers, *Reports on the Combustible Qualities of the Semi-anthracites of the Zerbes's Run Coal Fields* (1851); with Charles T. Jackson and J. G. Percival, *Reports on the Geological Relations, Chemical Analyses, and Microscopic Examination of the Coal of the Albert Coal Mining Co.* (1851); and articles in the *Boston Medical and Surgical Journal* 40 (1849), 45 (1852), 49 (1854), 63 (1861), and 64 (1861), and the *Annals of Scientific Discovery* 2 (1851), 3 (1852), 4 (1853), 9 (1858), 13 (1862), and 14 (1863). For an overview of practical chemistry as conducted by Hayes and his contemporaries, see Margaret W. Rossiter, *The Emergence of Agricultural Science: Justus Liebig and the Americans, 1840–1880* (1975). Obituaries in the *Boston Evening Transcript*, 23 June 1882; *Proceedings of the American Academy of Arts and Sciences* 18 (1882–1883): 422–27; and John M. Comstock, *Obituary Record of the Graduates of Dartmouth College* (1883), pp. 17–18, like most subsequent biographical sketches, derive essentially from David Ames Wells's somewhat embellished entries on Hayes in the *New American Cyclopaedia* (1858–1863; rev. ed., 1873–1876).

RICHARD L. KREMER

HAYES, Bully (1829–Mar. 1877), trader, adventurer, and blackbirder, was born William Henry Hayes in Cleveland, Ohio, the son of Henry Hayes, a bargeman in and around the Great Lakes; his mother's name is unknown. Little is known about Hayes's early life. His first maritime experience came as a saltwater sailor on voyages around Cape Horn to California. Hayes commanded a total of fifteen vessels over his lifetime.

Hayes's first job as a mate came in 1853 on a trip from New York to Australia, where he planned to search for gold. Failing to find gold or procure any business in Australia, Hayes began his history of questionable commercial practices. In 1854 he sailed to Singapore, where he managed to acquire his first ship. After purchasing merchandise using his craft as collateral, Hayes quickly sailed away without the proper authorization and without making arrangements to pay his debts—a tactic he repeated many times over the next two decades. Engaging in questionable transactions from the South Seas to San Francisco, Hayes frequently was chased by creditors. Conflicting jurisdictions with a mix of European and indigenous legal systems allowed Hayes to keep out of trouble until 1858, when he was forced into bankruptcy. Managing to recover financially, Hayes soon purchased another vessel.

Hayes's dynamic personality greatly contributed to his success. Strong and handsome, he had a beard, penetrating blue eyes, and a deep baritone voice. In August 1859, while in San Francisco, he bought and outfitted the *Ellentia*. As before, he managed to depart while owing large sums of money and sailed for Sydney with his creditors close behind. As described in an article in a San Francisco newspaper, Hayes "vamoosed" owing $3,794. Some of his contemporaries maintained that Hayes might have returned to pay those bills had he not run into trouble en route to Australia, but vamoosing remained a standard part of Hayes's routine.

Hayes took passengers on the *Ellentia* even though the craft was unseaworthy and uninsured, and in October 1859, before reaching Sydney, the *Ellentia* was lost. Hayes was sued for obligations and sent to debtors' prison. His actions attracted the notice of the local press, and he was chastised in the *Sydney Morning Herald*. Hayes was described as a "pirate," which marked the beginning of his legendary status. He was briefly incarcerated and for a time lived as an insolvent beachcomber in Sydney.

For several months in 1864 Hayes toured with a minstrel group in and around Sydney. After a short time he was able to purchase the brigantine *Black Diamond*. Soon defaulting on some commercial arrangements, Hayes sailed to the Croixelles. While his craft was being repaired, Hayes had a yacht accident in which his common-law wife, Rosetta Buckingham; their fourteen-month-old daughter; and her brother and nursemaid were drowned. Hayes survived the wreck only to be arrested again for financial misdeeds.

In the mid-1860s Hayes became involved in a variety of extralegal practices, the most sinister being "blackbirding"—the practice of kidnapping Polynesians and selling them as slaves in the Fiji Islands. Blackbirding had gone on for years in the South Seas, but the practice noticeably increased after the American Civil War. A worldwide cotton shortage led to the growth of plantations in the South Seas, which resulted in a labor shortage, and Hayes joined in the lucrative business of securing workers. When British officials became aware of his activities, Hayes was arrested but released after only a short prison stay.

In 1874 Hayes's ship, the *Leonora*, was lost in a storm. Settling in the Caroline Islands with several of his crew, he set up a trading system and generally terrorized the natives. When a British ship arrived, the claims against him were investigated, but before any action could be taken he fled to Guam. In 1875, while in Guam, Hayes was arrested by Spanish authorities and charged with aiding the escape of political prisoners; this time he spent several months in jail before being released.

In 1877 Hayes was back in San Francisco, where he managed to secure the yacht *Lotus*. Consistent with his history, he appears to have stolen not only the yacht but also the owner's wife. Hayes sailed the *Lotus* to Hawaii with a small crew. In March while en route to Samoa he got into an argument with his cook, and a fight ensued. The cook reportedly killed Hayes with a blow to the head, and his body was thrown overboard. A hearing was later held, and evidence was sent to Washington, but no action was taken.

Hayes's reputation was solidified in the writings of Louis Becke, who had sailed with him briefly in the 1870s and later wrote buccaneer tales in which Hayes is depicted as charismatic and charming—a romantic hero on the grand South Sea stage. While Becke chronicled the romantic side of Bully Hayes, others related darker accounts. He was especially notorious for his mistreatment of women. Documentation is lacking, but it is clear that Hayes was married several times. In 1857 he married Amelia Littleton, an Australian widow. In 1865 he married Emily Butler in New Zealand, while the first Mrs. Hayes was still living in San Francisco. Hayes and Emily Butler had three children. Hayes also lived for various periods with several different women in situations that resembled marriage. One of those women was Rosetta Buckingham, who died in the wreck of the *Black Diamond*. Hayes was also accused of taking indecent liberties with young girls—twice he had to defend himself against formal charges. The charges were dropped each time, but Hayes acquired a reputation for possessing a violent temper and treating women with little respect.

Although it is difficult to separate fact from fiction in accounts of Bully Hayes's career, several details of his life stand out. As a sailor, he was skilled; as a trader, crafty; and, just as an individual, unusually resourceful. Despite continual problems with money, he consistently managed to obtain both ships and trade commodities. But the strengths of his character were without a moral anchor. His defrauding of creditors, his highly questionable commercial transactions, his bigamous living arrangements, and his participation in the South Pacific slave trade all stamp him as a man unburdened by conscience or social consciousness. His notorious behavior is his most enduring legacy: he was a buccaneer of modern times and a classic rogue.

• Information about Hayes is sketchy and frequently unauthentic. The best attempt at a scholarly biography is Frank Clune, *Captain Bully Hayes: Blackbirder and Bigamist* (1971). While Clune includes an adequate bibliography, he prefaces his study with the warning that "this book may be classed as fiction because it includes numerous yarns about the career of Bully Hayes that cannot be verified." Other useful accounts of Hayes include A. T. Saunders, *Bully Hayes: Barrator, Bigamist, Buccaneer, Blackbirder, and Pirate* (1915; 2d ed., 1932); Alfred Basil Lubbock, *Bully Hayes: South Sea Pirate* (1931); and J. B. Musser, "Bully Hayes—Pirate de Luxe," *U.S. Naval Institute Proceedings* 53 (1927): 956–61. For the swashbuckling accounts of Hayes's career see Louis Becke, *By Reef and Palm* (1894) and *Bully Hayes: Buccaneer and Other Stories* (1913), and also Rolf Boldrewood, *A Modern Buccaneer* (1894). A valuable biography of Becke is Grove Day, *Louis Becke* (1966). Other references that discuss Hayes include Scott Russell, ed., "Of Wooden Ships and Iron Men: An Historical and Archaeological Survey of the Brig Leonora," *Micronesian Archaeological Survey Report* 15 (1982): 7–26, 103–7; W. B. Churchward, *My Consulate in Samoa* (1887); and A. R. Headland, *Adventures Afloat in Missionary Ships* (1929).

DAVID E. WOODARD

HAYES, Carlton J. H. (16 May 1882–3 Sept. 1964), historian, was born Carlton Joseph Huntley Hayes in Afton, New York, the son of Philetus Arthur Hayes, a physician, and Permelia Mary Huntley, a piano teacher. Hayes studied and made his career at Columbia University, which he entered as a freshman in 1900. He received a bachelor's degree with highest general honors in 1904, a master's degree in 1905, and a Ph.D. in 1909 after graduate study in medieval and American history. As a student, Hayes was greatly influenced by Professors James Harvey Robinson, James T. Shotwell, and William R. Shepherd, noted proponents of what was then called "new history," an approach that put greater emphasis on social and economic conditions than on political events. His dissertation, published as *An Introduction to the Sources Relating to the Germanic Invasions* (1909), challenged the tendency to make race a major factor in historical interpretation ("the strife of emperors eclipsed the strife of race" [p. 87]).

Having established close ties with Columbia's president, Nicholas Murray Butler, as well as with professors such as Robinson and Charles A. Beard, among others, Hayes became, in 1907, one of the youngest men to receive a lectureship in history at Columbia. After the completion of his dissertation, he rapidly climbed the academic ladder, from assistant professor in 1910 to associate professor in 1915 and full professor in 1919.

Hayes became a major force in the life of the university. He served on numerous committees and ad hoc panels dealing with academic, social, and athletic life and helped restructure and tighten Columbia's doctoral program in history. Early in his teaching career, Hayes shifted his interests to modern European history, in which field he became a stimulating, opinionated, and highly sought-after lecturer. He was awarded the Seth Low Professorship in 1935 and held this chair until his retirement in 1950. He supervised scores of graduate students; more than seventy of them completed dissertations—many about aspects of nationalism and some highly acclaimed—under his direction.

Of great importance to Hayes's outlook and life's work was his conversion to Roman Catholicism in 1904. His association with the church expressed and deepened his preference for the universal over discrete groups, whether Protestant denominations or national entities. Influenced heavily by Pope Leo XIII's encyclical *Rerum Novarum* (1891), Hayes became a critic of unfettered capitalism and, at least for a while, virtually a socialist, albeit one who looked more to medieval guild society for inspiration than to utilitarian and secular outgrowths of the Enlightenment, a distinction that left him somewhat out of step with many fellow reformers.

Hayes's widely used textbooks helped popularize the study of European history and brought him economic security. *A Political and Social History of Modern Europe* (2 vols., 1916), intended for use in colleges, marked Hayes's entry into the growing market for such texts. In the 1930s he reworked it as *A Political and Cultural History of Modern Europe* (1932; 1936). For high schools, he wrote, with Parker T. Moon, *Ancient History* (1921); the highly successful and controversial *Modern Europe* (1923); and *Ancient and Medieval History* (1929). The books went through many editions and helped spread aspects of "new history" across the country.

Opposed to U.S. entry into World War I, Hayes proposed ways in which the United States might encourage a cessation of hostilities. Once Congress declared war, however, Hayes lent his support to the effort. Taking a leave of absence from Columbia, he entered the army as a captain and worked in military intelligence for the General Staff. He also published articles calling for the establishment of constructive relations with a demilitarized Germany. He supported U.S. entry into the League of Nations and contributed "The Historical Background of the League of Nations" to *The League of Nations*, edited by S. P. H. Duggan (1919).

The war had a major influence on Hayes's subsequent career. It turned his interests increasingly toward nationalism and international relations rather than social issues. Tellingly, in 1913 he published *British Social Politics: Materials Illustrating Contemporary State Action for the Solution of Social Problems*, and in 1914 "The War of the Nations" (*Political Science Quarterly* 29, no. 4 [Dec.]: 687–707), in which he began to decry the nefarious effects of modern nationalism and the "pseudo-scientific obscurantism" that nourished it. Ever *au courant* in his field, Hayes published a well-received *Brief History of the Great War* in 1920.

As editor of a series of works on the social and economic conditions in postwar France under the auspices of Columbia University's Council for Research in the Social Sciences, Hayes was able to combine both his interests and to concentrate on the study of nationalism. His major contribution to the project was *France: A Nation of Patriots* (1930). That work was preceded by the pioneering *Essays on Nationalism* (1926) and soon followed by the influential *Historical Evolution of Modern Nationalism* (1931), in which he identified variants of the phenomenon (and warned about the threat posed by Hitler). He linked the growth of nationalism—from "blessing" to "curse"—primarily to the effects of industrialization and the decline of religious faith; indeed, he saw exclusivistic nationalism as a new form of religion. He drew a distinction between "original," or "liberal," nationalism, which he viewed as primarily cultural and liberal, and "derived," or "integral," nationalism, which he described as exclusive, bellicose, and intolerant.

An engaged citizen and effective speaker, Hayes often wrote for and spoke before nonacademic audiences, especially during the interwar years, on behalf of religious liberty, tolerance, and political pluralism. He also called on the country to face up to its international responsibilities. A member of the first editorial board of *Commonweal*, a lay Catholic journal of opinion founded in 1924, he occasionally published articles in its pages. Among them was a series, also published separately in 1924, titled "Obligations to America." He helped found the National Conference for Christians and Jews, and served as its Catholic co-chair from 1928 to 1946. He worked with the Catholic Association for International Peace and the Association of History Teachers of the Middle States and Maryland, among other groups, and in 1930 he served as president of the American Catholic Historical Association, a group that he had helped found late in 1919. He was, in addition, an active member of several professional and scholarly associations, and he received several honorary degrees and other honors. In 1920 he had married Mary Evelyn Carroll, like him an activist in Catholic lay circles; they had a daughter and a son. Their home near Columbia University became well-known for frequent, gracious, and purposeful entertainment.

During these years, Hayes became embroiled in controversy. In 1927 several chauvinists carped openly about his strictures against exclusivistic American nationalism, which Hayes claimed had been misreported, and in 1930 an Episcopal priest complained, in a communication to the New York Board of School Superintendents, that *Modern History* was too radical, internationalist, pro-Catholic, and antipatriotic. Eventually, he and Moon felt constrained to make minor revisions in an effort to keep the book on New York's list of approved textbooks.

In 1941 Hayes published a book that added to his reputation but that also offended some of his liberal colleagues: *The Generation of Materialism, 1871–1900*, part of a series on the "Rise of Modern Europe" edited by William L. Langer. In the artful and topically organized work, Hayes criticized "sectarian liberalism" for its support of nationalism and imperialism and raised disturbing questions about the values and direction of modern civilization. But some critics saw "a kind of semi-obscurantist, antiscientific thread running through" the book and questioned the genuineness of Hayes's own liberalism (Jefferson, p. 15).

Having called for U.S. intervention against the Axis powers after war began in Europe in 1939, Hayes played a significant wartime role as U.S. ambassador to Spain from the spring of 1942 to January 1945. His acceptance of the appointment, at the personal insistence of President Franklin D. Roosevelt, and his policies provoked considerable criticism from many fellow liberals. They objected to Hayes's call for recognition of and support for the strongly Catholic but quasi-fascist regime of Francisco Franco. In *Wartime Mission to Spain, 1942–1945* (1946), Hayes defended his efforts, in accordance with the administration's wishes, to pull Spain into the Anglo-American orbit, thus to keep it from joining the Axis powers that had helped Franco win the civil war (during which, ironically, Hayes had had his name removed from the masthead of *Commonweal* because of its pro-Franco stance). Hayes returned to the topic with *The United States and Spain: An Interpretation* in 1951, in which his negative views of the republican government destroyed during Spain's civil war further upset many fellow historians.

In an unusual contested election, Hayes was named president of the American Historical Association (AHA) for 1945, becoming the first Catholic to be so honored. Opposition to Hayes stemmed primarily from his support for Franco, but some observers suspected that anti-Catholic, not just antifascist, sentiment might also have contributed to it. That same year Hayes resigned his ambassadorship, more because of disagreements with the administration about policies toward Spain once the war was almost over than because of his new professional responsibilities. In his presidential address to the AHA in December 1945, Hayes used commentary about Frederick Jackson Turner's "frontier thesis" to champion a comparative approach to the study of history and to warn against the intellectual and political isolationism that he thought Turner's popular thesis fostered ("The American Frontier—Frontier of What?" *American Historical Review* 51, no. 2 [Jan. 1946]: 199–216).

Hayes returned to the classroom in September 1945 and spoke out publicly about international affairs, supporting especially organizations linking the countries of Western Europe and the Americas—what he called the Atlantic community. He continued to write and publish, notably (with others) *A History of Europe* (1949; revised in 1956, and expanded into *A History of Western Civilization* in 1962) and his own two-volume textbooks, *Modern Europe to 1870* and *Contemporary Europe since 1870* (1953; rev. ed., 1958). In 1954 he delivered at Stanford University the Raymond Fred West Memorial Lectures, published later that year as *Christianity and Western Civilization*. In 1960, ten years after retirement, he produced a final book about the topic whose study he had helped stimulate; in *Nationalism: A Religion*, he restated some of the themes of his earlier works and added prescient commentary about the effects of nationalism on emerging states in Asia and Africa.

When he retired in 1950, Hayes was honored with a festschrift, *Nationalism and Internationalism: Essays Inscribed to Carlton J. H. Hayes*, edited by Edward Mead Earle. Despite such well-deserved recognition, the growing distance between Hayes and the historical establishment of the day, especially over his emphasis on religion and his defense of the Franco regime, meant that his "last years could hardly have been pleasant" (Jefferson, p. 35).

Hayes typifies the historian who saw in his conception of the past direct relevance to the events of his own time. He had an enviable ability to bring historical figures and developments alive in his classroom, and wherever he wrote and spoke, he used lessons from the past to make trenchant comments about current events. He could also be preachy. The final sentence in several editions of *A Political and Social History of Modern Europe* provides a fitting summary of his overall message: he asserted that a solution to the world's ills "lies through . . . an education which will train the succeeding generation for right thinking and right doing, for coöperation and peace" (1931 ed., vol. 2, p. 866).

• A substantial collection of Hayes's papers in the Special Collections at Columbia University includes a short unpublished autobiography and the texts of several speeches, among other items. Hayes contributed autobiographical reflections to collections of essays, including *These Eventful Years* (1924), *Essays in Intellectual History* (1929), and *Columbia University Lectures: A Quarter Century of Learning, 1904–1929* (1931). The fullest published commentary about Hayes is Carter Jefferson, "Carlton J. H. Hayes," in *Historians of Modern Europe*, ed. Hans A. Schmitt (1971), pp. 15–35. Arthur Joseph Hughes, "Carlton J. H. Hayes: Teacher and Historian" (Ph.D. diss., Columbia Univ., 1970 [c. 1972]), is a lengthy examination of Hayes's career and provides a list of his varied publications. See also John Paul Willson, "Carlton J. H. Hayes in Spain, 1942–1945" (Ph.D. diss., Syracuse Univ., 1969). For a short appreciation of Hayes in the classroom, see Irwin Edman, "Former Teachers," in *Modern American Vistas*, ed. Howard W. Hintz and Bernard D. N. Grebanier (1940), pp. 357–71. Obituaries are in the *New York Times*, 4 Sept. 1964; *Catholic Historical Review* 50 (Jan. 1965): 677–79, *Time*, 11 Sept. 1964, p. 106; *Commonweal*, 18 Sept. 1964, p. 624; *Publishers Weekly*, 28 Sept. 1964, p. 97; *American Historical Review* 70, no. 2 (Jan. 1965): 640–41; and *Political Science Quarterly* 80, no. 3 (Sept. 1965): 516.

C. EARL EDMONDSON

HAYES, Charles Willard (8 Oct. 1858–8 Feb. 1916), geologist and administrator, was born in Granville, Ohio, the son of Charles Coleman Hayes, a tanner, and Ruth Rose Wolcott, formerly a schoolteacher. After graduating from Oberlin College in 1883, Hayes taught school for a year before attending Johns Hopkins University. He received a doctorate in 1887 with a major in chemistry and minors in geology and mineralogy. In mid-April of that year he joined the U.S. Geological Survey as a field assistant to I. C. Russell in Alabama, at $50 per month.

The prevailing plan was to establish the sequence of rock formations in the southern Appalachians by having geologists prepare three detailed cross-sections through the mountain chain; Russell had already devoted two years to this project. Unfortunately the detailed surveying and measuring turned out to be virtually useless, because the sequence was broken by many faults and further disrupted by lateral movement of rock masses for miles, a phenomenon not suspected at the time. In 1888 Russell moved to geologic studies in Alaska, and Hayes took over his Appalachian effort; almost immediately, Hayes demonstrated the large-scale overthrusting (the pushing of older rock units over younger ones) and published on its geological significance.

In his subsequent geologic mapping, Hayes was greatly hindered by the lack of adequate topographic maps and first had to make his own base maps. Despite that major handicap, he grasped the principal elements of the rock succession and the structural changes affected by mountain building. Hayes would complete the mapping of a large area, one degree of latitude by one degree of longitude, in a single field season, and he expected his subordinates to follow this same rigorous schedule. Notwithstanding his push to achieve results promptly, the mapping was accurate in detail. Hayes was both respected and liked by his colleagues and assistants, in part because of his insistence on high standards. He produced some of the earliest "Folios" for the *Geologic Atlas of the United States*.

As a change from the Appalachian Mountains mapping, Hayes explored in the Copper River region of Alaska during the 1891 field season. The party to which he was attached as geologist went up the Taka River through the Coast Range to the Yukon Plateau, then down the Lewis River. From there they traveled to the headwaters of the White River and across the divide to the Copper River basins, exploring territory virtually unknown to non-native people.

Hayes returned to the southern Appalachians in 1892 and in addition to regional mapping began to concentrate on surveying economically important mineral deposits in the "gold belt" of the Atlantic Piedmont and in the Tennessee phosphate mines. Out of this latter investigation came work on estimating reserves of phosphates, which eventually led to a USGS program of estimating the reserves of many nonmetal minerals. Hayes also worked on bauxite deposits in the South. Another aspect of his work was a study of physiography (the development of the present-day land surface) of the southern Appalachians.

In 1894 Hayes married Rosa E. Paige of Washington, D.C.; the couple had eight children. During December 1897 Hayes traveled on detail to the Nicaragua Canal Commission to Central America, where he remained for some months. He was charged with conducting both a general physiographic study of the region and with making detailed engineering studies. Despite a fever acquired upon landing, within ten days he had organized his first camp and was moving drilling equipment toward the interior. Logistic problems were exceedingly difficult, but Hayes showed masterful skill in keeping several drilling rigs operating while

moving others to new sites. Incidental to his daily work and his report on the physiography he prepared a geologic map of most of Nicaragua.

1 July 1900 the Geologic Division was reorganized into seven sections, and Hayes was placed in charge of the Nonmetals Section. During 1901 he spent five weeks in Cuba investigating nonmetal deposits. Hayes was very concerned with the U.S. need for fuels, and, following the 1901 Spindletop oil gusher in Texas, he rapidly increased the USGS research in oil geology, recognizing the relationship between structural geology and the accumulation of oil.

In 1902 Hayes was promoted to geologist in charge of geology and paleontology. In that position, he launched an annual *Contributions to Economic Geology* to speed the dissemination of data on mineral deposits derived from mapping and stratigraphic studies. Simultaneously, Hayes oversaw the collecting of train-car loads of coal from various fields in the United States. The coal was tested for BTU production and ash content in the plant established by the USGS at the 1904 Louisiana Purchase Exposition in St. Louis; this coal testing contributed to the establishment of the Bureau of Mines in 1910.

When C. D. Walcott retired as USGS director in 1907, the title of chief geologist was reinstituted, and Hayes held that office until 1911. Because of his interest in fuels and other geologic commodities, Hayes was a key adviser on nonrenewable raw materials to the "new conservation" movement of Theodore Roosevelt.

Hayes's success in the application of geology to engineering problems in Nicaragua led to work in 1910 in the Panama Canal Zone, despite his administrative duties. Several geologists were assigned to the Isthmian Canal Commission to resolve the problem of landslides. On an inspection trip, Hayes was so disgusted with the disreputable appearance of several field men that he designed a uniform for USGS geologists; although a few men bought uniforms, the geologists refused to wear them, and the uniform faded into agency mythology. Nevertheless, Hayes was generally regarded as an excellent chief geologist by his associates. His contributions to structural geology and to the geology of nonmetal economic deposits were significant accomplishments.

On leave from the USGS in 1909, he had worked in the Tampico area of Mexico and had located what turned out to be the most productive oil well in the world up to that time. Offered better pay, Hayes resigned from the USGS in 1911 to become vice president and general manager of the Eagle Oil Company, the largest oil company working in Mexico. In this new capacity, Hayes outlined the broad features of the Mexican coastal plain, made detailed stratigraphic studies of promising areas, and even supervised the drilling crews. He spent two years in Tampico before the turmoil of the Mexican revolution necessitated his leaving with his family. He spent the last three years of his life in Washington, D.C., where he died of cancer.

• Information about Hayes, including a portrait and a bibliography, can be found in A. H. Brooks, "Memorial of Charles Willard Hayes," *Bulletin of the Geological Society of America* 28 (1917); 81–123. A shorter account appears in Eugene C. Robertson, ed., *A Centennial History of the Geological Society of Washington, 1893–1993* (1993), pp. 66–67. Hayes is also mentioned in M. C. Rabbitt, *Minerals, Lands, and Geology for the Common Defence and General Welfare*, vol. 2, *1879–1904* (1980), and vol. 3, *1904–1939* (1986), both U.S. Government Printing Office publications.

ELLIS L. YOCHELSON

HAYES, Edward Cary (10 Feb. 1868–7 Aug. 1928), sociologist and eleventh president of the American Sociological Society, was born in Lewiston, Maine, the son of Benjamin Francis Hayes and Arcy Cary. His parents provided him with a home that combined intellectual rigor and a concern for social improvement. Hayes's father was a philosophy professor at Bates College and also a faculty member at Cobb Divinity School. His mother was a teacher and served as Edward's only educator until he was ten years old. She was also involved in community improvement activities and helped to create a number of local social welfare organizations.

After graduating from Bates College in 1887, Hayes studied for the ministry at Cobb Divinity School. He was ordained as a minister in 1893 and served as pastor of a congregation in Augusta, Maine, for three years. During his tenure with this church, he married Annie Lee Bean in 1895. The couple had three children. Hayes's career in the ministry was shortlived, however, because he discovered that his beliefs conflicted with those of many members of his congregation. He therefore turned to academics, following in his father's footsteps. He moved to Keuka College, in upstate New York, where he taught philosophy and served as dean for two years.

In 1899 Hayes decided to pursue a doctorate in philosophy and entered the recently created University of Chicago. He studied with George Herbert Mead, John Dewey, and James Tufts. During this time, he became interested in sociology; he entered the newly created department and became a student of Albion Small, whom he had known several years earlier when studying for the ministry. Small reportedly issued a call to the fledgling sociologist, telling Hayes that "I believe you are one of the men who can help to create a science of society" (Sutherland, p. 93). Hayes also spent a year in Germany studying at the University of Berlin with such scholars as Georg Schmoller, Adolph Wagner, Friedrich Paulsen, Alfred Vierkandt, and Georg Simmel.

Like other students of Small who became distinguished sociologists, including George E. Vincent, William Isaac Thomas, and Charles A. Ellwood, Hayes played an important role in the formative period of the discipline as it became institutionalized in American colleges and universities. He was one of a cadre of sociologists who transplanted the Chicago School's perspective, particularly in the Midwest and the West. His first academic appointment after completing his doctorate in 1902 was at Miami University in Oxford, Ohio. Former students remembered him as one of the most dynamic and erudite professors they had encountered at Miami. His skills in the pulpit carried over successfully into the university lecture hall.

In 1907 Hayes moved to the University of Illinois to become the head of a new department. Before his arrival, the few sociology courses offered at Illinois had been located in the economics department. He had to overcome considerable opposition to sociology at Illinois in order to build a successful program, but he succeeded. He remained at Illinois until his death; by that time the department had seven full-time faculty members and over 2,000 students enrolled in their courses each year. During these years, he also taught in the summer school sessions at several prominent universities, including Harvard, Columbia, the University of Chicago, and the University of Pennsylvania.

As he did at the University of Illinois, Hayes expended considerable time and energy getting sociology on a firm footing in the profession at large, promoting its acceptance as well as providing a clear sense of what the discipline was about. He served as secretary to the Social Psychology section of the World's Congress of Science, held at the St. Louis Exposition in 1904. In the following year he attended the organizational meeting of the American Sociological Society and became a charter member. He was an active and influential member of the organization throughout his career. In 1919 he was elected second vice president, the following year first vice president, and in 1921 he was elected to the presidency of the organization. Hayes served as the general editor of the Lippincott sociological series. His cosmopolitan interests were reflected in his memberships in such international organizations as the German Sociological Society, the Institut Internationale de Sociologie, and the Instituto Internazionale di Sociologia.

Hayes was especially interested in the teaching of sociology. He was selected as one of the American Sociological Society's Committee of Ten, a group charged with the task of developing a design for the introductory or foundational sociology course to be offered at the undergraduate level. Similarly, in working to get sociology accepted as part of the curriculum in secondary schools, Hayes represented the Society on the Joint Commission on the Presentation of Social Studies in Schools. He also produced a widely read textbook, *Introduction to the Study of Sociology* (1915).

This concern with the profession is reflected in his publications. Hayes did not engage in empirical research; instead, his work consisted largely of attempts to define and refine the object domain of sociology as well as to summarize the methodological and conceptual issues confronting practitioners of the discipline. Thus, while he saw that specialization was an inevitable trend, he warned against losing sight of the larger vision of sociology as expressed by early proponents of the science of society, such as Comte and Spencer. In relating sociology to other social sciences, he defined it as a "science of leftovers," by which he meant that its proper objects of inquiry consisted of a wide range of topics ignored by the other disciplines. Thus, he was more interested in finding a distinctive niche for sociology than in finding areas of overlap and mutual interest with the other social sciences.

Hayes was also concerned with articulating the connection between sociological knowledge and societal progress. His own political views were shaped by the progressive movement and were quite similar to those of his mentor, Albion Small. Some of his writings reflect a concern with radicalism and with conservatism, although he more frequently criticized the resistance of the latter to change. To address the social problems of the era, he urged an expanded role for government in the provision of social welfare. Like his lectures, his writings often had a hortatory quality to them. The continuing religious influence on his thought gave it what Robert Friedrichs, in *A Sociology of Sociology* (1970), characterized as a "prophetic mode."

The desire to put sociology to use in effecting societal improvements is evident in several articles and in his book *Sociology and Ethics* (1921). Hayes's own involvements in social reform activities included organizing and working with both the Family Welfare Society and the community chest in Champaign-Urbana. At the state level, he was a member of an advisory committee to the Illinois State Department of Public Welfare, and in 1910–1911 he served as president of the Illinois State Conference of Charities and Corrections.

Hayes died in Urbana. Today his work is largely unread, an indication of the fact that he was not the originator of a distinctive sociological perspective. His major contribution to the discipline lies in his work promoting it and securing a place for it in college and university curriculums.

• Hayes's publications include, in addition to the books cited above, an edited collection published a year before his death, titled *Recent Developments in the Social Sciences* (1927). His articles appeared in a number of social science journals, but his most important appeared in the *American Journal of Sociology*, including "Sociological Construction Lines," 10 (1904–1905): 623–42; 11 (1904–1905): 26–48, 623–45; 12 (1904–1905): 45–67; "The 'Social Forces' Error," 16 (1910–1911): 613–25; "Sociology as Ethics" 23 (1918–1919): 289–302; and "Were Comte and Spencer Wholly Wrong?" 33 (1927–1928): 14–27. For an overview of Hayes's life, see Edward Sutherland, "Edward Carey Hayes, 1868–1928," *American Journal of Sociology* 35 (1929): 93–99. Assessments of his scholarly work can be found in Pitirim Sorokin, *Contemporary Sociological Theories* (1928), Emory Bogardus, *A History of Social Thought* (1929), and Howard Odum, *American Sociology* (1951). The most in-depth treatment is contained in Harry Elmer Barnes, *An Introduction to the History of Sociology* (1948).

PETER KIVISTO

HAYES, Gabby (7 May 1885–9 Feb. 1969), actor, was born George Francis Hayes in Wellsville, New York, the son of Clark R. Hayes, a hotelkeeper, and Elizabeth Morrison. As a youth, Hayes appeared in local plays and developed a lifelong interest in sports, especially baseball and boxing. He left school after the eighth grade and joined a traveling show as a song-and-dance performer. He performed in burlesque and vaudeville on the Orpheum and Keith circuits, and in 1914 he married fellow performer Dorothy Earle, known also as Olive Dorothy Ireland, who subsequently retired from the stage. Their marriage produced no children.

Hayes moved to California in the late 1920s and first appeared on the screen in bit parts. His first sound film was *The Rainbow Man* (1929); in the same year he appeared as a reporter in *The Big News*. In 1931 Hayes began a long film career as character actor and helped define the sidekick persona in western films. At first his roles were small, and often he portrayed the heavy. In 1933 he began a series of comedic and serious roles in films starring John Wayne, produced by Paul Malvern for Lone Star Productions and released by Monogram Pictures. He also appeared with Bob Steele, Tom Tyler, Hoot Gibson, and Sunset Carson.

After completing eleven films with Wayne, Hayes worked with William Boyd in the Hopalong Cassidy series. They made twenty-two films in all, but it was not until their fifth that Hayes assumed his longtime role as Windy Halliday. Tension with series producer Harry Sherman caused Hayes to leave the Cassidy series and join Republic Pictures' new B-western star, Roy Rogers. Sherman went to court to prevent Hayes from using the familiar name of Windy Halliday; thus Hayes became "Gabby," but he continued the whiskered, toothless characterization.

Hayes's on-screen character sharply contrasted with his own personality, although they so blended over the years that he could move into the character at will, and his whiskers, which were real, always made him believable. He shaved his beard once and was so alarmed by the unfamiliar face that he refused to be seen in public until it grew back. Urbane and well read despite his lack of formal education, he was always well groomed offscreen and was considered a connoisseur of wines. He loved to travel and to talk with people about their work, saying that that was the way he learned. In politics, he was conservative.

Hayes and Rogers made twenty-seven films together (1939–1942). In 1943 Republic assigned Hayes to a new series starring Wild Bill Elliott, and they made ten films together, the last two in the Red Ryder series. He returned to work with Rogers, and they made fourteen more films from 1944 through 1946. In 1945 Hayes was rated by theater owners as the most popular western actor behind Rogers. From 1946 to 1950, Hayes appeared in seven more films, four of them starring Randolph Scott, perhaps his closest offscreen associate. His last film was *The Cariboo Trail* (1950). Hayes formed close relationships with all the stars to whom he played sidekick, and Rogers said that Hayes was "like my father, my buddy, my brother, all wrapped up in one."

Hayes performed on Rogers's weekly radio show for several years before moving to television in a Sunday afternoon children's show on NBC. Hayes appeared in the character of Gabby with guests, told tall tales, narrated dramatizations of American history, and delivered commercials. In 1951 he also hosted a daily screening of a western film, and in 1954 he replaced Buffalo Bob Smith on "The Howdy Doody Show" while Smith recovered from a heart attack.

Hayes also suffered from heart disease, frequently experiencing angina. Dorothy Hayes, whom he often called "Maw," died in 1957. Hayes spent his final years living in an apartment complex they had built, declining opportunities to appear as a talk-show guest. He died in Burbank, California.

• See David Rothel, *Those Great Cowboy Sidekicks* (1984); Ted Holland, *B Western Actors Encyclopedia: Facts, Photos and Filmographies for More than 250 Familiar Faces* (1989); Roy Rogers and Dale Evans, with Carlton Stowers, *Happy Trails: The Story of Roy Rogers and Dale Evans* (1979); and an obituary in the *New York Times*, 10 Feb. 1969.

ARCHIE P. McDONALD

HAYES, Helen (10 Oct. 1900–17 Mar. 1993), actress, was born Helen Hayes Brown in Washington, D.C., the daughter of Francis Van Arnum Brown, a wholesale meats salesman, and Catherine Estelle "Essie" Hayes, a sometime actress. A precocious child through whom her mother sought to realize her own ambitions, Hayes was on stage at the age of five and made her professional debut in 1909 as the boy prince in *A Royal Family* with the Columbia Players, a Washington stock company. Hayes was seen by the New York producer and vaudeville comedian Lew Fields, who invited Hayes and her mother to New York, where Fields immediately cast the girl in *Old Dutch*, a Victor Herbert musical comedy, and also shortened her name to Helen Hayes. While appearing in another Fields production in 1910, Hayes and her mother trekked to Brooklyn, where Hayes made her first film, a Vitagraph silent titled *Jean and the Calico Doll*, in which Hayes was rescued from a ravine through the efforts of a talented collie.

Hayes and her mother returned to Washington during 1911–1917, when Hayes played principal roles with the Columbia Players and at Poli's Theatre. She and her mother returned to New York in 1914 when Hayes was cast as John Drew's angelic adopted daughter in *The Prodigal Husband*. She also continued her education at the Academy of the Sacred Heart, from which she graduated in 1917. She soon set out on a national tour of *Pollyanna*, through 1918, playing the title character, who welcomes every hardship with gladness. This role was to prove a landmark in Hayes's career because it initiated her long sponsorship by the producer-director George C. Tyler. The role of the happy, innocent, and plucky character was Hayes's usual "type" throughout her career, though some of her best performances were in playing against the type. Her small stature (as an adult, she stood 5′ tall and weighed about 100 pounds) and unusually wideset eyes gave her an open and innocent appearance

that, Hayes said late in life, led people to "coddle and care" for her. While this image of perpetual happiness and charity would endear Hayes to generations of audiences, it led cynics to conclude that she was either a fool or a fraud. In what was perhaps the worst thing ever said about Hayes, Tennessee Williams accused her in his *Memoirs* of having somehow caused her husband's chronic alcoholism and early death by being too steadfastly virtuous.

Hayes soon graduated into more assertive ingenue roles, specializing in the light comedy-dramas of Booth Tarkington and Sir James Barrie. She appeared on Broadway in 1918 as the love interest for Tarkington's *Penrod* and as William Gillette's "dream daughter" in Barrie's *Dear Brutus*. In 1919 she was the love-stricken daughter in Tarkington's *Clarence*, a play that enhanced Hayes's reputation as a skilled comedic technician. Hayes's first starring role on Broadway came in 1920, as the title character in the comedy *Bab*, based on the popular novel by Mary Roberts Rinehart.

In 1924, frustrated over Tyler's domination of her and his refusal to cast her in anything but light comedy, Hayes severed her association with him. Her career did not suffer as a result. In 1925 she played Cleopatra in the elegant Theatre Guild production of Shaw's *Caesar and Cleopatra*. She enjoyed long runs in a revival of Barrie's *What Every Woman Knows* (1926–1927) and in the George Abbott melodrama *Coquette* (1927–1929). During the long run of *Coquette* (in Aug. 1928) Hayes married playwright Charles MacArthur, whose hard-boiled farce *The Front Page*, written with Ben Hecht, was the sensation of the 1928–1929 season.

The Hayes-MacArthur home, first a spacious apartment on Manhattan's Upper East Side and later a Victorian mansion on the Hudson River in suburban Nyack, became a center of witty conversation and monied entertainment. The couple brought together Hayes's actor friends Alfred Lunt, Lynn Fontanne, and Ruth Gordon with MacArthur's set from his days at the Algonquin Round Table, a wicked salon that included among its members George S. Kaufman, Harpo Marx, Dorothy Parker, Alexander Woollcott, and Robert Benchley.

The bicoastal careers of both partners flourished in the 1930s. Hayes won an Academy Award for the film *The Sin of Madelon Claudet* (1931), with a screenplay by MacArthur. She followed this with much-admired performances in *Arrowsmith* (1931) and what is often considered her best film, *A Farewell to Arms*, opposite Gary Cooper, in 1932. Hayes's stage portrayal of Mary Stuart in Maxwell Anderson's *Mary of Scotland* (1933–1934) was the prelude to what she came to value as her favorite stage role, Laurence Housman's *Victoria Regina*. In that play she aged from teenaged princess to elderly monarch in a memorable portrayal that captivated audiences (with some interruptions) between 1935 and 1939. In the meantime, MacArthur and Hecht had become the most highly paid screenwriting team in Hollywood.

During the war years Hayes appeared in Maxwell Anderson's anti-Nazi drama *Candle in the Wind* (1941–1942) and a stage biography of Harriet Beecher Stowe, *Harriet* (1943–1944). She won a Tony Award for best actress in 1947 for her performance in Anita Loos's *Happy Birthday*. Though Tennessee Williams would later blame Hayes for the "failure" of *The Glass Menagerie* in its 1948 London run, her performance was praised at the time as being equal to, though quite different from, Laurette Taylor's original creation of Amanda Wingfield. English actress Sybil Thorndike wrote to the play's director, John Gielgud, saying that "she fulfills all I feel about acting. . . . The funniness of her, the tragedy, the absurdity. . . . She has restored my faith. . . . Never for one moment does she let you see the wheels working though they are oiled marvelously" (Barrow, p. 154).

With the death of their only child, a nineteen-year-old daughter, from polio in 1949, both Hayes and MacArthur suffered personal and professional crises. Hayes was prodded from seclusion to perform in Joshua Logan's adaptation of *The Cherry Orchard* in March 1950, and, as time passed and roles accumulated, she slowly recovered. (The MacArthurs' adopted son, James MacArthur, born in 1938, had a brief career in films and a long-running role on television's "Hawaii Five-O.") Charles MacArthur found himself unable to write and slipped ever further into alcoholism, dying from related illnesses in 1956. Again emotionally shattered, Hayes kept working, keeping up a grueling pace of what was often simultaneous production in theater, film, and television. She was brought again to the attention of world audiences through her portrayal of the Russian grand duchess in the film *Anastasia* (1956) and was praised for her stage performances in Eugene O'Neill's *A Touch of the Poet* (1958) and repeated revivals of *The Skin of Our Teeth* and *The Glass Menagerie*.

Hayes surprised many observers when she joined the APA (Association of Producing Artists)–Phoenix Repertory Company at New York's Lyceum Theatre in 1966. The notion of the "First Lady of the American Theatre," as journalists often called her, appearing in small roles as part of a sustained company, was difficult for some to accept. Hayes embraced the experience, relishing the relief from the pressure of being the "star" on whose health and performance the livelihood of a full company and set of investors depended. The APA–Phoenix provided her the opportunity to play supporting roles such as Mrs. Candour in Sheridan's *The School for Scandal*, walk-ons such as Grand Duchess Olga in Kaufman and Hart's *You Can't Take It with You*, and the occasional large role, such as Mrs. Fisher in George Kelly's *The Show-Off*. Despite the presence of fine actors in good material, the APA–Phoenix did not survive in the New York commercial environment and dissolved after its second season. In 1971 Hayes became the first person to have won both best actress and best supporting actress Oscars when she was awarded the latter for her performance as a beguiling stowaway who is seated next to the mad bomber in the film *Airport*.

During rehearsals for a Washington production of O'Neill's *Long Day's Journey into Night* in 1971, Hayes suffered what was diagnosed as an allergic reaction to theater dust. She recovered sufficiently to complete the run of the play but announced at the closing performance that she would end her theatrical career in Washington, where it had begun.

Hayes continued to work, though less constantly, in television and film, appearing in three Disney films and starring in a television series ("The Snoop Sisters," 1973–1974). Hayes seemed to enjoy working wherever she could, regardless of the frequently obvious and quaint material that was offered to her. Her last performance was as Agatha Christie's Jane Marple, Hayes's third such project, in the television film *Murder by Mirrors* in 1985.

Hayes remained active in the charitable causes that she had championed since the 1940s, continuing as spokesperson for the March of Dimes (Jonas Salk had credited her with being a major contributor in the fight against polio). She died in Nyack.

Hayes's long life and career were, of course, intertwined, but they should not be confused with each other. The face that Hayes presented to the world—that of an amiable and generous nymph, matron, and then old lady—is surely distinguishable from the disciplined and resourceful artist who was repeatedly credited by critics with having avoided sentimentality in roles that invited it. Within the amiable and much-loved personality was an intuitive, resourceful, and highly skilled theater artist.

• Hayes's scrapbooks, photographs, programs, and other memorabilia comprise the Helen Hayes Collection in the Billy Rose Theatre Collection, New York Public Library for the Performing Arts, Lincoln Center. Hayes wrote three volumes of memoirs: *A Gift of Joy* (1965), *On Reflection* (1968), and *My Life in Three Acts* (1990). An outstanding source of information on Hayes is Donn B. Murphy and Stephen Moore, *Helen Hayes: A Bio-Bibliography* (1993), which contains an exhaustive and annotated bibliography, a comprehensive listing of Hayes's performances, and a concise biographical essay. Kenneth Barrow, *Helen Hayes: First Lady of the American Theatre* (1985), is a full-length biography that benefits from thorough research and interviews with Hayes. Hayes's mother wrote a biography of the young actress, *Letters to Mary: The Story of Helen Hayes* (1940). Jhan Robbins, *Front Page Marriage* (1982), details the relationship between Hayes and MacArthur. An obituary is in the *New York Times*, 18 Mar. 1993.

MARK FEARNOW

HAYES, Ira (12 Jan. 1923–24 Jan. 1955), soldier, was born Ira Hamilton Hayes on the Gila River Indian Reservation at Sacaton, Arizona, the son of Joe Hayes and Nancy (maiden name unknown), farmers. Hayes's father worried about providing irrigation for his crops, and his mother believed in providing her children with a good education. Both parents instilled in their children a pride for their Pima Indian heritage, a sense of duty to country, and a love of the land. The family moved from Sacaton to Bapchule, a town on the reservation forty miles from Phoenix, when Ira was nine years old. Their housing was a small one-room adobe hut whose doorway faced east to take advantage of the warmth of the morning sun. On one wall an American flag was tacked among a collection of religious pictures. Ira was educated at reservation schools.

After World War II erupted, Hayes enlisted in the marines in 1942. As was the tradition, Pima tribal elders, church leaders, and the choir spoke to Hayes before he left, telling him to never dishonor his tribe. Although discrimination was prevalent, Hayes overcame the cultural differences in the marines and formed friendships. Still, he was often teased, but he accepted his nickname "Chief" and felt proud to be a marine.

Hayes was sent overseas as part of the First Marine Division. After a campaign at Guadalcanal resulted in heavy casualties among paratroopers, the marines advertised for recruits and offered incentive pay of $50 extra per month. Hayes enthusiastically joined and became the first Pima Indian paratrooper and earned a promotion to private first class.

Assigned to the Third Parachute Battalion, Hayes fought through campaigns on Vella Lavella and Bougainville. His battalion was part of the forces that invaded the Japanese-held island of Iwo Jima in 1945. In the midst of the battle on 23 February 1945, a flag was raised on the summit of Mount Suribachi to hearten the fighting men and to send an image of victory back home. As the battle wore on, the commanders ordered a second, larger and more visible flag to be raised on Suribachi. As the men rushed to hold up the second flag, they called out for extra help. Ira Hayes was one of the two men summoned. He joined five other men, and in an instant Associated Press photographer Joe Rosenthal caught them on film. The picture had good composition, but the quality was not good and only one face could be seen, and yet the picture made headlines and changed Ira Hayes's life forever.

After weeks of fighting, Iwo Jima was secured. The marines suffered the worst casualties in their history, including three of the men who had helped raise the flag. Hayes received a Letter of Commendation with Ribbon and was recommended for a Bronze Star. The flag-raising photograph became a famous symbol of heroism, and the public clamored for the identities of the men to be revealed. Five of the six men were identified, but Hayes tried to remain anonymous. Marine officials eventually succumbed to increasing pressure and revealed Hayes as the sixth man; he was reassigned to civilian duty to promote war bonds. Overnight he became a hero, a title he did not wish to have.

Hayes joined the other two flag-raising survivors as they attended Red Cross drives and patriotic celebrations and spoke to church groups to pitch the sale of war bonds. Everywhere Hayes went, people shook his hand and passed him a drink. But privately many disparaging comments were made about the "Indian." A shy young man, Hayes wanted to be taken out of the limelight and said he wished that "that guy had never made the picture." After getting drunk on the tour,

Hayes was returned to active duty overseas. Before his discharge on 1 December 1945, the marines promoted him to corporal.

After World War II Hayes returned home to pick cotton. The celebrity status followed him though, as people stopped at the reservation to have him sign autographs and journalists badgered him for interviews. Sometimes he went into Phoenix, became drunk, and landed in jail. He tried to pull himself together numerous times and had a bit part in the filming of the *Sands of Iwo Jima* (1949), posed for the bronze statue of the flag raising that became the U.S. Marine Corps War Memorial, and took a job as a tool grinder at International Harvester in Chicago, Illinois. He kept drinking, made headlines, and was given help from Elizabeth Martin, the ex-wife of comedian Dean Martin. Feeling guilt for being a celebrity instead of dying on Iwo Jima and dodging the notoriety of the newspapers and facing prejudice, Hayes drifted from place to place, continued to drink, and was arrested fifty-one times.

Ira Hayes died of exposure and chronic alcoholism in Bapchule, Arizona. He was buried at Arlington National Cemetery, not far from the Iwo Jima Memorial, the bronze statue for which he once posed. In 1986 a memorial honoring the American Indian veterans was dedicated near his gravesite.

After his death, stories of the ill-fated Ira Hayes continued. A 1960 NBC television program, "The American," which highlighted the life of Hayes, aired despite protests filed by the Pima Indians and controversy over its accuracy and the image it portrayed of a drunken Indian. A subsequent movie, titled *The Outsider*, was filmed in 1961 intending to vindicate Hayes but instead emphasizing the division between races. In 1964 singer Johnny Cash recorded the best-known version of Peter La Farge's "The Ballad of Ira Hayes." Hayes became a victim symbolic of the American Indian who had been exploited and then neglected by white society.

Hayes never desired the notoriety that befell him and often even denied being one of the flag raisers on Iwo Jima that day. Claiming that he did not deserve to be a celebrity, he once told Elizabeth Martin that "the real heroes are still on Iwo Jima." Ira Hayes, who had only wished to serve his country with honor as a marine, remained doomed after death to be a convenient symbol of heroism and of victimization.

• No manuscript sources exist for Ira Hayes. A biographical work is Albert Hemingway, *Ira Hayes: Pima Marine* (1988). Other sources include "Suribachi to Skid Row," *Newsweek*, 26 Oct. 1953; "Heroes—Then There Were Two," *Time*, 7 Feb. 1955; "Ira Hayes—Our Accuser," *Christian Century*, 9 Feb. 1955; "This Be the Verse You Grave for Me," *Amerindian-American Indian Review*, Mar.–Apr. 1955; William Bradford Huie, *The Hero of Iwo Jima and Other Stories* (1962); Richard R. Newcomb, *Iwo Jima* (1965); Joseph Rosenthal and W. C. Heinz, "The Picture That Will Live Forever," *Fifth Marine Division Reunion Journal* (1978); and Karal Ann Marling and John Wetenhall, *Iwo Jima: Monuments, Memories, and the American Hero* (1991).

MARILYN ELIZABETH PERRY

HAYES, Johnny (10 Apr. 1886–23 Aug. 1965), Olympic marathon champion and professional runner, was born John Joseph Hayes in New York City, the son of poor Irish farming parents (names unknown) from the town of Nanagh, Tipperary, located near the river Shannon. He spent much of his youth running through the streets of Manhattan and was described as a 5′4″, 125-pound "nickled steel athlete, black-haired, blue-eyed, freckle-faced, with a ton of confidence in himself." He joined the St. Bartholomew's Club as well as the Irish-American Athletic Club and began his career as a long-distance runner.

Hayes finished third behind Canada's Tom Longboat and Bob Fowler in the prestigious Boston Marathon of 1907. The next year, after Hayes finished close to J. P. Morrisey in the 1908 Boston race, Michael Murphy, the legendary Yale University coach and leader of the American Olympic team, chose him to run in the Olympic marathon in London that same year. Hayes was just twenty-two, a startlingly youthful age for an international marathon runner.

Young Hayes faced formidable opposition in London, including the undefeated road runner Tom Longboat; six well-coached American marathoners; a team of resolute English veterans; the South African record holder C. C. Hefferon; and the European champion from Italy, the diminutive Dorando Pietri: seventy-five competitors altogether. The race began at Windsor Castle underneath the balcony of King Edward VII, exactly 26 miles and 385 yards (42 kilometers) from the finish line inside the Shepherd's Bush Stadium. Hayes later recalled standing restlessly at the starting line. It was an exceedingly warm day, 24 July 1908. "The castle grounds were exquisitely beautiful. I began to wonder if the interior of the castle was as beautiful as the view from its windows must be," Hayes wrote.

But there was little time for reverie as the starting cannon fired. From the beginning the calculating New Yorker was sure that Pietri was the man to beat, and he was determined to follow him throughout. England's Price and Lord passed 10 miles in 56 minutes, 53 seconds, with Hefferon in 57:12, Pietri in 57:13, and Hayes, eyes focused on the Italian, a hundred yards back. The Englishmen were gone at 15 miles, with Hefferon, Longboat, and Pietri leading and Hayes in close attendance. The temperature rose with each mile completed. Longboat collapsed at 17 miles; at 20 miles it was Hefferon (2 hours, 02 minutes), Pietri (2 hours, 06 minutes), and the little metronome Hayes close and focused on Pietri. At 25 miles, according to Theodore Andrea Cook, Pietri "made his fatal sprint," passed Hefferon, and entered the stadium "almost unconscious, turned right instead of left," and fell down on the cinder track. He was helped to his feet and turned around by British officials, staggered a few yards, and in full view of a huge, horrified audience, crumpled to the ground again. Hayes, having passed Hefferon, entered the stadium, and semisprinted around the track.

British officials picked up Pietri once again and dragged him across the finish line; he was the Olympic marathon champion but for just a few hours. The Olympic jury reluctantly disqualified Pietri for receiving illegal assistance. Hayes was declared winner of the gold medal. He returned to New York City to a ticker tape parade down Fifth Avenue and an audience with the president at his summer home at Sagamore Hill ("President Will See Athletes at Oyster Bay," *New York Daily Tribune*, 14 Aug. 1908). Theodore Roosevelt, addressing the entire victorious American team, selected the marathon victor for special commendation. "Johnny, you are a top-notcher," Roosevelt said, shaking Hayes's hand with all vigor.

Professional long-distance running in America, already an established and popular spectator sport, received an immense boost as a result of Hayes's dramatic victory in London. A marathon craze swept major eastern cities, and the little New Yorker earned a fortune, $35,000 in the years 1908–1911. He was the American marathon coach in 1912 and accompanied the team to Stockholm, Sweden, where his athletes took four of the top eight places, establishing the United States as an international force in marathon running. Hayes's contribution was significant. After the First World War and for many years, Hayes worked as a food broker in New York City. He died in Englewood, New Jersey.

• Hayes wrote "How I Won the Marathon Race," *Cosmopolitan*, Dec. 1908, pp. 113–18. Sir Arthur Conan Doyle wrote 2,000 words titled "Dorando Scene" in the *Times* (London), 25 July 1908. The 1896 Olympic gold medalist, James B. Connolly, wrote "The Shepherd's Bush Greeks," *Collier's Weekly*, 5 Sept. 1908, pp. 14–15; see also John Lucas, "The Professional Marathon Craze in America 1908–1909," *Quarterly Review of the U.S. Track Coaches Association*, Dec. 1968, pp. 31–36. The marathon is discussed in Theodore Andrea Cook, *The Fourth Olympiad Report 1908* (1909), pp. 67–86; the *New York Daily Tribune*, 14 Aug. 1908; the *New York Herald*, 9 Aug. 1908; and the *Boston Globe*, 23 Sept. 1908. Obituaries are in the *Times* (London), 26 Aug. 1965; the *New York Herald Tribune*, 25 Aug. 1965; and the *New York Times*, 26 Aug. 1965.

JOHN A. LUCAS

HAYES, Lucy Ware Webb (28 Aug. 1831–25 June 1889), wife of the nineteenth president of the United States, was born in Chillicothe, Ohio, the daughter of James Webb, a medical doctor, and Maria Cook. When Lucy was two, her father died during a cholera epidemic in Kentucky, where he had gone to free slaves he had recently inherited. Until Lucy and her two older brothers needed better schools, they lived with their mother in Chillicothe. In 1844 the family moved to Delaware, Ohio, where Lucy entered the preparatory department of what is now Ohio Wesleyan University. Later she took courses in the college department, where her brothers were enrolled, even though young women were not usually allowed to study there. It was near the popular sulphur spring on the school's campus that visiting Rutherford B. Hayes first met "bright-eyed," clever, and "sunny-hearted" Lucy, whom at fifteen he found "not quite old enough to fall in love with" (Geer, p. 7). A few months later Lucy transferred to Cincinnati Wesleyan Female College, one of the first colleges in the United States to give degrees to women. In 1850, during her last year, Lucy was asked to speak at her graduation, elected a member of the exclusive Young Ladies Lyceum, and visited by Hayes, who had become a lawyer and moved to Cincinnati.

Late that summer Lucy and Hayes were members of a wedding party, and seeing her "bright eyes and merry smile" again gave him such a "peculiar" feeling that he gave her the gold ring he was lucky enough to find in his piece of wedding cake. When they were secretly engaged the next summer, Lucy put the wedding-cake ring on his finger, and Hayes wore it the rest of his life. They were married in Lucy's home in Cincinnati on 30 December 1852. Before a year was over the first of their eight children was born. Influenced by Lucy's antislavery sentiments, Hayes, who had thought abolitionists too radical, began defending runaway slaves who had crossed the Ohio River from Kentucky. Influenced, in turn, by Rutherford Hayes's feelings against woman suffrage, Lucy, who had two aunts active in the women's movement and after hearing Lucy Stone had herself conceded that reform was needed, did not work for women's rights.

Thanks to the help of her mother, Hayes was freed from the constant care of her children. Taking an active part in her husband's political career, she accompanied him to Indianapolis to ride back to Cincinnati with President-elect Abraham Lincoln. After southerners attacked Fort Sumter, she enthusiastically supported his decision to volunteer for the Union army. Half a dozen times during the Civil War, Lucy Hayes—sometimes accompanied by her mother and children and always participating fully in camp life—joined her husband. Adored by young officers and common soldiers, she often helped her brother Joe, the surgeon of Hayes's regiment, care for the sick. She spent her "bitterest hour" in camp, when her infant son Joe sickened and died (Geer, p. 64). Sadly, the experience was not unique; two of her other boys would die in babyhood.

When Rutherford Hayes became a congressman, Lucy Hayes, wearing a checkered shawl he could easily spot, was often in the chamber's diplomatic gallery. During his terms as Ohio governor, she worked for children and veterans, securing state funding for an orphanage she had started for veterans' children. Rutherford Hayes acknowledged her support. "My life with you has been so happy—so successful—so beyond reasonable anticipations," he told her, "that I think of you with a loving gratitude that I do not know how to express" (Williams, vol. 3, p. 120).

On 2 March 1877, a few hours after the disputed presidential election had been decided, the Hayes family arrived in Washington, D.C. Reporters noted that Lucy Hayes, the first president's wife to have graduated from college, was striking and self-confident. Always fond of people and entertaining, she invited young friends and relatives from Ohio to help make large White House events more friendly and less formal. After angering temperance organizations by serving wine and liquor at a state dinner, Rutherford Hayes—who realized the importance of the temperance vote to the Republican party—decided not to serve alcohol at the White House. Because Lucy Hayes was a Methodist teetotaler, she was blamed for his decision. Although no one called her "Lemonade Lucy" at the time, the alliteration—made evident in a newspaper poem poking fun at the policy and called "Lemonade"—is probably responsible for the appellation, frequently used in the twentieth century.

Hayes was best at informal gatherings. "She has the reputation of fascinating her visitors," the New York *Graphic*'s correspondent observed on 18 March 1878, "because . . . she is so vivacious and so responsive that everybody leaves her presence with a vague idea that he is the one person whom she was longing to see." On Sunday evenings, Hayes, who had an unusually strong and sweet voice (and sometimes accompanied herself on the guitar), gathered friends and family to sing with her around a piano, usually played by Secretary of the Interior Carl Schurz. Vice President William Almon Wheeler—with whom Lucy Hayes sometimes went fishing—was almost always a member of this group.

Hayes continued her work for veterans and young people. She often visited the National Deaf Mute College and Hampton Institute in Virginia, where she furnished a scholarship for an American Indian girl. In the month of January 1880 alone, Hayes and her husband gave $990 of their own money to help the poor in Washington.

It chagrined Hayes to see from White House windows the abandoned, unfinished monument to George Washington, begun forty years earlier. Nudged by her interest, President Hayes consulted experts, had the foundation of the monument strengthened, and made its completion his "hobby" (Williams, vol. 4, p. 302). Wanting to combine elegance and American design in new dishes for the White House, Hayes asked Theodore R. Davis, an artist noted for his knowledge of American plants and animals, to design them. After dining on them, Marian Hooper "Clover" Adams, a celebrated Washington hostess and letter writer, complained, "To eat one's soup calmly with a coyote springing at you from a pine tree is intimidating" (Friedrich, *Clover* [1979], p. 262).

Hayes was the happiest when she was surrounded by young people and animals. With the White House usually crowded, the Hayes children and their visiting friends often had to sleep on cots in hallways, couches in reception rooms, or even in large bathtubs. Pets included the country's first Siamese cat, a loud-singing mockingbird, two dogs, and a goat, who hauled youngest son Scott around the White House grounds in a cart. Because Congress no longer permitted area children to roll eggs on the Capitol grounds, Lucy Hayes invited them in 1880 to use the White House lawn on Easter Monday, and this activity has become a tradition.

During her last months in the White House, Hayes was acclaimed "the most widely known and popular President's wife the country has known" (Geer, p. 232). In 1880 she had become the national president of her church's Woman's Home Missionary Society, an organization to improve the living conditions of destitute American women by operating small industrial homes and by supporting schools, especially for former slaves, American Indians, and Hispanic-Americans. After she and Rutherford Hayes left Washington for "Spiegel Grove," their Fremont, Ohio, home, Lucy Hayes remained the president of this organization and regularly addressed its annual meeting in cities such as Philadelphia and Detroit. While seated at a bay window sewing and watching her daughter play tennis, Hayes suffered a stroke and died at home a few days later.

• The Lucy Webb Hayes Papers are located at the Hayes Presidential Center in Fremont, Ohio. She is also frequently mentioned in other collections there, as she is in Charles Richard Williams, ed., *Diary and Letters of Rutherford Birchard Hayes: Nineteenth President of the United States* (5 vols., 1922–1926). The most complete assessment of her is Emily Apt Geer, *First Lady: The Life of Lucy Webb Hayes* (1984). An obituary is in the *New York Times*, 26 June 1889.

OLIVE HOOGENBOOM

HAYES, Max Sebastian (25 May 1866–11 Oct. 1945), labor editor and trade union leader, was born in Huron County, Ohio, the son of Joseph Maximilian Sebastian Hoize and Elizabeth Storer, farmers. His parents, immigrants from central Europe, had changed their name to Hayes and made their way to Ohio by ox team. Hayes attended grammar school in Fremont, Ohio, where he became an apprentice printer in 1879. In 1883 the Hayes family moved to Cleveland, and Hayes began a lifelong career in journalism by going to work on the *Cleveland Press*.

In 1891 Hayes and Henry Long founded the *Cleveland Citizen*, the oldest labor newspaper in America. It became the official instrument of the Cleveland Central Labor Union, and Hayes became its editor in 1892. In the early years of the *Citizen*, Hayes was a proponent of the eight-hour-day movement, populism, and the single tax. But, in 1896, the year he joined the Socialist Labor party (SLP), Hayes told his readers that such reforms were only ameliorative, urging them to join the working-class political movement and to vote in the "cooperative commonwealth." For several years the *International Socialist Review* featured Hayes's regular review of labor issues, but his fame in the circles of labor journalism came primarily through his continued editorial leadership of the *Citizen* until ill health forced him to step down in 1939.

Hayes played a prominent role in Socialist politics from 1899 to 1920. In 1899 he joined with Morris Hillquit and others in opposing the dominance of SLP leader Daniel DeLeon. The following year this "kangaroo" faction named Hayes as its vice presidential candidate. The typographer withdrew his nomination, however, when the dissident Socialist Laborites and the Social Democratic party agreed upon a joint ticket featuring Eugene Debs and Job Harriman. Instead, Hayes ran unsuccessfully for Congress that year. In 1900 Hayes also married Dora Schneider, a retail clerk, and the couple had one daughter.

Hayes's long association with the Socialist Party of America dated from its creation in 1901 as a result of the merger of the Socialist Labor insurgents with the Social Democrats, a merger in which Hayes played a large role. Hayes served as an SPA national committee member and developed a close friendship with party leader Eugene Debs. In 1912 Hayes declined an opportunity to run for the party's presidential nomination because he supported Debs. Although they initially differed on their view of the syndicalist Industrial Workers of the World, with Hayes remaining more critical of the organization, the two remained politically close during the heydey of American socialism.

Hayes's prominence as a Socialist editor grew as his influence in the labor movement rose. He joined Local 53 of the International Typographical Union (ITU) while working at the *Cleveland Press* and served as the Cleveland Central Labor Union's delegate to the American Federation of Labor's (AFL) annual conventions between 1898 and 1901. Later he regularly attended the AFL conventions as the representative of the ITU until 1937. Like many other Socialist party leaders, Hayes focused inordinately on political action. He argued incessantly for Socialists to work from within the trade union movement and for trade unionists to engage in radical politics. In the 1890s Hayes attacked the Socialist Trades and Labor Alliance for competing against established trade unions. Later he was critical of the short-lived American Labor Union, conceived as a national, radical labor center to challenge the AFL. In 1905 he rejected an invitation to the meeting at which the syndicalist Industrial Workers of the World was formed, preferring instead to remain "inside the [AFL] fort and take chances to secure the adoption of my plans than be outside and be regarded as an enemy" (Dubofsky, p. 77). It made no sense, Hayes asserted in 1907, for Socialists to waste their time "splitting hairs" over the question of whether to support industrial unionism or craft organizing. In fact, Hayes was a determined opponent of industrial unionism. Later his loyalty to the AFL's craft-based tradition propelled his opposition to the Congress of Industrial Organizations (CIO) as it revitalized the moribund labor movement in the 1930s.

Although Hayes remained an active proponent of socialism in the AFL in the 1910s, political developments caused him to distance himself from the Socialist party. In 1911 Hayes challenged Samuel Gompers's long tenure as president of the AFL. Hayes's campaign hoped to persuade the AFL to endorse socialism and political action, taking it beyond the conservative, "bread-and-butter" unionism favored by the long-reigning cigar maker. At the convention Hayes won 30 percent of the vote, a high-water mark of left-wing influence in the national labor body. American involvement in World War I weakened Hayes's commitment to the SPA. As a socialist he had been critical of the war in Europe, but when the United States entered the war in April 1917, he sided with the AFL and against the SPA by choosing to support the American war effort. The political tensions excited by the war were exacerbated by the Bolshevik Revolution. Hayes eventually broke with the Socialist party after Charles Ruthenberg, a left-wing Socialist who would become a cofounder of the Communist Party of America, won control of the leadership of the Ohio party in 1918.

In 1919 and 1920, Hayes played a leading role in the formation of the National Labor party, which merged into the Farmer-Labor party (FLP) in 1920. That year he was also named the FLP's vice presidential candidate; Hayes and Parley Christensen, a Progressive Utah lawyer, garnered 300,000 votes, largely in the rural West. Debs, running for the fifth time on the Socialist party ticket, racked up more than 900,000 votes. In 1924 Hayes worked with the Conference for Progressive Political Action and helped bring out the vote in Cleveland for its candidate, Robert M. LaFollette. During the 1930s Hayes enthusiastically supported the New Deal. He served on the Ohio state adjustment board of the National Recovery Administration and was a member of the Cleveland Metropolitan Housing Authority. Hayes suffered a stroke in 1939, which left him partially paralyzed; he died six years later in his Shaker Heights, Ohio, home.

• The Max S. Hayes Collection at the Ohio Historical Society contains the bulk of Hayes's correspondence and important papers. As a founding member of the Consumers League of Ohio, he is also represented in the records of that organization, which are held in the Western Reserve Historical Society in Cleveland. The pages of the *Cleveland Citizen* (1891–1939) offer the best view of Hayes's Socialist philosophy and view of trade unionism. Hayes's columns in the *International Socialist Review* (1910–1911) also offer a glimpse of his views on contemporary labor issues and radical politics. Morris Hillquit et al., eds., *The Double Edge of Labor's Sword* (1914), contains excerpts of his testimony before the U.S. Commission on Industrial Relations. Hayes's role in the founding and development of the Socialist party is discussed in Howard Quint, *The Forging of American Socialism* (1953); Ira Kipnis, *The American Socialist Movement* (1952); and Nick Salvatore, *Eugene V. Debs* (1982). Hayes's trade union philosophy is briefly discussed in David Montgomery, *The Fall of the House of Labor* (1989), and Melvyn Dubofsky, *We Shall Be All* (1969). An obituary is in the *New York Times*, 12 Oct. 1945.

Eric J. Karolak

HAYES, Patrick Joseph (20 Nov. 1867–4 Sept. 1938), cardinal archbishop, was born in New York City, the son of Irish immigrants Daniel Hayes, a longshoreman, and Mary Gleason, both natives of Killarney. His mother died when he was five, and about a year later his father married Mary Dunning. Young Patrick lived with his father and stepmother until he was about fifteen, when he went to live with his mother's sister and brother-in-law, Ellen and James Egan, who were childless.

Hayes's education from grammar school to college took place entirely in institutions conducted by the Christian Brothers in New York City—Transfiguration parochial school, De La Salle Institute, and Manhattan College, where he received the A.B. with high honors in 1888. After deciding to study for the priesthood, Hayes entered St. Joseph's Provincial Seminary in Troy, New York, the major seminary of the Archdiocese of New York, where he was a student from 1888 to 1892. After ordination to the priesthood by Archbishop Michael A. Corrigan on 8 September 1892, Hayes spent an additional two years studying at the Catholic University of America in Washington, D.C., where he received the S.T.L. in 1894.

After Hayes's return to New York, he was assigned as a curate to the Manhattan parish of St. Gabriel, whose pastor was Monsignor John Murphy Farley, one of the most prominent clerics in the archdiocese. Hayes won the confidence of Farley, who thereafter guided his ecclesiastical career. When Farley became New York's first auxiliary bishop in 1895, he selected Hayes as his secretary. Farley became archbishop of New York in 1902, and in the following year Farley appointed Hayes chancellor of the archdiocese and president of Cathedral College, the newly established archdiocesan preparatory seminary located in Manhattan adjacent to St. Patrick's Cathedral. Hayes filled both of these positions until 28 October 1914, when he was appointed auxiliary bishop of New York.

From 1915 until 1917 Hayes served as pastor of the large Manhattan parish of St. Stephen. On 24 November 1917 he was appointed military ordinary with responsibility for the Catholics in the armed forces, a newly created post made necessary by the rapid expansion of the armed forces after the entry of the United States into World War I. Within a year, for example, the number of Catholic army chaplains increased from twenty-five to almost nine hundred. As military ordinary, Hayes coordinated the activities of the Catholic chaplains and visited military installations throughout the United States.

While still military ordinary, Hayes played a key role in the establishment in 1917 of the National Catholic War Council, the first permanent national organization of U.S. Catholic bishops. Hayes served as one of four episcopal members of the original administrative committee, and, after the war, he was a strong supporter of the successor organization to the War Council, the National Catholic Welfare Conference. In 1919, as a member of the administrative committee of the NCWC, Hayes was one of four bishops who signed the progressive *Program of Social Reconstruction*, written by Catholic University professor John A. Ryan.

On 10 March 1919 Hayes succeeded Farley as the fifth archbishop of New York. The archdiocese was still the largest in the United States in population and reputed to be the wealthiest. During the 1920s and 1930s, however, the Catholic population in New York fell from about 1.25 million to about 1 million due to the decline in immigration and the movement of the middle class to the suburbs outside the archdiocese. However, there was still a need for additional parishes. Hayes established sixty-five new parishes, all but five of them before the onset of the Great Depression in 1929. By 1934 almost a million people in New York City were receiving government relief, and Hayes was known to be a discreet supporter of the social policies of the Franklin Roosevelt administration.

A shy man with a narrow range of interests, Hayes shunned the limelight and consistently refused invitations to public affairs. He presided over a largely decentralized archdiocese where the local pastors enjoyed wide autonomy, especially in financial matters. Hayes's episcopate was a halcyon period in New York Catholicism, an era of crowded churches, full convents, obedient clergy, deferential laity, and—at least until the onset of the Great Depression—generous collections. Tammany Hall, the local Democratic organization, was so responsive to Catholic wishes that the archbishop's residence at 452 Madison Avenue was popularly known as "The Powerhouse." One of Hayes's few administrative "problems" was the excessive number of vocations to the diocesan priesthood, which led him in the late 1930s to decrease by one-third the enrollment in the archdiocesan seminary at Dunwoodie.

Hayes demonstrated imaginative leadership during the restructuring of the charitable organizations and institutions of the archdiocese. Between 1910 and 1916 a series of city and state investigations had criticized the management of some Catholic institutions. In 1919 Hayes sponsored a careful survey of these institutions by a team of salaried professionals, which led in 1920 to the legal incorporation of the Catholic Charities of the Archdiocese of New York, a supervisory umbrella organization that set new standards of professionalism for Catholic social service agencies throughout the United States.

On 24 March 1924 Hayes was appointed a cardinal. He played an active role as a diocesan administrator until in 1932 he suffered a serious heart attack, which restricted his activities thereafter. He died in his sleep at St. Joseph's Camp in Monticello, New York. The *New York Times* commented, "The sincerest tribute that can be paid to any man is to be mourned by the poor. Cardinal Hayes will be so mourned. He had them always in his heart" (5 Sept. 1938).

• Hayes's papers are in the archives of the Archdiocese of New York. The best summary of his career is Florence D. Cohalan, *A Popular History of the Archdiocese of New York* (1983). Two popular hagiographical works are J. B. Kelly, *Cardinal Hayes* (1940), and Parish Visitors of Mary Immaculate, eds., *The Cardinal of Charities* (1927). An obituary is in the *New York Times*, 5 Sept. 1938.

THOMAS J. SHELLEY

HAYES, Roland (3 June 1887–31 Dec. 1976), singer, was born in Curryville, Georgia, the son of William Hayes and Fanny (maiden name unknown), tenant farmers and former slaves. Young Roland worked as a fieldhand from an early age alongside his mother and two brothers. William Hayes had become an invalid following an accident when Roland was an infant, and he died when Roland was twelve.

Although neither parent could read or write, Fanny Hayes was determined that her children would get an education. However, Roland was able to attend local country schools, which were inferior and segregated, only for a few months at a time, when he was not needed in the fields. At the age of fifteen, he and his family moved to Chattanooga, Tennessee, as part of a plan his mother had devised to have her sons educated. The three boys were to alternate school and work a year at a time, with one brother working to help support the family while the two others studied.

Hayes found employment as a laborer in a machine shop, and despite the harsh working conditions (in one of several accidents, hot iron splashed on his feet and left permanent scars) he rose to foreman. When his turn came to take a year off and attend school, he decided against it because he was making more than his brothers could earn. He therefore stayed at the machine shop and was tutored in the evenings by a local black teacher.

Like his fellow workers, Hayes often sang as he labored. At his church, his distinctive tenor voice attracted the attention of the choir director, a black man named W. Arthur Calhoun who was taking a year off from his studies at Oberlin College Conservatory in Ohio. Calhoun persuaded Hayes to sing in the choir and offered to help him develop his voice. Fanny Hayes refused to let Calhoun give her son singing lessons, however, believing that black musicians were trashy riffraff. Calhoun persisted, however, and one day took Hayes to the home of a prosperous white man who owned a phonograph. When the man played operatic recordings, including performances by the Italian tenor Enrico Caruso, Hayes was overwhelmed—he later described it as a mystical experience—and vowed that despite his mother's opposition he would become a singer.

With Calhoun's encouragement, Hayes set out for Oberlin, but when he reached Nashville he realized he did not have enough money to continue the journey. He enrolled instead at Fisk University, an all-black institution in Nashville, where he was placed in the preparatory division. Hayes studied at Fisk for four years and took singing lessons there; he supported himself by working as a servant. Then suddenly, in 1910, he was dismissed from the school—apparently because he had begun singing for organizations off-campus and had not received the required permission from school authorities to do so.

The dejected Hayes moved farther north, to Louisville, Kentucky, and became a waiter in a men's club. His voice again attracted attention, and he was asked to sing at various gatherings. Hayes had remained in touch with his singing teacher at Fisk, and in 1911 he was asked to join the university's famous performing group, the Fisk Jubilee Singers, in a concert appearance in Boston. Putting aside his bitterness, Hayes agreed. After the concert, he decided to stay in Boston, which became his home for the remainder of his life.

Hayes worked first as a hotel bellboy and then as a messenger at an insurance company while continuing his vocal studies with Arthur J. Hubbard, a teacher of same renown. When his brothers married, Hayes moved his mother to Boston; she lived with him there; and he supported her on his small wages. Their home was a tenement room, and they used packing boxes for furniture. Fanny Hayes was now supportive of her son's decision, and her encouragement, combined with Hubbard's, fueled Hayes's determination to be a great singer.

In 1917, with the help of Hubbard, Hayes rented Symphony Hall in Boston to give a recital—the first black musician ever to do so. His performance of Negro spirituals, lieder, and continental art songs was a notable success, and it launched his career. However, opportunities for black singers in the United States were limited, and Hayes knew that a climb to prominence would take time. After four years of local appearances, he had saved enough money to go abroad. In 1921 he gave several recitals in London, including a command performance for King George V and Queen Mary at Buckingham Palace. He then went on to appear in Paris, Vienna, and Prague, taking voice lessons in those cities.

Upon his return to the United States after a triumphal year in Europe, Hayes was hailed as a musical sensation. Singing a repertoire of spirituals, folk and art songs, and occasional operatic arias, he began what was to become a series of concert appearances throughout the United States and Europe during the next four decades. In addition to recitals, Hayes appeared with the Boston, Philadelphia, and Detroit symphonies, the New York Philharmonic, and leading orchestras in Paris, Amsterdam, Vienna, and Berlin. Many noted musicians of the twentieth century, including Ignace Paderewski, Serge Rachmaninoff, Pablo Casals, Fritz Kreisler, and Nellie Melba, championed Hayes, who became the first black to be recognized as a serious musician on the American concert stage.

A deeply religious man throughout his life, Hayes believed that God had given him his voice for a purpose: to express the soul of his race. Hayes's success served as an example to younger black singers, and his encouragement of Marian Anderson, Paul Robeson, and others helped launch their careers. Tragically, although some critics considered Hayes the equal of Lauritz Melchior, Giovanni Martinelli, and other renowned operatic tenors who were his contemporaries, his race deprived him of a career in opera. Black performers began to appear on the American operatic stage only after Anderson's debut with the Metropolitan Opera in 1955, and by then Hayes was in his late sixties.

Hayes refused to become embroiled in discussions about racism, even after a widely publicized incident in 1942: he and his family were arrested in a shoe store in Rome, Georgia, after they sat in chairs reserved for whites. "I am not bitter," he said after his release. "I am only ashamed that this should happen in my native state. I love Georgia."

Hayes continued to perform in public until the early 1960s. To mark his seventy-fifth birthday, in June 1962 he gave a recital at Carnegie Hall in New York City, and in a ceremony at City Hall he was honored by Mayor Robert F. Wagner and a number of distinguished black performers, including Robeson, Anderson, and Leontyne Price.

Hayes was married to Helen A. Mann (the exact date of the marriage is unknown); they had one daughter, who later became a concert singer under the name Afrika Lambe. The family maintained a home in Brookline, Massachusetts, a Boston suburb, as well as a 600-acre farm in Curryville, Georgia, which included his birthplace. One of Hayes's most valued possessions was the original phonograph from Chattanooga on which he heard operatic music for the first time. During his lifetime, Hayes received numerous awards, including the Spingarn Medal and eight honorary degrees. He died in Boston.

• Further information on Roland Hayes can be found in Mackinley Helm, *Angel Mo' and Her Son* (1942). See also Maud Hare, *Negro Musicians and Their Music* (1936), Benjamin Griffith Brawley, *Negro Genius* (1937), and William L. Stidger, *The Human Side of Greatness* (1940). An obituary appears in the *New York Times*, 2 Jan. 1977.

ANN T. KEENE

HAYES, Rutherford Birchard (4 Oct. 1822–17 Jan. 1893), nineteenth president of the United States, was born in Delaware, Ohio, the posthumous son of Rutherford Hayes, Jr., a farmer and distiller, and Sophia Birchard. Puny at birth, Hayes unexpectedly survived and grew strong, but his mother remained overly protective—especially after his older brother Lorenzo drowned while ice-skating—and would not let him join other boys in rough play. His precocious sister Fanny—with whom Hayes remained unusually close until her death in 1856—was his constant companion.

Although his tethered existence lasted until he was nine years old, it apparently did Hayes little harm; when finally his mother untied the apron strings, he excelled in sports and made friends easily. Hayes admired his carefree bachelor uncle, Sardis Birchard, who served as his surrogate father, visiting the household often after removing from it when Hayes was four. As Birchard prospered he helped his sister when her income, from lodgers and a rented farm, failed to cover unusual expenditures.

In 1838 Hayes entered Kenyon College at Gambier, Ohio, and in 1842 graduated at the head of his class. After a disappointing year of reading law in Columbus, he entered the Harvard Law School, studied under Simon Greenleaf and Supreme Court Justice Joseph Story, and received his bachelor of laws degree in 1845.

Hayes first practiced law in Birchard's little town of Lower Sandusky (now Fremont), Ohio, but in 1850 he moved to Cincinnati. There on 30 December 1852, as he began to make his mark, he married Lucy Ware Webb (Lucy Webb Hayes), a Methodist graduate of Wesleyan Female College, who had strong abolitionist and temperance beliefs. In contrast, Hayes had little interest in reform and had neither experienced conversion nor joined a church. A lifelong "worshipper" of Ralph Waldo Emerson (Hayes to Oliver Wendell Holmes, 21 Nov. 1885, Holmes Papers, Library of Congress), Hayes was a closet Unitarian who attended mainstream churches regularly, believing, "Where the habit does not Christianize, it generally civilizes" (*Diary and Letters*, vol. 3, p. 267).

A Whig in politics, Hayes was a conservative who upheld traditional values, but his commitment to reason and justice enabled Lucy to make him a moderate reformer. Beginning in 1853 he defended runaway slaves, and later, seeking to prevent the spread of slavery into western territories, he joined the Republican party. From 1858 to 1861 Hayes served as Cincinnati's city solicitor. When the lower southern states seceded following the election of Abraham Lincoln, Hayes was willing to "*Let them go*" (*Diary and Letters*, vol. 2, p. 4). The attack of Fort Sumter on 12 April 1861, however, infuriated him. On 27 June he was commissioned a major in the Twenty-third Ohio Volunteer Infantry, preferring to "*be killed in the course of it than to live through and after it without taking part in it*" (*Diary and Letters*, vol. 2, p. 17). An inspirational (and lucky) leader in battle, Hayes served four years, was wounded five times (once seriously), was brevetted major general, and emerged from the war a member of Congress.

In Congress from 1865 to 1867, Hayes consistently supported Radical Republican Reconstruction measures, and as chair of the Joint Committee on the Library, he worked to develop the Library of Congress into a great institution. Disliking the long separations from Lucy and their children (they would rear four sons and a daughter), in 1867 Hayes happily resigned from Congress to run for governor of Ohio. He was elected and served two terms from 1868 to 1872. He was primarily responsible for the ratification by Ohio of the Fifteenth Amendment and for the establishment of Ohio State University.

Hayes loyally supported Ulysses S. Grant for reelection in 1872 and ran for Congress to help the Republican ticket. Although Grant carried Ohio, Hayes was defeated and in May 1873 returned to Fremont. There he helped his ailing Uncle Sardis, who died in January 1874, leaving Hayes the bulk of his estate. After Hayes left politics the Republican party declined. In Ohio the Democrats triumphed in the 1873 gubernatorial race, and the financial panic of 1873, followed by a deepening economic depression, enabled the Democrats to take control of the U.S. House of Representatives in 1875. Pressure developed in Ohio and in the nation to inflate the currency with greenbacks. Plummeting land values threatened Hayes's private fortune—largely invested in real estate—but, although he was "one of the noble army of debtors" (*Diary and Letters*, vol. 3, p. 255), he considered inflation dishonest. As Radical Republican governments collapsed in the South, he also began to consider a policy that would allow local self-rule (without military intervention) there if white southerners would respect the political rights of blacks. Furthermore, revelations of corruption in the Grant administration led Hayes to affirm his bent for civil service reform. Despite these beliefs, Hayes was content to remain outside politics, but in 1875 Ohio Republicans, desperate to reverse their decline, nominated Hayes, their best vote-getter, for a third term as governor. When Hayes won in a close race, supporters advocated his nomination for president in 1876.

Obnoxious to no one, Hayes recognized that "availability" was his strength and did little to secure the nomination (*Diary and Letters*, vol. 3, p. 305). When more powerful candidates failed, availability worked, and Hayes received the nomination. The ensuing campaign was difficult for Republicans because of the severe depression, the reform reputation of the Democratic nominee, Governor Samuel Jones Tilden of New York, and the violence Democrats employed to prevent black and white Republicans in the South from voting. On election day Tilden appeared victorious, but Republicans in control of the official election returning boards in Florida, Louisiana, and South Carolina, citing intimidation, disqualified enough Democratic ballots to produce Republican majorities in those states, giving Hayes the electoral votes necessary for his election. Claiming they were defrauded, the Democrats sent rival sets of electors' votes to be counted, as the Constitution prescribed, by the president of the Senate in the presence of both houses of Congress.

To decide which votes to count, the Democratic House of Representatives and the Republican Senate created an Electoral Commission—five senators, five representatives, and five Supreme Court justices—that balanced seven Republicans with seven Democrats and relied on Justice David Davis, a political independent, to make a nonpartisan decision. Davis, however, disqualified himself after Democrats helped elect him senator from Illinois, and his Republican replacement, Joseph P. Bradley, gave the disputed votes to Hayes. With the presidency lost, the Democrats delayed the count by filibustering and threatened chaos unless Republicans removed the federal troops supporting Republican regimes in the South. When both President Grant and Ohio politicians close to Hayes agreed to the removal if the Democrats in those states pledged to respect the civil rights of blacks—assurances that did not go beyond Hayes's published letter accepting the nomination—enough Democrats voted with Republicans to complete the count, and on 2 March 1877 Hayes was finally declared president.

Despite his disputed election, Hayes proved a successful president. Other chief executives have confronted great crises upon entering office, but only

Hayes began his term with a vast segment of the population believing he had been elected by fraud. Additionally, Hayes had to govern with his own party factionalized and with the Democrats controlling the House of Representatives and, after the midterm election of 1878, the Senate as well.

Hayes overcame these handicaps as an individual, not as the head of an agglomeration of advisers called the presidency. His small staff merely handled visitors and correspondence. Twice weekly cabinet meetings provided counsel, and Hayes especially valued the opinions of Secretary of the Treasury John Sherman (1823–1900), Secretary of State William Maxwell Evarts, and Secretary of the Interior Carl Schurz.

In deciding issues, Hayes was principled yet practical, cautious yet courageous. Once he made up his mind he was firm and consistent. He did not panic under stress, endured criticism and hostility, was slow to anger, and bore few grudges. He was a patient reformer, confident that ultimately his goals would be achieved. Because of these attitudes, Hayes succeeded so far as the circumstances of his presidency allowed. He initiated new policies in the South and the civil service, arrested the erosion of executive power with victories over both the Senate and the House of Representatives, and left office with the nation prosperous and the Republican party united.

Harsh political realities, rather than any deal made during the count, determined Hayes's southern policy. Particularly after the panic of 1873, northern support for Radical Reconstruction had eroded, while southern opposition to it had become violent. When Hayes took office, only Louisiana and South Carolina had Republican governments, and they were challenged by rival Democratic governments. The legitimacy of these Republican governments was on a par with that of the Hayes presidency; the same Republican-controlled returning boards had declared them victorious. The problem was that the survival of these governments depended on the support of federal troops. Hayes knew that northern public opinion would not long sustain these troops, for whom congressional Democrats had already blocked appropriations. The question was not whether troops should be withdrawn, but when. From this weak bargaining position, Hayes extracted from the rival Democratic governments of Louisiana and South Carolina promises to guarantee the voting and civil rights of all black and white citizens. Hayes was naive in accepting these pledges at face value, but he had no viable option.

Seeking to eliminate the corruption that permeated the government under Grant, Hayes embraced civil service reform to a greater degree than had any of his predecessors. He sounded the death knell of the spoils system and helped lay the foundation of a modern bureaucracy. To divorce the civil service from politics, in June 1877 he ordered federal officers not to "take part in the management of political organizations, caucuses, conventions, or election campaigns," and he prohibited the assessment of federal officeholders to pay for political campaigns (*Diary and Letters*, vol. 3, p. 438).

Civil service reform alienated many Republican politicians but none more than Senator Roscoe Conkling. In September 1877 Hayes tried to replace Conkling's lieutenant, Collector Chester A. Arthur of the New York Customhouse, with a reform-minded collector. After a protracted struggle, he did so and thus defeated "senatorial courtesy," the notion that senators, not the president, controlled federal civil service appointments in their home states. By insisting that appointments be made on merit determined by open competitive examinations, Hayes showed that civil service reform was needed because of the complexity of the nation's bureaucracy. The example of Hayes's reform policy in the New York Customhouse (the nation's largest office) made possible the passage of the Pendleton Civil Service Reform Act (1883).

In his struggle with Conkling, Hayes enhanced the power and prestige of his office against great odds. After a spectacular battle in 1879, Hayes also defeated congressional attempts to force him to approve unwanted legislation. To necessary appropriation bills the Democratic Congress attached riders designed to destroy laws enforcing voting rights under the Fourteenth and Fifteenth amendments. Sensing that northern public opinion would support the federal supervision of congressional and presidential elections, Hayes vetoed these bills. Ultimately Congress—under the lash of public opinion—passed money bills without the obnoxious riders. In these battles Hayes eschewed the politics of organization—requiring the purchase of local machines by granting favors to their congressional leaders—and embraced the politics of reform. In his travels and speeches Hayes outlined his policies and appealed to a broad range of public opinion.

The depression caused additional problems. For those experiencing hard times, Reconstruction and corruption were not important issues. Wage cuts, unemployment, and shrinking incomes led to the Great Railroad Strike of 1877, to agitation against Chinese laborers in California, and to demands for currency expansion. The reaction of Hayes to these problems was tempered by moderation and practicality. His restrained, legalistic response to the Great Strike saved lives and property. He remained calm, responding with federal troops only when properly requested by local and state authorities who had exhausted their means to keep the peace. He avoided a confrontation between strikers and federal forces by refusing to call up volunteers to operate the railroads or to use the blocking of the mail as a pretext for intervention. While ordering small detachments of regulars to cooperate with local and state authorities to end rioting, looting, and burning, Hayes neither broke the Great Strike nor did the bidding of the railroads.

Hayes vetoed popular legislation spawned by hard times to expand the currency and exclude Chinese laborers from the United States. After his successful veto of the Chinese Immigration Bill (1879) outraged Californians, Hayes placated them by appointing a commission that negotiated a treaty with China permitting limits on immigration (ratified in 1881). Although Congress passed the Bland-Allison Silver-Coinage Bill (1878) over his veto, Hayes reduced its inflationary effect by coining the minimum number of silver dollars required.

Near the end of his administration, Hayes claimed that his hard-money stance and especially the resumption of specie payments, which in January 1879 placed the United States back on the gold standard, had restored the confidence of investors and the business community. With abundant capital and low interest rates, industries were thriving, railroads expanding, and foreign trade increasing. The business cycle was primarily responsible for this economic recovery, but the fact remains that his currency notions prevailed during a vigorous business revival.

Although his southern policy failed to secure obedience to the Reconstruction amendments, Hayes never abandoned his commitment to civil rights and to equal educational and economic opportunities for all Americans. He was conscientious, humane, and just, and he worked to help the disadvantaged. When he thought that justice had miscarried, he used the pardoning power, even when he was criticized for its use. He urged that federal subsidies be given to poor states and territories so that all children could receive a quality education. During his administration Hayes stopped the policy of uprooting Native Americans and moving them to Indian Territory. He reformed the Indian Bureau and reduced violence on reservations by creating the Indian Police and by making strenuous efforts to keep white settlers out of Indian Territory. Hayes wished to integrate Native Americans into the dominant society by promoting education, individual land ownership, and citizenship.

An advocate of arbitration, Hayes made peace his objective in foreign relations, but he was sensitive to national interests. Avoiding war did not preclude the pursuit of criminal trespassers into Mexico or the denunciation of the Panama Canal scheme of Ferdinand de Lesseps, which was not "under American control" (*Diary and Letters*, vol. 3, p. 589).

Fearing that presidents prostitute their office to secure reelection, Hayes refused to run again. His policies were popular, and the voters, enjoying prosperity in 1880, elected his lieutenant, James A. Garfield, as his successor. Hayes combined old virtues with new ideas; he took modest steps on the path that would be followed by the great presidential leaders of the twentieth century, yet his honesty, simplicity, and decency echoed the pristine values of the early American Republic.

In retirement Hayes vigorously advocated a larger role for the federal government in promoting the public welfare. Having as president signed the Arrears of Pension Act (1879), he continued his fight to better support needy veterans. While striving for an egalitarian society in which all Americans would enjoy equal political rights and educational and economic opportunities, he perceived that the United States was becoming a plutocracy, tending toward a "government of the rich, by the rich, and for the rich" (*Diary and Letters*, vol. 4, p. 551). His denunciation of giant monopolistic corporations and his support of federal regulation of industry (for example, the 1887 Interstate Commerce Act), make Hayes a precursor of progressivism.

Believing that education would ultimately cure most of the problems in American society, Hayes made it his "hobby" (*Diary and Letters*, vol. 3, p. 619). Even when president, he was a conscientious trustee of the Peabody Fund, which supported the education of southern blacks and whites. As the first president of the board of trustees of the Slater Fund, he worked diligently from its creation in 1882 to educate blacks. Hayes attended all meetings of these organizations, wrote numerous letters supporting them, made inspection tours, and continued to urge that the federal government subsidize the education of poor children. He also served on the boards of trustees of Ohio State, Ohio Wesleyan, and Western Reserve Universities. On all of these boards, he argued that from primary school through college traditional disciplines should be supplemented with courses in manual training and the mechanical arts. In 1883 he accepted the presidency of the National Prison Association, and for the remainder of his life, he worked for a penal system that would be just, rational, and humane. Thinking it possible to reform some of the most heinous criminals, Hayes was against the death penalty.

Lucy Hayes, who supported her husband in his reform and philanthropic activities, died after a stroke in June 1889. Though he continued his work for education, Hayes often felt ready to follow her. A few months after his seventieth birthday, an attack of angina pectoris felled him in Cleveland, where he was on Ohio State University business. The pain was intense, but, after some brandy, he insisted on returning home to "Spiegel Grove," where he died.

• Hayes's diary and correspondence and collateral collections relating to his life and administration are at the Hayes Presidential Center, Spiegel Grove, Fremont, Ohio. Much of the diary and some of the correspondence was edited and published (with language and punctuation tidied up) in the five-volume *Diary and Letters of Rutherford Birchard Hayes: Nineteenth President of the United States* (1922–1926) by Charles Richard Williams. In contrast, *Hayes: The Diary of a President, 1875–1881, Covering the Disputed Election, the End of Reconstruction, and the Beginning of Civil Service* (1964), meticulously edited by T. Harry Williams, includes every jot and tittle. C. R. Williams's laudatory two-volume *Life of Rutherford Birchard Hayes: Nineteenth President of the United States* (1914) is useful for information as well as for copious extracts of hard to find source materials. Kenneth E. Davison in 1972 and Ari Hoogenboom in 1988 published useful volumes identically titled *The Presidency of Rutherford B. Hayes*. Harry Barnard, *Rutherford B. Hayes and His America* (1954), emphasizes Hayes's ancestry and relationship with his sister, while Ari Hoogenboom in *Rutherford B. Hayes: Warrior and President* (1994) concentrates on his career as a soldier, politician, and reformer. An obituary is in the *New York Times*, 20 Jan. 1893.

ARI HOOGENBOOM

HAYES, Woody (14 Feb. 1913–12 Mar. 1987), college football coach, was born Wayne Woodrow Hayes in Clifton, Ohio, the son of Wayne Hayes, a school superintendent, and Effie (maiden name unknown). Born into a lower middle class family, Hayes was raised in Newcomerstown, Ohio. As a young boy he was influenced by the drive for education instilled by his father as well as the sports figures with whom he came in contact. Cy Young, the great baseball pitcher, retired to Ohio and, as manager of the town baseball team, became a role model for Woody. From 1930 to 1934 Hayes attended Denison College in Greenville, Ohio, where he studied English and history, played as a lineman on the football team, and prepared to study law. As a precaution in case he failed to gain admission to law school, he took a clinic in coaching after college graduation.

In 1935 Hayes accepted his first job, teaching social studies and coaching football as an assistant at a junior high school in Mingo Junction, Ohio. One year later he moved to Columbus, Ohio, to study for a master's degree in education at Ohio State University. During this time he also taught and coached at New Philadelphia High School in New Philadelphia, Ohio. In 1936 he was introduced to Anne Gross; they married in 1942, and they would have one son. Believing that the United States would soon enter World War II, Hayes joined the U.S. Navy in the late summer of 1941 and received an assignment to their training section. There he worked with heavyweight boxing champion Gene Tunney and Naval Academy football star Tom Hamilton. He was assigned to sea duty in 1942 first as executive officer, then as captain of a troopship, and finally as a destroyer escort; he finished the war with the rank of lieutenant commander.

Returning from the war in 1946, Hayes was offered the head coaching job at Denison College. His command training in the navy served him well in motivating a lackluster team that went from a 2–6 record in Hayes's first year to two consecutive undefeated seasons. That brought him to the attention of a larger school, Miami University in Oxford, Ohio. Replacing the popular Sid Gillman at Miami, Hayes faced a tough rebuilding year until his coaching style won over his players. As a result his Miami teams posted 5–4 and 9–1 records in 1949 and 1950. After his second year he took his team to his first postseason game, the Salad Bowl in Phoenix, where his team defeated Arizona State 35–21. While at Miami Hayes became known both for his recruiting prowess and for his authoritarian style of coaching.

In 1951 Hayes applied for the vacant head coaching position at Ohio State University. Although he was not highly ranked among the thirty applicants for the job, he gained an interview and impressed the committee. After the first choice for the job declined, Hayes was offered the position, beginning a career that spanned twenty-eight years. Many players had a difficult time adapting to his hard-driving coaching style, but his compassion for his players and the success they experienced on the field won them over. In 1954, Hayes's

fourth season, Ohio State won the Big Ten conference title, the Rose Bowl, and a national championship.

Hayes developed a mania for coaching; he would spend long hours watching films and preparing himself, his coaches, and his teams. Few coaches have ever been as dedicated or as successful. An avid military historian, Hayes looked at football as a military operation that could benefit from the tactics and attitudes developed by generals. His favorite general was George S. Patton, and Hayes's personality was virtually identical to the aggressive, flamboyant, and controversial World War II leader. Like Patton, Hayes believed that nothing was more important than motivation, and that desire for success was a great equalizer when faced with imposing enemies. He worked his teams hard and developed in them a pride in their abilities and a work ethic that few ever lost. In addition to the fundamental aspects of the game, Hayes placed a strong emphasis on defense and on a rushing offense. The forward pass was a tactic that he used only sporadically. Hayes's style of offense, which was described as "three yards and a cloud of dust," was emblematic of Big Ten football during the 1960s and 1970s.

Personally, Hayes was known to his closest friends as an extremely caring man. He was genuinely interested in the lives of his players and went out of his way to look after their welfare. To this end, he made sure that his players completed their degrees, and he hounded those who did not finish, often for years, until they returned to school. In some cases he took struggling students home with him and forced them to concentrate on their studies. He gave much and asked little other than dedication. He lived frugally, accepted nothing for free, and made sure his debts were always paid. He also read voraciously and could speak with almost anyone on any subject. He spent as much time as he could with other professors at Ohio State and almost never talked football with them.

Hayes's desire for perfection and his relentless pursuit of victory showed in his outbursts of temper. He often kicked chairs and threw his hat, coat, or glasses when he was angry. As frequent and notable as these outbursts became, they never lasted more than a few seconds before he had vented his frustration and moved on to the next issue. He often lashed out verbally at his players for their mistakes, but he was rarely physical with them. His temper ultimately ended Hayes's career, however. After having developed a reputation with the press as a difficult man to deal with, Hayes was occasionally accused of striking reporters and cameramen. In the 1978 Gator Bowl game against Clemson University, an opponent intercepted a pass late in the fourth quarter and was pushed out of bounds in front of Hayes and the Ohio State bench. Believing that the player had taunted his team after the catch, Hayes struck him in the face with his fist; the scene was shown and repeated on national television. As a result, Ohio State had no choice but to relieve him of his duties.

After his retirement Hayes remained closely connected to Ohio State; his rank as professor emeritus entitled him to an office, which he used frequently. He continued to involve himself in charity work and speaking engagements, but his health steadily declined. He died in Upper Arlington, Ohio, of a heart attack.

Hayes influenced an enormous number of people. His players were dedicated to him and he remembered them all, no matter how long it had been since they played for him. Among the many All-American players he coached were Howard Cassady, the 1955 Heisman Trophy winner, and Archie Griffin, the first player to win the Heisman twice (1974–1975). Moreover, among his 42 assistant coaches during his tenure at Ohio State, 14 became college head coaches (including Bo Schembechler and Lou Holtz), four became National Football League (NFL) head coaches, and six became NFL assistant coaches. Hayes's Ohio State teams won 13 Big Ten conference championships or co-championships; appeared in the Rose Bowl eight times, posting a 4–4 record; and played in three other bowl games, posting a 1–2 record. His dedication to hard work and excellence in football and life affected those with whom he came in contact, and his views on work and motivation were widely duplicated.

• Hayes wrote three books: *Football at Ohio State* (1957), *Hot Line to Victory* (1969), and *You Win with People* (1973). A major biography is Paul Hornung, *Woody Hayes: A Reflection* (1991). Two works on his coaching style, both published at the height of Ohio State's football prowess, are Robert Vare, *Buckeye: A Study of Woody Hayes and the Ohio State Football Machine* (1974), and Jerry Brondfield, *Woody Hayes and the 100-Yard War* (1974).

PAUL K. DAVIS

HAYFORD, John Fillmore (19 May 1868–10 Mar. 1925), geodesist, was born in Rouses Point, New York, the son of Hiram Hayford and Mildred Alevia Fillmore, farmers. Hiram Hayford died when his son was eight years old, and after several years during which the young John worked on the farm before and after school, he was sent to finish high school in Detroit, living with an older sister, Mrs. Emily Coates. He completed high school in 1885 and enrolled in the College of Engineering at Cornell University. Hayford worked his way through college, waiting on tables and caring for a local professor's horse, and graduated in 1889.

Except for a brief stint as an instructor of civil engineering at Cornell (1895–1898) Hayford's scientific career was spent as a geodesist with the U.S. Coast and Geodetic Survey. In the nineteenth century, geodesy—the study of the shape of the earth—was one of the most important of sciences, essential to the creation of accurate maps. In the United States in the early twentieth century, survey data became increasingly urgent as commercial and territorial expansion led to a huge demand for accurate topographic data. As chief of computing and later inspector of geodetic work, Hayford streamlined survey field work and data reduction through technical and methodological innovation, and thereby greatly increased the rate of data production.

In doing so, he was largely responsible for producing the United States Standard Datum (renamed the North American Datum when united with Canada and Mexico in 1913).

In accumulating geodetic data across the United States, Hayford incidentally amassed the world's largest data set on deflections of the vertical. By this is meant the difference between vertical as defined by a surveyor's plumb bob and the normal to the earth's surface. Previous workers had generally ignored small deflections of the vertical as inconsequential and treated large deflections as surveying errors to be discarded. Hayford realized that these "errors" were information: one could use them to obtain an improved value for the figure of the earth. But to use this information, one had first to correct for the effects of local topography. Hayford thus organized a team of "computers"—modestly paid, generally female, workers—to calculate the gravitational effect of local topography surrounding 507 geodetic stations around the United States.

When the results were compiled, the topographic effects were much less than expected. The calculated corrections were too big—or conversely, the observed deflections were too small. Hayford realized that this result could be explained by the principle of isostasy—first proposed by the mathematician John Pratt in 1855 and further developed by George Biddell Airy in Great Britain and Clarence Dutton in the United States—that the mass surfeit represented by topographic features was compensated by a mass deficit below, and therefore the crust must float in hydrostatic equilibrium upon a denser substrate. If isostasy applied, then surface topography would have little or no gravitational effect on a surveyor's plumb bob, which was precisely Hayford's result. Using Pratt's assumption of a uniform depth of isostatic compensation, Hayford recalculated the deflections of the vertical and produced a new model for the figure of the earth. In 1924 the "Hayford spheroid" was adopted as the International Geodetic and Geophysical Union's reference standard for the figure of the earth.

In 1909 Hayford left the Coast and Geodetic Survey to become the first dean of the College of Engineering at Northwestern University, where he remained until his death. As dean, Hayford supervised the expansion of the engineering curriculum into a five-year course leading to professional certification and emphasized the importance of the liberal arts to prepare students to use their technical knowledge in salutary ways and to live contented lives. He adamantly opposed early specialization and considered a broad training essential for success in later life. It was Hayford's belief, reflected in the innovations he pioneered at the Coast and Geodetic Survey and the curriculum he promoted at Northwestern, that engineering problems were human problems and their solutions therefore involved understanding people and personalities as much as instruments and equations. During his tenure at Northwestern, Hayford amassed many honors for his earlier scientific work, including the Victoria Medal of the

Royal Geographical Society, but perhaps his most enduring legacy is Mount Hayford, located in southwestern Alaska at a latitude of 55°44'. He died in Evanston, Illinois.

Hayford represents a scientific tradition that ended in part because of its own success and in part because of technological innovation. By the mid-twentieth century, the figure of the earth was known to a high degree of accuracy and geodetic control established in the industrialized nations; soon thereafter, satellite monitoring and electronic distance measuring rendered traditional survey practice obsolete. Hayford's work is, nevertheless, of lasting significance for several reasons. First, the acceptance of the Hayford spheroid marked a milestone in the history of American science—an indigenously trained scientist, working in a federal government agency, had outdone the greatest European scientists to produce a new international standard. The great British geophysicist Harold Jeffreys (who was not generally known for his admiration of Americans) thus called Hayford's work "one of the outstanding scientific achievements of our time." Second, although Hayford was by no means the first to apply engineering and mathematics to geological problems, his success in doing so deeply impressed his geological colleagues. The period of the 1920s to the 1950s saw a huge expansion in the application of physics and engineering to geological problems; in retrospect, Hayford's work marks a watershed in this trend. Third, and most important from the perspective of current scientific knowledge, Hayford's work constituted the first proof of isostasy. Subsequently, seismic studies confirmed the Airy model, involving a variable depth to the base of the earth's crust, rather than the Pratt model, which Hayford utilized, but the basic principle was nonetheless solidified. Isostasy is now considered an essential fact about the earth, a fact whose establishment can be largely credited to John Hayford.

• Hayford's personal papers have not been preserved, but letters from and about him can be found in the papers of T. C. Chamberlin, University of Chicago, and Bailey Willis, Henry E. Huntington Library, San Marino, Calif. Hayford's most important works are *The Figure of the Earth and Isostasy from Measurements in the United States* (1909) and, with William Bowie, "The Effect of Topography and Isostatic Compensation upon the Intensity of Gravity," *U.S. Coast and Geodetic Survey Special Publication* 10 (1912). Hayford also published several influential papers on the geological implications of isostasy, including "The Geodetic Evidence of Isostasy, with a Consideration of the Depth and Completeness of the Isostatic Compensation and of the Bearing of the Evidence upon Some of the Greater Problems of Geology," *Proceedings of the Washington Academy of Sciences* 8 (1906): 25–40, and "The Relations of Isostasy to Geodesy, Geophysics and Geology," *Science* 33 (1911): 199–208. For a contemporaneous discussion of Hayford's work, including Jeffreys's assessment, see William Bowie, "The Earth's Crust and Isostasy" *Geographical Review* 12 (1922): 613–27. For a full obituary, with a complete list of Hayford's published works, see William Burger, National Academy of Sciences, *Biographical Memoirs* 16, no. 5 (1936): 156–292.

NAOMI ORESKES

HAYGOOD, Atticus Greene (19 Nov. 1839–19 Jan. 1896), clergyman and educator, was born in Watkinsville, Georgia, the son of Greene B. Haygood, a lawyer, and Martha Ann Askew, a former teacher. In 1852 his family moved to Atlanta. He entered Emory College in nearby Oxford, Georgia, in September 1856, graduating with a bachelor's degree in 1859. In the summer of 1858 Haygood was licensed as a preacher in the Methodist Episcopal church, South, and served in several small churches in Georgia after his graduation from college. He married Mary Yarbrough in June 1859; they had eight children, four of whom survived to adulthood.

When the Civil War began in 1861, Haygood enlisted as the chaplain of the Fifteenth Georgia Regiment. Although he resigned in November 1861 and returned to civilian preaching, he later traveled as a missionary chaplain with the Confederate army of Tennessee during its campaign in Georgia in 1863 and 1864. After the war, he served at Trinity Church in Atlanta in 1865–1866, and between 1867 and 1870 he was a presiding elder of the North Georgia Conference. In 1870 Haygood was appointed secretary of the Southern Methodist Sunday schools at the denomination's headquarters in Nashville, Tennessee. During his tenure there, he sought to improve the content of Sunday school lesson materials and edited a number of publications that were used in church libraries. When his wife's deteriorating health forced the family to leave Nashville and return to Georgia, Haygood gave up his position in the fall of 1875. In December of that year, however, he was elected president of Emory College.

Haygood served at Emory for nearly a decade. Although the college was in poor physical condition and burdened with debts, he enlarged the endowment and was able to pay off most of the money the school owed. He also directed the construction and repair of Emory's buildings and saw the student body double in size. In addition, he assumed the role of editorial correspondent for the *Southern Christian Advocate* between October 1875 and May 1878 and edited the *Wesleyan Christian Advocate* (the major weekly newspaper of Southern Methodism) from June 1878 until the fall of 1882. He was elected a bishop of the church in May 1882 but declined the position to continue his service as college president.

Although Haygood did not coin the term "New South" (the phrase that touted renewed industrial growth in the southern states in the 1880s), he helped popularize the idea. At a worship service on Thanksgiving Day in 1880, he preached about the blessings God had bestowed on the southern people and asserted that white southerners should feel thankful that the Confederacy had been defeated in the Civil War. When this sermon came to the attention of a New York financier, it was published under the title *The New South* (1880) and given wide national circulation. The next spring, Haygood also published *Our Brother in Black* (1881), a book in which he continued to reflect on the end of slavery and the religious meaning of southern defeat. While arguing that divine providence had brought Africans to the United States to civilize and Christianize them, he also emphasized that the war's outcome had benefited white southerners as much as black southerners, for it had destroyed slavery—an economically backward system of labor.

Haygood's book won praise from philanthropists in the North, and in November 1882 he became agent of the Slater Fund, an organization dedicated to providing education for African Americans in the South. He remained president of Emory for nearly two years after this appointment but eventually resigned in 1884 to work full time for the fund. Believing that industrial training was more appropriate for African Americans than a classic academic curriculum, Haygood offered Slater money to schools that accepted this educational philosophy (such as Clark University and Tougaloo College). On the other hand, he withheld support from colleges such as Atlanta University and Fisk University, whose curricular emphases he considered to be both misguided and harmful to the progress of black southerners.

In 1889 Haygood published two significant books: *Pleas for Progress* (a collection of speeches urging support of industrial training and education for African Americans that he had delivered as the Slater agent) and *The Man of Galilee* (a study of the life of Jesus that argued for his divinity). In May 1890 he was again elected bishop. After accepting this appointment, he resigned from his position at the Slater Fund and moved to Los Angeles, California. However, he contracted an infection while visiting Mexico City in 1892 and returned to Oxford in 1893 hoping to recover from its effects. Struggling with poor health, crippling financial debts, and an increasing reliance on alcohol, Haygood died in Oxford three years later.

Despite his decidedly paternalistic racial attitudes, Haygood was one of the few white southerners in the late nineteenth century who was willing to identify himself publicly with the concerns of African Americans. As such, his ideas about interracial "brotherhood" were well in advance of his time. A leader in both educational and religious affairs, he was a key figure in the transitional "New South" era, when white southerners began to abandon romantic notions about the antebellum past and looked forward to financial expansion and development in their region.

• Haygood's papers are located at the Emory University Library. Elam F. Dempsey's centennial biography, *Atticus Green [sic] Haygood* (1939), while based on the Haygood papers, also contains material no longer available at Emory (Dempsey did not deposit all the documents he collected at the library there, and they have since disappeared from the public record). Marion L. Smith's doctoral dissertation, "Atticus Greene Haygood, Christian Educator" (Yale Univ., 1929), adds further useful background on his educational philosophy. A modern scholarly analysis of Haygood's career is Harold W. Mann, *Atticus Greene Haygood, Methodist Bishop, Editor, and Educator* (1965).

GARDINER H. SHATTUCK, JR.

HAYGOOD, Laura Askew (14 Oct. 1845–29 Apr. 1900), missionary of the Methodist Episcopal Church, South, was born in Watkinsville, Georgia, the daughter of Green B. Haygood, a lawyer, and Martha Ann Askew, a teacher. Deeply committed to Methodism, her parents sent their two sons and two daughters to Methodist educational institutions. One of Laura's brothers, Atticus Green Haygood, became president of Methodist-related Emory College in Oxford, Georgia, and a bishop in the Methodist Episcopal Church, South.

Laura Haygood's mother directed her early education, which prepared her to enroll in Wesleyan Female College in Macon, Georgia, in 1862. Diligent study during both the regular term and the vacation enabled her to graduate two years later. In 1865 she began the teaching career that she pursued for the rest of her life. Her first position was as an assistant at Palmer Institute, Oxford, Georgia. The following year she began a private girls' school in Atlanta. When the Atlanta Girls' High School was established in 1872, Haygood became a member of its faculty, and in 1877 she was appointed principal. She was highly esteemed by her colleagues and loved by the students. One of her pupils wrote, "Scholarly and dignified, yet ever ready to enter into our pleasures and amusements; gentle, yet commanding in its truest and best sense; above all teaching by daily example the noblest of life's lessons, her influence in the schoolroom alone cannot be estimated" (Brown and Brown, p. 31).

During her years in Atlanta Haygood joined Trinity Church, where she taught Sunday school and led the Woman's Home Missionary Society. This group, which nurtured the spiritual growth of its members, also raised funds to support mission efforts in the United States and dedicated itself to helping the poor. In a letter circulated to the Methodist women of Georgia in 1883, Haygood urged every Methodist congregation in the state to form a local unit of the Woman's Home Missionary Society. She also helped organize other Atlanta Sunday schools that later grew into two Methodist churches in the city, St. Paul's and St. John's.

Although she initially showed no unusual interest in foreign missions, Haygood became acquainted with Methodist missionaries in China and was moved by their pleas for additional workers. On 24 February 1884, while listening to a sermon at Trinity Church by W. H. Potter, editor of the *Wesleyan Christian Advocate*, she decided to devote her life to China missions. She later wrote to Potter: "I have come to feel that if the work of God in China needs women, there is no woman in all the world under more obligation to go than I am" (Brown and Brown, p. 102). She was convinced that her Christian commitment, based in traditional Methodist faith, would be enhanced and fulfilled if she devoted her whole life to mission work in China.

On 18 October 1884 Haygood embarked from San Francisco for China; she arrived in Shanghai on 17 November. While she was still becoming familiar with the Chinese language and culture, she took up teaching responsibilities in the Clopton School, a girls' boarding school, and organized two-day (nonboarding) schools. The curriculum of these schools included reading, writing, geography, arithmetic, music, and religious instruction. Under her direction Clopton evolved into a school for training Chinese women to teach. Haygood also developed a plan to extend the work of day schools in the Shanghai area. Her most celebrated accomplishment was the establishment of the McTyeire Home and School, named for southern Methodist bishop Holland N. McTyeire. The idea for the school had originated with Young J. Allen, Methodist missionary to China since 1860 and an influential personality in Haygood's life. After several years of exhausting planning and fundraising, to which Haygood devoted herself without reserve, the McTyeire school opened on 16 March 1892 as an institution where missionaries to China could learn the language and train for their work and where young Chinese women could receive a broad education in a Christian context. While preparations for the school were being completed, in May 1889 Haygood became a missionary agent of the Woman's Board of Missions of the Methodist Episcopal Church, South, for the Shanghai District. Her overwork for McTyeire and other mission causes may have contributed to a decline in her health. She journeyed to the United States in 1894 to recover, but she returned to China two years later when she became the sole agent of the Woman's Board in China. When she became seriously ill in 1899, she refused to travel back to the United States. In her dying words she proclaimed, "Had I a thousand lives, I would willingly give them to save China" (Brown and Brown, p. 488). She died and was buried in Shanghai. The Laura Haygood Home and School was opened in Soochow as a memorial to the commitment and energy of one of the most important Methodist missionaries of the nineteenth century.

Haygood's correspondence and missionary reports to her constituency reveal that throughout her life she sought a deeper relationship with God through reading and studying the Bible, praying regularly, and serving people wherever she could. She was revered as a model missionary not only in her own denomination but by other Protestant women who were devoted to mission work in the United States and overseas.

• Haygood is mentioned frequently in histories of nineteenth-century American Methodist missionary work. The most complete biography is Oswald E. Brown and Anna M. Brown, *Life and Letters of Laura Askew Haygood* (1904). Other sources include Edmund F. Cook, *Laura Askew Haygood* (1910), James Cannon, *History of the Southern Methodist Missions* (1926), and the *Christian Advocate* (Nashville), 3 and 10 May 1900.

CHARLES YRIGOYEN, JR.

HAYMAN, Al (1852?–10 Feb. 1917), theatrical manager, was born Raphael Heyman in Wheeling, West Virginia. The names of his parents are unknown. He received his early theatrical training in his hometown

and by 1875 managed the Languish and Glenn company of *The Black Crook*, a fantasy featuring scantily clad dancers, on a long tour through the American South, Mexico, and Central America. He next managed a world tour of the "Royal Illusionists." By 1876 Hayman had arrived in Australia, where with T. E. Hiscock he managed the leading theaters in Melbourne and Sydney. In 1881 he went to England, where he met producer Charles Frohman, who hired him to manage the Fifth Avenue Theatre in New York City. There Hayman learned from theatrical manager T. H. Haverly the business methods that later inspired the Theatrical Syndicate.

Hayman next left New York for San Francisco to manage the Bush Street Theatre. After also managing the Baldwin Theatre for a time, he gained control of it by 1883. He soon owned or leased theaters in San Francisco, Portland, Oregon, Denver, Salt Lake City, Chicago, and Brooklyn. Renewing his acquaintance with Charles Frohman in 1886, Hayman set up a booking agency that provided shows for theaters in the West, the genesis of the syndicate the two men formed later. Hayman moved to New York City, where he soon acquired the rights (with Charles Frohman) to Bronson Howard's script *Shenandoah*, the success of which made both men wealthy. With Frank Sanger, Hayman built the Empire Theatre in New York City for Frohman in 1893. He also acquired Abbey's Theatre and reopened it as the Knickerbocker.

In 1896 Hayman and Frohman joined Marc Klaw and Abraham Erlanger of New York City and S. F. Nixon (Nirdlinger) and J. Fred Zimmerman of Philadelphia to form the Theatrical Syndicate, effectively taking monopolistic control of the American theater for two decades. While a few especially well-known stars could reject Syndicate terms, most performers and managers were brought under the thumb of the Syndicate (sometimes called the Trust) and paid whatever fees were required. Called an "arrogant, ruthless, grasping monopoly," the Syndicate earned enormous fortunes for the six men.

The Theatrical Syndicate was Hayman's conception, and he gained a greater share of profits from it than did the other members. Although the Syndicate had stultifying effects on the American theater of the day, such as rejecting European playwrights of high quality (including Henrik Ibsen, August Strindberg, and George Bernard Shaw), it solidified the business aspects of the legitimate drama for the first time in America.

Hayman retired in 1911, passing his theatrical interests on to his brother, Alf Hayman, but it was widely felt that Al Hayman's money backed many subsequent ventures. Hayman died in the Waldorf Astoria Hotel in New York City, leaving an estate estimated at a half-million dollars. He had personally produced only about a half-dozen plays in his career and never made any pretense to artistry. Indeed, Hayman had no interest in theatrical art, except as it brought more money into the box office. One observer noted that "Hayman . . . dislikes theatres, plays and players, and worships art if the box office is of the same opinion." Hayman avoided the theater after he became the richest of the Syndicate members, spending much of his time on his yacht, cruising foreign waters. Performer Francis Wilson quoted Hayman as complaining to him, "Give [Frohman] and Maude Adams a chance, and they'd spend all the money in the world with their damned fool ideas about art!" Hayman excused his own crass commercialism by stating, "The fundamental idea in the syndicate is that the public is the best judge of what it wants." As historian Alfred Bernheim said of him, "His career [was] a shining example of the out-and-out business man in the theatrical world."

• Considerable material on the Theatrical Syndicate is held by the Billy Rose Theatre Collection at the New York Public Library for the Performing Arts, Lincoln Center. Edmond M. Gagey, *The San Francisco Stage: A History* (1950), describes Hayman's early career there, and a few details are included in Arthur Hornblow, *A History of the Theatre in America* (1919). See also Alfred L. Bernheim, *The Business of the Theatre: An Economic History of the American Theatre, 1750–1932* (1932), and Monroe Lippman, "The History of the Theatrical Syndicate: Its Effect upon the Theatre in America" (Ph.D. diss., Univ. of Michigan, 1937). A detailed version of the rise of the Syndicate was published serially in 1904–1905 in *Leslie's Monthly Magazine*. Brief obituaries for Hayman are in the *New York Times*, 10 Feb. 1917, and the *New York Dramatic Mirror*, 17 Feb. 1917.

STEPHEN M. ARCHER

HAYNE, Paul Hamilton (1 Jan. 1830–6 July 1886), poet and man of letters, was born in Charleston, South Carolina, the son of Paul Hamilton Hayne, a lieutenant in the U.S. Navy, and Emily McElhenny, members of families prominent in politics, law, and religion. Two of the elder Hayne's brothers were U.S. senators, one of whom, Robert Young Hayne, was Daniel Webster's redoubtable opponent in the debates on Nullification and young Hayne's guardian after yellow fever caused the early death of his father. Educated in a local preparatory school and at the College of Charleston (1847–1850), Hayne turned after graduation to the study of law with James Louis Petigru, former state attorney general, and in 1852 was admitted to the bar. Also in 1852 he married Mary Middleton Michel; they had one child. But literature prevailed over law, and Hayne became editor and owner of the *Southern Literary Gazette* late in 1852. Disheartened by the reception of the *Gazette*, he sold it in 1854 and later that year assembled his first book, *Poems*, from previously published verse.

Encouraged by the generally favorable response to *Poems*—the well-known critic Edwin Percy Whipple, for instance, noted the book's "general promise as well as fine performance"—Hayne set about writing and putting together two more volumes of poetry before the war: *Sonnets, and Other Poems* (1857) and *Avolio: A Legend of the Island of Cos; with Poems, Lyrical, Miscellaneous, and Dramatic* (c. 1859). Many of these early pieces are conventional in form, style, and content. They indicate Hayne's general acceptance of the An-glo-American poetic tradition rather than an interest in the radical changes then being advocated by Walt Whitman. During this time Hayne also contributed to the *Southern Literary Messenger, Graham's Magazine, Harper's New Monthly*, and the *Atlantic Monthly*, and served as editor of *Russell's Magazine* from 1857 to 1860, Charleston's last serious antebellum effort to establish a literary monthly. The Civil War brought an end to the journal, and Hayne applied himself to full-time support of the Confederacy. Unable to engage in field service because of poor health (he had suffered from lung and liver complaints since his youth), he managed to serve for four months in 1861–1862 as aide-de-camp to Governor Francis Pickens, a kinsman, but devoted himself primarily to writing as a means of defending his state and nation. In 1864 he collected his poems, including his best war lyrics, and sent the manuscript to England, but it was lost in the blockade.

The defeat of the Confederacy brought financial ruin to Hayne and his family, and in 1865 he was forced to seek a new home in the pine barrens near Augusta, Georgia. There at "Copse Hill," Grovetown, he remained until his death of a stroke, devoting himself to writing poetry, criticism, and a voluminous correspondence involving the exchange of literary ideas and the promotion of southern cultural interests. After the death in 1870 of William Gilmore Simms, an old friend and mentor, Hayne became the chief literary spokesman for the South, an unofficial postwar laureate for the late Confederacy, a role not unlike the one his lifelong friend Henry Timrod had assumed during the war. In poems and essays he expressed what he considered to be the southern view of such political matters as the disputed presidential election of 1876 and the plight of the region during Reconstruction. He also wrote tributes to the Confederacy and to the memory of Simms, Timrod, and Sidney Lanier. In 1885 Andrew Adgate Lipscomb, former chancellor of the University of Georgia and a new friend of Hayne's, observed that he had "given utterance to the Southern heart as no one else has done."

Meanwhile, Hayne enhanced his reputation with three more collections of verse: *Legends and Lyrics* (1872), *The Mountain of the Lovers; with Poems of Nature and Tradition* (1875), and *Poems, Complete Edition* (1882), a collection based on earlier books with a selection from pieces printed since his last volume. He also contributed to the best magazines of the day—the *Atlantic Monthly, Harper's Monthly, Scribner's Monthly, Lippincott's Monthly*, and the *Century* in the North and to the *Southern Review*, the *South-Atlantic*, and the *Southern Bivouac* in the South. He was recognized as a significant poet throughout the country, as invitations and commissions to compose commemorative songs and odes in honor of the centennials of the battles of Kings Mountain and Yorktown and the founding of Charleston, as well as the sesquicentennial of Georgia, readily testify. Moreover, Henry Wadsworth Longfellow and John Greenleaf Whittier accepted him warmly as a colleague (the latter declared after Hayne's death that he was assured a place in the "Valhalla of the country" with Longfellow, William Cullen Bryant, and others); E. P. Whipple and Edmund Clarence Stedman, both important contemporary critics, praised his work; and Tennyson and Swinburne each acknowledged his achievements, especially as a sonneteer.

Aside from his literary accomplishments, Hayne was well known as a gentleman of the Old South who lived by the credo of honor and noblesse oblige, a true son of Charleston and Carolina, "the knightliest of men," according to one friend, and the "last literary cavalier," according to another. His character and principles, indeed, manifest themselves in his work and are reflected in some of its facile, conventional, and traditional qualities. In the light of another day, his poetry appears derivative and unabashedly romantic, and even his better work in criticism and letters exhibits similar limitations. Nevertheless, in the versatility of technique and scope and bulk of his production, Hayne rivals Simms as a nineteenth-century southern poet, though his best work fails to equal that of Simms, Edgar Allan Poe, Timrod, or even Lanier. His real achievement is in his correspondence, especially his letters to Simms, Whittier, Lanier, Margaret Junkin Preston, Moses Coit Tyler, E. C. Stedman, Philip Bourke Marston, Charles Gayarré, and A. A. Lipscomb, which demonstrates the courage, commitment, persistence, eloquence, and magnanimity of the writer and the man. Hayne was a minor poet assuredly, but despite his faults he was a dedicated man of letters and an estimable human being.

• The largest collection of letters, papers, clippings, and memorabilia is in the Paul Hamilton Hayne Papers, Perkins Library, Duke University, and the remains of Hayne's library are also housed there. Another important collection of correspondence and papers is at the South Caroliniana Library, University of South Carolina. Published letters may be found in *A Collection of Hayne Letters*, ed. Daniel M. McKeithan (1944), and *A Man of Letters in the Nineteenth-Century South: Selected Letters of Paul Hamilton Hayne*, ed. Rayburn S. Moore (1982). As for Hayne's other separate publications, see *The Poems of Henry Timrod* (1873), *The Lives of Robert Y. Hayne and Hugh Swinton Legaré* (1878), and *The Broken Battalions* (1885). An important unpublished collection of his work, "Last Poems," edited by Mary Middleton Michel Hayne and William Hamilton Hayne, is in the Hayne Papers, Perkins Library, Duke University. There is no fullscale biography, but Jay B. Hubbell's chapter on Hayne in *The South in American Literature, 1607–1900* (1954) focuses on his life and career. Moore's critical study, *Paul Hamilton Hayne* (1972), offers a chapter of biography, and many of his articles on Hayne in literary reference books and professional journals (1968–1992) provide biographical information. Obituaries appear in the *Boston Evening Transcript*, 8 July 1886, the *New York Times*, 10 July 1886, and *Harper's Weekly*, 17 July 1886.

RAYBURN S. MOORE

HAYNE, Robert Young (10 Nov. 1791–24 Sept. 1839), U.S. senator, governor of South Carolina, and railroad president, was born on the Pon Pon rice plantation in the Colleton District of South Carolina, the fifth of fourteen children born to William Hayne, a planter and one of the youngest members of South Carolina's 1790 constitutional convention, and Elizabeth Peronneau. Owing to the large number of children in the Hayne family, a formal education for Robert was not feasible. After his initial years of educational preparation under Mr. William Mason and Dr. John Smith in Charleston, Hayne studied law in the office of State Senator Langdon Cheves, who later achieved prominence as Speaker of the U.S. House of Representatives and as president of the Bank of the United States. This self-preparation enabled Hayne to be admitted to the South Carolina bar in 1812.

Hayne devoted a brief period of time to military service. He achieved the rank of lieutenant in the Charleston Cadet Infantry, and he served in the Third South Carolina Regiment during the War of 1812. While in service, Hayne married Frances Henrietta Pinckney, the daughter of Governor Charles Pinckney, on 3 November 1813. Before the war concluded, Hayne's military status extended to include captain of the Charleston Cadet Riflemen in 1814 and quartermaster general of South Carolina in December 1814. In addition to advancing in military rank, Hayne was elected in 1814 to the South Carolina state legislature with support from Democratic Republicans. Though unpolished by a college education, Hayne was a gifted and popular orator. This talent, combined with a strong analytical ability, served the young state representative well, and after four years Hayne became speaker of the South Carolina House.

In 1818 Hayne was unanimously elected attorney general of South Carolina. During his time as attorney general, or a few years prior to his election, Hayne's wife died; the events surrounding her death have remained obscure. In 1822, during his last year as attorney general, the young widower married Rebecca Motte Alston. As before, Hayne's marriage represented a connection to influential people, and this time the addition of wealth; Alston was the half sister of Governor Joseph Alston.

In 1823, with support from John C. Calhoun, Hayne's political career ascended to the national level with his election to the U.S. Senate. Six years earlier, Calhoun had written confidentially to a relative that "Hayne is a man that ought to be elected [to national office]. He has talents and eloquence, and will honor the State." After five months in office Hayne assumed a leadership role among the southern congressional delegation.

Hayne entered into the realm of national politics when one of the major arguments over the protection of American industry was raging. After the War of 1812 the United States faced economic hardship. War had extracted a costly toll on the nation's trade. Infant industries that had appeared to fulfill the demand for manufactured goods, the supply of which had been disrupted by the embargo and war, were threatened by the flood of cheap English goods after the war. Demands for a protective tariff increased. In 1816 Calhoun had supported a tariff, but the panic of 1819 exacerbated sectional animosities such that, by the mid-1820s, he and other South Carolinians, like Hayne, became fervently opposed to protective measures.

From this political posturing came numerous speeches and debates. Hayne fought to secure checks against increasing protective tariff rates on American manufacturing; this brought him up against Senator Daniel Webster of Massachusetts. Hayne believed that the leaders of industry had an insatiable desire for control, which must be managed by enacting safeguards. Additionally, he thought that protective tariffs denied people the opportunity to achieve their full potential. In 1824 Hayne emphasized that the tariff measure was not "a measure intended for revenue, but on the contrary, had been devised by . . . political 'restrictionists,' . . . engaged in the dangerous experiment of promoting by law particular employments of labor and capital."

Over the next six years the issues of slavery, constitutional interpretation, and nullification further complicated the protective tariff controversy. In 1830 Senators Hayne and Webster crossed swords in an oratorical match that has often been referred to as one of the greatest debates in U.S. history. The debate, which began on 29 December 1829 and commenced again after the holidays on 13 January, started as a discussion of policy on public land sales. By 14 January the debate turned into an argument over nullification. From 21 to 25 January Hayne defended South Carolina's, and therefore Calhoun's, policy of nullification. (This policy refers to the Union as a voluntary compact of autonomous states that reserve the right to determine for themselves the validity of federal law. Therefore, nullification is the dissolution of the original compact.) Webster's anticipated response on 26 January drew a huge crowd. The masterful orator picked Hayne's points apart one by one, and his spectacular delivery brought audience members to their feet. In 1832 South Carolina adopted an ordinance of nullification, Calhoun resigned as vice president of the United States, and Hayne resigned from the Senate. Within the year, Hayne was elected governor of South Carolina. Since President Andrew Jackson publicly condemned South Carolina's actions, this put him at odds with Governor Hayne. To avoid conflict, import duties on selected items were lowered and concessions were made to the system of revenue collection; however, these measures were only temporarily useful in ending the conflict. After the two statesmen reached an arrangement and the ordinance was invalidated, Hayne retired from national politics.

In September 1831 Hayne's brother had died while in service of the U.S. Navy, and Hayne was appointed as guardian of his nephew Paul Hamilton Hayne. Hayne took the boy into his home and became an affectionate father figure, teacher, and adviser, lavishing upon Paul the educational opportunities that he himself was unable to enjoy. With the encouragement of his uncle, Paul grew into a well-educated man and a distinguished poet.

From 1835 to 1837 Hayne served as mayor of Charleston, and in 1836 he became president of the newly organized Louisville, Cincinnati & Charleston Railroad Company. While attending a meeting of railroad stockholders in Asheville, North Carolina, he came down with a fever and died there within a few days. Records do not indicate any children from either of his marriages.

• With the exception of the Webster-Hayne debate, historians in the twentieth century paid little attention to Hayne's life. In the aftermath of the Civil War a substantial part of Hayne's papers were lost. An attempt at a comprehensive examination is Theodore D. Jervey's *Robert Y. Hayne and His Times* (1909). This inadequate work is based primarily on files from the South Carolina press with minor references to Calhoun's correspondence, the Debates of Congress, pamphlets, and the few remaining Hayne letters. Some general sketches of Hayne appear in *Biographical Directory of the United States Congress 1774–1989* (1989) and Robert Sobel's *Biographical Directory of United States Governors* (1978).

For Hayne's role in the tariff and nullification issues, refer to David Franklin Houston's *A Critical Study of Nullification in South Carolina* (1896), Charles M. Wiltse's *John C. Calhoun: Nullifier, 1829–1839* (1949), George Rogers Taylor's selected readings on *The Great Tariff Debate, 1820–1830* (1953), and Lance Patterson's "The Battle of the Giants: Webster and Hayne, Orators at Odds," *American History Illustrated* 17 (1983): 18–22. Minor references to Hayne are in Kate Harbes Becker's *Paul Hamilton Hayne: Life and Letters* (1951), Rayburn S. Moore's *Paul Hamilton Hayne* (1972), and Joseph J. Ellis's *Passionate Sage: The Character and Legacy of John Adams* (1993).

APRIL D. FOLDEN

HAYNES, Elizabeth Ross (30 July 1883–26 Oct. 1953), social scientist, politician, and community leader, was born in Mount Willing, Lowndes County, Alabama, the daughter of Henry Ross and Mary Carnes. Elizabeth Ross's parents were hard workers who amassed some wealth through the purchase of land that eventually grew to become a 1,500-acre plantation. Little is known about her parents beyond their commitment to their only child's well-being and success. Elizabeth attended the State Normal School in Montgomery and later won a scholarship to Fisk University, where she was awarded an A.B. degree in 1903. She taught school in Alabama and Texas for several years after graduation, and during 1905 and 1907 she attended summer school at the University of Chicago.

In 1908 Ross was invited to work with "colored students" for the student department of the national board of the Young Women's Christian Association (YWCA). In this position, she traveled extensively throughout the country to college campuses and cities where branches of the "Y" were established for African Americans to evaluate their programs and commitment of resources. She paid special attention to the conditions under which the female students lived and noted that many had to work to pay for school. She was also alert to the leadership potential of these young women. On one occasion, when Ross met an exceptional young woman, she indicated that the student was "worthy of being kept in mind as a possible Association worker somewhere." Ross continued to work in this capacity for the YWCA until December 1910 when she married Dr. George Edmund Haynes at the Fisk University Chapel.

Dr. Haynes, the first African American to graduate from the New York School of Philanthropy, was cofounder and first executive director of the National League on Urban Conditions among Negroes (renamed the National Urban League in 1920). After their marriage, Elizabeth resigned from her position as "special worker" with the YWCA but continued to work in a volunteer capacity. In 1910 Dr. Haynes accepted a position at Fisk University to establish a department of social work and Elizabeth began to volunteer her time to various social service organizations throughout Nashville. They had one child.

In 1918 Dr. Haynes accepted a position as director of Negro Economics, a division of the Department of Labor in Washington, D.C. Elizabeth Haynes became his assistant director. She was also a "dollar-a-year" worker for the Labor Department's Women in Industry Service (later named the Women's Bureau). In addition, she served as domestic service employment secretary of the United States Employment Service from January 1920 to May 1922. During this time she became one of the leading authorities on issues of African-American women and labor. Elizabeth Haynes believed that African Americans' economic independence would "some day enable them [Negro women and girls] to take their places in the ranks with other working women." In her publication "Two Million Negro Women at Work" (1922), which was written while Haynes was with the Women's Bureau, she identified domestic and personal service, agriculture and manufacturing, and mechanical industries as the three main areas in which the majority of women were engaged. Haynes also recognized a need for the "standardization of domestic service" and for "domestic-training schools in connection with public employment agencies." In 1923, while pursuing a master's degree in sociology at Columbia University, Haynes wrote an outstanding analysis of domestic working women for her thesis titled "Negroes in Domestic Service in the United States," in which she also surveyed the living conditions, health, social life, and organizational affiliations of these domestic workers.

In 1924 Haynes was elected the first African-American member of the YWCA National Board, a position that she held until 1934. A highly segregated organization fraught with racial tension, the YWCA resisted full integration of African Americans and allowed white women to set policies and determine the involvement of African-American women and girls. Nevertheless, Haynes was committed to interracial harmony and social justice and decided to work for planned change from within the organization.

After the war, the Hayneses had moved to New York City in 1921. Elizabeth worked with her husband while he served as secretary of the Department of Race Relations of the Federal Council of the Churches of Christ in America from 1922 to 1946. During this time, Elizabeth Haynes also became very involved in the politics of the Harlem community. In 1935 she served as the coleader of the Twenty-first Assembly District and as an executive member of Tammany Hall. Haynes believed that the time was right for women to become "contenders for the choicest official plums." She stated that she had "no fears in urging the women of this country, irrespective of race, to awake, register, vote, work and enlarge the fight for equality of opportunity in jobs, [and] in office for women." Identifying with the New Deal wing of the Democratic party, Haynes worked to ensure more Works Projects Administration involvement for African Americans, cheaper rents, better schools and housing, decent hospitals, and honest relief for the needy.

Haynes joined the Alpha Kappa Alpha Sorority in 1923. She worked diligently for this woman's group and was described as a "guiding light and an inspiration" for building "more stately mansions for womanhood." Haynes was involved in numerous organizations and clubs that focused on equal access to opportunities for women. She was a member of the National Association of Colored Women and served as chair of the Industry and Housing Department. Her memberships also included the Harlem Branch of the YWCA, the Mary F. Waring Club, the National Advisory Committee on Women's Participation in the New York World's Fair, the Dorrence Brooks Ladies' Auxiliary, No. 528 of the Veterans of Foreign Wars (VFW), the New York Fisk University Club, and Abyssinian Baptist Church.

Governor Herbert H. Lehman appointed Haynes to serve on the New York State Temporary Commission on the Conditions of the Urban Colored Population in 1937; the commission was designed to study the economic and social conditions of urban African Americans in the state. She was also appointed by Mayor Fiorello La Guardia to serve on the New York City Planning Commission.

Committed to an accurate historical record of her people, Haynes wrote several books, including *Unsung Heroes* (1921), which she said was written to tell of the "victories in spite of the hardships and struggles of Negroes whom the world failed to sing about." In 1952 she published *The Black Boy of Atlanta*, the story of Major Richard Robert Wright, a community leader and banker. A "race woman" who dedicated her life to the uplift and complete involvement of African Americans in every sphere of American life, Haynes was a pioneer in many ways and never lost sight of her goals and her commitment to the African-American community. Her belief that women were ignored, discouraged, and humiliated in society provided the impetus for much of her work and became a hallmark of her struggle. Elizabeth Ross Haynes died in New York City.

• Several manuscript collections contain information on Elizabeth Ross Haynes, including the Schomburg Center for Research in Black Culture and the archives of the National

Board of the YWCA, both in New York City. The James Weldon Johnson Memorial Collection at Yale University and the Moorland-Spingarn Research Center at Howard University contain biography files. Her own writings include "Two Million Negro Women at Work," *Southern Workman* 51 (Feb. 1922): 64–72, and "Negroes in Domestic Service in the United States," *Journal of Negro History* 8 (Oct. 1923): 384–442. Also see Paula Giddings, *When and Where I Enter* (1984). An obituary is in the *New York Times*, 27 Oct. 1953.

IRIS CARLTON-LANEY

HAYNES, Elwood (14 Oct. 1857–13 Apr. 1925), inventor, metallurgist, and automobile manufacturer, was born in Portland, Indiana, the son of Jacob March Haynes, a judge and banker, and Hilinda Sophia Haines. Haynes graduated from the Worcester County Free Institute of Industrial Science (now Worcester Polytechnic Institute), Worcester, Massachusetts, in 1881 with a B.S. in chemistry. He returned to Portland and taught in the local public schools. To further his knowledge of chemistry, he began in 1884 a year of study at the Johns Hopkins University in Baltimore, Maryland. His efforts to secure a fellowship that would enable him to complete a graduate degree were unsuccessful, forcing him to resume teaching in the Portland schools in 1885. In 1887 he married Bertha Lanterman; they had two children.

During the 1880s, huge reserves of natural gas were discovered in Indiana. This was the latest in a series of discoveries that had begun some years earlier in a geological band that extended from New York westward through Pennsylvania and Ohio. Important strikes made in Portland and nearby towns in 1886 marked the onset of an exploitation that lasted almost two decades. Haynes joined in the boom when he became a partner in the Portland Natural Gas and Oil Company, along with his father and three other investors. He was named superintendent of the new company, and, as his participation became full-time, he resigned from his teaching position. Haynes managed the day-to-day operations and supervised drilling and pipeline construction.

The degree to which he devoted himself to his work, learning whatever he could about natural gas, soon made him a leader in the industry. The Indiana Natural Gas and Oil Company hired Haynes in 1890, and he became field superintendent in the village of Greentown the following year. This company was part of a trust created to supply the city of Chicago with natural gas. Haynes was responsible for the construction of one of this country's first long-distance high-pressure gas lines, and it transported gas to Chicago from the rich Indiana fields.

This work took Haynes to many distant and isolated areas. Because travel by horse or rail was slow and could be difficult, Haynes concluded that travel might be made easier by a fast, independent means of transportation. In his spare time he set about designing a motorized vehicle that would accomplish this. The Riverside Machine Works owned by Elmer Apperson in nearby Kokomo was willing to build a vehicle of his design. Although the majority of the mechanical parts were unique to his specifications, it was powered by a gasoline engine manufactured by the Sintz Gas Engine Company of Grand Rapids, Michigan. The vehicle was successfully run for the first time on 4 July 1894, but contrary to Haynes's later claims, it was not the first American-made automobile.

The success of Haynes's first vehicle led to the construction of other improved models and a more formal association with Apperson. Haynes designed, and the machine works constructed, what came to be called Haynes-Apperson automobiles, with the first marketed in 1897. Although the Haynes-Apperson Company was incorporated in 1898, the association lasted only until 1901, when differences between the principles led Apperson to break away to build his own vehicles. At that time, Haynes was forced to abandon the gas company in order to assume the management of his automobile business. The original company name continued in use until 1905, when after a reorganization it became the Haynes Automobile Company.

Unlike most of the pioneering auto manufacturers, Haynes had a college education and a formal knowledge of science. From his youth, he had been interested in metallurgy and continued its study throughout his life. His investigations as an adult were directed primarily toward metallurgy in the automotive field. Haynes pioneered the use of aluminum in his engines in 1895, and in the following year he introduced nickel steel axles.

During the 1890s, while searching for a material that would take an edge and would not tarnish, Haynes devised alloys of nickel chromium and cobalt chromium. He found that the latter could be substituted for mild tempered steel, and in 1907 it was patented and given the trade name Stellite. An improved Stellite was patented in 1912. By adding tungsten to the original formula, Haynes created a material so hard that it could not be readily forged into shape. It had to be cast and then ground to achieve the desired configuration. Harder than tool steel, Stellite proved invaluable in automotive machine work, enabling much faster cutting speeds and less down time for tool replacement. Also in 1912 the Haynes Stellite Works was established in Kokomo to manufacture industrial cutting tools.

Haynes went on to develop a stainless steel, but his efforts to secure a patent were not altogether successful. Englishman Harry Brearley sought a like patent at the same time. Despite independent invention, the stainless steels the two devised were similar. The Brearley application was approved first and Haynes could patent only those few aspects not already enumerated. By itself Haynes's patent was of limited usefulness. To improve its value, Haynes joined forces with Brearley and his backers in the American Stainless Steel Company in 1917. As a holding company for all stainless steel patents, it was in a position to sell the rights to produce products made from the material and collect royalties.

Although Haynes's businesses made him quite wealthy, the general economic downturn after World War I proved fatal to the Haynes Automobile Company and drained much of his fortune. An expansion program immediately after the war left the company in a vulnerable financial position and mounting debts forced its closure in 1924. Its assets were finally sold off in 1925.

As a successful businessman, Haynes achieved a standing in the community that made his name useful in a number of causes. For obvious reasons, his automotive enterprises led him to be an early supporter of the good roads movement. Haynes was always interested in education and he was made a member of the Indiana state board of education. Having been a strict prohibitionist since his youth, he permitted his name to be placed on the Prohibition party ballot in 1916 when he ran unsuccessfully for the U.S. Senate. He was an active supporter of peace and the League of Nations; this despite the fact that his factories and Stellite proved invaluable in the production of munitions during World War I. Haynes belonged to a number of professional organizations. Among them were the American Chemical Society, American Society of Mechanical Engineers, Society of Automotive Engineers, and the Iron and Steel Institute. He died at Kokomo.

• Much of the documentary material generated by his business ventures has been lost. The repository with the largest amount of primary material on his life and work is the Elwood Haynes Museum in Kokomo. The varied collections consist of miscellaneous business records, correspondence, and some personal papers. Haynes is credited with writing *The Complete Motorist* published in 1914 by the Haynes Automobile Company. It purports to be a story of the automobile but is more an encomium of Haynes and his company. His paper, "Materials for Automobiles," was published in the *Transactions of the American Society of Mechanical Engineers* 29 (1907): 209–16. Haynes's article, "Stellite, A New Alloy," appeared in *Scientific American*, 19 Nov. 1910, p. 398. Haynes was a well-known figure for many years and was written about in contemporary newspapers and journals. Ralph D. Gray wrote the most complete biography, *Alloys and Automobiles: The Life of Elwood Haynes* (1979). Haynes's obituary is in the *New York Times*, 14 Apr. 1925.

WILLIAM E. WORTHINGTON, JR.

HAYNES, George Edmund (11 May 1880–8 Jan. 1960), sociologist and social worker, was born in Pine Bluff, Arkansas, the son of Louis Haynes, an occasional laborer, and Mattie Sloan, a domestic servant. He was raised by devout, hard-working, poorly educated parents. His mother stressed that education and good character were paths to improvement. She moved with Haynes and his sister to Hot Springs, a city with better educational opportunities than Pine Bluff. Haynes attended Fisk University, completing his B.A. in 1903. His record at Fisk enabled him to go to Yale, where he earned an M.A. in sociology in 1904. He also won a scholarship to Yale's Divinity School but withdrew early in 1905 to help fund his sister's schooling.

In 1905 Haynes became secretary of the Colored Men's Department of the International (segregated) YMCA, traveling to African-American colleges throughout the nation from 1905 to 1908. During this period he encountered Elizabeth Ross, a Fisk alumna and sociologist who later became the first secretary of Negro youth with the YWCA. Haynes married Ross in 1910; they had one son.

Meanwhile Haynes studied for two summers at the University of Chicago, then left his YMCA work in 1908 to do graduate study in sociology at Columbia University and at its social work affiliate, the New York School of Philanthropy (later the New York School of Social Work). In 1910 Haynes became the first African American to graduate from this social work school, and two years later he became the first African American to earn a Ph.D. at Columbia. His doctorate was in economics and his dissertation, *The Negro at Work in New York City* (1912), became his first book. It called for greater attention to urban blacks, whose population was continuing to grow.

While in New York Haynes worked with groups seeking to aid African Americans in cities. One group was the National League for Protection of Colored Women (NLPCW), which was established in 1906 by merging branches of the Association for the Protection of Colored Women that had been formed in 1905 in cities such as New York and Philadelphia. The league sought to protect African-American women who migrated northward to cities from being exploited by unscrupulous recruiters. Another group with which Haynes worked was the Committee for Improving the Industrial Conditions of Negroes in New York (CIICN), which was also formed in 1906. This group sought to expand employment opportunities for African Americans and hired Haynes to do research through interviewing prospective employees.

Frances Kellor and Ruth Standish Baldwin, leaders in the NLPCW and the CIICN, shared Haynes's concern that many more black social workers needed college training and internships in agencies. Haynes hoped to have blacks work as equals with whites rather than having groups dominated by whites working on problems affecting African Americans. Along with Kellor and Baldwin, Haynes proposed that the CIICN expand its work to train and intern black social workers. When the CIICN declined, Haynes and Baldwin in 1910 led the effort to form a third group, the Committee on Urban Conditions among Negroes (CUCAN).

Overlapping leadership, membership, and programs led to a federation of all three groups in 1911 as the National League on Urban Conditions among Negroes, a title shortened in 1920 to the National Urban League. Haynes became its first executive secretary (1911–1917). The Urban League regards Haynes as its founder and considers its starting date as 19 May 1910, when the CUCAN was formed. Haynes was a moderate leader, more militant than Booker T. Washington but not as strident as W. E. B. Du Bois.

As part of his overall career design, Haynes had moved to Fisk University in the fall of 1910 to teach economics and to set up a sociology department to train black social workers for internships in cities. He had hired Eugene Kinckle Jones in April 1911 as assistant secretary of CUCAN to direct day-to-day operations in New York. Haynes commuted to New York every six weeks and spent his summers there, but eventually Jones won over the board and staff, becoming co-executive with Haynes in 1916 and becoming the executive secretary in 1917, with Haynes given a subordinate role. Urban League leaders increasingly deemed a full-time executive imperative, a need Haynes never met.

In a face-saving move, Haynes took a federal post in 1918, leaving first the Urban League then Fisk. His post, which he held until 1921, was the director of Negro economics, a special assistant to the secretary of labor. His main task was to allay friction arising from blacks migrating to factory jobs in the North. His research in this post resulted in another book, *The Negro at Work during the World War* (1921).

From 1921 until he retired in 1946, Haynes worked for the Federal (later National) Council of Churches, heading the council's race relations department. In 1923 he founded Race Relations Sunday, and in 1940 he initiated Interracial Brotherhood Month. His department fostered interracial conferences, clinics, and committees, and he published two more books, *The Trend of the Races* (1922) and *The Clinical Approach to Race Relations* (1946). In 1930 and again in 1947 Haynes conducted surveys in Africa on behalf of the YMCA, writing his final book, *Africa: Continent of the Future* (1950).

Haynes also wrote many articles and engaged in many civic activities. He organized and administered the Harmon Foundation Awards for black accomplishment from 1926 to 1931. He lobbied for antilynching laws and worked hard to save the Scottsboro boys (nine black youths unjustly charged—and some sentenced to lengthy jail terms—in Alabama for an alleged rape), forming the American Scottsboro Committee (1934). He helped form and chaired the Joint Committee on National Recovery (1933–1935) to secure a fair share of New Deal programs for African Americans. Together with A. Philip Randolph, he fought from 1937 to 1940 to prevent communists from taking control of the National Negro Congress. Haynes served on a commission on the need for a state university in New York and on the board of the state university system (1948–1954) when it was set up.

During the 1950s Haynes was at the City College of New York, teaching courses on black history, interracial matters, and Africa in world affairs. After his first wife died in 1953, Haynes married Olyve Love Jeter in 1955; they had no children. He died in New York City.

• The personal papers of Haynes are in the George Edmund Haynes Collection at Yale University. Additional papers are in the Erastus Milo Cravath Library at Fisk University in Nashville, Tenn. The National Urban League's Archives (covering 1910 to 1965) are in the Manuscripts Division of the Library of Congress. Haynes's work with the Race Rela-tions Department of the National Council of Churches is documented in the council's archives in New York City. Two scholarly books on the Urban League that shed light on Haynes are Guichard Parris and Lester Brooks, *Blacks in the City: A History of the National Urban League* (1971), and Nancy J. Weiss, *The National Urban League, 1910–1940* (1974). The most complete biography of Haynes is Daniel Perlman, "Stirring the White Conscience: The Life of George Edmund Haynes" (Ph.D. diss., New York Univ., 1972). An obituary is in the *New York Times*, 10 Jan. 1960.

EDGAR ALLAN TOPPIN

HAYNES, John (1 May 1594–Jan. 1654), governor of Massachusetts and Connecticut, was born at Old Holt, Essex County, England, the son of John Haynes, a wealthy country gentleman, and Mary Mitchell. Upon his father's death in 1605, Haynes inherited the family's estates. It is probable that he graduated from Cambridge University. Haynes sold one of his father's manors, "Walkfare," in 1622 and two years later purchased "Copford Hall" in Essex County, forty-five miles from London, which he made his home. Haynes married Mary Thornton (the date of the marriage is unknown); they had a daughter and two sons. His sons fought on different sides during the English Civil War. Haynes's wife died before he traveled to America in 1633. He married Mabel Harlackenden in Newtown (now Cambridge), Massachusetts (the date of the marriage is unknown); they had five children. From his English landholdings Haynes received an annual £1,100 income. John Winthrop referred to Haynes as "a gentleman of great estate."

Haynes was a leading Puritan in his Essex neighborhood, and he was a close friend of the Reverend Thomas Hooker, who preached at the church of St. Mary in Chelmsford, the shire town of Essex. Responding to an invitation from Winthrop, Haynes, Hooker, and the Reverends John Cotton and Samuel Stone were among the two hundred persons who boarded the 300-ton ship *Griffin* for America. Arriving in Boston on 4 September 1633, Haynes and Hooker for a while resided in the home of Thomas Dudley in Newtown. The Massachusetts General Court considered Haynes an important person and awarded him 1,000 acres. He built an impressive home that bordered the market place in Newtown. At the court of election on 14 May 1634, Dudley was chosen governor, and Haynes was elected an assistant, one of the men who sat with the governor as an upper house of legislature and as a court. Haynes was also one of a committee of seven who had charge of "all military affairs whatsoever" of the colony.

On 6 May 1635 Haynes was elected the third governor of the Massachusetts Bay Colony. He was an attractive candidate, because he had taken Winthrop, the first governor, to task for leniency toward wrong doers and had also made known his view in favor of reducing taxes. As governor, Haynes declined a salary, seeing "how much the people had been pressed lately with public charges, which the poorer sort did much groan under" (Hosmer, vol. 1, p. 150). In 1635–

1636 he served on two successive committees, to revise the colony's legal code, "agreeable to the word of God." Eventually, in 1648, a new and sterner code went into effect.

In 1635 Haynes presided over the trial of Roger Williams that led to William's banishment. After a period of grace had expired and Williams had not complied with the sentence, Haynes and the assistants sent a band of men to Salem to apprehend Williams and place him on a ship bound for England. Williams, however, had fled a few days before to the Rhode Island country. Supposedly Winthrop had warned Williams in revenge for a censure placed on Winthrop by Haynes and his followers. Many years after Haynes's death Williams, who had no enmity toward Haynes, recalled: "That heavenly Man Mr Hains" had told him in Hartford that God "hath provided, and cut out this part of his World for a Refuge and Receptacle for all sorts of Consciences. I am now under a Cloud" with the Massachusetts colony "as you have bene. We have removed from them thus farr and yet they are not satisfied" (La Fantasie, vol. 2, p. 616).

Haynes served out his term as governor and another year as an assistant in Massachusetts. In December 1636 he was appointed colonel of the Second Regiment for that colony. In June 1636 Haynes's longtime associate Hooker took his Newtown congregation along with some migrants from Watertown and Dorchester to the Connecticut River, where they founded the three river towns of Hartford, Wethersfield, and Windsor. Haynes joined them in May of the next year, as did several other distinguished Massachusetts leaders, including the ministers Samuel Stone and Peter Prudden and the lawyer Roger Ludlow. The three Connecticut towns had an ambiguous legal status, but it was generally agreed that they function as an adjunct to Massachusetts for three years. In Connecticut Haynes involved himself in American Indian affairs. He met with Massachusetts emissaries during the Pequot War of 1637 to coordinate measures against the Indians, although he himself did not engage in any of the military action. In June 1637 Williams commented, "I much rejoice" that Haynes and Ludlow "are almost averse to killing women and children." On 21 September 1638 Haynes was a signatory to the Treaty of Hartford between the Connecticut settlers and the Narragansett and Mohican Indians, whereby these tribes were prohibited from using former Pequot lands. From 1637 to 1643 Haynes was among those New England leaders trying to arrange a confederation of the Puritan colonies. After differences over the jurisdiction for Agawam (now Springfield) and the residual authority of each member colony, in September 1643 the United Colonies of New England (the New England Confederation) went into effect, binding the colonies of Massachusetts, New Haven, Plymouth, and Connecticut to certain forms of intercolonial policy and action. Haynes served as one of Connecticut's two commissioners during 1646 and 1650. He spent a year in England, from late 1646 through 1647, during which time he sold his Old Holt estate.

The new government created by the Fundamental Orders elected its first officers on 11 April 1639. Haynes was chosen the first governor of Connecticut in a court of election attended by the "admitted freemen." Since the term in office was limited to only one year at a time, he served as governor until his death in most of the alternate years, and during the interim years he was usually deputy governor.

As governor or deputy governor Haynes sat with the magistrates (who formed the upper house) as a court that tried cases affecting citizens at large and also on the Particular Court of Connecticut, which rendered judgment pertaining to misdemeanors and differences between persons. The latter court also heard witchcraft cases. Of four and possibly five witchcraft trials conducted by the Particular Court during his lifetime, Haynes participated in only one, which resulted, on 6 March 1651, in a sentence of death pronounced upon John Carrington and Joan Carrington. During Haynes's governorship, Connecticut adopted the Code of 1650, written by Ludlow, which was the most elaborate legal code created by any of the Puritan colonies.

While serving as governor, Haynes died in his sleep at his home in Hartford. His last public appearance was in attendance at the Particular Court in December 1653. Although his tombstone mentions the date of death as 1 March 1654, a letter of William Goodwin to Winthrop on 10 January 1654 reported Haynes's demise.

• Biographical sketches of Haynes are Arthur Adams, "John Haynes," in *Founders and Leaders of Connecticut, 1633–1783,* ed. Charles E. Perry (1934), and Charles E. Cuningham, "John Haynes of Connecticut," *New England Quarterly* 12 (1939): 654–80. The archival material for Haynes's service in colonial government includes Nathaniel B. Shurtleff, ed., *Records of the Governor and Company of the Massachusetts Bay in New England* (1853); J. Hammond Trumbull, ed., *The Public Records of the Colony of Connecticut, 1636–1776,* vol. 1 (1850); *Connecticut Historical Society Collections,* vol. 22, *Records of the Particular Court of Connecticut, 1639–1663* (1928); and David Pulisifer, ed., *Records of the Colony of New Plymouth in New England,* vols. 9–10, *Acts of the Commissioners of the United Colonies of New England* (1859). Haynes's will and his father's will are in *New England Historical and Genealogical Register* 16 (1862): 167–69, and 24 (1870): 422–24, respectively. Aspects from Haynes's life are in *Winthrop Papers,* vols. 2–5, ed. A. B. Forbes (1931–1947); *Winthrop's Journal: "History of New England," 1630–1649,* ed. James K. Hosmer (2 vols., 1908); *The Correspondence of Roger Williams,* ed. Glenn W. La Fantasie (2 vols., 1988); and Frank Shuffelton, *Thomas Hooker, 1586–1647* (1977). The witchcraft trials are discussed in John Taylor, *The Witchcraft Delusion in Colonial Connecticut, 1647–1697* (1908; repr. 1974). An analysis of the forming and actions of the New England Confederation is Harry M. Ward, *The United Colonies of New England, 1643–1690* (1961). Conn. government under Haynes's leadership is discussed in Alexander Johnston, *Connecticut: A Study of a Commonwealth Democracy* (1887); Mary Jeanne Anderson Jones, *Congregational Commonwealth: Connecticut, 1636–1662* (1968); and Robert J. Taylor, *Colonial Connecticut: A History* (1979).

HARRY M. WARD

HAYNES, Lemuel (18 July 1753–28 Sept. 1833), Congregational minister, was born in West Hartford, Connecticut, the son of a black father and a white mother, both unknown, and both of whom abandoned him at birth. He was indentured at five months of age to a white family named Rose, through whom he absorbed strong Calvinist theology and evangelical piety. He was educated in the local schools, but, a serious and diligent child, he also taught himself by the light of the fireside at night; he later said, "I made it my rule to know more every night than I knew in the morning." In 1783 he married Elizabeth Babbit, a white schoolteacher who had proposed to him; they became the parents of ten children.

Haynes fulfilled his indenture and came of age just as the American Revolution was beginning. He signed up as a Minuteman in 1774 and joined militia troops at Roxbury following the Lexington alarm. He joined the Continental army in 1776, marched to Ticonderoga, and was mustered out because he contracted typhus. Haynes remained a lifelong patriot, an admirer of George Washington, an ardent Federalist, and an outspoken critic of Jeffersonianism. He may even have been a member of the secretive Washington Benevolent Society.

Haynes who had poetic aspirations, is thought to be the author of a broadside poem [1774?] lamenting the death of Asa Burt, who was killed when a tree fell on him. He was the author of a patriotic ballad, "The Battle of Lexington" [1775?], which remained unpublished until 1985, after it was discovered by Ruth Bogin in the Houghton Library at Harvard. Although it demonstrates more sincerity than talent, the poem is not entirely without merit: "Freedom & Life, O precious Sounds / yet Freedome does excell / and we will bleed upon the ground / or keep our Freedom still."

Deciding on the ministry as a career, Haynes turned down an opportunity to attend Dartmouth College and instead studied privately with local ministers. He was licensed to preach in 1780, served the Granville, Connecticut, church for five years, and was ordained to the Congregational ministry on 9 November 1785 by the Association of Ministers in Litchfield County. Haynes was apparently the first African American ordained by a mainstream denomination in the United States. He moved to Torrington, Connecticut, where the congregation included the parents of John Brown. In the tradition of Jonathan Edwards and George Whitefield, Haynes was a New Light Congregationalist who favored revivalism but recognized and was critical of its excesses.

In 1788 Haynes became minister of the west parish in Rutland, Vermont, a conservative congregation he served for thirty years. An effective preacher, he was often invited to speak at ordinations, funerals, and public events. He later recalled that he preached 5,500 sermons in Rutland, 400 of them at funerals. He and the congregation remained a center of Calvinism in the midst of the Vermont frontier's rationalism of Thomas Paine and Ethan Allen.

In 1805 Haynes preached a sermon that made an impact far beyond his local circle. In the brief but witty response to visiting Universalist Hosea Ballou, Haynes satirically linked Ballou to the Garden of Eden's serpent, which, as the title of his homily claimed, also promised "Universal Salvation." The sermon was printed, and then reprinted, as late as 1865, until more than seventy editions had been issued throughout the Northeast.

Haynes's humor extended beyond religious satire. When the house of Reverend Ashbel Parmelee burned down, Haynes asked Parmelee if he had lost his sermon manuscripts in the fire. When Parmelee told him that he had, Haynes asked, "Well, don't you think that they gave more light than they ever had before?" Haynes once inadvertently walked into a hotel dining room where a private party was celebrating Andrew Jackson's election to the presidency. Handed a glass of wine and invited to offer a toast, Haynes lifted his glass to the new president and said "Andrew Jackson: Psalm 109, verse 8," then put down the glass and went on his way. When someone later looked up the Bible verse he discovered that it read "Let his days be few and let another take his office."

Eased out of the Rutland church when he was sixty-five, Haynes moved to Manchester, Vermont, where he became involved in a sensational murder case. Two brothers, Stephen and Jesse Boorn, were in prison, having been convicted of the murder of their mentally unstable brother-in-law, Russell Colvin. Colvin's body had not been found, but he had disappeared, and several clues (a found button, a bone unearthed by a dog) pointed to the brothers' guilt. Haynes befriended the Boornes and became convinced of their innocence. Colvin surfaced in New Jersey just before the brothers were to be executed and was brought back to Manchester in a moment of great local drama. Haynes wrote an account of the case, *Mystery Developed* (1820), which had all the shape of a short story, and he preached a sermon, *The Prisoner Released* (1820), which warned against convicting a person on the basis of circumstantial evidence. The British novelist Wilkie Collins later read about the case and used the dead/alive theme in his story *John Jago's Ghost*. Haynes moved once again in 1822, serving the Granville, New York, church, just across the border from Vermont, until his death there.

Haynes has been remembered chiefly as a revolutionary war veteran and has even been omitted from some accounts of African-American history, perhaps because he never lived among black people. Because his religious interests have long since been out of fashion, Haynes the theologian and preacher has been ignored, despite the remarkable publishing history of *Universal Salvation*. Haynes has often been criticized for his failure to speak out against slavery, but recent discoveries of Haynes material may alter that situation. In addition to Haynes's poem on Lexington, Bogin also found an unpublished manuscript, dating from about 1776, entitled "Liberty Further Extended." Composed by the young Haynes, probably while he was in the Continental army, it argues, on the basis of natural rights, for an expansion of the Revolution to encompass the liberation of the nation's African slaves. "Men were made for more noble Ends than to be Drove to market, like Sheep and oxen," Haynes wrote. "Even an affrican, has Equally as good a right to his Liberty in common with Englishmen." The incomplete manuscript was not published until 1983. A more recent discovery, by David Proper, reveals that Haynes preached the funeral sermon in 1821 for Lucy Terry Prince, the earliest known African-American poet. A contemporary newspaper account states that Haynes read a poem that seems to be his own composition and that includes the lines "How long must Ethaopia's murder'd race / Be doom'd by men to bondage and disgrace?"

Haynes clearly was more race conscious than has been realized; he even identified himself, the author of "The Battle of Lexington," as "a young Mollato." In a Fourth of July speech in 1801 marking the twenty-fifth anniversary of American independence, Haynes contrasted European monarchy with American Republicanism and spoke of the plight of "the poor Africans among us." "What has reduced them to their present pitiful, abject state?" he asked. "Is it any distinction that the God of nature hath made in their formation? Nay, but being subjected to slavery, by the cruel hands of oppressors, they have been taught to view themselves as a rank of being far below others."

• There is no collection of Haynes papers, but copies of his printed sermons and addresses are in the Congregational Library, Boston, Mass.; the American Antiquarian Society, Worcester, Mass.; Union Theological Seminary, New York City; and other depositories. Works by and about him are listed in Richard Newman, *Lemuel Haynes: A Bio-bibliography* (1984). His known writings are gathered in Newman, *Black Preacher to White America: The Collected Writings of Lemuel Haynes, 1774–1833* (1990). The previously neglected area of Haynes as theologian has been dealt with by John D. Saillant, "Lemuel Haynes and the Revolutionary Origins of Black Theology, 1776–1801," *Religion and American Culture* 2 (Winter 1993): 79–102.

RICHARD NEWMAN

HAYNES, Williams (29 July 1886–16 Nov. 1970), publisher, historian, and chemical economist, was born Nathan Gallup Williams Haynes in Detroit, Michigan, the son of David Oliphant Haynes, owner and operator of a publishing company, and Helene Dunham Williams. He spent some time finding what he wanted to do with his life. After six months in his early twenties as a reporter for the *New York Sun*, he enrolled in Johns Hopkins University and studied economics, biology, and chemistry from 1908 to 1911, but he did not earn a degree there. From 1911 to about 1916 he worked on the fringes of journalism: in 1911 he edited *Field and Fancy*; he worked as a special correspondent in Canada and Europe from 1911 to 1916; he edited the Northampton (Massachusetts) *Herald* in 1914 and 1915; and during these years he produced seven short

handbooks on dog breeding, dog keeping, and terriers. He also published works of light verse and collections of Americana.

On 10 June 1911 Haynes married Elizabeth Bowen Batchelor, with whom he had one child. After her death, he married Dorothy Farrand on 5 June 1926; they had two children.

In 1916 Haynes told his father that anyone could improve the industrial chemical journal that D. O. Haynes and Company published. His father responded to the challenge by naming him secretary and editorial director of the company's drug trade journals, particularly *Drug and Chemical Markets*. By 1920 Haynes was the publisher of the journal, and in 1926 he split it into two publications, *Drugs and Cosmetic Industry* and *Chemical Industries*. The same year, he also founded *Chemical Week* and *Modern Plastics*.

Haynes had now found his metier. Publishing for the chemical industry became his major work for three decades. In 1919 and 1920 he served on federal commissions on business and on chemical standards. In 1928 he began the series *Chemical Who's Who*, editing it through its fifth edition in 1951. *Chemical Economics* appeared in 1933, and *Men, Money and Molecules* in 1936. Two pamphlets were based on his addresses at New York and Princeton, *American Chemical Society: Our Chemical Heritage* (1935), and *Chemistry's Contributions: The Economics of New Materials* (1936).

In 1939 Haynes sold his interest in the trade magazines and moved into a 1750 farmhouse near Stonington in eastern Connecticut, to devote his full time to writing about the chemical industry. He began to pull together the material he had collected in his years of journal coverage of the field. Between 1939 and 1955 he wrote ten books on various aspects of the industry, including *Chemical Pioneers: The Founders of the American Chemical Industry* (1939), *Dyes Made in America* (1941), *Rationed Rubber and What to Do about It* (with Ernst A. Hauser, 1942); *The Stone That Burns: The Story of the American Sulfur Industry* (1942; rev. ed., 1959, with title *Brimstone: The Stone That Burns*), *This Chemical Age: The Miracle of Man-made Materials* (1942; rev. ed., 1945), *The Chemical Front* (1943), *Southern Horizons* (1946), *Chemical Trade Names and Commercial Synonyms: A Dictionary of American Usage* (1951; rev. ed., 1955), and *Cellulose, the Chemical That Grows* (1953). Many of these volumes were reprinted several times and translated into European languages.

In the midst of this activity, Haynes found time to produce his major work, the six-volume *American Chemical Industry*, published by Van Nostrand between 1945 and 1954. This work, supported initially by Willard H. Dow of Dow Chemical Company and Edgar M. Queeny of Monsanto Chemical Company, was eventually subsidized by most of the major chemical manufacturers. It begins with the earliest commercial enterprises of the colonial period and continues through 1948. Haynes's treatment ranged from broad, general business and economic history, through the way in which this affected major areas of chemical industry, down to detailed chronologies of individual chemical firms. Nothing like it had appeared before, and its importance to the historian of chemistry and technology cannot be overestimated.

After Haynes moved to Stonington, he gradually resumed his general historical studies. Moved by both the long history of the town and his own descent from colonial families, in 1949 he produced *Stonington Chronology, 1649–1949*. Between 1955 and 1963 he wrote a series of pamphlets about Stonington, its colonial personages, and its later manufactures; these appeared as Connecticut historical booklets, all reprinted or revised over the years. In addition, Haynes was always available to speak to civic groups, historical societies, and college audiences about the history of Connecticut, the chemical industry, or more general topics, delivering hundreds of talks.

Haynes's only major award, presented shortly after completion of *Americal Chemical Industry*, was the 1957 Dexter Award from the Division of History of Chemistry of the American Chemical Society. In his last years Haynes and his wife spent winters in Oaxaca, Mexico. Characteristically, he developed an interest in Mexican history and culture and studied them when he was in his eighties. He died in Stonington.

• A biography of Haynes is in Wyndham D. Miles, ed., *American Chemists and Chemical Engineers* (1976). No bibliography of his works appears in a single publication, but most of them can be found in the "Pre-1956 Imprints" section of the *National Union Catalogue*, with only a few in the next two sections. The Dexter Award presentation is reported in *Journal of Chemical Education* 34 (1957): 488. An obituary is in *Chemical Week* 107, no. 2 (Nov. 1970): 12.

ROBERT M. HAWTHORNE JR.

HAYNSWORTH, Clement Furman, Jr. (30 Oct. 1912–22 Nov. 1989), lawyer and jurist, was born in Greenville, South Carolina, the son of Clement Furman Haynsworth, an attorney, and Elsie Hall. Haynsworth graduated summa cum laude from Furman University (founded by his great-grandfather) in 1933 and received a law degree from Harvard in 1936. He then joined his father's Greenville firm where, after service in the naval reserve during World War II (1942–1945), he became senior partner in 1946. That year he had also married Dorothy Merry, a Georgia matron with two sons, whom Haynsworth adopted.

Under Haynsworth's direction, his firm became South Carolina's largest and wealthiest, numbering among its clients numerous major corporate interests. His political instincts proved equally fruitful. Like many southern Democrats increasingly disenchanted with the policies of the national Democratic party, he supported Dwight Eisenhower's Republican presidential candidacies in 1952 and 1956. He also enjoyed a close association with Charles E. Daniel, a construction magnate with substantial ties to the Eisenhower White House. Such connections led in 1957 to his appointment to the U.S. Court of Appeals for the Fourth Circuit. In 1964 he became the court's senior jurist in years of service and thus chief judge of the circuit.

Not surprisingly, given his professional, social, and political backgrounds, Judge Haynsworth developed a moderately conservative record in civil liberties cases, especially those involving racial issues. In 1968, for example, the Supreme Court reversed his decision upholding "freedom of choice" desegregation plans permitting parents to select their children's schools, even though such arrangements left segregated school districts largely intact. Even more predictable, perhaps, was his stance in labor-management litigation. By 1969, according to one count, seven labor cases in which Haynsworth participated had been appealed to the Supreme Court. He had taken an "anti-labor" position in each and was reversed every time, by a unanimous Court in six of the seven cases. One case in which the judge's involvement was to prove particularly controversial concerned the closing of the Darlington Manufacturing Company, a subsidiary of Deering Milliken, Inc., one of South Carolina's industrial giants. In 1963 Haynsworth joined a 3 to 2 majority that overturned a decision of the National Labor Relations Board and held that an employer's decision to close a plant to avoid unionization did not constitute an unfair labor practice forbidden by federal law. On appeal the Supreme Court agreed that a company could close its entire business for anti-union reasons, but it considered Darlington merely a part of Deering Milliken and rejected any right of a company to close a portion of its operations to discourage unionization elsewhere in the business.

Haynsworth's votes in racial and labor cases hardly endeared him to union or civil rights leaders. But the Nixon administration considered the Fourth Circuit jurist ideally suited to its "southern strategy" for luring dissident southerners into the Republican fold. When a Supreme Court vacancy arose in the spring of 1969, Haynsworth quickly emerged as a leading candidate for the position. On 18 August President Nixon submitted his nomination to the Senate.

The Haynsworth nomination provoked an immediate outcry from labor and civil rights groups. Initially, the White House remained confident that its choice could weather the storm. Even before the president's selection was announced, however, the Haynsworth nomination had begun to raise the same sorts of ethical concerns that had led to Justice Abe Fortas's resignation the previous spring. Initially, opponents charged that Haynsworth should have recused himself from participating in the Darlington Mills case since he was a director and one-seventh owner of a vending machine firm that did business with Darlington's parent company, Deering Milliken. Then, after a specialist in judicial ethics told the Senate Judiciary Committee that recusal had been unwarranted in the case, critics revealed that the nominee had purchased stock in the Brunswick Corporation after participating in a decision involving that firm, but before the ruling was announced. Other ethical complaints were also raised.

Prominent members of the legal community, including sixteen past presidents of the American Bar Association, supported the nomination; and the

ABA's judiciary committee, unanimously at first and later by a divided vote, assigned Haynsworth a positive rating. But the ethical concerns, along with complaints about his stance in labor and civil rights cases, persisted. The Senate Judiciary Committee recommended confirmation in a 10 to 7 vote, but a growing number of senators, among them several Republicans who had led the successful fight against President Lyndon B. Johnson's attempt to make Fortas chief justice, announced their opposition. On 21 November 1969 the Senate voted 55 to 45 to defeat the nomination. President Nixon condemned the "brutal, vicious and, in my opinion, unfair" attacks on his nominee and vowed to continue his campaign to appoint a "strict constructionist" southerner to the high Court. But Senator Albert Gore, Sr. (D-Tenn.), offered another assessment: "If a local judge in almost any town in America should do [what Haynsworth did], the local lawyers and citizens would rise up in indignation. And they should."

Following his defeat, Judge Haynsworth considered whether his usefulness as a judge had been so impaired by the confirmation battle that he should return to private life. Ultimately, however, he elected to remain on the circuit bench. In 1981 he became a senior judge of the circuit, serving in that capacity until his death in Greenville twenty years and a day after his rejection by the Senate.

• The Clement F. Haynsworth, Jr., Papers are in the Library of Congress. John P. Frank, *Clement Haynsworth, the Senate, and the Supreme Court* (1991), examines the controversy over his nomination. The published Senate judiciary committee hearings on his confirmation are an excellent collection of materials on his judicial record from 1957 to 1969. A revealing biographical sketch issued by his office when his nomination was announced is reprinted in Leon Friedman and Fred L. Israel, eds., *The Justices of the Supreme Court*, vol. 2 (1969). An obituary is in the *New York Times*, 23 Nov. 1989.

TINSLEY E. YARBROUGH

HAYS, Alexander (8 July 1819–5 May 1864), soldier, was born in Franklin, Venango County, Pennsylvania, the son of Samuel Hays, a sheriff of the county and member of the Pennsylvania House of Representatives, and Agnes Broadfoot. Educated at Venango Academy, Mercer Academy, and Allegheny College, he left college in his senior year to accept an appointment to West Point. Among his classmates were Simon B. Buckner and Winfield S. Hancock. In the class above Hays was Ulysses S. Grant, with whom he formed a lifelong friendship. Hays graduated in 1844, number twenty in a class of twenty-five.

After graduation Hays was posted to the Fourth U.S. Infantry for frontier duty at Natchitoches, Louisiana, and in the military occupation of Texas. In the Mexican War Hays won a brevet to first lieutenant for gallant conduct in the battles of Palo Alto and Resaca de la Palma. He was wounded in the leg at the latter battle and was sent to Buffalo, New York, on recruiting duty. Upon recovery he returned to Mexico and

served to the end of the war. Hays married Annie Adams McFadden in 1846; they had seven children.

Hays resigned from the military on 12 April 1848 and entered the iron business at Victory Forge near Franklin, Pennsylvania, an unsuccessful venture. In 1849 he and a party of "forty-niners" traveled to California to seek their fortunes. The gold fields yielded little, and in 1851 Hays returned to Pennsylvania, where he was employed in engineering, construction, and surveying work for various railroads and municipalities in the western part of the state.

In 1855, at the height of the troubles with the Mormons in Utah, Hays received a presidential appointment as a captain in one of the new regular army infantry regiments being formed. He declined the appointment, but in 1859 he enlisted as a private in a fashionable militia company named the "City Guards of Pittsburgh." When the Civil War broke out Hays was elected its captain, and the company became part of the Twelfth Pennsylvania Infantry, a three-month volunteer organization. Hays was offered a captain's commission in the Sixteenth U.S. Infantry in June. He declined it, sensing that higher rank in the volunteer service was possible. He wrote his wife, "I am determined to play second fiddle to no ambitious ignoramus." His stubborn persistence was rewarded. In August 1861 he was appointed the colonel of the Sixty-third Pennsylvania. The historian of the Sixty-third recalled that Hays "was a thorough soldier, hot and fiery and impetuous at times, but courteous and kindly withal . . . he was just to his men."

Hays's regiment served in the defenses of Washington, D.C., until March 1862 and was principally occupied in drilling and training. The regiment participated in the Peninsula campaign at the battles of Fair Oaks, the Peach Orchard, and Glendale. At Glendale Hays and his regiment behaved with great gallantry. General Hiram Berry congratulated Hays afterward, writing, "I have not in my career in military life seen better fighting or a work better done." In recognition of his services in the Seven Days battles, Hays was brevetted major and lieutenant colonel of the regular army.

Following the withdrawal of the army from the Peninsula, Hays participated in the battle of Second Manassas, where he was severely wounded in the leg. Once again his courage was conspicuous, and three prominent Union generals of the Third Army Corps recommended his promotion to brigadier general of volunteers to President Abraham Lincoln. Less than one month later, Hays received his promotion. After a convalescent leave for his wound, he assumed command of a brigade of infantry in the defenses of Washington.

On 24 June 1863 Hays was ordered to report with his brigade to the Second Army Corps, which was then marching through Maryland with the Army of the Potomac to meet Robert E. Lee's invasion of Pennsylvania. Hays reported on the twenty-sixth and was assigned to command of the Third Division, Second Corps, whose commander had been relieved for other duties. The Second Corps arrived upon the battlefield of Gettysburg, Pennsylvania, early on 2 July, and Hays's Third Division was posted on the right of the corps, on Cemetery Ridge. On 3 July the Third Division played a significant role in the repulse of "Pickett's charge," Hays once more distinguishing himself in the fight. Following the defeat of the Confederates, he rode across the front of his division, trailing a captured flag, "a mark for a hundred sharpshooters." A Third Division veteran wrote of Hays, "I reckon him the grandest view of my life. I bar not Niagara" (*General Alexander Hays at the Battle of Gettysburg*, p. 13). Of Gettysburg Hays wrote to his mother, "I was fighting for my native state, and before I went in thought of those at home I so dearly love. If Gettysburg was lost all was lost for them, and I only interposed a life that would be otherwise worthless."

Hays participated in the Rapidan campaign during the fall of 1863 and sought unsuccessfully to obtain promotion to major general of volunteers. In the reorganization of the Army of the Potomac in March 1864, the Third Corps was merged into the Second Corps. In the shuffling of officers, Hays lost command of the Third Division, based on seniority, and was reduced to command of the Second Brigade, Third Division, which included his old regiment, the Sixty-third Pennsylvania.

Hays led his brigade into the battle of the Wilderness on the afternoon of 5 May 1864. Early in the combat, as he rode to the Sixty-third Pennsylvania, "a bullet struck him just above the cord of the hat, crashing into his brain," according to a veteran. Hays died a few hours later. He was buried at Alleghany Cemetery in Pittsburgh and was posthumously promoted to major general of volunteers. Grant paid a fitting tribute to the life and character of Hays, when he wrote in his memoirs of his fallen comrade, "With him it was 'Come on, boys,' not 'Go.'"

• Hays's papers are located in the Historical Society of Western Pennsylvania in Pittsburgh. George T. Fleming, *Life and Letters of Alexander Hays* (1919), is a complete but uncritical biography that includes Hays's personal correspondence with his wife and family and some of his official correspondence. An early biography of Hays is Samuel D. Oliphant, "Brigadier General Alexander Hays," *United States Service Magazine* 2 (1864): 266–72. There are details about Hays's personality in Gilbert A. Hays, *Under the Red Patch: Story of the Sixty Third Regiment Pennsylvania Volunteers* (1908). For Hays at Gettysburg, see the pamphlet by Fleming and Gilbert A. Hays, *General Alexander Hays at the Battle of Gettysburg* (1913), which includes extracts from Fleming's biography and Gilbert Hays's regimental history. Also see G. W. Cullum, *Biographical Register of the Officers and Graduates of the United States Military Academy*, vol. 2 (1879); C. A. Babcock, *Venango County, Pa.*, vol. 1 (1919); and J. H. Newton, ed., *History of Venango County, Pa.* (1879). An obituary is in the *Pittsburgh Dispatch*, 9 May 1864.

D. SCOTT HARTWIG

HAYS, Arthur Garfield (12 Dec. 1881–14 Dec. 1954), lawyer and author, was born in Rochester, New York, to Isaac Hays and Laura Garson, both members of prosperous families in the clothing trade. When Hays was twelve the family moved to New York City, where, with brief exceptions he lived throughout his life.

Hays was remarkable for his energy, his garrulousness, and his argumentativeness. As a high school student he joined the debating club, athletic organizations, and the quasi-military American Guard. He entered the City College of New York but later transferred to Columbia University, where he earned a B.A. in 1902 and an LL.B. and M.A. in 1905. He was an editor of the *Columbia Law Review*, and according to one source was regarded by his classmates as a tough opponent with a tenacious intellect.

After graduating from law school, Hays joined a well-established law firm, Bowers and Sands. Within a year he struck out on his own, setting up Hays, Kaufmann & Lindheim with two friends. Thus began a colorful legal career. Although his fame is primarily the result of involvement in civil liberties issues, Hays had a large commercial practice, including the representation of financiers, brokers, and merchants. In 1908 Hays married Blanche Marks; they had one child. During World War I he engaged in litigation and arbitration on questions of international law, such as seizure of cargoes, contraband, and blacklisting. He lived in England 1915–1917 and became closely associated with U.S. Ambassador Walter Hines Page. Hays's firm had several clients with German connections, leading to charges during and after World War I of "pro-German" sympathies. His partners were indicted and convicted in 1921 (although later pardoned) of having been German agents. Hays was vigorous in their defense and the defense of other German Americans.

In 1920 Hays was a founder of the American Civil Liberties Union (ACLU) and a member of its National Committee. He became its general counsel in the late 1920s, a position he held until his death. He argued repeatedly that the value of freedom, especially free expression, far outweighed any dangers created by speakers or the substance of their speech. As counsel for the ACLU, Hays represented the Nazi-sympathizing German-American Bund in the late 1930s, the Communist John Strachey, and even the arch-conservative William Randolph Hearst, when a Senate committee attempted to subpoena Hearst's telegrams. He assisted Clarence Darrow in the Scopes "monkey trial" (1925), defending the right to teach Darwinism in Tennessee schools. In one of Hays's books he explained his commitment: "I hate to see people pushed around. I vent my emotions in trying to help them from being pushed."

Hays was a leader in getting the ACLU to attack censorship of the arts as well as political speech. In 1926 he successfully defended H. L. Mencken against a charge of selling racy material banned in Boston, and he advocated artistic freedom to discuss and portray sexuality openly. Hays was an early champion of sexual privacy and a supporter of easy access to divorce. He successfully represented the Countess Cathcart in the late 1920s after she was denied entry to the United States on the ground that a widely publicized love affair demonstrated her moral turpitude.

Hays also participated in many cases in which the ACLU defended the rights of African Americans, including the complex series of rape charges against the Scottsboro boys (1932). He consistently worked to uphold the rights of workers to organize, especially when the challenged rights overlapped, as they often did, with the rights of speech and assembly. In the late 1930s Hays himself was once pelted with eggs and tomatoes as he attempted to speak at a labor rally. It was typical of Hays to defend Henry Ford, who was known for union-busting, against government restrictions on antiunion literature distributed to Ford employees (1938).

Hays's career had a strong international flavor. During World War I he represented shipping interests as well as German businesses. He had become well known abroad soon after the Nazis came into power, when he appeared at the Reichstag fire trial (1933) on behalf of the defendants, all of whom but one, a self-confessed pyromaniac, were acquitted. In 1937 he conducted an investigation of civil liberties in Puerto Rico, and in 1946 he was a member of the commission of inquiry of the Committee for the Fair Trial of the Yugoslav leader, General Mihailovich.

Hays maintained a prosperous legal practice until his death in New York City. After his first law firm was dissolved in 1921, Hays founded the firm that eventually became Hays, St. John & Abramson, specializing in international corporate law, copyright, and litigation. In 1924 Hays divorced Blanche Marks and married Aline Davis Fleisher, with whom he had one child. That same year he expanded the practice to include domestic relations. His most famous case was a successful challenge on behalf of sixty heirs to the will of Ella Wendel, a recluse who left her $50 million estate to charities. Hays did not regard his work for corporate clients as inconsistent with a commitment to civil liberties. As he put it, he "hated censorship of business as well as of books." He argued that "producing more, not dividing up, is the road to prosperity." Even in the depression, he maintained, Americans earned more and worked less than they had in the previous century.

But Hays was not uncritical of American capitalism; he opposed what he considered excessive concentrations of capital and supported the graduated income tax when it was controversial. He also consistently defended the rights of unions to organize, represent, and bargain for workers, while at the same time inveighing against what he called "bad" unions that were tyrannical, corrupt, or unfair. His answer to every problem was "liberty," by which he meant universal suffrage, tempered by stringent protection for individuals against tyranny by the majority.

Hays claimed that democracy—when combined with free speech, free press, and the secret ballot—was the only sure source of liberty. He believed that liberty, an end in itself, would ensure progress and civiliza-tion. He also believed that America was the home of such progress, and that its peculiar mix of economic and political systems, although defying categorization, maximized both "freedom and abundance."

Beyond his legal and public careers, Hays was a vigorous and complex man. He was generous, sentimental, devoted to family, impatient (especially with bores), old-fashioned about women, and deeply loyal. He liked sports, disliked organized religion, and abhorred pomposity and pretention.

• The Hays papers are at Mudd Library, Princeton University. Hays wrote several books and many articles for periodicals, including the *Nation*, *New Republic*, and *Saturday Review*. His books include *Enemy Property in America* (1923), *Let Freedom Ring* (1925), and *Trial by Prejudice* (1933); his philosophy is most clearly outlined in *Democracy Works* (1939). There is no biography of Hays, but much information is contained in his autobiographical *City Lawyer, the Autobiography of a Law Practice* (1942). Helpful secondary works include Samuel Walker, *In Defense of American Liberties: A History of the ACLU* (1990); Alan Reitman, ed., *The Pulse of Freedom, American Liberties: 1920–1970s* (1975); and Charles Lam Markmann, *The Noblest Cry: A History of the American Civil Liberties Union* (1965). An obituary is in the *New York Times*, 15 Dec. 1954.

NORMAN DORSEN
SARAH BARRINGER GORDON

HAYS, Isaac (5 July 1796–12 Apr. 1879), physician and editor, was born in Philadelphia, Pennsylvania, the son of Samuel Hays, a merchant, and Richea Gratz. A successful merchant in the East India trade, Hays's father attained considerable wealth and provided his son with an excellent education and introduction to the cultural life of Philadelphia. Raised in the Jewish faith, Hays was for many years a pupil in the Philadelphia grammar school run by the eminent divine and classical scholar Samuel B. Wylie, who later became professor of ancient languages at the University of Pennsylvania. Hays entered the university in 1812 and graduated four years later with a B.A.

After completion of his studies at the University of Pennsylvania, Hays, following the wishes of his father, decided to pursue a career as a merchant. He worked for a year in his father's countinghouse but in 1817 concluded that the merchant life was not for him. Settling on a career in medicine, Hays began an apprenticeship under Nathaniel Chapman, professor of the theory and practice of physic and the institutes of medicine at the University of Pennsylvania. A close and long-lasting friendship between pupil and teacher soon developed, and in his later years Chapman referred many of his patients to Hays. Hays received his M.D. from the University of Pennsylvania in 1820. He wrote his medical dissertation on the concept of sympathy.

Hays had also developed an interest in natural history and paleontology, which brought him into contact with many of America's most eminent natural scientists. While still a medical student, Hays was elected a member of the Academy of Natural Sciences of Philadelphia in 1818. He served that institution as curator, as a member of the Library Committee, as a member and chair of the Publications Committee, and as president (1865–1869). Hays edited the 1828 printing of Alexander Wilson's *American Ornithology*. Three years later he read before the American Philosophical Society a paper describing the jaws and the teeth of the mastodon.

Early in his medical career Hays devoted much time to the study of ophthalmology, and at his death he was considered one of the leading eye surgeons in the United States. In 1826 he published three articles concerning diseases of the eye in the *Philadelphia Journal of the Medical and Physical Sciences*. He prepared the chapter on diseases of the eye for the 1830 edition of William Potts Dewees's textbook, *A Practice of Physic*. Hays also edited the first three American editions of William Lawrence's *Treatise on Diseases of the Eye* (1843, 1847, and 1854), which included numerous additions related to his own practice. The third edition of the *Treatise* included Hays's description of a case of astigmatism, the first such description published in the United States. Hays was one of the first experts to observe and investigate color blindness as a pathological condition. He also devised an operation to cure strabismus and invented a cataract knife, an instrument subsequently used by many American ophthalmologists. In addition to his appointments as surgeon to the Pennsylvania Infirmary for Diseases of the Eye and Ear (1822–1827) and the Wills Eye Hospital (1834–1854), Hays also served as a physician at Philadelphia Orphans' Asylum, Philadelphia Dispensary, Southern Dispensary, and Pennsylvania Institution for the Instruction of the Blind.

In 1834 Hays married Sarah Minis of Savannah, Georgia; they had four children. Hays, a devoted and loving husband, rarely spent evenings away from home. It was not until 1846, when he traveled to New York City to attend the convention that led to the founding of the American Medical Association, that he spent his first night outside of Philadelphia.

Despite his reputation as a skilled surgeon, Hays was best known as an editor. He edited Richard Dennis Hoblyn's *Dictionary of Medical Terms* (1846 and 1855) and Neal Arnott's *Elements of Physics* (1848). With Robert Eglesfeld Griffith he translated two works by François Broussais, *History of Chronic Phlegmasiae* (1831) and *Principles of Physiological Medicine* (1832). In 1832, during Philadelphia's cholera epidemic, he helped found and edited the weekly *Cholera Gazette* in order to communicate useful information concerning the clinical history and treatment of the disease.

Hays was the editor of the first two volumes—the only ones ultimately published—of a projected massive anthology of the medical literature of the time, *American Cyclopedia of Practical Medicine and Surgery* (1834–1836). Hays selected the contributors to the *Cyclopedia* and wrote several articles for it, but the work was never completed owing to a lack of funding.

Hays, whose cardinal virtue was punctuality, had been ideally suited to gather and edit the contributions to the *Cyclopedia*. Few physicians in the United States at that time possessed Hays's knowledge of the medical profession, much of it gained through his editorship of the *American Journal of the Medical Sciences*, the leading U.S. medical periodical of the nineteenth century. Hays's friend and former preceptor Nathaniel Chapman had founded the periodical in 1820 as the *Philadelphia Journal of the Medical and Physical Sciences*. Hays became the journal's editor in 1827, after a year as an associate editor. Wishing to make the quarterly more national in character, Hays changed its name to *American Journal of the Medical Sciences* and assembled a distinguished group of contributing editors from across the country. From the very beginning of Hays's editorship, the *American Journal* published the work of America's leading physicians, including numerous classics of American medical science. The *American Journal* soon became America's most respected medical periodical. Hays edited the journal until 1879; his son Isaac Minis Hays, also a physician, joined him as an assistant editor in 1869.

Hays was extremely active in national as well as local medical and scientific organizations. In 1846 he participated in the founding of the American Medical Association as a delegate from the Philadelphia Medical Society to the inaugural meeting of the association in New York City. He later served the AMA as a member of its committee on medical education and as a member of the committee that prepared the association's code of medical ethics. From 1847 to 1853 he chaired the publications committee, which published the AMA's *Transactions*, and was also treasurer of the association from 1848 to 1852.

Hays was a member of the American Academy of Arts and Sciences and a councilor, curator, and member of the publications committee of the American Philosophical Society, to which he was elected in 1830. He was elected a fellow of the College of Physicians of Philadelphia in 1835, was a member of the Philadelphia Medical Society, the Philadelphia County Medical Society, and the Kappa Lamda Society of Philadelphia, and was corresponding secretary of the Medical Society of the State of Pennsylvania. Hays was the first president (1870) of the Ophthalmological Society of Philadelphia, an honorary member of the American Ophthalmological Society, and a corresponding member of the Société Universelle d'Ophthalmologie. A founder of the Franklin Institute in Philadelphia, he later served as a manager, corresponding secretary (1828–1840), chairman of the library committee, and chairman of the publications committee (1832, 1837–1841).

Hays retired from active practice in 1865 but continued with his editorial duties throughout his last years, surrounded by his family and his extensive collection of medical books. At the time of his death, in Philadelphia, he was the oldest living editor in the United States.

• An extensive collection of Hays's correspondence is in the Library of the American Philosophical Society. Hays's activities in the College of Physicians of Philadelphia, Academy of Natural Sciences of Philadelphia, Franklin Institute, and American Philosophical Society can be documented in the archives of those institutions. Useful accounts of Hays's life and career include Alfred Stillé, "Memoir of Isaac Hays, M.D.," *Transactions of the College of Physicians of Philadelphia*, 3d ser., 5 (1881): lxxvii–cx; Samuel D. Gross, "Obituary Notice of Isaac Hays, M.D.," *American Journal of the Medical Sciences* 78 (1879): 281–92; and Daniel G. Brinton, "Obituary Notice of the Late Isaac Hays, M.D.," *Proceedings of the American Philosophical Society* 18 (1879): 259–60. See also Edward B. Krumbhaar, "The Early Days of the American Journal of the Medical Sciences," *Medical Life* 36 (1929): 240–56. An obituary is in the *Philadelphia Public Leger*, 14 Apr. 1879.

THOMAS A. HORROCKS

HAYS, Jacob (5 May 1772–21 June 1850), police officer, was born in Westchester County, New York, the son of David Hays, a farmer and trader, and Esther Etting. Little is known about his childhood or education. By the 1790s Hays was living in New York City, where he pursued various occupations, including those of conveyancer and grocer, and served as captain of the watch. In 1802 he was appointed high constable. Starting in 1810, after nearly a decade of exchanging the office with several other men, he began a career as high constable through an unbroken succession of reappointments for the rest of his life. Although the constabulary was abolished in 1845, along with its adjunct the night watch, in favor of a "day and night" police, the title and salary of high constable were reserved for Hays until his death. He was also for many years the sergeant at arms of the board of aldermen and the crier of the court of sessions.

Shortly before Hays began his first term as high constable, the common council had defined the responsibilities of the office in terms of the suppression of what would later be called "quality of life" offenses, such as obstructing the sidewalk; "victimless" crimes, such as Sabbath breaking; and the control of vagrants. However, the rapid expansion of New York City in the following decades as a business center and as a port of entry for European immigrants fostered the development of an underclass of professional criminals. The city was increasingly troubled by robbery and violence in the streets, burglaries of houses and stores, forgery and business fraud, and counterfeiting.

Hays met these new problems with a dedication to public service, unimpeachable honesty, personal courage, and a remarkable skill at thief taking that astonished his contemporaries. In his prime it was supposed—by Hays himself as well as by New Yorkers in general—that he could recognize and know the history of every criminal on the eastern seaboard. Stories were told showing his insight and powers of observation. Once, while investigating a major theft, Hays arrested the perpetrator, in the public room of a hotel, solely because he become ill at ease upon seeing Hays enter. When a family was poisoned with arsenic-laden pastries, Hays showed that the man thought to have a motive for the crime also possessed twine similar to that used to tie up the pastry.

Hays and the other constables worked out of the police office in the basement of city hall. He made it a practice to issue bulletins to the press from this center, sometimes warning citizens against a new counterfeit bill or a gang of pickpockets newly arrived in the city, sometimes asking for the public's help in checking crime. These latter requests were occasionally general, reminding citizens not to buy goods that they supposed to be stolen but to report the seller to the police office, but more often they were specific requests: for witnesses to an accident that had killed a little boy, for instance, or for evidence of merchants who had accepted counterfeit money. Another apparent innovation of Hays's early years as high constable was improved record keeping. There was a "loss book" in the police office, to record thefts and descriptions of the stolen goods, and a file on criminals, which on one occasion helped to identify a man found dead in New Jersey. Hays also developed an extensive network of informers who aided him in solving crimes and sometimes even in anticipating them. Newspaper reports of arrests often observed that Hays had acted "upon information received, the nature of which did not particularly appear."

Hays was also remembered as unusually skilled at crowd control. During an 1831 confrontation in a theater between an unruly mob and a squadron of constables, Hays, whose tact was "proverbial," dismissed the constables and then ordered the mob to disperse. The group left the building after giving him three cheers. in 1836 he was specifically praised by the *New-York Transcript* for calming the excited feelings of a group of striking stevedores by addressing them "mildly and rationally."

As a result of these efforts, and of the success that attended them, Hays became a celebrity. Indeed, late in his life, a St. Louis newspaper praised a local officer by comparing him favorably to Hays. It was believed that the city's "police, exceeding that of Paris or London, suffers the escape of no vagabond" (*New-York Gazette and General Advertiser*, 19 Aug. 1817). One of his obituarists supposed that at the height of his career he would have been the one New Yorker all New Yorkers would have known. Another remembered Hays's name having been used as a last resort by a teacher to quiet a noisy classroom. Certainly in the late 1810s and throughout the 1820s Hays was frequently named as the arresting officer in newspaper accounts of crime, often with an added garland of praise: "that vigilant officer" or the like. Occasionally his name was invoked as if a guardian spirit: "We hope that Hays may get hold of him" (*Morning Courier and New-York Enquirer*, 9 Jan. 1830).

By the mid-1830s, Hays, who had been commonly called "Old Hays" for nearly a decade, was reserving his energies for major cases. By the early 1840s, age and infirmities had reduced him to performing his merely ceremonial duties in the court of sessions and at the meetings of the board of aldermen.

Among his notable cases are the following. He established the identity of the body of a man found murdered in an alley in November 1823 as that of James Murray, a traveler from Boston, and he arrested John Johnson, a boardinghouse keeper, for the crime. When the City Bank was robbed of nearly $250,000 in a break-in in March 1831, Hays, acting on information furnished by a boardinghouse keeper, quickly made an arrest and recovered $185,000. The informant received a reward of $5,000; Hays received a one-third share of $2,000. After further investigation, Hays made additional arrests and succeeded in retrieving most of the rest of the money.

Hays's most intricate case was the great forgery on the Union Bank, in October 1827. A check for $7,760 purportedly issued by a local business was accepted by the bank. A few days later the bank's cashier thought he recognized the forger in a passerby, who proved to be Timothy Redmond, proprietor of the United States Hotel. Redmond was questioned, but the case was not then pursued, for lack of additional evidence. Shortly thereafter, however, when David Ware, a professional criminal, was arrested with a large sum of money that in fact he had stolen, he decided that his best way out of trouble was to admit falsely that he had been involved in the forgery and to identify Redmond as the leader. Redmond was rearrested, tried in January 1828, and acquitted, partly by proving a partial alibi and partly through the jurors' distrust of Ware's testimony. Redmond subsequently had Ware arrested for perjury. In the last moments of Ware's two-day trial, in March 1828, Hays brought into the courtroom the real forger, who denied the involvement of either Redmond or Ware. Ware's lawyers declared his case to be indefensible, the judge gave a teary summation to the jury in which all the credit was given to the finger of God, and Redmond's innocence was at last accepted by all.

Hays was the grandson of a rabbi, though he himself attended a Presbyterian church. He was married three times and was the father of eleven children. His first wife, whose name is not known, was the mother of two. With his second wife, Catherine Conroy, Hays had three children; she died in 1812. His third wife, the mother of six, was Mary Post; she survived him. Hays died after a brief illness at his home on Lispenard Street in New York City.

Hays's career grew out of the sudden transition of the United States in the early nineteenth century from an agrarian nation whose largest towns were still small, personal communities into a more commercial society with rapidly growing cities and an economy based on money. The government of New York City was ill adapted to cope with the resulting problems of urban crime, but Hays's skill as an investigator was important to his fellow citizens, and appreciated by them.

• Much of what was written about Hays after his death is to some degree inaccurate, but see Augustine Costello, *Our Police Protectors* (1885), and City of New York, *Minutes of the Common Council of the City of New York* (1784–1831). A detailed summary of the Redmond case is in a series of articles on the criminal career of Robert Sutton in the *National Police Gazette* (Oct.–Nov., 1845).

GEORGE A. THOMPSON, JR.

HAYS, Lawrence Brooks (9 Aug. 1898–12 Oct. 1981), politician and Protestant layman, was born in London, Arkansas, the son of Adelbert Steele Hays, an attorney, and Sarah Tabitha "Sallie" Butler. Although his first name was in fact Lawrence, he preferred to go by his middle name, Brooks. His family took its religion—Baptist—and its politics—Democratic—seriously. Later, Hays would write that his early life was a "quadrangle marked by a line from . . . home to the public school, to the courthouse, to the little Baptist church, and back to the home." He attended his first Democratic party convention at the age of ten.

As a young man Hays was torn between studying for the ministry and pursuing a career in politics. He entered the University of Arkansas at Fayetteville in 1915 and decided, after graduating in 1919, to attend George Washington University Law School in Washington, D.C. In 1922, a few months before receiving his law degree, Hays married his college sweetheart, Marion Prather. They would have two children. That same year, the couple returned to Arkansas, where Hays joined his father's law firm.

Hays served as assistant attorney general of Arkansas for two years from 1925 to early 1927 and then decided to run for governor in the 1928 election. His platform called for reform: a state income tax, aid to public schools, and adjustments in the financing of public highways. Hays, only twenty-nine when he filed, placed second in the Democratic primary. He ran again in 1930 and again lost. Throughout these years Hays remained active in the Second Baptist Church in Little Rock.

In 1932 Hays was elected Democratic national committeeman from Arkansas and served in that position until 1939. With the election of Franklin D. Roosevelt as president, Hays hoped to find a job in Washington. He returned to Arkansas to run for Congress when he discovered that the incumbent congressman from Little Rock was planning to accept an appointment as a federal judge. Hays campaigned hard to win the Democratic nomination to Congress but was opposed by party leaders in Arkansas, opposition organized in part by Governor J. M. Futrell. Hays led the ticket in the first primary but was forced into a runoff election. He then was defeated in the second primary in what many Arkansans believe was the most openly fraudulent election in Arkansas history. Sure that the election had been stolen from him, Hays filed suit in state court to have the result set aside, but the suit was dismissed on a technicality.

For the remainder of the 1930s Hays worked for several New Deal agencies in Arkansas and Washington, D.C. He made common cause with southern liberals in the Roosevelt administration and joined both the Southern Policy Committee and the Commission on Interracial Cooperation.

Hays was forced to resign as Democratic national committeeman in 1939 as a result of the newly enacted Hatch Act, which prohibited federal officials from actively participating in political campaigns, but he was still interested in pursuing elective office. When Congressman David D. Terry decided to run for the Senate in 1942, Hays resigned his federal position as attorney with the Department of Agriculture to run for Congress from the Fifth District, which included Little Rock and Russellville. Hays won the election and served in Congress until 1958. He sat on the House Banking and Foreign Affairs committees. In 1947 he introduced a resolution to establish a prayer room for members of Congress, and one was designated in the Capitol in 1955.

Although he signed the 1956 Southern Manifesto, which denounced the 1954 *Brown v. Topeka* decision of the U.S. Supreme Court, Hays was known as a moderate on the issue of race. He had counseled a go-slow approach on integration in hearings on the 1956 Democratic party platform.

In 1957, however, Hays became caught up in the crisis over the integration of Central High School in Little Rock and as a result was branded an integrationist. Arkansas governor Orval Faubus had called out the National Guard to prevent nine African-American students from enrolling at Little Rock's only white high school. Determined to do what he could to prevent violence, Congressman Hays initiated a meeting between Faubus and President Dwight D. Eisenhower. With Hays serving as mediator between the two men, Faubus agreed to withdraw the National Guard. However, when the black students were threatened by an angry mob, Eisenhower sent federal troops to Little Rock to protect them, and he placed the Arkansas National Guard under federal command.

The 1957–1958 school year was tense in Little Rock. Hays defeated a segregationist candidate in the summer Democratic primary and did not anticipate strong opposition in the November general election. He had urged support for the law during the crisis at Central High, but in the spring of 1958 he had called for a cooling-off period while Congress assessed the impact of the *Brown* decision. Although many Arkansans thought he had taken a moderate position, Hays was denounced by Dale Alford, a prominent local doctor, as being soft on segregation. Faubus, who had used the integration of Central High to win reelection easily, now backed Alford as a write-in candidate against Hays in the general election. With the help of the Faubus political machine, Alford defeated Hays by about 1,200 votes. Hays protested the election in court and in the House of Representatives but to no avail. He was seen as a martyr by his many supporters.

In 1957 Hays had been elected president of the Southern Baptist Convention, an unusual position for a layman, and he continued as leader of the Southern Baptists following his defeat in the congressional race. As president and as chairman of the convention's Christian Life Commission, Hays worked within the white convention to build bridges to African-Americans and to the wider Christian community.

In 1959 President Eisenhower appointed Hays a director of the Tennessee Valley Authority, but after John F. Kennedy was elected president in 1960 Hays resigned from the TVA in order to become assistant secretary of state for congressional relations. Dissatisfied with this position, he was appointed special assistant to President Kennedy in 1961. Hays spoke occasionally on racial matters but more often was used as a public relations man and humorist. After Kennedy's assassination President Lyndon B. Johnson asked Hays to stay on, but Hays did not have the same enthusiasm for Johnson that he had had for Kennedy. He did agree to serve as counsel to the president, a largely honorary role, and concurrently taught public affairs at Rutgers University in New Jersey.

Hays returned to Arkansas in 1966 to run his third and final race for governor. Placing third in a crowded field of candidates, he missed the runoff. After losing the governor's race he served for a year as a visiting professor of government at the University of Massachusetts and then became director of the Ecumenical Institute at the Southern Baptist–affiliated Wake Forest University in Winston-Salem, North Carolina. From 1970 to 1974 he served as chairman of the North Carolina Human Relations Council. In 1972 Hays ran for Congress from the Republican Fifth District in North Carolina; he campaigned hard but lost to the popular Republican incumbent. Subsequently he served as a consultant to the Ecumenical Institute at Wake Forest University but made his home in Chevy Chase, Maryland, where he died.

• The Hays collection, housed in the Special Collections division of the library of the University of Arkansas at Fayetteville, contains material dealing with Hays's political career in Arkansas. The Southern Baptist School Board Archives in Nashville, Tenn., holds papers relevant to his activities in the Southern Baptist Convention. The Brooks Hays Collection at the John F. Kennedy Presidential Library in Boston relates to Hays's White House years. The Wake Forest University Library in Winston-Salem, N.C., contains papers pertinent to his work with the Ecumenical Institute and his brief career in North Carolina politics.

Hays was a prolific author. Among his books are *A Southern Moderate Speaks* (1959), *The Baptist Way of Life*, with John Steely (1963), *This World: A Christian's Workshop* (1968), *A Hotbed of Tranquility* (1968), and *Politics Is My Parish* (1981). James T. Baker, *Brooks Hays* (1989), is an excellent biography. An obituary is in the *New York Times*, 13 Oct. 1981.

DAVID E. RISON

HAYS, Lee Elhardt (14 Mar. 1914–26 Aug. 1981), songwriter, singer, and political activist, was born in Little Rock, Arkansas, the son of the Reverend William Benjamin Hays, a Methodist minister, and Ellen Reinhardt, a court reporter. The youngest of four children, Lee Hays left home at age fourteen for Emory

Junior College Academy in Oxford, Georgia, a Methodist prep school from which he graduated in 1930. He had hoped to take a bachelor's degree, but during the depression none of his family members could help with tuition.

Hays worked at the Cleveland Public Library from 1930 to 1934—the longest period he held a regular job—and educated himself through books. He later credited the novels of Upton Sinclair and contemporary periodicals for introducing him to the use of art as a political weapon. Through documentary photographs he became aware of the lives of Dust Bowl refugees, sharecroppers, and coal miners. "Somewhere along in there, I became some kind of socialist. Just what kind I've never to this day figured out" (Willens, p. 20).

In 1934 Hays returned to Arkansas, where the Reverend Claude Williams became his mentor. Hays briefly studied for the ministry at the College of the Ozarks (Ark.). He spent time at the Highlander Folk School and worked with the Southern Tenant Farmers Union in Tennessee, about whom he made a documentary film, *America's Disinherited* (1937). Starting in 1937 Hays taught "Workers' Dramatics" at Commonwealth College (Ark.), where he integrated sharecroppers' songs and union-adapted hymns into his productions and union organizing.

Hays cut an imposing figure when he left Arkansas for New York City in 1939. Over six feet tall, weighing around 250 pounds, articulate, activist, and possessing a voice that lent rock-solid bass harmonies to every group he sang with, Hays soon met Pete Seeger, Millard Lampell, and Woody Guthrie, all of whom were interested in combining their musical talents with their union organizing. Together they formed the original Almanac Singers and made several moderately successful recordings.

After World War II a group of musicians and activists, including Hays and Seeger, formed a political song organization called People's Songs. For a few years (1946–1949), they booked performances and operated a clearinghouse of musical and political information. For the newsletter, *People's Songs*, Hays wrote topical songs, witty reviews, and practical articles such as "How to Lead Mass Singing" (July 1946, pp. 4–5) as well as a regular column.

In 1949 Hays, Seeger, Ronnie Gilbert, and Fred Hellerman formed the Weavers. From their first official public performance at the Village Vanguard in 1949 through their farewell performance at Carnegie Hall in 1980, the Weavers exerted a great influence on what became the folk music revival. They were the first popular group to draw much of their repertoire from folk songs. Their hits included songs by Leadbelly ("Goodnight Irene") and Woody Guthrie ("So Long, It's Been Good to Know You"), traditional songs not in English ("Tzena, Tzena, Tzena" in Hebrew), songs based on traditional songs ("Wimoweh," a South African song), and songs written by the members themselves. When the Cold War anticommunist scare started in the early 1950s, the Weavers suddenly found themselves unable to get bookings due to the practice of blacklisting. The group broke up in 1952, reunited from 1955 until 1963, then reconvened a final time for two performances in 1980, documented in a film, *Wasn't That a Time*. During and after his participation with the Weavers, Hays sang children's songs as a member of the quartet the Babysitters.

Hays composed songs throughout this period. Many of his songs were of the moment (he even wrote a few commercial jingles during the late 1950s), but some songs he wrote or coauthored gained enough popularity to eventually bring him a regular royalty income. Among his songs were "Wasn't That a Time" (with Walter Lowenfels), about which he was extensively questioned by the House Committee on Un-American Activities in 1955 because the committee was upset by some of the lyrics, "Lonesome Traveler," and "Kisses Sweeter than Wine" (an old Irish song that Leadbelly sang, to which Hays added seven verses). One of Hays's best-known songs is "The Hammer Song" or "If I Had a Hammer." Hays borrowed the "Warning!" chorus from Marc Blitzstein's "Airbourne Symphony"; then he and Seeger wrote the song by passing notes during a meeting of People's Songs.

Hays's second career, practiced throughout his musical career, was that of a writer. He wrote in a variety of genres, including pornography and a novel, using pseudonyms while he was blacklisted. "Banquet and a Half," published in several languages in *Ellery Queen Mystery Magazine* (1953) and based on a civil rights case he worked on, was one of his best short stories.

Hays died at Phelps Memorial Hospital, North Tarrytown, New York, after living a fairly quiet life in Croton-on-Hudson, New York, for the previous twelve years. He had never married. Lee Hays introduced young, idealistic, northern musicians to a southern hymn-singing tradition of political activism, which had roots in his childhood religion and his experience as a union organizer. He educated himself about the world and found his political direction outside the traditions of his family. His biographer wrote that "he questioned everything . . . and distrusted authority of every kind" (Willens, p. xxi), a trait he shared with many of his peers. He left a legacy of enduring songs, exciting recordings, and fiction writings.

• The Lee Hays Papers are housed in the archives of the Smithsonian Institution's Center for Folklife Programs and Cultural Studies. The only full-length biography, *Lonesome Traveler: The Life of Lee Hays* (1988), was written by neighbor and fellow member of the Babysitters Doris Willens and tends to be uncritical. Much of Hays's significant work can be found on recordings he made as a member of several singing groups. The Almanac Singers released five albums of union and political songs. The Weavers released recordings on Charter and Decca starting in 1949, then on Vanguard after 1955. They had several commercial hits before the group broke up in 1963. During this same period, the Babysitters recorded four albums for children. The Weavers' final album, *The Weavers Together Again* (1981), and a video documentary, *Wasn't That a Time* (1981), written by Lee Hays and directed by his friend Jim Brown, summed up the careers of the Weavers and focused on the influence of Lee Hays. An obituary is in the *New York Times*, 27 Aug. 1981.

ANTHONY SEEGER
LORI ELAINE TAYLOR

HAYS, Paul Raymond (2 Apr. 1903–13 Feb. 1980), educator and federal judge, was born in Des Moines, Iowa, the son of Everett Hollingsworth Hays and Fae Susan Hatch. The family moved to New York City, where Hays would spend the rest of his life. In 1924 he married Eleanor K. Williams. They had one child. He received his A.B. (1924), M.A. (1927), and LL.B. (1933) from Columbia College and its Law School. While still in graduate school, he also taught Greek and Latin at Columbia from 1926 to 1932.

On being admitted to the New York bar, Hays joined the Wall Street firm of Cravath, de Gersdorff, Swaine and Wood, where he practiced from 1933 to 1936. He served in 1934 and 1935 as legal counsel to the National Industrial Recovery and Resettlement Administration in Washington, D.C., before returning to join the Columbia law faculty in 1936. At Columbia, Hays was an assistant professor from 1936 to 1938, an associate professor from 1938 to 1943, a full professor from 1943 to 1957, and Nash Professor of Law from 1957 to 1961, the year he went to serve on the federal bench.

During his tenure at Columbia, Hays distinguished himself as a classical scholar, a public servant, and a labor arbitrator. Between 1936 and 1937 he was legal consultant to the New York State Banking Department, serving on its Law Revision Commission in 1937 and 1945. He was also a member of the U.S. Board of Legal Examiners from 1941 to 1944, and in 1944 and 1945 he held a temporary appointment in the Department of Justice. His first marriage having ended in divorce in 1943, Hays married Elinor Rice in 1949. They had no children.

Between 1940 to 1960 Hays served as labor arbitrator and impartial chair of mediation boards for many industries. The arbitration decisions he wrote covered disputes in transit, communications, newspaper publishing, shipping, and restaurant and building services. As both a member of the New York State Board of Mediation and a private consultant, he helped fashion wage agreements for many of these industries. In the 1952 dispute between the International Longshoremen's Association (ILA) and the New York Shipping Association, Hays secured a 17 cents-an-hour wage hike for the dockers and a total of $12,000 in retroactive pay for members of the ILA. While a professor at Columbia Law School, he was much sought after by both unions and management as a mediator. In 1959 and 1960 he was secretary of the American Bar Association's section on labor relations law.

In October 1961 Hays received a recess appointment from President John F. Kennedy, and his appointment as judge of the U.S. Court of Appeals for the Second Circuit was made permanent in March 1962. By the time Hays assumed senior judge status on that court in September 1974, he was known for his strong views on judicial restraint, having written nearly fourteen volumes of legal opinions that were indicative of a rigorous fidelity to the Constitution.

As a member of the U.S. Court of Appeals for the Second Circuit, Hays was party to many important federal cases and a few that were spectacular. He wrote the majority opinion in 1968 in a two to one ruling that found the Swedish film *I Am Curious—Yellow* not to be obscene. He was also recognized for his opinion in the so-called Storm King case, a suit that centered around a 1971 Federal Power Commission license. Hays initially ruled that Con Edison, the proprietor, was required to consider certain environmental factors in its quest to build a 2 million kilowatt power plant at Storm King Mountain on the western shore of the Hudson River. Later, Hays allowed the license, arguing that the utility had appropriately taken these factors into account. The decision frustrated environmentalists, who thought him to be an advocate of the antinuclear cause.

By far the most celebrated and politically important free speech case of the 1970s in which Hays participated was *New York Times Co. v. U.S.* (1971), better known as the Pentagon Papers case. The dramatic facts of the case served to keep it in the public eye even as it was litigated. The *New York Times* had begun publishing selected portions of a 47-volume Defense Department study and other sensitive documents dealing with U.S. involvement in the Vietnam War at a time when the United States was still engaged in the fighting. The government sought an injunction against any further publication of these papers, which it claimed would cause "grave and irreparable injury" to the United States, consequently damaging national security.

The federal district court issued a temporary restraining order against the *Times*, but it then denied the government's request for a preliminary injunction, claiming that revelation of these historical documents would not constitute a serious breach of national security. When the government appealed, Hays was on the three-judge panel that voted to extend the restraining order, in effect continuing to enforce it against the *Times*. When the case was heard by the entire eight-member court of appeals, Hays voted with the five-member majority to postpone publication of various parts of the series until hearings could discern whether or not the government's contention that the text jeopardized national security was substantial. Within seventeen days of the ruling, the Supreme Court, in a per curiam opinion, reversed the second circuit, affirmed the lower court's ruling rejecting the government's arguments, and removed all restraints on publication. The Court said that any system of prior restraint bore a heavy presumption against its constitutionality.

The professional associations to which Hays belonged included the American Bar Association, the New York State Bar Association, the Association of the Bar of the City of New York, Phi Beta Kappa, the

American Law Institute, the American Judicature Society, and the Institute of Judicial Administration.

Hays was the author of a number of books, including *The Judicial Function in Federal Administrative Agencies*, with Joseph P. Chamberlain and Noel T. Dowling (1942; rev. ed., 1970); *Cases and Materials on Labor Law*, with Milton Handler (1950; rev. ed., 1963); *American Casebook Series* (1955 supp., including federal legislation); and *Labor Arbitration: A Dissenting View* (1966).

As a lawyer and labor mediator, Hays took a lively interest in politics. In New York he was elected state chair of the Liberal party in 1958 and president in 1960–1961, before going on the bench. One of his major interests was the move toward the creation of administrative agencies. The extension of government controls over more and more aspects of the economy and society led Congress to give greater powers to existing agencies or to create new ones to administer the legislation that the movement toward closer government regulation had precipitated. Hays was willing to acknowledge that the powers with which many of these agencies were vested were very broad. Within statutory limits they laid down the law for the future by regulation, decided cases involving private parties, carried out extensive investigations, and exercised wide discretion in controlling the operation of individual businesses, entire industries, and industry as a whole.

In the preface to his first book, Hays wrote, "The judicial function is only one of many devices resulting from the increasing use of administrative action to fill the gap in the regulation of society which lies between Congress and the courts, and to supply government machinery to supplement, not to supplant both Congress and the courts in the administration of the law" (*The Judicial Function*, p. ix). In the transitional period in which federal agencies were multiplying at a bewildering rate, Hays pointed out that instead of depending on individuals to defend what they considered their rights in the courts or depending on the action of Congress to assure through legislation the fair and orderly functioning of the social and economic system, these agencies were being created to protect both private parties and the public interest by imposing a direct control over business management and social relations.

Hays lived in Manhattan, where he was a member of the Century Club. For his long and distinguished service as a legal educator at Columbia he was made professor emeritus from 1971 until his death in Tucson, Arizona, where he was vacationing at the Lodge on the Desert.

• In addition to those titles already cited, Hays was the author of *Cases and Materials on Civil Procedure* (1947). Biographical material can be found in Thomas Charles Kingsley, ed., *Second Circuit Redbook* (1980). The full judicial progress of the Pentagon Papers case through the lower federal courts is in *New York Times Co. v. U.S.*, 403 U.S. 713 (1971). Fuller legal analysis of the celebrated case is provided in Louis Henkin, "The Right to Know and the Duty to Withhold: The Case of the Pentagon Papers," *University of Pennsylvania Law Review* 120 (1971): 271–80. See also Peter Junger, "Down Memory Lane: The Case of the Pentagon Papers," *Case Western Reserve Law Review* 23 (1971): 3–75, and Harry Kalven, Jr., "Foreword: Even When a Nation Is at War," *Harvard Law Review* 85 (1971): 3–36. An obituary is in the *New York Times*, 15 Feb. 1980.

MARIAN C. McKENNA

HAYS, Will H. (5 Nov. 1879–7 Mar. 1954), motion picture industry official, lawyer, and politician, was born William Harrison Hays in Sullivan, Indiana, the son of John T. Hays, an attorney, and Mary Cain. He graduated from Indiana's all-male Wabash College in 1900 and privately studied law. Upon passing the Indiana bar, Hays opened a law office in Sullivan and became city attorney. He moved through a variety of political offices in Indiana before he was named chairman of the Republican National Committee in June 1918. When Warren G. Harding was elected president in a 1920 landslide, Hays was credited with having pulled together a divided Republican party (fortunately for Hays, the Democrats were also divided in 1920).

In gratitude for Hays's healing efforts among Republicans, Harding appointed him postmaster general of the United States, and Hays held this office for one year. During his time as postmaster general, Hays established the Post Office Welfare Department, extended rural free delivery of mail, restored second-class mailing privileges for newspapers, and reduced Post Office expenses by $15 million. In 1924 the Senate Committee on Public Lands and Surveys investigated the highly publicized Teapot Dome oil scandal that rocked the Harding administration in its last days (Harding died in office in 1923 at the height of the scandal). Hays was called before the committee to testify about various contributions by oil companies to the Republican party. He was recalled in 1928 but denied any improper actions during his tenure as Republican chairman. Hays emerged as one of the few untainted members of Harding's cabinet.

In 1922, as the result of several highly publicized Hollywood scandals, most particularly two sensational trials surrounding the death of starlet Virginia Rappe at a party given by screen comedian Roscoe "Fatty" Arbuckle (Arbuckle was accused and ultimately acquitted of raping Rappe), the drug-related death of matinee idol Wallace Reid, and the sensational unsolved murder of director William Desmond Taylor, the major film studios appointed Hays to serve as head of the newly formed Motion Picture Producers and Distributors of America, Inc. (MPPDA). Hays's charge was to improve the sagging public image of the movie community and to address increasing public pressure for some form of censorship of film content. The producers hoped that Hays could do for films what federal judge Kenesaw Mountain Landis, in the wake of the Black Sox World Series scandal of 1919, had done for baseball.

By 1930 Hays and the MPPDA, then commonly known as the Hays Office, created the Motion Picture

Production Code, a strict censorship code to guide film production. The code stressed that "loose habits" must not be glorified in films and that the sanctity of marriage must be upheld (although a husband and wife could not be depicted in the same bed in the early days of the code). Other regulations banned the depiction of revenge in a modern setting and considered "passion" a violation if not necessary to the plot ("Excessive and lustful kissing, lustful embracing, suggestive postures and gestures, are not to be shown"). Regarding race, the code specified that "miscegenation (sex relationships between the white and black races) is forbidden." Even religion was covered in the statement that "ministers of religion should not be used as comic characters or as villains."

Although the rules of the code were not specifically written by Hays himself, but by Reverend Daniel A. Lord, a Jesuit priest, with assistance by Martin Quigley, they reflected Hays's rural, small-town, "middle-America" values. Film scripts that Hays's office felt glorified evil practices, from sex and swearing to drinking and drugs, or tended to lower the morals of those witnessing the picture were censored. As such, the code was open to wide interpretation. When producer David O. Selznick wanted permission for Clark Gable, as Rhett Butler, to say, "Frankly, my dear, I don't give a damn," as the final line of the classic movie *Gone with the Wind* (1939), as had been the case in Margaret Mitchell's 1936 novel, he went through quite a lengthy battle. He finally succeeded by including several other violations of the code in the film and "compromising" by agreeing to remove those offenses if he would be permitted to keep the final line. Other more significant tests of the code occurred over Jane Russell's ample bosom in producer Howard Hughes's *The Outlaw* (1941) and the use of the word "virgin" in director Otto Preminger's *The Moon Is Blue* (1953). By the mid-1960s sweeping changes in American society and Hollywood rendered the code impotent.

It is important to note that the Hollywood studios reluctantly supported the code, hoping to sidestep federal legislation and possible city and state laws regarding film content that they felt might be more restrictive. Hays's often-repeated statement, "Good taste is good business," set the tone and guided movie production. The code forced writers and directors to invent various clever techniques to symbolically represent sexual and violent content in their films. Hays wielded significant power in Hollywood in this era, enforcing the code in the direction of making the Hollywood studio product a wholesome and entirely inoffensive form of entertainment. As a result, many great novels and plays that were made into films were significantly altered in content to adhere to the code's restraints, and many important stories were not told in cinematic terms.

However, the code claimed to promote education. Hays wrote, "When we understand, we do not hate and when we do not hate, we do not make war." He added that he hoped the film industry would promote "international understanding by sympathetically telling the story of the nationals of every country to the nationals of all others."

It is perhaps not surprising that during his tenure as president of the MPPDA Hays was often accused of being too strict by the studios and too permissive by straight-laced pillars of public morality. He succeeded in maintaining a sort of balance for over twenty years. He resigned his post on 19 September 1945 owing, in part, to increasing dissent from the film companies. Not long after his retirement, Hays worked as a special adviser to the Motion Picture Association of America (MPAA), using his powerful influence to support the anti-Communist movement that resulted from the post–World War II investigations of the House Committee on Un-American Activities. Even after Hays's death in Sullivan, Indiana, the code remained unchanged until 1966, when it finally collapsed in the face of the seismic social changes of the 1960s.

Hays maintained law offices in Sullivan and Indianapolis; he also had a ranch near Los Angeles and an apartment in New York during his long tenure as "Censorship Czar." He was married twice, first to Helen Louise Thomas, whom he wed in November 1902. They had a son, Will H. Hays, Jr., who also became a lawyer and worked in Hollywood as a writer. After divorcing his first wife in 1929, Hays married Jessie Herron Stutsman in November 1930. At the time of Hays's death, leaders of both the nation and the motion picture industry mourned his passing. Former president Herbert Hoover stated that Hays "was a good American who had served his country well," and producer Samuel Goldwyn issued a statement saying that "I had a great respect for Mr. Hays and so did almost everyone in the industry. He was a very fine American and a very able administrator of our motion picture association."

Hays's name will always be synonymous with the constraints of film censorship, but his goal was the betterment of the movie industry. As he wrote in the early days of the MPPDA, "The motion picture is the epitome of civilization and the quintessence of what we mean by 'America.'" Although it is true that the MPPDA restricted film artists well beyond the point of censorship, Hays's tenure spread across Hollywood's golden age when numerous classic films were made and there was enormous growth in the movie industry.

• The Will H. Hays Papers are held in the library at Indiana University, Bloomington, Ind. Hays's own writings include *Fifteen Years of Motion Picture Progress: Annual Report to the Motion Picture Producers and Distributors* (1937); *Memoirs* (1955); *Report of Will H. Hays, President, on Plans and Programs of Motion Picture Production for 1934–35 Submitted to Motion Picture Producers and Distributors of America, Inc., October 10, 1934* (1934); and *See and Hear: A Brief History of the Motion Pictures and the Development of Sound* (1929). A biography by Hays's son is Will H. Hays, Jr., *Come Home with Me Now: The Untold Story of Movie Czar Will Hays by His Son* (1993). For further information on Hays and the Motion Picture Production Code, see Raymond Moley, *The Hays Office* (1945); Henry Fowles Pringle, *Big Frogs* (1928); Stephen

Vaughn, "Morality and Entertainment: The Origins of the Motion Picture Production Code," *Journal of American History* 77 (June 1990): 39–65; Francis Couvares, "Hollywood, Main Street, and the Church: Trying to Censor the Movies before the Production Code," *American Quarterly* 44 (Dec. 1992): 584–616; John Gould Fletcher, *The Crisis of the Film* (1970); Gerald C. Gardner, *The Censorship Papers: Movie Censorship Letters from the Hays Office, 1934–1968* (1987); and Don Gordon, *Hollywood from the Inside* (1929). An obituary is in the *New York Times*, 8 Mar. 1954.

JAMES FISHER

HAYS, Will S. (19 July 1837–23 July 1907), songwriter, poet, and editor, was born William Shakespeare Hays in Louisville, Kentucky, the son of Hugh Hays, a successful manufacturer of farming equipment, and Martha Richardson, an amateur musician and writer. Although he early showed signs of musical aptitude, his formal training extended no further than a few violin lessons. He attended small colleges in Hanover, Indiana; Clarksville, Tennessee; and Georgetown, Kentucky, in 1856–1857. During this time he published his first song, "Little Ones at Home," for which he wrote only the text. Hays returned to Louisville and worked in a music store. There he began to compose melodies for his poems, among the first of which was "Evangeline" (1857), musically in a style that acknowledged an important debt to the vogue for Italian opera. This turned out to be his first hit, selling perhaps as many as 300,000 copies. It was during his time at D. P. Faulds's music store that Hays allegedly composed the original version of "Dixie," a claim made by Faulds himself more than thirty years later and corroborated then by Hays. (This story has never been supported by evidence other than hearsay, and Dan Emmett's authorship is generally accepted.)

His next position was with the *Louisville Democrat*, first as a clerk, then as a local editor. During the Civil War he served as a war correspondent. At the outbreak of the war, Hays had written the musical appeal "Let Us Have Peace" (1861), and many of his songs, such as "The Union Forever" (1861), unashamedly promoted the Unionist cause. Others appealed to both North and South—for instance, "The Drummer Boy of Shiloh" (1863), today his best-known song, was a sentimental war song about the innocent killed in bloody battle who "prayed before he died." And the popularity of his "My Sunny Southern Home" (1864) landed him in jail in federally controlled New Orleans as a rebel propagandist.

Toward the end of the war Hays fell in love with Belle McCullough of Louisville, and he married her on 4 July 1865. Their union resulted in two children. His career as a newspaperman was confirmed in 1868 when he became editor of the "River" column in the Louisville *Courier-Journal*. This column conveyed necessary information about water levels and river conditions but spiced it with anecdotes, songs, characters, news, and tall tales. It became one of the paper's most popular features. During this period, from about 1866 to 1876, Hays was most productive as a songwriter. He wrote dozens of publishable songs in a range of styles. Among the best known were "Write Me a Letter from Home" (1866), which was claimed to have sold 350,000 copies; "We Parted by the River" (1866), a love song with Hays's beloved river as the backdrop; "The Little Old Log Cabin in the Lane" (1871), written for the minstrel show; "Mollie Darling" (1871), perhaps the most popular love song of the time; and "Angels, Meet Me at the Cross Road" (1875), one of the first minstrel-spirituals. Hays continued to write songs and poems up to the turn of the century, but he began to devote more and more time to his newspaper column and to his business as a steamboat ticket agent. In 1904 he suffered a stroke. He died in Louisville, tended by his physician son.

Altogether Hays wrote 322 songs and nine piano pieces, which together were said to have sold over twenty million copies. Also a poet, he penned at least 546 poems and published three books of poetry. An anonymous critic wrote in 1869: "The great secret of Mr. Hays' success as a songwriter may be attributed to the blending of his words with his music . . . in such a way that his ballads, like [Stephen] Foster's, appeal at once to the heart." For two decades after the Civil War, no American's songs were heard more frequently nor loved more deeply.

• The Hays papers are collected in the Kentucky Library at Western Kentucky University. Three unpublished theses provide the best biographical information available on Hays: Fannie Elizabeth Stoll, "Will S. Hays: Kentucky Composer, Marine Editor, and Poet" (M.A. thesis, Univ. of Kentucky, 1943); George C. Grise, "Will S. Hays: His Life and Works" (B.A. thesis, Western Kentucky State Teachers Col., 1947); and Martha Carol Chrisman, "Will S. Hays: A Biography" (M.A. thesis, Univ. of Minnesota, 1980). Hays features prominently in Chrisman's "Popular Songs of the Genteel Tradition: Their Influence on Music Education in Public Schools of Louisville, Kentucky, from 1850 to 1880 (Ph.D. diss., Univ. of Minnesota, 1985). The best treatment of Hays's music is found in Charles Hamm, *Yesterdays: Popular Song in America* (1979).

DALE COCKRELL

HAYWARD, Leland (13 Sept. 1902–18 Mar. 1971), theatrical and literary agent and producer, was born in Nebraska City, Nebraska, the son of William Leland, a district attorney, and Sarah Irland Tappan. Hayward attended private schools in New England and was admitted to Princeton University, but he was asked to leave in his freshman year because of poor grades. In 1921 he married Inez "Lola" Gibbs. They divorced the next year but remarried in 1930; they divorced again in 1934.

Hayward began his career as a reporter for the *New York Sun* in 1923 but was fired in less than a year. His interest in popular entertainment led him to a job as a publicist for United Artists. He also worked briefly in the scenario department of First National. In 1930 he began selling production rights to books and scripts, working for the American Play Company, an endeavor in which he was highly successful, handling more than $3 million in sales in just one year.

Hayward opened his own theatrical and literary agency in New York sometime in the early 1930s. As an agent, he became an important figure in both the entertainment and publishing industries, representing an array of well-known clients, who included the actors Fred Astaire, Henry Fonda, Clark Gable, Judy Garland, and Katharine Hepburn and the writers Edna Ferber, Dashiell Hammett, Ernest Hemingway, Ben Hecht, Charles MacArthur, Howard Lindsay, and Russel Crouse. Hayward came to be seen as the archetypical deal-making agent. *Variety* called him "a real maestro of the telephone," claiming that he could carry on six calls simultaneously.

In 1936 Hayward married the stage and screen actress Margaret Sullavan. The couple had three children. They divorced in 1948.

Hayward closed his agency and embarked on a career as a Broadway producer in 1944. His early credits included *A Bell for Adano* (1944), *State of the Union* (1945), *Mister Roberts* (1948), and *Anne of the Thousand Days* (1948). The Pulitzer Prize was awarded for *State of the Union*, but his greatest popular and critical successes were yet to come.

Hayward married again in 1949, this time to Nancy "Slim" Hawks. They were divorced in 1960. His final marriage, to Pamela Digby Churchill in 1960, lasted until his death. No children were born of either marriage.

In 1949, in association with Joshua Logan and the songwriting team of Richard Rodgers and Oscar Hammerstein II, Hayward produced *South Pacific*. The show, which ran for 1,925 performances, won the New York Drama Critics' Circle Award for best musical. In 1959, again teaming with Rodgers and Hammerstein, he produced *The Sound of Music*, one of Broadway's longest-running hits (1,443 performances). That same year, in partnership with David Merrick, he produced *Gypsy*. Many critics consider all three shows to be classics of the American musical theater.

Hayward's on-the-job training in entertainment contract law proved useful in his career as a producer. In 1960 he brought suit against Rodgers and Hammerstein, claiming a share of the royalties from the cast recording of *The Sound of Music*; he and his partner, Richard Halliday, won a judgment in 1967 of more than $1 million.

Returning to film work after a long absence, Hayward produced three features for Warner Bros. in the 1950s. None was a musical, but each reflected his personal interests in some way. *Mister Roberts* (1955) starred Henry Fonda and James Cagney in a screen adaptation of the wartime comic drama that Hayward had produced on Broadway a decade earlier. *The Spirit of St. Louis* (1957), was a film biography of Charles A. Lindbergh (1902–1974), whom Hayward idolized. For the film of Hemingway's *The Old Man and the Sea* (1958), he exploited his connections to obtain rights to the novella and to sign Spencer Tracy for the title

role; Hayward received a Christopher Award in 1959 for his work on the project.

Hayward's efforts extended to television. In 1953 he produced a lavish variety show for the fiftieth anniversary of the Ford Motor Company, and, in 1960 he received an Emmy as producer of "The Fabulous Fifties," a documentary. Other Hayward TV shows included "The Gershwin Years" (1961) and "A Night in Samarkand" (1962), musicals for CBS. His "That Was The Week That Was" (1964–1965) was the only prime-time series to be entirely devoted to topical political satire.

Hayward had been taught to fly by his first wife, and flying small planes became a lifelong avocation. Commissioned as a lieutenant in the U.S. Naval Air Force during World War II, he became a military flight instructor before serving in the Pacific. This interest also led him to join the board of Trans World Airlines during the 1930s and to become a founding investor in Southwest Airways in 1946.

Hayward was a member of the board of governors of the League of New York Theatres and belonged to the River Club and the Winks Club. He remained active in New York theatrical production throughout the 1960s, with *The Trial of the Catonsville Nine* (1971), an anti-Vietnam War play written by Daniel Berrigan and performed off-Broadway, being his last production. He died in Yorktown Heights, New York.

• Information on Hayward appears in *The Biographical Encyclopedia* and *Who's Who in American Theater* (1966), *Who Was Who in American Theatre, 1912–1976* (1978), *Encyclopedia of the Musical Theatre* (1976), and *Halliwell's Filmgoer's Companion*, 6th ed. (1977). See also the memoir by Brooke Hayward, Hayward's daughter, entitled *Haywire* (1970). Further personal details can be found in *Slim: Memories of a Rich and Imperfect Life* (1990) by Keith Slim and Annette Tapert. Obituaries are in the *New York Times*, 19 Mar. 1971; *Variety* 24 Mar. 1971, which includes a feature article on Hayward's life; and *Current Biography*, Apr. 1971.

DAVID MARC

HAYWARD, Susan (30 June 1917–14 Mar. 1975), actress, was born Edythe Marrenner in Brooklyn, New York, the daughter of Walter Marrenner, a transit worker, and Ellen Pearson. She was sent to Girls' Commercial High School in Brooklyn to study stenography and dress design. After her high school graduation she became a photographer's model in 1937. During the highly publicized nationwide search for a Scarlett O'Hara for the much-anticipated screen version of Margaret Mitchell's novel *Gone with the Wind*, Hayward was brought to Hollywood by producer David O. Selznick to test for the role. The part went to Vivien Leigh, but Hayward was signed to a short contract by Warner Bros., where her name was changed and she appeared in small roles in a number of forgettable films and a few good ones, including *Hollywood Hotel* (1937), *The Amazing Dr. Clitterhouse* (1938), and *The Sisters* (1938).

In 1939 Hayward was signed by Paramount Pictures and continued her apprenticeship in mostly

B-films, with the occasional supporting role in an A-picture. She had her best opportunities in William Wellman's *Beau Geste* (1939), Cecil B. DeMille's *Reap the Wild Wind* (1942), and René Clair's *I Married a Witch* (1942).

Following a short stint with RKO, independent producer Walter Wanger signed Hayward to a contract in 1945, and her roles began to improve. She made a particularly outstanding appearance in the dramatic film *Smash-up: The Story of a Woman* (1947) playing the neglected wife of a popular singer. Her performance led to her first Academy Award nomination as best actress and, eventually, to a star contract with 20th Century–Fox. At Fox, Hayward scored a major success in the tearjerker *My Foolish Heart* (1950), based on a J. D. Salinger short story, which earned her another Oscar nomination and considerable critical praise. She also found a strong role in the screen biography of singer Jane Froman, *With a Song in My Heart* (1952), under the direction of Walter Lang, and won another Oscar nomination. Other excellent vehicles for Hayward in this era included *David and Bathsheba* (1951), *The Snows of Kilimanjaro* (1952), *The President's Lady* (1953), and *The Conquerer* (1956). In *I'll Cry Tomorrow*, another screen biography (this time of singer and recovered alcoholic Lillian Roth), Hayward supplied the vocals herself (although she had been dubbed in the Froman film) and earned a best actress award from the Cannes Film Festival and another Oscar nomination.

A strikingly beautiful redhead with a determined and tempestuous nature, Hayward had a rich, husky voice that served her well in a variety of roles. Her métier was melodrama, but she also turned in polished performances in occasional comedies and epics. Hayward smoked two packs of cigarettes a day and was known as a hard drinker, but she was well liked by co-workers and widely considered one of the most professional and talented stars of her time.

Hayward's greatest acclaim as an actress came in 1958 with her searing performance in *I Want to Live!* as real-life murderer Barbara "Bloody Babs" Graham, a party girl who had been sentenced to die in the gas chamber. Hayward won both the Academy Award for best actress and the New York Film Critics Award for her intensely emotional acting. Of her performance, *New York Times* critic Bosley Crowther wrote that "she moves onto levels of cold disdain and then plunges down to depths of terror and bleak surrender as she reaches the end. Except that the role does not present us a precisely pretty character, its performance merits for Miss Hayward the most respectful applause" (19 Nov. 1958).

Despite her personal triumph in *I Want to Live!*, Hayward rarely found a similarly worthy challenge on screen again, although she received praise for her solid performances as the noble mistress of a married man in the 1961 remake of the classic melodrama *Back Street* and as the promiscuous daughter of Bette Davis in *Where Love Has Gone* (1964), a tawdry Harold Robbins dramatization of the Lana Turner–Johnny Stompanato case.

Hayward was married twice. Her first marriage to actor Jess Barker in 1944 ended in divorce in 1954. The union produced two sons, and Hayward attempted suicide in 1955 during a bitter custody battle with Barker. She married F. Eaton Chalkley in 1957, and they lived quietly in a Georgia retreat. He died in 1966.

Hayward returned to the screen after a three-year hiatus following *Where Love Has Gone* to replace Judy Garland in the coveted role of Helen Lawson, an alcoholic singer, in the film version of Jacqueline Susann's popular novel *Valley of the Dolls*. That same year she also appeared in *The Honey Pot*. However, as she moved firmly into middle age, movie opportunities were no longer plentiful for Hayward. After her first stage appearance in a 1969 Las Vegas production of the musical *Mame*, Hayward turned to television for three TV movies in 1972, *Heat of Anger*, *The Revengers*, and *Goodbye, Maggie Cole*. A television series spinoff of the last was curtailed when Hayward was diagnosed with a brain tumor.

While suffering the last stages of her illness, Hayward, on the arm of frequent costar Charlton Heston, appeared at the Academy Awards ceremony as a presenter. The prolonged applause of the audience of her peers acknowledged both Hayward's skill as an actress and her courage in battling her devastating illness. She died at her Beverly Hills, California, home a few months after this final public appearance.

• For additional information on Hayward see Christopher P. Andersen, *A Star Is a Star, Is a Star, Is a Star! The Lives and Loves of Susan Hayward* (1980); Robert LaGuardia and Gene Arceri, *Red: The Tempestuous Life of Susan Hayward* (1985); Beverly Linet, *Susan Hayward: Portrait of a Survivor* (1980); Doug McClelland, "The Brooklyn Bernhardt," *Films and Filming*, Mar. 1965; McClelland, "Susan Hayward," *Films in Review*, May 1962; McClelland, *Susan Hayward: Divine Bitch* (1973); Eduardo Moreno, *The Films of Susan Hayward* (1981); and James Robert Parish and Don Stanke, *The Forties Gals* (1980). An obituary is in the *New York Times*, 15 Mar. 1975.

JAMES FISHER

HAYWARD, William Louis (2 July 1868–14 Dec. 1947), track and field athlete and coach, was born William Louis Heyward in Detroit, Michigan, the son of Thomas Heyward. His mother's name is unknown. In 1878 William, his brother, and three sisters went to live with their grandparents in Toronto, Ontario, Canada, when their parents left North America to manage a Peruvian rubber plantation. Hayward lived in Toronto until 1888, when he left to earn a living as a professional athlete and a vaudeville performer.

Touring throughout the United States, Canada, and Australia, he profited especially from his running speed, specializing in distances from 75 to 600 yards. Hayward often entered track and field meets such as the Caledonian Games, sponsored by transplanted Scots. During these meets he participated in 20 to 25 events and garnered up to $5,000 in prize money. Hayward also served as a trainer and sparring partner for boxer "Gentleman" Jim Corbett, who knocked out John L. Sullivan for the world heavyweight championship in 1892. As a member of Corbett's vaudeville show, Hayward gave wrestling and Indian-club swinging exhibitions. Despite earning an income as a runner, he played on the Ottawa Capitals, the 1893 world champion amateur lacrosse team.

In 1898 Hayward retired from competitive athletics and became a track and field coach. That year his friend and rival Walter Christie became the head track and field coach at Princeton University and the University of California, and he appointed Hayward as his assistant coach at both institutions. After joining the University of California, Hayward changed the spelling of his last name. In 1901 he became the head track and field coach at Pacific University in Forest Grove, Oregon. Hayward coached at Pacific for two years and then took a similar position at Albany College in Albany, Oregon. Under his direction, Albany, a school with an enrollment of less than 100 students, defeated the track teams of many of Oregon's more established four-year institutions. In 1904 the University of Oregon, which had fallen victim to tiny Albany College, hired Hayward as its first full-time track and field coach. An avid fisherman, he welcomed the move to Eugene, Oregon, situated close to the McKenzie River.

Hayward coached track and field at the University of Oregon from 1904 to 1947. In 1927 he led Oregon to the Pacific Coast track and field championship, and from 1930 to 1941 his teams achieved seven top-ten finishes in the National Collegiate Athletic Association (NCAA) track and field championships. In addition to his work at Oregon, Hayward was an assistant track and field coach for the six U.S. Olympic Teams from 1908 to 1932. Among the many outstanding individual performers that he coached, four were world record holders, six were American record holders, four were NCAA champions, and nine were Olympians. One of Hayward's first stars was Daniel J. Kelly, who established a world record of 9.6 seconds for 100 yards in 1906. Ralph Hill, Oregon's top middle-distance runner of the 1930s, garnered the Amateur Athletic Union (AAU) 5,000-meter title and an Olympic silver medal in 1932. Hayward also prepared Mack Robinson, the brother of baseball player Jackie Robinson, for a gold medal–winning performance in the 200 meters at the 1936 Olympic Games. Robinson captured AAU and NCAA titles in the 220-yard dash in 1938. Lester Steers, who established a world record of 6'11" in the high jump, won three AAU championships and one NCAA title under Hayward. Hayward remained the track and field coach at Oregon until his sudden death in Eugene. Bill Bowerman, who ran the 440-yard dash for Hayward in the 1940s, became Oregon's track and field coach following Hayward's death.

Under Hayward, the University of Oregon and the city of Eugene gained the reputation of being the track and field capital of the United States. Part of his legacy includes the Hayward Relays, a track and field meet started by Hayward to encourage the sport among Oregon high schools. The university honored Hayward by naming its track and field facility after him.

• Materials on Hayward are held by the Sports Information Department, University of Oregon, Eugene. Articles include Dennis Clark, "Bill Hayward's Legacy," *Sportscene* (June 1982); Janet Heinonen, "Bill Hayward: The 'Grand Old Man,'" *57th Annual NCAA Track and Field Championships Program* (1978); and Blaine Newnham, "Pages Out of Time," *Eugene Register-Guard*, 22 June 1980. A biography is Sally Mitchell, *The Life Story of Colonel William Heyward* (1941). For the history of track and field at the University of Oregon, see Bob Baum, *History of Oregon Athletics* (1973). An obituary is in the *Eugene (Oreg.) Register-Guard*, 14 Dec. 1947.

ADAM R. HORNBUCKLE

HAYWOOD, Allan Shaw (9 Oct. 1888–21 Feb. 1953), labor leader, was born in Monk Bretton, Yorkshire, England, the son of Arthur Haywood, a coal miner, and Ann (maiden name unknown). At age thirteen Haywood followed his father and three of his brothers into the mines, joining the British Miners Federation. In 1906 he immigrated to the United States, settling in Taylorville, Illinois, where he worked as a coal miner. He married Kate Dewsnap in 1909; they had three children.

As soon as Haywood arrived in the United States, he joined the United Mine Workers, the largest union in the country. Over the next three decades, he moved up the ranks of its leadership, serving as a local officer, subdistrict vice president and president, and district executive board member, as well as vice president of the Illinois Federation of Labor. In 1935, under the leadership of UMW president John L. Lewis, a group of unions affiliated with the American Federation of Labor formed the Committee for Industrial Organization to organize the mass production industries, helping to spark a dramatic revival and expansion of the labor movement. (In 1938, after the AFL expelled the unions belonging to the CIO, the group renamed itself the Congress of Industrial Organizations.) Haywood was one of a number of present or former UMW officials who Lewis chose to staff the new federation.

Haywood initially served as a roving CIO organizer, advising and assisting emerging unions. During 1936 and 1937 he worked closely with the United Rubber Workers, helping it negotiate its first major contract, and the United Automobile Workers, serving on its policy committee during the sit-down strikes against General Motors and Chrysler. He also assisted the Packinghouse Workers and a number of smaller unions. In 1937 he was appointed CIO regional director in New York City, where he served as spokesman for the national CIO, helped the Transport Workers Union, the Steel Workers Organizing Committee, and other unions in organizing drives and contract negotiations, and served as president of the New York State Industrial Union Council.

At the 1939 CIO convention, as part of a staff shakeup designed to check the influence of Communists and their sympathizers, Lewis appointed Haywood, a staunch anti-Communist, to the newly created post of director of organization, which he held for the remainder of his life. In his new position, Haywood supervised the CIO field staff (which grew to some 230 people), served as chairman of organizing committees for the utility, optical, paper, telephone, and insurance industries, helped resolve jurisdictional disputes among CIO affiliates, and assisted affiliates in organizing drives. He also occasionally intervened in internal union faction fights on behalf of the CIO leadership. Haywood participated in the World War II economic mobilization as a member of advisory committees to the Council of National Defense and the Office of Price Mobilization.

In 1942, when Lewis pulled the UMW out of the CIO, Haywood remained with the latter group. His friendship with Lewis's successor as CIO president, Philip Murray, dated back to 1919, when they were both young UMW officials. Under Murray, Haywood's importance in the CIO continued to grow. He was elected a CIO vice president in 1942, given the additional job of director of state and city industrial union councils in 1950, and named to the newly created post of executive vice president in 1951, which made him, along with Murray and Secretary-Treasurer James B. Carey, one of the top three leaders of the organization.

Although Haywood was not well known to the general public, he was a familiar figure to local union activists. Year in and year out he crisscrossed the country, addressing union meetings, serving as a troubleshooter for the national CIO, and building up a vast network of acquaintances. Within the political spectrum of the CIO, Haywood was a centrist; in national politics, a liberal Democrat. But neither politics nor theoretical issues held much interest for Haywood; unionism alone was his passion. "When you join a labor union," he liked to say, "it's like joining a church: you work for nothing else and believe in nothing else." Although not an effective speaker, Haywood's warm manner and delight in talk, drink, and company made him widely liked within the labor movement.

After World War II Haywood became involved in international labor affairs. In 1945 he attended the London World Trade Union Conference and visited Moscow on a goodwill mission for the CIO. Four years later he was a delegate to the founding meeting of the International Confederation of Free Trade Unions. Haywood's last years, however, were largely spent trying to recoup the loss of some 800,000 members that resulted from the CIO's expulsion of eleven Communist-led unions in 1949 and 1950. While some groups of onetime members were won back, the most important membership boost came from Haywood's successful wooing of the newly formed Communications Workers of America, which affiliated with the CIO in 1949.

At the December 1952 CIO convention, Haywood ran against UAW president Walter Reuther for the CIO presidency, made vacant by Murray's recent death. While there were ideological differences between the candidates—Haywood was thought of as a bread-and-butter unionist and Reuther a social democrat—the rivalry between the Steelworkers and Auto Workers, the CIO's largest affiliates, was at least as important in shaping the outcome of the contest. Haywood lost with 46 percent of the vote, garnered largely from the Steelworkers, CWA, Transport Workers, Packinghouse Workers, and Utility Workers. Following his defeat, he was unanimously reelected executive vice president, with enlarged powers. He died less than three months later while addressing a CIO meeting in Wilkes-Barre, Pennsylvania.

Haywood, who was sometimes called "Mr. CIO," was one of the few CIO leaders whose primary affiliation and loyalty was to the CIO itself rather than to one of its constituent unions. Haywood, Murray said, did "the pluggin' and the drudgery and the pick-and-shovel work" for the CIO. He deserves some of the credit for the CIO's initial success, which helped transform national industrial relations and politics. However, as the person in charge of organizing for most of the CIO's history, he bears some of the responsibility for its failure to make significant gains after World War II, except through the affiliation of already organized groups. By the time Haywood died, the CIO had lost the dynamism that during the 1930s and 1940s had made it one of the most important institutions in the country.

• A tribute to Haywood and Philip Murray published by the Philip Murray Memorial Foundation, *Human Dignity, A Legacy to Labor* (1953), contains useful biographical information, as does an entry in *Current Biography, 1951–1952*. The *Proceedings* of the CIO's 1952 convention, which Haywood chaired, provide numerous examples of his speaking style. His personality and political views are sketched in Elise Morrow, "The CIO's Hatchet Man," *Saturday Evening Post*, 4 Nov. 1950, pp. 34, 142–44, and Daniel Bell, "Every Man a Dark Horse," *Fortune*, Nov. 1951, pp. 54, 56. An obituary is in the *New York Times*, 22 Feb. 1953.

JOSHUA B. FREEMAN

HAYWOOD, Big Bill. *See* Haywood, William Dudley.

HAYWOOD, John (16 Mar. 1762–22 Dec. 1826), lawyer and historian, was born in Halifax County, North Carolina, the son of Egbert Haywood, a tobacco farmer, and Sarah Ware. Following a brief education at a local academy, he volunteered for service in the revolutionary war and became an aide to a North Carolina officer. Self-taught in law, he was admitted to the Halifax bar soon after the Revolution. Quickly distinguishing himself in legal contests with talented opponents including James Iredell, Haywood was chosen by the general assembly in 1785 as judge of the newly created superior court for Davidson County in what is now Tennessee. Although he declined the office in favor of local practice and marriage, his election was to prove strangely prophetic of his later career. In late 1785 or early 1786 he married Martha Edwards; they had at least six children. In 1790 the general assembly elected Haywood solicitor general, and the following year, attorney general (at that time, a life-tenured office). In 1794 the assembly named him a judge of the state's superior court. While on the bench, he reported the court's decisions in two volumes, known as Haywood's *Reports*, which were incorporated into the *North Carolina Reports* as volumes 2 and 3.

In 1800 resignation ended Haywood's judicial career in North Carolina. Secretary of State James Glasgow was indicted along with others for fraud in issuing land warrants, and Haywood was induced by the offer of a $1,000 fee to resign from the bench in order to defend the accused. His argument on appeal from a conviction was elaborate but unavailing (*State v. Glasgow*, 1800). The odium attached to Haywood for his part in the affair may have temporarily depressed his popularity: he lost resoundingly in his bid to be elected a presidential elector that year. His reputation for learning, however, soon restored his practice. For an example of his forensic skill in a complicated land case in which he matched wits with William Gaston (1778–1844), see *Wells v. Newbolt* (1802). In 1805 he served the Federalist cause, representing the University of North Carolina in a successful challenge to an Antifederalist state statute designed to strip the university of its assets (*University v. Foy*). Despite his active practice, he still found time to write and periodically update two works for practitioners: a handbook for North Carolina justices of the peace (1800) and a manual of the laws of North Carolina (1801). Uninspired and intensely practical, they spread Haywood's fame and usefully supplemented his income.

About 1807 he decided to migrate to Tennessee, where he purchased a farm, which he named "Tusculum." Located seven miles south of Nashville, it lay within the jurisdiction of the superior court to which Haywood had declined election as a young man. Specializing in cases involving land titles, he practiced law in a log cabin office on Tusculum. A second log cabin nearby served as a law school—probably the first in the southwest—where Haywood was sole preceptor. In 1816 he was chosen for the Tennessee Supreme Court of Errors and Appeals, the state's highest court, on which he served until his death. As he had in North Carolina, Haywood wrote useful manuals for practitioners, publishing his *Tennessee Justice of the Peace* in 1810. He also published the reports of his court: the three volumes of Haywood's *Reports* cover 1816 to 1818 and appear as volumes 4–6 of the *Tennessee Reports*. With Robert L. Cobbs he compiled the two-volume *Statute Laws of Tennessee*, which appeared posthumously in 1831. Despite his professional duties, Haywood found time to reflect on larger issues, publishing his idiosyncratic *Christian Advocate* in 1819, in which he intermingled credulous accounts of ghosts and supernatural occurrences with astute observations on natural phenomena, his aim being to convince "young men" of the compatibility of science and religion. In 1821 Haywood organized the Tennessee Antiquarian Society, a forerunner of the Tennessee

Historical Society. His historical research, including interviews with many early settlers, resulted in the companion volumes *The Natural and Aboriginal History of Tennessee* and *The Civil and Political History of Tennessee*. Both published in 1823, they trace the history of the territory to statehood in 1796. He was honored by having a frontier county named for him in 1823.

Haywood was of remarkable physical appearance and weighed over 350 pounds at his death. A colleague, Judge Nathaniel Baxter, has left this word picture: "His arms, his legs, and his neck were short, his abdomen came down over his lap and nearly covered it to his knees. His head, which rested nearly on his shoulders, was unusually large and peculiarly formed. His underjaw and his lower face looked large and strong, and his head above his ears ran up high and somewhat conical, and, viewed horizontally, it was square rather than round." Haywood died at Tusculum and was buried there, survived by his children, to each of whom he left a large estate.

• Haywood's books are rare, but his arguments as an advocate and his opinions as a judge, often reported by himself, lay the groundwork for the jurisprudence of two states and are available in law libraries. A biographical sketch is in Joseph B. Cheshire, *Nonnulla* (1930). The best single source on Haywood is Samuel C. Williams, "Judge John Haywood," *Tennessee Law Review* 17 (1942): 423–39.

JOHN V. ORTH

HAYWOOD, William Dudley (4 Feb. 1869–18 May 1928), labor leader and political radical, known as "Big Bill," was born William Richard Haywood in Salt Lake City, Utah, the son of William Dudley Haywood, an itinerant worker, and Elizabeth (maiden name unknown). The senior Haywood died when his son was three years old. Four years later Elizabeth married a hard-rock miner (name unknown). Haywood changed his middle name from Richard to Dudley in 1878. He received a rudimentary education and began working as a youngster at the odd jobs available in a small mining camp or in Salt Lake City, where his family occasionally lived. At the age of fifteen he became a miner, and that remained his primary occupation until 1901, when he became a full-time union official.

By 1889 Haywood was a skilled hard-rock miner working in the Bingham Canyon, Utah, copper mines. That same year he married "Nevada Jane" Minor. During the early years of the marriage he tried other vocations, none successfully. Three years after the birth of his first daughter in 1892, Haywood resumed steady work as a miner in Silver City, Idaho. From 1895 through 1900 he worked in the same mine, becoming a highly respected miner and citizen. A second daughter was born to the Haywoods in 1897, after which "Nevada Jane" grew ill and bedridden. Increasingly alienated from his wife and children, he built a life outside the family, although he never legally divorced his first wife.

In Silver City, Haywood joined the American labor movement. He became a charter member of the Silver City local of the Western Federation of Miners (WFM) in August 1896 and rose rapidly through its ranks, becoming president of his local in 1900. He also quickly ascended the national union's hierarchy. In 1900 he became a member of the union's general executive board and soon thereafter left Silver City permanently to work in Denver at the WFM's headquarters. There Haywood assumed the editorship of the official union journal, *Miners' Magazine*, and served as secretary-treasurer of the WFM. As a national officer in perhaps the most militant and radical union in the nation, he received an intensive education in the theory and practice of class struggle. In 1903, a committed socialist as well as a trade unionist, Haywood led a bitter and violent struggle between miners and mine owners in Colorado. The battle, which dragged on for nearly three years, brought him into conflict with the governor of Colorado, the state militia, and the judiciary. In 1905, as the conflict in Colorado ebbed, Haywood joined with other radicals to form a new labor organization, the Industrial Workers of the World (IWW). Chairman of the IWW's founding Chicago convention, Haywood personified that organization's commitment to making a revolution in the United States by organizing the masses of less skilled and powerless working people neglected by the mainstream labor movement. His role in the formation of the IWW made him nationally prominent as a radical, a person soon to be characterized by conservatives as the "most dangerous man in America."

In February 1906, less than a year after Haywood burst into national prominence, Pinkerton detectives arrested him as an alleged accomplice in the assassination of Frank Steunenberg, former governor of Idaho. The focus of one of the most sensational murder trials in American history, he and his two co-defendants were represented by Clarence Darrow. They were acquitted in 1907, but Haywood found himself a union leader without an organization because the WFM and the IWW had split over the issues of radicalism and revolution while he awaited trial.

Having stood as the Socialist Party of America's (SPA) candidate for governor of Colorado in 1906, Haywood decided to devote his energies to the party, which elected him to its national executive committee in 1908 and as a delegate in 1910 to the International Socialist Congress. Even within the SPA he found himself the center of controversy. He regularly condemned "bourgeois" laws and counseled practices considered violent and illegal by other Socialists—sabotage for example—and, as a result, in 1913 a majority of more moderate party members removed Haywood from the national executive committee.

Repudiated by Socialists, Haywood renewed his interest in the IWW, where he found more congenial colleagues. He quickly regained IWW prominence as a result of his roles in the Lawrence, Massachusetts, textile strike of 1912 and the Paterson, New Jersey, silk strike of 1913. By then, Greenwich Village intellectuals and bohemians sought him out as a favorite invitee to soirees and salons, where he starred as the proletarian revolutionary. The most famous of Wobblies by 1915, Haywood was the logical choice to serve as the highest official of the IWW. In that capacity he successfully organized migratory farm workers, loggers, and copper miners.

When the United States entered World War I in April 1917, the IWW had reached the peak of its power and membership. The war spelled promise and peril for Haywood and his organization. A scarcity of labor enabled the IWW to organize workers and improve conditions, but IWW strikes in vital war industries sparked resistance to labor radicals and precipitated a vigorous national government response. In September 1917 Justice Department agents raided IWW headquarters and soon thereafter arrested Haywood and more than 100 other IWW officers, charging them with violations of the wartime sedition and espionage acts. After a lengthy federal trial in Chicago from April to August 1918, Haywood and 110 co-defendants were found guilty and sentenced to long terms in federal prison, effectively ending Haywood's career as an IWW leader.

Released on bail while attorneys appealed his conviction, Haywood spoke out in defense of other "political" prisoners. When in April 1921 his last appeal failed, he disappeared, reemerging later that year as an exile in the Soviet Union. Haywood, the prototypical American frontier proletarian, proved a misfit in Lenin's new world. Failing in the tasks of building industries in the Urals, assigned to him by the Communists, he retired to a room in Moscow's Lux hotel where he entertained visiting American radicals with drink, stories, and song. He also married a Soviet woman (name unknown) with whom he could barely communicate. Increasingly ill from diabetes complicated by alcoholism, Haywood deteriorated physically. After a series of strokes, he died in a Moscow hospital. Soviet officials placed some of his ashes in the Kremlin Wall and shipped the remainder to Waldheim Cemetery in Chicago for placement near the graves of the Haymarket martyrs.

• No single body of Haywood papers exists. The most complete collection of IWW records, which includes many letters to and from Haywood, is at the Archives of Labor and Urban History, Walter Reuther Library, Wayne State University, Detroit, Michigan. Other Haywood correspondence and materials can be found in several Department of Justice files in the National Archives in Washington, D.C. *Bill Haywood's Book: The Autobiography of William D. Haywood* (1929; repr. 1958) is a complete autobiography. For Haywood's own ideas see Frank Bohn and William D. Haywood, *Industrial Socialism* (1911). The most complete and readable biography is Peter Carlson, *Roughneck: The Life and Times of Big Bill Haywood* (1983). A shorter, more accessible biography is Melvyn Dubofsky, *"Big Bill" Haywood* (1987).

MELVYN DUBOFSKY

HAYWORTH, Rita (17 Oct. 1918–14 May 1987), movie actress, was born Margarita Carmen Cansino in Brooklyn, New York, the daughter of Eduardo Cansino, a Spanish dancer, and Volga Hayworth, a Ziegfeld showgirl. Although she was shy and showed little interest in professional performing, Margarita was put into dancing classes at age four. For the rest of her childhood, dance training and performing took precedence over formal schooling. Only briefly, in New York, did the family settle down long enough for her to regularly attend school.

In 1927 the family moved to California, where Eduardo Cansino hoped to find fame and fortune in Hollywood. There, at age twelve, Margarita became her father's professional dancing partner. For the next five years she performed with him on offshore gambling ships and in Tijuana nightspots where child labor laws were not stringent. Cansino's exploitation of his daughter at this time may, by some accounts, have included sexual abuse; the "Dancing Cansinos" were often assumed to be husband and wife.

The Cansino family fortunes declined during the depression, and the family hoped that Margarita's beauty and dancing talent would attract the attention of the Hollywood figures who frequented the establishments where the Cansinos performed. In 1933, at the age of fifteen, Margarita was summoned to Hollywood for a screen test at Warner Bros., but nothing came of it. The following year, Winfield Sheehan, then production chief at Fox Film Corporation, also gave her a screen test; this time she was signed to a six-month contract. At Fox, her first name was shortened to Rita, and as Rita Cansino she had a dancing role in her first feature film, *Dante's Inferno* (1935), and was publicized as "a beautiful young Spanish-Irish dancer," with emphasis on the Spanish. (In many of her early films she played stereotyped foreign or exotic roles.) She was then set to play the lead in Fox's Technicolor remake of *Ramona*. In 1935, however, Fox merged with Twentieth Century, Sheehan was ousted, and Rita Cansino was replaced in *Ramona* by Loretta Young. After two more pictures at Fox (from one of which her footage was cut entirely), Rita Cansino's option was dropped.

Around this time the first of Hayworth's five husbands entered her life. Edward Judson had a shady background as a car dealer and was old enough to be her father, but he recognized a certain star quality and offered to take over her career. Judson helped to find freelance acting jobs for the starlet; most were low-budget westerns at poverty row studios, but they led to a seven-year contract with Columbia Pictures in 1937. In May of that year Judson and Rita Cansino eloped, and then the transformation of Rita Cansino began in earnest. At Columbia it was decided that the Cansino name and image limited her roles, so her name was changed to Hayworth, and the visual signifiers of her Spanish background began to be played down. To correct what was perceived as a too-low forehead, she underwent electrolysis on her hairline. The result of the quite public process of transformation and fabrication was that Rita Cansino, "Latin starlet," emerged as Rita Hayworth, "all-American glamour girl." But while Judson was successful in getting Hayworth's new name and face into magazines and newspapers, her films remained nondescript. In 1939, however, director Howard Hawks signed her to play the second female lead in *Only Angels Have Wings*, and her beauty and sensuality attracted considerable press and public attention. Then followed a series of loan-outs, including the second-lead title role in Warner Bros.' highly successful *The Strawberry Blonde* (1941). She was next called to replace Carole Landis as temptress Doña Sol in Rouben Mamoulian's remake of *Blood and Sand* (1941) for Twentieth Century-Fox. She had, at this point, made thirty-one films, more than half of her lifetime output.

Mamoulian was fascinated by Rita Hayworth's ability to move "like a great cat," but Hayworth's dance training had not yet been fully exploited in her films. This changed after the success of her first tailor-made star vehicle at Columbia, a Cole Porter musical called *You'll Never Get Rich* (1941), with Fred Astaire; it was among the first of Hollywood's many wartime musicals. Around the same time, Hayworth became a popular troop pinup girl. She appeared (for the second of four times) on the cover of *Life* magazine on 11 August 1941; the photograph inside of Hayworth in a satin negligee became one of the most popular pinups of the war years. Hayworth performed in various wartime fundraisers and camp shows, but although she danced and often sang at these events, for reasons that remain unclear, her singing voice usually was dubbed in her films. Now much in demand, Hayworth was again loaned out for the Fox musical *My Gal Sal* (1942), which was followed that same year by another successful Columbia musical with Astaire, *You Were Never Lovelier*.

Hayworth's personal life continued to make news. She divorced Judson in 1942, and in 1943, while making one of her biggest film successes, *Cover Girl* (1944, with Gene Kelly), she married Orson Welles. Hollywood wags quickly dubbed the pair "Beauty and the Brain." They had one child, a daughter. *Cover Girl* was followed by Hayworth's last wartime musical, *Tonight and Every Night* (1945).

Until this point the Hayworth screen persona had been either vampish, as in *Blood and Sand*, or all-American, as in her musicals. But in the title role of *Gilda* (1946) Hayworth combined the all-American forthrightness and spunkiness of her musical roles with the eroticism and exoticism of a Doña Sol. The effect was stunning; Gilda is, as film scholar Michael Wood has put it, a "roaring, sexy woman" who is also "decent," and the film grossed millions. Hayworth's danced rendition of "Put the Blame on Mame" is, in the words of its choreographer Jack Cole, "absolutely first-rate," and the film has become a film noir classic. *Gilda* was followed by a less successful fantasy musical with Larry Parks, *Down to Earth* (1947), in which Hayworth played Terpsichore, the muse of dance. This role helped to win her the title of "American Love Goddess," a limiting but resonant sobriquet that followed her for the rest of her life.

The flip side of Gilda turned out to be the promiscuous but evil (and platinum blonde) Elsa Bannister of Orson Welles's *The Lady from Shanghai* (1948), one of Hayworth's few forties' box-office failures. She divorced Welles the same year.

Exhausted after many years of almost solid film work, Hayworth was on a trip to Europe in 1947 when she met and was wooed by Prince Aly Khan; their romance was front-page news in Europe and America for several months. Because Aly Khan was still married, the couple's peripatetic courtship occasioned some press disapproval. When their engagement was announced in 1949, however, Rita and Aly became the couple of the year, and their May wedding made Hayworth a "Cinderella Princess." Hayworth was pregnant at the time of the wedding; a daughter was born the following December. Almost immediately, the marriage began to falter amid rumors of Aly's incorrigible womanizing, and by 1951 Hayworth set sail for home with daughters in tow. She was granted a divorce by default in January 1953.

Back in Hollywood for the first time in three years, Hayworth faced a conservative and fragmented postwar audience on whose allegiance she could no longer rely and whose knowledge of her was likely based more on publicity stories and scandal than on her film work. Nevertheless, or perhaps because of this, her first film after her return to Hollywood ("She's back!" screamed the ads for *Affair in Trinidad*, a 1952 rehash of *Gilda*) was even more successful than *Gilda* had been. *Salome* (1953), an unimpressive entry into the biblical epic cycle, was next, followed the same year by *Miss Sadie Thompson*, a quasimusical remake of *Rain*. Hayworth's private life continued to dominate her star image, however. Her marriage to singer Dick Haymes in 1953 seemed, after the opulence of the Hayworth-Khan nuptuals, to be what one columnist called a "skid into the rhinestones." Haymes was brutal, and the marriage was short, and again Hayworth was off the screen for several years. Her return this time, in *Fire Down Below* (1957), did not attract much attention. Hayworth's Columbia contract was played out with the "older woman" role of Vera Simpson to Frank Sinatra's *Pal Joey* (1957); ironically, Hayworth was two years younger than Sinatra.

Hayworth's fifth and last marriage was to producer James Hill in 1958, for whom she made one of her finest dramatic films, *Separate Tables*, the same year. Her acting, rather than her glamour, began to come in for serious attention with films like *They Came to Cordura* (1959) and Clifford Odets's *The Story on Page One* (1960). Hayworth and Hill were divorced in 1961 amid rumors of alcoholism and, again, brutality. In 1962 Hayworth's scheduled Broadway debut in a play called *Step on a Crack* was canceled. Stories circulated in the press that Hayworth was unable to remember her lines. In fact, by the late fifties Hayworth had begun to exhibit signs—forgetfulness, erratic, sometimes physically violent, behavior, often assumed to be alcohol-related—of the Alzheimer's disease that eventually killed her. Nevertheless, between 1963 and 1971 Hayworth made seven films, most of them in Europe. The first public connection of Hayworth to the then little-known disease was not made until June 1981; later that year her daughter Yasmin Khan was legally appointed Hayworth's conservator. Hayworth was moved to New York City, where she lived near her daughter until her death.

The potency of Hayworth's star image seems to have been closely aligned to what in some sense she "was"—a "tempestuous glamour queen caught by the camera," as Hedda Hopper once wrote, who was also "a nice, quiet girl"; a Love Goddess who was Rita Hayworth "up there," but who never forgot that she had been born Margarita Cansino. A fan magazine writer once called Rita Hayworth a "shy siren," and the oxymoron well describes the tensions in—as well as the enduring popularity of—her all-American but exotic, and erotic, image.

• Book-length biographies of Hayworth include John Kobal, *The Time, the Place and the Woman* (1977); Joe Morella and Edward Z. Epstein, *Rita: The Life of Rita Hayworth* (1983); and Barbara Leaming, *If This Was Happiness* (1989). Reliable information about Hayworth's films can be found in Gene Ringgold and Lawrence Quirk, *The Complete Films of Rita Hayworth* (1992). Two popular articles that are particularly useful in considering Hayworth's image in the 1940s are Jerome Beatty, "Sweetheart of the A.E.F.," *American Magazine*, Dec. 1942, pp. 42–43, 72–74, and Winthrop Sargeant, "The Cult of the Love Goddess in America," *Life*, 10 Nov. 1947, pp. 80–96. An obituary is in the *New York Times*, 16 May 1987.

ADRIENNE L. McLEAN

HAZARD, Caroline (10 June 1856–19 Mar. 1945), college president, author, and antiquarian, was born in Peace Dale, Rhode Island, the daughter of Rowland Hazard, an industrialist, and Margaret Anna Rood. Rowland Hazard, a descendant of Brown University founder Thomas Hazard, was a progressive whose Peace Dale estate was the seat of a workers' community, in which he shared his profits from the Peace Dale Woolen Mills with employees.

Educated largely at home, Caroline Hazard attended classes at Brown University but never graduated. Her interest in Rhode Island's and her family's history led her to become an author and editor of historical works, including *Life of J. L. Diman* (1886), *Thomas Hazard, Son of Robert* (1893), *Narragansett Ballads* (1894), *The Narragansett Friends' Meeting* (1899), and the four-volume *The Works of Rowland G. Hazard* (1889). She also learned the family business and took part in the workers' community. Like other educated or intellectual women of her time, as a young adult she experienced personal uncertainty. In an autobiographical essay, "At Eight and Twenty," she described the unease of a woman who, unmarried and without a vocation, sees "her own social and intellectual usefulness limited." But in 1889 she was invited by Alice Freeman Palmer, president of Wellesley College, to serve on Wellesley's Board of Visitors (1889–1893). In 1899

Hazard was offered the presidency and reluctantly accepted the position in March, feeling unqualified.

Hazard initially had to deal with divisions within the faculty resulting from a "purge" of less research-oriented professors under her predecessor, Julia Irvine. Hazard's dignified presence and deep commitment to intellectualism, Christian spirituality and the social gospel, and the arts gave her a good rapport with the faculty. Liberal in some aspects (she abolished compulsory chapel and instituted student self-government), she also publicly appealed to the "eternal feminine" in women in delineating their possible life choices. Unlike other women educators, such as her contemporary M. Carey Thomas, Hazard did not question the commonly accepted belief in fundamental differences between the genders nor did she call attention to gender-based inequities such as lack of equal opportunities in career choices or the barriers that faced academic women in claiming an equal place in their professions. Her ideal of college education was "a vision of public service combined with . . . gentle womanhood."

Hazard's social centrism and her administrative emphasis on financial stability were apparent during the so-called "tainted money" debate in 1899, perhaps the greatest controversy of her presidency. Several faculty protested and students debated the college's acceptance of Rockefeller money, based on their negative assessment of the labor practices of the Standard Oil Company. Hazard, who believed that some always lost out "in the march of civilization" accepted the funds. No faculty resigned and there was no permanent damage to her presidency.

During Hazard's administration, Wellesley's enrollment nearly doubled, with a complementary expansion of faculty. She oversaw the establishment of studies or departments in astronomy, economics, English, and hygiene and physical education. Music, a special interest of Hazard's, received its own endowed department, and she also helped launch the college choir. She erased the college's debt and began an endowment, which by 1910 totaled $1.3 million. She raised money from alumnae, friends, and major donors for endowed chairs, departments, and scholarship funds, as well as for five dormitories, five academic buildings, a new library, and a heating plant. Hazard herself gave the college $95,000.

Having no academic degree, Hazard believed herself ill suited to take a leadership role in Wellesley's academic life. She largely deferred to the faculty in academic matters, and in her "perplexity and anxiety" over administering the college relied heavily on Bible instructor Mary Woolley, who became president of Mount Holyoke College in 1900, and on college secretary, later dean, Ellen Fitz Pendleton. Hazard's anxiety over her intellectual role may have been at the root of her frequent illnesses, obliging her to take leaves of absence in 1906–1907 and for part of 1908–1909. In 1910, pleading continued ill health, she resigned and resumed her writing and research, producing several more volumes of essays, poetry, historical, and edited

works. One, *From College Gates* (1925), contained significant material about her educational ideas and experiences as Wellesley's president.

During World War I she participated in war work, chairing the South Kingston County (R.I.) Women's Committee for National Defense in 1916, and for six months that same year the Women's Committee for National Defense. She sat on the Liberty Committee (1916) and the World War Savings Corporation (1917). After the war she began spending her summers in Santa Barbara, California, becoming involved in local history and cultural efforts there as well. She continued to move between Peace Dale and Santa Barbara until her death, remaining connected to Wellesley events and fundraising efforts. She died in Santa Barbara.

Hazard represented a new kind of women's college leader: upper class, well connected, with an interest in women's education, whose access to money and influence and familiarity with business affairs helped build the institution's material base. Like Mary Garrett, trustee and major contributor to Bryn Mawr College in this period, such women had both a belief in women's education and access to the means to support such institutions, which had not been the case for an earlier generation of women educational leaders. Hazard put a material base under the plans others made for Wellesley, reversing a grave economic decline and beginning a permanent endowment to ensure the college's continued fiscal security; she was the first president of Wellesley to emphasize fundraising.

Hazard's concept of "knowledge for service" in women's education brought together both older beliefs about women's proper role and the new claims being made for women's higher education, still a controversial idea in some circles. The overall impact of this idea may have been to make college for women more acceptable to those still unsure of its merits or its relation to more traditional, home- and family-oriented female roles. Hazard likened herself to medieval educational patron Lady Margaret Beaufort, a "woman of position and influence [with] a keen interest in education." Of Beaufort, and of herself, she wrote, "Through that woman's thought / We stand today / A company of women." Despite her own self-doubts about her role as an academic leader—or perhaps because of them—maintaining the "company of women" that was the Wellesley community was perhaps her greatest legacy.

• Hazard's presidential papers are in the Wellesley College Archives, Wellesley, Mass. Papers of the Hazard family, including a partially processed collection of her papers, are in the Rhode Island Historical Society's manuscripts collection. Additional Hazard Family Papers are in Harvard University's Baker Library, Cambridge, Mass., and may assist in assessing the degree of her involvement with the family business. In addition to the works mentioned in the essay, Hazard also wrote or edited Esther Bernon Carpenter, *South Country Studies* (1924), *John Safflin His Book 1664–1707* (1928), *Nailer Tom's Diary 1778–1840* (1930), *A Scallop Shell of Quiet* (1907), *A Brief Pilgrimage in the Holy Land* (1909), *Anchors of*

Tradition (1924), *Songs in the Sun* (1927), *A Precious Heritage* [a joint biography of her parents] (1929), *Threads from the Distaff* (1934), *The Yosemite and Other Verse* (1917), *Songs in the Swing, Homing* (1929), *Shards and Scarabs* (1931), and *The Golden State* (1939). Hazard's views about education and culture appear in the essays collected in *The College Year* (1910) and *Some Ideals in the Education of Women* (c. 1900). Her presidency is covered in Florence Converse, *Wellesley College: A Chronicle of the Years 1875–1938* (1939), in Alice Payne Hackett, *Wellesley: Part of the American Story* (1949), and Patricia Ann Palmieri, *In Adamless Eden* (1995), which also delineates the power dynamics at work behind the scenes during this period in Wellesley's history. An obituary is in the *New York Times*, 20 Mar. 1945.

CINDY BROWN

HAZARD, Rebecca Ann Naylor (10 Nov. 1826–1 Mar. 1912), reformer, was born in Woodsfield, Ohio, the daughter of Robert F. Naylor and Mary B. Archbold. She spent her early years in Woodsfield, where she attended Monroe Institute and the Marietta Seminary, until the age of fourteen. The family soon moved to Cincinnati, Ohio, and then to Quincy, Illinois, where she married William T. Hazard in 1844. The couple had five children, two of whom died in infancy. In 1850 the family moved to St. Louis. There Hazard began to work with neglected young women. She became manager of the Girls' Industrial Home from 1855 to 1856 and later served as corresponding secretary of the home from 1858 to 1859. The home was founded in 1854 to teach girls a trade that would enable them to earn a living. It also provided a home and school for destitute and orphaned girls. Hazard contributed her time and money to erect a new school building in St. Louis.

An ardent Unionist during the Civil War, Hazard joined the efforts of the Freedmen's Relief Society of St. Louis and helped organize the Ladies' Union Aid Society. As treasurer of the Freedmen's Relief Society she helped raise funds, clothing, and medical supplies for the freed slaves who migrated to St. Louis in the summer of 1863. Through the Ladies' Union Aid Society she volunteered in military hospitals, helping care for sick and wounded soldiers. She also made bandages and clothing. Hazard served on the executive committee of ladies for the Mississippi Valley Sanitary Fair in St. Louis and managed the book and stationery department of the fair. The fair, which opened in May 1864, raised over half a million dollars for the Western Sanitary Commission.

Hazard also joined the Woman's Christian Temperance Union (WCTU) and worked for reform in prostitution. Although Hazard disapproved of prostitution, it was a bittersweet victory for her when St. Louis legalized prostitution in 1870, requiring medical examinations and the licensing of prostitutes. Along with Mrs. A. W. Clapp and others, Hazard founded the Guardian Home for unfortunate, homeless women, many of whom had been or were in danger of becoming prostitutes. With Mrs. Mary F. Henderson, she also helped form the St. Louis School of Design, which opened opportunities to women in the field of decorative art. The school later merged into the Woman's Exchange.

Like many other women of her era, Hazard recognized the important position women had played in the Civil War. When black men received the right to vote, women began to hope for like treatment. On 8 May 1867 Rebecca Hazard and other St. Louis women organized the Woman Suffrage Association of Missouri, the first organization in the world having as its sole purpose the political enfranchisement of women. Many notable persons gathered in St. Louis in October 1869 to hold the National Woman Suffrage Convention. Hazard and other St. Louis women were prominent in the proceedings, and they joined the National Woman Suffrage Association, an organization founded earlier that year in New York City by Elizabeth Cady Stanton and Susan B. Anthony. The NWSA emphasized the need for a federal woman suffrage amendment.

In 1869 members of the Woman Suffrage Association of Missouri circulated a petition asking for a woman suffrage amendment to the state constitution. Hazard was one of a delegation of ten that went to Jefferson City to present the petition to the legislature. The document contained some 2,000 names, including Missouri governor Joseph W. McClurg and approximately seventy-five senators and representatives. Lawmakers were friendly, but the petition went unheeded.

Again in 1879, Missouri women presented a petition to the Missouri House of Representatives, and Hazard spoke before the Committee on Constitutional Amendments. She noted that women had repeatedly presented their plea to the lawmakers with little success, commenting, "No time should be lost in making amends for the injustice of the long delay. . . . it is surprising that it should be a question at all" (quoted in Scott, p. 295). Despite her efforts, the bill did not pass. Nevertheless, for the next decade women carried their petitions to the state capital every year the legislature was in session.

When the National Woman Suffrage Association split into two groups in late 1869, Hazard joined the American Woman Suffrage Association (AWSA). The AWSA took a more moderate stand on the suffrage issue and avoided other more controversial feminist issues supported by the NWSA. As an active member of AWSA, Hazard held a number of committee appointments, served as a vice president-at-large and represented the local association at a number of conventions. In 1878 she was elected president of AWSA, the first in that office to live west of the Mississippi River. In recognition of her contribution to the early suffrage movements, Hazard was one of three honorary presidents of AWSA elected at an interstate suffrage convention, held in Kansas City, 8–9 February 1892.

Also a lover of books, Hazard was an active member of the Monday Evening Club, a weekly study group concentrating on literary subjects. As evidence of her scholarly abilities, she published *A View of Dante* (1887) and *New View of Dante* (1891).

Unfortunately, Mrs. Hazard did not live to see woman suffrage legislation enacted. Her death occurred in Kirkwood, Missouri, eight years before women received the right to vote. The League of Women Voters of Missouri later recognized her efforts by listing her as one of fifty-five women who contributed to the Missouri woman suffrage movement. A plaque, in their honor, was presented in the state capitol of Missouri in 1931.

• An account of Hazard's life appears in Patricia L. Adams, "Rebecca Naylor Hazard," in *Show Me Missouri Women: Selected Biographies*, vol. 1, ed. Mary K. Dains (1989); R. T. Bamber, "The Foremost Suffragist of Kirkwood," *Kirkwood Historical Review* 32 (Sept. 1993): 27–28; and William Hyde and Howard L. Conard, eds., *Encyclopedia of the History of St. Louis*, vol. 2 (1899). Her woman suffrage work is described in Monia Cook Morris, "The History of Woman Suffrage in Missouri, 1867–1901," *Missouri Historical Review* 25 (Oct. 1930): 67–82; in Mary Semple Scott, ed., "History of Woman Suffrage in Missouri," *Missouri Historical Review* 14 (Apr.–July 1920): 281–384; and in the League of Women Voters of Missouri Records, Joint Collection, Western Historical Manuscript Collection–State Historical Society of Missouri Manuscripts. Her activities at the Girls' Industrial Home can be found in Girls' Industrial Home, annual reports, 1855–1860, in St. Louis Protestant Orphans' Asylum Records, Joint Collection, Western Historical Manuscript Collection–State Historical Society of Missouri Manuscripts. An obituary is in the *St. Louis Globe-Democrat*, 3 Mar. 1912.

MARY K. DAINS

HAZARD, Samuel (26 May 1784–22 May 1870), historical editor and antiquarian, was born in Philadelphia, Pennsylvania, the son of Ebenezer Hazard, then postmaster general of the United States, and Abigail Arthur. He received his early education at the Second Presbyterian Church school in Philadelphia and, from 1793 to 1796, at an academy in Woodbury, New Jersey. He then spent two years at Princeton College but left in 1799 because of illness. Like his father, Hazard became a merchant and an editor of historical records. He took his apprenticeship in the prominent Philadelphia countinghouse of Robert Ralston, a family friend and a fellow "Old Light" Presbyterian. As a young man Hazard was involved in the formation of the American Literary Association in 1805 and the Phoenix Social Club in 1809. He also became a member of the Academy of Natural Sciences of Philadelphia in 1812 and the Philadelphia Society for Promoting Agriculture in 1814.

Hazard formed in December 1806 a partnership with Samuel Cabot of Boston. During the War of 1812 he made supercargo voyages to the West Indies, the Mediterranean, and the Near East. From 1818 to 1827 Hazard lived in Huntsville, Alabama Territory; there the firm of Hazard & Co. conducted a cotton brokerage and general mercantile business. In March 1819 he married Abigail Clark Hetfield; they would have nine children, four of whom would live to old age. After eight years, Hazard's business partnership faced unprofitable commissions and went bankrupt. At the age of forty-four, preferring books to countinghouse figures, Hazard returned to Philadelphia to pursue a new, less remunerative vocation.

Over the next four decades Hazard involved himself in historical, literary, and scientific pursuits. In 1829 the Historical Society of Pennsylvania named him its curator, a position he held until 1847. Reflecting the tangle of pious, patriotic, and civic sentiments held by many church-going Calvinist Presbyterians, Hazard was also active in a number of humanitarian or benevolent associations established for improving the material and social conditions of Philadelphia's poor. For instance, he was a member of the Society for Supplying the Poor with Soup, and in 1828 he was elected secretary of the Guardians of the Poor. Additionally, he was elected in 1836 as secretary of the board of trustees of the Second Presbyterian Church—whose membership included some of the most prominent families of the city—and he remained in this position until 1864.

Hazard's bookish pursuits led him to publish documentary tracts. In 1828 he established a weekly publication in Philadelphia known as *The Register of Pennsylvania*. The series contained a wide array of public documents and research materials relating to the history of the city of Philadelphia and the commonwealth of Pennsylvania. Of special note was the first-time publication of manuscripts in the American Philosophical Society relating to early colonization along the Delaware River (in volumes four and five). Unsuccessful financially, the periodical folded in 1836 after sixteen volumes. Three years later Hazard edited the *United States Commercial and Statistical Register* (July 1839–June 1842). Containing useful financial and economic material, this national publication depended on developing liberal arrangements with the secretaries of state for copies of public documents. Like his first publication venture, it ended in failure because it lacked a targeted audience. In 1850 Hazard published his third work, *The Annals of Pennsylvania, from the Discovery of the Delaware 1609–82*. Focusing on early Swedish and Dutch settlement, it was intended to be the first in a multivolume series that was never completed. It was based on primary material found in previously unpublished sources.

Shortly after the *Annals* appeared, Hazard's antiquarian and political friends at the American Philosophical Society and the Historical Society of Pennsylvania in Philadelphia persuaded the commonwealth of Pennsylvania to use its resources and patronage in support of history. In 1851, urged on also by provincial pride, Governor William F. Johnston commissioned Hazard to edit the *Pennsylvania Archives: Selected and Arranged from Original Documents in the Office of the Secretary of the Commonwealth*. To this end he supervised the publication of the sixteen-volume *Colonial Records* (1851–1853), which consisted of the minute books of the Provincial Council (1683–1775) and the Supreme Executive Council (1775–1790). He also served as the editor of what became known as the "first series" of the *Pennsylvania Archives*. Composed of loose original documents, letters, treaties, and other papers dating from before 1790, the *Archives* contained about 11,000 distinct papers. The editing for the twelve volumes, each numbering about 800 pages, was noted particularly for its consistency and simplicity. Hazard's editorial tasks included selecting and arranging the papers, taken mostly from the office of the Department of State; writing an appropriate heading for each document; producing hundreds of references to minutes of council; and supervising the printing of the bundles or packages of organized papers, all ordered by endorsement date, to be submitted to the state printer. Included also was the responsibility "to prepare all necessary notes, indexes, appendixes, and such other matter as may be necessary and proper." A "General Index" volume to cover both the *Colonial Records* and *Pennsylvania Archives* came out in 1860, but it was inferior in quality to the indexes of the individual volumes. To his credit, Hazard convinced the state legislature to expand the coverage, from 1783 to 1790, and to produce twelve volumes instead of five.

Hazard's editorial work was judged to be among the best produced during the mid-nineteenth century, when documentary history was very popular, and it contributed measurably to scholarship in state and national history. However, because the Pennsylvania state government was not prepared to fund any additional series of printed records, Hazard's antiquarian career ended. In 1862 Hazard returned to the Historical Society of Pennsylvania as its sixth librarian. For the next two years he prepared a statistical statement on the condition and extent of the library and developed the arrangement and classification system that was used during the next half-century. Additionally, in 1864 Hazard completed his history of the Second Presbyterian Church of Philadelphia. Hazard is considered by many to be one of the founders of the Presbyterian Historical Society.

After his wife died in 1864, Hazard sustained himself financially by selling his rather large library through an auction in 1868. He died at his home in Germantown, Pennsylvania. At the time he was eulogized as Pennsylvania's "most eminent historical student."

• There is no major collection of Hazard papers. Letters written by him are the following: The Hazard Family Papers at the Historical Society of Pennsylvania; the Bancroft papers and the Worcester papers at the Massachusetts Historical Society; the Miscellaneous and the Crosby holdings at the New-York Historical Society; and the State Archives at the Pennsylvania Historical and Museum Commission. A scientific tract titled "Observations of the Warmth of Sea Water, etc. . . . " is at the American Philosophical Society. An account of Hazard's life is Willis P. Hazard, "The Hazard Family of the Middle States," in *Recollections of Olden Times . . . ,* ed. Thomas R. Hazard (1879), pp. 247–53. Scattered references to Hazard are in Hampton L. Carson, *A History of the Historical Society of Pennsylvania* (2 vols., 1940). A more contemporary appraisal of Hazard's career is presented in Roland M. Baumann, "Samuel Hazard: Editor and Archivist for the Keystone State," *Pennsylvania Magazine of History and Biography* 107 (Apr. 1983): 195–216. See also Baumann's in-

troduction to the *Guide to the Microfilm of the Records of Pennsylvania's Revolutionary Governments, 1775–1790 in the Pennsylvania State Archives* (1978), and William A. Hunter, "Substitute for Truth: Hazard's 'Provincial Correspondence,'" *Pennsylvania History* 29 (1962): 278–90. For Hazard's place in the larger realm of historical activity, see Lyman H. Butterfield, "Archival and Editorial Enterprise in 1850 and 1950: Some Comparisons and Contrasts," *Proceedings of the American Philosophical Society* 98 (June 1954): 159–70, and Henry Howard Eddy and Martha L. Simonetti's introduction to the *Guide to the Published Archives of Pennsylvania* (1949; repr. 1976).

ROLAND M. BAUMANN

HAZARD, Thomas Robinson (3 Jan. 1797–26 Mar. 1886), manufacturer and reformer, was born in South Kingstown, Rhode Island, the son of Rowland Hazard, a manufacturer and merchant, and Mary Peace. Hazard's father established the Peace Dale Manufacturing Company, the first water-powered wool-carding and fulling mill in South Kingstown, about 1802, on the site of an eighteenth-century fulling mill. By 1814 the company had expanded to include spinning and perhaps the earliest power loom-weaving in the state. After limited formal education at Westtown in Pennsylvania, and after training in mill management and operations at the growing enterprise, Hazard worked in the family's woolen business between 1813 and 1842.

In 1821 Hazard purchased a mill privilege (riverine property with rapids or a dam capable of generating waterpower) from Abigail Rodman in South Kingstown and established his own woolen mill, which he operated while continuing to work in the family firm. The following year, he acquired seventy acres of prime pasture land contiguous with his woolen factory from his father. There Hazard raised sheep. His sizable herd earned him the sobriquet of Shepherd Tom. Once he had attained a reputation for raising sheep, Hazard wrote horticultural discourses for agricultural organizations.

Hazard married Frances Minturn, the daughter of Jonas Minturn of New York, in 1838. They had six children. Shortly after his marriage, Hazard sold the land and business in South Kingstown and bought "Vaucluse," the seventeen-acre, late-eighteenth-century Portsmouth, Rhode Island, estate of Garvais Elam. The estate included a two-and-a-half-story Georgian Revival mansion. Its formal gardens of imported and rare trees and shrubs with winding walkways overlooked the Sakonnet River. With wealth amassed from textile manufacturing and horticulture, Hazard retired from business at forty-five years of age to devote himself to his family and to social and political reforms.

Although Hazard had never held a public office, he promoted political ideals that effected his economic beliefs and ethical concerns. Like many ardent Whigs, he had long supported reforms for the working class. He promoted Henry Clay's American System and protection for American domestic manufacturing, which he saw as a solution to unemployment. While the public blamed President Martin Van Buren for the economic depression of 1837, Hazard used the presidential campaign of 1840 to delineate domestic policies. At that time, Hazard penned a series of articles called "Facts for the Laboring Man" in support of the Whig's economic platform. The series received acclaim after being published in a Newport newspaper and a volume of collected articles was published under the same title in 1840.

Hazard actively pursued social reforms that had interested him for years. The Quaker had already indicated concern for educational reform prior to his retirement from the South Kingstown woolen business. He had established the first night school in Rhode Island at his factory in Peace Dale. Once settled in Portsmouth, Hazard supported the establishment there of the first schoolhouse on the "improved plan," which involved pedagogical and methodological changes in the ways individuals were educated, with particular emphasis on language and reading. He was instrumental in calling for the first statewide meeting to study state educational institutions. The meeting led to the formation of the Rhode Island Institute for Instruction.

Hazard applied this same zeal and enthusiasm to his efforts to ensure adequate care and education of the poor and insane. In 1851 he published *Report on the Poor and Insane in Rhode Island*. To research this study he visited with a standard questionnaire each facility caring for the poor and insane in the state. After completing and publishing the report, Hazard sought improved treatment. He did not endeavor to better each and every institution in Rhode Island; rather, Hazard centered his efforts on ameliorating institutional conditions for the poor at Butler Hospital in Providence, Rhode Island. His petition to the state's General Assembly secured fixed state appropriations for the care of the insane poor and for the education of the deaf and blind. In addition to these reforms, Hazard campaigned successfully for the abolition of capital punishment in Rhode Island in 1852 and encouraged aid for Irish famine victims.

The deaths of two of his daughters during the 1840s and his wife in 1854 moved Hazard to seek solace in seances by 1856. He became a passionate supporter of spiritualism and wished to be remembered for his efforts. In his own words, "whatever may be his merits or demerits otherwise he has no higher ambitions than that his name should be handed down to the coming generations associated with that fact alone" (*Recollections of Olden Times* [1879], p. 192). During the 1870s Hazard wrote numerous essays on spiritualism. He compiled the *Ordeal of Life* (1870) based on information gathered by medium John C. Grinnell from his encounters with 1,500 souls.

Hazard's interest in spiritualism did not deter him from promoting reforms. Two years after his wife's death, he wrote a series of antislavery texts later collected for publication under the title *A Constitutional Manual: Negro Slavery and the Constitution* (1856). The publication encouraged the preservation of the Union while recognizing the horrors and wrongs of enslaving other humans. Rhode Island's Quakers had a long history of trying to abolish slavery and were foremost in the state's antislavery movement. The Hazard family, along with other Rhode Island Quakers, was among the first to free its slaves and worked hard to abrogate the institution in Rhode Island during the eighteenth century. Thomas Hazard continued to urge antislavery by taking pen in hand. He sought ways to end bondage without bloodshed while protecting the Union in the years before the Civil War. He believed strongly in the African colonization movement, which relocated former slaves to Liberia in Africa. He also was a member and an advocate of the American Colonization Society.

During the final years of his life, Hazard recorded Rhode Island folktales and local legends in a collection of articles that first appeared in the *Providence Journal* and were later published in book form, the *Jonny-Cake Papers of "Shepherd Tom"* (1915). This work, along with a genealogy of the Robinson branch of the Hazard family, the publication of family accounts, and the description of various Rhode Island traditions, documents a period of time and a locality that would have vanished otherwise.

Thomas Robinson Hazard died in New York City. His remains rest in the family plot on Vaucluse. Hazard wished to be remembered for his efforts promoting spiritualism, yet today his name recalls his contributions to educational and social reform, and his nickname brings to mind his fond documentation of Washington County, Rhode Island, history.

• Manuscript sources of information about Thomas Robinson Hazard include the Peace Dale Manufacturing Company records (1742–1919), housed at the Baker Library at Harvard University and at the Rhode Island Historical Society in Providence. Family genealogical information appears in the papers of Caroline R. Hazard, Special Collections, University of Rhode Island. For his involvement in the American Colonization Society, see society records (1792–1964) in the Manuscript Division of the Library of Congress; the Blake Family Papers (1792–1921) at Yale University's library also refer to him.

Hazard's works are not widely collected, but the Rider Collection at Brown University's John Hay Library has a very complete selection of his publications. The subjects are diverse. There are works on horticulture, including *Address Delivered before the Aquidneck Agricultural Society* (1853); spiritualism; the death penalty, including *Christianity Opposed to Death Penalty* (1852), *An Appeal to the People of Rhode Island in Behalf of the Constitution and the Laws* (1857), and *The Death Penalty a Failure* (c. 1850); antislavery; and politics, including, among others, *A Rare Vindication* (1886), *An Examination of the Bliss Imbroglio, Both in Its Spiritual and Legal Aspect* (1878), and *To the People of Rhode Island; Memorial of Mumford Hazard* (1858). Reminiscences include *Sundry Prices Taken from the Account Book of Thomas Hazard, Son of Robert (Called College Tom)* (1892). Other writings include *Family Medical Instructor: Civil and Religious Persecution in the State of New York* (1876), *The "Astounding Development" Ives vs. Hazard* (1859), *Eleven Days at Moravia* (1873), and *Sundry Communications to the Providence Journal and Other Papers* (1874–1877).

Published accounts of Hazard's life and work, which are few and terse, include Edward Mayhew Bacon, *Narragansett Bay, Its Historic and Romantic Associations and Picturesque Setting* (1904); Richard M. Bayles, ed., *History of Newport County, Rhode Island* (1888); Louise M. Hoxie, "The History of Peacedale, Rhode Island" (unpublished leaflet, c. 1968); Sally Latimer and Marjorie Vogel, "Historic Peach Dale Mill Legacy, Brief History of the Peacedale Mill and the Hazard Family Legacy" (unpublished leaflet, Narragansett Historical Society, 1988); *Representative Men and Old Families of Rhode Island*, vol. 2 (1908); and Caroline E. Robinson, *The Hazard Family of Rhode Island 1635–1894* (1895).

GAIL FOWLER MOHANTY

HAZELIUS, Ernest Lewis (6 Sept. 1777–20 Feb. 1853), Lutheran minister and educator, was born in Neusalz, Province of Silesia, Prussia, the son of Eric Hazelius, a watchmaker, and Christiana Brahtz. Hazelius's Swedish father originally studied to be a Lutheran pastor, as had several generations of his family before him, but eventually decided he did not have a call to such ministry. He traveled, settled in Neusalz, married Moravian Christiana Brahtz, and converted to her faith. Their son Ernest was raised in that tradition. Ernest's parents took him to Herrnhut, the cradle of Moravianism, when he was five to be blessed by an aged Moravian bishop, Polycarp Müller, who proclaimed his future life dedicated to the ministry. The entire experience, even at such an early age, made a profound impact on Ernest.

Had he so chosen, Hazelius could have enjoyed another fate: life at imperial court. Empress Catherine II of Russia had been a childhood friend of his mother, and at Ernest's birth the empress wrote to his parents, offering to adopt the child and raise him as her own. The parents delayed a decision as long as possible, finally putting the empress's request directly to Hazelius when he was twelve. He elected to forego her offer, as even at that age he had decided to devote his life to spiritual concerns.

Orphaned and impoverished by sixteen, Hazelius nevertheless managed to continue his education and completed his theological training at the Moravian institution at Niesky under Bishop Anders. In 1800, at the age of twenty-three, he was sent to the United States to teach classics in the Moravian seminary at Nazareth, Pennsylvania, and by 1807 was head of the theological department. In 1808, however, the seminary board precipitated a crisis for Hazelius when it would not approve his desire to marry, and he left the Moravian denomination for the Lutheran church of his ancestors. Although he remained on good terms with the Moravians, he was ordained a Lutheran pastor by the New York Ministerium in 1809 and assigned the united congregations of New Germantown, German Valley, and Spruce Run in New Jersey. In 1810 he married Hulda Cummings Bray of Lebanon, New Jersey. They had no children.

Hazelius held the distinction of serving as theological professor in the first three Lutheran seminaries established in the United States, and it was as educator that he made his most lasting contribution. In 1815 Hazelius accepted a call as principal and professor of theology at Hartwick Seminary in New York, the first Lutheran seminary founded in the United States. In 1824 he was awarded the degree of doctor of divinity from both Union College and Columbia College. He left Hartwick in 1830 to become the second professor at the Lutheran Theological Seminary in Gettysburg, Pennsylvania, but his tenure there was brief and not entirely happy. Three years later he accepted a call to the Theological Seminary of South Carolina in Lexington, where he taught for the next two decades, until shortly before his death in Lexington.

Hazelius combated what he saw as two disparate but equally destructive enemies to the Christian faith during his career: infidelity and denominational narrowness. Hazelius's conservative theology and concern regarding the rise of rationalism in America led directly to his translation from German to English of the *Life of John Henry Stilling* (1831), a popular work on the Continent. Hazelius noted in his preface that "during a season of the grossest infidelity" the original biography had turned "many from darkness to the light of the gospel," and he hoped that his translation would produce the same "wonderful effect" in America.

In his efforts against denominational divisiveness, and perhaps as a reflection of his Moravian upbringing, Hazelius was allied with the influential southern Lutheran pastor John Bachman of Charleston, South Carolina, and with Samuel S. Schmucker of Gettysburg in their attempts to create an ecumenical, inclusive Christian community for the New World. As opposed to Lutherans who emphasized a more confessional, sacramental theology, leaders such as Hazelius, Bachman, and Schmucker preferred to emphasize points of commonality between Lutherans and other denominations rather than points that divided them, a position they felt was consistent with that of the original sixteenth-century reformers.

In so doing, Hazelius labored against the rising tide of Lutheran confessionalism first expressed in North Carolina's Henkelite controversy of the 1820s, which spread and split the southern Lutheran church in two, and which later found expression elsewhere among American Lutherans. While both parties considered adherence to the Augsburg Confession central to their self-definitions as Lutherans, those allied with Hazelius were more willing to allow freedom from a "literal sense" of the document. Hazelius argued, in *Discipline, Articles of Faith and Synodical Constitution* for the South Carolina Synod (1841), that "the main principle of the reformation is not a slavish adherence to every sentiment of those great and learned men, who had to shape their course according to circumstances beyond their control" (p. 8) but rather adherence to the Bible alone. Hazelius believed that divergent interpretations on issues such as the Real Presence in the sacrament remained less important in the end than enforced uniformity, since "the main point in this as well as in every other religious observance, is the heart" (p. 22).

Even though he was a participant in the spirited confessionalist debates, Hazelius remained irenic in temperament, congenial in personality, pious in spirit, and humble in manner. Southerner Edwin Scott, an acute non-Lutheran contemporary, remarked that Hazelius remained one of only three people he had met throughout his life who came "as near perfection as human nature ever attains," although Scott also noted that Hazelius was the only German he ever knew who could "neither sing nor smoke" (Scott, p. 145). Hazelius was universally revered by his students, whom he treated as the children he never had, and he poured his full personal and academic attentions on them. Although the American Lutheran church eventually returned to its more confessional roots, he influenced an entire generation of Lutheran pastors, both northern and southern, with his vision of a more ecumenical Lutheranism, better able to meet what he saw as the needs of a new nation and a new age.

• Hazelius's additional published works include *Life of Luther* (1813), *Material for Catechisation on Passages of the Scripture* (1823), and a translation of *The Augsburgh Confession with Notes and Observations* (1828). Larger works include the first volume of a projected four-volume *History of the Christian Church: From the Earliest Ages to the Present Time* (1842) and *History of the American Lutheran Church, from Its Commencement in the Year of Our Lord 1685 to the Year 1842* (1846). He also served as editor of *Das Evangelische Magazin* (Gettysburg) for several years.

Contemporary evaluations of Hazelius, some of which point to his scattered published sermons and addresses, may be found in Ray Bost, "The Reverend John Bachman and the Development of Southern Lutheranism" (Ph.D. diss., Yale Univ., 1963); Egil Grislis, "Ernest L. Hazelius: Ecumenical Theologian of the Southern Lutheran Church," *Lutheran Theological Seminary Bulletin* 45 (Aug. 1965): 22–39; Paul McCullough, ed., *A History of the Lutheran Church in South Carolina* (1971); and Henry Hardy Heins, *Throughout All the Years: Hartwick 1746–1946* (1946). Informative obituaries and older considerations of Hazelius's life may be found in M. L. Stoever, *Evangelical Review* 7, no. 27 (Jan. 1856): 377–90; "Memoir," *Minutes of the South Carolina Synod* (1853): 67–70; W. B. Sprague, *Annals of the American Pulpit* 9 (1869): 132–41; J. G. Morris, *Fifty Years in the Lutheran Ministry* (1878); G. D. Bernheim, *History of the German Settlements and of the Lutheran Church in North and South Carolina* (1872); W. A. Schwarze, "History of the Moravian College and Theological Seminary," *Transactions of the Moravian Historical Society*, vol. 7 (1909); Edwin Scott, *Random Recollections of a Long Life* (1884); and A. R. Wentz, *History of the Gettysburg Theological Seminary* (1926).

SUSAN WILDS MCARVER

HAZEN, Moses (1 June 1733–5 Feb. 1803), army officer, landowner, and merchant, was born in Haverhill, Massachusetts, the son of Moses Hazen, a merchant, and Abigail White. Hazen was apprenticed to a tanner and later operated independently. The outbreak of the French and Indian War lured him away, and he remained in the military during two great wars. In 1755 he enlisted in a British colonial unit and served under Colonel Robert Monckton at Fort Beauséjour, Nova Scotia. In 1758 he was commissioned in Rogers's Rangers and served under General James Wolfe at Louisbourg. Hazen wintered at Fort Frederick (St.

John, New Brunswick) and led a raid brutal even by Ranger standards on St. Ann's (Fredericton): burning settlements, destroying livestock, and killing and scalping those inhabitants who lingered too long. Nevertheless, the raid earned him a captaincy before all of the details became known. In 1759 he assisted Wolfe in the capture of Quebec and was wounded at Sainte-Foy. Having purchased a lieutenant's commission in the British 44th Foot (Essex) Regiment in 1761, he retired at half pay for life in 1763.

Hazen settled in Montreal where Governor James Murray appointed him justice of the peace. He was also appointed assistant surveyor of the king's forests and developed a lumbering enterprise on Lake Champlain. He and Lieutenant Colonel Gabriel Christie purchased the seigniories of Sabrevois and Bleury, both on the east bank of the Richelieu River, and five farms on the site of St. John. During Christie's long absences Hazen developed their joint property.

After incurring large debts on the seigniory, in 1766 Hazen mortgaged his half to Christie. Undaunted, he continued to borrow heavily and obtained a second mortgage. Between 1766 and 1770 he was involved in several lawsuits, including the fulfilling of a naval contract for timber by cutting trees on land that did not belong to him on Lake Champlain; lost some of his goods at a sheriff's sale in 1770; and was publicly accused of seducing the wife of his neighbor, Captain Joseph Kelly, in 1766. The case never came to court because allegedly Kelly was imprisoned for debt in Montreal at the insistence of Hazen. In 1770 Christie insisted on a division of their property, and Hazen became Seignior of Bleury-Sud. In the same year he married Charlotte de la Saussaye of St. Thérèse; they had no children. His attention now focused on a single seignory, Hazen became a successful farmer. He also acquired land rights in several New England towns and New Brunswick.

At the outbreak of the American Revolution in 1775 Hazen's lands lay along the American invasion route. Because of his equivocal behavior he was arrested first by the Americans, then by the British, who placed him in close confinement in Montreal. Following the American capture of Fort St. John, Sir Guy Carleton, governor of Canada, fled toward Quebec, taking Hazen with him. En route, Carleton was forced to abandon him to the Americans, and Hazen joined them in the siege of Quebec. Sent to Philadelphia to seek reinforcements from the Continental Congress, he was commissioned colonel of the Second Canadian Regiment and promised compensation for the loss of his half pay. Returning to Canada to recruit his force, he was at first successful among the disaffected French. After serving briefly as commander at Montreal during the spring of 1776, he, and his regiment, joined the American retreat from Canada in June; about 175 men, mostly French, followed him into New York. His estate had been pillaged by both armies, and throughout his lifetime he tried, unsuccessfully, to collect from Congress for these losses. He was also plunged into courts-martial, which tried to adjudicate the accusations between Hazen and Colonel Benedict Arnold, chief of which was Hazen's charge that Arnold pilfered Montreal for his own profit before his retreat from that city. Successive courts cleared Hazen of Arnold's charges but failed to affix any blame on Arnold, who by that time was creating a navy on Lake Champlain. Hazen made a permanent enemy of Arnold in the process.

Hazen's regiment remained intact during the Revolution, supplemented by recruitment in the States. The families of many of his Canadians also left Canada, and Congress established refugee camps with rations for them at Albany and Fishkill, New York. His regiment saw action at Staten Island, Brandywine, Germantown, and Yorktown, and earned a high reputation for its fighting qualities. It built the Hazen military road across northeastern Vermont in 1779, but Hazen's hoped-for second invasion of Canada never took place. He struggled stubbornly for the prerogatives of his men by repeated petitions to General Washington and Congress. Since the regiment was created by Congress, it enjoyed few of the benefits, such as regular promotions and promises of land, that were enjoyed by state units. Without any commitments to further benefits, the men were furloughed in June 1783 and the unit was disbanded in November.

Hazen's Canadians joined their families at the refugee camps, where they also received rations from Congress. Some began to drift back to Canada. Before the end of the war Hazen had tried to get land grants for them and although Congress took no action, the state of New York created the Canadian and Nova Scotia Refugee Tract of 131,500 acres in northeastern New York. In 1786 the refugees moved there, and many of their descendants still live in the area.

After the war Hazen had expansive plans for land speculation and colonization. He was hampered first by his inability to collect the large sums owed him, and second by a stroke in 1786 which disabled him for the rest of his life. Even before his illness and particularly afterward, he became increasingly irrational in his impatient insistence on gaining more land and developing what he already had. His succession of agents resigned in frustration. He lost all of his prewar holdings in New England and New Brunswick, largely through nonpayment of taxes and the repayment of loans, while his Richelieu lands were declared forfeited by the Privy Council in London and bought by Christie. Settling first in New York City and then in Troy, New York, Hazen was arrested fourteen times for debt; he, in turn, instituted numerous suits against his creditors. A court in 1802 adjudged him of unsound mind; nevertheless, he was jailed for debt twice within the weeks before his death in Troy, New York. On paper he died a wealthy man, but his widow was unable to collect his claims of $42,000, against Congress and individuals, before her death in 1827. However, his executor in 1828 obtained compensation from Congress for Hazen's loss of British half pay to the amount of $3,998.89 at the rate of two shillings fourpence a day for the period between 25 December 1781 and his

death. Three years later Congress decided to pay for the disbursements Hazen made in raising his regiment fifty-five years earlier. The amount was $12,769.18. Only his heirs, mostly nieces and nephews, shared the bounty.

The career of Moses Hazen is one of sharp contrasts. He had great leadership qualities in uniform, marred only by several brutal campaigns as a Ranger. A buccaneer in an age of buccaneers, he might after the American Revolution have become one of the great colonizers of his generation—at Detroit, in northern New York, or in the Coos country, land astride the Connecticut River in northern Vermont and New Hampshire. He was prevented from fulfilling his dreams by circumstance, the collapse of his health, and his temperament, which was increasingly driven by uncontrollable personal forces—hungry for more land, increasingly irascible, and frustrated by his failure to collect from Congress and individual borrowers. He will be remembered for his military prowess and for his role in establishing the Refugee Tract.

• There is no major repository of Hazen papers, but three recently located collections are very useful for details of his career: the Bailey collection, the Kent-Delord collection, and the McLellan collection, all deposited in the State University library at Plattsburgh, N.Y. All three contain documents in Hazen's writing but many more by his nephew and adjutant, Benjamin Mooers of Plattsburgh. Other valuable collections are the Haldimand papers in the Public Archives of Canada at Ottawa; papers of the Continental Congress, microfilm of the originals in the Library of Congress, and *Journals of the Continental Congress, 1774–1789* (34 vols., 1968).

The only biography of Moses Hazen is Allan S. Everest, *Moses Hazen and the Canadian Refugees in the American Revolution* (1976). Helpful for Hazen's career in the Rangers is Burt Garfield Loescher, *The History of Rogers' Rangers* (2 vols., 1946, 1969). For the Canadian story, see Gustave Lanctot, *Canada & the American Revolution, 1774–1783* (1967), and Justin H. Smith, *Our Struggle for the Fourteenth Colony: Canada and the American Revolution* (2 vols., 1907).

ALLAN S. EVEREST

HAZEN, William Babcock (27 Sept. 1830–16 Jan. 1887), army career officer, was born in West Hartford, Vermont, the son of Stillman Hazen and Sophrona Fenno, farmers. In 1833 the family moved to Hiram, Ohio. Growing up on a farm there, Hazen became a friend and schoolmate of future president James A. Garfield. He received an appointment to the U.S. Military Academy at West Point in 1851, from which he graduated four years later. He married Mildred McLean in 1871, and they were the parents of one son.

Hazen's tendency to become involved in controversy showed in the assessments of his West Point years, one calling him a perfectionist, independent-minded, a serious student, and possessed of driving ambition and a capacity for growth—all traits set off by allegations of his frequent dogmatism and contentiousness. Finishing twenty-eighth in a class of thirty-four, he was charged with 150 demerits in his senior year and scored particularly poorly in military courses. Described as short and stocky, he was much later (1879) also likened to a martinet.

Hazen's initial assignment in 1855 as a brevet second lieutenant sent him to various posts in the Oregon Territory until 1858. He appeared to serve without incident or complaint and boasted that he completed a wide range of duties without stoppages of pay, a punishment for deficiencies then feared by young officers. Sent to the Southwest during 1858–1859, he fought against the Comanches on the Nueces River and was seriously wounded, permanently rendering him slightly disabled and earning him sick leave until February 1861. A ball (bullet) had entered the fingers of his left hand, passed into the right side of his chest, and lodged between the sixth and seventh ribs. It was never removed. In early 1861 he moved briefly to West Point as an instructor.

Hazen went on active duty after the Civil War began, earning promotions up to major general in 1865. He served capably at Shiloh, Stones River, Chattanooga, Chickamauga, Missionary Ridge, Atlanta, and Jonesboro and in the March to the Sea and the Carolinas campaigns. Nevertheless, he defied authority. For example, as disease spread among troops near Louisville in 1862, he secretly ordered his wounded men home to Ohio to better their chances of recovery. Hazen complained to Garfield, questioning General William T. Sherman's authority to remove two regiments from Hazen's brigade. As a thirty-year-old who had never tasted liquor, he deplored the army's whiskey ration as costly and injurious to military effectiveness. He chided the army for ignoring the press and not using field hospitals instead of the disease-ridden large hospitals. Hazen appeared to equate high battle casualties with success in comparing his losses with those of other generals.

After the war, Hazen reverted to the rank of colonel with the Thirty-eighth Infantry (1866) and the Sixth Infantry (1869). During the Franco-Prussian War (1870–1871), Hazen observed both the German and French military systems. In 1877 President Rutherford B. Hayes appointed Hazen military attaché to Vienna to observe the Russo-Turkish War.

Meanwhile, Hazen served again in the West in the late sixties and early seventies, the latter assignment at Fort Buford, 1,000 miles west of St. Paul. He clashed with his popular rival George Armstrong Custer. Hazen persuaded Custer not to attack the Kiowa Indians in the late 1860s. Custer obliged but found out after subsequent Kiowa raids that Hazen had misjudged them as friendly. The two generals clashed in the mid-seventies over the potential of the West, the concept of the great American desert. Hazen characterized the Northern Pacific Railroad route from west of the Missouri River to the Yellowstone River as land not worth "a penny an acre." Particularly galling to Hazen were the false claims land and railroad speculators made to lure settlers to the area. Custer assumed the opposite position, that the plains were valuable and fertile. Each general exaggerated his claim beyond all reason.

The wrath of the press and citizens in the region was aimed at Hazen.

Throughout 1869–1876, Hazen antagonized Secretary of War William Belknap, who had to resign in 1876 to avoid impeachment proceedings by the House of Representatives on charges of bribery involving army post traders. Hazen believed his testimony was secret, but it was leaked to the press. The battle with his opponents continued to fester and erupted in 1879 with numerous belated charges against Hazen at a general court-martial. Allegedly, Hazen deserted at Shiloh, kept out of danger at Pickett's Mills, falsified the capture of guns at Missionary Ridge, and gave false testimony in the Belknap investigation. His critics also disputed Hazen's assertion that the strict Prussian military model was superior to the more relaxed and undisciplined U.S. model. Completely exonerated, Hazen, even so, felt put upon and complained to Garfield, now an influential congressman.

President Hayes listened to Garfield instead of rival generals in naming Hazen to lead the Signal Service, which retained its military signal duties in addition to serving as the forerunner of the U.S. Weather Bureau. Hazen, called by one author the "irascible infantryman," enthusiastically met this challenge and imposed his strong work ethic on this rather loosely organized unit, which was torn asunder over the question of civilian versus military control over its new meteorological duties. His strict military rules did not suit the civilians in the Signal Service, which became a part of the civilian Department of Agriculture at the end of the decade. Hazen had consistently championed retention of military control.

In 1881 Hazen's disbursing officer was indicted for embezzling at least $90,000, mostly before Hazen's appointment. By 1886 Hazen withstood another long-term investigation of his actions, this time over charges of financial irregularities in the unit, and was vindicated again. He also tangled with the War Department under Robert T. Lincoln for its failure to rescue the Arctic scientific expedition (assisted in its organization by the Signal Service) at Lady Franklin Bay during 1881–1883. Only seven of the original twenty-five survivors were finally found in 1884. Hazen was reprimanded.

The enigmatic Hazen was refined, well informed, and dauntless in criticizing laxity and corruption within both the military and civilian governmental operations. He promoted scientific research and fairer treatment of the American Indians. His own record was exceedingly meritorious. Both Custer and Sherman praised his military experiences as a commander in battle and as an administrator in the military. His abrasiveness, controversial nature, and cantankerous manner blunted at times his positive side, as indicated by relatives and colleagues.

Hazen died suddenly in Washington, D.C., reportedly of kidney poisoning. Possibly contributing to his death were diabetic complications and the moving within his body of the bullet he had carried since his 1859 wound suffered in the West.

• Limited materials on Hazen are in army records and Congressional hearings and reports. Hazen's publications include *The School and the Army in Germany and France, with a Diary of Siege Life at Versailles* (1872); *Some Corrections of "Life on the Plains"* (1875); *Our Barren Lands: The Interior of the U.S. West of the 100th Meridian and East of the Sierra Nevadas* (1875); and *Narrative of Military History* (1885), on his service in the Civil War.

For a cogent and informative account of Hazen in the West, see Marvin E. Kroeker, *Great Plains Command: William B. Hazen in the Frontier West* (1976). A thorough description of the post–Civil War Hazen-Custer rivalry over the Northwest is available in Edgar I. Stewart, *Penny an Acre: Empire in the West* (1968). Hazen's role in the U.S. Signal Service is covered in Donald R. Whitnah, *A History of the United States Weather Bureau* (1961). An obituary is in the *New York Times*, 17 Jan. 1887.

DONALD R. WHITNAH

H.D. *See* Doolittle, Hilda.

H'DOUBLER, Margaret Newell (26 Apr. 1889–26 Mar. 1982), dance educator, was born in Beloit, Kansas, the daughter of Charles Hougen-Doubler, a photographer and inventor, and Sarah Todd. H'Doubler (a shortened form of her father's Swiss name) grew up in a well-to-do family that could offer her a good education and exposure to classical music and the other arts. In high school in Madison, Wisconsin (where the family resettled in 1903), she participated in sports and took classes in Dalcroze eurythmics, a movement-based approach to music training. She attended the University of Wisconsin at Madison from 1906 to 1910, graduating with a biology major and a philosophy minor. During her undergraduate years she took part in a variety of physical education activities including sports, particularly basketball and swimming, and dancing based on the Louis Chalif and Melvin Ballou Gilbert methods.

From 1910 to 1916 H'Doubler taught basketball and swimming in the Department of Physical Education for Women at the University of Wisconsin at Madison. She spent 1916–1917 in New York doing graduate work at Columbia University and, at the urging of Blanche Trilling, the director of her department, investigating the New York dance scene. Trilling wanted her to look for something that might be appropriate for the university physical education curriculum. H'Doubler attended performances of Isadora Duncan and the Ballets Russes and discussed dance education with two notable innovators in the field, Bird Larsen and Gertrude Colby. What H'Doubler found most stimulating, however, were the methods of Alys Bentley, who incorporated movement into her teaching of creative music to children.

When H'Doubler returned to Wisconsin in the summer of 1917, she began teaching a new kind of educational dance that was still very much in its formative stages. By 1919 the number of students in her classes had grown to 300 at the beginning level, 140 at the intermediate, and 46 in a special class for those interested in teaching. Performances were given from the first year, and soon, at her students' urging, she established an honorary student organization devoted to preparing annual productions and generally promoting the dance. It was called Orchesis, from the Greek word meaning "to dance." Over the next several years H'Doubler's ideas developed and the dance curriculum grew. Wisconsin established its first formal dance teacher–training courses in 1926 and the first dance major internationally in higher education in 1927. The university thus became the most influential educational dance center in the United States and the world, and the Orchesis idea as well as H'Doubler's dance curriculum spread far and wide.

In 1934 H'Doubler married Wayne L. Claxon, who was then teaching art education at Wisconsin and later became director of the arts department at Wayne State University. The couple had no children. In 1954 H'Doubler left her university post and was designated professor emeritus. During her tenure at Wisconsin she had frequently been invited to guest teach at other institutions in the United States, Canada, and Europe, and after retirement she remained active for many years, continuing to fulfill such engagements. She died in Springfield, Missouri.

H'Doubler brought a remarkable breadth of vision to her work in dance. She read widely not only in dance literature but also in the other arts, aesthetics, education, philosophy, religion, the physical sciences, and the social sciences. She was committed to the ideas and goals of progressive education, particularly John Dewey's concept of education for democracy. She believed in education as a means of improving life, rather than merely facilitating adaptation to an unchangeable world. She developed a sophisticated and detailed system and philosophy of educational dance based on scientific and aesthetic principles.

The work of Margaret H'Doubler has had a lasting influence on American dance, both in education and on the concert stage. She taught literally thousands of students, many of whom became teachers and dancers as well as leaders of the next generation. Her influence has extended even further through her writings, among which are three books that have been particularly important as university dance texts: *A Manual of Dancing* (1921), *Dance and Its Place in Education* (1925), and *Dance, a Creative Art Experience* (1940). H'Doubler's technical approach was based on a scientific understanding of the body and its movement and a philosophical commitment to encouraging individuality and creativity among her students. She developed exercises for every part of the body with attention to movement quality and body tension. Equally important in her approach was the use of the physical techniques to create dance works with attention to form, content, what she considered organic unity, and musicality. She believed that dance was a creative endeavor that could benefit all people, not just those who chose it as a profession.

H'Doubler received a number of honors including the Wisconsin Governor's Council Award for Distinguished Achievement in the Performing Arts (1964), the Dance Magazine Award (1965), and the Luther Halsey Gulick Award of the American Association of Health, Physical Education and Recreation (1971). She is recognized throughout the United States, in Canada, and in Europe as the leading theorist, innovator, and teacher of educational dance as it developed in the twentieth century.

• Archival material on H'Doubler may be found in Historical Files, Department of Physical Education for Women, University of Wisconsin at Madison, and in her clipping file in the Dance Collection of the New York Public Library for the Performing Arts.
Important studies include Mary Lou Remley, "The Wisconsin Idea of Dance: A Decade of Progress, 1917–1926," *Wisconsin Magazine of History* 58 (Spring 1975): 178–95; Judith Ann Gray, "To Want to Dance: A Biography of Margaret H'Doubler" (Ph.D. diss., Univ. of Arizona, 1978); Gray and Dianne S. Howe, "Margaret H'Doubler: A Profile of Her Formative Years, 1898–1921," American Association for Health, Physical Education, Recreation and Dance, *Research Quarterly for Exercise and Sport, Centennial Issue 1985* (1985), 93–101; Gray and Howe, "Margaret H'Doubler and the First Dance Major," *Progress and Possibilities*, Congress on Research in Dance Annual Conference, 9–11 Oct. 1987, Proceedings and Selected Papers (1989), 68–76. An obituary is in *Dance Magazine*, Aug. 1982.

NANCY LEE CHALFA RUYTER

HEAD, Edith (28 Oct. 1897–24 Oct. 1981), Hollywood costume designer, was born Edith Claire Posener in San Bernardino, California, the daughter of Max Posener, a mining engineer, and Anna Levy. During her long life, Head was curiously quiet about her parents, their divorce early in her life, and her stepfather. Even in her autobiography she did not illuminate her formative years; indeed, the index of *Edith Head's Hollywood* contains no reference pages for parents, childhood, or early education. Her narration suggests that her life began in 1923.

By that time Head had completed undergraduate work at the University of California at Berkeley and had earned her master of arts in Romance languages at Stanford University. With those credentials, she was teaching French and also art at a private school in Los Angeles. Untrained in the latter subject, she enrolled at a local art school. That decision led to changes in her personal and professional life. A classmate introduced her to Charles Head, whom she soon married. Also, she answered an advertisement for a sketch artist at Famous Players–Lasky Studios (later Paramount). Because her interest was in nature scenes, Head's accompanying portfolio contained human figure drawings "borrowed" from classmates. ("It never occurred to me that it was quite dishonest.") Howard Greer, the chief costume designer, hired her.

For the next fourteen years, Head was a pupil of Greer and of Travis Banton, who replaced him in 1927. As a rule, the chief designed for the stars (actresses), and Head did less important work. However, soon after Banton became chief, he gave her the job of dressing Clara Bow. The "It" girl ate what she pleased without considering the consequences. Banton decid-

ed to let Head deal with the frustration of altering Bow's costumes from one week or month to the next.

At about the same time, Banton assigned Head to a young supporting actress in *The Saturday Night Kid*. Thus she became one of the first designers to drape satin, cut on the bias, over the soon-to-be-famous curves of Jean Harlow. More than three decades later, Head designed clothes for Carroll Baker to wear in the film biography *Harlow*. Head's long career contained other instances of fashion déjà vu.

In 1933 Banton made one of his regular trips to the Paris couture shows. His absence soon jeopardized the production schedule. For example, *She Done Him Wrong* was ready for filming, but Mae West's trademark, waist-pinching gowns were not. Because of Banton's drinking problems, Head had stepped in on other occasions to do minor jobs even when he was in Los Angeles. His absence in 1933 provided her the opportunity to design West's gowns. *She Done Him Wrong* was Head's first solo screen credit. In 1938, when Banton resigned, Head became chief costume designer at Paramount Studios.

Changes in Head's personal life soon followed her professional success. In 1938 she and Charles Head divorced. A Catholic, Edith had tried to save their childless marriage. Her work schedule, his job as a traveling salesman, and his alcoholism made salvage impossible. Two years later she married Wiard Ihnen, an art director at Paramount. He understood the demands of the movie industry and of her fierce commitment to it. Additionally, he accepted Edith's desire to remain Edith Head and to be sensitive to the problems that Charles had in the final years of his life. The Ihnen-Head forty-year marriage, also childless, began with the busiest two decades of her career.

The history of fashion and Hollywood in the 1940s and 1950s is replete with Head's name. Working without an assistant and without a sewing machine, she costumed hundreds of movies. Her magic was such that some of the most striking images of her fashions are from black and white films. They linger also because the actresses who wore them were significant in the movie history of those two decades. A very short list includes Barbara Stanwyck, Olivia DeHavilland, Elizabeth Taylor, Bette Davis, Audrey Hepburn, Ingrid Bergman, and Grace Kelly. Taylor and Kelly were two whose relationships with Head transcended their professional lives. The former, named in Head's will, occasionally found solace from the press at the Ihnen-Head estate. Kelly wore Head originals in four movies and then on board the honeymoon yacht in Monaco's harbor as she prepared to sail away from Hollywood.

From 1940 to 1960 Head was also busy away from Paramount. She was a regular on Art Linkletter's radio show and, later, on his television show. She wrote books on fashion and an advice column in *Photoplay* magazine. Women seemed interested in the advice of Head, who looked more bookish than chic. Her signature outfit was a simple suit in a muted color. She almost never smiled in public, even after Stanwyck prodded her into cosmetic dental work. On television and in photographs she wore tinted glasses, and she usually wore her straight hair cut in bangs across her forehead. Nevertheless, she was an acknowledged fashion maven of the mid-twentieth century.

Other Head projects included the mass production of some of her film fashions. She wanted women in Any Town, U.S.A., to be able to buy Dorothy Lamour's sarong, Hepburn's *Sabrina* cocktail dress, and the strapless, tulle-over-satin gown worn by Taylor in *A Place in the Sun*. Additionally, Head traveled with fashion shows featuring clothes from Paramount movies. She assisted in the transfer of some of her designs to Vogue pattern books. She outfitted United Nations guards, Pan Am flight attendants, coast guardsmen, and Stork Club waitresses. Her interest in new challenges resulted in a role in the 1955 film *Lucy Gallant*. She portrayed a fashion designer named Edith Head. (The following decade she had a similar role in *The Oscar*.)

Head, who received thirty-five Academy Award nominations, won six of her eight Oscars in the 1940s and 1950s. To the surprise of many, including herself, she did not win the first award given for costume design in 1948. However, in 1949 she won for *The Heiress* (black and white) and for *Samson and Delilah* (color). In the next ten years Head received Oscars for four black and white films: *All About Eve*, *A Place in the Sun*, *Roman Holiday*, and *Sabrina*.

By the 1960s the female star system was as anachronistic as the black and white films that had spawned it. Also, Hollywood was losing its role as the fashion capital of the United States. Those changes affected Head and other costume designers. In 1966 Gulf and Western purchased Paramount Studios. A year later, with no public acknowledgment of her departure or her contributions, management decided not to renew her contract. Head soon accepted an offer from Universal Studios. For the remainder of her life, she was the only costume designer under contract to a major Hollywood studio.

In 1973 Head won her final Oscar (she had not won since *The Facts of Life* in 1960). By that time her original designs occasionally were redesigns from earlier decades. For *The Sting* she dressed Paul Newman and Robert Redford in newsboy caps, band collars, and chalk-stripe suits from the 1930s. It was the first time that a movie without a female lead won an Oscar for costume design.

In 1979 Ihnen died at age ninety-one. Although she was almost eighty, Head was not a typical octogenarian. For the next two years she worked regularly in her Oscar-decorated bungalow on the Universal lot. She did so despite a progressive bone marrow disease and anemia that required blood transfusions. In October 1981, after finishing Steve Martin's retro clothes for *Dead Men Don't Wear Plaid*, she collapsed and was hospitalized at Good Samaritan Hospital in Los Angeles, where she died. She left no immediate survivors.

• Edith Head, *Edith Head's Hollywood* (1983), is an autobiography completed by Paddy Calistro after Head's death. For additional information about Hollywood fashions and Academy Awards, see David Chierichetti, *Hollywood Costume Design* (1976); Mike Steen, *Hollywood Speaks* (1974); and Mason Wiley and Damien Bona, *Inside Oscar* (1986). See also Patrick Humphries, *The Films of Alfred Hitchcock* (1994), and Robert Lacey, *Grace* (1994). Obituaries are in the *Los Angeles Times*, 27 Oct. 1981, and the *New York Times*, 27 Oct. 1981.

SANDRA L. CLEMENTS

HEALD, Henry Townley (8 Nov. 1904–23 Nov. 1975), educator and professional administrator, was born in Lincoln, Nebraska, the son of Frederick De Forest Heald, a botanist who then taught at the University of Nebraska, and Nellie Townley. He was at first tutored by his mother and did not start school until the ninth grade. Part of his youth was spent in Pullman, Washington, where his father became head of plant pathology at Washington State College.

After taking a bachelor's degree at Washington State College (1923) and a master's degree in civil engineering at the University of Illinois (1925), Heald worked briefly as an engineer for the Illinois Central Railroad and the Chicago Board of Local Improvements before beginning a career in education that would last to the end of his life. In 1927 he became an assistant professor of civil engineering at Armour Institute in Chicago, where he rose through administrative positions to take on the presidency of Armour, then nearly bankrupt, in 1938. By 1940 he had transformed Armour's outlook, brought about a merger with another school, the Lewis Institute, and thus founded the Illinois Institute of Technology (IIT). Armour's campus had had only seven acres and a half-dozen old buildings; IIT's 85-acre campus was designed by Mies van der Rohe, whom Heald brought in as head of the architecture department, and ultimately had fifteen new or acquired buildings. By 1952, when Heald left IIT to become the president of New York University, he had built an institution with more than 7,000 students, a sound financial base, and greatly expanded research.

When Heald assumed the presidency of New York University, it was a sprawling institution with more students than any other university in the country. His tenure at NYU was brief (until 1956) but long enough to start its transformation from a loose collection of quite independent schools into a more coherent university with higher and shared standards. He brought major financial resources and new talents to the faculties and governance of the university. But one day in 1956 he told his colleagues there, "Gentlemen, they've offered me the presidency of the Ford Foundation and I don't see how anyone in education could turn it down."

The Ford Foundation in 1956 was by far the world's largest foundation, with major national and international programs. Its funding was linked to the prospering Ford Motor Company and would peak during Heald's presidency. Heald liked to call Ford an "educational" foundation. It had merited that label before Heald came. But in his time as much as three-quarters of its domestic expenditures were educational, and education was, moreover, the largest category in grants made abroad. Heald's leadership between 1956 and 1962 were years of exceptional opportunity for the foundation. Its arts and humanities program started in 1957, bringing uniquely large resources to a national program in these fields a full decade before there was federal funding for them. The inhibitions that had held back Ford funding for population control programs fell away in the late 1950s, and the delay for nearly another decade in federal funding for such programs gave exceptional opportunities and importance to Ford's programs. Heald was often uncomfortable with the responsible staff officer, Paul Ylvisaker, but gave him full credit for "inventing and putting together" Ford's Great Cities–Gray Areas program that became an influential forerunner and model for President Lyndon B. Johnson's Great Society programs. Heald was by no means satisfied with many of the foundation's international ventures and had sharp differences with some of his trustees about them; but he was a warm supporter of the foundation's initiatives in rice and wheat production that became decisive contributions to the Green Revolution of the late 1960s and 1970s.

Despite impressive achievements, Heald's years at the Ford Foundation were increasingly troubled by conflicts with trustees. In his previous positions in Chicago and at New York University, he had shown exceptional skill in recruiting and cultivating strong and supportive boards. At Ford, he felt that trustees were bent on promoting their own special interests, and they did not share his views on the proper roles of trustees and staff. Heald was also more disposed than some trustees to think that the proper role of a foundation lay in research and education rather than in more direct action on social problems. By the early 1960s the trustees had become seriously dissatisfied with Heald; he was dismissed at the end of 1965.

After leaving the Ford Foundation, Heald formed an educational consulting firm that was engaged in the merger of Case Institute of Technology and Western Reserve University, among other significant undertakings. He also served as acting president of Cooper Union in 1968–1969 and as a trustee of Rollins College in Winter Park, Florida, where he died.

Henry Heald was famous for working twelve hours a day, seven days a week. A colleague who saw much of his career called him "the ultimate in the effective administrator. . . . he could have administered anything, any organization." Some who knew him in his Ford Foundation years thought the confusing diversity and idealistic aspirations commonly met in a large foundation's programs were increasingly unsatisfying to a man of orderly executive talents. His industry and stamina enabled him to reach beyond his prime responsibilities and engage in much public service, for example, a 1946 study of the reform of Chicago schools and New York state commissions on school construction in New York City and the reorganization of the state university. He was a director of many ma-

jor corporations and a leader in national educational organizations, and he was early thought to be a prospective mayor of Chicago or governor of Illinois. He was famously accessible in his university years and gracious and charming in his social responsibilities. Not much time was left for private life. He married Muriel Starcher in 1928, and they remained childless and lived mostly without intimate friends. He was fortunate in being able to apply his talents to building educational institutions at a time when the nation was rising out of depression and war and entering an era of unprecedented enthusiasm for and expansion of higher education. The troubles in his years at the Ford Foundation may have reflected some of the American "unraveling" of the 1960s; but he also presided over what were arguably the years of Ford's greatest achievements.

• The archives of the Ford Foundation contain Heald's office files from the years of his presidency, his oral history of these years, and much other pertinent material. A general account of the Ford Foundation in Heald's years is Richard Magat, *The Ford Foundation at Work* (1979), which gives a chronology and summaries of activities in major fields. Ford's chief population officer, Oscar Harkavy, in *Curbing Population Growth: An Insider's Perspective on the Population Movement* (1995), describes Ford's role during Heald's presidency.

The archives of New York University in the Bobst Library contain records of Heald's presidency there, including newspaper clippings, a collection of his speeches, and a valuable interview with James W. Armsey, who came from the Illinois Institute of Technology with Heald and went on to the Ford Foundation with him. Quotations in the article on Heald's decision to leave NYU and on his administrative competence are from these materials. J. Victor Baldridge, *Power and Conflict in the University: Research in the Sociology of Complex Organizations* (1971), deals with NYU in the 1960s and contains brief observations on Heald's administration.

The university archives at Illinois Institute of Technology have not been cataloged or indexed. The Ford Foundation made a grant of $5 million to IIT in 1964, and the file on this grant in the Ford Foundation Archives gives much information on IIT and its place in American higher education at that time.

FRANCIS X. SUTTON

HEALEY, Edward Francis, Jr. (28 Dec. 1894–9 Dec. 1978), professional football player and coach, was born in Indian Orchard, Massachusetts, the son of Edward Healey, Sr., a farmer and road building contractor (mother's name unknown). Healey claimed that he learned his tackling technique by chasing stray pigs on the family farm. He credited his father, who employed immigrant laborers, with instilling in him a strong work ethic and a respect for other races and religions.

Healey began his athletic career at Classical High School in Springfield, Massachusetts; he also worked as a playground supervisor and coach in Springfield. In 1915, after briefly attending Holy Cross College, he was recruited by coach Frank Cavanaugh to play football at Dartmouth College, where he studied premedicine. With Healey at end, Dartmouth enjoyed five straight wins, but when an injury sidelined him, the team lost its final three games of the season. In 1917 Healey left school to join the army, serving with the cavalry in the Argonne Forest; he returned to Dartmouth to study business in 1918.

After graduating the following year, Healey faced a postwar business slump. He accepted a part-time coaching position at Creighton University in Omaha, Nebraska, and worked as a manual laborer in the railroad yards. Learning that a new professional football league had been formed, he left Creighton to join the Independents in Rock Island, Illinois, earning $100 per game. Playing end for Rock Island from 1920 through 1922, he distinguished himself by his size (6′3″ and 220 pounds), speed, agility, and rough style of play. George Halas, co-owner of the Chicago Bears and an end on the team where he was an unwilling recipient of Healey's ferocity, purchased Healey's contract from Rock Island after the 1922 season for $100. Although no money changed hands since the Rock Island team owed Halas a debt in that amount, Healey is generally considered to have been the first pro football player to be sold to another team.

Switched to tackle in 1922, Healey played five more seasons and was selected for the unofficial all-pro team each year. The Bears enjoyed winning seasons throughout his tenure, finishing in second place on four occasions. Noted primarily for his toughness, he also displayed uncommon speed for a big man of that era. During the 1924 season he caught a confused teammate from behind after a 30-yard sprint to prevent him from crossing the wrong goal line. On a barnstorming tour of the West Coast the following year, Healey startled 60,000 fans in Los Angeles by leaping over his own fallen teammates and catching a speedy halfback on an all-star team.

In 1926 Healey turned down a reputed $10,000 offer to join promoter C. C. Pyle's American Football League, an alternative professional organization designed to feature the great running back Red Grange. In making his decision, Healey cited his distrust of Pyle and his loyalty to the Bears. It proved a wise choice since the new league folded after one season. Healey married Louise "Luke" Falk in 1927 and retired after that season. They had two children.

Besides working as a salesman and manager during the off-season for the France Stone Company, a quarrying operation in Indiana, Healey assisted Knute Rockne as a coach at the University of Notre Dame for three years. During that period Notre Dame enjoyed three winning seasons, going undefeated throughout 1929 and 1930 and winning acclaim as national champions both years. Healey concentrated full time on business thereafter, serving as the quarrying company's regional manager for Indiana and Illinois. In 1937 he became the first president of the Bears' alumni association, but he retained a lifelong interest in affairs at Notre Dame. He retired to his farm on the St. Joseph River in Michigan, not too far from his beloved South Bend.

Kind, courteous, and well-liked off the field, Healey earned a reputation as a tough and tenacious competitor. He was inducted into the Pro Football Hall of Fame in 1964 and the College Football Hall of Fame a decade later. Notre Dame bestowed honorary alumni status on him, and the South Bend Football Hall of Fame named him its distinguished American of 1977. He died in Niles, Michigan.

• Information and news clippings on Healey can be found in the Healey File, Pro Football Hall of Fame. An insightful interview is provided by Myron Cope, *The Game That Was: The Early Days of Pro Football*, 2d ed. (1974), pp. 1–18. A brief account of Healey's Dartmouth career is presented by John S. Bowman, ed., *Ivy League Football* (1988), p. 83. An obituary is in the *South Bend Tribune*, 10 Dec. 1978.

GERALD R. GEMS

HEALY, Eliza (23 Dec. 1846–13 Sept. 1919), Roman Catholic religious sister, was born a slave in Jones County, Georgia, the daughter of Michael Morris Healy, a well-to-do plantation owner, and Mary Eliza, one of his slaves. Eliza Healy's father was a native of Ireland who had immigrated to Jones County near Macon, Georgia, where, after acquiring land and slaves, he became a prosperous planter. Michael Healy chose a light-skinned slave as his concubine. Nine of the children she bore him survived. Healy acknowledged his children and carefully made provisions for their eventual removal outside of Georgia, where at that time, the manumission of slaves was virtually impossible.

Eliza Healy's mother died in the spring of 1850 and her father in the summer of the same year. By that time, her five older brothers and one older sister had already been sent north to be educated. The youngest three children, including Eliza, were successfully brought out of Georgia and sent to New York.

Although he was a Catholic, Michael Healy did not have his children baptized. In the North, however, several of the Healy children pursued vocations in their father's faith. The three youngest siblings, including Eliza, were baptized in New York in 1851. Their eldest brother, James Augustine Healy, was at that time a seminarian in Montreal. In 1854 in Paris he was ordained a priest for the Diocese of Boston and in 1875 became the second bishop of Portland, Maine, and the first African-American bishop in the United States. Two other brothers also became Roman Catholic priests. Patrick Francis Healy was ordained a Jesuit priest in 1865 and became president of Georgetown University in Washington, D.C., in 1874. A third brother, Alexander Sherwood Healy, served as a priest for the Diocese of Boston beginning in 1858. A fourth brother, Michael Healy, chose a secular path; he became a sea captain in the U.S. Revenue Cutter Service.

Both Eliza and her younger sister, Amanda Josephine, studied in schools operated by the sisters of the Congregation of Notre Dame in Montreal. At the same time, their older sister, Martha, was professed a nun in the same community in 1855. (Martha left the community with a dispensation from her vows in 1863.) After finishing her secondary education in 1861, Eliza, with Amanda Josephine, rejoined other members of the Healy family in the Boston area. About a dozen years later both sisters chose to lead the religious life.

Eliza was twenty-seven when she entered the novitiate of the congregation of Notre Dame in Montreal in 1874, and she made her first profession in 1876. Following the custom of the sisters of the Congregation of Notre Dame, she received the religious name of Sister Saint Mary Magdalen. In the beginning of her religious life, she taught in various schools operated by the Congregation of Notre Dame in Canada. She was superior of a convent for the first time in Huntington, Quebec, from 1895 to 1897, during which time her administrative gifts first became apparent. She returned to the mother house of the Sisters of Notre Dame in Montreal, where she was put in charge of English Studies and then served as a teacher in the Normal School from 1900 to 1903.

Sister Saint Mary Magdalen served longest at Villa Barlow in St. Albans, Vermont. From 1903 to 1918 she was superior and headmistress of the school, and during that time she completely restored and reorganized the school and community. The annals of the congregation recount the precarious financial situation at Villa Barlow when she took over; the community was almost ready to abandon the site: "She had to struggle against the parish and even the diocesan authorities. Her wisdom enabled her to unravel the complicated problems, to assure the resources, to pay the debts, and to make this . . . mission one of our most prosperous houses in the United States." Sister Saint Mary Magdalen also paid close attention to issues of health and hygiene for both the pupils and the sisters in her charge.

In 1918 she was sent to be superior of the Academy of Our Lady of the Blessed Sacrament on Staten Island, New York. In a few months she was able to improve the financial situation of the college, but her stay was brief. Her health declined rapidly, and she returned to the mother house in Montreal, where she died of heart disease the following summer.

Notices on Sister Saint Mary Magdalen by members of her community describe her as an indefatigable and somewhat demanding superior with a gift for business and organization. Her leadership qualities and her spirituality, such as her devotion to prayer, were especially remarked on by the sisters who had lived with her. Her relationship with the other sisters was described in the annals: "The sisters loved this superior, so just, so attractive, so upright! . . . she reserved the heaviest tasks for herself . . . in the kitchen, in the garden, in the housework . . . She listened to everyone, . . . was equal to everything . . . spared herself nothing . . . so that nothing was lacking to make the family life [of the community] perfect."

What role did African Americans play in her life? Both Bishop Healy and his brother Alexander were visibly black, but Patrick Healy's racial identity was not well known. No extant photograph of Sister Saint Mary Magdalen or contemporary comment in the community files reveals her racial origins. The profession document drawn up before the notary in 1876 mentions her mother as having been the spouse of Michael Morris Healy, but such a marriage would not have been legal in Georgia in the nineteenth century. It seems that Bishop Healy never fully explained to the younger children the special circumstances of their family origins. None of the priest brothers involved themselves with the black Catholic community. In the same way, it seems that their gifted and dedicated sister lived out her life of leadership and service far removed from the world of her mother and the harsh circumstances faced by those of her mother's African heritage.

• Information about Sister Saint Mary Magdalen can be found in the archives of the Sisters of the Congregation of Notre Dame in Montreal, Canada, especially in the *Annales de la Maison Mère*, the *Annales de Saint Albans*, and other community documents. Secondary sources in which she is mentioned are Henry G. Fairbanks, "Slavery and the Vermont Clergy," *Vermont History* 27 (1959): 305–12, and the biographies of two of her brothers by Albert Foley, *Bishop Healy: Beloved Outcaste* (1954), the story of James Augustine Healy's priesthood, and *Dream of an Outcaste: Patrick F. Healy, S.J.* (1989).

CYPRIAN DAVIS

HEALY, George Peter Alexander (15 July 1813–24 June 1894), portrait painter, was born in Boston, Massachusetts, the son of William Healy, a merchant seaman, and Mary Hicks. He first received encouragement in his determination to become an artist from Jane Stuart, daughter of the great portraitist Gilbert Stuart, and from painter Thomas Sully. Inspired by ambition and an enormous capacity for work—qualities that were to distinguish him throughout his career—Healy opened his own portrait studio at the age of eighteen. The patronage of a leading member of Boston society, Mrs. Harrison Gray Otis, assured a modest success, but the young painter realized his limitations and within a few years left for Europe to obtain the professional training unavailable in the United States.

Healy entered the École des Beaux-Arts in Paris in 1834 to study with Antoine Jean Gros, a renowned pupil of Jacques-Louis David. Here he learned academic methods for depicting the human figure, basic techniques of composition and painting, and the discipline of completing a work within a specific time frame—which was to be essential for his enormous oeuvre. Equally important were contacts in Gros's studio with other artists, especially with French painter Thomas Couture, who became a lifelong friend and professional mentor.

Portraits of Healy's early period, from the late 1830s through the 1840s, include some of his finest works and suggest his yearlong tenure under Gros (terminated by the master's tragic suicide): the practice of silhouetting a figure against a light background, a sense of intensity in the subject, and the use of lively color, as in his 1841 full-length portrait of the minister of

France, *François Pierre Guillaume Guizot* (National Museum of American Art, Smithsonian Institution). From the 1850s to the 1870s Healy appropriated certain qualities from Couture, such as the delineation of forms with a bold outline, warm brown tones throughout a picture, and the composition of multifigure paintings. The 1859 portrait of President John Tyler (National Portrait Gallery, Smithsonian Institution) and *The Arch of Titus* (1871, Newark Museum, Newark, N.J.) are outstanding works from this period. The scene in Rome includes depictions of Henry Wadsworth Longfellow and his daughter and was painted in collaboration with Frederic Church and Jervis McEntee.

By the mid-1840s Healy was well on his way to international renown. Through exhibiting at the Paris salons, he established a reputation, won honors, and attracted important American and European patrons such as Lewis Cass, the American minister to France, and Louis-Phillipe, king of the French. His portrait *Mrs. Lewis Cass* won a third-class medal at the 1840 Salon. (Healy's *General Lewis Cass*, c. 1839, and an 1860 copy of his Salon painting of Mrs. Cass are in the Detroit Historical Museum; his portrait of Louis-Philippe, shown at the Salon of 1850, is unlocated.) The king's patronage served as a springboard to other commissions in Europe, from heads of state, members of royal families, diplomats, composers, and the socially prominent. Endowed with an amiable temperament, the American painter could effectively relate to the variety of personalities and levels of society he encountered in his extensive clientele.

Intensely interested in historical personages and events, Louis-Philippe requested Healy to make copies of portraits of royalty and other distinguished persons in Britain from the time of Elizabeth as well as copies of portraits of American presidents. While carrying out this commission in London and Washington, Healy also painted portraits for a host of English and American patrons. The projected series of copies was truncated when the king was deposed in 1848, but more than forty are located, as originally intended, in the historical collection of the galleries at Versailles.

Ambitious to depict important historical events in addition to portraits, Healy spent seven years on *Webster's Reply to Hayne* (Faneuil Hall, Boston), an immense canvas completed in 1851. Containing 130 individual portraits, it dramatizes a memorable congressional debate on the constitutional nature of the Union versus the independence of the states. The artist won a third-class medal at the Paris Universal Exposition of 1855 for *Franklin Pleading the Cause of the American Colonies before Louis XVI*, another composition with life-sized figures (destroyed in the Chicago fire of 1871; a study for the painting is in the American Philosophical Society, Philadelphia). Other subject-pictures followed these efforts, but none of such monumental size.

Healy and his wife, Louisa Phipps of London, whom he had married in 1839, had seven children. With his family the artist lived abroad for much of his career, alternating residence in European capitals with various cities of the United States. Following the invitation of William B. Ogden, a railroad financier who had served as the first mayor of Chicago, he visited that city in 1855, and the following year he settled his family there. During the decade that followed, he was much in demand as a portraitist and painted many of the best-known Americans of his time. Congress commissioned him to paint portraits of all U.S. presidents (provided the cost was not more than $1,000 each), and Healy continued to travel frequently to carry out other portrait assignments.

In 1866 Healy and his family returned to Europe to live in Rome for several years and then Paris, where they remained until 1892, when they moved back to Chicago. Their former home there was destroyed in the great fire of 1871, along with many of the artist's paintings. Healy's self-portrait of 1873 (Art Institute of Chicago) shows him at a confident moment, the mid-point of his professional life. In Paris for the late period of his career, Healy felt out of step when confronted by styles of painting that radically departed from the academic methods of his own experience. In certain of his own works he adapted the extended palette and looser brush technique of impressionist painting, sometimes attaining a measure of success in these efforts to keep up with modern trends.

Much in keeping with his own personality, Healy depicted his sitters with emphasis on an agreeable, pleasant portrayal. Even his images of Abraham Lincoln contain no hint of a troubled mind reflected in the visage of the great man. Like almost all artists of his time—conservative and avant-garde—he made use of photography as an essential aid in painting. Perhaps the mechanical technique at times proved too beguiling, for some works, especially those from the 1870s to 1890s, tend to look like colored photographs, lacking the interpretation of the artist's mind and hand that characterize Healy at his best. He died in Chicago.

Healy's portraits comprise an invaluable visual record of history makers of the nineteenth century on both sides of the Atlantic. His works are found in many art and history museums throughout the United States, with sizable collections in the Corcoran Gallery of Art, Washington, D.C.; the White House; the National Portrait Gallery, Smithsonian Institution; the Illinois State Museum at Springfield; the Chicago Historical Society; and the Newberry Library in Chicago.

• Healy's autobiography, *Reminiscences of a Portrait Painter* (1894), contains many anecdotes of his experiences with portrait subjects but little of his involvement with the art world in Europe and the United States. *Life of George P. A. Healy* (1913), by his daughter Mary Bigot, is a brief account of the artist's life and contains a selection of his letters. The artist's granddaughter Marie De Mare, *G. P. A. Healy, American Artist: An Intimate Chronicle of the Nineteenth Century* (1954), contains much information about the family and Healy's professional life but does not cite any sources. The letters and documents on which this work is based are located in the Manuscript Division of the New York Public Library, assembled with notations by historian Thomas Robson Hay, who acted as adviser to De Mare. A microfilm copy is available at the Archives of American Art, Smithsonian Institution. Relevant papers located in the Archives of American Art include the Healy Family Papers as well as the correspondence, notes, clippings, and draft compiled by De Mare in the process of writing her book. Both of these collections are available on microfilm. A recent and useful discussion of Healy's career is in Albert Boime, *Thomas Couture and the Eclectic Vision* (1980). For a record of Healy's paintings owned by the French government see Claire Constans, *Musée national du Château de Versailles: Catalogue des Peintures* (1980). Location of Healy's paintings is recorded in the Inventory of American Paintings before 1914, National Museum of American Art, Smithsonian Institution.

LOIS MARIE FINK

HEALY, James Augustine (6 Apr. 1830–5 Aug. 1900), Roman Catholic bishop, was born near Clinton, Georgia, the son of Michael Morris Healy, a planter, and Mary Eliza Clark. Healy's Irish father had married Healy's mother, a mulatto slave, despite strict Georgia law that made the union illegal and all of their children technically slaves. Healy's early years were spent in the insular world of the family's 1,600-acre plantation. When he reached school age, he and his brothers Hugh and Patrick were placed by their father in a Quaker school in Flushing, New York. There the boys, though possessing the same legal rights as their classmates, still endured the status of social outcasts because of their mixed race. This experience solidified Healy's already guarded nature and created in him an attachment to his family that he maintained throughout his life.

In 1844 Healy and his brothers transferred to the College of the Holy Cross in Worcester, Massachusetts, a new Jesuit school established by Bishop John Bernard Fitzpatrick of Boston. Healy thrived in his new environment, excelling academically and experiencing a spiritual awakening that led to his decision to enter the priesthood in 1848. The Jesuit novitiate was in Maryland, a slave state, so with the help of Fitzpatrick, Healy in 1849 entered the Sulpician Seminary in Montreal, Canada. After receiving his M.A. two years later, Healy entered the seminary of St. Sulpice in Issy, France, where he worked toward becoming a professor of theology and philosophy. However, following the deaths of his parents in 1850 and his brother Hugh in 1853, Healy felt called to return to the United States.

In Notre Dame Cathedral in Paris on 10 June 1854, Healy became the first African American to be ordained a Roman Catholic priest. He then returned to Boston, where he became an assistant pastor of the Moon Street Church and an administrator of the House of the Guardian Angel, a home for orphaned boys. Fitzpatrick soon brought Healy onto his staff and gave him the responsibility of organizing the chancery office. In June 1855 Healy officially became the first chancellor of the diocese of Boston, loyally serving Fitzpatrick and learning from him the subtleties of Catholic leadership in New England's anti-Catholic environment.

In 1857, after Fitzpatrick became ill, Healy took over many of the bishop's duties. Plans to build a new cathedral were delayed because of the Civil War, and in 1862 Healy became the rector of a makeshift cathedral that had been a Unitarian church. As the war climaxed, he helped found the Home for Destitute Catholic Children, bringing in the Sisters of Charity to run it in 1865.

After Fitzpatrick's death in 1866, the new bishop, John Joseph Williams, appointed Healy as the pastor of St. James Church, the largest Catholic congregation in Boston. Healy was deeply concerned that as a southerner of African descent he would be unacceptable to the predominantly Irish parishioners. He kept this concern to himself, however, and soon won over the congregation through firm spiritual leadership and a tender affection for those in need. As one parishioner said, if Healy "had any such thing as an inferiority complex concealed about his person, his Irish congregation never discovered it, for he ruled them—and they were not easy to rule" (Foley, p. 109).

A highlight of Healy's years as the pastor of St. James was the establishment in 1867 of the House of the Good Shepherd, a refuge for homeless girls. However, his success as an apologist for the Catholic church before the Massachusetts legislature in March 1874 was perhaps his most impressive achievement. The legislature was considering the taxation of churches and other religious institutions, and Healy defended Catholic institutions—including schools, hospitals, and orphanages—as vital organizations that helped the state both socially and financially. He also eloquently condemned the laws that were already in place, which were generally enforced only on Catholic institutions.

Healy's success in the public sphere and his exemplary service as pastor of St. James led to his election by Pope Pius IX as the second bishop of Portland, Maine, in February 1875. Again he was concerned that the color of his skin would undermine his authority, particularly in regard to the fifty-two priests of the diocese. His fears, however, were never realized. Although Healy's personal history was the source of some intrigue and prejudice among his flock, his ability and pastoral excellence reduced the matter to a nonissue. He took firm control of the diocese, which covered all of Maine and New Hampshire and was growing rapidly as a result of Irish and French-Canadian immigration. Relying on the savvy of John M. Mitchell, a prominent local lawyer well schooled in Maine's political and social intricacies, Healy helped unify his parishes in an era when Catholics were often divided by ethnic differences.

Healy oversaw the founding of sixty parishes, eighteen schools (including American Indian schools), and sixty-eight charitable institutions within the diocese. In 1884, at Healy's suggestion, the diocese was divided by state lines, and a separate diocese of Manchester, New Hampshire, was established. Healy helped set up his former chancellor, Denis Bradley, as its first bishop. He also oversaw the establishment of the state's first Catholic college in 1886, as St. Mary's College in

Van Buren opened its doors. Under Healy, dozens of religious congregations were established, many of French-Canadian origin. By 1900 the Sisters of Mercy, the Sisters of the Congregation of Notre Dame, the Dominicans, the Marist Brothers, and the Christian Brothers were all established in various educational and institutional positions throughout the state.

While the quality of Healy's career proves that a person's race is not the essential characteristic by which he or she can be judged, his desire to avoid the issue led to several lost opportunities to condemn the sin of racism on a national stage. Even after the Third Plenary Council of Baltimore in 1884, which placed Healy on the newly formed Commission on Negro and Indian Missions, he refused to participate in organizations that were specifically African-American. Three times, in 1889, 1890, and 1892, Healy declined to speak at the Congress of Colored Catholics. His legacy as the first African-American Catholic bishop is at least partially diminished by this reticence.

Although healy was haunted by racism throughout his life, he never allowed it to affect his duties. His graceful attitude toward the problem is exemplified by an encounter he had with a young parishioner during the sacrament of penance. The teenage girl, unaware that her confessor was Healy himself, admitted that she had "said the bishop was as black as the devil." Healy responded, "Don't say the bishop is as black as the devil. You can say the bishop is as black as coal, or as black as the ace of spades. But don't say the bishop is as black as the *devil!*" (Foley, p. 145).

Healy was a religious leader whose intelligence, spiritual conviction, and dedicated service inevitably defined him and created a devoted, if not wholly color-blind, following. He died in Portland, Maine.

• Healy's papers, including diaries, correspondence, travel journals, and sermons, are at the library of the College of the Holy Cross in Worcester, Mass., the Archives of the Archdiocese of Boston, and the Archives of the Diocese of Portland. Albert S. Foley, *Bishop Healy: Beloved Outcaste* (1954), is an informative, laudatory account of all aspects of his life. A more critical evaluation is in Donna Merwick, *Boston Priests, 1848–1910: A Study of Social and Intellectual Change* (1973). William Leo Lucey, *The Catholic Church in Maine* (1957), is also helpful. An obituary is in the *Portland Express*, 6 Aug. 1900.

JAY MAZZOCCHI

HEALY, Patrick Francis (2 Feb. 1834–10 Jan. 1910), Jesuit priest and university president, was born in Jones County, Georgia, the son of Michael Morris Healy, an Irish-American planter, and Elisa, a mulatto slave. The senior Healy deserted from the British army in Canada during the War of 1812 and by 1818 had made his way to rural Georgia where he settled, speculated in land, and acquired a sizable plantation and numerous slaves. He fathered ten children by an African-American woman he had purchased. Healy acknowledged Elisa as "my trusty woman" in his will, which provided that she be paid an annuity, transported to a free state, and "not bartered or sold or disposed of in any way" should he predecease her. Healy also acknowledged his children by Elisa, although by state law they were slaves he owned, and he arranged for them to leave Georgia and move to the North, where they would become free.

After first sending his older sons to a Quaker school in Flushing, Long Island, Michael Healy by chance met John Fitzpatrick, then the Roman Catholic bishop coadjutor of Boston, who told him about the new Jesuit College of the Holy Cross opening in Worcester, Massachusetts. Patrick, along with three of his brothers, was enrolled in Holy Cross in 1844. A sister, Martha, was sent to the Notre Dame sisters' school in Boston. Patrick graduated in 1850, the year after his older brother James was literally the first person to receive a diploma from the fledgling college. At Holy Cross the Healy brothers' race was fully known and generally accepted without incident. In one poignant letter, however, Patrick Healy wrote, "Remarks are sometime made which wound my very heart. You know to what I refer . . . I have with me a younger brother Michael. He is obliged to go through the same ordeal."

The Healy children were baptized as Roman Catholics and placed under the care of Catholic clergy, so it is not surprising that Patrick Healy decided to emulate his friends and protectors and enter the Society of Jesus. He matriculated at the order's novitiate in Frederick, Maryland, where his light skin apparently kept him from being identified as African American and thus in school contrary to the law. An unconfirmed rumor suggests that some Healy children who remained in Georgia were sold as slaves in order to help finance the educations of their siblings.

After making his Jesuit vows in 1852, Healy taught at St. Joseph's College in Philadelphia and was then assigned back to Holy Cross, where he taught a variety of courses. In 1858 he was sent to Georgetown University in Washington, D.C., to continue his own studies in philosophy and theology, but soon he was abruptly reassigned to Rome, probably because his race had become an issue. His brother James, who had decided to enter the secular priesthood, attended the Sulpician seminaries in Montreal and Paris because it was not possible for a black person to be enrolled in an American school.

Patrick Healy's delicate health did not long tolerate the weather in Rome, so he was sent to the Catholic University of Louvain in Belgium. He was ordained to the priesthood on 3 September 1864 by Bishop Lamont in Liége and then stayed on at Louvain to complete a doctorate in philosophy. He received his degree on 26 July 1865, apparently the first African American to earn a Ph.D. He returned to the United States the next year, after further spiritual training in France, and was assigned to teach philosophy at Georgetown.

Healy took his final vows as a Jesuit on 2 February 1867, the first African American to do so. If the illegitimacy of his birth made his ordination problematic, it may be that the records were altered within the church, as apparently had been the case with his brother James, the first African American ordained to the Roman Catholic priesthood (10 June 1854). Patrick Healy moved quickly through the administrative ranks at Georgetown, becoming prefect of studies, or dean, and then vice president. When the president, the Reverend John Early, died unexpectedly in 1873, Healy was named acting president. Following confirmation by authorities in Rome, he was inaugurated the twenty-ninth president of Georgetown on 31 July 1874.

Patrick Healy's influence on Georgetown was so far-reaching that he is often referred to as the school's "second founder," following Archbishop John Carroll. Healy did, in fact, transform a small nineteenth-century college into a major twentieth-century university. He modernized the curriculum by requiring courses in the sciences, particularly chemistry and physics. He expanded and upgraded the schools of law and medicine. He centralized libraries, arranged for scholastic awards to students, and created an alumni organization. The most visible result of Healy's presidency was the construction of a large building begun in 1877 and first used in 1881. The imposing Healy Hall, with its 200-foot tower, contained classrooms, offices, and dormitories; its Belgian Gothic style was clearly reminiscent of Louvain. Paying for the building became somewhat problematic, however, when stories of Healy's race, never a secret, circulated through Washington.

Healy's influence extended beyond Georgetown as he mixed in the nation's capital with presidents of the United States and other government officials as well as the parents of Georgetown students. He served as head of the Catholic Commission on Indian Affairs. He preached often in Catholic churches in the Washington area, including St. Augustine's, an African-American parish. He was present at the cornerstone laying of this church in 1874 and at the dedication of its new building in 1876. He spoke at congressional hearings in opposition to taxes on religious and educational institutions.

Healy's health was never robust, and he apparently suffered from epilepsy, which grew more serious with age. Upon the advice of his physician, he retired from the Georgetown presidency on 16 February 1882. Several assignments followed, but they existed largely in name only: St. Joseph's Church, Providence, Rhode Island; St. Lawrence Church, New York City; and St. Joseph's College, Philadelphia. In fact, in retirement he traveled extensively through Europe and the United States, often in the company of his brother James. He spent his last two years in the Georgetown infirmary, where he died, survived only by his sister Eliza.

Patrick Healy's brothers and sisters led equally significant lives. James became bishop of Portland, Maine. Alexander became a professor of moral theology and accompanied Boston archbishop John J. Williams to Vatican I as his personal theologian. Eliza became sister Mary Magdalene, a superior in the Notre Dame sisters. Michael, the only sibling not to follow a religious vocation, became "Hell Roaring Mike," captain of a U.S. revenue cutter in the Arctic and North Pacific; it is said that Jack London's novel *The Sea Wolf* is modeled on his life.

• Healy's papers, including his diaries, are in the Georgetown University Library. A biographical sketch is in Rev. Albert Foley, *God's Men of Color* (1955; repr. 1970). The standard history of Georgetown is Robert Emmett Curran, *The Bicentennial History of Georgetown University*, vol. 1: *1789–1889* (1993).

RICHARD NEWMAN

HEALY, William (29 Jan. 1869–15 Mar. 1963), psychiatrist, medical psychologist, and pioneer in the field of juvenile delinquency, was born in Buckinghamshire, England, the son of a farmer and brickmaker. He was the youngest of four children. His family emigrated to the United States when he was nine, and at age fourteen he dropped out of school to work as a clerk in a local Chicago bank in order to help support his family. He worked at this job for ten years, during which time he read widely, availed himself of the local public library, and, with the encouragement of numerous individuals who saw his potential, became a self-taught intellectual. During this time he fell under the influence of the Reverend William Salter, a liberal Unitarian minister, leader of the local branch of the Ethical Culture Society, and a relative by marriage of William James. Through connections Healy established with James, he entered Harvard in 1893, at age twenty-three, as a special student. There James became his teacher, mentor, and close friend. Healy spent three years at Harvard College and three years at Harvard Medical School, earning the A.B. in 1899. He received the M.D. from the University of Chicago the following year.

Upon graduation, Healy taught at Northwestern University and worked in various hospitals. He specialized first in gynecology and then in neurology until 1906, when he became interested in nervous and mental diseases, a subject he had previously surveyed at the graduate level under James at Harvard. During this time Healy married Mary Sylvia Tenney; the marriage produced one son, Kent Tenney Healy, later a professor at Yale. Contrary to popular belief, Healy was never married to psychologist Grace Fernald.

In 1906 Healy undertook postgraduate study at Vienna, Berlin, and London before returning to medical practice in Chicago. He then became director of the Juvenile Psychopathic Institute in 1909. The Chicago Juvenile Psychopathic Institute, which became the Institute of Juvenile Research in 1920, began as a treatment center for delinquents, but later it began admitting nondelinquent children with emotional disturbances. The institute developed out of the work of Hull-House, run by Jane Addams, in cooperation with Julia Lathrop, later head of the Children's Bureau in Washington, D.C.; James Rowland Angell, professor of psychology; and George Herbert Mead, the head of the Department of Philosophy at the University of Chicago. Searching for a director, Mead wrote to colleagues in the East, where both Adolf

Meyer and William James recommended Healy. Working in conjunction with the juvenile courts, Healy established the Child Guidance Movement on a scientific footing. He examined Witmer's clinic at the University of Pennsylvania, where retarded children were given mental tests and a physical examination, and he looked at H. H. Goddard's laboratory for the feebleminded in Vineland, New Jersey. Believing both these programs to be good but incomplete, Healy set out to chronicle individual cases of delinquency by combining physical exams with school reports, interviews with parents and relatives, and observation of the child while confined to determine the influence of heredity, developmental personality traits, and family relationships.

Hearing of his work, Harvard University invited Healy to give summer school lectures in Cambridge in 1912 and again in 1913. There he met his future second wife, Augusta Bronner, who had been an assistant to E. L. Thorndike at Columbia. Healy convinced her to move to Chicago and work in his Juvenile Psychopathic Institute. She remained with him for the rest of her life. Together, they coauthored numerous works, including *New Light on Delinquency and Its Treatment* (1936) and *Manual of Individual Mental Tests and Testing* (1938).

In 1915 Healy wrote *The Individual Delinquent*, which definitively launched the field of child delinquency and sounded the death knell of nineteenth-century theories of degeneration and the stereotype of the "born criminal." Heralded as ushering in a new era of criminology, it was an analysis of 800 cases in which Healy conceived of juvenile delinquency as a learned behavior of multiple causes, modifiable by examining the psychological and sociological conditions of a youth's upbringing. He included a study of intelligence tests with the search for focal infections of a medical nature common to delinquent children, and he emphasized the routine search for emotional trauma, incorporating numerous psychoanalytic ideas. It was an unprecedented integration for its time and a thoroughly Jamesean text in its pragmatic eclecticism.

Healy came to the Judge Baker Foundation in 1917, where he continued his research with the support of Judge Cabot and professionals such as Walter Fernald and James Jackson Putnam. Under Healy's direction, the Judge Baker Guidance Center eventually provided a major professional center for the development of generations of women psychologists and psychiatrists, including Molly Putnam, Beata Rank, and pediatrician Josephine Murray. Healy was also chairman of the board of trustees of the Boston Psychopathic Hospital for some twenty-five years, president of the Boston Society of Neurology and Psychiatry, and president of the American Psychopathological Association. Also in 1934, with Bernard Glueck, Karl Menninger, and Herman Adler, among others, Healy cofounded the American Orthopsychiatric Association.

Both Healy and Bronner had three months of analysis under Helena Deutsch in 1929, after which they published *The Structure and Meaning of Psychoanalysis* in 1930, an important text in the continued Americanization of Freud's ideas. In 1931, at the age of sixty-three, Healy undertook a formal analysis with Franz Alexander and, in 1935, coauthored with Alexander *The Roots of Crime*, a psychoanalytic interpretation of forensic science. Despite the fact that Healy had been exposed to Freud's ideas, first through James in the 1890s, and then had been the first to incorporate them into the psychology of juvenile delinquency before the First World War, both he and Augusta Bronner have remained insufficiently recognized as early American interpreters of Freud by current psychoanalytic historians.

In the area of mental testing, Healy began working with the Binet tests of intelligence in 1911. Early on he recognized the need for performance tests to complement the more verbal types of intelligence test tasks of the Stanford Binet. He developed the Healy-Fernald series of twenty-three tests, first used in 1911, and some of his measures remained in use at the end of the twentieth century, such as the Healy Picture Completion Test and the Healy Puzzle.

Healy retired as director of the Judge Baker Foundation in 1947 and spent the last sixteen years of his life in Clearwater, Florida, where he died.

• Healy's papers are at Rare Books, Countway Library of Medicine, Harvard Medical School. A valuable monograph-length autobiographical statement, created under the direction of historian John C. Burnham, is on deposit at the Houghton Rare Manuscript Library, Harvard University. Biographies include G. E. Gardner's in the *Journal of the American Academy of Child Psychiatry* 11 (1972): 1–29; D. M. Levy's in the *American Journal of Orthopsychiatry* 38 (1968): 799–804. See also Leonard Zusne, ed., *Biographical Dictionary of Psychology* (1984).

EUGENE TAYLOR

HEAP, Jane (1 Nov. 1883–16 June 1964), artist and editor, was born in Topeka, Kansas, the daughter of George Heap, an engineer, and Emma (maiden name unknown). Interested in art from an early age, Heap attended the Art Institute of Chicago from 1901 until 1905 and later studied mural design in Germany. By the century's second decade Chicago was in the midst of a "Renaissance" in art and literature. Writers and artists influenced by Nietzsche, Shaw, Picasso, and Gauguin attacked the straitlaced conservatism of the Victorian genteel tradition. Young midwesterners with artistic aspirations traveled to Chicago where they embraced and expressed an American modernism that owed much to European philosophies. Heap was among them.

In 1916 she met Margaret Anderson, who in 1914 had founded the *Little Review*, a journal that advanced the most daring recent trends in the arts. The two women fell in love and formed, in Anderson's words, "a consolidation that was to make us much loved and even more loathed." They were among a small number of early twentieth-century urban women who lived openly as lesbians. In her autobiography Anderson wrote that her "mind was inflamed" by Heap's ideas and conversation. Hoping to capture Heap's quality of thought for the *Little Review*, Anderson asked her to become coeditor. Heap agreed and insisted on retaining a low profile by signing her contributions "jh." Her articles generated praise and criticism from subscribers who were struck by the combination of her droll humor and biting insights.

During its Chicago years the *Little Review* created a great deal of controversy by advocating free verse, anarchism, and sexual radicalism. Early contributors included Amy Lowell, Emma Goldman, Floyd Dell, and H.D. (Hilda Doolittle). In 1917 Anderson and Heap moved the magazine to New York City, and in an effort to make it "an international concern," they took on Ezra Pound as foreign editor. While based in New York they published T. S. Eliot, Wyndham Lewis, and James Joyce. Their serialization of Joyce's *Ulysses* landed them in court on charges brought by the New York Society for the Suppression of Vice. In 1921 they were convicted of obscenity, fined $100, and forced to promise not to publish further chapters.

After the trial the two women ended their relationship and Heap became sole editor of the magazine. Under her direction the journal became more concerned with the visual arts; she reprinted works of Francis Picabia, Man Ray, Max Ernst, and Fernand Léger. Heap was particularly interested in European movements such as Dada, surrealism, constructivism, de Stijl architecture and "machine age" aesthetics. In addition to editing the *Little Review*, Heap organized the ambitious International Theatre Exposition (1926) and the Machine Age Exposition (1927), both in New York City.

During the early 1920s Heap embraced the philosophy of the Russian mystic George Gurdjieff. A controversial figure among bohemian intellectuals, Gurdjieff taught that each individual's true personality was asleep, hidden behind mechanical reactions to life. To awake to one's true "essence" it was necessary to practice a series of physical and mental disciplines that he taught. In 1924 Heap studied at Gurdjieff's Institute for the Harmonious Development of Man in Fontainebleau. While in France, she traveled in American expatriate circles and obtained contributions for the *Little Review* from Gertrude Stein and Ernest Hemingway as well as work from foreign contributors such as Tristan Tzara, Jean Cocteau, and André Breton. During the remainder of the decade Heap split her time between Paris and New York where she continued to publish the *Little Review* and operated the Little Review Gallery at 66 Fifth Avenue.

Heap's increasing immersion in the spiritual teachings of Gurdjieff led her to reevaluate the importance and the role of art in the modern world, prompting her to end publication of the *Little Review* in 1929. She wrote in her farewell editorial, "Self-expression is not enough; experiment is not enough; the recording of special moments is not enough. All the arts have broken faith or lost connection with their origin and function." In the 1930s Heap moved to London where she taught Gurdjieff's philosophy to small groups of devotees and became increasingly reclusive, communicating little with former friends. She died in London.

Of all the little magazines of the early twentieth century, the *Little Review* was the most enduring and influential. Heap's role in that record of success has been underestimated, partly because of her recalcitrance to discuss her early life, and in part because of the self-promotion of Anderson, who wrote three autobiographical works and enjoyed reminiscing about the *Little Review* years. A lack of Heap's personal papers compounded the mystery, until discovery of correspondence in 1991 that shed light on both Heap's complex personality and contribution to the magazine. Heap's unabashed lesbianism, and her promotion of the modern in art and literature, make her one of the more fascinating, if somewhat forgotten, figures of the early twentieth-century avant-garde.

• The Jane Heap Collection at the University of Delaware contains more than 100 letters, dozens of photographs, and other memorabilia. Some of that material was incorporated in Holly Baggett, "Aloof from Natural Laws: Margaret C. Anderson and the *Little Review*: 1914–1929" (Ph.D. diss., Univ. of Delaware, 1992). No biography of Heap exists; the most complete view of her is given by Anderson in her first autobiography, *My Thirty Years' War* (1930), and, to a lesser extent, her following ones, *The Fiery Fountains* (1951) and *Strange Necessity* (1969). The importance of Heap's career as an art critic was explored by Susan Noyes Platt, "Mysticism and the Machine Age: Jane Heap and the *Little Review*," *Twenty/One* (Fall 1989): 19–44. An obituary is in the *New York Times*, 23 June 1964.

HOLLY BAGGETT

HEARD, Dwight Bancroft (1 May 1869–14 Mar. 1929), investment banker, farmer, and publisher, was born in Boston, Massachusetts, the son of Leander Bradford Heard, a wholesale grocer, and Lucy Bancroft. His father died in 1882. After Heard finished high school in Brookline, Massachusetts, his mother moved the family to Chicago, where Heard began work at the hardware sellers Hibbard, Spencer & Bartlett. The wife of the firm's president, Adolphus Bartlett, was a distant relative of Heard, who quickly became Bartlett's protégé. Heard was the company's specialist in credit sales in Wisconsin and much of the Midwest. In 1893 he married Maie Pitkin Bartlett, Adolphus Bartlett's daughter; they had one child.

Doctors told Heard that he had a lung condition that necessitated a relocation to the Southwest. Within a year of their marriage, the Heards moved to Amarillo, Texas, where they lived briefly before settling in Phoenix, Arizona, in May 1895. Initially Heard made his living as a farmer, but he grew interested in mortgage financing. Through his Chicago connections, he began offering loans to a carefully selected group of farmers, chosen for their financial stability and their moral reputations. These loans, made at an unusually low 8 percent interest, angered many other area financiers, who could not compete. This business eventually became the Dwight B. Heard Investment Company.

In 1900 Heard bought the Wormser Ranch, 7,500 acres of land in South Phoenix on which to grow alfalfa and raise cattle. With the financial support of Bartlett, this project became the Bartlett-Heard Land and Cattle Company. Also with the backing of his father-in-law, Heard bought 160 acres of land in northern Phoenix and developed them into Los Olivos, a residential community with palm tree–lined roads and Spanish architecture.

Because of his wealth, his involvement in the development of Phoenix, and his Chicago connections, Heard played a leading role in the political and social worlds of Phoenix. A Republican and a staunch supporter of Theodore Roosevelt, Heard was concerned with protecting Arizona's rights as an independent state and with increasing federal spending to facilitate settlement of the West. He was a leading advocate of the 1902 Reclamation Act, which set aside revenue from the sale of public lands in western states to finance construction of dams and irrigation projects that would encourage small farmers to settle in the West. He was influential in the development of the Roosevelt Dam, completed in 1911, that stored and supplied water for the Phoenix area. At first Heard wanted to finance the dam privately, but he soon realized the need for federal involvement. He opposed admitting Arizona and New Mexico into the Union as a single state and defended Arizona's rights in the development of the Colorado River. In 1912 Heard bought the *Arizona Republican*, openly planning to use the magazine to campaign for Roosevelt's presidential candidacy. He served as a delegate at the 1912 Republican National Convention and backed the establishment of the Progressive Party Convention. He was the president of the American National Live Stock Association from 1914 to 1917. A longtime member of the U.S. Chamber of Commerce, he was a director and chairman of the agricultural division. In 1924 he ran as the Republican candidate for governor of Arizona, losing by only 800 votes.

Heard and his wife were respected in Phoenix society but were considered aloof and snobbish. Heard's house, "Casa Blanca," became a center of Phoenix high society and hosted many important visitors from the East, including Marshall Field, Herbert Hoover, Harvey S. Firestone, and Roosevelt. Roosevelt and Heard were close friends, exchanging nearly 150 letters in twenty years. The Heards traveled extensively in Europe and Egypt, bringing back mementos with which they decorated their home. The Heards acquired a sizable collection of Native American art and eventually opened the Heard Museum, which also housed a substantial collection of New England antiques. Heard was a trustee of the Art Institute of Chicago and devoted his later years to philanthropy. On land donated by his father-in-law's estate, Heard financed the construction of the Phoenix Civic Center, the Phoenix Public Library, the Phoenix Little Theatre, and eventually the Phoenix Art Museum. Heard died in Phoenix.

Heard led the economic development and settlement of much of Arizona, and his influence reached into neighboring states. Through his support of the Reclamation Act, his development of the Los Olivos residential community, and the jobs created by his investments and farming, he contributed significantly to the population of the West. His philanthropic and civic projects, including the Heard Museum and the public buildings he financed, are of enduring value. Active in politics and society, Heard and his wife were among the most prominent citizens of early Phoenix.

• A biographical article on Heard and his wife is G. Wesley Johnson, Jr., "Dwight Heard in Phoenix: The Early Years," *Journal of Arizona History* 18, no. 3 (Autumn 1977). Heard's early family history is detailed in J. H. Edwards, *A History of the Heard Family of Wayland, Mass.* (1880). See also J. H. McClintock, *Arizona*, vol. 3 (1916), and *History of Arizona*, vols. 3–4 (1930). An obituary is in the *Arizona Republican*, 15 Mar. 1929.

ELIZABETH ZOE VICARY

HEARD, Gerald (6 Oct. 1889–14 Aug. 1971), writer and mystic, was born Henry Fitzgerald Heard in London, England, the son of Henry James Heard, a clergyman, and Maud Bannatyne. He received a B.A., with honors, from Gonville and Caius College, Cambridge, in 1911 and did a further year of graduate work. He never married. In the first part of his life Heard worked with the Agricultural Cooperative Movement in Ireland (1919–1923), edited the *London Realist* (1929), and was deeply involved in the peace movement before the Second World War. He was also a science commentator for BBC Radio (1930–1934) and taught at Oxford University (1929–1931), Washington University in St. Louis (1951–1952; 1955–1956), and Oberlin College in Ohio (1958).

Heard is best remembered as a friend of Aldous Huxley and as a writer of popular fiction. He authored over forty books. His best-known work is a Sherlock Holmes-type novel, *A Taste for Honey* (1941). In science fiction circles he is remembered for the dystopian novel *Doppelgangers* (1947). But his most extensive literary output was in the arena of popular religious philosophy, where he explored such themes as the spiritual evolution of the human race—as in, for example, *Pain, Sex and Time: A New Hypothesis of Evolution* (1939). He even wrote a book on flying saucers, *The Riddle of the Flying Saucers* (1950), which was reissued as *Is Another World Watching?* (1951). Heard had an interest in parapsychology and, with Huxley, visited J. B. Rhine at Duke University.

Heard and Huxley met in 1929, became best friends, and worked together in the pacifist movement. In 1937 they moved to the United States and undertook a lecture tour together, eventually settling in California. Heard was a serious mystic who meditated regularly and who in other ways led a spiritually disciplined lifestyle. Like Huxley, he studied under Swami Prabhavananda of the Vedanta Society of Southern California, but, unlike Christopher Isherwood (whom he introduced to the Swami), he did not become a disciple. Both Huxley and Heard experimented with psychedelics.

For a period of four or five years in the mid-1940s, Heard organized and led a small monastic community, Trabuco College, located in Trabuco Canyon, southeast of Los Angeles. Although he and his wife enjoyed visiting Trabuco, Huxley never joined. Heard presumed to set himself up as the spiritual director of Trabuco College, and, perhaps as a consequence, the two friends became somewhat distant. When the community folded, a disappointed and chastened Heard regained some of his original closeness to Huxley. The college's property was eventually taken over by the Vedanta Society.

Heard's writing has been characterized as "voluminous" and "opaque." Even Huxley once described Heard's prose as "frightful." A sentence from Heard's *Is God Evident?* (1948) provides an example:

We have, then, seen that the view which has so vastly influenced men's defeatism, against there being any evidence for purpose in Nature and in Life, the doctrine which has proved its mistakenness by sanctioning such outbursts of the international anarchy that civilization is one step away from suicide, that view was never worked out, is full of inner inconsistencies, is insignificant as a philosophy and fatal in practice. (P. 109)

Although a significant literary figure, Heard's style may explain why he has received so little critical attention. In the latter part of his life he helped to lay the philosophical foundations for the gay movement. He was an invalid for the last five years of his life and died at his home in Santa Monica, California. According to David Dunaway, a recent biographer of Huxley, Heard "was at times lucid in his final coma, giving interviews as a theorist of gay spirituality to a new generation of gay historians."

• Heard is often mentioned in literary reference books, but such mentions are unsatisfyingly brief. Two references that at least cover all of the basic biographical information and give a complete list of Heard's publications are John M. Reilly, ed., *Twentieth-Century Crime and Mystery Writers* (2d ed., 1985), and Curtis C. Smith, ed., *Twentieth-Century Science-Fiction Writers* (2d ed., 1986). Although no book-length biographies have been written about Heard, it is possible to find much information in some of the biographies of Huxley and Isherwood, such as David King Dunaway, *Huxley in Hollywood* (1989), and Brian Finney, *Christopher Isherwood: A Critical Biography* (1979). An obituary is in the *New York Times*, 19 Aug. 1971.

JAMES R. LEWIS

HEARD, J. C. (8 Oct. 1917–27 Sept. 1988), jazz drummer, was born in Dayton, Ohio. His father was a factory worker; further details of his parents are unknown. Heard told interviewer Peter Vacher that he actually was named J. C. by his parents, and he invented the given names James Charles to satisfy authorities who would not believe that the initials should stand alone. He was raised in Detroit from infancy. A tap dancer by age five, he taught himself to play drums. At about age

ten he won an amateur tap dancing contest, and the prize was the opportunity to tour with Butterbeans and Susie. About five weeks after the tour started, the drummer was taken ill, and Heard took his place for the remainder of the show's run.

A year or two later Heard acquired his own set of drums. As a teenager he worked with bands throughout Michigan. After playing with Milt Larkin's band, he joined pianist Teddy Wilson's big band in New York in April 1939. In June 1940, at the end of this affiliation, Heard made several recordings with singer Billie Holiday under Wilson's direction, including "Laughing at Life." He then joined tenor saxophonist Coleman Hawkins's big band, which broadcast from the Savoy Ballroom in July and August. From December 1940 to the summer of 1942 he played at Café Society with Wilson's sextet, and during this period he again recorded with Wilson, including a trio version of "I Know That You Know" (Apr. 1941). Heard also played briefly with alto saxophonist Benny Carter's big band at the Savoy (Jan. 1941), performed in the film short *Boogie Woogie Dream* (1941), and made further recordings with Holiday (Aug. 1941 and Feb. 1942).

In the fall of 1942 Heard traveled to Los Angeles to replace Cozy Cole in singer Cab Calloway's big band. He remained with Calloway until September 1945, while also working with pianist Count Basie's big band in the spring of 1944 and recording with tenor saxophonist Ike Quebec (several sessions, 1944–1946), alto saxophonist Charlie Parker and trumpeter Dizzy Gillespie in vibraphonist Red Norvo's group (June 1945), and Parker in pianist Sir Charles Thompson's All Stars (Sept. 1945).

After working in late 1945 in the sextet of trombonist Benny Morton, who had been a fellow member of Wilson's groups, Heard formed his own group at the downtown location of Café Society. In January 1946 this sextet included trumpeter George Treadwell, trombonist Dicky Wells, saxophonist Budd Johnson, pianist Jimmy Jones, and bassist Al McKibbon. Later group members were trumpeter Joe Newman, trombonist Dicky Harris, and saxophonist Big Nick Nicholas, with singer Etta Jones added as well. Apart from his own group, Heard recorded "Mr. Drum Meets Mr. Piano" in a duo with pianist Pete Johnson and "J. C. from K.C." as a soloist in Johnson's group in a session during January 1946, and small group versions of "52nd. Street Theme," "A Night in Tunesia," and "Anthropology" with trumpeter Dizzy Gillespie the following month.

Heard claimed to have played in the first Jazz at the Philharmonic concert with Nat King Cole, but discographies identify the drummer as Lee Young (Lester's brother). In any event he performed regularly with Jazz at the Philharmonic in 1946. Heard substituted for Jo Jones in Basie's group in the summer of 1947, and for the 1947 movie *The Kiss of Death* he found himself in the rare position of recording the soundtrack for Jones, who appears on screen; Heard's performing in Jones's stead was, in itself, a testimony to his stature as a jazz drummer.

Heard worked with bassist Oscar Pettiford in pianist Erroll Garner's trio at the Three Deuces club in New York in April 1948 and continued with the group after pianist George Shearing subsequently took Garner's place. Around 1949 Heard briefly replaced Cozy Cole in Louis Armstrong's All Stars when Cole broke his arm; Heard may be seen performing with a related Armstrong group on an episode of the television series "Eddie Condon's Floor Show" (3 Sept. 1949). He recorded with pianist Earl Hines's trio in June 1950.

Heard toured with Jazz at the Philharmonic in the early 1950s, but during concerts in Japan in November 1953 he received such a lucrative offer that he decided to leave this all-star group to remain in Japan. He acted in movies, appearing once as a black Samurai warrior; he hosted a television show through an interpreter; he led a jazz group that included pianist Toshiko Akiyoshi; and he worked with a big band, the Sharps and Flats. He toured widely, playing in Hong Kong, Saigon, Manila, and Calcutta, while also continuing to perform in Japan, where he married Hiroko (maiden name unknown); they had a son. After working in Australia as a singer, dancer, and drummer, he brought his family to New York late in 1957.

A European tour with pianist Sam Price in October 1958 included performances in England and at a jazz festival in Cannes. Heard worked alongside Hawkins and trumpeter Roy Eldridge at the Metropole club in New York (1959). He played in Wilson's trio (1961) and then held residencies in New York and toured with pianist Dorothy Donegan (1962–1963). In 1964 he joined Norvo's small group at the Sands Hotel in Las Vegas and the London House in Chicago. He led his own quintet, which included the hard bop musicians tenor saxophonist Harold Land, trumpeter Carmell Jones, and pianist Phineas Newborn, at Memory Lane in Los Angeles in 1965. After further work in California, he settled in Detroit early in 1967 and gradually developed a big band for local touring and student workshops around Michigan.

In the mid-1970s Heard toured the Hilton Hotels circuit, leading a four-piece group that included Detroit-based trumpeter Marcus Belgrave. While in France for performances at the Nice Jazz Festival in 1978, he also appeared on tenor saxophonist Illinois Jacquet's album *God Bless My Solo*. He toured Europe annually in the 1980s while continuing to work in the Detroit area, and in 1985 he performed on a jazz festival cruise ship. He died in Royal Oak, Michigan.

Heard was one of those accomplished drummers who is little known to the general public but much in demand within the community of jazz musicians: toward the end of his career a European fan sent him a list of 1,100 albums on which he had performed. The vast majority of his work was as a reliable and sensitive accompanist in swing groups (both big and small), but the recordings from 1946 with Johnson and Gillespie demonstrate that when the occasion demanded he was also comfortable and accomplished as a soloist and as a bop musician.

• For interviews with Heard, see Philip Hanson, "Catching up with J. C. Heard," *Jazz Monthly* 157 (Mar. 1968): 18–20; Peter Vacher, "Heard about J. C.?" *Melody Maker*, 4 Nov. 1978, p. 44; Mark B. Lipson, "Portraits: J. C. Heard," *Modern Drummer* 7 (July 1983): 48, 51; James Doran, *Erroll Garner: The Most Happy Piano* (1985), pp. 70–71; and Stanley Dance, "J. C. Heard," *Jazz Journal International* 39 (Nov. 1986): 10–12. See also Arnold Shaw, *The Street That Never Slept* (1971; repr. in 1977 as *52nd Street: The Street of Jazz*); Dizzy Gillespie and Al Fraser, *To Be, or Not . . . to Bop: Memoirs* (1979); Morroe Berger et al., *Benny Carter: A Life in American Music* (1982); John Chilton, *Who's Who of Jazz: Storyville to Swing Street*, 4th ed. (1985); Sammy Price, *What Do They Want?: A Jazz Autobiography*, ed. Caroline Richmond (1989). An obituary is in the *New York Times*, 30 Sept. 1988.

BARRY KERNFELD

HEARN, Lafcadio (27 June 1850–26 Sept. 1904), journalist and author, was born on the Greek island of Leucadia (also known as Santa Maura), the son of Charles Bush Hearn, an Irish surgeon in the British army, and Rosa Antonia Cassimati. He moved to Dublin with his mother in July 1852 to join his father's relatives. His mother returned to Greece two years later, leaving her son in the custody of Sarah Brenane, a great-aunt. A convert to Catholicism, she enrolled her charge in the Institution Ecclésiastique, a church school near Rouen, France, in 1862, and in St. Cuthbert's College, a Catholic boys' school near Durham, England, in 1863. There young Hearn suffered a disfiguring injury when a knotted rope struck him in the face and destroyed the vision in his left eye. He was withdrawn from school in October 1867 when his great-aunt could no longer pay his fees, and after boarding in London for a few lonely months he was given passage money to America.

After landing in New York, Hearn arrived in Cincinnati in 1869, and after struggling at a number of menial jobs he learned to set type and was hired as assistant editor of a trade journal and later proofreader for the Robert Clarke Company. He also worked as a part-time stringer for the Cincinnati *Enquirer*, where he signed on as a full-time reporter in early 1874. He soon earned a local reputation for writing about lurid crimes in an elegant style, though during this "period of the gruesome" he also coedited a short-lived literary weekly, *Ye Giglampz*, with his friend Henry Farney, and translated several of Théophile Gautier's stories and Gustave Flaubert's *The Temptation of Saint Anthony*. In mid-1875 he was fired from the paper amid scandal sparked by his liaison with a biracial woman, Mattie Foley, though he was soon hired by the crosstown Cincinnati *Commercial*.

Weary of the Queen City and something of a social pariah there, Hearn moved in 1877 to New Orleans, where he lived for the next ten years. Broke and unemployed during his first months in the South, he nearly died of dengue during a yellow fever epidemic. Yet he wrote back to friends in Cincinnati that "the wealth of the world is here—unworked gold in the ore." In June 1878 he finally found work as assistant editor of a feeble daily paper, the *Item*, in whose pages he immediately began to print meditative essays he called "fantastics" as well as some of his hitherto unpublished translations from Gautier, Alphonse Daudet, and Émile Zola. He later collected six stories he had translated from Gautier in his first book, *One of Cleopatra's Nights and Other Fantastic Romances* (1882). The author Joel Chandler Harris averred at the time that "Hearn has imparted to his translations a sensitiveness, a delicacy, a spiritual essence not to be found in the originals."

In 1881, Hearn became literary editor of the New Orleans *Times-Democrat*, which printed his reviews and translations from French and Spanish authors, including Daudet, Pierre Loti, François Coppée, and Charles Baudelaire, in its Sunday editions. Finding his métier as a cultural interpreter, he also began to study Creole dialect and folkways, an avocation that eventually led to the publication of *Gombo Zhèbes* (1885), a collection of dialect proverbs, and *La Cuisine Créole* (1885), a cookbook. He also published an anthology, *Stray Leaves from Strange Literature* (1884), versions of folklore he gleaned from Eskimo, Polynesian, Hindu, Jewish, Arabic, and other traditions. Meanwhile, he befriended two fellow New Orleaneans, the writer George Washington Cable and the missionary priest Père Adrien Rouquette, and he began to place his sketches with *Harper's Bazar* and *Harper's Weekly*.

In 1887 Hearn published *Some Chinese Ghosts*, a collection of six legends of the supernatural adapted from Eastern sources; he also placed with *Harper's Monthly* his first novel, *Chita*. Heavily influenced by the French symbolists, it is the story of a tidal wave off Last Island. The same year he traveled to the West Indies to write a series of articles for *Harper's*, then moved to Martinique later in the year. His sketches of native life there were subsequently published under the title *Two Years in the French West Indies* (1890). While living in the Caribbean, he also penned *Youma* (1890), a novella about a West Indian slave insurrection. He returned to New York and Philadelphia in the spring of 1889 and over the next year wrote "Karma," an uncharacteristically modern tale of virtue rewarded, published in *Lippincott's* (Apr. 1890); translated Anatole France's *Le Crime de Sylvestre Bonnard*; and finagled a commission from *Harper's* to write a book about Japan. "The studied aim" of such a project, he explained, "would be to create, in the minds of the readers, a vivid impression of *living* in Japan,—not simply as an observer but as one taking part in the daily existence of the common people, and *thinking with their thoughts*." He left for the Orient, never to return, in March 1890.

His years in Japan, the last chapter in what Malcolm Cowley has called the most exotic life of any nineteenth-century American author, were by far his most productive. Basil Hall Chamberlain of Tokyo Imperial University helped him secure a position as an English teacher in the provincial city of Matsue. Early in 1891, by arrangement and respectable Japanese custom, he wed Setusko Koizumi, daughter of a poor samurai family; they had four children. In the same year he was transferred at his request to the National College of Kumamoto in Kyushu. His articles on Japanese life appeared in the *Atlantic Monthly* and other magazines and were widely syndicated in American, English, and Australian newspapers. In 1894 he published *Glimpses of Unfamiliar Japan* (2 vols.), the first two of his twelve books on Japanese culture. He resigned from the public schools in 1894 to join the editorial staff of an English-language paper in Kobe but broke down from overwork after only a few months. In 1896 he became a Japanese citizen and changed his name legally to Koizumi Yakumo. He also accepted the chair of English language and literature at Tokyo Imperial University, a position he held until 1903 when he chose to resign rather than accept a sharp reduction in salary. He planned to return to the United States in 1903 to lecture on Japanese topics at Cornell University, but an outbreak of typhoid fever in Ithaca prompted the cancellation of the series. The finished lectures became instead Hearn's final book, *Japan: An Attempt at Interpretation* (1904). Shortly before his death of heart disease on the island of Honshu, he began to teach English literature at Waseda University, a private school, and he received an invitation to deliver a course of lectures at the University of London similar to those he had readied for Cornell. Hearn was the foremost multiculturalist of his generation, an antiprogressive whose successive exiles typified the antimodernist rebellion of the fin de siècle. "Civilization is a cold and vapid humbug," he once wrote. Such a perspective served him well in his roles of translator and ethnographer.

• Modest collections of Hearn's letters and other manuscript material are located at the Huntington Library in San Marino, Calif., the Library of Congress, the Houghton Library at Harvard University, the New York Public Library, Butler Library at Columbia University, the Pierpont Morgan Library in New York, the Humanities Research Center at the University of Texas at Austin, and Alderman Library at the University of Virginia. There are also special Hearn collections at the Public Library of Cincinnati, the Howard-Tilton Memorial Library at Tulane University, the Department of Literature at Tokyo University, and the Tenri Central Library of Tenri College, Tenri, Japan. The most reliable memoirs and documented biographies are Elizabeth Bisland, *The Life and Letters of Lafcadio Hearn* (1906); Nina H. Kennard, *Lafcadio Hearn* (1911); Elizabeth Stevenson, *Lafcadio Hearn* (1961); Jonathan Cott, *Wandering Ghost: The Odyssey of Lafcadio Hearn* (1991); and Carl Dawson, *Lafcadio Hearn and the Vision of Japan* (1992). An obituary is in the *New York Times*, 29 Sept. 1904.

GARY SCHARNHORST

HEARST, George (3 Sept. 1820–28 Feb. 1891), mine owner and U.S. senator, was born in Franklin County, Missouri, the son of William G. Hearst and Elizabeth Collins, farmers. The family lived in a log cabin.

Since no public schools operated in the area until Hearst was about eight years old, his childhood education was very intermittent. As a youth he visited local lead mines and became fascinated with the operations. When his father died, George took over the farming operation, which consisted of three mortgaged farms, a few slaves, and a crossroads country store. He studied mining, borrowing books from a local physician and visiting the nearby Virginia Mine. Using his savings, Hearst leased lead and copper mines and turned a profit, later pointing out that the best mining school was his practical experience in Franklin County.

Hearing the news of the gold discoveries in California, Hearst set aside funds to provide for his family and then joined a westward-bound emigrant group in May 1850. Riding on horseback in company with an ox-drawn train, Hearst and a friend from Missouri followed the Overland Trail via Fort Laramie and Fort Bridger.

Arriving in California after a six-month trek, Hearst tried his hand at gold mining in the Sierra Nevada range with moderate success. In 1851 he became part-owner of the first theater in Nevada City, California, a bustling mining town of over 5,000 people who mostly resided in tents. He also briefly operated a wholesale merchandising business in Sacramento.

In 1859 Hearst moved to Nevada, then the western part of Utah, where in the 1860s he laid the groundwork for a vast mining empire. His mine holdings eventually included the Ophir silver mine near what became Virginia City, Nevada, the Anaconda copper mines in Montana, and the Homestake in South Dakota. In 1862 he married Phoebe Apperson. They had one child, William Randolph Hearst, who later used the mining fortune to build a newspaper empire.

Relocating to San Francisco, Hearst served briefly as a Democrat in the California state legislature, 1865–1866, where he was a member of the Committee on Mines and Mining Interests. In 1872 he acquired the Ontario silver mine in Utah, one of his first large acquisitions, and he also bought the Daly mine. These two mines established the fortune that enabled Hearst to acquire even more profitable mining operations and several massive ranch properties in California. In later years, he bought a 600,000-acre ranch in Yucatan, Mexico, and the Barbicoa Ranch in Chihuahua, Mexico, which eventually occupied over 900,000 acres.

In 1880 Hearst bought the San Francisco *Daily Examiner*, which he used to promote his political ambitions. In 1882 his name was placed before the state Democratic convention as a nominee for governor, but he lost to George Stoneman. In 1885 the Democrats in the state legislature supported Hearst for U.S. senator, but the post went to Leland Stanford. In 1886 Governor Stoneman appointed Hearst to fill the vacant seat when Senator John Miller died in office. Hearst served from 23 March 1886 to 4 August 1886, when a Republican successor, Abram P. Williams, was selected. The next year Hearst was elected by the state legislature for the full U.S. Senate term, and he served from 4 March 1887 until his death. In the Senate, Hearst spoke on

few topics, but he energetically represented California's interests. One of the first bills he introduced was to provide financial support for the University of California. On other bills affecting railroads, harbors, and mining in the West, he spoke from his personal experience and travels, earning the respect of his colleagues for his knowledge of conditions and routes. He opposed the dismemberment of Idaho to enlarge both Washington State and Nevada and a motion, favored by dairy interests, to outlaw oleomargarine.

When his son dropped out of Harvard College, George Hearst attempted to interest him in taking over the mining and ranching properties. Finally he acceded to his son's request to become the publisher of the money-losing *Examiner*.

Hearst was regarded as a colorful, self-made millionaire, and during his service in the Senate, his tall and striking appearance with a full beard reminded his colleagues of his background as a western miner. His personal friends included President Grover Cleveland and Samuel Clemens. He died in Washington, D.C.

• Several holdings in the Bancroft Library at the University of California, Berkeley, contain George Hearst Papers. A laudatory but accurate biography commissioned by William Randolph Hearst gives details of George Hearst's life, Fremont Older and Cora Older, *George Hearst, California Pioneer* (1933; repr. 1966).

RODNEY P. CARLISLE

HEARST, Phoebe Elizabeth Apperson (3 Dec. 1842–13 Apr. 1919), philanthropist, was born in Franklin County, Missouri, the daughter of Randolph Walker Apperson and Drucilla Whitmire, farmers. She was educated by her parents and in a rude common school near what is now St. Clair, Missouri, southwest of St. Louis. At age seventeen she spent a year with cousins in St. James where she studied French and began the wider reading that became a lifelong occupation. She taught for a year in the Reedville or Ironworks (District 93) School near Sullivan but reportedly was nursing the family neighbor for whom she was named—Elizabeth Collins Hearst—when George Hearst (1820–1891) returned from California to attend his dying mother. Phoebe and George were married in Steelville, Missouri, in 1862, although the Appersons initially opposed the union because of the age difference and the distance from the groom's residence in California. (She spelled her given name "Phebe" in her letters through the 1890s; hence, this was the spelling recorded both on her wedding certificate and later in her appointment letter to the Board of Regents of the University of California. She apparently added the "o" at the suggestion of a stranger who wrote to her that it would connote, by inference to classical Greek, the qualities of light, grace, and music, which the admirer believed she possessed.) The couple's only child, William Randolph Hearst, was born in San Francisco in 1863.

Phoebe Hearst was a doting and indulgent parent, deeply interested in her son's upbringing and education. Hearst's relationship with her son was generally good and quite close but not free of disagreements. The principal and longest-standing source of conflict between the two was the fact that she had financial control over his life until her death, whereupon he received the bulk of her estate. Her husband's frequent absences strengthened her independence. With the foundations of George Hearst's great wealth already laid in the California goldfields and Nevada's Comstock Lode, she satisfied her zeal for self-improvement through reading, language studies, widening circles of friends, and travel. She also developed her talents as a hostess and began the program of personal giving and fund-raising on behalf of various causes for which she became famous and admired.

Compassion motivated her gifts of mortgage money to widows, the schooling she provided whole families, the handiworks she commissioned from destitute workers, her personal involvement in Travelers' Aid, hospital endowments, orphanages, the Humane Society, and the reform of American Indian affairs.

But faith in the power of education shaped and drove the bulk of Phoebe Hearst's lifework in philanthropy. From about 1833 she was a major supporter of the kindergarten movement: giving funds for the Golden Gate Kindergarten Association; founding free kindergartens for the children of the poor in San Francisco and Washington, D.C., and for the children of mineworkers in Lead, South Dakota; financing training schools for kindergarten teachers in Washington and San Francisco; and lobbying to have kindergartens made part of the public school system. She provided a lifetime income for Emma Marwedel, a kindergarten pioneer, and financed the publication of her work as she did for other writers. The College Settlement House in San Francisco, the West Berkeley Settlement, the Boys' Clubs and Girls' Clubs, the YMCA and YWCA, and the Camp Fire Girls all had her interest and financial support because of their emphasis on active learning, social and moral improvement, and the development of leadership skills. She enabled numerous writers, singers, musicians, artists, and architects to further their studies, often in Europe.

From 1886 to his death, George Hearst was also U.S. senator from California. While living in the nation's capital, Phoebe Hearst donated to the Protestant-Episcopal National Cathedral campaign and provided the building for the National Cathedral School for Girls. A successful campaign by Mary Garrett for funds to endow the Medical School of the Johns Hopkins University, on condition that the school admit women, got her subscription. She also contributed to the repair and endowment of George Washington's Mount Vernon home as a national shrine, led a women's drive for a statue of Washington as a gift to France, and helped finance rebuilding of the rotunda of the University of Virginia. Her Washington home was the locus for the organization of the National Congress of Mothers (later the National Congress of Parents and Teachers—the PTA), which she founded with Alice Birney and others in 1897.

After Senator Hearst's death in 1891 (she was his sole heir), Hearst returned to California, where she became a benefactress of the University of California: a conservative estimate of the value of her contributions to the university was more than $1.5 million. Her first notable gift (1891) was five annual scholarships for needy, worthy young women "of noble character and high aims"; she pointedly specified that the recipients need not be the top performers on the entrance examination. These were the first undergraduate scholarships the university awarded. Many of the recipients became teachers, the only paid job she herself ever had. But Hearst is best known for the elaborate international architectural competition to choose a comprehensive plan for the university's buildings and grounds, which she funded. Completed in 1899, the competition brought worldwide attention and raised the young University of California out of relative obscurity; the publicity, along with the tents she provided to supplement overcrowded classrooms, stimulated the state legislature in 1897 to double the basis of its tax support of the university. Her gift of the Hearst Mining Building was the first permanent structure implementing the plan for Italian Renaissance buildings and walkways. She had earlier built Hearst Hall, a large assembly and social hall for students. The Greek Theatre, given in her son's name, and the Hearst Memorial Gymnasium for Women were subsequent gifts. She virtually founded the anthropology and anatomy departments, underwriting professors' salaries, graduate research, publications, and archaeological expeditions to Florida, the American Southwest, Mexico, Peru, Italy, Egypt, Greece, and Russia. The collections became the basis of the Lowie Museum of Anthropology (later renamed the Phoebe Apperson Hearst Museum of Anthropology) and of the university's medical department collections in San Francisco, as well as adding to the University of Pennsylvania's archaeological holdings. Especially interested in science, art, and history, she outfitted departmental laboratories and paid or supplemented faculty salaries. She also financed astronomical expeditions and fellowships through the university's Lick Observatory. Phoebe Hearst served as the first and only woman member of the university's Board of Regents from 1897 to 1919.

Women's hopes, ambitions, needs, and unexploited potential were a major focus of Phoebe Hearst's activities. She was first president of the Century Club for women of San Francisco, an organizer of the General Federation of Women's Clubs and its first treasurer. She established the Hearst Domestic Industries, which taught women needlecraft skills by which they could support themselves at the university, furnished their supplies, and purchased their products. She paid the salary of a women's physician so that "coeds" might use the gymnasium and then gave them their first gymnasium and swimming pool. To the university's women students she was a "fairy godmother," taking up residence among them, furnishing the boarding clubs that prompted others to improve the housing of women students generally. By entertaining them and exposing them to fine art, drama, and music, she taught often-raw country girls—as what she herself had once been—how to meet strangers and master the social arts. Although she aided both sexes, Hearst believed that men's needs would be taken care of while women's were ignored. One of her earliest charities was a small homeopathic hospital, which allowed women physicians to practice; she was president of its board. She privately aided Susan B. Anthony's suffrage work in California in the 1890s but came late to public support of woman suffrage, a position consistent with a nineteenth-century ethic of outward womanly deference and utter respectability. Her daily routine showed a woman with great self-discipline, a prodigious capacity for work, patience and organization, who scrupulously studied the worth of the projects she supported. She represents something of a bridge between the older generation of aloof, ladylike philanthropy and that of the modern professional or activist woman. She subscribed to the principle that "the finest gift of God is an indomitable purpose *to do*." Inducted into a public life by the experience of schoolteaching, like so many of her own and subsequent generations of women, her power to do good was enormously expanded by a marriage into wealth. Phoebe Hearst died in Pleasanton, California, ending a notable career in social reform through private philanthropy, organizational efforts, and personal example.

• The Bancroft Library of the University of California houses many of Phoebe Hearst's papers, much of it incoming correspondence. The large Hearst collection includes an uncompleted biography by Adele S. Brooks, "Phoebe Apperson Hearst: A Life and Some Letters," part of which were used in Winifred Black Bonfils, *The Life and Personality of Phoebe Apperson Hearst* (1928). The Bancroft also has *Newsletters* of the Phoebe Apperson Hearst Historical Society of Franklin County, Missouri, and Denise Howe, *Phoebe Apperson Hearst, the Pleasanton Years* (1986). Mrs. Hearst's work on behalf of the University of California is discussed in William Carey Jones, *The Illustrated History of the University of California* (1901); J. R. K. Kantor, "The Best Friend the University Ever Had," *California Monthly Journal* 1, no. 1 (1969): 4–5; Verne A. Stadtman, *The University of California, 1868–1968* (1970); and Lynn D. Gordon, *Gender and Higher Education in the Progressive Era* (1990). The University Archives, also in the Bancroft Library, hold the Regents' Papers and Academic Senate Files that record her financial contributions and their terms. A full scholarly biography and historical assessment in Alexandra Nickless, "Making Dreams Come True: Phoebe Apperson Hearst and the Female World of Success" (Ph.D. diss., Univ. of California at Davis). On the family, see Judith Robinson, *The Hearsts: An American Dynasty* (1991).

GERALDINE JONÇICH CLIFFORD

HEARST, William Randolph (29 Apr. 1863–14 Aug. 1951), publisher, was born in San Francisco, California, the son of George Hearst, a mine developer and U.S. senator, and Phoebe Apperson. His mother was the sole guardian of cultured Victorianism in the fami-

ly, and she took her only child on two art tours of Europe by the time he was sixteen. The boy became a connoisseur but also a rebel; because of raucous behavior he was asked to leave St. Paul's School and Harvard College, which he attended from 1882 to 1885.

Journalism, which Hearst had sampled while working for the *Harvard Lampoon* and Joseph Pulitzer's *New York World*, was his next opportunity to break conventions. At age twenty-three, he took charge of the *San Francisco Examiner*, a weak paper owned by his father. Senator Hearst, a Democrat, expected little beyond partisan support from the paper; his son was loyal to the party but ambitious to develop a newspaper people would talk about. He made the *Examiner* a commercial success, and in 1895 he challenged Pulitzer with acquisition of the *New York Morning Journal*.

Hearst matched any journalist of his time in frenetic energy and dedication, but his distinctive contribution to the field was money. His was the first fortune of the industrial era to be reinvested in the sale of information and entertainment. The Ontario, Homestake, and Anaconda mines that his father had developed funded the production of words and pictures for a vast public. Hearst spent more than $8 million of family money in his first decade of newspaper work, and he was the first publisher to become famous for lavish spending to hire journalists. Hearst lured the entire staff of Pulitzer's Sunday *New York World*, for example, by more than doubling their salaries. In 1898 the publisher paid one editor, Arthur Brisbane, nearly twice as much in salary as the recent sale price of the *New York Times*. Hearst was even more generous in rewarding himself, especially with art. He was an indefatigable collector who called dealers at all hours to buy more. Phoebe Hearst wrote a check for $10,000 every month for her son's household until her death in 1919. By the time Hearst turned fifty he owned seven dailies, five magazines, two news services, and a film company. He ran newspapers on both coasts that spanned the century, as did the eclectic Hearst magazines, *Cosmopolitan*, *Good Housekeeping*, *Harper's Bazaar*, and *Motor Boating*.

Hearst newspapers reached across class and ethnic lines in the polyglot cities. Their insistent headlines and abundant pictures beckoned people just learning English, and the folklore of many lands echoed through the advice to the lovelorn and sentimental stories in these papers. Developments in science and the arts were passed on to readers, as were the startling doings of celebrities. An editor at the *Examiner* said that the Hearst organization was after the "gee-whiz emotion." The papers probably achieved this even for many nonreaders who watched Hearst court the public by delivering coal, sweaters, and food to poor neighborhoods. Civic fetes staged by the publisher, invariably with fireworks, boosted public spirit and circulation. By the end of 1896 the circus antics of the press were called "yellow journalism" after the Yellow Kid cartoon figure created by Richard Outcault and used in circulation drives by both Hearst and his previous employer Pulitzer.

"The force of the newspaper is the greatest force in civilization," Hearst said in a signed editorial in 1898. "Under republican government, newspapers form and express public opinion. They suggest and control legislation. They declare wars." Cultural politics complemented this imperial ambition. He favored the Irish and Germans, condemned British influence, and encouraged fear of Asian immigration, a legacy of his California upbringing. Hearst papers championed the Cuban rebels and took credit for the U.S. declaration of war against Spain in 1898. The *Journal* was a match for political parties and statesmen in marshaling public opinion. Hearst employees collected 10,000 signatures in five days to protest Spanish treatment of the rebel Evangelina Cosio y Cisneros. Her jailbreak in Cuba was financed by Hearst, and he brought her to the United States under the fiction "the Cuban Joan of Arc." The publisher also played the part of a head of state. Hearst ordered one reporter to present a diamond-studded sword to a Cuban rebel leader and sent another journalist, James Creelman, to scuttle a ship in the Suez Canal to stop the Spanish fleet. Hearst waded ashore in Cuba to accept the surrender of Spaniards. More than a million copies of the *Journal* were sold each day at the height of the crisis.

Journalism was intended to be the springboard for Hearst's political career. He was in excellent standing with the American Left before World War I. His early magazines and newspapers favored labor unions, progressive taxation, and municipal ownership of utilities, and he was a leading opponent of businesses seeking government favors, such as the Southern Pacific Railroad. He also waged war on trusts that had squeezed out competition. The front page of many a Hearst paper (as well as *Cosmopolitan* magazine covers) arraigned an American plutocracy and portrayed these political enemies as corpulent beasts (a specialty of the cartoonists Frederick Opper and Homer Davenport). In 1903 the trade unions of Los Angeles asked Hearst to begin a paper there so that workers would have a voice. Labor held a parade when the *Los Angeles Examiner* began publication. The populist Tom Watson, the socialist Upton Sinclair, and the labor lawyer Clarence Darrow similarly counted on Hearst to help save the plain people. Hearst supported William Jennings Bryan for president in 1896 and 1900 at a time when many northern Democrats had abandoned him. No other Democrat began the new century with brighter prospects.

Hearst headed the National Association of Democratic Clubs in 1900 and with the aid of his papers doubled the membership in a few months. In 1904 he finished second in the voting for the presidential nomination at the Democratic National Convention. This was the closest he came to his dream of living in the White House. Critics combed his newspapers to demonstrate that he was too radical to be trusted with power. "If bad institutions and bad men can be got rid of only by killing, then the killing must be done," the

Evening Journal said (10 Apr. 1901), in welcome of the second term of a Republican president, and on 4 February 1900 Hearst papers printed a poem by Ambrose Bierce that joked about the death of William McKinley. Hearst was blamed when McKinley was assassinated by an anarchist in 1901.

But Hearst's political career was stalled by more than rhetoric. He refused to choose between party loyalty and insurgency and pursued both, displaying neither the steady habits of the regular nor the charisma of the rebel. He worked with the Tammany machine of New York City and served two terms in the U.S. House of Representatives (1903–1907). In Washington he introduced progressive legislation but set records for absenteeism; he stayed clear of the "chewed wind" of floor debate and was present for only two of one hundred and seventy roll calls in the Fifty-eighth Congress. He missed meetings of his favorite committee, Labor, for ten months in a row in the Fifty-ninth Congress.

In addition to running his papers, Congressman Hearst ran for mayor and governor in New York. He lost narrowly both times, first running against and then with the Tammany organization. He used his newspapers to create a national constituency for the Independence League in 1907, but this had no impact in the following election year. Hearst ran again and lost the New York mayoralty on the Civil Alliance ticket in 1909. He was an unsuccessful candidate for lieutenant governor in a third party in the New York election of 1910. In the next year he resumed work in the Democratic party. Too much the maverick and too much the pol, Hearst always made enough enemies to lose.

Hearst's belief that he had the common touch was not an illusion. He had genuine feeling for the pleasures and fears of the urban working class, and in the early years he guided his editors skillfully. He loved comic strips and vaudeville. He was thrilled by the crime stories his papers featured. "When peace brooded over the city and nobody was being robbed or murdered," a colleague noted, "he would come down to the office with despondence written on his face." Hearst's confidence in himself as an art connoisseur was also well founded. Whether it was paintings, sculpture, textiles, ceramics, or architecture, he was capable of fine judgments. Working with his architect, Julia Morgan, Hearst appointed his huge La Casa Grande estate at San Simeon with exquisite rooms and furnishings, including his twenty-foot-square bedroom, large enough to accommodate the Spanish Gothic ceiling he loved.

Hearst was an imposing 6′2″ tall. He liked being called "Chief" by top associates. No journalist called him by his first name, and those who worked for him feared his harsh judgments. He moved decisively in hiring and firing, buying and selling. A Hearst editor was doing well if he earned the title "werewolf," Walter Howey, for example, and the papers featured columnists such as Bierce, Westbrook Pegler, and Walter Winchell, who eviscerated their prey. Hearst championed stories based on stolen documents, which he used in a drawn-out torture of opponents. Thus he went after the Standard Oil Company with the John D. Archbold letters of 1905–1912 and attacked the Plutarco Elías Calles government with alleged proofs of Mexican subversion in 1926–1927. The Chief's methods in these exposés were always careless and sometimes fraudulent. Similarly, favorable reviews of entertainment in the Hearst press were frequently sold for advertising patronage or traded for cooperation. For all the bullying in his papers, however, the publisher was shy in face-to-face communication and often considerate of people who served him. He was usually polite and mild-mannered (he drank little and did not smoke), and his dress was a racy counterpoint (in San Francisco he carried a cane that whistled as he walked). He dressed formally in middle age in the pursuit of political office, but reverted to daring outfits when he stopped courting voters. Davenport sketched him, at age thirty-three, as an imp. Hearst had a high-pitched voice that was sometimes mistaken for a woman's. Thus, the Victorian antimony of the rowdy and the dandy came to life in his career.

Hearst's critics charged that he was disloyal to his country because of the radicalism of his newspapers at the turn of the century and his respect for Germany in the first years of World War I. His papers were banned in many communities and he was hanged in effigy on both coasts. Characteristically, he reacted with bellicose patriotism during these challenges, adding "American" to the mastheads and "Americanism" to editorial boasts. Foreign issues often did put him off balance. His papers praised the Bolshevik revolution in Russia and urged the United States to keep hands off the new soviet state. He was no more influential at this time than he was with strident anticommunist crusades in the 1930s. Hearst was called a fascist by the Left in this decade, in part because of his association with Adolf Hitler and Benito Mussolini. But although Hearst ran columns by the Nazi hierarchy and greatly admired Mussolini, he was not a fascist. At their only meeting in 1934, the publisher apparently tried to dissuade Hitler from anti-Semitism. His early respect for the Italian leader was common among Americans across the political spectrum. Hearst was a leading opponent of intervention in both World Wars but cared little about the ideologies of the countries the United States was preparing to fight.

Hearst was deeply engaged on the subject of Japan. Beginning in the 1890s, his papers warned of a Japanese military challenge. Readers frequently were told that Japan was planning to invade Mexico (where Hearst owned the nearly million-acre Babicora ranch) to attack the United States from the south. After the bombing of Pearl Harbor in 1941 he moved his household from San Simeon on the coast to his Wyntoon estate near Mount Shasta to be safe from Japanese attack. The epithet "Jap" remained a common usage in the *San Francisco Examiner* during Hearst's lifetime.

On the home front in the interwar years, all of Hearst's efforts were quixotic. He quarreled with his fellow Democrat, Governor Alfred E. Smith, and was eclipsed by this rising New York politician. Hearst's support of Franklin Roosevelt in 1932, both at the convention and in the campaign, was his last important move in electoral politics. *Gabriel over the White House*, produced by Hearst's Cosmopolitan Pictures and released as Roosevelt took office, suggested that radical measures were warranted. But Hearst fought the New Deal after 1935 as a "Raw Deal," the phrase he ordered his editors to use. The publisher was particularly concerned with his rising tax bill and new unions in his work force. The Hearst press demonstrated its impotence by supporting losers for president—Alfred M. Landon in 1936, Wendell L. Willkie in 1940, and Thomas E. Dewey in 1944 and 1948.

Hearst's romantic life was conducted with unusual openness and, under the circumstances, felicity. He kept a mistress, Tessie Powers, at Harvard and brought her to live with him in the San Francisco Bay Area without alienating his parents. He then married Millicent Willson, a dancer, in 1903. They had five sons, and she remained Mrs. William Randolph Hearst of New York until her death in 1974, although for nearly three decades Hearst lived with the actress Marion Davies in California. (In spite of their separate lives, the Hearsts always exchanged anniversary gifts.) Hearst used his papers to advance Davies's film career and took a hand in the production of her work. They entertained lavishly at San Simeon from 1926 until World War II. She was also a business partner who used her independent wealth to help him during the Great Depression, and she was with him when he died in Beverly Hills, after suffering crippling illness for four years.

San Simeon and the 110-room beach house that Hearst built for Davies in Santa Monica gave hints of the future alliance between political leaders and entertainers. Here the film colony met former President Calvin Coolidge and future British Prime Minister Winston Churchill. In 1934 Hearst worked with studio heads to help defeat the socialist author Upton Sinclair, who was the Democratic candidate for governor of California. Younger people in Hearst's circle, such as Joseph P. Kennedy, glimpsed how celebrities could be marshaled in a political campaign. (Marion Davies made her mansion available to John F. Kennedy when he came to Los Angeles to win the Democratic nomination for president in 1960.)

Hearst failed as an entrepreneur and for the last three decades of his life his organization only prospered when it was taken over by professional managers. The publisher entered the 1920s with an inheritance conservatively valued at $20 million only to begin a ruinous overexpansion. In Washington, for example, he refused to sell either of his money-losing dailies. He went broke setting records for market share, with 14 percent of all daily circulation in 1933 and nearly a quarter of the Sunday papers sold in 1935. In 1937, more than $125 million in debt, he lost control of his holdings. Clarence John Shearn of Chase National Bank began getting rid of the unprofitable media and real estate. Hearst's reckless spending on art, another source of his problem, was stopped. He agreed to sell two-thirds of his art collection and stopped construction on San Simeon. Hearst collections that had not reached California were offered to the public. For several years, the sale of his artworks in a New York department store filled more floor space than Hearst had built at La Casa Grande. Of the forty-two papers that he had bought or established, only seventeen remained by 1940.

Hearst lost touch with blue-collar readers when he reversed himself on labor and tax issues. He was an ogre to writers on the Left, who viewed him as a traitor. "Even school boys and girls by the thousands now scorn his aged image and cankered heart," the historian Charles A. Beard wrote in 1936. Polls at this time showed that Hearst newspapers were held in contempt by the working press because of their lack of integrity. Hearst editors were given long lists of people who were always to be praised and others who had to be ignored or condemned. Many news stories simply boosted the Chief's causes. During the debate on neutrality in the fall of 1939, for example, Hearst papers gave lavish coverage to the National Legion of Mothers of America, "grimly determined to fight any attempt to send their sons to fight on foreign soil." This group had been organized by his newspapers.

At the end of his life, Hearst still headed the largest news conglomerate in America with sixteen dailies, two Sunday-only papers, and nine magazines. He controlled 10 percent of daily circulation after World War II, a greater share than any newspaper group managed for forty years after his death. Hearst's power in the field was a measure of the capital he had brought to media in the first place and the professional management that was given more power in the 1930s. But after he turned fifty, his business acumen and his ability to inspire journalists had withered.

The 1941 film *Citizen Kane* was a masterful and mischievous summing up of the publisher's life. Orson Welles and Herman Mankiewicz, authors of the screenplay, offered a melodramatic view of power that was in keeping with the "gee-whiz emotions" of the Hearst press. The publisher Kane in the movie was the victim of psychological trauma and suffered anguish for his abuses of power. Hearst had neither problem. The film showed that a master of the press had flirted with radicalism, scoffed at business conventions, and failed as a leader; and in this it captured the Hearst persona precisely.

• The papers of Hearst, his mother, and several important newspaper colleagues are in the Bancroft Library at the University of California, Berkeley, and contain material that was not available for W. A. Swanberg's *Citizen Hearst* (1961), which is the best biography and has a comprehensive bibliography. However, Judith Robinson, *The Hearsts: An American Dynasty* (1991), makes use of these family documents through World War I, which is also the stopping point for Roy Everett Littlefield III, *William Randolph Hearst: His Role in American Progressivism* (1980), who used correspondence in the *New York Journal-American* morgue at the University of Texas, Austin, and in the Joseph Arthur Moore Collection at the Library of Congress. Rodney P. Carlisle, *Hearst and the New Deal: The Progressive as Reactionary* (1979), uses the Bancroft collections to go beyond earlier biographers. See also Edmond D. Coblentz, ed., *William Randolph Hearst, a Portrait in His Own Words* (1952). Lincoln Steffens, "Hearst, the Man of Mystery," *American Magazine*, Nov. 1906, pp. 1–22, is the most penetrating interview. A. J. Liebling's acidic essays in *The Press* (1975) are an important statement of criticism by reporters. James F. O'Donnell, *100 Years of Making Communications History: The Story of the Hearst Corporation* (1987), is the company's view of its founder. The most valuable books from those close to the man are Cora B. Older, *William Randolph Hearst, American* (1936); Marion Davies, *The Times We Had* (1975); and William Randolph Hearst, Jr., with Jack Casserly, *The Hearsts: Father and Son* (1991). The Hearst San Simeon State Historical Monument is open to the public and is furnished as its owner left it; see Thomas R. Aidala, *Hearst Castle, San Simeon* (1981), and Nancy E. Loe, *Hearst Castle: The Official Pictorial Guide* (1991). On the Hollywood vision of the publisher see Pauline Kael, *The Citizen Kane Book* (1971). An obituary is in the *New York Times*, 15 Aug. 1951.

THOMAS C. LEONARD

HEARST, William Randolph, Jr. (27 Jan. 1908–14 May 1993), journalist and newspaper publisher, was born in New York City, the son of William Randolph Hearst, a newspaper magnate, and Millicent Willson, a chorus girl. A mediocre student, Hearst attended private schools on the East and West coasts, eventually settling at the Hitchcock Military Academy in San Rafael, California. Hating both discipline and study, Hearst attended the University of California, Berkeley, in 1925. As a liberal arts major he failed to find a focus and left the college halfway through his sophomore year without a degree.

Not surprisingly, Hearst developed an early fascination with the newspaper industry, from the printing presses to the copy room. From age seventeen he spent his summer vacations as a "fly-boy" in the press room of *The Mirror*, a New York daily tabloid owned by his father. Pulling fresh newspapers from the rolling presses, Hearst gained a grassroots insight into the functioning of the family empire. In 1928 he married Alma Walker, a student at Berkeley, against the wishes of his father. They had no children.

Seduced by the romance of journalism, Hearst was given a position as a reporter on *The American*, one of the first papers founded by the elder Hearst. Starting as a cub reporter on the city beat, he was soon transferred to the police rounds, which offered a more exciting potential for sensational scoops. True to form, he managed to provide *The American* with coverage of the Lindbergh baby kidnapping in 1932, the same year he divorced his wife.

Hearst's career as a reporter continued without great distinction until he was removed from news coverage altogether and slotted into the management structure of his father's empire. By 1931, at the age of twenty-three, Hearst was made titular president of *The American* without protest. Because of his youth and lack of business savvy, Hearst was essentially a figurehead executive within the corporation and was continually bypassed by his father and other executives. In 1933 Hearst married his second wife, Lorelle McCarver, in Palm Beach, Florida. The marriage produced no children.

The Great Depression played havoc with many of the Hearst investments and newspaper holdings, eventually forcing a series of layoffs and consolidations within the corporation. Young Hearst was moved around the organization in the retrenchment process and was used as a controlling force at both company and board levels while being given the increasingly arduous tasks the elder Hearst sloughed off. In 1936 Hearst was promoted again and named as the publisher of *The American*, a position that would serve as an effective bridge for a merger with the *New York Journal* in 1937. Hearst would control the *Journal-American* until 1960.

Despite being relegated to an executive position, Hearst still continued his passionate interest in reporting, especially in the arena of international relations. After the outbreak of World War II, he became a foreign correspondent to the *Journal-American* and other family newspapers, following the progress of the Allies through Italy and most of Europe after D-Day. As the sole Hearst representative in Europe, he was able to carve out a niche for himself and attain a certain independence of spirit that was impossible under his father's watchful eye.

After the war, Hearst was also made publisher of two Sunday supplements, the *American Weekly* and *Puck—The Comic Weekly*, while maintaining his position at the *Journal-American*. Having divorced his wife in 1947, he married Austine McDonnell, the author of a society gossip column, in July 1948. They had two children.

By the 1950s Hearst took over where his father left off and developed a blend of hysterical hyperbole and fervent anticommunism that was to alienate many readers. In promoting a vicious form of Red-baiting, Hearst allowed columnists like Walter Winchell and Louella Parsons free rein to libel and smear suspected communists. Hearst was also an emphatic supporter of Senator Joseph McCarthy and his campaign and actively aided his witch-hunts by providing suspect lists of fellow-travelers and enemies of the Hearst empire.

Despite Hearst's enthusiastic anticommunism, he still maintained an internationalist outlook and in 1955 pulled off a reporting coup: within a period of two weeks he managed to interview not only the four highest-ranking officials in the Soviet Union (including Nikita Khrushchev) but also had meetings with Winston Churchill and Dwight D. Eisenhower. In the same year Hearst took over partial voting control of the family corporation and was promoted to the position of editor in chief, a role formerly filled by Hearst, Sr., who had died in 1951. As commentators pointed out, to "Hearst staffers, this was recognition of what has long been apparent: the emergence of Bill Hearst . . . as the organization's most powerful editorial figure" (Winkler, p. 298).

At the age of forty-six Hearst was heir apparent to the newspaper empire, and in 1956 he put an end to the old rivalry between the Hearst interests and those of Joseph Pulitzer: ironically, Hearst won the Pulitzer Prize for international reporting. His interviews with Soviet leaders landed him the award, which he shared with Frank Conniff and Bob Considine, by unanimous decision. His adventures were later coauthored with Conniff and Considine in *Ask Me Anything: Our Adventures with Khrushchev* (1960).

Hearst finally relinquished his place at the *Journal-American* in 1960, when he became the chairman of the board of the Hearst Corporation, a position he held until 1973. Generally, the Hearst family gained power and increased its access to corporate profits throughout the 1960s and continued to buy and sell several daily and weekly newspapers well into the 1980s. Hearst continued at the helm until his death in New York City.

William Randolph Hearst, Jr., never attained the kind of reach and power that belonged to his father, and he certainly failed to create the same levels of anger and animosity stirred up by the advent of earlier "yellow journalism." Despite being more professionally focused than his father, Hearst essentially remained a corporate pawn, and the real power belonged to appointees outside of the family. Nevertheless, the Hearst family continued to control more than fifteen newspapers and channeled resources into the development of the more profitable magazine chain and mass-communications outlets. Hearst's death brought to a close an extraordinary family saga that had shaped, controlled, and directed American newspaper journalism for more than a century.

• The largest collections of Hearst's letters and manuscripts are at the Bancroft Library, University of California, Berkeley, and the Henry E. Huntington Library, San Marino, Calif. General overviews of the Hearst family can be found in W. A. Swanberg, *Citizen Hearst: A Biography of William Randolph Hearst* (1961), and Judith Robinson, *The Hearsts: An American Dynasty* (1991). For a broader understanding of the Hearsts in politics see Ian Mugridge, *The View from Xanadu: William Randolph Hearst and United States Foreign Policy* (1995). See also Ferdinand Lundberg, *Imperial Hearst: A Social Biography* (1936; repr. 1970); John K. Winkler, *William Randolph Hearst: A New Appraisal* (1955); William Randolph Hearst, Jr., *The Hearsts, Father and Son* (1991); and Lindsay Chaney and Michael Cieply, *The Hearsts: Family and Empire—The Later Years* (1981). Obituaries are in the *New York Times*, 16 May 1993, and in *Newsweek* and *Time*, 24 May 1993.

PAUL HANSOM

HEATH, Fred Harvey (25 Feb. 1883–26 Jan. 1952), chemist, was born in Warner, New Hampshire, the son of Benjamin Franklin Heath and Julia Augusta Wadleigh, occupations unknown. At the New Hampshire College (now the University of New Hampshire), Heath's interest in rarer elements was aroused by Charles L. Parsons, a specialist on beryllium, and Charles James, a world-renowned authority on the rare earths (lanthanides), a sorely neglected field at the time. After receiving a B.S. in 1905, Heath began graduate work in analytical chemistry under Frank A. Gooch, inventor of the perforated Gooch filtering crucible, at Yale University. Heath worked as an assistant from 1906 to 1909 and received his Ph.D. in 1909. During the summer of 1909 he studied at the University of Marburg in Germany.

Heath was an instructor of theoretical chemistry at the Massachusetts Institute of Technology in 1909–1910, of general and analytical chemistry at the Case School of Applied Science in 1910–1911, and of analytical and physical chemistry at the Wesleyan University of Connecticut in 1911–1912. He then became assistant professor of general and analytical chemistry at the University of North Dakota (1912–1914) and from 1916 to 1923 served as an assistant professor of chemistry at the University of Washington (Seattle). During the summers of 1914 to 1916 he carried out analytical research on natural waters at the North Dakota Biological Station at Devil's Lake. He became assistant professor of chemistry at the University of Florida in 1923 and professor in charge of its general chemistry program in 1925, a post he held until his death.

In 1911 Heath married Winnifred A. Grant, with whom he had his only child. After his wife's death in 1918, he married in 1921 Ida M. Erickson, who died in 1928. In 1932 he married Errah Shannon Schindler. He was the author of *Laboratory Manual of Quantitative Analysis* (1910; rev. ed. 1921–1922); *Photographic Chemistry* (1916); *Laboratory Manual of General Chemistry*, with W. H. Beisler (1926; rev. ed. 1934); and *General Chemistry Text Book*, with others (1926; rev. ed. 1927).

Heath carried out research on the iodometric determination of copper (the subject of his doctoral dissertation in 1907), of arsenic and antimony in 1908, and of hydrogen sulfide in natural waters in 1923. A prominent authority on war gases, he was a major in the Chemical Warfare Service Reserves and was chemical warfare gas consultant for the Florida State Defense Council during World War II. He insisted that war gases were more humane than other weapons and emphasized the impossibility of prohibiting chemical warfare by legislation. Together with Waldo L. Semon, he synthesized for the first time symmetrical tetrachlorodiethyl selenide, the selenium analogue of mustard gas, in 1918.

Heath was an authority in several fields, including geology, photography, astronomy, sponges, phosphorescent materials, fluoroborates, the rare earths, platinum ores, secret and spy inks, determination of hydrogen sulfide in waters, and new analytical uses of salts of vanadium, chromium, and molybdenum. He undertook research for the U.S. Submarine Base at Key West, Florida, and was a consultant to many industrial firms. Long active in the American Chemical Society, he was chairman of the Puget Sound Section; secretary, alternate councillor, and chairman of the Florida Section; and a member of the Division of

Chemical Education's Committee on Tests and Examinations. Despite his varied research activities, his major interest lay in chemical education; he developed several analytical procedures for use in the undergraduate laboratory.

At the University of Florida campus, Heath's name was associated with the discovery of element 43. While at the University of Washington, between 1917 and 1923, Heath and electrical engineer J. D. Ross were reported to have successfully prepared compounds of a previously unknown element from ores they had received from British Columbia. They thought it to be element number 43, the elusive eka-manganese, whose existence had been predicted by Russian chemist Dmitri Ivanovich Mendeleev as early as 1872. Heath and Ross submitted their findings to the *Journal of the American Chemical Society*. The journal's editor, Arthur B. Lamb, requested proof of their discovery in the form of X-ray spectra. Because the necessary X-ray equipment was unavailable, their results were never published.

When Heath went to Florida, he began work on an emission spectrograph, but in June 1925, before he could produce the required information, Walther Noddack and Ida Tacke of the Physico-Technical Testing Office in Berlin, together with Otto Berg of the Werner-Siemens Laboratory, announced their discovery of elements 43 and 75, which they named masurium and rhenium, respectively. Despite extensive investigation, the Germans' discovery of element 43 was never confirmed and has not been accepted. Their discovery of rhenium, however, was recognized.

Because only about one-billionth gram of element 43 was isolated from 5,300 grams of Congo pitchblende by Kenna and Kuroda in 1961 and because Heath and Ross had isolated salts in weighable quantities, it is not likely that the element that Heath and Ross reported was technetium. This element might, however, have been rhenium, in which case their discovery would have antedated that of Noddack, Tacke, and Berg. On the other hand, because the chemical literature contains many unsubstantiated claims to the discovery of the long-sought element 43, their substance might have been a mixture of elements. Heath died in Gainesville, Florida.

• There is no known collection of Heath's papers. Heath and Semon's report of the discovery of selenium mustard gas is found in the *Journal of Industrial and Engineering Chemistry* 12 (1920): 1100–1101. Short accounts of Heath's life and work are in George B. Kauffman, *Quarterly Journal of the Florida Academy of Sciences* 26, no. 1 (1963): 1–3, and in *American Chemists and Chemical Engineers*, ed. Wyndham D. Miles (1976), pp. 207–8. An obituary is in the *New York Times*, 28 Jan. 1952.

GEORGE B. KAUFFMAN

HEATH, James Ewell (8 July 1792–28 June 1862), author and politician, was born in Virginia, probably in Northumberland County, the son of John Heath, first president of Phi Beta Kappa, and Sarah Ewell. Little is known about his early life. During 1814–1817 Heath represented Prince William County in the Virginia General Assembly, in his third term serving as a member of the Privy Council. In 1819 he became state auditor, a post he held for thirty years. From 1850 to 1853, he served as commissioner of pensions in President Millard Fillmore's administration. A founding member of the Virginia Historical and Philosophical Society and its first recording secretary, Heath was active in Virginia public life, befriending religious and educational causes. His first wife was his cousin Fannie Weems, daughter of Mason Locke Weems, known as Parson Weems, author of *The Life and Memorable Actions of George Washington*; his second wife was Elizabeth Ann Macon, daughter of Colonel William Hartwell Macon of Virginia, with whom he had two children.

Heath's literary endeavors were curtailed by his public responsibilities, but he is known to students of American literature as the author of a historical novel, *Edge-Hill; or, The Family of the Fitzroyals* (1828) and the play, *Whigs and Democrats; or, Love of No Politics* (published 1839; produced 1844). These works reveal his knowledge of Virginia history and traditions and, in the case of *Edge-Hill*, his deep attachment to the state. Set in Virginia during 1781, *Edge-Hill*, which portrays the historical figures Benedict Arnold, Banastre Tarleton, and the Marquis de Lafayette, depicts events leading up to Cornwallis's surrender at Yorktown. The book is especially important as an almost entirely neglected example of the plantation novel, anticipating such later works in the field as John Pendleton Kennedy's *Swallow Barn* (1832) and also as an early version of what has come to be called the "Virginia novel." In the opening pages of *Edge-Hill*, Heath stresses the splendor, the maturity, and the relative antiquity of Virginia plantation culture as represented by the mansion that gives the book its title. The "large commodious brick" estate, he remarks, "overlooked a spacious lawn, which was shaded by some of the finest forest trees of lower Virginia"; its "green clover paddocks, and fields of early wheat and corn, announced the owner's opulence, and presented a refreshing picture of rural beauty." Yet for all its freshness, it "seemed mellowed by the hand of time," with its "low gothic windows, and mouldered aspects of the walls" recalling the "distant period when the mansion . . . was first erected" (vol. 1, pp. 6–7).

Also noteworthy in *Edge-Hill* are Heath's lively portraits of social classes and his conviction that natural merit matters more than aristocratic lineage. In his words, no "illustrious line of kindred . . . ever existed, which could not be traced to some ancient and simple origin, undistinguishable from the common mass" (vol. 2, p. 18). Such convictions are reflected in the narrative when the patrician Charles, heir to Edge-Hill and the Fitzroyal fortune, defeats his villainous cousin Monteagle in their rivalry for the orphan Ruth Elmore, of modest birth but of educated, refined sensitivities. *Edge-Hill* was dramatized in 1829 and revived

in 1831, when such sentiments as those quoted above were praised by the press.

Heath's spirited comedy *Whigs and Democrats*, which reflects the influence of eighteenth-century British literature, contrasts political expediency with genuine ethics, satirizes the inconstancy of the electorate, and like *Edge-Hill* reflects Heath's belief in merit rather than aristocracy as the true criterion of worth. The politician General Fairweather, who instructs his son to flatter "men's humors, prejudices, and delusions" when "any advantage is to be gained," curries favor with the tavern keeper Major Roundtree, who controls the votes of such tellingly-named characters as Slang, Rowdie, and Bangall. In return for supporting Fairweather, Roundtree expects to take "a bite at the public crib" of political patronage. But he and his followers turn against the General when Fairweather denounces Roundtree's educated daughter Catharine as "the vulgar progeny of a tavern-keeper,—a low pothouse politician,—a clownish Major of Militia." Under the tutelage of his friend Worthington, Fairweather eventually renounces "the phantom of popular favor," admits his errors in flattering "the passions and follies of the multitude," and after his political defeat dedicates himself to the "enjoyment of domestic peace."

An ardent southerner, Heath gave generously of his time in writing for and helping to edit the *Southern Literary Messenger* (1834–1864) under its founder, his friend Thomas W. White. In the opening essay "Southern Literature" in volume one of the *Messenger*, Heath disparages the South's literary vassalage to the North and argues vigorously for a journal devoted to southern "letters and mental improvement." As adviser to White, Heath corresponded with Edgar Allan Poe when Poe submitted "The Fall of the House of Usher" to the *Messenger*, and though like White, Heath was lukewarm toward the narrative, he praised Poe's intellectual powers, especially in criticism.

One of the *Messenger*'s editors, Benjamin Blake Minor, described Heath as "a gentleman of literary culture and a pleasing and graceful writer." Such well-known antebellum authors as Poe and William Gilmore Simms commended Heath's writing. For the student of American literature and history, Heath's importance lies in his contributions to the emerging American novel, his dedication to the South, and his service to his native state. He died in Virginia.

• Information about Heath's life and writing may be found in Horace Edwin Hayden, *Virginia Genealogies* (1891); Benjamin Blake Minor, *The Southern Literary Messenger, 1834–1864* (1905); George Edward Woodberry, *The Life of Edgar Allan Poe, Personal and Literary* (2 vols., 1909); Richard Beale Davis, *Intellectual Life in Jefferson's Virginia, 1790–1830* (1964); and Davis, "The Virginia Novel Before *Swallow Barn*," in *Literature and Society in Early Virginia, 1608–1840*, ed. Davis (1973).

MARY ANN WIMSATT

HEATH, William (13 Mar. 1737–24 Jan. 1814), revolutionary war general, was born in Roxbury, Massachusetts, the son of Samuel Heath and Elizabeth Payson, farmers. Heath, as he himself said, "was brought up a farmer" and was educated at home and probably also at a town school in Roxbury. There is no indication that his formal education extended much beyond the elementary level. In 1759 he married Sarah Lockwood of Cambridge, Massachusetts; they had five children.

Heath took an early interest in military drill and immersed himself in reading military treatises. He joined the Roxbury militia as a drummer and rose to lieutenant. Denied a captaincy he resigned, and in 1765 he joined the Ancient and Honorable Artillery Company of Boston, which he eventually commanded. Heath served in the Massachusetts legislature in 1761 and from 1771 to 1774. In 1770 he published several essays in a Boston newspaper under the title *A Military Countryman*, which discussed military discipline and the use of arms. Heath was made a colonel of the Suffolk County militia in 1774. Declaring firmly for the patriot movement, Heath sat in the Massachusetts Provincial Congress (1774–1775) and was named to its committees of correspondence and of safety. The Provincial Congress commissioned him one of five brigadier generals of the militia on 9 February 1775.

Just after the fighting at Lexington and Concord, 19 April 1775, Heath was the only general to arrive to take charge of the American troops as they harassed the retreating British force. At Cambridge, Heath commanded the militia in making defense preparations until, after a few days, General Artemas Ward assumed the supreme command. On 20 June 1775 Heath was appointed a major general in the Massachusetts militia, and on 22 June 1775 he received a commission from the Congress as a brigadier general in the Continental army. During the battle of Bunker Hill, Heath and his troops were kept in reserve at Roxbury; for the remainder of the siege of Boston he had charge of further defense preparations on Charlestown Heights. With the British evacuation of Boston in March 1776, Heath, under orders from George Washington, took his brigade to New York City. Being stationed at the northern tip of Manhattan Island, he avoided the battles of Long Island, Harlem Heights, and White Plains. On 9 August 1776 Congress named him a major general in the Continental army. Heath was given command of the third division for the defense of the Hudson Highlands, along the lower Hudson River above Harlem.

After the battle of Trenton, Washington hoped to attack the British at Brunswick, New Jersey. He ordered Heath to attack the British at their fort, which the Americans called Fort Independence, on Valentine's Hill, just north of Spuyten Duyvil Creek, which separates Yonkers from Manhattan. Washington expected such an engagement to draw British troops out of New Jersey. Heath, with three divisions, almost all militia, moved close to the fort, and called on the garrison to surrender. His artillery was ineffective. After several small skirmishes, Heath, expecting a snowstorm, had his army retreat on 29 January 1777. The decision elicited derision from both the British and the Americans. Although not publicly rebuking Heath,

Washington, in a private letter, greatly reprimanded him: "Your conduct is censured . . . as being fraught with too much caution by which the Army has been disappointed, and in some degree disgraced. Your summons, as you did not attempt to fulfill your threats, was not only idle but farcical." Thereafter, Washington kept Heath in positions not likely to be involved in battle.

Heath had charge of the Convention army (prisoners of war from the battle of Saratoga) in Massachusetts until these troops were sent to Virginia in 1778. From 1777 to 11 June 1779 Heath commanded the eastern district (Boston) and then joined Washington's army on the Hudson, having command of the Highlands area. Congress offered him membership on the Board of War, which, consisting of two congressmen and three nonmembers of Congress, reported to Congress on military matters and set the agenda for congressional enactments affecting the army. Heath declined, preferring to remain on active army duty. Except for the period of 16 June–1 October 1780, when he assisted in the reception of Rochambeau's army in Rhode Island, Heath continued for the remainder of the war in his Highlands command, with headquarters at West Point (Oct. 1780 to Apr. 1781). On 1 January 1780 he quelled a mutiny among troops of the Massachusetts line. During Washington's Yorktown campaign, Heath commanded the half of the army that stayed behind in the Hudson Highlands. He supervised the furloughing of the Continental army and was the last to hold the routine duty rotation of "general of the day." On 1 July 1783 he left the army and returned to his farm at Roxbury.

Heath was a Federalist leader as a member of the Massachusetts convention that ratified the U.S. Constitution in 1788. He expressed the view in one of his two speeches that "Every thing depends on our union." He served in the state senate (1791–1792) and in 1792 became judge of probate for Norfolk County. Unlike most prominent citizens of Massachusetts, Heath became an ardent Jeffersonian, largely because he feared the reach of the power of taxation by the U.S. government. In 1793 he resigned his membership in the Society of the Cincinnati, considering this hereditary organization of revolutionary war officers too aristocratic. He chaired a Roxbury town meeting (1797–1798), which drew up a petition to Congress calling for prevention of the arming of American merchant vessels because it would be supported by federal property taxes. Heath ran for Congress in 1798. A Boston newspaper, the *Centinel*, which supported his opponent, Harrison Gray Otis, referred to Heath as "the ridiculous, despicable, weak-minded, weakhearted Jacobin, commonly distinguished by the appellation of the *Hero of Fort Independence*." Otis won easily, though Heath carried rural districts by two to one. In 1806 Heath was elected lieutenant governor but refused to serve. He opposed war with Great Britain in 1812 as "unwise and unpopular."

Heath was considered a solid but certainly not brilliant officer. His greatest ability lay in the area of logistics. He worked hard to obtain food supplies, and he was considered an officer who cared for his men. In his memoirs he described himself as being "of middling stature, light complexion, very corpulent, and bald headed." Heath died in the home where he had been born, the last surviving major general of the revolutionary war.

• A large collection of Heath papers is found at the Massachusetts Historical Society: correspondence (26 vols.), orderly books (2 vols.), pamphlets (6 vols.), and newspapers (11 vols.), the latter two sets bearing notations by Heath. Correspondence pertaining to the war is in *Collections of the Massachusetts Historical Society*, 5th ser., vol. 4 (1878), which is entirely Washington-Heath letters, and 7th ser., vol. 4 (1904) and vol. 5 (1905). An entry in the *Proceedings of the Massachusetts Historical Society*, vol. 4 (1860), pp. 287–308, has miscellaneous items, including the brief "Journal of Some Occurrences in the Camp at Roxbury." See also Worthington C. Ford, ed., *General Orders Issued by Major-General William Heath When in Command of the Eastern Department* (1890). Heath's recounting of his war experiences is in *Memoirs of Major-General William Heath*, ed. William Abbatt (1798; repr. 1901). For his biography see J. M. Bugbee, *Memorials of the Massachusetts Society of the Cincinnati* (1890), pp. 237–41, and Graham P. Dolan, "Major General William Heath and the First Years of the American Revolution" (Ph.D. diss., Boston Univ., 1966). Douglas S. Freeman, *George Washington*, vols. 3–5 (1951–1952), and Richard Frothingham, *History of the Siege of Boston and the Battles of Lexington, Concord, and Bunker Hill* (1849; rev. 1970), comment on Heath's military career. Mention of Heath's postwar political activities is found in Samuel E. Morison, *Harrison Gray Otis: The Urbane Federalist* (1969), and Samuel B. Harding, *The Contest over the Ratification of the Federal Constitution in the State of Massachusetts* (1896). An obituary is in the Boston *Daily Advertiser*, 26 Jan. 1814.

HARRY M. WARD

HEATHCOTE, Caleb (6 Mar. 1666–1 Mar. 1721), merchant, manor lord, and Anglican activist, was born in Derbyshire, England, the son of Gilbert Heathcote, a trader in hides and iron who served as mayor of Chesterfield, England, and Anne Dickens. While living in England Heathcote became a merchant specializing in trade with New York, where he settled in 1692 after the woman to whom he was betrothed fell in love with his brother Samuel and married him instead.

Heathcote rapidly assumed a position of commanding influence in New York society. He set himself up in New York City as a merchant and as a factor for London traders, establishing a far-flung trading network that encompassed the East and West Indies as well as the mother country. Success in commerce enabled him to branch out as a military contractor for New York's four independent companies of British regulars. While maintaining a house in the provincial capital and continuing his involvement in mercantile life, a quest for gentility led Heathcote in 1696 to move to Westchester County. In that year he used his influence with Governor Benjamin Fletcher to have part of the country chartered as the borough town of Westchester. From then until his death he served as the borough's mayor, and within its limits he established

an extensive estate, replete with various mills and worked by more than a hundred slaves, indentured servants, and tenant farmers. Heathcote's estate became the Manor of Scarsdale in 1702, the beneficiary of the last manorial grant issued by English authority in colonial America. Heathcote's growing economic success and social prestige led to his marriage in 1699 to Martha Smith, the daughter of William Smith, chief justice of the New York Supreme Court. The couple had six children, four daughters and two sons.

Heathcote's economic and social ascent in New York was facilitated by a succession of responsible appointive positions he received from English officials. In 1692, soon after his arrival in the province, Governor Fletcher had appointed him to a seat on the New York Council, an influential post in which he served until his death, except for the period 1698–1702. For those years his appointment was suspended by the earl of Bellomont, who opposed the anti-Leislerian (more Tory-oriented) party with which Heathcote was then aligned. At about the same time Fletcher also made Heathcote colonel of the Westchester County militia, as well as presiding judge of the county's court of sessions, court of common pleas, and prerogative court. At various times between 1695 and 1703 Heathcote also served as New York's collector and receiver general of revenues, and from 1711 to 1713 Governor Robert Hunter appointed him to three successive terms as mayor of New York City. Apparently through the influence of his powerful English Whig brother Gilbert, the imperial administration in 1715 capped Heathcote's career of public service by appointing him surveyor general of customs for the northern department and vice admiralty judge for New York, New Jersey, and Connecticut. Owing to an identical vice admiralty appointment bestowed by Governor Hunter on another political ally in New York, Heathcote never exercised the latter office.

In the recurrent conflict between imperial authority and local autonomy that was at the heart of colonial political life Heathcote was a staunch advocate of the primacy of imperial interests. Imbued with the mercantilist principle that colonies existed for the benefit of the mother country, Heathcote sought in vain at various times after 1700 to win English approval for an imaginative plan to produce naval stores and build light frigates in New York using the labor of local militiamen and English regulars stationed in the colony. Concerned by the danger posed to the English colonies by the French policy of encirclement, Heathcote, who believed that the survival of these provinces required their inhabitants to "believe themselves as they really are to be but one family," proposed in 1715 the convocation of a congress of all colonial governors to coordinate an intercolonial response to the French threat. Heathcote also was apprehensive that the growing quest for power of colonial assemblies was undermining royal authority in America. The following year he suggested to the imperial administration that Parliament should provide an independent revenue for royal officials in the colonies, to free them from their "slavish dependence . . . on the uncertain Humours of assemblys," advice not taken until 1767. Vexed by the widespread evasion of the navigation acts in Connecticut and Rhode Island, he called on imperial officials in 1719 to curtail sharply the charter privileges of those colonies.

Heathcote's support for effective imperial authority in America led him to espouse the cause of Anglican expansion in the colonies. He viewed the religious heterogeneity he had encountered on his arrival in New York as symptomatic of a "rude and heathenish country." Expansion of the Anglican church was necessary, he believed, to strengthen English control over the colonies and rescue Dissenters from serious religious errors. Heathcote realized, however, that in such a pluralistic society the conversion of Dissenters depended on the persuasive powers of Anglican clergy and laymen rather than on the coercive powers of the English state and its agents in America. Accordingly, he strongly supported Anglican proselytizing efforts in New York. At first Heathcote acted in his own right and then, after 1704, as an active member of the Society for the Propagation of the Gospel in Foreign Parts (SPG), the London-based Anglican missionary organization. Under his patronage Anglicans established four churches as well as a day school and a Sunday school in Westchester, and with the support of his imposing presence the SPG established the first Anglican congregation in Puritan Connecticut. Heathcote also insisted that the SPG focus on the Christianization of black and Indian slaves, a policy he courageously supported even after it came under heavy criticism in the wake of a serious slave revolt in New York City in 1712.

After Heathcote's sudden death in New York of a stroke, he was mourned in the Philadelphia *Weekly Mercury* as a "gentleman of rare qualities, excellent temper and virtuous life and conversation."

• Heathcote's surviving papers are in the records of the Society for the Propagation of the Gospel in Foreign Parts, in London, and in Edmund B. O'Callaghan, ed., *Documents Relative to the Colonial History of the State of New York*, vols. 3 and 4 (15 vols., 1856–1887). The standard biography remains Dixon Ryan Fox's delightful *Caleb Heathcote, Gentleman Colonist: The Story of a Career in the Province of New York, 1692–1721* (1926).

EUGENE R. SHERIDAN

HEATON, Hannah Cook (1721–1794), diarist and farm woman, was born in Southampton, Long Island, New York, the daughter of Jonathan Cook, a surgeon, and Temperance Rogers. Little is known of her early life or education. In 1743 she married Theophilus Heaton, Jr., of North Haven, Connecticut. They and their two sons lived on farms in North Haven for the rest of their lives.

In the 1750s Heaton began keeping a spiritual diary that vividly expresses the point of view of an ordinary woman about the better-known persons and events of her day. In the diary, she recalls hearing the preaching of George Whitefield and Gilbert Tennent in 1741 during the Great Awakening, and she describes her conversion experience. For several years thereafter she refused to attend the established church, a violation of the law, for which she was charged, courageously stood trial, and was fined. Eventually she joined with the Wallingford Separates and recorded in her diary the inspirational sermons of leading evangelical ministers, including Ebenezer Frothingham and Eleazar Wheelock. Heaton also recorded her spiritual reflections and religious reading and wrote poetry inspired by piety.

Heaton's diary is also a source of information about her family life, neighbors, and events related to the American Revolution. Although her husband worked hard and provided well for his family, his interests were more mundane than hers. Through careful husbandry and judicious purchases of land, Theophilus was able to increase the value of his estate from £52 in 1755 to £628 in 1791, but he remained an Old Light and a casual observer of the sabbath to the end. Even on his death bed, as Hannah observed, "he seemd loth to talk about his soul once i asked him if he was afraid to die he said yes i asked him if he had a heart to beg for mercy and i thought he said not much." Their marriage was a tempestuous one. Theophilus apparently resented the time his wife spent away from home with the Separates; on occasion, he hid her spectacles, threw her diary in the mud, and refused to catch the horse for her so that she could attend religious meetings.

Hannah also viewed her sons as trials of her faith, since they showed little interest in religious matters, although her eldest son did have a change of heart and became a Separate after the death of his first wife in childbirth. Heaton addressed her diary to her younger son, her favorite, hoping to stir his sense of guilt and prompt him to search his heart for God's grace. Her opinions about religion also strained her associations with female acquaintances. One relationship ended in a quarrel when a longtime confidante disclosed a derogatory remark Hannah had made concerning a minister who, she said, read over a "great pack of notes" to his people and called it preaching. Heaton sought refuge from these turbulent relationships in lengthy private reflection and prayer and by writing in her diary.

As relations between England and the colonies deteriorated in the 1770s, Heaton dwelled increasingly on political and military events. On 14 September 1774 she reported

hearing the great commotion there is in new england on account of the old england army at boston the king has sent to change our constitution and how our land rulers and people are set against it last night we hear there was a mob at new hauen and they abused some that had spoke for the kings conduct and they have raired up liberty poles as they call them in the towns around us and all the trading to england is agoing to be stopt.

After the battle of Lexington and Concord the following year, she lamented on "the sin of this land in refusing and trampling on an offered christ imprisoning christs ministers." She agreed at first with Separate ministers who interpreted the Revolution as retribution for New England's sins, but later concluded that the English were clearly in the wrong: "O has king george forfited his coronation oath o does lord north gouern king and perliment and must he gouern amarica twoo by papists laws."

Both of Hannah's sons took part in the war, joining the New England army in New York. While one son was recovering at home from camp fever, Heaton recorded a dream about a favorable future: "Now i dreamed i was talking to ionathan and caluin i thot i told them to pray to god that they might liue threw this deluge of war for when it was ouer i belieued there would be greater glory seen in new england than euer was before . . . " Finally, Hannah recorded the victory at Yorktown in October 1781, after she heard that "coronal walles and his army is taken," but she was quick to add: "o what shooting frolicking and heathenish reioysing is there in our towns instead of giueing glory to god for this smiling prouidence."

In the last years of her life, while in declining health, Heaton's interests retreated from the outer world and again turned within. She recorded deaths in her family and community, spent more time in pious reading, and noted when religious revivals (foreshadowing the Second Great Awakening) occurred in Long Island, New Jersey, and in the Connecticut towns of Wallingford, Meriden, and Middletown in the 1780s. She hoped for such a revival in North Haven, which she thought could be the beginning of the Second Coming: "it seems to me sometimes as if it [North Haven] would be the chief seat of christs kingdom." Yet she ended her diary with doubts about a millennium: "Here the law of sin and grace will iar both dwelling in one room the saints expect perpetual war till they are sent for home."

The autobiography illuminates both the inner and outer worlds of an eighteenth-century woman, although Heaton says little about childrearing, education, or household work. By excluding so much, Heaton could create in her writing a free and solitary self. Her act of self-examination and reflection on the workings of God's grace within her helped her to rise above a world of sin into union with God. It was also a way for her to describe her struggle to endure and overcome adversity, and in the process she established her strength and sense of rightness, both in her eyes and for future readers.

• The manuscript diary is owned by Winifred N. Lincoln and Maryann Lincoln of Bethany, Conn.; a typescript is at the North Haven Historical Society. Heaton's will is in the probate records at the Connecticut State Library, Hartford. The diary is discussed in Barbara Lacey, "The World of Hannah Heaton: The Autobiography of an Eighteenth-Century Connecticut Farm Woman," *William and Mary Quarterly* 45 (Apr. 1988): 280–304; and briefly in Lucy McTeer Brusic, *Amidst Cultivated and Pleasant Fields: A Bicentennial History of North Haven, Connecticut* (1986).

BARBARA E. LACEY

HEATTER, Gabriel (17 Sept. 1890–30 Mar. 1972), broadcast commentator, was born on the Lower East Side of New York City, the son of Henry Heatter, a tailor, and Anna Fishman. Both of Heatter's parents were immigrants from the Austro-Hungarian Empire. He grew up in a Jewish community in the Brownsville section of Brooklyn, leaving high school without a diploma. In 1915 he married Saidie Hermalin, a schoolteacher; they had two children. Heatter began his journalism career first as a part-time reporter for a Brooklyn newspaper and in 1909 as a full-time reporter for the *Brooklyn Times*, and then as a magazine writer and editor. He made his reputation, however, as a radio news commentator. His coverage in 1935 of the Bruno Hauptmann trial for the kidnap-murder of the Lindbergh baby for New York's WOR led to a nightly news commentary on the Mutual Network and to hosting "We, the People," a popular weekly CBS program in which Americans from all walks of life described personal experiences. Heatter's sympathic manner and deep, resonating voice won him a national following, but he was criticized for reading the commercials on his newscasts himself.

During World War II Heatter's unwavering support for the Allied cause, especially for Britain during its bleakest days, and his optimism that Britain would eventually emerge victorious cheered his nightly radio audience. A strong supporter of Prime Minister Winston Churchill, Heatter supported the policy of sending American arms and supplies to Britain, ignoring the angry telephone calls that followed such broadcasts. As a result, sources in the British Embassy, where he was a favorite, gave him news tips. Heatter did not like the Soviet government, considering Stalin an ally by grim necessity. Adolf Hitler, the Nazis, and the Axis powers were targets of Heatter's wrath. Of Hitler's reported death, Heatter said, "Ah, Hitler is in Hell tonight!"

Despite depressing news reports, he frequently began his program with what became his trademark phrase, "Good evening, everyone. There is good news tonight." Yet Heatter so often dwelt on tragedy that he was more than once called "the voice of doom." Author Irwin Edman came up with this bit of doggerel: "Disaster has no warmer greeter, / Than gleeful, gloating Gabriel Heatter." More than most commentators he simplified and personalized news events, telling stories of the triumph of individual courage, hope, or faith.

In addition to his political commentary, Heatter was also known for presenting human interest stories of heroism with a sympathy that verged on being cloying. Among his most memorable is a tale of a mother willing to work in an aerial circus to provide for her daughter's music lessons. Stories about the heroic feats of dogs—saving children, traveling long distances to get home, or performing in the K-9 corps—were his favorites. Such stories brought him considerable fan mail.

Contrary to some political opinion, Heatter correctly predicted the steadfastness of England and Russia and the triumph of Harry S. Truman over Thomas Dewey in 1948. His nightly audience reportedly included Supreme Court justices and many members of Congress. Neither clearly liberal nor conservative, Heatter was willing to take on causes to correct what he regarded as injustices. After the war, with inflation squeezing people on fixed incomes, he crusaded for better pay for white-collar workers and increased Social Security benefits. His was "the white collar microphone."

In 1946, when he was broadcasting each weekday evening to an estimated audience of 7 million, Heatter began a half-hour dramatic show on Sunday evenings. "A Brighter Tomorrow," which consisted of reenactments of events in the lives of ordinary people, used not only actors but also an orchestra. Heatter served as interviewer to dramatize his familiar, optimistic themes. Almost 400 Mutual Broadcasting Company stations carried the show.

Heatter preferred to do his newscasts from his home. A small radio studio was built in his house in Freeport, Long Island, where he worked with his wife, his brother, and a broadcast technician. Heatter also bought a farm in Connecticut. He gave up his broadcasts in 1965 and lived out his remaining years in Miami Beach.

During the "golden age" of radio, roughly spanning the decades of the 1930s and 1940s, the political opinions expressed nightly by radio commentators about the depression, World War II, and the immediate postwar years had an effect on public discourse and consequently on public policy. Heatter had addressed from 11 million to 14 million listeners regularly during World War II and the postwar years. On days when major events occurred, his audience swelled to an estimated 20 million. In the dark days of 1940 he encouraged confidence in America's future allies, England and the Soviet Union. Although he gave comfort to many in his audience, he was an extremely shy, fearful man beset by phobias, which he described in an autobiography. Yet he gave courage to Americans during some of the war's grimmest days. He once told an interviewer, "When I talk about conquering fear, for instance, I am talking about myself primarily. In effect, I am trying to lift myself by my own bootstraps. And in so trying, I seem to inspire others."

• Heatter's autobiography, *There's Good News Tonight* (1960), is filled with agonized comments about the phobias that beset his life. Heatter is one of fifteen commentators during the "golden age" of radio broadcasting, 1930–1950, profiled in Irving Fang, *Those Radio Commentators!* (1977). For additional information, see Jack Alexander, "The Great Gabbo," *Saturday Evening Post*, 15 Mar. 1947, pp. 15–17ff, a sympathetic look at the radio commentator at the height of his popularity that contains photos and anecdotes about his life and his personality, including his deep depressions; Philip Hamburger, "The Crier," *New Yorker*, 20 Jan. 1945, pp. 23–33, a profile of Heatter as eccentric and overwrought, living a relatively secluded life for someone with his occupation; Dixon Wecter, "Hearing Is Believing," *Atlantic Monthly*, July 1945, pp. 37–43, an analysis of the field of radio commentary that criticizes Heatter for his sentimental delivery and for reading his own commercials; "Doom Always Pays," *Newsweek*, 17 Sept. 1945, pp. 92–96, a brief review of the commentator's life; and "Forearmed," *New Yorker*, 24 Oct. 1942, p. 14, a description of the Long Island home from which Heatter broadcast.

IRVING FANG

HEBB, Donald Olding (22 July 1904–20 Aug. 1985), biological psychologist, was born in Chester, Nova Scotia, Canada, the son of Mary Clara Olding and Arthur Morrison Hebb, physicians. Hebb received a B.A. from Dalhousie University in 1925. During the ensuing nine years, he worked as a teacher and principal in the school systems of Nova Scotia and Quebec. Reading the works of Sigmund Freud in his spare time, Hebb developed an interest in psychology and enrolled at McGill University in Montreal as a graduate student, where he worked with disciples of Ivan Pavlov and received an M.A. in psychology in 1932.

Two years later Hebb entered the University of Chicago to study with Karl Lashley, who was then the preeminent North American psychologist working on brain-behavior relationships. When Lashley moved to Harvard University the following year, Hebb followed. In Lashley's laboratory, Hebb pursued studies of brain mechanisms and the effects of early experience on visual perception in laboratory rats. Hebb spent one postdoctoral year with Lashley following receipt of his Ph.D. in psychology from Harvard in 1936 and was then awarded a two-year fellowship at the Montreal Neurological Institute, where he was involved in assessment of the effects of brain lesions in human patients. Hebb's results challenged the common belief that lesions of the frontal lobes would have a devastating effect on intellectual function, although his primary data came from IQ tests, and subsequent research revealed substantial effects of such lesions when more subtle tests are employed.

After a period of teaching at Queens University in Ontario, Hebb joined the staff of the Yerkes Laboratories of Primate Biology in Orange Park, Florida, where Lashley was director. During these years (1942–1947) Hebb wrote the book that established his position in psychology, *The Organization of Behavior*, which was published in 1949, when Hebb was professor of psychology at McGill University. The contents of this highly speculative theoretical monograph reflect the succession of Hebb's experience with the development of perception in Lashley's laboratory, with human intellectual function following brain injury, and with the complex mental life of chimpanzees that he had observed at the Yerkes Laboratories.

From Hebb's perspective, any theory of psychology had to deal with mental phenomena such as set and attention, subjects that were largely neglected by the dominant behavioristic psychology of the 1940s, and to accommodate the basic facts of perception revealed by the Gestalt psychologists. Such a theory would also have to account for the nature of learning. Finally, in Hebb's view, these psychological concepts would have to be rooted in a plausible physiology of the nervous system. Hebb's first task was to rid psychologists of their attachment to a passive, switchboard model of the nervous system. He emphasized the spontaneous activity of the nervous system, which then provided a basis for selective perception of the environment and accounted for the psychological phenomena of set and attention. In addition, because a plausible physiology of the nervous system was one that was based on synaptic connections between individual nerve cells, Hebb's task became one of accounting for such phenomena as perceptual generalization—for example, the ability to recognize a friend's face from different perspectives, irrespective of the specific pattern of excitation on the retina of the eye—while maintaining a firm grounding in a nervous system linked by synaptic connections between individual cells. He achieved this goal by postulating a critical period of early perceptual learning, during which time connections were established in the nervous system that enabled the apparently instantaneous recognition capacities of the normal human adult.

In the course of developing his theory, Hebb suggested that there are neural representations of images (cell assemblies) and of thoughts, or ideas (phase sequences). Cell assemblies develop as the result of experience, and the contemporaneous activation of a sequence of cell assemblies will result in the formation of a phase sequence. Establishing these permanent representations in the nervous system required postulating a mechanism of memory storage in the brain. Hebb proposed a dual-trace mechanism, whereby information was stored in the form of reverberatory activity in the nervous system until lasting cellular changes had occurred. In *The Organization of Behavior* he offered a specific postulate: "When an axon of cell A is near enough to excite cell B and repeatedly or persistently takes part in firing it, some growth process or metabolic change takes place in one or both cells such that A's efficiency, as one of the cells firing B, is increased" (p. 62). He then went on to suggest that the cellular change might consist of growth of synaptic knobs (structures at the terminal portions of axons), increasing the area of contact and facilitating the interaction between two nerve cells. This was a prescient postulate, and in contemporary neuroscience, it is common to refer to synapses that change as the result of use or experience as "Hebb synapses." The impact of Hebb's theorizing was buttressed by a steady stream of significant, novel research from the laboratories at McGill. This work included the discovery of pleasure centers in the brain by James Olds and Peter Milner; a set of papers by various students and colleagues that emphasized the importance of early experience for the development of the adult mind; and research that contributed to contemporary understanding of localization of intellectual functions in various circuits within the brain.

Hebb was married three times. His first wife, Marion Isabel Clark, died in 1933. In 1937 he married Elizabeth Nichols Donovan, with whom he had his only children, two daughters, before she died in 1962. He then married Margaret Doreen Williamson Wright in 1966.

Hebb's contribution was to expand psychology beyond the dominant behavioristic views of his time, accommodate the facts of perception revealed by Gestalt psychologists, and provide a neural famework to understand how the brain processes and stores information. As a person, Hebb was that rarest of scientists: a tolerant, friendly revolutionary. His styles of writing and personal interaction indicated respect for the contributions of "opponents," even as he was suggesting that psychology needed to move in new directions. Many honors were accorded to Hebb in his lifetime, including election as president of the Canadian Psychological Association (1952) and the American Psychological Association (1960) and election to the Royal Societies of Canada and London, England. He died in Halifax, Nova Scotia.

• Hebb contributed an autobiographical piece to Gardner Lindzey, ed., *History of Psychology in Autobiography*, vol. 7 (1980). A brief discussion of his life and contributions, written by his friend Frank A. Beach was published in *American Psychologist* 42 (Feb. 1987): 186–87. A useful explication of Hebb's ideas is by Peter Milner in *Scientific American*, Jan. 1993, pp. 124–29.

STEPHEN E. GLICKMAN
JOE L. MARTINEZ, JR.

HÉBERT, Felix Edward (12 Oct. 1901–29 Dec. 1979), journalist and congressman, was born in New Orleans, Louisiana, the son of Felix J. Hébert, a trolley car conductor, and Lea Naquin, a schoolteacher. Hébert attended Tulane University (1920–1924, no degree), and throughout high school and college, he covered sports for local newspapers. His journalistic experience resulted in Hébert's appointment in 1929 as the political editor of the *New Orleans States*, which he used as a platform for attacking Governor Huey P. Long via his front-page column. In 1934 he married Gladys Bofill; they had one daughter.

In 1939 Hébert was promoted to city editor at the *States*. While city editor, he wrote a series of articles that exposed rampant political corruption in what became known as the "Louisiana scandals." Because of the series, Governor James A. Noe, an estranged member of the Long family machine who reportedly gave Hébert information for the investigative articles, encouraged Hébert's foray into politics as a Democrat.

In 1940 Hébert sought election to Congress from the First Congressional District, which included New Orleans. He easily bested longtime incumbent Joachim Octave Fernandez by a 2–1 margin in the Democratic primary, which resulted in his election, and he commenced a congressional career that extended until the late 1970s. Upon entering Congress, Hébert was placed on the Committee for the District of Columbia, where he investigated scandals in the district's police department, leading to an extensive reorganization. He was also a member of the Naval Affairs Committee, which merged in 1947 into the Armed Services Committee, where he conducted two major inquiries. First he investigated labor and financial disturbances at the Brewster Aeronautical Corporation. Next, at the end of World War II in Europe, Congressman Lyndon B. Johnson selected Hébert to tour the war-ravaged Continent. He published his diary of those travels under the title *I Went, I Saw, I Heard* (1976).

In the years following the war Hébert continued to operate in an investigative manner. His handling of the Hiss-Chambers controversy while a member of the House Un-American Activities Committee was generally applauded for its fair-minded thoroughness. He generated controversy in 1951, when, as an observer of the secret Eniwetok atomic test, he recorded his observations for exclusive publication in the *New Orleans States*. During the 1950s continuing to serve on the Armed Services Committee, he conducted investigations into Defense Department purchasing procedures.

Despite his examinations of the armed services, Hébert was a staunch supporter of a powerful military. His voting record on defense matters was universally hawkish in nature. Backing American involvement in Vietnam, he publicly endorsed sending 4 million troops to Southeast Asia if that action would win the war. A believer in limited government with a constituency that favored segregation, he strongly opposed civil rights and the social welfare legislation associated with the Great Society during the 1960s. His views alienated Hébert from liberal Democratic freshmen and led to his fall from tangible political power. Nonetheless, in 1970. Hébert won accolades even from some of his critics for his subcommittee investigation into the 1968 My Lai massacre in South Vietnam. He scathingly criticized the Pentagon and the State Department for concealing important details about the massacre.

Hébert used his congressional power to lavish federal projects on his district. Several military bases were placed there at his behest, the large F. Edward Hébert Naval Hospital was constructed despite little need, and naval land was transferred from federal authority to Tulane University. Also, a research center bearing his name was created at Tulane.

In 1971, following the death of L. Mendel Rivers of South Carolina, Hébert finally ascended to the chair of the Armed Services Committee after three decades of service. His tenure was marred by conflicts with vocal junior members, who questioned his and the committee's unflagging support of U.S. military involvement in Vietnam. In early 1975 the Democratic caucus stripped Hébert and two other congressmen of their chairmanships. This previously inconceivable move broke long-standing informal seniority rules determining committee chairs and had the practical consequence of removing the last of the "Old Bulls," senior conservative members from the South, from meaningful power.

After this rejection by his colleagues, Hébert suffered a serious fall that shattered his arm in 1975. With his eyesight also failing, he decided not to seek a nineteenth House term in 1976. In retirement, Hébert continued to voice support for conservative causes despite deteriorating health. He died in New Orleans.

Overall, Hébert's record reveals a lengthy archconservative pattern matched only by his flamboyant streak. He maintained an unusually extensive wardrobe, owning more than a hundred suits at one point in his congressional service, and he had a reputation for making frequent quips regarding pending business. This colorful personality often mitigated his strident voting record until the later days of his career. Ultimately, his eccentric style was unable to alleviate the impact of his substantive views at a time when the ideological composition of the House Democratic caucus was shifting in favor of more liberal members.

• The Hébert papers are at Tulane University. Hébert's autobiography, *Last of the Titans* (1976), is a significant and informative source. A biography by Glenn R. Conrad, *Creed of a Congressman* (1970), illuminates Hébert's career prior to his ascension as the Armed Services Committee chair. Material on events surrounding his dismissal as House Armed Services Committee chair is in the *Congressional Quarterly Weekly Report*, 18 Jan. 1975. Obituaries are in the *Washington Post* and the *New York Times*, both 30 Dec. 1979.

MICHAEL E. SABINE

HÉBERT, Paul Octave (12 Dec. 1818–29 Aug. 1880), Louisiana governor and Confederate general, was born on his family's sugar plantation, "Acadia," along the banks of the Mississippi River in Iberville Parish, Louisiana, the son of Paul Gaston Hébert, a planter of Acadian or Cajun ancestry, and Mary Eugenia Hamilton. Bilingual in French and English, he graduated from Jefferson College (La.) at the top of his class in 1836. He then entered the U.S. Military Academy, where he finished in 1840 ranked first among forty-two graduates, including Winfield Scott Hancock, William T. Sherman, and George H. Thomas. Hébert was commissioned as second lieutenant of the Corps of Engineers and taught engineering at the military academy for one year, 1841–1842, as an assistant professor. Transferred to Fort Livingston on Barataria Bay, he strengthened the defenses there guarding one of the main approaches to New Orleans. He married Cora Wills Vaughn in 1842; they had five children.

Hébert resigned from the U.S. Army Corps of Engineers in 1845 to accept a position as chief engineer for the state of Louisiana, but he returned to military service in 1847 during the Mexican War. As lieutenant colonel of the Fourteenth Infantry, he fought with the brigade commanded by Franklin Pierce in several battles leading to the capture of Mexico City, including Contreras, Churubusco, Molino del Rey, and Chapultepec. His gallantry at Molino del Rey won him promotion to colonel. He remained with the occupation forces until 1848.

Shortly after his return to his Louisiana sugar plantation, Hébert became active as a Democrat in state politics. His U.S. military service, combined with his French-speaking Catholic background, made him an attractive candidate in a state that was deeply divided by religion and ethnicity. Narrowly defeated in his first run for the state senate in 1849, he accepted an appointment as one of the U.S. commissioners sent to the 1851 Crystal Palace Exhibition in London and in 1852 won his first election as a delegate to the state's constitutional convention.

In 1852 Hébert also became the Democratic nominee for governor and won that office in a landslide that gave his party control of both houses of the state legislature. After he assumed office on 1 January 1853, he tried to develop programs for public education and internal improvements but accomplished little more than the creation of a state public library and the establishment of the Louisiana State Seminary, a military academy and precursor to the Louisiana State University. The severe yellow fever epidemic of 1853 and the sudden surge of the Know Nothing party, with its accompanying violence in New Orleans, diverted attention away from his legislative program. Ineligible to succeed himself under the state constitution, he was the last governor of French-speaking ancestry in Louisiana until the election of Edwin Edwards in 1972.

In 1856 Hébert returned to his plantation and stayed aloof from politics. He lived the life of a gentleman and in 1859 made a grand tour of Europe. He also raised racehorses and served as president of the Metairie Jockey Club, which ran a racetrack near New Orleans. In the 1860 census he was listed as the owner of ninety-four slaves and more than $200,000 worth of property. Hébert remained a conservative Unionist until the election of Abraham Lincoln in 1860. A hesitant secessionist, he nonetheless supported slavery and assumed various state military posts after Louisiana left the Union. In August 1861 he was commissioned as brigadier general in the Confederate army and placed in command of Louisiana. His first wife had died in 1859, and on 3 August 1861 he married Penelope Lynch Andrews, with whom he had six more children.

Throughout the Civil War, Hébert remained in the theater of operations west of the Mississippi River. At first he was given command of the entire Trans-Mississippi Department, but two actions diminished his reputation among Confederate authorities. On 30 May 1862 he declared martial law in Texas to carry out the Confederate draft, but Jefferson Davis quickly countermanded his order to quiet discontent in Texas. Later Hébert failed to stop the capture of Galveston on 5 October 1862. Within a month of that defeat he was replaced by John B. Magruder, who promptly recaptured the port city. Scorned by Texas leaders for his caution and upstaged by his successor's daring victory, Hébert requested transfer to the command of the subdistrict of north Louisiana, where he assisted in the defense of Vicksburg. He participated in only one major battle during the war, at Milliken's Bend, Louisiana, in June 1863. Despite his military experience, he never won further promotion. By August 1864 he had withdrawn his forces to Texas, where he remained in various minor military roles until the end of the war. As the last official commander of the Confederate forces in Texas and Arizona, he surrendered them to General Gordon Granger in June 1865.

After returning to his sugar plantation, "Home Place," Hébert tried to reestablish his antebellum lifestyle. In the fall of 1865 he received a pardon from President Andrew Johnson. He extended his landholdings by inheritance and resumed the presidency of the Metairie Jockey Club, but he suffered significant losses in the agricultural depression that followed the war. In 1872 he reentered politics as a leader of Democrats endorsing the state's conservative Liberal Republican fusion movement. After Ulysses S. Grant's reelection, Hébert made overtures to Grant, his former associate at West Point and fellow officer during the Mexican War. Grant responded to the friendship by securing state and federal appointments for Hébert. In 1873 the Republican governor, W. P. Kellogg, appointed Hébert to the Board of State Engineers, which oversaw Louisiana's constant flooding problems. In 1874, after Hébert supported a third term for Grant, the president put him on a federal commission investigating internal improvements along the lower Mississippi River. Despite Hébert's prewar experience as a civil engineer on various river projects, he seldom challenged the military engineers or diverged from traditional engineering methods. He ended his efforts by opposing the brilliant concept of James B. Eads for a system of jetties that eventually opened the river for deeper draft vessels.

Berated as a scalawag by fellow Democrats for his political apostasy, Hébert explained his financial need for public office and quietly returned to the Democratic fold in 1876. He died in New Orleans. Throughout the turbulent era of the Civil War and Reconstruction, his moderate political stance failed to draw much favor from his fellow Louisianans.

• The Paul Octave Hébert Collection at Tulane University contains some letters and a scrapbook related to his military and political activities. The only biography about him is a long journal article written by Albert L. Dupont, "The Career of Paul O. Hébert, Governor of Louisiana, 1853–1856," *Louisiana Historical Quarterly* 31 (1948): 491–552. A more recent biographical essay by Marius M. Carriere, Jr., adds some new information about Hébert's term as governor of Louisiana, "Paul Octave Hébert," in *The Louisiana Governors: From Iberville to Edwards*, ed. Joseph G. Dawson (1990). For obituaries see the *New Orleans Daily Picayune* and the *New Orleans Democrat*, both 30 Aug. 1880.

JOSEPH LOGSDON

HECHT, Ben (28 Feb. 1894–18 Apr. 1964), writer, was born on New York City's Lower East Side, the son of Joseph Hecht, a tailor and designer of women's dresses, and Sarah Swernofsky. Hecht attended schools in New York and later in Racine, Wisconsin, where the family moved when he was six. In 1910 he moved to Chicago and began working as a picture stealer (purloining victims' pictures from family homes for use in the newspaper) and factotum for the *Chicago Journal*. Hecht was soon a successful full-time reporter working for the *Journal* and, after 1914, for the *Chicago Daily News*. Starting as a crime reporter, he soon extended the range of his writing into more artistic areas. With his impressionistic columns about urban life, his poems, his plays, and his satires, Hecht became part of artistic bohemian circles and an integral part of their revolt against nineteenth-century social and artistic gentility, which became known as the Chicago Literary Renaissance. In 1915 he married Marie Armstrong; they had one child. Hecht contributed to and helped edit Margaret Anderson's avant-garde *Little Review* and in 1923 founded the *Chicago Literary Times*. Shortly after World War I he spent a year (1918–1919) as a correspondent for a syndicate headed by his paper in Berlin, where he discovered both European politics and European art movements such as German dadaism. Returning to Chicago, Hecht turned to more plays and novels. Some, such as the novel *Erik Dorn* (1921), displayed the influence of his European experience and reading through the decadent character of its artist hero and in its subjective point of view and exaggerated style.

Hecht's reputation as an important and daring modernist writer grew with the publication of novels such as *Gargoyles* (1922) and collections of his newspaper columns and was solidified with the obscenity trial that resulted from seizure of his erotic psychopathic study *Fantazius Mallare* (1922). He was charged and convicted of sending obscene material through the mail. Hecht was disillusioned by this not only because he lost his case but because of his literary friends, only H. L. Mencken offered to come to his defense. He moved to New York in 1924, where he continued writing drama, fiction, and articles. In 1925 he married Rose Caylor, for whom he had left his first wife. Caylor and Hecht had one child. Hecht was often short of money, and when in 1926 his friend and fellow writer Herman Mankiewicz telegraphed an invitation to work in Hollywood: "Will you accept three hundred per week to work for Paramount Pictures. All expenses paid. Three hundred is peanuts. Millions are to be grabbed out here and your only competition is idiots. Don't let this get around," he went to Los Angeles. There he wrote a story about Chicago gangsters that became the basis for Josef Von Sternberg's film *Underworld* (1927), for which Hecht received an Academy Award.

Hecht stayed in Hollywood only a short time before returning to New York. Over the course of his career Hecht would maintain homes and creative lives in both California, where, he contended, he went only to make money, and New York, which was the center of his artistic world. He thought of his fiction and plays as his important writing. His reputation today, however, rests largely on his screenwriting in the 1930s and 1940s, when the film industry was dominated by the studio system. And although he had success in almost every genre, including serious period literary adaptations such as *Wuthering Heights* (1939), his best work reflected the urban life he had known as a reporter on the streets of Chicago. Light, racy, energetic, and idiomatic, they shaped such distinctly American genres as

screwball comedies (*Design for Living* [1933], *The Twentieth Century* [1934], *Nothing Sacred* [1937], *It's a Wonderful World* [1939], and *His Girl Friday* [1940]) and crime and gangster films (*Underworld, The Scarface* [1932], and *Kiss of Death* [1947]) and defined the character of the reporter in both the newspaper film (*The Front Page* [1931]) and as an element in other films (*Viva Villa* [1934] and *Angels over Broadway* [1940]).

Hecht was a celebrity in Hollywood, an established author always irreverent toward his screenwork and his employers. His literary reputation and his reputation for quickness, creativity, and dependability made him popular with producers. He was often brought in to rewrite or rethink a script that was already in production, such as for David Selznick's *Gone with the Wind* (1939). Hecht reports that he worked for one week for $15,000 without having read Margaret Mitchell's novel. Highly paid for his scripts, Hecht believed that his film work's being less important or lasting than his other more literary endeavors allowed him an emotional distance in an industry where the writer had little final control over his work.

Hecht believed he could make more money and have more artistic freedom by remaining independent, and consequently he did not tie himself for long to any one studio. As a result he worked with almost all the major studios and many of the major directors of his era, including Howard Hawks, Ernst Lubitsch, Sternberg, Lewis Milestone, William Wellman, William Wyler, Orson Welles, and Alfred Hitchcock. Altogether he wrote or contributed to well over seventy screenplays, including *Gunga Din* (1939), *Foreign Correspondent* (1940), *The Shop around the Corner* (1940), *Roxie Hart* (1942), *Spellbound* (1945), *Gilda* (1946), *Notorious* (1946), *Monkey Business* (1952), and *Roman Holiday* (1953).

Hecht produced and directed a number of his own films, including *Angels over Broadway* and *Specter of the Rose* (1946). He and Charles MacArthur had full control over four films they produced, wrote, and directed for Paramount in their Astoria, Long Island, studio in 1934 and 1935. Their emphasis was always on the literary aspects of the projects, and the results were mannered and not overly successful, although *The Scoundrel* (1935) did develop a cult following and won an Academy Award for Best Original Story.

Hecht wrote plays throughout his career. His first New York production was *The Hero of Santa Maria*, written with Kenneth Sawyer Goodman and produced by the Washington Square Players in 1917. His play *The Egotist* was produced on Broadway in 1922. His greatest success, however, came in his work with MacArthur. Hecht had a long and close collaboration with MacArthur, a fellow reporter from a rival Chicago paper with whom he became friends in New York. Hecht had a home on the Hudson River in Nyack, close to MacArthur's. They shaped their shared memories of their days in Chicago newsrooms into their most successful play, *The Front Page* (1928), which firmly established the image of the reporter on stage and, through its numerous adaptations and imitations, on screen as well. The play remains an important and effective American comedy. Among their other stage collaborations was *The Twentieth Century* (1933), a send-up of the theatrical world, which has also endured through film adaptations and, more recently, revival as a stage musical (*On the Twentieth Century* [1978]).

Although Jewish, Hecht had never identified himself with Jewish causes. Some of his fictional characters had even been attacked as examples of Jewish self-loathing. His image of himself as an American and an artist who had shed his Jewish identity was radically altered by the growing anti-Semitism of the 1930s and then by German genocide of European Jewry and America's unwillingness to combat it. During World War II Hecht became involved in attempts to publicize Hitler's war against the Jews. These efforts led him to involvement in Zionist activities, principally as an American fundraiser and publicist for the Irgun (Menachem Begin's Jewish underground in Palestine)—efforts he continued during Israel's struggle for independence. He wrote pageants to promote these causes as he had for the general war effort, including *Fun to Be Free* (1939), *We Will Never Die: A Memorial Service to the Two Million Jewish Dead in Europe* (1943), and *A Flag Is Born* (1946). Because of his anti-British activities, his films were blacklisted for a period in the late 1940s.

In his later years Hecht wrote a number of memoirs and worked in the new medium of television. He died in his New York City apartment.

In many ways Hecht was "a child of the century," a phrase he used as the title of his 1954 autobiography. He worked in several of the new mass media and helped to define them. His prolific work was in general critically well received and financially well rewarded. While he felt that his serious reputation rested on his novels and short stories, his lasting legacy appears to have been much more in the ephemeral and collaborative arts of film and theater. Through *The Front Page* on the stage and through many of his screenplays he helped give an "American voice" (urban, colloquial, and fast paced) to the performing arts, defining indigenous screwball comedy and crime genres and shaping our fictional image of the reporter—dogged, irreverent, and sentimental. Through his work and his much-publicized life he became the prototype for our image of the scriptwriter under the studio system. As critic Richard Corliss has put it, "Ben Hecht was *the* Hollywood screenwriter."

• Hecht's papers are in the Newberry Library, Chicago. Few of Hecht's many publications are now available. His novels are best represented by *Erik Dorn* (1921; repr. 1924), *Fantazius Mallare: A Mysterious Oath* (1922; repr. 1978), and *Humpty Dumpty* (1924). His short stories appeared in two collections: *The Collected Stories of Ben Hecht* (1945) and *A Treasury of Ben Hecht: Collected Stories and Other Writings* (1959). For his newspaper writing, the best collection is *1001 Afternoons in Chicago* (1922). *A Guide for the Bedeviled* (1944), a polemical attack on anti-Semitism, is Hecht at his vitupera-

tive best. *The Front Page* (1928; repr. 1950) is widely available in script form. His best memoir is *A Child of the Century* (1954; repr. 1985). Many of his screenplays, including early drafts, are often available at major film-study centers and in studio archives. The most recent biography of Hecht is William MacAdams's anecdotal *Ben Hecht: The Man behind the Legend* (1990). More critical analysis is available in Doug Fetherling, *The Five Lives of Ben Hecht* (1977). Jeffrey Brown Martin, *Ben Hecht: Hollywood Screenwriter* (1985), assesses Hecht's contribution as a screenwriter. Hecht's work is also dealt with in a number of works devoted to Hollywood screenwriters, particularly Richard Corliss, *Talking Pictures* (1974). An obituary is in the *New York Times*, 19 Apr. 1964.

JEFFREY BROWN MARTIN

HECHT, George Joseph (1 Nov. 1895–23 Apr. 1980), publisher and philanthropist, was born in New York City, the son of Meyer Hecht and Gella Stern. He attended the Ethical Culture School from 1902 until he graduated in 1913, when he entered Cornell University. Hecht's early schooling along with his parents' interest in social welfare helped him develop his lifelong interest in helping others. It was at Cornell that he discovered his talent for publishing. He helped change the *Cornell Era* into one of the country's leading college publications by increasing advertising and circulation dramatically.

Hecht graduated in May 1917, just a month after the United States declared war on Germany. Postponing his publishing ambitions, he attempted to enter officer's training but was rejected because of his poor eyesight; he then enlisted and served in the American Ambulance Field Service and later the Statistical Division of the General Staff of the U.S. Army. While serving in Washington, D.C., Hecht became involved with developing the Bureau of Cartoons, U.S. Committee on Public Information, which distributed appropriate political cartoons to the nation's newspapers. His work with cartoons led to his book *The War in Cartoons*, published by E. P. Dutton. The work was named as one of the best books of 1919 by the *New York Times*.

After the war Hecht entered his father's hyde and skin business, and when New York City's settlement centers, United Neighborhood Houses, needed a venue for distributing information about their work he produced the publication *Better Times*, which first appeared on 29 December 1919 as a monthly. Hecht, who volunteered his time and wrote everything for the newspaper for its first two years after he finished his day job, saw it develop into a successful weekly. The paper's influence gradually grew to the point that the large city papers would follow its lead in reporting social issues. In 1925 Hecht founded the Welfare Council of New York City (which eventually changed its name to the Community Council of New York City); the organization coordinated the numerous welfare agencies and so avoided duplication of efforts. The council published *Better Times* as a way to keep people involved and informed. Hecht remained editor of the publication until 1931 and was secretary and director of the agency until 1945. Keeping with his devotion to the interest of children, he was also very involved with UNICEF (United Nations International Children's Emergency Fund) from the time of its conception.

Hecht felt that the various charity fund drives were duplicating efforts and so began in 1920 a campaign for a central fundraising, asserting that such a drive would be more practical and would result in more funds being raised. It was not until 1930 that the Greater New York Fund held its first campaign to raise funds. While numerous other people had become involved, Hecht was the secretary of the organization for five years and was considered a moving force in its creation. In 1974 the organization changed its name to the United Fund of Greater New York.

In 1926 Hecht began his publishing empire with the creation of *Parent's Magazine*. He sought and received funding from the Laura Spellman Rockefeller Memorial Fund to begin a magazine devoted to helping parents raise their children. The fund made grants to Yale University, the University of Minnesota, the University of Iowa, and to Teachers College of Columbia University so they could purchase stock in the proposed company. From the beginning Hecht stressed the connection with the four universities and prominent educators from around the country by listing them in the front of the magazine. The new periodical was extremely popular and had a circulation of 200,000 after only five years.

Parent's Magazine originally began with articles covering university research dealing with children as well as articles by leading doctors and educators. Later the editor, Clara Savage Littledale, added articles on "Love and Marriage," "Women at Work," "Money Lines," and other topics that had an impact on children.

In 1930 Hecht married Freda Epstein; the couple had two children. His interest in the well-being of children continued, and during the 1930s and 1940s he began more publications, including the *Metropolitan Mother's Guide*, an entertainment guide for families in the New York metropolitan area that was later incorporated into the eastern edition of *Parent's*. This was followed by *School Management* (1932), *The Boy's and Girl's Newspaper* (1935), *True Comics* (1941), *Real Heroes*, *Senior Prom*, *Sweet Sixteen*, *Twenty-one*, *Calling All Boys*, *Calling All Girls*, and numerous others aimed at providing young people with wholesome reading material.

Hecht bought the stock in his publishing firm from the four universities in 1949, which led to the formation of the Family Publications Service in 1952. Time, Inc., purchased 50 percent of the company in 1959 and the remaining 50 percent in 1965. This company handled fifty magazines and the Homemaker's Library League, which offered selected magazines and books in special editions. Parent's Magazine Enterprises, Inc., remained under Hecht's ownership. In 1958 he acquired the oldest wholesaler of books, Baker & Taylor, which he turned into the largest of its kind before selling it in 1970. In 1963 Hecht took on a different type of enterprise when his firm gained controlling interest in the famous toy stores F. A. O. Schwartz, which he later sold.

• For additional information on Hecht, see *Current Biography: Who's News and Why* (1947); *Current Biography Yearbook 1980*; and *Who Was Who among North American Authors, 1921–1939* (2 vols., 1976).

DIANE LOOMS WEBER

HECHT, Selig (8 Feb. 1892–18 Sept. 1947), physiologist and biophysicist, was born in the village of Glogow, in what was then Austrian Poland, the son of Mandel Hecht and Mary Mresse. His family emigrated in 1898, settling in the Lower East Side of Manhattan, where Mandel Hecht worked as a foreman in the men's clothing industry. Selig attended both local public schools and Hebrew school, also studying Hebrew at home under his father's tutelage. He worked as a bookkeeper throughout his high school and college years to help support himself.

Hecht attended the College of the City of New York, first majoring in mathematics and later switching to zoology. During the summer of 1912 he received a fellowship to work at the U.S. Bureau of Fisheries station in Beaufort, North Carolina. He returned to New York that fall and received his B.S. in 1913. Before entering graduate school at Harvard in 1915, Hecht worked as an industrial chemist and as a pharmacologist for the U.S. Department of Agriculture. He completed his Ph.D. in zoology under George H. Parker in 1917, winning the Bowdoin Prize for a part of his thesis. That June he married Celia Huebschman, whom he had known since his undergraduate days; they had one child. They spent the summer of 1917 in La Jolla, California, where Hecht worked at the Scripps Oceanographic Institute.

From the fall of 1917 until 1921 Selig Hecht held an appointment as assistant professor of physiology in the medical school at Creighton University, Omaha, Nebraska. He lacked the time and facilities to conduct research during academic terms while at Creighton and spent his summers doing research at Woods Hole, Massachusetts, at the Marine Biological Laboratory. During one of these summer sojourns Hecht met Jacques Loeb, editor of the *Journal of General Physiology*. Loeb published all but a few of Hecht's papers throughout his career; more important, he became Hecht's scientific sponsor. In part because of Loeb's influence, Hecht spent the period from 1921 until 1926, when he was appointed associate professor of physiology at Columbia University, working under the auspices of the National Research Council and the General Education Board, on fellowships that allowed him to work with photochemist E. C. C. Baly in Liverpool, with physiologist Joseph Barcroft at Cambridge University, with Lawrence J. Henderson at Harvard, at Woods Hole, and at the zoological station in Naples, Italy.

Hecht stayed at Columbia until his death, having been named professor of biophysics in 1928. The biophysics laboratory he organized became one of the most productive groups for physiological experimentation and training. Hecht and his students made strides in the understanding of visual functions, particularly in humans, including dark adaptation, visual acuity, brightness discrimination, the mechanism of visual threshold, and color vision. The productivity of the laboratory was fostered by its layout and by Hecht himself, who encouraged an extraordinary amount of social interaction at daily afternoon breaks for tea, weekly colloquia, and evening meetings in Hecht's home; the group members discussed not only their work but also the arts, literature, and politics. Many of Hecht's students went on to academic positions, and one, George Wald, received a Nobel Prize.

Hecht made major contributions in the experimental measurement of visual response in many types of organisms and in the application of those data to the development of mathematical models for visual function that could be applied in a global way. He was the first to show clearly that visual response is the result of chemical and physical processes that can be studied in a quantitative way. Hecht showed that all photoreception begins with the absorption of light by visual pigment (S) in the retina and that the visual pigment must be converted to products (P). In order for the system to maintain a steady state so that vision is continuous, P must revert to S. This regeneration of S from P in darkness Hecht described as the basis of dark adaptation. The most lasting contribution from Hecht's lab was the measurement of the quantum efficiency of the human eye—the finding that the dark-adapted eye can be excited by one photon (one quantum of light). During World War II Hecht worked on problems of night vision for the armed forces. He was a member of the National Research Council Committee on Visual Problems and of the executive board of the Army-Navy-OSRD (Office of Scientific Research and Development) Vision Committee.

Hecht also played a prominent role in the Optical Society of America and served as a director-at-large. He received the Frederick Ives Medal from that organization in 1941. He was elected to the National Academy of Science in 1944. He served on the editorial boards of the *Journal of the Optical Society*, the *Biological Bulletin*, and *Documenta Opthalmologica* and advised and supported many young scientists. After World War II Hecht became the only member of the Emergency Committee of Atomic Scientists who was not a nuclear physicist and was made that group's honorary vice president. His book *Explaining the Atom* (1947), one of the first books on atomic energy written for the lay public was praised by the *New York Times* (20 Sept. 1947) as "by far the best so far written for the multitude" and was translated into many languages.

Hecht had wide-ranging interests beyond his work. He was a talented painter in watercolors, had a deep understanding of and passion for music, and read widely. He taught courses for adults at the New School on sensory physiology, physics, and atomic energy. He died in New York City of a coronary thrombosis.

• Hecht's papers are held at the Butler Library, Columbia University, New York City. Hecht's most significant publications are "Rods, Cones, and the Chemical Basis of Vision," *Physiology Review* 17 (1937); with Charles Haig and Ahrin M. Chase, "The Influence of Light Adaptation on Subsequent Dark Adaptation of the Eye," *Journal of General Physiology* 20 (20 July 1937); and, with Simon Shlaer and M. H. Pirenne, "Energy, Quanta, and Vision," *Journal of General Physiology* 25 (1942). An obituary with a bibliography, by George Wald, is in the *Journal of General Physiology* 32 (20 Sept. 1948): 1–16.

M. SUSAN BARGER

HECK, Barbara (1734–17 Aug. 1804), "mother of American Methodism," was born in Ballingrane, County Limerick, Ireland, the daughter of Sebastian Ruckle, a farmer, and his wife (name unknown), descendants of Protestant Palatine refugees from the War of Spanish Succession. She experienced a Methodist-inspired conversion at age eighteen, possibly after hearing John Wesley preach in Limerick, and married Paul Heck in 1760. In the spring of 1760 the Hecks left Ireland with family members and other Irish and Irish Palatine emigrants forced out by high rents and land scarcity. Their ship landed at New York City on 10 August. The Hecks communed with other Methodists at Trinity Lutheran Church, where the first three of their seven children were baptized between 1761 and 1765.

In late 1765 another cohort of immigrants from Ballingrane arrived in the city, including Barbara Heck's older brother Paul Ruckle. According to tradition, about a year later Heck discovered her brother and assorted men, chiefly Irish Palatines, gambling at cards, perhaps in her kitchen, more likely at one of the men's houses. Heck swept the cards into her apron and tossed them into the nearby fire. She then entreated Philip Embury, not at the game, to renew Methodist preaching. In October 1766 Embury gathered a small Methodist prayer group initially made up of the Hecks and their slave woman Betty. In a short time Embury was leading a religious revival among a large number of New Yorkers, including many Irish immigrants and a number of blacks. The revival was assisted further by the dramatic preaching of Captain Thomas Webb, an English lay itinerant.

Heck remained instrumental in the movement when she encouraged the Methodists to build a permanent chapel, the plan for which she believed she had received by divine inspiration. In March 1768 Embury, Webb, and six other Irish and English Methodists purchased a lot on John Street, where they constructed a simple stone chapel according to Barbara Heck's design. The John Street Chapel opened on 30 October 1768 and was long considered the first Wesleyan Methodist preaching house in the colonies, although it is now known to have been built after Robert Strawbridge's log preaching house in Frederick County, Maryland. More significantly, John Street's supporters persuaded John Wesley to send the first Methodist "helpers," licensed itinerant preachers, to America in 1769.

In about 1770 the Hecks moved to a land grant in Camden Valley, Albany (now Washington) County, New York, close to tracts conveyed to Embury and other Irish Palatines. They joined the Methodist society at Thomas Ashton's Irish colony of Ashgrove near present-day Cambridge, New York. At the outbreak of the revolutionary war the Heck family emigrated with other Loyalists to the outskirts of Montreal, where in 1777 Paul Heck enlisted as a sergeant in the Corps of Volunteers in Canada for the period of one year. He was briefly held prisoner of war by the Americans. In 1785 the Hecks moved again, to Augusta, Grenville County, Upper Canada (now Ontario), to a land grant reserved for veterans. Here they helped found the Augusta Methodist Society and prospered from the income of the Heck farm. Paul Heck died in 1795, leaving his house to Barbara and the farm to their son Samuel. Barbara Heck died at Samuel's new farm near Prescott, Ontario.

Heck was remembered as a pious woman who experienced visionary impressions typical of early American Methodists. Her influence among the Methodists demonstrates the extraordinary authority of ordinary followers, particularly women, in the early movement, and she has been celebrated as one of the "foundresses" of American Methodism since the mid-nineteenth century. Her story reveals as well the pattern of early Methodist expansion in which Methodist societies emerged and attracted the attention of itinerant preachers wherever Methodist immigrants and converts made their livings and raised their families. An accomplished portrait depicts Heck as a housekeeper of serious demeanor and material comfort, wearing a lacework cap and collar and embroidered shawl over a black dress and holding what appears to be a devotional book.

• A small number of miscellaneous Heck and Embury family papers are in the Archives and History Center of the United Methodist Church, Drew University, Madison, N.J. The records of the John Street Church are on deposit at the Manuscripts and Archives Section, New York Public Library. Heck's portrait is located in the collection at the United Library, Garrett-Evangelical and Seabury-Western Theological Seminaries, Evanston, Ill. The best accounts of Heck's life can be found in Abel Stevens, *The Women of Methodism* (1866), and William Crook, *Ireland and the Centenary of American Methodism* (1866). More recent accounts are Ruthella Mory Bibbins, *How Methodism Came: The Beginnings of Methodism in America* (1945; repr. 1987), and Frank Baker, *From Wesley to Ashbury: Studies in Early American Methodism* (1976).

DEE E. ANDREWS

HECKER, Friedrich Karl Franz (28 Sept. 1811–24 Mar. 1881), German revolutionary and American politician and soldier, was born in Eichtersheim, Grand Duchy of Baden, German League, the son of Joseph Hecker, a civil servant, and Wilhelmine von Lüder. Born a Catholic, he was educated at the humanistically oriented Gymnasium at Mannheim, finishing in 1830. He studied law at Heidelberg University from 1830 to 1833, taking the summer semester of 1833 at Munich before returning to Heidelberg to complete his doctorate in law in June 1834. Although Hecker underwent training to be a civil servant (including half a year studying legal procedures in Paris in 1835–1836), he entered private practice as an attorney. In 1839 he married Josephine Eisenhardt; they had nine children, five of whom survived infancy.

In 1842 Hecker was elected to the Mannheim city council then to the lower chamber of the Baden state assembly (Landtag). Though the youngest member of the assembly, he became a leader of the opposition, playing an instrumental role in the fall of the ministry of F. L. K. von Bittersdorf in November 1843. Hecker won notoriety as a fiery orator identified with the left in the assembly as well as in the extraparliamentary opposition led by Gustav Struve. As the Baden government sought support from more moderate members of the opposition after 1846, Hecker found himself increasingly defined as an unconditional democrat and republican, though he criticized the terrorism and ethnic bigotry (particularly anti-Semitism) that marred German peasant uprisings and urban protests of the time. He was a severe critic of hereditary princes and of established churches, advocating a democratic republic in which equality and freedom of conscience would prevail. This eloquence at public speaking made him a Liberal hero.

The general revolution that swept Europe in February and March 1848 led to the installation of liberal governments in all German states and the calling of a "Pre-Parliament" in Frankfurt am Main to prepare the way for an elected general assembly for Germany. Hecker attended the Pre-Parliament as a member of the far left. Struve presented a social-revolutionary platform for the abolition of hereditary rule and the creation of a democratic, federal German republic; in this Hecker strongly supported him. When moderates in the Pre-Parliament refused to adopt a radical program, Hecker, Struve, and seventy-six other deputies walked out. On 12 April 1848, already fearing arrest for treason, Hecker and Struve called on citizens to take arms to fight for a German republic. Hecker led a column of revolutionaries from Constance across the Black Forest to recruit fighters. His small force was defeated and dispersed on 20 April by a force of Baden and Hessian troops commanded by General Friedrich von Gagern, who died in the skirmish.

Hecker found brief refuge in Muttenz, Canton Basel-Land, Switzerland, before departing for the United States in September 1848, where he was received as a hero. He purchased land for a farm in Summerfield, several miles from Belleville, Illinois, east of St. Louis. In spring 1849 a renewed revolt in Baden prompted Hecker to return to Europe, only to learn in Strasbourg that the revolt had collapsed. Hecker then returned to the United States permanently, as he was under threat of arrest in Germany.

In Illinois Hecker established himself as a farmer, but he also spoke and wrote for German-language audiences, particularly in John Frémont's campaign for president (1856), Abraham Lincoln's campaign for the U.S. Senate (1858), and Lincoln's campaign for president (1860). The burning of his farmhouse during the 1856 campaign was thought to be revenge for his abolitionist views. At the start of the secession crisis in April 1861, Hecker crossed the Mississippi to enlist as a private in the Third Regiment, Missouri Volunteers, under Colonel Franz Sigel (a former military leader in the Baden revolutions of 1848–1849). He was recalled to Illinois to lead a newly formed regiment of his own, the Twenty-fourth Illinois Infantry (organized 17 June 1861). In August 1861, while campaigning in Southeast Missouri, junior officers in the regiment protested against Hecker's authoritarian methods of command. When Hecker found he was unable to remove officers who displeased him, he resigned his commission, and the unit was dissolved in December 1861. In October 1862 the Eighty-second Illinois Infantry regiment was formed in Chicago with Hecker as colonel. Serving in eastern campaigns with this unit, Hecker was wounded at Chancellorsville, Virginia, on 2 May 1863. On recovery, Hecker participated in the battle of Missionary Ridge as well as in the captures of Chattanooga and Knoxville. He commanded a brigade at Lookout Mountain but resigned his commission in January 1864, claiming he had been unfairly treated by superiors and passed over for promotion.

Leaving military service, Hecker became more intensely involved in Republican party activities than before, and he became a regular columnist in the German-language daily press. He supported Ulysses Grant for president in 1868 and less enthusiastically in 1872 (after a brief alliance with the Liberal Republicans, which he ended after Horace Greeley's nomination) but opposed a third term for Grant in 1876. Although occasionally mentioned as a possible Republican candidate for public office in Illinois, he was never nominated. Alongside his strong, consistent support of the Republican party, he continued the anticlericalism that marked his career in Germany, and he vehemently opposed prohibition, Sabbath legislation, and the extension of suffrage to women. He was distressed by the end of Reconstruction in 1877 and denounced the Ku Klux Klan. In 1873 he returned to Germany for a tour that became a nostalgic celebration of the tradition of 1848, though German governments grew hostile when he attacked them for their lack of guaranteed rights as well as for their excessive public spending.

Hecker died at his farm in Summerfield, Illinois, and was buried in the Summerfield Cemetery in a freethinker service. A man of great personal courage, Hecker's efforts were perennially complicated by a short temper and an unwillingness to consider the consequences of his acts. In Germany Hecker remains a symbol of a willingness to risk all for free, democratic institutions.

• Hecker's papers are in the Western Historical Manuscript Collection, University of Missouri–St. Louis, and they are available on microfilm from that collection. The papers are given a preliminary analysis by Franz X. Vollmer, "Der Hecker-Nachlass von St. Louis/USA," *Zeitschrift für die Geschichte des Oberrheins* 136 (1988): 349–415. A recent treatment of his German career is Klaus-Peter Klingelschmitt, *Vivat! Hoch!—Die Freie Republik! Friedrich Hecker—ein deutscher Mythos* (1982). There is as yet no extensive treatment of Hecker's American career.

STEVEN ROWAN

HECKER, Isaac Thomas (18 Dec. 1819–22 Dec. 1888), Catholic priest and founder of the Society of Missionary Priests of St. Paul the Apostle (the Paulists), was born in New York City, the son of John Hecker and Caroline Freund, owners of a brass foundry. Isaac was born at a time when his German immigrant parents and maternal grandparents were relatively prosperous in the foundry business, living in the comfortable and desirable Hester-Forsyth-Christie Street section of New York City. Isaac's mother was the dominant influence in his early life. She provided him with a strong sense of personal dignity and security, which was reinforced by a warm Methodist piety to which she introduced him at an early age. Isaac's father was absorbed in his business and was an unstable element in the family because of his alcoholism, or some unspecified "wicked passion" as Isaac called it, that contributed to the failure of his business in the early 1830s. After only six years of formal education, Isaac was forced to quit the New York public schools and to work in various jobs to help support the family. By the mid-1830s he joined his brothers, John and George, who had established a prosperous bakery, and in 1842, following the depression of 1837, the Hecker brothers built a flour mill that eventually made them a substantial fortune.

In the mid-1830s, the Hecker brothers were involved in the Locofoco movement in New York City and by 1841 were responsible in part for inviting the Bostonian Unitarian reformer Orestes A. Brownson to New York to address workers and small businessmen on Christianity and the reform of the American economic and political system. Isaac, sixteen years younger than Brownson, developed a friendship with him that was to last throughout their lives. Brownson introduced him to the intellectual movements of the day, and in 1842 Hecker went to the Transcendentalist stronghold in Massachusetts, living for about a year at Brook Farm, Fruitlands, and with the Henry Thoreau family.

In 1844, after some years of religious searching, Hecker became a Roman Catholic. In 1845 he joined the Congregation of the Most Holy Redeemer (Redemptorists), going to the novitiate at St. Trond, Belgium, and to Witten, Holland, to receive his education for the priesthood. He was ordained in London in 1849. In 1851 he returned to the United States and served the next six years as a Redemptorist missionary, preaching to non-Catholics as well as Catholics along the East Coast and writing two books, *Questions of the Soul* (1855) and *Aspirations of Nature* (1857), which developed a new Catholic Romantic apologetic.

Influenced by Romanticism and post-Kantian idealism, Hecker tried to demonstrate that the external ministries of the Catholic church, such as confession and absolution, were, in fact, the sacramentalizations of basic human and cultural aspirations.

In the midst of Know-Nothing attacks upon Catholicism, Hecker went to Rome in 1857 to get permission to open an American branch of the primarily German immigrant Redemptorist order. He believed an acculturized Redemptorist house would be able to attract vocations from young men who would exhibit American values and develop more successful missions to American Protestants. This proposal did not have the support of Hecker's German Redemptorist superior, so when he went to Rome he was expelled from the order. Pope Pius IX released Hecker and four other Americans from their Redemptorist vows, but in 1858 he allowed them to found the Society of Missionary Priests of St. Paul the Apostle (the Paulists) in New York, an indigenous American religious order that was dedicated to the conversion of American Protestants. Hecker became the superior of the Paulists and remained in that post until his death. As a Paulist, Hecker established the *Catholic World* in April 1865, a monthly journal of religious thought and popular Catholic opinion, and the Catholic Publication Society in 1866, which eventually became Paulist Press. In 1869 he attended the First Vatican Council as the theologian of Baltimore's archbishop Martin John Spalding. After the council, he became ill and never regained his health completely.

Hecker was primarily interested in demonstrating the compatibility of *The Church and the Age* (1887), the title of an anthology of his significant essays. Such an approach departed from the traditional Catholic arguments based upon the church's authority, motives of credibility, or reason. After his death in New York, Hecker's views became the subject of an ecclesiastical controversy, which ended when Pope Leo XIII's encyclical *Testem Benevolentiae* (1899) condemned Americanism as a complex of heretical ideas that some European Catholics had exaggeratedly identified with Hecker.

Although the Paulists never attracted a large membership, the order Hecker founded did produce several significant religious leaders in the United States during the twentieth century. Hecker's legacy continued, too, in the order's Paulist Press, which in the twentieth century became a leading publisher of materials on the liturgical revival, the ecumenical movement, biblical studies, and social justice. Although Hecker's ideas on apologetics and spirituality had only a few followers immediately after his death, they received much scholarly attention after the Second Vatican Council (1962–1965).

• Hecker's letters, diary, and other unpublished papers are located in the archives of the Paulists, the Archdiocese of New York, the Redemptorists, and Propaganda Fide (Rome). His correspondence with Orestes A. Brownson has been published in Joseph F. Gower and Richard M. Leliaert,

The Brownson-Hecker Correspondence (1979). A bibliography of his published works is available in John Farina, ed., *Hecker Studies: Essays on the Thought of Isaac Hecker* (1983). Important biographies include Walter Elliot, *The Life of Father Hecker* (1891); Vincent F. Holden, *The Early Years of Isaac Thomas Hecker, 1819–1844* (1939) and *The Yankee Paul: Isaac Thomas Hecker* (1958); and David J. O'Brien, *Isaac Hecker: An American Catholic* (1992). Critical assessments of his life and thought are found in Charles Maignen, *Études sur l'Americanisme: Le Père Hecker. Est-il un Saint?* (1898); *Le Père Hecker, Fondateur des "Paulistes" Américains, 1819–1888* . . . (1898), a French translation of Elliot's biography with an important preface by Felix Klein; Joseph McSorley, *Father Hecker and His Friends* (1952); John Farina, *An American Experience of God: The Spirituality of Isaac Hecker* (1981); and William Portier, *Isaac Hecker and the First Vatican Council* (1985).

PATRICK W. CAREY

HECO, Joseph (1837–1897), government interpreter, merchant, and publisher, was born Hamada Hikozō in the village of Komiya, near Kobe, Japan, on the eastern shore of the Inland Sea, the second son of a well-to-do farmer. After his father's death his mother remarried, to a sea captain who adopted him. While on what should have been a brief internal voyage in late 1850, his ship was blown into the Pacific. He and sixteen other persons, after drifting for fifty-two days, were picked up by a U.S. ship that landed at San Francisco in February 1851. The American authorities, planning for Commodore Matthew C. Perry's 1853 mission to Japan, maintained the Japanese for nearly a year in San Francisco before sending them to Hong Kong. Young Hamada then arranged to return to the United States independently; in San Francisco he was befriended by Beverly C. Sanders, a customs official and merchant, who took him by ship to Baltimore via New York, arriving in August 1853. During a visit to Washington, Hamada met President Franklin Pierce; on later visits he met Presidents James Buchanan and Abraham Lincoln and other dignitaries.

In Baltimore, Hamada received a Catholic education, and on 1 November 1854 he was baptized Joseph Heco. Returning to San Francisco, he studied at the institution that is now the University of San Francisco and then returned to Washington in November 1857, in the employ of U.S. senator William M. Gwin. In June 1858 a naval officer, Lieutenant John M. Brooke, appointed him captain's clerk for a survey he was about to make of the coastal waters of Japan and China. Since at the time Japan sometimes executed subjects who had gone abroad, Heco was naturalized by a federal judge on 7 June 1858, becoming the first Japanese to be naturalized as an American citizen.

In Shanghai the following year, he was introduced to Townsend Harris, about to take up residence as minister to Japan, who arranged for his appointment as interpreter in the consulate to be established in Yokohama. He served until February 1860, when he went into business as a merchant. In September 1861, partly because of anti-foreign disorders in Japan, he again visited the United States, returning to Yokohama in October 1862, serving the consulate there as interpreter until September 1863, when, conditions in Japan having calmed somewhat, he again set up as a merchant, first in Yokohama and then in Nagasaki. In June 1864, while still in Yokohama, he began publication of the *Kaigai Shimbun (Overseas News)*, the first Japanese language newspaper that chiefly translated news from foreign papers but also printed materials about American history and a translation of the Book of Genesis. From 1872 to 1874 he was an official, largely in an advisory capacity, of the Japanese finance ministry. Heco died in Tōkyo. Since 1956 the Josefu Hiko Kinenkai (Joseph Heco Society) has held an annual memorial service at Heco's grave in Tōkyo's Aoyama Cemetery.

• Heco published two autobiographies, *Hyōryūki* (1863), translated as *Floating on the Pacific Ocean* (1955); and *The Narrative of a Japanese: What He Has Seen and the People He Has Met in the Course of the Last Forty Years* (1895). Katherine Plummer, *The Shogun's Reluctant Ambassadors: Sea Drifters* (1984), contains a chapter on Heco.

ROGER DANIELS

HEDBERG, Hollis Dow (29 May 1903–14 Aug. 1988), geologist, was born in Falun, Kansas, the son of Carl August Hedberg and Zada Mary Dow, farmers. He attended local public schools, helped on the farm, and enjoyed family evenings of music and reading aloud. He entered the University of Kansas in 1920, intending to major in journalism but was drawn into geology. When his father died in 1921, Hedberg left college to run the family farm but returned to the university the next year. He received an A.B. in 1925. During the summers of 1924 and 1925 he was field assistant for the Kansas State Geological Survey.

Hedberg entered Cornell University in 1925 and received an M.A. in geology the following June. He was then employed as a petrographer by Lago Petroleum Company, a Venezuelan subsidiary of Standard Oil Company of Indiana. He traveled considerably in Venezuela, then left the company in 1928.

In Venezuela Hedberg met Milton Nunn Bramlette, head of the geological laboratory there of Gulf Oil Company. On Bramlette's recommendation, Hedberg was hired by that company as a stratigrapher in May 1928, and he replaced Bramlette as head of the laboratory five months later.

Hedberg married Helen Frances Murray in 1932; they had five children. On leave from Gulf Oil, he attended Stanford University in 1934–1935 and received a Ph.D. in geology in 1937, with a dissertation on the stratigraphy of a region of northeastern Venezuela.

From 1935 to 1937 he continued as director of Gulf's geological laboratory and then was put in charge of geological operations in eastern Venezuela for Mene Grande Oil Company (formerly Venezuelan Gulf). In 1939 he became assistant chief geologist for the company and led it into extensive development of oil in Venezuela. At least twenty new oil fields were put into production by 1945. In 1945 Hedberg was appointed assistant chief geologist of Gulf Oil Company, with responsibility for all of its geologic operations in Venezuela.

A year later he became chief geologist for Gulf's foreign exploration division, with an office in New York City. This move put him in charge of all the company's geological activities outside the United States, except in Venezuela and Canada. He immediately visited western Africa and arranged concession agreements with several countries there. This led to the development of several oil fields in that area.

Hedberg was appointed chief geologist for Gulf Oil Corporation in 1952, exploration coordinator in 1953, vice president for exploration in 1957, and exploration adviser until his retirement in 1968, after which he continued as an adviser on exploration. In 1959 he accepted a part-time appointment at Princeton University, where he taught a graduate course until 1972.

During his years with Gulf Oil, Hedberg took a keen interest in stratigraphy, the interpretation of layering in sedimentary rocks. His theory was that stratigraphic units can be based on either specific rock types or on fossils and that these do not always coincide, resulting in uncertainty in correlations in scientific literature. Hedberg said in 1952: "Uniformity in the procedure and terminology used in classification is essential to worldwide understanding among geologists" ("Procedure and Terminology in Stratigraphic Classification").

He began his efforts to compile a stratigraphic guide in 1946 as a founding member of the American Commission on Stratigraphic Nomenclature and presented his views in 1948 as "Time-stratigraphic Classification of Sedimentary Rocks." He noted that fossils in strata may not be reliable in determining the age of a formation, a point on which some paleontologists did not agree. As chairman of that commission from 1950 to 1952, he proposed that an international organization be established. He served as chairman of the International Subcommission on Stratigraphic Classification from 1952 to 1976, and he conferred with geologists throughout the world. He created the *International Stratigraphic Guide*, published in 1976. Geologist Timothy A. Anderson said: "He was, finally, enormously successful; it is sometimes forgotten that much of what we accept today as normal, logical stratigraphic practice is a result of that success."

In 1962 Hedberg became chairman of the Mohole Committee of the National Academy of Sciences, which was sponsoring a project to drill a hole through the ocean floor to the earth's mantle, to the layer known to geophysicists as the Mohorovičić discontinuity, at least six kilometers beneath the ocean floor. Some geologists questioned whether the technology was available for such deep drilling, while others felt that the cost was prohibitive. Hedberg was among the latter, and he urged instead a program of drilling shallower holes in many places. He resigned from the Mohole Committee in 1963. Congress ended the project of drilling a single deep hole in 1966, but by that time a program of shallower drilling had been established in 1964 as Joint Oceanographic Institutions Deep Earth Sampling. Hedberg chaired its Panel on Safety and Pollution Prevention from 1970 to 1977.

Hedberg's interest in worldwide exploration for oil led him to encourage Gulf Oil's program of evaluating offshore sedimentary basins by ship. The research vessel *Gulfrex* carried out this program in many parts of the world from 1967 to 1975, and it continued with the research vessel *Hollis Hedberg* from 1974 to 1985.

When the United Nations debated an international Law of the Sea, Hedberg participated as chairman of the Technical Subcommittee on Petroleum Resources of the Ocean Floor of the National Petroleum Council, a position he held from 1968 to 1973. In 1969 he proposed that the boundaries of nations be established on the basis of the continental slope rather than sea-level geography, a concept that was not accepted. He spoke and wrote against U.S. ratification of the United Nations Law of the Sea Convention.

Hedberg was honored with many scientific awards, including election to the National Academy of Sciences in 1960. His most valuable contributions were in exploration for oil resources and establishing an international code for terminology in geologic stratigraphy. He died in Princeton, New Jersey.

• Hedberg published 177 papers during his career. Several of the papers on oil fields in Venezuela, written with colleagues, were published in the *Bulletin of the American Association of Petroleum Geologists* in 1944, 1947, and 1948. His definition of stratigraphic classification was published as "Time-stratigraphic Classification of Sedimentary Rocks," Geological Society of America, *Bulletin* 59 (1948): 447–62; "Procedure and Terminology in Stratigraphic Classification," *Comptes Rendus de la Dix-Neuvieme Session, 19th International Geological Congress, Algier 1952* 8 (1954): 205–22; and in other journals. Another significant paper is "Petroleum and Progress in Geology," *Journal of Geological Society of London* 127 (1971): 3–16. Some of the history of the Mohole Project is in Elizabeth N. Shor, "A Chronology from Mohole to JOIDES," *Geological Society of America, Centennial Special* 1 (1985): 391–99. Hedberg's point of view on that project is presented in "Drilling the Ocean Crust," with Creighton A. Burk, *International Science and Technology* (Oct. 1964): 1–10. Biographies of Hedberg are by Timothy A. Anderson in Geological Society of America, *Memorials* 20 (1990): 97–103; and by Georges Pardo in National Academy of Sciences, *Biographical Memoirs* 61 (1992): 215–44, which includes a bibliography.

ELIZABETH NOBLE SHOR

HEDDING, Elijah (7 June 1780–9 Apr. 1852), circuit rider and bishop of the Methodist Episcopal church, was born near Pine Plains, Dutchess County, New York, son of James Hedding, a farmer of some prominence. Neither of his parents belonged to a particular denomination at the time of Elijah's birth, but his mother (name unknown) directed his early moral and religious development. The Methodist Episcopal church began to win adherents in southeastern New York in 1789 under the fiery revivalist Benjamin Abbott. Among the reportedly 1,400 souls won to the Methodists in the Dutchess circuit during Abbott's

first year of ministry were Elijah's mother and grandmother. The boy made no profession of faith at that time, but the seeds of conviction were sown. In 1791 the Hedding family moved to Starksborough, a frontier settlement in western Vermont, about fifteen miles east of Lake Champlain. The remote setting deprived Elijah of a formal education, but he learned to read through the Methodist church services held at neighbors' homes—services that featured studies of sermons by the founder of Methodism, John Wesley. Initially the domestic piety had little effect on Elijah. As a youth he experimented with deism, atheism, and universalism before being converted to Methodism at a revival meeting on 27 December 1798.

Possessed of a strong reading voice, Hedding soon began to pray and to exhort publicly. He decided to enter the ministry a year later, after the eccentric revivalist Lorenzo Dow abruptly left the shepherding of his Essex circuit to Hedding. Thus began an arduous 24-year career as circuit rider in New York and New England, initially as a preacher (1800), then as a deacon (1803), and finally as an elder (1805). Although he was less well known than the powerful bishop Francis Asbury and the colorful itinerant Peter Cartwright, Hedding became an exemplary Methodist circuit rider. Traveling a circuit of up to 500 miles every two to five weeks, he suffered tremendous physical hardships as a soldier in Methodism's cavalry. Certainly he was a key figure in the spread of Wesleyanism throughout New England.

Admitted to the New York Conference in 1801, Hedding saw his field of itinerancy transferred to the New England Conference in 1805. After that he was headquartered at Barre, Vermont (1805–1807), as circuit rider and was appointed, in succession, presiding elder (a supervisor of preachers) of the New Hampshire (1807–1809) and the New London (1809–1811) districts. In the midst of his excruciating schedule he was married, in 1810, to Lucy Blish of Gilsum, Cheshire County, New Hampshire.

Hedding began to assume national prominence within the Methodist Episcopal church when he attended his first General Conference in 1808. In addition to increasing denominational responsibilities, he was given yearly pastoral appointments: Boston (1811–1812, 1815–1817, and 1821–1824), Nantucket (1812–1813), and Lynn, Massachusetts (1813–1815 and 1818–1820); Portland, Maine (1817–1818); and New London, Connecticut (1820–1821). During one of his stints in Boston, Hedding was instrumental in founding, on 9 January 1823, *Zion's Herald*, the first regularly circulated, wholly Methodist periodical.

Hedding began to serve as bishop in 1824, during a difficult period for the denomination. In an age of unparalleled expansion for American Methodism, he exerted strong leadership in addressing the organizational issues that troubled the denomination. On the rancorous question of representation at annual conferences, he favored granting delegates a greater voice in the administration of the church and diminishing the role of bishops. On the weightier matter of discipline, his decisions were considered sufficiently authoritative to be distributed widely in his *Discourse on the Administration of Discipline* (1842). In his *Discourse*, Hedding defended a strict interpretation of discipline within the Methodist church but one tempered by a pastor's concern for the ultimate redemption of the individual.

Of course the most contentious issue facing Methodism in the antebellum era was slavery. Although Hedding thought the "peculiar institution" was a moral and political evil, he opposed the extreme abolitionism espoused by his fellow Methodists Orange Scott and Luther Lee, and as bishop Hedding used his influence to keep the New England Conference from taking an explicitly antislavery stance at the General Conference of 1836, which formally condemned both slavery and crusading abolitionism. This course of action brought on Hedding a great deal of abuse from the clergy in his conference who became increasingly radicalized throughout the 1840s.

Far less contentious was Hedding's lifelong support for the education of ministers in the Methodist Episcopal church. While he had been a circuit rider, he supplemented his limited formal education by studying the books he carried as a colporteur of the Methodist Book Concern. The obstacles he had to overcome in order to achieve a minimum of education made Hedding a fervent champion of learning, practical as well as theological. It is a testimony to his advocacy that Hedding College in Abingdon, Illinois, was named after him at its founding in 1856. It is also somewhat ironic, given that he was self-taught, that Hedding received the honorary doctor of divinity degree from not one but three schools (Augusta College in 1829, Union College in 1837, and the University of Vermont in 1840) and that he served as president of the Methodist Biblical Institute in Concord, New Hampshire (c. 1847–1848).

After residing in Lynn, Massachusetts (1824–1837), and Lansingburg, New York (1837–1842), Hedding moved to Saratoga Springs in the hope that the medicinal waters there might offer him some respite from chronic health problems. Relieved of many of his episcopal duties after 1848, he spent his final year in Poughkeepsie, New York, where he died.

Hedding was routinely characterized by his contemporaries as a simple and practical man. Although he also was suffused by a warm piety and a sublime profundity, he was, preeminently, a person of action. Such was fitting for one shaped by the elemental forces of pioneer life. These same forces, however, eventually took their toll on his physical health. Hedding was thus typical of the thousands of antebellum circuit riders who willingly—even joyfully—wore themselves out in service to their god and their church.

• A good deal of correspondence between Hedding and his contemporaries as well as records of churches and circuits served by Hedding can be found in the New England Methodist Historical Society Library at Boston University. The standard biography is D. W. Clark, *Life and Times of Rev. Elijah Hedding, D.D.* (1855), which is based on no longer existant manuscripts by Moses L. Scudder, L. M. Vincent, and William H. Ferris. Most of the other, shorter summaries appear to be derived from Clark's work in some fashion. The most significant of these works are the reminiscences of Hedding's contemporary Daniel Curry, "Life and Times of Bishop Hedding," *Methodist Review* 37 (Oct. 1855): 589–614; Tobias Spicer et al., "Elijah Hedding, D.D.," in *Annals of the American Pulpit*, vol. 8, ed. William B. Sprague (1865); and Bradford K. Pierce, "Elijah Hedding," in *Lives of Methodist Bishops*, ed. Theodore L. Flood and John W. Hamilton (1882). Hedding's significant contribution to the expansion of Methodism in the northeastern United States receives mention in James Mudge, *History of the New England Conference of the Methodist Episcopal Church, 1796–1910* (1910).

ROBERT H. KRAPOHL

HEDGE, Frederic Henry (12 Dec. 1805–21 Aug. 1890), Unitarian minister and Harvard professor, was born in Cambridge, Massachusetts, the son of Levi Hedge, a Harvard professor, and Mary Kneeland. His early education came from his father, Alford Professor of Natural Religion, Moral Philosophy, and Civil Polity, and George Bancroft, future historian and diplomat who was then a student at Harvard, whom Levi hired to tutor the young Frederic. At the age of thirteen, Hedge accompanied Bancroft to Europe, where he studied for four years at Gymnasiums in Ilfeld (Hanover) and Schulpforta (Saxony). Hedge entered Harvard in 1823 and received his bachelor's degree in 1825. In 1829 he earned a master's degree from Harvard Divinity School. On 20 May 1829 Hedge was ordained at the Congregational church in West Cambridge (now Arlington), Massachusetts. Four months later he married Lucy Pierce, daughter of the Reverend John Pierce, of nearby Brookline.

While at West Cambridge, Hedge began to "unfold," as Ralph Waldo Emerson put it. He developed close ties with several progressive thinkers in the Boston area, including future fellow Transcendentalists Emerson and Margaret Fuller, both of whom he had met while a student at Harvard. In 1833 he published in the *Christian Examiner* the seminal article on Transcendentalism. "Coleridge's Literary Character," in which he reviewed Coleridge's transcendental ideas and expounded on their origins in the thought of the German philosophers Kant, Fichte, and Schelling. The article is often cited as the first positive recognition of Transcendentalism in the United States, helping to usher the movement into this country from Europe. Emerson hailed it as "a living, leaping logos."

In 1835 Hedge became minister of the Independent Congregational Church of Bangor, Maine. Emerson had encouraged Hedge to take the position, but other of his friends had had misgivings. Fuller wrote to Hedge that she believed accepting the position would take him into "mental solitude." Hedge himself shared much the same misgivings, only later allowing that his absence may have led to a greater independence of thought than would have been possible had he continued to reside among like-minded friends in Cambridge.

In 1836 Hedge organized the Transcendental Club, also referred to as the Hedge Club, and in 1840, at his urging, members of the club began publishing the *Dial*, the literary organ of American Transcendentalism. Soon thereafter, however, Hedge distanced himself from the more radical figures within the movement, such as Emerson. He believed that these radicals had "slipped their moorings" in leaving Unitarianism, and he criticized them for using Transcendentalism to destroy Christianity as a providential instrument rather than employing it as a creative force within the church. The best expression of the limits Hedge established for American Transcendentalism can be found in his *Conservatism and Reform* (1843), which Emerson rejected for publication in the *Dial*.

In 1848 Hedge made his first of several contributions to the dissemination of German literature in the United States with the publication of *Prose Writers of Germany*. *Prose Writers*, which contained English translations of twenty-eight "classics" of German literature, was the first large-scale effort to introduce the best of German letters to the American reading public. It was superseded only by Hedge's own *Hours with German Classics*, which appeared in 1886.

In 1849 Hedge resigned his position in Bangor for one at the Westminster Congregational Society in Providence, Rhode Island. In 1857 he moved to the First Parish in Brookline, Massachusetts, once the congregation of his father-in-law. With his return to the Cambridge milieu, his position within American intellectual circles and within the Unitarian church advanced rapidly. Also in 1857 Hedge was named professor of ecclesiastical history at Harvard Divinity School and editor of the *Christian Examiner*, a post he held for three years. In 1859 he began a four-year term as president of the American Unitarian Association. Upon resigning his position in Brookline in 1872, Hedge became a professor of German at Harvard.

In 1865 Hedge authored *Reason in Religion*, the most widely read book of its time on liberal religion. It is a classic statement of Transcendental Christianity, which reaffirms the importance of the intuitive insight by which truths, especially those related to moral law, are drawn directly from the divine within each person rather than being produced by the operations of the understanding on data gathered by the senses. Hedge's other major works include *Recent Inquiries in Theology* (1860), *The Primeval World of Hebrew Tradition* (1870), *Ways of the Spirit and Other Essays* (1877), *Atheism in Philosophy* (1884), and *Martin Luther and Other Essays* (1888).

Hedge resigned his position at Harvard in 1881, although he continued to teach for another three years. In 1886 the college awarded him an honorary LL.D. Hedge died four years later in Cambridge and was survived by his wife and three children. A collection of his sermons was published posthumously in 1891.

"Wherever new thought is marching onto the field," wrote Thomas Carlyle, "there we find Mr. Hedge in the front rank." This was an apt tribute for one of the leading exponents of liberal theology and progressive thought in nineteenth-century America. A leader of the Unitarian church in nineteenth-century America as well, Hedge led that body toward a consistent theology and defended it against its more orthodox critics. He is perhaps best known, however, for his role in the development of American Transcendentalism.

• Hedge's letters are in the Appleton, Bellows, Dall, and Washburn collections of the Massachusetts Historical Society in Boston, the Hedge and Emerson collections of the Harvard University Archives, the Cabot Collection of the Houghton Library at Harvard University, the Hedge papers of the Andover-Harvard Theological Library, and the Poor-Hedge Collection of the Schlesinger Library at Radcliffe College in Cambridge. Major holdings of Hedge's works can be found in the Boston Public Library, the Andover-Harvard Theological Library, and the New York Public Library. The most complete listing of Hedge's publications appears in Bryan F. Le Beau, *Frederic Henry Hedge: Nineteenth Century American Transcendentalist* (1985), the only full-length study of Hedge and his work. Useful shorter and more specialized studies include Orie W. Long, *Frederic Henry Hedge: A Cosmopolitan Scholar* (1940); Ronald Vale Wells, *Three Christian Transcendentalists: James Marsh, Caleb Sprague Henry, and Frederic Henry Hedge* (1943); and Doreen Hunter, "Frederic Henry Hedge, What Say You?" *American Quarterly* 32 (Summer 1980): 186–201.

BRYAN F. LE BEAU

HEDGE, Levi (19 Apr. 1766–3 Jan. 1844), professor of philosophy, was born in Warwick, Massachusetts, the son of Lemuel Hedge, a Congregationalist pastor, and Sarah White. Before entering Harvard College, Hedge spent several years, of necessity, as a mason's apprentice. He graduated from Harvard in 1792.

Hedge's teaching career began with an annual tutorship at Harvard that lasted from 1795 to 1800. In 1800 he was offered the first permanent tutorship in the college, made possible through the appropriation of funds from income from West Boston Bridge. Soon after receiving the position, Hedge successfully petitioned for an increase in salary that was justified by the prospect of his having a family after he married Mary Kneeland in 1801. They had one child, a son.

Under President John Thornton Kirkland, Hedge was promoted in 1810 to professor of logic, ethics, and metaphysics. He made his primary contribution to philosophy when he published his *Elements of Logick* (1816; rev. ed. 1835), which became used widely as a college textbook and was later translated into German. Hedge used the book as a text for his own students and in this capacity it had some influence on the direction of American philosophy. Although the book has been ignored for some time, a close reading shows that Hedge's work was in its general plan, if not in its detail, seminal. Indeed, it foreshadowed the pragmatists' interest in adapting experimental reasoning to general philosophy and to our dealings with everyday affairs. Besides attending to the standard matters of formal logic and philosophy of mind, he added a full section dealing with the modes of scientific inquiry. As he put it, logic should "teach the principles of every species of reasoning, which we have occasion to make use of, both in the pursuits of science, and in the ordinary transactions of life" (p. iv). In particular, drawing on the work of Scottish philosophers, Hedge addressed the nature of "intuitive evidences" that provide the basic judgments for scientific inquiry. Furthermore, he included a chapter dealing with probability in inductive reasoning. In all, his book foreshadowed much that became central in logic later in the century in the work of more noted philosophers such as Charles Peirce and Chauncey Wright.

The rest of Hedge's career was steady and esteemed. In 1827 he received the Alford Professorship of Natural Religion, Moral Philosophy, and Civil Polity, which he held until 1832. He continued to display an interest in Scottish philosophy when he edited Thomas Brown's two-volume *Treatise on the Philosophy of the Human Mind*. Hedge's role was central in making "Scotland dominant" in Harvard philosophy (Kuklick, p. 131). He died in Cambridge.

Hedge's position as teacher of logic and philosophy was enough to give him significant influence in the early development of American philosophy. His work in logic remains of historical interest because of its originality and because of its use of Scottish common-sense philosophy that continued to influence American thought to the end of the century. His career, however, should also be measured in light of the quiet contributions Hedge made to Harvard's gradual transition from an intellectual atmosphere grounded in religious doctrine to one grounded in scientific inquiry.

• The analysis of Hedge's logic above relies on the 1835 edition of his *Elements of Logick*. His life and work are discussed in Josiah Quincy, *The History of Harvard University*, vol. 2 (1860); Samuel Atkins Eliot, *Heralds of a Liberal Faith* (1910); and Bruce Kuklick, *Churchmen and Philosophers* (1985).

DOUGLAS R. ANDERSON

HEENAN, John Carmel (2 May 1835–Oct. 1873), boxer, was born in West Troy, New York, the son of Irish immigrants Timothy Heenan, a foreman at the federal arsenal, and Mary Morrissey. After completing elementary school, John Heenan trained as a machinist's apprentice. In 1852, while still a teenager, he set off for the gold rush in California. There he prospected and worked as a laborer in a foundry, swinging a sledgehammer twelve hours a day for the Pacific Mail Steamship Company in Benicia. The work produced a well-muscled body, and he began engaging in prizefights as the "Benicia Boy." In 1857 Heenan returned to New York and obtained work as a political strong-armer during elections. He was rewarded with a position in the customs office. His continued pugilistic endeavors won him acclaim as a local favorite.

On 20 October 1858 Heenan met John Morrissey, the American champion, in a prizefight at Long Point, Canada, for $2,500 a side. Despite sickness and a leg infection, Heenan refused to postpone the match; however, in the 11th round he struck the ring post, breaking his hand, and was forced to concede. Mor-

rissey retired shortly thereafter, and Heenan claimed the American championship. The modest, jovial, and popular young man enhanced his stature among his peers when he married the actress and poet Adah Isaacs Menken in 1859, but the union ended in divorce three years later.

In 1860 Heenan traveled to England to challenge the British champion, Tom Sayers, a London bricklayer who had already defeated a dozen contenders. Because boxing had been banned in England on account of previous fighters' deaths in the ring, Heenan moved about the countryside, training in secret to avoid arrest. Nevertheless, as the first great international match, the fight generated intense media coverage, with nationalistic sentiments prevalent on both sides. The *New York Clipper* claimed to have sold more than 200,000 copies of its account of the affair. The secretly staged fight took place at Farnborough on 17 April 1860 and was attended by an estimated 12,000 fans, including members of the British aristocracy, who had bought train tickets to an unknown destination. Heenan enjoyed a distinct advantage in size and youth. Over 6′ tall and weighing more than 190 pounds, he faced an opponent eight years older, who stood only 5′8″ and who weighed in at 152. Despite the seeming mismatch, Sayers inflicted significant damage to Heenan's face; but Sayers himself was knocked down several times and bloodied. Heenan controlled the fight after round 33. With Sayers in dire straits in round 37, English partisans began working on the ropes, and cries of "police" caused the referee to flee the scene. The ring collapsed completely in the 39th round as the competitors continued fighting among and with the pressing crowd, who interfered freely for three more rounds, after which Sayers departed the site. Despite objections from both sides, the match promoter finally reached an agreement with both competitors on 20 May, and the fight was ruled a draw. Sayers retired thereafter, and Heenan claimed the world championship.

After briefly returning to the United States after the fight, Heenan traveled back to England, where he remained for the balance of the American Civil War, engaging in boxing exhibitions with Sayers, touring with a circus, and taking on all challengers at $10,000 a side. He married the American actress Sarah Stevens during his English sojourn.

On 10 December 1863 Heenan lost his British title to Sailor Tom King in a match at Wadhurst, England. He remained in the country, operating a gambling business. After returning to the United States, he established himself as the proprietor of a gambling establishment in New York, and he occasionally served as a sparring partner for a new contender, Jem Mace. During an overland return trip in 1873 to California, Heenan became ill and died at Green River Station in Wyoming Territory.

Heenan is remembered as one who sparked the intense, nationalistic athletic rivalry between the United States and Great Britain. Lasting for more than half a century, such competition was based on mutual pretensions to cultural supremacy. Heenan was elected to the Boxing Hall of Fame in 1954.

• Sam Andre and Nat Fleischer, *A Pictorial History of Boxing* (1987), provides background information; and George Kirsch, ed., *Sports in North America: A Documentary History*, vol. 3 (1992), offers a balance of primary accounts drawn from the *New York Clipper, New York Times, London Times,* and *Bell's Life.*

GERALD R. GEMS

HEEZEN, Bruce (11 Apr. 1924–21 June 1977), geologist and oceanographer, was born in Vinton, Iowa, the son of Charles Christian Heezen, a farmer and Benton County agricultural advisor, and Esther de Schirding. He attended public schools in Muscatine, Iowa, and completed a B.S. at the State University of Iowa in 1948. He received his M.S. from Columbia University in 1952 and his Ph.D. in 1957. After hearing William Maurice Ewing give a lecture about the ocean floor at Iowa, Heezen became a protégé of Ewing.

Through Ewing's influence Heezen began his professional career in 1947–1948 at the Woods Hole (Mass.) Oceanographic Institution, sailing as chief scientist on an oceanographic cruise. In 1948 he was named a Roberts Fellow in Geology at Columbia University. When Ewing founded Columbia's Lamont Geological Observatory, later the Lamont-Doherty Geological Observatory, in 1949, Heezen transferred there to conduct his doctoral research with Ewing. From 1951 to 1953 he held an assistantship in geology at Columbia, and from 1955 to 1957 a research associateship. In 1957 he was appointed a senior research scientist in the Geological Observatory. In 1960 he joined Columbia's faculty as an assistant professor of geology; in 1964 he was promoted to associate professor, serving in that rank until 1977. Heezen was a frequent collaborator with Ewing until Ewing's retirement from Columbia in 1972.

Heezen's first major contribution was his discovery, as a consequence of his work on his master's degree, of submarine landslides and consequent turbidity currents. Turbidity currents, flowing masses of water made dense by suspended sediment, had been observed before, but their size and widespread occurrence on the continental margins was unknown before Ewing and Heezen's study. They explained the timing sequence of submarine cable breaks in the North Atlantic Ocean after the Grand Banks earthquake of 1929 as the result of a very large, extensive turbidity current triggered by a massive slump on the continental slope margin. The discovery of turbidity currents explained the origin of deep sea abyssal plains and peculiar "graded" sediments and required extensive modification of previous geologic doctrine.

In 1952 Heezen's colleague, Marie Tharp, noted what appeared to be the cross-section of a valley on the crest of the Mid-Atlantic Ridge on six ocean floor profiles she had constructed from echo-soundings. Heezen and Ewing then analyzed the distribution of earthquake epicenters in the world's oceans and found them concentrated in the centers of the ocean basins. From this they concluded that there was an axial valley or graben on top of the Mid-Atlantic Ridge resulting from tensional deformation. Tharp and Heezen then constructed submarine topographic maps from echo-sounding records, demonstrating the continuity of the linear valleys on the world's mid-oceanic ridges for more than 45,000 miles through the world's oceans and continuing into the African rift valleys. Discovery of the mid-oceanic rifts, which implied tensional deformation, was an essential element in establishing the global concept of shifting plates in the crust of the Earth—plate tectonics—generally considered the single most important advance in geologic science during the twentieth century. Heezen early accepted the concept of moving continents, which he ascribed to expansion of the Earth. This brought him into conflict with Ewing, who long maintained his own belief in fixed continents and ocean basins as plate tectonic theory developed. The theory of an expanding Earth failed to attract much support.

Heezen also intensively studied tektites, shards appearing similar to volcanic glass that are locally scattered in fields on the Earth's surface as well as in deepsea sediments. He explained them as the result of an asteroid about one mile in diameter exploding above the earth about 700,000 years ago. He also concluded that the explosion caused a reversal of the Earth's magnetic field and the extinction of many species. Although this work stimulated much interest and research on the part of others, his interpretation was not generally accepted.

Heezen also demonstrated the occurrence of a layer of volcanic ash extending over most of the Mediterranean sea floor. He ascribed the ash to an explosion about 1400 BCE of the island volcano of Thera in the Aegean Sea. He suggested that the ash-fall destroyed the Minoan civilization on Crete and was a possible explanation for the Atlantis legend.

From 1974 to 1977 Heezen was a consultant to the U.S. Naval Oceanographic Office and the Naval Research Laboratory. He was a member of a U.S. State Department advisory committee, the Law of the Sea Task Force. He was chairman of the National Academy of Sciences panel on oceanwide survey from 1964 to 1968; president of the International Union of Geological Sciences commission on marine geology (1965–1970), and coordinator for the Atlantic, Indian, and Pacific Oceans in the *Geologic Atlas of the World*; secretary of the International Commission on Marine Geophysics in 1969; and president of the International Association of Physical Sciences of the Ocean, Committee on Marine Geophysics. In 1959 he became president of the editorial committee for the *General Bathymetric Chart of the Oceans*, and in 1965 he was a member of the editorial committee for the *International Tectonic Map of the World* and convener for oceans.

In 1964 Heezen received the Woods Hole Oceanographic Institution's Henry Bryant Bigelow Medal and prize in oceanography for physiographic studies of the deep oceans. The American Geographical Society's Cullum Geography Medal was conferred upon him in 1973. His other honors included the American Association of Petroleum Geologists's Francis A. Shepard Medal (1975); the American Geophysical Union's Walter Bucher Medal (1977); and the National Geographic Society's Hubbard Medal, jointly with Tharp (1978). He was a fellow of the American Association for the Advancement of Science, the American Geographical Society, the Geological Society of America, the Iowa Academy of Science, the Marine Biological Association of the United Kingdom, and the Royal Astronomical Society, and a member of numerous specialized professional societies.

Heezen wrote *The Floors of the Oceans, I: The North Atlantic* (1959) with Marie Tharp and Ewing. *The Face of the Deep* (1959), a book on submarine photography he coauthored with Charles D. Hollister, was nominated for the National Book Award in 1972. A series of physiographic maps of the world's ocean floors, done with Tharp beginning in 1956, comprise his most visible scientific works. These are the *Physiographic Diagram of the South Atlantic Ocean, the Caribbean Sea, the Scotia Sea, and the Eastern Margin of the South Pacific Ocean* (1961), *Physiographic Diagram of the Indian Ocean, the Red Sea, the South China Sea, the Sulu Sea, and the Celebes Sea* (1964), *Physiographic Diagram of the North Atlantic* (1968), *Physiographic Diagram of the Western Pacific Ocean* (1971), and *Morphology of the Earth in the Antarctic and the Subantarctic* (1972). Heezen coauthored *Hawaii to Guam* (1971) and *Japan to Fiji* (1973), volumes 6 and 20 of the *Initial Reports of the Deep Sea Drilling Project*. In addition, he was author or coauthor of more than 300 scientific papers and editor or convener of six symposium volumes.

Heezen died of a heart attack on the navy's nuclear research submarine NR-1 while it was being towed to a dive site above the Rekjanes Ridge southwest of Iceland. He never married.

• Heezen's papers are held by the Smithsonian Archives, Washington, D.C. For biographical information see William Glen, *The Road to Jaramillo* (1982); William Wertenbaker, *The Floor of the Sea: Maurice Ewing and the Search to Understand the Earth* (1974); and "Presentation of the Society's Awards," *Geographical Review* 64 (1974): 264–65. An obituary is in the *New York Times*, 23 June 1977.

RALPH L. LANGENHEIM, JR.

HEFFELFINGER, Pudge (20 Dec. 1867–2 Apr. 1954), college football player, was born William Walter Heffelfinger in Minneapolis, Minnesota, the son of Christopher B. Heffelfinger and Mary Ellen Totton. His father, a Civil War veteran of the Union army, owned a shoe company and speculated in real estate. Nicknamed "Pudge" because he was taller and heavier than his peers, Heffelfinger attended Central High School in Minneapolis, where he played on the school's baseball team for four years and helped to establish the city's first high school football team, on which he starred as a back.

In 1888 Heffelfinger enrolled at Yale University, where he competed in boxing, track, crew, baseball, and football. A 6′3″, 188-pound guard, Heffelfinger soon achieved renown as one of the most dominating football players of his era. The 1888 Yale squad went undefeated, annihilating its opponents by a combined score of 698 to 0, as Heffelfinger teamed with such early standouts as George Woodruff, guard, and Amos Alonzo Stagg, end. The team's record during Heffelfinger's tenure was 13–0–0 in 1888, 15–1–0 in 1889, 13–1–0 in 1890, and 13–0–0 in 1891. Line play was important in the early era when forward passes were still illegal. Heffelfinger's size, compared to that of his lighter counterparts, and his speed allowed him to dominate interior line play. Walter Camp, recognized as the father of American football and originator of the All-America team, referred to Heffelfinger as "the fastest big man I ever saw."

Heffelfinger developed new tactics soon mimicked by other players and teams. He developed a "pulling guard" play whereby he left his line position to lead interference for the ball carrier on an end sweep. Heffelfinger also was able to disrupt one of the era's more vicious offensive strategies, the "flying wedge" or V formation. Fearlessly leaping over the offense's blockers, Heffelfinger disrupted his opponents' blocking and consequently the entire play. He created so many injuries with the tactic that the flying wedge was soon outlawed.

Yale lost only two games during Heffelfinger's four-year career. In 1889 he was named to Camp's inaugural All-America team, an honor he earned two more times. By the conclusion of his college playing, Heffelfinger was already a football legend. He received a bachelor's degree in 1891 from Yale's Sheffield Scientific School.

Not content to give up the game, Heffelfinger toured with semiprofessional teams during the 1891 season while he studied law and railroad economics at Yale. The following year he received $500 for playing one game with the Allegheny Athletic Association of Pittsburgh, Pennsylvania. Before that, claimed Heffelfinger, "they usually paid us off with silver pocket watches." He has been regarded by historians as the first professional football player because of a contract calling for a specified amount of money for particular services—in this case, playing one game for the Allegheny Athletic Association. Occasionally, Heffelfinger played other games for pay in the 1890s, but he did not do so on a regular basis. Because he never publicly acknowledged receiving money for playing, it is difficult to say precisely how many games he played as a professional.

After working briefly for the Great Northern Railroad in 1893, Heffelfinger accepted a coaching position at the University of California. He took a similar post at Lehigh University in 1894 and the University of Minnesota in 1895. While keeping his hand in football, Heffelfinger tried to establish himself in the business world. He returned to Minneapolis in 1894 to work in his father's shoe business and ten years later became the company's vice president and general manager. In the meantime, he married Grace Harriet Pierce in 1901; they had three children.

The shoe company dissolved in 1907, a result of that year's financial panic, but Heffelfinger soon became a successful building contractor. Active in local Republican politics, he won a seat as Hennepin County Commissioner in 1924, which he held until 1948. Heffelfinger also ran unsuccessfully for Congress in 1930. In the mid-1930s he began Heffelfinger Publications, which produced sports booklets for promotional use by manufacturing concerns.

Heffelfinger kept his status as a football legend alive well after his Yale playing days had ended. From 1896 to 1910 he volunteered as a line coach for the University of Minnesota and until 1917 helped to prepare Yale for its key contests against Princeton and Harvard. In 1922, at the age of fifty-four, Heffelfinger agreed to play in a charity game at Columbus, Ohio, against former Ohio State University players. Playing fifty-six minutes against much younger athletes, Heffelfinger performed well although, he allowed, "I'd have done better if I hadn't dislocated my shoulder early in the game." He played his last game at the age of sixty-five in another exhibition at Minneapolis. This time, however, an injured knee forced Heffelfinger to the sidelines after nine minutes of action.

Shortly before his death in Blessing, Texas, Heffelfinger collaborated with John McCallum to produce *This Was Football* (1954), a book of reminiscences and observations about his career and contemporary strategy. Heffelfinger criticized the modern game, particularly line play, believing the lineman should assume the upright position he had perfected with Yale rather than the crouching three-point stance preferred by modern coaches. That way, Heffelfinger maintained, the defensive lineman could always maintain eye contact with the ball carrier. Similarly, Heffelfinger believed coaches should turn over play-calling and strategy decisions to team captains, as Heffelfinger had experienced at Yale.

Heffelfinger is a member of the National Football Foundation Hall of Fame (inducted in 1951) and the Helms Athletic Foundation Hall of Fame.

• Walter Camp's papers at Yale University cover Heffelfinger's years at Yale. Heffelfinger is credited with writing two articles in collaboration with George Trevor, "Nobody Put Me on My Back," *Saturday Evening Post*, 15 Oct. 1938, pp. 14ff, and "Football's Golden Era," *Saturday Evening Post*, 29 Oct. 1938, pp. 16ff. Profiles of Heffelfinger and his Yale teammates can be found in McCallum, *Ivy League Football since 1872* (1977); Tim Cohane, *The Yale Football Story* (1951); and Allison Danzig, *Oh, How They Played the Game* (1971). For a description of Heffelfinger's professional contract with the Allegheny Athletic Association, see J. Thomas Jable, "The Birth of Professional Football: Pittsburgh Athletic Clubs Ring in Professionals in 1892," *Western Pennsylvania Historical Magazine* 62 (Apr. 1979): 131–47. Obituaries are in *Newsweek* and *Time*, 12 Apr. 1954, and the *New York Times*, 3 Apr. 1954.

MARC S. MALTBY

HEFLIN, James Thomas (9 Apr. 1869–22 Apr. 1951), U.S. congressman and senator, was born in Randolph County, Alabama, the son of Wilson Lumpkin Heflin, a physician, and Lavicie Catherine Phillips. In later years Thomas Heflin often said that his father had been one of the largest slaveholders in his section of Alabama before the Civil War, but his father owned only seven slaves in 1860. Nevertheless, the Heflins were quite prominent politically.

Heflin left Alabama Agricultural and Mechanical College (present-day Auburn University) in 1891, at the end of his junior year, to begin reading law in Lafayette, the county seat of Chambers County, in Alabama's hill country. After his admission to the bar in 1893, Heflin practiced in Lafayette, serving as the town's mayor (1893–1895), the county's register in chancery (1894–1896), and the county's state representative (1896–1899). In 1895 he married Minnie Kate Schuessler of Lafayette. They had three children, only one of whom survived infancy.

In 1901 Heflin was elected to the state constitutional convention, called primarily to disfranchise Alabama's black voters, and there he marked himself as one of the most virulently Negrophobic of the convention's members. He condemned delegates who wished to apply suffrage restrictions even-handedly to both races, and he urged that the constitution limit support for black schools to taxes collected from blacks themselves, warning that adequately funded black education would enable blacks to challenge white supremacy. He also opposed granting pensions to the widows of sheriffs killed defending black prisoners from lynch mobs.

The following year, Heflin became Alabama's secretary of state, and in 1904 he was elected to fill the seat of Congressman Charles W. Thompson, who had died. Taking his seat in December, he at once embraced virtually all of the legislative causes that were to occupy his sixteen years in the House of Representatives. He denounced the protective tariff, high railroad freight rates, and corporate monopolies and introduced bills to forbid speculation on cotton exchanges, to refund the Civil War cotton tax, and to promote the sale of cotton in the Orient. His frequent and passionate denunciations of trading in cotton futures earned him the nickname "Cotton Tom." Heflin urged racial segregation on railroad sleeping cars and on Washington, D.C., streetcars, and in 1908 he shot and badly wounded a black man who had cursed him following a confrontation on a streetcar. Heflin was indicted for assault with a deadly weapon, but the charges evidently were quietly dropped. In later years, Heflin cited this incident in his campaign circulars as one of his accomplishments.

Heflin supported a federal income tax and direct election of senators, strongly favored immigration restriction, and defended lynching as a natural response to interracial rape. A committed prohibitionist, he supported local rather than federal regulation but later opposed repeal of the Eighteenth Amendment. It was in his role as a leading opponent of women's suffrage that Heflin secured the one substantial legislative achievement of his quarter century in Congress, the joint resolution of May 1914 establishing Mother's Day as a permanent national holiday. In 1917 he strenuously supported American intervention in World War I and championed wartime conscription. Without it, he said, no blacks would volunteer, and since a disproportionate number of southern whites would volunteer, the South would be left defenseless before a German invasion, because northerners and westerners would likely refuse to come to the South's aid. Later, he was a zealous proponent of the League of Nations, whose detractors he considered tools of arms merchants.

In 1920, following the death of John H. Bankhead, Sr., Heflin was elected to the Senate, and in 1924 he was elected without opposition to a full term. While Heflin had supported the creation of the Federal Reserve System in 1913, saying that it "took away from Wall Street the power to produce a panic," as a freshman senator he launched a crusade against it. The Federal Reserve's deflationary policies, he argued, were robbing farmers of credit. He also opposed a constitutional amendment forbidding child labor, both as an infringement of states' rights and because it might deprive farmers of needed field-workers.

As late as February 1924, Heflin denied ever having been a member of the Ku Klux Klan. Immediately after the Klan's overwhelming victory in the Alabama elections of 1926, however, he enthusiastically embraced its anti-Catholicism and commenced the series of anti-Catholic tirades in the Senate that made him notorious throughout America. His initial allegation was that the Knights of Columbus, in league with large oil companies, were conspiring to compel the United States to intervene in Mexican affairs in order to restore reactionary elements to power. He opposed as a part of this plot the sending of American troops to Nicaragua. This hostility to Catholicism, together with his long-standing prohibitionism, led Heflin to oppose Alfred E. Smith's 1928 presidential bid and to direct a revolt that nearly carried Alabama for Herbert Hoover. This action so aroused the conservative leadership of the Alabama Democratic party that it banned Heflin and other "Hoovercrats" from participating in the party's 1930 primary. Heflin headed a ticket of bolters in the general election, but after a heated campaign, he was defeated by the regular Democratic nominee, John H. Bankhead, Jr. Heflin contested the election, alleging massive fraud, but the Senate voted to seat his opponent.

Heflin's defeat in 1930 effectively ended his political career. His attempts to regain a seat in the House of Representatives in 1934 and 1938 and in the Senate in a 1938 special election were all unsuccessful. During the 1930s he lived in part on New Deal patronage, serving as a special representative of the Federal Housing Administration from 1935 to 1936 and again from 1939 to 1942 and as special assistant U.S. attorney from 1936 to 1937.

Heflin's peculiar style of dress—wide-brimmed black hat, frock coat, ornate double-breasted vest, and string tie—became the model for editorial cartoonists' depiction of southern congressmen. His provincialism, vitriolic racial and religious prejudice, and nearly paranoid conviction of rampant conspiracies powerfully reinforced negative national stereotypes of the region's politicians. He died in Lafayette.

• Heflin's voluminous papers are housed in the library of the University of Alabama at Tuscaloosa. Heflin's early career has not been well studied, but on his senatorial years, see Ralph M. Tanner, "James Thomas Heflin, United States Senator, 1920–1931" (Ph.D. diss., Univ. of Alabama, 1967); Vincent J. Dooley, "United States Senator James Thomas Heflin and the Democratic Party Revolt in Alabama" (M.A. thesis, Auburn Univ., 1963); and J. Mills Thornton III, "Alabama Politics, J. Thomas Heflin and the Expulsion Movement of 1929," *Alabama Review* 21, no. 2 (1968): 83–112.

J. MILLS THORNTON III

HEGAMIN, Lucille (29 Nov. 1894–1 Mar. 1970), blues singer, was born Lucille Nelson in Macon, Georgia, the daughter of John Nelson and Minnie Wallace. In her youth Hegamin sang in church, and she also sang ragtime tunes and popular ballads at theaters in Macon. At about age fifteen she joined Leonard Harper's touring company until it was stranded near Chicago. As the "Georgia Peach," Hegamin found steady work in that city from 1914 to 1917, presenting popular songs in nightclubs, cafés, and restaurants. Among her piano accompanists were Bill Hegamin, whom she married around 1914, Tony Jackson, and Jelly Roll Morton. She followed Morton, her husband, and many other entertainers to the West Coast, performing in Los Angeles, San Francisco, and Seattle from 1918 to 1919.

Around November 1919 the Hegamins settled in New York City, where they performed in cabarets. Lucille gained further prominence through appearances in Happy Rhone's occasional all-star shows of dance and entertainment at the Manhattan Casino in Harlem on 30 April and 25 September 1920 and on 22 April 1921; at this third show she was billed as the Chicago Cyclone, perhaps owing to her vocal ability to fill a large casino in the era before microphones. Around November 1920 her recording career got under way with the pairing of "The Jazz Me Blues" and "Everybody's Blues"; Hegamin was the second blues singer to record, after Mamie Smith. On the strength of the popularity of this disc, the Hegamins began a tour of Pennsylvania, West Virginia, and Ohio in May, now billed as Lucille Hegamin and her Blue Flame Syncopaters [sic]. In the course of this tour "Arkansas Blues," which she had recorded in February, was released. It became her biggest hit, with the Arto label's master eventually being leased by and issued on ten other 78-rpm labels.

Hegamin held an engagement at the Shuffle Inn in Harlem from November 1921 to January 1922, and at the Manhattan Casino on 20 January she participated in a blues contest won by Trixie Smith. From February through May Hegamin toured in the second of three companies presenting *Shuffle Along*, the pioneering African-American musical comedy created by Flournoy E. Miller, Aubrey Lyles, Noble Sissle, and Eubie Blake. Smith was one of the stars, taking the position that the legendary Florence Mills held in company number one.

After the second company of *Shuffle Along* was disbanded in May, Hegamin began touring with her own Jazz Jubilee band, directed by pianist J. Cyril Fullerton. With the demise of Arto records—despite her blues hits—Hegamin worked briefly for Paramount and then initiated a four-year association with the Cameo label, for which she recorded "Aggravatin' Papa" (Sept. 1922), "He May Be Your Man, But He Comes to See Me Sometimes" (Oct. 1922), "Some Early Morning" (June 1923), and "Rampart Street Blues " (Oct. 1923).

The marriage to Bill Hegamin ended in 1923. Lucille toured that fall with a musical comedy, *Creole Follies*, and also in a duo with Fullerton on the Keith circuit from December 1923 through 1924. In January 1925 she was at the Cotton Club in New York, broadcasting on WHN radio three times weekly to the accompaniment of Andy Preer and his Cotton Club Syncopators. She resumed touring with Fullerton, working from February as a duo, from November 1925 to February 1926 with Fullerton leading a band, and then once again as a duo. Hegamin and singer Adelaide Hall were co-stars of *Lincoln Frolics* at Harlem's Lincoln Theater in March 1926. After further touring with Fullerton, Hegamin starred in shows at the Club Alabam in Philadelphia for four months in 1927; the accompanying band was led by George "Doc" Hyder. Later that year she appeared in the *Shufflin' Feet* revue at the Lincoln, and in 1928 she was at Harlem's Lafayette Theater in *The Midnight Steppers*.

Hegamin toured with Hyder in the late 1920s, and she sang with Claude Hopkins's Savoy Bohemians at the Lafayette for New Year's celebrations in 1930 and 1931. Her career ended at the Paradise Café in Atlantic City, where she appeared from 1933 to 1934. From 1934 into the 1950s she worked as a nurse. Details of a second marriage, to a Mr. Allen, are unknown. In August 1961, accompanied by pianist Willie "the Lion" Smith's band, Hegamin recorded four tracks on the album *Blues We Taught Your Mother*, and the next year she recorded the album *Basket of Blues*. Her last performance was at a benefit for Mamie Smith at the Celebrity Club in New York in 1964. She died in New York City, but despite her past fame and recent rediscovery, no obituary appeared in the *New York Times*.

Hegamin had a genuine feeling for the blues, but like her predecessor, Mamie Smith, she sang with a wholesomely full timbre and enunciated lyrics with clarity, sometimes throwing in exaggerated vaudevillian gestures as she did so. By contrast with the rough and unpretentious geniuses of the classic female blues style, Ma Rainey and Bessie Smith, Hegamin's sophisticated presentation fit reasonably well into the mainstream of American popular music. Thus it is not surprising that she would have been invited to record sooner than they, thereby establishing her position as a historical figure of note. Today Hegamin is largely forgotten and her recorded legacy unavailable, except to specialists in the areas of vaudeville and early blues.

• The definitive survey to 1927 is by Len Kunstadt, with an introduction by Victoria Spivey, "The Lucille Hegamin Story," *Record Research*, no. 39 (Nov. 1961): 3–7; no. 40 (Jan. 1962): 3, 19; no. 41 (Feb. 1962): 4–5; and no. 43 (May 1962): 6; the planned continuation of Hegamin's story never appeared. Kunstadt's work provides the basis for Derrick Stewart-Baxter's survey of her career, generically titled "Blues," *Jazz Journal* 20 (July 1967): 13, 16, and continued as "Blues: Lucille Hegamin, Part 2" (Aug. 1967): 25, 36. See also Ronald Clifford Foreman, Jr., "Jazz and Race Records, 1920–1932: Their Origins and Their Significance for the Record Industry and Society" (Ph.D. diss., Univ. of Illinois, 1968), which provided a substantial source for Robert M. W. Dixon and John Godrich, *Recording the Blues* (1970). Additional biographical information on Hegamin is in Sheldon Harris, *Blues Who's Who: A Biographical Dictionary of Blues Singers* (1979). An obituary is in *Jazz Journal* 23 (June 1970): 15.

BARRY KERNFELD

HEGEMAN, John Rogers (18 Apr. 1844–6 Apr. 1919), insurance executive, was born in the Flatbush section of Brooklyn, New York, the son of John G. Hegeman and Charlotte Owen Rogers. After an early education at neighborhood public schools, he studied at a private school in Poughquag, New York, before entering Brooklyn Polytechnic Institute. Leaving school after a year, Hegeman took a bookkeeping job at the Bank of the Republic of New York City. He then entered the industry in which he was to spend the rest of his career—insurance—becoming an accountant with the Manhattan Life Insurance Company. Hegeman rose to the position of secretary to the board of directors before leaving Manhattan to become company secretary for the Metropolitan Life Insurance Company in June 1870. On 26 October of the same year he married Evelyn Lyon of Brooklyn, with whom he would have one son. Elected as vice president of the company on the same day as his wedding (an event he ever afterward referred to as his "double anniversary"), Hegeman soon combined with company president Joseph F. Knapp to lead the Metropolitan during a period of solid growth.

A relatively new (founded in 1868) addition to the rapidly growing number of American life insurance companies, Metropolitan enjoyed a market niche. At a time when life insurance was largely a luxury for the wealthy, many companies desired to follow the 1875 lead of Prudential in writing coverage for industrial workers and small businessmen. The inherent problem of overhead (such policies required weekly visits from company agents in order to collect premiums due) was addressed by Metropolitan in a unique fashion. Employing aggressive German-American agents, the company soon wrote great amounts of business through the auspices of the Hildise Bund, a German-American fraternal lodge that assumed many of the onerous tasks associated with the carrying of small policies.

As a small company competing against giants, Metropolitan struggled in its early years. A breakthrough was achieved in 1879 when Hegeman and Knapp developed (with the aid of imported English salesmen who understood both the product and the customers) a sales force that could effectively service the so-called "industrial" market. These efforts expanded Metropolitan's potential market to all working-class individuals and provided a solid base for business growth. Upon the death of Knapp in 1891 Hegeman succeeded him as president of the company. Immediately insisting upon Haley Fiske as his vice president, Hegeman set out to revive the "ordinary" market (policies of large face value that were funded with quarterly or annual premiums). Utilizing the daring approach of using an industrial sales force to write ordinary insurance, the strategy paid immediate dividends, as did the 1896 move into an intermediate market of policies in $500 increments aimed at middle-class merchants. Metropolitan was also an early industry leader in the writing of group life insurance, which they began in 1917.

Under Hegeman's administration, Metropolitan liberalized its policy provisions. A more forgiving posture was taken on policy premium lapses, with policyholders often able to renew premium payments on their policies long after the stated lapse period had occurred. In periods of better-than-expected earnings, industrial policyholders received unscheduled and unexpected bonuses. In 1909 Metropolitan took the unorthodox step of becoming an advocate for better health care, diet, and sanitation among its policyholders. Nurses were employed to make home visits, and agents frequently carried literature (composed by the company) on combating various diseases directly to the policyholders. This altruistic outreach effort earned the company praise and proved profitable as well—healthy people lived longer and were able to pay premiums for a greater number of years. Metropolitan further involved itself in social issues by lending strong support in 1913 to the cause of workmen's compensation.

The Armstrong Investigation of 1905, precipitated by an internal squabble at rival Equitable, caused the entire New York–based life insurance industry to come under the scrutiny of the state legislature. Hegeman was called on to testify and immediately returned from a scheduled trip to Japan in order to alleviate suspicion that he had left to avoid testifying. While low-interest loans that he had received from New York Life received some opprobrium, the Metropolitan itself emerged from the hearings relatively unscathed. Hegeman was, however, indicted on three counts of perjury and seven counts of forgery in May 1907. Although the basis of the charges—Hegeman's altering of company annual reports—had been admitted, the forgery indictments were dismissed by the state supreme court later that year on account of a lack of evidence regarding fraudulent intent. The perjury indict-

ments were also dismissed in June 1910 for the same reason. Although Hegeman remained bitter about his treatment and suffered from increasingly poor health, the restrictions placed on Metropolitan's competitors allowed it to vault past the "Big Three" companies (New York Life, Equitable, and Mutual Life) to take the lead in total insurance in force.

In addition to his duties at Metropolitan, Hegeman was a trustee of the Union Dime Savings Bank and of the Hamilton Trust Company. He served as a director of the Metropolitan Bank & National Surety Company and with his wife also took an active interest in the Salem Baptist Church of New Rochelle, New York. Following Hegeman's death in Mamaroneck, New York, bequeathed funds resulted in the establishment of a tuberculosis research laboratory in Mount McGregor, New York, which was subsequently named the John Rogers Hegeman Memorial. A colorful figure, Hegeman proved effective in working with both Fiske and Knapp in building up Metropolitan Life to a position of industry leadership.

• No collection of Hegeman papers is known to have survived. Two excellent sources of information on Hegeman's life and career are Louis I. Dublin, *A Family of Thirty Million: The Story of the Metropolitan Life Insurance Company* (1943), and Marquis James, *The Metropolitan Life: A Study in Business Growth* (1947). An obituary is in the *New York Times*, 7 Apr. 1919.

EDWARD L. LACH, JR.

HEGGEN, Thomas (23 Dec. 1919–19 May 1949), author and playwright, was born Orlo Thomas Heggen in Fort Dodge, Iowa, the son of Thomas O. Heggen, the operator of a mortgage and loan company, and Mina Amelia Paulson. When the depression forced his father's company out of business in 1935, Heggen moved with his family to Oklahoma City, where he graduated from Classen High School the following year. Heggen attended Oklahoma City University, Oklahoma A & M University, and the University of Minnesota, from which he received a degree in journalism in 1941. Heggen, a slightly built young man with a sardonic wit, wrote for the student newspaper at all three universities.

After finishing his undergraduate studies, Heggen was recruited by the *Reader's Digest*. He worked for several months as an editor for the magazine at its headquarters in suburban New York City before joining the U.S. Navy shortly after American entry into World War II in December 1941. Prior to leaving for sea duty in August 1942 he married Carol Lynn Gilmer, a journalist who had been a classmate at Oklahoma A & M. They had no children. Heggen, who eventually rose to the rank of lieutenant, spent a year aboard the USS *Salinas*, a tanker operating in the North Atlantic. Severely injuring his hand in a fight with another officer, Heggen was sent to Chelsea Naval Hospital, outside Boston, to convalesce. He was then assigned to the USS *Agawam*, a New Orleans–based fuel tanker plying a Caribbean route, and finally to the USS *Virgo*, a cargo and troop ship in the South Pacific. While serving on the *Virgo*, Heggen began writing short stories based on day-to-day life aboard the ship.

Following his discharge from the navy in the autumn of 1945, Heggen brought his stories to his cousin, novelist Wallace Stegner, who recommended them to editors at the *Atlantic Monthly* and at the Houghton Mifflin Publishing Company. After concentrating on his fiction for several months, Heggen returned to his prewar job at the *Reader's Digest* in New York and to his wife, from whom he had been separated for two years. Three of Heggen's stories appeared in the *Atlantic Monthly* in the spring of 1946. Later in the year Houghton Mifflin published *Mister Roberts*, a collection of stories based on Heggen's experiences on the USS *Virgo* (ironically renamed the USS *Reluctant*). The vignettelike stories are loosely tied together by the character of Doug Roberts, a serious and high-minded but affable young lieutenant much admired by his crew. Offering no standard military heroics, *Mister Roberts* focused on the tedium and frustration endured by servicemen stationed far away from the front lines of combat and presented their forbearance as a kind of heroism. "A quiet, credible story of the corroding effects of apathy and boredom," said the *New Yorker* in its review (24 Aug. 1946). The short book garnered similar positive comments from a majority of critics, earned a place on the bestseller list, and established Heggen as one of the most promising writers to come out of World War II.

On 18 February 1948 a stage version of *Mister Roberts*, coauthored by Heggen and director Joshua Logan, opened at the Alvin Theatre in New York. Movie star Henry Fonda, making a return to Broadway after a long absence, played the title character. Although more broadly comic and slickly commercial than the brooding Heggen's melancholic book, the stage version of *Mister Roberts* received almost unanimously enthusiastic notices. "Warm, full-blooded, hilarious and moving entertainment . . . it is difficult to see how any theatregoer could fail to be delighted," wrote Richard Watts, Jr., in the *New York Post* (19 Feb. 1948). The play, which was produced by Leland Hayward, ran for 1,157 performances and was a highly lucrative enterprise for everyone involved.

Despite his newfound wealth and fame, Heggen was despondent over his divorce in 1946 and his inability to put his war experiences behind him and move on to a new project. He was also resentful that the lion's share of credit for the success of the stage version of *Mister Roberts* was going to Logan. Heggen began to drink heavily and abuse prescription drugs. His behavior became increasingly erratic and contentious, and his attempts to write another play progressed with difficulty. In May 1949 the 29-year-old Heggen was found dead in the Manhattan apartment he shared with Alan Campbell, a screenwriter and the estranged husband of writer Dorothy Parker. Heggen had drowned in his bathtub after having taken an overdose of barbiturates. He left no suicide note, and whether his death was deliberate or accidental was never established.

Heggen's demise did not affect the continuing success of *Mister Roberts*. A well-received movie version, directed by John Ford and Mervyn LeRoy, was released in 1955. Fonda repeated his stage role, and Logan cowrote the screenplay. Logan later directed and cowrote an unsuccessful sequel, *Ensign Pulver* (1964), based on a secondary character in *Mister Roberts*. A television situation-comedy version of *Mister Roberts* ran for a single season on NBC in 1965–1966.

• The most complete source of information on Thomas Heggen is John Leggett, *Ross and Tom: Two American Tragedies* (1974), a cobiography of Heggen and novelist Ross Lockridge, Jr., a contemporary of Heggen's who also came to an untimely end. See also Joshua Logan, *Josh: My Up and Down, In and Out Life* (1976), which discusses Logan's personal and professional relationship with Heggen; and Victor Cohn, "Mister Heggen," *Saturday Review of Literature*, 11 June 1949, p. 19. An obituary is in the *New York Times*, 20 May 1949.

MARY C. KALFATOVIC

HEGGIE, O. P. (17 Sept. 1876–7 Feb. 1936), actor, was born Otto Peters Heggie in Angaston, South Australia, the son of James Heggie, a rancher. His mother is not named in biographical sources. He spent several years in the Australian bush country where his father owned a "station." There he lived a rugged life of breaking horses. He completed his education at Winham College in Adelaide and at the Adelaide Conservatory of Music. He complied with his father's orders to study law but yearned for stage work. While his father was visiting his homeland, Scotland, Heggie obtained a small part in a play presented by the Charles Hawtrey touring company, *A Message from Mars* (1899). Thereafter until 1905 he acted in Australian stock companies on tour. He was billed professionally with the initials of his given names, though among friends he was known as Peter.

Heggie decided he had no future as an actor in Australia, since the good parts always went to actors imported from Britain or the United States. He went to London to break into the theater, knowing no one and having no funds. After a dreary job search, he got the small part of Pippy in *The Lemonade Boy* (1906), which was his first London appearance. Ellen Terry noticed his work in the play and hired him for her American tour (1907), where he had small parts in *Nance Oldfield* and *Captain Brassbound's Conversion*. Returning to the London stage, he played in varied roles, from the drama *Strife* (1909) to revivals and musicals. Heggie admired greatly the work of contemporary British playwrights and worked with a number of them, including G. K. Chesterton, Sir Arthur Conan Doyle, Granville Barker, John Galsworthy, Sir James Barrie, George Bernard Shaw, and Sir Arthur Wing Pinero.

Heggie returned to the New York stage in 1912 to perform the part of the drug-crazed younger brother in *The New Sin*, which he had previously played in

London. The play did not find an audience in New York, and he returned to London to perform in a Hippodrome revue, *Hullo, Ragtime!* His next Broadway appearance, to much acclaim, was as Uriah Heep in a dramatic version of *David Copperfield* titled *The Highway of Life.* Over the next few years he appeared in a succession of dramas by British playwrights that made his reputation as an actor of great ability and versatility. The *New York Herald* called him "one of the most finished and subtle actors on the American stage today" (7 Nov. 1915). Some of his most remembered Broadway performances during these years were Androcles in *Androcles and the Lion* (1915), the physician Sir Ralph Bloomfield-Bonnington in *The Doctor's Dilemma* (1915), the old lawyer's clerk Cokeson in *Justice* (1916), and The Conjuror in *Magic* (1917). In these and other roles he gained such American success that he never returned to the London stage.

At an unknown date he married Frances Rodgers. They had three children and lived in a home on Cape Cod near Hyannis, which he loved and returned to at every opportunity. As his base during theatrical appearances he used the Players Club in New York.

Heggie cared deeply about doing a good job of acting in a wide range of roles and avoided typecasting. He never stopped trying to improve his work and shied from personal publicity, preferring to be known only by the characters he created. He was less interested in promoting himself to stardom than in bettering the American theater. In 1919 he advocated establishing an endowed theater for the regular production of plays with literary worth but limited commercial appeal. The *New York Times* reported that Heggie had tried for eight years to attain a staging of *A Bit o'Love*, viewing it as "Galsworthy's second best play standing aside only for *Strife*" (10 May 1925). It was produced by the Actors Theatre that year, with Heggie as Michael Strangway. During the 1920s he became identified as a player of men much older than his actual age. In *The Truth about Blayds* (1922) he was a ninety-year-old, and in *Minick* (1924) and *This Woman Business* (1926) he appeared as men over seventy. The *New York Times* reviewer of the 1926 play said, "Mr. Heggie has one of his favorite parts as an old, white-haired, shuffling, nodding, gentle philosopher" (8 Dec. 1926). In the late 1920s, as the Broadway stage suffered from the competition of motion pictures and producers hesitated to present untried plays, he appeared in several revivals of old-time British comedies: *Trelawney of the Wells* (1927), *She Stoops to Conquer* (1928), and *The Beaux' Stratagem* (1928).

Talking pictures offered Heggie a new arena for displaying his skills. His first screen appearance was in *The Actress* (1928), a screen version of *Trelawney.* His success was immediate, and the *New York Times* reviewer declared, "The best performance of the picture is that given by O. P. Heggie as the grandfather" (9 July 1928). He made only occasional stage appearances in the years that followed; his last theatrical role was as a religious fanatic turned murderer in *The Green Bay Tree* (1933). On screen his many character roles were as varied as his stage roles had been. Sometimes he was in musicals, such as the well-received *Vagabond King* (1930), in which he played King Louis. He proved equally effective in thrillers such as *The Mysterious Fu Manchu* (1929), playing the implacable Inspector Nayland Smith, and *The Bride of Frankenstein* (1935), appearing as the old blind hermit who befriends the monster and teaches it to speak. His last film role was in *The Prisoner of Shark Island* (1936). Soon after completing this film, Heggie died suddenly of pneumonia in a Hollywood hotel. His ashes were flown back to Cape Cod to be scattered over the ocean.

Heggie's appearance has been described as square-faced and serious-looking, with the high forehead of the partially bald. A character sketch in *Theatre* speaks of his "large, prominent blue eyes" and says that offstage he "looks younger than one expects [because] Mr. Heggie frequently plays old men" (Oct. 1925). Later in the same sketch he is described as "the amiable hermit of Broadway . . . so shy that he does not like being interviewed for publication. . . . He is as fawnlike and elusive as Maude Adams." He holds a place in theatrical history as an actor who supremely wanted to be known only for his art as a performer. As such, from the time of his long-remembered portrayal of Androcles, he was lauded as an "actor of talent and charm and breadth" (*New York Times*, 7 Mar. 1915) and one who favorably introduced American audiences to early twentieth-century British playwrights.

• Materials on O. P. Heggie are in the Billy Rose Theatre Collection at the New York Public Library for the Performing Arts, Lincoln Center. A brief character sketch is "Mirrors of Stageland," *Theatre Magazine*, Oct. 1925. A list of his stage appearances is in *Who Was Who in the Theatre . . . 1912–1976.* For a list of film appearances see the *American Film Institute Catalog* indexes, 1921–1930 and 1931–1940. Portraits and production photographs are in Daniel C. Blum, *A Pictorial History of the American Theatre* (1960) and *A New Pictorial History of the Talkies* (1968). Obituaries are in the *New York Times, New York Herald Tribune,* and *Los Angeles Times,* all 8 Feb. 1936, and in *Variety,* 12 Feb. 1936.

WILLIAM STEPHENSON

HEIDBREDER, Edna Frances (1 May 1890–19 Feb. 1985), psychologist, was born in Quincy, Illinois, the daughter of William Henry Heidbreder, a druggist, and Mathilda Meyer. After earning an A.B. from Knox College in 1911, Heidbreder spent several years as a high school history teacher before taking up graduate study in 1917–1918 at the University of Wisconsin, where she was awarded an A.M. in philosophy in 1918. Heidbreder then went back to high school teaching for another few years before receiving her Ph.D. in psychology from Columbia University in 1924 with a dissertation entitled "An Experimental Study of Thinking."

Beginning as an instructor in 1924, Heidbreder spent the next ten years in the Department of Psychology at the University of Minnesota with a year's leave in 1930–1931 for study at the University of London. While at Minnesota, she began research in the area of personality, using rating scales to measure the traits of introversion and extroversion and inferiority attitudes. She also continued her research on thinking with studies of problem solving in children and adults.

Her participation in a federally funded research project on mechanical ability being carried out at the University of Minnesota secured Heidbreder's rapid advancement from assistant professor in 1926 to associate professor in 1928. Under the pressure of a deadline, the team of investigators had asked for her help in transforming their experimental results and research notes into a book. During the next several months she assembled, edited, and put into book form the materials that she received from the research team. Heidbreder thus became—along with D. G. Paterson, R. M. Elliott, L. D. Anderson, and H. A. Toops—a coauthor of *The Minnesota Mechanical Ability Tests* published in 1930.

Among the courses that Heidbreder taught at Minnesota was one on schools and systems of psychology, a subject that deeply interested her. In 1933 she published *Seven Psychologies*, in which she presented and analyzed seven contemporary schools of psychology in the United States with the intent of shedding light not only on "the function and significance of those particular seven, but to suggest the function and significance of systems in general" (p. vii). Highly acclaimed when it first appeared, it would subsequently be judged as a remarkably enduring contribution to the field of history and systems of psychology.

In 1934 Heidbreder left the University of Minnesota to become professor of psychology at Wellesley College, where she remained until her retirement in 1955. During her tenure at Wellesley, Heidbreder chaired the Department of Psychology from 1936 to 1946 and carried out research on concept formation, publishing the results of her studies in a series of nine papers between 1946 and 1955. She summarized the findings of her experiments as showing a general trend, namely, that conceptual achievements occurred more or less readily as more or less situational support was provided for effective perceptual participation in the performance of conceptual tasks. In addition, she noted the influence of the particular experimental conditions used to study concept attainment, for example, whether subjects were given instances of concepts in the form of drawings or of verbal phrases, which affected this general trend. Extending her work in systematic psychology, she continued to publish evaluations of various theoretical approaches, including Kurt Lewin's topological psychology (1937), Freudian psychology (1940), and functionalism (1969).

Professional activities figured prominently in the later part of Heidbreder's career. She was a member of the governing board of the American Psychological Association in 1939–1940 and again from 1942 to 1944. She was a representative of that organization to the National Research Council from 1944 to 1947 and again from 1952 to 1955. In 1943–1944 she served as president of the Eastern Psychological Association and in 1950 as president of the American Psychological Association's division on general psychology. Heidbreder also served as secretary for the section on psychology (1942–1945) and as vice president (1947–1948) of the American Association for the Advancement of Science. She was a consulting editor for the *Journal of Abnormal and Social Psychology* (1938–1949) and for *Psychological Monographs* (1946–1962).

Her accomplishments were recognized by the American Psychological Association, which, as part of its seventy-fifth anniversary in 1967, honored her along with other senior members who had made distinguished lifetime contributions to the field. A festschrift, *Historical Conceptions of Psychology*, dedicated to Heidbreder in appreciation for her contributions to systematic psychology and edited by Mary Henle, Julian Jaynes, and John Sullivan, appeared in 1973.

Following her retirement from Wellesley College, Heidbreder was on the faculty of the Radcliffe seminars from 1955 to 1961. Never married, she lived in the town of Wellesley from the time she arrived at the college in 1934 until 1982, when she moved to a retirement community in Bedford, Massachusetts, where she died.

Heidbreder was remembered by friends, students, and colleagues as a remarkable woman for her personal as well as her intellectual qualities. A friend recalled being charmed by "her friendliness, her graciousness, and her perceptiveness." She was an inspiring teacher and one who impressed her introductory students by giving polished lectures without the use of notes. For advanced students doing independent work under her direction, she was a source of sympathetic encouragement and insightful suggestions. Former colleague Virginia Onderdonk described her as "open to whatever came along to observe and enjoy . . . a witty, lively, and altogether delightful companion" (*Wellesley Alumnae Magazine* [Spring 1985]: 51). Committed to women's education, Heidbreder spent more than twenty-five years teaching at two institutions dedicated to that undertaking—Wellesley and Radcliffe. She was also an advocate of equal pay for equal work and equal representation by women in various kinds of work as a means of breaking down stereotypes that she believed put limits on the development of women's abilities and achievement.

Heidbreder's two major contributions to psychology are her work on cognition and on systems. Her research on cognition began in the 1920s with her Ph.D. dissertation on thinking and culminated in the 1950s with an important series of studies that explored various conditions of concept attainment. Heidbreder's investigations of cognition coincided with the era in which behaviorism dominated American psychology, when thinking was a topic most psychologists chose to ignore.

Her writings on systematic psychology—*Seven Psychologies* and several later papers—are what have brought Heidbreder the most lasting recognition. Praised at the time of its publication in 1933 for its clarity and its fairness to the systems presented and as a book without peer, *Seven Psychologies* received an additional tribute in 1974 by Mary Henle and John Sullivan, who wrote a retrospective review of the book. They were struck by how contemporary the work remained in a field where factual knowledge became outdated in a decade or less.

Heidbreder herself made a clear distinction between the facts of psychology and its systems. Of the latter she wrote that "they can best be understood not as statements of scientific fact, not as summaries of existing knowledge, but as ways and means of arriving at knowledge, as temporary but necessary stages in the development of a science, as creations of workers who, in a confusing and sometimes depressing enterprise, must keep not only their poise but also their verve" (*Seven Psychologies*, pp. 16–17). Heidbreder's penetrating analyses of seven schools of psychology as seven attempts to conceptualize and to reconceptualize the field has endowed the work with lasting significance.

• There is no known body of papers, but information on Heidbreder may be found in the Wellesley College Archives. For an account of Heidbreder's life, career, and reflections on being a woman in psychology, see Laurel Furumoto, "Edna Heidbreder: Systematic and Cognitive Psychologist," *Psychology of Women Quarterly* 5 (1980): 94–102. Mary Henle and John Sullivan, "*Seven Psychologies* Revisited," *Journal of the History of the Behavioral Sciences* 10 (1974): 40–46, is a retrospective evaluation of Heidbreder's most important work. An obituary by Mary Henle is in the *American Psychologist* 42 (1987): 94–95.

LAUREL FURUMOTO

HEIDE, Wilma Scott (26 Feb. 1921–8 May 1985), social reformer and activist, was born in Ferndale, Pennsylvania, the daughter of William Robert Scott, a railroad brakeman, and Ada Long, a schoolteacher and retail clerk. According to Wilma's friend and biographer, Eleanor Humes Haney, William Scott was a labor union activist who read the classics and discussed intellectual issues with his daughter. Wilma was an excellent student and a leader in her small town high school. She captained a girls' basketball team and after graduation played semiprofessional ball for a couple of years. Active in a church youth group, she left the Lutheran church in her teens when she discovered women could not be ordained. In June 1938 she graduated from high school and won a scholarship to Seton Hill, a local Catholic women's college. Her parents would not allow her to accept it, insisting that she contribute to the support of her family. Disappointed, Wilma worked as a clerk, played basketball, and for a brief time was engaged to a local youth. In 1940 she left home to take a job as an attendant in a state mental hospital. Two years later she took a factory job in Cleveland, Ohio, but soon left to pursue a nursing degree at Brooklyn State Hospital in New York.

From the beginning, Wilma resented the hierarchical nature of the nursing profession and its close relationship to what she would later identify as the male-dominated institutions of the military and religion. Bored with her courses and skeptical of nursing procedures, she attracted the attention of a sympathetic supervisor who arranged for her to meet with Eleanor Roosevelt to discuss social change. After she graduated, Wilma worked as a psychiatric nurse at a state institution in Torrance, Pennsylvania, where she protested the treatment of patients and was forced to resign after being falsely accused in a check cashing scandal.

Between 1948 and 1950 she worked as a nurse at Pennsylvania College for Women, finished an undergraduate degree at the University of Pittsburgh, and started a master's program in sociology. At Pittsburgh she also met her future husband, Eugene Heide. They were married in 1951 and later divorced in the early 1970s. Wilma Heide worked as a nurse while both she and her husband continued graduate studies. Then in 1953 she followed her husband to South Carolina and took a job as education director in the School of Nursing at Orangeburg. There she was active in the National Association for the Advancement of Colored People and the League of Women Voters. She aroused the ire of local league officials for registering black voters and reported receiving hate mail and threats. She also later told friends that a black man was killed as the two of them walked down the street together in a small southern town.

In 1955 the Heides returned to Pennsylvania where Eugene began a series of jobs as an administrator in the Pennsylvania state university system. Increasingly restless and frustrated, Wilma worked as a nurse, sociology instructor, and administrator of various programs at Pennsylvania State University facilities. She and her husband had two daughters in the late 1950s. During her second pregnancy she suffered from severe depression and contemplated suicide. Seeking psychiatric help, she told her doctor that she "wanted to be a man."

In the early 1960s Heide pursued her interests in social change and civil rights, forming an early prototype of the Head Start program and writing an award-winning series on race relations for a local Pennsylvania paper. In 1965 Heide served as vice chair of the Allegheny County Civil Rights Council and vice chair of the Westmoreland County Economic Opportunities Program. Eventually she became the only woman member of the Pennsylvania State Human Relations Commission. Shortly after its founding in 1966, she contacted the National Organization for Women (NOW) and arranged to attend the national board meeting. She founded the Pittsburgh chapter of NOW, which became under her leadership one of the strongest and most influential branches of the new women's rights organization. Within a year, Heide was on the national board of NOW and was Pennsylvania coordinator for the organization. Under her leadership, the Pittsburgh chapter held demonstrations in Washington calling for Senate passage of the Equal Rights Amendment (ERA), organized a one-day national boycott against Colgate-Palmolive to force lifting of discriminatory practices against women, and led the fight against sex segregated employment advertising in Pittsburgh papers. In 1971 Heide became the third president of NOW, succeeding Aileen Hernandez.

Heide served as president for two and a half tumultuous years. During the early 1970s NOW was a growing, lively organization but also a very contentious and divided one. There were ideological conflicts between lesbians and heterosexual feminists and also disagreements between those who saw NOW as a mainstream liberal rights oriented organization and those who envisioned it as a more radicalizing force. Even more serious, NOW grew too rapidly to allow for effective coordination between national and local efforts. By late 1973 these problems were surfacing in the form of conflict between regional NOW organizations, and in 1974 Heide announced she would not be a candidate for reelection. While she suffered from health problems (a brain tumor had been diagnosed in 1969, but she had chosen to eschew conventional treatments) and also felt isolated from many of the factions emerging in NOW, Heide had accomplished a great deal. During her term of office NOW managed to ensure congressional passage of the ERA, won a $38 million settlement from AT&T on employment discrimination, and successfully pressured the federal government to move on affirmative action programs in hiring and contract-letting. The one criticism made of Heide's presidency was that she had sometimes given too much freedom to warring groups within the organization.

In the mid-1970s Heide, who supported the moderates in NOW, withdrew from active membership to pursue academic interests, receiving a doctoral degree from the Union Graduate School of the Union for Experimenting Colleges and Universities. She taught briefly at Goddard College, and from 1978 to 1982 she was director of the women's studies program at Sangamon State University. She resigned in 1982, upset by the conservatism of the university and still suffering from the effects of a brain tumor. The last three years of her life were spent lecturing, attending peace conferences, and completing her book, *Feminism for the Health of It* (1985). She died of a heart attack in Norristown, Pennsylvania.

While Heide came to national prominence briefly in the early 1970s as president of NOW, her larger significance is as a hard-working social reformer who fought for the rights of mental patients in the early 1940s and then turned her attention to civil rights, educational issues, and women's issues.

• Heide's *Feminism for the Health of It* is a good source for her opinions on nursing as a profession, the female life cycle, and general health issues. A full biography is *A Feminist Legacy: The Ethics of Wilma Scott Heide and Company* (1985), written by her friend Eleanor Humes Haney. Roberta Stock discusses Heide's ideological beliefs in *Wilma Scott Heide: Her Embracement of Nurses and Nursing* (1991). Winifred D. Wandersee, *On the Move: American Women in the 1970s* (1988), provides valuable perspectives on Heide's tenure as NOW president.

BARBARA A. McGOWAN

HEIDELBERGER, Charles (23 Dec. 1920–18 Jan. 1983), biochemist, was born in New York City, the son of Michael Heidelberger, an organic chemist, and Nina Tachau. From his youth, Heidelberger was exposed to science, because his father was an established chemist at the Rockefeller Institute for Medical Research. Throughout his youth, except in the summers when on vacation or in a camp on Cape Cod, Heidelberger lived in New York City and attended the Birch-Wathen School at Ninety-fourth Street. Here he learned the fundamentals of language, history, and science. While in high school, he engaged in the extracurricular activities of drama, journalism, and music. He became a sufficiently accomplished musician on the violin and the trumpet to play in jazz bands as well as become a member of the musicians' union. In 1937 he entered Harvard College, where he majored in chemistry. After obtaining a B.S. in 1942, he started graduate work in chemistry at Harvard and earned an M.A. in 1944 and a Ph.D. in 1946, with Louis Fieser as his Ph.D. adviser. Studying for his doctorate during World War II, Heidelberger wrote his thesis on "The Synthesis and Antimalarial Activity of Some Naphthoquinones," substances of great importance for controlling malaria in the Pacific war theater. While working under Fieser, Heidelberger became familiar with arylhydrocarbons (polycyclic aromatic hydrocarbons—carcinogens). After finishing his work at Harvard, Heidelberger obtained a position in the laboratory of Melvin Calvin at the University of California, where he participated in pioneering work using $_{14}C$ for the elucidation of metabolic pathways. An important outcome of this work was Heidelberger's synthesis of the first $_{14}C$ labeled carcinogen dibenzanthracene 9, 10 $_{14}C$ (now 7,12-$_{14}C$) dibenz (a,h)anthracene and studied its metabolism. In 1943 he married Judith Werbel; they had two girls and one boy.

This use of radioactively labeled carcinogens to study their metabolic pathways brought Heidelberger as assistant professor of oncology to the McArdle Laboratory at the University of Wisconsin in 1948. Here he continued work on synthesizing radiolabeled arylhydrocarbon carcinogens and studying their fate after injection into animals. Working first with Van R. Potter, he in 1950 synthesized [$_{14}C$] orotic acid, which was to serve as a radioactive intermediate for study of the metabolic pathway for the formation of pyrimidines from citric acid. This work initiated Heidelberger's interest in pyrimidines, which, as it turned out, was a first step toward his most important work: development of the cancer chemotherapeutic agent 5-fluorouracil.

When K. E. Wilzbach at the Argonne National Laboratories reported his method for tritiating organic compounds, Heidelberger applied this method to polycyclic hydrocarbons (arylhydrocarbons). The higher specific radioactivity facilitated studies of the binding of aromatic hydrocarbons to DNA and RNA, which in 1962 resulted in Heidelberger's being the first to report these carcinogens bound to nucleic acids.

Heidelberger then turned his attention to developing a simpler method for studying the mechanism by which arylhydrocarbons produced cancer. For these studies he turned to tissue culture. In time he developed a system, reported in 1973, to transform cells grown in vitro, which, on implantation or injection into animals, became cancerous tumors. Although Heidelberger was not the first to accomplish this feat, he was the first to produce tumors by injecting an established line of transformed cells. The procedure was important because it allowed transfer of tumors by injecting cultured cells whose properties could be controlled.

Heidelberger's most significant work was on the cancer chemotherapeutic agent 5-fluorouracil. Rapidly growing cells require large amounts of thymidylate for the formation of DNA. Seymour S. Cohen gave the term "thymidineless death" to his discovery in 1954 that cells died when the amount of thymidylate was low. Robert Rutman, A. Cantarow, and K. Paschkis also reported in 1954 that more uracil is taken up by cancer tissue than by normal tissue. With this information, Heidelberger determined that the uptake of uracil by human tumor tissues behaved as that of normal animal cells did. Heidelberger reasoned that if he synthesized uracil with a fluorine atom substituted for a hydrogen at the 5 position of uracil, the tightly bonded fluorine atom could not be removed by thymidylic synthetase, and the formation of thymadylic acid would be blocked, thus preventing the formation of DNA. Heidelberger was able to synthesize 5-fluorouracil, which, when tested, inhibited the growth of tumors. After successful testing in humans, this compound became one of the frequently used cancer chemotherapeutic agents.

During Heidelberger's twenty-eight years at the McArdle Laboratories, he became a full professor at the University of Wisconsin in 1958 and the American Cancer Society Professor of Oncology in 1960. In 1973 he was appointed the associate director for basic research of the Wisconsin Clinical Cancer Center. He moved to the Los Angeles County–University of Southern California Comprehensive Cancer Center as director of basic research in 1976.

Although throughout his career Heidelberger did little lecturing to medical students, he was a good teacher, teaching by example and direct contact. He trained numerous Ph.D. students, in his laboratory. In addition to his musical pursuits, Heidelberger loved travel and, on his numerous trips throughout the world, took many slides of the scenery, people, and subjects that fascinated him. He was an avid sailor. In 1975 he married Patricia Boshell. Heidelberger died in Los Angeles, California, eighteen months after he was found to have cancer of the nasal sinus.

• Biographical information is in Elizabeth C. Miller, and James A. Miller, "Charles Heidelberger, December 23, 1920–January 18, 1983," National Academy of Sciences, *Biographical Memoirs* 58 (1989): 258–302.

DAVID Y. COOPER

HEIDER, Fritz (18 Feb. 1896–2 Jan. 1988), psychologist, was born in Graz, Austria, the son of Moriz Heider, an architect in the Styrian provincial government, and Eugenie von Halaczy. He was taught at home until the age of nine. An accident with a cap pistol that damaged his left eye kept him out of military service and later made it natural for him to be interested in perception. After studying architecture and law, he earned a doctorate in philosophy from the University of Graz in 1920 for research under Alexius Meinong on the representation of objects in consciousness—an issue on the border between cognitive psychology and the theory of knowledge that would concern him throughout his life.

After working briefly as an applied psychologist in Austria, Heider spent six years (1921–1927) traveling in Germany, Austria, and Italy and studying psychology at the University of Berlin. In Berlin he worked closely with Gestalt psychologists Wolfgang Köhler and Max Wertheimer, and also with Kurt Lewin. From 1927 to 1930 he studied in Hamburg, where he worked with William Stern, Ernst Cassirer, and Heinz Werner. All of these scientists were interested in the issues of psychology, perception, and knowledge that concerned him as well. In the latter period he published two important papers, "Thing and Medium" (1927) and "The Function of the Perceptual System" (1931). In these original theoretical studies, Heider carefully analyzed the mediating processes that convey information about things to our sense organs and helped establish the distinction now accepted in cognitive science between distant (physical) and proximal (organic) stimuli in perception.

In 1929, when Gestalt psychologist Kurt Koffka, then at Smith College, wrote to William Stern to recruit an assistant for his laboratory, Stern passed the offer to Heider, who accepted the next year. Although he encountered some culture shock, his reception at Smith was friendly. He married psychologist Grace Moore in 1930; they had three sons. His wife remained his closest intellectual companion and surely helped to complete his integration into American life.

Rising from assistant to associate professor, Heider did research on the perception of causal relationships at Smith and worked with his wife at the Clarke School for the Deaf on the psychology of deaf children. In a study of motion picture descriptions published with Marianne Simmel in 1944, he showed that movements of unchanging, seemingly neutral forms can give rise to lively impressions of interpersonal events and relationships. In 1946 he developed the "balance hypothesis" to account for the organization of the social attitudes stimulated by cognitive events.

Increasingly burdened by a heavy teaching load and a lack of graduate students, Heider in 1947 accepted an offer from the University of Kansas, where he remained for the rest of his life. Colleagues at Kansas included émigré cognitive psychologist Martin Scheerer and clinicians from the nearby Menninger Foundation. After being urged by others, Heider applied for and won a Guggenheim Fellowship to complete his most important work, *The Psychology of Interpersonal Relations* (1956). Extending his earlier research on cognitive representation to social psychology, he tried to create a full-scale, systematic account of naive, "common sense" experience and the principles by which it is organized. The book became a major contribution to understanding the relations of cognitive and social psychology and a founding document of attribution theory—the study of the assignment of social and personality qualities to humans as well as perceptual qualities to the external world.

Heider received a Distinguished Scientific Contribution Award from the American Psychological Association in 1965, and he became a fellow of the American Academy of Arts and Sciences in 1981. He died in Lawrence, Kansas. Like many other German intellectuals in America, he brought theoretical enrichment and sophistication to a field largely dominated by hard data and technocratic applications.

• Heider's papers are privately held in Lawrence, Kansas. Some correspondence and autobiographical remarks are at the Archives of the History of American Psychology in Akron, Ohio; career records are at the Smith College Archives and the Archives of the University of Kansas. Heider's most important theoretical papers have been published in English in "On Perception and Event Structure, and the Psychological Environment: Selected Papers by Fritz Heider," *Psychological Issues* 1, no. 3 (1959). He told his own story engagingly in *The Life of a Psychologist: An Autobiography* (1983). His notebooks and manuscript fragments are in Marijana Benesh-Weiner, *Fritz Heider: The Notebooks* (6 vols., 1987–1989). Brief summaries of his impact are in Edward E. Jones, "The Seer Who Found Attributional Wisdom in Naivety," *Contemporary Psychology* 32 (Mar. 1987): 213–16; and John H. Harvey, "Fritz Heider (1896–1988)," *American Psychologist* 44 (1989).

MITCHELL G. ASH

HEIFETZ, Jascha (2 Feb. 1901–10 Dec. 1987), violinist, was born in Vilna, Lithuania, the son of Reuven Heifetz, a violinist, and Anna (maiden name unknown). Jascha's exceptional and instinctive musical gifts were already evident at age three, when he began violin study with his father, who was concertmaster of the Vilna Symphony Orchestra. His father arranged Jascha's first public concert in order to convince officials of the Imperial School of Music in Vilna that the five-year-old Jascha was ready for admission. Once admitted, he studied with Ilya Davidovitch Malkin, a pupil of Leopold Auer. Heifetz played the Mendelssohn Concerto in Kovno at age six, and a year later he graduated from the Vilna school. Persuaded by Malkin to listen to Heifetz play, Auer declared that he had never heard such beautiful playing. By the autumn of 1910 Heifetz was enrolled in the St. Petersburg Conservatory, and after one term he became Auer's private student. On 30 April 1911 Heifetz performed with great success in St. Petersburg. His Berlin debut recital in May 1912 was considered "immaculate" and led to his performance of the Tchaikovsky Concerto later that year with the Berlin Philharmonic Orchestra un-

der Arthur Nikisch. Between 1913 and 1916 Heifetz continued studies with Auer in St. Petersburg and in Loschwitz, near Dresden, at Auer's summer studio. Heifetz performed numerous concerts, especially in Norway during the summer of 1916 and in Russia during the winter of 1916–1917.

In 1917 Heifetz accepted an American manager's offer to perform in the United States. During the turmoil preceding the Russian Revolution, Heifetz, along with his parents and sisters, escaped from Russia to New York via Siberia, Japan, and San Francisco. Heifetz made his American debut in Carnegie Hall on 27 October. His fantastic dexterity, dazzling perfection, and superior musicianship astonished his audience; he became an overnight sensation. At the time, Heifetz's main competitor was violinist Mischa Elman. In 1919, however, Fritz Kreisler, another major competitor, returned to the concert stage. Although Kreisler and Elman maintained positions of stature because of their individual stylistic appeal, Heifetz eclipsed them both, and his playing set a new standard for all who followed. He changed audience expectations and professional violin-playing standards, becoming *the* violinist of the twentieth century.

After three years of basking in the many professional and personal opportunities available to him in the United States, Heifetz made his London debut on 5 May 1920. A tour of Austria, Germany, Italy, and France followed, and his impeccable artistry became known throughout the world. In 1921 alone, Heifetz performed in Australia, India, Europe, Britain, Ireland, and Germany. Other tours took him to Japan (1923), Israel (then Palestine, 1933), and Russia (1934). Heifetz had become a U.S. citizen in 1925, and he returned to Russia only once, in 1934. During this trip, he retrieved his treasured quarter-size violin from his uncle's house.

During World War II Heifetz became a volunteer "musical soldier," performing for enthusiastic U.S. soldiers in California, the Panama Canal Zone, Central and South America, North Africa, and Europe. Heifetz also performed with Sir John Barbirolli and Vladimir Horowitz in a 1941 benefit concert for medical aid to the Soviet Union.

In April 1947, at the peak of his career, Heifetz sought the opportunity to rest and refill his personal and artistic reservoirs. He married Frances Spiegelberg that year, and their son was born a year later. Heifetz took a sabbatical from concertizing that lasted until January 1949. When Heifetz returned to the concert stage, the *New York Times* music critic Olin Downes reflected that "we have never heard him play in a more phenomenal manner or communicative spirit." Heifetz said, "I still play the same way. . . . I'm still trying to present pieces as I think the composer was thinking of presenting them."

Heifetz followed his return to the stage with several tours to Israel (1950, 1951, 1970 with Gregor Piatigorsky), but he never resumed his former demanding schedule of more than 100 concerts per year. In February 1960 Heifetz assumed a new role, as Distinguished Professor of Violin at the University of Southern California. In doing so, he followed in the footsteps of Auer, his beloved professor. Among Heifetz's numerous students, Erick Friedman and Eugene Fodor achieved wide recognition.

Film captured Heifetz's artistry in *They Shall Have Music* (1939), a drama he was in built around a famous violinist; he also played on the soundtrack. He was one of the all-star cast of musicians assembled for the movie *Carnegie Hall*, filmed in the summer of 1946. In 1971, to celebrate Heifetz's seventieth birthday, NBC-TV aired an hour-long special featuring Heifetz in performance with the French National Orchestra.

On 23 October 1972, almost fifty-five years after his New York debut, Heifetz played a recital in the Dorothy Chandler Pavilion to raise scholarship money for the USC School of Music. Heifetz performed a strenuous program, showing no hint of age. This turned out to be his last performance.

Heifetz was unrivaled in the elegance of his technical perfection—the exactness and clarity of pitch, articulation, and bow arm dexterity. Myriad gradations of speed enhanced his intense and vibrant vibrato, and he applied quickly ascending portamenti as an interpretive gesture. He was a master of expressive nuance, with a vast tonal palette. His preference for fast tempi demonstrated his unfailing technical security that allowed him to play with devilish abandon, yet replete with elegant refinement. His sound had radiance, brilliance, and "sizzle." A consummate violinist, Heifetz made violin playing look easy because, as he said, he worked very hard before coming to the concert stage and was committed to continual practice. Heifetz's renowned violin colleagues, such as Nathan Milstein, David Oistrakh, Oscar Shumsky, Isaac Stern, Henryk Szeryng, Itzhak Perlman, and Pinchas Zukerman, proclaimed him supreme among violinists, and in 1971 Stern declared, "Heifetz represents a standard of polished execution unrivaled in my memory by any violinist either by book or by personal knowledge."

Heifetz's artistry received thorough documentation through his exclusive recording contract with RCA, saving for posterity much of his vast repertoire, from concertos with major orchestras and conductors, among them Serge Koussevitzky and Arturo Toscanini, to collaborations with pianists Emanuel Bay and Brooks Smith. Heifetz's recorded legacy also includes his famous chamber music partnerships, which included duos with cellist Emanuel Feuermann, with cellist and close friend Piatigorsky, and with violist William Primrose; piano trios with Feuermann and pianist Artur Rubinstein or with Piatigorsky and Rubinstein; and string trios with Primrose and Piatigorsky.

To satisfy his own need for musical growth and to encourage twentieth-century composers, Heifetz commissioned and premiered concertos by William Walton, Mario Castelnuovo-Tedesco, Sergei Prokofiev, Erich Korngold, and Louis Gruenberg, in addition to Cyril Scott's *Fantasie Orientale*, Robert Russell Bennett's *Hexapoda*, and Castelnuovo-Tedesco's *The Lark*. The concertos of Jules Conus and Sibelius owe their popularity largely to Heifetz's championing of them.

Heifetz transcribed nearly 150 violin-piano pieces, starting with *Estrellita* (1927), a folk tune originally from Mexico. Popular favorites include transcriptions of Leopold Godowsky's *Alt Wien*, Grigoras Dinicu's *Hora staccato*, and songs from George Gershwin's *Porgy and Bess*. Heifetz also composed a hit song under the pen name Jim Hoyl and was a member of the American Society of Composers, Authors, and Publishers.

Heifetz, whose public career spanned approximately sixty-seven years, guarded his private life from the general public. When at his home in Beverly Hills, where he had settled in the 1940s, he enjoyed the company of family and friends, with whom he was witty and fun loving. Sailing, gardening, and ping-pong, at which he was expert, were among his favorite activities. A passionate reader, Heifetz also collected rare books.

Despite Heifetz's eminence, he was not a beloved figure. On stage, he was precise, patrician, and unemotional. Heifetz himself admitted a disdain for showmanship. Boris Schwarz describes Heifetz's unchanging stage manner: "the immobile stance, the unsmiling face showing his profile to the public, the violin held high and pushed far back, the bow arm with the elbow angled up, a minimum of fuss which disguised a maximum of self-discipline." Heifetz's father had advised him that the violin, not his face, should express his emotion, and his parents had shielded him from public adulation to guarantee that he would continue serious violin practice. For Heifetz, performing was serious business. He wanted to give audiences his best, and his supreme self-discipline and prodigious concentration were always evident. His critics called him cold, but as Joseph Wechsberg said, "He seems 'cold' only to concertgoers who follow the interpreter more with their eyes than their ears." Heifetz's incomparable violin mastery, musical élan, shimmering sound, and elegance of phrasing are legendary. In David Oistrakh's words, "There are many violinists—then there is Heifetz."

• The immensity of Heifetz's artistry is captured in Herbert R. Axelrod, ed., *Heifetz* (1976; 3d rev. ed., 1990), but an air of voyeuristic journalism pervades portions of the work, in which many of Heifetz's private papers are revealed and discussed. Artur Weschler-Vered, *Jascha Heifetz* (1986), portrays Heifetz's unique place in violin history and includes a bibliography with radio, television, and newspaper entries, along with book and magazine listings and a Heifetz discography compiled with Julian Futter. Joseph Wechsberg, "Heifetz," *The Heifetz Collection: A Retrospective in Six Volumes 1917–1955* (1975), summarizes Heifetz's renown as the supreme violinist of the twentieth century. Historical reissues of Heifetz recordings are available on compact disc from RCA (Red Seal and Victor Gold Seal), and Biddulph Leopold Auer, *My Long Life in Music* (1923), describes Auer's role in Heifetz's musical development. See also Samuel Applebaum and Sada Applebaum, *With the Artists* (1955) and *The Way They Play*, vol. 1 (1972), for information based on personal interviews with Heifetz. Also informative are

Schuyler Chapin, *Musical Chairs: A Life in the Arts* (1977); Harold C. Schonberg, *The Glorious Ones: Classical Music's Legendary Performers* (1985); Boris Schwarz, *Great Masters of the Violin* (1983); Henry Roth, *Great Violinists in Performance* (1987); Margaret Campbell, *The Great Violinists* (1981); James Creighton, *Discopaedia of the Violin: 1889–1971* (1974); Allan Kozinn, *Mischa Elman and the Romantic Style* (1990); Louis P. Lochner, *Fritz Kreisler* (1950; 3d rev. ed., 1981); William Primrose, *Walk on the North Side* (1978); Yehudi Menuhin, *Unfinished Journey* (1977); Robert Magidoff, *Yehudi Menuhin* (1955); and Richard Schickel and Michael Walsh, *Carnegie Hall: The First One Hundred Years* (1987). For magazine articles of note, see the special Heifetz issue of the *Strad*, Dec. 1988; Samuel Chotzinoff, "A Conversation with Jascha Heifetz," *Holiday*, Sept. 1963, pp. 89–97; and Roger Kahn, "Fiddler on the Shelf," *Life*, 31 Oct. 1969, pp. 58b–68.

JOANNE SWENSON-ELDRIDGE

HEIGHTON, William (1801–1873), labor radical and shoemaker, was born in Oundle in Northamptonshire, England, and shortly before the War of 1812, came to the United States with his family, settling in Philadelphia. Little is known of Heighton's early years. Around 1820 he married Ann Beckley, with whom he had at least four children. He supported his family on the paltry wage of a journeyman shoemaker.

Shoemaking in Philadelphia as in England proved a hothouse for trade unionism and political radicalism. Perhaps it was this tradition in conjunction with the fall of the craft that in the early 1820s turned the struggling shoemaker to Anglo-American radicalism. Though Heighton respected the work of Thomas Paine, the more recent work of English and American radicals left a deeper impression. He was particularly influenced by John Gray's *Essay and Human Happiness* (1825), which argued that poverty originated in economic exploitation, not in political oppression, as Paine had claimed. The middle of the decade found Heighton discussing his inchoate radicalism with fellow craftsmen in neighborhood pubs and lyceums. By spring 1827 he had emerged as a fully formed labor radical, as is revealed in his pamphlet, *An Address to the Members of Trades Societies, and to the Working Classes Generally . . . Together with a . . . Plan . . . by a Fellow-Labourer* (1827), which he followed with two more addresses on this subject (*An Address Delivered before the Mechanics and Working Classes Generally . . . by the "Unlettered Mechanic"* [1827] and *The Principles of Aristocratic Legislation . . . by an Operative Citizen* [1828]). He also issued a report on education reform in 1830 and produced several editorials for the *Mechanics' Free Press* between 1828 and 1830.

In his early speeches Heighton probed the sources of inequality and elaborated a reform program. He stressed glaring class distinctions, the contrast of want and misery amid abundance and plenty. To explain this paradox, he invoked both the labor theory of value and a theory of competition borrowed from Gray. The labor theory of value held that manual labor created all wealth and that all societies cleaved into producers, who produced wealth, and accumulators, who did not.

Inequality existed in part because accumulators appropriated wealth through interest, rent, and profit. In addition, as Gray had explained, competition in labor markets drove down wages to subsistence levels and limited production. Gray and Heighton maintained that after the American Revolution accumulators had quietly taken control of government and passed "aristocratic legislation" that rigged the market in their favor. Producers acquiesced, argued Heighton, because they were unaware of their true political interests.

Heighton made this question of political literacy the centerpiece of a remedial program with three organizational centers: a library with its own labor press to raise political consciousness; a citywide union to encourage unionism, coordinate economic activity, and amass a strike fund; and a labor party to field candidates who pledged to pursue worker interests. All three organizations took shape within a year of Heighton's November 1827 address. That same fall a dozen unions had formed the Mechanics' Union of Trade Associations, the nation's first significant city central union, which inspired similar unions in New York, Boston, and other urban places. The MUTA helped raise funds for the Mechanics' Library Company, whose board of directors doubled as the editorial committee of the *Mechanics' Free Press*. The weekly newspaper's initial edition in January 1828 coincided roughly with an MUTA meeting that laid the foundation of the Working Men's party. This party, the first such party in the United States, ran a poor third in state and local races in 1828 but had a banner year in 1829, when they had the balance of power. A year later, however, the party stalled badly, and it ran its last campaign in 1831.

The failure of the party to attract supporters hit Heighton hard. It probably prompted his departure from Philadelphia sometime after the election and from the labor movement itself. Settling down just outside Philadelphia in Salem County, New Jersey, he married Rebecca (maiden name unknown) in the 1850s after his first wife's death in the 1840s and continued to make shoes into the 1860s, when he turned to farming. During these years Heighton eschewed the labor movement for land reform activity and antislavery work. One surviving piece of his writing in behalf of these causes is an 1865 letter solicited by the prominent abolitionist George L. Stearns for inclusion in a short book with contributions from such antislavery luminaries as Wendell Phillips and Frederick Douglass. In it, Heighton predicted that unless the plantations of leading confederates were "broken up" and redistributed to former slaves, the North would leave intact resentful planters who "will vent their spleen on the innocent and helpless freedman, and, charging him with being the cause of their ruin . . . will grind him to powder." Heighton died in Elmer Village of Pittsgrove Township, Salem County, New Jersey.

An architect of the nation's first labor movement, Heighton is also notable for his contributions in the realm of thought. He was one of the first popular intellectuals to demonstrate the practical application of Ricardian socialism, a doctrine previously associated only with utopian retreat to the countryside. He also refined the Ricardian category of producer by making a distinction between "productive" (skilled) and "official" (unskilled) labor and by arguing, contrary to all labor radicals, that official workers were producers and therefore entitled to a place in the house of labor. This helps explain why the General Trades' Union, a central union of skilled workers, in the 1830s succeeded the MUTA, recruited casual laborers into its ranks. Finally, Heighton's shadowy work as an antislavery radical after 1845 may be seen as a thread running through a faction of the early labor movement to the later antislavery movement.

• Heighton left no personal papers. In addition to publishing his major speeches as pamphlets, Heighton was principal author of "Report of the Working Men's Committee on Public Education," *Mechanics' Free Press*, 4, 8, and 11 Feb. 1830, and reprinted in Philip S. Foner, *William Heighton: Pioneer Labor Leader of Jacksonian Philadelphia* (1991). The letter referred to in the text above is in George L. Stearns, ed., *The Equality of All Men before the Law Claimed and Defended* (1865). Until the appearance of Foner's useful biography, the standard work on Heighton was William H. Arky, "The Mechanics' Union of Trade Associations and the Formation of the Philadelphia Working-Men's Movement" (Ph.D. diss., Univ. of Pennsylvania, 1952), and an article by the same title in *Pennsylvania Magazine of History and Biography* 76 (Apr. 1952): 142–76. For a helpful intellectual biography, see David J. Harris, *Socialist Origins in the United States: American Forerunners of Marx, 1817–1832* (1966).

BRUCE LAURIE

HEIJENOORT, Jean van. *See* Van Heijenoort, Jean.

HEILMANN, Harry Edwin (3 Aug. 1894–9 July 1951), baseball player and announcer, was born in San Francisco, California, the son of Richard Heilmann, a German-immigrant ironworker, and Mary McVeigh. Raised in the Roman Catholic faith, Heilmann attended parochial schools until 1911, when he dropped out of Sacred Heart College, the preparatory school for St. Mary's College of California, after flunking mathematics and failing to make the varsity baseball team. While working as a bookkeeper for the National Biscuit Company, Heilmann started playing baseball for a semiprofessional club at Hanford, California. He was signed by a scout for Portland Oregon, in the Northwest League, where he showed a great deal of professional promise as an outfielder-first baseman. At the end of the 1913 season the Detroit Tigers of the American League (AL) purchased his contract. Paid $2,100 for the 1914 season, Heilmann appeared in 66 games and batted only .225. When he turned down the same amount in 1915, Detroit assigned him to San Francisco in the Pacific Coast League, where he batted a lusty .364.

Heilmann's big-league career began in earnest when he reported to the Tigers for the 1916 season. For several years, alternating at first base and right field, the good-natured Californian was a solid though unspectacular performer. Then in 1921 Ty Cobb, Detroit's great outfielder and newly named manager, began working to make Heilmann a stronger hitter. Under Cobb's coaching, Heilmann gripped his bat at the end, with hands slightly apart, and feet placed close together at the rear edge of the batter's box. With his altered style, the husky, right-handed Heilmann began to terrorize AL pitchers. He batted .394 to beat Cobb for the AL title in 1921 and then led the league three more times—curiously enough, every other year (1923, 1925, 1927). (Later Heilmann joked that because he was playing on two-year contracts in the 1920s he only bore down every other year.) Although he was basically a line-drive hitter, specializing in doubles and triples, he also hammered as many as 21 home runs one season (1922) and a total of 183 as a major leaguer.

Following the 1929 season, in which he batted .344 but failed to win another odd-year title, Detroit sold his contract to the Cincinnati Reds of the National League for $40,000. After still another productive year, he missed the 1931 season because of an arthritic condition in his right wrist. The next year, still unable to grip his bat or throw properly, he announced his retirement after appearing in only 15 games. His career average in the major leagues stood at .342; he also had driven in 1,552 runs and scored 1,291.

In 1920, Heilmann had married Harriet Maynes of Detroit; they had a daughter and a son. Heilmann's Detroit insurance agency, which he started during his last years with the Tigers, failed in the depths of the Great Depression. In 1933 he was an unsuccessful candidate for city treasurer. Heilmann finally found a steady means of supporting his family when H. Allen Campbell, who owned radio station WXYZ in Detroit, hired him to announce Tigers games. Eventually, a 28-station Michigan Network carried Heilmann's play-by-play accounts, and he became an extraordinarily respected and popular radio personality. In 1948 J. G. Taylor Spink, publisher of the weekly *Sporting News*, baseball's trade paper, described him as "a calm and accurate reporter, spicing his programs with a rich collection of anecdotes." That year he finished runner-up to Mel Allen, the New York Yankees play-by-play man, in the *Sporting News*'s rating of AL broadcasters.

A heavy cigarette smoker, Heilmann developed lung cancer early in 1951. Although able to leave Henry Ford Hospital to do a few innings of radio work, he was re-admitted in June and died there a month later. "People have been so nice to me," he said shortly before his death, "so generous and gracious that I feel ashamed, for I don't deserve all the grand things done in my behalf." In 1952 the Baseball Writers Association of America named him to the National Baseball Hall of Fame.

• For Heilmann's complete baseball record, see Craig Carter, ed., *Daguerreotypes*, 8th ed. (1990), p. 121. For biographical information, see *Sporting News*, 18 July 1951, p. 11; and the *New York Times*, 10 July 1951, p. 27. See also Fred Lieb, *The Detroit Tigers* (1946).

CHARLES C. ALEXANDER

HEILPRIN, Angelo (31 Mar. 1853–17 July 1907), geologist and explorer, was born in Satoralja-Ujhely, Hungary, the son of Michael Heilprin, a scholar and encyclopedist, and Henrietta Silver. His father was originally from Russian Poland. In 1856 Heilprin and his family immigrated to the United States, searching for the freedom that had evaded them in both Poland and Hungary. He grew up in New York City and attended the public schools of Brooklyn and Yonkers. At the age of fourteen he entered a hardware concern in New York City in conjunction with his younger brother Louis. He worked there for several years, but he had already decided to become a naturalist and enthusiastically pursued the opportunity to write articles for the *New American Cyclopaedia*, of which his father had become an associate editor in 1873.

After the completion of the encyclopedia in 1876, Heilprin went abroad to study with the masters in the field of natural science. He entered the Royal School of Mines in London (now known as the Normal School of Science). His distinguished teachers (including Thomas Henry Huxley) noticed his talents and encouraged him to further his studies on the Continent. He went to France and Switzerland, studied painting in Florence, Italy, and studied for a short time at the Imperial Geological Institute of Vienna, Austria. By the time he returned to the United States in 1879, he was certainly among the best-trained Americans of his generation in the natural sciences.

Heilprin was soon named as a correspondent of the Academy of Natural Sciences in Philadelphia. He served in that capacity for three years, from 1880 to 1883. He also held the position of professor of invertebrate paleontology at the academy starting in 1881, and he was selected as a professor of geology at the Wagner Free Institute of Science in Philadelphia in 1885. The culmination of his academic honors came in 1904, when he was elected as a lecturer at the Sheffield Scientific School at Yale University.

Heilprin was not essentially an academic, however. He loved the adventure of seeing nature in its pristine state too much to stay for long periods in a university setting. He therefore became best known as a traveler and explorer in the spirit of adventurers of the early nineteenth century. He explored the Florida Peninsula and the Everglades in 1886. He went to Mexico for the first time in 1888 and came to the mistaken conclusion that the Peak of Orizaba was the highest on the North American continent. He explored the physical geology of the Bermuda Islands in 1889 and then moved on to what was his most significant service in the field of exploration: his association with and assistance of Lieutenant Robert Peary.

In 1891 Heilprin headed the group of scientists that accompanied Peary on his first voyage to the Arctic. The group sailed from Brooklyn, New York, on 6 June 1891 aboard the steamer *Kite*. Heilprin was in charge of the West Greenland expedition, which gathered zoological, entomological, botanical, and ornithological data. The following year Heilprin led the Peary relief expedition to Greenland, once again

aboard the *Kite*. He had a dramatic meeting with Peary on the ice cap on 5 August 1892; the incident was recorded by Heilprin and others as being nearly as memorable as the meeting of Stanley and Livingstone in Africa.

Heilprin visited Morocco, Algeria, and Tunisia in 1896 and the Klondike River in 1898, when the Alaskan gold rush was in its full flower. In 1902 he went to Martinique and observed Mount Pelee, which had a violent volcanic eruption in May of that year. His calm and cheerfulness in the face of danger impressed all who observed him in this important work. He made his last expedition in 1906, a journey up the Orinoco River in British Guiana. In the course of that voyage he contracted a fever, and his health was never the same. He died from heart disease at the home of his sister in New York City. A significant tribute came in the form of a telegram from Peary, who wrote that "a man among thousands, Professor Heilprin's place can never be filled. . . . You and all your secretaries know that to him was due primarily the renewal of interest in Arctic work in this country" (Pollak, p. 387).

Heilprin was one of a small but significant number of Americans who undertook to expand the notion of the "frontier" toward the end of the nineteenth century. Keenly aware that the Pacific Ocean had been reached and that American continental expansion was at an end, they explored other areas of the Americas, the Arctic, and the Caribbean Islands. A discriminating scientist and a born explorer, Heilprin brought all his strongest qualities to his work. His work was important both for its own merits and for the encouragement it gave to other academics and explorers at the turn of the twentieth century.

• Heilprin's voluminous writings include *The Geological Evidences of Evolution* (1888), *The Arctic Problem and Narrative of the Peary Relief Expedition* (1893), and *The Earth and Its Story* (1896). The best biographical source is Gustav Pollak, *Michael Heilprin and His Sons* (1912). Information on Heilprin can be found in H. S. Morais, *The Jews of Philadelphia* (1894). An obituary is in the *New York Times*, 18 July 1907.

SAMUEL WILLARD CROMPTON

HEILPRIN, Michael (23 Feb. 1823–10 May 1888), writer, was born in Piotrkow, Poland, the son of Phineas Mendel Heilprin, a Jewish merchant and Hebrew scholar, and Hannah Lipschitz. He spent his early years in Tomaszow. The atmosphere of the Heilprin home reflected the humanism and rationalism of the Enlightenment and the impact of secular knowledge and liberalism on the hitherto isolated, traditional culture of the Jews of Central Europe.

Heilprin never attended a formal school. Under the direction of his father he studied languages, history, and philosophy and early on demonstrated a prodigious memory and an unusual facility with languages. Twice in his life Heilprin moved from one country to another—from Poland to Hungary and then to the United States—each time mastering a new language well enough to become a respected writer. He spoke

German and Polish at home and began studying Hebrew at the age of five. Greek, Latin, and French soon followed, and as an adult Heilprin spoke eight languages easily and read another ten.

National liberation was in the air, and in 1842, deciding they could no longer live in Poland under Russian domination, the Heilprin family left for Hungary. Michael, who by this time had married Henrietta Silver, spent two years learning the Magyar language. He opened a bookstore in Miskolc and began writing poetry. His poems dealt with the depressed status of Jews in Hungary and with the struggle of the Hungarians against the Austrian House of Hapsburg. The patriotic poetry brought him to the attention of Lajos Kossuth and other leaders of what soon developed into the revolution of 1848.

During the short-lived revolution, Heilprin spoke at public rallies and served as secretary to the literary bureau of the Interior Ministry in Kossuth's government. When the revolution was quashed, Heilprin fled in fear of reprisals from the Austrians and spent some months in France. There his eyesight became a problem that plagued him throughout his life. In later years when he worked constantly as writer and editor, he depended almost entirely on others, especially his wife and five children, to read aloud to him. The Heilprins returned to Hungary in 1850, and for several years Michael taught in a Jewish school in Ujhely; he also taught himself English in preparation for coming to the United States.

Heilprin arrived in the United States in 1856 as one of hundreds of political refugees from the failed Hungarian revolution of 1848, a well-educated, skilled, and politically liberal group. He spent his first two years in Philadelphia teaching in the schools of the Hebrew Education Society.

In the years leading up to the Civil War Heilprin fervently supported the antislavery movement. Shortly after his arrival in the United States he made an impassioned speech defending the abolitionists and barely escaped violence at the hands of proslavery hoodlums. And he wrote for the *New York Daily Tribune* a devastating attack on Rabbi Morris J. Raphall, who had assembled biblical passages to support the institution of slavery.

The family moved to New York in 1858, and Heilprin began a 23-year career as a journalist, encyclopedist, and political commentator, interrupted by a two-year stint in Washington, D.C. (1863–1865), where he operated an unsuccessful bookstore and edited a short-lived political weekly, the *Balance*. Through their years in the United States the family lived in modest circumstances, never financially secure, but their home was always a center for Hungarian exiles. The editors of Appleton's *New American Cyclopaedia* gave Heilprin the task of revising all their historical, geographic, and biographical material as well as preparing articles in areas of his expertise. He worked on a comprehensive revision of the encyclopedia from 1872 to 1876. Heilprin wrote extensively for the American press. As a contributor to the *Nation* for more than twenty years, he earned a reputation as a leading commentator on European politics, wars, literature, and linguistics.

Much of Heilprin's work was by its nature anonymous, but in 1879 and 1880, returning to the fascination he long had with Hebrew literature, he published his only book. This two-volume work, *The Historical Poetry of the Ancient Hebrews*, combined his original translations with the "scientific criticism" of the Bible that was then emerging, especially in Germany. Heilprin was not a practicing Jew, and he never joined a synagogue, though he felt a deep kinship with the Jewish people. Following the pogroms in czarist Russia in 1881 and 1882, he threw all his energies into helping Russian Jewish immigrants. He served as secretary of the Hebrew Emigrant Aid Society and helped establish agricultural settlements for Jewish immigrants from New Jersey to Oregon. Among those who worked closely with him at this time was the poet Emma Lazarus.

The tributes to Heilprin after his death in Summit, New Jersey, speak of him as an exceedingly modest man—erudite, very friendly, and eager to hear criticism of his own work. They stress his painstaking efforts to write truthful and fair accounts of complex and controversial subjects. But the editors of the *Nation* may have identified a deeper significance when they wrote that Michael Heilprin brought to the American public "countries and men and incidents hidden from the Western world by unfamiliar tongues."

• The only biography of Heilprin is Gustav Pollak, *Michael Heilprin and His Sons* (1912), which includes a large collection of his articles on topics ranging from "Panslavism" to Persian literature. Short accounts of his life and of his two sons appear in Emil Lengyel, *Americans from Hungary* (1948), and in Robert Perlman, *Bridging Three Worlds: Hungarian-Jewish Americans, 1848–1914* (1991). A tribute and a short biographical sketch of Heilprin was written by John W. Chadwick for the *Unitarian Review*, Sept. 1888, and was reprinted in Pollak's book cited above. Another tribute was published by the *Nation*, 17 May 1888. An obituary is in the *New York Times*, 11 May 1888.

ROBERT PERLMAN

HEIN, Mel (22 Aug. 1909–31 Jan. 1992), football player and coach, was born Melvin John Hein in Redding, California, the son of Herman H. Hein, an electrician, and Charlotte Wilson. As a small boy Hein moved with his family to Glacier, Washington, where his father managed a power plant in the Mount Baker region. The Heins later moved to Bellingham, Washington, where Hein completed grammar school; then to Fairhaven, Washington; and subsequently to Burlington, Washington, where Hein attended secondary school.

Standing 6′3″ and weighing 175 pounds, Hein planned to attend the University of Washington to try out for crew, but he first worked as a power lineman to save money for college. His older brother Lloyd, who was already attending Washington State College (later Washington State University), alerted coach Babe

Hollingberry to Hein's potential in football, Hollingberry thus persuaded Hein to enroll at Washington State. As a freshman Hein only made the third team as a center and had little playing time. He and his brother then obtained summer jobs with the forest service in order to toughen themselves up for football.

Hein's endeavors in cutting new trails and other outdoor activities helped him build up to over 200 pounds (as a professional he weighed about 235 pounds) and to claim the football team's starting center spot. As a junior he made All-Coast, and as a senior he was an All-American. He continued to play center on offense but when needed could line up at guard or tackle as well. Hein of course also played defense. Washington State had an undefeated season in 1930 and accepted an invitation to the 1931 Rose Bowl game. There it played an even better Alabama squad that won the game handily. While in college Hein also performed on the track and basketball squads and excelled academically.

In 1931 Hein signed a contract with the Providence Steam Rollers of the National Football League. When he heard that the New York Giants had belatedly mailed a contract to him offering $150 per game—which was higher than Providence's offer—Hein cabled the postmaster in Providence asking if his letter to the Steam Rollers could be intercepted and returned to him. It was and Hein instead signed with the Giants, the team for which he had preferred to play. Before he left for the East, Hein married Florence Porter. The couple would have two children.

Hein quickly moved into the Giants' starting lineup at center. He was an able blocker and a reliable long snapper on offense; this was essential in the single-wing offense, in which the tailback lined up about seven yards behind the line of scrimmage and took snaps directly from the center prior to running, passing, or punting the ball. Hein would also pull out of the line to block on running plays. Backing up the line on defense, Hein won a reputation as a ferocious but clean tackler who did not gouge, pile on, or engage in other unnecessarily rough practices. During this time a linebacker normally stayed close to the line of scrimmage, trying to stop any runs through the middle. But Hein's speed and agility led him to attempt things linebackers had normally not been expected to do, such as pursuing opposing runners on sweeps to the outside and falling back to defend against short passes. Hein's speed even enabled him to drop back deep enough to help cover the Green Bay Packers' immortal receiver Don Hutson in the 1938 NFL title game won by the Giants. As a result, Hein redefined the position of linebacker so that men who subsequently played this post would require greater speed and quickness to help out on pass coverage.

Hein made second team on the All-Pro squad his first two years in New York, and then for eight consecutive years he was named first-team All Pro. Hein played on several Giants' division winners and on two league championship teams: the 1934 team that defeated the Chicago Bears by switching to sneakers to have better traction on the frozen playing surface; and the 1938 team, rated by Giants' coach Steve Owen as his best ever. In 1938 Hein won the league's Most Valuable Player award, a rare achievement for a lineman.

In 1941 Hein slumped enough to be dropped to second string on the All-League team. He retired after the 1942 season to become head coach at Union College in Schenectady, New York. Union, however, dropped football because of World War II and the subsequent shortage of male students, but Hein stayed at Union to help train students in the U.S. Navy's V-12 program. He also returned to the Giants, skipping practice with the consent of coach Owen and taking the train from Schenectady to join the team for games. Hein ended his playing career for good following the 1945 season. He remained in football as an assistant coach with the Giants (1946–1950), and then as a line coach with three different professional teams, before finding a new home as line coach at the University of Southern California; he remained there until 1966. He then worked as a supervisor of league officials, first for the American Football League (1967–1970), and then for the American Football Conference of the NFL (1970–1974) after the two leagues had merged. In 1954 he was selected for the College Football Hall of Fame, and in 1963 became a charter member of the Professional Football Hall of Fame. He died at his home in San Clemente, California.

• Additional material on Hein is available at the Professional Football Hall of Fame, Canton, Ohio. See also Robert Shoemaker, *Famous Football Players* (1953), Murray Olderman, *The Defenders* (1973), Robert Curran, *Pro Football's Rag Days* (1969), Arthur Daley, *Pro Football's Hall of Fame* (1963), George Sullivan, *Pro Football's All-Time Greats* (1969), Dave Klein, *The New York Giants: Yesterday, Today, Tomorrow* (1973), and William Heumann, *Famous Pro Football Stars* (1967). An obituary is in the *New York Times*, 2 Feb. 1992.

LLOYD J. GRAYBAR

HEINEMAN, Daniel Webster (23 Nov. 1872–31 Jan. 1962), engineer and corporate executive, was born in Charlotte, North Carolina, the son of James Heineman, a businessman engaged in the chewing tobacco trade, and Minna Hertz. After attending elementary school in his hometown, Heineman relocated with his mother to her native Germany following his father's death in 1880. He became interested in the newly emerging field of electrical engineering and studied the subject upon entering the Technical College of Hannover. After graduating from the college in 1895, he went to work at Union-Elektrizitäts-Gesellschaft in Berlin. The firm, which was associated with General Electric, soon had Heineman out in the field directing the conversion of city transit systems from horsepower to electricity. Over the course of the next ten years, he oversaw the conversion process in a number of cities, including Liège, Naples, Brussels, and Koblenz.

In 1905 Heineman joined a Belgian-based firm, the Société Financière de Transports et d'Enterprises Industrielle (SOFINA), as its managing director. His lofty title was somewhat deceiving; the firm's entire staff consisted of two other employees. Nevertheless, under Heineman's guidance, the firm prospered. In the years preceding World War II, the firm developed or overhauled existing tramways systems in cities as diverse as Bangkok, Lisbon, Constantinople, Buenos Aires, and Barcelona and grew to include 40,000 employees among its various subsidiaries.

Although his firm was recognized as an industry giant, Heineman found time to develop a number of outside interests. He began collecting rare books and manuscripts around the time he joined SOFINA and soon possessed a collection that included works by Mozart, Rousseau, Heine, Maupassant, and Goethe. A man of culture and refinement, he cultivated friendships with numerous European heads of state and enjoyed early morning discussions of music or politics before setting himself to the day's tasks. His interest in politics turned to practical action with the outbreak of World War I when, fearing mass starvation among the Belgian people, he took a leading role in the formation of the Commission for Relief in Belgium. Awarded the Grand Cross of Leopold II and named a Grand Officer of the Order of Leopold for his wartime relief efforts, Heineman maintained his outside interests after the conflict ended. Intrigued by new economic possibilities, he advocated the formation of a United States of Europe (similar in concept to the European Common Market) and published *Outline of a New Europe* (1930). He also married Hettie Meyer; they had three children.

In 1924 Heineman and SOFINA purchased Société Internationale d'Énergie Hydro-Électrique (SIDRO), another electrical utility firm that had been formed in the previous year by Alfred Loewenstein, a flamboyant Belgian financier. Having fallen into financial difficulties, Loewenstein sold enough shares of SIDRO to SOFINA to give the latter firm effective control of the company. Significantly, among SIDRO's many holdings was Barcelona Traction, Light & Power Company, Ltd., a utility firm founded in Spain by an American engineer, Fred Stark Pearson, in 1911. Although the transaction was unremarkable at the time, the management of this firm would later provide Heineman with the greatest challenge of his career.

After World War II forced his relocation from Brussels to New York City, Heineman continued to direct SOFINA with a firm hand. SOFINA's many holdings, including Barcelona Traction (and its main subsidiary, the Elbro Irrigation & Power Company, Ltd.), emerged relatively unscathed from both the Spanish Civil War and World War II; indeed, by 1948 Barcelona Traction was supplying four-fifths of the electricity in the Spanish region of Catalonia, as well as 20 percent of Spain's total supply of electricity. Despite its prosperity, however, the firm faced criticism. As a foreign-held company (with its charter in Toronto, Canada, and its ownership largely Belgian), the firm was an easy target for jealous nationalists. It was also accused by many in Spain of tax evasion as well as the use of bribery among local officials in an attempt to crush native-born electrical cooperatives that had sought to compete with the firm. Barcelona Traction's biggest weakness, however, was financial. The company had issued bonds in 1911 and 1915 in order to raise capital but had been forbidden since 1936 from making interest payments, which had to be made in British pound sterling, to bondholders by the Spanish government's foreign-exchange regulations. The firm's weakness soon gained the attention of Juan March, a former tobacco smuggler whose wealth and assistance had been instrumental in bringing Francisco Franco to power.

Rebuffed by Heineman in attempts to purchase Barcelona Traction outright in both 1940 and 1944, March shifted tactics and quietly began purchasing the firm's bonds, which were selling at a deep discount because of the firm's technical default. The failure of the British Treasury—which March had assisted during World War II—to intervene on Barcelona Traction's behalf with the Spanish government helped kill a proposed Plan of Compromise that would have satisfied the bondholders' demands in 1946. March brought matters to a head in February 1948 when—despite the firm's previous year net profits of $3.7 million and ready cash on hand to pay all obligations, including bond interest payments—a court in Reus, Spain, placed the firm in bankruptcy on the basis of the defaulted interest payments. Blindsided by the decision, which gave March as a bondholder priority claims against the firm's assets, Heineman and the SOFINA directors attempted to fight back through the courts and also sought the assistance of the Canadian, Belgian, and British governments. Through a complex series of intrigues, March managed to thwart the company at every turn, and in January 1952 his holding company (Fuerzas Eléctricas de Cataluña—FESCA) acquired control of Barcelona Traction. Heineman's frustration turned to desperation when even the arguments of lawyer (and Franco brother-in-law) Ramoón Serrano Suñer fell on deaf ears. By the time of Heineman's retirement in 1955, the firm's prospects seemed hopeless. The case was eventually referred to the International Court of Justice at The Hague in 1958, and it dragged on for another eleven years until the court finally, in 1970, ruled in favor of Spain (and March). Neither principal lived to see the outcome; Heineman had died in New York City in January 1962, with March surviving him by less than two months, dying in Madrid as a result of an automobile accident.

In an effort to formalize his philanthropic efforts, Heineman created the Heineman Foundation for Research, Educational, Charitable and Scientific Purposes, Inc., which was meant to promote research in the fields of heart surgery and the physical sciences and to which he donated his collection of rare books. The American Institute of Physics also benefited greatly from his largess and established the Dannie Heineman Prize in Mathematical Physics in his honor. Heineman was also honored by the creation of the annual Heineman Lectures at the Mecklenberg Medical Society in his hometown of Charlotte.

Given his lifelong efforts at creation rather than manipulation, it seems cruelly ironic that Heineman is remembered today, if at all, for his failures in dealing with the machinations of a wily financial pirate. His life serves as a cautionary tale regarding the dangers of operating a multinational business firm in a variety of cultural and political climates.

• While Heineman's papers have not been located, his rare book collection resides at the Pierpont Morgan Library in New York City. The best secondary source of information on Heineman's life and career remains John Brooks's lengthy article "Annals of Finance: Privateer" in the 21 and 28 May 1979 issues of *New Yorker* magazine. The Barcelona Traction case also received continuing attention in the *New York Times* beginning in 1948, and March's career is discussed in B. Díaz Mosty, *La irresisible ascensión de Juan March* (1977), and Ramon Garriga, *Juan March y su tiempo* (1976). Heinemann's obituary is in the *New York Times*, 2 Feb. 1962.

EDWARD L. LACH, JR.

HEINEMANN, Barbara (11 Jan. 1795–21 May 1883), a spiritual leader of the Community of True Inspiration (Amana Society), was born in Leitersweiler, Alsace, the daughter of Peter Heinemann (Heynemann) and Anna (maiden name unknown), peasants. She received no formal education, and her early life was marked with hard work and poverty. At age eight she began factory work as a wool spinner and later became a household servant.

As a young woman she developed an intense desire to enter into the "presence of the true God." This search drew her to a radical Pietist sect, the Community of True Inspiration, which was formed in Wittgenstein, Germany, in 1714. Inspirationist leaders (the "Inspired") were guided by divine inspiration as latterday "New Prophets." Following the death of the first generation of prophetic leaders around midcentury, a period of gradual decline set in.

Renewal came in 1817 when three young people were recognized as inspired prophets, or "instruments" (*Werkzeuge*). These were Christian Metz, a cabinetmaker from Ronneburg; Barbara Heinemann; and Michael Krausert, a journeyman tailor from Strassburg who had introduced Heinemann to the group. Heinemann taught herself to read the Bible and write, and for more than a year she practiced the gift of written prophesy (*Einsprache*). Then, on Christmas Day in 1818 she experienced divine "illumination" and the gift of oral prophesy (*Aussprache*). Krausert pronounced her divinely inspired, although some of the sect's members had reservations.

Tension with the community's elders, however, soon developed. Krausert confessed doubts about his own inspiration and was forced to leave the sect. Heinemann's testimony also came under suspicion. Her written prophesies were burned in 1819, and for a brief period she too was banished. After being restored, however, she continued to prophesy, along with Metz. Then, in 1823, against the "will of God" (and Metz), Heinemann married George Landmann of Bischweiler, a schoolteacher. Like many other radical Pietists, Inspirationists considered marriage a less pure spiritual state than celibacy, so she lost her prophetic office. She lived with her husband as an ordinary member of the community for the next twenty-six years. They had no children.

Political pressures in the 1820s forced the Inspirationists to migrate to a few isolated centers in Hesse, whose government was more tolerant of religious dissenters. Eventually, however, high rents and renewed persecution forced approximately 800 Inspirationists, including Heinemann and her husband, to immigrate to Erie County, New York, in the early 1840s. Here Metz established the Ebenezer colony on 5,000 acres purchased from the Seneca Indians.

Heinemann's divine utterances at a feet-washing service preceding the Lord's Supper in 1849 convinced Metz and others that she was again God's chosen instrument. Restored as a *Werkzeug*, she worked with Metz to organize the colony on a communal basis with all property shared in common. She also confirmed Metz's divine command in 1854 to move the community to the Midwest. Their new home was a 3,000-acre tract (which grew to approximately 26,000 acres) near Iowa City, Iowa. Seven settlements were founded over the next two decades, all named with variations on the word Amana (with one exception, Homestead), taken from a word in the Song of Solomon. Heinemann and her husband moved to Amana in 1861.

Following the death of Metz in 1867, the spiritual leadership of the Amana Society's more than 1,200 colonists fell solely to Heinemann. Details of operating the extensive and prosperous Amana industries, however, were guided by a Great Council of the Brethren, with whom she regularly met. She alone, however, presided at the Lord's Supper and continued to speak inspired messages in which she exhorted the faithful to avoid worldliness and lead a life of quiet devotion, humility, and love. Concerned about the unity of the elders after Metz's death, she spoke: "I see the evil spirit, the independent spirit, the high-handed spirit and see how he will tear you apart and hurl one hither, the other thither. I see the murderer between brother and brother, the snake, how it divides the heart so that true love is lacking." She was also concerned about eternal judgment for those who slipped into worldliness. She forbade cameras, popular amusements, and "ornamental" rather than "useful" fruit trees, and she became increasingly suspicious of marriage, except those marriages sanctioned by prophetic inspiration.

Heinemann, who survived her husband by three years, died at main Amana and is buried there in a simple, unadorned grave. She was the Inspirationists' last *Werkzeug*; thereafter, no new inspired prophets were recognized and the sect's religious life slowly declined. Amana's communal organization was dissolved in 1932 when church and business affairs were legally separated. As of 1995, membership in the Amana Church Society was more than 500. Worship services in English and German were led by twelve lay elders on a rotating basis, and the revelations of Metz and

Heinemann continued to be an integral part of the service.

• The most important resource on Heinemann and the Amana Society is the archive in Amana, Iowa. Her oral prophecies may be found in *Jahrbücher der Wahren Inspirations-Gemeinden* (42 vols., 1842–1871); see also her *Kurze Erzählung von den Erweckungs-Umständen* (1885), and Janet Zuber, trans., *Barbara Heinemann Landmann Biography [and] E. L. Gruber's Teachings on Divine Inspiration* (1981). Her early years as an inspired prophet are briefly treated in Walter Grossman, "The European Origins of the True Inspired of Amana," *Communal Societies* 4 (Fall 1984): 133–49. Her leadership following Metz is evaluated in two essays by Jonathan G. Andelson, "Postcharismatic Authority in the Amana Society: The Legacy of Christian Metz" in *When Prophets Die*, ed. Timothy Miller (1991), and "The Community of True Inspiration from Germany to the Amana Colonies," in *America's Communal Utopias*, ed. Donald Pitzer (1997). An important English source for Heinemann and the society is Bertha M. H. Shambaugh, *Amana That Was and Amana That Is* (1932). Two excellent studies are Andelson, *Communalism and Change in the Amana Society, 1855–1932* (1974), and Diane Barthel, *Amana: From Pietist Sect to American Community* (1984). The most complete account of Amana in the nineteenth century is Gottlieb Scheuner, *Inspirations-Historie*, vol. 1, *1714–1728*, vol. 2, *1729–1819*, vol. 3, *1817–1850*, trans. Janet W. Zuber (1978; orig. pub. 1884–1891). Two works that also cover Heinemann's leadership are William F. Noe, *Brief History of the Amana Society, 1714–1900* (1904), and William Rufus Perkins and Barthinis L. Wick, *History of the Amana Society or True Inspiration* (1891).

DAVID B. ELLER

HEINLEIN, Robert Anson (7 July 1907–8 May 1988), writer, was born in Butler, Missouri, the son of Rex Ivar Heinlein, an accountant, and Bam Lyle. Heinlein attended the University of Missouri for one year in 1925, leaving to enter the U.S. Naval Academy, from which he graduated in 1929. Commissioned as an ensign in 1929, he was promoted to lieutenant in 1934 but was retired in the same year for physical disability caused by tuberculosis. He then completed graduate study in physics and mathematics at the University of California, Los Angeles. From 1934 to 1935 he owned and managed the Shively and Sophie Lodes Silver Mine in Colorado. He made a failed bid for the California State Assembly in 1938.

Heinlein's career as a writer began in 1939, when his first short story, "Life-Line," was bought by *Astounding Science Fiction* for $70. Consisting of disjointed, loosely connected scenes, it was immediately successful, and Heinlein acquired a strong popular following and much critical praise. He was the guest of honor at the World Science Fiction Convention in 1941. Yet despite his instant and unflagging popularity, Heinlein always insisted in interviews that he began writing solely as a means to supplement his naval retirement stipend; his only real ambition in life was to become an admiral.

During World War II Heinlein returned to technical work as an aviation engineer at the Naval Air Experimental Station in Philadelphia, Pennsylvania. At the end of the war he returned to writing, publishing his short stories in more selective national magazines like the *Saturday Evening Post*. He was one of the first science fiction writers to gain such broad exposure and to appeal to a more general fiction readership. In the late 1940s he also published a successful series of books for young adults. After his first marriage to Leslyn McDonald ended in divorce in 1947, Heinlein married Virginia Gerstenfeld in 1948. He had no children from either marriage.

Expanding into the new genre of television scripts, Heinlein adapted his novel *Space Cadets* for the television program "Tom Corbett: Space Cadet" (1948). He later worked as the technical adviser on "Destination Moon," a television drama about space exploration based on his short story "Rocket Ship Galileo," which foreshadowed and helped win public support for the Apollo space program. His novel *Double Star* (1956) won a Hugo Award in 1956, a prize given by the World Science Fiction Convention for the year's best science fiction novel.

Heinlein's writings during this period in his career tended to focus on scientific changes and the ways they could affect everyday human life. His predictions of coming technology were remarkably accurate, forecasting the atomic bomb, nuclear power plants, moving sidewalks, and waterbeds. The increasingly controversial novels Heinlein produced in the late 1950s marked a shift in his focus from purely technological innovations in society to issues of broader social change. *Starship Troopers* (1959) is a fascist vision of a world run under strict military law. Although attacked for its extreme right-wing vision, in 1960 it won for Heinlein another Hugo and remains one of his most successful and popular novels.

Stranger in a Strange Land (1961), Heinlein's best-known work, continued the success of *Starship Troopers*, creating perhaps even greater controversy. In it, a martian named Valentine Michael Smith settles on earth and establishes the Church of All Worlds, whose members live in small communes and practice group sex. The novel's unabashed questioning of sexual and religious conventions and its insistence on the overriding power of love caught the spirit of the 1960s. Garnering for Heinlein still another Hugo, it became a cult classic and sold more than 3 million copies.

Themes of sexual deviance remained central in Heinlein's novels that appeared after *Stranger in a Strange Land*. *The Moon Is a Harsh Mistress* (1966), which won the Hugo Award in 1967, portrays the group marriages that become common on the moon because of a shortage of women. In *I Will Fear No Evil* (1971), a businessman becomes impregnated with his own sperm after his mind is transplanted into the body of a young woman. Incestuous relationships occurring as a result of time travel and immortality are the subject of *Time Enough for Love: The Lives of Lazurus Long* (1973), in which the main character has sex with his mother, his adopted daughter, and two female clones of himself. These novels drew critical attack for being propagandistic vehicles of Heinlein's offbeat views of sexuality rather than artistic creations. Sales of Heinlein's books did not suffer, however. His widespread popularity prompted Heinlein's selection as a guest commentator with Walter Cronkite for the CBS television network during the Apollo 11 lunar landing in 1969. In the late 1970s Heinlein was honored with many awards, including the best all-time author in the *Locus Magazine* Readers' Poll in 1973 and 1975, the Nebula Grand Master Award from the Science Fiction Writers of America in 1975, and the Inkpot Award in 1977.

Heinlein's final major novels return to the more conventional framework of science fiction adventure stories. *Friday* (1982) relates the sexual, psychological, and interplanetary journeys of an artificial woman who works as a spy and document courier. *Job: A Comedy of Justice* (1984), adapted from the Old Testament, relates the difficulties that its protagonist, Alex Hergensheimer, incurs as his life violently and unpredictably shifts between alternate universes. The instability of history is the main theme of *The Cat Who Walks through Walls: A Comedy of Manners* (1985), as Colonel Colin Campbell and his wife flee earth for the moon to escape a wrongful murder accusation and eventually join the Time Corps, a group of time travelers who intervene in and alter human history.

Heinlein was a member of the American Institute of Astronautics and Aeronautics, the Author's League of America, the Navy League, the Air Force Association, the Air Power Council, and the American Association for the Advancement of Science. His outside interests included fiscal theory, cats, ballistics, and stone masonry. He died in Carmel, California.

Heinlein is remembered as perhaps the greatest modern science fiction author and one of the most prolific, having written thirty-six novels, ten collections of short stories, two screenplays, television and radio scripts, as well as numerous individually published short stories and articles. His major works have sold more than 40 million copies and have been translated into twenty-nine languages. Of his impact on the genre, there can be no doubt: eighteen of the most prominent science fiction writers of 1953 named Heinlein as the greatest influence on their writing in a poll taken that year by the magazine *Astounding Science Fiction.* Gerald Jonas, longtime reviewer of science fiction for the *New York Times Book Review*, has asserted that Heinlein "has probably influenced the development of science fiction more than any other writer."

Heinlein's success in popularizing the previously obscure genre of science fiction was due to his unique blend of the believable and the fantastic. Unlike the wildly improbable stories of other science fiction writers, Heinlein created familiar, understandable, realistic characters before sending them on wild adventures. Even the improbable "science" written into his books was often extrapolations of real research being done at the time, not fantasy.

The most consistent feature of Heinlein's work is its insistence on the overriding importance of human freedom and individualism. His heroes tend to be rugged and independent loners who struggle against bu-

reaucracy and organized authority. In its least subtle formulations, Heinlein's dogged emphasis on individualism and patriotism often reveals itself as a markedly right-wing political vision.

• Heinlein's papers are at the University of California, Santa Cruz. Other major works by Heinlein include *Sixth Column* (1949; reprinted as *The Day after Tomorrow*, 1951); *The Green Hills of Earth* (1951); *Double Star* (1956); *Citizen of the Galaxy* (1957), and *The Door into Summer* (1957). There are several full-length biographies of Heinlein, including H. Bruce Franklin, *Robert A. Heinlein: America as Science Fiction* (1980), and Peter Nicholls, *Robert A. Heinlein* (1982). Joseph D. Olander and Martin Harry Greenberg, eds., *Robert A. Heinlein* (1978), is a collection of articles on the writer. Critical analysis of his earlier work is available in Alexei Pushkin, *Heinlein in Dimension: A Critical Analysis* (1968), and Damon Knight, *In Search of Wonder: Critical Essays in Science Fiction* (1966). Perspective on the literary influence of Heinlein on science fiction as a genre is given in Brian Aldiss, *Billion Year Spree: The True History of Science Fiction* (1973); James Gunn, *The Road to Science Fiction: From Heinlein to the Present* (1979); and Sam Maskowitz, *Seekers of Tomorrow: Masters of Modern Science Fiction* (1966). Obituaries are in the *New York Times* and the *Los Angeles Times*, 10 May 1988.

ELIZABETH ZOE VICARY

HEINRICH, Anthony Philip (11 Mar. 1781–3 May 1861), composer, was born in Schönbüchel (now Krásný Buk), Bohemia, of German-Bohemian parents (names unknown). He was adopted by an uncle, from whom he inherited an import-export business. He visited the United States in 1805 and returned in 1810 in an unsuccessful attempt to establish the business in Philadelphia. At this time he was also an unpaid musical director of the Southwark Theatre. He married a Boston woman (identity unknown), whom he took to Bohemia in 1813, where their daughter Antonia was born. Leaving the daughter in Bohemia, Heinrich and his wife returned to the United States, where she died in 1814. Heinrich then decided to pursue a career in music. In 1816 he walked from Philadelphia to Pittsburgh to become musical director of a theater. When this venture failed, he voyaged down the Ohio River to Kentucky, where in Lexington, in 1817, he directed one of the first performances of a Beethoven symphony in the United States.

Heinrich lived near Louisville, teaching himself composition, and in 1820 the results were published in Philadelphia as *The Dawning of Music in Kentucky; or, The Pleasures of Harmony in the Solitudes of Nature*, op. 1, an extraordinary 269-page collection of works for piano, voice, and instruments. His second collection, *The Western Minstrel*, op. 2, appeared the same year. His op. 3, *The Sylviad; or, Minstrelsy of Nature in the Wilds of N. America* (1823–1826), 361 pages, was published in Boston, where he moved in 1823, and was dedicated to the Royal Academy of Music in London, where he went in 1826. His attempt to further his career in London was not successful, and he was reduced to playing violin in pit orchestras. He was in Boston again from 1831 to 1833 and then returned to Europe for concert tours. In 1837 he settled in New York, where, as in Boston, several concerts were devoted to his music, including orchestral works. After a final trip to Prague and other European cities from 1856 to 1859, he returned to New York, where he died a pauper. His music has remained unknown until recent years.

Heinrich was a pioneer of musical Romanticism. Nearly all of his works are programmatic. Whereas some dance music and songs in *The Dawning of Music in Kentucky* and elsewhere are rooted in traditional middle European classical principles, his piano sonata "La Buona Mattina," in the same collection, avoids the usual forms in its movements and even includes a voice part in its first and last movements. Extreme (for its time) complexity and pianistic virtuosity is represented in *Sylviad* by "Toccata capriciosa" and "Toccata grande cromatica," and in *Dawning* by "A Chromatic Ramble of the Peregrine Harmonist" (which includes a text). The "program" of this last piece describes the music, to be sung or presented in some other manner; it predates Hector Berlioz's programmatic *Symphonie fantastique* by ten years. Such an avantgarde musical language brings Franz Liszt to mind, yet Liszt was only nine when *Dawning* was published.

Heinrich wrote autobiographical compositions, such as "The Log House"—one of ten songs and piano works in *Sylviad* that describe his journey from Kentucky to London. He was a fervent American nationalist. The main section of *Sylviad*'s "Sylvan Scene in Kentucky; or, The Barbecue Divertimento, Comprising the Ploughman's Grand March, and the Negro's Banjo Quickstep" is not only an early representation of African Americans, but also of the instrument thirty years before Louis Moreau Gottschalk's "The Banjo." Heinrich was the first major composer to represent Native Americans in many works, such as *Pushmataha, a Venerable Chief of a Western Tribe of Indians* (1831), for thirty-three instruments, and *Pocahontas—The Royal Maid and Heroine of Virginia, the Pride of the Wilderness: Fantasia Romanza* (1837), for an orchestra unusually large for its time. In other works he foreshadowed Charles Ives in the use of distinctly American tunes, such as "Yankee Doodle" and "Hail Columbia." His interest in American nature—such as in the symphonies *The Columbiad; or, Migration of American Wild Passenger Pigeons* (c. 1857), *The Ornithological Combat of Kings; or, The Condor of the Andes and the Eagle of the Cordilleras* (1847; rev. 1857), and the orchestral capriccio *The War of the Elements and the Thundering of Niagara* (1840s?)—parallels that of Thomas Cole and Frederick Church in painting and James Fenimore Cooper and Henry David Thoreau in literature.

Heinrich was largely misunderstood during his lifetime for the strange and difficult nature of his works, even though in 1822 he was dubbed "the Beethoven of America" in one Boston journal and later "Father Heinrich." Once he attempted to obtain the patronage of President John Tyler (1790–1862) for a "grand musical work . . . illustrative of the greatness and glory of this republic, the splendor of its institutions and the indomitable bravery of its army and navy," but the president interrupted his demonstration at the White House piano with "can't you play us a good old Virginia reel?" (quoted in Howard, 4th ed., pp. 230–31). The New England advocate of traditional classical music John Sullivan Dwight wrote in 1846 that "Mr. Heinrich belongs to the romantic class, who wish to attach a story to every thing they do. . . . We are sorry to see such circumstances dragged into music as the 'Indian War Council,' the 'Advance of the Americans,' 'the Skirmish' and 'Fall of Tecumseh.' Music, aiming at no subject, . . . is sure to tell of greater things than these" (quoted in Upton, pp. 200–201). Nonetheless, Heinrich was also respected, as in Gustav Schilling's *Encyclopädie* (1836): "he is distinctly individual, particularly in regard to rhythm; and his descriptive notes, both in English and German, disclose something of genius scarcely to be expected from one of his education" (quoted in Upton, p. 144).

• An extensive collection of Heinrich's archives is in the Library of Congress. Da Capo Press reprinted *Dawning* and *Western Minstrel* together in 1972. His *Sylviad* was reprinted by Conners Publications in 1996, with an introduction by J. Bunker Clark. Heinrich's *Ornithological Combat of Kings* is recorded on New World NW 208 (1978). His piano works are included in *Anthology of Early American Keyboard Music, 1787–1830* (1977) and *American Keyboard Music through 1865* (1990), ed. J. Bunker Clark. "The Wildwood Troubadour" (1850–1852) is in *American Orchestral Music, 1800 through 1879*, ed. Sam Dennison (1992). Heinrich's friend F. A. Mussik wrote *Skizzen aus dem Leben des sich in Amerika befindenden deutschen Tondichters Anton Philipp Heinrich, nach authentischen Quellen bearbeitet* (1843), and a twelve-page booklet, *Anthony Philip Heinrich ("Vater Heinrich"): Zur Lebensgeschichte des Veteran Kompositeurs, unsers aus der neuen Welt heimgekehrten Landsmannes*, was published in Prague in 1857. The only biography is William Treat Upton, *Anthony Philip Heinrich: A Nineteenth-Century Composer in America* (1939; repr. 1967). Gilbert Chase, *America's Music*, 3d ed. (1987), includes a chapter on him. Two unpublished studies are Neely Bruce, "The Piano Pieces of Anthony Philip Heinrich Contained in *The Dawning of Music in Kentucky* and *The Western Minstrel*" (D.M.A. diss., Univ. of Illinois, 1971); and David Barron, "The Early Vocal Works of Anthony Philip Heinrich" (D.M.A. diss., Univ. of Illinois, 1972). Barron wrote the biographical entry in *The New Grove Dictionary of American Music* (1986). Wilbur Maust, "The American Indian in the Orchestral Music of Anthony Philip Heinrich," in *Music East and West: Essays in Honor of Walter Kaufmann*, ed. Thomas Noblitt (1981), is based on his Indiana University dissertation (1973). See also J. Bunker Clark, "A Bohemian Predecessor to Dvořák in the Wilds of America: Anthony Philip Heinrich" in *Dvořák in America*, ed. John C. Tibbetts (1993); Irving Lowens, "The Triumph of Anthony Philip Heinrich," in *Music and Musicians in Early America* (1964); and Betty E. Chmaj, "Father Heinrich as Kindred Spirit; or, How the Log-House Composer of Kentucky Became the Beethoven of America," *American Studies* 24 (Fall 1983): 35–57. The last chapter of J. Bunker Clark, *The Dawning of American Keyboard Music* (1988), is devoted to Heinrich's piano music to 1830.

J. BUNKER CLARK

HEINTZELMAN, Samuel Peter (30 Sept. 1805–1 May 1880), soldier, was born in Manheim, Pennsylvania, the son of Peter Heintzelman and Ann Elizabeth Grubb. Appointed to the U.S. Military Academy in 1822, he graduated in the class of 1826. He was commissioned a second lieutenant of infantry and initially served in the Second Infantry at Jefferson Barracks, Missouri, Fort Mackinac, Michigan, and Fort Brady, Wisconsin. Promoted to first lieutenant, he was a quartermaster during American Indian campaigns in Florida in 1835–1837. He was promoted to captain in 1838.

In 1844 Heintzelman married Margaret Stewart. During the war with Mexico, he joined General Winfield Scott's expedition to conquer Mexico City in 1847. For gallantry in action at the battle of Huamantla, he was promoted to brevet major on 9 October 1847. He then served with the infantry in the Southwest, and in 1851 he was brevetted to lieutenant colonel, however, he was not promoted to permanent major in the regular army until 1855, when he was assigned to recruiting duties.

At the outbreak of the Civil War, Heintzelman was on recruiting duty at Fort Columbus, New York. He was promoted to colonel and given command of the Seventeenth Infantry in May 1861 and served as inspector general of the Department of Washington, D.C. On 24 May, having become a brevet brigadier general the week before, he and his troops occupied Alexandria, Virginia, and were engaged in the defense of the nation's capital until July 1861.

In late July Heintzelman and a number of other Union officers began a series of fruitless battles against the better-led but numerically inferior Confederate forces in Virginia. Leading the Third Division, Heintzelman belatedly came to the support of a hard-pressed unit. Nevertheless, his men seized the Henry House, a position at the center of the battle of First Bull Run (First Manassas), on 21 July. Confederate attackers were mistaken for Federal troops, and before the error was discovered, a considerable contingent of Union artillery was captured. Heintzelman bravely but vainly tried to recover the artillery and suffered humiliation when the Third Division was driven from the field of battle. He was wounded in this struggle.

Recovered from his wound, Heintzelman was commander of the Third Corps in Major General George B. McClellan's failed effort to capture the Confederate capital Richmond in the Peninsula campaign of 1862. His corps led the Union advance on the Confederate works at Yorktown. Heintzelman's report to McClellan that the rebel defenses were too strong for assault colored his postwar reputation, since the Confederate defending forces were actually heavily outnumbered by McClellan's army. When the southerners gave up this line and withdrew to a line near Williamsburg, Heintzelman pursued and caught up with the defenders. On 5 May Heintzelman was at the front of a serious but uncoordinated Federal attack that was unsuccessful. During the battle of Seven Pines at the end of that month, other Union forces were routed, and

Heintzelman, once again demonstrating personal courage, led his troops in a futile attempt to halt the Federal retreat.

Heintzelman's Third Corps participated with meager success during the battles of Mechanicsville and Gaines's Mill in late June 1862. His efforts in the Seven Days' battle were nullified by Confederate gains elsewhere on the battlefield, and McClellan began his careful withdrawal from the peninsula. Heintzelman's performance during this period was uneven. By August, when Federal troops had been evacuated from their forward positions on the peninsula, Heintzelman was promoted to major general of volunteers.

Heintzelman again failed when he encountered General Thomas "Stonewall" Jackson on 29 August near Manassas. Launching an assault on what he assumed to be a retreating enemy, Heintzelman and his Union troops were almost immediately thrown back. A renewed effort the next day produced no better results, and Heintzelman found himself once again withdrawing in the face of inferior forces.

Heintzelman was never given the opportunity to face substantial Confederate forces again. Returning to the defensive works surrounding Washington, D.C., on 12 October 1862 he was subsequently given a command of the Northern Department in 1864 and then served on courts-martial until the war's end. Leaving volunteer service in late 1865, he regained command of the Seventeenth Infantry and served mostly in Texas. He retired from active service in February 1869. Congress, by a special act, allowed him to hold a major general's rank in retirement. He died in Washington, D.C.

Heintzelman was little different from a number of Union commanders who tried and failed to defeat Confederate forces in northern Virginia from 1861 to 1863. Like many Federal officers in the East, he often overestimated the Confederate battle strength. His bravery in battle was incontestable, but it was not complemented by initiative or by any particular ability to outmaneuver his more competent adversaries.

• Heintzelman's battle record is detailed in *The War of the Rebellion: A Compilation of the Official Records of the Union and Confederate Armies* (128 vols., 1880–1901) and U.S. Congress, *Report of the Joint Committee on the Conduct of the War*, 38th Cong., 2d sess. (3 vols., 1865). Another view that is considered accurate is in George B. McClellan, *McClellan's Own Story* (1887). The highlights of Heintzelman's entire military career are detailed in George W. Cullum, *Biographical Register of the Officers and Graduates of the U.S. Military Academy*, 3d ed., vol. 1 (1891). An obituary is in the *New York Times*, 2 May 1880.

ROD PASCHALL

HEINTZELMAN, Stuart (19 Nov. 1876–6 July 1935), army officer, was born in New York City, the son of Charles Stuart Heintzelman, an army officer, and Emily Bailey. A career in the military for Heintzelman was probable, and he became the third successive member of the family to graduate from the U.S. Military Academy at West Point and achieve the rank of general in the army. His grandfather was Major General Samuel P. Heintzelman, who served with distinction during the Civil War as a division and corps commander with the Army of the Potomac. The Heintzelman ancestry traced its military roots to the first American immigrant, Hieronimus (Jerome) Heintzelman, who came to this country from Germany through England in 1756 as a lieutenant in the "Royal Americans," a regiment of German riflemen serving the British colonials.

Heintzelman's formative years were marred by the death of his father when Heintzelman was five. His distraught mother took him abroad for his early education, but later he returned to the United States to attend the Groton School in Groton, Massachusetts. Heintzelman entered West Point in 1895 and graduated four years later with a commission as a second lieutenant in the Sixth U.S. Cavalry. An academy classmate of Heintzelman's described him as having "enthusiasm and inspiration and joy of life . . . with a fine mind and splendid physique." He was also a gifted sportsman and was elected president of the Cadet Athletic Association.

Known as "Tommy" among his fellow soldiers, Heintzelman's initial assignments after graduation consisted of garrison duty at Fort Riley, Kansas; commander of the post at Fort Sherman, Idaho; then another garrison detail at Fort Walla Walla, Washington. He was ordered to the Philippine Islands in 1900 for duty with the Fourth U.S. Cavalry, then to China to take part in suppressing the Boxer Rebellion. During this conflict, Heintzelman proved himself as a capable combat leader when he commanded the allied cavalry forces in the fighting near Tientsin on 19 August 1900. Returning to the Philippines from China, he was assigned as the aide-de-camp to Brigadier General Samuel S. Sumner and saw action in several engagements and expeditions during the Philippine insurrection. His success on the battlefield was rewarded with a promotion to first lieutenant in February 1901. Ordered back to the United States in 1903, Heintzelman served with troops stationed at the Louisiana Purchase Exposition in St. Louis, Missouri.

From 1904 to 1906 Heintzelman attended the Infantry and Cavalry School as well as the Army Staff College at Fort Leavenworth, Kansas. He graduated with honors and was promoted to captain on 20 October 1905. Once again he was assigned to his old regiment in the Philippines, the Sixth Cavalry, as an adjutant for two years. He later returned to Leavenworth for two tours of duty, 1909–1912 and 1914–1916, as an instructor at the Army Services Schools. His achievements as both a student and a teacher brought Heintzelman accolades from Major Generals Frederick Funston and Leonard Wood for his competency in practical military art, theoretical and practical engineering, law, and French. At this stage of Heintzelman's career his record included the Philippine, China, Mexican Border, and Victory campaign badges. Also at this time he met Rubey Bowling, whom he

married in 1910. They raised one daughter from his wife's previous marriage.

Through the influence of President Woodrow Wilson, Heintzelman was detailed in 1916 to Princeton University as a professor of military science and art. He remained at this post until 1917 and received an M.A. in the process. When the United States entered World War I, Heintzelman was ordered to France in July 1917 with the General Staff at the headquarters of the American Expeditionary Forces. He was attached to the French army as a military observer during the Chemin des Dames offensive of October 1917 and served with the French Tenth Army in their winter operations in northern Italy. He also took part in the St.-Mihiel offensive as chief of staff of the Fourth Army Corps before being assigned as chief of staff to General Robert Lee Bullard of the American II Army. He served with Bullard until demobilization in April 1919.

Heintzelman was highly decorated for his endeavors during World War I. He received from the French government the Commander of the Legion of Honor and the croix de guerre with palm and was awarded the Commander of the Order of the Crown by the grateful Italian government. His success in organizing the Fourth Corps as an effective fighting unit of the American Expeditionary Forces as well as his vigor, intelligence, and military expertise earned him the Distinguished Service Medal.

In July 1919 Heintzelman was ordered to Washington, D.C., to serve as director of the Army War College. He remained in this assignment until early 1921, when he was transferred to Fort Sheridan, Illinois, for duty on the staff of the Sixth Corps Area. Later that year he returned to Washington, D.C., where he served for four years in a variety of capacities on the War Department General Staff. His assignments included assistant chief of staff of the Military Intelligence Division, the Supply Division, and the War Plans Division.

From 1924 to 1927 Heintzelman commanded the Twenty-second Infantry Brigade at Schofield Barracks, Hawaii, and from 1928 to 1929 he was placed in charge of the harbor defenses of eastern New York with headquarters at Fort Totten, Long Island. He then returned to the Command and General Staff School at Fort Leavenworth as its commandant for six years and was promoted to major general. During the last year of his life he commanded the Seventh Corps Area. A few months before his own death, his wife passed away. Heintzelman died following a gall bladder operation at the Army-Navy Hospital, Hot Springs National Park, Arkansas.

Heintzelman is best remembered for his talents as a leader, organizer, and innovator in the army's system of military training. A former student, Colonel Stuart C. Godfrey, recalled: "The most outstanding quality of General Heintzelman as a teacher was his passion for reality. He did not attempt to introduce arbitrary changes into the course of instruction . . . but saw it as his task to break the molds before they set up too rigidly, to challenge dogma with the test of reality" ("Heintzelman: Soldier and Teacher," *Infantry Journal* 45, no. 3 [May–June 1936]: 259).

• The principle primary sources on Heintzelman are his War Department files in the National Archives in Washington, D.C., which include a personnel file, 1895–1917, in the Records of the Adjutant General's Office (RG 94) and general correspondence relating to his assignments with the War College Division in the Records of the War Department General and Special Staffs (RG 165). Personnel documentation on his service from World War I until the time of his death is in his military personnel record at the Military Personnel Records Center, St. Louis, Mo. Additional information on his military career is in Brevet Major General George W. Cullum, *Biographical Register of the Officers and Graduates of the U.S. Military Academy* (1901); Francis B. Heitman, *Historical Register and Dictionary of the U.S. Army* (1903); and U.S. Army, *Official Army Register* (1899–1935). Information on his life outside the military is in obituaries in the *Annual Report of the Association of Graduates of the United States Military Academy at West Point, New York*, 11 June 1936, and the *Leavenworth Times*, 7 July 1935.

MITCHELL YOCKELSON

HEINZ, Henry John (11 Oct. 1844–14 May 1919), industrialist, was born in the Birmingham section of Pittsburgh, Pennsylvania, the son of Henry Heinz, a brick manufacturer, and Margaretha Schmidt, German immigrants. He spent his childhood and youth in Sharpsburg, Pennsylvania. At age fourteen he attended the newly opened Allegheny Seminary in Sharpsburg, but he decided against a career in the Lutheran ministry.

Heinz decided to become involved in the world of business. In 1859 he completed a course in bookkeeping at Duff's Business College in Pittsburgh; he then served as the bookkeeper and the factotum of his father's brickyard business. At age twenty-one he bought a half interest in his father's brickyard. Heinz installed heating flues and drying apparatus in the plant and purchased and laid bricks for the buildings of the company. He was recognized as an expert on bricks and in later years frequently piled brick samples acquired during his travels on his office desk.

Heinz, however, gave up brick manufacturing to devote his attention to the food business, a field in which he displayed great business acumen. At age eight he had peddled surplus produce from the family garden to households in Sharpsburg; four years later his parents gave him three and a half acres of his own in the family garden to raise vegetables. By age seventeen Heinz was using hotbeds and intensive cultivation to increase production to two or three crops of vegetables per year. In his flourishing produce and grated horseradish business, Heinz, his younger siblings, and several other employees delivered goods three times a week to grocers in Pittsburgh. He was an imaginative merchandiser, for he sold horseradish in a clear glass bottle and recognized the importance of packaging and display. By 1861 his business demonstrated great potential, for he grossed $2,400.

As the business continued to expand, Heinz seven years later entered into partnership with his neighbor L. Clarence Noble, to make and distribute grated horseradish and to purvey other Anchor Brand products. In 1872 E. J. Noble joined Heinz, Noble, and Company, and the firm established its headquarters on the south side of Second Avenue in downtown Pittsburgh. The company also acquired a vinegar factory in St. Louis and a warehouse in Chicago. Heinz directed business operations in Pittsburgh; he did the firm's bookkeeping and supervised its manufacturing and distribution of horseradish, pickles, and sauerkraut. The firm experienced financial problems in 1875 as a result of excessive crop production, low agricultural prices, and tight credit. Despite the efforts of Heinz's friend the banker Jacob Covode, in December 1875 the partners filed for bankruptcy. Heinz capably handled one of the most difficult ordeals in his life and later fully paid his share of the firm's debts.

After this setback, Heinz became enormously successful in the food industry. With his brother John and his cousin Frederick Heinz as partners, Heinz established F. and J. Heinz Company in 1876 and served as the firm's manager. In 1877 Heinz acquired inexpensive food preparation equipment and gradually began to develop a profitable pickle business; in November of that year he displayed pickle samples at the food exposition in Pittsburgh. Profits from the pickle business allowed Heinz in 1879 to pay off large company loans, achieve solvency and stability, and begin "to be more comfortable in finances." Between 1881 and 1887 he increased the company's product offerings. By using newly invented tin-plate containers that enabled effective food preservation, Heinz met with great success as a canner of fruits and vegetables. Under his direction the company also manufactured and distributed such products as chili and tomato sauces, spaghetti, and baked beans with pork. In 1888 the H. J. Heinz Company was established when Heinz acquired the shares of his brother and cousin and became president of the new business.

Heinz's management and merchandising abilities brought the company to a position of leadership in the American food processing industry. Between 1889 and 1890 he built a huge factory and administrative complex in Allegheny City (today Pittsburgh's North Side). Fronting the Allegheny River and done in the Pittsburgh Romanesque style, the Heinz plant included a can and box factory, preserving kitchens, bottling and packing departments, a meeting hall, and comfortable facilities for employees. Heinz made changes in the selling and distribution of the company's products; salesmen were only to solicit orders, shipping was the responsibility of distributing branch and assistant managers.

Heinz as well demonstrated creative promotional and advertising talents. On his suggestion, pickle pins were given to visitors to the company's pavilion at the 1893 Chicago World's Columbian Exposition. He also insisted that his Pittsburgh plant give free tours and pickle samples and that his salesmen present demonstrations of products during food shows. During trips to New York City, Heinz studied advertisements. In 1896 he coined with an alleged magical number printed over a pickle, the company's well known slogan and logo of "fifty-seven varieties," which appeared on electrical signs in New York and in Atlantic City at Heinz pier and then was displayed on billboards and in newspapers throughout the nation. The use of effective advertising techniques, in some respects, explains how Heinz by the late 1890s developed his company into America's largest producer of pickles, ketchup, and vinegar and into the biggest grower and producer of horseradish, sauerkraut, and pickling onions.

Heinz believed that his workers constituted an integral part of the family operated company. He employed both men and women in his plants, paid employees decent wages, and provided them with an agreeable working environment. He built a restaurant, a gymnasium, an indoor swimming pool, and other facilities for his workers. He also encouraged them to take courses and to attend concerts and other cultural events sponsored by the company. Heinz also was a progressive in other respects. He and his son Howard supported the enactment of the 1906 Pure Food and Drug Act, for both believed that it was good business for a large manufacturer of quality foods to oppose those food operators who were engaging in dangerous and corrupt practices.

In 1905 Heinz incorporated the company and allowed the managing partners to become exclusive stockholders of the corporation. Heinz at this time became the president and general supervisor and appointed his son Howard as assistant to the president. In 1919 the company, with twenty-five branch plants, its own box, bottle, and can factories, and 6,523 workers, occupied a prominent place in the food processing business, both in the United States and abroad.

In 1869 Heinz had married Sarah Sloan Young, who was a Presbyterian and had come to Pittsburgh from County Down in Northern Ireland. The couple had five children, moved in 1892 into a mansion known as "Greenlawn," and lived near Pittsburgh aristocrats such as Richard Beatty Mellon, Henry Clay Frick, and George Westinghouse. After his wife's death in 1894, Heinz erected and funded a settlement house that bore her name. Heinz found religion to be meaningful and, more through accident than through doctrinal views, was affiliated successively with the Lutheran, Methodist Episcopal, Methodist Protestant, and Presbyterian churches. Heinz served as Sunday-school superintendent for twenty-five years and was appointed to the executive councils of the International Sunday-school Association and the World Sunday-school Association and served as president of the Pennsylvania State Sabbath School Association.

Heinz was quite civic-minded and was a refined Pittsburgh aristocrat with numerous interests. He was named as a life manager of the Pittsburgh Exposition Society and in 1905 was elected vice president of the Pittsburgh Chamber of Commerce. He adopted a progressive stance about major issues arising in the city;

he served in 1908 as president of the Pittsburgh Flood Commission and between 1910 and 1914 worked to resolve the city's sanitation and smoke problems. Heinz also supported educational and cultural institutions in Pittsburgh. He gave donations to the Carnegie Institute of Technology and to the University of Pittsburgh, was named a guarantor of the Pittsburgh Orchestra, and served as president of the Pittsburgh branch of the Egyptian Exploration Fund. He also traveled extensively in later life and brought back many items from his trips to Europe and Asia. His vast collection, which first was housed at Greenlawn and then was donated to the Carnegie Museum of Pittsburgh, included French and Chinese time pieces, Japanese ivories, and European and Asian paintings and textiles. Heinz died at Greenlawn.

Several major legacies are associated with Heinz's career. He was an advocate of the work ethic who effectively utilized machine technology to develop his company into one of the leading producers in the American food processing industry. Heinz assuredly is best remembered for his innovative marketing accomplishments; these contributions, in many regards, explain why the H. J. Heinz Company was able to evolve into a leader in its field.

• Diaries, letters, scrapbooks, and other significant primary sources concerning the founder are housed in the archives of the H. J. Heinz Company. Catalogs of the large personal collection of Heinz papers are to be found in the Pittsburgh Carnegie Library. A sketch of his life is in *Henry J. Heinz* (1919). E. D. McCafferty, who was the private secretary of Heinz and was secretary of the company, wrote the laudatory account, *Henry J. Heinz: A Biography* (1923). Based on family diaries and letters, Robert C. Alberts, *The Good Provider: H. J. Heinz and His 57 Varieties* (1973), is the most comprehensive biography and contains especially detailed chapters about his management and marketing achievements. For a discussion of his leadership role in the food processing business, consult Stephen Potter, *The Magic Number: The Story of "57"* (1959), Edward C. Hampe, Jr., and Merle Wittenberg, *The Lifeline of America: Development of the Food Industry* (1964), and Stefan Lorant, *Pittsburgh: The Story of an American City* (1964). For an examination of the institutional development of the H. J. Heinz Company, see Lisa Mirabile, ed., *International Directory of Company Histories*, vol. 2 (1990), pp. 507–9, and Eleanor Dienstag, *In Good Company: 125 Years at the Heinz Table* (1994). *The Story of the Sunday School Life of Henry J. Heinz* (1920) is one of the few works about this topic. An obituary is in the *Pittsburgh Post*, 15 May 1919.

WILLIAM WEISBERGER

HEINZ, Henry John, II (10 July 1908–23 Feb. 1987), business executive and philanthropist, was born in Sewickley, Pennsylvania, the son of Howard Heinz, a business executive, and Elizabeth Grainger Rust. He was the grandson of Henry J. Heinz, the founder of H. J. Heinz Company, one of the largest international food processing and distribution corporations. Heinz, known as Jack, attended Yale University and graduated in 1931 with a B.A. in English. He pursued post-graduate studies in economics at Trinity College, Cambridge University, England (1931–1932).

According to *Time*, British Prime Minister Winston Churchill once told Heinz, "You should begin at the top and work down" (30 Sept. 1946, pp. 92–93). Heinz did not accept Churchill's advice. Rather, his career up the corporate ladder followed his grandfather's belief that young Heinz would do well to advance from the ranks. He began his employment with H. J. Heinz Company on a part-time basis, working in various positions and learning different aspects of the family business. After his Cambridge days, Heinz worked as a full-time salesperson in England in 1932. Returning to the United States in 1933, he worked for several years in sales-related positions—salesman, branch manager to headquarters sales, and advertising.

In 1934 Heinz's father dispatched him to Australia to establish a manufacturing plant, Heinz-Australia, which became the largest processor of food in that country. In 1936 he became a member of Heinz's board of directors. One year later he was appointed assistant to the president, a position he held from 1937 to 1941. At the relatively young age of thirty-three, Heinz was elected president of the company after his father died of a stroke at age sixty-four.

In addition to serving as chief executive officer and leading the H. J. Heinz Company in the 1940s, Heinz involved himself in a variety of nonbusiness activities. For example, during World War II he vigorously participated in the war effort by serving as the chairman of the United War Fund, traveling to England five times, and directing his company to make K and C rations for troops engaged in battle. In 1942 Heinz was named Pittsburgh's Man of the Year. In 1946 he was responsible for H. J. Heinz Company's first public stock offering.

During his twenty-four year tenure in office, Heinz's corporate vision enabled the company to establish several major facilities in Canada, the United Kingdom, and Australia, and to acquire two major American companies, Star-Kist (1963), and Ore-Ida Food, Inc. (1965). Heinz was also responsible for making the company's presence felt in South America (Alimentos Heinz C.A., Caracas, Venezuela, 1959); Asia (Heinz Japan Ltd., Tokyo, Japan, 1961); Europe (Heinz, Italia S.P.A., Milan, Italy, 1963, and Industrias De Alimentacao, LDA, Lisbon, Portugal, 1965).

Advertising and public relations were among his many business strengths. Heinz did not rely solely on financial data in his evaluations: he also trusted his personal insights and intuition. As CEO, he appeared in television commercials and in print to promote Heinz products.

Heinz's distinguished career as a businessman was only surpassed by his interest and passion in collecting art, contributing to civic philanthropic causes, and establishing a nutrition foundation (1940). He took an avid interest in photography, architecture, and skiing

and was well-known as a wine connoisseur. William Buckley, the publisher of the *National Review* and a close friend, offered a brief vignette of Heinz in his *NR* eulogy. "He loved good food and good wine, but a discreet sense of frugality caused him to search out (and to find) fine wines that cost less than five dollars a bottle. He would arrive with great gusto to taste such wines at dinner, and leave a house present of a grand Château Lafite." His world travels, no doubt a remnant of years of traveling to conduct business, competed with his role as CEO of an international concern. At one time he owned twelve homes throughout the United States, France, England, and the Caribbean.

Although he retired in 1966, Heinz remained active in H. J. Heinz, serving as chairman of the corporate board of directors (1966–1987), and as chairman of the Howard Heinz Endowment, which distributed millions of dollars for public affairs. As an international businessman and jet-setter, he mingled with the likes of Aristotle Onassis, Aly Khan, and Truman Capote. Heinz was also interested in international affairs. An Anglophile like his father and his grandfather, he was knighted in 1979 by Queen Elizabeth for his many years of contributing to British-American relations.

Heinz was married three times. In 1935 he married Joan Diehl and had his only son, H. J. Heinz III, who became a U.S. senator from Pennsylvania. In 1947 he married Jane Ewing Jenney, and in 1953 he married Drue Maher. Heinz died in Hobe Sound, Florida.

Heinz, who revolutionized the manufacturing and distribution of food, was responsible for transforming the Heinz Company from a family-operated business to a major international professional corporation. His corporate vision enabled the company to compete globally. His philanthropic activities demonstrated his concern for less fortunate members of society. During the later part of his life, he contributed both time and money to revitalize the city of Pittsburgh.

• Eleanor Foa Dienstag, *In Good Company: 125 Years at the Heinz Table* (1994), is an excellent historical narrative of the H. J. Heinz Company. Her chapter "Henry J. Heinz, II: The Internationalist" (pp. 77–107) is an especially informative account of Heinz's life. Michael Patrick Allen, *The Founding Fortunes: A New Anatomy of the Super-Rich Families* (1987), touches on Heinz's background, inheritance, and philanthropy. An obituary is in the *New York Times*, 24 Feb. 1987.

JOSEPH C. SANTORA

HEISER, Victor George (5 Feb. 1873–27 Feb. 1972), medical doctor and public health administrator, was born in Johnstown, Pennsylvania, the son of George Heiser and Mathilde Lorenz. On 31 May 1889 both parents perished in the Johnstown flood, but Heiser, clinging to the roof of a barn, was swept to safety. Able to retrieve nothing more than his father's Civil War uniform and his mother's Bible, he left school to earn his living first as a plumber's assistant and then as a carpenter. At the age of eighteen Heiser, lonely and unhappy, entered engineering school in Chicago. Within a year, however, he decided that he wanted to be a doctor, and so, with characteristic dedication, he moved to New York and set about acquiring enough course credits to be awarded an A.B. degree from the University of the State of New York (1894). This permitted him to enroll in Jefferson Medical College in Philadelphia, where he completed the four-year course in three years, receiving his M.D. in 1897.

During his internship at Lankenau Hospital, Heiser passed the grueling examinations for admission to the U.S. Marine Hospital Service, forerunner of the Public Health Service. His success attests to his advanced knowledge of the new science of bacteriology. Sent immediately to Boston, Heiser was assigned to help improve the efficiency of hospitals overtaxed by an influx of veterans from the Spanish-American War; it was his first experience at managing tropical disease. When the crisis abated, Heiser joined his colleagues at Boston Harbor, where he worked out a system to expedite the medical examination of immigrants. Always more interested in the "prevention of disease on a wholesale basis" than in "retail" efforts—and thinking himself a "practical" man—he found public health duties very much to his taste.

In 1903 Heiser became chief quarantine officer and (from 1905) director of health in the American colonial administration in the Philippines. He remained in the islands until 1915. During this period he supervised the development of new public hospitals, expanded laboratory facilities, and organized successful smallpox vaccination programs, improvements in water supply and sewage disposal, as well as numerous health-education projects. His public health department became a model for other colonial governments. Heiser went about "washing up the Orient," using the tactics of the new public health movement. In the tropics this principally meant insect control and screening local human populations for carriage of disease organisms. To protect vulnerable Occidentals and to fortify the colonial labor force, Heiser ensured that Filipinos were tested, isolated, vaccinated, and medicated as never before. He claimed to have saved more than 100,000 lives in the process.

With a dedication he thought typically American, Heiser spread the "gospel of health" in the Philippines, seeking a thorough reformation of any Filipino customs and habits likely to transmit disease organisms. In the colonial context, such Progressive era ambitions for public health acquired a particularly authoritarian cast. Convinced of Filipino backwardness, Heiser did not hesitate to antagonize local physicians, nurses, and community leaders. To nurses he often seemed haughty and arrogant, and the association of Filipino physicians charged him with succumbing to the "evil prejudices of race." But Heiser was a relentless self-promoter, a prolific writer for the medical press, and he remained in favor with W. Cameron Forbes, governor general of the islands. Ever a convivial member of the American community, Heiser played tennis daily at the club and ventured out of Manila to hunt and fish with other single men from senior ranks of the colonial service. It was not until the appointment in 1914 of the new governor general, Fran-

cis Burton Harrison, that his position was successfully challenged. Harrison, who regarded the director of health as a "shrewd intriguer" and a principal opponent of the new filipinization policy, soon managed to obtain his resignation. Dean Worcester, Forbes's former secretary of the interior, publicly defended Heiser, arguing that he had been "shamefully maligned." Heiser himself later claimed that he decided to leave simply because he had achieved all his goals.

Wickliffe Rose, director of the International Health Board of the Rockefeller Foundation, immediately offered Heiser the post of director for the East of the new board, based in New York City. In addition to making surveys of health conditions in Asian and Pacific countries, Heiser was to report on the status of medical education and to advise on the establishment of public health programs. Over the next twenty years, he used Rockefeller funds to help organize health departments from Ceylon to Australia, to extend hookworm eradication projects, and to modernize medical training throughout the region. In 1920, as a respite from Rockefeller work, he attached himself to the Wood-Forbes mission, which reported critically on Harrison's filipinization policies, and Heiser took great satisfaction in briefly displacing the Filipino director of health from his office. But such pleasures were fleeting, and he increasingly came to regret his constant travel and the lack of family ties.

In 1934 Heiser retired from the International Health Board and began compiling his autobiography, using old reports and transcribed interviews. *An American Doctor's Odyssey*, published in 1936, proved immensely popular; it became a Book-of-the-Month Club selection, sold a half-million copies, and was translated into fourteen languages. Its success breathed new life into the genre of medical tales from the tropics. But some of Heiser's colleagues expressed disappointment with these curiously depopulated reminiscences. Sam Lambert, author of *A Yankee Doctor in Paradise*, wondered why it was not titled "Alone in the Orient."

In 1938 the National Association of Manufacturers (NAM) asked Heiser, by now a medical celebrity, to become its consultant on "healthful working conditions." Rarely hesitant to generalize his expertise, Heiser was quick to detect the continuity of tropical medicine with the new field of industrial hygiene. He had always argued that improvements in Filipino personal hygiene would lead to improved economic productivity. Applying the same principle to industry in the United States, Heiser urged workers to take personal responsibility for their health care. On behalf of the NAM, Heiser organized clinics for local manufacturers' groups where he extolled the benefits of vitamin supplementation, regular exercise, and avoidance of contagious disease. Accidents, he argued, were usually the result of carelessness, fatigue, and malnutrition. Heiser's goal was to help management use its personnel to greatest advantage in production. He believed that the doctor's mission in the factory was "as bold and as adventurous as in any of nature's jungles."

Thus the logic of his career united two apparently disparate medical specialties.

As chairman of the medical advisory committee of the New York World's Fair of 1939, Heiser was responsible for developing its memorable health exhibition. An admirer of German public health programs, he managed to obtain replicas of exhibits from the Dresden Museum of Hygiene, including the famous "transparent man." But his later efforts to establish a permanent American Museum of Hygiene failed, despite German support. During World War II, though, Heiser turned his attention to improving stamina on the home front, addressing radio audiences and writing a number of pamphlets, all urging Americans to enhance their diets and to "toughen up" to meet the Nazi challenge.

Well into his eighties and nineties Heiser continued to lecture on tropical medicine and industrial hygiene. In 1969 he received the Damien-Dutton Society Award for his work in the prevention and treatment of leprosy. The disease was a lifelong interest. In the Philippines he had demanded the segregation of lepers on Culion Island and had introduced treatment with chaulmoogra oil. From 1931 to 1938 he was first president of the International Leprosy Association.

In 1940 Heiser had married Marion Peterson Phinny, who predeceased him in 1965. He died in New York City, survived by a stepson. When asked to what he attributed his long life, Heiser replied, "Exercise, basic foods, no desserts."

• Heiser's papers are chiefly at the American Philosophical Society in Philadelphia, Pa., although the Rockefeller Foundation Archives in Tarrytown, N.Y., and the National Association of Manufacturers' papers at the Hagley Museum and Library in Delaware also contain important holdings. See also Heiser, *An American Doctor's Odyssey: My Life in Forty-Five Countries* (1936), and "Reminiscences on Early Tropical Medicine," *Bulletin of the New York Academy of Medicine* 44 (1968): 654–60. An obituary is in the *New York Times*, 28 Feb. 1972.

WARWICK ANDERSON

HEISMAN, John William (23 Oct. 1869–3 Oct. 1936), football coach, was born in Cleveland, Ohio, the son of John M. Heisman and Sara Lehr. In the 1870s the family moved to Titusville, Pennsylvania, where his father employed thirty-five workers in his barrel-making shop, which served the booming oil industry in the town. In 1887 Heisman graduated from the local high school, where he was a top student, captain of the baseball team, the school's gymnastics champion, and a member of the football team. Though his father disliked his participation in football, Heisman continued to play when he entered Brown University in the fall of 1887. After two years as a lineman for Brown he transferred to the University of Pennsylvania, where he played until 1891. Although he earned a law degree from Penn in 1892, Heisman accepted an offer to coach football at Oberlin that fall.

In his first year as a coach, Heisman exhibited the innovative strategy for which he would become well known. Influenced by the success of Yale University and its use of the great guard W. W. "Pudge" Heffelfinger, Heisman employed his guards to pull out of the line to lead interference for the runner. His team went undefeated (7–0), beating the Ohio State University team decisively on two occasions. Despite such success, and ever in search of more lucrative positions, Heisman became athletic director and coach at Buchtel College (later the University of Akron) in February 1893. Criticized for his alleged overemphasis on winning, Heisman returned to Oberlin the following year, although he did not completely sever his ties with Buchtel. Heisman's former players at Buchtel hired him to play against Ohio State in a state tournament game in September 1894. The resultant 12–6 victory allowed Buchtel to claim the state championship.

In 1895 Heisman moved to Alabama A & M (later Auburn University), where he coached football and baseball and taught speech for five years. Known as a precise, dramatic, even overstated orator, Heisman engaged in summer work as an actor. A stern taskmaster and perfectionist as a coach, his sarcasm and authoritarian style often grated on his players but produced winning teams. Faced with a lack of talent, Heisman sometimes resorted to trickery, and he was often accused of circumventing the rules. In an 1895 game against Vanderbilt he unveiled the hidden ball trick by having a player shove the ball under his jersey to confuse the opponents. Often considered the originator of such deception, Heisman probably witnessed an earlier variation of the ruse by Amos Alonzo Stagg's Chicago team.

Never given to modesty, Heisman produced a self-promotional pamphlet after the 1899 season, which contributed in 1900 to his being named coach at Clemson University at an increased salary. In his first season at Clemson his team went undefeated (6–0) and won the Southern Intercollegiate Athletic Association championship. In October 1903 Heisman married Evelyn Cox, a widow with a twelve-year-old son. They had no children together.

After the 1903 season Heisman moved to Georgia Tech, which guaranteed him a salary of $2,000 per year plus 30 percent of the football and baseball gate receipts for coaching its football, basketball, and baseball teams. The school's location, in Atlanta, the major metropolis of the South, and the growing popularity of football as a commercial spectacle promised a bright future for Heisman. There he enjoyed his longest tenure and greatest success; his Georgia Tech teams compiled a 101–28–6 record. In 1908 Heisman also assumed directorship of the Atlanta Athletic Club, and he served as president of the Atlanta Baseball Association from 1910 to 1914. John Grant, a local businessman, financed the expansion of the Georgia Tech stadium in 1913, and Heisman promoted his teams and attendance by running up huge scores against weaker opponents. Georgia Tech defeated Mercer 103–0 in 1913 and set the college football scoring record in 1916 when it defeated Cumberland 222–0. Heisman had offered the small school $500 to play his team in Atlanta, and, despite a 126–0 lead at halftime, Heisman exhorted his team not to let up, although he agreed to shorten the second half. In addition to such overwhelming victories, fans were often treated to Heisman's volatile outbursts directed at game officials with whom he disagreed.

Heisman emphasized discipline, teamwork, and precision. While at Georgia Tech he perfected an intricate shift that allowed backs to move into blocking positions before defenders could adjust, thereby giving the offense an advantage in momentum. An early proponent of the forward pass, which was legalized in 1906, Heisman used this new element of the game with success. (Until that time, passing had been limited to the lateral.) He also played a significant role in instituting the 1910 rule that a game be divided into four quarters.

As early as 1905 his Georgia Tech team went undefeated, but he gained national prominence during World War I. His team was unbeaten from 1915 to 1917. With four All-Americans on the 1917 squad, including Joe Guyon, a transfer from Carlisle Indian School, Georgia Tech went 9–0, even winning two games in one day, and claimed the national championship, the first southern school to do so.

Following his divorce in 1919 Heisman returned to Penn as its football coach from 1920 to 1922. There he helped to professionalize the intercollegiate game by adding seven assistant coaches to his staff. In 1922 he authored a book, *The Principles of Football*, which advocated a dictatorial coaching style and the character-building potential of the game. Heisman served as president of the American Football Coaches Association in 1923 and 1924. He spent the 1923 season as coach at Washington and Jefferson College in Washington, Pennsylvania, then in 1924 accepted a contract as the athletic director and football coach at Rice, where his salary of $9,000 per year greatly exceeded that of the top faculty members. That same year he married a former girlfriend, Edith Maora Cole. They had no children. While at Rice he installed an athletic dorm for football players, thus underscoring the team's importance, but he failed to match his past success. After a losing season in 1927 Heisman resigned and moved to New York, where he wrote a weekly column for *Collier's* magazine for two years and eventually entered the sporting goods business.

In 1929 Heisman became the athletic director of the New York Downtown Athletic Club. The organization's Touchdown Club began offering a trophy to the best college football player in the eastern United States. The award became a national one in 1935 and later was named for Heisman. He died in New York City; the funeral and interment took place in his wife's hometown of Rhinelander, Wisconsin. Heisman was elected posthumously to the National Football Federation, College Football, and Georgia Tech halls of fame.

Heisman is often credited with original strategies and techniques that may also be attributed to other early coaches. Even his official coaching record of 186–70–16 is in dispute. A biographer of Heisman's, Wiley Lee Umphlett, unearthed four additional wins and a reversed decision. There is no doubt that Heisman played an influential role in important rules changes. Nevertheless, Heisman left his most lasting mark on the game with the trophy that bears his name, the most prestigious award in college football.

• The University of Pennsylvania Archives contain materials on Heisman. Wiley Lee Umphlett, *Creating the Big Game: John W. Heisman and the Invention of American Football* (1992), is the first biography of Heisman, though some of its contentions may be considered faulty. Additional information is included in Ralph Hickok, *The Encyclopedia of North American Sports History* (1992); Tom Perrin, *Football: A College History* (1987); Edwin Pope, *Football's Greatest Coaches* (1956); and Allison Danzig, *The History of American Football: Its Great Teams, Players, and Coaches* (1956). John W. Heisman, "Signals," *Collier's*, 6 Oct. 1928, pp. 12–13, 31–32, provides an account of his early football career, innovative claims, and racial attitudes. An obituary is in the *New York Times*, 6 Oct. 1936.

GERALD R. GEMS

HEISS, Michael (12 Apr. 1818–26 Mar. 1890), Roman Catholic educator and bishop, was born in Pfahldorf, Germany, the son of a peasant couple, Joseph Heiss and Gertrude Frei. From 1835 to 1839, he attended the University of Munich, where he came under the influence of theologians such as Johann Adam Mohler and Johann Joseph von Gorres. He completed his studies for the priesthood at Eichstätt and was ordained in Nymphenburg in 1840.

After two years of pastoral work in Germany, Heiss immigrated to the United States, intrigued by the accounts of the new country from *Annals of the Propagation of the Faith* and the letters of an American friend, Rev. Charles Boeswald. In response to the pleas of Bishop Benedict Joseph Flaget of Bardstown, Kentucky, for German-speaking priests, Heiss volunteered for service in Covington, Kentucky, in 1842. A year later, disconcerted by the paucity of German-speaking Catholics there, he affiliated himself with the new bishop of Milwaukee, John Martin Henni, a champion of German-speaking Catholics. Heiss accompanied Henni to Milwaukee in 1844 and became pastor of St. Mary's Church. He went to Germany in the early 1850s for health reasons but returned to Milwaukee in 1856. He played a major role in the construction of St. Francis Seminary, where he was rector from 1856 to 1868 and taught theology, canon law, and scripture. Heiss was an able scholar, publishing books on matrimony (1861) and the scriptures (1863). Less weighty pieces appeared on the pages of the popular German-American journals *Pastoral-Blatt* and *Der Warheitsfreund*. He participated in the planning for the Second Plenary Council of Baltimore in 1866, and in 1868, he became the first bishop of LaCrosse, Wisconsin.

The LaCrosse diocese was carved out of the extreme western counties of the state of Wisconsin, and Heiss spent much time on the road, confirming, visiting missions, and attempting to organize the church in western Wisconsin. He attended the First Vatican Council in Rome (1869–1871), where he was a supporter of the definition of papal infallibility.

In 1878, Archbishop Henni's health rapidly deteriorated, and Henni clearly wanted Heiss as his coadjutor and successor in Milwaukee. However, the nomination of Henni's successor was caught in the crossfire of an internal dispute between English-speaking and German-speaking Catholic clergy. English-speaking clergy in Milwaukee petitioned Archbishop James Gibbons of Baltimore to persuade Rome to appoint another candidate. Gibbons suggested the appointment of John Lancaster Spalding, but Heiss had powerful friends as well, including Mother Caroline Friess of the School Sisters of Notre Dame and Rev. Peter Abbelen, the spiritual director of the Sisters. Rome delayed making a decision until the end of 1879 when Henni suffered a near-fatal stroke. In April 1880, the Vatican appointed Heiss to the post.

Heiss strongly believed in the need for more German-speaking bishops in the United States, and, in 1886, he approved the visit of the Reverend Abbelen to Rome with a petition for more German bishops. This request provoked a negative reaction among English-speaking prelates like Gibbons and John Ireland (1838–1918) and was disregarded by the Vatican. Heiss also led opposition to the Bennett Law of 1889, which mandated English-only instruction in Wisconsin schools.

Heiss served briefly on the committee to form the Catholic University of America, but he was not warmly disposed to the idea, believing instead that Catholic resources should go into local seminaries. He died in LaCrosse.

• There are fragments of Heiss's correspondence in the Archives of the Archdiocese of Milwaukee, St. Francis Seminary, and the Diocese of LaCrosse. Other evidence can be found in the Archives of the Archdioceses of Cincinnati, Baltimore, and St. Paul. Secondary sources include M. Mileta Ludwig's biography of Heiss, *Right Hand Glove Uplifted* (1968). Benjamin Blied, *Three Archbishops of Milwaukee* (1955), contains an essay on Heiss. See also Peter Leo Johnson, *Crosier on the Frontier: A Life of John Martin Henni* (1959); *Stuffed Saddle Bags: The Life of Martin Kundig, Priest* (1942); and *Halcyon Days: The Story of St. Francis Seminary* (1956). Marvin R. O'Connell, *John Ireland and the American Catholic Church* (1988), also contains information from a different perspective.

STEVEN M. AVELLA

HEIZER, Robert Fleming (13 July 1915–18 July 1979), archaeologist and anthropologist, was born in Denver, Colorado, the son of Ott Fleming Heizer, a mining engineer, and Martha Madden. Much of his youth was spent in the countryside, in particular in the semiarid region around Lovelock, Nevada. There he learned how to live off the land, and he acquired a deep interest in and affection for the Nevadan and, later, the Californian Indians, observing their way of life, history, social organization, and technology.

In 1934 Heizer entered the University of California at Berkeley, where for eight years he pursued a rigorous undergraduate and graduate program in anthropology. Under Alfred Kroeber, Robert Lowie, and Edward Gifford, he was required to develop competence in each of the subdisciplines of the subject. During these years Heizer began to study the archaeology of central California. His pioneer work in the delta of the Lower Sacramento River and the Central Valley, using stratigraphic excavation and sequence dating, laid the firm foundation for the chronology of Californian Indian archaeology on which all subsequent research has been based. Yet Heizer wrote his Ph.D. dissertation not on California archaeological research but on indigenous West Coast whaling practices. With his subsequent publications on whaling and fishing practices, the dissertation became a standard text.

In 1940 Heizer married Nancy Jenkins, with whom he had three children. In 1947 he returned to Berkeley to begin a career as a teacher and scholar. His scientific production was prodigious. He authored, coauthored, or edited twenty-four books and nearly four hundred scientific articles. He was known above all for his archaeological research and writing on western North American and Meso-American topics, but he made major scientific contributions to a broad range of subjects. His versatility is explained by his insatiable curiosity and the kind of training he received at Berkeley. This combination of basic intellect, curiosity, and broad training produced one of the country's last "general" anthropologists, who could talk and write knowledgeably in areas of the discipline far transcending his primary passion, archaeology.

Heizer made several important contributions to historic archaeology in the western states, particularly in *Francis Drake and the Californian Indians, 1579* (1947), which followed from his excavations of Indian mound sites on Drake's Bay and the recovery of evidence of Sebastian Rodriguez Cermeno's shipwreck of 1595 in the bay. Heizer's historical research included Spanish missions of the Southwest; the 1840s Russian settlement at Fort Ross, California; the excavation of Sutter's Mill, where gold was discovered in the California Sierra foothills in 1849; and mining towns of the gold rush days.

Heizer's work in prehistoric archaeology in California and Nevada also included a study of the trade in obsidian and shell beads, lithic technology, mines and quarrying methods, and, in particular, radiocarbon and other ways of dating prehistoric sites in the West. He was especially interested in the new scientific methods being used to identify trace elements in soils and in using quantitative methods for estimating population densities and settlement size. These interests, resulting in his several publications with the physiologist Sherburne F. Cook, which made use of chemical analysis of bone and soils and which were very influential in developing subsistence studies, were brought together in the volume he edited in 1960, *The Application of Quantitative Methods in Archaeology*. They are also evidenced in his excavations at Lovelock Cave by

Humboldt Lake in Nevada, where much basketry and other perishable remains were preserved. The cave contained numbers of human coprolites; these were painstakingly separated and studied by Heizer and Lewis Napton, and from them very precise information was obtained on dietary preferences. Heizer was also interested in prehistoric art, and his work with Martin Baumhoff, *Prehistoric Rock Art of Nevada and Eastern California* (1962), describes and reproduces the many rich engraving sites that were, Heizer thought, associated with game trails and seasonal hunting.

Early man in North America was another of Heizer's interests, and his publications did much to negate the dubious claims for human presence in the continent much earlier than 12,000 years ago. The exposure of so-called prehistoric hearths as pack-rat houses; the proof of the dissociation of artifacts and fossil fauna at Thule Springs, Nevada; and his use of excavation and radiometric dating all combined to provide the kind of cautionary approach needed in interpreting prehistoric archaeological contexts.

In 1955 Heizer began work in Mexico at the Olmec Civilization site of La Venta, a large, pre-Classic ceremonial center in the east coast lowlands. Working with Phillip Drucker and others, he directed several excavation seasons, mapping the structures, studying the rich stonework, and discovering the famous Jade Group of human figures buried in association with the main building complex. His last season at La Venta was in 1970, when he carried out a magnetometer survey of the pyramid and discovered evidence of a structure within it. Regrettably, political problems prevented his following this up.

La Venta triggered Heizer's interest in identifying the sources of the stone stelae and heads found there because no local stone existed; his work with Howell Williams, a vulcanologist at Berkeley, resulted in the identification of several of these distant sources. Thus began his interest in the methods used for transporting large stones, a research interest that stayed with him for the rest of his life and inevitably led him to Egypt. There, in the late 1970s, his collaboration with the chemist Fred Stross and the neutron-activation specialist Isadore Perlmann resulted in the identification of the quarry sources of the stone used for the Colossi of Memnon at Luxor. A secondary interest in Egypt was the methods used to make alabaster vases and bowls in dynastic and predynastic times. His study with his student and collaborator Thomas Hester showed that the same basic methods were still being used.

Heizer's work was always marked by great attention to detail; by the recognition that archaeological facts must be understood in the context of wider cultural systems of which they are only parts; and by his early use of new methods and techniques not primarily archaeological (for instance, x-ray fluorescence and neutron activation analysis). He also broke new ground with his collaborative research with colleagues in other fields. The remarkable breadth of his ethnographic and technological knowledge can be seen from the diverse titles of his ethnographic papers on, for example, fishing equipment, plank boats and the use of bitumen for caulking, salt production, domestic fuel sources, slings in prehistoric Nevada, the *milpa* system of swidden cultivation in Meso-America, and coiled and twilled basketry in the western United States. He was the author, coauthor, or editor of several books on the Californian and Nevadan Indians, in particular *The California Indians* (1971), *Ishi, the Last Yahi: A Documentary History*, with T. Kroeber (1979), and the *Handbook of North American Indians*, volume 8, *California* (1978). This volume became a standard classic. He also wrote feelingly of the political injustices suffered by the Indians as a result of broken treaties in *The Other Californians: Prejudice and Discrimination under Spain, Mexico, and the United States to 1920* (1971), among other works.

Heizer excelled in teaching at both the undergraduate and graduate levels. As in his excavation, he worked with exactitude, and he held his students to his own high standards. This endeared him to some but occasionally alienated him from others. Not content with existing texts, he produced his own manuals of instruction. *Field Methods in Archaeology*, with Hester Graham and John A. Graham, first published in 1949, went through six editions, while *An Introduction to Prehistoric Archaeology*, with Frank Hole, was published in 1965 and saw two later editions. His interest in the history of archaeology led him to research many original sources, an important selection of which he brought together and published as *Man's Discovery of His Past* (1962). Heizer's ability and success as a teacher can be gauged by the large enrollments in his undergraduate courses and by the number of professional archaeologists trained by him who went on to teach or engage in research at universities and other institutions around the country.

Heizer retired from Berkeley as professor emeritus in 1977. When he died in San Francisco, he was working on a volume titled *Heavy Transport*, based on his research in Egypt, which was completed by Thomas Hester in 1990.

To some extent Heizer was a solitary, work-addicted man whose prodigious production required rigid self-discipline. Yet he could be extremely witty and companionable. His many friends remembered him for his wry and often sardonic humor, for his willingness to share his knowledge and ideas, for the magnitude and depth of his scholarship, and for the stimulus that he gave to anthropology in general.

• A complete "Bibliography of the Published Writings of Robert F. Heizer, 1937–1978" was published in 1979 and received limited distribution; a copy is available in the Archaeological Research Facility at the University of California, Berkeley, where a collection of Heizer's papers is also to be found. Artifact collections made by Heizer are in the Phoebe Hearst Museum at Berkeley. Obituaries are in J. Desmond Clark, George M. Foster, and David Mandelbaum, *University of California in Memoriam* (1985), pp. 114-15, and the Texas Archaeological Society *Bulletin* 50 (1980): 151–52.

J. DESMOND CLARK

HEKTOEN, Ludvig (2 July 1863–5 July 1951), physician, was born in Westby, Wisconsin, the son of Peter P. Hektoen, a schoolteacher and farmer, and Olave Thoragaard. Hektoen graduated from Iowa's Luther College in 1883. Thereafter he studied at the University of Wisconsin, although he did not earn a degree there. He received the M.D. in 1887 from the College of Physicians and Surgeons in Chicago, which later became part of the University of Illinois. In the early 1890s he studied medical science, especially pathology, in Uppsala, Prague, and Berlin. The faculty of Luther College awarded him an A.M. in 1896 in absentia in recognition of the range of his academic work since receiving his undergraduate degree. He married Ellen Strandh on 7 July 1891, while in Europe; they had two children.

Hektoen's career progressed rapidly in the late 1880s and 1890s. In 1887 he earned the highest score on Cook County Hospital's competitive internship examination. While an intern at the hospital he worked under Christian Fenger, a pathologist and surgeon. Hektoen later emphasized other medical research fields, but pathology was his first specialty because of Fenger's influence. In 1907 the grateful former student edited Fenger's collected works.

In 1889 Hektoen accepted appointment as Cook County Hospital pathologist, a position he held until 1903. In December 1889 he began his long association with Rush Medical College on Chicago's west side. His initial appointment was as curator of the museum of medical specimens; within a year Rush promoted him to lecturer in pathology. Two years later the College of Physicians and Surgeons recruited him to be professor of pathologic anatomy, a position from which he resigned in 1894 to return to Rush. Between 1890 and 1894 he also served as physician for the Cook County Coroner's Office.

Hektoen began his teaching career at Rush as professor of morbid anatomy. In 1898 he was promoted to the pathology chair on the death of its incumbent. Although his work took other directions after 1900, Hektoen remained professor of pathology at Rush until he gained emeritus rank in 1933. From 1898 until 1942 Rush was affiliated with the University of Chicago; Hektoen was appointed head of Chicago's Department of Pathology in 1901, a position from which he retired in 1932. In 1902 he accepted appointment as the first director of the John McCormick Institute for Infectious Diseases, a research laboratory adjoining the Rush campus, which had been established by the McCormick family. Hektoen directed the institute until 1942. Its emphasis on infectious diseases and his administrative responsibilities established the direction of his career after 1900.

Hektoen was an important participant in the rapid changes occurring in medical education and research in the United States in the late nineteenth century and early twentieth. The term "scientific medicine" is often used to summarize the phenomenon. Its hallmarks included strong emphasis on laboratory research in medical schools, as well as residencies in German universities or institutes, which provided opportunities to study with important medical scientists and to observe the best research facilities. Hektoen participated in these and other aspects of the development of American scientific medicine.

After 1900 Hektoen's research turned toward bacteriology and immunology. As late as 1899 he published a typical pathology study, in this case devoted to pathogenic fungi and the lesions they produce. In 1903 he published his first paper on immunity. In the intervening years his research addressed varied topics, from aneurysms (reflecting interest in the categorizing observations of disease manifestations which had dominated his work since his internship) to bacteriological examination of blood and infectious disease of unknown origin. His approach toward aspects of tuberculosis illustrates the development of his research: in the 1890s his well-regarded analysis of blood-vessel changes in tuberculous meningitis and the fate of the disease's giant cells was typical pathologic or microscopical anatomy; by 1920 his tuberculosis work addressed whether ill rabbits would produce antibodies to blood cells obtained from sheep.

Four of Hektoen's contributions proved to be important. He confirmed that a protein of the lens of the eye is organ-specific rather than species-specific. Other work demonstrated that reintroduction of one of a group of antigens to which an animal is immune prompts the production of antibodies to all the antigens, a discovery useful in the treatment of certain infections. He introduced in Chicago, and perhaps in the nation, the important diagnostic tool of making blood cultures from patients. He was apparently the first researcher to recommend improving the success of blood transfusions by carefully matching recipient and donor for compatibility.

Hektoen participated actively in the network of institutions, organizations, and journals serving scientific medicine. In 1901 the Association of American Pathologists and Bacteriologists elected him president; in 1909 the American Association for the Advancement of Science made him vice president. In 1908 he became chair of the American Medical Association's Committee on Scientific Research. In 1927 Hektoen's quarter-century of work in bacteriology and immunology brought election to the presidency of the Society of Immunologists. In 1926 he agreed to become the first editor of *Archives of Pathology*. He was a member of the National Academy of Sciences and the Academy of Medicine.

In Hektoen's most active years scientific medicine looked to private philanthropy to support research. Hektoen worked effectively with the McCormick family and other Chicago philanthropists to develop the extensive facilities and generous endowment associated with the McCormick Institute during his directorship. In its early years Hektoen and two other institute researchers shared space with other Rush faculty and students in the college's laboratory building; however by the World War I era, Hektoen and his McCormick associates had established a hospital for low-income

Chicagoans suffering from infectious diseases next to a building dedicated to the institute's research. The institute sponsored the founding in 1904 of the *Journal of Infectious Diseases*, which Hektoen edited for thirty-seven years.

One of Hektoen's honorary citations described him as "a pioneer pathologist of the middle border." This is an appropriate description, although his career evolved to include research and teaching in immunology and bacteriology as well as pathology. He also edited several medical journals and led medical societies. In 1942 the American Medical Association recognized his accomplishments with its Distinguished Service Award. In that year Chicago's McCormick Infectious Diseases Institute, a research facility he directed for forty years, was renamed for him.

Chicago remained Hektoen's home for the rest of his life, and he died there. Ernest Irons, his colleague and contemporary and a former dean of Rush Medical College and president of the American Medical Association, described Hektoen: "His life exhibited the serenity of intellectual power [and as] an originator of ideas and a builder of men, he served well the science and art of medicine."

• The Rush-Presbyterian-St. Luke's Medical Center Archives in Chicago holds a biographical file on Rush which includes some correspondence and bibliographies. Rush Medical College's archives within the Medical Center Archives also reflects Hektoen's career. Hektoen authored *Technique of Postmortem Examination* (1894) and edited *Durcks General Pathological Histology* (1904), *Contributions to Medical Science by Howard Taylor Ricketts* (1911), *Collected Works of Christian Fenger* (1907), and *American Textbook on Pathology* (1901). Among his many articles, "Introduction to the Study of Infectious Diseases," in *Osler's Modern Medicine*, vol. 2 (1925) is of interest. The Oregon Printing Department published "Old and New Knowledge of Immunity," his 1920 Noble Wiley Jones Lecture at the University of Oregon. Obituaries appeared in the *Journal of the American Medical Association* 146 (1951): 1057; *American Journal of Clinical Pathology* 21 (1951): 1065–7; *Archives of Pathology* 52 (1951): 390–4, an analysis of Hektoen's research; and *Proceedings of the Institute of Medicine of Chicago* 19, no. 1 (Jan. 15, 1956), an obituary written by James B. Herrick, Rush Medical College colleague and friend, quoting at length from other obituaries and Rush Medical College dean Ernest E. Irons's funeral eulogy. A more recent biographical study is William K. Beatty, "Ludwig Hektoen—Scientist and Counselor," *Proceedings of the Institute of Medicine of Chicago* 35, no. 1 (Jan.–Mar. 1982): 7–9.

STUART W. CAMPBELL

HELBURN, Theresa (12 Jan. 1887–18 Aug. 1959), playwright and theater producer, was born in New York City, the daughter of Julius Helburn, a Boston leather merchant, and Hannah Peyser, a primary school teacher. Helburn acquired a love of literature and culture from her mother, who educated her in the experimental elementary school she had established at home. When her mother took her at age nine to see Ada Rehan's stock company perform four Shakespear-ean plays in repertoire, Theresa knew she had found her life's work. "The theatre was not a dream, or a goal—it was home," she later wrote.

As an undergraduate at Bryn Mawr College she acted in, produced, and directed college plays, keeping herself so busy that after graduating in 1908 she suffered a nervous collapse. Recuperating on a farm she began to write plays, determined to become a writer. She entered graduate school to study English at Radcliffe College, and she was a member of George Pierce Baker's English 47 Workshop for playwriting at Harvard.

In 1910 Helburn returned to New York City, made a modest social debut, and supported herself in various occupations. Her poetry and short stories were published in *Century*, *Harper's*, and *New Republic*; she taught drama at Miss Merrill's Finishing School in Mamaroneck, New York; and she worked as governess for the Herter family in New York and Paris. Helburn studied at the Sorbonne and met Gertrude Stein, Alice B. Toklas, Isadora Duncan, and others in Paris. In New York she joined the Poetry Society of America and met Edwin Arlington Robinson and Vachel Lindsay. In 1911 she also met a young teacher of high school English, John Baker Opdycke, whom she married in 1920; the couple had no children. Opdycke, a graduate of Franklin and Marshall College, wrote more than twenty books on the art of commercial prose before he died in 1958.

Also in 1911 Helburn joined a weekly play-reading group that included Lawrence Langner, Lee Simonson, Edward Goodman, and Philip Moeller. This amateur group called itself the Washington Square Players and was dedicated to presenting new American plays. The group's first production, *Licensed*, featured Helburn as an actress until family objections to her role in this play about birth control forced her to withdraw. The Players next produced her one-act play, *Enter the Hero* (1916), starring Edna St. Vincent Millay, but it was withdrawn early in the production process because Millay was a "better poet than player." In 1915 Helburn collaborated with Katharine "Kit" Cornell (a former student) to direct *Twelfth Night* at the Oaksmere School, and in 1918 she served as drama critic for the *Nation*.

Helburn's true working life began in 1919 when Langner (an English patent attorney in love with the theater) formed the Theatre Guild from the nucleus of people who had begun the Washington Square Players. It was Langner's dream to build an art theater that would offer beauty in every aspect of the stage, including in the kind of drama performed, something often lacking on Broadway. Helburn joined the Theatre Guild as a play reader and, when asked to sign on as secretary pro tem, stayed for life. "All I had to give them was my inexperience," she wrote.

Helburn was the Theatre Guild's executive director from 1919 to 1932 and the administrative director with Langner and Armina Marshall from 1933 to 1953. She was also a member of the board of managers—an organizational structure unique to the Theatre Guild that ruled by collective decision—which also included Langner, Helen Westley, Rollo Peters, Moeller, Simonson, Justus Sheffield, and Maurice Wertheim.

For forty years the Theatre Guild was America's foremost art theater. It presented new European and American plays by George Bernard Shaw, John Howard Lawson, Eugene O'Neill, Elmer Rice, Georg Kaiser, Maxwell Anderson, Paul Claudel, Ernst Toller, Franz Werfel, Luigi Pirandello, William Saroyan, Philip Barry, S. N. Behrman, and William Inge. (Helburn fought bitterly against attempts to censor O'Neill's *Strange Interlude* and *A Moon for the Misbegotten*.) The Guild's prestigious and honorable evolution included the creation of a subscription audience; maintenance of a permanent professional acting company performing in weekly alternating repertoire; development of a generation of playwrights, directors, and designers; and seven Pulitzer prizes.

Helburn was also a director—*Mary of Scotland* and *Chrysalis*—and a playwright—*Crops and Croppers* (1918), *Allison Makes Hay* (1919), *Other Lives* (1921) in collaboration with Goodman, *Denbigh* (1921), *A Hero Is Born* (1937), and *Little Dark Horse* (adapted from the French in 1941). These plays were successful community theater properties. Helburn reappeared on stage as an actress after a twenty-year hiatus to play in *Suzanna and the Elders* at the Westport Country Playhouse in 1938.

In 1947 Bryn Mawr named a chair in her honor. In 1957 she established the Theresa Helburn Award in commemoration of those in Hungary who rose against Soviet rule in 1956. She retired from the Theatre Guild in 1958 and died a year later in Norwalk, Connecticut.

Helburn's contribution to the Theatre Guild and to the American theater was enormous. In a day when women producers were rare, she helped produce more than 100 plays and encouraged the writing of many more. She is credited with founding both the short-lived Theatre Guild School and the Bureau of New Plays. Her writing seminars formed the foundation for the Dramatic Workshop of the New School. In 1943, when the Theatre Guild was nearly bankrupt, she decided to turn Lynn Riggs's *Green Grow the Lilacs* into a drama with music and dancing. This effort was called "Helburn's Folly" until Rodgers and Hammerstein added their music and lyrics, and it was renamed *Oklahoma!*, the hit that both saved the Theatre Guild financially and changed the direction of American musical theater.

In the New York theater of the twenties, thirties, and forties, Helburn was "the power behind the throne . . . the terror of actors, the bane of playwrights, and the thorn of agents, managers and kindred mortals." Langner recalled, "Her nerves were like whipcord and her power like steel."

• Helburn's personal and professional papers, correspondence, clippings, and photos are in the Theatre Guild Collection at the Beinecke Library, Yale University; the Billy Rose Theatre Collection at the New York Public Library for the Performing Arts, Lincoln Center; the Harvard Theatre Collection; and the Radcliffe College Archives. Bryn Mawr College has typescripts of her unpublished plays. Helburn's autobiography, *A Wayward Quest* (1960), was completed after her death by her assistant Elinore Denniston. Two of her plays, *Allison Makes Hay* (1919) and *Enter the Hero* (1918) have been published. Other important sources are Walter Eaton, *The Theatre Guild: The First Ten Years* (1929); Roy Waldau, *Vintage Years of the Theatre Guild* (1972); Lawrence Langner, *The Magic Curtain* (1951); and Marya Mannes, "Profiles: The Power Behind the Throne," *New Yorker*, 6 Dec. 1930. An obituary is in the *New York Times*, 19 Aug. 1959.

KATHLEEN M. ROBBINS

HELD, Anna (18 Mar. 1865?–13 Aug. 1918), actress and singer, was born in Warsaw, Poland (although she often claimed to have been born in Paris, France), the daughter of Maurice Held and Yvonne Pierre. Her true birthdate is a matter of considerable conjecture. Most sources give 1873 or 1877 as the year, but more recent research has provided evidence that Held was actually born in 1865. Her father was a glovemaker, but after he became seriously ill the family moved from Warsaw to Paris and opened a restaurant. Held worked in the restaurant, as did her siblings, and she also worked in Parisian shops sewing buttonholes, making curled ostrich feathers, and constructing fur caps. She occasionally sang in her father's restaurant and was clearly drawn to the stage at an early age. She made her debut in a café concert in 1889, impressing her audience by singing in Spanish, French, German, and Polish. After her father's death, Held moved with her mother to London where she sought chorus work and made her legitimate theater debut at London's Princess Theatre in 1889. She also performed in London's Yiddish Theatre. She slowly moved up to featured roles both in England and on the Continent, where she performed in the elegant El Dorado and La Scala cabarets in Paris. While starring in other top-notch European cabarets in Germany, Amsterdam, Hungary, and Scandinavia, Held also performed in the palaces of royalty and the mansions of the rich. Her celebrity was such that at this time she was the model for two Toulouse-Lautrec lithographs. Also at about this time, Held secretly wed a fifty-year-old South American named Maximo Carrera in 1894. They were separated after a short time.

Although several distinguished American producers, including Oscar Hammerstein and the Kiralfy brothers, had attempted to engage Held for her American debut, she signed with the lesser-known Florenz Ziegfeld, Jr., who brought Held to America with great fanfare. The two were known as Mr. and Mrs. Ziegfeld, but it is unclear when (or if) they were actually married. Once in America, the flamboyant Ziegfeld cast Held in a leading role in his production of *A Parlor Match*, which opened in New York's Herald Square Theater on 21 September 1896. The combination of Held's coquettish talents and Ziegfeld's canny showmanship transformed her into one of the most popular Broadway celebrities of her day. Critics were particularly taken with Held's voluptuous figure and formidable charm. They regarded her delivery of the song "Won't You Come and Play wiz Me?" (which became her trademark) as a memorable moment in the history of musical theater. For eleven seasons, between 1897 and 1908, Held appeared in an array of successful Ziegfeld shows, which increasingly became celebrated for their lavish spectacle and taste. The best of these shows were *La Poupée* (1897), *Papa's Wife* (1899), *The Little Duchess* (1901), *Mam'selle Napoleon* (1903), *Higgledy Piggledy* (1904), *The Parisian Model* (1906), and *Miss Innocence* (1908). In these productions Held popularized many songs, most memorably "It's Delightful to Be Married" and "I Just Can't Make My Eyes Behave," both of which became permanently associated with her name. As a rule Held's songs emphasized her carefully projected Parisian panache and made much of her thick accent ("It's delightful to be married, to be, be, be, be, be, be, be married"), which was frequently mistaken for French. Despite the accent, critics were impressed by the quality of her precise diction. A small, slightly plump woman, Held was known more for her vivacity in light comedy than for any particular prowess as a vocalist. Ziegfeld's aggressive promotion of Held's sexy image led to a variety of outlandish marketing ploys, including Anna Held corsets, face powders, and even cigars.

It is thought that Held suggested to Ziegfeld the idea of producing an annual revue that ultimately became known as the *Follies*, beginning a long and legendary run in 1907. Certainly, her lighthearted vehicles, which were more like revues than musical comedies, served as a prototype for the *Follies*, which immediately found unprecedented success. Oddly, Held herself never appeared in any edition of the *Follies*, but Ziegfeld featured a chorus of beauties known for a time as the Anna Held Girls before his celebrated slogan "Glorifying the American Girl" was coined. As Ziegfeld's predominance as the producer of the Broadway stage grew to phenomenal heights, Held's popularity slowly declined. This was due in part to rapidly changing tastes in popular music and the fact that audiences were becoming increasingly resistant to European tastes. More to the point, Held was aging, and critics began to carp about the lack of variety in her shows, which seemed to slavishly repeat the successful formula of her early, and most popular, New York shows. Perhaps inevitably, Held sued for divorce from Ziegfeld in 1913, although it was revealed in court that they had never legally married. Ziegfeld was widely known as a ladies' man, but it may be that Ziegfeld's interest in Held waned as her stardom declined.

Following her break with Ziegfeld, which generated considerable publicity, Held appeared mostly in vaudeville where she was able to capitalize on her former association with Ziegfeld and the shows and songs of her past. She returned to the musical stage under the management of the Shubert brothers for *Follow Me* (1916), in which she sang yet another of a long series of "eye" songs, "I Want to Be Good But My Eyes Won't Let Me." She was well received in the production and her occasional vaudeville appearances but was never able to recapture the extraordinary fame she had achieved during her Ziegfeld years.

Held's health weakened after the Shubert production, and she died in New York City. She remains one of the legendary figures of the musical stage. Her image was unquestionably aided by *The Great Ziegfeld*, a 1936 Metro-Goldwyn-Mayer movie biography of Ziegfeld. Luise Rainer's Academy Award–winning performance as Held ably captured her stage charm and provided a sympathetic offstage portrayal. Rainer's depiction of a vivacious and flighty Held, who, according to the screenplay, lost Ziegfeld as a result of her unreasoning jealousy about the beautiful women surrounding her misunderstood husband, was clearly fictitious, but it is the image of Held that has prevailed. In a 1970s television biographical film on Ziegfeld, Held was again portrayed in this vein, this time by Barbara Parkins, and in 1988 an English stage musical called *Ziegfeld* featured French actress Fabienne Guyon as Held. Held was survived by a daughter, Liane Carrera, who later wrote about her mother's life with Ziegfeld.

• Held's version of her life is *Memoires* (1954). For information on Held, see Eddie Cantor and David Freedman, *Ziegfeld: The Great Glorifier* (1934); Liane Carrera, *Anna Held and Flo Ziegfeld*, trans. Guy Daniels (1979); Randolph Carter, *The World of Flo Ziegfeld* (1974); M. Farnsworth, *The Ziegfeld Follies* (1956); "A French Maid," *Dramatic Magazine* 6 (Mar. 1899): 233–40; and Martin Gottfried, *In Person: The Great Entertainers* (1985). Other sources include Felix Isman, *Weber and Fields* (1924); Ethan Mordden, *Broadway Babies* (1983); Cecil Smith and Glenn Litton, *Musical Comedy in America* (1981); and Bernard Sobel, *Broadway Heartbeat* (1953).

JAMES FISHER

HELD, John, Jr. (10 Jan. 1889–2 Mar. 1958), cartoonist and illustrator, was born in Salt Lake City, Utah, the son of John Held, Sr., an artist, engraver, and amateur bandmaster, and Annie Evans. Held began sketching and painting at a very early age, and at the age of nine, he was paid for a block print he produced, his first earnings as an artist. In high school he worked on the school paper with Harold Ross (destined to found the *New Yorker* in 1925), and by the time he was fourteen, he was cartooning for the *Salt Lake City Tribune*, where Ross was working as a reporter. The two frequently spent their off hours together roaming the seedier sections of town. Held's biographer, Shelley Armitage, speculated that the cartoonist's comic sensibility was fostered by his perceiving the contrast between the noble vision of his Mormon faith and the seamy life of the red-light district.

In 1908 Held married the *Tribune*'s society editor, Myrtle Jennings (they would have no children), and sold his first cartoon to the humor magazine *Life*. Two years later he went to New York City to become a serious artist, intending to send for his wife once he became established. He studied and lived with the sculptor Mahonri M. Young (one of Brigham Young's

160-odd grandsons) for a short while until he needed money, whereupon he found work doing posters for the Collier's Street Railway Advertising Company. Soon he left to become a display designer for the United Lithographic Corporation, where he stayed for more than a year. When Myrtle joined him, she took his cartoons and sketches around to magazines, selling some to *Vanity Fair*. In 1913 Held joined the advertising department at the New York City office of John Wanamaker Company, continuing at the same time to freelance illustrations and cartoons to various magazines. In 1917 he was hired as an artist on a Carnegie Institute archeological expedition to Central America and spent a year documenting the explorations by making maps and paintings and sketches of the sites visited. When he returned to New York in June 1918, he resumed his freelance career, and before the end of the year he was selling cartoons and covers regularly to *Judge*, *Life*, *Puck*, and *Vanity Fair*.

Before his trip to Central America, Held's style of drawing had been rather conventional for the time, distinguished by a spindly line, elongated and somewhat stiffly stylized figures, and lavish use of solid black and geometric patterns. After the trip, Held began drawing plumper figures with disproportionally large round heads, a maneuver that made the people in his drawings seem youthful, almost childlike. Afterward, Held specialized in cartoons about young people, a choice of subjects that placed him in the public eye at precisely the right moment: a youth culture was emerging in America in the postwar years, and Held was soon seen as its spokesman, capturing its insouciance with the simple elegance of his line. His style continued to evolve, however, and his characters became more realistically proportioned until about 1923, when the style for which he is most remembered reached its maturity. Skinny approximations of their sex, Held's belles were emblematic of a sort of perpetual adolescence. As skirts became shorter, he exaggerated the effect by making his girls' legs longer and slenderer, giving them the gangling coltish appearance of youth. Humorist Corey Ford maintained that Held actually invented the flapper by supplying the young people with a prototype: "Each new Held drawing was pored over like a Paris fashion plate, girls cropped their hair and rouged their cheeks and shortened their skirts to be in style, galoshes and raccoon coats were indispensable to every male undergraduate wardrobe. So sedulously did we ape his caricatures that they lost their satiric point and came to be a documentary record of our times" (*The Most of John Held, Jr.*, p. 19).

Without question, Held defined the spirit of the 1920s, capturing in his graphic abstractions the fashions and fads of the collegiate jazz age. His leggy flappers with noses in the air and hose rolled at the knee and his bell-bottomed sheiks with their hair plastered tight to cue-ball heads personified the younger generation to a nation of readers. Sophisticated and vaguely dissolute, his skimpily skirted cuties were insatiable neckers, and their tuxedo-clad escorts inveterate social bootleggers, a flask on every hip. The drawings were rendered with matching élan—delicate, thin lines in bold contrast against arresting solid blacks. Susan E. Meyer notes that Held's work was unique: "His work was idiosyncratic, bearing no stylistic resemblance to that of any other artist before him" (p. 283).

Held's cartoons, advertisements, and covers appeared regularly throughout the Roaring Twenties in all the most popular magazines. In 1924 Held started a weekly half-page comic strip called *Oh! Margy!* for United Feature Syndicate; lured away to King Features in 1927, Held continued the strip under an assortment of titles (*Merely Margy* and *Rah Rah Rosalie* among them) until the mid-thirties. In 1925, for Ross's infant *New Yorker*, he began producing a series of woodcutlike drawings of the "gay nineties." Fashioned from his fond recollections of life in Salt Lake City's demimonde, these cartoons reflected obliquely upon the manners and mores of Flaming Youth in the 1920s.

Held was well known and wealthy by 1921. At one time during the decade, he owned a small working farm near Westport, a penthouse apartment in Manhattan, a beach house in Florida, and a second country estate (this one 163 acres) in Connecticut where he played at being a gentleman farmer, maintaining a kennel of blooded dogs, a stable of blue-ribbon saddle horses, and a staff of dozens of servants. His domestic life, however, was not successful: he had divorced his first wife in 1919 and married Ada "Johnnie" Johnson, a woman animated very much by the spirit of the jazz age, whose frequent demand for lavish and populous house parties kept her husband at the drawing board for long hours every day, earning the wherewithal to support her social life. The couple adopted three children. At the peak of his fame from 1923 until the end of the decade, Held could earn thousands of dollars with a single drawing; editors begged for his work. And then came the stock market crash of 1929 and the aftermath in which Held lost a fortune. The accumulated pressure took its toll: by March 1931 Held was in a Stamford sanitarium suffering from nervous exhaustion. In the fall he and his second wife were divorced, and in November he married Gladys Moore. She preferred the social whirl of the smart set in the city while Held yearned for the country life; they separated in 1936, having produced a daughter.

In the 1930s Held's spherical-headed sheiks and shebas lost their appeal, and Held began writing short stories and novels (some of which he also illustrated) about those bygone days of the jazz age. Often bleak in the naturalistic manner, Held's narratives aimed at exposing the shallowness of the Flaming Youth of yesteryear, but they never achieved the popularity of his cartoons and drawings. During this decade, Held illustrated several books, produced and hosted a collegiate talent radio program ("Tops Variety Show"), designed sets for the successful Broadway comedy *Hellzapoppin*, and became (at last) a serious artist in watercolor and bronze. In 1940 he was artist in residence at Harvard University and then at the University of Georgia.

In December 1942 Held married Margaret Schuyler Janes, and during World War II they both worked for the Signal Corps, making pictures of radar apparatus then being designed. In 1943 they purchased the Conover Farm near Belmar, New Jersey, where Held became, again, a farmer. He also occasionally drew magazine illustrations, and he produced several children's stories. Before he died on the farm of throat cancer, he had been "rediscovered" and enjoyed considerable reputation.

A satirist whose comedy depended upon irony, Held's career is itself riven with ironies. Aspiring to be a serious artist and sculptor, he achieved fame and fortune beyond his most extravagant expectations with simple cartoon drawings, undertaken initially to earn enough money to support his other artistic ambitions. His success was so great that he was virtually a prisoner of it; only economic and personal disaster freed him to resume artistic pursuits. The supreme irony, however, was that his cartoons of the twenties, caricatures that he intended as satirical comment on the faddish foibles of youth, became instead their fashion bible and brought him wealth and celebrity; but his fiction of the thirties, satirizing the very era his cartoons had helped to create, was scorned. His place in the pantheon of American cartoonists is nevertheless secure: his cartoons virtually define that period now known as the Roaring Twenties.

• Held's papers are at the Archives of American Art in Washington, D.C. Held's novels are *Women Are Necessary* (1931), *Crosstown* (1933), *I'm the Happiest Girl in the World* (1935), and *The Gods Were Promiscuous* (1937); his short story collections are *John Held, Jr.'s Dog Stories* (1930), *Grim Youth* (1930), *The Flesh Is Weak* (1931), and *A Bowl of Cherries* (1932). His illustrated books include *Frankie and Johnny* (1930), *Outlines of Sport* (1930), *The Wages of Sin and Other Victorian Joys and Sorrows* (1931), and *The Works of John Held, Jr.* (1931). He also illustrated several books for Frank Shay (such as *My Pious Friends and Drunken Companions*, 1927) and for Walter Pritchard Eaton (*Nantucket* and *Rhode Island Shores*, both 1925, and *Cape Cod*, 1927); perhaps the most representative of his 1920s style is his work in Frank B. Gilbreth's *Held's Angels* (1952), which reprints as illustrations many of Held's drawings and cartoons from the Jazz Age. Many of the details of his life are in *The Most of John Held, Jr.*, introduced by Carl J. Weinhardt (1972); and in Susan E. Meyer, *America's Great Illustrators* (1978). However, the most thoroughgoing biography is Shelley Armitage, *John Held, Jr.: Illustrator of the Jazz Age* (1987), which includes an extensive bibliography.

ROBERT C. HARVEY

HELLER, Maximilian (31 Jan. 1860–30 Mar. 1929), Reform rabbi, was born in Prague, Bohemia, the son of Simon Heller, a men's fabric merchant and Talmudist, and Mathilde Kassowitz. The family's bourgeois circumstances and Simon Heller's love of Jewish learning enabled Max Heller to obtain both a liberal European education as well as traditional training in Hebrew sources. The Kassowitz family had established Simon Heller in business, but severe financial reverses in the late 1870s motivated the family's immigration to Chicago, leaving Max Heller to remain in Prague at the Neustadter Gymnasium, where he completed preparatory studies for a proposed medical career. The family's financial situation, however, did not improve sufficiently to allow Heller to continue with his European education. After his graduation from Gymnasium in 1879, he followed his family to Chicago. Within months he had moved to Cincinnati, where he enrolled in the recently established Hebrew Union College, the first permanent rabbinical seminary in the United States. There he came under the direct tutelage of Isaac Mayer Wise, self-appointed leader of American Reform Judaism and the institution's founder. Although he probably knew no English before his arrival in the United States, Heller simultaneously pursued a secular course of study at the University of Cincinnati. He graduated Phi Beta Kappa with a B.L. degree in 1882 and received his M.L. degree in philosophy as well as rabbinical ordination two years later.

Heller began his career by serving as associate rabbi under Bernhard Felsenthal at Chicago's Zion Congregation. Although Heller remained in Chicago for only two years, Felsenthal's zealous embrace of Reform and his sympathy for Eastern European Jews made a significant impact on his younger colleague. Both men, however, had strong personalities, which inevitably clashed, and by August 1885 Houston's Congregation Beth Israel had offered Heller a pulpit of his own. He remained in Houston just over a year and a half; the following year James Gutheim, the South's leading rabbi, died, leaving vacant the pulpit of New Orleans's Temple Sinai, the major pulpit in that region's largest city. In February 1887 Temple Sinai elected Heller its rabbi, and he remained in that position until 1927, when he retired. Marrying Ida Annie Marks, a native New Orleanian, in March 1889 further solidified ties to his adopted home. The Hellers raised four children, two sons and two daughters; their older son, James Gutheim Heller, also became a leading Reform rabbi.

Heller's influence ranged far beyond the congregation he served. In the early 1890s he aligned himself with the elite ministerial and lay leadership of the city in the successful fight to defeat the infamous Louisiana Lottery, and from there he moved onto the State Board of Education. While thus identifying himself as a civic activist, he also spearheaded efforts to make German Jewish secular institutions, such as the city's Touro Infirmary/Hebrew Benevolent Association, more compassionate in their treatment of recently arriving Russian Jews. His courage in championing these immigrants led him to take other, less popular stands on behalf of the beleaguered in the United States and abroad.

At the turn of the century he joined Felsenthal and the tiny minority of American Reform leaders who espoused Zionist beliefs. At about the same time, in a period when white voices were notoriously silent, Heller began to condemn, carefully yet openly, the region's injustices against its African-American citizens. Both positions garnered much criticism, but censure only tended to reinforce Heller's resolve and did not diminish his influence as a more typical southern progressive on such issues as public health or prostitution. Although Reform Judaism officially opposed political Zionism, Heller remained loyal to Reform institutions. From 1909 to 1911 he served as president of the movement's Central Conference of American Rabbis while also serving as vice president of the Federation of American Zionists—quite a feat considering the chasm between the two groups. Similarly, his Jewish nationalism did not inhibit his devotion to internationalism, and he fully supported Woodrow Wilson's efforts to fashion the League of Nations in which the United States would play a major role.

Heller publicized his opinions through extensive journalistic writings, including editorship of the New Orleans *Jewish Ledger* from 1896 to 1897. Throughout his career he contributed sermons and articles to the New Orleans dailies and frequently wrote letters to the editor on many issues. From 1902 to 1914 he was the leading editorial writer for the *American Israelite*, the Reform Jewish organ published in Cincinnati. Other forums for his articles included the *American Hebrew*, the *Maccabbean*, and the *Menorah Journal*. After World War I Heller became a special correspondent for *B'nai B'rith News*. Following his retirement from the pulpit, Heller achieved his lifelong dream and visited Palestine, sending weekly observations back to the New Orleans *States Item*, which featured them prominently each Sunday. After his death in New Orleans, the Heller family published these articles as *My Month in Palestine: Impressions of Travel* (1929). Heller also was the first chronicler of New Orleans Jewish history as compiler of a series of sketches, *Jubilee Souvenir of Temple Sinai, 1872–1922* (1922), which covered and well documented far more than the congregation's history and thus has served as a source for all succeeding students of the region's Jewish experience. His Hebrew scholarship also achieved for Heller the position of professor of Hebrew language and literature at Tulane University, which he held from 1912 until the year before his death.

Heller's significance lies in his divergence from the stereotypical image of the American Reform rabbi or southern Jew of his time. That he was able to champion unpopular causes yet remain in a southern pulpit and earn a well-respected reputation as a national Jewish leader is a testament not only to his political skills and personal charm but to the degree of tolerance he was able to wrest from an often ungenerous environment. Esteemed even by those who fought against him, Heller left a legacy of "standing unswayed" on issues of social justice that challenged American Jews as well as citizens of the American South.

• The American Jewish Archives of Hebrew Union College–Jewish Institute of Religion in Cincinnati houses Max Heller's extensive and well-indexed papers and correspondence. Gary B. Zola, "Reform Judaism's Pioneer Zionist: Maximilian Heller," *American Jewish History* 4 (June 1984): 375–97, examines Heller's dual leadership in the American Reform

movement and in American Zionist circles. Barbara S. Malone, "Reform and Dissent: The Americanization of Max Heller, 1860–1898" (M.A. thesis, Tulane Univ., 1989), documents Heller's European background, American rabbinical training, and early career. Malone, " 'Standing Unswayed in the Storm'; Rabbi Max Heller, Zionist and Southerner, 1887–1929" (Ph.D. diss., Tulane Univ., 1994), is a full biographical account of his life. Other works that include information about Heller or clarify the evolution of Reform Judaism during the late nineteenth and early twentieth centuries are Michael A. Meyer, *Response to Modernity* (1988); and David Polish, "The Changing and the Constant in the Reform Rabbinate," in *The American Rabbinate: A Century of Continuity and Change: 1883–1983*, ed. Jacob R. Marcus and Abraham J. Peck (1985), and Polish, *Renew Our Days: The Zionist Issue in Reform Judaism, 1885–1948* (1976). An obituary is in the New Orleans *Times-Picayune*, 31 Mar. 1929. The most helpful eulogies are by Ephraim Lisitzky in the *Jewish Ledger*, 12 Apr. 1929, and by Joseph Stolz in the *Reform Advocate*, 18 May 1929.

BOBBIE MALONE

HELLER, Walter Wolfgang (27 Aug. 1915–15 June 1987), chairman of the Council of Economic Advisers, was born in Buffalo, New York, the son of Ernst Heller, a civil engineer, and Gertrude Warmburg. Both parents were German immigrants. In 1935 Heller received an A.B. from Oberlin College, where he earned election to Phi Beta Kappa. He did his graduate work in economics at the University of Wisconsin and received his M.A. in 1938 and a Ph.D. in 1941, specializing in finance and taxation. At the time, Heller received a Social Science Research Council grant to study income tax laws in thirty-one states, the District of Columbia, and Canada. Heller married Emily Karen Johnson, also a graduate student at the University of Wisconsin, in 1938. They had three children.

Barred from military service because of poor eyesight, Heller served in the tax research division of the U.S. Treasury Department during World War II, helping implement a new tax withholding system tailored along the lines of the Canadian model he had studied as a graduate student. He left the Treasury Department in 1946 to teach economics at the University of Minnesota's School of Business Administration, becoming a full professor in 1950. He continued to serve in a number of public advisory positions throughout the 1950s, including service to the U.S. Treasury Department, work as an economic adviser to Minnesota's Democratic governor Orville Freeman, and consulting for the Minnesota Department of Taxation. In 1957 he became chairman of the Department of Economics in the University of Minnesota's School of Business Administration.

During John F. Kennedy's campaign for the presidency in 1960, the candidate pledged to "get the country moving again," specifically calling for higher rates of economic growth than the 2–3 percent under President Dwight D. Eisenhower. After the election, on the recommendations of Governor Freeman and economist Paul Samuelson, President-elect Kennedy appointed Heller chairman of his Council of Economic

Advisers (CEA). As chairman of the CEA, Heller became the chief architect of Kennedy's antirecession strategy and was responsible for pushing many of the administration's initial economic measures through Congress.

Heller argued that current economic problems stemmed not so much from technological displacement as from insufficient demand. High taxes were stalling the recovery by slowing down purchasing power and draining investment capital. He also believed that the recession of 1960–1961 and its accompanying 7 percent unemployment level stemmed from an incomplete recovery from the deeper recession of 1957–1958. He recommended that the application of a classical Keynesian stimulus, such as a tax cut, would produce higher levels of economic growth and reduce unemployment. Much of his faith in Keynesian central planning was based on his stint as a young administrator at the Treasury Department during the Second World War.

Heller's most significant contribution to the Kennedy administration's economic policy was in the area of tax reduction. Tax cuts, he argued, would stimulate economic growth, and the deficit created by such cuts would be offset by the increase in taxable income. Heller, Samuelson, and John Kenneth Galbraith made up a Keynesian group in the administration known as the "new economists." They favored the direct use of government fiscal and monetary policy to maintain full employment and increase the rate of economic growth. However, the Keynesians themselves were divided, as Heller disagreed with Galbraith over the question of spending. Galbraith advocated an increase in government spending to improve public services, while Heller wanted to increase aggregate demand with a substantial tax reduction. Such a program of tax cuts, Heller argued, would have the effect of putting investment and spending decisions in the hands of individuals and businesses.

President Kennedy did not immediately sign on to Heller's recommendations on taxation. During the August 1961 Berlin crisis, for example, Kennedy supported a $3 billion tax increase to finance military mobilization. By mid-1962 the president was persuaded that the tax cuts outlined by Heller were necessary to stimulate faster growth. In his January 1963 State of the Union Address, Kennedy called for extensive tax cuts totaling $13.6 billion and the closing of various tax loopholes. The so-called Kennedy tax cut, ultimately totaling $11.5 billion, passed the House in September 1963 but had not reached the Senate floor when Kennedy was assassinated in Dallas in November. The subsequent Revenue Act of 1964 included most of the tax cuts Heller had recommended and was signed into law on 26 February 1964 by President Lyndon Johnson. The act reduced personal income tax rates from a range of 20–90 percent to 14–70 percent, while the corporate tax rate was reduced from 52 percent to 48 percent. By mid-1964, fearing that inflation would rise with the surge in government spending, Heller reversed position and advised President Johnson to raise taxes. Johnson refused.

Heller was also an influential member of a select group of advisers assigned to draft Kennedy's legislative program for 1962, and he played a key role in designing the Trade Expansion Act, giving the president authority to reduce trade barriers. Heller and the Council of Economic Advisers led the administration's effort in April 1962 to force U.S. Steel to rescind its price increases. Working with Labor Department economists, Heller and the CEA prepared the administration's response to the rate increase by arguing that it would fuel inflation and undermine American competitiveness. While the steel industry avoided raising prices in 1962, the largest steel companies did so in 1963. Heller counseled President Kennedy to temper his response to the 1963 price hike because, he argued, the increases were selective and not across the board.

Heller left the Council of Economic Advisers in November 1964 and returned to the University of Minnesota to teach economics. Throughout the mid-1960s he continued to be a leading advocate of a plan to share federal revenues with the states. President Johnson supported this plan, which Heller called "revenue sharing," but was unable to secure congressional approval. Johnson's successor, President Richard M. Nixon, succeeded and in October 1972 signed the measure into law, providing more than $30 million to the states over five years. Heller also served as a member of the Trilateral Commission from 1978 to 1984. He died in Seattle, Washington.

Heller is remembered as one of the fathers of modern economic policy making. His advocacy of tax cuts while heading the CEA and his later promotion of revenue sharing had significant impacts on the economic life of the nation. Many of his books on economics and public policy continue to be widely read and discussed in academic circles.

• Heller's papers repose in the John F. Kennedy Presidential Library. During his long career in academia and government, Heller published numerous books. Heller's *State Income Tax Administration* (1959) highlights his early views on taxes and spending that helped bring him to the attention of Kennedy and his inner circle. His *New Dimensions of Political Economy* (1966) is an important discussion of the Keynesian approach to the economic circumstances of the 1960s. Heller wrote *Revenue Sharing and the City* (1968), which helped promote that scheme during both the Johnson and Nixon administrations, and he was the author of *Monetary vs. Fiscal Policy* (1968), *Economic Growth and Environmental Quality* (1973), *The Economy: Old Myths and New Realities* (1976), *Economic Policy for Inflation* (1981), and *Activist Government* (1986). For an incisive account of the Kennedy economic policies with a discussion of Heller's role, see Hobart Rowen, *The Free Enterprisers: Kennedy, Johnson and the Business Community* (1964). Rowen argues that Kennedy's economic policies were essentially conservative and probusiness. Seymour Harris, *Economics of the Kennedy Years* (1964), offers an analysis by a member of the Kennedy economic team, as does James Tobin, *National Economic Policy* (1966). See also Edward S. Flash, *Economic Advice and Presidential Leadership* (1965); E.

Ray Canterbery, *Economics on a New Frontier* (1968); and Jim F. Heath, *John F. Kennedy and the Business Community* (1969). An obituary is in the *New York Times*, 17 June 1987.

CHRISTOPHER D. O'SULLIVAN

HELLMAN, Lillian (20 June 1905–30 June 1984), playwright, was born Lillian Florence Hellman in New Orleans, Louisiana, the daughter of Max Hellman, a shoe salesman, and Julia Newhouse. When Max Hellman's shoe business failed, the family moved to New York City, where five-year-old Lillian attended school. Her studies, however, were constantly interrupted by trips to New Orleans (for six-month intervals), as her father, a traveling salesman, attended to business. Hellman describes the disconcerting impact of her bifurcated childhood in her memoir *An Unfinished Woman*; she suggests that her temperamental, impatient character was formed by her different experiences in the North and the South and exacerbated by the fact that her mother's family was wealthy. This group of shrewd bankers and businessmen—described in *An Unfinished Woman* and *Pentimento*—appealed to Hellman because of their power over other people, but the ruthless Newhouses also disgusted her and later became the subjects of two of her most successful plays, *The Little Foxes* and *Another Part of the Forest*, which portrayed the rapacious careers of the fictional Hubbards in the post–Civil War South.

In 1922 and 1923 Hellman attended classes at the Washington Square branch of New York University and summer sessions at Columbia University. A desultory student, she considered a writing career, proposing to write biographies of Dante and Lewis Carroll, but she left college in her junior year for a job with the New York City publisher Liveright in the autumn of 1924. Although this should have been an exciting opportunity—Liveright was then publishing some of America's most distinguished authors—Hellman quickly became bored with her low-level assignments and proved to be an unreliable worker. At Liveright, she met Arthur Kober, a struggling writer, and became pregnant by him. Not wanting the pregnancy, she submitted to an abortion. She and Kober married six months later in December 1925.

The next five years were a restless period for Hellman. While her husband established himself as a short-story writer and playwright, she tried to write fiction, producing short stories of uneven quality and abandoning her attempt at a novel. The couple lived in Paris for four months in 1926. After they returned to the United States, Hellman took on various jobs, including stints as a publicist and reader of plays for a theatrical agent and as a book reviewer for the *New York Herald Tribune*. On her own in the summer of 1929, she traveled to Germany, studying at the university in Bonn. While there, she experienced the kind of anti-Semitism that she would later dramatize in *Watch on the Rhine* and *The Searching Wind*.

By the fall of 1930, when Hellman joined Kober in Hollywood, where he was employed writing movie scripts, their marriage seemed tenuous. Hellman had been involved in at least one love affair in New York City, and she was upset by her uncertain status in Hollywood—the wife of a screenwriter who got her a job at MGM reading and summarizing books for scenarios. Kober was patient with his wife but did not know how to help her achieve her goals.

Casting about for some outlet, Hellman saw her opportunity in a liaison with the handsome and successful detective story writer Dashiell Hammett. Well known as a prodigious drinker and womanizer, Hammett seemed intrigued by the aggressive Hellman, a stylish, articulate woman who wanted to write. Noting her dramatic flair, he suggested she write a play based on the case of two teachers in nineteenth-century Edinburgh who had been accused of lesbianism.

The story appealed to Hellman's melodramatic imagination. Through several drafts of *The Children's Hour* (1934), she fashioned an account of two teachers, Karen and Martha, who successfully set up their own school only to be ruined by a malevolent child, Mary, who, refusing to be disciplined, strikes back by telling her grandmother, a powerful member of the community, that her teachers have an "unnatural" love for each other. An enormous success (the play ran for over seven hundred performances on Broadway), *The Children's Hour* established Hellman as a promising playwright with a keen eye for both individual and social psychology. She balances the blindness of the teachers to their own feelings and the equally blind hysteria of society, which tends to take the word of authority figures and to be swayed by the emotional impact of an accusation, which, in this case, cannot be overcome even by the rational objections of Dr. Joseph Cardin, who tries to expose Mary's manipulative attack on Karen and Martha.

The Children's Hour also dramatizes a love triangle: both Martha and Joseph Cardin are in love with Karen, and Cardin—despite his defense of the women—cannot entirely allay his suspicion that perhaps Karen is in love with Martha. Variations on this triangle would appear in much of Hellman's theatrical writing, in her film scripts, in her memoirs, and in her private life, for she would continue to involve herself in triangles: she did not divorce Kober until 1932, and she later had an affair with publisher Ralph Ingersoll while maintaining her relationship with Hammett.

Hellman's success as a playwright brought her an offer from Samuel Goldwyn to write screenplays. Throughout the 1930s Hellman worked for Goldwyn, producing superior scripts for her version of *The Children's Hour*, retitled *These Three* (1936), and *Dead End* (1937) as well as collaborating on other projects. She had unusual creative control over her own scripts and a reputation in Hollywood for independence. Instrumental in forming the Screen Writers' Guild, she became involved in leftist politics and was briefly a Communist party member (1938–1940).

After the disastrous failure of her second play, *Days to Come* (1936)—in which she lost control of her story of a strike in a midwestern factory town, meandering between psychological and political implications—

Hellman regained her form in *The Little Foxes* (1939), a classic of American theater, set in the South just after the Civil War. Her main character, Regina, holds her own with her brothers, Ben and Oscar, in capitalizing on the family business. Although the play can be analyzed as a critique of capitalism, it is equally the story of a family in which each member struggles for dominance. One of the most striking features of this play is its lack of sentimentality, a hardheadedness Hellman herself exemplified.

Until his death in 1961, Hammett was at Hellman's side, proferring advice on her scripts, though not always living with her—as Hellman admits in terming theirs an on-again, off-again relationship. Hammett's philandering, his terrible drinking, and his service in World War II meant separations and estrangements. Hellman never dropped Hammett, but she felt free to engage in love affairs and to maintain her own residences.

A staunch supporter of the Soviet Union, which seemed to offer the hope that socialism might eventually lead to a truly egalitarian society free of ethnic strife and economic imbalances, Hellman would later defend herself in *Scoundrel Time* against charges of Stalinism. Although she initially defended Stalin's 1939 pact with Hitler, by the writing of *Watch on the Rhine* (1941), she had seen the need for the United States to enter World War II before Hitler abrogated the pact by invading the Soviet Union. Like *The Searching Wind* (1944), *Watch on the Rhine* focuses on the innocence of Americans and their blindness to the advance of fascism during the 1930s. In Kurt Muller, a German antifascist fighter seeking refuge in America, Hellman creates a vulnerable hero. A fragile man with broken hands, he is constrained to strangle a foreign national who threatens to reveal Kurt's presence and to expose the network of antifascist groups. That Fanny Farrelly, the mother of Kurt's American wife, Sarah, must condone this killing in her own household and allow Kurt to escape reinforces Hellman's message that Americans must take some responsibility for combating the world's evils, even at the price of losing their innocence.

Although Hellman managed to complete *Another Part of the Forest* (1947), a second successful play about the Hubbards, she began to sense that her resources as a playwright were diminishing. Her final plays, *The Autumn Garden* (1951), *Toys in the Attic* (1960), and her adaptation of a Burt Blechman novel, *My Mother, My Father, and Me* (1963), show that she was moving toward the more flexible and more open memoir genre and away from tightly wound melodramas. *The Lark* (1955), a crisp adaptation of Anouilh's play *L'Alouette*, was a great success, but the comic operetta *Candide* (1957), written with Leonard Bernstein, Richard Wilbur, and others, was not, and Hellman found herself tiring of the collaborative efforts required of a playwright.

Hellman had also begun teaching at several universities, the most notable being Harvard, Yale, Hunter College, and the City University of New York, some-times conducting classes on playwrighting but just as often teaching fiction and poetry. Called on to explain her career in numerous interviews, energized by the contentious campus life of the 1960s, and disgusted by the terrible failure of *My Mother, My Father, and Me*, Hellman found it necessary to present some record of herself, explaining not only the origins of her character, but also revealing to a later generation what it was like growing up in the 1920s, making her way among the writers and the politics of the 1930s and 1940s, and coping with her blacklisting in the 1950s for her leftist sympathies.

Hellman's first two volumes of memoirs, *An Unfinished Woman* (1969) and *Pentimento* (1973), were enormous successes, garnering her the best reviews of her life. She became a cult figure, lionized by young people, especially women, who saw in her a role model who had held her own in a man's world while remaining feminine. There was criticism of her long-term relationship with Hammett—some women viewed Hellman as the subordinate partner—but on the whole she was praised for confronting the temper of her times with courage and candor. The style of the memoirs, particularly *Pentimento*, was much admired, for chapters read like short stories, especially her account of her childhood friend Julia, who had become part of the antifascist underground in Europe and whom Hellman claimed to have aided at considerable risk to herself by smuggling money into Nazi Germany for use by the resistance.

When Hellman's third memoir, *Scoundrel Time* (1976), appeared, it was initially greeted with rave reviews, but the response grew hostile as her enemies of the 1930s and 1940s disputed her accounts. In the *Paris Review* (1981), Martha Gellhorn, Ernest Hemingway's third wife, ridiculed the contradictions and inaccuracies of *An Unfinished Woman* and made a compelling case for Hellman's having lied about many incidents to aggrandize her own life. Other attacks followed, pointing up the self-serving quality of *Scoundrel Time* and its deficiencies as history. The culmination of this criticism came in Mary McCarthy's allegation on national television that every word Hellman wrote was a lie.

Hellman received little sympathy when she decided to sue McCarthy. Since she had built her reputation on candor, the likelihood that the stories in *Pentimento*, especially "Julia," were fiction came as devastating news to Hellman's readers, and she did not deign to reply to the charges. When she died on Martha's Vineyard, the suit against McCarthy was still pending, but Hellman's reputation had been significantly damaged.

The events of Hellman's last years did not overshadow her importance as an American playwright—one of the best this country has produced. Several of her plays—*The Children's Hour, The Little Foxes, Another Part of the Forest, The Autumn Garden, Toys in the Attic*—are regularly revived and comprise a significant addition to the American repertory. Although the quality of the writing in her memoirs is high, their place in American letters may yet be determined by how Hellman's political views are interpreted over time.

• The most important collection of Hellman's papers is housed in the Harry Ransom Humanities Research Center, University of Texas, Austin. Other significant collections of her correspondence and manuscripts can be found in Special Collections, New York Public Library; the Billy Rose Theatre Collection, Lincoln Center Library for the Performing Arts, New York Public Library; Special Collections, Mugar Memorial Library, Boston University; the Wisconsin Center for Film and Theater Research, University of Wisconsin, Madison; the Library of Congress; the University of Southern California Library, Los Angeles; and the Academy of Motion Picture Arts and Sciences, Beverly Hills. Two full-length biographies of Hellman are William Wright, *Lillian Hellman: The Image, the Woman* (1986), and Carl Rollyson, *Lillian Hellman: Her Legend and Her Legacy* (1988). Both biographies are based on important interviews; Rollyson works from a much broader grasp of the archival sources. Robert P. Newman, *The Cold War Romance of Lillian Hellman and John Melby* (1989), is an important contribution to an understanding of her politics and her personal life, concentrating on her love affair with Melby, an American foreign service officer, as a result of which he was dismissed from his position in the 1950s. Peter Feibleman, *Lilly* (1988), is an effective memoir of his close association with Hellman.

CARL ROLLYSON

HELLRIEGEL, Martin Balthasar (9 Nov. 1890–10 Apr. 1981), clergyman, was born in Heppenheim, Germany, the son of Martin Hellriegel II, a furniture maker, and Eva Kohler. Hellriegel grew up in Heppenheim, a town in the southern part of the province of Hesse near the Rhine River, in a traditionally Catholic part of the German Empire. The Emperor Charlemagne had once worshipped at the local church of St. Peter's where Hellriegel would be baptized a thousand years later. After finishing high school and college in his home town, Hellriegel came to the United States early in 1906 and prepared for the Catholic priesthood at St. Meinrad's Abbey-Seminary in southern Indiana. He was ordained for the archdiocese of St. Louis in 1914. Later on, he took advanced studies in liturgical theology in Rome and his native Rhineland.

During his twenty-two years (1918–1940) as chaplain of the Sisters of the Precious Blood at their central headquarters in O'Fallon, Missouri, Hellriegel put the nuns in touch with the latest liturgical thought of Western Europe, celebrated feasts with solemnity, and urged the nuns to promote the liturgy in the many parishes where they taught. He read widely on liturgical topics in German, French, and Flemish. As early as 1926 he concluded that the vernacular had to be introduced into the Mass, and he drew up musical settings for liturgy in English. He also composed a hymn, "To Jesus Christ, Our Sovereign King," for a new church feast. When Dom Virgil Michel began the liturgical publication *Orate Fratres* (Pray Brothers) at St. John's Benedictine Abbey in Collegeville, Minnesota, in 1926, he invited Hellriegel to be a contributing editor. Over the years Hellriegel, a pioneer among American Catholic diocesan clergy in promoting the liturgical movement, published 100 articles and a column titled "Merely Suggesting." He also was one of the founders of the National Liturgical Conference in 1940.

That same year Hellriegel became pastor of Holy Cross Parish at the north end of St. Louis. He set out to make this predominantly German-American congregation a model of advanced liturgical practice. In 1944 he published *The Holy Sacrifice of the Mass*, a small book that called for congregational participation in church worship, vernacular in the liturgy, the deployment of the altar so that the priest would face the people, and the transference of the Easter Vigil from Holy Saturday morning to night.

At that time the liturgical movement in the United States was almost entirely a midwestern, German-American development. Few Irish-American pastors and even fewer bishops paid much attention to the movement. But Archbishop John J. Glennon of St. Louis, recognizing that Hellriegel centered his attention on the worship of God, not on ritual procedures, encouraged Hellriegel in his work. Like all prophets, Hellriegel saw beyond his time. He tried to make his fellow Catholics appreciate the church's liturgical treasures that he believed were hidden beneath a dead language and bounded by excessive restrictions. In response he met suspicion, ridicule, and condemnation. Fortunately he had the support of outstanding leaders in the St. Louis cultural community, among them, Emil Frei and Emil Frei, Jr., in art glass and mosaic art, Frederick Kenkel in progressive publishing, and Monsignors Frederick Howleck and John Rothensteiner in church history. The interests and achievements of these men complemented Hellriegel's work.

Although there is no evidence that Hellriegel aspired to a position in church administration, as historian John Jay Hughes wrote, "The opposition which Hellriegel's liturgical apostolate encountered disqualified him for the position for which (as we can now see by hindsight) he was uniquely qualified at the age of 56: Archbishop of St. Louis (upon the death of Cardinal Glennon in 1946)" (*The Priest*, Sept. 1981, p. 14). Such a choice would have been more likely in a Northern European diocese where administrative problems were less central and where many bishops were scholarly religious leaders. Glennon's successor, Archbishop Joseph E. Ritter of Indianapolis, who had attended St. Meinrad's Seminary at the same time as Hellriegel, faced many immediate administrative problems, such as parish and school integration; the liturgy was not then high on his list of concerns.

Gradually the liturgical movement spread beyond the Midwest through the writings and lecturing of Hellriegel, Virgil Michel, and the Jesuit Gerald Ellard. The magazine *Orate Fratres* took the name *Worship* in 1951. The Liturgical Conference grew to more than a thousand members. The United States was catching up with Europe. When the Second Vatican Council convened in 1962, the Constitution on the Sacred Liturgy was the first document completed. The statement approved many changes Hellriegel had sought: the vernacular in church worship, a wider choice of scriptural readings, a variety of prayers, and participation by the congregation. Hellriegel's hymn, "To Jesus Christ, Our Sovereign King," became a part of the liturgical prayer on appropriate feasts.

Hellriegel's joy was temporarily clouded by a wave of "desacralization" that occurred in many places: a casual approach to the service at the altar, a denigration of the Blessed Eucharist, the singing of songs that called inappropriate attention to themselves, and a preference by some to worship any place except in a church. Although he deplored these excesses, Hellriegel remained serene, convinced that this period would pass without the total destruction of his life work. It was on its way out by the time he died in O'Fallon, Missouri. The riches of the liturgy that he had worked for all his life endured.

• Hellriegel's papers are in the Liturgical Collection in the Burns Library at Boston College. Hellriegel's articles appeared regularly in the magazine *Orate Fratres* (later called *Worship*) from 1925 to 1965. Noel Schattman Barrett, *Martin B. Hellriegel: Pastoral Liturgist* (1990), is the best book on Hellriegel. Obituaries are in the *St. Louis Review*, 17 Apr. 1981, and the *St. Louis Globe-Democrat*, 13 Apr. 1981.

WILLIAM BARNABY FAHERTY

HELM, John Larue (4 July 1802–8 Sept. 1867), governor of Kentucky, was born near Elizabethtown, Kentucky, the son of George Helm and Rebecca Larue. The son of a prosperous farmer, Helm received a common school education. After studying in the law offices of Samuel Haycraft and Duff Green, two prominent Elizabethtown attorneys, he was admitted to the bar in 1823. The following year he was appointed Meade County attorney, a position he held for sixteen years. His law practice flourished, partly because of family connections and partly because of his legal skill, especially as counsel in litigation stemming from the entanglement of Kentucky's land titles.

In 1826 Helm commenced a long career as a Kentucky legislator; he served in both chambers, including five sessions as Speaker of the House and two as Speaker of the Senate. While in the legislature he supported internal improvements, especially turnpikes and railroads, and became a leader of the Whig party. In 1848 he was elected lieutenant governor and assumed the governorship on 31 July 1850, when John Jordan Crittenden resigned to accept President Millard Fillmore's appointment as attorney general.

As governor, Helm continued his advocacy of railroad building. He succeeded in gaining legislative approval for a state census of manufacturing and agricultural resources, a survey of mineral reserves, and laws against vote fraud, but he failed in his efforts to increase judicial salaries and to toughen laws against carrying concealed weapons. A fiscal conservative, except on transportation projects, Helm vetoed a plan to use money from the sinking fund, established to pay off the state debt, to cover deficits in the state school fund, though the legislature overrode his veto.

In 1835 Helm first advocated the construction of a railroad connecting Kentucky to the South and, while lieutenant governor, helped secure a charter for the Louisville and Nashville Railroad. He became that railroad's president in 1854 and almost immediately found himself embroiled in controversy and financial crisis. Helm successfully promoted the building of a branch line to Memphis, despite fierce opposition from Louisville merchants who feared losing trade to rivals in Memphis. A chronic shortage of cash prompted Helm himself to invest heavily in the enterprise, and once he personally redeemed $20,000 of the railroad's bonds. Critics, including some of the railroad's directors, accused Helm of incompetence and poor financial management, but he refused to leave office until several months after completion of the initial line in October 1859. Despite his detractors, Helm appears to have played a significant role in the development of Kentucky's most powerful and important economic institution of the nineteenth century.

During the Civil War, Helm endorsed neutrality for Kentucky, but when that policy failed he leaned heavily toward the Confederacy. In 1865 he was again elected to the state senate, where he successfully fought for amnesty for ex-Confederates. Like many other ex-Whigs, Helm joined the Democratic party during the Civil War and, in 1867, ran as its candidate for governor. He was overwhelmingly elected but died of complications from diabetes only five days after his inauguration.

In 1830 Helm married Lucinda B. Hardin, the daughter of Ben Hardin, a famous Kentucky lawyer. They had eleven children, including Ben Hardin Helm, a Confederate general, who was killed at Chickamauga.

• There is no significant collection of Helm papers. For an updated biographical sketch see Tom Owen, "John Larue Helm," in Lowell H. Harrison, ed., *Kentucky's Governors, 1792–1985* (1985). See also Jennie C. Morton, "Sketch of Governor John L. Helm," *Register of the Kentucky Historical Society* 3 (Sept. 1905): 11–14. Helm's presidency of the Louisville and Nashville Railroad is discussed in Maury Klein, *History of the Louisville and Nashville Railroad* (1972).

ROBERT M. IRELAND

HELMPRAECHT, Joseph (14 Jan. 1820–15 Dec. 1884), Catholic priest and prelate, was born at Niederwinkling, Bavaria. He received secondary schooling at the Benedictine abbey at Metten, where one of his teachers was Boniface Wimmer, who was to establish the Benedictine order in the United States. Helmpraecht aspired to be a diocesan priest and studied theology at the University of Munich. Concerned about the pastoral care of German immigrants to the United States, he decided to join the Congregation of the Most Holy Redeemer, commonly called the Redemptorists, an order that had ministered to Germans in American cities since 1832. Helmpraecht entered the Redemptorist novitiate at Altötting, Bavaria, in 1843 and that same year was sent to Baltimore, where he was ordained to the priesthood in 1845 and assigned to St.

James Church. He could then expect to engage in ministry at the order's German-speaking congregations and in the traditional Redemptorist activity of conducting missions that featured a week or more of spirited preaching in Catholic churches. These missions aimed to renew the fervor of faithful Catholics and to bring back those who had fallen away from regular religious practices.

In 1848 Helmpraecht took charge of St. Mary Church in Buffalo and served there until 1854. In this assignment he directed the completion of the church's construction and built a school and orphanage. He then became pastor of the larger Church of the Most Holy Redeemer serving Germans on the Lower East Side of New York. One of the Redemptorists whom he came to know there was the noted American-born convert Isaac Hecker, who later left the order to establish the Paulist community of priests.

In 1860 officials of the Redemptorist order found that Helmpraecht's building program for the school and orphanage had produced a large debt. He was abruptly transferred to St. Peter Church in Philadelphia, then assigned to St. Philomena Church in Pittsburgh. In 1863 he was appointed to the Redemptorist novitiate and House of Studies at Annapolis, Maryland. In 1865 he accompanied the superior of the Redemptorists' American province, John De Dycker, on a trip to Rome to conduct business with the Redemptorist superior general. Helmpraecht succeeded De Dycker as superior of the Redemptorists' American province in 1865.

As provincial superior, Helmpraecht sought to implement the superior general's policy of preferring to establish so-called mission houses as bases for preaching rather than staff parish churches. Accordingly, mission houses were started at St. Louis and Boston, and several parishes were relinquished at Detroit, Baltimore, Cumberland, Maryland, and Rochester, New York. Helmpraecht accepted the invitation of bishops to staff parishes in Philadelphia and Quebec City but declined similar requests from fifteen other dioceses. He promoted the physical development of existing Redemptorist parishes at New York, Philadelphia, Detroit, Buffalo, Baltimore, and Chicago by encouraging the construction of larger churches and schools.

To train Redemptorist priests, Helmpraecht replaced the House of Studies at Annapolis with a major new seminary at Ilchester, Maryland, completed in 1868, and he opened a minor seminary there in 1872 for boys aspiring to the priesthood. In the 1870s he renewed the practice of recruiting Redemptorists from Europe to augment personnel at the new seminaries and for other works. In 1870 the Dutch moral theologian Anthony Konings, whose works were influential in the Catholic world, arrived to join the seminary faculty. The German Joseph Putzer, noted canon law scholar, began teaching at the seminary in 1876. The seminaries and attention to studies resulted in a more thorough intellectual preparation of Redemptorist seminarians.

At Helmpraecht's urging, the superior general formed a new Redemptorist province for the western United States in 1875 with headquarters at St. Louis. After serving twelve years as provincial superior, Helmpraecht was allowed to relinquish the position in 1877. He then became pastor successively of St. Michael's in Baltimore and of Most Holy Redeemer Church in New York City, where he died. His activities as Redemptorist superior reflected the close attention given to organizational and administrative matters during a period of rapid growth of the immigrant Catholic community and its religious institutions.

• The Redemptorists and Helmpraecht's work are discussed in John F. Byrne, *The Redemptorist Centenaries; 1732: Founding of the Congregation of the Most Holy Redeemer; 1832: Establishment in the United States* (1932); Michael J. Curley, *The Provincial Story: A History of the Baltimore Province of the Congregation of the Most Holy Redeemer* (1963); and Thomas L. Skinner, *The Redemptorists in the West* (1933). Obituaries are in the *New York Times*, 17 Dec. 1884, the *Baltimore Sun*, 18 Dec. 1884, and *New York Freeman's Journal*, 27 Dec. 1884.

JOSEPH M. WHITE

HELMUTH, Henry (16 May 1745–5 Feb. 1825), minister, was born Justus Heinrich Christian Helmuth in Helmstedt, Duchy of Brunswick, Germany, the son of Johann Christoph Helmuth, a baker, and Justina (maiden name unknown). Following Johann Helmuth's death in 1756, the family house and garden were sold to satisfy debt, and Helmuth relied entirely on charitable help to fund his education. This he received from Karl Heinrich von Bogatzky, one of the patrons of the Francke Foundations in Halle, through the intervention of the count von Boetticher, a local nobleman. Admitted in 1759 to the orphanage and in 1762 to the Latin school at the pietist center in Halle, Helmuth distinguished himself as a good but independently minded student. He worked as a tutor in the school and later in the academy, the elite school run by the Francke Foundations for sons of the nobility from 1765 to 1767. A good speaker, Helmuth prepared for the ministry but hoped to remain a teacher in Halle. Instead, in 1768 he was urged to accept a call to Trinity Lutheran Church in Lancaster, Pennsylvania.

Like many pastors from Halle who were sent to the United States, Helmuth was ordained at Wernigerode, another renowned pietist center. He then traveled to England with fellow Halle-trained pastor Johann Friedrich Schmidt and on to Philadelphia in April 1769. He succeeded Johann Siegfried Geroch as Lutheran pastor in Lancaster, and in 1770 he married Maria Barbara Keppele, the daughter of Johann Heinrich Keppele, one of the most powerful and influential merchant-traders among the German speakers of Pennsylvania. The couple had five children. While in Lancaster Helmuth invited the British revivalist George Whitefield to preach at Trinity in 1770 and witnessed a revival of religious sentiment among his members. Consistent with his pietist determination to instill proper behavior in his congregation, Helmuth introduced compulsory confession and registration of prospective communicants.

Helmuth was generally positive about the fight for American independence. Like most pietists, he frowned on the frivolities of dance and theater, especially during the war. Helmuth and his longtime friend and associate Reformed pastor Johann Conrad Albert Helfenstein published a denunciation of such an assembly held in Lancaster in February 1778.

In 1779 Helmuth accepted a call to Philadelphia's St. Michael's and Zion parish, the largest Lutheran parish in the United States. He remained there until his retirement in 1820. As he informed his teachers in Halle shortly after arriving in the United States, the education of youth was the cause to which he felt himself called. The revolutionary war had not yet ended when he joined forces with fellow Lutheran pastor Johann Christoph Kunze to revive the latter's abortive 1773 effort to found a Lutheran seminary. The author of many hymn texts, Helmuth helped to organize the 1786 Lutheran Hymnal (*Erbauliche Liedersammlung*) and composed numerous poems for children. He and Kunze used the parochial school and by 1780 a Gymnasium-like German-Latin school to prepare German Lutheran children for admission to a residential college within the new University of Pennsylvania, where they were also able to take courses from the broader curriculum. A more comprehensive plan could not be realized, which envisioned feeder schools that would supply the best and brightest candidates to a central Lutheran college at the university. However, his hopes for a separate German college did not materialize and had foundered by 1788. For adults Helmuth founded in 1789 the von Mosheim Society, a literary club dedicated to promoting the cultivation of German language and literature. In 1784 he succeeded Kunze as professor of German at the university and remained in that post until 1796.

Helmuth garnered considerable contemporary fame for his ministrations to the stricken in Philadelphia's 1793 yellow fever epidemic, in which he buried 625 members and attendees of St. Michael's and Zion. He recounted his efforts in a pamphlet published in both German and English. Less well known were his cantata texts and a defense of the sacraments and the pastoral office that was published in 1793 at the behest of his parish's Society for the Relief of the Needy Poor. His scholarly interests secured him election to the American Philosophical Society.

By 1794 Helmuth's conviction that the French Revolution and radical deism were destroying faith in Germany and in the United States placed him at odds with powerful friends of Thomas Jefferson's Democratic-Republicans in his own parish. Led by General Peter Mühlenberg and other wealthy allies, these members initiated a campaign that lasted until 1807 to abolish German as the language of worship and to exclude recent immigrants from voting membership in the congregation. Helmuth fought their efforts and attacked Jeffersonianism, publishing a denunciation of German-American support for John Fries's rebellion against the federal direct tax of 1798 in Northampton County in 1799. But he later worked tirelessly to secure a pardon for Fries from President John Adams, arguing that Fries was misguided but not a threat to the government.

Discouraged by the election of Jefferson to the presidency, after about 1800 Helmuth devoted his life to the affairs of the Ministerium of Pennsylvania, which he served as president. He proposed a curriculum for seminary education for the organization, and in addition to publishing small pieces of pietist literature for children, in 1811 he and his colleague Schmidt established the *Evangelisches Magazin*, the first church magazine in German in the United States. Helmuth continued contact with Halle after the Francke Foundations were forced to close in 1806 by Napoleon; he helped to collect donations in Maryland and Pennsylvania to aid in the reopening of the orphanage and schools at the foundation by 1815. On 31 October 1817 Helmuth preached and published a sermon on the 300th anniversary of the Reformation. By 1820 Helmuth was forced into retirement by a coalition of younger parishioners who blamed slow parish growth on his continuing attachment to German. Helmuth was given $100 for past services. By 1823 he had left Philadelphia and was unable to attend services regularly. In January 1825 the parish ordered that a carriage be dispatched to carry Helmuth to church and back each week, but he died at his home in Germantown before the plan was implemented. Buried before the altar in St. Michael's Church with three of his predecessors, Helmuth was eulogized for his work during the yellow fever epidemic of 1793. One year later Helmuth's educational dream was partially realized with the founding of a Lutheran seminary in Gettysburg. He was remembered even in the late 1890s as one of the most influential pastors, having personally trained some sixteen persons for the ministry. Helmuth was among the last of the Halle pastors sent to North America to minister to German-speaking Lutherans; his educational and confessional dreams were not realized until a generation after his death.

• Helmuth's diaries and voluminous correspondence are in the Lutheran Archives Center in Philadelphia; the archives of the Francke Foundations, Halle, Germany; Gettysburg Theological Seminary archives; Muhlenberg College; and Trinity Lutheran Church, Lancaster, Pa. Secondary literature includes Theodore G. Tappert, "Pastoral Heroism in a Time of Panic: Helmuth and the Yellow Fever Epidemic in Philadelphia," *Lutheran Church Quarterly* 13 (1940): 162–75; Tappert, "Helmuth and the Fries Rebellion in 1799," *Lutheran Church Quarterly* 17 (1965): 265–69; Edward C. Wolf, "Music in Old Zion, Philadelphia, 1750–1850," *Musical Quarterly* 58 (1972): 622–52; A. G. Roeber, "Citizens or Subjects? German-Lutherans and the Federal Constitution in Pennsylvania, 1789–1800," *Amerikastudien/American Studies* 34 (1989): 49–68; and Roeber, "The von Mosheim Society and the Preservation of German Education and Culture in the New Republic, 1789–1813," in *German Influences on Education in the United States to 1917*, ed. Henry Geitz et al. (1995), pp. 157–76.

A. G. ROEBER

HELPER, Hinton Rowan (27 Dec. 1829–8 Mar. 1909), publicist, was born in Rowan County, North Carolina, the son of Daniel Helper and Sally Brown, farmers. Helper's family owned 200 acres of land and possibly a slave family. He was educated at home by his widowed mother and at nearby Mocksville Academy. In 1850, after serving out his apprenticeship to a storekeeper in Salisbury, North Carolina, he used money embezzled from his master (and apparently later repaid) to travel to New York City, where he was unable to find satisfactory employment. He went to California in early 1851 and remained there for two and a half years, returning to North Carolina after failing to find gold.

Helper's career as a writer began with the publication in 1855 of *Land of Gold*, a little-noticed account of how California had failed to live up to his expectations. His next book, *The Impending Crisis of the South: How to Meet It* (1857), became the center of a national controversy. The book called for the abolition of slavery because it was retarding the economic development of the South and limiting the opportunities of its nonslaveholding white majority. Helper argued that slavery was responsible for a one-crop system of plantation agriculture that benefited the slaveholding minority but denied to lower class whites the range of opportunities that a more diversified economy, like that of the North, would have provided. Since it appeared in the midst of the national debate over the fate of slavery in the federal territories, Helper's book attracted great public attention, being praised by northern free soilers and condemned by southern sectionalists. In 1859 an inexpensive *Compendium*, or digest, of *The Impending Crisis* was published with the endorsement of some leading members of the Republican party, who hoped to use it as a campaign document. Approximately 75,000 copies of the book and the *Compendium* were sold or distributed. Helper's work became a central issue in the bitter and prolonged contest for the Speakership of the House of Representatives that began in December 1959 and lasted for two months. The Republicans had a plurality but not an absolute majority in the House, and their original candidate for Speaker, John Sherman (1823–1900) of Ohio, failed to win election because he had endorsed the *Compendium*. Helper's doctrines, according to the resolution declaring Sherman unfit to be Speaker, were "insurrectionary and hostile to the domestic peace and tranquillity of the country." Only after the Republicans withdrew Sherman's name and put up a candidate who had not endorsed the *Compendium* did they succeed in organizing the House.

The uproar over *The Impending Crisis* was one in a sequence of events pushing the nation toward civil war between 1857 and 1860. Like the Dred Scott decision, the controversy over the proposed admission of Kansas to the Union under a proslavery constitution, and John Brown's (1800–1859) raid, it helped to polarize opinion on the slavery issue. It confirmed many northerners in their belief that the introduction of slavery anywhere would deprive white workers and farmers of economic opportunities, but its impact on southern opinion was even greater. Helper's call to the nonslaveholding whites to work for the abolition of slavery and the endorsement of his views by prominent Republicans aroused fears that the North would promote a class conflict among southern whites. Federal patronage might even be used to create within the South a nonslaveholders' party based on "Helperism." Such fears help to explain why many upper-class southerners who had previously resisted secessionism embraced it fervently after the victory of Abraham Lincoln in 1860.

Helper's subsequent career repeated the pattern of failure and relative obscurity that had been his lot before *The Impending Crisis* brought him to the attention of the country. After the Republican victory in 1860, he was rewarded for his services to the party with an appointment as American consul in Buenos Aires, where he served from 1861 to 1866. While in Argentina he married Maria Louisa Rodriguez in 1863. They had one child. After returning to the United States in early 1867, he embarked on a career as a fanatical propagandist for white supremacy. In a series of hastily written books—*Nojoque* (1867), *The Negroes in Negroland* (1868), and *Noonday Exigencies* (1871)—he argued for the radical and permanent inferiority of African Americans and demanded that all blacks be expelled from the United States.

Strongly opposing Congressional Reconstruction, Helper now put his pen at the service of the opponents of equal rights for blacks. But southern critics of Reconstruction could not forgive his earlier apostasy and generally found his views too extreme to be politically useful. Consequently, his racist writings attracted relatively little attention. Although he was sometimes described as an abolitionist who had seen the error of his ways, Helper's racist views of the Reconstruction era did not in fact contradict his earlier antislavery writings. He had attacked slavery for the harm it allegedly did to whites, not out of sympathy for blacks. In fact, *The Impending Crisis* had insisted that elimination of slavery be accompanied by the deportation of blacks from the United States. As he made clear then and later, one of his principal objections to slavery was that it brought blacks and whites into proximity. Helper's racial phobia even made him unwilling to patronize hotels and restaurants that employed blacks as servants or waiters.

During the last thirty years of his life, Helper devoted most of his attention to the promotion of a railroad linking North and South America, a project that he believed would lead to the civilization and racial purification of a continent that suffered from the intermingling of whites with "cumbersomely base black and brown elements." Failing to interest businesses or governments in his enterprise, he spent the last years of his life in poverty and frustration. He died, a suicide, in Washington, D.C. At the time of Helper's death, the historian John Spencer Bassett summed up his career succinctly but effectively: "He wrote a book which stated a very patent fact in a striking way, but, aside from that, he was neither wise nor attractive."

• The only available collection of Helper papers is the William Henry Anthon Book of Letters Relevant to the Publication of *The Impending Crisis* in the New York Public Library. Information on his life can be found in David Barbee, "Hinton Rowan Helper," *Tyler's Historical Quarterly and Genealogical Magazine* 15 (1934): 135–72; Hugh T. Leffler, *Hinton Rowan Helper, Advocate of a White America* (1935); and Hugh C. Bailey, *Hinton Rowan Helper: Abolitionist-Racist* (1965). For an annotated text of *The Impending Crisis* and an essay on his thought, see the John Harvard Library edition, ed. George M. Fredrickson (1968). Insight into his historical significance can be derived from Oliver Crenshaw, "The Speakership Contest of 1859–60," *Mississippi Valley Historical Review* 29 (1942): 323–39, and Clement Eaton, *The Mind of the Old South* (1964). Obituaries are in the *Nation*, 11 and 18 Mar. 1909, and the *Washington Post*, 10 Mar. 1909.

GEORGE M. FREDRICKSON

HEMENWAY, Mary (20 Dec. 1820–6 Mar. 1894), philanthropist, was born Mary Porter Tileston in New York City, the daughter of Thomas Tileston, a merchant, and Mary Dudley Porter. Her parents shared a New England ancestry. Her father's commerce in shipping, banking, and insurance provided a privileged life. Educated in private schools, she cultivated lifelong intellectual interests in art, history, literature (especially biography and sermons), and music. Unitarianism, in particular, provided the philosophical moorings for the projects she supported.

In 1840 Mary Porter Tileston married Edward Augustus Holyoke Hemenway, a distant cousin on her mother's side and her senior by fifteen years. The couple then moved to Boston, the site of Augustus's business. Her marriage to a successful, self-made shipping merchant like her father solidified her elite position, yet she never took her wealth for granted. The Hemenways had five children, one of whom died in infancy. In 1853 they moved to the impressive Beacon Hill residence that her husband built, and in the next two decades they acquired significant properties on Boston's exclusive South and North shores.

Hemenway's friends and associates included notable women and men in fields akin to her own interests, among them Mary E. Dewey, the daughter of Hemenway's childhood Unitarian minister and an Indian rights' activist and author; philosopher Ralph Waldo Emerson; the U.S. Commissioner of Education William T. Harris; and Sophia Peabody Hawthorne. Hemenway's involvement in public affairs, which began after the Civil War, developed from the private training she provided for talented youth. She entered public life at middle age after raising her family and suffering through her husband's confinement in a sanatorium from 1860 to 1874 and death in 1876, and the deaths of her father in 1864 and eldest daughter in 1865.

Hemenway's economic, social, and cultural privilege provided the fulcrum for her philanthropic work. She approached her work with commitment and quiet

dedication on a small scale at first, being actively and continuously involved with the projects for which she provided the financial seed and helped germinate with her enthusiasm. After demonstrating its worth and receiving public recognition, the project typically was taken over by a public agency such as a school board. Many of her projects were emulated by others and hence had national influence.

Although self-effacing, Hemenway's prominent position ensured that her work would have a profound impact on the urban poor and middle class whom it principally addressed. She was known for her executive abilities, possessing in Charles Gordon Ames's words a "judicial habit of mind," and for her deeply held belief that public institutions should provide a moral education, instilling patriotism and democratic values and teaching practical skills. Concern that the past inform the present and that education unify the nation motivated her support of philanthropic projects. Her work contributed to the creation of an American identity and ideology for the emergent nation state.

Hemenway sponsored projects that addressed issues stemming from the social upheavals of her day, including reconstruction, industrialization, immigration, and urbanism. A politically conservative woman, her work was forward-looking nevertheless and included assisting with schooling for poor whites and blacks in the South and founding an orphanage on her South Shore estate. Her principal projects for improving urban life were based in Boston but proved of enduring interest in American public education. In 1865, 1885, and 1888 respectively, she sponsored programs of sewing, cooking, and gymnastics instruction for girls in the Boston public schools that were later integrated into national public school curricula. She established the Boston Normal School of Cooking in 1887 and the Boston Normal School of Gymnastics in 1889 for teacher training in these areas. In 1876–1877 she provided generously to save the Old South Meeting House as a national symbol and instituted educational programs to promote popular interest in American history.

In 1886 Hemenway sponsored the Hemenway Southwestern Archaeological Expedition, which pioneered the four-field approach to the scientific investigation of human societies and cultures by combining the perspectives of archaeology, ethnography, linguistics, and physical anthropology. This approach became the foundation of twentieth-century American anthropology. Sponsorship of the expedition was the most advanced and complex of Mary Hemenway's endeavors in a philanthropic career of nearly thirty years. She apparently proposed the expedition, and Frank Hamilton Cushing, its first director, gratefully named it in her honor. Organized at her North Shore estate, bearing the imprint of her characteristic foresight, and undertaken before anthropology became a professional discipline, the expedition was intended to be a comprehensive exploration of Pueblo cultures as America's ancient, indigenous civilization. The work of the expedition, it was hoped, would culminate in the founding of both a museum and school in Salem, Massachusetts, whose focus on Pueblo cultures would foster public education in American history. But Hemenway's intentions were not realized; neither the museum nor the school was established. The expedition closed with her death, its material collections deposited at Harvard University's Peabody Museum and written records dispersed among individuals and institutions including the National Museum of the American Indian (formerly the Heye Foundation). Some of the expedition's findings were published in five volumes of the *Journal of American Ethnology and Archaeology* between 1891 and 1908.

Although she provided for the publication of materials related to her public work, she did not publish and left little of her own writing behind. In a memorial tribute soon after her death, the *Boston Gazette* described Hemenway as a woman of deeds with a "rare genius of expression through action." At her death, Mary Hemenway was reported to be the richest woman in Boston. Yet her legacy lies not in her means but in the fact that through her philanthropy she enhanced the development of professional disciplines and built national institutions.

• The Hemenway family papers are housed at the Phillips Library of the Peabody and Essex Museum in Salem, Mass. Biographical information on Mary Hemenway is in Charles G. Ames, "A Memorial Tribute," *Boston Gazette*, 18 Mar. 1894. Mary W. Tileston, *A Memorial of the Life and Benefactions of Mary Hemenway, 1820–1894* (1927), provides reminiscences of family and associates. See also the article by Lea S. McChesney on Hemenway in *International Dictionary of Anthropologists*, ed. C. Winters (1991); Curtis M. Hinsley and David R. Wilcox, eds., *A Hemenway Portfolio* (1995), on the Hemenway Expedition; and Betty Mary Spears, *Leading the Way: Amy Morris Homans and the Beginnings of Professional Education for Women* (1986), for discussion of the Boston Normal School of Gymnastics. An obituary is in the *New York Times*, 7 (and 15) Mar. 1894.

LEA S. McCHESNEY

HEMINGS, Sally (1773–1835), enslaved lady's maid and seamstress whose given name probably was Sarah, was born in Virginia, the daughter of the slave Elizabeth "Betty" Hemings and, allegedly, John Wayles, a merchant and planter. (Family members spell the surname both *Hemings* and *Hemmings*.) After Wayles's death in 1773, Betty Hemings and her children became the property of Thomas Jefferson and his wife, Martha Wayles Skelton Jefferson. From an early age Sally Hemings was a personal servant of Jefferson's daughter Mary (later Maria), whom she accompanied to France in 1787, when Sally was fourteen and Mary nine.

It is not known whether Sally, while in Paris, lived at Mary's convent school or at Jefferson's residence on the Champs-Elysées, where her brother James Hemings was chef de cuisine. Jefferson's expenditures during her two-year residence in Paris indicate that Sally received further training in the skills of a lady's maid,

and she acted in that capacity for Jefferson's older daughter, Martha, when the latter began going out in Parisian society in 1789. She intermittently received a small monthly wage during this period.

Jefferson, his two daughters, and his two slaves returned to Virginia at the end of 1789. Despite her long association with Jefferson's younger daughter, Sally Hemings remained at Monticello after Maria Jefferson's marriage and departure in 1797. Her son Madison Hemings remembered that she took care of Jefferson's chamber and wardrobe and did "such light work as sewing, &c." Jefferson's records reveal only that she was one of the "house-maids," that she bore six children, two of whom died as infants, and that, at Jefferson's death in 1826, she was still a slave, valued in the appraisal of his property at $50.

There is no certain information on Sally Hemings's status after Jefferson's death. It seems likely that she was unofficially freed by Jefferson's daughter Martha Randolph, whose 1834 will asked that "Sally" be given her "time." This may have been intended to legitimize an existing situation. She appears in an 1833 "List of Free Negroes & Mulattoes" with her son Madison, who recalled that his mother lived with him in Charlottesville until her death.

Madison Hemings, freed in Jefferson's will, related his life story to an Ohio journalist in 1873. It is this account, selectively accepted by historians, that contains most of what is known about the Hemings family. Hemings is the main source for the allegation that John Wayles was the father of Sally Hemings and five of her siblings. He also stated that he and his own brothers and sisters were Thomas Jefferson's children, the result of a relationship that began in Paris. When Hemings's account was published in 1873, the story of a possible sexual relationship between Jefferson and Sally Hemings had long been part of the public discourse. It had been transformed from local gossip to national news in the fall of 1802, when an article in the Richmond *Recorder* began, "It is well known that the man, *whom it delighteth the people to honor*, keeps, and for many years past has kept, as his concubine, one of his own slaves. Her name is SALLY." The author was James Thomson Callender, a disgruntled convert to the Federalist cause after his former heroes on the Republican side failed to "reward" him with a postmastership. Other Federalist writers quickly incorporated the tale in their attacks on President Jefferson and his administration. Jefferson himself was silent on the issue. In accordance with his practice in regard to personal attacks, he never publicly denied a connection. One private letter, which might be interpreted as a denial, remains ambiguous. His own family members were consistent in their disbelief but made their denials privately.

For the rest of the century the allegation that the author of the Declaration of Independence kept his own children in slavery was taken up by critics of Jefferson's party, his region, and his country. Skeptical British travelers, highlighting the hypocrisy of the American experiment, repeated and embellished the story, and antislavery activists of the antebellum period used the relationship to emphasize the exploitation of the slavery system.

In the meantime, more quietly, a belief in their Jefferson ancestry passed from generation to generation of Sally Hemings's descendants. Their side of the story was first given wider circulation in 1974 in *Thomas Jefferson: An Intimate History* by Fawn M. Brodie, one of the very few Jefferson biographers to accept the Hemings-Jefferson connection. At the center of Brodie's psychological portrait is an enduring relationship between master and slave, romantic rather than exploitative. It is her version that captured and has held the public imagination since that time.

In the absence of conclusive evidence to prove or refute its existence, the possible relationship between Thomas Jefferson and Sally Hemings has been the subject of vigorous and shifting debate for almost two centuries. The story has been a convenient symbol for some of the anomalies of American history and complexities of American society, and African Americans in the twentieth century viewed its denial by historians as symbolic of the negation of oral traditions—often the only possible link to their ancestors in slavery. At the center of the controversy—often eclipsed by the debate—is the still-elusive figure of Sally Hemings herself.

• It is not known whether, like several of her family members, Hemings was literate; if so, nothing in her hand has survived. A brief account of the known facts of her life appears in James A. Bear, Jr., "The Hemings Family of Monticello," *Virginia Cavalcade* 29 (1979): 84–85. See also Annette Gordon-Reed, *Thomas Jefferson and Sally Hemings: An American Controversy* (1997). Fawn M. Brodie, who accepted the truth of the liaison with Jefferson, makes Hemings a major character in her biography, *Thomas Jefferson: An Intimate History* (1974). The relationship is also the basis for two fictional reconstructions of Hemings's life, Barbara Chase-Riboud, *Sally Hemings* (1979), and Minnie Shumate Woodson, *The Sable Curtain* (1987).

References to Hemings in British travel literature were gathered by Sidney P. Moss and Carolyn Moss, "The Jefferson Miscegenation Legend in British Travel Books," *Journal of the Early American Republic* 7 (1987): 253–74. Merrill D. Peterson summarized the public life of the story of the liaison in *The Jefferson Image in the American Mind* (1960). The raging scholarly debate of the last half of the twentieth century is discussed in Scot A. French and Edward L. Ayers, "The Strange Career of Thomas Jefferson: Race and Slavery in American Memory, 1943–1993," in *Jeffersonian Legacies*, ed. Peter S. Onut (1993). Hemings family oral tradition appears in Minnie Shumate Woodson, *The Woodson Sourcebook* (privately printed, 1980) and Judith Justus, *Down From the Mountain: The Oral History of the Hemings Family* (1990).

LUCIA C. STANTON

HEMINGWAY, Ernest (21 July 1899–2 July 1961), writer, was born Ernest Miller Hemingway in Oak Park, Illinois, the son of Clarence Edmonds Hemingway, a doctor, and Grace Hall, a musician and voice teacher. Oak Park sits foursquare on the Illinois prairie, eight miles west of downtown Chicago, where it

was developed to hold at bay the corruption of the city. With its insistence on constant vigil against corrupting forces, the Village of Oak Park, as it called itself, put tremendous pressures on its sons and daughters. In the village of his youth, Hemingway was theoretically protected by city ordinances from uncensored movies, boxing matches, any information on venereal disease or birth control, all forms of gambling and prostitution, and all consumption of alcohol. Until he turned eighteen, Hemingway could not legally buy cigarettes, play billiards, drive a car, or own a cap gun within the village limits. Unless accompanied by a parent or responsible adult, young Hemingway, governed by the village curfew, could not be out of the house after 8:00 P.M. in fall and winter or after 9:00 P.M. in spring and summer. That Hemingway rebelled against these pressures is not surprising; had the first generation of the twentieth century not rebelled, it would have been strange indeed.

Hemingway grew up in the bosom of a well-known, extended, and respected family, college educated at Wheaton, Oberlin, and Rush Medical School, a family whose sense of civic responsibility was strong and whose interests were divided among medicine, the Congregational church, and real estate. Although Hemingway was sometimes embarrassed by his mother's free spirit and frightened by his father's retreat into depressions, his early years were not scarred by divorce or abuse; he grew up among his four sisters and one brother respecting his elders, submitting to discipline, and behaving like a good bad boy. With plenty of parental and community rules, it was easy to be bad in Oak Park and just as easy to be forgiven, for the Hemingway name was a substantial one within this well-to-do community.

When Grace Hall-Hemingway, as Ernest's mother hyphenated her last name, designed their house on North Kenilworth, she included a music studio and recital hall thirty feet square with a vaulted ceiling and a narrow balcony. Here she gave music and voice lessons, scheduled student recitals, and composed and practiced her own music, which was marketed by two different publishing houses. Incurably optimistic, she was the energy source in the Hemingway household, a woman always onstage, with a personality that could not be ignored—a woman not unlike her eldest son, Ernest. After he left home, Hemingway obscured his mother's talents and personality by professing to hate her and to hold her responsible for his father's 1928 suicide. Yet it was from his mother that Hemingway's boundless energy and enthusiasm came. No one who met mother or son ever forgot either of them.

Balanced against the propriety and culture of Oak Park were Hemingway's northern Michigan summers, where the family cottage was on one side of Walloon Lake and, later, his mother's farm was on the other. Every July and August from his birth through the summer of 1917, Ernest explored the woods, the streams, and the lake. For the first twelve years his father was with him, teaching him to hunt and fish, but after 1911, when Clarence Hemingway began to retreat into his deepening depressions, the boy was left to his own devices. Besides his sisters for company (his brother was not born until 1915), there were other summer people living in cottages all along the lake, summer friends from Horton Bay and Petoskey, and the last of the Ojibwa Indians who lived in the woods close to Horton. Those summers of trout fishing, camping out, hiking, baseball games, and awakened sexuality were as important to the education of young Hemingway as were his school years in Oak Park.

Whatever else his culture taught him, young Hemingway learned early that perseverance and winning were Oak Park virtues. Like his boyhood hero, Theodore Roosevelt, Ernest was determined to excel in physical activities: twice he ran the high school cross-country race; twice he finished last. He played lightweight football until his late growth got him onto the varsity team his senior year. Slow afoot and a little clumsy, he was a second-string interior lineman. He managed the swimming team, where his event was the "plunge," swimming underwater for distance. He captained the water polo team. When he got his height, he also got boxing gloves. Later in Europe he took up tennis, skiing, and the luge. He always admired professional boxers, baseball players, and, later, bullfighters.

In high school Hemingway took the then-standard precollege curriculum: six semesters of science, four of math, six of Latin, eight of English literature and composition, four of history, two of applied music, and another two years of orchestra. Whatever the course, humanities or science, there were always written assignments: weekly book reports, essays, and term papers. Hemingway translated Cicero; wrote about Greek tyrants, the Marathon campaign, and the Punic Wars; outlined his reading of *Macbeth* and *Hamlet*; and reported on the anatomy of grasshoppers, the necessity of life insurance, the need for a standing army, and the causes of the American Revolution. He also wrote humorous pieces for the school newspaper and the literary magazine. "Bill 3127 Introduced by Senator Hemingway" put the hunting of policemen under the game laws, making it a misdemeanor to kill them out of season. Like any Oak Parker, Hemingway could easily roll out his biblical parody:

It is written that in the Library thou shalt not chew gum. Thou shalt not covet thy neighbor's magazine orally. Thou shalt not play tic tac-toe with Toots Johnson. Thou shalt not match pennies with Reed Milliken. Thou shalt not throw paper wads with Jim Adams. . . . Thou shalt not kid the Jane that sitteth upon thy right hand, nor kick the boob who sitteth across from thee.
(John F. Kennedy Library)

Most of Hemingway's courses required collateral reading in both the high school library and the Scoville Institute. Besides required texts, Hemingway also found time to read the books he most enjoyed at age sixteen, the short stories of O. Henry, Rudyard Kipling's tales of empire, and Stewart Edward White's version of the strenuous life. From the Scoville's collection Hemingway borrowed books, particularly during the summer, and frequently had late fees to pay. He may never have gone to college, but in Oak Park he acquired the cultural background he needed for the next step in his life.

In June 1917, two months after the United States entered World War I, Hemingway graduated from high school and began his last completely idyllic summer at Walloon Lake, where he turned eighteen, still too young to enlist in the army. In October, with help from his Missouri relatives, he signed on as a cub reporter for the Kansas City *Star*, where he said he learned to write a "simple, declarative sentence." He also learned the *Star's* style sheet: short first paragraphs, vigorous language, no superfluous words, few adjectives, no trite phrases. For seven months young Hemingway covered the usual beats assigned to raw recruits: city council, train station, police station, and hospital emergency room. In March 1918 he wrote home, "We are having a laundry strike here and I am handling the police beat. The violence stories. . . . For over a month I have averaged a column a day" (John F. Kennedy Library). The romance of the newsman as crime fighter was part of what pulled young Hemingway into journalism. Three years later he would write stories about a young reporter, Punk Alford, solving violent crimes.

As eager as most American males of his age to experience the Great European War, Hemingway joined the Missouri Home Guard, which was eventually called to active duty. By that time Hemingway was already in Italy, serving as a volunteer ambulance driver for the American Red Cross. After two weeks of limited action at Schio he volunteered to man a rolling canteen on the Piave River front. There, on the night of 8 July 1918, after barely a month in the war zone, young Hemingway was wounded by an Austrian trench mortar. He was not yet nineteen. All that summer and fall he recovered from his leg wounds in the Milan Red Cross hospital, where his nurse was Agnes Von Kurowsky, an attractive young American woman eight years his senior. Although she found Hemingway handsome and entertaining, their relationship loomed larger in his mind than in hers. When he returned to America on 21 January 1919 he thought they were engaged to be married, but in March she wrote and broke off whatever the relationship might have been, saying that she was far too old for him.

In January 1920, still limping from his war wound and trading on his apprenticeship in Kansas City, Hemingway appeared at the Toronto *Star* desk looking for part-time work. The city editor agreed to buy Hemingway's stories on a piece by piece basis as they suited the needs of the paper. This arrangement produced Hemingway features on dental schools, prizefights, free shaves, and trout fishing. When Hemingway left Toronto in May 1920 to return to Chicago, his loose arrangement with the *Star* remained in place; over the next twenty months the paper regularly printed Hemingway features on rum-running and Chicago gangsters. During this same period Hemingway was courting Hadley Richardson, a St. Louis woman eight years older than himself. They were married at Horton Bay in September 1921 and immediately began planning to move to Italy.

In Chicago the new couple enjoyed the company and storytelling of Sherwood Anderson, who advised Hemingway that a would-be writer should go to Paris, not Italy. At the time, Hemingway was churning out copy for the short-lived *Cooperative Commonwealth* magazine, for which he was editor, writer, and general factotum. The magazine soon went bankrupt in a scandal, leaving the Hemingways free to leave Chicago for Paris. Traveling as a special correspondent to the Toronto *Star* allowed him to submit features on a per-piece basis and occasionally to work for weekly wages and expenses while covering major European news events. In January 1922 they moved into an inexpensive, fourth-floor walk-up apartment in the heart of Paris's Latin Quarter.

That first year in Paris Hemingway had little time to work on the novel he had begun in Chicago. Not only were there the distractions of the city (galleries, cafés, racetracks, boxing matches) and the demands of new-found friends (Sylvia Beach, Gertrude Stein, Ezra Pound, Bill Bird); there were also the demands of his newspaper work. During a twenty-month period in Europe, Hemingway filed more than eighty-eight stories with the Toronto *Star*, all but a few of which were printed. Between January 1922 and September 1923 the *Star* printed Hemingway submissions ranging from local color ("American Bohemians in Paris a Weird Lot") to winter sports ("Try Bob-Sledding If You Want Thrills") to the Great War ("A Veteran Visits Old Front, Wishes He Had Stayed Away"). The *Star* also sent Hemingway to cover four important events: the Genoa Economic Conference (6–27 Apr. 1922), the brief but intense Greco-Turkish War (29 Sept.–21 Oct. 1922), the Lausanne Peace Conference (21 Nov.–15 Dec. 1922), and the French military occupation of the German Ruhr (30 Mar.–9 Apr. 1923).

At the Genoa conference Hemingway was an early witness to the conflict between the fascist right and the Bolshevik left that would dominate much of his century. "The Fascisti," he wrote, "make no distinctions between socialists, communists, republicans or members of co-operative societies. They are all Reds and dangerous" (*By-Line*, p. 28). Less than a year later at Lausanne, Hemingway described the new fascist dictator of Italy, Benito Mussolini, as "the biggest bluff in Europe" (*By-Line*, p. 64). There was something permanently wrong, he said, with any man who would wear a black shirt and white spats. In September 1922 the *Star* sent Hemingway on a five-day train trip to Constantinople, where he covered the Greco-Turkish War that culminated with the Turks burning Smyrna and the Greeks retreating hopelessly from Thrace. "It is a silent procession," he wrote. "Nobody even grunts. It is all they can do to keep moving" (*Dateline*, p. 232).

These events began Hemingway's serious political education, giving him a privileged view of the postwar political leaders setting Europe's agenda: Georges Cle-

menceau, Georgi Tchitcherin, Jean-Louis Barthou, Lloyd George, and Mussolini. Hemingway wrote about anarchists, anti-Semitism, fascism, power politics, disarmament, German inflation, Paris nightlife, Spanish bullfights, and German trout fishing. Wherever he went, he always told his readers how to live well in another country: where to stay, what to eat, which wine to choose, how to get the most for their money. While covering the stories, Hemingway developed his admiration for the insider, the experienced man who knows the language, food, and customs of the country. As a foreign correspondent, such expert knowledge was expected of him. When he had it, he used it; when he lacked firsthand experience, he pretended so persuasively to have it that we later believed he wrote nothing that was not autobiographical. The bilingual insider, adept at European travel, became the trademark of his later fiction, which frequently was set in a foreign country.

Hemingway's short journalistic course in the socio-political aftermath of the Great War rubbed his Oak Park Republicanism up against European socialism. The impact added to his sense of being a man without a political home, a man more opposed to fascism than socialism but distrustful of all government. The experience also provided him with character types, themes, and images that would appear regularly in his fiction to the very end of his life. Jake Barnes's journalism (*The Sun Also Rises*), the socialist subtext in *A Farewell to Arms*, Harry's story of Constantinople in "The Snows of Kilimanjaro," Colonel Cantwell's return to the site of his first wound (*Across the River and into the Trees*), and the Paris streets of *A Moveable Feast* are firmly rooted in Hemingway's Toronto journalism.

While covering the Lausanne Peace Conference in the early winter of 1922, Ernest asked Hadley to join him for a vacation at Chamby. Packing up most of her husband's Paris fiction, including the novel begun in Chicago, Hadley booked a seat on the night train to Switzerland. While buying mineral water at the station, she left her luggage unattended in her compartment. She returned to find that a thief had stolen the valise containing Ernest's writing. In tears, she arrived in Lausanne to face him with what he later reconstructed as one of his most painful experiences. Evidence now indicates that it was less traumatic than he remembered, for he apparently did not immediately return to Paris to check with the police or the station's lost-and-found; nor did he post a meaningful reward. Shortly after he returned from Paris to Chamby, Hadley became pregnant, and they began talking of his moving back to a full-time newspaper job in Canada.

Despite the loss of his unfinished novel, Hemingway was not deeply discouraged about his creative future. Two of his best new stories—"My Old Man" and "Up in Michigan"—were not lost, and Hemingway was committed to be part of Bill Bird's inquest into the state of contemporary letters, a project begun by Ezra Pound to publish modernist prose. In January 1923 six of his poems appeared in *Poetry* magazine; in February Robert McAlmon agreed to publish a limited edition of Hemingway's poems and stories. By March Hemingway had produced six vignettes, which he sent to Jane Heap's *Little Review*, where, with another of his poems, they were published the following October. In August, two weeks before their ship sailed for Canada, McAlmon's edition of *Three Stories & Ten Poems* appeared in the Shakespeare and Company bookstore, and Hemingway finished the last short sketches that would complete his book that Bill Bird was to publish as *in our time* (1924).

Returning to Toronto, Hemingway expected to be welcomed as the *Star*'s foreign correspondent. Instead he found himself working with a new editor, who generally disliked prima donnas and particularly disliked Hemingway. No sooner did Ernest report for work than he was put on the night train to Kinston to cover the prison break of four convicts, including the bank robber Red Ryan. Two years later, while making notes for a novel, Hemingway vowed to write a picaresque novel about Ryan's escape from prison. "It will be the story of a tough kid," he said, "lucky for a long time and finally smashed by fate" (Princeton).

Although he never wrote the Red Ryan novel, his next fiction—the unpublished and unfinished "A New Slain Knight"—has a criminal breaking from custody and a central character who is a professional revolutionary with criminal tendencies. In *To Have and Have Not*, Hemingway gave us the fishing guide turned criminal in Harry Morgan, who is gut-shot while killing three Cuban bank robbers. Many of his male characters live lives apart from the social norm, men without family, without homes; lonely, self-reliant men; men not so distantly related to Red Ryan.

Hemingway's first son, John Hadley Nicanor, was born that October in Toronto while Ernest was returning from another out-of-town assignment. Furious with his editor, with Toronto, and with his inability to write for two masters—himself and the *Star*—Hemingway quit his last full-time job in January 1924; he, Hadley, and their son returned to Paris that same month to live on her small trust fund and whatever money he could make writing. They found an inexpensive, cold-water flat above a sawmill, close to Ezra Pound's apartment and near the heart of Montparnasse.

With Ezra Pound as his mentor, Sylvia Beach as his friend, and Gertrude Stein as his surrogate mother and godmother to his son, Hemingway was as well connected as a young writer could be. Pound convinced him to work as an unpaid assistant for Ford Madox Ford, who was then publishing the short-lived but important *Transatlantic Review*. From that vantage point, Hemingway connected with every expatriate American writer in Paris. Through Gertrude Stein's salon, he fell in love with Cezanne's landscapes and met young painters on the rise—Juan Gris, Joan Miró, and Pablo Picasso. At Sylvia Beach's bookshop and lending library, he extended his education and his circle of acquaintances, including George Antheil, Adrienne Monnier, Archibald MacLeish, and James Joyce.

Outwardly confident, vibrant with energy, interested in everything and anyone, and laughing and joking among his café friends, young Hemingway became a featured attraction along the Americanized Left Bank of Paris. Continuously moving with his curious, slow-footed gait, he was a man on his way somewhere else, always. He was six feet tall, broad shouldered, mustached, and handsome, a man who set his own style. Whatever the activity—hunting, fishing, walking, or writing—he was intense and competitive. Whether it was the bullfights at Pamplona, the ski slopes at Schruns, or an evening at a Paris dance hall, the Hemingway experience always demanded unexpected emotional resources. Few of his male friendships lasted longer than five years, but to whatever he touched in those days he added scale and a sense of importance. Yale-educated American painter Gerald Murphy said, "The lives of some of us will seem, I suppose by comparison, piddling. . . . For me, he has the violence and excess of genius."

Between 1924 and 1929 Hemingway rose from an undiscovered writer known only to the expatriate crowd to one of the best-known American writers of his generation. His limited edition publications were followed by *In Our Time* (1925); his breakthrough novel, *The Sun Also Rises* (1926); a second collection of stories, *Men without Women* (1927); and his first war novel, *A Farewell to Arms* (1929). Thanks to his lifelong New York publisher, Charles Scribner's Sons, he worked under the forgiving eye of editor Max Perkins, who seldom changed anything Hemingway wrote. During this period, although Hemingway spent his summers in Spain following the bullfights and his winters in Switzerland skiing, Paris remained his base of operations. His newfound success was not without its costs. In April of 1927 Hadley divorced him, allowing him to marry, in May, Pauline Pfeiffer, with whom he had begun an affair more than a year earlier. In their divorce settlement, he gave Hadley lifelong rights to all of the income from *The Sun Also Rises*.

In 1928 Ernest and Pauline returned to America for the cesarean birth of his second son, Patrick. During this visit they discovered the then-isolated pleasures of Key West fishing and Wyoming dude ranches. After spending most of 1929 in and out of their Paris apartment, in 1930 the Hemingways moved back to Key West, where Ernest began writing his vade mecum and explanation of the bullfight, *Death in the Afternoon* (1932). On 1 November 1930, while driving John Dos Passos from their Wyoming hunting trip into Billings, Montana, to catch the east-bound train, Hemingway, confused by the lights of an approaching car, swerved sharply on a newly graveled road and ended up in the ditch; his right arm was badly broken. While he recuperated in Billings, the sale of the film rights to *A Farewell to Arms* brought him a $24,000 windfall. During the Great Depression the Hemingways were supported by Pauline's trust fund; by gifts from her wealthy uncle, Augustus Pfeiffer, who paid for their home in Key West and their African safari; and by income from Hemingway's writing. For the last thirty years of his life, that income was richly supplemented first by Hollywood and later by television. During his lifetime, the sale of movie rights for five of his novels and numerous short stories gave him an independence enjoyed by few American writers.

Hemingway experimented freely with genre, voice, and subject matter, going ten years (1929–1939) before writing anything like a traditional novel. *Death in the Afternoon*, with its multiple voices, its stories within the narrative, and its factual framework, was a book before its time. Unclassifiable, it was and remains largely ignored by Hemingway critics but is pilfered freely for its pithy quotes. In 1933 Hemingway published his third collection of short stories, *Winner Take Nothing*, followed two years later by his seminonfictional account of his 1933 African safari, *Green Hills of Africa* (1935). Mixing humor, flashbacks, literary pontification, and self-exposure with his fable on aesthetics, Hemingway once again wrote outside the reception range of the critics. In 1936 he published his most experimental short story, "The Snows of Kilimanjaro," which contained a collection of vignettes similar to those of *in our time* embedded in a larger story. Written in tandem with what was to become his most popular short story, "The Short Happy Life of Francis Macomber," Hemingway presented, among other things, two contrasting views of American men and women.

During this period (1933–1936) he was also writing a series of personal essays, called "Letters," for the newly founded *Esquire* magazine. This forum allowed him to create a public persona that became as well known as that of many movie stars. His subject matter was himself in situ: Africa, the Gulf Stream, Paris, Spain, Cuba, Key West; wherever his interests took him. The voice was personal and frequently humorous, combative, or prophetic. In September 1935 he warned his audience about the next war, which he said would begin within two years. In September 1937 he was in Madrid reporting on the Spanish Civil War.

That October, Hemingway was on the cover of *Time* magazine, and his last experimental work from the Key West years, *To Have and Have Not*, was published to tepid reviews. What had begun as two stories about Harry Morgan, a Key West fishing guide and rumrunner, expanded in the planning stage to be a complex novel comparing a Cuban revolution with a parallel revolution in Spain. The book he intended to write was abandoned, the revolutions were reduced to a whisper, and the remainder was cobbled together as well as he could manage.

Hemingway was under self-imposed pressure to reach the war and to find a safe haven for his recently begun affair with 29-year-old Martha Gellhorn. With Pauline confined to Key West with their two sons—Gregory had been born in 1931—what safer place to conduct a love affair than Madrid under siege? There he covered the war for the North American News Alliance and the short-lived *Ken* magazine. He also contributed a narrative to the film *The Spanish Earth* and wrote his only play, *The Fifth Column* (1938).

In February 1939, with his marriage to Pauline essentially over, Hemingway took his fishing boat, the *Pilar*, to Havana, where, living in his favorite room in the Hotel Ambos Mundos, he began writing what would be received as his finest novel, *For Whom the Bell Tolls*. In April Gellhorn rented and made habitable a property outside of Havana, "La Finca Vigia," where she and Hemingway set up their writers' workshop. He worked steadily on his Spanish Civil War story of an American dynamiter, Robert Jordan, and his epic task of destroying a bridge behind Republican lines. She, who had seen almost as much of Spain as had he, wisely chose to write instead about her recent stay in Prague as it prepared to face the approaching Nazi invasion.

On 24 December 1939 Hemingway left his empty Key West house for the last time as Pauline's husband. Taking with him eight hundred books and his personal belongings, including several paintings by Miró, Fernand Léger, and Juan Gris, he moved permanently into La Finca. In Europe, Hitler's blitzkrieg had overrun Poland; the war Hemingway had predicted had begun, but America was not yet a part of it. That March, Martha's new novel, dedicated to Ernest, was published as *A Stricken Field*, the title taken from a pseudo-medieval quote written for her by Hemingway. That same month *The Fifth Column*, rewritten to make it work onstage, opened in New York to mixed reviews.

At the end of July 1940 Hemingway delivered his completed typescript of *For Whom the Bell Tolls* to Max Perkins. The novel appeared on 21 October to ecstatic reviews; four days later Paramount Pictures offered Hemingway $100,000 for the film rights. In early November Pauline's divorce suit against her husband on grounds of desertion was granted, leaving Hemingway free to marry Gellhorn a few weeks later.

Although the last two decades of Hemingway's life produced seven volumes of fiction and nonfiction, these years remain the murkiest and the least understood by his literary biographers. The first five years of this period were subsumed by Hemingway's various war efforts. Cuba, ruled by dictator Fulgencio Batista, was a haven for spies and intelligence agencies of every stripe. When Germany declared war on the United States in December 1941, German submarines operated freely up and down the Atlantic Coast and throughout the Caribbean, sinking freighters and oil tankers at will. In 1942 Hemingway organized a group of amateurs he called the Crook Factory to gather intelligence on German operatives, which he passed on to the American ambassador. The details of this operation remain buried in government archives. By July 1942 Hemingway was running Nazi submarine patrols with his fishing boat, which was rigged with machine guns and explosives. After several sightings but no contact, Hemingway took himself off the *Pilar*'s roster in November.

Drinking heavily and arguing with his new wife, Hemingway was suffering through the longest hiatus he had ever experienced in his writing career. Since finishing *For Whom the Bell Tolls* thirty months earlier, he had written nothing but an introduction to *Men at War* (1942). During this same period Martha published a short-story collection, *The Heart of Another* (1941), and began her next novel, *Liana* (1944), which she finished in June 1943. All that year and into 1944 Hemingway stayed in Cuba, where he returned to his self-appointed submarine patrols and wrote nothing. At the end of 1943 Martha left the Finca to cover the European war for *Collier's* magazine; she urged her husband to come with her. He brooded alone at the Finca, where his typewriter continued to gather dust until 1945. At the peak of his career, the foremost American male novelist went six years without writing any new fiction. Only later would students of his work recognize this hiatus as the onset of the severe depression that eventually would destroy Hemingway just as it destroyed his father before him. By this point, the Hemingway-Gellhorn marriage was finished in all but name. In April 1944 Hemingway signed on as a war correspondent for *Collier's*, displacing Martha; by the end of May he had met Mary Welsh Monks, soon to be his fourth wife, and Martha had closed the door behind her.

Between June and December 1944 Hemingway explored the European war with manic energy, deliberately putting himself in dangerous situations. On D-Day, 6 June, rather than observe the Normandy landing from the relative safety of the correspondents' ship, Hemingway went aboard a landing craft to get a closer view. The result was his essay "Voyage to Victory," which remains vintage Hemingway:

I saw a ragged shell hole through the steel plates forward of her pilothouse where an 88-mm. German shell had punched through. Blood was dripping from the shiny edges of the hole into the sea with each roll of the LCI. Her rails and hull had been befouled by seasick men, and her dead were laid forward of her pilothouse. (*By-Line*, p. 351)

At the end of that month he flew twice on Royal Air Force missions intercepting German rockets headed for England. In July he was attached briefly to George Patton's Third Army before transferring to Colonel Charles "Buck" Lanham's Twenty-second Regiment of the Fourth Army. By August, when *Collier's* published "London Fights the Robots," Hemingway was leading a small group of French irregulars and unattached GIs toward the liberation of Paris and the Ritz Bar.

In and out of Paris all that fall, Hemingway alternated between the battlefields of France and the bedroom of the Ritz Hotel, where his affair with Mary Welsh Monks was proceeding as well as the war effort. When he was not sick with colds and sore throats or suffering from recurring headaches from a severe concussion he sustained in London, Hemingway was by turns brave, gentle, obsessive, foolhardy, loving, and brutal: a man surfing on the crest of his manic drive. That fall *Collier's* published two of his essays, "Battle for Paris" and "How We Came to Paris." In October a U.S. Army court-martial cleared Hemingway of conduct forbidden to correspondents as noncombatants, conduct such as carrying weapons, shooting Germans, and behaving like a field officer. Under oath, Hemingway lied about his field activities prior to the liberation of Paris, lies for which he suffered deep remorse.

On 15 November 1944 Hemingway rejoined Lanham's Twenty-second for nineteen days of the bloodiest fighting of the war. On the German-Belgian border, in rolling, thickly forested hills cut by muddy logging roads, the German defense had prepared thick bunkers and thousands of mines. Heavy artillery zeroed in on all crossroads. Fighting in snow and winter mud, both sides suffered incredible losses; 33,000 Americans were casualties of the action they called Hurtgenwald. Here Hemingway verifiably killed a German soldier who was charging across the clearing toward Lanham's command post.

Sick, weary, his speech slurred from concussion, and his memory temporarily damaged, Hemingway had seen enough of the war. He returned to New York and then to Cuba, where Mary Welsh Monks joined him in May. The following month Hemingway wrecked his car, cutting Mary's face while breaking four of his ribs and reinjuring his head. That summer of 1945, as the war on both fronts came to an end, Hemingway began putting his writing life back together, working on what he said would be his "trilogy." In September he filed an uncontested suit for divorce from Martha on the grounds of her desertion. In November a $112,000 sale of movie rights to two short stories provided him the financial freedom to write without pressure to publish.

In March 1946 Hemingway and Mary Welsh Monks, both recently divorced, were married in Havana. By mid-June he claimed to have finished one thousand pages of a new novel; by December he said it was twelve hundred pages but would not be finished for several months. The first seven months of 1947 Hemingway remained in Cuba, writing steadily through March. In June Max Perkins died suddenly in New York; in August, Hemingway, morose, overweight, and with his ears buzzing, was diagnosed with high blood pressure. From this point to his death, he was to fight a holding action against hypertension, diabetes, depression, paranoia, and perhaps hemochromatosis—many of the same problems that led to his father's suicide and would, years later, lead to his younger brother's suicide.

The Hemingways spent the fall and winter of 1947, as they frequently did, hunting game birds in and around Ketchum, Idaho. Returning to Cuba in February, Hemingway continued writing on what may have become *Islands in the Stream*. Because the bulk of his writing during these later years was unpublished by the author, and because he seems to have been working simultaneously on what were later treated as discrete texts that he saw as a trilogy (*Islands*, *Garden of Eden*, and *A Moveable Feast*), nothing definitive can yet be said about the work from this period. It is becoming increasingly evident, however, that these three posthumous texts, mixing fact and fiction, engage thematically the role of the artist in modern times and have at their core, for good or ill, the experience of Paris in the 1920s. It was to be a trilogy unlike any other, bringing to closure the experiments begun in Paris twenty-five years earlier.

From September 1948 through April 1949 Ernest and Mary lived in northern Italy, principally Venice and Cortina, and visited sites from Hemingway's first war. Nostalgic returns to previously good places—Italy, Pamplona, Africa, Paris—became a feature of Hemingway's later years, and each return was less than happy. In Italy, between duck hunting in the Venetian marshes and skiing in the Dolomites, Hemingway became infatuated with eighteen-year-old Venetian beauty Adriana Ivancich. Mary tolerated her husband's behavior with what grace she could manage. Before they returned to Cuba at the end of April, Hemingway had begun the story of a Venetian duck hunt.

For six months at the Finca, Hemingway, having put aside his trilogy, used the duck-hunt story as a framing device for a novel, *Across the River and into the Trees* (1950). Aaron Hotchner, acting as Hemingway's sounding board and agent, negotiated an $85,000 price for the novel's serial rights. Hemingway took Mary, Hotchner, and the manuscript back to Paris, where he finished the story in a hotel room at the Ritz. Just before Christmas 1949, the group drove through the south of France, revisiting, among other places, Aigues Morte and Grau-du-Roi, where Ernest and Pauline once honeymooned. The Hemingways spent two months in Venice before returning to Paris and eventually to Cuba in early April. There Hemingway revised the book galleys for *Across the River*; in September the courtly love story of the dying American colonel and the teenage Venetian beauty received overwhelmingly negative reviews. By the end of 1950, Ivancich and her mother were visiting at the Finca, where Hemingway finished *Islands in the Stream* and may have begun *The Old Man and the Sea*. Mary, reduced to household drudge and the object of her husband's ridicule, wanted out of her marriage but did not act on it.

Fifty-one years old, sicker than most knew, and eleven years without a successful novel, Ernest Hemingway seemed to have reached the end of his career. Would-be biographers and scholars were in general agreement that this was the end of the line. Meanwhile, in a two-month burst of writing, Hemingway completed the first draft of *The Old Man and the Sea* and returned to add Thomas Hudson's last sub chase to the *Islands* manuscript, which he declared finished in May 1951. What was looking like a banner year turned to sorrow when Grace Hall-Hemingway died at the end of June and Pauline Hemingway, after a violent phone argument with Ernest, died unexpectedly in October. These two losses were followed by Charles Scribner's mortal heart attack in February 1952.

Each of these deaths diminished Hemingway's reserves but contributed to his art in ways that a writer can feel but not explain, refueling what seemed to be exhausted supplies. No matter how much he claimed to have hated his mother, he was ever the dutiful son, caring for her financially, writing occasionally, and telephoning her regularly. At the heart of him, he could not avoid seeing her face in his mirror. In March he began a story, "The Last Good Country," in which the mother stoutly stands up to authority in defense of her son. Pauline's death, coming on the heels of his Grau-du-Roi revisit, took him back to the *Garden of Eden* manuscript. Charles Scribner's death may have been the hardest of all to bear, for with him Ernest lost his last father surrogate to whom he could take his work seeking approval. At fifty-two and about to receive his greatest public adulation, Ernest Hemingway was more alone than he had ever been in his life.

Life magazine, having paid $40,000 for the serial rights, published and sold five million copies of its 1 September 1952 issue containing *The Old Man and the Sea* in its entirety. Book-of-the-Month Club bought the novella, and Scribners sold out its 50,000-copy first run. Critics and readers delighted in the simple, moving story of an old fisherman's losing battle with sharks over the carcass of his giant marlin. In early April 1953 a film crew arrived in Havana to begin filming Hemingway's pocket-sized epic. In May, Hemingway was awarded the Pulitzer Prize for fiction, which had been denied to *For Whom the Bell Tolls*.

In June, with a sizable advance from *Look* magazine to do a series of articles on a return safari to the Serengeti, Ernest and Mary left Havana for Europe and eventually Africa. Beginning with the Pamplona feria, Hemingway returned for the first time since 1933 to the Spanish bullfight circuit, which he and Mary followed for a month. By September they were in Kenya on safari, which did not end until 21 January, when Ernest treated Mary to a small-plane trip to see Africa from the air. Two days later at Murchison Falls, the plane struck a telegraph wire and crash landed. Newspapers worldwide headlined Hemingway's death. Soon afterward, the Hemingway party, bruised but alive, boarded another small plane, which crashed in flames on takeoff. More death notices appeared, but Hemingway again survived, badly injured internally and with serious burns. The couple returned to Venice to recuperate until Ernest was ready to drive back to Spain in May. In June 1954 they departed Europe for Havana, where on 28 October Ernest received news that he had been awarded the Nobel Prize for Literature, but he could not make the trip to Stockholm because of poor health.

From 1955 to 1961 Hemingway's life alternated between ever-shortening cycles of euphoric writing and paranoia-ridden depression. His weight rose and fell alarmingly; his hypertension worsened. Medication for his blood pressure exacerbated his depressions. The public did not see his vulnerability, but close friends became increasingly concerned. Yet, when his health did not prevent him, Hemingway wrote steadily on his trilogy. *Garden of Eden* expanded in several drafts, and he was now working alternately on *A*

Moveable Feast. This pattern continued well into 1958. In January 1959, when the Batista government was brought down by the Castro revolution, Hemingway bought a house in Ketchum, Idaho, where he could safely watch the revolution, for which he had a good deal of sympathy.

During the summer of 1959 Hemingway returned to Spain to cover for *Life* magazine the *mano-a-mano* bullfights of the young Ordóñez and the veteran Dominguín. All that summer and into the fall, Hemingway's behavior became more erratic, unpredictable, and uncontrollable. His mood shifts frightened Mary and bewildered his male friends. That winter and into the next year, Hemingway worked on his contracted 10,000-word feature for *Life* magazine. By May 1960 he had written 120,000 words, which he asked Hotchner to edit. *Life* paid $90,000 for the shortened version but printed only part of it.

When Hemingway insisted on returning to Spain during the summer of 1960, Mary remained in New York. From Spain he wrote her plaintive letters about his fears of cracking up. That November, under the care of his Ketchum doctor, Hemingway entered the Mayo Clinic to be treated for hypertension, enlarged liver, paranoia, and severe depression. He received extended treatments of electroshock therapy before being released in late January 1961. By the end of April, after two suicide attempts, he was back at Mayo for more electroshock. Discharged on 26 June, he was driven back to Ketchum, where he soon brought his story to its seemingly inevitable, sad conclusion. On the morning of 2 July Hemingway slipped two shells into his favorite shotgun and quite deliberately blew the top of his head away. He was survived by three wives, three sons, numerous rumors, five unpublished books, and a distinguished if frequently misunderstood body of work. In *Death in the Afternoon*, the character of the Old Lady is told that all stories, if followed far enough, end sadly and that no true writer would tell you otherwise. The words could have been put on Hemingway's tombstone.

In his junior year notebook at Oak Park and River Forest High School, Hemingway recorded his boy's hopes for the future:

I desire to do pioneering or exploring work in the 3 last great frontiers[:] Africa[,] southern central South America[,] or the country around and north of Hudson Bay. I believe that the Science, English and to a certain extent the Latin that I am now studying in high-school will help me in this object. I intend to specialize in the sciences in college and to join some expedition when I leave college. I believe that any training I get by hiking in the spring or farm work in the summer or any work in the woods which tends to develop resourcefulness and self reliance is of inestimable value in the work I intend to pursue. I have no desire absolutely to be a millionaire or a rich man but I do intend to do something toward the scientific interests of the world. (John F. Kennedy Library)

He read it over, and then he signed it: Ernest M. Hemingway—a binding contract with himself made on that first day of spring, a contract he kept with the world as well as he was able.

Hemingway never enrolled at college, but he never gave up his studies in natural history, ichthyology, or unencumbered spaces. His language studies broadened: Italian, French, Spanish, and a smattering of German. He never got to Hudson Bay or South America, but he took his readers with him to Africa, the heart of which beats deep within his writing in ways not always obvious. He studied trout streams in several countries, studied Gulf Stream marlin, studied Spanish bulls and African game. He studied the flight of birds, the bends of rivers, and the flow of country. But what he studied first, last, and always was that strange animal, his fellow man, rampant in his natural setting. Like his mother, Hemingway was an artist; like his father, he was a natural historian. Like both, he found his calling in Oak Park.

Like neither parent, however, he was a child of the twentieth century, born too late for the frontier and too soon for outer space, leaving only that dark country within himself and his readers to explore. He responded to every pressure of his time, recording its progress and aging as it aged. His life seemed to embody the promise of America: with good fortune, hard work, talent, ambition, and a little ruthlessness a man can create himself in the image of his choosing. As a young man in Paris, Hemingway dedicated himself to his writing, and he let nothing interfere with his goal. He created a public persona to match his prose, becoming the person he wanted to be. Like that of other self-made Americans, however, Hemingway's invented self was a mask that he wore with less and less ease as he grew older. Despite his public image, despite his raucous life and several wives, and despite the critics who turned on him, he left stories and novels so starkly moving that some have become a permanent part of the American cultural inheritance.

Before he turned twenty-five Hemingway was a friend of James Joyce, Ezra Pound, and Gertrude Stein and had written most of the stories to be published as *In Our Time*. Before he was thirty he had buried his father and written two of the best novels to come from his generation, *The Sun Also Rises* and *A Farewell to Arms*. At thirty-eight he reported the Spanish Civil War to neutral Americans. At forty-four he reported on the Normandy invasion from a landing craft off Omaha Beach. At forty-six he married his fourth wife. At fifty-three he won the Pulitzer Prize for fiction. At fifty-four he survived two plane crashes in Africa. At fifty-five the Nobel Prize was his. His legacy includes several of the finest short stories written in the twentieth century, at least three—possibly four—major novels, and an example of a writer's life carried out on an epic scale. His style has, at some point, influenced most American writers of the twentieth century. That he self-destructed affirmed his humanity; that he wrote as well as he did promises his permanence.

• Hemingway's letters and papers are located in several repositories, the most important of which is the Hemingway collection at the John F. Kennedy Library (Boston). Other significant collections are at Princeton, the University of Texas, the University of Virginia, Stanford University, the University of Illinois, the University of Delaware, and the Hemingway Museum in Oak Park. Hemingway's texts are available through his publisher, Charles Scribner's Sons, including *Dateline Toronto* (1985), *By-Line: Ernest Hemingway* (1967), and *Ernest Hemingway, Selected Letters* (1981). A helpful analysis of Hemingway's journalism is Robert O. Stephens, *Hemingway's Nonfiction* (1968). The most reliable guide to Hemingway studies up to 1974 is Audre Hanneman, *Ernest Hemingway, a Comprehensive Bibliography* (1967), and *Supplement* (1975). Several single-volume biographies exist, the most comprehensive but most general of which is Carlos Baker, *Ernest Hemingway: A Life Story* (1969). Other useful one-volume biographies include Matthew Bruccoli, *Fitzgerald and Hemingway: A Dangerous Friendship* (1994); Scott Donaldson, *By Force of Will* (1977); Kenneth Lynn, *Hemingway* (1987); James Mellow, *Hemingway: A Life without Consequences* (1992); and Jeffrey Meyers, *Hemingway, a Biography* (1985). Hemingway family memoirs also are numerous: Gregory Hemingway, *Papa* (1976); Leicester Hemingway, *My Brother, Ernest Hemingway* (1962); Marcelline Hemingway Sanford, *At the Hemingways* (1961); and Mary Hemingway, *How It Was* (1976).

Three volumes of Michael Reynolds's comprehensive five-volume biography are in print: *The Young Hemingway* (1986), *Hemingway: The Paris Years* (1989), and *Hemingway: The American Homecoming* (1992). Two more volumes are forthcoming. See also Reynolds, *Hemingway's First War: The Making of* A Farewell to Arms (1976), *Hemingway's Reading* (1981), and *Hemingway: An Annotated Chronology* (1991).

MICHAEL REYNOLDS

HEMMENWAY, Moses (15 Sept. 1735–5 Apr. 1811), Old Calvinist and Congregational minister, was born in Framingham, Massachusetts, the son of Ralph Hemmenway, occupation unknown, and Sara Haven. He was tutored by his uncle Phineas Hemmenway before entering Harvard College (B.A. 1755; D.D. 1785; D.D., Dartmouth, 1792). In 1759, after pulpit supply work in Massachusetts and New Hampshire, Hemmenway became the minister at the Fourth Congregational Church in Wells, Maine. He was ordained in 1759 and remained at Wells until his death. In 1762 he married Mary Jeffords, the daughter of his predecessor, Samuel Jeffords. The Hemmenways had eleven children. Unlike most of his peers, Hemmenway was a staunch Whig during the Revolution. During his tenure at Wells, he attended the Constitutional Convention in 1788, where he labored for its ratification.

In the 1760s Hemmenway emerged as a leader of the "Old Calvinists"—a general term for ministers whose moderate Calvinism provoked the wrath of strict followers of Jonathan Edwards, known as the "New Divinity Men." Hemmenway valued the writings of the standing orthodox theologians Francis Turretin, John Owen, and Edwards. However, as an "intellectualist" in debt to the commonsense philosophy taught at Harvard, Hemmenway broke with Edwards over questions of church membership. In *Seven Sermons, on the Obligation and Encouragement of the Unregenerate, to*

Labour for the Meat Which Endureth to Everlasting Life (1767) and *Vindication of the Power, Obligation and Encouragement of the Unregenerate to Attend the Means of Grace . . .* (1772), Hemmenway repudiated the position that only those who made a public profession of saving faith could partake of the Lord's Supper. He rejected the New Divinity claim that people could have such certainty of their standing; instead he urged a credible profession of faith, some evidence of "actual fitness for communion," and "no known bar in the way" as the only qualifications for access to the sacrament. The New Divinity spokesman, Samuel Hopkins of Newport, Rhode Island, responded to *A Vindication*, and Hemmenway completed the exchange with *Remarks on the Rev. Mr. Hopkin's Answer* in 1774.

As an outgrowth of his support for liberal church membership and his opposition to the rising number of Baptists in the area, Hemmenway championed infant baptism in *A Discourse on the Nature and Subjects of Christian Baptism* (1788). His regard for children led him to write *Discourse to Children* (1792), in which he celebrated Christ's love for them. Hemmenway's *Discourse Concerning the Church* (1792) continued his debates with the New Divinity Men. In a reply the next year, Nathanael Emmons of Franklin, Massachusetts, argued that none but the truly converted ought to partake of the Lord's Supper. In 1794 Hemmenway responded arguing that many of New England's founders had held liberal views on church membership. Although liberals generally welcomed his position on church membership, Hemmenway was critical of some liberal trends, such as Arianism, Socinianism, and Unitarianism. He died at Wells.

• Sermons by Hemmenway are included in the Sermon Collection of the Library of Congress. Hemmenway's career is discussed in W. B. Sprague, *Annals of the American Pulpit*, vol. 1 (1857), pp. 541–47, and John L. Sibley, *Sibley's Harvard Graduates*, vol. 13 (1873–1975), pp. 609–18.

STEPHEN CROCCO

HEMMINGS, Sally. *See* Hemings, Sally.

HEMPEL, Charles Julius (5 Sept. 1811–24 Sept. 1879), homeopathic physician, was born in Solingen, Germany. Little is known of his parentage and early life. After completing his college education, Hempel was compelled to take the Prussian military examination, which he passed, enabling him to defer service until age twenty-four. He took the opportunity to study at the Collège de France and the University of Paris, supporting himself by translating. He attended lectures by chemist Joseph Gay-Lussac, physician François Broussais, and Jules Michelet. Hempel lived with Michelet's family for six months while assisting the historian with his *Historie de France*.

Americans attending the lectures encouraged Hempel to emigrate to America, and he did so in 1835. Shortly thereafter he spent two years with the family of a Signor Maroncelli and became intimate with other members of the Carbonari who had sought asylum in

America. He returned to translating, greatly influenced by the revolutionary and literary thought of the Carbonari. He later became associated with David E. Sickles, Parke Godwin, Charles Henry Dana, John Bigelow, and other noted scientific and literary figures. Hempel was particularly influenced by Albert Brisbane, a social theorist, and Swedenborgian theologian George Bush. He became an ardent Swedenborgian and in 1840 published, in German, *Christianity and Civilization*, and *Life of Christ: The True Organization of the New Church as Indicated in the Writings of Emmanuel Swedenborg and Demonstrated by Charles Fourier* appeared in 1848 and reflected the views of Brisbane, an advocate of Fourier's utopian philosophy.

Hempel began to admire the new system of homeopathic medicine in early boyhood. This school, which treated disease by administering drugs that caused similar syndromes in the healthy, had become extensively practiced in Europe after success against cholera epidemics. The new school of medicine had a few practitioners in New York, among them John F. Gray, with whom Hempel became acquainted. With Gray he edited *The Homoeopathic Examiner* in 1843. Two years later he received an M.D. from the University of the City of New York. His thesis, *Eclecticism in Medicine*, was published in 1845 by William Radde, for whom Hempel was to work for many years as a translator and editor of European homeopathic literature. After graduating, Hempel began translating from German the major works of Samuel Hahnemann and other leading homeopaths. Errors in his early translations, particularly in Johann G. Jahr's *Symptomen Codex* and Hahnemann's *Chronic Diseases*, brought Hempel into conflict with many in the profession, notably Constantine Hering and Adolph Lippe.

Hempel's *Homoeopathic Domestic Physician* was published by Radde in 1846, with French and German editions in 1854. It reveals a preoccupation with the drug aconite, which, one British reviewer claimed, Hempel thought would cure all the ills of humanity. His later college teaching was once referred to as "hobbyism" for its focus on this drug.

From 1846 to 1870 Hempel translated twenty-five major works in addition to his busy practice, teaching, and writing of journal articles, books, and nonmedical works. His translations were often enriched with additions from other authors and from his own experience, earning him the title of the "father of homeopathic literature" in America. Still, he was criticized by Hering and Lippe for his renderings of Hahnemann and Jahr's works, especially for the unauthorized addition of his own views. In 1848 Hering and Lippe devoted the journal *Homoeopathic News* to expounding on the errors in Jahr's *Codex*. In 1854, when Hempel's own *Organon of Specific Homoeopathy* appeared, Lippe charged that the book promoted free love and that most of the few copies printed went to the paper mill unsold; however, this was Hempel's only work to be found in print late in the twentieth century.

Hempel married Mary Calder of Grand Rapids, Michigan, in 1855, and the next year moved from New York to Philadelphia to chair the department of materia medica and therapeutics at the Homeopathic Medical College of Pennsylvania (now the MCP-Hahnemann School of Medicine). He began to teach his divergent views rather than the methods of Hahnemann and his followers.

In 1859 Hempel's *A New and Comprehensive System of Materia Medica and Therapeutics* was published, elaborating his theories, some of which—such as the use of the strongest doses for "provings" (drug tests on the healthy)—he presented as the minority report of the Central Bureau of the American Institute of Homeopathy that year. His arguments were dismantled by Carrol Dunham, a leader of the more fundamentalist wing of the school. Hempel held to his views, however, clashing particularly with Lippe, throughout his career. He authored another book on philosophy, *Homeopathy—A Principle in Nature*, in 1860.

After the death of his father-in-law, Hempel moved to Grand Rapids in 1861 to manage the estate. He soon built a large and lucrative practice. In June 1866 the homeopathic physicians of Michigan petitioned the regents of the University of Michigan for a chair of homeopathic materia medica at Ann Arbor, recommending that Hempel fill the position. Lippe sent an influential politician some Canadian newspaper accounts of Hempel's inept expert testimony in a murder trial, thwarting Hempel's appointment. Subsequently he chaired materia medica at the Central Michigan Homeopathic Institute at Lansing, which held only one session, in 1871.

In 1870 Hempel went to Europe for ophthalmic consultations for his failing vision. By 1874, however, progressive paralysis and failing sight—results of a spinal injury—confined him to his home, and in two years he became an invalid, totally blind. Still lucid, he dictated to his wife the manuscript of his last work, *The Science of Homoeopathy* (1874; 2d ed., 1876). With the aid of Hugo Arndt, he was able to revise *Materia Medica and Therapeutics* before his death at Grand Rapids. Arndt saw the work through the press in 1880–1881.

The acknowledged father of homeopathic literature was also homeopathy's most misunderstood individual. From his early life freedom of thought was dear to Hempel, perhaps leading him to deviate from Hahnemann's teachings, leading to condemnation by most homeopaths even in the late twentieth century. Hempel classified drugs into physiological groupings, thereby destroying the strict individualization required by homeopathy; he defended the use of palliatives, including morphine, which could confuse symptoms and prevent accurate prescribing; he defended the use of massive doses and alternation of medicines; and he was long criticized for his errors in translation. Nonetheless, Samuel Jones, professor of homeopathic materia medica at Ann Arbor, stated, "No Paul more completely *felt* his mission, and Hempel gave his very life to homeopathy" (*Medical Publisher's Record*, Jan.

1884). Hempel felt the law of homeopathy to be a universal natural law, and this conviction, along with his coloring of homeopathic principles with the theology of Swedenborg, alienated many in his profession. His practical efforts, however, led to a resolution by the American Institute of Homeopathy in 1868 and began the process of standardization of homeopathic medicines that resulted in 1897 in a homeopathic pharmacopoeia, which became official in 1938. The dissemination of homeopathic literature, however imperfect, and the official recognition of the homeopathic pharmacy can be credited to his efforts. His physiological basis for the study of drugs lends a perfect counterpoint to what some see as the idealism of Hahnemann's method. Many of his translations continued to be used throughout the world into the late twentieth century.

• A list of Hempel's works, with the exception of *The True Organization of the New Church* (1848), is found in Thomas Lindsley Bradford, *Homoeopathic Bibliography of the United States, 1825–1891* (1892). Egbert Cleave, *Biographical Cyclopedia of Homoeopathic Physicians and Surgeons* (1873), offers a complete biography to that date. Bradford's *History of Hahnemann Medical College and Hospital of Philadelphia* (1898) and William Harvey King's *History of Homoeopathy and Its Institutions in America* (1905) give ample biographies. A short review of his life appeared in *Medical Advance* 5 (1878): 440–41. The *Medical Publisher's Record* 1 (1884) carries an insert of reviews of the third edition of Hempel and Arndt's *Materia Medica and Therapeutics*. Hempel's views on the theory and practice of medicine are discussed in Harris L. Coulter, *Divided Legacy: A History of the Schism in Medical Thought*, vol. 3: *Science and Ethics in American Medicine, 1800–1914* (1982). Obituaries are in the *Detroit Post and Tribune*, 26 Sept. 1879; *American Institute of Homoeopathy Transactions* 33 (1880): 150–52; *British Journal of Homoepathy* 38 (1880); *Medical Advance* 7 (1879): 378; *Homoeopathic Times* 7 (1879): 185; and *North American Journal of Homoeopathy* 28 (1880): 441–48.

CHRISTOPHER D. ELLITHORP

HEMPHILL, John (18 Dec. 1803–4 Jan. 1862), jurist and U.S. senator, was born in Chester District, South Carolina, the son of the Reverend John Hemphill and Jane Lind, both of Scotch-Irish descent and of the Presbyterian faith. Raised primarily by his father after his mother's death, and by his stepmother Mary Nixon after 1811, young John attended local schools before enrolling at Jefferson College (now Washington and Jefferson College) in Pennsylvania. In 1825 he graduated second in his class and returned to South Carolina, where he taught in various classical academies. After a few years he abandoned teaching to take up the study of law and in 1828 entered the office of D. J. McCord, a prominent attorney in Columbia. A year later the two of them established their own practice in Sumterville.

The youthful Hemphill took a vociferously partisan role in his state's growing crisis over slavery and nullification. In 1831 he began to write newspaper essays for the *Sumter Gazette* and soon became one of the most prominent proslavery, pronullification voices in local politics. The next year he became embroiled in a two-month-long debate over nullification with another local newspaperman, with whom he eventually brawled in front of the Sumter courthouse. Later that year Hemphill became editor of the *Gazette* and took an oath swearing to enforce John C. Calhoun's Ordinance of Nullification. Hemphill's partisan editorials continued to arouse opposition, and in 1833 he dueled with a local merchant using smooth-bore pistols and received a wound on the hand that scarred him for the rest of his life. In 1836, with characteristic zeal, Hemphill headed off to Florida to fight the Seminole Indians but returned home within a few months after taking ill in the Florida swamps.

In 1838 Hemphill left his home state for new opportunity on the Texas frontier. After settling in a tiny village called Washington, along the Brazos River, he received a license to practice and opened up his law office. According to Texas lore, however, Hemphill immediately went into seclusion to learn both the Spanish language and Spanish civil law, which was at that time still in general operation throughout the republic. Because of his intense study of Spanish and Spanish law, Hemphill was regarded highly for his legal learning. In January 1840, after only a two-year residence in the republic, President Mirabeau B. Lamar appointed him judge for the fourth district of Texas. Eleven months later, after further impressing his countrymen by disemboweling a Comanche chief during a famous fracas known as the Council House Fight, Hemphill succeeded Thomas J. Rusk as the chief justice of the Republic of Texas. In two short years Hemphill's career had soared. No longer known more for his journalistic diatribes than his legal abilities, he had simultaneously earned distinction as a studious lawyer, brave warrior, and community leader.

During his eighteen years as chief justice, Hemphill made a number of significant contributions to Texas law. He deeply admired Spanish civil law and frequently incorporated Spanish principles into his decisions. Although in 1840 the Congress of the Republic enacted legislation establishing the common law in Texas, both as a framer of the new state constitution of 1845 and as chief justice Hemphill continually advanced civil law principles, most evident in two areas: debt and rights of married women.

Hemphill favored the expansion of the homestead exemption for debtors, an idea with deep roots in Spanish and Mexican law. He helped to incorporate an exemption provision into the state constitution that protected the homestead of a family from "forced sale" for payment of debts. He then broadly applied this constitutional guarantee by expanding the value of the property eligible for exemption and by applying the provision to all inhabitants of Texas, not just heads of families or citizens of the state. Hemphill also vigorously championed the property rights of married women. He failed to convince his fellow delegates at the constitutional convention that Texas's already liberal civil law–based protections for married women needed to be expanded to include the right to control separate property. Nevertheless, even after the state passed legislation in 1848 specifically conferring on husbands the power to manage their wives' separate property, Hemphill used the constitution's ambiguous language to carve out exemptions that expanded the rights of married women. At a time when many states passed married women's property laws simply for purposes of debtor relief, Hemphill's crusade to allow women greater control over their property was significant.

While Hemphill handled the majority of the court's cases involving debtors, homestead exemption, and marriage, he wrote almost no opinions in cases regarding slaves, and his statements about slavery, aside from his early journalistic pronouncements, were few. Still, Hemphill apparently embodied southern orthodoxy when it came to sectional politics, for in 1858 the Texas legislature sent him as a consensus candidate to replace the Unionist-leaning Sam Houston in the U.S. Senate. There Hemphill delivered a passionately prosecession speech in January 1861, which was later circulated throughout the South. After Texas left the Union later that winter, he resigned his Senate seat to join the Confederate Congress and to help write the Confederate Constitution and compile a digest of laws for the new nation, but he declined appointment as Confederate judge for the District of Texas. Hemphill did not live to witness the future of the Confederacy, for he died in Richmond less than a year after the start of the Civil War.

Hemphill never married, but there is compelling evidence that he had a slave mistress, named Sabina, as well as two mulatto daughters whom he enrolled in the abolitionist-run Wilberforce University in Ohio. Hemphill's personal life may help to explain not only why contemporaries frequently described him as "reclusive" but also why he wrote so few opinions in slave cases. At the same time, though not unique among advocates of slavery, the existence of Hemphill's slave family certainly makes paradoxical his devotion to the Confederate cause.

Yet, Hemphill's life was full of incongruities. From a South Carolina past characterized by a volatile mix of passions and politics, Hemphill earned a reputation as a learned authority in Spanish law and acquired the nickname "the John Marshall of Texas." Despite an undistinguished early career, Hemphill became arguably the most important legal figure in nineteenth-century Texas.

• The Hemphill Family Papers (Duke University Special Collections Department, Durham, N.C.) and the John Hemphill Papers (South Caroliniana Library, Columbia) both contain useful bits of information about Hemphill, although neither is a substantial collection of his letters. The best source of information about Hemphill is his judicial opinions, found in *Dallam's Decisions* (1840–1844) and the *Texas Reports* (1844–1858). A book-length nonscholarly treatment of Hemphill is Rosalee Morris Curtis, *John Hemphill: First Chief Justice of the State of Texas* (1971). See also James P. Hart, "John Hemphill—Chief Justice of Texas," *Southwestern Law Journal* 3 (Fall 1949): 395–415. A substantive obituary is in the *Richmond Enquirer*, 10 Jan. 1862.

TIMOTHY S. HUEBNER

HEMPHILL, Joseph (7 Jan. 1770–29 May 1842), lawyer, judge, and congressman, was born in Thornbury Township, Chester (later Delaware) County, Pennsylvania, the son of Joseph Hemphill and Ann Wills, prosperous Quaker farmers. Hemphill attended West Chester preparatory school. In 1791 he graduated from the University of Pennsylvania at Philadelphia, afterward studying law. He was admitted to the bar in 1793. The same year Hemphill's father died, bequeathing to Joseph his entire estate. Hemphill magnanimously divided the inheritance among his brothers and sisters in the belief that he could make a respectable living. In 1806 he married Margaret Coleman, daughter of Robert Coleman, one of the richest iron manufacturers in Pennsylvania; the couple had two sons.

Hemphill's political career began in 1797 with his election to the state assembly. During his three-year tenure he helped resolve the Wyoming Controversy, a land dispute between Connecticut and Pennsylvania. He also secured the passage of the first state law authorizing the erection of a poorhouse.

Hemphill emerged on the national scene in 1800 with his election to the U.S. House of Representatives as a Federalist. He gave an impressive first speech in opposition to the repeal of the Judiciary Act, which had created the system of circuit courts and had broadened the jurisdiction of the federal courts. Hemphill argued that the resolution of too many court cases depended upon the prior expansion of the judicial system and any effort to reduce its size was inexpedient. That this was his only speech earned him the nickname "Single-Speech Hemphill." In 1804 Hemphill moved to Philadelphia to resume his law practice. One year later he won reelection to the state legislature and assisted in the reorganization of the judiciary.

Despite the virulent partisanship of the time, Hemphill was held in high esteem by both his Federalist allies and the Democratic Republicans. In 1811 Governor Simon Snyder, a staunch Democratic Republican, appointed Hemphill the first president-judge of the district court for the city and county of Philadelphia. To accept this appointment, he retired from the state legislature after nearly six years of service. In 1817 Hemphill was recommissioned as president-judge, but poor health and weak eyesight forced him to resign two years later.

After a hiatus of nearly twenty years, Hemphill was reelected to the House of Representatives from Philadelphia in 1819; there he opposed the expansion of slavery into Missouri. He also argued that Missouri's discriminatory treatment of free blacks and mulattoes was unconstitutional. The same year Hemphill was appointed chairman of the committee on the slave trade. In 1821 he coauthored a report with Charles Fenton Mercer of Virginia on the enormities of the African slave trade. The report received international recognition when the *Edinburgh Review* eulogized it as an important step in raising awareness about the continuing issue.

While in Congress, Hemphill supported the establishment of a national system of internal improvements funded and constructed by the central government. He advocated a federal transportation network of roads and canals to facilitate the political and economic development of the growing nation. Hemphill speculated that "the shores of the Great Lakes would one day be dotted with some of the richest cities in the nation."

Hemphill also served on a congressional committee to continue the construction of the Cumberland Road in 1822. He helped secure the passage of the General Survey Act in 1824, which authorized funding for topographical surveys of projects conducted by the Army Corps of Engineers. One year after its passage, Congress funded the construction of its first canal project, the Chesapeake and Ohio Canal. Three years later the Corps completed surveys of possible routes for two national roads. Both roads were to begin at the nation's capital, one extending northward to Buffalo, and the other southward to New Orleans.

In 1829 Hemphill was reelected to the House of Representatives as a Jacksonian Democrat. One year later he introduced legislation for the most ambitious transportation improvement considered by Congress up to that time—a 1,500-mile road extending north-south from Buffalo to New Orleans by way of the nation's capital. The legislation, Hemphill declared, "will hold out full assurance that national improvements are intended to be prosecuted by the General Government." The bill was defeated. Jackson's open rejection of a federal program of transportation improvements, shortly thereafter, left Hemphill bitter toward the president he had once supported. Although he did not run for reelection to Congress in 1831 he was reelected instead to the Pennsylvania state assembly, where he continued his struggle for state sponsored internal improvements.

After his retirement from political life in 1832, Hemphill engaged in porcelain manufacturing, but the business failed in 1834. He died in Philadelphia.

• Hemphill's papers are at the Chester County Historical Society, West Chester, Pa. Biographical sketches are included in Gilbert Cope and H. G. Ashmead, *Historical Homes and Institutions and Genealogical and Personal Memoirs of Chester and Delaware Counties, Pennsylvania*, vol. 1 (1904), and J. S. Futhey and Gilbert Cope, *History of Chester County, Pennsylvania* (1881). Other sources include Sarah Dickson Lowrie, *Strawberry Mansion: The House of Many Masters* (1926), and the *Edinburgh Review* (Oct. 1821): 50–51. The *Register of Debates*, 21st Cong., 1st sess., 1830, covers the debate on the Buffalo-Washington-New Orleans Bill. *House Report* 59, 16th Cong., 2d sess., 1821, contains the report on the slave trade. An obituary is the *North American and Daily Advertiser*, 30 May 1842.

PAMELA BAKER

HENCH, Philip Showalter (28 Feb. 1896–30 Mar. 1965), physician, was born in Pittsburgh, Pennsylvania, the son of Jacob Bixler Hench, a preparatory school teacher, and Clara John Showalter. In 1916 he received a B.A. from Lafayette College and enrolled in the University of Pittsburgh Medical School. When the United States entered World War I the next year he enlisted in the U.S. Army with the intention of serving with the Medical Corps but was assigned instead to the Medical Enlisted Reserve Corps so that he could continue his medical studies. After receiving his M.D. from Pittsburgh in 1920 he interned at St. Francis Hospital in Pittsburgh, and in 1921 he became a fellow at the Mayo Foundation for Medical Education and Research, part of the University of Minnesota Graduate School in Rochester, Minnesota.

In 1923 Hench joined the Mayo Clinic as a first assistant in medicine and was promoted to associate two years later. In 1926, the year before he married Mary Genevieve Kahler, with whom he had four children, he was made chief physician of its newly established department of rheumatic diseases and began studying disorders such as rheumatism and arthritis that cause inflammation of the muscles and joints. In 1929 he returned to Mayo from conducting postgraduate research on rheumatic fever at the German universities of Freiburg and Ludwig-Maximilians and was appointed instructor of medicine at the foundation. There he devoted the bulk of his research effort to diagnosing and treating rheumatoid arthritis, a chronic and painful condition that often results in deformed joints and that at the time could be neither cured nor treated.

Hench received an M.S. in internal medicine from the University of Minnesota in 1931 and was promoted to assistant professor in 1932. In the course of his investigations he noted that arthritic pain diminished considerably to the point of disappearing completely in arthritic patients who also suffered from jaundice, a condition characterized by yellowish skin that is caused by too much bilirubin, the yellowish pigment in bile, in the blood. In 1934, the year before he was promoted to associate professor, he hypothesized that bilirubin contains a "substance X" that relieves the pain of arthritis, but his efforts to prove this hypothesis by administering bilirubin to his patients failed. In 1938, after observing the temporary remission of arthritis in twenty pregnant women, he realized that the blood of patients with these two seemingly unrelated conditions contain unusually high amounts of steroids, organic compounds synthesized from cholesterol that play important roles in a number of physiological activities.

Shortly thereafter Hench began collaborating with Edward C. Kendall, a biochemist at the foundation who had recently isolated and identified the chemical structure of six steroids produced by the adrenal cortex. After Hench tried unsuccessfully to relieve arthritic pain by administering one of these compounds, he and Kendall in 1941 decided to proceed with an experiment involving "Compound E." The experiment was delayed by the extreme difficulty involved in producing sufficient amounts of the compound and by American involvement in World War II; from 1942 to 1946 Hench, a lieutenant colonel in the Army Medical

Corps, served as chief of medical service at Colorado's Camp Carson and as director of the army's rheumatism center at the Army and Navy General Hospital in Hot Springs, Arkansas. In 1948, the year after Hench's promotion to full professor, he and Kendall acquired enough of both Compound E and adrenocorticotropic hormone (ACTH), a hormone produced by the pituitary gland that stimulates the adrenal cortex, to proceed with the experiment. They enlisted the aid of Charles H. Slocumb and Howard F. Polley, two Mayo Clinic physicians, and began testing the effects of both substances on patients whose arthritic conditions were so severe that they were confined to bed. The results of the experiment demonstrated that, although neither substance was capable of effecting a cure, the continued administration of either Compound E, which Hench christened cortisone, or ACTH alleviated the painful symptoms of the disease to a remarkable degree. The magnitude of their effort, discovering a treatment for a hitherto untreatable disease, resulted in Hench and Kendall sharing with Tadeus Reichstein, the Polish-Swiss biochemist who had duplicated independently Kendall's work with steroids, the 1950 Nobel Prize in physiology or medicine.

Hench was a founding member of Ligue International Contre le Rheumatisme and the American Rheumatism Association and served as president of the latter organization in 1940–1941. He also served as secretary of the American Committee for the Control of Rheumatism from 1931 to 1938, chief editor of *American Rheumatism Reviews* from 1932 to 1948, consultant to the army's surgeon general from 1946 to 1957, chairman of the National Institutes of Health's arthritis and rheumatism study section from 1949 to 1950, and member of the National Institute of Arthritis and Metabolic Diseases' advisory council from 1950 to 1953. He was awarded the Heberden Society of London's Medal in 1942; the American Public Health Association's Albert Lasker Award in 1949; the American Pharmaceutical Manufacturers Association's Scientific Award, and the Passano Foundation's Award in Medical Science in 1950; special citations from the American Rheumatism Association and the Regents of the University of Minnesota, the Northwestern University Centennial Award, and the Masonic Foundation for Medical Research and Human Welfare's Award of Merit in 1951; and the Mississippi Valley Medical Society's Honor Award in 1952. He was made a senior consultant at the Mayo Clinic in 1953 and retired in 1957. He died while on vacation in St. Ann's Bay, Jamaica.

Hench's primary contribution to the development of medicine involved the application of the adrenal hormones as pain relievers. Although modern-day synthetic steroids do not produce the undesirable side effects of either cortisone or ACTH and for the most part have taken their place, it was the work of Hench and his collaborators that initiated the development of these synthetics and made possible the treatment of a variety of previously untreatable conditions.

• Hench's papers are located in the Archives of the Mayo Clinic in Rochester, Minn. A biography is "Philip S. Hench," *Nobel Prize Winners*, ed. Tyler Wasson (1987), pp. 433–35. Obituaries are in the *New York Times*, 1 Apr. 1965, *Nature*, 19 June 1965, and *Arthritis and Rheumatism*, Aug. 1965.

CHARLES W. CAREY, JR.

HENDERSON, Alice Corbin (16 Apr. 1881–18 July 1949), poet and author, was born in St. Louis, Missouri, the daughter of Fillmore Mallory Corbin and Lulu Hebe. After her mother died from tuberculosis in 1884, Alice moved frequently among family members. Educated in schools in Illinois, Missouri, and Virginia, she became at an early age enamored with the works of Victorian English and American poets. Her first book of poems, *Linnet Songs* (1898), was published by Wind-Tryst Press in a limited edition of fifty copies when she was a junior in high school. These early poems reflect the melancholy moods of nature, homespun sentiment, and the poet's subjective reactions that were standard in the popular verse of that era. Her most influential teacher was Harriet C. Brainard, later the wife of William Vaughn Moody, and an active member of the Chicago arts community.

In the fall of 1899, Alice Corbin entered the University of Chicago. Chest inflammation in the winter of 1902 prompted her move south to Sophie Newcomb College in New Orleans. There she became acquainted with southern black folksongs and traditions, which she subsequently incorporated into her writings. She worked for a time with the *New Orleans Times-Picayune* and then returned in 1903 to Chicago, where she wrote reviews for the *Evening Post* and the *Chicago Tribune*. There she met William Penhallow Henderson, an art instructor from Boston who had traveled widely throughout Europe and the American West. They were married in 1905; their only child was born in 1907.

The couple collaborated on Alice's next work, *Adam's Dream and Two Other Miracle Plays for Children* (1909), for which William supplied the woodblock illustrations. Royalties from that work enabled the Hendersons to tour Europe in 1910–1911. Soon after returning to their home in Lake Bluff, Illinois, Henderson published her translation of *Andersen's Best Fairy Tales*, which featured several of her husband's color lithographs. In 1912 she cofounded *Poetry* magazine, with Harriet Monroe as editor and herself as associate editor. This magazine featured several of her poems, reflecting her painterly sensitivity to light and color. In addition, Henderson is credited with discovering the talents of other young poets published in *Poetry*, including Edgar Lee Masters, Ezra Pound, Robert Frost, and Carl Sandburg. In December 1912 she published her first major collection of poetry, *Spinning Woman of the Sky*. Many of her Imagist lyrics reflect an attempted return to poetry's organic and religious sources, as expressed by the biblical Psalms, classic Greek poets, Italian sonneteers, French symbolists, and Eastern writers. With Harriet Monroe she edited the anthology *The New Poetry* (1917), which included some of her own writings as well as poems by Frost, Sandburg, T. S. Eliot, Wallace Stevens, and other contemporaries.

While helping her husband finish his commissioned murals in the cold, damp environment of Frank Lloyd Wright's Midway Gardens in 1915, Henderson fell seriously ill. Diagnosed as having tuberculosis and given only one year to live, she and her family hastily made plans to move to the drier climate of New Mexico, where they arrived in March 1916. Following treatment at Sunmount Sanitarium in Santa Fe, she regained her health and was completely won over by the desert mountain landscape and its native inhabitants. The Hendersons purchased a house on Santa Fe's Telephone Road, which William soon rechristened Camino del Monte Sol. However, she retained her position as associate editor of *Poetry* magazine until 1922. In Santa Fe, the Hendersons raised horses and in 1919 added a studio. While her husband launched his career as an architect, furniture maker, and painter of southwestern themes, Henderson experienced a literary rebirth, as New Mexico's natural and cultural surroundings gave her new inspiration and brought about dramatic changes in her writing. Spanish-American motifs, Indian life and ceremonies, and her love for the land itself figured prominently in what is considered her finest volume of poetry, *Red Earth* (1920).

Like those of her contemporaries in the growing Santa Fe and Taos colonies, Henderson's aesthetic viewpoints contrasted sharply with traditional, mainstream American perceptions of the West as a virgin wilderness to be "tamed"; instead, she envisioned it as a masterless, fragile, ecological system, "primal and liberating." She vehemently defended the New Mexico artist colonies against charges of "bolshevism" brought on in the wake of the 1919 "red scare." In 1926 she compiled *The Turquoise Trail: An Anthology of New Mexico Poetry* (1928), which was a community effort to promote the new genre. She also wrote the foreword to Mary R. Van Stone's *Spanish Folksongs of New Mexico* (1928). Another volume of Henderson's poems, *The Sun Turns West*, appeared in 1933. Her *Brothers of Light: The Penitentes of the Southwest* (1937), which her husband illustrated, was the first sympathetic, supportive study of that mysterious and often maligned religious sect. In addition, Henderson collaborated with Mary Morley to produce a collection of children's songs, *A Child's Bouquet* (1935). In the late 1930s she also served as editor in chief of the New Mexico project for the American Guide Series. As always, she published her poetry under her maiden name and her prose under her married name.

The demands of her household and various community activities occupied much of Henderson's time. She was on the executive committee of Writers' Editions, founded as a cooperative effort in 1933 by the Santa Fe colony to provide more publication opportunities for regional writers during the depression. In addition, Henderson was one of the founders of the Exposition of Indian Tribal Arts, which promoted the production and exhibition of Native-American art. Over the years she befriended the Navajo and Pueblo tribes and collected from them native ceramics that were subsequently purchased for the Indian Arts Fund of Edgar L. Hewitt's Laboratory of Anthropology in Santa Fe. In 1941 she chaperoned eight young Tewas on a tour to New York City, where they performed tribal ceremonial dances at its Institute of Modern Art. Overall, she provided leadership in the formation of several literary and civic enterprises beneficial to Santa Fe.

Henderson's wide correspondence advertising the region's natural charm and beauty drew several nationally known writers such as Witter Bynner and John Gould Fletcher to northern New Mexico. The Henderson home on Camino del Monte Sol became a popular gathering place for authors to read poetry, essays, and synopses of novels for peer evaluation; often it was the scene of the annual Poets' Roundup, held to raise funds for the New Mexico Association on Indian Affairs. Even after her husband's death in October 1943, Henderson and her daughter continued as a sustaining influence in the Santa Fe colony. Her last years were spent at the family's El Cuervo Ranch in the Tesuque Valley, where she died.

• Primary source materials on Alice Corbin Henderson and her central role in the Santa Fe colony may be found in the Zimmerman Library at the University of New Mexico in Albuquerque and at the State Records Center and Museum of New Mexico in Santa Fe. The Hendersons' daughter, Alice Rossin, has continued to maintain her parents' home, studio, and extensive library collection in Santa Fe. See Shelley Armitage, "Red Earth: The Poetry and Prose of Alice Corbin," *El Palacio* 93 (Winter 1987): 36–44; Arrell M. Gibson, *The Santa Fe and Taos Colonies: The Age of the Muses, 1900–1942* (1982); T. M. Pearce, *Alice Corbin Henderson: A New Voice in Poetry*, Southwestern Writers Series, no. 21 (1969); and Lois Rudnick, "Re-Naming the Land," in *The Desert Is No Lady*, ed. Vera Norwood and Janice Monk (1987). Obituaries are in the *Santa Fe New Mexican* and the *New York Times*, 19 Apr. 1949.

H. ALLEN ANDERSON

HENDERSON, Archibald (21 Jan. 1783–6 Jan. 1859), commandant of the U.S. Marine Corps, was born in Colchester, Prince William County, Virginia, the son of Alexander Henderson, a merchant and politician, and Sarah Moore. Raised in northern Virginia, Henderson began his education with a family governess and continued through a series of private academies in Maryland. His father's military experiences in the revolutionary war and subsequent political activities as a state delegate led young Henderson to choose a life of public service. He applied to the Thomas Jefferson administration for an appointment in the marines and received a commission as a second lieutenant on 4 June 1806.

Henderson's early assignments included command of marine detachments on board the frigates *Wasp* and *President* and shore-based command of the marine barracks at Charleston and Boston. He attained the rank of captain within the first five years of service. In that rank, while commanding the marines on board the USS *Constitution*, he distinguished himself during the ship's victorious engagement with the British warships *Cyane* and *Levant*, the final battle of the War of 1812. From this action Henderson received a Silver Medal from Congress, an engraved sword from the state of Virginia, and a brevet promotion to major.

In the fall of 1820 President James Monroe selected Henderson to assume the rank and position of lieutenant colonel commandant in place of the scandal-ridden incumbent, Anthony Gale. Henderson became the fifth commandant on 17 October 1820 but faced immediate threats to the continued existence of his small corps. Internally, many of his senior officers resented his appointment, citing his relative youth (age thirty-seven) and general inexperience in Washington. Externally, Henderson encountered a series of threats from the army, the navy, and a cost-conscious Congress to disestablish the corps. The Washington political leadership also looked askance at the corps's recent scandals of private misconduct and public mismanagement as well as its hybrid mission as "soldiers of the sea."

Henderson responded to these challenges by first putting his own house in order, demanding professional conduct, ethical behavior, and full accountability on the part of all officers and noncommissioned officers in their public and private lives. He then sought out his counterparts in the War and Navy departments and among the military and naval committees of Congress to establish a legitimate operational mission for the Marine Corps. Much of this was codified in the legislation enacted by Congress in 1834 "for the better organization of the United States Marine Corps," which corrected rank and pay inequities, increased personnel levels, and specified equal treatment of shipboard marines with sailors. However, Henderson found himself having to justify the roles and missions of the marines time and again to each new administration. In all, Henderson served under eleven presidents and eighteen secretaries of the navy.

Nothing better personifies Henderson's commitment to professionalism than his swift decision in 1836 to offer to President Andrew Jackson the immediate services of fully half the Marine Corps in support of the U.S. Army's campaign against the Creeks and Seminoles in Georgia and Florida. The commandant underscored this abrupt commitment with a personal flourish, closing down his Washington headquarters to lead his troops in the field. While the campaign itself proved unsatisfactory, the prompt availability of a trained body of marine regulars as a "force-in-readiness" established a tradition of national utility for such missions "as directed by the President." Henderson, for his part, received a brevet promotion to brigadier general. Eleven years later he repeated this offer of a force of trained regulars to President James K. Polk early in the Mexican War (although this time Henderson, by then sixty, remained in Washington).

Henderson also sought to integrate his Marine Corps headquarters within the greater Washington community. As early as 1822 he ordered the commander of the Marine barracks (located at Eighth and Eye streets in Southeast Washington continuously since 1803) to conduct parades, reviews, and band concerts, open to the public, on a weekly basis. In 1823 Henderson married Anne Marie Casenove; they had six children. The couple thereafter hosted a series of military reviews on the grounds, beginning a tradition that continues to this day.

For all his insistence on professionalism, General Henderson was slow to recognize the impact of technology on the naval service. The advent of steamships and rifled cannons obviated the traditional need for marine sharpshooters manning the "fighting tops" of sailing ships. Similarly, improvements in the quality of seamen in the U.S. Navy reduced the historic role of marines as enforcers of discipline on warships. Henderson's counterparts in the fleet urged him to retrain his marines as seagoing cannoneers and landing forces. Indeed, marines executed more than thirty landing operations during the Henderson years, including opposed assaults in Mexico, China, and Sumatra. However, his defining moment as a junior officer had occurred during the 1815 clash of sailing ships, and he rarely mentioned landing operations in his annual reports to the secretary of the navy and did very little to foster the organization, training, and weaponry needed to support an amphibious role for his marines. This was Henderson's major shortcoming. As an immediate consequence, the Marine Corps entered the Civil War two years after Henderson's death with but marginal benefits to offer the Union navy in its massive coastal and riverine operations.

An Election Day riot in Washington in 1857 caused President James Buchanan to call out the marines. General Henderson deployed two companies from the barracks to the mission, then went downtown in civilian clothes to observe the action. Seeing a group of rioters aiming a small cannon at his advancing troops, the 74-year-old commandant, according to several contemporary news accounts, strode to the muzzle, collared the group's ringleader, and helped restore order.

On 2 January 1859 General Henderson presided over a meeting of the Washington National Monument Committee. Four days later he died in Washington. He was buried in Washington's Congressional Cemetery in a service attended by the president and his entire cabinet. Henderson's fifty-two years of service as a marine officer and his thirty-eight years as commandant set records of longevity. More significantly, he dedicated his adult life to shaping the Marine Corps as a disciplined, multimission force in readiness, rich in customs and traditions and a distinctly naval service of abiding utility to the nation.

• The best single repository of material on Henderson is the Henderson collection, Reference Section, Marine Corps Historical Center, Building 58, Washington Navy Yard, Washington, D.C. Henderson was a prolific letter writer, and his official correspondence is in the National Archives, Washington, D.C., in RG 80, Navy Department, "Letters from Marines"; RG 127, U.S. Marine Corps, Office of the Commandant, "Letters Sent," "Orders Issued and Received," and "Miscellaneous Records of the Adjutant and Inspector"; and *American State Papers*, vol. 1, *Naval Affairs* (1834). See also Ralph W. Donnelly, "Archibald Henderson, Marine," *Virginia Cavalcade* 20 (Winter 1971); Allan R. Millett, *Semper Fidelis* (1980); Robert D. Heinl, *Soldiers of the Sea* (1962); and Clyde H. Metcalf, *A History of the United States Marine Corps* (1939).

JOSEPH H. ALEXANDER

HENDERSON, Charles Richmond (17 Dec. 1848–29 Mar. 1915), sociologist and minister, was born in Covington, Indiana, the son of Albert Henderson and Loraine Richmond. Henderson received an A.B. from the University of Chicago in 1870 and a B.D. (1873) and a D.D. (1875) from the Baptist Union Theological Seminary. After graduating from the seminary, he was ordained and became the pastor of the First Baptist Church in Terre Haute, Indiana, in 1873. In 1882 he became the pastor of Detroit's Woodward Avenue Baptist Church, where he remained for ten years. He served these churches with distinction.

Henderson's interest in sociology, coming at the middle of his career, stemmed from his personal exposure to the dire urban problems of Chicago while he was a theological student serving as an intern minister to a small stockyards church. An intensely religious man, Henderson came to see sociology as a tool to help better the living conditions of the poor. Henderson felt it was the moral obligation of educated and wealthy people to do something for the less fortunate. While a minister in Terre Haute and Detroit, he had led members of the clergy in various charitable efforts focused on service to those in poverty. Continuing his charitable work, he served as the president of the Twenty-sixth National Conference of Charities (1898–1899) and of the United Charities of Chicago (1913). Henderson became a well-known authority in penology after doing a path-breaking study of prisons and prison management while still a minister. Additionally, he often served as a mediator in social disputes in every community he served, once settling a potentially bitter strike on the Detroit streetcar lines.

Henderson was invited to join the newly opened University of Chicago in 1892 as the university chaplain, an assistant professor of sociology, and the university recorder. He became an associate professor in 1894 and a full professor of sociology in 1897. In 1901 Henderson received his Ph.D. from the University of Leipzig. He was the head of the Department of Practical Sociology at Chicago from 1904 until his death. In addition, he served as the university chaplain throughout his career at the university.

Of primary importance to Henderson was his belief that sociologists must actively utilize their skills and knowledge in service to the community, defined in both a local and global sense. To this end, he often participated in various national and international commissions and task forces that tackled the social problems endemic to modern industrial society. Penology was always one of his major interests; Henderson was a U.S. delegate member to the International Prison Commission in 1909 and the president of the National Prison Association (1901–1902) and the International Prison Congress (1910). He held numerous other state, national, and international posts, including the secretary of the Illinois Commission on Occupational Diseases (1907).

Henderson was a prodigious writer, with more than sixteen books and 100 articles to his credit. He specialized in the areas of penology, industrial insurance, and industrial public policy. Also, as might be expected given his background, he produced interesting books on the sociology of religion. His major works were *Introduction to the Study of the Dependent, Defective, and Delinquent Classes* (1893), *The Social Spirit in America* (1896), *Social Settlements* (1897), and *Industrial Insurance in the United States* (1907). In addition to his writings and community service, Henderson served as the associate editor of the *American Journal of Theology* and the *American Journal of Sociology* (1895), as well as the *Journal of the American Institute of Criminal Law and Criminology* (1911). He died in Charleston, South Carolina.

Henderson is typical of sociology's early pioneers in several respects. His interest in the new discipline of sociology stemmed from his religious beliefs, and he employed sociology's tools and techniques to attempt to rectify the pressing urban problems that characterized Chicago in the early industrial age. While he saw urbanism as a disease and its dwellers as victims of illness, Henderson's religious orientation also led him to emphasize society's obligation to better social conditions. His work helped establish the University of Chicago as one of the premier centers for sociological research. Henderson tirelessly endeavored to use academia's insights to help a suffering humanity.

• Henderson's other works include *Development of Doctrine in the Epistles* (1894); *Social Elements* (1898); "Modern Prison Systems," 57th Cong., 2d sess., H. Doc. 452 (1898); and *Modern Methods of Charity* (1904). An obituary is in the *New York Times*, 30 Mar. 1915.

WILLIAM P. KLADKY

HENDERSON, David (26 Apr. 1853–27 May 1908), journalist and theatrical manager and producer, was born in Edinburgh, Scotland, the son of William Henderson and Elizabeth Bissett. Educated in Edinburgh, Henderson became apprenticed in the printing business at the age of twelve after his parents died. He began his journalistic career working for the *Edinburgh Courant*, a newspaper founded by Daniel DeFoe. Henderson immigrated to the United States in 1871 with his older brother Wemyss, seeking his fortune and a career in the news business. Upon arrival in the United States, Henderson became the news editor of the *Scottish American* and worked there for four years. In 1875 he joined the staff of the *New York Herald* and three years later became the foreign correspondent for the *Chicago Tribune*, covering General Ulysses S. Grant on portions of his world tour. In 1877 Henderson's interest in entertainment led him to become the drama critic for the *Chicago Tribune* and the *Inter Ocean*. He served in this capacity until 1880, when he and partners General John A. Logan, W. D. Eaton, Slason Thompson, and John Ballantyne turned the *Evening Telegraph* into a morning newspaper—the paper they created became the *Chicago Herald*. After two years with the *Chicago Herald*, Henderson became the managing editor of the *Chicago Daily News*.

In 1884, after a little over a year at the *Daily News*, Henderson resigned as managing editor to pursue his interests in theater. He became manager of the newly built Chicago Opera House, which opened with a performance of Thomas Keene in *Hamlet*. In the beginning Henderson was determined to feature famous performers in their own productions; for example, the Opera House hosted Edwin Booth's last performance in Chicago. However, Henderson soon turned to producing his own events. By 1887 he had come to national prominence as a producer and introduced the first of his famous extravaganzas, *The Arabian Nights*. Based on English pantomime, Henderson's shows were elaborate theatrical displays that cost between $30,000 and $40,000 per production—a lavish amount before the turn of the century. *The Arabian Nights; or, Aladdin's Wonderful Lamp*, which opened on 5 June 1887, was called by the *Chicago Tribune* "a gorgeous spectacle" that exceeded all anticipation as hundreds of people were turned away on the sold-out opening night (6 June 1887). The *New York Times* reported that the scenery made for the production was "the finest ever seen in Chicago" (6 June 1887). The production included 120 performers, more than 220 costumes designed by New York designer Wolf Dazian, and innumerable stagehands to operate the elaborate scenery. The show had a lengthy run in Chicago and then went on the road, an amazing feat considering its size.

In the meantime, Henderson matched the success of *The Arabian Nights* with his second extravaganza, *The Crystal Slipper*, a version of the fairy tale *Cinderella*, which opened 12 June 1888. The *Chicago Tribune* praised the performance, writing "a more sumptuous spectacle has never been seen in Chicago—never, indeed, in America—than *The Crystal Slipper* . . . it is glittering without being brazen, it is rich without vulgarity, and both the figures and the masses of color are used, not as ends, but as means to a general artistic effect" (13 June 1888). As with Henderson's previous production, *The Crystal Slipper* played through the fall and then began a nationwide tour while he began preparations to top it in his next production.

According to Eddie Foy, a vaudevillian who earned great success in Henderson extravaganzas, "It was always a mooted question in Chicago, when a new Henderson show was opened, as to whether or not it was better than the last one. . . . so Henderson and his co-workers were kept busy cudgeling their brains and scouring Europe for new ballets, new ideas in cos-tumes, new effects" (*Clowning through Life*, p. 238). He apparently succeeded when *Bluebeard, Jr.* opened on 11 June 1889, with the *New York Times* hailing the production as "the best thing the Chicago Opera House has produced yet, and undoubtedly the best-mounted spectacle ever put on stage in this country" (13 June 1889). *Bluebeard, Jr.* included a wedding scene in which more than 200 performers appeared, half of them in shining armor, and a giant show from which swarmed dozens of children. Henderson spared no expense in making his extravaganzas—the armor was designed and imported from England; the settings and costumes were designed by some of the most famous theatrical artists of the time; Monsieur Bibeyran, a famous European ballet master, choreographed the dances; and Richard Barker, an Englishman who had staged all the Gilbert and Sullivan operettas, directed.

For *Ali Baba* Henderson imported all the costumes from England and the armor from France. The last of Henderson's spectacles, *Ali Baba*, "a series of gorgeous stage pictures, dazzling the eye with their brilliancy and glitter, appealing to the aesthetic sense by their beauty of coloring and delicacy of light effect" (*Chicago Tribune*, 3 June 1892), began its run in June 1892. It played during the World's Colombian Exposition in Chicago, where it became as important for visitors to visit the Opera House as other Exposition events. In spite of warnings from his associates, Henderson spent lavishly on the spectacle, estimating to the *New York Times* a cost of $87,000, which did not include the performers' salaries. Over the next year Henderson ran revivals of previous spectacles, but the nationwide economic slump following the World's Fair hit him hard. During the 1893–1894 season it was estimated that he was losing $7,000 each week. During this slump Henderson also lost many of his star performers, including the popular Foy, because he could not pay what they thought their performances demanded. All told Henderson had lost more than $250,000 in his failing effort to revive interest in his spectacles.

According to critic Burns Mantle, Henderson was not discouraged by his turn of bad luck and was determined to make another fortune. Over the next five years he brought back some of the glory of the spectacles working with John McCaull to stage McCaull's comic opera productions in the Midwest. During the 1895–1896 season Henderson managed the Auditorium Theatre in Kansas City, Missouri, but moved back to Chicago the following season to manage both the Great Northern and the Schiller theaters for one season. In 1901 Henderson moved to New York for one year to manage the Savoy Theatre but returned to Chicago. By this time the disappointments of his failed ventures had broken his spirit, according to Mantle, although "he spoke often of the day that was surely coming when he again would take a hand in the fascinating gamble of amusements and prove to certain conceited youngsters just how a really good man played his hand" (*Chicago Tribune*, 27 May 1908). Just prior to his death, a benefit for Henderson was sponsored by the Chicago Press Club and local managers in appreciation for his achievements. Henderson died in Chicago after a long battle with Bright's disease.

In Henderson's *Chicago Tribune* obituary, Mantle called him "first and last, an American showman. . . . the first American manager to combine a shrewd managerial sense with a reproduction of the London pantomime idea in entertainment and make it pay." Foy, whose career was made through his association with Henderson, called Henderson a "clever, canny Scotchman" (p. 231) and praised him for his nerve in locating his spectacle in Chicago, rather than New York. Herein lies Henderson's importance to the American theater. Henderson stole theatrical attention from New York by producing in Chicago and began a trend that grew over the following decades. The *Oxford Companion to the American Theatre* (1992) credits Henderson with reestablishing Chicago as a theatrical power and initiating a golden age of Chicago theatrical preeminence that lasted until 1916. His extravaganzas set the example for musical theatre and burlesque for more than ten years, enhancing the careers of stars like Foy, May Yohe, Ida Mulle, and Henry Norman.

• David Henderson appears in the *Biographical Encyclopedia and Who's Who in the Theatre* (1981) and in the *Oxford Companion to the American Theatre* (1992). Various clippings in the *New York Times* and the *Chicago Tribune*, and Eddie Foy's autobiography *Clowning through Life* (1928), provide useful information on individual productions produced by Henderson. His obituary is in the *New York Times*, 28 May 1908, and the *Chicago Tribune*, 27 May 1908.

MELISSA VICKERY-BAREFORD

HENDERSON, David Bremner (14 Mar. 1840–25 Feb. 1906), Speaker of the U.S. House of Representatives, was born at Old Deer, Aberdeenshire, Scotland, the son of Thomas Henderson and Barbara Bremner, farmers. In 1846 he immigrated to the United States with his parents. The family first settled in Winnebago County, Illinois; then in 1849 they moved to Fayette County, Iowa, where Henderson worked on the family farm and studied in the local schools. He attended Upper Iowa University until he enlisted in the Union army in 1861. As first lieutenant of Company C, Twelfth Iowa Infantry, he participated in the battles of Fort Henry, Fort Donelson, Shiloh, and Corinth. He sustained a severe injury in the neck at Donelson, and in 1862, at Corinth, he endured a serious leg wound that necessitated partial amputations over the years, requiring Henderson to wear an artificial limb. After working in 1863 as commissioner of the Board of Enrollment of Iowa's Third Congressional District, Henderson reenlisted in the army in June 1864 as colonel of the Forty-sixth Iowa Infantry, serving in this capacity until the close of the war.

Upon the conclusion of the Civil War in 1865, Henderson read law in Dubuque, Iowa, before being admitted to the bar later that year. In 1866 he married Augusta A. Fox; they had three children. During the next several years, Henderson held a variety of positions, including collector of internal revenue for the Third District from 1865 to 1869 and assistant U.S. district attorney for the northern district of Iowa from 1869 to 1871. He was a member of the law firm of Shiras, Van Duzee, and Henderson and later a member of the firm of Henderson, Hurd, Lenehen, and Riesel. Henderson, who chaired several Republican State Conventions, also kept a close eye on Iowa politics. At the Republican National Convention in 1880, he, as chairman of the Iowa delegation, endorsed James G. Blaine for the presidential nomination. Eight years later, at the 1888 Republican National Convention, Henderson functioned as the chief spokesman and manager of the presidential candidacy of Senator William B. Allison of Iowa. When former senator Benjamin Harrison of Indiana captured the presidential nomination that year, Henderson quickly announced his support of the ticket. In a letter to Harrison he revealed his strong partisanship, writing "Your great work will be in seeing to it that every Greek Warrior is in the field and fighting to reduce the modern Troy."

Henderson's twenty years of service in Congress began in 1882 with his election to the U.S. House of Representatives. Representing a primarily agricultural district, he served in the lower chamber from 1883 to 1903. His closest encounter with defeat occurred in 1890, the year of a Democratic congressional triumph, when he won another term with the slender margin of only 198 votes. During his career, Henderson advocated liberal pensions for Civil War veterans, widows, and orphans. He also favored tariff protectionism, railroad safety legislation, laws to curb the growth of monopolies, and rural mail delivery. His committee assignments included Banking and Currency, Militia, and Appropriations.

When Congressman Thomas B. Reed of Maine, Speaker of the House of Representatives, announced his intention in 1899 to retire from politics, Henderson announced his candidacy for the Speakership. He contacted numerous political allies, including Senator Allison and Congressman Gilbert N. Haugen of Iowa, who pledged their support. "From all that I can gather from all points of the compass, if the Iowa delegation is earnest and united we can win the prize," Henderson wrote Haugen. Henderson's efforts culminated in his unanimous election as Speaker in December 1899. The first man from a state west of the Mississippi River and the first Iowan to serve as Speaker, Henderson, a standpat conservative and strict partisan, used his position to issue rulings beneficial to his party. He considered it his duty as Speaker not only to promote national interests but also to serve as the titular head of Republicans in the House.

During Henderson's tenure as Speaker, the House passed several important pieces of legislation. The Gold Standard Act of 1900 declared the gold dollar the standard unit of value, thereby placing all forms of money issued by the government on a parity with gold. This legislation resulted in part from the work in 1899 of a caucus committee on which Henderson played a leading role. In 1901 Congress passed legislation that established a licensing system designed for using water power on public lands. The National Reclamation Act of 1902 allowed money from public land sales in various western states to be earmarked for financing irrigation projects. The Department of Commerce and Labor, an executive department headed by a secretary holding cabinet rank, was created in 1903, and in that same year the Elkins Act strengthened the authority of the Interstate Commerce Commission by providing punishments of railroad officials and shippers for offering or accepting rebates. Also in 1903, in an attempt to reorganize the War Department, Congress established the Army General Staff Corps to prepare and execute military plans.

After President William McKinley's assassination and the elevation of Theodore Roosevelt to the presidency in 1901, Henderson came to be regarded by progressives as a conservative holdover from an earlier time. In September 1902 he stunned the nation with the sudden announcement of his retirement, effective upon the conclusion of his term. Defending his record of having fought for what he believed to be best for the farm, labor, and business interests of his district and state, Henderson justified his decision to retire in a letter to Allison, writing, "I feel a growing repugnance and conviction against the doctrine that free trade medicine will cure the trusts, and cannot permit myself to be a candidate when I know that there is a growing sentiment of that kind in my District among the Republicans."

Although he listed the upsurge of antiprotectionist sentiment in his district as his reason for leaving politics, other factors contributed to his departure from Washington. He had become the target of the progressive reform faction in Iowa led by Governor Albert B. Cummins. Sniping at the Speaker's protectionist tariff views and charging him with drunkenness, progressive Republicans in Iowa had tried unsuccessfully to sidetrack Henderson's renomination in May, but they did succeed in snatching political patronage away from him. Henderson, feeling the effects of poor health, resigned rather than proceed with intraparty squabbling that he concluded would jeopardize his political effectiveness. Moreover, he harbored bitterness at his omission from a tariff conference at President Roosevelt's Oyster Bay home in September 1902. These affronts to his proud character, combined with the pain stemming from his leg surgeries and ill-fitting artificial limb, exhausted his tolerance and diminished his enthusiasm for politics. A man who disliked criticism, Henderson gradually grew more irascible as the demands of the office took their toll.

Prohibition politics also contributed to Henderson's discomfort. Iowa Republicans were torn apart by the passionate and controversial Prohibition issue in the 1880s and 1890s. The matter cut across progressive and conservative lines, divided political allies, and created new coalitions within the party. Henderson personally opposed prohibiting the sale and use of alcoholic liquors as beverages, a position that lined him up

with former Iowa governor Samuel Charcot. Yet in his speeches Henderson tended to endorse the idea of Prohibition. The Prohibitionist element was dominant within the Iowa Republican party, and Henderson had to balance himself carefully on this political tightrope. Like Allison, who had mastered the art of double-talk, Henderson at times issued vague statements that both friends and foes of Prohibition could interpret as favorable to their cause. Nevertheless, this explosive state quarrel and all the commotion kept Henderson ever cautious regarding his political base.

After leaving Congress, Henderson practiced law for a brief time in New York before returning to Iowa. His health declined rapidly over the next two years. He suffered from paresis, a form of insanity characterized by progressive degeneration of the brain. His mental impairment became obvious. Richard P. Clarkson, a prominent Iowa journalist, wrote to Illinois congressman Joseph G. Cannon, the new Speaker of the House of Representatives, describing Henderson's condition: "Poor Col. Henderson has gone down in darkness and gloom—never to rise again. He is an utter imbecile in all respects—cannot even sign his pension checks." Henderson died at Dubuque's Mercy Hospital.

Henderson had been a powerful fixture in the Iowa Republican leadership in the 1890s, culminating in his successful election to Speaker of the Fifty-sixth and Fifty-seventh Congresses. His short tenure as Speaker fell between the longer Speakerships of his predecessor Reed and successor Cannon. In contrast to them, Henderson managed affairs as Speaker in a more businesslike fashion. He chose a middle path, emphasizing his own style, which made him less feared by colleagues than Reed or Cannon. As Speaker, Henderson was less powerful than either Reed or Cannon, and his influence rested mainly upon his character and convictions.

• Henderson left no sizable collection of papers. Most of his extant letters are in the Dubuque County Historical Society in Dubuque, Iowa; the State Historical Society of Iowa at Des Moines; the University of Iowa Libraries at Iowa City; the William Larrabee Papers at Montauk in Clermont, Iowa; and the manuscript collections of contemporaries, especially those of William B. Allison at the State Historical Society of Iowa and Benjamin Harrison, William McKinley, and Theodore Roosevelt in the Manuscripts Division of the Library of Congress. Henderson's speeches are in the *Congressional Record* from 1883 to 1903. The major work on Henderson is Willard L. Hoing, "Colonel David Bremner Henderson: Speaker of the House" (M.A. thesis, Iowa State Teachers College, 1956). An informative article is "David B. Henderson," *Independent* 55 (1903): 651–55. A bibliography of contemporary articles and later studies relating to Henderson's career is in Donald R. Kennon, ed., *The Speakers of the U.S. House of Representatives: A Bibliography, 1789–1984* (1986). Additional insights are in Leland L. Sage, *A History of Iowa* (1974) and *William Boyd Allison* (1956). Obituaries are in the *New York Times* and the *Des Moines Register and Leader*, 26 Feb. 1906.

LEONARD SCHLUP

HENDERSON, Fletcher (18 Dec. 1897–29 Dec. 1952), musician, was born Fletcher Hamilton Henderson, Jr. in Cuthbert, Georgia, the son of Fletcher Hamilton Henderson, Sr., a Latin and mathematics teacher, and Ozie Lena Chapman, a pianist. His middle-class family disapproved of jazz and blues, and Henderson studied piano with his classically trained mother. He graduated from Atlanta University in 1920 with a chemistry degree and then moved to New York City to pursue postgraduate studies. For a short time he was a laboratory assistant in a chemical firm, but with few opportunities for black chemists he became a part-time song demonstrator for the Pace-Handy Music Company. He subsequently worked as house pianist and recording manager for Black Swan Records, where his duties included accompanying Ethel Waters and Bessie Smith and arranging tours for Waters and the Black Swan Troubadours. He married Leora Meoux in 1924; they had no children.

Henderson eventually began to lead his own small groups in engagements at clubs and dances. He successfully auditioned for an opening at the Club Alabam on West 44th Street in late 1923, and the following summer the band took up residence at the Roseland Ballroom, which Henderson used as a base for the next decade. At first, the group was little more than an ordinary dance band, playing watered-down blues and pop tunes. But Henderson also hired the best talent he could find, including Coleman Hawkins on tenor saxophone and Don Redman as musical director. Redman's arrangements in particular had a profound and lasting impact on big band jazz. He separated reed and brass sections and played them off against each other. One section would play the melodic lead, for instance, and the other would answer during pauses, or it would punctuate the playing with brief, rhythmic figures. In the group's recording of "Copenhagen" in late 1924, the music moved from one section or soloist to another twenty-four times in three minutes. Still, the band at this stage played stiffly, with little jazz feeling.

Also in 1924 the group's style took another major step forward when Henderson hired Louis Armstrong. Although Armstrong stayed with the band for only a short while, his lyrical style and propulsive sense of swing strongly influenced Henderson's men, who now began to play with more feeling and a more inventive sense of melody. During the next two years they broke through to become the first great big band in jazz history. Their recording of "Stampede" in May 1926 marks an early peak. Hawkins in particular was vastly improved over his initial recordings, playing with a powerful expressiveness and a rich, full-bodied sound. The trumpeter Rex Stewart contributed fiery solos, while Redman himself was writing fuller, better-integrated section passages. Recordings show the band continuing to improve over the next nine or ten months. Then in March 1927 Redman left to co-lead McKinney's Cotton Pickers. Henderson gradually lost interest in the band, his focus further blurred by an auto accident in the summer of 1928 in which he suf-

fered head injuries. Between 1927 and 1930 the group made only a dozen or so recordings, mostly ponderous efforts that showed a steady deterioration from the advances of 1926 and early 1927.

Henderson's own weakness as a leader proved to be the last straw. In 1929 the band went to Philadelphia to rehearse for a musical review. The director, Vincent Youmans, brought in about twenty white musicians, mostly string players, to augment the band, and he suggested that an outside conductor also be hired. Henderson agreed, and the new conductor began to fire Henderson's players, giving their positions to white musicians. Henderson said nothing. Disillusioned, most of the musicians never worked for him again.

Henderson rebuilt the band, and by 1931 they were recording again. This time the group was more of a showcase for individual players, built on exchanges between the sections and the soloists. The young saxophonist Benny Carter contributed swinging, spare arrangements; Walter Johnson on drums and John Kirby on bass provided strong rhythmic support. Carter's composition, "Keep a Song in Your Soul," is a fine example of the band's playing from this period. In December 1932 the band recorded an arrangement of "King Porter Stomp" that mightily swung, the solos seamlessly integrated with the ensembles. Hawkins's playing was masterful, and he dominated the band for the next two years before leaving for England. Henderson also had become his own arranger, turning to sparer arrangements than Redman's that created a light, unpretentious sound. His tunes were set in unusual keys, and his tempos more consistently swung. The band's 1934 recording of "Wrappin' It Up" perfectly illustrates this style, one which influenced the entire big band era. The piece opens with a call-and-response pattern; as the brass section states a fanfare, the saxophones respond, and the two sections engage in a brief exchange. In the first chorus the saxes state the main theme, and the brasses comment, joined at one point by the trumpets. The pattern continues through the arrangement, creating one of the early swing era masterpieces.

Unfortunately, by this time Henderson had lost much of his drive. He dissolved the group in 1934, and in 1935 he sold the arrangements for "Wrappin' It Up" and several other pieces to Benny Goodman, who used them to help fuel the swing craze of the later thirties.

Henderson's last great band was a 1936 ensemble that included the trumpeter Roy Eldridge. Throughout the 1930s he also maintained a close relationship with his brother Horace, who often served as pianist and arranger for the band and later led an important group of his own. Henderson worked briefly as an arranger for Goodman in 1939, and he failed several times to establish new bands. In 1950 he wrote music for the short-lived New York show *The Jazz Train* and led the accompanying band. He settled in that same year at Cafe Society in New York with a sextet. He suffered a stroke in December and another in 1952, dying from a heart attack in New York City.

Henderson's influence on jazz and particularly on the development of big bands was pervasive and lasting. Although personally withdrawn and lacking leadership qualities, he was a superb judge of talent, an excellent pianist, and an outstanding musician. Through the musical innovations he introduced in his various groups, he profoundly influenced the work of Duke Ellington, Goodman, Count Basie, and other big bands of the swing era, thereby laying an important foundation beam for an entire genre of jazz playing.

• Henderson's personal papers are located at the Amistad Research Center at Tulane University. Further reading should begin with the fine study by W. C. Allen, *Hendersonia: The Music of Fletcher Henderson and His Musicians: A Bio-discography* (1973). The most thorough and perceptive analysis of Henderson's music is Gunther Schuller, *Early Jazz: Its Roots and Musical Development* (1968), pp. 252–79; also see Schuller, *The Swing Era: The Development of Jazz, 1930–1945* (1989), pp. 323–26. Good, brief overviews can be found in James Lincoln Collier, *The Making of Jazz: A Comprehensive History* (1978), pp. 177–85, and Albert McCarthy, *Big Band Jazz* (1974), pp. 64–74. See as well Nat Shapiro and Nat Hentoff, eds., *The Jazz Makers* (1957); Rex Stewart, *Jazz Masters of the Thirties* (1972); J. R. Taylor, album notes to *Fletcher Henderson: Developing an American Orchestra* (1977); and Frank Driggs, *The Fletcher Henderson Story* (booklet accompanying CBS record collection, 1961). Also consult the first few chapters of John Chilton, *The Song of the Hawk: The Life and Recordings of Coleman Hawkins* (1990). An obituary is in the *New York Times*, 31 Dec. 1952.

RONALD P. DUFOUR

HENDERSON, Horace W. (22 Nov. 1904–29 Aug. 1988), jazz and popular arranger, bandleader, and pianist, was born in Cuthbert, Georgia, the son of Fletcher H. Henderson, Sr., a teacher, and Ozie Lena Chapman. He studied piano formally from about age fourteen to seventeen, when he left home to finish high school at the preparatory school of Wilberforce University in Ohio and then attend the university. In 1924 he visited his older brother, bandleader Fletcher Henderson in New York City during summer vacation. On returning, he formed an eight-piece school orchestra called Horace Henderson's Collegians. The band played locally for dances; trumpeter Freddie Jenkins was an early member.

In the summer of 1925 the Collegians traveled to New York City, where Fletcher secured a job for them at the Bamville Club in Harlem. Alto saxophonist Benny Carter joined the band in Pittsburgh, Pennsylvania, on its way back to school and remained with Henderson into 1926 (though Carter did not, as often reported, attend Wilberforce). Following Carter's departure from the band, cornetist Rex Stewart joined, having deemed himself incapable of replacing Louis Armstrong in Fletcher's orchestra. Saxophonists Elmer Williams, Castor McCord, and Ted McCord were also members during this period.

While at Wilberforce Henderson studied music for two years, disappointing his father by earning a bachelor of arts rather than a degree in science. He then followed his brother into a career in music. During these years Henderson borrowed freely from Fletcher's musical library, and his band often worked under Fletcher's name. Carter rejoined the band for a residency at the Savoy Ballroom, beginning in February 1928, and largely took over the band during the summer while Henderson played with bandleader Sammy Stewart in Chicago, Illinois, and on tour in Ohio.

Henderson reorganized his band, now known as the Stompers, in Ohio in October 1928. The group included trumpeter Roy Eldridge, a teenager he had discovered in Pittsburgh. The Stompers toured throughout 1929 with many changes in membership, most notably the replacement of Eldridge by Jonah Jones. The band was routinely billed under Fletcher's name.

Henderson formed a third new band for a ballroom engagement at the Dunbar Palace in New York City from 1930 into 1931. With trombonist Sandy Williams in the band, Henderson's men battled Fletcher's at the Dunbar on 19 October 1930. One published account rated the battle a tie, which attests to the quality of Henderson's ensemble. Apart from his band, he recorded as pianist with the Chocolate Dandies in December 1930 and in Fletcher's big band, which recorded two of his compositions and arrangements, "Hot and Anxious" and "Comin' and Going," in March 1931. After a period of difficulty finding work, Henderson remained as pianist and arranger for his own group but gave the band's direction over to Don Redman for a job at Connie's Inn in Harlem early in 1932. The association with Redman proved uncomfortable, but Henderson remained in the band until the spring of 1933. In November 1932 he played in the pit orchestra at Loew's State Theater in New York as the pianist in Duke Ellington's orchestra, under Ellington's direction.

From about May 1933 to November 1934 Henderson worked with Fletcher's big band as pianist and writer. Under Henderson's nominal leadership, the band recorded several titles on 3 October 1933, but his recorded contributions under Fletcher's name were more significant. These include his 1933 arrangements of "Yeah Man!" "Queer Notions," and "Nagasaki," as well as the original compositions and arrangements of 1934, "Big John's Special" and "Rug Cutter's Swing." After a well-publicized dispute between the brothers, the band appeared under either Henderson's or Carter's direction at the Apollo Theater in November 1934, while Fletcher led a new band at the Harlem Opera House; accounts of this incident are conflicting and unclear.

Henderson supplied a few arrangements to Benny Goodman early in 1935 and joined Vernon Andrade's orchestra during that spring and summer. He rejoined Fletcher intermittently during 1935 and full time in January 1936 at the Grand Terrace in Chicago. The band's big hit of this period—saxophonist Chu Berry's riff tune "Christopher Columbus," recorded in

March—is one of several arrangements credited to Fletcher but claimed by Henderson. Fletcher's biographer Walter C. Allen speculates that the misattribution was made when Fletcher supplied these arrangements to Goodman, who presumed they were Fletcher's own; in an oral history taken for the Smithsonian Institution, Horace gives an account of bringing "Christopher Columbus" into the band after hearing Berry perform it with a small group.

In July 1937 Henderson left to lead his own band for a year at Swingland in Chicago. The band was televised on CBS and expected to embark on a successful tour, but the tour failed because of poor management. During a fourteen-month stand at the 5100 Club in Chicago, Henderson's big band included trumpeter Emmett Berry, tenor saxophonists Dave Young and Elmer Williams, and trumpeter and violinist Ray Nance. (Nance is featured on a February 1940 recording of Henderson's composition "Kitty on Toast," which Nance subsequently brought into Duke Ellington's repertory.) After a brief stay at the Tropical Room in Chicago, Henderson reorganized and improved his group by retaining Berry but otherwise taking over most of Nat Towles's big band. In New York City in October 1940 they recorded an acclaimed but seldom heard session that produced "Smooth Sailing" and "You Don't Mean Me No Good."

Henderson remained in New York from late 1940 into 1941 as house arranger for bandleader and saxophonist Charlie Barnet, for whom he wrote "Charleston Alley" and "Ponce de Leon," recorded by Barnet in 1941. Henderson claimed to have discovered singer Lena Horne at the Apollo Theater in Harlem and to have brought her into Barnet's band; in her autobiography Horne credits Apollo choreographer Clarence Robinson and makes no mention of Henderson, but their stories are otherwise consistent, and it seems plausible that he transmitted Barnet's request to Robinson. Henderson also wrote arrangements for Jimmy Dorsey's big band around this time. Horace served as a substitute in Fletcher's band early in 1942 and returned with his own band to Swingland, renamed the Rhumboogie, only to be drafted into the army in November 1942. As a sergeant in charge of musical activities at Camp Des Plaines in Joliet, Illinois, he directed a 45-piece field band and three dance bands until he was discharged for being over age in August 1943.

Upon his release Henderson rejoined Fletcher, serving as pianist, musical director, and arranger. During this period Jimmie Lunceford's big band recorded his composition and arrangement "Jeep Rhythm" (Feb. 1944). While in California in May 1944, Henderson left Fletcher to form a small group. Horne was grateful for the boost that Henderson had given to her career, and although he occasionally worked with Fletcher on tour from 1945 to 1947, he mainly served as Horne's accompanist, arranger, and road manager for a tour of RKO theaters and army camps and for engagements in Chicago and New York City. At this last venue the stellar band accompanying Horne comprised trumpeter Dick Vance, trombonist

Benny Morton, reed players Edmond Hall and Earl Bostic, pianist Henderson, guitarist Al Casey, bassist Billy Taylor, and drummer Sid Catlett. When Horne left for Europe in 1947, Henderson took a job in Idaho leading a quartet. He led a band that included trumpeter Teddy Buckner in Los Angeles, and in 1949 he replaced pianist Bobby Tucker as Billie Holiday's accompanist.

Henderson was based in Minneapolis, Minnesota, in the early 1950s but then began leading bands regularly in Las Vegas, Nevada, including one featuring trumpeter and singer Clora Bryant. He led small combos and in 1962 briefly tried to revive his late brother's big band in Long Beach, California. He lived in Glendale, California, until about 1964, and then moved to Denver, Colorado, continuing to lead bands. At the time of a 1975 interview he was still playing regularly, but as an electric organist, having taken up the instrument around 1969. In the interview he hotly denied resentment of Fletcher's achievements and charges of his having filched some of Fletcher's scores, as had been reported by Allen and others. He said he idolized his older brother, who had put him through college and freely shared big band arrangements. Henderson died in Denver, survived by his wife, Angell, and a daughter from a previous marriage. Details of his marriages are unknown.

Henderson obviously had a fine ear for talent, to which the careers of Carter, Eldridge, Nance, and Horne testify. Although not a renowned pianist, he played with a better sense of swing than Fletcher—hence his usefulness as a sideman, taking Fletcher's place in many performances—and he was better able to adapt to changing styles. He is most important as an arranger and writer. His own preference was for his arrangement of Coleman Hawkins's composition "Queer Notions," an aptly titled piece that explores whole-tone scales and features an unusual accompaniment based mainly on an oscillation between two dissonant chords. But the eccentricities of this piece are unrepresentative of Henderson's work, which is otherwise firmly based on conventions of the big band era. "Yeah Man!" (1933; recycled as "Hotter then 'ell" in 1934) features perhaps his most memorable use of the classic device of trading an idea between sections of the big band, as the instruments toss back and forth a chord that slides downward. "Big John's Special" is his best-known piece, subsequently made into a toe-tapping anthem of the swing era by Goodman, who presented it in the "Let's Dance" radio broadcasts of 1935, used it as the encore at his celebrated Carnegie Hall concert in January 1938, and recorded a studio version in May 1938.

• Sharon A. Pease surveys Henderson's career and includes a notated musical example of his piano playing in "Horace Henderson's College Band Started Him to the Top," *Down Beat* 7 (1 Sept. 1940): 16, and "Little Smack Has Unique Style on Piano Keyboard," *Down Beat* 12 (1 Jan. 1945): 9. Henderson figures prominently in Walter C. Allen, *Hendersonia: The Music of Fletcher Henderson and His Musicians: A Bio-discography* (1973). Albert McCarthy, *Big Band Jazz*

(1974), traces his activities apart from Fletcher. Considerable additional material is in an oral history from an interview conducted by Tom MacCluskey in Denver in April 1975 for the Smithsonian Institution, which is now housed among the oral histories at the Institute of Jazz Studies in Newark, N.J. Gunther Schuller, *The Swing Era: The Development of Jazz, 1930–1945* (1989), supplies detailed musical analysis of Henderson's writing and recordings. See also Morroe Berger et al., *Benny Carter: A Life in American Music* (1982). An obituary is in the *New York Times*, 16 Sept. 1988.

BARRY KERNFELD

HENDERSON, James Pinckney (31 Mar. 1808–4 June 1858), governor and U.S. senator from Texas, was born in Lincolnton, Lincoln County, North Carolina, the son of Lawson Henderson, a lawyer, and Elizabeth Carruth. He attended Lincoln Academy and then the University of North Carolina at Chapel Hill, studied law, and was admitted to the North Carolina bar in 1829. He returned home to practice law. Henderson quickly emerged to prominence, marked in his militia service by his promotion to major in 1830 and his ultimate rise to the rank of colonel. He moved to Mississippi in 1835 but within the year decided to go to Texas, which at the time was in revolt against Mexico. Henderson helped Memucan Hunt raise a company for service in Texas, then went on to the republic ahead of his men, arriving after the battle of San Jacinto. He received a commission from president of the Republic of Texas David G. Burnet as brigadier general in the Texas army and was sent back to the United States to recruit more volunteers. He raised another company in North Carolina and returned to Texas in November 1836.

When Henderson came back, President Sam Houston appointed him attorney general in his first cabinet in 1836, then at the end of December named him secretary of state. Henderson remained in that position until June 1837, when Houston sent him to Europe as a special envoy to seek the recognition of Texas independence from France and Great Britain and to secure commercial treaties with the European powers. Henderson successfully secured accords that encouraged trade but was unable to obtain recognition of independence until the French signed such a treaty on 25 September 1839. The French treaty made it possible for Henderson to obtain two more treaties from Great Britain, in which that government promised to work for Mexican recognition of Texas independence. In Paris in 1839 Henderson met Frances E. Cox of Philadelphia, and they were married in London that year; they had three children.

The couple returned to Texas in February 1840. Henderson left government service and began practicing law in partnership with Thomas J. Rusk and Kenneth L. Anderson, vice president of the republic during the administration of Anson Jones. In the spring of 1844 Houston, who had been elected president for a second time in 1841, sent Henderson to Washington to assist Isaac Van Zandt in negotiating a treaty to bring Texas into the Union. On 12 April 1844 the two men signed a treaty of annexation with John C. Calhoun, but the U.S. Senate subsequently rejected it. Ultimately the U.S. Congress annexed the republic by joint resolution on 1 March 1845.

Returning to Texas following his success, Henderson was a member of the state constitutional convention of 1845 and in November was elected the first governor of Texas by an overwhelming vote. Much of Henderson's term as governor was spent in the military service. Inaugurated on 19 February 1846, Henderson received permission from the state legislature on 9 May 1846 to command the four Texas regiments sent to join the army of General Zachary Taylor in the Mexican-American War. Only three of the units arrived, and the First Texas Infantry Regiment returned home, but Henderson claimed the rank of major general. His claim was allowed, possibly because Taylor needed cavalry regiments, and he headed what was known as the Texas Division. The Texans played a prominent role in the battle of Monterrey. Along with General William J. Worth and Colonel Jefferson Davis, he negotiated the terms of surrender by Don Pedro de Ampudia, Mexican commander of the city. Returning to Texas, Henderson finished his term of office.

Following the war, Henderson suffered from poor health and decided not to seek reelection. He remained involved in politics, however. In his last message to the legislature he expressed his increasing concern with northern aggressiveness against the South on the slavery issue and called on Texans to join with other southerners to resist. That same year (1847) his longtime friendship with Houston ended over the issue of states' rights, and Henderson became a leader of the anti-Houston group within the state Democratic party. In 1850 his position on the slavery question led the state legislature to send him to the Nashville Convention. The only Texan who attended, Henderson opposed disunion, but he argued for constitutional amendments to gag antislavery petitions, guarantee slavery in the territories and the District of Columbia, and protect the slave trade. A major success for Henderson in the convention was his securing of southern support for Texas's claim to New Mexico, where the federal government was considering organizing a state.

On 9 November 1857 the state legislature elected Henderson to fill the position in the U.S. Senate left vacant by the death of Rusk, his old law partner, but his poor health (probably tuberculosis) continued to limit his activities. Before going to Washington, he traveled to Cuba to try to recover and was unable to take his seat until 1 March 1858. His health problems worsened shortly after taking his seat, however, and he was forced to seek medical treatment in Philadelphia, where he died.

• Henderson's papers are in the archives of the Texas State Library, Austin. The best biography is Robert G. Winchester, *James Pinckney Henderson: Texas' First Governor* (1971). An early biographical account is F. B. Sexton, "J. Pinckney

Henderson," *Quarterly of the Texas State Historical Association* 1 (1898): 187–203. A view of the politics of his gubernatorial administration is in Ralph G. Wooster, "Early Texas Politics: The Henderson Administration," *Southwestern Historical Quarterly* 73 (1969): 176–92.

CARL H. MONEYHON

HENDERSON, John Brooks (16 Nov. 1826–12 Apr. 1913), U.S. senator, was born in Danville, Virginia, the son of James Henderson and Jane Dawson, farmers. He moved with his family to Lincoln County, Missouri, in 1832. Orphaned before the age of ten, he nevertheless obtained a good education from the common schools while he worked on a local minister's farm. At age fifteen he began teaching school in Pike County while also reading law. He was admitted to the bar in 1848 and began his law practice in Louisiana, the Pike County seat. That same year he was elected to the Missouri House as a Democrat. In 1850 he made the first of three unsuccessful runs for Congress (the others were in 1858 and 1860). He served again in the Missouri House in 1857–1858. Having built a successful law practice, he then invested in local real estate and several banks and acquired a small fortune. Henderson served as a James Buchanan presidential elector in 1856, but his opposition to the president's support for proslavery forces in Kansas revealed an independent streak that would later dominate his political career. In 1860 he served as a Stephen Douglas delegate at both the Charleston and Baltimore Democratic conventions and as a presidential elector for the Douglas ticket, which carried Missouri.

In the aftermath of Abraham Lincoln's election, Henderson was chosen as a Unionist delegate to the Missouri secession convention where he served on the federal relations committee, which brought in a recommendation against secession. Upon the outbreak of war he organized a local militia company and was appointed brigadier general by Governor Hamilton Gamble. The unit saw brief service in central Missouri, but Henderson's military career quickly ended when Gamble appointed him to the U.S. Senate on 17 January 1862 to replace the ousted Trusten Polk, who had gone with the Confederacy. That fall the legislature elected Henderson to fill out the term ending in 1863 and a year later reelected him to a full six-year term. Although he was a slaveholder, he supported Lincoln's plan for compensated emancipation in the border states and urged it unsuccessfully in Missouri. In the state convention of 1863 he supported Gamble's plan of uncompensated gradual emancipation to take effect in 1870. He declined to join the Radical wing of the Republican party in Missouri, which now emerged to demand immediate, uncompensated emancipation; but after the Radicals gained control of the state government in the election of 1864, he cooperated with them.

Henderson favored the enlistment of blacks in the Union army, and in January 1864 he introduced the resolution in the Senate that culminated in the Thirteenth Amendment the following year. Although he was generally supportive of Lincoln's policies, he voted for the Wade-Davis Bill, which proposed a stronger congressional role in Reconstruction. Increasingly critical of President Andrew Johnson's leniency toward former Confederates, he voted in 1866 for the extension of the Freedmen's Bureau and the Civil Rights Bill mandating black citizenship. He also favored making the Fourteenth Amendment stronger to specifically include national black suffrage. In mid-March 1866, at the request of Governor Thomas C. Fletcher, Henderson argued Missouri's case before the U.S. Supreme Court in defense of ironclad test oaths for ministers (Cummings v. Missouri). That proscription, which required past as well as future loyalty, had been passed by the Radical state constitutional convention of 1865. He lost the case by a five-to-four vote.

As chair of the Senate Committee on Indian Affairs, Henderson favored policies that would bring about the cessation of hostilities with the Plains Indians and strengthen the reservation system to help the Indians adapt to white culture. In 1867 he served on the Indian peace commission with Generals William T. Sherman and William S. Harney. The group negotiated the treaties of Medicine Lodge and Fort Laramie, which were designed to accomplish the goals of the Indian affairs committee.

In the continuing controversy between President Johnson and Congress that same year, Henderson voted for the Tenure of Office Act, which limited the president's powers to remove federal officials, yet he voted against the Command of the Army Act, which required the president to issue military orders through his general in chief. In the impeachment proceedings against Johnson, Henderson wavered in his decision but finally, as a matter of conscience, believing that the action was politically rather than constitutionally motivated, joined six other Republicans in voting against the president's conviction, thereby helping to save Johnson by one vote. This proved his undoing in Missouri, where the controlling Radical Republicans in state government were staunchly anti-Johnson. In his ensuing attempt to secure a second Senate term in 1868, he was roundly defeated by Carl Schurz. A subsequent attempt against Democrat Francis Preston Blair (1821–1875) also failed. Henderson remained generally aloof from the Liberal Republican split from the Radicals in Missouri in 1870. He worked increasingly thereafter for the reconciliation of both wings of the state's Republican party and in 1872 ran unsuccessfully as its candidate for governor. His final Senate race was in 1873, when he was defeated by the Democrat Lewis V. Bogy. In 1875 Henderson was appointed special federal district attorney to help investigate and prosecute the notorious Whiskey Ring, which was defrauding the government of millions of tax dollars, but he was removed shortly thereafter when President Ulysses S. Grant took offense at certain remarks he had made. In 1884 he chaired the Republican National Convention.

After his defeat by Schurz in 1868, Henderson had returned to his law practice and settled in St. Louis with his new bride, Mary Newton Foote of New York. They had one child. He strongly supported his wife's endeavors on behalf of woman suffrage in the years that followed, as well as her establishment of the St. Louis School of Design in 1876 and the St. Louis Women's Exchange in 1879. They traveled widely and acquired an extensive art collection. Henderson added to his fortune through speculation in local railroad bonds.

Henderson retired from his law practice in 1889 and moved to Washington, D.C., where he spent the rest of his life. He and his wife acquired extensive real estate holdings along 16th Street and developed much of the area along what came to be known as "Embassy Row." He chaired the United States delegation to the Pan-American Congress of 1889–1890, during which he proposed the establishment of a permanent inter-American court to help settle disputes among the nations of the Western Hemisphere. He served as a regent for the Smithsonian Institution from 1892 to 1911. In his later years he wrote extensively on a variety of public issues for numerous magazines. He died in Washington, D.C.

• There are no published biographies of John B. Henderson, but he is the subject of an excellent Ph.D. dissertation by Arthur H. Mattingly, "Senator John Brooks Henderson, United States Senator" (Kansas State Univ., 1971). Biographical sketches are available in J. Thomas Scharf, *History of Saint Louis City and County* (1883), and William Hyde and Howard L. Conard, *Encyclopedia of the History of St. Louis* (1899), which also includes a biographical sketch of Mrs. Henderson. Henderson's relationships within the Missouri Republican party are covered in William E. Parrish, *A History of Missouri, vol. 3* (1973). Henderson discussed his dilemma in the Johnson impeachment trial in "Emancipation and Impeachment," an article in *Century Magazine*, Dec. 1912. His efforts in the Whiskey Ring trials are covered in David P. Dyer, *Autobiography and Reminiscences* (1922).

WILLIAM E. PARRISH

HENDERSON, Lawrence Joseph (3 June 1878–10 Feb. 1942), biochemist and physiologist, was born in Lynn, Massachusetts, the son of Joseph Henderson, a businessman, and Mary Bosworth. Henderson attended high school in Salem, Massachusetts, and graduated from Harvard University in 1898. He received his medical degree from the Harvard Medical School in 1902 and then spent two postdoctoral years in Strassburg in the laboratory of Franz Hofmeister, a pioneer in the application of physical chemistry to biochemistry. Upon returning to the United States in 1904, Henderson joined the Harvard faculty as a lecturer in biological chemistry. He also carried out research in the laboratory of the chemist T. W. Richards. In 1910 he married Edith Thayer, the sister of Richards's wife; the couple had one child.

As Henderson began to teach biochemistry his research interests became more focused on biological problems. In 1908, during the course of his work on the acid-base equilibrium of the body, he developed the mathematical treatment of buffer solutions that still bears his name and that of Karl Hasselbalch, the Danish biochemist who put Henderson's equation into the now familiar logarithmic form in 1916. The Henderson-Hasselbalch equation helped to explain why carbonic and phosphoric acids served so efficiently to preserve neutrality in the body fluids of living organisms.

Henderson was deeply impressed by the fact that the substances that seemed to be mainly responsible for regulating the acid-base balance of the body had almost ideal properties for this task. His research on neutrality regulation led him into broader philosophical speculations about the fitness of the environment for life. Encouraged by philosopher Josiah Royce, his friend and Harvard colleague, Henderson wrote *The Fitness of the Environment* (1913). In this work and its sequel, *The Order of Nature* (1917), Henderson concluded that the chemical elements and their compounds critical for life possessed properties that uniquely favored the evolution of complex physicochemical systems such as living beings, and that this relationship could not be a result of chance. Cosmic and biological evolution seem to be linked in a single, orderly process, and matter and energy apparently have an original property that organizes the universe in space and time. This order cannot be explained in mechanistic terms. The universe, according to Henderson, must be viewed from two complementary points of view, mechanism and "teleology" (a word that the agnostic Henderson used to denote order or harmonious unity rather than design or purpose). Henderson's concept of the fitness of the environment was favorably received by many scientists and philosophers, although his comments on "teleology" were more controversial.

Henderson had historical as well as philosophical interests, and in 1911–1912 he introduced a general course on the history of science at Harvard. In 1916 he played the key role in bringing the noted historian of science George Sarton to Harvard. Henderson was also a founding member and the first president (1924–1925) of the History of Science Society.

In an effort to dissuade Henderson from accepting an offer from Johns Hopkins University in 1920, Harvard promoted Henderson to full professor and created a laboratory of physical chemistry in the medical school for him. He soon turned over the actual supervision of the laboratory, which would make many significant contributions to biomedical science over the next few decades, to his protégé, Edward Cohn. Henderson meanwhile devoted his attention to another project that evolved out of his research on the acid-base equilibrium of the organism, a study of blood as a physicochemical system. He and his co-workers studied the interaction of the variables involved in the respiratory changes of blood and used a device called the nomogram to graphically depict the mathematical relationships between variables. Henderson's research on blood, summarized in *Blood: A Study in General Physiology* (1928), provided an excellent example of biological organization and of what the French physiologist Claude Bernard called the constancy of the internal environment.

In the late 1920s the entomologist William Morton Wheeler introduced Henderson to the work of the Italian engineer-turned-sociologist Vilfredo Pareto. Pareto emphasized the equilibrium of social systems and compared this equilibrium to that of the organism, views that struck a responsive chord with Henderson. Through several seminars he offered at Harvard, and a book on *Pareto's General Sociology: A Physiologist's Interpretation* (1935), Henderson helped to spread the concept of social equilibrium to colleagues and students in sociology and related fields. Among those influenced by his ideas were the Harvard sociologists George Homans and Talcott Parsons.

Henderson also played a key role in the creation of two other important institutions at Harvard in the latter part of his career. In 1927 he was responsible for the establishment of the Fatigue Laboratory in the School of Business Administration. The scope of the research conducted by the laboratory staff extended well beyond the study of the physiology of fatigue itself to include work in respiratory, muscular, environmental, nutritional, and blood physiology. Henderson was also one of the principal founders in 1932 of the Society of Fellows, designed to nurture young men of outstanding promise by providing them with a secure stipend and maximum freedom to pursue their own ideas for a period of three or more years.

Although Henderson's interests were diverse, a fundamental unity emerged in his work. Throughout his career, he was interested in the organization of systems, whether physicochemical, biological, or social. He stressed the need to take a holistic view of such systems and to recognize the mutual dependence of variables within a system. Henderson's holistic, organismic viewpoint was not unique to him but was representative of a popular approach in the science and philosophy of his time, as reflected in such theories as emergent evolution, gestalt psychology, and organismic biology.

In his later years, particularly after reading Pareto, Henderson grew increasingly skeptical of metaphysics and came to regret the tone of certain parts of his earlier works. He never rejected the concept of fitness, but he thought that the philosophical speculations he had derived from it were meaningless. He preferred to regard the apparent existence of fitness as a basic but inexplicable fact. He believed that all metaphysical statements, such as "the external world really exists," are nonlogical and hence meaningless for science. Conceptual schemes are useful because they are convenient, but they cannot be proven true or false in the sense of facts.

Henderson's biological research contributed significantly to our understanding of the acid-base equilibrium of the body, of the blood as a physicochemical system, and of biological organization. His work on fitness helped to clarify the restrictions that inorganic nature placed on the direction of organic evolution. Henderson may have given a greater impetus to the diffusion of equilibrium concepts among American social scientists than any other individual. His impact on Harvard University, exerted through the programs that he helped create and through his influence on students and colleagues, was substantial. After thirty-seven years on the Harvard faculty, Henderson died in Boston.

• Substantial collections of Henderson papers are in the Harvard University Archives and the Manuscripts and Archives Division of the Harvard Graduate School of Business Administration. Both of these collections include copies of Henderson's "Memories," an unpublished autobiographical typescript. For an overview of Henderson's career, see John Parascandola, "L. J. Henderson and the Mutual Dependence of Variables: From Physical Chemistry to Pareto," in *Science at Harvard University: Historical Perspectives*, ed. Clark A. Elliot and Margaret W. Rossiter (1992). See also Parascandola, "Organismic and Holistic Concepts in the Thought of L. J. Henderson," *Journal of the History of Biology* 4 (1971): 63–113. On Henderson's research on neutrality regulation, see Parascandola, "L. J. Henderson and the Theory of Buffer Action," *Medizinhistorisches Journal* 6 (1971): 297–309. On Henderson's sociological work and influence, see L. J. Henderson, *On the Social System: Selected Writings*, ed. Bernard Barber (1970); Cynthia Russett, *The Concept of Equilibrium in American Social Thought* (1966); and Barbara Heyl, "The Harvard 'Pareto Circle,'" *Journal of the History of Behavioral Sciences* 4 (1968): 316–34. The most detailed account of Henderson's philosophical views is Iris Fry, "L. J. Henderson's Theory of the Fitness of the Environment for Life: Historical Aspects and Current Parallels" (Ph.D. diss., Tel-Aviv Univ., 1992). An obituary, which includes a bibliography of Henderson's publications, is Walter Cannon, "Lawrence Joseph Henderson, 1878–1942," *Biographical Memoirs of the National Academy of Sciences* 23 (1943): 31–58.

JOHN PARASCANDOLA

HENDERSON, Leon (26 May 1895–19 Oct. 1986), economist and government official, was born in Millville, New Jersey, the son of Chester Henderson, a glass factory worker, and Lida Beebe. When Leon was twelve years old, his father bought a farm with the family's savings, leaving nothing for Henderson's further education. While working odd jobs, Henderson graduated from Millville High School in 1913. After a semester at the University of Pennsylvania (having dropped out because of money problems), and with the help of a scholarship, he enrolled at Swarthmore college in 1915. When the United States entered World War I, Henderson enlisted in the army. Discharged in 1919, he returned to Swarthmore, graduating in 1920. From 1920 to 1922 he was a graduate student in economics at the University of Pennsylvania and then became an assistant professor of economics at Carnegie Institute of Technology. Next he joined the administration of Pennsylvania governor Gifford Pinchot. Between 1923 and 1925 Henderson served in multiple capacities, including deputy secretary of the commonwealth. Among his achievements, he organized a pension system for the state's 15,000 employees.

In 1925 Henderson married Myrlie Hamm, with whom he had three children. That year he began a new job with the Russell Sage Foundation, directing its

Department of Remedial Loans. In that position between 1925 and 1934 he spearheaded a drive against loansharking that prompted several states to pass or strengthen usury laws.

Henderson's commitment to protecting consumers brought him into President Franklin D. Roosevelt's administration. In December 1933 Henderson led a delegation of consumer advocates into the Washington office of General Hugh Johnson, National Recovery administrator. The general responded to their complaints that National Recovery Administration (NRA) codes sanctioned price fixing and hurt consumers with shouting and desk pounding. To Johnson's amazement and apparent admiration, the pugnacious Henderson yelled back and pounded harder. Johnson forthwith hired Henderson as an NRA adviser on consumer problems, and within two months the general elevated him to NRA's chief economist and head of its Research and Planning Division. Operating from within the NRA, Henderson objected repeatedly to unnecessary price increases and planned scarcity perpetrated in many industries. As early as 1934 Henderson called for an antitrust investigation to uncover monopolistic practices that resulted in inflexible prices.

After the Supreme Court in 1935 declared the NRA unconstitutional, Henderson briefly became economic adviser to the U.S. Senate Committee on Manufactures. During the 1936 campaign, he was consulting economist for the Democratic National Committee. Following the election, Harry Hopkins hired Henderson as his leading economist for the Works Progress Administration. Early in 1937 Henderson wrote a memorandum to Hopkins predicting the "Roosevelt recession" that began later that year. Henderson's analysis showed prices were rising faster than purchasing power, and reduced government outlays had not been offset by heightened private-sector investment. In November 1937, with the economic slump in full swing, Hopkins arranged a meeting with Roosevelt for Henderson and fellow Keynesian economists Isadore Lubin and Lauchlin Currie. They urged the president to increase government spending on relief, public works, and housing and to undertake an antitrust investigation. In spring 1938 Roosevelt asked Congress for a $3.75 billion supplemental appropriation and establishment of the Temporary National Economic Committee (TNEC) to probe monopoly in the United States.

Between 1938 and 1941 Henderson, as executive secretary, guided the TNEC, composed equally of congressmen and administration members, in one of the most thorough studies of the economic and financial structure of American business ever conducted. In 1939 Roosevelt also appointed Henderson to the Securities and Exchange Commission (SEC). Henderson left the SEC and the TNEC in 1941. Few reforms resulted from his TNEC findings.

Henderson and the president had by 1940 switched their attention to mobilizing the economy for World War II. In May Roosevelt created the National Defense Advisory Commission (NDAC) with Henderson as one of its seven members. Serving on the NDAC and its successor agencies during 1940 and 1941, Henderson constantly battled for rapid conversion of the economy for war, a greatly expanded arms program, and holding down inflation with price controls and rationing. Henderson warned that to beat Adolf Hitler the United States must produce "more and faster than any nation has ever produced before. You can't have 500 bombers a month and business as usual." In April 1941 Roosevelt put Henderson in charge of the Office of Price Administration and Civilian Supply, which was to provide for an adequate supply of civilian goods, curtail production of nonessentials, and curb inflation. But Henderson lacked legislative authority to set prices. His jawboning, a term he invented, against price hikes had limited success. Only after Pearl Harbor did Congress pass the Price Control Act that empowered the renamed Office of Price Administration (OPA) to set prices and impose rationing. However, at the insistence of the farm bloc, the law denied OPA the right to cap agricultural prices. Quickly Henderson issued a General Maximum Price Regulation, imposing wholesale and retail price ceilings on most products. The Washington office set up and staffed thousands of district and state OPA agencies to enforce the regulations. Still, skyrocketing food prices threatened to undermine the anti-inflation effort. Finally, in October 1942 Henderson and Roosevelt convinced a reluctant Congress to grant OPA power to control agricultural prices and rents. Also, by the end of 1942 rationing had been extended to ten items, including sugar, coffee, shoes, and gasoline.

Armed with real power, the abrasive, wisecracking Henderson grew most unpopular. Farmers and their congressmen blamed him for denying agriculture its deserved rewards; motorists and oil producers denounced gasoline rationing; businesspeople complained of red tape and confusing regulations; Democratic senators fumed at nonpartisan appointment of district OPA staffs and attributed Democratic losses in the November 1942 elections to Henderson's OPA. With Capitol Hill threatening to kill OPA unless Henderson went, Roosevelt accepted his resignation in December 1942.

Henderson held no subsequent government office. He dabbled in business, worked as an economic consultant, and was one of the founders of Americans for Democratic Action, but according to John Kenneth Galbraith, his OPA colleague, Henderson was "never completely happy again. Divorced from public concerns, he did not wholly exist."

Henderson died in a hospital in Oceanside, California. He was one of the most dedicated New Dealers, and he played a crucial role in preparing the U.S. economy for combat. The OPA he launched kept the rise in the cost of living during the four years of World War II to 28 percent, as opposed to the 62 percent jump experienced during the year and a half of World War I.

• The Leon Henderson Papers are in the Franklin D. Roosevelt Library in Hyde Park, N.Y. Many comments on Henderson are in the oral histories of other members of the Roosevelt administration in the Columbia University Oral History Collection (COHO). Especially useful are the reminiscences of Henry A. Wallace, Thomas I. Emerson, and Bernard L. Gladieux. Henderson wrote articles intended to build public support for war preparations and price controls, including "We Only Have Months," *Fortune*, July 1941, pp. 68–69; "The War and Your Pocketbook," *American Magazine*, Oct. 1941, pp. 24–25, 116; and "Preview of Life in '43—by Leon Henderson," *New York Times Magazine*, 19 July 1942, pp. 3–4. Brief biographical sketches are in Samuel Lubell, "The Daring Young Man on the Flying Pri-cees," *Saturday Evening Post*, 13 Sept. 1941, pp. 12–13, 78–86; Robert Coughlin, "Leon Henderson," *Life*, 14 Sept. 1942, pp. 104–19; Walter Davenport, "What Price Henderson," *Collier's*, 6 Sept. 1941, pp. 18, 51–53; and Delbert Clark, "Hard Hitting Boss of Prices," *New York Times Magazine*, 27 Apr. 1941, pp. 6, 25. The best discussion of Henderson's fight to prepare the economy for war and to control inflation is in John Kenneth Galbraith, *A Life in Our Times: Memoirs* (1981). His role in the 1930s is discussed in Joseph P. Lash, *Dealers and Dreamers: A New Look at the New Deal* (1988); and Arthur M. Schlesinger, Jr., *The Coming of the New Deal* (1958) and *The Politics of Upheaval* (1960). An obituary is in the *New York Times*, 8 Oct. 1986.

BARBARA BLUMBERG

HENDERSON, Leonard (6 Oct. 1772–13 Aug. 1833), chief justice of the North Carolina Supreme Court, was born in what is now Vance County, North Carolina, the son of Richard Henderson, a lawyer and land speculator, and Elizabeth Keeling. Privately educated in Greek and Latin by the local Presbyterian minister, he was raised along with his five siblings by his mother after his father's death in 1785. When his mother died five years later, he moved to nearby Williamsboro, where he lived and studied law with a distant relative, Judge John Williams. Admitted to the bar in 1794, Henderson moved to Hillsborough and secured the remunerative post of clerk of the district court. At this time he was an active Freemason. In 1795 he married Judge Williams's niece, Frances Farrar; they had six children.

In 1800 Henderson entered the private practice of law. Soon thereafter he and his family returned to Williamsboro, where he made his home for the rest of his life. Native ability and family connections soon brought recognition; in 1802 the general assembly appointed him to a one-year term on the Council of State, and in 1808 it elected him a life-tenured judge of the Superior Court, filling a vacancy created by the death of his brother-in-law Judge Spruce McKay. Although a staunch Federalist and particular admirer of U.S. Chief Justice John Marshall, Henderson was chosen by the Republican legislators, a testament to his character but also evidence of the enduring conception of common law judging as nonpolitical. To supplement his income, Henderson offered tuition in law and attracted a steady stream of students, which included such distinguished future judges and legal educators as Richmond M. Pearson and William Horn Battle.

To support his growing family, Henderson resigned his judgeship in 1816 to resume the practice of law and to conduct his law school. In 1817 the general assembly appointed him a trustee of the University of North Carolina, a post he held until he resigned in 1828.

In 1818 the North Carolina Supreme Court was created by statute. (Prior to that date appeals had been decided by a conference of superior court judges.) Henderson was elected to the new three-member court by general assembly, again securing the votes of his political opponents. He and his associate Judge John Elihu Hall chose their colleague John Louis Taylor as chief justice, apparently because his judicial service was the longest. On Taylor's death in 1829, Henderson was chosen chief justice and served until his own death four years later. His judicial opinions, which are reported in volumes four to seventeen of the *North Carolina Reports*, are unornamented common law decisions. He was known by his contemporaries more for his practical common sense than for his use of precedents, although his law students could testify to his mastery of case law. A fair specimen of his judicial style can be found in *Taylor v. Shuford* (1825), a property case involving the technical question of whether delivery of a deed with covenants of title precluded a grantor then actually without title from asserting an after-acquired title. Brusquely dismissing the massed authorities who favored the grantor, Henderson ruled against him on the ground that his claim lacked substantial justice. While inferior in industry to his successor as chief justice, Thomas Ruffin, Henderson equaled him in pure legal cogitation. He had the ability quickly to isolate the legal issue in a case, succinctly to explore its technical ramifications, and convincingly to apply his moral judgment in its resolution. His former pupil Richmond M. Pearson, when himself chief justice, rated Henderson even higher, asserting that his "powers of reflection exceeded that of any man who ever had a seat on this bench, unless Judge [John] Haywood be considered his equal in this respect" (*N.C. Reports* 64 [1870]: 273).

In religion a freethinker for most of his life, Henderson was remembered by his student William Horn Battle as lacking "that purity of manners and morals which the genuine spirit of christianity alone can produce" (*North-Carolina University Magazine* [Nov. 1859]). Late in life he professed Christianity and joined the Episcopal church. His final words upon his death at his home in Williamsboro, North Carolina, were reported to be "I have passed the portals and see nothing terrifying" (*N.C. Reports* 149 [1909]: 614). Hendersonville, the county seat of Henderson County, and Henderson, the county seat of Vance County, North Carolina, are named for the judge. A portrait of Henderson, which showed a large man with dark hair and gray eyes, was presented to the North Carolina Supreme Court in October 1908.

Henderson's legacy to North Carolina legal culture was twofold: on the bench he upheld the state's tradition of strong common law judging, and in the classroom he helped to initiate the practice of legal instruction apart from pure apprenticeship. Of the two, the latter was perhaps the more significant. While Henderson's best pupils continued to develop the common law, they even more assiduously cultivated professionalism in legal education.

• Henderson's judicial contributions are assessed by Walter Clark, a later chief justice, in a series of articles on the history of the North Carolina Supreme Court that was published in the *Green Bag* in Oct., Nov., and Dec. 1892, pp. 457–74, 521–40, and 569–91; Clark briefly resurveyed the field in an address that was reported in the *North Carolina Reports* 177 (1919): 617. An address on Henderson by Judge R. W. Winston on the occasion of the presentation of his portrait appears in the *North Carolina Reports* 149 (1909): 436. All of the above rely heavily on the memoir by Judge William Horn Battle in the *North-Carolina University Magazine* 9 (Nov. 1859): 192–202, based on personal recollection and material supplied by one of Henderson's sons.

JOHN V. ORTH

HENDERSON, Loy Wesley (28 June 1892–24 Mar. 1986), diplomat, was born in Rogers, Arkansas, the son of Methodist minister George Milton Henderson and schoolteacher Mary May Davis. After graduating from Northwestern University in 1915, Henderson entered Denver University Law School but dropped out after the United States entered World War I. Rejected for military service because of a childhood injury to his arm, Henderson joined the Red Cross and worked in France and Germany.

After the Armistice, Henderson served with the Inter-Allied Commission to Germany, involved in the repatriation of prisoners and inspection of prisoner of war camps. During 1919 and 1920 he served with the American Red Cross Commission to Western Russia and the Baltic States, and was appointed head of the Red Cross in Germany during 1920–1921.

Henderson joined the U.S. Foreign Service in 1922. His first posts were as vice counsel in Dublin, Ireland, and then Queensland, Ireland, during 1923–1924. He was promoted to counsel in 1925 and later that year transferred to the State Department's Division of Eastern European Affairs in Washington, D.C. When the department debated whether the United States should establish diplomatic relations with the Soviet government, Henderson argued strongly against recognition. In a 1925 memo to his superiors, he stated that his study of the department's records concerning the Soviet Union led him to conclude that that nation's leaders were "united in their determination to continue to promote chaos and revolution in the noncommunist world until they could achieve their ultimate objective of a communist world with headquarters in Moscow."

In 1927 Henderson was posted as third secretary to the U.S. delegation in the Baltic States, the nation's "listening post" on the Soviet Union. While serving in Riga, Henderson met Elise Marie Heinrichson, a music student and outspoken anticommunist. The couple married in December 1930; they had no children.

Henderson returned to a Washington post at the Eastern European Division from 1930 to 1934 and was appointed to the newly opened American embassy to the Soviet Union under Ambassador William Bullitt. He served successively as second secretary, first secretary, chargé d'affaires ad interim, and counselor, under Bullitt and his successor Joseph E. Davies, until 1938 when he returned to Washington.

In October 1938 Henderson became assistant chief of the Division of European Affairs, in charge of Russian and East European matters. He remained an outspoken critic of the Soviet Union, since he continued to believe, as he stated in his memoirs, "that . . . leaders of the Kremlin were intending to contribute eventually to the violent overthrow of all the countries with which the Soviet Union maintained relations." He later served briefly as an inspector of diplomatic missions and consular offices in 1942, and he was appointed counselor and chargé d'affaires at the Moscow embassy, where he attended the August 1942 Churchill-Stalin conference. He returned to Washington in early 1943 to his post as assistant chief of the Division of European Affairs until he was appointed envoy extraordinary and minister plenipotentiary to Iraq in June 1943.

Iraq was within the British sphere of influence, and Henderson devoted his initial efforts to analyzing the methods by which the officials of the British empire exerted control over a nominally independent state. He described an extensive paragovernmental network run by the British embassy in Baghdad, constructed "to safeguard British interests in practically every field of Iraqi national life and to direct the trends of Iraqi internal and external policies into channels which will serve the well-being of the British Empire."

In March 1945 Henderson returned to Washington, to become the chief of the State Department's Division of Near Eastern and African Affairs. During the following three years Henderson played a key role in the development of the Truman Doctrine, working closely with Dean Acheson to determine the types and amount of economic and military aid that Greece and Turkey needed to stave off Soviet intrusions. He also developed a keen appreciation of the growing importance of Middle Eastern oil and warned: "An unfriendly foreign power in possession of these reserves would be in a position to hamper, if not prevent, the rehabilitation of Western Europe and to retard the economic development of Africa and southern Asia."

Henderson's fears of postwar Soviet aggression led him to revise and then discard his earlier hostility toward British colonialism. He now perceived the British empire as a source of political stability, a strong bulwark against turmoil in the Middle East. He participated in the negotiations that facilitated the British departure from Palestine but feared that American support for the creation of a Jewish homeland would result in the Arab nations aligning themselves with the Soviet Union. His support for the British position—which opposed the creation of an independent Israel—drew strong criticism and accusations of his being "pro-Arab" from American Jewish leaders. Henderson based his stand upon cold war considerations, particularly the danger of Soviet-aligned Arab nations cutting off American access to Middle East oil, and he declared: "There is one fact facing both the United States and Great Britain. That is the Soviet Union. It would be wise to bear that in mind when you consider the Palestine problem."

Mounting criticism of Henderson prompted Truman to remove him from Washington before the 1948 presidential election by appointing him ambassador to India in July 1948 and later ambassador to Iran in 1951. At this time the United States, Great Britain, and the Soviet Union were contending for control over Iran, and Mohammed Reza Shah Pahlevi fled the country after an unsuccessful attempt to remove the Communist-supported prime minister Mohammad Mussadiq. During Henderson's tenure, the Central Intelligence Agency station head, Kermit Roosevelt, in close cooperation with British intelligence agencies, planned and financed a coup against Mussadiq, which led to the reinstallation of the shah in 1953. Afterwards, Henderson headed negotiations by which an international consortium took over control of the Iranian oil fields.

Henderson returned to Washington in late 1954 and was appointed deputy undersecretary of state for administration in January 1955. He helped Secretary of State John Foster Dulles implement the recommendations of the Wriston Committee, which called for a merger of the Civil Service and Foreign Office personnel into a single diplomatic corps. He also continued to advise President Dwight D. Eisenhower on Middle Eastern matters. He received an appointment as Career Ambassador in 1956 and represented the United States in the negotiations that followed the Suez Canal crisis in that same year.

During the late 1950s Henderson headed a State Department committee that determined U.S. representation at the newly decolonized nations in Africa and Asia. He retired from the Foreign Service in 1961. He taught courses in foreign policy at the School of International Service of American University, founded the Washington Institute of Foreign Affairs, and worked on his memoirs. He was a firm supporter of U.S. involvement in the Vietnam War and attributed the nation's defeat to a "lack of determination and decisiveness." He died in Bethesda, Maryland.

Henderson's career and beliefs embodied and helped shape the main trends of American diplomacy during the mid–twentieth century. During the interwar period his traditional American concerns and suspicions about the British empire were superseded by hostility toward the Soviet Union and its declared revolutionary intentions. In the period following the end of World War II he came to regard the rapidly fading British empire as America's most reliable ally in containing Soviet aggression, which he considered the major threat to American interests. He supported a wide range of Anglo-American initiatives, particularly the close cooperation between the two nations' intelligence agencies that had begun during the war, and discarded traditional American opposition to the Western European nations' colonialism in exchange for their support of anti-Soviet and anticommunist policies.

• Most of Henderson's papers, including a transcript of his memoirs, are at the Library of Congress, but the 1,600-page manuscript of his memoirs is at the Hoover Institution on War, Peace, and Revolution, Palo Alto, Calif. Oral history interviews are located at the Truman Presidential Library, Independence, Mo. and at Columbia and Princeton Universities. A shortened version of his memoirs was published as George W. Baer, ed., *A Question of Trust: The Origins of U.S.—Soviet Relations: The Memoirs of Loy W. Henderson,* (1986), and a good biography is H. W. Brands, *Inside the Cold War: Loy Henderson and the Rise of the American Empire 1918–1961* (1991). His early career is covered in Thomas R. Maddux, "Loy W. Henderson and Soviet-American Relations: The Diplomacy of a Professional," in *U.S. Diplomats in Europe, 1919–1941,* ed. Kenneth Paul Jones (1981; repr. 1983); Martin Weil, *A Pretty Good Club: The Founding Fathers of the U.S. Foreign Service* (1978); and George Kennan, *Memoirs, 1925–1950* (1967). Henderson's postwar role is discussed in Dean Acheson, *Present at the Creation: My Years in the State Department* (1969); John Snetsinger, *Truman, the Jewish Vote and the Creation of Israel* (1974); Mark H. Lyle, *Origins of the Iranian—American Alliance, 1841–1953* (1987); Kermit Roosevelt, *Countercoup: The Struggle for the Control of Iran* (1979); and Mohammad Mussadiq, *Mussadiq's Memoirs* (1988). Postwar abandonment of traditional anti-colonialism in exchange for support of anti-communist policies is discussed in Christopher Hitchens, *Blood, Class and Nostalgia: Anglo-American Ironies* (1990). Obituaries are in the *New York Times* and the *Washington Post,* both 26 Mar. 1986.

STEPHEN G. MARSHALL

HENDERSON, Paul (13 Mar. 1884–19 Dec. 1951), airline executive, was born in Lyndon, Kansas, the son of Clark Ebenezer Henderson and Flora Anne Waddle (occupations unknown). Henderson grew up in Chicago. Following his graduation from South Division High School, he worked as a salesman in Chicago for the Turner Brass Works and, later, for the Olds Motor Works of Detroit. In 1907 he joined the Western Stone Company of Lamont, Illinois. Over the next ten years he rose from salesman to general manager to president of Western Stone, one of the world's largest producers of building stone. In 1910 Henderson married Mabel Madden, his high school sweetheart and the daughter of Martin B. Madden; the marriage produced five children. Henderson's father-in-law, who had preceded him as president of Western Stone, was a U.S. congressman and the powerful chairman of the House Appropriations Committee. Henderson joined the army in 1917 and served in France as an ordnance officer. Discharged as a major in 1919, he remained in the army—later, Air Service—reserves and reached the rank of colonel. He favored the military title in his civilian career.

Henderson returned to Western Stone after the war. On 14 April 1922 he was appointed second assistant postmaster general in the Warren G. Harding administration. Henderson's selection no doubt represented a gesture to Congressman Madden, who had been an outspoken critic of the post office's Air Mail Service.

Begun as an experiment in 1918, the Air Mail Service had come under attack for spending too much money and for killing too many pilots (with twenty-two deaths in three years of operation).

Responsible for the delivery of all mails in the United States and its territories, Henderson devoted most of his time to the Air Mail Service. A talented administrator, he compiled an outstanding record. Building on the work of his predecessor, he sharply reduced fatalities. Indeed, the Air Mail Service won the prestigious Collier Trophy in 1922, awarded for the year's greatest achievement in aviation, for operating the New York–San Francisco air route for one year without a fatal accident. Henderson went on to spearhead the development of a lighted airway, which permitted day and night operations along the transcontinental route. This pioneering effort, which gave the United States world leadership in night flying, brought a second Collier Trophy in 1923.

In 1925 Henderson resigned from the post office to become general manager of National Air Transport (NAT). The best-funded of the new airlines that appeared after the government enacted legislation to privatize airmail delivery, NAT in October 1925 secured the contract for the airmail route between Chicago and Dallas. Two years later it took over the Chicago–New York portion of the government's transcontinental route. By 1929 NAT ranked as the nation's largest airline, flying over 2.6 million miles and carrying more than 2 million pounds of mail. Henderson, who became vice president of NAT in 1928, had charge of the airline's expanding operations. Under his direction, NAT took over from the Air Mail Service the leadership in technological pioneering and did important work in developing instrument flying and radio aids to navigation.

In 1929 Clement M. Keys, the Wall Street financier who controlled NAT, selected Henderson to start a coast-to-coast passenger-carrying airline. On leave from NAT, Henderson supervised the start of Transcontinental Air Transport (TAT), which began a combination air-rail service between New York and Los Angeles on 7 July 1929. Plagued by financial problems with the onset of the Great Depression, TAT in 1930 became part of Transcontinental & Western Air, progenitor of Trans World Airlines (TWA).

Henderson returned to NAT in 1930 as president of the company. The following year he added the duty of vice president of United Air Lines, a management company (later, an operating company) for the airlines—NAT, Boeing Air Transport, Stout Air Services, and Varney Air Lines—owned by United Aircraft and Transport Corporation, the aviation industry's largest holding company.

Henderson's promising career ended in 1934, when he was scrutinized by a special Senate investigating committee, headed by Hugo L. Black of Alabama. After Henderson admitted his reluctant participation in a so-called Spoils Conference held in 1930 by Postmaster General Walter F. Brown to allocate airmail routes, he was forced to sever all connections with the airline industry. Henderson tried his hand at real estate development, boat building, and other business enterprises in years that followed his departure from aviation; however, as his daughter recalled, the penalty imposed by the Black committee "broke his heart." In 1942 he retired to a farm near Chapel Hill, North Carolina. Four years later he suffered a devastating family tragedy when his son was killed in an air crash. He died in Washington, D.C.

• Considerable information on Henderson's career is in the Records of the United States Post Office, Record Group 28, National Archives, Washington, D.C., and in the papers of Clement M. Keys at the National Air and Space Museum, Smithsonian Institution, Washington, D.C. Henderson's years with the post office are detailed in William M. Leary, *Aerial Pioneers: The U.S. Air Mail Service, 1918–1927* (1985). His later career is discussed in Henry Ladd Smith, *Airways: The History of Commercial Aviation in the United States* (1942); Nick A. Komons, *Bonfires to Beacons: Federal Civil Aviation Policy under the Air Commerce Act, 1926–1938* (1978); and Frank J. Taylor, *High Horizons: Daredevil Flying Postmen to Modern Magic Carpet, the United Air Lines Story* (1951).

WILLIAM M. LEARY

HENDERSON, Ray (1 Dec. 1896–31 Dec. 1970), composer, author, and pianist, was born Raymond Brost in Buffalo, New York, the son of William Brost and Margaret Baker. His mother was his first piano teacher. He later studied organ, piano, music theory, harmony, and counterpoint with private tutors and sang in the choir at the Episcopal church in Buffalo. From 1911 to 1914 he did advanced study at the Chicago Conservatory of Music. Later he studied composition privately with English composer Benjamin Britten.

His first job was in Tin Pan Alley in New York City as an accompanist for vaudeville and cabaret performers who demonstrated Leo Feist's songs. He subsequently worked as staff pianist and arranger for the publishing house of Fred Fisher and later for the Shapiro-Bernstein Company. Brost married Florence Hoffman in 1918. Two years later, he began to use Ray Henderson as his professional name, a common practice in musical theater at the time.

Lyricist Lew Brown and Henderson wrote a song, "Georgette," that became part of the *Greenwich Village Follies* of 1922. In 1923 Henderson became a member of the American Society of Composers, Authors, and Publishers (ASCAP). Then followed a series of successful collaborations with many lyricists that resulted in seven highly popular and memorable songs of that decade: "Annabelle" (1923), with Lew Brown; "That Old Gang of Mine" (1923) and "Follow the Swallow" (1924), with Billy Rose and Mort Dixon; the million-copy seller, "Alabamy Bound" (1925), with B. G. "Buddy" De Sylva and Bud Green; and "I'm Sitting on Top of the World" and "Five Foot Two, Eyes of Blue" (both 1925), with Sam M. Lewis and Joe Young. Also from 1925 was "Bye, Bye, Blackbird," with lyrics by Dixon.

In 1924 Henderson replaced George Gershwin as the composer for George White's *Scandals* musical revue, where he worked again with Buddy De Sylva and Lew Brown in the first collaboration of this trio that soon became known as De Sylva, Brown, and Henderson. This team started a music publishing firm in 1925. They wrote music and lyrics for the *Scandals* of 1926, with hits "Lucky Day," "The Girl Is You," "The Birth of the Blues," and "Black Bottom." The next year their first Broadway musical comedy, *Good News*, ran for over 550 performances and included the song, "The Best Things in Life Are Free." They went on to write the score for George White's *Scandals* of 1928. A musical comedy from 1928, *Hold Everything!* premiered on 10 October and featured such spectacular hits as "You're the Cream in My Coffee," "Don't Hold Everything," and "To Know You Is to Love You." *Follow Thru* came in 1929 with the cheerful "Button Up Your Overcoat" as its crowd pleaser and the songs "You Are My Lucky Star," and "I want to Be Bad." The next year their fourth collaboration for the musical stage was *Flying High* in which the song "Red Hot Chicago" identified that city as the birthplace of jazz. Three other titles from *Flying High* that stood out were "Without Love," "Thank You Father," and "Wasn't It Beautiful While It Lasted?"

Henderson's film career began with songs for *The Singing Fool* (1928), *Say It with Songs* (1929), and *Sunny Side Up* (1929), which were created along with his collaborators De Sylva and Brown. "Sonny Boy" from *The Singing Fool*, a song purposely designed to be highly sentimental, ended up becoming a bestseller in sheet music and in a recording by Al Jolson, the singer who also helped popularize Henderson's earlier tunes, "Alabamy Bound" and "I'm Sitting on Top of the World." *Sunny Side Up* starred Janet Gaynor and Charles Farrell, who enchanted audiences with renditions of "Keep Your Sunny Side Up," "I'm a Dreamer, Aren't We All," and "If I Had a Talking Picture of You." They also wrote songs for a few less successful movies, *Follow the Leader* (1930) and *Just Imagine* (1930), and for *Manhattan Mary*, which was produced on the Broadway stage in 1927. During the years from 1925 until 1928, they wrote several songs that were popular but were not written for the stage, including "It All Depends on You," "Broken Hearted," "Just a Memory," and "Together." They sold their music publishing business in 1929.

In 1930 they went to Hollywood under contract with 20th Century–Fox to work in film, but they broke up within a year. Brown and Henderson returned to Broadway to do George White's *Scandals* of 1931. That score included an array of hits among its musical numbers: "Life Is Just a Bowl of Cherries," "The Thrill Is Gone," "My Song," "This Is the Missus," and "That's Why Darkies Were Born," the latter a tribute to the courage of African Americans in the face of injustice. The next two scores were for the Broadway show *Hot-Cha!* (1932) and a musical revue, *Strike Me Pink* (1933), with Jimmy Durante. Brown and Henderson worked on *Say When* in 1934, which

featured Bob Hope and Harry Richman, but Henderson worked with other lyricists, including Ted Koehler and Irving Caesar, in New York City after Brown went back to Hollywood in 1934. With Koehler and Caesar he created the familiar "Animal Crackers in My Soup" from the film *Curly Top* (1935), popularized by child star Shirley Temple. Jack Yellen and Henderson worked on George White's *Scandals* for 1936, and Henderson, Yellen, and Caesar wrote the songs for the 1943 film version of the musical. Henderson's last theater score was for the 1943 edition of the Ziegfeld *Follies*, which was filled with nostalgia in such songs as "Love Songs Are Made in the Night," "Come Up and Have a Cup of Coffee," and "Hold That Smile."

From 1942 until 1951, Henderson was the director of ASCAP. The film, *The Best Things in Life Are Free* (1956), with the title taken from their 1927 song, tells the story of the famous Henderson–Brown–De Sylva music-and-lyrics team and features their most well-known songs from their successful collaborations of the 1920s, a decade whose musical styles were especially idiomatic for Henderson.

Henderson's historical significance lies in his talents as a songwriter who flourished in the decades of the twenties and thirties. The songs he wrote in collaboration with others were enduring and, in many ways, defined the major popular music song styles of that time. Henderson died in his home in Greenwich, Connecticut, where he had lived the last twenty years of his life.

• A clippings file on Henderson is in the Music Division of the New York Public Library for the Performing Arts, Lincoln Center. Henderson's accomplishments are listed in several directories and dictionaries that contain composers of American popular music. Additional information can be found in Cecil Smith and Glenn Litton, *Musical Comedy in America* (1950), David Ewen, *Great Men of American Popular Song* (1970), Ethan Mordden, *Better Foot Forward* (1976), and Stanley Green, *The World of Musical Comedy*, 4th ed. (1980). Obituaries are in the *New York Times*, 2 Jan. 1971, and *Variety*, 13 Jan. 1971.

CAROLYN L. QUIN

HENDERSON, Richard (20 Apr. 1735–30 Jan. 1785), land speculator, judge, and politician, was born in Hanover County, Virginia, the son of Samuel Henderson and Elizabeth Williams. Samuel Henderson, who had served for a time as sheriff of Hanover County, moved his family to North Carolina around 1742 and settled on Nutbush Creek in Granville County; within a few years he became sheriff. Little is known of Richard Henderson's childhood, but it must have been a happy one. Under the watchful eye of his mother his education was guided toward a law career. He studied under a private tutor before getting his first job as a deputy sheriff under his father. He then read law under John Williams, his mother's cousin and a gifted attorney who became a lifelong friend. After being admitted to the bar, Henderson joined Williams in law practice. Their association grew closer after 1763, when Henderson married Elizabeth Keeling, Williams's stepdaughter who was the daughter of an English peer, Lord Keeling. They had six children.

In March 1768 Royal Governor William Tryon appointed Henderson a superior court judge, describing him as a "gentleman of candor and ability . . . for whom [the inhabitants] entertain an esteem." Henderson soon found that not all the inhabitants shared that esteem. The naysayers were back-country farmers who called themselves Regulators and who had organized to protest high taxes and extortionate legal fees. In September 1770, while Henderson was holding court at Hillsborough, the Regulators stormed the courthouse. Henderson escaped by the back door, but several others, including Williams, were roughed up. Two months later, the Regulators burned Henderson's house.

The Regulator troubles were climaxed by the battle of Alamance, in which Governor Tryon led an army of colonial militia that defeated the Regulators. Henderson was one of the presiding justices who convicted twelve of the Regulators of treason. Six of these were hanged, and the others were pardoned. When his term ended in 1773, Henderson retired from the bench to pursue his real interests.

The West had always held a fascination for Henderson, and his interest was intensified when he met a young man named Daniel Boone at Salisbury, probably in the mid-1760s. Boone had such glowing reports of a place called "Cantucky" that Henderson sent him back to explore and locate sites suitable for settlement. In 1774 Henderson formed the Louisa Company, consisting of six prominent men, including Williams, to make plans for a large purchase of land from the American Indians. Later, after the association was renamed the Transylvania Company, Henderson summoned the American Indians to a meeting at Sycamore Shoals on the Watauga River. There a treaty was reached for the purchase of a huge tract of land—an estimated 20 million acres, which comprised nearly all of present-day Kentucky, a large slice of Tennessee, and a sliver of Virginia.

However, the deal was doomed from the start, when it was denounced by the royal governors of North Carolina and Virginia. North Carolina's governor Josiah Martin called Henderson and his associates "land pirates" and thundered that the proposed sale would be a "lawless undertaking" and "an infraction of the royal prerogative." In addition, when Henderson sent James Hogg, a prominent North Carolinian and a member of the Transylvania Company, to Philadelphia to ask the Continental Congress to admit Transylvania as the fourteenth American colony, he got a flat "no." The Congress was then appeasing Great Britain and wanted no part of angering the British by recognizing the proposed "New Independent Government" of Transylvania. Later North Carolina and Virginia each granted Henderson 200,000 acres of western land. In its grant of a tract between the Ohio and Green rivers, the Virginia Assembly noted that the Transylvania Company had incurred great expense in purchasing the land and settling it "by which the Commonwealth is likely to receive great advantage by increasing its inhabitants and establishing a barrier against the Indians." The tract given by North Carolina was between the Powell and Clinch rivers in what is now Tennessee.

Meanwhile, Henderson had proceeded with his plans to colonize the purchased lands. He sent Boone with thirty axmen to cut a path through the wilderness to "Cantucky" that was called the Wilderness Road. Henderson followed with another party. The trip was perilous, as Henderson wrote in his diary on 7 April 1775, "About Brake of day began to snow. . . . Received a letter from Mr. Luttrells camp that were five persons kill'd on the road to Cantuckie by Indians. Cap't Hart, upon the receipt of this News Retreated with his Company, & determined to Settle in the Valley to make corn for the Cantucky people. The same day received a letter from Dan'l Boone that his company was fired upon by Indians, kill'd Two of his men—tho he kept the ground & saved the Baggage &c." On his birthday, Henderson wrote, "Thursday the 20th [of April] Arrived at Fort Boone on the Mouth of Oter Creek where we were Saluted by a running fire of about 25 guns; all that was then at Fort." In Kentucky, Boone's men erected Fort Boonesborough, using a plan prepared by Henderson. Around it people settled, forming a town of the same name (now Boonesboro). In time, millions of people poured into Kentucky over the Wilderness Road, now a segment of U.S. 25, the Dixie Highway. They settled in towns like Boonesborough or pushed on to colonize other states. Among those who paid tribute to Henderson and Boone for the part they played in colonizing the Midwest was Theodore Roosevelt (1858–1919). "Had it not been for Henderson and Boone," he wrote in his *Winning of the West*, "it is most unlikely that the land would have been settled at all until after the Revolutionary War, when perhaps it might have been British soil."

Henderson took an active role in the fight for freedom during the revolutionary war. In 1778 he was nominated as a delegate to the Continental Congress but withdrew on learning that his friend Williams was also being considered. In the same year he declined appointment to the Council of State. He served again as a judge but soon resigned.

In 1779 Henderson served on a commission that completed running the boundary between Virginia and North Carolina. The boundary showed that the land on which the Tennessee state capital of Nashville stands was then part of North Carolina and not in Virginia as that state had claimed. Nashville was then known as French Lick—a name it got from brackish springs that attracted huge herds of buffalo. Under the aegis of Henderson this area of Tennessee was settled. Henderson founded a town at French Lick, which he named Nashborough—later changed to Nashville—in honor of his friend, General Francis Nash, who was killed leading a charge during the revolutionary battle of Germantown.

In 1780 Henderson was appointed to the North Carolina War Board and served until the end of hostilities in 1781. He was also a militia colonel and assisted in recruiting and procurement of supplies. After the war he served in the general assembly in 1781 and on the Council of State in 1782–1783. He died a few years later and was buried in an unmarked grave on his Nutbush Creek farm.

• Henderson is mentioned in Archibald Henderson, *The Conquest of the Old Southwest* (1920), and a series of articles by Archibald Henderson in the *Charlotte Observer*, 16 Mar.–1 June 1913. See also *North Carolina Dictionary of Biography*, vol. 3 (1979), and an article in the *Durham* (N.C.) *Herald*, 17 Oct. 1934.

NOEL YANCEY

HENDERSON, Yandell (23 Apr. 1873–18 Feb. 1944), physiologist, was born in Louisville, Kentucky, the son of Isham Henderson, a politically-active businessman, and Sally Nielson Yandell. His father died when Yandell was three, and he was raised in his mother's family, which included an uncle, David Yandell, who had been a high-ranking medical officer in the Confederacy and who was an influential medical teacher and journalist. Henderson and his mother moved to New Haven, Connecticut, in 1891 when Henderson enrolled at Yale College. As a student he displayed an interest in travel and adventure. He vacationed with his mother in Europe, spent the summer of 1894 climbing and hunting in the Canadian Rockies, and in 1897 joined the naval militia. He served during the Spanish-American War on the U.S. cruiser *Yale* as naval aide to General Nelson Miles.

From 1895 to 1898, guided by the physiological chemist Russell Chittenden, Henderson pursued graduate work at Yale's Sheffield Scientific School. He received his Ph.D. for a dissertation on the metabolism of the popular food supplement peptone. He then rounded out his education with two years in Germany, working in the laboratories of the medical chemists Albrecht Kossel and Carl Voit. On his return to the United States he was hired as an instructor in physiology at the Yale Medical School. In 1903 he became assistant professor, and in 1911 professor of physiology. In 1903 he married Mary Gardner Colby; they had a son and a daughter.

Henderson was a self-confident and dogmatic scientist. His ideas were often poorly grounded and sharply criticized by scientific colleagues, but he influenced many aspects of medical practice and social policy. A crusading reformer during the first half of his career, he operated after World War I as an authority-wielding technocrat.

Henderson gained a reputation as an iconoclast with his first independent research. Although trained as a chemist, in 1903 he began to study circulation and respiration in living mammals. He soon questioned the longstanding consensus that blood circulation depended primarily on contraction of the heart and the resistance of the arteries and tissues. He claimed instead that the veins, through a yet-unknown "venopressor mechanism," played an active role in determining the flow of blood into the heart. A few years later he questioned the dominant belief that carbon dioxide was merely a respiratory waste product; he argued, rather, that CO_2 blood levels played a major role in regulating breathing, and that surgical shock was a consequence of "acapnia," or a deficiency in blood CO_2.

Most of Henderson's American colleagues believed that his theories were overstated, if not entirely wrong. He gained confidence, however, from the support of the prominent British physiologist John Scott Haldane. In 1911 the two men organized the Oxford–Yale Pikes Peak Expedition. Operating out of a hotel on the mountain's summit, they performed five weeks of stress tests on each other and two associates to determine how humans acclimated to high altitude. Henderson came to adopt both Haldane's conviction that the pain and danger of self-experimentation made science a modern form of heroism, and his interest in using laboratory science for immediate medical and social improvement.

During the 1910s Henderson was associated with a wide range of reforms in clinical medicine, industrial safety, and politics. He urged physicians to adopt such laboratory tools as the sphygmomanometer and recommended that anesthesiologists use an oxygen-carbon dioxide mixture to prevent shock during surgery. As a consultant to the U.S. Bureau of Mines he helped to develop self-contained breathing apparatus which rescuers could use in mines containing carbon monoxide. He also worked to improve techniques to resuscitate victims of carbon monoxide poisoning. He argued that high rates of asphyxiation occurred in areas supplied with heating gas because municipal utilities had watered their stock. "Few facts," he noted in the *Journal of the American Medical Association* in 1916, "are more significant than this in indicating how deeply we must cut into social problems in order to apply preventive medicine."

Henderson's conviction that scientists and the state should unite to combat selfish businessmen, and thereby improve peoples' lives, led him into electoral politics. In 1912 he was chairman of the Progressive party in New Haven and of the Connecticut delegation to the party's national convention; he ran for Congress in both 1912 and 1914.

Events during and after World War I altered Henderson's reformism. He publicly sympathized with Germany, which he considered a highly progressive country, before 1917, but he became deeply involved in military research after the American declaration of war. Working largely within the Bureau of Mines, he tested gas-mask designs, volunteering to be the first experimental subject for a new American-made mask; he supervised toxicity tests for new gases and participated in plans to manufacture bullets tipped with the powerful poison ricin. He also adapted his Pikes Peak experiences to devise ways to test potential pilots for altitude endurance.

With the decision by Yale's leaders in 1920 to use Rockefeller philanthropy to build up the university's medical school, Henderson saw one of his long-sought goals realized. He had antagonized so many colleagues, however, that his removal from the chair of physiology was the price of reform. He became a professor at large, without responsibilities and with minimal institutional support. He responded to this situation by taking on contract research from both government and industry. He also prepared a report for the American Association of University Professors, *Incomes and Living Costs of a University Faculty* (1928), which showed that the incomes of Yale professors were not comparable to those of other professionals.

Henderson's most important project during the 1920s was to determine the safe concentration of carbon monoxide in New York City's new Holland Tunnel. The maximum allowable level he recommended, which was four times higher than that earlier proposed for tunnels by Haldane, was adopted throughout the United States. He also investigated monoxide levels in enclosed garages and on city streets. With funding from the American Gas Association, he developed apparatus for resuscitating victims of monoxide poisoning. In *Noxious Gases and the Principles of Respiration Influencing Their Action*, with Howard W. Haggard (1927), he provided a compendium on the toxicity and management of numerous industrial chemicals. His view—that substances such as carbon monoxide were inevitable byproducts of industrial civilization, and that the responsibility of industry and government was to keep exposure below what would cause acute injury under normal circumstances—dominated industrial hygiene for the next half-century. During this period he also wrote a number of papers in which he unsuccessfully attacked Harvard biochemist Lawrence J. Henderson's ideas about acid-base equilibrium in the blood.

In 1932 Henderson utilized his expertise to influence federal alcohol policy. Testifying before Congress that alcohol, like carbon monoxide, was not "intoxicating" when sufficiently diluted, he provided the scientific justification for the legalization of 3.2 percent beer. *A New Deal in Liquor* (1934) argued that alcohol policy should be based on a sharp distinction between fermented and distilled beverages. Henderson's Laboratory of Applied Physiology became the nucleus for the Yale Center for Alcohol Studies, the major locus for science-based alcohol policy in the mid-twentieth century.

Henderson retired from Yale in 1938; he died in La Jolla, California. He was one of a small group of scientists who gained positions of influence at the boundary between experimental physiology and social policy during the first third of the twentieth century. He helped to establish that the central problem of industrial hygiene was to determine what concentrations of the various poisons produced by modern technology humans could absorb without definite injury. This perspective predominated until the 1960s.

• Small collections of Henderson's papers are at the National Library of Medicine and in the administrative files of Yale. He was the author of more than 100 scientific papers and reports, the books mentioned in the text, and *Adventures in Respiration* (1938), an autobiographical defense of his ideas, which contains an incomplete bibliography. He described his experiences in the Spanish-American War in "Cruise of the Yale," *Yale Alumni Weekly*, 29 Sept. 1898. On Henderson generally see Howard W. Haggard's obituary in the *Yearbook of the American Philosophical Society* (1944), pp. 369–74. Herbert F. Janick, *Government for the People: The Leadership of the Progressive Party in Connecticut* (1993), uses correspondence in private hands to discuss his political activities during the 1910s. His opposition to Prohibition is analyzed in Philip J. Pauly, "Is Liquor Intoxicating? Scientists, Prohibition, and the Normalization of Drinking," *American Journal of Public Health* 84 (1994): 305–13.

PHILIP J. PAULY

HENDRICK (1680?–1755), Mohawk chief, was the son of a Mohegan father and a Mohawk mother. The names of his parents are not known. Hendrick's Mohawk name was Tiyanoga, also spelled Thoyanoguen, and he was also known as Henry Peters. Throughout the first half of the eighteenth century, Hendrick was perhaps the Mohawks' most influential sachem as well as a leading voice within the Iroquois Conferacy (that is, the Five Nations of New York: the Mohawks, Oneidas, Onondagas, Cayugas, and Senecas). A convert to Christianity in his youth, Hendrick became a close personal friend of William Johnson (Sir William Johnson), the New York trader who served as the official liaison between the English and the Iroquois and other northern tribes, and he was a longtime British ally.

Hendrick gained fame as one of four Iroquois sachems who accompanied Peter Schuyler to London in 1710 on a mission to attract British support for Indian affairs and against New France. The "Four Kings" were enthusiastically received by London officialdom. The queen outfitted them with expensive clothes and feted them; officials escorted them on guided tours of arsenals and landmarks; and officers saluted them with cannons on her majesty's ships. When Hendrick and the other sachems were presented at court, Queen Anne was so impressed by the Indians' pledges of loyalty and requests for missionaries that she instructed her government to dispatch Anglican ministers, Bibles, communion plates, and prayer books for her "Chapel of the Mohawks" and "Chapel of the Onondagas."

Before leaving London, the four sachems had their individual portraits painted in colorful costumes. In Hendrick's portrait, done by the London artist I. Verelot, the Mohawk sachem is dressed in an elegant European-style suit, draped in a flowing, regal cape. In his right hand is a belt of wampum signifying peace. A tomahawk is at his feet, while a wolf—the symbol of his clan—lurks behind him.

On his return, Hendrick was often referred to by the colonists as "King" or "Chief" Hendrick. As the leading sachem and spokesman for his Mohawk village at

Canajoharie, Hendrick took part in numerous conferences with British officials in New York, Massachusetts, and Pennsylvania. In 1740 he made a second visit to England (where he again had his portrait painted).

Hendrick's impressive oratorical skills, astute political leadership, and keen sense of military strategy earned him respect among Indians and whites. The Mohawk sachem demonstrated his flair for the dramatic in 1753, when he boldly chastised the governor of New York for ignoring the Mohawks and allowing French encroachments in the Ohio country. Dissatisfied with the governor's evasive reply, the defiant Hendrick shouted, "The Covenant Chain is broken between you and us!" The sachem and his followers then stormed out of the meeting.

Hendrick's actions stunned officials back in England. Fearing the loss of their Indian allies to the French, the Board of Trade immediately ordered the convening of the Albany Congress in 1754. At the meeting between the British colonies and the Five Iroquois Nations, Hendrick served as one of the Indians' main speakers, challenging the colonists to strengthen themselves and support the Indians against the French. At one point, Hendrick bluntly told the assembled delegates, "Look at the French, they are men, they are fortifying—but we are ashamed to say it, you are like women bare and open without any fortifications." The colonial delegates acceded to the demands of the Iroquois for payment of lands, restrictions on the sale of alcohol, and the building of an Anglican church in the Mohawk village of Canajoharie. The officials also promised to protect the Iroquois and check French advances onto Indian lands.

Within two years, Hendrick and many other Mohawks were fighting alongside their British allies in the French and Indian War. In 1755 Hendrick, along with other Mohawks, joined William Johnson's expedition to Crown Point. The old chief, by then in his seventies, was killed in an ambush at Lake George, as British and Indian forces were marching to intercept the enemy.

The death of Hendrick was a tremendous loss for both the Mohawks and the British colonists. The man whom Johnson called "the great Mohawk sachem" had been a dedicated patriot chief and a staunch British ally. His leadership enabled the Mohawks to retain their political, economic, and military strength and facilitated Britain's imperialistic goals throughout the Great Lakes country. Hendrick's many achievements have earned him recognition as one of the greatest and most successful Native-American leaders in history.

• Information about Hendrick's life and public actions can be found in a variety of places. Two of the best sources for primary documents are *Iroquois Indians: A Documentary History of the Diplomacy of the Six Nations and Their League*, ed. Francis Jennings et al. (1984), and *The Papers of Sir William Johnson*, ed. James Sullivan et. al. (14 vols., 1921–1965). Perhaps the most accurate and complete secondary source that contains information about Hendrick is Milton W. Hamilton, *Sir William Johnson: Colonial American, 1715–1763* (1976). This can be supplemented with additional information found in Richard Aquila, *The Iroquois Restoration: Iroquois Diplomacy on the Colonial Frontier, 1701–1754* (1983), and Francis Jennings, *The Ambiguous Iroquois Empire* (1984).

RICHARD AQUILA

HENDRICK, Burton Jesse (8 Dec. 1870–23 Mar. 1949), journalist and biographer, was born in New Haven, Connecticut, the son of Charles Buddington Hendrick, a watchmaker and inventor, and Mary Elizabeth Johnston. Hendrick worked to earn money for his tuition before entering Yale University at age twenty. He received his B.A. in 1895. In 1896 he married Bertha Jane Ives; they had two sons.

While at Yale, Hendrick was editor of the student newspaper and financial editor of the literary magazine. In 1896 he began working as a reporter at the *New Haven Morning News* while doing graduate work in literature at Yale; he received his M.A. in 1897. At the *Morning News*, Hendrick moved up to the editorship, but the newspaper ceased publication in 1898. He also wrote occasionally for the *New York Evening Post* and the *New York Sun* and was New Haven correspondent for the *Sun* briefly in 1899. In March 1899 he was hired as a reporter at the *New York Evening Post* and worked there until 1905, spending the last two years as an editorial writer. He also wrote occasional magazine articles. After submitting two of them to *McClure's Magazine*, he was asked in 1905 to join the magazine's staff.

From 1905 to 1913 Hendrick was one of the stalwarts of S. S. McClure's distinguished company of writers, contributing several notable works to the "literature of exposure" of those years. Historian David Chalmers included him among the thirteen writers who constituted the core of the movement that became known as "muckraking," with Hendrick on the conservative side of that group. His major achievement was a seven-part series, "The Story of Life Insurance" (May–Nov. 1906), which took several months of research and portrayed in extensive detail the schemes company executives used to pile up huge reserves of cash that they used for their own purposes. It was republished as a book by McClure in 1907. Of that work, Louis Filler wrote that "not many of the lesser muckrakers left so substantial a memento of youthful enthusiasm" (p. 199). Another series in 1907–1908 examined how great American fortunes had been made. Besides business and finance, Hendrick during his years at *McClure's* also wrote on politics, health, medicine, and science.

In 1913 Hendrick went to work at the *World's Work*, the monthly public-affairs magazine founded by Walter Hines Page, who had just been appointed U.S. ambassador to Great Britain. Hendrick remained at the magazine as associate editor until 1927, writing about many of the subjects of his earlier work but with a new emphasis on national defense and diplomacy and writing most of the magazine's editorials. He also continued to write for *McClure's* (1914–1915) and for *Harper's Magazine* (1914–1918).

While at the *World's Work* and largely through his work there, Hendrick achieved notice and success in biography, winning three Pulitzer Prizes. He collaborated in 1920 with Rear Admiral William Sowden Sims, commander of U.S. naval forces in the Atlantic in World War I, to write *The Victory at Sea*, Sims's account of the naval war, which had been serialized in the magazine under Sims's byline. It won the 1920 Pulitzer Prize for history. Earlier, he had ghostwritten Henry Morgenthau's memoirs, *Ambassador Morgenthau's Story* (1918), which also had run as a series in the *World's Work*.

In 1920 Arthur W. Page, editor of the *World's Work* and son of Walter Hines Page, who had died in 1918, assigned Hendrick to write the elder Page's biography. He continued to receive his regular salary from the magazine for two years while working only on the biography, which told Page's life story largely through his letters. Historian John Milton Cooper noted that Hendrick, late in his life, downplayed his role. Cooper, however, attributed part of the book's success to Hendrick's "assiduous research," which included "gathering voluminous papers . . . and collecting a great deal of collateral information and description from interviews" (p. 398). The work was serialized in the magazine, appearing in fourteen parts (Sept. 1921–Oct. 1922), and published in two volumes as *The Life and Letters of Walter Hines Page* in September 1922. It sold well in the United States and Great Britain in its first year and continued to do so for several years. Hendrick earned his second Pulitzer Prize when the work was recognized as best American biography of 1922. After Woodrow Wilson's death in 1924, Page's letters to the president were made available, and Hendrick produced a third volume, which was published in September 1925, after being serialized in the *World's Work*. It also sold well. A third Pulitzer Prize came to Hendrick for *The Training of an American: The Earlier Life and Letters of Walter Hines Page, 1855–1913* (1928).

In 1927 Hendrick left the *World's Work* and worked full time on biography. He spent five years in research for *The Life of Andrew Carnegie* (2 vols., 1932), for which he was paid a salary and expenses by Carnegie's widow. (A similar arrangement in the 1940s with the Mellon family to write a biography of Andrew W. Mellon was ended by the family after the work was completed but before publication.) He also edited *Miscellaneous Writings of Andrew Carnegie* (1933). His final project was *Louise Whitfield Carnegie: The Life of Mrs. Andrew Carnegie*, for which he was paid a commission by the Carnegies' daughter. The book was published posthumously in 1950 after being completed by Daniel Henderson.

Between 1935 and 1946, Hendrick produced four major works epitomizing his approach to telling history through group biography. *The Lees of Virginia: Biography of a Family* (1935) was followed by *Bulwark of the Republic: A Biography of the Constitution* (1937), which told the story of the document through the lives of key figures. Hendrick's final major works, *States-*

men of the Lost Cause: Jefferson Davis and His Cabinet (1939) and *Lincoln's War Cabinet* (1946) portrayed both sides of the great conflict through the men who directed it. *Bulwark* and *Statesmen* sold especially well. Hendrick died in New York City.

As a "scholarly biographer-historian-journalist," which is how *Time* (4 Apr. 1949, p. 83) remembered him, Hendrick merged in his work the research and writing skills of journalism with the scholarship of history to produce accurate and detailed biographies. Some pointed to a lack of critical evaluation of his subjects, but most recognized his skill in appealing to readers. "His historical studies were substantial, if not definitive," the *American Historical Review* commented, "and he had the gift to reach and interest a large public" (54 [July 1949]: 989).

• Hendrick's papers are privately held in Winfield, Illinois. His reminiscences are in the Oral History Collection of Columbia University. The American Academy of Arts and Letters Library, New York City, has a collection of correspondence (1923–1949) relating to the National Institute of Arts and Letters, of which Hendrick was secretary for many years. Other relevant collections are the Walter Hines Page Papers at Duke University Library and Houghton Library, Harvard University; the Arthur W. Page Papers at the State Historical Society of Wisconsin, Madison; and the S. S. McClure Papers at Lilly Library, Indiana University. Hendrick's other books are *The Age of Big Business: A Chronicle of the Captains of Industry* (1919), a volume in Yale University Press's Chronicles of America series; *The Jews in America* (1923), a series published in the *World's Work*; and *William Crawford Gorgas: His Life and Work* (1924), written with Marie Doughty Gorgas, which also first appeared in the *World's Work*. Various works on *McClure's* and Progressive Era journalism that mention Hendrick include Peter Lyon, *Success Story: The Life and Times of S. S. McClure* (1963); David Chalmers, *The Social and Political Ideas of the Muckrakers* (1964); Harold S. Wilson, *McClure's Magazine and the Muckrakers* (1970); and Louis Filler, *The Muckrakers* (1976). See also John Milton Cooper Jr., *Walter Hines Page: The Southerner as American, 1855–1918* (1977). An obituary is in the *New York Times*, 25 Mar. 1949.

RONALD S. MARMARELLI

HENDRICKS, Sterling Brown (13 Apr. 1902–4 Jan. 1981), physical chemist, was born in Elysian Fields, Texas, the son of James Gilchrist Hendricks, a physician, and Martha Daisy Gamblin, a schoolteacher. Hendricks received his elementary education both in a local one-room school and from his mother. There not being a high school in Elysian Fields, he moved to Shreveport, Louisiana, living with an aunt there until his graduation from Shreveport High School in 1918. He then attended the University of Arkansas, earning a bachelor of science degree in chemical engineering in 1922. After receiving a master's degree in chemistry in 1924 from Kansas State University, he undertook doctoral studies at the California Institute of Technology. There a new faculty member, Linus Pauling, directed his dissertation, and Hendricks received a Ph.D. in chemistry in 1926, one year after Pauling had received his doctorate from Caltech. Hendricks and Pauling maintained a close friendship that lasted until the former's death.

Hendricks was at Caltech when physics and chemistry were in ferment as a result of revolutionary ideas of quantum mechanics and the Lewis-Langmuir electronic theory of the chemical bond and valency, which proposed that chemical bonds form by electron sharing between atoms instead of the then accepted theory of bond formation by electrostatic attraction. He absorbed both Pauling's enthusiasm for the new ideas and his interest in the structural organization of matter. Pauling, who was using X-ray diffraction analysis to determine the atomic arrangements in crystalline solids, assigned Hendricks the task of determining the molecular structure of the minerals corundum and hematite. These had been investigated in Europe, but Hendricks proved that some of the assigned atomic positions were incorrect, his refined structures providing a clearer understanding of the interatomic forces in these crystals. He left Caltech an expert on X-ray diffraction and full of enthusiasm for advancing the understanding of molecular structure.

After one-year research assistantships at the Geophysical Laboratory of the Carnegie Institution and the Rockefeller Institute of Medical Research, Hendricks in 1928 joined the U.S. Department of Agriculture as an associate chemist in the Fixed Nitrogen Laboratory and became a member of the Soils Research Group, a division within several subsequent units of the USDA. From 1957 to 1970 he was chief scientist of the Mineral Nutrition Pioneering Research Laboratory of the USDA's Agricultural Research Service, founded in Beltsville, Maryland, to conduct the basic research needed to solve agricultural problems.

Hendricks married Edith Ochiltree in 1931. The couple resided in Silver Spring, Maryland, and had one child. In 1970 he retired but remained active in research. He claimed that he chose government service out of a conviction that to serve people through science his research had to be of direct human benefit and that with the USDA he could do basic research on soils, minerals, and plants that might result in the improvement of crops and human nutrition. He never regretted his decision to join the federal government, finding with the USDA all the freedom and satisfaction that he could desire.

Hendricks's researches in his first years with USDA were a continuation of his Caltech work on X-ray diffraction of minerals and his interest in the concept of the hydrogen bond, a part of Gilbert N. Lewis's valence theory. His first major contribution appeared in an article on the nature of soil colloids, "The Results of X-ray and Microscopical Examination of Soil Colloids" (*Soil Science* 29 [1930]: 457–79). He established that the colloidal particles in clay were really crystalline minerals and not amorphous material, as believed. His X-ray diffraction studies revealed that these minerals had a variety of lattice structures. He determined the size, shape, opacity, and other physical properties of the particles and used the chemical composition of the colloids to classify soils based on their silicon-oxygen ratios. Many soil scientists regard his 1930 paper as the most important ever published on the nature and properties of soils.

During the 1930s and 1940s Hendricks demonstrated how the properties of silicate minerals, such as kaolinite, montmorillonite, and halloysite—the predominant inorganic constituents of soil—were a consequence of the atomic arrangements in their crystal structures. The silicates were of immense variety because silicon and oxygen atoms formed stable compounds, the basic unit being the silicon-oxygen tetrahedron, in which a central silicon atom bonded tetrahedrally to four oxygen atoms. This arrangement gave rise to structures of indefinite extent in all dimensions by the sharing of the corners and edges of tetrahedra. Enhancing the variety of structures was the ability of aluminum to replace silicon in the tetrahedron. Hendricks elaborated these extended structures and established the mineral groups, crystal structures, and method of identification of all the clays in soil, and related the properties of clays to the structures. He showed that the overall negative charge of the tetrahedral units was balanced by cations of different metallic elements dispersed between the linear chains or layered structures. In some lattice structures he found that hydrogen bonds, formed by the linking of hydroxyl (OH) groups in a silicate layer to oxygen atoms in an adjacent layer, increased the stability of the layered structures.

Hendricks's study of hydrogen bonding within lattice structures began with his finding ways to detect the presence of such bonds. A bond between the hydrogen of a hydroxyl or amine (NH) group with entities having unpaired electrons, such as oxygen or nitrogen atoms, would be much weaker than a covalent bond but could have a cumulative effect on large molecules, such as the silicates, and play a decisive role in the formation and maintenance of a highly organized structure. In the early 1930s Hendricks was a pioneer in the detection of such bonds by using infrared spectroscopy for this purpose. His research led to some of the most informative and characteristic manifestations of the hydrogen bond.

Infrared spectroscopy in the 1930s was in a primitive state. The devices used were difficult to build and operate. Nevertheless, Hendricks published in the *Journal of the American Chemical Society* a series of papers in 1935 and 1936 in which he reported finding that the characteristic hydroxyl or amine absorption in the infrared was absent in alcoholic or amino compounds because of hydrogen bonding. His research produced an immense volume of research by other scientists and a vast expansion of knowledge about hydrogen bonds in a variety of molecules.

In the early 1940s Hendricks explored the process by which soils made their mineral nutrients available to plants. He discovered that ion exchange in soil minerals was essential to soil fertility. Cation exchange by silicates required the existence of channels in the lattice structure large enough for ionic migration, with soil fertility the result of the hydrogen ions produced by plants being exchanged for cation nutrients in the soils, such as calcium and potassium ions. Physical scientists regarded these studies on mineral structures of the 1930s and 1940s as monumental contributions to mineralogy and soil science. One indication of his studies' importance was the award of the Day Medal of the Geological Society of America in 1952 to Hendricks, the first nongeologist so honored.

From 1945 Hendricks's research moved in new directions. He became an expert radiochemist in order to take advantage of the postwar availability of radioisotopes produced by nuclear reactors. He realized the value of radiophosphorus for agriculture as a tracer to study the uptake of soil phosphate by plants, phosphate being essential to the physiology of every living cell. In 1946 he introduced the phosphorus-32 radioisotope into his research to determine the extent to which increasing the phosphorus content of soil improved plant growth. He found that all crops obtained their phosphorus from both the soil and fertilizer. The proportions, however, varied greatly, depending on the character of the root system. Corn, for example, with an extensive system was capable of storing large amounts of soil phosphorus, whereas potatoes, with a limited system, relied more on fertilizer phosphorus. He traced the path followed by the nutrient through the soil, into the plant, and through the plant, as well as determining the differing needs of plants for fertilizer during their growth cycle. His research greatly benefited farmers, since the purchase of fertilizer was one of the farmer's largest cash expenditures in crop production. Agricultural scientists' demand for radiophosphorus became so great that the USDA prepared fertilizer containing the radioisotope to meet the needs of investigators throughout the country.

Another new direction in research led to Hendricks's most striking accomplishment. In 1945 he began to study photoperiodism, the process by which plants respond to the length of day and night in their physiological activity. USDA scientists knew that the length of day or night was a critical factor in determining when a plant would flower. In the mid-1930s two USDA scientists, Harry Borthwick and M. W. Parker, investigated the photocontrol of flowering. They asked Hendricks to join them in a study of short-day plants (plants that flower on a short-day, long-night regime). In 1945 Hendricks introduced the use of absorption spectroscopy as a means of measuring a plant's response to radiation at different wavelengths when its leaves are exposed to short periods of light during the long-night period. He built a spectrograph from parts of his infrared device that he had used in his hydrogen bond work. He obtained a powerful carbon arc from a Baltimore movie theater, and other parts from a variety of sources, including old streetcar systems. The spectrograph produced an intense beam from the carbon arc that then passed through a prism to break light into specific bands and irradiated leaves with different parts of the spectrum. Within a year he obtained an action spectrum for short-day soybean

plants, a spectrum derived from the absorption of light by plant leaves and the concomitant effect on flowering. The maximum absorption and inhibition of flowering took place with red light of a specific wavelength.

By 1952 the research team had extended action spectra to other short-day plants and to other phenomena, such as seed germination and stem elongation, again finding maximum absorption with red light. Hendricks concluded that there was a single red-absorbing pigment functioning in plants. However, with seed germination another discovery emerged. Seeds displayed maximum growth with brief periods of red radiation, but with red light at the edge of the visible spectrum there was an inhibition of germination. The photocontrol process was reversible, a finding that also applied to flowering and stem elongation.

Hendricks, finding that the photoperiodic effects were repeatedly reversible, inferred the pigment existed in two interchangeable forms, one having maximum absorption within the red region of the spectrum and the other having a maximum in the far-red. He found a way to estimate the concentration of the pigment in plant leaves from a comparison of the intensity of light falling on and transmitted by the leaves. The result indicated that the pigment functioned at very low intracellular concentrations. By 1956 he and Borthwick had also proved that the critical aspect of photocontrol was in the dark transformation of the far-red form back to the red-absorbing form, providing a timing mechanism, or biological clock, that enabled photoperiodic plants to distinguish long nights from short ones.

Hendricks's next task was to establish the nature of the entity in plants that reacted to light. In the mid-1950s two new members joined the group, Karl Norris, an agricultural engineer, and Harold Siegelman, a plant biochemist. Norris had developed spectrophotometers capable of measuring very small changes in light absorption. Hendricks knew that a bioassay or chemical assay was not possible with the pigment at such low concentrations, but a spectrophotometric assay might work. Hendricks, Norris, and Siegelman examined plant tissue in the spectrophotometer for the photoreversible absorbance changes in the red and far-red spectral regions. However, all attempts were unsuccessful, presumably because of the very low concentration of the pigment. But in 1959 with seeds of dark-grown turnip plants they found the absorbance changes.

Siegelman then used protein extraction methods to obtain highly purified cell-free extracts and produced the same spectrophotometric results as with plant tissue. By heat denaturation, Hendricks and Siegelman proved that the pigment was a protein and cleaved from the protein its associated chromophore, the chemical group responsible for the color of the pigment. They named the pigment "phytochrome." The chromophore had a structure that isomerized under the action of light from a red-absorbing blue pigment to a far-red absorbing, less colored green-blue form of the pigment by a shift of hydrogen atoms within the structure.

Through the 1970s Hendricks continued to study phytochrome. He discovered that phytochrome was involved in photocontrol at the level of cell membranes and proposed that the far-red pigment form bonded to membranes and influenced their permeability to ions, which in turn affected the synthesis and secretion of plant hormones, a hypothesis still under investigation at his death. Other scientists demonstrated that phytochrome regulated many plant growth and development processes.

The recipient of many honors and awards for both his mineralogical and biological studies, Hendricks was elected to the National Academy of Sciences in 1952 and to the presidencies of the Mineralogical Society of America in 1954 and the American Society of Plant Physiologists in 1959. In 1958 President Dwight Eisenhower bestowed on him the Presidential Award for Distinguished Civilian Service, the highest honor given to a career civil servant. From President Gerald Ford he received the 1976 National Medal of Science.

Hendricks was an active outdoorsman, being both a long distance swimmer and a highly regarded alpinist. Growing up in east Texas, he developed a love of nature as he explored the countryside of rolling hills and pine forests. In California in the 1920s he attempted to swim around Catalina Island and backpacked 100 miles through the Santa Lucia Mountains. As an alpinist in the 1930s, he scaled four previously unclimbed peaks in the British Columbia Rockies and received official recognition from Canadian authorities. In 1942 he was a member of the third party to climb Mount McKinley, the highest peak in North America. For the last seven years of his life he was a member of the Committee for Research and Exploration of the National Geographic Society and made field trips for the society to Africa and the Middle East. On a 1980 Christmas visit to his daughter in Novato, California, he came down with the flu and took a vaccine to minimize the symptoms. The inoculation, however, resulted in the Guillain-Barré syndrome and his death there a few days later.

Hendricks was a warm, lively, and responsive person who remained young in spirit and engaged in creative and productive research to the end of his life. What characterized his research was its interdisciplinary nature, depth of penetration, and incredibly broad scope. In seeking causes for phenomena involving soils and plants he drew on all the physical sciences to reach his goal of understanding.

• Hendricks provided two autobiographical essays, "The Passing Scene," *Annual Review of Plant Physiology* 21 (1970): 1–10, and a more technical statement in *McGraw-Hill Modern Scientists and Engineers* 2 (1980): 43–44. Among his important articles are "X-rays in Agriculture," *Journal of Applied Physics* 9 (1938): 237–43; "Lattice Structures of Clay Minerals and Some Properties of Clays," *Journal of Geology* 50 (1942): 276–90; "Base Exchange of Crystalline Silicates," *Industrial and Chemical Engineering* 37 (1945): 625–30; "Recent Developments in the Control of Flowering by Photope-riod," *American Naturalist* 84 (1950): 117–34; "Radioisotopes in Soils Research and Plant Nutrition," *Annual Review of Nuclear Science* 1 (1952): 592–610; and "Phytochrome and Its Control of Plant Growth and Development," *Advances in Enzymology* 26 (1964): 1–33. He wrote on photoperiodism for the nonscientist in "The Clocks of Life," *Atlantic Monthly*, Oct. 1957, pp. 111–15. A detailed biographical study is by Warren L. Butler and Cecil H. Wadleigh in the National Academy of Sciences, *Biographical Memoirs* 56 (1987): 181–212, which includes a bibliography of his publications. Two perceptive essays with personal recollections are by Linus Pauling, "Memorial of Sterling Brown Hendricks," *American Mineralogist* 67 (1982): 406–9, and Cecil H. Wadleigh, "Sterling Brown Hendricks," *American Philosophical Society Yearbook* (1981), pp. 458–62. An obituary is in the *Washington Post*, 6 Jan. 1981.

ALBERT B. COSTA

HENDRICKS, Thomas Andrews (7 Sept. 1819–25 Nov. 1885), twenty-first vice president of the United States, was born in Muskingum County, Ohio, the son of John Hendricks and Jane Thomson, farmers. Hendricks's grandfather, Abraham Hendricks, served in the Pennsylvania legislature, and an uncle, William Hendricks, was governor of Indiana and twice its U.S. senator. Another uncle and a cousin also held state and local offices. His father served as a deputy surveyor of public lands after he took his family to Shelby County, Indiana, in 1822. Following graduation in 1841 from Hanover College in Indiana, where he studied a classical curriculum and excelled as a debater, Thomas read law, first under the tutelage of a local attorney and then with Alexander Thomson in Pennsylvania. In 1845 he married Eliza C. Morgan; they had one son who survived three years. Hendricks practiced law in Shelby County until 1860, when he moved to Indianapolis, where he formed a legal partnership with Oscar Hord. Raised a Presbyterian, Hendricks joined the Episcopal church as an adult.

An accomplished politician and a lifelong Democrat, Hendricks pursued public life as his avocation as well as an occupation from his entrance into government at age twenty-eight until his death. In 1848 he won election to the Indiana General Assembly, where he chaired the committee on banks and advocated free public education. He took an active role in the convention (1850–1851) that rewrote Indiana's state constitution, successfully urging prohibition of state indebtedness and of African-American settlement in the state. He also supported state operated banks and the replacement of annual meetings of the state legislature with biennial sessions limited to sixty-one days. As a member of Congress from 1851 to 1855, Hendricks sided with Douglas Democrats in opposing antislavery agitation and supporting the Kansas-Nebraska Act, a vote that contributed to his defeat for reelection in 1854. In Congress he voted with Whigs in favor of internal improvements and joined westerners in support of cheap land policy. Between 1855 and 1859 he served as commissioner of public lands; in this position his principal duty was the registration of land titles.

Defeated in the race for governor in 1860, Hendricks's fortunes rebounded in 1862 when Democrats won control of the state legislature and elected him to the U.S. Senate (1863–1869). In Washington he anchored the small band of Democrats who opposed the Radical Republicans during the Civil War and Reconstruction. Although critical of secession, he objected to the conscription of men into the army, the use of African-American troops, and the overthrow of slavery under the animus of war. During Andrew Johnson's administration he adopted the Democrats' lenient posture toward the former Confederate states, which he argued had not technically left the Union because secession was illegal. For his vote against the impeachment of the president and other prosouthern, antiblack positions, Republicans labeled him an "apologist of slavery" and a "traitor." Their control of the state legislature barred Hendricks from a second term in the Senate.

Hendricks nevertheless remained popular with Indiana Democrats, who nominated him once again for governor in 1868. Narrowly defeated in this contest, he won the gubernatorial post in 1872. As was customary for executives at the time, he preferred to defer to the will of the legislature during his four-year term. He sidestepped confrontation with temperance advocates by signing a bill that impeded liquor sales, but he favored a less-restrictive substitute act that the legislature passed two years later. He recommended the elimination of the fee method of compensating public officials and closer regulation of elections. As depression settled across the state, Hendricks authorized the militia to intervene in labor disturbances among coal miners in 1873 and among railroad workers who were angered by wage cuts and the use of black strikebreakers in 1874.

Hendricks was an aspirant for the presidential nomination in 1868 and 1876. He accepted the second spot on the ticket in the latter race, when Samuel Tilden won a majority of the popular vote but lost the election because twenty disputed electoral votes were awarded to Republican Rutherford Hayes. Rebuffed in an attempt for the presidency in 1880, Hendricks disavowed interest in becoming a candidate for president in 1884. He consented, however, to run as the vice presidential nominee when Democrats sought a regional counterweight to a ticket headed by Grover Cleveland of New York. As in 1876, strategists hoped that Hendricks would tip Indiana, where partisan loyalists were closely balanced, into the Democratic column. They also conjectured that his ties to politicos in Tammany Hall would aid the party in New York and that his support of "honest" government and "Greenback" currency would attract voters elsewhere. By holding the "Solid South" and by edging out Republicans in four northern states, including Indiana and New York, Democrats captured the White House for the first time since 1856.

Hendricks was one of the more tenacious politicians of his age. Counting his several considerations as a potential presidential nominee, he was a candidate for elective office on thirteen occasions. He won seven of these elections, which placed him in legislative and executive offices at both the state and national levels. When not campaigning for himself, he lent his talents as an orator to Democrats in his home state and across the country. To admirers such as David Turpie, a Democratic politician in Indiana, Hendricks had a "practical and constructive" mind. Detractors such as the editors of the *Indianapolis Daily Journal* described him as a "bundle of very convenient negatives" (13 June 1872). The vice president epitomized the Democratic party's outlook of limited government and resistance to federal encroachment on "states' rights." Like Cleveland, Hendricks's reputation rested heavily on denouncing corruption and political favoritism in government. Nine months into office he died unexpectedly at his home in Indianapolis. The vacancy in the vice presidency prompted Congress to enact a law specifying presidential succession.

• No major collection of Hendricks papers exists. John W. Holcombe and Hubert M. Skinner, *Life and Public Services of Thomas A. Hendricks* (1886), is a useful review of his life. The political background of his career is discussed in Emma Lou Thornbrough, *Indiana in the Civil War Era, 1850–1880* (1965); Allan Bogue, *The Earnest Men: Republicans of the Civil War Senate* (1981); Allan Nevins, *Grover Cleveland: A Study in Courage* (1932); and David Turpie, *Sketches of My Own Times* (1903).

BALLARD C. CAMPBELL

HENDRICKS, William (12 Nov. 1782–16 May 1850), Indiana congressman, governor, and senator, was born in Westmoreland County, Pennsylvania, the son of Abraham Hendricks and Ann Jamison, farmers. In 1810 Hendricks graduated from Jefferson College at Canonsburg, Pennsylvania, and migrated to Cincinnati, Ohio, where he taught school, read law, and was admitted to the bar. He arrived at Madison, Indiana Territory, during the early months of the War of 1812, and Madison remained his home until his death. There he practiced law and in 1813 cofounded the *Western Eagle*, the second newspaper in the territory. In 1816 Hendricks married Ann Parker Paul, the daughter of John Paul (1758–1830), founder of Madison. To them were born six sons and three daughters.

By the time Indiana became a state in 1816, Hendricks had held several political offices, including representative to the territorial house of representatives from Jefferson County, Speaker of the territorial house, U.S. attorney for Indiana Territory, and secretary of the constitutional convention. In 1816 he was elected Indiana's representative to the second session of the Fourteenth Congress; he was reelected in 1817, 1818, and 1820. In 1818 his margin of victory was almost nine to one; in 1820 it was more than ten to one. In 1822 he was elected governor of Indiana without opposition. In 1825 and 1830 the Indiana General Assembly elected Hendricks to the U.S. Senate.

Though few politicians surpassed him in careful attention to the needs and desires of their constituents, and though he had been the most popular politician in

Indiana, he was not reelected in 1836. Hendricks always had maintained his freedom of action without regard to party politics, but his nonalignment had become unpopular in an era of intense partisanship, and he could not muster enough support on personal grounds to be reelected. Though he remained active in politics, he never again held public office. He spent his latter years managing his extensive properties and practicing law at Madison.

As a public official, Hendricks supported federally constructed or financed internal improvements, backing the Cumberland Road, a road across Indiana from the Ohio River to Lake Michigan, and a canal around the Falls of the Ohio on the Indiana side of the river. He urged that Indians whose presence obstructed white settlement or resulted in friction between Indians and whites be removed to lands west of the Mississippi River. He also worked for legislation making it easier for settlers to acquire land and urged that all public lands be ceded to the states in which they were located.

Hendricks was not a partisan legislator, nor could he be identified as a nationalist or as a states' rights advocate. He opposed the extension of slavery into the territories but agreed that Congress had no right to interfere with slavery in the states; he believed that a well-managed national bank was essential for maintaining a stable monetary system, but he was not committed to the Second Bank of the United States; he sought economy in government but did not believe that this should be at the expense of national security or public welfare; and he applauded the revolutions in Latin America but did not advocate intervention. He defended the protective tariff, however, and rejected the doctrines of states' rights and nullification.

Though Hendricks represented the people of Indiana on Capitol Hill for eighteen years, he made little lasting impact on the national political scene. Even in Indiana his name is almost unknown. He long was popular with his constituents, however, because he diligently and faithfully defended and promoted their interests, both public and private, without regard to their politics. He died at a farm he owned that was near his home in Madison.

• Hendricks's views on national and state matters are readily accessible in Frederick D. Hill, ed., "William Hendricks' Political Circulars to His Constituents," *Indiana Magazine of History* 70 (Dec. 1974): 296–344; and 71 (June 1975: 124–80; Dec. 1975: 330–74). Small collections of Hendricks's papers are located in the Indiana Historical Society Library and in the Indiana Division, Indiana State Library, both at Indianapolis. Additional items are scattered in other collections. These are cited in the bibliography of Frederick D. Hill, "William Hendricks: Indiana Politician and Western Advocate, 1812–1850" (Ph.D. diss., Ind. Univ. 1972), the only comprehensive account of Hendricks's life. Frederick D. Hill, "William Hendricks: Popular Nonpartisan," in *Their Infinite Variety: Essays on Indiana Politicians, Indiana Historical Collections*, vol. 53 (1981), is a brief survey of Hendricks's political career.

FREDERICK D. HILL

HENDRIX, Eugene Russell (17 May 1847–11 Nov. 1927), bishop of the Methodist Episcopal Church, South, was born in Fayette, Missouri, the son of Adam Hendrix, an educator and banker, and Isabelle Jane Murray. A Pennsylvania transplant who worked as a teacher before migrating to Fayette in 1840, Adam Hendrix became a leading citizen of the community, achieving prosperity and prestige as town banker for almost forty years. Family, education, and religious service intertwined to form the defining triad in Eugene's life where, as the second of five children, he grew up in a close family. As a younger teenager, he was nurtured religiously by the Methodist Episcopal Church, South (MECS), the denomination of his mother and despite an early interest in business, his commitment to the Methodist ministry developed during vacations spent with his pious paternal grandfather in Pennsylvania.

Precocious and wealthy, Eugene followed the example of his older brothers and traveled east for college. In preparation for the ministry beginning at the age of sixteen he attended in succession Wesleyan University in Middletown, Connecticut, where he received an A.B. in 1867, and Union Theological Seminary in New York from which he graduated in 1869. Residence in a cosmopolitan venue was a heady experience for Hendrix, yet he retained a deep affection for the Midwest ethos, which eventually drew him back to his native region.

From its inception, Hendrix viewed his ministry as one of reconciliation. This emphasis was especially significant in Missouri, a border state during the Civil War where northern and southern branches of American Methodism had battled one another openly. He was ordained in 1870, and one year later he was admitted to the Missouri Conference of the MECS. An ambition to pursue advanced studies and a desire to live near his elderly parents kept Hendrix on the move for most of his short pastoral career. Successively, he served as pastor at Leavenworth, Kansas, from 1869 to 1870; Macon, Missouri, from 1870 to 1872; and St. Joseph, Missouri, from 1872 to 1876. Despite such brief stays, however, during his Macon tenure he became a close friend of Dr. Nathan Scarritt of Kansas City, Missouri, and in June 1872 he married the oldest of Scarritt's nine children, Ann Eliza Scarritt. The couple would have four children.

Hendrix was already a rising star in the MECS when he accompanied Bishop Enoch M. Marvin on a survey of Far Eastern missions in 1876. Hendrix's impressions were subsequently published in 1878 under the title, *Around the World*. The trip not only demolished Hendrix's last vestiges of parochialism, it also nurtured his incipient advocacy of ecumenism. From this small spark, a great fire would eventually rage.

In 1878 Hendrix gave up the pastorate to assume the presidency of Central College in Fayette, Missouri. This appointment surprised few as Nathan Scarritt had led Central since its opening in 1857. During his eight years of service to Central College, Hendrix proved to be a superb administrator who updated and enlarged Central's facilities, increased its endowment, and enhanced the institution's academic reputation.

Hendrix's successful stint at Central lasted until 1886, giving him substantial promise of an illustrious career in academic education. In fact, Hendrix had previously received offers for the theological deanship of Vanderbilt and the presidency of the University of Missouri in 1885. He declined to accept both offers, however, mainly because his attachment to the church was stronger than his tie to the academy.

Consequently, Hendrix yielded to the call of the MECS to its episcopacy in May 1886. For more than forty years, he distinguished himself as bishop, dedicating 287 churches, ordaining over 1,600 ministers, and presiding over every annual conference held during his tenure. His influence was felt not only locally, but also nationally and worldwide. During this time period he maintained his scholarly credentials through lectureships at Vanderbilt (1903), Emory (1903), Trinity College (1916), and Syracuse (1916). He also authored various texts, including *Skilled Labor For the Master* (1901), *The Religion of the Incarnation* (1903), *The Personality of the Holy Spirit* (1903), *Christ's Table Talk* (1908), and *If I Had Not Come* (1916). Likewise, Hendrix published numerous articles in various Methodist journals. Hendrix could best be characterized as a "theological liberal," although in the moderate sense of the term. His overriding concerns were pastoral, and he was interested in theological constructs only to the extent that they affected the execution of pastoral duties. Still, as Ivan Lee Holt noted, there is a definite "mystical and theological" dimension to Hendrix's preaching (p. 78). Other concerns of Hendrix were missions and the reunion of American Methodism.

Throughout Hendrix's adult life, his conviction that the Methodism of his youth must transcend its regional and sectarian boundaries in order to thrive in the twentieth century continued to grow. Consequently, he took every opportunity to promote ecumenism among the clans of Methodism, as well as within the larger Protestant family. In 1900 he served as messenger to the British Wesleyan Conference, and his tireless advocacy of interdenominational cooperation was capped by his election in 1908 as the first president of the Federal Council of the Churches of Christ in America. It was a post he held for four years. After his association with the Federal Council, Hendrix then served on Andrew Carnegie's ill-fated Church Peace Union for a time after 1914. Hendrix remained extraordinarily active until infirmities began to overtake him in the early 1920s. He died at his home in Kansas City, Missouri.

Although he was an administrator, educator, and pastor, ultimately, Hendrix's value to his denomination exceeded even the sum of these impressive titles. Certainly, he was one of Southern Methodism's first truly modern leaders. Exhibiting an attitude rare among his contemporaries, he was largely responsible for guiding the MECS out of the narrow regionalism that gave the denomination birth. In doing so he laid the groundwork that led to the reunion of the northern and southern branches of American Methodism in 1939 and the larger involvement of Methodists in various ecumenical efforts throughout the first half of the twentieth century.

• Hendrix's diary, along with other papers, can be found in the Western Historical Manuscript Collection of the University of Missouri Library at Columbia. The standard biography of Hendrix is Ivan Lee Holt, *Eugene Russell Hendrix: Servant of the Kingdom* (1950), which was compiled using many quotations from Hendrix's diary. Hendrix's role in the Federal Council of Churches is mentioned briefly in Elias B. Sandford, *Origin and History of the Federal Council of the Churches of Christ in America* (1916). For an extensive obituary see Alfred F. Smith, "Eugene Russell Hendrix: A Bishop in the Methodist Episcopal Church, South," *Methodist Quarterly Review* 77, no. 2 (Apr. 1928): 205–16. Other obituaries are in the *Kansas City Journal*, 12–13 Nov. 1927, and the *Christian Advocate* (New York ed.), 24 Nov. 1927.

ROBERT H. KRAPOHL

HENDRIX, Jimi (27 Nov. 1942–18 Sept. 1970), rock guitarist, singer, and songwriter, was born into a working-class black family in Seattle, Washington, the son of James Allen Ross Hendrix, a gardener, and Lucille Jetter. Named Johnny Allen Hendrix at birth by his mother while his father was in the service, his name was changed to James Marshall Hendrix by his father upon his return home. Self-taught as a left-handed guitarist from an early age, Hendrix played a right-handed guitar upside down, a practice he maintained throughout his life since it allowed for unusual fingering patterns and quicker access to tone and volume controls. His early influences ranged from jazz guitarist Charlie Christian to blues guitarists and honking rhythm and blues saxophone soloists. He attended elementary school in Vancouver, British Columbia, and Seattle and went to Garfield High School in Seattle. In his senior year, he left high school to become a paratrooper with the 101st Airborne Division of the U.S. Army.

At Fort Campbell, Kentucky, Hendrix formed a rhythm and blues band, the Casuals, with bassist Billy Cox, who would rejoin him years later at the height of his fame. Following his discharge from the army in 1962, he moved to Nashville, where he played with some locally successful rhythm and blues groups and recorded a demonstration tape with the soul guitarist Steve Cropper, one of many guitarists to have an influence on Hendrix's maturing style. After a brief tour in 1963 with Little Richard, Hendrix was in great demand as a sideman, performing with a number of established figures and groups such as Solomon Burke, Ike and Tina Turner, Jackie Wilson, B. B. King, and, later, the Isley Brothers and Curtis Knight. In 1963–1964 Hendrix's guitar playing was increasingly influenced by traditional bluesmen such as Robert Johnson (1911–1938), T-Bone Walker, B. B. King, Muddy Waters, and especially Albert King, although the relatively few available recordings from this period reveal only that he was a fluent and idiomatic rhythm and blues guitarist and capable sideman.

Leading his own group, Jimmy James and the Blue Flames, in a Greenwich Village club in late 1965, Hendrix began to exhibit increasing signs of an original, even eccentric approach that incorporated feedback and other electronic sounds as an integral part of his style as well as overt sexual posturing and a further development of the showmanship techniques (such as playing his guitar behind his back and with his teeth) that he had displayed while touring with the Isley Brothers. Among the influences that took root in this period were Bob Dylan, whose mannered vocal style and sometimes mystical and visionary lyrics Hendrix admired, and the guitar playing of Mike Bloomfield, the inventive lead guitarist for the Paul Butterfield Blues Band and Bob Dylan.

Impressed by Hendrix's formidable technique, distinctive playing style, and charismatic stage presence, Chas Chandler, former bass guitarist of the British rock group the Animals, convinced Hendrix to return with him to England to launch a new career. Under Chandler's guidance, the new Jimi Hendrix Experience, also featuring bassist Noel Redding and virtuoso drummer Mitch Mitchell, quickly became a favorite on the British and European pop scenes, releasing its first single, "Hey Joe," in December 1966 and its first album, *Are You Experienced?* (Reprise 6267), in September 1967. Consisting mostly of original songs, the album was characterized by extensive multitracking and electronic manipulation of sound (for example, phase shifting, tape reversed effects, and a variety of feedback sounds), the result of a collaboration between Hendrix and recording engineer Eddie Kramer. The album demonstrated that Hendrix's virtuoso guitar style had by this point successfully assimilated and adapted techniques from an unusually wide variety of sources ranging from soul guitarists to traditional and contemporary urban bluesmen and even jazz players such as Wes Montgomery. His vocal style had developed into a highly individualistic blend of mannerisms derived from blues, soul, and Dylan's half-spoken narrative style.

The *Are You Experienced?* album and associated singles did much to propel Hendrix to the forefront of the emerging British psychedelic rock movement, one of few black performers associated with that style. His popularity in the United States was guaranteed by his electrifying performance at the prestigious First International Monterey Pop Festival in June 1967, in which he burned his guitar and destroyed his equipment onstage.

Hendrix released his second album with the Experience, *Axis: Bold as Love* (Reprise 6281), in January 1968. This album exhibited an even more elaborate use of multitracking and electronic manipulation than the first, with some songs demonstrating more complex structures and more ambitious and visionary lyrics, some of which appear to have been inspired by drug experiences. In 1968 he was named artist of the year in both *Billboard* and *Rolling Stone* magazines.

Following this album, Hendrix began various attempts to expand the basic "power trio" format of the Jimi Hendrix Experience. The double album issued in September, *Electric Ladyland* (Reprise 6307), employed various other artists along with Redding and Mitchell and was the most intricately textured to date. Some songs, however, such as the hit single version of Dylan's "All along the Watchtower," showed an unusually straightforward, almost austere style, and others, such as "Voodoo Chile," suggested a return to the earlier urban blues style of Muddy Waters.

After the release of this album, Hendrix continually expressed the desire to shed his "psychedelic wizard" reputation and further develop his musical style, speaking on a number of occasions of his interest in jazz and his eagerness to perform with major jazz figures such as Miles Davis, who had shown some interest in Hendrix's music. Hendrix disbanded the Experience in 1969, envisioning a fluid "Electric Sky Church" made up of various musicians performing in different styles. His performance at the August 1969 Woodstock Festival, in which Billy Cox, a friend from his army days, replaced Noel Redding on bass, included a particularly dynamic and violent performance of the "Star Spangled Banner" that became famous as a demonstration of his unique guitar style. Under some pressure from black militants to make outspoken political statements, Hendrix shied away from active involvement in politics but did launch an all-black trio, the Band of Gypsys, featuring bass player Billy Cox and drummer/vocalist Buddy Miles, which in 1970 released an album of tracks (*The Band of Gypsys*, Capitol 0472) from a concert at the Fillmore East in New York City. But Hendrix remained dissatisfied, and the group quickly disbanded, with Hendrix walking offstage during a performance in early 1970. Hendrix was briefly rejoined by the original members of the Experience, but Noel Redding was soon replaced by Cox once again. In this period, he devoted considerable time to planning for and working in his new studio, Electric Lady Studios. His final live performances were erratic, with Hendrix sometimes appearing to be out of control or distant. He died in London in his sleep, asphyxiated following a presumably accidental overdose of sleeping pills. By then he had become a figure of gigantic proportions in the pop music world, not only as the first major black artist in the psychedelic style, but as a guitarist and composer whose work was considered strikingly original and distinctive.

Despite his great fame, his influence on later rock musicians was expressed more in terms of inspiration than direct imitation. Few if any of his followers appeared able to duplicate many of Hendrix's guitar-derived or studio-generated electronic effects with the finesse that he had demonstrated. His compositional approach was sufficiently unique that his songs were largely inimitable as well. But the Hendrix legacy remains strong, if for no other reason than because he is seen as a musical free spirit who expanded the potential of the electric guitar and the boundaries of rock music in general in the late 1960s to a degree matched by few others.

• The most comprehensive biography is David Henderson, *'Scuze Me while I Kiss the Sky: The Life of Jimi Hendrix* (1980). Also useful are Curtis Knight, *Jimi: An Intimate Biography of Jimi Hendrix* (1974), for its personal anecdotes revealing insight into Hendrix's personality and aspirations; Chris Welch, *Hendrix: A Biography* (1972), for excerpts of interviews with a number of Hendrix's friends and associates; and Jerry Hopkins, *Hit and Run: The Jimi Hendrix Story* (1983), for its treatment of Hendrix's childhood and relationship with his father. Of interest for its analysis of Hendrix's guitar style is Steve Tarshis, *Original Hendrix* (1982). Some of the earliest available recordings of Hendrix are found on the Isley Brothers, *In the Beginning* (T-Neck 3007), *Roots of Hendrix* (Trip Records 9501), and *Rare Hendrix* (Trip Records 9500). Other important albums released posthumously include *The Cry of Love* (Reprise 2034 [1971]), *Rainbow Bridge* (Reprise 2040 [1971]), *War Heroes* (Reprise 2013 [1973]), and *Nine to the Universe* (Polydor 1023 [1980]). An obituary is in the *New York Times*, 19 Sept. 1970.

TERENCE J. O'GRADY

HENIE, Sonja (8 Apr. 1912–12 Oct. 1969), figure skater and film actress, was born in Oslo, Norway, the daughter of Hans Wilhelm Henie, a wealthy fur trader, and Selma Lochman-Nielsen. In her autobiography Henie described herself as sometimes feeling like a "lottery winner." If by that she meant that she was born into circumstances allowing her the opportunity to develop into a world-class athlete, she was certainly correct. Her father was a champion sportsman himself and encouraged her to skate and ski from an early age. Once her talent for figure skating became apparent, her parents invested a portion of their wealth in her skating career, providing her with the coaching, dance lessons, costumes, and tutors that allowed her to quit school and concentrate on her sport.

Along with Norway's premier figure-skating coach, Oscar Holte, Henie's parents spent many hours at the rink dissecting her performances and encouraging her to perfect her skills. After her first successful international competitions she also worked with the American coach Howard Nicholson. Henie later described her experience of skating as a "state of intoxication," as she pushed her body to go faster and faster over the ice. That ice speed, coupled with her grace and musicality, allowed her to become a major innovator in her sport.

From the beginning, Henie was successful in competition. She won her first senior Norwegian National Championship at age nine. When figure skating was added to the program of the first Olympic Winter Games held in 1924 at Chamonix, France, Henie competed. The eleven-year-old finished last but gained what she considered to be valuable experience that helped prepare her for the level of competition she would encounter at future international events. Her first World Championship victory, occurring in her hometown of Oslo, in front of the Norwegian king and queen, was remarkable both because Henie was only thirteen and because she and her family established a unique training regimen in the months leading up to the competition. She followed a strict schedule of skating for three hours in the morning and two hours in the afternoon, with her nutritious meals set at precisely scheduled intervals.

The intensity of her training, along with the attention paid to her diet and to the incorporation of ballet into movement over ice, established Henie as one of the most important innovators in the sport. Before her career ended she had made the choice of the skater's music and costume, along with the skater's choreography, a critical part of skating competition. This emphasis on the more graceful and athletic aspects of the sport led to the deemphasis and ultimate abandonment of the traditional school-figure test (a method of determining a skater's control and ability to cut an edge by requiring the skater to trace a curved pattern on the ice derived from a basic figure eight) as part of major world and Olympic figure-skating competitions.

The 1927 figure-skating World Championships began Sonja Henie's unprecedented stretch of world and Olympic victories. Before she retired from amateur skating following her third Olympic and tenth world championship, Henie had proved that she had the discipline and imagination to continue moving her sport forward while meeting the challenges of new competitors. And Henie also revealed her competitive fire in other pursuits. She played tennis and, like her father, became an excellent driver, competing in amateur sportscar races. But with her Olympic victories at St. Moritz in 1928, Lake Placid in 1932, and Garmisch-Partenkirchen in 1936 came controversy. Henie's appearances in figure-skating exhibitions, and the means by which they were financed, led to charges that she and her father had profited from her athletic success, again revealing the tensions between the code of amateur athleticism and the realities of international sport. Furthermore, Henie's apparent friendship with Adolf Hitler and other Nazi leaders, a consequence of her victories at the World Championships in Berlin and the subsequent Olympic Winter Games at Garmisch, would later lead many to suspect that she had tacitly cooperated with the German regime, undermining her status as a Norwegian and American heroine.

Having achieved all she could in amateur figure skating, Henie retired from competition in 1936 to concentrate on her dream of achieving success in film and of creating new ice shows in which to perform. She was tired of the strict rules governing amateur championships and believed that it was time that she be financially compensated for her talents. Henie, her parents, and her brother Leif moved to the United States and took up residence in Los Angeles. Wishing to do more than just skate in films, she had to persuade important figures in the motion-picture industry of her acting ability. After signing a contract with Arthur Wirtz, the owner of the Chicago Stadium and other venues, to perform in a series of ice shows, in May 1936 Henie appeared in a skating spectacular designed to show off her talents at the Polar Palace in Hollywood.

She impressed Darryl F. Zanuck of 20th Century–Fox studios and soon agreed to appear in a series of film musicals, both as an ice skater and as a featured player. She was as successful in the movies as in the rink, trailing only Clark Gable and Shirley Temple as a fan favorite in 1939. Although her first film, *The Peach Edition* (1937), was a quick, formulaic movie in which she played a Swiss girl who became a figure-skating champion, Henie dedicated herself to learning the particulars of filmmaking, studying the process by discussing their jobs with everyone from the grips to the cameramen. Even though she often skated in later films, such as *One in a Million* and *Thin Ice* (both released in 1937), and *Sun Valley Serenade* (1941), Henie prided herself on her improving acting skills and on her enhanced ability to get each scene down in the fewest takes possible. Nevertheless, her talents as an actress never matched her ambition. Her last feature, *The Countess of Monte Cristo*, was released in 1948.

Despite settling in the United States, Henie maintained her ties to her homeland until the German occupation of Norway made it impossible to visit. She owned a residence outside of Oslo and lived there summers until the war. Recognizing her contributions to Norwegian life, King Haakon of Norway awarded Henie the Knighthood of St. Olav in 1937. In later years Henie was accused of doing too little during World War II to alleviate the suffering of the Norwegian people and failing to financially support the underground opposition to Nazi rule. She was also criticized during and after the war because the Nazi troops occupying Norway made a point of preserving her home and possessions. This sense that she had betrayed Norway perhaps was exacerbated by Henie's decision to become a United States citizen. Her naturalization was completed in 1941.

After the war Henie spent less time making movies, yet continued her figure skating, ultimately producing her own ice shows. In doing so she undertook the responsibility of booking venues, arranging transportation, and hiring and firing cast and crew. As had been true before the war, Henie continued to be a hard-headed businesswoman, dedicated to making a profit from the shows. This became virtually impossible after a March 1952 collapse of temporary bleachers at a Baltimore performance led to numerous fan injuries and subsequent litigation. A 1953 tour of Europe did much to restore her love of performing and her financial security.

Henie was married three times. Her first husband was Dan Topping, a wealthy sportsman and owner of the Brooklyn Dodgers football team, whom she married in Chicago in 1940. After her divorce in 1946 from Topping, she married Winthrop Gardiner, heir to a substantial New York fortune, in 1949. Gardiner was an alcoholic, and life with him exacerbated Henie's own drinking; they were divorced in 1956. That same year she was married, for the final time, to Niels Onstad, a fellow Norwegian. She had no children.

Later, with Onstad, Henie became an important collector of modern art. In 1968 she and her husband established the Sonja Henie, Niels Onstad Art Center, just outside Oslo, as a gift to the Norwegian people. Shortly after the dedication of the art center, Henie was discovered to have leukemia, from which she died en route to Oslo.

Henie's contributions to the sport of figure skating are well recognized. By bringing elements of dance into the free program, she set in motion the process by which skaters were allowed to express themselves on ice. Through her efforts, and those of successors such as Janet Lynn, Peggy Fleming, and Dorothy Hamill, figure skaters would eventually be freed from the requirement to meticulously perform figure patterns to be successful. Henie also established a standard of training and discipline for future female athletes.

• Memorabilia and scrapbooks from Sonja Henie's career are in the collection of the Sonja Henie, Niels Onstad Art Center in Norway. Her autobiography, *Wings on My Feet* (1940), contains her own assessment of her early life and competitive career as well as chapters devoted to figure-skating technique. Raymond Strait and Leif Henie, *Queen of Ice, Queen of Shadows: The Unsuspected Life of Sonja Henie* (1985), provides an intimate look at Henie's personal life, along with a filmography. For another assessment of her career, see Edward Z. Epstein, "One in a Million: The Amazing Story of Sonja Henie," *Scandinavian Review* 81 (Winter 1993): 67–72. See also Allen Guttmann, *Women's Sports: A History* (1991), which examines Henie's accomplishments along with those of other female athletes of the first part of the twentieth century. An obituary is in the *New York Times*, 13 Oct. 1969.

WANDA ELLEN WAKEFIELD

HENING, William Waller (1767?–1 Apr. 1828), lawyer and legal editor, was born on the family farm about five miles west of Fredericksburg, Culpeper County, Virginia, the son of David Hening and Mary Waller. Hening received his earliest education at a school conducted by the Reverend John Price in Culpeper County. He studied under Adam Goodlett, whom he styled as his "preceptor of the classics." He read law in Fredericksburg, where he was admitted to the bar in April 1789.

Hening had a reasonably successful law practice. In June 1790 he was admitted to the bar of Stafford County Court, and by 1793 he had extended his practice as far away as Fauquier County. He purchased land in Spotsylvania County; he may have acquired additional means when in 1790 he married Agatha Banks. The Henings had seven children.

Early in 1793 Hening moved his law practice to Charlottesville, where he dealt in real estate and acquired a major interest in a distillery. He also became sufficiently acquainted with Thomas Jefferson to ask him to revise several sheets of the manuscript of *The New Virginia Justice*, a handbook for Virginia justices of the peace. This volume was widely distributed throughout Virginia; a second edition appeared in 1799. Numerous and significant later changes in state law, including the penal code, dictated a revised edition by 1810; the legislators codified the laws again in 1820. The popularity of the work required still another edition in 1825.

Hening joined the Masonic order as an entered apprentice on 18 March 1796 and was raised to master mason the next day. He rose rapidly in the Masonic hierarchy. Between 1801 and 1811 members elected him to the state organization's major offices—senior warden, grand master, and grand high priest. His interest in Masonic work waned in about 1813.

Hening was elected to represent Albemarle County in the Virginia House of Delegates in 1804; here he was particularly active. Near the end of his second term he was elevated to the Executive Council, an office designed as a check on the powers of the governor. He moved to Richmond in 1807 to facilitate attending council meetings. He served as a councilman until 1810, when he became clerk of the Superior Court of Chancery for the Richmond District, a post he held until his death.

Between 1808 and 1814 Hening served as deputy adjutant general of Virginia. This post offered no particular political or social prestige and was probably desired by him to supplement his income. In this capacity he published a pamphlet, *The Militia Laws of This Commonwealth and the United States*, in 1808.

In collaboration with William Munford, Hening published *The Reports of Cases Argued and Determined in the Supreme Court of Appeals of Virginia* (1810). Under the supervision of Benjamin Watkins Leigh, the two men also worked on the *Revised Code of the Laws of Virginia (1819)* and *The American Pleader and Lawyer's Guide* (1811), which had been collected for years. Volume one was issued in 1811, volume two in 1826. A third projected volume never appeared. In addition, Hening edited three treatises on law and equity. His edition of Richard Francis's *Maxims in Equity* appeared in 1824; a year later he published editions of Thomas Branch's *Pricipia Legis et Aequetates* and William Hoy's *Grounds and Maxims of the Law of England*.

Shortly after Hening moved to Richmond he joined the Amicable Society, an organization for the relief of strangers and wayfarers. Membership was limited to sixty residents of the city. About this time, he also began to make arrangements for his major work, *The Statutes at Large; Being a Collection of All the Laws of Virginia, from the First Session of the Legislature in the Year 1619*. Thomas Jefferson offered his collection of manuscripts and printed materials to the proposed project. The state treasury promised financial support in the form of subscriptions. After examination and approval by at least two Executive Council members, the work would have the force of law. The first volume appeared in 1809 and the last in 1823. A second edition of the first four volumes followed in 1820–1823, and a reprint edition of the entire thirteen volumes in 1969. Hening died at the home of his son in Richmond.

• No collection of Hening's papers exists, but the Alderman Library of the University of Virginia, Virginia State Library and Archives, and Virginia Historical Society hold significant manuscripts. Reports to British Merchants in the British Public Record Office microfilm in the Library of Congress (microfilm reel 121) refer to incidents in his early life. Biographical sketches appear in William Hamilton Bryson's *The Virginia Law Reporters before 1880* (1977). Details of his Masonic activities are in William Moseley Brown, *Freemasonry in Virginia* (1936), and the *Virginia Masonic Herald*, Aug. 1976. Waverly Keith Winfree's M.A. thesis, "Acts Not in Hening's Statutes, with a Biographical Sketch of William Waller Hening" (1959), with the author's notes are on file at the Virginia Historical Society. Obituaries are in the *Constitutional Whig*, 5 and 12 Apr. 1828, and the *Richmond Enquirer*, 4 Apr. 1828.

WAVERLY K. WINFREE

HENKEL, David (4 May 1795–15 June 1831), Lutheran clergyman, was born in Staunton, Virginia, the son of the Reverend Paul Henkel, a Lutheran minister, and Elizabeth Nagley. Along with four of his brothers, David Henkel, one of seven children, seemed committed to following his father's calling at an early age, and together the Henkels devoted themselves to spreading and strengthening German Lutheranism throughout the South and West. As a youth, Henkel studied Lutheran theology and the classics. In 1811 he began working at his brother Solomon's print shop, and in 1812 he sold religious publications in South Carolina and pursued his theological education with Godfrey Dreher. He preached his first sermon on 1 November 1812 at the age of seventeen in South Carolina and in 1817 was sent by the Synod of North Carolina as a missionary to Tennessee, where he would help to organize St. Paul's Church in Monroe County. Henkel's progress, however, from catechist to deacon to pastor was delayed by the synod. When he applied for ordination at the North Carolina Convention in 1819 he was denied; instead, he was disciplined by the synod after being charged with "exercising improper communication, teaching transubstantiation, claiming the power to forgive sins, and acting unfriendly toward ministers of other denominations" (Wolf, p. 73). When his brother, the Reverend Philip Henkel, went ahead and ordained him anyway, the Henkel family and their sympathizers (the "Henkelites") disavowed the authority of the synod and in 1820 formed the separate Conference of Tennessee, which in 1825 became known as the German Evangelical Lutheran Synod of Tennessee.

Henkel's ordination was only the trigger of a synodical schism that had far deeper roots. One historian, in fact, has seen the Henkels and the leadership of the North Carolina Synod as representing the two major contending forces within American Lutheranism (Kuenning, *Rise and Fall*). North Carolina's Gottlieb Shober, an "American Lutheran" Pietist, was leading the movement for the establishment of an American General Synod, a national organization that Shober hoped would unite American Lutherans, promote ecumenical cooperation with Reformed Protestant denominations, and focus on benevolence, moral reform, and general evangelization rather than on doctrinal squabbling. The "Old Lutheran" Henkels vigorously resisted such efforts. They championed strict adherence to the Augsburg Confession (1530), retention of German as the language of worship, and opposition to any latitudinarian dilution of Lutheran identity. In 1820 the

Tennessee Conference, led by David Henkel, issued a scathing attack against the General Synod's constitution. Henkel's "Objections," which opened a decade of controversy, declared that the General Synod was too ecumenical, too hierarchical, too expensive, and in its avoidance of the Augsburg Confession, un-Lutheran. "We do not expect finally to prevent the establishment of this General Synod," the document concluded apocalyptically, " . . . because we believe, agreeable to the divine predictions, that the great falling away is approaching, so that Antichrist will set himself into the temple of God. . . . We also believe that the establishment of General Synods are preparing the way for him" (Wolf, p. 77).

The Henkels continued to travel, preach, and organize churches, but in the 1820s they also wrote letters to pastors and laymen and orchestrated opposition to the General Synod throughout Tennessee, Ohio, Virginia, Indiana, and Kentucky. David Henkel, described by one historian as "the most brilliant and aggressive of Paul Henkel's six sons" (Nelson, p. 117), published essays and tracts that instructed "misguided" Lutherans and non-Lutherans with equal vigor. In the *Carolinian Herald* (1821) he defended religious and political liberty against the ecclesiastical designs of those who would arbitrarily usurp local power. In 1822 he published a short treatise on baptism called *The Heavenly Flood of Regeneration*; three years later he defended his position against the arguments of Joseph Moore, a Methodist, and added some remarks on the doctrine of justification. He drafted the Tennessee Synod's constitution, attached a treatise on prayer to the synod's minutes, and translated Luther's *Small Catechism* from the German. In 1830 his brother Solomon published *David Henkel against the Unitarians*, a 119-page treatise arguing for the divinity of Jesus Christ. Henkel was an energetic preacher, though even his father had to admit that his four-hour sermon on "Baptism and the Lord's Supper" was too long. Henkel traveled in all kinds of weather, often preaching two or three times a day in both German and English. In nearly eighteen years in the pulpit, he is said to have preached more than 3,200 sermons. His last sermon was delivered on 12 August 1830 in Lincoln County, North Carolina, near the home town of his wife, the former Catherine Heyl or Hoyle (the date of their marriage is unknown). He was ill for nine months with what was diagnosed as dyspepsia and died in Lincoln County the following June at the age of thirty-six. The Henkels had eight children, seven of whom survived him.

• The David Henkel Papers are housed in the Abdel Ross Wentz Library, Lutheran Theological Seminary, Gettysburg, Pa. On the activities of the Henkel family, see Jens Christian Roseland, *American Lutheran Biographies* (1890); Socrates Henkel, *History of the Evangelical Lutheran Tennessee Synod* (1890); C. W. Cassell et al., *History of the Lutheran Church in Virginia and East Tennessee* (1930); and William Edward Eisenberg, *The Lutheran Church in Virginia* (1967), pp. 132–38. Selections from the Tennessee Conference's 1820 "Objections" to the General Synod can be found in Richard C. Wolf, ed., *Documents of Lutheran Unity in America* (1966), pp. 72–77. For the Henkel family's broader significance within American Lutheranism, see E. Clifford Nelson, ed., *The Lutherans in America* (1975), chap. 2, and Paul P. Kuenning, *The Rise and Fall of American Lutheran Pietism* (1988), pp. 53–60.

CHRISTOPHER GRASSO

HENKEL, Paul (15 Dec. 1754–17 Nov. 1825), evangelist and cooper, was born in Rowan County, North Carolina, the son of Jacob Henkel and Barbara Teter (or Dieter). Little is known about his early life. He was confirmed in 1768 and spoke of having had a "jolly" youth, giving little thought to religion until he was a young man. In 1775 he served fifty-six days with a company of rangers in the revolutionary war.

While supporting himself as a cooper, pioneer Lutheran evangelist Henkel put most of his energies into leading his church in areas of the new nation where it was just establishing footholds. His audiences, who came largely from German-speaking frontier settlements, had little acquaintance with the Lutheran doctrines that he found so important. The orthodox versions that he worked to impress upon the congregations took shape in environments in which Germans and Lutherans were outnumbered.

In 1776 he married Elizabeth Negley (or Negeley); they had nine children. In the same year, Henkel was drawn to a religious vocation. He schooled himself in Latin and Greek under the tutelage of a Maryland pastor, who also indoctrinated him in Lutheran ways. In 1783 the ministerium of Pennsylvania gave him a license to preach, and through that ministerium he received ordination in 1792. By this time the pattern of Henkel's work was set for decades to come. Though he often used New Market, Virginia, as a base, one locale could not confine the restless preacher. His son Andrew, also a pastor, concluded that "having no inclination to confine himself to any single charge, he resolved to become an independent missionary." He would earn some of his own keep as a cooper and then set out on evangelizing trips. But Henkel had energies and passion left over, and these he put to work providing order, structure, and definition to the new Lutheran communities.

Among his legacies was the North Carolina Synod, which he helped found in 1803, at a time when highly emotional revivals were sweeping the frontier. Hyperemotionalism did not match the Lutheran style, Henkel thought, so he set out to help develop ways to combine Lutheran orthodoxy with rhetorical approaches that would be effective in new communities. The new rhetoric was infused with emotional intensity and conviction, in contrast to the drily dogmatic approach most of the Lutheran orthodox employed, while avoiding the appeal to "enthusiasm" that characterized revivalists. Continuing his founding activity, he helped organize the Joint Synod of Ohio in 1818 and the Evangelical Lutheran Synod of Tennessee in 1820. During the intervening period, after 1806, Henkel linked with two of his sons to promote the first

Lutheran publishing house in the hemisphere. Solomon, a physician turned printer, and Ambrose, a printer and minister, were the key to the publishing enterprise. Most notable was Henkel's production in 1810 of a German hymn book, which he followed in 1816 with an English-language counterpart. He also published a crudely rhymed book of satire, which was aimed at providing what Andrew called a "rebuke of fanaticism and superstition, vice and folly."

From this publishing base the Henkels promulgated their distinctive blend of teachings. Distinction, the Henkels thought, was necessary because their great rivals, headed by Samuel S. Schmucker of the more powerful General Synod, seemed overeager to adapt to American ways. These ways, in Henkel's eyes, would seduce Lutherans to blend into a generalized Protestant "evangelical" ethos that would allow for little attention to central Lutheran doctrines. If the Schmuckerites foresaw an evangelical coalition, a genus of which Lutheranism would be a mere species, the Henkels wanted to forestall it in the name of a Lutheranism that was marked by devotion to charter documents of the tradition derived from sixteenth-century Reformation Germany. Turbulence therefore followed Henkel wherever he went, and he seemed to go everywhere that there was a potential for organizing Lutherans, including Virginia, Kentucky, Indiana, and Ohio. While in open confrontation neither the Henkelites or the Schmuckerites prevailed, the followers of both groups characterized Lutheranism for decades to come, and Lutheranism did not become a part of the evangelical coalition. Later nineteenth-century immigrations, particularly to the Midwest, provided hundreds of congregations with worshipers who felt more at home with the approach Henkel had already established in the East.

Henkel continued studying Lutheran dogma, itinerating, converting, organizing congregations, and contending for his view of what American Lutheranism should be until he was felled by a stroke in 1823. Characteristically, he did not let the hardships it imposed end his career, and he continued to organize and preach until just over a month before he died in New Market, Virginia.

• Two boxes of Henkel papers and materials are in the Wentz Memorial Library of the Lutheran Theological Seminary at Gettysburg, Pa. Henkel's many published works, journals, and controversial booklets were chiefly in German. Best remembered is a hymn book, *Das Neu Eingerichtete Gesang-Buch* (1810). An influential book of instruction in English, for which he served as colporteur, *The Christian Catechism* (1811), also survives. No biography exists. An article that locates him in Lutheran controversy is R. H. Baur, "Investigation of an Early Nineteenth Century Expression of Confessionalism," *Lutheran Quarterly* 22 (May 1970): 172–84. See also Baur, "Paul Henkel, Pioneer Lutheran Missionary," *Essays and Reports, 1978, The Lutheran Historical Conference* 8 (1979): 57–83.

MARTIN E. MARTY

HENLEY, Robert (5 Jan. 1783–6 Oct. 1828), naval officer, was born in Williamsburg, Virginia, the son of Leonard Henley and Elizabeth Dandridge, the sister of Martha Dandridge Custis Washington. His older brother was John Dandridge Henley, also a naval officer. Although Henley briefly attended the College of William and Mary, he preferred to serve in the navy. His appointment as a midshipman is dated 8 April 1799, but he did not actually receive the warrant and take the oath until October of that year. Upon returning his oath Henley was ordered to report to Norfolk for duty aboard the frigate *Chesapeake*. Because the *Chesapeake* had just recently been launched and would not be ready for sea for several months, Henley was ordered to join the crew of the frigate *Constellation* under the command of Thomas Truxtun. Henley was aboard when the frigate sailed in December for the West Indies.

Sailing at the time of the Quasi-War with France, the *Constellation* was to protect American shipping against attacks from French warships and privateers then active in the West Indies. On the evening of 1 February 1800 the *Constellation* sighted and engaged the French frigate *La Vengeance*. Although the French vessel took the worst of the battle and, according to American reports, actually struck her flag, it managed to slip away under cover of darkness and evade capture. During the battle Henley fought gallantly, and according to family tradition Truxtun was reported to have remarked about him, "That stripling is destined to be a brave officer."

Following the end of the Quasi-War Henley took leave from the navy and returned to Williamsburg, where he studied navigation and naval science. He returned to active duty in time to join the frigate *Adams* for service in the Mediterranean. In September 1803, thanks to the influence of his brother-in-law Tobias Lear, the U.S. consul in Algiers, Henley transferred from *Adams* to the larger frigate *Constitution*. During the winter of 1803–1804, while the *Constitution* remained at Syracuse, Henley was allowed to join Lear in Algiers. Henley rejoined the *Constitution* in time to receive his commission as lieutenant, dated 1 June 1804.

In March 1805 John Rodgers, captain of the *Constitution*, took his squadron in toward Tripoli to bombard the city. During the engagement Henley commanded a gunboat assigned to cut out an enemy guard boat. Henley remained with the *Constitution* until August 1805; suffering from ill health he then received permission to return home. For the next several years Henley remained at Norfolk, occupying a shore billet and commanding a gunboat.

When the War of 1812 began Henley was at Norfolk commanding a division of gunboats that in June 1813 successfully drove a small squadron of enemy frigates away from the town. Henley was then transferred to Lake Champlain to serve as Commodore Thomas Macdonough's second in command. With the British advancing down the lake, Macdonough took up a strong defensive position at Plattsburg, New York. He arranged his vessels in line on a north-south axis and awaited the enemy attack. While Macdonough himself was aboard the flagship *Saratoga*, Henley established the brig *Eagle* at the front of the American defense. In the ensuing battle the *Eagle* was badly damaged, with thirteen of its crew killed and twenty wounded. Henley's demeanor during the battle caused Macdonough to remark after the Americans' victory that Henley behaved "like a brave man." For his role in the battle Congress voted Henley a gold medal and the Virginia legislature voted him their thanks. He also received a handsome sum in prize money and was promoted to the rank of master commandant.

Following the war Henley returned to Virginia and took command of the naval station at Norfolk. During these years American commerce was increasingly distressed by pirating activity in the West Indies. With the acquisition of Florida in 1819, the Navy Department assigned vessels to new naval stations at Key West and Pensacola from which they could patrol these waters. Henley was assigned command of the brig *Hornet* and ordered to Key West. On 29 October 1821, while sailing off the coast of Santo Domingo, the *Hornet* captured the pirate schooner *Moscow*.

Subsequent to his command of the *Hornet* Henley returned to shore assignments, first in North Carolina and then to the naval station at Charleston, South Carolina, where he died. Henley married at an early age but his wife's name is not known. Apparently they had no children.

• For additional information see the following: U.S. Government Printing Office, *Naval Documents Related to the United States Wars with the Barbary Powers* (6 vols., 1939–1944); Wilson Miles Cary, "The Dandridges of Virginia," *William and Mary Quarterly*, 1st ser., 5 (1896): 30–39; and William M. Fowler, Jr., *Jack Tars and Commodores: The American Navy 1783–1815* (1984).

WILLIAM M. FOWLER

HENNEPIN, Louis (7 Apr. 1640–1705?), author and explorer, was born at Ath in the province of Hainaut in present-day Belgium, the son of Gaspard Hennepin, a butcher, and Robertine Lelup. Hennepin was baptized as Jacques. As the son of a butcher, Hennepin could experience social and educational advancement only through the Catholic priesthood. He began preparing for the priesthood by attending the *École latine*, where he pursued a curriculum of classical studies. Around the age of seventeen Hennepin joined the Franciscan order at the Convent of Bethune in the present Department of Pas-de-Calais, France. He continued his religious studies in the present French Department of Loiret at the Convent of Montargis, where he was eventually ordained a Catholic priest.

While preparing for the priesthood, Hennepin became imbued with missionary fervor, and after his ordination he traveled to the Vatican to apprise ecclesiastical authorities of his desire to serve in the foreign missions. Hennepin then returned to the Low Countries and conducted a preaching ministry at Hal in the province of Brabant. One year later he moved to the French province of Artois, where his imagination was fired by stories of exploration related by French seamen returning from the New World. After the war between France and the United Provinces of the Netherlands began in 1672, Hennepin returned to the Low Countries to provide medical assistance to military casualties. He remained in the Low Countries until 1675, when he was one of five young French-speaking priests selected for missionary duty in New France.

Hennepin sailed to Quebec aboard the same vessel that carried René Robert Cavelier de La Salle to the New World. Hennepin served as an itinerant missionary in New France in the winter of 1675–1676, preaching at the colonial settlements of Cap-Tourmente, Trois-Rivières, Sainte-Anne de Beaupré, and Bourg-Royal. In the spring of 1676 he traveled to Fort Frontenac on Lake Ontario and helped establish a mission there. In 1678 Hennepin was reassigned to Quebec. In the fall of 1678 La Salle, who had just returned to the colonial capital from France with royal authorization to engage in North American exploration, presented Hennepin with a letter from his superior asking the missionary to accompany the explorer into the Great Lakes region. Hennepin accepted the challenge, and on 18 November 1678 he set sail for the Niagara River with La Salle's advance party.

In 1680, after establishing an outpost on the present site of Peoria, Illinois, La Salle left his companions and returned to Canada for supplies. Before his departure La Salle assigned Michel Accault to explore the upper Mississippi Valley; Hennepin accompanied Accault. During the exploratory expedition, the Franciscan priest was taken prisoner by Sioux. Hennepin traveled extensively with his captors, encountering and naming St. Anthony Falls at the present site of Minneapolis, Minnesota. Hennepin was rescued in 1681 by a small party of French explorers led by Daniel Greylsolon, sieur du Lhut.

Hennepin returned to France in 1682 and entered the cloister at St. Germain-en-Laye. He served as guardian of the Recollets at Renty, France, from 1684 to 1687. During his residence at Renty, Hennepin published *Description de la Louisiane* (1683), a detailed account of his North American adventures that gained him considerable literary notoriety in Europe. As a result of this notoriety, Hennepin was named vicar of the convent at Le Cateau-Cambrésis in 1683. He then served as superior of the convent at Renty from 1684 to 1687. In 1687 Hennepin fell into disgrace for reasons that have never been disclosed. He subsequently fled to Hainaut, where he served from 1687 to 1692 as chaplain of the Recollet nuns at Gosselies. In 1692 Hennepin was again forced to leave his post under mysterious circumstances.

Hennepin then sought the protection of King William III of England, to whom the former missionary proposed colonization of the Mississippi Valley. Through the assistance of the British secretary of war Hennepin was permitted to travel to Amsterdam for the dual purposes of publishing works on North

America and preparing to participate in possible British colonization of the American interior. Unable to publish his proposed works in Amsterdam, Hennepin subsequently traveled to Utrecht and with British assistance published there two major works on early North America, *Nouvelle découverte d'un très grand pays, situé dans l'Amérique* (1697) and *Nouveau Voyage d'un païs plus grand que l'Europe*. In these works Hennepin falsely claimed to have made a voyage of discovery along the lower Mississippi River before La Salle's famous descent of the river in 1682; in both books, the former missionary claimed that he urged the British monarchy to colonize the Mississippi Valley.

Hennepin traveled to Rome around July 1698; while in Rome the following year, he received permission to retire to the convent of Saint-Bonaventure-sur-le-Palatin. Hennepin's twilight years are veiled in obscurity. He was in modern-day Belgium in 1701. Hennepin is thought to have died sometime before 1705.

Hennepin is noteworthy primarily because of his three book-length publications that were translated into numerous European languages in more than forty editions. The first established his reputation as a major figure in the European exploration of the North American interior; it also helped to focus the attention of the major European powers and the European scientific community on the importance of Mississippi Valley exploration and development. The latter two books, based as they were on fallacious information, largely destroyed Hennepin's reputation both as a writer and as an authority on North American exploration. The works nevertheless had a profound impact on North American colonization. Fearing that William III would follow Hennepin's advice, France organized a major colonization expedition to the mouth of the Mississippi River. In 1699, two years after publication of Hennepin's notorious Utrecht books, French forces established Fort Maurepas near present-day Biloxi, Mississippi, to safeguard France's interests in the lower Mississippi Valley.

• Louis Hennepin's *A New Discovery of a Vast Country in America*, ed. Reuben Gold Thwaites (2 vols., 1903), provides important commentary on Hennepin's fabricated voyage of discovery along the lower Mississippi. Jean-Roche Rioux provides the best available overview of Hennepin's life in the *Dictionary of Canadian Biography* (1969), whereas Narcisse E. Dionne, *Hennepin: Ses Voyages et ses oeuvres* (1897), provides the most thorough biography to date. Jean Delanglez's now dated *Hennepin's Description of Louisiana: A Critical Essay* (1941) remains the most complete modern assessment of the missionary's life and writings. See also Isaac Joslin Cox, *The Journeys of René-Robert Cavelier, Sieur de la Salle, as Related by His Faithful Lieutenant, Henri de Tonty; His Missionary Colleagues, Fathers Zenobius Membré, Louis Hennepin, and Anastasius Douay . . .* (1922).

CARL A. BRASSEAUX

HENNESSY, John (20 Aug. 1825–4 Mar. 1900), Roman Catholic archbishop, was born in the village of Bulgaden in Limerick County, Ireland, the son of William Hennessy and Catherine Meaney, farmers. When John was twelve years old, he decided that he would become a priest. He thus began studies in various private schools. Through this education Hennessy became proficient in both Latin and Greek, subjects that prepared him well for his entrance into All Hallows College in Dublin, where he would train as a missionary priest.

Hennessy studied for only a short time at All Hallows, however, as the Great Famine forced him out of Ireland in 1847. The future for the son of a poor farmer in Ireland was not promising during these years. Therefore, at the age of twenty-two, Hennessy headed for the United States. Six of his nine siblings would eventually follow him. Upon his arrival he traveled to St. Louis, Missouri, where he met Archbishop Peter R. Kenrick, who placed Hennessy at St. Vincent Seminary in Cape Giradeau, Missouri. In 1848 he was then transferred to the new diocesan seminary at Carondelet, near St. Louis, where he studied philosophy and theology.

Hennessy was ordained a priest on 1 November 1850, and his first parish was located in a vast wilderness near the town of New Madrid, Missouri, about ninety miles south of St. Louis along the Mississippi River. Although the parish centered around a town, it also contained 6,000 miles of uncharted and unpopulated territory. Fever and fatigue eventually forced Hennessy back to St. Louis, where in 1851 he accepted the pastorate at Grovois. He remained there until 1854, when he was installed as vice president and professor of dogmatic theology and ecclesiastical theology at Carondelet Seminary. Upon the retirement of the president of Carondelet Seminary, Father Patrick Feehan, Hennessy became president in 1857.

Hennessy spent 1858–1859 in Rome, to which he had been sent by his archbishop to carry decrees made in the archdiocesan synod of 1858. There he came under the eyes of Vatican officials, making a favorable impression. Later in life he would return to Rome to attend the historic First Vatican Council in 1868. By 1860, however, he was back in the United States, where he was installed as pastor in St. Joseph, Missouri. This city was a place of divided allegiance during the Civil War as well as the scene of bloodshed. Hennessy served there until 1866 when, upon the death of the bishop of Dubuque, Clement Smyth, he was chosen by Rome to serve as the diocese's next bishop. It was here that Hennessy made a lasting impression in the United States.

Work in Catholic education, specifically primary and secondary, but also in higher education, would soon become Hennessy's most important achievement for American Catholicism, eventually earning him a reputation as the apostle of American Catholic education. Hennessy began by establishing a quality Catholic educational system on the local level in his own diocese. He then developed a detailed plan for a free school association in the city of Dubuque. Although it was an admirable plan, it lacked support beyond Hennessy and unfortunately was never implemented.

Instead, Hennessy turned his attention to reviving Mount St. Bernard College and Seminary, which was originally founded in 1850 and temporarily closed in 1863. Hennessy reestablished the institution in 1873, naming it St. Joseph's College. Now named Loras College, this institution remains his most important contribution to Catholic higher education.

After 1873 Hennessy focused on primary and secondary Catholic education, making his most famous stand for Catholic private schools in 1884 at the Third Plenary Council of Baltimore, where he made an argument for the establishment of a school in every parish. He was a powerful orator who was able to convincingly portray the public schools as "dens of iniquity" and the "gates of hell." His support for Catholic private schools should not be understood in isolation, however, but as part of an overall trend within Catholicism toward centralization during the nineteenth century. It is also notable that Hennessy stuck to his belief in private Catholic education against heavy criticism from both Catholics and non-Catholics who believed private schools would undermine American public education.

Hennessy made a notable contribution to the growth of Catholic education in America; however, his name is surprisingly missing from scholarly accounts of the Third Plenary Council and histories of Catholic education in America. Despite such an absence, during Hennessy's tenure as bishop there was tremendous growth of Catholic education in Iowa. In 1866, when he took office, only twenty-nine schools were under Catholic control. By 1900 there were 187 Catholic schools in Iowa.

Hennessy's work was not confined to education. In 1873 he helped found the first English-speaking community of Benedictines at Malleray Abbey in the Dubuque archdiocese. He also enlisted the help of the Sisters of Mercy to establish Mercy Medical Center in Davenport, Iowa. After a tremendous life of accomplishment, Hennessy was named the first archbishop of Dubuque when it was made an archdiocese in 1893. Hennessy died in Dubuque.

• Hennessy burned most of his letters and papers before his death; however, some of his sermons, letters, and papers can be found in the Dubuque archdiocesan archives. A summary of his episcopal activities can be found in F. J. Sheridan, *Souvenir-Volume, Silver Jubilee Rt. Rev. John Hennessy, D.D., Bishop of Dubuque* (1891). A modern presentation and assessment of Hennessy is M. Jane Coogan, "The Redoubtable John Hennessy, First Archbishop of Dubuque," *Mid-America* 62 (1980): 21–34. Nineteenth-century accounts of his life can be found in John Dawson Gilmary Shea, *The Hierarchy of the Catholic Church in the United States* (1886), and John F. Kempker, *History of the Catholic Church in Iowa* (1887). A history of his activities at Loras College is in Mathias Martin Hoffmann, *Story of Loras College, 1839–1939* (1939).

MATTHEW E. BRANDT

HENNI, John Martin (15 June 1805–7 Sept. 1881), editor and Catholic missionary, was born in Misanenga, Switzerland, the son of Johann George Henni and Maria Ursula Henni, farmers. He was educated at the Gymnasium of St. Gall, Switzerland, the Lyceum and Gymnasium of Lucerne, and the Urban College of the Propaganda in Rome. While a student in Rome he met Father Frederick Résé, a co-worker of Bishop Edward Fenwick, Order of Preachers of Cincinnati, and agreed to become a missionary to German Catholics in Ohio and Kentucky. In 1828 he immigrated to the United States and completed his theological studies at St. Thomas Seminary in Bardstown, Kentucky.

Henni was ordained to the priesthood on 2 February 1829 by Bishop Fenwick and engaged in itinerant pastoral work in Ohio, settling for a time in Canton and then moving to Cincinnati. In 1834 he was appointed vicar-general of the diocese. He became pastor of German-speaking Holy Trinity Parish in Cincinnati and in 1837 founded *Der Wahrheitsfreund*, the first German Catholic newspaper published in the United States. He established bilingual schools in Cincinnati, wrote a German catechism, and laid plans for a bilingual seminary for German-speaking candidates for the priesthood. His proposed seminary did not meet with approval from the Irish-dominated American Catholic hierarchy. Henni pressed on, even buying land in Kentucky for the school, but his plan was thwarted and the seminary never opened.

When the Holy See established the diocese of Milwaukee in 1843, Henni was selected as the first bishop of the jurisdiction, which included all of the territory of Wisconsin and a small portion of eastern Minnesota. Although French Catholic missionaries had worked among the Native Americans in the seventeenth century, there had been no significant Catholic population in the region until the 1820s, when Indian claims were extinguished and land surveys were made. Steamships on the Great Lakes opened the region to settlement, prompting the outbreak of "Wisconsin Fever." Before long the area had evolved from a missionary territory to a large local church ripe for formal ecclesiastical organization. Much of the groundwork had been laid by itinerant missionaries, especially Henni's friend and companion Father Martin Kundig. When Henni arrived in Milwaukee in May 1844 he found a thriving city, and subsequent travels around the state revealed a total Catholic population of around 9,000, mostly located in the fertile farmlands south of the Wisconsin and Fox rivers.

Henni immediately began to build on the firm foundation of earlier Catholic efforts in Wisconsin and recruited several religious orders to establish Catholic schools and minister to the spiritual needs of the growing Catholic flock. He also renewed his editorship of a German Catholic press by establishing *Der Seebote* (1852) and a successor *Die Columbia* (1872). The crowning jewel of his building activities was the construction of St. Francis de Sales Seminary on land south of the city. The opening of the seminary in 1856 realized Henni's dream for a German-language seminary that would train young men to minister to the swelling numbers of German immigrants to the United States. In addition, he encouraged the Jesuits to found what later became Marquette University in Milwaukee.

In public debates and in print, Henni battled vigorously against both nativists and German rationalists and defended Catholic interests in Wisconsin and beyond. To aid his fledgling diocese he traveled to Europe several times to solicit funds from missionary societies in Bavaria and Austria. Present at Vatican Council I (1869–1870), he opposed adding the infallibility question to the council's agenda, but he voted in favor of the definition adopted. Meanwhile, his jurisdiction had grown large enough to be subdivided in 1868 into two new dioceses, Green Bay and La Crosse. In 1875 Milwaukee was raised to the status of an archdiocese, and Henni became its first archbishop.

Henni's health began to deteriorate in the late 1870s. After suffering a series of mild strokes, he petitioned Rome for a coadjutor bishop to help him with his duties and ultimately succeed him. Henni's selection, Bavarian-born Michael Heiss, did not sit well with the English-speaking priests of the diocese or with "Americanist" bishops like John Ireland (1839–1918) or James Gibbons, who feared a growing German dynasty in the Middle West. They mounted an effective campaign against Heiss with Roman officials and temporarily derailed the effort to have him appointed coadjutor. However, Henni suffered an even more debilitating stroke in 1880, and with the help of the mother general of the School Sisters of Notre Dame and their chaplain, Father Peter Abbelen, Rome approved Heiss. Henni died peacefully in Milwaukee. His long tenure provided Milwaukee with the stability necessary for a firm foundation.

Henni can rightly be acknowledged as one of the founders of Catholicism in Wisconsin. Although committed to making Milwaukee a haven for the increasing numbers of German Catholics coming to the United States, he successfully accommodated the diversity of newcomers that moved to Wisconsin between 1850 and 1880. He left a strong diocesan infrastructure, including a prospering seminary, social welfare institutions, and a strong and growing network of parishes. His longevity in office assured a secure and stable beginning for the Archdiocese of Milwaukee.

• Henni's papers are in the Archives of the Archdiocese of Milwaukee. There are also records pertinent to his years in Ohio in the Archives of the University of Notre Dame. See also Peter Leo Johnson, *Crosier on the Frontier* (1959); Johnson, *Halcyon Days: The Story of St. Francis Seminary* (1956); M. Mileta Ludwig, *Right Hand Glove Uplifted: A Biography of Archbishop Michael Heiss* (1968); and Timothy Walch, *Catholic Education in Chicago and Milwaukee, 1840–1890* (1988).

STEVEN M. AVELLA

HENNINGSEN, Charles Frederick (21 Feb. 1815–14 June 1877), filibuster and author, was born in either England or Belgium. The names and occupations of his parents are unknown. As "a man apparently without a country" (*New York Times*, 15 June 1877), Henningsen began his career fighting for the Carlists in Spain in 1834, serving under general Thomas Zumalacarregui. In 1835 he was awarded the title Knight of St. Ferdinand and Knight of Isabella for his service. Following his Spanish campaign, Henningsen joined the revolutionary Schamyl in Circassia. He was a fugitive in Asia Minor, when in 1848 the Magyars, under the leadership of Louis Kossuth, rebelled against Austrian control. Offering his services to Kossuth, who was in exile following the failure of the revolution, Henningsen was appointed plenipotentiary. He followed the Hungarian leader to America as his personal secretary in 1851. Remaining in the United States, he married Williamina Belt Connelly, a widow and niece of Georgia senator John McPherson Berrien, and settled in New York City.

During his tenure in New York, Henningsen worked to improve the technology of weaponry, an interest that acquainted him with steamship magnate and Know Nothing politician George Law. Enlisting Henningsen to convert out-of-date arms into Minie rifles, Law involved the munitions expert with the filibuster movement. Favoring the expansion of the United States, and more specifically, slavery, into Central America, filibusters invaded Central American countries that were at peace with the United States. Serving under filibuster William Walker, who had proclaimed himself president of Nicaragua after leading a military expedition into the country in 1855, Henningsen journeyed to Central America in October 1856. Henningsen was not motivated by ideas of expansion and adventure alone; with his wife he raised $30,000, which ostensibly was for the cause, but which he used to purchase lands in Nicaragua. As an experienced soldier with an expertise in firearms, Henningsen served as brigadier general under Walker and was appointed artillery commander. In the ensuing war against the rival Nicaraguan faction, Henningsen carried out orders to burn the capital of Granada, the capital of the opposition, in late 1856. Walker's fortunes in Nicaragua declined, however, after he alienated Cornelius Vanderbilt in a contest for control of the Accessory Transit Company, which had initially supported Walker's efforts. In turn, Vanderbilt impeded Walker's supply transports and backed neighboring republics in resisting Walker's leadership. On 1 May 1857 Walker and his supporters, including Henningsen, surrendered to the U.S. Navy and returned to the United States.

When he arrived in New York, Henningsen was met by a torchlight procession and endorsed by Democratic Tammany Hall. After accompanying Walker on a tour of the South to garner support for another Nicaraguan expedition, Henningsen organized the Central American League in New York City for the same purpose. Henningsen did not confine his expansionist ideas to Nicaragua. He traveled to Mexico in 1858 in the hope of forming a Sierra Madre Republic. He pursued filibuster schemes the following year when he organized the New York–based Arizona, Mexican and Central American Colonization Company. At the outbreak of the Civil War, Henningsen not surprisingly fought for the Confederacy, as he supported the expansion of slavery and had illegally invaded countries to make it possible. Appointed colonel of the Fifty-ninth Regiment, Virginia Infantry, known as the Wise Legion, on 14 October 1861, Henningsen resigned his commission on 5 November 1862.

Henningsen's European military adventures provided material for his vocation as an author in the years preceding his filibustering. While he wrote both poetry and prose, the greater part of his work consists of observations and analysis of European societies. His most important works, most of which were published in both Europe and America, include *The Most Striking Events of a Twelvemonth's Campaign with Zumalacarregui* (2 vols., 1836); *Eastern Europe and the Emperor Nicholas* (3 vols., 1846); *Kossuth and the Times* (1851); and *The Past and Future of Hungary* (1852). Largely abandoning his career as a writer for his Central American exploits, Henningsen's only work pertaining to America is his *Letter from General C. F. Henningsen in reply to the letter of Victor Hugo on the Harper's Ferry Invasion* (1860). In addition to his nonfictional works, Henningsen penned two novels, *The White Slave* (1845), and the futuristic novel *Sixty Years Hence* (1847). His prolific writing and capacity for languages prompted one eulogist to conclude that "among his associates Gen. Henningsen was known as a gentleman of urbanity, liberality, and cultivation" and that he was "an accomplished linguist" (*New York Times*, 15 June 1877). After the Civil War, Henningsen led a life largely removed from the public eye. He died in Washington, D.C.

As an international adventurer, Henningsen championed European nationalist movements and gained military expertise that he would later utilize as a filibuster. Thus, his career and fame in the United States rested on American expansionism and southern efforts to strengthen slavery, two causes united in the filibustering that preceded the Civil War.

• Primary sources on Henningsen's life can be found in the papers of William Walker, Tulane University, and the Authors Collection, University of Virginia. Contemporary accounts of the filibusters in Nicaragua include "The Nicaraguan Leaders," *Harper's Weekly*, 23 May 1857, p. 332, and "Nicaragua and the Filibusters," *Blackwood's Magazine*, 3 Mar. 1856, p. 314. For Henningsen's burning of Granada, see "Official Report of General Henningsen," *New Orleans Picayune*, 17 Jan. 1857. William Walker, *The War in Nicaragua* (1860), is an account by Henningsen's commander. The most information compiled on Henningsen's life in a secondary account is Alejandro Bolanos-Geyer, *William Walker: The Gray-Eyed Man of Destiny*, vols. 4 and 5 (1990). For filibusters see Thomas Chaffin, " 'Sons of Washington': Narciso Lopez, Filibustering, and U.S. Nationalism, 1848–1851," *Journal of the Early Republic* 15 (1995): 79; Craig L. Dozier, *Nicaragua's Mosquito Shore* (1985); Charles H. Brown, *Agents of Manifest Destiny: The Lives and Times of the Filibusters* (1980); Robert E. May, *The Southern Dream of a Caribbean Empire, 1854–1861* (1973); Albert H. Z. Carr, *The World of William Walker* (1963); and W. O. Scroggs, *Filibusters and Financiers* (1916). A history of Henningsen's regiment in the Civil War is George L. Sherwood, *59th Virginia Infantry*

(1994). Obituaries are in the *New York Times*, 15 June 1877, the *Washington Evening Star*, 14 June 1877, and the *Washington National Republican*, 15 June 1877.

CHRISTINE DOYLE

HENNOCK, Frieda Barkin (27 Sept. 1904–20 June 1960), attorney and federal official, was born in Kovel, Poland (now Ukraine), the daughter of Boris Hennock, a banker and real estate broker, and Sarah Barkin. In 1910 the family moved to the United States, settling in New York City. Hennock graduated from Morris High School in the Bronx and then enrolled in Brooklyn Law School, receiving her Bachelor of Laws degree in 1924. In 1926 she was admitted to the New York bar.

After joining the bar, Hennock began her legal practice in the office of a friend. In 1927 she founded a firm with Julius Silver and quickly became one of the most successful criminal defense attorneys in New York. In 1934 Hennock terminated her partnership with Silver and moved into corporate law. From 1935 to 1939 she served as assistant counsel and directed studies of low-cost housing for the New York Mortgage Commission. In 1941 Hennock joined the prestigious law firm of Choate, Mitchell and Ely, the first female attorney to do so.

Through the 1940s Hennock was active in New York Democratic party politics, both as a campaigner and as a financial contributor. She worked with the Women's Division of the Democratic National Committee to urge President Harry S. Truman to appoint more women to federal positions. Largely as a result of that pressure and her longstanding support of the party, in 1948 Truman appointed Hennock as the first woman commissioner of the Federal Communications Commission (FCC). Despite a Republican majority in the Senate, Hennock was confirmed with little difficulty, making her the first woman to serve as a commissioner of any federal regulatory agency. Following her confirmation Hennock stated, "it seems fundamental that in this field [communications]—so peculiarly affecting women—the viewpoint of this sex should be represented."

Hennock's tenure as FCC commissioner was distinguished by her vigorous advocacy of the educational potential of radio and television. In 1952 she proposed, without success, that at least 500 television channels be reserved for noncommercial use; however, the commission eventually set aside 242 channels for that purpose. Hennock then mounted a personal, nationwide campaign to promote educational television and urge educators to apply for channels. Partly due to her efforts, the first educational television station in the United States, KUHT-TV in Houston, Texas, was established in 1953.

Hennock took a number of other stands while at the FCC that were unpopular with both broadcasters and her colleagues. Fearing the existence of monopolies in the communications industries, she attacked several of the commission's grants that gave control of multiple broadcast facilities to a single owner. She also opposed excessive violence on television. Before a Senate investigating subcommittee Hennock argued for stricter controls on children's programming and proposed that licenses should be revoked for stations that broadcast excessive violence. At the core of her advocacy was her firm belief that stations operated on behalf of the general public and thus broadcasters were trustees of an important public resource.

In 1951 Hennock became the center of a controversy when President Truman nominated her for a federal district judgeship. She was endorsed by several women's legal organizations and her colleagues on the FCC, but the American Bar Association and the New York City Bar Association both opposed the nomination. During Senate Judiciary Committee hearings, she was repeatedly questioned about her relationship with a married judge. Despite her insistence that the relationship was nothing more than a platonic friendship, Hennock failed to stem the controversy and ultimately withdrew her name.

After President Dwight D. Eisenhower declined to offer her a reappointment as FCC commissioner in 1955, Hennock resumed her corporate law practice in Washington, D.C. She later commented: "Having fought the interests, I was not the least bit surprised that I was not reappointed. Monopolistic forces control the entire field of TV" (*New York Times*, 21 June 1960). In 1956 she married William H. Simons, a real estate broker in Washington. Hennock died in Washington after surgery for a brain tumor.

Hennock was both a pioneer for women in government service and a major force in the history of American mass communications. As the first woman commissioner of the FCC, she was one of only a few women to hold a federal appointment in the postwar period. Hennock was also a trailblazer of sorts with regard to the use of television for the public good, and she is credited with greatly helping to establish noncommercial and educational television through her relentless lobbying as FCC commissioner.

• The Frieda Hennock Simons Papers are deposited at the Harry S. Truman Library in Independence, Mo., and at the Schlesinger Library at Radcliffe College. For her work on the FCC, see Hennock's written opinions in *FCC Reports* from 1948 to 1955. See also Cary O'Dell, *Women Pioneers in Television: Biographies of Fifteen Industry Leaders* (1997). Obituaries are in the *New York Times* and *Washington Post*, both 21 June 1960.

THADDEUS RUSSELL

HENNY, David Christian (15 Nov. 1860–15 July 1935), civil engineer, was born in Arnhem, Holland, the son of David Henny and Berendina Lorentz. Henny attended schools in Holland and matriculated at the Polytechnic Institute in Delft, where he studied civil engineering. He graduated in 1881. He worked briefly in the Netherlands in general engineering, gaining experience in drainage projects and railroad bridge construction, before emigrating to the United States in 1884.

Although Henny began his American engineering career with the Chicago & Northwestern Railroad, he moved fairly quickly into a specialization in waterworks and drainage systems. Drawing on his experience with drainage systems in the Netherlands, Henny worked on waterworks projects in Menominee, Michigan; Sterling, Illinois; and Oberlin, Ohio. After a series of short-term contracts that took him to various sites throughout the United States, in 1892 he began a thirteen-year association with Excelsior Wooden Pipe Company of San Francisco, California. Having obtained a degree of security in what were then uncertain times for engineers, he married Julia Antoinette Hermanie Wetzel-Brown in 1893; they had three, possibly four, children.

After ten years as manager of Excelsior Wooden Pipe (later known as Redwood Manufacturers Company), Henny left the firm in 1905 to become a supervising engineer for the northwestern district of the U.S. Reclamation Service. As a supervising engineer Henny oversaw drainage, irrigation, and flood control projects throughout the states of Washington and Oregon. These projects included work at Umatilla, Sunnyside, and Klamath. In 1910 Henny established a private practice as a consulting engineer with a special expertise in dam design and construction. Over the next twenty-five years Henny was involved with almost every major work undertaken by the U.S. Bureau of Reclamation that required the construction of a dam. As an active member of both the American Society of Civil Engineers and the American Concrete Institute, Henny participated in research undertaken by those organizations to determine the safety of designs for large concrete dams. In 1925, for example, Henny was a member of the special subcommittee of the Engineering Foundation that arranged for a concrete arch dam to be tested to destruction on Stephenson Creek in central California. Data obtained from these tests were later used by Henny in his work with Bureau of Reclamation engineers in designing large dams such as Owyhee Dam in Oregon (1932) and Hoover Dam on the Colorado River (1935). The question of the safety of thin arch dams divided the engineering community during the 1920s, and Henny's belief that gravity dams were inherently safer than thin arch continued to influence engineering designs on large federal projects even after his death in 1935. Henny was one of a number of engineers who believed the safest dam design would be a gravity arch, which combined the best features of gravity and arch construction. That view was influential, but mistaken.

Henny was a strong believer in the value of participation in professional societies and served two terms as president of the Technical Society of the Pacific Coast, a local technical club in San Francisco, as well as one term as a director and one term as a vice president of the American Society of Civil Engineers. As an ASCE member, he was appointed to numerous committees in addition to serving as chairman of the irrigation division of that society for a number of years. He served on the Committee on Mass Concrete while a member of the American Concrete Institute. Henny wrote numerous papers on dam construction, which were published in professional journals such as *Proceedings of the American Society of Civil Engineers*, as well as writing research reports for the Bureau of Reclamation and the Federal Power Commission. While he was little known outside engineering circles, Henny's numerous activities in research, publication, and professional societies helped him to exercise a strong influence within the professional community.

As is typical of many consulting engineers, Henny remained active in the profession until he died. At the time of his death, in Portland, Oregon, he was chairman of the Bonneville Dam Commission (Columbia River, Oregon) as well as a member of the consulting board for the Fort Peck Dam project (Missouri River, Montana) and an engineer for the Los Angeles County Flood Control District.

• Henny has been largely overlooked by historians of engineering, although Donald C. Jackson, *Great American Bridges and Dams* (1988), does note that Henny's design for the Owyhee Dam in eastern Oregon served as a model for construction of Hoover Dam a few years later. An obituary in *Engineering News-Record*, 18 July 1935, p. 102, mentions some of Henny's most notable professional accomplishments and provides a brief biographical sketch.

NANCY FARM MANNIKKO

HENRI, Robert (24 June 1865–12 July 1929), artist and teacher, was born Robert Henry Cozad in Cincinnati, Ohio, the son of John Jackson Cozad, a riverboat gambler and land speculator, and Theresa Gatewood. His father invested in 50,000 acres in Nebraska to found a city, and in 1873 or 1874 he moved the family to the frontier, where he formed the agricultural community of Cozad. Young Robert spent his next few years on the family ranch, attending school intermittently in Cozad and at the Chickering Classical and Scientific Institute in Cincinnati, to which he returned each fall in 1875, 1877, 1878, and 1879. The Cozads moved to Denver in 1881, and on a visit to his Nebraska property the next year John Cozad killed one of his workers in a fight over wages. The family fled an arrest warrant, settling in Atlantic City under assumed names. John and Theresa became Mr. and Mrs. Richard Henry Lee, their older son John took the name Frank L. Southrn [*sic*], and Robert simply dropped "Cozad" and changed the spelling of his middle name to the French form "Henri" to identify himself with his Huguenot forebears. Although his father was later exonerated, Robert kept the alias but always insisted (though with little success) that it be given the "American" pronunciation *Hen*-rye.

From a young age Henri was devoted to drawing, and in 1886, with his family's support, he enrolled in the Pennsylvania Academy of the Fine Arts in Philadelphia. There he had his first exposure to the realistic style introduced at the academy by Thomas Eakins, who had taught at the school until the semester before Henri's arrival, and came under the tutelage of Thomas P. Anshutz and Thomas Hovenden. Henri's brother Frank, a student at Jefferson Medical College, enabled him to observe operations and autopsies, which gave him the opportunity to further his study of anatomy. Already an independent thinker, Henri organized a private portrait class among his fellow students and participated in the formation of separate sketching sessions in which he emphasized quick, spontaneous work. Though he was often in personal conflict with Anshutz and Hovenden, both of the older artists recognized his talent and encouraged him warmly.

Henri was a natural leader and was popular with his classmates. In 1888 he organized a trip to Paris, then a rite of passage for art students, with four others: Harry Finney, James R. Fisher, William Haefeker, and Charles Grafly. He enrolled at the Académie Julian, where he studied under the well-known academicians William-Adolphe Bouguereau and Tony Robert-Fleury. He found their instruction so dry and formal that he transferred to the École des Beaux-Arts, but the manner of teaching there was no more to his liking. Nevertheless, he persevered in the rigid academic discipline, devoting as much of his free time as he could to studying the masterpieces in the Louvre and to attending the many salons and international expositions the city offered. Frustrated by the repeated rejections of his submissions to the national Salon, he began to travel in the spring of 1889, spending the next two years in the south and the west of France, in Italy, and in Spain, where he was deeply impressed by the work of Diego Velázquez.

In 1891 Henri and his friends returned to the United States. He studied at the academy again for a time, but in 1892 he secured a job teaching at the Philadelphia School of Design for Women (later Moore College of Art). His reputation as both an artist and a teacher grew rapidly, and he became the center of a group of art students, teachers, and illustrators drawn to his forceful personality and liberal ideas. Their spirited weekly sessions included eating, drinking, and horseplay but were essentially devoted to earnest conversation about art. Among the artists in this lively group were a number of young newspaper illustrators including John Sloan, George Luks, William Glackens, and Everett Shinn, all later to become famous as realistic painters. In 1895 Henri and Glackens, with whom he was then sharing a studio, went to Paris, and with Edward Redfield they toured Belgium and the Netherlands. In Paris he had already been deeply influenced by the "graphic impressionism" and realistic subject matter of Edouard Manet; his visit to the Low Countries gave him the opportunity to examine the work of Frans Hals, in whose robust realism he found the spirit and the technique toward which he had been moving. That experience proved a lasting inspiration for him.

Henri returned to Paris in 1895, and the next year he finally succeeded in participating in a Salon show there. In 1897 he was accorded his first solo exhibition at the Pennsylvania Academy. The following year Henri married Linda Craige of Philadelphia, and the two traveled to Paris, where he exhibited four paintings at the Salon. One of them, *La Neige*, was purchased by the French government for the Musée National du Luxembourg in 1899, an honor that greatly enhanced his professional status. The next year Henri and his wife returned to the United States and settled in New York, where he lived for the rest of his life.

Although Henri had begun to mount solo exhibitions in commercial galleries, he still depended on teaching as his main source of income and resumed it with a job at the Veltin School. In 1902 he accepted an offer from noted portrait painter William Merritt Chase to join the faculty of Chase's New York School of Art, where he taught drawing, portrait painting, and composition until 1908, turning increasingly to portraiture and figure painting as the major subject matter in his personal work. His human figures were greatly admired for their insight as well as for the vigor and dash of their technique. John Sloan compared Henri's portraiture favorably with that of Chase, observing in 1951, "The difference between Henri's greatest portraits and Chase's people was a feeling of appreciation for the personality, the human style he re-created" (Helen Farr Sloan, "Robert Henri: An Appreciation," in Perlman, *Robert Henri, Painter*).

Henri's career advanced swiftly, bringing him both financial success and numerous honors. He was elected to the Society of American Artists in 1903, and the next year he exhibited at the National Arts Club in New York, won a silver medal at the Universal Exposition in St. Louis, and made his first sale to an American institution when the Carnegie Institute purchased *Girl in White Waist*. In 1905 he became a member of the jury of Carnegie International and won the Norman W. Harris Prize of the Art Institute of Chicago for *Lady in Black*. Although long a rebel against the conservative spirit of the National Academy of Design, which he called "a cemetery of natural art instincts," Henri accepted membership in that august body in 1906.

Henri's wife Linda died in 1905, but he did not interrupt his work. He left the New York School of Art in 1908 and early the next year founded the Henri Art School, which he operated through 1910. Subsequently he taught at the Modern School (1911–1918) and intermittently at the Art Students League (1915–1928). In his teaching, as in the informal gatherings he had conducted in Philadelphia, he stressed painting from real life in a natural, spontaneous style.

Henri was a dynamic exponent of truth and honesty in art and a rebel against the upper-class subject matter of the academics of his time. Already prominent enough to be included in the jury of the National Academy of Design, he withdrew his own work from the academy's 1907 show when it refused to include that of Luks, Shinn, Glackens, and others of his group, and the next year he was dropped from membership in the jury. In protest against the judge's narrow aesthetic standards, he organized a competitive show. Declaring in the press that "the Academy is hopelessly against what is real and vital in American art," he filled New York's Macbeth Gallery, which had given him solo shows since 1902, with the vigorous realistic work of Glackens, Sloan, Luks, Shinn, and three new members of Henri's circle, Maurice Prendergast, Arthur B. Davies, and Earnest Lawson, as well as his own. The exhibition of The Eight, as the group was known, opened in May 1908. It was attacked by conservative critics for its "vulgarity" but was a huge success with the public. Only seven paintings were sold (two by Henri), but the event had a powerful democratizing effect on the art world, which became more open to exhibitions organized by independent galleries and by artists themselves rather than by committees of critics. Although The Eight did not work in particularly similar styles and never exhibited together again, they have remained linked in art history by their defiance of the genteel tradition. Inspired and led by Henri, they became the nucleus of what was to be called the Ashcan School because of their deliberate rejection of the refined subjects and styles that dominated the art of the time in favor of commonplace, even sordid, aspects of the life of American cities.

A few months after the exhibition of The Eight, Henri married Marjorie Organ, a popular newspaper caricaturist and comic artist. They spent the summer in Spain, where he painted pieces such as *Spanish Gypsy*, later acquired by New York's Metropolitan Museum, and returned to help launch his second major assault on the elitist tradition of the art establishment, the organization of the Exhibition of Independent Artists. For it he dispensed with the academy's practice of selection by a jury and the presentation of prizes. From 1 April to 17 April 1910 more than a hundred artists, including Henri, Glackens, Sloan, Davies, George Bellows, Guy Pène Du Bois, Rockwell Kent, Walt Kuhn, and Dorothy Rice, presented some 600 paintings in a New York loft building rented by Henri. It was the largest exhibition of progressive art yet seen in America. Again the critical reception was generally hostile, and again the public response was wildly enthusiastic. On opening night a police patrol was necessary to maintain order.

In an effort to establish a permanent venue for the work of the artists to whom he had given such spectacular exposure, Henri created the MacDowell Club of New York to perpetuate his democratic system of exhibition. The club lasted from 1911 to 1919, presenting the work of many of Henri's friends and students. In 1912 Henri participated in the organization of the controversial International Exhibition of Modern Art, known as the Armory Show, which introduced the American public to modernism in art. In the planning of this exhibition, Henri opposed Sloan and others on the proportion of space to be given to avant-garde European artists, preferring to keep the emphasis on the emerging American art tradition, but he was outvoted, and more than one-third of the 1,600 artworks presented were by Europeans. Despite Henri's relative exclusion from the organization of the show, five of his paintings were presented in it. That summer he and his wife made their first visit to Ireland, where he painted *Himself* and *Herself*, later purchased for the permanent collection of the Chicago Art Institute.

From 1911 to 1916 Henri experimented with abstraction, creating a series of what he called "color notes" based on a mathematical system of color harmonies propounded by Hardesty Maratta, who worked with him in the Henri School in 1909 and 1910. In these innovative nonrepresentational pieces, such as *Color Notes*, he reduced the natural form of human figures, still lifes, and landscapes to planes of pure, flat color. Although the small paintings on bristol board were intended as private investigations in chromatic theory, they were subsequently to be regarded as important abstract compositions. It was characteristic of Henri's adventurous spirit that he never ceased exploring new methods of personal expression.

Henri continued to paint and teach, earning new honors during the remaining years of his life. He was awarded a silver medal at the Panama Pacific Exposition in San Francisco in 1915 and another for best portrait from the Wilmington Society of Fine Arts in 1920. In 1929 he received the Temple gold medal for *Wee Woman*, a portrait of an Irish child painted in 1927. He died in New York City after returning from a visit to Ireland.

Henri was an imposing figure, more than six feet tall, with high cheekbones and dark, slanted eyes that gave him a mysterious, somewhat Oriental look. A well-known etching by John Sloan, *Robert Henri* (1931), is at the Delaware Art Center in Wilmington. A charismatic personality, he was an influential teacher who led a generation of artists away from sterile academicism. In 1923 his student Margery Ryerson collected his classroom and personal notes in *The Art Spirit*, which sold widely. In it he expressed his devotion to human dignity and to the primacy of real life as a source in art. "I am not interested in one school or movement, nor do I care for art as art," he stated. "I am interested in life."

• The best account of Henri's philosophy of art is in his own *The Art Spirit* (1923) and in his articles "Progress in Our National Art Must Spring from the Development of Individuality of Ideas and Freedom of Expression: A Suggestion for a New Art School," *Craftsman* 15 (Jan. 1909): 387–401, "The New York Exhibition of Independent Artists," *Craftsman* 18 (May 1910): 160–72, and "My People," *Craftsman* 27 (Feb. 1915): 459–69. Discussion of his life and influence can be found in almost every history of American art since his own time, but authoritative full-length studies of the man and his work are William Yarrow and Louis Bouche, eds., *Robert Henri: His Life and Works* (1921); Nathaniel Poussette-Dart, *Robert Henri* (1922); Helen Appleton Read, *Robert Henri* (1931); William Innes Homer, *Robert Henri and His Circle* (1969); and Bennard B. Perlman, *Robert Henri: His Life and Art* (1991). A novel based on Henri's early years is Mari Sandoz, *Son of the Gamblin' Man: The Youth of an Artist* (1960). Essays on Henri's art can be found in many exhibition catalogs, including American Academy of Arts and Letters, *Robert Henri and His Circle* (1964); Chapellier Galleries, *Robert Henri, 1865–1929* (1976); and Perlman, *Robert Henri, Painter: Delaware Art Museum* (1984). See also Mary Fanton Roberts, "Robert Henri—Great American," *Century Magazine*,

Spring 1930, pp. 271–77; Guy Pène Du Bois, "Robert Henri," *Arts* 17 (Apr. 1931): 495–99; Perlman, "Practicing Preacher: Remembering Robert Cozad," *Art and Antiques* 7 (Nov. 1990): 84–89, 108; and Henri's obituaries in the *New York Times* and the *New York Herald Tribune*, both 13 July 1929.

DENNIS WEPMAN

HENROTIN, Ellen Martin (6 July 1847–29 June 1922), woman's club leader and social reformer, was born in Portland, Maine, the daughter of Edward Byam Martin and Sarah Ellen Norris. Following her birth the family moved to New Haven, Connecticut, and after Ellen's thirteenth birthday they were transplanted to the British Isle of Wight, where Edward Martin had acquired land. The status and wealth of the family enabled Ellen to be educated in London, Paris, and Dresden schools and to learn many foreign languages. In 1868 the family returned to the United States, making their home in Chicago where her father had numerous investments.

At a dance Ellen happened to meet Charles Henrotin, the 26-year-old son of a Belgian doctor who had emigrated to America. The couple married in 1869, and they would have three sons. Her husband became president of his own bank and of the Chicago Stock Exchange; he was also a consul for Belgium and Turkey. The couple led an active social life and rose in Chicago society.

In 1874 Ellen Henrotin had her first exposure to clubs when she joined the Fortnightly Club, which met for the purpose of mixing intellectual discussion with a social atmosphere. Henrotin contributed by writing and presenting papers on literary topics. In 1887 she coauthored *The Social Status of European and American Women* with her sister Kate, and she cofounded the Friday Club, which operated along the same lines as the Fortnightly. She also joined the Chicago Woman's Club in the 1880s, working on various reforms and serving as president between 1903 and 1904.

Henrotin earned greater status when she became vice chair of the Board of Lady Managers for the World's Columbian Exposition held in Chicago in 1893. Hoping to further the recognition of women, she persuaded officials to include a Woman's Branch with the Congress Auxiliary, which organized conferences for cultural and scholarly congresses. Henrotin took on the organizational duties, selecting women as representatives, and addressed most of the 1,200 sessions where women had the opportunity to speak publicly at the exposition. The Board of Lady Managers also set up safe, inexpensive housing for women arriving from outside the city.

In 1892 the first biennial convention was held for the General Federation of Women's Clubs, an organization to bring together all the unrelated women's clubs that had sprung up across the country. Two years later Henrotin took over the presidency, a title she held for four years. Her principal aims were to enlarge the federation and to expand the membership into more areas of public service. In pursuit of these goals, Henrotin traveled to twenty-four states, speaking to women of various backgrounds. By 1898, when her term ended, thirty-one state federations were in existence with a membership of about 160,000 women. A century later these federations continued to be strong.

Henrotin believed that women's clubs were "the most democratic of institutions" and that in joining clubs women had heightened their educational possibilities through classes offered there that gave them the opportunity to become active citizens. She thought every club should incorporate the study of civics and social economics into its programs. She sought to create possibilities for women with more educational opportunities, better labor conditions, and the institution of a bureau for national health. She was made official representative of the General Federation to serve on the executive board of the American Peace Society in 1910 and retained this position permanently.

Between 1904 and 1907, as president of the National Women's Trade Union League, Henrotin fought to improve conditions for women workers through unionization. Under her direction and sponsored by the Chicago Women's Club, a "Women in Industry" conference was held in 1904. Hoping to bring about protective legislation for women and child workers, she helped to organize the "Chicago Industrial Exhibit," which demonstrated the problems associated with sweatshops, such as child labor and improper equipment. She also helped garment workers come to a settlement by publicizing their grievances during a 1910 Chicago strike. Additionally, she gave her support to the Industrial School for Girls in Illinois.

Since women workers often found themselves in financial need because of their low wages, they sometimes turned to prostitution. Henrotin joined the move to end the problem of "white slavery" after the mayor named her to the Chicago Vice Commission in 1910. With her help, a report called *The Social Evil in Chicago* was published in 1911. Stressing that education was the clue to changing the situation, she sought to have sex hygiene training in public schools and acted as chair of the executive committee of the Amanda Smith School for dependent girls. Because of her strong belief in education, in 1912 Henrotin was elected as trustee of the University of Illinois and vice president of the international commission that sponsored a Congress on Home Education in 1914.

After Henrotin's husband died in 1914, her activities lessened. She spent much of her remaining time at the home of her son Edward in Cherryplain, New York, where she died. A representative link between rich and poor, Henrotin's effective writing and persuasive voice convinced others to join with her in working toward reforms. Upon becoming president of the General Federation of Women's Clubs, Henrotin stressed that "the Federation represents the sum and soul of all causes, the home and society." She felt that the club movement would bring together the forces needed for the greater good of all women.

• Henrotin's papers are at the Schlesinger Library, Radcliffe College. Henrotin wrote several articles detailing her involvement in woman's clubs, including those in *Review of Reviews*, Mar. 1896 and Oct. 1897; *Arena*, Dec. 1896; *Outlook*, 6 Feb. 1897; and National Education Association, *Proceedings* (1897): 73–83. Information regarding her connection with the World's Fair is in Henriette G. Frank and Amalie H. Jerome, *Annals of the Chicago Woman's Club* (1916): 112–16; and *Review of Reviews*, May 1893. General histories of the women's club movement written during Henrotin's time include Jane C. Croly, *History of the Woman's Club Movement in America* (1898), and Mary I. Wood, *History of the General Federation of Women's Clubs* (1912). More recent studies are Mildred W. Wells, *Unity in Diversity* (1953), Mary Jean Houde, *The Clubwoman: A Story of the Illinois Federation of Women's Clubs* (1970), and Houde, *Reaching Out: A Story of the General Federation of Women's Clubs* (1989). Information about her suffrage activity is in "The Suffragist and the G.O.P.," *Harper's Weekly*, 4 July 1908, p. 16; and Susan B. Anthony and Ida H. Harper, eds., *History of Woman Suffrage*, vols. 4–6 (1902–1922). Obituaries are in the *Chicago Daily Tribune*, 30 June 1922, and the *Chicago Herald and Examiner*, 1 July 1922.

MARILYN ELIZABETH PERRY

HENRY, Alexander (Aug. 1739–4 Apr. 1824), fur trader and merchant, was born probably in New Brunswick, New Jersey, possibly the son of Alexander Henry, a merchant, and Elizabeth (maiden name unknown). Nothing is known of Henry's childhood. However, at age twenty, in 1760, he was transporting merchandise along Lake Ontario's southern shore to supply British Major General Jeffery Amherst's attack on French Montreal during the French and Indian Wars. When Montreal surrendered, Canada was open to English merchants. Henry immediately returned to Albany, New York, to purchase merchandise. Selling the goods at Fort William Augustus near Ogdensburgh, New York, in January 1761 he journeyed toward Montreal, stopping at Les Cedres. There he learned of the potential of Indian trade at Michilimackinac (now Mackinaw City, Mich.) and the Lake Superior region. Intrigued by the opportunity, Henry secured the second fur trade pass given to an Englishman to trade in the upper Great Lakes.

Disguised as a Frenchman, Henry took his canoes up the Ottawa River, Lake Nipissing, French River route. Despite Canada's surrender, England and France remained at war, and France's Indian allies were hostile. In September Henry arrived at Michilimackinac, the major trading center for the upper Great Lakes. Sixty Ojibwa warriors, not fooled by his disguise, confronted Henry. The tall chief threatened; then, because the Ojibwa needed the trade goods Henry brought, offered friendship. When British soldiers arrived to garrison the fort, the British traders were relieved.

During the winter of 1761–1762 a minor Ojibwa chief, Wawatam, adopted Henry as a brother. In May 1762 Henry paddled to Sault Ste. Marie, where he met

French fur trader Jean-Baptiste Cadot. When the fort at the Sault burned in December, Henry helped the surviving British soldiers return to Michilimackinac.

On 2 June 1763 Ojibwa warriors inspired by Chief Pontiac surprised the British garrison. Henry hid, was discovered and captured, but later was rescued by Wawatam. During the next year he lived with his Ojibwa family and followed their seasonal hunting and fishing cycle. In 1764 he accompanied the local Ojibwa to Sir William Johnson's peace conference at Niagara. Now free, Henry eagerly returned to Michilimackinac to recover his property. Accompanying Colonel John Bradstreet's expedition from Niagara to Detroit, he joined the troops who reoccupied Michilimackinac in September.

In 1765 Henry secured a license to trade in the Lake Superior area in partnership with Cadot. During 1767–1768 he wintered at Michipicoten and in 1768 joined a consortium headed by Alexander Baxter to mine Lake Superior copper. The unprofitable venture folded in 1774.

Henry, primarily an Indian trader, took canoes in 1775 northwest of Lake Superior. There he and other peddlers from Montreal challenged the Hudson's Bay Company. From his post on Beaver Lake, Henry set off in January to Fort des Prairies on the Saskatchewan River to see the Great Plains. Having satisfied his curiosity, he returned, and early in the spring he purchased beaver skins on the Churchill River. Laden with prime furs, Henry set off in July for Montreal. There he sold his furs and presented to governor Sir Guy Carleton a map of the western region.

Captivated by the potential of the Northwest, Henry sailed to England in the autumn of 1776 to propose that the Hudson's Bay Company employ Canadian canoeists. Bearing a letter of introduction, Henry crossed to France and was introduced at court to the young queen, Marie-Antoinette.

In the spring of 1777 Henry returned to Canada and went to Michipicoten in partnership with Jean Baptiste Blondeau. Selling his post, he traded at Sault Ste. Marie in 1778 in association with Cadot. Henry sailed to England in the fall of 1778 and again in 1780 to promote his idea of a transcontinental overland exploring expedition to the Pacific. After Henry's return to Canada, he sent Sir Joseph Banks in 1781 a detailed plan for the expedition.

Henry became a general merchant in Montreal, making occasional trips to Detroit and Michilimackinac. In 1785 he married a widow, Julia Kittson; they had five children. Henry and eighteen other traders active in the Northwest founded the Beaver Club in February 1785. In the spring of 1786 Henry apparently suffered a severe financial setback. To recoup his losses, Henry again traded actively at Michilimackinac until 1790.

During the mid 1780s Henry eagerly watched American efforts to open trade with China. Fascinated by the prospects of sending vessels to the Pacific Coast to acquire furs, Henry discussed his ideas with New York merchant John Jacob Astor, whom he had introduced into the Canadian trade. Astor stayed with Henry during his visits to Montreal. During the 1790s Henry and Astor assisted the North West Company ship furs to China.

Henry maintained close ties with John Askin, whom he met early in his career at Michilimackinac. During the mid 1790s they speculated in several unsuccessful land schemes in northern Ohio.

In 1792 Henry, in company with his nephew Alexander Henry, Jr., obtained one six-year share in the North West Company. Henry sold his interest in 1796 but continued to buy furs and export to England. When an uninsured shipment was lost in 1801, he suffered a financial crisis. Although in ill health, Henry recouped in 1802 by becoming a commission merchant and an auctioneer. Despite his reverses, Henry maintained a secure place in Montreal's society. He served as captain in the militia and justice of the peace, entertained leading merchants in his home, attended parties, and regularly signed petitions and memorials. He was the senior member of the Beaver Club, reactivated in 1807.

By then, new men were taking over the fur trade and many of Henry's former associates had died. To recapture his exciting past he wrote a memoir of his early life. Published in New York in 1809, *Travels and Adventures in Canada and the Indian Territories between the Years 1760 and 1776* became an adventure classic and is one of the best descriptions of Great Lakes Indian life.

During his later years Henry continued to trade, and in 1812 he was appointed king's auctioneer for the district of Montreal. His partner and nephew Norman Bethune lived with him at 14 St. Urbain Street. A middle-sized man, easy yet dignified, Henry was called by the Ojibwa "the handsome Englishman." Henry died in Montreal esteemed by all who knew him.

• Manuscript sources relating to Henry are scattered. Significant items are found in the "Beaver Club Minutes, 1807–1827" in the McCord Museum, McGill University; "Consolidated Return of Licenses Granted to Trade 1774, 1777, 1778, 1785, 1786, 1787, 1788, 1789, 1790" and "Forest Oakes Account Book 1765–1780" in the Public Archives of Canada; and the William Edgar Papers in the Toronto Public Library. The most important sources for Henry's career are his *Travels and Adventures in Canada* and the *Canadian Magazine and Literary Repository* 2 (Apr. 1824) and 2 (May 1824). Edited editions of Henry's book were published by James Bain (1901) and Milo M. Quaife (1921). Henry's involvement with John Askin in various land speculation projects is found in Quaife, *The John Askin Papers*, vol. 1 (1928) and vol. 2 (1931). His connections with John Jacob Astor are discussed in Kenneth W. Porter, *John Jacob Astor, Business Man*, vol. 1 (1931); his China trade figures in Grace Parker Morris, "Some Letters from 1792–1800 on the China Trade," *Oregon Historical Quarterly* 42 (1941): 48–87.

DAVID ARTHUR ARMOUR

HENRY, Alice (21 Mar. 1857–14 Feb. 1943), labor reformer, was born in Richmond, a suburb of Melbourne, Australia, the daughter of Charles Ferguson Henry, an accountant, and Margaret Walker, a seamstress. Henry's parents, educated Presbyterian immigrants from Glasgow, Scotland, tried farming for three years in the outpost of Pakenham, near Melbourne, where she grew up freely. Back in Melbourne, her father sent her to high school, rare then for girls, and introduced her to the community-oriented "new liberalism" movement, which would become the basis of Henry's political beliefs.

After graduation, Henry taught grade school until hired as a journalist by the local daily *Argus* and the *Australasian*, its weekly edition. She became active in reform organizations such as the Women's Writers' Club and the National Council of Women. Without family save her brother after her parents died, she formed close friendships with such militants as Catherine Spence, who influenced her thought. Like many Australian feminists, she supported the Labor party despite its antifeminist culture. To protect her job from the conservative owners of the *Argus*, she wrote on reform under pseudonyms such as "Wyuna" and worked in the office rather than as a street militant, an experience that only strengthened her belief that to seek equal opportunity for women was not enough. In 1901 Australia became a federation, and the coalition between middle-class feminists and labor succeeded in gaining female suffrage, labor laws, and wage boards able to force employers to give reasonable work conditions.

The success of the coalition raised interest abroad in Australian reformers. Henry went to London in 1905 and to New York in January 1906, speaking across the United States on the Australian and British suffrage campaigns. In 1907 she became secretary of the Chicago office of the Women's Trade Union League (WTUL). Founded in 1903 to organize unskilled women workers and lobby for labor laws, it was headed by Margaret Dreier Robins, a wealthy German-American. Most militants were middle-class women, as in other American reform groups, but a number of ethnic working-class women had joined the organization and WTUL had been accepted as a member by the American Federation of Labor (AFL).

Henry found the WTUL ideologically and personally congenial, especially after she was joined in October 1907 by the Australian novelist Stella Miles Franklin, who became her closest friend. Henry wrote for American, British, and Australian newspapers, studied women in the Milwaukee brewery industry, was active in the Socialist party and the National American Woman Suffrage Association, edited the WTUL's page in Chicago's *Union Labor Advocate*, and after January 1911 the new WTUL monthly, *Life and Labor*. During the 1909–1910 textile strikes in New York and Chicago, she stood in the picket lines. Weary from many brutally suppressed strikes, AFL leaders such as Samuel Gompers distrusted WTUL's approach. The AFL held that under existing conditions only skilled workers could extract better conditions, if only the American government, which had usually sided with employers, would withdraw entirely from labor disputes and allow both sides to fight it out alone. Mid-

dle-class feminists complained that to ask for labor laws specifically for women betrayed the fight for equal opportunity and interfered with their right to work. Henry attacked this "mere manufacturers' argument" that forgot that most working women were unskilled and vulnerable. Considering their misery, she argued, it was callous to insist on ideological purity.

Life and Labor never became self-supporting. Robins, who paid its bills, blamed Henry and also wanted a newsletter instead. Henry resigned in June 1915. She went on to campaign for WTUL's industrial legislation, wrote *The Trade Union Woman* (1915), and represented WTUL at the 1917 Trades and Labor Congress in Ottawa. World War I shattered Henry's faith in human progress and created personal strains. During the Boer War, she had supported the Australian Peace and Humanity Society and its fight against war guilt and atrocity propaganda. During her stay in London, she had further been shocked by the power of the English oligarchy, "built upon the wealth and misery of the world." She did not idealize Great Britain, which now hurt her relations with Anglo-American reformers who did. Like Robins, Henry fervently opposed American intervention, but, unnerved by superpatriotic attacks against Robins, Henry confined her sorrow to her friends and pacifist magazines in remote Australia.

The war and the postwar reaction destroyed the basis of WTUL's work. The Progressive coalition had been shattered, and although women gained the national right to vote in 1920, suffrage also destroyed the need for a feminist-labor alliance. The WTUL decided to focus its dwindling resources on lobbying for workers' education. Henry took charge of the campaign. She also taught union organizing at the Bryn Mawr Summer School, edited from 1921 to 1924 the newsletter *Life and Labor Bulletin*, and published *Women and the Labor Movement* (1923) to justify unions for women. She retired in 1927. In 1933 she moved to Melbourne to live with her brother and his family, and she died there in her sleep. She never married. Her friends Nettie Palmer and Isabel Newsham finished her memoirs. Then she was forgotten.

A militant rather than a thinker, Henry's contributions to American reform are difficult to assess, especially as WTUL failed, disbanding in 1950 after two decades as a small labor lobby. Its ideology, at odds with mainstream feminism, whose individualistic, procapitalist outlook focused on equality of opportunity, led to neglect by historians of American women and reform, while labor historians focused on proletarian organizations. Recent interest in the feminist-labor alliance represented by WTUL has led to new interest in the life of its main publicist, Alice Henry.

• Henry's papers are in Australia, at the National Library in Canberra, and the Mitchell Library in Sydney. Important sources are the papers of Stella Franklin and Catherine Spence, at the Mitchell Library, of Margaret Dreier Robins at the University of Florida, and of the WTUL archives at the Library of Congress and the University of Illinois. See also the mimeographed *Memoirs of Alice Henry*, ed. Nettie Palmer (1944). Extended studies of WTUL and Henry's work are Elizabeth Payne, *Reform, Labor and Feminism: Margaret Dreier Robins and the Women's Trade Union League* (1988), Diane Kirkby, *Alice Henry: The Power of Pen and Voice, the Life of an Australian-American Labor Reformer* (1991), and Robin Miller Jacoby, *The British and American Women's Trade Union Leagues, 1890–1925* (1994).

THOMAS REIMER

HENRY, Andrew (c. 1775–10 June 1833), miner, fur trader, and explorer, was born in Fayette County, Pennsylvania, the son of George Henry and Margaret Young, farmers. Before 1800 Henry left Pennsylvania for Nashville, Tennessee. He moved in 1800 to the Upper Louisiana village of Ste. Genevieve, a Mississippi river town in present-day Missouri. Henry returned to Nashville in 1802 or 1803 before resettling in Ste. Genevieve, where he formed Andrew Henry & Co. in 1804.

In December 1804 Henry was appointed to the grand jury of the Court of Common Pleas for the Cape Girardeau District. A year later he married Mary Villars, whom he left within a month. Around this time, Henry formed a mining partnership with William H. Ashley. In 1806 the two men bought 640 acres near Little Mine Creek, in present-day Washington County, and established Henry's Diggings. In Ste. Genevieve, Henry engaged in other businesses, served as a justice of the peace, and was one of the original trustees of the town's first academy.

In 1809 Henry became a partner of Manuel Lisa and other traders in the St. Louis Missouri Fur Company. He led the company's first fur trade expedition of some 300–400 men up the Missouri River. They encountered trapper John Colter, who convinced the fearless Henry to strike out for the rich, fur-bearing waters of the Missouri River's Three Forks area. Henry's trappers successfully harvested beaver but faced deadly Indian attacks, intemperate weather, and lack of food. He led his men over the Continental Divide, and in 1810 they built a fort on the north fork of the Snake River, now known as Henry's Fork. The next year, after discovering Lake Henry in present-day Idaho, he split his weary party into three groups, leading his followers toward St. Louis. Near the Mandan villages, Henry's party met up with Lisa, who had enlisted other trappers to search for Henry's group.

Lisa and Henry's men commenced down the Missouri in the fall of 1811. At Cedar Island, to placate the Sioux, the men reconstructed a burned-out fort. After reaching St. Louis, Henry, disappointed with the lack of profit from the fur trade, returned to southeast Missouri. There he pursued his business enterprises and once again participated in community and civic affairs. When his land became part of Washington County in 1812, Henry was asked to serve as foreman of the new county's first jury.

During the War of 1812 Henry served as a major in the Missouri militia. Major Henry, as he became known, provided lead from his mines for the Ameri-can military effort. After the war he was nominated as a Washington County commissioner to assist with military claims against the government.

From 1817 on, Henry joined other citizens to advocate Missouri's statehood. He speculated in lots in the new town of Caledonia in 1818. Around this time he married Mary Fleming, daughter of an owner of Washington County's Mine a Joe; she eventually bore him four children.

A slaveholder, Henry administered his Missouri business activities until 1822, when the urge to profit from the fur trade again found him joining his former mining partner and militia commander, William H. Ashley. On 6 March 1822 the St. Louis *Missouri Republican* published Ashley's advertisement to hire one hundred "Enterprising Young Men" for up to three years to trade and trap the Upper Missouri River and its sources. Those interested were to contact Major Henry in Washington County. Henry spent weeks interviewing and training inexperienced young men who would join seasoned trappers selected for the expedition. To reduce costs, Ashley and Henry paid the trappers on commission and operated a company store to supply them. The expedition attracted notable explorers and trappers whose exploits became a part of the annals of the American West, among them Jim Beckwourth, Jim Bridger, Thomas Fitzpatrick, Hugh Glass, David Jackson, Edward Rose, Jedediah Smith, and William Sublette.

To get a head start on competitors, Henry left St. Louis in early April 1822, bound for the mouth of the Yellowstone River. Henry's Fort was constructed at the Yellowstone's confluence with the Missouri. To circumvent the need for a trading post the trappers planned to rendezvous at predetermined sites. The laborious trip up the Missouri forced Henry's party to face dwindling food supplies. Desertions occurred. Assiniboin Indians attacked Henry's land party, taking supplies and horses. Even so, in mid-October those who remained with the major moved to the beaver country of the Missouri and Yellowstone rivers.

Henry's contingent searched for beaver that fall and winter, but unnavigable rivers and the party's inability to replace stolen horses hampered their efforts. Ashley, leading trappers to join Henry, clashed with the Arikaras (Rees) and sent Jedediah Smith to find the major. In early July 1823, Smith and Henry returned to Ashley's camp at the mouth of the Cheyenne River. When Colonel Henry Leavenworth decided to mount an expedition against the Rees, Henry, Ashley, and other trappers joined the ill-fated campaign as members of the Missouri Legion. They were later discharged in time to plan for the fall hunt.

Around early September, Henry left Fort Kiowa for the Rockies with one group of trappers. Jedediah Smith's contingent planned to leave later. By October, after skirmishes with Mandans and Assiniboins, Henry's party entered Crow country. News of their activities finally reached Ashley in June 1825. Henry had built a fort and sent out trapping parties on the Yellowstone and Big Horn rivers, focusing on the Wind River area. He had located Smith and instructed him to trap the Rockies' western slopes. His June express to Ashley told of fur trade competition, hostile Indians, and unsafe river travel. When Henry finally returned to St. Louis in late August, he brought back tales of hardship and danger. The pelts he delivered after twenty-eight months in the field brought only $10,000, an insufficient amount to pay company debts.

Disconsolate, Henry returned to southeast Missouri and eked out a living. Known for his fondness for drink, he opened a tavern in 1826, but the majority of his time was spent mining and occasionally serving as an election judge. Dying at home in Harmony Township shortly after the birth of his last child, Henry left his family virtually penniless, despite his prominent part in the fur trade in the American West.

• A brief sketch on Henry by Louis J. Clements is found in LeRoy R. Hafen, ed., *The Mountain Men and Fur Trade in the Far West*, vol. 6 (1968), pp. 173–84. Other sources to consult are Richard Edward Oglesby, *Manuel Lisa and the Opening of the Missouri Fur Trade* (1963); Donald McKay Frost, *Notes on General Ashley, the Overland Trail and South Pass* (1945); Richard M. Clokey, *William H. Ashley: Enterprise and Politics in the Trans-Mississippi West* (1980); Dale L. Morgan, *The West of William H. Ashley, 1822–1838* (1964); Hiram M. Chittenden, *The American Fur Trade of the Far West* (2 vols., 1902, 1935); and Adella Breckenridge Moore, "A Rock Was Found," typescript, Western Historical Manuscript Collection, a joint collection of the University of Missouri-Columbia and the State Historical Society of Missouri.

JAMES W. GOODRICH

HENRY, Caleb Sprague (2 Aug. 1804–9 Mar. 1884), educator, pastor, and author, was born in Rutland, Massachusetts, the son of Silas Henry and Dorothy Pierce. Henry received his A.B. from Dartmouth in 1825 and later studied at Andover Theological Seminary. At twenty-four years of age, Henry was ordained a pastor in the Congregational denomination and served at churches in Greenfield, Mississippi (1829–1831), and in West Hartford, Connecticut (1833–1835). Henry was a proponent of the peace movement and in 1834 wrote the pamphlet *Principles and Prospects of the Friends of Peace*. In that same year, he launched a quarterly publication, the *American Advocate of Peace*, which became a component of the American Peace Society.

In 1835, for an unknown reason, Henry changed his denominational orientation and the next year was ordained a priest in the Protestant Episcopal church. Also in 1836, Henry received an appointment as the professor of intellectual and moral philosophy at Bristol College in Pennsylvania and taught there until 1837. Henry left Bristol to become one of the first four professors at the University of the City of New York (later New York University) and taught there until 1852. He held the position of professor of history, belles-lettres, and philosophy. Henry married Cornelia M. Heard in 1838.

Soon after arriving in New York, Henry joined with several others to start a literary journal, the *New York Review*, of which he served as editor until 1840. From 1847 to 1850 he accepted the editing responsibilities of a monthly publication of the Protestant Episcopal church, the *Churchman*. Henry also was the political editor for the *New York Times* for several years. During his later years at U.C.N.Y., Henry served as the rector of St. Clement's Church (1847–1850). In 1852 financial problems at the fledgling university led Henry to depart from the institution. After 1852, except for the position of rector at St. Michael's Church in Litchfield, Connecticut (1870–1873), Henry focused on his literary projects.

Although Henry worked as both a pastor and an educator, he was best known for his writing and editing. For one of his first well-known publications he was the editor and translator of Victor Cousin's significant work of the time, *Elements of Psychology* (1834). He also edited W. Hazlitt's translation of Guizot's work, *A General History of Civilization in Europe* (1842), and translated Bautain's *Epitome of the History of Philosophy* (1841).

In addition to editing, Henry wrote more than fifteen books, which are mostly collections of his essays and publications of his addresses and include *Moral and Philosophical Essays* (1839), *Dr. Oldham at Greystones and His Talk There* (1860), *About Men and Things* (1873), and *Satan as a Moral Philosopher* (1877).

Henry maintained various interests, as is evidenced in his writing, which spanned such topics as the biblical figure of Job, politics in the church, the value of higher education, a critique of utilitarian ethics, a philosophical analysis of dreaming, the providence of God, and the historical significance of the acquisition of California. As an author and editor, Henry was well thought of and received numerous kind reviews.

Henry was an ardent supporter of public higher education and had a meaningful influence on many of his college students. An 1850 graduate of the City College of New York describes Henry in this way:

He was an intellectual force, charged to the full with animal vitality, sparkling vivacity, mental activity, and literary enthusiasm. We felt him, whether he said anything or not. . . . Dr. Henry was an omnivorous reader, and in the departments of history, the mental sciences and general literature was one of the most thoroughly furnished Americans of his day. He was a great conversationalist. . . . And into his talk he threw, or rather tumbled his entire personnel—body, mind, heart and spirit. (Chamberlain, p. 39)

In the mid- to late nineteenth century, the American intellect was undergoing a time of transition and construction. The dividing lines between conservative Christianity and secularism were beginning to be drawn. While a portion of the Protestant church was settling into a defense of orthodoxy, Henry sought to merge the Christian religion with a rising philosophical trend of his day, Transcendentalism. Part of this integration of Transcendentalism and Christianity took the form of what has been called the "social gospel," in which churches took an active and leading role in prison reform, workers' rights, the abolition of slavery, and other social and political concerns of the time. Henry attempted to maintain orthodoxy while endeavoring to guide the Protestant church into the mainstream of political life with hopes of permeating society with a Christian social ethic.

Henry's motivation for his moral enthusiasm was what he saw as the betterment of the human race. He writes in *Politics and the Pulpit* (1860): "God has many present uses for such souls besides going to church and sacrament, praying in their families and in their closets . . . among which uses we reckon eminently the standing up for truth and righteousness against fraud and corruption, for justice and mercy against oppression and wrong in public conduct" (p. 324).

Henry played a small but needed role as a religious and philosophical thinker in a period of American history that necessitated the skills of both disciplines. As an educator, he attempted to help his students think freely and critically, rather than indoctrinate them. As a churchman, he sought to integrate his Christian faith into all areas of life. As an editor and author, he brought his clarity of thought and organizational abilities to bear on the editing of several significant and timely works, as well as contributing his own thoughts on various issues of his era. While Christian Transcendentalism was not embraced by many adherents, Henry was a part of a movement to encourage the Protestant church to activate its faith in the political and public arena. Henry died in Stamford, Connecticut.

• The vast majority of Henry's writings can be found in the New York University Archives. Some of Henry's published works not mentioned above are *A Compendium of Christian Antiquities* (1837), *On the Foundations of Morals* (1839), *The Gospel: A Formal and Sacramental Religion* (1846), *The True Idea of a University* (1853), *Plain Reasons for the Great Republican Movement* (1856), *Considerations on Some of the Elements and Conditions of Social Welfare* (1861), *The Endless Future of the Human Race* (1879), and *The Christian Doctrine of Providence* (1885). The most recent assessment of Henry's life and a list of his writings can be found in Ronald Vale Wells, *Three Christian Transcendentalists* (1943). See also Joshua L. Chamberlain, *Universities and Their Sons: New York University* (1901), and Theodore Francis Jones, *New York University 1832–1932* (1933), on Henry's time at the University of the City of New York; F. N. Zabriskie, *Christian Intelligencer*, 7–21 May 1884, and Lyman Abbott, "Reminiscences," *Outlook* 106 (1914): 676–95, on his influence as a professor; Evert A. Duyckinck and George L. Duyckinck, *Cyclopedia of American Literature*, vol. 2 (1880), and "Professor Henry's Writings," *North American Review* 94 (1862): 525–40, for reviews of his writings; and "Transcendentalism," *Princeton Review* 11 (1839): 37–101, and O. B. Frothingham, *Transcendentalism in New England* (1959), on his contribution to Transcendentalism.

STEVEN L. PORTER

HENRY, Guy Vernon (9 Mar. 1839–27 Oct. 1899), soldier, was born at Fort Smith in Indian Territory, the son of Major William S. Henry, a soldier in the Third Infantry, and Anetta Livingston Thompson. Henry was appointed to the U.S. Military Academy at West Point as a cadet from New York on 1 July 1856 and graduated on 6 May 1861. He was assigned as a second lieutenant in the First Artillery and saw his initial Civil War combat at the battle of Manassas on 21 July 1861. After brief service in Washington, D.C., he was transferred with his company to the South Atlantic theater of the war.

During fighting in Florida and South Carolina, Henry proved to be a man of iron will and utter fearlessness. Promotions came rapidly, and on 9 November 1863 he was appointed colonel of the Fortieth Massachusetts Volunteers. In the summer of 1864 Henry and his unit were ordered to Virginia and took part in the battle of Cold Harbor and the siege of Petersburg. Henry was awarded a Medal of Honor and three brevets for gallant and meritorious service in these actions.

After Appomattox, Henry served on routine duty at various posts, primarily in the Northeast, for some four years. On 15 December 1870 he was assigned as a captain in the Third Cavalry and took station at Fort McDowell, Arizona Territory. For the next two years Henry experienced the difficulty of achieving success against elusive Apache bands. In 1873 he was ordered to Fort D. A. Russell in Wyoming Territory.

On 26 December 1875 Henry led a small column into the Black Hills, Dakota Territory, to drive out miners who were in the area illegally. The miners were not found, and on the march back to their base, Henry's troops encountered plunging temperatures and a blinding snowstorm. Only Henry's grim determination to save his small force from freezing to death brought them to safety. His left hand was frozen, one finger had to be amputated, and for the rest of his life he had only partial use of that hand. He was forced to take a long leave of absence.

Late in May 1876 Henry, commanding a battalion of the Third Cavalry, formed part of a strong force under General George Crook, whose objective was to strike the camps of Sioux and Northern Cheyennes known to be in unceded American Indian lands in southeastern Montana Territory. On 17 June a large body of warriors struck Crook's bivouac on Rosebud Creek and launched one of the fiercest actions in the history of American Indian warfare. During the fighting, much of it at close quarters, Henry was struck in the face by a bullet and suffered a nearly fatal wound that cost him the sight in his left eye. He was again required to take an extended leave of absence.

On 26 June 1881 Henry was promoted to major in the Ninth Cavalry, an all-black unit except for its officers. In the Sioux War of 1890–1891, Henry again distinguished himself. After the slaughter at Wounded Knee, hundreds of hostile Sioux converged on the Pine Ridge Agency and were met by eight companies of the Seventh Cavalry near Drexel Mission. Henry and four companies of the Ninth had been scouting the badlands for hostiles when a courier reached him urging a swift march to the Pine Ridge Agency to reinforce troops already there. Henry's battalion had just settled into camp after a fifty-mile scout when the courier arrived. He reached Pine Ridge after another fifty-mile march in blizzard conditions. It was an extraordinary accomplishment, a march of 100 miles in a single day. Hardly had the weary troopers had time to boil coffee when they were in the saddle again and riding to assist the Seventh Cavalry, who were under heavy fire in a narrow valley. Henry ordered a charge and drove off the warriors. The action at Drexel Mission ended the war.

In 1892 Henry was promoted to lieutenant colonel in the Ninth and the following year returned to the Third Cavalry. Four years later he became colonel of the Tenth Cavalry. With the outbreak of the Spanish-American War, Henry was appointed brigadier general of volunteers and shortly thereafter was promoted to brigadier general in the regular army. He commanded a brigade under General Nelson A. Miles in the invasion of Puerto Rico. Following the war he served as military governor of the island until May 1899. While awaiting assignment in New York City, he died of pneumonia. Henry was married, but the date of his marriage and his wife's name are unknown; the couple had four children.

• A biography of Henry has yet to be published, but two summaries are helpful. See George W. Cullum, *Biographical Register of Officers and Graduates of the United States Military Academy at West Point, 1802–1867*, vol. 2 (1868); and Francis B. Heitman, *Historical Register and Dictionary of the United States Army*, vol. 1 (1903). A brief treatment of Henry's career can be found in Cyrus T. Brady, *Indian Fights and Fighters* (1971). The best account of the battle on Rosebud Creek is in chapter 14 of Robert M. Utley, *Frontier Regulars: The United States Army and the Indian, 1866–1891* (1973). For Henry's ride after Wounded Knee, see William H. Leckie, *The Buffalo Soldiers* (1967).

WILLIAM H. LECKIE

HENRY, John (1746–16 or 23 Oct. 1794), actor and theatrical manager, was born in Dublin, Ireland. Nothing is known about his parents except that, according to William Dunlap in *A History of the American Theatre* (2 vols., 1832), they provided Henry with a liberal education. His professional acting career began as early as 1761, in Dublin, Belfast, or London (depending upon the source consulted). Henry evidently accompanied Irish performer Charles Storer and his family on their journey from Ireland to Jamaica in 1762, where they played for several years. Henry married Helen Storer (sometimes called Jane), one of Charles Storer's seven daughters, some time between 1762 and 1767. They had two children. In 1767 Henry and the Storer family (which no longer included Charles Storer, who died in Jamaica) sailed for America to join David Douglass's American Company of Comedians, the first professional theatrical troupe in the colonies. During the voyage a fire broke out aboard the brig *Dolphin*. Henry's wife and his children died in the blaze; he was among the few survivors. Henry's American debut occurred on 5 or 6 October 1767 in Phila-

delphia, where the American Company offered a short season while the John Street Theatre in New York was being built. Following Helen's death, her sister Ann was advertised on the company's posters as "Mrs. Henry." Although no marriage seems to have taken place, Ann became the mother of Henry's third child. Later still, perhaps in 1788, Henry married yet another Storer sister, Maria, who eventually gained recognition as a leading actress in the company. Henry's relations with the three Storer sisters "furnished scandalous gossip at every Colonial tea-table," in theater historian Arthur Hornblow's words (*History of the Theatre*, p. 125), and perhaps added to Henry's mystique as an actor.

Although initially confined to small roles because of the presence of Lewis Hallam, Jr., the company's leading player, Henry gradually established himself as one of the troupe's finest actors and was hailed as "one of the best performers in the colonies" (Dunlap, vol. 1, p. 52). Henry began playing leading roles, including Othello, Shylock, Sir Peter Teazle in Richard Brinsley Sheridan's *The School for Scandal* (1777), Jaffeir in Thomas Otway's *Venice Preserv'd* (1682), and Aimwell in George Farquhar's *The Beaux' Stratagem* (1707). Dunlap noted that "his Irishmen were very fine and he had great merit in serious and pathetic fathers" (vol. 1, p. 155). Henry's skills as a musician and an acrobat made him especially valuable to the company. Henry gained experience in management when he served as treasurer for the American Company in 1773 and as acting manager in Douglass's absence the same year.

During the Revolution, the American Company played in Jamaica, with Henry serving briefly as comanager with Lewis Hallam, Jr., after Douglass's retirement. Henry also performed in London from the summer of 1777 until 1780, appearing at the Drury Lane and other theaters. He returned to Jamaica in 1781, where he and Hallam again acted as comanagers of the company.

In 1782 Henry returned to the United States, gave some solo performances and then a series of full productions, and kept busy with theatrical activities until the Old American Company (as it became known) was reunited in New York in 1785, again under the dual management of Hallam and Henry.

Although New York continued to be the center of its activities, the Old American Company played in Philadelphia, Washington, D.C., Richmond, and elsewhere, and the company opened a new theater in Baltimore in 1786. The company experienced considerable success and prosperity in the years to follow, a tribute to Henry and Hallam's managerial skills. Owing to personal differences, the comanagers were frequently at odds, at least once coming to blows, but they continued their partnership until 1794. Periodically, Henry traveled to England to recruit new performers for the company, among them John Hodgkinson, known in England as "the provincial Garrick," who became widely regarded as the leading actor in the United States.

One specific contribution Henry made to theatrical management was his role in ending the sharing system, the method by which American actors had been paid since the first professional troupe was established in 1752 (under which all members of the company shared in an unequal distribution of the profits), replacing it with the salary system (under which each member was paid an agreed-upon salary).

Henry's play *School for Soldiers; or, the Deserters* (first performed in 1781, printed in Jamaica in 1783), was adapted from Michel de Sedaine's *Le Deserteur*. The play, now lost, was acted in New York at least until 1788. Henry also wrote *The Convention; or, the Columbian Father*, staged in 1787, and two unpublished plays, *The American Soldier, a Comedy* and *True Blue; or, the Sailor's Festival: A Farce*.

A vain man, Henry was, according to Dunlap, "the only actor in America who kept a carriage" (vol. 1, p. 150), which he decorated with a coat of arms—an affectation regarded as presumptuous. He was "tall and uncommonly handsome" (Hornblow, p. 124) and athletic. As comanager of the company, he rejected a play of Dunlap's simply because there were—in Henry's opinion—no suitable roles for Henry and his wife; when Dunlap wrote another play with roles particularly written for them, the play was immediately accepted. Hornblow characterizes Henry as eccentric and refers to his "choleric outbursts" (p. 126). Henry also appears to have been quarrelsome. His feuds with Hallam, Hodgkinson, Thomas Wignell (the leading comic actor in the United States after 1785, who left the Old American Company as a result of his arguments with Henry and Hallam), and others were both intense and legendary. On the other hand, Henry displayed an enlightened outlook when he freed three slaves in 1788.

Hodgkinson had little regard for the way in which the company was managed or for Henry's abilities as an actor. Hodgkinson, conspiring with Hallam, began playing Henry's best roles. The frequent and vehement quarrels between Henry and Hodgkinson eventually resulted in Henry's selling of his interest as comanager to Hallam—who thereupon transferred it to Hodgkinson—for $10,000 in 1794. Shortly thereafter, Henry sailed for Rhode Island, perhaps hoping to begin a rival company, but he died of consumption aboard ship.

As an actor, Henry was among the best of his time. Under his effective, albeit stormy, management of the Old American Company, the company held its position as the leading theatrical troupe in the United States from 1785 to 1794.

• Henry's unpublished plays are in the library of the Player's Club in New York City. Most accounts of Henry, such as Arthur Hornblow, *A History of the Theatre in America from its Beginnings to the Present Time* (1919); Glenn Hughes, *A History of the American Theatre, 1700–1950* (1951); and Howard Taubman, *The Making of the American Theatre* (1965), rely heavily upon William Dunlap's account mentioned in the text. Philip H. Highfill, Jr. et al., *A Biographical Dictionary of Actors, Actresses, Musicians, Dancers, Managers & Other Stage Personnel in London, 1660–1800* (1982), is a valuable source, offering material that does not derive directly from Dunlap. George O. Seilhamer, *History of the American Theatre* (3 vols., 1888–1891), also provides material not found in Dunlap's account. Errol Hill provides information about Henry's activities in Jamaica in *The Jamaican Stage* (1992). Henry's association with the American Company is chronicled in Hugh F. Rankin, *The Theater in Colonial America* (1964). Details concerning Henry's career can also be found in William B. Wood, *Personal Recollections of the Stage* (1855), and in George C. D. Odell, *Annals of the New York Stage*, vol. 1 (1927). Obituaries are in the *New York Daily Advertiser*, 27 Oct. 1794, and the *Columbian Centinel*, 1 Nov. 1794.

JARED BROWN

HENRY, John (1776?–1820?), adventurer, was born in Ireland, the son of a prominent family. Little is known about his early life. He was sent to the United States in 1792 to work for his uncle Daniel McCormick, a New York merchant, and by 1795 he was an editor for the *Philadelphia Gazette*.

In 1798 Henry, by this time a naturalized American citizen, was a captain in the U.S. Army. Serving about four years, he commanded an artillery company at Fort Jay (Governor's Island) and Fort Wolcott (Newport, R.I.). In 1799 Henry, although a Roman Catholic, married a daughter of the Reverend Jacob Duché, an Anglican clergyman, of Philadelphia. She died shortly after the birth of their second daughter. Henry resigned from the army in 1801, went to Massachusetts, and became active in the Federalist party. Soon, however, he bought a farm of 330 acres, just north of the village of Windsor, Vermont. During his five years in Windsor, Henry studied law, engaged in real estate, and held part ownership of a tannery. He attained high office in the Masons, and became editor of the *Post Boy*, a paper supporting the most avid Federalists.

Henry moved to Montréal, Lower Canada (later Quebec, Canada) in the spring of 1806, "because he preferred a monarchial government" (Waldon, p. 116). Before the end of 1807, he became acquainted with Herman Ryland, civil secretary to the governor general of Canada, through whom he continually but unsuccessfully petitioned the government of Lower Canada for a civil service position. Henry became so friendly with leaders of the North West Company that he was invited to their prestigious Beaver Club. In letters to the *Montréal Herald*, Henry defended the "fur barons" against attacks that they were forming a monopoly and supported their opposition to increased customs duties. At the Club, and in private homes, Henry ingratiated himself with civil and military figures; due to his former military rank, and to distinguish him from others of the same surname, he became "Captain" Henry.

Henry became a central figure in an international intrigue, the disclosure of which "helped to pave the way" for President James Madison's war message against Great Britain on 1 June 1812 (Adelson, p. 100). Henry's presence in Montréal was at a critical time in Anglo-American relations, due to the British warship *Leopard* having fired on the American *Chesa-*

peake; three of the American crew were killed and four impressed. President Thomas Jefferson, hoping to avoid war, pursued a policy of economic sanctions, and Congress passed the Embargo Act in December 1807. In New England such restrictions on trade did not sit well and resulted in an increase in Federalist activity; in Canada, Governor General James Craig grew suspicious of Jefferson's pro-French sympathies and envisioned a French plan to conquer Canada with American help. But, he surmised the New England Federalists would not support such a war. This was the background for Henry's legacy to history: the "Henry Letters."

During March and April 1808 Henry traveled to Vermont and Massachusetts on private business. He offered to write Ryland to inform him on the political situation south of the border. From Swanton (a "port" of entry on the Vermont-Quebec border), Windsor, and Boston he wrote letters "on the embargo, on the growing anti-British feelings, on the war spirit in the United States at large and on the supposed pro-British sentiment of New England" (Morton, p. xii). Henry predicted that men of power in Boston were determined to avert war with Great Britain, and even that the "mob" were on their side; that, should war be declared, northern Vermonters would "convene and endeavour to negotiate with the Governor of Lower Canada for his protection" (quoted in Cruikshank, pp. 21 and 24). Ryland handed the letters over to the governor general, who sent them to Secretary of State Lord Castlereagh in London.

The following year Governor General Craig sent Henry back to the New England states on a secret mission of inquiry. Henry was charged with informing Craig of American public opinion, the strengths of political parties, and the likelihood of war with England. As requested, Henry detailed the situation in the states and in Washington, not without hyperbole resulting from his own enthusiasm. He estimated that the states of New England had "transferred their political power from the friends to the enemies of the [Jefferson] Administration" (quoted in Cruikshank, p. 55).

Although Craig had confidence in Henry's reports from the United States and forwarded some letters to his superiors in London, he recalled Henry. Anglo-American relations had eased somewhat and President Madison's proclamation of April 1809 had reopened trade. Henry again sought preferment as a reward for his services in transmitting information to Craig. In this regard he had no success either in Canada or in London, so in the fall of 1811 Henry sailed, with his letters, to America. On shipboard Henry befriended another adventurer, the self-proclaimed Count Edward de Crillon, who was not a count at all. Henry confided his situation to de Crillon, who advised his new "friend" to sell his valuable letters to the U.S. government. He implied an intimacy with the French minister in Washington, thus providing an avenue to the White House, and therefore Henry's need for de Crillon's services.

By February 1812 President James Madison and Secretary of State James Monroe were addressing the increasing likelihood of war with England. Eager to discredit the opposition Federalists, Madison and Monroe accepted "Count" de Crillon's claim of possessing information that would blow apart Anglo-American relations. They collected $50,000 (in those days, enough to build a sizeable frigate) and, through de Crillon, purchased the "Henry Letters."

On 9 March 1812, Madison presented the letters to Congress, stating "they prove" that the British government had sent a secret agent to stir up antagonism against the "constituted authorities of the nation," to destroy the Union, and to form the "eastern part thereof into a political connection with Great Britain" (Richardson, vol. 2, p. 483). As Madison and Monroe had hoped, the letters played into the escalation of war fever. Although Federalists generally remained opposed, the Republican administration may have gained support for its forthcoming declaration of hostilities. Opinions differ as to the value of Henry's letters: they revealed no names of pro-British Federalists and little unknown information. They reflect, however, certain temperaments in a time of tension, and "except for the overestimate of his own services, . . . were reasonably exact." The adventurer himself, it is generally agreed, was a "political blackmailer" and "more or less of a liar" (Adams, p. 52).

Henry, accompanied by his two daughters, was placed on a ship and guaranteed safe passage to France before Madison revealed his letters to Congress. Little is known of his life in France; he was disappointed to find that an estate promised him by his friend the "Count" did not exist, and he continued the life of an adventurer. In 1820 Henry was in Italy, employed to gather information to be used against Queen Caroline of England. Details regarding Henry's life after 1820 have remained unknown.

• Primary sources on Henry are held at the Library of Congress and the Public Archives of Canada and are published in the *Vermont State Papers*, vols. 39, 44, 46, 79, and 80. For details and a sense of adventure, Ernest Alexander Cruikshank, *The Political Adventures of John Henry: The Record of an International Imbroglio* (1936), is essential; it includes facsimiles of letters and a physical description of Henry. Some "Henry Letters" are in *Niles' Weekly Register*, 14, 21, and 28 Mar. 1812. Richard A. Adleson, "Politics and Intrigue: John Henry and the Making of a Political Tempest," *Vermont History* 52 (Spring 1984): 89–102, summarizes Henry's life while focusing on his Vermont activities. Freda F. Waldon's article on Henry in the *Encyclopedia Canadiana*, vol. 5 (1977), pp. 116–17, summarizes his life and cites two other Canadian sources. *The Journal of Duncan M'Gillivray of the North West Company at Fort George on the Saskatchewan, 1794–95*, with introduction, notes, and appendix by Arthur S. Morton (1929), has a lengthy preface that details Henry's association with the fur trading barons. Three biographies of James Madison discuss the "Henry Letters" within the context of the problems leading up to the War of 1812: Irving Brant, *James Madison: The President 1809–1812* (1956); Ralph Ketcham, *James Madison: A Biography* (1971); and Robert A. Rutland, *James Madison: The Founding Father* (1987).

Madison's message to Congress concerning the letters is in James D. Richardson, *A Compilation of the Messages and Papers of the Presidents*, vol. 2 (1987). Charles S. Blue, in "John Henry The Spy," *Canadian Magazine*, May 1916, pp. 3–10, discussed Henry's "strange and romantic" career about which "our historians are somewhat reticent." For more about the role of Henry's "friend" de Crillon, see Henry Adams, "Count Edward de Crillon," *American Historical Review* 1 (Oct. 1895): 51–69. Adams also treated the blunder of the Henry affair in his *History of the First Administration of Madison*, vol. 2 (1891).

Sylvia B. Larson

HENRY, Joseph (17 Dec. 1797–13 May 1878), physicist and first secretary of the Smithsonian Institution, was born in Albany, New York, the son of William Henry, a teamster, and Ann Alexander. At around the age of seven, he went to live with his uncle John Alexander and his maternal grandmother in the nearby village of Galway. His father died when Henry was thirteen. As a teenager, he returned to Albany and served a failed apprenticeship with a watchmaker and silversmith. His great enthusiasm at this time was the stage, and he contemplated a career as an actor.

According to Henry's recollection, the turning point in his life occurred when he was sixteen. By accident he came upon a copy of George Gregory's *Lectures on Experimental Philosophy, Astronomy, and Chemistry* (1808), a popular exposition of science. He later wrote that this book "opened to me a new world of thought and enjoyment, invested things before almost unnoticed with the highest interest, fixed my mind on the study of nature and caused me to resolve at the time of reading it that I would immediately commence to devote my life to the acquisition of knowledge." Between 1819 and 1822 he attended the Albany Academy as an overage student, although he would later describe himself as "principally self educated." After working as a tutor and surveyor, he returned to the Albany Academy in 1826 as professor of mathematics and natural philosophy. He married his cousin, Harriet Alexander, in 1830; they had four children.

In 1832 Henry was named professor of natural philosophy at the College of New Jersey (now Princeton University), in spite of the fact that he had no college degree. At Princeton he became extremely popular with the students and was described by one as "a splendid old fellow to talk with," who "excites within one, an emotion akin to Awe!" In addition to natural philosophy, Henry also lectured on geology and architecture and informally discussed metaphysics and other subjects. He spent most of 1837 on a trip to Britain, France, and Belgium, which demonstrated his acceptance by the international scientific community.

In 1846 Henry was elected secretary (chief executive officer) of the newly established Smithsonian Institution and remained secretary until his death in Washington, D.C. From 1868 until his death he also served as president of the National Academy of Sciences, saving it from extinction by recasting it into a symbol of impartiality and scientific excellence. He also served as president of the American Association for the Ad-

vancement of Science (1849–1850), president of the American Association for the Advancement of Education (1854), an original member of the Light-House Board (1852–1871), and chair of the Light-House Board (1871–1878).

Although he was a lifelong Presbyterian, Henry did not formally become a member of the church until 1844. He had no problem finding a harmony between religion and science. In his lectures on geology he attempted to reconcile scientific discoveries with the biblical account of creation and found satisfaction in superficial agreement. But as a scientific elder statesman, he publicly supported Darwin's theory of evolution. His approach to religion was more rationalistic than emotional. In his lectures at Princeton he ridiculed evangelicals, dismissing the participants in revivals as sufferers of sympathy-induced hysteria. Yet he could also be ecumenical. He was much more sympathetic toward Catholics than were many of his fellow Protestants, as was evident by his rejection of the widespread nativist hostility to Catholics in the 1840s. His championing of the British mathematician J. J. Sylvester for a position at Columbia University in 1843, an effort that failed because Episcopalian Columbia would not hire a Jew, was an example of his view that scientific excellence took precedence over creed or nationality.

Henry's research career can be divided into three phases, each associated with a different institutional home. His letters and notebooks show a man driven by curiosity about the world around him. Seemingly trivial incidents, such as heating water for shaving or watching children blow soap bubbles, led to research programs that investigated evaporation, capillarity, and molecular cohesion. His wide-ranging and intense curiosity gave rise to his distinctive pattern of research: the investigation of topics in short bursts of activity with frequent shifts between topics. Despite the breadth of his research, there was a central theme for most of it—understanding and testing the relationships between electricity, magnetism, light, and heat.

During his years at the Albany Academy, he focused primarily on electromagnetic phenomena. By utilizing many layers of insulated wire, he produced an electromagnet of previously unmatched power. It was this discovery, announced in 1831, that first brought him to the attention of other scientists. He also demonstrated how such magnets could be electrically activated over long distances, in essence creating a telegraph. Also announced in 1831 was his invention of the first electric motor. (It was, however, a reciprocating motor, and modern motor technology has followed a path broken by William Ritchie's 1833 invention of a rotary motor.) Most importantly, he discovered (independently of Michael Faraday in England) mutual electromagnetic induction—the generation of an electric current by magnetism—and electromagnetic self-induction.

Electromagnetism remained important to him at Princeton. He explored the phenomenon of lateral discharge, the tendency of electricity to diverge from its most direct course. Because lightning paths were viewed as instances of lateral discharge, this was a topic of both theoretical and practical interest, and Henry was frequently consulted about more effective ways of protecting buildings from the effects of lightning strikes. He also investigated the theory of induction, especially the screening of induction by conductors, the creation of higher order induced currents, and induction over long distances. By using lightning storms as his source of electricity, he was able to demonstrate induction over distances of an estimated twenty miles. Among his other discoveries were the concept of the transformer and the oscillatory nature of the discharge of a capacitor.

At Princeton, Henry's research program broadened considerably. The research he conducted outside the field of electromagnetism included experiments on ultraviolet light, the use of soap bubbles to explore molecular cohesion, work on the capillarity through solids, and the demonstration of the interference of heat. He also took the first empirical measurements of the temperature differences between the solar surface and sunspots by utilizing thermoelectric apparatus. Not only did he demonstrate that sunspots were cooler than the surrounding surface, but he also found evidence of the phenomena of limb darkening, the apparent coolness of the sun at its limb. Continuing an interest begun while at the Albany Academy, Henry conducted research in geophysics, including meteorology, terrestrial magnetism, and auroras. While at Princeton he also provided advice, support, and encouragement to Samuel F. B. Morse's efforts to develop a practical telegraph. Subsequently, Henry became embroiled in Morse's patent disputes and, as a recipient of attacks and slights, changed from admirer to embittered enemy.

When Henry was selected to be the first secretary of the Smithsonian on 3 December 1846, its future path was unclear. There had been years of debate and considerable confusion in Congress over the meaning of James Smithson's bequest to establish an institution for "the increase and diffusion of knowledge." The legislation that established it in August 1846 provided for a building to house a museum, a library, an art gallery, a chemical laboratory, and lecture rooms; a system of governance; but no definitive program. Three distinct visions of the Smithsonian were represented among the members of the board of regents: a significant local presence as a school and/or museum, a national library, or an international research center. Henry, the candidate of the last group, envisioned the Smithsonian as a supporter of research through grants and publication subventions. Skillfully playing off the other two groups against each other, Henry won partial victories that ensured that the Smithsonian would be a force in American science.

In the original legislation, the Smithsonian had been designated a copyright depository. Having succeeded in firing the librarian of the Smithsonian, Charles Coffin Jewett, in 1854, for insubordination, after they clashed over the relative roles of the library and research functions within the Smithsonian, Henry had the copyright provision removed in 1857. Three years later, most of the institution's library was transferred to the Library of Congress, and the Smithsonian retained only a working collection.

Henry's approach to the museum function was different. He recognized the need to house the great natural history collections being brought back east by the government surveys of the 1850s and offered the Smithsonian as curator of the national collections on the condition that the federal government paid the direct costs. The initial appropriation was passed in 1857, and in 1859 the Great Hall of the Smithsonian building was designated the "National Museum of the United States." Subsequently, the federal appropriation increased to meet the rising costs of exhibition and conservation.

By ridding the Smithsonian of its library function and obtaining federal support for the museum, Henry was relatively free to support research in a diversity of fields, including anthropology, archaeology, botany, zoology, meteorology, geophysics, and astronomy. His publication strategy was to accept, after a careful refereeing process, what commercial publishers refused to publish and learned societies could not afford. He chose as the first volume in the series Smithsonian Contributions to Knowledge, Ephraim George Squier and Edwin Hamilton Davis's *Ancient Monuments of the Mississippi Valley: Comprising the Results of Extensive Original Surveys and Explorations* (1848), a work on archaeology, a subject in which he had neither expertise nor direct interest. Its publication demonstrated that the Smithsonian would support topics other than Henry's own fields of research. This landmark work proved to be a catalyst in the transformation of American archaeology. Thanks in large part to Henry's editorial control over the publication, it furthered the movement of American archaeology from an arena of unfounded speculation to one of empirical evidence.

Meteorology proved to be an example of Henry's use of the Smithsonian for coordinating research in a field, then eliminating the activity when an alternative patron appeared. In cooperation with the federal government, he established a national network of observers in 1849. At its peak in 1870, there were over 500 participants. In the same year, Congress established a national weather service in the War Department. Three years later, the Smithsonian turned its activities over to the government.

While secretary of the Smithsonian, Henry set aside his personal research program to become an administrator and spokesman for the value and necessity of basic scientific research. He also served as a consultant for the government on a number of occasions and at least three times for the Capitol alone: concerning protection from lightning, building materials for an extension, and its interior acoustics. During the Civil War he was a member of the Permanent Commission of the Navy Department, which advised the department on innovations in military technology. While with the

Light-House Board he conducted investigations of fog-signals and illuminants during his summers in an attempt to find an inexpensive substitute for the sperm oil burned in the lighthouse lamps.

Contemporaries often compared Henry to Benjamin Franklin (1706–1790). Like Franklin, Henry became a larger-than-life symbol of American accomplishment in science. At the end of the nineteenth century, Henry was enshrined as one of the sixteen representatives of human development and civilization memorialized in the Main Reading Room of the Library of Congress, along with such notables as Isaac Newton, Herodotus, Michelangelo, Plato, and William Shakespeare. His name was given to the standard unit of inductance. There arose a hagiographic literature written by scientists and engineers that treated Henry as the father of modern electrical technology and an isolated example of American excellence. He was renowned as the greatest American physicist of the mid-nineteenth century.

In the late twentieth century, historians have shifted their focus to Henry's role as a leader of American science and as an institution builder. Without denying that he was America's foremost scientist in the 1840s, they view his success as an experimenter as important not only because of the discoveries he made, but because these discoveries gave him the prestige and respect necessary for success as a science administrator and spokesman. Along with his friends Alexander Dallas Bache and Louis Agassiz, he was one of the major figures in the Lazzaroni, an informal group of scientists and science administrators who attempted to establish standards for the American scientific community and increase the level of public support for research. The study of Henry has become part of the wider study of the range and interconnections of mid-nineteenth-century American science and government.

• The Joseph Henry Papers Project at the Smithsonian Institution has identified and indexed almost 100,000 extant Henry manuscripts. A selection of these manuscripts will appear in a fully annotated fifteen-volume edition, *The Papers of Joseph Henry* (1972–). The project also maintains Henry's personal library. Most of Henry's publications are collected in *The Scientific Writings of Joseph Henry* (2 vols., 1886). Despite its many problems, the standard biography of Henry remains Thomas Coulson, *Joseph Henry: His Life and Work* (1950). Modern assessments by Nathan Reingold, former editor of the Henry Papers, include "The New York State Roots of Joseph Henry's National Career," *New York History* 54 (1973): 133–44, and, with Arthur P. Molella, "Theorists and Ingenious Mechanics: Joseph Henry Defines Science," *Science Studies* 3 (1973): 323–51. For studies of Henry as an institution builder, see Robert V. Bruce, *The Launching of Modern American Science 1846–1876* (1987); James Rodger Fleming, *Meteorology in America, 1800–1870* (1990); and Curtis M. Hinsley, Jr., *Savages and Scientists: The Smithsonian Institution and the Development of American Anthropology, 1846–1910* (1981). Memorial addresses are collected in *A Memorial of Joseph Henry* (1880).

MARC ROTHENBERG

HENRY, O. *See* Porter, William Sydney.

HENRY, Patrick (29 May 1736–6 June 1799), revolutionary statesman, orator, and lawyer, was born at Studley, Hanover County, Virginia, the son of John Henry, a Scottish-born and prosperous planter, and Sarah Winston Syme, a young widow, also from a family of substantial means. Often mistakenly thought to have been of more humble origins, Patrick Henry was, by birth and estate, a member of the gentry of the colony, if not of the highest rank. After attending a local school for a few years, he received the remainder of his formal education from his father, who had attended King's College, University of Aberdeen.

Rather than continuing his education, Henry began to work at age fifteen as a clerk for a nearby merchant. A year later he and an older brother, William, opened their own store, which promptly failed. In 1754, at age eighteen and still without means of his own, Henry married Sarah Shelton, a sixteen-year-old from a family of comparable social status to his own; they had six children. Provided three hundred acres of land and slaves by his father-in-law, Henry began a brief career as a planter until fire destroyed his new home. He then made a second unsuccessful attempt at storekeeping and worked for a time in his father-in-law's tavern.

By 1760, nearing his twenty-fourth birthday, Henry decided to become a lawyer. Essentially self-taught and woefully unprepared, he nonetheless demonstrated an intelligence that persuaded the panel of distinguished Virginia attorneys who examined him to approve his admission to the bar. He seemed at last to have found the right arena for his talents. By his industry and ability—and with some help from his in-laws—Henry quickly built a successful practice in the courts of Hanover and nearby counties.

On 1 December 1763 Henry won a spectacular victory in a case that formed a key part of the controversy known as the Parsons' Cause. A few years earlier the Virginia assembly had passed legislation that prevented the clergy of the legally established Anglican church, who were paid by public taxation in tobacco at its market price, from collecting a fortuitous increase in their stipend that resulted from unusually high tobacco prices in two years of short crops. When the laws commuted the payment to the customarily lower price of tobacco, several clerics brought suit to recover the additional amount, an action that compounded their increasing unpopularity at a time when religious dissent was growing rapidly in the colony. Their appeal to British authorities at home brought further censure on the colony.

Only one minister, the Reverend James Maury, had won his suit. Henry belatedly became counsel for the defendants, the tax collectors of Louisa County, when the case went before a jury convened to fix the amount to be awarded the cleric. Delivering an impassioned plea that criticized the clergy and challenged the authority of the home government, Henry persuaded jurors to grant token damages of one penny. The popular acclaim that he won throughout much of the colony both enhanced his legal practice and launched his political career. It also helped to make the Parsons' Cause an important precursor of the revolutionary controversy that was soon to follow.

Henry began that political career in equally dramatic fashion. Winning a by-election for a seat in the House of Burgesses, the lower house of the Virginia legislature, he began his service in the first session to convene after news of the passage of the Stamp Act of 1765 reached the colony. There was no essential disagreement between Henry and the established leadership on the constitutional grounds for opposing the law, but to the debate over how best to contest its passage he brought a more outspoken, direct style and a willingness to act more forcefully. The consequence was the adoption, on 30 May 1765, of his Stamp Act Resolves, which attacked the legality of taxation of the colonies by the British Parliament and seemingly endorsed resistance if the imperial government persisted.

If the exact nature of Henry's actions is, as one historian has aptly remarked, "clear in legend but cloudy in history" (Morgan, p. 89), passage of his Stamp Act Resolves was enough to establish his place among the leaders of the American Revolution. It was the occasion for one of his most famous orations, the "Caesar-Brutus" speech in which he suggested that the British monarch might be inviting the same fate that awaited Julius Caesar at the hand of Brutus if he and his government persisted in their disregard of American liberty. By one account Henry backed down when some of his opponents raised cries of treason, but his spirited remarks had already achieved their effect. With attendance at the session thinned by the early departure of many members, Henry introduced and carried five of an intended seven resolutions, finding it necessary to hold back two of the stronger ones that faced defeat. When one was later repealed, the official record listed only four, but newspaper accounts in other colonies printed versions with six or all seven resolutions, including the ones not passed. Not only in Virginia but across the mainland British colonies, Henry quickly established his reputation as an uncompromising opponent of imperial policy.

Over the next few years, as tensions between the colonists and the British government continued to mount, Henry remained a member of the Burgesses, continuing on occasion to challenge the older leaders but joining on them in opposition to British policies. For a time, however, he appeared more preoccupied with the needs of a growing family, with his law practice, and with speculation in western lands. His advancement as an attorney proceeded, in fact, to the point that in 1769 he gained admission to practice before the General Court, the highest judicial body in the colony.

In 1773, taking a renewed interest in the imperial crisis, Henry joined the group spearheading an effort to establish a network of intercolonial committees of correspondence. With the Boston Tea Party in December of that same year and Parliament's subsequent enactment of the Coercive Acts, especially the closing of the port of Boston to all trade on 1 June 1774, the colonies drew closer together in their resistance. When the first session of the Continental Congress convened in Philadelphia in September 1774, Henry was in attendance, one of seven Virginia delegates. His reputation had preceded him, and he initially received several important committee assignments. Early in the session he gave delegates a demonstration of his powers as a speaker when he asserted that the old governments and colonial boundaries were swept away. "The distinction between Virginians, Pennsylvanians, New Yorkers, and New Englanders, are no more," he declared. "I am not a Virginian, but an American." While he won praise for his oratory, he turned out not to be an especially influential member of the body. In the following year, on 18 May 1775, Henry took his seat in the Second Continental Congress, again not playing a major part in its deliberations. After the session adjourned on 1 August, he set out for Virginia, never again to hold a continental or national office.

For a few months between the two sessions of Congress in late 1774 and early 1775, Henry was back in Virginia, busy with the organization of a volunteer militia company for Hanover County and also with a difficult personal problem, Sarah Henry's severe mental illness. When she died sometime in early 1775 from unknown causes, Henry resumed an active role in the leadership of the Revolution in Virginia, in particular at the second Virginia Convention, which opened at Richmond on 20 March 1775. The delegates were divided on whether to concentrate on a continued search for a peaceful solution to the imperial dispute or to proceed as well with military preparations. Henry led the call for preparedness, introducing resolutions to that effect and concluding with the legendary exhortation, "Give me liberty or give me death!" However apocryphal is this wording of one of his most famous orations, Henry again carried the day, though by no more than a half dozen votes.

The royal governor, the earl of Dunmore, was quick in his response to the threat of armed resistance. On 20 April 1775 he dispatched a small contingent of British marines to seize powder and guns stored in the Public Magazine in Williamsburg. The force was only partially successful before being discovered, but the incident stirred popular protests that threatened to explode in violence against the governor. Some of the more cautious Virginia leaders, men who had often opposed Henry, succeeded in quieting citizens of Williamsburg and heading off a proposed march on the capital by several volunteer military companies that had gathered at Fredericksburg. Henry, however, was not to be dissuaded; he led his Hanover company within a few miles of Williamsburg to demand payment for the seized powder and arms before finally agreeing to turn back.

During Henry's brief absence from Virginia while attending the Second Continental Congress, the military preparations that he advocated had come to fruition. Another Virginia Convention had formed two provincial regiments and, in a close contest, had agreed to make the inexperienced Henry commander of the first and the senior officer of the entire force. Henry set out to organize his regiment; he had little difficulty recruiting troops from his growing body of loyal supporters, but in the end his opponents were able to thwart his military ambitions. The Committee of Safety, which they dominated, sent the second regiment, freed of Henry's command, to fight against Dunmore and his forces at Great Bridge, near Norfolk, on 9 December 1775. Then in early 1776, the two regiments were incorporated into the newly organized Continental army with Henry left as a colonel in command of his old regiment but placed under former subordinates. He declined to serve, and his regiment threatened to leave military service in protest. In one of his finest moments he refused to let his personal disappointment hurt the cause, and he persuaded his men to remain under their new officers.

If his short-lived military career was at an end, Henry's political career had just begun. Even those who opposed him often stressed that he was needed in the political arena. With Virginia and most of the colonies moving by early 1776 toward independence, Henry won election to the last of the extralegal provincial conventions, which met in Williamsburg on 6 May. Over the course of the following two months delegates adopted a resolution for independence that instructed its delegates at the Continental Congress to call for a declaration of independence; the delegates also wrote a new constitution for the state and adopted the Virginia Declaration of Rights, an important influence on the Bill of Rights, the first ten amendments to the Federal Constitution. Henry was initially reluctant to support independence without assurance of stronger intercolonial union and foreign support, such as an alliance with France. Reassured on these questions, he introduced one of three proposed versions of the resolution for independence. The ultimately successful fourth and compromise version incorporated his language for proposing independence to the Congress. Henry also served on a large committee chosen to draft the Declaration of Rights but was not especially active in its work. He seemed generally to have approved of its content and that of the new, generally conservative constitution, although he disliked the weak powers granted to the governor, who was elected by the legislature for a maximum of three successive one-year terms and denied a veto over legislation.

As it turned out, Henry had immediate reason to rue the establishment of a governorship he had termed a "mere phantom," for before the convention adjourned, he found himself elected as the first occupant of the office. He served for the allotted three years, from 6 July 1776 to 1 June 1779, and later from 30 November 1784 to 30 November 1786. The weakness of the office was a continuing problem for him, especially in his efforts to raise and equip soldiers for the prosecution of the war. In 1778 he approved the raising of state troops under the command of George Rogers Clark and secretly authorized their use in a risky effort to hold the Old Northwest against the British and their Indian allies. The expedition was initially successful but after 1781 went awry.

After Henry left the governorship in 1779, his political base in the interior sections of the state remained as strong as ever. He had also continued to build his estate and his social prestige, adding to the latter by his marriage, on 9 October 1777, to Dorothea Dandridge, who was from an old and prominent family and with whom he had ten children. Moving his residence to a plantation of ten thousand acres in a newly created distant county that was named for him, he declined election to the Continental Congress but in 1780 won a seat in the House of Delegates, the lower house of the legislature. Despite sporadic attendance, he quickly emerged as one of its most influential members. In a body marked by shifting factions, Henry led the opposition to James Madison and his followers, who advocated reforms in the state constitution and legal system propounded by Thomas Jefferson, measures to strengthen the government of the Articles of Confederation, and pursuit of a tighter, more creditor-oriented fiscal policy. Henry and his backers passed only an occasional law, primarily to provide debtor relief. Their success lay more in defeating almost every bill that Madison and his allies introduced. A key exception was the enactment, under Madison's sponsorship, of Jefferson's Statute for Religious Freedom. Henry, although committed to religious freedom, consistently opposed the provision in the law for total separation of church and state, favoring instead the continuation of public taxation for the support of all recognized religious groups. The measure passed, however, in 1786 while Henry was again serving as governor and lacked a direct voice in the legislature.

Late in that same year, Henry declined reelection and retired from the governorship, citing reasons of health and the need to look after his private affairs. It was a critical period when the movement for strengthening the central government of the new nation was rapidly gaining force, culminating in the convention that gathered at Philadelphia in May 1787 to draft the new Federal Constitution. How Henry would react to the proposed creation of a strong central government was not entirely predictable. Many of his past stands, a growing hostility between him and Thomas Jefferson, his recent disagreements with Madison, and the lack of concern that his immediate constituents in the Virginia interior felt for the problems faced by the nationalists all pointed toward his likely rejection of the new constitution. Yet he had not uniformly opposed efforts to assure adequate revenues and increase the effectiveness of the confederation. Virginia Federalists retained some hope that he might be won over, and he was among those chosen as members of the delegation to the Philadelphia convention.

Henry declined his appointment, claiming a lack of funds. He was clearly suspicious, for his opposition to a stronger national government had hardened after John Jay concluded an agreement with Spain in 1786 that, had it been ratified, would have sacrificed the right of settlers on the southern frontier to free navigation of the Mississippi River while protecting commercial advantages for northern mercantile interests. When George Washington sent him a copy of the new constitution with a letter outlining its advantages in September 1787, just after the convention had adjourned, Henry composed a cryptic reply that made his deep reservations clear: "I have to lament that I cannot bring my Mind to accord with the proposed Constitution. The Concern I feel on this account, is really greater than I am able to express." By the end of the year James Madison regarded him as the greatest threat to ratification by Virginia.

Henry ran as a delegate to the state ratification convention from Prince Edward County, to which he had recently moved. Although it was a safe Anti-Federalist seat, Henry crowned his victory with a typically stirring speech against the constitution. At the opening of the convention in Richmond on 2 June 1788, its members were closely divided. As the leading spokesman for the Anti-Federalists in the debates, Henry laid out at length his objections to the document, on occasion pausing to appeal in more ringing terms to the liberty for which Virginians had fought and their ability to sustain it without a federal government. One unifying theme undergirded almost everything he said (though at times it was obscured by the sheer diversity of his specific arguments): an abiding fear of a powerful government that was too centralized and too far removed from its citizens. Henry made his initial attack at the very beginning of the debate when he denounced the constitution as "clearly a consolidated government," one that would destroy the rightful power of the states. Its principles, he continued, were "extremely pernicious, impolitic, and dangerous." Here, he asserted, "is a revolution as radical as that which separated us from Great Britain." The willingness of Federalists to accept ratification with proposed amendments, however, won over a small but critical group of moderate Anti-Federalists. Henry was outmaneuvered, and ratification carried by a vote of 89 to 79.

Henry did not willingly accept his defeat, remaining the most uncompromising of all the Virginia leaders. In the session of the general assembly in the fall of 1788 he commanded a strong majority of former Anti-Federalists and continued the fight by such strategies as blocking Madison's election to the first U.S. Senate and promoting a second convention to overturn or amend the Federal Constitution. He could not, however, stop the launching of the new government and had to recognize that most of the people of the state were now willing to accept it. Virginians, however, were largely opposed to the economic policies advanced by Alexander Hamilton, and as a result, the state underwent a major political realignment, one that drew together many who had originally supported ratification and many former Anti-Federalists, thereby creating the new Republican party of Jefferson and Madison.

Somewhat isolated and in declining health, Henry retired from the legislature at the end of 1790. Once again he devoted himself to a busy law practice, winning cases in some of his most successful courtroom appearances, and to a new round of land speculation, including acquisition of some of the Yazoo lands sold off by the state of Georgia at bargain prices. By the middle of the decade, however, his political allegiance took a surprising turn. Expressing a desire for "order" in government, and seeing the Republican opposition led by his old enemies Jefferson and Madison as the more disruptive force, he proved receptive to the overtures made by such leading Virginia Federalists as Washington, Henry Lee, and John Marshall. Although he was offered and declined appointments as secretary of state, attorney general, justice of the Supreme Court, and minister to Spain, he reentered politics in the crucial battles of 1798 and 1799 over the alien and sedition laws that Federalists had enacted in an effort to counter Republican attacks. It is not clear that Henry ever endorsed the repressive legislation, but he supported Marshall, a moderate Federalist, for Congress and in March 1799 once again ran for the state legislature. Although easily winning, he was already seriously ill and died at his last home, "Red Hill," in Charlotte County before taking his seat.

Of the numerous leaders who were active largely at the state level and who generally opposed ratification of the Federal Constitution, Henry was one of the few who came to be ranked among the truly major figures of the American Revolution. Unlike most who achieved that status, he held no high national office. Yet, by his unmatched oratorical powers, by employing a certain common touch to win the unwavering loyalty of his constituents, and by closely identifying with their interests, he almost certainly contributed to making the Revolution a more widely popular movement than it might otherwise have become. Too, as his career unfolded, he increasingly expressed a distrust of centralized political authority that has remained a persistent theme in American political culture.

• No significant body of Patrick Henry papers has survived, but the three-volume work by a grandson, William Wirt Henry, *Patrick Henry, Life, Correspondence, and Speeches* (1891), reprints much of the source material that does exist. The most-detailed modern biography is Robert D. Meade, *Patrick Henry* (2 vols., 1957–1969). Richard R. Beeman, *Patrick Henry: A Biography* (1974), is a briefer study, particularly useful for putting Henry's career in its full context. The best examination of Henry's Stamp Act Resolves is in chapter 5 of Edmund S. Morgan and Helen M. Morgan, *The Stamp Act Crisis: Prologue to Revolution* (1953). David J. Mays, *Edmund Pendleton: A Biography* (2 vols., 1952), although sometimes critical of Henry, provides one of the best accounts of the major events of the revolutionary crisis in which Henry was involved. For Henry's role in state politics after 1776, John E. Selby, *The Revolution in Virginia, 1775–1783* (1988), and Norman K. Risjord, *Chesapeake Politics, 1781–1800* (1978), are helpful. The full and carefully edited documentary evidence for Henry's part in the contest over ratification of the Constitution is in John P. Kaminski et al., eds., *The Documentary History of the Ratification of the Constitution*, vols. 8–10 (1988–1993). Even though the two men were at times opponents, Edmund Randolph presents the most judicious estimate of Henry by a contemporary in his *History of Virgin-*

ia, ed. Arthur Shaffer (1970). Bernard Mayo, *Myths and Men: Patrick Henry, George Washington, Thomas Jefferson* (1959), includes a very perceptive essay on Henry.

THAD TATE

HENSHAW, Henry Wetherbee (3 Mar. 1850–1 Aug. 1930), ornithologist, ethnologist, and government official, was born in Cambridge, Massachusetts, the son of William Henshaw and Sarah Holden Wetherbee. His interest in natural history was demonstrated from early childhood, and he began focusing has attention on birds. He completed his primary and secondary education in the local public schools, but poor health compelled him to defer plans to take the entrance examination at Harvard in 1869. While in high school, Henshaw met William Brewster, another local ornithologist, and a lifelong friendship was soon cemented by their deep interest in the study and collection of birds.

In the summer of 1869 Henshaw was invited to join the captain of a Coast Survey schooner on a trip to Louisiana. There he recovered his health and began to develop his skills as a field naturalist. By the time of his return to Cambridge in 1871, he had given up plans for college study. Henshaw became acquainted with a number of other young men in the Cambridge area who shared his fascination with birds. Soon Brewster, Henshaw, and several other like-minded young men in the Cambridge area began meeting periodically at Brewster's home to read Audubon's Birds of America and to discuss their avocation. In 1873 they were the core of a larger group that formed the Nuttall Ornithological Club, whose members met regularly to compare notes about the birds they had observed and collected.

In the summer of 1872 Spencer F. Baird, then the assistant secretary of the Smithsonian Institution, invited Henshaw to serve as naturalist with U.S. Army lieutenant George M. Wheeler's geographical explorations and surveys west of the 100th meridian. He began work at the end of July 1872, remaining with Wheeler until the end of the latter's program in 1879. Summers were spent collecting and making observations in the western United States, while the remainder of the year was devoted to research, writing, and office work in Washington, D.C.

Late in the 1870s Henshaw took an evening course in anatomy at Columbian (now George Washington) University in Washington, with the thought of beginning the study of medicine, but this plan was soon abandoned. With the amalgamation of all survey efforts into the new U.S. Geological Survey in 1879, all work in natural history was abandoned, except for paleontology. Henshaw then accepted the invitation of his friend Major John W. Powell to join the newly organized U.S. Bureau of Ethnology as an ethnologist. He remained with Powell for some years, taking over day-to-day administration of the bureau's activities from 1888 to 1892. Powell offered to make him his successor as chief of the Ethnology Bureau, but Henshaw declined the responsibility, owing in part to his

sensitivity to criticism and to his unwillingness to exercise any control over the work of his associates. For four years (1889–1893) Henshaw served as editor of the *American Anthropoligist*, in addition to his regular government responsibilities. A bout with influenza in 1891 led to a breakdown in health and to his being given lighter duties studying California Indians in 1893.

Late in 1894 Henshaw was obliged to request a leave of absence from his responsibilities with the Bureau of Ethnology, and he spent the next decade in Hawaii, recovering his health. During this period he made extensive studies of Hawaiian birds and natural history, and a list of Hawaiian birds that he had compiled was published in 1902. In 1904 he sold his collection of 1,100 bird specimens to the Bishop Museum. By this time he had begun to develop considerable skill as a photographer. Many years later some 300 of his negatives were sold and came into the hands of the National Geographic Society.

Henshaw returned to California in 1904, and in June of the next year he rejoined the U.S. Biological Survey (with whom he had collaborated in Hawaii) as administrative assistant to his old friend Clinton Hart Merriam. Six months later he was appointed assistant chief of the survey. When Merriam resigned his post in 1910, Henshaw was named his successor. Much of his attention was given to the control of predatory mammals and birds, to continuing work on the food habits of birds, and to the enforcement of recently enacted conservation legislation. Field research into the nature and geographical distribution of vertebrates was another important element in the work of the survey. The passage of a federal migratory bird protection law in 1913 and ratification of a treaty with Great Britain dealing with the protection of migratory birds in the United States and Canada in 1916 had Henshaw's full and active support. Members of the survey's staff were soon busily engaged in the enforcement of these new enactments.

In 1913 Henshaw proposed and published a Department of Agriculture *Farmer's Bulletin* titled "Fifty Common Birds of Farm and Orchard." An initial printing of 200,000 copies rapidly sold out, and additional printings and revisions continued to come out in later years. Henshaw's felicitous text accompanying the pictures in this publication led to a suggestion by the editors of the *National Geographic Magazine* that additional birds be described in several articles for that periodical. This was done, and all of the articles, with others, were subsequently combined in a book about American birds published by the society. This popular publication was revised several times in subsequent decades.

Henshaw's *Report on the Ornithology of Nevada, Utah, California, Colorado, New Mexico, and Arizona* was published in 1875, and his *Birds of the Hawaiian Islands* came out in 1902. He contributed a number of articles to ornithological journals and to the two-volume *Handbook of American Indians*, published by the Bureau of Ethnology in 1907 and 1910. He also prepared an autobiography, appearing in successive issues of the *Condor* between May 1919, and June 1920. A fellow of the American Ornithologists' Union, he twice served as its vice president (1891–1894 and 1911–1918). Henshaw's other scientific interests included diatoms and Hawaiian land and tree shells.

A kindly, scholarly, and considerate man of regular habits, Henshaw was popular with his staff, who nicknamed him "Uncle Henry." He was a graceful writer and wielded a constructive editorial pencil when called upon to do so. Declining health obliged him to retire as chief ot the Biological Survey in 1916. He never married. He was largely inactive in his later years, and he died in Washington, D.C.

• An unpublished assessment of Henshaw during his years as Biological Survey chief is included in the Waldo Lee McAtee Papers, Manuscript Division, Library of Congress. These same notes provide insights on many of the men with whom Henshaw worked. Edward William Nelson, friend and successor to Henshaw at the helm of the Biological Survey, published "Henry Wetherbee Henshaw—Naturalist" in the *Auk*, Oct. 1932. Henshaw described the work of the Biological Survey in "The Policemen of the Air: An Account of the Biological Survey of the Department of Agriculture," *National Geographic Magazine*, Feb. 1908. See also Jenks Cameron, *The Bureau of Biological Survey: Its History, Activities, and Organization* (1929), and Keir B. Sterling, *Last of the Naturalists: The Career of C. Hart Merriam*, rev. ed. (1977). Obituaries are in the *Washington, D.C., Evening Star*, 2 Aug. 1930, and the *New York Times*, 3 Aug. 1930.

KEIR B. STERLING

HENSON, Jim (24 Sept. 1936–16 May 1990), puppeteer and entertainment industry entrepreneur, was born James Maury Henson in Greenville, Mississippi, the son of Paul Henson, an agronomist, and Elizabeth Brown. Henson studied art and stage design part time at the University of Maryland. At college, he met his future wife, Jane Nebel, an art student. The two worked together in creating puppet segments on local Baltimore and Washington, D.C., childrens' shows. They married in 1959 and were to have five children. Henson graduated from college in 1960. Soon afterward, Jane Henson essentially withdrew from her involvement in Henson's puppetry work.

In the mid-1950s and 1960s, Henson and his creations appeared on numerous television variety shows, notably "The Steve Allen Show," "The Today Show," and "The Ed Sullivan Show." Starting in 1969, however, he became famous for his enlarged cast of Muppet characters for the educational Children's Television Workshop program "Sesame Street." Through the use of warm humor, Henson and his puppets helped children learn numbers, letters, and simple lessons of life. Since its inception, the program has been seen in 120 countries and produced in dozens of languages. Toys, stuffed animals, books, a theme park, and other licensed products have become spinoffs from Muppet creations.

In September 1976 the one-hour "Muppet Show" was introduced on TV. It featured Henson's Muppets and a well-known guest star in a series of zany skits.

Among those who appeared were Diana Ross, Ethel Merman, George Burns, and Candice Bergen. The program was produced in partnership with Lord Lew Grade, a British independent producer, and it became one of the first truly global programs. At its height in the late 1970s, it was seen by some 235 million viewers in more than 100 countries, and it is reported that Henson grossed some $40 million from the show. Never before had a cast of puppets and the art of puppetry attracted such a large audience.

Henson then brought the Muppets to the big screen. His first film was *The Muppet Movie* (1979). It was a success, and in August 1980, Kermit and Miss Piggy were featured on the cover of *Life Magazine*. It was followed by *The Great Muppet Caper* (1981; Henson's directorial debut). In 1982, Henson established the Henson Foundation to promote, develop, and encourage public interest in the art of puppetry. His next movie, a more somber film without the traditional Muppet characters, *The Dark Crystal* (1982; co-directed with Frank Oz), had a lukewarm reception at the box office. In 1983 the TV program "Fraggle Rock" premiered on HBO; it was on the air for four years. In 1984 the animated Saturday morning "Muppet Babies" program was launched; it lasted eight years. Henson's next movie, *The Muppets Take Manhattan* (1984), was well received. His next major project, the film *Labyrinth* (1986; directed by Henson), did not use the traditional Muppet figures and was not successful. Also in 1986, Henson and his wife legally separated after living apart for some years. Henson then made another foray into the prime-time TV market with "The Jim Henson Hour," a family entertainment program that premiered on 14 April 1989. It lasted only five episodes.

In August 1989 an agreement in principle for Disney to acquire Henson Associates, Inc., was announced, but because of Henson's unexpected death the following May the attempt to merge foundered and in December 1990 was abandoned.

Henson died in New York City of complications of pneumonia caused by Group A *Streptococcus* bacteria. Although suffering from severe symptoms, Henson did not seek treatment until it was too late. Jane Henson attributed his failure to get help to his Christian Science upbringing; others said it was due to his natural reticence. In response to Henson's request for a "friendly little service of some kind," a vibrant memorial tribute, attended by some five thousand colorfully dressed colleagues and fans, was held at the Cathedral of St. John the Divine in Manhattan. A Dixieland band played "When the Saints Go Marching In." Mourned by the world, Henson had been known for his gentle, unpretentious manner, his dynamic energy, and, among his imperfections, according to Stephen Harrigan, "a wandering eye for women and a cheerful lust for material objects" ("It's Not Easy Being Blue," *Life*, July 1990, pp. 92–98).

Henson is perhaps chiefly remembered for his creation of the Muppets. Among the best-known figures are Kermit the Frog (operated solely by Henson until his death), Miss Piggy (operated solely by his longtime associate Frank Oz), Bert, Ernie, Cookie Monster, Oscar the Grouch, the Count, and Big Bird. They have been seen worldwide on TV, in film, and in animation. What makes Henson a thoroughly modern puppetmaster is the fact that he never performed on a traditional live puppet stage; all his work was for television and film. He and his colleagues developed and perfected techniques never used before. As one writer described it,

Standing below an elevated set both men held their characters over their heads so the camera could see the Muppets, but not Jim and Frank. They kept track of what their Muppets were doing by watching a small monitor below the stage. Often Jim and his fellow Muppeteers had to twist themselves into pretzel shapes to create some of the complicated Muppet routines. Yet what viewers saw on the screen were Muppets moving with astonishing grace (John Culhane, "Unforgettable Jim Henson," *Reader's Digest*, Nov. 1990, pp. 124–29).

Henson, whose characters and productions have received Emmy, Oscar, Peabody, and Grammy awards, is hailed as an imaginative artist and innovator in the design, development, presentation, marketing, and distribution of puppetry as an educational force and as family entertainment worldwide—his plots and use of puppets with live actors were entertaining for adults while the action was easily understood by children; his comedies were affirming of traditional family values, produced with technical mastery and intelligent dialogue.

• The Theatre Collection at the New York Public Library for the Performing Arts houses clipping files on Henson. "Dialogue on Film: Jim Henson," *American Film*, Nov. 1989, pp. 18–21, contains an interview with Henson in which he discusses some working techniques and his plans for the future. Diana Loevy, "Inside the House That Henson Built," *Channels*, Mar. 1988, pp. 52–61, has a business and management slant on Henson and his work. David Owen, "Looking Out for Kermit," *The New Yorker*, 16 Aug. 1993, pp. 30–43, provides detailed biographical material on Henson and his family, a view of Henson from his children's viewpoint, and information on his empire since his death. Susan Schindehette and J. D. Podolsky, "Legacy of a Gentle Genius," *People*, 18 June 1990, pp. 88–96, offers excellent photographs, informative quotes by Henson's colleagues, and a readable overview of his life. An obituary is in the *New York Times*, 17 May 1990.

TINA MARGOLIS

HENSON, Josiah (15 June 1789–5 May 1883), escaped slave and preacher, was born in Charles County, Maryland, on a farm owned by Francis Newman. As a child, Henson frequently saw his parents abused and severely beaten. On one occasion, as a punishment for defending his wife, Henson's father was sentenced to a physical mutilation that left him permanently scarred. Although he was raised without religion, Henson was immediately converted to Christianity after his first exposure to it at a revivalist camp meeting. As a young boy, he was sold to Isaac Riley.

Because of his unusual strength and intelligence, Henson was made superintendent of the farm at a young age. He managed the plantation well, doubling the annual crop production. One day, during an argument at a neighboring farm, Henson defended his master in an argument with the other plantation's overseer. In revenge, the overseer and three of his slaves waylaid Henson one evening soon afterward, beating him and shattering his shoulder blade. For the rest of his life, he could not raise his arms above shoulder level. At age twenty-two Henson married another slave (name unknown); they had twelve children.

Isaac Riley, the master of Henson's plantation, went bankrupt in 1825 and was forced to sell his farm and to transfer his twenty slaves to his brother's farm in Kentucky. After making Henson swear to their safe passage, Riley entrusted him with the care of the slaves. The route to Kentucky took the party through Ohio, a free state, where many implored Henson to allow them their freedom, but Henson kept his word and brought them intact to their new owner. In 1828 Henson became a preacher for the Methodist Episcopal church. He then attempted to buy his freedom from his owner. A price of $400 was settled on, but at the last minute the owner reneged on his agreement, deciding instead to sell Henson to a new owner in New Orleans. Journeying south with his master's son, who had instructions to transact some business and then to sell Henson before the return voyage, Henson's trepidation grew as he saw the terrible conditions in which slaves in the Deep South lived. Midway through the journey, the master's son developed a serious fever, rendering him weak and helpless, and he begged Henson to bring him home safely. Though he could easily have deserted his young master and made a bid for freedom, Henson remained to escort the son back to his father. His loyalty met with neither reward nor gratitude. Henson's growing desire for freedom, augmented by outrage at this ingratitude, propelled him to escape with his wife and four young children in the summer of 1830. In two weeks he had reached Cincinnati, from there he sailed to Buffalo, New York, and, in October, he crossed the U.S. border into Canada.

Henson settled in Dresden, Ontario, near Lake St. Clair and south of the Sydenham River, and he became a preacher. His oldest son, then in school, taught him to read. Quickly establishing himself as a leader in the Afro-Canadian community, Henson made several trips back to the United States and across the Mason-Dixon line to help other slaves escape. During the Canadian Rebellions of 1837–1838 Henson served the British as a captain in a troop of Afro-Canadian volunteers. With the support of sponsors from England and America, Henson began laying the foundations for an Afro-Canadian community and industrial school. The British American Institute, begun in 1842, encompassing two hundred acres of wooded land, was intended as a refuge for escaped slaves. However, the community never grew large or self-sufficient enough to survive, and by the end of the Civil War almost all of the colony's remaining members had returned to the United States. In 1849 Henson published his autobiography, *The Life of Josiah Henson, Formerly a Slave, Now an Inhabitant of Canada, as Narrated by Himself*. Reprinted in 1858, its name was changed to *Truth Stranger Than Fiction: Father Henson's Story of His Own Life*, and the next edition was titled *"Truth Is Stranger Than Fiction": An Autobiography of the Rev. Josiah Henson* (1879). Both later editions contain a foreword by Harriet Beecher Stowe.

On three journeys to England, in 1849, 1851, and 1876, Henson received much attention from members of high society there, including the archbishop of Canterbury. He was honored at a private party given in 1851 by Prime Minister Lord John Russell and invited by Lord Grey to travel to India to supervise cotton plantations. Soon after his return from England, Henson met Stowe. After *Uncle Tom's Cabin* was published in 1852, the public began to believe that Henson's life story was the basis for the character of Uncle Tom in the novel. Following the death of his first wife, Henson married a Boston widow. His final trip to England, a preaching and lecturing tour in 1876, was highlighted by Queen Victoria's personal gift of her photograph encased in a gold frame. Henson died in Dresden, Ontario.

Henson's life story is that of a daring early leader of slaves and escaped slaves, a man of high moral principles who endured great suffering. Although the British American Institute was small and unsuccessful, Henson's work as an ambassador to England for African Americans did much for their perception overseas. His greatest achievement was the example he offered of a man born into slavery, illiterate and handicapped by vicious physical abuse, who gained his freedom, learned to read, and became a preacher and a leader of a community of escaped slaves.

• Harriet Beecher Stowe's account of Henson's life and his role in *Uncle Tom's Cabin* is described in her work, *A Key to Uncle Tom's Cabin* (1853). Other sources include Robin Winks, *Blacks in Canada: A History* (1971); William Pease and Jane Pease, *Black Utopia: Negro Communal Experiments in America* (1963); and W. B. Hargrove, "The Story of Josiah Henson," *Journal of Negro History* 3 (Jan. 1918): 1–21. See also Penelope Johnston, "Canada's Uncle Tom," *History Today* 40 (Sept. 1990): 3–4. An obituary appears in the *New York Tribune*, 6 May 1883.

ELIZABETH ZOE VICARY

HENSON, Matthew Alexander (8 Aug. 1866–9 Mar. 1955), arctic explorer, was born in Charles County, Maryland, the son of Lemuel Henson, a sharecropper, and Caroline Gaines. Contradictory information exists about the details of his early life, but most accounts, including his autobiography, *A Negro Explorer at the North Pole* (1912), agree that Henson was orphaned at an early age, spent several years at the N Street School in Washington, D.C., and went to sea on the three-masted sailing vessel, *Katie Hines*, from Baltimore, when he was twelve or thirteen.

Henson, who signed on as a cabin boy and later became an able-bodied seaman, spent six years on the ship under a Captain Childs. After Childs's death Henson held several jobs ashore including that of a stock clerk for B. H. Steinmetz & Sons, a hatter and furrier in Washington, D.C. In 1887 the store owner recommended Henson to Lieutenant Robert E. Peary of the Navy Corps of Civil Engineers, recently returned from his first arctic expedition, who hired Henson as a valet to accompany him on the Nicaragua Ship Canal survey. Peary also included Henson as a member of all his succeeding arctic expeditions—two North Greenland expeditions, 1891–1892 and 1893–1895, two summer expeditions to retrieve meteorites, 1896 and 1897, and three North Pole expeditions, 1898–1902, 1905–1906, and 1908–1909.

On the expeditions Henson worked variously as a sledge builder, driver, hunter, carpenter, blacksmith, and cook. Described by Peary as "more of an Eskimo than some of them," Henson developed expertise in Inuit customs and native language. As Donald MacMillan, one of the 1908–1909 expedition members later wrote, Henson, with his years of experience and skills, "was of more real value than the combined services of all of us." Henson, four Inuit sledge drivers—Ootah, Seeglo, Egingwah, and Ooqueah—and Peary were the first to reach the North Pole on 6 April 1909. In between expeditions Henson held various positions—as a Pullman porter, as a messenger for Peary at the League Island Navy Yard in Philadelphia, and as an aide for arctic exhibit production at the American Museum of Natural History in New York. In connection with the expeditions Henson worked periodically for Peary, in 1905 and again in 1908–1909, for example, he organized the expeditions' equipment on Peary's arctic ship, the *Roosevelt*. He accompanied Peary on a three-month lecture tour after the 1891–1892 expedition, went on the road with a William A. Brady arctic stage show in 1896, and went on his own Brady-run slide lecture tour in 1909.

After the North Pole success, Henson received some recognition from African-American organizations and publications. He had few further contacts, however, with Peary and worked in a Brooklyn, New York, garage. In 1913, after New York black politician Charles Anderson wrote to President William Taft, Henson received a civil service appointment as a messenger boy at the New York Customs House, where he worked until mandatory retirement in 1936. His contributions to arctic exploration increasingly garnered official recognition; he received Explorers' Club membership in 1937, a congressional medal in 1944, honorary degrees from Morgan State College and Howard University, and a citation from President Dwight D. Eisenhower in 1954. Henson married Eva Helen Flint in 1891 (it is unknown how this marriage ended); fathered a child, Anaukaq, with Akatingwah, an Inuit woman, in 1906; and married Lucy Jane Ross in 1907. He died in New York City. Originally buried in a New York City cemetery, Henson was reburied with military honors in Arlington National Cemetery in 1988.

• Henson's brief North Pole diary and other artifacts are located in the Matthew Henson Collection, Morgan State University Library, Baltimore, Md. The Robert E. Peary Papers, National Archives, Washington, D.C., include some correspondence between Henson and Peary. Scattered letters are also located in the archives of the Explorers' Club, N.Y. In addition to the 1912 autobiography, Henson authored "The Negro at the North Pole," *World's Work* 19 (Apr. 1910): 12825–37. Articles based on extensive interviews with Henson include Lin Bonner, "First to Reach the Pole," *Liberty Magazine*, 17 July 1926, pp. 15–21; Robert H. Fowler, "The Negro Who Went to the Pole with Peary," *American History Illustrated* 1 (Apr. 1966): 4–11, 52–55, and (May 1966): 46–52. Peary's published expedition accounts include numerous references to Henson: *Northward over the "Great Ice"* (1898), *Nearest the Pole* (1907), and *The North Pole* (1910). Several biographies have been published, most notably, Bradley Robinson, *Dark Companion* (1947), and Floyd Miller, *Ahdoolo: The Biography of Matthew A. Henson* (1963). See also the introduction by Susan A. Kaplan to Henson's autobiography republished in 1989. S. Allen Counter, who facilitated a 1987 reunion of Henson's and Peary's Eskimo offspring with their American family members, reexamines the Peary and Henson arctic expeditions in *North Pole Legacy: Black, White & Eskimo* (1991). An obituary is in the *New York Times*, 10 Mar. 1955.

KATHERINE G. MORRISSEY

HENTZ, Caroline Lee Whiting (1 June 1800–11 Feb. 1856), sketch writer and novelist, was born in Lancaster, Massachusetts, the daughter of John Whiting, a bookseller, and Orpah Danforth. Her father served in the revolutionary war, and several of her brothers followed military careers. Very little is known about Caroline's early life and schooling, except that she was a precocious reader and writer who evidently cultivated her literary skills in her father's bookshop. The family reported that Caroline composed poetry and drama before age twelve and wrote a novel when a teenager.

In 1824 Caroline Whiting married Nicholas Marcellus Hentz, a French-born entomologist, engraver, and miniature painter who spoke several languages and studied medicine in Paris and at Harvard. He was also the author of several school texts, a treatise on alligators, and a novel, *Tadeuskund, the Last King of the Lenape* (1825), a fictionalized account of the Paxton massacres on the Pennsylvania frontier. His posthumous *Spiders of the United States* (1875), a collection of scholarly papers on the subject, long remained a standard in the field. Once married, Caroline Hentz embarked on a life of raising children and assisting her husband as he moved through the South and Midwest from teaching position to teaching position. When the couple married, Nicholas Hentz was a French instructor at the Round Hill School in Northampton, Massachusetts, under the direction of historian George Bancroft. In 1826 the family moved to Chapel Hill, North Carolina, where he had accepted a professorship in modern languages and belles lettres. Four years later the Hentzes moved to Covington, Kentucky, where Nicholas conducted a female academy for two years. He found similar employment in Cincinnati, Ohio, 1832–1834; Florence, Alabama, 1834–1843; Tusca-

loosa, Alabama, 1843–1845; Tuskeegee, Alabama, 1845–1848; and Columbus, Georgia, 1848–1849. During these years Caroline Hentz gave birth to five children, four of whom grew to maturity, and performed various functions connected to her husband's teaching career: assisting in the performance of classroom duties, running a household for numerous boarding students, and performing the farm chores required of frontier homesteads. She also helped her husband collect insect specimens. Such duties left little leisure for literature.

Nevertheless, Hentz began writing a verse drama, *De Lara; or, The Moorish Bride*, while living in North Carolina. Entering the play in a contest sponsored by the actor-manager William Pelby, Hentz won the first prize of $500 and saw her play produced to favorable reviews in Boston and Philadelphia in 1831. In Chapel Hill Hentz also came into contact with poet George Moses Horton, a slave and the first professional African American of letters. Hentz edited and helped promote his work by sending two of Horton's poems to her hometown newspaper, the *Lancaster Gazette*, which published them with her cover letter on 8 April 1828. In gratitude Horton praised Hentz effusively and composed a poem in her honor in the preface to his *Poetical Works* (1845). While living in Kentucky, Hentz wrote two other dramas, *Constance of Werdenberg; or, The Heroes of Switzerland*, which was produced in New York in 1832, and *Lamorah; or, The Western Wilds*, produced in Cincinnati in 1832 and New Orleans in 1833. She also wrote a number of sketches in James Hall's *Western Monthly Magazine*. In Cincinnati, Hentz published her first novel, *Lovell's Folly* (1833), which her family attempted to suppress as too personal, and belonged to the Semi-Colon Club, a literary society that included Harriet Beecher. Nicholas Hentz's violent display of jealousy may help account for the family's departure from Cincinnati and the prevalence of the theme of uncontrolled passion in Caroline Hentz's mature work.

Life in rural Alabama in the 1840s provided even less opportunity for writing, and Hentz produced only occasional poems and prose pieces in magazines. First published serially in 1844 in the *Philadelphia Saturday Courier*, Hentz's sketches of the Worth family were collected in 1846 as *Aunt Patty's Scrap-Bag*, which appeared in five editions before 1873. Additional sketches were collected in *The Mob Cap* (1848), which appeared in three editions before 1852. Hentz turned her attention to literature full time only after her husband retired from teaching in 1849 because of poor health, leaving Hentz to support the couple with her income from writing. Fortunately for her family, Hentz was a facile writer, producing eight novels and seven story collections in the seven years before her death.

The earliest and most popular of Hentz's novels of the 1850s was *Linda; or, The Young Pilot of the Belle Creole* (1850), a tale of domestic travail and improbable adventure that saw thirteen editions in two years. Hentz explored its theme of the misery caused by undisciplined emotion in later novels as well. The plot of

Robert Graham: A Sequel to Linda (1855), in which the heroine marries a previously rejected suitor after her first husband dies, suggests that males are worthy of female admiration and devotion only after they fully master their emotions. The plight of Mittie in *Helen and Arthur; or, Miss Thusa's Spinning-Wheel* (1853) intimates that unfettered passion is as self-destructive in females as it is in males. *Rena; or, The Snow Bird* (1851), which is set in New England, and *Eoline; or, Magnolia Vale* (1852), while developing earlier themes, are notable for their positive portrayals of independent and strong-willed older women, Aunt Debby and Miss Manly, respectively. Hentz is best known, however, for her favorable depictions of plantation culture in *Marcus Warland; or, The Long Moss Spring* (1852), the only novel by Hentz with a male protagonist, and *The Planter's Northern Bride* (2 vols., 1854), which was written in response to Harriet Beecher Stowe's *Uncle Tom's Cabin* (1851–1852). *Ernest Linwood* (1856), Hentz's most autobiographical novel, examines not only the destructiveness of jealousy but also the potential conflict between domestic duty and literary creativity and productivity. Although the heroine-narrator Gabriella admits that she "once thought it a glorious thing to be an author," she subsumes her career goal to "the measured duty, the chained down spirit, the girdled heart" of domestic life, much as Hentz appears to have subordinated her early literary ambitions to married life. Although in *The Banished Son, and Other Stories of the Heart* (1856) Hentz criticized the notion of female intellectual inferiority, she nevertheless insisted that men and women were intended for different life work, despite her own commercial success as an author. "Were woman to leave her own, for man's more sun-like sphere," asked Hentz, "what account can she render to her own neglected duties, to her own deserted orbit?"

Hentz lived her last years in Marianna and St. Andrews, Florida, with her ailing husband and grown children. She died in Marianna of pneumonia. An immensely popular writer of her own day, Hentz remains of interest for her role in the development of domestic fiction, the professionalization of authorship, and the study of nineteenth-century southern culture.

• Unpublished documents relating to Caroline Hentz, including her 1836 diary, family letters, her husband's notebooks, and an autobiography by her physician son Charles are contained in the Hentz Family Papers, Southern Historical Collection, University of North Carolina. Other collections of essays and sketches by Hentz include *Ugly Efie; or, The Neglected One and the Pet Beauty, and Other Tales* (1850?); *Wild Jack; or, The Stolen Child: and Other Stories* (1852); *The Victim of Excitement. The Bosom Serpent, etc., etc., etc.* (1853); *Courtship and Marriage; or, The Joys and Sorrows of an American Life* (1856); *The Lost Daughter, and Other Stories of the Heart* (1857); and *Love after Marriage; and Other Stories of the Heart* (1857). *The Planter's Northern Bride* and *Eoline* were reprinted by Arno Press in the 1970s. The fullest accounts of Hentz's life and works are contained in Helen Waite Papashvily, *All the Happy Endings* (1956); Nina Baym, *Woman's Fiction* (1978); and Mary Kelley, *Private Woman, Public Stage* (1984). See Arthur Hobson Quinn, *A History of the American Drama from the Beginning to the Civil War* (1923), for an account of Hentz's plays, and Rhoda C. Ellison, "Mrs. Hentz and the Green-Eyed Monster," *American Literature* 22 (Nov. 1950): 345–50, for a discussion of jealousy in Hentz's life and fiction. An obituary is in the *Columbus (Ga.) Times and Sentinel*, 20 Feb. 1856.

JEANNE M. MALLOY

HENTZ, Nicholas Marcellus (25 July 1797–4 Nov. 1856), entomologist, educator, and miniaturist, was born in Versailles, France (although he is also recorded as being a native of Metz), the son of Nicholas Hentz, a lawyer, and Marie-Anne Thèrese Daubrée. Around 1816, when Hentz was in his late teens, the Hentz family left France for the United States, allegedly for reasons connected to Hentz's father's political activities. Given the situation in France between 1814 and 1816—the fall and rise and fall of Napoleon, the restoration of the French monarchy—emigration was probably expedient for a number of people. Further, if the family did have a connection to Metz, which is on the Moselle River and part of Alsace-Lorraine, the Hentzes' decision to leave their homeland could have been affected by German as well as French political fluctuations.

As a youth in France, Hentz studied miniature painting and attended the Hospital Val-de-Grâce. Upon arrival in the United States, he attended medical lectures at Harvard College (it is unclear whether he was a matriculant) before joining his family in Wilkes-Barre, Pennsylvania. He began teaching school in Philadelphia around that time. Hentz's talent as an artist was first publicly noted in 1819, when his miniature portrait of a Creole woman was exhibited at the Pennsylvania Academy. His skill in detailed drawing would stand him in good stead in his later work. He eventually left Philadelphia to teach in Boston and from there went to Northampton, Massachusetts, where in 1823 he became part of the faculty at George Bancroft's innovative and ill-fated boys' academy, the Round Hill School. Also in 1823, Hentz met Caroline Lee Whiting, a descendant of the Reverend Samuel Whiting, who had settled in Massachusetts in 1636. In the autumn of 1824 Hentz and Caroline Whiting were married and were eventually to have four children.

The year after the Hentzes' marriage saw two major events in Hentz's life: first came the publication of his novel, *Tadeuskund, the Last King of the Lenape, an Historical Tale* (1825). Though overwritten and highly sentimental by today's standards, the novel is a sympathetic consideration of the Delaware Indian group known as the Lena Lenape and the incited clashes between colonials and Indians that preceded the American Revolution. (James Fenimore Cooper's comparable consideration, *The Last of the Mohicans*, would be published one year later.) *Tadeuskund*'s opening paragraph hints not only at Hentz's command of English (probably his third language, after French and German) but also his concern for accuracy and his attachment to his adopted homeland: "As a landscape painter, collecting subjects for the exercise of his art, roams over the plains of ancient Ausonia; . . . so has the author of the following tale endeavored to collect such traits and scenes in the history and aspect of his country, as may, in their fictitious arrangement, give a representation of truth, from which he has endeavored never to depart" (p. 3).

The second major event was the Hentzes' departure from Northampton to North Carolina, where Hentz took a position as professor of modern languages and belles-lettres at the University of North Carolina. From the beginning, Bancroft's Round Hill School had seemed doomed to failure. While the idea had looked good on paper, the curriculum (based on Swiss-German educational models) had proved unmanageable—partly because it was unfamiliar territory and partly because Bancroft seems to have been singularly inept at handling and teaching schoolboys. Hentz abandoned the Round Hill experiment early; the school would finally close, after eight excruciating years, in 1831. Whether it was the Round Hill students or Bancroft's administration that made Hentz decamp to North Carolina cannot be determined.

In 1830, after four years at the university, Hentz left North Carolina (the reason is unclear) and moved his family to Coventry, Kentucky, where he took over the directorship of a girls' school. Apparently his interest in educating children had not diminished; his Round Hill experience (with boys) may or may not have had a bearing on his choice of schools. Two years in Kentucky were followed by two years in a similar position in Cincinnati, Ohio. In his memoirs, Hentz's son Charles speculated that an impolitic challenge to a duel may have prompted the Hentzes' move from Ohio—Hentz seems to have been jealously protective of his wife and resented what he considered untoward attentions. Leaving Ohio in 1834, the Hentzes next settled in Florence, Alabama, where Hentz headed the girls' school there for almost ten years. After Florence, Hentz filled more two- and three-year directorships at girls' schools in Tuscaloosa, Tuskegee, and finally Columbus, Georgia.

One benefit of running girls' schools may have been the opportunity for Hentz to indulge his several academic interests, rather than being limited to one teaching subject. Hentz was very much a polymath, accomplished in many fields. In 1825, the same year his novel *Tadeuskund* was published, his engraving of an American alligator had accompanied the publication of his paper on that animal in the *Transactions of the American Philosophical Society* of Philadelphia. His first scholarly love, though, was entomology, and his skill as miniaturist translated well to his insect studies: his engravings are small works of art. Within the world of entomology, Hentz established as early as the 1830s a reputation as an expert on spiders (though his earliest work was on beetles, of which he discovered several new species). When the noted naturalist Edward Hitchcock of Amherst compiled his *Catalogues of the Animals and Plants of Massachusetts* in 1835, the chapter on Araneides was written by his former Northampton neighbor, Nicholas Hentz.

Hentz did not enjoy living in the Deep South; he missed the scientific camaraderie and the insects of New England and the Middle Atlantic states. He kept wishing to return to some place "nearer the seats of science," he wrote to Samuel Haldeman, a co-member of the Entomology Society of America, of which Hentz was a corresponding member. Such was not to be the case geographically, but Hentz still managed to be seminally and singularly influential in his field.

Hentz's publications throughout his teaching career centered on spiders, whose variety seems almost infinite. By 1842 he had become America's leading and first authority on arachnology. His knowledge was so expert that nearly one hundred years after its publication, his serial monograph "Descriptions and Figures of the Araneides of the United States," in the *Boston Journal of Natural History* (BJNH, 1843–1857), was still being consulted. (The monograph was finally published as a whole in 1875 as *The Spiders of the United States: A Collection of the Arachnological Writings of Nicholas Marcellus Hentz*, edited by Edward Burgess and J. H. Emerton.) Though essentially a concise but informative list of the plethora of spiders Hentz had observed in the numerous places he lived, the monograph also gives a little insight into his personal life and character. In several instances he credits spiderly discoveries and descriptions to his son Charles A. Hentz, implying that bug-hunting was a family avocation.

Drawing on his storytelling inclinations, Hentz imbues the spiders with individuality, not exactly anthropomorphizing, but helping to make them distinct. For example, in describing the *epeira cornigera*: "This very singular little spider obstinately holds its legs folded up" (*BJNH* 6:20). And in detailing particular araneides, he offers (perhaps unconsciously) offhand commentary on relations between the sexes and the condition of his house: The *linyphia communis*—"I have observed two males on a web, fighting an obstinate battle; they strove to grasp each other with their cheliceres, and when exhausted by the conflict, they retired at some distance to rest themselves, and presently renewed the combat. I know not how the contest terminated, but I believe it was without bloodshed. During this, the female, who was the lady of the manor, remained quiet and apparently unconcerned" (*BJNH* 6:28). The *epeira rugosa*—"It is the only subgenus in which the male and female may be seen harmoniously dwelling together" (*BJNH* 6:28). And the *mimetus interfector*—"This singular depredator is not rare, and is usually found in houses. This has enabled me to make many curious observations upon its manners. The first specimen I found was a female, which had made two cocoons under a table in my study. . . . *Habitat*. Alabama" (*BJNH* 6:32–33). In this last case, the image of Hentz down on all fours, circumnavigating his study looking for spiders, is hard to resist.

Hentz's wife Caroline was also well educated, and, along with raising their four children, she assisted Hentz with his teaching and educational supervision. A friend of Harriet Beecher Stowe, she was also a successful and popular writer, contributing poems and stories to numerous magazines and writing at least three plays that achieved public performance. Her writing skills became of paramount importance in 1849 when Hentz fell ill and was invalided. Hentz's illness meant he could no longer work, and they had to give up the life of girls' schools to which they had become accustomed. The nature of Hentz's illness is unknown, but it seems to have been debilitating. The family moved from Columbus, Georgia, to Marianna, Florida, where some of the grown children lived, and Caroline Hentz took over the support of the family. In the course of six years, she wrote more than a dozen highly popular novels and stories.

Hentz's research and writing career stopped with the American spiders monograph, written prior to 1850 although published serially over the course of a decade. In February 1856, worn down by caring for her husband, Caroline Hentz succumbed to pneumonia. Nine months later, Nicholas Hentz himself died in Marianna, Florida.

While devoting so much of his life to teaching young minds, Nicholas Hentz is known mainly, and justly, for his pioneering work in entomology. He was the first American authority on arachnology. Working and writing at a time when advanced professional degrees were not the norm for defining a scholar, the "amateur" Hentz made invaluable contributions to the study of the natural sciences. Indeed, his name is immortalized in such species as the *Dugesiella hentzi* (a "short-sighted," nocturnal Texas spider) and the *Lycosa hentzi* (a yellowish, "hunting" spider of Florida). Combined with that scientific acumen was a draftsman's skill for detail and an artist's heart. The care with which he pursued his spiders, his drawings, and his writing (both scientific and fictional) makes one want to believe that while Hentz may have been a demanding, formal, and difficult personality, he was also concerned, caring, and appealingly eccentric. He brushed away the cobwebs and illuminated and illustrated a corner of natural history no one had explored before.

• Little is written in depth about Hentz, the majority of information coming from biographical material on his wife, Caroline Lee Whiting Hentz, and from his son Charles A. Hentz's "Autobiography" (North Carolina Collection, Library of the University of North Carolina at Chapel Hill). See also Rhoda Coleman Ellison's introduction to Caroline Lee Hentz's *The Planter's Northern Bride* (1970). Hentz's name, however, is well known among entomologists, and his own writings and correspondences with other entomologists can be tracked down, with some picture of the man being garnered from his own words. Especially valuable are the Haldeman/Hentz correspondence in the Samuel S. Haldeman Collection, Academy of Natural Sciences of Philadelphia, and the Harris/Hentz correspondence in *Entomological Correspondence of Thaddeus William Harris, M.D.*, ed. S. H. Scudder, Occasional Paper of the Boston Society of Natural History 1 (1869). The best secondary sources for information about Hentz and about entomology are Arnold Mallis, *American Entomologists* (1971), and W. Conner Sorensen, *Brethren of the Net: American Entomology, 1840–1880* (1995).

E. D. LLOYD-KIMBREL

HEPBURN, Alonzo Barton (24 July 1846–25 Jan. 1922), banker and philanthropist, was born in Colton, New York, the son of Zina Earl Hepburn and Beulah Gray, farmers. He attended St. Lawrence Academy in Potsdam from 1861 to 1867. For lack of funds, he left Middlebury College early in his sophomore year (1868). He was a mathematics instructor at St. Lawrence Academy for one term and principal of the Ogdensburg Educational Institute for a year. He studied law in the Ogdensburg office of Stillman Foote and Edward C. James. Admitted to the bar in November 1871, he enjoyed a busy practice until his home town's fortunes declined when the New York Central Railroad bypassed it. Hepburn married Hattie A. Fisher in 1873; she died eight years later. The couple had two children.

In the fall of 1872 he was appointed a school commissioner for the second assembly district to fill an unexpired term and then won election for the full term. He took a seat in the New York Assembly in January 1875 as a Republican. Reelected four times with increasing majorities, he served on the committees on cities, insurance (chair), ways and means, judiciary, and apportionment (chair). Known for talking to the point, he had great influence on his colleagues. In February 1879 he chaired a special committee "to investigate alleged abuses in railroad management" that led to creation of a state railroad commission in 1882, as well as to increased regulatory activity in other eastern states.

Hepburn was named superintendent of New York's banking department by Governor Alonzo R. Cornell, was confirmed on 13 April 1880, and served three years. To prevent mismanagement, he advocated regular examination of state-chartered institutions. Failure of the Merchants Bank in Watertown (1882) pointed to the need, he argued. Regular examinations became law in May 1884. Hepburn declined reappointment when Grover Cleveland became governor.

Hepburn had paid $15,000 for 30,000 acres of timberland in St. Lawrence County. From 1883 to 1889 he busied himself making a market for his timber, the basis of his fortune. In 1887 he married Emily Lovisia Easton; they had two children.

Named national bank examiner for New York City, Brooklyn, and Jersey City in June 1889, Hepburn urged banks to use analytical methods to determine the profitability of their accounts. On 27 July 1892 Hepburn became comptroller of the currency, filling Edward S. Lacey's unexpired term. He served until 25 April 1893, so that Cleveland could secure confirmation of his successor. Hepburn's brief Washington stay "was marked by the same characteristic ability and forcefulness that was shown in every public position he had held," observed Thomas P. Kane, who was associated with the office for more than a generation (*Romance and Tragedy of Banking* [1922], p. 175).

Hepburn was president of New York City's Third National Bank from 1893 until it was voluntarily liquidated on 20 May 1897. National City Bank acquired it in order to secure its business—particularly out-of-town banks' deposits—and to gain Hepburn as a vice president. "His ability, experience and reputation will strengthen our staff," stated James Stillman. Hepburn resigned after two years, preferring a smaller bank.

Chase National Bank's Henry W. Cannon personally solicited Hepburn and named him vice president on 24 January 1899. Hepburn became president on 9 February 1904, following Cannon's resignation from the post. Hepburn was elected chair of the board on 11 January 1911 when Cannon retired altogether from management. The board of directors authorized him "to bind the Bank by his acts and signature with the same effect as if he were President." The board recorded its pleasure that under Hepburn, Chase "has grown steadily in importance, in strength, in public confidence, and in reputation for stability and conservative progress," praising his "untiring application, capacity for searching analyses, foresight, breadth of view, rare judgment, and the wise courage which has made him a leader of men."

Hepburn himself attributed his success to "hard, systematic work directed by every ounce of intelligence in me." Hepburn resigned the chairmanship on 12 September 1917 but continued to enjoy the same legal powers as before as chair of the advisory board (a post created for him). Bylaws adopted 28 November 1917 made the chair of the board, the chair of the advisory board, and the president all the chief executive officers of Chase with "like powers." This innovation reflected the directors' unwillingness to lose Hepburn's counsel; the position disappeared after his death.

In 1897 Chase had some 2,000 accounts from banks all over the country—more than any other in the city. Its very substantial correspondent banking activity represented about 75 percent of Chase's deposit volume. It had almost 3,200 correspondent accounts in 1912, but by then National Park Bank had 4,200. Total deposits grew from $41 million in 1899 to $315 million by January 1922 as National City went from $105 million to $584 million. Fourth in size among banks in the New York Clearing House Association in 1899, Chase under Hepburn's leadership was never smaller than sixth place in New York. It stood in third place from 1920 until the time of Hepburn's death.

Hepburn had a long-standing interest in monetary reform. He wrote in the *North American Review* (Mar. 1893) that "every currency should be sound, safe, elastic and as good as gold." He served as treasurer and general secretary of the National Sound Money League, organized at the time of the 1896 campaign to combat efforts to restore bimetallism. His *History of Coinage and Currency in the United States and the Perennial Contest for Sound Money* (1903) was widely distributed by the league. An updated, revised edition under the title *A History of Currency in the United States* appeared in 1915. In the revised and enlarged edition published posthumously in 1924, Hepburn cautioned that "the time will never come when the sound banker and economist will not need to combat the idea that governmental fiat can create something out of nothing" (p. 487).

Hepburn was chair of the American Bankers Association's currency commission from the time it was established (1906) until he died. In October 1907 he noted that "a government-controlled central bank of issue, where the banks . . . can . . . discount their receivables, receiving the proceeds in bank-notes, [would] afford the best solution of the currency question, the interest rate and bank reserves" (*Moody's Magazine*, p. 483). Congressmen, as well as Carter Glass's expert adviser H. Parker Willis, consulted with Hepburn on the Federal Reserve bill. Hepburn convinced President Woodrow Wilson that the twelve Federal Reserve Banks should have the right and obligation to rediscount for one another, in keeping with the principle of consolidation of reserves. In 1919 the directors of the Federal Reserve Bank of New York elected Hepburn to the Federal Advisory Council of the Federal Reserve Board. He gave his council duties priority over other matters during his two-year term.

Of all his achievements Hepburn was perhaps proudest of his prowess as a big-game hunter. Returning from salmon fishing in Quebec in the last summer of his life, he suffered a stroke of paralysis, from which he never fully recovered. He died at his Park Avenue home.

Hepburn's benefactions came to $5 million. Ogdensburg Hospital and Middlebury College each got $1.1 million. A total of $535,000 went to the building of libraries in seven St. Lawrence County towns from 1913 to 1920. Williams College received $301,250 and St. Lawrence University, $276,500; lesser amounts were donated to Princeton, Wellesley, and New York University. Convinced that commercial education was important for the prosperity of New York City, Hepburn was instrumental in the establishment of the Columbia University School of Business, with a gift of $500,000 in February 1919 and later a bequest of $350,000.

He was "sincere, modest, strong and simple" and respected for "an exceptionally sound judgment," wrote *Bankers Magazine* (1922). In New York it was said that he was "president of everything worthwhile but the United States": the Clearing House Association, the Chamber of Commerce of the State of New York, the Academy of Political Science, the New England Society of New York, the St. Andrews Society of New York, Bankers Club, and University Club, among others. He served as director of many corporations, including New York Life Insurance, American Car and Foundry, Woolworth, Studebaker, Great Northern Railway, and Sears, Roebuck.

• Hepburn's papers are at Columbia University and Chase Manhattan Bank. For additional information on Hepburn's business activities, see his *Annual Report of the Superintendent of the Banking Department of the State of New York* (1880, 1881, 1882); the *Annual Report of the Comptroller of the Currency* (1892); *The Story of an Outing* (1913); *Artificial Waterways of the World* (1914); and "Government Currency vs. Bank Currency," in *The Currency Problem and the Present Fi-*

nancial Situation (1908), pp. 41–59. Also useful are "Credit and Banking," an address delivered in the Page Lecture Series at Yale University and published in *Morals in Modern Business* (1909), pp. 74–101; *Financing the War . . .* , a published lecture delivered at Princeton University (1918); and *Address . . . at the Conference of the Currency Commission of the American Bankers Association* (1913). For more information see Joseph Bucklin Bishop, *A. Barton Hepburn* (1923), and B. C. Forbes, *Men Who Are Making America* (1917). An obituary is in the *New York Times*, 26 Jan. 1922.

BENJAMIN J. KLEBANER

HEPBURN, Audrey (4 May 1929–20 Jan. 1993), film and stage actress, was born Edda Kathleen van Heemstra Hepburn-Ruston in Brussels, Belgium, the daughter of Joseph Victor Anthony Hepburn-Ruston, a financial adviser, and Baroness Ella van Heemstra. Because of her mother's wealth and aristocratic background, Hepburn's early childhood was affluent and secure despite the traumatic breakup of her parent's marriage when her father left home in 1935 and returned to London. As part of the divorce settlement, it was agreed that Hepburn would attend school in England so that her father could visit her regularly. Hepburn was a good student and a voracious reader, but her interest lay in creative pursuits, chiefly ballet, which she began at the age of nine.

At the outbreak of World War II, Hepburn was sent to live with her mother in Arnhem, Holland, in hopes that Holland's neutral status would ensure a safer environment. Within a year, however, Germany invaded Holland and seized the assets of aristocratic families, forcing the van Heemstras into poverty. In September 1944 her family fled when the occupation government forced the residents of Arnhem out of their homes and into the countryside. Nearly 3,000 of Arnhem's 100,000 citizens perished from hunger, exposure, and disease; in the spring of 1945 Hepburn nearly died from infection and malnutrition, but relief shipments of food and medicine enabled her to survive.

Once she regained her health, Hepburn resumed her dance training and got her first acting job in 1947 when her excellent English won her the role of a bilingual flight attendant in a promotional film for KLM airlines. In the same year she was awarded a scholarship to the Ballet Rambert, the most important school of dance in London. Hepburn's intensive study of ballet convinced her that she did not have the gifts for a career in dance, so she began to take on work as a model, a file clerk, and a dancer in nightclub revues and musical comedies. She appeared as a chorus girl in West End musicals such as *High Button Shoes*, *Sauce Tartare*, and *Sauce Piquante*; she also took lessons in elocution and appeared as a model in print advertisements, which led to bit parts in several British-made motion pictures.

Hepburn landed her first significant supporting role in *The Secret People* (1952), a film about European refugees in pre–World War II England. Soon afterward, a leading role in the Anglo-French farce *Monte Carlo Baby* (1952) brought her to the Riviera and to the attention of Colette, the French author, who was looking for an actress to play the title role in the Broadway version of her novel *Gigi*, a Cinderella story about the daughter of a courtesan. Hepburn politely refused Collete's offer on the grounds that she knew nothing about acting. Nevertheless, she was sent to audition for producer Gilbert Miller, who signed her for the role and hired Hepburn's costar, Cathleen Nesbitt, as her acting and voice coach. Hepburn's novice acting got her fired twice during rehearsals, but her performance gradually improved, and by the time the play opened critics called Hepburn "an actress of the first rank" and "the acting find of the year." Her success led to a national tour of *Gigi* and a starring role in 1953 in Paramount Studios' *Roman Holiday*, her first major motion picture, for which she won an Academy Award for best actress.

Eager to capitalize on the sudden fame of its new star, Paramount signed Hepburn to a long-term contract in 1954, allowing her script approval and the right to work in stage plays, freedoms that few film stars enjoyed in those days. For an actress as young and inexperienced as Hepburn, such terms were extraordinary. Yet she managed to justify such special treatment, for in the same year she received her second Oscar nomination for *Sabrina* and won a Tony Award in the best dramatic actress category for her performance as the title character in Jean Giraudoux's *Ondine*. Shortly afterward she married her costar, Melchior Gaston (Mel) Ferrer. They had a son in 1960 and divorced in 1968.

In the first decade of her career, Hepburn acted in a series of films that characterized her as the young naïf who reaches maturity through a difficult and exciting adventure or as the charming, virginal ingenue who warms the heart of a worldly older man. William Wyler, who directed her in three films, said she embodied "the spirit of youth," combining the poise and grace of her aristocratic background with the eagerness and passion of a young girl. In *Roman Holiday* (1953), *Sabrina* (1954), *War and Peace* (1956), *Funny Face* (1957), *Love in the Afternoon* (1957), *The Nun's Story* (1959), and *Green Mansions* (1959), she appeared opposite Hollywood's major stars, including Gregory Peck, Humphrey Bogart, William Holden, Henry Fonda, Fred Astaire, Gary Cooper, Peter Finch, and Anthony Perkins. Because of her unusual contractual arrangement, Hepburn chose films that featured her as the central character rather than a mere love interest like most actresses of her day. In fact, most of her costars served as her satellites, much to their dismay. By 1959, with an Academy Award, a Tony, and two more Oscar nominations, she had become a top box-office attraction of the 1950s, and in 1964 her million-dollar salary for *My Fair Lady* made her the highest-paid actress in the world.

Hepburn's celebrity also extended to the world of fashion. With her short, dark hair, tall frame (5′7″), thin figure, and dancer's grace, she was a designer's dream. Though she immortalized the fashions of such famous designers as Edith Head, Cecil Beaton, and

Christian Dior, Hepburn is most identified with the designs of Hubert de Givenchy. The pair's lifelong friendship and professional collaboration had a salutary effect on both their careers, earning international recognition for Givenchy and putting Hepburn into the role of trendsetter. An editorial in the *New York Times* paid tribute to her unique image. "What a burden she lifted from women! Here was proof that looking good need not be synonymous with looking bimbo. Thanks to their first glimpse of Audrey Hepburn in *Roman Holiday*, half a generation of young females stopped stuffing their bras and teetering on stiletto heels" (23 Jan. 1993). Commenting on her sophisticated look, director Billy Wilder voted her "the girl most likely to make bosoms a thing of the past."

In the second decade of her career, Hepburn's film image shed some of its innocence and emphasized her independence and womanliness. In her Oscar-nominated performance as Holly Golightly, the free spirit of Truman Capote's *Breakfast at Tiffany's* (1961), she played a sexually liberated bohemian who comes to recognize her need for stability and love; as Eliza Doolittle in *My Fair Lady*, she played a vulnerable waif transformed into a lady of spirit and elegance. Her fifth Academy Award nomination came with her performance as Susy Hendrix, a blind woman terrorized by drug dealers in *Wait until Dark* (1967). Other films of note in this period are *The Children's Hour* (1961), *Charade* (1963), *Paris When It Sizzles* (1964), *How to Steal a Million* (1966), and *Two for the Road* (1967). In 1969 she retired from films to marry Italian psychiatrist Andrea Dotti and in 1970 gave birth to their son. In 1982 the couple divorced. Meanwhile, Hepburn had returned to the screen to act in *Robin and Marian* (1976), then starred in Sidney Sheldon's *Bloodline* (1979), *They All Laughed* (1981), and in the television film *Love among Thieves* (1987). In the next year, she played a cameo as an angel in her final film, *Always*, released in 1989.

In 1988 Hepburn took on the role of Good Will Ambassador for the United Nations International Children's Emergency Fund (UNICEF), an unpaid position she held until her death from cancer. With Robert Wolders, her companion for thirteen years, Hepburn traveled to countries plagued by war, famine, and disease; in hundreds of speeches and interviews she raised awareness about the plight of impoverished children and lent her celebrity to numerous benefits that raised millions of dollars in relief funds. Asked why she dedicated herself to such punishing work, Hepburn said simply, "My childhood made me more receptive to the ravages of war. It's that wonderful old-fashioned idea that others come first and you come second. This was the whole ethic by which I was brought up." Quoting her mother, she added, "Others matter more than you do, so 'don't fuss, dear; get on with it'" (quoted in Harris, p. 279). Her work for UNICEF earned her the Presidential Medal of Freedom in 1992 and the Jean Hersholt Humanitarian Award, presented posthumously in 1993 by the Academy of Motion Picture Arts and Sciences. She died in Tolochenaz, Switzerland.

• A recent biography of Hepburn is Barry Paris, *Audrey Hepburn* (1996). Other comprehensive biographies include Warren G. Harris, *Audrey Hepburn: A Biography* (1994), Diana Maychick, *Audrey Hepburn: An Intimate Portrait* (1993), and Alexander Walker, *Audrey: Her Real Story* (1994). Other works of interest are Charles Higham, *Audrey: The Life of Audrey Hepburn* (1984), Robyn Karney, *Audrey Hepburn: A Star Danced* (1995), and Ian Woodward, *Audrey Hepburn* (1984). An obituary is in the *New York Times*, 21 Jan. 1993.

STACEY CONNELLY

HEPBURN, James Curtis (13 Mar. 1815–21 Sept. 1911), medical missionary, oculist, and lexicographer, was born in Milton, Pennsylvania, the son of Samuel Hepburn, a lawyer, and Ann Clay, the daughter of the Reverend Slator Clay. Hepburn received his early education at home and at the Milton Academy. At the age of fourteen he matriculated as a junior in Princeton College, from which he graduated in 1832. He began his medical studies with Dr. Samuel Pollack of Milton, Pennsylvania, and then attended the University of Pennsylvania Medical School, from which he graduated with an M.D. in 1836. In 1835 he was awarded an A.M. by Princeton College.

Hepburn began his general practice of medicine in Norristown, Pennsylvania. There he met Clarissa Leete, a teacher at the Norristown Academy, whom he married in October 1840; only one of their five children survived infancy. Clarissa Hepburn would become a pioneer of women's education in Japan.

While in medical school Hepburn made a commitment to devote his life to Christianity and the Presbyterian church. Accepting an assignment from the American Board of Commissioners for Foreign Missions to work among the Chinese people, Hepburn arrived with his wife in Singapore in July 1841. The end of the Opium War in August 1842 opened China to foreign trade and influence. The Hepburns left Singapore for Macao, a Portuguese enclave on the China Sea, and then for the island of Kolongsu, near Amoy off the China coast. There malaria was endemic and taking its toll on missionaries and English soldiers stationed on the island. Hepburn and his wife succumbed to the disease, and the illness forced them to return to the United States. The couple arrived in New York City in March 1846, disappointed that the five years spent as missionaries had not met their high expectations of becoming productive emissaries for the church. For Hepburn the end of his first missionary experience was a personal letdown in that he thought he would not be able to do Christ's work as a medical missionary but would have to spend his life as a medical practitioner in New York City. He resumed his medical practice and became a successful oculist (an ophthalmic surgeon) and remained active in church affairs. He nevertheless looked forward to his return to the Orient as a medical missionary.

In 1853 the United States began negotiations to open Japanese ports to American trade. A treaty with

Japan was signed in 1854, and in 1859 four ports were opened to Americans for commercial enterprises. In January 1859 Hepburn requested permission to go to Japan; a week later his offer was accepted. In April 1859 Hepburn and his wife left for Japan; their son Samuel was sent to boarding school.

Arriving at Kanagawa, Japan, in October 1859, Hepburn immediately opened a dispensary and began to study Japanese. As early as 1861 Hepburn was asked by the Edo government to teach English to nine young Japanese men of rank; later Western culture and science were added to the program. A political crisis in 1862 forced the cancellation of the program and the closing of the dispensary but did not prevent Hepburn from continuing to care for those in need of medical care.

Hepburn reopened the dispensary when he moved to Yokohama in 1863. His daily schedule included medical practice and medical training for Japanese students, Bible and language study and translations, exercise, and his social and public service obligations. The dispensary was open every day for three to five hours. There he was surrounded by a group of devoted students, anxious to learn the healing art, who served as his assistants. Three days a week he conducted medical classes. In Japan Hepburn worked as an ophthalmologist, surgeon, and general practitioner, but he was especially renowned as an oculist.

Illness forced Hepburn to leave his dispensary in 1879, allowing him more time as lexicographer and translator of biblical works. In 1867 he had published his first Japanese-American dictionary, an improvement on the limited content and narrower focus of earlier such dictionaries. Three new editions of his dictionary appeared, and in 1886 a revision to the third edition was printed. Alone and in conjunction with missionary colleagues, he had also published religious tracts in Japanese. On 19 April 1880 at a public meeting held in Tokyo, Hepburn and his co-workers were honored by members of the foreign missionary societies and private Japanese citizens for their efforts in completing the translation of the New Testament into Japanese. After sixteen years of his labor in translating, revising, providing transliterations, and preparing the text for publication, on 31 December 1887, at a special church service, one set of the Holy Scriptures in five volumes was presented to Hepburn by the National Bible Society of Scotland.

In April 1887 the faculty of the Meiji Gaku-in (Hall of Learning of the Era of Enlightened Government), a college and theological school in Tokyo, appointed Hepburn president of the school and chair of physiology and hygiene. He remained with the institution until his return to the United States in 1892. In the years that Hepburn served as a medical missionary he aided in the growth of both the Protestant church and the medical profession in Japan. At the October 1884 meeting of the Tokyo Medical Society, some seventy Japanese doctors attended, and Hepburn admitted that he had never expected to see that degree of progress during his career.

Hepburn was honored by his colleagues in Japan and in the United States for his contributions to lexicography and education. Mutsuhito, the Emperor of Japan, awarded him "The Third Order of Merit of the Rising Sun" for services to spiritual and educational causes in Japan.

In 1892 the Hepburns returned to the United States and settled in East Orange, New Jersey. Hepburn was elected an elder in the Brick Presbyterian Church and became an active congregant. He died in his home in East Orange.

• After Hepburn's death, his son Samuel D. Hepburn gave Hepburn's personal papers to biographer William Elliot Griffis, who wrote *Hepburn of Japan and His Wife and Helpmates: A Life Story of Toil for Christ* (1913). See also *Journal of the American Medical Association* 57 (7 Oct. 1911): 1221. An obituary is in the *New York Times*, 22 Sept. 1911.

SAM ALEWITZ

HEPBURN, Katharine Martha Houghton (2 Feb. 1878–17 Mar. 1951), women's rights activist, was born in Buffalo, New York, the daughter of Alfred Houghton, a businessman and son of founders of the Corning Glass Works, and Caroline Garlinghouse. After the deaths of her parents—her father of suicide in 1892 and her mother of stomach cancer in 1894—the teenager and her two sisters were sent to Corning, New York, to live with their mother's cousin Mack Smith in Canandaigua, New York. Katharine attended Bryn Mawr College and earned her B.A. in 1899 and an M.A. in chemistry and physics in 1900. After a European tour, she took a teaching job in Baltimore, where she met Thomas Norval Hepburn, a student at Johns Hopkins Medical School, whom she married in 1904.

Like many young women of her day, Hepburn was struck by the inequities of American life. Though wealthy and well-connected, she had been taught by her mother to question the status quo, to think independently, and to conduct a socially useful and personally fulfilling life. Shortly after her marriage, she and her husband moved to Hartford, Connecticut, where she soon entered the public sphere, joining prominent local women in their efforts to end the white slave trade and close the houses of prostitution. At the same time, Thomas Hepburn had become a national figure in the campaign to eliminate venereal disease. The couple also started a family. They had six children, the second of whom, Katharine Houghton Hepburn, born in 1907, was to become a celebrated movie actress.

In 1909 England's veteran suffragist, Emmeline Pankhurst, spoke to a small group of women in Hartford. Inspired by Pankhurst's appeal, Hepburn became convinced that enfranchisement was not only a basic human right but also a potentially useful tool in the movement for social, political, and economic justice. After 1909 she turned her full attention to the woman suffrage movement. In the final decade of that struggle, Hepburn became Connecticut's foremost spokesperson for women's rights and a national suffrage leader. As president of the Connecticut Woman Suffrage Association (1910–1911 and 1913–1917), she turned a moribund organization into one of the most active in the United States. With the help of a number of talented women, she built an organization of over 32,000 members.

An early advocate of enfranchisement by constitutional amendment and supporter of the militant, partisan tactics of Alice Paul, Hepburn resigned her office in the CWSA in 1917 in sympathy with the National Woman's party's Washington picketing campaign. Hepburn was appalled by National American Woman Suffrage Association president Carrie Chapman Catt's refusal to condemn the treatment of the jailed pickets. She felt she could no longer preside over an organization with an official connection to NAWSA. Although she herself never joined the Washington picket lines, she admired the "honesty . . . self-forgetfulness, and . . . practical wisdom of the pickets." Because she was pregnant and unable to risk arrest, she paid a young Hartford working woman, Edna Purtell, to march in her place. Purtell was arrested and jailed for several days.

Alice Paul appointed Hepburn to the National Executive Committee of the National Woman's party. Hepburn became chairman of the Connecticut branch of the NWP in 1918, serving in that capacity until ratification of the Nineteenth Amendment in 1920. Her strong leadership and enthusiastic support of party tactics helped to make Connecticut a particularly active branch of the NWP. Although Connecticut's leading politicians remained adamant in their opposition to the federal amendment, the suffragists succeeded in attracting a wide range of followers, including working-class women and labor unions.

Striving to keep controversial matters in the background, Connecticut suffrage leaders managed to keep the suffrage movement united. Although Hepburn's support of the NWP alienated some of Connecticut's more conservative suffragists, by and large relations between the state's two organizations remained cordial. The two groups at times even coordinated their activities. When the Nineteenth Amendment became national law, they gathered together to celebrate their victory.

Like many suffragists, Hepburn continued to advance social causes in the postsuffrage era. A founder of the Connecticut Birth Control League, she was particularly concerned that not only health but also economic reasons be considered in any legislation allowing physicians to dispense birth control information. Connecticut was notorious for its strict regulations on the dissemination of information and its prohibition of the sale of birth control devices. Hepburn was quick to point out that birth control was not accessible to poor women but was easily available to women who could afford private, sympathetic physicians. She was instrumental in setting up an illegal birth control clinic in Hartford in 1935, although, despite her protests, the clinic was closed in 1939 after several of its supporters expressed fear of arrest.

For more than two decades, Hepburn spoke regularly before the Connecticut state legislature for liberalization of birth control laws, though she was attacked widely throughout the United States. With Margaret Sanger, Hepburn appeared before the Judiciary Committee of the U.S. Congress, and she was an active member and legislative chairman of Sanger's National Committee on Federal Legislation for Birth Control. The struggle continued long after Hepburn's death. A legal battle over the closing of another illegal birth control clinic in New Haven finally resulted in the laws being declared unconstitutional by the U.S. Supreme Court in *Griswold v. Connecticut* (1965).

In her struggles for political equality and reproductive freedom, Hepburn was an effective leader and organizer and a courageous public speaker. By the time of her death in Hartford, she had earned a wide reputation for her women's rights activities and was considered one of the most prominent birth control advocates in the United States. Hepburn was an outstanding example of the many suffragists who continued to work throughout their lives toward the creation of a more just and humanitarian society.

• Hepburn left few papers, but materials relating to her activities can be found in the archives of the Connecticut Woman Suffrage Association, Connecticut State Library, Hartford; the National Woman's Party and the National American Woman Suffrage Association, Library of Congress; the Planned Parenthood League of Connecticut, New Haven Historical Society; the American Birth Control League, Harvard University; and the Planned Parenthood Federation of America, Smith College. Hepburn figures prominently in Carole Nichols, *Votes and More for Women: Suffrage and After in Connecticut* (1983); on two radio programs, "The Suffragists" and "The Birth Control Movement," produced by Connecticut Public Radio and the Connecticut Humanities Council (1983); a video documentary, *The Roots of Roe*, co-produced by Connecticut Public Television and the Connecticut Humanities Council and directed by Andrea Haas-Hubble (1993); and an oral history interview of Hartford birth control activist Hilda Crosby Standish conducted by Carole Nichols (1980). Hepburn is profiled in *Bryn Mawr* 66, no. 1 (Fall 1984): 6–7. An obituary is in the *New York Times*, 18 Mar. 1951.

CAROLE ARTIGIANI NICHOLS

HEPBURN, William Peters (4 Nov. 1833–7 Feb. 1916), congressman, was born in Wellsville, Columbiana County, Ohio, the son of James Schmidt Hepburn, an artillery officer and physician, and Ann Fairfax Catlett, a teacher. His father died before William was born, and his mother married George S. Hampton, a prosperous merchant, who in 1841 moved the family to a farm near Iowa City, Iowa. The youth lived there for three years until his parents relocated to Iowa City for professional employment. After attending private schools and serving an apprenticeship in the printing office of the *Iowa Republican*, Hepburn, who read law in Chicago with William Penn Clarke, was admitted to the bar in 1854. The following year, in 1855, he married Melvina Annette Morsman, with whom he raised five children. They settled in Marshalltown, Iowa.

Hepburn's political career began in 1856, when he attended Iowa's first Republican State Convention and was elected prosecuting attorney of Marshall County. In 1858 he became chief clerk of the Iowa House of Representatives and district attorney of the Eleventh Judicial District. Upon entering the Civil War in 1861, Hepburn, captain of the Second Iowa Cavalry, gained the ranks of major and lieutenant colonel, earning distinction at the battle of Corinth. He served much of his time on the staffs of Generals Philip H. Sheridan and William S. Rosecrans.

Upon the conclusion of the Civil War in 1865, Hepburn practiced law in Memphis, Tennessee, until 1867, when he returned to Iowa to open a law office in Clarinda. There he also engaged in journalism and purchased a half interest in the *Page County Herald*. Hepburn's interest in politics expanded as well during this time. Disgusted with the scandals of the Ulysses S. Grant administration, Hepburn, supporting the Liberal Republican movement in 1872, favored Horace Greeley, a New York editor, for the presidency. In 1876 he was a Republican presidential elector in Iowa for Rutherford B. Hayes, the party's standard-bearer.

Hepburn entered national politics in 1880. After a prolonged deadlock between Hepburn and Congressman William F. Sapp at the Republican State Convention in Council Bluffs that year, Hepburn ultimately emerged on the 385th ballot as the party's congressional nominee. In the general election he won a seat in the U.S. House of Representatives, serving six years. Defeated for reelection in 1886 by Albert R. Anderson, a Sidney lawyer who ran as an Independent Republican, Hepburn returned to his law practice in Clarinda. He still maintained his interest in politics, attended various conventions, and was a Republican presidential elector in 1888 for Benjamin Harrison, the party's nominee for the White House. In 1889 President Harrison appointed Hepburn to the post of solicitor of the treasury, in which capacity he served until the end of Harrison's administration.

Hepburn's political career accelerated in 1892 with his election once again to Congress to represent the Eighth Iowa District. Serving eight consecutive terms, he gained seniority and public attention. He was for fourteen years the influential chairperson of the Committee on Interstate and Foreign Commerce and for a decade sat on the Committee on Pacific Railroads. Long interested in American transportation, Hepburn was a major force in this area in the House of Representatives.

In 1896 Hepburn's fierce partisanship momentarily overshadowed his congressional work. He served as temporary chairman of the Republican State Convention in Des Moines, where he vigorously denounced Democrats for having surrendered everything but their name to the Populist party. Blaming the Democratic administration of Grover Cleveland for the panic of 1893 and the ensuing severe economic depression, Hepburn rapidly sketched by way of contrast the achievements of the Republican party, which included the emancipation of slaves, the preservation of the Un-

ion, homesteads, a good labor system, and a sound financial structure for the nation. He next journeyed to St. Louis in June to attend the Republican National Convention, which nominated William McKinley for president. Although Hepburn would have preferred the nomination of Senator William B. Allison of Iowa, he acquiesced in the decision of the delegates. Regarding the controversial money issue, he claimed that Republicans had been better friends of silver than Democrats. Because of his national reputation, Hepburn was impressed into the presidential campaign in Iowa and other states. On one occasion he accompanied Senator Joseph B. Foraker of Ohio on a political sojourn across Iowa.

Hepburn's work in the field of transportation culminated in the Hepburn Act of 1906, one of the major achievements not only of the Iowa congressman but also of the presidency of Theodore Roosevelt. The Hepburn Act represented a compromise between President Roosevelt on the one hand and congressional conservatives on the other. It increased from five to seven the membership of the Interstate Commerce Commission (ICC) and gave that body the authority to adjust maximum railroad rates. The act, which prohibited rebates, broadened the jurisdiction of the ICC to include safety regulations for terminal facilities, oil pipelines, and bridges. Moreover, the act also restricted the granting of free passes and incorporated various prohibitions on railroads carrying their own commodities. In addition, the ICC gained the authority to set maximum railroad rates and outline more standard accounting methods.

In addition, Hepburn played a role in the making of other legislation. He favored the bill to construct the Panama Canal and advocated measures to prevent the manufacture or transportation of fraudulently labeled foods and drugs. Hepburn was the joint author of the Pure Food and Drug Act of 1906, signed by President Roosevelt, who noted that that Congress would be remembered in history for its constructive legislation. Although progressive in some areas, including his desire to reduce the powers of the House speaker and promote the regulation of interstate commerce, Hepburn remained conservative on other matters, such as his opposition to civil service reform and trade unions. Fiercely opposed to pork barrel legislation, he was just as firmly committed to his advocacy of pensions for war veterans.

Hepburn won his party's renomination in 1908 for another term in Congress, but he narrowly lost the general election. This defeat closed his political career. He remained in the nation's capital for a time to practice law before returning to Iowa, where he died in Clarinda. Although not known for flowery eloquence, Hepburn earned a reputation as a powerful debater in Congress. He was frequently referred to as the "Long Tom" and "Big Gun" of the Republican side. His friends and opponents recognized his parliamentary skills and masterful command of diction. A product of the midwestern heartland during the late nineteenth and early twentieth centuries, Hepburn was a leader in Iowa politics.

• Hepburn left no collection of papers. His letters are scattered in the manuscript collections of contemporaries, including those of Ulysses S. Grant, Benjamin Harrison, William McKinley, Theodore Roosevelt, and William Howard Taft in the Manuscript Division of the Library of Congress and those of Samuel J. Kirkwood, Grenville M. Dodge, and William B. Allison at the State Historical Society of Iowa at Des Moines. A biography of Hepburn, now outdated, is John Ely Briggs, *William Peters Hepburn* (1919), a book in the Iowa Biographical Series published by the State Historical Society of Iowa. Hepburn's name surfaces from time to time in various articles published in the *Annals of Iowa*. Insights into the period may be gleaned from Robert Cook, *Baptism of Fire: The Republican Party in Iowa, 1838–1878* (1994); Leland L. Sage, *William Boyd Allison* (1956); Sage, *A History of Iowa* (1974); and Stanley P. Hirshson, *Grenville M. Dodge* (1967). Obituaries are in the *Des Moines Register and Leader* and the *New York Times*, 8 Feb. 1916.

LEONARD SCHLUP

HERBER, Arnold (2 Apr. 1910–14 Oct. 1969), professional football player, was born in Green Bay, Wisconsin. He was a star in basketball and football at Green Bay West High School. On Sundays during the fall, he sold programs outside Packers games to earn the price of admission to watch Green Bay's National Football League (NFL) team.

After graduating from high school, Herber attended the University of Wisconsin for one year and then transferred to tiny Regis College in Denver, Colorado. Almost immediately, the Great Depression brought an end to his college career. He returned to Green Bay where he found a job as a handyman around the Packers' clubhouse. Remembering Herber's high school reputation, Packers head coach Earl "Curly" Lambeau gave the stocky youngster a tryout at tailback and signed him for $75 a game. Although the Packers had won the 1929 league championship, money was tight, and an important part of Lambeau's thinking was that a "local hero" might prove a drawing card. In his first appearance as a professional, Herber threw a touchdown pass to help earn a Green Bay victory over the Chicago Cardinals. The Packers repeated as NFL champions in 1930 and 1931.

After substituting for two seasons, Herber blossomed as a starter in 1932, the first year the NFL compiled official statistics. He became the league's first passing champion, completing 44 of 110 passing attempts for 774 yards and nine touchdowns. That year he was named to the official All-NFL team. At that time the ball, more rounded than today's football, did not lend itself to the aerial game. Most coaches used the forward pass only in emergencies or a few times a game as a surprise strategy. Herber's continued success with the pass throughout the 1930s began to change this way of thinking. He led the league in passing again in 1934 and 1936, and the Packers ranked consistently among the highest-scoring teams in the NFL. By the end of the decade the football had been

made more tapered, and nearly every NFL team had, or was seeking, an ace passer.

Herber had short, stubby fingers that led him to grip the football in an unusual way when passing. Instead of holding the ball with his fingers across the laces as most passers do, he kept the ball from wobbling by putting his thumb on the laces. Though odd, this technique allowed him to throw tight, accurate spirals. He was particularly adept at throwing long. Proud of his talent, he once fell prey to a clever teammate who bet him that he could not throw the ball from one goal line to the other even if the roll was included. Herber confidently fired the ball 80 yards; but when it landed, its angle of descent coupled with its shape caused it to bounce backward toward him.

In addition to his passing skills, the 6-foot, 200-pound Herber—nicknamed "Flash" by the local press—was an excellent punter and, until a mid-career leg injury slowed him down, a fine runner. In one game against the Staten Island Stapletons during the 1932 season, he did all the Green Bay punting, ran for 85-yard and 45-yard touchdowns, and completed nine of 11 passes for three more touchdowns.

In 1935 receiver Don Hutson joined the Packers. Herber and the speedy rookie immediately combined to form the league's most devastating long-distance punch. On the second play of Hutson's first game, he and Herber connected for an 83-yard touchdown against the Chicago Bears. The pair clicked for six more touchdowns that year.

In 1936 the Packers won the NFL championship, and Herber enjoyed his best season, completing 77 passes for 1,239 yards, and 11 touchdowns. Reportedly Herber's prowess with the pass in the championship game victory over the Boston (later Washington) Redskins convinced Redskins owner George Preston Marshall to draft Sammy Baugh the following year. While Baugh, who was instantly hailed as football's foremost passer, led the Redskins to the 1937 championship, Green Bay slumped when Herber suffered a leg injury that was to hamper him the rest of his career. The Packers lost the championship game to the New York Giants in 1938 and then came back to win the title over New York in 1939. By then, however, Herber had been reduced to a substitute's role because of his lack of mobility. He retired after the 1940 season.

During World War II, when a large number of athletes were in the service, teams brought back many retired players. Herber was signed by the Giants in 1944. Although he was overweight and unable to run at all, he could still throw. Herber's passing helped take New York to the championship game, where they lost a close contest to, ironically, Green Bay. After one more season with the Giants, Herber retired for good. In his next-to-last game, he came off the bench in the third quarter with the Giants trailing the Philadelphia Eagles, 21–0. He threw four touchdown passes to bring New York a 28–21 victory.

Official statistics are unavailable for Herber's first two seasons, but in the 11-year period from 1932 to

1945 he passed for 8,033 yards and 79 touchdowns, by far the best record in the NFL until Baugh's arrival.

After his final retirement, Herber ran a soft drink business in Green Bay. He also hosted a radio show once a week. In 1966 he was named to the Pro Football Hall of Fame. He died in Green Bay.

• There is an Arnold Herber file at the Pro Football Hall of Fame in Canton, Ohio. Unofficial rushing, passing, and kicking statistics for 1930–1931 culled from newspaper accounts and yearly official statistics from 1932 onward are in David S. Neft and Richard M. Cohen, eds., *The Football Encyclopedia* (1991). See also "Hall of Fame Profile," *Pro!* (San Francisco–Pittsburgh football game program), 1 Nov. 1981; George Sullivan, *Pro Football's All-Time Greats: The Immortals in Pro Football's Hall of Fame* (1968); and Jack Yuenger, "He Came to Play," *Green Bay Packers Yearbook, 1962* (1962).

BOB CARROLL

HERBERG, Will (30 June 1901–26 Mar. 1977), Jewish intellectual and social critic, was born in Liachovitzi, near Minsk, Russia, the son of Hyman Louis Herberg, an electrical contractor, and Sarah Wolkov, a housekeeper and beltmaker. In 1904 Herberg's parents emigrated from Russia to the United States, where they settled in a poor Jewish neighborhood in Brooklyn, New York. Herberg's father began to neglect his business, and when he deserted the family in 1910 its economic condition deteriorated. Eventually, his parents were divorced. Sarah Herberg raised her two sons on a limited income. They occasionally attended synagogue on high holy days, but by his own choice Will Herberg did not have a bar mitzvah. After attending Brooklyn elementary schools, he entered Boys' High School in 1915, graduated three years later, and entered the College of the City of New York (CCNY) in September 1918.

As an undergraduate, Herberg was a diligent student of foreign languages, literature, mathematics, and physics. He completed two-thirds of the requirements for graduation, but his failure to meet a requirement in physical education, poor grades in hygiene and military science, chronic absence from the latter, and a fight with the military science instructor led to his suspension from CCNY in November 1920. It was the end of his formal education. During the next five years Herberg became active in the Communist Young Workers League (YWL). By 1925, when he married Anna Thompson, the daughter of Russian Jewish immigrants who settled in Brooklyn, Herberg was a delegate to the YWL's national convention, a member of its national executive committee, its director of "agitprop" (agitation and propaganda), and a contributor to its publication, *Young Worker*. Believing that the workers' cause demanded their undivided attention, Will and Anna Herberg chose to have no children.

Because of his opposition to Joseph Stalin's purge of Nicholai Bukharin, Herberg was dismissed from his position in the American Communist Party (CPUSA) in the summer of 1929. With other "right deviationists," including Jay Lovestone, Benjamin Gitlow, and Bertram Wolfe, who were also expelled, he organized the CPUSA-Majority, later known formally as the CPUSA-Opposition and the Independent Labor League of America (ILLA) and informally as the "Lovestonites." They maintained that the particular circumstances of the American situation required a uniquely American interpretation of the workers' struggle. In 1929 Herberg became the managing editor of the Lovestonite publication *Revolutionary Age*, later known as *Workers' Age*. In December 1933 Charles S. Zimmerman, a Lovestonite who led a New York local of the International Ladies' Garment Workers Union (ILGWU), hired Herberg as its education director. During the 1930s he was the foremost intellectual spokesman for the Lovestonite faction of American communists, equally critical of Stalinist communism, Trotskyite communism, and democratic socialism as deviant from the teachings of Karl Marx and Nicholai Lenin. Herberg's affiliation with the ILLA continued until its dissolution in 1941, and his employment by the ILGWU continued until 1948.

Disillusioned by the purges, the Nazi-Soviet Pact, Russia's invasion of Finland, and the continued subservience of the CPUSA to the vagaries of Stalinist policy, Herberg began an ethical critique of Marxism by 1938 and increasingly thought of himself as a democratic socialist. His reading of Reinhold Niebuhr's *Moral Man and Immoral Society* (1932) led him to think that behind the moral bankruptcy of Stalinist policy lay Marxism's failure to acknowledge the corrupting influence of sin on all collective human action. Briefly, he considered the possibility of becoming a Christian, but at Niebuhr's recommendation he explored the theological roots of his own tradition. Submersing himself in study at the Jewish Theological Seminary of the sources of historic Judaic faith and contemporary Jewish theology, the prolific Marxist writer published nothing between December 1940 and the spring of 1943. From this time of intense study, Herberg emerged as an articulate democratic socialist and conservative Jewish theologian.

Deeply influenced by the thinking of Martin Buber, Franz Rosenzweig, and Solomon Schechter, as well as Christian theologians such as Søren Kierkegaard, Karl Barth, and Niebuhr, Herberg published his first book, *Judaism and Modern Man: An Interpretation of Jewish Religion*, in 1951. After analyzing the false expectations offered by scientism, Marxism, and psychoanalysis to human despair in the mid-twentieth century, he outlined the hope that he saw for modern man in an existential interpretation of historical Judaism. The book ended with a meditation on the mystery of Israel's unique election as a people of God. Herberg's second major book, *Protestant-Catholic-Jew: An Essay in American Religious Sociology* (1955), was a more broadly influential interpretation and critique of religion in America. By the mid-twentieth century, he argued, the grandchildren of immigrants were assimilating into a mainstream American culture in a "triple melting pot," largely defined by the three major religions of their immigrant heritage. While they maintained the forms of their distinct religious traditions, Herberg warned, American Protestantism, Catholicism, and Judaism all tended to promote a religion of the "American Way of Life," which had little to do with biblical faith. At best, the religion of the American Way of Life could inculcate values that would help to bind a multicultural society together; at worst, it was a vain, idolatrous celebration of the national experience.

Widely published and very active on the college lecture circuit, Herberg joined the faculty of Drew University as professor of Judaic studies and social philosophy in 1955 and was awarded an honorary doctorate by Park College in 1956. In the next few years, he edited three important anthologies: *The Writings of Martin Buber* (1956), *Four Existentialist Theologians* (1958), and *Community, State and Church* (1960). Herberg's empathy with American Catholicism was signaled by his support of John F. Kennedy's presidential campaign in 1960, but its deeper tendency was reflected in his becoming an editor of William F. Buckley's *National Review* in 1961. For the next fifteen years, he contributed to the intellectual renaissance of American conservatism. In 1962, when Herberg first appeared in *Who's Who in America*, he falsely claimed to have been born on 7 August 1907 in New York City and to have earned bachelor's, master's, and doctoral degrees from Columbia University. In his later years, Herberg carried in his jacket a clipping of Confucius's epitaph: "He is this sort of man: so intent upon teaching those eager for knowledge that he forgets to eat, so happy in doing so that he forgets his sorrows and does not realize that old age is creeping up on him." Anxious to extend his vocation, he amended subsequent entries in *Who's Who* to cite a birth date in 1909. Because of Herberg's encyclopedic knowledge and intellectual brilliance, neither his students nor his colleagues doubted his claims until his last years. Herberg died in Chatham, New Jersey.

• The archive of Will Herberg's papers and his personal library are in Rose Memorial Library at Drew University in Madison, N.J. Among his few autobiographical pieces is "From Marxism to Judaism . . . ," *Commentary*, Jan., 1947, pp. 25–32. The standard biography, Harry J. Ausmus, *Will Herberg: From Right to Right* (1987), includes a bibliography of his books, pamphlets, and articles. On Herberg's claims about his birth and academic degrees, see Douglas G. Webb, "From Old Left to New Right," *Canadian Review of American Studies* 8 (Fall 1978): 223–40; and Lewis S. Feuer and Webb, "Reasoning Together," *Canadian Review of American Studies* 10 (Fall 1980): 262–68. See also *From Marxism to Judaism: The Collected Essays of Will Herberg*, ed. David G. Dalin (1989). Obituaries and tributes are in the *New York Times*, 28 Mar. 1977; *National Review*, 5 Aug. 1977, pp. 880–86; and the *American Jewish Year Book* 78 (1978): 529–37.

RALPH E. LUKER

HERBERT, F. Hugh (29 May 1897–17 May 1958), dramatist, screenwriter, and novelist, was born Frederick Hugh Herbert in Vienna, Austria, the son of Lionel Frederick Herbert, a stockbroker, and Paula Knepler. His family moved to London when he was young, and he was educated at Gresham Public School. He entered the London School of Mines with the intention of becoming an engineer, but his schooling was interrupted by World War I, during which he served with the Royal Garrison Artillery in London and Jamaica.

Herbert's father had emigrated to the United States during the war, and Herbert decided to join him in 1920. Despite his previous training, Herbert set out almost immediately to earn his living as a writer. His short stories and essays began appearing in *Smart Set* and the *Saturday Evening Post*. Although he harbored ambitions from the first to be a playwright, big bucks lured him to write for Hollywood in 1921. After he moved there in 1924, he began to create a steady output of original screenplays and adaptations of the stories of others for the movies. Because he was skillful with dialogue, his services became even more in demand when the film industry turned to sound, and more than fifty motion pictures bear evidence of his work as a writer. Herbert married Arline Appleby in 1927, and they had two daughters prior to their divorce in 1937. He subsequently married Mary Alice Lankey in 1938.

Herbert's screen writing covered a broad range of subject matter, but he was at his best when writing comedies. For example, many historians and critics of motion pictures have termed *Sitting Pretty* (1948) the funniest picture of its decade. Other examples of his work that are well known to the movie buff are *Vanity Fair* (1932), *Hotel Continental* (1932), *The Secret Bride* (1935), *Traveling Saleslady* (1935), *Three Faces West* (1940), *Home Sweet Homicide* (1946), and *Scudda Hoo! Scudda Hay!* (1948).

Still, Herbert's reputation rests largely on one of his Broadway plays that he adapted for the screen. *The Moon Is Blue*, which opened in March 1951 and had a respectable run of 924 performances at Henry Miller's Theatre in New York, was the vehicle that would thrust Herbert relentlessly into the limelight, usually in a vortex of controversy. The play seems innocent enough by today's standards. A young, successful architect "picks up" a likable young woman who goes back with him to his apartment where they talk openly and frankly, usually about sex. The play survived on Broadway practically without incident, but when Otto Preminger and Herbert filmed the story in 1953, the ensuing public outrage brought both no end of trouble. The Legion of Decency objected to the shocking use of such words as "virgin," "mistress," and "seduction," and the Hollywood Production Code Administration refused to grant its approval. In a bold act of defiance, United Artists released it anyway, and the picture did six million dollars worth of business, a huge return for that time. More importantly, this refreshing film cleared the path for several other similar pictures, and when the dust had settled the production code had been battered into a new attitude.

Although Herbert's talents were in constant demand in Hollywood, he still found time to write occasionally for Broadway, and one of his plays, *Kiss and Tell* (1943), also had a hit run of 962 performances. The play followed, and was based on, Herbert's highly successful group of short stories about a teenaged girl named Corliss Archer. These stories also became the basis for a popular and long-running radio program ("Meet Corliss Archer"). Herbert's other works for the New York stage included *For Love or Money* (1947), the book for the musical *Out of This World* (1950), *A Girl Can Tell* (1953), and *The Best House in Naples*, an unsuccessful effort of the 1956 season. He died in Beverly Hills, California, of lung cancer.

Although Herbert never again achieved the success (and certainly not the notoriety) of *The Moon Is Blue*, his career output places him high among writers specializing in romantic comedy. He was a master of subtle nuance and of dialogue that fell pleasantly on the ear of the ordinary American moviegoer and patron of the theater. The latter trait was all the more remarkable since Herbert had spent his formative years in London. His dialogue was so natural and free-flowing that he could have his characters talk about previously taboo subjects and get away with it. His influence on the subject matter today allowed on the motion picture screen was immense and undeniable.

• The Herbert papers and manuscripts reside in the University of Wyoming Library, Laramie. Interesting accounts of the production of *The Moon Is Blue* as a motion picture are contained in Otto Preminger, *Preminger: An Autobiography* (1977), and Willi Frischauer, *Behind the Scenes of Otto Preminger, an Unauthorized Biography* (1973). An obituary is in the *New York Times*, 18 May 1958.

LARRY D. CLARK

HERBERT, Frank (8 Oct. 1920–11 Feb. 1986), science fiction writer, was born Frank Patrick Herbert, Jr. in Tacoma, Washington, the son of Frank Herbert, a bus-line operator, and Eileen M. McCarthy. He graduated from high school in 1938 and later attended the University of Washington (1946–1947) without receiving a degree. In 1940 Herbert married Flora Parkinson, with whom he had one child. The following year he enlisted in the U.S. Navy and joined the Seabees but received a medical discharge after six months. His first marriage ended in divorce in 1945. He married Beverly Ann Stuart in 1946; they had two children. She died in 1984. His third wife was Teresa Shackleford, whom he married in 1985.

In 1939 Herbert began his journalism career with a position at the *Glendale* (Calif.) *Star*. His first published story, "The Survival of the Cunning," appeared in *Esquire* in 1945. Also in 1945 he moved to Seattle and began working for the *Seattle Post-Intelligencer*. *Startling Stories* published his first science fiction story, "Looking for Something," in 1952. Herbert's first novel, *Under Pressure* (formerly titled *The Dragon in the Sea*), was published in 1956. His most famous work, *Dune*, was published in 1965.

Herbert continued to work as a newspaper reporter and editor until 1969, when his success as a science fiction writer made it practical for him to make a living from his books. In addition to the *Dune* novels: *Dune* (1965), *Dune Messiah* (1969), *Children of Dune* (1976), *God Emperor of Dune* (1981), *Heretics of Dune* (1984), and *Chapter House Dune* (1985), he published twenty-seven books. Besides his writing, he was very interested in ecology and the environment. At his farm in Port Townsend, Washington, which Herbert referred to as an "ecological demonstration project," he experimented with alternative energy sources and other ecological ventures while attempting to maintain high material as well as ecological standards of living. He died in Port Townsend.

Dune won the two most prestigious science fiction awards, the Nebula Award from the Science Fiction Writers of America in 1965 and the Hugo Award from the World Science Fiction Convention in 1966. In 1984 *Dune* was made into a motion picture starring Kyle MacLachlan and Sting. The cult status of the *Dune* sextet ranks it with other epic science fiction series such as J. R. R. Tolkien's *Lord of the Rings*, Isaac Asimov's *Foundation*, Gordon Dickson's *Dorsai* novels, and Philip Jose Farmer's *Riverworld*.

Dune is remarkable both because of its focus on ecology (centering on the planet Arrakis) and because of its treatment of religious demagogues and personal charisma. The ecology of Arrakis, a desert planet with limited plant and water sources, is conceived of as something that people can change if they conserve water and make intelligent use of technology. William Touponce has suggested that, despite Herbert's deep interest in ecology, he had a fear that "ecology might be the next banner for demagogues" (p. 12). The hero of *Dune*, Paul Muad'Dib, is the illegitimate son of Duke Leto, who took control of Arrakis. Herbert sets Paul up as the biological heir to centuries of careful inbreeding and genetic engineering conducted by a women's religious order. He is also the product of an advanced intellectualism called mentat thinking, which requires the hyperdevelopment of logic and inferences. The strength of mentat thinking lies in its evolving into a paranoid-based military stratagem, much like U.S. Cold War strategy.

The novel's treatment of religious demagogues and personal charisma as they interact within the political structure of the intergalactic civilization of *Dune* seems to reflect American society and politics in the late 1950s and early 1960s. The intergalactic society is ruled by the Imperial Household, called the Federated Great Houses of the Landsraad, and the intergalactic transportation company, called the Guild. The imperial nature of *Dune* seems to correspond to the imperial quality of the John F. Kennedy administration. Touponce has remarked on Herbert's fascination with Kennedy and with George Patton, both of whom worked as charismatics within a mythic structure of American thought (p. 12). The language of "Camelot," which was derived from Kennedy's short but mythical presidency, suggests, as a cultural construct, a too-close connection between ideology and an individual's charisma, which Herbert believed posed a threat to human society. With the assassination of the charismatic Duke Leto, as with the assassination of Kennedy, new social and economic resources had to be developed and new alliances had to be made.

Representing the new alliances in *Dune* are the Fremen of Arrakis, whom Herbert based on the "premier" guerrilla fighters of modern history, the Apaches of the American Southwest and the nomads of North Africa and the Arabian Peninsula. Tim O'Reilly has emphasized the Apache connection, but Herbert seemed to have a particular need to recognize the power of the Arab guerrillas fighting for independence, such as the Algerian nationalists who defeated the French in July 1962. Of course, any mention of guerrilla forces in the early 1960s would necessarily invoke the followers of Fidel Castro and Che Guevara who toppled the government of Fulgencio Batista in Cuba in 1959.

Herbert's contributions and lasting significance are hard to assess, as scholarly research about him and his work is limited. However, his focus on the environment and his discussions of the implications of demagoguery have opened up important topics within American cultural studies, including issues of power and control in American society. Herbert's work is an area of study full of potential.

• Frank Herbert's papers have been collected at California State University at Fullerton. William Touponce, *Frank Herbert* (1988), discusses the *Dune* books in terms of Herbert's ecological views. David Miller, *Frank Herbert* (1980), is a guidebook with plot summaries of the novels, diagrams of characters and their alignments within the novels, and some minor analysis. Tim O'Reilly, *Frank Herbert* (1981), is both a biography and a critical discussion of Herbert's work. O'Reilly carefully follows Herbert's major themes and, significantly, also locates Herbert in connection with important events in twentieth-century American history. Obituary notices are in the *Los Angeles Times* and the *New York Times*, both 13 Feb. 1986.

GEOFF COHEN

HERBERT, Henry William (7 Apr. 1807–17 May 1858), writer and sportsman, was born in London, England, the son of William Herbert, dean of Manchester, and Letitia Emily Dorothea Allen, daughter of Joshua, Fifth Viscount Allen. Herbert's father imbued him with a lifelong passion for field sports. Herbert attended Caius College, Cambridge, where he gained a modest reputation for scholarship and a greater one for convivial social life. Completing his studies in 1830, he became embroiled in "difficulties" of an undisclosed nature, which were serious or embarrassing enough for the family to take stern measures: emigration to North America. Initially, Herbert went to Canada. Although he gained knowledge of Canadian field sports, he did not find social life there to his liking. He settled in New York City in the early 1830s, a seemingly unlikely place for him but one where he found a group of men whose values and interests, including journalism and literature, were congenial and where he had ready access to New York State's and New Jersey's sporting counties.

To support himself, Herbert first taught school; when he found teaching repugnant, he determined to make his way as a professional writer. He apparently always hoped and intended to return to Britain someday, but at the same time—the contradictory impulses are characteristic—he insisted that he wished to become an American writer. He had a high opinion of American writing in this period, especially the work of two writers associated with New York State and New York City, James Fenimore Cooper and Washington Irving. Herbert's first venture was as the editor of a giftbook. A popular form of contemporary publishing, giftbooks were elaborate annual volumes made up of articles and stories, many of them English reprints, with illustrations. Herbert's, called *The Magnolia*, appeared twice (1836 and 1837) and contained original work by Irving, Cooper, and N. P. Willis, among others. Henry Inman supervised the engravings.

After that beginning, Herbert wrote prolifically, including works of poetry, biographies of military leaders, translations from the French, and fiction. He always believed he would make his reputation as a historical novelist. Ironically, especially in light of his aspirations to be known as an American writer, his historical novels, which sold fairly well in England, failed in the United States. He was forced to turn to hackwork, such as historical adventure stories, some of which were derisively noticed by Edgar Allan Poe. Such work did not even afford Herbert a decent living, and so, reluctantly, he turned to field sports as a subject.

In the late 1830s Herbert began writing articles about horses, hunting, and fishing for the *American Turf Register* and for the *Spirit of the Times*. (George Porter, brother of the *Spirit*'s editor, William Trotter Porter, was one of his close friends.) These pieces were carefully developed and scholarly. Herbert also began writing sporting sketches, although most American publishers of the time believed no audience existed for such writing. As sporting literature was thought to be beneath the dignity of a serious writer, Herbert adopted the pseudonym Harry Archer. In 1842 he edited a collection of sketches by a friend, William P. Haws, who wrote under the pseudonym J. Cypress, Jr., and who had died a year earlier. These appeared as *Sporting Scenes and Miscellaneous Writings*. Herbert accepted George Porter's suggestion to do this kind of work on his own, and he adopted the pseudonym Frank Forester as appropriate for the American scene.

In 1845 Herbert collected and published these sporting sketches under the title *The Warwick Woodlands; or, Things as They Were Twenty Years Ago*. The book was a great success, both in terms of critical reception and of sales. As Frank Forester, Herbert did as a writer what he had been unable to do under his own name: find an audience and create a literary genre in the United States. Two more collections followed, *My Shooting Box* (1846) and *The Deerstalkers* (1849).

All three volumes recount the sporting adventures of a group of American and English sportsmen. Set more or less in the 1820s and in the southeastern counties of New York State, the sketches achieve a loose but effective closeness in tone and style, tied together by Forester's presence. Their essential unity was most apparent when they were published in England in one volume as *Frank Forester and His Friends*.

The primary theme of the stories is that of transformation, the often subtle but persistent and, in the end, unstoppable way in which English sporting culture became American. This theme is never crudely forced on readers as a general proposition but emerges out of Herbert's detailed disquisitions on proper hunting and fishing techniques, equipment, food, and drink and in his often delicate comparisons of the English and American countryside. In addition, Herbert showed a genuine capacity for creating character among his fictional sportsmen. He was especially interested in capturing the emerging types of American sportsmen. Transcending the limitations of his own class and aesthetic values, he was able to sympathize with the appearance of the American frontier sportsman, crude but vital, something of a social outcast, but with the frontiersman's passion for freedom from social convention. Something in this type deeply appealed to Herbert, who was himself an outcast. A pervasive sense of melancholy also pervades the stories, stemming from his dismayed observation of the spoliation of the countryside, reckless slaughter of animals, and triumph of commercial over sporting values.

Herbert's own life was haunted by a sense of tragedy, or at least of ineradicable guilt, no doubt connected with his exile from Great Britain. In 1857 he published his major work of nonfiction, *Horse and Horsemanship of the United States*, in two volumes. But neither this work nor the success of his sporting sketches could appease his melancholy. He became morose and secluded, living alone in a gothic cottage, "The Cedars," near Newark, New Jersey. He had been married twice; both wives had died. There were no children. In the Stevens House Hotel, in New York City, he committed suicide by shooting himself in the heart. He was buried in Mount Pleasant Cemetery in New Jersey, leaving instructions in his will that on the headstone of his grave should be the single word *infelicissimus*, "most unhappy."

• A complete list of Herbert's works may be found in William Mitchell Van Winkle, *Henry William Herbert: A Bibliography of His Writings, 1832–1858* (1936). Studies of Herbert's life and career include William Southworth Hunt, *Frank Forester: A Tragedy in Exile* (1933); Luke M. White, Jr., *Henry William Herbert and the American Publishing Scene, 1831–1858* (1943); and Thomas Picton, "The Story of His Life," in *The Life and Writings of Frank Forester*, ed. D. W. Judd (2 vols., 1882). Thomas Picton, "Reminiscences of a Sporting Journalist," *Spirit of the Times*, 1 Apr. 1882; Charles Hemstreet, *Literary New York: Its Landmarks and Associations* (1903); E. B. Hornby, *Under Old Rooftrees* (1908); and John

Dizikes, *Sportsmen and Gamesmen* (1981), provide further information. An obituary is in *Porter's Spirit of the Times*, 22 May 1858.

JOHN DIZIKES

HERBERT, Hilary Abner (12 Mar. 1834–6 Mar. 1919), Confederate soldier, congressman, and secretary of the navy, was born in Laurensville, South Carolina, the son of Thomas Edward Herbert and Dorothy Teague Young, teachers and slaveholding farmers. The Herberts moved to Alabama in 1846, and Hilary matriculated as a sophomore at the state university in 1853 only to quit that same year, along with most of his class, in protest against harsh discipline. He attended the University of Virginia from October 1854 to February 1856 before a stomach ailment forced his withdrawal. Eventually he read law in Alabama, practicing in Greenville until 1861.

A second lieutenant in the Greenville Guards, Herbert was sent to capture Pensacola's naval station. With the opening of the Civil War, Herbert was captain of the Guards, then a militia unit but later reorganized as part of the Eight Alabama Infantry Regiment. Gallantry in the Peninsular campaign earned him the oak leaf insignia of a major. After fighting at Manassas, Fredericksburg, Antietam, and Gettysburg, Herbert was promoted to lieutenant colonel. At the battle of the Wilderness, while commanding the regiment, he was severely wounded, losing the use of an arm. Promoted to his field rank upon leaving the Confederate army, Colonel Herbert resumed his law practice in Greenville. He married Ella B. Smith in 1867; they had three children.

In 1872 the Herberts moved to Montgomery, where the colonel practiced law until he won election to the U.S. House of Representatives in 1876. A "Bourbon" Democrat, he earnestly supported the redemption of the South from Reconstruction policies in force after the Civil War, although he despaired of success. He wrote his brother-in-law, "This country I cannot believe will prosper in our day. First the free negro is a roguish vagabond & therefore an incubus upon the country" (Hammett, p. 49). While Herbert campaigned on a platform of "home rule," he did not seek majority rule in his own district, which had slightly more blacks than whites.

Although these were notoriously ineffective Congresses, and despite his opposition to the locally popular bill providing federal support for the construction of the Texas and Pacific Railroad, his seat remained solid until the 1890 challenge of the Farmers' Alliance, which he overcame. Herbert opposed the alliance because it promoted blacks and sought what he considered to be special privileges for a class or sector of the economy. In that same year, he also gained distinction in Congress for his staunch opposition to Henry Cabot Lodge's (1850–1924) "Force" Bill, which called for stationing federal observers at southern polling stations to prevent fraud and to ensure the doctrine of "one man, one vote." To combat this effort, Herbert edited and coauthored with several other southern congressmen a volume entitled *Why the Solid South? Or Reconstruction and Its Results* (1890). This propaganda tract detailed the alleged woes inflicted upon the South by "black Republican" Reconstruction. Though hastily prepared and based on dubious facts, it helped defeat the Force Bill and contributed fodder for an emerging group of historians, who used such distortions to support the New South's restoration of white supremacy.

Herbert was appointed to the House Naval Affairs Committee in 1885 and immediately made a name as the leading Democratic navalist—a believer that a strong blue water fleet would strengthen the nation morally and strategically, a notion more generally held by Republicans. He later wrote, "My task with my own party was not an easy one, and it soon became apparent that to 'go sure' it was necessary to 'go slow'" (Hammett, p. 118). He chaired that crucial committee in the Forty-ninth, Fiftieth, and Fifty-second Congresses, overseeing and frequently guiding the naval revolution. He consistently pushed for more and larger ships. He fought for cruisers, then worked for armored cruisers, and finally in 1890 obtained support for the construction of large battleships.

Herbert became secretary of the navy in 1893 in Grover Cleveland's second administration, serving through four years of naval buildup, increased international tensions, and domestic crises (about which the president consulted Herbert only infrequently). Though Herbert was a relatively minor figure in the administration, with his help the authorizations for warships increased by 65,942 tons, to be capped by the building of the world's largest battleships.

Cleveland and Herbert had inherited the Hawaiian annexation crisis after sailors and marines from the *Boston* had assisted in *haole*, the white planter minority overthrow of Queen Liliuokalani. Much of the administration's earliest efforts concentrated on remedying the situation without annexing these islands. While he was pronavy, Herbert was no colonialist; he could not see non-Caucasian Hawaiians ever participating in the American governing process. Herbert longed for the Old South, replete with slavery, small government, and a courtly governing class. As the increasingly expensive navy brought the nation into contact and eventual control over differing peoples, his vision of America was challenged by the very institution he had so lovingly nurtured.

Herbert retired from government service somewhat grudgingly in 1897. With his son-in-law Benjamin Micou, he founded a successful Washington law firm, in which he practiced until his retirement in 1910.

• The major collection of works by and about Herbert is at the University of North Carolina Library, Chapel Hill. Hugh B. Hammett, *Hilary Abner Herbert: A Southerner Returns to the Union* (1976), is a solid biography covering Herbert's entire life. One might also consult Herbert's own writings, including *The Abolition Crusade and Its Consequences* (1912).

MARK R. SHULMAN

HERBERT, Victor (1 Feb. 1859–26 May 1924), composer and conductor, was born in Dublin, Ireland, the son of Edward Herbert, a businessman, and Fanny Lover. When he was three years old, his father died in Paris, and he was taken by his mother to the estate of his maternal grandfather, the Irish poet and novelist Samuel Lover, in Kent, England. Lover noticed his grandson's obvious aptitude for music and determined that he should have a musical education. Accordingly, at age seven young Victor was taken to Germany for musical training. He studied in Leipzig, Munich, and Berlin and developed exceptional proficiency on the cello.

Herbert began his musical career in his early twenties as a cello soloist with ensembles in Germany, France, and Italy and in 1882 was appointed first cellist of Johann Strauss's orchestra in Vienna. A year later he joined the Stuttgart court orchestra as first cellist and remained there for three years. In Stuttgart he also studied composition and wrote his first work, the Suite in F for Cello and Orchestra.

A turning point in Herbert's life came in 1886, when he met and married Therese Förster, a prominent Viennese opera singer; they later had two children. At the time of their marriage, Förster had a far more distinguished career than that of her husband. Förster was engaged by the Metropolitan Opera in New York City that year, and Herbert was given the position of first cellist with the opera. He subsequently occupied the first cellist's chair in several New York orchestras, including the New York Philharmonic, where he served as assistant conductor. From 1888 to 1891 Herbert was also the associate conductor of summer music festivals in Worcester, Massachusetts.

During his first decade in the United States, Herbert combined performing and conducting careers while continuing his activities as a composer. For much of that time he wrote classical music for both instrumental ensembles and voice. The performance of his pieces received respectful attention from critics, most notably the premieres of his oratorio *The Captive* at the 1891 Worcester summer festival, under his direction, and of his Second Cello Concerto with the New York Philharmonic, with himself as soloist, in the spring of 1894. That same year he was appointed bandmaster of the Twenty-second Regiment Band, an ensemble affiliated with the New York National Guard, and he remained their conductor for the rest of his life.

Another turning point in Herbert's life occurred in the fall of 1894 with the performance in New York of *Prince Ananias*, a comic opera that he had been commissioned to write by the Bostonians, a light opera company. Its success led Herbert to concentrate on writing other works in this popular genre, and in quick succession he composed the music for *The Wizard of the Nile* (1895), *The Serenade* (1897), *The Idol's Eye* (1897), and *The Fortune Teller* (1898). All were hits, and Herbert was hailed as the American answer to Sir Arthur Sullivan.

At the same time that his career as a composer was flourishing, Herbert's conducting talents were also in demand. In 1898 he was appointed the conductor of the Pittsburgh Symphony, a post he held for six years while he continued to compose operettas. His most notable works include *Babes in Toyland* (1903), which became one of the most beloved musicals of the twentieth century; *Mlle. Modiste* (1905), which featured the popular song "Kiss Me Again"; *The Red Mill* (1906); *Little Nemo* (1908); *Naughty Marietta* (1910), which equaled *Babes in Toyland* in popularity; *The Madcap Duchess* and *Sweethearts* (both 1913); *Princess Pat* (1915); and *Her Regiment* (1917).

Despite these successes, Herbert believed that he had to justify his early musical training by making his mark as a serious composer. Thus, while his reputation soared as the premier creator of operettas in the United States, Herbert also wrote several grand operas, including *Natoma*, staged in Philadelphia in 1911, and *Madeleine*, presented at the Metropolitan Opera in 1914. Contemporary and later critics praised Herbert's music for these works while lamenting the inferior quality of their librettos, written by men with limited talent, which doomed them to obscurity.

In the second decade of the twentieth century, Herbert lent his talents to the infant motion picture industry, believing that he would find there an outlet for serious composition. His movie credits include the musical score for the groundbreaking film *Birth of a Nation* (1915) and for the later silents *Little Old New York*, *The Great White Way*, and *Yolanda*. Herbert's forte was popular stage music, however, and his final compositions were musical scores for the Ziegfeld *Follies* of 1919, 1921, and 1924; he was helping to rehearse the 1924 show at the time of his death.

Herbert was a gregarious man who made friendships with ease. He was loved and admired by millions who were grateful for the joy that his music brought into their lives. Touring companies of his operettas gave performances throughout the country, sheet music for his songs found permanent residence on thousands of parlor pianos across the United States, and phonograph records of his melodies were played over and over again. With the advent of radio broadcasts in the 1920s, Herbert's music became ubiquitous.

That ubiquity led Herbert to help found the American Society of Composers, Authors, and Publishers (ASCAP), which worked for passage of legislation that required radio stations to pay for broadcast rights to copyrighted music. At the time, the sale of sheet music was a major source of revenue for popular composers, and frequent broadcasting diminished the demand for that product. In testimony before the Senate Patents Committee a month before his death, Herbert voiced a complaint echoed by many composers: "I have heard one of my compositions, 'A Kiss in the Dark,' played eight or nine times in one night over the radio. They play and play that *ad nauseam*. How can you expect anybody to buy it in printed form?" Thanks to Herbert's efforts, protective legislation was ultimately passed, and today ASCAP continues to collect royalties for broadcast performances, which it then redistributes to composers.

Herbert was active in the Friars and other associations of musicians and performers in New York City. Another Herbert passion was a lifelong love for Ireland, though he had left the country when barely out of infancy. He was an active member of many Irish societies, including the Friendly Sons of St. Patrick and the Sons of Irish Freedom, and was a strong supporter of home rule for Ireland. During the 1916 rebellion he even abandoned his musical activities for a time to write articles and letters in an effort to enlist U.S. support.

Severely overweight at a time when girth was equated with flourishing health, Herbert died suddenly of a heart attack while climbing the stairs to his doctor's office in New York City for a routine checkup. His untimely passing was announced on the front pages of newspapers across the United States, and he was mourned by millions.

The *New York Times* article on Herbert's death called him "America's Leading Composer of Light Opera," a title that he retains to this day. Yet some critics and scholars of American music, envious of a European operatic tradition that U.S. composers have failed to create, have decried Herbert's focus on popular music. He had the potential to be a Verdi or Puccini, they bemoaned, yet he chose to squander his talents on the creation of what they considered ephemera. What such critics choose to ignore is Herbert's role as the godfather of the American musical that emerged as a unique art form in the decades following his death, especially the "feel good" musicals of the 1940s from such composers as Rodgers and Hammerstein. Far from ephemeral, his place in the history of American music is assured.

• For biographical information on Victor Herbert, see Edward N. Waters, *Victor Herbert: A Life in Music* (1955; repr. 1978), and Joseph Kaye, *Victor Herbert: The Biography of America's Greatest Composer of Romantic Music* (1931; repr. 1955). See also Rupert Hughes and Arthur Elson, *American Composers* (1914), and an obituary notice in *Musical America*, 31 May 1924. Obituaries are in the *New York Times*, 27 and 29 May 1924, and the *New York Herald Tribune*, 27 May 1924.

ANN T. KEENE

HERBST, Josephine Frey (5 Mar. 1892–28 Jan. 1969), novelist, biographer, and radical journalist, was born in Sioux City, Iowa, the daughter of William Benton Herbst, a salesman of farm equipment, and Mary Frey. Herbst graduated from high school in 1910 and earned her own college tuition. Alternating schooling with stints as a teacher, secretary, and clerk, she attended classes at Morningside College, the University of Iowa, and the University of Washington before completing her B.A. in English at the University of California, Berkeley. Her first poems were published in an undergraduate magazine at Berkeley.

In 1919 Herbst moved east and began to frequent Greenwich Village. While working as an editorial reader at H. L. Mencken's magazine *Smart Set*, she published her first story, "The Elegant Mr. Gason," under the pseudonym Carlotta Greet. She became friendly with radical writers and intellectuals, including Genevieve Taggard, Floyd Dell, and Mike Gold. An affair with Maxwell Anderson ended unhappily in 1920 after an abortion. In the early 1920s, she lived in Berlin and Paris. While enjoying café friendships with Ernest Hemingway, Nathan Asch, and Robert McAlmon, Herbst worked on her unpublished novel, "Following the Circle," the story of a young woman's sexual adventures. In Paris Herbst also met John Herrman, an aspiring writer whom she married in 1926. Herbst and Herrmann returned to the United States in 1924 and lived in writers' communities in rural Connecticut and New York City. They had no children.

Herbst's life changed in 1927 with the execution of Italian-American anarchists Sacco and Vanzetti. "So far as I am concerned," she wrote in her memoir "A Year of Disgrace" (published in *The Noble Savage* in 1961), "what had been the twenties ended that night. . . . It would be three years before we took down a volume of *Kunstgeschichte* from our shelves, to be replaced by a thin narrow book in red entitled *What Is to Be Done?*, by V. I. Lenin." After 1927 she and Herrmann bought a farmhouse in rural Pennsylvania and became more politically active.

Herbst's first published novel, *Nothing Is Sacred* (1928), is a spare family drama set in the Midwest and written with a Hemingwayesque attention to everyday language. The novel was favorably reviewed, although some left-wing critics found the portrayal of middle-class American anomie too unfocused. *Money for Love* (1929) has an artsy, urban setting, but the blackmail plot also presents a grim portrait of a decaying society. Both novels combined fragmented modernist structures with naturalist content.

In 1930 Herbst and Herrmann were unofficial delegates to the Kharkov conference on revolutionary literature in the Soviet Union. Although Herbst's reaction to the proletarian aesthetic was mixed, during the early 1930s she avidly reported on labor and midwestern agrarian issues for *Scribner's*, *American Mercury*, and the *New Masses*. In 1933 she articulated her own radical aesthetic in *Pity Is Not Enough*, the first volume of a trilogy. Based loosely on Herbst's family history, the trilogy portrays the struggles of middle-class midwesterners between the Civil War and the Great Depression. The first volume focuses on Joe Trexler, a romantic figure involved in carpetbagging and the closing of the frontier. The second volume, *The Executioner Waits* (1934), contrasts the farmers' struggles with the frantic consumerism of urban prosperity on the East Coast. The volume closes ominously with a graveyard scene and echoes of a Wobblie tune mourning fallen comrades.

In the late 1930s Herbst's marriage disintegrated, in part because of her affair with the young painter Marion Greenwood. However, she received a Guggenheim Award (1936) for the first two volumes of her trilogy and continued her journalism. In Cuba she documented labor conditions and in Germany the underground resistance to Hitler. In 1937 she made a dangerous journey to Spain, visiting the front lines of the civil war and coming away disheartened about the integrity of the Communists. Traces of her reportage were included in the most successful volume of her trilogy, *Rope of Gold* (1939). This novel sets the breakdown of a marriage in an increasingly crisis-ridden international scene.

After her break with the Communist party and her divorce in 1940, Herbst's political involvement lessened, as is illustrated in *Satan's Sergeants* (1941), which explores the isolation and moral ossification of a rural Pennsylvania town. Nonetheless, in 1942, she lost a position as government propagandist for political reasons. In "Yesterday's Road," a memoir published in *New American Review* in 1968, Herbst describes her resistance to McCarthyism; she chose not "to reduce some of [her] best yesterdays to outworn slogans; telephone numbers of people who were no longer there, or were dead; and foxed files." Herbst also applied this ethic of silence when FBI investigators interviewed her about Herrmann's possible involvement in the Alger Hiss case.

After World War II Herbst wrote two more works—a novel looking back to the 1930s, *Somewhere the Tempest Fell* (1947), and a biography of Pennsylvania naturalists John and William Bartram, *New Green World* (1954). Her relationship with the poet Jean Garrigue, like her earlier romances with women, was not something she mentioned in her writings, although memoirs were her primary project in later years. She published essays on Spain, the 1920s, the 1930s, and her friend Nathanael West, and she received prizes in the late 1960s, including grants from the Rockefeller Foundation (1965) and the National Institute of Arts and Letters (1966). Despite this somewhat belated attention, Herbst died relatively unknown in New York City.

Throughout her life, Josephine Herbst devoted herself to writing responsibly about American social history. Her works are distinguished by their experiments with collective voice and their imaginative recasting of semipersonal material, such as family narratives. Her reputation waned with that of depression-era radicalism during the mid-century, but a revival of interest in women writers led to the reprinting of many of her novels during the 1980s and 1990s. In all, her career remains an important example of the difficult compromises made by literary radicals during the 1930s.

• Herbst's papers are located in the Beinecke Rare Book Library at Yale University. Her memoirs have been reprinted in *The Starched Blue Sky of Spain* (1991). The two major works on Herbst are Elinor Langer's original, feminist biography, *Josephine Herbst* (1984), and Winifred Farrant Bevilacqua's well-balanced critical study, *Josephine Herbst* (1985). Another rediscovery of Herbst is Walter Rideout's "Forgotten Images of the Thirties: Josephine Herbst," *Literary Review* 27, no. 1 (Fall 1983): 28–36. Comparisons of Herbst and her feminist contemporaries are in Nora Ruth Roberts, *Three Radical Women Writers: Class and Gender in Meridel Le Sueur, Tillie Olsen, and Josephine Herbst* (1996), and Paula Rabinowitz, *Labor & Desire: Women's Revolutionary Fiction in Depression-Era America* (1991). At least nine dissertations have been written on Herbst since her death. See also Alfred Kazin's warm obituary in the *New York Review of Books*, 27 Mar. 1969.

CAREN IRR

HERFORD, Oliver (1 Dec. 1863–5 July 1935), poet, illustrator, and wit, was born Oliver Brooke Herford in Sheffield, England, the son of Brooke Herford, a Unitarian minister, and Hannah Hankinson. His father, a noted clergyman, editor, and author of hymns, brought his wife and nine children to the United States on a visit in 1875 and was persuaded to remain as minister of the Church of the Messiah in Chicago. In 1882 or 1883 the family moved to Boston, where Dr. Herford served at the Arlington Street Church and as a preacher at Harvard until returning to England in 1893. Oliver studied at a boarding school in Lancaster, England, before coming to the United States, and he attended Antioch College in Yellow Springs, Ohio, from 1877 to 1879. He withdrew to study at the Art Institute of Chicago and later at the Museum of Fine Arts School in Boston. He continued his art studies in Germany, at the Slade School in London, and at the Académie Julian in Paris.

Back in the United States, Herford supported himself doing illustrations for magazines in New York but, according to legend, had little success until he sent a batch of submissions to *Century Magazine* editor Richard Watson Gilder with a note complaining that the magazine's office boy had been rejecting "these masterpieces." Gilder was amused and bought some, initiating a long and fruitful relationship between Herford and the monthly. In 1898 he and fellow light-verse writers Carolyn Wells and Gelett Burgess collaborated on a magazine of their own called *Enfant Terrible* but gave it up after one issue. Herford later became a member of the editorial staffs of the humor magazine *Life* and *Harper's Weekly*. For some years he had a page of his own in *Leslie's Weekly* called "Pen and Inklings," which later appeared in *Everybody's Magazine* and *Harper's*. From the 1890s to the 1930s he also provided numerous illustrations, caricatures, verses, and short humorous essays to many other magazines, including the *Ladies' Home Journal* and *St. Nicholas*. In 1904 he married Margaret Regan, an English actress, poet, and playwright, with whom he sometimes collaborated. The marriage was childless.

Herford's whimsical writing and delicate pencil drawings, washes, and watercolors found a wide audience and were collected into many small volumes, beginning with *Artful Anticks* in 1888. He himself kept no records or copies of his output, and the total number of his separate books has been variously estimated at from thirty-four to fifty, including collaborations and illustrations of others' work. His independent publications of humorous poetry and prose, often self-illustrated, included *Jingles from Japan and Other Rhymes by Peter Simple* (1891), *Pen and Inklings* (1893), *The Bashful Earthquake, and Other Fables and Verses* (1898), *Overheard in a Garden* (1900), *Rubáiyát of a Persian Kitten* (1904), *A Little Book of Bores* and *A Bold Bad Butterfly* (1906), *This Giddy Globe, by Peter Simple* (1919), and *Sea Legs* and *The Deb's Dictionary* (1931). He also adapted Ferenc Molnár's play *The Devil* (1908) and wrote at least five of his own that were successfully produced in New York: *McAdam & Eve; or, Two in a Garden* (1900), *The Love Cure* (1909), *The Danse Macabre: A Pantomime* (as Gustave Schehl, 1912), *The Florist Shop* and *Con & Co.* (both n.d.).

Herford's caricatures were genial, and his writing was never sharply satiric, but under the fanciful nonsense of his playful little verses often lay something of a bite. Among the chaste limericks in *A Little Book of Bores* is the often-quoted example:

> E is the Egotist dread
> Who as someone has wittily said,
>   Will talk till he's blue
>   About *himself* when you
> Want to talk about *yourself* instead,

and in *The Jingle-Jungle Book* (1913) appears the ironic observation:

> Said an envious erudite ermine,
> "There's one thing I cannot determine:
>   When a man wears my coat
>   He's a person of note
> While I'm but a species of vermin."

A *New York Times* editorial (7 July 1935) described Herford's humor as "odd, unexpected, his own brand" and the man himself as "an old-fashioned gentleman, a painstaking artist, whose work had edge, grace, and distinction."

Herford was considered one of the wittiest talkers in America and reputedly was called the Charles Lamb of his day by William Dean Howells. A member of the National Institute of Arts and Letters, Herford also belonged to the Players' Club, where he frequently spent his evenings. It was there that he was heard to describe his wife as having "a whim of iron" and to rebuff an intrusive boor, who demanded, "You remember me?" with the words, "I don't recall your face, but your manner is very familiar," a remark frequently quoted by Woodrow Wilson. An urbane, slightly eccentric figure who wore old-fashioned high collars and used a monocle, Herford led an active social life. Often referred to as "elfin" (a characterization that he said made him feel elf-conscious), he reflected the sprightly quality of his work in his personality. Carolyn Wells described him as "quicksilver-witted" and wrote, "The great charm of Oliver Herford lies in the fact that instead of following the main-traveled roads of wit and humor, he strays into bypaths of whimsical fancy and fantastic imagination" (*Atlantic Monthly*, p. 62).

Herford had become a legend, already viewed as belonging to another generation, by the time of his death, after a long illness, in New York City. Most of his quaint little volumes were out of print and valued by bibliophiles as much for their preciosity as for their wit.

• Other books by Herford, who sometimes published more than one a year, include *Alphabet of Celebrities* and *A Child's Primer of Natural History* (1899), *More Animals* (1901), *The Fairy Godmother-in-Law* (1905), *The Peter Pan Alphabet* and *The Astonishing Tale of a Pen and Ink Puppet* (1907), *The Simple Geography* and *The Smoker's Yearbook* (1908), *The Kitten's Garden of Verses* (1911), *The Mythological Zoo* (1912, 1914), *Confessions of a Caricaturist* and *A Cynic's Calendar* (1917), *The Laughing Willow* (1918), *The Herford Aesop: Fifty Fables in Verse* (1921), *Neither Here nor There* (1922), and *Excuse It, Please* (1929). Additional information on Herford can be found in Thomas Lansing Masson, *Our American Humorists* (1922); Grant Overton, *When Winter Comes to Main Street* (1922); and Carolyn Wells, *The Rest of My Life* (1937). For affectionate recollections of Herford, see Wells, "Oliver Speaking," *Atlantic Monthly*, Jan. 1936, pp. 61–69, and William Rose Benét, "Exit of a Humorist," *Saturday Review of Literature*, 13 July 1935, p. 8. Extensive obituaries are in the *New York Times* and the *New York Herald Tribune*, both 6 July 1935, and an appreciative editorial is in the *New York Times*, 7 July 1935.

DENNIS WEPMAN

HERGESHEIMER, Joseph (15 Feb. 1880–25 Apr. 1954), novelist and short story writer, was born in Germantown, Pennsylvania, the son of Joseph Hergesheimer, an employee of the U.S. Coast and Geodetic Survey, and Helen Janet MacKellar. Recalling his childhood in *The Presbyterian Child* (1923), Hergesheimer pictured himself as frequently ill and lonely, in part because his father was often away working and seemed distant even when he was at home. Likewise, his mother seemed withdrawn, largely, he inferred, because of the loss of three children in infancy. In response, feeling he "wasn't widely cared for," he "closed in on" himself by taking long walks alone and by reading, especially Romantic literature of the nineteenth century, in hopes of discovering "the secret of love" and "the beauty of passion" in a "sordid" world.

Hergesheimer's schooling consisted of three undistinguished years at the Germantown Friends School and three uneven years at the Pennsylvania Academy of Fine Arts, where he studied painting. In 1901, after receiving a considerable inheritance from his maternal grandfather, he left for Europe, where he spent a year living extravagantly until he exhausted his funds. He then returned to the academy virtually penniless and resumed his study of painting. But his interest in painting was waning, and when a popular English novelist known as Lucas Cleeve, the pen name of Adelina Kingscote, asked him to read proof for her, he decided to end his formal education and become a writer.

Over the next several years Hergesheimer worked in virtual isolation, producing thousands of words of prose each day, most of it fiction, and developing habits of productivity that lasted for years. But it was not until 1913, when he sold three short pieces to *Forum*, that his fortunes began to change. In 1914 he published his first novel, *The Lay Anthony*. A year later his second, *Mountain Blood*, appeared, and on 22 May 1915 one of his stories was published in the *Saturday Evening Post*. Of these developments, only the story accepted by the popular and lucrative *Post* signaled what would soon become the dramatic improvement in Hergesheimer's financial fortunes. It was the first of many stories that he would publish there, including another in 1915. His first two novels, which did not sell well, nevertheless attracted the attention of critics such as H. L. Mencken, establishing him as a promising new writer. In 1917 he published both his most famous story, "Tol'able David," in the *Post* and his third novel, *The Three Black Pennys*, thus beginning one of the most remarkable rises to commercial success and critical acclaim in the history of American literature.

Earlier, Hergesheimer had begun corresponding with Dorothy Hemphill, whom he met through a student at the Academy of Fine Arts, and in November 1907 the two married. They had no children. When Hergesheimer's fortunes began to rise, they bought the Dower House, an elegant estate located in West Chester, which Hergesheimer later described in loving detail in *From an Old House* (1926). The years following his initial breakthrough were years of meteoric rise in fortune and fame. *The Three Black Pennys* was followed in the next seven years by ten books, including *Gold and Iron* (1918), *The Happy End* (1919), *Java Head* (1919), *Linda Condon* (1919), *San Cristobal de la Habana* (1920), *Cytherea* (1922), *The Bright Shawl* (1922), and *Balisand* (1924).

Taken together, these early writings illustrate the defining characteristics of Hergesheimer's work: keen attention to atmosphere that creates a sense of mood; lavish descriptions both of place and of the rich, elegant surfaces that help to create a sense of place; female characters who play traditional roles; and heroes who, though varied in appearance, manner, and circumstance, remain loyal to some ideal of life and beauty. For Hergesheimer's characters such ideals are defined in terms of style as much as virtues or values; their commitment is absolute, and they are more often than not prepared to risk everything, including life itself. More varied than his female characters, his heroes are "natural" aristocrats even when they are not social aristocrats, and they belong, whether consciously or not, to the remnant of special people who keep alive, even in degraded or diminished times, a sense of courage, beauty, and style on which civilization depends. Although these works established Hergesheimer as an astonishingly prominent writer, they also defined the limits of his achievement and took him to the edge of decline. For some, including fellow aesthetes such as his friend James Branch Cabell, his appeal began with his highly mannered prose—or what Alfred Kazin in *On Native Grounds* (1942) called his "splendor of style" and described as "devotional estheticism." Others were drawn by his defense of "aristocratic" values and traditions against the rise of those individuals whom Mencken called the "booboisie." Still others liked Hergesheimer's way of taking them out into exotic places such as the Caribbean or Mexico or back into an American past—in Virginia, Pennsylvania, or Massachusetts—made simpler by the loss of detail. Many also liked his devotion to a world where men remained dominant and where women, whatever else they might be, were not rivals—the prospect he denounced at Yale University in his 1921 Bergen lecture entitled "The Feminine Nuisance in American Literature," which was later published in the *Yale Review* (July 1921).

In 1922, at the height of Hergesheimer's reputation, the *Literary Digest* surveyed opinions among thirty-three widely respected critics and editors in order to select the five outstanding figures in American literature of the past ten years. Hergesheimer finished first by a wide margin; Eugene O'Neill finished second. Following the publication of *Balisand* in 1924, however, Hergesheimer experienced a decline that accelerated in the late 1920s, when a literature bleaker in its disillusionment and more aggressive in its formal experimentation took hold, making his work seem dated, escapist, and even quaint. His novels continued to come—*Tampico* (1926), *The Party Dress* (1930), *The Limestone Tree* (1931), *Tropical Winter* (1933), and *The Foolscap Rose* (1934). But they found fewer readers and attracted less praise. Then, as the bleakness of the Great Depression deepened, Hergesheimer's productivity began to decline. By 1945 income from his writings had fallen to almost nothing, and he was forced to sell the Dower House. He died in Sea Isle City, New Jersey, a largely forgotten figure.

• An outstanding collection of Hergesheimer's manuscripts and papers is in the Humanities Research Center at the University of Texas. Victor E. Grimmestad, *Joseph Hergesheimer* (1984), provides a good survey of his career. Ronald E. Martin, *The Fiction of Joseph Hergesheimer* (1965), also gives a good assessment of his achievement. An obituary is in the *New York Times*, 26 Apr. 1954.

DAVID MINTER

HERGET, Paul (30 Jan. 1908–27 Aug. 1981), astronomer, was born Paul Frederick Ernst Herget in Cincinnati, Ohio, the son of Conrad Frederick Herget, a skilled machine-tool maker, and Clara Brueckner. His father had emigrated from Germany at the age of eighteen, and his mother was the daughter of German immigrants. As soon as he could read and write, Paul dropped the middle names and always signed himself Paul Herget. A good student, he was inspired to go on by his high school mathematics teacher, Helen Swineford, whom he later considered the greatest single influence on his career. After graduation, he entered the University of Cincinnati Engineering College but soon dropped out; he worked a year as a surveyor, then re-entered in the College of Liberal Arts as a mathematics student. In 1931 he received his A.B. and got a job as an assistant at the Cincinnati Observatory, a part of the university located in a different part of the city from the main campus. Herget continued as a graduate student in mathematics, learned orbit theory on his own,

and was encouraged by mathematics professor Louis Brand to put it entirely into vector form, instead of the more complicated component form then used. Herget received his M.A. in 1933 and his Ph.D. in mathematics and astronomy in 1935, then spent a year at the University of California, Berkeley, astronomical department as a postdoctoral research fellow, working with noted orbital expert Armin O. Leuschner. Herget returned to Cincinnati as an instructor in astronomy in 1936 and stayed on its faculty all his life, rising to assistant professor in 1940, then to full professor and director of the observatory in 1943. In 1935 Herget married Harriet Louise Smith, his high-school classmate and the daughter of Elliot S. Smith, the director of the Cincinnati Observatory. They had one daughter.

In the 1930s orbital calculations, requiring high numerical accuracy, were carried out by human beings, chiefly assistants like Herget, using mechanical computing machines and recording their results with pencil and paper. He made himself an expert numerical calculator. His first published paper was a table of sines and cosines that he had calculated, accurate to eight decimal places and perfectly adapted for precise numerical interpolation. Herget became an authority on the orbits of the outermost satellites of Jupiter, whose large, elongated orbits about the giant planet are strongly perturbed by the Sun and by Saturn. Studying on his own, he was attracted by the papers of Leslie J. Comrie, the leading early exponent of using punch-card machines to do orbital calculations faster and more accurately at the Nautical Almanac Office in Great Britain.

During World War II Herget went on leave to the Nautical Almanac Office of the U.S. Naval Observatory in Washington, D.C., where Wallace J. Eckert had introduced IBM punched-card computing machines. Herget worked closely with him, adapting the formulas and programs used for calculating the positions of planets from human to machine computation. Eckert and Herget also used these same machines to calculate tables for locating the precise positions of German submarines in the Atlantic Ocean, from radio directional fixes obtained by a network of Allied stations. After the war Herget returned to Cincinnati, where he now had standard IBM equipment available at the observatory, but he did most of his astronomical calculations with the more powerful computing equipment that large industrial concerns were acquiring, mostly for accounting applications. He arranged to use these machines at night, when they were not otherwise in demand, in exchange for his lectures and advice to the company employees on how to use them. Herget directed the Minor Planet Center of the International Astronomical Union from 1947 until 1978, calculating orbits and predicted positions by these methods for all asteroids then known and adding previously unknown ones to them each year as they were discovered. Herget also kept close ties with the Nautical Almanac Office and did many of his calculations of the precise orbits of Earth, Venus, and the four largest asteroids there. He followed the development of each new generation of electronic computers very closely and quickly worked out the best ways to use them most effectively for orbital calculations.

Thus when the space age dawned in the 1950s, Herget was very well equipped to be a leader in the calculations of the orbits of intercontinental ballistic missiles, artificial satellites, and manned spacecraft. He was a consultant on many such projects and was always able to develop new methods to get the best predicted trajectory or orbit from measured data quickly and accurately. Herget's textbook, *The Computation of Orbits* (1948), written in vector notation, became one of the early bibles of the field. He was elected to the National Academy of Sciences in 1962, and in 1965 he received the academy's James Craig Watson Gold Medal for his research on the orbits of asteroids. The University of Cincinnati set up an Institute of Space Sciences, with Herget as director, and a related graduate teaching program. Within a few years it turned out several excellent dynamical astronomy theorists. But, as better funded universities with larger research faculties entered the field, the Cincinnati program proved too small to survive. Nevertheless, Herget remained there and retired in 1978. In 1965 Harriet Herget was diagnosed with cancer; after several remissions and renewed bouts of illness, she died in 1972. Later that year Herget married Anne Lohrbach, the long-time secretary of the observatory. Nine years later he died at his home, in sight of the observatory at which he had spent his entire working life.

Herget was an outstanding practitioner of a very specialized but highly important branch of astronomy. His orbit calculations were widely known and used. He was an expert numerical computer and a skilled theorist with the insight necessary to put practical problems into forms well suited for solution with available technology.

• The main collection of Herget's scientific correspondence is at the U.S. Naval Observatory, Washington, D.C. The most complete published memorial biography is Donald E. Osterbrock and P. Kenneth Seidelmann, "Paul Herget 1908–1981," National Academy of Sciences, *Biographical Memoirs* 57 (1987): 59–86; it includes a bibliography listing all his published scientific papers. Most of these papers are highly technical, but he described part of his own work in "The Minor Planet Center at the Cincinnati Observatory," *Bulletin of the Cincinnati Historical Society* 24 (1966): 175–87, and published a brief summary of his and other astronomers' research in "The Outer Satellites of Jupiter," *Astronomical Journal* 73 (1968): 737–42. Obituaries are in the *New York Times*, 29 Aug. 1981, and the *Cincinnati Post* and the *Cincinnati Enquirer*, both 28 Aug. 1981; the latter newspaper also published a follow-up editorial on Herget's career on 5 Sept. 1981.

DONALD E. OSTERBROCK

HERING, Constantine (1 Jan. 1800–23 July 1880), homeopathic physician and educator, was born in Oschatz, Saxony, the son of Christian Gottlieb Karl Hering, a school headmaster and church organist, and Christiane Friedericke Kreutzberg. After receiving "classical schooling" in Zittau, Saxony, he began studying medicine in Dresden in 1817. While taking courses in medicine at the University of Leipzig in 1820, he was asked by his teacher to write a paper denouncing homeopathic medicine (a system of therapeutics developed by Samuel Hahnemann, based on the principle that a substance that is capable of causing symptoms in a healthy person is capable of curing similar symptoms when they occur as a part of a natural illness). Hering investigated the system and became convinced of its efficacy. He transferred to the University of Wurzburg and received his medical degree in 1826. Hering worked for a short time as a teacher of mathematics and natural sciences in Dresden. An avid naturalist and botanist, he was commissioned as a naturalist by the king of Saxony and was sent to Surinam to collect specimens. After contributing articles to several homeopathic journals in Europe, Hering was asked by the king to cease his involvement in medicine while in Surinam. In response to this request, Hering resigned his commission and stayed on to practice medicine. He remained in Surinam until 1833, at which time he was invited to join a colleague in the United States and settled in Philadelphia.

With his boundless energy for the cause of homeopathy, he became a leading proselytizer for homeopathy in Pennsylvania and in the United States. In 1835 he was invited to Allentown to organize the North American Academy for the Homeopathic Healing Art (commonly called the Allentown Academy)—the first school in the world to teach homeopathy. It was in existence for five years (1836–1842). While in Allentown Hering wrote *The Homoeopathist or Domestic Physician* (1835), the first homeopathic self-care manual. It became the standard homeopathic self-care manual during the westward migrations. It was eventually translated into nine languages and was still in print at the end of the twentieth century.

In 1844 Hering became one of the founders and the first president of the American Institute of Homeopathy, the first national medical organization in the United States. In 1848, with two other physicians, Jacob Jeanes and Walter Williamson, Hering founded the Homeopathic Medical College of Pennsylvania in Philadelphia—a direct descendant of the Allentown Academy.

The debate over the need to teach pathology at the school led Hering (who believed that understanding pathology was necessary in a medical education) to leave the college in 1867 to form a second school—the Hahnemann Medical College of Pennsylvania. In 1869 the two schools merged under the latter name. Hering was dean from 1867 until 1871, when he retired from formal teaching but continued his private practice, tutorials, and writing until his death in Philadelphia.

Hering married Charlotte Van Kemper in Surinam in 1829; they had one child before her death in 1831. He married Marianne Husmann in 1834, shortly after his arrival in the United States. Of this marriage there were four children, two living past infancy. His second wife died in 1840, and Hering returned to Germany in 1845, intending to stay. While there he met Therese Bucheim, married, and returned to the United States in 1846 after hearing that the homeopathic movement was in disarray. Of this marriage there were eight children, six of whom survived him.

Hering was active as an editor and prodigious as an author. From 1851 to 1853 he was the editor of the *North American Homeopathic Journal*; from 1854 to 1856 he edited the *Homeopathic News* and from 1867 to 1871 the *Homeopathic Materia Medica*. Under Hering's name, Thomas Lindsley Bradford's *Homeopathic Bibliography of the United States* (1892) lists, in addition to 325 articles, six books: *Domestic Physician* (1835), *Comparative Materia Medica* (1867), *Materia Medica* (1873), *Analytical Therapeutics* (1875), *Condensed Materia Medica* (1877), and *The Guiding Symptoms of Our Materia Medica* (10 vols., 1879–1891). He was working on the third volume of the massive *Guiding Symptoms* at the time of his death; the remaining seven volumes were edited by pupils of his. It remains one of the major reference sources in homeopathy and in 1992 was developed for electronic retrieval.

Hering was the first to introduce the use of snake venoms into homeopathic practice (*Lachesis muta* in 1828), the first to use products of disease (*Psorinum*, made from the discharge of a scabies vesicle, 1828), and the first to use nitroglycerine, in 1856, as a treatment for angina. He was responsible for the introduction of over 80 medicinal substances into the homeopathic materia medica and tested on himself 104 remedies.

Always a scholar and collector, Hering was particularly interested in the works of Paracelsus, the Swiss physician (1493–1591) whose writings anticipated many of the ideas later formulated by Hahnemann. Hering's private library of Paracelsus's work, one of the finest collections in the world, is housed in the Hahnemann University Archives in Philadelphia. Hering was a member of the Academy of Natural Sciences in Philadelphia, to which he presented his large botanical and zoological collection from South America.

Hering has been credited as the person who brought the Christmas tree to the United States. Although he was probably one of several German immigrants to do so, his was the first "German Christmas Tree" in Philadelphia. In politics he supported the abolitionist cause and offered training in medicine at his home to many black students from the United States and Jamaica, who were denied admission to medical schools at the time. In religion he was a follower of Swedenborg and the Church of the New Jerusalem. He was physician to many of the society elite in Philadelphia, and patients came long distances to see him. He was the physician to the American politician Henry Clay.

Said a colleague, "Always a student, endowed with indomitable will and untiring industry, he seemed to infuse everyone with whom he came in contact with the spirit of work. 'Change of occupation is rest,' was his oft repeated expression." Many mentioned his "hearty, genial laugh" and his straightforward manner. In his later years, those who knew him referred to him as "Papa." A student wrote, "I studied medicine from a homeopathic standpoint while at college; I really learned homeopathy from Dr. Hering in that back-office of his." His home on North Twelfth Street was a central meeting place for physicians, students, and friends.

Hering has often been referred to as "the Nestor" of American homeopathy. When he arrived in the United States, homeopathy had no formal organization. Within fifteen years of his arrival, homeopathy had a school, a national organization, and a core group of people who were to carry it into the next century, many of whom were his students. A tireless worker, his vibrant personality drew people to him and to his cause. He was a charismatic teacher and a prolific writer. He introduced many of the most important medicines used in homeopathy. His monumental ten-volume *Guiding Symptoms* is still a major reference work to homeopathic physicians worldwide.

• Many of Hering's papers and memorabilia are in the archives at Hahnemann University in Philadelphia. Carl Hering, "The Chronology of Events in the Life of Constantine Hering," in *Transactions of the International Hahnemannian Association* (1918), provides the major milestones. Charles Raue, ed., *A Memorial to Constantine Hering* (1880), gives a brief biography and presents the eulogies delivered at his funeral. Calvin B. Knerr, *The Life of Hering* (1940), includes the previously mentioned work as well as Dr. Knerr's memory of Hering and is a trove of detailed information. Two other pamphlets are Arthur Eastman, *Reminiscences of Constantine Hering* (1915), and Herman Faber, *Constantine Hering: A Biographical Sketch* (1917). Thomas Lindsley Bradford, *Pioneers of Homoeopathy* (1897); Egbert Cleave, ed., *Biographical Cyclopaedia of Homoeopathic Physicians and Surgeons* (1893); and William Harvey King, ed., *History of Homoeopathy and Its Institutions in America* (4 vols., 1905), gives some information that is not in the other sources. Hering's place in American homeopathy is best understood through Harris Coulter, *Divided Legacy: The Conflict between Homeopathy and the American Medical Association* 2d ed., (1982), and Martin Kaufman, *Homeopathy in America: The Rise and Fall of a Medical Heresy* (1971).

JULIAN WINSTON

HERKIMER, Nicholas (1728–16 Aug. 1777), soldier in the American Revolution, was born near what is now Herkimer, New York, the son of John Jost Herkimer (formerly Herchheimer or Erghemer) and Katharine (maiden name unknown), modestly wealthy landowners. His father had emigrated from the Rhine Palatinate in 1725 to the Mohawk Valley, where he received a large tract of land through the royal governor. Nicholas grew up under the primitive living conditions of frontier life. At the age of thirty, during the Seven Years' War, he was commissioned a lieutenant of militia and served at Fort Herkimer. After hostilities ceased, he secured a substantial tract of land in the Canajoharie District, where he settled to farm. He was married first to Lany Dygert (or Tygert), then to Lany's niece Myra. In 1775, at the beginning of the American Revolution, Herkimer was commissioned a colonel in the New York militia and elected chairman of the Committee of Safety of Tryon County. A year later he was promoted to brigadier general and ordered to defend his district against hostile Indian and Tory raids.

Herkimer was an energetic, well-respected citizen who gave strength to the rebel cause at a time when his region was bitterly divided between patriots and Loyalists. His first military action was as leader of a successful expedition to suppress Sir John Johnson's Tory and Indian forces. His first real challenge arose in 1777, when British General John Burgoyne invaded New York by way of Lake Champlain, ordering Colonel Barry St. Leger to support him in the Mohawk Valley by attacking eastward from Lake Ontario toward Albany. On 2 August, St. Leger's army besieged Fort Schuyler, which was under the command of Colonel Peter Gansevoort, and General Herkimer was ordered to come to Gansevoort's assistance. Having issued a stirring call to mobilize the militia two weeks before, Herkimer now set out with an army of about 800 patriots and 1,000 Indians to rescue Gansevoort's garrison.

On the march, Herkimer sent word to Gansevoort to prepare for a sortie against the enemy when he arrived, but delays along the trail doomed his plan. After he was reproached by his younger officers for moving too slowly, Herkimer incautiously proceeded toward his goal, and on 6 August, in a wooded ravine near Oriskany, he was ambushed by a portion of St. Leger's army. After a protracted and bitter battle with the enemy force, which consisted chiefly of Tories and Indians, Herkimer's men were compelled to retreat. During the fight, Herkimer had been wounded in the leg and had conducted the battle while seated under a tree calmly smoking his pipe. He was carried on a litter to his home thirty-five miles away, where an unskillful surgeon amputated his leg. Ten days later he died of complications from the operation, without knowing that he had slowed St. Leger's advance and given Benedict Arnold time to march to Fort Schuyler's relief, where he compelled St. Leger's withdrawal, thereby contributing to the defeat of John Burgoyne's army at Saratoga.

• Sources on Herkimer's life are not abundant, particularly primary sources. Information about the siege of Fort Schuyler and the battle of Oriskany is in Colonel Marinus Willet's descriptions and St. Leger's report to Burgoyne, both published in Henry B. Dawson, *Battles of the United States by Land and Sea*, vol. 2 (1858). See also Phoebe Strong Cowen, *The Herkimers and the Schuylers* (1903), and Christopher Ward, *War of the Revolution*, vol. 2 (1952).

PAUL DAVID NELSON

HERMAN, Augustine. *See* Herrman, Augustine.

HERMAN, Billy (7 July 1909–5 Sept. 1992), baseball player and manager, was born William Jennings Bryan Herman in New Albany, Indiana, the son of William Herman, Sr., a machinist; his mother's name is not known. Named for the perennial presidential candidate, William Jennings Bryan, he was the ninth of ten children. Like many farm boys of his generation, Herman played baseball for his school team and on occasional weekends for semiprofessional teams. Pitching his church team into a championship in 1927 won him a pair of World Series tickets. That same year Herman married Hazel Jean Steproe; they would have one child before they divorced in 1960. Also in 1927 he took a job with a Louisville, Kentucky, veneer manufacturing plant and played for the company team. This experience led to his being signed in 1928 by the Louisville Colonels of the Class AA American Association; he played a few games for the Colonels that season but spent most of the season farmed out to Vicksburg, Mississippi, of the Class D Cotton States League. Here he played second base and hit .332 in 106 games.

In 1929 Herman batted .329 in 138 games for Dayton, Ohio, of the Class B Central League and then returned to Louisville for 24 games in which he hit .323. This performance was enough to promote him to Louisville again for the entire 1930 season, in which he hit .305. The next year he was hitting .350 in September when he was purchased by the Chicago Cubs of the National League to replace Rogers Hornsby, who was in his last full year as a player. Hornsby, who was also the Cubs' manager, was fired in the summer of 1932, and Herman became the regular second baseman.

From 1932 through 1940 Herman was both the star and the stabilizing influence in the Cubs' infield. Most seasons he played every game. He made the National League All-Star team each year from 1934 through 1940, and his batting average for those games was a superb .433. In 1935 he led the league in total hits with 227, in doubles with 57, and in fielding average among the league's second basemen with .964. He led in fielding again in 1936 and 1938. He was not a home run hitter, but he amassed an abundance of extra-base hits, and in 1939 he led the league in triples with 18.

Herman's World Series record was unspectacular. The Cubs won the National League pennant three times during Herman's nine years in Chicago. In the 1932 World Series he hit only .222 in the New York Yankees' four-game sweep of the Cubs. In 1935 he led the Cubs in hitting (.333) as they lost to the Detroit Tigers, and in 1938 he hit only .188 in another loss to the Yankees.

Herman's contemporaries considered him to be far above average in the mental aspects of the game. His teammates often benefited from his uncanny ability to steal other teams' pitching signals and to hit behind the runner in hit and run situations. He was particularly adept at positioning himself against opposing hitters. Statistical evidence confirms the belief; Herman led the league's second basemen in total putouts seven times and in assists three times. Herman, paired with shortstop Billy Jurgis, was invariably among the leaders in double plays.

In 1941 Herman was traded to the Brooklyn Dodgers. Many reporters believed that the trade took place because the Cubs' manager, Jimmy Wilson, resented

Herman's close friendship with the Cubs' owner, William Wrigley, Jr. Herman played three full seasons with the Dodgers, hitting .291 in 1941, .256 in 1942, and .330 in 1943. Brooklyn won the National League pennant in 1941; but once again Herman hit poorly against the New York Yankees' pitching, hitting only .125. But in 1943 he was second only to Stan Musial for the league's batting championship. In 1942 and 1943 he was again chosen to the league All-Star team.

Herman served in the U.S. Navy in 1944 and 1945 and then played part of 1946 with Brooklyn. Later that season the Dodgers traded him to the Boston Braves, for whom he hit .306 in 75 games. In 1947 he served as playing manager of the Pittsburgh Pirates, playing in only 15 games and finishing in last place. By his own admission he tried too hard to be "one of the boys," and many on the team took advantage of his good nature. He lasted just one year at Pittsburgh.

For the next thirty years Herman coached in the major leagues, managed several minor league teams, and even played for teams in Minneapolis (1948) and Oakland (1950). In 1961 he married Frances Ann Antonucci. Late in the 1964 season he was given one more chance to manage a major league team, the Boston Red Sox. In two full seasons at Boston (1965–1966) he again had a losing record. His overall record as a major league manager was 189–274, with an unsatisfactory winning percentage of .408. After scouting for the Oakland Athletics from 1968 to 1974, he retired. He resided comfortably in Florida, enjoying his four grandchildren and pursuing his hobbies of golf and bridge. He was chosen for the National Baseball Hall of Fame in 1975. Several studies placed Herman among the ten best second basemen of all time and perhaps the best of all in the era of the 1930s and early 1940s.

Herman died of cancer in West Palm Beach, Florida.

• The best sources on Herman are the clipping file at National Baseball Library in Cooperstown, N.Y., and Martin Appel and Burt Goldblatt, *Baseball's Best: The Hall of Fame Gallery* (1977). Gene Karst and Martin J. Jones, Jr., *Who's Who in Professional Baseball* (1973), contains much on Herman's early playing days. John Thorn and Pete Palmer, eds., *Total Baseball*, 3d ed. (1993), has an abundance of statistical data. Lowell Reidenbaugh, *Cooperstown* (1983), stresses Herman's baseball intelligence. An obituary is in the *New York Times*, 7 Sept. 1992.

THOMAS L. KARNES

HERMAN, Pete (12 Feb. 1896–13 Apr. 1973), prizefighter, was born Peter Gulotta in New Orleans, Louisiana, the son of a Mississippi River banana carrier. When he was twelve years old, he worked as a shoeshine boy in a barbershop. The conversation of the shop's patrons sparked his interest in boxing, and he was encouraged to enter the ring by a local promoter, Dominick Tortorick, and a matchmaker, Red Walsh. Walsh became Herman's first manager. (In that era, boxers changed managers frequently, and Jerome Gargano, Doc Cutch, and Sammy Goldman would later manage Herman.) Pete adopted the ring name of a popular lightweight of the day, Kid Herman, and without any amateur boxing experience fought his first public bout as a professional on 30 September 1912 in New Orleans, holding Eddie Coulon to a six-round draw.

As was to be expected from someone so inexperienced, Herman's career started slowly, with one victory, two losses, and two draws in his first five bouts. The two losses were to Johnny Fisse, a local boxer who never attained championship caliber. Herman subsequently met Fisse six more times during the next two years, losing three more times before winning the last three. The diminutive (5′2″, 118 pounds) pugilist's first major opportunity came on 30 June 1914 when he fought Kid Williams, the world's bantamweight champion. Although the ten-round nontitle bout resulted in no decision, Herman won in the opinion of the newspaper reporters. Boxing primarily in New Orleans and in Memphis, Tennessee, Herman compiled a record of 38 wins, eight losses, five draws and two no decisions in 53 bouts by the end of 1915, earning him a rematch with Williams on 7 February 1916—this time with the title at stake. The 20-round bout ended in a draw. Eleven months later, in a third bout, Herman knocked Williams down twice, winning a close 20-round decision and the world bantamweight championship.

After winning the title, Herman stayed active in the ring, fighting 61 bouts from 1917 to 1920. Only one of those fights was for his title—a 20-round decision over Frankie Burns in New Orleans on 5 November 1917. Among his opponents in the nontitle matches were Johnny Coulon, Kid Williams, Jack Kid Wolfe, Memphis Pal Moore, Johnny Ertle, Joe Lynch, and Johnny Buff, all of whom were world champions at one time or another. In one of those bouts, both his boxing career and his life were severely altered. On 21 May 1917 he met Gussie Lewis in a six-round no-decision bout in Philadelphia, during which Herman was thumbed in the right eye and began losing his sight. Although the loss was gradual at first, it eventually led to total blindness in both eyes. After obtaining an exemption from the draft in 1917 as sole support of his family, he was reclassified in February 1918 and was accepted in the U.S. Naval Reserve by somehow passing the physical examination.

On 22 December 1920, in only his second title defense, Herman lost the championship to Joe Lynch on a 15-round decision at Madison Square Garden in New York City. Prior to the Lynch bout, Herman had signed to meet the world flyweight champion, Welshman Jimmy Wilde, on 13 January 1921 at the Royal Albert Hall in London. Wilde had an outstanding record with only one loss in 143 bouts and 99 of his victories by knockout. Herman traveled to England only to encounter a reluctant Wilde who had expected to fight for the bantamweight championship. Told that the prince of Wales was among the spectators, Wilde finally agreed to fight. Herman knocked out Wilde in the 17th round of the scheduled 20-round bout. The prince, who later became the duke of Windsor, became friendly with Herman and later visited him in New Orleans.

After winning five of seven bouts in the United States, Herman returned to London where he stopped Jim Higgins in 11 rounds, although he weighed in at one-half pound over the limit and forfeited $1,500 of his $10,000 purse. After the bout he immediately boarded a ship back to New York. On 25 July 1921, only three days after landing, he met Lynch in a rematch at Ebbets Field in Brooklyn and won back the title with a 15-round decision, earning $22,500 of the total gate receipts of $103,315. This was the first world bantamweight title bout to be broadcast on radio. Two months later Herman lost the title to Johnny Buff in New York by a 15-round decision. He fought six more times, after which his failing eyesight caused him to retire. In his last bout on 24 April 1922 he won a 10-round decision over Roy Moore in Boston, although he had lost most of his sight by this time.

Following his retirement, Herman purchased a nightclub in the French Quarter of New Orleans and managed it successfully for the remainder of his life, residing in an upstairs apartment. He also served as a member of the Louisiana State Athletic Commission. During his later years he spent quite a bit of money in futile attempts to restore his sight. An avid baseball fan, he claimed in a 1956 interview to have attended every World Series for the past 20 years accompanied by his best friend, Sam Saia, who would describe the action to him.

In 1959 he was elected to *The Ring* Boxing Hall of Fame and was rated by *The Ring* publisher and editor, Nat Fleischer, as one of the greatest bantamweights of all time, second only to George Dixon. His complete ring record is 144 bouts, 94 wins (21 by knockout), 26 losses, 14 draws, and 10 no decisions. Herman died in a hospital in New Orleans.

• Herman's complete ring record is in Herbert G. Goldman, ed., *The Ring 1986–1987 Record Book and Boxing Encyclopedia* (1987). Although contemporary newspaper reports are the best sources of details of his bouts, two articles in boxing periodicals provide insights into his life and some of his major bouts: Stanley Weston, "They Don't Build 'em That Way Anymore," *Boxing and Wrestling*, Apr. 1956, pp. 16–19, 62–64, and Ike Morales, "Pete Herman, at 71, Recalls," *The Ring*, May 1967, pp. 22–25, 35. Peter Heller, *In This Corner* (1973), includes an interview with Herman recorded in Oct. 1970 in which he reminisces about his career. Bert Randolph Sugar, *The 100 Greatest Boxers of All Time* (1984), presents an interesting one-page sketch of Herman's life. Jimmy Wilde, *The Art of Boxing* (c. 1925), contains a brief section in the preface describing his views of the controversial bout with Herman. For obituaries see Nat Loubet, "Ring Great Herman Dies at 77," *The Ring*, July 1973, pp. 26, 47; and the *New York Times*, 13 Apr. 1973.

JOHN GRASSO

HERMAN, Woody (16 May 1913–29 Oct 1987), jazz bandleader, reed player, and singer, was born Woodrow Charles Thomas Herrmann in Milwaukee, Wisconsin, the son of Otto C. Herrmann, a shoemaker,

and Myrtle Bartoszewicz. With his father's encouragement, the young Herrmann began performing in a kiddie revue at age eight. He tried playing piano and violin before settling on alto saxophone and clarinet. He also studied dance. Billed in vaudeville as the Boy Wonder of the Saxophone, he was performing regularly by age ten while attending a public school. He transferred to St. John's Cathedral Preparatory School, where teachers and administrators were willing to encourage a boy who sometimes worked late hours in show business.

By 1925 he became seriously interested in jazz, though it would be over a decade before his career turned in that direction. Throughout high school he played frequently throughout the Milwaukee area; during this period the spelling of his surname as "Herman" first appeared. In 1930 he added tenor saxophone to his reed instruments, influenced in particular by Coleman Hawkins.

In 1931 Herman dropped out of school to join Tom Gerun's dance band. Herman left Gerun's band in 1934 and played briefly with the dance bands of Harry Sosnick and Gus Arnheim before he joined bandleader Isham Jones, for whom he sang and played clarinet and saxophones, principally baritone. When Jones retired from touring in 1936, Herman and other of Jones's sidemen organized a cooperative ensemble called the Band That Plays the Blues. Herman, its leader, married Charlotte Neste in 1936; they had a daughter.

After an initial success at the Roseland ballrooms in Brooklyn and New York City, the Band That Plays the Blues became just another of the numerous not-quite-major big bands touring frequently. They had a long-standing contract with the Decca label, but their function was mainly that of dull house band, accompanying singers and making versions of pieces already recorded by better-known groups. The principal exception was the energetic blues "Woodchopper's Ball," recorded in April 1939; Herman's most requested, bestselling piece, it was a part of his musical identity, though, as he noted in his characteristically wry manner, he grew rather tired of it after the first 1,000 performances.

From November 1939 through the early 1940s, Herman held engagements at many prestigious locations, including the Panther Room of the Hotel Sherman in Chicago, the New Yorker Hotel and Paramount Theater in New York, and the Hollywood Palladium. He first recorded "Blue Flame," the band's theme song, in March 1941 and that September had a hit with a cover version of "Blues in the Night," which had just been recorded by Jimmie Lunceford's orchestra. The band also performed in the movies *What's Cookin'?* (1942), presenting a version of "Woodchopper's Ball," and *Wintertime* (1943).

A substantial overhaul of his personnel during the winter of 1943–1944 marked the end of the Band That Plays the Blues and the establishment of a big band that came to be known as Woody Herman's Herd, and retrospectively as his First Herd. In late 1943 bassist

Chubby Jackson joined the group and became its associate leader as well as a catalytic force. Between 1944 and 1946 Herman hired trumpeter, arranger, and composer Neal Hefti; trumpeters Pete Candoli, Conte Candoli (later replaced by trumpeter, composer, and arranger Shorty Rogers), and Sonny Berman; trombonist Bill Harris, whose eccentric improvisatory style was one of the band's greatest assets; tenor saxophonist Flip Phillips; pianist, arranger, and composer Ralph Burns; vibraphonist Margie Hyams (replaced by Red Norvo); guitarist Billy Bauer; drummer Dave Tough (replaced by Don Lamond); and singer Mary Ann McCall.

By this time Herman was together with Charlie Barnet, one of only two white bandleaders regularly playing black theaters. The First Herd secured a weekly network radio show for several months beginning in June 1944 and again from mid-October 1945 through July 1946. In the interim, they signed with Columbia Records and made a series of fine recordings. Sessions from late February 1945 included Herman's rough ballad singing on "Laura" and his joyful cover version of singer and saxophonist Louis Jordan's rhythm-and-blues song "Caldonia," together with the vigorously swinging instrumentals "Apple Honey" and "Northwest Passage."

As their popularity soared, the First Herd appeared in more films, and Igor Stravinsky composed the *Ebony Concerto* for Herman, who premiered the piece in March 1946 at Carnegie Hall and then recorded it, with Stravinsky conducting.

After a brief interlude to deal with personal problems, Herman established the Second Herd in October 1947. Financially, the Second Herd proved to be a disaster. The public evidently wanted tuneful swing, not an incorporation of bebop into a big-band setting, and Herman estimated that he lost more than $175,000 in a little over two years. Personally, it was a nightmare, with several of Herman's leading sidemen addicted to heroin, including the "four brothers": baritone saxophonist Serge Chaloff and tenor saxophonists Stan Getz, Zoot Sims, and Al Cohn. But musically, the Second Herd was arguably the greatest jazz big band of its era, achieving a reasonably consistent and timelessly fresh amalgamation of big-band swing and bebop that even Dizzy Gillespie's rival big band could not match.

The Second Herd's key pieces were Jimmy Guiffre's "Four Brothers" (1947) and Burns's "Early Autumn" (1948). "Four Brothers" derived from an orchestral experiment by Gene Roland, who had utilized the sound of four tenor saxophones; Giuffre's orchestration featured three tenors—Getz, Herbie Steward (soon replaced by Cohn), and Sims—plus baritone player Chaloff. "Early Autumn," a revision of Burns's rather pretentious "Summer Sequence" suite for the First Herd, featured Getz delivering the definitive cool jazz tenor saxophone solo. The four brothers (including Cohn), Herman, and trombonist Earl Swope may be seen soloing in the film short *Woody Herman and His Orchestra* (1948). Other key figures in this virtual all-star ensemble were Harris, Rogers, Lamond, McCall, trumpeter Ernie Royal (the first African American in Herman's band), and such later members as tenor saxophonist Gene Ammons, pianist Lou Levy, guitarist Jimmy Raney (replaced by vibraphonists Terry Gibbs, first, and then Milt Jackson), bassist Oscar Pettiford, and drummer Shadow Wilson (replaced by Shelly Manne).

After disbanding the Second Herd, Herman toured Cuba from December 1949 to January 1950 and the United States with a small group. He formed a Third Herd in spring 1950; among its later members was pianist and arranger Nat Pierce, whose orientation toward Count Basie's music helped make the Third Herd more accessible and acceptable to contemporary audiences than the Second Herd had been. Herman toured Europe for the first time in 1954, and in 1958 he took the band on a tour of South America sponsored by the State Department. In 1959 he toured widely with several small groups, briefly led an Anglo-American big band in England, and also assembled an alumni big band for the Monterey Jazz Festival in 1959.

Herman formed yet another big band, known as the Swinging Herd, in 1961. Key members were Pierce, trumpeter Bill Chase, drummer Jake Hanna, and tenor saxophonist Sal Nistico. The Swinging Herd's finest album is *Woody Herman 1963* (recorded in 1962), and this band may be seen in two self-titled television shows, "Woody Herman and his Swingin' Herd" (both 1963), hosted by jazz writer Ralph Gleason for KQED in San Francisco. In 1966 the group secured another State Department tour, visiting Africa and Eastern Europe.

At this point Herman became the object of an Internal Revenue Service prosecution that by all accounts could be described only as a vendetta. Manager Abe Turchen, a shady gambler who nonetheless had been vitally helpful in securing jobs for the band for over two decades, caused Herman's downfall by not paying Herman's income taxes or the bandmembers' withholding taxes from 1964 to 1966. Basing the undocumented earnings on Herman's best years of 1944 to 1946 and adding penalties, the IRS assessed Herman an absurdly large amount: $1.6 million. He paid weekly thereafter and was often destitute throughout the remainder of his life. But Herman accepted his predicament and kept at his career. The Herd toured England annually from 1966 into the mid-1970s and visited the Far East in 1970. Touring incessantly and maintaining a fondness for working with twentyish players, he acquired the nickname "Road Father."

Herman won a Grammy award in 1973 for the album *Giant Steps*, with its title track adapting John Coltrane's blisteringly fast and harmonically complex bebop composition to a big band setting. In 1974 the University of Houston established the Woody Herman Music Archives at its School of Music. In the following year a new rhythm section, including keyboard player Lyle Mays, helped to establish a pipeline for graduates of North Texas State University to join the band. Herman had been skeptical at first about jazz education, but he became more enthusiastic as he found such fine new instrumentalists.

A Carnegie Hall concert in 1976 celebrated Herman's fortieth anniversary as a bandleader. He toured Poland annually from 1976 to 1979 and visited other European countries during this period. His activities were interrupted in March 1977, when he fell asleep while driving and seriously crushed his leg in the ensuing accident. Still in a wheelchair that May, he received an honorary doctorate from the Berklee College of Music in Boston and resumed bandleading in June.

In 1980 Herman toured South America again, and he became the first white man to be honored as king of the Zulus during Mardi Gras in New Orleans. From late 1981 into 1982 he attempted to sustain his own nightclub at the Hyatt Regency Hotel in New Orleans, but that venture failed. He toured Europe and Australia in 1985, even as his health was deteriorating and the IRS was in the process of seizing his house and then renting it back to Herman and his daughter. The indefatigable Herman celebrated his fiftieth anniversary of bandleading with a concert in the Hollywood Bowl in July 1986. He collapsed and was hospitalized that November but resumed playing intermittently. The IRS nearly evicted him from his home in September 1987, during his fifth hospitalization because of heart disease and emphysema; he died seven weeks later in Los Angeles. The band continued to perform under Tiberi's leadership.

Musical analyst Gunther Schuller argues strongly and perhaps excessively for Herman's talents as a singer and instrumentalist. Most jazz fans would not rate Herman as an exceptional performer. Rather, his special gifts were less tangible, although no less substantial: a persistent youthfulness and hence musical freshness; the ability to give direction to a large and sometimes contentious group of instrumentalists; and an uncanny on-the-spot sense for musical editing, a talent to which his arrangers repeatedly testified. The outstanding documents of his work are the recordings of the sensationally energetic First Herd, blending swing and bop with some rather dated vaudeville antics thrown in, and those of the Second Herd, widely regarded as one of the finest jazz big bands ever.

• Tapes and transcripts of Herb Wong's interviews with Herman (Dec. 1978 and Jan. 1979) are at the Institute of Jazz Studies, Newark, N.J. For additional information on Herman's life and career see Woody Herman and Stuart Troup, *The Woodchopper's Ball: The Autobiography of Woody Herman* (1990); William D. Clancy, with Audree Coke Kenton, *Woody Herman: Chronicles of the Herds* (1995); Robert C. Kriebel, *Blue Flame: Woody Herman's Life in Music* (1995); and Gene Lees, *Leader of the Band: The Life of Woody Herman* (1995); Clancy, Kriebel, and Lees include numerous detailed remembrances from Herman's former sidemen. For a survey of his tenor saxophone soloists, see Alun Morgan, "Woody's Tenors," *Jazz Monthly* 6 (Sept. 1960): 4–7, (Oct. 1960): 13–15, 31, (Feb. 1961): 9–10. See also Amy Lee, "Will Keep Progressing: Woody," *Down Beat*, 3 Nov. 1950, pp. 1–4; Arnold Shaw, *The Street That Never Slept* (1971; repr. as *Fifty-second Street: The Street of Jazz*, 1977); Herb Nolan, "Woody Herman: Forty Years of the Nomadic Herd," *Down Beat*, 4 Nov. 1976, pp. 12–15, 37–39; Gary Giddins, *Rhythm-a-ning: Jazz Tradition and Innovation in the '80s* (1985); and Steve Voce, *Woody Herman* (1986). For musical analysis see Gunther Schuller, *The Swing Era: The Development of Jazz, 1930–1945* (1989). Catalogs of recordings are in James A. Treichel, *Keeper of the Flame: Woody Herman and the Second Herd, 1947–1949* (1978), which includes a detailed chronology of the band's activities. A discography is Dexter Morrill, *Woody Herman: A Guide to the Big Band Recordings, 1936–1987* (1990). An obituary is in the *New York Times*, 30 Oct. 1987.

BARRY KERNFELD

HERNDON, Alonzo Franklin (26 June 1858–21 July 1927), barber and businessman, was born in Social Circle, Georgia, the son of a white father (name unknown) and a slave mother, Sophenia Herndon. Born on a farm in Walton County, forty miles east of Atlanta, he was a slave for the first seven and a half years of his life and, in his own words, "was very near it for twenty years more." After emancipation, he worked as a laborer and peddler to help his family eke out a living in the hostile rural environment, where he was able to acquire only a few months of schooling. In 1878, with eleven dollars of savings, Herndon left his birthplace to seek opportunities elsewhere.

Settling in Atlanta in the early 1880s, he obtained employment as a journeyman barber and soon purchased his first barbershop. Herndon began building a clientele composed of the city's leading white lawyers, judges, politicians, and businessmen. By 1904 he owned three establishments; his shop at 66 Peachtree Street, outfitted with crystal chandeliers and gold fixtures, was said to be the largest and best barbershop in the region. According to the *New York World*, Herndon and his all-black barbering staff were "known from Richmond all the way to Mobile as the best barbers in the South." Herndon's success in barbering was spectacular and, as his earnings grew, he invested in real estate in Atlanta and in Florida.

In 1905 Herndon entered the field of insurance, placing his growing resources behind a failing mutual assistance association set up initially by a local minister to benefit his congregation and other black Atlantans. Herndon and several other men reorganized the association and incorporated it as the Atlanta Mutual Insurance Association. With Herndon playing a pivotal role as president and chief stockholder, the company expanded its assets from $5,000 in 1905 to over $400,000 by 1922 and achieved a reputation for safety and reliability. The firm reorganized as the Atlanta Life Insurance Company in 1922, and that same year achieved legal reserve status, a position enjoyed by only four other black companies at that time. With the added status of having met the state of Georgia's requirements for capitalization, Herndon was able to increase the size and variety of policies offered by the company and by 1924 had expanded its operations into seven other states. More than any other individual, he set the Atlanta operation on the way toward becoming one of the largest insurance enterprises among African Americans in the country.

Herndon's growing wealth and business position placed him among a group of progressive African Americans in Atlanta and elsewhere involved in economic, social, and civic endeavors to advance blacks. Although not widely heralded as a race leader, he was deeply interested in the economic and social welfare of African Americans. Herndon was particularly influenced by the ideas of Booker T. Washington and others who espoused hard work, thriftiness, and business development as means of race progress. In 1900 he was among the founding delegates of the National Negro Business League formed to promote entrepreneurship among African Americans. In 1913, in an address at Tuskegee Institute, Herndon insisted on the necessity of cooperative business efforts among African Americans, extolling the possibilities of amassing capital and providing job opportunities for youth. He told the audience, "My aim has been for several years to get as many of our people together to cooperate in business and along all lines as possible."

Herndon also demonstrated his concern for progress among African Americans in areas other than business. He shared, on some level, many of the aims of black leaders such as W. E. B. Du Bois for social and political advancement. Herndon was among the twenty-nine African Americans from throughout the country who assembled in 1905 near Buffalo, New York, to organize the Niagara Movement, the forerunner of the National Association for the Advancement of Colored People. In Georgia, he and other African-American leaders signed a memorial to protest disfranchisement measures passed by the state legislature in 1907. Herndon made donations to a host of local institutions and charities devoted to uplifting and advancing the black community.

Herndon's impact as businessman and civic leader was distinctively felt in Atlanta. He rose from slavery to become the head of a growing black enterprise and overcame poverty and illiteracy. In addition to Atlanta Life, located on Atlanta's famed Auburn Avenue, which was described by *Fortune Magazine* (Sept. 1956) as "the richest Negro Street in the World," Herndon's investments ranged from the first black-owned cemetery and loan association to the first black-owned bank and drug store. A visible reminder of his entrepreneurship is the three-story Herndon Building, which he built to help facilitate the settlement and growth of black businesses and professionals in the community.

A family man, Herndon married twice. His first marriage, in 1893, was to Adrienne Elizabeth McNeil, a professor at Atlanta University who died in 1910. This marriage produced Herndon's only child, Norris, who succeeded him as chief executive of the company and for forty years continued its solid growth as a respected enterprise. The second marriage, in 1912, was to Jessie Gillespie, a Chicago businesswoman. Both marriages had far-reaching impact on his life, bringing culture, refinement, and education into his household and enhancing his community standing and business position.

After Herndon's death in Atlanta, the *New York World* compared his life to that of Booker T. Washington, stating, "It was another whimsical tale of adventure and conquest, another graphic story of spectacular rise from abject poverty to a position of financial security and unquestioned influence, another arresting and gripping 'Up From Slavery.'" He was praised in the *Atlanta Independent*, a local black-owned paper, as a man "who was as great in the uses of his wealth as he was in accumulating it." Writing in *Crisis* magazine (Sept. 1927), Du Bois described him as "an extraordinary man [who] illustrates at once the possibilities of American democracy and the deviltry of color prejudice." Also noting Herndon's status as the wealthiest black man in Atlanta, Du Bois wrote, "This representative of Negro America lies dead today and buried in a separate Negro cemetery, which he helped found, but if ever an American 'burst his birth's invidious bar' that man was Alonzo Herndon."

• The Herndon Family Papers, consisting of photographs, letters, business receipts, and other items, are in the Herndon Home, a house museum in Atlanta. Complete assessments of Alonzo Herndon are in Alexa Benson Henderson, *Atlanta Life Insurance Company: Guardian of Black Economic Dignity* (1990), and "Alonzo Herndon and Black Insurance in Atlanta," *Atlanta Historical Bulletin* 21 (1977): 34–47. See also "Postscript by W. E. B. Du Bois," *Crisis* 33 (1947): 234, and the article in the *New York World*, 31 July 1927.

ALEXA BENSON HENDERSON

HERNDON, William Henry (25 Dec. 1818–18 Mar. 1891), lawyer and biographer, was born in Greensburg, Kentucky, the son of Archer G. Herndon, a farmer, tavern keeper, and merchant, and Rebecca Day Johnson. Herndon's family moved to Illinois in 1820; in 1825 his father opened a tavern in Springfield, later expanding his business to include a general store. In 1836 Herndon briefly attended the preparatory department of Illinois College in Jacksonville, Illinois. Later, he worked as a clerk at a store in Springfield, joining Abraham Lincoln and others as roommates in a large room above the store. Herndon married Mary J. Maxey in 1840; they had six children before she died in 1861. He married Anna Miles in 1862; they had two children.

Herndon read law with Lincoln and his partner, Stephen T. Logan. Lincoln and Herndon became law partners almost immediately after Herndon was admitted to the Illinois bar in December 1844. Their partnership lasted until 1861 when Lincoln left for Washington to become president. During those seventeen years, Herndon complemented Lincoln in almost every way—a Democratic newspaper would later describe him as "Lincoln's Man Friday." Herndon was the office manager, attending to the details Lincoln disliked; he tended to stay in Springfield while Lincoln rode circuit; he favored philosophical discourse while Lincoln preferred an earthy anecdote. It is difficult to specify Herndon's influences on Lincoln; theirs was a relationship that drew its closeness from daily contact, not from singular conversations. Herndon himself would later describe their partnership as one in which he did the reading while Lincoln did the thinking.

Herndon was active in Illinois politics in his own right, and later on behalf of Lincoln. Initially, he was a Whig, concerned about the underprivileged, slaves, and women. He was a staunch advocate of temperance, in spite of his own later problems with excessive drinking. As mayor of Springfield in 1854 he supported the beginning of a public school system and local prohibition, being so strongly in favor of temperance that he was not reelected. He moved to the Republican party in 1856, which he supported with great public enthusiasm though he had private doubts about the choice of John C. Frémont as its presidential candidate. The first Republican governor of Illinois, William H. Bissell, appointed Herndon one of three state bank commissioners in February 1857, an office he held until its abolition in 1865.

Herndon was an avid reader and letter writer. He corresponded with a number of leading reformers, including Theodore Parker, Charles Sumner, and Lyman Turnbull. He appeared to advocate whatever philosophy he had read most recently, and he seemed to need the correspondence with eastern leaders to ratify his own importance.

For more than a decade after Lincoln's death in 1865, Herndon could find little direction for his life. He struggled to define his own life in terms of Lincoln's. At first he was driven to collect information about Lincoln, primarily through interviews of people in Illinois, Indiana, and Kentucky who had known the assassinated president. He proposed to some publishers a full-length biography based on a series of lectures in 1865 and 1866, the fourth of which provoked a torrent of criticism. In it Herndon reported that Lincoln had loved only one woman in his life, Ann Rutledge; her death drove Lincoln into a depression that led to his lifelong struggle with melancholy. Herndon insisted that his version was a truth that he told to protect Lincoln from inappropriate hagiography. Herndon also believed that Lincoln's greatness came from his "westernness." But the hostile reaction to his lectures prompted Herndon to lose interest in the biography. With Herndon's initial interest in and time spent speaking about Lincoln, his law practice was diminishing to almost nothing. He now turned to farming on land he inherited on his father's death. But poor management, excessive drinking, and the depression of 1873 forced him to sell off most of his land and much of his Lincoln material to pay debts.

In 1881 Herndon stopped drinking and tried in vain to resume his law practice. Fortuitously, he began writing to Jesse W. Weik, who had expressed an interest in Lincoln. Together they agreed to complete a biography of Lincoln. Weik traveled and researched to fill the gaps in Herndon's memory; he also edited Herndon's extravagant prose. The three-volume biography, *Herndon's Lincoln: The True Story of a Great Life*, finally appeared in 1889. Unfortunately, the publisher went bankrupt shortly afterward for other reasons. Although the initial public reaction was favorable, Herndon disliked the edition, saying that it contained many errors. He died on his farm just outside of Springfield before a second edition could be published.

The biography is almost entirely a book of Herndon's reminiscences of his association with Lincoln in the prepresidential years. Herndon wrote to tell the truth about Lincoln, believing that the truth would only ensure the president's greatness. Evaluations of the work have changed as the craft of writing history has evolved. Professional historians have castigated the book for factual errors, in particular in reporting that Lincoln's mother was illegitimate, that Lincoln loved only Ann Rutledge, that Lincoln failed to appear at his first wedding to Mary Todd, and that Lincoln was not a Christian. Others have seen the work as the forerunner to oral histories because it relied so heavily on Herndon's interviews with people who had known Lincoln personally. The book remains an unmatched source of descriptions and anecdotes about Lincoln. No other writer has contributed as much to the public's image of the sixteenth president; no one has so vividly described his personal characteristics.

• The Library of Congress holds the William Henry Herndon–Jesse William Weik Collection of correspondence between the two authors. The best source of additional information about Herndon is David Donald's biography, *Lincoln's Herndon* (1948), which contains a list of manuscript sources and of Herndon's published writings. For a detailed account of Herndon's financial setbacks see Gary Lee Erickson, "The Last Years of William Henry Herndon," *Journal of the Illinois State Historical Society* 67 (1974): 101. An obituary is in the *Chicago Tribune*, 19 Mar. 1891.

WALTER F. PRATT, JR.

HERNE, Chrystal Katharine (16 June 1882–19 Sept. 1950), actress, was born in Dorchester, Massachusetts, the daughter of James A. Herne (originally A'Herne), a playwright, actor, and director, and Katharine Corcoran, an actress. Herne's father was dubbed the American Ibsen for his pioneer work in bringing realism to theater. Herne's Irish-born mother was his adviser, leading lady, and inspiration. Chrystal was named after the heroine of *Hearts of Oak* (1879) and its star, her mother. The melodrama, written by her father in collaboration with David Belasco, catapulted the struggling actor-playwright to fame and financial security. With its proceeds he purchased Herne Oaks, the family estate near Boston where Chrystal spent her early childhood. When she was about ten, the family's income decreased, and they relocated to Convent Avenue in upper Manhattan.

Despite their limited schooling, Herne's parents were well read, especially in contemporary literature. Among their close friends they counted Hamlin Garland, who won a Pulitzer Prize in 1922, Augustus Thomas, and Israel Zangwill. Chrystal was the model for Zangwill's portrait of the high-spirited Allegra in

Mantle of Elijah; the pointed chin, quick emotions, "fascinating femininity," and half-awakened ambition were all reminiscent of Chrystal.

At sixteen, Herne joined her parents and older sister, Julie, on the professional stage as "the lovely and lovable" Sue Hardy in the premiere of *The Reverend Griffith Davenport*, her father's Civil War melodrama. The play opened at the Lafayette Square Theatre in Washington, D.C., on 16 January 1899 and had a short run. On 24 October 1899, Herne's father's *Sag Harbor* premiered at the Park Theatre in Boston. Chrystal (as Jane Cauldwell) and Julie played supporting roles. For the New York premiere at the Republic Theatre on 27 September 1900, Lionel Barrymore joined the cast as Jane Cauldwell's love interest.

Her "tall lily" beauty (according to Thomas), clear diction, and subtle expression of emotions won critical acclaim. Coached in the new realism, she approached the script with intelligence and imagination, inventing scenarios for the character's offstage life. George Tyler was so impressed with her acting that he invited her to join his touring company, but she declined.

After her father's death in 1901, the family troupe dissolved. In the 1901–1902 season, Herne performed in her father's *Shore Acres*, played the lead in *Sag Harbor*, and agreed to join E. H. Sothern's company. She was assigned understudy and bit parts, then graduated to the Player Queen in *Hamlet* and Huguette in *If I Were King*. But she rankled at these secondary roles and accepted Nat C. Goodwin's invitation to play Hippolyta in *A Midsummer Night's Dream*. Clyde Fitch cast her as his leading lady in *Major André* in November 1903 opposite Arnold Daly. Both plays had disappointing runs.

Daly remembered her when he assembled his innovative Shaw repertory (1905–1906) and offered her star billing. Although *Candida*, *You Never Can Tell*, and *John Bull's Other Island* were well received, *Mrs. Warren's Profession* was closed in New Haven, and in New York Daly was arrested for indecency. Herne left for a London debut at the Lyric Theatre in *The Jury of Fate* (1906), a short-lived drama, but returned to rave reviews as Raïna in Daly's production of Shaw's *Arms and the Man*. Late in 1906 the Chicago New Theatre invited the actress to star in *Margaret Fleming*, her father's masterpiece, which had been neglected for seventeen years. The role of the woman who adopts her husband's illegitimate child had been written expressly for Herne's mother.

Chrystal Herne proved her versatility and talent in a series of popular dramas including Zangwill's *The Melting Pot* (1909), Thomas's *As a Man Thinks* (1911; opposite John Mason) and *Arizona* (1913), and Harley Granville-Barker's production of *The Trojan Women* (1915), in which she played Cassandra. In George Scarborough's *At Bay* (1913) and Harvey O'Higgins and Harriet Ford's *Polygamy* (1914), she was a much-put-upon heroine, what she called a "sobbing lady." In W. Somerset Maugham's *Our Betters* (1917), a satire on title-hunting American women, she became a "'perfectly ripping' little siren" (*Herald*). She pre-

pared for months to play a rural black washerwoman, the tragic lead in *Roseanne* (1923). She believed that the subject matter would open the theater for African Americans. Although white actors premiered on Broadway, two all-black troupes, one with Charles Gilpin, toured this "play with spirituals." In *Expressing Willie* (1924), a popular farce by Rachel Crothers about a music teacher and a toothpaste manufacturer, she impressed the critics with her rendition of a Liszt rhapsody.

She lived for the theater, with "no friends, no parties, no beaux" ("I Remember Me") until she met Harold Stanley Pollard, a Boston Brahmin. After a passionate courtship, they married in Los Angeles in August 1914, while she was touring. Pollard, a Harvard graduate and longtime aide to Joseph Pulitzer, became a noted editorial writer with the *Evening World* and the *World-Telegram*. They remained devoted to each other. They had no children.

Stardom arrived with *Craig's Wife*, a Pulitzer Prize–winning drama by George Kelly (1887–1974), about an indomitable, manipulative wife whose dedication to appearances destroys her marriage. The drama opened on 12 October 1925 at the Morosco Theatre. James Herne's innovation in *Shore Acres* had been a three-minute silent close as Uncle Nat Berry, played by the playwright, tidied up the room for the night. *Craig's Wife* ended with three silent minutes as Mrs. Craig, played by Herne, crumbled rose petals on her immaculate carpets.

Although critical reaction to her performances remained positive, her last productions were not even minor successes. In Lynn Starling's *Skin Deep* (1927) she was a shrew. Lawrence Langner's *These Modern Women*, a caricature of feminists that opened on 14 February 1928, was followed by *The Gray Fox* (1928), a biodrama of Prince Machiavelli, in which she played the strong-willed Caterina Sforza. Her last role was Beatrice Crandall in *A Room in Red and White* in January 1936. She died in Boston of cancer.

Chrystal Herne loved comedy, but she was best known for her cold aristocrats. Alexander Woollcott wrote that this "beautiful, unfailing actress . . . [was] distinguished by the . . . platinum fineness of her every performance" (*World*, 13 Oct. 1925). George M. Cohan, playing opposite her in *The Acquittal*, judged her "one of the greatest emotional actresses on our stage." Critics blamed mediocre plays for her indifferent fame.

• The major biographical source, Chrystal Herne's unpublished autobiography, "I Remember Me," and miscellaneous documents are in the Art Library, a division of the Benjamin S. Rosenthal Library, Queens College, City University of New York. Photographs, reviews, programs, and articles are on file at the Billy Rose Theatre Collection of the New York Public Library, Performing Arts Research Center at Lincoln Center. Daniel Blum's *A Pictorial History of the American Theatre* (1953) offers an impressive photographic record. Herne family documents are located in the Harvard Theatre Collection at the Widener Library, Harvard University, and the Herbert J. Edwards Collection, Folger Library, University of Maine, Orono. Other sources for the Herne family are John Perry, *James A. Herne: The American Ibsen* (1978); Herbert J. Edwards and Julie A. Herne, *James A. Herne: The Rise of Realism in the American Drama* (1964); and Julie Herne's biographical essay in *Shore Acres and Other Plays* (1928). Obituaries are in the *New York Times* and *Boston Herald*, both 20 Sept. 1950.

GLENDA FRANK

HERNE, James A. (1 Feb. 1839–2 June 1901), actor and playwright, was born James A'Herne in Cohoes, New York, the son of Patrick A'Herne and Ann Temple, Irish immigrants. At age thirteen James was put to work in the hardware store that employed his father, and later he worked in a brush factory. In 1859, after a stint with the barnstorming Coney and Webb Company, who produced "dog dramas" starring well-trained canines, he was hired by Troy's Adelphi Theater, playing in *Uncle Tom's Cabin* and a variety of other plays. At this time he changed his name to James A. Herne when a theater manager suggested that removing the apostrophe would make his name more suitable for the stage.

Over the next few years, Herne acted in supporting roles in Albany, Washington, D.C., and Baltimore. From 1863 to 1866 he remained at Ford's New Theater in Washington, D.C., and developed a specialization in sailor parts. In 1864 he also played at Philadelphia's Walnut Street Theater and toured the West with the Susan Denin Company.

At Walnut Street Theater he performed opposite Lucille Western, and in 1866 he married Lucille's sister, Helen. He played Helen's leading man for several seasons, but he and Helen divorced in 1868. He then performed with Lucille from 1868 to 1870. The precise nature of his relationship with Lucille remains clouded; they may have been married.

One of Herne's greatest roles at this time was the villainous Bill Sykes in an adaptation of *Oliver Twist* by Charles Dickens, Herne's favorite author. Herne played a number of colorful Dickensian roles throughout his career, and the British novelist influenced the nature of the plays he later wrote.

In 1869 Herne became actor-manager at New York City's Grand Opera House, where he shared the stage with Lucille until they parted in 1870. In 1874 Herne moved to San Francisco, where impresario Tom Maguire hired him to manage and act at the New Theater. Herne's first play, *Charles O'Malley, the Irish Dragoon* (1874), based on Charles Lever's novel, premiered there. After the theater closed, in 1876 he managed another Maguire venture, the Baldwin Academy of Music. Two years later Herne married Katharine Corcoran, a talented and intelligent actress who had a positive effect on his career and starred in most of his later plays. They had four children, two of whom became famous actresses.

Herne collaborated with another Californian, David Belasco, on a series of adaptations from novels and plays. These included *Marriage by Moonlight* (renamed *Hap-Hazard*), *Within an Inch of His Life*, *The Millionaire's Daughter*, and their biggest success, *Chums*, a sentimental melodrama of New England life, all written in 1879. (Herne did not know that Belasco had taken the story for *Chums* from an 1865 British script and was later surprised to find himself caught in a plagiarism suit.) The realistic touches of *Chums* included a baby and an actual multicourse dinner, both of which became familiar Herne devices. A failure in San Francisco, the play became a hit in Chicago, where it was titled *Hearts of Oak*. It toured widely, earning Herne $100,000. Although conventionally melodramatic in most regards, its realistic depiction of average Americans suggests an improvement in American playwriting.

Herne and Belasco parted company following a dispute; henceforth Herne wrote alone. His next play was *The Minute Men of 1774–1775* (1886), a melodrama starring Katharine Herne as a feminist individualist. (In the face of public discomfort, Herne revised the ending in which the white heroine married an Indian.) The play ultimately lost Herne his *Hearts of Oak* fortune.

In 1881 the Hernes moved to Ashmont, Massachusetts. After about a decade, they moved to New York City, where Herne was hired to direct Broadway plays for Abraham Erlanger. During the last two decades of his life, Herne wrote a number of essentially antiromantic plays, most of them set in New England. The best include *Drifting Apart* (1888), a temperance drama involving fisherfolk; *Margaret Fleming* (1890); *Shore Acres* (1892); *The Reverend Griffith Davenport* (1899), an antiwar Civil War drama that dealt seriously with the slavery issue; and *Sag Harbor* (1899), which began as a new version of *Hearts of Oak* but evolved into an independent work. The most commercially successful were the realistic domestic comedy-dramas with Yankee character roles, *Shore Acres* (which made Herne a millionaire) and *Sag Harbor*.

Herne's plays included a substantial complement of his socially progressive—even radical—ideas, including his belief in the single-tax theory of Henry George (1839–1897), whose philosophy he expounded in public lectures. In all his work he was an activist. He fought for women's rights and the establishment of an actors' union and against the Theatrical Syndicate.

Herne may be considered a leader in the development of American realism because of his believable representation of average American citizens, his strikingly naturalistic stage representations, his abandonment of conventions such as soliloquies, asides, and overtly villainous characters, the relative plotlessness of his plays, and his preoccupation with important, if subtly stated, ideas. *Shore Acres*, for example, deals with feminism, agnosticism, and evolutionism. In his essay, "Art for Truth's Sake in the Drama," Herne described the purpose of drama as the expression of "some *large* truth. . . . Truth is not always beautiful, but in art for truth's sake it is indispensable."

Margaret Fleming was the first so-called "Ibsenist" American play, although Herne probably was not influenced directly by Ibsen. The realist writer Hamlin

Garland, an important promoter of Herne's work, introduced him to the work of the major European writers of the day. Many Victorian-era spectators and critics were shocked by *Margaret Fleming*, which not only revealed a character suffering from delirium tremens but also depicted a woman who, after discovering that her husband has had an affair, accepts his illegitimate child. Audiences gasped at the scene in which she began to unbutton her blouse to suckle the offspring.

Herne was famous for his restrained acting style. At a time when black characters (typically played by white actors) were broadly burlesqued, he brought three-dimensionality to a black character in Clay M. Greene and Joseph R. Girsmer's *The New South* (1893). One of the finest directors of his day, he was remarkable for his convincingly realistic mise-en-scenes, atmospheric lighting (in which he was a pioneer), and beautifully integrated ensembles. He directed not only his own nonconformist plays, but also those of other playwrights, including successful commercial fluff such as *The Country Circus* (1891), a Klaw (Marc Klaw) & Erlanger–produced spectacle, which offered the novel touch of creating a circus atmosphere by seating spectators in onstage bleachers. He also directed Israel Zangwill's *Children of the Ghetto* (1899), noteworthy for its depiction of Orthodox Judaism.

Herne was acting in *Sag Harbor* in Chicago when illness forced him to return to New York City, where he died. Although his plays do not justify his being called "the American Ibsen," when contrasted with the plays of his contemporaries, they stand out for their realistic qualities.

• Herne's papers were destroyed in a fire, but there are Herne letters in the Arthur Hobson Quinn Collection, University of Pennsylvania Library; the Hamlin Garland Collection, University of Southern California Library; and the Houghton Library, Harvard University. Herne's plays are collected in Mrs. James A. Herne, ed., *Shore Acres and Other Plays* (1928), and Arthur Hobson Quinn, ed., *The Early Plays of James A. Herne* (1963). The best biography is John Perry, *James A. Herne: The American Ibsen* (1978). See also Herbert A. Edwards and Julie J. Herne, *James A. Herne: The Rise of Realism in the American Drama* (1964).

SAMUEL L. LEITER

HERON, Matilda Agnes (1 Dec. 1830–7 Mar. 1877), actress, was born in County Londonderry, Ireland, the daughter of John Heron, a lumber merchant, and Mary Loughlin. In 1843 John Heron brought his wife and five children to Philadelphia, Pennsylvania, where Matilda attended a private academy and was taught elocution by Peter Richings. She convinced him to train her for the stage and at age twenty-one made her acting debut as Bianca in Henry Hart Milman's tragedy *Fazio* at the Walnut Street Theatre in Philadelphia. For the next two years she had moderate success in stock companies in places like Washington, D.C., and Boston. Her first role on the New York stage was that of Lady Macbeth at the Bowery Theatre in August 1852. She remained at that theater for several months in various leading roles.

In 1853 Heron went to California, where she was extremely successful, despite the difficulty of the journey in that day (there are indications that her manager may have died along the way). Afterward she went to London and Paris, where she saw *La Dame aux Camelias* and was inspired to do her own translation. Heron returned to the Walnut Street Theatre to debut her *Camille* but had little success with it there or elsewhere until she went to St. Louis in January 1856. Her success thereafter was such that a year later, on 22 January 1857, Heron debuted *Camille* at Wallack's Theatre in New York City, where the response was astounding. The *New York Times*, which spoke almost exclusively of Heron's performance rather than of the play as a whole, said, "In every careless word, there is the inspiration of genius, the vivifying power and grace of originality" and proclaimed her "the greatest actress of the age," comparing her favorably to the popular French actress Rachel (23 Jan. 1857).

It was the role of Camille that propelled Heron to fame and the one on which her reputation rested for the remainder of her life. Her acting style, always considered emotional and unpredictable, was perfectly suited to Camille. Heron's performance, according to theater historian T. Allston Brown, "showed morbid passion in its deepest form, unrelieved by French graciousness and French charm" (p. 491). *Camille*'s initial run went forty-five nights, but it was revived many times over the next few years before the public tired of it. By Heron's own account she had performed the role over seven hundred times before the end of 1860, and she considered it a work of "powerful fascination, poetic interest, and immortal life" (quoted in Hutton, *Plays and Players*, p. 163).

Riding on the success of *Camille*, Heron was able to make herself known in other roles as well, including Medea in her own translation of Legouvé's play. She also wrote several of her own plays, the most successful of which was *The Belle of the Season*, called one of the original "society plays" of the 1860s. Despite its mediocre popularity, *Belle* was Heron's personal favorite, and she even said that she wanted "Belle of the Season" written on her tombstone.

Heron continued acting in other traditional stock heroine roles and in the 1860s had several successful tours across the country and in Europe. *Camille* was her biggest hit everywhere, except in London, where she did only slightly better as Rosalie Lee in *New Year's Eve* at the Lyceum.

Romantic acting was the style when Heron first took the stage, and her passion and tempestuousness, as well as her unpredictability and disdain for tradition, captured the country's attention and helped to usher in a new style. She has been labeled "naturalist" by more recent scholars, and she paved the way for the twentieth-century "realist" actors who were to follow. More uncontrolled and wild than those actresses who preceded and followed her, Heron was characterized by "an intensity and passion in her performances which, at times, were magnificent and carried everything before them" (Hutton, *Curiosities*, pp. 83–84).

Her impulsive departures from traditional style prompted one critic to call Heron "a superb *artiste* who holds the traditions of the stage in the palm of her hand, and strangles them when they strive to impede the free exercise of her genius."

Heron was married twice, the first time in 1854 in California to Henry Herbert Byrne, a marriage that lasted about a month. In 1857, at the height of her career, she married Robert Stoepel, shortly after he debuted his "Matilda Heron March" during a production of *Camille*. This marriage also eventually ended in divorce, but their daughter Hélène (known on stage as Bijou Heron) became a successful actress in her own right.

Heron's fortunes went downhill in the late 1860s and 1870s. Her popularity among her fellow performers is evidenced by their attendance at a benefit in her honor given in 1872. The third and fourth acts of *Camille* were presented; Edwin Booth, Augustin Daly's company, Lester Wallack's company, Charles Backus, Sheridan and Mack (sketch artists), Rollin Howard, and the Majiltons, an eccentric vaudeville dancing act, all performed. The performance lasted more than five hours.

Unfortunately, the goodwill of her friends and the large amount of money she made from *Camille* was not enough to support her in her later years, and Heron was forced to teach acting, influencing young actresses such as Agnes Ethel and her own daughter Bijou. Her last performance was in 1876, when she played Medea in a benefit for her daughter. At the age of forty-six Heron died in New York City after an unsuccessful hemorrhoid operation.

• Laurence Hutton, *Curiosities of the American Stage* (1891) and *Plays and Players* (1875), and T. Allston Brown, *A History of the New York Stage* (1903), are very informative as to Heron's career, as is Alberta Lewis Humble, "Matilda Heron, American Actress" (Ph.D. diss., Univ. of Illinois, 1959). George C. D. Odell, *Annals of the New York Stage*, vols. 6–10 (1931–1938), documents Heron's New York appearances. Obituaries are in the *New York Times*, the *New York Herald*, and the *New York Sun*, all 8 Mar. 1877.

SUSAN KATTWINKEL

HERR, Daniel (11 Feb. 1917–28 Sept. 1990), journalist and publisher, was born in Huron, Ohio, the son of William Patrick Herr, a worker in the railroad industry, and Wilhelmina Stryker. Herr was raised in a devoutly Roman Catholic family and graduated from Fordham University, receiving a B.A. in 1938. He served in the U.S. Army in World War II, rising from the rank of private to major; severely wounded in action in the Buna campaign in 1942, he was awarded the Silver Star for gallantry. Following the war he worked as a reporter for the *New York Daily News* while freelancing for *Life*, *Coronet*, and the *Saturday Evening Post*. In 1948 he was named vice president of the Thomas More Association, a nonprofit organization founded in Chicago in 1938 by John C. Tully "to promote wider distribution of Catholic books and to combat the vicious effects of modern literature." The Thomas More Association sponsored a book club along with a book shop in Chicago, but it was best known as the publisher of *Books on Trial*, a monthly journal offering reviews of religious and secular literature from a Roman Catholic perspective.

In 1950 Herr launched a monthly column, "Stop Pushing," that became a highly popular yet often controversial feature in *Books on Trial*. The following year he replaced Tully as president of the Thomas More Association. In his column as in other forums, he persistently urged Catholics to turn from critiques of American culture to a more positive, even apostolic commitment to their own traditions. "When Catholic organizations and newspapers beat the drums against bad literature," he wrote in 1950, "let them also sound off for more parish libraries, for more reading and study groups, for planned efforts to induce more Catholics and non-Catholics to read worthwhile books. . . . we won't accomplish much if we try to promote badly-written pious literature, simply because it is not morally bad." Herr's position was characteristic of the liberal Catholicism that emerged in the the 1950s. While publications such as *Commonweal* and the *Catholic Worker* had flourished for several decades, the "Catholic revival" they promoted was largely indebted to European sources or to American converts to Catholicism. An Irish-American, Herr belonged to a generation of Catholics who had demonstrated their full "Americanism" in World War II yet remained committed to the unique traditions of the church, even when they seemed to clash with secularist values.

Like many other liberal Catholic writers, educators, and politicians of the 1950s, Herr conducted campaigns on several fronts. He objected to the militant, triumphalist Catholicism and conservative political views of many prominent Catholics, including Thomas More Association founder Tully. At the same time, while condemning the postwar neo-nativism associated with Paul Blanshard, author of several bestselling attacks on the church, Herr cautioned his readers not to react "smugly to this new propaganda drive and work ourselves into a position of resenting and fighting all discussion and criticism." Although the middle ground sought by Herr and many Catholic liberals in the 1950s proved elusive, the period witnessed a renaissance in American Catholic literature that Herr staunchly encouraged.

In 1957 *Books on Trial* was renamed the *Critic*; over the next five years the magazine heralded the work of a new generation of authors, including Brian Friel, Daniel Berrigan, S.J., and Andrew M. Greeley, while continuing to provide a forum for the work of well-established writers such as Caroline Gordon, Flannery O'Connor, and Thomas Merton.

Herr assumed the duties of publisher of the *Critic* in 1962, just as Vatican Council II was convening in Rome. Under his leadership, the magazine staunchly advocated the reforms endorsed by the council. In the heady days of the mid-1960s the *Critic* was one of the liveliest, feistiest publications of any kind in the United States. While maintaining its Catholic identity, the

Critic explored issues of racism and poverty and provided a forum for Catholic critics of the escalating U.S. presence in Southeast Asia. Yet throughout the tumultuous 1960s and beyond the *Critic* remained primarily a journal of literary and cultural criticism. At the height of its popularity, in the late 1960s, the magazine boasted a circulation of 35,000. By the 1970s, however, the *Critic's* increasingly irreverent tone—a reflection of Herr's curmudgeonly sense of humor—alienated many of its readers who, like American Catholics generally, harbored ambivalent views as to the legacy of Vatican II. Some readers were particularly offended by the *Critic's* satirical editorial cartoons.

Despite its identity as a journal of lay opinion, the *Critic* had always enjoyed a large readership among priests, nuns, and other religious. "Our biggest readers were nuns," Herr reported in 1985. "One of the reasons is that they couldn't do much else. But then their whole lives opened up, and they went and did everything else, and books became a smaller part of their life. Then a lot of nuns and priests left the church." In a 1976 *New York Times* commentary, Herr argued that many American nuns had grown frustrated from a lack of appreciation; he concluded that the issue of women's ordination had to be resolved before other challenges facing American Catholicism could be addressed. The rise of neoconservatism among many formerly liberal Catholics further eroded the *Critic's* readership base in the late 1970s. In 1981 the magazine suspended publication but was revived in a more limited format in 1985.

While Herr's national reputation was founded on his stewardship of the *Critic*, in Chicago he was deeply respected as well for his leadership of the Thomas More Association. "They live by their wits," Greeley noted of Herr and his associates in 1985, "and they try things that are original, that a religious publishing house would be afraid to try because it might offend readers or church authorities." In evaluating Herr's contribution, Joel Wells, the long-time vice president of the Thomas More Association and coeditor with Herr of several books, explained in 1990, "He really stirred things up, especially in the Catholic press. His real genius was as a literary football coach. He got more out of people than they knew they had in them." Wells also observed that at its peak, under Herr's leadership, the *Critic* "had gathered perhaps the most sophisticated and highly educated general readership of any Catholic magazine in the history of the country."

Herr died in Chicago. He had never married.

• Herr's *Stop Pushing* (1961) offers a representative sample of his columns for the *Critic* from the 1950s. He also coedited several books with Joel Wells, including *Harvest* (1960), *Bodies and Souls* (1961), and *Through Other Eyes: Some Impressions of American Catholicism by Foreign Visitors from 1777 to the Present* (1965). An obituary is in the *Chicago Tribune*, 30 Sept. 1990.

JAMES T. FISHER

HERRESHOFF, James Brown (18 Mar. 1834–5 Dec. 1930), inventor, was born at Popasquash Neck near Bristol, Rhode Island, the son of Charles Frederick Herreshoff and Julia Ann Lewis. He and his brothers, John Herreshoff and Nathaniel Herreshoff, became famous for their many contributions to the design and construction of sail and steam yachts, including five defenders of the America's Cup from 1893 to 1903. At the age of nineteen James entered Brown University, where he majored in chemistry. He graduated in 1853 and found an outlet for his creative aptitude at the Rumford Chemical Works outside Providence, Rhode Island. In two years he rose to superintendent, having developed an acid phosphate and a baking powder; the patent rights to the latter became the foundation of his financial success. In 1863 he began the manufacture of fish oil and fertilizer on Prudence Island, using an oil press of his own invention. He exported the fish oil and sold the fertilizer in New England. Soon he added other products—paints, dyes, toothpaste, and pharmaceuticals.

John and Nathaniel Herreshoff founded their boatbuilding company in 1878. While the Herreshoff yards were expanding, James contributed a number of ideas. A sliding seat for rowboats, still used in racing shells, was not of much help, but an antifouling paint and lapstreak construction for small hulls enhanced the speed and durability of Herreshoff yachts. His fertile mind also produced an improved process for making nitric and hydrochloric acids and a thread-tension regulator for sewing machines, which he patented. In 1869, always restless and by now well-to-do, he decided to go abroad, and for the next fourteen months he traveled in Europe. During this period he devised a bicycle driven by a gasoline engine and an apparatus for measuring the specific heat of gases.

After his return to Bristol Herreshoff perfected a new type of steam boiler for light vessels, made in the form of a beehive with coils of iron pipe, which heated water quickly while saving fuel. It was first tried on a 48-foot launch, *Vision*, which attained a speed of fifteen miles per hour. Its success led the Herreshoffs to be deeply involved with steam-powered vessels for the next decade. The coil-type boiler was adopted for the first torpedo boat built for the U.S. Navy. Five years later, in 1879, James went one step further by devising an engine that could be operated with super-heated steam.

In 1875 Herreshoff married Jane Brown (no relation) of Dromore, Ireland. He became the family firm's representative in England, and he and his wife took up residence in London, where the first of their five children was born. For the baby he invented a lightweight, collapsible, four-wheeled carriage, which caught the eye of Queen Victoria as her entourage was passing through Hyde Park. Her approval, it is said, led to a demand for similar baby carriages all over England and spawned a lucrative business.

During this period James Herreshoff began experimenting with a revolutionary idea for racing yachts—a fin keel which would, by virtue of its depth and weight, allow the yacht to carry unconventionally large sails. Returning to Bristol in 1883, he perfected this concept, undeterred by his brothers' skepticism.

In their eyes James had always been an impractical dreamer when it came to yachting design, but Nat Herreshoff finally adopted the knifelike fin keel and incorporated it to great advantage in his America's Cup defenders. His brother never received credit for this invention.

Estranged from his younger brothers, James Herreshoff moved his family to Coronado, California, in 1893, never to return to Rhode Island. Without financial cares, he played with such inventions as a "row cycle," a three-wheeled vehicle with handlebars that propelled it like the oars of a rowboat. Eleven years later he left California and settled in a hilltop home in Riverdale on the Hudson, New York. There, in his declining years, he filled countless notebooks with plans for solar-powered engines, swept-back airplane wings, amphibious vessels, and similar fantasies, some of which others would turn into real inventions. One newspaper account portrayed him as an impressive, white-clad figure "who still looked out upon the world with clear blue eyes, in which there burned the fire of genius." Even in his ninety-fifth year he kept busy hybridizing roses and making model gliders. He died in Riverdale.

The Herreshoff firm thrived until John's death in 1915. It was sold two years later, with Nat remaining president, but it was shut down and auctioned off in 1924. James never resented that most of the family glory centered around the achievements of John and Nat. As a Herreshoff biographer, Samuel Carter III, wrote, "It was enough to know that he had improved the lot of millions of American families, with fertilizers for their gardens, flour and baking powder for their kitchens, plants for their homes, fabrics for them to wear, and sporting devices for their amusement" (p. 179).

• Herreshoff's contributions to boat design are discussed by Samuel Carter III, *The Boatbuilders of Bristol* (1970). Obituaries are in the *New York Times*, 7 Dec. 1930, and the *Providence Journal*, 8 Dec. 1930.

ELLSWORTH S. GRANT

HERRESHOFF, Nathanael Greene (18 Mar. 1848–2 June 1938), steam engineer and yacht designer, was born in Bristol, Rhode Island, the seventh of nine children of Charles Frederick Herreshoff (pronounced Herr-es-off, with the stress on the first syllable), a gentleman farmer whose paternal grandfather had emigrated to Rhode Island from Prussia in 1787, and Julia Ann Lewis. Herreshoff escaped the disease that early blinded five of his siblings. But when his consumingly ambitious older brother John Brown Herreshoff became blind at age fourteen, Herreshoff was compelled to assist him in his sailing and boat-building endeavors. By twelve he was a proficient draftsman and boat modeler as well as a skilled yacht racing helmsman and navigator. By the time he graduated from high school (1865), he was playing an important role in the design of small craft being built at his brother's newly formed Herreshoff & Stone boat works.

By 1870, a year after he left the Massachusetts Institute of Technology (he did not choose to graduate) to become a draftsman and engineer at Corliss Steam Engine Company, Providence, Rhode Island, he was, according to a son, the noted yacht designer L. Francis Herreshoff, "responsible for designing all yachts, their parts, and machinery in toto that were built" by John Herreshoff. Nathanael Herreshoff left Corliss in 1878 to become his brother's business partner in Herreshoff Manufacturing Company (HMCo.) at Bristol. He had full charge of the company's engineering and design departments until 1915; thereafter he superintended most design work until his full retirement in 1930.

Although the 33′5″ racing sloop *Shadow* (1871) and the revolutionary catamaran *Amyrillis* (1876) brought him early fame as a designer of fast sailing yachts, Herreshoff's main work through 1891 was with light high-performance steam engines and steam-driven hulls for naval and recreational use. He brought to its highest development the coil boiler that had been introduced in 1873 by his oldest brother, the inventor James Brown Herreshoff. He designed *Lightning*, the first purpose-built U.S. Navy torpedo boat, in 1875 and, in 1885, the 90′ *Stiletto*, arguably America's first high-speed steam yacht. HMCo. built no naval vessels between 1897 and the war year of 1917. But its production of outstanding Herreshoff-designed steam yachts and launches, for such customers as J. Pierpont Morgan (1867–1943), George Vanderbilt, and William Randolph Hearst, continued steadily (and profitably) throughout the partnership of Herreshoff and his brother John. In 1891 Herreshoff designed the sloop *Gloriana* for the then hotly competitive 46′ yacht racing class; in construction and rigging detail, as well as in hull form, the *Gloriana* was well ahead of its time and became, perhaps, Herreshoff's single most influential design.

The death of Edward Burgess, Herreshoff's good friend and chief American design rival, and the great racing success of Herreshoff's 26′6″ sloop *Dilemma* (the first bulb-keeler, 1891) and, in 1892, of his 46′ sloop *Wasp* and his 84′ sloop *Navahoe* (the first Herreshoff racing yacht built of metal) made Herreshoff a logical choice to design a boat for the 1893 America's Cup trials. He actually designed two—*Colonia* and *Vigilant*. His 86′ *Vigilant* successfully defended the Cup against the British challenger, *Valkyrie* (II). Over the next twenty-six years there were five more challengers for America's Cup. And five more times (with *Defender*, 1895; *Columbia*, 1899 and 1901; *Reliance*, 1903; and *Resolute*, 1920), huge (up to 150 tons displacement, up to 80 crewmen, up to 15,000 square feet of sail area), gaff-rigged Herreshoff sloops prevailed.

In a period of unprecedented popular interest in yachting, the austere, taciturn, secretive Herreshoff soon became internationally famous as the "Wizard of Bristol" or, to his workmen and customers, "Captain Nat." His wizardry was amply displayed in a succession of sailboat classes of uniform design and construction in waterline lengths from 12.5 to 70 feet that pioneered and for years dominated yacht racing in the

United States. He also devised the Universal Rule for yacht measurement (1903), which became the dominant American measurement rule of the period. And in the years before World War I he designed a series of large racing schooners, of which the 87′3″ *Ingomar* (1903), the 92′6″ *Queen* (1906), and the 96′ *Westward* (1910) were among the most celebrated.

Despite the death of John Herreshoff in 1915, the sale of HMCo. to outside investors in 1916 (the business was subsequently resold at auction and refounded in 1924, then closed forever in 1946), and the adverse economic impact of World War I on America's traditional yacht-owning class, Herreshoff remained active and productive as a yacht designer until his mid-eighties. He had been married, first in 1883 to Clara Anna DeWolf, with whom he had six children, and then, following Clara's death, to Ann Roebuck in 1915. He died in Bristol. Herreshoff had produced more than 600 individual naval, yacht, and small craft designs during his seventy-year career, all of them derived from wooden half-models shaped and carved by his own hand. Ever a believer that form should follow function, he created forms that were pleasing to the senses; fast and able enough to satisfy his most demanding patrons; and, in finish, durability, and technological detail, equal or superior to the products of the competition. His influence on yachting as a sport, art, and science was and will always remain incalculably great.

• Herreshoff Marine Museum, Bristol, R.I., has an outstanding collection of yachts, small craft, and marine hardware designed by Nathanael Herreshoff. Construction plans and other N. Herreshoff-related materials from the files of Herreshoff Manufacturing Company are in the Hart Nautical Collection, MIT Museum, Cambridge, Mass. Important correspondence in the archives of the New York Yacht Club has been edited, but not yet published, by John Streeter. Herreshoff contributed "Rules for the Construction, the Scantlings, and the Other Proportions of Wooden Yachts" to New York Yacht Club, *Rules and Regulations for the Construction of Racing Yachts* (1928). The standard biography of N. Herreshoff is L. Francis Herreshoff, *Capt. Nat Herreshoff, the Wizard of Bristol* (1953). For a first-rate pictorial review of Herreshoff's life and work, see Maynard Bray and Carlton Pinheiro, *Herreshoff of Bristol: A Photographic History of America's Greatest Yacht and Boat Builders* (1989). See also Samuel Carter III, *The Boatbuilders of Bristol* (1970), and, for younger readers, Constance Buel Burnett, *Let the Best Boat Win: The Story of America's Greatest Yacht Designer* (1957).

LLEWELLYN HOWLAND III

HERRICK, Christine Terhune (13 June 1859–2 Dec. 1944), cookbook author and household affairs writer, was born in Newark, New Jersey, the daughter of Edward Payson Terhune, a minister, and Mary Virginia Hawes, a writer. Christine was educated primarily at home by tutors. Her mother, a respected author whose pen name was Marion Harland, stressed the importance of a woman's financial independence to her daughter. Christine's education was supplemented by studies in Europe, where the family moved in 1876 because of her mother's illness. She studied first in Rome

and then in Geneva and became proficient in both Italian and French. Her family traveled to a large extent throughout France and England before returning to the United States and settling in Springfield, Massachusetts, in 1878. In the winter of that same year, Christine made her debut in Richmond, Virginia.

Upon returning to her family in Springfield, Christine pursued the study of English and began to teach at a private girls' school. She remained in that job until her marriage to James Frederick Herrick, editor of the *Springfield Republican*, in 1884. Following her marriage Christine was encouraged by both her husband and her mother to begin a career of advising housewives in the "proper" ways of performing household chores and handling domestic matters. Christine was able to keep a relative balance in her two separate roles as housewife and prolific writer.

Immediately successful, Herrick in May 1885 published her first article, "The Wastes of the Household," in the premier issue of *Good Housekeeping*. Three years later Herrick's first book, *Housekeeping Made Easy*, appeared. She also contributed to such popular women's magazines as *Ladies' Home Journal* and *Demorest's Monthly*.

Believing that "there is no department of domestic science to which attention may be more profitably devoted than to the proper selection of food," Herrick sought to offer balanced and affordable recipes for her women readers. She also aspired to a grander conception of household efficiency, arguing that the "art of cooking [can] become an exact science." She promoted this idea in such books as *Housekeeping Made Easy*, *The Cooking School* (1908), and *Lose Weight and Be Well* (1917). She was also the editor of the *Letters of the Duke of Wellington to Miss J.* (1889).

Her husband's death possibly precipitated much of Herrick's productivity. It left her the single mother of two sons. Two other children had died before the age of three. Herrick was able to support her family and send her boys to private schools, college, and on trips abroad. Because she was well paid for her work, she was able to live independently. Herrick was probably unique in her field in that she did become the sole family supporter on account of her husband's early death; it is quite likely that part of her motivation to improve on women's roles stemmed from the freedom offered by her widowhood.

Although the sole breadwinner for her family and a supporter of woman suffrage, Herrick was not a "feminist." Her books conceived of the home as the chief arena for women's work. To her a woman was her husband's business partner, whose job it was to ensure that the home was pleasant and well-ordered and that "every dish, however simple, [was] as perfect as possible." Because her status in the home was "director of the housekeeping department," a woman was to be mortified and humiliated if she failed her family by not serving a perfect meal, or disregarding her housekeeping responsibilities.

Above all, Herrick and others in the domestic science movement sought to legitimize and draw increased recognition to the function of the housewife, by likening her training to that required for jobs primarily held by men. No longer was a woman merely a "housewife"; calling her a domestic scientist or manager would put her on par with other trained professionals. The simple housewife would become the economist, scientist, and administrator of her household. By applying the concepts of system and efficiency to her kitchen and home, a woman could "achieve the best results for the smallest expenditure of labor or money—in fact, [realizing] the scientific ideal of the minimum cost of production." Though a woman still was in the home, her role and importance there was greatly magnified by the ideals of this movement.

In 1928 Herrick moved from her home in New York City to Washington, D.C., where her son Horace served as a governmental official. She remained there until her death. Through her writings Herrick helped shape the ideal of a well-ordered home at the turn of the twentieth century, a "home [that] was capacious, orderly and clean" (Cowan, p. 159). Indeed, Herrick was among those who created a "decent" lifestyle for those who were able to live comfortably. Her readers may have lived lives within the homes, but with Herrick's instruction and encouragement they could envision themselves as important parts of an increasingly scientific and progressive age.

• Herrick's writings, including the aforementioned books, are located in various college libraries across the United States. Her most famous works not mentioned above are *Cradle and Nursery* (1989), *Liberal Living upon Narrow Means* (1890), *What to Eat, How to Serve It* (1891), *The Little Dinner* (1893), *The Chafing-Dish Supper* (1894), *National Cook Book*, written with her mother, Marion Harland (1896), *First Aid to the Young Housekeeper* (1900), *In City Tents* (1902), *The Expert Maid-servant* (1904), *Sunday Night Suppers* (1907), *The Helping Hand Cook Book*, written with Harland (1912), and *The New Common Sense in the Household* (1915). She is mentioned in Francis E. Willard and Mary A. Livermore, eds., *A Woman of the Century* (1893). Ruth Schwartz Cowan's *More Work for Mother* (1983) is another useful source. An obituary is in the *New York Times*, 3 Dec. 1944.

STEPHANIE LYN STRAJCHER

HERRICK, Clarence Luther (22 June 1858–15 Sept. 1904), and **Charles Judson Herrick** (6 Oct. 1868–29 Jan. 1960), neuroscientists and editors, were born in the area of Minneapolis, Minnesota, the oldest and youngest sons of Henry Nathan Herrick, a Free Baptist minister and chaplain during the last year of the Civil War, and Ann Strickler.

During his freshman year of high school, Clarence Herrick and some of his school friends formed what they called the Young Naturalists Society (1875–1878). Some of the research conducted by these neophyte scientists, led and inspired by Clarence, was eventually published in national and state journals, and several society members went on to distinguished careers in medicine and science. In the fall of 1875, and after only one year of high school, Herrick entered the University of Minnesota. He received a B.S. in

1880, having completed a six-year program in five years. In addition to pursuing his university studies, Herrick had been working as an assistant in the Minnesota State Geological Survey since 1876. After his graduation, realizing the value of advanced study, he took leave of his job at the geological survey in 1881 and spent one academic year (1881–1882) in advanced study at Leipzig, Germany. He studied zoology under the great scientist Rudolf Leuchart, studied psychology and theology with Zirkel, and attended lectures by Hermann Helmholtz in Berlin. He returned to the geological survey in 1882 and completed his studies for an M.S. from the University of Minnesota (1885). He married Alice Keith in 1883; they had two daughters and one son.

Clarence Herrick began his academic career in 1884 when he took a temporary position at the rank of instructor at Denison University. By all reports he was a talented and inspiring teacher of great energy and enthusiasm. Recognizing this fact, Denison University appointed him to the position of professor (and chair) of geology and natural history beginning in the fall of 1885. By this time Herrick had already published a number of papers on the fossils of Minnesota, including one 192-page report with thirty plates, all drawn by his own hand. He had a growing reputation as a geologist but would soon branch into new areas of investigation. In late 1885 Herrick founded the *Bulletin of the Scientific Laboratories of Denison University* (published from 1885 to 1990) and followed this effort in 1887 by founding the Denison Scientific Association. It was during this period that he published his first effort in neuroscience: a translation of a small book (brought back from Leipzig) titled *Grundzüge der Psychologie*, by Hermann Lotze. He added a short chapter on brain anatomy and published this work at his own expense. Although a small press run initially resulted in limited distribution of this book, it was reprinted in 1973 by Arno Press in the series Classics in Psychology. For a variety of reasons, personal as well as professional, Herrick left Denison University and took a temporary position in the fall of 1888 in the Department of Biology at the University of Cincinnati, where in 1889 he became the department chairman. At Cincinnati, his research in the field we now call neuroscience blossomed. His research at this time focused on the structure of the nervous system with special emphasis on lower vertebrate forms and on how experiments might be designed to elucidate the correlation between behavior and brain structure. He attracted enthusiastic students, presented papers at national meetings, published his data in national and international journals, and, most significantly, founded in 1891 the *Journal of Comparative Neurology*. Until this time comparative neuroanatomical studies in the United States had been published in a hodge-podge of local, state, and national journals. Herrick's new journal, offering a focal point for all scientists interested in comparative aspects of the nervous system, quickly attracted an international audience and continues to be one of the most influential neuroscience journals in the world.

In early 1891 Clarence Herrick was contacted by William Rainey Harper, the president of a newly reorganized University of Chicago, who encouraged him to consider a position at Chicago and offered several inducements. Based on promises made by Harper, Herrick resigned his chair at Cincinnati in December 1891, but by spring 1892 it had become clear that Harper had completely reneged on these promises, and Herrick resigned in June 1892 a position he had never occupied at Chicago.

Denison University welcomed Clarence Herrick back as professor of biology in June 1892. Tragically, however, he had a serious pulmonary hemorrhage (indicative of tuberculosis) in December 1893 and left for New Mexico in early 1894. In New Mexico, Herrick returned to geology research as a way to make a living and a way to express his academic interest, continued his writings on a variety of topics, and in 1897 was appointed president of the University of New Mexico. In spite of progressively declining health he served in this position until 1901. During his tenure Herrick worked to develop strong academic, research, and graduate programs at New Mexico. He made special efforts in geology and psychology and founded two scientific bulletins, one in biology and one in geology. This brought the total of scientific journals founded by Herrick during his lifetime to four.

Clarence Luther Herrick died in Socorro, New Mexico, at age forty-six of the complications of pulmonary tuberculosis. He had published 150 papers, seventy-four of which were on neural-related topics. Left unfinished were six papers (later published) and a never-completed book manuscript. Although Clarence Herrick's academic career spanned only about ten years (1884–1893), followed by a brief period (1897–1901) as university president, he was remarkably productive and made substantial and lasting contributions to the field of neuroscience. These include the founding of the *Journal of Comparative Neurology*, seminal studies on the brains of lower vertebrate forms, and advancement of the now common concept of studies on the nervous system that integrate structure and function. German neurologist Ludwig Edinger named a commissure in the forebrain of Teleost fish (commissura minor of Herrick) in recognition of Herrick's observations.

Charles Judson Herrick (C. Judson Herrick in his writings) was introduced to science in his eleventh year of age, by his brother Clarence. In 1885 when Clarence became a professor at Denison, Judson enrolled in its preparatory department. Although he initially undertook a course of study in the classics, by his second college year he had committed himself to science. C. Judson Herrick also followed (in 1889) his brother to the University of Cincinnati to continue his studies in biology and there in 1891 received a B.S. For the academic years 1891–1892 and 1892–1893, C. Judson Herrick was, respectively, an instructor in the preparatory department at Denison University and

professor of natural science at Ottawa University in Kansas. He married Mary E. Talbot in 1892; they had one daughter.

In the fall of 1893, C. Judson Herrick returned to Denison as a teaching fellow and enrolled in a master's program. While he completed requirements for the M.S. (1895), his brother's sudden illness in December 1893 profoundly affected his life and future career. By early 1894, when his older brother left for New Mexico with tuberculosis, C. Judson Herrick found himself in charge of the histology course his brother had been assigned to teach (and in which he was also enrolled) and the editor, for all practical purposes, of the *Journal of Comparative Neurology*. His willingness, in spite of inexperience, to assume this great responsibility saved the journal from certain extinction. A contributor to earlier volumes, he now found himself the moving force behind this journal, which at the time was solely owned by the Herrick brothers and ran deficits every year.

C. Judson Herrick remained on the faculty of Denison University until 1907, achieving the rank of professor in 1898. He spent 1896–1897 at Columbia University conducting research toward a Ph.D. (received in 1900), primarily in the laboratory of Oliver Smith Strong. His dissertation, winner of the Cartwright Prize in 1899, was published simultaneously in *Archives of Neurology and Psychopathology* and *Journal of Comparative Neurology* as "The Cranial and First Spinal Nerves of Menidia. A Contribution upon the Nerve Components of the Bony Fishes" in the same year, foretelling of a long series of publications by Herrick on cranial nerves and their functional components and on the central nervous systems of a wide range of lower vertebrates. Herrick's extensive research on the tiger salamander covered many years, produced numerous papers, and resulted in what is probably his most famous book, *The Brain of the Tiger Salamander, Ambystoma tigrinum* (1941).

C. Judson Herrick became professor of neurology at the University of Chicago in 1907 and served in this position until he retired in October 1934. In January 1908 Herrick transferred ownership of the *Journal of Comparative Neurology* to the Wistar Institute, a renowned research and publishing enterprise. During the First World War (1918–1919), he served as a major in the U.S. Army Sanitary Corps at the Army Medical Museum. Also, for about three months before his retirement, he served as chairman of the Department of Anatomy at Chicago. During his long career at Chicago, Herrick was tremendously productive, publishing numerous papers and several books. His text *An Introduction to Neurology* first appeared in 1915 and eventually went through five editions. Collectively Herrick's research papers and books brought him great recognition and fame, making him, in the words of the great Dutch neuroanatomist C. U. Ariëns Kappers, a "great pioneer in American comparative neurology." Herrick was a member of a number of U.S. and foreign scientific societies and was elected a member of the National Academy of Sciences in 1918.

Clarence Luther Herrick, based on his founding of the *Journal of Comparative Neurology* in 1891 and on his propagation of the concept of an integrative neuroscience (bringing techniques from various fields to the study of neural structure and function), is arguably the father of comparative neuroanatomy/neuroscience in the United States. His journal was continued, nurtured, and brought to a level of maturity by his younger brother Charles Judson after Clarence contracted tuberculosis in December 1893. The role played by C. Judson Herrick in the eventual success of the *Journal of Comparative Neurology* is undisputed. His identification with this journal became so strong that he is frequently, though incorrectly, credited as being its founder. Between 1894 and 1904, while Clarence Herrick was listed as editor, the day-to-day responsibilities nevertheless fell to C. Judson Herrick, who became the journal's managing editor in 1905. Although he formally stepped down from this position in 1927, he was identified as emeritus editor for many years and was actively involved in the journal almost until his death, in Grand Rapids, Michigan.

• The Herrick Collection in the Spencer Research Library at the University of Kansas, Lawrence, contains most of the papers of both brothers; a smaller collection is at Denison University. The most detailed and accurate information on Clarence Luther Herrick and C. Judson Herrick can be found in the following accounts: H. H. Bowden, "Clarence Luther Herrick," *Journal of Comparative Neurology and Psychology* 14 (1904): 515–34; "Charles Judson Herrick—Editor, Teacher, Scientist," *Journal of Comparative Neurology* 56 (1932): 1–14; C. J. Herrick, "Clarence Luther Herrick, Pioneer Naturalist, Teacher, and Psychobiologist," *Transactions of the American Philosophical Society*, n.s., 45, part 1 (1955): 1–85; P. G. Roofe, "Charles Judson Herrick, 1868–1960," *Anatomical Record* 137 (1960): 162–64; G. W. Bartelmez, "Charles Judson Herrick, October 6, 1868–January 29, 1960," National Academy of Sciences, *Biographical Memoirs* 47 (1973): 77–108; W. F. Windle, *The Pioneering Role of Clarence Luther Herrick in American Neuroscience* (1979), published by Exposition Press, N.Y.; S. L. Palay, "The Founding of the *Journal of Comparative Neurology*," *Journal of Comparative Neurology* 314 (1991): 1–8; D. E. Haines, "The Contributors to Volume 1 (1891) of the *Journal of Comparative Neurology*: C. L. Herrick, C. H. Turner, H. R. Pemberton, B. G. Wilder, F. W. Langdon, C. J. Herrick, C. von Kupffer, O. S. Strong, T. B. Stowell," *Journal of Comparative Neurology* 314 (1991): 9–33; and D. E. Haines, *Clarence Luther Herrick on the Organization of the Motor Cortex*, Kopf Carrier No. 38 (1994), pp. 1–5.

DUANE E. HAINES

HERRICK, James Bryan (11 Aug. 1861–7 Mar. 1954), cardiologist, was born in Oak Park, Illinois, the son of Origen White Herrick, a banker, and Dora Kettlestrings. James graduated from Oak Park High School in 1877; to prepare for college, he attended the Rock River Seminary. In 1878 he entered the University of Michigan, where he specialized in English literature and classical languages and obtained his A.B. in 1882.

At his father's suggestion, Herrick became a teacher, first at Peoria High School for a year; he returned to Oak Park to teach at the high school from 1883 to 1886. His choice of medicine as a career became settled during the winter of 1885–1886, when he took evening and Saturday courses at Rush Medical College. He enrolled full time at Rush in the fall of 1886, obtaining his M.D. in 1888. He finished first in the Cook County Hospital intern examination, completed his eighteen-month internship in September 1889, and became assistant to Charles W. Earle. After a year he left to start his own general practice. In 1889 Herrick married Zellah Pavey Davies of Oak Park, the daughter of a physician; they had two children.

Herrick joined the attending staff at Cook County Hospital in 1890, beginning a twenty-year affiliation. That same year he became a member of the internal medicine staff at Presbyterian Hospital, where he remained until 1924, serving as vice president of the medical board (1903–1907) and as its president (1908–1913). He also served on the medical staff of the Central Free Dispensary from 1890 to 1927. Returning to Rush in 1890, he was on the faculty until 1927 (1890, instructor; 1894, adjunct professor; 1900, professor of medicine).

Three trips to Europe provided Herrick with a postgraduate education. In 1894 he spent three months in Prague, studying diagnosis with the pathologist Hans Chiari. Returning to Chicago, he resumed his practice and wrote *A Handbook of Medical Diagnosis* (1895). In 1899 he and Arthur R. Edwards traveled to Italy, Germany, and Austria; at Würzburg they benefited from Wilhelm von Leube's experience in diagnosis. Finally, in 1905 Herrick spent three months in Emil Fischer's laboratory in Berlin.

After ten years in general practice, Herrick limited his work to internal medicine and cardiology and closed his office to become a consultant and hospital practitioner. His skill as a diagnostician soon brought him much work. Herrick, however, always urged physicians seeking to specialize to spend some years in general practice first.

Herrick was one of the first physicians in Chicago (around 1906) to use the diphtheria antitoxin. In 1912, through the gratitude of a patient, he acquired one of Einthoven's string galvanometers, the forerunner of the electrocardiograph, the first in use in his area; in 1918 he had a second one installed at Presbyterian Hospital.

The first of Herrick's two major contributions to medicine, his description of sickle-cell anemia, appeared in *Archives of Internal Medicine* 6 (1910): 517–21. A Jamaican patient had entered Presbyterian Hospital in 1908. Herrick noticed the peculiar shape of the blood cells and carried out many tests to be sure that this was not an artefact before he submitted his report for publication. Herrick's acute observation and careful study alerted physicians to a new clinical entity, discovered through detailed laboratory work.

Herrick's interest in the heart resulted in his second major contribution, reported in the *Journal of the American Medical Association* 59 (1912): 2015–20. Physicians in the nineteenth century had believed that acute occlusion of a coronary artery by a blood clot (first reported in the 1840s) automatically resulted in sudden death. Herrick's article showed that this was not necessarily so; the condition could be recognized in a live patient, and suitable therapy after even a severe attack could give the patient many useful years of life. Herrick saw this article as "missionary work," because the condition had often been diagnosed incorrectly as angina pectoris, acute indigestion, or ptomaine poisoning. Although Herrick's original report in 1912 stimulated little discussion, when he added experimental work with dogs, revised the text, and presented it again in 1918, the response was favorable and widespread. Indeed, Herrick soon had to remind his colleagues that a similar condition could be caused by a ruptured peptic ulcer, a ruptured gall bladder, or pancreatitis. Herrick's work brought about the recognition of coronary thrombosis as a common medical condition and stimulated considerable clinical and research study; it was a milestone in cardiology. Although he became known as a heart specialist as a result of this work, Herrick resisted the categorization, stressing that he was an internist with a particular interest in the heart, not a narrow specialist.

During Herrick's medical career he wrote more than 160 articles and three books. *A Short History of Cardiology* appeared in 1942, and his autobiography, *Memories of Eighty Years*, was published in 1949.

The importance of lifelong medical learning led Herrick to active work with several organizations. His favorite was the Association of American Physicians, which he joined in 1898; he served as its president in 1923. In 1930 the association bestowed its Kober Medal on him. He was also president of the Congress of American Physicians and Surgeons (1938), the American Heart Association (1927–1928), the American Association for the History of Medicine (1933), and the Institute of Medicine of Chicago (1925). His enjoyment of literature led him to membership in the Chicago Literary Club and its presidency (1931–1932). He served the American Medical Association's Judicial Council for six years; the association honored him with its Distinguished Service Medal in 1939.

Herrick's interests in education were not limited to his professional colleagues. In the early 1920s, impressed with the work of the Association for the Prevention and Relief of Heart Diseases in New York, he took an active role in founding the Chicago Heart Association, which also included both lay and professional members. In addition, he supported the work of Sunset Camp in Antioch, Illinois, a summer camp for heart patients. When this developed into a year-round home for those suffering from rheumatoid heart conditions, the board renamed it Herrick House.

During World War I Herrick served on both a local draft advisory board in Chicago and a district appeal board for the state. In 1918 Governor Lowden appointed him chairman of a commission to study the condition of women in industry, with special attention to the influence of hours of work on health.

Herrick's pioneering descriptions of sickle-cell anemia and of the survival of patients with coronary thrombosis were major contributions to medicine. He was a hard worker, a logical and practical physician, and a skilled diagnostician. His efforts in medical and lay education benefited many. He died in Chicago.

• The University of Chicago Library, Department of Special Collections, holds a large collection of Herrick papers, including correspondence, photographs, publications, and patient records. William H. Holmes, "James Bryan Herrick: An Appreciation," delivered before the Central Interurban Club in 1935 and later expanded, contains a bibliography of Herrick's work and is in this archive. The Rush-Presbyterian-St. Luke's Medical Center Archives in Chicago also has valuable Herrick materials. Herrick's autobiography, *Memories of Eighty Years* (1949), is a major source of information. Also of interest is Richard S. Ross, "A Parlous State of Storm and Stress: The Life and Times of James B. Herrick," *Circulation* 67 (1983): 955–59. Obituaries are in the *New York Times*, 9 Mar. 1954, and the *Journal of the American Medical Association* 154 (1954): 1016.

WILLIAM K. BEATTY

HERRICK, Myron Timothy (9 Oct. 1854–31 Mar. 1929), banker, governor of Ohio, and diplomat, was born near Huntington, Ohio, the son of Mary Hulbert Herrick and Timothy R. Herrick, farmers. He attended local schools and at age sixteen began teaching in nearby Brighton. Two years later he enrolled in Oberlin Academy for a year and a half, and he later attended Ohio Wesleyan University for two years. In 1875 Herrick began reading law in the Cleveland offices of G. E. Herrick and J. F. Herrick and became active in the Cleveland Grays, a local militia group. In 1878 he opened his own law office. In 1880 he married Carolyn M. Parmely; they had one son. Until her death in 1918, Herrick considered his wife his closest adviser.

Herrick took advantage of the opportunities provided by Cleveland in the late nineteenth century. Representing a hardware manufacturer in a bankruptcy proceeding in 1880, he kept control of several patents for his client. During liquidation Herrick and his client organized a new company and purchased the factory for one-fourth its value. He thus became a member of the board of the new Cleveland Hardware Company. He was also a successful real estate speculator, earning $70,000 in his first development. In 1885 he won the first of two terms on the city council, and in 1888 he was elected, the first of eight times, as a delegate to the Republican National Convention.

Politics eased Herrick's way into banking. In 1886 industrialist and Ohio Republican leader Mark Hanna recommended the young lawyer for the position of secretary-treasurer of the Society for Savings, Cleveland's largest bank. After leading the bank through the panic of 1893, Herrick became chairman of the board in 1894. In that position he made the decision to build Cleveland's first steel-frame skyscraper to house the bank and considered it "the best investment the bank ever made."

As a prominent banker, Herrick grew in political importance. When Ohio governor William McKinley went bankrupt in 1893, Herrick raised $130,000 to pay off the governor's debts. He also solicited contributions, both in and out of Ohio, for McKinley's electoral campaigns. When McKinley was reelected and emerged as a presidential candidate in 1896, Herrick and Hanna helped him secure the Republican nomination. During the campaign Herrick strenuously advocated the gold standard and helped shape the candidate's position on the money question. Following his victory, McKinley offered Herrick the post of secretary of the treasury, but he declined, citing his business commitments. In 1901 he became president of the American Bankers Association.

In 1903 Herrick was elected governor of Ohio. During the campaign his opponent, Cleveland reform Democrat Tom L. Johnson, criticized corporate influence in politics and pressed Herrick to debate him. Herrick refused, but he did campaign throughout the state. As governor, Herrick opposed local option saloon legislation, vetoed legislation to allow betting at race tracks, established a program to invest state funds in banks throughout Ohio, and created a state highway department. In 1905 he sought reelection but lost. Returning to private life, he helped reorganize several railroads and participated in the business merger creating the Union Carbide Corporation, of which he became chairman of the board.

In 1912 William Howard Taft appointed Herrick ambassador to France. While in France he completed *Rural Credits* (1914), a study of the use of bank credits to stabilize farm economies that had some influence on the Federal Farm Loan Act of 1916. At President Woodrow Wilson's request, Herrick remained as ambassador until December 1914. After World War I broke out, he helped repatriate Americans stranded in Europe, and when the French government moved to Bordeaux in September 1914, Herrick kept the U.S. embassy in Paris open, intending to protect churches, museums, and monuments should the city fall to the invading German army. He took over the interests of Germany, Austria, Serbia, Japan, and Turkey by working with citizens of those countries who were stranded in France and by serving as a channel of communication between the warring governments. He also established the American Relief Clearing House to care for widows, orphans, and the disabled. For his efforts the French government awarded him the Grand Cross of the Legion of Honor.

After returning to the United States, Herrick lost a bid for the U.S. Senate in 1916. He worked in the presidential campaign of Senator Warren G. Harding, who, after becoming president, returned Herrick to France as U.S. ambassador in 1921. Because of the postwar economic settlement, his second tour of duty was marked by considerable antagonism toward the United States. Herrick wanted the Allied war debts scaled down to ease the European economic crisis, but sentiment at home precluded it. In 1922 France occupied the Ruhr Valley when Germany defaulted on its reparations payments, and Herrick openly advocated U.S. economic intervention. In 1924 he helped implement the Dawes Plan, which was intended to revive the German economy through American investments and tied reparations payments to German economic recovery. Remaining convinced that the economic situation in Europe undermined U.S. moral influence, Herrick in 1925 failed in efforts to have the debt question reopened. He also doubted that U.S. membership in the League of Nations would guarantee European peace, believing that French, British, and U.S. statesmen rightfully distrusted Germany for failing to endorse "full and faithful execution of the [Versailles] Treaty." In Herrick's view, Europe and the United States would not be able to "disarm down to bed-rock necessities" and establish a lasting peace until Germany admitted starting the war and abided by the treaty.

Herrick viewed his diplomatic service as important and willingly spent his energy and wealth to advance the cause of good relations with France. He used personal resources to purchase a home in Paris, which later became the permanent U.S. embassy. Throughout the 1920s, in the face of anti-American sentiment, he took every opportunity to remind France of past American support. In March 1929, when Marshal Ferdinand Foch died, the frail 74-year-old ambassador marched and stood, exposed to the elements, for five hours during the French hero's funeral. Five days later, on Easter Sunday, Herrick died at the U.S. embassy in Paris.

• Herrick's official papers for his term as governor are at the Ohio Historical Society in Columbus, Ohio. His personal papers are at the Western Reserve Historical Society in Cleveland, Ohio. T. Bentley Mott, *Myron T. Herrick: Friend of France* (1929), is a biography by his military attaché based on extensive conversations with Herrick during his second term as ambassador. Hoyt Landon Warner, *Progressivism in Ohio: 1897–1917* (1964), is the most detailed account of Herrick's governorship. Margaret Leech, *In the Days of McKinley* (1959), sympathetically deals with Herrick's friendship with McKinley. An obituary is in the *New York Times*, 1 Apr. 1929.

JAMES E. CEBULA

HERRICK, Robert Welch (26 Apr. 1868–23 Dec. 1938), writer and university professor, was born in Cambridge, Massachusetts, the son of William Augustus Herrick, an attorney, and Harriet Peabody Emery. Both parents came from long-settled New England families. After growing up in genteel near-poverty, he managed in 1885 to enroll in Harvard University with the help of his uncle George Herbert Palmer. His interests there centered on the literature and writing courses dominated by Barrett Wendell, renowned as a teacher though not yet as a literary historian, and he emerged as editor in chief of the *Harvard Monthly* for half a year. After graduating in 1890 with a B.A. degree, he taught courses in writing and in modern literature at the Massachusetts Institute of Technology for three years before moving to the newly founded University of Chicago to help organize its program in composition. *Composition and Rhetoric for Schools* (1899), of which he was coauthor, would go through many reprintings; with frequent leaves for travel and writing he spent the rest of his academic career in Chicago until his early retirement in 1923. In 1894 he had married Harriet Peabody Emery (his first cousin). Of their three children only one outlived infancy. The marriage survived shakily until a formal separation in 1913 and divorce in 1916. Though gossip about his philandering had a basis in fact, he firmly upheld a code of ethical behavior. Though austerely reserved, even snobbish in the opinion of some, he attracted and held such distinguished friends as his colleague and literary historian Robert Morss Lovett, who would compile a long record of activity as a sociopolitical liberal.

During his undergraduate years Herrick had decided to aim at becoming a self-supporting writer. His very first stories reflected the avant-gardism of the 1890s with an art-for-art's sake aestheticism and a wavering preciosity of characters, motives, and style imitating current European models. But his sense of ethical, disciplined integrity soon asserted itself. Literature, like other forms of discourse, he believed, must lead the individual toward self-realization, that is, toward the richest development of his or her talents, satisfied best through intellectual or spiritual rather than material ways; furthermore, that goal required contributing to the positive goals of the ongoing society. Later generations may find the title of his first novel, *The Gospel of Freedom* (1898), a misnomer because Herrick ends by preaching duty to society rather than self-liberation; while it presented an Ibsenian wife who demands genuine equality with her husband, the novel nonetheless stressed everyone's responsibility for the good of humankind.

This principle of responsibility to one's immediate society led Herrick into the realistic mode of fiction, though he would stop short of Dreiserian naturalism. *The Web of Life* (1900) explored objectively the major economic classes of Chicago before ending with a tempered hopefulness. Though *The Real World* (1901)— with the clashing subtitle *An Allegory for Today*— exalted the power of steady, uncompromising idealism, *The Common Lot* (1904) again explored urban poverty as well as the career of an architect corrupted by fast-profit builders. Surprisingly, *The Memoirs of an American Citizen* (1905) avoided both the intrusive rhetoric and moralizing of the preceding novels by means of a terse first-person narrator who defends his essentially ruthless climb to wealth and the U.S. Senate. Again surprisingly, his story "The Master of the Inn" (1907) was a fervent parable about a physician who is essentially a faith-healer; republished as a novelette in 1908, it became his best-selling book. Disciplined by a tone of urbane irony, *Clark's Field* (1914) would also achieve effective socioeconomic criticism with its interplay of the leisured rich, scheming corporate attorneys, and the mass of workaday men and women.

Herrick's contemporaries identified him with novels about the city, especially Chicago, as the arena in which the gospel of financial success, the rising professional classes, the so-called New Woman, and the ideas of the Progressive movement played out their conflicts. The melodramatic *Together* (1908), which sold briskly, was praised as a multidimensional exhibit of modern (upper middle-class) marriage, though the almost cynical *One Woman's Life* (1913) and the warm, quietly feminist *Homely Lilla* (1923) have worn better. Too often, Herrick's ethical strenuousity drove him to what later critics perceive as purple prose and blatant symbolism broadening into allegory, as again in *A Life for a Life* (1910). Still, before 1914 his admirers, some beyond the United States, considered him the leading serious American novelist, who approached a sexual honesty that then seemed valiant, especially in allowing women to express physical desire without being punished somehow.

Regularly, Herrick's career made unpredictable turns. After a burst of patriotic, militant fervor as special correspondent in Europe for the *Chicago Tribune*, he probed World War I skeptically. While deploring the Jazz Age, he showed a stronger, better-grounded interest in current politics with essays for the *New Republic* and the *Nation* ranging from national elections to foreign policy. After losing substantially from the stock market crash of 1929, he met the Great Depression not with bewilderment but with open-ended analysis. *Sometime* (1933), his cosmopolitan, utopian fantasy, surprised all but his close friends. Almost as unpredictably, 1935 he accepted the post of government secretary in the Virgin Islands. His travel essays about the Caribbean had helped bring the offer, especially because they broke through the current racial stereotypes. When serving as acting governor, he handled administrative problems with reasonable patience and impartiality until his sudden death in Charlotte Amalie, St. Thomas.

Nobody is likely to reproclaim major stature for Herrick, nor will the general reader rediscover any of his twenty-five books of fiction, even if *The Memoirs of an American Citizen* and *Clark's Field* deserve to escape oblivion. Collectively, his novels are repetitious in plot and characters partly because he could not move far past his own experiences or compromise his personal and social ethics, though his essays during the 1920s signaled a greater tolerance and flexibility of mind. Still, he is now read mainly by literary historians who are tracing motifs such as urbanization or middle-class domesticity and political historians who are examining fellow-travelers of the Progressive movement between the turn of the century and World War I.

• For the major collection of personal materials, see Phyllis Franklin, "A Handlist of the Robert Herrick Papers at the University of Chicago," *American Literary Realism 1870–1910* 8 (1975): 109–54. The collections at the Newberry Library (Chicago) and Princeton University are at the next level of importance. *Waste* (1924) is the most richly autobiographical of his novels, though *Wanderings* (1925), a collection of four long stories, deftly uses his current life and travels, and *Chimes* (1926) wryly reflects his academic career. *The End of Desire* (1932) resignedly chronicles a late love affair.

The best critical biography remains Blake Nevius, *Robert Herrick: The Development of a Novelist* (1962); drawing on it, Louis J. Budd's *Robert Herrick* (1971) is briefer within the format of a series. Authoritative general essays are by Tom

H. Towers, "American Realists and Naturalists," in *Dictionary of Literary Biography*, vol. 12 (1982), and by Richard J. Thompson, "American Short-Story Writers, 1880–1910," in *Dictionary of Literary Biography*, vol. 78 (1989). An obituary is in the *New York Times*, 24 Dec. 1938.

Louis J. Budd

HERRICK, Sophia McIlvaine Bledsoe (26 Mar. 1837–9 Oct. 1919), editor and writer, was born in Gambier, Ohio, the daughter of Albert Taylor Bledsoe, a lawyer and professor of mathematics, and Harriet Coxe. Sophia, or Sophie, grew up in Springfield, Illinois, where her father practiced law, and in Mississippi and Virginia, where he taught at the state universities. She was educated at boarding schools in Cincinnati and Dayton. In 1860 she married James Burton Herrick, an Episcopal clergyman, and moved with him to New York City. Between 1862 and 1865 Sophia and James had three children. In 1868 they separated, and Sophia and the children moved to Baltimore to join her father, who had served as assistant secretary of war in the Confederate government.

From 1868 to 1872 Sophia Bledsoe Herrick headed a Baltimore girls' school; thereafter she contributed to the *Southern Review*, which her father edited, as writer and associate editor. Always interested in the natural sciences, she took a biology course at Johns Hopkins in 1876 and became fascinated with the microscope. Soon her articles on cell biology appeared in the *Southern Review*, otherwise often devoted either to defending the South or to dogmatic feuds between her father and other Methodist Episcopal theologians. Herrick also wrote on the religion and history of India and about prominent women, including the novelist George Eliot and the astronomer Caroline Herschel. When her father died in 1877, Herrick replaced him as editor.

In 1879 Herrick returned to New York and joined the editorial staff at *Scribner's Monthly*, which had already published a series of her illustrated articles on plants, insects, and microscopic studies. At *Scribner's Monthly* and its successor the *Century*, Herrick reviewed manuscripts, edited copy, and continued to write articles on subjects from marine biology to home economics to literature. A colleague at the *Century*, Robert Underwood Johnson, described her as "an intellectual woman of keen literary perceptions and of a scientific training and cast of mind." James Russell Lowell, an occasional correspondent, recognized the quality of her mind and pen. But Herrick made her most valuable contribution as an author of science books for children. *The Wonders of Plant Life Under the Microscope* (1883), *Chapters on Plant Life* (1885), and *The Earth in Past Ages* (1888) are notable for their forthright, clear style.

Herrick had a gift for explaining complex processes using simple, everyday images that her young readers would understand. Her tone is friendly and never condescending. In *Chapters*, for instance, she explains single-cell plant life using the example of yeast in baking. "If you have never watched the mixing of bread, I would advise you to go and look at it the first chance you have, for it is a very curious and entertaining bit of gardening." In the same book she attributes Charles Darwin's popular preeminence to his writing style. Although other scientists made comparable discoveries, she explains, "he wrote about what he had studied in such a clear and simple and interesting way that anybody could understand him." Herrick follows Darwin's example. In *The Earth in Past Ages*, a narrative geological history, she discusses why clear, logical hypotheses are important in a field beset by religious controversy: "I have been so very particular about this because many people who are ignorant of geology—that is, the science of earth-making—are fond of speaking of it with contempt, calling it mere guesswork; and I want you to see just what sort of guesswork it is." Besides her science books, Herrick wrote the introduction to *Essays and Reviews of George Eliot* (1887) and compiled *A Century of Sonnets* (1902).

Sophia Herrick never remarried. During the 1870s she apparently had an affair with Allen C. Redwood, an illustrator and colleague who specialized in scenes from Confederate army life. In a letter to Redwood, Herrick said she preferred her legal separation, which upheld the letter if not the spirit of her marriage vows, to the stigma of a divorce, despite its freedom. Her introduction to George Eliot's *Essays* concentrates largely on Eliot's steadfast moral purity. "Again and again she tells us, that it is not only wickedness, but folly, to make happiness the supreme object of our lives; that no direct and unscrupulous search after pleasure will ever be crowned with success; that abiding happiness lies nowhere but in the path of honor and duty." As a single mother Herrick felt keenly the responsibility to set a moral example for her children; she once advised mothers that children "see through your flimsy disguises which sometimes deceive yourself—of feeling that it is your 'duty' to do what you want to."

Though most of her career unfolded behind the scenes, Herrick succeeded in a field where few women ventured. Her social views reflected her era and her conservative background, yet her separation from her husband and her passion for science mark Herrick as a quiet pioneer among independent women. Her children's books, her strongest achievement, remain refreshing among contemporary efforts.

Herrick retired from the *Century* in 1906, after more than thirty years in the magazine business. In 1915 she published a memoir of her father, discussing his ties to both Abraham Lincoln and Jefferson Davis. She died in Greenwich, Connecticut.

• Sophia Bledsoe Herrick's papers, including letters and unpublished memoirs, are in the Bledsoe-Herrick Family Papers in the Schlesinger Library at Radcliffe College. "Personal Recollections of My Father and Mr. Lincoln and Mr. Davis" appeared in the *Methodist Review Quarterly* (Oct. 1915): 665–79. Stephen Davis and Robert Pollard III published "Allen C. Redwood and Sophie Bledsoe Herrick: The Discovery of a Secret, Significant Relationship" in *Maryland Historical Magazine* 85, no. 3 (Fall 1990): 256–63. Robert Underwood Johnson included Herrick in his *Remembered*

Yesterdays (1923). The *Letters of James Russell Lowell*, ed. Charles E. Norton, vol. 2 (1894), chronicles Lowell's side of their friendship. Herrick's work in the *Southern Review* is unsigned; however, Albert Taylor Bledsoe listed her 1873–1874 articles when he introduced her as associate editor in the Jan. 1875 issue. Subsequent articles on science and literature are invariably hers. Much of her work in *Scribner's Monthly* appeared in 1877–1879. While working at the *Century*, Herrick wrote articles for *Popular Science Monthly* and *Cosmopolitan*. An obituary is in the *New York Times*, 10 Oct. 1919.

AARON M. LISEC

HERRIMAN, George Joseph (22 Aug. 1880–25 Apr. 1944), cartoonist, was born in New Orleans, Louisiana, the son of George Herriman, Jr., a tailor, and Clara Morel. There is uncertainty about Herriman's ethnic background. His birth certificate identified him as "Colored," his parents were listed in the 1880 New Orleans federal census as "Mulatto," but his death certificate noted that he was "Caucasian." During his lifetime, friends often thought he was Greek or French because of his Adonis-like appearance, and he has been called a "Creole." The family moved to Los Angeles when Herriman was a child, and his father opened a barbershop and then a bakery.

Herriman attended St. Vincent's College, a Roman Catholic secondary school for boys. When he finished school in 1897 he followed his artistic bent and began to contribute illustrations to the *Los Angeles Herald*. After the turn of the century he moved to New York City and began to contribute cartoons to *Judge, Life*, and other humorous periodicals and comic strips to various newspaper syndicates, including several sequential series such as *Musical Mose, Professor Otto and His Auto, Acrobatic Archie*, and *Two Jolly Jackies* for the Pulitzer Syndicate and *Major Ozone's Fresh Air Crusade, Alexander the Cat, Bud Smith*, and *Rosy Posy* for the World Color Printing Company. In 1902 he returned briefly to Los Angeles to marry Mabel Lillian Bridge, his childhood sweetheart; they had two children.

The great variety and skill of Herriman's numerous efforts soon attracted the attention of William Randolph Hearst, who hired him for several of his papers, including the Los Angeles *Examiner*. Herriman lived in Los Angeles from 1905 until 1910, when Hearst brought him back to New York City to draw for the *New York Evening Journal*. Here, Herriman created his first widely successful feature, which would become known as *The Family Upstairs*, a domestic comic strip about the Dingbat family and their noisy neighbors in the apartment above. On 26 July 1910 this study in urban paranoia was interrupted by the appearance of the family cat, which is hit in the head by a rock thrown by a mouse. Therein lay the genesis for Herriman's most successful strip, *Krazy Kat*, which began as an independent feature on 2 July 1911.

In the world of *Krazy Kat*, Ignatz the Mouse is the object of Krazy Kat's affection, but instead of returning this love, Ignatz is disposed to hit the cat in the head with a brick. The cat naively believes that these clouts are meant as tokens of love. Meanwhile, the benevolent presence of Offissa Pup, himself in love with Krazy, operates to thwart Ignatz and keep the mouse behind jailhouse bars as much as possible. This situation of fully unrequited and androgynous love (Krazy's sex changes from time to time) is acted out against a surrealistic shifting background in the Arizona desert, while the characters speak a poetic dialogue and richly mixed dialect unique in literature outside the fiction of James Joyce or the poetry of E. E. Cummings. Both Cummings and T. S. Eliot wrote in praise of *Krazy Kat*, which has remained the most admired comic strip in newspaper history. No other strip has matched its genius in humorous whimsy, abstract style, and metaphoric power.

Several series of animated cartoons have been based on *Krazy Kat*, two stage ballets have been inspired by it, Jay Cantor has used the characters in a novel under the same title, and any number of modern artists have created paintings and sculptures in homage to Herriman. While Herriman produced *Krazy Kat* on a daily basis, he also created other comic strips, most notably *Baron Bean, Stumble Inn, Us Husbands*, and *Embarrassing Moments* (or *Bernie Burns*). He illustrated the anthologies of Don Marquis's columns about the poetic cockroach Archy and the feline vamp Mehitabel, giving an indelible visual stamp to the characters almost as endearing as Marquis's comic verse.

In 1922 Herriman settled permanently in Hollywood. He has been described as a handsome, slender, short man with twinkling gray eyes and curly black hair, given to wearing a Stetson hat. He once wrote of his creation, "Be not harsh with 'Krazy.' He is but a shadow himself, caught in the web of this mortal skein." A shy and private man, and more given to visual than verbal communication, he seldom commented on his art. He died in Los Angeles.

At the time of his death Herriman had penciled a week's worth of *Krazy Kat* comic strips, which were to remain uninked on his drawing board. Given the limited circulation of the feature by then, Hearst permanently retired the strip rather than allow other artists to continue it. Legend has it that *Krazy Kat* was a personal favorite of Hearst's, and no one could have imitated the Herriman style and whimsy, anyway. Like Pablo Picasso in painting, Herriman changed the visual style of his art form and influenced generations of cartoonists to come; like James Joyce in fiction, he stretched the traditional limitations of language; and like Samuel Beckett in drama, he captured the absurdities of efforts to communicate on the larger stage of life.

• A brief biography of Herriman is found in *Krazy Kat: The Comic Art of George Herriman* (1986), by Patrick McDonnell, Karen O'Connell, and Georgia Riley de Havenon. Other useful essays on Herriman are those by Bill Blackbeard in *The World Encyclopedia of Comics* (1976), ed. Maurice Horn; Ron Goulart in *The Encyclopedia of American Comics* (1990); Richard Marschall in *America's Great Comic-Strip Artists* (1989); Judith O'Sullivan in *The Great American Comic Strip* (1990);

and M. Thomas Inge in *Comics as Culture* (1990). Informative introductions to anthologies of Herriman's work include those by E. E. Cummings to *Krazy Kat* (1946 and 1969); M. Thomas Inge to *Baron Bean, 1916–1917* (1977); and Bill Blackbeard to *The Family Upstairs: Introducing Krazy Kat 1910–1912* (1977) and *Krazy & Ignatz: The Komplete Kat Comics* (1988–).

M. THOMAS INGE

HERRING, Augustus M. (3 Aug. 1867–17 July 1926), airplane designer, was born in Covington, Georgia, the son of William F. Herring and Chloe Conyers, occupations unknown. He was married to Lillian Mellen and had two children.

In his early teenage years, Herring's interest in the air was aroused by a toy helicopter butterfly. He began to make large model helicopters, then took a four-year engineering course at the Stevens Institute of Technology in Hoboken, New Jersey. He left in 1888 without graduating when the school rejected his thesis on flying machines as impractical.

Herring is credited, in his *New York Times* obituary, with having developed in 1889 the "aerofoil," a curved surface—such as an aircraft wing, aileron, or rudder—designed to obtain reaction from the air through which it moves. In 1889 he sent his first model plane into the air, using a compressed-air motor. After a brief stint in 1895 with the Smithsonian Institution's Samuel P. Langley, who was to build the highly publicized but unsuccessful "aerodrome" that crashed into the Potomac River, Herring began a series of collaborations that placed him on the periphery of great events and earned him a reputation as "the perennial thorn in the budding aviation industry's side" (Combs, p. 356).

In December 1895 he was hired by French-born Octave Chanute to help design and test gliders that would remain stable even in gusty winds. With Herring doing the flying, Chanute and a tiny group of engineers experimented in 1896 with a wide variety of multiple-winged gliders on the Indiana shore of Lake Michigan. They eventually made some 700 flights of the most successful pre–Wright brothers glider—the Chanute biplane, with braced wings and a fixed tail unit on a semiflexible outrigger. Chanute and Herring soon fell out over Herring's insistence that the biplane was ready for an internal combustion engine. Meanwhile, in 1896, Herring filed a patent application on his own "curved wing" flying machine, but it was rejected. (Seven years later, the Wright brothers filed their successful application.) In 1898 Herring failed in an attempt to fly a compressed-air-powered biplane glider. Chanute later turned down his request for money to build a motor-driven flying machine.

The two were drawn back together in fall 1902 when Chanute hired Herring as pilot to try out one of Chanute's gliders at Kitty Hawk, North Carolina, where the Wrights were also working. Annoyed at being interrupted in the midst of what would be the most famous design and development program in aviation history, the Wright brothers felt obligated to watch Chanute's test flights. They turned out to be a disaster; even on a steep sand dune, Herring could do no more than come downhill in brief hops and jumps.

By this time, Herring had developed a "reputation in aeronautical circles of exaggerating the credit due him for his share in the experiments of others" (Morris and Smith, p. 68). Leaving Kitty Hawk, he went straight to Washington, D.C., and tried to see Langley, apparently ready to give him information about the Wrights' plane. Langley refused to see him.

In 1904, the year after the Wrights' first powered flight, Herring proposed that the brothers give him a one-third interest in their invention. He suggested that some of their patents infringed patents he claimed to have, and he implied that expensive litigation might be avoided if they accepted his proposal. The Wrights did not reply and learned later that Herring's claims appeared to be bogus. About that time, Jerome Fanciulli, a newspaper and wire service reporter who covered aviation from its infancy, got to know Herring. Here is his assessment (quoted in Combs, p. 308): "He was a very clever fellow, a faker. . . . I went to New York when he was trying to get a Signal Corps contract. [I] visited his shop. He had a beautiful shop, beautiful propellers, and all that sort of thing. But as young as I was then, I immediately sized him up as a faker."

The next great aviation pioneer approached by Herring was Glenn Curtiss. Trying to generate interest in commercial applications for his aircraft design, he was put in touch with the persuasive Herring, who said he had government contracts and aeronautical patents antedating the Wright brothers' patents. Not bothering to investigate, Curtiss agreed to form the Herring-Curtiss Company, capitalized at $360,000, mostly from wealthy New Yorkers. In 1909 Herring-Curtiss built the Gold Bug, or Gold Flyer, which immediately set distance records and won prestigious prizes in France. Its ease of handling was attributed to mounting the ailerons—used for directional control—between the wings, an alternative to the Wrights' use of wing-warping.

That same year, however, in the first legal action in American aviation, the Wrights alleged that Herring-Curtiss's aileron was an infringement of their patent. Curtiss hoped to base his defense in part on patents supposedly held by Herring. After much wrangling, a court order requiring Herring to turn over the patents produced nothing more than patent applications, none of which had ever been granted. Angry at being defrauded, Curtiss convinced the directors of Herring-Curtiss to put the firm in bankruptcy, which allowed him to regain control. In 1914 the U.S. Court of Appeals found in favor of the Wright Company.

By then, Herring had associated himself with a yacht builder named William Starling Burgess, and in 1910 the Herring-Burgess airplane, which closely resembled the Curtiss design, appeared. In 1918 he resurrected the bankrupt Herring-Curtiss Company and sued "Glenn Curtiss and others" for $5 million, charging that the bankruptcy had been contrived to ruin him. Herring claimed during the litigation that he had built craft that flew "before the Wrights ever commenced to experiment." The court decided for the defendants, and Herring appealed. But while the appeal was pending, he died of a stroke in Brooklyn.

Modern aviation historians do not support Herring's claims to being one of the key players in the earliest days of flying machines. At best, he was a clever engineer and able pilot who stood in the wings, stepping forward at times to help the trailblazers, and at other times to annoy and frustrate them.

• One of the best modern assessments of Herring can be found in Harry Combs, *Kill Devil Hill: Discovering the Secret of the Wright Brothers* (1979). Herring's years with Chanute are described in Howard C. Scamehorn, *Balloons to Jets: A Century of Aeronautics in Illinois, 1855–1955* (1957). Also useful are Enzo Angelucci, *The World Encyclopedia of Civil Aircraft, from Leonardo Da Vinci to the Present* (1982); Lloyd Morris and Kendall Smith, *Ceiling Unlimited: The Story of American Aviation from Kitty Hawk to Supersonics* (1953); Charles H. Gibbs-Smith, *The Aeroplane: An Historical Survey of Its Origins and Development* (1960); and Archibald Black, *The Story of Flying* (1940). An obituary is in the *New York Times*, 19 July 1926.

DAVID R. GRIFFITHS

HERRING, James (12 Jan. 1794–8 Oct. 1867), portraitist and art promoter, was born in London, England, the son of James Herring, a teacher, and Mary Holland. He came to the United States with his parents, arriving and settling in New York City in October 1805. Herring attended Erasmus Hall Academy in Flatbush (now part of Brooklyn), New York, where drawing, he wrote years later, was his best subject. As a young adult he pursued various occupations, working as a teacher, a clerk, and a distiller of alcohol.

Sometime between 1812 and 1814 Herring married Ann Golden. They had two children, one of whom, Frederick William, also became a portraitist. Around the time of his marriage Herring started to pursue a livelihood in the arts, first coloring mezzotints for John Wesley Jarvis, a printmaker and one of New York City's leading portraitists, and later coloring maps for Philadelphia publisher Mathew Carey.

In early 1816 Herring became a member of Solomon's Lodge No. 1, in Somerville, New Jersey, thus beginning a lifelong commitment to the fellowship of Freemasonry. Later that year he was back in New York, where he was listed in the city directory as a portrait painter with a studio on Greenwich Street. Several portraits of New Jersey subjects dating to the late 1810s show that Herring at least worked as an itinerant artist in that state even if he did not reside there. His portraits of the Reverend and Mrs. Jacob Kirkpatrick (1817) represent residents of Somerset County, New Jersey. Mr. and Mrs. Martin J. Ryerson, shown in a pair of portraits dating to about the same time, were residents of Pompton Plains in neighboring Morris County.

Herring's portraits of John and Sophia Pitkin, painted in New York in 1824, represent the full flowering of his early style. Generally, subjects are portrayed in waist-length format. Clothing of men and women is kept to black and white with the exception of shawls with colorful floral borders occasionally worn by his female sitters. While costume may have been somber, Herring often would enliven a portrait with a crimson curtain drawn back to reveal a background landscape glimpsed through a window. The subjects gaze placidly and directly at the viewer. These portraits are forthright likenesses carefully drawn and highly finished. In addition to portraits, Herring painted banners and transparencies. He had one known student in this period, William Page, who became a prominent portrait and figure painter. Herring's wife died in 1829. By 1835 he had married a woman named Emily (maiden name unknown), and their only child, a daughter, had been born.

Herring's position in the New York art community was well established by the beginning of the 1830s. In 1831 he was secretary of the American Academy of the Fine Arts. He conceived the idea of publishing in periodical format a collection of biographies of men and women of note in the United States, both historical and contemporary figures. Each biography would be accompanied by an engraved portrait. Herring found a partner for this enterprise in James B. Longacre, a Philadelphia engraver and portraitist, and secured the sponsorship of the American Academy of the Fine Arts. The resulting publication, *The National Portrait Gallery of Distinguished Americans*, was published in four volumes between 1834 and 1839. For much of the 1830s Herring was occupied in painting portraits either from life or from works by other artists for the engravers of the *National Portrait Gallery* to copy. Herring's brush provided the artwork for nineteen of the 151 engravings in the *National Portrait Gallery*, and he was also the author of twenty-four of the biographical essays. The style he used for his portraits represented a departure from his decorative style of the 1820s. He employed a plain background that emphasized the face of the subject and made the portrait quicker for the engraver to copy and cheaper to produce. Herring's subjects included Noah Webster, painted from life in 1833, and James Monroe, copied from a portrait by John Vanderlyn.

With fellow artist John G. Chapman, Herring developed the concept of a gallery where artists could exhibit and sell their work. He envisioned that revenues from the gallery could be put toward establishing a permanent public collection in New York City. Accordingly, Herring rented a hall one flight above his own studio, located at 410 Broadway, where 260 works, including two portraits and a landscape by Herring, were shown in the First Fall Exhibition of the Work of Modern Artists at the Apollo Gallery, which opened in October 1838. Receipts generated from admission fees to the gallery failed to cover the expenses, however, so in January 1839 Herring called a meeting of persons interested in the fine arts that resulted in the formation of the Apollo Association for the Promotion of the Fine Arts in the United States. The association, like the Apollo Gallery, sponsored periodic art exhibitions, but since it was a membership organization, dues covered the costs of exhibiting and publishing catalogs, posing less of a personal financial risk for Herring. Herring was elected the group's first corresponding secretary, in which capacity he traveled extensively in an attempt to garner members outside New York City.

The Apollo Association purchased some of the paintings from its exhibitions, which in turn it distributed by means of a lottery among its members. In return for an annual fee each member had a chance to win an original work of art in the lottery. In 1842 the Apollo Association changed its name to the American Art Union. Until its dissolution by court order ten years later, when its method of distributing works of art by lottery was declared illegal and unconstitutional by the New York Supreme Court, the American Art Union was the greatest force in the United States promoting a market for American art. Further, it served as the model for art unions in other American cities.

The American Art Union owed its existence to Herring's efforts, but the rent of exhibition space for its predecessor, the Apollo Association, had imposed such a financial burden on him that he was forced to give up both his studio and the gallery space on Broadway in 1840. That same year Herring moved to Brooklyn, although he maintained a portrait studio in New York at various addresses until 1863. Portraits by Herring were included in annual exhibitions of the National Academy of Design for the years 1845, 1848, 1849, and 1855.

Herring devoted much energy to Freemasonry throughout his adult life. The year after his initiation in New Jersey, he was initiated into a New York City chapter. In 1827 he became master of Clinton Lodge in New York. Off and on between 1829 and 1858, he was grand secretary of the Grand Lodge of the State of New York. When Freemasonry came under fierce attack during the anti-Masonry movement of the late 1820s, Herring in large part kept the organization alive in New York state.

Herring spent the last year of his life at the home of his daughter Ann in Paris, France, where he died. He is buried in Greenwood Cemetery in Brooklyn, New York.

• James Herring's unpublished autobiography is in the Manuscripts Collection, New-York Historical Society. See also the article by Cynthia Seibels, "James Herring, American Portraitist," *Magazine Antiques* 113 (Jan. 1978): 212–20. For more information on *The National Portrait Gallery of Distinguished Americans*, see Robert G. Stewart, *A Nineteenth-century Gallery of Distinguished Americans* (1969); and Gordon M. Marshall, "The Golden Age of Illustrated Biographies: Three Case Studies," in *American Portrait Prints*, ed. Wendy Wicks Reaves (1984). For a history of the American Art Union, see Maybelle Mann, *The American Art Union* (1977). For Herring's involvement in Freemasonry, see Charles T. McClenachan, *History of the Most Ancient and Honorable Fraternity of Free and Accepted Masons in New York, from the Earliest Date* (4 vols., 1888–1894). An obituary is in the *New York Tribune*, 23 Oct. 1867.

CYNTHIA SEIBELS

HERRMAN, Augustine (1605?–1686?), merchant, attorney, ambassador, and mapmaker, was born in Prague, Bohemia, thought to be the son of Ephraim Augustin Herrman, a shopkeeper and city councilman, and Beatrix Redel, but possibly the son of Abraham Herrman, a Hussite minister in Mseno who was exiled to Zittau in Saxony because he was not Roman Catholic, and eventually settled in Amsterdam (wife's name unknown).

Augustine Herrman probably studied law and surveying and may have served in the army before emigrating to the Dutch colony in America in the employ of the Dutch West India Company. In 1633 he witnessed the signing of the treaty with Native Americans for the purchase of the land where Philadelphia now stands.

Based in New Amsterdam, Herrman shipped furs to Europe; salt from Curaçao to New Amsterdam; and, in 1634, cattle, horses, pottery, glassware, wines, and African slaves to Virginia for tobacco. He successfully defended himself in a suit over delivery of spoiled tobacco and later claimed to have started the Virginia tobacco trade. The Dutch often sued one another, providing excellent training for Herrman in the law.

In New Amsterdam Herrman acquired rental properties, a farm on which he successfully raised indigo, a house on Pearl Street next to the West India Company's warehouse, and a large orchard in what is now the Bowery, known in the eighteenth century as Herrman's Orchard. He also owned vast tracts of land in present-day New Jersey. The earliest known drawing of Manhattan, inset in Nicholas Vissher's 1651 map, is attributed to Herrman.

Herrman was elected in 1647 to the governor's Council of Nine Men, which made the day-to-day, local administrative decisions and advised Governor Peter Stuyvesant on major policies. On 28 July 1649 Herrman signed a document reconfirming the 1633 treaty he had witnessed.

By 1649 he owned shares in two privateers that preyed on Spanish, but not English, ships. That year he was sent by Stuyvesant as ambassador to the governors of Rhode Island and Massachusetts to protest charges of Dutch encroachment and to negotiate trade agreements.

In New Amsterdam on 10 December 1651, he married Jannetje Varlett (also spelled as Verleh or Varleth), who had been born in Utrecht. Her brother had married Governor Stuyvesant's sister, and her sister had married a wealthy Virginia tobacco grower whose connections became very important to Herrman. The Herrmans had five children before Jannetje died around 1664. Herrman is thought to have married Catherine Ward from Maryland in 1666.

As there seem to have been between Stuyvesant and other influential men, there were many serious quarrels between Stuyvesant and Herrman over trading rights, real estate, and possibly a love rivalry. Nonetheless, Stuyvesant chose Herrman for many difficult and delicate situations.

In August 1659 Maryland governor Josias Fendall sent word to the Dutch that everyone along the Delaware Bay was within Lord Baltimore's province and would have to leave. Stuyvesant sent Herrman and Resolved Waldron to see Lord Baltimore's brother and secretary, Philip Calvert, to settle the dispute.

When three conflicting maps of the province failed to resolve the boundary question, Calvert brought out the 1632 charter itself, which stated that the province was composed of land hitherto uncultivated. Since crops had been planted and harvested in 1631 at the Dutch settlement near present-day Lewes, Delaware, Herrman successfully argued that Maryland's boundary lay to the south of that settlement. Otherwise, the area that became the Three Lower Counties of Pennsylvania on Delaware, and eventually the state of Delaware, would have been part of Maryland. The protection of William Penn's colony of Pennsylvania and the fate of the city of Philadelphia twenty years later made those three counties vitally important in the control of pirates who were raiding ships on the river.

Herrman spent the winter of 1659 with his wife's family in Virginia, and, having realized that the English would eventually prevail over the Dutch in New Amsterdam, decided to move his family to the gentler climate of Maryland. He was granted denization in 1660 in order to own property in the English province.

Herrman offered to map the province in return for a land grant and was granted 26,000 acres over the next twenty-five years. His map, "Virginia and Maryland As it is Planted and Inhabited this present year 1670 Surveyed and Exactly Drawne by the Only Labor & Endeavour of Augustin Herrman Bohemiensis," was published in London in 1673, but the result displeased him as being ineptly done and "slobbered over." However, the king of England and Lord Baltimore praised the map, and George Washington described it as "admirably planned and equally well executed." The map was the authority for accurate and detailed information on the Chesapeake Bay area for seventy years.

Herrman named his manor and the river beside it "Bohemia" after the country of his birth. He was granted the title of lord of the manor and awarded his own seal. His deepest desire, confided to Lord Baltimore, was to found a landed aristocracy such as the one in England, and he hoped to start a settlement on his property.

He continued to own property and make investments in New York after the English had taken it from the Dutch in 1664, serving on a jury there in 1666. During that time he was also a commissioner, justice of the peace, and gentleman of the quorum in Upper Baltimore County, which at his urging became Cecil County in 1674.

When he found squatters on his New York property, his actions to try and oust them resulted in his imprisonment by Stuyvesant, who was annoyed that Herrman had deserted him to live in Maryland. According to legend, Herrman refused to give up his huge white horse and rode him upstairs into his cell; that night he jumped the horse through the window onto the cobblestone street, swam him across to New Jersey, and rode him home. Herrman had his portrait painted with the horse and had him buried in the manor graveyard.

In 1671 he instigated the building of a cart road from his manor east and then north to New Castle, Delaware. A part of his road is now Route 299 through Middletown and Odessa, Delaware. He was appointed in 1678 by the governor of Maryland to keep peace with the Native Americans, a job he managed well until 1683 when he became too weak to continue. Although Herrman was not known to have had strong religious beliefs, he was enticed by his son to give 3,700 acres in 1684 to the Labadists, a sect with some beliefs similar to those of the Quakers.

It is not known where Herrman died. His will was probated in 1686. His remains may still be buried on the site of the manor. Although only the name of the area, still called Bohemia Manor, and the name of the river remain from Herrman's vast holdings, the existence of his road, his map, and the state of Delaware attest to his vision and capacity in the law, in diplomacy, and in surveying and drafting.

• Herrman's 1678 commission to treat with the Native Americans and many important records in the Proceedings of the Council of Maryland are kept in Maryland's state archives in Annapolis. The Library of Congress and Brown University have 1673 copies of his map. A copy of Herrman's portrait with his white horse and a portrait of Jannetje are kept at the Maryland Historical Society. A translation of his 1659 journal appears in Clayton Colman Hall, *Narratives of Early Maryland* (1910). Excerpts from letters by Lord Baltimore and Herrman are included in Lee Phillips, *The Rare Map of Virginia and Maryland* (1911). The only comprehensive biography is Earl W. Heck, *Augustine Herrman* (1941).

DOROTHY ROWLETT COLBURN

HERRMANN, Bernard (29 June 1911–24 Dec. 1975), composer and conductor, was born in New York City, the son of Russian immigrant parents. His father, an optometrist, was born Abraham Dardick but changed the family name to Herrmann after he arrived in the United States about 1880. His mother's name was Ida Gorenstein. Even though he was not a musician, Abraham Herrmann insisted that his three children take music lessons. In 1924, when he was only thirteen, Bernard, or "Benny" as he was known by family and friends, won a prize for one of his first compositions, "The Bells," a song based on a poem by Verlaine. In 1927 he had his first lessons in music composition with Gustav Heine.

The following year he met composer Aaron Copland, who encouraged Herrmann to continue his composition studies. While still a student at DeWitt Clinton High School, Herrmann enrolled at New York University (NYU), where he studied composition with Philip James and conducting with Albert Stoessel. In 1930, when Stoessel left NYU to become head of the opera and orchestra department at the Juilliard School of Music, he invited Herrmann to continue his studies there. Herrmann spent the next two years studying conducting with Stoessel and composition and harmony with Bernard Wagenaar. But he was not satisfied with his teachers. With his father's encouragement, in 1931 he returned to NYU to earn a teaching degree. But he left after only one term to pursue a career as a conductor and composer.

In 1932 Herrmann joined the Young Composers Group, led by Copland. Later that year Herrmann returned to NYU, this time to study with Australian pianist and composer Percy Grainger. Herrmann greatly admired Grainger's eclectic musical interests and unorthodox method of teaching and remained an admirer throughout his life. In 1933 Herrmann assembled a group of thirty unemployed musicians to form the New Chamber Orchestra. With the assistance of Grainger and Vladimir Dukelsky (whose name was later Americanized by George Gershwin to Vernon Duke), the ensemble gave its first concert in May 1933 at the New School for Social Research in New York. The program consisted primarily of little-known works by Sir Edward Elgar, Henry Purcell, Charles Ives, Jerome Moross, and Herrmann.

Thanks to the efforts of songwriter and arranger Johnny Green, in 1934 Herrmann was hired by CBS radio as a conductor and arranger. He also began to compose original scores for radio dramas, culminating in his association with Orson Welles and the Mercury Theater on the Air. The most famous of these broadcasts, the one-hour dramatization of H. G. Welles's *The War of the Worlds*, aired on 30 October 1938 and created public hysteria. In that famous broadcast, Herrmann conducted the CBS orchestra playing dance music as background to the radio play.

Owing to the resulting publicity, in 1939 RKO invited Welles to come to Hollywood. Welles took with him many actors from the Mercury Theater and also asked Herrmann to join him and to compose the score for his first movie. That movie, *Citizen Kane* (1941), was the most auspicious film debut of any director or composer. It has been called one of the greatest films of the twentieth century. Herrmann's score, containing a multitude of music styles, contributed to the film's success. He explained that to impart "unity to the film's time-jumping narrative . . . I decided that I would use the old musical form of the leitmotiv, in other words a theme that is transferred incessantly" (*New York Times*, 25 May 1941; quoted in Smith, p. 78). In his review, *New York Times* movie critic Bosley Crowther singled out "the stunning manner in which the music of Bernard Herrmann has been used" (2 May 1941).

Also in 1941 Herrmann composed a score for director William Dieterle. The film, *All That Money Can Buy*, was based on the Stephen Vincent Benét story "The Devil and Daniel Webster." The score to that movie earned Herrmann his first and only Academy Award. From the 1940s to the 1970s he composed forty-eight movie scores and received four additional Academy Award nominations, beginning with *Citizen Kane* and followed by *Anna and the King of Siam* (1946), the latter directed by John Cromwell. Thirty

years later he was again nominated, for his last two scores, *Obsession*, directed by Brian De Palma, and *Taxi Driver*, directed by Martin Scorsese, both released in 1976.

Between 1955 and 1966 Herrmann composed the scores for eight movies directed by Alfred Hitchcock, beginning with *The Trouble with Harry* (1955), Herrmann's only comic movie score. He also composed the scores for Hitchcock's *Vertigo* (1958), *North by Northwest* (1959), and *Psycho* (1960). Besides the scores for Hitchcock movies, other important scores by Herrmann include those for *Hangover Square* (1945), *The Ghost and Mrs. Muir* (1947), *The Day the Earth Stood Still* (1951), *The 7th Voyage of Sinbad* (1958), *Mysterious Island* (1961), *Fahrenheit 451* (1966), and *Sisters* (1973).

During the 1950s and 1960s Herrmann wrote music for television as well as for the screen. He composed the themes for the well-known 1950s TV series "Gunsmoke," "Have Gun Will Travel," and "The Twilight Zone." Herrmann wrote highly evocative scores for "The Twilight Zone" (1959–1964) and "The Alfred Hitchcock Hour" (1963–1965). His only TV movie score was for *Companions in Nightmare* (1968). Herrmann also composed concert works for radio, movies, and television. Among these are *Sinfonietta for Strings* (1935); *Moby Dick* (1938), a cantata for male voices, soloists, and orchestra; his only symphony (1941); and *Wuthering Heights* (1951), his only opera.

Herrmann was married three times, first to Lucille Fletcher in 1939. They had two daughters (his only children) before they were divorced in 1948. His second marriage, to Lucille Anderson in 1949, ended in divorce in 1965. In 1967 he married Norma Shepherd; their union lasted until his death in Los Angeles.

In his book *Film Score*, film historian and record producer Tony Thomas wrote that "a good case can be made for him [Herrmann] as the most important of all American film composers, and it is possible to support that claim with a generous amount of his work on recordings" (p. 169). He also wrote that Herrmann "bitterly resented the suggestion that to write for films was of less value than writing for the concert hall or the opera house, and the quality of his scores makes it difficult for critics to prove their points" (p. 171). In a lecture given at Eastman College in 1973, Herrmann claimed that what "music can do in a film is something mystical. The camera can only do so much; the actors can only do so much; the director can only do so much. But the music can tell you what people are thinking and feeling, and that is the real function of music."

In *A Heart at Fire's Center*, biographer Steven C. Smith wrote this evaluation of Herrmann's career:

Herrmann remains the most imitated and influential composer in film. . . . His music, almost all of it programmatic, embodied the German Romanticism of Wagner and Mahler as well as the psychological impressionism of the French school (Debussy and Ravel especially)—perceived through the Anglo-American culture Herrmann adored. His music for films, radio and television not only gave temporal and emotional focus to its subject; it imparted a point of view that was distinctly Herrmann's own. . . . A strong element of nostalgia pervades Herrmann's writing, along with a brooding melancholy: the music reflects a divided man who sought more than he could find but reveled in the quest. It is this sensitivity for the separation between possibility and reality . . . that gives Herrmann's music its enduring emotional resonance. (pp. 2–4)

Though he was very difficult to deal with at times and very demanding of others, Herrmann always maintained a highly professional approach to his music. Music and film critics alike held him in high regard as a master of his craft. Working diligently and creatively for over forty years in radio, television, films, and the concert hall, he remained an individual voice in the crowded and often critical world of music. It was his long associations with Orson Welles and Alfred Hitchcock that made Herrmann famous, but it is for his inventive film music that he is most appreciated and best remembered.

• Herrmann's music manuscripts and papers are located in the Bernard Herrmann Archive at the University of California at Santa Barbara Music Library. For the fullest account of his career, see Steven C. Smith, *A Heart at Fire's Center: The Life and Music of Bernard Herrmann* (1991). Also recommended is the chapter on Herrmann in Tony Thomas, *Film Score: The Art & Craft of Movie Music* (1991). An earlier book by Thomas, *Music for the Movies* (1973), also contains a chapter on Herrmann. An interview with Herrmann is included in Irwin Bazelon, *Knowing the Score: Notes on Film Music* (1975). Herrmann's views on his first film score are expressed in "Score for a Film" in Ronald Gottesman, *Focus on Citizen Kane* (1971). An obituary is in the *New York Times*, 25 Dec. 1975.

ROGER L. HALL

HERRMANN, Eduard Emil (18 Dec. 1850–24 Apr. 1937), violinist, composer, and string quartet director, was born in Oberrotweil, duchy of Baden (now Baden-Württemberg, Germany), the son of Eduard Stephan Herrmann, a schoolteacher, and Amalie Knoebel. At an early age Eduard was trained musically by his father and later was given a stipend by the duke of Baden for his further education. In Freiburg he studied violin, then in 1864 enrolled at the Stuttgart music conservatory, where he was encouraged to continue by Franz Liszt. His quest for advanced musical training and broadened intellectual opportunities brought him in 1868 to the Berlin conservatory (Hochschule für Musik), where he became a protégé of the renowned violinist Joseph Joachim.

Intense, disciplined study in composition, violin technique, and quartet playing with Joachim prepared Herrmann for a professional career. Years of musical activity led to positions at the Schwerin Opera in 1871, where he met Richard Wagner, and in 1875 as concertmaster at the Hamburg Opera. With his brother Carl, a pianist, he made extensive concert tours in Germany and Holland. As a soloist in Berlin, then in Warsaw, Stockholm, Reval (Estonia), Helsingfors, and St. Petersburg, Herrmann featured a repertoire that included the Paganini violin concerto and Max Bruch's newly composed Concerto in G Minor (op. 26).

Herrmann accepted a permanent post as concertmaster in the Russian Imperial Ballet orchestra in St. Petersburg. As a composer, teacher, and instrumentalist, he was deeply involved in the city's rich musical life, playing in a string quartet with the noted Russian cellist Karl Davidov and establishing friendships with the composer Anton Rubinstein and with Leopold Auer. For several years he was the music critic of a German-language newspaper, the *Petersburger Herold*. In 1881 he auditioned for the post of concertmaster of the prestigious Imperial Opera orchestra with a superb performance of Joachim's difficult Hungarian Concerto. He won the position, then was informed by the judges that only a native Russian could be hired. Incensed at the blatant Slavophilism, Herrmann determined not to return to Germany but to immigrate to the United States, long a cherished dream of his.

On arriving in New York in September 1881, Herrmann continued his newspaper column, "The Travel Letters of a Musician," for the *Herold*. In it he described the transatlantic crossing and his positive reactions to the vibrant American lifestyle. Settling in New York City, he and his brother Carl gave successful joint concerts, with the endorsement of Liszt and the support of the impresario William Steinway. At their first appearance, Eduard played the Bach Chaconne and selections from Wieniawski and Paganini, while Carl performed the Beethoven Piano Sonata, op. 67 ("Appassionata"), to the delight of their audience.

Despite the intense musical competitiveness—there were more than 600 violinists listed in an 1882 New York musical directory—Herrmann entered into the tempo of the city's cultural activities. As he wrote to his fiancée in Russia, "In every way I prefer the Americans (to the Europeans) and you have to respect their industriousness." He responded to the individualistic approach of Americans, which enabled him to be fully independent. Critical of the lack of appreciation of the aesthetic and philosophic values of music and of the high standards of European musical performance, he worked tenaciously to transform the American attitude toward music through his own rigorous violin teaching. With a concept of music as an art rather than a business, he had the faith of many nineteenth-century intellectuals that the transforming power of music would result in societal progress. He imparted his philosophic and musical values to a large coterie of students, among them such accomplished professionals as Alexander Bloch and Amelia Galloway.

In 1881 Herrmann joined the orchestras of Leopold Damrosch and Theodore Thomas, dominant Germanic figures and giants in New York's emerging musical culture. Observing these archrivals, he noted that Damrosch was the better musical interpreter but that Thomas, "with an iron will and tenacious endurance, achieved his objective of making New York . . . the musical center of America" ("Autobiography," p. 71).

Herrmann accompanied Theodore Thomas's orchestra on its pathbreaking 10,000-mile tour in 1883, the first transcontinental trek of a symphony orchestra across the Midwest to San Francisco and back. This difficult undertaking nevertheless had notable results in stimulating civic musical awareness. With increasing family obligations (he had returned to St. Petersburg in 1882 to marry Ida von Bernhard, with whom he had two children), he left solo and orchestral playing to develop chamber music in New York and to continue teaching.

In the mid-1880s Herrmann took over the direction of the Standard Quartet as first violin. But by 1890 he had started his own group, the String Quartet Society of New York, with A. W. Lilienthal, Carl Hauser, and Emil Schenck. In 1900 these instrumentalists were the first to perform the complete cycle of the sixteen Beethoven quartets for New York audiences. Playing at the music salon of the sculptor Augustus Saint-Gaudens or at the homes of business patrons and intellectuals, Herrmann educated musical devotees through his own erudite and enthusiastic approach to the repertoire of chamber music from Mozart to Richard Strauss. To introduce the general public to chamber music, his quartet performed free concerts at the New York Masonic Hall.

Herrmann's most productive years as a composer were between 1901 and 1930. His Violin Concerto in C Minor was inspired by his affinity for the Adirondack Mountains, so reminiscent of his native Black Forest in Germany. It was first performed in 1905 at the People's Symphony Concerts in Carnegie Hall. In his compositions Herrmann emphasized the violin, producing quartets, quintets, and a sextet with woodwinds among his more than forty works.

With a lifelong interest in religious philosophy, Herrmann turned to theosophy and to spiritualism, especially after the death of his young son in 1900. He was greatly influenced by the works of William Quan Judge and translated his 1893 volume *The Ocean of Theosophy* into German. Later Herrmann published his own *Popular Theosophy* in Leipzig. He died in Miami, Florida.

Herrmann's career in Germany, Russia, and the United States offers insight into the influence of European-trained musicians on the development of late nineteenth-century American musical culture, especially that of New York City. Overcoming the inherent differences in American and European cultures confronting an immigrant, he quickly became rooted in a new milieu at a critical period in the growth of New York's musical life. Through incessant work and absorption in his profession, he responded, as a creative artist, to the public thirst and enthusiasm for instrumental music.

• Herrmann left a manuscript autobiography in German, now in private hands, which presents details of his life, his cultural focus, and his philosophic outlook. His extant correspondence, likewise privately held, reveals vividly the New York City musical world of the late nineteenth century. Copies of some of Herrmann's compositions are in the Music Division, Library of Congress; the Boston Public Library; and the Music Library, Yale University. Among his published works are Concerto for Violin with Orchestra, op. 25 (1904); Quintet for Two Violins, Viola, and Two Cellos, op. 31 (1911); Quartet for Two Violins, Viola, and Cello in F Major, op. 32 (1913); and Thirty-nine Violin Etudes for the Systematic Study of Double Stops (1913). Further details are in Wanda MacDowell, "Miami Men and Music," *Miami Daily News*, 26 Apr. 1936, and Henry Cavendish, *Miami Herald*, 26 Apr. 1936. Obituaries are in the *New York Times*, 26 Apr. 1937, and *Miami Herald*, 25 Apr. 1937.

WINFRED E. A. BERNHARD

HERRON, Carrie Rand (17 Mar. 1867–11 Jan. 1914), philanthropist and socialist activist, was born in Burlington, Iowa, the daughter of Caroline Amanda Sherfy, also a noted philanthropist, and Elbridge Dexter Rand, a lumber baron and banker. After her father's death in 1887, the young high school graduate became her mother's close friend and companion. Together they managed "The Pines," the family's estate in Burlington, and were involved in local civic affairs and the Burlington Congregational Church.

In 1891, George Davis Herron, who had been touring the country giving his highly acclaimed sermon "The Message of Jesus to Men of Wealth," accepted an offer to become the assistant pastor at the Rands' church. Herron was a fiery proponent of a social gospel message that insisted that the relationship between capital and labor be changed in order to give workers a better life; almost immediately, however, it became clear that Herron's message disturbed the head pastor, William Salter, and several prominent members of the church. George A. Gates, the president of Iowa College, in Grinnell, became aware of this untenable situation through Mrs. Rand, and in 1893 Gates negotiated a gift from the Rands to the college for $35,000 to endow a chair in Applied Christianity for Herron.

When Herron and his wife and four children moved to Grinnell that autumn, Carrie and her mother built a house for themselves in Grinnell and followed him. President Gates was an advocate of both the social gospel and of muscular Christianity, a belief that Christians should be active and virile, and so he happily arranged an appointment for Carrie as an instructor of physical education for women. She traveled to Chicago for special training and the next year was named principal of women. In this capacity she spent her mornings giving physical exams to female students and four afternoons a week leading them in exercise. In 1897 the E. D. Rand Women's Gymnasium was opened through a gift of $8,000 from the Rands.

During his tenure at Grinnell, Herron's message became more and more radical, and each year the pressure increased on him to resign. Finally, in October 1899 he tendered his resignation, effective January 1900. Upon his resignation, he and the Rands took an eight-month trip together to Europe. After they returned, Mrs. Herron asked for a divorce, claiming that

Herron had not lived at home for five years. This confirmed rumors that had connected Carrie and Herron since his time in Burlington. The Rands provided a $60,000 settlement to Mrs. Herron, and several newspaper accounts reported that they also paid for her lawyer, Clarence Darrow.

In January 1901 Carrie and Herron moved together to Chicago to begin working in a Christian group called the Social Apostolate. Herron served as the group's leader and worked to establish ministry to the poor through various cooperatives. Mrs. Rand helped to bankroll the group, and Carrie served as its treasurer. This project was short-lived, however, as following his divorce in March, Rand and Herron moved to New York City and were married on 25 May 1901 in a highly publicized wedding. The wedding was considered highly unorthodox because the couple wrote their own vows and performed the service themselves in the Rands' apartment. By this time, Herron had been deposed by the Congregationalist church in Iowa because of his divorce: he had been forced to admit to neglect and mental cruelty, and the church could not accept this publicly in a minister.

The new Mr. and Mrs. Herron worked tirelessly for socialist causes for the next four years. In July 1901 they served together as delegates to the Indianapolis convention at which the Socialist Party of America was founded. Carrie and her mother donated money to socialist organizations during these years, and Carrie became a regular part of the socialist intellectual circles in New York City.

The couple continued to receive sensational coverage in the national press, and, tiring of this, they moved with Mrs. Rand to Florence, Italy, in 1904. They settled in a sixteenth-century villa, "La Primola," where Mrs. Rand died the following year. Carrie Rand Herron's last great act of socialist patronage came in 1905 in carrying out the terms of her mother's will, which stipulated that a trust fund be created "to carry on and further the work to which I have devoted the later years of my life." Mrs. Herron administrated this trust together with socialist leader Morris Hillquit, and they chose to endow the Rand School of Social Science in New York City, which served to educate people about the principles of socialism and to support the creation of socialist propaganda. (The Rand School no longer exists.) Carrie remained in Florence, however, where she led a quiet, though isolated, life with her husband and raised their two children.

Carrie Rand Herron's life reflects the "two-party Protestantism" that emerged at the end of the nineteenth century. One "party" of the Protestant churches wanted to redeem the nation by changing the social institutions that created and fostered poverty and inequality, whereas the other "party" wanted to redeem the nation by focusing on individual salvation and personal sanctity. Carrie's devotion to reform and socialist causes was spurred by her early life in the Congregational church as well as by the emerging social gospel movement, but her husband's divorce and their controversial marriage combined with the prevailing power of the conservative majority to make her a social pariah in almost all circles. She died of cancer at her villa in Florence.

• Good source materials are in the Grinnell College Archives, the Hillquit papers in the State Historical Society of Wisconsin, and the George Herron Papers in the Hoover Institute at Stanford University. Useful information about Carrie Rand Herron's father and their life in Burlington is in *The Biographical Dictionary and Portrait Gallery of Representative Men of Chicago and Iowa* (1893). Her time in Grinnell is covered most extensively in John Nollen, *Grinnell College* (1953). Morris Hillquit, *Loose Leaves from a Busy Life* (1934), contains an account of the creation of the Rand School.

BRADLEY W. BATEMAN

HERRON, Francis Jay (17 Feb. 1837–8 Jan. 1902), major general, was born in Pittsburgh, Pennsylvania, the son of John Herron and Clarissa Anderson, a prominent Pittsburgh couple. He entered the Western University of Pennsylvania (now University of Pittsburgh) but left at sixteen without taking a degree to become a bank clerk. In 1855, seeking business opportunity in the West, he joined his three brothers in Dubuque, Iowa, where they established a bank. In 1859 he organized and was elected captain of a militia company known as the "Governor's Grays," which Herron offered to President-elect Abraham Lincoln in January 1861, two months prior to Lincoln's inauguration. On 14 May 1861 Herron resigned from the bank and, at the head of his militia company, joined the First Iowa Volunteer Infantry Regiment. Assigned to Brigadier General Nathaniel Lyon's army in Missouri, the First Iowa served at the battle of Wilson's Creek, 10 August 1861, where Herron so distinguished himself as to win promotion to lieutenant colonel of the Ninth Iowa Infantry. Commanding his regiment at the battle of Pea Ridge, Arkansas, 7–8 March 1862, Herron was taken prisoner when a Confederate artillery projectile shattered his right ankle. For his exploits at Pea Ridge, Herron was promoted to brigadier general of volunteers to rank from 16 July 1862 and, thirty-one years after the event, was awarded the Congressional Medal of Honor.

After being exchanged on 20 March 1862, Herron was given command of the Second and Third Divisions of John M. Schofield's Army of the Frontier. Encamped on Wilson's Creek in December 1862, Herron received an urgent request for assistance from Brigadier General James G. Blunt, whose 7,000 Federals were being menaced by 11,500 Confederates under Major General Thomas C. Hindman. Herron force-marched his 6,000 Iowa, Illinois, Indiana, Wisconsin, and Missouri troops more than 100 miles in less than three days, arriving at Prairie Grove, Arkansas, on 7 December in time to save Blunt's command and turn an apparent disaster into a decisive Union victory. Despite what he called "a terrible trip," Herron was able to report, "We have bearded the tricky rebel, General Hindman, in his den." On 28 December, following the battle of Prairie Grove, Herron and Blunt captured

Van Buren, Arkansas, forcing Hindman to evacuate Fort Smith and subsequently all of Northwest Arkansas. "I think this section is rid of Hindman," Herron reported to Major General Samuel R. Curtis.

For these deeds—his finest achievements of the war—Herron was promoted to major general of volunteers on 10 March 1863, to rank from 29 November 1862, and on 30 March 1863 he superseded Schofield as commander of the Army of the Frontier. With the war in Arkansas substantially won for the Union, however, Herron was transferred to command of the Army of the Tennessee on 11 June 1863 and sent to aid Major General U. S. Grant at the siege of Vicksburg. There his division occupied the extreme left wing of the Union army, and with the city's capitulation on 4 July, Herron was appointed as one of the three generals to take possession of the city.

On 7 August 1863 Herron was transferred to Port Hudson, arriving soon after the fall of the last Confederate bastion on the Mississippi. For the remainder of the war Herron was stationed in the Department of the Gulf, in Louisiana and Texas. From Brownsville, Texas, during the winter of 1863–1864, he aided Mexican president Benito Juárez in his civil war against the forces of Ferdinand Maximilian. From 1 May until 9 June 1864 Herron commanded the Military Division of West Mississippi. From 6 August 1864 until 3 October 1864, he commanded XIX Corps, District of Port Hudson, and from 9 February 1865 through July 1865 he commanded the Northern District of Louisiana, with headquarters at Baton Rouge. Both of those commands were districts of the Department of the Gulf. At the close of the war Herron was appointed commissioner to negotiate treaties with the Indians, but he resigned from the army on 7 June 1865.

In Baton Rouge at the war's end, Herron remained in Louisiana, where for a time he was tax collector for a district in New Orleans and from 1867 to 1869 was U.S. marshal. In 1871 Governor Henry Clay Warmoth appointed Herron, a strong Radical, as secretary of state. When Herron broke with the governor in 1871, however, Warmoth revealed charges that Herron had failed to settle accounts as tax collector and removed him from office. In 1877, with the end of Radical Reconstruction and the removal of U.S. troops from Louisiana, Herron moved to New York City, where he was reportedly connected with a manufacturing establishment, but may also have practiced law. The 1900 federal census lists him as a banker. He died a pauper in a tenement on West Ninety-ninth Street. His death certificate records, "Occupation: None." He was survived only briefly by his second wife, Adelaide Wibray Flash. Whether there were children from either marriage is not known.

• For more information on Herron's career see Patricia Faust, ed., *Historical Times Illustrated Encyclopedia of the Civil War* (1986); Alvin M. Josephy, Jr., *The Civil War in the American West* (1991); William L. Shea and Earl J. Hess, *Pea Ridge, Civil War Campaign in the West* (1993); A. A. Stewart, *Iowa Colonels and Regiments: Being a History of Iowa Regiments in the War of the Rebellion* (1865); Joe Gray Taylor, *Louisiana Reconstructed, 1863–1877* (1974); Ezra J. Warner, *Generals in Blue: Lives of the Union Commanders* (1964); and John D. Winters, *Civil War in Louisiana* (1963).

THOMAS W. CUTRER

HERRON, George Davis (21 Jan. 1862–9 Oct. 1925), social reformer and author, was born in Montezuma, Indiana, the son of William Herron, a teacher and newspaper publisher, and Isabella Davis. A sickly lad, he was educated at home by his father. Compelled to shift for himself by the age of ten because of his family's financial difficulties, Herron followed the printer's trade for seven years. He then resolved to seek further education. Supporting himself by editing a college newsletter, he undertook his only formal schooling in the preparatory department of Ripon College in 1879, dropping out in 1881 because of ill health. He then became involved in other newspaper ventures. In 1883 he married Mary V. Everhard of Ripon; they had four children.

Herron decided to enter the ministry in 1883, pastoring a small Congregational church in the Dakota Territory. He then moved through a series of short pastorates, and at his second, in Atlanta, Georgia, he was ordained in 1884. He undertook extensive reading in theology, philosophy, sociology, and economics. In 1890 he rose to prominence after delivering the address, "The Message of Jesus to Men of Wealth," to the Minnesota Congregational Club. Identifying himself with the emerging social Christian movement, he maintained that the teachings of Jesus contained the solution to all social problems and proved to be a dramatic, popular, magnetic speaker. Driven by a guiding sense of destiny, he published a collection of four sermons entitled *The Larger Christ* (1891) and accepted a pastorate at the prominent First Congregational Church of Burlington, Iowa. In 1892 he was awarded an honorary D.D. by Tabor College, a small Congregational institution in Iowa, and henceforth was known as "Dr. Herron" throughout his varied career.

Among his new parishioners was Caroline Amanda Rand, a wealthy philanthropist, who in 1893 arranged an endowment for Herron as professor and head of the new Department of Applied Christianity at Iowa College (later Grinnell College). Herron's classes became quite popular, and from this base he traveled widely, spoke often, published frequently, and became the center of what came to be known as the "Kingdom movement," an effort to call the churches to the reform of society at a time of depression and labor strife. Winning support from those influenced by Populist and other reform movements, Herron became increasingly judgmental and censorious of the complacency in church and society concerning social and economic evils and injustices in his many addresses, sermons, and books. He was a factor in the spread of the Social Gospel in the 1890s as he sought to motivate people to undertake reform activities by accepting the ideal of self-sacrifice, but as he moved increasingly to the left theologically, he became a highly controversial figure. By the time he attracted public attention, he had already moved from the conservative, revivalistic frontier Congregationalism that had first shaped him to a liberal Social Gospel position. By mid-decade he had moved from that moderate reformist stance to espouse a more rigorous Christian socialist position, and his messages became increasingly critical of church life. He also displayed an increasing social radicalism as he espoused socialist views on many matters and with growing frequency addressed radical reformist rather than church audiences.

By 1899 his position at the college was under attack because of his controversial views; in October he presented his resignation and was given leave for the second semester. He spent it traveling in Europe with Caroline Rand and her daughter Carrie Rand, who had been an instructor in Iowa College's social and physical education program. Returning in September 1900, Herron threw his support to political socialism, working toward a unification of several of the small socialist parties. His activities involved extensive traveling; he spent little time at home and repeatedly asked his wife for a divorce. In March 1901, at a time when divorce was widely viewed with great distaste by the church and in much of the wider culture, Mary Herron sued for divorce on the grounds of cruelty and desertion. The divorce was uncontested; Mary was awarded custody of the children and given a cash settlement in an action that attracted national attention. In May Herron married Carrie Rand; they located in New York City and were to have two children. Early in June he was defrocked as a Congregational minister.

That summer Herron played an important role in the formation of the Socialist Party of America, wrote for many socialist publications, and appeared destined to occupy a major place in what was then a rapidly growing avant-garde movement. But as newspapers relentlessly exploited the Herron-Rand scandal, not only accusing the former minister of being a cruel and faithless husband and father, but also calling him an advocate of free love and making other irresponsible charges, the couple went abroad for a year. Returning late in 1902, Herron had adopted a Marxist position, though his views of class struggle were moderate, emphasizing a religious, gradualist, revisionist interpretation of socialism rather than the strict scientific socialism of Marx. The high point of Herron's leadership in American socialism came in 1904 when he nominated Eugene Debs for the presidency and prepared the party platform. The barrage of criticism continued, however, and the Herrons fled to Italy, permanently settling in a villa overlooking Florence in 1905. Caroline Rand died later that year, leaving a trust fund for causes dear to her, used in part by trustees Carrie Herron and Morris Hillquit to found the Rand School of Social Science in New York City. Although now Herron's work was largely focused on socialism in Europe, his speeches and writings continued to be characterized by sweeping generalities, utopian overtones, and the search for messianic figures and movements to rescue humankind from destructive forces. Seeking to be a mediator among socialist and reform movements, he cultivated his wide European contacts, entertained frequently, and became well known for his intellectual and literary interests and output. Carrie died in 1914, and in 1915 he married Frieda B. Schoeberle; they had three children.

Disgusted with the factionalism of socialism, and rejecting the pacifistic tendencies of many of its supporters when World War I erupted, Herron severed all political ties with the movement and relocated to Geneva to be better able to support the Allies. There he played the role of mediator among contending minorities through his network of friendships and soon became employed by the U.S. State Department as a secret negotiator and an unofficial diplomatic adviser, keeping in close contact with British and American foreign offices.

Herron had found his new enemy in Prussianism, and in Woodrow Wilson, his new hero. In a stream of letters and articles, he presented the American president to Europe as one who, at the right moment, would lead the United States into the struggle. By the time his book *Woodrow Wilson and the World's Peace* (1917) appeared, his explanations of Wilson's actions before the American entry into the war proved to be quite accurate, and he became known as "Wilson's man of confidence." He was disillusioned, however, by the results of the peace conference, setting forth his views in *The Defeat in the Victory* (1921).

Moving back to Italy after the war, Herron briefly identified an Italian politico-cultural renaissance as pointing to that country as civilization's last hope but soon returned to placing his final hopes on the League of Nations. His last years were troubled by ill health. He died in Munich, Bavaria, where he was seeking a health cure.

George Herron was an early important figure in the rise of the Social Gospel in American Protestantism, and though he moved into its radical wing and beyond, where few of his earlier followers were willing to go, many whom he had influenced remained in the mainstream of social Christianity after he had left it. His activities in the early twentieth century cast light on the history of socialism in the United States and Europe, and his role as a significant interpreter of Woodrow Wilson to Europe during World War I provides insight into diplomacy of the period. Although he shifted from one cause to another during his varied career, Herron remained an articulate idealist, judging the present in the light of his high hopes, always seeking a new leader or movement to save civilization.

• Some of Herron's papers from his Iowa career are at Grinnell College. The most complete collection of his papers and correspondence, with much attention to his work during and after World War I, is at the Hoover Institution of War, Revolution, and Peace, Stanford University. In addition to the works mentioned above, Herron's most notable works include *The New Redemption: A Call to the Church to Reconstruct Society according to the Gospel of Christ* (1893), *The*

Christian Society (1894), *The Christian State: A Political Vision of Christ* (1895), *Between Caesar and Jesus* (1899), *The Menace of Peace* (1917), *Germanism and the American Crusade* (1918), *The Greater War* (1919), and *The Revival of Italy* (1922). On Herron's role in World War I, see Mitchell P. Briggs, *George D. Herron and the European Settlement* (1932). For detailed doctoral dissertations on Herron, see Robert T. Handy, "George D. Herron and the Social Gospel in American Protestantism, 1890–1901" (Univ. of Chicago, 1949); Phyllis Ann Nelson, "George D. Herron and the Socialist Clergy, 1890–1914" (State Univ. of Iowa, 1953); and Herbert R. Dieterich, "Patterns of Dissent: The Reform Ideas and Activities of George D. Herron" (Univ. of New Mexico, 1957), all of which provide extensive bibliographical information. An obituary is in the *New York Times*, 11 Oct. 1925.

ROBERT T. HANDY

HERSEY, John Richard (17 June 1914–24 Mar. 1993), writer, was born in Tientsin, China, the son of Roscoe Hersey, an employee of the Young Men's Christian Association, and Grace Baird, a missionary. Hersey attended British and American schools in Tientsin and continued his education in the United States after his family left China in 1924. As an undergraduate at Yale University, he held a variety of jobs, including waiter, tutor, lifeguard, and electrician's assistant. He was also a football letterman and vice chair and music critic for the *Yale Daily News*. He received his B.A. in 1936. The following year Hersey attended Clare College of Cambridge University in England on a Mellon Fellowship, but he never completed an advanced degree.

After working as a secretary for writer Sinclair Lewis during the summer of 1937, Hersey joined the staff of *Time* magazine, and from 1937 to 1944 he covered the events of World War II in China, Japan, Russia, the South Pacific, and the Mediterranean. This experience inspired his first two books, *Men on Bataan* (1942), which dealt with American troops in the Philippines during World War II, and *Into the Valley* (1943), which concerned a small group of marines in a battle at Guadalcanal. Hersey married Frances Ann Cannon in 1940; they had four children.

In his third book, *A Bell for Adano* (1944), Hersey ventured into a form that he later called the "novel of contemporary history." This wartime novel about Italians and the U.S. Army became a bestseller and won a Pulitzer Prize. It was translated into more than ten languages and rewritten as a movie and a Broadway play.

Throughout his career Hersey experimented with many genres and techniques, such as short stories, traditional novels, histories, science fiction, and literary criticism. Regardless of his form, however, he focused upon the effect of significant—often horrifying—events on individual lives while retaining the journalist's flair for detail, sense of place, and fluent style.

Nowhere are these traits more apparent than in Hersey's best-known book, *Hiroshima*, hailed by one reviewer as "one of the great classics of the war" (*New Republic*, 9 Sept. 1946). Hersey completed this work after a trip to Japan in 1945–1946; the trip was cosponsored by *Life* magazine, for which he had worked as an editor and a correspondent in 1944–1945, and by the

New Yorker. An account of six survivors of the atomic bombing of Hiroshima, the work was first printed as an issue of the *New Yorker* (31 Aug. 1946) and later read in its entirety on ABC radio.

Always concerned with social and moral issues, Hersey immersed himself in the study of another tragedy of World War II: the destruction of the Warsaw ghetto by the Nazis. The novel that resulted from his study, *The Wall* (1950), is considered by some as Hersey's finest achievement. Like *A Bell for Adano*, *The Wall* was adapted for the stage. In 1982 it was also filmed for television by CBS.

Hersey's essay "The Novel of Contemporary History" (*Atlantic Monthly*, Nov. 1949) illuminates his position as a writer. Most people, he contends, learn more about history from historical novels than from textbooks. Thus, a historical novel "should make anyone who reads it better able to meet life in his generation."

Hersey's canon reflects this vision and suggests why he abandoned journalism. Fiction, he believed, "is a clarifying agent [that] makes truth possible." His own work follows his prescription for promoting truth:

The image of a single protagonist, in which the reader may see his own image—this is far more moving, more persuasive, and more memorable than the most raucous headlines and the most horrible statistics and the most authoritative editorials that could possibly be published in a newspaper. Journalism allows its readers to witness history; fiction gives its readers an opportunity to live it.

Although Hersey continued to write prolifically until his death, his reputation as a writer hinges almost entirely on his early work. He was also active in public affairs. In 1948 he joined the Authors League of America and worked on problems of copyright and censorship. From 1949 to 1955 he served as the vice president of this organization, and from 1975 to 1980 he was its president. He was also a prominent member of the Authors Guild. In 1952 he chaired an organization of Connecticut volunteers in support of the Democratic presidential hopeful Adlai Stevenson and was a member of Stevenson's campaign staff in 1956. In two books, *The President* (1975) and *Aspects of the Presidency: Truman and Ford in Office* (1980), he further pursued his interest in national politics. Hersey publicly opposed America's involvement in the Vietnam War.

An educator as well as a writer, Hersey joined the Yale faculty in 1950, attaining the rank of professor in 1976. After retiring, he continued to teach as an adjunct professor. He also held visiting appointments at the American Academy in Rome (1970–1971) and at the Massachusetts Institute of Technology (1975).

Hersey's interest in education extended beyond his classroom. In the mid-1950s, as a member of the National Citizens' Commission for the Public Schools, he observed classes and prepared reports, including a pamphlet for the Woodrow Wilson Foundation in 1959 titled *Intelligence, Choice, and Consent*.

In addition to the Pulitzer Prize, Hersey received many awards, including a naval citation in 1942 for his work with the wounded on Guadalcanal; the Anisfield-Wolf Award (1950); the Daroff Memorial Fiction Award of the Jewish Book Council of America; the Sidney Hillman Foundation Award (1951) for *The Wall*; the Howland Medal from Yale (1952); and the Sara Josepha Hale Award (1963). At age thirty-nine he was elected to the National Academy of Arts, the youngest writer ever to receive this honor.

Hersey's first marriage ended in divorce in 1958. In June of that year he married Barbara Day Addams Kaufman; they had one child. Hersey died at his home in Key West, Florida, only six weeks after sending a new manuscript to his publisher. The work, *Key West Tales* (1994), was published posthumously.

Hersey intended his work to be read and enjoyed by an educated general readership; he had no qualms with using his books to present a moral message that may have labeled him as a traditionalist in the minds of the academic elite. This literary focus likely accounts for the diversity of opinion expressed by his reviewers, some of whom objected to what they considered his moralistic or simplistic stance. Nevertheless, Hersey was highly regarded for his "compassion without sticky sentimentality, an almost monumental integrity, an eloquent simplicity, a basic respect for his craft" (Norman Cousins, "John Hersey," *Saturday Review of Literature*, 4 Mar. 1950).

• Hersey's papers are at the Beinecke Library of Yale University. A bibliography of Hersey's work through mid-career is found in Nancy Lyman Huse, *John Hersey and James Agee: A Reference Guide* (1978). Three critical studies are David Sanders, *John Hersey* (1967); Huse, *The Survival Tales of John Hersey* (1983); and Sanders, *John Hersey Revisited* (1990). Hersey's work is also analyzed in Samuel B. Girgus, "Against the Grain: The Achievement of John Hersey" (Ph.D. diss., Univ. of New Mexico, 1972), and Huse, "John Hersey: The Writer and His Times" (Univ. Ph.D. diss., Univ. of Chicago, 1975). A personal reminiscence is in D. W. Faulkner, "John Hersey," *Sewanee Review* 101 (1993): 636–37, and an obituary is in the *New York Times*, 25 Mar. 1993.

CARROLL VIERA

HERSHEY, Lewis Blaine (12 Sept. 1893–20 May 1977), military officer and director of the Selective Service System, was born in Steuben County, Indiana, the son of Rosetta Richardson and Latta Freleigh Hershey, a farmer. Hershey was raised in northeast Indiana by his father after the death of his mother in 1898. Showing little interest in the family farm, he entered Tri-State College in Angola, Indiana. Working part time as a deputy sheriff, he also played varsity basketball and belonged to several college dramatics clubs. He received a bachelor of science degree in 1912, and he graduated with honors in 1914 with bachelors degrees in arts and pedagogy. His first professional job was as principal of Flint High School in rural Indiana.

Although successful as a teacher, Hershey cut short his pursuit of a graduate degree in education at Indiana University to participate in World War I. He had joined the Indiana National Guard in 1911 and by 1916 had been elected first lieutenant. In 1916 his unit served in Texas, patrolling the Mexican border as part of President Woodrow Wilson's pacification policy. Events in Europe forced a recall of these troops, and Hershey's unit was federalized on 29 December 1916. The United States entered the European war on 6 April 1917.

Acting as a first lieutenant in Battery "C" of the 137th Field Artillery, Hershey began training at Camp Shelby, Mississippi. Before departing for Europe, he married Ellen Dygert of Angola, Indiana, on 29 November 1917. Arriving in France as a captain in October 1918, Hershey had no opportunity to see combat. But he enjoyed the comradeship as well as the travel and adventure of military life. With little desire to return to rural Indiana, he volunteered for an extension of his tour and served for eleven months as an embarkation officer. He returned to the United States in September 1919 and obtained a regular army commission on 1 July 1920.

Moving from one isolated army post to another for the next sixteen years, Hershey and his wife had four children. A polo accident in November 1927 at Fort Bliss, Texas, permanently blinded Hershey in the left eye. After attending Command and General Staff College in August 1931 and the Army War College in August 1933, Hershey obtained the rank of major in July 1935.

Called to Washington in September 1936 for duty with the General Staff of the War Department, Hershey left the artillery and began his long career in manpower mobilization. As secretary of the Joint Army and Navy Selective Service Committee, he supervised manpower mobilization plans for war. After the United States adopted a peacetime draft in October 1940, Hershey became deputy director of the new Selective Service System. In July 1941 President Franklin D. Roosevelt appointed him director, a post he held until February 1970.

The successful mobilization of the armed forces in World War II, including the drafting of 13 million men, enhanced Hershey's reputation. Promotions followed rapidly: to lieutenant colonel in August 1940, to temporary brigadier general in October 1940, and to major general in April 1942. In March 1947 the draft ended, but Hershey continued as director of the Office of Selective Service Records. The Cold War and the failure of volunteer enlistments soon forced the Department of Defense in early 1948 to call for a renewal of the draft and Selective Service.

President Harry S. Truman refused even to consider a new director. By this time the entire Congress had become captivated by the expert manpower knowledge and homespun wit of the Hoosier general who looked like a farmer. The president quickly reappointed Hershey to lead the reborn system in July 1948. During the Korean War the system again functioned efficiently. Responding to pleas for special treatment from the scientific and educational community, Hershey appointed a committee of civilian leaders in these fields to design a system of deferments that would ensure the most efficient use of specialized manpower.

Once the Korean War ended in 1953, Hershey's main responsibility became supervising an increasingly liberal deferment system. Draft calls dropped as authorized strength for the armed forces diminished. As the number of eighteen-year-old males in the population increased, the military participation rate declined. Selective Service found itself offering deferments to channel the surplus manpower into colleges and defense-related jobs.

After a decade of relative inactivity, except for managing the expanding deferments, the system was again called upon to deliver men in 1965 to meet the needs for troops in the Vietnam War. As the war became increasingly unpopular with the American public, Hershey's reputation began to suffer. Over the preceding twenty-five years he had helped to shape the character of the draft. Operating under general guidelines from the president and Congress, Hershey had promoted a decentralized draft system with major power residing in local draft boards. As the man who had been present at the design and creation of the system in the late 1930s, who had personally visited hundreds of local boards, and who had defended the prerogatives of these civilian volunteers against centralization threats by the federal government, he now enjoyed an unprecedented popularity among draft officials and in Congress. When he offered "advice" to the local boards, they generally followed his leadership. His position was reenforced by his winning personality and unparalleled knowledge of the system.

By 1966, however, this system seemed riddled with inequity. Local board classification authority led to lack of uniformity in classifications. The draft risk for men in different sections of the country depended upon a myriad of local circumstances, but critics complained about what appeared to be capricious classifications. While Hershey and others argued that it was impossible to guarantee an equal risk for men with different physical and personal circumstances living in different communities, critics demanded more equity than the system could deliver. There was simply no way in which a decentralized draft system could achieve the kind of national uniformity demanded by draft opponents. This inconsistency had always been part of the draft; indeed Congress had frequently praised decentralization. But never before had the system been forced to draft so many men for so long for such an unpopular war. The period of automatic deferments that preceded Vietnam also ensured a new attitude toward being called to the colors against an enemy who did not seem to threaten the nation.

Hershey had weathered other periods of criticism. He had accommodated some earlier critics by adopting specialized deferments. In Congress he disarmed opponents with his wit and homespun philosophy about the wisdom of local citizens in contrast to faceless Washington bureaucrats. Senators as diverse as Republican Jacob Javits and Democrat Richard Russell insisted that "General Hershey knows best" when it came to military manpower. And for more than a quarter century, he had won endorsements from five sitting presidents, from Roosevelt to Johnson.

But the Vietnam War was a different struggle for the general. As a firm believer in the principles of America's containment policy, with a son serving in Vietnam, and as a representative of an older ethos of patriotism and discipline, he had little sympathy for the new wave of draft protest and counterculture. At first he limited his reaction to verbal scorn, but as the protest grew, he took action. Under oral instructions from President Lyndon Johnson, Hershey threatened to use the draft to silence war protesters, by removing student deferments from those who participated in illegal antiwar protests.

In the 1968 election Hershey became a political liability. After Richard Nixon took office as president, one of his first priorities was to reform and then end the draft, as a means of ending antiwar protest. As someone whose entire life had centered on the value of the citizen soldier and who believed firmly in the local boards and the decentralized draft, Hershey opposed the president's attempt to centralize and nationalize draft classifications. Seeking to avoid an open struggle with Hershey, who still had support in Congress, Nixon awarded the general a fourth star and reassigned him to the position of presidential adviser on manpower. Left to wither away, and disregarded by the White House, Hershey retired from the army in April 1973.

His major significance to the nation lies in his almost thirty years of directing the Selective Service System. Six different presidents found Hershey indispensable in running the draft. By the time of his retirement the system reflected his Jeffersonian views of decentralized authority, with considerable autonomy being exercised by local draft boards. The sixty thousand volunteers who operated these boards eventually inducted over 14.6 million young men. But the autonomy led to inconsistency of classification. When the Vietnam War grew unpopular, the draft system became a convenient scapegoat for protesters. The entire deferment system, which had been erected in response to demographic pressure and to demands of special interest groups, now seemed a source of inequity rather than a sign of scientific selection of manpower. As the draft grew unpopular in the 1960s, Hershey's political astuteness failed, and he allowed the system to become a political instrument. When he left office, his name was a scourge among protesters. Yet his great personal charm, integrity, and political skill had allowed him to serve his country with efficiency and success. After his retirement Hershey lived in Bethesda, Maryland. He died in Angola, Indiana.

• The Hershey papers, including considerable material on the operation of Selective Service, are found at the Military History Institute, Carlisle Barracks, Carlisle, Pennsylvania. Additional papers useful in a study of his career may be found in Record Group 147, National Archives, Washington, D.C. Some cursory material is also available at the Hershey Museum, Tri-State College, Angola, Indiana. The most comprehensive study of the general is George Q. Flynn, *Lewis B. Hershey, Mr. Selective Service* (1985). For the operation of Selective Service under Hershey see Flynn, *The Draft, 1940–1973* (1993). R. E. Seiverling, *Lewis B. Hershey: A Pictorial and Documentary Biography* (1969), is uncritical but useful for photographs. More substantive on conscription issues is James M. Gerhardt, *The Draft and Public Policy* (1971). An obituary appears in the *New York Times*, 21 May 1977.

GEORGE Q. FLYNN

HERSHEY, Milton Snavely (13 Sept. 1857–13 Oct. 1945), candy manufacturer, was born at his family's homestead in Derry Church, Dauphin County, Pennsylvania, the son of Henry H. Hershey and Fannie B. Snavely. In search of elusive wealth and success, Henry Hershey moved his family numerous times, always failing at his varied business ventures, including farming, cough drop manufacturing, and sales. As a result of the instability, Milton's formal education was haphazard, and he never went beyond the fourth grade.

At age fourteen his father apprenticed Hershey to Sam Ernst, a printer in Lancaster, Pennsylvania, but within months he had been fired for his poor performance. Hershey's mother then arranged an apprenticeship with Joseph H. Royer, a confectioner in Lancaster. From 1872 to 1876 Hershey worked with Royer in his confectionery and ice cream parlor, learning many of the skills and tools that would later enable him to build his candy empire.

After finishing his apprenticeship, Hershey decided to open his own candy business. He chose Philadelphia, the site of the Great Centennial Exposition established to celebrate the one-hundredth anniversary of the Declaration of Independence. With the help of loans from his uncle, Abraham Snavely, he opened his first candy shop, M. S. Hershey, Wholesale and Retail Confectioner, in June 1876. He made candy at night and during the day sold his freshly made caramels and taffy from a pushcart to the crowds at the exposition. His mother, a frugal, hardworking Mennonite who had separated from his impractical father during Hershey's apprenticeship, moved to Philadelphia with her sister Mattie Snavely to help in the fledgling confectioner's store. For six years Hershey barely managed to keep his business viable. In February 1882, however, after a winter dogged by illness and mounting debts, Hershey sold the business and returned to Lancaster.

Hershey next decided to join his father in Colorado, where the elder Hershey had moved after a short stint helping in his son's Philadelphia store. In Denver, Hershey worked briefly for a candy manufacturer where he learned that adding fresh milk to candy greatly improved its quality. This knowledge would be crucial to him in later years.

Nevertheless, failure continued to haunt Hershey. After his stay in Denver he and his father attempted to open a candy business in Chicago, but the venture fell through after his father endorsed a friend's bad note. A trip to explore business possibilities in New Orleans proved futile, so Milton Hershey decided to try New York City, where he moved in the spring of 1883 to work for the candymaking firm of Huyler and Company while arranging to open another shop, Hershey's Fine Candies. Despite his efforts, his lack of capital combined with high sugar prices caused his business to falter. In the fall of 1885, after failing to make payments on a $10,000 note, he lost his candymaking machinery and once again returned to Lancaster, where his persistence finally paid off.

Hershey was determined to succeed in the candymaking business. Because of his successive failures, however, both his aunt and uncle refused him further financial assistance. Consequently he joined forces with a man he had employed in Philadelphia, William Henry Lebkicher. Together they scraped up enough cash to start the Lancaster Caramel Company. As he had learned in Denver, Hershey developed a recipe using fresh milk for a candy he called "Hershey's Crystal A" caramels. An English importer who appreciated the quality and freshness of the caramels placed the company's first large order—£500 sterling worth of the candy—enough to provide a foundation for Hershey's company's growth.

This success enabled Hershey to secure a $250,000 loan from the Importers and Traders Bank of New York City. Using this capital, he quickly began to expand his candy business. By 1893 he had opened plants in Mount Joy, Pennsylvania, and Chicago and Geneva, Illinois, all of which joined the original Lancaster plant in producing his trademark Crystal A caramels. In 1894 a local history, *The Portrait and Biographical Record of Lancaster County*, claimed that Hershey's business had "grown to wonderful proportions," doing "over a million dollars' worth of business in a year." About Hershey, the volume declared that "no man stands higher in business and social circles in the city of Lancaster."

On a business trip to Europe in 1892, Hershey learned that the Swiss were dipping caramels in chocolate and that they were using milk not only to make caramels but also in their chocolate coatings. He returned home determined to put these discoveries to use. In 1893, therefore, on a trip to the World's Columbian Exposition in Chicago, he ordered chocolate-rolling machinery manufactured by the J. M. Lehmann Company of Dresden, Germany. The next year he opened the Hershey Chocolate Company, which was to produce cocoa, baking chocolate, and sweet chocolate coatings for his caramels; in the spring of 1895 the new company recorded its first commercial sale of chocolate. Hershey soon expanded his new business to include many novelty items such as chocolate cigars and chocolate bicycles. Deciding to concentrate on his chocolate business, in 1900 Hershey sold the Lancaster Caramel Company for $1 million to the rival American Caramel Company, but he retained exclusive rights as its supplier of dipping chocolates.

The turn of the century yielded another landmark in the Hershey annals. In February 1900 his chocolate company began marketing its milk chocolate Hershey Bar. Previously manufactured only in Switzerland and Germany, milk chocolate was new to the United

States. Hershey had experimented for several years before devising the formula that would allow him to mass produce the chocolate. Meanwhile, in 1897 he had purchased his birthplace, the Derry Church homestead. Originally planning to reunite his parents on the old farm, he realized instead, in his quest to manufacture affordable milk chocolate, that the rich dairy land surrounding his Dauphin County farm provided an ideal location for his chocolate plant. Not only did the area provide an abundant supply of the requisite fresh milk, it also offered plenty of fresh water for cooling purposes in the factory as well as surplus land for expansion. By buying adjacent properties he soon accumulated more than 1,500 acres of prime farm land. In 1903 he broke ground in the village of Derry Church for his new chocolate plant. Realizing that workers would need places to live, shop, worship, and educate their children, he also began construction of an entire community.

Both the company and the community prospered. In 1908 the Hershey Chocolate Company incorporated; by 1915 its plant covered thirty-five acres. Company sales rocketed from just $600,000 in 1901 to $20 million twenty years later. In both 1918 and 1919 stockholders earned 120 percent on their investments. The community, renamed Hershey in 1905, provided affordable housing, sewerage, electricity, schools, stores, trolley transportation, a hospital, a park, and even a zoo. Determined to keep his employees working during the lean years of the depression, Hershey launched a large-scale building project in the 1930s that included a hotel, a high school, a community building, a sports arena, and an innovative windowless, air-conditioned office building.

As the depression ended, Hershey could claim that no one working for him in Hershey had been laid off. Nevertheless, Hershey was not immune to labor organization. In 1937 the Congress of Industrial Organizations (CIO) organized a sit-down strike that was only ended when dairy farmers protesting the plant's inactivity caused a near riot. By 1940 the American Federation of Labor (AFL) had organized a union at the Hershey plant.

Hershey's concern for the community did not end with his employees. He and his wife, Catherine Elizabeth "Kitty" Sweeney, a former candy shop employee from New York, whom he had married in 1898, had no children of their own. In 1909 they founded a school for orphaned boys. Originally established as the Hershey Industrial School by its deed of trust, its charge was to train "young men to useful trades and occupations." Over time its vocational emphasis gradually shifted to include college preparatory and business curricula. In 1918, three years after the death of his wife, Hershey donated an estimated $60 million in trust to the school. By the latter part of the century the school, renamed the Milton Hershey School, annually provided housing and Kindergarten through twelfth-grade education for more than 1,000 children of both sexes whose family life had been disrupted. Through its trustee it also owned more than 40 percent of the

common stock of the chocolate company's successor, Hershey Foods, and controlled more than 75 percent of the corporation's voting shares.

Hershey's persistence, innovative ideas, insistence on quality, and concern for his employees and others in the community were both the reason for and the hallmark of his success. His ability to judge the market and produce a fresh, affordable taste treat were all evident in his original five-cent Hershey Bar and later successes—the Hershey Kiss (1907), Mr. Goodbar (1925), the Krackel Bar (1938), and Hershey's Miniatures (1939). During World War II Hershey again demonstrated his inventiveness by developing the Field Ration D, a four-ounce bar that packed 600 calories. Because it did not melt, soldiers could carry it to sustain them if no other food was available. In 1942 Hershey was awarded the Army/Navy E award for this contribution to the war effort. Hershey's concern for quality was apparent from the first when he set standards for the industry by integrating fresh milk into his candy recipes. The community and school he funded and built testify to his concern for others.

Milton Hershey died in Hershey Hospital one year after retiring as chairman of the board of Hershey Chocolate Corporation. Because he had given most of his fortune to the town and school that bore his name, a public sale of his effects after his death raised less than $20,000. Gordon Rentschler, chairman of the board of the National City Bank of New York, wrote shortly after the candy manufacturer's death that Hershey was a man who "measured success, not in dollars, but in terms of a good product to pass on to the public, and still more in the usefulness of those dollars for the benefit of his fellow men."

• The Hershey Community Archives and the Milton S. Hershey School, both in Hershey, Pa., maintain archives of Hershey's personal and corporate papers and effects. Biographies of Hershey tend to be popularized and often sentimental. Charles Schuyler Castner, *One of a Kind* (1983), contains numerous photographs. Also see Samuel F. Hinckle, *Hershey* (1964); Katherine B. Shippen and Paul A. W. Wallace, *Milton S. Hershey* (1959); and Joseph R. Snavely, *An Intimate Story of Milton S. Hershey* (1957). The public relations office of Hershey Foods has two concise, fact-filled booklets available, *The Man behind the Chocolate Bar* (1982) and *Hershey's 100 Years: The Ingredients of Our Success* (1994). An obituary is in the *New York Times*, 14 Oct. 1945.

JANE M. GILLILAND

HERSKOVITS, Melville Jean (10 Sept. 1895–25 Feb. 1963), anthropologist, was born in Bellefontaine, Ohio, the son of Herman Herskovits, a clothing merchant, and Henrietta Hart. After a series of moves during childhood, he attended high school in Erie, Pennsylvania, graduating in 1912. He then enrolled at both the University of Cincinnati and Hebrew Union College.

During his time at Hebrew Union College, Herskovits began doubting his faith in God. After brief service in the U.S. Army Medical Corps during World War I, he enrolled at the University of Chicago, where he received a bachelor's degree in history in 1920. He then moved to New York City and began studying at the New School for Social Research, including taking anthropology classes with Alexander Goldenweiser. Goldenweiser introduced him to Franz Boas's anthropology seminars at Columbia, and Herskovits soon enrolled at Columbia, receiving his A.M. in 1921 and his Ph.D. in 1923, both in anthropology. In 1924 he married Frances S. Shapiro. They had one daughter.

Throughout the 1920s Herskovits argued that African-American culture would eventually be assimilated into European-American culture. In "The Negro's Americanism," an article he wrote for Alain Locke's anthology, *The New Negro: An Interpretation* (1925), Herskovits argued that African culture had been decimated by slavery and that African Americans would soon be totally assimilated into the larger, white culture.

Locke, a central figure of the Harlem Renaissance, helped Herskovits secure a teaching position at Howard University in Washington D.C., in 1925. While at Howard, he received a National Research Council grant that enabled him to investigate the effects of "race crossing" in African Americans. As a topic for scientific investigation, this choice was influenced by Boas, who had long fought the notion that the mulatto inherited the bad traits of each of the parental stocks. Over the next four years Herskovits measured various physical traits of African Americans living in Harlem and West Virginia, as well as those attending Howard University.

Herskovits's conclusions were published in two books: *The American Negro* (1928) and *The Anthropometry of the American Negro* (1930). In these works, he argued that African Americans represented a new "homogenous population group" that could be considered distinct from either of the parental stocks. African Americans, in his view, were a new racial group, physically different from their European and African ancestors. He argued that this type had arisen recently, indicating that interbreeding was decreasing. Consequently, he began to question his earlier convictions regarding assimilation. From 1930 onward he turned his scientific study to the process of acculturation of Africans into the Americans.

The center of Herskovits's new project was his belief that it was possible to trace cultural patterns found in the "New World Negro" back to Africa. He became convinced that if cultural traits survived the trip from Africa to the New World, then they could be found in folklore, religion, and music, for these, rather than commercial or political activities, were the center of African culture.

In 1927 Herskovits took a position in the Department of Sociology at Northwestern University. As the sole anthropologist within the Department of Sociology, he was isolated scholastically, and his sense of isolation was underscored by the pervasive anti-Semitism on the campus. Despite these handicaps, he established a Department of Anthropology at Northwestern

in 1938. He was joined in his studies by his wife, who taught African literature.

The Herskovitses conducted a series of field studies between 1927 and 1935. These included two trips to Surinam (1928 and 1929), one to Dahomey (1931), and one to Haiti (1934). The result of these field trips was a series of books that began exploring the ethnography of those areas as well as the links between cultural traits in the New World Negro and the West African. As suspected, the Herskovitses discovered a large number of West African words that appeared in the New World, as well as parallels in music, art, and, especially, folklore.

The Surinam and Haiti trips were the foundation for a massive study that Herskovits planned to undertake on the New World Negro with the help of a grant from the Carnegie Foundation. However, Carnegie had already decided to fund a project headed by Swedish economist Gunnar Myrdal that would eventually result in the publication of *An American Dilemma: The Negro Problem and Modern Democracy* (2 vols., 1944). For this project, Myrdal recruited nearly every American social scientist with any experience in race relations or the study of African Americans. Although Myrdal considered Herskovits a major researcher he was extremely skeptical of his claims about African survivals. Nevertheless, in 1940 Myrdal asked Herskovits to prepare a study of African survivals in the United States. The result was Herskovits's *The Myth of the Negro Past* (1941).

The myth referred to in Herskovits's title was that the "Negro is a man without a past" because his culture was decimated by the slave experience. This myth, Herskovits claimed, was "one of the principal supports of race prejudice in this country." To a far greater extent than in his previous works, he set out to trace the patterns of survivals in African-American culture, arguing that most slaves were taken from areas of West Africa that had rich and complex cultures. These cultures were similar enough to allow the slaves to build up a synthetic African culture in the New World. He noted that it was possible to trace African survivals in family life, economic patterns, and, especially, in religious and spiritual life.

Although certain scholars, notably W. E. B. Du Bois and Carter G. Woodson, welcomed Herskovits's claims about the extent of African survivals, the general social science community of the 1940s was skeptical. The dominant views were those of E. Franklin Frazier and Ruth Benedict, who argued that slavery had destroyed any vestiges of African culture. Even Alain Locke thought that Herskovits had gone too far in his claims for African-American culture. With the rise of black nationalism in the 1960s, however, Herskovits's views began to gain adherents, and by the 1970s his views were almost universally accepted by scholars of the African-American experience.

During World War II Herskovits served as the chief consultant for African affairs of the Board of Economic Warfare. After the war he continued to do fieldwork, making trips to Africa in 1953, 1954, 1955, 1957, and

1962. In his postwar publications, he began to argue for a particular vision of anthropology as a science that grew out of his studies of the process of culture change. In 1938 he had developed a comprehensive theory of acculturation in his book *Acculturation*, and in 1948 he published *Man and His Works*, later abridged as *Cultural Anthropology* (1955). In these works, he used his studies of particular cultures to frame an outlook for the entire science of anthropology. Central to his outlook were his strong views on the value of cultural relativism as the proper methodological outlook for anthropologists. His strong stance in favor of cultural relativism thrust him into the center of a wide-ranging controversy, both inside and outside anthropology, on the dangers of relativism.

Despite Herskovits's continued scholarly output, much of his time after the war was consumed by administrative tasks. He served as president of the American Folklore Society in 1945, founded the Program of African Studies at Northwestern, the first interdisciplinary program of its kind in the United States, in 1948, and edited the *American Anthropologist* from 1949 to 1952. He was president of the African Studies Association for 1957–1958. He became a member of the National Academy of Sciences in 1959 and the following year prepared a major report for the U.S. Senate Foreign Relations Committee that helped forge relations between the United States and the countries of Africa. In 1962, the year before his death in Evanston, Illinois, he organized the First International Congress of Africanists.

Herskovits enjoyed great success in building institutions during his lifetime, making the study of Africa part of the academic agenda. However, he remained an iconoclastic scholar, whose published works made him, in his own words, a "lone wolf."

• Herskovits's papers are in the Northwestern University Archives and the Schomburg Center for Research in Black Culture, New York Public Library. The Northwestern archives also contain the records of the Program of African Studies. Most of the papers of Frances S. Herskovits are in the Schomburg Center, which also holds the notes for the research memoranda prepared for *An American Dilemma*, including Herskovits's work on *The Myth of the Negro Past*. A complete bibliography of Herskovits's writings was published by Anne Moneypenny and Barrie Thorne in *American Anthropologist* 66 (1964): 91–109.

Brief biographical sketches include Alan P. Merriam, "Melville Jean Herskovits," *American Anthropologist* 66 (1964): 83–91, and Joseph H. Greenberg, "Melville Jean Herskovits," National Academy of Sciences, *Biographical Memoirs* 42 (1971): 65–75. A work that examines Herskovits in a larger historical context is Walter Jackson, "Melville Herskovits and the Search for Afro-American Culture," in *Malinowski, Rivers, Benedict, and Others: Essays on Culture and Personality*, ed. George W. Stocking, Jr. (1986), pp. 95–126. For more extended treatments see George Eaton Simpson, *Melville J. Herskovits* (1973), and Robert Baron, "Africa in the Americas: Melville J. Herskovits' Folkloristic and Anthropological Scholarship, 1923–1941" (Ph.D. diss., Univ. of Pennsylvania, 1994).

For Herskovits's relationship with Alain Locke and the Harlem Renaissance see Mark Helbling, "Feeling Universality and Thinking Particularistically: Alain Locke, Franz Boas, Melville Herskovits, and the Harlem Renaissance," *Prospects* 19 (1994): 289–314.

JOHN P. JACKSON

HERTER, Christian Archibald (3 Sept. 1865–5 Dec. 1910), physician and biochemist, was born in Glenville, Connecticut, the son of Christian Herter, an artist and highly successful interior decorator, and Mary Miles. He was educated privately under the direction of his father, who chose a medical career for him. Herter received an M.D. from Columbia University in 1885, after which he undertook postgraduate work with pathologist William H. Welch at Johns Hopkins University and on the Continent with August Forel, from whom he gained an interest in nervous disorders. During this period, Herter became imbued with the European spirit of laboratory-based, scientific medicine, which Welch was pioneering at the new Johns Hopkins. In 1886 he married Susan Dows; they had five children.

Herter began a private medical practice in New York City in 1888. He also organized one of the nation's first medical research laboratories in his home and became increasingly drawn to scientific investigation. A large family fortune (besides his own family's wealth, his wife was the daughter of the nation's largest grain merchant) enabled Herter to employ as many as six or more chemists, bacteriologists, and physicians in his laboratory, whose work soon attracted widespread attention. In order to stay in touch with clinical medicine, Herter affiliated himself with various medical institutions throughout his life, including New York City Hospital, Presbyterian Hospital, and Babies' Hospital. Herter's laboratory investigations mainly evolved out of medical problems seen at the bedside of patients.

In 1898 Herter accepted the chair of the pathological chemistry faculty at University and Bellevue Hospital Medical College of New York University. In 1903 he left Bellevue to become a member of the pharmacology and therapeutics faculty at his alma mater, the (Columbia) College of Physicians and Surgeons, which he headed until his death.

Herter's early research interests culminated in the publication of *The Diagnosis of Diseases of the Nervous System* (1892). He then shifted his attention to the biochemical study of disease. Examining the biochemistry of metabolic disorders and the formation of gallstones and glycosuria, he published a textbook, *Lectures on Chemical Pathology in Its Relation to Practical Medicine* in 1902. He then explored the process of digestion and the chemistry and pathology of diseases caused by intestinal bacteria, which he elucidated in his third book, *The Common Bacterial Infections of the Digestive Tract and the Intoxication Arising from Them* (1907). In the following year Herter described a condition of physical infantilism in children that arose from chronic intestinal infection ("celiac disease" or "Herter's infantilism").

Through his friendship with John D. Rockefeller, Jr., Herter exerted considerable influence in assembling, and in 1901 becoming a charter member of, the board of directors of the Rockefeller Institute for Medical Research in New York City; he also acted as the board's treasurer in administering research grants. Under the leadership of pathologist and bacteriologist Simon Flexner, this distinguished board of directors oversaw the creation of one of the world's foremost biomedical research centers. After the institute commenced operations in 1901, Herter arranged for the early opening of an associated teaching and research hospital. As his increasing infirmity prevented him from directing the hospital's affairs, he agreed to accept a position with less responsibility. In 1908 he was appointed physician to the Hospital of the Rockefeller Institute, which opened in 1910.

Because the growing volume of American biomedical research suggested the need for a new periodical, Herter began publication of the *Journal of Biological Chemistry* in 1905. He subsidized the venture and coedited the journal with pioneer pharmacologist John Jacob Abel of Johns Hopkins until 1909, when Herter assumed its sole editorship.

Around 1905 Herter and his wife endowed lectureships at Johns Hopkins and Bellevue that helped to advance medical science in the United States by making it financially feasible for several of Europe's leading researchers, including Paul Ehrlich and William Ostwald, to come to America to lecture.

In 1906 Ira Remsen, the president of Johns Hopkins University, asked Herter to become a member of a government board, the Referee Board of Consulting Experts, to assist in the enforcement of the country's first pure foods and drug act, which had been enacted that year. President Theodore Roosevelt had asked Remsen to establish the board because of the opposition of some food companies to the efforts of the U.S. Department of Agriculture, which had the responsibility for enforcing the act, to ban the use of benzoate of soda and saccharin. Subsequently, Harvey W. Wiley, chief chemist of the Department of Agriculture, and the board became involved in a clamorous and protracted dispute about the safety of these food additives. At his own expense, Herter published and distributed a critique of the department's work. Ultimately, the board's finding that low levels of benzoates are harmless was accepted but not before Herter and other board members were pilloried in the press for endangering the public health.

Herter was an accomplished cellist and played occasionally with the professional musicians who regularly performed in his home. The Herters' home frequently contained visiting scientists, students, friends, and neighbors. Summers were usually spent out of the city, first at Saranac Lake, and after 1900, at Mt. Desert Island, Maine. Herter died in New York City from a wasting nervous disorder, possibly myasthenia gravis.

Through his research and editorial labors, Herter helped establish the discipline of biochemistry in the United States. He also participated actively in the creation and early development of the Rockefeller Institute for Medical Research.

• Valuable biographical sketches are in Howard A. Kelly and Walter L. Burrage, eds., *Dictionary of American Medical Biographies* (1928), pp. 560–61; and Robert M. Hawthorne, Jr., "Christian Archibald Herter, M.D. (1865–1910)," *Perspectives in Biology and Medicine* 18 (Autumn 1974): 24–39. An obituary is in the *New York Times*, 6 Dec. 1910.

STUART GALISHOFF

HERTER, Christian Archibald (28 Mar. 1895–30 Dec. 1966), governor of Massachusetts and U.S. secretary of state, was born in Paris, France, the son of Albert Herter and Adele McGinnis, artists and expatriates. Educated at the École Alsatienne in Paris (1901–1904), he went to New York City and studied at the Browning School (1904–1911) before entering Harvard, from which he graduated cum laude in 1915. He enrolled in Columbia University's School of Architecture for a short time, then turned his attention to the U.S. Foreign Service. He served as an attaché in Berlin and Brussels in 1916 and was a special assistant for the Department of State when the United States became involved in World War I (1917–1918). In 1917 he married Mary Caroline Pratt, a wealthy heiress. They became the parents of four children.

In 1918 Herter negotiated a prisoner-of-war agreement with Germany, and Secretary of State Robert Lansing called on him to serve as secretary to the Paris Peace Commission in 1919. He then became special assistant to Herbert C. Hoover, who was in charge of the European Relief Council (1920–1921), and continued as his assistant (1921–1924) when Hoover became secretary of commerce in 1921.

Retiring into private life in Boston in 1924, Herter pursued a career in journalism and maintained his interest in foreign affairs. As coeditor of the *Independent* (1924–1928), he defended the League of Nations and criticized isolationism. After the publication was sold to *Outlook*, Herter continued his interest in journalism as associate editor of the *Sportsman* (1927–1936). He retained his grasp of diplomatic issues by spending a year as a lecturer on foreign affairs at Harvard (1929–1930). Republican Henry Parkman, Jr., a shrewd politician, encouraged Herter to enter politics in Massachusetts.

Even though the Herters were not Boston Brahmins, like the Lodges and the Saltonstalls, in 1930 Herter, whose grandfather had migrated from Stuttgart, Germany, won a seat representing Boston's Ward Five, the center of the city's social elite, in the Massachusetts House of Representatives. Serving for thirteen years from 1931 to 1943, he rose within a decade to Speaker (1939–1943). Herter was in the Massachusetts House when Thomas P. O'Neill, Jr., later Speaker of that body and of the U.S. House, entered as a young legislator. At the time, O'Neill was impressed by the way in which Herter used his parliamentary expertise to dominate the state legislature.

In 1942 Herter campaigned for the congressional seat held by George Holden Tinkham, whose isolationist views made him vulnerable during World War II. Once Herter entered the contest, Tinkham withdrew and thereby opened the way for Herter to be elected from the Tenth Massachusetts District to the U.S. Congress. Although he was critical of Franklin D. Roosevelt's New Deal, Herter distinguished himself during 1943–1953 primarily for his stand on foreign affairs, especially owing to the so-called Herter Committee in 1947 whose report initiated proposals that led to Harry Truman's Marshall Plan. In those years, he had helped to found the School of Advanced International Studies at Johns Hopkins and refused to support a permanent congressional committee investigating un-American activities.

Urged by such Massachusetts Republicans as Henry Cabot Lodge, Jr., Leverett Saltonstall, and Joseph W. Martin, Jr., to enter the contest for governor of Massachusetts in 1952, Herter, with the support of Dwight D. Eisenhower, defeated incumbent Paul A. Dever by a narrow margin of about 15,000 votes. Herter worked effectively with a Democratic legislature to bring about social, political, and economic reforms, and his unusual blend of conservatism and liberalism made him a potential candidate for the Republican nomination for the vice presidency in 1956. However, he was unwilling to become the tool of liberals like Harold Stassen, who wanted to unseat Richard M. Nixon, the controversial incumbent, whom Herter himself eventually nominated. For this loyalty, Herter was rewarded in 1957 with appointment as under secretary of state, replacing Herbert Hoover, Jr.

Upon the death of John Foster Dulles in 1959, Herter became the obvious choice to replace him as secretary of state. His nomination by President Eisenhower was so popular that the Senate unanimously approved it, enabling Herter to take office in record time, on 22 April. Though Herter had greater authority and prestige in his new office, he followed the policies of his predecessor, which were actually those approved by the president himself, rather than break new ground in the crises that the nation faced around the globe. During his tenure, U.S. relations with Cuba and the Soviet Union deteriorated.

When Fidel Castro came to power in Cuba in February 1959, he began seizing American properties in that country. Though this created a new situation, Herter acted according to the precedents set by Dulles, and on 30 September of that year the State Department advised Americans to stay away from Cuba unless it was absolutely necessary to travel there. On 19 October 1959 Herter approved an embargo on most exports to Cuba while trying to preserve the system of alliances with a Latin America struggling to overcome its economic, political, and social problems. Castro retaliated by demanding that the United States cut down drastically on its personnel in Havana, and, as a logical consequence, diplomatic relations between the countries ruptured on 3 January 1961.

Similarly, in the crisis over the invasion of Soviet territory by the American U-2 plane on 1 May 1960, Herter followed policies established by Dulles. Herter's response reflected U.S. determination to continue espionage surveillance. Characterizing the practice as "outrageous," Soviet premier Nikita S. Khrushchev proceeded to scuttle the Paris Summit Conference, which had been scheduled to open on 16 May.

Likewise, in other parts of the world the problems appeared more distressing at the end of Herter's tenure as secretary of state than they had at the start, with Africa emerging from colonialism, Asia developing in the shadow of mainland China, and the Middle East reacting to the evenhanded policy of the United States, especially when the Cold War continued to shape American foreign policy. Yet, in the face of those challenges, Herter reflected more flexibility than Dulles and was somewhat more confident in the ability of the United States to deal effectively with them as long as the nation maintained its economic as well as its military strength. Significantly, his vision of the future did not exclude a time when the United States might eventually be able to collaborate with Russia and even China for the development of all nations.

Tall in stature (six feet six inches), Herter was a mild but tough person who did not have much time to leave his imprint on American diplomacy, especially since Eisenhower felt more confident directing his own foreign policy during the closing years of his presidency. Plagued for more than twenty years with arthritis, Herter carried on conscientiously and dutifully but without any demonstration of the aggressiveness and showmanship that had characterized his controversial predecessor, who had a closer working relationship with Eisenhower.

In brief, Herter was a model of courage and courtesy as a diplomat. His credentials and qualifications were recognized by President John F. Kennedy, who in 1962 appointed him special U.S. representative for trade negotiations with Europe, a position that Herter held until his death in Washington, D.C. Throughout his career, Herter gained the respect of those who came to know his exceptional talents in both politics and diplomacy. "When you just look at him," President Eisenhower supposedly declared, "you know you are looking at an honest man."

• Papers covering Herter's years at the State Department have been published on microfilm by University Publications of America from the Dwight D. Eisenhower Library in Abilene, Kans. The Houghton Library at Harvard University has forty-four boxes of Herter's papers covering his life since 1929, including his gubernatorial years. Francis W. Tully, Jr., his press secretary, compiled *Addresses and Messages . . . Governor Christian A. Herter . . .* (1956). Herter's legislative work on the state and national levels is in government publications, including *Journal of the House of Representatives of the Commonwealth of Massachusetts* (1939–1943) and the *Congressional Record* (1943–1953). See also Dwight D. Eisenhower, *Mandate for Change* (1963); G. Bernard Noble, *Christian A.*

Herter (1970), more a study of his diplomacy than a biography; and U.S. Congress, *Memorial Addresses and Other Tributes in the Congress of the United States on the Life and Contributions of Christian Archibald Herter* (1967). An obituary is in the *New York Times*, 1 Jan. 1967.

VINCENT A. LAPOMARDA

HERTER, Gustave (14 May 1830–29 Nov. 1898), and **Christian Herter** (8 Jan. 1839–2 Nov. 1883), craftsmen, were born in Stuttgart, Germany, the sons of Johanna Christiana Maria Barbara Hagenlocher and Christian Herter, a cabinetmaker and woodworker.

Gustave's full name at birth was Julius Gustav Alexander Hagenlocher; his mother was unmarried at the time. When she married Christian Herter, Sr., he adopted Gustave, who eventually added the extra letter to his first name. Gustave immigrated to New York in 1848 at the age of eighteen, renounced his German citizenship two years later, and quickly distinguished himself among a burgeoning population of immigrant craftsmen. Although unsubstantiated, it is said that he was employed by Tiffany, Young & Ellis as a silver designer until 1851. He then established a short-lived cabinetmaking concern, called Herter, Pottier & Co., with a young French émigré craftsman named Auguste Pottier; this partnership lasted only until 1853. Concurrently, Herter seems to have been associated with Erastus Bulkley, a well-established New York cabinetmaker, and from 1853 until 1858 their firm, Bulkley & Herter, is listed in the local directories. From 1854 the firm was located at 547 Broadway, then at the heart of the carriage trade, an address at which Herter remained until 1869.

The three extraordinary pieces of furniture designed by Gustave Herter displayed in New York City at the 1853 Crystal Palace Exhibition of the Industry of All Nations attracted much public attention. One, an immense alter-like "buffet," architectural in scale, featured a figure of Ceres on the crest and a fully sculpted dead stag as its centerpiece. It was a calculated rejoinder to the celebrated sideboard shown in London at the Great Exhibition of 1851 by the prodigious Parisian cabinetmaker Alexandre-Georges Fourdinois. Young Herter no doubt profited from the comparison.

Herter was one of the first American cabinetmakers to expand his practice to include the full spectrum of interior decoration. The formation of his own firm in 1858, styled as Gustave Herter from 1858 to 1864, coincided with his first documented interiors commission, the summer residence of Ruggles Sylvester Morse in Portland, Maine, which survives almost entirely intact. Herter employed the eighteenth-century revival and neo-Renaissance styles then fashionable in Paris under the Second Empire and used imported goods to augment American craftsmanship, such as French silks and fringes for upholstery and draperies, and decorative elements such as the resplendent floral marquetry top on the center table he designed for the drawing room. The table was part of a large suite of richly carved rosewood furniture with winged figural supports, cabriole legs, hoofed feet, and gilt-bronze

mounts in the so-called Louis XIVth style, which contrasted with the delicate ivory, gold, and pastel palette of the room. The console table bears a pencil inscription that confirms Herter's authorship, and stylistically his hand can be discerned in the furnishings and decorations throughout the house.

By 1860 the U.S. Products of Industry Census recorded that Herter employed 100 men and generated an annual product of $121,500, indicating a successful business. His younger brother, Christian (in full, Christian Augustus Ludwig Herter), had immigrated to New York by 1859 and was probably employed by Gustave soon after he arrived. In 1861, at the outset of the Civil War, R. G. Dun & Co., an early credit reporting agency and the predecessor to Dun & Bradstreet, reported that Gustave Herter had secured a lucrative contract for making gun stocks. Clients in the early 1860s included Henry Probasco of Cincinnati, whose house survives in private hands, and J. Pierpont Morgan of New York City. But certainly Gustave Herter's most impressive accomplishment during these years, however, was the sixty-foot-high sculpted organ case for a 6,000-pipe organ commissioned for the Boston Music Hall in 1860. Completed in 1863, it was eventually sold and moved to Methuen, Massachusetts, where it remained in use at the end of the twentieth century.

Gustave's 1863 marriage to Anna F. Schmidt was followed by the birth of the first of five sons the following year. Also in 1864 Christian married Mary Miles of Cleveland; they had two sons. When Christian Herter formally joined Gustave's firm in 1864, the name was changed to Herter Brothers.

In the years following the Civil War, the scale of Herter Brothers' business expanded considerably. In 1869 the firm moved its showrooms to the Hoyt Building at 877–79 Broadway, a fashionable location on Ladies' Mile near Union Square, and in 1874 replaced its workshops on Mercer Street, where they had been since the early 1850s, with a large manufactory built on First Avenue at Twenty-eighth Street. The completion of the transcontinental railroad in 1869 permitted the development of a truly nationwide clientele, which included a coterie of wealthy patrons in San Francisco and environs.

Around 1869 Herter Brothers decorated several reception rooms in "Elm Park," the French Second Empire–style residence of LeGrand Lockwood in Norwalk, Connecticut, which survives. Here the firm essayed the "néo-grec" style promoted at the Paris International Exposition of 1867, exemplified by rosewood and maple woodwork and furniture, characterized by allusions to classical architecture, painted decoration, highly refined marquetry patterns, and portrait medallions inspired by ancient coinage and Renaissance medals.

In 1870 Gustave Herter retired from active participation in the firm and, probably early in 1871, returned to Germany with his family; his departure coincided with the defeat of France by Germany in the Franco-Prussian War. The end of the Second Empire also marked a noticeable lessening of Continental influences on Herter Brothers during the 1870s. Nevertheless, it was in "Thurlow Lodge," the well-documented Menlo Park, California, home of Milton Slocum Latham (destroyed in 1942), which Herter Brothers decorated in 1872–1873, that the firm's interpretation of Second Empire taste was most clearly articulated. A monumental rosewood console with mirror nearly fifteen feet high (Los Angeles County Museum of Art), with carved, painted, gilded, and marquetry decoration, conveys the scale of the rooms and illustrates the extraordinary craftsmanship typical of the Herter firm. That the surviving woodwork from the dining room and the library is marked by the Parisian firm Gueret Freres, however, is evidence of the close commercial and artistic connections between New York and Parisian firms during this period.

Under Christian Herter's artistic direction during the 1870s, the firm was strongly influenced by the British design reform, or Aesthetic, movement. One of the earliest commissions to reflect this was the parlor designed for Major James Goodwin and his wife, Lucy Morgan, of Hartford, Connecticut, in 1871 (completed 1874); the room has been installed in the Wadsworth Atheneum. Other important commissions from this decade include the Red Room in the White House (1875) and the Mark Hopkins house in San Francisco, (1878–1880). The firm's signature style from this decade is epitomized by its Anglo-Japanese furniture, such as the bedroom suite owned by Jay Gould (The Metropolitan Museum of Art). Typically, it is rectilinear in form, made of ebonized cherry (an allusion to Japanese lacquer), and embellished with spindles, low-relief carving, and contrasting marquetry veneers featuring abstract floral patterns rendered in light-colored woods. Alexandre Sandier, a French architect, joined Herter Brothers as a designer in the mid-1870s and contributed to the definition of the company's reform style.

Around 1880 Herter Brothers commenced a host of major commissions in New York City. The design and decoration of William H. Vanderbilt's house began in 1879; the decoration of Darius Ogden Mills's residence, J. P. Morgan's residence, and several rooms in the Seventh Regiment Armory, in 1880; and the Robert Leighton Stuart and Jacob Ruppert residences, in 1881, to name but a few. The architect William B. Bigelow headed Herter Brothers' design department during these years and oversaw several of these projects.

The Vanderbilt house was Christian Herter's magnum opus, an undertaking unprecedented in the United States. Six to seven hundred workmen, including several hundred sculptors and carvers, labored to finish this luxurious domicile by 1882. Herter drew on myriad artistic sources—Pompeiian, Renaissance, Japanese, Chinese, and Moorish—to create interiors and furnishings of stunning originality and richness. Exemplary is the table fashioned for Vanderbilt's library (The Metropolitan Museum of Art). Although loosely based on ancient Roman furniture made of stone, it, like the paneling and woodwork of the room

in which it was situated, is made of carved rosewood painstakingly inlaid with mother-of-pearl and brass. One-half of the terrestrial globe appears at either end, while the top is a field of stars arranged in the configuration of the constellations over the northern hemisphere on the day that Vanderbilt was born.

Christian Herter died prematurely of tuberculosis the following year, no doubt exhausted by the sheer volume and artistic intensity of his recent work. From 1883 until 1891 the firm was led by William Baumgarten, who had been hired by Herter Brothers in 1871, and by William Gilman Nichols, who had become a partner in 1882. After Baumgarten left in 1891, Nichols presided over the company until it closed in 1906. During this last phase, although still actively involved in interior decoration, Herter Brothers increasingly subcontracted work to other firms and, conversely, became a subcontractor itself, executing architectural woodwork designed by architects such as McKim, Mead and White. In 1892 Gustave Herter and his wife returned to New York, where he died a few years later. He is buried in a mausoleum of his own design in Kensico Cemetery in Valhalla, New York.

Although they were trained as craftsmen in Europe, it was as impresarios of the artistic interior that Gustave and Christian Herter achieved their reputation in the United States. Their projects were ambitious and sophisticated in scale and scope, and they summoned from Europe whatever decorative vocabulary, materials, or objects they needed to render their complex interiors complete. Whether the objects manufactured in their own workshops bear the stamp of the French Second Empire, the British design reform movement, or the spirit of cosmopolitanism around 1880, the interpretation is distinctly Herter Brothers' own. Few artists or designers of any century attain a level of originality and superior craftsmanship that distinguishes their work from the mainstream. Certainly the achievements of Gustave and Christian Herter can be numbered among the significant contributions to the history of late nineteenth-century decorative arts and interior design.

• There are no business or personal papers from the period between 1848 and 1883 when Gustave and Christian Herter were active in New York. A large archive of Herter Brothers records pertaining to the latter part of the firm's history, from about 1891 until the closing of the firm in 1906, is at the Winterthur Library in Delaware. The book published in conjunction with a retrospective exhibition organized by the Museum of Fine Arts, Houston, and the Metropolitan Museum of Art in 1994–1995 contains essays on Herter Brothers' European heritage, the history of the firm, the New York furniture trade, patronage, and the construction and decoration of Herter furniture and commission entries, a detailed chronology, and a selected bibliography: Katherine S. Howe, Alice Cooney Frelinghuysen, Catherine Hoover Voorsanger, Simon Jervis, Hans Ottomeyer, Marc Bascou, Ann Claggett Wood, and Sophia Riefstahl, *Herter Brothers: Furniture and Interiors for a Gilded Age* (1994). The principal authors supplied articles to *The Magazine Antiques* that contain additional illustrations and information. See Howe, "Gustave and Christian Herter: The European Connection," Sept. 1994;

Frelinghuysen, "Christian Herter's Decoration of the William H. Vanderbilt House in New York City," Mar. 1995; and Voorsanger, "Gustave Herter, Cabinetmaker and Decorator," May 1995.

CATHERINE HOOVER VOORSANGER

HERTS, Henry Beaumont, II (23 Jan. 1871–27 Mar. 1933), architect, was born in New York City, the son of Henry Beaumont Herts, the director of Herts Brothers, decorators and antiquarians; his mother's name is unknown. After briefly attending the City College of New York, Herts began his career in the office of architect Bruce Price. Impressed by Herts's nascent artistic abilities, Price arranged for him to enroll in the architecture program of the School of Mines at Columbia University in 1889. He received no degree. In 1892 Herts won the design competition for a temporary memorial arch that was erected in Central Park in celebration of the Christopher Columbus quadricentennial. The following year Herts journeyed to Paris to enter the renowned École des Beaux-Arts and to study in the atelier of Henri Deglane.

Returning to New York in 1897, Herts formed an architectural firm in partnership with fellow École student Hugh Tallant. An 1891 Phi Beta Kappa graduate of Harvard, Tallant attended the École from 1893 to 1896 and was the recipient of the Prix Jean Leclare and the Grande Medaille d'Honneur, the institution's highest awards open to non-Frenchmen. Early works by the firm of Herts & Tallant include New York City commissions for the remodeling of the Harmonie Club (1898, demolished), the Aguilar Free Library (1899), the Isaac Rice mansion (1901–1903), and the Corem Library at Bates College in Lewiston, Maine (1901).

Herts and Tallant's plans for the renovation of Daly's Theatre in New York for producer Daniel Frohman (c. 1899, demolished 1920) led to the 1902 commissions for the Lyceum Theatre and the New Amsterdam Theatre, which both opened in 1903 in New York's developing Times Square theater district. A rare American example of the Art Nouveau style, the New Amsterdam was New York's largest theater in terms of seating capacity and stage size, and it was further hailed for its innovative planning and technical facilities. Writing in the *Architectural Record*, Abbot Halstead Moore noted that

the complete diversity of the New Amsterdam and New Lyceum Theatres lies in the well-defined fact that the architects have stamped the significance of each playhouse with distinction. The former, gay and whimsical, properly lends itself to the production of large pictorial effects, the latter in its quiet elegance appeals eminently to a more cultured audience and stands as a fitting frame for the conservative works of the most distinguished living dramatists. The New Amsterdam is throughout picturesque, playful, teeming with movement and color; the New Lyceum is quietly rich in tone, and, while individual, at the same time displays the strictest regards for the essential groundwork and grammar of architecture. (pp. 68–70)

Both the Lyceum (exterior in 1974 and interior in 1987) and the New Amsterdam (in 1979) were designated official New York City landmarks.

In 1904 Herts & Tallant designed the Liberty Theatre on Forty-second Street, a companion to the nearby New Amsterdam, and won the design competition for the new Brooklyn Academy of Music, a major performing arts facility whose predecessor had been destroyed by fire in 1903. Completed in 1908, the Brooklyn Academy contains both a 1,400-seat concert hall and a 2,200-seat opera house, as well as banquet and meeting facilities and the headquarters of the Brooklyn Institute of Arts & Sciences. The year 1908 also witnessed the opening of Herts & Tallant's Gaiety Theatre (demolished 1982) in the Broadway district and the new German Theatre (demolished 1929) on Fifty-ninth Street near Madison Avenue, designed in the modern German Art Nouveau style. In 1911 work was completed on both the Atlanta Theatre (demolished) in Atlanta, Georgia, and Broadway's Folies-Bergere, a theater restaurant that Herts later transformed into a conventional theater. The contention arising from the demolition of this theater in 1982, by which time it was known as the Helen Hayes, led to the New York City Landmarks Commission's granting protective status to Broadway's remaining playhouses.

In 1911 Herts and Tallant dissolved their partnership, Tallant departing to join the firm of Lord & Hewitt. Herts continued to practice on his own, designing Broadway's Longacre, Booth, and Sam S. Shubert theaters, all in 1913, and planning alterations to the Knickerbocker Theatre (demolished 1930) in 1914. The departure that same year of his chief associate, Herbert J. Krapp, signaled an end to the association of the Herts firm with the design of theaters.

Prominent nontheater designs by Herts & Tallant and by the office of Herts alone include those for the New York City Fire Department headquarters (1908); the City Athletic Club (1909); new grandstands for the Polo Grounds, home of the New York Giants baseball team (1912, demolished 1964); the Rice Memorial Stadium in Pelham Bay Park, Bronx (1916); buildings for Yeshiva College on Amsterdam Avenue in New York City (1925–1928, in association with architect Charles Meyers); and the Ochs Memorial Chapel in Chattanooga, Tennessee (1928). Outside the United States, Herts is credited for the design of the Palatina Brewery in Havana, Cuba, and of several branches of the Lyon's Restaurant chain in London. He also served as special consultant to fire chief Richard Croker on the 1904 revision of New York City's fire safety code as it related to theaters and places of public amusement.

Herts was married in 1901 to actress Cynthia Frances Harris, and they had two children. Herts retired in 1928 and died in New York City. In their work "Setting the Stage: Herts & Tallant," architectural historians Robert Stern, John Massengale, and Gregory Gilmartin characterize the theaters designed by Herts and his associates as "a unique, if seminal, synthesis between the image of the theatre as a public monument and as a temple of vernacular pleasures" (*Skyline* [Dec. 1981]: 32–33). Combining the sophistication of Beaux-Arts technique with the ebullient individuality of the Victorians, the surviving Herts playhouses continue to be landmarks of American theater design and treasured additions to the urban scene.

• Herts's business and personal records were apparently destroyed, but copies of theater plans and correspondence between him and some of his clients are housed in the Shubert Archive in New York City. An examination of the firm's early works can be found in Abbot Halstead Moore, "Individualism in Architecture: The Works of Herts & Tallant," *Architectural Record* (Jan. 1904): 54–91. For more detailed analyses of Herts's contribution to theatrical architecture, see Bill Morrison, "The Theatres of Herts & Tallant," *Marquee: The Journal of the Theatre Historical Society* 22, no. 4 (1990): 3–22. Obituaries are in the *New York Times*, the *New York Herald-Tribune*, and the *New York World-Telegram*, all 28 Mar. 1933.

BILL MORRISON

HERTY, Charles Holmes (4 Dec. 1867–27 July 1938), chemist, was born in Milledgeville, Georgia, the son of Bernard Ritchie Herty, a druggist, and Louisa Turno Holmes. Before Herty was eleven years old, he and his sister were orphaned and subsequently reared by an aunt, Florence I. Holmes, of Athens, Georgia. In 1886 Herty graduated from the University of Georgia with a degree in chemistry. Planning to follow his father as a druggist, he enrolled in the newly opened graduate program of the Johns Hopkins University for additional work in chemistry. Professor Ira Remsen persuaded Herty to reorient his efforts toward a career in chemistry and supervised his dissertation on the double halides of lead and alkali metals.

After obtaining his Ph.D. in 1890, Herty returned to Georgia to become assistant chemist for the state experiment station. A year later he began his nine-year teaching career at the University of Georgia. In 1895 Herty married Sophie Schaller; they had three children. In 1899 he took leave to study at the Universities of Zurich and Berlin, where he worked, respectively, with the future Nobel laureate in chemistry, Alfred Werner, and with the synthetic dye chemist Otto N. Witt. After he returned to the United States in 1900 or 1901, Herty adapted their training in applied chemistry to the southern turpentining industry. He developed the cup-and-gutter method of obtaining turpentine to replace the traditional method of cutting a large box into trees. Herty's technique reduced the evaporation of turpentine, decreased the incidence of forest fires, and increased the quality of lumber from the pines. Production of "Herty cups" for this process, moreover, made Herty financially independent.

In 1905 Herty was named chair of the department of chemistry at the University of North Carolina. Briefly he returned to basic chemical research, publishing in 1908 on the double halides. His focus had shifted, however, toward promoting applications of chemistry that he believed would improve the lives of people. Herty's engaging personality and ability to forge consensus within a group facilitated his success as a booster of the nascent chemical industry in the United States. He was active in the American Chemical Society (ACS), becoming chairman in 1909 of its Division of Physical and Inorganic Chemistry. In 1915 and 1916 he served as the ACS president and cooperated with the National Research Council in producing a census of American chemists. This effort was prompted by the German use of gas warfare in World War I, even though the United States at that time was not yet involved in the hostilities. In 1916, also during Herty's term as president, the ACS News Service was launched.

By 1917, when the United States entered the war, Herty had become the first full-time editor of the ACS *Journal of Industrial and Engineering Chemistry* in New York City. From this position, which he held for five years, he promoted greater cooperation between universities and industry and advocated high tariff protection to stimulate the nascent U.S. synthetic organic chemical industry. He also publicized the work of chemists in the war, especially the contributions of the Chemical Warfare Service organized in 1918 to assist the military in preparing to defend against gas warfare.

In 1919 President Woodrow Wilson appointed Herty to represent the United States in arranging for the purchase of impounded German dyestuffs. This led to the organization of the Textile Alliance for protecting the domestic dye industry. From 1921 to 1926 Herty served as president of the Synthetic Organic Chemical Manufacturers Association (SOCMA), a post in which he turned his persuasive gifts to securing favorable federal legislation. During this period also, Herty chaired an ACS committee that sought to promote chemistry in medicine by raising funds for a privately endowed institute for "chemo-therapeutic" research. In 1926 he resigned his SOCMA lobbying post to devote much of his time to this undertaking. He became an adviser to the Chemical Foundation, an organization chartered in 1919 to purchase German chemical patents captured during World War I and to license them to American firms. Its president, Francis Garvin, had lost a daughter to a systemic streptococcal infection and thus was personally interested in the potential of chemistry for medical advancement.

By 1926 the lack of a private patron for the proposed institute caused Herty to consider federal support. His experiences with government-supported research during World War I had been favorable and convinced him that federal funding was not necessarily inimical to freedom of scientific inquiry. He was thus receptive to a proposal by Senator Joseph E. Ransdell of Louisiana to introduce a bill that would create the proposed institute as an entity within the U.S. Public Health Service. In 1930 Congress agreed to rename the existing Hygienic Laboratory of the Public Health Service the National Institute of Health. After World War II multiple institutes were created, and this agency became the National Institutes of Health, the principal funding agency for medical research in the United States.

From 1928 to 1935 Herty consulted on new industrial projects in his native South. Most notably, he convinced the Chemical Foundation, the state of Georgia, and the city of Savannah to support a research laboratory for the production of pulp and paper from southern slash and other pine trees. Although derided by supporters of northern evergreens as unsuitable for paper production, southern pines proved satisfactory, and in 1933 a weekly newspaper was printed on this newsprint. By 1936 sufficient capital had been raised to erect a plant near Lufkin, Texas, to manufacture the newsprint.

In addition to chemistry, sports were Herty's great passion. While teaching chemistry at the University of Georgia, Herty also served as the university's physical director, bringing Glenn "Pop" Warner and the game of football into Georgia academic life. He likewise served as director of athletics while chairing the chemistry department at the University of North Carolina. An active Episcopalian, Herty established a pension system for clergy while serving as a vestryman in Chapel Hill, North Carolina. Because it worked so successfully, the Episcopal church adopted it in 1917 as a model for its national pension program.

By the time of his death in Savannah, Georgia, Herty had received many honors, including six honorary degrees, the medal of the American Institute of Chemists in 1932, and the first ACS Herty medal, named in his honor, in 1934. A town in Texas was named for him, and he was "starred" in *American Men of Science* as one of the outstanding chemists in the United States.

• The Charles Holmes Herty Papers, Special Collections Department, Robert W. Woodruff Library, Emory University, Atlanta, Ga., comprise 153 manuscript boxes of materials with an excellent descriptive inventory. A list of Herty's publications, with the exception of his unsigned editorials in the *Journal of Industrial and Engineering Chemistry*, is in Frank K. Cameron's obituary, *Journal of the American Chemical Society* 61 (1939): 1619–24. Additional biographical materials can be found in "A Crusader," *Journal of Industrial and Engineering Chemistry* 24 (1938): 963–64; A. V. H. Morey, "Charles Holmes Herty," *Journal of Industrial and Engineering Chemistry* 24 (1932): 1141–42; Florence E. Wall, "Charles H. Herty—Apostle to the South," *Chemist*, Feb. 1932, pp. 123–31; and Wyndham Miles, ed., *American Chemists and Chemical Engineers* (1976), pp. 217–18. Additional information on Herty's role as a professional chemist is in Charles Albert Browne and Mary Elvira Weeks, *A History of the American Chemical Society: Seventy-five Eventful Years* (1952).

VICTORIA A. HARDEN

HERTZ, John Daniel (10 Apr. 1879–8 Oct. 1961), transportation entrepreneur and investment banker, was born in Ruttka, a village in the Austro-Hungarian Empire to the north of Budapest (now a part of Slovakia), the son of Jacob Hertz and Katie Schlessinger. The family immigrated to the United States in 1884 and settled in Chicago. The family was poor and parental discipline strict.

At age eleven, after completing the fifth grade, Hertz left home and supported himself as a newsboy, living in the Newsboys' Home. He became a night office boy at the *Chicago Record* soon after, but the night hours affected his health and he left to drive a delivery wagon. At the same time he joined a gym and took up boxing. From this association he began to supply sports news to the *Record*, which led to reporting assignments on boxing and thoroughbred horse racing. Not a championship athlete, Hertz gave up boxing to manage two boxers, traveling about the country from match to match.

While working at Washington Park racetrack Hertz met Frances L. Kesner, who attended the races with her family, and they were married in 1903. They had three children. Before the couple married, her family objected to his work managing boxers, so Hertz took employment as a salesman in a Columbia Electric automobile agency. Offering his customers emergency service whenever and wherever needed, Hertz built up a large clientele and in his second year earned commissions exceeding twelve thousand dollars. Twenty years later he recalled his success: "I went to work two hours before anybody else and worked five or six hours longer. There were thirteen salesmen . . . and I was selling more than seventy per cent. of the cars. I had the desire to work and to make good. I had an incentive. That's all you need in this country" (*New York Times*, 6 July 1924).

In 1907 he paid $2,000 for a one-quarter interest in a debt-ridden automobile dealership and quickly turned it into a highly profitable enterprise. To generate earnings from excess used-car inventory, Hertz put several vehicles on the streets as taxicabs. A success, the sideline soon took on a life of its own and by 1910 Hertz supplied a fleet of private cabs to the Chicago Athletic Association. Following a drivers' strike he took more interest in labor relations and established a profit-sharing program as an incentive for good work. Partly for health reasons, Hertz toured Europe in 1915 and also used the time to study the taxi business in several European cities. He found European cabs to be smaller, cheaper, and operated without extending credit to customers; he returned home determined to revamp his cab business.

Reorganizing his cab company as Yellow Cab in 1915, Hertz halved fares, accepted only cash, and painted his cabs a distinctive bright orange-yellow. Yellow cabs did not wait at stands; they cruised the streets seeking fares. Cheaper prices greatly expanded the market for service, and Yellow prospered. Dissatisfied with available vehicles, Hertz organized the Yellow Cab Manufacturing Company and built his own rugged taxicabs. To increase cab sales, Yellow sold cabs on credit to operators nationwide and provided them with full business consulting services to assure their success and ability to pay. By the mid-1920s Yellow vehicles and business methods dominated the industry. The *Wall Street Journal* (25 Apr. 1924) estimated that except for New York City, where Yellow was not a factor, the company sold more than 95 percent of all cabs in use. In Chicago alone Yellow Cab operated 1,750 vehicles and employed 3,600 drivers.

In October 1922 Hertz led a group of investors in the purchase of the struggling Chicago Motor Coach Company. Formed in 1917, the company primarily served north-side elite residential districts. Hertz raided New York's Fifth Avenue Coach Company, the nation's oldest motor bus system, and hired away top operating and design personnel. Expanding rapidly into other areas of Chicago, the company quickly became profitable, and Hertz followed this success by establishing the Yellow Motor Coach Manufacturing Company to manufacture and market buses. In 1924 he acquired controlling interests in Peoples Motor Bus of St. Louis and Fifth Avenue Coach in New York City. He grouped all three operating companies under the newly formed Omnibus Company of America, a $40 million holding company.

Believing the motor bus superior to urban and intercity rail transport in many operating environments, Hertz envisioned buses eventually replacing most streetcar and steam railroad passenger service, and in July 1924 he announced that the Omnibus Company would work with urban street railways, interurban railways, and steam railroads to convert rail lines to bus lines, and would provide equity capital for equivalent ownership interests. "We have enough confidence in the future of this new industry to match our capital against that of local interests," Hertz told *Bus Transportation* (Aug. 1924, p. 383), "and we will provide the enterprise, the energy and the operating experience to make such companies a success."

Although Hertz clearly intended to duplicate with motor buses his previous successes with taxicabs, events took a different turn. In 1925 he accepted an attractive offer from General Motors to merge the Yellow coach and cab manufacturing units into its truck division. Hertz and his associates received preferred stock and seats on the board of the newly constituted Yellow Truck and Coach Manufacturing Company, the forerunner of GMC. Hertz was elected chairman of the board. Included in the merger was the Hertz Drive-Ur-Self Company, formed by Hertz a year earlier following his purchase of a local Chicago auto rental business, which he was then rapidly transforming into a nationwide franchised rental network. Under General Motors management (1925–1953), however, the rental company achieved limited success.

In 1925 Hertz also began to sell off his taxicab operating assets, withdrawing from the business completely by the end of the decade. In 1926 Hertz and his Chicago associates sold a majority interest in the Omnibus Corporation to a consortium of New York investment bankers. While Hertz remained as chairman of the board, the company curtailed its grandiose expansion plans and concentrated instead on the Chicago and New York City transport markets. In 1926 Omnibus bought a controlling interest in New York Railways, the bankrupt operator of a 72-mile streetcar system in Manhattan, and proposed to change the service to bus. This involved the company in a nine-year struggle for bus operating rights; not until 1935–1936 did Yellow-built buses replace aging streetcars on Manhattan's West Side.

Many times a millionaire, Hertz retired in 1929 at age fifty, in part to spend more time on what had become his and his wife's avid avocation, the breeding and racing of thoroughbred horses. His stables, which eventually included farms in Illinois, Kentucky, and California, raced under bright yellow "taxicab" colors and produced two Kentucky Derby winners, Reigh Count (1928) and Count Fleet (1943), the latter of which went on to win racing's Triple Crown.

Hertz's retirement did not last long. Still an active member on the boards of the Omnibus Company and its various subsidiaries, Hertz became involved in the Paramount-Publix company in 1931, restructuring its finances and retiring again two years later. In 1934 he was offered and accepted a partnership in Lehman Brothers, a New York investment banking firm. Specializing in transportation, Hertz in 1935 brokered the sale of General Motor's 13 percent interest in Transcontinental and Western Air to Floyd Odlum's Atlas Corporation, giving Atlas and Lehman Brothers together working control. In the same year he convinced Lehman partners and Odlum to invest in Keeshin Motor Express, a Chicago-based regional trucking firm and a pioneer in rail piggyback service, to provide the capital for acquisitions and route extensions that quickly expanded the company's service area east to New York City and west to Kansas City.

During World War II Hertz served as assistant to the under secretary of war and chaired the Hertz Committee on Automotive Maintenance, for which he received the Medal for Distinguished Public Service. In the 1950s the Omnibus Company restructured. Buying the Hertz auto and truck rental system from General Motors in 1953, the company subsequently sold its increasingly marginal urban transport systems in New York and Chicago, renamed itself the Hertz Corporation, and used the proceeds from the sales to expand the rental business. Now in his mid-seventies, Hertz accepted the largely symbolic position of honorary chairman of the board but was not active in the corporation after 1954. The company bought numerous regional rental companies and established outlets at more than fifty airports; its automobile fleet grew from about 2,400 cars in the early 1950s to more than 30,000 by the end of the decade. In 1967 the company was acquired by RCA.

Hertz continued as a partner in Lehman Brothers but devoted most of his time to his stables. He served on several corporate boards, including the Baltimore and Ohio Railroad and the Studebaker Corporation. Concerned about Russian technological superiority following the launch of Sputnik, he used a substantial portion of his fortune in the late 1950s to establish the Fannie and John Hertz Engineering Scholarship Fund.

The foundation was a fitting capstone to Hertz's career. His fortune, after all, was the product of his unique ability to apply automotive technological advances commercially, and he played a major role in shaping the taxicab, motor bus, and auto rental industries in the United States between 1910 and 1960. John Hertz died at his Amarillo—Spanish for "yellow"—Ranch in Los Angeles.

• Hertz's papers are not known to exist. Hertz discussed his business methods and ideals in several trade journal articles: "We Wouldn't Make as Much Money if We Raised Prices," *System* 38 (Sept. 1920); "Write Your Own Paycheck," *Illustrated World* 38 (Jan. 1923); "Why Our Business Has Grown to the Largest of Its Kind," *System* 43 (May 1923); "Three Methods That Doubled Our Sales," *System* 46 (Nov. 1924); and in "Getting On in the World," an article in *Saturday Evening Post*, 4 June 1927. His role in the cab industry is discussed in Gorman Gilbert and Robert E. Samuels, *The Taxicab: An Urban Survivor* (1982), and in "John Hertz Makes Millions Building Cabs and Selling Dime Bus Rides," *Current Opinion*, Jan. 1925, pp. 30–32. His role in the auto rental industry is portrayed in Harris Saunders, *Top Up or Down? The Origin and Development of the Automobile and Truck Renting and Leasing Industry—56 Years* (1972). His participation in the motor bus industry is discussed in "Yellow Truck and Coach," *Fortune*, July 1936, p. 61. A good source for his life through 1924 is "Once Immigrant Boy Buys Fifth Avenue Buses," *New York Times*, 6 July 1924. Unfortunately, his racing interests have received more detailed treatment than his business career. See Evan Shipman, *The Racing Memoirs of John Hertz as Told to Evan Shipman* (1954), and a three-part series, Mrs. John Hertz as told to Bozeman Bulger, "Thoroughbreds and Thrills," *Saturday Evening Post*, 9 Apr., 23 Apr., 7 May 1932. Both contain useful biographical information. An obituary is in the *New York Times*, 10 Oct. 1961.

DOUGLAS SHAW

HERTZLER, Arthur Emanuel (25 July 1870–12 Sept. 1946), physician, surgeon, and pathologist, was born in the Mennonite community of West Point, Iowa, the son of Daniel Hertzler, a farmer, and Hannah Krehbiel, the first Mennonite child born west of the Mississippi River. Hertzler's parents grew to hold divergent religious beliefs, separating their family, according to Hertzler, "as completely broken as it would have been by divorce," and leaving Hertzler a lifelong skeptic about organized religion.

Hertzler attended Denmark Academy, a Congregationalist school, for four years, graduating in 1887, and received an A.B. from Southwestern College in Winfield, Kansas, in 1890. After a yearlong medical preceptorship with S. S. Haury in Moundridge, Kansas, he began medical studies at Northwestern University Medical School in Chicago, Illinois, from which he received his M.D. on 24 April 1894. Upon graduation he married Myrtle Arnold in 1894; they had three children. After their divorce in 1905, he married Edith D. Sarrasin in 1909; after a second divorce, he married Irene A. Koeneke in 1935. Hertzler earned three additional degrees—a B.S. from Southwestern College in 1896, an M.A. from Illinois Wesleyan in 1897, and a Ph.D. from Illinois Wesleyan in 1902.

Hertzler established a medical practice in Halstead, Kansas, in 1897. During his horse-and-buggy trips to attend patients, later chronicled in his autobiography, *The Horse and Buggy Doctor* (1938), he contemplated

furthering his medical education. Having learned German as a child, he added French, Spanish, and Italian to his repertoire and traveled to Berlin in 1899 to study anatomy and surgical pathology with Hans Virchow and Wilhelm V. Waldeyer. Under Virchow, Hertzler began a study of the peritoneum which resulted in a two-volume publication, *The Peritoneum* (1920).

Hertzler returned to the United States in 1901 and declined an offer of the chair of anatomy at Northwestern University in favor of returning to Halstead. One year later he accepted a lectureship in histology and pathology at the University Medical College of Kansas City, a position he held until the school closed in 1907. He then accepted an assistant professorship in surgery at the University of Kansas School of Medicine, Rosedale, becoming full professor in 1919 and professor emeritus in 1944. Hertzler also served as attending surgeon to the Swedish and General hospitals in Kansas City and traveled by rail on the weekends to attend his Halstead practice.

Hertzler's lifelong publishing career began with *Laboratory Guide in Bacteriology* (1903) and *Laboratory Guide in Histology* (1904). In *Surgical Operations with Local Anesthesia* (1912), he discussed the value of cocaine as an anesthetic; this was the first work in English to describe local anesthesia. Hertzler's renown as a skillful and quick surgeon spread throughout the country. Publications, including *Principles of Abdominal Surgery* (1918), *Clinical Surgery by Case Histories* (1921), and *Diseases of the Thyroid Gland* (1922), helped establish him as an authority on abdominal and thyroid surgery. From 1930 to 1938 Hertzler published his most ambitious project, a ten-volume set of monographs on surgical pathology. His preparation of this work was aided by his careful preservation, from his first patient onward, of all records, photographs, microscopic slides, and even gross anatomical specimens of anything pathological.

Hertzler traveled throughout much of Kansas on what he called his "kerosene circuit," often operating in his patients' homes on their kitchen tables. As his reputation spread, he found a need in 1913 to incorporate a hospital in Halstead. The simple structure was repeatedly enlarged for two decades until Hertzler found himself unable to keep up with the management of both the hospital and his Kansas City duties. In 1933 he transferred the title of the Agnes Hertzler Memorial Clinic to the Sisters of St. Joseph.

Later in life Hertzler turned to writing for a more general audience, beginning with *The Horse and Buggy Doctor* in 1938. This "record of the old country doctor by one of the species" was a Book-of-the-Month-Club success; it was translated into German, French, Spanish, and fifteen Asian languages, and adapted into a radio play. Later autobiographical works, including *The Doctor and His Patients: The American Domestic Scene as Viewed by the Family Doctor* (1940), *Grounds of an Old Surgeon's Faith: A Scientific Inquiry into the Causes of War* (1944), *Ventures in Science of a Country Surgeon* (1944), and *Always the Child: A Scientific In-*

quiry into Influences Which Harm the Child (1945), met only moderate success.

Hertzler belonged to a number of professional organizations, including the Kansas State Medical Society, the Missouri Medical Association, the American Medical Association, the Western Surgical Association, the Association of American Anatomists, the American Association of Obstetricians and Gynecologists, the Mississippi Valley Medical Society, and the American Microscopical Society, serving the last as president in 1911–1912. Hertzler found his Colt Peacemaker pistol an indispensable companion on his long horse-and-buggy journeys and during the evenings between closing his practice and beginning his writing. His expert marksmanship won him the National Championship of the U.S. Revolver Association for several years around 1930.

Hertzler amassed many other awards, including fellowships in the American College of Surgeons (1913) and the American College of Anatomists (1938).

Railway travel restrictions during World War II forced Hertzler to abandon his weekly Kansas City travels in 1942. He retired on 22 February 1946 and died in Halstead.

• Hertzler's papers are located in the Hertzler Archives of the Hertzler Clinic, Halstead, Kansas. Hertzler's articles most often cited by his contemporaries are "Studies in the Anatomy and Physiology of the Hip-Joint," *Anatomical Record* 3 (1909): 41–46; "Quinine and Urea Hydrochloride as a Local Anesthetic," with R. B. Brewster and F. B. Rogers, *Journal of the American Medical Association* 53 (1909): 393–95; "Pseudoperitoneum, Varicosity of the Peritoneum and Sclerosis of the Mesentery," *Journal of the American Medical Association* 54 (1910): 351–56; and "The Present Status for the Treatment of Diffuse Peritonitis," *Transactions of the Western Surgical and Gynecological Association* 19 (1909): 87–104. His respected series of pathological surgery was composed of *Surgical Pathology of the Diseases of the Bone* (1930), *Surgical Pathology of the Genito-urinary Organs* (1931), *Surgical Pathology of the Skin, Fascia, Muscles, Tendons, Blood and Lymph Vessels* (1931), *Surgical Pathology of the Female Generative Organs* (1932), *Surgery of General Practice* (with Victor E. Chesky, 1934), *Surgical Pathology of the Diseases of the Peritoneum* (1935), *Surgical Pathology of the Gastro Intestinal Tract* (1936), *Surgical Pathology of the Thyroid Gland* (1936), and *Surgical Pathology of Diseases of the Neck* (1937). In addition to Hertzler's autobiographical accounts, see Jerrad J. Hertzler, "Arthur E. Hertzler: The Kansas Horse and Buggy Doctor, A Biographical Sketch," *Journal of the Kansas Medical Society* 63 (1962): 424–33, and Edith C. Coe, *Hertzler Heritage: Irene A. Koeneke, M.D., and the Hertzler Research Foundation* (1975).

PHILIP K. WILSON

HERZFELD, Karl Ferdinand (24 Feb. 1892–3 June 1978), chemical physicist, was born in Vienna, Austria, the son of Karl August Herzfeld, a gynecologist and obstetrician, and Camilla Herzog. The Herzfeld family, originally Jewish, was well established in the professions and had converted to Catholicism. Herzfeld's love of learning and devout religious beliefs had their foundation in his early education at the Benedictine Schottengymnasium.

Herzfeld studied physics at the University of Vienna, with terms spent in Zurich and Göttingen. He completed his degree in July 1914 with a dissertation that applied the old quantum theory to the electron theory of metals. At this time he began to use the methods of statistical mechanics to analyze a variety of physical and chemical systems. Statistical mechanics, a mathematical theory of the aggregate behavior of systems of large numbers of particles, was part of the tradition in physics at the University of Vienna. Because he was a theorist, Herzfeld was able to continue his research through World War I while serving in an artillery regiment in the Austrian army; unlike many of his contemporaries, he was positive about his military service. As he wrote later in his unpublished autobiography, "The war taught me to live in community with others, often under primitive conditions, to make decisions and take responsibilities. I was able to write and publish four papers while at the front."

After the war Herzfeld served as Arnold Sommerfeld's assistant for six years in Munich. Although his work spanned a variety of topics, his greatest interest was in the intersection of chemistry and physics. Chemists in the 1920s were just beginning to formulate a rigorous mathematical theory of chemical reaction rates, and Herzfeld demonstrated that statistical methods originated by physicists Josiah Willard Gibbs and Ludwig Boltzmann could be invaluable in solving this problem. For example, in 1919 he derived an expression for the rate constant of a first-order reaction by estimating the probability of collision of two atoms to form a diatomic molecule. Although Herzfeld's was essentially a classical derivation, his result matched that derived fifteen years later by Henry Eyring using quantum mechanics. Herzfeld also wrote *Kinetische Theorie der Wärme* (Kinetic theory of heat) in 1925; it was extremely influential in the German-speaking scientific world but was never translated into English. The book was a systematic survey of statistical mechanics with many applications to chemistry and was one of the first to describe the use of partition functions, mathematical expressions based on the distribution of energy within a system of particles.

In 1926 Herzfeld accepted an invitation to come to the United States as Speyer Visiting Professor at Johns Hopkins University in Baltimore; at the end of the term he was offered a permanent appointment as professor of physics. Over the next ten years he was instrumental in bringing an emphasis on theoretical physics into a department that had been essentially experimental in nature. He worked closely with members of the chemistry department, continuing his work in chemical reaction rates. In particular, in 1931 he and F. O. Rice demonstrated the role of free radicals in organic chemical reactions. Herzfeld was able to mathematize the result in a way that yielded experimentally verifiable results.

At Hopkins Herzfeld also began a related research program. He and Rice found that ultrasonic absorption measurements could be used to determine the rate of energy transfer between molecules in chemical reactions. This technique, widely used and modified thereafter, gave a way to evaluate the intermolecular interactions taking place in reactions, something that was not directly detectable by other means. The theoretical study of the behavior of ultrasonic waves remained a long-term interest for Herzfeld.

When Herzfeld left in 1936 to take over leadership of the physics department at Catholic University, his colleagues in chemistry at Hopkins mourned "the loss of a very effective and fruitful connecting link between physics and chemistry" (Chemistry Department Archives, Johns Hopkins Univ.). At Catholic University Herzfeld turned a quiet department that had offered only undergraduate physics into a productive, research-oriented graduate department. By offering graduate courses at night he created a special niche for the department, and over the years dozens of scientists working in government laboratories in the Washington, D.C., area were able to complete doctorates in physics at Catholic University. Herzfeld married Regina Flannery, an anthropologist at Catholic University, in 1938; he accompanied her on a number of research trips to study Native American peoples in Canada and the western United States. They had no children.

When World War II broke out, Herzfeld's contribution to the war effort consisted of teaching an increased number of courses for officer-training programs; he also studied elastic stress in artillery shells and the use of ultrasound to measure the effects of the explosion of underwater mines. He declined to serve on the Manhattan Project after ascertaining from R. C. Tolman that there was little chance that the Germans would succeed in developing a nuclear weapon, and he never participated in any form of nuclear research after the war.

Through the 1950s and 1960s Herzfeld continued to teach, served on the navy's Mine Advisory Committee, and focused his scientific attention on the nature of the liquid state. Statistical physicist Elliott Montroll wrote of him, "For many years he was the capital area's wise theoretical physicist to whom local researchers went with their problems, which he generally clarified and frequently resolved." Herzfeld retired in 1968, although he continued to teach occasional courses; he died in Washington, D.C.

Herzfeld's scientific career spanned many areas of physics, including the theory of liquids, crystal dynamics, and optics, as well as those mentioned above, and demonstrated that classical physics still had a place in twentieth-century science. This classical approach was essential to his success in forging strong links between the disciplines of chemistry and physics before quantum mechanics was widely accepted by chemists. He published more than 130 scientific papers during his career, as well as numerous essays on science and religion. In the tradition of many scientists of the seventeenth through the nineteenth centuries, Herzfeld's deep religious commitment was not independent of his scientific work but was an essential part

of it. He brought a strong moral sense to all of his endeavors and was widely respected for it.

• A small collection of Herzfeld's correspondence and other papers is in the American Institute of Physics Niels Bohr Library, College Park, Md. It includes his unpublished family history "The Herzfeld Family: A Documented Illustrated History," with extensive autobiographical material and the transcript of an interview with Herzfeld conducted shortly before his death. Herzfeld contributed chapters to a variety of physics handbooks, such as *Handbuch der Physik* (1924; 2d ed., 1933), and was author, with T. A. Litovitz, of *Absorption and Dispersion of Ultrasonic Waves* (1959). The most comprehensive assessment of Herzfeld's role in science is Karen E. Johnson, "Bringing Statistical Mechanics into Chemistry: The Early Scientific Work of Karl F. Herzfeld," *Journal of Statistical Physics* 59 (1990): 1547–72. See also E. W. Montroll, "On the Vienna School of Statistical Thought," *American Institute of Physics Conference Proceedings*, no. 10g (1984). Obituaries are in the *Washington Post*, 7 June 1978, and *Physics Today*, Jan. 1979.

KAREN E. JOHNSON

HESCHEL, Abraham Joshua (11 Jan. 1907–23 Dec. 1972), theologian and social activist, was born in Warsaw, Poland, the son of Moses Mordecai Heschel, a Hasidic rebbe, and Rivka Reizel Perlow. Both parents were descended from distinguished Hasidic dynasties. A child prodigy, Heschel mastered the classic Jewish texts. At age fifteen he published his first Talmud commentaries in a Warsaw Orthodox monthly. Around that time he was ordained as a rabbi.

Heschel's Jewish learning was immense, but he wanted a secular education as well. At age eighteen he studied at the secular Yiddish-language Real-Gymnasium in Vilna (Vilnius), Lithuania. There he associated with a group of writers and artists soon known as Yung Vilna. Heschel published his first Yiddish poem in the noted anthology *Varshaver shriftn* (Warsaw writings) (1926–1927). In June 1927 he graduated from the Real-Gymnasium and moved to Berlin, where he completed his studies at the Friedrich Wilhelm University (now Humboldt University) and at the Hochschule für die Wissenschaft des Judentums, a liberal rabbinical and teachers' college. In Berlin Heschel was deeply influenced by the Russian Jewish social philosopher David Koigen.

In 1931–1932 Heschel taught the Talmud to advanced students as assistant to Dr. Hanoch Albeck at the Hochschule. In 1933, the year Hitler came to power, he completed his doctorate at Berlin University with a phenomenological study of prophetic consciousness. The same year he published his first book, a collection of Yiddish poems entitled *Der shem ham'forash: mentsh* (Mankind: God's Ineffable Name).

In 1934 Heschel completed his academic work at the Hochschule, where he continued to teach Talmud. The next year he published a biography of Maimonides, the medieval philosopher. In 1936, his dissertation, "Die prophetie" (On prophecy), established his reputation as a biblical scholar and original theologian. Defining a "theology of pathos"—that is, God's active, emotional concern for humankind—it introduced themes that he continued to develop throughout his life. Martin Buber invited Heschel to Frankfurt in 1937 to replace him as co-director of the Central Organization for Jewish Adult Education and the Jüdisches Lehrhaus. Through his teaching and writing, Heschel contributed to the spiritual resistance to the Nazis.

In 1938, with thousands of other Polish Jews, Heschel was expelled from Germany. He returned to Warsaw and taught at the modern Institut Nauk Judaistyczynch (Institute for Jewish Science). About six weeks before the 1 September 1939 German invasion of Poland, he left for London. There he founded the Institute for Jewish Studies, modeled after the Frankfurt Lehrhaus. At the invitation of Julian Morgenstern, president of the Hebrew Union College in Cincinnati, he emigrated to the United States in March 1940.

In Cincinnati, confronted with the threat of the destruction of European Jewry, Heschel sought to work toward the redemption of civilization by emphasizing the divine reality in religious practice. While teaching in theological seminaries, he devoted his main energies to writing. Heschel taught at the Reform Jewish Hebrew Union College until 1945, when he joined the faculty of the Conservative Jewish Theological Seminary in New York City as professor of Jewish ethics and mysticism. His numerous publications soon established him as the leading modern exponent of (non-Orthodox) traditional Judaism in the United States—some would say in the entire world. In 1945 he was naturalized an American citizen, and the next year he married Sylvia Straus of Cleveland, Ohio, a concert pianist; they had one child.

Heschel sought to encourage sensitivity to "the presence of God in the Bible." His works in English appeal to Jews and Christians both inside and outside observant religious communities as they evoke the "ineffable" dimension of reality, an intuition of the sacred as beyond human thought and language. His extraordinary mastery of literary English, in a dynamic style that is both intellectually incisive and poetic, makes concrete his intimacy with holiness and his full-blooded ethical judgments.

The books Heschel published in the 1950s define a model of spirituality and led to his adopting the role of *zaddik* (righteous man) or "apostle to the Gentiles" (in Protestant biblical scholar James Sanders's terms). *The Earth Is the Lord's: The Inner Life of the Jew in East Europe* (1950) explains the values intrinsic to Heschel's Hasidic origins and maps out his theological system. *The Sabbath: Its Meaning for Modern Man* (1951) both evokes and analyzes this weekly ritual of holy consciousness. Heschel achieved national prominence with *Man Is Not Alone: A Philosophy of Religion* (1951), as Reinhold Niebuhr had accurately predicted in an influential review: "He will become a commanding and authoritative voice not only in the Jewish community but in the religious life of America." People of all faiths found in Heschel an authentic biblical voice. *God in Search of Man: A Philosophy of Judaism*

(1955), Heschel's masterwork, reinterprets the entire Jewish tradition in modern terms. It follows the path from universal religious insight or "radical amazement" through God's Revelation at Mount Sinai in order to interpret Jewish observance and ethical imperatives.

All of Heschel's works address Orthodox, Conservative, and Liberal Judaism, for he maintains Judaism's various and sometimes contradictory elements. *Man's Quest for God: Studies in Prayer and Symbolism* (1954) focuses on Jewish prayer as a polarity between halakhah (prescribed law) and spontaneity or inwardness. He maintains that prayer is as necessary as faith, for God is not a symbol but a living reality.

Heschel's specialized scholarship, written in German, Hebrew, Yiddish, and English, covers a remarkably wide range of subjects: Bible, medieval Jewish philosophy, Kabbalah, Hasidic masters, theology, and ethics. Of particular interest is his three-volume work of talmudic interpretation, *Torah min ha-shamayim ba-ispaqlaryah shel ha-dorot* (Torah from heaven in the light of the generations [3 vols., 1962, 1965, 1990]; the English title page reads *The Theology of Ancient Judaism*), in which he defines the opposing schools of Rabbi Akiva, who considered the Torah as mystically revealed, and Rabbi Ishmael, who emphasized the human elements of biblical interpretation.

Heschel was a prophet for the 1960s, combining spiritual sensitivity and moral activism. In 1960 he delivered a stirring address at the White House Conference on Children and Youth, and the following year he spoke at the Conference on Aging. In Chicago in 1963, at the first national conference on religion and race, he proclaimed, "It was easier for the children of Israel to cross the Red Sea than for a Negro to cross certain university campuses." There he met the Reverend Martin Luther King, Jr., and in 1965 he participated with King in the Selma, Alabama, civil rights demonstration. A famous photograph of him marching with King has enriched black-Jewish relations. His picturesque appearance, prematurely gray hair, beard, dignified rabbinic bearing, and biblical oratory, accented with the intonations of his native Yiddish, all contributed to an effective public persona.

Heschel's sometimes controversial activism stood on a firm scholarly foundation. The Hebrew prophets remained his ethical model from the beginning of his academic career. His massive study, *The Prophets* (1962), expands his doctoral dissertation, defining a type of consciousness that identifies with the living God's active—and, as it were, emotional—involvement with human deeds. Heschel's career confirmed his biblical theology, namely, that the "purpose of the prophecy is to conquer callousness, to change the inner man as well as to revolutionize history."

Beginning in 1961 Heschel acted as theological consultant to the American Jewish Committee in preparation for the Second Vatican Council. He began by submitting a memorandum to Augustin Cardinal Bea, a venerable Old Testament scholar whom Pope John XXIII charged with formulating a declaration on non-

Christian religions. Heschel's 1962 document called upon the Vatican to accept the autonomous existence of Judaism; to stop considering Jews as candidates for conversion; to absolve Jews of the charge of deicide; and to eliminate other anti-Semitic allusions in the liturgy and church teachings. Cardinal Bea and his commission, already devoted to the new openness, energetically fought for ratification of a favorable declaration on the Jews. Heschel met privately with Pope Paul VI on 14 September 1964 and helped influence the *Nostra Aetate* (1965), which, despite shortcomings, has revolutionized Jewish-Christian relations by accepting the spiritual integrity of Judaism.

Heschel's speeches and essays evoked with searing immediacy his prophetic judgments on contemporary issues, including religious and moral education, medical ethics, racism, the drug culture, Soviet Jewry, Israel, and the Vietnam War. Many are collected in *The Insecurity of Freedom: Essays on Human Existence* (1966). Beginning in 1965, as a cofounder of Clergy Concerned about Vietnam (later Clergy and Laity Concerned), he participated in many interreligious demonstrations against the American war in Vietnam. After the June 1967 Arab-Israeli war, he published *Israel: An Echo of Eternity* (1969), a passionate book explaining the value of the state of Israel to Christians. That same year he experienced a massive heart attack from which he never completely recovered. However, he maintained his intense antiwar activities, his teaching, and his efforts to complete two books, one in English and the other in Yiddish, on the Hasidic dissident Rabbi Menachem Mendl of Kotzk.

His autobiographical confession, *A Passion for Truth* (1973), was delivered to the publisher just days before his death in New York City. In that work, he expresses the central conflict of his sensibility: "To live both in awe and consternation, in fervor and horror, with my conscience on mercy and my eyes on Auschwitz, wavering between exaltation and dismay."

Abraham Heschel was a hypersensitive person, both energized and oppressed by contradictions: he was a Hasidic prince in a world of talmudic formalism or agnostic rationality; an observant Jew in the secular United States; a prophetic radical and a prayerful mystic. He was never completely at home, whether in Warsaw, Vilna, Berlin, Frankfurt, or the United States, although he absorbed culture. However, he was able, through his writings and public appearances, to bring to people of varied backgrounds a sense of the living God. Despite the unsystematic structure of his body of work, Heschel has defined a biblical theology for the twenty-first century. His works justify the living God and face the complexities of contemporary civilization—its anguish and despair and its yearning for ultimate meaning.

• Heschel's library and personal papers remain in the possession of his family. Major works by Heschel in English not mentioned in the text include *Who Is Man?* (1965) and *Maimonides: A Biography*, trans. J. Neugroschel (1982). His works appear in the following collections: *Between God and Man*, ed. Fritz A. Rothschild (1959; rev. ed., 1976), *The Circle of the Baal Shem Tov*, ed. Samuel Dresner (1985), and *Moral Grandeur and Spiritual Audacity: Essays*, ed. Susannah Heschel (1996). Notable articles by Heschel include "The Quest for Certainty in Saadia's Philosophy," *Jewish Quarterly Review* (1943 and 1944); "The Mystical Element in Judaism," in *The Jews: Their History, Culture, and Religion*, ed. Louis Finkelstein (1949); "No Religion Is an Island," *Union Seminary Quarterly Journal* 21 (Jan. 1966): 117–34; "The Moral Outrage of Vietnam," in R. M. Brown et al., *Vietnam: Crisis of Conscience* (1967); "The Jewish Notion of God and Christian Renewal," *Renewal of Religious Thought*, ed. L. K. Shook (1968); "Conversation with Martin Luther King, Jr.," *Conservative Judaism* 22 (Spring 1968): 1–19; "Teaching Jewish Theology at the Solomon Schechter Day School," *Synagogue School* 28 (Fall 1969): 4–18.

The most comprehensive studies of Heschel's thought are John Merkle, *The Genesis of Faith: The Depth Theology of A. J. Heschel* (1985); John Merkle, ed., *Abraham Joshua Heschel: Exploring His Life and Thought* (1985); Lawrence Perlman, *Abraham Heschel's Idea of Revelation* (1989); Harold Kasimow and Byron Sherwin, eds., *No Religion Is an Island: A. J. Heschel and Interreligious Dialogue* (1991); and Edward K. Kaplan, *Holiness in Words: Abraham Joshua Heschel's Poetics of Piety* (1996). Articles on Heschel include Jakob Petuchowski, "Faith as the Leap of Action: The Theology of A. J. Heschel," *Commentary* 25 (May 1958): 390–97; Marvin Fox, "Heschel, Intuition, and the Halakhah," *Tradition* 3 (Fall 1960): 5–15; Fritz Rothschild, "A. J. Heschel," in *Modern Theologians*, ed. Thomas Bird (1967); Edmond Cherbonnier, "Heschel as a Religious Thinker," *Conservative Judaism* 23 (Fall 1968): 25–39; Eugene Borowitz, *A New Jewish Theology in the Making* (1968): 147–60; Seymour Seigel, "Abraham Heschel's Contributions to Jewish Scholarship," *Proceedings of the Rabbinical Assembly* 32 (1968): 72–85; Edward Kaplan, "Mysticism and Despair in A. J. Heschel's Religious Thought," *Journal of Religion* 57 (Jan. 1977): 33–47; Steven Katz, "A. J. Heschel and Hasidism," *Journal of Jewish Studies* 31 (Spring 1980): 82–104; Samuel Dresner, "The Contribution of A. J. Heschel," *Judaism* 32 (Winter 1983): 57–69; Arnold Eisen, "Re-Reading Heschel on the Commandments," *Modern Judaism* 9 (Feb. 1989): 1–33; Jeffrey Shandler, "Heschel and Yiddish," *Journal of Jewish Thought and Philosophy* 2 (1993): 245–99; Edward Kaplan, "A. J. Heschel," in *Interpreters of Judaism in the Late Twentieth Century*, ed. Steven Katz (1993).

Obituaries are in the *New York Times*, 24 Dec. 1972, and the *American Jewish Yearbook* (1973), pp. 533–44.

EDWARD K. KAPLAN

HESS, Alfred Fabian (19 Oct. 1875–5 Dec. 1933), pediatrician and clinical investigator, was born in New York City, the son of Selmar Hess, a successful publisher, and Josephine Solomon. Hess graduated in 1897 from Harvard College and received his M.D. from the College of Physicians and Surgeons of Columbia University in 1901. He did postgraduate clinical work at Mount Sinai Hospital until 1904. In 1904 he married Sara Straus, with whom he had two daughters. Hess and his wife traveled to Prague and Vienna, where he was a postgraduate student. Upon their return, Hess worked at the Rockefeller Institute and began a private practice, caring for children up to age five. He was associated with the laboratories of the Department of Health in New York City (1908–1920), the department of pathology of the College of Physicians and Surgeons (1920–1933), and, as clinical professor of pediatrics, with New York University and Bellevue Hospital Medical College (1915–1931).

Around 1911 Hess began a lifelong association as chief medical officer and trustee of the Hebrew Infant Asylum in the Bronx, New York. He frequently used infants and children in the orphanage as subjects in investigations, recognizing the value of the "systematic study of a group of infants over a long period of time" (*Collected Writings*, vol. 1, p. 607). Topics of study emerged from his medical experience in the asylum.

In the early twentieth century considerable attention was focused on the bacteriology of communicable disease. Hess investigated tuberculosis and other communicable diseases of childhood. He founded a preventorium to care for infants and children whose parents were afflicted with tuberculosis. However, his interest turned to the nutritional diseases after he studied in Berlin with Heinrich Finkelstein in 1910. From that time he focused on scurvy and rickets. Some believed that these diseases might be the result of bacterial toxins produced in the intestine, but at the same time they recognized that nutritional diseases could be cured by eating certain foods. Hess subscribed to the hypothesis of the Polish researcher Casimir Funk that nutritional diseases could result from deficiencies of specific substances in the diet, which came to be called vitamins.

Scurvy is a disease of nutritional deficiency characterized by hemorrhaging of the gums, under the skin, and within the joints. For centuries it was known that certain foods cured scurvy in adults. Scurvy was not thought to exist in infants—its signs were believed to be evidence of advanced rickets—but by careful observation and studies of treatment, Hess established the existence of infantile scurvy. In 1914 he studied effects on infants at the Asylum when orange juice was discontinued; in a 1921 article in *The Nation*, the social worker Konrad Berkovici harshly criticized Hess for this use of "orphans as guinea pigs." Hess discovered that the heart was also affected in scurvy. He found that the antiscorbutic factor (vitamin C) was destroyed in the presence of oxygen, under too high or too prolonged heating of food, and when other foods added to it were too alkaline. He recommended tomatoes as a readily-available, inexpensive source of the vitamin.

Hess recognized that scurvy and rickets were often found in the same infant, so his investigation of scurvy naturally led him to study rickets. A nutritional deficiency causing retarded growth of the bones and bending of weight-bearing bones, rickets was endemic among children in large cities in temperate climates. In 1920 Hess estimated that 75 percent of children in New York City were afflicted with it. By X-ray examination of joints, he found rickets in 90 percent of children in the Hebrew Infant Asylum, but he discovered that children in the tropics were rarely afflicted.

From the 1920s Hess carried out investigations of sunlight and artificial light as therapy for rickets in human infants and animals. In 1918 he exposed infants with rickets to rays of a mercury vapor lamp but found inconclusive results. A German researcher, Kurt Huldschinsky, confirmed by X-ray that such treatment with ultraviolet light cured rickets. By the 1920s cod liver oil had been discarded as a remedy for rickets, yet Hess demonstrated its curative value in animals and in human infants. More importantly, he demonstrated its value as a preventive in an experimental intervention using infants in an African-American community.

In 1924 Hess published his discovery that cholesterol in some foods could become a potent antirachitic if irradiated with ultraviolet rays. Searching in vain for the active component of cholesterol, he twice took his findings to an expert German chemist, Adolf O. R. Windaus. Using Hess's laboratory findings and at Hess's urging, Windaus discovered ergosterol as the active factor in cholesterol; irradiating the ergosterol in milk with ultraviolet light converts part of the ergosterol to vitamin D. Windaus received the Nobel Prize in Chemistry (1928) for this discovery. Throughout this laboratory phase of his career, Hess continued to address practical issues as well. He compared the curative powers of sunshine and artificial lamps. He investigated antirachitic powers in irradiated foods. He searched for the simplest preventive for rickets—whether it was to treat pregnant mothers, nursing mothers, the food given to cows, the cows themselves, or infants and children. The *New York Times* (11 Nov. 1933) reported that Hess urged the irradiation of milk as an "automatic method" of preventing rickets by providing vitamin D to infants and children during the winter months when there was not adequate sunshine. Implementation of this measure largely eliminated rickets in the United States; its use continues today.

Hess died in the Bronx after giving a speech to graduating nurses at the Hebrew Infant Asylum. Remembering Hess in a biographical memoir (*Collected Writings*, vol. 1), Abraham Flexner found it astonishing that although not "a bacteriologist, a chemist, a histologist, or a physiologist," Hess nevertheless was "one of the very foremost investigators of his time in medicine." Some of his discoveries were preempted by or shared with others, but Hess was "a great skirmisher on the forefront of scientific progress, with an almost uncanny eye for the point at which the next attack should be made," Health Department researcher William H. Park told Flexner. Park found Hess, a clinician by training, author of 227 research reports, a text on scurvy and one on rickets, "the best example of what can be accomplished in science by the ability to think alone and unaided."

• Biographical information, reprints of many of Hess's research reports, and a complete list of his published research reports are in Alfred Fabian Hess, *Collected Writings* (2 vols., 1936). Hess wrote two books, *Scurvy: Past and Present* (1920) and *Rickets: Including Osteomalacia and Tetany* (1929). Obituaries are in the *American Journal of Diseases of Children* 47

(1934): 635–39; *Science* 79 (1934): 70–71; *Medical Life*, 41 (1934): 615–17; and the *New York Times*, 7 Dec. 1933. An account of his funeral is in the *New York Times*, 9 Dec. 1933.

BERNADINE COURTRIGHT BARR

HESS, Harry Hammond (24 May 1906–25 Aug. 1969), geologist and oceanographer, was born in New York City, the son of Julian S. Hess, a stockbroker, and Elizabeth Engel. In high school in New Jersey he was interested in foreign languages. In 1923 he entered Yale University, where he began with a major in electrical engineering but soon changed to geology, for which most of his courses were in the graduate department.

After receiving a B.S. in 1927, Hess worked as a geologist for Loangwa Concessions for two years in remote areas in northern Rhodesia with local African helpers. On his return to the United States he entered Princeton University for graduate study in geology. There Edward Sampson urged him into a field and laboratory study of soapstones from Schuyler, Virginia. Reluctant at first, Hess later said that this work started him on a fascinating career of research on ultramafic rocks. He received an M.A. in 1931 and the Ph.D. in geology in 1932. He taught at Rutgers University for a year, was a research associate at the Geophysical Laboratory of the Carnegie Institution of Washington in Washington, D.C., for the next year, and in 1934 became an instructor in geology at Princeton, where he advanced to professor and remained for the rest of his life. He served as department chairman from 1950 to 1966. Also in 1934 he married Annette Burns; the couple had two children.

While a graduate student in 1931, at the urging of Princeton professor Richard Montgomery Field, Hess participated in a study of seafloor gravity, in a U.S. Navy submarine in the West Indies, with Dutch geophysicist Felix Andries Vening Meinesz. To facilitate the work, Hess joined the Naval Reserve as a lieutenant.

On 8 December 1941 he reported for active duty in the U.S. Navy. Given responsibility for detecting German submarines in the Atlantic Ocean, he worked out their patterns of operation until he could estimate their daily positions, which led to a high rate of destroying submarines. He later became commanding officer of the USS *Cape Johnson* and participated in four troop landings on Pacific islands.

At sea on the *Cape Johnson*, although it was not navy policy to do so, he continuously maintained use of the ship's sounding equipment and was able to obtain considerable information on bathymetry. He observed that a number of deep, submerged peaks on the sea floor had flat tops and deduced that these "drowned ancient islands" had been eroded by wave action before becoming submerged. He proposed the name "guyot" to distinguish these from cone-topped submerged volcanoes, in recognition of Arnold Henry Guyot, who had established the geology department at Princeton in the 1850s. After returning to Princeton at the end of World War II, Hess stayed in the Naval Reserve and retired with the rank of rear admiral in the Research Reserve.

In 1947 Hess expanded a program at Princeton of geologic studies in the Caribbean. Over the years it was supported by the university, the National Science Foundation, the Office of Naval Research, several oil companies, and the governments of Venezuela, Puerto Rico, and Colombia, providing research opportunities for many students from a dozen nations.

Hess's own researches included both geology and oceanography. He published a number of papers on the plutonic rocks and minerals that originate at great depth in the earth, and he proposed that metamorphosed peridotite from the mantle has been forced upward along the axes of major mountain systems. His paper on "Pyroxenes of Common Mafic Magmas" (*American Mineralogist* 26 [1941]: 515–35 and 573–94) is considered a classic and "the foundation for all modern studies" on these rocks, according to his biographer Harold L. James.

Combining his two broad interests, Hess was drawn into the program proposed in 1957 to drill a hole to the earth's mantle that became known as the Mohole project. He worked intensely toward having the program established and was chairman of the site selection committee. Congress ended the project in 1966, but it eventually led to an extensive continuing program of drilling to lesser depths throughout the oceans.

In oceanography, Hess's most widely known idea was that convection cells in the earth's mantle moved material upward under the mid-ocean ridges, outward, and finally downward at the oceanic trenches and under the continents. This theory of sea-floor spreading implied that, while continents are "permanent," ocean basins are impermanent features. When Hess proposed his idea in 1960, he called it "an essay in geopoetry" and considered it "a useful framework for testing various and sundry groups of hypotheses relating to the oceans." Other scientists soon worked out the details, and the ocean drilling program provided essential tests.

Hess served effectively on many committees at Princeton and as an adviser to various federal offices. He was chairman of the Committee for Disposal of Radioactive Wastes (connected to the National Research Council), chairman of the Earth Sciences Division of the National Research Council, and chairman of the Space Science Board of the National Academy of Sciences, whose role was to advise the National Aeronautics and Space Administration on its scientific programs. Hess died in Woods Hole, Massachusetts, while chairing a committee meeting of the Space Science Board. He had earlier been designated a NASA principal investigator for some of the samples obtained from the moon. NASA awarded him the Distinguished Public Service Award posthumously (1969).

Hess was elected to the National Academy of Sciences in 1952. He was president of the Mineralogical Society of America (1955) and of the Geological Society of America (1963), from which he received the Penrose Medal in 1966. Among his other honors was the

Feltrinelli Prize of the Accademia Nazionale dei Lincei in Rome, Italy (1966). One of the many Pacific Ocean guyots was named Hess Guyot. His final field trip was only a month before his death: to South Africa to observe igneous rocks of the kind that had become his specialty years earlier.

• Hess's archival records are in the Manuscripts Unit of the Department of Rare Books, Firestone Library, Princeton University. Among his significant publications is *Stillwater Igneous Complex, Montana, a Quantitative Mineralogical Study*, Geological Society of America Memoir No. 80 (1960). His paper on the movement of continents was "Evolution of Ocean Basins," a widely circulated report on a contract from the Office of Naval Research (1960); he submitted the idea also as "History of Ocean Basins," in *Petrologic Studies: A Volume to Honor A. F. Buddington*, ed. A. E. J. Engel et al. (1962). Biographical accounts are by William W. Rubey in *Yearbook of the American Philosophical Society of Philadelphia* (1970), pp. 126–29; A. F. Buddington in *Geological Society of America Proceedings for 1969* (1970), with bibliography; and Harold L. James in National Academy of Sciences, *Biographical Memoirs* 43 (1973): 109–28, with bibliography. An obituary is in the *New York Times*, 26 Aug. 1969.

ELIZABETH NOBLE SHOR

HESS, Seymour Lester (27 Oct. 1920–15 Jan. 1982), meteorologist and planetary scientist, was born in Brooklyn, New York, the son of Morris J. Hess, a linoleum company operator, and Rose B. (maiden name unknown). He grew up in Brooklyn in a Jewish family. Hess received a bachelor's degree in chemistry at Brooklyn College in 1941. During World War II he entered the U.S. Army Air Corps at the University of Chicago, where he took a nine-month course that trained weather forecasters for the war effort. One of his teachers was Carl Rossby, a pioneer in the study of global atmospheric circulation. Hess studied how temperatures in the troposphere (the lowest layer of the atmosphere) decline toward the pole. He obtained a master's degree from Chicago in 1945 and remained at the university as an assistant meteorologist and meteorology instructor until 1948.

In the 1940s some scientists grew interested in the atmospheres of other planets. They hoped to refine terrestrial circulation models by seeing how atmospheres behaved on other planets. The planet Mars held special interest because of its relative closeness and the clarity of its air. Among the numerous late nineteenth-century astronomers to have studied, sketched, photographed, and spectrally analyzed Mars, the best known was Percival Lowell, who in the 1890s had founded Lowell Observatory in Flagstaff, Arizona. Like a number of other astronomers, Lowell claimed to see long, thin "lines" on Mars. In a number of popular books, he argued that the lines were canals built by Martians.

Hess came to Lowell Observatory in the summer of 1948, intending to study martian meteorology. Unfortunately, the available astronomical observations of Mars were limited and of low resolution. Astronomers still debated elementary meteorological issues, such as the temperature of the martian surface and the amount of water vapor on Mars. Hess managed nevertheless to calculate that the martian surface air pressure is less than 1 percent that of Earth at sea level. He also determined that the planet is so dry that the diffuse martian clouds are the equivalent of four-tenths of a millimeter of water spread over the planet. In 1949 Hess's dissertation on the martian atmosphere earned him a Ph.D. from the University of Chicago.

In 1950 Hess joined the meteorology department at Florida State University, where he remained for the rest of his career, with the exception of visiting lectureships in the Soviet Union, England, and elsewhere. From 1966 to 1971 he served as associate dean of the university's College of Arts and Sciences. He chaired the meteorology department from 1958 to 1963 and from 1977 to 1978. He married Eugenia E. Legrande in 1966; they raised four children, including three from Hess's first marriage, other details of which are not known.

In the mid to late 1960s U.S. space probes flew by Mars and sent back close-up photos of the planet. Mars proved to be crater-scarred, and its "canals," optical illusions, as most astronomers had suspected. Even so, some scientists still thought Mars might house simple life forms such as microorganisms. Planning to send two robot landers—Viking One and Viking Two—to the martian surface to look for such life, the National Aeronautics and Space Administration picked Hess to head the Viking meteorology team and to design the landers' meteorological gear. In this role Hess envisioned each Viking's weather station as "a net stretched in time rather than space" (Burgess, p. 56). Each probe, he hoped, would regularly transmit to Earth data on temperature, air pressure, and wind speed and direction.

Viking scientists disagreed about where the probes should land. For meteorological reasons, Hess wanted to land the probes in a flat, elevated area. But the life scientists wanted to land in a low-lying region. They also hoped to place at least one probe at a martian pole. They argued that a low-lying area would probably be warmer and wetter and have higher air pressure; therefore it was likelier to be inhabited. Likewise, the pole might be water-rich. Hess characterized the polar scheme as "fiscal recklessness" and successfully opposed it.

The Vikings landed in the summer of 1976 in the martian northern hemisphere, in regions with fairly flat terrains. Each probe extended a boom, with weather sensors attached, several feet above the surface. On 21 July, Hess issued a bulletin:

This is the first weather report from Mars in the history of mankind, the weather in Chryse on sols [martian days] zero and one. Light winds from the east in the late afternoon, changing to light winds from the southwest after midnight. Maximum wind was 15 miles per hour. Temperature ranged from −122 degrees Fahrenheit, just after dawn, to −22 degrees Fahrenheit, but we believe that was not the maximum. Pressure is steady at 7.70 millibars. (Burgess, p. 93)

The martian atmosphere proved to be less dynamic than Earth's. One reason is the almost total lack of water, which on Earth profoundly affects atmospheric heat flow. Also, on Mars the air pressure varies seasonally because of seasonal fluctuations in the amount of carbon dioxide gas frozen at the poles. Hess's instruments and other Viking sensors confirmed that Mars is a world more hostile to man than Antarctica. Orbital photos of Mars taken through the 1970s, however, showed show huge features that resemble dried riverbeds. These may have been carved by flowing water billions of years ago. If so, then Mars may once have had a more habitable surface.

Hess and his team won a Special Award from the American Meteorological Society in 1977 "for the scientific and engineering achievement which has brought us daily weather reports from Mars. This new capability to compare the atmospheric dynamics of two planets marks a major and historic step forward in the science of meteorology." Thanks considerably to Hess, the domain of meteorology had been extended from Earth to other planets. He died in Tallahassee, Florida.

• Some significant early papers by Hess include "A Meteorological Approach to the Question of Water Vapor on Mars and the Mass of the Martian Atmosphere," *Proceedings of the Astronomical Society of the Pacific* 60 (1948): 289–302; "Some Aspects of the Meteorology of Mars," *Journal of Meteorology* 7 (1950): 1–13; and "Atmospheres of Other Planets," *Science* 128 (1958): 809–14. See also Hess and Hans Panofsky, "The Atmospheres of the Other Planets," in *Compendium of Meteorology*, ed. Thomas F. Malone (1951), pp. 391–98. Hess's *Introduction to Theoretical Meteorology* (1959), was an important textbook in the field.

Pre-Viking theories of Mars life are described in Walter Sullivan, *We Are Not Alone* (1964), and William Graves Hoyt, *Lowell and Mars* (1976). Hess's early research at Lowell Observatory is detailed in Ronald E. Doel, *Solar System Astronomy in America: Communities, Patronage, and Interdisciplinary Science, 1920–1960* (1996). An official NASA history of its Mars programs, including Hess's role, is Edward Clinton Ezell and Linda Neuman Ezell, *On Mars: Exploration of the Red Planet 1958–1978* (1984). See also Eric Burgess, *To the Red Planet* (1978). Hess and his Viking team's earliest findings appeared in *Science* 193 (27 Aug. 1976): 759–815. The results of the 1983 "Seymour Hess Memorial Symposium" in Hamburg, Germany, plus a brief biographical account of Hess by his longtime associate W. A. Baum, are in Garry E. Hunt, ed., *Recent Advances in Planetary Meteorology* (1985). An obituary is in the *New York Times*, 16 Jan. 1982.

KEAY DAVIDSON

HESS, Victor Franz (24 June 1883–17 Dec. 1964), physicist, was born at Waldstein Castle, Styria, Austria, the son of Vinzenz Hess, director of forests to the prince of Oettingen-Waldstätt, and Serafine Grossbauer-Waldstätt. Hess studied physics, mathematics, and astronomy at the University of Graz, where he received his doctorate degree in 1906. After teaching physics at Vienna Veterinary College from 1908 to 1910, he taught and conducted research at the University of Vienna and its Institute for Radium Research. In 1920 Hess accepted a position at the University of Graz, remaining only a short time before leaving the following year to serve for two years as director of research at the U.S. Radium Corporation in Orange, New Jersey. In 1923 he returned to the University of Graz, where he advanced to the rank of full professor in 1925. In 1931 he left again, this time to found a cosmic-ray observatory on Hafelekar Peak in Innsbruck.

Hess returned to the University of Graz in 1937, but he was dismissed by the Nazi government in March 1938 after the German occupation of Austria. His dismissal resulted in part from the fact that his wife, Mary Bertha Warner, whom he had married in 1920, was Jewish. Furthermore, Hess was a devout Roman Catholic and had been a science adviser to the independent Austrian government. Following his dismissal, Hess received offers from Manchester University in England and Fordham University in New York. He accepted the latter offer, and he and his wife arrived in New York in November 1938. He immediately began teaching at Fordham, where he remained until his retirement in 1956. After retiring, he continued his experimental research there as professor emeritus. Hess became an American citizen in 1944. Following the death of his first wife in 1955, he married her nurse, Elizabeth M. Hoenke. He had no children and died at Mount Vernon, New York.

Hess had originally planned to do research in physical optics, but around 1906, following the suicide of his professor at Graz, he decided to study radiation instead. He began doing advanced research under Franz Exner, who was famous for his work in atmospheric electricity and ionization, a subject much studied and discussed throughout the nineteenth century. A common idea in 1910 was that the atmosphere had become ionized because of something within the earth, perhaps radium traces in the earth's crust. But in 1910 Father Theodor Wulf noted that atmospheric ionization was greater at the top of the Eiffel Tower than at its base. With the help of the Austrian Aeroclub and using an airtight ionization chamber that he designed, Hess, an amateur balloonist, made a series of ten high-altitude balloon flights (maximum altitude 5,350 meters) to test Wulf's findings. Carrying multiple instruments to ensure reliable measurements, he made both daylight and nighttime flights to investigate the sun as a possible source of ionization. By 1912 he concluded that ionization increased markedly at distances greater than about 150 meters above the earth and that powerful penetrating radiation came from outside the earth. Hess's experimental flights were soon followed by those of others. His theory of cosmic radiation was controversial until at least 1926, however, largely because of the apparently contradictory findings of Robert A. Millikan at the California Institute of Technology, whose initial experiments failed to confirm Hess's idea that the penetrating radiation originated outside the earth. By 1926, however, Millikan, who coined the term "cosmic rays" in 1925, concurred with Hess's ideas. Hess's work on cosmic rays stimulated the development of elementary particle physics, thereby contributing to Carl D. Anderson's discovery of the positive electron (*positron*), and the two shared the Nobel Prize for Physics in 1936.

Hess published more than 130 papers and reports and several books. In his later career he also concentrated on the biological effects of radiation, including tests of radioactive fallout and radiation effects on living tissue.

• A very brief autobiographical sketch of Hess is at the Niels Bohr Library of the American Institute of Physics in New York City. His books are *Die elektrische Leitfähigkeit der Atmosphäre und ihre Ursachen* (1926), translated as *The Electrical Conductivity of the Atmosphere and Its Causes* (1928); the monograph-length "Luftelektrizität," in *Müllet Pouillets Lehrbuch der Physik*, vol. 5, 11th ed. (1928), written with H. Benndorf; and *Die Weltraumstrahlung und ihre biologischen Wirkungen* (1940), written with Jacob Eugster and rewritten, enlarged, and translated as *Cosmic Radiation and Its Biological Effects* (1949). Additional biographical information is in Frank N. Magill, ed., *The Nobel Prize Winners: Physics*, vol. 1 (1989), including a portrait. Good discussions of the birth and overall development of cosmic ray physics are in Bruno Rossi, *Cosmic Rays* (1964); Martin A. Pomerantz, *Cosmic Rays* (1971); and Michael W. Friedlander, *Cosmic Rays* (1989). An obituary is in the *New York Times*, 19 Dec. 1964.

C. STEWART GILLMOR

HESSE, Eva (11 Jan. 1936–29 May 1970), artist, was born in Hamburg, Germany, the daughter of Wilhelm Hesse, a criminal attorney, and Ruth Marcus. In 1938, to escape the Nazis, she and her sister, Helen, were sent on a children's train to Amsterdam, where they were placed in a Catholic orphanage. In 1939 the family reunited and emigrated to New York City, where Hesse's father became an insurance broker. Very soon thereafter her mother, probably depressed as a result of the war and subsequent relocation, was hospitalized. Her parents were divorced in 1945, and in 1946 her mother committed suicide, an event that shaped Hesse's vision of herself and her art. Hesse attended therapy sessions most of her adult life, kept private diaries and datebooks, and wrote autobiographical letters to friends. Her desire for personal expression ultimately extended to the visual arts, initially painting but finally culminating in a significant body of sculptural work that alluded to, but did not illustrate, her emotional and physical anguish.

Hesse's art education took place at several schools. She studied at the Pratt Institute of Design in Brooklyn, New York (1952–1953), the Art Students League (1954), Cooper Union (1954–1957), and the Yale School of Art and Architecture (1957–1959), where she earned a B.F.A. Her teachers at Yale included Josef Albers, Rico Lebrun, and Bernard Chaet. Although she is best known today for her sculpture, in which she experimented with unusual materials and forms, Hesse actually studied painting while at school. She married sculptor Tom Doyle in 1961; they had no children together. Soon after her marriage she made

her first three-dimensional work. However, it was not until an extended visit to Germany in 1964 and the beginning of her friendship with Sol Lewitt that Hesse truly turned to sculptural materials, making a series of reliefs in response to difficulties she was having with her painting. Over time and through Lewitt, she became friends with a growing number of significant sculptors, including Robert Smithson and Nancy Holt. Lewitt acted as a mentor and sounding board, and he and Hesse appear to have influenced each other in their work. Additional friends in Hesse's circle included important artists, artist couples, and writers, such as Donald and Julie Judd, Dan and Sonja Flavin, Robert and Sylvia Mangold, Robert Ryman, Al Held, and Lucy Lippard.

In her relief sculptures from this period, such as *Oomamaboomba* (1965, Robert Miller Gallery), Hesse combined painting and sculpture into carefully controlled compositions in which she built up forms with plaster, painted them, and then added found objects. Already demonstrating her fascination with organic forms that tangentially represent body cavities and extremities, these works demonstrated Hesse's exploration into the visceral quality of paint. This interest in surface transferred later in the three-dimensional pieces to the actual support material, the body of the sculpture itself.

On her return to the United States Hesse developed a unique style that melded together many sources, ideas, and influences: autobiography and psychological introspection, new materials, and minimalist structure. Her sculpture was a change from her earlier paintings, which had been fairly small in scale and abstract with expressively applied paint. In January 1966 she completed *Hang Up* (Art Institute of Chicago), which she later considered her first important work. It was also during this period of intense artistic exploration that her marriage to Doyle disintegrated (they remained separated until her death but did not divorce) and that her father died in August 1966. Hesse's sculpture was included in several important group shows: Abstract Inflationism and Stuffed Expressionism (Mar. 1966), curated by Joan Washburn at the Graham Gallery, and Eccentric Abstraction (Sept.–Oct. 1966), curated by critic Lucy Lippard at the Fischbach Gallery. Hesse's work was greatly admired by other artists, but among those initially writing on her work Lippard most understood the complex and personal themes of Hesse's pieces.

In 1967 Hesse joined the Fischbach Gallery, preparing for a one-person show that took place there in November 1968. During this period she began to experiment with factory fabrication, fiberglass, and latex. Unfortunately, it was also during this tremendously prolific year that she first experienced the symptoms of serious illness: fatigue, headaches, and nausea. By 1969 she required help to complete her work. In April of that year she underwent surgery to remove a brain tumor. Despite her illness Hesse continued to work, finishing a number of important pieces. She participated in a series of influential shows at this time, including A Plastic Presence at the Jewish Museum in New York (Nov.–Jan. 1969) and Anti-Illusion: Procedures/Materials at the Whitney (May–July 1969). During the final year of her life she exhibited work at the Owens-Corning Fiberglass Center and in String and Rope at the Sidney Janis Gallery.

Figural associations were primary to Hesse's work; despite the abstractness of the forms, her constructions often contained an explicit sexuality saturated with abstract references to human anatomy. Textural surfaces and shapes that alluded to body parts explored the role of women as object and subject in art. In *Repetition Nineteen III* (Museum of Modern Art), created in July 1968, nineteen individual forms, each a container with a textured surface and organic torso-like form, alluded to the concept of woman as container. Additionally, they spoke of the minimalist preoccupation with repetition, except that here the forms were repeated with unique variation, not mechanical precision. In *Accession V* (1968, Wadsworth Athenaeum) and *Accession II* (1969, Detroit Institute of Art), Hesse created galvanized steel boxes, but each had highly textured surfaces and plastic or rubber tubing that pushed out into the center, recalling the simbria of human fallopian tubes. Even when using the strong, industrial materials employed by her peers, she altered them, denying her creations the anonymity typical of minimalist work.

Content remained important to Hesse's work, and she always retained a sense of emotional or physical pain in her imagery. She had been sickly as a child and struggled with emotional problems that formed her work in the same way that Frida Kahlo's work derived its inspiration from Kahlo's emotional anguish and physical suffering. Seemingly melting forms, organic materials, and structural isolation contribute to the emotional context of Hesse's pieces. Limp, malleable elements hang in strands, perhaps alluding to Hesse's inability to stand emotionally independent. Her attention to the content of the three-dimensional pieces can be traced to her early paintings, which were expressionist in character and paralleled, though never overtly or specifically represented, Hesse's internal struggle with the Holocaust and its effects on her family. Some scholars believe these issues continued to play a role in Hesse's mature sculpture as well. However, Hesse's exploration of her psyche contrasted with minimalism's denial of a human presence, as well as with her own training in purely abstract art, resulting in a tension and uniqueness that separates her work from many of her contemporaries and set up the opposing themes of exterior/interior, multiple/singular, and hardness/softness that remained at the core of her work.

Despite Hesse's training with Albers, the grand master of modern color theory, she was not interested in color in her three-dimensional works. In fact, her forms are structured, yet organic, with color reduced to the inherent color of her materials. For instance, in *Tori* (Philadelphia Museum of Art), completed in August 1969, Hesse experimented with fiberglass and polyester resin, leaving the work the unadulterated color of the materials. Again, container-like forms, with their anthropomorphic characteristics and interior/exterior allusions, demonstrate the abstract yet allegorical nature of Hesse's vision. Moreover, their reduced color and avant-grade use of materials contributed to Hesse's interest in organic form and demonstrated her attention to experimental media. For Hesse, finding a unique voice was imperative. She noted in her diary in 1964, "It just seems to me that the 'personal' in art if really pushed is the most valued quality and what I want so much is to find it in and for myself" (quoted in Berger et al., p. 111).

Hesse fell into a coma on 22 May 1970, and she died seven days later at the age of thirty-four. Her premature death, coming at the end of the turbulent sixties, symbolized for many later artists the role of the woman artist as both heroine and uncelebrated creator within a male-dominated hierarchy. However, Hesse herself publicly denied gender-based art and asserted that excellence was the true definer of one's work. Nonetheless, privately she felt keenly the struggles of women artists. Hesse became a central figure for female artists and feminists who were to follow, and her imagery and its allusions foretold of later related imagery by women artists interested in the problem of woman as subject. While her imagery and ideas were contained within a more abstract structure, Hesse's investigation into content and new materials placed her work in the forefront of contemporary sculpture.

• Hesse's original diary and other materials are in the Eva Hesse Archives at the Allen Memorial Art Museum, Oberlin College, Ohio. There has been much interest in Hesse's work in recent years, including an important retrospective exhibition at Yale University Art Gallery; see the catalog by Maurice Berger et al., *Eva Hesse: A Retrospective* (1992). Another important publication, which concentrates on her sculpture, is Bill Barrette, *Eva Hesse: Sculpture* (1989). A recent work that examines her art within a social context is Anne Middleton Wagner, *Three Artists (Three Women): Modernism and the Art of Hesse, Krasner, and O'Keeffe* (1996). An earlier work by Lucy R. Lippard, *Eva Hesse* (1976), provides an account from an art critic who both knew the work and had access to many of the artist's friends and her writings. Other sources include *Eva Hesse: Drawing in Space*, the catalog of the exhibition of Hesse's work held at the Ulmer Museum in Ulm, Germany (1994), and the artist's obituary in the *New York Times*, 30 May 1970.

J. SUSAN ISAACS

HESSELIUS, Gustavus (1682–23 May 1755), painter, was born in Falun, Sweden, the son of Andreas Olai Hesselius, a Lutheran clergyman, and Maria Bergia. When Gustavus was four years old, the family moved to Folkarna, where his father served as pastor until his death in 1700.

Hesselius was for a period at the University of Uppsala, where he was known as a *conterfejare*, suggesting that he was already a trained portrait painter. With whom he studied is unknown, but he was probably aware of the portrait style of David von Krafft, who came to Sweden from Hamburg and eventually served as court painter to Charles XII, painting portraits of a type Hesselius was to produce in America.

In October 1711 Hesselius set out for the New World with his older brother Andreas, who had been commissioned pastor to the Swedish community on the Delaware. They sailed first to England, where they stayed for several months awaiting passage to America. In England, Hesselius undoubtedly came into contact with the portrait style of leading painters such as court painter Godfrey Kneller. Hesselius probably had contact in London with Michael Dahl, a Stockholm-born painter who settled in England and enjoyed the patronage of English nobility and royalty.

On 23 February 1712 the Hesselius brothers sailed from England with a letter of introduction from Governor William Penn to the government of Pennsylvania. In May they reached Christiana (now Wilmington, Delaware). After a few weeks there, Hesselius moved to Philadelphia, which offered more opportunities for patronage. In a letter of 1714 to his mother in Sweden, he wrote of his "rich livelihood," indicating that he was the only portrait painter in Philadelphia. On 14 April 1714 he married Lydia Gatchell at the Lutheran church in Wicaco (South Philadelphia); they had at least six children. By early June 1715 Hesselius had painted an altarpiece for the Wicaco church, but it is not known to exist. This work was perhaps the first painting other than a portrait commissioned in the colonies.

In January 1719 Hesselius was in Annapolis; in the summer of 1721 he and a daughter were naturalized in Maryland, where the family remained until the late 1720s. During their stay, Hesselius and his wife were members of an Anglican parish, for which he painted a now lost *Last Supper*. He also did general painting and repairs for the church and produced portraits of notable citizens.

Returning to Philadelphia, Hesselius apparently developed a profitable business as a general and easel painter, but few of his works are known to survive. Many have undoubtedly vanished. The attribution of others is difficult because of extensive overpainting and because Hesselius signed few if any of his works (no known painting by him bears his signature). His activity, however, is indicated in the account books of Benjamin Franklin, which list large amounts of silver and gold leaf as well as oil that the painter purchased from the printer. Hesselius's work in Philadelphia enabled him in 1735 to purchase property on High Street, near Fourth, which remained his residence until his death.

Hesselius's most important commission as a general painter was probably the interior of the Pennsylvania State House, known today as Independence Hall. Between 1738 and 1741, he or his assistants painted the interior and furnishings of Thomas Penn's estate at Springettsbury.

Among Hesselius's finest easel paintings are his portraits of *Tishcohan* and *Lapowinsa*, two Delaware Indian chiefs. These portraits, painted for Thomas Penn about 1735, reveal an unflinching realism as well as a sense of human nobility and character. They can be regarded as the earliest realistic likenesses of Native Americans painted in the New World. Portraits of *Mrs. William Penn* (Hannah Callowhill) and *Mrs. Thomas Freame*, the daughter of William and Hannah Penn, are today known only through small copies. His *Self-Portrait* and a portrait of his wife, *Lydia Hesselius*, painted about 1740, are comparable to the portraits of the Indian chiefs in their characterizations. His portrait of his daughter Mary, *Mrs. Ericus Unander*, painted about 1750, reflects a growing interest in fashionable portraiture toward the end of his career.

Hesselius's close contact with clergymen provided him with significant patronage, and portraits exist of *Reverend George Ross*, *Reverend Peter Tronberg*, and *Reverend Israel Acrelius*. Other prominent figures portrayed by Hesselius were *James Logan*, a Pennsylvania statesman and scholar, and *Thomas Bordley*, the attorney general of Maryland. Hesselius's portraits of *Gustavus Brown* and *Mrs. Gustavus Brown*, the former Frances Fowke of Maryland, are dated 1742.

Two small paintings of mythological subjects, *Childhood of Bacchus* and *Bacchus and Ariadne*, have traditionally been ascribed to Hesselius and are probably based on engraved prototypes. They are the earliest known classical subjects painted in America.

Hesselius was one of the earliest European-trained painters to introduce the full-blown Baroque style into the English colonies. In contrast to the hard-edged linearity and naïve vision of earlier painters, his works display softer edges and a more refined sense of atmosphere and of potential movement. Moreover, his freer handling of pigment reflects the Baroque awareness of the aesthetic appeal of the painted surface. The work of Hesselius and other European-trained painters exhibit a more visually based use of color, characterized by interpenetrating and interacting hues that express greater realism and vitality, than the decorative local color of other colonial artists.

From the mid-1740s until 1751, Hesselius was a member of the Moravian church in Philadelphia, and during that time he supervised installation of an organ for the Moravian Brethren in Bethlehem, Pennsylvania. It is probable, however, that he retained his affiliation with the Lutheran church, for it was then possible to hold dual membership. Hesselius died in Philadelphia.

• The fullest studies of Hesselius's work are the catalogs of exhibitions in celebration of the anniversary of the founding of New Sweden in 1638: Christian Brinton, *Gustavus Hesselius* (Philadelphia Museum of Art, 1938), and Roland E. Fleischer, *Gustavus Hesselius, Face Painter to the Middle Colonies* (New Jersey State Museum, Trenton, 1988). Some attributions to Hesselius in the 1938 exhibition are questioned by H. E. Keyes, "Doubts Regarding Hesselius," *Antiquities* 34 (1938): 144–45, and by E. P. Richardson, "Gustavus Hesselius," *Art Quarterly* 12 (1949): 220–26. The relationship of Hesselius to the extant portraits of Mrs. William Penn and Mrs. Thomas Freame is clarified in Fleischer, "Gustavus Hesselius and Penn Family Portraits: A Conflict between Visual and Documentary Evidence," *American Art Journal* 19, no. 3 (1987): 4–18. A letter written by Hesselius in 1714 describing conditions and his life in Philadelphia, along with essays by Carin K. Arnborg and Fleischer discussing the letter's discovery and significance, is in "With God's Blessings on Both Land and Sea," *American Art Journal* 21, no. 3 (1989): 4–17. A discussion of the characteristics of Hesselius's art is in Fleischer, "Gustavus Hesselius: A Study of His Style," in *American Painting to 1776: A Reappraisal*, ed. I. M. G. Quimby (1971).

ROLAND E. FLEISCHER

HESSELIUS, John (1728?–9 Apr. 1778), portrait painter, was born probably in Philadelphia, Pennsylvania, the son of Gustavus Hesselius, a Swedish immigrant who was also a painter, and Lydia Gatchell. No record of the date or place of John's birth survives. He is first recorded in July 1739, when he bought some paper on his father's account at Benjamin Franklin's printing shop. Years later, in 1758, Franklin referred to him as "young Hesselius" when discussing his portrait of Franklin's daughter Sarah (the portrait is unlocated).

Hesselius learned the painting trade from his father. The dark shading of flesh that Gustavus used is visible in his son's work throughout his career. His earliest surviving work is his 1749 portrait of attorney Lynford Lardner (private collection). At about this time Hesselius met New England portraitist Robert Feke, then on his second painting trip to Philadelphia. He and Feke may have traveled together to Virginia, where Hesselius painted portraits of members of the Gordon family of Lancaster County in 1750 and in 1751 made six portraits for the Fitzhugh family of "Bedford," Stafford County. Hesselius also painted portraits in 1751 in Maryland, where his sitters included Margaret Black Brown, the second wife of Gustavus Brown, a physician, of "Rich Hill," Charles County (Baltimore Museum of Art). For some, Hesselius copied existing family portraits; these included his father's portrait of Brown (1742, National Museum of American Art; copy, Baltimore Museum of Art).

In the 1750s Hesselius lived in Philadelphia and painted portraits there as well as in Maryland, Virginia, and Delaware. One of the few portrait painters in the middle colonies at this time, he seems to have attracted patrons through personal recommendations. No newspaper advertisements are known, and many of his sitters were related. These early portraits reveal Feke's influence in their poses, bright colors, depictions of lush fabrics, and background landscape settings. Some also appear to be indebted to engravings of English portraits or to the portraits he was commissioned to copy.

At his father's death in 1755 Hesselius inherited his house as well as his "chamber Organ, Books, Paints, Oils, Colours, and all my other painting materials and tools, and my unfinished Pictures" (Gustavus Hesselius's will, quoted in Fleischer [1988], p. 25). Hesselius's style changed in the late 1750s in response to the work of John Wollaston, a London-trained artist, who visited Philadelphia in 1752 and again in 1757–1758. Hesselius's new manner combined Wollaston's elegant compositions and sophisticated modeling with Feke's colorful fabrics and bright landscape settings.

Hesselius probably moved to Maryland in the late 1750s. By 1761 he had settled in Anne Arundel County. He joined the Anglican parish of St. Anne's, near Annapolis; vestry minutes listed his modest worth at about £300. That year he was awarded an important commission from Benedict Calvert, the son of Charles Calvert, the fifth Lord Baltimore, to paint four of his children (three portraits are at the Baltimore Museum of Art, the fourth is at the Maryland Historical Society). In 1763 Hesselius married Mary Young Woodward, the widow of Henry Woodward of "Primrose Hill," a marriage that brought him financial security. His stepdaughter Mary later recalled that he treated his stepchildren "with great tenderness and friendship" (quoted in Doud [1969], p. 142). He bought an estate near Annapolis, which he named "Bellefield." He and his wife had seven children.

Hesselius continued to work as a painter while managing Bellefield and Primrose Hill. In 1763 he demonstrated his portrait painting technique for Charles Willson Peale, who gave him a saddle and fittings. The younger artist's earliest work is similar to Hesselius's, especially in the tonality and the shapes of the sitters' faces. Peale also seems to have adopted Hesselius's pictorial honesty in capturing the personalities of older sitters, a manner that Hesselius learned from his father. The similarity of their work is indicated by the attribution of Hesselius's portrait of Maryland planter John Paca (c. 1765, Maryland Historical Society) to Peale before cleaning revealed the older artist's signature.

Also in the 1760s Hesselius acquired a copy of Robert Dossie's *Handmaid to the Arts*, published in London in 1758, which was the most popular art manual in the colonies. He continued to travel to paint portraits; among his later sitters were Gavin Lawson, a Falmouth, Virginia, merchant, and his wife Susanna, painted in 1770 (Colonial Williamsburg Foundation). His last signed work, dated 1777, probably represents Mrs. Thomas Gough (Sophia Dorsey) of Baltimore (Washington County Museum of Fine Arts, Hagerstown, Md.). This portrait is notably similar to Peale's portraits of older women of the mid-1770s, despite changes in Peale's style after his two-year study of painting in London.

Hesselius died "in the 50 year of his age," according to an entry in a family Bible. The cause and place of death are not known. Hesselius referred to himself in his will as a limner, an archaic term for portrait painter. The inventory of his estate, with a value of more than £3,400, reveals a moderately high standard of living. It lists an assortment of both elegant and plain furniture, household goods, silver plate, a gold watch, and "Wearing Apparel much worn." In addition to artists' supplies and numerous prints and paintings, Hesselius owned an old camera obscura and a microscope. A harpsichord, three violins, and music books indicate that he shared his father's musical interests. His estate included thirty-one black slaves, listed by name, age, and monetary value. "Family Pictures" probably included his paintings of his stepdaughter Eleanor Woodward and his son Gustavus, Jr., who is depicted with a black nurse (both c. 1767, Baltimore Museum of Art); no self-portrait is known. Later, in 1796, his wife's portrait (Baltimore Museum of Art) was painted by Swedish painter Adolph-Ulrich Wertmüller, who in 1801 married Hesselius's niece Elizabeth Henderson.

Hesselius painted more than 100 portraits during his 28-year career. He was one of the few artists at work in Maryland and Virginia in the decades before the Revolution. His portraits are especially appreciated today for their decorative qualities and for their careful documentation. Hesselius signed and dated many of them on the reverse, often adding the sitter's name and age, as well as the place the portrait was painted.

• Only one letter from Hesselius is known to survive, written on 26 June 1755 to his friend Henry Callister of Oxford, Md. (Archives of the Episcopal Diocese of Maryland, Baltimore). His will and an inventory of his estate are at the Hall of Records, Annapolis, Md. Richard K. Doud's research on Hesselius is the major source of biographical information and artistic assessment; see "John Hesselius: His Life and Work" (master's thesis, Univ. of Delaware, 1963), "The Fitzhugh Portraits by John Hesselius," *Virginia Magazine of History and Biography* 75 (Apr. 1967): 159–73, and "John Hesselius, Maryland Limner," *Winterthur Portfolio* 5 (1969): 129–53. Recent brief discussions include that by Dorinda Evans in *Philadelphia: Three Centuries of American Art* (exhibition catalog, Philadelphia Museum of Art, 1976), pp. 48–49; Sona K. Johnston, *American Paintings, 1750–1900, from the Collection of the Baltimore Museum of Art* (1983), pp. 73–81, 177–78; and Richard H. Saunders and Ellen G. Miles, *American Colonial Portraits: 1700–1776* (1987), pp. 47, 228–29, 250–53. Research on his father by Roland E. Fleischer includes the correct identity of Hesselius's mother as well as information on the son's career; see *Gustavus Hesselius: Face Painter to the Middle Colonies* (exhibition catalog, New Jersey State Museum, Trenton, 1988), and "Gustavus Hesselius's Letter of 1714 and Its Contribution to Current Scholarship," *American Art Journal* 21, no. 3 (1989): 14–17. The letter is translated and discussed by Carin K. Arnborg, "'With God's Blessings on Both Land and Sea': Gustavus Hesselius Describes the New World to the Old in a Letter from Philadelphia in 1714," *American Art Journal* 21, no. 3 (1989): 4–13.

ELLEN G. MILES

HESSOUN, Joseph (8 Aug. 1830–4 July 1906), Roman Catholic priest, was born in Vrcovice in the present Czech Republic, the son of Albert Hessoun, an overseer of a Bohemian estate, and Marie Strabochova. Although his father died while he was a small boy, his family supported his desire to become a priest. After completing his seminary studies at Budejovic (Budweis), ranking fourth in his class, he was ordained to the priesthood on 31 July 1853 by Archbishop John Valerian Jinsik of Budejovic. Hessoun served the archdiocese of Budejovic in the towns of Sedlic and then Jinin. But after his mother's death, he answered a plea to minister to his fellow countrymen in America from Monsignor Joseph Melcher, the vicar general of

the archdiocese of St. Louis, Missouri, in 1865. In his appeal to the Bohemian hierarchy for Czech-speaking priests, Melcher estimated the number of Czechs in St. Louis to be 5,000.

The Czech community in St. Louis needed an able leader. The economic and linguistic limitations of these new immigrants reduced their opportunities for advancement and threatened the survival of their culture and faith. Remnants of the religious debates from the old country and certain secularist assumptions of the European Enlightenment found echos in the St. Louis Bohemian community. Among the Catholic Czechs there was disillusionment stemming from inconsistent and arbitrary pastoral leadership that was soon compounded by the lack of a priest who could speak Czech. The mission of St. John Nepomuk, the first Czech parish in the United States, teetered on the verge of extinction. Established in 1854 in south St. Louis, the congregation dwindled as the bills mounted.

Hessoun's deep love for the Czech traditions and language, his passionate concern for the spiritual welfare of his flock, especially the poor, his considerable talent as a preacher and administrator marked him as the leader able to maintain a sense of dignity and pride in the Czech heritage while easing the immigrant's transition to the new American situation. Hessoun's coming to St. Louis had been delayed by the final stages of the Civil War and the difficulty of traveling from New York to St. Louis in those troubled days. He arrived in the city on 30 September 1865 and accepted the pastorate of St. John Nepomuk's mission the next day. He reflected on his reception in a letter to his family penned in 1865: "Words could not express the joy of these people in their reception of me. . . . Our fellow countrymen here were very unhappy . . . and had practically given up every hope in this world and in themselves."

The people's confidence in their new pastor was not misplaced. In the forty-one years that this vital man pastored St. John's, he not only brought the church from a simple mission to one of the finer congregations in the city, but after 1880 when immigration from Eastern Europe began to escalate, made it a hub and support for the many Czech communities that were arising in the United States. This was especially true in the Midwest and Southwest.

Three months after his arrival, the mission was debt-free. By 1866 he had a small school reopened in the basement of the church, and by the spring of 1867 he was arranging for the construction of a school. After the dedication of this building on 22 August 1869, Hessoun boasted that the school "ranks with the best in St. Louis." Another school followed in 1884. In the fall of 1885 there was an enrollment of 465 children in the two schools. Hessoun held that the Czech language and culture were the life-sustaining force for the immigrant. In the early years of St. John's school, he personally taught the Czech language to the older students. His concern that the youth have an awareness and pride in their Czech origin and culture can be seen in his establishment of a Czech library of about 1,500 volumes covering a wide variety of subjects.

In 1868 Hessoun joined several priests in publishing a Chicago-based Czech paper, *Katolicke Noviny* or *The Catholic News*. The paper failed, but in 1873, after a false start in 1871, Hessoun successfully began publishing the *Hlas* or *Voice* from St. John's in St. Louis. *Hlas* soon became a respected national voice for the Catholic Czech community. Hessoun also reached out personally to that community. It is said that there was hardly a Czech-Catholic celebration where he did not speak. He offered missions in the Czech settlements and raised money for them especially in times of emergency. Hessoun offered sound advice on community organization, and he made frequent visits to the Bohemian communities of the United States.

Among his other achievements was the organization of the First Roman Catholic Central Union at a meeting held in St. Louis on 5 June 1877. The First Central Union, as it is now known, is still serving its members. It was the first among the Czech Catholic Benevolent Unions whose lodges offered emergency aid as well as social and moral support to their members in the difficult days of cultural adjustment. Hessoun was a strong believer in clubs and associations. By 1904 St. John's sponsored twenty-four associations serving a broad spectrum of needs of the members of the church.

Hessoun directed the building of three churches during his tenure at St. John's. On 5 May 1870 the cornerstone was laid in St. Louis for the first brick church dedicated to St. John Nepomuk. This church was destroyed by the "great tornado" of 26 May 1896. Hessoun built again, and on 7 November 1897 his second church was dedicated. In 1895 a debate as to whether St. John's should be enlarged to meet the needs of the growing Czech immigration was settled by the decision to build a new church, St. Wenceslaus, several miles to the southwest of St. John's. Hessoun had the responsibility of directing this building also.

In December 1899 Hessoun suffered a paralytic stroke. He could not continue his duties, and the parish was administered by the assistant pastor, Rev. Charles Bleha. In his later years, Hessoun witnessed the full flowering of his missionary efforts. Pope Leo XIII appointed him a domestic prelate with the title of right reverend monsignor in July 1896. He died in St. Louis.

Historians rightly speak of Hessoun as "the Apostle to the Slavs in America." To Czech-Americans, however, he was "Tàticek," the affectionate form of father, which is poorly rendered in English as "Little Father" or, better, "Daddy."

• The few important papers relating to Hessoun are in the Archives of the Archdiocese of St. Louis, Mo. There is no fully developed biography of Hessoun, although several rather good profiles exist. See Ant. Petrus Houst, *A Short History of Czech-Catholic Parishes and a List of Them in the United States of America, Published on the Occasion of the 25th Jubilee of Father Joseph Hessoun* (1890). The work contains several valuable letters reflecting on the early state of Hessoun's ministry. John Habenicht, *History of the Czechs in America*

(1904), was translated by the St. Louis Genealogical Society as *History of the Czechs in Missouri, 1845–1904* (1988). Another primary source in Czech is the *Golden Jubilee Book of the First Central Union of St. Louis* (1927). These Czech sources are in the Archives of the Archdiocese of St. Louis, where there are also many booklets. Among the more complete and historically accurate of these booklets is Albert Prokes, *The Czechs and Their First Diamond Jubilee in the New World* (1929).

DONALD F. MOLITOR

HESTON, William Martin (9 Sept. 1878–9 Sept. 1963), college football player, was born on a farm near Galesburg, Illinois. Details about his parents are not known. While Heston was a small boy, his family moved to southwestern Kansas, where he grew up herding open-range cattle on horseback for nine months each year. During the other months, he attended a nearby country school, but he did not finish the eighth grade until he was sixteen. Soon after the family moved west to Grants Pass, Oregon, where Heston completed high school with high honors in 1898. His family then urged him to continue his education, and he chose to go to California's San Jose Normal College that same year, working his way through school.

Heston began his athletic career at San Jose. He apparently had never seen a football game before he began college, but the coach, struggling to build a team, saw potential and taught him the game's rudiments. Heston began as a guard, but the coach soon had him occasionally carrying the ball. In his senior year when he was elected captain, San Jose tied for a league championship. Against their captain's wishes, the team recruited the coach from nearby Stanford, Fielding Yost, to lead them in a playoff game against rival Chico State Normal School. With Heston playing at halfback, San Jose won the game 46–0. More important, it was the beginning of his lifelong friendship with Yost, who was about to move on to the University of Michigan.

After working the summer of 1901 on the San Francisco docks, Heston abandoned his plans to return to Oregon to become a teacher and entered the University of Michigan to play football under Yost and to seek a law degree. Yost was on the threshold of a brilliant career, and Heston, one of his brightest stars, was one of the first players from the Midwest to gain national recognition. In Heston's four years, 1901–1904, Yost's "point-a-minute" teams had a 43–0–1 record, with the 1901 team going 11–0–0 and outscoring opponents 550–0. Michigan won or shared the Western Conference title from 1901 through 1904 and, in testimony to the growing prominence of western football, it shared the national title with Harvard in 1901 and Yale in 1902.

Heston at 5'8" and 190 pounds ran from left halfback in Yost's famed "hurry-up" offense, and during his career he scored 93 five-point touchdowns. Records of individual performances were rarely kept in those days, and Heston's total yardage gained cannot be determined. But he was known to run for better than 200 yards in games, and in the 1903 victory over Chicago he gained 237 of Michigan's 260-yard total. He probably averaged more than 130 yards per game during his career, according to some estimates. Contemporaries spoke in awe of his "rolling, hurdling and smashing" of opponent's lines as he ran around the ends or off tackle. He had phenomenal speed for forty yards, and in informal match sprints he beat Michigan's Archie Hahn, an Olympic gold medalist in 1904.

Heston's feats in individual games became legendary. In the first Rose Bowl game against Stanford on 1 January 1902, played in 85-degree heat and shortened because Stanford ran out of substitutes, Heston made a mockery of West Coast critics by gaining 170 yards in Michigan's 49–0 victory. In 1903 in the first Little Brown Jug game with Minnesota, which ended in a 6–6 tie, Heston was knocked unconscious, one of the few times he was removed from a game because of injuries. He also hurdled over the University of Chicago's famous Walter Eckersall on his way to a 75-yard touchdown in Michigan's 28–0 victory over Chicago that year. Heston played before the development of the forward pass, which could have given him greater opportunity to run in the open field.

Heston, whom Yost called the "greatest and gamest football player he ever saw or coached," was selected for Walter Camp's 1901 and 1902 All-America third teams and for the first teams in 1903 and 1904. He was captain of the Michigan team in 1904, and he was chosen the Helms Athletic Foundation's player of the year. Camp also selected him for an all-time all-player team in 1910, and his name appeared on similar lists in 1911 and 1920. A 1924 listing of all-time all-star football players put him at fullback, but he was subsequently named as a halfback on Grantland Rice's all-star list in 1928 and on a Football Writers Association of America list in 1969. He was elected to the Helms Athletic Foundation Hall of Fame in 1954, and that same year he was inducted into the National Football Foundation College Football Hall of Fame.

Heston received his law degree from Michigan in 1905. He then stayed for an additional postgraduate year before coaching football at Drake University in 1905 (4–4–0) and at North Carolina State (3–1–4) in 1906. In 1906 he played one game for the professional Canton Bulldogs before retiring after breaking his leg in an all-star game.

In 1908 he began practicing law in Detroit, and he also went into real estate. In 1911 he became assistant prosecuting attorney, and from 1916 until 1963 he was on the bench of the recorder's court. After 1926 he developed and ran a cemetery, the management of which he turned over to a son. He had three children by his first wife who died in 1953 (her name and the marriage date could not be ascertained for this entry). His two sons, William, Jr., and John P., played varsity football at the University of Michigan in the early 1930s. In 1956 Heston married his longtime secretary, Sarah E. Williams, and they lived in retirement at his homes in Ana Maria Island, Florida, and in Detroit. Always a believer in the active life, he ran at least a half-mile daily until a few years before his death in Traverse City, Michigan.

• The files of the University of Michigan Athletic Office in Ann Arbor contain material on Heston. L. H. Baker, *Football: Facts and Figures* (1945), lists the many Heston honors. Richard M. Cohen et al., *The University of Michigan Football Scrapbook* (1978), gives contemporary descriptions of him as a player. Allison Danzig, *The History of American Football: Its Great Teams, Players, and Coaches* (1956), describes the nature of the game at the time Heston played. Ralph Hickok, *Who Was Who in American Sports* (1971), illuminates the problem of summarizing Heston's records. Will Perry, *The Wolverines: A Story of Michigan Football* (1980), places Heston in the context of Michigan football history. An obituary appears in the *New York Times*, 11 Sept. 1963.

DANIEL R. GILBERT

HETH, Henry (16 Dec. 1825–27 Sept. 1899), soldier, was born at Blackheath, Chesterfield County, Virginia, the son of John Heth and Margaret L. Pickett. His father was a midshipman in the navy during the War of 1812 and served until 1822, when he resigned his commission, returned to Blackheath, and joined the family businesses—manufacturing, mining coal and iron, and farming. He died in April 1843 and with him his family's comfortable financial situation. Henry had received an excellent early education and in 1843 won an appointment to the U.S. Military Academy at West Point. He was an indifferent student and graduated last of thirty-eight cadets in the class of 1847.

Heth was commissioned in the First Infantry but arrived in Mexico in January 1848, too late for the war and possible honors or promotion. He spent the next thirteen years at various posts and assignments and, impressing his superiors, was promoted to first lieutenant in 1854 and to captain in 1855, ahead of his classmates. As a company commander in the Tenth Infantry, he saw his first combat in the destruction of a Sioux village on 3 September 1855. He handled his company with competence if not distinction.

In 1857 Captain Heth married Harriet Selden, his first cousin. They had three children. In 1857–1858 Heth developed a system of training in marksmanship that was adopted by the army. After returning to the West, he took part in Albert Sidney Johnston's Mormon expedition of 1858 and remained in Utah until October 1860.

Heth was saddened by the prospects of civil war, but on 17 April 1861, when Virginia seceded, he resigned his commission and offered his sword to the Confederacy. Jefferson Davis endorsed his application, commenting, "This is a first rate soldier and of the cast of man most needed." Heth was soon promoted to lieutenant colonel in the quartermaster service and in August 1861 was posted to western Virginia as a staff officer in John B. Floyd's command. He also attracted the attention of Robert E. Lee, who had replaced the inept Floyd. Davis wanted to send Heth to take command of Confederate forces in Missouri, but resentment of Heth's West Point background by political generals prevented the appointment. On 18 January 1862 Heth, now a brigadier general, took command of the Lewisburg Military District in western Virginia. He led his force successfully at Gile's Court House on 9 May 1862 but was defeated by George Crook and the Thirty-sixth Ohio at Lewisburg on 23 May. In July Heth angered the locals with a harshly worded order to males between the ages of eighteen and thirty-five to report for active service or to be "shot as deserters wherever found." Under intense political pressure, Heth was ordered to Chattanooga to serve as a division commander under Edmund Kirby Smith. He missed the actions at Cumberland Gap and Richmond, Kentucky, and notwithstanding General Smith's praise, he asked for a transfer to the Army of Northern Virginia, a request that Lee endorsed.

Heth reported on 5 March 1863 and took command of a brigade in A. P. Hill's "Light Division" of Thomas J. "Stonewall" Jackson's corps. His first test was at Chancellorsville, where Union general Joseph Hooker was positioning the Army of the Potomac. On 1 May the Light Division made heavy contact with Union forces and halted for the night. On 2 May Jackson's corps made the famous flank march that caved in the Union right. In the intense fighting that evening, Jackson and Hill were wounded (Jackson mortally), and Heth took command of the Light Division. In the fighting on 3 May Heth was slightly wounded but stayed on the field. Hill commended Heth's service, and on 23 May 1863, when the army was reorganized, Heth was given his own division and the rank of major general.

Then came Gettysburg and the demise of Heth's military reputation, at least in his own mind. Lee's strategy was to seize Harrisburg and threaten Philadelphia, Baltimore, or Washington. If challenged by the Army of the Potomac, he would defeat it piecemeal or in pitched battle. However, Lee's own army was "piecemeal" and without an adequate cavalry screen, thanks to J. E. B. Stuart's ill-considered "raid." The knowledge that Union forces were under a different and steadier commander, George G. Meade, and that they were farther north than expected led Lee to begin to concentrate near Gettysburg. On 1 July Heth dispatched a brigade toward Gettysburg in an untimely quest for supplies, especially shoes. The brigade halted when its commander, James J. Pettigrew, found that Union cavalry, under John Buford, was already there. Heth, with Hill's consent, pushed his entire division forward, still after shoes, but without due regard for reconnaissance or security. Thus the fighting began to the disadvantage of Heth's division and Lee's army. The casualties were severe, and Heth himself was *hors de combat* with a head wound. The blame for the defeat at Gettysburg lay properly with Lee and his senior commanders, but Heth had mishandled his division on 1 July. He recovered in time to command the rear guard on Lee's retreat. On 14 July, at Falling Waters, he allowed his division to be surprised by Federal cavalry, who killed Pettigrew and captured some 700 Confederates.

Heth's next action was at Bristoe Station on 14 October 1863, and his division was again severely bloodied when Hill ordered an attack against concealed and prepared Federal units. In the early fighting in the Wilderness campaign on 5 May 1864, Heth's division withstood seven assaults, and then Heth ordered a counterattack. His outgunned and exhausted men took a beating. Heth blamed himself for the misstep and conducted himself well enough in subsequent fighting in the Wilderness, at Cold Harbor, and around Petersburg. He received praise for personal bravery at Reams Station, and he showed tactical ability at Jones Farm and Hatcher's Run. By the winter of 1864–1865, the Confederate cause was lost.

Heth was both a veteran and a novice in 1861, a well-regarded professional who had commanded no unit larger than a company. He did well enough in the Civil War, but others of similar experience did better. He tended toward rashness, acting without forethought and without a grasp of what the other side was doing or might do. Yet he seldom took the initiative when a veteran officer should have done so. He was personally courageous, devoted to his cause and his soldiers, and withal a man of charm and presence who never lived up to his early promise.

After the war, Heth left the army and settled in Richmond but could never cope with life beyond the army and the war. He suffered business failures, notwithstanding the aid of friends from the old army. He held government jobs, wrote about the war, and served on commemorative committees. He also wrote his memoirs, a historical document both valuable and to be handled with care. Heth died in Washington, D.C., while on a trip, and was buried in Richmond, where he lies under the epitaph "In Action Faithful and in Honor Clear."

• Heth's memoirs are in manuscript form at the Alderman Library of the University of Virginia. The published version is *The Memoirs of Henry Heth*, ed. James L. Morrison, Jr. (1974). Heth's military career is in Douglas Southall Freeman, *Lee's Lieutenants* (3 vols., 1942–1944); Edwin B. Coddington, *The Gettysburg Campaign* (1968); and James I. Robertson, Jr., *General A. P. Hill: The Story of a Confederate Warrior* (1987).

JOHN T. HUBBELL

HEWAT, Alexander (1740?–3 Mar. 1824), historian and minister, was born in Scotland. Nothing is known of Hewat's parentage and birth. He attended the 1755–1756 session at the University of Edinburgh where he studied logic and metaphysics. In November 1763 he was called to Charleston, South Carolina, to minister to one of the leading, dissenting Scottish First Presbyterian congregations in South Carolina.

Hewat's theology was most closely aligned with Old Side Presbyterianism, the conservative branch of the Presbyterian church in the colonies that adhered to the Calvinist-inspired Westminster Articles and opposed George Whitefield's evangelicalism. On a broader scale, Old Side Presbyterianism's quest for social as well as religious coherence and stability manifested itself in a distrust of extreme religious enthusiasm and radical social change. Given his extensive land holdings and his desire to return to his church after the American Revolution, it appears that his fourteen-year ministry was satisfying both financially and professionally.

Soon after arriving in Charleston, he was elected to the prestigious St. Andrew's Society, a social and philanthropic organization of native-born Scots, whose members included John Stuart, superintendent of Indian affairs for the Southern District; James Wright, royal governor of Georgia; and Robert Wells, editor of the *South-Carolina Gazette*. As a leading member of the community, Hewat also became acquainted with many royal officials and members of the council and general assembly, including Lieutenant Governor William Bull II. Thus Hewat was provided access to official documents and had ample opportunity to talk to colonists who had personally participated in, or at least possessed oral descriptions of, the events he would later write about in his *An Historical Account of the Rise and Progress of the Colonies of South Carolina and Georgia* (1779), the first extended historical treatment of South Carolina (Georgia is given only cursory coverage in Hewat's *Account*). In addition, he traveled extensively through the Lower South observing firsthand the peoples and customs therein, including the lives of Native Americans and slaves. And on his own, "he was at some pains to pick up such original papers and detached accounts of the past transactions of that colony" as were available to him.

Hewat, initially writing only "for the sake of private amusement," began writing in earnest amid the political turbulence of the 1770s. In the preface to his *Account*, he laments that "being in a town agitated with popular tumults, military parade, and frequent alarms" had not only created a situation "very unfavourable for calm study and recollection" but excluded him from data before he had "finished the collection necessary to complete his plan." The "tumult" to which he referred was the 1774 installation of the revolutionary provisional government in South Carolina. Indeed, he terminates his *Account* with the repeal of the Stamp Act in 1766, before the colonies, "infected with pride and ambition, aspiring after independence," threatened "a total dissolution of all political union and commercial intercourse." Hewat remained loyal to the Crown throughout the conflicts and was forced to flee to England in 1777 when he refused to renounce his loyalty to the king and pledge allegiance to the new Congress. In London in 1779 he anonymously published his *Account*.

Hewat's *Account* reflects the influence of William Robertson and the Scottish school of historiography. Less concerned with a strict chronology of events, Hewat instead focused on the interrelatedness of those events and their various causes and effects. His goal in doing so was to provide moral, political, and practical instruction to the colonists and to those in England—both of whom he hoped would see the importance of continuing South Carolina's close ties to the Crown.

Initial reaction to Hewat's *Account* was mixed. A contemporary reviewer in the *London Monthly Review* complained that the book was "extremely deficient in the graces of historical composition" and "often tedious." The reviewer did admit, however, that Hewat's *Account* "will probably be preserved as a valuable collection of materials." Subsequent colonial historians such as David Ramsey, Robert Mill, William Gilmore Simms, William James Rivers, and Yates Snowden seemed to share the reviewer's opinion. They alternately mined large sections of the *Account* for their own works while simultaneously condemning it for its prolixity and Tory sympathies. Thus a book that Hewat feared would be "deemed useless and unprofitable" remained a major source of historical data for one and a half centuries.

After publication of his *Account*, Hewat spent the remainder of his life unsuccessfully seeking to regain his former congregation in Charleston and extract compensation from the English government for loss of property. He received an honorary doctor of divinity degree from the University of Edinburgh in 1780, married a Mrs. Barksdale, a widow from South Carolina (they had no children), and published a number of religious texts. He died presumably in London.

Although Hewat has been criticized for his uncritical use of sources, failure to quote correctly or provide a bibliography, and occasional lapses in his dispassionate tone engendered by his fierce opposition to slavery and his loyalist sympathies, it is worthwhile to note that Hewat, a first-time author and amateur historian, was able to incorporate successfully sources as diverse as firsthand observations, eyewitness accounts, official government documents, and previous historical works. Indeed, Hewat's source material, which he often quoted verbatim, as well as his careful observations of daily life, are his most important contribution to colonial history. His accomplishments are especially remarkable when we consider the turbulent political conditions under which he labored.

• Hewat's papers and letters are in the Memorial of Alexander Hewat, Public Record Office, Loyalist Transcripts, Manuscript Division, New York Public Library. In addition to his *Account*, Hewat also published *The Firm Patriot* (1795), *Religion Essential to the Being and Happiness of Society* (1796), and *Sermons on Various Subjects* (1803–1805). The best critical assessment of his work is Geraldine Meroney, "Alexander Hewat's *Historical Account*," in *The Colonial Legacy*, ed. Lawrence H. Leder (1971). For an extended discussion of his relation to other historians, see Elmer D. Johnson, "Alexander Hewat: South Carolina's First Historian," *Journal of Southern History* 20 (1954): 50–62.

SCOTT HERSTAD

HEWES, Joseph (23 Jan. 1730–10 Nov. 1779), politician and signer of the Declaration of Independence, was born in Kingston, New Jersey, the son of Aaron Hewes and Providence Worth, planters.

Hewes grew up in a Quaker family but later drifted away from Quakerism. After serving an apprenticeship to Joseph Ogden, a Philadelphia merchant, he moved to Edenton, North Carolina, in 1755. There he became a successful merchant, owning ships that sailed regularly to Europe and the West Indies. Portraits of Hewes show a man with thin, short hair, large, wide-set eyes, a narrow forehead, and a long, slightly hooked nose. His contemporaries noted his unusually pleasant personality: jurist James Iredell called him "one of the best and most agreeable men in the world." His betrothed, Isabella Johnston, died before their wedding date, and apparently he never again considered marriage.

In 1760 and 1766–1774 Hewes served in the North Carolina General Assembly, representing the borough of Edenton. In 1774 the revolutionary First Provincial Congress elected him to the First Continental Congress, in which Hewes did not distinguish himself. Even so, in 1775 he was elected to the Second Continental Congress. Never prominent in debate, he was nonetheless appreciated by his fellow congressional delegates for the excellent work he did on committees and standing boards.

During the early months of 1776 Hewes, the only North Carolina delegate present in Philadelphia, served on numerous committees while simultaneously sitting on the Marine, Claims, and Treasury boards, plus the Secret Committee, which was actually a standing board charged with securing war material for the Continental army.

As Congress moved in 1776 toward abandoning resistance in favor of independence, Hewes hesitated, as did his fellow North Carolina delegates William Hooper and John Penn (1740–1788). Hewes believed that the colonies could not afford a costly war that would lead to financial chaos. Yet by May, when American sentiment shifted firmly toward the new objective, Hewes followed and never regretted the decision to withdraw from the British Empire. It was he who laid before Congress in May 1776 North Carolina's Halifax Resolves, which instructed that colony's delegation to join a movement for independence if somebody else proposed it.

Once independence was declared, Hewes seized the opportunity to augment his considerable financial fortune. His membership on the Secret Committee led to his being named its agent. From that position he arranged to rent his own ships to Congress with the understanding that the rent would be paid in Spanish gold dollars, not inflated paper currency. Like many other revolutionary leaders, Hewes saw nothing wrong with using his office to promote his own business interests.

An overworked and weary Hewes left Congress in September 1776 for a rest and to carry out his duties as an agent of the Secret Committee. He fully expected to return to Congress, but when the first general assembly under the new North Carolina constitution met in the spring of 1777, another candidate, John Penn (who had recently lost his own seat), contended that Hewes held two important positions at the same time—delegate to Congress and agent of the Secret Committee—and that this violated the new state constitution. The general assembly agreed and ousted Hewes in favor of Penn. Hewes did not regain his seat in Congress until 1779.

On his return to Congress in July 1779, he was a frail man near death. His habit of sitting in Congress in 1776 from "six in the morning till five, and sometimes six in the afternoon without eating or drinking" was in part to blame. Hewes clearly used the Revolution to his financial advantage, but he also worked indefatigably for the cause. Ill health prompted his resignation from Congress on 29 October 1779. He died in Philadelphia, where he was buried at Christ Church. His funeral was attended by many members of Congress.

Hewes is remembered today as a signer of the Declaration of Independence. Yet, ironically, he would never have chosen independence if Great Britain had been willing to compromise on American rights. Nevertheless, Hewes deserves praise because once committed he served the American cause with unusual dedication.

• Letters from Hewes are in the Cupola House Papers, Southern Historical Collection, University of North Carolina, Chapel Hill; the Emmet Collection, New York City Public Library; the Hayes Collection, North Carolina State Archives, Raleigh; and the Joseph Hewes Papers, Duke University Library, Durham, N.C. They are published in *Letters of Members of the Continental Congress*, ed. Edmund C. Burnett (8 vols., 1921–1936); *Journals of the Continental Congress*, ed. Worthington C. Ford (35 vols., 1904–1937); and *Letters of Delegates to Congress, 1774–1789*, ed. Paul H. Smith et al. (1976–). A biographical sketch by Michael G. Martin, Jr., is in *Dictionary of North Carolina Biography*, ed. William S. Powell, vol. 3 (1988). See also David T. Morgan and William J. Schmidt, *North Carolinians in the Continental Congress* (1976) and "From Economic Sanctions to Political Separation: The North Carolina Delegation to the Continental Congress, 1774–1776," *North Carolina Historical Review* 52 (Summer 1975): 215–34.

DAVID T. MORGAN

HEWETT, Edgar Lee (23 Nov. 1865–31 Dec. 1946), educator and anthropologist, was born in Warren County, Illinois, the son of Harvey Hanson Hewett and Tabitha Stice. Although originally a participant in the California gold rush of 1849, Hewett's father eventually became a farmer in Illinois, where he also raised stock and later engaged in land speculation in Chicago. Hewett's mother's family had befriended Chief Black Hawk and his Sauk band, and it was this fact that first stirred young Edgar's interest in and sympathy toward American Indians. Energetic and precocious, the boy possessed a remarkable intellectual hunger and knack for research. Reverses in the family's fortune led the Hewetts to move to Hopkins, Missouri, where Edgar attended high school. There he became acquainted with the early works of Lewis Henry Morgan and Adolph Bandelier, and his interest in anthropology was aroused.

After graduating (probably in 1886) from Tarkio College in Fairfax, Missouri, Hewett launched his teaching career in the rural schools of Missouri and

Iowa. That same year he was appointed a professor of literature and history at Tarkio. Although he briefly studied law, Hewett chose to remain in academics; in 1889 he accepted a school principal's position in Fairfax and later was superintendent of schools at Florence, Colorado. In 1891 he married Cora Whitford, a fellow schoolteacher whom he had met in Missouri; they had no children. The couple shared not only a common interest in education but also a mutual love for horses and the outdoors. In 1894 Hewett accepted a faculty position at the new State Normal College (now Northern Colorado University) at Greeley.

In 1896 Hewett made his inaugural summer field trip into New Mexico, where he conducted his first archaeological studies of Indian pueblo ruins in the Pecos Valley and the Pajarito Plateau. This research led to an invitation from Frank Springer, a member of the board of regents of New Mexico Normal University, in 1897 to give a series of lectures in Santa Fe on his findings, and in October 1898 Hewett was appointed first president of the newly opened New Mexico Normal (now New Mexico Highlands) University in Las Vegas, New Mexico, where he also offered courses in archaeology. During this period he helped to organize the Archaeological Society of New Mexico and led the movement toward the preservation of pre-Columbian sites throughout the United States. His efforts resulted in the passage of the Lacey Law, spearheaded by Congressman J. F. Lacey and designed to protect archaeological sites on public lands, in 1906.

Beginning in 1903 Hewett periodically journeyed overseas to the University of Geneva to study for a doctorate in anthropology, which he successfully completed in 1908. During these years he also conducted studies at the National Museum in Washington, D.C., made field trips to Mexico and Central America, and did surveys of the Indian ruins in Frijoles Canyon and Mesa Verde National Park. His efforts garnered him the friendship and support of other pioneer anthropologists, such as Adolph Bandalier, Francis W. Kelsey, Alice C. Fletcher, Charles F. Lummis, and Frederick W. Putnam. In January 1907 Hewett was made director of the School of American Archaeology (later the School of American Research) for the Archaeological Society of New Mexico. Between 1910 and 1913 he and his protégé, archaeologist Jesse Nusbaum, conducted the remodeling of the old Governors' Palace in Santa Fe and made it the headquarters of the Museum of New Mexico (which Hewett and Judge John R. McFie created), as well as the society.

In addition to his duties as director of the museum and of the School of American Research, Hewett was made director of exhibits for the Panama-California Exposition in San Diego, California, from 1911 to 1916. Under his leadership the exposition's New Mexico Indian Building was erected and subsequently turned into a branch museum and school of archaeology, which Hewett directed until 1929. In Santa Fe he helped begin the New Mexico Museum of Fine Arts and revive the Santa Fe Fiesta in 1919. From 1922 to 1927 Hewett was professor of anthropology at San Diego State Teachers College. He then became head of the newly organized anthropology department at the University of New Mexico in Albuquerque, a position he held until 1935; in 1928 his School of American Research became affiliated with the university.

As his teaching staff at the School of American Research increased, Hewett was able to direct more attention to his field trips, writings, and other interests of the school. In 1930 he was elected president of the managing board of the school in Santa Fe. That year he took steps to establish the American School of Archaeology in Mexico City, which became the School of Middle American Studies in 1934. In 1932 he established a third branch of the school at the University of Southern California in Los Angeles, headed its new anthropology and archaeology department for two years, and afterward continued as that university's director of research. His extensive field trips took him to South America, Spain, Greece, and the Middle East.

In addition to numerous archaeological reports and journal articles, Hewett published several books in his field, including *Ancient Life in the American Southwest* (1930), *Ancient Life in Mexico and Central America* (1936), *The Chaco Canyon and Its Monuments* (1936), *Pajarito Plateau and Its Ancient People* (1938), *Ancient Andean Life* (1939), *Campfire and Trail* (1943), *Man and Culture* (1944), and an autobiography, *Two Score Years* (1946). He also collaborated with other authors in producing several works.

Six years after the death of his wife in 1905, Hewett married Donizetta "Doni" Jones; they likewise had no children. Over the years Doni was her husband's constant traveling companion and a gracious hostess. In the summer of 1923 the Hewetts were injured in an automobile accident in the Syrian desert, but their determination enabled them to complete their planned expedition through the Holy Land to Egypt, a tour funded in part by the Oriental Museum of Yale University.

Despite token opposition from New Mexico Republican party leader Bronson Cutting and other conservative political leaders, Hewett received firm backing for his work from the Santa Fe Railroad and the local chamber of commerce. He was instrumental in promoting Indian arts and crafts and in turning Santa Fe into a major southwestern cultural center, which attracted well-known artists and writers such as Carlos Vierra, Kenneth Chapman, Gerald Cassidy, Sheldon Parsons, William and Alice Corbin Henderson, Mary Austin, and Ernest Thompson Seton. His efforts resulted in the preservation of several ancient pueblo sites as state and national monuments. The Hewett's adobe-style home on Lincoln Avenue became an informal gathering place for many of Santa Fe's muses and intellectuals. Hewett died in Albuquerque, New Mexico.

• Hewett's papers are in the State Records Center, the Laboratory of Anthropology, the Museum of New Mexico in Santa Fe, and the Zimmerman Library at the University of New Mexico in Albuquerque. The Hewett home in Santa Fe continues to be maintained as a center for the New Mexico Archaeological Institute. Additional sources include Donald D. Brand and Fred E. Harvey, eds., *So Live the Works of Men* (1939); Beatrice Chauvenet, *Hewett and Friends: A Biography of Santa Fe's Vibrant Era* (1983); and Arrell M. Gibson, *The Santa Fe and Taos Colonies: Age of the Muses, 1900–1942* (1983). Obituaries are in the *Santa Fe New Mexican* and the *Albuquerque Journal*, both 1 Jan. 1947, and in *El Palacio* 54 (Jan. 1947): 3–12.

H. ALLEN ANDERSON

HEWIT, Augustine Francis (27 Nov. 1820–3 July 1897), Catholic priest and Paulist superior, was born Nathaniel Augustus Hewit in Fairfield, Connecticut, the son of Nathaniel Hewit, a prominent Congregationalist minister, and Rebecca Hillhouse, the daughter of U.S. senator James Hillhouse. Hewit was educated at Phillips Academy and Amherst College, graduating from the latter in 1839. Shortly after college he studied for the Congregationalist ministry at the Theological Institute of Connecticut (Hartford) and was licensed as a Congregationalist minister in 1842. He left the institute before finishing his theological education because, as he noted in a brief autobiographical account in 1887, he found the "whole system [of Calvinist theology] to break to pieces under my feet."

In the early 1840s Hewit moved to Baltimore, where he became an Episcopalian after reading what he called the "rich literature of the Oxford school," which led him to examine primitive Christianity and apostolic succession. From his early youth, though raised in a Congregationalist household, he was attracted to Episcopalianism, and by the time he moved to Baltimore he believed that Presbyterian church order was a departure from the primitive order of episcopacy. Under the guidance of Baltimore's Bishop William Rollinson Whittingham, he studied for the Episcopalian ministry and was ordained a deacon in 1843.

In November 1845, for reasons of health, Hewit moved to Edenton, North Carolina, where he preached to slaves and continued to read the Oxford school's publications. His study, though, made him troubled with the Oxford position, and by the end of 1845 he had become convinced that he must become a Catholic. At the end of Holy Week in 1846, he was received into the Catholic church in Charleston, South Carolina, and in March 1847, after studying Catholic theology with Father Patrick Lynch of Charleston, he was ordained to the Catholic priesthood. He wrote *A Few Thoughts concerning the Theories of High-Churchmen and Tractarians* (1846) as an apology for joining the Catholic church. For Hewit the continuity, infallibility, and development of the primitive church could be found in no other denomination, and he saw his own movement toward Catholicism as the logically consistent consequence of his studies of the Oxford school.

After his ordination, from 1847 to 1849, Hewit preached in the Charleston Cathedral parish, taught in the Charleston Catholic seminary, and was primarily responsible for collecting and editing *The Works of the Right Rev. John England, First Bishop of Charleston* (5 vols., 1849). In 1849, moreover, he entered the Redemptorist (i.e., the Congregation of the Most Holy Redeemer) novitiate in Baltimore because he felt called to the religious life. In April 1851, having finished his novitiate, he joined a small band of Redemptorists who were giving parish missions to Catholics on the East Coast. From 1851 to 1858 the American Redemptorists carried on their missionary enterprise and in the process attracted many Protestants to their parish missions. But American Redemptorists such as Hewit, Isaac Hecker, Clarence Walworth, and Francis A. Baker, all converts to Catholicism, clashed with the German Redemptorist superiors over the nature of the mission work and the need to Americanize. In 1858, therefore, these American converts sent Hecker to Rome to iron out the problem.

Hecker was dismissed from the order but was allowed to organize the other convert Redemptorists into a new religious community, the Paulists (founded in 1858), one of whose missions was the conversion of American Protestants to Catholicism. Hewit left the Redemptorists and became one of the charter members of the new religious community. While residing in New York City he helped to draft the community's first constitution.

Hecker became the Paulists' first superior, but Hewit was always his second in command and the one primarily responsible for the organizational efficiency of the new order. In 1865 Hecker established the *Catholic World*, a journal of Catholic opinion on religious and cultural issues, and Hewit became the assistant editor. In fact, Hewit managed the journal and performed many of its editorial duties until Hecker's death in 1888, when he became in title, as well as in fact, the chief editor. He wrote profusely for the *Catholic World* and other journals of Catholic opinion and in the process became one the chief apologists for Catholic theology during the second half of the nineteenth century. Theologically and philosophically conservative (he enthusiastically supported the revival of scholastic philosophy and theology in the 1870s and 1880s), Hewit was progressive in his view that the Catholic church must adapt itself to American institutions and methods of evangelization.

After Hecker's death, Hewit was elected superior of the Paulists in 1889, a position he retained until his death. Like a number of other Paulists, Hewit had supported the efforts of the Third Council of Baltimore for the Americanist establishment of the Catholic University of America in 1884. In 1889 he moved himself and the Paulist House of Studies from New York City to Washington, D.C., the location of the new Catholic University of America, so that those studying for the priesthood among the Paulists would have a first-rate American university education. In 1897, because of illness, he returned to the Paulist motherhouse in New York City, where he died.

• Hewit's correspondence and personal papers are located primarily in the Paulists' archives in Washington, D.C. Hewit's "How I Became a Catholic," *Catholic World* 46 (Oct. 1887): 32–43, and *Sermons of the Rev. Francis A. Baker, Priests of the Congregation of St. Paul. With a Memoir of His Life by Rev. A. F. Hewit* (1865 and subsequent editions) have autobiographical importance. His articles and editorials in the *Catholic World* from 1865 to 1897, his *Problems of the Age; with Studies in St. Augustine on Kindred Topics* (1868), and *The King's Highway; or, The Catholic Church the Way of Salvation as Revealed in the Holy Scriptures* (1874) are particularly important for an insight into his philosophical and theological positions. The most complete biographical information is in Joseph Flynn's "The Early Years of Augustine F. Hewit, C.S.P., 1820–1846" (M.A. thesis, Catholic Univ. of America, 1945) and in Joseph McSorley's *Father Hecker and His Friends* (1972). An obituary is in *Catholic World* 65 (Aug. 1897): 706–7.

PATRICK W. CAREY

HEWITT, Abram Stevens (31 July 1822–18 Jan. 1903), iron manufacturer, congressman, and mayor, was born near Haverstraw, New York, the son of John Hewitt, a machinist and cabinetmaker, and Ann Gurnee. After attending the public schools of New York City, Abram, at the age of thirteen, entered the Grammar School of Columbia College. Three years later he won a scholarship to Columbia College, where he ranked first in his class in academics. Upon graduation from Columbia in 1842, he began the study of law while also teaching mathematics at Columbia's grammar school. At this time he tutored Edward Cooper, the son of inventor and manufacturer Peter Cooper. In 1843–1844 Hewitt traveled to Europe with Edward Cooper, and the two were shipwrecked on their return voyage. This harrowing adventure strengthened their friendship, and henceforth Hewitt was regarded as virtually a member of the Cooper family. In 1845, with Peter Cooper's backing, the two friends established the Trenton Iron Works. They proved highly successful, manufacturing not only rails and wire but also iron beams used widely in building construction. In 1855 Hewitt cemented his relationship with the Cooper family when he married Sarah Amelia Cooper, Peter Cooper's only daughter. The couple had six children.

Though a Democrat and consequently not totally in accord with President Abraham Lincoln's policies, Hewitt contributed to the Union cause during the Civil War by manufacturing gun barrel iron for the government at virtually production cost. After the war, President Andrew Johnson appointed Hewitt as one of the American commissioners to the Paris Exhibition of 1867, and while in Europe Hewitt surveyed the latest techniques in iron and steel manufacturing. He recorded his findings in a highly acclaimed report to the U.S. government. As a result of his investigations, Hewitt introduced the open-hearth process for manufacturing steel into the United States in 1867–1869.

By the early 1870s Hewitt's interests were turning from manufacturing to politics. Together with Edward Cooper he helped topple the corrupt Tweed Ring, which had ruled New York City, and he endeavored to reform Tammany Hall, the New York City Democratic organization. In 1874 he was elected to the U.S. House of Representatives from New York City and served in that branch of Congress for ten of the next twelve years. As a congressman he favored moderate tariff reform, especially seeking lower tariffs on raw materials. He also sponsored the legislation that established the U.S. Geological Survey. Though Hewitt was frustrated by his inability to achieve more in Congress, most notably to reduce tariffs, others viewed him as one of the nation's leading legislators. In his autobiography, *The Education of Henry Adams* (1907), Henry B. Adams pronounced Hewitt "the most useful public man in Washington," and he claimed to know of "no other man who had done so much."

In 1876 Hewitt was chairman of the Democratic National Committee and managed New York governor Samuel Tilden's unsuccessful race for the presidency. Two years later, disgruntled Tammany boss John Kelly (1822–1886) deprived Hewitt of renomination to Congress, and in 1880–1881 Hewitt and Cooper retaliated by joining with others in founding a rival party faction known as the County Democracy. Despite continued factional feuding, Hewitt was reelected to Congress in 1880, 1882, and 1884.

In 1886 Hewitt's career took a new turn when he accepted the Democratic nomination for mayor of New York City. The radical reformer Henry George (1839–1897) was running on the United Labor party ticket, and to thwart George, Tammany and the County Democracy joined in support of Hewitt. On election day Hewitt handily defeated George as well as the Republican party candidate Theodore Roosevelt (1858–1919).

As mayor Hewitt sought to ensure honest administration and eliminate corruption. In the process he became embroiled in patronage battles with Tammany, refusing to appoint some Tammany men to office. He also endeavored to enforce the law that prohibited saloons from operating on Sundays. This earned him the enmity of many saloon keepers and imbibers. He further outraged many New Yorkers when he refused to take a place in the reviewing stand at the St. Patrick's Day Parade of 1888. Critical of the divided national loyalties of many immigrants, Hewitt would not participate in this Irish celebration. In the heavily Irish city, this decision proved unpopular and contributed to Hewitt's defeat for reelection in 1888.

Mayor Hewitt also urged some more farsighted initiatives. He supported the creation of small parks in the city's congested neighborhoods, and he introduced a plan for building an underground mass transit system. His scheme for the financing and construction of a subway system was not implemented until a decade after he stepped down as mayor.

Following his defeat for reelection by Hugh Grant, the Tammany candidate, Hewitt devoted an increasing amount of his time to philanthropy. In the 1850s Peter Cooper had founded Cooper Union, an educational institution for the working classes. During the decade before his death in New York City, Hewitt endeavored to put Cooper Union on a sound financial footing, donating much of his own money to the Union endowment.

As a manufacturer and a public official, Hewitt epitomized Victorian America and its values. Throughout his business career, he demonstrated a boundless, positive faith in economic growth and technological progress. He was also a model of moral rectitude whose rigid devotion to principle damaged his political fortunes. Honest to the point of bluntness, he was a pillar of righteousness in a political world demanding compromise and pragmatism.

• Hewitt's papers are in the New-York Historical Society, New York City Municipal Archives and Record Center, and the Cooper Union. Some of Hewitt's writings have been compiled in Allan Nevins, ed., *Selected Writings of Abram S. Hewitt* (1937). The standard, and highly laudatory, biography of Hewitt is Nevins, *Abram S. Hewitt, with Some Account of Peter Cooper* (1935). Other articles on Hewitt include Thomas J. Condon, "Political Reform and the New York City Election of 1886," *New-York Historical Society Quarterly* 44 (1960): 363–93, and Matthew J. Downey, "Grover Cleveland and Abram S. Hewitt: The Limits of Factional Consensus," *New-York Historical Society Quarterly* 54 (1970): 223–40. An obituary is in the *New York Times*, 19 Jan. 1903.

JON C. TEAFORD

HEWITT, James (June 1770–2 Aug. 1827), conductor, composer, and publisher, was born in Dartmoor, England, the son of John Hewitt, a captain in the British navy. (His mother's name is unknown.) Details of his childhood are sketchy, but sources indicate that he occupied 12 Hyde Street in the Bloomsbury section of London during 1791–1792. Although it is impossible to verify his family's claim that Hewitt was leader of the King's Band of Musick, it is known that around this time he was a member of the orchestra at Astley's Amphitheatre in London, one of the forerunners of the modern circus. In 1790 Hewitt married Louisa Lamb; they had one child, but both mother and child died shortly after the baby's birth.

Hewitt came to the United States in 1792, arriving in New York on 5 September aboard the brig *Bristol*, with a group of actors and musicians hired by the Old American Company, a theatrical agency active in the United States at that time. He played first violin and conducted the orchestra for the company at the Park Theatre until 1808, when he was dismissed because of a dispute concerning rehearsals for a special production. In 1792 or 1793 Hewitt married a woman named Charlotte, who died in 1795. Before her death, they had one child, who died in infancy. In 1796 Hewitt married Eliza King, by whom he had six children, all of whom made music their vocation.

Hewitt's tenure in New York was the most productive time of his career and marked the years during which he had the greatest influence on the musical life of the new nation. Besides being the orchestra conductor of virtually the only theater in the city, he was also the leader of the band for nearly all of the concerts in

New York during this period. In addition to these activities, he arranged music for some of the Old American Company's productions, composed music, and published his own music and that of other composers. Hewitt is known to have composed at least 160 works, which he published himself, along with approximately 480 editions of compositions by other composers. These editions include some works by Handel, Haydn, and Mozart, but the vast majority are songs by English composers, such as William Shield, Stephen Storace, and James Hook. Hewitt's own compositions include secular songs, marches, variations, and sonatas. Among his vocal compositions, *The Primrose Girl* and *The Wounded Hussar* were quite popular, each going through several editions. *Mark My Alford, Governor Lewis's Waltz*, and *Hewitt's Quick Step* are instrumental works that, judging by the number of editions for each, also were very popular. He authored pedagogical works for keyboard and violin as well. Hewitt sold the compositions at his music store at 59 Maiden Lane, where he also sold musical instruments and supplies. He somehow found time in the midst of his busy schedule to give string, voice, and harpsichord lessons at his store or in his pupils' homes. Hewitt served for a brief time in 1796 as the organist at Trinity Episcopal Church; and, as a member of the New York State Militia, he was in charge of all military music for the city.

Hewitt became conductor of the Federal Street orchestra in Boston beginning with the 1808–1809 season. He moved there in 1810 and by 1812 had moved his family there as well. In Boston Hewitt pursued essentially the same musical activities that he had undertaken in New York. In addition to conducting the orchestra at the Federal Street Theatre, he served as organist at Boston's Trinity Episcopal Church. He continued to compose and publish music, which he sold, along with the music of other composers, at his music store at 58½ Newbury Street. Hewitt also taught vocal and instrumental music lessons.

In 1816 Hewitt returned to New York, where he resumed his conducting, concertizing, and music publishing activities. He once again conducted the orchestra at the Park Theatre and was also the organist at St. Peter's Catholic Church. It was at this time that he published his own setting of "The Star Spangled Banner." During the last years of his life Hewitt toured the mid-Atlantic and southern states with various theatrical troupes, leading the orchestra for stage works and presenting concerts. He died of facial cancer in Boston.

By virtue of his key positions and his many areas of activity in the field, Hewitt was the dominant figure in the musical culture of New York during the years 1792–1808. He was influential in the hiring and firing of musicians in the theater orchestra and in the selection of music and performers for the concert programs. His own compositions and his music publishing further determined what music was available for the general public to purchase and play in their homes. Although he pursued the same activities in Boston and in the South during his later years, Hewitt's influence on the musical life of the United States was by far the strongest during his earlier New York tenure, when the quality and quantity of his work were at their best and his competitors were comparatively few.

• Almost no music in manuscript form or correspondence by Hewitt survives. Printed editions of his music are in the Library of Congress, the Boston and New York public libraries, and the library of the American Antiquarian Society in Worcester, Mass. The most convenient sampling of his compositions is contained in John W. Wagner, ed., *James Hewitt: Selected Compositions* (1980). The most comprehensive collection of biographical data and musical analysis concerning Hewitt is found in Wagner, "James Hewitt: His Life and Works" (Ph.D. diss., Indiana Univ., 1969). A seminal article for research on Hewitt and his musical descendants is John Tasker Howard, "The Hewitt Family in American Music," *Musical Quarterly* 17 (Jan. 1931): 25–39. Vera Brodsky Lawrence, "Mr. Hewitt Lays It on the Line," *19th-Century Music* 5 (Summer 1981): 3–15, is an excellent article dealing with Hewitt's dismissal as conductor of New York's Park Theatre orchestra in 1808.

JOHN W. WAGNER

HEWITT, John Napoleon Brinton (16 Dec. 1859–14 Oct. 1937), ethnologist and linguist, was born on the Tuscarora Indian reservation in New York, the son of David Brainard Hewitt, a doctor, and Harriet Brinton. His mother was of Tuscarora, French, English, and Oneida descent. His father, of Scotch and English descent, had been orphaned as a boy, adopted by a Tuscarora family on the Tuscarora reservation, and raised as an Indian. Although both parents spoke fluent Tuscarora, they did not teach it to their children. Not until Hewitt—taught to read and write by his parents—entered the district school at the age of eleven did he begin to learn Tuscarora from his classmates. At sixteen, he entered the union school in Wilson, New York, where he studied for two years. He next attended the union school in Lockport, New York, but was unable to finish his last term there, as overstudy and a sunstroke had affected his health. After he returned to the reservation, he became a farmer and newspaper correspondent and established a private night school for Tuscarora men.

In 1880 Hewitt met Erminnie A. Smith, who was then collecting Iroquois tales and myths and data on the Iroquois languages for the Bureau of (American) Ethnology, and she hired him as her assistant. He continued to work for her, accompanying her on trips to various Iroquois reservations in New York State and Canada in the summer and in the winter assisting her at her home in Jersey City, New Jersey, until her death in 1886. After Smith's death, he applied for and received a position at the bureau to complete the work they were then engaged in, a Tuscarora-English dictionary. He remained on the staff of the bureau as ethnologist until his death.

During these years Hewitt studied the languages, culture, and history of North American Indians, especially those of the Iroquois. A year after joining the bu-

reau, he wrote a manuscript establishing the relationship of Cherokee to the Iroquois languages, a relationship long suspected but not fully proven. A few years later, in 1893, he wrote two papers, also unpublished, on the relationship between the Shahaptian (Sahaptian), Waiilatpuan, and Lutuamian language families, what he termed the Shahapwailutan family (now known as Plateau Penutian). In another manuscript, he tested and found wanting the claim of a relationship between the Mayan and Polynesian languages. For W J McGee, he compared Seri to the Yuman and Waicurian languages, finding no relationship between them, a report published by McGee in his "The Seri Indians" (*Annual Report of the Bureau of American Ethnology* 17, no. 1 [1898]: 299–344). In this period he also published some articles, including "Legend of the Founding of the Iroquois League" (*American Anthropologist*, o.s., 5 [1892]: 131–48), "Polysynthesis in the Languages of the American Indians" (*American Anthropologist*, o.s., 6 [1893]: 381–407), and what is perhaps his best-known article, "Orenda and a Definition of Religion" (*American Anthropologist* 4 [1902]: 33–46). He subsequently contributed a number of entries to the two-volume *Handbook of American Indians North of Mexico* (*Bureau of American Ethnology Bulletin* 30, 1907 and 1910).

Hewitt's most important work, however, was his transcriptions in the native languages and English translations of the great oral traditions and ritual speeches of Iroquois, including the origin myth (as Hewitt more aptly termed it, the cosmology), the traditional account of the founding of the League of the Iroquois, and the rites of the Condolence ceremony for raising up chiefs of the league. Hewitt had an almost obsessive concern with accuracy and completeness and constantly revised his manuscripts. As a result, although he published some of these materials, notably *Iroquois Cosmology* (in two parts, *Annual Report of the Bureau of American Ethnology* 21 [1903]: 127–339 and 43 [1928]: 449–819), and edited "Seneca Fiction, Legends, and Myths" (*Annual Report of the Bureau of American Ethnology* 32 [1918]: 37–813), a collection made by Hewitt and Jeremiah Curtin, most of the texts he collected remain unpublished.

Hewitt was active in the Anthropological Society of Washington, serving as its treasurer from 1912 to 1926 and president from 1932 to 1934, and was a charter member of the American Anthropological Association. He also was active in the Society of American Indians. From 1918 until his death he was the Smithsonian Institution's representative on the United States Board of Geographic Names.

A deeply religious man and much interested in biblical scholarship, Hewitt was a member of the Ingram Memorial Congregational Church until 1925 when he joined the All Souls Unitarian Church in Washington. He also was a member of the La Fayette Lodge of Masons. Hewitt was married twice. His first wife (name and marriage date unknown) died in 1918. Seven years later, in 1925, he married Carrie Louise Hurlbut, who outlived him. Neither marriage produced children. Hewitt died in Washington, D.C.

• Hewitt's papers, including his unpublished manuscripts, are in the National Anthropological Archives, Smithsonian Institution, Washington, D.C. The two best biographies of Hewitt are John R. Swanton's obituary notice, "John Napoleon Brinton Hewitt," *American Anthropologist* 40 (1938): 286–90, and Marie L. B. Baldwin's "John N. B. Hewitt, Ethnologist," *Quarterly Journal of the Society of American Indians* 2 (1914): 147–50.

ELISABETH TOOKER

HEWITT, Peter Cooper (5 Mar. 1861–25 Aug. 1921), inventor, mechanical and electrical engineer, and manufacturer, was born in New York City, the son of Abram Stevens Hewitt, an iron manufacturer, merchant, and politician, and Sarah Amelia Cooper. Hewitt attended Stevens Institute of Technology at Hoboken, New Jersey, and Columbia University School of Mines in New York City. The fortune amassed by his father and his maternal grandfather, Peter Cooper, enabled him to pursue his own interests. As a result, he devoted much of his adult life to scientific investigation and experimentation, for which he received numerous patents. An orderly and determined individual, his strict work regimen was to attend to business interests in the morning while his afternoons and evenings were devoted to experimentation and investigations in his laboratory, located in the tower of the old Madison Square Garden. This intense schedule continued for three-quarters of the year and was followed by three months totally devoid of work and devoted to relaxation, travel, and sports.

His first major invention came about in the late 1890s, when he was deeply involved in electrical experimentation. With only about 5 percent of the energy used in the incandescent electric lamp actually going to the production of light and the rest given off as heat, he sought ways of providing a better light source. By proving that a gas could conduct an electrical charge, he was able to pass an electric current through mercury gas sealed in a quartz tube. The Cooper Hewitt mercury-vapor lamp produced an intense, cool, bluish-green light. Because a greater part of the energy consumed by the lamp went into the production of light, it was more efficient and thus less expensive to operate. Its one drawback was its strange color. Lacking the elements that produced red light rays, the strong, albeit ghastly, light was ideal for shop work and situations where color differentiation was not critical. Hewitt proved this problem could be overcome by devising a transformer that added those parts of the color spectrum that were lacking. A powerful source of ultraviolet light, the mercury lamp was useful in a number of therapeutical, sterilizing, and chemical applications.

Hewitt and George Westinghouse formed the Cooper Hewitt Electric Company in 1902 to manufacture and sell the new lamp. The partnership was broadened when the firm of Westinghouse Cooper-Hewitt was formed in England for the manufacture and distribution of a variety of electrical equipment. By 1914 the General Electric Company had assumed a controlling interest in the Cooper Hewitt Electric Company.

Hewitt in 1904 introduced the static converter or mercury arc rectifier, which was based in large part on research that produced the mercury-vapor lamp. A simple transformer, it converted alternating electric current into direct current. Weighing only a few pounds, it could replace expensive and massive rotary converters weighing many hundreds of pounds. This important advance meant that direct current, which cannot be easily transmitted over long distances, could be economically converted from alternating current at its destination. In recognition of this development, Hewitt was nominated for and received the prestigious Elliott Cresson Medal of the Franklin Institute in 1914.

Shortly after the turn of the century, Hewitt's interests came to include the automobile. Working on a machine purchased in Europe, his major contribution was an improved method of controlling the engine's speed. He also provided some of the technical details for the Hewitt automobile manufactured by his brother, Edward Ringwood Hewitt.

Hewitt developed in 1907 what was referred to as a gliding craft. A small hydroplane motorboat, in some respects, it was a precursor of later high-speed hydrofoil watercraft. Only by lessening or freeing altogether a ship's hull from the friction of the water through which it passes could it be made dramatically faster and more efficient. Powered by a large eight-cylinder engine of his own design, the hull of his craft, as its speed increased, would break loose from the water. It rose up and planed on four small wing-shaped hydrofoils that extended from the hull below the waterline.

Among his other interests was powered flight, both lighter and heavier than air. He wrote articles for the popular press and in 1908 predicted that aircraft would one day be more plentiful and cheaper than automobiles. During this period, he launched investigations into the possibility of helicopter flight. In 1915 he received U.S. Patent No. 1,134,386 for an aerostat (balloon) envelope and supporting truss.

Hewitt worked on behalf of all inventors when in 1910 he became a supporter and member of the newly formed Inventor's Guild, which was formed in New York City to further the interests and secure the rights of those who made contributions in the fields of science and technology. Believing that more could be accomplished by a small dedicated membership, entry into the guild was difficult and limited to successful inventors who it was felt would be able to exert some influence on industry as well as government. Extensive recommendations were required for membership, and participation was limited to fifty individuals. Peter Cooper Hewitt served on the first board of governors.

A measure of the guild's success was evident in 1915 when it, along with professional engineering societies, was asked by the secretary of the navy to recommend individuals to the new Naval Advisory Board created in response to the war in Europe. The guild named

Hewitt. Chaired by Thomas Edison, the board comprised eleven prominent individuals from the fields of science and technology who were to advise the government on what value a variety of inventions might be to it.

Although the War Department had expressed an interest in his plans for a helicopter at the time the United States entered World War I, no actual device had been constructed. In 1920 he received three patents (Nos. 1,350,454, 1,350,455, and 1,350,456) for a helicopter. In that same year Hewitt, along with Francis B. Crocker of Columbia University, constructed a full-size working example. Its two counter-rotating wings or blades were able to provide sufficient lift to support the craft and as much as 225 pounds.

Married twice, his first marriage in 1887 to Alice Work ended in divorce. His second marriage, to Maryon J. (Andrews) Bruguiere, took place in 1918. He died at the American Hospital in Paris.

• Charles W. Price, "Peter Cooper Hewitt," *Cosmopolitan*, Mar. 1904, provides a good sense of the man. Another view of his character comes from Michael I. Pupin, *In Memoriam of Peter Cooper Hewitt* (1921). Hewitt's association with Westinghouse is discussed by Henry G. Prout in *A Life of George Westinghouse* (1922). Articles by Francis B. Crocker in *Aerial Age*, 22–29 Nov. 1920, thoroughly describe his efforts in the field of aviation. Articles by others on his electrical inventions and the hydroplane appear in *Scientific American*, 7 Feb. 1903, 11 Feb. 1905, 3 Aug. 1907, 24 Dec. 1910, 30 Dec. 1910, and 2 Oct. 1915. His nomination for the Cresson Medal is published in the *Journal of the Franklin Institute*, Jan.–June 1914. Thorough descriptions and illustrations of his inventions are available in the records of the U.S. Patent Office. Obituaries are in *Transactions of the Society of Naval Architects and Marine Engineers* 29 (1922), and the *New York Times*, 26 Aug. 1921.

WILLIAM E. WORTHINGTON, JR.

HEWITT, Sophia Henriette (1799?–31 Aug. 1846), organist, pianist, and music teacher, was probably born in New York, the daughter of James Hewitt, a violinist, composer, and conductor, and Eliza King. Sophia's first music teacher was her father, and she made her performing debut at the age of seven in New York City on 14 April 1807, playing a piano sonata. She continued to play in public from time to time until she was twelve, when her father moved the family to Boston. There she occasionally appeared as a pianist and studied organ with George K. Jackson.

Hewitt moved back to New York, where she taught music at Mrs. Brenton's Boarding School. She also sang at the New York Oratorios (concerts) and frequently performed with the Euterpian Society. During this period she took harp lessons with a Mr. Ferrand and piano lessons with Peter K. Moran. In 1817 Hewitt gave a number of performances in Boston, playing the piano and singing, and the following year the Handel and Haydn Society offered her the position of organist, a remarkable honor for such a young woman. She refused, for reasons that are unknown, and during the next few years she continued to perform in

both Boston and New York. In 1819 she played Beethoven's Piano Sonata in A-flat, op. 26, believed to be the first performance of a Beethoven sonata in the United States.

By the spring of 1820 Hewitt had again moved to Boston and was teaching piano, voice, and harp, as well as performing with the Philharmonic Society and accompanying singers in recital. The Handel and Haydn Society repeated its earlier offer, and this time Hewitt accepted, becoming the organist on 26 September 1820. At that time she was the leading professional pianist in Boston and a highly regarded organist. Hewitt continued to teach organ as well as the other instruments and voice, and she gave an important solo recital, a public benefit concert, in 1822.

Later in 1822 Hewitt married violinist Louis Ostinelli, the concertmaster and conductor of the Philharmonic Society and the theater orchestra; they were to have one child. The couple was in demand for recitals, and they performed throughout New England for the next few years. Despite Hewitt's favorable reputation and enthusiastic reviews of her playing, and disregarding popular protest, the Handel and Haydn Society decided to replace her in 1830 with a more formally educated musician. Evidence suggests that for the next two years she may have served as a church organist in Portland, Maine, and she continued to teach in Boston. Her last public performance in Boston took place on 5 August 1834. It is believed that she was by then separated from her husband and that she spent the last decade of her life in Portland, probably teaching and working as a church organist. Hewitt died in Portland.

Hewitt was the first American woman instrumentalist to achieve such renown and to be considered on a par with much older and highly esteemed male musicians. Moreover, she was the first American woman, and one of relatively few since her time, to become a recognized outstanding organist.

• The fullest available account of Hewitt's life and career is in Christine Ammer, *Unsung: A History of Women in American Music* (1980), which is based on periodicals and records from the period. More about her family may be found in John Tasker Howard, "The Hewitt Family in American Music," *Musical Quarterly* (Jan. 1931).

CHRISTINE AMMER

HEWLETT, James S. (fl. 1821–1831), actor and singer, is said to have been born on Long Island, New York, presumably toward the end of the eighteenth century. His parents are unknown, and nothing is known about his childhood. As a young man he worked as steward on passenger ships, and he is said to have been an avid playgoer. In 1820 New York City had a black population of about 11,000, out of a total of about 125,000. The one theater in town, the Park, admitted African Americans to only a section of one of the balconies. When William A. Brown established a theater by and for New York's black community (originally called the African Theatre), in the fall of 1821, Hewlett quickly became its star, beginning with its second performance, when he played Richard III. The theater's third performance saw Hewlett repeating the role of Richard as well as singing seven songs and choreographing and dancing in the ballet. He later played the lead in the theater's productions of *The Poor Soldier* and *The Drama of King Shotaway*, a play written by Brown, and no doubt he took other roles as well. During the 1823–1824 season, Hewlett was listed as the manager of the African Theatre, but it was to be its last season.

At some point during the 1822–1823 season, Charles Mathews, an English comedian touring the United States, saw a performance of the African Theatre and interviewed Hewlett. Flattered, Hewlett began to offer a full show of adaptations of Mathews's comic sketches in imitation of Mathews's style. When news reached New York that Mathews had written a skit on the African Theatre that showed an actor called "the Kentucky Roscius" in an absurd performance of Hamlet, Hewlett was deeply hurt, as New Yorkers assumed him to be its butt. After the closing of the African Theatre in the summer of 1824, Hewlett sailed for England, to confront Mathews and to find work as an actor. Succeeding in neither, he returned to New York at the end of the year and soon signed on a ship as steward for what proved to be an exceedingly unpleasant nine-month voyage to the Caribbean and Europe.

Back in New York, Hewlett resumed his performing career in November 1825, giving recitals of familiar English songs in imitation of the styles of popular singers and of speeches and soliloquys from classic plays in imitation of the styles of notable actors. He billed himself as the "New York and London Coloured Comedian," though he had almost certainly not played in London and particularly not at the Coburg Theatre, as was his claim. Within two months he had appeared in New York, Brooklyn, Philadelphia (in a series of three concerts), and back in Brooklyn. Reports of his performances become more scattered thereafter, but he is known to have appeared in concert in Albany and Saratoga Springs, New York, and in York, Pennsylvania, in the next few years.

In 1829 a British traveler in New York saw a troupe of black actors doing *Julius Caesar*; the actor who played Brutus, though unnamed, was no doubt Hewlett. Other details in this account suggest that this company represented a revival of the African Theatre and that it had been active for the theatrical season of 1828–1829.

After 1829 there is no record of Hewlett's theatrical activity until March 1831, when several New York newspapers carried advertisements for his appearance at a minor museum. He returned to the museum in July of the same year, when he was obliged to supplement his usual repertory of imitations of singers and actors by making a spectacle of himself by inhaling "exhilarating gas," or nitrous oxide. Two months later he advertised that he had rented a hall in order to give a concert backed by a full band. However, there are no further notices to indicate whether this concert ever took place.

Nothing more is known of Hewlett's activities as a performer. In June 1834 he was arrested for a petty theft and sentenced to six months in jail. It appears that he did not attempt to resume his career after his release. Martin Delany reported having seen Hewlett demonstrate his talents in a private rehearsal in 1836. His name last appeared in the newspapers in March 1837, when a young white woman who identified herself as his wife was arrested for theft. The stories referred to Hewlett as a former actor. Delany indicated that Hewlett died in the late 1840s but does not say where.

Hewlett is described as light skinned and of middle height. There is an undated illustration of him costumed as Richard III, his favorite role. Testimony from several sources suggests that his manner of pronouncing English was incompatible with the fluent delivery of blank verse but that he was a perceptive mimic and comedian and an excellent singer, with a voice in the tenor range. He took serious and comic roles with the African Theatre and as a recitalist favored speeches and soliloquys from Shakespeare and other classics and from popular recent plays. As a singer he specialized in English light classical songs and opera arias. Several glimpses of his private life show him to have had a warmhearted and beguiling personality. He was undoubtedly the first African American to attempt a career as a stage performer.

• For more information see the *National Advocate*, the *Commercial Advertiser*, and other New York City newspapers for the period from 1821 to 1837; Errol Hill, *Shakespeare in Sable: A History of Black Shakespearean Actors* (1984); and George C. D. Odell, *Annals of the New York Stage*, vol. 3, *1821–1834* (1928).

GEORGE A. THOMPSON, JR.

HEXAMER, Charles John (9 May 1862–15 Oct. 1921), civil engineer and political advocate for German-American causes, was born in Philadelphia, Pennsylvania, the son of Ernest Hexamer, a civil engineer, and Marie Klingel. His father was a prominent "forty-eighter," one of the wave of educated, liberal German immigrants who came to the United States after the European revolutions of 1848. Hexamer attended the University of Pennsylvania, receiving a B.S. in 1882, an A.M. in 1884, and a Ph.D. in 1886. He also received an LL.D. from the National University in 1899. He married Annie Josephine Haeuptner in 1891 and worked as an engineer in Philadelphia from 1882 until his retirement in 1917. He authored *Spontaneous Combustion* (1885); *Fire Hazards in Textile Mills, Mill Architecture and Means for Extinguishing Fire* (1895), and *Finely Divided Organic Substances and Their Fire Hazard* (1896). He received several awards for inventions, including the Scott Legacy Medal of the Franklin Institute.

Hexamer is best known for his political advocacy for the German-American community during the first two decades of the twentieth century. He was president of the National German-American Alliance from its inception in 1901 until 1917. The Alliance, which was called the DANB after its German name, Deutsch-Amerikanischer National-Bund, was a confederation of state and local cultural and social organizations. Although it was an influential organization of high profile, the DANB was organized and run by an affluent and elite small group rather than being a grassroots organization. Its large membership (2.5 million in 1901) was due more to the practice of counting as members of the DANB all the members of the local and state associations than the desire of millions of German Americans to join a national organization devoted to cultural preservation. The diversity of the German-American population in the United States during the first part of the twentieth century makes the accuracy of most of the DANB's articulation of German-American interests difficult to gauge. Prohibition, however, was the one issue against which German-Americans united. The fight to prevent Prohibition provided the impetus for the formation of the DANB.

The DANB declared the Prohibition movement to be discriminatory against German-American culture. German-American social life in the early part of the twentieth century centered on participation in various ethnic social organizations, including benevolent aid societies, religious organizations, choral groups, and gymnastic clubs. Most of these groups sponsored festivals at which alcohol was served. A ban on alcohol, argued the DANB, would seriously undermine German-American social and cultural life and was more an affirmation of the values of the dominant Anglo-American culture than merely a neutral pursuit of the public good. The Prohibition movement, whether by design or by accident, promoted a uniformity of culture which, argued the DANB, violated the spirit of the Constitution. By linking Prohibition with the threat of a monoculture, Hexamer enlarged the role of the DANB from merely an antiprohibitionist institution to a preserver and defender of German culture in the United States. Prohibition was a vehicle by which the assimilation of various ethnic groups into the mainstream Anglo-American culture would be hastened. Fear of assimilation, or at least fear of the rapid acceleration of the assimilation process, fueled the antiprohibitionist fight for the leaders (though evidence suggests not the membership) of the Alliance. Frederick C. Luebke notes in *Bonds of Loyalty: German Americans and World War I* (1974) that Hexamer's most quoted and most criticized remark on the subject was made in 1915: "No one . . . will find us prepared to step down to a lesser *Kultur*; no, we have made it our aim to draw the other up to us" (p. 185).

Remarks such as this underscore the increasing difficulty facing Hexamer and the DANB in the years immediately preceding the United States' entry into the First World War. The difficulty was to continue to try to preserve German culture while asserting the loyalty to the United States of German-Americans and protesting the discrimination and harassment of German-American citizens. Hexamer's tactlessness regarding German culture drew criticism from many quarters,

including his own constituency and Theodore Roosevelt, and it did nothing to quell the anti-German sentiment in the popular press. Still, Hexamer managed to keep the DANB politically active. In addition to testifying before Congress on the evils of Prohibition, Hexamer organized a campaign to protest the selling of Allied war bonds during the period of American neutrality. He noted that financial support of Great Britain was, like the Prohibition movement, an expression of Anglo-American bias rather than a strictly neutral transaction. Hexamer also led the DANB in its support of Charles Evans Hughes's presidential campaign in 1916 and organized letter-writing campaigns to the popular press protesting anti-German prejudice in that medium. Dr. Hexamer retired as president of the German-American Alliance in 1917 due to poor health and died in Atlantic City, New Jersey.

• Information regarding the details of Hexamer's life can be found in *Who Was Who in America*, vol. 1 (1943). Frederick C. Luebke, *Bonds of Loyalty: German Americans and World War I* (1974), is an excellent analysis of Hexamer's political activity. A useful source written during Hexamer's lifetime is Albert Bernhardt Faust, *The German Element in the United States* (1909). An obituary is in the *New York Times*, 16 Oct. 1921.

JANE FREIMILLER

HEYWARD, DuBose (31 Aug. 1885–16 June 1940), novelist, dramatist, and poet, was born Edwin DuBose Heyward in Charleston, South Carolina, the son of Edwin Watkins Heyward, a mill hand from an old and distinguished southern family ruined after the Civil War, and Jane Screven DuBose, also descended from once-prosperous plantation owners. His father died when Heyward was two, and his mother was reduced to taking in sewing to support the family. He attended a private school until he was nine and entered public school in the fourth grade but was, as he later described himself, "a miserable student," uninterested in schoolwork. He dropped out in his first year of high school, at the age of fourteen, to work as a clerk in a hardware store and later worked among African-American stevedores as a checker for a steamship company. Often sick as a child, he got polio when he was eighteen; two years later he contracted typhoid fever and the next year pleurisy. At twenty-one, Heyward and his friend Henry T. O'Neill organized a real estate and insurance company. A skilled salesman of great personal charm, he succeeded in making himself financially independent.

Always interested in literature, the young Heyward had passed the time in his sickbed writing verses and stories. In 1913 he wrote a one-act play, *An Artistic Triumph*, which was produced in a local theater. A derivative farce about mistaken identity, it showed little promise, but its success sharpened the young author's appetite for a literary career. Heyward never fully recovered from the illnesses of his youth. In 1917, while convalescing, he began to devote himself seriously to writing fiction and poetry. In 1918 his first published short story, "The Brute," appeared in *Pagan, a Maga-*

zine for Eudaemonists. The next year he met Hervey Allen, then teaching at the nearby Porter Military Academy. The two became close friends and together formed the Poetry Society of South Carolina, which helped spark a revival of southern literature. Heyward edited the society's yearbooks until 1924 and contributed a good deal of their content. His poetry was well received, earning him a Contemporary Verse award in 1921. With Allen he published a collection, *Carolina Chansons: Legends of the Low Country,* in 1922. That same year the two edited a southern issue of *Poetry* magazine.

While spending the summer at the MacDowell Colony in New Hampshire, Heyward met Dorothy Hartzell Kuhns, a student in George Pierce Baker's playwriting workshop at Harvard; they were married in 1923. They had one child. In 1924 his first independent book, a volume of poems titled *Skylines and Horizons,* appeared. Largely based on themes from Charleston history, it established his local reputation as a poet. With the encouragement of his wife, Heyward determined to make a living by writing. In 1924 he gave up the business that had supported him for eighteen years, resigned as president of the Poetry Society, and moved with his wife to the Great Smokies to work on a novel. Between stints of writing, he supported himself by lecturing on southern literature at college campuses.

Porgy, published in 1925, was a powerful story of a crippled African-American beggar, set in a black waterfront neighborhood of Charleston called Catfish Row. A poignant picture of a culture seldom before depicted without quaintness or condescension, *Porgy* was an immediate success, described in the *New York Times Book Review* (7 Sept. 1925) as "a noteworthy achievement in the sympathetic interpretation of negro life by a member of an 'outside' race," and conveying "an intimate and authentic sense of the dignity, the pathos . . . the very essence of his chosen community."

Heyward's next novel, *Angel* (1926), dealt with mountaineers in North Carolina. It was not a popular success, but the following year he renewed his large audience with a dramatization of *Porgy* done in collaboration with his wife. The first major Broadway play with an all African-American cast, it was a great hit, running for a total of 367 performances in 1927–1928 and earning the Heywards a Pulitzer Prize. The play was later turned into an opera, titled *Porgy and Bess* (1935), with music by George Gershwin and libretto by Heyward and Gershwin's brother Ira. Hailed as the first great American folk opera, it was influential in opening the American theater to African-American musical forms and was made into a successful motion picture in 1959.

"The Half Pint Flask," a short story dealing with the conflict between white science and supernatural forces in the African-American community, appeared as a separate volume in 1929. Later that year Heyward returned to Catfish Row as a setting for *Mamba's Daughters,* his longest novel, which chronicled the social ele-

vation of an African-American girl in white society as an opera singer. In 1931 he published *Jasbo Brown and Selected Poems.* A play, *Brass Ankle,* dealing with the problems of a mulatto in small-town white society, was produced that same year but was a commercial failure. Abandoning the theme of race in 1932, Heyward published *Peter Ashley,* a romantic novel set in pre–Civil War Charleston. The next year he answered the siren call to Hollywood, where he wrote screenplays for Eugene O'Neill's *The Emperor Jones* (1933) and Pearl Buck's *The Good Earth* (1934). In 1936 he published the novel *Lost Morning.* Set in the Piedmont region, the story is about the competing values of business and the artistic life. In the year before his death of a heart attack in Tryon, North Carolina, he published *Star-Spangled Virgin,* a novelette about a society of blacks whose harmony with nature in the Virgin Islands is disrupted by the effects of the New Deal. That year the Heywards' dramatization of *Mamba's Daughters,* starring Ethel Waters, was produced on Broadway; he also published a children's book written for his nine-year-old daughter Jenifer.

A slight, graceful figure with courtly manners, Heyward was personally popular and widely admired. He was a member of the Poetry Society of America and the National Institute of Arts and Letters. Although his poetry has been largely dismissed as fragmentary and conventional and the plots of his fiction criticized as melodramatic, his sensitivity to the rhythms of African-American life has retained its vitality and given him, and the society he so keenly observed and so sympathetically celebrated, a lasting place in American fiction.

• Heyward's correspondence and manuscripts can be found in the DuBose Heyward Papers and the John Bennett Papers at the South Carolina Historical Society in Charleston, in the Yates Snowden Papers at the University of South Carolina in Charleston, and in the Hervey Allen Papers at the University of Pittsburgh Library. Heyward's life is detailed in Frank Durham, *DuBose Heyward: The Man Who Wrote Porgy* (1954), and his work is critically examined at length in William Slavick, *DuBose Heyward* (1981). See also Emily Clark, "DuBose Heyward," *Virginia Quarterly Review* 6 (Oct. 1930): 546–56, and Harlan Henthorne Hatcher, *Creating the Modern American Novel* (1935). Obituaries are in the *New York Times* and the *New York Herald Tribune,* both 17 June 1940.

DENNIS WEPMAN

HEYWARD, Nathaniel (18 Jan. 1766–10 Apr. 1851), planter and legislator, was born in Charleston, South Carolina, the son of Daniel Heyward, a planter, and Jane Elizabeth Gignilliat. As a boy Heyward served as a powder monkey in the Charleston Battery of Artillery during the American Revolution. His formal education consisted only of academy training. Coming of age, he traveled for a year in Europe and returned home to settle down to the life of a rice planter. As a younger son, he inherited only a few small inland swamp tracts from his father, who had many thousands of acres of land and 1,000 slaves. Heyward's acres were subject to unwanted flooding, and it took the loss of only one crop to convince him that the future of rice culture lay in the tidal swamps then being developed. Tidal swamps had two advantages over inland swamps: tidal swamps were not subject to unwanted flooding, and more important, they had ample water to kill most of the grass and weeds.

In 1788 Heyward married Harriet or Henrietta Manigault, daughter of the extremely wealthy Peter Manigault. They had nine children. Harriet's dowry of $50,000 enabled Heyward to buy a large tideland tract, on which he erected four plantations. He became the largest and most successful rice planter in the antebellum South, and eventually he possessed 5,000 acres of prime rice land and 30,000 unimproved acres on seventeen plantations, most on the Combahee River in Colleton District, and 2,087 slaves.

A number of Heyward's plantations, averaging about 300 acres of rice land and a little over 100 slaves, bore Dutch names, such as "Amsterdam" and "Rotterdam," doubtless influenced by his travels and observations of the Dutch system of water control. Others included "Silk Hope" on the Cooper River in Charleston District, the principal Manigault seat, sold to Heyward by his brother-in-law in 1805. On this plantation silk production proved a failure in the late 1600s, but there rice was first grown with real success in South Carolina. "The Bluff," Heyward's residence, was located on a rise above the Combahee. He maintained a very fashionable home on East Bay Street in Charleston and owned eight other houses elsewhere in the city. Upon being approached to subscribe to stock in an industry in Charleston, he replied that Charleston should not be an industrial center but rather a summer residence for the rice planters.

Heyward was not only the largest antebellum rice planter, but he was also one of the most skilled. Indeed, he was registered as a "model" planter. He was ever seeking for new and better techniques and methods of planting. He was intimately associated with the perfection of the "point" or "stretch" flow, the second of several floodings of the rice crop. Heyward was noted for keeping all of his plantation facilities in the best working condition. He was also genuinely interested in the welfare of his slaves, selecting the best possible overseers and drivers and working through them to ensure the best of treatment. He concerned himself with the most minute details in plantation management. He was a most paternalistic master, and in turn he was respected by all of his slaves.

According to the 1850 federal census, Heyward produced 16.7 million pounds of rice on his plantations in 1849, by far the largest amount grown by a single American planter to that date. On his seventeen plantations, he had in 1850 100 working oxen, 600 milch cows, 2,000 other cattle, 1,000 sheep, 1,000 swine, and 80 horses, mules, and asses, further illustrating the size and scale of his operations. When Heyward died, he left an estate worth $1 million in slaves and another million in land, stocks, and bonds.

Heyward's public service began when he represented St. Peter Parish in the Eighth South Carolina General Assembly (1789–1790). He represented the same parish as a delegate at the state constitutional convention in 1790. He was a representative for St. Thomas and St. Dennis parishes in the Seventeenth and Eighteenth South Carolina General Assemblies (1807–1810). He was vice president and president of the South Carolina Association, an organization formed in 1823, in the wake of the abortive Vesey uprising, to combat slave insurrections and enforce race control. In November 1832 Heyward was a delegate at the Nullification Convention, where he signed the Ordinance of Nullification that voided the federal tariff acts of 1828 and 1832. He was also a member and vice president of the Agricultural Society of South Carolina, a militia captain, and a trustee of the Medical College of South Carolina.

Heyward died at his home, the Bluff. He died before any significant crises arose between the North and South and before the Civil War and emancipation, which would have hit him harder than most other southern planters. Heyward's extensive holdings were divided up among the four children who survived him, and these holdings survived as rice producing tracts after emancipation.

• Heyward plantation papers are in the South Carolina Historical Society, Charleston; the South Caroliniana Library of the University of South Carolina, Columbia; and the Southern Historical Collection of the University of North Carolina Library, Chapel Hill. A manuscript biography of Heyward written by his grandson, Gabriel E. Manigault, is in the possession of the Manigault family in Charleston. For a good account of Heyward's rice planting, see Duncan Clinch Heyward, *Seed from Madagascar* (1937). See also Irvine Walker, *History of the Agricultural Society of South Carolina* (1919?). Obituaries are in the Charleston *Courier* and the Charleston *Mercury*, both 13 Apr. 1851.

JAMES M. CLIFTON

HEYWARD, Thomas (28 July 1746–22 Apr. 1809), signer of the Declaration of Independence, was born in Saint Helena Parish, South Carolina, the son of Daniel Heyward, a rice and indigo planter, and Maria Miles. He was known as Thomas Heyward, Jr., because others in his family had the same name.

In 1765 Heyward entered the Middle Temple in London and studied law there until 1770, when he was admitted to the English bar. In a revealing letter to his father written in 1767, Heyward admitted that he found legal studies and the pleasures of London city life equally diverting. He spent time among "the courts at Westminster Hall, the Parliament, my private tutors, my closet and my friends."

On 22 January 1771 Heyward was admitted to the Charleston bar and thereafter divided his energy between a city law practice, rural planting concerns, and civic duties. He established a plantation, which he named "White Hall," on land inherited from his father on the Combahee River in Saint Helena Parish (portions of St. Helena Parish, including White Hall, later became part of Saint Luke Parish). He represented St.

Helena Parish in the South Carolina Commons House of Assembly from 1772 to 1775.

From the beginning Heyward played an active role in South Carolina in the political and military events of the Revolution. He served in the First Provincial Congress of 1775 and the Second Provincial Congress in 1775–1776. Both bodies elected him to the Council of Safety, which supervised defense efforts in South Carolina. Considered a political moderate, he preferred a passive military strategy and apparently hoped for a reconciliation with Britain. As a captain in the Charleston artillery company, he helped defend the city from British warships in late 1775. In the second session of the Second Provincial Congress, which convened on 1 February 1776, Heyward served on a committee of eleven that prepared the state constitution adopted on 26 March.

In early 1776 the Second Provincial Congress chose Heyward as a delegate to the Continental Congress. At Philadelphia Heyward was one of four South Carolinians to sign the Declaration of Independence. He remained in Congress until late 1778, with the exception of a temporary hiatus between November 1777 and June 1778, when he returned to South Carolina to oversee business concerns. In Congress he served on several committees, most notably the Committee for Foreign Affairs, and apparently helped persuade the South Carolina delegation to endorse the Articles of Confederation.

At the conclusion of his tenure in Congress, Heyward returned to South Carolina and resumed his political and military roles. Beginning in 1779 he served as a judge of the Court of General Sessions and Common Pleas. As a jurist Heyward took special interest in legal training and helped initiate educational standards for the state bar. He was elected to the third general assembly, 1779–1780, but he declined the office of lieutenant governor proffered by the assembly. In February 1779 he helped lead a successful attack against the British position on Port Royal Island near Beaufort, and he was wounded in that action. The following year he participated in the defense of Charleston and was captured by the British when the city surrendered on 12 May. The British first paroled Heyward as a prisoner of war, but in August he was among thirty-three leaders who were arrested and exiled to St. Augustine, where he remained until his exchange in July 1781.

Heyward served intermittently in the state legislature from 1782 to 1790, and until 1789 he continued as circuit judge. He supported the federal Constitution and served at the state ratifying convention in 1788. In 1790, after taking part in the state constitutional convention, he retired from an active role in politics.

Heyward devoted the remainder of his life to agricultural innovation. An organizer and the first president of the Agricultural Society of South Carolina, founded in 1785, Heyward was noted for his pioneering experiments in tidal rice irrigation, which utilized estuarial flows to irrigate the crop. This procedure killed most weeds, required fewer slaves for cultivation, and resulted in greater grain yields.

Heyward was married twice, first to Elizabeth Mathewes in 1773; that union lasted nine years and produced five children, none of whom survived him. In 1786 Heyward married Elizabeth Savage, with whom he had three children.

Heyward's exact place of death is unknown, but he was buried in a family cemetery on his father's plantation in Saint Luke Parish. As a jurist and agriculturalist, Heyward made his most lasting contributions to his native state. Owing to the paucity of his surviving correspondence, however, it is difficult to evaluate his political achievements at the state level and as a delegate to the Continental Congress.

• Heyward's experiences in London are briefly traced in George C. Rogers, Jr., *Evolution of a Federalist: William Loughton Smith of Charleston (1758–1812)* (1962). His service in the Continental Congress can be followed in Paul H. Smith, ed., *Letters of Delegates to Congress, 1774–1789* (1976–); vol. 7 contains an engraving of Heyward and a short summary of his tenure in Congress. Edward McCrady, *The History of South Carolina in the Revolution, 1775–1780* (1901), remains a valuable account. For a detailed biographical sketch see Walter B. Edgar and N. Louise Bailey, *Biographical Directory of the South Carolina House of Representatives*, vol. 2 (1977). On Heyward's agricultural interests consult Chalmers S. Murray, *This Is Our Land: The Story of the Agricultural Society of South Carolina* (1949), and Joyce E. Chaplin, *An Anxious Pursuit: Agricultural Innovation and Modernity in the Lower South, 1730–1815* (1993).

GREGORY D. MASSEY

HEYWOOD, Angela Fiducia Tilton (1840–1935), feminist and social reformer, was born in Deerfield, New Hampshire, the daughter of Daniel Tilton and Lucy Locke, farmers. By her own account, Angela's family was impoverished when she was a young girl. Forced to work at the age of ten as a domestic servant, Angela began her long career as a dressmaker, store clerk, farm worker, and innkeeper. But these occupations only comprised half of her public life. While she had little formal education, she read widely and was part of a circle of abolitionists and transcendentalists that included William Lloyd Garrison, Wendell Phillips, Theodore Parker, Ralph Waldo Emerson, and Bronson Alcott. It was in this circle that she met her future husband, Ezra Hervey Heywood, and formed a relationship that would make her a part of the historical record.

Angela and Ezra Heywood were married in Worcester, Massachusetts, in 1865; they would have four children. Their initial interest in labor reform and the abolition of slavery continued when they moved to Princeton, Massachusetts, in 1871. At Princeton, which by the 1870s had become a popular summer resort, they established the "Mountain Home," a large hotel that was the principal source of their income and the center of their reform activities. While year-round guests included reformers such as Stephen Pearl Andrews and Josiah Warren, during the summer months the Heywoods hosted annual conferences where, according to one Princeton neighbor, "long haired men & short haired women discussed various subjects," including dress reform, land reform, labor reform, the abolition of taxes, interest, and rent as well as free thought, women's rights, spiritualism, and free love. Their home in Princeton also housed the Co-operative Publishing Company, which published their newspaper, *The Word*, along with a series of radical pamphlets and books that reflected their reform interests. While they assumed a traditional division of labor—Angela raised their four children and ran the hotel while Ezra penned treatises and edited *The Word*—as Stephen Pearl Andrews observed, they were "far more comrades in a common cause" than husband and wife. Lucien Pinney, another contemporary, seconded this view, noting that "the commotion of thought raised by *The Word* is as much due to her as to anybody." Placing Angela at the center of activity, Pinney described her as "the light, the life, . . . the motive power of the establishment."

Andrews and Pinney were correct in their observations. Angela was instrumental in helping Ezra organize a host of reform organizations that forwarded the causes they championed, including the New England Labor Reform League, the New England Free Love League, the New England Anti-Death League, and the Union Reform League. Angela also played an active role in shaping the tone and perspective of both *The Word* and Ezra Heywood's popular reform tracts, encouraging him to be as concerned with the rights of women as with those of men, and shifting his attention from labor reform to sexual radicalism.

Angela Heywood, however, provided far more than a goading conscience for the reform efforts of her husband. In the many articles she wrote for *The Word* from the mid-1870s until the early 1890s, in the "Leaflet Literature" series she edited, as well as in her public speeches at conferences and conventions, her feminist concerns led to distinctive and fearless attacks on many of the fundamental beliefs and institutions of Victorian society.

In her struggles for women's rights, for example, Heywood argued for greater economic opportunities for women as well as for equal pay for equal work. Like many feminists who came out of the abolitionist movement, Angela also insisted that the marital rights granted to husbands and denied to wives by the church and state transformed women into slaves. Within marriage—an institution based on inequality, compulsion, and force—women lost control of their property, their bodies, and their identities. Unlike most abolitionist feminists, however, who wanted to reshape marriage, Heywood, an ardent free lover, called for its immediate and total destruction.

In addition to the economic system that impoverished women and the marriage system that enslaved them, Heywood attacked the prudery, reticence, and hypocrisy of Victorian culture by openly discussing sexual issues in her writings and in her speeches. Central to this effort was her desire to bring sexuality un-

der the control of conscious thought. Like many nineteenth-century feminists, Heywood identified male sexual desire as the source of many of the wrongs suffered by women. "Man loves woman enough," she wrote in 1876, "but recklessly and selfishly; he should not only feel, but think—consider responsibility, not gratification merely, drawing his heart up through his intellect as a bucket from a well." While many feminists wanted to severely restrict male desire, however, Angela rejected the beliefs of the "Suffering Sisters" who viewed man as a "monster" and argued for the rehabilitation rather than the repression of male sexuality. She further alienated herself from mainstream feminists with her rejection of the ideal of female passionlessness. Heywood insisted that the sexual desires of women were equal in strength to those of men when properly approached. "There are times when woman wants man's fingers to pass through between every two hairs on Mt. Venus," she confided to the readers of *The Word* in 1889.

Heywood not only challenged the conventions of Victorian society; she also expanded the limits of free speech. As a result, she incurred the attention, and the wrath, of Anthony Comstock, the special agent charged with enforcing an 1873 federal law popularly known as the "Comstock Act," which prohibited the sending of "obscene, lewd, or lascivious" material through the mail. Heywood, for example, defended the advertising, sale, and use of vaginal syringes as contraceptives, which were prohibited by the 1873 law. Decrying Comstock's efforts to control women by limiting their access to sexual knowledge, she ardently fought for a woman's "natural right to wash, rinse or wipe out her own vaginal body opening." By visualizing Comstock's self-appointed role as the "inspector and supervisor of American women's wombs," she framed the debate over birth control in the late nineteenth century as a struggle over who would control a woman's right to sexual pleasure as well as her right to reproductive self-control.

Heywood also ran afoul of the Comstock law by using "obscene" words to describe the sexual organs and sexual intercourse. Her goal in taking this stand was not limited to piercing the hypocritical cant of Victorian prudery. She believed that the use of plain language was an important part of her program for the conscious exploration of sexuality because it would transform erotic desire, rendering it the basis for social harmony and individual happiness. When "plain words" bring sexuality "under the jurisdiction of intelligence and good sense," she concluded, "love will be free, honor reign, and calamity cease."

Angela Heywood's ideas and actions gained her great notoriety in the late nineteenth century. While lying in wait to arrest Ezra Heywood in 1877, Comstock was forced to listen to Angela address a meeting of the Free Love League in Boston. In *Traps for the Young* (1883), Comstock described her as lacking any sense of shame as she walked onto the stage and "delivered the foulest address" he had ever heard. He claimed to be so sickened by her "offensive tirade against common decency" that he was forced to flee the noxious atmosphere of the auditorium and rushed to the streets for fresh air. In 1878 the Reverend Joseph Cook, a prominent Boston minister, also singled Heywood out as a "brazen woman" whose "leprous language [filled] with profanity" had worked to corrupt the morals of the community. After Ezra Heywood's death in 1893, however, *The Word* ceased publication, and Angela disappeared from the speaker's platform and historical memory. Although she outlived Ezra by more than four decades, very little is known about her final years.

Angela Heywood's thoughts clearly placed her beyond the pale of respectability in Victorian America. Not only moral conservatives, but many fellow reformers in the feminist and socialist ranks were shocked by her ideas and by her language. Yet these ideas also make her of interest to succeeding generations of Americans. Her concern with free speech, her celebration of women's sexuality, her struggle for reproductive freedom, and her ideas on the connection between language, sexuality, and social change anticipated many of the concerns of modern feminists and cultural radicals. Even more significant, however, because she disregarded the moral and legal restrictions prohibiting the public discussion of sexual issues, Heywood's writings provide important insights into the social and sexual conflicts that shaped the private lives of American women and men in the last half of the nineteenth century.

• Both the originality of Angela Heywood's thought and her unique style of expression are evident in the many articles she wrote for *The Word* from 1872 to 1893, the years of its publication. A few of her personal letters, as well as comments on her life by her daughter Ceres H. Bradshaw can be found in the Labadie Collection of the University of Michigan Library. Ezra Heywood's papers at the John Hay Library of Brown University also contain several interesting but less reliable accounts of Angela Heywood written by her Princeton neighbors. A complete run of *The Word* is available on microfilm from the State Historical Society of Wisconsin. The most colorful and insightful descriptions of Angela Heywood's personality and politics were written by her contemporaries, such as Stephen Pearl Andrews, "Co-operation," *The Word*, Oct. 1883, and Lucien V. Pinney, "The Man and the Woman of Princeton," *The Word*, June 1890. For more recent efforts to explore her ideas and her contributions to the history of reform, see Hal Sears, *The Sex Radicals* (1977), Page Smith, *The Rise of Industrial America* (1984); Alden Whitman, ed., *American Reformers* (1985); Jesse Battan, "'The Word Made Flesh': Language, Authority, and Sexual Desire in Late Nineteenth-Century America," *Journal of the History of Sexuality* 3 (1992): 223–44; and Martin Blatt, *Free Love and Anarchism: The Biography of Ezra Heywood* (1989).

JESSE F. BATTAN

HEYWOOD, Charles (3 Oct. 1839–26 Feb. 1915), ninth commandant of the U.S. Marine Corps, was born in Waterville, Maine, the son of Charles Heywood, a naval officer, and Antonia H. Delgarde. At the age of eighteen, the younger Heywood received a commission as a second lieutenant of marines with date of rank of 5 April 1858. Heywood distinguished himself as a troop leader during the Civil War. After the war, in 1866, with the brevet rank of lieutenant colonel but permanent rank of captain, Heywood married Caroline Bacon. They had no children. In 1873–1874, during the crisis with Spain over the seizure of the American ship *Virginius*, he commanded the marines assigned to fleet maneuvers off the Florida Coast. During the labor unrest of 1877, newly promoted Major Heywood led a marine battalion into Baltimore to maintain public order. In 1885 Heywood headed a marine brigade that deployed to Panama.

Long identified with the marine reform element, Heywood, now a lieutenant colonel, in 1889 took over the Marine Barracks in Washington, D.C. Two years later the secretary of the navy appointed him to be the new colonel commandant of the Marine Corps. Immediately on his assumption of office on 10 February 1891, Heywood pushed a reform agenda, which included expanding the Marine Corps, increasing enlisted morale, carefully defining the marine mission on board ship, further professionalizing the officer corps, and founding a marine "School of Application" for both officers and noncommissioned officers.

From 1891 through 1897 the new marine commandant was able to implement many of his reforms. One of his first actions was the establishment of the School of Application to raise officer standards. In 1892, with the support of the Navy Department, Heywood persuaded Congress to require every marine officer below the rank of commandant to pass both a physical and a professional examination before promotion. At the same time, as a result of other initiatives, he reduced the marine enlisted desertion rate by 20 percent. Finally, in 1896, he obtained from Congress a 500-man increase in the size of the Marine Corps, the first substantial increase since the Civil War.

As part of an attempt to redefine the marine mission, Heywood worked unstintingly to assign his marines to the secondary batteries of the new armored warships then coming into commission, the pride of the "new" navy. He nevertheless encountered resistance from certain naval "progressives," who waged a continuous bureaucratic sub rosa campaign against the marines. These so-called naval "young Turks" believed that the marines belonged to a naval past and were no longer required for modern navies. Their efforts culminated in 1897 with the establishment of a Navy Personnel Board, which considered removing marines from ships and integration of marine officers with those of the navy. Although the board rejected these extreme proposals, the role of marine guards remained a sore point between the marines and the navy reformers throughout the Heywood commandancy.

In 1898 other more pressing matters were to attract the attention of both the navy and the Marine Corps, as the nation prepared for war with Spain. While the wartime role for the Marine Corps remained somewhat vague, in contingency planning as early as 1890, Captain Alfred Mahan, the U.S. Navy theorist, advocated the formation of a marine landing force. While not yet fully articulated into doctrine, other naval planners called for the establishment of advanced bases for the fleet. The only practical force to carry out either mission was the Marine Corps.

At the start of the Spanish-American War, the Navy Department ordered Heywood to organize a marine battalion. Under his personal supervision, the Marine Corps formed a battalion of over 600 men from the marine guards at the various navy yards on the East Coast. Deploying first to Key West, Florida, and then reembarking, the marine battalion seized Guantánamo as an advance base for the American warships blockading Santiago de Cuba. The Guantánamo battalion captured the public imagination and foreshadowed future marine operations.

With the American commitment to overseas colonies in both the Caribbean and in the Pacific as a result of the Spanish-American War, naval strategists emphasized the need for a mobile force to establish advanced bases for the fleet. In October 1900, with marines already assigned to the newly acquired Philippines and to the "Boxer" campaign in China, the navy's General Board recommended the establishment of a marine advanced base force to consist of both fixed defense and mobile elements. The following month Heywood accepted the new mission for the Marine Corps.

While originally looking to the Pacific for the establishment of the Advanced Base Force, the Marine Corps experimented with the concept in the Caribbean and on the Atlantic Coast. Excluding the marine battalion in the Spanish-American War, the first tests occurred in 1901 at Newport, Rhode Island, where the marines formed the nucleus of an advanced base force that participated in the North Atlantic Squadron's summer maneuvers. During the winter maneuvers of 1901–1902, the detachment of approximately 100 men participated in landings and in establishing the defenses on the island of Culebra near Puerto Rico. The following year a regiment of nearly 700 marines landed at Culebra, taking part in the largest U.S. fleet maneuvers up to that time. Although not specifically stated, this demonstration of American naval prowess apparently related directly to the crisis then existing between Venezuela and several European powers, especially Germany.

Throughout the period following the Spanish-American War, Heywood presided over not only an expansion of mission but also an increase of forces. From 1899 through 1903 Congress increased the Marine Corps prewar strength of 75 officers and 2,600 enlisted men to over 270 officers and 7,500 enlisted men. As a result of the new legislation, Heywood received the rank of a major general with the title major general commandant of the Marine Corps. Despite this growth in size and mission, General Heywood insisted on and largely succeeded in maintaining fairly high standards for both officers and enlisted men. While never foregoing the traditional marine missions on board ship, including service at the secondary batteries that remained a bone of contention between marines and their naval counterparts, Heywood both literally and figuratively brought the Marine Corps into the twentieth century. He retired from the Marine Corps in 1903 at the age of 64 and died in Washington.

• Heywood left no personal papers and published no articles or books. Still, several primary sources, both published and unpublished, relate to his official duties: Letters Sent by the Commandant of the Marine Corps to the Secretary of the Navy, Record Group 127, Records of the U.S. Marine Corps, National Archives; Commandant of the Marine Corps, *Annual Reports* (1890–1903); and various congressional published documents for the same period relating to the Marine Corps. Two contemporary compilations also are useful: Richard S. Collum, *History of the United States Marine Corps* (1903), which contains much primary material; and Lewis R. Hamersly, *The Records of Living Officers of the U.S. Navy and Marine Corps*, 4th ed. (1890). The Reference Section, Marine Corps Historical Center, Washington Navy Yard, Washington, D.C., maintains a small biographical file on Heywood. Brief biographical sketches are in Charles Lee Lewis, *Famous American Marines* (1950), and Karl Schuon, *Home of the Commandants*, rev. ed. (1974). Extensive treatment of the Heywood commandancy is in the following secondary works: Robert D. Heinl, *Soldiers of the Sea: The U.S. Marine Corps, 1775–1962* (1962); Allan R. Millett, *"Semper Fidelis," The History of the United States Marine Corps* (1980); and Jack Shulimson, *The Marine Corps' Search for a Mission, 1880–1898* (1993).

JACK SHULIMSON

HEYWOOD, Ezra Hervey (29 Sept. 1829–22 May 1893), social reformer, was born Ezra Hervey Hoar in Westminster, Massachusetts, the son of Ezra Hoar and Dorcas Roper, farmers. In 1848 the family name was changed from Hoar to Heywood. Ezra's parents were devout Baptists and raised him on their family farm in Princeton, Massachusetts.

After studying at Westminster Academy, Heywood left his family and familiar surroundings in 1852 for Providence, Rhode Island, to attend Brown University, receiving his undergraduate degree in 1855 and a master's degree in 1856. He then remained at Brown for two more years while preparing for the ministry.

Interactions with the abolitionist movement in Providence changed the course of Heywood's life. He decided in 1858 to leave the church, describing his decision as a conversion experience: "I 'fell' from well-dressed and full-stomached religion to abolition 'infidelity.'" Heywood moved to Boston and joined the radical Garrisonians, serving as a general agent for the Massachusetts Anti-Slavery Society. In the later years of the Civil War, however, Heywood broke with William Lloyd Garrison because he felt that Garrison had abandoned nonresistance in his support of the North's war effort.

Later Heywood embraced the individualist anarchist philosophy of Josiah Warren, whom he met in 1863. Individualist anarchists placed primary emphasis on economic issues. They believed that a free and unregulated society of autonomous individuals would achieve a natural state of harmony through voluntarism. Heywood organized the New England and

American Labor Reform Leagues in 1869 and 1871, respectively. However, the individualist anarchists never made a substantial impact among American workers because most were not workers themselves.

In 1865 Heywood married Angela Fiducia Tilton; they had four children. Angela was a major influence on Heywood's radicalism, especially concerning women's rights. She argued forcefully for the rights of working women and addressed the economic, social, and political plight of all women.

Heywood moved in 1871 to Princeton, the town where he grew up. Here he published his own newspaper, *The Word*, from 1872 to 1893, and he established his own publishing venture, the Co-Operative Publishing Company. These two projects, along with the many reform leagues that he guided, provided Heywood with the means to express his politics to a national audience.

Heywood initially published booklets focusing on economic issues. Advocacy for women's rights, however, was the arena in which he had the most impact and gained the greatest notoriety as a social reformer. His first major statement on women was a book arguing for woman suffrage titled *Uncivil Liberty* (1870). Six years later, alarmed by the governmental harassment of sex reformers, Heywood wrote *Cupid's Yokes*, in which he denounced marriage as a form of slavery and argued that neither church nor state should have an influence on the relations between men and women. He believed that individuals should determine when, where, how, and why they would use their sexual organs. Heywood directly challenged Anthony Comstock who, with the backing of the Young Men's Christian Association, the New York Society for the Suppression of Vice, and the U.S. Post Office, was waging an unrelenting campaign to enforce a rigid social purity. He branded Comstock a "religious *monomaniac*" who acted with the "spirit that lighted the fires of the Inquisition."

Heywood was a more prolific writer than his wife, because she was often engaged with maintaining the "Mountain Home," a summer resort in Princeton from which they derived much of their income, and tending to the children. His writing style tended to be wordy and scholarly, while hers was much more dramatic. For example, in an article in *The Word* in March 1893 she declared that a man "should have solemn meeting with, and look seriously at, his own penis until he is able to be lord and master of it, rather than it should longer rule, lord and master, of him, and of the victims he deflowers."

On 2 November 1877 Comstock arrested Heywood at a Boston convention of the New England Free Love League. This was the first of five arrests Heywood was to endure at the instigation of Comstock. He was convicted of two counts of obscenity for selling R. T. Trall's *Sexual Physiology* and his own *Cupid's Yokes*, and he served six months in prison before a spirited defense effort won a pardon from President Rutherford B. Hayes.

Comstock arrested Heywood again in 1882 for publishing and selling *Cupid's Yokes* and a sheet called the *Word Extra*, which contained two allegedly obscene poems by Walt Whitman, and for advertising a contraceptive device in *The Word*. The trial judge, however, allowed Heywood to argue the broad issues of the case, and he was acquitted. Two other arrests, in 1883 and 1887, did not lead to convictions.

Heywood's final arrest occurred in May 1890 when he stood trial on three federal counts of obscenity for pieces published in *The Word*. The first count was based on Richard O'Neill's "A Physician's Testimony," a letter that explicitly discussed oro-genital sex. The second count stemmed from an anonymous letter from a mother to her daughter that clearly explained the meaning of the word *fuck*. An article written by Angela Heywood, in which she defended a woman's right to use birth control devices, was the evidence in the third count. Heywood was found guilty and served his full two-year term at Charlestown State Prison. Weakened and ill from his prison experience and worn out from years of persecution and financial hardship, Heywood died in Boston a year after his release from prison.

Free love, for Heywood and many advocates, meant that a woman had the right to deny herself sexually to anyone. The "sexual abuses" issue, which often meant excessive sexual demands by men, was one of the most frequent subjects of correspondence in free-love journals. The true aim of free-love advocates was the end of the institution of marriage and the achievement of social, economic, political, and sexual equality between men and women. Ezra and Angela Heywood were key figures in a small post–Civil War group of Victorian sex radicals who sought to realize the free-love vision.

Heywood was a leader among nineteenth-century American individualist anarchists. His dedication to liberty, free speech, nonviolent struggle, the rights of working people, and women's emancipation inspired many. Emma Goldman, the fiery anarchist agitator, called Heywood one of the trailblazers in the fight for birth control rights in the United States.

• The Labadie collection at the University of Michigan, the largest holding of materials on American anarchism in the United States, has significant archival materials on Heywood, as does the Heywood collection at Brown University. The State Historical Society of Wisconsin, which has an excellent collection of American radicalism materials, has every issue of Heywood's paper, *The Word*. Heywood's major published works are collected in a single volume, *The Collected Works of Ezra H. Heywood*, ed. Martin Blatt (1985). A full-length biography is Blatt, *Free Love and Anarchism: The Biography of Ezra Heywood* (1989). The comprehensive collection of free-love documents, Taylor Stoehr, ed., *Free Love in America: A Documentary History* (1979), is useful. A thorough narrative account of free love in the United States is Hal D. Sears, *The Sex Radicals: Free Love in High Victorian America* (1977). Several works by Paul Avrich provide the best overview of the history of anarchism in the United States; see his *Anarchist Portraits* (1988) and *An American Anarchist: The Life of*

Voltairine deCleyre (1978). Obituaries are in the *Boston Herald*, 23 and 25 May 1893, and the *Providence Journal*, 28 June 1893.

MARTIN HENRY BLATT

H.H. *See* Jackson, Helen Hunt.

HIACOOMES (?–1690), member of the Pokanauket band of the Narragansetts who became a Calvinist minister, lived near Martha's Vineyard in Massachusetts. Little is known about his early life, but he had one son who also became a minister.

In 1641 Thomas Mayhew, Sr., received a grant of land at Nantucket and Martha's Vineyard, and in 1642 a group of Puritans colonized Martha's Vineyard under his proprietorship. Mayhew originally had arrived at Salem in 1630 and had settled in Watertown before moving to Martha's Vineyard. Mayhew's adopted son Thomas worked as a missionary among the tribes around Martha's Vineyard. In 1643 Hiacoomes approached the Mayhews and asked to be instructed in the Puritan form of Calvinism. The elder Mayhew agreed, and under the direction of the younger Mayhew, Hiacoomes learned to read and write English. At the same time he was given religious training within the Puritan church. Afterward, Hiacoomes volunteered to serve as Mayhew's interpreter in his ministry among local tribes. His presence and advice enhanced Mayhew's ability to overcome opposition from non-Christian Indian leaders such as Josias and Wannamanhutt. Eventually, Hiacoomes began preaching on his own and was very successful in converting many of the Gay Head Indians on Martha's Vineyard.

In 1645 a plague swept the region. Because of the younger Mayhew's ability as a physician, however, most of the Christian converts were spared; other Indians believed it was a miracle. This helped overcome the reluctance of several local chiefs and medicine men to embrace the new religion, and by 1651 Hiacoomes and Mayhew were ministering to almost 200 converts spread among two congregations. The preaching of both men was needed to serve the adherents, and under Mayhew's direction Hiacoomes delivered two sermons every Sunday.

Other reasons for the success of their mission was the Mayhews' insistence on respecting the authority of tribal leaders and their equal treatment of the Indians regarding land titles, actions that were ignored by other New England officials. When he first arrived the elder Mayhew, who served as governor of the area, pledged to local Indians that "he would in no measure invade their Jurisdiction," a promise he kept. While the government of the Christian villages was left to Mayhew, the non-Christian Indian leaders administered their own affairs outside the settlements. Likewise Mayhew and Hiacoomes insisted that Native American land rights be respected. Whenever the missionaries requested additional land from the Indians for a Christian Indian settler, the convert was required to pay an annual rent to the local chief. Christian Indians who did not pay their rent had their land reclaimed by non-Christian tribal elders.

As their missionary efforts grew, schools were established for Indians, and in 1670 an Indian church was opened. Although he had been preaching under the younger Mayhew's direction for more than a quarter of a century, Hiacoomes officially was ordained on 22 August 1670 by John Eliot and John Cotton of Plymouth Plantation. He continued to preach until his death.

• Accounts of Hiacoomes's missionary work can be found in Francis Jennings, *The Invasion of America: Indians, Colonialism, and the Cant of Conquest* (1975); Lloyd C. M. Hare, *Thomas Mayhew, Patriarch to the Indians, 1593–1682* (1932); Eleanor Ransom Mayhew, *The Christiantown Story, 1659–1959* (1959); Cotton Mather, *Magnalia Christi Americana* (1702); and Experience Mayhew, *Indian Converts* (1727).

FRED S. STANDLEY

HIAWATHA (fourteenth century), Onondaga warrior and orator, was spokesman for Deganawidah in the campaign for the formation of the League of the Hau-De-No-Sau-Nee, or People of the Longhouse. In the absence of contemporary sources, our current information is based on oral traditions handed down by the elders, some of which were recorded and published only in the late nineteenth century. Oral tradition is transmitted through storytelling, ritual reenactments, and sacred symbols carved on wooden sticks or embroidered on wampum belts. The so-called myths are of historical importance because they reflect the traditional values of the past and are called on to resolve present issues.

According to the original forms of the Deganawidah legend, Hiawatha was an evil-intentioned Onondaga warrior and cannibal whom Deganawidah, a Huron mystic, first met on his arrival at Onondaga (Syracuse, N.Y.) to fulfill his prophetic mission. Deganawidah had arrived miraculously at the south shore of Lake Ontario from the Bay of Quinte in a white stone canoe to institute peace among the warring Iroquoian nations. The second miracle was the conversion of Hiawatha, whom Deganawidah found returning to his lodge with a human victim that he proceeded to make into a stew. In that brew Hiawatha suddenly saw the luminous tranquil face of Deganawidah and fell into deep remorse over his evil deed. Thus Hiawatha became the first convert to the new rule of peace and brotherhood and very soon the chief spokesman for the propagation of the Great Peace.

Deganawidah suffered from a speech impediment, and therefore it was Hiawatha, through his eloquence, who acted as spokesman for the peace mission. He appears to have been adopted by the Mohawks, although the reason for this remains unclear.

The Mohawk, Oneida, Cayuga, and, after some dialogue, the Seneca were persuaded to join together to espouse the Great Peace. The Onondaga held out, largely because of the influence of their aggressive chief, Atotarho. He cast an evil spell on Hiawatha's wife and children. Their deaths undermined Hiawatha's faith so that he abandoned the path of peace for a time. According to one tradition, in his melancholy wanderings Hiawatha discovered the importance of shells or *porcelaine* beads as mnemonic devices that could be incorporated into belts or collars, or *wampum*, as symbols to help recall events and revive promises and agreements. Ultimately the good spirit of peace prevailed, Hiawatha was restored, Atotarho was converted, and the Great Law of Peace was adopted to bind the five nations together in a union symbolized by the planting of the great Tree of Peace at Onondaga.

The Hiawatha story was used by the Five Nations of Iroquois as an explanation of the foundation of their league, its vision of strength in unity and harmony, and its role in extending this concord to other nations. Through events in Hiawatha's life the Five Nations were held to have come to a realization that both cannibalism and witchcraft were antisocial. The various symbols and metaphors that characterized their social and political actions were related to his extraordinary experiences. Ceremonies such as condolence and requickening, which have continued to mark Iroquois practices and beliefs, have been attributed to Hiawatha's experiences in the context of Deganawidah's mission, although there is no conclusive historical evidence to confirm such an association.

The Hiawatha legend fascinated nineteenth-century Euro-Americans. Henry Wadsworth Longfellow wrote a long poem reciting many of the episodes of Hiawatha's fascinating career. In 1907 the Independent Motion Picture Company filmed Longfellow's poem in dramatic fashion. Hiawatha became a cultural hero not only for the Iroquoian peoples but to a degree for all North Americans.

• The most recent scientific work dealing with this aspect of Iroquois history is Matthew Dennis, *Cultivating a Landscape of Peace: Iroquois-European Encounters in Seventeenth-Century America* (1993). Of equal importance is Daniel K. Richter and James H. Merrell, eds., *Beyond the Covenant Chain: The Iroquois and Their Neighbors in Indian North America* (1987), for an understanding of early Iroquois history and the search for regional peace and harmony. There are no biographies of either Hiawatha or Deganawidah, and it was not until the late nineteenth century that a full account of what has come to be known as the Deganawidah epic was published by Horatio Hale, *The Iroquois Book of Rites* (1883). Valuable information about Iroquois social and political organization and beliefs can be found in such early works as C. T. Gehring and W. A. Starna, eds., *A Journey into Mohawk and Oneida Country, 1634–35: The Journal of Harmen Meyndertz van den Bogaert* (1988); Father J. F. Lafitau, *Moeurs des sauvages Amériquains, comparées aux moeurs des premiers temps* (1724); and John Heckwelder, *An Account of the History, Manners, and Customs of the Indian Nations* (1819). Still useful as an overview is Elizabeth Tooker, "The League of the Iroquois: Its History, Politics, and Ritual," in *Handbook of the North American Indians: Northeast*, ed. Bruce G. Trigger (1978).

CORNELIUS J. JAENEN

HIBBEN, John Grier (19 Apr. 1861–16 May 1933), philosopher, educator, and president of Princeton University, was born in Peoria, Illinois, the son of the Reverend Samuel Hibben and Elizabeth Grier. Born in the first year of the Civil War, Hibben was a year old when his father, a volunteer chaplain, died in a Union army camp. Brought up alone by a mother who worked hard to educate her only child, he graduated in 1882 from Princeton University as both valedictorian and class president. He studied at the University of Berlin for a year and then at the Princeton Theological Seminary; he was ordained in 1887. In that same year, he married Jenny Davidson of Elizabeth, New Jersey; they had one daughter. They moved to Chambersburg, Pennsylvania, where he served the congregation of Falling Spring Presbyterian Church as minister.

Hibben gave up the ministry after only four years, apparently as the result of a throat malady, and returned to Princeton as instructor of logic in 1891. He received the Ph.D. in 1893 and rose through the academic hierarchy, becoming assistant professor of logic in 1894, professor of logic in 1897, and Stuart Professor of Logic in 1907. During this period, he wrote *Inductive Logic* (1896), *The Problems of Philosophy* (1898), *Hegel's Logic* (1902), *Logic, Deductive and Inductive* (1905), *The Philosophy of the Enlightenment* (1909), and *A Defense of Prejudice and Other Essays* (1911). He also edited a twelve-volume work, *Epochs of Philosophy*, that included essays by American and British authors. In 1912 Hibben became president of Princeton, succeeding Woodrow Wilson who had resigned in 1910 to run for governor of New Jersey.

Hibben took control of a university split by internal politics. In 1905 he had agreed with his predecessor's introduction of the preceptorial system, an arrangement in which lecture classes were supplemented by small discussion groups. But he, along with a bitterly vocal faction of the faculty, disagreed with Wilson's proposal to reorganize the campus into quadrangles, a plan that would have eliminated both dormitory-style living and the eating clubs that defined student social life. Nevertheless, the trustees appointed Hibben, who was well liked and had a reputation for fairness.

A fervent patriot and internationalist, which was reflected in his work, *The Higher Patriotism* (1915), Hibben called for American preparedness and early intervention in World War I. During the war he invited military training schools on campus and volunteered university resources for the war effort. He belonged to the advisory board of the American Defense Society and the advisory commissions of the National Security League and the United States Junior Naval Reserve, and was a member of the executive committee of the League to Enforce Peace. After the armistice Hibben continued to be active in the nonpartisan work of the League of Nations. His attitude toward public service was based upon his strong belief in duty, loyalty, honor, self-control, service, and sacrifice.

During his presidency Hibben spearheaded Princeton's development in almost every area of undergraduate and graduate life. Immediately after the end of the war, he expanded the preceptorial system to include sophomores. In 1923 he introduced the Upperclass Plan of Study, emphasizing independent work for juniors and seniors through a senior thesis and comprehensive examinations. In addition, to encourage student life on campus, Hibben oversaw the construction of eight new dormitories and a student center, took steps to regulate the eating clubs, and appointed a Council on Undergraduate Life. Thirty-one new college buildings were constructed during his presidency, including the Graduate College (1913), Palmer Memorial Stadium (1914), the University Chapel (1928), and Fine Hall of Mathematics (1931). He also provided for increases in professors' salaries and gave faculty members a greater voice in university matters.

Working with research-oriented professors, Hibben oversaw the founding of the School of Architecture (1919), the Department of Oriental Languages (1922), the School of Engineering (1921), and, in 1930, the School of Public and International Affairs (later named for Woodrow Wilson). In 1925 he announced a $20 million endowment campaign that evolved into a full-scale commitment to create a prestigious modern program in the sciences. A million-dollar grant from the General Education Board, matched by gifts from alumni, led in 1928 to the investment of $3 million in research and graduate education in the sciences and mathematics.

By the time Hibben retired in 1932, the university's endowment had increased by almost 400 percent, the faculty by 75 percent, and the student body from 1,200 to 2,200. Under his leadership, Princeton University had emerged as an internationally renowned research university.

After his retirement in 1932, Hibben continued to be active in university affairs. On a rainy spring day in May 1933, driving the car the trustees had given him as a retirement gift, he was killed in an automobile accident; a month later, Mrs. Hibben died of the injuries she sustained in the same accident. They are buried next to one another in "Presidents' Row" in Princeton Cemetery.

• Hibben's papers are in the Seelye G. Mudd Manuscript Library at Princeton University. Other relevant material in the archives includes *Reports of the President* as well as trustee and faculty minutes, which are available for restricted use. The *Princeton Alumni Weekly* and the *Princetonian* provide a wealth of information about Princeton during Hibben's years there. Alexander Leitch, *A Princeton Companion* (1978), offers a vital compendium of university history for this period. An obituary is in the *New York Times*, 17 May 1933.

LAURA SMITH PORTER

HIBBEN, Paxton Pattison (5 Dec. 1880–5 Dec. 1928), journalist, was born in Indianapolis, Indiana, the son of Thomas Entriken Hibben and Jeannie Merrill Ketcham, dry goods wholesalers. He earned a bachelor's degree at Princeton University in 1903 and a master's at Harvard the following year. He studied law for a year at Harvard and was admitted to the Indiana bar in 1906 but never practiced law. Instead, after short-

term newspaper jobs in Philadelphia and Indianapolis, he entered the diplomatic service and was appointed third secretary of the U.S. embassy in St. Petersburg, Russia. There he devoted himself to aiding Japanese troops captured in Russia's war against Japan and won decorations from both countries. He also witnessed the first phases of the unsuccessful Russian Revolution of 1905.

For a half dozen years thereafter, Hibben followed an upward career path in the Department of State. Promoted to the rank of second secretary in 1906, he was transferred to the embassy in Mexico City. In mid-1908 he was named secretary of the legation in Bogota, Colombia, and two years later was appointed to the same post in the Netherlands, meanwhile serving as secretary on behalf of the United States at the International Court of Permanent Arbitration at The Hague. After one more transfer—to the embassy in Chile—he resigned in 1912 and returned to the United States to work in the third-party Progressive presidential campaign of Theodore Roosevelt. Two years later, at the urging of Indiana senator Albert J. Beveridge, he ran as a Progressive for Congress in an Indiana district. He lost.

After the election Hibben, transforming himself into a war correspondent, rushed to Europe, where World War I had begun. With credentials from *Collier's Weekly*, he reported from Germany. Then the Associated Press hired him as a staff correspondent and assigned him to cover fighting in northern Greece involving Allied forces against the Austrians and Bulgarians. While in Greece in 1916, he married Cecile Craik of Montgomery, Alabama; they had one daughter. Hibben warmed to the efforts of King Constantine I of Greece to maintain his country's neutrality against Allied pressure to enter the war, and in 1917 the Century Company published his book *Constantine I and the Greek People*, which was recalled after publication and suppressed until 1920. At the same time his stories were suppressed by censors, and ultimately he was recalled by the AP.

Shortly before the United States entered the war in April 1917, Hibben returned home and volunteered for army service. He was commissioned a first lieutenant in November 1917, was assigned to a field artillery unit in France, and was promoted to captain. After the armistice, he filled several desk jobs. Working in the office of the inspector general, he aided in an exposé of financial misfeasance among the welfare societies that had offered behind-the-lines services to the U.S. forces during the war.

Discharged on 21 August 1919, Hibben joined an American military mission to Russian Armenia, then torn by fighting between Bolsheviks and anti-Bolsheviks. When the mission ended in 1920, Hibben wrote numerous magazine articles calling attention to the plight of the Armenians and the next year returned to the area as secretary of the Russian branch of Near East Relief. Here again he exposed inefficiency in a report that was submitted to a Senate investigating committee and subsequently suppressed. However, his findings were ultimately published as the pamphlet *An American Report on the Russian Famine* by the *Nation*. The major focus of his concern by this time had become the hunger in Russia. He became secretary for the Russian Red Cross in America, organized a committee for the relief of Russian children, and wrote a brief book, *The Famine in Russia* (1922).

Given American hostility to the Soviet Union—the United States refused for sixteen years to recognize the Communist government—his relief activities placed Hibben under suspicion. Moreover, he went beyond advocating relief and made the unpopular argument that the Soviet Union should be rehabilitated in the interest of the world's economic stability. Early in 1923 the National Republican Club barred him from giving a scheduled address. Later, John Dos Passos recounted the story that inebriated classmates at his twentieth-anniversary Princeton reunion set about, half-seriously, to lynch him.

In 1923 the army set in motion an investigation to decide whether Hibben's reserve commission, which he had held since 1920, should be revoked. Hibben requested a court of inquiry to clear his name; the issue, it soon became clear, was less the assortment of vague charges than a test of Hibben's right, as a reserve officer, to voice views on Russia contrary to official policy. The army appeared embarrassed by the vigor of Hibben's defense and the support he received. The result was a standoff: the charges were neither upheld nor dismissed, but no official action was taken against Hibben.

In 1927 Hibben stimulated a different kind of controversy with publication of his *Henry Ward Beecher: An American Portrait*, an exposé of the famed clergyman as a fraud and hypocrite. He finished twenty-one chapters of a similar biography of William Jennings Bryan before he died in New York City on his forty-eighth birthday of pneumonia that developed from influenza. The Bryan biography, completed by his friend C. Hartley Grattan was issued in 1929 under the title *The Peerless Leader*.

Hibben was well characterized in the title—"A Hoosier Quixote"—of the tribute by Dos Passos that appeared in the *New Republic* (27 Jan. 1932, pp. 294–96) and was later incorporated in the novelist's trilogy *U.S.A.* Hibben spent his brief career taking up difficult, even impossible, causes and defending them against the tide of popular opinion. Suzanne La Follette, appraising his growing radicalism after the war, wrote, "Perhaps the most significant thing about his public career lies in the fact that he had the strength to break the social mold which cramps the spirit of most Americans of his class, and to emerge into a triumphant individualism which many of his compatriots, no doubt, never understood, but which they were nevertheless forced to respect" (La Follette, p. 711).

• Sources on Hibben's life are scattered. The Princeton class of 1903's *Twenty-Year Record* (1923) contains his brief "Autobiography of a Rolling Stone." Besides the John Dos Passos sketch in *Nineteen Nineteen* (1933), the second volume of the *U.S.A.* trilogy, Anna Strunsky Walling in *Labor Age*, Jan. 1928, p. 29; Suzanne La Follette in the *Nation*, 26 Dec. 1928, pp. 711–12; and Oswald Garrison Villard in *World Tomorrow*, Mar. 1929, pp. 119–20, wrote memorial tributes. An obituary is in the *New York Times*, 6 Dec. 1928.

JAMES BOYLAN

HIBBINS, Ann (?–19 June 1656), was an early and unusually prominent victim of witchcraft persecution in colonial New England. Her place of birth, parents, and maiden name are unknown. She came to New England in the 1630s during the Puritan Great Migration and settled with her husband, William Hibbins, in Boston. (It is not known if the couple had children.) William quickly grew to prominence as a merchant and political figure. He was elected as a deputy to the lower house of the Massachusetts General Court in 1641–1642 and in 1643 rose as an assistant to the upper house, where he remained until his death. During this time William Hibbins also served as the colony's agent in England. His rapid advancement in affairs of state was matched by the family's quick acceptance into the religious community. In 1639 Hibbins and her husband were together admitted to the Boston church, presumably by demonstrating their abilities to make orthodox confessions of faith and relate convincing descriptions of the work of God's grace on their souls.

Despite these illustrious beginnings, Hibbins's security within this newfound community quickly began to dissipate, and she gained a reputation for contentious behavior that would haunt her years in New England. The early Massachusetts economy, geared to satisfy the needs of a booming immigrant population, was extremely turbulent. Imported commodities and skilled labor were in great demand and consequently fetched higher prices than they had in England. In 1640 Hibbins became embroiled in controversy over just these issues when she accused a carpenter of overcharging her for work done on her house. At her husband's request, an independent expert and fellow church member was called in to settle the matter. When he confirmed the original carpenter's price, Hibbins refused to accept his judgment and accused him of conspiring against her, cursing him and calling him a liar. Since both Hibbins and "Brother Davis" (the expert) were church members, the matter was taken up by the Boston church.

After a lengthy inquiry, during which William Hibbins unsuccessfully encouraged his wife to see her error and mend her ways, the church voted to excommunicate her. A transcription of her church trial survives and reveals several interesting facts about her case, especially in light of the Boston church's 1638 excommunication of Anne Hutchinson for her heretical antinomian beliefs. Like Hutchinson, Hibbins was accused of acting in ways unbecoming to a woman, "in usurping authority over him whom God hath made her head and husband, and in taking the power and authority which God hath given to him out of his hands." Surprisingly enough, this accusation was made by "Sergeant Savidge," a Boston merchant who had been censured and disarmed by the colony two years earlier for his support of Hutchinson. But where great pains were taken to convince Hutchinson of the error of her beliefs in the hope of restoring her to the church, Hibbins was excommunicated quickly. Governor John Winthrop (1588–1649), also a Boston church member, rejected the need for further admonitions in Hibbins's case because of the nature of her sins and the obstinacy of her response: "If it had been [a] matter of opinion or error, then a second admonition might have followed the former; but this is a matter of fact which is plain and manifest to every eye" (Demos [1972], p. 233). Heretical opinions were slippery and required careful handling, but obstinately sinful behavior could be easily identified and dispatched. Hibbins was expelled from the religious community without further ado, and her reputation as a contentious and unruly woman was fixed.

Nothing is known of Hibbins's life from her excommunication in 1640 until the death of her husband in 1654. From his behavior during the church proceedings one might guess that William Hibbins served as a buffer between his wife and the world and that his prominent position in the community protected her from further conflicts with neighbors. Although he may have suffered occasional substantial losses in his mercantile business during the 1640s, such losses were common in the turbulent colonial economy, and by the time of his death the estate Ann Hibbins inherited was quite considerable. This inheritance, combined with her reputation as a difficult, argumentative woman, may well have been the cause of her downfall.

In 1655 Hibbins was accused of witchcraft and convicted by a jury, but the upper house of the General Court, on which her husband had so recently sat, refused to accept the verdict and its attendant death sentence. The case was then retried before the entire General Court, and although the upper house continued to oppose her prosecutors, they were outvoted by the deputies in the lower house. Hibbins was convicted and sentenced to hang. Among those who were acquainted with the victim and her late husband, the verdict was regarded as a travesty. John Norton, then minister of the Boston church, explained that she was "hanged for a witch, only for having more wit than her neighbors, . . . she having . . . unhappily guessed that two of her persecutors, whom she saw talking in the street, were talking of her" (Hutchinson, pp. 187–88).

The fact that Hibbins *had* persecutors among her neighbors can perhaps be blamed on her reputation for contentious behavior after the 1640 excommunication case. But the charge of witchcraft gained popular support and legal prosecution only after her husband's death and her inheritance of his fortune. These events point to the anomalous place of women who possessed power and property in a society that expected them to be under men's control. While her husband lived, Ann Hibbins's "strange carriage" may have annoyed her neighbors, but after he died, her potential economic and social power made her "turbulent passions" seem a threat to community order. Consequently, the vox populi denounced and destroyed her.

• An abridged transcript of Hibbins's excommunication proceedings is printed in John Demos, ed., *Remarkable Providences, 1600–1760* (1972); the original is found in Robert Keayne, *Notes on John Cotton's Sermons,* manuscript in the Massachusetts Historical Society, Boston. The few surviving documents and near-contemporary references to Hibbins's witchcraft prosecution can be found in *Records of the Governor and Company of Massachusetts Bay,* vol. 4, part 1 (1854), p. 269; *New England Historic and Genealogical Register* 5 (1852): 283; William Hubbard, *A General History of New England,* 2d ed. (1848), p. 574; and Thomas Hutchinson, *History of the Colony and Province of Massachusetts Bay,* vol. 1 (1764), pp. 187–88. Several of these are reprinted in David D. Hall, ed., *Witch-Hunting in Seventeenth-Century New England: A Documentary History, 1638–1692* (1991), pp. 89–91. The best modern treatments of Hibbins's life are Demos, *Entertaining Satan: Witchcraft and the Culture of Early New England* (1982), pp. 87–88, and Carol Karlsen, *The Devil in the Shape of a Woman: Witchcraft in Colonial New England* (1987), pp. 1–5, 150–52, where the argument for the relationship between Hibbins's economic status and her personal character is most fully laid out.

MARK A. PETERSON

HIBBS, Ben (23 July 1901–29 Mar. 1975), magazine editor, was born Benjamin Smith Hibbs in Fontana, Kansas, the son of Russell Hibbs, an accountant and manager of a lumber company, and Elizabeth Smith, a math teacher. Hibbs had a happy childhood and carried rural values with him years later when he edited the *Saturday Evening Post.* Hibbs worked for his father's lumber business in Pretty Prairie to earn money sufficient to enter the University of Kansas in 1919. He graduated as a member of Phi Beta Kappa in February 1924. He reported for several papers in Colorado and Kansas and taught English and journalism for two years at Fort Hays State College (Kans.), then returned to journalism. As managing editor of the *Arkansas City Daily Traveler,* his fresh writing drew the notice of the larger *Kansas City Star,* which labeled him "the most quoted young squirt in Kansas." The notoriety brought an offer in 1929 from the major publisher Curtis Publishing to become associate editor of the *Country Gentleman,* a rural interest magazine. Hibbs moved to Philadelphia. He married Edith Kathleen Doty, a teacher, in 1930. They had one child. Hibbs traveled widely, writing general interest and agricultural stories. He was named fiction editor in 1934 and advanced to editor in chief in 1940.

The *Saturday Evening Post,* a sister Curtis magazine and the most widely read periodical in the country, asked Hibbs in 1942 to replace editor Wesley Winans Stout. Stout had resigned in a furor over a series of articles widely considered anti-Semitic.

Curtis expected that Hibbs would not only calm the storm but, as he had with *Gentleman,* make graphic changes and enliven the prose to turn around a *Post* circulation and revenue plunge. The *Post*'s advertising income had reached $52 million in 1929 under the editorship of George Horace Lorimer but stagnated under Lorimer's successor, Stout. Revenues—despite gradually increasing circulation to 3.3 million copies in 1942—stood at about $24 million when Hibbs arrived.

Hibbs faced a temporarily hostile staff, some of whom had hoped for his position. With Robert Fuoss as managing editor, Hibbs changed the magazine's typography. "Post" was emphasized in the new cover logo. Broadened editorial focus meant fewer business stories, more family emphasis, personality profiles, and sports stories. Hibbs refocused long-standing *Post* fixtures. He asked the illustrator Norman Rockwell to begin the patriotic "Willie Gillis" cover series, which depicted a typical American GI. Rockwell's "Four Freedoms," realistic depictions of the security of life in America, went on national tour to raise war funds for the country.

"Despite the fact that the war was already flaming on many fronts throughout the world," Hibbs said in *A Short History of the Saturday Evening Post* (1949), "I found we had only one foreign correspondent—and he was in New York." The magazine quickly organized a solid staff of war correspondents, including Edgar Snow, Demaree Bess, Ernest Hauser, and Samuel Lubell. It was recognized with the University of Pennsylvania's 1947 annual Award for Meritorious Achievement in Journalism for its war coverage.

Fiction remained a staple for the *Post*'s loyal readers. "We did without Tugboat Annie for seven years and the complaints never let up," Hibbs observed. But complementing the gruff skipper and William Hazlett Upson's Alexander Botts, bulldozer salesman, were nonfiction articles intended to attract new readers. Hibbs paid a hefty $175,000 to Captain Harry C. Butcher, the general's aide, for "My Three Years with Eisenhower" and $125,000 for the memoirs of Casey Stengel. Pete Martin authored a well-read series of personality profiles. An ambitious "Adventures of the Mind" presentation of scholarly, thoughtful articles proved a big success; Hibbs refused to underestimate his readers' intelligence.

Business Week (28 Sept. 1946) reported the *Post* ranked number one nationally in advertising pages: "Under Hibbs' direction it became more sensitive to current thinking, shortened its articles and stories so that more varied subjects could be included, added to and pepped up cartoons, and reached out for women readers and younger readers of both sexes." Advertising revenues grew back to the $50 million level in the late 1940s. Circulation was more than 4 million in 1949.

"We're conservative, but I don't think blindly so," the *Post*'s $74,519-a-year editor said (*Newsweek*, 26 May 1947). The *Post* had gone through some uncomfortable years during Franklin D. Roosevelt's presidency; Lorimer despised New Deal politics and fought Roosevelt editorially and in articles. Conservative Hibbs and the *Post* were more comfortable in the less tumultuous Dwight D. Eisenhower years.

Hibbs offered "Some Thoughts on Magazine Editing" at the tenth annual William Allen White Memorial Lecture at the University of Kansas in 1959. He said that the development of color printing, changing tastes in reading matter, competition, and challenges by television and radio made editing and publishing far more complex than in previous decades. Hibbs told *Newsweek* (23 Feb. 1959), "If a magazine is to be vital, I think it must deal with dangerous material—material which may bring subscription cancellations or even involve troublesome and expensive lawsuits." The remark refers more to independence from a magazine's advertising department than to brash investigative reporting. Despite changes in appearance, the editor from Kansas held strongly to the *Post*'s well-established, conservative values.

Despite solid revenue figures, "there was something hollow about Ben Hibbs's rural, familial, conservative *Post*," in the view of journalism historian Otto Friedrich. "By 1960, in the era of Jack Kennedy, Fidel Castro, the civil rights struggle, and rock 'n' roll, the viewpoint of Ben Hibbs began to appear somehow irrelevant."

The magazine was healthy, and its circulation neared 7 million in 1962, but Curtis fortunes had diminished, and executives dictated changes in the *Post*. Hibbs decided to leave. A *Post* editorial (23 Dec. 1961) remarked, "Ben Hibbs has been a great editor. . . . His editorial judgment and sense of fair play have been lauded by countless commissions, movements, foundations and institutions of learning—and by our ever-growing audience." The magazine itself ceased publishing in 1969, then in 1971 it was revived as a monthly.

Hibbs became senior editor for *Reader's Digest* in 1962, remaining until 1971. He also returned to writing. He died at his home in Narberth, Pennsylvania. The *Saturday Evening Post*, an American publishing icon in Lorimer's hands, solidified its old-fashioned values under the skillful editorial hand of Hibbs.

• Hibbs's papers are in the Spencer Research Library archives at the University of Kansas. See also Deryl R. Leaming, "A Biography of Ben Hibbs" (Ph.D. diss., Syracuse Univ., 1969). *Newsweek* discusses Hibbs's appointment in "Post Shake-Up," 23 Mar. 1942, pp. 60–61. *Time* surveys his achievements in "Shiny New Post," 26 May 1947, pp. 71–72. *Business Week*'s "Hibbs and the Satevepost: A Happy 10-year Marriage" appeared 15 Mar. 1952, pp. 66–82. *Post* history is covered in *A Short History of the "Saturday Evening Post"* (1949), Theodore Peterson, *Magazines in the Twentieth Century* (1964), John Tebbel, *The American Magazine: A Compact History* (1969), and Otto Friedrich, *Decline and Fall: The Death Struggle of the "Saturday Evening Post"* (1970). An obituary is in the *New York Times*, 30 Mar. 1975.

BERNARD A. DREW

HICHBORN, Philip (4 Mar. 1839–1 May 1910), naval officer and shipwright, was born in Charlestown, Massachusetts, the son of Philip Hichborn and Martha Gould. After he graduated from high school in 1855, Hichborn took work as a shipwright apprentice at the U.S. Navy's shipyard at Charlestown. His reputation for excellent craftsmanship won him recognition from the navy in the form of special instruction in naval construction. After brief employment as a ship's carpenter aboard the clipper ship *Dashing Wave*, Hichborn again took employment with the U.S. Navy, this time in the navy yard at Mare Island, California. Again, the superior quality of his workmanship attracted favorable attention, and after promotion through several civilian positions, on 26 June 1869 he was appointed assistant naval constructor with a commission in the U.S. Navy. In 1870 the navy transferred Hichborn to its navy yard at Portsmouth, New Hampshire.

In 1875 Hichborn finished in first place on a competitive examination, and on 12 March he was commissioned as a naval constructor. That same year the navy reassigned him to the League Island Navy Yard near Philadelphia. Also in 1875 he married Jennie M. Franklin. The couple had two children. In 1883 Hichborn became a member of the navy's board of Inspection and Survey. The next year he was sent on an extended trip to Europe to visit and report on European naval designs, construction methods, and fabrication techniques. In October 1884 he made his report, which was about 100 pages in length. Filled with charts and innovative designs, *Report on European Dock-Yards* was published in 1886 and used by the navy as a textbook.

In November 1884 Hichborn was transferred to Washington, D.C., in another promotion, becoming the assistant to the U.S. Navy's chief of the Bureau of Construction and Repair. While he was in this position, the navy produced a number of modern, steam-powered cruisers and battleships, all-metal warships with gun turrets and substantial armor that were a dramatic departure from the age of wooden sailing warships. On 7 September 1893 he was elevated to bureau chief, thus becoming the U.S. Navy's senior constructor with the rank of commodore. Subsequently, Hichborn was promoted to rear admiral. The U.S. Navy's stunning performance against the Spanish fleet in 1898 owed much to the superior designs that Hichborn had advocated and brought to fruition. In 1900 he published *Standard Designs for Boats of the United States Navy*, and he held the position of chief of the Bureau of Construction and Repair until he retired in Washington, D.C., on 4 March 1901.

Hichborn remained active in naval design and construction in his retirement. The navy often called on him for advice and consultation in its progressive modernization efforts. From the 1880s on, the United States offered a friendly but nonetheless serious challenge to Britain's Royal Navy for first place among the globe's naval forces. The acquisition of an overseas, colonial empire during the Spanish-American War and the elevation of former assistant secretary of the navy Theodore Roosevelt to the presidency prompted the pumping of more and more funds into U.S. warship construction. Hichborn's wide naval engineering knowledge and his lengthy experience was a national asset, particularly because the decade following his retirement was the height of the great European battleship and dreadnought construction race. He belonged to several patriotic societies and readily offered his services to the navy, even though younger men had taken over his previous duties.

Hichborn was a key figure in America's rise to become the world's superior naval power. Even though he did not live to see the U.S. Navy overtake the Royal Navy, he did see many of his innovations and ideas put into service. Perhaps the most familiar Hichborn invention was the common Franklin life buoy. But his most notable contribution was a solution to a serious problem in the early designs of gun turrets, which, being heavy, caused the ship to roll when they were rotated to one side or the other. This effect not only cost the crew excessive time in training the guns on a target, it caused another roll when the guns were fired and went into and out of recoil. Hichborn's solution was a smoothly balanced turret that always poised the turret's center of gravity, no matter what the gun orientation or whether it was in firing position or recoil position, directly over the ship's keel. Internationally, the turret was known as the Hichborn balanced turret, a fitting tribute to a man who had risen from laborer to a world-class chief of naval construction. He died in Washington, D.C.

• A family history of Hichborn's maternal heritage is in B. A. Gould, *The Family of Zaccheus Gould of Topsfield* (1895). Much of Hichborn's career is traced in L. R. Hamersly, *The Records of Living Officers of the U.S. Navy and Marine Corps*, 5th ed. (1894). Obituaries are in the *Army and Navy Journal*, 7 May 1910); and the *Washington Post*, the *Washington Evening Star*, and the *New York Times*, all 2 May 1910.

ROD PASCHALL

HICKENLOOPER, Bourke B. (21 July 1896–4 Sept. 1971), lawyer and politician, was born in Blockton, Iowa, the son of Nathan C. Hickenlooper and Margaret Blackmore, farmers. On completing high school in 1914, he enrolled at Iowa State College (now Iowa State University), Ames, but following American intervention in the European war, he enlisted in the U.S. Army's Officer Training Camp at Fort Snelling, Minnesota. Commissioned a second lieutenant, he was assigned to the Third Battalion, 339th Field Artillery, serving in Europe from August 1918 to February 1919. Following his return to Iowa, he resumed his studies at Iowa State, earning a B.S. degree in industrial science in 1920. The next year he enrolled in the College of Law at the State University of Iowa (now the University of Iowa in Iowa City), where he earned a J.D. degree in 1922. He then moved to Cedar Rapids, where he was a member of the firm Johnson, Donnelly and Lynch in 1925. He then proceeded to solo practice until 1937, at which time he joined with M. F. Mitvalsky to form the partnership of Hickenlooper & Mitvalsky, where he continued his practice intermittently even after entering politics. In 1927 Hickenlooper married Verna E. Bensch, with whom he had two children.

After his first run for public office ended in defeat, he came to believe that voters simply could not relate to a name so cumbersome as Hickenlooper. He then decided, with pride, to tell the voters to think of him simply as "Hick," a ploy that worked remarkably well in rural Iowa. During the next three decades Hick became the winningest Republican in Iowa history as he won successive elections often by whopping majorities. He was elected to a seat in the Iowa General Assembly (1934–1937), the office of lieutenant governor (1939–1942), governor (1943–1944), and the U.S. Senate (1944–1969). He was not a candidate for reelection in 1968. Although Hickenlooper's somewhat dour persona lacked political charisma, he quickly learned how to use the state's media—newspapers, radio, later television—and to work with political columnists and editors in communicating his views to the voters. His conservatism, which emphasized strong national security, resistance to big and powerful federal bureaucracy, and fiscal responsibility with minimal taxation, appealed to the Iowa electorate.

As governor, Hickenlooper is probably best remembered for his leadership at the Republican Conference at Mackinac, Michigan, in the summer of 1943. It was at this crucial meeting that Republicans steered the party away from its posture of political isolationism and toward support of U.S. membership in a postwar international organization. Hickenlooper was instrumental in persuading many midwestern Republican leaders to abandon the party's isolationist values.

Throughout Hickenlooper's long service in the Senate, his name was attached to only a few statutes, notably, the Atomic Energy Act of 1954 and the Hickenlooper Amendment to the Foreign Aid Act of 1963, which was intended to curtail U.S. aid to foreign countries that expropriated the property of U.S. companies without providing compensation. He did, however, exercise remarkable influence on government policies. As a member of the Joint Committee on Atomic Energy, he was an early advocate of civilian rather than military control of the Atomic Energy Commission, and he favored conferring on the federal government exclusive rights to nuclear patents. Through his leadership on the Senate's Foreign Relations Committee, he led fellow Republicans in providing bipartisan support for much of President Harry S. Truman's foreign policy initiatives, including the Truman Doctrine committing U.S. military and economic assistance to Greece and Turkey; the Marshall Plan and its European Recovery Program; and U.S. participation in the North Atlantic Treaty Organization. In 1951 he was appointed to the U.S. delegation that formally negotiated the end to the Asian-Pacific War with the Japanese Empire. Later, in the 1960s, as one of the sponsors of the Gulf of Tonkin Resolution, he became a steadfast defender of U.S. military involvement in Vietnam.

Hickenlooper's terms in the U.S. Senate paralleled the years of the Cold War, and his views and general outlook coincided with the conservatism associated with midwestern republicanism. He was forever railing against the threat posed to the United States, and the rest of the free world, by a monolithic Communist conspiracy centered in Russia. He was concerned about internal subversion undermining American institutions. He opposed increasing the powers of the federal government in Washington. And he sought to strengthen the armed forces of the United States as the best means for maintaining national security. Hickenlooper expressed strong reservations about the effectiveness of President Truman's loyalty program. He was a sharp critic of Secretary of State Dean Acheson. During the Truman-MacArthur controversy in the early 1950s, he sided with the general.

Hickenlooper opposed allowing U.S. trade to flow to Communist countries, extending his opposition to countries that traded with Fidel Castro's Cuba after 1958. Hickenlooper served on Senator Joseph McCarthy's ad hoc subcommittee that investigated charges of Communist infiltration in the U.S. State Department. He believed that McCarthy and McCarthyism provided a useful service to the nation, but Hickenlooper opposed McCarthy's political style and his methods. He voted against censure of McCarthy.

Hickenlooper was a member of the Free and Accepted Masons, the American Legion, the Independent Order of Odd Fellows, the Benevolent and Protective Order of Elks, and the Loyal Order of Moose. He died at Shelter Island, New York, and was buried in Cedar Rapids, Iowa.

• Hickenlooper's papers are in the Herbert Hoover Presidential Library, West Branch, Iowa. See also Edward L. Schapsmeier and Frederick H. Schapsmeier, "A Strong Voice for Keeping America Strong: A Profile of Senator Hickenlooper," *Annals of Iowa*, ser. 3 (1984): 362–76. Obituaries are in the *Chicago Tribune* and the *New York Times*, 9 May 1971.

LAWRENCE E. GELFAND

HICKEY, Edgar Sylvester (20 Dec. 1902–5 Dec. 1980), college basketball coach, was born on a farm near Reynolds in Thayer County, Nebraska, the son of Christopher Hickey, a real estate broker, and Fern (maiden name unknown). He played four sports in high school and captained the football, basketball, and baseball teams. At Creighton University in Omaha, he played two years of basketball and four years of varsity football before graduating cum laude with a law degree in 1926. In 1924 Hickey had married Hariette Pinkerton of Omaha. They had two sons.

Hickey intended to move to Denver to start a law practice allied with his father's real estate business, but just before he graduated his father was killed in an automobile accident. Hickey therefore remained in Omaha, joined a law firm, and simultaneously agreed to coach at Creighton Prep High School. Having coached there while in college, he was now appointed director of athletics and head coach of the baseball and football teams. He added basketball a year later.

Hickey worked out an arrangement to spend mornings and evenings at the law offices of John A. McKenzie and afternoons at the athletic facilities that Creighton Prep shared with the university. For several years he balanced both careers, but coaching took precedence after he took a summer course to earn a Nebraska teaching certificate. "Finally I had to make a choice between law and coaching," he recalled. "The Depression was on, and getting started in law figured to be tough, so I picked coaching" (*Creighton Prep Alumni News*, Fall 1981, p. 3).

Hickey remained at Creighton Prep for nine years and was successful in all three sports. In football his teams won 36 games, lost 24, and tied four. His basketball teams won 115 games, including 27 in a row at one point, and lost 26. In baseball his teams won two city championships and one state title.

In 1934 Hickey was named football coach at Creighton University. He remained in this position only one year and then switched to basketball. Over the next eight seasons, the Bluejays won 113 games against 64 defeats. Creighton broke the stranglehold of Oklahoma A&M (now Oklahoma State) on the Missouri Valley Conference (MVC) championship despite the university's desire to strengthen its football program at basketball's expense. Hickey was forced to house some of his players, including All-American Ed Beisser, in his own basement and attic. Without Hickey's assistance, these players could not have stayed in school.

Creighton won a pair of MVC titles outright (in 1940–1941 and 1942–1943) and shared two others (1935–1936 and 1941–1942). Twice, in 1941–1942 and 1942–1943, the Bluejays advanced to the National Invitational Tournament (NIT), then a major postseason affair played in New York's Madison Square Garden. In 1940–1941 the Bluejays played in the National Collegiate Athletic Association (NCAA) tournament but lost in the first round.

After the 1942–1943 season, Creighton suspended its athletic programs for the duration of World War II. Hickey decided to enter the navy. He coached basketball teams at naval flight schools in Iowa and after three and a half years left the service with the rank of lieutenant commander.

Returning to Omaha for the 1946–1947 season, he coached the Bluejays to a 19–8 record. But, in 1947, when Creighton decided to deemphasize basketball further, Hickey accepted the head coaching job at St. Louis University. "I always considered St. Louis more centrally located than Omaha, and figured we might build up a great team here," he said at the time (*Sporting News*, 14 Jan. 1948, sec. 2, p. 2).

Hickey, known as Eddie but nicknamed the "Little General," brought to the Billikens' basketball program three attributes for which he became famous: an intense devotion toward work and long hours; a solid commitment to seeing his players succeed as students as well as athletes; and a defensive scheme that stifled and frustrated many opponents. Hickey described this "Creighton defense" as a zone alignment, with players picking up their opponents as if they were in a man-to-man and switching as necessary.

However, Hickey found his first St. Louis squad so talented that he abandoned the Creighton defense for a traditional man-to-man. The Billikens, led by 6′8″ center "Easy" Ed Macauley, were a closely knit team that featured dazzling passing and Hickey's innovative fast break with three players running the length of the court simultaneously. They defeated NCAA champion Holy Cross and six other nationally prominent teams early in the season and earned a bid to the NIT. St. Louis defeated Bowling Green, Western Kentucky, and New York University to claim the New York version of national honors with a record of 24–3.

Hickey coached the Billikens for ten more seasons. In all, his St. Louis teams won 212 games and lost 89, in the process establishing the Jesuit university as a national basketball power. St. Louis shared the MVC title in 1954–1955 and won it outright in 1951–1952 and 1956–1957. The Billikens advanced to the NCAA tournament in each title year and made six other appearances in the NIT after their 1948 championship.

Hickey's teams were noted for their tough, intense defense and their discipline. He put his players through repetitive drills at long practices and demanded precise execution. "You've done it again," Hickey warned a player once. "You're not where you're supposed to be. You made that mistake twice before. In this game you shouldn't make the same mistake more than once."

Hickey was also an active member of the National Association of Basketball Coaches throughout his career. A long series of committee assignments culminated in a term as president in 1953–1954, following which he chaired the All-America Selection Committee until his retirement.

After the 1957–1958 season, Hickey left St. Louis to become head basketball coach at Marquette University in Milwaukee because he wanted to move to a new opportunity and start again and because he was attracted to Wisconsin's recreational areas. He cited his age, then fifty-five, as the principal reason he accepted Marquette's offer to coach at no reduction in salary without the additional duties of athletic director he bore at St. Louis. However, Billikens' officials had been willing to let Hickey drop the athletic director's job, and he later assumed these duties at Marquette anyway.

Hickey remained at Marquette for six seasons, during which his teams compiled a record of 92 wins and 70 losses. His best year was his first. The Warriors finished at 23–6 and earned a bid to the NCAA tournament. Hickey was named Coach of the Year by the U.S. Basketball Writers' Association and the National Association of Basketball Coaches. Two other Hickey teams made postseason appearances. The 1960–1961 squad (16–11) went to the NCAA, and the 1962–1963 team (20–9) finished third in the NIT.

Marquette fired Hickey as coach after the 1963–1964 season. That year the Warriors had finished at 5–21, at one point losing fifteen games in a row, but this poor showing was not blamed for his dismissal. The university president acted on a recommendation of the athletic board based in part on Hickey' heavy-handed discipline, including his decision to dismiss four players in January 1964 for missing a curfew. His overall collegiate record stood at 436–231.

After suffering a heart attack in November 1964, Hickey moved to Terre Haute, Indiana, to work for the Automobile Association of America. In 1965 he married Ethel Miller of Wellston, Missouri. He held various positions in Terre Haute before retiring to Mesa, Arizona, in 1978.

Hickey was elected to the Naismith Memorial Basketball Hall of Fame in 1979. At the time of his induction, he was remembered as a tough, dedicated coach with a strong, aggressive personality and a great love for teaching basketball. He died in Mesa.

• There are clippings files on Hickey at the Basketball Hall of Fame, the St. Louis University Archives, the Marquette University Archives, and the *Sporting News*. Obituaries are in the *New York Times*, 8 Dec. 1980, and the *Sporting News*, 27 Dec. 1980.

STEVEN P. GIETSCHIER

HICKMAN, John James (26 May 1839–29 Apr. 1902), temperance reformer, was born in Lexington, Kentucky, the son of James L. Hickman. His mother's name is unknown. When his father died, the family moved to the southern part of the state. His mother inspired "J. J." Hickman's commitment to teetotalism. There are few details available about his family other than that his uncle Thomas Metcalfe had served as governor of Kentucky (1828–1832) and as a Whig member of the U.S. Senate (1848–1849). At age nineteen Hickman married Lizzie Hollingsworth, whose father was prominent in business. After an early attempt at farming, Hickman studied law and medicine. He was twenty-one when the Civil War broke out, but he apparently did not serve in the military, perhaps because of his chronic poor health. Although the state did not secede, many whites in Kentucky supported the Confederacy. Hickman's wartime sympathies are unknown.

While still in his twenties, Hickman became a leader in the Independent Order of Good Templars (IOGT), a fraternal temperance society that admitted both men and women. In May 1867 he joined a western Kentucky lodge. Quickly appointed a state deputy, he moved to Louisville. In October 1868, at the first session of the Grand Lodge of Kentucky that he attended, he was elected its head with the title Grand Worthy Chief Templar. About this time the Templar Order claimed 500,000 members in the United States and Canada but few in the former slave states. Hickman made the IOGT important in the South and the South important in the IOGT. Inheriting a state organization with fewer than 3,000 members and 60 working lodges, he left office three years later with nearly 25,000 members and more than 500 lodges. Personal character, the sanctity of the family, and evangelical Protestantism dominated Hickman's message. Although he worked for local option, he opposed identification of the IOGT with the Prohibition party.

In 1870–1871 the Kentucky Templars paid him a salary of $3,000.

Like other white southerners, Hickman insisted on the right of the Grand Lodges in the former slave states to exclude blacks from Templar membership. In 1871 he recommended the creation of a separate fraternal temperance society for men and women of African descent, eventually called the True Reformers. In 1872, after the international organization (the Right Worthy Grand Lodge) rejected a proposal to force black Templars to transfer to a segregated order, Hickman called for the Councils of Temperance, a federation of southern organizations that he recently had helped found, to be turned into a fraternal society for white southerners. In the following year he demanded the secession of the southern Grand Lodges when it appeared that the Right Worthy Grand Lodge would insist they allow black lodges to affiliate with them. In both cases the storm cleared when successive heads of the Templars, anxious to avoid a schism, let each Grand Lodge make its own policy on race.

Hickman already was a major figure in the Templar Order where he had built a position as a liaison between the international organization and whites in the American South. He forged a close alliance with the Templars in the Canadian province of Ontario. As early as 1869 Hickman was named to a minor international office. In 1871 and 1872 he was elected to the second-highest international office.

As part of northern appeasement of white southerners, Hickman was elected to the supreme Templar office (Right Worthy Grand Templar) in 1874 and was reelected in 1875 and 1876. In that year at a convention held in Louisville the IOGT split in two, with a predominantly British faction setting up a rival organization, the Right Worthy Grand Lodge of the World. In part this was a struggle over power. In contrast with a decline in numbers in the northern states, the IOGT had grown substantially in the southern states and even more dramatically in England and Scotland. Hickman's opponents depicted the schism as a fight for the right of African Americans to join the IOGT in the former slave states. In response Hickman conceded segregated Dual Grand Lodges of black Templars in the southern jurisdictions.

Hickman declined renomination in 1877, probably because a virtually bankrupt organization could not pay a salary, but he was elected to the highest Templar office again in 1879 and 1880. In 1881 he was defeated for reelection in a straw vote, which the official records omit.

Although his influence declined with the collapse of the southern lodges in the late 1870s and the 1880s, Hickman remained an active Templar until his death. Prior to 1880 Hickman moved to Columbia, Missouri, where his only surviving children, two sons, attended the state university. In 1886 or 1887 he was elected head of the Grand Lodge of Missouri. He represented Missouri in 1887 at the meeting in Saratoga Springs, New York, that ended the international schism. In later life he served as a paid organizer for the IOGT.

Hickman was a charismatic and colorful figure. A renowned orator, he delivered more than 10,000 speeches. He was a lifelong abstainer from tobacco, coffee, and tea, as well as from alcoholic drink. In religion he was a Baptist. Despite his failure to join the fighting in 1861–1865, he called himself Colonel Hickman, an honorary title awarded him by a Kentucky governor in 1873. Hickman supplemented his Templar salaries as a sales agent for a St. Louis–based fire and life insurance company.

By the time that Hickman died in Columbia, Missouri, he had slipped into obscurity. Despite this neglect, Hickman deserves to be remembered as a leading American temperance reformer for the dozen or so years from the late 1860s until the early 1880s and for his role in the international controversy over African-American membership in the Templar Order.

• The principal source of what scanty biographical information survives is by Tim Needham in *Good Templar Gem* (July 1880), repr. in Thomas F. Parker, *History of the Independent Order of Good Templars* (1882; rev. ed., 1887). Hickman's date of death is noted in Ernest Hurst Cherrington, ed., *Standard Encyclopedia of the Alcohol Problem* (6 vols., 1926–1930). For the years when Hickman headed the Grand Lodge of Kentucky only the *Journal of Proceedings* for 1871 survives, but all issues of the Right Worthy Grand Lodge, *Journal of Proceedings*, are available. A detailed account of the controversy over African-American membership is in David M. Fahey, *Temperance and Racism: John Bull, Johnny Reb, and the Good Templars* (1996).

DAVID M. FAHEY

HICKOK, Laurens Perseus (29 Dec. 1798–6 May 1888), philosopher, was born in Bethel, Connecticut, the son of Ebenezer Hickok and Polly Benedict, farmers. He taught school in Bethel (P. T. Barnum was, briefly, one of his pupils) and entered Union College in Schenectady, New York, in 1819 as a junior. He was "particularly noted for his activity, agility, and strength in all athletic exercises," including "base-ball playing," and graduated from Union in 1820. In the same year, he was admitted to membership in the Congregational church of Bethel, and undertook studies for the Congregational ministry under the oversight of William Andrews of Danbury and Bennet Tyler of South Britain, Connecticut. In 1822 he married Elizabeth Taylor; they had no children.

Hickok was ordained pastor of the Congregational church in Kent, Connecticut, on 10 December 1824, and then installed as pastor of the Congregational church in Litchfield, Connecticut, on 3 July 1829 as the successor to Lyman Beecher. His pastorate in Litchfield was remarkably successful: 214 new members joined the church, 95 of them in a revival of religion in Litchfield conducted by Hickok in 1831.

Hickok's career as a parish clergyman ended in November 1836, when he was elected professor of Christian theology at Western Reserve College in Hudson, Ohio. But he stayed in Ohio only until 1844, when he was elected professor of Christian theology at the Auburn Theological Seminary in Auburn, New York,

which emphasized "New School" Presbyterian theology. He delivered his inaugural lecture at Auburn, "Theology as a Science," on 8 January 1845. He published the first in his quartet of philosophical works, *Rational Psychology; or, the Subjective Idea and the Objective Law of all Intelligence* in 1845, followed by *A System of Moral Science* in 1853. That same year he became professor of mental and moral philosophy at Union College, serving also as vice president and publishing *Empirical Psychology; or, The Human Mind as Given in Consciousness* (1854) and *Rational Cosmology; or, The Eternal Principles and the Necessary Laws of the Universe* (1858). In March 1866 he became president of Union.

The roots of Hickok's intellectual career are located firmly within the boundaries of the Edwardsean, or "New Divinity," Calvinism of the so-called New England theology associated with the followers of Jonathan Edwards. The first editions of his *Rational Psychology* and his *System of Moral Science*, as well as his lectures at Auburn Theological Seminary, all reflect many of the conventional Edwardsean formulas on psychology and volition. His tenure at Western Reserve placed him within the same circle of New England emigrés who founded Lane Theological Seminary and the Oberlin Collegiate Institute to win the Ohio River valley for evangelical Protestantism. But, in contrast to "Old School" Presbyterianism, which sought to ground theology and conversion in the presentational realism of the Scottish "common sense" philosophers, Hickok found intellectual reinforcement for New Divinity Calvinism's immaterialist ontology and ethic of "disinterested benevolence" in the manipulation of Kant and Kantian forms of a priori rationalism. He categorized all human knowledge under the two headings of "empirical" (knowledge derived from the senses, such as physical science or even psychological introspection) and "rational" (the discovery of the suprasensory mental principles that organize the data supplied by the "empirical"). For Hickok, the inherent rationality of human knowing confirms the existence of an "aesthetic Standard of Taste," a "Philosophic Law of Truth," and an "Ethical Rule of Right," and ultimately of the existence of God. In fact, only on the assumption that the mind contains such organizing features can we intelligibly comprehend empirical data or rise to supraempirical truths about God. "The human mind is not a mere aggregation of states and exercises," he told his Auburn students in 1850, "but an organization held together by one law of unity."

Hickok was even willing to suggest that the mind not only contained organizational categories but also used them to obtain complete knowledge of itself. This assured him that both the mind and the will are consciously self-directed and therefore can be held morally accountable. While all of this certainly owed a great deal to Kant (as Hickok acknowledged in the revised edition of *Empirical Psychology* in 1882), it also echoed many of the theological imperatives of Edwardseanism: the priority of perception over sensation, the comprehensive self-awareness of minds, and the demand for full moral accountability in volition. But in using Kant as his principal aid, Hickok carved out a position of considerable originality in nineteenth-century American collegiate philosophy, especially in contrast to the hegemony of Scottish "common sense" thinking before 1860 and the post–Civil War attractions of neo-Hegelianism for George S. Morris, Josiah Royce, and the early John Dewey.

Hickok occupied the presidency of Union College for two years, only to find that the animosities that had grown up under President Nott between the faculty and trustees were beyond his abilities to resolve. In November 1868 he resigned and moved to Amherst, Massachusetts, where with his nephew Julius H. Seelye of Amherst College, he reworked *Moral Science* (rev. ed., 1880) and *Empirical Psychology*. He occasionally lectured and preached at Amherst College and sat as a member of the Congregationalist Hampshire East Association. He died in Amherst.

• Hickok's papers are in the Special Collections of the Frost Memorial Library at Amherst College and include his correspondence, lectures, sermons, and the unpublished text of one book, "Comprehensive Evolution in Three Distinctive Grades." A substantial file on him as an alumnus and former president of Union College is at the Schaffer Library at Union College; the file includes a lengthy reminiscence by a former student, William M. Johnson. In addition to his major philosophical writings, Hickok also published several sermons and addresses, most notably an address to the Connecticut Peace Society, *The Sources of Military Delusions, and the Practicability of Their Removal* (1833), and a sermon for the ordination of Julius H. Seelye, *The Essential Element in Good Preaching* (1853). He also published in later life several theological works, *Humanity Immortal; or, Man Tried, Fallen and Redeemed* (1872; 2d ed., 1876), *Creator and Creation; or, The Knowledge in the Reason of God and His Work* (1872), and *The Logic of Reason, Universal and Eternal* (1875). He was the subject of a small but well-informed study in the series on "Union Worthies" by Harold A. Larrabee et al., published by Union College in 1947. The best analyses of Hickok's thought are in the sections devoted to him in Joseph L. Blau, *Men and Movements in American Philosophy* (1952), and Bruce Kuklick, *Churchmen and Philosophers: From Jonathan Edwards to John Dewey* (1985). Obituaries are in the *Boston Transcript*, 7 May 1888, and the *Amherst Sentinel*, 9 May 1888.

ALLEN C. GUELZO

HICKOK, Lorena Alice (7 Mar. 1893–1 May 1968), journalist, was born in East Troy, Wisconsin, the daughter of Addison J. Hickok, a buttermaker, and Anna Waite, a dressmaker. (There is confusion about her name; a birth record gives it as Alice Loraine Hickok.) Her father was a violent, abusive man and lost one job after another, forcing the family to move throughout the upper Middle West as he searched for employment. Consequently, Lorena's schooling was frequently disrupted. Her father's cruelty, which included whipping his daughters and killing Lorena's kitten by throwing it against a barn, marred her childhood. Her mother, who had run away from her home in a moderately prosperous farming family to be mar-

ried, tried ineffectively to protect Lorena from his beatings. She died in Bowdle, South Dakota, when Lorena was thirteen.

Forced to leave home, Hickok began work at the age of fourteen as a domestic, staying with nine different families in the next two years. Although the work was hard, she was relieved to be independent of her father. Finally she was employed by the kind wife of a saloonkeeper who felt sorry for Hickok and arranged for her to move into the home of her mother's cousin, Ella Ellis, in Battle Creek, Michigan. There she received much-needed affection and, under Ellis's guidance, finished high school, displaying intellectual gifts that surmounted her lack of preparation. Her literary aspirations were encouraged by an English and Latin teacher.

In 1912 she enrolled at Lawrence College in Appleton, Wisconsin. A large woman, she found herself referred to as "Fatty" by her classmates. To avoid ridicule, she clerked in a grocery to earn money to eat off campus, attended class sporadically, and refused to wear bloomers for a required gym course. After flunking out at the end of her freshmen year, she began her newspaper career as a $7-a-week reporter for the Battle Creek *Evening News*, reporting on train arrivals and collecting personal news items. The following year she tried attending Lawrence again but left when no sorority invited her to pledge.

Hoping to follow the path of Edna Ferber, the popular writer who had started her career as a Milwaukee reporter, Hickok landed a job on the *Milwaukee Sentinel*. Faced with the customary sex discrimination of her period, she was hired as society editor—the only position available to most women on newspapers. Uninterested in society reporting, she managed to transfer to the city staff, establishing a reputation as an excellent interviewer. Hickok so impressed singer Ernestine Schumann-Heink during an interview that she removed her sapphire ring and gave it to the reporter, who would later give it to Eleanor Roosevelt.

Hickok moved on to the *Minneapolis Tribune* in 1917 but dreamed of going to Europe as a war correspondent. She got as far as New York City, where she worked for a month on the *New York Tribune* before being fired because of her unfamiliarity with the big city. This experience prompted her to return to Minneapolis and enroll in the University of Minnesota while doing rewrite work for the *Tribune*.

Running afoul of a dean of women who tried unsuccessfully to make her live in a dormitory, Hickok soon quit college to concentrate on her newspaper career. She became the protégée of Thomas J. Dillon, the managing editor of the *Minneapolis Tribune*, who promoted her to Sunday editor and then chief bylined reporter. Hickok called him "the Old Man" and later credited him with teaching her "the newspaper business, how to drink, and how to live." Dillon gave her assignments rarely offered to women, including coverage of politics and sports.

In 1926 Hickok, who suffered from diabetes, left Minneapolis for San Francisco to regain her health and to try to become a writer. After her money ran out she decided to return to journalism and to give New York City another try. Far better prepared at this point, she worked on the Hearst tabloid, the *Daily Mirror*, in 1927.

The next year she became one of the first women to be hired by the Associated Press. At first restricted to features because she was a woman, she soon out-did her male competitors and won a byline. According to Ishbel Ross, who wrote the first history of American women journalists in 1936, Hickok achieved "standing with the AP that no other woman has matched," covering politics as well as sensational stories like the Lindbergh baby kidnapping.

Assigned at her own suggestion to cover Eleanor Roosevelt during Franklin D. Roosevelt's successful 1932 presidential campaign, Hickok soon became Eleanor Roosevelt's confidante, writing stories that introduced her as a "different kind of First Lady" who would be more active than her predecessors. She also advised Eleanor Roosevelt to hold press conferences for women reporters only and give them exclusive news items. The two women became intimate friends, corresponded daily, and traveled together, leading to later speculation that they may have had a lesbian relationship, although this possibility is discounted by the Roosevelt family.

Leaving the AP because her friendship with Eleanor Roosevelt compromised her journalistic independence, Hickok became chief investigator for the Federal Emergency Relief Administration, making fact-finding trips through thirty-two states from 1933 to 1936. Her colorful, often angry, reports on conditions confronting ordinary people during the Great Depression went to Harry L. Hopkins, head of the administration, and Eleanor Roosevelt, both of whom passed her findings on to the president. Her reports focused on individuals trying to cope with the depression, for example, " . . . the Negro woman in Philadelphia who used to walk eight miles every day over the scorching pavements just on the chance of getting, perhaps, a little cleaning to do, at 10 cents an hour"; " . . . the little Mexican girl, aged 6, in Colorado, who said, sure, she'd worked 'in the beets' two Summers already and, yes, sometimes she did get pretty tired"; and "the farm woman in South Dakota who had a recipe for Russian thistle soup and said, 'It don't taste so bad, only it ain't very filling.'" Hickok's reports helped officials gauge the depth of public need and provided feedback on the effectiveness of relief efforts.

From 1937 to 1940 Hickok worked as a publicist for the New York World's Fair. She subsequently joined the staff of the Democratic National Committee, first as a publicist, then as executive secretary of the Women's Division, a position she held for four years until 1945. During that period she lived in the White House as Eleanor Roosevelt's guest and developed a passionate friendship with Marion Janet Harron, a judge of the U.S. Tax Court.

After working for the New York State Democratic Committee from 1947 to 1952, Hickok, now partially blind, moved to Hyde Park, New York, to be near Eleanor Roosevelt. Hickok collaborated with her on *Ladies of Courage* (1954), a book about women in politics. To support herself, she also wrote *Reluctant First Lady* (1962), a biography of Eleanor Roosevelt, and six biographies of famous Americans for juveniles. She died in Rhinebeck, New York, of pneumonia following the amputation of a leg.

Although late twentieth-century scholarship has centered on her relationship with Eleanor Roosevelt, Hickok's historical significance lies primarily in her own achievements. She proved that a woman could succeed in journalism in the early twentieth century in spite of overwhelming sexual discrimination. Her reports on the depression, circulated to key policymakers, showed her to be a keen observer and may have played a part in setting policy.

• Hickok's papers, including portions of an unfinished, unpublished autobiography and correspondence with Eleanor Roosevelt and Marion Harron, are in the Franklin D. Roosevelt Library, Hyde Park, N.Y. Hickok's reports to Harry Hopkins were published in Richard Lowitt and Maurine Beasley, eds., *One Third of a Nation: Lorena Hickok Reports on the Great Depression* (1981). Hickok's six biographies for juveniles are *The Story of Franklin D. Roosevelt* (1956), *The Story of Helen Keller* (1958), *The Story of Eleanor Roosevelt* (1959), *The Touch of Magic: The Story of Helen Keller's Great Teacher, Anne Sullivan Macy* (1961), *The Road to the White House* (1962), and, completed after her death by Jean Gould, *Walter Reuther: Labor's Rugged Individualist* (1972). Her biography is Doris Faber, *The Life of Lorena Hickok, E. R.'s Friend* (1980). See also two chapters on Hickok in Blanche W. Cook, *Eleanor Roosevelt: 1884–1933* (1992). An obituary is in the *New York Times*, 3 May 1968.

MAURINE H. BEASLEY

HICKOK, Wild Bill (27 May 1837–2 Aug. 1876), western lawman and gambler, was born James Butler Hickok in Homer, Illinois, the son of William Alonzo Hickok and Polly Butler, farmers. As a young man, Hickok spent most of his time working on—and, after the death of his father in 1852, managing—the family farm. The availability of land in newly organized Kansas Territory was enticing to Hickok, and in June 1856 he and his brother Lorenzo moved westward. His mother's illness soon prompted Lorenzo to return to Homer. Hickok remained, but he did not settle into an agrarian lifestyle. Various events offered other opportunities to him. In the pre–Civil War years, he served in General James Lane's Free State army. In the succeeding years, he was elected constable of Monticello Township, Johnson County; worked as a teamster on the Santa Fe Trail; and served as a spy and special detective in numerous skirmishes along the Missouri border during the Civil War.

The event that brought Hickok both fame and notoriety and earned him his nickname was the killing of David McCanles at Rock Creek, Nebraska, in 1861. McCanles was engaged in a dispute over money owed to him for some land. Hickok, who was not a party to the dispute, intervened, then stepped back from the scene, but was called to return by McCanles. McCanles gestured, and Hickok killed him as well as James Woods, a McCanles employee, who was shot in the ensuing fight. A dramatized recounting of McCanles's death written by George Ward Nichols appeared in an 1867 issue of *Harper's Weekly*. This story catapulted Wild Bill Hickok into the national limelight and made him the central figure of many dime novels.

After the Civil War, Hickok put his experiences and connections to various uses as an army scout, guide, and U.S. marshal in Kansas. More important, by the end of the 1860s he had achieved considerable fame in the region for his expertise in the use of handguns. He did not boast of his skill, but for the rest of his life many men tested him only to fall victim to his uncanny speed and accuracy.

Hickok resumed his law enforcement career in 1869 when he was appointed sheriff in Ellis County, Kansas. Combating the rampant state of lawlessness was his principal task, and Hickok proved himself tough enough for it. His superb marksmanship and striking physical appearance made Hickok an effective officer and a formidable opponent. However, local residents criticized his heavy-handed methods. As a result, Hickok was not reelected sheriff.

In April 1871 he was appointed marshal of Abilene, Kansas. It would mark the climax of his career in law enforcement. For eight months, he succeeded in bringing civil order to the raucous cattle-trail town. A celebrated civil affair occurred when Hickok, acting on orders, physically carried a councilman back into the council chambers. The dramatic event later turned to satire in the surrounding communities and quickly became an embarrassment to the town. Subsequent events soon worked against Hickok. When the cattle drive was finally concluded in 1871, the citizens voted to ban cattlemen from using Abilene as a shipping terminal in the future. Now that the principal threat to civil order was forever curtailed, the town had no further need for Hickok's kind of law enforcement administration and dismissed him.

After Abilene, Hickok led a transient existence. He acted in several Wild West shows, including Buffalo Bill's Wild West Show from 1873 to 1874. In each case, he proved up to the task, but his career as dramatic actor was cut short by his own impatience with static character portrayals and his desire to live rather than act the part. Between acting engagements he traveled about the West and eventually made Cheyenne, Wyoming, his second home. During this period, he found solace in frequenting gambling saloons. His shooting prowess soon gave way to guile as an expert gambler.

In 1876 Hickok married Agnes Lake Thatcher. Reflecting on his newfound responsibilities, Hickok considered undertaking a more sedentary life. Upon hearing news about gold in the Black Hills, Hickok believed he could make a good living as a mine owner. That summer, he escorted a party of people, which included such notable figures as Calamity Jane and White-Eye Jack Anderson, to Deadwood, South Dakota. As elsewhere, his reputation preceded him, and he quickly became a public celebrity. After his death, the presence of him and Calamity Jane together aroused speculation that the couple were not merely casual riders but also lovers and that he had a child with her. Although these stories are not true, they added a romantic dimension to the Wild Bill legend.

Hickok did not find a gold mine but instead settled back into a comfortable daily routine of gambling. While playing poker in the No. 10 saloon in Deadwood, he was shot and killed by Jack McCall. McCall was probably angry and embarrassed because, the day before, he had lost in a poker game to Hickok, who had given him money for breakfast and advised him not to play if he could not cover his losses. At the time of his death, Hickok was supposedly holding two black aces, two black eights, and a jack of diamonds, and a hand that would be known as "aces and eights—the dead man's hand." That detail, however, may have been added later as part of the local lore that grew out of fascination with Hickok's fate. McCall was captured, tried before Judge William Kuykendall, and hanged 1 March 1877 for Hickok's murder.

In later years, films and stories would characterize Hickok's life in dramatic dimensions similar to those in the dime novels of his own age. In truth, Wild Bill Hickok was for the most part an unassuming, pragmatic figure. He took advantage of opportunities whenever they presented themselves and never thrust himself upon situations. He did not actively seek personal fame, but toward the end of his life he did live off a mixture of hyperbole and fact about his own legendary personality.

• Hickok's letters are at the Kansas State Historical Association. The best book about Hickok and one with an impressive bibliography is Joseph G. Rosa, *They Called Him Wild Bill: The Life and Adventures of James Butler Hickok* (1964). An interesting pictorial book is Rosa, *The Wild West of Wild Bill Hickok* (1982). See also Rosa, *Wild Bill Hickok: The Man and His Myth* (1996).

CARL V. HALLBERG

HICKS, Edward (4 Apr. 1780–23 Aug. 1849), folk artist, was born in Attleboro (now Langhorne), Bucks County, Pennsylvania, the son of Isaac Hicks and Catherine Hicks. (His parents were first cousins; his mother's maiden name was Hicks.) The Hicks family were Anglicans, and Isaac Hicks had sided with the British during the American Revolution. He eventually was forced to flee from Bucks County, leaving his family behind. His wife died not long after, and Edward Hicks, then eighteen months old, was taken in by family friends David and Elizabeth Twining, who raised him in the Quaker faith. When he was thirteen, Hicks was apprenticed to coachmakers William and Henry Tomlinson of Langhorne. He displayed a talent for painting, and in 1801 he became a partner of coachmaker and carriage painter Joshua Canby of Milford, Pennsylvania. In 1803 he married Sarah Worstall; they had a son and four daughters.

Hicks was a successful carriage painter and branched out into the equally lucrative business of sign painting. Around 1810 he and his family moved to Newtown, Pennsylvania, where he continued to enjoy success as a carriage and sign painter. He was as devoted to his faith as he was to his business, and in 1812 he became a Quaker preacher, an unsalaried post that required constant travel to preach. His frequent absences from his decorating business, coupled with his growing uneasiness that painting was incompatible with what was expected of a Quaker minister, led Hicks to abandon the arts for agriculture. This was a mistake, as he later admitted, "I quit the only business I understood, and for which I had a capacity, *viz.* painting, for the business of a farmer, which I did not understand and for which I had no qualification whatever" (Mather and Miller, p. 17). He went deeply into debt but was saved from bankruptcy by family and friends. He resumed painting and allayed his doubts about the fitness of such an occupation by choosing thereafter to paint primarily themes of a religious or highly moral nature.

Hicks's best-known and most popular paintings are his representations of the prophecy of Isaiah 11 ("The wolf also shall dwell with the lamb, and the leopard shall lie down with the kid; . . . and a little child shall lead them"), known as *The Peaceable Kingdom*. Exactly when he began painting this subject is unknown, but it was probably around 1820 or 1821. The composition is based on an engraving after a design by British artist Richard Westall, but from the beginning Hicks contributed his own touches: the Natural Bridge of Virginia (copied from an 1822 engraving by Henry S. Tanner) and a vignette of William Penn negotiating a peace treaty with the Indians, copied from John Hall's engraving of the well-known painting by Benjamin West. Hicks included the Natural Bridge as a symbol of God's handiwork on Earth and Penn's treaty with the Indians as a depiction of the Quaker attributes of peace and brotherly love. He altered the design of his *Peaceable Kingdom* works over the years, and the Natural Bridge ceases to appear after the 1820s, but Penn's treaty can be seen in most versions. (Hicks painted more than sixty versions of *The Peaceable Kingdom*, the last one on the day before his death.)

One group of *Peaceable Kingdom* paintings illustrates the schism that occurred between the mainstream Society of Friends and the followers of the artist's cousin, Elias Hicks. Elias felt that the mainstream Quakers had strayed from the teachings of the society's founder, George Fox. Edward supported his cousin but was deeply distressed by the animosity that resulted when the so-called "Hicksite" Quakers broke away from the main body of Friends. In the several versions of *The Peaceable Kingdom* painted in the aftermath of the break, Hicks coupled Elias with Fox, William Penn, and other early Quakers, and with George Washington, a hero of Edward's. Later versions feature groups of animals and children placed against a landscape of the Delaware River (taken from an engraving by Aher B. Durand) with Penn's treaty in the background at left.

Hicks also painted historical scenes. *Washington at the Delaware* was a subject close to his heart not only because the general was a hero of his but also because the crossing had taken place not far from the artist's home. He based his composition on an engraving after Thomas Sully's 1819 painting (Museum of Fine Arts, Boston). His first depictions on this theme were a pair of paintings intended for the two ends of a bridge spanning the Delaware near the site of the crossing, and he subsequently made three more paintings of the event. Hicks executed three paintings of *The Declaration of Independence*, based on an engraving after the well-known painting by John Trumbull (Yale University Art Gallery) and a painting of *The Landing of Columbus*, done around 1837 and copied from M. I. Danforth's engraving after a painting by John Gadsby Chapman.

Hicks expressed his Quaker beliefs not only in the *Peaceable Kingdom* paintings, but also in paintings of *Penn's Treaty with the Indians*, based on the Benjamin West painting, and *The Grave of William Penn*. The latter, painted in 1847, was copied from an engraving after a painting by Hendrik Frans de Cort and depicts a group of Quakers paying their respects at Penn's grave in England. Hicks painted several versions of both these subjects.

The historical works, while indicative of Hicks's interests, are more or less straightforward copies after other artists. Of greater interest, and on an equal level artistically with the *Peaceable Kingdom* paintings, are his farmscapes of Bucks County. These all date from the latter part of his career. The first, *The Residence of Thomas Hillborn* (1845, Abby Aldrich Rockefeller Folk Art Center, Williamsburg, Va.) shows a neighbor plowing his field and the six Hillborn children performing various chores. *The Cornell Farm* (1848, National Gallery of Art) depicts a large group of prize livestock milling about in the foreground and the farmhouse, barn, and other farm buildings in the distance beyond. (Hicks also executed a portrait of James Cornell's prize bull.) *The Leedom Farm* (1849, Abby Aldrich Rockefeller Folk Art Center), one of Hicks's last paintings, portrays farm buildings and farm animals set within a view of the Bucks County landscape. Hicks also painted four similar retrospective paintings of the farm where he was raised by David and Elizabeth Twining. In them he depicts his foster parents, their daughter and son-in-law, a farmhand plowing, various animals, and himself, aged seven, at Mrs. Twining's knee. (The last and best of the four, painted 1846–1847, is owned by the Abby Aldrich Rockefeller Folk Art Center.)

Hicks continued to paint signs, of which the best known is that painted for the Newtown Library in 1825 and still owned by the library; it includes a likeness of Benjamin Franklin reading, taken from a portrait by Scottish artist David Martin. His shop often employed many assistants including, at one point, his cousin Thomas Hicks and a local boy, Martin Johnson

Heade, both of whom became well-known artists, albeit (unlike Edward) in the academic tradition. Edward Hicks also continued to preach and travel widely, making frequent journeys through eastern Pennsylvania, Virginia, New York, and New Jersey; and he even traveled as far as Canada and Ohio. On one of these trips he visited Niagara Falls, which made such an impression on him that he subsequently painted two pictures (1825, one at the Abby Aldrich Rockefeller Folk Art Center, the other at the Metropolitan Museum of Art). Hicks never sketched from nature, and, although he had seen the falls, he based his paintings on an engraving by Tanner.

Hicks died at his home in Newtown and was buried in the burying ground of the Friends' Meeting House in Newtown. He was remembered within the Quaker community as an outstanding preacher, but his work as a painter was virtually forgotten until the early 1930s, when there was an awakening of interest in American folk art. Hicks had an excellent feel for design and color that contributes greatly to the strength and originality of his paintings. Although he never advanced technically to the level of the academic painter, within the confines of the folk art tradition his work evolved from primitive sign painting to visionary depictions of God's kingdom on earth and charming but realistic portrayals of the farms of his beloved Bucks County.

• The Friends Historical Library, Swarthmore College, Swarthmore, Pa., owns the manuscript of Hicks's memoirs, written in 1843–1849, and a collection of his letters. The Bucks County Historical Society in Doylestown, Pa., owns a group of Hicks's letters and his shop ledger. He was painted by his cousin Thomas Hicks in 1837 or 1838; the life portrait is owned by the National Portrait Gallery, Smithsonian Institution, and a replica belongs to the Abby Aldrich Rockefeller Folk Art Center in Williamsburg, Va., which also owns the largest collection of Hicks's work. The National Gallery of Art in Washington and the Bucks County Historical Society likewise have important collections of his paintings. The standard biography is Alice Ford, *Edward Hicks: Painter of the Peaceable Kingdom* (1952). Eleanore Price Mather and Dorothy C. Miller, *Edward Hicks: His Peaceable Kingdoms and Other Paintings* (1983), contains a catalog of all his known works.

DAVID MESCHUTT

HICKS, Elias (19 Mar. 1748–27 Feb. 1830), Quaker minister, was born in Hempstead, Long Island, New York, the son of John Hicks and Martha Smith, farmers. The Hicks family had Anglican roots, but Elias's father became a member of the Society of Friends not long before Elias was born; his mother was uncomfortable with the mysticism of Quaker meeting and never joined. Elias received only a minimum of formal education, although he was apprenticed for a time to a carpenter, learned surveying, and taught occasionally in the village school. After marrying Jemima Seaman in Westbury meeting in 1770, he moved to her family's farm in nearby Jericho. The couple had eleven children, but none of their four sons lived to adulthood, all dying of mysterious illnesses. In 1777 Hicks inherited the farm. Within a year he was formally recognized as a minister by his meeting, and in 1779 he went on the first of fifty-nine journeys of what Quakers called "traveling in the ministry." Cultivating the habit of harkening to his inward leadings, a characteristic of Quakers of his age, marked him as a potential leader within the Society of Friends.

Hicks read widely in the Bible, writings of early Quakers, and religious history generally, but his thought seldom rose above the unsophisticated and intuitive. Although he was a farmer all his life, Hicks's reputation came to rest on his controversial religious activities and theology, particularly his appeals to fellow Quakers to separate themselves from the habits of the secular world. Until he was seventy years old, his ministry was seldom gainsaid and remained acceptable to many of those who would presently come to resist his ideas. An early and forceful opponent of slavery, he used the retreat of New York Yearly Meeting from its strictures against the use of products made with slave labor to write *Observations on the Slavery of the Africans* (1811). This pamphlet vigorously attacked the ownership of Africans, asserting that they were "prize" goods, stolen by violence and war, and had as much right to liberty as anyone else. Determined to be consistent, he refused therefore to use slave-produced goods, wearing linen or woolen clothes and eschewing sugar and rice. Hicks sometimes evinced a self-righteous air, a fact explaining why he occasioned little neutrality among people who came in contact with him.

Hicks was tall, austere in his dark shadbelly coat, stern-looking with piercing eyes, and determined. His appearance underlined his traditional and stubborn opposition to many modern developments of the day. Banks, chemistry, railroads, the Erie Canal, foreign trade, and fine arts were all targets of his ire; he even, it was charged, distrusted civil government. His strong opinions brought him into conflict with some of his fellow believers, especially the urban Quakers who were amassing wealth and increasing their influence in the modern world. Such prosperity and acclaim, he asserted, might give comfort to one's body but certainly lent none to the soul; instead they led the rich into "grinding the faces of the poor." Well-to-do Friends in New York and Philadelphia might help organize Bible, colonization, temperance, and other "mixed" societies to seek reform from the top down; Hicks preached, however, that Quakers should remain aloof from the "world's people" and keep themselves untainted as leaven in the larger community.

Hicks likewise rejected newer interpretations of Quakerism infiltrating American yearly meetings from England. These evangelical ideas, influenced by Methodism, stressed the primacy of the Bible over the sometimes ineffable leadings of the divine spirit within each individual, the traditional Quaker belief. Hicks spoke widely through the Northeast and Midwest where he traveled with letters of commendation from his home meeting. He went as far south as Alexandria, Virginia, and westward to Richmond, Indiana. Beginning in the second decade of the nineteenth century, Hicks clashed with more cosmopolitan Friends, who had come to accept evangelical theology as one of the givens of the world in which they moved.

This opposition first emerged publicly in Philadelphia in October 1819, when Hicks visited the city. An evangelical elder, Jonathan Evans, forced a quick adjournment of the men of Pine Street Meeting as a rebuke to the visitor. The incident took on almost mythic importance as both sides bruited about word of this open affront to the New Yorker. A group of Quakers in Wilmington, Delaware, more rationalistic than Hicks, now took up the cudgels of what they began calling a "reformation" and added an important new dimension to already existing rural distrust of powerful Philadelphia elders. One of these Wilmingtonians, Benjamin Ferris, agreed to bear one-half the burden of a long-running theological dialogue in the pages of the local *Christian Repository* which was dubbed the "Paul and Amicus" debate and was later published separately. Ferris sought advice from Hicks as well as other reformers as he contrasted Quakerism with Presbyterianism, particularly stressing his objection to what he termed the "vulgar" doctrine of the Trinity. Hicks, failing to find a scriptural basis for this hallowed doctrine, also opposed it. Viewed by evangelicals as the fount of this heresy, he received the most direct fallout from the disagreement.

Arriving again in Philadelphia in December 1822, just as the Paul and Amicus series was ending, Hicks was informed by the elders that his views were unsound and that he could not make his usual visits among them. Combative as always, the now-unwelcome minister pursued his trip anyway, abrading his opposition at every turn. He told an audience of young people that God would "lead them off from all dependence on man . . . and they will have no need that any man teach them." At another stop he quoted Job Scott, an eighteenth-century minister from Rhode Island who had also run afoul of the evangelical element, that the outward blood of Christ had no more efficacy for believers than the blood of bulls and goats. These were sentiments, needless to say, hardly calculated to calm angry Friends. Charges and countercharges flew back and forth, with Hicks adding his bit by returning to the Philadelphia area in 1824 and 1826. Visiting ministers from Great Britain contributed to the turmoil; they naturally gravitated to the side of their fellow evangelicals and plotted how to embarrass the old man. Pamphlets soon inundated the Quaker communities of the mid-Atlantic states and Ohio. Only one meeting of the five in Penn's City, and that in a working-class area, sided with the Long Islander, but the rural meetings nearby were firmly in his camp.

Hicks's followers in Philadelphia Yearly Meeting determined in 1827 to wrest control from the evangelicals—now universally known as Orthodox—but succeeded only in splitting it during the late April sessions. In October the reformers set up their own schismatic body. Hicks himself led the charge in his home territory of New York the following May, and

the yearly meeting divided. In September the eighty-year-old appeared again in Ohio, where the yearly meeting, after dissolving into fisticuffs over his ideas and the heresy they supposedly embodied, separated into two groups, each claiming to be the authentic one. The same thing, minus the violence, occurred in Indiana. Baltimore Yearly Meeting split in October, but Hicks had not yet returned from the West. Nearly eighteen months later five of the eight North American yearly meetings had split into "Hicksite" and Orthodox factions. Hicks died at his home in Jericho.

However unintentional, Hicks gave his name to the reformation effort, the most pivotal series of events in American Quaker history. Rooted to a major extent in his rural background, his negative response to the new world he saw unfolding represented the last stand mainstream Quakers would make against modernity. His subsequent followers tended, on the contrary, to embrace the modern world. Neither careful in his use of language nor very politic, Hicks sometimes let the enthusiasm of the moment carry him beyond where he preferred to go. Thus his iterated stress on "reason" was an unlikely representative of traditional Quakerism; much of his theology, especially when filtered through the rationalists in Wilmington, seemed to verge too close to the Unitarianism that was emerging about the same time. His opposition to the authority of the elders also added significantly to the individualistic strain within Quakerism and helped produce one major modern version of that faith. The geographical extent of the Hicksite reformation bore a direct relationship to the places he visited through the years. His remarkable "human magnetism," as described by the poet Walt Whitman, who as a child heard him preach, built a following willing to forsake old landmarks to support him and his cause. His reputation, much of it colored by polemics, made him controversial in Quaker circles long after his death.

• The major body of Hicks manuscripts, including unpublished parts of his journal, may be found in the Friends Historical Library at Swarthmore College; other collections in that library also contain letters to and from him. Hicks's posthumous *Journal of the Life and Religious Labours of Elias Hicks* (1832) contains useful details but little of its author's reflections. For his sermons and a flavor of the contemporary controversy they engendered, see *Letters and Observations Relating to the Controversy respecting the Doctrines of Elias Hicks* (1824); *A Series of Extemporaneous Discourses* (1825); M. T. C. Gould, ed., *Sermons by Thomas Wetherald and Elias Hicks* (1826); and [Isaac Hopper, ed.,] *Letters of Elias Hicks* (1834). A kind of periodical, the *Quaker* (1827–1828), ed. M. T. C. Gould, contains numerous sermons by Hicks and went to four volumes. For a somewhat dated but still the most complete biography, see Bliss Forbush, *Elias Hicks, Quaker Liberal* (1956). The only full account of the separation is H. Larry Ingle, *Quakers in Conflict: The Hicksite Reformation* (1986).

H. LARRY INGLE

HICKS, Granville (9 Sept. 1901–18 June 1982), literary critic and author, was born in Exeter, New Hampshire, the son of Frank Steven Hicks, the superintendent of a small factory, and Carrie Weston. Active as a young man in the Universalist church in Framingham, Massachusetts, Hicks attended Harvard College, where he studied English. After graduating summa cum laude in 1923, he entered Harvard Theological School for two years before giving it up to teach and write. He married his high school sweetheart, Dorothy Dyer, in 1925 and became an instructor in religion and English at Smith College. There he met and was influenced by his colleague Newton Arvin's antibusiness views and Van Wyck Brooks's ideas about the role of the artist in society. Brooks had championed the creation of a society that would be compatible with and would foster the work of artists; he felt that the artist suffered in an industrial, mass society like that of the United States.

Following publication in 1927 of an article in the *American Mercury*, which dealt with how hawkish church ministers had been in World War I, Hicks continued to write articles and reviews for this and other journals, including *American Literature, Forum, Nation, New Republic,* and *South Atlantic Quarterly.* He wrote about literature and social values especially, as well as political and social topics. After earning an M.A. in English from Harvard in 1929, he became a professor of English at Rensselaer Polytechnic Institute. He had been feeling increasingly alienated from American society because of such perceived injustices as the execution of Nicola Sacco and Bartolomeo Vanzetti in 1927. In 1932 he openly espoused communism in the journal *New Masses* and became its literary editor in 1934. Because of his Communist party activities, he was let go from his teaching position in 1935.

Following his dismissal, Hicks worked principally from his home near the village of Grafton, New York. Like many other leftists of the time, he believed that the task of literature was to expose social injustice and to celebrate proletarian solidarity. Art was to be a weapon for revolution. He criticized such writers as Pearl Buck, Willa Cather, William Faulkner, Henry James (1843–1916), Ernest Hemingway (until Hemingway published *To Have and Have Not* in 1937), Thomas Mann, Thornton Wilder, and Thomas Wolfe for failing in this task. He approved of such writers as John Dos Passos, James T. Farrell, Sinclair Lewis, and John Steinbeck, and he was enthusiastic about various "proletarian" writers including Jack Conroy, Kenneth Fearing, Horace Gregory, Albert Halper, B. Traven, and Richard Wright.

Hicks and others on the left were united during the 1930s in their opposition to the rising threat of fascism in Germany, Italy, and Spain. Shocked by Stalin's nonaggression pact with Hitler in August 1939, Hicks quit the *New Masses* and in a letter of 4 October in the *New Republic* resigned publicly from the Communist party. He underwent a period of profound soul-searching, and he subsequently wrote about the failure of literary Marxism and communism. In the 1940s he worked as a publisher's reader and occasional book reviewer and wrote a utopian novel, *The First to Awaken*

(1940), and three tolerable novels on life in small towns as well as on his experience with radical politics. The first one, *Only One Storm* (1942), sold well, but the other two did not. Also based on his experiences and on some research, Hicks wrote a nonfiction social study, *Small Town* (1946), which received good reviews. It is in my opinion a wise and humble book. Hicks no longer believed that the weight of reforming the world lay on his shoulders. The book also deals with his preference for the small town and with the trends toward urbanization in the United States.

During the 1950s he wrote a column, "Living with Books," for the *New Leader.* In April 1958 he began a similar column, "Literary Horizons," for the *Saturday Review,* which he continued writing until 1969 and which received considerable acclaim. Hicks felt that he and other leftist critics had been wrong in their preoccupation with the political uses of literature during the 1930s, and he recanted many of the attacks he had made on important writers during his Marxist days. He remained concerned, nevertheless, with the social and moral aspects of literature and was impatient with the excesses of academic formalism, especially the New Criticism, which he called "the New Pedantry." Hicks insisted on an eclectic, flexible approach to literature and focused on the concerns of readers, not scholars, although he acknowledged that a close reading of a literary text could be useful. Hicks considered Edmund Wilson to be America's best critic. During his later years Hicks wrote hundreds of reviews and covered the new writers emerging after World War II, praising Saul Bellow, James Gould Cozzens, Herbert Gold, Carson McCullers, Bernard Malamud, Wright Morris, Flannery O'Connor, Philip Roth, and John Updike, among others.

Hicks called himself a "critical liberal" after 1939, but in the 1960s he rejected the liberal label because many liberals until the second half of the decade had supported the Vietnam war. In 1973 he described himself as "a radical with no place to go." He resented being labeled an ex-Communist, since he had done most of his literary work after his rejection of Marxism. Hicks suffered a severe seizure or stroke in 1975, and he and his wife went to live with their only child in Kendall Park, New Jersey. He died in a convalescent home in Franklin Park, New Jersey.

• Hicks's letters and papers are deposited at Syracuse University. Autobiographical works are *Where We Came Out* (1954) and *Part of the Truth* (1965). Leftist works from the 1930s are *The Great Tradition* (1933, 1935; paperback reprint with important new afterword, 1969); *John Reed: The Making of a Revolutionary* (1936); *Figures of Transition* (1939); and *Granville Hicks in the New Masses,* ed. Jack Alan Robbins (1974). Hicks's later criticism is sampled in *Literary Horizons: A Quarter Century of American Fiction* (1970). For critical commentary, see Terry L. Long, *Granville Hicks* (1981); Daniel Aaron, *Writers on the Left* (1961); and Malcolm Cowley, *Think Back on Us* (1967). An obituary is in the *New York Times,* 19 June 1982.

TERRY L. LONG

HICKS, Otis. *See* Lightnin' Slim.

HICKS, Thomas Holliday (2 Sept. 1798–13 Feb. 1865), governor of Maryland and U.S. senator, was born in Dorchester County, Maryland, where his parents Henry Hicks and Mary Sewell were prosperous Eastern Shore farmers. Hicks attended a district school and was briefly a merchant, a shipowner, and a slaveholding farmer before establishing his career in politics. He married three times—to Anne Thompson, Leah Raleigh, and Mary Wilcox.

In 1824 Hicks was elected sheriff of Dorchester County and from then until his death was a public official. From 1830 to 1838 he served in the Maryland state legislature as an assemblyman. During that time he was also a member of the state electoral college that, until a change in the Maryland constitution, elected state senators. Hicks was a member of the influential Governor's Council for a year until it was abolished in 1838, meanwhile retaining his post as Dorchester County registrar of wills from 1838 to 1851.

Representative of a new group of professional politicians who made their living from politics, Hicks was elected a member of his county's delegation to the state's 1850 constitutional convention. Like many Maryland slaveholders during this period, Hicks changed parties from the Democrats to the Whigs in the 1840s, and during a period of party realignment during the 1850s, when the Whig party collapsed, he became a Know Nothing.

As a member of the Maryland constitutional convention of 1850, Hicks earned notoriety by opposing the election of judges, by sponsoring a resolution to guarantee every head of household in Maryland an inheritance of $500, and by proposing a procedure for the secession of the Eastern Shore from Maryland. While the last idea attracted many residents of the Eastern Shore who took seriously the possibility of separation from Maryland's Western Shore, his political opponents believed Hicks's other suggestions to be frivolous.

Hicks is best known for his governorship of Maryland during the Civil War. Under a constitutional provision that required the governorship to rotate among residents of the Eastern Shore, the Western Shore, and Baltimore, he was elected governor for a three-year term as a Know Nothing, taking office in 1858. At the time the principles of nativism appealed to Marylanders like Hicks who worried about the impact of immigration on American workers and who wanted to retain a Protestant, English-based culture, which they believed was threatened by Irish and German immigrants. Accordingly, Hicks supported extending the period of naturalization and ending public support of Catholic schools. In the presidential election of 1860 he voted for the Constitutional Unionist candidate John Bell.

During the secession crisis of 1860–1861, Governor Hicks took several crucial steps to keep the border slave state of Maryland in the Union. First he refused to meet officially with the agents of seceded southern states intent on persuading Maryland to join the Confederacy. Then, following the sentiments of the Unionist majority of Maryland, he refused to call a special session of the legislature, which met biennially and was not scheduled to meet until 1862. Staunchly he resisted a move to organize a state convention to consider the issue of secession. Throughout the winter Hicks remained convinced that the critical issue for Marylanders was that they choose for themselves their future, and he reminded the governor of South Carolina "that Maryland should not convene her legislature at the bidding of South Carolina."

While Hicks sympathized with southern opposition to the North's personal liberty laws that freed fugitive slaves, he continued to resist a Confederate conspiracy to force Maryland out of the Union. Appealing before the start of the war for peace and reason, he represented a moderate body of thought in Maryland, which believed that the border states of Kentucky, Delaware, Missouri, and Maryland could serve as territorial buffers between the North and South. Such a confederation might prevent war and serve as a force to adjudicate sectional differences peacefully.

Once the war began, Hicks negotiated with President Abraham Lincoln to keep Maryland's militia in the state. When a Baltimore mob attacked Massachusetts troops on their way to defend Washington in April of 1861, Hicks may have accepted a plan of the neutralists to burn railroad bridges north of Baltimore in order to isolate the state and prevent Union troop movements through Maryland. The square-jawed governor pleaded for calm and assured Marylanders that any troops traveling through Maryland were only for the defense of Washington from Confederate attack. To the crowds in Baltimore he delivered a stirring speech that concluded, "I am a Marylander. I love my state and I love the Union."

On 22 April 1861 Hicks called the legislature into special session to deal with issues raised by the Civil War. He did not convene the legislature in the state capital of Annapolis but instead chose Frederick, a town in the northwest part of the state. His probable intention was to remove lawmakers from Annapolis where Union troops landed on their way to Washington, a situation that would irritate legislators who believed in Maryland's neutrality.

When the possibility of his state brokering negotiations between the North and the South collapsed, the governor was ready to give firm allegiance to the Lincoln administration, which offered him a brigadier generalship in the army. Hicks refused, but when his gubernatorial term ended and Maryland senator James Pearce died, Hicks was appointed for a year to fill the term. In 1864 the legislature elected him to a full term. Supporting Lincoln's reelection in 1864, Hicks the Unionist generally voted with the Republicans in the Senate, and he was appointed to the Committee of Naval Affairs. Hicks had injured his leg in 1864, and a year later he died in Washington, D.C., from an infection following its amputation. Never an influential U.S. senator, his historical significance rests in his support, as a border state governor, of the Union during a critical period.

• Very few letters and documents relating to Thomas Hicks's life have survived. The best study is that of George Radcliffe, *Governor Thomas H. Hicks of Maryland and the Civil War* (1901). See also Heinrich Buchholz, *Governors of Maryland* (1908), and Roy Glashan, *American Governors and Gubernatorial Elections, 1775–1975* (1975). There is material on Hicks in Jean H. Baker, *The Politics of Continuity: Maryland Political Parties from 1858–1870* (1973–1977); and Robert Brugger, *Maryland: A Middle Temperament* (1988). See the obituaries in the *Congressional Record*, 38th Cong.

JEAN H. BAKER

HIDALGO, Francisco (1659?–Sept. 1726), Franciscan friar, was born in Spain. Neither his birthplace nor his parents are known. At age fifteen he completed the requisite study and took the religious habit. At age twenty-four he sailed for New Spain (Mexico) as one of the founders of the missionary college of Santa Cruz de Querétaro. From Querétaro Hidalgo joined other priests on missions to neighboring parishes and quickly won a reputation for preaching against vice. The Franciscan historian Juan Domingo Arricivita describes, from his own religious perspective, the fruits of Hidalgo's discourse in the bishopric of Puebla: "Indecent costumes were abandoned, thefts and usuries were restored, ancient enmities reconciled, illicit and dishonest trade stopped; and above all, general confessions and public penitence were seen on every hand" (p. 208).

In 1688 Hidalgo and two of his religious brothers left the missionary college to undertake conversion of native peoples beyond the northern frontier. Barred from going past Monclova, they worked among the Alasapa Indians at Boca de Leones (present-day Villadama, Nuevo León). Hidalgo's chance to seek conversion of the "pagan" tribes of the north resulted from the threat to Spanish interests seen in the Frenchman Robert Cavelier de la Salle's landing on the Texas coast.

After Spanish soldiers had found the French settlement and captured its survivors, a Franciscan mission was placed in eastern Texas to secure the Spanish claim by occupying the territory. Such missions served as instruments of both church and state, attempting to make the natives useful Spanish subjects while converting them to Christianity. Hidalgo entered the frontier province with the expedition of Domingo Terán de los Ríos in 1691, to work among the Hasinai Confederacy. This Caddoan group occupied an extensive area of eastern Texas centered on the Neches and Angelina river valleys. Its population at this time has been estimated at 4,000 to 5,000. Hidalgo remained at the Mission San Francisco de los Tejas, in present-day Houston County, Texas, until it was abandoned in 1693, as the Indians, falling victim to the white man's diseases and believing the baptismal waters fatal, threatened a massacre. Hidalgo, reluctant to leave the unfinished task, pledged to return to begin anew. The resolution guided his actions for twenty-

three years before he finally saw the opportunity for its fulfillment.

From the missionary college at Querétaro, Hidalgo was sent in 1698 to establish missions on the borders of Coahuila and Nuevo León. The first mission began with a chapel of straw at Lampazos de Naranjo, Nuevo León. The following year he and his companion, Fray Diego de Salazar, were requested by Coahuiltecans to found a mission among them on the Río de Sabinas, ten leagues farther north. In response the Mission San Juan Bautista was placed on the Río de Sabinas with Father Hidalgo in charge. On 1 January 1700 the mission was transferred to a new location near the Río Grande at present-day Guerrero, Coahuila, and there became the gateway to the region beyond: the Spanish province of Texas.

Two months later Hidalgo and Fray Antonio de San Buenaventura y Olivares established nearby a second Coahuiltecan mission called San Francisco Solano. Together the two priests worked toward material improvement of the site while struggling against cultural differences, the language barrier, and hostility. In time the enclave was expanded to include a third mission, San Bernardo, and a presidio, or military garrison, for the settlement's protection. Hidalgo, however, was called to Querétaro late in 1700 as guardian of the Colegio de la Santa Cruz. Not until late 1703 did he return to the Río Grande to serve as president of the three missions.

In all this time, as Arricivita tells it, Hidalgo longed and planned to take up the unfinished task among the Hasinai. His petitions to his superiors went unheeded. At last, in January 1711 he sent a letter to the French governor of Louisiana asking about the Indians' welfare and whether he might be permitted to establish a mission for them. It was a provocative move that bore great implications for the future of Texas and the United States. In response, the French governor, Antoine de La Mothe, Sieur Cadillac, with commercial motives, sent the veteran soldier and explorer Louis Juchereau de Saint-Denis to find the Spanish friar. Saint-Denis, having come from Mobile, reached San Juan Bautista in July 1714. The threat implicit in his journey across the vacant province of Texas stirred Spanish officials to action. In late April 1716 a new missionary expedition left San Juan Bautista, destined for the permanent occupation of eastern Texas. By early the following year six missions and a fort had been founded among the Caddoan tribes of eastern Texas and western Louisiana. Father Hidalgo himself headed the mission, called Nuestro Padre San Francisco de los Tejas, successor to the 1690 endeavor. In the coming months his letters spoke eloquently of the nature of the Hasinai, the hardships of the missions, and the activities of the French.

In 1720, following temporary withdrawal from the region because of war with the French, Hidalgo was assigned to the Mission San Antonio de Valero. This mission, formerly San Francisco Solano, had been moved from the Río Grande in 1718 to the San Antonio River in Texas. It is remembered in history as the Alamo.

The San Antonio missions were sorely afflicted by Apache raids during their early years. Spanish military forces responded with bloody retaliation. Advocating more peaceful means, Hidalgo blamed the failure to settle the Apaches on improper management of the presidios. On 25 March 1725 he and a lay brother sought leave from their superiors to go into Apache country, armed only with a desire to spread the Christian gospel. Permission was denied. Father Hidalgo, in despair, retired to San Juan Bautista, where he died. He had served the religious calling for fifty-two years, thirty-five of which were on the frontiers of Coahuila and Texas.

Although often frustrated in his effort to convert native peoples to Catholicism, Fray Francisco Hidalgo put in motion forces that bore results far beyond his expectations. His hope for an Apache mission ultimately was realized, albeit with disappointing results. More important, he brought about the lasting Spanish occupation of Texas and thereby influenced development of the region well beyond the end of the Spanish regime.

• Important Hidalgo letters are found in the Archivo General y Público de la Nación México, vol. 181, and in Archivo San Francisco el Grande, vol. 10. Juan Domingo Arricivita, *Crónica seráfica y apostólica del Colegio de propaganda fide de la Santa Cruz de Querétaro en la Nueva España, segunda parte* (1792), pp. 206–26, provides a useful but somewhat eulogistic biographical sketch of Hidalgo. Hidalgo's part in the actual founding and operation of missions in northern Mexico and Texas is brought into focus by Isidro Félix de Espinosa, *Crónica de los colegios de propaganda fide de la Nueva España* (1746; new ed., 1964), pp. 685, 751–56; see also Lino Gómez Canedo's introduction to the new edition. Espinosa was closely associated with Hidalgo, both at San Juan Bautista and in the East Texas missions founded in 1716, and therefore wrote with considerable authority. Hidalgo's letters were drawn upon by Robert S. Weddle in *San Juan Bautista: Gateway to Spanish Texas* (1968), which offers a fairly comprehensive view of the missionary priest.

ROBERT S. WEDDLE

HIESTER, Joseph (18 Nov. 1752–10 June 1832), merchant and politician, was born in Bern Township, Berks County, Pennsylvania, the son of John Hiester and Mary Barbara Epler, farmers. In 1737 his father and three brothers had emigrated from Silesia, then part of the Hapsburg Empire, to the colony of Pennsylvania. Eventually buying several thousand acres of land in Berks County, his father and two brothers moved to Bern Township, where Joseph was born. From an early age, Joseph worked hard on the farm. He obtained his formal education under the minister at the Bern church but could attend classes for only a few months of the year, during the intervals of farm labor. When he grew up, he was apprenticed as a clerk in the general store of Adam Whitman in Reading. He became a partner in the business in 1771, when he married Whitman's daughter, Elizabeth Whitman. Together they had six children.

Opposed to the elitist politics of the colony's proprietary government, Hiester became an enthusiastic Whig patriot and was soon heavily engaged in the revolutionary cause. He was a delegate to the provincial congress at Philadelphia, which in June 1776 suspended the proprietary authority, assumed the government of the colony, and called a convention to frame a state constitution. Returning to Reading, he helped to raise and equip troops for the fight against the British army and was chosen captain of the militia. In the battle of Long Island he commanded a company in Colonel Henry Haller's battalion. On the night of 26 August, after losing several of his men, Hiester was captured by the British. Together with many other American officers he spent several weeks on the infamous prison ship *Jersey*. He was then moved to a prison in New York City; his health further deteriorated until he was paroled and exchanged. Soon he rejoined George Washington's army, was promoted to lieutenant colonel, and was slightly wounded at the battle of Germantown on 4 October 1777. In 1779 he served as a commissioner of exchange for prisoners of war and as a member of a committee charged with the confiscation of Loyalist property. The following year he returned to his family in Reading and took sole possession of the mercantile business.

During the 1780s Hiester became involved in the intensely partisan politics of the state of Pennsylvania. He represented his predominantly German neighbors in Berks County and joined the radical Constitutionalist party, which defended Pennsylvania's revolutionary constitution against the more conservative Republicans led by Robert Morris and James Wilson. Between 1780 and 1790 Hiester served five one-year terms in the Pennsylvania assembly. He was elected to the Pennsylvania state convention, which met from 20 November to 15 December 1787 to discuss and ratify the new federal constitution. In accordance with his radical convictions, he opposed ratification and signed the Antifederalist "Address and Reason of Dissent of the Minority of the Convention of the State of Pennsylvania to Their Constituents." The dissent summarized the arguments against adoption of the Constitution, such as the fear of losing essential state rights, and presented a number of amendments to the public, thus giving sanction to the growing demand for a bill of rights.

After ratification of the new federal constitution, Hiester participated in the state constitutional convention of 1789–1790, which brought the Pennsylvania constitution of 1776 into line with the new federal system. Like most Constitutionalists, Hiester was now ready to admit that the revolutionary frame of government had been defective. Following this convention he served four years in the newly created state senate, and in 1792 as well as in 1796 he was a presidential elector. In 1797 he became a representative in Congress from Berks County. He was reelected as a Republican six times and served a total of fourteen years (1797–1805 and 1815–1820). In Congress he gained a reputation as a pragmatist, and Jefferson regarded him as "disinterested, moderate and conscientious."

From 1807 to 1810 Hiester commanded the Pennsylvania state militia, with the rank of major general. After the War of 1812 he sided with the Independent or "Old School" wing of the Republican party, which opposed the policy of Governor Simon Snyder and championed traditional Jeffersonian values. In 1817 he entered the gubernatorial race in Pennsylvania on the Independent Republican ticket but was defeated by William Findlay, a Snyderist. After resigning from Congress in 1820, he was renominated by his party on a platform that attacked nominations by legislative caucus and that advocated various political and economic reforms. With the additional support of Federalists, he beat Governor Findlay by a narrow margin to become the fifth governor of Pennsylvania. In his inaugural address he declared, "Considering myself elected by the people of this Commonwealth, and not by any particular denomination of persons, I shall endeavour to deserve the name of Chief Magistrate of Pennsylvania, and to avoid the disgraceful appellation of the Governor of a Party" (Vaux, p. 18).

Hiester was true to his word. While in office, he surprised friend and foe by making appointments according to merit and without regard to party line. He pushed for a liberal, state-supported system of education and for internal improvements, advocating the chartering of numerous canal and turnpike companies. During his term the great highway across the Allegheny Mountains to Pittsburgh was completed. In accord with the one-term principle of old republican spirit, Hiester refused to stand for reelection in 1823. Concluding a career of nearly fifty years in public life, he retired to his home in Reading to take care of his business interests. When he died he left a considerable estate of $460,000.

Hiester was not among the first-rate, nationally renowned politicians of his time. However, he translated his firm republican beliefs and principles into day-to-day politics. Moreover, as a successful state politician he contributed in an important way to the integration of Pennsylvania's German minority into the state and federal political processes.

• Primary records are included in the Hiester Family Collection and the Orbison Family Papers, both located at the Pennsylvania State Archives. There exist only a few biographical essays on Hiester, dating back to the turn of the last century: Henry M. M. Richards, "Governor Joseph Hiester; a Historical Sketch," Pennsylvania-German Society, *Proceedings and Addresses* 16 (1907); "The Hiester Family," Pennsylvania Archives, 4th ser., 5 (1900); and Richard Vaux, *Sketch of the Life of Joseph Hiester, Governor of Pennsylvania* (1887). Some additional information about Hiester's stand in the ratification debate can be derived from John B. McMaster and Frederick D. Stone, eds., *Pennsylvania and the Federal Constitution, 1787–1788* (1888). Also informative are David M. Gregg, "Governor Joseph Hiester," *Berks County Historical Review* 1 (1936): 99–106, and Sandford W. Higginbotham, *The Keystone in the Democratic Arch: Pennsylvania Politics 1800–1816* (1952).

JÜRGEN HEIDEKING

HIGGINBOTHAM, J. C. (11 May 1906–26 May 1973), jazz trombonist, was born Jay C. Higginbotham in Social Circle, Georgia. Little is known of his parents or early family life other than that he was the thirteenth of fourteen children, all of whom were raised in a musical environment. A sister and one brother played trombone, another brother played trumpet, and his niece was a composer.

Higginbotham attended school in Cincinnati, where he apprenticed as a tailor at the Cincy Colored Training School and worked at the General Motors factory before joining Wesley Helvey's band as a professional musician in 1924. After two years with Helvey, he left for Buffalo, New York, to work with Eugene Primos and trombonist Jimmy Harrison (1926–1927). He then settled in New York in 1928. There, while sitting in with the Chick Webb orchestra at the Savoy Ballroom, he was hired by bandleader Luis Russell; he remained with Russell until 1931. Higginbotham developed into an especially strong soloist during this period, and he was frequently featured in Russell's band, soloing after Louis Armstrong on such recordings as "Mahogany Hall Stomp" and "Dallas Blues" (both 1929). During the next few years Higginbotham migrated through many of the prominent black swing bands of the 1930s, including those led by Webb, Fletcher Henderson, Lucky Millinder, and Benny Carter, before rejoining Russell in 1937 for three years in which Russell's orchestra again provided the backing for Armstrong.

Higginbotham's reputation during the swing years (1930s and early 1940s) continued to grow, culminating in his selection as the winner of the *Down Beat* poll (1941–1944), the *Metronome* poll (1943–1945), and the *Esquire* gold award in 1945. But the arrival of bebop and the rise of younger trombonists (J. J. Johnson, Benny Green, Kai Winding) began to detract from Higginbotham's stature in the late 1940s and early 1950s. With the demand for his skills as a sideman considerably lessened, he began working a succession of modest engagements in Cleveland, Boston, and New York. A recording that he made with trumpeter Buck Clayton in March 1956 was his first in ten years.

Throughout much of his career Higginbotham was closely associated with trumpeter Henry "Red" Allen. Few partnerships in jazz have been so successful, for the two began working together in 1929 while in the Russell orchestra and continued to play together intermittently for more than thirty years in such groups as the Blue Rhythm Band (1934) and the Russell orchestra (while backing Armstrong, 1937–1940), and at such places as the Garrick Stage Bar in Chicago (1942), the Onyx Club, the Apollo Theatre (early 1940s), and Kelly's Stables in New York City (1946). In late 1956 Higginbotham was back with Allen for a stay at the Metropole Cafe in New York and remained there intermittently until the summer of 1959. During the 1960s Higginbotham fronted a succession of small groups, most of them with a New Orleans revival tinge, but although he continued to play until the early 1970s, these were difficult years for him. Writer Paul

Hemphill in 1966 related how the trombonist had fallen on hard times and even had to borrow cab fare in order to participate in a jam session at Eddie Condon's New York club during the mid-1960s.

Higginbotham remained active as a performer almost until his death in New York City, but his contributions as a pioneering jazz trombonist were made early in his career. His powerful tone, surefooted technique, and legato style—a style introduced by Jimmy Harrison but refined by Higginbotham during the 1930s—placed him in the vanguard of jazz trombonists who gradually overcame the problems of technical agility that afflicted the first generation of players. He transformed the trombone into a modern instrument, closer in dexterity to that of other horns, and his consistent ability as an improviser made him the dominant model for an emerging group of younger trombonists that included Trummy Young, Bill Harris, and Eddie Bert.

• Higginbotham's early recordings of his own original compositions include "Higginbotham Blues" and "Give Me Your Telephone Number" (both in 1930), but during the 1930s and 1940s he also recorded with many well-known jazz artists, including Lil Armstrong, Mezz Mezzrow, Coleman Hawkins, Fletcher Henderson, Henry "Red" Allen, Louis Armstrong (his most consistently featured sideman on Armstrong's large band recordings of the late 1920s), Lionel Hampton, Cootie Williams, Rex Stewart, and Tiny Grimes. A selected discography spanning 1930 until 1966 is listed in Walter Bruyninckx, *Sixty Years of Recorded Jazz, 1917–1977* (1977–1983). Additional titles can be found in Roger D. Kinkle, *The Complete Encyclopedia of Popular Music and Jazz, 1900–1950* (1974), and in the standard jazz discographies of Brian Rust, *Jazz Records, 1897–1942* (1970), and Jorgen Grunnet Jepsen, *Jazz Records: A Discography* (1963–). Most of the information outlining Higginbotham's career is currently available only in introductory articles that appear in standard jazz reference works and in a few periodicals. Brief biographical sketches can be found in Leonard Feather, "Jay C. Higginbotham," *Down Beat* 8, no. 6 (1941), pp. 10–11, and Bernard Houghton, "Higginbotham Blues," *Jazz Journal* 31, no. 1 (1968): 4–5. Higginbotham's 1967 return to Atlanta for a homecoming recording session and an appearance at the Atlanta Jazz Festival is described in two articles from the *Atlanta Journal and Constitution*, Paul Hemphill, "Repaying Higgy," 24 Nov. 1966, and Richard Hughes, "Atlanta Movin', Says Higgy As He Brings Sliphorn Home," 16 June 1967. The most complete assessment of Higginbotham's musical contributions can be found in Gunther Schuller, *The Swing Era: The Development of Jazz, 1930–1945* (1989). The C. Jones monograph, *J. C. Higginbotham* (1944), is out of print. An obituary is in the *New York Times*, 28 May 1973.

CHARLES BLANCQ

HIGGINS, Alice Louise. See Lothrop, Alice Higgins.

HIGGINS, Andrew Jackson (28 Aug. 1886–1 Aug. 1952), industrialist and shipbuilder, was born in Columbus, Nebraska, the son of John Gonegal Higgins and Annie Long O'Conor. His father, a judge and newspaper editor, was a close friend of Grover Cleveland. Intense loyalty to the Democratic party inspired Judge Higgins to name his son after the seventh president. Andrew Jackson Higgins attended public schools in Columbus and Omaha and then Creighton Preparatory School from 1900 to 1903.

In 1906, after stints in the National Guard, in logging, and in truck driving, Higgins purchased a timber farm and launched a lumber company in Mobile County, Alabama. There he met Angele Leona Colsson; they married in 1908 and had six children.

A combination of hurricane and economic depression ruined Higgins's business, and in 1910 he moved to New Orleans, where he became general manager of a German-owned lumber company. He quit in 1915 over philosophical differences with his employers after Germans sank the *Lusitania*. He then again started his own lumber company, which wholesaled logs imported from Central America, Africa, and the Philippines. After that enterprise failed in 1923, Higgins made shipbuilding an integral part of his subsequent business operations.

Higgins transported the lumber for his new enterprise, Higgins Lumber and Export Company (formed in 1922), with a small fleet of sailing ships and built a repair yard to service his ships. When the market for mahogany logs dried up, Higgins cut up the logs and built barges, then embarked on small-boat design and construction, which he had studied as a correspondence student in naval architecture at the National University of Sciences in Chicago. By 1926 he was manufacturing boats as his primary business. Indeed, by 1931 Higgins Lumber and Export was defunct, a year after the formation of Higgins Industries, which focused on the manufacture and sale of a variety of boats. The same year he formed the new enterprise, one of his boats, *And How III*, beat the record of ninety hours for the run from New Orleans to St. Louis that had stood for more than fifty years. In 1931 Higgins's *Dixie Greyhound* lowered the record to seventy-two hours.

Oil drillers and lumbermen used Higgins's motorboats, tugs, and barges; his speed boats were used both by rum-runners and by their Coast Guard pursuers. The most innovative of the boats was the *Eureka*, a shallow-craft vessel whose propeller and shaft were housed in a semitunnel to protect it from submerged obstacles. The boat was fast, durable, and maneuverable and could operate in less than a foot of water. Higgins adapted the *Eureka* into various forms of landing craft for wartime use, the most significant of which featured a ramp that replaced the rounded bow. This design allowed the craft to unload personnel or vehicles in shallow water.

Both the navy and the marines tested Higgins's boats in 1938, and he received his first navy contract the same year. In 1940 his 36-foot *Eureka* outperformed an entry by the navy's Bureau of Construction and Repair, resulting in a contract for 335 boats. Higgins caught the attention of military brass the following year, when the navy asked him to begin designing an experimental tank carrier. When Marine Corps and navy officials arrived at Higgins's place of business in

New Orleans a couple of days later they were shown a completed 45-foot boat rather than just the drawings they had expected to see. The boat had been designed, built, and launched in sixty-one hours. Higgins received an immediate contract for fifty of the tank carriers. With war raging in Europe and fears of possible conflict in the Pacific, Higgins soon found his steadiest customers in the armed forces.

During the war Higgins Industries built torpedo boats, patrol boats, and other small craft. Most important, though, were his various amphibious boats, which saw action in North Africa, Europe, and the South Pacific. More than 1,500 Higgins landing craft participated in the D-Day invasion of Normandy. The press dubbed Higgins "today's Noah" and a "shipyard Bunyan."

Reflecting his rapid rise, Higgins was called, along with three other shipbuilders, to appear in 1943 before the Senate committee investigating the United States's war effort. Instead of grilling Higgins and the others about problems or mistakes, the committee sought to understand their secrets of success at achieving efficiency and speed, in hopes that similar production records could be attained at other yards.

Higgins Industries became one of the nation's most striking examples of war-related industrial growth. Sales rose from a 1937 level of $422,000 to a peak of $94 million in 1944; the number of workers Higgins employed rose from 300 in 1939 to a wartime peak of more than 20,000. Higgins Industries ultimately built more than 20,000 boats during World War II, a greater number than any other American shipbuilder.

Higgins attracted the attention of the national press not only through his firm's performance but also through contracts he was first granted and then denied—including the largest single contracts in both shipbuilding and aviation history. The shipbuilding cancellation was the more controversial. In July 1942 the Maritime Commission canceled the Higgins contract to build 200 "Liberty" ships—10,500–ton cargo vessels—on the grounds of a shortage of steel. The cancellation caused a public outcry and a congressional investigation. Higgins accused eastern industrialists of engineering the cancellation as a means of avoiding postwar competition. African-American leaders argued that the cancellation destroyed "one of the biggest opportunities ever given to the Negro race"; two of the four assembly lines were to employ all-black crews. Perhaps the biggest factor in the cancellation, however, was the increased efficiency of existing shipyards; the president's production goals for 1943 could be achieved without using additional yards.

Brimming with energy, Higgins worked long hours and pushed his workers, including his four sons, to do the same. His belief in collective bargaining—a rarity in southern industry at the time—helped develop a relationship with President Franklin D. Roosevelt (Higgins headed "Businessmen for Roosevelt" during the 1944 campaign). During the war, however, his work force grew so rapidly that thirteen craft unions represented his workers, and jurisdictional disputes presented Higgins with increasing difficulties. In 1945 he liquidated Higgins Industries and established Higgins, Incorporated, in an attempt to avoid union problems, which persisted nevertheless.

More important to Higgins, the market for merchant shipbuilding dried up after the war. The American government contributed to producers' difficulties by putting surplus army and navy boats on the market. Higgins returned to building commercial craft and pleasure boats and dabbled in the production of housing materials. He was innovative in design and in his willingness to try new mass-production methods. Throughout his career, his boats were tremendous examples of form following function. His enterprises, however, which had taken off as a consequence of increased government demand for boats, declined as quickly as they had risen. Higgins was better at building boats than at building—and sustaining—a business. Yet other organizations with equally primitive management structures (such as Kaiser and Howard Hughes) thrived after the war as markets for their products took off rather than dried up. Higgins's fortunes simply rose and fell with the government's demand for boats.

Andrew Jackson Higgins was a popular symbol of the can-do spirit associated with the American production effort during World War II. Indeed, General Dwight D. Eisenhower later referred to Higgins as "the man who won the war for us." Higgins died in New Orleans.

• A biography of Higgins is Jerry E. Strahan, *Andrew Jackson Higgins and the Boats That Won World War II* (1994). On the significance of Higgins's boats, see George Garland and Truman R. Stronbridge, *Western Pacific Operations*, vol. 4 of *History of U.S. Marine Corps Operations in World War II* (1971); Benis M. Frank and Henry I. Shaw, Jr., *Victory and Occupation*, vol. 5 of *History of U.S. Marine Corps Operations in World War II* (1968); Ronald W. Charles, *Troopships of World War II* (1947); and Frederic C. Lane, *Ships for Victory: A History of Shipbuilding under the U.S. Maritime Commission in World War II* (1951). See also Herman B. Deutsch, "Shipyard Bunyan," *Saturday Evening Post*, 11 July, 1942, p. 22; Don Eddy, "Mr. Higgins Builds a Navy," *American Magazine*, Sept. 1942, p. 22; "The Boss," *Fortune*, July 1943, p. 101; and "Mr. Higgins and His Wonderful Boats," *Life* 16 Aug. 1943, p. 100. On the Senate's investigation of Higgins, see Donald H. Riddle, *The Truman Committee: A Study in Congressional Responsibility* (1964).

STEPHEN B. ADAMS

HIGGINS, Frank Wayland (18 Aug. 1856–12 Feb. 1907), businessman and politician, was born in Rushford, Allegany County, New York, the son of Orrin T. Higgins, a storekeeper and businessman, and Lucia Cornelia Hapgood. He attended the Rushford Academy and, with a youthful interest in soldiering, the Riverview Military Academy in Poughkeepsie, New York, from which he graduated in 1873. He supplemented his education with a commercial course in a business college and extensive travel through various parts of the United States. Higgins worked briefly as a salesman in Denver, Chicago, and then in Stanton,

Michigan, where for three years he was a partner in Wood, Thayer, and Company, a mercantile firm. In 1878 he married Catherine Corrinne Noble; they had three children. The next year he returned to New York state and joined his father in Olean in the grocery firm of Higgins, Blodgett, and Company. Later he acquired additional stores in Olean and had large holdings in pine timberlands and iron ore fields in the West, some of which he inherited from his father. He became head of a half-dozen corporations in Michigan, Minnesota, Oregon, and Washington and often visited their operations to see that they were functioning properly. Contemporaries attributed Higgins's business successes to sound judgment, shrewd investment practices, and solid administrative abilities.

Higgins early developed an interest in politics. Although his father was a staunch Democrat, Higgins as a youth espoused Republican principles such as tariff protection, civil rights, and pensions and benefits to Civil War veterans. He attended the 1888 Republican National Convention as a delegate and cast his ballot for the presidential nomination of Benjamin Harrison (1833–1901). For several years he resisted encouragement in Olean to run for public office but in 1893 succumbed to the entreaties of local Republican officials and accepted the nomination for the New York State Senate seat from a district that comprised Cattaraugus and Chautauqua counties. He easily won the election and was reelected thrice thereafter (1896, 1898, and 1900), each time by substantial pluralities. In the senate Higgins chaired major committees, including Finance and Taxation and Retrenchment. His devotion to governmental economy and efficiency and his leadership in the passage of important legislation earned him, in 1902, the Republican nomination for lieutenant governor, to which he was elected. Two years later, with the backing of President Theodore Roosevelt (1858–1919) and state GOP chairman Benjamin B. Odell, Jr., Higgins was nominated for governor. In the ensuing campaign he emphasized his independence from all political bosses and the need to continue the state's indirect tax system. He won the governorship by a plurality of 80,560 votes over Democrat D. Cady Herrick following a tough, hard-fought campaign.

As governor Higgins pressed hard for the extension of the civil service to county government, reform of the state tax structure by phasing out direct taxation and developing further indirect taxes such as those on stock transfer, and generally a businesslike administration of executive offices. His economy-mindedness left New York with a treasury surplus of $11 million by the end of his two-year term. Most important, however, was his constructive response to the joint legislative committee investigations in 1905 first of the gas and electric utilities in New York City and then of insurance companies doing business in the state. Conducted by the brilliant attorney Charles Evans Hughes, these investigations revealed large-scale corporate wrongdoing and mismanagement and have been considered the catalyst for the introduction of progressive government in Albany. They promoted much corrective legislation. Higgins strongly supported a measure that established a statewide public commission to supervise utilities and to regulate rates charged to customers. This 1905 law served as a model for the Public Service Commissions Act (1907) and similar legislation in fifteen other states. In 1906 he helped steer to passage several bills that would curtail abuses in the insurance industry, prohibit corporate contributions to political campaigns, and regulate campaign solicitations and expenditures.

Governor Higgins also began the process of reorganizing the Republican party of the state of New York, a move deemed necessary because the insurance investigation had publicized the existence of a corrupt politico-business alliance that discredited both the aging Republican U.S. senator Thomas C. Platt and State Chairman Odell, who were personally linked to insurance company wrongdoing. In late 1905 Higgins used his influence to replace an Odell man with Herbert Parsons as chairman of the New York County Republican Committee and in the selection of the youthful James W. Wadsworth, Jr., as Speaker of the state assembly. He stopped short of removing his old ally Odell for fear that deepening factionalism in the Republican party might threaten his renomination as governor in the summer of 1906. This failure, in turn, angered President Roosevelt, who had spurred the reorganization program, and Roosevelt pressured the state Republican nominating convention to dump Higgins in favor of the newcomer Hughes. Higgins graciously accepted his fate, in part because he was suffering from declining health and his physician had advised him to leave public life. He retired to his Olean home, attended Governor Hughes's inauguration, and suffered a fatal heart attack in Olean only six weeks after he left office.

As a politician Higgins was widely known for his candor, honesty, and probity. On the whole, he worked well with public figures of divergent persuasions, and his moderate Republicanism allowed him to tread a political path between regularity and independence. Although he was unspectacular in demeanor and style, his pragmatic approach to governing helped smooth the way toward the interventionist and regulatory state in New York that is often associated with twentieth-century progressive government.

• A small collection of Higgins papers is in the George Arents Research Library at Syracuse University. His gubernatorial papers are available in *Public Papers of Frank W. Higgins, Governor* (2 vols., 1906–1907). A biographical sketch appears in Ray B. Smith, ed., *Political and Governmental History of the State of New York*, vol. 4 (1922). The major features of his governorship are covered in Robert F. Wesser, *Charles Evans Hughes: Politics and Reform in New York, 1905–1910* (1967); and Richard L. McCormick, *From Realignment to Reform: Political Change in New York State, 1893–1910* (1981). An obituary is in the *New York Times*, 13 Feb. 1907.

ROBERT F. WESSER

HIGGINS, Marguerite (3 Sept. 1920–3 Jan. 1966), journalist, was born in Hong Kong, the daughter of Lawrence Daniel Higgins, an Irish-American freight company agent, and Marguerite Godard, a Frenchwoman. In 1923 her father became a stockbroker in Oakland, California, where the family settled. In 1937 she graduated from Oakland's exclusive Anna Head School and in 1941, from the University of California at Berkeley with a bachelor of science degree in French, with honors. Awarded a master of science degree from Columbia University's Graduate School of Journalism in 1942, she joined the *New York Herald Tribune* as a full-time reporter; she had been a part-time campus correspondent.

Higgins established her professional reputation early by working feverishly, exercising ingenuity, and gleaning interviews with public figures reportedly hostile to the press. She lobbied fiercely for an overseas assignment and in 1944, after having gained the support of Helen Rogers Reid, the wife of the *Herald Tribune*'s publisher, was dispatched first to London and Paris and then to the front in Germany.

Front-page stories earned Higgins international recognition and awards. *Herald Tribune* editorial executive and newspaper historian Harry W. Baehr, Jr., called her early career "exceptional," assessing her as "a great newspaperwoman." Higgins was among the first correspondents to reach Dachau and Buchenwald as the Allies were liberating the concentration camps, and her stories from the camps stunned readers. The New York Newspaper Women's Club recognized her reporting as the best foreign correspondence of 1945, and the army presented her with its campaign ribbon for "outstanding service with the armed forces under difficult conditions," a preview of the more than fifty awards she would eventually garner.

In 1947, age twenty-six, she was named the *Herald Tribune*'s Berlin bureau chief, the youngest woman ever selected for such a post. Higgins covered the 1948 Berlin Airlift and the Nuremberg war trials before being assigned to Tokyo as Far East bureau chief in May 1950. When her freelance articles appeared in popular magazines, such as *Mademoiselle* and the *Saturday Evening Post*, her audiences grew. She relished her role as a journalist, later recounting, "I have never lost this sense of excitement about newspapering. If I ever do, I'll quit" (*News Is a Singular Thing*, p. 16).

When the Korean War erupted in June 1950, Higgins was among the first reporters there and the only woman. Although the *Herald Tribune*'s senior military correspondent, Homer Bigart, arrived soon after to cover the conflict, Higgins was determined to report the story herself and refused to leave the area. The paper, to Bigart's annoyance, acquiesced. Their competition became legendary, some said driving them both to Pulitzer Prizes the following year; hers was the first ever awarded to a woman for foreign correspondence.

Ordered out of Korea by Eighth Army lieutenant general Walton H. Walker because the front "was no place for a woman," Higgins was reinstated after appeals to General Douglas MacArthur. Before 1950 was out, she had gone fearlessly ashore with the Fifth Marines at Inchon; administered blood plasma to dying troops; and trudged through mud, filth, snow, and ice with beleaguered GIs. Higgins, a tall, attractive blonde, drew both positive and negative attention. A six-page *Life* magazine article assured her fame, though colleagues, whether envious or jealous, were often critical. GIs held her in high esteem both for her beauty and bravery.

A celebrity on her return from Korea, Higgins received extraordinary honors and speaking invitations. Her bestselling book, *War in Korea: The Report of a Woman Combat Correspondent* (1951), was serialized in the *Woman's Home Companion*, further assuring her celebrity.

Higgins's 1942 marriage to Stanley Williams Moore, a philosophy professor, ended in divorce in 1948. They were childless. In April 1952 she married Major General William Evans Hall in Reno, Nevada. She had known him from Berlin when he was intelligence director for the army's European Command during the Berlin Airlift. Higgins and the general had three children; the first, prematurely born, lived only five days.

Settling in Novato, California, Higgins in 1952 launched a one-woman television interview program with WPIX, a West Coast CBS affiliate. She proved effective on radio and television as repeated appearances on "Meet the Press" and other programs attest. Her 1954 Guggenheim Fellowship to study in Russia resulted in a book, *Red Plush and Black Bread* (1955), and her autobiography, *News Is a Singular Thing* appeared later that year. By September she had reestablished the *Herald Tribune*'s Moscow bureau. Upon returning to the United States in 1958, she and her family settled in Washington, D.C., where she covered Washington diplomacy and the White House. In 1959 she accompanied Richard Nixon to Russia and Siberia and, though eight months pregnant, joined the press contingent covering Soviet premier Nikita Khrushchev's tour of the United States.

Higgins obtained exclusive stories from the Congo and was one of the earliest to observe an ominous military buildup in Cuba. In 1962 she published a children's book, *Jessie Benton Fremont*, and in 1964 her *Overtime in Heaven: Adventures in the Foreign Service*, jointly written with news colleague Peter Lisagor, was published.

A Far East expert, Higgins went to Vietnam in July 1963 to assess reported religious disturbances. Her six-part series concluded that Buddhist immolations were politically rather than religiously motivated. In October 1963, impatient for more freedom and the opportunity to write opinion pieces, she joined Newsday Syndicates, writing a thrice-weekly column, and continued to secure exclusives. In 1965 her sixth book, *Our Vietnam Nightmare*, objected to U.S. policies in Vietnam, and her numerous magazine articles expanded on those views.

In November 1965, Higgins returned from her tenth visit to Vietnam racked with fever, entered Walter Reed Hospital in Washington, but died of complications from leishmaniasis, a tropical disease she probably contracted from an insect bite during her last Far Eastern tour.

As a pioneering twentieth-century woman journalist, Higgins's life and career dramatically demonstrated that women could perform the most physically and intellectually challenging demands of being a foreign correspondent and a war correspondent.

• Marguerite Higgins's papers are in the George Arents Research Library for Special Collections at Syracuse University. Antoinette May, *Witness to War: A Biography of Marguerite Higgins* (1983), gives background on friends and relationships. See also Kathleen Kearney Keeshen, "Marguerite Higgins: Journalist 1920–1960" (Ph.D. diss., Univ. of Maryland, 1983); and Marion Marzolf, *Up from the Footnote: A History of Women Journalists* (1977). Carl Mydan, "Girl War Correspondent," *Life*, 2 Oct. 1950, describes Higgins in Korea; and Michael Charles Emery, "The American Mass Media and the Coverage of Five Major Foreign Events 1900–1950" (Ph.D. diss., Univ. of Minnesota, 1968), discusses her Korean reporting. Also helpful are Barbara Belford, *Brilliant Bylines* (1986); Julia Edwards, *Women of the World: The Great Foreign Correspondents* (1988); and Kay Mills, *A Place in the News: From Women's Pages to the Front Pages* (1988). Richard Kluger, *The Paper: The Life and Death of the* New York Herald Tribune (1986), treats Higgins's relationships with the paper and her peers. Obituaries are in the *New York Herald Tribune*, *New York Times*, and *Washington Post*, all 4 Jan. 1966.

KATHLEEN KEARNEY KEESHEN

HIGGINSON, Francis (1586–6 Aug. 1630), Puritan writer and clergyman, was born in Claybrooke, Leicestershire, England, the son of Rev. John Higginson and Elizabeth (maiden name unknown). Baptized on 6 August 1586, he earned a B.A. from Jesus College, Cambridge, in 1610 and his M.A. in 1613. He was ordained a deacon on 26 September 1614 and then a priest of the Church of England on 8 December by the archbishop of York. Conferred the rector of Barton-in-Fabis, Nottinghamshire, he was instituted 20 April 1615 but apparently never formally inducted. Instead, he settled in Claybrooke, probably as curate to his father. He married Anna Herbert at St. Peter's, Nottingham, on 8 January 1616. The couple had nine children, all of whom survived infancy.

After his return to Claybrooke, Higginson became a protégé of Arthur Hildersham, the leader of the Puritan movement in Leicestershire, who probably helped him gain a lectureship at St. Nicholas's, Leicester. There he became a highly popular preacher. His nonconformity tolerated by John Williams, bishop of Lincoln, to whose diocese he belonged, Higginson remained at Leicester for a decade, becoming a noted Puritan lecturer. In 1627 Archbishop William Laud suspended him and suppressed the lectureship at St. Nicholas's. Higginson was then part of the Puritan underground, preaching illegally without a formal living.

Recruited by the Massachusetts Bay Company, Higginson, his wife, and eight children embarked from Gravesend aboard the *Talbot* on 25 April 1629.

During the passage he kept a journal that was immediately published in London as *A True Relation of the Last Voyage to New England* (1630). He interpreted this tempestuous voyage ending in a delightful summer landfall metaphorically as a recapitulation of the Exodus story. Thus Higginson was among the first to view Massachusetts as the New Israel entering another Canaan, "our new paradise of New England." This vision of religious and social renewal was further developed in his *New-Englands Plantation; or, A Short and True Description of the Commodities and Discommodities of that Countrey* (1630), which went through three editions in its first year. Echoing Captain John Smith (1580–1631), Richard Hakluyt, and other promoters of colonization, Higginson observed that "great pitty it is to see so much good ground for Corne & for Grasse as any is under the Heavens, to ly altogether unoccupied, when so many honest Men and their Families in old England through the populousnesse thereof, do make very hard shift to live one by the other." His sense that the landscape itself might have morally redemptive value for "honest Men and their Families" who farm it made him one of the founders of the great agrarian myth of early America.

Soon after arrival in Salem in June 1629, Higginson, together with his colleague, Samuel Skelton, founded the Salem church on 6 August 1629, the first formed in New England beyond the jurisdiction of separatist Plymouth. The decision to adopt the congregational policy of the Plymouth church without its separatist rationale marked a crucial juncture in the history of American Puritanism, as subsequent churches in Massachusetts Bay followed the Salem precedent. The object, in Higginson's view, was to reform, not repudiate, the Church of England. His sense of an inclusive, biblically based, yet flexible religious community was embodied in the church covenant he wrote that simply read, "We Covenant with our Lord, and one with another; and we do bind ourselves in the presence of God, to walk together in all his ways, according as he is pleased to reveal himself unto us in his blessed word of truth."

This decision initially provoked controversy in Salem and among the officers of the Massachusetts Bay Company still in England. To settle the matter, John Endecott, the resident governor, held a public debate in 1629 during which some colonists complained that Higginson and Skelton were "departing from the orders of the Church of England, that they were Separatists, and would be anabaptists, etc." Particularly galling was the abandonment of the Book of Common Prayer. The ministers replied with the argument that was to characterize Massachusetts nonseparatism through the rest of the colonial era, claiming that they were not separating from the Church of England "but only from the corruptions and disorders there." They won the debate in the eyes of the "governor and council, and the generality of the people" present. Ironically, despite this victory for nonseparatism, the Salem church did, in fact, drift into separatism under the pastorate of Roger Williams in the mid-1630s, which provoked a major crisis in the history of the town and the colony.

Higginson himself did not live to see these bitter fruits of his efforts. After his death, perhaps of tuberculosis, his widow moved with their children to New Haven, Connecticut, where she died in 1640. Their eldest son, John Higginson, returned to Salem in 1659 to become a highly influential pastor there until his death in 1708. Despite his brief time in America, Francis Higginson profoundly influenced the ecclesiastical and intellectual history of early New England.

• The two best biographies are Cotton Mather, *Magnalia Christi Americana* (1702), bk. 3, pp. 70–76, and Thomas Wentworth Higginson, *Life of Francis Higginson* (1891), which reprints both *A True Relation* and *New-Englands Plantation*, among other documents. See also Richard P. Gildrie, "Francis Higginson's New World Vision," *Essex Institute Historical Collections* 106 (1970): 182–89. A convenient edition of *A True Relation* is in *Massachusetts Historical Society Proceedings* 62 (1930): 281–99, while *New-Englands Plantation* has been more recently reprinted in Edmund S. Morgan, ed., *The Founding of Massachusetts: Historians and the Sources* (1964), pp. 138–49, together with a letter of advice to immigrants from Higginson, pp. 154–57.

RICHARD P. GILDRIE

HIGGINSON, John (6 Aug. 1616–9 Dec. 1708), clergyman, was born at Claybrooke, Leicestershire, England, the son of the Reverend Francis Higginson and Anna Herbert. He emigrated to Massachusetts with his parents in 1629. His father, the teacher of the church at Salem (a post akin to assistant pastor), died the next year. Although Higginson was apprenticed to a surgeon, Governor John Winthrop and the Reverend John Cotton oversaw his education, which included learning Indian languages and shorthand. Higginson became a freeman of Massachusetts in 1636 and was put to work almost at once trying to reconcile Indians who had committed depredations against the colonists. He soon served as army chaplain in the Pequot War (1636–1637) and was so caught up in his duties that he urged Massachusetts to delay building Harvard College until the enemy was totally vanquished. Higginson's shorthand proved useful as well when he recorded the interrogation of the Antinomians, supporters of Anne Hutchinson who believed God still revealed himself to saints and held private religious services to compensate for those of "dead" ministers. When his friend and tutor John Cotton was implicated, Higginson found excuses not to present a transcription to the Massachusetts General Court, although he was offered £50 for it.

After teaching school for a while in New Haven (a separate colony until 1644; now part of Connecticut), Higginson moved between 1641 and 1643 to Guilford, Connecticut, where he became assistant to the Reverend Henry Whitfield. He married Whitfield's daughter Sarah, although when he did so is not known. The couple had seven children, one of whom, Nathaniel, became a prominent merchant and governor of Fort St. George for the British East India Company. While at Guilford, Higginson prepared the collected sermons of Connecticut's founder, the Reverend Thomas Hooker, for publication. He rose to be teacher after his father-in-law and most of Guilford's leading inhabitants returned to England with the establishment of the Commonwealth in 1649. Thereafter, Higginson's salary of £80 per year was frequently in arrears, and he sought other employment. He considered emigrating to the West Indies and turned down a job as a missionary to the Indians before departing for England in 1659.

Providentially, Higginson's ship was driven back by a storm to his old home of Salem, where the minister, Edward Norris, was old and infirm. Higginson was invited to preach, appointed Norris's assistant, and became his successor in 1660, a post he retained for forty-eight years. Salem was a troubled community, and Higginson faced repeated crises during his tenure. One of the most notable was with the Quakers, whom he despised. He termed Quakerism "the doctrine of the Devil" and fought it at every opportunity. Higginson was nearly as contemptuous of all dissent, and in 1668 he was one of six Massachusetts clergy chosen to dispute publicly with the Anabaptists, who hoped to make inroads into New England.

Higginson also had troubles with his own congregation. In 1672 Charles Nicholet was appointed his assistant. When the church refused to continue Nicholet after a trial year thanks to Higginson's objections, the congregation split in two until Nicholet departed in 1676. Higginson faced another schism in the 1680s when the people of Salem Village, the poorer, rural interior of what was becoming a prosperous commercial town, sought their own church and government. The objections of Higginson, Salem Town, and Massachusetts may have fueled the witchcraft trials of 1692, where Salem Village inhabitants accused many worldly people from Salem Town, including Higginson's daughter Anna Dolliver, of consorting with Satan. Higginson remained aloof from the trials, although in 1698 he wrote, in a preface to the Reverend John Hale's "Modest Inquiry into the Nature of Witchcraft," that "there is a question yet unresolved, whether some of the laws, customs, and principles used by the judges and juries in trials of witches in England (which were followed as patterns here) were not insufficient."

Higginson was an upholder of the traditional New England Puritan order. Although he sought to admit all baptized members to full fellowship in his church, his intent was to extend church discipline and achieve more general involvement. He stood up to Sir Edmund Andros, who asked him whether the lands of New England were or were not the king's, saying, "No, they are the lands of the king's subjects," lawfully bought by them from the original inhabitants. While he sometimes tried to reconcile disputes, Higginson did not hesitate to speak fearlessly or recommend suppression of dissent—as with the Quakers—when he thought arbitration would do no good.

During the course of his ninety-two years, Higginson confronted any challenge—Indian war, Quakers, Anabaptists, internal strife, witchcraft, and royal authority—that he thought threatened the New England way. He died in Salem.

• Simeon E. Baldwin, "John Higginson," *Massachusetts Historical Society, Proceedings,* 2d ser., 16 (1902): 478–521, is the most complete source for Higginson's life as well as a list of his writings. See Richard P. Gildrie, *Salem, Massachusetts, 1626–1683: A Covenant Community* (1975) and "Contention in Salem: The Higginson-Nicholet Controversy, 1672–76," *Essex Institute Historical Collections* 113 (1977): 117–39. Paul Boyer and Stephen Nissenbaum, *Salem Possessed: The Social Origins of Witchcraft* (1974), touches on Higginson's role in this dispute. See Thomas W. Higginson, *Descendants of the Rev. Francis Higginson* (1910), for information on his family.

WILLIAM PENCAK

HIGGINSON, Nathaniel (11 Oct. 1652–31 Oct. 1708), colonial administrator and merchant, was born in Guilford, Connecticut, the son of Sarah Whitfield and John Higginson, a clergyman. Higginson moved with his family to Salem, Massachusetts, in 1659 when his father took over that parish. He graduated from Harvard College in 1670. He had no inclination for the ministry; two years after receiving his master's degree in 1672 he left for England, where he tutored the children of Lord Wharton, a prominent Dissenting Whig, and worked at the royal mint in the Tower of London.

Higginson's career took off when he entered the British East India Company's service in 1683. Beginning as a writer who performed clerical tasks at Fort Saint George in Madras, he rose through the ranks, becoming a customs agent, a factor, a municipal judge, and eventually a member of the city's council, which advised its governor. In 1688 Higginson became first mayor of the newly incorporated city. He did not remain there long, returning to England the next year, but once again removed to Madras as governor of the colony in 1692, succeeding Elihu Yale, for whom Yale College was named. (That same year Higginson married Elizabeth Richardson, the orphaned daughter of John Richardson, a British merchant of Bengal. They had three sons and two daughters.) Sir Josiah Child, head of the company, accounted for Higginson's advancement: "We do not do it out of any partiality to him, for he has no relation here to speak for him, nor ever had the ambition to think of such a thing [the governorship] for himself . . . but sincerely we apprehend for the public good, knowing him to be a man of learning, and competently well-read in the ancient histories of the Greeks and Latins which, with a good stock of natural parts only, can render a man fit for government and political service."

In the late seventeenth century the East India Company was interested primarily in trade rather than in occupation of territory, and it ruled merchant communities that survived thanks to profits that accrued to local native rulers. In 1694 Higginson became lieutenant general of India and directed a limited war with the Mahratta invaders who were challenging the power of the reigning Moguls, upon whom the British depended for smoothly flowing trade. In 1698, when Higginson was the first governor of Madras, his advisory council succeeded in having him recalled; however, the circumstances seem to offer a testimony to his professional integrity. Because East India's officials had much opportunity to do business on their own, corruption was commonplace. But Higginson was the first governor of Madras to retire without having any charges of corruption brought against him. The likely conclusion, therefore, is that his subordinates were dissatisfied with him because he was unwilling to countenance exploitative and illegal schemes to make money.

Higginson had maintained contact with his relations and friends in Massachusetts over the years. Although only one letter of his correspondence during his years in India survives, it indicates he was sending money to his family in Salem from the prosperous mercantile business he developed and transferred to England upon his return there. He also contributed to the Congregational—not to be confused with the more famous Anglican—Society for the Propagation of the Gospel in New England. Since Higginson held the highest overseas position ever attained by a transplanted New Englander, it was logical for the opponents of Massachusetts governor Joseph Dudley to choose him to present their famous petition to Queen Anne in 1706 asking for Dudley's removal for a "horrid reign of bribery," which they asserted but could not prove. (Dudley was accused of trading with the French in Canada while New England was launching military expeditions against them.) Massachusetts councillor Samuel Sewall, a close friend of Higginson's brother John, hoped that Higginson would apply for the governorship himself, but he had no intention of leaving his lucrative business at home. Higginson died soon thereafter of smallpox in London. His career illustrated the worldwide and transatlantic commercial and political connections of British and colonial merchants during the seventeenth century and the generally overlooked fact that there was migration out of, as well as into, New England.

• Some of Higginson's letters are in the *Collections* of the Massachusetts Historical Society, vol. 27 (1838): 196–222. B. C. Steiner, "Two New England Rulers of Madras" appeared in the *South Atlantic Quarterly,* July 1902; the material on Higginson has been separately published. Mrs. Frank Penny, *Fort St. George, Madras* (1900), and company records in London have the most material on his governorship.

WILLIAM PENCAK

HIGGINSON, Thomas Wentworth (22 Dec. 1823–9 May 1911), minister, reformer, soldier, and author, was born in Cambridge, Massachusetts, the son of Stephen Higginson, Jr., a Boston merchant, and Louisa Storrow. Higginson enrolled at Harvard in 1837 and graduated second in his class. Unsure about his future, he matriculated in Harvard Divinity School, dropped out, and then reenrolled. He graduated in 1847. In the same year he married his second cousin, Mary Elizabeth Channing, the daughter of the dean of the Harvard Medical School.

In September 1847 Higginson became pastor of the First Religious Society (Unitarian) of Newburyport, Massachusetts, a conservative town whose residents had shunned William Lloyd Garrison and prevented John Greenleaf Whittier from speaking. Only the acute shortage of Unitarian ministers moved the conservative church proprietors to hire Higginson. To deliver his ordination address, he invited radical Transcendentalist minister William Henry Channing, who believed that the clergy must help bring a "heaven on earth," while the Reverend James Freeman Clarke, an advocate of "rational and liberal religion," presented the charge, emphasizing the godlessness of slavery.

Higginson welcomed Theodore Parker from Boston's Free Church to speak from his pulpit and Ralph Waldo Emerson to deliver a Lyceum lecture. The new minister supported the Essex County Antislavery Society, invited fugitive slave William Wells Brown to speak at the church, and preached against northern apathy in the face of slavery's evils. Higginson also criticized long hours and low wages at Newburyport cotton factories and the high tariff endorsed by his Whig parishioners. He also backed the Free Soil Party and opposed capital punishment. A local newspaper soon concluded: "Mr. Higginson is a young man of much intellectual and moral power" but "seems tinctured with those radical and imaginative notions . . . which would fain seek to govern society at large more wisely than God has seen fit to guide it ever since the dawn of creation" (*Herald*, 16 Sept. 1847). Though supported by "women, the young men, the poor men, the Democrats and the Come-outers," he was asked to resign his pulpit after serving for only two years.

Congressional passage of the Compromise of 1850, including provisions that demanded the return of escaped slaves to the South, stimulated Higginson to seek political office. He ran in the Massachusetts Third Congressional District as a Free Soil party candidate. Referring to the Fugitive Slave Act, he counseled citizens to "DISOBEY IT . . . and show our good citizenship by taking the legal consequences! . . . If Massachusetts is not free, I know at least of one house that shall be" (*Address to the Voters of the Third Congressional District*, Newburyport, 1850).

The first major test of the new law came when warrants were issued for the arrest of William and Ellen Craft, who had been living in Boston since 1848. Higginson responded by asking "whether the law of God or man is to prevail" (*Newburyport Union*, 12 Nov. 1850). Abolitionists helped the Crafts to flee to Canada and freedom.

Defeated in the election, Higginson remained in Newburyport for two more years, teaching in an evening school for adult factory workers and writing newspaper articles challenging the promise of economic mobility. In September 1852 he assumed the pulpit at the Free Church in Worcester, where he promoted abolition, temperance, and the rights of labor and women. His "Woman and Her Wishes" (1853), first published in *Una*, a women's rights journal, was one of the earliest published feminist tracts. He also joined Lucy Stone, Abby Kelley Foster, Susan B. Anthony, Wendell Phillips, and William Lloyd Garrison in organizing temperance conventions during the 1850s.

Radical action was central to Higginson's efforts. His unequivocal opposition to the fugitive slave law was evident as he participated in freeing fugitive slave Thomas Sims and participating in attacking the Boston Courthouse, where fugitive slave Anthony Burns was held. Recruiting and leading armed men to the Kansas territory after passage of the Kansas-Nebraska Act (1854), Higginson helped organize the Massachusetts Kansas Aid Committee, the militant arm of the Emigrant Aid Society. "A single day in Kansas," wrote Higginson from Lawrence, "makes the American Revolution more intelligible than all [historians] Sparks and Hildreth can do." He praised "Old Captain John Brown . . . who has prayers every morning, and then sallies forth, with seven stalwart sons, wherever duty or danger calls, who swallows a Missourian whole and says grace after the meat" (*Liberator*, 16 Jan. 1857). In January 1857 he organized the Worcester Disunion Convention, which declared that abolition must be the primary goal: "peace or war is a secondary consideration" (*Proceedings of the State Disunion Convention*, Boston [1857], p. 18).

Higginson was one of the "Secret Six"—abolitionists who raised money for Brown's planned slave insurrection at Harpers Ferry, Virginia. Unlike some other radical abolitionists, he supported Lincoln's presidential candidacy. But his wife's poor health prevented him, at the war's outset, from joining the army. Instead, he became a man of letters, publishing frequently in the *Atlantic Monthly*. In "Letter to a Young Contributor" (Apr. 1862), Higginson encouraged women to write and seek publication, and in response Emily Dickinson sent him four of her poems. Her letter led to a relationship that would, after the war, be of primary importance to Dickinson and of haunting significance to Higginson.

By the time Dickinson wrote this letter, however, Higginson had abandoned seclusion for social action, finding suitable lodgings for his invalid wife so that he could enlist in the army. In early August, chosen to recruit and lead a Worcester regiment, he published a large newspaper announcement: "What will you say to your children's children when they say to you, 'a great contest was waged between Law and Disorder, Freedom and Slavery, and you were not there?'" (*Worcester Spy*, 16 Aug. 1862). Then in November 1862 he accepted a request from Brigadier General Rufus Saxton, military governor of the Southern Department, to become colonel of the First South Carolina Volunteers, composed of slaves freed by Union forces, thereby becoming commander of the first federally authorized African-American regiment.

Leading his troops on skirmishing and raiding expeditions in Georgia and Florida, Higginson freed, enlisted, and trained former slaves. His regiment played a secondary role in the attack on Fort Wagner, South Carolina, where the Fifty-fourth Massachusetts Regiment, composed of free northern black troops, was repulsed with heavy losses. He remained in the South until a battle wound and malaria caused him to leave the army in May 1864. While never engaged in a major Civil War battle, the well-publicized success of Higginson's black troops helped stimulate Union recruitment of African Americans. By the war's end, 175,00 black soldiers had enlisted, comprising a higher percentage of the northern black population than white soldiers did of the northern white population. His moving account of his wartime experiences, *Army Life in a Black Regiment* (1870), differed significantly from his manuscript war diaries and was written too late to influence the fierce public debates over radical Reconstruction. Earlier, he edited and contributed to *Harvard Memorial Biographies* (1866), declaring, despite extensive Civil War participation of African Americans, that American "patriotism comes most promptly and surely from its highest educated class." Nonetheless, he advocated free land and immediate enfranchisement for former slaves and initially supported radical Reconstruction. By 1876, however, he defended the complete withdrawal of northern troops from the South. He also backed the growing Mugwump movement in its attack on political corruption. Although retaining his deeply paternalistic concern about African Americans and women, he retreated from social activism to devote himself to writing.

His prolific writing included essays, history, literary criticism, and fiction. *Malbone: An Oldport Romance* (1869), his only novel, was serialized in the *Atlantic Monthly* but proved to be a commercial and aesthetic failure. More successful were *Young Folks' History of the United States* (1875), which sold 200,000 copies, and *Larger History of the United States* (1885), which deftly synthesized the work of Jared Sparks, James Parton, George Bancroft, Hermann Von Holst, and Lewis Henry Morgan while exploring in some detail the role of women in American history. Following the rift among woman's rights advocates that developed when the Fifteenth Amendment enfranchised only black men, Higginson joined the American Woman Suffrage Association led by Lucy Stone, rather than Susan B. Anthony's and Elizabeth Cady Stanton's National Woman Suffrage Association. He became a contributing coeditor of the *Woman's Journal* (1870–1884) and later wrote regularly for the widely circulated *Harper's Bazaar*.

Relationships with women—personal and political—were central to his development. His first wife died in 1877. Higginson then moved to Cambridge, Massachusetts, in 1879 and married 33-year-old Mary Potter Thacher, the daughter of Cambridge lawyer Peter Thacher. They had two daughters, one of whom died in infancy. Aspiring women writers, such as Helen Hunt Jackson, Rose Terry, and Harriet Prescott

Spofford, often spoke with Higginson in Boston, but Emily Dickinson declined to join him there. She met him for the first time, during the summer of 1870, in the Dickinson parlor after she invited him to Amherst. He reported that "she talked soon and thenceforward continuously . . . and seemed to speak absolutely for her own relief, and wholly without watching its effect upon her hearer." While thankful "not to live near her" (*Letters of Emily Dickinson*, vol. 2 [1958], pp. 473–76), their correspondence spanned twenty-four years, and when she died in 1886, he spoke at her funeral.

Higginson discouraged Dickinson from publishing her poetry during her lifetime, but he deserves much of the credit for bringing it to public attention after her death. He coedited two volumes of her work (1890 and 1891) and enthusiastically reviewed the third in the *Nation* (1896). In publishing her poetry, he employed the license common to the era's editors by adding titles, moving stanzas, and "correcting" grammatical oddities. There were enormous differences between Higginson's and Dickinson's ideas about democracy, nature, children, women, death, and immortality, as well as about literary symbolism and poetic form. Yet he still supported Dickinson, unlike any other of the century's notable literary figures, reflecting his uniqueness as a critic. He also wrote the first sympathetic biography of Margaret Fuller Ossoli (1884), and praised Sidney Lanier's poetry, Henry David Thoreau's essays, and the novels of Hart Crane and William Dean Howells.

Higginson never retreated from his concern with social issues. Elected in 1879 and 1880 as Republican representative from Cambridge to the Massachusetts legislature, he unsuccessfully ran for Congress in 1888 as a Mugwump Democrat. His commitment to religious pluralism, evident in his early pastorate with the Worcester Free Church, continued during his tenure as president of the Free Religious Association of Boston. He spoke against anti-Catholicism and anti-Semitism and for free immigration. He initially trusted Southern paternalism to provide racial justice after Reconstruction, but the spread of lynchings, Jim Crow legislation, and disfranchisement moved him in the 1890s to praise the leadership of Booker T. Washington. In the final days of his life, he welcomed the racial activism advocated by W. E. B. Du Bois and the newly established National Association for the Advancement of Colored People.

Higginson's social activism spanned the antebellum and Progressive eras. His literary criticism touched upon the era's major writers, and he produced some thirty books of his own and ranked third only to Oliver Wendell Holmes and James Russell Lowell in the number of articles published in the *Atlantic Monthly*. Reviewing Higginson's autobiography, *Cheerful Yesterdays* (1898), Henry James aptly noted that his life "reflected almost everything that was in the New England air" (quoted in Anna Mary Wells, *Dear Preceptor*, p. 316). At his death in Cambridge, Massachusetts, he was given a military funeral. The worn flag of the First South Carolina Volunteers draped his coffin.

• Higginson's manuscripts are primarily in the Houghton Library, Harvard University. An incomplete list of his more than five hundred published titles are in Winifred Mather, *A Bibliography of Thomas Wentworth Higginson* (1906); Mary Thacher Higginson, *Thomas Wentworth Higginson, The Story of His Life* (1914); and *Letters and Journals of Thomas Wentworth Higginson, 1846–1906* (1921). Footnote references to additional published items and manuscript locations are in Tilden G. Edelstein, *Strange Enthusiasm: A Life of Thomas Wentworth Higginson* (1968). Other biographies are Anna Mary Wells, *Dear Preceptor: The Life and Times of Thomas Wentworth Higginson* (1963); Howard N. Meyer, *Colonel of a Black Regiment: The Life of Thomas Wentworth Higginson* (1967); and James W. Tuttleton, *Thomas Wentworth Higginson* (1978).

TILDEN G. EDELSTEIN

HIGHET, Gilbert (22 June 1906–20 Jan. 1978), classicist and critic, was born Gilbert Arthur Highet in Glasgow, Scotland, the son of Gilbert Highet, a superintendent of telegraphs, and Elizabeth Boyle. He matriculated at Glasgow University in 1925, receiving a B.A. with highest honors in Greek and Latin (1928) and an M.A. (1929). From Glasgow he went up as Snell Exhibitioner to Balliol College, Oxford. At Oxford he was strongly influenced by three distinguished classicists, Gilbert Murray, C. M. Bowra, and Cyril Bailey. Here, as at Glasgow, he demonstrated the range of his interests by publishing poetry, fiction, and reviews in university literary magazines and was also active in experimental theater. He took the Oxford B.A. with a double first in classics in 1932.

In the same year he won appointment as fellow and lecturer in classics at St. John's College, Oxford, and married fellow Glaswegian Helen MacInnes, who would herself become a bestselling novelist. They had one child. Highet taught classics for five years at St. John's, receiving the Oxford M.A. in 1936. Among his publications for this period were translations from the German, done in collaboration with his wife, of Otto Kiefer's *Sexual Life in Ancient Rome* (1934) and Gustav Mayer's *Friedrich Engels: A Biography* (1936). The Highet who later turned moral and political conservative was then something of a radical.

The major turning point in his career came in 1937. Highet accepted an invitation to serve for one year as visiting associate in Greek and Latin at Columbia University, New York. The following year he received a permanent appointment as professor of Greek and Latin. He spent the remainder of his academic career at Columbia. The only hiatus was his leave for war service (1941–1946), spent partly at British Security Coordination headquarters in New York and later in occupied Germany, where he was involved in tracking down loot taken by the Germans from occupied countries. Commissioned in the British army in 1943, he left as a lieutenant colonel.

Highet wrote constantly. Even during the war he continued his translation from the German of Werner Jaeger's massive three-volume work, *Paideia: The Ideals of Greek Culture* (1939–1944). His own best-known books on classical subjects are *The Classical Tradition: Greek and Roman Influences on Western Literature* (1949) and *Juvenal the Satirist* (1954). But his impact as a scholar was overshadowed by that as a teacher—both of his own students and of the wider public. He wrote in *The Classical Tradition*:

It is the fundamental fault of modern classical scholarship that it has cultivated research more than interpretation, that it has been more interested in the acquisition than in the dissemination of knowledge, that it has denied or disdained the relevance of its work in the contemporary world, and that it has encouraged the public neglect of which it now complains.

Virtually his entire career was a response to this perception. He saw literature—particularly that of Greece and Rome—as embodying permanent moral and intellectual standards, and he felt it his duty to help others enjoy and learn from it—in translation, if need be. Highet's classroom performances were all but scripted from entrance to exit, and his lectures, delivered in a rapid, clipped burr, were enlivened by anecdotes, songs, gestures, and even props; they were unabashedly theatrical but effective, and behind them lay solid scholarship. He shared some of his principles and methods in *The Art of Teaching* (1950), a book that enjoyed repeated English printings and was translated into sixteen languages. The decade of the 1950s, during which Highet published eight books while maintaining a full teaching schedule, was his busiest. Named Anthon Professor of Latin in 1950 and naturalized as a U.S. citizen in 1951, he was awarded the D.Litt. by Glasgow (1951) and Oxford (1956) and elected fellow of the Royal Society of Literature (1959). Even as his scholarly achievements were being recognized, he was also becoming a public figure through his role in the popular media. He was chief literary critic for *Harper's Magazine* from 1952 to 1954, served as judge for the Book-of-the-Month Club from 1954 on, and in 1958 was appointed first chairman of the editorial advisory board of the new upscale periodical, *Horizon*, to which he became a frequent contributor. But he reached by far the widest audience through his series of weekly fifteen-minute radio talks, "People, Places, and Books." Begun in 1952 on WQXR in New York, they were eventually carried by more than 300 stations in North America as well as the BBC until their discontinuance in 1959. They dealt with an astonishing variety of subjects, chiefly literary, but also musical, artistic, and philosophical. "Flavorsome" and "charming" were the words chosen by John Crosby of the *New York Herald Tribune* (21 May 1952) to describe these talks by the "overwhelmingly erudite" Anthon Professor.

Graduate classics enrollments at Columbia surged in the 1960s, and Highet now spent much of his time directing doctoral dissertations. The student riots of 1968 were an appalling blow. He saw them as typifying the barbarism he had fought against all his life, and they were a factor in his decision to retire in 1972. His remaining years, spent partly in travel with his wife, partly at their Park Avenue apartment or East Hampton summer home, were among his most productive of scholarly articles for classical journals. He died in New York City.

For all the prominence of his public persona, Highet was a very private person. Michael Crosby, one of his student admirers, described him as "a hearty but not a friendly man." It cannot have pleased him that he was never fully accepted by many members of his profession, who tended to dismiss his efforts as superficial popularization. Yet he had not only been a principal mover in revitalizing classics at Columbia, but had helped to lead and legitimize the classics-in-translation movement that had proved and would continue to prove the salvation of nearly every classics department in the country. And during his apogee in the 1950s he had provided the extraordinary example of a classicist who was a force in American culture as arbiter of literary taste for the immediate postwar generation.

• Highet's other books on classical subjects not mentioned in the text include *Poets in a Landscape* (1957), *The Anatomy of Satire* (1962), and *The Speeches in Vergil's Aeneid* (1972); on teaching, *The Immortal Profession* (1976). Many of his radio talks were reworked and published in five volumes of essays: *People, Places, and Books* (1953), *A Clerk of Oxenford* (1954), *Talents and Geniuses* (1957), *The Powers of Poetry* (1960), and *Explorations* (1971). For a complete bibliography, see Highet's student R. J. Ball, *The Classical Papers of Gilbert Highet* (1983), pp. 349–78; see also Ball's portrait of Highet, pp. 1–11.

Numerous autobiographical details are to be found scattered throughout Highet's essays on general subjects. A good portrait by another of his students is M. Crosby, "Gilbert Highet: A Remembrance," *College Board Review* 108 (Summer 1978): 28–30. For assessments by younger Columbia colleagues, see W. M. Calder III, *Classical World* 66 (1972–1973): 385–87, and Calder, *Gnomon* 50 (1978): 430–32; also T. A. Suits in *Classical Scholarship: A Biographical Encyclopedia*, ed. W. W. Briggs and W. M. Calder III (1990), pp. 183–91. Obituaries are in the *New York Times*, 21 Jan. 1978, and the *Times* (London), 26 Jan. 1978.

THOMAS A. SUITS

HILDEBRAND, Joel Henry (16 Nov. 1881–30 Apr. 1983), chemist and educator, was born in Camden, New Jersey, the son of Howard Ovid Hildebrand, who was in the life insurance business, and Sarah Regina Swartz. He was reared in Camden and later in Wayne, Pennsylvania, where he attended high school. His interest in natural science was aroused by reading such texts as Josiah P. Cooke's *Chemical Philosophy*. In high school Hildebrand carried out numerous experiments and proved that nitric oxide reacted with oxygen to form N_2O_4 rather than N_2O_3 as stated by Cooke, which gave him "confidence in the experimental method and a disrespect for authority," attitudes that contributed to his philosophy of education.

In 1898 Hildebrand won the entrance prize in mathematics at the University of Pennsylvania, where he majored in both chemistry and physics in the College of Arts and Sciences rather than in a more professional chemistry curriculum "devoted largely to descriptions and recipes for analysis." He thus not only learned more physics but also literature, history, and mathematics, while avoiding the details of chemistry that he considered "untrue or unimportant." After graduating in 1903 (as class president), he earned a Ph.D. in chemistry at Pennsylvania in 1906. His doctoral dissertation, "The Determination of Anions in the Electrolyte Way," was followed for several years by articles on electrochemical methods of analysis, but his primary interest soon shifted to physical chemistry.

Hildebrand spent 1906–1907 as a postdoctoral fellow at the University of Berlin, where he attended lectures by Jacobus Henricus van't Hoff, the first (1901) Nobel Prize winner in chemistry, and Walther Nernst, the future (1920) Nobel chemistry laureate, under whom he also carried out research on solubility and electrolysis. After learning the principles of physical chemistry, he returned as instructor in the fall of 1907 to his alma mater, where he was the first to offer lectures and laboratory sections in this then new field of chemistry. His article, "Some Applications of the Hydrogen Electrode in Analysis, Research, and Teaching" (*Journal of the American Chemical Society* 35 [1913]: 847–71), attracted much attention and earned the electrode the nickname of the "Hildebrand electrode." This article brought him offers of $3,000 per year from the National Bureau of Standards at Washington, D.C., and of $2,000 per year from Gilbert Newton Lewis of the University of California, Berkeley. He accepted the second offer.

At Berkeley, Hildebrand was assistant professor (1913–1917), associate professor (1917–1918), professor (1918–1952), and professor emeritus (1952–1983). After his formal retirement he continued to teach and published more than thirty scientific articles, many of them papers on education, and popular books such as *Science in the Making* (1957) and *Is Intelligence Important?* (1963). As professor emeritus he had many postdoctoral students and considered these years "the most productive period of his life." He served as dean of men (1923–1926), faculty research lecturer (1936), dean of the College of Letters and Sciences (1939–1943), chairman of the Department of Chemistry (1941—1943), and dean of the College of Chemistry (1949–1951). In 1950, during his last-mentioned deanship, he was an articulate leader in opposition to the "loyalty oath" (a non-Communist declaration) required for faculty members, an issue on which the California Supreme Court decided in favor of the faculty in 1952. He also played a major role in the Academic Senate and served as chairman of several of its committees.

Hildebrand married Emily J. Alexander in December 1908; they had four children. Hildebrand died in his home in Kensington, California.

The author of more than 300 articles and books, Hildebrand considered his lifelong work on liquids and nonelectrolytes his most important contribution to chemistry. He was an internationally recognized authority on intermolecular forces, the theory of regular solutions, solubility, and the structure of liquids, but he also carried out studies of fluorine chemistry, electroanalysis, emulsions, fused salt mixtures, vapor pressure of metals, and liquid alloys. He was interested in the causes of solubility or insolubility of different substances in different solvents, and he theorized that the cohesive forces of the molecules of solute and solvent cause the interaction between the two. Hildebrand's Rule (1915) states that for "normal" liquids boiling near or below room temperature the entropy of vaporization is more nearly constant if measured at constant volume rather than constant pressure.

Throughout his career Hildebrand was fascinated by the color of iodine solutions, publishing his first article on this topic while still at the University of Pennsylvania (*Journal of the American Chemical Society* 31 [1909]: 26–31). In 1920 he noted that positive deviations from Raoult's law of vapor pressures in iodine solutions follow a regular pattern, which led him to a general theory of "regular solutions." His last article on this subject (*Proceedings of the National Academy of Sciences U.S.A.* 76 [1979]: 6040–41) appeared only a few years before his death. In addition to numerous articles on solubility in various journals, he summarized the current state of knowledge about nonelectrolyte solutions in the monograph *Solubility* (1924; 2d ed. published as *Solubility of Non-Electrolytes* [1936]; 3d ed. published as *The Solubility of Nonelectrolytes*, with Robert L. Scott [1950]). He then left to others the task of reviewing the general knowledge of nonelectrolyte solutions and concentrated on shorter books on his areas of particular interest—*Regular Solutions*, with R. L. Scott (1962), and *Regular and Related Solutions: The Solubility of Gases, Liquids, and Solids*, with J. M. Prausnitz and R. L. Scott (1970).

In a series of articles with H. A. Benesi (1949–1950) Hildebrand ascribed an intense ultraviolet absorption in the spectra of iodine solutions to the formation of electron donor-acceptor complexes, now known as charge-transfer complexes. From 1970 to 1977 Hildebrand carried out studies of viscosity of liquids, which were collected in a small monograph, *Viscosity and Diffusivity: A Predictive Treatment* (1977).

Hildebrand served his country during leaves of absence in both world wars. He was a captain in the Officers' Reserve Corps (1917) and then major (1918) and lieutenant colonel (1919) in the U.S. Chemical Warfare Service. He directed the CWS laboratory near Paris and was commandant at Hanlon Field near Chaumont, which included the Experimental Field and Allied Expeditionary Forces Officers' Gas Defense School, and he received the U.S. Army's Distinguished Service Medal (1922). As a consultant for the U.S. Bureau of Mines (1924–1926) he suggested that a mixture of helium and oxygen be substituted for ordinary air (a mixture of nitrogen and oxygen) for divers and caisson workers to prevent caisson disease (the "bends"), the painful formation of nitrogen bubbles in the blood during ascent. This practice was adopted by the U.S. Navy, permitting deeper and safer underwa-

ter descents. During World War II he was a member of the Chemical Referee Board of Production Research and Development of the War Production Board (1942–1943) and an expert consultant for the military planning division of the Quartermaster Corps (1942–1945). For his service as a scientific liaison officer for the Office of Scientific Research and Development attached to the American Embassy in London (1943–1944) he was cited by the U.S. Army and Navy (1948) and received the United Kingdom's King's Medal for Service in the Cause of Freedom (1948).

Hildebrand's impact as a teacher was in many respects as important as his contributions to research. Although most of Berkeley's faculty were involved in the freshman chemistry course, a policy instituted by Lewis, Hildebrand presented the lectures, wrote the quizzes and examinations, and was in general charge of the course. In his own words, "Freshmen are more dependent upon good teaching than at any later period. It is, therefore, more of a challenge to teach at this stage and more of an art to do it well." From 1913 through his "pseudoretirement" in 1952, this enthusiastic lecturer is estimated to have had about 40,000 students in his freshman lectures. The course at Berkeley developed by Hildebrand, William C. Bray, and Wendell M. Latimer differed from the usual practice of the time by emphasizing general principles with reduced attention to the memorization of specific factual material. In 1918 Hildebrand wrote the challenging textbook for this course, *Principles of Chemistry*, the seventh edition of which (coauthored with Richard E. Powell) appeared in 1964. To encourage students to look up rather than memorize experimental facts, Hildebrand, together with Wendell M. Latimer, wrote *Reference Book of Inorganic Chemistry* (1929), which was revised twice (1940, 1951) and was available combined with *Principles of Chemistry* as a single volume.

Hildebrand was a lifelong campaigner for scientific education and an outspoken critic of schools of education, which he thought were promoting "social adjustment," where conformity to the peer group was considered more important than scientific competence. He was appointed to the Citizens Advisory Commission to the Joint Committee on Education of the California Legislature (1958–1960), where he spoke widely on the need for basic education and warned that the "life adjustment" theory of education championed by the California Department of Education has "repelled many able college students from becoming school teachers and driven competent teachers from their profession."

Hildebrand was elected to the National Academy of Sciences in 1929 and the American Philosophical Society in 1951. He received numerous awards, including the highest award of the American Chemical Society, the Priestley Medal. He held various positions in the ACS but declined being nominated for president until after his retirement from regular teaching. He served as ACS president in 1955. On the occasion of his one hundredth birthday, the University of California renamed Berkeley's chemistry building in his honor;

thereafter he enjoyed the unusual honor of having an office in a building bearing his name.

Actively interested in athletics throughout his life, he learned to ski at age forty and was chosen to manage the U.S. skiing team at the 1936 Winter Olympic Games in Bavaria. An avid mountain climber, he served as president of the Sierra Club (1937–1939) and published books on mountaineering, backpacking, skiing, hiking, and camping, including *Camp Catering*, with his daughter Louise (1938).

Hildebrand had a long, distinguished career and was as highly regarded by educators for his methods of teaching science as he was among scientists for his theoretical and experimental contributions to the solubility of liquids, gases, and nonelectrolytes.

• Hildebrand's papers (six cartons and one box) at the Bancroft Library of the University of California, Berkeley, include correspondence, articles, bibliography, lecture outlines, biographical materials, book reviews, grant files, and varied writings. Biographical articles include Rudy Baum, "ACS Celebrates Hildebrand's 100th Birthday," *Chemical and Engineering News* 59, no. 49 (7 Dec. 1981): 33–34; "Hildebrand in the Alpha Chi Sigma Hall of Fame," *The Hexagon* 75, no. 3 (Sept. 1984): 43; Kenneth S. Pitzer, "Joel Henry Hildebrand," National Academy of Sciences, *Biographical Memoirs* 62 (1993): 224–57, which contains an autographed portrait and selected bibliography; and Robert F. Gould, "Joel Henry Hildebrand," in *American Chemists and Chemical Engineers*, vol. 2, ed. Wyndham D. Miles and Robert F. Gould (1994), pp. 128–30. Obituaries include the *New York Times*, 3 May 1983; "Joel Hildebrand: Noted Chemist Dies at Age 101," *Chemical and Engineering News* 61, no. 19 (9 May 1983): 4–5; and Glenn T. Seaborg, *Physics Today* 36, no. 10 (Oct. 1983): 100–101.

GEORGE B. KAUFFMAN

HILDRETH, Samuel Prescott (30 Sept. 1783–24 July 1863), physician, naturalist, and historian, was born in Methuen, Massachusetts, the son of Samuel Hildreth, a physician and farmer, and Abigail Bodwell. At age fifteen he entered Phillips Academy in Andover, Massachusetts; he spent four terms at Andover and Franklin academies. He studied medicine first under his father and then for two years under Thomas Kittredge of Andover. To complete his education, he attended an eight-week course at Harvard Medical School, after which he received a diploma from the Medical Society of Massachusetts in 1805.

Hildreth began the practice of medicine at Hampstead, New Hampshire, then moved to Ohio in October 1806. After a brief sojourn at Belpre, he lived at Marietta from 1808 until his death, remaining active in his profession until 1861. While in Belpre he married Rhoda Cook in 1807; they had six children.

Hildreth was a versatile man. Besides practicing medicine, he took a keen interest in the natural world, especially in geology. Throughout much of his life he kept records of the weather; his exhaustive report, "Results of Meteorological Observations Made at Marietta, Ohio, between 1826 and 1859, Inclusive," was published in *Smithsonian Contributions to Knowledge* 16 (1870). He was a frequent contributor, beginning

in 1826, to the *American Journal of Science and Arts*. He helped to establish the Geological Survey of Ohio, organized in 1837.

Hildreth was elected to the Ohio state legislature in 1810, at the age of twenty-seven. He left his mark by drafting the Hildreth Act, passed 14 January 1811. It divided Ohio into medical districts, each with a board of three examiners. The act thus provided for the regulation of the practice of medicine as well as for the organization of medical societies.

Hildreth often wrote on medical subjects, including "Notes on the Epidemic Fever, As It Appeared at Marietta, in the State of Ohio, and Its Vicinity, in the Years 1822 and 1823" (*Philadelphia Journal of the Medical and Physical Sciences* 9 [1824]). That fever was malaria, a scourge of the frontier.

Hildreth took an early interest in petroleum. In "Facts Relating to Certain Parts of the State of Ohio" (*American Journal of Science and Arts* 10 [1826]), he remarked, "The petroleum affords considerable profit, and is beginning to be in demand for lamps, in workshops and manufactories." In the same journal (24 [1833]) his "Observations on the Saliferous Rock Formation, in the Valley of the Ohio" recorded one of the earliest treatments of oil and gas associated with salt wells. "Observations on the Bituminous Coal Deposits of the Valley of the Ohio, and the Accompanying Rock Strata; with Notices of the Fossil Organic Remains and the Relics of Vegetable and Animal Bodies, Illustrated by a Geological Map, by Numerous Drawings of Plants and Shells, and by Views of Interesting Scenery" (*American Journal of Science and Arts* 29 [1836]) described an anticline, a prime site for the accumulation of oil and gas, and suggested what became known in the twentieth century as the carbon-ratio theory, whereby the occurrence of petroleum is related to the amount of volatile matter in coal.

As a historian Hildreth preserved a record of the early events of the Old Northwest. In 1848 he published *Pioneer History: Being an Account of the First Examinations of the Ohio Valley, and the Early Settlement of the Northwest Territory*. He followed that with some local history, including "Biographical Sketches of the Early Physicians of Marietta, Ohio" (*New England Historical and Genealogical Register* 3 [1849]); one of the sketches was of himself. As a companion piece to *Pioneer History*, he wrote *Biographical and Historical Memoirs of the Early Pioneer Settlers of Ohio, with Narratives of Incidents and Occurrences in 1775* (1852), and *Contributions to the Early History of the North-West, Including the Moravian Missions in Ohio* (1864).

Hildreth treated his patients according to the dictates of the time, resorting to bleeding, purging, and sweating. When he contracted malaria, though, he knew enough to prescribe quinine for himself. He also noted the value of yeast and charcoal for fevers.

Hildreth came to be considered one of Ohio's greatest frontier doctors. Perhaps his greatest contribution to posterity, however, along with his histories, was his work on petroleum. His treatments of petroleum in the *American Journal of Science and Arts* presaged a time when the world would demand that mineral in ever greater amounts. Although he did not recognize the exact connection between geological structure and petroleum accumulation, his description of an anticline deserved attention. He died in Marietta, Ohio.

• For a list of Hildreth's works on the natural world, including geology, see John M. Nickles, *Geologic Literature on North America, 1785–1918* (1923). An interesting account of Hildreth's life and writings is Erman Dean Southwick, "Doctor S. P. Hildreth and His Home," *Ohio Historical Quarterly* 64 (Jan. 1955): 30–54. For Hildreth's contributions to petroleum geology, see Edgar Wesley Owen, *Trek of the Oil Finders: A History of Exploration for Petroleum* (1975).

KEITH L. MILLER

HILGARD, Eugene Woldemar (5 Jan. 1833–8 Jan. 1916), geologist and pedologist, was born in Zweibrücken in the Rhine-Palatinate (then under Bavarian control), the son of Theodor Erasmus Hilgard, chief justice of the provincial court of appeals, and Margarethe Pauli. His family emigrated in 1836 to a farm near Belleville, Illinois, settling amongst a number of cultured German families. Hilgard and his siblings were educated mostly by their father. At an early age he acquired a strong interest in both the sciences and humanities, including, specifically, soils and their chemistry. At age sixteen he was sent to Washington, D.C., for treatment of failing eyesight and chronic malaria. There his brother Theodore introduced him to the scientific community, including Joseph Henry, the first secretary of the Smithsonian Institution. After four months he moved to Philadelphia to attend chemistry lectures at the Homeopathic Medical College and later at the Franklin Institute. In 1849 he enrolled in the university at Heidelberg, Germany, where he studied chemistry under Karl Christian Gmelin. Later, as political unrest intervened, he shifted to Zurich, Switzerland, and from there to the Royal Mining Academy at Freiburg. Finally returning to Heidelberg, he completed his doctorate summa cum laude under Robert Bunsen in 1853.

Returning from Germany in 1855, Hilgard established a chemical laboratory in the Smithsonian Institution at Joseph Henry's suggestion. That same year he was appointed assistant state geologist of Mississippi. His work there was interrupted when the survey was suspended in 1857; he then returned to the Smithsonian and began lecturing in chemistry at the National Medical College. When the survey was reauthorized in 1858, he returned to Mississippi as state geologist. During the Civil War, he was made custodian of the University of Mississippi's library and laboratory equipment. He served with the "Confederate Nitre Bureau" collecting nitre for munitions. He also served at Vicksburg, attempting to install calcium lights on the Vicksburg bluffs to illuminate the Federal fleet in its attempts to run past the city. In August 1860 Hilgard married Lenora J. Alexandrina Bello in Madrid, Spain; they had two children. In 1866 he resigned as state geologist to become professor of chemistry at the University of Mississippi, but concurrently with this position he resumed his post as state geologist, without recompense, in 1870.

Hilgard spent the first half of his career investigating the geology, soils, and agriculture of Mississippi and Louisiana. His *Geology and Agriculture of the State of Mississippi* (1860) and *Geology of the Mississippi Delta* (1870) comprise the first comprehensive description and interpretation of Gulf Coast Mesozoic and Tertiary geology. In his application of geology to soils, he has been credited as the first to describe soils as independent, dynamic entities resulting from both chemical and biological processes. He also first noted the chemical and physical layering of soils and the relation of soils to bedrock.

After leaving the University of Mississippi in 1873, Hilgard became a professor of geology and natural history at the University of Michigan. Two years later he was invited to become professor of agriculture at the University of California at Berkeley. He accepted and spent the next twenty-four years teaching before becoming professor emeritus in 1904. While at Berkeley, Hilgard established experimental fields in 1875; these evolved into the California Agricultural Experiment Station, of which he was director from 1888 to 1904. In this role, he organized and developed a major research facility, the first of its kind according to Hilgard, a claim contested by the state of Connecticut, where a similar facility was founded at approximately the same time. Hilgard staunchly advocated incorporation of scientific and scholarly instruction in the colleges of agriculture established under the Morrill Act against those who would have established "farm schools" emphasizing practical instruction in farming operations. His *Agriculture for Schools of the Pacific Slope*, written with W. J. V. Osterhout (1909), summarizes much of his philosophy of agricultural education and research.

Another area in which Hilgard made advances was regional soil mapping. From 1879 to 1883 he was special agent in charge of cotton production for the Tenth Census. His *Cotton Culture in the U.S.*, Tenth Census (1880), includes the first significant regional soil maps.

Later in his career, Hilgard concentrated on problems of alkaline soils, irrigation, plant nutrition, organic matter in soils, estimation of soil values, and crop introduction. He developed techniques for bringing alkaline soils into production, thus opening large regions to agriculture. These efforts led to the establishment of a major wine production and olive culture in California.

A recipient of honorary degrees and other awards at home and abroad, Hilgard had numerous affiliations with honorary societies and professional organizations, including the U.S. National Academy of Sciences, the American Academy of Arts and Sciences, the Geological Society of America, the Society for the Promotion of Soil Science, the American Association for the Advancement of Sciences, and the American Geographical Society. In addition to the books he wrote, he published almost 300 journal articles.

Hilgard's contribution to soil science led to his being dubbed the "father of pedology." His contributions to geology, such as defining the stratigraphic succession on the Gulf Coast, were equally impressive. Hilgard died in Berkeley, California.

• The Bancroft Library of the University of California at Berkeley contains a collection of Hilgard family papers including his autobiographical notes. In addition, a few Hilgard family personal papers from 1833 to 1911 are in the Illinois Historical Survey Collection in the University of Illinois Library at Urbana. For Hilgard's career in Mississippi, see Bahngrell W. Brown, "The First Hundred Years of Geology in Mississippi," *Southern Quarterly* 13, no. 4, (1975): 295–302; and Walter S. Pittman, Jr., "Eugene W. Hilgard and Scientific Education in Mississippi," *Earth Science History* 4 (1985): 26–31. For a comprehensive review of Hilgard's career on the Gulf Coast, including Mississippi, see Henry V. Howe, "Hilgard as a Geologist," in *Mississippi Geologic Research Papers*, Bulletin 104, Mississippi Geological Survey (1965). For an overview of Hilgard's entire career, see Hans Jenny, *E. W. Hilgard and the Birth of Modern Soil Science* (1961), and Frederick Slate, "Biographical Memoir of Eugene Woldemar Hilgard," National Academy of Sciences, *Biographical Memoirs* 9 (1919): 93–155. Eugene A. Smith, "Memorial of Eugene Woldemar Hilgard," *Bulletin of the Geological Society of America* 28 (1917): 40–67, details Hilgard's personal and professional life. An obituary appears in the *New York Times*, 9 Jan. 1916.

RALPH L. LANGENHEIM, JR.

HILGARD, Josephine Rohrs (12 Mar. 1906–16 May 1989), psychologist and psychiatrist, was born in Napoleon, Ohio, the daughter of Henry F. Rohrs, a practicing physician and surgeon, and Edna Irene Balsley. Her subsequent education after high school led to an A.B., magna cum laude, from Smith College (1928); an M.A. (1930) and a Ph.D. (1933) from Yale University in child psychology; and an M.D. from Stanford University Medical School (1940). This education was followed by psychoanalytic training at the Chicago Psychoanalytic Institute in Washington, D.C., and at the Washington-Baltimore Psychoanalytic Institute, completed in 1946. Each of her academic degrees led to honor society membership: Smith, Phi Beta Kappa; Yale, Sigma Xi; Stanford, Alpha Omega Alpha.

While at Yale she met and married Ernest R. Hilgard, then an instructor in psychology, in 1931. They moved to Palo Alto, California, site of Stanford University, in 1933. With her husband, on sabbatical leave, she spent the year 1940–1941 in Chicago, where she served as a staff psychiatrist at the Institute for Juvenile Research. She joined her husband for the years 1943–1945 in the Washington, D.C., area, where he had gone to serve in civilian war agencies. There she joined the staff of the Chestnut Lodge Sanitarium in Rockville, Maryland, where she worked closely with Harry Stack Sullivan and Frieda Fromm-Reichmann in the treatment of disturbed adolescents.

With their two children, they returned to reside again in Palo Alto, where from 1945 to 1948 she was director of the Child Guidance Clinic at Children's Hospital in San Francisco. She also opened a private office in Palo Alto for the practice of psychiatry and psychoanalysis, which continued on a part-time basis from 1945 to 1975. She served also as an associate clinical professor of psychiatry at the Stanford University Medical School, 1947–1962, and as a clinical professor, 1962–1972.

During the early postwar years she became active in research. Her most widely read publications were concerned with what came to be called "anniversary reactions," that is, significant events in later life (including mental illness) that could be traced to an influence of childhood events, including events that were triggered by age-related occurrences in a later generation reflecting events in an earlier generation (hence having "anniversary" characteristics). This series of studies, including case studies and large-scale community studies, was published (with collaborators) in fourteen articles that appeared between 1953 and 1969. The results demonstrated that functional or psychogenic factors were involved in the genesis of mental illness, including schizophrenia, depressive psychoses, and psychoneuroses.

She added a new dimension to her developmental studies by accepting appointment as a research associate in the Laboratory of Hypnosis Research that her husband had founded. In this role, from 1964 to 1980, she interviewed hundreds of Stanford students participating in studies of hypnotic responsiveness. Her goal was to determine personality factors related to their hypnotizability. This study resulted in her first published book on hypnosis, *Personality and Hypnosis: A Study of Imaginative Involvement* (1970; 2d ed., 1979), in which she showed that absorption in imaginative experiences in daily life was a predictor of hypnotic responsiveness. Her second book, published jointly with her husband, reviewed the clinical and experimental studies of pain relief through hypnotic procedures, *Hypnosis in the Relief of Pain* (1975; 2d ed., 1983). Her third book on hypnosis, *Hypnotherapy of Pain in Children with Cancer* (with Samuel LeBaron, 1984), reported the results of investigating the use of hypnosis with children suffering the pain of bone marrow aspiration in the treatment of leukemia. These and others of the eighteen research reports she published on hypnosis led to six major awards from the Society of Clinical and Experimental Hypnosis. Three of these were for her books, each of which was recognized as "the best book on scientific hypnosis published in the preceding year." These signs of recognition culminated in a Gold Medal Award from the International Society of Hypnosis in 1985. This award is given at each triennial International Congress on Hypnosis to an outstanding contributor to scientific hypnosis. Also in 1985, a special symposium in her honor was held at the annual convention of the American Psychological Association.

She died in a retirement residence in Palo Alto, where she and her husband had lived since 1981.

Josephine Hilgard faced the complex problems of being a wife, a mother, and an active professional woman. She managed, however, to fulfill her personal obligations, along with her many professional duties, with good grace and to do significant research throughout her career.

In an obituary in the *American Psychologist* (45 [Dec. 1990]), a former colleague, Kenneth S. Bowers, wrote that the research published in Hilgard's *Personality and Hypnosis* "has had a major impact on the understanding of hypnosis" (p. 1382), chiefly in showing why some individuals are more responsive than others to hypnotic suggestions. The value to psychiatry of her anniversary studies was affirmed again in the year following her death, when a group of her colleagues and others now practicing psychiatry who had been supervised by her, returned to Stanford for what they called "a first anniversary." Using the play on words at the first anniversary of her death, they validated the importance of her teaching and case supervision, especially with regard to the influence of the anniversary reactions she had documented during her lifetime.

• Josephine Hilgard left a short autobiography in unpublished form, prepared three years before her death. A copy has been deposited in the Archives of the History of Psychology, in the library of the University of Akron. It contains a complete listing of her published writings, except for the following summary of her anniversary studies that appeared late in the year of her death: Josephine R. Hilgard, "The Anniversary Syndrome as Related to Late-appearing Mental Illnesses in Hospitalized Patients," in *Psychoanalysis and Psychosis*, ed. Ann-Louise S. Silver (1989). Her autobiography includes a curriculum vitae, plus a listing of a number of professional experiences (such as consultant to the Veterans' Administration) not included in the curriculum vitae. There is no archival collection of her books and papers.

ERNEST R. HILGARD

HILGARD, Julius Erasmus (7 Jan. 1825–8 May 1891), geodesist, was born in Zweibrücken, Rhine-Palatinate, the son of Theodor Erasmus Hilgard, a judge, and Margaretha Pauli. His formal education consisted entirely of the first three grades of the local Gymnasium. In 1835 his family immigrated to the United States and settled the following year on an established farm in Belleville, Illinois. Hilgard was then taught at home by his father until 1843, when he moved to Philadelphia, Pennsylvania, to live with a married sister and study civil engineering.

Hilgard began his career later that year by surveying potential rights-of-way for the Bear Mountain Railroad. In 1844 he was recruited by Alexander Dallas Bache, superintendent of the U.S. Coast Survey, to join that agency as a computor after pointing out to Bache, whom he knew socially, several formulaic errors in its calculations of geographical positions. In 1845 Hilgard began surveying coastline in the lower Chesapeake Bay, and between 1846 and 1850 he divided his time between taking part in surveys of the Mississippi Sound and the Florida Keys and making computations in the office. In 1848 he married Katherine Clements, with whom he had four children. From 1850 to 1855 he supervised the work of the USCS computing department, and after 1853 he also discharged a number of special assignments, such as testing equipment or assisting with a particularly difficult survey. Between 1855 and 1860 he was charged primarily with publishing the results of the USCS's work in the *Annual Reports of the U.S. Coast Survey*.

In 1860 Hilgard left the USCS to go into business for himself in Paterson, New Jersey, but he returned to the agency two years later as de facto superintendent because Bache was too ill to continue in the day-to-day performance of his duties. Hilgard's first task was to save the agency from wartime budget cuts. To this end he found it necessary to lobby for its continued existence, and his impassioned pleas for funding to prominent Republican congressmen, such as Schuyler Colfax and Roscoe Conkling, achieved this goal. Thereafter, the USCS contributed to the war effort against the Confederate States of America by providing maps and charts to Union troops and naval units operating or stationed along the Confederate coastline. In 1863 he played a prominent role in organizing the National Academy of Sciences to advise the U.S. government on matters related to science and technology and became one of its first fifty members. Appointed the USCS's acting superintendent in 1864 when Bache retired, he continued in this capacity until 1867, when Benjamin Peirce, an eminent mathematician and astronomer and Hilgard's senior by fifteen years, was appointed superintendent.

Retained as the agency's assistant superintendent, Hilgard oversaw the work of the U.S. Office of Weights and Measures, and in that capacity he drafted standards and legislation intended to establish the metric system in the United States. In 1872 he traveled to Paris, France, to determine by means of telegraph the exact difference in transatlantic longitude between the Naval and Harvard Observatories in the United States and the observatories in Greenwich, England, and Paris, a determination required by astronomers who were updating star catalogs by comparing observational data obtained on both sides of the Atlantic Ocean. In 1874 he returned to Paris to represent the United States at an international conference called to standardize the measurement and use of the meter and create an international bureau of weights and measures. He also served as the conference's vice president, but, when the directorship of the new bureau was offered to him in 1875, he declined it and returned to his duties at the USCS and the Office of Weights and Measures. In 1877 he was made the inspector of Standard Weights and Measures and was elected president of the American Association for the Advancement of Science. That same year he invented a device that determined optically the density of sea water, for which he won a gold medal at the London International Fisheries Exposition in 1883, and served as a judge of scientific and mechanical devices at the Centennial Exposition in Philadelphia. Between 1877 and 1878 he gave a series of twenty lectures at Johns Hopkins University titled "Extended Territorial Surveying," in which he proposed and offered suggestions on how to proceed with an accurate geodetic survey of the interior of the

United States. In 1878 he traveled a third time to Europe in an official capacity, visiting London, Hamburg, and Paris, this time to assist in organizing the International Committee on Weights and Measures.

By 1881, when Hilgard became superintendent of the USCS, he was suffering from nephritis, a debilitating malady of the kidneys that causes fatigue and loss of mental concentration. Consequently, he was unable to oversee the activities of the agency with either his customary vigor or the necessary rigor. Four years later, during a high-profile congressional investigation into corruption in the federal government's major scientific bureaus, he was suspended from those duties for mismanaging the USCS amid widespread, but unsubstantiated, rumors that he was an alcoholic. Shortly thereafter he retired from public service and remained in Washington, D.C., where he died.

Hilgard contributed to the development of science in the United States by vitalizing the work of the U.S. Coastal Survey for a period of over forty years. His willingness and ability to supervise some or all of its activities during times of transition enabled the agency to survive and contribute to a better understanding of American physical geography.

• Hilgard's papers are located in the Hilgard Family Papers in the Bancroft Library at the University of California at Berkeley. A biographical account is by his brother, E. W. Hilgard, "Memoir of Julius Erasmus Hilgard," National Academy of Sciences, *Biographical Memoirs* 3 (1893): 327–38. Obituaries are in the *New York Herald* and the *Washington (D.C.) Evening Star*, 9 May 1891.

CHARLES W. CAREY, JR.

HILGARD, Theodor Erasmus (7 July 1790–26 Jan. 1873), jurist and "Latin farmer," was born in Marnheim near Kirchheimbolanden in the Rhenish Palatinate, the son of Jakob Hilgard, a Protestant clergyman, and his wife, Maria Dorothea Engelmann. Growing up in wartime in a family that strongly sympathized with the principles of the French Revolution, he spent part of his childhood with his maternal grandparents in Bacharach; his uncle Peter Engelmann continued to take a special interest in the boy's education. Hilgard read law at the universities of Heidelberg (1807), Göttingen (1808–1809), and Paris (1810), completing his studies at the law academy at Koblenz in 1811 as *licencié en droit*. He settled down as a successful lawyer at the French court of appeals in Trier (1812–1815), moving with the court to Kaiserslautern after the end of the French rule on the left bank of the Rhine and finally to Zweibrücken (1816), where he also served in the provincial council of Rhenish Bavaria (1821–1826). In 1816 he married Margaretha "Gretchen" Pauli, the daughter of a Protestant minister. In 1826 he accepted an appointment as associate justice at the court of appeals, having previously declined a professorship for French law to be established at a Bavarian university (1824).

At the height of his professional career, however, Hilgard found himself increasingly dissatisfied with the political situation in Bavaria, especially after the revolutionary year of 1830 and the subsequent backlash. Hoping that future generations of his family might find a more congenial atmosphere and personal independence in a country with democratic institutions and ample opportunities, he decided to sell most of his property and emigrate to the United States. Other members of the Hilgard-Engelmann clan had already settled in America when Hilgard, his wife, and their nine children left Zweibrücken in September 1835, traveling via Le Havre and New Orleans. In February 1836 Hilgard bought a large farm near his relatives in Belleville, Illinois, which he afterwards subdivided, laying out the town of West Belleville. His real estate investments turned out to be decidedly more profitable than his farming endeavors, in part because he tried unsuccessfully to establish viticulture in St. Clair County. Finding the Illinois climate and farm life less to his liking than he had expected, he devoted much of his time to scholarly pursuits and the classical education of his children. Although he never completely mastered the English language, he was proud to become an American citizen in 1841.

Yet Hilgard never severed his ties to Europe. Some of his children returned to Germany to live or to study, and he crossed the Atlantic in 1850 and again for an extended stay in 1851–1852. A widower since 1842, he married his 25-year-old niece, Marie Theveny, in 1854 and spent the rest of his life as a gentleman scholar in Heidelberg with his second wife, with whom he had three children. He returned briefly to the United States in 1864–1865 to settle his financial affairs.

Before his emigration Hilgard had edited a law journal, *Annalen der Rechtspflege in Rheinbayern* for two years (1830–1831); in the United States and after his return to Europe he continued to take a lively interest in German affairs and published pamphlets on political, social, and legal questions. His *Zwölf Paragraphen über Pauperismus und die Mittel ihm zu steuern* (1847) advocated governmental aid to emigration to solve the problem of pauperism. He joined the political debate of 1848, deliberating about Germany as a nation in *Fünf Paragraphen über Deutschlands National-Einheit und ihr Verhältnis zur Freiheit* (1849) and expressing his preference for a republican form of government with *Eine Stimme aus Nordamerika. Zehn Paragraphen über verfassungsmäßige Monarchie und Republik* (1849). In spite of his democratic convictions he was always rather conservative in outlook, arguing against woman suffrage (*Frauenrechte* [1869]) and for the death penalty (*Über Beibehaltung oder Abschaffung der Todesstrafe* [1868]).

Hilgard also enjoyed writing poetry. In Hilgard's youth, Goethe had praised some of his poems; in later years Hilgard wrote occasional verse and German adaptations of part of Thomas Moore's *Lalla Rookh* (*Die Feuer-Anbeter* [1851]), *King Lear*, and Ovid's *Metamorphoses*. His last lengthy publication, *Die Hundert Tage. Ein Epos* (1868), dealt with Napoleon's return from Elba. Much of Hilgard's literary production remained unpublished, and little that he wrote is read today. He died in Heidelberg.

Hilgard's most remarkable work is his autobiography, *Meine Erinnerungen*, written for his family and friends and published privately in 1860, in which he detailed his experiences as a citizen of two worlds. Reflecting on his life on both continents, he concluded that American institutions, while not ideal, were "still the best and most enlightened existing on earth" and that his hope in the future of the New World had been justified.

• Some of Hilgard's papers have survived in the Hilgard Family Papers in the Illinois Historical Survey Collections, University of Illinois, Urbana, and at the Bancroft Library, University of California, Berkeley. Aside from Hilgard's autobiography, the most important source for his life in the United States is his *Briefe an seinen Freund Philipp Heinrich von Kraemer 1835–1865*, ed. Wolfgang Krämer (1935), with a good biographical introduction. Hilgard's thesis as *licencié en droit, Traité sur la question de savoir si, et en quel sens, les donations entre-vifs de biens présens font passer au donataire les dettes et charges du donateur*, was printed privately in 1812; it was also published in Mauguin and Dumoulin, *Bibliothèque (ou journal) du barreau* 5 (Feb. and May 1812). His life and writings are discussed in two articles by Helmut Hirsch, "Theodor Erasmus Hilgard, Ambassador of Americanism," *Journal of the Illinois State Historical Society* 37 (1944): 164–72, and "Die beiden Hilgards. Ein biographischer Beitrag zur Geschichte der achtundvierziger Revolution und des Deutschamerikanertums," *Zeitschrift für die Geschichte des Oberrheins* 98 (1950): 486–97.

MARIE-LUISE FRINGS

HILL, Abram (20 Jan. 1910–6 Oct. 1986), theatrical director and playwright, was born in Atlanta, Georgia, the son of John Hill and Minnie Hill. His father, a fireman on the Seaboard Air Line Railroad, participated in salary protests that forced him to leave the railroad after World War I; he then became a house painter.

Hill appeared at the Morehouse College Chapel at the age of seven but did not pursue an interest in the stage. At the age of fourteen he fell ill with a severe case of pneumonia and spent two months in a hospital. The experience inspired Hill to become a surgeon, and in 1925 the Hill family moved to New York City to provide Abram with more educational opportunities. He attended Theodore Roosevelt High School and graduated from DeWitt Clinton High School in 1929. Hill then spent three years working at Macy's department store as an elevator operator while taking premedical courses at the College of the City of New York. According to Mary Braggiotti of the *New York Post*, Hill also supported himself as a photographer's assistant, hotel clerk, sandhog in the Westchester water tunnel, factory worker, and delivery boy. During this time Hill began writing short stories and even a novel entitled *The Crystal Casket*, but these were never published. In 1932 Hill became the drama coach at both St. Philip's Protestant Church and the Abyssian Baptist Church.

Still interested in the medical profession, Hill went to Lincoln University in Pennsylvania in 1932 to continue his education, but a drama professor, J. Newton Hill, recognized Abram Hill's talents and allowed him to run the school's Little Theater, for which Hill wrote and directed plays. In 1937 he received his B.A., was awarded the Charles W. Conway Prize in English, and stayed on a semester as a faculty assistant in drama. During summer vacations from Lincoln, he worked as drama director for a Temporary Emergency Relief Association (TERA) at Camp Upton, Long Island, adapting plays to reflect a black worldview, and during the summers of 1935 and 1936 he acted as assistant state supervisor of the TERA camps.

After graduating from Lincoln, Hill joined the Federal Theatre Project (FTP). Assigned to work with the national director, Hallie Flanagan, in writing a Living Newspaper–style play depicting the black experience, Hill also became a censor of sorts, reviewing all plays with black characters considered for production by the FTP. Hill kept a number of plays from production that he felt presented a distorted view of black life, and his own play, *Liberty Differed*, did not reach the stage due to the withdrawal of government funds for the project.

Despite the FTP's demise, Hill continued to write plays. In 1937 Hill's *Hell's Half-Acre* was produced both by the Unity Players in the Bronx and by Joseph Ornato. Intent on studying playwriting, Hill took courses at the New School of Social Research and did summer work in theater at Columbia and Atlanta Universities. His gifts brought him to the attention of Theresa Helburn of the Theatre Guild, who awarded Hill a scholarship to the school. At the school he and another promising playwright, Tennessee Williams, studied under John Gassner. With the end of the FTP in 1939, venues for young playwrights were scarce, so Hill tried to sell his plays in the commercial arena. While producers agreed on his talent and promise, few were willing to risk money on an unknown. Erwin Piscator, a German director, wanted to produce one of Hill's plays, but the lack of black actors made casting difficult, and the project was dropped.

Desperately trying to make a living in the theater, Hill approached the National Association for the Advancement of Colored People's Public Relations Council, which advised him to organize the black playwrights into a production company the civil rights organization could sponsor. Hill did so, and along with two other prominent black playwrights, Theodore Ward and Langston Hughes, founded the Negro Playwrights' Company. Hill stayed with the venture only two months, leaving "quite brokenhearted over the Negro Playwrights' Company's lack of vision and practical planning" (*Current Biography 1945*, p. 284). Hill thought the group too willing to sacrifice artistic quality for propaganda. While the group was one of the first to challenge the traditional black representation on the stage, it disbanded after one production. That same year Hill's satire *On Strivers' Row* was produced by the Rose McClendon Players and ran for sixteen performances.

Encouraged by this success, Hill applied to and was accepted at the Yale School of Drama, but he was unable to afford the tuition. Disappointed, he considered founding his own theater group in New York. Establishing a black theater group had been tried before, but a determined Hill studied these groups and their failures so as not to repeat them. In the spring of 1940 he gathered together other interested parties, and the group founded the American Negro Theatre (ANT). According to Hill the ANT "had no money—only enthusiasm." Hill acted as director, and Frederick O'Neal, who had founded the Aldridge Players in St. Louis, became the manager. Its members comprised both professionals and amateurs, including Ruby Dee. The ANT made its home at the 135th Street Library Theater in the basement of the Harlem branch library with a threefold purpose: to develop art, to develop a vital black theater, and to develop pride and honor among the black community.

The first major production of the new company was Hill's *On Strivers' Row*, and, although not a critical success, the play ran for 101 performances and came to be considered Harlem's favorite play. The story of the racial and social issues faced by a young prizefighter trying to make it out of Harlem struck a familiar chord with Harlem audiences. The ANT produced eighteen plays over the next decade, including Henry and Phoebe Ephron's *Three's a Family* (1943), a show imported from Broadway that had the distinction of being the only play to run in New York simultaneously with a white and a black cast. The lack of black scripts became a problem for the new company, so Hill began to adapt established and new plays to the ANT's needs. The most important of these adaptations was Philip Yordan's *Anna Lucasta*, originally about Polish Americans. The play had been rejected by forty-four Broadway producers before Hill secured permission to adapt it for the ANT. It opened in June 1944 under director Harry Wagstaff Gribble and starred Hilda Simms, Canada Lee, Alice Childress, and Earle Hyman. *Billboard* (June 1944) called the cast "excellent without exception."

The success of *Anna Lucasta* became both the apogee and the perigee in the life of the ANT. It led to a grant of $9,500 from the Rockefeller Foundation General Education Board in 1944 and another $12,000 in 1945. It also brought the ANT to the attention of the general theatergoing public. Critics praised the play, particularly for its nontraditional portrayal of the black characters. Burton Rascoe of the *New York World-Telegram* wrote that *Anna Lucasta* was important not only for the quality of the production but also because "it is not the usual white theatrical exploitation of the Negro as a . . . 'colorful,' 'quaint,' or 'charming' character, but is a serious story of average human beings . . . who happen to have pigmented skins." The play's success led to its transplantation to Broadway with its cast, which included Frederick O'Neal. It was equally acclaimed on Forty-seventh Street, but the ANT would not long survive the loss of O'Neal and the others.

The ANT had been founded on the principle that it was a company with no stars, but when part of the *Anna Lucasta* cast went to Broadway while the others stayed behind in Harlem, the company began to fall apart. The ANT, which had become known for its experimentation, now became a tryout theater for those trying to get to Broadway. In 1947 the Rockefeller grant expired, and financial difficulties settled in for the company. Hill resigned the following year. By 1950 the ANT had stopped producing plays except for the occasional variety show.

From 1951 to 1955 Hill served as director of dramatics at Lincoln University. The remainder of his life was spent teaching and writing plays. He worked as a professor of English at the New York City schools from 1957 to 1980. The best of Hill's later plays include *Power of Darkness* (1948), *Miss Mabel* (1951), and *Split down the Middle* (1970). Hill died in New York City.

Hill's contribution to the American theater through both his own plays and the American Negro Theatre is unquestionable. In his writing, Hill was one of the first American playwrights to move away from the stereotype and present a realistic picture of the black experience. In 1945 he received a Schomburg Award and an award from the Riverdale Children's Association, both for promoting interracial understanding. Unwavering in his desire for quality black theater, Hill's vision helped create in the ANT an opportunity for black actors, directors, writers, and technicians to learn and practice their craft that the commercial theater often did not allow. While the ANT suffered in its later years, it provided an important step in the development of the black theater movement.

• Sources on Hill include C. W. E. Bigsby, *A Critical Introduction to Twentieth Century American Drama*, vol. 1 (1982); Edith J. R. Isaacs, *The Negro in the American Theatre* (1947); Errol Hill, ed., *The Theatre of Black Americans* (1987); and Doris Abramson, *Negro Playwrights in the American Theatre, 1925–1959* (1959). Hill's obituary is in the *New York Times*, 11 Oct. 1986.

MELISSA VICKERY-BAREFORD

HILL, A. P. (9 Nov. 1825–2 Apr. 1865), Confederate lieutenant general, was born Ambrose Powell Hill on the family estate near Culpeper, Virginia, the last of four sons of planter Thomas Hill and Fannie Russell Baptist. Privately tutored as a youth, Hill entered the U.S. Military Academy in 1842. A summer furlough at the end of his second year at West Point brought the tragedy of his life: Hill contracted gonorrhea. The disease did not run its normal course and disappear; instead, the gonorrhea bacteria lodged in the urinary tract and in the years to come would attack vital organs. The illness held Hill back a year at West Point. He graduated fifteenth in a class of thirty-eight cadets in 1847 and was assigned as a lieutenant in the First Artillery. Hill arrived in Mexico too late to see significant field action. For the next seven years his duty assignments alternated between Mexico and Florida. In

1855 Hill transferred to the U.S. Coastal Survey service in Washington. Hill and his former roommate, George B. McClellan (1826–1885), courted the same young woman for a time. Hill lost the contest but in 1859 married Kitty Morgan McClung, the widowed sister of future Confederate cavalryman John Hunt Morgan. Four daughters came of the union.

Strongly attached to his native state and convinced that civil war was inevitable, Hill resigned from the army on 1 March 1861 to await Virginia's call. It soon came with the colonelcy of the Thirteenth Virginia Infantry Regiment. From the moment he entered Confederate service, "Little Powell" was a familiar figure. He stood five feet, nine inches tall but weighed only 145 pounds. His chestnut hair was wavy and worn long. Catching immediate attention were his hazel eyes, which stared intently and assumed a steely glint in anger or in battle. Hill disdained uniforms and ornaments. He customarily wore calico shirts made by his wife; one, bright red in color, was his favorite battle attire. Trousers stuffed into boots, a shapeless, black hat, sword, revolver, and field glasses completed his dress. Hill regularly smoked a pipe.

The colonel and his regiment missed the battle of First Manassas. Hill's abilities in organization, drill, and discipline were so outstanding, however, that on 26 February 1862 he was promoted to brigadier general and given command of a Virginia brigade. Barely two months later, the new brigadier led his men into battle at Willamsburg. Hill attacked at a critical moment, swept Union forces from his front, and emerged from the engagement as the most conspicuous Southern brigade commander on the field. This success led to Hill's promotion on 26 May to major general. He took command of the largest division the Army of Northern Virginia ever had: six brigades of infantry (twice the size of a normal division). The new unit went into battle exactly a month later. When General Robert E. Lee launched his Seven Days counteroffensive against McClellan's Union army east of Richmond, Hill's troops were to attack in concert with Stonewall Jackson's forces coming in from the Shenandoah Valley. On 26 June Hill became impatient with Jackson's tardiness and late in the day led the assault on his own.

The battle of Mechanicsville was a sharp setback for the Confederates. Hill's units took equally heavy losses in subsequent fighting on 27 June at Gaines' Mill and on 30 June at Glendale. Yet the Virginian had fully demonstrated his prowess in combat. Lee came to regard him as the best division commander in the southern army. A month later, Hill's timely arrival at Cedar Mountain swung that battle into a Confederate victory. At Second Manassas (29–30 Aug.), Hill's troops anchored Jackson's left and beat back repeated Federal assaults until the full Confederate army arrived on the field and sent General John Pope's forces reeling in defeat.

Meanwhile, a growing estrangement had developed between Hill and his immediate superior, Jackson. Hill considered Jackson inexcusably tardy in three of the battles of the Seven Days campaign; Jackson regarded Hill as lax in discipline and lackadaisical in performance. Lee's army had just invaded Maryland early in September when Jackson placed Hill under arrest for disrespect to a superior and failure to obey orders. Hill gained temporary release, and his arrival on the Antietam battlefield late in the afternoon, when the Confederate line was about to snap, saved Lee's army from almost certain destruction. Hill and Jackson continued their vendetta through the battle of Fredericksburg to Jackson's death from wounds received at Chancellorsville. In the 26 May 1863 reorganization of Lee's army, Hill was appointed lieutenant general and assigned command of the newly created Third Corps. This elevation was probably one step above Hill's abilities. He never seemed able to adjust his strategic thinking up from utilizing brigades to divisions in combat. That weakness, plus illness, hampered his performance in July at Gettysburg. Hill's costly repulse at Bristoe Station in October was his greatest tactical mistake and underscored his tendency to launch assaults with brigades.

On 5 May 1864 Hill's corps was half of Lee's two-pronged attack against Ulysses S. Grant's forces in the Wilderness. Hill acted capably throughout the struggle but had to relinquish command a few days later when he fell seriously ill. Recent deductions by a number of physicians unanimously find that the gonorrhea contracted years earlier had become active and was leading to kidney blockage. This hydronephrosis would grow progressively worse. Hill returned to duty too soon and performed poorly in late May fighting along the North Anna River. Two weeks later he made solid reparations at Cold Harbor. Yet it was during the ten-month besiegement of Lee's army at Petersburg that Hill rose to his most brilliant heights. He commanded the southern half of the Confederate army with a corps that was no more than division-size. Sickness prostrated him from time to time as nephritis slowly developed into potentially fatal uremia. Still, a high-ranking southern officer noted that from June 1864 through March 1865 "every Federal effort to break Lee's right was met and defeated by General Hill with promptness and heavy loss."

Brilliant battle direction at Jerusalem Plank Road, Weldon Railroad, the Crater, Reams' Station, Peeble's Farm, Jones's Farm, Hatcher's Run, and White Oak Road made Hill the subaltern on whom Lee most depended in the last year of the Civil War. But by the spring of 1865, Hill was unknowingly dying. Only two days after returning to the front lines from sick leave, Hill had to rush into the fury of an all-out attack from the Federal army. It was barely dawn on 2 April when Hill, frantically trying to repair his shattered lines, died instantly from a Federal soldier's bullet. His body was twice exhumed before the remains were placed beneath the statue to his memory in Richmond, Virginia, in 1891. Courageous but impetuous, dedicated but too often dogmatic, congenial but extremely sensitive to any affront, Powell Hill epitomized the short-lived nation to which he gave his own life.

• Few of Hill's personal papers survive. The only collection of note is in the Virginia Historical Society. Two biographies exist, of which the most recent and thorough study is James I. Robertson, Jr., *General A. P. Hill: The Story of a Confederate Warrior* (1987). William Woods Hassler, *A. P. Hill: Lee's Forgotten General* (1957), was a pathbreaking study based on limited sources. For a work on Hill's troops, see Martin Schenck, *Up Came Hill: The Story of the Light Division and Its Leaders* (1958).

JAMES I. ROBERTSON, JR.

HILL, Benjamin Harvey (14 Sept. 1823–16 Aug. 1882), Confederate senator and U.S. senator, was born in Jasper County, Georgia, the son of John Hill and Sarah Parham, farmers. When he was ten, the family moved to Troup County in western Georgia, where he worked on the family farm and attended school intermittently. He entered the University of Georgia at seventeen, graduating with honors in 1843. He was admitted to the bar the next year and soon developed a prosperous practice in La Grange. In 1845 he married Caroline Holt. They had six children.

In 1851 Hill served a one-year term in Georgia's lower house. Although a Whig, he aligned with the Constitutional Union party, a coalition led by Howell Cobb, Alexander Stephens, and Robert Toombs that hoped to sustain the Compromise of 1850 as the final settlement of the major differences between the North and South. Hill served on the party's executive committee until it disbanded in 1853. The Kansas-Nebraska debate prompted him to run for Congress in 1854, losing only by twenty-four votes. With the disintegration of the Whig party, he affiliated with the American or Know Nothing party and was the leading campaigner for Millard Fillmore in Georgia during the 1856 presidential race. Although little known at the time, Hill gained notoriety through his bitter debates with Toombs and Stephens, both former Whigs, whom he rebuked for joining the Democrats. When Stephens, stung by the criticism, challenged Hill to a duel, he declined, ridiculing the idea of his fighting the frail congressman.

Hill's reputation as an orator grew, and he soon became a leading opponent of the Georgia Democrats and of secession. In 1857 he ran for governor on the Know Nothing ticket, losing by almost 10,000 votes to Joseph E. Brown. He was elected to the state senate in 1859, and in the 1860 presidential election he campaigned for John Bell of the Constitutional Union party. A few months later, he was elected to Georgia's secession convention, where he led the fight to keep the state in the Union. When it became apparent that secession was inevitable, however, he signed the ordinance of secession, while arguing for cooperation among the southern states. Despite his opposition, he was appointed to Georgia's ten-member delegation to the Provisional Congress in Montgomery, Alabama, to form the Confederate government and then was elected to the Confederate senate. Throughout the war he was one of the most consistent and vigorous defenders

of President Jefferson Davis, despite strong opposition to his administration in Georgia.

After the war Hill, along with many other leading Confederates, was arrested and imprisoned for three months at Fort Lafayette, New York. After his release he withdrew from politics until July 1867, when he made a famous speech in Atlanta urging southern states to resist the newly passed Reconstruction Act. He followed the speech with a series of long articles in the Augusta *Chronicle* entitled "Notes on the Situation" attacking Reconstruction as unconstitutional. His vitriolic speeches in the 1868 campaign marked him as one of the most outspoken opponents of Reconstruction in the South. In December 1870, however, he reversed his position, urging Georgia Democrats to accept Reconstruction as an accomplished fact and to turn their attention to economic development. As a practical demonstration of this shift, he then participated in the Republican administration's highly controversial lease of the state-owned Western & Atlantic Railroad to a consortium of private investors who were politically connected to both parties, among whom was Hill himself. Despite the outcry at his self-interested collaboration with the Republicans, he was able to maintain his credibility as a Democrat and soon became a leader of the moderate New Departure wing of the party, which joined with Liberal Republicans in 1872 to endorse the presidential bid of Horace Greeley, running as the Democratic nominee against U. S. Grant, the Republican.

By 1873 Hill's position in the Democratic party was so secure that he was a leading contender for the U.S. Senate. Finding himself unable to get the necessary majority in the state assembly, he threw his support to John B. Gordon, denying his nemesis, Alexander H. Stephens, the seat. But in 1875 Hill was elected to Congress, where he saw himself as spokesman for the resurgent Democratic South, and in January 1876 he gained national attention by defending Jefferson Davis once again, this time against charges leveled by James G. Blaine that Davis was responsible for the inhumane treatment of Union captives at Andersonville prison during the Civil War. The following winter, Hill played a significant role in bringing about the bargain between northern Republicans and southern Democrats that gave Rutherford B. Hayes the presidency and formally ended Reconstruction. In 1877 Hill was finally elected to the U.S. Senate and was now, after a tortuous political career in which he was usually aligned with the minority party, a dominant figure in Georgia politics and in the South's ascendant Democratic party.

But in July 1881 he was diagnosed as having cancer of the tongue, and he died a year later at his home in Atlanta.

• The main sources are Benjamin H. Hill, Jr., *Senator Benjamin H. Hill of Georgia: His Life, His Speeches, and Writings* (1891), and Haywood J. Pearce, Jr., *Benjamin H. Hill: Secession and Reconstruction* (1928). There is no collection of Hill's personal papers. He gave his own account of his career in the

Civil War and Reconstruction eras in his testimony to Congress in its investigation of the Ku Klux Klan, in *House Reports*, 42d Cong., 2 sess., 1872, no. 22, pts. 6–7. W. J. Northern, *Men of Mark in Georgia* (1911), contains an entry on Hill, and there is a long obituary by Henry W. Grady in the *Atlanta Constitution*, 17 Aug. 1882.

MICHAEL PERMAN

HILL, Charles Andrew (28 Apr. 1893–8 Feb. 1970), pastor and civil rights activist, was born in Detroit, Michigan, the son of Edward Hill and Mary Lance. He attended local public schools before graduating from Cleary Business College in Yipsilanti (1914) and Lincoln University near Philadelphia (1919). He also attended Moody Bible Institute in Chicago and in 1918 entered the ministry. Hill assisted at the Second Baptist Church and within two years he became pastor of Hartford Avenue Baptist Church, expanding it from thirty-five to several hundred congregates nearly fifty years later. In 1919 he wed Georgia Roberta Underwood and began a family of eight children.

A social gospel advocate, Hill combined religious beliefs and community action during the late 1930s. He helped Snow F. Grigsby pressure the Detroit Edison Company into hiring more black utility workers, and, before most other ministers, helped the United Automobile Workers (UAW) organize black automobile workers. By the early 1940s he recruited blacks for the Civil Rights Federation, served on the mayoral Inter-Racial Committee, and presided over the state conference of the National Negro Congress (NNC).

Hill came to the forefront during World War II. Believing in Double Victory (saving democracy abroad while extending it at home), he chaired committees seeking specific redress. None proved more important than the Sojourner Truth Citizens Committee of 1942, which successfully fought for black occupancy of the federally-funded defense project named after the famed abolitionist and feminist. Overseeing this biracial coalition of church, civic, and labor groups, Hill coordinated its inner circle and linked it with community leaders and rank-and-file supporters, respectively, through luncheons at the Lucy Thurman YWCA and meetings among the black churches. He also contributed to the committee's newspaper, headed rallies, and led delegations to municipal, federal, and congressional offices. Historically, he advanced many of the techniques that would be used by civil rights activists in the postwar era.

Hill became popular among militants and leftists. In late 1942 he transformed the housing group into the Citizens Committee for Jobs in War Industries and, encouraged by members of Ford Local 600 and the local NNC, sought to unseat Dr. James J. McClendon as president of the local National Association for the Advancement of Colored People (NAACP). He failed, and paid the price of losing association funding and office space for his committee. Undaunted, he led an unsuccessful effort to bring the Fair Employment Practices Committee into Detroit for public hearings on racial discrimination in war industries in 1943. The combined pressure of his committee, labor leaders, and federal officials fostered improvements in employment. However, following the worst riot of the war, which claimed thirty-four lives and destroyed $2 million worth of property in late June, his organization, along with others, adopted less volatile strategies.

Even as the riot raged, Hill sponsored a community-wide meeting with Mayor Edward J. Jeffries, Jr., which criticized the police while suggesting ways to end the bloodshed. Thereafter, he and others clashed with local, county, and state officials who blamed the violence on black leaders and organizations, especially the NAACP and the *Michigan Chronicle*. When the report of the Governor's Fact-Finding Committee became available, he labeled it a "white wash" of the Detroit Police Department, and he held the mayor and police commissioner responsible for having done nothing to avert the disorder. He initiated a petition for a federal grand jury probe of the outburst, unsuccessfully insisting upon it as a member of the Mayor's Peace Committee. Hill also aligned his jobs committee with other organizations in the Vote Mobilization Committee. That fall, under state senator Charles C. Diggs, it failed to spoil the re-election of Mayor Jeffries or elect a black candidate to common council.

In 1944 Hill mobilized black voters and joined unionists to deny William E. Dowling, former chair of the governor's committee, renomination as the Democratic candidate for Wayne County Prosecutor. During the following year, he participated in a similar coalition that failed to elect both a former UAW official for mayor over Jeffries and new councilmen (including himself). Believing that better conditions would come "only to those who use the ballot," he ran for council and lost again in 1947, 1949, and 1951. He also fell short in special primaries for council and congressional vacancies, respectively in 1948 and 1955.

Upon the retirement of McClendon, Hill became president of the Detroit NAACP in 1946. He soon gained the reputation of being not just a poor administrator but, more troubling to executive board members in the growing reactionary climate, an advocate of communist organizations and causes. As a result, he lost his election for a second term and moved even more to the left, participating in efforts to free Earl Browder, former president of the U.S. Communist Party.

By the end of the decade, Hill was a target of anticommunism. In 1949 his eldest son and namesake, a decorated pilot in World War II and reserve officer, faced charges of disloyalty by the United States Air Force for having read the *Daily Worker* and assisted in the 1945 councilmanic campaign. Clearly, Hill's son was being punished for his father's politics—"guilt by relationship"—although his own appeal of the flimsy accusations did force an official apology. Still, he never flew missions again, and in 1951 his father was subpoenaed by the House Un-American Activities Committee (HUAC) to answer, among other charges, that of having criticized the Korean War.

No charges were brought against Reverend Hill, who denied ever having been a communist and continued his activism until retiring in 1968. He died shortly thereafter in Detroit, a native son who combined protest tactics, religious faith, and independent thought. A fearless coalition-builder who inspired others to act, he believed that the struggle for equality required sacrifice and assistance from everyone; like the flight of a bird, to use his own metaphor, it needed a right wing and a left wing. Indeed, his was a lifelong commitment to activism that created opportunities for more radical members of the black and white communities and promoted the ideal of a colorblind society.

• Only sketchy information exists about Hill's family and upbringing. His collection in the Archives of Labor and Urban Affairs, Wayne State University, Michigan, is disappointing, although information about him for the war years is in several other collections like the Civil Rights Congress of Michigan. His oral history in the same depository's Blacks in the Labor Movement Collection, as well as those of Sheldon Tappes, Jack Raskin, and others in that and the Unionization of the Auto Industry Collection, which provide additional data about him and his philosophy of race relations. August Meier and Elliott Rudwick, *Black Detroit and the Rise of the UAW* (1979), and Dominic J. Capeci, Jr., *Race Relations in Wartime Detroit: The Sojourner Truth Housing Controversy of 1942* (1984), detail Hill's role in those subjects. Mary Penick Motley, ed., *The Invisible Soldier: The Experience of the Black Soldier, World War II* (1975), provides first hand accounts of his son's mistreatment by the United States Air Force. Richard W. Thomas, *Life for Us Is What We Make It: Building Black Community in Detroit, 1915–1945* (1992), mentions Reverend Hill in several places. Most of his activities, particularly during his most significant period from 1940 to 1951, can be gleaned from the *Detroit Tribune* and the *Michigan Chronicle*. Obituaries appear in the *Detroit Free Press*, 10 Feb. 1970, and the *Michigan Chronicle* and the *Detroit Tribune*, both 14 Feb. 1970.

DOMINIC J. CAPECI, JR.

HILL, Chippie (15 Mar. 1905–7 May 1950), dancer and singer, was born Bertha Hill in Charleston, South Carolina, the daughter of John Hill and Ida Jones. From the age of nine she sang in church. The family moved to New York City sometime around 1918, and the following year Hill danced at Leroy's Club in Harlem in a show led by Ethel Waters. The owner of Leroy's nicknamed Hill "Chippie" because of her youth.

Hill toured as a singer and a dancer with the Rabbit Foot Minstrels in the early 1920s and as a featured blues singer on the Theater Owners' Booking Association circuit. In St. Louis her "wardrobe was stolen, and several nights later Chippie spotted the thief sitting in the front row. 'I knew her,' says Chippie, 'because she was wearing my best dress.' There was nothing for Chippie to do but leap off the stage in the middle of the show and attack the culprit. 'I tore that rag right off that bitch's back'" (Aurthur, p. 3).

Hill settled in Chicago in the mid-1920s. She participated in recording sessions with cornetist Louis Armstrong in November 1925 and February 1926, recording "Low Land Blues," "Trouble in Mind," and

"Georgia Man." She performed at the Race Records Ball at the Chicago Coliseum in February 1926, and she also won a talent and recording contest at the coliseum. Hill commenced regular performances at the Plantation Café, where she worked with cornetist King Oliver's band in August 1926, and at the Dreamland Café. Hill recorded "Pleadin' for the Blues," "Pratts [*sic*] City Blues," and "Lonesome Weary Blues" (again with Armstrong) in November 1926; "Weary Money Blues" and "Christmas Man Blues" in 1928 (with pianist Georgia Tom Dorsey and guitarist Tampa Red); a new version of "Trouble in Mind" in 1928; and "I Ain't Gonna Do It No More" in 1929. Hill sang at Chicago's Elite No. 2 Club before touring with pianist Lovie Austin in 1929. That year she married John Offett; they had seven children. Hill continued to work part time at clubs around Chicago, including engagements at the Annex Café (1934–1937), the Cabin Inn with clarinetist Jimmie Noone (1937), and the Club DeLisa (1939–1940).

During the 1940s Hill left music to devote herself to her family, but early in 1946 writer and promoter Rudi Blesh found her in Chicago and immediately recorded nine tracks, including versions of "Trouble in Mind," "Careless Love," "How Long Blues," and "Around the Clock Blues," all with Austin's band. Hill resumed working at the Club DeLisa (1946–1947), and she participated in a jazz concert in Chicago before moving to New York, where she starred in Blesh's "This Is Jazz" concert at the Ziegfeld Theater in June 1947 and on his weekly radio series "This Is Jazz" in July and August of that year. In late 1947 and early 1948 Hill appeared at the Village Vanguard in Greenwich Village, and she also sang at Jimmy Ryan's club in midtown.

In the spring of 1948 Hill worked with trombonist Kid Ory in a concert at Carnegie Hall, and she performed in Paris. She held engagements at New York's Central Plaza Club (1949) and Riviera Club (1949–1950), and she performed with pianist Art Hodes's quintet at the Blue Note in Chicago (1950) and again in New York at the Stuyvesant Casino (1950). Hill's strong personality remained intact during these final years: "When she arrived in New York she slyly informed the press that she was forty-two. This year [1949] she is forty-one." Although already a grandmother, she could "outcurse and outdrink any truck driver you can dig up, and if you ever get up the nerve to ask her to dance, she'll jitterbug you into exhaustion" (Aurthur, p. 4). Hill died in a hit-and-run traffic accident in New York.

Like the better-known singers Ma Rainey and Bessie Smith, Hill emphasized a southern, African-American, "downhome" blues vocal style more than the mainstream mannerisms of vaudeville singing—although the latter may be heard in a song such as "Lonesome, All Alone and Blue" (recorded with Armstrong in February 1926). Sliding blue notes abound in her work; she often moves out of her mid-range voice into a strained, piercing, shout-singing; and she sometimes muffles lyrics, as in her first recording,

"Low Land Blues." Of the discs from her second career in the 1940s, Blesh writes that "in these she reveals . . . a rhythmic shouting more forceful than will be found on any of the known records of Ma and Bessie, and a clipped, hot phrasing that barely appears in her earlier work."

• For further information on Hill's life and work see "Singing for the Devil," *Time*, 15 Sept. 1947, pp. 78, 80; Carter Harman, "Portrait of a Blues Shouter," *New York Times*, 16 Nov. 1947; Bob Aurthur, "Let the Good Times Roll: An Impression of Chippie Hill," *Playback* 3 (Feb. 1950): 3–4; Rudi Blesh, *Shining Trumpets: A History of Jazz*, 2d. ed. (1958); and Ronald Clifford Foreman, Jr., "Jazz and Race Records, 1920–1932: Their Origins and Their Significance for the Record Industry and Society" (Ph.D. diss., Univ. of Illinois, 1968). Also see Derrick Stewart-Baxter, *Ma Rainey and the Classic Blues Singers* (1970); Sheldon Harris, *Blues Who's Who: A Biographical Dictionary of Blues Singers* (1979); Dempsey J. Travis, *An Autobiography of Black Jazz* (1983); Jack Litchfield, *This Is Jazz* (1985); Laurie Wright, *Walter C. Allen and Brian A. L. Rust's "King Oliver"* (1987); and Daphne Duval Harrison, "'Classic' Blues and Women Singers," in *The Blackwell Guide to Blues Records*, ed. Paul Oliver (1989; rev. ed., 1991). An obituary is in *Melody Maker*, 24 June 1950, p. 9.

BARRY KERNFELD

HILL, Daniel Harvey (12 July 1821–24 Sept. 1889), soldier, educator, and editor, was born at Hill's Iron Works, York District, South Carolina, the son of Solomon Hill, a farmer, and Nancy Cabeen. Signally influenced by the military and religious traditions of his forebears, Hill was descended from Scotch-Irish and Scottish Presbyterians who had settled in the Carolina upcountry before the American Revolution. Both grandfathers had fought with distinction under General Thomas Sumter during the revolutionary war, and William Hill, his paternal grandfather, was a South Carolina legislator and noted ironmaster who manufactured cannon for the revolutionary armies. Because of his father's early death, Hill's mother, a devout Presbyterian, was the predominant influence in his upbringing.

Despite a spinal affliction from which he suffered throughout life, Hill was admitted to West Point in 1838. He graduated twenty-eighth in the class of 1842. After graduation Hill did garrison duty as a second lieutenant in artillery until the outbreak of the Mexican War in 1846. A participant in all the major actions of the war, he was promoted to first lieutenant in March 1847. In that same year he received brevet promotion twice, first as captain for "gallant and meritorious conduct" in the battles of Contreras and Churubusco, and then as major for bravery in the storming of Chapultepec. In recognition of Hill's distinguished war record, the state of South Carolina presented him with a gold sword of honor.

On 2 November 1848 Hill married Isabella Morrison. From this marriage there were nine children, five of whom lived to maturity. Resigning from the army in February 1849, Hill was appointed professor of mathematics at Washington College (now Washington and Lee University) at Lexington, Virginia, where he remained until 1854. While in Lexington, Hill recommended Thomas J. "Stonewall" Jackson for a teaching position at the Virginia Military Institute; he later became Jackson's brother-in-law when Jackson married Anna Morrison, the younger sister of Hill's wife.

Because of Hill's Presbyterian loyalties and his father-in-law's connection as a trustee and former president of Davidson College, in 1854 he became professor of mathematics at that struggling Presbyterian institution in North Carolina. During his five years at Davidson, Hill led in restoring discipline and raising academic standards and was credited with having saved the college from collapse. A successful and admired classroom teacher, while at Davidson he published *College Discipline: An Inaugural Address* (1855), which received widespread attention, and two theological expositions, *A Consideration of the Sermon on the Mount* (1858) and *The Crucifixion of Christ* (1859), as well as a textbook, *Elements of Algebra* (1857); the last was acclaimed for its excellence and celebrated for the anti-Yankee bias evident in its exercises. Recognizing the need for a military school in Charlotte, Hill left Davidson in 1859 to become the founding superintendent of the North Carolina Military Institute.

In spring 1861 the governor of North Carolina invited Hill to establish a camp at Raleigh for the instruction of state troops. On 11 May of that year Hill was elected colonel of the First North Carolina Volunteers, known as the "Bethel Regiment." After secession the regiment was sent to the lower Virginia Peninsula, where at Big Bethel on 10 June Hill led it to victory in the first battle of the Civil War. Promoted to brigadier general on 10 July, Hill performed administrative duties until September, when he was ordered to strengthen defenses in the Pamlico district of North Carolina. After this assignment, he served under General Joseph E. Johnston in northern Virginia until spring 1862. Commissioned major general on 26 March, he led his division during the Peninsular campaign, rendering distinguished service at Seven Pines, and was commended by General Robert E. Lee for his performance during the Seven Days, especially at Malvern Hill.

During July and August 1862, Hill commanded the military department of North Carolina and southern Virginia. Having disappointed Lee in the administration of that department, he was recalled to the Army of Northern Virginia in time for the invasion of Maryland. He was charged after the war (E. A. Pollard, *The Lost Cause* [1867], p. 314) with having carelessly allowed a copy of Lee's plan for the Maryland campaign to fall into enemy hands; Hill stoutly denied that he had directly received the dispatch from Lee's headquarters. In the Maryland campaign Hill displayed great skill and uncommon bravery in delaying McClellan's army at South Mountain and in leading his division in the "Bloody Lane" at Sharpsburg.

Suffering ill health and resentful at not being promoted to lieutenant general in Lee's reorganization of October 1862, Hill decided to resign from the army at the beginning of 1863, but he was dissuaded by Jackson. From February to July 1863, he again commanded the department of North Carolina and Southern Virginia. Although he had clashed with Lee over the allocation of troops and assignment of officers, Hill effectively defended Petersburg and Richmond during Lee's Gettysburg campaign.

Having previously volunteered for service in the west, Hill was nominated lieutenant general on 11 July 1863 by President Jefferson Davis and was assigned to a corps command in the Army of Tennessee under General Braxton Bragg. Critical of Bragg's generalship after the battle of Chickamauga, in September Hill and other generals petitioned Davis to remove him. Erroneously believing that Hill was the author of the petition, Bragg prevailed on Davis to relieve Hill of his command. Moreover, Davis declined to submit Hill's nomination as lieutenant general to the Confederate Senate for confirmation. Failing in efforts to clear his record or to obtain reassignment, Hill was without military employment until early 1865. For a few months in 1864 he was a volunteer aide-de-camp to General Beauregard at Petersburg. In the last months of the war he commanded, as major general, a division under General Joseph E. Johnston; and in the battle of Bentonville, North Carolina, on 19–21 March 1865, he temporarily commanded a corps. Hill concluded his military career when Johnston surrendered to Sherman at Durham Station on 26 April.

As a soldier, Hill was recognized as a fearless and courageous leader in combat. Although popular with his troops and subordinate officers, he was not esteemed by his superiors, whose judgment he openly and tellingly criticized. No admirer of Robert E. Lee, Hill questioned the wisdom of Lee's strategic and tactical decisions during the Seven Days' battles around Richmond, the invasion of Maryland, and the Gettysburg campaign; Lee praised Hill as a fighter and division commander but doubted his capability for higher or independent command. Although the sincerity and depth of Hill's devotion to the Southern cause was never disputed, he alienated many by his intemperate language, sarcasm, and irascibility, which may be attributed to his frequent ill health and constant pain. Intellectually, Hill was one of the most gifted and best-read of the Confederate generals.

Returning to Charlotte after the war, from 1866 to 1869 Hill edited *The Land We Love*, a monthly magazine devoted to literature, military history, and agriculture. From 1870 to 1877 he was the editor of a Charlotte weekly newspaper, the *Southern Home*. As an editor, he did much of the writing; he sought not only to vindicate the South in history and to restore home rule to white Southerners, but also to broaden the cultural interests of the South and to strengthen educational opportunities in the region by giving more attention to agricultural and industrial training.

In 1877 Hill became president of the Arkansas Industrial University (now the University of Arkansas) at Fayetteville. Until his resignation because of ill health in 1884, he struggled with considerable success to maintain the independence of the university from political interference, to improve standards, and to maintain discipline. After a year's rest in Macon, Georgia, in 1885 Hill accepted the presidency of the Middle Georgia Military and Agricultural College (now the Georgia Military College) at Milledgeville.

While carrying out his administrative duties in Arkansas and Georgia, Hill continued to teach and write. In addition to public addresses and other occasional pieces, he wrote four articles on Civil War campaigns for the *Century Magazine* (1885–1887), which were later published in *Battles and Leaders of the Civil War* (vols. 2 and 3, 1887, 1888). Compelled to resign the Georgia presidency in 1889 because of stomach cancer, Hill died in Charlotte.

Remembered mainly for his military career, Hill also made noteworthy contributions to the educational and intellectual life of the South, though his influence was lessened by the devastation and impoverishment of the South after the Civil War. Hill's stern and unbending integrity was fortified by his strong religious convictions as an active Presbyterian churchman.

• The most important collections of Hill's papers are in the North Carolina Department of Archives and History, Raleigh; the Southern History Collection of the University of North Carolina Library, Chapel Hill; the Duke University Library, Durham, North Carolina; and the Virginia State Library, Richmond. Hal Bridges, *Lee's Maverick General* (1961, repr. with a useful introduction by Gary W. Gallagher in 1991) is the best account of Hill's military career. A work by Hill's son, Daniel Harvey Hill, Jr., *Bethel to Sharpsburg* (2 vols., 1926) also gives a full account of his father's military career from the beginning of the Civil War to the close of the Maryland campaign in 1862. The fullest biographical sketches are in pamphlets by A. C. Avery, *Memorial Address on the Life and Character of Lieutenant General D. H. Hill* (1893), and Joseph M. Hill, *A Biography of Daniel Harvey Hill* (1948). Articles dealing with Hill's work as an author and educator are Hall Bridges, "D. H. Hill and Higher Education in the New South," *Arkansas Historical Quarterly* 15 (1956): 107–24, and his "D. H. Hill's Anti-Yankee Algebra," *Journal of Southern History* 22 (1956): 220–22; Marguerite Gilstrap, "Daniel Harvey Hill, Southern Propagandist," *Arkansas Historical Quarterly* 2 (1943): 43–50; and Henry Elliott Shepherd, "General D. H. Hill as a Teacher and Author," *North Carolina Booklet* 16 (1917): 191–208.

MALCOLM LESTER

HILL, David Bennett (29 Aug. 1843–20 Oct. 1910), lawyer and politician, was born in Havana (now Montour Falls), New York, the son of Caleb Hill, a carpenter, and Eunice Durfey. After graduating from public school, Hill began reading law in the office of Marcus Crawford, a local attorney. At the age of twenty he moved to Elmira, New York, where he continued his studies at the firm of Thurston, Hart & McGuire. Hill was admitted to the bar in 1864 and, though only twenty-one, was appointed city attorney within a year. Thereafter he devoted his life to law and politics. From 1868 through 1881 he served as a delegate to the New York Democratic State Conventions and presided over the meetings of 1877 and 1881. In 1870 he began copublishing the *Elmira Gazette*, which he used to popularize his views and those of the Democratic party. Hill was elected to the New York State Assembly in 1870 and 1871 (serving in 1871 and 1872). There he developed a close personal and political friendship with Democratic leader Samuel Tilden. During the 1872 session he and Tilden served on the Judiciary Committee, which secured the impeachment of New York Supreme Court judge George Barnard, a member of the Tweed ring. By 1875 Hill firmly controlled the Democratic party in Chemung County, wielding his power on behalf of the Tilden reform wing of the party.

Following his 1871 election to the assembly, Hill did not run again for public office until 1881, when he was elected alderman from Elmira's Third Ward. In 1882 he was elected mayor of Elmira, and soon afterward he began lobbying for the post of lieutenant governor on the 1882 Democratic state ticket. He received the nomination and, along with gubernatorial nominee Grover Cleveland, was swept into office by a large plurality. Always willing to promote others in order to clear a path for himself, Hill was among the first to urge Cleveland to run for president in 1884. Following Cleveland's victory, Hill succeeded to the governorship in January 1885. He was elected governor in his own right in November 1885 and reelected to a second three-year term in 1888, serving a total of seven years.

Hill's gubernatorial administrations were characterized by administrative efficiency. In traditional Democratic fashion, he promoted himself as an economy-minded advocate of limited government. In one of his most celebrated acts, Hill vetoed the 1885 State Census Bill when Republican legislators refused to heed his request to save money by limiting the census only to the enumeration of inhabitants. Yet while his policy positions often made good sense, they were first and foremost calculated to advance the interests of the Democratic party. As his biographer noted, Hill was less concerned with governing than with political strategy and the maneuvering necessary to perpetuate party success. In his positions on the important issues of the day, Hill opposed civil service reform, which reduced the amount of patronage available to party leaders, and only in the face of overwhelming public demand did he eventually support limited measures to reform the ballot. Prohibition and labor reform were also recurring issues during Hill's tenure. The governor steadfastly opposed Republican efforts to raise excise taxes on liquor. By shrewdly keeping the issue alive, however, he perpetuated the life of the Prohibition party, which drew votes away from the Republican party and gave him his margin of victory in 1885 and 1888. Hill also established himself as a friend of labor, advocating measures to facilitate the organization of labor unions, establish a system of arbitration to settle labor disputes, set maximum work hours, end prison labor contracts, and regulate tenement houses.

Hill was a dedicated partisan. In 1885 he coined the phrase "I am a Democrat!" by which he was identified throughout his career. Hill's talent for political organization and meticulous attention to detail enabled him to build up a strong personal machine, making him the dominant leader of the New York Democratic party from 1885 through the early 1900s. While he was governor, Hill's partisanship and political ambition quickly brought him into conflict with the Cleveland-Mugwump wing of the Democratic party. From 1885 through the mid-1890s Hill and Cleveland battled for control of the New York party as well as for the Democratic presidential nomination. Hill generally succeeded in controlling the Democratic state organization but failed to capture the presidential nomination he coveted. He came closest in 1892, when he pegged his nomination hopes on his support for the free coinage of silver. However, the issue failed to generate the appeal among delegates that it would in 1896, and Hill finished a distant second behind Cleveland in the balloting. A contributing factor to his defeat may have been his election to the U.S. Senate in 1891. Hill chose himself to be the Democratic candidate and was duly elected by the Democratic legislature, conveying the impression that he was an excessively ambitious office seeker. This was compounded by his decision to serve out his final year as governor before assuming his Senate seat in January 1892, for which political opponents dubbed him the "governor-senator." Hill's legendary "steal of the senate" following the 1891 election, in which he engineered a successful scheme to overturn the elections of three Republican state senators and replace them with Democrats, thus securing a Democratic majority in the state senate, demonstrated the senator-elect's disregard for political ethics and further plagued his quest for the presidential nomination.

The 1892 Democratic National Convention represented the apex of Hill's career. Thereafter, his political influence gradually declined. In the U.S. Senate (1892–1897) he was known as an excellent orator. Though he constantly battled with President Cleveland for control of New York patronage, Hill generally defended the Democratic administration against Republican and Populist attacks. In 1894 Hill was nominated once again as the Democratic candidate for governor of New York, this time against his will. Battling a wave of anti-Democratic sentiment, he lost decisively, the only electoral defeat of his career.

Following his 1894 defeat, Hill never ran again for public office, but he remained politically active. He retreated from his earlier endorsement of the free coinage of silver toward a more orthodox defense of the gold standard. He opposed the Democratic party's populistic platform in 1896 and 1900, as well as the nomination of William Jennings Bryan for president, but he remained loyal to the party. Hill's lack of faith in the party's free-silver policy, among other factors, led him to withdraw himself from consideration for the vice presidential nomination at the Democratic National Convention in 1900, after a strong movement began on his behalf. In 1904 he managed the presidential campaign of Democrat Alton B. Parker. Thereafter Hill retired from active politics and devoted himself to his Albany law practice. A successful and well-respected lawyer, he served as president of the

New York State Bar Association from 1885 to 1887. His most famous case, eventually decided by the U.S. Supreme Court in 1890, was the McGraw-Fiske suit against Cornell University.

Hill's political career is best characterized by his partisan disposition and devotion to the Democratic party. He was a firm believer in party discipline and party government at a time when these traditional nineteenth-century values were coming under increasing attack by proponents of bipartisan and nonpartisan government. Despite his adherence to the "practical" school of politics, Hill was regarded as personally honest. Unlike many party bosses, he did not use his power to line his own pockets. He was a man of simple tastes who neither smoked nor drank. Often cold and aloof, he avoided large social gatherings and never married. Hill died at "Wolfert's Roost," his country home outside Albany.

• The largest collections of Hill papers are in the Department of Manuscripts and Special Collections at the New York State Library, the George Arents Research Library at Syracuse University, and the New York Public Library. The New York State Archives contains material relating to Hill's gubernatorial administration in the Factory Inspector Appointment Files, 1885–1890, and Appointment Correspondence Files, 1883–1936. Additional manuscript material is scattered among several repositories, as listed in Karen D. Paul, ed., *Guide to Research Collections of Former United States Senators, 1789–1995* (1995). Hill's annual messages and other communications to the state legislature are published in Charles Z. Lincoln, *Messages from the Governors*, vol. 8 (1909). A published biography is Herbert J. Bass, *"I Am a Democrat": The Political Career of David Bennett Hill* (1961), which focuses on the period from 1885 to 1892, when Hill was at the height of his power. Hill's political career is treated more broadly in DeAlva S. Alexander, *Four Famous New Yorkers: The Political Careers of Cleveland, Platt, Hill and Roosevelt*, vol. 4 of *The Political History of the State of New York, 1882–1905* (1923). Obituaries are in the *New York Times*, the *New York Tribune*, and the *New York Herald*, all 21 Oct. 1910; and the *Albany Evening Journal*, 20 Oct. 1910.

JOHN F. KIRN, JR.

HILL, David Jayne (10 June 1850–2 Mar. 1932), diplomat and college president, was born in Plainfield, New Jersey, the son of Daniel Trembley Hill, a Baptist minister, and Lydia Ann Thompson. Hill lived in various places during his youth as his father followed calls to a number of pulpits in the Middle Atlantic states. In 1870 Hill enrolled at the University of Lewisburg in Lewisburg, Pennsylvania, graduating as valedictorian in 1874. That year he married Anna Liddell; they had one son. Hill was to asked to join the faculty, rising quickly to professor of rhetoric in 1877. A battle for control of the college between traditional rural, small-town Baptists in the Lewisburg region and modernists in the metropolitan Philadelphia area soon elevated him further. The latter group won, ousted the president, and replaced him with the 29-year-old Hill. He quickly legalized fraternities, reduced restrictions on student lives, permitted elective courses, and encouraged faculty to play a greater role in governance. To lessen fiscal pressures Hill virtually put the college's name up for sale and persuaded William Bucknell, a wealthy Philadelphia Baptist, to effectively purchase the University of Lewisburg, which was renamed Bucknell University. Bucknell, in turn, placed money and power in the young president's hands.

Despite such success, Hill sought a career in the newly emerging research universities. The death of Hill's wife in 1880 added to his sense of isolation in Lewisburg. In 1886 he married Juliet Lewis Parker; they had one daughter. Although his second marriage gave him a social life, both partners desired a larger stage. Hill planned to study psychology at Johns Hopkins University when another opportunity beckoned. Martin Anderson, longtime president of the Baptist-dominated University of Rochester, named Hill as his successor. Rochester enticed him with a raise and a year's study in Europe. But when he assumed duties in 1889 he discovered that Rochester was not embracing the new academic world. Although popular with Rochester businessmen and students, Hill was undercut by denominationalism. Rochester proved to be more directly under the control of Baptists than Bucknell had been. Threatened by Hill's insufficient denominational enthusiasm, the trustees passed a requirement that two-thirds of the board be Baptist. Hill responded by scheduling graduation at a Presbyterian church and publishing *Genetic Philosophy* (1893), which lessened the role of divine influence in human biology. In turn, the Genesee Baptist Ministerial Association rebuked him. Surrounded by controversy, his fundraising floundered, and Hill resigned.

Hill's career then took a dramatic turn. A high-tariff Republican, Hill had impressed William McKinley, who said that with more college presidents like Hill there would be fewer freetraders. Thus, after Hill spent two years in Europe studying public law, McKinley appointed him assistant secretary of state to John Hay in 1898. He served in the post longer than all but one of his twenty-four predecessors, and his wife became a leading Washington hostess. After an initial conflict over the Hay-Pauncefort treaty fanned by the press, Hay and Hill worked well together. Hill's academic interest in international arbitration quickly found practical application at the First International Peace Conference convened in The Hague in 1899. His article "International Justice," published in the *Yale Law Review* in 1896, had received international attention. While armaments limitation, the original purpose of the meeting, was stillborn, Hill's vision of international juristic arbitration of disputes helped form the Permanent Court of Arbitration, the first international judicial organization with an ongoing administrative framework.

Hill's support of and skill in arbitration scored several further successes. He played an influential role in settling the Samoa Islands conflict with Great Britain and Germany. Charged with oversight of the Second Pan-American Congress, scheduled for 1902 in Mexico City, Hill expertly defused a long-standing Chilean-

Peruvian dispute that threatened to torpedo the meeting. This permitted a productive conference to take place.

By 1903 Hill yearned to leave Washington and openly sought an ambassadorial post in Berlin. Instead President Theodore Roosevelt sent him to Switzerland. The quiet posting permitted Hill to begin work on his long-delayed *A History of Diplomacy in the International Development of Europe* (2 vols., 1905–1906). After aiding Roosevelt's 1904 reelection campaign, Hill was named minister to the Netherlands and moved to The Hague. There Hill acted as intermediary between Andrew Carnegie and Dutch officials over Carnegie's plans to build a permanent home for the Court of Arbitration. He also served as a delegate to the Second Hague Conference in 1905.

In 1907 Hill attained a longtime ambition when Roosevelt named him ambassador to Germany. But the appointment became an international controversy that even drew the attention of the "Mr. Dooley" newspaper cartoon when the Kaiser temporarily withdrew his approval and sought a wealthier candidate who would entertain in the lavish fashion of his predecessor. Seen as an affront to national honor, the imbroglio briefly made Hill a famous national figure. Hill's presence in Berlin—he assumed the post in 1908—fortuitously presented the opportunity to move the Kaiser's government, the most resistant major power, toward accepting international arbitration. Although he developed a close relationship with the Kaiser, Hill made little progress in lessening Germany's resistance to arbitration. In 1911 Hill was recalled by President William Howard Taft, apparently in connection with domestic political maneuvers.

The departure from Berlin ended Hill's diplomatic career, but he remained a prominent spokesman in international affairs. He supported American intervention in World War I, because he was convinced that Germany was the leading obstacle to an international legal system. Despite his commitment to internationalism he also fervently opposed the League of Nations, preferring a more juridical structure. On less consistent and very partisan grounds he also opposed the World Court, which was the subject of his last book, *The Problem of a World Court* (1927). On domestic as well as foreign affairs Hill remained a leading spokesman of Old Guard Republicanism and exercised some influence in the Harding administration, although he turned down several proffered positions.

Hill was a highly competent and intelligent public servant in education and diplomacy who exerted surprising influence on world affairs and leaders for some one who became virtually forgotten. He died in Washington, D.C.

• There is a small collection of Hill's papers at Bucknell University. The principal collection, covering the years 1876–1932, is held in the Special Collections of the Rush Rhees Library, University of Rochester. It also holds manuscripts of Hill's unpublished autobiography, "The Confidences of a Grandfather." Both universities that Hill headed have excellent histories covering his period. For Bucknell see J. Orin Oliphant, *The Rise of Bucknell University* (1962). For the University of Rochester see Arthur J. May, *A History of the University of Rochester, 1850–1962* (1977). For a work that puts Hill's Bucknell years in a comparative context see W. Bruce Leslie, *Gentlemen and Scholars: College and Community in the "Age of the University," 1865–1917* (1992). For information on Hill's diplomatic career and later public life see Aubrey Parkman, *David Jayne Hill and the Problem of World Peace* (1975). An obituary and an editorial about Hill appear in the *New York Times*, 3 Mar. 1932.

W. BRUCE LESLIE

HILL, George Handel (8 Oct. 1809–27 Sept. 1849), actor, known as "Yankee," was born in Boston, Massachusetts, the son of Ureli K. Hill, a musician, and Nancy Hull (the couple separated during Hill's infancy). He attended the Bristol Academy at Taunton, Massachusetts, but ran away from home at about age fifteen. In New York City he found work as an apprentice in a jewelry shop, but he also served as a theatrical supernumerary at the Chatham Street Theatre. Always attracted to the stage, Hill determined his future line of business when in 1825 he saw Alexander Simpson playing a Yankee role, Jonathan, in *The Forest Rose*.

Yankee characters on the American stage appeared as early as 1787 but achieved their greatest popularity in the generation before the Civil War. The stage Yankee—from which derived America's emblematic Uncle Sam—was based on rural New Englanders, also known as "down-easters," simple but shrewd characters, with eccentric speech patterns, great ability as raconteurs, and a suspicious dislike of urban lifestyles.

Hill first appeared in a Yankee persona in Brooklyn in 1826, then began an engagement as a low comedian, specializing in roles featuring horseplay and the representation of low life. In 1828 he married Cordelia Thompson and quit the stage; the couple had at least one child. But he failed as a shopkeeper and returned in 1831 to the stage in Albany, New York. For the next several years Hill wandered up and down the eastern seaboard, finally signing on as a minor actor at the Arch Street Theatre in Philadelphia in 1832. After seven years of preparation he became an overnight star when he appeared as Jonathan Ploughboy there, playing the same role in Baltimore and Boston before opening at the Park Theatre in New York City on 14 November 1832. He immediately rose to star status, in great demand all over the United States.

Hill soon began to develop a repertory distinct from other Yankee actors; his first important original script, written for him by Joseph Jones, was *The Green Mountain Boy*, which he premiered in Philadelphia in March 1833. Hill had met Jones, also a New Englander, in Boston in 1832; the playwright supplied several of Hill's more important roles. In *The Green Mountain Boy*, Hill played Jedediah Homebred, a shrewd bargainer and an uneducated and unaffected country boy. Other similar roles followed in productions such as *Josh Horseradish; or, The Lying Yankee* (1833), *Ovid and Obid; or, Yankee Blunders* (1834), and *Jonathan*

Doubikins (1835). A script by John Augustus Stone (author of *Metamora*, Edwin Forrest's starring role), *The Knight of the Golden Fleece*, contained one of Hill's most-played roles, Sy Saco. Unfortunately the script was never printed, and no copy exists.

In this first portion of his career Hill successfully sought to distinguish himself as the most authentic of the stage Yankees. In 1836 he sailed for England, following James Hackett's engagement there and Charles Mathew's earlier delineations of Yankees in London. He opened at Drury Lane with *Old Times in Virginia; or, The Yankee Pedlar* as Hiram Dodge. London reviewers lauded Hill but condemned the script. Critics applauded his naturalistic style; audiences deemed his appearance good and his dry, quaint, witty Dodge a true Yankee, devoid of vulgarity. Hill toured the provinces, played a few other roles, and returned home as a conquering hero.

While Hill's success continued in America, his personal fortunes did not. Henry Dickinson Stone, in *Personal Recollections* (1873), suggests that Hill had an affair in London with a young actress whom he later brought back to America and concluded that women and wine destroyed Yankee Hill. Francis Wemyss, a manager who had greatly admired Hill's early endeavors, also lamented his striving for "an unenviable notoriety out of his profession" and claimed that an "overweening vanity" proved detrimental to his fame (*Twenty-six Years*). In any event, Hill returned to Europe in 1838, this time accompanied by his wife. He successfully played the Haymarket Theatre in London, visited Paris in January 1839, and returned to London until September.

In the midst of a highly successful acting career Hill took up theater management, leasing the Franklin Theatre in New York City in 1840 and renaming it Hill's Theatre. In this capacity he competed with Edmund Simpson at the Park Theatre and J. W. Wallack at the National; his season there was short and disastrous. Two years later he reattempted management at Peale's Theatre in New York; again he failed. Discouraged and influenced by a physician friend, Hill set out to become a doctor (some sources suggest he practiced dentistry for a time), but the rigors of his new profession forced him back to the stage. In 1842 he created Solon Shingle in Jones's *The People's Lawyer*, which became one of his most successful roles and marked a change in the Yankee character. Shingle offered the sagacity of age rather than the vivacity of the country boy of Hill's earlier roles. It also marked Hill's last significant contribution to the American stage; illness, debts, and legal problems began to erode his personal life, and he died in Saratoga, New York, barely forty years old.

During the nineteenth century the American theater converted from an English colonial theater to a uniquely American form, using the various native characters available to it: American Indians, African Americans, urban slum-dwellers, frontiersmen, and the Yankee character. Increasing use of these characters demonstrated a move toward greater realism in theater in the United States. In developing the Yankee to its most naturalistic form, Hill led the way by anticipating the evolution of American drama toward the realism that would peak later in the century. American theater historian Francis Hodge could thus justifiably call Hill the "most perceptive and authentic impersonator of the Yankee character on the American stage." Hill's range was narrow, to be sure, but his ease, quaintness, and detailed characterizations disarmed his critics.

• As early as 1834 the *New York Mirror* (22 Nov.) published a profile of Hill as a successful young actor. The first full biographical treatment of him was written in 1850 by William Knight Northall, *Life and Recollections of Yankee Hill: Together with Anecdotes and Incidents of His Travels*. Drawing heavily on newspaper criticism, Northall supplied a detailed account of Hill's Yankee characters as well as a 97-page biographical sketch. Three years later Hill's widow, Cordelia, arranged her husband's manuscripts for publication with the aid of their son; the document appeared as *Scenes from the Life of an Actor*. Gaylan Collier published a brief extract from his dissertation on stage dialects, "George Handel Hill: The Yankee of Them All," in *Southern Speech Journal* 24 (1958): 91–93. For a detailed analysis of Hill's career and contributions to the American stage, see Francis Hodge, *Yankee Theatre: The Image of America on the Stage, 1825–1850* (1964).

STEPHEN M. ARCHER

HILL, George Washington (22 Oct. 1884–13 Sept. 1946), tobacco entrepreneur, was born in Philadelphia, Pennsylvania, the son of Percival S. Hill, a carpet jobber and retailer, and Cassie Rowland Milnes. In the year that Hill was born North Carolina tobacco executive James B. Duke went to New York City determined to corner the American tobacco trade. By 1889 he had succeeded in assembling five of the largest tobacco companies in the United States into a single business concern, the American Tobacco Company. In an attempt to bring other opposition to heel, Duke then launched an intensive advertising campaign. As Duke anticipated, the marketing barrage forced many of his competitors into bankruptcy. Faced with the prospect of insolvency, other executives instead sold out to Duke.

Hill's father, a partner in the Blackwell Durham Tobacco Company, followed this course. In 1892, while still involved in carpet selling, he joined Blackwell Durham as a sales manager. Two years later he sold his share of the carpet business to department store pioneer John Wanamaker. Over time, Percival Hill increased tobacco sales substantially at Blackwell Durham and bought into the firm. Around 1898, however, American Tobacco acquired Blackwell Durham, and Hill became an executive at American Tobacco. The Hills moved to New York, where they enrolled their son George in the Horace Mann School. In 1902 Hill graduated and went on to attend Williams College, but after two years he left school and began to work for American Tobacco. Initially he played a minor role, working in the South first in factories and later in the leaf department.

In 1907 father and son bought Butler & Butler, a small New York tobacco company, and George gained greater responsibility. As president of the newly acquired firm, he exhibited a talent for marketing. Like other tobacco companies of the period, Butler & Butler sold a wide array of tobacco products, including various cigarette lines. Hill chose, however, to focus much of his marketing attention on a single brand, Pall Mall, a premium Turkish cigarette. the resulting campaign proved highly successful, so much so in fact that Pall Mall became the leading brand in that market segment.

Based at least in part on his success selling Pall Mall, Hill obtained a more prestigious position at American Tobacco. In 1911 the U.S. Supreme Court ordered the tobacco trust dissolved. During the reorganization that followed, Duke stepped down, appointing Percival Hill president and George Hill vice president responsible for cigarette merchandising. The American Tobacco name remained that of the parent firm.

As vice president, Hill inherited an inefficient decentralized sales network organized by brand. Determined to streamline the system, he retired the least popular cigarettes American Tobacco manufactured. He then promoted his most successful brand managers to district sales managers to supervise the merchandising of every brand in a given region. This centralized management proved more effective for selling cigarettes on a national scale.

To maintain quality and reduce spoilage, Hill also instituted new cigarette packaging and inventory controls. To keep cigarettes fresher longer, he used vacuum tins and then glassine paper carton wrappers. Over time Hill also instituted product dating and the practice of traveling in automobiles to systematically inspect dealers to encourage the sale of older merchandise before newer stock.

In 1913, however, R. J. Reynolds revolutionized the tobacco business when he introduced the first modern cigarette—a blended smoke known as "Camel"—with a nationwide advertising campaign. At the time the cigarette market remained fragmented with different machine-made brands popular locally. By concentrating his marketing effort on the new cigarette, however, Reynolds made Camel a national brand by 1914.

By 1916 Hill recognized the ramifications of Camel. Over Duke's objections, he convinced his father that American Tobacco must follow Reynold's lead by introducing and concentrating on a blended cigarette. For the new product they chose the name "Lucky Strike," formerly a brand of pipe tobacco.

Almost from the start, Hill's involvement with "Luckies" became a passion, an obsession likened by a contemporary to a "missionary's devotion to Jesus" (quoted in Fortune, p. 154). As was his style of management, Hill played a direct role in promoting Lucky Strike. With commercial artists, he redesigned the Lucky Strike package. Then, in search of some attribute on which to build an advertising campaign, he haunted the factory, later sharing his impressions with his father, who devised the slogan "It's Toasted," a reference to the aroma of drying tobacco. By 1917 Lucky Strike sales constituted more than 10 percent of the domestic cigarette market.

But Camel sales continued to surpass those of Lucky Strike. Indeed, by the middle of 1918 Luckies had even lost ground. Part of the problem was that during World War I federal policies encouraged cigarette smoking in general but stymied Hill's efforts. Before the war, many Americans considered smoking immoral, unmanly, and un-American. The military cigarette ration not only prompted the troops to smoke but also eliminated the moral stigma attached to smoking and the social prejudices smokers faced. But government officials shipped cigarettes to the doughboys in quantities based on prewar sales, figures that strongly favored Camels. To make matters worse, George Hill had gone off to war—first with the Red Cross in France and later with the Motor Transport Corps in Washington—robbing American Tobacco of his sales expertise.

As a result, in 1923 Percival Hill approached Albert D. Lasker of the Lord & Thomas advertising agency to request his help in marketing Lucky Strike, and for a substantial fee, Lasker accepted the offer. Lasker ranked as one of the most powerful and respected individuals in the field of mass marketing. Earlier, he had helped to pioneer the simple but revolutionary advertising concept of "salesmanship in print." Advertising, Lasker insisted, must sell merchandise, not merely announce its availability.

George Hill and Lasker worked together closely. Even after ascending to the presidency following Percival's death in 1925, George continued to play a major part in Luckies merchandising by maintaining final say over every phase. Clearly, Hill appreciated the power of advertising to sell cigarettes. The substantial funds he lavished on advertising—$20 million in 1931, the largest outlay of any firm—support this contention. Hill was also an early, if hesitant, national radio advertiser.

Contemporaries acknowledged Hill's keen understanding of the wants and needs of average Americans. Indeed, he employed advertising tactics geared to the common man, relying on repeated slogans and inflated claims. Beginning in 1926, Hill and Lasker employed testimonials to sell Luckies to women, drawing a direct link between women and smoking in their advertisements, a connection deemed unseemly at the time.

Hill possessed a fertile advertising imagination, one he applied frequently to Luckies merchandising. In 1928, in one particularly controversial campaign attributed to Hill, the cigarette maker admonished consumers to "Reach for a Lucky Instead of a Sweet." The campaign infuriated confectioners but raised Lucky Strike sales substantially. When wartime shortages forced Hill to change the color of Luckies packaging, he helped devise the memorable slogan: "Lucky Strike Green Has Gone to War." At one time or another, the Federal Trade Commission, Better Business Bureau, and American Medical Association all contested the validity of Hill's bombastic claims. But in 1930 Lucky Strike finally surpassed Camel sales.

In 1904 Hill had married Lucie Langhorn Cobb; they had three children. George W. Hill, Jr., eventually succeeded his father as vice president in charge of sales for the American Tobacco Company. In 1920 the Hills divorced. Two years later he married Aquinas M. Heller, with whom he had two children; she died in 1925. In 1935 Hill wed Mary Barnes, his secretary.

Even away from the office, Hill surrounded himself with reminders of the tobacco business to the point of eccentricity. Tobacco plants and a bronze statue of the Durham Bull graced the garden of his home in Irvington, New York. Even the names of his dachshunds, "Mr. Lucky" and "Mrs. Strike," testified to the nature of his passion. He had few outside interests, except dancing and fishing. Hill died while vacationing at his private fishing camp outside Matapedia, Quebec. He is buried in North Tarrytown, New York.

Evaluations of Hill's management style and historical significance have varied over time. During the thirties and forties contemporaries portrayed him as an enigmatic marketing genius responsible almost single-handedly for the achievements of the American Tobacco Company. As early as the mid-1940s, however, his reputation began to deteriorate. In 1946 Frederic Wakeman published *The Hucksters*, a less than flattering fictional portrayal of Hill. More recent writers claim that while he allowed Hill to take the credit, Lasker actually was responsible for the success of Lucky Strike advertising. Hill remains, nonetheless, an important figure in American social and business history. He stimulated tobacco use throughout the United States and thus contributed to the social, medical, and economic ramifications that smoking entailed. The success of Lucky Strike stemmed less from some secret tobacco blend than from effective merchandising. The tactics Hill employed were not entirely new, but his aggressive marketing methods encouraged other businesspeople to advertise.

• A full-length biography of Hill has yet to be published. Hill relates his advertising theories, however, in *Selling Principles of Demonstration*, a manual he published privately in 1917. He also discusses his management style and advertising techniques in H. L. Stephen, "How Hill Advertises Is at Last Revealed," *Printers' Ink*, 17 Nov. 1938, pp. 11–14, 89–103; and Edward H. Pearson, "Gone—One of Advertising's Great Teachers," *Printers' Ink*, 4 Oct. 1946, p. 156. Other helpful sources are George H. Allen, "He Makes Americans Sit Up and Buy—George Washington Hill," *Forbes*, 1 Jan. 1933, pp. 12–14; "The American Tobacco Company, Which Is More Than Two-Thirds Lucky Strike: A Story of Advertising, Which Is Nine-Tenths George Washington Hill," *Fortune*, Dec. 1936, pp. 96–102, 154, 156, 158, 160; and William L. Day, "George Washington Hill as I Knew Him," *Advertising and Selling*, Oct. 1946, pp. 43, 94. "*Sold American!*": *The First Fifty Years* (1954), the official company history, describes Hill's efforts on behalf of American Tobacco. On Hill's place in the history of American advertising, see Roland Marchand, *Advertising the American Dream: Making Way for Modernity, 1920–1940* (1985). In *They Satisfy: The Cigarette in American Life* (1978), Robert Sobel evaluates

George Hill's contribution to the cigarette industry as well as the nature of Hill's relationship with Albert D. Lasker; John Gunther, *Taken at the Flood: The Story of Albert D. Lasker* (1960), is another source. As to the widely held theory that in *The Hucksters* (1946) Richard Wakeman based the villainous soap executive Evan Llewelyn Evans on Hill, see, for example, "Love That Account," *Time*, 9 Sept. 1946, pp. 86, 88. Useful obituaries are in the *New York Times*, 14 Sept. 1946; *Printers' Ink*, 20 Sept. 1946; and *Newsweek*, 23 Sept. 1946.

LAWRENCE F. GREENFIELD

HILL, George William (3 Mar. 1838–16 Apr. 1914), mathematical astronomer, was born in New York City, the son of John William Hill, an artist and engraver, and Catherine Smith. In 1846 his family moved to a farm near West Nyack, New York, and he received his secondary schooling there. Although his preparatory education was rudimentary, Hill showed a marked aptitude for mathematics and entered Rutgers College in 1855.

While at Rutgers, Hill studied under Thomas Strong, an exceptionally able teacher and a friend of Nathaniel Bowditch, the noted commentator and translator of Pierre S. Laplace's great work on celestial mechanics. An ardent enthusiast for classical mathematics, Strong gave Hill access to his personal library and guided his independent studies of the French masters. Under Strong's guidance, and while still an undergraduate, Hill read and mastered the following books: *Traité du calcul différentiel et intégral* of Sylvestre F. Lacroix, *Mécanique analytique* of Joseph L. Lagrange, *Mécanique céleste* of Pierre S. Laplace, *Fonctions elliptiques* of Adrien M. Legendre, *Théorie analytique du système du monde* of Phillippe G.D. de Pontécoulant, and the *Traité mécanique* of Siméon D. Poisson. Such a reading program, which was highly unusual, gives graphic testimony of Hill's remarkable ability and youthful precocity.

Hill received his A.B. in 1859 and his A.M. in 1862. In the meantime he had begun doing research, and in 1861 he won the first prize in a competition, held by *Runkle's Mathematical Monthly*, for his essay "On the Confrontation of the Earth," in which Hill attempted to extend Laplace's work on the constitution and figure of the Earth. The paper attracted such widespread attention that at the time of Hill's death it was still deemed worthy of study. Hill then took a job as an assistant in the Office of the American Ephemeris and Nautical Almanac in Cambridge, Massachusetts, and after a few years he was permitted to do his calculations for them in his home in West Nyack. Upon the move of the office to Washington, D.C., Hill resided there from 1882 to 1892. This offered him the opportunity of association with Simon Newcomb, the leading astronomer of his day as well as the superintendent of the office.

Hill conducted his initial research at the Almanac Office, where by virtue of his unselfish help to others, he was regarded as the "spirit" of the office. His first major effort was concerned with the calculation of tables for the transit of Venus, but he also mastered the two-volume treatise, *Théorie du mouvement de la lune* (1860, 1867), of Charles Delaunay. Delaunay's methods would profoundly influence Hill's subsequent work on the three-body problem, concerned with the motion of three bodies in space that attract each other according to the Newtonian law of gravitation. It was first considered by Isaac Newton in his *Principia* (1687), but the first particular solutions were those discovered by Lagrange in 1772. The problem greatly exercised the imagination and ingenuity of eighteenth- and nineteenth-century mathematical astronomers, greatly influenced the development of mathematics, and remained an open challenge during the twentieth century. Hill's work represented the first significant advance in over 100 years and was incorporated in two articles: "On the Part of the Motion of the Lunar Perigee Which Is a Function of the Mean Motion of the Sun and Moon" and his "Researches in Lunar Theory." The former, which he regarded as his greatest work, was privately published at his own expense in 1877 (it was later reprinted in *Acta Mathematica* in 1886), while the latter appeared in the first volume of the *American Journal of Mathematics* (1878).

The two offered a bold new approach to the problem. Previous investigators first solved a two-body problem and then attempted to solve the three-body problem by varying their solution. Hill instead solved a "restricted three-body problem" and then proceeded to the general problem by varying his solution. The restricted three-body problem involves two bodies, moving in a circle around their center of mass, which attract each other. They are not affected by the third body, which moves in the plane of the two revolving bodies and whose mass is assumed to be negligible. The problem is then to determine the motion of the third body; for astronomical purposes the situation occurs when one takes the bodies to be the Sun, the Earth, and the Moon. Hill's solution replaced the usual Keplerian ellipse of the Moon's orbit by an intermediate (the so-called variational) orbit. In doing so he was led to consider periodic orbits and a second order homogeneous differential equation with periodic coefficients (now called Hill's differential equation), whose solution involved infinite determinants. Hill also introduced as a byproduct the useful notions of curves and surfaces of zero relative velocity. These notions completely revised scientific thinking regarding the three-body problem, and remained of contemporary interest throughout the twentieth century.

Following the appearance of these publications, Hill was thrust into the study of the theory of Jupiter and Saturn by his supervisor Newcomb, and hence he was unable to complete his work on lunar theory. Hill worked on the theory of Jupiter and Saturn for eight years, and he believed that his calculations were among the most extensive ever done by one man alone. His tables for Jupiter and Saturn were published in 1890. In addition Hill published numerous smaller papers concerning other problems in celestial mechanics. However, ill health significantly curtailed his activities after 1908.

Upon Hill's retirement he returned to the family farm in West Nyack. A special lectureship in celestial mechanics, which carried no specified duties, was endowed for him at Columbia University by Catherine Wolfe Bruce, and Hill officially held the position from 1898 to 1901. However, few students were capable of taking his courses, and it is believed that he actually taught only during the academic year 1898–1899. It is an indication of his character and simple life style that, although the position was created for five years, he was unwilling to accept the stipend after 1900; and he donated his 1900–1901 salary of $1,000 to the Department of Astronomy at Columbia.

Nothwithstanding his rather modest positions of employment, Hill's research had brought him such international recognition that in 1903 when *American Men of Science* conducted a poll of the leaders in American science, Hill was rated second out of eighty in mathematics and tied with Newcomb as first out of fifty in astronomy. Newcomb called Hill "the greatest master of mathematical astronomy during the last quarter of the nineteenth century," and next to Newcomb himself he was one of the most internationally honored American astronomers of his age. Upon personally meeting him in 1904, the French savant Henri Poincaré, whose own work owed much of its inspiration to Hill's research, hailed him as "the one man I came to America to see." Later Poincaré lauded him as "one of the most original workers in the American scientific community." Referring to Hill's great memoir of 1878, Ernest William Brown said that "in it we may perceive the germ of all the progress which has been made in celestial mechanics since its publication." Subsequently Brown would perfect Hill's ideas on lunar theory into a form that remained the basis of the modern theory throughout the twentieth century. A model of clarity and conciseness, Hill's exposition truly broke new ground in celestial mechanics. Hill applied his talents freely in the fullest measure to the progress of science and his fellow man asking only the opportunity to pursue his work unhindered.

During his lifetime Hill was elected a member of the National Academy of Science (1874); a foreign associate of the Royal Astronomical Society (1878); a foreign member of the Royal Society (1902); a corresponding member in astronomy of the French Academy of Science (1903); a corresponding member of the Bavarian Academy of Sciences (1908); an associate member of the Royal Belgian Academy (1909); and a foreign member of the Society of Sciences in Christiannia (1910), the Swedish Academy (1913), and the Accademia dei Lincei in Rome (1913). In addition, he received the Gold Medal of the Royal Astronomical Society (1887); the Damoiseau Prize of the French Academy of Sciences (1898); the Schubert Prize of the Imperial Academy of Sciences in St. Petersburg, Russia (1905); the Bruce Gold Medal of the Astronomical Society of the Pacific (1908); and the Copley Medal, the Royal Society's highest honor (1909). He was also president of the American Mathematical Society in 1895–1896.

Hill never married and spent most of his life on the family farm at West Nyack. His income was small, but so were his needs, and several of his brothers lived nearby. Although a virtual recluse, he was happiest there among his large library, where he was free to pursue his research. He died in his home in West Nyack. The mathematical sciences building at Rutgers was named the Hill Center in his honor.

• A four-volume work, *The Collected Mathematical Work of George William Hill* (1905–1907), contains all but six of his papers, together with a glowing introduction by Poincaré. Apparently at Hill's suggestion, the volumes do not contain the transcript that he prepared for his lectures on celestial mechanics at Columbia. This transcript is in the archives at Columbia University. Personal recollections of Hill are included in Simon Newcomb, *Reminiscences of an Astronomer* (1903), pp. 218–23. Hill wrote very little of an expository character; however, his presidential address for the American Mathematical Society, "Remarks on the Progress of Celestial Mechanics Since the Middle of the Century," *Bulletin of the American Mathematical Society* 2 (Feb. 1896), is noteworthy. An excellent survey of his early work is contained in "Address Delivered by the President J. W. L. Glaisher, on Presenting the Gold Medal of the Society to Mr. G. W. Hill," *Monthly Notices of the Royal Astronomical Society* 47 (Feb. 1887). Hill's contributions to celestial mechanics are treated in every advanced book on the subject, but two modern accounts are especially detailed: Victor Szebehely, *Theory of Orbits—The Restricted Problem of Three Bodies* (1967), and Christian Marchal, *The Three-Body Problem* (1990). Obituaries are in the National Academy of Sciences, *Biographical Memoirs* 8 (1916): 275–309, and the *American Mathematical Society Semicentennial Publications* 1 (1938), both of which contain portraits and a complete list of publications. There is also a detailed notice in the *Bulletin of the American Mathematical Society* 21 (July 1915), which is a reprint of the entry in the *Obituary Notices of Fellows of the Royal Society* 91A (1915). The obituary in the *New York Times*, 18 Apr. 1914, is a subdued piece, illustrating Hill's relative obscurity among the American public at large.

JOSEPH D. ZUND

HILL, Grace Livingston (16 Apr. 1865–23 Feb. 1947), novelist, was born in Wellsville, New York, the daughter of Charles Montgomery Livingston, a Presbyterian minister, and Marcia MacDonald, a short story writer. Her family background and childhood led naturally to the career she pursued. Her father, who came from a wealthy, established New York family, accepted the relative poverty of the ministry and moved frequently from one parish to another rather than compromise his principles. Her mother's sister, Isabella MacDonald Alden, was also a writer. Her aunt, writing under the pseudonym "Pansy," produced highly successful religious fiction.

Encouraged by her mother and her aunt, Hill began writing as a child but initially concentrated on art, first at the Cincinnati Art School and then at Elmira College in New York State. In 1887 she published *A Chautauqua Idyl*, which appeared with an introductory letter from Edward Everett Hale, chaplain of the U.S. Senate and author of the famous *The Man without a Country*. Although she continued to write and pub-

lish, writing did not become her main concern until she was faced with financial pressure. In 1892 she married Thomas Guthrie Franklin Hill, a Presbyterian minister with whom she had two daughters. Her husband died in 1899, making it necessary for her to earn a living. Her first major success, *Marcia Schuyler* (1908), brought her a popularity that she never lost.

Hill thought of her work as light fiction, but her books are so saturated with Christian doctrine that her publisher, J. B. Lippincott, broke with her when she refused to be more moderate, only to publish her again after her most popular novel, *The Witness* (1917), appeared. Her heroes and heroines are wholesome, intelligent, and physically attractive, and although they may be spoiled or temporarily misguided, they emerge as staunch examples of Christian principles in a secular world—a world that Hill knows well and describes realistically. Her success lay in simple characterization, clear narrative, and a very skillful maintaining of suspense, especially suspense over the fate of deserving lovers not yet united.

For example, the heroine of *The Man of the Desert* (1914) is lost and is rescued by a missionary to the Indians with whom she falls in love, only to overhear his prayers and learn that although he loves her, he considers her unfit and unworthy for the life he leads. Through rigorous self-discipline she becomes worthy and through unblushing use of coincidence on the author's part finds him again and becomes his wife. The hero of *The Witness*, Paul Courtland, participates in the brutal hazing of Stephen Marshall, whom his fellow college students have found too pious. Marshall, who has been forced to attend a risqué play, loses his life in a theater fire while saving Courtland's. The temporarily blinded Courtland has a vision he knows to be Stephen Marshall's Christ, and this Presence, now always with him, protects him while he is innocently attracted to a depraved girl, leads him to the girl he should love, and guides him to a career as an independent Christian minister. Passages like the following from *The Man of the Desert* are common:

And then at night he told them of the God who set the stars above them; who made the earth and them, and loved them; and of Jesus, His only Son, who came to die for them and who would not only be their Saviour, but their loving companion by day and by night; unseen, but always at hand, caring for each one of His children individually, knowing their joys and their sorrows. . . . He saw the humanity in them looking wistfully through their great eyes, and gave himself to teach them. (p. 134)

Hill produced novels like these until her death, often writing as many as three a year. Her personal life was troubled for a time by a marriage in 1904 to Flavius Lutz, from whom she separated but would not divorce for religious reasons. She settled into a pattern of writing, public speaking, and church work and found herself at odds with the postwar mood, her work appealing in the 1920s to those who shared her religious views. Through the years the subjects, mood, and tone of her work remained substantially the same. She avoided seeing movies and reading the works of such modernist writers as Hemingway and Fitzgerald. Settled in her home in Swarthmore, Pennsylvania, she dedicated herself to establishing the abandoned Old Leipert Church as a functioning Presbyterian mission. She died in Swarthmore.

It is doubtful that Hill's novels will ever be taken seriously by scholars and critics, but she survives as a popular novelist in part because, in the words of her adulatory biographer, "Mrs. Hill's novels present the kind of idealism that is a real need in the world today. . . . They set forth situations in which there is a distinct line between good and bad, right and wrong. They depict characters who meet these situations with exemplary courage and dignity" (Karr, p. 6). Hill published more than 100 novels, many of which are still in print.

• The Henry E. Huntington Library, San Marino, Calif., has two letters by Hill, the University of Illinois one, New York University one, and the University of Texas one. The Pennsylvania Historical Museum Commission of Harrisburg has one manuscript. A brief account of Hill's life appears in Jean Karr's *Grace Livingston Hill: Her Story and Her Writings* (1948).

MARYJEAN GROSS
DALTON GROSS

HILL, Henry Aaron (30 May 1915–17 Mar. 1979), chemist and businessman, was born in St. Joseph, Missouri, the son of William Anthony Hill II, the head waiter at a local hotel, and Kate Anna Evans. Hill attended public elementary and secondary schools in St. Joseph and graduated from Bartlett High School in 1931. After completing his first year of college at Lewis Institute in Chicago (later a part of the Illinois Institute of Technology), he attended Johnson C. Smith University, an all-black institution in Charlotte, North Carolina. He graduated in 1936 with a B.S. cum laude in mathematics and chemistry.

Hill spent the 1937–1938 academic year as a special student at the Massachusetts Institute of Technology. The following year he studied at the University of Chicago, where he was one of two African-American graduate students in the chemistry department. While the other black student, Warren Henry, went on to earn a Ph.D. at Chicago (1941), Hill returned in 1939 to MIT to complete his doctoral work. The reason for this move is uncertain; it has been suggested that both Hill and Henry were in need of "work-study" assistance to carry them through the program and that the Chicago chemistry department was unwilling to support more than one African-American student in this way.

Hill received a Ph.D. in chemistry from MIT in 1942. His work was supported by fellowships from the Julius Rosenwald Fund, a private foundation with a special interest in educational and other needs of African Americans. One of his mentors at MIT was the chemist James Flack Norris, whom Hill admired for his refusal to make an issue of race. According to Hill,

Norris was "the first big man whom I met who was more interested in my ability to learn chemistry than in the identity of my grandparents."

Race proved to be a barrier, however, in the search for employment. Hill's job applications were declined by forty-five companies before North Atlantic Research Corporation in Newtonville, Massachusetts, hired him onto their staff in 1942 as a research chemist in charge of organic research. This job offer coincided with offers from several other firms, all of which occurred after the United States entered World War II. "The impenetrable barrier of race prejudice," Hill wrote to the Rosenwald Fund in 1942, "has been lowered under the pressure of the war effort, and some employers are accepting Negroes in the industries as laborers and even in the so-called professional positions." At North Atlantic, he helped develop water-based paints, protein fibers, rubber adhesives, surface coatings, fire-fighting foams, and several types of synthetic rubber. He became director of research in 1943 and company vice president in 1944 and held both positions until his departure in 1946 to join Dewey & Almy Chemical Company in Cambridge, Massachusetts, as a group leader in polymer research. During the war he worked for a brief period as a civilian chemist attached to the Office of Scientific Research and Development. He married historian Adelaide McGuinn Cromwell (later Gulliver) in 1943; they had one child.

In 1952 Hill cofounded National Polychemicals, Inc., a manufacturer of chemical intermediates used in elastomer and polymer production. He served as the company's assistant manager from 1952 to 1956 and vice president from 1956 to 1961, and was in charge of the company's technical operations in chemistry, engineering, research, and production. He resigned in 1961 to establish his own company, Riverside Research Laboratory, Inc., in Watertown, Massachusetts (later moved to Haverhill, Mass.), and was its president until his death. This enterprise provided research, development, and consulting services in the field of organic chemistry, particularly resins, rubbers, textiles, and plastics. Hill was the author of a number of related patents, including "manufacture of azodicarbonide" (1961), "barium azocarbonate as a blowing agent for high melting plastomers" (1963), and "urea-formaldehyde condensates" (1967).

A noted authority on polymer chemistry and fabric flammability, Hill was appointed in 1968 by President Lyndon B. Johnson to the National Commission on Product Safety, on which Hill served for two years. Thereafter, the focus of his work was on product liability and product safety. He devised and conducted tests for compliance with federal, state, and local safety standards. He was a consultant on product safety to various firms and testified in court as an expert witness in product liability cases—usually on behalf of plaintiffs injured by substandard products. Hill also served in 1969 as a member of the advisory council to the Subcommittee on Consumer Affairs of the U.S. Senate Committee on Commerce. He was a member of the

National Motor Vehicle Safety Advisory Council (1970–1973, 1977) and chairman of its compliance committee, as well as a member of an evaluation panel of the National Bureau of Standards (1972–1976). In this latter stage of his career, he played an integral role in the modern consumer-rights movement.

Hill was active in the American Chemical Society. First elected to office in 1958, as chairman of the membership committee of ACS's Northeastern Section, he went on to play a prominent role in regional ACS affairs and served on the national council (beginning in 1964) and board of directors (1971–1978). In line with his evolving interest in community and consumer affairs, he became involved in labor, educational, and other issues of special concern to chemists and chemical engineers. He served, for example, as chairman of ACS's Committee on Professional Relations in 1968 and established an Economic Status Subcommittee and a Division of Professional Relations within ACS. Through these programs, he helped formulate guidelines that became a widely accepted protocol of employment and termination conditions for chemists and chemical engineers; in addition, he investigated periodic mass layoffs in the chemical industry and assisted in the resolution of employment problems faced by individual ACS members. Elected president of ACS in 1976, Hill was the first African American to hold this post.

Hill became a fellow of the American Association for the Advancement of Science in 1964. Other professional affiliations included memberships in the American Association of Textile Chemists and Colorists, New York Academy of Sciences, and American Institute of Chemists. He died in Haverhill, Massachusetts.

• A file on Hill's work as a graduate student, along with related career information, is in the Julius Rosenwald Fund Archives, Special Collections Department, Fisk University, Nashville, Tenn. Hill's doctoral thesis, "A Test of Van't Hoff's Principle of Optical Superposition," in the Institute Archives at MIT, contains a biographical note (p. 56) that provides information on Hill's early schooling. For a brief assessment of Hill's life and work, see Samuel P. Massie, "Henry A. Hill: The Second Mile," *Chemistry* 44 (Jan. 1971): 11. Regarding the reason for Hill's transfer from the University of Chicago to MIT, see Kenneth R. Manning, "Henry C. McBay: Reflections of a Chemist," in *Henry C. McBay: A Chemical Festschrift: Proceedings of a Symposium in Honor of the First Martin Luther King, Jr., Scholar at the Massachusetts Institute of Technology*, ed. William M. Jackson and Billy Joe Evans (1994), p. 20. An obituary is in *Chemical and Engineering News* 57 (26 Mar. 1979): 6–7.

KENNETH R. MANNING

HILL, Isaac (6 Apr. 1788–22 Mar. 1851), editor and politician, was born in Cambridge, Massachusetts, the son of Isaac Hill and Hannah Russell, farmers. Hill had a difficult childhood because his family was poor, his father became insane, and he himself was left permanently lame by an early accident. In 1798 his mother moved the family to Ashburnham on the New

Hampshire border, where Hill received a few months of formal schooling before being apprenticed in 1802 to the publisher of the *Farmer's Cabinet* in Amherst, New Hampshire. By 1809 he had saved enough money to become the owner and editor of the *American Patriot*, a struggling newspaper in Concord, New Hampshire, which he renamed the *New-Hampshire Patriot*.

The growing influence of Hill's newspaper and his marriage to Susanna Ayer, the daughter of a well-to-do Concord family, in 1814 made him a prominent civic figure. (Hill and his wife were to have four children.) A committed Republican, he used the *Patriot* to defend the administration of James Madison (1751–1836) and to arouse the upland farmers of New Hampshire against the Federalists, who controlled the state. His rhetoric helped the Republicans win the election of 1810, but three years later they lost control of the government because of the unpopularity of the War of 1812. When the Republicans finally regained power in 1816, Hill intensified his assault on the Federalists and their Congregationalist supporters. The Republicans quickly passed a bill changing Dartmouth College, a Federalist-Congregationalist stronghold, into a state university, only to have Chief Justice John Marshall in 1819 declare the act unconstitutional. Hill also backed the Toleration Act of 1819, which weakened the Congregational church by giving all Christian denominations in a town the right to be supported by taxes. Passage of the act roughly coincided with the demise of the Federalist party in New Hampshire.

Between 1820 and 1823, while Hill was serving in the state senate, the reigning Republican party split into factions, and a new party system began to evolve. Hill's faction suffered a setback in the presidential election of 1824 when its candidate, William Harris Crawford, lost both New Hampshire and the presidency to John Quincy Adams (1767–1848). Seeking a new candidate, Hill turned to Andrew Jackson, whom he had praised as a "dauntless warrior" after the battle of New Orleans. Hill's views were similar to those of Jackson; both men, for example, blamed the panic of 1819 on banking excesses. By 1827 Hill had formed a Jackson party in New Hampshire that returned him to the state senate and elected Benjamin Pierce, who came from the uplands, as governor. In the new party system the Jackson party was strongest in Hill's backwater, non-Congregational towns in the interior uplands, while the Adams party prevailed in the up-and-coming Congregational towns near the seacoast and in the Connecticut Valley. Hill's organization, a forerunner of modern political parties, made good use of nominating conventions, a party press, party patronage, and the policy of rotation in office.

Hill, a master of invective, was unbridled in his efforts to carry New Hampshire for Jackson in 1828. He published lurid stories, including the ridiculous charge that Adams had once "procured" a woman for the czar of Russia. Adams managed to carry the state, but Jackson won the presidency. The Jacksonians, soon known as Democrats, did not lose another election in New Hampshire until 1846. Hill failed to win a seat in the U.S. Senate in 1828, but in March 1829 Jackson appointed him second comptroller of the Treasury. After the appointment was rejected in April 1830, the president helped Hill win election to the U.S. Senate in June. When he first appeared in that body in December 1831, dressed in "the humble garb of a printer" (Bradley, p. 109), Hill made a great stir.

A member of Jackson's Kitchen Cabinet, Hill played an important role in the party. In 1829 he helped start the war against the Bank of the United States by attacking the lending policies of the bank's branch in Portsmouth. In June 1831 he arranged to have the New Hampshire legislature call for the first national Democratic nominating convention. Although an indifferent public speaker, he gave an important Senate speech on 8 June 1832 against the recharter of the Bank of the United States and another on 3–4 March 1834 in favor of removing the federal deposits from the bank. When the abolitionist movement threatened to divide the northern and southern wings of the Democratic party in 1835, Hill sought to soothe the South in September by presiding over an antiabolitionist meeting in Concord.

On 30 May 1836 Hill gave up his Senate seat to become governor of New Hampshire. Unlike his predecessors, who had sent brief messages on state affairs to the legislature, Hill sent a thirty-page message on national issues, which was read to the legislature on 3 June. Elaborating his Jacksonian ideals, he called for states' rights and strict construction of the Constitution and opposed abolitionism, the Bank of the United States, and federal internal improvements. He was perfectly willing, however, to have the state spend money on railroads, including one in which he had heavily invested. During his three years as governor he sided with conservative Democrats, who wanted the state to support railroads, as against radical Democrats, who opposed the railroads. The conservatives won, but Hill's obvious conflict of interest so weakened his support that in 1838 he barely won a third term.

By the time Hill left office in 1839, he had lost control of the state Democratic party, which had shifted toward the radicals. Unable to win election to the U.S. Senate, he served as receiver general of the Boston subtreasury from 1840 to 1841. He also started a new newspaper in Concord, *Hill's New Hampshire Patriot*, to oppose the *New-Hampshire Patriot*, which he had sold. No longer a mainstream Democrat, he supported the administration of John Tyler (1790–1862) and wrote occasionally for Tyler's newspaper, the Washington *Daily Madisonian*. He died in Washington.

Hill was a skilled journalist, a wily politician, and a prosperous businessman, with investments in a wide range of activities. He is best remembered, however, as one of the nation's leading political organizers, rivaled at the time only by Martin Van Buren and perhaps a few others.

• There are small collections of Hill papers at the New Hampshire Historical Society, the Library of Congress, the Houghton Library of Harvard University, and the New York Public Library. The most extended modern treatment of Hill is in Donald B. Cole, *Jacksonian Democracy in New Hampshire, 1800–1851* (1970). For a campaign biography see Cyrus P. Bradley, *Biography of Isaac Hill* (1835). See also Lynn W. Turner, *The Ninth State: New Hampshire's Formative Years* (1983), and Francis E. Robinson, "Isaac Hill" (Ph.D. diss., Univ. of New Hampshire, 1933). Other sources include Nathaniel Bouton, *The History of Concord* (1856); E. S. Stearns et al., *Genealogical and Family History of the State of New Hampshire*, vol. 4 (1908); and Thomas W. Baldwin, comp., *Vital Records of Cambridge, Mass. to the Year 1850*, vol. 1 (1914). Obituaries are in the *New Hampshire Patriot and State Gazette*, 27 Mar. 1851, and the Amherst, N.H., *Farmer's Cabinet*, 3 Apr. 1851.

DONALD B. COLE

HILL, James Jerome (16 Sept. 1838–29 May 1916), railroad developer, was born near Rockwood, Ontario, Canada, the son of James Hill and Anne Dunbar, farmers. Early plans to become a physician were disrupted by a childhood accident, which destroyed the sight in one eye, and by the death of his father when Hill was fourteen. After moving to St. Paul, Minnesota, in 1856, Hill held a variety of wholesale and retail jobs in the dry goods and grocery trades. From this experience, he developed an appreciation for the importance of efficient transportation in the Northwest. In 1865 he became an agent for both the Northwestern Packet Company and the Milwaukee and Mississippi Railroad, thanks to the influence of a friend and business associate, William E. Wellington. The next year he established the James J. Hill Company (which became Hill, Griggs & Company in 1869), specializing in the transfer and warehousing of freight. In 1870 he began steamboat operations on the Red River and, in partnership with Norman Kittson, he established the Red River Transportation Company in 1872.

Hill also invested in the fur, land, timber, and coal trades, activities that deepened his commitment to transportation development. In 1867 he arranged to supply the St. Paul and Pacific Railroad with coal, rather than the more traditional wood, for use as locomotive fuel. This contract eventually led to the creation of the Northwestern Fuel Company in 1875.

Hill married Mary Theresa Mehegan in 1867. Like her husband, she was of Irish descent. Nine of their ten children survived into adulthood.

Hill's business dealings brought the St. Paul and Pacific Railroad to his attention and launched his career as one of America's preeminent railroad builders. This line showed tremendous potential, even though poor construction quality and financial mismanagement drove it into bankruptcy in 1873. In 1878 Hill, Kittson, and several of their business associates gained control of the railroad from its Dutch bondholders. Rehabilitation and expansion followed, and the reborn company soon completed a link between St. Paul and Winnipeg, Manitoba, Canada. In 1879 Hill became general manager of the line, newly reorganized as the St. Paul, Minneapolis, and Manitoba Railway. During the next decade the company built extensive main and branch lines to develop farmland in Minnesota, North Dakota, and eastern Montana. Hill assumed the presidency of the railroad in 1882, a position he held until 1907. In 1890 his Great Northern Railway (created a year earlier) leased the St. Paul, Minneapolis, and Manitoba.

During the early 1880s Hill became involved in the construction of the Canadian Pacific Railroad. He believed that the Canadian Pacific should concentrate its resources on the development of the Canadian prairies, rather than on the construction of its own line through the difficult terrain north of Lake Superior. Hill's suggestion that all traffic from the Canadian prairies be funneled through the United States on its way to eastern Canada would naturally have benefited his own railroad, but it did not mesh with Canadian dreams for a transcontinental railroad entirely within their own country. As a result, Hill resigned from the board of directors of the Canadian Pacific in 1883.

Throughout his career in the railroad industry, Hill maintained a reputation for caution and integrity in his business dealings. Unlike the rival Northern Pacific, built hastily as a speculative venture by Wall Street financier Henry Villard, Hill intended the Great Northern to increase its profitability as the territory through which it traveled slowly matured. He authorized construction to the Pacific only after he had established a rail network in the central Plains. The Great Northern completed this 900-mile extension to Seattle, Washington, on 6 January 1893.

In order to increase settlement and rail traffic, Hill and the railroad financed crop and livestock breeding programs and dispatched classroom trains to promote better farming techniques. Hill's efforts to cultivate and maintain a stable traffic base ensured that the Great Northern weathered periodic economic downturns (particularly the 1893 depression) far better than other, speculatively financed western railroads.

Hill's interest in the economic development of the northern Plains and the Pacific Northwest paid other dividends as well. Although he, like many of his contemporaries, could be ruthless in his business dealings, he stood apart from eastern financiers such as J. P. Morgan in that he expressed interest in and concern for the people of the region. His climb to personal fame and fortune paralleled the growing economic success of the American Northwest, and many people felt that the first occurrence had caused the second. One story, perhaps apocryphal, describes his conduct as Great Northern construction crews pushed the railroad westward through a brutal Great Plains winter. Observing exhausted shovelers clearing the line of snow, Hill left his railroad car and, cloaked by darkness and heavy clothing, went anonymously to work alongside his men. Accounts such as these ensured that many in the Northwest viewed him as a benevolent developer of the region, rather than a distant and rapacious Wall Street manipulator.

Increasing grain production encouraged the further expansion of the Great Northern and the creation of subsidiary shipping operations on the Great Lakes and the Pacific Ocean. In 1900 Hill organized the Great Northern Steamship Company in an attempt to increase westbound grain shipments (Hill once remarked that the only American export that Asians could afford to buy was food). This venture did not live up to expectations, however, and had become moribund by 1905.

Like most other contemporary railroad executives, Hill bemoaned vicious price competition, caused by overbuilding in the 1870s and 1880s. He had little use for voluntary pooling efforts, such as the Western Traffic Association. The 1887 Interstate Commerce Act, with its restrictions on rebates and short-haul discrimination, had the potential to aid railroads as much as it did their customers, particularly since most members of the Interstate Commerce Commission were former railroad executives. This potential remained unfulfilled, however, and railroads continued to suffer from excess capacity and cutthroat competition.

The parallel Northern Pacific continued to be particularly irritating, until Hill and Wall Street financier J. P. Morgan acquired control of this financially troubled rival in 1896. In 1901 Hill and Morgan purchased the strategically located Chicago, Burlington & Quincy (CB&Q), whose mainline linked Minneapolis-St. Paul with Chicago. The Great Northern and the Northern Pacific each received a half share of the CB&Q. Railroad financier Edward H. Harriman, who controlled the Illinois Central, Union Pacific, and Southern Pacific railroads, also coveted the CB&Q, however. Harriman began purchasing Northern Pacific stock in order to acquire that railroad's share of the CB&Q. Both the Hill-Morgan and Harriman parties purchased large blocks of Northern Pacific stock. The bidding war that ensued caused a panic on Wall Street in May 1901 and eventually led to the creation of the Northern Securities Company in November 1901.

As president of the Northern Securities Company, Hill controlled the Great Northern, Northern Pacific, and CB&Q, and thus effectively monopolized railroad transportation in the north central and northwestern United States. As a result, the federal government filed suit against the company in March 1902. In March 1904 the U.S. Supreme Court ruled that the combination constituted a violation of the 1890 Sherman Act and ordered the Northern Securities Company to be dissolved. In spite of the Supreme Court's decision, the Great Northern and the Northern Pacific remained closely allied under Hill's influence, an alliance that was strengthened by the construction of the jointly owned Spokane, Portland, and Seattle Railroad in 1905. In 1970 the Great Northern, Northern Pacific, and CB&Q were again combined, the result of a merger approved by the Interstate Commerce Commission.

In 1907 Louis Warren Hill replaced his father as president of the Great Northern. The elder Hill then became chairman of the board of directors, a position he held until 1912. He continued to play an active role in the management of the Great Northern and in St. Paul civic life until shortly before his death. In 1915 seventy-four of Hill's friends and business associates honored him with the creation of the Hill Professorship of Transportation at the Harvard University School of Business Administration. After his retirement, Hill continued to pursue his interests in books (he established the Hill Reference Library in St. Paul in 1912) and in the collection of art until his death at his St. Paul home.

Hill's career spanned the pivotal decades of the late nineteenth century, a time when the establishment of a comprehensive, coordinated railroad network facilitated the settlement of the Northwest and enabled the creation of a true mass market for manufactured goods. In his position as president of one of the leading companies in one of the most important segments of the American economy, he was both praised and condemned—praised by those who benefited from the economic expansion created by an efficient transportation network and condemned by those who feared the financial, and potentially monopolistic, power of his railroad empire. Still, he never acquired the reputation for vicious or unscrupulous behavior often applied to J. P. Morgan, John D. Rockefeller, Jay Gould, and other nineteenth-century capitalists. Fellow railroad executive Daniel Willard, president of the Baltimore & Ohio, believed that Hill possessed "a strong constitution . . . a wonderful memory . . . together with a keen intellect . . . able to form a clear understanding concerning whatever matters were brought to his attention." Willard went on to describe him as "more than a railroad builder—he was a philosopher and a statesman in the broadest sense." Throughout his career, he was reputed to be exacting and demanding—a domineering yet tireless and supremely confident promoter of the region to which he had tied his own future. His faith in economic development was encapsulated in his book *Highways of Progress*, published in 1910. His colleagues praised his detailed knowledge of every aspect of railroad construction and operation and his willingness to become personally involved in all matters pertaining to the Great Northern and to the region it served. His contemporaries, many of whom felt that he had done more than any other individual to encourage economic development in the Northwest, often referred to him as the "empire builder."

• The James J. Hill Reference Library in St. Paul, Minn., houses Hill's personal papers and correspondence and provides a wealth of information about his varied economic activities. Studies of Hill include Stuart Bruchey, ed., *Memoirs of Three Railroad Pioneers* (1981); Albro Martin, *James J. Hill and the Opening of the Northwest* (1976); and Joseph G. Pyle, *The Life of James J. Hill* (1917). Hill's obituary is in *Railway Age*, 2 June 1916, pp. 1164–65, 1181–84.

ALBERT J. CHURELLA

HILL, Joe (7 Oct. 1879–19 Nov. 1915), labor radical and troubadour, was born Joel Hägglund in Gävle, Sweden, the son of Olof Hägglund, a railway conductor, and Margareta Katarina (maiden name unknown). Raised in a devout Lutheran home with many siblings, he enjoyed considerable exposure to music but none to politics or labor affairs. When he was eight his father died as a result of a work accident, and the Hägglund family was left penniless. All the children had to work for wages, and young Joel found employment in a rope factory and later as a stationary fireman. Stricken with skin and joint tuberculosis in his late teens, he traveled alone to Stockholm where he received treatments for the disease, including a series of operations that left him scarred for life. Outside the hospital he worked at odd jobs. His mother died in January 1902, prompting all the surviving children to leave home. In the fall of 1902 he and a brother emigrated from Sweden to the United States.

Arriving in New York City, Hill apparently worked at odd jobs there for the better part of a year. Most of what he did during the next twelve years, prior to his arrest in Utah, remains shrouded in obscurity. By 1905 he had been in Chicago and Cleveland and had changed his name, first to Joseph Hillstrom and then to Joe Hill. The name change may have been an attempt to escape an employer blacklist, but more likely it was part of the Americanization process experienced by many immigrants. Between 1906 and 1910 Hill traveled widely, visiting Philadelphia; San Francisco, where he arrived in time for the earthquake of 1906; the Dakotas; Portland, Oregon; and even the Hawaiian Islands. Sometime in 1910 he took out a membership card in the San Pedro, California, local of the Industrial Workers of the World (IWW). Later that year he traveled north to Portland, where he agitated for the IWW and sent a letter under the name Joe Hill to the *Industrial Worker*. Over the next couple of years he traveled up and down the West Coast, perhaps even crossing the border into Baja California to participate in the Mexican Revolution. Of those experiences Hill personally recollected, "I am just one of the rank and file—just a common Pacific Coast wharfrat—that's all."

Two things, however, distinguished Hill from other common laborers. First, he behaved more radically than most, not just by working actively for the revolutionary principles of the IWW but also by condemning in print the electoral process, suggesting instead that workers "may find out that the only 'machine' worthwhile is the one which capitalists use on us when we ask for more bread. . . . the one that works with a trigger." Second, and more important, Hill used his musical talent to become the most famous troubadour of labor radicalism. During his travels and his agitating he composed several of the most frequently sung songs of labor protest, especially "The Preacher and the Slave" and "The Rebel Girl." As an IWW comrade wrote, "Wherever rebels meet, the name of Fellow Worker *Joe Hill* is known. Though we may not know him personally, who among us can say that he is not on speaking terms with 'Scissor Bill,' 'Mr. Block' . . . the famous 'Casey Jones' . . . and many others in the little red song book." Hill's songs were easy to learn and to sing, as they appropriated the tunes of familiar hymns and popular songs.

However well known were his songs, Hill himself remained relatively unheard of outside IWW circles until his arrest in January 1914 in Salt Lake City, where he was charged with the murder of a local grocer and the grocer's son during an armed robbery. Whether or not Hill committed the crime for which he was charged, convicted, and executed will never be known for certain. He never offered an alibi, and damaging circumstantial evidence strengthened the prosecution's case against him. His arrest and trial, however, transformed a "common wharfrat" into a martyr. Hill's defenders within and outside the IWW portrayed him as the victim of a conspiracy by Utah copper mine owners and their political allies to destroy trade unionism and labor radicalism in the state. Hill played the role of martyr to the hilt. The more a protest movement of international proportions urged the governor of Utah and the president of the United States to spare his life, the more the condemned man relished the attention. To Elizabeth Gurley Flynn he stressed his own insignificance, stating that his own life was not as vital as the survival of the IWW and that "as the war news puts it . . . one more or less does not count any more than it does in the European War." On the eve of his execution he wired Big Bill Haywood: "Good-bye, Bill. I will die like a true blue rebel. Don't waste any time in mourning. *Organize.*" The next morning a firing squad executed Hill.

An obscure migratory worker on his arrival in Utah in 1913, Hill departed the state as a corpse two years later; he had become an internationally proclaimed martyr to labor's cause. In the words of the famous folk song by Alfred Hayes and Earl Robinson ("I Dreamed I Saw Joe Hill Last Night"), he was now the Joe Hill who had "never died." Whatever he may have been in life, Hill was transformed by his death into a symbol of the individual sacrifice that made a revolutionary and free society possible.

• There are no Hill papers, although the official records of the IWW are housed at the Archives of Labor History and Urban Affairs, Walter P. Reuther Library, Wayne State University. The most complete and accurate biography is Gibbs M. Smith, *Joe Hill* (1969). A briefer though more tendentious and less accurate biography is Philip S. Foner, *The Case of Joe Hill* (1965). A wonderful novel, albeit one that paints a rather unflattering portrait of its protagonist, is Wallace Stegner, *The Preacher and the Slave* (1950). Stegner's book was republished in 1990 as *Joe Hill: A Biographical Novel*. The most complete history of the IWW remains Melvyn Dubofsky, *We Shall Be All: A History of the Industrial Workers of the World* (1969).

MELVYN DUBOFSKY

HILL, John (9 Sept. 1770–6 Nov. 1850), aquatint engraver, was born in London, England, of unknown parentage. He served an apprenticeship under one Martin (first name unknown), a printmaker and publisher of illustrated books on conchology, and began work over his own signature in 1798. The intaglio art of aquatint, to which Hill devoted a lifetime of activity, is an etching process in which areas in tone are bitten into a copperplate by nitric acid through a porous ground. In the London printshops, Hill encountered the creative geniuses of his craft, with whom he associated and collaborated for eighteen productive years. These men included John Claude Nattes, Augustus Charles Pugin, Thomas Rowlandson, William Henry Pyne, with whom he lodged and boarded in 1801–1802, and the great publisher Rudolph Ackermann, for whom he worked on the *Microcosm of London* (3 vols., 1808–1811) and handsome plates that bear evidence of his mastery of the engraver's art. Hill married Ann Musgrove in England about 1802; they had seven children, one of whom, John William Hill (1812–1879), was also an artist who produced a number of illustrations that were engraved by John Hill.

In 1816, sensing the end of his livelihood in England, Hill immigrated to the United States, where aquatint was still relatively undeveloped. He settled in Philadelphia, where he remained for six years. Hill's early work was modest; he spent much of the first three years working for Moses Thomas, a Chestnut Street bookseller and publisher. He engraved several small landscapes for Thomas in 1817, and some of his book illustrations culminated in 1819 in a large aquatint of the burning of the Masonic Hall in Philadelphia. That some year, Hill's wife and children joined him in the United States.

In 1819 Hill undertook his first major American commission, the engraving of *Picturesque Views of American Scenery*, an album of large, hand-colored aquatints of scenes taken by Joshua Shaw. Initially sponsored by Thomas but relinquished to another publisher, the work was a milestone in American printmaking of views essentially scenic in effect. Only twenty of the intended thirty-six aquatints were published during the two years Hill worked on the project, but they opened the eyes of Americans to the beauty of aquatint when handled by an expert; the work's appeal was such that it was republished in 1835.

Upon completion of the *Picturesque Views*, Hill was engaged in 1821 by Henry J. Megarey, a New York stationer and print publisher. Hill was hired to engrave the *Hudson River Portfolio* (original printing, 1821–1825), a projected series of large landscape aquatints from watercolors by William Guy Wall, which was promised to be the equal of anything in Europe. Hill devoted four years of work to engraving, printing, and coloring twenty plates, and he continued to pull and color additional prints until 1833. The prints are among the best-known and most sought-after examples of nineteenth-century Hudson River views, and the portfolio was praised in 1826 as an elegant, splendid, and "superb collection," and by I. N. P. Stokes in his monumental *The Iconography of Manhattan Island* (1918) as the "finest collection of New York State views ever published."

In 1822 Hill moved from Philadelphia to New York. The *Picturesque Views* and the *Portfolio* remain his best-known works but are by no means his only works worthy of merit. Even while at work on the *Portfolio*, Hill found time to engrave famous panoramas of New

York, taken from Brooklyn and Weehawken, also from originals by Wall, and a large study of the New York City Hall, which is lauded as the finest engraved view published of that building. During the late 1820s and into the 1830s, Hill engraved cityscapes, country scenes, scenic natural wonders, whaling scenes, an incomplete series of charming Erie Canal views, and a rare set of equestrian prints, which are the only sporting prints engraved in aquatint in early nineteenth-century America.

Among Hill's least-known but loveliest plates are those engraved for popular drawing manuals: *A Series of Progressive Lessons Intended to Elucidate the Art of Flower Painting in Water Colours* (1818), *The Art of Drawing Landscapes* (1819–1820), *Drawing Book of Landscape Scenery* (1821), and *Lucas' Progressive Drawing Book* (1827–1828).

Hill's last-known engraving is dated 1838. In more than twenty years of activity in the United States, he engraved a notable array of prints that have become an integral part of America's artistic and iconographic heritage and are prized items in private collections, libraries, and museums. The popularity of his work in his own day is evidenced by reissues of many of his prints and widespread public demand. Hill helped to instill in the American public an appreciation of the landscape as an art form and contributed to a public acceptance of the emerging painters of the Hudson River School of landscape art. Together with William James Bennett, another of Ackermann's engravers who emigrated from England, Hill ranks preeminent among engravers who flourished in the Golden Age of American aquatint in the 1820s and 1830s. He was a capable and dependable craftsman, and his eye for the engraved composition was such that, if need be, he could improve the engraved version of an artist's original rendition with creative touches of his own to the copperplate, such as with the Wall panoramas of New York, whereon his added details strengthened and enhanced the published views.

Hill spent his last years at Clarksville (now West Nyack), New York, where he had purchased property in 1837 and where he died.

• The art of three generations of Hill artists was carefully preserved by the family until the early twentieth century when it began to be disposed of and sold piecemeal. Hill's manuscript account book of his English years (1798–1816) is in the print department of the Metropolitan Museum of Art. His combination diary and account book written in the United States (1820–1834), is in the New-York Historical Society. The major study on Hill is Richard J. Koke, "John Hill, Master of Aquatint, 1770–1850," *New-York Historical Society Quarterly* 43 (1959): 51–117; and Koke, comp., *A Checklist of the American Engravings of John Hill (1770–1850), Master of Aquatint* (1961).

RICHARD J. KOKE

HILL, John Henry (28 Apr. 1839–18 Dec. 1922), artist, was born in Clarksville (now Nyack), New York, the son of John William Hill, a painter and etcher, and Catherine Smith. His grandfather, John Hill, was an aquatint engraver. Hill attended the one-room school in Clarksville and received lessons in painting and etching from his father. Hill's father had begun as a painter of topographical views, but after reading the first volume of John Ruskin's *Modern Painters* (1849), he abandoned conventionalized landscape painting for closely focused depictions of the natural world. John Henry Hill's first entries in the National Academy of Design exhibition of 1856 were direct studies from nature. By the following year both father and son had given up tonal washes in favor of a meticulous stipple technique in both oil and watercolor. They spent the next few summers in outdoor painting in the White Mountains of New Hampshire and on the Maine coast as well as along the Hackensack River and in the vicinity of Clarksville. During winters they were part of the New York City art community, showing their work in the monthly receptions at the Dodworth Building as well as the National Academy, where Hill was named an associate in 1859.

About this time Hill befriended young Thomas Charles Farrer, who had recently arrived in New York after studying with Ruskin in London. Farrer was full of reforming zeal and firsthand knowledge of the English pre-Raphaelites. By the beginning of 1863 he, both Hill and his father, and a few like-minded realists had formed the Society for the Advancement of Truth in Art, an organization dedicated to uncompromising truth to nature. In July 1863 Hill painted the *Study of Trap Rock* (Metropolitan Museum of Art), which he called "the most elaborately literal study from nature I ever made" (letter, 14 May 1911, MMA Archives). His large-scale landscapes of the next few years were more loosely painted, however, and he gradually abandoned the nearly imperceptible brushwork and prismatic color characteristic of his father's watercolors.

Hill spent the winter of 1864–1865 in London studying the work of J. M. W. Turner and writing letters about English painting for *The New Path*, the American pre-Raphaelite publication. Following his return to the United States he prepared a group of twenty-five etchings, which he published himself in 1866 as *Sketches from Nature*, intended as examples of close observation and outdoor drawing. The last appearance of the American pre-Raphaelites as a group was in an 1867 exhibition at the Yale School of Fine Arts, where it was pointed out by the critic for the *New York Times* that the members "sacrifice effect to accuracy and prefer elaboration of detail to the sketchy and suggestive style now so generally popular" (22 July 1867). Not only was close-focus realism out of style, but landscape painting itself was losing ground to genre and figure subjects. That year Hill and his father took part in the first exhibition of the newly formed Watercolor Society at the National Academy, although neither became a member.

In 1868 Hill joined the U.S. Geological Survey of the fortieth parallel for several months—his watercolors from this western trip served as the basis for large landscapes he exhibited at the National Academy for a few years after his return. In the fall of 1870 he built a two-room cabin on unoccupied Phantom Island in Lake George near Bolton, New York. Here he spent the next five winters making etchings and large paintings from his watercolor studies done in the summer months. These etchings were very different from the finely drawn ones of *Sketches from Nature*, making use of both aquatint and drypoint for more subtle gradations of tone. Concurrently in his large paintings he was less concerned with specificity of form, aiming instead for color effects and suggestive treatment of light and shade, although he never abandoned his conviction that a work of art ought to be true to nature.

In 1876 Hill returned to Clarkstown, but he was off again in 1878 to visit Thomas Farrer, who had returned to England, and to embark on a walking tour of Switzerland following an itinerary suggested by Ruskin. He was called home by his father's death in September 1879 and was not to leave Clarkstown again except for infrequent trips to visit friends. Hill gradually withdrew from the art world after his five entries to the 1882 Watercolor Society exhibition were refused. By this time the popularity of a sketchy tonalist treatment meant that even his more loosely painted outdoor studies were unacceptable. The critic of the *New York Tribune* lamented that "one of the men who, with his father . . . did more to create a love for water-color in this country than anyone else who can be named, is absolutely refused a representation" (15 Feb. 1882).

Hill's focus turned to the preservation of his father's work. In 1883, in a studio behind the house in Clarkstown where he lived with his sister Emma (he never married), he began etchings after his father's work destined to illustrate *An Artist's Memorial*. The twenty-two etchings, ten full page plates and ten vignettes included within the fifteen-page biographical text, were published in New York in 1888. In his etchings of both landscape and still life, he showed acute sensitivity to his father's particular style, combining delicacy of touch with breadth of vision. His own tendencies can be seen in an intensified contrast of light and dark that occasionally created a more moody and dramatic composition than his father's original one.

In addition to the forty-seven etchings in his two published books, more than forty other etchings by John Henry Hill are known. The sale of impressions from these plates, with the occasional painting, must have been the main financial support for the last four decades of his life. In 1884 he opened the studio to the public as a gallery showing the work of his grandfather, father, and himself, and in 1917 he published a catalog of the 112 works on view. He received belated if brief recognition when Frank Weitenkampf, curator of prints at the New York Public Library, recounted a visit to the studio in the *New York Times Magazine*, noting that "the pictures collected form a continuous chain of artistic growth and development, a series of documents illustrating the history of an artist family" (8 Dec. 1901).

Hill's hundreds of landscapes in oil and watercolor are remarkable for their meticulous, close-focus real-ism combined with breadth of vision and brilliant outdoor light and color. Hill was a leader of the short-lived Ruskinian landscape movement in the mid-1800s, and his etchings, ranging from an early linear to a more tonal style, place him among the first American painter/etchers and point to his status as a pioneer in the etching revival of the 1880s.

• John Henry Hill's diary from 25 Dec. 1870 to 25 Mar. 1874 is in the collection of the Adirondack Museum, Blue Mountain Lake, N.Y. Letters from John William and John Henry Hill to fellow artists of the American pre-Raphaelite group are in the Gordon Lester Ford Collection of the New York Public Library. The most complete study of Hill's life and work is an unpublished manuscript by May Brawley Hill, "Landscapes of Rockland County" (1991), commissioned by the Historical Society of Rockland County, N.Y., and available there. John Scott wrote "The Hill Family of Clarksville," *South of the Mountain* 19 (Jan.–Mar. 1975): 5–18. Hill's work is included in Linda S. Ferber and William H. Gerdts, *The New Path: Ruskin and the American Pre-Raphaelites* (1985).

MAY BRAWLEY HILL

HILL, John Wiley (26 Nov. 1890–17 Mar. 1977), public relations executive, was born near Shelbyville, Indiana, on the farm owned by his parents, Theophilus Wiley Hill and Katherine Jameson. After graduating from high school in 1909, he started working as a reporter for a local newspaper. Then for two years he studied journalism at Indiana University. Without graduating, he returned to newspaper work as a reporter in Akron, Ohio. In 1916, while working as a newspaper reporter in Cleveland, he married Hildegarde Beck. They had no children and would eventually divorce after more than thirty years of marriage.

For a decade beginning in 1917 Hill worked in Cleveland, editing a steel industry trade journal. The pay was better than what he earned as a newspaper reporter, and the work he found not at all dull. During that period he also published a bulletin that compiled business and economic information for the Cleveland Trust bank. Inspired by his reading of Ivy Lee's *Publicity*, a collection of speeches by the pioneer of public relations, Hill decided in 1927 to embark on a career as an independent specialist in "corporate publicity." His first client, the Union Trust Company, Cleveland's biggest bank, helped him to acquire other local businesses as clients. Hill built his own business by cultivating favorable newspaper coverage for clients. But when the Union Trust Company closed during the national banking crisis early in 1933, that success was threatened.

After the loss of his most important client, Hill formed a partnership with Don Knowlton, who had been director of advertising and public relations at the Union Trust Company. Hill and Knowlton were only in business a few months when they got their big break: the American Iron and Steel Institute (AISI) hired them to handle its public relations. The trade association needed help responding to New Deal regulations and greater press scrutiny. Hill, a staunchly conservative Republican committed to corporate management and opposed to the New Deal, quickly won the confidence of the industry's top executives. From then until he retired, the steel industry employed him as its public relations advocate against labor unions and government regulation.

Hill's work on behalf of the steel industry during the 1930s lifted him from provincial obscurity. Regularly attending the AISI's board meetings in New York City, he planned and directed the campaign to win over public opinion for management and against the Congress of Industrial Organizations's attempt to establish collective bargaining in the steel industry. When the Senate Civil Liberties Committee in 1938 investigated the "Little Steel" strike of the previous year, it uncovered evidence that Hill's firm had sought to gain favorable editorial opinions by threatening newspapers with the loss of advertising revenues. In response, Hill testified that such behavior was an aberration contrary to the firm's policies. Press coverage of the Senate investigation may have embarrassed him, but it did not hurt his career.

Hill's work for AISI made him aware of the potential for expanding his operations to New York City. As the nation's financial and communications hub and headquarters for many of the largest corporations, New York was already the center of the advertising and public relations businesses. In 1938 Hill opened a branch office there and, without resorting to self-promotion and high-pressure "selling," began to attract a desirable clientele. By 1947 business at the New York office had grown so large that the partners reorganized. Knowlton, who had remained in Cleveland, became principal owner and chief executive of Hill and Knowlton of Cleveland, serving a regional clientele. Hill, who retained only a small ownership share and no operating role in that firm, established an entirely separate firm in New York, Hill and Knowlton, Inc., of which he was principal owner and chief executive.

Measured by volume of annual billings, Hill and Knowlton, Inc., became the largest public relations firm in the country. As its founder, owner, and chief executive, Hill was one of the profession's towering figures, proud that his firm never had to solicit business. With a reputation for effective and sincere advocacy for conservative causes, he promoted the free-enterprise system for an extensive list of corporate and political clients.

While business leaders became more conscious of the benefits of public relations after the Second World War, Hill tried to enhance his own profession. In 1948 he joined the Public Relations Society of America, a struggling new organization of practitioners seeking professional status. Also during the late 1940s he began to support public relations education at Boston University, endowing a chair there in 1950. Meanwhile, shortly after a divorce from his first wife, in 1949 he married Elena Karam, and they adopted two children.

As his firm grew by mergers, Hill pushed for expansion abroad. In 1954, despite the reservations of his associates who doubted the potential of business in

Europe, the firm became Hill and Knowlton International. Adding a former assistant secretary of state to its executive staff, it opened a successful European branch in Geneva, Switzerland. By 1958 it operated offices in Düsseldorf, The Hague, and Sydney and had associates in as many as eight other foreign cities.

By the time Hill retired in 1962, he could point with pride to the size and outstanding education, experience, talent, and linguistic capabilities of the expert staff that the firm had assembled under his direction. Rated by peers as the best public relations agency in the country, Hill and Knowlton, the "PR factory," then employed a staff of about 250 employees and reportedly had gross annual billings of over $3.5 million. Hill had brought to public relations practice the kind of corporate organization that resembled the structure of its major clients. Health conscious and committed to a careful diet and regular exercise, Hill remained vigorous well past retirement, going regularly to his office until a month before his death in New York City.

• The John W. Hill Papers are deposited in the State Historical Society of Wisconsin in Madison. His autobiography, *The Making of a Public Relations Man* (1963), contains little personal information. An obituary is in the *New York Times*, 18 Mar. 1977.

ALAN R. RAUCHER

HILL, Joshua (10 Jan. 1812–6 Mar. 1891), lawyer and U.S. representative and senator, was born in the Abbeville District of South Carolina, the son of Joshua Hill, a farmer of Irish descent and moderate means, and Nancy Ann Wyatt Collier. Educated in the common schools and tutored by John Gray and Moses Waddell, Hill is said to have walked at about the age of seventeen to Monticello in Jasper County, Georgia, where his older brother was practicing law. In 1836 he married Emily Reid, with whom he would have eight children. He moved to Madison, Georgia, sometime before 1848 and established himself as a lawyer and planter. By 1860 he owned approximately sixty slaves.

In 1844, as a delegate to the Whig National Convention, Hill backed Henry Clay for the presidency. In 1856, although he denied accepting all the tenets of the American party, he was elected to Congress on the Know Nothing ticket, defeating Linton Stephens, the brother of Alexander H. Stephens, in a contest that marked him as an ideological outsider among Georgia's political elite. First seated on 4 March 1857, Hill was reelected in 1858. An opponent of secession, in 1860 he was a delegate to the Constitutional Union Convention at Baltimore, where he supported John Bell's presidential candidacy. After Georgia seceded from the Union, he resigned his congressional seat and returned to Madison.

Hill took no active role in the Civil War but allowed his name to be advanced as incumbent Joseph E. Brown's opponent for the Georgia governorship in 1863. Winning support primarily among Atlanta-area reconstructionists and North Georgia Unionists, he ran ahead of a third candidate but far behind Brown. In 1864, after visiting Union general William Tecumseh Sherman to solicit the return of the body of his second son, Hugh Legare, he agreed to act as intermediary in Sherman's scheme to detach Georgia from the Confederacy. Although he and his associates met with Governor Brown and others, and although the peace movement enjoyed some popularity in Georgia, particularly in the mountain areas of the state, nothing came of these efforts.

After the war, Hill favored cooperation with federal authorities and quick reconstruction of the South, and he was among southerners early professing their loyalty to President Andrew Johnson. He was chosen a delegate to Georgia's 1865 constitutional convention and hoped to be elected senator, but he was disappointed when Herschel V. Johnson and Alexander H. Stephens were elected to the Senate instead. He was offered federal appointments but declined them. In 1868 he was elected to the Senate by a coalition of conservative Republicans and former Democrats seeking primarily to prevent the election of former Georgia wartime governor Joseph E. Brown, but all Georgia representatives-elect were rejected by Congress. Finally seated on 1 February 1871, after Georgia had undergone what is commonly called its "second military reconstruction," Hill served until 3 March 1873. During his term he successfully opposed the seating of Foster Blodgett, the candidate of Georgia's Radical Republican faction, as Georgia's second senator and vigorously challenged federal civil rights legislation.

Hill did not seek reelection and returned to his law practice in Madison. Except for serving in Georgia's constitutional convention of 1877, he avoided any further active political involvement. He died in Madison and was buried in the family plot there.

By the time of his death, the bitterness of prominent midcentury Georgia politicians like Stephens and Brown, as well as memories of Hill's often unpopular opinions and alliances, had been blunted by time. He was memorialized in fulsome if conventional terms as a politician of firm opinions, who, though never charismatic, was steady in his purposes and in his associations.

• No major collection of Hill's papers has survived, but some small collections are found at the Georgia Department of Archives and History in Atlanta, and letters from and about Hill are scattered among papers of prominent national and state politicians, including Andrew Jackson (Library of Congress) and Alexander H. Stephens (Manhattanville College, Library of Congress, and Emory University). There is no complete biography, but Lucien E. Roberts, "The Political Career of Joshua Hill, Georgia Unionist," *Georgia Historical Quarterly* 21 (1937): 50–72, is valuable. Information on various aspects of Hill's career also appears in Horace Montgomery, *Cracker Parties* (1950); Joseph H. Parks, *Joseph E. Brown of Georgia* (1976); Thomas Conn Bryan, *Confederate Georgia* (1953); Alan Conway, *The Reconstruction of Georgia* (1966); and Elizabeth Studley Nathans, *Losing the Peace: Georgia Republicans*

and Reconstruction, 1865–1871 (1969). A useful biographical sketch appears in Kenneth Coleman and Charles Stephen Gurr, eds., *Dictionary of Georgia Biography* (1983).

ELIZABETH STUDLEY NATHANS

HILL, Lister (27 Dec. 1894–20 Dec. 1984), U.S. congressman and senator, was born Joseph Lister Hill in Montgomery, Alabama, the son of Luther Leonidas Hill, Jr., a prominent physician, and Lilly Lyons. Dr. Hill named his son for the world-renowned British surgeon Sir Joseph Lister, under whom he had studied in London. At his mother's insistence, Lister Hill—as he preferred to be known—attended a Catholic grade school and was reared in the Catholic church. Before embarking on a political career in overwhelmingly Protestant Alabama, Hill publicly announced his conversion to Methodism, the faith of his paternal ancestors.

After graduating from Starke School, an elite prep school in Montgomery, Hill attended the University of Alabama (1911–1915), where he earned A.B. and law degrees, and Columbia University Law School (1915–1916), where he earned a second law degree. Returning to Montgomery, he entered the practice of law. During World War I he served eighteen months in the Seventeenth U.S. Infantry, rising from private to first lieutenant. Although hostilities had virtually ended by the time he reached France, Hill acquired the valuable political credential of war veteran.

Thanks in large measure to his father's wide acquaintance with physicians, nurses, hospital administrators, and grateful patients, Hill was elected in 1923 on the Democratic ticket as representative of Alabama's Second Congressional District, which encompassed the infertile piney hills of south central Alabama as well as Montgomery and a strip of rich Black Belt soil. Unlike many politically ambitious Alabamians in the 1920s, Hill did not affiliate with the then-powerful Ku Klux Klan, perhaps in part because of his Catholic upbringing and because some of his maternal ancestors had been Jewish.

When he took the oath of office at the age of twenty-eight, Hill became the youngest member of the U.S. House of Representatives. He retained his House seat with ease, running unopposed in seven Democratic primaries and encountering only token opposition in 1932 and 1936. A highly eligible bachelor during his early years in Washington, D.C., Hill married Henrietta Fontaine McCormick, member of a socially prominent southern family, in 1928; they became the parents of two children.

When Democrats took over the presidency and leadership of Congress in 1933, Hill came under the charm and influence of Franklin D. Roosevelt, who inspired the young congressman with the spirit of noblesse oblige. Originally cautious about expanding the role of the federal government, Hill became in 1933 the House sponsor of a bill that embraced the sweeping concept, originated by Nebraska senator George Norris, of the Tennessee Valley Authority. Joining the congressional majority that authorized the New Deal,

Hill supported its public works and employment programs, the National Industrial Recovery Act, and federal subsidies to cut back agricultural production; he even took political risks by opposing a bonus for war veterans and by supporting Roosevelt's plan to enlarge the Supreme Court. Following Roosevelt's reelection in 1936, the president named Hill to head the steering committee that in 1937 helped frame and enact the Farm Security Administration, which offered government loans to aid small farmers in becoming landowners.

In 1938 Hill won the Senate seat vacated by Hugo L. Black, Roosevelt's first nominee to the U.S. Supreme Court. Campaigning against former Alabama senator J. Thomas Heflin, Hill vigorously supported the principle of a federally mandated minimum wage and maximum work week, the major issue in this contest. His victory, closely followed by that of Senator Claude Pepper in Florida, helped bring about passage of the Fair Labor Standards Act of 1938. Hill's ardor for New Deal programs won him the honor of placing Roosevelt's name in nomination for a third term at the 1940 Democratic National Convention.

In 1946, however, faced with the prospect of having to rally support for President Harry S. Truman's civil rights proposals, Hill resigned as Democratic whip, thereby relinquishing his chance to succeed Kentucky senator Alben Barkley as majority leader. A political pragmatist, Hill, in order to keep his Senate seat, had opposed attempts by Congress to abolish the poll tax, outlaw lynching, and curb the filibuster. After the Supreme Court's 1954 *Brown* decision, he publicly supported the Alabama legislature's futile gesture, a resolution declaring the decision null and void within their state, and he joined one hundred other members of Congress in signing the Southern Manifesto of protest. Referring to another politician who had made a similar compromise, Hill once remarked to a friend, "Do you want him to stick his neck out and get beat, or stay here and get something done?" (Hamilton, p. 291).

Having thus deflected the politics of race, Hill won easy reelection over token opposition in 1950 and 1956. Thereafter he concentrated his enormous power and influence on sponsoring legislation in the less controversial fields of health and education. In 1946, with Ohio senator Harold Burton as titular cosponsor, he had won passage of the Hill-Burton Act, which forestalled Truman's proposal for national health insurance by providing federal funds for a vast hospital construction program, particularly in rural areas. In 1956 Hill and Alabama representative Carl Elliott cosponsored the Library Services Act, which provided federal funds to upgrade the nation's libraries.

In 1958 Hill and Elliott succeeded in persuading Congress to enact the so-called National Defense Education Act, passed amid the national hysteria that followed the Russian launch of Sputnik. Invoking the need to educate more scientists for national defense, this legislation pioneered federal loans for college students in all fields of study. Hill, occupying the powerful post of chairman of the Senate Committee on Labor and Public Welfare, also convinced Congress to commit billions to expand the National Institutes of Health into a medical research empire funding thousands of projects concerned with the causes and control of major diseases and other health problems.

But as the civil rights movement became stronger and parts of it more militant during the 1960s, Hill's longtime opponents—leaders of big business, agriculture, and the timber industry—sensed the opportunity to lure Alabama's white, working-class majority, heretofore loyal Democrats due to the economic benefactions they had received from the New Deal, into the ranks of the Republican party. By fielding a vigorous, young candidate, James D. Martin, and inciting the emotions of white voters over issues such as school prayer and the integration of the neighboring University of Mississippi, Republicans almost defeated Hill in 1962. George C. Wallace, obsessed by his presidential ambitions, encouraged further defections from the New Deal wing of the Alabama Democratic party during his first term as governor (1963–1967).

Rather than face a reelection campaign centered on the issue of race, Hill retired in 1968, having served forty-five years in the House and Senate. On the Senate floor, colleagues paid high tribute to Hill's long and productive career; Texas senator Ralph Yarborough declared that Hill ranked among the top five members who had rendered "the greatest service to the people" in the history of the Senate (Hamilton, pp. 280–81). Numerous organizations in the fields of medicine, education, and librarianship honored Hill; he received a special Lasker Foundation Award for his sponsorship of health research, and in 1980 the Lister Hill National Center for Biomedical Research was dedicated on the campus of the National Institutes of Health in Bethesda, Maryland.

Hill lived quietly in his unpretentious bungalow in Montgomery until his death there a week short of his ninetieth birthday. Although he deliberately chose political survival over the championship of civil rights, Hill, because of his major legislative achievements in the areas of education and health, indirectly benefited all Americans.

• Hill's papers, a collection of more than 1.8 million pieces containing detailed files on all aspects of his long congressional career, are housed at the University of Alabama, Tuscaloosa. An immense clipping file, located in the Alabama Department of Archives and History in Montgomery, complements the papers. Further materials related to Hill can be found in the papers of the presidents under whom he served: Hoover, Roosevelt, Truman, Eisenhower, Kennedy, and Johnson. For a comprehensive overview of his career, see Virginia Van der Veer Hamilton, *Lister Hill: Statesman from the South* (1987).

Virginia Van der Veer Hamilton

HILL, Louis Clarence (22 Feb. 1865–5 Nov. 1938), civil and hydraulic engineer, was born in Ann Arbor, Michigan, the son of Alva Thomas Hill, a jeweler, and Frances Bliss. Hill's decision to pursue an engineering career was influenced by a great-uncle who served in the U.S. Engineer Office in St. Paul, Minnesota, during Hill's boyhood.

Hill attended the University of Michigan and received a B.S. in civil engineering in 1886. His first employment opportunities came with railroads. He worked as an assistant engineer for the Duluth, Redwing & Southern Railroad in 1887–1888 and became division engineer for the Great Northern Railway in 1888. Much of this work involved strenuous outdoor activity, locating railroad construction sites in North and South Dakota and Minnesota. Hill returned to the University of Michigan and in 1890 obtained a second B.S., this one in electrical engineering. That same year he married Gertrude B. Rose of Ann Arbor; they had two children. Within a month of his marriage Hill and his wife moved to Golden, Colorado, where he spent the next thirteen years as a professor of hydraulic and electrical engineering at the Colorado School of Mines. In 1902 he served as acting president of the school.

Hill entered government service in June 1903, joining the U.S. Geological Survey's new Reclamation Service under the leadership of Frederick H. Newell. From August 1903 to January 1905 Hill supervised the construction of the Salt River Project in Arizona Territory, which culminated in the building of Roosevelt Dam. At the time the Reclamation Service had no policy regarding the use of electrical power in its construction projects. With the benefit only of a survey for a twenty-mile-long power canal ending just below the dam site, Hill constructed a power plant to hoist stone blocks from the quarry, operate a tramway, and supply other power uses. He made good use of his background in electrical engineering, bringing attention to the need for a hydroelectric policy to the Reclamation Service. Congress responded in 1906 by passing an act authorizing the Reclamation Service to produce hydroelectric power as well as irrigation projects. During Hill's time on the Salt River Project he was in charge of the construction of the cement mill, oversaw the design and construction of Roosevelt Dam, helped design the power plant, and saw to the construction of 147 miles of mountain road.

In 1905 Hill was appointed supervising engineer of the southern district, including Arizona, New Mexico, Texas, Utah, and southern California. Under his direction, Roosevelt Dam was completed, and Elephant Butte Dam, Strawberry Valley Dam, and Granite Reef Dam were built. He also saw to the construction of several hundred miles of canals, three power plants on the Salt River Project, and the Strawberry Valley Tunnel under the Wasatch Mountains in Utah. Of particular significance was his involvement in the Yuma Project and the construction of Laguna Dam on the Colorado River, a task that also called for the building of an inverted siphon under the river. Other assignments included the Rio Grande Project, in which he designed and was involved in the initial construction of Elephant Butte Dam and other diversion dams on the Rio Grande, plus a system of canals and drainage

works. Beginning in 1908, Hill served as the U.S. representative negotiating the division of Colorado River water between the United States and Mexico. The Mexican Revolution delayed agreement until the 1920s.

Hill resigned from the Reclamation Service in 1914 to enter private engineering practice. He joined the firm of Quinton, Code & Hill in Los Angeles; the firm merged with Leeds & Barnard in 1930. Hill's reputation as a consulting engineer brought him many important assignments. Projects included Gibraltar Dam on the Santa Ynez River in Santa Barbara County, the Pine Flat Reservoir and Dam at Fresno, and the Otay Dam in San Diego County. He was also associated with flood-control projects in Los Angeles County, including Big Tujunga Dam in Tujunga Canyon, Bouquet Canyon Dam for the Los Angeles Department of Water and Power, and Morris Dam for the City of Pasadena. In 1924 he coauthored a report on water distribution in the Owens Valley–Los Angeles water dispute. Hill also was consulted on projects in Canada and Mexico. The Reclamation Service frequently called on him for consultation in western hydroelectric projects, as did the Army Corps of Engineers, which used his expertise on the Fort Peck Dam on the Missouri River and the Bonneville Dam on the Columbia River. Hill's expertise was also used in the construction of Boulder Dam, Imperial Dam, and the All-American Canal. During World War I he advised in the construction of Camp Kearney, Nebraska, for the U.S. Army.

The Hills settled in Los Angeles and participated for many years in civic and social affairs. Hill joined the American Society of Civil Engineers in 1906 and belonged to the organization for more than thirty years. From 1928 to 1929 he served as vice president and director of the society, and he became its president in 1937. His son Raymond, who also became an engineer, served as vice president at the same time his father was president, the first time this occurred in the ASCE. Hill also held memberships in the National Geographic Society, the Shriners, the American Forestry Association, the University of Michigan Union, the California Club of Los Angeles, and the Scottish Rite Masons, in which he attained the Thirty-second degree. He died in Los Angeles.

Hill enjoyed a long and successful engineering career in both public and private service. Known during his lifetime as one of the foremost civil and electrical engineers in the United States, he lent his expertise, either through direct involvement or consultation, to many of the most important dam projects in the first third of the twentieth century.

• Profiles of Hill include "Past-President Louis C. Hill," *Civil Engineering* 8 (Dec. 1938): 851; Edwin O. Palmer, *History of Hollywood*, vol. 2 (1938), pp. 215–17; W. C. Wolfe, ed., *Men of California*, p. 58; and John S. McGoarty, *Los Angeles from the Mountains to the Sea*, vol. 2 (1925), pp. 37–38. See also William E. Warne, *The Bureau of Reclamation* (1973), p. 88.

ABRAHAM HOFFMAN

HILL, Mary Elliott (5 Jan. 1907–12 Feb. 1969), organic and analytical chemist, was born in South Mills, North Carolina, the daughter of Robert Elliott and Frances Bass. Little is known about the early part of her life, except that she lived with her parents and two brothers in modest circumstances. After completing elementary and secondary education, she enrolled in Virginia State College, where during her sophomore year, she married Carl McClellan Hill, who in addition to being an honor student at Hampton Institute was also class president and an All-America guard on the school football team. Over the course of their 41-year marriage the couple had three children.

In 1929 Hill received a bachelor of science degree from Virginia State College Laboratory School, where from 1930 to 1937 she was instructor and critic teacher in high school sciences. As critic teacher, Hill advised other staff members, mediated conflicts or disagreements related to the attainment of teaching goals, familiarized herself with the most current books, teaching ideas, and so on, and suggested in-house changes, improvements, and course additions when appropriate. At various times between 1932 and 1936, while also teaching at the laboratory school, she taught chemistry at Hampton Institute, where from 1937 to 1940 she was a full-time faculty member and associate professor of chemistry.

Recognizing the practical benefits of advanced study, Hill enrolled in the Graduate School of Arts and Sciences at the University of Pennsylvania, where in 1941 she was awarded a master of science degree in analytical chemistry. For the next six years she was an instructor in chemistry at Dudley High School in Greensboro, North Carolina. Until about 1950 intractable racial barriers kept blacks from finding technical employment in the chemical industry or academia outside of black colleges and universities. In the South of Hill's day, gifted, science-minded black students who did not aspire to medicine, dentistry, or agriculture were not encouraged to seek professional careers in science. The conventional wisdom was that unless a student's ambition was to teach in an all-black school, there was no work in science. This philosophy derived from the well-known and widely publicized negative experiences of several world-class black scientists, such as chemist Percy Julian, cell biologist Ernest Everett Just, and chemistry textbook writer Lloyd Ferguson. In the South, white college graduates with a doctoral degree in chemistry could choose to work in the chemical industry or to teach at either the high school or college level. Such options did not exist for black graduate students with a similar degree, there were no opportunities in the chemical industry, and teaching opportunities existed only in all-black high schools or colleges. If there were no vacancies in a college, the only options for the black Ph.D. were to teach high school or switch fields.

In 1944, after serving one year as an assistant professor at Bennett College in Greensboro, Hill accepted a teaching position at Tennessee A & I College, a historically black college in Nashville now known as Ten-nessee State University, where for the next eighteen years she was an associate professor of chemistry; in 1951 she became acting head of the chemistry department. In 1962 her husband, who was dean of Tennessee A & I's School of Arts and Sciences, accepted the position of president of Kentucky State College in Frankfort. Relocating with him, Hill accepted a position as professor of chemistry. With her husband, she collaborated in the writing of *General College Chemistry* (1944), a textbook which Carl Hill coauthored with Myron B. Towns, and *Experiments in Organic Chemistry* (1954), a laboratory manual; the latter volume went through four editions. As an analytical chemist on her husband's research team, she was one of the coauthors of their forty-plus published papers.

Both a skilled classroom teacher and analytical laboratory chemist, Hill preferred the classroom because she enjoyed interacting with students, from whom she always demanded excellence. On college campuses where she taught, Hill established and supervised student-affiliate chapters of the American Chemical Society, which influenced many students to consider careers in science and teaching. A conservative estimate is that at least twenty of her students became college professors. Her powerful influence on students is reflected in her having been designated as one of the top six chemistry teachers in the United States and Canada by the Manufacturing Chemists Association.

Until the early 1950s Europe, in particular Germany, was recognized as being the center of work in theoretical and experimental organic chemistry, the thrust of which is to create entirely new substances—preferably with commercial applications—out of existing raw materials. The cutoff in scientific communication between German and U.S. chemists during World War II caused the American chemical industry to grow, and this led in the 1950s and 1960s to the ascendance of brilliant, creative, innovative chemists. Both Mary Hill and Carl Hill were in that category. Among other things the Hills used ketenes, which are very reactive chemical substances with great potential as starting materials for creating new types of ethers, and for helping a chemist to better understand complex chemical reactions. In much of their work they used the then relatively new chemicals known as Grignard Reagents (named after the inventor, Nobel laureate Victor Grignard), which in controlled chemical reactions promote rearrangements of atoms to positions desired by the synthesis chemist and confirmed by an analytical chemist.

In her role as analytical chemist for her husband's research team, Hill pioneered efforts to create new methods, as well as to modify existing methods, of organic chemical analysis using such instruments as the ultraviolet spectrophotometer. She also established procedures for monitoring the progress of chemical reactions by determining the degree of solubility of reaction species in non-waterbased (nonaqueous) reaction systems. This ability to isolate, identify, and quantify such reaction products enabled synthesis chemists on her team, aided by the Grignard Reagents, to design new materials, including plastics.

The Hills were longtime, active members of St. Andrews Presbyterian Church in Nashville; Mary Elliot Hill was a member of the Women of St. Andrews, a church auxiliary, and also served for a time as church historian. She belonged to several professional and civic organizations, including Alpha Kappa Alpha National Honor Society, the American Chemical Society, the Tennessee Academy of Science, the National Institute of Science, and Beta Kappa Chi Sorority; she was also assistant editor of The Bulletin, the Beta Kappa Chi newspaper. After moving to Frankfort, she became an active member of the Women's Circle of the South Frankfort Presbyterian Church. She died in Frankfort and was interred at Norfolk, Virginia.

• Among the papers that Hill coauthored are Carl M. Hill et al., "Grignard Reagents and Unsaturated Ethers: The Synthesis, Properties, and Reactions of beta-Substituted Vinyl Ethers with Aliphatic and Aromatic Grignard Reagents," *Journal of the American Chemical Society* 80 (1958): 4602–4; "The Cleavage of Diallyl Ethers by Aliphatic and Aromatic Grignard Reagents," *Journal of the American Chemical Society* 80 (1958): 3623–25; and "Lithium Aluminum Hydride Reduction of Aryloxyalkylketene Mers and Dimers," *Journal of the American Chemical Society* 81 (1959). For brief biographical sketches see Jacques Cattell, *American Men of Science*, 10th and 11th eds. (1960; 1968); Julius H. Taylor, *The Negro in Science* (1955); Vivian Ovelton Sammons, *Blacks in Science and Medicine* (1990); and Marianna Davis, ed., *Contributions of Black Women to America* (1982). For an insightful look at Hill as a teacher, wife, and mother, see the feature article "Many Components Equal Mary Hill," Louisville *Courier-Journal*, 11 Oct. 1963. Obituaries are in the *(Frankfort) Kentucky State Journal*, 12 Feb. 1969, and the *Norfolk Virginian-Pilot*, 13 Feb. 1969.

BILLY SCOTT

HILL, Nathaniel Peter (18 Feb. 1832–22 May 1900), U.S. senator and mining entrepreneur, was born in Montgomery, New York, the son of Nathaniel Peter Hill, a farmer and state legislator, and Matilda Crawford. After managing the family farm in New York for several years after his father's death, Hill graduated from Brown University in 1856 and remained with the university as a professor of chemistry. In 1860 he married Alice Hale, with whom he had three children. He supplemented his academic position by serving as a consultant and chemical analyst for numerous corporations in Rhode Island. In 1864 Hill accepted an opportunity to go west and investigate the mines of Colorado. He was employed by a group of eastern capitalists to report on the prospects of opening new mines in the San Luis Valley. While faithfully carrying out his duties for his employers, he also kept an eye open for opportunities of his own. Sufficiently impressed, he resigned from Brown, deciding that his future lay in the West.

The prospects for success in Colorado were not entirely self-evident in the mid-1860s, as Colorado's mines were running into difficulties. The initial boom had depended on placer deposits and stamp milling,

i.e., crushing the mineral-bearing rocks and recovering gold through amalgamation with mercury. However, when miners were forced to dig for ore, the sulphide or pyritous ores found below the surface proved resistant to this process. Consequently, the recovery of gold fell to less than one-fourth of the ore's assayed value, and production fell dramatically. Hill believed that a new high-heat process called "smelting" might increase that proportion. In 1866 he toured Europe, studying the smelting process in Swansea, Wales, and Freiburg, Saxony. The trip convinced him that smelting was the key to successful gold mining, and on returning to the United States in 1867, he gained the backing of wealthy Boston industrialists to form the Boston and Colorado Smelting Company. The results were astounding. According to historian James E. Fell, Jr., "During its first ten years in business the Boston and Colorado company processed one-quarter of the precious and base metals mined in the high country" (Fell, p. 331). It would be twenty-five years before another change in technology allowed other companies to challenge Hill's dominance. In 1872 Hill added a refinery to his mining operations and began processing ores from all over the Southwest. The Boston and Colorado company would remain in operation until 1910. Hill's success reflects his ability to obtain capital, his administrative skills, and his willingness to hire expert European metallurgists with whom he worked.

Like some other mining entrepreneurs in Colorado, Hill's economic success soon translated into political success. In 1871 he was elected mayor of Black Hawk, and one year later he entered the territorial council. The state legislature elected him to the U.S. Senate in 1879 as a Republican, and he was appointed chairman of the Committee on Mines and Mining. His election in 1879 engendered a heated factional feud with fellow Republican Henry M. Teller that would dominate party politics for years afterward. During his term, Hill was the leading advocate of a federal telegraph system. He was most conspicuous, however, as an ardent proponent of the free coinage of silver. While his stand as a "Silver Republican" was no doubt influenced by his own financial interests, Hill consistently defended this position with arguments about the need to relieve what he termed "the debtor class." A further rationale for his positions on money and the telegraph was his belief (shared by a growing number of citizens) in the increasing danger of monopolies. Finally, he later fought against the influence of the anti-Catholic American Protective Association in Colorado's Republican party. In 1885 Hill was defeated for reelection by his rival Teller in a raucous interparty battle.

Hill returned to Colorado and became active in businesses ranging from petroleum to ranching while remaining general manager of his mining company. He also purchased the *Denver Republican*, using it to continue campaigning for "free silver" and to carry on his running feud with Senator Teller. Thus, in 1890 Hill's newspaper did not endorse all Republican candidates, but he remained fundamentally loyal to the

GOP. In 1891 President Benjamin Harrison (1833–1901) appointed Hill to the International Monetary Commission, and Hill served as a delegate to the Bimetallic Conference two years later. He also served as a regent of the Smithsonian Institution. Hill remained active in his business ventures until his death in Denver, Colorado.

Hill was well known as a prominent innovator who became a successful entrepreneur. Using his professional training as a chemist, he found new ways of solving the dilemmas of deep-rock mining. His greatest fame resulted from bringing a successful smelting process to Colorado's gold mines. He revived a moribund industry and sparked another boom in the Colorado economy. His political career was dominated by his support for the coinage of silver, a position based on both self-interest and ideology. However, it was his entrepreneurial prowess that made Hill a success and gave him a position of prominence in Colorado's history.

• Hill's papers are located at the State Historical Society of Colorado. For Hill's views on politics, see N. P. Hill, *Speeches and Papers on the Silver, Postal Telegraph, and Other Economic Questions* (1890). The most informative work is James E. Fell, Jr., "Nathaniel P. Hill: A Scientist-Entrepreneur in Colorado," *Arizona and the West* 15 (1973): 315–32. Also useful for information on state politics are Duane A. Smith, *Horace Tabor: His Life and the Legend* (1973), and James Edward Wright, *The Politics of Populism: Dissent in Colorado* (1974). Obituaries are in the *Denver Republican* and the *Colorado Springs Gazette*, 23 May 1900.

WILLIAM T. HULL

HILL, Patty Smith (27 Mar. 1868–25 May 1946), kindergarten educator, was born in Anchorage, outside of Louisville, Kentucky, the daughter of William Wallace Hill and Martha Jane Smith. Her father, a Princeton graduate, Presbyterian minister, and one-time editor of the *Presbyterian Herald*, had by the time of Patty's birth become involved in the education of young women, first as headmaster of a school for girls in Anchorage, Kentucky, and later as president of colleges in Missouri and Texas. The Hills encouraged all six of their children, including four daughters, to pursue higher education and a career. Following the death of William Hill, the family returned to Kentucky, where Patty graduated from the Louisville Collegiate Institute in 1887.

From an early age Hill expressed a desire to work with young children, aspiring to become the director of an orphanage. When in 1887 a kindergarten training school opened in Louisville, she enrolled as one of five women in its first class. The training school and kindergarten, attached to a philanthropic mission, were under the direction of Anna Bryan, a Louisville native recently returned from study in Chicago. Bryan was to be Hill's chief mentor. Apparently trained in a conventional manner, Bryan was not wedded to prevailing notions of kindergarten theory or practice, and she encouraged Hill to adopt her own experimental and pragmatic approach to the field. Following completion of her training program in 1889 Hill was appointed director of one of the mission's branch kindergartens. In 1893 she succeeded Bryan as director of the training school and superintendent of what had developed into the Louisville Free Kindergarten Association. Under Hill's leadership the association's kindergartens became increasingly tied to the Louisville public schools.

Throughout the 1890s Hill devoted summers to furthering her own formal education, leaving Louisville to study under a number of the nation's preeminent educational thinkers. She enrolled in courses taught by Francis Parker, John Dewey, G. Stanley Hall, and Luther Gulick. The efforts of Bryan and Hill to develop a kindergarten program consistent with current educational thinking increasingly brought visitors to Louisville's kindergartens. Hill also gradually attracted national attention to herself, beginning with a presentation at the 1890 National Educational Association. With her sister and fellow teacher Mary she began in the same year a series of articles for the *Kindergarten Review*. With her musician sister Mildred she published *Song Stories for the Kindergarten* (1896).

During the same years that Hill was gaining a national reputation, the kindergarten movement was becoming increasingly polarized. The kindergarten had been brought to the United States from Germany, where it originated in the work of Friedrich Froebel. By the turn of the century kindergartens were well established in American cities. Leaders in the movement were divided, however, over the degree to which Froebel's system, with its clearly delineated "gifts" and "occupations," was to be considered fixed for all time. Hill emerged as a leader of the reform faction within the International Kindergarten Union (IKU). When the IKU established a commission in 1903 to address the division in its ranks, Hill was asked to draft that section of the report representing the progressive perspective. Against the "uniform system" of her opponents, Hill argued for accommodating the kindergarten to changing conditions, for applying the insights gained from empirical study of children's development, and for a less authoritarian role for the teacher. Such emphases, she insisted, were more in the spirit of the kindergarten's original intentions than the letter-of-the-law programs of Froebel's defenders.

Having established a reputation not only as an advocate of kindergarten reform but as a lively and persuasive speaker, Hill was asked to represent the progressive point of view in a series of lectures at Teachers College, Columbia University, in 1905. Hill's lectures were alternated with those of Susan Blow of St. Louis, translator of Froebel's work and leader of the IKU's conservative faction. Hill was asked that same year to join the faculty on a permanent basis. She was to remain at Teachers College for thirty years, retiring in 1935 as a full professor (conferred in 1922) and the recipient of an honorary Columbia University doctorate (1929).

Under Hill's leadership Teachers College became one of two major national centers for graduate study in kindergarten education. Programs developed for the college's Speyer School and Horace Mann School kindergartens were emulated worldwide. Hill continued to speak and write prolifically. She was a consistent advocate of childcare education for parents and for the provision of medical care for preschool and school-age children. Conceiving early childhood education and later schooling as part of a continuous process, Hill worked to coordinate the kindergarten program with that of the primary school. She upheld a broadly professional role for the kindergarten teacher, one that demanded a rigorous education and enabled the teacher to engage in ongoing research in her own classroom.

Teachers College afforded Hill continuing opportunities to interact with leading educational thinkers. The work of colleague Edward Thorndike particularly influenced her outlook. Hill actively embraced the movement to define educational outcomes in precise terms, a movement reflected in her *A Conduct Curriculum* (1923). Attempting to preserve the best in Froebelian thinking, she nonetheless helped to legitimate an emphasis on the external manipulation of behavior, a significant departure from the thinking that brought the kindergarten into being.

At home with educational theory, quoting freely from Dewey, Hall, and Froebel, Hill was primarily interested in kindergarten practice. One of her concrete contributions to the field was, characteristically, a new product for children's play. Insight on children's development gained from Hall, Gulick, and her own observation led Hill to develop large interlocking construction blocks that demanded greater group cooperation and less fine motor coordination than existing blocks. An even more widely known legacy was a children's song, "Good Morning to You," which became popular as "Happy Birthday to You." Hill's copyright was established following a successful plagiarism suit in 1935.

After her retirement from Teachers College, Hill was an active supporter of preschool education, devoting particular attention to the Hilltop Community Center serving poor neighborhoods adjacent to Columbia University. She never married, sharing her final years with a sister. She died in New York City after a long illness. Hill's most enduring contribution was to bring kindergarten theory and practice into the mainstream of American education. Her colleague William Heard Kilpatrick gave Hill primary credit for the transformation of the kindergarten from a "mysterious cult . . . to what we know it now to be."

• The major repository for Hill's unpublished material is the Filson Club in Louisville, Ky. Some correspondence and papers may also be found in the Special Collections of Teachers College, Columbia University. Hill's "Some Conservative and Progressive Phases of Kindergarten Education," in the *Sixth Yearbook* of the National Society for the Scientific Study of Education, part 2 (1907), is useful as a sample of her many short pieces and as an introduction to the professional tensions she lived through. The most complete study of Hill's career is M. Charlotte Jammer, "Patty Smith Hill and Reform of the American Kindergarten" (Ed.D. diss., Teachers College, Columbia Univ., 1960). A succinct and substantive, but relatively uncritical, treatment of Hill is Agnes Snyder, *Dauntless Women in Childhood Education, 1856–1931* (1972). For the larger context in which Hill worked, see Evelyn Weber, *The Kindergarten: Its Encounter with Educational Thought in America* (1969). An obituary is in the *New York Times*, 26 May 1946.

ANDREW MULLEN

HILL, Pete (12 Oct. 1880–Dec. 1951), Negro League baseball player, was born Preston Hill in Pittsburgh, Pennsylvania. His parents' names and other details about his early years are unknown, though he reportedly was part American Indian. Hill started his career with the Pittsburgh Keystones in 1899, but no statistical records are extant. He left in 1903 to join the Cuban X-Giants, a team of American blacks that starred pitcher Rube Foster, the so-called "father of black baseball." The club also featured second baseman Charlie Grant, who had just failed to pass with the Baltimore Orioles as an "Indian," Chief Tokahoma. That autumn the Giants won the informal black championship over the Philadelphia Giants.

The next year Hill and most of his teammates jumped to the Philadelphia Giants, winners of the unofficial 1904 championship. The Giants played mostly against white semipro outfits, occasionally facing other black teams. In two games against the Philadelphia Athletics in 1904, Hill got three hits against future Hall of Fame pitchers Rube Waddell and Eddie Plank. For the years 1903 to 1906 only fourteen box scores have been found for games against other top black teams; in these games Hill batted .414.

In 1906 Hill and Foster moved to the Chicago Leland Giants, which played at Seventy-ninth and Wentworth. As in Philadelphia, most of their competition came from local semipro teams that often starred former and future major leaguers. In 1907 the Leland Giants reportedly won 110 games (48 in a row) and lost just 10. Hill was the star batter and center fielder, and the Giants was the best black team of its era.

Veteran catcher Frank Duncan (later Jackie Robinson's first manager) recalled Hill as "a great hitter, a lot like Yogi Berra. He was built like Berra. Yogi wasn't as tall, and Pete was kind of bow-legged. Like Berra, he'd spray the ball to all fields." Added veteran black pitcher Arthur Hardy, "He wasn't a long-ball hitter, but he was a clever base-runner. He moved so easily that it didn't look like he was putting much effort into it. He had perfect muscular control."

In the spring of 1908 the Lelands were prosperous enough to become the first black team to hire its own private Pullman car to travel to spring training. In the winter of 1909–1910 the players sailed to Cuba, where they met the American League champion Detroit Tigers, who arrived without their star, Ty Cobb. Hill got eight hits in twenty-five at bats as his team won four of the six games. The Tigers were followed by an all-star team that included pitchers Mordecai Brown of the Chicago Cubs and Howie Camnitz of the Pittsburgh Pirates, and the black team beat them two out of three.

Rube Foster broke with owner Frank Leland in 1910 and formed the American Giants, bringing along Hill, John Henry, Lloyd, pitcher Frank Wickware, catcher Bruce Petway, and others. The Giants dominated black teams in the Midwest. Heavyweight boxing champion Jack Johnson occasionally played first base. Hill batted .522 against other Negro League teams in the few games for which we have box scores, and the American Giants claimed an overall won-lost record of 123–6.

That winter Hill and Lloyd were back in Cuba for another series of games with the Tigers; this time Cobb came along. Although the Tigers won the series, Cobb vowed never to play against blacks again and never did. The Cubans, with Hill and Lloyd in the lineup, then beat the world champion Philadelphia Athletics in three straight games. In all, Hill had eight hits in twenty-seven at bats against the big leaguers; his lifetime average against major league opponents was .303.

In 1913 the Giants journeyed to the West Coast and beat the recently retired Cy Young. Based on sketchy records, Hill batted .361 that year. On another jaunt in 1914 the American Giants beat a club that included shortstop Honus Wagner. However, Hill's average for the full year fell to .231. Three more subpar years followed, his batting average falling to as low as .207 in 1917.

In 1919 Hill managed the Detroit Stars, who joined Foster's new Negro National League the following year. Hill's average shot up to .310 that year and to .391 the following year. After a year of managing the Milwaukee Bears in 1923, when he batted .326, Hill moved to Baltimore in 1924 to take over the Baltimore Black Sox in the Eastern Colored League.

Hill dropped out of big-time black baseball after the 1924 season. Details of his later life are cloudy, but he reportedly worked for the Ford Motor Company in Detroit and managed the semipro Buffalo, New York, Red Caps. He died in Buffalo.

• Hill's statistical record is found in the Macmillan *Baseball Encyclopedia*, 9th ed. (1992), p. 2632. See also Larry Lester, *The Ballplayers* (1990), pp. 473–74, and "The Passing of Pete Hill," *Half-Century*, 1 May 1919, p. 8.

JOHN B. HOLWAY

HILL, Richard (?–1700), mariner and legislator, was born probably in England shortly before 1640. In his will, dated 20 October 1700, he gives his age as "over Three score years." His antecedents are unknown, although at the time of his death he had a sister, Abigail Parr, in Worcestershire. Hill first appears definitively in Maryland records when he assisted his wife, the former Milcah Clarkson, in the probate of her deceased husband's estate in May 1666. Milcah's first husband, Robert Clarkson, a Quaker, had died earlier that year leaving, besides his widow, three children, a personal estate valued at more than 78,000 pounds of tobacco,

and real property totaling more than 500 acres in Anne Arundel County near the present site of Annapolis. Hill and his wife had three children.

By 1675 Hill was a justice of Anne Arundel County and had an ordinary, probably on Clarkson's land. He was given the titles of captain and gentleman in the records of the 1670s. In 1681 Hill was elected to the lower house of the General Assembly, beginning a fifteen-year career in the legislature, one of the longest of his era. The following winter, Charles Calvert, Lord Baltimore, governor and proprietor of Maryland, sent Hill to negotiate with the governor of New York for cooperation in controlling the activities of the northern American Indians, who had recently broken a peace treaty of several years' standing. Hill made the trip in something under six weeks, returning without particular satisfaction from the governor, who blamed the problem on Maryland's not having renewed the treaty annually.

Hill was appointed quorum justice of the Anne Arundel County Court in 1676 and president of the court in 1686, the same year that he was also appointed to collect duties on shipping for the new town on the Severn River, later called Annapolis. By this time, Hill had acquired more than 1,700 acres of land and was frequently mentioned in county wills as overseer or witness. He had become a man of considerable reputation in his locale, a fact that soon became his undoing and almost cost him his life.

In the spring of 1689 revolutionary John Coode frightened Marylanders with tales of Catholic-inspired Indian uprisings and accused the proprietor's followers of treason against the new British monarchs, William of Orange and his wife Mary; Hill spoke out publicly against Coode and his band of agitators. When in the summer of 1689 Coode captured the government and called for the election of a new assembly, only Anne Arundel County refused to elect delegates. The refusal is largely credited to Hill, whom historians Lois Carr and David Jordan call the rebellion's "foremost opponent" in the county. The revolutionaries, called Protestant Associators, issued a proclamation denouncing Hill as a rebel and traitor to the Crown. He was dismissed from office as justice. Hill wrote to Lord Baltimore, by then back in England, of the dangerous situation in Maryland and begged his return to the province "for as hitherto noe blood hath been spilt altho' we are in great fear and terror that it will not end without; except some speedy meanes from your Lordship to prevent the same."

In May 1690, immediately after receiving a letter authorizing them to act on behalf of the Crown in Maryland, the associators sent a force of almost forty men to arrest Hill for treason. For two days and nights the men attacked Hill's property, terrifying his family, seizing his new ship, rifling his house, and destroying his cornfields. Hill was forced to flee to "the Wilderness" from which he wrote a frantic letter to friends, captains of ships of the convoy forming in the bay, asking for their intervention in his name before William and Mary. He was, he said, "an Englishman and their

Majesties' Loyall and obediant subject." Three of the captains obliged him with a letter of endorsement, saying that the commander of the forces "in whose hands the bloody warrant was, the purpose of which was to bring him the said Hill alive or dead" refused to tell them what Hill's crimes were. In the opinion of the ship captains, Hill's greatest crime was "he is apt to talk what others tho' of his opinion dare hardly think." Hill escaped to Virginia and from there to England, where he successfully defended himself before the lords of the Committee of Trade and Plantations and testified against Coode and his associates.

Soon after Francis Nicholson became governor of Maryland in 1694, he appointed Hill naval officer of Annapolis and a justice of the provincial court. Hill was elected to represent Anne Arundel County in the second Royal Assembly that began that year and continued to serve in the legislature from then until his death six years later. When Nicholson moved the capital of the province from St. Mary's City to Annapolis in 1695, Hill was well placed to profit from the growth of the town. He had given 30 acres of land toward formation of the town in 1683 and sold at least another 90 acres to the government for its enlargement in 1695. His house near the dock of the new town was used by the provincial government for meetings and court sessions prior to the building of the new state house. Hill was one of the largest benefactors of the new Free School in Annapolis, contributing 4,000 pounds of tobacco in 1694.

Hill continued to patent and purchase land in the area of the Severn River as well as in Baltimore, Cecil, and Talbot counties. By 1700 he owned almost 5,000 acres of land in Maryland. Throughout his career in Maryland, Hill also engaged in overseas trade, both as master and as shipowner. At his death, his storehouse contained fabrics and laces, buttons, knives, and other imported goods. His total personal estate was valued at more than £1,100 sterling. Hill's primary dwelling remained the Clarkson plantation across Spa Creek from Annapolis, and it was there that he was buried sometime between 20 October and 5 November 1700.

• Primary sources with essential information on Hill can be found at the Maryland State Archives. They include records of the Provincial Land Office (patents and rent rolls), Prerogative Court (wills, inventories, and accounts), Provincial Court Land Records, Anne Arundel County Land Records, and the proceedings of the council and assembly of Maryland printed in William Hand Browne et al., eds., *The Archives of Maryland* (1883–1990), esp. vols. 5, 8, and 17. Also helpful are materials in filing case A at the Maryland Historical Society. Very little has been written on Hill. His biography in Edward C. Papenfuse et al., eds., *A Biographical Dictionary of the Maryland Legislature, 1634–1789* (1979), outlines his career and family. His troubles with John Coode and the Protestant Associators are described in Lois Green Carr and David William Jordan, *Maryland's Revolution of Government, 1689–1692* (1974). J. Thomas Scharf, *History of Maryland*, vol. 1 (1879; repr. 1967), is also helpful for that period. I am indebted to Rouse Todd of Annapolis for his research on Hill's land and involvement with the early history of Annapolis.

JANE WILSON MCWILLIAMS

HILL, Robert Thomas (11 Aug. 1858–28 July 1941), geologist and explorer, was born in Nashville, Tennessee; details of the lives of his parents are not known. Hill was born into a family of eight children just before the Civil War. He was orphaned at the age of five, raised by his grandmother in the war-torn city. He began work when very young, helping to support his family; at the age of sixteen, he finally completed the sixth grade. An older brother invited him to come to Comanche, Texas, 100 miles from the nearest railroad, and the youth eventually arrived there in 1874, penniless.

For the next seven years Hill assisted his brother, printer of the *Comanche Chief*; one of his few entertainments was to read the newspapers received in exchange. He also worked on a surveying party in north-central Texas and spent six months on the trail on one of the great cattle drives from Texas to Dodge City, Kansas. He accompanied traveling salesmen and learned the lay of the land through much of south and central Texas.

From a schoolbook a friend brought to Comanche, Hill learned of the science of geology; he managed to obtain a copy of Dana's *Manual of Geology*. Even before that, he had observed and extensively collected the local fossils, and now he had the means of beginning to interpret them and the rock strata in which they occurred. After writing to a newspaper editor for assistance with his self-taught geologic studies, he was put in contact with A. D. White, president of Cornell University.

Despite his lack of formal education, Hill was accepted at Cornell, where he obtained a bachelor's degree in 1886. His principal teacher was H. S. Williams, and under his mentorship Hill's description of the fossils he had collected from the Cretaceous rocks of Texas formed the basis for U.S. Geological Survey *Bulletin* 45. After graduation, Hill received an appointment to the U.S. Geological Survey as an assistant paleontologist at $50 per month. The USGS was then headed by John Wesley Powell. Powell became Hill's idol; partially in an attempt to emulate his mentor's exploration of the Colorado River, in 1900 Hill organized a river expedition through the three canyons of the Rio Grande between Texas and Mexico.

Hill began his Geological Survey career assisting in a study of the Cretaceous rocks of Arkansas, 1886–1887, and then transferred his activities to Texas, where he laid the groundwork of a state geological survey. He left the USGS in the fall of 1888 to establish the teaching of geology at the University of Texas, but conditions were unsatisfactory at that institution and after two years he returned to Washington, as secretary of the Fifty-second Congress Committee on Irrigation of Arid Lands. Throughout this period Hill continued to study the Cretaceous outcrops of Texas, and the results of his investigations formed the basis for six important papers. In 1890 he studied underground water for the Department of Agriculture in Texas, New Mexico, and the Indian Territories. In 1892 Hill rejoined the Geological Survey.

From 1892 until 1902, Hill made extensive studies of the Cretaceous geology of Texas during the summer field seasons. In the winters, he did field work in the Caribbean islands under the general direction of Alexander Agassiz of Harvard's Museum of Comparative Zoology, under a cooperative arrangement with the Geological Survey. He published reports on Cuba, Puerto Rico, Jamaica, Panama, and Costa Rica; Hill has been called "the father of Antillean geology." In 1901 he was one of the first American geologists to visit the volcanically destroyed city of Saint-Pierre, Martinique, and the first to observe a Pelean cloud. Unfortunately, his major report on the Windward Islands, revised after the eruption of Mount Pelée, was not completed, in part because of a disagreement with Agassiz.

Hill's efforts in Texas included studies of the stratigraphic sequence and the naming and interpreting the Balcones fault zone. He wrote basic papers on the Grand Prairie and Black Prairie areas of Texas and produced a physiographic atlas of the state, as well as conducting investigations on the Edwards Plateau. As a result of his work on the Gulf Coast Cretaceous outcrops, the term "Comanchean" became generally applied to the Upper Cretaceous series of rocks.

Hill was sometimes quick to take offense, and in part because of friction with Agassiz and with Director Charles Doolittle Walcott, who succeeded Powell in 1894, Hill left the government in 1902. He spent the next decade in New York and worked as a consulting mining geologist, but he was not successful. About 1912 he moved to California, where he remained until 1931. He studied the geology of southern California, supported in part by the USGS, concentrating on the Los Angeles area; much of that work remains unpublished. He consulted for the Board of Water Engineers, taught for a year, and in 1928 published a book on earthquakes to allay the fears that had lowered real-estate values in Los Angeles. During World War I and for several years after it, he consulted in the oil business in Texas and recouped much of the money he had earlier lost in Mexican mining ventures. His knowledge of physiography played a key role in resolving a dispute over the boundary of the Red River, the border between Texas and Oklahoma, where oil discoveries had been made.

Hill returned to Texas in 1931 and was engaged to write articles for the *Dallas News*. He first wrote on the East Texas Field, then just being developed, and other aspects of the geology of oil but gradually broadened the scope of his articles to include other aspects of geology. He reinterpreted the route of Cabeza de Vaca and other early explorers in the Southwest. His first scientific paper was published in 1886, and he had produced more than 200 titles before his venture into newspaper writing. About fifty of his articles appeared in newspapers nationwide.

Hill was married twice, to Justina Robinson and later to Margaret McDermott; a daughter by each marriage survived him. Hill received a number of honors, including two honorary degrees, a medal from the So-

ciété Geologique de France, and honorary membership in the American Association of Petroleum Geologists. He died in Dallas, and his ashes were scattered on Round Mountain, Comanche County, Texas. Despite great disadvantages, Hill made such significant advances in regional geology that he has been called "the father of Texas Cretaceous geology."

• A book-length biography is N. S. Alexander, *Father of Texas Geology: Robert T. Hill* (1976). An extensive obituary is W. E. Wrather, "Robert Thomas Hill (1858–1941)," *American Association of Petroleum Geologists* 25 (1941): 2221–28.

ELLIS L. YOCHELSON

HILL, Thomas (7 Jan. 1818–21 Nov. 1891), Unitarian clergyman, college president, and scientist, was born in New Brunswick, New Jersey, the son of Thomas Hill, a judge, and Henrietta Barker. Hill's father died when Hill was ten, leaving the family only a modest amount of money. In his early years, Hill apprenticed himself to a printer and to an apothecary, but he was not happy in either of these professions. With the financial help of his older brothers, Hill hired a tutor in Latin and Greek and was accepted into Harvard in 1839. In his senior year he published a pamphlet, *Christmas and Poems on Slavery* (1843), and distinguished himself in astronomy by inventing a device called an "occultator," which was used for predicting eclipses. He received his B.A. in 1843. Despite having impressed his professors with his mathematical and scientific aptitude, Hill decided to study for the ministry and graduated from Harvard's Divinity School in 1845.

That fall Hill married Anne Foster Bellows and moved to Waltham, Massachusetts, where he had been offered a parish. Devoted to and well liked by his parishioners, Hill also found time to write on education, science, and religion. In 1849 he wrote *Geometry and Faith*, a book that detailed Hill's abiding belief that science revealed God's laws, a view held by many mid-nineteenth century scientists. During this time he also wrote a number of papers on mathematics and astronomy that were accepted by the American Association for the Advancement of Science as well as Appleton's Encyclopedia. It was Hill's interest in education however, that determined his future. In a Harvard Phi Beta Kappa address entitled "Liberal Education" (1858) and in a series of articles, Hill elaborated a detailed theory of education that was applicable from elementary school to college. Hill proposed that students be schooled in five main areas of study, mathematics, natural history, history, psychology, and theology. Hill believed that each of these subjects served to enhance the student's overall cognitive powers. He wrote, "In a varied course of study . . . the progress of the pupil is actually greater in each branch, than it would be if he had not pursued the other studies. . . . Each man will be the better qualified to labor. . . . In proportion to the breadth and depth of his acquaintance with all other departments" (*The True Order of Studies*). This commitment to the liberal arts eventually brought Hill to the attention of administrators at Antioch College, who were searching for a new president to take the place of the recently deceased Horace Mann.

To the deep regret of his parishioners, Hill accepted the Antioch presidency in September 1859. At Antioch, Hill tried to carry on Mann's work while at the same time implementing his own educational theories. However, Hill was hampered by the lack of an endowment and by the fact that donors became increasingly frugal with the advent of the Civil War. The college suspended operations in 1862, and the Harvard Overseers stepped in to offer Hill the presidency at his alma mater. Frustrated by the lack of funds at Antioch, Hill accepted.

In comparison with his famous successor, Charles William Eliot, Hill's tenure at Harvard is hardly striking, and yet he did attempt to implement a variety of changes. Presaging many of Eliot's efforts, Hill sought to establish a graduate school, electives, and more stringent entrance requirements. Long-standing educational traditions, however, frustrated his reforming efforts. The intransigence of many faculty members combined with personal misfortune and a lack of administrative prowess contributed to Hill's short tenure. In 1864 his wife died shortly after giving birth to their fifth child. In 1866 Hill married Lucy Shepard, but she suffered from ill health and died in 1869. These events, combined with his own failing health, impelled him to resign the Harvard presidency in September 1868.

While the years of the Harvard presidency were Hill's most prominently public ones, he remained active after his resignation. In 1871 he traveled with zoologist Louis Agassiz on a sea voyage to South America. The ten-month voyage was primarily devoted to scientific research, and Hill participated in the capacity of botanist, physicist, and photographer.

In 1873 Hill began a Unitarian parish in Portland, Maine, to which he ministered until his death. Hill also continued to pursue his varied interests. In 1876 he invented the "nautrigon," which was used for nautical navigation. Unconvinced by the new views of science, he spoke out against Darwinism in "The Duty of Unitarians in Regard to Scientific Thought" (*Unitarian Review*, Sept. 1874), republished a number of primers on mathematics that he had written earlier (*Practical Arithmetic* [1881]), and compiled many of his essays on the value of a liberal arts education into *The True Order of Studies* (1876). He died in Waltham.

Hill's career was a varied one, and like many mid-nineteenth-century generalists he was able to make notable contributions to more than one field. Hill's prominence, however, is due mostly to his Harvard presidency. Although he tried to institute some of the innovations that would turn Harvard College into a modern university, almost all of these changes were achieved by his successors.

• Hill's papers, which include his personal correspondence as well as his college addresses, are located in the Harvard Archives at Harvard University Library. Hill wrote a number of practical works on arithmetic and geometry, including *An Elementary Treatise on Arithmetic* (1845), *Puzzles to Teach Geometry* (1848), and *First Lessons in Geometry* (1855). Additional insight into Hill's skepticism of Darwinism can be found in his "Geometry and Biology," *Unitarian Review* 9 (1878): 129–57. Hill's understanding of the relationship between nature and theology is well represented in his *Postulates of Revelation and of Ethics* (1895), *Jesus, the Interpreter of Nature* (1860), and *A Statement of the Natural Sources of Theology* (1877). William G. Land, *Thomas Hill: Twentieth President of Harvard* (1933), provides a comprehensive account of his life and includes lengthy excerpts from Hill's diaries, letters, and published treatises as well as an informal bibliography written in a discursive style. For a memorial, see *Tributes to the Memory of Rev. Thomas Hill* (1892). An obituary is in the *Portland (Maine) Daily Eastern Argus*, 23 Nov. 1891.

LUKE FERNANDEZ

HILL, Ureli Corelli (1802–2 Sept. 1875), violinist and conductor, was born in Connecticut, the son of music teacher and composer Uri K. Hill and Nancy Hull. Hill was named Ureli after his father and his father's physician friend, "Eli," and Corelli after the seventeenth-century Italian violinist. When Hill's parents separated in 1811, each parent agreed to take one son (another sibling had died earlier). Hill lived with his father in New York City and began studying violin. His brother, George Handel "Yankee" Hill, became a comedic actor famous for his portrayals of comic New England characters.

Hill played violin in different bands as a youth and in orchestras throughout his life, but hard work and dedication never surmounted what many considered the lack of a "natural gift." His true talent was demonstrated in leadership roles. From 1828 to 1835 Hill headed the most important choral organization at the time, the New York Sacred Music Society. According to historian Frédéric Louis Ritter, "due to the efforts of this energetic and enthusiastic musician," the society progressed from singing anthems and psalm tunes to performing pieces such as Handel's *Messiah*, the first oratorio presented by the society (and conducted by Hill) on 18 November 1831. The society gained popularity, members, and profit, allowing for yearly performances. In 1843 Hill edited *The New York Sacred Music Society's Collection of Church Music*.

After studying violin and composition from 1835 to 1837 at Louis Spohr's school in Kassel, Germany, Hill returned to New York City and became a successful violin teacher. "With all his eagerness he inculcated a taste for good music" (Krehbiel [1892], p. 55). This taste, however, was rarely satisfied; at the time there was no permanent orchestral society or organized concert series in which students could expect to gain posts or from which audiences could gain pleasure. The Euterpean Society, established about 1799, was composed of amateur instrumental musicians (including Hill, in 1839), and music critics were disappointed with its yearly concerts. "[P]ublic exhibitions were, time and time again, marred, either by insufficient rehearsing, or by a want of practical musical skill, on the part of the performers" (Ritter, p. 221). Furthermore, the society seemed to play more for itself, family, and friends than for the public. Hill sensed America's need for a permanent orchestral society of professional musicians, an orchestra that could guarantee accompaniment to musical societies and operas as well as perform works of the master composers. European opera companies performing in America had long complained of the lack of quality orchestral accompaniment available for their productions. They had either to bring their own orchestras from overseas or gather makeshift ones for each performance.

This situation began to change on 25 June 1839, when Hill organized, then conducted, the best and largest ensemble of musicians (sixty in all) ever gathered in New York. They played a "Musical Solemnity" for the funeral of leading musician Daniel Schlesinger. Although the performance might suffer by today's standards, "for its day it was little short of marvelous, and the musicians themselves were astonished at the effect produced by the music upon the two thousand people in the audience" (Krehbiel [1892], p. 37). The positive response to Weber's overture "Der Freischutz" and the last movement of Beethoven's Second Symphony convinced Hill that the city could support a symphonic society capable of performing several concerts yearly.

Backed by reputable musician friends, in April 1842 Hill accomplished his mission. The first orchestra in America, the New York Philharmonic Society was established with the aim of advancing instrumental music and assuring the performance of the highest quality concerts. Hill conducted the orchestra in its first five seasons, beginning with the society's inaugural concert on 7 December 1842. The performance of Beethoven's Fifth Symphony in C Minor under his direction met with audience approval, and as a result, society membership, audience, and receipts grew, as did the number of New York music clubs and schools. In addition to conducting and playing violin, Hill served as society president from 1842 to 1848, was vice president for seven years, and was a member of the board of directors.

Not all of Hill's ventures proved as successful as the Philharmonic. In 1843 he attempted to make private performances of chamber music (soirées) available to the public. Although some credited Hill with success, one society member condemned the effort as a failure "artistically and financially." Hill also invented a piano that he claimed would not fall out of tune, due to his substitution of bells for wires, but despite exhibitions in New York and London, his piano failed to sell. In 1847 Hill moved to Cincinnati, where he hoped to profit from real estate investments. Three years later he moved back to the New York area and to the Philharmonic as a violinist. An unsuccessful real estate investment in Paterson, New Jersey, left Hill impoverished, and he was forced to request from the society loans he had difficulty repaying.

Hill taught for many years at the Conservatory of Music in Newark, New Jersey, while remaining with the New York Philharmonic Society, until aging and the pressures of orchestral playing led to his resignation in 1873. Penniless at seventy, Hill took a job as an extra at Wallack's Theater in New York but could not survive on his earnings. Hill's wife's name is unknown, but he did have at least one daughter. After an attempt to organize a concert for her merely proved the deterioration of his reputation in the music world, Hill committed suicide at his home in Paterson by taking an overdose of morphine.

For several years the "financially and artistically strong" New York Philharmonic Society found it "not convenient to commemorate by a suitable monument the enthusiastic musician's noble, disinterested deed" (Ritter, p. 356). The plight of Philharmonic players who retired due to illness or age was finally addressed in 1891, when a fund was started, the interest from which was divided among them. In his 1905 article on Hill, Henry Edward Krehbiel stated that only now "New York is enjoying abundant realizations of the dreams of the man to whom . . . more than any American musician who ever lived the present state of instrumental music is due."

• Although he mistook Hill's name (Uriah instead of Ureli) and possibly his place of birth, Frédéric Louis Ritter, *Music in America* (1890), provides an account of Hill's life and contribution to the development of music in America. Ritter also includes a short biography furnished by Anthony Reiff, a member of the New York Philharmonic Society, whose father was one of its most active members when it was first established. See the *New York Atlas*, 3 Feb. 1846, for details concerning Hill's naming and place of birth as well as Henry Edward Krehbiel's article "The Founder of the Philharmonic: His Relations with Mendelssohn, Spohr and Hauptmann" in the *New York Daily Tribune*, 29 Oct. 1905. Numerous references are made to Hill in Howard Shanet, *Early Histories of the New York Philharmonic* (1979), which contains Krehbiel's *The Philharmonic Society of New York: A Memorial* (1892), James Gibbons Huneker's *The Philharmonic Society of New York and Its Seventy-fifth Anniversary* (1917), and John Erskine's *The Philharmonic-Symphony Society of New York: Its First Hundred Years* (1943). Hill's brother, George Handel "Yankee" Hill, mentions his brother briefly in his autobiography, *Scenes from the Life of an Actor* (1853). See also R. O. Mason, *Sketches and Impressions* (1887). Obituaries are in the *New York Times* and the *Newark Daily Advertiser*, both 4 Sept. 1875.

BARBARA L. CICCARELLI

HILL, William (1741–1 Dec. 1816), ironmaster and politician, was born in Belfast, Ireland. Information is unavailable on Hill's parentage. While still a child, he immigrated with his family to York County, Pennsylvania, but moved to New Acquisition (later York County), South Carolina, having learned the trade of iron manufacturing. Hill was probably attracted to this section by the then prevalent belief that land around Nanny's Mountain (on Allison's Creek near the Catawba River) contained extensive iron deposits. He built a home, saw and grist mills, and a bloomery (a forge capable of producing only bar iron). He also acquired more than 5,000 acres of land before the Revolution.

In August 1777 South Carolina governor John Rutledge persuaded Hill to accept a ten-year state loan of £1,000 currency to erect a furnace for the production of cannonballs, grape shot, camp kettles, and other utensils for the revolutionary army. When "Aera" furnace was completed sixteen months later, Hill and Isaac Hayne (who became a co-partner in March 1778) became the sole manufacturers of heavy weapons and munitions south of Virginia. By June 1780 Hill's Iron Works had provided over 106 tons of ironware for the revolutionary forces, as well as farm implements, anvils, hammers, pots, kettles, skillets, and Dutch ovens for settlers in the surrounding region.

The munitions produced by Aera furnace attracted the attention of the enemy. On 18 June 1780 a detachment of British and Tory soldiers burned Hill's ironworks, home, saw and grist mills, and the dwellings of his free and enslaved workers. They also confiscated ninety slaves. The destruction infuriated Hill, prompting him to join Thomas Sumter's brigade as a lieutenant colonel. Hill served 286 days in the militia, participating in local battles at Williamson's Plantation, Rocky Mount, Hanging Rock (where he was wounded in the arm), King's Mountain, Fishdam Ford, and Blackstock's Plantation.

Hill was also active in local and state politics. He represented the area known as New Acquisition in the General Assembly (1776–1778, 1782–1784) and state senate (1778–1780, 1785–1790). In 1788 Hill served as a delegate to the state convention, voting against ratification of the federal Constitution. He represented New Acquisition again at the state Constitutional Convention two years later. Hill returned to the General Assembly in 1800, where he served until 1808 and again from 1812 to 1813. Other offices he held include justice of the peace for Camden District (1783) and York County (1785–1799) and commissioner for inspection of tobacco (1789).

To facilitate the sale of his products throughout the backcountry, Hill supported various transportation schemes: he was a member of the House committee that considered the improvement of inland navigation of the state (1782), a commissioner for clearing a portion of the south fork of the Edisto River (1783), a member of both the Santee (1786) and the Catawba and Wateree canal companies (1787), a commissioner to superintend the opening of the Broad and Pacolet rivers (1801), and a commissioner to superintend the opening of the navigation of the Broad River (1805).

Realizing the importance of iron manufacturing to the state, the South Carolina legislature provided Hill with fifty slaves (obtained from confiscated estates) in 1782 to assist him in rebuilding his ironworks. Four years later he received additional assistance from two Charleston merchants who loaned him £4,350 sterling to renovate and enlarge his enterprise. With such support, Hill was able to rebuild Aera furnace by 1787 and open a second furnace ("Aetna") the following year. These facilities produced mainly pig and bar iron, mill machinery, and nails, as well as household and farm tools. In addition the South Carolina government occasionally contracted with Hill to provide cannon, shot, and swords for the state's arsenals and fortifications.

Hill's furnaces created iron using the Catalan plan, a process that reduced the ore by directly fusing it with charcoal. Instead of using the customary bellows, Hill became one of the first iron manufacturers in the United States to utilize the *trompe*, a European device that used falling water to force a more even flow of air to the furnace. Hill employed over one hundred laborers—the vast majority slaves trained in all aspects of iron manufacturing—to operate the ironworks. A lack of men skilled in iron manufacturing in the region forced Hill to hire workers from Virginia to serve as founders, fillers, and colliers; a farm on site provided food and supplies.

Financial difficulties continually plagued Hill's Iron Works. His troubles began during the war when paper money received from the revolutionary government depreciated rapidly. Furthermore, he was not properly compensated for supplies furnished to the state. Unable to repay the loans he received after the war to rebuild and expand his facility, Hill was forced in 1796 to sell his entire operation to William Edward Hayne, a lowcountry planter and son of Isaac Hayne. Nevertheless, Hill continued to manage the works. Recognizing his losses and contributions during the Revolution, the legislature in 1812 forgave the balance of Hill's debt. Despite his financial troubles, Hill remained a wealthy and influential leader in his community. Shortly before his death he owned a plantation, a 500-acre tract, household items, twenty-one slaves, and livestock—all valued at $5,910.

A man of imposing presence and dignified manner, Hill was reputed to have been a charming conversationalist as well as a forceful orator. Often regarded as the extraordinary company in the state during the eighteenth century, Hill's Iron Works helped to lay the foundation for the development of a modest iron industry in antebellum South Carolina. Married to Jane McCall (date unknown), Hill was the father of six children. Hill died in his home in York County.

• Hill's petitions to the South Carolina General Assembly in 1791, 1793, and 1812, located in the South Carolina Department of Archives and History (SCDAH), provide detailed information regarding the history of his enterprise. In the same archives, York County Deeds, book B, 152–55, 167–71, 177–93, and book E, 132–34, 138–41, 143–44, contain additional information regarding Hill's financial difficulties. For a detailed inventory of Hill's ironworks, its operations, and items manufactured, see (Charleston) *South Carolina and American General Gazette*, 3 Dec. 1779; (Charleston) *City Gazette and Daily Advertiser*, 12 May 1795; (Columbia) *South Carolina State Gazette and Columbian Advertiser*, 20 Dec. 1806; and Articles of Co-Partnership between Isaac Hayne and William Hill, 3 Mar. 1778, subject file (Iron Industry), SCDAH. Thomas Cowan, "William Hill and the Aera Ironworks," *Journal of Early Southern Decorative Arts* 13 (Nov. 1987): 1–32, provides the most thorough description and analysis of Hill's ironworks, while Ernest M. Lander, Jr., "The Iron Industry in Ante-Bellum South Carolina," *Journal of Southern Industry* 20 (Aug. 1954): 337–55, places his business in a larger perspective. Alexander Salley, ed., *Colonel William Hill's Memoirs of the Revolution* (1921), and Daniel P. Hill, *Colonel William Hill and the Campaign of 1780* n.d., describe Hill's military service.

KEITH KRAWCZYNSKI

HILL, Yankee. *See* Hill, George Handel.

HILLARD, George Stillman (22 Sept. 1808–21 Jan. 1879), lawyer, politician, and author, was born in Machias, Maine, the son of John Hillard and Sarah Stillman, whose family was prominent in Massachusetts society. Hillard graduated with first honors in his Harvard class (1828), studied law in Northampton and taught at George Bancroft's experimental Round Hill School, returning to Cambridge for his A.M. (1831) and LL.B. (1832). He entered law practice in 1833 and the next year established a partnership with Charles Sumner that lasted until 1856. Their office was a gathering place for Boston literati, politicians, and assorted hangers-on, to the detriment of the practice. Hillard's law career was busy (Nathaniel Hawthorne and Henry W. Longfellow were clients) but unspectacular. While his peers considered him capable, he was praised more for conscientiousness and integrity than for legal ability. He served as the first dean of the Boston Law School.

Hillard was politically ambitious, and over the years he held a number of offices: state representative (1835), member of the Boston Common Council (1845–1847), state senator (1850), delegate to the state constitutional convention (1853), and Boston city solicitor (1853–1855). A leader, with Sumner, of the Massachusetts "conscience Whigs" who favored a stronger antislavery stand, he did not follow Sumner into radicalism; when the Whig party divided over the slavery question in the 1850s, Hillard was left in the middle, personally esteemed but without a political identity. His removal as Boston city solicitor by the Know Nothings in 1855 ended his public career, although he remained on the sidelines as part owner and editor of the *Boston Courier* (1857–1861). His appointment as U.S. attorney for Massachusetts (1866–1871) was due to his personal connections and literary reputation, as he was no longer aligned with either party.

Hillard was a multitalented man of letters. A polished and elegant occasional orator, his eulogies (e.g., Daniel Webster, 1852) and graduation orations were celebrated. Sumner reports that John Quincy Adams, "Old Man Eloquent" himself, pronounced Hillard's "The Relation of the Poet to His Age" (Phi Beta Kappa address, Harvard, 1843) " 'the finest piece of eloquence he had ever heard.' " Hillard wrote numerous articles, chiefly book reviews for periodicals, including the *North American Review* (twenty-three between 1831 and 1864) and the *Christian Register*, of which he was also an editor. His reviews and criticism covered a wide range of topics in keeping with Hillard's many interests, including law, literature, oratory, and histo-

ry (he was a member of the Massachusetts Historical Society for thirty-six years). Other publications included occasional poems, translations, a series of school readers, a critically praised edition of the works of Edmund Spenser (1839), an uncritical biography of Captain John Smith (1834), and a rather defensive campaign biography of George McClellan (1864). Hillard was admired as a conversationalist by his friends, among whom were Longfellow, Hawthorne, and virtually everyone else on the Boston literary scene. He could be relied on for thoughtful yet invariably warm reviews of their work and help in dealings with publishers. A faithful and entertaining correspondent, his most popular book, *Six Months in Italy* (1853), was based on letters from his trip to Europe in 1847–1848. It remained in print until 1881 and was "probably the most popular book about Italy by an American" (Paul R. Baker, *The Fortunate Pilgrims: Americans in Italy, 1800–1860* [1964]).

His contemporaries, and probably Hillard as well, considered his life a disappointment. His marriage, to Susan Howe in 1834, was apparently not happy. Their only child died in 1838, aged two. Hillard was pale, slight, and prone to minor illnesses; his persona was not warm; his mannerisms and voice, while "musical" and refined, were considered effeminate; and he was, thus, never an effective popular speaker. These were significant liabilities for an aspiring politician, and the offices Hillard held were essentially party appointments. He never escaped having to work for a living; his literary friends saw this as distracting him from his true calling as a man of letters, while his legal friends thought his literary predilections crippled his career. Yet, as an exemplary Brahmin, with his catholicity of interests, tireless efforts on behalf of Boston writers, and integration of a literary and political career, Hillard was both a vital component and a creator of the "atmosphere" that made Boston the American cultural capital of his day. Hillard died at his home in Longwood, Massachusetts.

• Other published works by Hillard include a translation of M. Guizot's *Essay on . . . Washington* (1840); *The Connection between Geography and History* (1846); "Letters of Silas Standfast to his Friend Jotham," in *Discussions on the Constitution Proposed to the People of Massachusetts by the Convention of 1853* (1854); *Selections from the Writings of Walter Savage Landor* (1856); and several memoirs. Letters from Hillard can be found in Julian Hawthorne, *Nathaniel Hawthorne and His Wife* (1884); Edward Pierce, *Memoir and Letters of Charles Sumner* (1878); and in the Francis Lieber Papers in the Henry E. Huntington Library (San Marino, Calif.). The most substantial biography is Francis Palfrey, "Memoir of the Hon. George S. Hillard," Massachusetts Historical Society, *Proceedings* 20 (1882), which includes remarks by Oliver Wendell Holmes and others. Hillard's relationship to Hawthorne is discussed extensively by Thomas Woodson in his introduction to vol. 15 of the centenary edition of Hawthorne's works (1984), and his political career figures in David Donald, *Charles Sumner and the Coming of the Civil War* (1960). An obituary appears in the *Boston Transcript*, 21 Jan. 1879, and a memorial from the Massachusetts Bar Association appears in the same paper, 23 Jan. 1879.

CHARLES H. BRICHFORD

HILLE, Einar (28 June 1894–12 Feb. 1980), mathematician, was born Carl Einar Heuman in New York City, the only son of Carl August Heuman, a civil engineer in Sweden, and Edla Eckman. His parents separated before his birth, and he would not meet his father until forty-three years later. The name Hille was a mistranslation of Heuman and was subsequently adopted by his mother. At the age of two Hille returned with his mother to Sweden, where he remained for the next twenty-four years.

From 1900 to 1911 Hille attended the private school Palmsgrenska Samskola in Stockholm, after which he entered the University of Stockholm. His initial intention was to become a chemist, and for two years he worked in the laboratory of future Nobel Prize–winning chemist Hans von Euler-Chelpin. However, after publishing his first paper in 1913 (with von Euler), Hille felt he lacked the manual dexterity and patience for laboratory work, and he thus switched his studies to mathematics. He studied with the distinguished mathematicians Ivar Bendixson and Helge von Koch and received his Cand.Ph. and M.Ph. (the equivalents of a B.A. and M.S., respectively) in 1913 and 1914. Further study with Marcel Riesz and a thesis on conformal mapping led to a Lic.Ph. in 1916. During 1916 and 1917 Hille served in the Swedish army as a typist, and during that time he decided to study for a Ph.D. in mathematics. Unassisted, he embarked on his own program of mathematical research and produced a dissertation, "Some Problems concerning Spherical Harmonics," for which he was awarded a Ph.D. in 1918. The following year he received the Mittag Leffler Prize and attained Docent status at the University of Stockholm. From 1918 to 1920 Hille worked in the Swedish civil service.

Upon being awarded a fellowship from the Swedish-American Foundation, Hille spent the 1920–1921 academic year at Harvard University. There he studied primarily with George David Birkhoff and Oliver Dimon Kellogg, and during the following year he was the Benjamin Peirce Instructor at Harvard. He then moved to Princeton University, where he was successively an instructor from 1922 to 1923, an assistant professor from 1923 to 1927, and an associate professor from 1927 to 1933. Hille then moved to Yale University, where he was professor from 1933 to 1962 and director of graduate studies in mathematics from 1938 to 1962. During his years at Yale he directed twenty-four doctoral students. An inveterate traveler both before and after his retirement in 1962, he also held visiting positions in Stanford, Chicago, Uppsala, Nancy, Paris, Mainz, Canberra, Haifa, Bombay, Irvine, Eugene, Albuquerque, and San Diego.

Hille was president of the American Mathematical Society (1947–1948) and its colloquium lecturer in 1944. He served as an editor of *Annals of Mathematics* (1929–1933) and the *Transactions of the American Mathematical Society* (1937–1943). He was elected a member of the National Academy of Sciences in 1953 and the Royal Academy of Sciences of Stockholm. In 1951 he was made a knight of the Order of the North Star (Sweden).

Hille's research may be divided into two major periods. From 1917 to 1938 his primary interests were in classical analysis, which included special functions, Dirichlet series, and linear differential and integral equations. During the years 1928–1935 he also had a noteworthy collaboration with Jacob David Tamarkin on the summability of Fourier series. From 1938 to 1953 his primary activity focused on functional analysis, particularly the theory of semi-groups. This led to his Colloquium monograph, *Functional Analysis and Semi-Groups* (1948; rev. ed. with Ralph S. Phillips, 1957). The first American book specifically devoted to modern functional analysis, it was both a textbook and a research monograph. It included notable accounts of the calculus of vector-valued functions, a function theory of vector-valued functions, an operational calculus, and the theory of Banach algebras. In addition, it contained Hille's most famous result: the Hille-Yosida Semi-Group Theorem. Hille was one of the few mathematicians who brought to his study of functional analysis–operator theory some twenty years of experience in classical analysis. Moreover, he was almost unique among mathematicians in applying functional analysis to investigate classical problems, rather than simply considering abstract situations for their own sake. On one occasion, while addressing a younger generation of mathematicians who were imbued with the spirit of abstract ideas, he admonished that their work—if successful—was also destined to become "classical." Hille never lost his love of classical mathematics and wrote the textbooks *Analytic Function Theory* (2 vols., 1959, 1964), *Analysis* (2 vols., 1964, 1966), *Lectures on Ordinary Differential Equations* (1969), *Methods in Classical and Functional Analysis* (1972), and *Ordinary Differential Equations in the Complex Domain* (1976). Through his boundless enthusiasm, prolific research, and inspiring teaching, Hille made a significant contribution to the mathematical program at Yale, as well as to the American mathematical community at large.

On 10 August 1937 he married Kirsti Ore (the sister of his Yale colleague Oystein Ore); they had two sons. His final years were spent in La Jolla, California, and he remained mathematically active until his death there. Indeed, a few weeks before his death, the terminally ill Hille left the hospital to address a conference being held in his honor in Laguna Beach, California.

• Hille wrote a personal account, entitled "Accomplishments" (dated Oct. 1953), which is held in the Archives of the National Academy of Sciences. His most influential papers were published as *Einar Hille: Classical Analysis and Functional Analysis—Selected Papers*, ed. Robert R. Kallman (1975). This contains the text of a lecture given at the Yale Mathematical Colloquium in 1962. A brief autobiographical sketch is given in *McGraw Hill Modern Scientists and Engineers* 2 (1980). Additional personal recollections may be found in the following articles: Nathan Jacobson, "Einar Hille, His Yale Years, A Personal Recollection," and Kôsaku Yosida, "Some Aspects of E. Hille's Contributions to Semi-

Group Theory," both in *Integral Equations and Operator Theory* 4 (1981). Obituaries, which include a list of his publications, appear in National Academy of Sciences, *Biographical Memoirs* 63 (1994): 219–44, and in the *Bulletin of the American Mathematical Society* 4 (May 1981).

JOSEPH D. ZUND

HILLEBRAND, William Francis (12 Dec. 1853–7 Feb. 1925), geochemist, was born in Honolulu, Hawaii, the son of Wilhelm Hillebrand and Anna Post. His father, a physician and commissioner of immigration from the German state of Westphalia, was also an expert on the botany of the Sandwich Islands. Young Hillebrand traveled extensively with his parents, visiting the United States, Europe, China, Java, and India. Unsure of what career to pursue, he studied from 1870 to 1872 at the newly established Cornell University in Ithaca, New York, as preparatory work for a proper German university education. In 1872, at his father's suggestion, he chose to study chemistry at the university in Heidelberg with Robert Wilhelm Bunsen and Gustav Robert Kirchoff, who had become famous scientists for their collaborative development of spectral analysis in 1859–1861.

Hillebrand's doctoral research and early publications, work begun in collaboration with his friend Thomas Herbert Norton, were on the rare earth metals cerium, lanthanum, and "didymium" (later found to be a mixture of neodymium and praseodymium). Hillebrand took his Ph.D. from Heidelberg in March 1875, then broadened his chemical education with study at the University of Strassburg (in 1876–1877) and at the Mining Academy at Freiburg (in 1877–1878).

In the fall of 1878 Hillebrand returned to the United States, where he perceived a great opportunity in the mineral exploitation of the Rocky Mountain West. In the summer of 1879 he moved to Leadville, Colorado, where he became a partner in an assaying firm. As an assayer, he apparently impressed Samuel Franklin Emmons, chief of the Rocky Mountain Division of the newly established U.S. Geological Survey. In 1880 Hillebrand joined the survey as a mineral chemist in Denver, Colorado, where he remained for five years. As the sole chemist with the Rocky Mountain Division, he used his training in new methods of analysis, coauthoring several papers with geologist Whitman Cross on minerals not previously known to occur in the Rockies. These discoveries included baryta and the lanthanoid minerals gadolinite and samarskite. In 1881 he married Martha May Westcott; they had two children.

In November 1885 Hillebrand was transferred to the USGS laboratory in Washington, D.C. There he earned a reputation for thorough and accurate mineral analysis, achieved largely through his development of standardized and systematized methods of analysis. He was especially skilled at discovering faulty analyses caused by contaminants in apparatus and reagents. This interest in analytical methods led to several publications between 1897 and 1907 and culminated in a posthumously published textbook, *Applied Inorganic Analysis* (1929). Beginning in 1904–1905 Hillebrand led a cooperative effort of the USGS, the National Bureau of Standards, and the American Chemical Society's Committee for Uniformity in Technical Analysis to develop a standard collection of reference ore samples. This effort was rewarded in 1909 when Hillebrand was appointed chief chemist of the Bureau of Standards.

Hillebrand's precision analyses led to his near discovery of terrestrial helium. Undertaking spectral analysis of the mineral uraninite during the late 1880s, he detected anomalous spectral lines. Too busy to procure and test another sample, he attributed the lines solely to nitrogen, which was present in the sample. Sir William Ramsay, searching for compounds of argon, read Hillebrand's published paper and repeated the analyses. After chemically removing the nitrogen, Ramsay recognized the remaining gas as helium. Hillebrand's congratulatory letter to Ramsay provides a revealing glimpse into the process of discovery and near-discovery in science.

Around 1902 Hillebrand undertook two other series of analysis, both leading to commercial developments. In a study of the Portland cement industry, he suggested that potash could be profitably recovered from the manufacturing process. His discovery that some jarosite contained lead, instead of potassium, resulted in several new lead mines being opened.

Hillebrand was active in the early growth and consolidation of the American Chemical Society. Following a revolt led by his friend Frank Wigglesworth Clarke, Hillebrand resigned in 1879 because he was fed up with the parochial overemphasis on the New York City area. He rejoined in 1893, after the schism was healed by George Chapman Caldwell, who had been ACS president in 1892. After rejoining, Hillebrand was extremely active and led a successful effort to represent the interests of technical chemists and industry, beginning with the ACS's absorption of the *Journal of Analytical and Applied Chemistry* in 1893. As ACS president in 1906, he promoted strongly the idea that the ACS must represent all facets of the chemical profession, including technical interests. Finally, his efforts led to the establishment of a new ACS publication, the *Journal of Industrial and Engineering Chemistry*, in 1909.

Narrow in his professional interests and focused in his pursuits, Hillebrand was not an innovative chemist. He did, however, utilize his management skills, leadership ability, and technical competence to further the interests of the chemical profession. In addition to the American Chemical Society, Hillebrand was a member of the American Association for the Advancement of Science, the American Society for the Testing of Materials, the American Philosophical Society, the Geological Society of Washington, the Göttingen Gesellschaft, the National Academy of Sciences, and the Washington Academy of Sciences. He served as chair of general chemistry from 1892 to 1910 with the National College of Pharmacy, which after 1906 was affiliated with George Washington University. His protégés at the USGS honored him by naming a mineral, hydrated calcium silicate, Hillebrandite in 1909. He received the Chandler Medal from Columbia in 1916. He received an honorary doctorate from Heidelberg in 1925 and died in Washington, D.C.

• Hillebrand's *Applied Inorganic Analysis*, with G. E. F. Lundell (1929), went through at least nine printings and is a testament to the lasting influence of Hillebrand's standard methods and rigorous expectations. Details on Hillebrand's near discovery of terrestrial helium are in Hillebrand, "Occurrence of Nitrogen in Uraninite," *Science* 40 (1890): 384–94; and "New Analyses of Uraninite," *Science* 42 (1891): 390–93. Hillebrand stated his aspirations as president of ACS in "The Present and Future of the American Chemical Society (Presidential Address)," *Journal of the American Chemical Society* 29 (1907): 1–18. Several brief biographical accounts of Hillebrand were published by his contemporaries following his death. These include Frank W. Clarke, "Biographical Memoir of William Francis Hillebrand," National Academy of Sciences, *Biographical Memoirs* 12 (1929): 43–70, which includes a complete bibliography of Hillebrand's works; E. T. Allen, "Pen Portrait of William Francis Hillebrand," *Journal of Chemical Education* 9 (Jan. 1932): 73–83; and Charles E. Waters, "Hillebrand," *Science* 61 (1925): 53. Virginia Bartow, "W. F. Hillebrand and Some Early Letters," *Journal of Chemical Education* 26 (1949): 367–72, is based on letters discovered by Hillebrand's son. On Hillebrand's role in the ACS see Charles Albert Browne and Mary Elvira Weeks, *A History of the American Chemical Society* (1952).

PAT MUNDAY

HILLEGAS, Michael (22 Apr. 1729–29 Sept. 1804), colonial merchant, revolutionary, and first treasurer of the United States, was born in Philadelphia, Pennsylvania, the son of Michael Hillegas, a naturalized Palatine German and Philadelphia merchant, and Margaret (maiden name unknown). Orphaned at age twenty-one, Hillegas by the following year had taken control of his father's business interests and begun a career that continued to expand and prosper throughout his life. He sold metal goods, including stoves and stills; had interests in iron manufacturing, sugar refinement, and real estate; and owned at least partial interest in the ship *Henrietta*. In 1753 he married Henrietta Boude; they had ten children.

Hillegas also developed an interest in music and musical instruments that spanned his personal and professional lives. Hillegas's shop in Philadelphia, on Second Street between Race and Arch, was reputedly the first to specialize in musical merchandise in British North America. His advertisements in Philadelphia newspapers from the 1750s through the 1770s make frequent mention of his selling flutes, harpsichords, stringed instruments, pump organs, sheet music, and musical composition books. He purchased one of Benjamin Franklin's glass armonicas, an instrument Franklin invented, while Franklin was serving as provincial agent in London. Hillegas's interests in music went beyond selling. In 1775 John Adams accompanied him on a boat excursion and reported in his diary: "Hillegas is . . . a great Musician—talks perpetually of

the Forte and Piano, of Handel & c. and Songs and Tunes. He plays upon the Fiddle."

Hillegas played civic roles that befitted his growing importance as a leader in the merchant community. He was elected assessor for Philadelphia County in 1759 and county commissioner in 1761. In 1762 he was a member of the commission that laid out Fort Mifflin in Pennsylvania. In 1764 the Quaker party suffered a political defeat that unseated Assembly Speaker Franklin. Stung by its setback, the party nominated Hillegas as representative to the Pennsylvania Assembly from Philadelphia County in 1765, hoping that his ethnicity would be an olive branch to Pennsylvania's German community. As a member of the assembly from 1765 to 1776, Hillegas served on numerous committees, including Account and Audit; addressed issues of night watches and street lighting for Philadelphia; revised methods of collecting taxes; and worked on civic improvements, such as roads, highways, and dams.

Beyond his elected offices, Hillegas was active in numerous social and philanthropic activities. "Am well satisfied that nothing in this World affords you more pleasure Than when you can render service to the Community, be it in whatsoever way Possible," Hillegas wrote to Franklin in 1769 (*Franklin Papers*, ed. Leonard Labaree, et al. [1959–] vol. 16, pp. 235–36). In that letter he asked Franklin for advice on securing towns from house fires, using Enlightenment ideas of observation and discussion in scientific work to ascertain which roofing material was most fire resistant and cost effective. In many instances, Hillegas used his business acumen to support community activities. He subscribed to the creation of the Pennsylvania Hospital; was a member of committees to distribute money to the poor and run lotteries to build a public school in Germantown, Pennsylvania, and Anglican churches in Philadelphia's Northern Liberties; was a director of the Philadelphia Contributionship for the Insurance of Houses from Loss by Fire; and was a member of the vestry of Christ Church (Anglican). He was elected a member of the American Society for the Promotion of Useful Knowledge (later merged with the American Philosophical Society) in 1768 and was also a member of the St. John's Masonic Lodge of Philadelphia.

Hillegas's involvement in the events that led to the Revolution began in 1774, when he was elected a member of the Committee of Correspondence, which sought to redress the Boston Port Act. His vantage point as a merchant prompted his advocacy of free trade for American mercantile interests and colored his beliefs on Parliament's actions. From 1774 to mid-1776 Hillegas shifted from being a pro-British to a radical revolutionary member of the Pennsylvania Assembly, and by the summer of 1776 he was an important swing vote in the cause of independence. He used his considerable business skill and community understanding to support the cause of the Revolution. He was appointed treasurer of the Pennsylvania Committee of Safety in July 1775 and was elected to the committee in April 1776. Congress appointed Hillegas and George Clymer Continental treasurers on 9 August 1775, and Hillegas assumed the position of sole treasurer on 6 August 1776 after Clymer took his seat in the Continental Congress. Hillegas was appointed provincial treasurer of Pennsylvania in May 1776. On 6 September 1777 he was appointed treasurer of the United States and continued in the position until 11 September 1789, when the Treasury Department was created under the new federal government. In July 1780, in order to secure currency and ensure regular supplies for the American military, The Bank of Pennsylvania was founded "in order to raise supplies for Continental troops"; Hillegas subscribed £4,000 to its creation. Hillegas also supported and helped organize the Bank of North America in December 1781.

The Hillegas household exemplifies women's role in the affairs of the Revolution. Henrietta Hillegas raised money and prepared clothing for troops and cared for the sick. George Washington wrote to Henrietta Hillegas and the four other members of her committee that their work "embellishes the American character with a new trait; by proving that the love of country is blended with those softer domestic virtues, which have always been allowed to be more peculiarly *your own*" (John C. Fitzpatrick, ed., *The Writings of George Washington*, vol. 21 [1937], p. 221).

After the Revolution Hillegas continued in a number of civic roles. In 1781 the Pennsylvania Assembly asked Hillegas to prepare its wartime journals for publication, along with other important papers, and he corresponded with governors of other states asking that they preserve their revolutionary records in a similar manner. He took an active interest in Mathew Carey's magazine, the *American Museum*, and recommended pieces to the editor that he thought would inspire morality or patriotism. In 1793, he was elected an alderman of Philadelphia and was appointed an associate judge in the mayor's court, holding both offices until his death. His business interests also continued to grow in the 1790s. He was an original investor in the Lehigh Coal Mining Company, the Pennsylvania Land Company, and the Martin Forge in Lancaster, Pennsylvania. Hillegas died in Philadelphia.

• Hillegas's papers are in the collections of the Historical Society of Pennsylvania and the American Philosophical Society. His business and political careers can be traced through the advertisements and news items in the *Pennsylvania Gazette* and *Pennsylvania Packet*. A standard biography of Hillegas is Edna St. Clair Whitney, *Michael Hillegas and his Descendants* (1891). A. G. Roeber's study of Pennsylvania's German settlers *Palatines, Liberty, and Property: German Lutherans in Colonial British America* (1993) explicates the Hillegas family's move to North America and Hillegas's early career. For studies of his era in colonial American politics, see Gary B. Nash, *The Urban Crucible: Social Change, Political Consciousness, and the Origins of the American Revolutions* (1979); Richard Alan Ryerson, *The Revolution Is Now Begun: The Radical Committees of Philadelphia 1765–1776* (1978), and Ryerson, "Portrait of a Colonial Oligarchy: The Quaker Elite in the Pennsylvania Assembly, 1729–1776," in *Power and Status: Officeholding in Colonial America*, ed. Bruce C.

Daniels (1986). Hillegas's nonpolitical interests are considered in JoAnn Taricani, "Musical Commerce in Eighteenth-Century Philadelphia: The Letters of Michael Hillegas," *Pennsylvania Magazine of History and Biography* 113, no. 4 (Oct. 1989): 609–25, and Steven Bullock, "The Revolutionary Transformation of American Freemasonry, 1752–1792," *William and Mary Quarterly* 47, no. 3: 347–69.

GEORGE BOUDREAU

HILLENBRAND, Reynold Henry (19 July 1905–22 May 1979), priest and social activist, was born in Chicago, Illinois, the son of George Hillenbrand, a dentist, and Eleanor Schmitt. Reared in a comfortable, middle-class setting near Chicago's Lincoln Park, Hillenbrand attended St. Michael's Church, run by the German Redemptorists. He was educated by the School Sisters of Notre Dame and the Brothers of Mary. In 1920 he followed his elder brother, Frederick Hillenbrand, to Chicago's Quigley Preparatory Seminary, where he developed a lifelong love for English literature and served as the editor of the seminary newspaper. In 1924 he continued his studies for the priesthood at the newly built St. Mary of the Lake Seminary in Area (now Mundelein), Illinois. He completed his studies for ordination with the Jesuits, who directed the academic program at the seminary. He was ordained to the priesthood on 29 September 1929 and completed a doctorate at St. Mary of the Lake, writing a dissertation on the indwelling of the Holy Spirit. Upon completion of his doctoral work in 1931, his superior, Cardinal George Mundelein, sent him abroad for a one-year stay in Rome. Hillenbrand returned in 1932 and took up a position at Quigley Seminary as a teacher of English literature.

When Hillenbrand returned, the Great Depression had fallen on Chicago with full force. Near his residence was a "Hooverville" inhabited by homeless men, symptomatic of the larger economic and social distress of the city. He resided with Monsignor Joseph Morrison, the rector of Chicago's Holy Name Cathedral, who exercised an enormous influence over the young priest. Morrison was a lively and volatile man who literally opened the church doors to the poor and homeless and apparently challenged Hillenbrand to consider the larger context for the economic disarray in the city and nation. Morrison also had a great passion for the Roman Catholic liturgy and saw in a reformed Roman Catholic liturgy, emphasizing popular participation, an antidote to the excessive individualism of American life. Hillenbrand integrated these twin themes of social justice and liturgical reform into his own priestly career, and they became the controlling motifs of his life.

From 1933 to 1936 Hillenbrand headed the Diocesan Mission Band, a group of traveling priests who preached missions or retreats in the various parishes of the city. He also conducted a class for the young women of Rosary College, preparing them for street preaching work in the South under the auspices of the Catholic Evidence Guild. In 1936 Cardinal Mundelein appointed Hillenbrand to take over St. Mary of the

Lake Seminary. From 1936 until his dismissal in 1944, Hillenbrand exercised a tremendous influence over the lives of hundreds of Chicago priests. As seminary rector, he introduced a series of reforms that constituted a dramatic departure from previous seminary regimen.

Hillenbrand's constant point of reference was papal teaching, which he invoked as the inspiration and authority for his actions. At the seminary he moved vigorously to reform both liturgical formation and practice for the seminarians while urging them to be aware of and involved in ameliorating many of the social problems of the day. Hillenbrand insisted that the seminarians congregate in the seminary's main chapel and pray the responses of the Mass together, as opposed to the older custom of separate house chapels and silence at the Mass. He revivified the practices of Holy Week, making them more accessible to popular participation, and introduced the students to the writings and periodicals of the Liturgical movement emanating from Collegeville in the 1920s and 1930s. Hillenbrand's interest in liturgical reform, particularly in cultivating intelligent and vocal participation from the congregation, anticipated the reforms of Vatican II in 1964 and afterward. Moreover, Hillenbrand also moved into leadership roles in national organizations of like-minded reformers, helping to host the first National Liturgical Week at Holy Name Cathedral in Chicago. He was a major force in the organization of the National Liturgical Conference, which stimulated energies for reform nationwide.

In addition to his liturgical reforms, Hillenbrand took pains to acquaint the cloistered seminarians with the vexatious social issues of the day along with the distinctively Catholic solutions to the problems. Through a series of speakers, including Catholic Worker founder Dorothy Day, labor priest Francis Haas, and Hispanic advocate Robert Lucey, and summertime experiences in parishes and urban neighborhoods, the seminarians were exposed to some of the most dynamic and effective social activists in the American Catholic church of the 1930s and 1940s. As a result, a significant number of priests devoted themselves to labor organizing, work with minorities, and the cause of liturgical reform on the parish level.

After Mundelein's death in 1939, a more conservative and less sympathetic successor, Samuel A. Stritch, ultimately dismissed Hillenbrand. Hillenbrand's difficulties with Stritch probably emanated from the prelate's discomfort with the rector's liturgical innovations as well as his increasingly vocal critique of Chicago's business community. Hillenbrand often denounced the forces of laissez-faire capitalism and materially assisted in the organization of industrial unions, which took place at a rapid pace during the 1930s and 1940s. Deeply committed to social justice and unwilling to cultivate favor among some of the powerful clerical figures of Chicago, Hillenbrand had no base of support. Consequently, when he actively participated in a strike against Montgomery Ward in the summer of 1944, Stritch abruptly dismissed him

and assigned him to an affluent parish on Chicago's North Shore in the city of Hubbards Woods.

The departure from the seminary came as a blow to Hillenbrand and to his students. However, he continued to be a force within diocesan life through Specialized Catholic Action, a variant of a larger movement begun by Pope Pius X and Pope Pius XI to encourage Catholic lay activity in a variety of endeavors to re-Christianize society. Although Catholic Action included a wide array of groups, Hillenbrand seized on a model developed by a Belgian priest, Joseph Cardijn, who worked to re-Christianize French factory workers by forming small cells, or groups, differentiated by gender, age, and occupation, all devoted to the transformation of their immediate environment through the methodology "observe, judge, and act." This method, operating under the influence of Christian teaching and liturgical participation, would bring about the desired regeneration of social life. Just as important was the essentially lay character of these movements. Although they all had clerical guidance and instruction, the leadership and the work was done by lay "apostles" at work, school, or home.

The formation of small groups devoted to social regeneration, formed by a practical grasp of church teaching, especially papal encyclicals, and energized by active participation in the liturgy, became the passion of Hillenbrand's life. Even after his dismissal from the seminary, he continued to work closely with the groups of Young Christian Workers and Students that were forming around Chicago and the nation, largely responding to the urgings of Hillenbrand and the many young priests and others who came under his influence. Throughout the country, but particularly in Chicago, cells of priests, sisters, young adults, workers in various industries and professions, and teenagers met continually to observe-judge-act according to the challenges of their respective environments. By 1946 the number of these cells was so great that Cardinal Stritch appointed a priest to direct the various Catholic Action movements in the archdiocese.

In the late 1940s Hillenbrand brought his vision and organizational skills to the formation of the Christian Family Movement (CFM), a popular Catholic program that appealed to the growing number of young families who were looking for direction and guidance from the church in raising their families. As with the cells, Hillenbrand insisted on the predominance of the lay character of the organization, and Chicago lawyer Patrick Crowley and his wife Patricia Crowley assumed major roles in leading the group. Although the CFM spread throughout the nation, Chicago was acknowledged as the unofficial capital of the movement.

In 1949 Hillenbrand was severely injured in an automobile accident while traveling in Oklahoma. After nearly one year in the hospital, he was somewhat disabled and subject to severe migraine headaches. As he aged, his irascibility and unwillingness to compromise became more entrenched. He had major quarrels with many of his former clerical supporters and protégés and eventually broke with the Crowleys when they urged a change in the papal ban on artificial contraception in 1967.

The Second Vatican Council (1962–1965) seemed to ratify many of the initiatives for which Hillenbrand had worked and suffered. In the first session the council mandated sweeping liturgical reforms that restored the use of the vernacular in the Mass and Sacraments and insisted on popular participation in the Mass by all congregants. The council's Constitution on the Church in the Modern World insisted on Catholic engagement with the major social issues of the day. A host of other ideas long pressed by Hillenbrand, from adult education to seminary reform, also seemed to vindicate his earlier initiatives. By the mid-1960s many referred to him reverentially as a prophet of the post-conciliar era.

Yet because of his deteriorating health and his distress at what he perceived to be a lack of respect for the authority and teaching of the popes, Hillenbrand did not adjust to this new era of Catholicism smoothly or happily. He was especially offended at the extent and level of opposition to Pope Paul VI's encyclical banning artificial birth control. His devotion to papal utterance was unbending. Moreover, his administrative style in his parish, characterized at times by a heavy-handed authoritarianism, was out of step with many newer initiatives demanding wider consultation with younger clergy and with laity. In 1973 Hillenbrand was removed from his parish by an edict of Cardinal John P. Cody. He spent the last six years of his life a virtual recluse, apart from many of the friends and people who had once looked on him as an idol. When he died in Chicago, his obituary in Chicago's Catholic newspaper was terse and uninformative.

• Hillenbrand's personal papers are at the archives of the University of Notre Dame. For information on Hillenbrand see Steven M. Avella, *This Confident Church: Catholic Leadership and Life in Chicago, 1940–1965* (1992); "Reynold Hillenbrand and Chicago Catholicism," *U.S. Catholic Historian* 9 (Fall 1990): 353–70; and Robert L. Tuzik, "The Contribution of Msgr. Reynold Hillenbrand (1905–1979) to the Liturgical Movement in the United States" (Ph.D. diss., Univ. of Notre Dame, 1989).

STEVEN M. AVELLA

HILLENKOETTER, Roscoe Henry (8 May 1897–18 June 1982), first director of the Central Intelligence Agency (CIA), was born in a German-speaking district of St. Louis, Missouri, the son of Alexander Hillenkoetter, a postal inspector, and his French wife, Olinda Du Ker. He served with the Atlantic Fleet in World War I, graduated from the U.S. Naval Academy in 1919, and then returned to duties on both submarines and surface craft. In 1928 he became involved in intelligence operations when he helped to supervise elections in Nicaragua. His interest and expertise in intelligence increased when he traveled to Europe as a naval courier, meeting with William C. Bullitt, the newly appointed American ambassador in Moscow, who persuaded Hillenkoetter to become assistant naval attaché in Paris in 1933. That same year he married

Jane E. Clark; they had one child. By this time "Hilly," as his friends called him, spoke Spanish and Italian as well as the English, German, and French he had learned in St. Louis. Already well equipped as a foreign intelligence officer, he served several tours of duty as naval attaché in France. In 1940–1941, during the Vichy government, he worked with the French underground and was instrumental in organizing the escape to safety of men hunted by the German authorities.

Hillenkoetter was wounded on board the *West Virginia* when the Japanese sunk the battleship at Pearl Harbor in December 1941. He subsequently took an even keener interest in intelligence matters. Under Commander in Chief Admiral Chester W. Nimitz, he organized naval intelligence in the Pacific area.

In 1945 President Harry S. Truman disbanded the Office of Strategic Services (OSS), the wartime intelligence agency, and dismissed its director, William J. Donovan, a forceful bureaucratic expansionist whom the president disliked. Instead, Truman set up the Central Intelligence Group (CIG) as a small-scale holding operation. On 1 May 1947 Hillenkoetter took charge of the CIG, which became the CIA on 18 September under the terms of the National Security Act of that year. The new agency was an essential part of the American plan to contain Soviet expansionism at the start of the Cold War and was intended to eradicate duplication of effort in the foreign intelligence areas by the Federal Bureau of Investigation, the State Department, the air force, the army, and the navy. The CIA was established to coordinate the activities of the other agencies, to develop the capability to collect information using its own resources, and to produce integrated and objective intelligence estimates to help the president in making national security decisions.

The CIA expanded under Hillenkoetter, but slowly. To the annoyance of admirers of Donovan's secret operations, Hillenkoetter did not seem to throw his weight behind an increase in the agency's covert operational capabilities. On the one hand he sanctioned "psychological warfare," the use of clandestine propaganda and secret subsidies. He even went against the advice of the agency's lawyers by intervening in elections in France and Italy, and in 1949 he secured from Congress the Central Intelligence Act, which allowed the CIA to engage via unvouchered funds in worldwide operations concealed from Americans and foreigners alike. On the other hand Hillenkoetter, like President Truman, avoided schemes with a paramilitary dimension and plans to overthrow democratically elected governments. He fought to contain the activities of Frank G. Wisner, the director of the CIA's Office of Policy Coordination. The office, set up in 1948, was nominally under Hillenkoetter's control, but in practice it was a hotbed of covert activism supported by Donovan and powerful factions in the Truman administration.

Hillenkoetter attempted to develop the capabilities of another important branch of the CIA, the Office of Research and Evaluation (ORE). Meant to meet the informational needs of a president who had to make critical decisions about national security, ORE ran up against the jealous obstructionism of other intelligence agencies that were supposed to cooperate with it. To his critics, Hillenkoetter seemed to be incapable of managing Washington's intelligence bureaucracy, an opinion based partly on his relatively lowly naval rank. His inadequacies were blamed for the CIA's failure to predict the Bogota riots of 1948, to correct the CIG estimate that the Soviets would not have the nuclear bomb until 1951 (in fact they exploded a device in 1949), and to forewarn President Truman of North Korea's attack on South Korea in 1950. But even in ORE's early days, its analysts began to enjoy success. They were alert to divisions in the Soviet leadership, they predicted the outbreak of serious trouble in the Philippines, and they exposed as unfounded a dangerous report from air force intelligence that the Soviets were about to invade Scandinavia. Moreover, some of the criticism would have been better directed at the CIA's political masters in the executive branch of government, who turned deaf ears to intelligence warnings they did not want to hear. Yet the criticism was politically damaging to Hillenkoetter, and when he returned to his beloved navy on 7 October 1950 he did not take with him an unblemished reputation.

From November 1950 to September 1951 Hillenkoetter was in command of the heavy cruiser *St. Paul* and of the Seventh Task Force of the U.S. Navy in the Korean War. He was responsible for the protection of Taiwan, and his force provided cover for the South Korean forces as they advanced up the east coast to the north and then retreated before the Chinese onslaught. Hillenkoetter's ships also protected General Douglas MacArthur's forces during the Inchon landings. After the war Hillenkoetter served as inspector general of the navy and retired in 1957 with the rank of vice admiral. Thereafter he entered private business, serving in senior executive positions with a shipping company, a construction firm, and a defense contractor. He died in Mount Sinai Hospital, New York City.

Hillenkoetter has been both neglected and maligned by historians. His tenure came between the reputed glories of Donovan's OSS in World War II and the so-called Golden Age of the CIA under Allen W. Dulles, who served as director from 1953 to 1961. Hillenkoetter's reputation suffered at the hands of contemporary rivals pushed aside by the new CIA, frustrated expansionists within the agency, historians dedicated to the defense of Hillenkoetter's predecessors and successors, and ideologically committed critics of the CIA and those associated with it. His reputation or lack thereof was also self-inflicted; as Truman observed in a private set of valedictory notes, Hillenkoetter was "self-effacing" and characterized by "extreme modesty," in contrast to other U.S. intelligence chiefs like Donovan, Dulles, and the FBI's J. Edgar Hoover. Hillenkoetter's critics are divided between those who believe he expanded the CIA too much and those who think he did too little. In reality he pursued a moderate course and was a pioneer who made some mistakes yet overcame difficulties in exceptionally harsh and confusing times.

• Much of the information relating to Hillenkoetter's activities that is housed in the Harry S. Truman Presidential Library in Independence, MO., is classified, though some scattered documents are available in the president's office files, the National Security Council Papers, and especially the George M. Elsey Papers. *The Central Intelligence Agency: An Instrument of Government to 1950* (1990), was prepared in 1952–1953 by the CIA's official historian, Arthur B. Darling. Based on privileged access to documents, the account provides information on Hillenkoetter's attempts to build up the CIA and is stubbornly objective in spite of the anti-Hillenkoetter feeling among Darling's superiors in the CIA. For a detailed though not wholly reliable portrait of Hillenkoetter, see "St. Louis Admiral, Who Didn't Want the Job, Takes Over as Director of Central Intelligence," *St. Louis Post-Dispatch*, 11 May 1947. A brief sketch of his career by Stephen Flanders is in *Political Profiles: The Truman Years*, Eleanora W. Schoenebaum, ed. (1978). Rhodri Jeffreys-Jones, *The CIA and American Democracy* (1989), deals with the main episodes of Hillenkoetter's career with the CIA, especially the Bogota incident. An obituary is in the *New York Times*, 21 June 1982.

RHODRI JEFFREYS-JONES

HILLHOUSE, James (20 Oct. 1754–29 Dec. 1832), attorney and public office holder, was born in Montville, Connecticut, the son of William Hillhouse, a judge, and Sarah Griswold, a member of a powerful family in the state. For reasons that are not clear, in 1761 Hillhouse was adopted and subsequently raised by the family of his uncle James A. Hillhouse, an attorney. After attending Hopkins Grammar School, he graduated in 1773 from Yale College, of which he became treasurer in 1782 and served in that capacity until his death. After his graduation Hillhouse studied law, was admitted in 1775 to the bar in New Haven (where he spent the rest of his life), and took over the legal practice of his deceased uncle in 1775. He prospered at the law and from investments in real estate.

Soon after independence was declared in 1776, Hillhouse became a lieutenant, first in a company of New Haven volunteers, then in 1777 in a company of the Governor's Foot guards, of which he became captain in 1779. His principal action as a military leader was in successfully repelling an attempted British invasion of New Haven in that year. In 1779 he married Sarah Lloyd, who died the following year. He was remarried in 1782 to Rebecca Woolsey. The couple had five children.

Hillhouse entered politics upon his election in 1780 to the Connecticut House of Representatives, to which he was reelected for annual terms until 1785. The legislature subsequently elected him three times to annual terms in the Confederation Congress; he did not attend, however, thus revealing the relative insignificance into which service in that body had fallen. From 1789 to 1791 he served as a member of the Governor's Council, the upper house of the Connecticut General Assembly, and in 1790 he accepted election to the second federal Congress as a member of the U.S. House of Representatives, in which he served from 1791 to 1796. Upon the resignation of Oliver Ellsworth from the U.S. Senate, Hillhouse was elected in 1796 to that body; he remained in the Senate until 1810, being reelected twice.

Hillhouse pursued conventional Federalist party stances in both houses of Congress. He backed the Jay Treaty in the House and in 1798 introduced in the Senate the Alien Act, one of the four notorious Alien and Sedition Acts. The Alien Act—or Alien Friends Act, as it is sometimes called—authorized the national government to deport any aliens, even citizens of friendly powers, thought to be involved in subversive activities. Hillhouse also served briefly in 1801 as president pro tempore of the Senate. While accused at the time of being involved in discussing plans for the formation of a confederation of northeastern states in 1804, no evidence of his participation exists.

Hillhouse's most memorable legislative initiative was his introduction in 1808 of a Senate bill proposing seven amendments to the Constitution, the most significant proposal for structural constitutional change since the inauguration of the new government in 1789 and the adoption of the Bill of Rights. In so doing Hillhouse sought to limit the power of the federal government, controlled since 1801 by the Democratic-Republican party of Thomas Jefferson, and to make it more responsive to the people. These amendments, some of which had been proposed in the late 1780s by Antifederalist opponents of ratification, included such alterations as the annual election of congressional representatives, three-year terms for senators, the limitation on presidential service to one four-year term, and confirmation by both the House and the Senate of all presidential appointments. While none of these amendments were accepted by the Congress and sent to the states for ratification, they can be seen as the basis for the constitution of a separate confederacy of New England states had one ever been established. Similar proposals for constitutional amendment have been revived from time to time ever since.

Hillhouse became widely respected for his skills in banking and finance, serving, for example, as a founding director of the Eagle Bank of New Haven in 1812. In 1810, despite his stature in the Senate, Hillhouse resigned to accept appointment to the new position of commissioner of the Connecticut School Fund, a post he retained until 1825. In that capacity, he reorganized funding for Connecticut public education and reestablished stable accounting of monies derived from the sale of lands in the old Western Reserve of Connecticut, by then part of Ohio. He then resigned that position to supervise the construction of a new Connecticut canal.

Yet Hillhouse did not give up Federalist politics. The state legislature elected him in 1814 a member of the ill-fated Hartford Convention. Though frequently arraigned since then for harboring secessionists among its members, most delegates sought either to protest the prosecution of the War of 1812 or propose changes in the structure and operation of the federal government. One of the convention's most outspoken members, Hillhouse was known from the start to want the meeting to propose constitutional amendments not unlike those he had introduced six years earlier in the Senate. Probably for this reason, more moderate members, seeking merely to protest policies of the James Madison administration rather than advance proposals for more extensive changes in government, kept Hillhouse off the committee authorized to bring in proposals for action. Yet in the end, the convention followed his lead and, in its final report, proposed a number of constitutional amendments. While, for reasons not clear, Hillhouse seems to have wished to issue a minority report, in the end, no doubt because the convention report issued a call for constitutional amendments, he acquiesced in its unanimous adoption.

Hillhouse remained an active partisan as chairman of the Federalist party in Connecticut until the overthrow there of the Federalist oligarchy in the election of 1817 and the adoption of the new state constitution of 1818. He died in New Haven.

Though an advocate of conventional Federalist party policies, Hillhouse was distinctive among Federalists in seeing his party's difficulties in constitutional—that is, national and structural—terms. His proposals for constitutional amendment thus had more than provincial and contemporary significance. It may be said that, by reinforcing in partisan terms earlier, analogous, Antifederalist criticisms of the Constitution of 1787, Hillhouse gave such initiatives a fresh life and pertinence, which they have retained ever since.

• The major collection of Hillhouse papers is at Yale University. The political and social context of Hillhouse's public life is examined in Richard J. Purcell, *Connecticut in Transition, 1775–1818* (1918). The standard history of the Hartford Convention, in which Hillhouse played an important role, is James M. Banner, Jr., *To the Hartford Convention: The Federalists and the Origins of Party Politics in Massachusetts, 1789–1815* (1969).

JAMES M. BANNER, JR.

HILLIARD, Francis (1 Nov. 1806–9 Oct. 1878), lawyer and author, was born in Cambridge, Massachusetts, the son of William Hilliard and Sarah Lovering. His father was a senior partner in the publishing house of Hilliard, Gray, & Co., a predecessor of Little, Brown, & Co. Hilliard graduated from Harvard College in 1823 and attended, for a short time, Harvard Law School. He was admitted to the bar in 1830, after which he practiced law in Lowell and Roxbury, Massachusetts. His public service included a term for the Massachusetts legislature (1848) and positions as judge of the Roxbury Police Court (1855) and commissioner of insolvency for Norfolk County and judge of insolvency for Norfolk County (1856). He married Catherine Dexter Haven, and they had at least two children. When he moved to Worcester in 1862 he was suffering from unspecified "impaired" health.

Hilliard's primary professional recognition came through his writings. In addition to articles in publications such as the *Central Law Journal* of St. Louis, Hilliard published at least sixteen law books. Several of his books were published in multiple editions. The first of these, *Elements of Law*, appeared in 1835 and sought to provide a comprehensive summary of American law. With the exception of *A Digest of Pickering's Reports* (1837), all of his works were treatises. From 1838 until 1875 he published works on real property, the sale of personal property, mortgages, torts, bankruptcy, injunctions, new trials, contracts, and taxation. In 1877 he returned to the subject matter of his first work: *American Law* sought to provide a comprehensive summary of the law in the United States.

English common law was "received" in the thirteen colonies and continued as the foundation of the American legal system after independence was established. The common law could be changed by American judges to suit American conditions; it could also be modified by statute. Hilliard provided lawyers with treatises on American common law. Moreover, by utilizing cases from a variety of states he promoted a more general, rather than parochial, view of law.

Hilliard's most noteworthy accomplishment was the publication, in 1859, of *The Law of Torts*. This was the first treatise in torts in the English language. To some extent his treatise responded to the tremendous growth in accidents, injuries, and conflicts caused by industrialization and urbanization. But it was also an intellectual accomplishment. The novelty of the idea is shown by the fact that twelve years later Oliver Wendell Holmes, Jr., writing in *The American Law Review* on Charles Addison's treatise on torts, claimed that torts was "not a proper subject for a law book." In his search for general principles that could unify and explain tort law, Hilliard was successful in changing the focus of the analysis from the procedural writs, through which remedies were sought, to the nature of the wrong itself—that is, the substantive requirements to state a claim for relief.

The contemporary critics were divided on the quality of Hilliard's work. An 1865 review of his treatises in *The Monthly Law Reporter* praise Hilliard for his ability, accuracy, and originality. Later reviews in the *American Law Review* were less than enthusiastic about the quality of his work and, on at least one occasion, took him to task for "grave" omissions of cases it considered indispensable for his topic. He was, however, a success with the publishers and purchasers of his books. Acknowledging his popularity when reviewing the first volume of his 1877 *American Law*, *The American Law Review* stated, with what appears to be exasperation and resignation: "It is useless, therefore, to criticize Mr. Hilliard." Hilliard died in Worcester, Massachusetts.

• Hilliard's articles appear in *Central Law Journal* 1 (1874) and 2 (1875). Reviews of his work appear in *Monthly Law Reporter* 27 (1865); and *American Law Review* 1 (1866), 3 (1869), 4 (1869), and 12 (1878). Hilliard's books not mentioned in the text include: *An Abridgment of the American Law of Real Property* (1838); *The American Law of Real Property* (1846); *The Law of Mortgages of Real and Personal Property* (1853); *Law of Vendors and Purchasers of Real Property* (1858); *Law of Sales of Personal Property* (1841); *A Treatise on the Law of Bankruptcy and Insolvency* (1813); *Law of Injunctions* (1864); *The Law of New Trials, and Other Rehearings* (1866); *Law of Remedies for Torts or Private Wrongs* (1867); *Law of Contracts* (1872); and *The Law of Taxation* (1875). General references to Hilliard are in William T. Davis, *History of the Judiciary of Massachusetts* (1900), and David M. Walker, *The Oxford Companion to Law* (1980). His importance in the development of law is discussed in G. Edward White, *Tort Law in America* (1980), and Kermit L. Hall et al., *American Legal History* (1991). Obituaries appear in the *Worcester Daily Spy*, 11 Oct. 1878; *American Law Review* 13 (1878); and *Legal News* 1 (1878).

RICHARD L. AYNES

HILLIARD, Henry Washington (4 Aug. 1808–17 Dec. 1892), congressman and diplomat, was born in Fayetteville, North Carolina, and raised in Columbia, South Carolina. His parents' names are unknown. Hilliard graduated from South Carolina College at age eighteen and read law under the orator and politician William C. Preston. He then moved to Athens, Georgia, and after further legal study was admitted to the bar in 1829. It was at about this time that he married Mary Bedell of Georgia. The couple would have children, including a son, William Preston Hilliard.

Hilliard was also a student of literature, and in 1831 he was chosen as professor of English literature at the newly opened University of Alabama. On the Tuscaloosa campus he taught literature, rhetoric, history, mathematics, and other subjects. A well-regarded orator, he eulogized Charles Carroll, signer of the Declaration of Independence, before the state legislature. The early University of Alabama was a troubled and unruly institution, however, and in 1834 Hilliard resigned his post. He traveled to Montgomery, Alabama, where he practiced law with Joseph J. Hutchinson. By the mid-1830s he had been ordained an itinerant minister in the Methodist church, and he often preached in Montgomery before attentive crowds.

By the late 1830s Hilliard had found a home in politics. After publishing a series of letters against the subtreasury system, he was elected as a Whig to the state legislature in 1838. The next year he attended a national Whig convention and nominated John Tyler for vice president. Back in Alabama, Hilliard campaigned for the Harrison-Tyler ticket, was an owner-editor of the Montgomery *Alabama Journal*, and in 1841 ran unsuccessfully for Congress. His services to the party stood him in good stead, especially when Tyler succeeded to the presidency. In fact, Hilliard asked for a political version of the grand tour, and after turning down diplomatic posts in Portugal and Holland, in May 1842 he accepted that of chargé d'affaires at Brussels.

In two years abroad Hilliard furthered his education, traveled, and conversed with important people, including Belgium's King Leopold. The possible U.S. annexation of Texas was an international issue at the time, and Hilliard maintained that the union of the two republics was inevitable. Almost certainly, he learned that antislavery sentiment in Europe was widespread, and he may have experienced an awakening of his own conscience on the subject as a result of reading abolitionist literature or as part of the development of his strong religious principles. (He did not yet fully reject slave ownership, however, as he was noted to possess fourteen slaves in 1860.) In any case, he returned to the United States in 1844, in time to campaign for Henry Clay.

In 1845 Hilliard won a seat in Congress from Alabama's Second District and served three terms. Encompassing the state capital Montgomery, the district was a center of both Whig and southern-rights sentiment. Hilliard was torn by his loyalty to the national Whig party, his need to defend the sectional interests of his constituents, and his conviction that congressmen should exercise independent judgment. Scholars have called him an "Antebellum Alabama Maverick" and a "Nationalistic Rebel of the Old South." Many of his stands were controversial at home. As a pacifist and a student of international law, for example, he criticized taking Mexican territory by conquest. Like most southern Whigs, he refused to sign John C. Calhoun's 1849 "Address of the Southern Delegates," but in February 1849 admitted: "There is a domestic institution in the South which . . . insulates us from all mankind. The civilized world is against us."

On the other hand Hilliard was a consistent opponent of the Wilmot Proviso, believing that the slave states should be given equal access to the territories. He was willing to extend the Missouri Compromise line to the Pacific; but he supported the Compromise of 1850 as a means by which southerners might secure their position in the Union. During the Alabama congressional elections of 1851, he defended the compromise in a celebrated series of debates with states' rights firebrand William Lowndes Yancey and had the satisfaction of seeing the Second District reject secessionism for the time being. Hilliard was not a candidate for reelection that year. He was tired of congressional strife, and he hoped that the Millard Fillmore administration would give him a diplomatic appointment.

No post abroad was forthcoming, and in the 1850s Hilliard floundered politically. He was a Whig during the presidential election of 1852 and a member of the American or Know Nothing party during the election of 1856. When the latter party fell apart, he joined the Democrats and supported the James Buchanan administration. In the crisis of 1860 he vacillated but ended by campaigning in the North for the Bell-Everett ticket. In Alabama, after Abraham Lincoln's election, he spoke in Montgomery against immediate secession, urging instead a convention of southern states to demand constitutional changes. Yet he supported the Confederacy once it was formed and, angered by Lincoln's call for volunteers to defend the Union, served in May 1861 as Confederate emissary to the state of Tennessee.

In late 1861 Hilliard asked for a Confederate diplomatic appointment. Failing that, he raised a "legion" of three thousand troops and commanded them in combat in Tennessee. In 1862, Mary Bedell Hilliard having died, he married Eliza Ann Glascock Mays in Montgomery. Leaving military service in December 1862, he briefly returned to Montgomery before moving to Augusta, Georgia, where he lived for several years. There he sketched out plans for ending the war and penned a religious novel, *De Vane, a Story of Plebians and Patricians* (1865). Over the next decade he supported the Republicans intermittently, notably as an unsuccessful candidate for Congress in 1876. Ironically, this loss, like his defeat in 1841, seemed to entitle him to the foreign posting he had so long desired. President Rutherford B. Hayes made Hilliard his ambassador to Brazil.

Hilliard's most important work in Brazil was his encouragement of that country's antislavery forces. In a speech before an abolitionist meeting, he emphasized the benefits, to white and black, of emancipation, and by this undiplomatic behavior he created a brief political furor. Nonetheless Hilliard served out a four-year term and in 1881 returned to Atlanta, where he practiced law and wrote a memoir of his congressional and diplomatic careers, *Politics and Pen Pictures* (1892). He died in Atlanta.

Suave, persuasive, and astonishingly versatile, Hilliard followed his own path while in office. The fact that such a man could serve three stormy terms in Congress without once defending the morality of slavery was a testimony to his political skills but may also indicate that Alabama voters were more tolerant of divergent opinions than has been thought. Though Hilliard's later fence straddling made contemporaries throw up their hands, he was a persistent lover of the Union and a man of genuine moral purpose, as shown by his late venture into abolitionism.

• Small collections of Hilliard papers are at the Alabama State Department of Archives and History and at the Special Collections Department of the Duke University Library. Aside from the books cited above, Hilliard published a volume of *Speeches and Addresses* (1855). Several nineteenth- and early twentieth-century works contain information on Hilliard, including Willis Brewer, *Alabama: Her History, Resources, War and Record, and Public Men* (1872); William Garrett, *Reminiscences of Public Men in Alabama for Thirty Years* (1872); John Witherspoon DuBose, *The Life and Times of William Lowndes Yancey* (2 vols., 1892); Toccoa Cozart, "Henry W. Hilliard," *Transactions of the Alabama Historical Society, 1899–1903* 4 (1904): 277–99; and Thomas M. Owen, *History of Alabama and Dictionary of Alabama Biography* (4 vols., 1921). A thorough treatment of Hilliard is Evans C. Johnson, "A Political Life of Henry W. Hilliard" (M.A. thesis, Univ. of Alabama, 1947). Journal articles on Hilliard include J. William Rooney, Jr., "The Diplomatic Mission of Henry Washington Hilliard to Belgium, 1842–1844," *Alabama Historical Quarterly* 30 (Spring 1968): 19–31; Carlton Jackson, "Alabama's Hilliard: A Nationalistic Rebel of the Old South," *Alabama Historical Quarterly* 31 (Fall and Winter 1969): 183–205; and Johanna Nicol Shields, "An Antebellum Alabama Maverick: Henry Washington Hilliard, 1845–1851," *Alabama Review* 30 (July 1977): 191–212. Benjamin Buford Williams, *A Literary History of Alabama: The Nine-

teenth Century (1979), discusses Hilliard's worth as a writer. Obituaries are in the *Montgomery Daily Advertiser* and the *Birmingham Age Herald*, both 18 Dec. 1892.

PAUL M. PRUITT, JR.

HILLIARD, Robert (28 May 1857–6 June 1927), actor, was born Robert Cochran Hilliard in New York City, the son of Robert Bell Hilliard, a coffee and tea broker, and Caroline Matilda Cochran. His socially prominent parents moved to Brooklyn soon after his birth. He was educated in private schools, New York Free College, and Bishop's College School in Canada. In 1872 Hilliard began a career in business, working for a bank and for stockbrokers. He had had acting ambitions since adolescence and was coached by retired actress Matilda Heron, who saw in him a handsomeness like that of her beloved John Wilkes Booth. "Handsome Bob," as his friends called him, took leading roles with the Brooklyn amateur dramatic societies during the 1870s and 1880s. In 1881 he married Cora Bell; they had one child.

In 1886, using money he had amassed on Wall Street, Hilliard leased a theater in Brooklyn and there cast himself in the starring roles of three plays, beginning with *False Shame*. This appearance led to his first professional engagement in New York City later that year, in *A Daughter of Ireland*. Other parts followed. In a review of *The Golden Giant* (1887), the *New York Times* critic seemed hardly able to decide if Hilliard was an amateur or a true professional: "Mr. Robert Hilliard, as the gambler, did so well as to astonish even his friends" (12 Apr. 1887). Also in 1887, his handsome face and physique enabled him to succeed Maurice Barrymore as leading man in Lillie Langtry's company. There he won praise for his role of Lord Dolly Dasey in *As in a Looking Glass*, but he was fired before year's end. Langtry accused him of brawling while on tour in Montreal, Canada, and of quarreling with members of New York's Union Club over a supposed slur to his wife. In addition, Hilliard denied Langtry's statement that he had kissed Langtry's shoes and "annoyed" her by "continually running to her dressing room door" (*New York Times*, 17, 18, and 19 Nov. 1887).

Hilliard soon became as much known for his offstage flamboyance as for his dramatic skills. He presented himself as a dandy. In many cases, audiences came to see in person the man they had read about in the papers. Hilliard's career was aided by his role as the stalwart hero in a hugely successful melodrama of 1890, *Blue Jeans*. He was one of a new style of stars emerging in the 1890s, who charmed the public by their display of personality rather than by heavy dramatic acting. Hilliard's histrionic skill in *The Balloon* (1890) appeared to surprise the *New York Times* reviewer (5 Aug. 1890).

Most often in this period he played in comedies, where he could show himself off as the bluff, virile, high-spirited man of action who makes things happen. A matinee idol to young female playgoers, during the 1890s Hilliard was voted the handsomest man on the stage. He was a public favorite rather than an esteemed actor, and his personality came across as well in vaudeville sketches as in Broadway plays. Between stage appearances, he toured the variety circuits profitably for years, beginning with a one-act play he wrote himself, *Adrift* (1892).

Hilliard's first wife divorced him in 1894. In 1896 he married Nellie Estelle Whitehouse Murphy. By the later years of the decade, he was becoming known for his pugnacity in private life. He was mentioned in the papers in August 1896 for his arrest for verbal threats to a streetcar conductor. Also that year, during a backstage quarrel with his costar in *The Mummy* (1896), Amelia Bingham, he "grossly insulted" her and "set upon" her husband. During the fistfight that followed, the husband knocked Hilliard unconscious. The *New York Times* (19 Dec. 1896) reported that Bingham's triumph was generally commended by theater professionals; Hilliard became known to the profession as "Fighting Bob." Despite his belligerence Hilliard maintained a wide circle of friends and drinking pals in show business. Comedian James T. Powers, in his memoirs, concedes that Hilliard "generally spoke his mind with itching knuckles." Witty himself, he appreciated wit in others. His "witty curtain speeches" over the years were recalled in his *New York Herald Tribune* obituary.

In 1896 Hilliard wrote another one-act play, *The Littlest Girl*, which was a curtain-raiser for a longer, starring piece. He made his London debut in the play that year and toured with it in vaudeville for years. *Sporting Life* (1898) added a sporting, raffish element to his stage personality. A one-act convict drama, *No. 973* (1903), became another vaudeville vehicle. On Broadway, a series of "personality" roles maintained his popularity into the first decade of the new century. He was especially successful with the role of the road agent in *The Girl of the Golden West* (1905). He wrote two more one-act sketches for his vaudeville tours: *As a Man Sows* (1906) and *The Man Who Won the Pool* (1907). Hilliard's greatest Broadway success came with *A Fool There Was* (1909), a dramatization of Kipling's "The Vampire." The play ran in New York City and on tour until 1912. Another success followed, with the role of a detective in *The Argyle Case* (1912).

In 1913 Hilliard's second wife died. By the end of the year, when *The Argyle Case* was on tour in New Orleans, he was back in the news owing to a lawsuit brought by his valet, who claimed he had been beaten by the actor.

The next June, Hilliard married Olga Everard Williams. He was fifty-seven; she, twenty-three and newly divorced, was the heiress of $14 million from the estate of her father, a wealthy brewer. After the marriage Hilliard became president of the brewery and was not seen on Broadway for two years. He returned to the stage in *The Pride of Race* (1916), where he shocked public sensibilities of the time by playing a man one-sixteenth black, who marries a white woman of the South and who has by her a "throwback" dark-skinned son. The play was a scandalous success for Hilliard.

The *New York Review* (12 Feb. 1916) observed that "not for several seasons has there been such a notable example of the value of a strong personality in furthering the success of a play opening in the face of a storm of hostile criticism."

His last starring appearance, in *A Prince There Was* (1918), brought his career to an embarrassing end. The play was in difficulties at an out-of-town tryout, and Hilliard called on his friend George M. Cohan to rewrite it. Though Hilliard complained that the starring role was no longer suited to him, he opened in it. After three weeks of bad box office in New York City, Cohan took over the starring role himself and made a success of it. Hilliard was incensed, and rather than use his fists now that he was in his sixties, he sued Cohan, claiming Cohan had not kept his promise to provide Hilliard another starring vehicle. The case was settled in 1922 in Cohan's favor.

Apart from a brief return to vaudeville in *The Littlest Girl* in 1921, Hilliard's career was over in 1918. For a few years "the Beau Brummel of actors" was a regular first-nighter at play openings, a "striking and handsome figure, an invariable white carnation matching the silver whiteness of his hair" (*New York Times*, 8 June 1927). In 1922 he became ill with diabetes. That same year, he and his third wife separated. In the next few years Hilliard went through all his financial resources to pay for medical and dietetic aid. He was nearly blind and had suffered repeated heart attacks before his death in New York City. His entire estate of $10,000 went to a friend to repay a loan in that amount.

A *New York Times* editorial (9 June 1927) commented that Hilliard's death marked the disappearance of "the old-fashioned matinee idol" of the turn-of-the-century theater: the tall, handsome hero, wearing a full mustache and always perfectly dressed. He was a sparkling character to read about in the newspapers, with his fights, his wit, and his trademark boutonnieres. In theatrical history, Hilliard stands as a prototype of the personality stars who arose in the 1890s and who sold tickets on the strength of the charm and real-life character they showed in their stage vehicles.

• Materials on Hilliard's career are in the Billy Rose Theatre Collection at the New York Public Library for the Performing Arts, Lincoln Center. Details of his early life are in Ada Patterson, "Robert Hilliard—A Versatile Actor," *Theatre Magazine*, May 1913, with portrait. Anecdotes can be found in James T. Powers, *Twinkle Little Star* (1939). Portraits and production photographs are in Daniel C. Blum, *A Pictorial History of the American Theatre* (1960). Obituaries are in the *New York Times*, the *New York Herald-Tribune*, and *Variety*, all 8 June 1927.

WILLIAM STEPHENSON

HILLIS, Newell Dwight (2 Sept. 1858–25 Feb. 1929), Presbyterian and Congregational clergyman, was born in Magnolia, Iowa, the son of Samuel Ewing Hillis and Margaret Hester Reichte, farmers. Samuel Ewing Hillis was an ardent abolitionist who was also interested in higher education and social reform. Young Newell

studied at academies in Magnolia and Grinnell, Iowa, but when a fire destroyed their property in Iowa, the family moved to Nebraska, where Hillis attended public school in the intervals between farm work. In 1876 he became a missionary for the American Sunday School Union to organize Sunday schools and Congregational/Presbyterian churches in the West. While attending Lake Forest College in Illinois, Hillis surveyed frontier Nebraska, Utah, Wyoming, and Nevada for the Union, finding shelter in dugouts and deserted dwellings and organizing Wyoming's first Sunday school in a saloon. In 1884 Hillis graduated from Lake Forest with a B.A. and entered Chicago's McCormick Theological Seminary. He married Annie Louise Patrick of Marengo, Illinois, in 1887. They became the parents of three children.

Ordained in the Presbyterian ministry in May 1887, Hillis received a B.D. from McCormick with highest honors and was called to the pastorate of First Presbyterian Church of Peoria, Illinois, that same year. From 1890 to 1895 he was the pastor of First Presbyterian Church in Evanston, Illinois. In these congregations of increasing prominence in the Midwest, Hillis gained a reputation as an eloquent and powerful preacher. In 1895 he succeeded David Swing as the pastor of Chicago's Central Church, an independent congregation that met in the city's Central Music Hall. There Hillis drew huge crowds to hear his sermons and published his first books, including *A Man's Value to Society* (1896), *The Investment of Influence* (1898), and *Great Books as Life-Teachers* (1899).

In 1899 Hillis accepted a unanimous call to become the pastor of Plymouth Congregational Church in Brooklyn, New York. Succeeding two of the most influential pulpit orators of nineteenth-century American Protestantism, Henry Ward Beecher and Lyman Abbott, he extended their tradition of popular liberal Protestant preaching. During his early ministry in Brooklyn, Hillis published *The Influence of Christ in Modern Life* (1900), *Building a Working Faith* (1903), and *The Quest of John Chapman* (1904). By 1903, however, Hillis had begun to feud with Abbott, who continued to edit the *Outlook*, a popular national magazine. When Abbott defended the disenfranchisement of black voters in the South, Hillis invoked Beecher's witness against racial discrimination. He confirmed his local influence by publishing one sermon per week in the *Brooklyn Eagle* and an article per week for the press. Later books by Hillis included *The Contagion of Character* (1911) and *The Story of Phaedrus* (1914). He also edited works by two of his illustrious predecessors: *The Message of David Swing to His Generation* (1913) and *Lectures and Orations by Henry Ward Beecher* (1913).

By 1914 Plymouth Church had become increasingly isolated from its membership as congregants left Brooklyn for the suburbs. Such isolation prompted Hillis to secure a generous endowment for Plymouth Institute from the estate of John Arbuckle, a wealthy member of the congregation. The endowment confirmed Plymouth Church's Brooklyn location as an institutional church offering day and night classes in business, fine arts, foreign languages, home economics, and physical education to residents of the central city. Other wealthy members of the congregation donated the church's stained glass windows, which celebrated events, heroes, and heroines in the history of freedom.

When Hillis began to preach about the European war in October 1914, he drew upon his widespread travels in Europe, an admiration for the "New Germany," and a familiarity with political economies of the contending powers in an effort to develop an even-handed analysis of the war's causes and origins. As Hillis concluded his *Studies of the Great War* (1915) in December 1914, however, he became convinced that overwhelming responsibility lay with Germany. In 1915 his interest in the war was deflected by a series of embarrassing lawsuits stemming from his endorsement of and investment in the Albertini Lumber Company, a Canadian timber landowner. Public embarrassment was compounded by Hillis's tearful pleas for forgiveness from the pulpit of Plymouth Church. Soon, however, he began repairing his image by publicly imploring the United States to enter the war on the side of the Allies.

By 1917 Hillis had upbraided the Woodrow Wilson administration's "dillydallying" about the war and attacked German soldiers as "mad dogs," "hyenas," "insane men," and "rattlesnakes." When the United States entered the war, Hillis took a leave of absence from Plymouth Church to work for the American Bankers' Association, selling liberty bonds with his platform skills. After a tour of European battlefronts in the summer of 1917, this "raconteur of atrocities" gave 400 lectures in 162 U.S. communities that he published as *German Atrocities, Their Nature and Philosophy* (1918). His most notorious story told of syphilitic German soldiers cutting off the breasts of Belgian and French women whom they had ravished as a warning sign against the disease to other German soldiers. His campaign sold $100 million in liberty bonds in forty-six days. After a similar European tour in the summer of 1918, his lectures entitled *The Blot on the Kaiser's 'Scutcheon* (1918) included "The Black Soul of the Hun," "The German Sniper behind the Crucifix," "The Judas among the Nations," "Polygamy and the Collapse of the Family in Germany," and "Must German Men Be Exterminated?" which contemplated the sterilization of 10 million German soldiers.

After the war, Hillis returned to his Plymouth Church pulpit. He published *The Better America Lectures* in 1921. His sermons on the civic duty of beautifying the city prompted a city planning movement in Brooklyn and the appointment of a planning committee by the borough president in 1922. A cerebral hemorrhage in January 1924 incapacitated Hillis for eight months. By then, a million copies of his twenty-five books had been sold, and the British government had circulated 9 million copies of a single wartime lecture. Hillis recovered to preach and travel for several years. He died in Bronxville, New York.

• There is no known collection of Hillis's papers. Among the secondary sources on Hillis, Ray Abrams, *Preachers Present Arms* (1933), severely indicts his martial enthusiasm; John Franklin Piper, Jr., *The American Churches in World War I* (1985), puts the same record in a broader historical context; and Ralph E. Luker, *The Social Gospel in Black and White: American Racial Reform, 1885–1912* (1991), takes note of Hillis's relatively enlightened attitude in domestic race relations. In addition to the standard biographical sources, obituaries are in the *Brooklyn Eagle*, the *New York Times*, and the *New York Herald Tribune*, all 26 Feb. 1929.

RALPH E. LUKER

HILLMAN, Bessie Abramowitz (15 May 1889–23 Dec. 1970), labor leader, was born in Grodno, Russia, the daughter of Emanuel Abramowitz, a merchant, and Sarah Cherechevsky. She left home at fourteen to look for work, and a year later, fleeing a wave of anti-Jewish pogroms, she immigrated with several relatives to the United States. The family settled in Chicago, where Abramowitz found work in a sweatshop, earning only $3 for a sixty-hour week. When she formed a committee of co-workers to complain about a dishonest foreman, she was fired and blacklisted. She took a job in another town for several months, then returned to Chicago and, using a false name, found work at the Hart, Schaffner and Marx clothing factory. Once again the conditions were very bad, and when the already meager piece-rate was cut back in September 1910, Abramowitz appealed for help to a men's local that had already been established in the factory by the United Garment Workers (UGW). They showed no interest, so Abramowitz acted on her own, leading more than a dozen of her female co-workers out on strike. Gradually other employees joined the walkout; by October, 8,000 of them were on strike, and within another month the action had spread across Chicago, drawing in 45,000 workers.

Meanwhile, Abramowitz had turned for assistance to the Women's Trade Union League, an alliance of middle-class volunteers and working women that had been established to encourage unionization among women factory workers. The league responded with alacrity, as did the Chicago Federation of Labor. Once the strike ended, Margaret Dreier Robins, the head of the league, hired Abramowitz as an organizer. Abramowitz showed herself a natural; a colleague described her as "a power among the women workers and a friend and counselor to the young girls in the industry." She always remembered Robins's role in her life; when Robins died years later, Hillman said that it was she who "enabled me to become what I am today." Abramowitz became increasingly influential in league circles; she also served as business agent for one of the new locals formed at Hart, Schaffner and Marx as a result of the strike.

During the strike, Abramowitz had met Sidney Hillman, a young cutter who emerged as one of the leaders. She later recalled that her first impression was unfavorable. "He was too prudent, too nice, and I felt suspicious of him." But the two became friends and then sweethearts. By 1914, when Hillman left Chicago to take up a new job with the Cloakmakers' Union in New York, he and Abramowitz were secretly engaged. Within the year, a number of garment-workers' locals seceded from the UGW and established a new organization, the Amalgamated Clothing Workers of America. Abramowitz was among the delegates at the founding convention in Nashville, Tennessee, and, as an influential member of the Chicago delegation, played an important part in the decision to offer the Amalgamated presidency to Hillman. Three decades later, a colleague reminded her of that night "when you walked me up and down the streets of the city arguing that Sidney was the only logical person to be president of the Amalgamated" (Josephson, p. 99). Hillman accepted the position, which he would hold the rest of his life. For two years the couple maintained a long-distance courtship between New York, the site of the Amalgamated headquarters, and Chicago. Meanwhile, in 1915 Abramowitz became the only woman on the Amalgamated's general executive board. On 1 May 1916 she and Hillman headed a joyful parade of thousands of clothing workers through the streets of Chicago to a festive bridal celebration at the Amalgamated offices. The couple was married in a synagogue two days later, after which they went on their honeymoon—to their union's annual convention.

Giving up her job, Hillman moved to New York. She resigned from the Amalgamated board a year later when she had the first of their two daughters. She would not hold another formal union position for nearly twenty years, but her life was dedicated to the Amalgamated as surely as her husband's. She shared his austere standard of living despite the union's growing prosperity over the years, and she accepted his consuming preoccupation with the Amalgamated, his punishing schedule, and his long absences on union business. Once her daughters were older, she joined the Amalgamated's campaign to organize shirt workers in sweatshops in Connecticut, Pennsylvania, and New York. She acted as education director of the Laundry Workers' Joint Board from 1937 to 1944 and served as codirector of the union's War Activities Department during World War II, helping to organize plants doing war work and to build solidarity between white Amalgamated members and newly hired black women. "She knew what she was talking about," recalled her codirector, Esther Peterson, "and the women in the shops loved her." She also served on the advisory board of the Office of Price Administration in New York City during the war, and she was a member of the Child Welfare Committee of New York.

After her husband's death in 1946, Hillman became a vice president of the Amalgamated. In this position she worked to build up the union's education program and maintained an active speaking schedule at union conferences, seminars, and conventions. She also became active in the campaign on behalf of equal rights for women, noting in 1961 that unions were "the greatest offenders as far as discrimination against women is concerned" (Gabin, p. 231). She served on President John F. Kennedy's Comission on the Status of Wom-

en and in 1962–1963 attended the meetings of the United Nations Commission on the Status of Women as a delegate from the International Confederation of Free Trade Unions. She died in New York City.

It was a running joke between Hillman and her husband that women, not men, had started the strike that paved the way for the founding of the Amalgamated. He once laughingly assured a union convention that this fact had "given what I consider a completely unfair advantage to Bessie Hillman over me, even in our household" (Josephson, p. 436). In truth, Hillman lived much of her life in her husband's shadow, and she did so gracefully. But she never lost her sense of herself as an independent member of the labor movement. The separate persona she fought to preserve can clearly be heard in her periodic observation, "I was Bessie Abramowitz before he was Sidney Hillman."

• References to Bessie Hillman's career are in the combined papers of Sidney Hillman and the Amalgamated Clothing Workers of America at the New York State School of Industrial and Labor Relations, Cornell University. See also Steven Fraser, *Labor Will Rule: Sidney Hillman and the Rise of American Labor* (1991); Matthew Josephson, *Sidney Hillman: Statesman of American Labor* (1952); Brigid O'Farrell and Joyce L. Kornbluh, *Rocking the Boat: Union Women's Voices, 1915–1975* (1996); Elizabeth Anne Payne, *Reform, Labor and Feminism: Margaret Dreier Robins and the Women's Trade Union League* (1988); James J. Kenneally, *Women and American Trade Unions* (1978); Nancy Gabin, *Feminism in the Labor Movement* (1990); and Philip S. Foner, *Women and the American Labor Movement: From the First Trade Unions to the Present* (1979). An obituary is in the *New York Times*, 24 Dec. 1970.

SANDRA OPDYCKE

HILLMAN, Sidney (23 Mar. 1887–10 July 1946), labor leader, was born in Zagare, Lithuania, the son of Samuel Hillman and Judith Paiken. Because Hillman's father, a merchant, devoted himself to religious study, his mother's grocery shop was the family's main support. In 1901 the boy moved to Kovno to study for the rabbinate, but he was soon caught up in the revolutionary ferment of the time. In less than a year he left the seminary for a job in a chemical laboratory; after hours he studied economics and organized typesetters for an illegal Jewish trade union. Soon after the failure of the 1905 revolution, Hillman (who had twice been imprisoned for political activism) fled the country, first to Manchester, England, and then in 1907 to the United States.

Hillman went to Chicago, where he worked as a stock clerk at Sears, Roebuck. Laid off after two years, he took a job in the clothing factory of Hart, Schaffner and Marx. He started as an apprentice cutter, working fifty-four hours a week under terrible conditions. Many workers shared his dissatisfaction, and when a dozen women employees went on strike in September 1910, the rest of the workforce soon joined them. Within weeks 45,000 garment workers all over Chicago had walked off their jobs. The strike ended with few gains in most factories, but Hillman, who had emerged as one of the leaders, managed to persuade his employers to accept arbitration. When the new Local 39 of the United Garment Workers of America (UGW) was formed, he became its business agent.

In 1914 Hillman moved to New York to serve as chief clerk of the Cloakmakers' Union. Meanwhile, his local in Chicago joined an uprising within the UGW; the radically inclined immigrants felt little connection with the conservative native-born men who headed their union. The insurgents were barred from attending the UGW's 1914 convention, so they held a separate gathering and founded a new organization, the Amalgamated Clothing Workers of America (ACWA). When they offered Hillman the presidency, he immediately gave up his job and accepted despite the uncertainty of the dissidents' future. "The tailors made me," he said. "They can have me." Two years later Hillman married Bessie Abramowitz, one of the ringleaders of the 1910 strike. She resigned her job as business agent of the vestmakers' local in Chicago and moved to New York City, the ACWA headquarters. The couple had two daughters.

In building his new union, Hillman faced the challenge of organizing workers in an industry characterized by ferocious competition, thousands of small employers, and sharp seasonal fluctuations. Moreover, he could not count on the support of organized labor because the American Federation of Labor (AFL) viewed the ACWA as an illegitimate rival of the UGW. He gradually expanded the union, however, combining occasional bitter strikes with a generally conciliatory style. During World War I he lobbied successfully for the creation of a federal Board of Control and Labor Standards for Army Clothing, under whose regulatory wing his union flourished. By 1920 the ACWA had contracts with 85 percent of the country's garment manufacturers, had 177,000 members, and had established the 44-hour week as an industry standard.

In his dealings with management Hillman was as committed to "constructive cooperation" as the most conservative members of the AFL old guard; on occasion the ACWA even sponsored loans and efficiency studies to help financially shaky employers. Hillman was more adventurous inside his union, building a pioneering structure of educational and social programs, including low-cost housing cooperatives, banks, medical clinics, recreational facilities, union restaurants, and unemployment insurance. This approach, which came to be known as the "new unionism," made Hillman enormously popular among his own rank and file and led him to be regarded as one of the more progressive labor leaders of the day. But Hillman expressed no interest in the socialist views of many of his members, systematically resisted Communist influence in the union, and strenuously denied that the ACWA program might offer a blueprint for broader social reform.

The crisis of the Great Depression led Hillman to seek a new partnership between government and labor. A strong supporter of the New Deal, he served on the Labor Advisory Board of the National Recovery Administration (NRA) in 1933 and on the National Industrial Recovery Board in 1934. By then he had become convinced that, with the Franklin D. Roosevelt administration behind it, the labor movement could reach out to unprecedented numbers of workers. Only one obstacle stood in the way. The leadership of the AFL (to which the ACWA had finally been admitted in 1933) remained resolutely committed to organizing each craft separately and to focusing primarily on skilled workers. By the mid-1930s Hillman joined a growing insurgency within the AFL, led by John L. Lewis, which insisted that this traditional approach could not possibly succeed in the mass-production industries that now dominated the economy.

Hillman and Lewis maintained that the AFL must switch its emphasis to industrial unionism so that all the workers within a given industry—unskilled as well as skilled—could be enrolled in a single union. (The ACWA was already an industrial union, as was Lewis's United Mine Workers, but they remained a minority within the AFL.) When their proposal went down to defeat at the 1935 AFL convention, Hillman and Lewis led a group of dissident unions to found the Committee for Industrial Organizations, which in 1938 became the Congress of Industrial Organizations (CIO). Over the next several years Hillman participated as the CIO organized one mass-production industry after another; he became first vice president in 1937. Hillman himself headed the CIO's Textile Workers Organizing Committee, which scored extraordinary gains in 1937. He faced sharp criticism from affiliated union leaders when he felt obliged to accept wage cuts during the recession of 1938, and by 1939 there was growing pressure for a more democratic structure. These demands led to the formation in 1939 of the Textile Workers Union of America, an organization whose size—100,000 members—bore eloquent testimony to what Hillman and the CIO had accomplished in just two years.

Recognizing the close connection between the CIO's future and the fortunes of the Democratic party, Hillman and Lewis founded Labor's Non-Partisan League in 1936 to organize union support for Roosevelt's reelection campaign. (Hillman also helped establish the American Labor party in New York State to accommodate independents and Socialists who favored Roosevelt but were disinclined to vote Democratic.) Labor's considerable role in Roosevelt's victory helped Hillman win passage of the Fair Labor Standards Act two years later. The New Deal was already winding down by then, but Hillman's star continued to rise, especially after Lewis broke with Roosevelt in 1940. As the senior union figure in Democratic circles, Hillman was chosen that year to serve as the labor member on the National Defense Advisory Commission and was soon made an associate director general of the Office of Production Management (OPM). He did not prove particularly effective in the OPM job, however, and his reluctance to confront business interests drew increasing fire from union leaders. Discredited with his own constituency, shadowed by a procurement scandal that appears to have been orchestrated by Lewis, and struggling to do a difficult job while in poor health, Hillman was let go by Roosevelt in 1942 and returned to the presidency of the ACWA deeply depressed.

Hillman rallied in 1943 when he was named to chair and direct the CIO's new Political Action Committee (PAC), established to get out the labor vote for Roosevelt's fourth-term run in 1944. So effective was the project that Hillman gained considerable influence in Democratic circles. When he and the PAC leaders saw that their candidate for vice president, incumbent Henry A. Wallace, could not win party acceptance, their acquiescence in Harry S. Truman's candidacy helped clinch the nomination for him. Allegations that Roosevelt would respond to each suggestion about the vice presidency by saying "clear it with Sidney" became so well known that Hillman found himself a target of Republican venom during the fall campaign.

In 1945 Hillman helped found the World Federation of Trade Unions; his tireless efforts at conciliation succeeded in bringing the representatives of Communist and non-Communist countries into one organization, though they subsequently split apart. Hillman had been in ill health since a serious case of pneumonia in 1937, and starting in 1942 he suffered a series of heart attacks. He died at his summer home in Point Lookout, New York.

Hillman ran the ACWA with an iron hand. "You couldn't change Hillman's mind on things," recalls one union worker. "He was not easy to work with." Yet much of Hillman's eminence came from his role as conciliator, from his ability to mediate between business and labor in his early days, between the right and left wings in his union and the CIO, and between government and labor during his years serving Roosevelt. Although this balancing act sometimes strained his relations with other union leaders, he was convinced that labor's greatest gains would come through pragmatic collaboration. Defending the NRA against its critics, for instance, he insisted that if the program continued "and we have a labor movement vital and moving, we will make more progress than the dreamers can look to." The NRA proved a disappointment, as did many of the initiatives on which Hillman pinned his hopes. Nevertheless, through a lifetime of practical coalition-building Hillman managed to forge a group of fractious locals into a strong and innovative union, play a major part in the CIO's most productive years, and win labor a temporary place at the very center of national power.

• The combined papers of Hillman and the ACWA are at the New York State School of Industrial and Labor Relations, Cornell University. See also an essay by Hillman, "Labor Attitudes," in *American Labor Dynamics*, ed. J. B. S. Hardman (1928); Steven Fraser, *Labor Will Rule: Sidney Hillman and the Rise of American Labor* (1991); Jean Gould, *Sidney Hillman, Great American* (1952); Matthew Josephson, *Sidney Hillman: Statesman of American Labor* (1952); George Soule, *Sidney Hillman* (1939); Melech Epstein, *Profiles of Eleven* (1965) and *Jewish Labor in the U.S.A., 1914–1952* (1953); Melvyn Dubofsky and Warren Van Tine, eds., *John L. Lewis: A Biography* (1986); and Fraser, "Sidney Hillman: Labor's Machiavelli," in *Labor Leaders in America*, ed. Dubofsky and Van Tine (1987). An obituary is in the *New York Times*, 11 July 1946.

SANDRA OPDYCKE

HILLMAN, Thomas Tennessee (2 Feb. 1844–4 Aug. 1905), industrialist, was born in Montgomery County, Tennessee, son of Daniel Hillman, an ironmaster, and Ann Marable. Hillman was descended from a long line of iron makers; his father, originally from Trenton, New Jersey, moved west, where he was a pioneer in the iron industry of Tennessee and Kentucky. Young Hillman grew up around his father's iron furnaces, and as a result he developed a lifelong attachment to the business so strong that a business associate claimed that Hillman had been "born and bred in a blast furnace." At the age of seven Hillman was badly injured in a riding accident; it took years for him to recover from the accident and even then, his recovery was never really complete, leaving him with a permanent "spinal weakness."

After a brief stint at a rolling mill in Louisville, Kentucky, Hillman spent two years in study at Vardusia Academy, located in Edgefield near Nashville, Tennessee. On returning home Hillman was given a job in his father's Empire Iron Works in Twigg County, Tennessee, whose boilerplate and bar iron products were well recognized. During the Civil War Hillman managed the Empire Iron Works and the Center Iron furnace, which was also owned by his father. On his twenty-first birthday Hillman was given a $50,000 interest in his father's business, and in the following year the business was renamed D. Hillman and Son. In 1867 Hillman married Emily S. Gentry; they had no children. Hillman managed D. Hillman and Son through the uncertain years of the Reconstruction and the difficult years of the depression that began in 1873 and persisted through most of the 1870s. In 1879 he sold his interest in the business and entered the mercantile business in Nashville. Within a year he sold this business as well and moved to Birmingham, Alabama.

Hillman had been invited to Birmingham by Henry Fairchild De Bardeleben, with whom he formed a partnership, the Alice Furnace Company. The company built the iron furnace Alice No. 1, which went into blast in 1880. Soon De Bardeleben left for Mexico to seek a cure for imagined tuberculosis, leaving Hillman as president; under his management a second furnace, Alice No. 2 (or "Big Alice"), was constructed, and it went into blast in 1883. In the following year Enoch Ensley (formerly of Memphis) bought De Bardeleben's interest in Pratt Coal and Coke Company—which soon thereafter became the Pratt Coal and Iron Company—and then took control of Alice Furnace Company, reducing Hillman to a minority stockholder.

Hillman got his revenge against Ensley in 1886, when in league with Alfred Montgomery Shook and Nat Baxter, and with the financial backing of Wall Street manipulator John Hamilton Inman, he arranged the acquisition of the Pratt Coal and Iron Company by the Tennessee Coal, Iron and Railroad Company (TCI). Hillman was made vice president and general manager of TCI, which, capitalized at $10 million, was the largest industrial corporation in the South. Through Hillman's initiative TCI simultaneously built four blast furnaces in the largest expansion yet undertaken by a single company. As first vice president, Hillman was the operating manager of TCI until his retirement in 1889. In 1891 he returned to TCI as second vice president and a director.

Hillman's other business interests included serving as director for the First National Bank of Birmingham and Birmingham Railway, Light and Power Company and as president of the Ensley Railway Company. In addition, the Hillman Hospital and Hillman Hotel were named for him.

In 1904 Hillman, along with the brothers George B. and H. E. McCormack, Erskine Ramsey, and others, formed the Pratt Consolidated Coal Company (not connected with the earlier Pratt Coal and Iron Co.). Hillman served as president of this firm at the time of his death in the following year. Never of vigorous health, he died while on vacation in Atlantic City, New Jersey, leaving an estate worth an estimated $2 million.

• As there are no known papers associated with Hillman, details of his life must be pieced together through the following secondary sources: George M. Cruikshank, *A History of Birmingham and Its Environs* (2 vols., 1920); Ethel Armes, *The Story of Coal and Iron in Alabama* (1910, 1972); and W. David Lewis, *Sloss Furnaces and the Rise of the Birmingham District: An Industrial Epic* (1994). Two obituaries add only details to the information in the above sources: the *Birmingham Age-Herald*, 5 Aug. 1905, and the *Nashville Banner*, 7 Aug. 1905.

STEPHEN GOLDFARB

HILLQUIT, Morris (1 Aug. 1869–7 Oct. 1933), attorney and socialist leader, was born Morris Hillkowitz in Riga, Latvia, then a part of the Russian Empire, the son of Benjamin Hillkowitz, a schoolteacher, and Rebecca Levene. His father sent Morris to elementary and secondary schools in Riga, where he learned Russian and German. The family immigrated to the United States in 1886 and soon after changed its name to Hillquit. In New York City, Morris resumed his education and learned English, a language that he always spoke with a foreign accent. As was the case with most Jewish immigrant families, the Hillquits required contributions from all members to survive. Hence Morris found work in a shirt factory, where he met other young immigrant workers and became acquainted with the infant Jewish-American labor movement. He began to learn Yiddish in order to communicate with fellow immigrant Jews for whom it was the language of choice. He also read socialist literature in its original German. As a result of his reading and personal experiences in the United States, Hillquit joined the Socialist Labor Party (SLP) in 1887. That year he became a staff member of the first Yiddish-language socialist newspaper in the United States, *Arbeter Zeitung*. While working to support himself, participating in an incipient labor movement, and playing an active role in the SLP, Hillquit attended New York University Law School, from which he earned an LL.B. in 1893; that year he also married Vera Levene, with whom he had two children.

As an active member of the SLP and a leading American Marxist theoretician, Hillquit opposed the policies and practices of party leader Daniel De Leon. Unlike De Leon, who condemned immediate reforms as palliatives that diluted revolutionary élan and who waged a tireless struggle against "class collaborationist" trade unions, Hillquit believed that reform and revolution were two sides of the same coin and that socialism would not succeed unless the party built amicable relations with the trade unions. Unable to sway De Leon or weaken his control of the SLP, Hillquit in 1899 led a group of insurgents who sought to seize control of the party. Failing in that effort, Hillquit and his group seceded from the SLP, formed their own socialist party, and subsequently amalgamated with other non–De Leonite socialists to found the Socialist Party of America (SPA) in 1901.

For the remainder of his life Hillquit served as the SPA's leading theoretician, an influential member of its national executive committee, and a regular delegate to international socialist conferences. Not only did he write the first major history of socialism in the United States, *History of Socialism in the United States* (1903), and the SPA's first and principal theoretical work, *Socialism in Theory and Practice* (1909), Hillquit also ran for Congress in 1906, 1908, 1916, 1918, and 1920. As a candidate in districts with a large Jewish immigrant population, he polled substantial numbers of votes and on one occasion lost only because the Democrats and Republicans united behind a single candidate. Hillquit shaped the SPA's relations with the trade unions, seeking always to influence trade unionists to a socialist perspective and never to condemn their leaders as "labor fakirs." As he said in 1900, labor unions "are the best fields for propaganda in so far as they are organized on the basis of class struggle. It makes them more accessible to the teaching of Socialism." He also stressed how such immediate reforms as municipal ownership of public utilities, public health clinics, and the regulation of wages and hours would pave the path to socialist revolution. "We do not expect the Socialist order to be introduced by one sudden and great political cataclysm," Hillquit wrote to a progressive reformer in 1908, "nor . . . expect it to be established by a rabble made desperate by misery and starvation."

Because of his oratorical skill and good relations with trade unionists and Progressive reformers, Hillquit frequently represented the SPA in public forums. His most famous such appearance featured a debate with Samuel Gompers in 1915 before the U.S. Commission on Industrial Relations about the principles and practices of trade unionism and socialism. The SPA published it as *The Double Edge of Labor's Sword* (1915). When World War I erupted Hillquit drafted the SPA's official position on the war, first in 1915 and then at a special emergency party convention in 1917, called after the United States entered the conflict. Both resolutions condemned the war as a capitalist conflict. Hillquit became a leader of the antiwar People's Council for Democracy and Peace. In 1917 he ran for mayor of New York City on an antiwar platform, winning more votes than any previous socialist candidate. His tireless mayoral campaign caused Hillquit to develop a serious case of tuberculosis, a disease that plagued him thereafter.

Hillquit's socialist activities did not conflict with his career as an attorney. He maintained a law practice that represented working people and trade unions, serving, for example, as general counsel for the International Ladies' Garment Workers' Union from 1913 until his death. As the union's counsel he helped negotiate and administer the women's clothing industry's famous collective-bargaining contract known as the "Protocol of Peace" (1910–1916). Later he acted as the legal adviser to the Soviet Government Bureau in the United States (1918–1919), and in 1920 he defended the five socialist members suspended by the New York State Assembly, as well as other radicals and dissenters.

The Bolshevik Revolution in Russia affected Hillquit enormously. At first a warm defender of Lenin and the Bolsheviks, Hillquit soon fought with U.S. supporters of Lenin over their condemnation of reformist socialism. He also refused to accede to the demands set by the Bolsheviks for membership in their Third International, or Comintern. Between 1918 and 1920 the SPA split, with its secessionists forming independent communist parties. Throughout the 1920s Hillquit sought new allies for socialism. In 1922 he allied with trade unionists and social reformers to create the Conference for Progressive Political Action, which two years later endorsed the third-party presidential candidacy of Robert LaFollette. For the remainder of the 1920s, however, Hillquit led a socialist party in disarray and decline. The Great Depression led to Hillquit's final major political foray, a second campaign for mayor of New York in 1932 in which he polled over 250,000 votes. The campaign weakened his health, and less than a year later he died at home in New York City.

For more than three decades Hillquit served as the foremost party leader, theoretician, and public spokesperson for socialism in the United States. Abroad, he was also perhaps the best-known American socialist in the era of the Second International (1881–1914) and after World War I among those socialists who declined to submit to the authority of the Comintern and the Soviet Union.

• The main body of Hillquit papers is at the State Historical Society of Wisconsin, Madison, and available in a microfilm edition. A smaller collection of papers is held by the Tamiment Institute Library, Robert F. Wagner, Sr., Archives, New York. Hillquit's autobiography, *Loose Leaves from a Busy Life* (1934), offers glimpses into his life and career. Among other publications of his, one might consult *Socialism Summed Up* (1913), *Socialism, Promise or Menace* (1914), and *From Marx to Lenin* (1921). The best available biography is Norma F. Pratt, *Morris Hillquit: A Political History of an American Jewish Socialist* (1979). The *New York Times* has an obituary (9 Oct. 1933) and a feature article (15 Oct. 1933).

MELVYN DUBOFSKY

HILLYER, Robert Silliman (3 June 1895–24 Dec. 1961), poet, novelist, and critic, was born in East Orange, New Jersey, the son of James Rankin Hillyer and Lillian Stanley Smith. After graduating from the Kent School, he entered Harvard College. In 1916, while still an undergraduate, he won Harvard's Garrison Prize for poetry and published his first poem in the *New Republic*. Then, in the eventful year of 1917, he received his B.A. cum laude; published his first book of poetry, *Sonnets and Other Lyrics*; married Dorothy Stewart Mott; and volunteered for the American Field Service, which was one of two World War I ambulance corps (the other being Norton-Harjes) then appealing to the patriotism of young graduates of Harvard, including E. E. Cummings and John Dos Passos. After performing ambulance duty with the French army and for it receiving the Verdun Medal, Hillyer transferred to the army of the United States, where he held the rank of lieutenant and served as a courier during the Versailles Peace Conference.

Following his discharge from the army, Hillyer joined the faculty of Harvard as an instructor of English. In 1920–1921 he studied in Copenhagen and developed an interest in Danish verse that resulted in his translating and coediting, with S. Foster Damon and Oluf Friis, *A Book of Danish Verse* (1922). In 1926, his first marriage having ended in divorce, he married Dorothy Hancock Tilton, with whom he had a son, his only child. He served two years as assistant professor at Trinity College, returning to Harvard in 1928 as associate professor. Later he was named Boylston Professor of Rhetoric and Oratory; later still, following his retirement from Harvard in 1945, he taught at Kenyon College (1948–1951) and at the University of Delaware (1952–1961). He also lectured widely and gave readings of his poetry, particularly in the 1920s and 1930s, when he was most productive as a poet. He was Phi Beta Kappa Poet at Tufts in 1924, at Harvard in 1929, at Columbia and Harvard in 1936, at William and Mary in 1938, and at Goucher in 1940.

In 1920 he published two volumes of poetry—*The Five Books of Youth* and *Alchemy: A Symphonic Poem*—and followed them with a series of collections, including *The Hills Give Promise* (1923), *The Halt in the Garden* (1925), *The Seventh Hill* (1928), *The Gates of the Compass* (1930), *Collected Verse* (1933), which won the Pulitzer Prize in 1934, *A Letter to Robert Frost and Others* (1937), *In Time of Mistrust* (1939), *Poems* for Music, 1917–1947 (1949), The Suburb by the Sea (1952), The Relic and Other Poems (1957), and Collected Poems (1961). In 1949 he published a narrative poem, The Death of Captain Nemo. In addition, he was the author of three autobiographical novels—The Happy Episode (1927), Riverhead (1932), and My Heart for Hostage (1942)—written in studied, highly mannered prose. He also published a successful textbook, First Principles of Verse (1938), and a collection of essays, In Pursuit of Poetry (1960).

Throughout his life Hillyer remained a loyal conservative. In politics he was a Republican; in religion, an Episcopalian; and in art, a traditionalist heavily influenced by the poetry he had studied in college. A serious yet restrained critic of the "new poetry" associated with T. S. Eliot and Ezra Pound and the "new criticism" associated with Eliot, among others, he sought in his textbook, his essays, and his public appearances to defend traditional verse that dealt nobly with nature or familiar themes of love, death, and honor. He was active in literary politics, serving as a member of the New England Poetry Club, as chancellor of the Academy of American Poets in 1942, as president of the Poetry Society of America in 1949 and again from 1951 to 1953, as Phi Beta Kappa Poet six times, and as a member of the American Academy of Arts and Sciences and the National Institute of Arts and Letters. In addition he used his influence to promote traditional religious and aesthetic values in an age he thought increasingly radical and decadent. In the 1930s, when his conservatism provoked the ire of left-wing critics, he persisted in espousing his views without personally attacking his adversaries. But in 1949, when the Library of Congress announced that the prestigious Bollingen Prize was being awarded to Ezra Pound for the Pisan Cantos, he responded with a "protest" that was widely quoted in newspapers and then with three essays—"Treason's Strange Fruit" and "Poetry's New Priesthood" in Saturday Review of Literature (June 1949), and "The Crisis in American Poetry" in American Mercury (Jan. 1950)—in which he attacked not only Pound and his poetry but also the selection committee and the drift of modern literature as influenced by the poetry and criticism of T. S. Eliot. He described Pound's poems as "vehicles of contempt for America" and as containing "ruthless mockery of our Christian war dead"; he accused Eliot of having gained a "stranglehold on American poetry" through the example of his own dense, allusional, obscure poetry and by the authority of "the so-called 'new criticism'" created to decipher it. In his second essay Hillyer asserted that "an uncompromising assault on the new estheticism" was "long overdue."

In September 1953, his second marriage having ended in divorce, Hillyer married Jeanne Hinternesch Duplaix. An avid sailor, he continued to sail as well as teach and advocate the kind of verse he had spent his life reading, writing, and defending. But the assault on Eliot and Pound that he called for, though it found scattered supporters, did not succeed. After Hillyer's death in Wilmington, Delaware, in 1961, Eliot and Pound remained major forces both in American literature and in modern literature generally, whereas Hillyer faded farther from sight. Ironically, when more formidable foes than he later began attacking the poetry and criticism of Pound and Eliot, they did so in terms that were even more hostile to Hillyer's traditional verse than to the experimental work he so loathed.

• Hillyer's other works include another book of poetry, Pattern of a Day (1940), and one critical work, Some Roots of English Poetry (1933); he edited Eight Harvard Poets (1917) and, with S. Foster Damon, Eight More Harvard Poets (1923), and, with others, Prose Masterpieces of English and American Literature (1931). An obituary is in the New York Times, 25 Dec. 1961.

DAVID MINTER

HILPRECHT, Herman Vollrath (28 July 1859–19 Mar. 1925), Assyriologist, was born in Hohenerxleben (Anhalt), Germany, the son of Robert Hilprecht, a tax official, and Emilie Wielepp. He spelled his name differently at various periods of his life, preferring "Hermann" for his first name in Germany but "Herman" in America; his middle name is spelled "Volrath" or "Vollrat" in some sources. After attending local schools in Hecklingen and Hoym and the Herzogliches Karls Gymnasium in Bernburg, Hilprecht entered in 1880 the University of Leipzig, where he studied theology, law, and Semitic languages. He received his doctorate under Friedrich Delitzsch in Assyriology in 1883 with a dissertation on a Babylonian boundary stone of the time of Nebuchadnezzar I in the British Museum. After spending two years in Switzerland for health reasons, he was appointed teaching assistant in Old Testament theology at the University of Erlangen. The following year he moved to Philadelphia, Pennsylvania, to become oriental editor of the Sunday School Times.

Hilprecht was an important figure in the expansion of Semitic studies in the United States to include Akkadian and Sumerian, the languages of ancient Mesopotamia. At the end of the nineteenth century, Harvard, Johns Hopkins, and Yale Universities, as well as the Universities of Chicago and Pennsylvania, had created programs in the languages and civilizations of the ancient Near East. Competition among them was intensified by a race to determine which would be the first to launch an archaeological excavation in Mesopotamia.

The University of Pennsylvania had three Semitists on its faculty by 1886: John P. Peters, Morris Jastrow, Jr., and Hilprecht. Hilprecht began as a lecturer in Egyptology but was subsequently appointed to the Clark research professorship of Assyriology and comparative Semitic philology. Largely through Peters's efforts, the university received an excavation permit from the Ottoman government for the site of Nippur, a Sumerian city that had been occupied for at least three millennia. The first three seasons were under the directorship of Peters and John Henry Haynes, with

Hilprecht present in 1888–1889 as epigrapher. When Peters left the university in 1895, Hilprecht took over as scientific director and was present when thousands of cuneiform tablets were discovered. Asserting that the excavations had been grossly mismanaged and lacking in regard for architecture in the effort to uncover documents and other artifacts, Hilprecht gave himself credit for putting the project on a sounder scientific basis. He claimed discovery of a Sumerian library that was far older than the famous library of Assurbanipal found at Nineveh a half-century before. Hilprecht's version of the excavation and his harsh judgments of the other members of the Nippur team appeared in *Explorations in Bible Lands during the Nineteenth Century* (1903).

A storm of controversy broke in Near Eastern circles in America over this publication. Peters and Jastrow, among others, accused Hilprecht of falsification of facts, misuse of evidence, claiming to have made discoveries that were made before his arrival at the site, and referring to tablets he had bought from antiquities dealers as if they came from the library at Nippur, the very existence of which they questioned. Hilprecht answered that the existence of the library was "assured" and questioned the integrity of his critics. Hilprecht's critics also asserted that he had improperly retained as his personal property objects excavated at Nippur that rightfully belonged to the University of Pennsylvania.

In response to the uproar, the university convened a judicatory committee, which issued a confidential report exonerating Hilprecht; this was widely denounced as a "whitewash." Most of the major figures in American Near Eastern studies united against Hilprecht, who published in response *The So-called Peters-Hilprecht Controversy* (1908); this included the proceedings of the judicatory committee. Further dispute arose when Hilprecht published in 1910 a Sumerian document that he argued confirmed the biblical flood story, *The Earliest Version of the Babylonian Deluge Story and the Temple Library of Nippur*. Again, he seemed to be going beyond the evidence, perhaps for nonscholarly reasons, although he was by no means the only scholar of his day prone to enthusiastic presentation of biblical "discoveries" in Babylonian texts. Because Hilprecht's main backers on the scholarly level were European Assyriologists, the debate began to assume a nationalistic character, with American scholars complaining of foreign interference in the American university scene.

Simultaneously with his professorship, Hilprecht held the position of curator of the Babylonian section of the University Museum. Between 1893 and 1901 he also helped to reorganize the Mesopotamian collections of the Imperial Ottoman Museum at Constantinople. The sultan presented to Hilprecht numerous tablets and other objects excavated at Nippur or purchased while the expedition was in the field. Although his critics maintained that this was a legal fiction, making possible under the Turkish antiquities law division of the Nippur expedition's finds, Hilprecht chose to regard these artifacts as his property. He claimed to have presented the University Museum with its collection of fifty thousand Mesopotamian antiquities, as if the findings of the Nippur expedition were his to bestow.

In 1910 Hilprecht alleged that his office had been opened in his absence and that the cases containing the Nippur tablets had been broken open and the contents removed. He demanded a university investigation, but the trustees voted instead to accept his resignation. He left the museum in 1911 embittered and with a strong sense of betrayal.

Although the controversy obscured Hilprecht's scholarly merits at the time, his superb publications of the Nippur clay tablets have had great long-term value. His *Old Babylonian Inscriptions, Chiefly from Nippur* (1893), containing 152 inscriptions in hand copies of extraordinary beauty and faithfulness to the original, was a pioneering publication of "archaic" third millennium inscriptions that established Hilprecht's reputation as a first-rate epigrapher. In 1906 he published a volume of mathematical, metrological, and chronological tablets. A gifted linguist and a demanding, if tyrannical, teacher, he trained a generation of Assyriologists to decipher and copy with precision cuneiform documents.

Hilprecht was a proponent of the "exact" method of publishing cuneiform tablets, in contrast to the cuneiform type or freehand representation typical of much Assyriological work of the time. He edited four series of publications from Nippur, of which the text series alone ran to fourteen large volumes, an inestimable service to Assyriology and the first American scholarly enterprise of its kind. He was the author of a large number of other publications on theology, history, and epigraphy, mostly focused on the Bible and discoveries from Mesopotamia. Hilprecht's "temple library," however, was proved by later excavations at Nippur to be a group of private houses belonging to scribes and their families.

Hilprecht married in 1886 Ida Haufe, who served as coauthor of the first part of his *Explorations*. She died in 1902. In 1903 he married Sallie Crozer Robinson, whose wealth and social standing made possible for him a way of life not typical of a university professor of the time. They traveled extensively in Europe and the Far East and collected ancient bronzes, Greek vases, Chinese ceramics, and other objects d'art. There were no children by either marriage.

After his resignation, Hilprecht settled in Munich, Germany. Torn in his allegiance by the First World War, he remained in Germany with his wife and stepson, devoting considerable energy and money to assisting German war wounded and civilian victims. After the armistice, he returned to Philadelphia and became a U.S. citizen, contributing no more to Assyriology. Hilprecht died in Philadelphia.

Hilprecht willed the Nippur tablets he had retained to the University of Jena, Germany, where they were eventually installed as the Frau Professor Hilprecht

Collection. Other antiquities were willed to the University of Pennsylvania and the city of Philadelphia.

Hilprecht's substantial strengths as a scholar and success as a teacher were undoubtedly undermined by his inordinate vanity, inability to admit mistakes, ungenerous treatment of his associates, and free manipulation of evidence. He embroiled the leading scholars of the ancient Near East of the time in a lengthy and debilitating controversy that could easily have been avoided. These unhappy contradictions were not lost on his contemporaries; an anniversary volume of thirty-two studies in his honor (1909) contained only one contribution by a scholar living in America, his student Hugo Radau.

• Hilprecht's papers and field diaries are at the University of Jena, Germany. Portions of his correspondence are in the Nippur files, Museum Archives, University of Pennsylvania. His annual reports as curator of the University Museum provide details on his professional activities. His early years are sketched in the vita to his dissertation (Leipzig, 1883). A bibliography of his publications of Babylonian tablets and inscriptions is found in Rykle Borger, *Handbuch der Keilschriftliteratur*, vol. 1 (1967), pp. 190–94; there is a detailed study by Ferdinand Hestermann, "Die Bibliographie Hilprechts über Nippur," *Wissenschaftliche Zeitschrift der Friedrich-Schiller-Universität Jena* 4 (1954–1955): 35–47. The Hilprecht controversy has been studied in detail by Paul Ritterband and Harold Wechsler in "A Message to Lushtamar: The Hilprecht Controversy and Semitic Scholarship in America," *History of Higher Education Annual* 1 (1981): 5–41, which includes extensive references to unpublished material in the archives of the University of Pennsylvania, the University Museum, and Harvard and Columbia Universities, as well as a bibliography. For a review of the personal side of the Nippur excavations, see A. Westenholz, "The Early Excavators of Nippur," in *Nippur at the Centennial*, ed. M. deJ. Ellis (1992), pp. 291–95. Hilprecht's holograph will is on file at City Hall in Philadelphia. Additional information on Hilprecht's family appears in a sketch by D. O. Edzard in *Neue Deutsche Biographie*, vol. 9 (1972), pp. 160–61. Obituaries include Heinrich Zimmern, *Zeitschrift für Assyriologie* 36 (1925): 309–10; the *Philadelphia Public Ledger* and the *New York Times*, both 20 Mar. 1925; and the *Journal of Biblical Literature* 45 (1926): iii–iv. Discrepancies will be found in these sources for his date of death; the one given here is drawn from the death certificate signed by his attending physician on file in the Pennsylvania Department of Health, Division of Vital Records, New Castle.

BENJAMIN R. FOSTER

HILTNER, Seward (26 Nov. 1909–19 Nov. 1984), theological educator, was born in Tyrone, Pennsylvania, the son of Clement Seward Hiltner, a railroad mail clerk, and Charlotte Porter. Graduating from Lafayette College in 1931 with a degree in psychology, Hiltner studied theology at the Divinity School of the University of Chicago (1931–1935), bypassing the bachelor of divinity degree to begin Ph.D. studies. Recruited by clinical pastoral pioneer Anton T. Boisen for a summer program of pastoral training in clinical settings, an experimental concept in theological education at the time, Hiltner spent three summers in hospital-based programs under the supervision of two other pioneering figures, Donald C. Beatty and Carroll A. Wise, and developed an enduring commitment to the value of supervised clinical experience in theological education. He also became deeply committed to Boisen's revolutionary proposition that theology itself can be learned from the crucible of psychological conflict and struggle.

In 1935 Hiltner was ordained to the Presbyterian ministry and became the second executive secretary of the Council for Clinical Training of Theological Students in New York under Flanders Dunbar, M.D. There he organized clinical pastoral programs, introduced clinical pastoral education to the federal prison system, and forged institutional relationships between the fledgling clinical pastoral movement and numerous theological seminaries. Hiltner emphasized the theological and pastoral aspects of the emerging clinical programs against pressures for a more secular and multiprofessional orientation and worked to integrate clinical training into the theological curriculum, coining the term "clinical pastoral training" to emphasize its pastoral orientation. In 1936 he married Helen Margaret Johansen; they had two children.

In 1938 Hiltner became executive secretary of the Commission on Religion and Health (later the Department of Pastoral Services) of the Federal Council of Churches of Christ in America (New York), working to strengthen and unify the clinical pastoral education movement. He organized the First National Conference on Clinical Training in 1944 and edited its proceedings in a seminal volume, *Clinical Pastoral Training* (1945). In 1950 he formed the Association of Seminary Professors in the Practical Fields (now the Association for Practical Theology).

During World War II Hiltner organized and chaired the New York Psychology Group, a monthly gathering of distinguished theologians, psychotherapists, and social scientists, including (among others) Erich Fromm, Rollo May, Carl Rogers, Ruth Benedict, and Paul Tillich. Hiltner's later writing reflected the influence of these figures, especially Fromm's socially and culturally oriented revision of Freudian theory; and Hiltner in turn influenced them (for example, Tillich's theory of the "transmoral conscience"). In 1949 Hiltner published his classic text, *Pastoral Counseling*, which advocated a method of pastoral counseling similar to Rogers's "nondirective" psychotherapy (though developed independently of Rogers). Hiltner's approach emphasized, like all of his work, the minister's ethical commitments and pastoral identity.

In 1950 Hiltner became associate professor (later professor) of pastoral theology at the University of Chicago Divinity School, completing his Ph.D. dissertation on "Psychotherapy and Christian Ethics" in 1953. At Chicago Hiltner formed the first doctoral program in religion and personality. This program educated many who were to become the nation's academic leaders in the fields of pastoral care and counseling and interdisciplinary studies in psychology and religion. He authored scores of articles (many appearing in the popular journal *Pastoral Psychology*, for which he was editorial consultant) that introduced a generation of ministers to clinical theories and methods of counseling. He also produced a succession of books that gave clinical pastoral education a significant literature of theory and research.

Hiltner's most creative and important book, *Preface to Pastoral Theology* (1958), drew from field theory and process philosophy to develop a new way of conceptualizing the practice of ministry in terms of three "perspectives" ("shepherding," "communicating," and "organizing"), which he hoped would replace the traditional way of conceiving ministry in terms of objective, sharply differentiated "offices" (or roles) such as preaching, liturgics, and pastoral care. Hiltner's perspectives flexibly interpenetrate and combine attitudinal and situational dimensions, arguably offering ministry a more insightful and nuanced way of conceiving its work as a differentiated unity. Hiltner developed his theory of perspectives, however, principally as a means of reconceiving the discipline of pastoral theology. In his proposal, the task of pastoral theology is expanded from the narrowly practical work of discovering ways to "apply" theological principles to ministry to a fundamental theological enterprise capable of developing original theological insights out of pastoral practice (when practice is examined in conjunction with authoritative revelation). Thus, in theory, Hiltner integrated clinical pastoral perspectives and insights into theology and theological education.

In 1961 Hiltner joined the faculty of Princeton Theological Seminary as professor of theology and personality. Notable among his achievements at Princeton were the development of a doctor of ministry curriculum based on the analysis of pastoral cases, significant developments in the Ph.D. program, and a book, *Theological Dynamics* (1972), which seeks to interpret theological doctrines by construing them as dynamic systems open to psychological analysis.

Though Hiltner is popularly associated with his early work on pastoral care and counseling, his later work turned more broadly to ministry as a whole and to general topics in pastoral theology, such as anxiety and aging. Hiltner was critical of the development of specialized pastoral counseling (or "pastoral psychotherapy") in the early sixties, which he believed would isolate pastoral counseling from the churches and divide the ministry as a profession (a concern that history has largely confirmed). In his later years, however, he served as consultant to the Trinity Counseling Service in Princeton and received the annual award of the American Association of Pastoral Counselors at his retirement in 1980.

Hiltner was highly regarded as a theological consultant in the psychiatry and mental health fields and enjoyed a long relationship with Karl Menninger and the Menninger Foundation (1957–1972), where he was Sloan visiting professor in 1957. Hiltner was also a Fulbright Research Fellow in New Zealand in 1958 and visiting professor at the University of Utrecht (Netherlands) in 1970. He served on the advisory boards of numerous journals, including the *Journal of Religion and Health, Journal of Suicidology, Quarterly Journal of Studies on Alcohol, American Imago, Pastoral Psychology, Medical Aspects of Human Sexuality*, and *Journal of Pastoral Care*.

In seminars and case consultations Hiltner's ability to synthesize complex data, perceive and express essential points clearly, and identify relationships between psychology and theology, often with wry wit and humor, was legendary. At the same time he was notorious for expressing insightful critical judgments on the work of others and drawing shrewd connections in seminars between conceptual or methodological difficulties in a paper and its author's personality, a habit which earned him a fearsome reputation for candor and critique among colleagues and students.

Hiltner's theory of the discipline of pastoral theology has, in itself, so far failed to gain a wide following (there have been few significant attempts to write exactly the kind of pastoral theology Hiltner proposed). His theory of ministry is also commonly misunderstood or misapplied (the "perspectives" become fixed roles), and his resistance to the development of a specialized profession of pastoral counseling has gone unheeded. He has also been charged, wrongly, with reducing American pastoral care to a nontheological pragmatism. Yet there is no question that Hiltner was the major intellectual theorist of the postwar pastoral care movement in the United States, that he played a leading role in legitimating clinical pastoral care and counseling in theological education, and that he was one of the most influential figures in bringing clinical theories and methods into modern ministry and promoting ministry's concern for human health and development. He died in Princeton, New Jersey.

• Hiltner's papers are in the Robert E. Speer Library of Princeton Theological Seminary. His other major books include: *Religion and Health* (1943), *Sex Ethics and the Kinsey Reports* (1953), *The Christian Shepherd* (1959), *The Context of Pastoral Counseling* (with Lowelle G. Colston) (1961), *Constructive Aspects of Anxiety* (with Karl Menninger) (1963), *Ferment in the Ministry* (1969), *Pastoral Care in the Liberal Churches* (with James Luther Adams) (1970), and (as editor) *Toward a Theology of Aging* (1975). Major articles by Hiltner include "The Psychological Understanding of Religion," in *Readings in the Psychology of Religion*, ed. Orlo Strunk, Jr. (1959); "Pastoral Psychology and Christian Ethics," *Pastoral Psychology* 4, no. 33 (1953): 23–33; "Clinical and Theological Notes on Responsibility," *Journal of Religion and Health* 2, no. 1 (1962): 7–20; and "The Future of Christian Anthropology," *Theology Today* 20, no. 2 (1963): 242–57. Hiltner's bibliography through 1967 appears in *Pastoral Psychology* 19, no. 180 (1968): 6–22. Hiltner's role in the history of clinical pastoral education is described in Edward E. Thornton, *Professional Education for Ministry: A History of Clinical Pastoral Education* (1970); Allison Stokes, *Ministry after Freud* (1985); and E. Brooks Holifield, *A History of Pastoral Care in America: From Salvation to Self-Realization* (1983). For articles assessing Hiltner's significance see *Pastoral Psychology* 29, no. 1 (1980), and LeRoy Aden and J. Harold Ellens, eds., *Turning Points in Pastoral Care: The Legacy of Anton Boisen and Seward Hiltner* (1990). See also John H. Patton, "Toward a Theology of Pastoral Event: Reflections on the work of Seward Hiltner," *Journal of Pastoral Care* 40, no. 2 (1986): 129–41. Obituaries are in *Pastoral Psychology* 34, no. 1 (1985): 3–8, and the *Princeton Seminary Bulletin*, n.s., 7, no. 1 (1986): 76–78.

RODNEY J. HUNTER

HILTON, Conrad (25 Dec. 1887–3 Jan. 1979), businessman, was born Conrad Nicholson Hilton in San Antonio, Socorro County, New Mexico Territory, the son of Augustus Holver "Gus" Hilton, an entrepreneur, and Mary Laufersweiler. Hilton's early life was spent on the frontier of the Southwest, where his father ran a variety of businesses, including a general store. He learned Spanish from his playmates and spent a great deal of time assisting his father in his various enterprises. After early study at a local school, he attended Goss Military Institute in Albuquerque (1899–1900), New Mexico Military Institute (1900–1901, 1902–1904), and St. Michael's College, Santa Fe (1901–1902). Hilton dropped out of the New Mexico Military Institute in 1904 and went to work full time in his father's increasingly prosperous store. There he learned to haggle with all types of customers, thereby honing the negotiating skills that were to serve him well in the future. Selling off part of his business (coal mines), Hilton's father, now a wealthy man, moved the family to Long Beach, California, in 1905 due to his wife's poor health.

The family finances suffered severely in the panic of 1907, and the Hiltons returned to San Antonio; Conrad's plan to attend Dartmouth was permanently shelved. Instead he entered the New Mexico School of Mines (now the New Mexico Institute of Mining and Technology) in Socorro in the fall of 1907, finding time on weekends to assist in his father's newest enterprise—a hotel. Hilton's job was to meet the incoming trains (at noon, midnight, and 3:00 A.M.) that came into San Antonio and to drum up trade. Business soon thrived, yet Hilton remained restless.

Hilton left the School of Mines in 1909 and served a term in the lower house of the first New Mexico state legislature (1912–1913); in 1913 he helped organize the New Mexico State Bank of San Antonio, of which he was named vice president. Passed over for president and instead awarded the position of cashier as a sop, Hilton conducted a vigorous proxy fight and gained the presidency of the bank in 1915. He had previously earned a partnership with his father in A. H. Hilton & Son, and in August 1917, with the advent of U.S. entry into World War I, Hilton left banking and entered the U.S. Army as a second lieutenant, serving first in San Francisco and later in France with the 304th Labor Battalion. While Hilton was in France, his father died; he left the army in February 1919 with no definite plans.

Hilton returned to San Antonio intending to resume banking, but instead he took a dying friend's advice to move to Texas, where he envisioned greater opportunities in the oil-rich state. Hilton was frustrated in his attempt to buy a bank in Cisco and instead bought the Mobley Hotel from an owner who was eager to leave the business. This purchase, in the summer of 1919, was followed closely by the purchase of the Hotel Melba in Fort Worth, launching Hilton into his ultimate and most successful career.

Hilton's first hotels were worn-down existing structures, and he initiated several managerial practices that proved successful. Seeking to maximize profits, he scrutinized every inch of his properties and often squeezed several additional rooms or a novelty shop into previously unused space. Remembering his own frustration with his father's interference while in his employ, Hilton insisted on finding first-rate managers for his properties and then left them in peace to do their jobs. Business expansion always required capital, and Hilton financed his operations with a mix of bank loans, funds from friends and family, and his own money. He mixed an aggressive expansion policy with shrewd negotiation, good timing, and a stubborn refusal to overextend his finances (he never asked investors for funds without putting his own money in a property). Hilton never attempted to standardize the appearance of his hotels; instead, he sought to bring out the best possible appearance in each property.

Using the management slogan "minimax" (minimum cost, maximum hospitality), Hilton switched strategies in the mid-1920s, and he built his first hotel in Dallas in 1925. That same year he married Mary Barron in Dallas; they had three sons. Other newly erected hotels (in Waco, Abilene, Marlin, Plainview, San Angelo, and Lubbock) soon followed, and Hilton had just announced plans to build a hotel in El Paso when the stock market crashed in the fall of 1929.

Even as the El Paso hotel opened in November 1930, Hilton, along with other hotel owners, began to feel the effects of the depression. Revenue steadily dropped, and debts mounted. Attempts at economy, such as closing off unused hotel floors and removing guest room phones, provided only temporary relief. Reduced at one point to borrowing $300 from a bellboy for food, Hilton managed (after complex negotiations and frantic fundraising) to regain control of his El Paso property. Badly needed funds were also forthcoming from an oil lease that Hilton had taken as a gamble. Slowly Hilton began to reduce his debts and regain his business footing. His marriage, a casualty of depression-era stress, ended in divorce in 1934.

In 1938 Hilton purchased his first hotel outside of Texas, the Sir Francis Drake in San Francisco. As the national economy recovered, Hilton took advantage of his improving situation, and other hotels soon followed: Albuquerque in 1939 and the Town House in Los Angeles and Hilton's first foreign venture, the Palacio Hilton in Chihuahua, Mexico, both in 1942. That same year he married Zsa Zsa Sari Gabor, with whom he had one daughter; they divorced in 1946.

With the acquisition of the Roosevelt and the Plaza hotels in 1943, Hilton expanded his growing empire into New York City. He bought the Palmer House and the Stevens Hotel (the world's largest) in Chicago in 1945 and in 1946 formed Hilton Hotels Corporation, with himself as president. The company stock was listed on the New York Stock Exchange—the first hotel firm on the exchange. His greatest acquisition, however, had been years in the making. In the depths of the depression Hilton had cut out a magazine picture of the New York Waldorf-Astoria, written "the greatest of them all" across it, stored the photo, and allowed himself to dream. After a long period of negotiation, Hilton purchased the hotel on 12 October 1949—becoming "the man who bought the Waldorf."

A tall, active, gregarious man who rarely lacked energy, "Connie" Hilton refused to slow down. His first European hotel, the Castellana Hilton, opened in Madrid, Spain, in 1953. He acquired the Statler chain of hotels in 1954, and his autobiography, *Be My Guest*, was published in 1957. Hilton assumed the role of chairman of the board in 1960 but turned over the presidency of Hilton Hotels to his son Barron in 1966. A devout Roman Catholic, Hilton also enjoyed dancing and golf and remained active until just before his death in Santa Monica, California. His third wife, Mary Frances Kelly, whom he had married in 1977, survived him. At the time of his death, Hilton Hotels operated worldwide and continued to expand operations.

Conrad Hilton combined ambition, intelligence, and an uncanny business sense to create a hotel empire. The Hilton Hotels Corporation is the legacy of his perseverance and dreams.

• Conrad Hilton's papers are at the archive of the University of Houston School for Hotel and Restaurant Management. As a leading business figure, Hilton was covered extensively by the press; see, for example, "Hilton's Texas Connection," *Houston Chronicle Magazine*, 28 June 1987, pp. 6–9, and "Conrad Nicholson Hilton (born: 1887)," *Fortune*, 30 Jan. 1978, p. 96. An obituary is in the *New York Times*, 4 Jan. 1979.

EDWARD L. LACH, JR.

HILTON, Edward (1596–1670?), entrepreneur and judge, was baptized at Witton chapelry in Northwich, Chester County, England, on 9 June 1596, the son of William Hilton, a gentleman farmer. His mother's name is unknown. Very little is known about Hilton's childhood and early adult years. Sometime after his father's death in 1605, he was apprenticed to a fishmonger's widow, Marie Hilton, in London. In 1621 he was admitted to the aristocratic Fishmongers Guild—the same year his brother William, who had been admitted to the guild in 1616, immigrated to the Plymouth colony in New England.

The date of Hilton's arrival at Hilton's Point, seven miles up the Piscataqua River, establishing the settlement of Dover, is also a mystery. What appears to have happened is that sometime between 1623 and 1626 both Edward and William Hilton (not necessarily together) joined a settlement established by David Thomson at Little Harbor (now Rye, New Hampshire) that he called Pannaway. The brothers set up fishing stages and an Indian trading post at Hilton's Point (later Dover) on the Piscataqua; when Thomson abandoned the Pannaway settlement for an island in Massachusetts in 1625 or 1626, the remaining settlers moved with or joined the Hiltons to establish what became the first permanent settlement in New Hampshire, with houses, cornfields, a fishery, and an Indian trading post.

In the meantime, Sir Ferdinando Gorges and Captain John Mason, the dominant individuals in the Council for New England, received at least seven council grants in northern New England between 1621 and 1635, many of which overlapped or duplicated one another and the Hilton settlement. After the arrival on the Piscataqua of Laconia Company agents representing Gorges and Mason in 1630, Edward Hilton went to England to secure land titles for his settlement. In March 1631 the council granted to him and his associates (some Bristol merchants) Hilton's Point "with the south side of the said River up to the fall of the River, and three miles into the Maine Land by all the breadth aforesaid." This grant, known as either the Hilton or the Squamscott patent, assured Dover's land titles; but its ambiguities touched off a series of land controversies that would not be settled for almost thirty years, and it helped Hilton become one of the richest and most influential men in the Piscataqua region.

The boundaries of Hilton's patent became controversial as settlers sponsored by the Laconia Company (especially Gorges and Mason), the Massachusetts government, and various Puritan groups migrated into the Piscataqua region during the 1630s and found Hilton a central figure to be accommodated. By the time this controversy was resolved, Hilton owned Hilton's Point, a large farm encompassing Newfields just north of Exeter, sawmills, and timber grants from the town of Exeter. By the mid-1650s, Hilton had progressed from exploiting the fisheries and Indian trade to exploiting the land and timber and was carrying on a significant trade in lumber and fish with English merchants, a general pattern of economic activity that would dominate the region for at least another century.

As an ambitious Anglican friendly to Gorges and Mason on the chaotic frontier, Hilton coped effectively with escalating pressures. Dissident Puritan ministers as well as settlers were immigrating; Massachusetts's leaders had designs to assert legal jurisdiction, and there were various conflicting land claims. Moreover, piracy, crime, and lawlessness had become significant problems in the region. Hilton responded by corresponding with Massachusetts governor John Winthrop about the problems and by helping the Massachusetts government extend its law and order into the region. In return, in 1641 it promised to exempt all his property from taxes and appointed him as one of the two Piscataqua magistrates. This agreement also guaranteed all "liberties of fishing, planting, and felling timber as formerly enjoyed" and protected the land claims and political rights of the Piscataqua settlers.

This agreement brought a long-needed stability to the Piscataqua and reveals the respect and distinction that Edward Hilton held in the region. Having moved from Dover to his large farm near Exeter, he continued to be chosen as an associate justice during the 1640s and was selected to help determine town boundaries between Exeter and Hampton in 1652 and between Dover and Exeter in 1657. In 1661 and 1664 he again served as an associate justice. Hilton served as Exeter selectman in 1645, 1646, and 1651. In 1646 he helped the town finance a parsonage, and in 1650 he served as the town's negotiator, persuading the Reverend Samuel Dudley to become its pastor. In 1652 he received a large timber grant from the town as a partial return for his services.

While there is no evidence regarding the identity of Hilton's first wife or wives, he and one wife had seven children between 1630 and 1642. However, sometime before 1655 his wife died, and in that year he married the widow Catherine Treworgy, a daughter of Nicholas Shapleigh of Kittery. Shapleigh was a converted Quaker and the New England agent of Gorges.

As the Massachusetts government increased its persecution of Quakers in the 1650s and 1660s, Hilton grew unfriendly toward Massachusetts's control over the Piscataqua region. After the restoration of King Charles II, when his royal investigating commission appeared on the Piscataqua in 1665, Hilton welcomed its presence. The commission declared that both the Piscataqua and Maine were beyond the boundaries of Massachusetts and needed royal protection. Hilton helped prepare a petition to the Crown and obtained signatures from inhabitants of three of the four towns in support of the commission's claims and authority. The petition denounced Massachusetts for denying the commission's powers to set boundaries and to establish governments in the region, declared that the petitioners were "much transported with joy" at the Crown's concern for them, and called for the Piscataqua towns to be placed under "royal protection" and joined to the "province of Maine." Undoubtedly, Hilton's Anglican tolerance and new family connections led him to this change of heart. By 1666, he was taking out 1,000-year leases from his father-in-law Shapleigh, now the agent of Mason as well as Gorges. This petition and another from Portsmouth proved to be significant parts of an initial effort that culminated in the royal colony of New Hampshire in 1679.

Hilton died on his farm near Exeter, a rich man by seventeenth-century colonial standards with an estate worth over £2,200. Today there is a small monument dedicated to him in Hilton Park at Dover Point. It honors him as the "founder of Dover, 1623" and as the "father of New Hampshire." While both claims are somewhat overdrawn, nevertheless, as the first permanent settler of one of the original New Hampshire towns, as an entrepreneur who followed economic activities that became the major patterns of the Piscataqua region, and as an Anglican nonconformist with a vision of a separate province under royal auspices in a Puritan-dominated sphere, Hilton prefigured colonial New Hampshire's future.

• There are no unpublished Hilton manuscripts in New Hampshire repositories. Published primary sources relating to him are in the *New Hampshire Provincial and State Papers*, vols. 1, 17, 29, 31, and 40 (1867–1943), and *Winthrop's Journal*, ed. James K. Hosmer (2 vols., 1908). Biographical information and background are in Charles H. Bell, *History of the Town of Exeter, New Hampshire* (1888); Sybil Noyes et al., *Genealogical Dictionary of Maine and New Hampshire* (1928–1939); and John Scales, *History of Dover, New Hampshire* (1923). The best general discussions of Hilton and the seventeenth-century Piscataqua region are Jere Daniell, *Colonial New Hampshire: A History* (1981); John S. Jenness, *Notes on the First Planting of New Hampshire and on the Piscataqua Patents* (1878); Elwin L. Page, *Judicial Beginnings in New Hampshire, 1640–1700* (1959); Frank Sanborn, "Churchmen on the Piscataqua, 1650–1690," *Proceedings of the Massachusetts Historical Society* 45 (1911): 211–43; Everett S. Stackpole, *History of New Hampshire* (4 vols., 1916); and David E. Van Deventer, *The Emergence of Provincial New Hampshire* (1976). Also see Bernard Bailyn, *The New England Merchants in the Seventeenth Century* (1955); Elwin L. Page, "A.D. 1623," *Granite Monthly* 54 (1922): 208–11; and Scales, "The Date of the First Permanent Settlement in New Hampshire," *Granite Monthly* 54 (1922): 269–77.

DAVID E. VAN DEVENTER

HILTON, William (1617–c. 1675), seventeenth-century explorer of the Carolina coast, was born in Northwich, Cheshire, England. His father, William Hilton, immigrated to New Plymouth colony in 1621, followed two years later by the six-year-old William and his mother (name unknown). The Hilton family settled in Piscataqua, and as an adult the younger William moved to Massachusetts Bay colony, living in Newbury and Charlestown. Following the custom of going to sea as a youth, Hilton gained extensive experience on transatlantic and Caribbean voyages. His first marriage was to Sarah Greenleaf of Newbury. After her death he married Mehetabel Nowell of Charlestown, who was the daughter of Increase Nowell, a former secretary of Massachusetts Bay colony and one of the governor's assistants. Hilton had at least one child, a daughter Sarah, who became the wife of Edward Winslow, a companion on Hilton's first exploratory voyage.

By midcentury the town lands in New England were occupied to such an extent that the younger generation of New Englanders looked to the developing southern colonies on the mainland and to the rich Caribbean colonies, hoping to establish trading partnerships. An influential Massachusetts Bay merchant family, the Vassalls of Scituate, with relatives in London and Barbados, had already been involved in an attempt to colonize in the Carolana grant, as the area at that time was identified, and they were influential in organizing investors in both Boston and London for settling on the southeastern coast, also known as Florida. A "Committe for Cape ffaire at Boston" sponsored the first of William Hilton's exploratory voyages to the present Carolinas as well as a second expedition to establish a colony.

Hilton, commanding the *Adventure*, embarked from Charlestown, Massachusetts Bay, on 14 August 1662 and returned in November with a glowing report on his exploration of the Cape Fear River, which he named the Charles River. Despite severe storms that kept the *Adventure* from entering the river for nearly a month, Hilton succeeded the next month in sailing some thirty-five miles up the Cape Fear and its tributaries, recording "vast meddows" ideal for cattle, rich upland fields, and "a summer Contry" climate. The few American Indians in the area appeared to be friendly. From the information gathered on this voyage, the first detailed map of the Cape Fear was drawn by Nicholas Shapley, a Charlestown navigator. The Shapley map contained a reference to a James Fort on the east bank of the river that probably marked either a temporary camp of Hilton's expedition or a site for a future colony. Inspired by Hilton's narrative, another group from Massachusetts Bay unsuccessfully attempted to seat a colony on the river in the spring of 1663.

On 24 March 1663, as the New Englanders were leaving the Cape Fear, a new proprietary patent to the land south of Virginia called Carolina was granted by Charles II to eight Lords Proprietors, including Barbadian Sir John Colleton. Joining the New England and London groups interested in colonization of Carolina was the Corporation of Barbadian Adventurers, an association of merchants and planters initially organized by the Vassalls and the Colletons. Hilton, at the time sailing from Barbados, was engaged to command a second exploration of the southeastern mainland. Again commanding the *Adventure*, Hilton, accompanied by Captain Anthony Long and Peter Fabian, set sail from Speights Bay on 10 August 1663. An uneventful sixteen-day voyage brought them to the southern coast of what is now South Carolina in the vicinity of St. Helena Sound and the Combahee River. Contacts with the local American Indians revealed news of English castaways, whom Hilton succeeded in rescuing through complicated negotiations with both the natives and a band of Spaniards sent to capture the English. As usual, Hilton reported rich soil, "clear and sweet" air, and "a very pleasent and delightful" country.

After sounding the entrance to Port Royal Sound, Hilton sailed toward the Cape Fear into a gale that blew the ship north almost to Cape Hatteras. Anchoring at last on 12 October at the entrance to the Cape Fear River, Hilton began an extensive exploration of the area that lasted until 4 December. The *Adventure* was sailed upriver, and then the ship's longboat was used to extend the explorers' movements into the interior. As on his earlier voyage, Hilton's report was promotional, as illustrated by his concluding statement that the Cape Fear River had "as good Land, and as well Timbered, as any we have seen in any other part of the world, sufficient to accomodate thousands of our English Nation."

The most interesting aspect of this narrative was the more extensive description of the area's American Indians. Although a little hostility was encountered, which led to some mistrust, most of the contacts with the natives were friendly. The local tribe, who were keeping the cattle and swine left by the New Englanders on the Cape, several times traded fresh beef and pork to Hilton's men. The publication in London of Hilton's narrative, *A Relation of a Discovery lately made on the Coast of Florida* (1664), aroused interest in the colonizing proposals from New England and Barbados. When the New Englanders could not get their desired terms from the proprietors, the Barbadians, now divided into two groups, forged ahead, with John Vassall establishing Charles Town on the Cape Fear on 29 May 1664. Although this colony failed within three years, it was the initial effort that led directly to the establishment of Charles Town (later Charleston, S.C.) on the Ashley and Cooper rivers in 1670.

Following his voyages of exploration, Hilton disappeared from the record. Although there is a brief mention of a William Hilton in Barbados in 1671, it is presumed that he returned to New England. Hilton's role in history is brief but significant. His two voyages to the Carolina coast preceded two colonization attempts that culminated in the permanent settlement of modern South Carolina. His narratives are the first detailed descriptions of the Carolina coast, inspiring the important Nicholas Shapley map. His name is commemorated on the South Carolina coast at Hilton Head and Hilton Head Island.

• The accounts of Hilton's voyages are in Louise Hall, "New Englanders at Sea: Cape Fear before the Royal Charter of 24 March 1662/3," *New England Historical and Genealogical Register* 124 (Apr. 1970): 88–108, and Alexander S. Salley, Jr., ed., *Narratives of Early Carolina, 1650–1708* (1911). Secondary studies of value are Charles M. Andrews, *The Colonial Period of American History*, vol. 3 (1937); Enoch Lawrence Lee, *The Lower Cape Fear in Colonial Days* (1965); and Cornelius M. D. Thomas, *James Forte* (1959).

LINDLEY S. BUTLER

HIMES, Chester Bomar (29 July 1909–12 Nov. 1984), African-American author, was born in Jefferson City, Missouri, the son of Joseph Sandy Himes, a teacher of blacksmithing and wheelwrighting at Lincoln Institute, and Estelle Bomar. The family moved several times during Chester Himes's childhood, settling finally in 1923 in Cleveland, Ohio, where Himes graduated from high school. In 1926 Himes enrolled at Ohio State University on a disability pension; earlier that year, while working as a busboy at a Cleveland hotel, he had fallen down an elevator shaft, suffering serious head and back injuries. At Ohio State, Himes tried to be the Jazz Age collegian, complete with "a knickerbocker suit, a long-stemmed pipe, and a Model T Ford," as he states in his autobiography, *The Quality of Hurt* (1972). By the end of the academic year, he was cutting classes and spending time in the poolhalls and saloons in the black section of Columbus. Himes left Ohio State for home in the spring of 1927, suffering from poor health and failing grades.

Returning to Cleveland in 1927, Himes drifted to the city's underworld of gambling and prostitution. It was in the area of Cleveland known as the Bucket of

Blood that he encountered the characters and violent milieu that he would describe in his crime fiction. Himes was arrested three times in 1928 for robbery; in December 1928 he was sentenced to twenty to twenty-five years of hard labor at Ohio State Prison in Columbus. He observes in *The Quality of Hurt*: "I was nineteen years old when I went in and twenty-six years old when I came out. I became a man, dependent on no one but myself." Himes began to write while in prison, sending stories to black newspapers and national magazines like *Esquire* and *Abbott's Monthly Magazine*. In 1934 *Esquire* published "To What Red Hell," a story based on the 1930 Easter Monday fire at Ohio State Prison in which more than 330 inmates died.

Following his parole in 1936, Himes returned to Cleveland. He married an old friend, Jean Lucinda Johnson, in 1937, the same year he began a prison novel, *Black Sheep*, which was not published until 1952, under the title *Cast the First Stone*. Unabashedly autobiographical, the novel set the tone for the highly personalized approach to fiction that Himes took in the first half of his career. While writing, Himes held numerous jobs in the 1930s and 1940s. He was employed as a laborer and then as a research assistant for the Works Progress Administration in 1937–1938, worked as a butler on author Louis Bromfield's Malabar Farm in Ohio in 1939, and found employment in various wartime industries in Los Angeles and San Francisco from 1940–1944. In 1944 Himes was awarded a Rosenwald Fellowship to finish *If He Hollers Let Him Go* (1945), his first published novel. This novel and his next, *Lonely Crusade* (1947), are "protest novels" that express Himes's disillusionment with life in California, a state that struck Himes as more virulently racist than anyplace he had encountered back east.

Himes moved to New York City in 1946 and for the next seven years worked as a porter, an estate caretaker, a bellhop, and a janitor in the greater metropolitan area while revising his prison novel and writing *The Third Generation* (1954). This book, the most explicitly autobiographical of his novels, traced the conflicts that ultimately destroyed his parents' marriage. In 1950, Himes's own marriage had ended in separation, and in 1953, disappointed with his personal life and hostile reviews of his novels, Himes left the United States for relatively permanent exile in Europe.

In Paris, Himes established himself as a member of the expatriate group that formed loosely around his friend Richard Nathaniel Wright, whom he had known in New York. Himes, however, was too suspicious of groups and of people in general to remain attached to them and often argued with other expatriates like Wright and James A. Baldwin. Consequently he spent most of his European years wandering from place to place, accompanied by a succession of women. Much of his bitterness over his life in the United States is poured out in a novel, *The Primitive* (1955), that Himes wrote while living in Majorca; the novel recounts a destructive interracial affair that Himes himself had experienced and represents his most virulent attack on American racism. It was the last autobiographical novel that Himes wrote.

In 1956, having returned to Paris, Himes set aside the autobiographical style he had used until then and began writing detective fiction for Marcel Duhamel, who had created the enormously popular *Série Noire* crime fiction editions for the publisher Gallimard. Duhamel offered the continually impoverished Himes $1,000 for a hard-boiled detective novel, which the author produced in short order. Himes's first attempt at detective fiction, *For Love of Imabelle* (1957), written in English and translated and published in French as *La Reine des Pommes*, won the 1958 Grand Prix for the year's best crime novel. It made Himes instantly popular in France and soon throughout Europe, but not in the United States. Subsequently Himes created a cycle of detective fiction—*The Crazy Kill* (1959), *The Real Cool Killers* (1959), *All Shot Up* (1960), *The Big Gold Dream* (1960), *Une Affaire de Viol* (*A Case of Rape*) (1963), *Cotton Comes to Harlem* (1965), *Run Man Run* (1966), *The Heat's On* (1966), and *Blind Man with a Pistol* (1969)—that was highly innovative within the genre and that ultimately provided him with a degree of financial security and fame in the United States.

The center of Himes's detective fiction, as well as of his comedy of manners, *Pinktoes* (1961), is Harlem, which for the author is an absurd landscape governed by violent, apocalyptic forces. Himes had never lived in Harlem, but he said he found it the perfect literary landscape to write about "blacks with their extreme absurdity." Trying to control the grotesque world of Harlem are two black detectives, Coffin Ed Johnson and Grave Digger Jones, prototypes for many other black heroes who would follow them into American fiction and film. Essentially Himes had managed to create a unique genre of detective fiction that incorporated an assault on the absurdities of American racism. For Himes, during the second major phase of his career, detective fiction had become a decidedly valid literary form.

Chester Himes moved to Alicante, Spain, in 1968 with Lesley Packard, an Anglo-Irish woman whom he had married in 1965. In a house they built in Moraira, he spent the last years of his life working on his autobiography. Finally some measure of American success came to him when the film version of *Cotton Comes to Harlem* was released in 1970, followed by *Come Back Charleston Blue* in 1974. Always difficult and irascible, uncompromising in his disgust for all forms of racism, and combative in his personal and literary opinions, Himes died in Moraira.

• Letters from Himes are in the John A. Williams Collection at the University of Rochester and in the Beinecke Collection at Yale University. His two-volume autobiography also contains long extracts from his correspondence. For biographical and critical commentary, see James Lundquist, *Chester Himes* (1976); Stephen Milliken, *Chester Himes* (1976); and Gilbert H. Muller, *Chester Himes* (1989). For Himes's career in the context of African-American expatriation, see Michel Fabre, *From Harlem to Paris: Black American Writers in France, 1840–1980* (1991).

GILBERT H. MULLER

HINDMAN, Thomas Carmichael (28 Jan. 1828–27 Sept. 1868), general and congressman, was born in Knoxville, Tennessee, the son of Thomas Carmichael Hindman and Sallie Holt. His father moved to Jacksonville, Alabama, in 1832 as an Indian agent of the federal government and then to Ripley, Tippah County, Mississippi, in 1841, where he operated a large plantation. As the son of a well-to-do family, Hindman attended a variety of local private schools and graduated in 1846 from the Lawrenceville Classical and Commercial Institute located near Princeton, New Jersey.

Hindman exhibited an early interest in military affairs and demonstrated skills as a leader. Only eighteen years old, during the Mexican-American War he raised a company in his home county that became a part of the Second Mississippi Regiment. Hindman held the ranks of lieutenant and captain in this regiment.

After the war, Hindman returned to Mississippi and studied law. He was admitted to the bar in 1851 and opened his practice in Ripley, Mississippi. Almost immediately he jumped into politics. He was an active Democrat and, in 1851, vigorously supported Jefferson Davis against Henry S. Foote in the dramatic Mississippi gubernatorial contest by speaking for Davis in northern counties. He was elected a member of the Mississippi House of Representatives in 1853 and served in the 1854 session.

In 1856 Hindman moved to Helena, Arkansas, where he established a law practice. In 1856 he married Mary Watkins Biscoe, the daughter of a prominent local planter, a connection that provided allies for continued political activity. The couple had three children. As a newcomer, Hindman found his political ambitions blocked by the influence of the regular Democratic party leadership, a group known as "the family," tied to U.S. Senator Robert W. Johnson. Hindman confronted them head-on, using a variety of demagogic appeals to attract voters. In 1858 he was elected to the Thirty-sixth Congress as a Democrat without the regular party's support, and he was reelected in 1860.

A strong advocate of states' rights, Hindman became a leading proponent of Arkansas's secession following the election of 1860 and the withdrawal of South Carolina from the Union. In January 1861 Hindman joined Senator Johnson in calling for state action. He campaigned for secessionist candidates to the state convention, although that body refused to take the state out of the Union until after the attack on Fort Sumter. In the meantime, Hindman turned his attention to war and helped organize the Second Arkansas Infantry, which he commanded for a short time.

Hindman's ambitions, his connections, and his previous military service helped him initially to rise rapidly in the army. On 28 September 1861 he received a commission as brigadier general. He was serving as a brigade commander with the Army of Mississippi at Corinth when he was promoted to major general on 18 April 1862 and was sent to Arkansas to attempt to re-

pel an invasion by General Samuel Curtis. As army commander, Hindman practiced total war, paying little attention to the fine points of constitutionality in marshaling resources, conscription of soldiers, or combat tactics. His course may have prevented Curtis's success, but it also provoked widespread opposition to Hindman locally, including outspoken criticism from Albert Pike and Douglas H. Cooper. His course led ultimately to his removal and replacement by General Theophilus H. Holmes. Holmes arrived at Little Rock in August to find that he agreed with much that Hindman had done and kept Hindman in the department, assigning him to command an army that marched into northwestern Arkansas in an effort to drive the Federals out of that section. Hindman's command fought the Federals at Prairie Grove on 7–8 December 1862. The battle ended in a practical defeat for the Confederate forces, and Hindman requested that he be relieved of his command and transferred to the Army of Tennessee.

Hindman was unable to secure the command that he sought and instead was assigned as the senior officer to the court of inquiry investigating allegations of Major General Mansfield Lovell's negligence of duty at New Orleans, an assignment that lasted until 9 July 1863. Six days later Hindman was assigned to command a division under Lieutenant General Leonidas Polk in Braxton Bragg's army at Chattanooga. Hindman's career in the Army of Tennessee was filled with personal conflicts that characterized his time in Arkansas and hindered his career. Although he performed well at the battle of Chickamauga, his earlier failure to attack an isolated division of Federals on 11 September led Bragg to remove him from command. After a lengthy contest, he returned to his command when Bragg was removed in December 1863, but under General Joseph E. Johnston, Hindman felt he was repeatedly overlooked for command. His support of General Patrick Cleburne's proposal, made in January 1864, to arm slaves for use in the Confederate army did not help his political position in the army. Blaming an injury to his eye received when thrown from a horse on 4 July at Chickamauga, Hindman frequently absented himself from his division and ultimately was removed just prior to Kennesaw Mountain. He finally left the Army of Tennessee without another assignment and moved back to the Trans-Mississippi, where he spent the rest of the war.

Following the war Hindman left the United States, intending to develop a coffee plantation in Mexico, and settled for a time in Mexico City. He joined other Confederate immigrants at Carlota but failed to make enough money to maintain his family. In 1867 he returned to Helena, Arkansas, resumed his legal practice, and entered once again into politics. He aggressively fought the Republicans in the 1867 state elections and helped reorganize the Democratic party. On 27 September 1868 he was assassinated in Helena. The assailant was never found, and the cause of the murder remains one of speculation.

• A scholarly biography is Diane Neal and Thomas W. Kremm, *Lion of the South: General Thomas C. Hindman* (1993), but for an older treatment see Charles E. Nash, *Biographical Sketches of Gen. Pat Cleburne and Gen. T. C. Hindman, Together with Humorous Anecdotes and Reminiscences of the Late Civil War* (1895; repr. 1977). See also Bobby L. Roberts, "Thomas Carmichael Hindman: Secessionist and Confederate General" (M.A. thesis, Univ. of Arkansas at Fayetteville, 1972).

CARL H. MONEYHON

HINE, Lewis Wickes (26 Sept. 1874–4 Nov. 1940), photographer, was born in Oshkosh, Wisconsin, the son of Douglas Hine, the operator of a coffee shop, and Sarah Hayes. Hine left Oshkosh after graduating from high school and working at a variety of menial jobs. In 1900 he enrolled at the University of Chicago for one year. In 1901 he began teaching nature study in New York City at the Ethical Culture School, upon the invitation of recently appointed superintendent Frank A. Manny, formerly a professor at the Oshkosh State Normal School. Within three years Hine was in touch with key figures in New York's reform community, including Felix Adler (1851–1933), founder of the humanist religion of ethical culture and first head of the National Child Labor Committee (NCLC); John Spargo, author of *The Bitter Cry of the Children*; Florence Kelley, of the National Consumers' League; and Paul Kellogg and Arthur Kellogg, of *Charities* magazine. Hine added photography to his school teaching in 1903 or 1904. In 1904 he married Sara Ann Rich. While teaching he attended New York University's School of Education and received a Pd.M. (education) degree in 1905.

Frank Manny first suggested that Hine take students to photograph immigrants arriving through Ellis Island. By 1906 he was also taking pictures as a freelance photographer for NCLC. In the summer of 1908 he left the school to do photography full time, beginning a career built around a sympathetic portrayal of workers' humanity and dignity. Urban immigrants, child laborers, and steelworkers and their families in Pittsburgh comprised Hine's major prewar projects.

In 1907 the recently formed Russell Sage Foundation had employed Paul Kellogg to head a massive investigation of life and work in the steel industry in Pittsburgh. In 1908 Hine joined Kellogg as the Pittsburgh Survey's staff photographer, at the same time joining the staffs of *Charities and the Commons* and the NCLC. In hiring Hine, Kellogg arranged for a graphic supplement to his own sympathetic portrait of immigrant steelworkers. In contrast to the people in many of his later pictures, Hine's subjects typically posed face-front, showing head and shoulders, without the work context. Typical of Hine's captions are those that identify individuals by nationality, such as "a young millworker: Slav." "Immigrant Types in the Steel District," a photoessay in *Charities and the Commons*, listed all subjects simply by nationality. Even "a leader in the Homestead Strike" remains nameless. At best the workers are "types." Nevertheless, Hine's photo-

graphs established the image in readers' minds of the workers' humanity and thereby contributed to the considerable impact of the Pittsburgh Survey.

The results of the Pittsburgh project were widely disseminated, first through three special issues of *Charities and the Commons* in 1909. The journal was subsequently renamed the *Survey*, an indication of the profound significance of the Pittsburgh study: the survey had become the model for virtually all Progressive reform activity. The Russell Sage Foundation published six volumes of the Pittsburgh findings, all with photographs by Hine. Public speeches, press releases, and articles in popular magazines spread the information, accompanied by Hine's photographs, and set the stage for state and federal reform legislation limiting hours of work on government steel contracts, along with reforms instituted by US Steel itself.

The years after the Pittsburgh Survey were among Hine's most prolific and successful. When he left his teaching position to do social (that is, reform-oriented) photography full time, he had ignored a warning from a philanthropist, according to art critic Elizabeth McCausland, that he did not have a sufficiently "broad sociological background." Nevertheless, Hine wrote Manny in 1910, "I'm sure I am right in my choice of work. . . . My 'sociological horizon' broadens hourly" (Trachtenberg, p. 200). By 1918 he had taken several thousand pictures, most for the NCLC. As its staff photographer, Hine toured the United States for almost ten years, investigating, photographing, and publicizing the issues that surrounded child labor. Unlike the Pittsburgh Survey work, these projects entailed frequent encounters with hostile employers, forcing Hine to obtain information and photographs surreptitiously. Also unlike the Pittsburgh Survey, where he was part of a large team of investigators, Hine himself gathered a major portion of the information. He talked to the children, learned their ages and work histories, and presented his findings in the captions, lectures, and poster displays that accompanied the photos.

One of Hine's early NCLC assignments investigated child labor in the textile mills of the Carolinas. In unstudied but formal group portraits, Hine repeatedly lined children up outside the mills. He named the mills in the captions—Kesler Manufacturing Co., Salisbury, North Carolina; Loray Mill, Gastonia, North Carolina; Wampum Manufacturing Co., Lincolnton, North Carolina—while the children remained anonymous. The series documented what was important for the reform effort: the number of children (thus the repetition), their heights and ages, how long they had been working, and how much they were paid.

Photographs showing the children working inside the mills and highlighting their small size and long work hours accompanied this documentation. Ten pages of Hine's photographs appeared in January 1909 in *Charities and the Commons*, one of eleven periodicals to publish the series. In an editorial in the same issue, Florence Kelley praised Hine: "The Department of

Labor, the Department of Education, the census leave us to the ingenuity of a young photographer for current knowledge of the sad lot of the most unfortunate of our little fellow citizens" (30 Jan. 1909, p. 742). Nevertheless, Hine remained a background figure, as he did throughout his career. The article was credited to A. J. McKelway, the director of the project. Hine himself never became a part of the inner circle of reformers, such as Kelley, McKelway, Homer Folks, Paul Kellogg, and Owen Reed Lovejoy, for whom he worked.

Hine continued working for the NCLC, studying Colorado beet farms, Connecticut cranberry fields, Pennsylvania coal mines, Gulf Coast canneries, and glass, tobacco, and clothing manufacturers as well as further investigating southern mills. His photographs played a crucial role in rousing public opinion against child labor. Like the Pittsburgh Survey, in the 1910s the campaign to mobilize public support met with remarkable success as reflected in changes in legislation and public concern.

In 1917 Hine settled in Hastings-on-Hudson, New York, with his wife and five-year-old son. When he sought to reduce his extensive traveling investigations, the NCLC responded with a salary reduction, and Hine quit. The next year he crossed the Atlantic to photograph conditions faced by civilian refugees. Working for the American Red Cross under the direction of Homer Folks, he captured the health, hunger, and sanitation problems that confronted postwar Europe.

When Hine returned to Paris in 1919, he decided that he had done enough "negative documentation." While he continued some freelance work for the NCLC, he branched out in a new direction, accommodating his prewar progressivism to the "normalcy" of the new decade. The "work portraits" that evolved during this period formed the core of his last two decades of photography. Paul Kellogg, now editor of the *Survey*, published the work series in the new monthly supplement, *Survey Graphic*, starting in late 1921. By this time, Hine's photography was providing only an intermittent income, a living that was further threatened when, after a year, Kellogg cut back the frequency of publication of Hine photographs.

From 1923 through 1927 the most regular publisher of Hine's pictures, with the occasional exception of *Survey Graphic*, was the employee magazine *Western Electric News*. Hine's Hawthorne Works photographs, unlike his prewar work, emphasized the harmony of worker and machine, worker and company. They were used by Western Electric to boost employee morale through recognition of workers' contributions and were thus part of the same corporate strategy that made *Hawthorne effect* a staple term in industrial psychology.

He obtained several other contracts for "work portraits" during the 1920s. Though he was recognized with a medal at the Exhibition of Advertising Art in 1924 and showings at the Advertising Club in 1928 and the Russell Sage Foundation in 1929, these honors failed to lead to more than sporadic financial comfort. In 1930 an assignment to photograph the construction of the Empire State Building generated several dramatic publication series, generally recognized as the best of his postwar work. Two years later Hine used many of the construction images in *Men at Work* (1932), a picture book aiming to show children the central role of human labor in industrial society. In his introduction Hine explained: "We call this the Machine Age. But the more machines we use the more do we need real men to make and direct them."

Subsequently he worked on several projects with the New Deal through the Tennessee Valley Authority, the Rural Electrification Administration, and the National Research Project of the Works Progress Administration. These undertakings, however, were short lived and riddled with conflict between Hine and his bureaucratic superiors.

In 1938 Hine was rediscovered by Berenice Abbott and Elizabeth McCausland as the predecessor of New Deal documentary photography, but the interest was generated by his older photographs. Hine remained on the brink of financial insolvency through the decade, struggling with a foreclosure on his home in September 1939 and the death of his wife three months later. He died in Dobbs Ferry, New York.

Hine was a pioneer in demonstrating the efficacy of photography as an instrument of social reform. Hine's ability to convey the human qualities of his subjects gave his documentary photographs their power, both for his Progressive-era contemporaries and as enduring historical records. His work is rightly seen as the precursor of New Deal documentary photography, and his pictures, those of child labor in particular, continue to be widely published as demonstrations of social conditions in early twentieth-century America.

• The most complete collection of Hine's negatives and photographs is located at the International Museum of Photography–George Eastman House, Rochester, N.Y. Other collections include the Library of Congress, Prints and Photographs Division and Manuscript Division; the University of Maryland–Baltimore County Library; the National Archives, Prints and Photographs Division; and Columbia University Library, Avery Library, New York, N.Y. Hine's written words survive in correspondence located in the *Survey* Associates Records, Social Welfare History Archives, University of Minnesota, Minneapolis, and in the McCausland Papers, Archives of American Art, Washington, D.C. Selected correspondence has been published, with photographs, in Daile Kaplan, ed., *Photo Story: Selected Letters and Photographs of Lewis W. Hine* (1992). Jonathan Doherty, ed., *Lewis Wickes Hine's Interpretive Photography: The Six Early Projects* (1978), includes microfiches of the Eastman Collection prints with Hine's captions, through World War I. Walter Rosenblum et al., *America and Lewis Hine: Photographs 1904–1940* (1977), includes a thorough bibliography, a powerful selection of Hine prints, biographical notes, and an essay by Alan Trachtenberg. Recent assessments include Trachtenberg, *Reading American Photographs: Images as History, Mathew Brady to Walker Evans* (1989); Peter Seixas, "Lewis Hine: From 'Social' to 'Interpretive' Photographer," *American Quarterly* 39, no. 3 (1987): 381–409; and Maren

Stange, *Symbols of Ideal Life: Social Documentary Photography in America, 1890–1950* (1989). Also see Judith Mara Gutman, *Lewis Hine and the American Social Conscience* (1967) and *Lewis W. Hine, 1874–1940: Two Perspectives* (1974). Studies of particular segments of Hine's photographic career include Verna Posever Curtis and Stanley Mallach, *Photography and Reform: Lewis Hine and the National Child Labor Committee* (1981); Daile Kaplan, *Lewis Hine in Europe: The Lost Photographs* (1988); and Judith Mara Gutman, "Lewis Hine's Last Legacy," *New York Times Magazine*, 17 Apr. 1983.

PETER SEIXAS

HINES, Duncan (26 Mar. 1880–15 Mar. 1959), author, editor, and publisher of travel and restaurant guidebooks for motorists, was born in Bowling Green, Kentucky, the son of Edward L. Hines, a former Confederate army captain, schoolteacher, lawyer, and housebuilder, and Cornelia Duncan. Hines was raised by his grandmother after his mother died, and he attributed his appreciation of the art of dining to his grandmother's southern cooking. Though he would achieve widespread name recognition as a restaurant critic, his career did not involve food until he reached his mid-fifties. In 1896 he enrolled in Bowling Green Business University but left after two years. For the next forty years he worked in a variety of jobs, mostly public relations; he designed, wrote, and produced corporate brochures, traveling widely from his home in Chicago to visit clients around the country. In 1905 he married Florence Chaffin; they had no children.

Hines, whose hobby was eating well, became expert at sniffing out good food while he was on the road. Because of the dearth of clean restaurants serving tasty food, Hines applied himself assiduously to the search; he sought recommendations and filled notebooks with his findings. Traveling with his wife on weekends, he took busman's holidays, driving as much as 500 miles on gastronomic safaris. His reputation as a restaurant hunter began to spread, and a growing contingent of Chicago business travelers consulted him before daring to venture out of town.

Beleagured by queries, he came up with a scheme to silence his phone. In 1935 he printed a list of 167 favorite spots in thirty states and mailed off 1,000 copies as Christmas greetings. But the gesture failed to accomplish its goal; the barrage of requests for restaurant reconnaissance only escalated. In self-defense, Hines expanded the card into an inexpensive, pocket-sized guidebook called *Adventures in Good Eating*, adding more restaurants with short descriptions for each; the price is variously reported to have been $1.00 or $1.50. From this modest beginning would erupt a quarter-century publishing phenomenon that would make "Recommended by Duncan Hines" a household—or, rather, a car-seat—phrase.

Hines was an advocate of plain American cooking, which, in his view, could be "the best in the world" and also "the worst." He liked simple, wholesome fare true to its geographic origins. The author grumbled publicly about restaurants that served "leathery eggs or vegetables in billboard paste or dishwater soup,"

and he railed against inns that ignored regional specialties in favor of steak and chicken. Once, when asked how he made his menu selections, he snapped, "I steer clear of hashes and meat loaves with fancy names, and from dishes disguised with French names that don't mean anything in a Midwest hotel."

Even more demanding were his standards of cleanliness. Before entering a restaurant, Hines often surveyed the back door, using his nose to detect malodorous garbage and other sanitary lapses. He then asked to inspect the kitchen. If satisfied, he entered the dining room and ordered a half-dozen entrées. Restaurants that pleased his sensibilities and his palate were added to the annual (eventually semiannual) update of *Adventures in Good Eating*. Although Hines included some well-known big-city restaurants in the book, he focused on uncharted territory—the uncelebrated small-town establishments that his urban readers needed to know about in order to eat well when driving from one city to another. He reviewed these places without a trace of snobbery or literary affectation in a style that exuded humor and humility. Restaurants included in the book could hang his seal of approval: a sign that boasted "Recommended by Duncan Hines." Hines retained ownership of the signs and would retrieve one when he judged that a restaurant's quality had fallen. He snubbed all offers of advertising, fiercely guarding his independence and his anonymity. The only photograph he used was a twenty-year-old portrait.

Financially, *Adventures in Good Eating* was at first a disaster, netting the author-publisher a $1,500 loss on 5,000 copies sold. But in 1938 a feature article in the *Saturday Evening Post* helped put him in the black. After publishing *Lodging for a Night* (for travelers seeking a bed) and *Duncan Hines' Vacation Guide*, he quit his job and moved back to Bowling Green. His books catered to motorists at a time when owning a car was coming to be regarded as an American birthright. By the end of 1939 Hines's books were moving at a brisk 100,000 copies a year. Eventually, with the addition of *Adventures in Good Cooking* and *The Art of Carving in the Home*, combined annual sales would reach half a million. According to a chef cited in *Scribner's Commentator* in 1941, Hines had done "more in four years to raise the level of the American cuisine than chefs had done in the previous forty." As business soared and mail poured in (over 50,000 letters a year), Hines found it necessary to assemble a volunteer corps of several hundred "dinner detectives" who pioneered new ground and revisited the old. His army of culinary lieutenants included bank presidents, university professors, corporate chiefs, and many well-known personalities.

Hines's first wife died in 1939, and his second marriage, to Emelie Elizabeth Daniels, that same year ended in divorce. In 1946 he married Clara Wright Nahm, a widow who embraced his hobby-turned-profession. He had no children with any of his wives. The two of them toured the United States, Mexico, the Caribbean, Hawaii, and Western Europe for gastronomic pleasure. Hines claimed to have logged over two million miles for the love of food.

In 1948 Duncan Hines was approached by Roy H. Park, a businessman in upstate New York who was seeking a brand name for clients interested in marketing food products. Park broke down Hines's resistance to endorsements, and the two men established Hines-Park Foods to license the Duncan Hines name. It soon appeared on 200 different items from bread and jam to canned fruit, ice cream, and cake mix. To administer publication of Hines's books, the partners established the Duncan Hines Institute at Ithaca, New York, in 1953. Two years later the institute brought out the *Duncan Hines Food Odyssey* and the *Duncan Hines Dessert Book*, which included his thoughts on courtesy, safe driving, and cooking methods. After a vigorous promotional campaign complete with television appearances and the proclamation of "Duncan Hines Days" in dozens of cities, the food champion slowed down. In 1956 Procter & Gamble purchased all the Duncan Hines interests, and Hines went into semiretirement.

The guidebooks outlived their creator, who died of lung cancer in Bowling Green eleven days before his seventy-ninth birthday. Procter & Gamble discontinued the book series in 1962 and later dropped most products bearing the Duncan Hines name. The notable exception was cake mixes, and for these, rather than guidebooks or restaurant recommendations, the name Duncan Hines has lived on. Highway travelers, who now take for granted the availability of appetizing food prepared in sanitary kitchens, owe a debt of gratitude to Duncan Hines. He demanded a level of quality and cleanliness that was uncommon in his day. Gradually it became the norm, perhaps because, for more than two decades, the nation's best-known advocate of fine dining would accept nothing less.

• For more on Hines, see Milton MacKaye, "Where Shall We Stop for Dinner?" and Duncan Hines and Frank J. Taylor, "How to Find a Decent Meal," *Saturday Evening Post*, 3 Dec. 1938 and 26 Apr. 1947; Marion Edwards, "They Live to Eat," *Better Homes & Gardens*, Mar. 1945, pp. 30–31; and David M. Schwartz, "He Cultivated Our Culinary Consciousness," *Smithsonian*, Nov. 1984, pp. 86–97. Obituaries are in the *New York Times* and the *Park City* (Ky.) *Daily News*, both 16 Mar. 1959.

DAVID M. SCHWARTZ

HINES, Earl "Fatha" (28 Dec. 1905–22 Apr. 1983), jazz pianist and bandleader, was born Earl Kenneth Hines in Duquesne (later absorbed into Pittsburgh), Pennsylvania, the son of Joseph Hines, a foreman on the coal docks. His mother, whose name is unknown, died when he was an infant. From the age of three he was raised by his stepmother, Mary (maiden name unknown), an organist. His father played cornet and led the local Eureka Brass Band, an uncle was an accomplished brass player, and an aunt sang light opera. Thus immersed in musical influences, Hines commenced classical piano studies in 1914. He possessed an immense natural talent. While making rapid progress through the classics he also began playing organ in the Baptist church and covertly entertaining at parties, this last activity a consequence of his ability to learn popular songs by ear. His life, like his music, moved fluidly between middle-class proprieties and wild pleasures.

Hines lived with his aunt Sadie Phillips from the age of twelve and attended Schenley High School. Continuing to perform brilliantly, he nevertheless also learned to be a barber and attempted other trades, none holding his lasting interest. During summer vacation from high school in 1922, he played at the Leader House in a trio under the direction of singer and saxophonist Lois Deppe. Hines was with Deppe's group that in 1923 became a big band and toured the region and recorded for the Gennett label. During this period the rambunctious Hines tried his hand at being a pool shark and a pimp, and he fell into a disastrous and brief marriage to singer Laura Badge, who used his already considerable reputation to advance her career.

Banjoist Harold Birchett taught Hines always to keep a set tempo steady, a requirement of the dance-band world that was at odds with his training in the rhythmic freedoms of the European romantic piano tradition. Hines learned the lesson well but retained in his soloing a penchant for rhythmic flights of fancy. Advised that his skills were too great for the Pittsburgh area, in 1924 he left his hometown for an engagement in Chicago, a cradle of jazz in the 1920s.

While working at an after-hours club around 1925, Hines concurrently played with Carroll Dickerson's orchestra at the Entertainer's Club. When the club was padlocked by police—a routine occurrence in Chicago of the 1920s—Dickerson secured a 42-week tour on the Pantages theater circuit, taking the band to the West Coast and Canada. On their return to Chicago in 1926, Dickerson's band began an engagement at the Sunset Cafe, where Louis Armstrong joined. Earlier each evening Hines and Armstrong also played in Erskine Tate's Vendome Theater Symphony Orchestra. When Dickerson was fired from the Sunset in February 1927, Armstrong was made nominal leader and Hines, music director. Also around this time Hines worked as an accompanist for singer Ethel Waters.

In late 1927 in Chicago Hines joined clarinetist Jimmie Noone's Apex Club Orchestra, one of the most important bands in early jazz. He eventually left the group after a dispute with Noone. Meanwhile in May 1928 Hines began recording a succession of discs that collectively document his stature in early jazz. A good number of these titles were made under Noone's leadership, even as their personal relationship was disintegrating. Perhaps the finest, from the perspective of Hines's contribution, are "Sweet Sue (Just You)," "Four or Five Times," "Every Evening," "Monday Date," "Oh! Sister, Ain't That Hot!," "King Joe" and "Sweet Lorraine" with Noone; "Skip the Gutter" and "A Monday Date" as a member of Armstrong's Hot Five; "Savoyagers' Stomp" alongside Armstrong in Dickerson's orchestra; the duo "Weather Bird" with

Armstrong; and the pianist's unaccompanied solos on the popular song "I Ain't Got Nobody" and on his own compositions "Caution Blues" (also known as "Blues in Thirds"), "A Monday Date," and "Fifty-Seven Varieties" (a punning reference to his surname and his home, from the advertising slogan of the Pittsburgh food corporation, Heinz). These last sides were recorded in December 1928, just after a trip to Long Island City, New York, where he punched eight piano rolls for the QRS company.

Also by 1928 Hines had entered into a relationship with entertainer and violinist Kathryn Perry, who became his second wife by common-law marriage. On his birthday he brought a new big band into the Grand Terrace, where, apart from numerous regional tours, he held an engagement through the end of 1939. Stories abound—humorous, nostalgic, and ugly—from these eleven years. Ballroom owner Ed Fox offered Hines considerable musical opportunities and an unusually stable job in the world of entertainment, while simultaneously taking great advantage of him. Hines seemed unconcerned with developing expertise in the business aspects of music. Gangsters (notably Al Capone) frequented the club and around 1931 took it over, demanding a 20 percent share for "protection" and for preventing Hines's sidemen from leaving for other bands. Some musicians expressed their pleasure at belonging to a band that felt like a happy family (in contrast to the cutthroat devisiveness of many swing-era big bands), owing in no small part to Hines's joyful leadership.

Hines's explanation of how he got his nickname is indicative of how he was viewed by his band members and others who worked with him. One night after he had written the band's theme song, "Deep Forest," in collaboration with English jazz composer Reginald Foresythe, Hines gave a fatherly scolding to the master of ceremonies for drinking too much. The in-house broadcast on NBC then opened: "Here comes Fatha Hines through the deep forest with his little children." Hence he was thereafter known as "Fatha."

Prominent among artistic highlights at the Grand Terrace, apart from Hines's ever-present piano playing, were the performances of dancer, singer, and trumpeter Valaida Snow from 1933 to 1934. When Snow left for Europe in 1935, she was replaced by Hines's wife, Perry. During these years his band featured trumpeters Walter Fuller and George Dixon, trombonist Trummy Young, alto saxophonists and clarinetists Omer Simeon and Darnell Howard (who doubled on violin as well), and tenor saxophonists and arrangers Jimmy Mundy and Cecil Irwin. The rhythm section provided a wonderful push, with Hines working in conjunction with guitarist Lawrence Dixon, bassist Quinn Wilson, and drummer Wallace Bishop. Their recordings, never especially innovative, were nonetheless characteristically sparky, clean, and swinging, except for the somewhat pretentious mood piece "Harlem Lament" from 1933, which afforded Hines his greatest opportunity as a soloist with the orchestra.

The band's overall level of performance evidently dipped after Irwin died in May 1935. He was immediately replaced by tenor saxophonist and arranger Budd Johnson, who helped bring the band to another peak a few years later with such prominent new members as drummer Alvin Burroughs, singer Billy Eckstine (both joining in 1939), and alto saxophonist Scoops Carry (1940). A second spate of high-quality recordings included "Grand Terrace Shuffle" and "G. T. Stomp," made before a financial dispute with Fox led to Hines's final departure from the ballroom at the end of 1939; the hit songs "Jelly, Jelly" (1940) and "Stormy Monday Blues" (1942); and "Skylark" (also 1942), on which for the first time an African-American singer (Eckstine) was allowed to debut a romantic ballad. Less inspiring musically but highly profitable was "Boogie Woogie on St. Louis Blues" (1940). Independent of the big band, Hines recorded unaccompanied improvisations in 1939 and 1940, including "The Father's Getaway" and "Reminiscing at Blue Note."

Hines was divorced from his second wife by June 1940. The big band, having lost its home base, toured continuously from that year onward. New members included drummer Shadow Wilson (who joined in 1942), the two future giants of bop, Charlie Parker (playing tenor rather than alto saxophone) and trumpeter Dizzy Gillespie (both from late 1942 into 1943), and singer Sarah Vaughan (from Apr. 1943). Because of a recording ban, no documentation of their contribution survives. They had all left Hines by the fall of that year and soon would form a big band under Eckstine's leadership. Shifting directions considerably, Hines formed a short-lived, 24-piece orchestra in October 1943, imitating another popular trend by adding a string section (in this instance, all women) and a vocal group (also women) to the standard big-band instrumentation. In March 1944 he briefly led the Duke Ellington orchestra while Ellington was suffering from tonsilitis.

In 1946 Hines was in a serious automobile accident that left his right eye permanently damaged. The following year he disbanded the big band and married Janie Moses, who had sung with the group for two years. They had two daughters. After a losing venture running a nightclub from April to August 1947, he joined Jack Teagarden and Sid Catlett in Louis Armstrong's newly formed All Stars in January 1948. The group toured Europe in 1948, giving an acclaimed appearance at the Nice Jazz Festival, and again in 1949. Apart from Armstrong he recorded a fine trio session with bassist Al McGibbon and drummer J. C. Heard in 1950. Hines remained with Armstrong until the fall of 1951, when he quit in a controversy over publicity. Also in 1951 Hines had a small role in a feature film, *The Strip*. During the 1950s and later he appeared occasionally on television as well.

From 1952 to 1954 Hines led small swing groups that included at various times trumpeter Jonah Jones, drummer Art Blakey, and trombonist Dickie Wells. Having interrupted these affiliations to play with a sparky dixieland band at the Hangover in San Francisco (June 1952 and Feb. 1954), he began a long engagement there in September 1955. He took his family to San Francisco the following year and settled across the bay in Oakland in 1960. Among his sidemen were trumpeter Muggsy Spanier, clarinetist Darnell Howard, trombonist Jimmy Archey, and bassist Pops Foster. During this period Hines also toured England as co-leader of a group with Jack Teagarden (Sept. 1957) and led a swing group at the Embers in New York City (1959).

The dixieland group moved into the Black Sheep in San Francisco in 1961–1962 and then disbanded. In 1964 writer Stanley Dance convinced a reluctant Hines—who thought of himself as an entertainer rather than a concert-giver—to present three concerts at the Little Theatre in New York. Performing alone and in a trio with bass and drums, he surprised the audience with the quality of his playing and thereby launched the final portion of his career, during which he toured internationally from 1965 into the early 1980s. In these last two decades his working group was usually a quartet in which, initially, he was reunited with Budd Johnson and to which he often added a singer, such as Alberta Hunter. Two LPs in the boxed set *The Father of Modern Piano*, recorded at a later reunion in 1977, capture well the quartet of the mid-1960s to the end of the decade, with bassist Bill Pemberton and drummer Oliver Jackson joining Hines and Johnson. Hines divorced Janie Hines in 1980; their daughters had died. He died in Oakland.

It is in his unaccompanied performances that Hines made his greatest contribution, offering profound and original interpretations of American popular songs. The essential qualities of his playing since the 1920s were an extraordinary speed and independence of hands; the ability to reharmonize and to ornament melodies in infinitely varied ways; a hammer-like tone, enhanced further by the presentation of melodies in octaves; the use of left-hand techniques of ragtime and stride piano playing, but in quicksilver, unpredictable sequences. Hines's irrepressible swing rhythms might suddenly give way to impossibly difficult and seemingly irrational rhythmic figures and then, just as suddenly, resume; he could command showy tremolos in either hand and stark and pointed registral contrasts. During the first four decades of his career, Hines often used his talents in a flighty and superficial manner (especially during the big band decades), as if he were bursting with so many brilliant ideas that he could not control and shape the music. In his later years, however, he was more disciplined and managed to attain high levels of artistic achievement along with commercial success. On his solo work of the 1960s and 1970s Hines was, arguably, the finest jazz pianist ever.

• The indispensable comprehensive source is Stanley Dance, *The World of Earl Hines* (1977; repr. 1983), which brings together Hines's autobiography, interviews with many of his sidemen, numerous photographs, a bibliography of general articles on him in jazz books and periodicals, and a documented chronology by Dance and Walter Allen that in some instances corrects Hines's autobiographical memories. Perhaps the only crucial omission from Dance's list of general articles is the survey of recordings in Albert McCarthy, *Big Band Jazz* (1974), pp. 237–40. Later sources include Kent Hazen, "A Talk with 'Fatha,'" *Mississippi Rag* 4 (May 1977): 10–13; David Keller, "Earl Hines: Fatha on Down the Road," *Down Beat*, 17 May 1979, pp. 14–15, 42; and stories and photos scattered through Dempsey J. Travis, *An Autobiography of Black Jazz* (1983). Eckstine recounted the big band era in "Crazy People Like Me," *Melody Maker*, 14 Aug. 1954, pp. 3–4; 21 Aug. 1954, p. 5; and 28 Aug. 1954, p. 13 (repr. in Max Jones, *Talking Jazz* [1987], pp. 233–44). Eckstine supplied further stories in Eileen Southern, "'M. B.' of Ballad and Bop," *Black Perspective in Music* 7 (1979): 182–98 and 8 (1980): 54–64.

The finest musical analyses are by Gunther Schuller, *Early Jazz: Its Roots and Musical Development* (1968), pp. 120–30, and *The Swing Era: The Development of Jazz, 1930–1945* (1989), pp. 263–92; and Jeffrey J. Taylor, "Earl Hines's Piano Style in the 1920s: A Historical and Analytical Perspective," *Black Music Research Journal* 12, no. 1 (1992): 57–77, and "Earl Hines and Black Jazz Piano in Chicago: 1923–1928" (Ph.D. diss., Univ. of Michigan, 1993). The comprehensive catalog of Hines's recordings is Lionel Moxhet, *A Discography of Earl Hines, 1923–1977: Records, Festivals and Concerts* (1978). His occasional film and television appearances are documented in David Meeker, *Jazz in the Movies* (1981). An obituary is in the *San Francisco Chronicle*, 23 Apr. 1983.

BARRY KERNFELD

HINES, James J. (18 Dec. 1876–26 Mar. 1957), politician, was born on the Lower East Side of New York City, the son of Mary (maiden name unknown) and James F. Hines, a blacksmith. The Irish Catholic Hines family supported Tammany Hall, the city's Democratic political machine. Dominating New York City politics from the early 1870s to the late 1920s, the machine maintained political power via the functional centralization of the boss system and geographical decentralization provided by electoral support from city districts. Machine politics were often extragovernmental and legally dubious in nature. They were characterized by informal negotiation with city businesses to secure political and monetary support for machine politicians in return for kickbacks in the form of construction and public utility contracts and the "quid pro quo vote-service exchange mechanism" (Pecorella, p. 42), which came to symbolize Tammany's relationship with the New York City immigrant community.

Hines's father had captained an election district for Tammany Hall boss Richard Croker. In 1884 the family moved to the Upper West Side of Manhattan, where Hines's father received profitable contracts from Croker for shoeing horses for the police and fire departments. Leaving school at the age of fifteen, Hines took a job in his father's business and inherited the business four years later when his father died. Hines's inheritance also included captaining the election district, which led the ambitious young man to take an active role in Democratic city politics. His political career was assisted by his general demeanor. Standing at five feet, eleven inches, the blue-eyed, broad-shouldered Hines rarely smoked or drank alcohol. His charming personality led New York judge Samuel Seabury to call Hines "the most likeable rogue I know" (Smith, p. 253). In 1904 Hines married Geneva E. Cox; they had three children.

In 1907 Hines won election as alderman, and in 1912 he took charge of the Eleventh Assembly District, after conducting failed bids in 1910 and 1911. That same year he was sold the family shop and moved into the trucking business, using his influence to secure city contracts for rubbish and snow removal. A year later he became chief clerk to the board of aldermen.

In 1918 Hines and Tammany leader Charles F. Murphy went into partnership to sell glucose to the British government. However, a business dispute permanently divided the two men. Determined to remove his former partner from power, Murphy seized on the opportunity to exploit Hines's absence from the city, due to his military service as a lieutenant in the Motor Transport Corps during World War I. Returning in 1920, Hines was greeted by a party of more than 2,000 well-wishers and set out to defeat the new organization that Murphy had created. His efforts paid off in the primary election that year in the Eleventh Assembly District, when Hines won forty-three of forty-five election precincts. Although in 1921 Hines narrowly missed winning election as Manhattan's borough president, losing to a Murphy supporter, he won the respect of many people both within and outside the Tammany organization.

The following decade saw Hines expand both his political influence and wealth. Working from his office at the Monongahela Democratic Club, he ensured political support by serving his constituents, at times doing so beyond the boundaries of the law. He frequently made it easier for privileged businesspeople to conduct their affairs by circumventing the city's cumbersome bureaucratic machinery. The practice of handing out dollar bills to faithful voters each election day in Hines's Eleventh District was also well known. Despite Hines's charming manner, honest civil servants who queried his methods faced a vindictive and powerful foe. Potentially troublesome police officers were switched to unfavorable beats to prevent interference. The extent to which Hines was rewarded financially is unknown; his wife managed the family finances, and Hines did not even maintain a bank account. Yet he spent far more than he legally earned, playing the stock market and gambling heavily, particularly at the racetrack. His sons attended Harvard and Yale, and he set one of them up in an office furniture company that prospered on city contracts.

Hines's extravagant life style brought him into contact with known criminals, and he was often accompanied by Frank Costello, Charles "Lucky" Luciano, and Dutch Schultz, among other gangsters. Hines was also linked to Arnold Rothstein when his telephone number was found in a police raid on the racketeer's apartment. Aware of the value of the support of such underworld figures, Hines is said to have protected them from criminal prosecution, often exerting pressure upon the New York Police Department to drop cases. Despite his underworld links, Hines regularly exhibited displays of generosity that made him popular with constituents, most notable among them the June Walk, a party for 25,000 children in Central Park held annually for twenty-six years.

After Murphy's death in 1924, Hines consolidated his political power. A backer of New York Democratic governor Alfred E. Smith, he came to believe that Smith's efforts to improve Tammany's public image were adversely affecting his own income and patronage. In 1932 Hines supported Franklin D. Roosevelt for the Democratic presidential nomination, splitting with the Tammany organization in the process. This support earned Hines the control of Manhattan's federal patronage opportunities after Roosevelt's election.

In the late 1930s Hines's criminal links became the focus of Thomas E. Dewey, the aggressive young district attorney who in 1944 was the Republican candidate for president. Dewey was determined to convict Hines of complicity in the numbers game and for selling protection to the Dutch Schultz gang. In September 1938 a New York grand jury indicted Hines, but the hearing ended in a mistrial. In February 1939, he was retried and convicted on a thirteen-count indictment for selling protection to Schultz and sentenced to four to eight years in jail. Hines was paroled on 12 September 1944, in part under the condition that he refrain from active political participation of any sort. He spent the rest of his life in the family's Long Island home, far from the political power he once enjoyed. He died in Long Beach, New York.

While his supporters and many New York City residents chose to forget his criminal associations, preferring to fondly remember him for his displays of generosity, Hines was first and foremost a product of the Tammany machine, a system within which the retention of political power and creation of wealth overrode other considerations. Although New York bossism is often commended for instigating progressive social legislation, such as child labor regulations, workmen's compensation laws, and factory safety codes, it can be seen not simply as the product of a desire for social change but rather as a practical response to liberal challenges to machine hegemony from within the state Democratic party. Personifying the Tammany approach to city politics, Hines appreciated how ostensibly progressive political actions and grandiose populist gestures helped guarantee grass-roots electoral support. Thus, despite his philanthropic work, Hines followed the path of machine politicians in never "being overly generous in the allocation of resources and tending when possible to provide symbolic rather than material incentives to his constituents" (Pecorella, p. 37).

• The Oral History Project of Columbia University contains materials related to Hines, particularly his trial; these include the memoirs of Thomas E. Dewey and Supreme Court justice Ferdinand Pecora. Further records of the Hines trial include *New York State v. James J. Hines* in the New York County District Attorney's Files, New York City Records Administration; and the Thomas E. Dewey Papers, University of Rochester. A three-part profile in the *New Yorker*, 25 July, 1, 8 Aug. 1936, provides a useful overview of Hines's life up to that date. Useful secondary accounts of the Hines trial are in Mary M. Stolberg, *Fighting Organized Crime: Politics, Justice, and the Legacy of Thomas Dewey* (1995), and Richard N. Smith, *Thomas E. Dewey and His Times* (1982). Good starting points for background to the issue of bossism and New York City machine politics include Robert F. Pecorella, *Community Power in a Postreform City: Politics in New York City* (1994); Raymond Wolfinger, *The Politics of Progress* (1973); and Alfred Connable and Edward Silberfarb, *Tigers of Tammany* (1967). Obituaries are in the *New York Times*, 26 Mar. 1957, *Time*, 8 Apr. 1957, and *Newsweek*, 8 Apr. 1957.

DAVID R. BEWLEY-TAYLOR

HINES, John Leonard (21 May 1868–13 Oct. 1968), officer, general, and chief of staff of the U.S. Army, was born in Greenbrier County, West Virginia, the son of Irish immigrants Edward Hines, a merchant and postmaster, and Mary Leonard. His early formal education began at a small private school (now Concord College) in Athens, West Virginia, where he studied to become a teacher. However, his education was cut short by an epidemic of smallpox in 1886. His desire for a better education—not martial glory—led him to take the competitive examinations for an appointment to the U.S. Military Academy at West Point.

Hines received an appointment in 1887 and graduated forty-eighth in a class of sixty-five in June 1891, receiving a commission as a second lieutenant in the infantry. During his cadet years at West Point Hines acquired the nickname "Birdie," given by his fellow cadets for his springing gait.

Hines's initial army assignments were at various frontier posts and Indian agencies in the West. The outbreak of the Spanish-American War in 1898 offered an opportunity to lead men in battle, and he immediately volunteered. In Cuba he participated in the fighting at San Juan Hill and Santiago, earning a Silver Star and a War Department citation for "gallantry in action."

Returning to the United States, Hines married Harriet Schofield Wherry in 1898; they had two children. After a short tour in Cuba with the Army of Occupation the next year, Hines was assigned to the Philippines. This was the first of many tours of duty there. Promoted to captain, he saw action in the Philippine insurrection and, later, against the Moros.

In 1912 Hines was promoted, and in 1914 he was detailed to Fort Leavenworth, Kansas, to take the field officers course at the Army Service School. He served in 1916 as adjutant and, in the closing stages, acting chief of staff during the punitive expedition to catch Pancho Villa in Mexico. This experience enabled him to establish what became a lifetime friendship with John J. Pershing, commander of the American Expeditionary Force during World War I and, later, chief of staff of the U.S. Army.

Because of Hines's service record, experience in the field, and their friendship, Pershing chose Hines, who had been promoted to lieutenant colonel in May 1917, to serve on his staff for the American Expeditionary Force in France during World War I. Hines attained the height of his battle experience during that war. He received an accelerated promotion to colonel in August 1917 and was given command of the First Division, Sixteenth Infantry, that October. During the course of the war Hines rapidly rose both in rank and leadership.

Promoted to brigadier general in May 1918, Hines received command of the First Brigade, First Division; he commanded the brigade during the second battle of the Marne. For his actions in the fighting at Soissons—part of the American counteroffensive at Aisne-Marne—he was awarded the Distinguished Service Cross for "extraordinary heroism in action."

In August 1918 Hines achieved the rank of major general and simultaneously was given command of the Fourth Infantry Division. During the operations at St. Mihiel and in the Meuse-Argonne offensive, Hines's division remained on the attack for twenty-five consecutive days, a record, according to Major General Fox Connor, that was "unsurpassed by any division" during the war. That October Hines assumed command of the Third Corps, where he remained until the end of the war, in November. He thus became the only American officer during World War I to command in battle a regiment, brigade, division, and corps. Only one other American military leader could claim this distinction—the famous Confederate general of the Civil War, Thomas "Stonewall" Jackson.

After serving briefly with the Army of Occupation in Germany, Hines returned in September 1919 to the United States, where he held a series of divisional commands. In 1922 General Pershing, the new chief of staff, chose Hines as his deputy, and when Pershing completed his appointment two years later, he nominated Hines as his successor.

Hines's fine service record, and no doubt their close personal friendship, enabled Pershing to advance Hines over other general officers who were senior to him. Pershing characterized his successor as being "able, efficient, conscientious, and loyal . . . An exceptionally fine officer . . . No. 1 on the list of general officers known to me." Formally appointed chief of staff by President Calvin Coolidge in 1924, Hines took up the challenge of trying to maintain a standing peacetime army when neither the president, the administration, nor Congress was interested in expenditures for the military.

Hines continually sought all that he could for the army, but increased appropriations were out of the question and troop strengths reached record lows. In *The American Year Book*, for 1925 and 1926, editor Albert Bushnell Hart observed that at one point the regular army of the United States became the smallest in the world in relation to "population, wealth, or area."

One area that Hines turned his attention to was upgrading and improving the various army schools. In this way he felt that while the army was being downsized it could, at least, ensure that the officer corps was well trained. He urged interservice cooperation through the Grand Joint Army-Navy Maneuvers, which were held annually. The Signal Corps, the Engineers, the Army Air Corps, and the Medical Department all made advances. Hines ended his tenure as chief of staff on 20 November 1926.

Relieved to be free from the confines and restrictions of a desk job in Washington, Hines was given command of the Ninth Corps Area in San Francisco and, in 1930, returned to familiar territory—the Philippines—to succeed Major General Douglas MacArthur as commanding general of the Philippine Department. Hines held this command, his last, until 1932.

On 31 May 1932, after forty-one years of military service, Hines retired with his wife to their home in White Sulphur Springs, West Virginia. In July 1940 he received two additional stars with rank (dating from June 1940), but he was denied any increase in pay or allowances. When Hines died at Walter Reed Army Hospital in Washington, D.C., at age one hundred, he was then the oldest living graduate of West Point.

Though largely ignored by historians, John Leonard Hines was a professional soldier, a knowledgeable officer, and a competent leader who devoted his life to serving the army and his country. His command experience before the First World War had prepared him for his greatest test—leading large groups of men in battle. He had learned to lead, to direct, and, above all else, to soldier—the qualities that also enabled him to succeed as chief of staff of the army.

• Letters from Hines are in the John L. Hines Papers in the Library of Congress and in the John L. Hines Collection in the U.S. Army Military History Institute, Carlisle Barracks, Penn. His diary is in the possession of his family. Hines's "Statement of the Military Service of John Leonard Hines" is located in the Office of the Adjutant General, Department of the Army, Washington, D.C. For a brief biographical statement see General Charles L. Bolte, "John Leonard Hines" in the U.S. Military Academy publication *Assembly* 29 (Spring 1970). See also Jim Comstock, ed., *The West Virginia Heritage Encyclopedia* (1976). For an article Hines wrote while he was chief of staff see *Army and Navy Journal* (Dec. 1926): 342, 355. For an essay concerning Hines, see *Dictionary of American Military Biography* (1984). An obituary is in the U.S. Military Academy publication *Assembly* 26 (Winter 1968) and the *New York Times*, 14 Oct. 1968.

LOUIS ARTHUR PEAKE

HINES, Walker Downer (2 Feb. 1870–14 Jan. 1934), lawyer, was born in Russellville, Kentucky, the son of James Madison Hines, a lawyer and journalist, who had been an officer in John Morgan's Confederate brigade, and Mary Walker Downer. When Hines was almost eleven, his father died, and his mother became a public schoolteacher. While attending nearby Ogden College, Hines first worked as a stenographer in a law office before becoming at age sixteen the official stenographer of the Circuit Court of Warren County. After his graduation from college in 1888 at age eighteen, he did similar work in Trinidad, Colorado. Returning to Kentucky in 1890, he was secretary to Judge Horatio W. Bruce, assistant chief attorney of the Louisville & Nashville Railroad Company (L&N) in Louisville. Two years later Hines began studying law at the University of Virginia, where he distinguished himself and completed the three-year course in a year. Returning to the L&N as an assistant attorney, he became assistant chief attorney in 1897 and, in 1901, first vice president, responsible for financial and operational problems as well as legal matters. In 1900 he married Alice Clymer Macfarlane; they had one child.

In the long-and-short-haul cases in Kentucky, Hines challenged the McChord law, which gave the Kentucky Railroad Commission power to fix rates. He became the main spokesperson for railroads in a public debate over how much they should be regulated by states and the federal government, advocating a weak Interstate Commerce Commission (ICC) merely empowered to investigate and report, with the courts enforcing its judgments. His chief adversary, whose views he countered in the media and on the lecture platform, was Charles A. Prouty, who served on the ICC from 1896 to 1914. Their conflict and the publicity given it polarized public opinion on the subject of railroad regulation and fueled many fiery discussions before the passage of the Hepburn Act (1906), which strengthened the ICC and resulted in stricter railroad regulation.

In 1904 Hines joined the firm of Judge Alexander P. Humphrey, one of the South's most prominent lawyers. Two years later he moved to New York City, where he joined the Cravath, Henderson and de Gersdorff law firm, becoming a partner the next year and remaining with the firm until 1914. Hines was the general counsel of the Atchison, Topeka & Santa Fe Railroad, one of the country's most prominent railroads. By 1908 he was chair of its executive committee, and by 1916 he was chair of its board of directors. A gifted lawyer, Hines was vehemently opposed to railroad legislation. He was a spokesman for railroads and other carriers before the ICC, the Supreme Court, and various congressional committees. His persuasive briefs, which he carefully prepared from the extensive research of his large staff of lawyers, dominated the proceedings in which he participated, but he was invariably gracious both to his aides and his opponents.

In December 1917, when the Woodrow Wilson administration took over operation of the nation's railroads in the transportation emergency caused by World War I, Hines was appointed the assistant director general of the U.S. Railroad Administration. A lifelong Democrat, he became the director in January 1919, when his chief, William G. McAdoo, resigned. Hines formulated and enforced plans mandating the flow of rail traffic and pooling freight cars and other facilities that made unified control of railroads and other carriers successful. He began with an overworked, run-down, chaotic transportation system, dealt successfully with an unhappy labor force and demanding politicians, and returned the railroads to private management in better condition than he had found them. In his *War History of American Railroads* (1928), Hines detailed the difficulties the Railroad Administration had surmounted and defended it against charges of wasteful operation, deteriorating service, and high wages for inefficient workers. He showed that wage increases under the Railroad Administration, which at about 33 percent had been called excessive, were consistently less than those in privately controlled industries, which ranged from 60 to 150 percent.

Hines's government service had convinced him, despite his railroad involvement, that regulation of private railroad management was necessary. He advocated compulsory consolidation of railroads into a few large systems, but he did not back public ownership of railroads. The country "is far too vast," he insisted, "its railroad mileage too extensive." Public regulation of private ownership to encourage competition, he suggested, "gives initiative, elasticity, efficiency, responsiveness to public needs, and a minimum strain on the political system of our government." Wartime control of railroads, he maintained, was "not a sound argument either for or against permanent peace-time government ownership and operation" (*New York Times*, 15 Jan. 1934).

Hines completed his railroad work in May 1920 and the next month traveled to Europe to arbitrate shipping disputes on its international rivers. There, as in his own country, he displayed his "unfailing fairness and his extraordinary impartial approach to questions submitted for his decision" (*New York Times*, 15 Jan. 1934). With his headquarters in Paris and a branch office in Vienna, he spent fifteen months making decisions, which were unanimously accepted.

Hines resumed his law practice upon his return from Europe in 1921, but he interrupted it again in 1925 to travel to Europe, study waterways, and write *Report on Danube Navigation* (1925) for the League of Nations. When he returned to the United States, he became the director and a member of the executive committee of the Chicago, Burlington & Quincy Railroad, a director of the Colorado & Southern Railroad, and counsel for the Great Northern Railroad. In 1926 he also assumed the presidency of the Cotton-Textile Institute, which had been formed to promote the progress and development of the cotton industry. Three years later he became chair of the institute's board, and he continued with this organization until 1931. From 1927 to 1934 he was a partner in the Hines, Rearick, Dorr, Travis and Marshall law firm, which specialized in interstate commerce and railroad law. He was also a director of the Chicago, Burlington & Quincy Railroad from 1930 to 1934. From 1932 until his death Hines was the vice president of the New York City Bar Association, on whose committees he had often served. He was also active in the state and national bar associations.

In 1933, before he assumed the presidency, Franklin D. Roosevelt called Hines to Warm Springs, Georgia, to consult with him on ways to cut government spending. Favoring strict economy, Hines suggested withdrawing government support from inland waterways and opposed the St. Lawrence Seaway project. Although he was mentioned as a possible budget director or coordinator of railroads, neither job was offered to him. In June of that same year he headed a group of business experts assembled to study economic conditions in Turkey and to make suggestions on how to restore prosperity to that country. Hines suffered a stroke a month after his arrival in Europe and died in Merano, Italy.

• Hines's papers from 1912 to 1927 are at the Hoover Institution on War, Revolution, and Peace, Stanford University. Some of his correspondence is in the Records of the United States Railroad Securities Commission, Yale University Library. For an evaluation of Hines and a partial list of his letters to newspapers and journals and his speeches and articles, see Bernard Axelrod, "Railroad Regulation in Transition, 1897–1905: Walker D. Hines of the Railroads v. Charles A. Prouty of the ICC" (Ph.D. diss., Washington Univ., 1975). Hines's life story is told in Robert T. Swaine, *The Cravath Firm and Its Predecessors, 1819–1947*, vol. 2 (3 vols., 1946–1948). See also "Where Hines Stands as the Director-General of Railroads," *Current Opinion* 66 (Mar. 1919): 154–55; and Gerard C. Henderson, "The Railway Policy of Walker D. Hines," *New Republic*, 3 Mar. 1920. For further information on Hines, see William R. Doezema, "Walter D. Hines," in *Railroads in the Age of Regulation, 1900–1980*, ed. Keith L. Bryant, Jr., a volume of the *Encyclopedia of American Business History and Biography* (1988), pp. 201–12. A family history is in James Davis Hines, *Descendants of Henry Hines, Sr., 1732–1810* (1925). An editorial about Hines was printed in the *New York Times*, 16 Jan. 1934. An obituary is in the *New York Times*, 15 Jan. 1934.

OLIVE HOOGENBOOM

HINKEY, Frank Augustus (23 Dec. 1871–30 Dec. 1925), college football player, known variously as "Hink," "Gussie," or "The Living Flame," was born in North Tonawanda, New York, the son of German-born Lewis Hinkey, a partner and manager of a building supply–hardware business, and Mary Ann Nice. Hinkey was educated at local schools and from 1889 to 1891 attended Phillips Academy in Andover, Massachusetts. He began his athletic career at Andover, where he starred as a 135-pound end on the football team. Unheralded when he went out for football at Yale in the fall of 1891, he was a regular on the varsity squad by the middle of the season and was chosen the Helms Athletic (later Citizens Savings Bank) Foundation player of the year. During his four-year career, 1891 to 1894, Yale had a record of 52–1–0; won the mythical Ivy League championship in 1891, 1892, and 1894; and outscored opponents 1,738 to 15.

Records list Hinkey as standing 5'9" and weighing 155 pounds, but contemporaries recalled he played much of his career at less than 150 pounds. While primarily known as an "end rush" (defensive end), he also ran back punts and, "slippery as an eel," occasionally played in the backfield on offense. He was effective at returning punts and kickoffs. With his long arms and large hands, Hinkey moved on defense from an unusual crouch. He had an uncanny ability to anticipate the opposing team's tactics, and Walter Camp said he "drifted through interference like a disembodied spirit" to deliver a tackle that drove the runner back into the ground.

In spite of his small stature and the fact that he played without a helmet, Hinkey approached the game with a rare intensity. He was sometimes accused of going out of his way to injure opponents, and there were several games in which he got into fistfights. His rough play particularly attracted attention in the 1894 Harvard game. But his teammates noted that he sometimes took the blame for the rugged play of others, and the press noted "Hinkey's gentlemanly game" against Princeton later in the season.

Hinkey's individual exploits in games were legion. In Yale's 1891 victory over Harvard, he forced a fumble that led to a touchdown and blocked a field goal attempt. In Yale's legendary 1892 victory over Princeton, the *New York Times* reported, "Hinkey, the lively end, was a marvel in the way of intelligent action" (13 Nov. 1892). The next year against Dartmouth he made a sensational touchdown after snatching a loose ball out of a scrimmage, and that season he scored five touchdowns in ten games. There were occasions in the 1893 season, such as Yale's rugged 12–4 victory over Harvard or their 6–0 loss to Princeton, when opponents were able to turn his end, which only brought Hinkey to new levels of intensity and fierce play. The 1893 Princeton contest marked the only time he was forced out of a game with an injury. Hinkey also played baseball briefly as a freshman and his younger brother Louis played football with him on the 1893 and 1894 teams.

Taciturn, shy, morose, and reclusive, Hinkey was frequently called "the Silent One" or the "Silent Man." Yale's famed literature professor, William Lyons Phelps, remembered later that "he was as silent in class as on the gridiron." He added that Hinkey's reclusiveness made him "unpopular with newspapermen." But Hartford alumni responded enthusiastically to Hinkey's articulate defense of football in a speech at the Hartford Yale Alumni Banquet in early 1895, in which Hinkey took exception to Harvard president Charles William Eliot's remarks concerning excessive rough play and quoted from a book by Camp to refute the charges, and he clearly had the respect of teammates. From his first varsity appearance, it was recognized that he had unusual knowledge of the game. His captaincies in 1893 and 1894, in an era in which that post entailed the organization and coaching of the team, were high honors. By his graduation in 1895 he had been selected to Walter Camp's All-American teams for four straight years (1891–1894). He was subsequently named to All-Time All-American teams by Camp in 1910, by the Helms Athletic Foundation in 1950, and by the Football Writers of America in 1969. He was a charter selection for the National Football Foundation College Football Hall of Fame in 1951 and also was chosen for the Helms Athletic Foundation College Football Hall of Fame. Pop Warner said simply, "He was the greatest football player of all time."

Life was never the same for Hinkey after 1895. Friends recalled that he could not watch a Yale game without becoming ill from nervous excitement. From 1895 to 1903 he tried selling real estate in Tonawanda and working with a brother to revive the family's building supply business. He then moved on to manage a zinc smelting works in Iola, Kansas, from 1903 to 1910, and another zinc works in Springfield, Illinois, from 1910 to 1913. In 1912 he married Elizabeth Thomas of Springfield; the couple had no children.

In 1913 Yale made a historic decision to hire paid coaches, and Hinkey, who had always been one of the football alumni who informally helped to coach the team each year, served as a paid assistant coach in 1913 and head coach in 1914 and 1915. He made his mark by bringing in a Canadian rugby team, the Hamilton Tigers, to teach a wide open offensive game utilizing lateral passes, and his 1914 team went 7–2–0. But contemporaries said he did not teach the fundamentals of football or an effective defense. Worse, the team lost to Harvard. After his 1915 team lost early season games to Colgate, Virginia, and Washington and Jefferson, he was replaced as head coach by Tom Shevlin, another former Yale star. Some said Hinkey's dismissal was due in part to Camp's dislike for his smoking, heavy drinking, and swearing, yet Camp had less influence in Yale athletics after 1910. Contemporary press accounts suggested that the taciturn Hinkey had lost the confidence of the team, its captains, and the Old Blue alumni.

Hinkey had begun to work for a New York brokerage house in 1913 and remained there until 1920, after which he was a stockbroker in Dayton, Ohio, from 1920 to 1922 and coach of the Dayton Triangles football team of the American Professional Football Association in 1921. Known to have been consumptive since his youth, he entered a sanatorium in Southern Pines, North Carolina, in 1922 and died there three years later.

• For Hinkey's exploits as player and head coach, see the *New York Times*, 1891–1895 and 1914–1915. See also "Silent Frank Hinkey—The Living Flame," in *College Football, USA, 1869–1971*, ed. John D. McCallum and Charles H. Pearson (1971). Tim Cohane, *The Yale Football Story* (1951), contains chapters on Hinkey as a player and his years as a coach. For Yale football in the Hinkey era, see Walter Camp and L. S. Welch, *Yale: Her Campus, Class-Rooms and Athletics* (1899); Allison Danzig, *The History of American Football* (1956); Parke H. Davis, *Football: The American Intercollegiate Game* (1911); and Harford Powel, Jr., *Walter Camp* (1926). For a contemporary Princeton view of the Hinkey years, see William H. Edwards, *Football Days* (1916). An obituary is in the *New York Times*, 31 Dec. 1925.

DANIEL R. GILBERT

HINKLE, Beatrice Moses (10 Oct. 1874–28 Feb. 1953), psychoanalyst and feminist, was born in San Francisco, California, the daughter of Benjamin Frederick

Moses, a physician, and Elizabeth Bechley Van Geisen. She was educated at home and in 1892 married Walter Scott Hinkle, an assistant district attorney. They had two children. Her desire to study law met with her husband's derision, and she enrolled instead at Cooper Medical College, later part of Stanford University, where she received her M.D. in 1899. That same year her husband died, and Hinkle became the city physician of San Francisco, the first woman to hold such a public health post.

Like many of the first generation of American psychoanalysts, Hinkle's interest in the new science derived from experiences with the various forms of psychotherapy and mind cure then popular throughout the United States. As city physician during an epidemic of the bubonic plague, she noticed that patients responded positively to her, and she speculated about the reason for her unusual success in curing some victims of the plague. She began to experiment with suggestive therapy and hypnosis.

Hinkle moved to New York City in 1905, spent 1906 at the New Thought sanatorium in Kingston, New York, and by 1907 had become clinical assistant in the Department of Neurology at Cornell University Medical College. In 1908, collaborating with Cornell neurologist Charles L. Dana, she established what is thought to be the first psychotherapeutic clinic in the United States. Her first published article, "Psychotherapy, with Some of Its Results," appeared in the *Journal of the American Medical Association* (May 1908). The article was part case study and part defense of psychotherapy against charges of quackery. Hinkle made clear the mind-body connection, distinguished between suggestive therapy and faith healing, and argued that therapy deserved a place in American medical practice. Her lifelong belief in the power of the individual to transform his or her life emerges in these early writings.

In 1909 Freud and Jung made their well-known visit to Clark University, and Hinkle read Freud's *Studien über Hysterie* for the first time. Later in 1909 she traveled to Europe to "study the new work." As she recalled in *The Re-creating of the Individual* (1923), "my own personal analysis was conducted in the most approved Freudian style," but "in my first discussion on the subject, with C. G. Jung at Zurich, I knew that I had found the key." While Freud's study addressed Hinkle's interest in a scientific explanation of the workings of the human mind, Jung's rejection of Freud's "rigid sexual hypothesis" attracted her more. In 1911, now working with Jung, Hinkle joined Freud and Emma Jung at the Weimar psychoanalytic congress.

Hinkle rejoined Cornell's neurology department as assistant physician in 1912 and remained there until about 1915, when she divorced her second husband, variously identified as Phillip or Percy Eastwick, believed to have been a banker. (The couple, married in 1909, had no children.) She subsequently became the key figure in the diffusion of Jungian ideas in the United States through her 1916 translation of Jung's *Psychology of the Unconscious*, originally published as *Wandlungen und Symbole der Libido* (1912). The book contained Hinkle's lengthy introduction to Freudian and Jungian ideas and translations of German poetry by Louis Untermeyer, a friend of Hinkle's analysand, James Oppenheim. Oppenheim (later a Jungian lay analyst) was founder of the *Seven Arts* magazine for which Hinkle secured financial backing from another analysand, Mrs. A. K. Rankine.

Sometime before World War I Hinkle opened her private practice at 31 Gramercy Park in New York City. She was consulted professionally by a number of Greenwich Village's literary avant-garde and joined New York City's feminist network, Heterodoxy (founded in 1912), where she met such feminist activists and intellectuals as Marie Jenney Howe, Charlotte Perkins Gilman, Crystal Eastman, and Fola La Follette.

In 1923 Hinkle published her major work, *The Re-creating of the Individual*, an eclectic study drawing on the ideas of Freud and Alfred Adler as well as Jung and inspired by philosopher Henri Bergson's optimistic notions of creative energy and self-transformation. Though expanding on Jung's categories of psychological types, Hinkle's most original contribution was her early feminist critique of Freudian assumptions about female psychosexual development. She questioned all of Freud's basic theories, noting that they were "worked out entirely from the standpoint of male psychology" and have "absolutely nothing to do with women or girl children." The problem, she observed, was that no analyst had "given any consideration to the special psychology of woman as distinct from man." She also offered a penetrating assessment of masculine psychology, which, she argued, was based on the male "fear and dread of woman," an insight that anticipated by almost a decade Karen Horney's much better known 1932 article, "The Dread of Woman."

In a series of articles during the 1920s and 1930s Hinkle explored gender relations, masculine psychology, and what she called the "psychic bondage" of women to men. Along with a growing group of female Jungians in the United States, including Eleanor Bertine, M. Esther Harding, and Kristine Mann, Hinkle founded the Analytical Psychology Club of New York in 1936. Following her death, the club established the Beatrice M. Hinkle Scholarship to assist analysts wishing to study at the Jung Institute in Zurich. *The Re-creating of the Individual* was reissued in 1949, and Hinkle's translation of *Psychology of the Unconscious* was reissued in 1991.

Hinkle maintained a summer home and small sanatorium, "Smokey Hollow Lodge," in Washington, Connecticut. There, she enjoyed her dogs, cats, and elaborate gardens. Bertine described her as "spicy rather than sweet" and "frank to the point that one sometimes gasped" but with "an essential good humor" that "left no barb" (*Analytical Psychology Club Bulletin* [May 1953]). A former patient recalled Hinkle as "the last person in the world to sound her trumpet," perhaps accounting for her undeserved absence from most accounts of the early history of psychoanalysis in the United States. She died in New York City.

Hinkle was the first American practitioner of Carl Gustav Jung's analytical psychology and a pioneering feminist critic of Sigmund Freud.

• Hinkle's personal correspondence did not, for the most part, survive. However, the Nancy Hale Papers at the Sophia Smith Collection at Smith College contain forty letters from Hinkle to Hale written in the 1940s. Hale, a novelist, Hinkle's former patient, and her biographer in the *Dictionary of American Biography*, published *Heaven and Hardpan Farm* (1957), a collection of sketches based loosely on her time at Smokey Hollow Lodge. The Kristine Mann Library at the C. G. Jung Center, New York City, and the Library of the C. G. Jung Institute, San Francisco, hold Hinkle's unpublished works, including "The Evolution of Woman and Her Responsibility to the World of Today" (1940). The Mann Library has photographs of Hinkle and issues of the *Analytical Psychology Club Bulletin* that contain biographical information. Hinkle's 1927 *Nation* essay, "Why Feminism?" is reprinted in *These Modern Women: Autobiographical Essays from the Twenties*, ed. Elaine Showalter (1978). The fullest treatment of Hinkle's work is Kate Wittenstein, "The Heterodoxy Club and American Feminism, 1912–1930" (Ph.D. diss., Boston Univ., 1989). For information on Hinkle's San Francisco years, see Anne O'Hagan, "Beatrice Hinkle, Mind Explorer," *Woman Citizen*, July 1927, pp. 13, 46–48. See also William McGuire's introduction to C. G. Jung, *Psychology of the Unconscious*, trans. Beatrice M. Hinkle (1991), and John C. Burnham, *Psychoanalysis and American Medicine, 1894–1918* (1967). Obituaries are in the *New York Times* and the *New York Herald Tribune*, both 1 Mar. 1953.

KATE WITTENSTEIN
BENJAMIN HARRIS

HINKLE, Samuel Forry (9 June 1900–19 Apr. 1984), manufacturer, was born in Columbia, Pennsylvania, the son of Samuel Wisler Hinkle, a pharmacist, and Elizabeth Forry. He graduated from Pennsylvania State College (later Pennsylvania State University) in 1922 with a B.S. in chemical engineering. He immediately took a job as chemist with the Norton Company in Chippewa, Ontario, Canada, a manufacturer of electric furnaces. In 1923 he moved to a position as chief chemist at another Canadian firm, National Abrasive Company of Niagara Falls, Ontario. One year later he returned to the United States to work for Hershey Foods Corporation in Hershey, Pennsylvania, where he spent the rest of his career. In 1935 he married Margaret Joseph in Harrisburg, Pennsylvania. They had two sons.

Hinkle started with Hershey as chief chemist and director of research, positions he held until he became plant manager in 1947. From 1948 he served on the company's board of directors. In 1956 he accepted appointment as president of the firm. He took on the role of chair of the board in 1962, holding both the presidency and chairmanship until he retired in 1965. He played a major role in the growth of the Hershey Foods Corporation from the principal product company that Milton S. Hershey founded in 1893 to the diversified company it became under Hinkle's tenure.

As chief executive officer, he improved operations within the company by instituting personnel-training programs and enhancing quality control methods. He oversaw a major expansion entailing large capital expenditures. These involved the modernization of manufacturing methods and equipment and the construction of new state-of-the-art facilities for storage as well as for research and product development. For employees, he advanced benefits including pensions, life insurance plans, liberalized vacation and paid holiday schedules, and scholarship plans to assist with tuition for children's higher education. He supervised the extension of manufacturing operations into Smiths Falls, Ontario, Canada, in 1961 and Oakdale, California, in 1963. He promoted diversification of operations, from the purchase in 1963 of the H. B. Reese Candy Company, Inc., also located in Hershey, Pennsylvania, to the manufacture of pasta, the leasing of coffee vending machines, and the development of a large chain of Friendly Ice Cream Company restaurants. To recognize his many achievements on behalf of the company, Hershey dedicated its new technical center to him in 1979.

Hinkle contributed personally to the enlargement of Hershey's product line. He was the principal developer of Hershey's Syrup, Krackel, and Mr. Goodbar. During World War II he collaborated with the U.S. Army Quartermaster Corps on research toward producing a chocolate bar capable of sustaining life under extremely adverse environmental conditions. The emergency ration chocolate bar that resulted from this partnership withstood melting under tropical heat and provided 600 calories and 150 units of vitamin B1 to guard against disease. As soon as positive field test results were reported, the Hershey company began to manufacture these bars in quantities sufficient to supply U.S. military forces. They were first issued as K, C, and D rations. For his role in the development of this product, Hinkle received a certificate of appreciation from the army's Quartermaster Subsistence Research and Development Laboratory.

In addition to his executive responsibilities for the Hershey company, Hinkle became extensively involved with philanthropic and civic organizations, some of which had been founded by Milton Hershey. Hinkle sat on the boards of the M. S. Hershey Foundation and the Milton S. Hershey School for orphans. He directed the Hershey National Bank, Tri-County United Way, and Tri-County Heart Association. He also sat on the board of the American Heart Association. He served as a governor for Hershey Hospital and Harrisburg Hospital. He was director of the Pennsylvania Manufacturers' Association Casualty Insurance Company and the Pennsylvania Manufacturers' Association Fire Insurance Company. His most significant philanthropic achievements occurred in his role as board member of the M. S. Hershey Foundation. For example, he secured funding from Hershey Corporation for a scholarship program to send secondary school teachers to Ghana and Nigeria. Most notably, Hinkle motivated a $50 million grant from the legacy of Milton Hershey to Pennsylvania State University for the construction of a medical center named after Hershey that was opened in 1971. Thereafter he served as a trustee of Pennsylvania State University for fifteen years. He was also a trustee of Gettysburg College, also in Pennsylvania.

Hinkle's activities in professional organizations rivaled his involvement in community and charitable enterprises. He served as chair of the board of directors for the American Cocoa Research Institute and as president of the Chocolate Manufacturers Association of the United States. He sat on the boards of the Pennsylvania Manufacturers Association, the Pennsylvania State Chamber of Commerce, and the Pennsylvania chapters of the Grocery Manufacturers of America, Inc., and Americans for Competitive Enterprise Systems, Inc. A charter member of the Institute of Food Technologists, he was also a member of the National Confectioners Association, the American Association of Candy Technologists, the American Chemical Society, and the Newcomen Society, among others. In addition, he wrote for trade journals. In 1961 Hinkle received the Stroud Jordan Medal of the American Association of Candy Technologists.

Hinkle remained in Hershey after his retirement in 1965. By then he had not only diversified and modernized Hershey Foods Corporation, but he had also played an active role in community ventures that transformed the town of Hershey into a major tourist area. Hinkle died in a nursing home in Hershey.

• Some archival material related to Hinkle's work at Hershey and his community activities is located in the Hershey Community Archives in Hershey, Pa. Hinkle published his Newcomen Society address on Milton Hershey, the company, and the town as *Hershey: Farsighted Confectioner, Famous Chocolate, Fine Community* (1964). An obituary is in the *New York Times*, 21 Apr. 1984.

HELEN M. ROZWADOWSKI

HINSON, Eugene Theodore (20 Nov. 1873–7 June 1960), pioneering black physician, was born in Philadelphia, Pennsylvania, the son of Theodore C. Hinson, and Mary E. Cooper. Hinson grew up in Philadelphia, where he attended the O. V. Catto public schools. After his family moved to Camden, New Jersey, across the Delaware River from Philadelphia, where his father was employed at an iron foundry, Hinson was influenced by his principal at the Mt. Vernon School, William Powell, later a U.S. minister to Haiti.

Returning to Philadelphia, Hinson then studied at the Quaker Philadelphia Institute for Colored Youth, where noted educator Fannie Jackson Coppin was principal. He graduated in 1892 and taught in Hartford County, Maryland, and then Philadelphia. By 1894, he had decided to pursue a career as a physician and enrolled in the medical school at the University of Pennsylvania. Specializing in gynecology, he received his medical degree in 1898 with honors and ranked twelfth in his class.

Because he was black, Hinson was unable to secure an internship at the University of Pennsylvania Hospital even though the top fifteen graduates usually were accepted. He also was refused employment at the Philadelphia General and Presbyterian Hospitals. Hinson was welcomed to join the staff at the Frederick Douglass Memorial Hospital, an African-American facility established in 1895 by Dr. Nathan F. Mossell, a University of Pennsylvania Medical School alumnus.

Hinson was invited to be on the hospital's board of directors, and he served through 1905. Friction between black physicians and "difficulties of existence" in Philadelphia resulted in the decision to establish another black hospital. Health care for blacks was limited, and often inferior to that for whites, and African-American medical professionals sought to improve services.

Hinson led a group of doctors to create Mercy Hospital on 12 February 1907. He was the first member appointed to the new hospital's board of directors and was named chief of gynecological service. He also had a private practice until 1955, when he retired as a result of failing health.

A 1948 merger with the Douglass Hospital resulted in the Mercy-Douglass Hospital, considered the city's second oldest black hospital. At a June 1948 banquet, the Mercy-Douglass staff recognized Hinson's role in establishing the health care facility and his dedication to bettering health care for the black community. Four years later, a testimonial banquet was held in his honor, at which he was toasted as "one of Philadelphia's most distinguished and beloved practitioners."

A gifted surgeon as well as a medical pioneer, Hinson belonged to a variety of local, state, and national professional organizations. He was a member of the Philadelphia Academy of Medicine, the Philadelphia County Medical Society, the Pennsylvania State Medical Society, the National Medical Association, and the Academy of Medicine. He was pictured on the cover of the May 1956 *Journal of the National Medical Association*.

Hinson married Marie E. Hopewell in November 1902; they had no children. A civic leader and reformer, Hinson participated in a variety of activities to enrich his community. He was a lifelong member of the Lombard Central Presbyterian Church and chairman of the Philadelphia National Association for the Advancement of Colored People's Committee on Public Schools. A dedicated educator, Hinson donated part of his family's farm at Oxford, Pennsylvania, to Lincoln University, which built its campus on the site. Interested in athletics and student life, he was a member of the fraternity Alpha Phi Alpha and co-founder of Sigma Pi Phi, the first black American Greek fraternity.

Hinson died in 1960 in the hospital that he founded. The *Journal of the National Medical Association* lauded his contributions to the African-American medical community: "He is one of the early pioneers to whose vision and benefactions the present Mercy-Douglass Hospital stands as a monument."

• A biographical account is "Eugene Theodore Hinson, M.D., 1873–," *Journal of the National Medical Association* 48 (May 1956): 213. A secondary source is Herbert M. Morais, *The History of the Afro-American in Medicine* (1976). An obituary is in the *Journal of the National Medical Association* 52 (Nov. 1960): 454.

ELIZABETH D. SCHAFER

HINTON, Carmelita Chase (20 Apr. 1890–13 Jan. 1983), educator, was born in Omaha, Nebraska, the daughter of Clement Chase, an editor of financial newspapers, and Lula Belle Edwards. Carmelita cared little for the conventional social life of Omaha's upper crust, but prairie camping trips with her brother and her Campfire Girls troop absorbed some of her brimming energy. Between serving customers at her father's bookstore, she read the entire works of Charles Dickens, sitting on the floor. She regularly cared for five children living next door. She became a competitive tennis player, as though to compensate for the dullness and lack of purpose that seemed to her intrinsic to her classical education in Omaha's Episcopal School for Girls.

Carmelita Chase's four years at Bryn Mawr College were much more stimulating. She warmed to the faculty's commitment to women's equality and the idealism of many of her classmates. Though she excelled only in athletics and theater, she read William James and Friedrich Froebel with rapt attention. She began to assume the progressive movement's confidence that a new kind of education could transform the nation's future. After graduating in 1912, she worked for her father as a writer, but within a year, she decided that above all she wanted to know one of her heroes, Jane Addams. She went to Chicago and persuaded Addams to allow her to live at Addams's renowned settlement, Hull-House, as her part-time secretary.

Among the many education reformers who came to dine and talk with Hull-House residents was Neva Boyd, a leading educator of nursery and kindergarten teachers. Already one of Hull-House's playground volunteers, Carmelita enrolled in Neva Boyd's two-year playground course. Boyd's conviction that "the play group is society epitomized" and Carmelita's continuing work with immigrant children focused her mind on the larger contexts of teaching and learning. Noting the power of children's natural curiosity, she worried about the grinding inequalities surrounding her. She could hardly wait to start a nursery school of her own, a small, firm step toward a new society.

In 1916 Carmelita Chase married Sebastian Hinton, a patent lawyer and a passionate amateur naturalist. Almost immediately, she opened her own nursery playschool in the couple's Chicago apartment, one of the first of such schools in the nation. The school would continue for six years, interrupted only briefly by the birth of the three Hinton children and the family's move to a much larger home and yard in Winnetka. Like all Hinton's teaching, this school became a family affair with the Hinton children as pupils; Sebastian Hinton invented and constructed playground equipment (taking out a patent on the first "jungle gym"), and he occasionally taught shop. His sudden death in 1923 left his wife and children stunned.

Hinton decided on a new start. Following two years of kindergarten teaching at the North Shore Country Day School, she moved her family to Cambridge, Massachusetts, where she enrolled the children in Shady Hill School and became the second-grade teacher. Shady Hill made an ideal setting for her experiments in teaching. Her pupils learned social studies and mathematics by building a small town, with houses furnished by their own handmade chairs, rugs, and pottery; they learned geography by building a huge concrete contour map of Boston harbor.

The Hinton household in Cambridge, then in Weston, Massachusetts, became a progressive experiment in itself as the family took in young boarders and their horses, which they rode to nearby schools or on weekend camping trips. After nine years, however, Hinton's discontent with the secondary schools available to her own growing children impelled her to wonder why the eagerness to learn ended, so often, with elementary school. She began to plan a high school of her own.

Hinton shared John Dewey's admiration for traditional farm life, especially the natural induction into adult responsibility it provided rural children. But far from thinking such a rural life an anachronism, she envisioned a working farm as the ideal setting in which adolescents could gain the competence and independence they would need to be useful citizens in a complex urban-industrial society. A college preparatory curriculum would be powerfully enriched, she argued, by the social discipline of cooperative work that a farm demands, by the responsibility of care for animals, by the self-discipline required to produce the music, dance, visual arts, and theater that would be essential enrichments for an isolated community, and by the healthy exercise natural to outdoor life.

With much help from Edward Yeomans, Sr., an education reformer whom she had come to know at Hull-House, Hinton secured the gift of a 300-acre farm in Putney, Vermont. But she wanted five acres for each of the 180 students she expected to enroll in her school, so she sold her Weston house and some jungle gym stock to add approximately 600 acres more. When Putney School opened in 1935, fully coeducational boarding schools were almost unknown. To begin one in the middle of the Great Depression seemed madness even to Hinton's admirers. Yet the depression helped more than it hindered. Gifted neophyte teachers were happy to sign on for room and board and $50 a month; experienced, out-of-work teachers, artists, and engineers welcomed the challenge of pioneering for a Putney School whose catalog promised to "lift civilization up." Local men and women became the essential teachers of farm and household skills. The children of New Deal idealists signed on as students; musicians, writers, and prosperous nearby farmers sent their children to the school or to the Putney Labor Camp (in 1935, one of the first work camps in the nation; later the Putney Work Camp), which accomplished the summer farm and construction work.

Hinton and her children had led travel groups to Scandinavia and Germany for the new Experiment in International Living during the summers of 1933 and 1934. Several of the travelers became Putney students, while young assistant leaders left Nazi Germany to join the teaching staff. Soon refugees from the Spanish Civil War joined them; Putney took on the international flavor it would keep for decades.

By the end of World War II Putney School seemed well established. The student body had increased from 55 to 180. The school's commitments to rigorous (though ungraded) intellectual study matched its pledge to teach farmwork, skiing, crafts, and arts. Colleges had learned that Putney's unconventional students made successful undergraduates. Milk sales from the school's dairy supplemented scholarships supporting one-third of the student body. But low salaries and spartan living conditions began to grate on many faculty, and others objected to the lack of faculty participation in the formal governance of "Mrs. H.'s" school. In the fall of 1948 one interesting but weak history teacher was in danger of losing his job: Edwin Smith, a labor activist who had found Putney School a haven from the postwar crusade against radical labor leaders and Soviet sympathizers. Smith organized his willing colleagues—twenty-four of the twenty-eight classroom teachers—into a union, which demanded redress of all faculty grievances. In March the little union went on strike. Classes virtually halted, and the reopening of school looked doubtful. Parent intervention finally led to a contract specifying that an elected faculty-staff council would share in the administration of the school and an independent board of trustees would provide more distant supervision. The union teachers, however, were worn and bitter. One by one they left.

Putney School did not fully recover for several years, but on the whole, the new arrangements strengthened it. The refusals of both principal and teachers to be cowed by criticism of Putney's "left wing" tendencies throughout the McCarthy era may have helped increase applications. Hinton threw herself into further educational projects. She persuaded the Putney School trustees to sponsor a Putney graduate school of education farther up the mountain; later, as an independent corporation, the graduate school would be absorbed by Antioch College. She promoted an elementary school on Putney's Lower Farm (which she still owned) and richly encouraged several former teachers and students who were starting innovative schools of their own.

In 1955, when Hinton retired from a flourishing Putney School, she went to work as a full-time volunteer for the Women's International League for Peace and Freedom, becoming chief organizer of its Jane Addams centennial celebrations. She defied State Department travel bans to enter China by way of the Soviet Union in 1961 to visit her youngest daughter, whom she had not seen for thirteen years. Though her passport was confiscated on her return, she got it back ten years later, when the Chinese government invited her to lead the first American youth tour of the People's Republic. Hinton continued organizing peace marches and skiing expeditions into her mid-eighties. She died in Concord, Massachusetts.

Carmelita Hinton is chiefly known as the founder of the Putney School in Vermont. Innovative for its time, the Putney School continued during her twenty-year tenure as its head to inspire other progressive schools both public and private.

• Hinton's papers are in the Putney School archives and include early prospectuses and catalogs as well as some personal correspondence. Jane Arms, *Putney School Aborning* (1947), is a lively personal account of Putney's beginnings. Nearly two hundred interviews (including five of Hinton herself) and a study of Hinton's favorite books are the main resources for Susan M. Lloyd's *The Putney School: A Progressive Experiment* (1986). An obituary appears in the *New York Times*, 23 Jan. 1983.

SUSAN M. LLOYD

HINTON, William Augustus (15 Dec. 1883–8 Aug. 1959), physician and clinical pathologist, was born in Chicago, Illinois, the son of Augustus Hinton, a railroad porter, and Marie Clark; both parents were former slaves. His formal education was completed in Kansas City, Kansas, where his parents moved before his first birthday. After attending the University of Kansas from 1900 to 1902, he transferred to Harvard College, where he received a B.S. in 1905.

Postponing a medical-school education because of lack of funds, Hinton taught the basic sciences at colleges in Tennessee and Oklahoma and embryology at Meharry Medical College between 1905 and 1909. While teaching at the Agricultural and Mechanical College in Langston, Oklahoma, he met a schoolteacher, Ada Hawes, whom he married in 1909; they had two daughters. During the summers Hinton continued his studies in bacteriology and physiology at the University of Chicago.

Hinton entered Harvard Medical School in 1909 and was awarded an M. D. in 1912. Scholarships and part-time work in the Harvard laboratories of Richard C. Cabot and Elmer E. Southard allowed him to attend medical school and support his family.

Because of racial discrimination, Hinton was prevented from gaining an internship in a Boston hospital. Unable to acquire the specialty training in surgery that he desired, he turned to the laboratory aspect of medicine. In 1912 he began working part time as a volunteer assistant in the department of pathology of the Massachusetts General Hospital. During the three years he spent at Massachusetts General after medical school graduation, he was asked to perform autopsies on all persons known or suspected to have syphilis. He also acquired a paid position as an assistant in the Wassermann Laboratory (the Massachusetts state laboratory for communicable diseases), based at the Harvard Medical School complex. (This laboratory had been named for August Von Wassermann, who devised the first blood serum test for the detection of syphilis in 1906.) Southard was so impressed by Hinton's knowledge of syphilis that he arranged for him to teach its laboratory diagnostic techniques to Harvard medical students. Within two years of his medical school graduation, Hinton had published his first scientific paper on the serology of syphilis in Rosenau's *Textbook of Preventive Medicine.*

In 1915, when the Wassermann Laboratory was transferred from Harvard to the Massachusetts Department of Public Health, Hinton was appointed assistant director of the Division of Biologic Laboratories and chief of the Wassermann Laboratory. He served as the head of the Wassermann Laboratory for thirty-eight years. At the Peter Bent Brigham Hospital he observed both inpatients and outpatients, correlating serologic tests with the clinical manifestations and treatment of patients with syphilis. For twelve years, from 1915 to 1927, he immersed himself in the search for a more effective test for syphilis; the Wassermann test and others for syphilis yielded a high percentage of false positive results, and many doctors had lost confidence in the Wassermann test. Because the treatment of syphilis was long, painful, and dangerous, and it was a seriously debilitating disease, a more accurate test was badly needed.

In 1918 Hinton was appointed instructor of preventive medicine and hygiene at the Harvard Medical School, the beginning of a 34-year teaching career at Harvard. In 1921 his instructional responsibilities were expanded to include bacteriology and immunology.

During the 1920s Hinton carried on intensive research on the pathology of venereal diseases. He was responsible for all syphilis testing in Massachusetts and had responsibility for the diagnosis of rabies for the State Division of Animal Husbandry. When Massachusetts established blood tests for syphilis as a requirement for marriage licenses and for mothers before birth, Hinton supervised the expansion of state laboratories from ten to 117. His laboratories also conducted research on tuberculosis and influenza for the state.

Hinton's signal, most important contribution to medical science came in 1927, when he perfected what was judged to be the most accurate and sensitive blood serum test for syphilis. His test drastically reduced the percentage of false positives. It also met the requirements of mass screening, quick results, simplicity, replicability, and unambiguity. For the next quarter of a century the Hinton test was universally used, replacing the Wassermann test. Even though the Hinton test was 98 percent accurate, Hinton was not completely satisfied, and he collaborated with John Davies in perfecting his test. By 1931 he had developed an improved version that could be done with smaller amounts of the patient's blood. Known as the Davies-Hinton test, this was adopted as the official test of the disease by the Massachusetts Department of Public Health. In 1934 the U.S. Public Health Service reported that its evaluation showed the Hinton test to be the best available, using sensitivity and specificity as evaluative standards.

In 1934 Hinton began writing his classic textbook, *Syphilis and Its Treatment* (1936). In this book, praised in both Europe and the United States, Hinton sought to provide "a clear, simple, relatively complete account of syphilis and its treatment for physicians, public health workers and medical students." The book became a standard reference in medical schools and hospitals. Documenting Hinton's years of research and "his experience in clinics with patients and the disease from their point of view," it is believed to be the first medical textbook written by an African-American doctor.

Recognition came slowly and late to Hinton. In 1946 he was promoted to the rank of lecturer in bacteriology and immunology at the Harvard Medical School. Three years later, a year before he retired and twenty-two years after he had developed his first test for syphilis, he was elevated to the position of clinical professor—the first African American to attain the title of professor at Harvard.

Hinton was a member of the American Society of Clinical Pathologists, the Society of American Bacteriologists, the American Medical Association, and the American Association for the Advancement of Science, and a fellow of the Massachusetts Medical Society. In 1948 he was elected a life member of the American Social Science Association. He lectured frequently to the medical specialty groups of the National Medical Association. He contributed twenty-one medical-scientific articles to professional journals. He also served as a special consultant to the U.S. Public Health Service.

Hinton died in his home in Canton, Massachusetts. His legacy to American medicine was not forgotten. In 1974, fifteen years after his death, when the new State Laboratory Institute Building of the Massachusetts Department of Public Health in Boston was dedicated, it was named the William A. Hinton Serology Laboratory.

• The most extensive treatment of Hinton's life is Barbara Nabrit, "A Question of Merit: A Study of Willian A. Hinton" (Honors thesis, Radcliffe College, 1972). Biographical articles include W. Montague Cobb, "William Augustus Hinton, M.D., 1883–," *Journal of the National Medical Association* 49 (Nov. 1957): 427–28; and Robert C. Hayden, "William A. Hinton: Pioneer against Syphilis," in *Eleven African-American Doctors* (1992), pp. 36–51. Hinton is also mentioned in Harvard Medical School's *Fiftieth Anniversary Report, Class of 1912* (1962), pp. 12–13.

ROBERT C. HAYDEN

HIRES, Charles Elmer (19 Aug. 1851–31 July 1937), manufacturer and businessman, was born on a farm near Roadstown, New Jersey, the son of John Dare Hires and Mary Williams, farmers. After a meager early education, Hires, similar to many of his generation, moved away from his parents' farm and began a four-year apprenticeship in 1863. He clerked at a pharmacy in Bridgeton, New Jersey, and then, at age sixteen, journeyed to Philadelphia with little more than fifty cents in his pockets. There he combined working for a physician-druggist with night classes at both Jefferson Medical College and the Philadelphia College of Pharmacy. An unsuccessful return to Bridgeton—in which he attempted with two associates to open his own pharmacy—caused him to travel once again to Philadelphia where, at the age of eighteen, he began his own pharmacy. An early indication of his entrepreneurial talents was a business venture involving the purchase and resale of a clay that Hires identified as fuller's earth. Renaming the substance Hires' Potter's Clay, he sold it to various wholesale drug houses, proclaiming it a successful grease and spot remover. All told, he made several thousand dollars profit from these transactions. In 1875 Hires married Clara Kate Smith; they had five children.

Hires first tasted the drink that would bring him both fame and fortune while staying at a New Jersey boardinghouse during his honeymoon. Served to him by his landlady, so the story goes, the beverage was a mixture made from sassafras bark and herbs. After conversations with several chemist friends and experimentation with sarsaparilla root and other ingredients, he concocted what became known as root beer. Initially he intended to call the beverage a tea. Hoping, in the interest of the temperance movement, to sell it among Pennsylvania miners, he was dissuaded by his friend, the Reverend Dr. Russell H. Conwell, who reportedly told Hires: "The miners would never drink it if it were called a tea. Let's call it a beer—root beer." The Philadelphia Centennial Exposition of 1876 offered Hires the opportunity to sell his root beer to the millions of visitors attending the fair. Their response was extremely positive and led Hires to begin marketing and packaging his root beer. At first he sold the beverage in bulk, dried form, offering a packet of dried roots for twenty-five cents. Brewed at home, the contents would produce about five gallons of root beer. In 1893 he began selling his product in liquid form in three-ounce bottles.

Selling the beverage to soda fountains increased its popularity among both industrial workers and members of the middle class, but extensive use of advertising brought him his greatest gains. Advertisements in local newspapers like the *Philadelphia Public Ledger* as well as national periodicals like the *Ladies' Home Journal* increased sales dramatically. Ironically, his soft drink also caught the attention and ire of the Woman's Christian Temperance Union (WCTU), which disparaged Hires's use of the term "beer." (When he began bottling his root beer in 1893, making it even more accessible to consumers, he created further anxiety for the WCTU.) In 1890 he reorganized his business and named it the Charles Elmer Hires Company. With a capital investment of more than $300,000, Hires watched his company's worth rise to more than $2 million by 1921. He remained the company's chairman of the board until his death.

In addition to root beer, Hires made a considerable sum of money from the manufacture and distribution of condensed milk. Begun in 1899, the Hires Condensed Milk Company blossomed into a wholly separate business venture. By the time he sold his majority interest in the company to Nestle Company in 1918, he had built more than twenty milk plants in various regions of the United States and Canada.

Among Hires's many leisure activities was his profound interest in the Society of Friends. Indeed, throughout the second half of his life, Hires spent a great deal of time, energy, and money restoring Quaker meeting houses. In 1934 he refurbished and reopened the Merion Meeting House, where William Penn had worshipped. Hires's interest in the meeting house is documented in his 1917 book *A Short Historical Sketch of the Old Merion Meeting House*. A lifelong Republican, Hires was also director of the Merchants Bank of Philadelphia and a one-time president of the Philadelphia Drug Exchange. He was also active in several clubs and associations, such as the Merion Cricket Club, the Poor Richard Club of Philadelphia, the Philadelphia Board of Trade, and many yachting clubs. His favorite leisure activities were yachting and deep-sea fishing, which he often did off the coast of Florida.

Two of Hires's sons, John Edgar Hires and Harrison Streeter Hires, became vice presidents of the Hires Root Beer Company, while Charles Elmer Hires, Jr., succeeded his father as company president. Clara Smith Hires died in 1910, and Hires married Emma Waln the following year. They had no children. Hires died at his home in Haverford, Pennsylvania.

• Hires left no personal papers, and biographical materials are limited. In addition to the book previously noted, Hires wrote *Hires' Puzzle Book of Unnatural History* (n.d.). See also Joseph J. Fucini and Suzy Fucini, *Entrepreneurs: The Men and Women behind Famous Brand Names and How They Made It* (1985), and John N. Ingham, *Biographical Dictionary of American Business Leaders* (1983). Obituaries are in the *New York Times* and the *Philadelphia Public Ledger*, 1 Aug. 1937.

STEPHEN A. BROWN

HIRSCH, Emil Gustave (22 May 1851–7 Jan. 1923), rabbi and civic leader, was born in the Grand Duchy of Luxembourg, the son of Samuel Hirsch, a rabbi, and Louise Michols. In 1866 Hirsch immigrated with his family to Philadelphia, where his father had been called to the pulpit of Reform Congregation Keneseth Israel. Upon graduation from the University of Pennsylvania in 1872, he returned to Europe to pursue advanced work in philosophy and theology at the University of Berlin and then at the University of Leipzig, where he received a doctorate in 1876. At the same time, he embarked upon rabbinical training at the Hochschule für die Wissenschaft des Judentums in Berlin, studying with such prominent liberal Jewish scholars as Abraham Geiger and Moritz Lazarus. Upon completion of his studies, Hirsch briefly served congregations in Baltimore (1877–1878) and Louisville (1878–1880), before being called to the prestigious pulpit of Sinai Congregation in Chicago, a position he held until his death. In 1878 he married

Mathilda Einhorn in Louisville; her father was Rabbi David Einhorn, the leading religious radical in American Judaism. The couple had five children.

Hirsch soon gained a widespread reputation as an eminent preacher; he regularly drew crowds numbering well over a thousand to his intellectually demanding sermons. The religious services that he conducted were held—contrary to Jewish tradition—on Sunday mornings and drew gentiles as well as Jews. Hirsch and his brother-in-law, Rabbi Kaufmann Kohler, represented a "classical" Reform Judaism that stressed full acceptance of modern science, demanded intellectual rigor, and showed little regard for religious nostalgia. Biblical criticism, to Hirsch's mind, undermined the literal authority of the text but not the religious and moral messages it contained. He defined God in Judaism as the "ideal of progressive humanity." Influenced by anthropological studies, he rejected Jewish dietary laws as "a survival of a species of totemism." He regarded ceremonialism as generally characteristic of religious primitivism and therefore eliminated virtually all religious symbols from his congregation and its liturgy. Instead, Hirsch used services to preach a prophetic Judaism of social concern and specifically to draw attention to injustices in American society. At his initiative, a conference of American Reform rabbis, meeting in Pittsburgh in 1885, adopted a statement that called upon Jews "to participate in the great task of modern times, to solve, on the basis of justice and righteousness, the problems presented by the contrasts and evils of the present organization of society." As a universalist, Hirsch could not identify with the Zionist movement, although he favored the survival of the Jews as a religious people. Hirsch's influence as a Jewish religious leader spread beyond Chicago through the *Reform Advocate,* a periodical that he edited from 1891 to 1923.

As a scholar of the Jewish religion, Hirsch was appointed editor for the Department of the Bible of the *Jewish Encyclopedia* (1904), the first major work of Jewish scholarship produced in the United States. For that work he also wrote many articles on the Bible, rabbinics, theology, and ethics. He was likewise a contributor to the fourth volume of the *Hastings Encyclopedia of Religion and Ethics* (1922). In addition to his congregational duties, Hirsch regularly taught rabbinic literature and philosophy at the newly created University of Chicago, beginning in 1892. In each of his various capacities, Hirsch sought to instill a better appreciation for Judaism among non-Jews.

Hirsch also played a prominent role in the civic life of Chicago. He served as a member and later as president of the board of the Chicago Public Library (1888–1897); as a member of the Illinois State Board of Charities; and as president of the board of examiners of the Civil Service Commission in Chicago. He was active in the movement for welfare reform and became a champion of the right of labor to organize. He advocated a more enlightened capitalism that would treat workers more humanely and provide them with such benefits as unemployment insurance. He often served on labor arbitration boards. Within the Jewish community, Hirsch helped to organize the Associated Jewish Charities and participated in various Jewish and general philanthropic activities.

Hirsch was noted for his biting sarcasm and was a formidable opponent in political or religious polemics. He was highly esteemed by those who shared his intellectualism and social activism. Among his admirers was Rabbi Stephen S. Wise, perhaps the most significant Jewish communal leader of the next generation. However, Hirsch's views on social reform, which were advanced for the time, soon became conventional. His radical understanding of the Jewish religion became less influential in the decades after his death as the Reform movement in Judaism reincorporated many of the traditions it had earlier abandoned.

• Hirsch's principal work is *My Religion* (published posthumously, 1925; repr. 1973). A collection of his articles from the *Jewish Encyclopedia, Theology of Emil G. Hirsch* (1977), was published by his son David Einhorn Hirsch, who produced the only book-length biography *Rabbi Emil G. Hirsch: The Reform Advocate* (1968). For Hirsch within his religious context see Michael A. Meyer, *Response to Modernity: A History of the Reform Movement in Judaism* (1988).

MICHAEL A. MEYER

HIRSCH, James Gerald (31 Oct. 1922–25 May 1987), physician and biomedical research scientist, was born in St. Louis, Missouri, the son of Mack J. Hirsch, a merchant, and Henrietta B. Schiffman. Hirsch was raised in Pinckneyville, Illinois, graduating from the coal-mining town's one-room grammar school. He then attended Western Military Academy in Alton, Illinois, before beginning undergraduate study at Yale University at the age of sixteen. During his freshman year Hirsch injured his knee playing basketball, which restricted him to scholarly pursuits, including editing the *Yale Scientific*. Hirsch graduated magna cum laude from Yale in December 1942 with a degree in chemical engineering. He married Marjorie Manne in June 1943; the couple had two children before they divorced in 1974. He later married Beate Kaleschke, with whom he had another child.

The post-depression economy and the absence of job prospects for chemical engineers led Hirsch to enter medical school at Columbia University, even though his only biological training was a zoology course he had taken at Yale. He obtained an M.D. in 1946. While applying for internship positions, Hirsch and his wife were visiting family in St. Louis, the location of Barnes Hospital. After meeting with the head physician, Barry Wood, Hirsch accepted his offer of an internship and residency training in internal medicine. At Barnes the young physician first became interested in the clinical aspects of infectious disease, an area that became his life's work. Beginning in 1948 Hirsch served as chief of medicine and pediatrics at Warren Air Force Base in Cheyenne, Wyoming. There he organized a research project on rheumatic fever. This study led to the development of the use of penicillin following streptococcal infection for the prevention of cardiac damage.

Following his first clinical experiences, Hirsch planned to continue as an internist with a desire to advance in academic medicine. Realizing that laboratory experience was necessary for such a career move, he elected to spend some time doing research. This proved to be a career-altering decision. In 1950 he began his three-decade tenure at the Rockefeller Institute for Medical Research (now Rockefeller University) in New York City as a National Research Council fellow. His initial project, in the lab of René Dubos, led to the conclusion that extensive bed rest was not necessary for tuberculosis patients undergoing drug treatment. This finding fundamentally altered the clinical treatment of tuberculosis and resulted in the closing of most sanatoriums worldwide. In later years, in a Yale alumni publication, Hirsch reminisced, "I had intended to stay [at Rockefeller] for only a couple of years . . . but within six months I had fallen head over heels in love with research."

Hirsch rose through the academic ranks and in 1960 became professor, senior physician, and director, along with his colleague Zanvil Cohn, of the Laboratory of Cellular Physiology and Immunology at Rockefeller. Hirsch's research focused on the cells in the human body that target the destruction of infectious agents. Hirsch was intrigued by state-of-the-art technology, which he referred to as "toys." This led him to the use of time-lapse photography for the study of phagocytosis, the process by which cells recognize and destroy invading microorganisms. These interests eventually led to his structural studies of white blood cells and the general immune response. During this time Hirsch wrote numerous scientific articles and was the editor of the *Journal of Experimental Medicine* (1963–1981). According to Cohn, Hirsch's studies "laid the groundwork for all that was to follow" in the field of cellular immunology.

Hirsch was recognized for his achievements by election to the National Academy of Sciences in 1972, the same year that he was named dean of graduate studies at Rockefeller. During his tenure as dean, Hirsch instituted a combined M.D.–Ph.D. program with Cornell Medical College. In 1974 he was also elected a member of the Institute of Medicine, a component of the National Academy of Sciences. Hirsch was a member of numerous scientific organizations, including the Harvey Society, the American Academy of Microbiology, the Society for Experimental Biology and Medicine, and the American Association of Immunologists. He was chair of the Medical Sciences section of the NAS and chair of the Assembly of Life Sciences of the National Research Council. He was also for many years a consultant to the surgeon general of the United States.

Hirsch continued his efforts to combine basic research with clinical application. In 1981, while continuing as adjunct professor at Rockefeller, he became president of the Josiah R. Macy, Jr., Foundation, an organization concerned with medical care and physi-

cian training. In this capacity, in which he served until his death, Hirsch developed medical curricula directed toward minority groups and guided graduate researchers in the basic sciences toward the study of human physiology and disease.

Hirsch was also an amateur science historian, writing biographies for the National Academy of Sciences' *Biographical Memoirs* of his internship mentor Barry Wood (51 [1980]: 387–418) and his research mentor René Dubos (58 [1989]: 133–61). At the time of his death in New York City, Hirsch was working with his wife on a manuscript about the German immunologist Paul Ehrlich. A physician, scientist, educator, and historian, Hirsch is remembered as an individual who combined the compassion of the clinician with the curiosity of the researcher for the betterment of the human condition.

• Hirsch's scientific writings (more than 100 articles) are in the Rockefeller University Archives, which also has collected biographical information. Hirsch produced several films during his research career at Rockefeller to illustrate the processes he studied. These include *Phagocytosis and Degranulation* and *Pinocytosis and Granular Formation in Macrophages* (with Z. A. Cohn). Hirsch coedited, with René Dubos, *Bacterial and Mycotic Infections of Man*, 4th ed. (1965). A short biographical essay of Hirsch is found in Don Herbert and Fulvio Bardossi, *Secret in the White Cell: Case History of a Biological Search* (1969). Obituaries are in the *New York Times*, 26 May 1987, and the National Academy of Sciences' newsletter, *Letter to Members* 17, no. 3 (Jan. 1988).

DAVID S. GOTTFRIED

HIRSCH, Louis A. (28 Nov. 1881–13 May 1924), popular composer, was born Louis Achille Hirsch in New York City, the son of Isidore Hirsch, a businessman, and Henrietta Hayman. Hirsch grew up on East Fifty-sixth Street, next door to future composer Jerome Kern, who was his senior by three and one-half years. Hirsch reportedly taught himself piano and, like many of the era's popular composers, planned a career as a concert pianist. After graduating from the City College of New York with a bachelor's degree, he completed his musical education under Rafael Joseffy at Berlin's Stern Academy.

By the age of nineteen Hirsch was the staff pianist at Shapiro-Bernstein, a publishing firm; he began contributing songs to Lew Dockstader's Minstrels and the Gus Edwards variety shows. Within a year his songs were being interpolated into the conventional book musicals of the time. He composed some of *The Golden Window* (1909) and shared the score of *The Girl and the Wizard* (1909) with Kern and Irving Berlin.

As staff composer for producers Jake and Lee Shubert between 1910 and 1912, Hirsch produced several noted lilting revue scores, including *The Revue of Revues*, *Vera Violetta*, *The Whirl of Society* (for Al Jolson and English star José Collins), and *The Passing Show* (for Charlotte Greenwood and Willie Howard). His first major hit, "The Gaby Glide," saluted *Vera Violetta*'s tempestuous star, Gaby Deslys, and typified the demands of the dancing craze. Choreographed by

Deslys's impassioned partner Harry Pilcer, the "Glide" was a "jazzed-up Apache number."

The ragtime craze hit London in September 1912, when the American Ragtime Octette made a memorable debut at the Hippodrome. Hirsch resigned his position with the Shuberts and shortly thereafter wrote the score for Albert de Courville's Hippodrome revue, *Hullo, Ragtime!* (1912). In composing a ragtime theatrical score, he preceded Berlin by almost two years. Hirsch also served as musical director for the show, and Great Britain came to recognize him as an innovator of ragtime. Ragtime historian Ian Whitcomb particularly praised Hirsch's "How Do You Do, Miss Ragtime?" Noting Hirsch's Jewish-German background, Whitcomb said, "With its characteristic minor dips, [he took] Miss Ragtime America through *schule* without destroying her corn-fed eyes" (p. 160).

In 1913 and 1914 Hirsch scored four more London revues: *Come Over Here*, which included a filmed segment showing the American members of the company departing from New York and arriving at Southampton, *Hullo, Tango!*, *The Honeymoon Express*, which, in differing versions, also played on Broadway and in Paris, and *Dora's Doze*. His collaborators included ragtime composer J. Rosamond Johnson. *Dora's Doze*, "a musical slumber in seven nightmares," according to the show's program, was a response to the London public's demand for jaunty, French-influenced revues.

Returning to New York after the outbreak of World War I, Hirsch became one of the founding members of the American Society of Composers, Artists and Publishers (ASCAP). Between 1915 and 1918 he wrote three editions of Ziegfeld's *Follies*. The 1915 edition includes Hirsch's hit "Hello, Frisco!" His songs continued to be interpolated into London shows such as *Three Cheers* (1916).

By 1916 the New York Princess Theatre shows, in which musical numbers were unusually well employed to advance the story line, were changing the form of musical comedy. Although Kern was the nominal composer of the shows, in collaboration with P. G. Wodehouse and Guy Bolton, Hirsch replaced him for *Oh, My Dear!* (1918) and began writing this kind of integrated score.

Hirsch's score for *Going Up* (1917) was thoughtful and memorable. Starring Edith Day, *Going Up* introduced "The Tickle Toe," a dance song simultaneously humorous and tinkling, flirtatious and exuberant. His sonorous, nearly operettic "The Touch of a Woman's Hand" subtly incorporates interior syncopation. *Going Up* repeated its success in London. Hirsch's six scores in 1918 and 1919 are less interesting, but *Mary* (1920), with lyrics by Otto Harbach, displays a varied score perfectly integrated with the plot.

The score for *Mary* includes "Love Nest," Hirsch's best-remembered standard, which is a tribute to inexpensive housebuilding. The song's uncomplicated melodic and rhythmic line is in the conversational tradition of good theater songs, on a level with Kern's best. (The song remained popular for decades as the theme song for the radio and television shows of comedians George Burns and Gracie Allen.) In *American Musical Theatre: A Chronicle*, theatrical historian Gerald Bordman writes that *Mary* had "all the types of song a 1920s show could be expected to have—a dance ('Tom Tom Toddle'), a celebratory chorus ('We'll Have a Wonderful Party'), an emotional exchange ('Anything You Want To Do, Dear'), and a fine title song." *Mary* proved equally successful in London, where it was lauded as a "dancing comedy."

Hirsch's score for *The O'Brien Girl* (1921), written with Harbach, includes another hit, "Learn to Smile." For a 1922 John Murray Anderson revue, Hirsch wrote incidental music to an Oscar Wilde poem. A consummate professional whose talent continued to develop throughout his career, Hirsch died in a New York hospital from cancer of the jaw, just several months before the opening of his last show, *Betty Lee* (1924). He and his wife, Genevieve L. Hall, whom he had married in 1918, had no children. Hirsch was one of the most prolific theatrical composers of his transitional era, quickly adapting to the demands of minstrel shows, large-scale revues, and musical comedy.

• Hirsch's papers and manuscripts remain in the hands of his family. Sheet music for Hirsch's songs and scores is held in various places, such as the University Library, Cambridge, England, the later shows were copyrighted by Victoria Publishing Co., N.Y., of which Hirsch was a director. Although Hirsch's theater music was very popular, American practice in his time did not include "original cast" recordings: some recordings of the English productions are on file at the British Library's National Sound Archive branch in London. There is no biography of Hirsch. Ian Whitcomb, *Irving Berlin and Ragtime America* (1987), briefly sets him within the context of his time. Some biographical material is found at ASCAP. Theatrical reviews mentioning Hirsch's work can be found in various libraries, particularly the Performing Arts Library of the New York Public Library, the British Library, and the archives of the Victoria and Albert Theatre Museum, London.

JAMES ROSS MOORE

HIRSCHBEIN, Peretz (7 Nov. 1880–16 Aug. 1948), playwright, producer, and director, was born in a mill near Klestchel, Grodno Province, Belarus, the son of Lippe der Milner, a miller, and Sheyne Hollander. He studied in a traditional religious school in Klestchel and in yeshivas in Brest-Litovsk and Vilna. By age twenty he had decided to abandon a rabbinical career and remained in Vilna, supporting himself by tutoring.

Although his early plays, such as *Miriam* (1905), were written in Hebrew, Hirschbein translated these into Yiddish and from 1906 on wrote exclusively in Yiddish. In 1907 he went to Warsaw to see Y. L. Peretz, who influenced his thinking and his career. He moved to Odessa in 1908, where he met with Chaim Bialik and Mendele Mokher Sforim. Since the 1883 Russian imperial edict forbidding the performance of plays in Yiddish had been revoked in 1908, he was able to gather a clutch of young actors, dedicated theater students, with whom he founded the Hirschbein Troupe in order to present Yiddish dramas of high literary quality. This ensemble traveled throughout Belarus, Poland, Russia, and Ukraine for two years, presenting the plays of Sholem Aleichem, Sholem Asch, Jacob Gordin, David Pinski, and Hirschbein. It provided the model in successive years for the longer-lived Vilna Troupe, which toured Europe and America, the Warsaw Yiddish Art Theatre, and the Young Theatre, all of which trained a generation of actors while developing more sophisticated audiences.

In 1911 Hirschbein was in Vienna, Paris, London, and New York. He returned to Russia in 1913, remaining there for a year, after which he traveled first to Argentina, then to Brazil, and finally to New York. From 1915 on he earned his living by contributing to the Yiddish press, especially to *Der Tog*. In 1918 he married Esther Shumiatsher, a distinguished poet. They had one son. New York City was their permanent residence until 1940, when they relocated to Los Angeles, the West Coast magnet for Yiddish literati. Between 1920 and 1924 Hirschbein made a world tour that included Australia, South Africa, the Crimea, and India, where he met Mahatma Gandhi and Rabindranath Tagore.

Hirschbein's two idyllic rustic comedies, *The Haunted Inn* and *A Forsaken Nook*, introduced a new momentum and direction into the Yiddish stage. *The Haunted Inn*, written in 1913 and produced on Broadway in 1922, attracted wide critical attention and became a staple of the Yiddish stage. *A Forsaken Nook*, a folk play with the theme of a miniature *Romeo and Juliet*—in a shtetl setting and with a happy ending—appeared in 1916. That year he began an important trilogy, *Green Fields, Two Towns* (1919), and *Levi Isaak* (1923), a multigenerational epic. Critics date the genesis of professional dramatic art in the American Yiddish theater from the staging of *A Forsaken Nook* in Maurice Schwartz's Irving Place Theatre on 16 November 1918.

Hirschbein's work was both accessible and broadly appealing, describing a world of simplicity, directness, and compassion. In creating this world he became a worthy successor to Avrom Goldfaden and a major force in elevating the level and quality of theatergoing on the Yiddish rialto. Realism was Hirschbein's dominant approach to dramaturgy, although the influence of Leonid Andreyev (who befriended him) and Maurice Maeterlinck are evident in the symbolism of some of his later plays. Hirschbein's impact on early twentieth-century Yiddish drama was enormous, on both the creative and the pragmatic levels. His gift for composing arresting dialogue and creating vivid characterization guaranteed a perennial place for his plays. Not the least of his contributions is his significant involvement in the establishment of Schwartz's Yiddish Art Theatre in New York in 1921.

While the success of Hirschbein's plays established him as the first major Yiddish playwright in the West, he also wrote volumes of poems, children's stories, and a classic autobiographical reminiscence of his ear-ly years, *Years of Childhood* (1932), arguably his best literary accomplishment. His most highly regarded novel, *Red Fields* (1935), dealt with agriculture collectives in Crimea; in 1942 he wrote another novel, entitled *Babylon*, a roman fleuve about Jewish life in the United States. A five-volume collection of his writing (containing twenty-six pieces) came out in 1917; an edition of nine volumes appeared in Poland in 1930, followed by another five-volume anthology in 1951. His writings have been translated into English, German, Hebrew, Polish, and Russian.

The author of more than fifty full-length and one-act plays, Hirschbein is firmly established as a major figure in the golden age of the Yiddish theater. He died in Los Angeles.

• Hirschbein's papers are at the YIVO Library in New York City. Biographical information dealing with Hirschbein can be found in Isaac Goldberg, *The Drama of Transition* (1922); Joseph C. Landis, ed., *The Great Jewish Plays* (1972); David S. Lifson, ed., *Epic and Folk Plays of the Yiddish Theatre* (1975); and Lifson, *The Yiddish Theatre in America* (1965). His life is also treated in Sol Liptzin, *A History of Yiddish Literature* (1985) and *The Maturing of Yiddish Literature* (1970), and Charles Madison, *Yiddish Literature: Its Scope and Major Writers* (1971).

THOMAS E. BIRD

HIRSCHENSOHN, Chaim (25 Aug. 1855–16 Sept. 1935), Orthodox rabbi and author, was born in Safed, Palestine, the son of Yaacov Mordecai, a rabbi, and Sarah Bayla of Pinsk in Belorussia (now Russia). His parents had emigrated from Pinsk to the land of Israel in 1847. They lived in Safed until 1864, at which time they moved to Jerusalem. Hirschensohn's father was a noted scholar and educator as well as his primary teacher. In 1875 Hirschensohn married Hava Sarah, daughter of Rabbi Shaul Binyamin ha-Cohen. He engaged in business but with limited success.

In 1885 Hirschensohn visited relatives in Russia and Germany. The vibrant intellectual life in Frankfurt inspired him to found the Hebrew-language journal *ha-Misderonah* (The Corridor), which he published for four years following his return to Jerusalem in 1885. The journal focused on the need for a renewal of religious studies in order to meet the demands of the influx of Jewish immigrants and the associated movement to establish a modern Jewish state. Hirschensohn believed that Jewish law should not be limited to small groups of pious Jews but rather should be viewed as the means to a dynamic religious way of life that could serve as the foundation for a modern and complex Jewish state. He also believed that the Hebrew language should be the cornerstone of modern Jewish education and worked tirelessly to spread its use, speaking only Hebrew in his own home and associating with other pioneers of the revitalized Hebrew language, such as Eliezer ben Yehudah. These pioneers wanted Hebrew to become a living language and adapted classical Hebrew words to modern life. Hirschensohn's progressive and nationalistic educational ideas were opposed by inflexible religious traditionalists, who preferred to reserve Hebrew for sacred studies.

Hirschensohn also set for himself the task of applying classical Jewish law to the needs of modern times. He believed that halakhah (Jewish law) should govern the newly emerging Jewish state but that, in order for it to do so, it needed to be interpreted in light of modern conditions. The task was to apply halakhah to the contemporary situation and not to consider it as a frozen, inflexible system. As he wrote: "'The ways of the Torah are ways of pleasantness and all its pathways are peace.' There is no law or rule in the Torah which opposes the ways of true civilization, nor demands of us ever to do something contrary to reason and understanding" (*Malki ba-Kodesh*, vol. 1, pp. 21–22). He offered innovative halakhic opinions relating to expanding the rights of women, creating a democratic framework for the Jewish state, and using technology in halakhically appropriate ways on the Sabbath and during festivals.

In 1901 Hirschensohn went to Constantinople, where he became principal of two Jewish schools. While there he developed modern curricular and text materials and insisted that all classes be taught in the Hebrew language. One of the first members of Mizrachi, the movement of religious Zionism, Hirschensohn attended the Zionist Congress held in Basel in 1903. He came into contact with the American delegates there and by the end of the year had decided to move his family to the United States. He became rabbi of the Orthodox synagogues in Hoboken, New Jersey, where he served until his death.

Hirschensohn expressed his opinions not only in his journal but also in many books focusing on the nature of Jewish law, biblical exegesis, education, and theology. In his compilation of a series of volumes of responsa under the title *Malki ba-Kodesh* (1919–1928), he offered his own legal decisions on a wide variety of topics. His originality and outspokenness made him something of a religious revolutionary, although he was absolutely dedicated to Jewish Orthodoxy.

Hirschensohn and his wife were advocates of high-quality education, both religious and secular, for males and females. Their son Benjamin was an engineer. Their daughters became prominent intellectuals and leaders in their own rights. Nima Adlerblum was a philosopher and author; Tehilla Lichtenstein, together with her husband Morris, was a leader in the Jewish Science movement; Tamar de Sola Pool, wife of Shearith Israel's rabbi David de Sola Pool, was national president of Hadassah and coauthor of a number of works with her husband; and Esther Taubenhaus, with her husband Jacob, was involved in Jewish research and intellectual life.

One of the few Orthodox rabbis to grapple with religious issues connected with the establishment of a modern Jewish state, Hirschensohn actively advocated his positions through his writings, educational work, and community leadership. At his death in Hoboken, he was still a controversial figure in Orthodox Jewish circles, but he had many supporters and admirers both in his community and beyond.

• Little has been written about Hirschensohn aside from short articles in various encyclopedias. Information about his life can be culled from his various works, in particular *Malki ba-Kodesh* (1919–1928). Eliezer Schweid, *Democracy and Halakhah: A Study in the Thought of Rabbi Chaim Hirschensohn* (1978), includes some biographical information but focuses primarily on Hirschensohn's philosophy of Jewish law and its consonance with democratic principles. Yosef Gabrieli, Hirschensohn's nephew, wrote a biographical sketch of his great-uncle in the Jerusalem-based Hebrew newspaper *Ha-Tsofeh*, 5727 (Sept. 1966).

MARC D. ANGEL

HIRSCHFELDER, Arthur Douglas (29 Sept. 1879–11 Oct. 1942), pharmacologist and cardiologist, was born in San Francisco, California, the son of Joseph Oakland Hirschfelder, a physician, and Clara Honigsberg. Joseph Hirschfelder, who was professor of medicine at Cooper Medical College (later Stanford University School of Medicine), had done postgraduate studies in Germany and was active in clinical research. His example influenced the choice of career of his son Arthur, who greatly admired his father.

Arthur Hirschfelder was a brilliant student, graduating from high school at age thirteen. He obtained his B.S. from the University of California at Berkeley in 1897 as the institution's youngest graduate. Hirschfelder then studied medicine for two years in Germany before entering the Johns Hopkins University School of Medicine, where he received his M.D. in 1903. He remained at Johns Hopkins the following year to serve as an intern under William Osler and then spent the next year as a resident under his father at San Francisco General Hospital.

In 1905 Hirschfelder returned to Johns Hopkins to head the newly established physiological laboratory of the Department of Medicine. This laboratory was one of three full-time clinical research divisions established that year by Lewellys Barker, Osler's successor as professor of medicine, and these units were the first of their kind in the United States. In that same year Hirschfelder married Mary R. Strauss, with whom he had two children.

Hirschfelder's research at Johns Hopkins focused on problems of the heart and blood circulation. With physiologist Joseph Erlanger, he studied the action of the cardiac nerves during complete heart block, when the two parts of the heart are functioning independently of each other. He investigated methods for determining blood pressure, variations in the venous pulse, paroxysmal tachycardia (recurrent attacks of rapid beating of the heart), and other topics in cardiovascular medicine. Hirschfelder was one of the first in the United States to conduct electrocardiographic studies in humans. In 1910 he published his influential treatise *Disease of the Heart and Aorta*, which has been referred to as "the first comprehensive monograph on the subject published in the United States" (Harvey, p. 133).

At the meeting of the American Medical Association in Minneapolis in the spring of 1913, Hirschfelder delivered a paper on "Diuretics in Cardiovascular Disease." The paper greatly impressed Charles Lyman Green, who was chair of the search committee to recommend a professor of pharmacology for the University of Minnesota College of Medical Sciences. Minnesota had created a joint department of physiology and pharmacology in 1907 and in 1913 wished to establish a separate department of pharmacology, a science that was just coming into its own as an independent discipline in the United States. Green, who wished to have a clinician teach pharmacology, was obviously favorably influenced by Hirschfelder's close ties to clinical medicine in his research. Hirschfelder was offered and accepted the professorship in pharmacology at Minnesota in the summer of 1913.

Soon after Hirschfelder arrived in Minneapolis, he initiated collaborative studies with Merrill C. Hart, an organic chemist in his department. Hirschfelder admired the work of German scientist Paul Ehrlich, who pioneered the field of chemotherapy by synthesizing chemicals that could be used to attack pathogenic microorganisms. Ehrlich's introduction in 1910 of the arsenical compound Salvarsan to treat syphilis greatly stimulated interest in chemical drugs. Hirschfelder was therefore eager to work with a chemist in the development of new drugs. Hart synthesized a series of organic compounds that Hirschfelder tested for their antiseptic and local anesthetic properties. The major accomplishment of Hart and Hirschfelder in this research was the synthesis and discovery of the local anesthetic action of saligenin—the least toxic of all local anesthetics that had yet been developed. Unfortunately, the anesthesia was of too short a duration for the drug to be useful clinically.

After moving to Minnesota, Hirschfelder's research shifted from clinical medicine toward pharmacology, although he continued to make use of his clinical training in his approach to teaching and research and was an early proponent of clinical pharmacology (research on the effects of drugs in humans). This shift to research in experimental pharmacology was probably aided by the fact that Hirschfelder could not obtain a license to practice medicine in Minnesota. The Minnesota Medical Practice Act required a course in physical diagnosis, and there was no formal course in this subject at Johns Hopkins when Hirschfelder attended medical school there. The Board of Medical Examiners would not grant Hirschfelder a license by reciprocity or on the basis of taking the state board examination.

During the First World War Hirschfelder became actively involved in the war effort. He helped to organize and taught in a school for navy pharmacist mates held at the University of Minnesota. He also developed brominated and chlorinated cresol compounds for impregnating cloth, which, when worn next to the skin, produced louse-killing vapors. These compounds retained their ability to produce such vapors for up to thirteen days, whereas ordinary cresol and naphthol lost this ability in one day. In 1918 he served as a pharmacologist in the Chemical Warfare Service research unit at Johns Hopkins. After the war, he was a member of the Board of Consultants of the Chemical Warfare Service at Edgewood Arsenal (1922–1925).

Hirschfelder's research interests also included studies on the pharmacology of digitalis, magnesium and calcium salts, and various chemotherapeutic agents. In 1929 he developed a cardiovascular problem that restricted his ability to work and eventually led to his death in Minneapolis, although he remained head of the pharmacology department at Minnesota up until the time of his death. His major contribution to medicine and science was as one of the pioneers in the establishment of full-time clinical research, the field of cardiology, and the discipline of pharmacology in the United States.

• Although there are few of Hirschfelder's personal papers at the University of Minnesota, relevant materials are in the Department of Pharmacology Papers and the Raymond N. Bieter Papers in the university archives. Copies of a few family items related to Hirschfelder may be found in the Kremers Reference Files, F. B. Power Pharmaceutical Library, University of Wisconsin, Madison, filed under Hirschfelder's name in the biographical section of the files. The best biographical article is A. McGehee Harvey, "Arthur D. Hirschfelder: Johns Hopkins's First Full-Time Cardiologist," *Johns Hopkins Medical Journal* 143 (1978): 129–39, which includes a partial bibliography of Hirschfelder's publications. Other useful sources are J. Arthur Myers, *Masters of Medicine: A Historical Sketch of the College of Medical Sciences, University of Minnesota 1888–1966* (1968), pp. 553–57; and Solomon R. Kagan, *Jewish Contributions to Medicine in America from Colonial Times to the Present*, 2d ed. (1939).

JOHN PARASCANDOLA

HIRSCHFELDER, Joseph Oakland (27 May 1911–30 Mar. 1990), chemist and physicist, was born in Baltimore, Maryland, the son of Arthur Douglass Hirschfelder, a physician and professor of pharmacology, and May Rosalie Straus. He received his B.S. degree from Yale University in 1931 and a double Ph.D. in theoretical chemistry and theoretical physics from Princeton University in 1936. Following a year as a postdoctoral fellow with John von Neumann at Princeton's Institute for Advanced Studies, in 1937 he took a position as research associate at the University of Wisconsin. He became an instructor in physics and chemistry in 1940 and assistant professor of chemistry in 1941. Between 1942 and 1946 he was involved with several war-related projects as head of the interior ballistics group for the National Defense Research Council, as chief phenomenologist for the Bikini atomic bomb tests (responsible for predicting all effects of the atomic bomb), as group leader at Los Alamos (N.M.) Scientific Laboratory, and as head of theoretical physics at Naval Ordnance Test Station, China Lake, California. In 1946 he returned to Madison, Wisconsin, as professor of chemistry and established the Naval Research Laboratory (NRL), whose main activities included the study of flames and explosions. In 1959 the

NRL was, at the invitation of NASA, reorganized as the Theoretical Chemistry Institute, chartered to investigate intermolecular forces and chemical dynamics. In 1971 Hirschfelder began his association with the University of California at Santa Barbara, where he spent part of each year after his retirement from Wisconsin in 1981.

During the 1930s theoretical chemists at the forefront of their discipline were concerned with the application of new ideas of quantum mechanics to the fundamental problems of theoretical chemistry. They sought how to predict the structures and properties of individual molecules, and how to relate these characteristics to the macroscopic physical and chemical properties of bulk systems. Hirschfelder's years at Princeton brought him in contact with the world's most eminent theoretical physicists and chemists and early established his reputation—as well as his long-term interest in understanding and predicting the magnitudes of the interaction forces between molecules. Under the direction of Edward U. Condon, he tackled the problem of calculating the parallel and perpendicular polarizability parameters of molecular hydrogen—a laborious calculation in those days, before the advent of high-speed computers. Because Hirschfelder, a mere graduate student, obtained results in disagreement with those of Bernhard Mrowka, an established scientist in Germany, Condon did not allow him to publish them until three years later, when Mrowka discovered his own methods were erroneous. With Eugene P. Wigner, Hirschfelder next commenced work on how to facilitate calculations (by separating out rotational coordinates) on an arbitrary number of elementary particles described by Schrödinger's equation. This work continued, with significant refinements, into the 1960s. In the following years Hirschfelder went to work with Henry Eyring on the new activated complex theory, a novel approach to the problem of predicting *a priori* the rates of chemical reactions. The first step in this approach requires calculating the energy of interactions (potential energy surfaces) of individual atoms at all possible interatomic distances. He continued work on this problem when he went to the University of Wisconsin as a research associate for Farrington Daniels. There he developed some simple approximate relationships (later known as Hirschfelder's Rule) for predicting the energy barrier to a chemical reaction as a function of the chemical bonds of the two reacting molecules.

In the course of studying the problem of predicting chemical reaction rates, which involves describing the interactions of atoms and molecules undergoing very violent collisions, Hirschfelder reasoned that a useful first step would be to study the behavior of particles undergoing much gentler collisions—the kinds of events that are responsible for transport properties (viscosity, diffusion, and heat conductivity) of gases and liquids. A major achievement of his was in developing practical methods of applying existing mathematical formalisms so they could be compared directly with experimental data. His extensive work in this field led to the treatise *Molecular Theory of Gases and Liquids* (1954), written with two colleagues and former students, C. F. Curtiss and R. B. Bird. For many years this compendium served as a veritable bible for physical scientists and engineers; it was listed as the fourth most cited scientific reference during the period 1961–1972. Its great utility was owed in part to its lucid compilation and presentation of techniques for predicting many properties, unmeasured or unmeasurable, of fluids. One of countless practical applications of Hirschfelder's work in this area was the estimation of the heat transferred to the nose cone of a satellite on reentry into the Earth's atmosphere, work for which he was made a lifetime honorary member of the American Society of Mechanical Engineers.

Hirschfelder's earliest wartime efforts were devoted to the systemization of the thermochemistry of powder gases in order better to predict the performance of rockets and guns. His studies led to the development of the system of interior ballistics, the first theory that took into account the transfer of heat from the powder gas to the surface of the bore of the gun. This theory's greatest success was in explaining quantitatively the performance of recoilless guns within a few days after the first such German weapon was discovered by the Allied Forces.

As group leader at Los Alamos in the development of the atomic bomb in 1943 to 1946, Hirschfelder was one of the first (with John Magee) to predict radioactive fallout from atomic weapons—predictions that proved to be quantitatively accurate. In developing these predictions, Hirschfelder and Magee pulled together a number of highly diverse technical studies: Goodrich Rubber Company documents on the kinetics of formation of industrial carbon black in rubber tires provided data on particle nucleation; Department of Agriculture Soil Conservation reports on dust behavior, and a treatise on the physics of windblown sands of the Sahara gave them the basis for understanding particle behavior under various conditions; and a volume on air pollution from industrial smokes and particulates explained how particles would spread and descend with time. In spite of all this work, many of Hirschfelder's scientific colleagues doubted that there would even be radioactive fallout. After the war Hirschfelder was one of several scientists involved in the project who felt it was essential that they tell the complete scientific story of the atomic bomb (without compromising production secrets); he was selected to chair the editorial board that produced, from 237 contributing experts, *The Effects of Atomic Weapons* (1950).

Between 1946 and 1962 Hirschfelder, along with other distinguished scientists including John von Neumann, Eugene Wigner, and Peter Debye, served as a consultant to Humble Oil Company, addressing problems of oil exploration, production, and refining.

In the 1960s, under Hirschfelder's direction, the Theoretical Chemistry Institute at Wisconsin grew rapidly, attracting graduate students, postdoctoral fellows, and visiting faculty. Hirschfelder and his wife, mathematician Elizabeth Stafford Sokolnikoff, whom he had married in 1953 (they had no children), created a hospitable atmosphere for visiting and resident scientists. Important advances were made in the areas of the theory of intermolecular forces, the theory of reactive and non-reactive molecular collisions, and the statistical mechanics of real gases.

At the same time, recognizing that new experimental techniques were producing new data of unprecedented precision, Hirschfelder applied himself to developing new mathematical techniques for solving the equations of molecular quantum mechanics. In the 1970s he made numerous contributions to the quantum electrodynamics of molecular systems interacting with electromagnetic fields.

Reflecting in 1983 on his long career in science, Hirschfelder saluted the theoreticians of the 1930s for their "imagination and guts," contrasting the scene of the 1980s: "Unfortunately, now there are too few theoretical chemists with sufficient vision to take the giant step of exploring completely new techniques. Instead, scientists in the 1980s get so immersed in a maze of computational detail that they lose sight of the simple, elegant theories."

Writing about the "scientific and technical miracle" that was the atomic bomb, Hirschfelder took the opportunity to castigate society's use of the discoveries of science: "As a result of public apathy, greed, and ignorance, many of the scientific discoveries have been technologically misused . . . The future for our children and their children looks very bleak—that is, unless we can produce a set of new scientific-technological miracles which are need to solve our present problems."

Hirschfelder was the recipient of many distinguished awards. He received the American Chemical Society's highest honor, the Debye Award, in 1966. In 1976 he received the National Medal of Science from President Gerald Ford. He also received the Edgerton Gold Medal of the Combustion Institute (1966) and the Silver Medal of the American Society of Mechanical Engineers (1981). He was elected to the National Academy of Sciences (1953), the American Academy of Arts and Sciences (1959), the Norwegian Royal Society (1965), and the Royal Society of Chemistry of Great Britain (1981). He is remembered as one of the founders of modern physical chemistry. He died in Madison.

• For more information, see Hirschfelder's "My Adventures in Theoretical Chemistry," *Annual Reviews of Physical Chemistry* 34 (1983): 1–29; his autobiographical entry in *Modern Scientists and Engineers* (1980); his "The Scientific and Technical Miracle at Los Alamos," in *Reminiscences of Los Alamos: 1943–1945,* ed. Lawrence Badash et al. (1980), pp. 67–88; a eulogy by R. Byron Bird, Phillip R. Certain, and Charles F. Curtiss, *Theoretica Chimica Acta* 82 (1992): 3–6; and Bird, "Joseph Oakland Hirschfelder, 1911–1990," National Academy of Sciences, *Biographical Memoirs* 66 (1995). An obituary is in the *New York Times,* 31 Mar. 1990.

NORM COHEN

HIRSHHORN, Joseph H. (11 Aug. 1899?–31 Aug. 1981), financier and art collector, was born Joseph Herman Choneh Hirshhorn in the village of Jukst, near Mitau (now Jelgava), Latvia, the son of Lazar Hirshhorn, a grain broker and owner of a general store, and Amelia Friedlander. One year after Joseph's birth (which some sources list as 1900), his father died of heart disease. His mother and two of his sisters fled Latvia for the United States in 1906. By 1907 Amelia Hirshhorn could afford to send for Joseph and her five other children, who joined her in Brooklyn. She supported the family by working in a sweatshop. Hirshhorn was raised in a succession of railroad flats in the Williamsburg section of Brooklyn. After his mother was injured in a tenement fire, he learned to fend for himself. Determined to escape poverty, he left school at age twelve or thirteen to make his fortune on Wall Street. Employed initially as an office boy and Western Union messenger, Hirshhorn took his first step into the world of finance by charting stock for the influential *Magazine of Wall Street.* He began buying stock with a few hundred dollars in savings, and by age eighteen he had earned $168,000 and a seat on the New York Curb Market. In 1922 he married his childhood sweetheart, Jennie Berman; they had four children.

Naturally shrewd, Hirshhorn developed into a financial wizard and maverick investor. During the 1920s he amassed a $4 million fortune as a stock broker and securities trader. Anticipating the stock market crash, he withdrew from trading in August 1929. As the Great Depression deepened, Hirshhorn realized that untapped natural resources in Canada offered the key to untold wealth. In 1933 he opened a small office in Toronto, and after several speculative mining investments he acquired the abandoned Preston East Dome mine in northern Ontario in 1936. His new drilling operation struck a major gold deposit. Hirshhorn preferred the adventure of such creative speculation to the security of more conservative businesses: "What I believe in . . . is *resources,*" he told Emmet John Hughes, "They're *creative.* They're *different.* They're *imaginative*" (*Fortune,* Nov. 1956).

Those were the qualities that Hirshhorn came to prize in the art he collected. Neither an aesthete nor a man of social ambition, he developed a genuine interest in art and artists. His earliest acquisitions—two prints by Albrecht Dürer and paintings by Israels and Bougereau, among others—mirrored the art reproduced on the Prudential Insurance company calendars that had decorated his Brooklyn tenement. By the mid-1930s he began to collect contemporary American art and to befriend artists and dealers. "These guys . . . had to worry about plenty," he told Aline Saarinen, "I'd take 'em out and buy 'em proper nourishing food and lend them money. And I'd buy their pictures. But I wouldn't buy what I didn't like. I'd give a guy two hundred bucks, but not buy his things" (p. 280). In the 1940s he acquired social realist paintings by Philip Evergood, William Gropper, and Gregorio Prestopino. While he purchased modern French paintings, his unconventional taste and unorthodox methods were evident in his wholesale acquisition of works by artists as disparate as Milton Avery, Louis Eilshemius, and Arshile Gorky. Art filled Hirshhorn's offices in New York and Toronto, his estates in Great Neck, Miami, and the Poconos, as well as a New York warehouse. Hirshhorn's family life suffered as a result of his preoccupation with business and art: his first marriage ended in divorce in 1945. He married painter Lily Harmon in 1947, and they adopted two daughters. In 1948 Hirshhorn sold his impressionist and school of Paris paintings in order to concentrate on contemporary art and modern sculpture.

As a financier and art collector, Hirshhorn attained international renown during the 1950s, when his daring investments in Saskatchewan and northern Ontario gave him controlling interest in the largest uranium deposits outside South Africa. He hired geologist Franc Joubin, whose research led to the development of uranium mining in Blind River and the Algoma Basin. In 1955 Hirshhorn sold his mining interests to the British firm Rio Tinto in exchange for majority interest and the chairmanship of the company's Canadian subsidiary. In 1956 his personal fortune was said to exceed $60 million.

With such vast wealth at his disposal, Hirshhorn expanded the scale of his collecting. Unlike other postwar collectors who concentrated on painting, Hirshhorn assembled an unparalleled collection of nineteenth- and twentieth-century sculpture, including major works by Jean-Baptiste Carpeaux, Medardo Rosso, Auguste Rodin, Constantin Brancusi, Alberto Giacometti, Jacques Lipchitz, Henri Matisse, and Pablo Picasso. He also focused on overlooked areas such as early American modernism and American realism from Thomas Eakins to Raphael Soyer and the Bay Area figurative painters. His adventurous acquisitions also encompassed work by lesser-known artists such as Arthur B. Carles, John Flannagan, and John Storrs. Although he eschewed expert advice, Hirshhorn hired Abram Lerner, a painter and the director of New York's ACA Gallery, as curator of his collection in 1956.

Mindful of his humble origins, Hirshhorn developed a sense of obligation to the public about his growing collection, and he planned to found a town for miners in Blind River, Canada, where his art would be displayed in a public arena. Opposition from neighboring communities forced him to abandon the plan, so Hirshhorn loaned works to museum exhibitions throughout the 1950s. In 1957 the National Gallery of Canada arranged a circulating exhibition of his American paintings. Traveling exhibitions organized by the Detroit Institute of Arts and the American Federation of the Arts followed within two years. The Solomon R. Guggenheim Museum's 1962 exhibition of Hirshhorn's sculpture collection garnered broad critical acclaim.

While his career as financier and art patron flourished, Hirshhorn's second marriage failed. One year after his 1955 divorce, he married socialite Brenda Hawley Heide. That marriage ended in divorce in 1963. The following year Hirshhorn married Olga Zatorsky Cunningham, the proprietor of an employment agency who had helped staff his new estate, "Round Hill," in Greenwich, Connecticut. Having conducted hundreds of tours of his collection, Olga Hirshhorn grew to share her husband's passion for art. Hirshhorn had no children with his last two wives.

During the 1960s Hirshhorn's enormous collection attracted overtures from municipal and national governments in Switzerland, Israel, Italy, England, Canada, as well as several American cities. S. Dillon Ripley, secretary of the Smithsonian Institution, convinced President Lyndon B. Johnson of the international importance of the collection. Through the personal intervention of the president and first lady, Ripley secured Hirshhorn's 6,000-work collection for the people of the United States in May 1966 and thereby fulfilled a long-standing congressional mandate to establish a national museum of modern and contemporary art. The Hirshhorn Museum and Sculpture Garden, designed by Gordon Bunshaft of Skidmore, Owings, and Merrill, opened in October 1974. Hirshhorn's founding gift included master works by then living artists, notably Balthus, Francis Bacon, Willem de Kooning, and Henry Moore. Artists of the caliber of Josef Albers, Stuart Davis, Barbara Hepworth, and David Smith were represented in depth.

During the 1970s, as he continued collecting, Hirshhorn and his wife maintained residences in Naples, Florida, and Washington, D.C. Hirshhorn died in Washington, D.C. He bequeathed his remaining personal collection and remainder interest in his estate to the Hirshhorn Museum and Sculpture Garden. While opinion remains divided over his unorthodox collecting habits, Hirshhorn's achievements as an art patron cannot be underestimated. Critic Harold Rosenberg, lauding the egalitarianism of his eclectic collection, dubbed Hirshhorn a "folk collector." He was a self-made man and self-taught art patron who amassed a contemporary art collection of such breadth and depth that it became the nucleus of an international museum of modern and contemporary art.

• Joseph and Olga Hirshhorn's papers are in the Smithsonian Institution Archives. The records of Hirshhorn's art collection reside in the Collection Archive of the Hirshhorn Museum and Sculpture Garden. A transcript of an oral history interview with Hirshhorn (1976) and an untranscribed recorded interview (1981) are in the Archives of American Art. The best biographical account remains "Little Man in a Big Hurry: Joseph H. Hirshhorn," in Aline B. Saarinen's *The Proud Possessors* (1958). For a profile of Hirshhorn the financier see Emmet John Hughes, "Joe Hirshhorn: The Brooklyn Uranium King," *Fortune*, Nov. 1956, pp. 154–58, 160, 164, 166, 171–72. Other useful articles include Jo Ann Lewis, "'Every Day Is Sunday' for Joe Hirshhorn," *Art News* (Summer 1979): 56–61; Harold Rosenberg, "The Art World: The Hirshhorn," *New Yorker*, 4 Nov. 1974, pp. 156–61; and Judith Zilczer, "Artist and Patron: The Formation of the Hirshhorn Museum's Willem de Kooning Collection," *Journal of the History of Collections* 8, no. 1 (1996): 117–25. For the history of the collection, see Abram Lerner et al., *The Hirshhorn*

Museum and Sculpture Garden (1974), and James T. Demetrion's introduction to *The Hirshhorn Museum and Sculpture Garden: 150 Works* (1996). An obituary is in the *New York Times*, 2 Sept. 1981.

JUDITH ZILCZER

HISE, Elijah (4 July 1801–8 May 1867), lawyer and diplomat, was born in Allegheny County, Pennsylvania, the son of Frederick Hise, a merchant. His mother's name is unknown. Hise was raised in Russellville, Kentucky, and attended Transylvania University, where he was graduated from the law department in 1822 or 1823. He then returned to Russellville, the county seat. Hise was one of the first lawyers in Logan County, and that, combined with his keen mind, legal aptitude, and speaking ability, quickly brought him professional recognition and success. Over the years he also acquired considerable wealth. He married Elvira Stewart in 1832; the marriage was childless.

A staunch Democrat who volunteered to "battle valiantly" to get Whigs to switch their party allegiance, Hise soon became prominent in local and state politics. He served in the state legislature, but lost a bid for a congressional seat in 1839. Hise was briefly considered the leading candidate for governor in 1848, but like many other Democratic hopefuls he withdrew from the race when the divided Whig party united behind the unbeatable John Crittenden. Hise was appointed to the Kentucky Court of Appeals and retained his seat in 1851, when the new constitution made the office elective. In August 1852 he was selected chief justice of the court, serving until 1854. He showed independence on the bench and rendered an important dissenting opinion in the case of *Slack v. Maysville and Lexington Railroad Company*. Standing firmly with the new forces of laissez-faire, Hise denied virtually every argument used by the court's majority to uphold the validity and propriety of the city of Maysville's subscription to the stock of the railroad. Hise then returned to private law practice, but he remained the most influential Democrat in southern Kentucky.

In October 1866 Hise won a special election to fill out the term of Congressman Henry Girder, who had died in office. Although the district had voted staunchly Whig before the Civil War, Hise won reelection to a full term in May 1867. His back-to-back victories signaled the success of Democrats and conservatives in capturing political control of Kentucky and vigorously opposing the Fourteenth Amendment and other objectives of Radical Reconstruction. However, they could not reverse the national political and social upheaval stemming from the Union triumph in the Civil War and the abolition of slavery, which greatly disturbed Hise.

From a national perspective, Hise is best remembered for his brief diplomatic career and the unratified treaty that bears his name. In early 1848 President James Polk appointed him chargé d'affaires to Guatemala, just when the United States was sparring with Great Britain over isthmian transit rights. Secretary of State James Buchanan authorized Hise to negotiate commercial treaties with Guatemala and El Salvador. He was also to report on the general situation so that the administration could revive the Central American confederation as a means of resisting British encroachments. When Hise discovered that the British had established de facto control over the Nicaraguan canal route, he asked Washington for power to negotiate transit treaties. Despairing of a timely reply, on 21 June 1849 Hise signed a treaty (Hise-Selva) that granted the United States or its citizens the right of way for a canal in return for American protection of Nicaragua's territorial integrity. Hise had no power to conclude such an agreement, and he had already been recalled by the new Taylor administration. His treaty was never submitted to the Senate, and it was subsequently superseded by the Clayton-Bulwer Treaty of 1850. Yet the treaty was useful in persuading the British to accept a truce in the rivalry for transit rights. Hise's treaty was also championed by opponents of Clayton-Bulwer and by Democratic expansionists, such as Stephen A. Douglas.

Hise's life ended tragically. A few days after his reelection to Congress, Hise shot himself in his Russellville home. His suicide note ("I am weary of the world, and intend to leave it.") admitted to physical illness, infirmities of age, and despair over the increased Radical control of Reconstruction. Although he was often uncompromising and nervously tense, his friends and admirers remembered him for his high principles, devotion to public service, and personal integrity.

• There is no known collection of Hise papers, but there are a few of his letters in the papers of major political figures of the mid-nineteenth century, such as James K. Polk, James Buchanan, and Stephen A. Douglas. See also "Letters of Bancroft and Buchanan on the Clayton-Bulwer Treaty, 1849, 1859," *American Historical Review*, Oct. 1899, pp. 95–102; E. Merton Coulter, *The Civil War and Readjustment in Kentucky* (1926); Albert D. Kirwan, *John J. Crittenden: The Struggle for the Union* (1962); Mary W. Williams, *Anglo-American Isthmian Diplomacy 1815–1915* (1916; repr. 1965); and Robert Johannsen, *Stephen A. Douglas* (1973). For obituaries and press stories on his suicide, see the *Louisville Daily Journal*, 9 and 10 May 1867; *Lexington Observer and Reporter*, 4 Dec. 1867; and *Congressional Globe*, 40th Cong., 2d sess., pt. 1:732–33.

NOEL H. PUGACH

HITCHCOCK, Alfred (13 Aug. 1899–29 Apr. 1980), motion picture director, was born Alfred Joseph Hitchcock in Leytonstone, England, the son of William Hitchcock, a greengrocer, and Emma Jane Whelan. His lower middle-class, Cockney Catholic parents enforced a strict upbringing. His main interests as a youth included maps and timetables; at one point he memorized the schedules of most of England's train lines. Hitchcock attended a Jesuit day school for boys but spent most of his adolescence working to help support his family, particularly after his father died in 1914. He eventually found steady employment at the

Henley Telegraph and Cable Company, allowing him to take night courses in economics, drawing, art history, and painting.

With England at war, Hitchcock increasingly found escape in the arts. He was fascinated by the mystery fiction of Edgar Allan Poe and spent much time at the local cinema; American films, such as those made by D. W. Griffith and Buster Keaton, particularly appealed to him. Learning that an American film company, Famous Players–Lasky, was opening a studio in London, Hitchcock generated a portfolio of artwork and in 1920 was hired as an illustrator to design the title cards, drawings, and lettering styles for the Famous Players–Lasky films produced in England. He became a man of all trades around the studio, and when a newly formed British company, Gainsborough Pictures, headed by Michael Balcon, took over the facility in 1924, Hitchcock had already become an assistant director. During an assignment in Germany, he saw the filmmaker F. W. Murnau at work—an experience that made a lasting impression on him. He later said, "My models were forever after the German filmmakers. . . . They were trying very hard to express ideas in purely visual terms" (Spoto, p. 75).

In 1925 Balcon gave Hitchcock his first feature film to direct, *The Pleasure Garden*. He also directed a second film, *The Mountain Eagle*, that year and *The Lodger* the following year. By the end of 1926, Hitchcock found himself "the most sought-after" British director, despite the fact that none of the films had actually been released. However, the studio held a special screening of *The Lodger* for the press and film exhibitors. It was a huge success. Ecstatic trade reviews proclaimed *The Lodger* as possibly "the finest British production ever made" (*Bioscope*, 16 Sept. 1926) and "one of the first real landmarks in the coming advance of British pictures" (*Kinematograph*, 23 Sept. 1926). These reviews prompted the distributor to schedule release dates for all three of Hitchcock's completed films. In December of this busy year, Hitchcock and screen editor Alma Reville were married. They had one child.

The first Hitchcock film to be shown publicly was *The Pleasure Garden*, which opened in London on 24 January 1927. However, *The Lodger*, premiering three weeks later, attracted crowds. *The Lodger* was the first film in which Hitchcock made an uncredited cameo appearance, something that became a trademark of his films.

Hitchcock's reputation as a thriller director evolved more slowly than his reputation as England's finest director. During his first decade of filmmaking, he worked in whatever genres were popular at the time, including middle-brow theatrical adaptations (*Easy Virtue* [1927], *Juno and the Paycock* [1930], *The Skin Game* [1931]), romances (*Rich and Strange* [1932]), and even a musical (*Waltzes from Vienna* [1933]). Although the thrillers *The Lodger* and *Blackmail* (1929) were among his most critically acclaimed early films, *The Ring* (1927), a boxing melodrama based on an original story by Hitchcock, and *Juno and the Paycock*,

a surprisingly faithful and uncinematic adaptation of the Sean O'Casey play, were also well received.

In 1934 Hitchcock filmed *The Man Who Knew Too Much*, a spy thriller that marked a turning point in his career. It was the first of six consecutive thrillers made between 1934 and 1938, including *The 39 Steps* (1935), *Sabotage* (1936), and *The Lady Vanishes* (1938). However, it is not clear that Hitchcock's "classic thriller sextet" reflected the director's growing realization that the thriller genre best suited his temperament. It was probably box office success and organizational factors that led him to concentrate on the thriller format during this period of his career.

By the late 1930s the New York critics had joined the Hitchcock bandwagon. Applauding his "mastery of the melodramatic film," they concluded that his reputation as "one of the greatest directors in motion pictures" was richly deserved (*The Lady Vanishes* Scrapbook, Hitchcock Collection). Impressed with his consummate craftsmanship in the comedy-thriller *The Lady Vanishes*, the New York film critics voted Hitchcock the best director of 1938. Press clippings and reports about the director eventually reached Hollywood (many sent by Hitchcock's own camp), and a number of Hollywood film studios, including that of producer David Selznick, became interested in "Alfred the Great." Hitchcock was a consummate self-promoter.

In 1939 Hitchcock signed a long-term contract with Selznick International, thus alienating his most ardent critical supporters, the British press, who for years maligned Hitchcock's American work as inferior to his output in Britain. He was, however, welcomed warmly in the United States; *Rebecca*, his first film for Selznick, was both a popular and critical success, winning the Oscar for the best film of 1940. During the 1940s Hitchcock continued to have commercial and critical success with thrillers (including *Foreign Correspondent* [1940], *Suspicion* [1941], *Saboteur* [1942], *Shadow of a Doubt* [1943], and *Notorious* [1946]). On occasion, however, he worked in other genres, making a screwball comedy (*Mr. and Mrs. Smith* [1941]), a costume drama (*Under Capricorn* [1949]), and a war film (*Lifeboat* [1944]). It was during this period that Hitchcock began fruitful professional relationships with Cary Grant and James Stewart, both of whom starred in many of his films, as well as with Ingrid Bergman, his favorite female star during the 1940s.

After the spectacular success of the spy thriller *Notorious* in 1946, Hitchcock hit a bit of a lull. The last of his Selznick films, *The Paradine Case* (1947), disappointed both critics and fans. Hitchcock and a business associate and friend, Sidney Bernstein, then set up an independent production company, Transatlantic Pictures, that produced only two films, *Rope* (1948) and *Under Capricorn*, both directed by Hitchcock. Neither film did particularly well at the box office or with the critics. The director enjoyed somewhat more success during his four-year stint at Warner Bros. (1949–1953), especially with the psychological thriller *Strangers on a Train* (1951).

In 1952 Hitchcock entered the most productive period of his career. Between 1952 and 1960 he completed three feature films for Warners, six for Paramount, and one for MGM. His first major box office hit of this period was *Rear Window* (1954), starring James Stewart and Grace Kelly, who had replaced Ingrid Bergman as Hitchcock's principal leading actress. The movie, his first for Paramount, was also popular with critics, who praised its clever blending of suspense, comedy, and romance—qualities that had made Hitchcock's early works so successful. *Rear Window* helped to strengthen Hitchcock's reputation as a master entertainer, a view that his subsequent 1950s films—*To Catch a Thief* (1955), the remake of *The Man Who Knew Too Much* (1956), and *North by Northwest* (1959)—reinforced.

In 1955 the director launched "Alfred Hitchcock Presents," the television show he hosted for ten years. Hitchcock's actual involvement in the show was peripheral; he directed only 20 of the 372 episodes. He offered only occasional suggestions to Joan Harrison and Norman Lloyd, who were the real creative powers behind the show. Nevertheless, the program made him a household name all over the world.

Hitchcock energetically promoted himself during the 1950s. Press releases, staged interviews, and newspaper and magazine articles reportedly written by him instructed audiences on what to expect in a typical Hitchcock feature film. "After a certain amount of suspense," said Hitchcock, "the audience must find relief in laughter." Suspense and laughter he saw as part of a "basic pattern—mounting suspense and then final catharsis in laughter" (Kapsis, p. 36).

While Hitchcock cultivated the view of himself as a master entertainer, he hoped the critical press would perceive the serious intent behind his films. After *Psycho* in 1960, he began to speak out about criticism of his work. His usual showmanship and cunning marketing strategy made *Psycho* an enormous hit but led to occasional hostile reactions from critics (many found the now legendary shower murder sequence disgusting). Hitchcock felt the critics missed the point, which was his use of film art to precipitate an identical emotional response from audiences the world over—"something of a mass emotion," as he liked to put it. He defended himself against claims that his films were too formulaic. "They may be all corpse-thriller and suspense pictures," Hitchcock would remark, "but there's a vast difference between—we'll say, *Rebecca* and *Psycho* and *The Trouble with Harry* . . . and *North by Northwest* or *The Birds*. Look at the difference in all these pictures. Not one of them resembles another in any form except suspense" (Kapsis, p. 74).

While all of Hitchcock's later works (especially *Marnie* [1964]) were driven by his ambition to be taken seriously as an artist, *The Birds*, coming three years after *Psycho*, represented his most ambitious attempt to reshape his reputation. In 1963 he achieved a major promotional coup when the Museum of Modern Art sponsored a press screening of *The Birds* and hosted a large-scale retrospective of his work as well.

Hitchcock became increasingly preoccupied with undermining audience expectations of what to anticipate in his films. Whether shooting in a grim, documentary style (*The Wrong Man*), killing the lead character off in the middle of the film (*Psycho*), or ending a film without a clear-cut resolution (*The Birds*), Hitchcock made daring, revolutionary choices for nearly a decade—and *within* the Hollywood studio system.

The first to notice were influential French critics, including François Truffaut and Claude Chabrol, who launched a campaign to advance the view that Hitchcock was a cinematic genius who had a distinctive moral vision of the human condition. Contrary to many American critics, they believed his Hollywood films surpassed those he made in England; they saw his career as a proof of their conviction that cinematic art could flourish within the Hollywood studio system. When this film aesthetic became established in American film circles during the late 1960s and early 1970s, Hitchcock's standing with the critics improved dramatically.

Hitchcock's reputation was further advanced when, in spring 1968, the Academy of Motion Picture Arts and Sciences presented him with the Irving G. Thalberg Award "for the most consistent high level of achievement by an individual producer." Hitchcock had been nominated four times for a directorial Oscar, but, as he frequently put it, he had "always been the bridesmaid." The Directors Guild of America also honored Hitchcock that spring with the prestigious D. W. Griffith Award for his directorial achievements. Hitchcock's reputation received another shot in the arm when the English edition of Truffaut's influential book on Hitchcock was finally published in late 1967. A few weeks before the summer 1972 release of his next to last film, *Frenzy*, Hitchcock received an honorary doctorate from Columbia University. According to his biographer Donald Spoto, that event was "only the beginning of the greatest outpouring of adulation America gave Hitchcock in over a decade." The outpouring continued as critics nearly unanimously praised *Frenzy*.

By the time of *Frenzy*'s release, a significant number of influential U.S. critics had come to accept the "new" view of Hitchcock as a great artist. Reflected in their reviews were many of the values that the new generation of critics now looked for: hidden meanings, personal vision, universality, reflexivity, and thematic and stylistic consistency and coherence. While these values could be successfully applied to many of his earlier works, *Frenzy* was the first recent work (following the disappointing *Torn Curtain* [1966] and *Topaz* [1969]) that critics could hold up as a shining example of Hitchcock as the "auteur."

By the mid-1970s, Hitchcock's artistic stature and renown had become so established among American critics that even with a film that is viewed as inferior, such as his final film, *Family Plot* (1976), Hitchcock could accumulate more fame. This was achieved in two ways: through critics who praised the film and through those highly critical of it who used their reviews as an occasion for commenting on Hitchcock's illustrious career, highlighting his greatness as a cinematic artist. When Hitchcock died at home in Los Angeles, he had accomplished professionally what he had always been attempting to achieve—worldwide respect as both a premier popular entertainer and a true artist of the cinema.

Hitchcock is taught in every university filmmaking program not only as a master of the thriller but also as the master of cinematic form. His reputation has survived because of the great range of his work but also because many of his films have been able to sustain a diversity of interpretations. For example, *Marnie*, an underappreciated film when released, is regarded among Hitchcock's most profound works. To some critics, *Marnie* was an old-fashioned psychological melodrama about a female thief, while others highlighted the film's purely cinematic qualities. It has also been seen as an exploration of male dominance in a patriarchal social system, or even lesbian desire. Hitchcock's films have endured due to their variety, ambiguity, and adaptability to changing social, cultural, and aesthetic norms. Yet his films are also unmistakably the work of a single person—Hitchcock.

• The Alfred Hitchcock Collection (including scripts, papers, production notes, publicity files, correspondence, and memorabilia spanning Hitchcock's entire career) is at the Margaret Herrick Library, Academy of Motion Picture Arts and Sciences, Beverly Hills, Calif. Donald Spoto, *The Dark Side of Genius: The Life of Alfred Hitchcock* (1983), is the most comprehensive Hitchcock biography to date; see also John Russell Taylor, *Hitch: The Life and Times of Alfred Hitchcock* (1978); Tom Ryall, *Alfred Hitchcock and the British Cinema* (1986); and Leonard Leff, *Hitchcock and Selznick* (1987). Important critical interpretations can be found in Robin Wood, *Hitchcock's Films Revisited* (1989); Eric Rohmer and Claude Chabrol, *Hitchcock* (1957); William Rothman, *Hitchcock: The Murderous Gaze* (1982); Maurice Yacowar, *Hitchcock's British Films* (1977); Lesley Brill, *The Hitchcock Romance: Love and Irony in Hitchcock's Films* (1988); Thomas M. Leitch, *Find the Director and Other Hitchcock Games* (1991); Robert J. Corber, *In the Name of National Security: Hitchcock, Homophobia, and the Political Construction of Gender in Postwar America* (1993); and David Sterritt, *The Films of Alfred Hitchcock* (1993). For a provocative feminist reading of *Blackmail*, *Murder* (1930), *Rebecca*, *Notorious*, *Rear Window*, *Vertigo* (1957), and *Frenzy*, see Tania Modleski, *The Women Who Knew Too Much* (1988). For analysis of Hitchcock's ever evolving reputation, see Robert E. Kapsis, *Hitchcock: The Making of a Reputation* (1992). Absolutely indispensable is François Truffaut, *Hitchcock* (1967; rev. ed., 1984), fascinating book-length interview with Hitchcock; see also Sidney Gottlieb, ed., *Hitchcock on Hitchcock: Selected Writings and Interviews* (1995). Also invaluable is Jane E. Sloan, *Alfred Hitchcock: A Guide to References and Resources* (1993). Obituaries are in the *New York Times*, 11 May 1980, *Time*, 12 May 1980, and the *New Republic*, 27–31 July 1980.

ROBERT E. KAPSIS

HITCHCOCK, Charles Henry (23 Aug. 1836–5 Nov. 1919), geologist, was born in Amherst, Massachusetts, the son of Edward Hitchcock, a geologist, professor, and minister, and Orra White. Hitchcock followed in his father's footsteps both figuratively and literally. Even before he graduated from Amherst College (B.A., 1856; M.A., 1859), he had spent several years assisting his father in the field on geological assignments and in cataloging the natural history collections at the college. He shared not only his father's scientific interests but also his theological leanings, pursuing studies at Yale Divinity School for a year and then attending Andover Theological Seminary for two years in the 1850s. Throughout his career he published papers dealing with the relationship between religion and science, especially geology.

It was probably due to his father's intercession that Hitchcock was employed as curator of the Amherst museum (1858–1866) and as lecturer in zoology at Amherst (1858–1865). Edward Hitchcock was a longtime professor at the college (1825–1864) and its president as well (1844–1854). Geology, not zoology, however, was Hitchcock's science, and he moved on to a nonresident professorship of geology and mineralogy at Lafayette College in Pennsylvania in 1866, retaining that position until 1870. After supplementing his own geological education with a year at the Royal School of Mines in London and travel on the Continent in 1866 and 1867, Hitchcock was named professor of geology and mineralogy at Dartmouth College in 1868, teaching there until he became emeritus professor in 1908. During his tenure at Dartmouth he also lectured on geology at Mt. Holyoke College (1870–1896) and held professorships of geology and zoology at Williams College and the Virginia College of Agriculture and the Mechanical Arts in 1880 and 1881.

Hitchcock served as assistant to his father on the state geological survey of Vermont (1857–1861). The expertise he developed in northern New England geology while working with his father stood him in good stead as he moved on to surveys of his own. He was state geologist of Maine (1861–1862) and state geologist of New Hampshire (1868–1878). His thorough survey, *The Geology of New Hampshire*, appeared in four quarto volumes (1874–1878).

Hitchcock applied his geological expertise to numerous private surveys in the mid-1860s, working for mining and oil companies in Canada, Pennsylvania, New York, and Kentucky. Such work was common for geologists in this period and usually paid well compared to teaching or state survey work. State and private survey work provided Hitchcock with the raw material for his numerous scientific publications on glacial phenomena and the geological particulars of the northeastern United States. Late in life he developed an interest in volcanology, particularly the volcanoes of Hawaii. He visited the islands several times, retired to Honolulu in 1908, and published *Hawaii and Its Volcanoes* in 1909.

Hitchcock contributed to the general advancement of the science of geology in several ways. He educated several generations of geologists at Dartmouth. He provided ready access to a wealth of geological information by preparing a number of geological maps of the United States, including one prepared, with William P. Blake, in 1874 for *Walker's Physical Atlas* and another issued in 1886 by the American Institute of Mining Engineers. He was also instrumental in organizing the Geological Society of America in 1888.

Hitchcock had married Martha Bliss Barrows in 1862; they had five children, of whom two died young. Two years after Martha's death in 1892 Hitchcock married her sister, Charlotte Malvina Barrows. He died in Honolulu.

• Correspondence and a collection of Hitchcock's pamphlets are in the archives of the Dartmouth College Library. Most of the obituary notices published at the time of Hitchcock's death are limited to a single sentence and highlight his length of tenure at Dartmouth. One of his students, Warren Upham, prepared a memorial for the *Bulletin of the Geological Society of America* 31 (1920): 64–80; while very laudatory, it contains many of the basic facts of Hitchcock's life and a bibliography of his works through 1907. Newspaper obituaries are in the *Honolulu Star-Bulletin*, 6 Nov. 1919, and the *Pacific Commercial Advertiser*, 7 Nov. 1919.

JULIE R. NEWELL

HITCHCOCK, Edward (24 May 1793–27 Feb. 1864), geologist, was born in Deerfield, Massachusetts, the son of Justin Hitchcock, a poor farmer and hatter, and Mercy Hoyt. He supported himself while attending Deerfield Academy and afterward served as its preceptor from 1815 to 1819. In 1821 Hitchcock married Orra White; she assisted him and illustrated his works. The union yielded six children, of whom two became eminent in science.

Hitchcock exhibited an early strong interest in science, starting in 1811 with his observations of a comet, but problems of eyesight forced his attention to other areas. Sometime during his tenure at Deerfield, he met Amos Eaton, the notable American geologist and natural historian, who was then an itinerant lecturer. This encounter resulted in Hitchcock redirecting his energies into botany and geology. He corresponded with Yale College professor of chemistry and natural history Benjamin Silliman, Sr., and exchanged mineral specimens with him. Thus began a lifelong interest in geology.

Hitchcock's career did not immediately turn to geology. After a youthful conversion to Unitarianism, he had returned to his parents' Congregational denomination and left Deerfield Academy to study for the ministry at Yale, graduating in 1820. He then took up his pastoral responsibilities at Conway, Massachusetts, from 1821 to 1825. But in 1825 he became the professor of chemistry and natural history at Amherst College, where, as part of his duties, he also taught courses on geology and mineralogy. He spent the rest of his life at the college, changing his title to professor of natural theology and geology in 1845. He served as president of the college from 1844 until 1854.

Hitchcock was noteworthy in three areas: as a state geologist, as a teacher and popularizer of geology, and as a spokesman on issues of science and religion in the pre-Darwinian debates that often centered on geology.

He held two appointments as state geologist of Massachusetts, 1830–1833 and 1837–1841, and also served as the Vermont State geologist, 1856–1861. The first of these appointments was the most crucial, for his *Report on the Geology, Mineralogy, Botany, and Zoology of Massachusetts* (1833) was the first of the state geological reports to be completed, and it became the standard.

An outgrowth of Hitchcock's service as state geologist of Massachusetts was his cofounding of the Association of American Geologists. He had earlier been a member of two short-lived geological societies, the American Geological Society, founded by Silliman and George Gibbs in New Haven, active from 1819 to 1826, and the Geological Society of Pennsylvania, active from 1834 to 1836. Hitchcock saw the benefits of regular meetings among state geologists and other competent naturalists. From 1837 on, he lobbied Silliman and Henry Darwin Rogers, the state geologist of Pennsylvania, to aid in the formation of a national organization. Although at first envisioning a comprehensive scientific society, in 1840 Hitchcock became the cofounder, with Rogers, and the first president of a group concerned exclusively with geology and allied sciences, the Association of American Geologists (from 1842 known as the Association of American Geologists and Naturalists). In 1848, and independent of Hitchcock's efforts, his first idea was realized. This society reorganized as the American Association for the Advancement of Science (AAAS), which remains the chief general scientific society in the country; in 1859 Hitchcock was its vice president.

As a popularizer of geology, Hitchcock had no equal in his time. He was the single most effective person in making geology part of the American college curriculum. From 1828 on, his course was required for graduation from Amherst. His report on Massachusetts geology sparked general interest in the subject and led other colleges to emphasize the geological sciences. One result was his *Elementary Geology* (1840), based on his Amherst teaching, a phenomenally successful textbook that went through thirty-one editions by 1860. This was only the second such textbook produced in the United States and the first that was not an Americanized edition of a British text, as was Silliman's edition of Robert Bakewell's *Introduction to Geology* (1829). Hitchcock's book soon replaced Silliman's at most colleges throughout the United States.

As a reconciler of science and religion, Hitchcock had few peers in antebellum America. In the 1820s and 1830s, mainly on account of work by geologists in Britain and France, there had been a revolution in the classification and dating of the geological strata, through examination of the fossil record. This dramatic work came to the attention of the public, and, as it presupposed a great antiquity to the earth as well as the existence of species that had never interacted with humankind, it posed a problem to biblically based accounts of creation. Hitchcock's first remarks on this problem came in 1835 in a series of articles in a Congregationalist review, the *Biblical Repository*. Pointing out the many features that the geological and scriptural accounts had in common (both referred to fire and water as agents of change, for example), he reconciled the six-day account of creation by interpreting each day as an epoch. Overall, he promoted the idea of a concordance of the two books, of nature and of scripture. As he later put the matter, "the principles of science, rightly understood, should not contradict the statements of revelation, rightly interpreted" (*Elementary Geology*, 1840 ed., p. 264). Though these ideas were not new, they were forcefully argued.

He returned to the subject a decade later, becoming involved in a related controversy. In his inaugural lecture as president of Amherst, *The Highest Use of Learning* (1845), Hitchcock, like many other natural scientists, reacted strongly and negatively to Robert Chambers's anonymously published work *Vestiges of the Natural History of Creation* (1845). That popular book's argument—that natural physical laws could explain the progressive development of organic life—provoked Hitchcock to insist on the miraculous creation of human life, by processes unapprehendable to human reason. This and subsequent lectures were collected into *The Religion of Geology and Its Connected Sciences . . .* (1851). As Stanley Guralnick, the leading historian of Hitchcock's religious thought, stated, his positions became irrelevant, on the one hand to those who believed in the literal truth of the Bible and, on the other, to critical biblical scholars and to those who sought moral instruction alone there. It was primarily relevant to those for whom the modern science of the times seemed vaguely irreligious and who needed "the blessing of a scientist upon religious belief" (Guralnick, p. 537). The numerous editions of the *Religion of Geology*, on both sides of the Atlantic, emphasized that this was a sizable audience.

Beyond his survey reports, Hitchcock produced two notable geological works. *Illustrations of Surface Geology* (1857), a classic paper, showed a just regard for numerous different geological processes shaping surface topography, including the effect of glaciers, championed by Louis Agassiz and others. His *Ichnology of New England* (2 vols., 1858; *Supplement*, ed. Charles H. Hitchcock, 1865) detailed his investigations into fossil footprints, which he ascribed to ancient birds, but which paleontologists have since considered to have been made by dinosaurs.

In 1862 Hitchcock was elected a charter member of the National Academy of Sciences. He died the following year in Amherst.

• Hitchcock's manuscript papers are in the Special Collections Room, Robert Frost Library, Amherst College; a full bibliography of published work is in the biographical sketch by his son, Charles Henry Hitchcock, *American Geologist* 16 (1895): 139–49. Hitchcock included autobiographical details in his *Reminiscences of Amherst College* (1863). Other works by Hitchcock include his *Final Report on the Geology of Massachusetts* (2 vols., 1841) and *A Report on the Geology of Vermont* (2 vols., 1861). The best brief account of Hitchcock's geological ideas is Michele L. Aldrich's article in the *Dictionary of Scientific Biography*. A careful account of Hitchcock's relig-

ious views is found in Stanley Guralnick, "Geology and Religion before Darwin: The Case of Edward Hitchcock, Theologian and Geologist (1793–1864)," *Isis* 63 (1972): 529–43. The same author's *Science and the Antebellum American College* (1975) briefly considers Hitchcock's role in the college curriculum. For an account of his role in the founding of the Association of American Geologists, see Sally Gregory Kohlstedt, *The Formation of the American Scientific Community: The American Association for the Advancement of Science, 1848–1860* (1976). See also Dennis R. Cohen, "Hitchcock's Dinosaur Tracks," *American Quarterly* 21 (1969): 639–44; and Jordan D. Marché II, "Edward Hitchcock, *Fucoides*, and the Ichnogenus *Scoyenia*," *Earth Sciences History* 11 (1992): 13–20.

PAUL THEERMAN

HITCHCOCK, Ethan Allen (18 May 1798–5 Aug. 1870), soldier and author, was born in Vergennes, Vermont, the son of Samuel Hitchcock, a U.S. Circuit Court judge, and Lucy Caroline Allen, the daughter of Ethan Allen. Though raised in affluence, Ethan Hitchcock was compelled to make a career decision at the age of sixteen because of the death of his father. With family connections to the army, Hitchcock sought appointment to the U.S. Military Academy. He entered the academy on 11 October 1814 and graduated as a third lieutenant of artillery on 17 July 1817. He was in garrison duty for the next seven years.

Always interested in scholarly pursuits and an avid reader and diarist, Hitchcock was appointed to the faculty of the Military Academy on 31 January 1824 as assistant instructor of infantry tactics. On 31 December 1824 he was promoted to captain. During his tenure, Hitchcock embarked on a personal study of religious philosophy in an attempt to answer the basic questions of existence and the nature of the human soul. He found special meaning in the works of Benedict de Spinoza and Emanuel Swedenborg. This led Hitchcock to accept the fundamental dogma of pantheism, which he summarized in his own maxim: "The great Whole is one, and all the parts agree with all the parts."

Hitchcock's nonconformist nature affected his military career. In 1827 he refused to take part in a court of inquiry at the Military Academy, maintaining that the court had overstepped an accepted interpretation of military law. For this he was dismissed from the faculty and ordered to duty at Fort Snelling, Minnesota. Captain Hitchcock appealed to President John Quincy Adams. A subsequent investigation upheld Hitchcock's original assertion, and in 1829 he was reinstated at the academy, this time as commandant of cadets. Hitchcock, however, found disfavor with President Andrew Jackson over the issues of discipline and political interference. Hitchcock would allege that his promotion to major was withheld several years as a result of his stand.

From 1833 to 1836 Hitchcock served with his company at Fort Crawford, Wisconsin, and then he joined the staff of Brigadier General Edmund P. Gaines, engaged in the Second Seminole War in Florida. Hitchcock sat on a court of inquiry in 1837 to investigate the failure of the campaign against the war chief Osceola. The findings of the court criticized the operations of both Gaines and Brigadier General Winfield Scott.

In 1837–1838 Hitchcock acted as disbursing officer for American Indian funds at St. Louis. His conscientious and equitable handling of government funds brought him promotion to major on 7 July 1838. In 1841 the War Department detailed Hitchcock to look into charges of profiteering and fraud committed against the Cherokee Nation by white contractors. Hitchcock subsequently submitted a well-documented report, which showed that the corruption was far greater than anticipated. Congress tried to subpoena the report, but the secretary of war refused to make the document public, and after much chicanery and political maneuvering, the report "disappeared."

Promoted to lieutenant colonel in 1842, Hitchcock returned to Florida. By now a veteran of many encounters with American Indians, both hostile and friendly, Hitchcock was moved to write, "I have been much with Indians and look upon them as a part of the great human family, capable of being reasoned with and susceptible of passions and affections which, rightly touched, will secure moral results with almost mechanical certainty." In Florida until 1843, Hitchcock then received orders for Jefferson Barracks, near St. Louis. Here he wrote his first book of philosophy, *The Doctrines of Spinoza and Swedenborg Identified* (1846). He was next assigned to duty with Major General Zachary Taylor's army of occupation in Texas in 1845. Hitchcock wrote in his diary, "I have said from the first that the United States are the aggressors. We have outraged the Mexican government and people by an arrogance and presumption. . . . My heart is not in this business, . . . but, as a military man, I am bound to execute orders." Following a season of ill health, which he spent on leave in St. Louis, Hitchcock returned to Texas, where General Scott requested him on his staff as inspector general. Hitchcock served with distinction throughout Scott's campaign from Veracruz to Mexico City, March–September 1847, and received promotion to brevet brigadier general.

Although Hitchcock's antiwar conviction mellowed somewhat during the Mexico City campaign, he remained aloof from the typical pleasures and pastimes of army life. In his journal he wrote, "I find so little to interest me in the military profession that I had rather study or read books of philosophy. I fear I am not in my proper vocation." Following the Mexican War, Hitchcock was appointed as commander of the Military Division of the Pacific, where he was instrumental in forcing the arrest of William Walker, an American adventurer who had attempted to establish an independent republic in Baja California. Hitchcock ordered the seizure of Walker's brig, *Arrow*, an act that reportedly angered Secretary of War Jefferson Davis. In 1855—perhaps spitefully—Davis refused Hitchcock's request for a leave of absence due to ill health; Hitchcock reacted by submitting his resignation from the army on 18 October 1855.

Hitchcock moved to St. Louis and devoted himself to writing. He published *Remarks upon Alchemy and the Alchemists* (1857), which advanced his pantheistic philosophy; *Swedenborg, a Hermetic Philosopher* (1858); and *Christ the Spirit* (1861), in which he argued that the Savior was a symbolic creation of Jewish writers.

At the outbreak of the Civil War, Hitchcock, now past sixty, attempted to return to military service but was not accepted until 10 February 1862. With the rank of major general of volunteers, he was assigned to staff duties under the direction of the secretary of war. On 15 May 1862 he was ordered to inspect the conditions and wants of northern prisoner of war camps. On 15 November 1862 Hitchcock was appointed commissioner for the exchange of prisoners. Thereafter he directed the activities of agents in obtaining the exchange and return of captives. In December he was made president of a board of officers formed to propose amendments to the *Rules and Articles of War*. On 24 April the board issued "Instructions for the Government of Armies of the United States in the Field," a lengthy document that delineated the nature of warfare to be carried on against the Confederacy. On 3 December 1863, in response to criticism that the exchange process had become hopelessly mired, Hitchcock offered to resign, stating that he "would not upon any consideration in the world be supposed to stand in the way of any arrangement which might promise the relief to the sufferers in Richmond prisons." For the remainder of the war Hitchcock stayed at his post, rendering opinions in unusual situations and reviling Confederate authorities for their refusal to treat captured black troops as legitimate prisoners of war. On 3 November 1865 Hitchcock was appointed as commissary general of prisoners, responsible for the accounting, provisioning, settling of claims, and final disposition of all prisoners of war, North and South. He continued in this activity until his retirement on 1 October 1867.

Hitchcock continued his literary pursuits throughout the war. His later works included *Spensers's Poem Entitled Colin Clouts Come Home Againe Explained* (1865), *Remarks on the Sonnets* (1865), and *Notes on the Vita Nuova* (1866). He had married Martha Rind Nicholls in 1868; they had no children. Hitchcock moved to Charleston, South Carolina, and later to Sparta, Georgia, where he died.

• The major papers of Hitchcock are in the Thomas Gilcrease Institute of American History in Tulsa, Okla., and in the Library of Congress. Hitchcock's journals were published posthumously as *Fifty Years in Camp and Field* (1909) and *A Traveler in Indian Territory* (1930), the latter detailing his visit to the Cherokee Nation in 1841–1842. Hitchcock's lengthy correspondence as commissioner of prisoner exchange is published in *The War of the Rebellion: A Compilation of the Official Records of the Union and Confederate Armies* (128 vols., 1880–1901), especially in those volumes that comprise series 2 and 3. In addition, John E. Weems, *To Conquer a Peace* (1974), makes good use of Hitchcock's diaries in the context of the Mexican War.

HERMAN HATTAWAY
ERIC B. FAIR

HITCHCOCK, Ethan Allen (19 Sept. 1835–9 Apr. 1909), secretary of the interior, was born in Mobile, Alabama, the son of Henry Hitchcock, a Vermonter by birth who became chief justice of the Alabama Supreme Court, and Anne Erwin. He was the great-grandson of Ethan Allen, nephew of General Ethan Allen Hitchcock, and brother of Henry Hitchcock. After the death in 1839 of his father, who suffered economic reverses in the panic of 1837, the family relocated to Knoxville, Tennessee, where Hitchcock attended school. He was sent east to complete his education at a private military academy in New Haven, Connecticut, after which he followed his brother Henry to St. Louis, Missouri, and entered the mercantile business. His firm sent him to the Far East as its representative in 1860. By 1866 he was a partner in the firm of Olyphant and Company in Hong Kong; six years later he returned to the United States a wealthy man. He married Margaret Collier of St. Louis, the sister of his brother's wife, in 1869. They had three children.

After traveling abroad for two years he settled in St. Louis in 1874, and over the next two decades, as director of several corporations, including mining, railroad, and manufacturing companies, greatly expanded his personal fortune. A staunch Republican he contributed heavily to campaign funds, acquiring a wide acquaintance among the party's politicians. He became a good friend of William McKinley, whom he assisted by drafting the glass schedule, which fixed the duties to be imposed on foreign glass, for the tariff of 1890 (Hitchcock had established the first plate-glass factory near St. Louis). After McKinley became president he appointed Hitchcock minister to St. Petersburg (raised to embassy status during his tenure) in the hopes that he would foster trade between Russia and the United States. In December 1898 he was called home to become a member of McKinley's cabinet as secretary of the interior.

Hitchcock brought strength and integrity to a department long in bad repute. His commissioner of Indian affairs, Francis Leupp, safeguarded valuable coal, oil, and mineral lands for the Five Civilized Tribes, and Hitchcock manfully stood up to the enormous pressures of powerful interests that had hoped to acquire these resources. Hitchcock's term coincided with the emergence of the conservation movement. He supported transfer of the forest reserves from the control of the General Land Office in the Department of the Interior to Gifford Pinchot's Division of Forestry (subsequently the Forest Service) in the Department of Agriculture.

Hitchcock also backed the sweeping withdrawals carried out by President Theodore Roosevelt in 1906 that vastly expanded the forest reserves and set aside valuable mineral lands. During his tenure the Geological Survey in the Department of the Interior carried out a vast inventory of resources in the public domain and improved administrative procedures for disposing of resources, especially through leasing. Timber cutting was limited and the conduct of Indian Affairs, a bureau often viewed in about equal parts as inefficient and corrupt, was much improved.

Hitchcock secured his name as an outstanding cabinet officer by his handling of the extensive land fraud prosecutions, which, beginning in 1903, cast a shadow over the department. In the number of persons involved, the land fraud was larger than all the major corruption scandals of the nineteenth century combined, dwarfing even the Teapot Dome scandals of the Harding administration.

The cumulative sweep of the land frauds was breathtaking. Before Hitchcock left office in 1907, 1,021 people had been indicted in twenty-two states and the District of Columbia, 126 had been convicted, and more were convicted after his departure. The affair was put in motion when Hitchcock was convinced by an in-house investigation that the government had been defrauded of valuable lands and natural resources. He fired Binger Hermann, the commissioner of the General Land Office, and instituted relentless investigations that led directly to the prosecutions. Powerful people were involved. Hermann—one of those indicted, though ultimately not convicted—had served in both branches of the Oregon legislature and had been a deputy collector of internal revenue, judge advocate of the Oregon militia, and a six-term member of Congress (and was again elected to Congress after Hitchcock forced him to resign as commissioner).

A senator, a house member, a Montana state senator, state officials, and numerous westerners prominent in their communities were among those indicted. With so much influence at bay, incredible pressure was brought to bear on Hitchcock, but his cold, formal demeanor and deliberate temperament—always a trial to his impetuous contemporary Pinchot—stood him in good stead. He was unbending, equally impervious to cajolery, geniality, or threats, answering all criticism with stony silence. President Roosevelt also resisted pressures, numerous and intense, to remove the secretary of the interior; but the president was said to be privately relieved when Hitchcock, worn down by four years of unremitting strain, finally submitted his resignation, having served longer than any of his predecessors.

Hitchcock served as campaign manager for William Howard Taft in the presidential election of 1908 and was traveling in the West when illness struck. He died in the Washington, D.C., home of his son-in-law, Lieutenant Commander (later Admiral) William S. Sims.

• For additional information on Ethan Allen Hitchcock's life and work, see *Fifty Years in Camp and Field* (1909) by his uncle General Ethan Allen Hitchcock, and the *Annual Reports of the Secretary of the Interior*, especially the years 1903 to 1907. See also Henry S. Brown, "Punishing the Land-looters," *Outlook* 85 (1907): 426–39; Lincoln Steffens, "Discovery of the Land Fraud System," *American Magazine* 64 (1907): 489–98; and Gifford Pinchot, *Breaking New Ground* (1947). An obituary is in the *New York Times*, 10 Apr. 1909.

JAMES L. PENICK

HITCHCOCK, Frank Harris (5 Oct. 1867–5 Aug. 1935), politician and postmaster general, was born in Amherst, Ohio, the son of Henry Chapman Hitchcock, a Congregational clergyman, and Mary Laurette Harris. He attended public school in Boston and entered Harvard in 1887. Interested in politics and sports, he participated in collegiate boxing matches and was a Republican precinct committeeman in Boston. After graduation in 1891, he began a career in public service, holding several minor jobs in Washington, D.C., including that of a biologist in the Department of Agriculture. During this time he studied at the Columbian law school (now George Washington University), where he earned an LL.B. degree in 1894 and the LL.M. in 1895. He was admitted to the District of Columbia bar in 1894. In 1897 he was made chief of the Agriculture Department's Division of Foreign Markets.

Hitchcock's major break came in 1903, when Secretary George B. Cortelyou appointed him chief clerk of the recently created Department of Commerce and Labor. He became Cortelyou's right-hand man, helping to organize the department. His frequent travels on departmental business helped him establish numerous political contacts. In July 1904 Cortelyou, now chairman of the Republican National Committee, made Hitchcock the party's assistant secretary in charge of Theodore Roosevelt's presidential election campaign in the eastern United States. After the election, Roosevelt appointed Cortelyou postmaster general, and Hitchcock became the first assistant. In 1905 the president placed him on the (Charles H.) Keep Commission to study the executive branch and streamline it by recommending efficient and economical ways to conduct business.

In February 1908, at the urging of Roosevelt, Hitchcock resigned from the post office to manage William Howard Taft's preconvention campaign. Despite Hitchcock's success in steamrollering Taft's nomination and later in leading the party to victory as chairman of the Republican National Committee, both Taft and Roosevelt complained about his methods. Roosevelt felt that Hitchcock was making himself more prominent than the candidate. Taft and Roosevelt criticized Hitchcock for hurting the party by giving too many conservatives important, public roles in the election. Taft, who said he considered Hitchcock "far and away the ablest organizer that we can get" (Anderson, p. 45), complained of Hitchcock's imperious ways and later said, "The trouble with Hitchcock is, he does not understand me or my aims" (Butt, p. 463).

Nevertheless, when Taft became president, Hitchcock joined the cabinet as postmaster general. Even though he used the office in its traditional way to fulfill patronage needs of the administration, he had a notable tenure. In 1911 he began the postal savings bank system and started airmail as an experimental service, which earned him the sobriquet "father of the United States air mail." He introduced business management practices to the post office, cutting out wasteful processes, simplifying methods of handling mail, and raising the efficiency of employees; in so doing he erased a reported $17 million deficit. He was accused of hurting mail delivery in cities, but he defended his economy, asserting that it had been done without cutting a single job, lowering a single salary, or closing a single post office. He helped inaugurate parcel post, instituted COD (Cash on Delivery) service, added RFD (Rural Free Delivery) routes, extended franking privileges to former presidents and their wives, cut excessive government payments to railroads for carrying mail, and raised rates for second class postage, a decision that caused considerable political discomfort for the administration, since magazine and newspaper owners opposed the increases.

During 1911, as Roosevelt and Taft became politically estranged, Taft grew increasingly suspicious of Hitchcock, fearing that he supported Roosevelt. In an embarrassing confrontation before the cabinet, Hitchcock assured the president of his loyalty. Hitchcock used his influence with southern delegates to help Taft win renomination at the 1912 convention, which Roosevelt bolted because of "stolen delegates." Still, goaded by his closest advisers, Taft replaced Hitchcock as party chairman, choosing Congressman William B. McKinley of Illinois to run the 1912 campaign.

After Hitchcock left office in March 1913, he practiced law in New York City and engaged in various business dealings on Wall Street. Politics continued to be his paramount interest. Charles Evans Hughes employed him to conduct his successful preconvention canvass in 1916. In 1920 he performed the same preconvention function for General Leonard Wood, who failed to secure nomination when a longtime antagonist of Hitchcock, Frank O. Lowden, released his delegates, giving Warren G. Harding the nomination.

Hitchcock moved to Arizona in 1928. He had invested in mining activities and was coowner of the Tucson *Daily Citizen.* An advocate for the state since he toured it as first assistant postmaster general, he was elected as its Republican national committeeman for 1932–1933. Hitchcock had a lifelong interest in aviation. He served as a colonel in the Army Air Corps Reserve and was an active member of the National Aeronautical Association. Because he did not allow publicity about his health and would not print information about aircraft accidents, when he died of pneumonia in Tucson, reports circulated that he had suffered a chest injury in an airplane crash and died of ensuing complications. He had never married.

Hitchcock was a hard-working, loyal party politician, a big man with an amazing memory, who operated effectively at the highest levels of government. Accused of being a cynical but not bitter manipulator, he was defended after his death by friends, including Victor Rosewater, editor and publisher of the *Omaha* (Nebr.) *Bee,* who remembered him as a trustworthy leader whose "success rested on the faith and reliance which his assurances inspired" (*New York Times,* 11 Aug. 1935).

• Hitchcock's correspondence is scattered among various collections cited in the *National Union Catalog of Manuscript Collections*, vols. 1961, 1965, and 1979. He is mentioned frequently, or correspondence is directed to him, in Archibald Butt, *Taft and Roosevelt: The Intimate Letters of Archie Butt, Military Aide* (2 vols., 1930); and Elting E. Morison, ed., *The Letters of Theodore Roosevelt* (8 vols., 1951–1954). Several studies in which he is discussed are Donald F. Anderson, *William Howard Taft: A Conservative's Conception of the Presidency* (1973); Henry F. Pringle, *The Life and Times of William Howard Taft: A Biography* (2 vols., 1939); and Norman M. Wilensky, *Conservatives in the Progressive Era: The Taft Republican of 1912* (1965). Much useful information may be found in the *Post-Office Department Annual Reports, 1909–1912*, and the *New York Times*, including his obituary on 6 Aug. 1935.

ROBERT S. LA FORTE

HITCHCOCK, Gilbert Monell (18 Sept. 1859–3 Feb. 1934), lawyer, publisher, and politician, was born in Omaha, Nebraska, the son of Phineas W. Hitchcock, a lawyer and politician, and Annie M. Monell. Educated in Omaha and in Baden-Baden, Germany, he studied law at the University of Michigan. Graduating in 1881 with an LL.B., he passed the bar exam and practiced law in Omaha for four years. The young lawyer married Jessie Crounse in 1883; they had two children.

From active law practice, Hitchcock turned to publishing, which involved him increasingly in politics. He founded the *Omaha Evening World* in 1885 and served as its editor. In 1889 he purchased the *Omaha Morning Herald* and merged the two newspapers as the *World-Herald*, which he continued to publish until his death. A Democrat, he supported William Jennings Bryan during the agrarian revolt of the 1890s, appointing Bryan editor of the *World-Herald*. For a time Bryan and Hitchcock promoted each other's political careers, but by 1900 the two Nebraskans, both highly independent, had alienated each other.

Hitchcock's connections with Bryan and the *World-Herald* assisted his transition into politics. In 1898 he ran as a Democratic candidate for the U.S. Congress from the second district around Omaha. Although defeated, he tried again and won in 1902. He served in the Fifty-eighth Congress (1903–1905), experienced defeat in 1904, and reclaimed the seat in the Sixtieth and Sixty-first Congresses (1907–1911). A defender of western agriculture, he criticized Wall Street banks for financial centralization and "trusts" for monopolistic tendencies.

In the House of Representatives Hitchcock served at first on committees dealing with irrigation of arid lands, Indian affairs, and Pacific railroads and eventually joined the Foreign Affairs Committee. He advocated more economical government, lower tariffs, and postal savings banks and became a strong critic of William Howard Taft's presidency. Although a staunch Democrat, he worked closely with "insurgent" midwestern Republicans.

In 1911 Hitchcock was elected to the U.S. Senate, where he served two terms (1911–1923). He joined the Foreign Relations, Military Affairs, and Philippines committees, as well as some minor ones. An advocate of free trade, he favored the 1911 Canadian reciprocity treaty. But he opposed the 1911 arbitration treaty with the United Kingdom, denouncing it as the first step toward an Anglo-American alliance and seeing in it the undesirable influence of industrialist Andrew Carnegie. He wanted no political connection with foreign nations, but only good commercial relations. Hitchcock continued to oppose the Taft administration on both foreign and domestic issues in the Senate.

Hitchcock also displayed political independence toward Woodrow Wilson. He rebelled against the new Democratic president's use of the party caucus to organize congressional support for his tariff and banking reforms. During legislative struggles in 1913 over the Underwood Tariff and the Federal Reserve System, he resisted Wilson's appeal for Democratic unity and, as a member of the Banking and Currency Committee, advocated more governmental control over private banks than Wilson had proposed. Eventually he voted for the tariff and banking bills, but his independence left doubts about his loyalty in Wilson's mind.

Hitchcock's greatest political prominence came in foreign affairs. He supported Wilson's handling of the Mexican Revolution and, as chair of the Philippines Committee, played a key role in the passage of the 1916 Jones Act that promised eventual independence for the Philippines. "The American occupation of the Philippines Islands," he believed, "is the finest example of an altruistic effort by a great country to bring the blessings of civilized government to a weak people" (*World-Herald*, 12 Jan. 1916). Like Wilson, Hitchcock thought that the United States should help other peoples achieve the kind of self-government that the United States already enjoyed.

World War I brought Hitchcock to the peak of his Senate career. His membership on the Military Affairs and Foreign Relations committees placed him in crucial leadership positions. Seeking to avoid an alignment with the British Empire, he advocated strict neutrality, and in December 1914 he introduced a bill to prohibit the sale of arms and munitions to belligerents. The Wilson administration, including Secretary of State Bryan, opposed the arms embargo, but Hitchcock continued to champion it even after imperial Germany announced unrestricted submarine warfare in February 1917. Still hoping to keep the United States out of the war, Hitchcock on Wilson's behalf sought the Senate's approval for armed neutrality. A filibuster by Robert La Follette, however, prevented a vote on a bill that would have authorized the arming of U.S. merchant ships.

Despite his earlier advocacy of neutrality, Germany's unrestricted submarine warfare led Hitchcock to support Wilson's request for a declaration of war against Germany in April 1917. Hitchcock in fact introduced the Senate Foreign Relations Committee's war resolution, being next in line after chair William Stone of Missouri, who refused the task. Hitchcock also favored war against Austria-Hungary in December 1917. In 1918 he replaced Stone as chair. Although some accused him of being pro-German, Hitchcock called for total defeat of the Central Powers. He criticized the Wilson administration for failing to wage all-out war. In the Military Affairs Committee he advocated the creation of a war cabinet, but Wilson successfully resisted the proposal.

After the war Hitchcock emerged as the Senate's foremost champion of the Versailles Treaty, including Wilson's League of Nations. He responded to criticism from Henry Cabot Lodge and other Republican senators of Wilson's peacemaking at the Paris Peace Conference of 1919. Throughout the treaty fight in 1919–1920, Hitchcock did his best on Wilson's behalf in the Republican-controlled Senate. To secure a two-thirds majority for the treaty, Hitchcock wanted to compromise, but because Wilson rejected any amendments or reservations compromise was impossible. All the president would approve were Hitchcock's interpretive reservations, which were unacceptable to Republicans. Hitchcock suffered final defeat in the treaty fight in March 1920.

Landslide Republican victories in 1920, including Warren G. Harding's election as president, shoved Hitchcock to the margins. He opposed the Knox resolution to end the war but acquiesced in the separate 1921 peace treaty with Germany. He denounced as a Pacific alliance the Four Power Treaty with the United Kingdom, Japan, and France, but the Senate approved it along with the other 1921–1922 Washington Conference treaties. He lost his Senate seat in 1922 and failed to regain it in 1930. After his first wife's death in 1925, he married Martha Harris in 1927. He died at home in Washington, D.C.

• The Library of Congress holds the major collection of Gilbert M. Hitchcock Papers, but the Nebraska State Historical Society also has a small one. There is no full-scale biography or study of Hitchcock. Aspects of his career are covered in Paul C. Polmantier, "The Congressional Career of Gilbert M. Hitchcock" (M.A. thesis, Univ. of Nebraska, Lincoln, 1935); Paolo E. Coletta, *William Jennings Bryan* (3 vols., 1964–1969); Lloyd E. Ambrosius, *Woodrow Wilson and the American Diplomatic Tradition: The Treaty Fight in Perspective* (1987); August Heckscher, *Woodrow Wilson: A Biography* (1991); and Jan Willem Schulte Nordholt, *Woodrow Wilson: A Life for World Peace* (1991). An obituary is in the *New York Times*, 3 Feb. 1934.

LLOYD E. AMBROSIUS

HITCHCOCK, Henry-Russell (3 June 1903–19 Feb. 1987), architectural historian, was born in Boston, Massachusetts, the son of Henry Russell Hitchcock, a physician, and Alice Davis. Hitchcock added the hyphen to his name at some point before 1929. Raised in Plymouth, Massachusetts, he traced his ancestry back to the Mayflower. He entered Harvard in 1921 and received an A.B. in 1924. The art history program at the Fogg Art Museum at Harvard trained its students to scrutinize art objects; this formalistic approach usually was reserved for painting and sculpture, but Hitchcock applied it to architecture. He was awarded a mas-

ter's degree at Harvard in 1927 and began a doctorate in architectural history of the Romanesque period, but he did not earn a Ph.D.

Like that of most historians, Hitchcock's scholarship developed in an academic atmosphere. He held a number of positions at respected small colleges. From 1929 to 1941 he taught at Wesleyan University, moving to Northampton in 1948 to teach at Smith, where he was the Sophia Smith Professor from 1961 to 1968. He also held temporary visiting professorships at Massachusetts Institute of Technology, Cambridge University, and his alma mater, Harvard. In 1949 he became director of the Smith College Museum of Art, and through extensive contacts in the art world, most dating back to his college days, he was able to purchase high-quality paintings for relatively little money. Some credit goes to Hitchcock for Smith College's excellent teaching museum and highly regarded undergraduate major in art history.

Hitchcock's first article, published when he was twenty-four in the Harvard University magazine *Hound and Horn*, marked his early promotion of avant-garde architecture. Titled "The Decline of Architecture," the article reveals that Hitchcock valued the work of Le Corbusier and Erich Mendelssohn at a time when it was hardly known in the United States. His first substantive study, published when he was twenty-six, was *Modern Architecture: Romanticism and Reintegration*. In it he put forth a novel interpretation of nineteenth-century architecture by suggesting that late nineteenth-century architects were either "New Traditionalists" (Hendrik Berlage and Peter Behrens) or "New Pioneers" (J. J. P. Oud, Le Corbusier, Ludwig Mies van der Rohe, and Walter Gropius), a division indicating that architects from this period were either informed by vernacular traditions or had turned their backs on history altogether. Not surprisingly, it was the New Pioneers who, in Hitchcock's teleology, forged a path toward twentieth-century modernism.

Although he had a successful career as a teacher and scholar with wide-ranging interests, Hitchcock is best known as the historian of modernism. His collaboration with Philip Johnson on Modern Architecture: International Exhibition, held at the Museum of Modern Art in 1932, and the accompanying catalog, *The International Style: Architecture since 1922* (1932), made him the preeminent advocate of modernism in architecture in America. The exhibition and the book presented the previous decade of architecture in Europe, the United States, and Japan as embodying an international movement that had cast aside what the collaborators viewed as the falsehood of much nineteenth-century architecture. The already existing, coherent style of architecture that Johnson and Hitchcock claimed to have recognized was simplified in the catalog's introduction by Alfred H. Barr, Jr., as an emphasis on volume over mass, regularity as opposed to symmetry, dependence on the intrinsic qualities of materials, the use of fine proportions, and a rejection of applied ornament. Hitchcock's identification of an "actual set of monuments" that proved the existence of this International Style was not idle speculation about futuristic projects but advocacy of what he saw as successful, functional architecture. In keeping with his training at Harvard, Hitchcock evaluated and scrutinized discrete objects, in this case buildings, to assess artistic merit.

Although the exhibition introduced contemporary architecture to a wide audience, especially in the United States, and although the term "International Style" gained immediate acceptance, and even though it is still possible to identify buildings as "International Style" by distinctive formal qualities, the catalog met with harsh criticism. One of the most valid objections was that the book lacked social commentary; its formalist approach neglected to include a description of the political context of much modern architecture, especially the socialist housing projects of the 1920s. Furthermore, Hitchcock did not recognize regional influences on architects, and he chose photographs that stressed similarities between the buildings rather than differences. Nonetheless, by the age of twenty-nine, Hitchcock had completed two major works, one in architectural history and the second in contemporary criticism.

In 1936 another aspect of Hitchcock's career came to fruition, that of partisan Americanist. Hitchcock's New England heritage predisposed him to admire things American at a time when many art historians valued European art and architecture. An exhibition, again at the Museum of Modern Art, on the architect Henry Hobson Richardson commended this American's architecture for its simple massing and honest, rugged use of materials. The significance of the exhibition catalog, *The Architecture of H. H. Richardson and His Times* (1936), lies not so much in Richardson's times as in the times that followed: Richardson was made the grandfather of modern American architecture, the precursor of Louis Sullivan and, more importantly, Frank Lloyd Wright.

Wright scholars owe a special debt to Hitchcock, whose *In the Nature of Materials* (1942), a monograph published in connection with another exhibition at the Museum of Modern Art, was the first major work on the architect. In the Pelican edition, *Architecture: Nineteenth and Twentieth Centuries* (1958), Hitchcock praises Wright's Falling Water (the Kaufmann house, 1936–1937) in his typical prose, laden with concise visual detail and artistic judgment:

The completely unified living space is closed in by stone walls on the inner or dining side. It also extends out over the waterfall; the all-glass walls on that side, with their thin metal mullions, hardly seem to separate the interior space at all from that of the open terraces outside. . . . Never before had Wright exploited the structural possibilities of concrete so boldly. (P. 445)

Summarizing Wright's influence up to 1937, Hitchcock compared the American architect's career to the sweep of art history, declaring that his early work had a "serenity of . . . expression, a classic if hardly a Classical quality," while his middle period showed a "Ba-

roque exuberance in the proliferation of the ornament," but that Wright finally came into his own at Falling Water, where "his Romantic or anti-Classical tendencies—call them what you will—reached an intensity of purely architectonic expression comparable to the musical intensity of the late quartets of Beethoven that Wright so much admired" (pp. 445–46). The book not only lent authority to Wright's architecture, it quickly became a standard art historical text, thus extending Wright's importance to a broad audience.

As a true connoisseur, Hitchcock never wrote about buildings he had not seen, and as a leading critic of modernism he was personally acquainted with Wright, Le Corbusier, J. J. P. Oud, and other architects. His modernist bent cast a shadow on the study of all earlier architecture. For example, his belief that the structure of a building should be honestly expressed led him to admire the Crystal Palace, the technologically advanced ferrovitreous structure that housed the 1851 Great Exhibition in London (now demolished), more than other Victorian buildings. However, his dedication to the study of nineteenth-century architecture (see *Early Victorian Architecture in Britain* [1954] and the first half of *Architecture: Nineteenth and Twentieth Centuries*) allowed later scholars to seriously engage the subject, and his tenure as president of the Victorian Society in the United States (1969–1974) demonstrates that he was not an orthodox modernist. Some other major works, indicating the breadth of his interests, are *Rhode Island Architecture* (1939), *Latin American Architecture since 1945* (1955), and *Rococo Architecture in Southern Germany* (1968).

In his later years Hitchcock continued to travel, examining both well-known and noncanonical buildings. He served as president of the Society of Architectural Historians from 1952 to 1954. He received an award of merit from the American Institute of Architects in 1978, a similar award from the Council of Learned Societies, and the Benjamin Franklin Award of the Royal Society of Arts (London). His last book was *German Renaissance Architecture*, published in 1981. He ended his career with a professorship at the Institute of Fine Arts at New York University; he was ill with cancer for many years, and his lover, Robert Schmitt, cared for him until his death in New York City. At the time of Hitchcock's death, Philip Johnson called him the "leader of us all. He set a new standard of architectural scholarship and accuracy of judgment." He was memorialized in obituaries by nearly every prominent architectural historian, all of whom appreciated his perfectly trained eye and passion for architecture.

• The Papers of Henry-Russell Hitchcock are held by the Archives of American Art, Washington, D.C.; not all of them are open to the public. The most thorough accounts of his career can be found in Helen Searing, "Henry-Russell Hitchcock: The Architectural Historian as Critic and Connoisseur," in *The Architectural Historian in America*, ed. Elizabeth Blair MacDougall (vol. 35 of Studies in the History of Art, 1990), and Reyner Banham, "Actual Monuments," *Art in America*, Oct. 1988, pp. 172–76, 213, 215. On the International Style exhibition and book, see Terence Riley, *The International Style: Exhibition 15 and the Museum of Modern Art* (1992). Obituaries include Helen Searing, *Progressive Architecture*, Apr. 1987, pp. 27, 31; William Jordy, *New Criterion* 5 (Apr. 1987): 81; Andrea Oppenheimer Dean, *Architecture*, Apr. 1987, p. 28; Brendan Gill, *Architectural Digest*, July 1990, pp. 33, 36; John Summerson, *Architectural Review*, May 1987, p. 5; and the *New York Times*, 20 Feb. 1987.

CARLA YANNI

HITCHCOCK, Lambert (28 May 1795–3 Apr. 1852), chair and cabinet manufacturer, was born in Cheshire, Connecticut, the son of John Lee Hitchcock, a veteran of the American Revolution, and Eunice Hudson. Although his master is not known, Hitchcock is thought to have been apprenticed in the furniture trade in Cheshire. By 1814 he had begun work as a journeyman in the shop of Silas E. Cheney of Litchfield, Connecticut, where he would remain for four years (minus an unsuccessful semester of study at the Episcopal Academy of Connecticut in Cheshire).

In 1818 Hitchcock went to Barkhamsted (later Hitchcocks-ville, and then Riverton in 1865), Connecticut, at the fork of the Farmington and Still rivers in the northwestern part of the state, to take up chairmaking. Taking advantage of an abundant supply of local timber and an operating sawmill, and perhaps driven by the Yankee propensity for technological innovation and entrepreneurship, he embarked on a career in the chairmaking business. He is generally credited with being among the first to apply mass-production concepts to furniture making.

Hitchcock began his operation by making component chair parts for export to markets in Charleston, South Carolina, and other areas of the South and Midwest, but within a few years he was making and selling completed chairs, decorated with stenciling, striping, and banding, and employing a workforce of more than one hundred people. The business prospered for a few years, producing cabinet wares as well as chairs, but Hitchcock was forced into bankruptcy in 1829, the first in a series of reversals that would characterize his business. A group of trustees took over operation of the firm, but by 27 November 1832 Hitchcock had regained control of the company "on his own account and responsibility" and continued "to manufacture chairs . . . made after the latest fashions, and finished in the best manner" (*Hartford Courant*) in partnership with Arba Alford. Hitchcock's recurrent business problems were largely due to a shortage of labor in an isolated part of the state, poor roads to Hartford and elsewhere, and difficulties with cash flow. These problems, however, did not deter Hitchcock from opening a retail store in Hartford and continuing to pursue his goals.

The firm of Hitchcock, Alford, and Company remained in business until 1841, when Hitchcock opened another chairmaking company, the Hitchcocks-ville Company, in partnership with Alford and Josiah Sage of Massachusetts. The partnership dissolved in 1843. Beginning in 1844 Hitchcock ran his own furniture-making factory in Unionville, Connecticut, which did not prosper and which went out of business after his death. Hitchcock died in Unionville of "brain fever" (probably cerebrospinal meningitis). His estate totaled $12,420.54, but his debts came to $13,758.02.

Hitchcock had married Eunice Alford in 1830; they had no children. After her death in 1835, he married Mary Ann Preston of Cazenovia, New York, in August 1836; they had four children. He was a member of the local Whig party and served as a member of the state legislature for three terms in 1834, 1840, and 1841.

Although Hitchcock produced a variety of chairs and other objects, the typical Hitchcock chair followed a standard formula. It had a one-piece crest rail in a rolled-top, crown-topped, bolster-topped, or pillow-topped form. A horizontal crosspiece in the center of the back was decorated with a cornucopia, eagle, or so-called turtle- or button-back shape. The chairs have a rectangular seat with a rolled front edge. The rear stiles are continuations of the back legs, while the front legs and stretchers were turned in a variety of fashions and decorated with striping and banding on their fronts. Their final embellishment was grain-painted decoration in various colors or bronze-powdered stenciled ornaments, primarily fruits and flowers. Hitchcock used local native woods such as birch and maple for his frames, and the seats were of rush, cane, or plank. The rear seat rails were often, but not always, inscribed "L. Hitchcock. Hitchcocks-ville. Conn. Warranted.," or a variation reflecting his current partners, including "Hitchcock. Alford. & Co Hitchcocks-ville. Conn. Warranted."

The inventory of Hitchcock's factory in Unionville, taken after his death, provides a significant look at his late work (repr. in Kenney, pp. 317–30). His stock included supplies of cherry, whitewood (probably yellow poplar), white pine, maple, chestnut, black walnut, and mahogany veneer, along with glues, varnish, paint, and other finishing materials. An extensive array of tools and machinery, including circular saws, a dovetailing machine, a "squaring up mortising machine with cutters and Mandrels," a double tenoning machine, and a table butt machine (a device with planing cutters on the face of a disk, used for rounding and smoothing the ends of small pieces) indicate Hitchcock's use of the latest woodworking technology. As also befits a nineteenth-century manufacturer, he had a variety of goods on hand, both finished and in parts, including many forms in addition to chairs, such as bureaus, bureau washstands, tables, French bedsteads, boxes, looking glasses, and shaving boxes. The chairs on hand included plain wood chairs, banister wood chairs, chamber chairs, best birch chairs, plain cane chairs, round post cottage chairs, table chairs, children's chairs, officer chairs, flag chairs, round foot rockers, sewing chairs, cane rockers, and other types (as revealed in excerpts from an account book of 1851–1853, repr. in Kenney, pp. 331–32).

After Hitchcock's death, his fame and reputation passed from the public eye. Hitchcock's habit of stenciling his name on his chairs attracted the attention of twentieth-century collectors and scholars, who resurrected Hitchcock and eventually made his name virtually synonymous with factory-made painted seating furniture and "Hitchcock chair" a generic collector's term that has been misapplied to the products of many factories. They praised the beauty, natural materials, and "honest" craftsmanship of Hitchcock chairs and regarded Hitchcock as the prototypical small entrepreneur in the Golden Age prior to total industrialization. John Tarrant Kenney, author of a rambling, filiopietistic biography of Hitchcock, revived the Hitchcock Chair Company in 1946, and the mass production of reproduction Hitchcock chairs has cemented their reputation in the public's mind as *the* form of early American seating. But despite his admirable personal characteristics and the undoubted qualities of his chairs, Hitchcock was but one of thousands of chairmakers in nineteenth-century America who produced similar designs and forms.

• John Tarrant Kenney, *The Hitchcock Chair: The Story of a Connecticut Yankee—L. Hitchcock of Hitchcocks-ville—and an Account of the Restoration of His 19th-Century Manufactory* (1971), which mythologizes its subject, nevertheless contains a good deal of useful information, including a summary of Hitchcock's career and transcriptions of his estate papers and inventory. Kenney relies heavily on Mrs. Edward Hitchcock, Sr., *Genealogy of the Hitchcock Family* (1894). Also useful are Mabel Roberts Moore, *Hitchcock Chairs* (1933), a small booklet (no. 15) issued by the Tercentenary Commission of Connecticut and published by Yale University Press, and the entry in Ethel Hall Bjerkoe, *The Cabinetmakers of America* (1957). Some pioneering articles are Mrs. Guion Thompson, "Hitchcock of Hitchcocks-ville," *Antiques* 4, no. 2 (Aug. 1923): 74–77, and Esther Stevens Fraser, "Random Notes on Hitchcock and His Competitors," *Antiques* 30, no. 2 (Aug. 1936): 63–67, which addresses the inflation of Hitchcock's reputation. The connoisseurship of Hitchcock chairs is addressed in Ruth Berenson, "Hitchcock Furniture," in her *Nineteenth Century Furniture: Innovation, Revival, and Reform* (1982), pp. 18–25, and they are placed in context in Robert Bishop, *Centuries and Styles of the American Chair, 1640–1970* (1972), and Dean A. Fales, Jr., *American Painted Furniture, 1660–1880* (1972, repr. 1979). Hitchcock's stenciling is also discussed in Janet Waring, *Early American Stencils on Walls and Furniture* (1968).

The Hitchcock Museum in Riverton, Conn., founded in 1972, is governed by the Hitchcock Chair Company and maintains a collection of painted and decorated furniture from the early and mid-nineteenth century. Hitchcock chairs are in many museums, historic houses, and private collections. Beginning in 1946 the modern Hitchcock Chair Company started to produce replicas of the original Hitchcock chairs.

GERALD W. R. WARD

HITCHCOCK, Raymond (22 Oct. 1865–25 Nov. 1929), actor, was born in Auburn, New York, the son of Charles Hitchcock and Celestia Burroughs. Educated locally, Hitchcock left his job as a Philadelphia shoe clerk in 1887 to join a local troupe specializing in Gilbert and Sullivan. By 1890 he had made his New York debut in the chorus of Henry W. Savage's shows.

After supporting roles in such comedies as *The Brigand* (1891), *The Golden Wedding* (1893), *Charley's Aunt* (1894), *A Dangerous Maid* (1899), *The Belle of Bridgeport* (1900), and *Wiener Blut* (1901), the straw-blond Hitchcock, a studiously nonchalant performer, became a star in *King Dodo* (1901), which ran for two years on Broadway. In the same year he married Izabelle Mangasarian (who went by the stage name Flora Zabelle), an actress with whom he subsequently co-starred in several plays, including the musical *The Yankee Consul* (1904). They had no children.

Hitchcock's subsequent comic portrayals were cut from much the same pattern as his *Yankee Consul* role as Abijah Booze, the straight-faced and dense American posted to "Puerto Plata." Wearing chalk-white makeup, hair askew, Hitchcock regularly engaged in raspy asides to the audience that regularly knew more about what was going on than he did. He sang the hit song "Ain't It Funny What a Difference Just a Few Hours Can Make."

After *Easy Dawson* (1905) and *The Student King* (1906), Hitchcock again took up his *Consul* character in *The Galloper* (1906) and its musical version *The Yankee Tourist* (1907), coping ineffectually with blackmailers and corrupt policemen. Starring roles in *The Merry Go Round* (1908), *The Man Who Owns Broadway* (1909), and *The Red Widow* (1910) preceded *The Beauty Shop*, which toured during 1913, played Broadway in 1914, was produced in London in 1916, and eventually became a silent film in 1922. In *The Beauty Shop* Hitchcock played Dr. Arbatus Budd, a beauty doctor dogged by creditors who runs away to "Bolognia," where he is fêted as the land's lost baron. The happy ending occurs when a smitten, ugly Bolognian lass named Cremo Panatella is made gorgeous by Budd's beauty paste.

In 1915 Hitchcock starred in two forty-minute film comedies, *My Valet*, alongside Mack Sennett and Mabel Normand, and *The Ringtailed Rhinoceros*, a drunk's dream. A 1916 London musical comedy built around him, *Mr. Manhattan*, proved a personal triumph. As a rich American bachelor in London and France, Hitchcock was called by the *Times* (London) critic "so quaint, so winning, so confidential, so endearingly comic." *The Stage* called him "curiously angular" and explained his particular charm as "consistent imperturbability."

At the top of his fame, a member of all the theatrical clubs, in 1916 Hitchcock was credited with selling $152,800 in Liberty Bonds in twelve minutes. He starred in the New York version of the London musical comedy *Betty* (1916) and in 1917 launched a producing career, teaming with E. Ray Goetz in the first of the frothy *Hitchy-Koo* revues as well as *Words and Music*.

By 1918, when he returned to London to appear in the second version of the revue *Hullo, America!*, Hitchcock was the sole producer of the American

Hitchy-Koo series. *Hitchy-Koo of 1919* included several songs by the youthful Cole Porter, including his first "standard," "An Old-Fashioned Garden." The 1920 version included a score by Jerome Kern and Anne Caldwell, a reigning Broadway musical star in Julia Sanderson, and the light-footed dancing Mosconi Brothers. Theater critic Alexander Woollcott praised its check-suited producer-star as "old reliable Raymond Hitchcock."

It was the last *Hitchy-Koo*; Hitchcock declared bankruptcy in 1921 and returned to performing, first in the Ziegfeld *Follies* of 1921, one of that series' most acclaimed. Outshone by Fanny Brice and W. C. Fields, Hitchcock had "moments of hilarity," but here it was first noted that he was really no better than his material, which was somewhat outdated.

By 1922 Hitchcock, an accomplished after-dinner speaker, was appearing in benefits for such professional organizations as Equity and the Friars. He produced *Raymond Hitchcock's Pinwheel Revue* (1922), a failed assortment of international dances punctuated by comic turns. In 1923 he toured in the nonmusical *The Old Soak*, remaining in San Francisco in 1924 in *The Caliph*. Hitchcock returned to film in the background of *Broadway After Dark* (1923), as a member of real-life New York showbiz royalty.

A Broadway comeback in *Hassard Short's Ritz Revue* (1924) was overshadowed by Short's gorgeous staging. Hitchcock's personality, "unctuous and persuasive," was again his main asset. The show was also unfavorably compared with its contemporary rival, the stylish *Charlot's London Revue*. Hitchcock returned to straight comedy, playing an "ingratiatingly amusing" village good-for-nothing in *The Sap* (1925). In a club production, the *Lambs Gambol*, he spoofed Gilbert and Sullivan's *Trial by Jury*.

Hitchcock next appeared in a series of one-hour films: *Everybody's Acting* (1926), as one of five "fathers" of an orphaned daughter of traveling actors; *Redheads Preferred* (1926), a typical farce; *The Monkey Talks* (1927), as a circus performer; *The Tired Business Man* (1927), as an alderman; and *Upstream* (1927), as the star boarder in a theatrical boardinghouse.

In New York once more, Hitchcock developed a nightclub act and served as master of ceremonies in a 1927 Palace bill. Appearing in the musical comedy *Just Fancy!* (1927), he gave a "stump speech" between acts rallying support for its embattled producer. Hitchcock's last New York appearance came in the Players' club version of Farquar's *The Beaux' Stratagem* (1928). Clad in his taproom apron, the sidelong-faced Hitchcock won praise from critic Brooks Atkinson for his "gambolling humor," which went "beyond the text" in a production that celebrated the original's "volatile spirit in bubbling merriment."

On his way West once more, Hitchcock played Dudley Dixon in a Chicago production of the comedy *Your Uncle Dudley* (1928). A member of an earlier era's theatrical establishment, Hitchcock died of a heart attack in an automobile in Beverly Hills, California.

• Information regarding Hitchcock's career may be gleaned from playbills and reviews of his performances found in the Theatre Museum, London, and the Billy Rose Theatre Collection at the New York Public Library for the Performing Arts, Lincoln Center. An obituary is in the *New York Times*, 26 Nov. 1929.

JAMES ROSS MOORE

HITCHCOCK, Roswell Dwight (15 Aug. 1817–16 June 1887), church historian and seminary president, was born at East Machias, Maine, the son of Roswell Hitchcock and Betsey Longfellow. He prepared for college there at Washington Academy and entered Amherst as a sophomore in 1833, graduating three years later. After two years as the principal of an academy, he attended Andover Theological Seminary but after a year was called back to Amherst as a tutor and only in 1842 returned to seminary, graduating in two years. In 1845 he married Elizabeth Anthony Brayton (three children were born of the union) and was ordained as pastor of the First Congregational Church of Exeter, New Hampshire. After a leave of absence to study at Halle and Berlin (1847–1848), he returned to his parish but was appointed professor of religion at Bowdoin College in 1852. Three years later he was elected to the newly endowed Washburn Chair of Church History at Union Theological Seminary in New York City, a post he held for the rest of his life. Once at Union he transferred his ministerial credentials to the New School Presbyterian church and showed loyal devotion to the Westminster Confession, interpreting it in the light of the demanding intellectual trends of his times.

Hitchcock devoted his major energies to teaching and preaching. Those who heard him speak often mentioned the clarity and brilliance of his addresses, his effective delivery and personal magnetism. Through his classroom lectures he interpreted ecclesiastical developments against the background of general history in a broad fashion, yet with careful attention to authoritative detail. Eminently suited for such special occasions as ordinations, anniversaries, dedications, and memorials, he was much in demand as a preacher and speaker. Many of his sermons and addresses were published in periodicals, collections, or pamphlets; some of his favorites filled his posthumously published *Eternal Atonement* (1888), which displayed his basically orthodox theology in progressive terms. His concern for the pressing problems of the day was displayed in a small volume, *Socialism* (1879), which was highly critical of radical socialism but argued for increased wages for working people.

Hitchcock accepted heavy editorial responsibilities throughout his career. During the years when he edited the *American Theological Review* (1863–1870), he also prepared *Hitchcock's New and Complete Analysis of the Holy Bible* (1870 and later editions), a thorough recasting of previous works by Matt Talbot and Nathaniel West. In collaboration with others he edited *Hymns and Songs of Praise* (1874); it too was published in later editions, notably as *Carmina Sanctorum* (1885). He and his colleague Francis Brown edited the then recently discovered manuscript of *The Teaching of the Twelve Apostles* (1884).

In 1880 Hitchcock was elected president of Union and served with competence. Proving to be an effective fundraiser, he played a key role in enabling the seminary to move in 1884 from 9 University Place (just north and east of what is now Washington Square Park) to a new set of buildings at 700 Park Avenue. Through his will he endowed the Hitchcock Prize in Church History, to be awarded annually. He died suddenly while at his summer home in Somerset, Massachusetts.

• Most of Hitchcock's published writings are in the Union Theological Seminary library; in its archives are four boxes of miscellaneous manuscript materials, including three sets of notes of his classroom lectures taken by students. For brief treatments of his life with an emphasis on his Union career, see William G. T. Shedd et al., *Addresses in Memory of Roswell Dwight Hitchcock, D.D., LL.D.* (1887); George L. Prentiss, *The Union Theological Seminary in the City of New York: Historical and Biographical Sketches of Its First Fifty Years* (1889); and Robert T. Handy, *A History of Union Theological Seminary in New York* (1987).

ROBERT T. HANDY

HITCHCOCK, Thomas, Jr. (11 Feb. 1900–19 Apr. 1944), sportsman, was born in Aiken, South Carolina, the son of Thomas Hitchcock, a horse trainer and sportsman, and Louise Mary Eustis, a horsewoman. He was fortunate to have well-to-do parents who were very involved in the game of polo. His grandfather was a financial writer and part-owner of the *New York Sun*. His father bred horses, founded a golf club, trained hunting dogs, and became an ardent huntsman. Hitchcock's mother was the granddaughter of William W. Corcoran, who founded the Corcoran Art Gallery.

Nicknamed "Tommy," Hitchcock grew up at "Mon Repos," his parents' winter home in Aiken, and "Broad Hollow," his parents' estate in Old Westbury, New York. He learned to ride horses at age three and began swinging a polo mallet from the back of a pony at age five or six. Hitchcock started playing polo by 1913 and belonged to both the junior and senior foursomes (four members of a polo team who compete against four other players) in 1916.

Hitchcock continued a family tradition of involvement with polo. His father was a top rated player until 1920 and then continued to contribute to American polo by training all of his son's polo ponies. His mother also influenced Hitchcock's early training. She founded and operated Meadow Larks, a training ground for young people interested in polo, and she is credited with having helped to train the polo team captained by her son for many years. Tommy played in his first tournament at age thirteen at Narragansett Pier, New York.

Upon American entry into World War I, Hitchcock volunteered for military service. The military rejected him because of his age, although the seventeen-year old student at St. Paul's school in Concord, New Hampshire, had passed the 100 hours' endurance test. He then received training and an assignment to the Lafayette Escadrille in the French aviation service, which consisted of American volunteers. In 1918, while flying an aerial combat mission, he was wounded in the thigh and was forced to land behind enemy lines. The Germans imprisoned him at Lecheld, but he escaped five months later by jumping from the train as he was being transferred to another prison. Eventually, he walked eighty miles to the Swiss border and then to France, where he transferred to the American Air Service. He left the military later in 1918 as a second lieutenant and returned home as a holder of the Croix de Guerre with two palms for valor for downing three German planes.

Upon returning to the United States after the war, Hitchcock enrolled at Harvard University and resumed his polo playing. He played on the U.S. Polo Association's teams that won championships in 1919, 1920, and 1921, and he led the U.S. foursome in 1921 to a victory over the British. In 1921 he was elected a member of the "Big Four" (the U.S. polo team selected for international competition) while studying at Oxford. He received an A.B. from Harvard in 1922.

Hitchcock's entry into polo on the international scene helped interest the American public in the game. Crowds as large as 40,000 watched international matches, which were publicized in journals such as *Vanity Fair* and the *New Yorker*. Large crowds witnessed the international championship matches with Great Britain and Argentina held at Meadow Brook Club in Jericho, New York. His involvement changed American polo, both in public interest and in those participating in the sport. The Meadow Brook polo set always had provided the main crops of the international four, but Hitchcock believed that polo should be open to all riders and players. To this end, in 1927 he captained American polo and opened it to any players, not just those from his inner Meadow Brook polo set. He insisted that the development of players for international competition include individuals from other parts of the country. As a result, by 1930 two cow punchers from the Texas Panhandle had become eligible to play against Great Britain. That year Hitchcock chaired the defense committee and captained the U.S. squad.

Hitchcock was raised to ten-goal status (the highest ranking available for a polo player) in the American handicap list of polo in 1922, and he kept that top ranking for thirteen years. In 1935 he was dropped to a nine goal but remained the nation's top player. His ten-goal ranking was restored in 1936, and he retained it until he retired from active competition in 1940. Many considered Hitchcock the greatest No. 2 position player in the game that the United States had ever fielded.

Owing in part to Hitchcock's superb play, the United States successfully defended the Challenge Cup against British teams in 1924, 1927, 1930, and 1939. In fact, he never lost to the British in international competition during his career. The 1941 yearbook of the U.S. Polo Association referred to Hitchcock's retirement in a summary of the 1940 season, stating that "this year's annual carries his name on the inactive list at the ten-goal rating he has so well deserved most of the time since his first international appearance on the team of 1921."

In 1928 Hitchcock married Margaret Mellon Laughlin; they had four children. In 1932 he became associated with Lehman Brothers Bankers and became a partner in 1937. Until that time he was also with Bankers Company and in business for himself. He was also director of the Electric Shovel Coal Corporation.

During World War II, Hitchcock was commissioned shortly after the Japanese attacked Pearl Harbor, and he began serving as assistant military attaché of the U.S. embassy in Great Britain in 1942. He headed the tactical research section in the Ninth Air Force Fighter Command, and in 1944 he was approved for combat flying even though he was forty-four years old. He was killed in a plane crash at Salisbury, England, on a routine flight, having served his country in two world wars.

Hitchcock was a brilliant polo player and one of the few ten-goal men recognized by the U.S. Polo Association, a ranking he held for a total of eighteen years. The American polo successes during Hitchcock's playing days helped raise interest to the American public.

• For information on Hitchcock, see John Durant, "Four Tough Gentlemen," *Collier's*, 10 June 1939, pp. 11ff; and Robert Harron, "Ten-Goal; Tommy," *Collier's*, 11 Aug. 1938, pp. 16ff. An obituary is in the *New York Times*, 20 Apr. 1944.

MIRIAM F. SHELDEN

HITE, Les (13 Feb. 1903–6 Feb. 1962), jazz alto saxophonist and bandleader, was born in DuQuoin, Illinois. His parents' names are unknown. While attending school in Urbana, he played alongside his parents and siblings in a family band. He studied at the University of Illinois, Urbana; details of his education are unknown.

After local work with the obscure Detroit Shannon band, he toured with a little-known singer named Helen Dewey in a revue that failed in Los Angeles late in 1924. Hite, trumpeter George Orendorff, and saxophonist Jimmy Strong decided to stay there. Hite worked with the bands of Reb Spikes, Mutt Carey, Paul Howard, Curtis Mosby, and Sonny Clay, these last two concurrently in 1928. By early 1929 he was working with Henry "Tin Can" Allen, and when he died Hite took his place as bandleader.

The pool of excellent big-band musicians in the Los Angeles area at this time was not large, and one would expect much interchange among them. By one account the band that Hite was hired to form at the Cotton Club late in 1929 was a continuation of Paul Howard's Quality Serenaders. It may be the case, however, that the band that Hite brought into a second Cotton Club the following year was Howard's old band. Some sources say Howard played in 1930 at this new location with Orendorff and drummer (and soon to be vibraphonist) Lionel Hampton, both of whom then joined Hite.

Hite's California Syncopators began their stand at the new Cotton Club in an auspicious way by accompanying Louis Armstrong, with whom they also made recordings, including "Body and Soul," "Shine," and "Sweethearts on Parade." New bandsmen in 1931 included trombonist Lawrence Brown, who also had worked with Howard, and alto saxophonist Marshall Royal, who took over leadership of the saxophone section. Probably by this point Hite had suffered the auto accident in which he severely injured his lower lip. He rarely played thereafter.

In a profession in which changes in personnel are commonplace, Hite's was one of the most stable big bands of the 1930s. Trumpeter Dizzy Gillespie explained that Hite had a sponsor, an affluent white woman who kept the band on a modest salary even when there was no work. Through the decade Hite held residencies at Los Angeles's Cotton Club, including a show with Fats Waller in the summer of 1935. The band also contributed to sixty-five films while in Hollywood, although not one of the films in which they appear is a classic; these include *Taxi* (1932), *Sing, Sinner, Sing* (1933), *The Music Goes Round* (1936), *Gangsters on the Loose (Bargain with Bullets)* (1937), *Fools for Scandal* (1938), and three soundies (for video juke boxes of the 1940s).

In September 1939 Hite disbanded in order to take over alto saxophonist Floyd Turnham's band, with Turnham remaining as Hite's sideman. At the band's first engagement, in Dallas late that month, Hite hired T-Bone Walker, whose singing was admired during performances at New York's Golden Gate Ballroom and Apollo Theater in January 1940. Recordings in New York around June 1940 and in March 1941 included versions of "That's the Lick" and "T-Bone Blues," which are pioneering discs in the contribution of Los Angeles–based musicians to the development of rhythm and blues. Despite Walker's forthcoming role as one of the most important early electric blues guitarists, he is strictly the singer on "T-Bone Blues"; the guitarist is Frank Pasley.

Hite reorganized his band in New York City in March 1942, when Gillespie and pianist Gerald Wiggins joined, and again in July of that year, now with trumpeter Gerald Wilson, saxophonist Buddy Collette, trombonist John Ewing, and Wiggins as the notable sidemen. Trumpeter Snooky Young joined in October, remaining into 1943. In 1945 Hite left music, and from 1957 he was a partner in a booking agency. He died in Santa Monica, California.

• The principal survey of Hite's musical career is Albert McCarthy, *Big Band Jazz* (1974). See also Tony Burke and Dave Penny, "Les Hite's Orchestra 'T. Bone Blues,' 1935–42," *Blues and Rhythm: The Gospel Truth* no. 9 (May 1985): 8–11; Dizzy Gillespie and Al Fraser, *To Be, or Not . . . to Bop: Memoirs* (1979; repr. 1985); James Lincoln Collier, *Lou-*

is *Armstrong: An American Genius* (1983); Frank Driggs and Harris Lewine, *Black Beauty, White Heat: A Pictorial History of Classic Jazz, 1920–1950* (1982); Klaus Stratemann, *Negro Bands on Film*, vol. 1, *Big Bands, 1928–50: An Exploratory Filmo-Discography* (1981); and David Meeker, *Jazz in the Movies*, 2d ed. (1981).

BARRY KERNFELD

HITT, Robert Roberts (16 Jan. 1834–20 Sept. 1906), journalist, congressman, and diplomat, was born in Urbana, Ohio, the son of Thomas Smith Hitt, a Methodist minister, and Emily John. The family moved to Mount Morris, Illinois, in 1837. Hitt studied at the Methodist Rock River Seminary, which his father helped to establish. In 1855 Hitt graduated from Indiana Asbury University (now DePauw University) and two years later began working as a shorthand reporter in the Chicago court system and for area newspapers. In 1874 he married Sallie Reynolds; they had two sons.

Because of Hitt's shorthand skills, Abraham Lincoln selected him to record the famous Lincoln-Douglas debates in 1858. Hitt favored Lincoln's position against federal interference with slavery in the southern states and against slavery's extension westward. From 1857 until 1860 Hitt worked as the official stenographer of the Illinois state legislature. During the U.S. Civil War, Hitt was a reporter on several Federal government investigatory commissions. The most notable was the inquiry into General John C. Frémont's military activities in Missouri in the first year of the war, when the general was at odds with Washington over the need for supplies and men and the objectives of his command, particularly with regard to emancipation policy. In 1872 Hitt served as a reporter for congressional committees looking into the activities of the Ku Klux Klan against the civil rights of freed blacks.

Hitt played a brief but unimportant role in international affairs after the Civil War. He went to the Dominican Republic in 1871 with a commission to investigate that nation's resources in anticipation of its annexation. U.S. naval officials had long been interested in Samaná Bay on the northeast coast with its command of the Mona Passage into the Caribbean Sea, but in the late 1860s Congress was not in an expansionist mood. In 1874 Hitt was appointed secretary to the U.S. legation in Paris, where he remained for seven years and served as chargé d'affaires on several occasions. However, during this time the United States had little interest in the affairs of Europe. Upon his return to the United States, Hitt served as assistant secretary of state for the ten months of James G. Blaine's first secretaryship in 1881 and supported Blaine's call for Pan-Americanism.

Hitt began his congressional career in 1882, when he was elected to fill the vacancy created by the death of Robert M. A. Hawk. He was reelected for twelve consecutive terms, serving until his death and earning a reputation as an able debater. He chaired the House Committee on Foreign Affairs during those terms that the GOP gained control of the House, the Fifty-first, Fifty-fourth, and Fifty-eighth Congresses. Despite his position, Hitt did not become a prominent policy maker in international affairs, but he was a spokesman for the growing U.S. influence in the world. In the minority report on the anti-Chinese immigration policy, 3 May 1884, he charged that a bill to impose a ten-year ban on Chinese immigration violated the 1880 Angell Treaty.

Always interested in Latin American affairs, Hitt introduced a bill in 1895 to pay the expenses of the U.S. commission that proposed a settlement of the Orinoco River valley dispute between Venezuela and Great Britain. In 1896, responding to Spain's brutal efforts to suppress the Cuban independence movement, Hitt reported the resolution Congress approved recognizing Cuba's belligerent status. He defended U.S. recognition of the newly independent Panama in 1903, and he encouraged reciprocity with the Latin American republics, recommending improved consular and diplomatic service. Elsewhere in the hemisphere, Hitt advocated a commercial union with Canada largely because of the loss of tariffs on goods brought into the United States via railroads. In 1889 he gained House approval for the commercial union, but nothing materialized.

Hitt was an ardent supporter of U.S. annexation of Hawaii. In 1894 he introduced a resolution on the House floor that supported U.S. expansion in Hawaii and criticized President Grover Cleveland's restoration of the island's monarchy. Hitt supported U.S. annexation of the islands in 1898, and for his efforts, President William McKinley appointed him to the commission that established a government in the Hawaiian Islands.

At home Hitt favored reform of the civil service system, which was bloated with incompetent political appointees. From 1893 until his death he served as a regent of the Smithsonian Institution, and he was a meaningful contributor on the committee that secured the 1898 Chicago World's Fair. He died at his summer home in Newport, Rhode Island.

• A collection of Hitt's speeches and resolutions is in F. L. Davis, ed., *Legislative History of Robert R. Hitt* (1907). A comprehensive survey of U.S. policy in the Caribbean during Hitt's congressional career is David A. Healy, *Drive to Hegemony: The United States in the Caribbean, 1898–1917* (1988). A readable account of the annexation of Hawaii is Julius W. Pratt, *Expansionists of 1898: The Acquisition of Hawaii and the Spanish Islands* (1936). An obituary is in the *Chicago Tribune*, 21 Sept. 1906.

THOMAS M. LEONARD

HO, Chinn (26 Feb. 1904–12 May 1987), financier, developer, and newspaper owner, was born in Honolulu, Hawaii, the son of Ho Ti Yuen, a clerk at the segregated British Pacific Club, and Kam Lan. In the "Chinn Ho Oral History Project" Ho said a sickly childhood delayed his elementary schooling and made him a "runt" who was "pushed around" when he did begin regular classes. In the meantime, having become an avid reader of the Pacific Club's discarded business periodicals brought home by his father, Ho realized that he had to extend his boundaries and perform better than expected to gain recognition. Through sports he improved physically. He sold soft drinks, newspapers, school supplies, and advertising gimmicks. He was a 20-year-old senior at McKinley High School (class of 1924) when he motivated a small group of classmates to stage school events, including a carnival that paid off the $38 class debt for breaking windows. After graduating, they organized a social and business *hui* (limited partnership) known as the Commercial Associates to pool their savings and invest in stocks and real estate under Ho's sole management.

Unable to afford college, Ho joined Bishop Bank in 1924 as ledger boy for $75 a month. Trading profitably in penny stocks at Duisenberg, Wichman & Co. (later Dean, Witter in Hawaii), the firm hired him as a broker at $110 a month in 1924. From 1925 to 1926 Ho took University of Hawaii extension courses. In 1934 he married Betty Nyuk Moy Ching, a secretary; the couple raised six children. Except for 1935 spent in the Philippines with Swan, Culbertson & Fitz brokerage, Ho was with Dean, Witter until 1943. Starting work at 4:30 A.M., he beat the competition by making same-day trades in New York despite the time difference with Honolulu.

World War II brought profound changes to Hawaii. Property owners fearing Japanese invasion sold at depressed prices that Ho could afford. He liquidated Commercial Associates in 1943 to form his own *hui*, Capital Investment Company (CIC), in 1944 with $150,00 in stock and three employees. He developed and financed new projects separately, but always under the parent CIC, and always under his control. Foreseeing tourism as central to Hawaii's economy, Ho in 1946 became the first Chinese-American director of the Hawaii Visitors Bureau. It was the beginning of his many "firsts" in surmounting some of the historic barriers erected by the Caucasian, land-based oligarchy that controlled enterprise, labor, and politics as well as social and cultural life and prevented ethnic minorities from achieving their potential.

When Ho bought 9,150 acres of Waianae Sugar Co. for $1.25 million in 1947, he became the first Chinese American to own so much fee-simple acreage. That he took only one weekend to research, finance, and complete the transaction so impressed the community that investors large and small quickly joined CIC. Selling off some portions, he earned millions of dollars while reserving the Makaha Valley for residential and resort development. Native Hawaiians among others appreciated his restoration of a *heiau* (ancient Hawaiian shrine) at Makaha.

Ho's lifelong business philosophy was to apply the human equation, "kill the competition with kindness," permit others to profit, treat business like a game, and exit a bad venture quickly. In 1954 Ho paid Mark Robinson $450,000 for 136 acres that the Oahu Sugar Co. (OSC) did not re-option; Ho told Robinson he would sell at $600,000. When OSC realized that Ho's land fronted their sugar mill and he controlled access to it, they needed to buy him out. Robinson was not interested. Refusing advice that he profit up to a million dollars, Ho let OSC have it for $600,000. He had established his reputation as a shrewd but fair entrepreneur. Later that year Ho became the first Asian-American managing trustee of the Mark A. Robinson Trust & Estate, a medium-sized, land-based, private, Native Hawaiian estate. In 1955 Ho became the first Asian-American court-appointed guardian (with two Caucasians) of a "non-competent" heiress of the Victoria Ward Estate, a private, land-based Native Hawaiian estate. Invited to join the exclusive Commercial Club, in 1956 he was its first Chinese-American president. Two years later he was a director of Victoria Ward, Ltd. A fervent advocate of equality, Ho celebrated when Hawaii became the fiftieth state of the United States in 1959. Also that year, Ho was the first ethnic-minority director and board member of the morning daily newspaper, the *Honolulu Advertiser*, and president of Latipac, Inc., developer of an upscale residential development in Marin County, California. In his epic novel *Hawaii* (1959), James Michener used his friend Ho as the model for the character Hong Kong Kee, the wily moneyman who outsmarted the oligarchy.

Ho was the first Asian-American chairman of the Hawaii Visitors Bureau from 1960 to 1962. Acquiring the option for the Ilikai, a large cooperative apartment building planned for Waikiki, Ho was stymied without local funding. Yet mainland sources such as Equitable Life Assurance Society of New York saw opportunities, and by 1961 Ho had started construction. Sylvia Porter, syndicated newspaper financial columnist with a potential 23 million readership, concluded after a week in Hawaii that Ho was the nation's most impressive bridge between East and West. Ho opened the Marin Bay subdivision in 1961. When Ho joined Theo. H. Davies as its director in 1962, at long last the oligarchy's boardrooms were open to minorities. He was the first Asian-American chairman of the U.S. Olympic Fundraising Committee in Hawaii from 1960 to 1962. While vacationing with his wife on a trip around the world in 1962, Ho took ten days off to conclude an $11 million purchase that made him the primary owner and director of the *Honolulu Star-Bulletin*, the daily afternoon newspaper. In 1962 Ho and the *Honolulu Advertiser* established the Hawaii Newspaper Agency, the state's first joint-production arrangement that ensured the community of two separate editorial voices under local control. His *hui* soon acquired the *Pacific Daily News* on Guam and two newspapers in West Virginia. As president of the Hawaii Islanders, Ho brought in first-class Pacific Coast League baseball between 1963 and 1974. He lobbied the Hawaii legislature to pass the pioneer condominium law in 1963 that enabled buyers to purchase condos in fee simple and allowed the thirty-story Ilikai to open in 1964 as a unique hotel and condominium apartment complex. Then the tallest building, the Ilikai featured Hawaii's first exterior glass elevator. By 1965 Makaha Valley resort was a million-dollar project funded by East Coast and other monetary sources.

The recipient of many local awards, Ho also won wider recognition. He was the first Chinese-American civilian aide to the secretary of the army in Hawaii from 1965 to 1971. He won the Golden Eagle Award from the Invest-in-America Council in 1967 and the Golden Plate Award of the American Academy of Achievement in 1968. The Chinn Ho Foundation in 1968 donated $8,500 to build an elementary school library named after him in Cheju City, South Korea. In 1971 Ho sold the *Honolulu Star-Bulletin* for $35 million to the Gannett Corporation. Ho was chairman of the board of the Gannett Pacific Corporation from 1971 to 1978. He won the National Jewish Hospital Honor Award in 1972. During an economic downturn, he sold the Ilikai in 1974. Japanese investors bought the Makaha resort in 1979 and the Makaha East golf course in 1982. CIC's board chairman since 1975, Ho named as chairman his son Stuart effective 1982. In 1976 Ho donated $200,000 for books to Harvard University's Harvard-Yenching Library, whose reading room became the Chinn Ho Reading Room in 1978. In 1977 Ho helped to establish the Law Library Microfilm Consortium, a Hawaiian nonprofit publishing company to duplicate older and scarce legal materials on microfiche; by 1985, 1.5 million volumes had been sent to some fourteen foreign countries. One of Ho's international *huis* bought, updated, and reopened the Empress Hotel in Hong Kong in 1974 before selling it a few years later.

Not everyone appreciated Ho's vision and methods of operation. In the 1970s, accused of ruining the Waikiki skyline, he suggested that future hotels be built at the base of Diamond Head but was not taken seriously. Most property owners in Kahala, a choice residential area, opposed his ideas for increasing the density of lots.

The National Association of Chinese Americans gave Ho the Distinguished Achievement Award in 1982. Ho was deeply interested in China's progress and traveled frequently there after the 1970s. He was part of an international *hui* that helped to fund the Great Wall Hotel, which opened in 1984 in Beijing. Ho won the 1985 Distinguished Citizen Award from the Aloha Council of the Boy Scouts of America. After Ho died in Honolulu, the Gannett Corporation and Foundation in 1990 established in his honor the Freedom Foundation, a $100,000 endowment to acquire Chinese-language materials in the humanities for the University of Hawaii library.

• Ho's tape-recorded, transcribed interviews with Michaelyn P. Chou, "The Chinn Ho Oral History Project" (1978–1987), are the primary unpublished sources, privately held. See also George Cooper and Gavan Daws, *Land and Power in Hawaii* (1985), on Ho's strong political connections and business dealings; Sylvia Porter's columns appeared nationwide; see *Honolulu Advertiser*, Feb. 1961. For business and finance coverage, see Julius Spellman, "Chinn Ho," *Finance*, June 1970, pp. 8–13; "Capital Investment Company," *Hawaii Business and Industry*, Apr. 1963, pp. 22–30; and "Future of the Dailies," *Hawaii Business and Industry*, Apr. 1963, pp. 36–39. For local color, see A. A. Smyser, "Charisma," "Hawaii," "Chinn Ho's," and "Hotels," *Honolulu Star-Bulletin*, 18–21 Apr. 1972, and reprint booklet, "The Saga of Chinn Ho," 20 Sept. 1973. See also Lloyd Shearer, "Chinn Ho," *Parade*, 1 Nov. 1970, pp. 4–5, and Charles C. Keely, Jr., "A Touch," *Western's World*, Aug. 1984, pp. 64–67, 102–5, for popular treatment. An obituary is in the *Honolulu Star-Bulletin*, 13 May 1987.

MICHAELYN P. CHOU

HOADLEY, David (29 Apr. 1774–7 July 1839), builder and architect, was born in Waterbury, Connecticut, the son of Lemuel Hoadley and Urania Mallory, farmers. Although he received little formal education, he must have become apprenticed in his early teens to a joiner and learned the craft of house building. His earliest works were the Congregational and Episcopal churches in Waterbury, both under construction in 1795. Hoadley was twenty-one at the time, which indicates that he proved himself early to be an accomplished craftsman in his community. Some documents suggest that he also designed buildings. For example, the congregation of the United Church in New Haven thanked him in November 1815 as the "architect" and praised him "for the substantial, elegant, and workmanlike manner in which he has performed his contract, and that he be recommended to the Public for his skill and fidelity in his profession." The congregation thanked the contractors separately, which suggests that Hoadley was indeed the designer of the church. In 1798 he married Jane Hull, who died shortly thereafter.

It is possible that early in his career Hoadley acquired one or more pattern books popular in eighteenth-century America and began to incorporate into his own architectural vocabulary the classical forms and details illustrated in the books. Some historians assert that Hoadley designed the house of Judge William Bristol on New Haven Green in 1800, the entrance of which is now preserved in the New York Metropolitan Museum. If Hoadley did indeed design the Bristol house, it shows that he already had a thorough knowledge of the classical rules of composition. There is evidence that in 1819 Hoadley furnished a plan for and supervised the construction of Yale's Philosophical Building. Most documentary evidence suggests, however, that Hoadley's role in building was limited to joinery, plastering, and supervision of construction.

Without doubt, Hoadley worked in the vernacular tradition of house builders who, in a collaborative effort with their clients, often designed and directed construction. Hoadley was not, however, an architect in the modern sense of the word. The term architect had little specific meaning in the late eighteenth and early nineteenth centuries and was usually ascribed to anyone who could conceive and execute a building's plan and its ornament.

In the 1920s and 1930s local antiquarians in Connecticut and elsewhere, inspired by the early twentieth-century Colonial Revival, began to look more closely at buildings they thought to date from the eighteenth and early nineteenth centuries. These antiquarians were especially eager to assign authorship to those buildings which showed signs of being designed by someone with an academic training. Thus they asserted that Hoadley was also an architect, using as evidence building contracts such as the one Hoadley won for the United Church. He was the Connecticut representative for the New York architectural firm of (Ithiel) Town and (Alexander Jackson) Davis in the early 1830s, and this association helped confirm his design abilities in the minds of some historians.

Clearly, Hoadley's role as an architect in Connecticut is still open to interpretation. Nevertheless, the formal aspects of the buildings associated with his name suggest the continuity and artistic expression of a regional style that Hoadley probably influenced if not directed. Hoadley died in Waterbury, Connecticut.

• Hoadley is first mentioned in two local histories and one genealogy: Henry Bronson, *The History of Waterbury, Connecticut* (1858); Edward E. Atwater, *History of the City of New Haven* (1887); and F. B. Trowbridge, *The Hoadley Genealogy* (1894). One of the persons responsible for his elevation from builder to designer was George Dudley Seymour, who wrote "David Hoadley: The 'Self-Taught' Architect, 1774–1839," catalog of the Third Annual Exhibition, the Architectural Club of New Haven (1922). Seymour also published "David Hoadley, Architect," *Art and Progress* 3, no. 4 (Apr. 1912). J. Frederick Kelly continued Seymour's adulation of Hoadley in his *Early Connecticut Meetinghouses* (1948), attributing authorship of several buildings to Hoadley. Elizabeth Mills Brown began a reevaluation of Hoadley's design career in her books *The United Church on the Green, New Haven, Connecticut: An Architectural History* (1965) and *New Haven: A Guide to Architecture and Urban Design* (1976). Neither of these books focuses on Hoadley exclusively, but they do embody Brown's findings on his career. Brown's own documentary research is concisely stated in the *McMillan Encyclopedia of Architects* (1982), which includes a list of the buildings with which Hoadley is associated.

CLIFTON C. ELLIS

HOADLY, George (31 July 1826–26 Aug. 1902), lawyer and politician, was born in New Haven, Connecticut, the son of George Hoadley, a merchant and one-time mayor of New Haven, and Mary Ann Woolsey. (At some time, Hoadly dropped the *e* in his name.) In 1830 the family moved to Cleveland, Ohio, where the older Hoadley served as mayor and where Hoadly grew up. Despite close ties to Yale University, of which his mother's younger brother would become president, Hoadly attended Western Reserve College, graduating in 1844. For a year Hoadly attended Harvard Law School, where the faculty included Justice Joseph Story and Simon Greenleaf, and he then studied for a year in the Zanesville, Ohio, office of future Ohio Supreme Court judge, Charles C. Convers. Following another year in the Cincinnati office of Salmon P. Chase and Flamen Ball, Hoadly was admitted to the bar in August 1847. One of a coterie of young antislavery lawyers who gathered around Chase, Hoadly was significantly influenced by Chase.

In 1849 Hoadly became a junior partner of Chase's firm, stepping into the vacancy created that year by Chase's election to the Senate and his removal to Washington. Chase held young Hoadly in high esteem, perhaps partly because of their shared political beliefs. As antislavery Democrats, they were in a minority and would leave the party over the slavery question. Owing to his political skill and talents, Chase rose to prominence, and Hoadly was his trusted political lieutenant, first in the Free Soil movement of 1848 and then in Chase's unsuccessful pursuit of the Republican presidential nomination in 1856.

In 1851 Hoadly married Mary Burnet Perry, and that year he was selected to fill out an unexpired term on Cincinnati's superior court. He formed a partnership with Edward Mills and served as Cincinnati's city solicitor in 1855–1856. He was elected to the new superior court in 1859 and was reelected in 1864 but resigned in 1866 to form the firm of Hoadly, Jackson & Johnson. The firm quickly became one of the nation's leaders, but despite a busy schedule Hoadly taught for many years at the University of Cincinnati Law School and was a trustee of both the university and the Cincinnati Museum. Along with Stanley Matthews, he served as counsel for the Cincinnati Board of Education in 1869–1870, when its action abolishing the morning religious exercises was challenged. His argument in 1869 in *Minor v. Board of Education* was a forceful statement for the separation of church and state. The board lost at the trial level but won on appeal. Like many Democrats who had left the party and had become Republicans over the slavery issue, Hoadly became disenchanted with the Republican party's post–Civil War probusiness course. In 1872, with Matthews, he played an active role in the Liberal Republican convention that convened in Cincinnati in May, but when the convention nominated high-tariff advocate Horace Greeley, Hoadly gave his support to Ulysses S. Grant's reelection.

Ohio's constitutional convention of 1873–1874 provided a forum for Hoadly to set forth his political credo, even to his thoughts on government service. He had set aside a period of time from his law practice to engage in the convention's deliberations, much as though it were pro bono work. He was an unequivocal advocate of laissez faire. "I believe . . . in free trade in money, and in everything else, without let or hindrance of any government, national, State, or municipal." He believed only gold or silver coin should constitute money. In short, he found common cause with Democrats like Samuel L. Tilden and later Grover Cleveland. In the disputed presidential election of 1876, Tilden designated Hoadly as one of his counsel to argue before the special fifteen-member commission. James A. Garfield thought Hoadly's position untenable but his argument brilliant, and with Republicans comprising an 8 to 7 majority of the commission, Tilden and Hoadly's defeat was understandable.

In the gubernatorial election of 1883, Hoadly eked out a victory over Joseph B. Foraker of just over 12,000 votes out of almost 700,000 cast. Two years later Foraker reversed the results, although again the count was close. Hoadly lost by 17,500 votes of 700,000 cast, so it is difficult to draw any significance from it. Throughout the Gilded Age the Democratic party was usually in the minority in Ohio, and Hoadly's victory can be considered an aberration. His term in office was marked by violence, most notably a strike against the Ohio Coal and Iron Company in the Hocking Valley in April 1884. Hoadly unsuccessfully urged the company president, since "the great body of the locked-out miners are law-abiding," to make a fair adjustment in their wages. Ultimately he had to send in the National Guard, although he kept the force to a minimum. He was very circumspect about granting pardons and gave close scrutiny to every case.

Hoadly unsuccessfully sought the Democratic presidential nomination in 1884. With Cleveland's success that year, Hoadly requested Tilden's help in gaining the attorney generalship, but the appointment went elsewhere. After his governorship, Hoadly returned to his law practice in 1885. He soon incurred self-imposed financial obligations. As a bondsman for a $50,000 defaulted debt, he felt morally responsible, though not legally so, and paid off the debt. In the mid-1880s, to improve his financial position, he moved to New York City, where he founded the highly successful firm of Hoadly, Lauterbach & Johnson. Hoadly died at his summer home in Watkins, New York.

• Little biographical material is available on Hoadly. The sketch in C. T. Greve, *Centennial History of Cincinnati* (1904), is useful. His Cincinnati background is in John Niven, *Salmon P. Chase: A Biography* (1995). For a beginning to Hoadly's governorship, see Philip D. Jordan, *Ohio Comes of Age: 1873–1900*, vol. 5 of *The History of the State of Ohio*, ed. Carl Wittke (1943). Hoadly's involvement in the constitutional convention is in *Official Report of the Proceedings and Debates of the Constitutional Convention of Ohio* (2 vols., 1873–1874).

DONALD M. ROPER

HOAG, Joseph (22 Apr. 1762–21 Nov. 1846), Quaker minister, was born in Oblong, Dutchess County, New York, the son of Elijah Hoag and Phebe (maiden name unknown), farmers. As a child Hoag experienced many "divine visitations" and felt that he was called to preach. Despite uncertainties and some opposition, he began speaking in Quaker meetings when about eighteen years of age and was acknowledged as a minister a few years later. In 1782 Hoag married Huldah Case, who later became a well-known Quaker minister herself. Quakers regarded the ministry as a free gift from God and therefore disapproved of paid ministry. Hoag, like other Friends, rejected any suggestion that he receive payment or other support for his work in the ministry.

On several occasions during the American Revolution and the War of 1812, Hoag defended Quaker Pacifism. During the Revolution his father had been imprisoned for refusing to take up arms. Joseph Hoag said at that time that "it was impossible for a true Quaker to be either Whig or Tory, for that implied opposite parties, and both believed in war, and Friends did not" (*Journal*, 1861 ed., p. 30).

After their marriage, Joseph and Huldah Hoag began farming in Dutchess County, but they soon ran into debt and for several years were in reduced circumstances. About 1790 the family moved to Charlotte, Addison County, Vermont, to uncleared land; there they farmed for the rest of their lives. The couple had at least ten children, and of the eight who survived to adulthood, all were acknowledged as ministers.

Hoag traveled extensively in the ministry, first within the New York Yearly Meeting, which at that time included the Quaker meetings in Vermont, and later throughout North America. Between 1801 and 1844 he visited almost every Quaker meeting in North America. His journeys took him north to Prince Edward Island and Nova Scotia, south to the Carolinas and Tennessee, and as far west as Iowa. On several occasions he was absent from home for more than a year. His wife also traveled in the ministry, though not as extensively as he did.

Hoag considered the ministry a divine gift and was troubled when he felt he had been inattentive or disobedient to divine guidance. Beginning in childhood, he had prophetic visions. The most notable was his vision in 1803 of divisions in American society, beginning in the Presbyterian churches, continuing through the Society of Friends and the Freemasons, and ending in a great civil war. This civil war was to be followed by the rise of a "monarchial power" that would oppress Quakers and others. These tribulations were caused by "iniquity, and the blood of Africa." Although the text of Hoag's report of this vision was reportedly known among Quakers as early as the 1820s and 1830s, the earliest datable published version was in *Frederick Douglass's Paper* in 1854. The text circulated widely in manuscript, as a broadside, and after 1854 in periodicals. Hoag spoke frequently against slavery, particularly during his travels in Virginia, North Carolina, and Tennessee in 1812–1813 and 1816–1817.

In 1845 Hoag, with the help of his granddaughter, Narcissa Battey, compiled his earlier writings and travel journals into a narrative of his life, and gave explicit instructions that his writings not be allowed to fall into the hands of the followers of his doctrinal foes Elias Hicks and Joseph John Gurney. In the 1850s the Wilburite New York Yearly Meeting at Poplar Ridge arranged for the editing and publication of the journal; however, disagreements over its editing stirred a division between the Wilburite Friends of New York and Vermont. The so-called "Otis" faction published an edition of Hoag's *Journal* in 1860, and the "King" faction published their version the following year. The 1861 edition was reprinted in London in 1862, and in a slightly shortened version in Philadelphia in 1909.

Hoag's *Journal* is unusually candid in its descriptions of the religious controversies among Friends in the nineteenth century. By 1815 Hoag was opposing the ministry of Long Island Quaker Elias Hicks, which he felt tended toward deism and rationalism. During the Orthodox-Hicksite schism of 1827–1828, Hoag was in the Orthodox Camp, as were the majority of Vermont Quakers. In the 1830s and 1840s Hoag was equally opposed to the evangelical influences represented by an English Quaker, Joseph John Gurney. In 1837 and 1845 Hoag predicted another schism in the Society of Friends. Although Hoag died before the separation affected the Vermont Quakers, his opposition to Hicks and Gurney clearly identified him with the Wilburite or Conservative Friends in the religious controversies of the 1840s.

Hoag was well known among Quakers during his active life as a minister, and his extensive travels served to connect the scattered network of Quaker meetings. Among non-Friends, he was best known for his "Vision," which seemed to prophesy the Civil War. His *Journal* remains one of the best examples of the beliefs and sensibilities of the Wilburite branch of the Society of Friends.

• There are two manuscript versions of Hoag's *Journal*, one in the Friends Historical Library, Swarthmore College, and the other in the Quaker Collection at Haverford College. Hoag's "Vision" of 1803 circulated widely in manuscript and print; copies are at the Friends Historical Library at Swarthmore College and the Quaker Collection at Haverford. Albert J. Edmunds, *The Vision in 1803 of Joseph Hoag* (1915), traces the textual variations of the "Vision." In the 1880s and 1890s the Periodicals *Friend* and *Friends Intelligencer* published personal recollections of Joseph and Huldah Hoag. See also Christopher Densmore and Doris Calder, "Joseph Hoag: A Quaker in Atlantic Canada, 1801–1802," and Densmore, "Joseph Hoag and Traveling under Quaker Concern," both in Albert Schrauwers, ed., *Faith, Friends and Fragmentation: Essays on Nineteenth Century Quakerism in Canada* (1995).

CHRISTOPHER DENSMORE

HOAGLAND, Dennis Robert (2 Apr. 1884–5 Sept. 1949), plant physiologist, was born in Golden, Colorado, the son of Charles Breckenridge Hoagland and Lillian May Burch, occupations unknown. He spent his first eight years in his birthplace, but then the family moved to Denver, where Hoagland graduated from East Denver High School in 1903. He began his education as a chemistry major at Stanford University and received the A.B. in 1907. In 1908 he took a position as assistant chemist in the Laboratory of Animal Nutrition at the University of California, Berkeley, and in 1910 he became an assistant chemist in the Food and Drug Administration of the Department of Agriculture. Hoagland was awarded a graduate scholarship in animal biochemistry at the University of Wisconsin in 1912 and graduated with the M.A. in 1913. At Wisconsin, he worked with E. V. McCollum in the field of animal nutrition; years later, Hoagland looked back on his year of graduate study with McCollum as the true source and inspiration of his future life of scientific research. However, instead of remaining in the specialty of animal nutrition, in 1913 Hoagland accepted an appointment as assistant professor of agricultural chemistry at Berkeley at the invitation of Professor John S. Burd of the College of Agriculture. In 1922 Hoagland was promoted to associate professor of plant nutrition and to professor in 1927.

In 1913 the Division of Agricultural Chemistry at the University of California was chiefly interested in immediate, practical solutions to the problems of soil chemistry and fertilizers. However, Burd, its director, was dedicated to a search for underlying principles as well and encouraged the fundamental research that was Hoagland's real interest. In his first project, Hoagland made a study of the inorganic and organic composition of kelps, a study that was brought about by the shortage during World War I of German sources of potash fertilizers. There was an idea that the giant Pacific kelps might be a possible source of supply and, hence, Hoagland's project. The conclusion reached was that any commercial exploitation of these kelps was problematic, but Hoagland's work led him into the study of ion accumulation by plants. This became a lifelong interest.

At the time, the established theory about plant growth was that plants would only do well in a pH environment that was either neutral or slightly alkaline. In studying barley plants, Hoagland showed that they flourished in solutions that were acidic (pH 5), and he came to the conclusion that previous generalizations about plant nutrition were unreliable—largely because of the complexity of soils and a lack of understanding of plant–soil relationships. This assumption led Hoagland to emphasize research on plants growing in artificial cultures; the "water–culture" technique served as a major tool for researching problems in plant physiology. However, along with this emphasis, Hoagland urged a close collaboration between investigators in the two related fields of plant research: "Soil chemistry and plant physiology cannot be divorced and the practical art of soil management must have as its scientific basis a definite concept of the chemical and physiological interrelation between soil and plant." The practical application of this concept was the establishment in 1922 of the Division of Plant Nutrition in the College of Agriculture. Hoagland was appointed head of the new division.

He now returned to the subject that had attracted him during the kelp project: absorption and accumulation of ions by plants. For his new research, he used a freshwater alga, *Nitella*, and showed that absorption of ions by plants is a metabolic, rather than a physical (for example, osmotic), process. In the process, ions of different elements reacted reciprocally and were able to create, within the organism, concentrations of free ions far higher than those existing in the surrounding medium. From this point, Hoagland began a long study in the absorption of nutrients by the roots of higher plants, and eventually his research provided an enormous amount of data on the influence of light, temperature, hydrogen ion concentration, oxygen supply, and other factors on plant nutrition. This led to greatly increased understanding of the effects of fertilizer treatments and other chemical changes in soils and of the importance of soil aeration. The results of his research were published in many articles in scientific journals and in *Lectures on the Inorganic Nutrition of Plants* (1944).

Hoagland and his associates also conducted research on the movement of solutes in plants. As radioactive isotopes became available, they were used so that the course of various nutrient elements could be followed through the different plant parts. This research gave strong support to Hoagland's theories concerning the complex relationships among water absorption, nutrition, and plant environment. For Hoagland, to ignore these complex relationships always resulted in generalizations that could not be experimentally upheld. "Inherent in the green plant itself," he wrote, "are all the complexities common to living organisms and to these must be added the complexities of the soil medium in which the plant is anchored and finds some of the substances essential for its nourishment."

Under Hoagland's guidance, the Division of Plant Nutrition was also involved in practical problems. For example, in cooperation with the Division of Pomology, studies were made of nutritional deficiencies in fruit trees, and remedies were found that were of great benefit to California fruit growers. He also prepared a circular on artificial nutrients and crop production in soil, thousands of copies of which were distributed throughout the state. Hoagland believed absolutely in the importance to agriculture of basic research regardless of whether that research provided immediate practical results. Principles discovered in the laboratory, he claimed, would, at some time, help the farmer in solving the practical problems in the field.

The honors, as well as outside responsibilities, that came to Hoagland in his lifetime were numerous and demonstrated the worldwide recognition that he had achieved. In 1929 the American Society of Plant Physiologists gave him its highest honor, the Stephen Hales Award. He was also president of that society and of the Western Society of Soil Science; the Western Society of Naturalists; the Botanical Society of America, Pacific Division; and the American Association for the Advancement of Science, Pacific Division. In 1940 the American Association for the Advancement of Science awarded him $1,000 for one of his papers, and he gave the John M. Prather Lectures at Harvard in 1942. Hoagland was also consulting editor for *Soil Science, American Journal of Botany, Plant Physiology,* and *Plant and Soil* and was one of the organizers of the *Annual Review of Biochemistry.*

Hoagland was one of the most distinguished plant physiologists and the "world's leading authority in the broad field of plant and soil interrelationships (Arnon, p. 129)." He inspired numerous students and colleagues, and his own researches were unique and of major significance. He was held in high esteem by those who studied and worked with him and was noted for his generosity, integrity, and objectivity.

Hoagland was in poor health the last four years of his life. Because of his failing eyesight, he asked for retirement in 1949. He had married Jessie A. Smiley in 1920, but she died in 1933, leaving him with the sole responsibility of raising three children. Hoagland died in Oakland, California.

• A list of the principal publications of Hoagland can be found in his *Lectures on the Inorganic Nutrition of Plants* (1944). In addition, Walter P. Kelley, "Dennis Robert Hoagland, 1884–1949," National Academy of Sciences, *Biographical Memoirs* 29 (1956): 123–43, contains eight pages of bibliography. For comprehensive biographical essays, see D. I. Arnon, "Dennis Robert Hoagland, 1884–1949," *Plant and Soil* 2, no. 2 (1950): 129–44, and "Dennis Robert Hoagland, 1884–1949," *Plant Physiology* 25 (1950): iv–xvi. Those essays are abridged in *Soil Science* 69 (1950): 1–5, and *Science* 112 (1950): 739–42, respectively.

ROBERT F. ERICKSON

HOAN, Daniel Webster (12 Mar. 1881–11 June 1961), socialist leader and mayor of Milwaukee, was born in Waukesha, Wisconsin, the son of Daniel Webster Hoan, a well digger, and Margaret Hood. Upon completing seven years of school, he worked as a chef in Waukesha, Milwaukee, and Chicago hotels and restaurants. In 1901 he entered the University of Wisconsin as an "adult special" student. There he organized a Socialist society and regularly attended meetings of the Socialist party members of the state legislature. Following graduation in 1905, Hoan opened a restaurant in Chicago and attended night classes at Kent College of Law, passing bar examinations in Illinois and Wisconsin in 1908. In the following year he married Agnes Bernice Magner; they had two children before her death in 1941.

In 1908 Hoan became the attorney for the Wisconsin Federation of Labor, and he played an important role in the passage of the nation's first constitutional workmen's compensation act. Led by Victor Berger, the Milwaukee Social Democratic party swept to victory in 1910, and Hoan was elected city attorney. He was reelected in 1914. In state and federal courts and before the Wisconsin Public Service Commission, Hoan won important decisions involving railroad, street railway, and utility fares and services. Out of his experiences as city attorney, he published *The Failure of Regulation* (1914), one of the earliest left-wing attacks on regulatory commissions.

The Milwaukee Socialist party had lost control of the mayor's office and the Common Council in 1912, leaving Hoan as the party's most prominent elected official. He became the party's choice for mayor in 1916, and in a close election he won, running ahead of his party. In spite of limited mayoral powers allocated by the city of Milwaukee, Hoan was able to obtain publicly owned street lighting and improvements in sewage and water systems, and he inaugurated city planning programs. The Socialist party's St. Louis platform of April 1917 committed it to "active and public opposition" to World War I, placing Hoan and the Milwaukee Socialists in a quandary. Fearing to lose the mayor's office in 1918, Berger urged Hoan to obey all wartime governmental decrees. Hoan's legal support of the Socialist party became an issue in the election of 1918. He was deposed from the board of the Milwaukee County Council of Defense and was bitterly opposed by prominent Milwaukeeans as a mayoral candidate. Again Hoan ran ahead of his party, carrying 18 of 25 wards. With the cooling of wartime passions, he reaffirmed his commitment to municipal reform and in 1920 was again reelected handily.

Following his election in 1920, Hoan put forward his goals for Milwaukee. He called for improved health measures, construction of a filtration plant, a tighter building code, municipally sponsored cooperatives, city planning, equitable tax assessments, extension of the merit system, development of a municipally operated port, establishment of public marketing facilities, extension of equal protection to labor, and careful scrutiny of expenditures. These objectives became the basis of his program for the next two decades, and he was successful in meeting all of them save the establishment of city sponsored cooperatives. However, he had to obtain his goals without a majority in the Common Council. Hoan's record as a reform politician was verified by his easy victory in 1924 over David Rose. A combination of prosperity and Hoan's popularity led him to victory in 1928. He was chairman of the Socialist party presidential committee in 1928 and 1932 and was considered a possible presidential candidate in 1932.

The Great Depression put additional burdens on Hoan and at the same time propelled him into the national limelight. In 1932 he won the mayor's race and carried with him Socialist aldermen, city attorney, and treasurer. Faced with pressure from the Taxpayers' Council, Hoan was forced in 1933 to curtail expenditures and public services. He had bonds issued that were secured by tax certificates, which successfully allowed city services to be maintained. In 1932 he was chosen to a national Committee of Mayors, which petitioned President Herbert Hoover for federal aid to cities. In the following year Hoan was one of the founders of the U.S. Conference of Mayors, and he became its first vice chairman. He published *City Government* (1936), which emphasized his role in Milwaukee reforms. Milwaukee came to be recognized as a model of municipal government and Hoan as its chief spokesman. On a regional basis, Hoan played a significant leadership role in the Great Lakes Harbor Association, and he advocated the construction of the St. Lawrence Seaway.

By 1935 Hoan and the Milwaukee Socialists realized that they had failed to exploit gains made early in the depression. Hoan turned to the idea of a farmer-labor party. Others were receptive, and the Wisconsin Socialists, the La Follette-sponsored Wisconsin Progressive party, and other liberal organizations joined to form the Farmer-Labor Progressive Federation. Hoan was reelected in 1936, but his large majority of 1932 dropped to 13,000. In 1937 he resigned from the Socialist party's National Executive Committee and took

little part in further party quarrels. In 1940, after twenty-four years in the mayor's office, he was defeated by Carl Zeidler. In September 1940 Hoan was appointed associate director of state and local cooperation for the National Defense Commission, and for two years he spoke on civil defense in North and South America.

Until 1940 Hoan never wavered in his support of the Socialist party, which in turn basked in his success as America's highest elected Socialist party official. Hoan resigned from the Socialist party in December 1941 and joined the Wisconsin Progressive party, where he remained active in the Farmer-Labor Progressive Federation. He became a member of the Democratic party in 1944, and that year he was the Democratic gubernatorial candidate. He again campaigned unsuccessfully for governor in 1946. He also lost races for mayor (1948), congressman (1948), U.S. senator (1950), and state senator (1952). He was a delegate to the Democratic National Convention in 1952, but owing to the sudden death of his second wife, Gladys Townsend, whom he had married in 1944, he took little part in the proceedings. He remained on the Milwaukee Harbor Commission until 1958. Hoan died in Milwaukee.

• The extensive Daniel W. Hoan Papers are in the Milwaukee County Historical Society Museum. Robert C. Reinders, "The Early Career of Daniel W. Hoan: A Study of Socialism in the Progressive Era" (M.A. thesis, Univ. of Notre Dame, 1949), covers the years to 1920. Broader in scope is Floyd John Stachowski, "The Political Career of Daniel Webster Hoan" (Ph.D. diss., Northwestern Univ., 1966). Less scholarly is Edward S. Kerstein, *Milwaukee's All-American Mayor: Portrait of Daniel Webster Hoan* (1966). An excellent study that discusses Hoan is Frederick I. Olson, "The Milwaukee Socialists 1897–1941" (Ph.D. diss., Howard Univ., 1952). An obituary is in the *Milwaukee Journal*, 12 June 1961.

ROBERT C. REINDERS

HOAR, Ebenezer Rockwood (21 Feb. 1816–31 Jan. 1895), judge and attorney general, was born in Concord, Massachusetts, the son of Samuel Hoar, a lawyer and congressman, and Sarah Sherman. Hoar was a mischievous and precocious lad whose scholarship was enhanced by keeping up with his older sister Elizabeth. Although he was ready to enter college at fourteen, his father suggested that he work on a farm for a year. During his first day's work, Hoar (who was nearsighted) stepped on a scythe and permanently injured his foot, but he was able to participate in the interclass mayhem known as football when he entered Harvard in 1831. After graduating third in the class of 1835, Hoar taught Latin to young girls for a year in Pittsburgh, Pennsylvania. Returning home, he read law under his father's tutelage, entered Harvard Law School in 1837, received his LL.B. in 1839, and on 30 September of that year was admitted to the Massachusetts bar. Hoar began to practice in Concord, where he married Caroline Downes Brooks in 1840; they had seven children.

Entering politics during the 1840 presidential campaign of William Henry Harrison, Hoar was both a delegate and the secretary of the Whig Young Men's Convention of Middlesex County. Four years later he supported Henry Clay's unsuccessful bid for the presidency. Hoar's antislavery proclivities were heightened in November 1844, when South Carolina expelled his father, who was in that state challenging—on behalf of Massachusetts—its practice of jailing free black sailors while their vessels were in port. In 1845 Ebenezer Hoar helped organize opposition to the annexation of Texas and its admission to the Union as a slave state, and later, in defeat, he resolved with Charles Francis Adams (1807–1886), Charles Sumner, and William Lloyd Garrison to continue the fight until slavery was destroyed. In 1846 Hoar served in the Massachusetts State Senate, where he opposed the Mexican War and originated widely accepted names for the divided wings of his party by declaring he would rather be a Conscience Whig than a Cotton Whig. Supporting neither major party candidate for the presidency in 1848, Hoar led other dissatisfied Whigs in forming the Free Soil party in Massachusetts.

Never robust and overworked and overwrought by politics and the cases he tried, Hoar in July 1849 was glad to become judge of the court of common pleas. He opposed the 1850 alliance of Free Soilers and Democrats (whom he despised) that elected George S. Boutwell governor and Sumner senator, even though they were his friends. He was outraged by the 1850 Fugitive Slave Law and in 1854 charged the Suffolk County grand jury to inquire into the militia's actions that returned the runaway Anthony Burns to slavery following an unsuccessful rescue attempt by a group of abolitionists. If those actions were not warranted, Hoar insisted that everyone involved, from the "highest official . . . to the last private," should be indicted.

Hoar's resignation from the bench in 1855 was probably inspired by the evolution of the Massachusetts Republican party. That year, at their second convention, the Republicans nominated him for attorney general, but he lost, even though he campaigned vigorously, to a combination of nativist Know Nothings and conservative Whigs. Hoar attended the 1856 Republican National Convention, helped write its platform (attacking, in his memorable phrase, "those twin relics of barbarism, polygamy and slavery"), and wholeheartedly campaigned for its presidential nominee John Charles Frémont, who carried Massachusetts but not the country. In 1859 Hoar withdrew from politics. Governor Nathaniel P. Banks named him to the Massachusetts Supreme Court, which he dominated for a decade with his quick mind, his impatience—accentuated by dyspepsia—with long-winded lawyers, and his short, pointed, commonsense opinions.

In March 1869 Hoar was "astonished" to be named by President Ulysses S. Grant (whom he had impressed at a recent dinner) as attorney general, succeeding his cousin William M. Evarts in that position. A loyal, strong, and independent adviser, Hoar was painfully honest, and Grant appreciated his candor. Helping Grant select judges was Hoar's greatest contribution. Congress in 1869 created a new judgeship in each federal circuit and a vacancy on the Supreme Court by increasing its number to nine. Many senators had candidates for these positions, but Hoar (who did not suffer senators gladly) only backed candidates whom he thought possessed superior character and fitness. Grant nominated virtually all of Hoar's choices, and the Senate took vengeance on 3 February 1870 by rejecting Hoar, whom Grant had nominated for the Supreme Court. Hoar continued in the cabinet until 23 June 1870. Anxious over his scheme to annex Santo Domingo, Grant sought support in Congress—especially among southern Republicans, who felt that Hoar had not moved with dispatch against white terrorists in their region—by asking Hoar to resign to make way for a southerner. Although he was a hero of the civil service reformers who were becoming disillusioned with Grant, Hoar remained loyal to the president, refusing to publicize the circumstances that eased him out of the cabinet.

Hoar returned to private practice in Concord and Boston but retained his commitment to public service. He served on the joint high commission that negotiated the 1871 Treaty of Washington with Great Britain which provided for the arbitration of serious difficulties (including the *Alabama* claims). In 1872 he opposed the Liberal Republican movement (which advocated civil service reform, free trade, hard money, and abandoning radical Reconstruction), supported a second term for Grant, and was elected to the Forty-third Congress, where he joined his youngest brother, George Frisbie Hoar, in the Massachusetts delegation. As a representative, Hoar opposed any inflation of the currency, voted for the Civil Rights Act of 1875, and helped revise the U.S. statutes into a more convenient format. Rather than run for a second term in 1874 he sought election to the Senate in 1875, but the legislature chose Henry Laurens Dawes from western Massachusetts. Hoping to defeat Benjamin F. Butler (1818–1893), whom he despised as a spoilsman, inflationist, and personal enemy who frustrated Hoar's judicial and political ambitions, Hoar unsuccessfully ran for Congress in 1876 as an independent Republican. After his retirement from politics, he was so regular a Republican in subsequent elections that he probably did not vote for his son Sherman Hoar, who was elected to Congress as a Democrat in 1890. Hoar served his profession as president of the Boston Bar Association (elected in 1879); his college with three decades of service beginning in 1857 as either an overseer or a member of the Harvard Corporation; and his denomination as presiding officer of the National Conference of Unitarian Churches. A gregarious man of wit and wisdom, Hoar loved to smoke cigars and play whist with friends, and during close to four decades preceding his death in Concord, he more than held his own with the literati, savants, and gourmands of Boston's Saturday Club.

• Some of Hoar's papers are in the various manuscript collections of the Massachusetts Historical Society. For additional information see Moorfield Storey and Edward W. Emerson,

Ebenezer Rockwood Hoar: A Memoir (1911); Massachusetts Historical Society, *Proceedings*, 2d ser., vol. 9 (1895): 301–31; George F. Hoar, *Autobiography of Seventy Years* (2 vols., 1903); and Jacob Dolson Cox, "How Judge Hoar Ceased to Be Attorney-General," *Atlantic Monthly*, Aug. 1895, pp. 162–73. An obituary is in the *New York Times*, 1 Feb. 1895.

ARI HOOGENBOOM

HOAR, George Frisbie (29 Aug. 1826–30 Sept. 1904), U.S. congressman and senator, was born in Concord, Massachusetts, the son of Samuel Hoar, a lawyer, politician, and, later, U.S. congressman, and Sarah Sherman. A grandson of Roger Sherman, signer of the Declaration of Independence and the U.S. Constitution, Hoar was imbued with filial piety and the New England tradition of "simple living and high thinking." He graduated from Harvard College (B.A., 1846) and the Harvard Law School (LL.B., 1849) and subsequently practiced law in Worcester, Massachusetts. On two occasions in later years he declined appointment to the supreme court of Massachusetts.

Early in his legal career Hoar became involved in politics. He was elected to the Massachusetts House of Representatives in 1852 and the state senate in 1857. Initially a Free Soiler, in 1856 he joined the Republican party, through whose ranks he rose, becoming particularly adept in procedural and administrative matters. He frequently chaired the party's state conventions in the 1870s and 1880s and in the same decade regularly attended its national conventions, presiding in 1880. Two presidents, Rutherford B. Hayes and William McKinley, unavailingly offered him top diplomatic posts in England.

Hoar's career in Congress began in 1868 when he was elected to the House of Representatives from the Eighth District of Massachusetts. His district was the birthplace of the state's Republican party organization, and the city of Worcester, where he lived, exemplified the industrial growth of modern America. Accordingly, Hoar called for tariff protection and the establishment of a federal labor commission. Solicitous, too, of the civil rights of freed people, he supported the Fourteenth and Fifteenth amendments, referring to the latter (prohibiting the denial of the right to vote on racial grounds) as "the crowning measure of Reconstruction." Hoar, however, became increasingly disillusioned with a legalistic approach to eradicating southern racism and urged public education—supported by the federal government if need be—as an agent of social transformation. Distancing himself from the fast and loose politics of Ulysses S. Grant's administrations, he denounced the congressional "salary grab" in 1873 and, as a member of the Judiciary Committee, helped manage the impeachment proceedings against William Belknap, the secretary of war, pressing the matter even after Belknap had resigned. In 1877 Hoar sat on the electoral commission that considered the disputed Hayes-Tilden contest, though he was not involved in the discussions leading to the broad compromise by which Democrats accepted Hayes's election in return for the abandonment of the remaining Reconstruction governments in the South.

Elevated to the U.S. Senate that same year and reelected four times, Hoar became prominent in the "Half-Breed" faction of his party. He believed his greatest contribution in the Senate came with his work on the Committee on Claims that directed the larger body's disposition of individual, corporate, and state claims arising from the Civil War. To promote sectional reconciliation he pressed President Benjamin Harrison to sign a bill to rebuild parts of the College of William and Mary destroyed during the war. For twenty years Hoar served on the Senate Judiciary Committee, chairing it from 1891 to 1893 and from 1895 to 1904. He employed his legislative craftsmanship in drafting the presidential succession act of 1886 and an 1887 law that fully restored a president's power to remove executive department officials by repealing what remained of the Tenure of Office Act. He claimed authorship of the Sherman Antitrust Act of 1890 and twelve years later drafted an abortive amendment to the law that would have set up an informal federal licensing system for corporations engaged in interstate trade.

Hoar remained a Republican partisan, claiming his party was made up of "the men who do the work of piety and charity in our churches . . . who administer our school systems . . . who own and till their own farms . . . who perform skilled labor . . . who went to the war and stayed all through . . . who paid the debt, and kept the currency sound, and saved the nation's honor." The Democrats' constituency, by contrast, was "the old slave-owner and slave-driver, the ballot-box-stuffer, the Kuklux, the criminal class of the great cities, and men who cannot read or write" (John A. Garraty, *The New Commonwealth, 1877–1890* [1968], p. 236). But he would not allow his partisanship to compromise the Senate's integrity. He upheld the highest standards of conduct, authoring two rules requiring decorum in floor debate, and for more than twenty-five years served on the Committee on Privileges and Elections. Nor would Hoar countenance the spoils system. In 1882 he worked for the passage of the Pendleton Civil Service Act, which set up a bipartisan commission to oversee the new merit system of federal appointments.

Forward-thinking on a number of other issues, Hoar wrote pamphlets for the New England Woman's Suffrage Association and publicly denounced the anti-Catholicism of the nativist American Protective Association. However, he opposed the popular election of U.S. senators, arguing that it would lead to electoral corruption and result in the public's selection of inferior talent as well as subvert the masterful system of checks and balances in the Constitution.

During the Philippine–American War (1899–1902), Hoar was a leading anti-imperialist. Imperialism, he feared, would endanger the sacred principle of "consent of the governed" proclaimed in the Declaration of Independence. Among the Senate anti-imperialists he was nearly alone in urging self-determination not only for Filipinos but also for Puerto Ricans. He believed the United States had a moral duty not to abuse its might in dealing with weaker powers. "The Moral Law and the Golden Rule are for nations as well as individuals," he told the Massachusetts legislature in February 1901. Curiously, he did not show a similar regard for the self-governing rights of Polynesians when he supported Hawaiian annexation in mid-1898. Though at odds with President McKinley and the Republican leadership in his own state on the issue of empire, Hoar nevertheless won reelection in 1901.

Beyond the Senate chamber, Hoar served as a Harvard College overseer for twelve years and was a trustee for both the Worcester Polytechnic Institute and Clark University. Deeply interested in U.S. history, he also served as a regent of the Smithsonian Institution and president of the American Antiquarian Society and the American Historical Association. In later life resembling Charles Dickens's Mr. Pickwick, the bespectacled, white-haired, and round-figured Hoar relaxed by preparing his own translation of Thucydides's history of the Peloponnesian Wars. A faithful supporter of his Unitarian church, Hoar's religious creed stressed tolerance and individual responsibility.

Hoar was married twice. He fathered two children by his first wife, Mary Louisa Spurr, whom he married in 1853. Their marriage ended with her death in 1859. Hoar wed Ruth Ann Miller in 1862. Their childless marriage lasted forty-one years. Less than a year after his second wife's death, Hoar—still a member of the U.S. Senate but sick and "feeling like a man strangely lost and empty"—died in Worcester.

George Frisbie Hoar's career served as an ideological bridge between the human rights principles of the early Republican party and the GOP's turn-of-the-century identification with industrial growth. Certainly not a progressive by outlook or temperament, Hoar's support for merit-based civil service appointments, the women's movement, and trust regulation nevertheless anticipated the reforms of the twentieth century.

• Hoar's voluminous papers, including accessions in 1991, are in the Massachusetts Historical Society. Among his writings see also *Autobiography of Seventy Years* (2 vols., 1903) and a genealogical study, although published under the name of Henry S. Nourse, done largely by Hoar, "The Hoar Family in America and Its English Ancestry," *New England Historical and Genealogical Register* (Jan., Apr., July 1899). The most seminal and balanced biography is Richard E. Welch, *George Frisbie Hoar and the Half-Breed Republicans* (1971); compare Frederick Gillett, *George Frisbie Hoar* (1934). For Hoar's anti-imperialism, see Robert L. Beisner, *Twelve against Empire: The Anti-Imperialists, 1898–1900* (1968), and Welch, *Response to Imperialism: The United States and the Philippine-American War, 1899–1902* (1979), "Opponents and Colleagues: George Frisbie Hoar and Henry Cabot Lodge, 1898–1904," *New England Quarterly* 39 (June 1966): 182–209, and "Senator George Frisbie Hoar and the Defeat of Anti-Imperialism, 1898–1900," *The Historian* 26 (May 1964): 362–80. For eulogies see *Congressional Record*, 58th Cong., 3d sess. (28 Jan. and 12 Feb. 1905), pp. 1503–23 and pp. 2434–45, respectively, and Thomas Wentworth Higginson, "George Frisbie Hoar," American Academy of Arts & Sciences, *Proceedings* 15 (May 1905): 761–69. An obituary is in the *New York Times*, 30 Sept. 1904.

THOMAS J. OSBORNE

HOAR, Leonard (1630?–28 Nov. 1675), Puritan minister and president of Harvard College, was born in Gloucestershire, England, the son of Charles Hoare, a brewer, and Joanna Hinksman. Charles Hoare was wealthy enough to provide in his will for Leonard to be sent to Oxford University, but after his father's death in 1638, Leonard's mother moved the family across the Atlantic to New England, where they settled in Braintree, Massachusetts. Instead of Oxford, Leonard Hoar enrolled at Harvard College, where he received an A.B. in 1650 and an A.M. in 1653.

By this time the success of the Puritan faction in the English civil war had begun to lure many Harvard graduates and New England clergymen back to England, and Hoar joined the exodus. In July 1654 he was granted an M.A. from Cambridge University and soon thereafter was made rector of Wanstead, Essex. But the Restoration of Charles II in 1660 and the subsequent Act of Uniformity forced Hoar and many of his fellow Puritans from their clerical posts. Throughout the 1660s Hoar maintained close ties to other dissenters, especially through his marriage (probably in the late 1660s) to Bridget Lisle, daughter of John Lisle, one of the regicide judges who passed sentence on Charles I. The couple had two daughters. Hoar also strengthened his connections to England's scholarly and scientific communities. He published an abridgement and guide to the historical books of the Bible, studied botany and medicine, and in 1671 was made a "Doctor of Physick" by Cambridge University. Hoar's intense piety and scholarly ambition were reflected in a letter to his nephew, Josiah Flint, a student at Harvard College. He instructed Flint not to do only what is "expected of you; but daily something more than your task. . . . [W]hen the classes study only logick or nature, you may spend some one or two spare hours in languages, rhetoric, history, or mathematics, or the like." In addition to this formidable plan of study, Hoar recommended that Flint "read every morning a chapter in the old testament, and every evening one in the new," and meditate on the meaning of these daily scriptural passages.

In the early 1670s Hoar's reputation for scholarship and piety raised considerable interest in New England. The newly formed Third Church of Boston recruited him to be its minister, and in 1672 Hoar returned to Massachusetts intending to take up the post. At the time the advanced age of Charles Chauncy, the Harvard College president, was worrying Puritans on both sides of the Atlantic. A group of English dissenting ministers sent letters of introduction strongly recommending Hoar's "gifts of learning and the grace of his spirit" as suitable qualifications for Chauncy's successor. Chauncy died while Hoar was crossing the ocean, and shortly after his arrival Hoar was elected to the Harvard presidency and formally installed on 10 December 1672.

Hoar approached the Harvard presidency with vigor and enthusiasm. He planned to revive the impoverished and underenrolled college by introducing experimental science to the curriculum and by providing equipment for agricultural, chemical, and physical experiments. He pushed through a new college charter to strengthen the hand of the corporation, made up of the president and teaching fellows, against the influence of the outside board of overseers. He also used his transatlantic connections to raise money for a new college building to replace the rapidly decaying "Old College." But for reasons that remain obscure, Hoar's presidency quickly degenerated and ended in disgrace. Shortly after his inauguration, the resident teaching fellows and student body turned sharply against the new president. Cotton Mather, a very young student at the time, later wrote that "the *Young Men* in the Colledge [*sic*] . . . set themselves to *Travestie* whatever he *did* and *said*, and aggravate everything in his Behaviour disagreeable to them, with a Design to make him *Odious.*" In 1673 the four teaching fellows resigned their posts, many students dropped out, and vague complaints about Hoar's "untruthfulness" were brought before the Harvard Overseers and the Massachusetts General Court. These bodies gave some measure of support to Hoar, but their encouragements were only half-hearted, and the students continued their steady withdrawal from the college. Hoar finally resigned on 15 March 1675. His health rapidly declined, and less than nine months later he died in Boston of a "consumption."

The reason for Hoar's rapid downfall was the subject of considerable controversy at the time and has never been fully resolved. Some blamed the affair on the jealousy of other aspirants for Hoar's position, notably Urian Oakes, the minister of Cambridge who was passed over for the presidency. In addition, Boston's churches had recently been riven with contention over issues of ecclesiastical authority. In this context, Hoar's sudden departure from his English dissenting church without a formal dismissal, together with the breach of his implied promise to become the minister of Boston's Third Church, may have turned some supporters against him. Thomas Danforth, a Third Church member who was glad not to have Hoar as his minister, believed "he will be a better pr[e]sid[ent], than a pulpit man (at least) as to vulg[a]r acceptation," hinting at the possibility of Hoar's general unpopularity. But supporters like Cotton Mather and John Hull insisted that he was a "worthy man" wronged by enemies, and that if "those that accused him had but countenanced and encouraged him in his work, he would have proved the best president that ever yet the college had."

Samuel Eliot Morison, Harvard's tercentennial historian, blames "some fault in Hoar's character or conduct," perhaps "something unfortunate in Hoar's manner, repellent in his personality, harsh in his discipline, or unreasonable in his policy." Yet as recently as 1976 a resolution was passed by the Massachusetts State Senate defending Hoar against the "contumacious and envious displeasure" of the college fellows who forced him to resign and proclaiming his "innocence of any misdeed while president of Harvard College." Judged by his scholarly promise and the strength of his plans for the curriculum, it does seem possible that Hoar could have revived the rapidly deteriorating college. But whether the trouble was caused by his personal shortcomings or by a conspiracy of his enemies, Hoar's presidency was a disaster, perhaps the low point in the early history of Harvard.

• Some of Hoar's papers, along with the Massachusetts State Senate resolution exonerating him, are in the Harvard University Archives. His letter to Josiah Flint, 27 Mar. 1661, is printed in Massachusetts Historical Society, *Collections*, 1st ser., vol. 6 (1800): 100–108; correspondence regarding Hoar's qualifications for the Harvard presidency are in Thomas Hutchinson, *Collection of Papers* (1769), pp. 429–31. Contemporary comments include Cotton Mather, *Magnalia Christi Americana* (1702), bk. 4, p. 129; "The Diary of John Hull," in *Transactions . . . of the American Antiquarian Society* 3 (1857): 233; and Thomas Danforth to John Winthrop, 1 Aug. 1672, Massachusetts Historical Society, *Proceedings* 13 (1875): 235–36. Hoar's publications include his *Index Biblicus* (1668), two funeral sermons published under the title *The Sting of Death and Death Unstung* (1680), and the first catalog of the graduates of Harvard College, reprinted in Massachusetts Historical Society, *Proceedings* 8 (1864): 9–75. The best accounts of Hoar's life are in Samuel Eliot Morison, *Harvard College in the Seventeenth Century*, vol. 2 (1936), pp. 390–414, and John Langdon Sibley, *Biographical Sketches of Graduates of Harvard University*, vol. 1 (1873), pp. 228–52. For a vivid description of the low state of the college during Hoar's tenure, see David Levin, *Cotton Mather: The Young Life of the Lord's Remembrancer* (1978), pp. 23–56.

MARK A. PETERSON

HOBAN, James (1758?–8 Dec. 1831), architect, was born in County Kilkenny, Ireland, the son of Edward Hoban and Martha Bayne. He studied architecture with Thomas Ivory in Dublin, winning a medal in 1780 from the Dublin Society for "Drawings of Brackets, Stairs, Roofs, etc." The date of his emigration to America is unknown, but on 25 May 1785 he advertised his services as an architect in the *Pennsylvania Evening Herald*.

Most of Hoban's papers and drawings were lost in a fire in the 1880s, and therefore the picture of his career must be pieced together from other sources. During his residence in Charleston, South Carolina, from 1787 to 1792, he designed Savage's Green Theater and a plan for an orphan asylum, both in 1792, and several private houses. The South Carolina State House in Columbia (begun in 1788 and completed in 1795) has been erroneously attributed to Hoban.

In 1792 Hoban submitted plans in the design competitions for the "President's House" and the Capitol. George Washington, to whom he had been introduced the previous summer in Charleston, gave Hoban a letter of introduction to the commissioners in charge of overseeing construction of the nation's capital. On 18 July 1792 they awarded Hoban a prize of $500 for his design of the White House. Hoban based his design on the Leinster House in Dublin (1745–1751), following incorrect engravings in Robert Pool and John Cash's *Views of the Most Remarkable Public Buildings, Monuments, and other Edifices, in the City of Dublin* (1780). Late Georgian in style, with a giant portico bisecting a rectangular, three-story building, its facades were organized according to a traditional Renaissance-derived palace type with the principal story raised above ground, its tall windows surmounted by pediments marking its importance. Hoban spent the remaining forty years of his life working in Washington, throughout which constructing, rebuilding, and altering the White House occupied much of his time.

The White House established the architectural typology that Hoban utilized in the design of his other principal known work, Blodget's Hotel (1793–1800) in Washington. Between 1793 and 1802, Hoban also served from time to time as superintendent in charge of construction of the Capitol. Two drawings in the Maryland Historical Society, generally attributed to Stephen Hallet (Étienne Sulpice Hallet), probably are Hoban's 1795 scheme to complete the Capitol using Hallet's foundations. Beginning in 1815, Hoban repaired the two extant executive department offices (originally designed by George Hadfield in 1798 and burned by the British in August 1814) and erected two additional offices following Hadfield's model, which had been greatly influenced by Hoban's White House. He is also known to have advised George Washington on the design of "Mount Vernon" in 1797 and James Monroe on "Oakhill" in 1821.

Hoban was an active member of the community as well. He has been credited with establishing the first Catholic church, St. Patrick's, in Washington in 1792 and in 1820 served on the committee to erect St. Peter's Church on Capitol Hill. In 1793 he was a founding member of Washington's first lodge of Freemasons. Beginning in 1797 he served as captain of the Washington Artillery. In 1802 he was elected to the Washington City Council and served intermittently for many years. Hoban was also a member of the Columbian Institute, founded in 1817.

In 1799 he married Susannah Sewell of Massachusetts, with whom he had ten children. She died in 1822. Hoban died several years later in Washington. His known works show him to have been a competent designer whose forte was his organizational ability to oversee and implement construction.

• The majority of surviving Hoban papers are in the National Archives and in the Office of the Architect of the Capitol. Biographical details of Hoban's life can be found in Martin I. J. Griffin, "James Hoban, the Architect and Builder of the White House," *American Catholic Historical Researches* 3, no. 1 (1907): 35–52. Recent studies include William Ryan and Desmond Guinness, *The White House: An Architectural History* (1980); William Seale, *The President's House: A History* (1986); and Egon Verheyen, "James Hoban's Design for the White House in the Context of the Planning of the Federal City," *Architectura* 11, no. 1 (1981): 66–82.

Pamela Scott

HOBART, Alice Tisdale (28 Jan. 1882–14 Mar. 1967), writer, was born Alice Nourse in Lockport, New York, the daughter of Edwin Henry Nourse, a musician and music teacher, and Harriet Augusta Beaman. Her family moved to Chicago when Alice was two, and she attended school in nearby Downer's Grove. She lost her mother when she was ten and her father when she was seventeen. At an early age she contracted spinal meningitis, later aggravated by a fall, and suffered pain for the rest of her life. She attended two semesters at Northwestern University but left to teach elementary school for a year, then worked as an organizer for the Young Women's Christian Association at Kansas State University for two years before resuming her formal education. She attended the University of Chicago from 1904 to 1907, but ill health forced her to withdraw without graduating.

She went to China in 1908 to visit her older sister Mary Nourse, a teacher in Hangchow, the capital of Chekiang province. After two years there she took an extended trip through Russia and Western Europe and returned to Hangchow to join her sister as a teacher. There she met Earle Tisdale Hobart, an executive with Standard Oil stationed in China. The two were married in Tientsin in 1914 and spent their honeymoon in Peking. They had no children. Earle Hobart's work took them to many areas, rural and urban, throughout the country, and Alice Hobart was exposed to a cross section of Chinese life as well as to the turmoil of the social revolution then taking place. She began to record her impressions around 1916 and reworked some of her letters home into a series of articles that were published in the *Atlantic Monthly*. These essays were later expanded into three books: *Pioneering Where the World Is Old: Leaves from a Manchurian Notebook* (1917), *By the City of the Long Sand: A Tale of New China* (1926), and *Within the Walls of Nanking* (1928).

The Hobarts were living in the Hunan capital of Changsha when that city fell to the Nationalists in 1927. They fled to Nanking, where Earle was made manager of his company's office. When Nanking was taken the next year, they lost their home and most of their belongings, including the manuscript of Alice's first novel, *Pidgin Cargo* (1929). It was providentially recovered by their Chinese houseboy and returned to its author. The Nationalist government expelled the foreign community that year, and Earle resigned from Standard Oil. The couple returned briefly to the United States before relocating in Germany, where Earle worked as the manager of an export company. In 1929 they went back to America and settled in Virginia, near Washington, D.C.

Alice Hobart's first novel, reissued as *River Supreme* in 1934, dealt with the beginnings of Western-style industrialization in China, describing an American entrepreneur's efforts at introducing steamboats to the Yangtse River. In 1933 she wrote her most popular book, *Oil for the Lamps of China*, the story of an idealistic young American mining engineer and his wife in China and their conflicts with both the large, impersonal company that employs him and the foreign culture in which they live. Described by the *Saturday Review of Literature* (21 Oct. 1933, p. 201) as "the most humanely vivid book on China since Pearl Buck gave us her 'Good Earth,'" it was a bestseller for two years and was made into a successful film in 1935 and again, as *Law of the Tropics*, in 1941.

In 1933 Hobart went to China alone to observe the changes in the country and returned to write *Yang and Yin* (1936), a philosophical novel contrasting the American goal of material progress with the Eastern ideal of harmony between opposing forces. *Their Own Country* (1940) is a sequel to *Oil for the Lamps of China*, portraying the young couple's return to America during the depression and their discovery of many of the same social and moral problems they had encountered in China. In 1935 Hobart and her husband moved to California, where she was able to indulge her lifelong passion for gardening. From her experience in growing grapes she wrote her first work set entirely in America, *The Cup and the Sword* (1942), a saga of three generations of vintners and the effects of Prohibition on the family business. It was made into a film as *This Earth Is Mine* in 1959.

Earle Hobart's knowledge of Eastern culture brought him a government assignment in India in 1942. Alice Hobart spent the next two years in Mexico, where she wrote *The Peacock Sheds His Tail* (1945). Another study of a family and its struggle to maintain its traditional values, it is a revealing account of social and economic change in Mexico. In *The Cleft Rock* (1948), a story of the exploitation of water rights in California's Central Valley, Hobart returned to the theme of the conflict between big business and the individual. She challenged the medical profession, with which her long personal experience of illness had made her intimately familiar, in *The Serpent-Wreathed Staff* (1951). Although admired for its critical examination of ethical questions, it was criticized as too cerebral. *Venture into Darkness* (1955), an account of an American businessman's attempt to rescue a compatriot from the Communist Chinese, took a strongly pro-Western political stand. Hobart's autobiography, *Gusty's Child* (1959), was praised for both its social philosophy and its personal insight. In her last book, *The Innocent Dreamer* (1963), a tale of interracial marriage in China, she once again contrasted Eastern and Western culture.

Hobart was criticized for diffuse plotting, pedestrian style, and solemn treatment of her material, but she was popular for her sympathetic spirit and her gift for vivid detail. The first American novelist to depict the Western business community in China, she was always a commercial success, and sales of her books in many languages exceeded 4 million by the time of her death in Oakland, California.

• Accounts of Hobart's life and work are in the *Wilson Bulletin*, Nov. 1933, p. 146; Henry R. Warfel, *American Novelists of Today* (1951); and her autobiography. Her first books are examined at length in Ruth Moore, *The Work of Alice Tisdale Hobart* (1940). See also the *New York World Telegram*, 5 Dec. 1942; the *New York Herald Tribune Book Review*, 7 Oct. 1951; and the *New York Times Book Review*, pt. 1, 11 Nov. 1951. An obituary is in the *New York Times*, 15 Mar. 1967.

DENNIS WEPMAN

HOBART, Garret Augustus (3 June 1844–21 Nov. 1899), vice president of the United States, was born in Long Branch, New Jersey, the son of Addison Willard Hobart, a schoolteacher, and Sophia Vandeveer. He attended local schools and graduated from Rutgers College in 1863. After teaching school briefly, he read law in the office of Socrates Tuttle in Paterson, New Jersey. He became a member of the New Jersey bar in 1866 and a law partner with Tuttle in 1869. He married Tuttle's daughter, Jennie, the same year. The couple had two children, a son and a daughter.

Hobart quickly became active in local politics. After serving as city counsel in Paterson in 1871, he was elected as a Republican to the New Jersey Assembly in 1872, was reelected twice and became Speaker in 1874. He went on to the state senate in 1876, was again reelected twice, and was president of the upper house during his last term.

As his political and business career prospered, Hobart moved into national Republican affairs as chair of the party's state committee from 1880 to 1891. He was chosen as a member of the Republican National Committee in 1884. That same year he made an unsuccessful bid for the U.S. Senate.

Hobart's business interests were diverse. He was on the board or held offices in sixty corporations. These included banks, water companies, electric utilities, and railroads. From 1895 to 1897, he was one of the three arbitrators resolving disputes among the railroads that formed the Joint Traffic Association.

In 1895 Hobart directed the Republican campaign that enabled his party to win the New Jersey governorship for the first time in thirty years. His role in helping to carry an important eastern state that the Democrats had long dominated gave Hobart visibility among national Republicans as the presidential election of 1896 approached. When the party chose William McKinley of Ohio as its presidential nominee, delegates felt a need to balance the ticket by selecting an eastern figure to go with McKinley's western affiliation. The vice presidency was first offered to Thomas B. Reed of Maine, and when he declined Hobart was designated. Hobart believed strongly in the gold standard, which was one of the central issues in the 1896 race. "The money standard of a great nation should be as fixed and permanent as the nation itself," he said in his letter of acceptance. He also proved an effective fund-raiser in the East among corporations fearful of William Jennings Bryan and the Democrats.

After McKinley's victory, Hobart and his wife purchased a home in Washington close to the White House, where they expected to carry on the social activities assigned in those days to the vice president. Because of the physical infirmities of Mrs. McKinley, Jennie Hobart often stood in for her as a White House hostess. The Hobarts also surmounted a small protocol crisis when in 1897 the vice president successfully asserted his precedence at social gatherings over the British ambassador.

Relations between President McKinley and Hobart were very close, and the two men often consulted about foreign and domestic policy. Hobart played an important part in relations with Congress during the weeks before the outbreak of the war with Spain in 1898, when he acted as a quiet, behind-the-scenes negotiator for the administration in steering Congress toward intervention in Cuba along lines that the president approved. Hobart brought his friend John William Griggs into the cabinet as attorney general in 1898 and secured other patronage appointments from the president for New Jersey allies. During the battle over the peace treaty with Spain in February 1899, a resolution in the Senate in favor of Philippine independence resulted in a tie vote. Vice President Hobart cast the deciding vote against the proposal.

By early 1899 Hobart's health had begun to fail, and he returned to New Jersey to convalesce. During the summer the issue of replacing Secretary of War Russell A. Alger was before the administration. The secretary visited Hobart at his New Jersey home and learned that the president wanted him to resign. It was Hobart's last act for the McKinley administration. During the rest of the year Hobart gradually weakened, and he died of heart disease in Paterson, New Jersey. Hobart's death opened the way for a new vice president to be chosen in 1900, with the resulting boost to the fortunes of Theodore Roosevelt (1858–1919). Despite the historical obscurity into which he has fallen, Hobart was a successful vice president who played a significant role in the McKinley administration.

• No large collection of Hobart's papers appears to have survived. There are small collections of his letters at the New Jersey Historical Society in Trenton and other documents related to his life in collections such as the McDowell Family Papers at the Historical Society. His role in the McKinley administration is covered in the McKinley and George B. Cortelyou papers at the Library of Congress. There are some letters from him in the Russell A. Alger Papers, William L. Clements Library, University of Michigan. The only biography is David Magie, *Life of Garret Augustus Hobart* (1910). *Memories, by Mrs. Garret A. Hobart* (1930), is an engaging memoir. The *Official Proceedings of the Eleventh Republican National Convention, 1896* (1896) contains Hobart's official acceptance of the vice presidential nomination. W. E. Sackett, *Modern Battles of Trenton* (1914), provides a New Jersey perspective on Hobart's career. "Vice President Hobart," *Public Opinion,* 9 Nov. 1899, p. 581, and "Death of Vice President Hobart," *Literary Digest,* 2 Dec. 1899, pp. 669–70, describe his final illness. *New York Tribune,* 22 Nov. 1899, is an excellent obituary.

LEWIS L. GOULD

HOBART, George V. (16 Jan. 1867–31 Jan. 1926), playwright and librettist, was born George Vear Hobart Philpot in Ship Harbour (now Port Hawkesbury), Nova Scotia, Canada, the son of Angus Philpot, a mar-

iner carpenter, and Amelia (maiden name unknown). George apparently received no more than a high school education. He worked for a time as a cable operator in Newfoundland but eventually sought an opportunity to escape the severely cold weather. He had published small comic articles in local papers, and he sent samples of his work to American newspapers. His writings were accepted, and Hobart initially moved to Cumberland, Maryland, in 1895 to run the *Sunday Scimitar.* The following year he went to Baltimore, working first for the *Morning Herald* and then as sporting editor for the *Baltimore News.* He later wrote humorous pieces for the *Baltimore American.* Hobart earned a certain celebrity for his "Dinkelspiel" and "John Henry" stories. (The latter he eventually turned into a farce and then into a musical comedy, but both productions failed.) In 1897 Hobart married Sarah De Vries of Cumberland; they had two children.

New York playgoers probably first came across Hobart's name in a playbill when he was listed as librettist of the 1897 musical *Miss Manhattan.* The show was not a major success, but it taught Hobart that even a middling Broadway hit paid better than most journalism jobs and that musicals were usually more remunerative than straight plays. Both alone and with collaborators, he served as librettist and/or lyricist for popular shows such as *Broadway to Tokio* (1900), *The Wild Rose* (1902), *Sally in Our Alley* (1902), *The Ham Tree* (1905), *The Boys and Betty* (1908), *Old Dutch* (1909), and *Buddies* (1919). He also contributed sketches and lyrics to revues, including numerous editions of famous annuals such as the *Ziegfeld Follies,* the *Greenwich Village Follies,* and *Hitchy-Koo.* Hobart's nonmusical collaborations include *Wildfire* (1908), the story of a beautiful woman who becomes the reluctant owner of a famous stable, which he wrote with George Broadhurst as a vehicle for Lillian Russell; and *Our Mrs. Chesney* (1915), which recounts the misadventures of a traveling saleswoman and which he wrote with Edna Ferber for Ethel Barrymore. Hobart's most unusual and most celebrated work is *Experience* (1914), an allegorical morality play centering on the trials and tribulations of the hero, Youth. To everyone's amazement, including Hobart's, this offbeat show had a tremendously successful eight-month run in New York. Perhaps wisely regarding its success as a freak, he never tried to write a second similar work, but he did name the mansion he built in Greenwich, Connecticut, with profits from the show "Xperience Court." Hobart directed many of his own works and those of others and was a respected doctor of other playwrights' efforts.

In later years Hobart also worked on film screenplays, including that for *The White Sister* (1923), a very popular melodrama starring Lillian Gish and Ronald Colman. Hobart died of heart and kidney failure while visiting Cumberland, Maryland.

• No collection of Hobart's personal papers is known to exist, and his biography has yet to be published. An obituary is in the *New York Times,* 1 Feb. 1926.

GERALD BORDMAN

HOBART, John Henry (14 Sept. 1775–12 Sept. 1830), Protestant Episcopal bishop and author, was born in Philadelphia, Pennsylvania, the son of Enoch Hobart, a commander of a merchant ship, and Hannah Pratt. Hobart, whose father died when he was one year old, was reared by his mother, who also began his education at home. After attending a number of schools, including the Episcopal Academy of Philadelphia under the direction of John Andrews, he entered the College and Academy of Philadelphia (now the University of Pennsylvania) in 1788. In 1791 he transferred to the College of New Jersey (now Princeton University) and received a B.A. in 1793. After a short essay in a counting house he accepted a position as tutor at the College of New Jersey in 1795. He served as tutor between 1796 and 1798 and received the A.M. degree in 1796. During this time he also did extensive reading in Anglican theology under the direction of William White (1748–1836), bishop of Pennsylvania. On 3 June 1798 he was ordained deacon by White and was ordained priest by Samuel Provoost in 1801. In 1800 he married Mary Goodin Chandler, daughter of the Anglican missionary clergyman Thomas Bradbury Chandler; they had seven children.

Hobart's rise in the Episcopal church was rapid, owing both to his energy and talent and to the depressed state of his church in the decades after the American Revolution. After serving congregations in Oxford and Perkiomen, Pennsylvania, New Brunswick, New Jersey, and Hempstead, New York, between 1798 and 1801, he was chosen as assistant minister of Trinity Church, New York City, at the time the most important parish in the Episcopal church in the United States. There, in addition to his clerical duties, he involved himself in numerous church organizations such as the Protestant Episcopal Society for Promotion of Religion and Learning, the Protestant Episcopal Theological Society, and the New York Protestant Episcopal Bible and Common Prayer Book Society. He was also secretary to the House of Bishops and on the Board of Trustees of Columbia College. In 1811 he was elected assistant bishop of the diocese of New York to aid the ailing Benjamin Moore, and in 1816 he was made bishop of the diocese as well as rector of Trinity Church. From 1811 to 1815 he also had episcopal responsibility for the diocese of New Jersey, and between 1816 and 1819 he was provisional bishop of the diocese of Connecticut.

Hobart was only thirty-six years old when he was elected assistant bishop (so young that he occasionally powdered his hair to look more distinguished), and he breathed new vitality into the office. He traversed his almost 50,000-square-mile diocese in a way no American Episcopal bishop—indeed no Anglican bishop—had ever attempted. At times he traveled between 4,000 and 5,000 miles a year in his episcopal visitations, and through his labors the Episcopal church increased almost eightfold. He was known as a vigorous preacher who usually spoke without notes. Hobart also rejuvenated the role of bishop as teacher. His annual episcopal addresses transcended the usual brief chronicling of official activities and became extended discussions of the state of the diocese. He inaugurated the use of formal pastoral charges on the diocesan level to instruct on key issues. He was dedicated to the idea of education and labored to establish the General Theological Seminary for the training of Episcopal clergy, founded in 1817 and after 1821 located permanently in New York City.

Hobart gained great fame and notoriety as an apologist for the high church vision of the Episcopal church, and during the early decades of the nineteenth century he was the leading advocate of this position. He described this vision as "evangelical truth apostolic order." In numerous books, sermons, and tracts he argued that the true church must be governed by bishops who were part of an unbroken succession from the apostles. This claim involved him in numerous controversies, the most famous being the "*Albany Centinel* controversy" of 1805–1808, which pitted him and his supporters against defenders of Presbyterianism, including the intellectual historian Samuel Miller (1769–1850). A product of this debate was Hobart's most famous theological treatise, *An Apology for Apostolic Order and Its Advocates* (1807). He also set forth his theology in his works *The Churchman* (1819) and *The High Churchman Vindicated* (1826). Hobart's exclusive ecclesiology provoked opposition within his own denomination as well, particularly on account of his unwillingness to participate in the American Bible Society. This precipitated a tract controversy with the noted jurist and Episcopal layman William Jay (1789–1858). Hobart attempted to instill his high church vision within his diocese, and his episcopacy was marked by a number of conflicts with Episcopalians sympathetic toward Protestant evangelicalism.

Hobart was known for his many works of devotion and catechesis, including *A Companion for the Altar* (1804) and *A Companion for the Festivals and Fasts of the Protestant Episcopal Church* (1805). Some of these volumes were based on earlier English works, but Hobart reworked them to set forth Episcopal piety and devotion in contrast with current Protestant practices.

For years Hobart suffered from dyspepsia, and in 1822–1823 his health deteriorated. As a result he journeyed to Europe for two years (1823–1825), visiting Britain, France, Switzerland, and Italy. In Britain he became a celebrated figure among many of the high church clergy of the Church of England, and some have claimed that he indirectly influenced the rise of the later Oxford movement. After his return to the United States he continued in his active ministry, and while on a missionary journey he became ill and died in Auburn, New York.

Hobart's career and ministry, though controversial, has been credited with rejuvenating the Episcopal church in the early nineteenth century and revitalizing an interest in a distinctive Episcopal theology and vision. A number of his younger associates, including Henry U. Onderdonk, Levi S. Ives, and George Washington Doane, later became bishops.

• Hobart's correspondence can be found in the Archives of the Episcopal Church, Austin, Tex., and in the New-York Historical Society. There are two main collections of Hobart's sermons, *The Posthumous Works of the Late Right Reverend John Henry Hobart* (3 vols., 1832–1833) and *Sermons on the Principal Events and Truths of Redemption* (2 vols., 1824). His other works include *The Clergyman's Companion* (1806), *The Origin, the General Character, and Present Situation of the Protestant Episcopal Church in the United States of America* (1814), and *The State of the Departed* (1816). Some of his correspondence has been published in Arthur Lowndes, ed., *Archives of the General Convention: The Correspondence of John Henry Hobart* (6 vols., 1911–1912). The most complete biography is still John McVic[k]ar, *The Early Life and Professional Years of Bishop Hobart* (1838). The best modern treatments of Hobart's thought are E. C. Chorley, *Men and Movements in the American Episcopal Church* (1946), and R. B. Mullin, *Episcopal Vision/American Reality: High Church Theology and Social Thought in Evangelical America* (1986).

ROBERT BRUCE MULLIN

HOBART, John Sloss (6 May 1738–4 Feb. 1805), revolutionary committeeman and justice of the New York state supreme court, was born in Fairfield, Connecticut, the son of Rev. Noah Hobart and Ellen Sloss. After graduation from Yale College (1757) he resided in New York City. There he married Mary Greenill (Grinnell) (d. 1803) in 1764 and moved to the manor of "Eaton's Neck," Long Island, which he had inherited from his mother's family. In 1765 Hobart was a member of the Sons of Liberty in Huntington, Suffolk County, and served as justice of the peace. In 1774 he was a member of the town and county committees of correspondence. He served in the four New York provincial congresses from May 1775 through May 1777. Hobart was an active participant in the last congress, called the "Convention," served on several of its committees, and contributed proposals to the state constitution. In April 1777 he was one of six committeemen assigned to prepare a draft of the document. He also was a member of the state council of safety. In May 1777, even though he admitted "not having been educated in the profession of the law," Hobart was appointed one of two associate justices of the state supreme court, serving with Abraham Yates under Chief Justice John Jay (1745–1829). Chancellor James Kent posthumously applauded Hobart's efforts as a jurist, remembering him as "a faithful, diligent and discerning judge during the time he remained on the bench."

In August 1775 the second provincial congress placed Hobart on a committee to create the revolutionary militia for Suffolk County. Six months later he served on a committee to apprehend Loyalists. In June 1776 he was granted permission to return home to secure his cattle from the British and was an envoy to General Nathaniel Woodhull and other military commanders on the island. He arrived there just after the battle of Long Island and found Suffolk revolutionaries in disarray. Hobart helped evacuate his family and other revolutionaries to southern New England. Later he was involved in unsuccessful attempts to attack the British on the north shore of Long Island and obtain provisions in privateers' raids. Hobart served on the sixteen-member committee that acted as the state-appointed temporary government for the Southern District; this committee was empowered to act until the British evacuated the region.

The wartime destruction of Hobart's estate severely undercut the economic base for his gentlemanly situation, but he retained his social prominence. From then until his death he lived on the salaries of offices he held. He supported the move to strengthen the Articles of Confederation and was a delegate to the 1786 Annapolis convention. In 1788 he served as a Federalist in New York ratifying convention held in Poughkeepsie and developed a close friendship with John Jay. At this time Hobart sold the Eaton's Neck manor and moved to New York City, where he invested in a few pieces of urban property and bought a farm on Throgg's Neck, on the south shore of the Bronx on Long Island Sound. Hobart remained on the state bench for almost twenty-one years, until January 1798. When Philip Schuyler resigned from the U.S. Senate, Hobart was chosen by the state legislature to serve in his place. He was a Federalist senator only from 11 January to 16 April 1798, resigning to become a U.S. judge for the New York District, probably because the costs of his legislative office, which required that he maintain a temporary residence at the national capital, were more than he could afford. Also, he possessed a judicial temperament and probably disliked the tumble of politics during the undeclared naval war with France. Hobart served on the federal bench until his death in New York State.

John Sloss Hobart was a typical politically active revolutionary whose labors made the new nation possible, although he was economically ruined by the fortunes of war. Hobart served on prewar committees and helped to form the New York state government as a highly respected layman in a sea of lawyers. A successful state legislator and Federalist, Hobart served for over a generation as a New York and a federal judge when common sense and integrity were prized as much as legal training.

• L. John Tooker, "John Sloss Hobart," *Long Island Forum*, Jan. 1952, pp. 9 and 15, is a brief exposition of his life. Mary Voyse, *John Sloss Hobart, Forgotten Patriot* (1959), is a longer biographical sketch that reconstructs Hobart's life from scattered letters, documents, and reminiscences. A discussion of Hobart's membership in the Sons of Liberty appears in Carl Lotus Becker, *The History of Political Parties in the Province of New York, 1760–1776*, 2d printing (1960), p. 46, n. 95. Also useful are F. B. Dexter, *Biographical Sketches of Graduates of Yale College*, vol. 2 (1896); J. D. Hammond, *The History of Political Parties in the State of New York*, vol. 1 (1842); F. G. Mather, *Refugees of 1776 from Long Island to Connecticut* (1913); and U.S. Congress, Senate, *Biographical Dictionary of the American Congress, 1774–1971*, 92d Cong., 1st sess., 1971, S. Doc. 92–8, p. 1126.

EUGENE R. FINGERHUT

HOBBS, William Herbert (2 July 1864–1 Jan. 1953), geologist, was born in Worcester, Massachusetts, the son of Horace Hobbs, a grocer and later a dairy farmer, and Mary Paine Parker. His mother died when he was a year old, and his father and stepmother encouraged his academic pursuits. At Worcester Academy he became interested in industrial design because of his talent for drawing. Hobbs attended Worcester Free Institute of Industry and Design (later Worcester Polytechnic Institute) and in 1883 was its youngest recipient of the B.S. degree to that time. For the next year he taught in local schools. He then entered Johns Hopkins University for graduate work in chemistry, but he was diverted to geology by the mineralogist George Huntington Williams. Hobbs spent the summer of 1886 doing geologic fieldwork in New England with Raphael Pumpelly; his return to Johns Hopkins was delayed by the extended field season, and he studied instead for two terms at Harvard under Nathaniel Southgate Shaler. Back at Johns Hopkins, Hobbs received both an A.M. and a Ph.D. in geology in 1888. He spent the next year in Europe, primarily at the University of Heidelberg; he also visited other countries to observe the geology.

In 1889 Hobbs became instructor in mineralogy and metallurgy and curator of the geological museum at the University of Wisconsin. He advanced to professor the next year and to professor in 1900. In addition to teaching, he edited the *Transactions of the Wisconsin Academy of Science* and the *Bulletin of the University of Wisconsin* from 1900 to 1905. His publications were chiefly on geologic structure, faults, diamond sites in the United States, and tungsten deposits. Through appointments from the U.S. Geological Survey, he continued to spend his summers doing fieldwork in New England until 1906. His summary of the fault pattern in Connecticut, "The Newark System of the Pomperaug Valley" (*Twenty-first Annual Report of U.S. Geological Survey for 1900*, pt. 3, 1901, pp. 1–162), was contested by some geologists, but Hobbs's conclusions were verified by the director of the USGS, George Otis Smith. Hobbs married Sara Kimball Sale in 1896; they had one daughter.

Having become more interested in structural geology than in mineralogy, Hobbs spent a sabbatical year (1905–1906) in Europe and Morocco. Arriving in Italy following an earthquake in Calabria, he concluded that there were many intersecting subsurface lines that caused shocks, where one crossed another (*Earthquakes: An Introduction to Seismic Geology*, 1907), an idea that was not accepted by others. He also observed an eruption of Mount Vesuvius and studied glaciers in the Swiss Alps.

During his year abroad, Hobbs resigned from the University of Wisconsin. In 1906 he accepted a position as professor of geology at the University of Michigan, where geology, previously taught solely by Israel Cook Russell, was a separate department from mineralogy. Called "an unusually able administrator" by his biographer George D. Hubbard (p. 522), during his twenty-eight years as chairman Hobbs increased the faculty to ten, and the student enrollment in geology courses increased almost tenfold to more than a thousand annually. Students found him inspiring in class, a person of "infectious and unquenchable enthusiasm" (Gould, p. 134). Hobbs brought the geographer Carl O. Sauer to the University of Michigan in 1915 and urged that geography be established as a separate department, which took place in 1923.

Hobbs's interest in glaciers continued during several summer trips to Europe and led him to an interest in polar exploration. He severely denounced Frederick A. Cook's claim in 1909 that he had reached the North Pole a year before Robert Edwin Peary. From 1926 to 1928 Hobbs organized and led three privately funded expeditions by himself and students of the University of Michigan to Greenland, as recounted in his book *Exploring about the North Pole of the Winds* (1930). He recognized that very fine soil was deposited on outwash areas from glaciers and that this was later carried by winds far from its source to fall as loess deposits. He had proposed that the presence of the ice cap was responsible for atmospheric circulation in the Northern Hemisphere (*The Glacial Anticyclones, the Poles of the Atmospheric Circulation*, 1926), and his group traced air currents with meteorological balloons; however, his concept of the cause of this circulation was not widely accepted. His establishment of an airfield at his Greenland base camp led to his recommendation that air defense fields be established there as World War II approached; this was done.

In 1921 Hobbs visited many western Pacific islands, including some under Japanese mandate, traveling on Japanese navy ships, a tour summarized in *Cruises along By-Ways of the Pacific* (1923). His interest was in the nature of island arcs, which he considered sources of future mountain ranges. During World War II his photographs of some rarely visited islands were useful to the U.S. military.

After reaching emeritus status in 1934, Hobbs wrote a biography, *Peary* (1936), and devoted time to the history of antarctic exploration. He dismayed his British colleagues by insisting that the American sealer Nathaniel Brown Palmer had first sighted Antarctica, rather than the Britons Edward Bransfield and James Weddell. In other studies of early explorers, Hobbs concluded that Antonio Zeno of Venice had reached Nova Scotia in 1390 ("The Fourteenth Century Discovery of America by Antonio Zeno," *Scientific Monthly* 72 [1951]: 24–31).

Hobbs was an intense patriot with strong political opinions. He enjoyed arguments in person and in print, often writing letters to newspapers. He published about four hundred articles and fifteen books, including his autobiography, *An Explorer-Scientist's Pilgrimage* (1952). Although some of his geologic ideas were not fully accepted, he encouraged students to find their own solutions. Hobbs participated in many international meetings, where he relished acquaintance with explorers and well-known scientists. Students and colleagues gave Hobbs's name to five glaciers, three mountains, and an area of coastal Antarctica. He died in Ann Arbor, Michigan.

• Hobbs's personal correspondence and manuscripts are at the University of Michigan. Biographies are J. D. M. Blyth, "Prof. W. H. Hobbs," *Nature* 171 (1953): 416–17; George D. Hubbard, "William Herbert Hobbs: 1864–1953," *Science* 117 (1953): 521–22; Laurence M. Gould, "Memorial to William Herbert Hobbs (1864–1953)," *Geological Society of America Proceedings, Annual Report for 1953* (1954), pp. 131–40; and Harley H. Bartlett, "William Herbert Hobbs (1864–1953)," *American Philosophical Society Yearbook 1955* (1956), pp. 442–60. An obituary is in the *Detroit News*, 4 Feb. 1953.

ELIZABETH NOBLE SHOR

HOBBY, William Pettus (26 Mar. 1878–7 June 1964), newspaper publisher and governor, was born in Moscow, Texas, the son of Edwin E. Hobby, a state senator and district judge, and Eudora Adeline Pettus. The family lived in Livingston, Texas, until 1893 when they moved to Houston. Hobby quit school in 1895 to work as a circulation clerk for the Houston *Post*, where one of his co-workers was William Sydney Porter (O. Henry). Soon Hobby was covering the growing business community in Houston. He was promoted to city editor in 1902 and in 1905 to managing editor. In 1907 he became publisher of the Beaumont *Enterprise*.

Hobby plunged into the turbulent politics of the Democratic party in Texas. He identified with the conservative, antiprohibition wing of the party and was a strong supporter of Senator Joseph Weldon Bailey. He organized a young Democrats club in Houston and served as secretary of the State Democratic Executive Committee in 1904. In 1914 Hobby announced his candidacy for lieutenant governor, running as an opponent of liquor control and advocate of relief for tenant farmers. Aided by the gubernatorial candidacy of James E. Ferguson, who rallied antiprohibition voters, Hobby was easily elected. In 1915 he married Willie Cooper, the daughter of a Democratic congressman; they had no children.

Hobby had an uneventful first term and was reelected in 1916. After Ferguson was impeached in 1917 because of accusations that he had interfered in the administration of the University of Texas, mismanaged state funds, and accepted a large loan from an unknown source, Hobby became governor for the remainder of Ferguson's two-year term. To win election in 1918, Hobby had to overcome his previous alliance with antiprohibition forces and win the support of the dry leaders who had orchestrated Ferguson's ouster.

Hobby proved to be a skillful political operator. He aligned his administration with support for U.S. involvement in World War I and argued that regulation of alcohol was necessary to protect soldiers from unhealthy influences during their training. He cooperated with the Wilson administration in running the draft in Texas. He also organized opposition to Ferguson, who sought reelection even though the impeachment judgment barred him from running again.

Hobby called a special session of the legislature in late February 1918 to push through his program. The lawmakers passed measures to regulate the sale of alcohol around military bases and to bar its consumption in the rest of the state. They also enacted Hobby's bills mandating a run-off or majority election in the Democratic primary and allowing women to vote in these contests. The reform legislation of the special session convinced the drys, women, and other progressive reformers among Texas Democrats that Hobby was the best choice to head off a Ferguson comeback in the party primary. Ferguson launched a free-swinging campaign in which he attacked Hobby as a latecomer to the prohibition cause and denounced the friends of the University of Texas. Hobby supporters feared that he would be no match for the magnetic Ferguson.

Hobby found a winning strategy in the issue of patriotism, assailing Ferguson for undermining the war effort because of his ties with the brewing industry. The Hobby campaign charged that a $156,000 loan to Ferguson, the source of which he had refused to disclose during his impeachment proceedings, must have come from German agents and the Kaiser. A coalition of women voters, drys, and progressives swept Hobby to victory in the Democratic primary of July 1918. Victory in the general election was a foregone conclusion in heavily Democratic Texas.

During his second term, Hobby faced problems arising after the end of World War I, including a drought in the western part of the state and an infestation of the pink bollworm that threatened the cotton crop. Public education in the state confronted low teacher salaries, underfunding of rural schools, and an inadequate revenue base. Hobby's administration made a start on dealing with these issues. A dockworkers strike in Galveston in 1920 brought Hobby national attention when he declared martial law in the city. Regulation of the state's oil and gas industry, under the Texas Railroad Commission, also came during Hobby's tenure. As governor, Hobby embodied a "business progressivism" that mixed the application of methods from the private sector to the operation of state government with a mild and cautious approach toward education, public health, and regulation of business.

Hobby left office in 1921 and returned to the newspaper business in Beaumont. In 1924 his friend Ross Sterling persuaded him to become president of the Houston *Post-Dispatch*. Hobby guided the fortunes of the newspaper during the 1920s and into the 1930s as the city prospered. In 1931, two years after the death of his first wife, he married Oveta Culp; they had two children. Oveta Hobby worked with her husband at the *Post*; at the time of his death she had become president and editor. She headed the Women's Army Corps (WACs) during World War II and later served in President Dwight D. Eisenhower's cabinet as secretary of health, education, and welfare.

Hobby became the owner of the *Post* in 1939 and also presided over its television and radio holdings. By 1937 he had broken with the New Deal and President

Franklin D. Roosevelt over the president's campaign to reshape the U.S. Supreme Court in a more liberal direction. The *Post* endorsed Wendell Willkie in 1940. In 1952 the Hobbys campaigned enthusiastically for Eisenhower. During the last decades of his life, Hobby was a key supporter of the conservative trend among Texas Democrats that led to the growth of the Republican party during the 1950s. After undergoing surgery in 1957 for a hemorrhaging ulcer, Hobby's health declined. He died in Houston.

• Hobby's papers as governor are in the Archives Division of the Texas State Library, Austin. The papers of Joseph Weldon Bailey and Thomas B. Love, at the Dallas Historical Society; Will C. Hogg and M. M. Crane, at the Center for American History, University of Texas at Austin; and Lyndon Johnson, at the Lyndon B. Johnson Presidential Library, contain some relevant materials. James A. Clark, with Weldon Hart, *The Tactful Texan: A Biography of Governor Will Hobby* (1958), is the only biography. Nancy C. Beck, "The Origins of Business Progressivism in Texas: William Pettus Hobby and the 1918 Gubernatorial Election" (master's report, Univ. of Texas at Austin, 1989), examines the key election in Hobby's career. For the background on Hobby's governorship, see Lewis L. Gould, *Progressives and Prohibitionists: Texas Democrats in the Wilson Era* (1973), and Norman D. Brown, *Hood, Bonnet, and Little Brown Jug: Texas Politics, 1921–1928* (1984). See also, William P. Hobby, Jr., "William Pettus Hobby," in *The Handbook of Texas*, vol. 3, ed. Eldon Branda (1976), p. 396. Obituaries are in the *Congressional Record*, 23 June 1964, pp. 1740–48.

LEWIS L. GOULD

HOBSON, Laura Keane Zametkin (19 June 1900–28 Feb. 1986), writer, was born in New York City, the daughter of Michael Zametkin, a labor organizer and Yiddish-language newspaper editor, and Adella Kean, a Yiddish-language newspaper columnist. Hobson's father was a Russian-Jewish immigrant, a central figure in the world of progressive politics based in New York, as well as in the national network created by the foreign-language press. As both a liberal and a fiction writer, she took a different direction from her father, yet he remained a formative influence on her career as a socially engaged writer.

After graduating from Cornell University in 1921, Hobson worked in New York as an advertising copywriter and subsequently as a journalist, first for the *New York Evening Post* and then for *Time*, *Life*, and *Fortune* magazines. Her first experience as a fiction writer was on the two pulp western novels she coauthored in 1933 and 1934 with her husband, publisher Thayer Hobson, whom she had married in 1930, under the joint pseudonym "Peter Field." Even after she began writing mainstream fiction under her own name, Hobson continued to take intermittent magazine and copywriting jobs, until her first bestseller was published. The impact—for better or for worse—of these other forms of writing may be observed in Hobson's fiction.

Hobson and her husband were divorced in 1935. In the late 1930s, as a single parent, Hobson adopted a son, Michael. She found herself unexpectedly pregnant a few years later, at the age of forty by a man whose identity she never revealed. To avoid public acknowledgment that she was an unwed mother, she went into seclusion for the later months of her pregnancy and gave birth to her son Christopher in secret. She then formally adopted him as if he were a child provided, as Michael had been, by the adoption agency.

It was when she was the mother of two small children that Hobson published her first work of fiction, a children's book called *A Dog of His Own* (1941). Her first adult novel, *The Trespassers* (1943), centers on a political question, the challenge to immigration quotas for refugees from Hitler's Europe and its impact on the love affair of a man and a woman who take different sides in the conflict over U.S. policy on the matter.

The Trespassers began a pattern that Hobson was to follow in her other social-problem novels: the real victims of the injustices she addresses in these novels are never her protagonists. Rather, the central figure is typically someone who takes on another person's fight, usually with a growing realization that what appears to be the oppression of one particular group actually engages us all. Hobson's most successful novel, *Gentleman's Agreement* (1947), typifies this approach. The theme of the novel and its Academy Award–winning film adaptation is the survival of anti-Semitism in postwar America, and its hero is not a Jew but a Gentile journalist who learns about and combats the prejudice by pretending to be Jewish.

Hobson's tendency to place her most important characters outside the causes she is advocating coexists with a strong autobiographical strain in her fiction. *First Papers* (1964) is the story of an immigrant family much like Hobson's own, centering on the parents' public careers—especially that of the father, who is a socialist editor for Yiddish newspapers—and the education of the daughter of the family, who is in college by the end of the narrative. *The Tenth Month* (1971) is a fictionalized version of Hobson's decision to bear a child out of wedlock and proceed to adopt him. By moving her story of an unplanned single pregnancy to 1968 and incorporating a number of contemporary events—the Columbia University strike and the assassinations of Martin Luther King and Robert Kennedy—Hobson makes the solution she worked out for herself in 1940 into something of an anachronism. Similarly, Hobson confronted the question of her son Christopher's homosexuality in the late 1950s, but her *Consenting Adult* (1975), which deals with a mother's coming to terms with having and loving a gay son, was not written until there was a large and active gay liberation movement.

Hobson's ability to invest social causes with human interest won her a wide readership. In addition to the enormously popular *Gentleman's Agreement*, *First Papers*, *The Tenth Month*, and *Consenting Adult* were all commercial successes; both *The Tenth Month* and *Consenting Adult* were made into TV movies, in 1979 and 1985, respectively. Hobson's fiction served to introduce a mass audience to issues that were already public but were discussed principally by members of the groups affected or by progressive activists. The popularization of such issues remains her principal contribution to American life and letters.

Like many bestselling authors, Hobson won mixed reviews from critics, who admired her ability to breathe life into the problems of contemporary society but disliked her overwritten style and distrusted her popularity itself.

Hobson was a lifelong liberal, involved in speaking on behalf of and otherwise publicizing social justice causes, as well as making them the subjects of her fiction. In the Cold War period, she opposed the McCarthy witch-hunts, but selectively, since she herself was extremely anti-Communist. Her attacks on Soviet policy and its U.S. exponents led to a decade-long estrangement from her left-wing sister and brother-in-law, Alice and Milton Milvey.

Hobson had many close friends and lovers and claimed to have been engaged, for a time in the late 1930s, to Ralph M. Ingersoll, publisher of the left-liberal newspaper *PM.* She remained physically active, jogging and bicycling in Central Park well into her eighties. She stayed professionally active in old age as well, beginning to write her memoirs when she was eighty-one. The first volume, *Laura Z: A Life*, appeared in 1983. She was at work on the sequel when she died in New York City. This unfinished volume was published later in 1986 under the title *Laura Z: The Early Years and Years of Fulfillment*, with commentary by her son Christopher.

• In addition to those works already mentioned, Hobson's major publications include *The Other Father* (1950), *The Celebrity* (1951), *I'm Going to Have a Baby* (1967), *Over and Above* (1979), and *Untold Millions* (1982).

LILLIAN S. ROBINSON

HOBSON, Richmond Pearson (17 Aug. 1870–16 Mar. 1937), naval officer and congressman, was born in Greensboro, Alabama, the son of James Marcellus Hobson, a lawyer, and Sarah Croom Pearson. He received an appointment to the U.S. Naval Academy at Annapolis in May 1885. The youngest member of his class, he was put "in Coventry" (ostracism via the silent treatment) by his classmates for placing some of them on report and spent the balance of his second- and all of his first-class years under the ban. Never lower than third academically, he graduated in 1889 first in his class. The ostracism was to cast a long shadow on the active naval career of one who, in his own words, "*had* to be first and . . . *had* to carry out his resolves."

Following his midshipman's cruise aboard the USS *Chicago* in the Mediterranean and South Atlantic (July 1889–Oct. 1890), Hobson was offered the opportunity to study naval architecture abroad. He spent the next three years in Paris, France, first attending the *École National-Superieur des Mines* (1890–1891) and then the *École d'Application du Génie Maritime* (1891–1893). Returning to the United States, he served with the Bu-

reau of Construction and Repair for eighteen months. In the summer of 1895 Hobson was detailed to the armored cruiser *New York,* the flagship of the North Atlantic Squadron, following his suggestion that naval constructors be permitted sea duty, the better to observe vessel performance. He served at the Brooklyn Navy Yard (1895–1896) and subsequently at Newport News (1896–1897). In the spring of 1897 he ran afoul of Naval Constructor Joseph J. Woodward, who accused him of neglect of duty because some defective metal castings had passed his inspection. Hobson defended himself in a 47-page memorandum addressed to Secretary of the Navy John Davis Long and received vindication at the hands of Acting Secretary Theodore Roosevelt (1858–1919).

Hobson's suggestion that a three-year, postgraduate course in naval construction be established at Annapolis was approved in 1897. Hobson himself designed the program and was selected to run it. He let it be known that he wanted to transfer from a staff to a line position and be assigned duty afloat should war loom, as it did with Spain following the destruction of the USS *Maine* in Havana Harbor early in 1898. Hobson was permitted to take his students to join the North Atlantic Squadron at Key West, Florida. He was aboard the USS *New York,* Admiral William T. Sampson's flagship, when the conflict began.

Sampson established a blockade of Santiago de Cuba, where Admiral Pascual Cervera's squadron had sought refuge. His plan to sink the collier *Merrimac* in the entrance was designed to bottle up Cervera until the arrival of the army expeditionary force could compel the surrender of both the town and the squadron. Hobson and a carefully selected crew took the *Merrimac* in during the early morning of 3 June. The attempt miscarried when the vessel's rudder was shot away and explosive charges rigged on the hull failed to detonate. Captured by the Spanish, Hobson and his associates later were exchanged under cartel. The exploit lost nothing in the retelling and made Hobson a national hero. Hobson's picture appeared in virtually every paper and magazine; correspondents and reporters vied with each other to find new adjectives to describe the act of "splendid daring and magnificent courage" he and his men had performed. His account of the venture was serialized in *Century Magazine* (Dec. 1898–Mar. 1899).

Appointed inspector of Spanish wrecks, he succeeded in raising the *Reina Mercedes* (which later became the station ship at Annapolis) and the *Infanta Maria Teresa*. His next posting was to the Far East, where he supervised the reconstruction of the former Spanish gunboats *Isla de Cuba, Isla de Luzon,* and *Don Juan de Austria* at Hong Kong. As a result of some of the adulation he had received stateside, he endured another spell "in Coventry" at the hands of his fellow officers.

While stationed at the Cavite Naval Yard in the Philippines, he began to suffer from inflammation of the retina. Seeing this condition as career threatening if he remained a contractor in the navy, upon his return to the states in September 1900 he began to wage a campaign for a medical discharge. In February 1901 a joint resolution of Congress (introduced in June 1898) was approved, formally thanking Hobson for his *Merrimac* exploit and authorizing his promotion. He was advanced three grades from lieutenant to captain, becoming the youngest man ever to achieve captain's rank in the navy, and was advanced ten numbers on the seniority list in the Construction Corps. This undoubtedly earned him a fresh helping of enmity, especially within the Construction Corps. A posting to the Brooklyn Navy Yard was followed by a brief stint (May-June 1902) as superintendent of naval construction at the Crescent shipyard in Elizabeth, New Jersey. His request for a medical discharge refused, he reluctantly resigned his commission on 6 February 1903.

Hobson's heroic public image, his oratorical skills, and his concern for the nation's naval strength made it easy for him to undertake a series of lecture tours in 1903 and 1904. He began to consider seriously a political career. In 1904 he challenged longtime incumbent John Hollis Bankhead (1842–1920) in the Democratic primary for Alabama's Sixth Congressional District but was defeated. Undaunted, Hobson decided to try again two years later. This time he was successful and entered Congress for the first of four consecutive terms in 1907. In May 1905 he married Grizelda Houston Hull; they had three children. His wife's southern ties (General Leonidas Polk (1806–1864) was her great-great-uncle; General Joseph Wheeler was her cousin) proved an asset to Hobson politically, and she became an expert political campaigner in her own right.

As a member of the House Naval Affairs Committee, Hobson was a consistent advocate of strengthening the navy. He supported those elements in the service critical of the entrenched power of the existing bureaus in matters of ship design and construction. An advocate of a naval general staff, Hobson pushed for the adoption of the naval aide system proposed by Secretary of the Navy George von Lengerke Meyer in 1909. From 1911 on, he annually sponsored legislation calling for the creation of a Council of National Defense. Hobson authored the bill providing for a chief of naval operations in December 1914; it passed both houses of Congress in amended fashion as part of the appropriations bill for fiscal year 1915. In debates early that year he helped defeat a challenge from "little navy" Democrats, preserving the building program substantially intact, granting authority for the office of naval operations, and establishing a naval reserve. He ran unsuccessfully for the Senate seat held by Oscar Underwood in 1914; a failed attempt to regain his congressional seat two years later ended his political career.

In later life Hobson maintained an interest in drug and alcohol abuse. He served as general secretary of the American Alcohol Education Association (1921), was president of the International Narcotic Education Association (1923), organized the World Conference on Narcotic Education held in 1926 in Los Angeles, and served as president of the World Narcotic Defense Association (1927).

In 1933 Hobson was awarded the Congressional Medal of Honor for his exploits with the *Merrimac*. The following year he was made a rear admiral on the retired list and granted a naval pension. Hobson died in New York City. He was buried with full military honors in Arlington National Cemetery.

Hobson served the navy well as an officer and perhaps even better as a congressman. The *Merrimac* episode unfairly overshadows a more enduring claim to recognition as a protagonist for an expanded modernized navy and the office of chief of naval operations. Naval preparedness for war was his guiding vision, and Hobson helped to bring this vision closer to realization. The Hobson papers are in the Manuscript Division of the Library of Congress. Hobson's *The Sinking of the "Merrimac"* (1899; repr. 1987), remains a classic. Two of Hobson's books intended for younger readers, *Buck Jones at Annapolis* (1907) and *In Line of Duty* (1910), contain much of an autobiographical nature. There is no extant biography of Hobson; see Richard Neal Sheldon, "Richmond Pearson Hobson: The Military Hero as Reformer during the Progressive Era" (Ph.D. diss., Univ. of Arizona, 1970). See also David F. Trask, *The War with Spain in 1898* (1981); Barton C. Shaw, "The Hobson Craze," *United States Naval Institute Proceedings* 102 (Feb. 1976): 54–60; and the essays "George von Lengerke Meyer" and "Josephus Daniels" by Paolo Coletta, in *American Secretaries of the Navy*, ed. Paolo Coletta (1980). An obituary is in the *New York Times*, 17 Mar. 1937.

RICHARD W. TURK

HOCKING, William Ernest (10 Aug. 1873–12 June 1966), professor, was born in Cleveland, Ohio, the son of William Francis Hocking, a homeopathic physician, and Julia Carpenter Pratt, a teacher. Since his family of seven had only modest means, Ernest, a high school graduate at fifteen, made it his singular responsibility to earn money for college and accordingly worked as a surveyor, mapmaker, printer's assistant, and illustrator. Following his initial interest in engineering, he enrolled in Iowa State College of Agriculture and the Mechanic Arts in 1894. But, a chance reading of William James's *Principles of Psychology* (1890) served as a refreshing counterbalance to Hocking's earlier reading of Herbert Spencer and motivated him to attend Harvard and study with this psychologist-philosopher.

Then in its "golden age," Harvard included among its faculty, in addition to James, John Dewey, Josiah Royce, George Santayana, Hugo Münsterberg, and the incomparable teacher George Herbert Palmer. As it happened, James was on leave preparing his Gifford Lectures when Hocking arrived. But Hocking found a kindred spirit in Royce, who conceived of philosophy as having a comprehensive task of understanding human experience in its broadest reach.

After receiving his B.A. (1901) and his M.A. (1902) from Harvard, he accepted a Walker Fellowship in Germany. This enabled him to study in Göttingen, Berlin, and Heidelberg. He had the advantage of history of philosophy with Wilhelm Windelband, psychology with George Elias Müller, theoretical physics with Max Abraham, and phenomenology with Edmund Husserl. Although Hocking's contact with Husserl was brief, Husserl the man and philosopher left an enduring mark. By his intense concern as a thinker dedicated to expressing the mental anguish and striving of an age, he exemplified for Hocking a creativity manifest through suffering.

On his return to Harvard in 1903, Hocking completed his dissertation, "The Elementary Experience of Other Conscious Being in Its Relation to the Elementary Experience of Physical and Reflexive Objects," which argued that our social experience or experience of other minds has the same metaphysical basis as our experience of physical and reflexive objects. He received his Ph.D. in 1904.

That year Hocking took a job teaching comparative religion at Andover Theological Seminary. In 1905 he married Agnes Boyle O'Reilly who, as he notes, was his "unfailing source of insight." They had three children, one of whom, a son, collaborated with his father in later years to write the book *Types of Philosophy* (1929).

Hocking next spent two years at the University of California (Berkeley), before accepting a post at Yale University, where he spent six productive years. During these years he completed his magnum opus, *The Meaning of God in Human Experience* (1912). This catapulted him into prominence and secured him the position of professor of philosophy at Harvard. In this book he develops the thesis that man's primal knowledge of God is the presupposition of man's knowledge of nature, other minds, and self. This discovery of a prior acquaintance with God is always made in media res. In this same book Hocking unfolds his view that religious living is enhanced and enriched by an alternation between mystical experiences and prophetic activities. This rhythm between the radically different but complementary experiences gives genuine religion its vitality.

This book was only the first of eighteen books and more than 270 articles written by Hocking, and half a dozen additional volumes edited by him during an active career that spanned sixty-seven years. It was an auspicious beginning for scholarly writings that were to cover the full range of philosophy: philosophy of religion, human nature, political and social philosophy, ethics, comparative religion, and philosophy of law.

From an idealist perspective strongly influenced by Royce, Hocking appropriated elements from James's "radical empiricism" (taking facts as experienced as one's basic referent) and fused these with the chief insights of Christian mystics. Hocking believed that primitive experience, involving a knowledge of other minds, reflected an immediate awareness of God as Other Mind. In this view, our experience in its most primal form is already social, and mystical experience is more truly conceived as a recognition of this Other Mind. This understanding removes the threat of solipsism.

During World War I Hocking served as captain in the army and as a teacher of military engineering for the Reserve Officers Training Corps at Harvard. Having studied military morale firsthand on the British and French fronts at the request of the British Foreign Office, he wrote *Morale and Its Enemies* (1918), which explores the psychological effects of warfare on soldiers.

Without loss of depth Hocking's interests have been broader in scope and relevance than almost any other twentieth-century thinker. He disavowed philosophy as an armchair endeavor and insisted that it was inescapably practical. He himself was not reluctant to apply his views and repeatedly took action in the public realm. He participated as a volunteer in the rebuilding of San Francisco after the earthquake and fire damage of 1906. He tried to get the United States to accept and support the League of Nations. He was participant and cofounder with his wife of the Shady Hill elementary school in Cambridge, Massachusetts. Supporting the Arab cause against Israel, he wrote a book, based largely on firsthand acquaintance, to help unravel some of the sociopolitical problems of the Middle East. As leading spokesman for the national Commission on Freedom of the Press, he wrote a book indicating what philosophy had to say about a free and responsible press. Publishing a book after a firsthand study of U.S. efforts to educate Germany in the post–World War II era, he boldly indicated ways to improve our perspective and enrich our approach. His last book, entitled *Strength of Men and Nations* (1959), encouraged dialogue and active cooperation between the U.S. and the U.S.S.R. As a person who never lost touch with ordinary people, he admired the stark honesty of laborers and enjoyed speaking to labor union schools in both Oakland and Boston.

Hocking's spirit as a teacher is captured in the tribute paid him by a former student and later prominent philosopher in his own right, Brand Blanshard of Yale:

I remember well his appearance in the metaphysics classroom [at Harvard, 1920] and the atmosphere he carried with him. He was a commanding personal presence—a little above middle height, with a frame that was broad and solid but not stout, a massive head, a ruddy face with a clipped moustache, and deep-set, thoughtful gray eyes. . . . He was a philosopher in the traditional and etymological sense of a "lover of wisdom"; and along with something of the collectedness of the mystic he had the judgment of the reflective man of the world. (*The Wisdom of William Ernest Hocking*, ed. John Howie and Leroy S. Rouner [1978], p. xiii)

The scope and depth of his interests, his active and thoughtful participation in the whole range of public activities, and his incredible productivity as a philosopher all combine to assure him an enduring place in

American history and philosophy. These concerns together with his creative energy make the narrow empiricism and linguistic analysis of present-day philosophy seem by comparison pathetic and anemic.

• Hocking's numerous writings include *Human Nature and Its Remaking* (1918; rev. ed., 1923), *The Present Status of the Philosophy of Law and of Rights* (1926), *Man and the State* (1926), *The Self: Its Body and Freedom* (1928), *The Spirit of World Politics: With Special Studies of the Near East* (1932), *Re-Thinking Missions: A Layman's Inquiry after One Hundred Years* (1932), *Thoughts on Death and Life* (1937), *The Lasting Elements of Individualism* (1937), *Living Religions and a World Faith* (1940), *What Man Can Make of Man* (1942), *Science and the Idea of God* (1944), *Freedom of the Press: A Framework of Principle* (1947), *Experiment in Education: What We Can Learn from Teaching Germany* (1954), *The Coming World Civilization* (1956), and *The Meaning of Immortality in Human Experience* (1957). An almost complete bibliography is Richard C. Gilman, "The Bibliography of William Ernest Hocking from 1898–1964," in *Philosophy, Religion and the Coming World Civilization, Essays in Honor of William Ernest Hocking*, ed. Leroy S. Rouner (1966). Biographies of Hocking include Richard C. Gilman, "William Ernest Hocking," in *The Encyclopedia of Philosophy*, vol. 4, ed. Paul Edwards (1967); Leroy S. Rouner, "The Making of a Philosopher: Ernest Hocking's Early Years," in *Philosophy, Religion and the Coming World Civilization*, ed. Rouner (1966); and Rouner, *Within Human Experience: The Philosophy of William Ernest Hocking* (1969). Obituaries are in the *New York Times*, 13 June 1966, and *Time*, 24 June 1966.

JOHN HOWIE

HOCTOR, Harriet (1903?–9 June 1977), dancer, was born in Hoosick Falls, New York, the daughter of Timothy Hoctor, a stonecutter and tombstone maker, and Elizabeth Kearney. She was a naturally precocious dancer, able to stand on her toes and take off her hair ribbon with her feet. Her mother's sister, Anna Kearney, who had seen ballet while traveling in Europe, offered to take twelve-year-old Harriet to New York for training. Hoctor's weekly class at the Louis H. Chalif Russian Normal School of Dance quickly became a daily class that she attended for more than three years. Chalif's standard was perfection, and very early in her career Hoctor became known as a perfectionist.

In 1921 Hoctor began to train with Ivan Tarasoff, a former Diaghilev Ballets Russes dancer who was particularly noted as a teacher of revue specialty dancers. Hoctor remained with him throughout her professional career. The dance team of Nelson Snow and Charles Columbus invited her to join their act; however, she had no public performing experience and asked them to wait. After four months in the back row of the "Moth" chorus of the "Butterfly Ballet" in the long-running hit *Sally*, Hoctor went into rehearsal with Snow and Columbus. For a year, they toured as a vaudeville act of stunt and ballroom dancing plus her ballet number.

While Hoctor was able to perform in a variety of dance techniques, classical toe dancing was her preferred form and the one in which she established her reputation. On 8 July 1923 *Topsy and Eva* opened in San Francisco, starring, written, and produced by the Duncan Sisters, Vivian and Rosetta, and featuring Hoctor as Eva's brother Henrique. From San Francisco the show moved to Chicago, where Hoctor studied with Merriel Abbott, a dance director known for her stagings of precision acrobatic routines. On 23 December 1924 *Topsy and Eva* opened in New York, running for six months before moving to Boston, where in October 1925 Hoctor left the company. Her three numbers were hailed as showstoppers, and the Act II "Bird Dance" introduced the movements that were to become her signature: after traveling and turning around the stage in a deep sweeping backbend on pointe, she would appear to hover in the center of the floor and then delicately lift one foot at a time to touch the top of her head. She often used the sequence to climax her dances, and Florenz Ziegfeld insisted she use it when she worked for him.

Hoctor was a featured class act in vaudeville and on the Broadway musical stage for the next fifteen years. In addition to her first partners, Snow and Columbus, she was teamed in various acts with William Holbrook, Theodore Sherer-Bekefi, Billy Bradford, and Simeon Karavaeff. In 1927 she played the Palace, vaudeville's most prestigious stage, for the first time and returned for increasingly lengthy stays later that same year and again in 1930. She was in demand for Broadway revues and musicals, appearing in *A la Carte* (1927); *The Three Musketeers* (1928), with the Albertina Rasch Dancers; *Show Girl* (1929); *Simple Simon* (1930); *Bow Belles* (1932), in London; *Earl Carroll Vanities* (1932); and the Ziegfeld *Follies* (1936), in which she performed two dances choreographed by George Balanchine. Hoctor received her first program credit for staging the ballets for *Hold Your Horses* (1933). For her 1934 vaudeville season, she toured with a corps of twenty dancers and a symphony orchestra.

Hoctor's Hollywood career was brief, but it left two valuable records of her typical and popular performances. She appeared in a circus ballet as a toe-dancing lion tamer in MGM's *The Great Ziegfeld* (1936). And in *Shall We Dance* (RKO, 1937), Hoctor, not Ginger Rogers, danced with Fred Astaire in the film's final ballet versus tap-dancing production number. While Astaire, as a ballet dancer who would rather be a hoofer, searches among the masked chorus girls for his missing nightclub star played by Ginger Rogers, Hoctor shimmers and swirls on her toes. She is the physical embodiment of ballet, the cool otherworldly art that Astaire rejects for the hot and earthy world of jazz.

In the late 1930s Hoctor began to choreograph and stage the elaborate production numbers that were the hallmark of Billy Rose's nightclubs, the Case Mañana Revue in Fort Worth, Texas, and his Diamond Horseshoe in New York City. She stopped performing in 1945 to teach full time at the Harriet Hoctor School of Ballet in Boston, which she had established in 1941 with Jerry Cragin. Hoctor never married. She retired to Lorton, Virginia, in the late 1960s and died in Arlington, Virginia.

Harriet Hoctor was one of a very few American dancers of her era who believed in ballet as a serious art form. She chose to work on the American stage in vaudeville and musical comedy. Before the formation of American ballet companies, individual ballet dancers made their professional careers as specialty acts on the musical stage. A performer who combined the grace and precision of classical technique with popular appeal, Hoctor was named prima ballerina in *Dance Magazine*'s "All-American Choice of Dancers" for both 1928 and 1929. The Dancing Masters of America awarded her a Medal of Distinction in 1930. She was hailed by her contemporaries for raising the standards of dance on the musical comedy stage. To her audiences, Hoctor was an American première danseuse, an ethereal being floating magically on her feathery toes.

• Clipping files on Hoctor exist at the Billy Rose Theatre Collection and the Dance Collection, New York Public Library for the Performing Arts, Lincoln Center. In addition to contemporary reviews of Hoctor's performances and personal interviews to promote her appearances, the most detailed and perceptive appraisal to appear during Hoctor's career is Walter Ware, *Ballet Is Magic: A Triple Monograph [of] Harriet Hoctor, Paul Haakon, Patricia Bowman* (1936). More recent biographical investigations include Ginnine Cocuzza, "An American Premiere Danseuse," *Dance Scope* 14, no. 3 (1980): 36–51, and Doris Hering, "Don't Forget the Backbend, Harriet!" *Dance Magazine*, Dec. 1965, pp. 112–17. Obituaries are in *Dance Magazine*, Aug. 1977, p. 18, and the *New York Times*, 11 June 1977.

GINNINE COCUZZA

HODDER, Jessie Donaldson (30 Mar. 1867–19 Nov. 1931), women's prison reformer, was born in Cincinnati, Ohio, the daughter of William Donaldson, a tradesman, and Mary Hall. Her mother died when she was two, and her father remarried. Following physical abuse by her stepmother, Jessie was rescued and taken in by her paternal grandmother. Later an uncle, Andrew Donaldson, joined and supported the household. In 1883 Andrew Donaldson's career with the Erie Railroad took the family from Cincinnati to New York City, where Jessie studied music. Either there or possibly in Cambridge, Massachusetts, she met Alfred LeRoy Hodder, whose family also had ties to Cincinnati and who was a favored doctoral student of Harvard University philosopher William James. Alfred told Jessie that he was already married and could not divorce; the two held a personal ceremony, and Jessie took his name. In 1891–1893 they were in Germany and Switzerland, where both studied; their daughter Olive was born in the Jameses summer flat in Florence, Italy, in 1893.

Returning to the United States, Alfred joined the English faculty at Bryn Mawr College. Jessie accompanied him, and in 1897 their second child, a son, was born. Alfred began a relationship with fellow English faculty member Mary "Mamie" Gwinn, companion of Bryn Mawr president M. Carey Thomas. Jessie and the children returned to Leipzig, Germany, in 1898, and Alfred promised to join them. The family moved to Switzerland in 1901. Jessie kept house and may have taught music and English to local students. She was friendly with Hans Kellerhels, a leading Swiss penal reformer, her first known contact with a person in that field. Alfred Hodder did not keep his promises to join his family; instead he eloped with Mamie Gwinn in June 1904. In November, as Jessie pondered her choices, her daughter became ill and died. Prostrate with grief and contemplating suicide, Jessie sent death announcements to some of her old friends, including Alice Gibbons James, William James's wife.

Recognizing her desperate straits, Alice James and her friend Elizabeth Glendower Evans corresponded with Jessie and urged her to return to the states. She did so in early 1906, and Evans, a Boston philanthropist, helped her procure a job as matron at the Industrial School for Girls in Lancaster, Massachusetts. James and Evans urged her to sue Alfred for support. Before the case came to trial, he died under somewhat mysterious circumstances in New York City in March 1907. Though Jessie did not benefit from Alfred's estate, she was eventually reconciled with his family and continued to cherish his memory.

Jessie Hodder's success in working with the girls at Lancaster led to her appointment in 1908 as a worker in the pioneering social services department of Massachusetts General Hospital. She developed counseling guidelines and was especially adept at working with unwed mothers, whom she believed should be encouraged to keep their children. In December 1910, despite self-doubt, Hodder was appointed superintendent of the Massachusetts Prison and Reformatory for Women in Sherborn (now Framingham). Stressing rehabilitation rather than punishment, she believed that inmates should "use their time" rather than serve it. She succeeded in eliminating "prison" from the institution's name, abolished the women's uniforms, and gave them everything from windows and paid labor programs to regular education at all levels. She liberalized work-release policies and created recreational programs, always with an eye toward the eventual return of inmates to society.

Hodder's work led to a new professional understanding of prisons and delinquency in Massachusetts. She maintained case records, required medical and psychiatric examinations, and expanded social services for the inmates. She petitioned successfully for the women to be allowed to keep their young infants with them at the prison, a step she considered vital in maintaining their ties to their children. A trustee of the Judge Baker Foundation in Boston, she supported university research into criminality and rehabilitation.

Hodder's compassionate nature and absorption in her career impressed those who worked with her, and her empathy with the women inmates was often noted. She became a tireless voice for reform of a system in which women's relationships to criminal acts was poorly understood and had often been ignored. Her intense manner and belief in her work made up for her lack of speaking skills and formal higher education as she worked her way into leadership in her field.

Among Hodder's contributions was the classification system, which she used in part to distinguish between inmates with organic and mental disabilities and those whom she termed "morally sick," who needed to be "returned to the community morally well." Prisoners of like classification could then live in self-contained cottages on prison grounds, further stressing the rehabilitative rather than the penal aspects of incarceration. Though she never succeeded in implementing the cottage system, she did put in place most of the other reforms and innovations she sought, and with the help of others in Boston reform circles she was able to experiment with new ideas and continue those that succeeded.

Hodder's professional activities were largely prison-related and included membership in the National Prison Association, service as the only American woman delegate to the International Prison Congress in 1925, and appointment by two presidents to national crime commissions, in 1927 and 1929. She had some interest in the ethical culture movement as well, frequently summering with movement devotees. At the time of her last illness in 1930, she had been appointed a delegate to the International Prison Conference. She died at her residence on the reformatory grounds.

Of the prominent women's prison reformers of the time, Hodder was the least academically oriented, which may account in part for why her reputation has been eclipsed by those of others such as Katharine Bemont Davis and her own successor at Framingham, Miriam Van Waters. Yet her pioneering work was well regarded by important scholars of penal reform and deserves to stand on its own. Her life before her prison reform career remains somewhat shrouded but possibly holds the keys to her reform contributions. As both a personal and a public story, Jessie Donaldson Hodder's life stands as a testament to the changes and challenges of the Progressive Era generation in American life.

• Hodder's papers are in the Schlesinger Library, Radcliffe College. They should be read in conjunction with the papers of Elizabeth Glendower Evans, also at the Schlesinger. Alfred Hodder's papers at the Alfred and Mary Gwinn Hodder Collection, Princeton University Libraries, include correspondence to and from Jessie. Jessie Hodder's published articles include "Indenture of Prisoners: An Experiment," *Journal of the American Institute of Criminal Law and Criminology* (May 1920), and "The Next Step in the Correctional Treatment of Girl and Women Offenders," *Proceedings of the National Conference of Social Work*, 45th Annual Meeting (1918): 117–21. A feature article about Hodder's work appears in the *New York Times*, 21 June 1914. See also Sheldon Glueck and Eleanor T. Glueck, *Five Hundred Delinquent Women* (1934); Estelle Freedman, *Their Sisters' Keepers: Women's Prison Reform in America, 1830–1930* (1981); Barbara Brenzel, *Daughters of the State: A Social Portrait of the First Reform School for Girls in North America, 1856–1905* (1983); and Helen Lefkowitz Horowitz, *The Power and Passion of M. Carey Thomas*

(1994). Obituaries appear in the *Boston Transcript*, 19 Nov. 1931, the *New York Times*, 20 Nov. 1931, and the *Springfield (Mass.) Sunday Republican*, 22 Nov. 1931.

CYNTHIA FARR BROWN

HODES, Art (14 Nov. 1904?–4 Mar. 1993), jazz pianist and writer, was born in Nikolaev, Russia, the son of William Hodes, a tinsmith, and Dorothy (maiden name unknown). "I'm not completely correct on when I was born. It was . . . somewhere between 1904 and 1906. We left hurriedly, and we had no papers," he told writer Whitney Balliett. He moved with his family to New York City at the age of six months and then to Chicago at age six. Hodes took piano lessons at Hull-House from 1916 to 1920. He attended Crane High School, a vocational school, but dropped out to take on a variety of day jobs, none lasting very long. He then enrolled at Medill High School and graduated.

With experience playing for parties and dances, Hodes secured his first full-time job performing for eighteen months at the Rainbow Gardens Cafe. He continued working in Chicago clubs over the next twelve years. While playing at a resort at Delavan Lake in Wisconsin in 1927, he first heard jazz on records by trumpeter Louis Armstrong and cornetist Bix Beiderbecke. On returning to Chicago, Hodes and his friend and roommate for two years, trumpeter Wingy Manone, frequented jazz-oriented venues to listen to the great African-American players, including especially Armstrong but also pianist Earl Hines and the brothers Johnny Dodds and Baby Dodds, whose ensemble work Hodes particularly admired. He had an opportunity to hear blues singer Bessie Smith in concert, and he spent considerable time listening to solo blues pianists and trying to replicate the intimacy and emotional depth of their unaccompanied performances. He made his first recordings in December 1928 with Manone.

While continuing a still obscure career in Chicago clubs, Hodes married Thelma Johnson early in 1938; they had six children. They moved to New York City, but Thelma returned to Chicago after their first child was born. He recorded "South Side Shuffle," a boogie woogie, in August 1939. While leading bands or playing as a soloist, he hosted a jazz radio show, "The Metropolitan Review," six days per week on the nonprofit station WNYC radio.

With Dale Curran, Hodes copublished and edited the *Jazz Record*, which published sixty issues from February 1943 to November 1947; Harold Hersey replaced Curran for the last year. The magazine mainly offered insider portraits of musicians playing in early jazz styles.

At the same time, Hodes began recording prolifically, especially for the Blue Note label and often in the company of reed player Sidney Bechet. His discs included "Maple Leaf Rag," "Doctor Jazz," "M. K. Blues," "Apex Blues," "Blue Horizon" (all 1944; the last title under Bechet's leadership), "Save It, Pretty Mama," and Baby Dodds's "Feelin' at Ease" (both

1945). In January 1946 Hodes led his Blue Note Jazz Men at the Stuyvesant Casino in New York City. He continued playing in New York through 1949, when he and clarinetist Pee Wee Russell founded Pee Wee and Art's Backroom at the Riviera on Seventh Avenue south.

Early in January 1950 Hodes returned to Chicago, initially to work with Russell and singer Chippie Hill at the Blue Note club. He decided to stay in Chicago to be with his family. Engagements at Rupneck's (June 1950 to July 1951), Jazz Ltd. (1953, late 1956, and 1957), and the Brass Rail (July–Nov. 1955 and Feb.–Sept. 1956) alternated with midwestern touring. From 1957 to 1959 Hodes taught piano at the Park Forest Conservatory. While holding further engagements in Chicago nightclubs as a member of trumpeter Bob Scobey's group for four years from late 1959 onward, Hodes began to contribute a semimonthly column to *Down Beat*, excerpts of which appear in his autobiography. He also wrote for *Jazz Report, Second Line*, the *Chicago Tribune*, the *New York Times*, and *Esquire*.

Hodes recorded the duo albums *Plain Old Blues* (1962) with bassist Truck Parham, and *Mama Yancey Sings, Art Hodes Plays Blues* (1965). He gave lecture-concerts in public schools during the academic year 1963–1964. On local station WTTW he hosted an educational television show, "Plain Ol' Blues," winning an Emmy Award for the 1965–1966 season. Portions of another television series from the years 1969 to 1971 were distributed via National Education Television throughout the United States and Canada, and this in turn led to a national tour by the Stars of Jazz, including trumpeter Wild Bill Davison, clarinetist Barney Bigard, and guitarist Eddie Condon from 2 October 1971 into 1972.

Having made his first trip to Europe in 1970 to perform in Denmark, Hodes returned regularly thereafter, appearing at the Grande Parade du Jazz in Nice, France, in 1975. He held another residency at Jazz Ltd., and he toured the United States, giving community concerts until 1978, also the year in which he first performed at the Newport Jazz Festival, then held in New York.

Thelma died of cancer in late 1979. In February 1981 Hodes came back to New York to perform at Hanratty's, where he recorded the album *Someone to Watch over Me: Live at Hanratty's*. Great reviews led to a 22-month stand at the Mayfair-Regent Hotel in Chicago. In 1981 he also performed again at New York's summertime Newport festival, by that time renamed the Kool Jazz Festival. Hodes married "Jan" (Georgeann, her maiden name unknown), a classical pianist, in 1983. He recorded the album *South Side Memories* in 1983 and returned to the Nice festival in 1985. A series of strokes ended his career in 1991. He died in Harvey, Illinois.

Hodes was a casual, unremarkable writer, and his autobiographical material is exceedingly repetitive and automatic, as if he had given scarcely any new thought to the matter since the mid-1940s. But many of his short essays on people and places are wonderfully evocative of that period. Among leading jazz pianists, he was a master of tasteful understatement, offering an approach that was, if it is possible, even more economical than that of Count Basie late in his career. Indeed the first two Blue Note sides mentioned above are to be admired for Hodes's ability to organize and underpin driving performances in the style of the New Orleans jazz revival, with the understanding that the piano is scarcely to be heard in ensemble passages, though Hodes does have a bouncy solo on "Doctor Jazz." He excelled in moderate- to slow-tempo blues, such as "M. K. Blues" and "Blue Horizon," in which his fondness for tremolos (the little finger and thumb oscillating rapidly between two notes an octave apart) added motion and tension to his solos and accompaniments.

• Hodes's autobiography, written with Chadwick Hansen, is *Hot Man: The Life of Art Hodes* (1992), which includes a discography by Howard Rye. Other writings by Hodes include "From Twenty Years Ago," *Storyville* 1 (Feb. 1966): 2–5; the liner notes to *Jazz Classics: Sittin' In*, vol. 1: *Art Hodes* (c. 1969); and "Jazz: The Sweet Slow Comeback," *Esquire*, Dec. 1972, pp. 161–64, 268, 270. Hodes also edited, with Hansen, *Selections from the Gutter: Jazz Portraits from "The Jazz Record"* (1977). See also Dale Curran, "Art Hodes," *Jazz*, 15 Jan. 1945, pp. 3–6; Dave Helland, "Two-Fisted Chicago Pianist," *Contemporary Keyboard* 5 (Mar. 1979): 24, 62, 66; Whitney Balliett, *American Musicians: Fifty-six Portraits in Jazz* (1986); Sam Freedman, "Hodes' Blue: Still Art after All These Years," *Down Beat*, June 1982, pp. 23–25; Ray Horricks, "Custodian of the Blues," *Jazz Journal International* 38 (Dec. 1985): 14–16; Dan Morgenstern, pamphlet notes to *The Complete Art Hodes Blue Note Recordings* (1986); John Norris, "Art Hodes: South Side Memories," *Coda*, no. 213 (Apr.–May 1987): 10–11; Sid Bailey, "Art Hodes: 1989," *New Orleans Music* 1 (Feb. 1990): 5–9; and "Art Hodes: 1946," *New Orleans Music* 1 (Feb. 1990): 10–12. A notated example of Hodes's soloing appears in Eli H. Newberger, "Refinement of Melody and Accompaniment in the Evolution of Swing Piano Style," *Annual Review of Jazz Studies* 1 (1982): 87–88. Obituaries are in the *Chicago Tribune*, 5 Mar. 1993, and *New York Times*, 6 Mar. 1993.

BARRY KERNFELD

HODGE, Archibald Alexander (18 July 1823–11 Nov. 1886), theologian, was born in Princeton, New Jersey, the son of Charles Hodge, a professor in the Theological Seminary at Princeton, and Sara Bache. Hodge was named for Archibald Alexander, mentor and colleague to his father at the seminary. The name proved apt, for the views taught at that Presbyterian institution shaped Hodge's career and thought.

After graduating from the College of New Jersey (later Princeton University) in 1841, Hodge served there as a tutor and also taught in the Lawrenceville School (New Jersey). He enrolled at Princeton Seminary in 1843 and completed his studies in 1847. That same year he married Elizabeth B. Holliday of Winchester, Virginia, received ordination into the Presbyterian ministry, and set sail for Allahabad, India, where he served as a missionary. Due to ill health, Hodge returned to the United States with his wife and two children in 1850. He assumed successive pastorates in Lower West Nottingham, Maryland (1851), in Fredericksburg, Virginia (1855), and in Wilkes-Barre, Pennsylvania (1861). A series of Sunday evening lectures delivered to the Fredericksburg congregation provided the basis of Hodge's *Outlines of Theology* (1860). He acknowledged that the book was primarily an abridgment of lectures he had heard his father deliver in the 1840s. The book bore the characteristic marks of the theology associated with Princeton: adherence to Reformed orthodoxy, especially as manifested in the Westminster Confession of Faith; belief that external evidences attested the veracity of Christian revelation; commitment to the Bible as the infallible authority in all theological matters; and conviction that theology was a science based on the facts of scripture and thus was capable of rendering its conclusions as propositional truths fully consonant with the findings of other sciences. Despite the treatise's derivative nature, *Outlines* established Hodge as a theologian of eminence and was widely used as a textbook in conservative divinity schools. Hodge considerably expanded the book in 1878.

He accepted an appointment in 1864 as professor of didactic theology at Western Theological Seminary in Allegheny, Pennsylvania; in 1866 he additionally began serving as pastor of the North Presbyterian Church in Allegheny. After the death of his first wife, he married Margaret McLaren Woods in 1869.

Hodge returned to Princeton Seminary in 1877 as an associate to his father and, upon the latter's death the following year, acceded to the chair of Didactic and Polemic Theology. In 1880 he published *The Life of Charles Hodge*. Although he generally perpetuated the theological legacy of his father, the younger Hodge differed from him in minor ways. Without rejecting his father's contention that Darwinism was atheistic, Hodge allowed that evolution might be presented in a fashion consistent with orthodox Christianity. In this respect, Hodge stood closer to the theistic evolutionism of Princeton University's James McCosh than to the views of his father. Hodge also developed a teaching style that some favorably contrasted to that of Charles. Shy by nature, Hodge nevertheless possessed a wit that endeared him to friends and students. Listeners appreciated his ability to condense difficult theological arguments, to provide vivid illustrations, and to offer pointed asides in lectures. Hodge employed these talents to good advantage in *Popular Lectures on Theological Themes*, posthumously published in 1887. His skill as a learned popularizer stood in curious juxtaposition to the elitist sentiments that he sometimes expressed in private conversation or correspondence. During his years in India, he acquired an admiration of the British Empire and subsequently was prone to offer negative contrasting assessments of America's republican institutions. Hodge's Princeton friend and colleague Francis Landey Patton observed that "aristocratic sympathies were very strong in him, and they found expression sometimes in an extravagant avowal of Toryism that was partly jest, and partly based upon a real conservatism of sentiment respecting the philosophy of social life."

In 1881 Hodge published in the *Presbyterian Review*, where he was one of the two managing editors, an article entitled "Inspiration," coauthored with Benjamin B. Warfield of Western Seminary. Later reprinted and widely disseminated by the Presbyterian Board of Publication, the essay has received more attention from subsequent historians than any of Hodge's other writings. The article crystallized the conservative Presbyterian position on the inerrancy of the Scriptures. It contended that God, without suppressing the diverse styles or idioms of the various writers, superintended their compositions so that the original biblical texts (the autographs) were without error. This freedom from error included "the affirmations of Scripture of all kinds, whether of spiritual doctrine or duty, or of physical or historical fact, or of psychological or philosophical principle." In framing this position, Hodge and Warfield sought to erect a bulwark against the rising tide of modern biblical criticism and to assure that Christians would have in the Scriptures the sure and reliable authority so essential to the objective, scientific theology to which the Princeton theologians aspired. The Hodge-Warfield doctrine became a rallying cry for many conservatives. After Hodge's death, the Presbyterian General Assembly in 1892 declared this view to be the official confessional position of the denomination. This sparked a generation of struggle, which led to the departure from the church in 1893 of Charles A. Briggs, the other, more liberal managing editor of the *Presbyterian Review*. The debate culminated in the so-called Fundamentalist-Modernist controversy of the 1920s when the church, fearful of schism, retreated from its 1892 pronouncement. Princeton Seminary was reorganized, thus preparing the way for the demise within Presbyterianism of the theology that Archibald Alexander Hodge had represented.

Though a brilliant thinker, Hodge stood for most of his career in the shadow of his illustrious father. His chief contribution to the Princeton theology was to enunciate with brevity, clarity, and effective illustration the thought of the elder Hodge. For that contribution, however, he was greatly esteemed by fellow conservatives, who regarded his sudden death in Princeton as a sore loss.

• The papers of the Hodge family are located in Firestone Library, Princeton University. For information concerning Hodge's life, see Francis Landey Patton, *A Discourse in Memory of Archibald Alexander Hodge* (1887); William M. Paxton, *Address Delivered at the Funeral of Archibald Alexander Hodge* (1886); and C. A. Salmond, *Princetoniana, Charles and A. A. Hodge: With Class and Table Talk of Hodge the Younger* (1888). The larger setting of Hodge's work is admirably portrayed in Lefferts A. Loetscher, *The Broadening Church* (1954).

JAMES H. MOORHEAD

HODGE, Charles (27 Dec. 1797–19 June 1878), conservative Presbyterian theologian, was born in Philadelphia, Pennsylvania, the son of Hugh Hodge, a physician and merchant, and Mary Blanchard, a native of Boston and descendent of prominent patriots. Hodge and his brother were raised by their mother, who was widowed when Charles Hodge was less than seven months old. His lifelong attachment to Whig politics may have begun when his mother's small legacy was wiped out in President Thomas Jefferson's embargo of European commerce. Mary Hodge eventually moved to Princeton to secure the education of her sons at the College of New Jersey (later Princeton University). Hodge began his studies there in 1812 at the same time that his Philadelphia minister, Rev. Ashbel Green, was being called to the college as its new president. Under Green, Hodge had learned the Westminster Catechism in Philadelphia; now at Princeton he was guided by Green to pursue practical piety, respect physical science, and practice the philosophy of common sense realism. Hodge professed his personal Christian faith and joined the Presbyterian church in Princeton on 13 January 1815, an event connected with a large-scale revival at the college. He graduated the following September.

The major early influence on Hodge was Archibald Alexander, the first professor of the Presbyterians' new theological seminary. A native of Virginia who had been an itinerant preacher, pastor, and college president, Alexander took a special interest in the young Hodge. He encouraged him to study Greek and, after Hodge entered Princeton Seminary in 1816, took him along on preaching tours. From Alexander, Hodge learned the combination of biblical fidelity, seventeenth-century Calvinist theology, intense practical piety; and common sense reasoning that would mark his own career. Hodge revered Alexander as the father he had never known and named his own first son Archibald Alexander.

Hodge graduated from the seminary in September 1819 and then, at Alexander's request, prepared to return as a teacher of biblical languages. While studying Hebrew privately in Philadelphia, he was licensed by the Presbytery of Philadelphia in October 1819. He then supplied pulpits in the Philadelphia area while continuing his study until in May 1820 he was appointed by the Presbyterian General Assembly to a one-year position at Princeton as instructor of Greek and Hebrew. That October he traveled throughout New England, where he met several leading Congregationalists, including Moses Stuart of Andover Seminary and Nathaniel W. Taylor of the Yale Divinity School, with whom he later engaged in vigorous theological polemic. In November 1821 Hodge was ordained by the Presbytery of New Brunswick; in May 1822 the General Assembly appointed him a professor of Oriental and biblical literature (at an annual salary of $1,000); in June he married Sarah Bache, great-granddaughter of Benjamin Franklin (1706–1790); and in September he delivered his inaugural address at Princeton. Its theme, as much of Hodge's later work, concerned the proper use of Scripture. Its argument stressed the spiritual character of biblical study: "The moral qualifications of an Interpreter of Scripture may

all be included in Piety: which embraces humility, candor, and those views and feelings which can only result from the inward operation of the Holy Spirit" (*Life*, p. 94).

The course of Hodge's life was now set. Over the next fifty-six years he instructed more than 3,000 students, including many who became notable theologians in their own right. In 1825 he founded a journal that, under different official titles, was widely known as the *Princeton Review*. As its editor and principal author, Hodge organized a committed band of colleagues who with him used its pages to defend the confessional Presbyterian faith as they understood it. By the time Hodge relinquished the editorship in 1871, it was the second oldest quarterly in the United States. That same year the *British Quarterly Review* called Hodge's journal "beyond all question the greatest purely theological Review that has ever been published in the English tongue" (*Life*, p. 257). Early in his career at the seminary Hodge also embarked on a publishing career that, from his first pamphlet in 1822, *On the Importance of Biblical Literature*, to a last collection of meditations for seminary students, published posthumously in 1879 as *Conference Papers*, eventually covered almost all of the major theological controversies and many of the practical religious questions of his day.

Hodge's one lengthy absence from Princeton occurred from October 1826 through September 1828 when he traveled to Europe. Into early 1827 he was at Paris studying French, Arabic, and Syriac, but the bulk of his sojourn was spent in Halle and Berlin, where he studied new developments in German theology. He came away with a deep respect for the thoroughness of German scholarship, the power of preachers like Friedrich Schleiermacher, and the moving character of German church music. At the same time, he found German speculative theology most uncongenial. To him, post-Kantian philosophy overestimated the creative power of the human spirit, and the vogue for Hegel he found entirely unfathomable. He also thought that the theology of Schleiermacher, which grounded religion on a feeling of utter dependence, debased sound thinking as well as sound theology. In Europe he sharpened an earlier sense that proper Christian theology could be undermined by overemphasizing either philosophical rationalism or inner subjectivity.

During the 1830s Hodge experienced a debilitating pain in his thigh (he called it "rheumatism") that immobilized him for several years. For the period 1833 to 1836 he met seminary classes in the study of his house. He also endured heroic treatments on his leg, including the application of galvanism from a machine created by his friend and chess partner Joseph Henry, a professor at the College of New Jersey who later founded the Smithsonian Institution. Despite this physical debility, Hodge's pen did not flag. During the years he was confined to bed he published twenty-eight articles in the *Princeton Review* (some up to sixty pages in length), a major commentary on the book of

Romans (1835), and a lengthy history of the Presbyterians in America. He also lent his support to the Old School, or conservative, wing of the Presbyterian church in a dispute that split the denomination in 1837. While Hodge was not as rabidly opposed to the New England influences and the social activism of the New School party as were Ashbel Green and some other Old Schoolers, he nonetheless wanted Presbyterians to define their doctrine carefully and to eschew radicalism in society. In 1846 he was elected the moderator of the Old School General Assembly.

Hodge directed his polemics in this period largely against moderating influences in American Calvinism, such as the New Haven Divinity of N. W. Taylor, other Congregationalists at Andover Seminary like Moses Stuart, and the New School party in his own Presbyterian church that promoted beliefs similar to the New England Congregationalists. Especially in his commentary on Romans and in a review of Moses Stuart's commentary on the same book, Hodge defended what he took to be the teaching of both the Bible and the historic creeds of the English-speaking Reformed tradition. Against the New England and New School views, which held that sinfulness was constituted only by the individual's own sinning, Hodge contended that Adam acted as a covenant representative of the whole human race. All humans were therefore born with an inherent tendency to sin that only divine grace could overcome. Humans were active in their own redemption but in no sense the cause of it. These notions offended conceptions of individual dignity and abstract notions of equity that had gained tremendous power in the wake of the American Revolution. Hodge stuck to the traditional view most of all out of a concern for divine grace—if Adam's sin was not imputed to later generations, neither could the saving work of Christ be imputed to believers. His opponents were worried about fair play; Hodge was worried about redemption.

Hodge regained the use of his leg in the late 1830s, though he continued to require a cane. In 1840 he became Professor of Exegetical and Didactic Theology. By this time he was also presiding over a busy household; eight children survived infancy, of whom two would later become professors at the seminary. When his wife, Sarah, died on Christmas Day 1849, Hodge was grief-stricken. In 1852 he married Mary Hunter Stockton, the widow of a navy lieutenant. To his household, which usually embraced several collateral relatives and charity cases as well as his immediate family, Hodge was a warm, indulgent guide. For a defender of rational Reformed theology and an opponent of theological subjectivity, Hodge's intimate friendships were unusually passionate. His grandson William Berryman Scott left this record: "It is the fashion nowadays to decry the Calvinistic theology and to paint its professors as gloomy and austere fanatics. . . . I can truthfully say that never, in any part of the world, have I met such sunny, genial, kindly and tolerant people as my Grandfather and his children. He

stands in my memory as the ideal of a perfect saint and gentleman" (1939, p. 8).

As a theologian, Hodge contended for a Calvinism that had been defined by its sixteenth- and seventeenth-century development. He proclaimed the dangers of unchecked religious experience, whether as sophisticated European Romanticism or the rough-hewn revivalism of America's frontier. About the latter he once cautioned that a "too exclusive dependence on revivals tends to produce a false or unscriptural form of religion" (*Princeton Review* 19 [Oct. 1847]: 520). Hodge shared his age's enthusiasm for scientific method, understood in terms of Francis Bacon's empiricism, and so could introduce his three-volume *Systematic Theology* (1872–1873) by saying, "The Bible is to the theologian what nature is to the man of science. . . . In theology as in natural science, principles are derived from facts, and not impressed upon them" (vol. 1, pp. 10, 13). Hodge summed up a lifetime of classroom instruction in *Systematic Theology*, a work that dominated Presbyterian theological education until the 1930s and that has continued to be used as a text in some conservative seminaries.

But the heart of Hodge's interest was an Augustinian picture of the human condition as defined by the Protestant reformers. The defense of this theology inspired his weightiest polemics. What most troubled him were positions that undercut dependence upon divine sovereignty in salvation or that valued too highly the moral capacities of human nature. So he criticized Schleiermacher, the Roman Catholic church, the English Oxford Movement, and his American contemporaries Horace Bushnell, Nathaniel W. Taylor, and Charles G. Finney for substituting principles of innate spiritual capacity in the place of proper dependence upon God's grace. Hodge's most memorable intellectual battle was an exchange of weighty articles with Edwards Amasa Park of Andover Seminary in the early 1850s on the relationship of traditional theological language to the realities of religion. While Park advanced the mediating position that Calvinistic categories should be considered an emotional expression that did not correspond precisely to an external reality, Hodge held determinedly to the identity of "the theology of the intellect" and "the theology of the feelings." As an old man, Hodge justified the course of his polemics by contending that "when it was taught . . . that men, since the fall, are not born in a state of sin; . . . that in conversion it is man, and not God, who determines who do, and who do not, turn unto God, . . . the vital principles, not of the Reformed faith only, but even of Catholic Christianity [i.e., the historic faith as a whole] were involved" ("Retrospect of the *Princeton Review*," pp. 12–13).

Against those who argued for the nineteenth-century's customary exaltation of internal religious capacity, Hodge himself sometimes fell prey to a sterile rationalism. Upon occasion he also misread his opponents to their disadvantage. On the whole, however, the level on which Hodge and his various opponents conducted their exchanges marked the highpoint of public theological discussion in American history. After Hodge's death the Lutheran Charles Porterfield Krauth said that "next to having Hodge on one's side is the pleasure of having him as an antagonist" (*Life*, p. 616).

Although Hodge exerted his greatest efforts in defense of God's centrality in human salvation, his interests ranged widely. He wrote commentaries on several New Testament books and regularly on Presbyterian ecclesiastical affairs. He penned numerous expositions for lay people, of which *The Way of Life* (1841) was notable for its limpid prose and clear exposition: When he was more than seventy-five he wrote a book on evolutionary theory that the best modern student of religious reactions to Darwin called "a trenchant theological analysis" (Moore, p. 193). This book, *What Is Darwinism?* (1874), condemned notions of random biological change (though not evolution itself or even natural selection as an explanation for evolution) as atheism. Despite the anti-Catholic sentiment that was common in the United States, Hodge defended Roman Catholic baptism as a valid Christian sacrament. Hodge also commented regularly on public affairs in the pages of the *Princeton Review*. He held that slavery as such was not condemned by Scripture but that the way it was practiced in the South perpetuated great evil. In the heated days before the outbreak of the Civil War he won the ire of many northern Presbyterians by arguing against Unionism as a requirement for church fellowship. Once the war began, however, he urged that it be fought vigorously, and he wholeheartedly supported President Abraham Lincoln (who regularly worshiped at the New York Avenue Presbyterian Church in Washington, where Hodge's student, Phineas D. Gurley, was the minister).

Through a long career at Princeton Theological Seminary, Hodge's theological determination, tireless pen, breadth of interest, and favorable social connections made him one of the century's best-known theologians as well as a major public influence. When he celebrated his fiftieth anniversary as a Princeton professor in 1872, Hodge personally had instructed more students than had attended any other theological institution in the United States. After his death, a Methodist journal, the *National Repository*, called him "not only *par excellence* the Calvinistic theologian of America, but the Nestor of all American theology . . . the grandest result of our Christian intellectual development" (*Life*, p. 585).

Hodge did not integrate the various aspects of his thought smoothly; neither did he have much sympathy for the shifting intellectual climate of his own century, but the body of his work remains the most powerful nineteenth-century American example of the Calvinist theology that for three centuries had figured large in Anglo-American civilization. Although Hodge's point of view has passed from favor in the West's dominant culture, it remains alive in a number of smaller ecclesiastical bodies.

Hodge's last public duty was a prayer at the funeral of his friend Joseph Henry, in Washington, D.C., in May 1878. He died a month later in Princeton.

• Hodge's papers, including much recently catalogued material, are at the Speer Library, Princeton Theological Seminary, and the Firestone Library, Princeton University. In addition to Romans, Hodge wrote commentaries on Ephesians (1856) and First and Second Corinthians (1857). Among other separately published works not mentioned above, the most important are *The Constitutional History of the Presbyterian Church in the United States of America* (1840), *Essays and Reviews: Selected from the Princeton Review* (1857), and "Retrospect of the History of the *Princeton Review*," *Biblical Repertory and Princeton Review: Index Volume* (1870): 1–39. A. A. Hodge, *The Life of Charles Hodge* (1880), is still the fullest biography. William Berryman Scott, *Some Memories of a Palaeontologist* (1939), contains revealing glimpses of Hodge's household.

Of modern discussions, see Andrew W. Hoffecker, *Piety and the Princeton Theologians* (1981), for the best general work on Hodge's theological stance; David F. Wells, "Charles Hodge," in *Reformed Theology in America*, ed. Wells (1985), on the main themes of his theology; William S. Barker, "The Social Views of Charles Hodge (1797–1878)," *Presbyterion: Covenant Seminary Review* 1 (Spring 1975): 1–22, for attitudes to American society; James R. Moore, *The Post-Darwinian Controversies: A Study of the Protestant Struggle to Come to Terms with Darwin in Great Britain and America* (1979), and Jonathan Wells, *Charles Hodge's Critique of Darwinism* (1988), for Hodge's views on religion and science; and Mark A. Noll, ed., *The Princeton Theology, 1812–1921* (1983), for excerpts and a full bibliography.

Much of the best writing on Hodge is in the form of dissertations, among which the most illuminating are John Oliver Nelson, "The Rise of the Princeton Theology: A Genetic History of American Presbyterianism Until 1850" (Yale Univ., 1935); Earl William Kennedy, "An Historical Analysis of Charles Hodge's Doctrines of Sin and Particular Grace" (Princeton Theological Seminary, 1968); Marion Ann Taylor, "The Old Testament in the Old Princeton School" (Yale Univ., 1988); and John William Stewart, "The Tethered Theology: Biblical Criticism, Common Sense Philosophy, and the Princeton Theologians, 1812–1860" (Univ. of Michigan, 1990).

MARK A. NOLL

HODGE, Frederick Webb (28 Oct. 1864–28 Sept. 1956), anthropologist and museum director, was born in Plymouth, England, the son of Edwin Hodge and Emily Webb. Hodge's family came to the United States in 1871, when he was seven years old; he became a naturalized citizen that year. His father was an employee of the postal service, and the family settled in Washington, D.C. In 1879 Hodge took a job as secretary in a local law firm, and from 1883 to 1886 he attended Columbian (now George Washington) University night classes. In 1884 he joined the U.S. Geological Survey as a stenographer, working for John Wesley Powell, who headed both the survey and the Bureau of American Ethnology.

In 1886, at the major turning point in his life, Hodge was hired by Frank Hamilton Cushing of the Smithsonian Institution as field secretary for the Hemenway Southwestern Expedition. Financed by Mrs.

Mary Hemenway of Boston, the expedition was an ambitious effort to study the past and present Native American cultures of Arizona and New Mexico. During his three-year association with the expedition, Hodge served not only as secretary, but also as an assistant in archaeology, learning a great deal about the nascent discipline. Perhaps more important was his exposure to the many cultures of the Southwest; Hodge became an acknowledged expert on the Native Americans of that region, as well as on the various Spanish expeditions of the early historical period. These were to be his major research subjects for the next seven decades.

Hodge returned to Washington in 1889 as an employee of the Bureau of American Ethnology, although he was still working for Powell. Hodge undertook a variety of tasks in his new position, including field archaeology, editing most of the many publications issued by the bureau, and, after 1893, acting as its librarian as well. He also began his lifelong pattern of prolific publication of anthropological and historical papers. His full bibliography includes over 400 items on a wide variety of topics.

In August 1891 Hodge married Margaret W. Magill, Cushing's sister-in-law. They had three children before the marriage ended in divorce. During the summer of 1893 Hodge served as acting director, or ethnologist in charge, of the Bureau of American Ethnology.

As an employee of the bureau, and as part of Washington's anthropological scene, Hodge found an outlet for his organizational abilities. He took on increasing responsibilities within the bureau over the years, and became a major participant in the influential Anthropological Society of Washington. The emergence of the bureau as the premier research institute for Americanists, and the concentration in Washington of a high proportion of the country's professional anthropologists, gave the city a dominance in anthropology for several decades around the turn of the century.

Hodge grew with the discipline, largely due to his willingness to take on difficult and often thankless jobs. His editorial work at the bureau led to his becoming editor of the *American Anthropologist* from 1899 to 1902. When, in March 1902, the Anthropological Society of Washington and other groups amalgamated into the modern American Anthropological Association (AAA), Hodge was one of the founders. In the early years of the AAA Hodge served on a number of important committees. These included the committees for policy, preservation of American antiquities, archaeological nomenclature, linguistic families north of Mexico, and editorial management. He chaired the latter two committees.

Hodge continued as editor of the *American Anthropologist* (new series) for another decade (1902–1911), under conditions that can best be described as amateurish. For much of this period he received little or no help, acting as editor, secretary, and in many other capacities. After a year away from the position during 1911–1912, Hodge was lured back by assurances of more professional working conditions. He remained as editor of the journal, and also continued to edit most of the association's *Memoirs*, until he began his two-year term as president of the AAA (1915–1917).

In 1901 Hodge had transferred from the Bureau of American Ethnology to its parent organization, the Smithsonian Institution. There he put his extensive editorial and bibliographic expertise to good use as executive assistant in charge of international exchanges, an important role. By 1905 he was back in the bureau, however, working hard to complete the project that has remained most closely associated with his name. Begun a number of years earlier under Powell as a comparatively simple linguistic guide, the *Handbook of American Indians North of Mexico* (Bureau of American Ethnology, Bulletin 30, 1907, 1910), as developed and edited by Hodge, resulted in over 2,000 pages of encyclopedic information concerning every known Native American group.

Hodge succeeded William Henry Holmes as director of the Bureau in January 1910, at the age of forty-five. He remained in that post just over eight years, continuing the bureau's pattern of intensive research and prolific publication on Native American topics, and maintaining his own impressive efforts in both areas. It was during his directorship that the bureau offices were moved into the Smithsonian Institution.

In 1917 Hodge was invited to become assistant director of the Museum of the American Indian in New York City; he accepted and joined the museum staff in February 1918. The museum was operated by the Heye foundation, and its director at that time was George Heye. The new position allowed Hodge to spend considerable time in the field, excavating archaeological sites in the Southeast and, to a greater extent, the Southwest. In addition to his regular duties as assistant director, Hodge became editor of the museum's publication series, Indian Notes and Monographs. In 1919 Hodge participated in the museum's Hendricks-Hodge Expedition, excavating the abandoned Zuni villages of Hawikuh and Kechipauan.

While on the staff of the Museum of the American Indian, Hodge remained an active member of the American Anthropological Association. In 1918 he served on a committee to develop sound fiscal policies for the *American Anthropologist* and chaired a similar committee to find financing for the *Journal of Physical Anthropology*. He was named a representative to the National Research Council (1921–1923, 1927–1930), and in 1923 he was appointed to a committee to examine the status of anthropology in various branches of the federal government.

In 1932, at the age of sixty-seven, Hodge was invited to become the director of the Southwest Museum in Los Angeles, California. The museum was founded in 1907 by Hodge's friend Charles Lummis; its focus on the peoples of the American Southwest perfectly suited Hodge's lifelong interests, and he accepted. He was an active director, extensively reorganizing the museum and taking on the role of editor of its popular publication *The Masterkey*. In Los Angeles Hodge continued his pattern of involvement in a variety of organizations and tasks. He had also been one of the founders (in 1929) of the Quivira Society, dedicated to publishing rare Spanish documents, and he served as advisory editor of its publication series. In 1934 came the death of Hodge's second wife, Zarah H. Preble, after seven years of marriage, and in 1936 he married artist and author Gene Meany.

Hodge remained director of the Southwestern Museum for an astonishing 23 years. He took sabbatical leave in 1955, working on several new projects, including the beginnings of an autobiography. He formally retired in January 1956 and moved to Santa Fe, New Mexico, where he died.

• A major collection of Hodge's personal papers is located in the Southwestern Museum in Los Angeles. Hodge's major contributions to anthropological literature were editorial, but he published a tremendous number of articles and books as well. Some of the most important are *The Nagoochee Mound in Georgia*, with George G. Heye and George H. Pepper, Contributions of the Museum of the American Indian, vol. 4, no. 3 (1918); *Hawikuh Bonework*, Museum of the American Indian, Indian Notes and Monographs, vol. 3, no. 1 (1920); and *History of Hawikuh, New Mexico, One of the So-called Cities of Cibola*, Southwest Museum, Publications of the Frederick Webb Hodge Anniversary Publication Fund, vol. 1 (1937). Discussions of his life are in obituaries by Fay-Cooper Cole, *American Anthropologist* 59 (1957): 517–20; Arthur J. O. Anderson, *Hispanic American Historical Review*, 38 (1958): 263–67; and Neil Judd, Mark Harrington, and Samuel Lothrop, *American Antiquity* 22 (1957): 401–04.

DAVID LONERGAN

HODGE, Hugh Lenox (27 June 1796–26 Feb. 1873), physician, was born in Philadelphia, Pennsylvania, the son of Hugh Hodge, a physician, and Maria Blanchard. He gained his early education under the tutelage of Mr. Thompson at the grammar school of the University of Pennsylvania and later attended boarding schools in Summerville and New Brunswick, New Jersey. He received an A.B. from the College of New Jersey (now Princeton University) in 1814. Upon graduation, he began a medical apprenticeship with the renowned anatomist Caspar Wistar in Philadelphia and in 1818 received his M.D. from the University of Pennsylvania, having written a dissertation on digestion. He then sailed as a ship's surgeon for Calcutta, where he gained much insight in his work at the Indian cholera hospitals. At the time, Asiatic Cholera was unknown in the United States, and the experience he gained into its successful treatment later proved invaluable during the 1832 cholera epidemic in America.

Returning to Philadelphia in 1820, Hodge began practice as physician to the Southern Dispensary and the Philadelphia Dispensary. He accepted the job of teaching anatomy as a substitute for William E. Horner at the University of Pennsylvania in the summer of 1821. Two years later, Hodge was appointed to a surgery lectureship at Nathaniel Chapman's summer school (later the "Medical Institute" of the University of Pennsylvania). Gradual failure in his eyesight led him to abandon a career in surgery; he choose to pursue the specialty of obstetrics instead. In 1826 Hodge was a founding editor of the *North American Medical and Surgical Journal*, a publication of the Kappa Lambda Society of Aesculapius, an organization of physicians with members throughout the United States. In 1828 he married Margaret E. Aspinwall; they had seven sons.

Hodge was appointed physician-in-charge of the lying-in department of the Pennsylvania Hospital in 1832. Three years later, Hodge was selected as professor of obstetrics and the diseases of women and children at the University of Pennsylvania. At the time, obstetricians in the United States were challenging the more traditional use of women midwives trained only through an informal apprenticeship as the primary assistants of childbirth. A "midwife debate" ensued in which, according to medical historian Jane Donegan, obstetricians sought to convince women patients that "the superior training of doctors equipped with instruments meant safer and shorter parturition" (p. 141). With an increasing number of medically trained male obstetricians, the need for women midwives was seriously questioned. Hodge worked to ensure a perceived necessity of obstetricians by inculcating the view that, according to Donegan, "parturition was *always* dangerous" (p. 152). If this "information can be promulgated," Hodge declared in his 1838 *Introductory Lecture to the Course on Obstetrics and the Diseases of Women*, and if "females can be induced to believe that their sufferings will be diminished, or shortened, and their lives and those of their offspring be safer in the hands of the profession, there will be no further difficulty in establishing the universal practice of obstetrics. All the prejudices of the most ignorant or nervous female, all the innate and acquired feelings of delicacy so characteristic of her sex, will afford no obstacle to the employment of male practitioners" (p. 11).

Hodge made several lasting contributions to the practice of obstetrics. His studies on the influence of variations of female pelvic architecture on disrupting the mechanism of natural labor prompted him to further the practice of inducing labor before full term when the pelvic structure was found to be contracted or deformed. His serious attention to deformities of the pelvis prompted him to encourage the development of Caesarean sections to be "far more successful than in times past, and, perhaps [they] may be justified even in cases of moderate [pelvic] deformity." Hodge adamantly opposed abortion, was apprehensive about the use of anesthesia in childbirth, and did not agree with Harvard professor Oliver Wendell Holmes's claim that physicians were, in part, responsible for the spread of childbed fever. Hodge also initiated a novel method, which became widespread, of using external manipulation in order to remove the placenta. According to Hodge, the practitioner may "facilitate the contraction of the uterus by placing his hand . . . [on] the relaxed walls of the abdomen, over the fundus of the uterus, and by making firm pressure direct the whole organ" toward the pelvis (Thoms, p.

891). However, like many male practitioners who heralded instruments as professional symbols of obstetrics and gynecology, Hodge advocated overall an interventionist approach to his practice. He promoted the use of forceps in childbirth as an "addition or substitute for the natural powers by which the child is expelled," and he argued that a "very large proportion" of vesico-vaginal fistulae, an opening between the urinary bladder and the vagina, resulted "not from the use, but from the neglect of the forceps" (Thoms, p. 891).

In addition to lecturing, Hodge built a sizable private practice and gradually relinquished his obstetrical duties in favor of the wider variety of "diseases peculiar to women." He recounted much that he had learned about this special group of diseases in his *On Diseases Peculiar to Women, Including Displacements of the Uterus* (1860). In this work he addressed what has become his most lasting contribution to the field, a pessary used to support a displaced or inverted uterus. Like many male practitioners of his day, Hodge viewed women's diseases as arising from nervous disorders that owed their origin to the displacement of the uterus. His obsession with this organ's responsibility for causing the vast number of women's disorders led him in 1860 to design a method to stabilize the womb. One biographer recounts Hodge's serendipitous mental formulation of this mechanical device as follows: After countless unsuccessful experiments, "Sitting one evening in the University [Hodge's] eyes rested on the upright steel support designed to hold the shovels and tongs, which were kept in position by a steel hook, and as he studied its supporting curve, the longed-for illumination came, and the lever pessary was the result" (Thoms, p. 889). Hodge, using the rubberized vulcanite recently discovered by the inventor Charles Goodyear, composed an oblong ring molded in a way as to fit the curvature of the birth canal. One contemporary claimed that no other discovery "has ever been made in the treatment of female diseases which has done more good than this original" device (Penrose, p. 15). This widely adopted invention soon gained eponymous status and became known as Hodge's Pessary; it remained in use throughout the twentieth century.

The continual worsening of Hodge's eyesight caused him in 1863 to resign his chair in obstetrics, having achieved emeritus status. Unable to read and write for himself, he relied on the assistance of one of his sons to compile a massive obstetrical work, which Hodge claimed was "in opposition to the most admired authors." This work, *Principles and Practices of Obstetrics* (1864), met with wide acclaim. As one biographer noted, from this work's "philosophical character" as well as "its original teachings and illustrations" it "ranked among the very first" of its kind both in America and abroad (Penrose, p. 21).

Hodge was a fellow of the College of Physicians (Philadelphia) and of the American Philosophical Society. He died in Philadelphia.

• Much of the material Hodge used to compile his works is located in the College of Physicians of Philadelphia. His other important writings include *On the Pathology and Therapeutics of Cholera Maligna* (1833), *On the Non-contagious Character of Puerperal Fever: An Introductory Lecture* (1852), and *Foeticide, or Criminal Abortion* (1869). Contemporary biographical accounts include William Goodell, *Biographical Memoir of Hugh L. Hodge, M.D.* (1874), and R. A. F. Penrose, *A Discourse Commemorative of the Life and Character of Hugh L. Hodge* (1873). See also T. G. Morton and Frank Woodbury, *The History of the Pennsylvania Hospital* (1895). Herbert Thoms, "Hugh Lenox Hodge," *American Journal of Obstetrics and Gynecology* 33 (1937): 886–93, remains a most useful brief account of Hodge's life. For a general historical description of the shift from female midwifery to male obstetrics, see Jane B. Donegan, *Women and Men Midwives: Medicine, Morality, and Misogyny in Early America* (1978), and Judith Walzer Leavitt, *Brought to Bed: Childbearing in America, 1750 to 1950* (1986).

PHILIP K. WILSON

HODGE, John Reed (12 June 1893–12 Nov. 1963), army officer, was born in Golconda, Illinois, the son of John Hardin Hodge, an educator, and Melissa Caroline Steagall. Hodge attended Southern Illinois Teachers College from 1912 to 1913 and later the University of Illinois, where he studied architectural engineering. After the United States entered World War I in April 1917, Hodge was commissioned a second lieutenant in the Officers' Reserve Corps, and in October 1917 he was commissioned a second lieutenant in the regular army. On 6 October 1917 Hodge married Lydia Gillespie Parsons; they had one daughter. In early 1918 Hodge went to France with the Fifth Division and saw action in the St.-Mihiel and Meuse-Argonne offensives.

Hodge returned to the United States in the summer of 1919, and over the next two decades he rose slowly in rank while holding a variety of assignments, reaching the rank of lieutenant colonel in 1940. His assignments included a professorship in the Reserve Officers' Training Corps (ROTC) program at Mississippi Agricultural and Mechanical College from 1921 to 1925, service with the Twenty-seventh Infantry Regiment and the Twenty-second Infantry Brigade in Hawaii from 1926 to 1929, and a tour with the Operations and Training Division of the War Department General Staff from 1936 to 1941. Hodge also graduated from the Infantry School in 1926, the Line and Staff Officers' Course of the Chemical Warfare Service in 1932, the Command and General Staff School in 1934, the Army War College in 1935, and the Air Corps Tactical School in 1936. At the time of the Japanese attack on Pearl Harbor in December 1941, he was serving as operations officer of the VII Corps in Birmingham, Alabama. When the corps was transferred to the West Coast in late December, Hodge was named chief of staff.

In June 1942 Hodge was appointed assistant commander of the Twenty-fifth Division, then training in Hawaii, with the temporary rank of brigadier general. At the end of 1942 the division was sent to Guadalcanal in the South Pacific to reinforce the marines, who had been struggling with the Japanese for control of the island since the previous August. In the final stages of the campaign in early 1943 Hodge proved himself to be a tough and aggressive leader, and in April 1943 he was promoted to the temporary rank of major general and given command of the Americal Division. At the end of July 1943, when the commander of the Forty-third Division was relieved during the heavy fighting on New Georgia island, Hodge was appointed temporary commander and led the division through the mopping up operations in early August. Hodge then returned to the Americal Division. In December 1943 he led the division to Bougainville island, where it took up a defensive position along the eastern sector of the American beachhead at Empress Augusta Bay. When the Japanese launched a major counterattack in March 1944, Hodge's division saw heavy action before the Japanese were repulsed.

Hodge's performance in these campaigns earned him a reputation as one of the best combat commanders in the Pacific area, and in April 1944 he was named commander of the newly created XXIV Corps. Attached to the Sixth Army, Hodge's corps landed at Leyte island in the Philippines on 20 October 1944. By the end of the campaign two months later, it had engaged in almost continuous fighting as it advanced across the southern part of the island. On 1 April 1945 Hodge's corps, now attached to the Tenth Army, landed on Okinawa island, and during the next three months it participated in some of the bloodiest fighting in the Pacific war before the Japanese defenders were practically annihilated. Near the end of the campaign, Hodge, whom the press had now dubbed "the Patton of the Pacific" because of his hard-driving style, was promoted to the temporary rank of lieutenant general.

In September 1945 Hodge and his XXIVth Corps went to Korea to take the surrender of the Japanese forces south of the thirty-eighth parallel, the Soviet Union under an arrangement with the United States having already taken control of the area to the north, and to administer the military occupation of the southern part of the country. For the next three years, Hodge as commander of U.S. Army Forces in Korea was the highest-ranking American official in Korea. From the outset, he was frustrated in carrying out American policy, which initially called for an interim four-power trusteeship over all Korea followed by eventual independence. The Soviets undermined trusteeship by establishing a Communist administration in the North, while conservative nationalists in the South led by Syngman Rhee demanded immediate independence. Matters were made worse by severe economic problems, often violent conflict between the political left and right, and Hodge's political inexperience, blunt style, lack of familiarity with Korean history and culture, and reliance on wealthy Korean landlords and businessmen for administrative personnel.

Hodge, a visceral anti-Communist and convinced that rightest political power offered the only certain bulwark against complete Communist domination of Korea, sought to restore order to the South and promote political stability by suppressing Communists and Fostering a pro-American coalition made up of moderate conservatives. Hodge's actions angered the left, which favored wideranging economic and social reform. At the same time, Hodge's strong personality differences with Rhee strained his relations with the right. Ultimately, the United States resolved the Korean conundrum through elections in the South that resulted in the establishment of the Republic of Korea in 1948 and, despite Hodge's search for a moderate alternative, the selection of Rhee as president. Recalled to the United States in August 1948, Hodge thereafter held various assignments, including command of the V Corps and the Army Field Forces, before retiring in June 1953 with the rank of full general.

A stocky, direct, and pugnacious individual, Hodge stands out as an able field commander in World War II and as a military administrator who grappled with almost intractable problems to secure American interests in Korea. He died in Washington, D.C.

• Hodge's records for his service in Korea are located in the National Archives. His service during World War II is discussed in John Miller, Jr., *Guadalcanal: The First Offensive* (1949) and *Cartwheel: The Reduction of Rabaul* (1959); M. Hamlin Cannon, *Leyte: The Return to the Philippines* (1960); and Roy A. Appleman et al., *Okinawa: The Last Battle* (1948). Extensive, and somewhat critical, discussions of his work in Korea are in Bruce Cumings, *The Origins of the Korean War* (2 vols., 1981, 1990); James Irving Matray, *The Reluctant Crusade: American Foreign Policy in Korea, 1941–1950* (1985); Robert T. Oliver, *Syngman Rhee and American Involvement in Korea, 1941–1960: A Personal Narrative* (1978); Michael C. Sandusky, *America's Parallel* (1983); and William Whitney Stueck, Jr., *The Road to Confrontation: American Policy toward China and Korea, 1947–1950* (1981). An obituary is in the *New York Times*, 13 Nov. 1963.

JOHN KENNEDY OHL

HODGE, William Thomas (1 Nov. 1874–30 Jan. 1932), actor and playwright, was born in Albion, New York, the son of Thomas Hodge, a businessman and real estate agent, and Mary Anderson. He began his education in the Albion public schools and continued in the public schools of Rochester, New York, after his family moved there early in his childhood. In 1891, at the age of seventeen, he ran away from home determined to go on the stage. He began his career as a property man for the Hill Repertoire Company, which was managed by his brother Joseph. During his stay with this company and all through his apprentice years he gained experience in virtually all aspects of the theater, becoming a member of a number of lesser touring companies that frequented the small towns in New York. These early days also found him performing with companies in Canada and appearing in vaudeville in Chicago, Illinois.

Hodge's first appearance in New York City was at the People's Theatre in January 1898 in a play called *The Heart of Chicago*. In 1900 he received good reviews for his performance of the role of Freeman

Whitemarsh in James A. Herne's popular *Sag Harbor*, and in 1904 he was a part of the immensely successful production of *Mrs. Wiggs of the Cabbage Patch*, a play by Anne Crawford Flexner based on the stories of Alice Hegan Rice. In 1907 he landed the role that made him a star—Daniel Vorhees, the shrewd, witty, truly American hero of *The Man from Home*, by Booth Tarkington and Harry Leon Wilson. This play, with Hodge as star, was in continuous performance, either in New York City or on the road, for the next five years. In 1909 Hodge married Helen P. Cogswell, a musical comedy actress (stage name Helen Hale?); they had three children.

In a way, Hodge played the Vorhees role for the remainder of his life. Failing to find other plays with similar characters, he began to write them for himself. His first was *The Guest of Honor* (1920). This was followed by *Beware of Dogs* (1921), which Hodge described as a "satirical tale in three wags"; *For All of Us* (1923); *The Judge's Husband* (1926); *Straight through the Door* (1928); and *The Old Rascal* (1930).

Hodge continued to find a strong following in the small towns of the country. Buoyed by that success, he would repeatedly and optimistically bring his work back to New York, only to discover once again that the door had been closed to his character's brand of crafty, slick, double-dealing humor. Writing in the *New York Times* of Hodge's *The Guest of Honor*, Alexander Woollcott said, "There are hundreds of thousands of people in New York who would be enchanted by [that production], but whether they are in the habit of theatregoing at all is a matter of some doubt."

The tall, craggy, redheaded Hodge was called the "Lincoln of the stage" as an actor and the "Harold Bell Wright of the stage" as an author. He carried on the Yankee tradition several decades after its heyday. His plays are often rags-to-riches stories in which his character always shrewdly straightens out the most intricate and implausible plot machinations. Many supporting characters appear to be right off the vaudeville circuits, with Irish washerwomen and Cockney Brits making frequent appearances. The plays are structural disasters, with people coming and going for no apparent reason and with the main purpose of the action being to get Hodge's character onstage as much as humanly possible. His final appearance was as Joe Adams in *The Old Rascal* in 1931. He died of pneumonia the following year at his home near Greenwich, Connecticut.

• Hodge was interviewed about his decision to write his own plays in the *Literary Digest*, 16 Oct. 1926. His plays were collected and published in two volumes by Samuel French in 1928. Mary B. Mullett provides a particularly comprehensive, if chatty, biographical article about Hodge in *American Magazine*, Apr. 1924. An obituary is in the *New York Times*, 31 Jan. 1932.

LARRY CLARK

HODGES, Courtney Hicks (5 Jan. 1887–16 Jan. 1966), army officer, was born in Perry, Georgia, the son of John Hicks Hodges, a newspaperman, and Katherine

Norwood. Hodges attended local schools and North Georgia College prior to entering the U.S. Military Academy in 1904. He was deficient in mathematics, however, and was dismissed from West Point after one year. Hodges returned to Perry and worked as a grocery clerk for a year before enlisting in the army as a private. In 1909 he qualified on competitive examinations for a commission as a second lieutenant. Hodges then had tours of duty at Fort Leavenworth, Kansas, at two posts in Texas, and in the Philippines. Promoted to first lieutenant in 1916, he served with General John Pershing's Punitive Expedition in Mexico until it was withdrawn early in 1917. The following year Hodges was ordered to France, where he served in the Sixth Infantry Regiment, Fifth Division. He received brevet promotions to major and lieutenant colonel and won the Distinguished Service Cross for his performance commanding a detachment along the Meuse River in eastern France. The war ended less than two weeks later.

Hodges served with occupation forces in Germany and in 1920 was confirmed in the permanent rank of major. Although a surfeit of officers kept Hodges from receiving another promotion until 1934, his leadership abilities and knowledge of infantry tactics were recognized with teaching assignments at West Point (1920–1924) and at the Infantry School at Fort Benning, Georgia (1929–1933). In tours at the Field Artillery School and at the Air Corps Tactical School (where he taught infantry tactics), Hodges gained insight into the importance of coordinating infantry operations with artillery and air support. Hodges himself attended the Command and General Staff School (1924–1925). He spent 1925–1926 as an instructor at the Infantry School, Fort Benning; in 1926–1929 attended the Air Corps Tactical School, Langley Field, Virginia; and attended the Army War College in 1933–1934. He also put in two-year stints with the Seventh Infantry at Vancouver Barracks (1934–1936), as a staff officer in the Philippines (1936–1938), and as commander of the Seventh Infantry Regiment (1938–1940) at Vancouver Barracks in the state of Washington. In 1928 Hodges married Mildred Lee Buchner, a widow. The couple had no children.

In 1940, as correspondent Gladwin Hill put it, "Hodges' head started appearing above the crowd" when he was named commandant of the Infantry School. Promoted to brigadier general in 1940, Hodges was next assigned to Washington, D.C., as chief of infantry. In this capacity Hodges oversaw the development of infantry doctrine appropriate to the conditions of World War II and also fostered the adoption of new weapons and equipment, such as the bazooka (an antitank weapon that could be handled by an individual infantryman), the jeep, a new helmet to replace an unsatisfactory design dating to the First World War, and the rapid-fire carbine. After a year as chief of infantry, Hodges headed the new Ground Forces Replacement and School Command. He left Washington in mid-1942 to command the training of the Tenth Corps, after which he headed the Southwest Defense Command.

In March 1944 Hodges, now a lieutenant general, was ordered overseas to become deputy commander of the First Army under his longtime friend, General Omar Bradley. The latter had already had combat experience in North Africa and Sicily and commanded the First Army during the Normandy landings in June 1944 and the crucial buildup period that followed. When sufficient American troops were ashore, the Third Army was activated under the command of General George Patton, and Hodges took over the First Army on 1 August 1944. By then the offensive was under way, and the two American armies as well as British and Canadian armies broke out of Normandy. In less than six weeks the four Allied armies had liberated much of France and were advancing swiftly across Belgium and eastern France.

As the Allied forces approached German borders, the First Army had the difficult task of moving toward the Ruhr, the center of the German steel industry. Several natural barriers, including the Huertgen Forest, the Roer (Rur) River, and the Rhine, had to be breached before the First Army could threaten the Ruhr. In addition, Germany had erected a series of concrete pillboxes and other obstacles known as the West Wall. By mid-September all the Allied armies became bogged down, in part because of these and other obstacles but also because of the shortage of critical supplies.

In October First Army divisions took Aachen, the first German city of any importance to be conquered, but the fight there was bitter. It was soon followed by a gruelling campaign in the dense Huertgen Forest. By the end of November Hodges's spearheads had just cleared the forest. However, before more offensive operations of any consequence could be undertaken, both Hodges and his superiors were taken by surprise, when major German forces unleashed a counteroffensive that became known as the Battle of the Bulge. German forces far outnumbered the four First Army divisions then manning the Ardennes region of Belgium. Once he realized the gravity of the German attack, which had begun on 16 December, Hodges called on Bradley for reinforcements and directed them to occupy such key road junctions as Bastogne and St.-Vith. Hodges also ordered into the Ardennes other First Army divisions that had been engaged north of the threatened area. Although British general Bernard Montgomery considered recommending Hodges's relief, Bradley and General Dwight Eisenhower, Supreme Commander of the Allied Powers, retained faith in his leadership.

By early 1945 Allied forces had eliminated the Bulge and could prepare to advance into Germany. Once again the First Army made impressive gains. It first crossed the Rhine in force at Remagen then joined the Ninth Army in encircling the Ruhr and capturing hundreds of thousands of German troops. The First Army finally moved directly across Germany and met Soviet forces on the Elbe River on 25 April 1945.

For Hodges the war was not over, for Washington planners had already concluded that, to subdue Japan, another American army would be needed to join the two already in the Far East under General Douglas MacArthur. The First Army was assigned the task of capturing Tokyo. Although the reasons Hodges was chosen for this command are not entirely clear, it is likely his experience in large-scale mechanized warfare and his reliable, self-effacing leadership in Europe gained him this assignment. With his staff, Hodges proceeded to the Philippines in the summer of 1945 to begin planning for the First Army's landings in Japan. The war ended, however, in August 1945, and Hodges was not again called to lead what would have been, in effect, a new First Army in combat. Instead, Hodges returned to the United States to command the First Army, which reverted to its prewar status as a training command. Hodges retired in February 1949 and moved to San Antonio, where he died.

Hodges's accomplishments prior to and during World War II are impressive but not as widely known as those of Patton, who commanded the Third Army and sought the attention of the press. In the opinion of many observers, Hodges resembled a small-town banker more than a hard-driving and successful general. He made mistakes, especially in trying to batter through the Huertgen Forest in a manner reminiscent of World War I leaders. Nevertheless, his First Army was impressive in victory and resilient in containing the German onslaught in the Ardennes. Undoubtedly these were among the factors that led to his subsequent assignment in the Pacific.

• Materials relating to Hodges's commands are found primarily in the Eisenhower Library in Abilene, Kans., and at the National Archives and the Washington National Record Center in Suitland, Md. Hodges has been profiled on several occasions. The most useful are Gladwin Hill, "For Hodges History Repeats," *New York Times Magazine*, 25 Mar. 1945, pp. 834–35; and G. Patrick Murray, "Courtney Hodges: Modest Star of World War II," *American History Illustrated* 7 (Jan. 1973): 12–25. Virtually every book about ground warfare in Western Europe mentions Hodges. Helpful overviews are Charles B. MacDonald, *The Mighty Endeavor: American Armed Forces in the European Theater in World War II* (1969); and Russell F. Weigley, *Eisenhower's Lieutenants* (1981). On Pacific planning see John Ray Skates, *The Invasion of Japan: Alternative to the Bomb* (1994). An obituary is in the *New York Times*, 17 Jan. 1966.

LLOYD J. GRAYBAR

HODGES, Edward (20 July 1796–1 Sept. 1867), organist, writer, and composer, was born in Bristol, England, the son of Archelaus Hodges, a paper merchant, and Elizabeth Stephens. The death of his father in 1811 ended his formal schooling; however, he continued educating himself by reading widely throughout his life. For a brief period after his father's death, Hodges carried on with the family paper business. His interests lay in music rather than commerce, however, and sometime during the early 1820s he resolved to devote himself to church music.

In 1819 Hodges became organist of St. Nicholas Church in Bristol, and in 1821 he assumed the same post at St. James's Church, also in Bristol. In May 1825 he matriculated at Sydney Sussex College in Cambridge, not for course work but rather to certify his abilities. In July of that year he was awarded the Mus. Bac. and Mus. Doc. degrees in quick succession, submitting for the latter an original piece for chorus and orchestra.

Over the next decade Hodges maintained his posts at the two Bristol churches, contributed articles on church music and organ design to music periodicals, and composed church music. At the same time, he sought an appointment as organist of either a cathedral or a large collegiate church. As it turned out, Hodges was unable to attain such a position because he had been raised a Nonconformist Independent. Even though he had converted to Anglicanism and held a Cambridge doctorate, Hodges lacked the requisite background and connections. Candidates for such posts were expected to have begun their training as choir boys and to have spent a period of years under the tutelage and sponsorship of a prominent cathedral organist.

In 1818 Hodges had married Margaret Robertson, the daughter of a leading Moravian layman in nearby Malmsbury. Hodges and his wife had eight children, six of whom survived infancy. Margaret died in October 1835, and shortly thereafter, Hodges decided to seek a position in North America. In 1838 he was offered the post of organist at St. James Cathedral in Toronto, and in August of that year he set sail with his eldest son. The two stopped briefly in New York before continuing on to Canada, and Hodges apparently made several contacts in New York that proved useful less than a year later. The economic and political situation in Canada was precarious, and Hodges stayed only through October. He returned to New York, and on 14 January 1839 was appointed organist of Trinity Parish. At the time, Trinity was the largest Episcopal church in the United States and was about to undergo construction of its third edifice. Hodges served as organist at St. John's Chapel until the completion and dedication of Trinity's new building in 1846. His innovative design for Trinity's new organ, the largest in the United States at the time, aroused much public and professional interest.

In 1844 Hodges was married again, to Sarah Moore, the sister of the president of Columbia University and the member of a prominent family; they had no children together. Her private income enabled Hodges to bring his remaining children to the United States from England. Moreover, he was able thereafter to work for the establishment of an English cathedral-style music program at Trinity against official indifference, and even opposition, without having to fear for his family's livelihood and well-being. Hodges added boys to the Trinity choir (while retaining the women), instituted Anglican chant for the canticles in place of metrical psalmody, and introduced anthems into the services. He founded and directed the Church Choral Society, which presented English cathedral-style sung services in several New York–area churches. Hodges remained at Trinity for the rest of his career. He also contributed regular articles, mostly on aspects of church music, organ building, and choir organization, to the *New York Musical World*. During 1856 and 1857 he was listed as one of the publication's three editors.

Hodges suffered a mild attack of paralysis owing to a stroke in the spring of 1854 but recovered quickly. In September 1855, however, he was stricken again by paralysis and forced to take a three-month leave. In September 1858 he suffered a third stroke, this time of moderate severity. Once again he took leave; however, for all practical purposes, Hodges never returned to Trinity's organ loft.

Following the death of his second wife in July 1861, Hodges lived for two years with his son the Reverend J. S. B. Hodges, rector of Grace Church in Newark, New Jersey. In May 1863 Hodges resigned his appointment at Trinity and, shortly thereafter, returned to England. His last years were spent in the Bristol suburb of Clifton, where he died.

Hodges's compositions are of uneven quality, and his music has not stood the test of time, although several pieces are well worth reviving for performance. Although most of his writings are either practical or polemic on aspects of church music, several show a surprisingly sophisticated command of music history and historical theory, especially for the period. Hodges's main significance lies in his influence on the course of American church music. He was one of the first church musicians in the United States to view his work as a profession, rather than as an adjunct to teaching, theater music, or music merchandising. More important, he was a reformer, as opposed to others who accepted the musical status quo and merely worked within its limited artistic parameters. Hodges worked toward the establishment of English cathedral-style service music both at Trinity and as the norm for Episcopal churches in the United States. His attitudes and standards, passed on through his students, became the model for the professional practice of church music in many, if not most, American denominations well into the twentieth century.

• Hodges's manuscripts of his own music were given to the Bristol Public Library by his son J. S. B. Hodges, to whom they were bequeathed at his father's death. Much, if not all, of Hodges's music collection is now at the Library of Congress. Another collection of letters, two diary volumes, and other written memorabilia are in the American Organ Archives of the Organ Historical Society at Westminster Choir College, Princeton, N.J. Hodges's life and career are discussed at length in John Ogasapian, *English Cathedral Music in New York City: Hodges of Trinity Church* (1994). Hodges's daughter Faustina Hasse Hodges wrote a memoir of her father, *Edward Hodges* (1896). See also Ogasapian, "New Material on Edward Hodges," *Tracker* 35, no. 1 (1991): 13–18. On Hodges's work at Trinity, see Arthur H. Messiter, *A History of the Choir and Music of Trinity Church* (1906). On his ideas in organ design, see Nicholas Thistlethwaite, *The Making of the Victorian Organ* (1990).

JOHN OGASAPIAN

HODGES, George (6 Oct. 1856–27 May 1919), clergyman and educator, was born in Rome, New York, the son of George Frederick Hodges and Hannah Elizabeth Ballard. Hodges received his bachelor's degree from Hamilton College in 1877. After teaching for a year in London, Ontario, Canada, he entered St. Andrew's Divinity School in Syracuse, New York. Dissatisfied with the instruction he received there, he transferred to Berkeley Divinity School in Middletown, Connecticut, from which he graduated in 1881. During his final year in seminary, he also served at a small Episcopal parish in South Glastonbury, Connecticut. He was ordained a deacon in the Episcopal church in 1881 and a priest the next year. Called to be an assistant minister at Calvary Church in Pittsburgh, Pennsylvania, in 1881, Hodges was placed in charge of St. Stephen's, a mission congregation under Calvary's care. He married Anna Sargent Jennings in 1881, and they had two children. After the death of his first wife in 1897, he married Julia Shelley in 1901. They had three children.

When Calvary's rector left in 1888, Hodges was chosen to succeed him and was officially installed in that office in January 1889. He was deeply influenced by the writings of Charles Kingsley and Frederick Denison Maurice, Anglican clergy who had developed and spread "Social Gospel" theology in England in the mid-nineteenth century. Maurice and Kingsley emphasized that the Christian idea of salvation pertained not simply to the afterlife but to everyday human experience as well. During Hodges's tenure at Calvary, the parish took a leading role on behalf of political and social reform in Pittsburgh, and it supported the ecumenical venture that founded a settlement house named after Kingsley. Although Hodges was elected bishop coadjutor (assistant bishop) of the diocese of Oregon in June 1893, he chose not to accept that appointment. Instead, he left Calvary six months later to become dean of the Episcopal Theological School (now the Episcopal Divinity School) in Cambridge, Massachusetts. He assumed those duties in January 1894.

As Hodges observed in a sermon he delivered at the seminary early in 1894, the typical clergyman was often more interested in the history of Jerusalem than in the history of his own city or state. That trend, he thought, had to be reversed, and future students for the ministry needed to be thoroughly trained in both sociology and theology. Hodges also believed in the need to teach students modern critical methods of biblical interpretation, and he warmly welcomed non-Episcopalians as speakers on the seminary campus. As a result of this openness to new ideas and emphases in theological education, many conservative church members began to question whether students at the seminary were being introduced to unorthodox or even heretical beliefs. Hodges responded to these charges, however, by arguing that the Episcopal church ought to broaden its outlook and recognize truth wherever it existed. He insisted, furthermore,

that Christians had nothing to fear from the diligent scholarly exploration of the Bible.

Hodges functioned at the seminary in a number of capacities besides that of dean. He was a professor of homiletics and pastoral care, a lecturer on liturgics and church polity, and a teacher of courses on the English Bible. A prolific writer as well, he composed more than thirty books and numerous journal articles. His works include popular studies of church history, theology, and scripture; several collections of sermons; textbooks about the beliefs and practices of the Episcopal church for both adults and children; and introductions to Christian sociology. Hodges was also in great demand as a preacher and lecturer at church gatherings. He suffered a physical collapse in 1915 and struggled thereafter with poor health, but he remained as dean until his death. He died while vacationing at his summer home in Holderness, New Hampshire.

Hodges was regarded as one of the foremost educational figures in the Episcopal church in his day. Although he was by no means a profound thinker or theologian, he brought significant leadership to the academic affairs of his denomination during a period of intellectual transition and adjustment. Through his emphasis on the Social Gospel while he was a parish minister and through his openness to new approaches to the Bible and Christian belief during his tenure as a seminary dean, Hodges helped the Episcopal church come to terms with many of the cultural and religious challenges of the early twentieth century.

• Hodges's manuscript papers are at the Episcopal Divinity School Library in Cambridge, Mass. The essential published source about his career is Julia Shelley Hodges, *George Hodges* (1926), the biography written by his second wife. James Arthur Muller, *The Episcopal Theological School, 1867–1943* (1943), also offers a full description of Hodges's work as dean. An obituary is in *Proceedings of the Massachusetts Historical Society* 53 (Oct. 1919–June 1920): 131–39.

GARDINER H. SHATTUCK, JR.

HODGES, Gil (4 Apr. 1924–2 Apr. 1972), baseball player and manager, was born Gilbert Raymond Hodges in Princeton, Indiana, the son of Charles Hodges, a coal miner, and Irene Horstmeyer. A three-sport letterman in high school, he was recruited by major league baseball clubs after graduating in 1941, but chose instead to attend St. Joseph's College in Indiana. He only played one year of college baseball, playing instead in a semiprofessional industrial league in the summers after his freshman and sophomore years. In that second summer, after enlisting in the U.S. Marine Corps and while awaiting assignment to active duty, Hodges was signed as a third baseman by the Brooklyn Dodgers and was placed directly on the club roster.

He made his major league debut in the last game of the 1943 season, after which he reported to the marines. During World War II Hodges saw combat action in the Pacific, including the invasion of Okinawa, and rose to the rank of sergeant.

During his initial stay in the majors Hodges was identified by Dodger management as a catching prospect. After his discharge from the marines in 1946, he spent a year in the minor leagues learning the new position, at Newport News, Virginia, of the Class B Piedmont League. Promoted to the major league club in 1947, he saw limited service as a catcher. In 1948, his catching career diverted by the arrival of Roy Campanella, Hodges was moved to first base. Through hard work and natural athletic ability, he developed into one of the steadiest and most graceful first basemen of his day, setting fielding records for his position. Hodges received the Gold Glove Award at first base in each of the first three years the award was made, 1957–1959.

In December 1948 Hodges married Joan Lombardi in Brooklyn. Unlike most of the other Dodgers, Hodges lived in Brooklyn year round, earning even more affection and loyalty from the local fans. The couple had four children.

Hodges played through 1961 with the Dodgers, the last four years in Los Angeles following the team's move. His fielding at first base was a defensive asset for the club, and his batting was an important part of a heavy-hitting lineup that was largely responsible for the emergence of the Dodgers into a National League power during the 1950s. In the years he played for the Dodgers, the team was in seven World Series, and Hodges batted over .300 in three of them. In the seventh game of the 1955 Series, he batted in the two runs that gave the Dodgers their first World Series championship.

At the time he left the Dodgers, Hodges had hit 361 home runs, more than any other Dodger player. He was given an award after the 1959 season by the Los Angeles Baseball Writers Association as the player who most typified the Dodger spirit. Hodges ended his playing career with the New York Mets. He joined the National League expansion team in its inaugural 1962 season but appeared in only fifty-four games. He retired early in the following season.

After his playing career ended, Hodges managed two different teams, leading one of them to the first World Series victory by an expansion team in baseball's modern era. His first managing opportunity was with the Washington Senators, an American League expansion club established after the original Senators moved to Minnesota in 1961. He took over the last-place team on 22 May, forty-one games into the 1963 season, and managed them through 1967. Although they never rose into contention under Hodges, the Senators improved their won-lost record each year, finishing the 1967 season tied for sixth place in the ten-team league.

Hodges's managing triumph came in his next position, returning in 1968 to the Mets as the fourth manager in the club's history (although his immediate predecessor managed only eleven games). Hodges took over a team that finished in last place in five of its first six years of play, including 120 losses in its opening season of 1962. In his first year as manager, the Mets finished in ninth place (out of ten teams) for only the second time in their history.

The team's prospects for the 1969 season looked as dismal as its previous record would suggest, but Hodges skillfully managed a team that included players nearing the ends of their careers as well as two young pitchers—Tom Seaver and Nolan Ryan—who would later dominate their position. The Mets won the Eastern Division in the first year of divisional play in the major leagues; they then swept the Atlanta Braves in three straight games in the first National League Championship Series. The Baltimore Orioles, their American League opponents in the World Series, had a record that was superior to the Mets in nearly every category. To the surprise of most baseball observers and the delight of their long-suffering fans, the Mets defeated the Orioles in five games.

Hodges was named baseball's Manager of the Year for 1969. He managed for two more seasons with the Mets; in both years the team compiled the same record and finished third in the Eastern Division. While preparing the Mets for the 1972 season, Hodges suffered a heart attack and died in West Palm Beach, Florida.

Considered among the physically strongest players in baseball, Hodges had a lifetime .273 batting average, with 370 home runs and 1,274 runs batted in over eighteen years. He was named to the All-Star team eight times. Although he had a losing record as a manager, he regularly elicited a level of play that enabled his clubs to finish better than expected, culminating in the "miracle" of the 1969 Mets.

Hodges was widely respected as an extraordinarily decent person throughout his career. He took his responsibilities and his talents seriously, most notably in mastering new positions and in working out of extended batting slumps. The steadying influence he provided to his clubs as a player continued during his managerial career. With Hodges as manager, players knew that there were rules to be followed and expectations about the effort to be given. Undoubtedly his character combined with his understanding and appreciation of the game enabled him to make what is often a difficult transition from star player to manager. Contrary to the famous cynical remark made by his first major league manager, Leo Durocher, Hodges proved with his 1969 season that nice guys can finish first.

• The National Baseball Library in Cooperstown, N.Y., contains a file on Hodges. Hodges published his reflections on the sport and on his career in *The Game of Baseball* (1970), written with Frank Slocum. A biography of Hodges by Milton J. Shapiro, *The Gil Hodges Story* (1960), was published as his career with the Dodgers was coming to an end. Hodges's statistics are published in *The Baseball Encyclopedia*, 9th ed. (1993). A biographical tribute, containing reminiscences by a number of former teammates, is Marino Amoruso, *Gil Hodges: The Quiet Man* (1991). The flavor of the Dodgers during their years in Brooklyn when Hodges played for the club is captured in Roger Kahn, *The Boys of Summer* (1972). The story of the Met's championship season of 1969 and Hodges's managing of the team to a World Series victory is told in Stanley Cohen, *A Magic Summer* (1988). An obituary is in the *New York Times*, 3 Apr. 1972.

PAUL A. LeBEL

HODGES, Johnny (25 July 1907–11 May 1970), jazz musician, was born Cornelius Hodges in Cambridge, Massachusetts, the son of John Hodges and Katie Swan. The family moved to Boston when Hodges was an infant, and he grew up in a rich musical environment. His neighbors included Harry Carney, the future baritone saxophonist with the Duke Ellington band, and both his mother and sister played piano. Hodges's mother taught him enough piano so that he could play at house hops; throughout his career he often worked out musical ideas at the keyboard.

During his early teens Hodges began to play both soprano (curved) and alto saxophone. He met Sidney Bechet in 1920 when the soprano saxophonist came to Boston with a burlesque show, and Bechet and Louis Armstrong on records became Hodges's chief influences. He gained early experience playing in groups led by Bobby Sawyer and pianist Walter Johnson, and he began to visit New York City on weekends, playing with pianist Luckey Roberts's society band, with Willie "the Lion" Smith at the Rhythm Club, and in various cutting contests. But his most important early experience was with Bechet, who adopted Hodges as his protégé and introduced him to the straight soprano saxophone. At Bechet's Club Pasha, Hodges played soprano duets with his mentor and often led the group when Bechet was late or absent.

From 1925 until 1928 Hodges spent time in both Boston and New York, playing with groups led by Lloyd Scott (1926) and Chick Webb (until 1928). Duke Ellington's early group, the Washingtonians, spent summers in New England, and at times Hodges heard them in person. Ellington heard Hodges in both Boston and New York. Twice, Ellington invited him to join the band, but Hodges felt he needed more experience. Finally, in 1928, on Webb's recommendation and after Otto Hardwicke (Ellington's alto and soprano saxophonist) had been injured in an automobile accident, Hodges joined Ellington for a stay that, with only one interruption, lasted until his death.

Hodges immediately became a star attraction, and Ellington often turned to him for compositional and melodic ideas, contrasting his smooth tone with the "jungle" sounds of Tricky Sam Nanton, Bubber Miley, and Cootie Williams. During the 1930s Hodges developed the sensuous, deeply lyrical sound that became his trademark, "a tone so beautiful," Ellington later wrote, "it sometimes brought tears to the eyes"; his playing sounded like "poured honey" that could "melt the melody to smoldering." Hodges's deeply sensual sound is evident in such specialties as "Warm Valley" and "Passion Flower" and in the later Ellington compositions "Isfahan," "Come Sunday," "Star-Crossed Lovers," and Billy Strayhorn's masterpiece, "Blood Count." But Hodges's playing stayed rooted in the blues, clearly so on such pieces as "Jeep's Blues"

and on the sextet album he recorded with Ellington in 1959, *Back to Back*. His solos also never failed to convey a propulsive sense of swing. Pieces like "The Jeep Is Jumpin'," "Things Aint What They Used to Be," and "On the Sunny Side of the Street" are forever marked as swinging Hodges vehicles.

By 1940 Hodges had tired of the burden of playing lead and solos on both alto and soprano saxophones, and he decided to concentrate on the alto. He also began a long series of recordings with small groups drawn largely from Ellington's band. He recorded nine sextet sessions in 1938 and 1939 under the name of Johnny Hodges and His Orchestra, with Ellington on piano, and in 1947 he recorded with the Johnny Hodges All-Stars. In 1948, while Ellington was in Europe convalescing from surgery, Hodges, Strayhorn, vocalist Al Hibbler, and five others enjoyed great success in a seven-week engagement at the Apollo Bar on 125th Street. Hodges also recorded with an octet in Paris in 1950.

By 1951, economic conditions had deteriorated for big bands. Even Ellington, one of the few leaders who held a band together without interruption, was forced to cut salaries. A dispirited Hodges and several others struck out on their own, Hodges signing a contract with impresario Norman Granz for Verve Records. Immediately he had a huge recorded hit with "Castle Rock," a piece with a strong rhythm and blues feeling that featured the new group's manager, Al Sears, on tenor saxophone. The band enjoyed continued success; a summer 1954 session, *Used to Be Duke*, is particularly noteworthy. But Hodges disliked a leader's responsibilities. In 1955 he returned to Ellington.

Hodges continued to record with smaller groups: a septet under the pseudonym "Cue Porter" (for contractual reasons) with Strayhorn on piano in 1958, an early 1959 sextet with Ellington, and 1959–1960 sessions with a ten-piece orchestra. In 1961 he toured Europe with an octet from the band while Ellington worked on the film *Paris Blues* (1961) in France. Hodges recorded one of his best albums, *Everybody Knows Johnny Hodges* in 1964, with both a big band and a smaller group. Ellington crafted the beautiful "Isfahan" movement of the *Far East Suite* with Hodges in mind. Although Hodges's health deteriorated during the 1960s, he continued to play inspirationally. He died in New York City.

Although some found him personally brusque and aloof, in truth Hodges was painfully shy. In fact, he often mediated disputes between band members. He was a dedicated family man. After a failed early marriage, he married Edith Cue Fitzgerald, a dancer in the Cotton Club chorus, in 1957; the couple had two children. Never a good sight reader (Harry Carney and Barney Bigard often had to guide him through new orchestrations during rehearsals), Hodges possessed a powerful sense of swing, a fluid, graceful way of phrasing, and among the most softly beautiful sounds in jazz history.

• The best extended essay, followed by session commentaries, is by Stanley Dance in *The Complete Johnny Hodges Sessions, 1951–1955* (Mosaic Records, 1989). Ellington's commentary in *Music Is My Mistress* (1973) is essential. Also see the analysis in Gunther Schuller, *The Swing Era: The Development of Jazz, 1930–1945* (1989), and the comments on Hodges in Ellington studies by John Edward Hasse, *Beyond Category: The Life and Genius of Duke Ellington* (1993); James Lincoln Collier, *Duke Ellington* (1987); and Derek Jewell, *Duke: A Portrait of Duke Ellington* (1977). Mark Tucker, ed., *The Duke Ellington Reader* (1993), contains many contemporary comments on Hodges and his work; see in particular the article by Helen Oakley and the interview with Hodges and Harry Carney by Don DeMichael. An obituary on Hodges is in the *New York Times*, 12 May 1970.

RONALD P. DUFOUR

HODGKINSON, Francis (16 June 1867–4 Nov. 1949), mechanical engineer and inventor, was born in London, England, the son of Francis Otter Hodgkinson and Margaret Thompson, occupations unknown. Hodgkinson attended the Royal Naval School, New Cross, in his youth. His practical engineering training began in 1882 with a machinist's apprenticeship at Clayton & Shuttleworth, an agricultural engineering firm that produced farm equipment and steam engines. In addition, Hodgkinson continued to pursue a formal education by taking night courses at the Department of Science and Art at New Kensington in London and at the Rutherford College of Durham University.

In 1885 Hodgkinson secured employment at Clarke, Chapman, Parsons & Company, the partnership where engineer Charles Parsons was developing his early steam-turbine designs that would revolutionize the industrial and maritime world. This firm initially manufactured steam-turbine generators for ships. When Parsons sought to expand into other markets, the resulting disagreements caused the partnership to collapse. In 1889 Parsons established his own company, C. A. Parsons & Company, where Hodgkinson became the superintendent of field construction. In 1890, however, he accepted a commission as an engineering officer in the Chilean navy and fought in Chile's civil war between congressional and presidential forces. Hodgkinson then worked for Percy Burbank, a representative of Thomson Houston Company, in Lima, Peru, where he operated a small electrical utilities plant and installed telephone lines. Hodgkinson also served as a master mechanic for a silver and copper mining company in Cordillera, Peru. When he returned to England in 1894, he became the shop superintendent for C. A. Parsons & Company.

In 1895 American inventor and manufacturer George Westinghouse sent his company's vice president, E. E. Keller, to negotiate the purchase of the U.S. patent rights for the Parsons turbine. Although the steam-turbine principle received considerable skepticism from most engineers of that age, Westinghouse was attracted to its promise of direct, high-speed rotational motion—a problem into which he had already invested considerable attention. The genera-

tion of high-speed rotational motion was becoming increasingly critical following Westinghouse's commitment to the development and manufacturing of alternating-current electrical machinery. In addition to acquiring the patent rights, Keller persuaded an initially reluctant Parsons to allow Westinghouse to hire Hodgkinson as their principal turbine engineer, thereby minimizing the risk of this significant technology transfer. Hodgkinson left for the United States in 1896 to direct the design and construction of Parsons turbines for Westinghouse. He briefly returned to England in 1897 to marry Edith Marion Kate Piercy; they had three children.

At Westinghouse Machine Company (later known as the machine works of the Westinghouse Electric & Manufacturing Company), Hodgkinson was the project leader on virtually all of the early turbine projects. These included a 120-Kilowatt, 180-volt, direct-current turbine generating system for the Nichols Chemical Company (1896); an electrical generating system for Westinghouse's Air Brake Company, which involved three 300 kw, 3600 revolutions per minute turbines (1899); a 2000 kw, 1200 rpm turbine for Hartford Electric Light Company (1900); a 1250 kw, 1200 rpm tandem compound turbine for the Interboro Rapid Transit Company (1903); and a set of 5500 kw turbine generators for the Pennsylvania, New York, and Long Island Railroad to power electric trains (1905). In 1914 Hodgkinson's efforts resulted in the first installation of a reduced-gear turbine on a ship, the U.S. collier *Neptune*. Before this breakthrough, steam turbines that powered ships had been restricted to high-speed applications. In addition to such speed-reduction gearing, some of the significant design issues that Hodgkinson helped resolve involved turbine-blade attachments; condensing apparatus; thrust bearings; rotors, glands, and packing; low-pressure and tandem-turbine systems; and the use of stainless steel as a turbine-blade material. His 101 patents reflect the innovative nature of such work. Hodgkinson remained as Westinghouse's chief turbine engineer until 1916, when he was promoted to chief engineer. In 1927 he assumed the position of consulting mechanical engineer and advised Japan's Imperial Navy following its purchase of Westinghouse turbines. He also assisted in designing the mountings for Mount Palomar's 200-inch reflecting telescope. He formally retired from Westinghouse in 1936 but maintained an engineering consulting practice.

Although Hodgkinson's reputation rested primarily on his engineering design and construction work for Westinghouse, he did much more. He published numerous articles on mechanical engineering topics such as boiler tubes, nozzles, bearings, and power plants, in addition to those on steam turbines. The British Institution of Mechanical Engineers awarded him the Willans Premium in 1931 for his paper "Journal Bearing Practice" (1929). Hodgkinson's theoretical sophistication, especially in thermodynamics, is reflected in papers such as "Theoretical and Practical Considerations in Steam Turbine Work" (1904), which he presented to the BIME, and "Steam Turbine Efficiencies," which he published in *Mechanical Engineering* (1939). Active in the American Society of Mechanical Engineers, he served as chair of the ASME's Power Test Codes Committee in 1937 and two terms as the society's vice president. Hodgkinson also served as the ASME's representative on the International Electrotechnical Commission, where he pushed through the implementation of international codes for steam-turbine and internal combustion testing. In recognition of his contributions to mechanical engineering, Hodgkinson received the silver medal at the Louisiana Purchase Exhibition in 1904, the Elliot Cresson Gold Medal of the Franklin Institute in 1925, an honorary degree from the Stevens Institution of Technology in 1935, and an honorary professorship at Columbia University in 1936. The ASME honored him with the Holley Medal in 1938 and by making him a fellow in 1939. He died in Toledo, Ohio. A pioneer in the development of steam turbines for large-scale energy generation, Hodgkinson has been called the dean of American turbine engineering.

• There is no known collection of Hodgkinson papers. Two articles that Hodgkinson coauthored that provide important biographical details are "The Steam Turbine in the United States: Developments by the Westinghouse Machine Company," *Mechanical Engineering* 58 (Nov. 1936): 683–96, and "The Steam Turbine," *Mechanical Engineering* 59 (Apr. 1937): 271–74. Obituaries are in the *New York Times*, 6 Nov. 1949, and *Mechanical Engineering* 71 (Dec. 1949): 986.

BRETT D. STEELE

HODGKINSON, John (c. 1767–12 Sept. 1805), stage actor and comanager of the Old American Company, was born John Meadowcroft, or Meadowcraft, near Manchester, England. His parents' names are unknown, although records show that his father was a farmer of modest means who became an ale-house keeper soon after Hodgkinson's birth. Apprenticed to a Manchester manufacturer, Hodgkinson ran away to Bristol when he was fourteen or fifteen, changing his name in order to avoid being identified as a runaway apprentice. There he joined a theatrical troupe, impressing the manager with his fine singing voice. As he gained experience with various provincial companies, Hodgkinson rose through the ranks, becoming a leading player in Joseph Shepherd Munden's troupe. He ran off with Munden's common-law wife, Mary Ann Jones, in 1789; they had no children of their own. It is not certain if they were legally married, but she was known as "Mrs. Hodgkinson."

The Hodgkinsons joined the theater in Bath the following year, where Hodgkinson became recognized as a "provincial celebrity." The engagement won him a highly favorable notice from the critic for the London *Gazeteer*, indicating that he was on the verge of a distinguished London career. However, Hodgkinson wrote to Lewis Hallam, Jr., and John Henry, managers of the Old American Company, in 1791, asking employment for himself and for Frances Brett, an actress in the Bath company. When Henry visited England the following year, he saw Hodgkinson and Brett perform and engaged them both for the troupe. They sailed for the United States (Hodgkinson deserting his wife and her four children by Munden) in August 1792.

Soon after their arrival in September, Brett and Hodgkinson were married. They had three children. Hodgkinson debuted with the Old American Company in Philadelphia on 26 September 1792. He made a good impression and continued to demonstrate his skill and versatility throughout the season. Hallam and Henry gave up many of their roles to Hodgkinson, acknowledging that he was the superior performer. He was, in fact, incomparably the best actor seen in the United States at the time of his arrival, and he retained that distinction until Thomas Abthorpe Cooper began to overtake him in popularity around 1800 (Bernard, pp. 26, 257; Dunlap, vol. 1, p. 170). Hodgkinson came to the United States with a reputation as "the provincial Garrick" (David Garrick, recognized as the greatest actor in the English-speaking world until his retirement in 1776), and he did not disappoint. The *Federal Gazette* called him "the American Kemble" (John Philip Kemble, Garrick's acknowledged successor in England) in 1793. He was remarkably versatile, an excellent singer, and he was able to memorize a role simply by reading it over a few times. John Bernard, who saw him perform, said "Hodgkinson was a wonder. In the whole range of the living drama there was no variety of character he could not perceive and embody, from a Richard or a Hamlet down to a Shelty or a Sharp." Although not handsome and tending to corpulence, he "passed for handsome" on the stage. He dressed ostentatiously offstage and lived in considerable luxury, in the manner of America's leading actor.

Hodgkinson attempted to insure his supremacy in the Old American Company by conspiring against both managers. His most effective tactic against Mr. and Mrs. Henry was to recommend the importation of performers from England, then to arrange a redistribution of the Henrys' roles to the newcomers. He also took some of Henry's best roles for himself, with Hallam's approval. In 1794, Henry, wearying of the constant friction, sold his half of the company's management to Hodgkinson, who immediately began attacking Mr. and Mrs. Lewis Hallam, Jr., sparing no effort to discredit them. In this attempt he was helped greatly by Mrs. Hallam's habit of public intoxication (whether from alcohol, or, as Hodgkinson suggested, from laudanum); sometimes she appeared at the theater in no condition to perform. A monumental feud erupted. Time and again Mrs. Hallam was withdrawn from the cast because of her drunkenness, incurring Hodgkinson's ire; she mocked and upbraided him; Hallam promised to keep his wife under control, but he was invariably unsuccessful. Despite Hodgkinson's best efforts to sever Mrs. Hallam's relationship with the company, her behavior became "if possible, worse than ever." In April 1796 Hodgkinson sold half of his share in the management of the company to William

Dunlap, who became acting manager while Hodgkinson continued as director of the stage department.

The feud with Mrs. Hallam erupted into a near-riot on 29 March 1797 when she burst onto the stage in the midst of one of Hodgkinson's scenes. She addressed the audience directly, calling Hodgkinson a villain and a liar, which charges were supported by her husband. Hodgkinson appealed to the audience, eventually calming them. Later that year Hodgkinson published a pamphlet that consisted almost entirely of his account of his grievances against the Hallams, including a description of the events leading up to the public disturbance.

On 25 May 1797 Hallam quit as comanager, selling his interest to Dunlap and Hodgkinson. Despite finally achieving his goal of forcing Hallam out, Hodgkinson remained as comanager only for another year and a half, resigning in the fall of 1798.

During Hodgkinson's tenure, the company played in Boston, Hartford, and Philadelphia, as well as its base, New York. Its longtime theater on John Street was replaced—partly through Hodgkinson's efforts—by the finest, most comfortable theater in America, the Park, in 1798.

After leaving the Park Theatre company, Hodgkinson managed one theater in Boston and controlled another, but he did not fare well, and in April 1799 he wrote to Dunlap offering to return to the Park as an actor. Dunlap accepted the offer, but he often regretted it, for Hodgkinson's insistence on additional salary, perquisites, and roles was never ending. He also stole a short play of Dunlap's, using it as the basis for his full-length drama, *The Man of Fortitude* (1797). At one point the tension between them became so great that Hodgkinson threatened Dunlap with violence.

Hodgkinson, whose star began to decline as Cooper's was ascending, declared bankruptcy in 1803. His wife died of consumption that year. In September 1803 Hodgkinson, having left the Park Theatre, settled in Charleston, South Carolina, where he played for two seasons. In the spring of 1805 he obtained the lease of the Park from the bankrupt Dunlap. However, while recruiting a new company, he contracted yellow fever and died in Maryland.

Little good can be found to say of Hodgkinson's character (except by S. C. Carpenter, who, in a biographical essay, expresses almost unalloyed admiration). He conspired to ruin the careers of the Henrys and the Hallams, achieving considerable success in his aim. He made life miserable for Dunlap, always behaving irascibly and often ruthlessly. He lied shamelessly about his background and accomplishments. One can say in his favor that he was, by and large, an able manager and that he did not succeed as an actor on talent alone but worked hard to improve himself and maintain his lofty position.

• Hodgkinson himself provided the information for S. C. Carpenter's wholly admiring biographical sketch printed in the *Mirror of Taste*, Mar.–Nov. 1810; the general belief, however, is that Hodgkinson liberally embroidered some facts and invented some material. Hodgkinson wrote *Narrative of His Connection with the Old American Company* (1797), which consists primarily of a defense of his behavior vis-à-vis the Hallams; here, too, Hodgkinson exercised imagination and selectivity in his account. William Dunlap, *History of the American Theatre* (1832), and John Bernard, *Retrospections of America, 1797–1811* (1827, published 1887), provide the reader with observations about Hodgkinson by those who saw him perform and, in Dunlap's case, who worked with him. Dunlap's account is particularly valuable, as is George O. Seilhamer, *History of the American Theatre*, vol. 3 (1891), which offers much additional information and a valuable perspective. Other sources of interest include William B. Wood, *Personal Recollections of the Stage* (1855); Glenn Hughes, *A History of the American Theatre, 1700–1950* (1951); and Oral Sumner Coad and Edwin Mims, Jr., *The American Stage* (1929).

JARED BROWN

HODUR, Francis (1 Apr. 1866–16 Feb. 1953), founder and first prime bishop of the Polish National Catholic church, was born Franciszek Hodur in Zarki (near Krakow) in the Austrian Partition of Poland, the son of John Hodur and Mary (or Maria) Hodur (her maiden name as well as her married name), poor farmers. Hodur graduated with high merit from a Gymnasium in Krakow in 1889, then entered the Roman Catholic seminary. Late in 1892 he was dismissed from the seminary, apparently because of his participation in a protest involving the institution's food. He then emigrated to the United States and completed his theological studies at St. Vincent Seminary in Latrobe, Pennsylvania. He was ordained on 19 August 1893 by Bishop William O'Hara for the diocese of Scranton.

For eighteen months he served with great success as assistant pastor in Scranton at a Polish parish headed by Richard Aust, then at other ethnic parishes in Scranton and Nanticoke. By 1896 Aust's standoffish manner and allegedly high lifestyle had polarized the parishioners and led to rioting. The public disorder repeated a pattern that was common among first-generation Catholic Polish immigrants when disagreements arose within parishes over hiring practices, the disbursement of funds, and the relative status of Polish Americans within the Catholic church. In Scranton, both disaffected parties refused the compromises proposed by church officials, and the dissidents organized a new parish, St. Stanislaus Bishop and Martyr. In March 1897 Hodur accepted their invitation to become pastor, incurring canonical suspension from diocesan authorities for his disobedience.

To publicize his views, Hodur quickly founded a weekly, *Straż* (the Guard), which advocated ecclesial reforms, including lay trusteeship and freedom from "foreign" domination in religious matters, and criticized some of the Polish-American clergy for what Hodur judged to be their scandalously affluent lifestyle. The paper also reflected his early leanings toward socialism by supporting labor unions and the claims of the working class. After a journey to Rome in a futile effort to gain vindication, Hodur was excommunicated by Bishop O'Hara in a letter dated 29 September 1898. Denouncing the warrant as a judgment of the Irish-American bishops against the Poles, Hodur burned the document and, after 1900 abandoned further efforts at reconciliation.

By 16 December 1900, when Hodur's parishioners voted formally to constitute themselves as a church independent of Rome, about ten congregations in Pennsylvania, New Jersey, and Massachusetts had affiliated with his movement. In 1904 the first church synod in Scranton adopted a formal constitution and elected Hodur to be bishop. As organizer of the Polish National Catholic church, Hodur faced three primary challenges: gaining episcopal consecration to validate his leadership within the Catholic tradition, winning followers, and defining the teachings and practices of his church. The first two tasks were complicated by the rivalry of Polish-American church movements in Buffalo and, especially, Chicago, where another independent Polish movement had been founded by Anthony Kozlowski. Kozlowski claimed a large following and had already been consecrated in Europe in 1897 by bishops of the Old Catholic communion who had left the Roman Catholic church in disagreement with the teachings of Vatican Council I. In 1899 and again in 1904 Hodur requested consecration from the Old Catholics, but they refused until 1907, when Kozlowski died without a successor. On 29 September of that year Hodur was consecrated at St. Gertrude's Old Catholic Cathedral in Utrecht. He now had more than 15,000 adherents, including former followers of Kozlowski, whose support he sought.

Starting in 1904 a series of synods considered church governance, discipline, and theological positions. Under Hodur's leadership the delegates affirmed the concept of ownership and administration of parish properties through lay trustees and mandated the opening of a seminary (1904); assumed the name of Polish National Catholic church for all its congregations (1909); adopted the Confession of Faith and resolved to expand to Poland (1914); abolished mandatory clerical celibacy and authorized churchwide general confession for adults (1921); erected geographic dioceses with additional bishops and designated Hodur as prime bishop (1924); and agreed to intercommunion with the Protestant Episcopal church (1946). Bishop Hodur's liturgical innovations included Mass in the vernacular (1901), the introduction of several new feasts, such as the feasts of brotherly love and of the poor shepherds (1904), and Mass wherein the priest faced the people (1931).

Following the Old Catholic and Orthodox churches, Hodur accepted the teaching of the seven ecumenical councils of the undivided Catholic church. His theological teaching is summarized in the Confession of Faith (adopted by the third synod, 1914) and the Eleven Great Principles (published in 1923). He characterized Jesus as regenerator of humanity, the Son of God who communicates life to individuals and affirms their potential for good. He taught that baptism and confirmation are two facets of a single sacrament, and he defined preaching and hearing the word of God as a sac-

rament. He rejected papal infallibility and the notion of hell as a place of everlasting punishment. He also insisted that a national church is the appropriate expression of interaction between religious faith and the particular culture and history of a nation. As he expressed it in the Confession of Faith, "God . . . influences chosen spirits of nations, who in a given epoch of human development, are the creative agent in the building of God's Kingdom on earth."

A charismatic leader, Hodur worked ceaselessly on behalf of his church. He composed hymns, wrote polemical pamphlets, contributed articles to church journals, and preached frequently, even during his later years when, blind and infirm, he spoke to his congregation from his sickroom via loudspeaker. He journeyed to Poland eighteen times, ordained more than 200 priests, and consecrated nine bishops. At the time of his death in Scranton, he had about 270,000 church members in the United States and Canada and an unspecified following in Poland. In 1990 the number of contributing members in the United States was estimated at about 100,000.

• Holdings associated with the life and work of Francis Hodur are located at the archives of the Polish National Catholic church in Scranton, Pa. His basic writings, including *Nowe Drogi* (New Roads, 1901) and *Nasza Wiara* (Our Faith, 1913), exist only in Polish, but English extracts of many of his writings appear in Stephen Wlodarski, *The Origin and Growth of the Polish National Catholic Church* (1974). A biography of Hodur has yet to be published. Good biographical articles by Joseph Wieczerzak, Laurence J. Orzell, and others have appeared in *PNCC Studies*, an annual published since 1980 by the PNCC Commission on History and Archives, and in *Polish American Studies*, the journal of the Polish American Historical Association since 1942. See also Orzell, "The 'National Catholic' Response: Franciszek Hodur and His Followers," in *The Polish Presence in Canada and America*, ed. Frank Renkiewicz (1982). The best secondary source on Hodur's life is Hieronim Kubiak, *The Polish National Catholic Church in the United States of America from 1897 to 1965* (1982).

ANTHONY J. KUZNIEWSKI

HOE, Richard March (12 Sept. 1812–7 June 1886), manufacturer and inventor, was born in New York City, the son of Robert Hoe, a manufacturer, and Rachel Smith. He attended the New York public schools and at age fifteen went to work in his father's machine shop. The main products of the shop were printing presses and long and circular saws. The elder Hoe retired in 1830, leaving his son and his nephew Matthew Smith in charge of the plant. At that time the Hoe company built two hand-operated printing presses: the Smith, with a cast-iron frame and a platen that the pressman raised and lowered over a flatbed that held the type, and the Washington, an improved platen press with automatic inking rollers that printed 250 pages an hour. Upon his father's death in 1833, Hoe became the senior member of the firm. When Smith died in 1842 Hoe's brothers, Robert Hoe II and Peter

Smith Hoe, joined him in the enterprise under the firm name of R. M. Hoe & Co., a name it retained, with changing members of the firm, until Hoe's death.

Hoe took over the company in the age of Jackson, when newspapers were proliferating and publishers were demanding faster presses. He enlarged the shop and expanded the manufacture of all kinds of machines to order, but he devoted his inventive skills to improving the Hoe printing presses. Around 1833 he brought out a single small cylinder press, based on English models. This press retained the flatbed principle but replaced the platen with an impression cylinder that held the sheets of paper, turning as the type-bed moved back and forth beneath it. In 1837 the Hoe double small cylinder press appeared and shortly thereafter a single large cylinder "perfecting" press that printed on both sides of a sheet.

In the 1840s Hoe departed from the flatbed press and experimented with placing type on a cylinder, not a new idea but one that he refined and incorporated in the most efficient printing press of the time, the Hoe Type Revolving Machine, which he patented in 1846. It is this machine, later described by the British Privy Council as "the greatest step ever made in the printing art," that Hoe's reputation principally rests. First installed at the Philadelphia *Public Ledger* in 1847, this rotary press revolutionized newspaper printing in the United States. A central horizontal cylinder holding cast-iron type-beds revolved against four to ten impression cylinders grouped around it. Boys stationed on platforms at the machine fed in sheets of newsprint, one feeder for each impression roller, at the rate of 2,000 an hour by each feeder. Including machinists and helpers, the largest of these presses—twenty feet high and more than thirty feet long—required a crew of fourteen to sixteen men and boys.

For more than twenty years the Hoe company supplied these machines to many of the leading newspaper publishers in the United States and abroad. Newspapers that had been technologically limited in their output rapidly increased their circulation and many new ones appeared. A Hoe type-revolving machine especially designed for printing books and sold to D. Appleton & Co. in 1852 was still in use a half-century later. In 1859 Hoe acquired the Isaac Adams Press Works in Boston, and the firm continued to operate the factory there until 1869, when the works were removed to New York to be combined with the parent plant. By that time R. M. Hoe & Co. occupied an entire block in Manhattan.

In 1865 a competitor, William Bullock of Philadelphia, received the first American patent for a press that printed from a continuous roll of paper, known as a web. Originally unreliable, the machine was improved and adapted to an extent, but the rapid machine delivery of a completed newspaper awaited the appearance in the 1870s of a Hoe web press that embodied a gathering and delivery device, the invention of Stephen D. Tucker, a member of the firm. In 1873 the first of these machines went to *Lloyd's Weekly Newspaper* in London; a few years later the first in the United States went to the New York *Tribune*. Operated at top speed, this press could print, cut, and deliver 18,000 newspapers an hour. In 1875 Tucker patented a device that folded papers as fast as they came off the press. The exhibit of R. M. Hoe & Co. won two awards in class 540, printing presses, at the Centennial Exhibition in Philadelphia in 1876.

To service the many Hoe presses in Great Britain, the Hoe company maintained a repair shop in London as early as 1865. Later the shop was expanded into a manufactory. The company also opened branch offices in Chicago and San Francisco. Through the years Hoe remained involved in the day-to-day operation of this large enterprise. Concerned that the industry should have a steady supply of trained craftsmen, he set up an apprentices' evening school at the New York plant, where the boys were given a common school education and taught mathematics and mechanical drawing. He established an employee benefit society that included a consumer cooperative, supported the New York House of Refuge, was a director of the Magnetic Telegraph Company, and invested in real estate.

A frequent traveler to Europe, Hoe died suddenly in Florence, Italy, while on a trip with his wife and a daughter. He had been married twice, first to Lucy Gilbert, with whom he had two children; and, after her death, to Mary Gay Corbin, with whom he had three children. The dates of the marriages are unknown. His nephew, Robert Hoe, succeeded him as head of the Hoe company.

• Records of R. M. Hoe & Co., including patent records, are in the Library of Congress. Indispensable sources are Robert Hoe, *A Short History of the Printing Press* (1902), and S. D. Tucker, "History of R. Hoe & Company, 1834–1885," *Proceedings of the American Antiquarian Society* 82, pt. 2 (1972): 351–453, both with many illustrations. Obituaries are in the *New York Times* and the *New York Tribune*, both 9 June 1886.

IRENE D. NEU

HOE, Robert (10 Mar. 1839–22 Sept. 1909), manufacturer and bibliophile, was born in New York City, the son of Robert Hoe, a manufacturer, and Thyrza (or Thirza) Mead. He was educated at the Quackenbush School in New York and by private tutors.

About 1856 Hoe entered the family business, R. M. Hoe & Company of New York, makers of printing presses, industrial saws, and other machines to order. The firm was known worldwide for the "Hoe Type Revolving Machine," a rotary printing press that was the invention of Hoe's uncle, Richard March Hoe, the company's president. Robert Hoe worked in all departments of the company and in 1863 became a partner in the firm. In the 1870s the Hoe company put out a continuous-roll, or web, press that superseded the earlier rotary press, which printed only one page at a time. When Hoe became the senior and managing partner in 1886, the company was producing a press that cut, folded, and delivered 18,000 newspapers an hour. Still the demand for faster presses continued.

Not himself an inventor, Hoe worked closely with the firm's draftsmen and other specialists to speed up the newspaper-printing process. "It is not I [who am the inventor]," *Cosmopolitan* (Nov. 1902) quoted him as saying, "it is the corporation." The *New York Genealogical and Biographical Record* (Apr. 1910) cited an English writer who stated not long before Hoe's death that "under his regime, every year in the history of the firm has been marked by the perfecting of some new style of newspaper press that involved a new principle, or combination of principles." One employee of the company was said to hold more than sixty patents for printing press devices. By 1902 the Hoe company was manufacturing the "Octuple Perfecting Press with Folders," a machine that printed on both sides of the paper from four rolls, each four pages wide. The press turned out 96,000 four-, six-, or eight-page papers—or 24,000 24-page papers—an hour.

With few exceptions the printing of books continued on hand or cylinder presses until 1890 when the Hoe company developed the rotary art press, which, Hoe boasted, could do work as fine as it was possible to do on the earlier presses. A machine built in the Hoe company's London works for English weekly journals simultaneously printed text and covers of different colors. During the years around 1900 Hoe interested himself in the development of color printing, directing the preparation of inks and plates and the adaptation of the web press to the purpose. Magazines began to use colored illustrations and the leading city dailies to publish colored supplements. The largest of the Hoe newspaper color presses could print in six colors on one side of the sheet and five colors on the other, at a rate commensurate with demand.

Robert Hoe remained head of the Hoe firm, which changed its name to R. Hoe & Company in 1886, until his death, at which time the company was the largest manufacturer of printing machinery then in operation. The New York plant, with 2,500 employees, spread over 20,000 square feet, and the London factory, with 600 to 800 workers, was one of the largest in Great Britain. There were branch offices in Boston, Chicago, and Paris.

Hoe presses printed some of the world's greatest newspapers, including the *Herald*, *World*, and *Times* in New York and *The Times* (London), as well as *Century Magazine*. Under Hoe the company continued the apprentice school founded by his uncle. Here several hundred youths at any one time received a basic education and training in mechanics and drafting. For many years some of the leading pressmen in New York City began their careers as Hoe apprentices.

Aside from business, Hoe was a well-known figure in New York's cultural life. He was a founder and trustee of the Metropolitan Museum of Art and of the industrial arts school that was attached to it. An avid collector, he assembled one of the greatest private rare book libraries of his day, including two Gutenberg Bibles. The catalog of only those of his books published before 1700 ran to six volumes. When his entire collection was sold in 1911–1912, it brought almost $2 million. Hoe's holdings included examples of bookbinding through the centuries, an interest that prompted him to aid in organizing the Club Bindery, a small custom bindery of which he served for a time as president. In 1884 he was one of the founders of the Grolier Club, an association of bibliophiles. He was its president from its inception to 1888. An address of his to the club, "Bookbinding as a Fine Art," was published in 1886, and in 1902 he brought out *A Short History of the Printing Press*, in which he placed the history of the Hoe company within the larger framework of the history of mechanical printing.

In addition to his New York City residence, Hoe had a stock farm at Lake Waccabuc, New York, and a house in London. In 1863 he had married Olivia Phelps James; they had nine children. He died in London.

• Manuscript records of Robert Hoe and R. Hoe & Company are in the Library of Congress, Columbia University Rare Book and Manuscript Library, and the Bronx County Historical Society. Robert Hoe, *A Short History of the Printing Press* (1902), and S. D. Tucker, "History of R. Hoe & Company, 1834–1885," *Proceedings of the American Antiquarian Society* 82, pt. 2 (1972), are important sources. James H. Bridge, "Captains of Industry, Part VII, Robert Hoe," *Cosmopolitan*, Nov. 1902, pp. 85–88, and Walter Gillis, "Robert Hoe," *New York Genealogical and Biographical Record* 41, no. 2 (Apr. 1910): 67–72, are laudatory but useful contemporary accounts. See also *Catalogue of the Library of Robert Hoe of New York* (8 vols. bound in 4, 1911–1912). Obituaries are in the *New York Times* and *The Times* (London), 23 Sept. 1909.

IRENE D. NEU

HOEN, August (28 Dec. 1817–20 Sept. 1886), lithographer, was born in Hoehn, Duchy of Nassau, Germany, the son of John Martin Hoen, a farmer and village burgomaster, and Elizabeth Schmidt. Educated in the neighboring town of Dillenburg, Hoen emigrated with his family to Baltimore, Maryland, in 1835. There, at the age of eighteen, he began what became a lifetime career in the recently introduced trade of lithographic printing. With his cousin Edward Weber, who had been trained in Germany by Alois Senefelder, the inventor of lithography, Hoen helped found the commercial lithography company of E. Weber & Company. The printing presses and lithographic stones that they used had been brought over from Germany when they immigrated to the United States.

Although other lithographic firms had been established earlier in Boston, New York City, and Philadelphia, Weber and Hoen's business became one of the most prominent of its day. While they received numerous commissions from private businesses for such items as theatrical posters, political broadsides, and book and magazine illustrations, their financial success was increasingly a result of their work for the federal government. In the 1840s they printed the maps and illustrations that appeared in government reports for several western surveys, including John C. Frémont's explorations in the Rocky Mountains, Oregon, and California. These prints represent the earliest application of lithography to the reproduction of illustrations in government reports.

Weber's sudden death in 1848 led to several important changes in Hoen's life. Professionally, Hoen came into his own as a commercial lithographer. Although he waited five years before changing the company's name to A. Hoen & Company, the thirty-one-year-old printer and his brother Ernest assumed the leading roles in the business. August Hoen was the innovator and technician, taking the lessons learned from Weber and developing the lithographic process well beyond what Senefelder had accomplished. He was also directly involved in creating graphic designs. Ernest Hoen, on the other hand, acted principally as the firm's business manager. Both men hired trained artists to assist in the process of drafting and executing the great variety of printed material that the company produced. Weber's death also brought about changes of a personal nature. Less than a year later, Hoen married his former partner's widow Caroline Muth Weber; they had seven children.

Hoen possessed both a keen business sense and a scientific curiosity that kept the firm at the forefront of progress in the commercial printing business. Throughout his career he experimented with the medium and its various applications. This work led to several new advances, including the invention of the so-called Lithocaustic process, patented in 1860. A forerunner of the half-tone process, it created highly detailed prints using a system of cross-ruled lines on a lithographic stone, which was then etched. However, as the process needed to be executed by an individual artist, it proved too expensive and was soon abandoned.

Under Hoen's direction, the printing of scientific illustrations and maps became a specialty, the lithographic process proving much more adaptable than the older raised-type and block-cut printing. Hoen also made important contributions in the field of map symbolism, developing a color-coded system that made it possible to differentiate subdivisions of geological periods. The U.S. Geological Survey later adopted Hoen's system as a standard practice. In addition to producing multicolored maps, posters, and charts, Hoen's firm also introduced the printing of ornamental labels for manufacturers. Responding to the large amount of business they were doing with tobacco and cotton companies, the firm opened up a branch office in Richmond, Virginia. Managed by Hoen's son Ernest, this plant soon rivaled the size and activity of the Baltimore house.

In the field of commercial printing after the Civil War, A. Hoen & Company was recognized as an industry leader, both in terms of its profitability and its reputation. As a testament to the firm's success, a large sampling of its work was exhibited in Memorial Hall during the Philadelphia Centennial Exposition in 1876. Because of its national prominence, the company attracted business from well beyond the immediate vicinity. One of Hoen's best known customers, William "Buffalo Bill" Cody, in fact, made a special trip to Baltimore to oversee the printing of advertising posters for his "Wild West" show. This series of lithographic prints for Cody represented some of Hoen's most popular work.

Away from his business, Hoen cultivated an appreciation for the fine arts, horticulture, and music. He played the violoncello and later formed an orchestra with his children. He was also a public-spirited individual who worked as a member of the school board and the city planning commission in Baltimore. Following his death in Baltimore in 1886, control of the business was passed on to his sons. The firm continued in the same line of work for nearly a hundred years after Hoen's death. In 1981 it ceased operations owing to bankruptcy following a protracted dispute over labor practices with the Graphic Arts International Union. At the time it closed, A. Hoen & Company was the oldest commercial lithographic company in the country.

• The most complete catalog of Hoen's work is Lois McCauley, *A. Hoen on Stone, Lithographs of E. Weber & Co. and A. Hoen & Co., Baltimore, 1835–1969* (1969). All extant financial and personal papers, business equipment, and historically significant prints were either sequestered for legal reasons by a Baltimore court, sold away at auction, or simply thrown out at the time of the firm's closing in 1981. Hoen's career is discussed in several books on the history of lithography, including Domenico Porzio, ed., *Lithography: 200 Years of Art, History, and Technique* (1983), and Harry T. Peters, *America on Stone* (1931). An obituary is in the *Baltimore American*, 21 Sept. 1886.

FRANK H. GOODYEAR

HOEY, Clyde Roark (11 Dec. 1877–12 May 1954), politician, was born in Shelby, North Carolina, the son of Samuel Albert Hoey, a planter and Confederate army captain, and Mary Charlotte Roark. A prosperous family at one time, the Hoeys lost their fortune during Reconstruction. When his father's health failed in 1890, the younger Hoey quit school to work as a printer's devil, later becoming a journeyman printer for the *Charlotte Observer*. In 1894 he purchased the financially ailing *Shelby Review* and transformed it into a thriving concern. He remained its publisher until 1908.

Journalism soon led Hoey into politics. In 1898 he ran successfully for the North Carolina legislature, becoming at age twenty-one its youngest member. During the 1899 session Hoey supported Prohibition, increased funding for education, and, as he put it, "disenfranchising all the Negroes possible." Two years later he won reelection, campaigning for a constitutional amendment that would limit black suffrage. In 1903 Hoey moved to the state senate, where he served one term as that body's youngest member. In 1900 he married Margaret Gardner, the sister of O. Max Gardner, the future North Carolina governor. The couple had three children.

Meanwhile, Hoey had taken up the study of law, passing the bar in 1899. He was soon recognized as one of the state's top trial lawyers. President Woodrow Wilson appointed him assistant U.S. attorney for the western district of North Carolina in 1913. Hoey held this position until 1919, when he won election to the U.S. House of Representatives. As a freshman Democrat, Hoey found he could accomplish little in the Republican-controlled House, though he loyally supported the League of Nations and other Wilson policies. He did not seek reelection and returned to his law practice in March 1921. In 1929 Hoey participated in two trials that received national attention. In October he won the acquittal of eight deputy sheriffs charged with killing six persons during a textile strike in Marion, North Carolina. Later that month, in a private capacity, he aided in the successful prosecution of several Communist strikers accused of murdering a police chief during similar labor unrest in Gastonia. At this time, Hoey also served as a lobbyist for Duke Power, demonstrating the kind of antiunion, probusiness stance taken by many politicians who made up the state's "progressive plutocracy."

In 1930 Hoey, fearing charges of nepotism, declined Governor Gardner's appointment to a vacant Senate seat. Still, he gladly accepted the support of his brother-in-law's political machine in his 1936 run for governor. At Gardner's suggestion, Hoey "liberalized" his rhetoric during the primary campaign—one of the most bitterly contested in state history—to undercut the appeal of his opponent, Ralph McDonald, an avid New Dealer. Wrapping himself in the Roosevelt mantle and benefiting from Gardner's tightly organized political army "putting pressure on everywhere," Hoey captured the Democratic nomination. In November he won the general election easily. During his administration, the legislature increased educational funding by 30 percent, approved the distribution of free textbooks to elementary schools, raised teacher salaries, and authorized the state-run black colleges to offer graduate and professional courses. The state expanded its highway system and launched a successful publicity campaign to draw business and tourism to North Carolina. New labor laws banned employment of children under sixteen, though Hoey and the assembly rejected any attempt to introduce minimum wage legislation. The governor also condemned the widespread sit-down strikes of 1937, declaring that such activities would not be tolerated under his watch. Only reluctantly did he implement a limited welfare program in accordance with the Social Security Law. Despite his liberal campaign rhetoric, Hoey's instincts were basically conservative. A staunch supporter of states' rights, he resented the encroaching power of the federal government and expressed concern that the New Deal had gone "so far to the left."

Uninterested in building a political organization, Hoey relied on his personal charm and "silver-tongued" oratory to maintain support. Known as the "gadabout governor," he made two trips a day to the local drugstore for a "Coca-Cola break," engaging in friendly conversation all those he met along the way. Hoey's rafter-rattling speeches, peppered with verses from the Bible and often concluding with the last stanza of "My Country 'tis of Thee," held Tar Heel audiences spellbound. By the time he left office in 1941, the governor had become one of the most popular figures in twentieth-century North Carolina politics.

Three years later Hoey won the Democratic nomination for senator by a record margin and swept to a landslide victory in November. Resplendent in his swallowtail English walking coat complete with red carnation boutonniere, winged collar, striped trousers, high laced shoes, and gray fedora atop long, flowing white hair, Hoey, "a near physical prototype of the Civil War era," struck quite an incongruent pose in "the Washington of the atomic age" (Hatcher, "A Last Gasp," p. 29). Still, "the Duke," as his colleagues called him, became one of the Senate's most respected members (as well as a favorite of the Washington photographers). Hoey generally voted with his party on legislative questions, though he adamantly opposed any federal challenges to segregation or states' rights. Breaking with President Harry Truman on the poll tax issue, the establishment of a permanent Fair Employment Practices Commission, and the passage of an antilynching bill, he argued that such measures were merely a "smokescreen" for enhanced federal control over the states. Retaining his long-held antiunion views, Hoey voted for the Taft-Hartley Bill in 1947. He won reelection in 1950.

Hoey gained national attention as chair of the Senate Investigations Subcommittee, later renamed the Government Operations Committee, during its 1949 inquiry into the "five percenters," influence peddlers who orchestrated the awarding of government contracts for a fee. Barring television and newsreel cameras from the subcommittee's hearings, Hoey (in contrast to his successor, Joseph McCarthy) insisted that the proceedings not become a public spectacle. The senator also won acclaim for treating those who testified with dignity and respect. Likewise, Hoey's 1950 investigation to determine if homosexuals employed by the federal government posed a security risk was a victory for restraint, compared to the witch hunts that would follow.

The first North Carolinian to serve as governor and in both houses of the state and federal legislature, Hoey died at his Senate office desk. Although a committed defender of segregation, which he sincerely believed benefited both races, Hoey was not a southern demagogue. Holding that the "race issue" should be discussed without rancor, his rhetoric was neither aggressive nor inflammatory. Not a powerful senator nor a party leader, Hoey was nonetheless admired by his constituents as an honest conservative of noble character, devoted to preserving the familiar world of the Old South. Ironically, coverage of his funeral shared the headlines with the announcement of the Supreme Court's *Brown v. Board of Education* decision, marking the demise of a man and his political era.

• Hoey's papers are at Perkins Library, Duke University, and at the North Carolina Department of Archives and History, Raleigh. Some of his correspondence and speeches have been published in David LeRoy Corbitt, ed., *Addresses, Let-*

ters, and Papers of Clyde Roark Hoey, Governor of North Carolina, 1937–1941 (1944). James Free and Ann C. Free, "You Know He's a Senator," Colliers, 2 Feb. 1952, pp. 32, 67–69, offers a colorful contemporary sketch of Hoey. Elmer L. Puryear, Democratic Party Dissension in North Carolina 1928–1936 (1962), Anthony J. Badger, North Carolina and the New Deal (1981), and Douglas C. Abrams, Conservative Constraints: North Carolina and the New Deal (1992), provide detailed analyses of Hoey's career in Tar Heel politics. Joseph L. Morrison, Governor O. Max Gardner (1971), contains information on Hoey's relationship with his powerful brother-in-law. Susan Tucker Hatcher, "A Last Gasp: Clyde R. Hoey and the Twilight of Racial Segregation, 1945–1954," in The South Is Another Land, ed. Bruce Clayton and John A. Salmond (1987), examines Hoey's views on civil rights issues. Hatcher, "The Senatorial Career of Clyde R. Hoey" (Ph.D. diss., Duke Univ., 1983), is a biographical account. Andrew J. Dunar, The Truman Scandals and the Politics of Morality (1984), recounts Hoey's tenure as chairman of the Senate Investigations Subcommittee. Obituaries are in the New York Times and the Raleigh News and Observer, both 13 May 1954.
THOMAS W. DEVINE

HOEY, Jane Margueretta (15 Jan. 1892–6 Oct. 1968), social worker, was born in Greeley County, Nebraska, the daughter of John Hoey and Catherine Mullen, who had immigrated to New York City from Ireland shortly after the Civil War. Twenty years later the family moved west, where John Hoey tried his hand at ranching. When this proved unsuccessful, the Hoeys returned to New York City around 1898. Hoey claimed that growing up in this urban environment she learned about poverty from her mother who "had a deep concern for people, especially those in trouble." Although John Hoey worked as a laborer, the eight older children quickly found jobs that greatly improved the economic status of the family and ensured Jane's education.

Hoey graduated from Wadleigh High School in 1910 and then attended Hunter College until 1912. She transferred to Trinity College in Washington, D.C., where she studied under prominent Catholic clergymen John A. Ryan and William J. Kerby. After receiving her undergraduate degree from Trinity, Hoey earned a master's degree in political science from Columbia University and also studied at the New York School of Philanthropy under Mary Richmond, one of the foremost social workers in New York.

Her education completed in 1916, Hoey's first job was as assistant to Harry Hopkins who was then secretary of the New York City Board of Child Welfare (BCW), an agency that administered a widows' pension program to help needy mothers care for their children at home. Her professional relationship to Hopkins established during this time proved to be important, and their career paths took similar routes. Hoey's older brother James served in the New York State legislature and his friends Al Smith, Robert Wagner, and Franklin D. Roosevelt also exerted an important influence on her social work career.

Hoey resigned from the BCW in late 1917 and went to work for the American Red Cross (ARC). From January 1918 to June 1921 Hoey was field director for the Atlantic Division of the ARC Civilian Relief, providing services for the families of soldiers and sailors. When the ARC ended its Civilian Relief program, Hoey returned to New York and was recruited by the National Information Bureau to make a study of the local units of national welfare organizations. As assistant director of the project, Hoey studied social services in twelve cities and two rural counties and surveyed forty-six organizations. The project report took two years to complete and was published in 1926.

In 1923 Hoey took a post with the New York Tuberculosis Association heading the Bronx Division, where from 1923 to 1926 she supervised the clinic and the children's camps and organized public relations programs for the association. During this time Hoey also helped organize the influential Welfare Council of New York City, a clearinghouse of leading social service agencies. It was during her decade of work with the council that she made good use of her association with Smith, Wagner, and Roosevelt. In 1926 Governor Smith named Hoey to the New York State Crime Commission, which investigated the causes of crime and assisted in new legislation, and to the New York State Correction Commission, which supervised state prisons and county jails and promoted rehabilitation programs. In this work she began a lifelong interest in penology and juvenile delinquency.

In 1936 Hoey was appointed to the Social Security Board, a federal agency created to administer the Social Security Act's programs. She served as director of the board's Bureau of Public Assistance, where she was responsible for the welfare provisions of the act. She administered federal contributions to and supervision of the joint state-federal programs providing financial aid to the needy aged, to dependent children, and to the blind. It was the task of her bureau to determine whether individual state programs met federal standards and to allot federal funds to those approved. As director of the Bureau of Public Assistance, Hoey drew on her past experiences and brought to her work a coherent attitude toward welfare that combined fiscal responsibility and a strong commitment to social justice. She favored cash over in-kind payments to enable recipients to maintain their dignity; she advocated sound accounting methods to ensure sound financial management; and she insisted on the use of well-trained, professional social workers. Dwight D. Eisenhower removed Hoey from the board in 1953 when he replaced Democrats who held top administrative positions.

In 1940 Hoey was appointed president of the National Conference of Social Work, and she also represented the United States at several sessions of the United Nations Social and Economic Commission. Toward the end of her career she became the director of social research for the National Tuberculosis Association and vice chair of Mayor Robert Wagner's Advisory Board of Public Welfare. She was also active in many other organizations concerned with social work, education, health, child welfare, race relations, and Catholic culture. She received the first Florina Lasker

Social Work Award in 1955, the René Sand Award for her contribution to international social work in 1966, and the James J. Hoey Award for her work as an advocate of the rights of minorities from the Catholic Interracial Council of New York, which her brother had founded.

Hoey died in New York City. Never married, she died a wealthy woman, having been left an insurance business by her brother for which she had managerial responsibility. She left the bulk of her estate to Trinity College and to the Columbia University School of Social Work. Her commitment to social justice combined with her formidable administrative ability led to a varied and successful social work career. As one of the key federal executives in the New Deal, Hoey helped pave the way for women in high-level government work.

• Hoey's papers are at Trinity College in Washington, D.C. *The Reminiscences of Jane Hoey* (1965) is at the Columbia University Oral History Collection. See also Robert Trisco, ed., *Catholics in America, 1776–1976* (1976); Roy Lubove, *The Struggle for Social Security, 1900–1935* (1968); and Edwin Witte, *The Development of the Social Security Act* (1962). An obituary is in the *New York Times*, 7 Oct. 1968.

JUNE HOPKINS

HOFF, John Van Rensselaer (11 Apr. 1848–14 Jan. 1920), U.S. Army medical officer, was born in Mount Morris, New York, the son of Alexander H. Hoff, also a medical officer, and Ann Eliza Van Rensselaer. He received an A.B. from Union College in New York in 1871 and an M.D. in 1874 from the College of Physicians and Surgeons in New York City. Some accounts suggest that he also received an M.D. from the Albany Medical College in New York in 1871 and an A.M. from Union College in 1874. In 1874 he was given a contract as acting assistant surgeon, in which capacity he served in action against the Sioux Indians. When a vacancy occurred in the Army Medical Department in November 1874, he was commissioned assistant surgeon and first lieutenant.

Hoff's first post was Fort Omaha, Nebraska, where he was serving in 1875 when he married Lavinia Day; no record can be found of any children from this marriage. In 1879 he was promoted to captain. He continued to serve at posts in the West and in 1885 gave a course in ophthalmology at the University of California. In 1886 he took a leave of absence to examine the medical services of armies in Europe and to study at the University of Vienna, Austria. After his return to the United States, he was initially stationed at Fort Reno in Indian Territory. There, despite his initial skepticism about the potential of the newly created Hospital Corps—an organization composed of the medical department's enlisted men and noncommissioned officers—in 1887 he organized the first Hospital Corps detachment. As a result of the drill regulations he designed and the training he gave this unit, in 1891 a Hospital Corps detachment under his command gave the wounded of the battle of Wounded Knee prompt and efficient emergency care on the field and rapidly evacuated them.

In 1891 Hoff was promoted to major and surgeon. In 1898, with the outbreak of the Spanish-American War, he received a commission as lieutenant colonel and chief surgeon with the volunteers. After assisting in the necessarily hasty design of plans for the work of the medical service in the field, in May he was assigned to serve as surgeon for the III Army Corps at Camp George A. Thomas at Chickamauga, Georgia, at a time when a typhoid epidemic was causing heavy casualties. In September 1898 he was sent to Puerto Rico, where in November of that year he reverted to his rank and status of major and surgeon in the regular army. He continued to serve in Puerto Rico, where he organized health services for the island. He brought a prompt end to a serious smallpox epidemic, despite the near-inaccessibility of many communities, through an aggressive vaccination campaign. He also directed disaster relief in the wake of a catastrophic hurricane that struck the island in August 1899.

From 1901 to 1902 Hoff served as a professor at the Army Medical School in Washington, D.C., and as president of the Association of Military Surgeons. In 1902 he was promoted to lieutenant colonel and deputy surgeon general. He served from 1902 to 1905 as an instructor in military hygiene at the General Service and Staff College at Fort Leavenworth, Kansas. In May 1905, shortly after his promotion to colonel and assistant surgeon general, he served as an observer in the Russo-Japanese War. Returning the following year to assignment as chief surgeon of the Department of the Missouri, he also taught military hygiene for a year at the University of Nebraska.

Beginning in December 1906 Hoff was assigned to duty as chief surgeon of the Department of Luzon in the Philippine Islands, then as chief surgeon of the Philippines Division. Upon his return to the United States, he became chief surgeon of the Department of the Lakes in 1909. His final assignment before his retirement because of age in 1912 was as chief surgeon of the Department of the East.

After leaving the army, Hoff was active with the American Red Cross and served as secretary of the Association of Military Surgeons and editor of its publication *Military Surgeon*. In 1916, when U.S. troops were positioned along the border with Mexico, Hoff volunteered for duty in the Surgeon General's Office. In July 1918, in his capacity as editor of *Military Surgeon*, he published an editorial criticizing the appointment of two medical reserve officers rather than regular army surgeons to serve with the general staff. His article was regarded as undermining the cooperation necessary among organizations in time of war, and Hoff received an official reprimand and was relieved from active duty. In December 1919, however, in response to his appeal, Secretary of War Newton D. Baker withdrew the reprimand, noting Hoff's long and honorable efforts on behalf of the Army Medical Department and the good intentions that inspired the article. Hoff's request for restoration to duty was denied, however, because, hostilities having ended, his services were no longer needed. He died at Walter Reed General Hospital in Washington, D.C.

Hoff was a soldier's soldier, described by Merritte W. Ireland, surgeon general at the time of Hoff's death, as "a happy warrior . . . who lived a busy, earnest life," an officer with "a set and unshakable standard of honor." The medical department and the army itself relied heavily on Hoff's tireless devotion to duty and the example he set to others; however, perhaps more soldier than physician, he lacked the tact of some of his colleagues and the scientific brilliance of others. Thus he worked in their shadow, greatly respected without receiving popular acclaim and passed over in favor of his juniors when new surgeon generals were selected.

• Hoff's papers are in two collections at the National Library of Medicine in Bethesda, Md.; one contains his correspondence, principally letters from other medical officers in the period of the Spanish-American War, and the other contains the manuscript of a brief history of the Army Medical Department from 1775 to 1898. References to Hoff are also found among the papers of Merritte W. Ireland at the National Library of Medicine. His publications include *Outlines of the Sanitary Organization of Some of the Great Armies of the World* (1895), *The Medical Department in the Field* (a brief booklet containing a lecture he gave at the Infantry and Cavalry School at Fort Leavenworth), and *Military Government of Porto Rico from October 18, 1898, to April 30, 1900* (1901), as well as *Notes on Bearer Drill with Hand-litter, Ambulance Wagon, etc., Supplementary to a Provisional Manual of Instruction for the Hospital Corps, U.S.A., and Company Bearers* (1889). He also wrote many articles, most concerning the management and organization of evacuation or sanitation, which were published in the series of journals of the Association of Military Surgeons. See also *The Golden Jubilee of the Association of Military Surgeons of the United States* (1941), in which Edgar Erskine Hume discusses the situation that led to Hoff's reprimand in 1918. Information concerning Hoff's contributions to work of the Army Medical Department are also in Mary C. Gillett, *The Army Medical Department, 1865–1917* (1995). A lengthy obituary is in *Military Surgeon* (1920): 204–7, and a brief notice of death is in the *Journal of the American Medical Association* 74 (1920): 339.

MARY C. GILLETT

HOFF, Max (29 May 1893–27 Apr. 1941), bootlegger and boxing manager and promoter, was born in South Philadelphia, Pennsylvania, the son of Harry Hoff and Sara (maiden name unknown). He attended the local Horace Binney elementary school and was a newsboy in the city's downtown. As a teenager, Hoff (known as "Boo-Boo") became part of a group of largely Jewish young men involved in the boxing and gambling world that centered in gyms on the southern edge of the downtown. There he developed ties central to his successes during the 1920s, including one to Charlie Schwartz, with whom Hoff probably ran small gambling establishments in South Philadelphia before Prohibition. In 1917 he married Helen Flynn. They had one son.

In the 1920s Hoff managed one of the nation's largest stables of boxers. As his stable grew, Hoff established the Arcadia Gym in a large building on North Thirteenth at Cherry Street (near the downtown) and outfitted it as perhaps the finest gym in the city. There Jack Blackburn—the former black boxer and later Joe Louis's trainer—trained Hoff's aspiring fighters. By 1924 Hoff scheduled his boxers each summer for bouts at Philadelphia stadiums. In 1928, for instance, he rented Baker Bowl, the Philadelphia Phillies baseball field, for several evenings of outdoor fights. Each winter his fighters performed in the Arena at Forty-sixth and Market Streets in West Philadelphia—the center for boxing in a city then noted for its boxing fans. Periodically, he took members of his stable on well-publicized trips as far as California to compete in important matches.

A footnote to Hoff's boxing career emerged from the famous Philadelphia bout of September 1926 in which Gene Tunney won the heavyweight championship from Jack Dempsey. In January 1927 Hoff's attorney revealed that, on the day before the fight, Tunney and his manager had signed a contract that Hoff would receive 20 percent of Tunney's earnings for that fight and subsequent fights if he defeated Dempsey. Amid charges that Hoff had obtained the signatures by improper promises, his attempts to collect dragged through the courts until he withdrew his suit in January 1931.

By the mid-1920s, Philadelphia was the major center for the diversion of industrial alcohol for bootleg liquor. Hoff and his partners, including Schwartz and Samuel Lazar, were early investors in alcohol and chemical companies and soon dominated the market. Eventually they incorporated the Franklin Mortgage and Investment Co., with headquarters in the business district, from which to operate their various alcohol companies. Their attorney was U.S. congressman Benjamin M. Golder. The alcohol was not only diverted for use in Philadelphia but was shipped as oil, lumber, or bricks to midwestern cities such as Chicago and Minneapolis. Hoff invested in several prominent gambling houses in the 1920s. Both he and Schwartz had social and business ties to the Jewish gamblers, boxers, and bootleggers of New York. In the 1920s Hoff invested in real estate in Atlantic City and Ocean City on the New Jersey shore, and he moved into a large home in a fine West Philadelphia neighborhood.

A series of shootings during a bootleg war led in August 1928 to the convening of an investigative grand jury. Until the grand jury, Hoff was a prominent fight manager whose bootlegging was largely unknown to the public. After several months of well-publicized hearings, in which his name appeared regularly in the headlines, the grand jury issued a report that, with some exaggeration, labeled Boo-Boo Hoff "the King of the Bootleggers." The report exposed Hoff's numerous presents of money and Christmas baskets to the police. It revealed his ownership of various alcohol companies, including the Quaker Industrial Alcohol Company and the Glenwood Industrial Alcohol Company. Indirectly, it linked him to some of the shootings through his purchases of guns, including machine guns, from the Military Sales Co. on Market Street. The grand jury also mentioned his ownership of gambling houses and of the Piccadilly nightclub. While many policemen, including the director of public safety and the captain of detectives, were fired or forced to resign, Hoff himself escaped indictment.

After 1928, however, Hoff's fortunes declined. His winnings from his fight management were attached by the court to cover debts incurred from his investments on the Jersey shore. His fine home in West Philadelphia was sold at sheriff's auction in 1929. His bootleg interests were harmed by the publicity of the grand jury and by more effective law enforcement. His fight business waned, perhaps because his rivals in the Philadelphia fight business were linked to the racketeers like Frankie Carbo who came to dominate prizefighting by the 1930s. In 1929 his first wife died. He married Margaret Kaher (or Kaier) in 1929 or 1930. They had one son.

In the 1930s Hoff continued to operate a gym in downtown Philadelphia and to manage a declining stable of fighters. He owned several clubs, including The 1214 (on Spruce Street), where Jimmy Durante and Sophie Tucker performed. He continued to operate gambling clubs. One of his most prominent businesses was the Village Barn, a chaperoned dance hall that was a popular teenage hangout. He was also among the partners who owned the Philadelphia Warriors professional basketball team. A diminutive man and less flamboyant than his associates, Hoff was for two decades a central figure in the sports, gambling, and nightclub scene in Philadelphia. He died, probably of a heart attack, while sleeping at home.

• The best source for Hoff's life is the morgue of Philadelphia newspapers, located in the Urban Archives, Paley Library, Temple University, which contains clippings and photographs concerning Hoff from the 1920s and 1930s. The Urban Archives, in addition, has a copy of the "Report of Special Grand Jury" (1929) in the Committee of Seventy Papers, series 3, folder 1. There is a folder on Hoff in the Coast Guard Intelligence Files, box 63, in the National Archives. This biographical sketch also benefited from interviews with Hoff's son and grandson. Mark H. Haller, "Philadelphia Bootlegging and the Report of the Special August Grand Jury," *Pennsylvania Magazine of History and Biography* 109 (Apr. 1985): 215–33, places Hoff's bootlegging activities in the context of Philadelphia bootlegging generally. Steven Riess, "Only the Ring Was Square: Frankie Carbo and the Underworld Control of American Boxing," *International Journal of the History of Sport* 5 (May 1988): 29–52, analyzes the control of boxing during Hoff's years. Obituaries are in the *Philadelphia Bulletin* and the *Philadelphia Record*, both 28 Apr. 1941.

MARK H. HALLER

HOFFA, Jimmy (13 Feb. 1913–c. 30 July 1975), trade union leader, was born James Riddle Hoffa in Brazil, Indiana, the son of John Cleveland Hoffa, a coal driller, and Viola Riddle. Following the death of his father in 1920, Hoffa moved to Detroit, Michigan, where his mother found work as a radiator cap polisher at the Fisher Body Plant. After an education that ended with the ninth grade and a $12-a-week, sixty-hour-a-week

job as a department store stock boy, Hoffa worked as a warehouse freight handler for the Kroger grocery chain in Detroit in 1930, organizing an American Federation of Labor (AFL) federal labor union local, 19341, with four co-workers. From then until his disappearance forty-five years later, Hoffa's life was the labor movement. He brought local 19341 into the International Brotherhood of Teamsters (IBT) in 1934 and became a full-time organizer for the IBT and president of the local in 1937. In 1936 he married Josephine Poszywak; the couple had two children.

In 1937 Hoffa, as an IBT organizer, worked with Farrell Dobbs, a dissident Minneapolis Teamster leader whose small group of Trotskyist organizers had led the 1934 Minneapolis general strike and had played a major role in the growth of the IBT from a membership of 75,000 in 1933 to 277,000 in 1938. Learning from Dobbs the importance of organizational centralization, Hoffa also took from the Minneapolis activist a commitment to craft a master contract for all Teamsters in the United States.

Although he admired Dobbs and later claimed to have offered the latter a high salary to leave the Socialist Workers party and rejoin the union, Hoffa, at the behest of national IBT leader Dan Tobin, led goon squads in 1941 to Minneapolis to fight Dobbs and his supporters as they sought to take the powerful Central Conference of Teamsters out of the AFL and into the more militant Congress of Industrial Organizations (CIO). In this conflict, which also included a counterattack by CIO forces against Hoffa's Detroit base (he had been elected president of the Michigan Conference of Teamsters in 1940), Hoffa, it is alleged, first turned to Detroit gangsters Santo Perrone and "Scarface Joe" Bommarito to acquire the troops to defeat the left-led CIO in the internal labor wars.

For the rest of his career, Hoffa represented the contradictory traditions of militant trade unionism, which had peaked in the 1930s, and corrupt business unionism, which, at its worst, spawned in the United States the kind of labor racketeering largely absent in other industrialized countries.

Supporting the campaign of conservative Seattle business unionist Dave Beck to replace Dan Tobin as Teamsters president in 1947, Hoffa strengthened his position in the national union, becoming a vice president of the IBT and president of the Central Conference of Teamsters in 1953.

Earlier, in 1946, Hoffa had been tried for extortion in Detroit in a scheme to compel small grocers to purchase "permits" from the Teamsters to make deliveries with their own trucks. He received two years' probation as part of a plea bargain that reduced the charges in exchange for his making restitution to the grocers. In 1951 the Kefauver crime commission unearthed evidence that a Detroit Teamster local had acted as a front for organized crime to extort money from jukebox distributors.

The 1950s saw the stagnation of the labor movement, beset by the restrictions of the Taft-Hartley Act (1947), the destructive effects of anti-Communist internal purges, and popular exposés in the press and the cinema of labor racketeering, which engendered the Landrum Griffin Act (1959), providing for further legal restrictions on trade unions.

When Democrat John McClellan replaced the censured Republican Joseph McCarthy as chair of the Permanent Investigations Subcommittee of the Senate's Committee on Government Operations in 1955, he sought to clean the committee's tarnished reputation by investigating mismanagement and corruption in government, which soon led to investigations of labor racketeering in the garment industry and in the IBT. The committee's televised hearings introduced Hoffa, John Kennedy, and Robert Kennedy to national audiences and contributed to the downfall of IBT president Dave Beck, who was convicted of grand larceny in 1957 and replaced by Hoffa as IBT president. The hearings also led to Hoffa's indictment for attempting to bribe an individual to act as a spy on the McClellan committee staff, although he was subsequently acquitted. The McClellan committee hearings also transformed Hoffa into both a national celebrity and a stereotypical 1950s antihero, becoming the basis for a personal conflict with committee counsel Robert Kennedy that would eventually pass into American political folklore.

As president of the IBT, however, Hoffa centralized union leadership and won praise from many labor militants by greatly expanding union organizing, substantially raising the wages of his members as he reduced competition from nonunion drivers, and taking the Teamsters into campaigns to organize white-collar employees and other unorganized workers that had largely fallen by the wayside with the anti-Communist political purges and the passage of the Taft-Hartley Act. At the same time, Hoffa's activities played an important role in revitalizing the labor movement in the 1960s by encouraging the conservative AFL-CIO leadership, which had expelled the Teamsters for labor racketeering in 1958 (largely in response to media coverage of Hoffa's leadership), to revive in a limited way its organizing drives. In 1964 Hoffa achieved his greatest victory, accomplishing the thirty-year-old goal of his mentor Farrell Dobbs when he negotiated the first national contract in the trucking industry.

In 1964 Hoffa was also convicted in federal court of jury tampering, fraud, and conspiracy in the disposition of union funds, a personal triumph for Robert Kennedy and a posthumous victory for the Kennedy administration. After exhausting appeals, Hoffa left the Teamsters to his handpicked successor, Frank Fitzsimmons, and began in 1967 to serve a thirteen-year prison sentence in the federal penitentiary at Lewisburg, Pennsylvania.

Pardoned by President Richard Nixon in 1971, with the provision that he keep out of union affairs until 1980, Hoffa received the title president emeritus and an award of $1.7 million in lieu of a pension. However, he soon sought legal action to invalidate the provision that he keep out of union affairs, believing that it had been drawn up by White House counsel Charles Colson at the behest of Fitzsimmons, who later made Colson chief counsel of the Teamsters. While feuding with Fitzsimmons and attempting unsuccessfully to gain the right to run for Teamsters president in 1976, Hoffa became active in the National Association for Justice, a prison reform group. He also published works reflecting his own account of his career and conflicts with the government.

James Riddle Hoffa disappeared without a trace on 30 July 1975, leaving his family and the mass media to speculate about his fate. After leaving a restaurant in the Detroit area, Hoffa called his wife to tell her that he had been "stood up" for a meeting by Anthony Giacolone, an alleged Detroit underworld figure; he was never heard from again. Although his case has remained open, the FBI, his biographers contend, believes that he was murdered by underworld figures who considered him less trustworthy than Fitzsimmons in protecting their control over Teamster locals and particularly their influence over the Central States Teamsters Pension Fund. There are also many other theories of the disappearance. All are connected to some underworld group and/or the Teamster leadership, and all are in agreement only on the point that Hoffa was the victim of foul play.

Portrayed as the quintessential labor racketeer in American media and popular culture since the 1950s, in much the same way that Al Capone became the ultimate gangster after the 1920s, Hoffa has since his disappearance been portrayed in television miniseries recounting his life and his battles with Robert Kennedy, in Sylvester Stallone's fictionalized film *F.I.S.T.*, and in endless jokes speculating about his final resting place.

However, his success both in building the Teamsters and in reviving labor's commitment to organize the unorganized in the 1960s, along with a notoriety born of his underworld connections' strong-arm methods and the mystery of his disappearance, made him the best-known and most controversial U.S. labor leader of the second half of the twentieth century.

• The best recent biographical treatment of Hoffa is Arthur A. Sloane, *Hoffa* (1991). See also Steven Brill, *The Teamsters* (1978), and Walter Sheridan, *The Fall and Rise of Jimmy Hoffa* (1972). For Hoffa's own account of his experiences, see James R. Hoffa, as told to Oscar Fraley, *Hoffa: The Real Story* (1975). For a useful account of Hoffa's struggles with the Kennedy administration, see Victor S. Navasky, *Kennedy Justice* (1971). An article on the memorial service held for Hoffa by his family twenty years after his disappearance is in the *Detroit News*, 31 July 1995.

NORMAN MARKOWITZ

HOFFER, Eric (25 July 1902–20 May 1983), social philosopher and longshoreman, was born in the Bronx, New York, the only child of Alsatian immigrants whose names are unknown. He spoke German before he spoke English, and his English was heavily accented. Blinded by a fall when he was nine years old, his eyesight was inexplicably restored when he was fifteen. He never attended school.

Hoffer's mother died when he was a boy; when his father also died in 1920, he left New York for southern California, which he believed would be his land of opportunity. For ten years he lived on Los Angeles's skid row and worked odd jobs, occasionally close to starvation, borrowing books from the public library to further his self-education. For another ten years he picked crops in the valleys of California, borrowing books from libraries along the rail lines. During those years he discovered the father of the modern essay, Michel de Montaigne, memorized his works line for line, and began writing essays of his own in Montaigne's style. From his experiences, his reading, and his efforts to put his ideas into written form came the themes, conclusions, and style that would characterize the body of his own work.

With U.S. entry in World War II in 1941, Hoffer became a longshoreman on the San Francisco waterfront, explaining that he wanted to do his part to defeat Adolf Hitler, and worked there until his retirement in 1967. A settled life and the security of a regular paycheck gave him the time and opportunity to begin organizing the scattered thoughts and notes accumulated during the two decades of poverty and the road. By 1950 he had written, in longhand, the book that would introduce him to a national audience. In 1951 Harper's published it under the title *The True Believer*. It was praised by critics as a rare, penetrating analysis of the radical individual in public life (the most dangerous of men, said Hoffer), and its author was hailed as the embodiment of intellectual America's long-awaited dream of the self-educated citizen philosopher.

In 1951 Hoffer met Lili Osborne. Although they never married, she was his closest companion and confidant for the last thirty years of his life. Her youngest son, Eric Osborne, bore the names both of her former husband and of his real father. Hoffer's relations with young Eric were stormy. In the 1960s, when Hoffer conducted seminars as an adjunct instructor at the University of California at Berkeley, he met Stacy Cole, who became his pupil, disciple, and surrogate son for his last fifteen years.

The secure three decades, with Lili as companion and Stacy as attendant, gave Hoffer time to write another ten books, all of them widely reviewed and read. Even President Dwight D. Eisenhower, whose literary tastes usually ran to western thrillers, let it be known that he read and admired Hoffer. Each succeeding book, most of them collections of essays after the tradition of Montaigne, added to his image as the genius of great common sense. His works include *The Passionate State of Mind* (1955), more about true believers and how to deal with them; *The Ordeal of Change* (1963), probably his best single volume, about man's fear of the new; *The Temper of Our Time* (1967), social commentary, based on previously published articles; *Working and Thinking on the Waterfront* (1969), a daily journal that captured Hoffer's personal and work life during his active years; *First Things, Last Things* (1976); *Before the Sabbath* (1979), comments on the world he was aware he might soon leave; *Between the*

Devil and the Dragon (1982), selections from previous works; and *Truth Imagined* (1983), random memories of his life and work. All his books were published by Harper's, although he frequently complained of inadequate compensation.

Among the topics Hoffer found intriguing, mulled over during his years following the crops and on the waterfront, and eventually served up in his books with vivid, sometimes startlingly unique, analyses and interpretations were the nature of mass movements and the types of personalities attracted to lead and serve them; the place of the misfit in society, his or her potential destructiveness and enormous capacity for positive creativity; and the painful ordeal of individuals and groups forced to adapt to changing conditions and circumstances.

Hoffer's fame and influence were vastly enhanced in 1967 when Eric Severeid interviewed him on a CBS television special. In the course of their conversation, Hoffer praised an embattled Lyndon Johnson; as a reward he was invited for a chat with the president in the Rose Garden, which further increased his fame and the sale of his books. For more than a year after his trip to Washington he wrote a syndicated column; but he abruptly broke his lucrative contract, complaining that he was spending himself in small change. His image with liberal pundits was somewhat tarnished when he publicly scolded black witnesses before Johnson's Commission on the Causes and Prevention of Violence, of which Hoffer was a member in 1968–1969. Still he remained until his death in San Francisco a fascinating, perhaps unique, figure in American letters and a widely quoted commentor on national and world affairs.

• James T. Baker, *Eric Hoffer* (1982), is based partly on personal conversations with Hoffer on his life and work. James D. Koerner, *Hoffer's America* (1973), is a vivid portrait of a salty Hoffer by someone who seemed to find Hoffer's more pessimistic side. Calvin Tomkins, *Eric Hoffer: An American Odyssey* (1968), is a brief treatment of Hoffer's life and thought based on a single visit with him; aphorisms of Hoffer's and excellent photographs by George Knight buttress the work. An obituary is in the *New York Times*, 22 May 1983.

JAMES T. BAKER

HOFFMAN, Abbie (30 Nov. 1936–12 Apr. 1989), radical activist, was born Abbott Howard Hoffman in Worcester, Massachusetts, the son of John Hoffman, the founder of the Worcester Medical Supply Co., and Florence Schanberg. Hoffman's family had emigrated to the United States from Russia around the turn of the century. Growing up in Worcester, he identified less with his Jewish roots than he did with American culture. Priding himself as a rebel, he hung out with street toughs, playing sports, gambling, and hustling pool. At the same time, he excelled academically and worked as a salesman for his father.

At Brandeis University, class of 1959, Hoffman majored in psychology and was influenced by Professor Abraham Maslow, a founder of humanist psychology. "A hundred years of examining the dark side of human experience . . . would be set in perspective by Maslow's insights regarding healthy motivation," Hoffman wrote in his autobiography. "Maslovian theory laid a solid foundation for launching the optimism of the sixties. Existential, altruistic, and upbeat, his teachings became my personal code."

In the autumn of 1960, after a year of graduate work in psychology at the University of California at Berkeley, Hoffman became a staff psychologist at Worcester State Hospital. He also helped organize the first ban-the-bomb and civil rights demonstrations in the Worcester area. In 1964 Hoffman began work as a salesman for a manufacturer of pharmaceutical drugs. His major involvement, however, was Friends of SNCC, the northern support group of the Student Nonviolent Coordinating Committee, an organization of civil rights activists, started in 1960, that brought the civil rights struggle into Mississippi and other states of the Deep South where white resistance to integration was especially violent. In 1965 he was hired by the Mississippi Poor People's Corporation to establish retail outlets for its cooperatively produced craft products in the Northeast. Hoffman spent pharmaceutical company time doing civil rights work and organizing the first demonstrations in Worcester against the Vietnam War. Fired from his sales position in 1966, he then joined the campaign staff of Thomas Boyleston Adams, an unsuccessful antiwar candidate in the 1966 Massachusetts Democratic primary for the U.S. Senate. That autumn, Hoffman moved to New York City to establish Liberty House, a retail outlet for the Poor People's Corporation.

The counterculture was then emerging in New York City, and in the alienation of hippie youth Hoffman saw seeds of a deeper social rebellion. In the spring of 1967, he set out to merge the hippie youth rebellion with the radical New Left activists who were then in the forefront of the movement against the Vietnam War.

In order to attract positive media coverage and publicly link the hippie lifestyle to radical politics, Hoffman staged political demonstrations in the form of political theater. To publicize the connection of hippies and the antiwar movement, Hoffman, in May 1967, led a contingent of hippies in a right-wing-sponsored "Support Our Boys" parade. As he anticipated, the right-wingers attacked the "flower brigade," and this became the major news story of the parade. To portray the ethics of capitalism, in August 1967 he led a group of hippies to the visitors' gallery of the New York Stock Exchange and threw dollar bills down to the trading floor. The spectacle of stockbrokers crawling on the floor to pick up the money drove home the message that Hoffman wanted to convey. In these and other demonstrations, Hoffman advanced the art of news manipulation, using the media to generate free publicity for his radical ideas.

In 1968, Hoffman and a group of friends, including Jerry Rubin, founded the Youth International Party, "Yippie" for short. The Yippies existed as an idea rather than as a formal membership organization. Hoff-

man's intention was to promote the illusion of a mass-based youth organization in order to attract media attention and publicize plans for demonstrations at the Democratic National Convention in Chicago in August 1968. Hoffman planned a hippie "Festival of Life" to contrast the values of the counterculture with the hawkish attitudes of President Lyndon B. Johnson. The Democratic convention "will be a political circus," Hoffman announced, but "ours will be the real thing complete with sawdust and laughing bears." Chicago authorities took Hoffman's tongue-in-cheek threats to organize public love-ins and put LSD in Chicago's water supply as serious plans and refused to permit the Yippies to hold a festival in Lincoln Park, where the Yippies planned to gather. During the convention, the police drove the Yippies out of Lincoln Park and into Chicago's hotel district, where television cameras recorded police attacks on the Yippies and other peace demonstrators, Democratic delegates, journalists, and innocent bystanders alike. But creating cultural conflict in order to further political antiwar goals backfired on Hoffman. Many Americans, even those who opposed the war and were shocked by the brutality of the Chicago police, were offended by the Yippies' flamboyant disdain for mainstream values.

After Chicago, Hoffman and the Yippies pursued a confrontational course, opposing antiwar Democrats and trying to polarize the nation along generational and cultural lines. In March 1969, Hoffman and seven other leading radicals were indicted for conspiring to commit violence during the Chicago demonstrations. Hoffman took the lead in transforming the trial of the "Chicago Seven" into a showcase for antiwar politics and countercultural values. In February 1970, he and four other defendants were found guilty of crossing state lines to incite a riot and were sentenced to five years in prison. For his mockingly defiant, verbal assaults on the way the presiding judge, Julius Hoffman (no relation), was conducting the trial, Hoffman was sentenced to an additional eight months for contempt of court. In November 1972 the conviction was overturned on appeal, and in November 1973 the sentence for contempt was reduced to time served.

The conspiracy trial made Hoffman a popular speaker on college campuses. A funny and electric performance artist (even before such a term existed), Hoffman was a successful pitchman for radical causes. But the delight he took in his media fame violated the egalitarian spirit of the radical movement, and increasingly he came under attack for his egotistical conduct. In 1972 Hoffman again led demonstrations at the Democratic National Convention. Wanting desperately to end the Vietnam War and respecting Democratic candidate George McGovern's antiwar credentials, Hoffman and his Yippie cohorts tried to moderate more militant activists who wanted to embarrass the Democrats by re-creating the confrontational politics of Chicago 1968.

Criticized by the militants eager to pursue the self-described revolutionary tactics that he himself had promoted in 1968, Hoffman withdrew from activism. In the summer of 1973 he was arrested for selling cocaine to New York undercover police. Faced with a minimum sentence of fifteen years and wanting to reestablish his radical credentials, Hoffman went underground in 1974, occasionally surfacing in public places to twit the authorities who were looking for him.

While underground and using the pseudonym Barry Freed, Hoffman settled in the Thousand Islands of New York. In 1978 he learned that the U.S. Army Corps of Engineers was planning to dredge the river for winter navigation. Believing that this would upset the ecological balance of the region, Hoffman organized Save the River, a grass-roots organization that led a successful fight to block the proposal. During his Yippie days Hoffman had used cultural issues to polarize society. Now he sought to find common ground with all the residents in the area. New York senator Daniel Patrick Moynihan, speaking against the project during a visit to the Thousand Islands, commended Hoffman/Freed for his organizing abilities and said, "Now I know where the sixties have gone. Everyone owes Barry Freed a debt of gratitude for his organizing ability."

Convinced that his identity was going to be exposed, and wanting also to take public credit for Freed's success and publicize his autobiography, *Soon to Be a Major Motion Picture*, Hoffman gave himself up to authorities in September 1980. After serving less than a year in jail, he resumed his career as a radical activist, again becoming a popular speaker on college campuses, serving as a consultant to grass-roots environmental organizations, and organizing demonstrations against U.S. policy in Central America.

Early in 1980 Hoffman was diagnosed as suffering from bipolar disorder, a metabolically caused mental illness more commonly known as manic-depression. Preferring the high energy he felt during the hypomanic stages of the disease, Hoffman often stopped taking his prescribed medicine. As a result he was subject to recurring episodes of manic behavior and severe depression, one of which, in the spring of 1983, led to a suicide attempt. Injured in an auto accident in June 1988, Hoffman fell into another deep depression and committed suicide at his home in Solebury Township, Pennsylvania.

Hoffman was married to Sheila Karklin from 1960 to 1966 and with her had two children. He and Anita Kushner were married in 1967 and had one child. Johanna Lawrenson was his companion from 1974 until his death.

In death, as in his earlier life, Hoffman has come to symbolize again the activist spirit of the 1960s. In his last public speech at Vanderbilt University, Hoffman summed up the accomplishments of his activist generation, saying, "We were young, we were reckless, arrogant, silly, headstrong—and we were right. I regret nothing."

• Major portions of Hoffman's first three books, *Revolution for the Hell of It* (1968), *Woodstock Nation* (1970), and *Steal This Book* (1972), are included with essays from the 1970s and 1980s in the anthology *The Best of Abbie Hoffman* (1990). Hoffman's other books are: with Jerry Rubin and Ed Sanders, *Vote!* (1972); with Anita Hoffman, *To America with Love* (1976); a collection of essays, *Square Dancing in the Ice Age* (1982); and, with Jonathan Silvers, *Steal This Urine Test* (1986). A critical but sympathetic biography that places Hoffman in a historic context is Marty Jezer, *Abbie Hoffman: American Rebel* (1992). See also John Murray Cuddihy, "A Tale of Two Hoffman's," in *The Ordeal of Civility* (1974), for a discussion of Hoffman's role in the conspiracy trial, his use of political satire, and his understanding of ethnic identity; and David Farber, *Chicago '68* (1988), for a full account of Hoffman's role in the Chicago demonstrations. An obituary is in the *New York Times*, 14 Apr. 1989.

MARTY JEZER

HOFFMAN, Charles Fenno (7 Feb. 1806–7 June 1884), writer and editor, was born in New York City, the son of Josiah Ogden Hoffman, a prominent judge, and his second wife, Maria Fenno. At the age of eleven, Hoffman was seriously injured in an accident along the New York docks, resulting in the amputation of his right leg above the knee. In spite of the accident, he was an avid athlete and outdoorsman. In 1821 he entered Columbia College, where he was active in student life but never rose above the bottom fifth of his class. He left Columbia after two years, and in 1823 he began to study law in the Albany office of Harmanus Bleeker. Admitted to the bar in 1827, he returned to New York and began to practice law. Soon after, he began contributing essays, reviews, and poems to the *New York American*, and in 1830 he gave up his law practice entirely to become a coeditor of the *American*.

Hoffman entered into the social and literary life of the "Knickerbocker" set and was enlisted as the first editor of the *Knickerbocker* monthly magazine, the first issue of which appeared in January 1833. Ill health forced him to resign the editorship after only a few months, however (after which the magazine's name was changed to *Knickerbocker*). In October 1833 he departed alone on horseback for an extended tour of the West that took him through Pennsylvania, Ohio, Michigan Territory, Indiana, Illinois, Missouri, and back through Kentucky and Virginia. Returning to New York in June 1834, he collected his travel letters into the two-volume *A Winter in the West* (1835), an extremely popular volume that was highly praised by reviewers.

In 1835 Hoffman became coeditor of the *American Monthly Magazine*, which in February 1837 began serializing his novel *Vanderlyn*. When he broke with the magazine at the end of 1837 in a dispute over payments, the novel remained unfinished. At the end of 1836, Hoffman agreed to edit a volume of poems by New York writers. Produced in only two weeks in order to be out for the holiday season, *The New-York Book of Poetry* (1837) included selections by fifty-three authors; among Hoffman's own contributions were such popular songs as "Rosalie Clare" and "Moonlight on the Hudson." After severing ties with the *American Monthly*, Hoffman began contributing to the *New York Mirror* and for at least a part of 1837 acted as its editor. A trip to the upper Hudson River Valley provided material for several sketches first printed in the *Mirror* and later included in his second book, *Wild Scenes in the Forest and Prairies* (London, 1839; New York, 1843). Whereas *A Winter in the West* had been a personal travel narrative, *Wild Scenes* was a collection of Indian and Gothic tales for which Hoffman's own travels provided only a very loose frame.

From 1838 to 1840, Hoffman devoted himself primarily to the writing of his only published novel, *Greyslaer; A Romance of the Mohawk* (1840). The plot of the romance draws loosely on the celebrated Beauchamp-Sharp abduction-murder incident that he had recounted in *A Winter in the West* (and that William Gilmore Simms used in two of his novels), but Hoffman changed the setting from Kentucky to the Mohawk Valley during the first years of the American Revolution, and the emphasis of the romance remains firmly on the historical drama. The novel was highly praised by reviewers and was dramatized at the Bowery Theater in August 1840. Three editions had been printed by 1841, and a fourth was printed in 1849.

Shortly before the publication of *Greyslaer*, Hoffman accepted a three-month contract as associate editor of Horace Greeley's *New-Yorker*. When his contract was not renewed, he accepted in May 1841 an appointment as third chief clerk in the New York Customs House. He was promoted to deputy surveyor at the beginning of 1843 and remained until July 1844, when the new Democratic administration and the political spoils system compelled Hoffman, a Whig, to resign. While working at the customhouse Hoffman published *The Vigil of Faith and Other Poems* (1842), the title work being a long narrative poem based on an Indian legend of the Adirondacks. The volume went through four editions in three years and was generally well received by reviewers. Rufus Griswold's first edition of *Poets and Poetry of America* (1842) included more poems by Hoffman than by any other writer. Griswold's anthology was sharply attacked by the British press, however, and Hoffman in particular was targeted as a poor imitator of British poets. Nevertheless, the American press defended Hoffman, who subsequently issued another volume of poems, *The Echo; or, Borrowed Notes for Home Circulation* (1844), which included a preface defending himself against the British attacks.

In March 1845 Hoffman joined the editorial staff of the newly established *Evening Gazette*, to which he contributed stories, essays, and poems until he took over as editor of the *Literary World* from Evert Duyckinck in May 1847. Hoffman successfully edited the *Literary World* for seventeen months, contributing regular reviews and essays, until Duyckinck was reinstated in October 1848. During this time, Hoffman also published *Love's Calendar, Lays of the Hudson, and Other Poems* (1847). At the end of 1847 Hoffman delivered a highly regarded lecture on the early settlers of New York, subsequently published as *The Pioneers of New York* (1848).

At the end of 1848 Hoffman began to suffer a physical and mental breakdown, apparently suffering from a manic-depressive psychosis, and in January 1849 he entered into the care of a specialist in mental disorders. By late April he was discharged and accepted a clerkship in the consular bureau of the State Department, but by the end of the year his declining health forced him to resign and reenter treatment. After a brief second recovery, his condition worsened, and he was admitted to the state hospital at Harrisburg, Pennsylvania, where he remained until his death more than thirty years later.

Hoffman is more often remembered for his role as editor and contributor to the magazines of the 1830s and 1840s than for his own prose or poetry, but his account of his western travels and his historical romance *Greyslaer* still merit the attention of literary historians.

• The principal holdings of Hoffman's manuscripts and letters are in the collections of Yale University, the Boston Public Library, Harvard University, the New York Public Library, Haverford College, and the Historical Society of Pennsylvania. Homer F. Barnes, *Charles Fenno Hoffman* (1930), is the only full-length biography, which includes in its appendices Hoffman's correspondence, his uncollected poems (supplementing the 1873 *Poems of Charles Fenno Hoffman*), and a bibliography of his collected and uncollected writings.

STEVEN FINK

HOFFMAN, Clare Eugene (10 Sept. 1875–3 Nov. 1967), U.S. representative, was born in Vicksburg, Pennsylvania, the son of Samuel D. Hoffman, a wagonmaker, and Mary V. Ritter. His family moved to a farm near Constantine, Michigan, when he was a year old. Though he graduated from Northwestern University law school in 1895, he was too young to be admitted to the Michigan bar. While waiting to join the bar, which he did in 1896, he enrolled at Valparaiso University in Valparaiso, Indiana, to take some business courses before returning to southwest Michigan. In 1899 he married Florence Wason. They had two children and settled in Allegan, Michigan, in 1904. In 1906 Hoffman won the first of his two terms as Allegan prosecutor. Afterward he served as an attorney for the city and as chair of the local and county GOP. As an attorney, he was known throughout the state for his real estate and malpractice cases.

In 1932 the Democrats won control of the Fourth District for the first time in history. Hoffman, who regained the seat for the Republicans in 1934, stressed individual initiative and saw business, unencumbered by the federal government, as the best means to end the depression. His views appealed to the largely agrarian and small-town constituents who reelected Hoffman to the House for the next twenty-eight years by large majorities, except for a close race in 1936, which he won by a narrow margin. One of the most vocal members in the House, Hoffman proved tough in debate and skilled in parliamentary maneuvering. A harsh New Deal critic, he voted against the major pieces of New Deal legislation, including Social Security, the Wagner Act, and both Agricultural Adjustment acts. He opposed big government spending to the end of his career, even refusing to sign up for Medicare benefits.

Labor issues dominated Hoffman's career. His response to the 1937 sit-down strike in Flint, Michigan, gained him national attention as "the most vociferous Congressional critic of the sit-down" (Fine, p. 333). Preferring the use of troops, Hoffman attacked Michigan governor Frank Murphy's peaceful tactics. After the sit-down had ended he shifted his criticism to the Congress of Industrial Organizations (CIO) and its head, John L. Lewis. Hoffman's labor views led the *Detroit News* (13 Jan. 1949) to label him "Enemy No. 1" on union lists from 1937 to 1947. Hoffman, viewing domestic Communist activities as the greatest danger to the United States, opposed measures that he feared would involve the nation in World War II. He voted against Lend-Lease, the 1941 Selective Service Act extension, and most defense spending. After the Japanese attack on Pearl Harbor in December 1941, he supported defense measures but also saw the war as an opportunity to dismantle many of the New Deal agencies.

During World War II Hoffman was regarded by many as being pro-fascist. Broadcaster Walter Winchell and prominent national publications such as the *Nation*, the *New Republic*, and *Life*, called for his defeat in the 1942 elections. The suspicion about Hoffman's possible connections to American fascists stemmed from his quoting their remarks, his prewar isolationism, his criticism of the government's handling of the sedition case against various American fascists, and the fascists' use of his speeches, particularly his Judas speech. This was actually two speeches of January 1942 printed together as "Don't Haul Down the Stars and Stripes," which criticized the concept of world government. Hoffman testified before a federal grand jury four times regarding his possible ties to American fascists before the matter was dropped. The actual connection between Hoffman and the fascists seems to have been one of shared opposition to the interventionist policies of President Franklin D. Roosevelt.

Hoffman was critical of many of President Harry S. Truman's policies. An unabashed supporter of Republican senator Joseph McCarthy, he bitterly criticized Truman for not aggressively rooting out Communists within the government. He also opposed Truman's efforts to establish a Fair Employment Practices Commission, abolish the poll tax, and pass an antilynching law, seeing these as infringements on the power of the states.

The year 1947 was the high point in Hoffman's career. As chair of the House Committee on Expenditures in the Executive Departments, he was responsible for the National Security Act, which dealt with the reorganization of the military. Convinced that the army sought to dismantle the marine corps, he advocated retaining the marines as a separate military branch. He considered this law his most impressive legislative accomplishment. Party leaders, wanting Hoffman's help in writing new labor legislation, waived the rule that members could only serve on one standing committee, thereby allowing Hoffman to retain his position on the Education and Labor Committee. Although he was unable to get some of his ideas, such as abolishing the union shop, into the 1947 Taft-Hartley Act, Hoffman was proud of his involvement in drafting the law, even though he considered it barely adequate.

Time (17 Nov. 1952) correctly called Hoffman "a bitter lone wolf." He proved no more able to get along with the Republican president, Dwight Eisenhower, than he had with Democratic ones. He remained concerned about the possibility of a dictatorship and about excessive spending. Hoffman resisted Eisenhower's plan to reorganize the government, noting, "Today's grant of unconstitutional power to a liberty loving President may be tomorrow's weapon in the hands of a now unknown tyrant."

Hoffman's last major battle with the labor movement came in 1953 when as chair of the Government Operations Committee (formerly the Expenditures Committee), he investigated Jimmy Hoffa of the Teamsters. Democratic senator John Kennedy noted that Hoffman's work "had come dangerously close to the truth" about Hoffa (*Look*, 12 May 1959). In 1964 some of Hoffman's evidence helped to convict Hoffa of misusing union pension funds. After the Republicans lost control of Congress in 1955, Hoffman was reduced to the role of critic, taking some solace from the 1959 Landrum-Griffin Act, which limited the use of secondary boycotts and picketing, ideas he had long advocated. Republican senator Barry Goldwater praised Hoffman for being a "pioneer in the labor reform movement" who deserved "special recognition," both for what he had done and for remaining "in the van of crusading legislators" (*Congressional Record*, 86th Cong., 1st sess., 10 Sept. 1959, appendix, p. 7924). Hoffman remained in the House until his health forced him to retire in 1963. He died in Allegan.

Hoffman was an ultraconservative who resisted the changes that characterized the first sixty years of the twentieth century, including the growth of organized labor, the increasing role of the federal government in people's lives, and the greater involvement of the U.S. government in international affairs. *Time* (17 Nov. 1952) once called Hoffman "the most reactionary man in Congress," a statement that would have been applicable at any time during his career.

• The Hoffman family retains his papers, but they have not been made available to scholars. Some of his scrapbooks and copies of his speeches, bills, and resolutions are in the Allegan Public Library, Allegan, Mich. There are also some letters in the Bentley Historical Library at the University of Michigan. Of less value, but still important for his labor views, is the material at the Walter P. Reuther Library, Wayne State University. The single best source on Hoffman is the *Congressional Record*, vols. 79–108 (3 Jan. 1935–13 Oct. 1962).

Both major Detroit newspapers, the *Detroit News* and the *Detroit Free Press*, are valuable, especially the *News*, which contains more out-of-state material. Local papers are generally pro-Hoffman; the most useful is the *Benton Harbor News-Palladium*. Because of the widespread attention that he received, newspapers of national standing (e.g., the *New York Times* and *Washington Post*) and news magazines (e.g., *Time*, *Newsweek*, and *U.S. News & World Report*) are good sources. A sampling of relevant articles includes "Berserk Republican," *Time*, 28 June 1937; "Hoffman's Challenge to NLRB Raises a Fundamental Issue," *Newsweek*, 8 Aug. 1938; "Voices of Defeat," *Life*, 13 Apr. 1942; "The Obstructionists," *New Republic*, 18 May 1942; "Republicans in Congress," *Life*, 30 Oct. 1944; "Two Fascist Members 'Nailed to the Floor' of Congress," *In Fact*, 14 May 1945; and Richard Tregaskis, "The Marine Corps Fights for Its Life," *Saturday Evening Post*, 5 Feb. 1949.

The only look at his congressional career is Donald E. Walker, "The Congressional Career of Clare E. Hoffman, 1935–63" (Ph.D. diss., Michigan State Univ., 1982). There are several general works that show the role Hoffman played. For the sit-down strikes, the best book is Sidney Fine, *Sit-down: The General Motors Strike of 1936–1937* (1969). Hoffman's activities in the Truman years are in Demetrios Caraley, *The Politics of Military Unification: A Study of Conflict and the Policy Process* (1966); and William E. Pemberton, *Bureaucratic Politics: Executive Reorganization during the Truman Administration* (1979). An obituary is in the *New York Times*, 5 Nov. 1967.

DONALD E. WALKER

HOFFMAN, David (24 Dec. 1784–11 Nov. 1854), lawyer and legal educator, was born in Baltimore, Maryland, the son of Peter Hoffman, a prominent merchant, and Dorothea Stierlin Lloyd. He attended St. John's College in Annapolis, an institution patronized by the Maryland elite, from 1800 to 1802 but left without taking a degree. A voracious reader throughout his life, he later claimed to have been almost wholly self-taught. While several older brothers joined the family's importing business, Hoffman instead entered the legal profession and became a leading Baltimore attorney by 1812. He further enhanced his professional status through marriage in 1816 to Mary McKean, daughter of a Philadelphia merchant and granddaughter of a former Pennsylvania governor and judge. They had three children.

Hoffman's scholarly interests led to his appointment in 1814 as professor of law in the embryonic University of Maryland, a state institution he had helped to establish in 1812. For three years he worked on a suitable curriculum, which he published in 1817 as *A Course of Legal Study*. Immediately acclaimed by reviewers in the United States and abroad, Hoffman's *Course* provided students with a comprehensive bibliographical guide to every branch of Anglo-American law, as well as substantial references to Roman law and modern Continental jurisprudence. Since Hoffman thought of law as a network of interrelated principles that underlay all human activities, he insisted that

students should familiarize themselves with the sciences and humanities before proceeding to specific legal subjects. His herculean reading program, which required six years to complete, sought to produce statesmen and legislators as well as practitioners and judges.

Such an ambitious design could not be realized in practice, especially at a time when most prospective lawyers gained admission to the bar by clerking for two or three years in a law office. Hoffman delivered the first of 301 projected lectures at the Maryland Law Institute in 1822, but low enrollment and limited state support soon forced him to admit students at any stage of the syllabus, provided they agreed to remain at least three months. Despite increasing setbacks, Hoffman persevered as the sole proprietor of the institute until 1832 and developed some innovative ideas and practices. An early advocate of historical jurisprudence, he related legal doctrines to evolving societal needs and anticipated the sociological jurists of the early twentieth century in arguing that law must be informed by the social sciences. He also emphasized the importance of statutory construction and draftsmanship and acquainted students with the codification efforts of Jeremy Bentham and other reformers, who argued that all law in a republican society should be formulated by popularly elected legislatures. Finally, he used moot courts, which normally functioned as debating societies, to teach students how to prepare and argue cases according to the procedures followed in both state and federal courts. In *Legal Outlines* (1829), an introductory textbook that reprinted his first nine lectures, he drew upon extensive reading in philosophy, psychology, and political theory to identify the principles of "universal morality" that in his view informed all systems of jurisprudence.

After years of strained relations with the university's trustees, Hoffman quit teaching in 1832, though he did not formally resign his professorship until 1836. The advent of Jacksonian democracy, with its leveling tendencies in law and politics, filled him with dismay. In an expanded edition of his *Course* published in 1836, he included a lengthy code of ethics for practitioners, *Fifty Resolutions in Regard to Professional Deportment*. Rejecting any distinction between professional and lay standards of morality, he insisted that a lawyer's primary duty was to obey his conscience, not to help an unworthy client prevail by means of legal technicalities. Through such ethical prescriptions Hoffman sought to preserve an elite tradition of gentlemanly conduct at a time when many state legislatures were scaling back requirements for admission to the bar.

A Federalist in his early years, he became a staunch Whig by the 1830s and wrote two books of social criticism—*Miscellaneous Thoughts on Men, Manners, and Things* by "Anthony Grumbler of Grumbleton Hall, Esq." (1837) and *Viator; or, A Peep into My Note Book* (1841)—in which he attacked the excesses of "ultra democracy." He continued to practice law and was admitted to the Philadelphia bar in 1843. From 1844 to

1847 he conducted a second law institute in Philadelphia, but mounting debts again forced him to abandon the venture.

In 1847 he traveled to England to complete work on a final grandiose project: the six-volume novel *Chronicles Selected from the Originals of Cartaphilus, the Wandering Jew*, which purported to describe the evolution of religion and government in the Western world as seen through the eyes of the Wandering Jew. The first three volumes appeared in 1853 and 1854; the rest remained unpublished. During a residence of six years in London, Hoffman also served as land agent for California impresario John Charles Frémont. When controversy developed over Frémont's claims, Hoffman returned to the United States in 1853 to investigate. He died of apoplexy in New York City.

Hoffman was ahead of his time in attempting to teach law as a rigorous intellectual discipline. A humanistic scholar, he did much to improve the ethics of legal practice, and he bequeathed to future generations through his *Course of Legal Study* an invaluable guide to the major sources from which the American legal tradition has developed.

• Letters from Hoffman are in the Hoffman Family Papers at the Maryland Historical Society; the John Pendleton Kennedy Papers at the Peabody Institute, Baltimore; the Charles Sumner Papers at Harvard University; and the papers of the Galloway-Maxcy-Markoe families in the Library of Congress. For Hoffman's account of his rancorous dispute with the University of Maryland trustees, see the series of letters he published with his *Introductory Lectures* (1837). In "David Hoffman and the Shaping of a Republican Legal Culture," *Maryland Law Review* 38 (1979): 673–88, Maxwell Bloomfield reassesses Hoffman's contributions to legal education in the light of recent scholarship. An obituary is in the *New York Tribune*, 13 Nov. 1854.

MAXWELL BLOOMFIELD

HOFFMAN, Frederick John (21 Sept. 1909–24 Dec. 1967), professor of English and literary critic, was born in Port Washington, Wisconsin, the son of Henry George Hoffmann, owner of a small family hotel, and Celia Rose Goldammer. He was brought up a Roman Catholic in a family of nine children, all of whom worked in the family hotel during their formative years. Frederick J. Hoffman, as he came to be known through his writings, dropped the second "n" from his surname as a young man.

Hoffman left Wisconsin and the church (he thought of himself in his mature years as a lapsed Catholic) when he went off to Stanford University. He received his B.A. in 1934, and two years later he completed the M.A. in philosophy at the University of Minnesota. After teaching stints at Pasadena Junior College (1936–1938) and at the University of Chicago (1938–1940), he entered the graduate program at Ohio State University from which he received the Ph.D. in English in 1942. His revised dissertation was published three years later by the Louisiana State University Press as *Freudianism and the Literary Mind*.

Hoffman's first book skillfully negotiates the uncertain tightrope stretched between literature and psychology as it examines the impact of Freud's theories on a number of twentieth-century writers, including James Joyce, D. H. Lawrence, Thomas Mann, Franz Kafka, and Sherwood Anderson. The interdisciplinary nature of his interests, his firm commitment to modern literature, and his eagerness to elucidate it set a standard for the remainder of his writing career.

Hoffman collaborated with Charles Allen and Carolyn F. Ulrich on *The Little Magazine: A History and a Bibliography*, published in 1946 by the Princeton University Press. Hoffman and Allen wrote the text; Ulrich was responsible for the bibliography, Hoffman for the incisive commentary on each item. Although the collaboration was apparently an uneasy one, with Hoffman's share disproportionately large, the book has remained a standard reference tool for scholars interested in those periodicals which had limited circulation but which published many experimental writers, including Ezra Pound and T. S. Eliot, early in their careers.

Hoffman taught at Ohio State for five years after he received his Ph.D., spent the academic year 1947–1948 at the University of Oklahoma, and then moved to the University of Wisconsin, where he remained until 1960. His first two books were the product of his apprenticeship years in Columbus. The maturing of his talents as writer and teacher were the result of the dozen years in Madison.

Hoffman managed to exert considerable influence in reshaping the curriculum in the traditionally oriented English department of the University of Wisconsin. He introduced courses in twentieth-century literature, which at the time were virtually unheard-of in American universities. He commented on this phenomenon years later in the *Nation* (8 Nov. 1965): "I am, of course, also a teacher of modern literature, and I happen to believe that it can and should be taught. . . . It is quite possible to teach *Naked Lunch* and *Corydon* and *Death in Venice*."

While at Wisconsin he was primarily responsible for launching *Wisconsin Studies in Contemporary Literature* (now published under the shorter title *Contemporary Literature*) and served as its advisory editor for the first two issues, both published in 1960. He also directed more than a dozen doctoral dissertations, each concerned with some aspect of modern literature; virtually all were later published in whole or in part, with Olga Vickery's *The Novels of William Faulkner: A Critical Interpretation* (1959) and Joseph N. Riddel's *The Clairvoyant Eye: The Poetry and Poetics of Wallace Stevens* (1965), both published by Louisiana State University Press, being perhaps the most notable.

Aside from his roles as teacher, editor, and mentor, Hoffman was enormously productive as a scholar during the Wisconsin years. The centerpiece of this period was *The Twenties: American Writing in the Postwar Decade* (1955), which offers a unique "strategy of presentation" (words from the preface to the 1962 second edition). In each chapter Hoffman moves from the "raw material" of the historical or social documents to the end product, the literary text. Thus in a chapter entitled "Forms of Experiment and Improvisation" he makes his way through a vast amount of literary and quasi-literary history on his way to a close reading of Hart Crane's *The Bridge*.

Hoffman joined the faculty at the University of California, Riverside, in the fall of 1960 and remained there for the next five years. He was instrumental once again in shaping the curriculum and asserting the respectability of modern literature as a scholarly discipline and as a legitimate subject for serious discussion in the classroom. In a two-year period he published two books in Twayne's United States Authors Series, *William Faulkner* (1961) and *Conrad Aiken* (1962); one in the University of Minnesota Pamphlets on American Writers series, *Gertrude Stein* (1961); and one in the Crosscurrents/Modern Critiques series at the Southern Illinois University Press, *Samuel Beckett: The Language of Self* (1962). These monographs contain a sophistication and critical acumen rare in introductory studies of this sort.

The central book of Hoffman's Riverside years was *The Mortal No: Death and the Modern Imagination* (1964), which attempts a redefinition of modern literature in terms of a new set of metaphors. It reveals once again Hoffman's flexibility as a critic, his ability to change method to suit his literary needs. An interdisciplinary study, it demands not only a knowledge of Western literature since 1830 but also more than a passing acquaintance with psychology, anthropology, theology, and even painting. Its vastness and originality suggested to reviewers seminal works like Erich Auerbach's *Mimesis* and Northrop Frye's *Anatomy of Criticism*.

Hoffman's final two years were spent as Distinguished Professor of English at the University of Wisconsin–Milwaukee where he started the Center for Twentieth Century Studies. During this period he divorced his first wife, the former Eleanor Thompson, whom he had married in 1936 and with whom he had one child; in 1967 he married Mary Charlotte Holm, with whom he did not have children. His writing continued at a furious pace in Milwaukee as he produced an uncommon number of essays and book reviews. Two books appeared in 1967, a few months before his death from a heart attack on Christmas eve. The first of these, *The Imagination's New Beginning: Theology and Modern Literature*—based on the first annual Ward-Phillips Lectures in English Language and Literature he gave in May 1966 at the University of Notre Dame—Hoffman always considered as a kind of extended appendix to *The Mortal No*. Both titles are indeed taken from the same Wallace Stevens poem, "Esthétique du Mal," and the books share a preoccupation with the secularization of religious experience in modern literature. The other 1967 study, *The Art of Southern Fiction: A Study of Some Modern Novelists*, treats a group of southern writers, including James Agee, Flannery O'Connor, Eudora Welty, Carson McCullers, and William Styron, who wrote in the shadow of Faulkner. Hoffman did not live long enough to update *The Little Magazine: A History and a Bibliography*, which was to be his next major project.

John B. Vickery ended his preface to *The Shaken Realist* by praising Hoffman for offering "a surpassing professional example." He was indeed a central presence among commentators on twentieth-century literature for more than two decades. William Ronald Tanksley grouped him with three other major critics, Lionel Trilling, Edmund Wilson, and Kenneth Burke, placing him closest to Trilling. There is no doubt that Hoffman, whom Tanksley characterized as "a skeptical humanist," belongs in this august company.

• There is, unfortunately, no collection of Hoffman's papers. At the time of his death his personal library, which John B. Vickery described as "in all likelihood . . . the most distinguished and complete working library for scholars in modern literature in America," was sold to Rice University. An item in *Journal of Modern Literature* 1 (1971): 660 speaks of the University of Tulsa as having purchased from Rice "the bulk of the late Frederick Hoffman's personal library."

Another important book by Hoffman is *The Modern Novel in America* (1951; 2d ed., 1956; 3d ed., 1963), which seems to have had the widest popular appeal of all of his works and to have been translated into the most foreign languages, including Italian, Greek, Arabic, Spanish, Korean, and Japanese. Among his many edited volumes, *William Faulkner: Two Decades of Criticism* (1951) and *William Faulkner: Three Decades of Criticism* (1960), both in collaboration with Olga Vickery, attracted the most attention.

The only complete study of Hoffman's career is William Ronald Tanksley's "Frederick J. Hoffman as Literary Scholar and Critic" (Ph.D. diss., Univ. of Illinois, 1969). This useful work includes an extensive list of Hoffman's published writing and a list of selected reviews of his books. See also *The Shaken Realist: Essays in Modern Literature in Honor of Frederick J. Hoffman*, ed. Melvin J. Friedman and John B. Vickery (1970), which contains biographical and critical material in the preface and introduction and offers a reasonably complete year-by-year listing of Hoffman's publications from 1943 through 1968, including foreign translations of his books. Brief obituaries are in the *New York Times*, 26 Dec. 1967, and in *Poetry*, Mar. 1968.

MELVIN J. FRIEDMAN

HOFFMAN, Frederick Ludwig (2 May 1865–23 Feb. 1946), statistician and public health author, was born in the town of Varel, in the former Duchy of Oldenburg (near the North Sea, not far from the port city of Bremen), in present-day northwestern Germany, the son of Augustus Franciscus Hoffman, an accountant, and Antoinette Marie Elise von Laar. In 1876 Hoffman's father died. A few years later, at age fifteen, Hoffman left school to become an apprentice in a mercantile business because there were not sufficient funds to provide for his university education. The work did not suit him; after six months, he left. After working at several other unsatisfactory jobs, he decided to emigrate to the United States. He arrived at New York City on 28 November 1884, and he became a U.S. citizen on 25 October 1893.

After several years of wandering and of working at various short-term jobs, in 1887 Hoffman became a shipping clerk for the Standard Oil Company at their office in Brunswick, Georgia. In Georgia he met Ella George Hay, whom he married in 1891; they had six children.

Hoffman resigned his post in 1888 and went to Boston, where he secured a position as an agent for the Metropolitan Life Insurance Company, beginning his life's work in the field of insurance. In 1890 he moved to Chattanooga, Tennessee, as co-manager of an independent insurance agency. He next became first assistant superintendent of the Life Insurance Company of Virginia at Norfolk. In 1894 he was invited to join the actuarial department of the Prudential Life Insurance Company at its headquarters in Newark, New Jersey; there he would make his career.

Several of Hoffman's first published studies in the 1890s dealt with racial issues, as in his article "Vital Statistics of the Negro" in *The Arena* (1892). His book *Race Traits and Tendencies of the American Negro* (1896), published by the American Economic Association, grew out of his humanitarian interest in the status of African Americans in the American South. He wrote extensively about American Indians, as in his article "Health Conditions among the Indians" (*Journal of the American Medical Association* [1920]), and in numerous other articles and in letters to the editor of newspapers such as the *New York Times*. He wrote especially about the Navajo, whose society he greatly admired. He maintained a lifelong interest in minority groups.

In 1901 Prudential appointed Hoffman statistician, and he began to establish a vast library of statistical materials for use in his research. He also was instrumental in the founding of the Prudential Press, which published many of his works. In 1918 he was appointed third vice president of Prudential. In his work for the company, he traveled all over the United States and abroad, to investigate questions related to the insurance industry and to inspect industrial conditions in mining, lumbering, and other activities. His main purpose was to gather information that would help to establish accurate actuarial statistics about occupational hazards and thus about life expectancies. He also gave countless speeches and presentations at conventions, congresses, and meetings of professional associations; he represented Prudential at world fairs, such as the Panama-Pacific Exposition in San Francisco (1915). Many of his addresses were published in the proceedings of various organizations and collected for reprinting by the Prudential Press.

In the early years of the twentieth century Hoffman wrote works concerning the so-called "dusty trades"—that is, manufacturing occupations in which organic or mineral dust was generated. The incidence of tuberculosis and pneumoconiosis was notably higher among workers in such industries, and Hoffman, through his important publications brought out by the U.S. Department of Labor, campaigned for amelioration of labor conditions and for legislation to regulate sanitary conditions in the workplace.

Another of Hoffman's major interests was national health insurance, which had been introduced in Germany in 1883; in the late nineteenth and early twentieth century similar plans were being considered in Britain and elsewhere. Hoffman was resolutely opposed to such public welfare programs, since he thought that they encouraged dependency rather than self-sufficiency and responsibility. His numerous critiques were not only statements of his own beliefs but also attempts to protect the viability of the private-sector insurance business, which he considered threatened by the introduction of such programs.

In 1913 Hoffman delivered to the American Gynecological Society his influential address "The Menace of Cancer." This was the first of many works on cancer by him, some of them of major importance, such as his extensive study, *The Mortality from Cancer throughout the World* (1915), his *San Francisco Cancer Survey* (9 vols., 1924–1934), and *Cancer and Diet* (1937), his last major publication. Hoffman was instrumental in the founding of the American Cancer Society, and in 1943 he received the Clement Cleveland Award of the New York City Cancer Committee of the ACS.

Hoffman's published work was influential in combating malaria (his publishing of statistical research on malaria and his campaigning for public awareness of strategies of prevention helped eradicate the disease in the United States) and leprosy (he was instrumental in the founding of a national leprosarium at Carville, La.). He also wrote extensively on suicide and homicide. He wrote about his travels in Mexico, Central America, and in the Bolivian and Peruvian Andes, as well as his exploration of the headwaters of the Amazon River during the Mulford Expedition of 1921. He made pioneering airplane trips all over the United States (which he reported on at length in the *New York Times* in 1928) and flew extensively in Russia, reporting on those trips in a series of articles in the *Peoria Star* in 1927. Hoffman also wrote lengthy typewritten (unpublished) analyses and statistical reports for Prudential. He was a frequent contributor of letters to the editor to newspapers and magazines, and his writings and speeches were widely reported on and summarized in newspapers such as the *New York Times*. He wrote original poetry (mostly unpublished).

Resigning from Prudential in 1922, Hoffman continued to do consulting work for the company. He was appointed to teach at Babson Institute, in Wellesley Hills, Massachusetts, where he remained until 1927 as dean of the Advanced Research Course in business. Later, as a research consultant, he joined the Franklin Institute in Philadelphia. He moved in 1938 to San Diego, California, where he was living at the time of his death.

Hoffman's influence is as extensive and varied as his interests and activities. His public health crusade is carried on, for example, by the American Cancer Society, the Tuberculosis Association, the Hansen's Disease Center at Carville, Louisiana, and in legislation concerning healthful conditions for workers. Among his most enduring achievements were his tireless campaigns for healthful work conditions and his constant pleas for comprehensive and accurate systems of statistical registration of data relating to mortality and public health issues, his studies of cancer and tropical diseases, his geographical explorations, and his pioneering aviation journeys. His enormous body of writing (he is said to have published more than 1,200 articles and books) both published and unpublished and his many legacies ensure his lasting reputation.

• A major collection of manuscript and published material by Hoffman is at the Rare Book and Manuscript Library of Columbia University, which also contains an unpublished biography by Hoffman's daughter Ella Hoffman Rigney. Other important collections of material relating to Hoffman are at Tulane University; Prudential Insurance Company of America in Newark, N.J.; College of Physicians of Philadelphia, National Library of Medicine, Bethesda, Md.; and American Cancer Society, Atlanta, Ga. Hoffman published twenty-eight major books (of 100 pages or more in length) and hundreds of articles, lectures, and statistical analyses. Among his important titles not already named in the text are *History of the Prudential Insurance Company of America* (1900); "The Mortality from Consumption in the Dusty Trades," *Bulletin of the Bureau of Labor* 17, no. 79 (Nov. 1908); "Mortality from Consumption in Occupations Exposing to Municipal and General Organic Dust," *Bulletin of the Bureau of Labor* 18, no. 82 (May 1909); "Fatal Accidents in Coal Mining," *Bulletin of the Bureau of Labor* 21, no. 90 (Sept. 1910); *Insurance Science and Economics* (1911); *Care of Tuberculous Wage Earners in Germany*, Bulletin of the U.S. Bureau of Labor Statistics, whole no. 101 (1912); *The Statistical Experience Data of the Johns Hopkins Hospital, Baltimore, Md., 1892–1911* (1913); *Industrial Accident Statistics*, Bulletin of the U.S. Bureau of Labor Statistics, whole no. 157 (1915); *Facts and Fallacies of Compulsory Health Insurance* (1917); *Mortality from Respiratory Diseases in Dusty Trades (Inorganic Dusts)*, Bulletin of the U.S. Bureau of Labor Statistics, whole no. 231 (1918); *The Problem of Dust Phthisis in the Granite-stone Industry*, U.S. Department of Labor, Bureau of Labor Statistics, no. 293 (1922); *The Homicide Problem* (1925); *Windstorm and Tornado Insurance*, 4th ed. (1926); *Health Survey of the Printing Trades 1922 to 1925*, Bulletin of the U.S. Bureau of Labor Statistics, no. 427 (1927); *Earthquake Hazards and Insurance* (1928); *Malaria Problems* (1928); *Some Problems of Longevity* (1928); and *Suicide Problems* (1928). More than 200 of Hoffman's publications are listed in "Bibliographie Frederick L. Hoffman," *Archiv für soziale Hygiene und Demographie* 3, pt. 1 (1928). Hoffman is discussed in two *New Yorker* articles: Alva Johnston, "The Fifteen Biggest Men in America," 25 Jan. 1930, and James Thurber, "Behind the Statistics," 1 July 1933. An obituary is in the *New York Times*, 25 Feb. 1946.

F. J. SYPHER

HOFFMAN, John Thompson (10 Jan. 1828–24 Mar. 1888), mayor of New York City and governor of New York, was born in Sing Sing (subsequently renamed Ossining), New York, the son of Adrian Kissam Hoffman, a physician, and Jane Ann Thompson. Hoffman graduated from Union College in Schenectady, New York, in 1848 and returned to his home town to study law with two local attorneys. Admitted to the bar in early 1849, he moved to New York City later that year to form a legal partnership with Samuel M. Woodruff and Judge William Leonard. In 1854 Hoffman married Ella Starkweather of New York City; the couple had one child.

Even before his move to New York City, Hoffman, who claimed kinship with both the Livingstons and Kissams, two of the state's more prominent families, had begun making a name in politics. In 1848 he had traveled throughout the state to speak on behalf of the Democratic presidential candidate, Lewis Cass, and was also elected to the party's central committee in New York. He continued to participate in politics after he was established in New York City. Hoffman became a member of the Young Men's Tammany Hall General Committee in 1854, and in 1859 he was elected to the Tammany Society's General Committee. Riven by factional strife over many of the same issues that were dividing the nation, the Democratic party in the state of New York was unable to campaign with its usual vigor. The party was also hurting in New York City, where Tammany Hall's ability to mobilize voters had held the key to Democratic success since the 1820s. Dissident factions, primarily Mozart Hall (named for the group's meeting place), were drawing away votes that normally went to Tammany-backed candidates. Tammany's efforts to secure Hoffman an appointment as a U.S. district attorney were ignored by the James Buchanan administration, which at the time was not particularly inclined to heed its requests for patronage.

In 1861, however, Hoffman's prospects improved dramatically when he was elected to the office of recorder, a position that gave him authority comparable to that of a police judge. Hoffman's win contrasted sharply with the fate of other Tammany candidates. Republican George Opdyke won the mayoralty, and William Tweed, not yet established as the organization's boss, lost his bid for sheriff. Oakey Hall, who had had the backing of the Mozart Hall faction in his race for district attorney but who soon made his peace with Tweed, also won. Their victories in this otherwise gloomy year earned Hoffman and Hall recognition as two of the city's most promising men in the Democratic party.

Two years later Hoffman and Hall (as district attorney) occupied the key positions in the trial of participants in the New York City draft riots of 1863. The trials began in late July and continued into September, winning praise for both Hoffman and Hall, who were seen as firmly committed to law and order—and to union. Their efforts played an important symbolic role in Tweed's rise to supremacy in New York City's factionalized politics, for Tammany was positioning itself as a pillar of the wing of the Democratic party that was identified with support of the Union's war effort. The so-called War Democrats were by no means uncritical of the Abraham Lincoln administration, but they endeavored to stress support for the preservation of the Union.

Hoffman's record as an upholder of law and order and of nationalism also won praise from Republicans, and in 1863 he was reelected with bipartisan support. He gained the mayoralty in 1865 in a hotly contested four-way race. Although he apparently did not seek pecuniary gain from Tammany's graft, his popularity and respectability served as a front for the Tweed ring, which was then solidifying its dominance of Tammany Hall and undermining Mozart Hall's credibility as a rival within New York City. In his zeal to end the Civil War, Fernando Wood, leader of the Mozart faction, had allowed himself to be perceived as someone who would sacrifice the Union to bring about peace. Hoffman, who had been defeated for the governorship in 1866 by the incumbent Republican Reuben Fenton, was reelected overwhelmingly to the mayoralty in 1867. As mayor, Hoffman facilitated the machine's operations by naming Tweed henchman Peter B. Sweeny to the office of comptroller in 1867, but on occasion he also vetoed extravagant spending measures that the ring wanted. However, the extent of the Tweed ring's corruption would not be fully revealed for several years, and in the meantime Hoffman was able to increase his stature by stressing long-standing Democratic principles such as home rule and government noninterference with private morality.

Hoffman, the most visible and articulate opponent of Republican centralism, again received the Democratic nomination for governor in 1868. He won and resigned the mayoralty of New York City a few weeks before his inauguration in January 1869. Widespread voting fraud in the city had resulted in tens of thousands of fraudulent votes being cast for Hoffman and other Tammany candidates by repeaters, by individuals who existed only on paper, and by illegally naturalized immigrants. Without these votes Hoffman might well have been defeated. The pall cast by the election scandal on Hoffman's prospects for a successful administration did not last long, however, because Hoffman disarmed his critics with a masterful inaugural message to the state legislature. In it he emphasized the need for frugal government, for localism, and for an end to special legislation for favored lobbyists. Fortunately for Hoffman, a vote-buying scandal that erupted amid factional strife within the Republican party in New York diverted attention from the Democrats' problems and from his own failure early in his administration to veto the Erie (Railroad) Classification Bill that Tweed and the notorious financier Jay Gould wanted enacted.

As his term advanced, Hoffman continued his advocacy of Jacksonian principles and in 1870 won much praise for his part in helping bring about charter reform that gained New York City a greater measure of home rule than it had enjoyed in a generation. An 1847 charter bill had given Albany considerable say in New York City affairs. Home rule also played into the hands of Tweed by enabling him to pack New York City's various governmental agencies with his men. Although Hoffman often deferred to Tammany on patronage matters (his own father-in-law held the finan-

cially rewarding position of collector of assessments in the city), Hoffman's record as governor won applause in several quarters. His emphasis on traditional Democratic principles helped him retain the support of old Jacksonians, and he handled the controversial temperance issue adroitly by advocating decentralization of authority over excise taxes and license fees. That is, the state of New York could retain the tax law passed by a Republican-dominated legislature in 1866 but shift the emphasis to localism by allowing locally chosen boards to set the rates for their respective communities. The amended laws governing license fees were sufficiently ambiguous on Sunday closing so that both drys and wets could claim victory. Genteel reformers were impressed by his fiscal responsibility as well as by the special commission he named to eliminate obsolete statutes. To many in cosmopolitan New York City, Hoffman's stress on tolerance and localism was preferable to what historian Iver Bernstein refers to as "the aristocratic, nativist, and coercive style" offered by the Republican party.

Hoffman's achievements and the continued backing of the Tammany machine gained him reelection in 1870, this time unmarred by voting scandals. Eager to eradicate the stigma of disunion and to carry New York's large electoral vote, some northern Democrats began to look to Hoffman as a national standard-bearer. For several months he continued to enjoy the good fortune that had enabled him to overcome the stigma of the corrupt 1868 elections. Although he continued to make opposition to special interests a theme of his administration, Hoffman was nevertheless able to give Tammany much of what it wanted because large-scale construction projects often had advocates within the business community. To some, construction meant plunder; to others it meant civic improvement and commercial development. For instance, in 1871 Hoffman signed into law legislation for an elevated railway that would run the length of Manhattan on a massive stone viaduct. Financed by a combination of public and private funds, the viaduct plan had its critics but it also had the backing of reputable citizens such as merchant William Martin, editor Horace Greeley, and businessmen August Belmont and Peter Cooper. (The downfall of the Tweed ring discredited the Viaduct Railway before it could be built.)

Hoffman, who had presidential aspirations, began to dissociate himself from Tammany later in 1871 when he persuaded New York City authorities to withdraw their ban on the 12 July parade of the Loyal Order of Orangemen. Violence ensued when Irish Catholics clustered at the parade's assembly point to harass the marchers and the troops ordered by Hoffman to protect them. When stones were hurled and a shot fired, the militia retaliated by firing indiscriminately at the Catholic crowd. Several dozen people were killed. Hoffman's decision to permit the parade that ring insiders had initially opposed was risky for it could well cost him Irish support in any subsequent campaigns. The slayings made matters worse. But the question of the Catholic vote became moot when reports of the

Tweed ring's enormous graft began to gain attention. Hoffman was by no means the only ranking Democrat to remain quiet as journalists and civic reformers bore the initial burden of protest, but he lost respect by delaying comment too long.

In the meantime, attorney Samuel Tilden, long prominent in Democratic party affairs, stepped forth as the chief spokesman for those who wished to prosecute Tammany leaders for graft. Hoffman finally seemed to join ranks with Tilden in the fall of 1871 by naming Charles O'Conor, a widely respected lawyer, as a special attorney general to recapture public funds in the civil courts. O'Conor was a member of the Tilden wing of the Democratic party who could be counted on to diligently pursue the investigation of the Tweed ring's graft. Satirized by the political cartoonist Thomas Nast as a wooden Indian (an Indian had often been used as the Tammany Society's emblem) mounted on wheels so he could be pushed and pulled toward the White House by the Tweed ring, Hoffman did not immediately disclose his intentions about running for reelection in 1872. Democrats, however, were relieved when Hoffman chose not to seek the party's nomination for governor and instead returned to the practice of law, first in Albany and later in New York City. He did head the New York delegation to the 1872 Democratic convention, where he promoted the nomination of Greeley for president, but rarely spoke out on politics thereafter. Hoffman had been suffering from heart disease for several years when he was stricken on his annual trip to Wiesbaden, Germany, where he died. At the time of his death he was affiliated with the law firm of Johnes, Willcox & Purdy.

From 1868 through 1892 every Democratic nominee for the presidency but one (General Winfield Scott Hancock in 1880) was a New Yorker: Horatio Seymour, Greeley, Tilden, and Grover Cleveland, who was elected president in 1884 and again in 1892. Whether the ambitious Hoffman would have tried to bid for the Democratic presidential nomination (that went to the liberal Republican Greeley) in 1872 is uncertain, for at age forty-four he might have preferred to run again for the governorship or seek some other office before trying for the presidency. In any event, it was not the tarnished Hoffman who became the Democratic candidate in 1876 but Tilden, the man who had humbled Boss Tweed.

• No substantial body of Hoffman's papers survives. The Manuscript Division of the New York Public Library has about sixty items (mainly letters to Hoffman) that comprise one of the collections in the Personal Miscellaneous file. Papers of his contemporaries can be used in gaining insight into Hoffman's career in politics. Among the relevant collections are the papers of Manton Marble at the Library of Congress in Washington, D.C., and the papers of Samuel J. Tilden at the New York Public Library. Personal information about Hoffman can be found in two laudatory profiles, Hiram Caulkins and De Witt Van Buren, *Biographical Sketches of John T. Hoffman and Allen C. Beach* (1868), and Adrian Hoffman Joline, "John Thompson Hoffman," *New York Genealogical and Biographical Record* (Apr. 1911): 111–28. The *Public Papers of John T. Hoffman* (1872) should also be consulted. Much insight into the politics of Hoffman's times can be found in Iver Bernstein, *The New York City Draft Riots* (1990); Adrian Cook, *The Armies of the Streets: The New York City Draft Riots of 1863* (1974); Leo Hershkowitz, *Tweed's New York: Another Look* (1977); and James C. Mohr, *The Radical Republicans and Reform in New York during Reconstruction* (1973). Three books by Jerome Mushkat, *Tammany: The Evolution of a Political Machine* (1971), *The Reconstruction of the New York Democracy, 1861–1874* (1981), and *Fernando Wood: A Political Biography* (1990), are essential. Also pertinent are Alexander Flick, *Samuel J. Tilden* (1939); Alexander B. Callow, Jr., *The Tweed Ring* (1966); and Mark W. Summers, *The Era of Good Stealings* (1993). Charles F. Wingate, "An Episode in Municipal Government," *North American Review* (Oct. 1874), and DeAlva S. Alexander, *A Political History of the State of New York, 1861–1882*, vol. 3 (1909; repr. 1969), provide more detail on Hoffman than is common in more recent works. An obituary is in the *New York Times*, 25 Mar. 1888.

LLOYD J. GRAYBAR

HOFFMAN, Malvina (15 June 1885–10 July 1966), sculptor, was born Malvina Cornell Hoffman in New York City, the daughter of Richard Hoffman, a pianist, and Fidelia Marshall Lamson. Her early years were spent in a handsome brownstone on West 43d Street in New York City. Her father, born in England, was an internationally recognized pianist who first came to the United States as an accompanist to Jenny Lind, the Swedish soprano. Richard Hoffman's home was filled with works of art and artists, inspiring his daughter's interest in art.

Hoffman attended classes at the Woman's School of Applied Design and the Art Students League while still in her teens. She studied painting privately with John White Alexander. In 1906 she began to study sculpture with Herbert Adams and George Grey Bernard at the Veltin School. The young artist received private instruction in sculpture with Gutzon Borglum before traveling to Paris in 1910. That summer Hoffman worked as an assistant in the Parisian studio of American sculptor Janet Scudder. For the following two years she also benefited from critiques by Auguste Rodin. In 1911 she completed her first figure group, *Russian Dancers* (Detroit Institute of Arts), which was based on Anna Pavlova and Mikhail Mordkin, whom Hoffman saw in a London performance the previous year.

Hoffman spent the winters of 1911 through 1913 in New York City, attending anatomy classes at Columbia University's College of Physicians and Surgeons. In order to overcome the prejudices against women artists, she developed superb technical skills and produced many anatomical drawings. In 1914—until the fall, when she returned to the United States—Hoffman resided in Paris, where she met Gertrude Stein, Henri Matisse, Romaine Brooks, Frederick MacMonnies, Mabel Dodge, and Constantin Brancusi. Her study with Rodin developed into a lasting friendship, and he was a dominant influence on her early work. She also became acquainted with dancers Anna Pavlova and Vaslav Nijinsky, who were to inspire many sculptures of dancing figures. In 1924 Hoffman's polychrome portrait mask of Pavlova (1924; Metropolitan Museum of Art) won the Watrous Gold Medal of the National Academy of Design.

Dance was a major theme in the oeuvre of Hoffman. Her inspiration stemmed principally from Anna Pavlova, whom she first saw perform with Sergei Diaghilev's Ballet Russe in 1910. The bronze group *Bacchanale Russe* (1912; Metropolitan Museum of Art) depicts Anna Pavlova and Mikhail Mordkin in the opening moments of "The Bacchanale," a dance choreographed by Michel Fokine. Energy emanates from this sculpture, which depicts both dancers raising their arms to grasp a billowing drapery as they begin their pas de deux. Hoffman captured brilliantly a single moment in the dance. When she modeled this sculptural group, Hoffman acknowledged her study with Rodin, who inspired her interest in depicting figures in motion. She presented a more realistic likeness of her subject than did Rodin, but the attention to movement and the attempt to capture a fleeting moment can be compared to the French master's depictions of dancers. In 1917 the *Bacchanale Russe* was exhibited at the National Academy of Design and won the Shaw Memorial Prize. It was enlarged to a "heroic-size bronze" and acquired by the French government for the Luxembourg Gardens in 1918—the only work by a woman in either the garden or the interior galleries of the Luxembourg Museum. The sculpture was seized by the Nazis in 1941.

Hoffman made studies of Anna Pavlova as early as 1910, but she did not meet the famous Russian ballerina until 1914. The two women became close friends, and Hoffman made hundreds of sketches of the dancer. In addition to many studies of Pavlova with her partners, Hoffman also represented the dancer in a solo role. *Pavlova Gavotte* (1915; Metropolitan Museum of Art) is a fluid and sensitive depiction of a trained body in motion. Hoffman's technical proficiency allowed her to capture a realistic likeness of the gesture and movement of the renowned dancer. In her autobiography Hoffman recalled Pavlova's posing for this sculpture in her small studio on Thirty-fourth Street in Manhattan: "Once inside the studio she would disrobe and reappear 'in costume,' as he insisted on calling it . . . a snug little suggestion of short tights, long-heeled golden slippers, and the famous yellow poke bonnet with long streamers. . . . The diaphanous clinging yellow satin dress, which I added as drapery after the nude figure was completed, served to accentuate the grace and rhythmic silhouette of her figure" (p. 144).

In June 1924 Hoffman married Samuel B. Grimson but continued to use her own name professionally. They were divorced in 1936; they had no children. Active as a sculptor for more than forty years, Hoffman produced fountains, statuettes, and architectural sculpture. She was renowned for her portrait studies. Among her portraits are those of Ivan Mestrovic, Katharine Cornell, and Ignace Paderewski.

Hoffman's proficient naturalism and her penetrating study of character found its best expression in a major commission from the Field Museum of Natural History in Chicago: studies of the ethnic groups of the world. A series of figures, referred to as the "Living Races of Man," was to be displayed in the Hall of Man in the Field Museum. With her husband, Hoffman traveled around the world in 1931 and 1932, gathering information for her commission. By 1933 she had cast 102 original bronzes and had created other full-length figures and sculptural groups related to the Field Museum bronzes. Examples of Hoffman's ethnographic works were exhibited in a number of American cities following the acclaim she received for her remarkable commission.

When the Hall of Man opened at the Field Museum in 1933, about eighty of her sculptures were exhibited; by 1935 all of them were on display. In her world travels, Hoffman had been assisted by anthropologists who found "pure" ethnic types to be her models. The sculptor tried to create likenesses that exemplified the diverse races, but she always considered her assignment "art" rather than "anthropology." Her ethnographic portraits lack much of the spontaneity and suggestion of character that viewers sense more readily in Hoffman's busts of her friends.

Ni-Polog (1931; Metropolitan Museum of Art), a portrait of a Balinese temple dancer, is a small study (one-third of life-size) related to her life-size portrait for the Races of Man series in the Field Museum. The sculpture features variations in the patination to emphasize the black hair contrasting with the warm brown flesh. In her book *Heads and Tales* (1936) Hoffman mentioned her trip to Bali and her completion of a head of Ni Polog, who is shown in a photograph (p. 258). While in Bali, Hoffman also worked on a full-length statuette of the same Balinese dancer in elegant regalia.

Hoffman mastered marble carving, plaster casting, and the building of armatures. She experimented with lost-wax casting in her own studio and wrote a book about sculpture techniques. She was elected to membership in the National Institute of Arts and Letters in 1937 and was made a fellow of the National Sculpture Society. In 1939 Hoffman exhibited a sixteen-foot relief of dancing figures at the New York World's Fair. After 1940 she continued to make portraits. In 1948 she was given a commission for a World War II memorial. In 1964 she was awarded the National Sculpture Society's Medal of Honor. She died of a heart attack in her studio at 157 East 35th Street in New York City.

In the latter part of the twentieth century Malvina Hoffman's sculpture has been received as competent academic work in an age identified with modernism. Her reputation has benefited from the critical attention given to women artists of the past and present.

• Papers of Malvina Hoffman are at the Archives of History of Art, Getty Center for the History of Art and the Humanities, Los Angeles. Her autobiography is *Yesterday Is Tomorrow: A Personal History* (1965). She was also the author of several books with technical information about the creation of sculpture, among which are *Heads and Tales* (1936) and

Sculpture Inside and Out (1939). There are no monographs on Malvina Hoffman, but see Linda Nochlin, "Malvina Hoffman: A Life in Sculpture," *Arts Magazine* 59 (Nov. 1984): 106–10, and "Malvina Hoffman," in Janis Conner and Joel Rosenkranz, *Rediscoveries in American Sculpture: Studio Works, 1893–1939* (1989).

JOAN MARTER

HOFFMAN, Ogden (3 May 1793–1 May 1856), lawyer and politician, was born in New York City, the son of Josiah Ogden Hoffman, a noted lawyer, and Mary Colden. For generations his family on both sides had been among New York's political and economic elite, and he enjoyed many advantages as a child. Hoffman graduated from Columbia College in 1812; he afterward kept close ties to his alma mater, giving talks to the alumni and serving on the board of trustees. Although his Federalist father opposed the 1812 war with Great Britain and wanted his son to study law, the nationalistic young man preferred to join the U.S. Navy, which had won glorious victories early in the conflict. In December 1814 Hoffman finally received an appointment as midshipman aboard the powerful, 52-gun frigate *President*, commanded by Stephen Decatur. By this time, however, Great Britain had placed a tight blockade around American ports. When the *President* tried to run the blockade, it was pursued and captured, and Hoffman was taken as a prisoner of war to Bermuda. Released in 1815 after the peace treaty was signed, Hoffman continued to serve under Decatur in the Mediterranean against the Barbary states until 1816.

Upon resigning his navy commission, Hoffman moved to Goshen, New York, to begin a law career. After a period of reading law in a law office, he was admitted to the bar and became a partner of his former mentor. In 1819 he married Emily Burrall, who died in 1830 after bearing five children. In 1823 he secured an appointment as Orange County district attorney and was elected to the state legislature in 1825. Returning to New York City in 1826, he became a partner of then district attorney Hugh Maxwell, whom he succeeded in that post in 1829, serving to 1835. He rapidly rose to the top of his profession.

Hoffman had a keen mind and quick understanding of legal principles. His kindness, generosity, and outgoing, genial personality made him universally liked, even by those he opposed in the courtroom or in politics. His courteous, gentlemanly manner and full, mellifluous voice, attested to by contemporaries such as the diarist Philip Hone and confirmed in the grandiloquent eulogies after his death, complete the general picture of Hoffman as the ideal lawyer of the time. Specializing in criminal law but accepting many civil cases as well, he served as counsel in many of New York City's most celebrated trials during the first half of the nineteenth century, including a sensational 1836 murder case where it appears that Hoffman's eloquence alone secured his client's release. Yet for all his brilliance in the courtroom, Hoffman made little lasting contribution to the law itself. And while he be-longed to exclusive New York clubs like the St. Nicholas Society and Union Club, his income, based on legal fees, never kept pace with the growing fortunes based on commerce and trade, and he was continually in debt despite his professional successes.

Hoffman's intelligence, personal and professional contacts, legal training, and oratorical gifts were valuable assets in politics as well as law, but in an era of mass-based, popular parties his "aristocratic" demeanor did not make him an ideal candidate for high positions. This, together with his own natural disinclination, limited Hoffman's political career. His most typical political contribution was to make rousing speeches for others. After the disintegration of the Federalist party left New York with only various Republican factions, Hoffman was elected as a Tammany man to the 1828 legislature, where he helped revise the criminal statutes during his service on the judiciary committee. He gravitated toward the National Republican opposition to President Andrew Jackson as he became increasingly disenchanted with the latter's handling of the Bank of the United States. He was defeated for Congress running as a Whig in 1834 but elected to the Twenty-fifth and Twenty-sixth Congresses, serving from 1837 to 1841 on the foreign affairs committee. While his oratorical efforts opposing Martin Van Buren's independent treasury bill won plaudits locally, he was not a leader in Congress and did not seek reelection following his second term. The Harrison-Tyler administration rewarded Hoffman's 1840 campaign efforts for the party by appointing him U.S. district attorney for the Southern District of New York from 1841 to 1845. As a favor to Whig leader Thurlow Weed, he ran for state attorney general in 1852 and, in return, received control of applications for canal patronage. His presence on the ticket symbolized tradition and respectability as the Whig party entered its final decline. He was elected to the post despite the Whig party's general failure. Hoffman was never outspoken on the slavery issue, and, unlike most New York Whig leaders, he showed little interest in the fusion movement in 1854 that began the transition toward the Republican party. His death in New York City in 1856 ended speculation on his future political course. He was survived by his second wife, Virginia E. Southard, whom he married in 1838; they had three children.

• Legal papers from Hoffman's tenure as United States district attorney are at the New-York Historical Society. The *New York Times*, 2 May 1856, carried an obituary and reported several eulogies in its columns. The latter appeared in *Ogden Hoffman, 1793–1856: A collection of Tributes from the Daily Journals of May, 1856* (n.d.). Short, biographical sketches appear in *Biographical Directory of the American Congress* (1928) and Charles E. Fitch, *Encyclopedia of Biography of New York* (1916).

PHYLLIS F. FIELD

HOFFMAN, Paul Gray (26 Apr. 1891–8 Oct. 1974), automotive executive, government official, and international administrator, was born in Chicago, Illinois, and spent his childhood in a nearby suburb. His parents—George Hoffman, a successful inventor, corporate executive, and entrepreneur, and Eleanor Lott—provided a comfortable family environment oriented toward modern business and civic responsibility. He ended his formal schooling in 1909 after a year at the University of Chicago.

Starting work for a Chicago car dealership, Hoffman quickly found success as a car salesman. In 1911 he moved to southern California and joined the sales staff of a Studebaker dealership. From salesman he rose to become a district sales manager. He married Dorothy Brown in 1915; they had four children and adopted two others, while also providing for a ward.

After eighteen months in the army during World War I, Hoffman returned to civilian life in 1919 and, with capital borrowed from relatives and friends, bought Studebaker's southern California distributorship. As a car dealer he tried to employ the most modern business methods. For example, to advertise his business, in 1921 he launched the KNX radio station from his Hollywood showroom. A millionaire by his mid-thirties, he took an active part in Republican politics and civic affairs in Los Angeles. Yet despite his prominence there, he accepted when the president of Studebaker, Albert Russel Erskine, asked him in 1925 to become the corporation's vice president for sales and a board member, even though it required moving to company headquarters in South Bend, Indiana.

As vice president for sales, Hoffman created a distinctive corporate image for Studebaker as the "Friendliest Factory." Publicizing the firm's good labor-management relations, he claimed that it produced better cars than did its competitors' brutal production pace. In the process, he acquired much greater public visibility than Studebaker's size and his own rank should have warranted. However, the combination of hard times and mismanagement by Erskine nearly put Studebaker out of business. Unable to meet its immediate obligations in 1933, the corporation was placed into receivership by a federal court.

Hoffman, in tandem with Harold S. Vance, who became chairman, lifted Studebaker from its receivership, and after it reorganized in 1935, he served until 1948 as its president. During that time, he gave Studebaker the kind of positive public exposure it needed to win over investors, car dealers, employees, and customers. At the "Friendliest Factory," he and Vance worked well with the labor union, which started there in 1934, both because they believed that it could represent workers' legitimate grievances and because they knew that in its weakened position Studebaker could not withstand labor strife. For those efforts Hoffman gained a reputation as a strong advocate of the so-called human relations approach to labor management.

To make Studebaker profitable, Hoffman and Vance adopted strategies to sell more cars. Accordingly, they promoted the development of a new lightweight, fuel-efficient, and distinctively designed car.

Beginning with the 1939 Champion, Studebaker sales for the next few years increased at a faster rate than did the rest of the industry. While the corporation earned profits, Hoffman and Vance won recognition as innovative business leaders.

Meanwhile, Hoffman had also become known as the industry's "apostle of safety." Earlier than most automotive leaders, he recognized that public concern about traffic problems and accidents could hurt sales and lead to harmful government interference. In 1937 he persuaded other industry leaders to create and finance the Automotive Safety Foundation. While he served as its first president, the organization lobbied for better streets and highways and law enforcement aimed at unsafe drivers.

During the 1940s, while Studebaker earned good profits from military production and then a return to automotive production, a variety of other public causes increasingly pulled Hoffman away from South Bend. In 1942 he became national chairman of United China Relief and the first chairman of the Committee for Economic Development. The latter, an organization of progressive businessmen, sponsored research by economists aimed at influencing public and private policy making. Besides expanding his network of contacts among top corporate leaders and government officials, those experiences broadened his outlook and convinced him that the expansion of international trade was essential for world peace and prosperity. By 1946 he had also come to believe that the Soviet Union represented the major threat to those goals.

During the early stages of the Cold War, Hoffman joined with other prominent Republicans in supporting the Truman administration's foreign policy. President Harry Truman, needing bipartisan approval in Congress, returned the favor by appointing him to several important committees of businessmen, who provided advice and help in gathering public support for U.S. foreign aid to reconstruct war-torn countries. It was no surprise, therefore, when the president in 1948 nominated Hoffman to serve as the first head of the Economic Cooperation Administration (ECA), the agency responsible for implementing the Marshall Plan. Although Hoffman preferred to stay at Studebaker, which then enjoyed its greatest successes since the early 1920s, he accepted the call to public service.

Affable, low-key, but energetic, he proved ideal for the job. First, he was able to recruit effective administrators who operated the ECA efficiently and honestly without scandal. Second, as the program's most visible public advocate, he was especially effective in presenting reasons why Americans had to give away several billion dollars to reconstruct the economy of Europe. He urged American taxpayers and Congress to overcome their fears about the recovery of European competitors and to resist efforts by special interest groups to use the Marshall Plan to acquire trading advantages. Finally, he worked to persuade European aid recipients to replace their piecemeal national efforts at recovery with one based on cooperation with one another and with his agency. Although the Marshall Plan failed to achieve full economic integration, it did foster the kind of cooperation that helped to revitalize European economies.

The favorable publicity generated by the Marshall Plan thrust Hoffman into the public limelight and opened a new phase in his career. Though no intellectual, he was intelligent, articulate, serious-minded, and committed to public service. He impressed many contemporaries as a man who could lead without scheming or self-importance. Subordinates appreciated that he gave them credit for the program's success, and they responded with admiration and loyalty.

In 1950 Hoffman resigned from the ECA to become the first president of the enormously wealthy Ford Foundation. He started by assembling a competent staff, including veterans of the ECA, which launched many innovative programs within the United States and abroad for studying and trying to solve contemporary social problems, such as racial conflicts and poverty. Meanwhile, Hoffman personally worked to persuade General Dwight D. Eisenhower to seek the Republican presidential nomination and then worked to secure Eisenhower's election. Thereafter, he remained a friend and adviser to the president. Unfortunately for Hoffman, some of the Ford Foundation's programs during his tenure angered political conservatives, and the adverse publicity stemming from the political controversies led Hoffman into clashes with the foundation's chief patron, Henry Ford II. In 1953 the foundation discreetly camouflaged Hoffman's dismissal as a resignation so that he could return to Studebaker as its chairman.

Back in the automotive business after an absence of nearly five years, Hoffman quickly discovered that rising costs and declining sales in a highly competitive market threatened Studebaker's survival. Vance, who wanted to reduce his own burdens, willingly relinquished the chairmanship, while retaining the title of president. Soon the two collaborators disagreed over what Studebaker needed to do: Vance wanted it to continue on its own, but Hoffman concluded that it could survive only by joining with another automaker. Rebuffed by other possible merger partners, Hoffman negotiated a merger with the Packard Motor Company, whose leaders had concluded that their firm lacked sufficient size to survive as an independent.

Starting in October 1954 as the industry's fourth largest firm, the new Studebaker-Packard Corporation faced the overwhelming problems that had plagued each partner company. Its president, James Nance of Packard, blamed Hoffman and Vance for excessive labor costs and low productivity and took a tougher stand with the union. He also replaced Studebaker's distinctively designed, fuel-efficient models with bigger and flashier cars to match competitors. Except to obtain military contracts through their political connections with President Eisenhower, he otherwise ignored Hoffman and Vance. Without executive authority, Hoffman remained chairman until 1956, when Curtiss-Wright bought out the corporation.

Although sixty-five years old and well-off financially, Hoffman was unwilling to retire. For a while he busied himself with the management of Hoffman Specialty Manufacturing Corporation, which his father had started in 1913. Mostly he concentrated on trying to persuade President Eisenhower to provide more economic aid to Third World countries. In 1956, over the objections of Senate conservatives, the president appointed him a member of the U.S. delegation to the United Nations General Assembly. That experience expanded Hoffman's personal network and reinforced his conviction that wealthy and industrialized countries had to extend economic assistance so that Third World countries could escape their poverty. In December 1958 UN Secretary-General Dag Hammarskjöld gave him a chance to put those beliefs into practice when he appointed Hoffman to head a new Special Fund created to assist the economic development of poor countries.

In 1959 Hoffman moved to New York and started a highly successful career as a UN administrator. His wife Dorothy, who stayed behind at their home in southern California, died in 1961. The following year he married an old friend, business associate, and prominent Democrat, Anna Rosenberg. Until he retired in 1971, Hoffman concentrated on raising money for his agency and negotiating development projects with recipient countries. In all, his agency, renamed the UN Development Program, raised and distributed about $3.4 billion of "seed money" for development projects. However, with limitations beyond his control, it suffered from excessive bureaucracy and donor bias. In 1973 President Richard M. Nixon awarded him the Medal of Freedom. Hoffman died in New York, leaving an estate of about $4 million.

Although never at the very top of the power elite, Hoffman often stood close to those with greater power, sharing many of their values, attitudes, and limitations. During a long and multifaceted career as the head of important institutions in business and public affairs, he demonstrated a capacity for recognizing modern trends and new ways of coping with them. His managerial skills and his talents as a publicist gave wider currency, especially within the Establishment, to progressive ideas and what he called enlightened self-interest about corporate behavior and international economic relations.

• Hoffman's papers are located in the Harry S. Truman Library in Independence, Mo. The evolution of his views on international relations can be found in two of his books, *Peace Can Be Won* (1951) and *World without Want* (1962). Alan R. Raucher, *Paul G. Hoffman, Architect of Foreign Aid* (1985), covers his entire career. Obituaries are in the *Washington Post*, 9 Oct. 1974, and the *New York Times*, 9 Oct. 1974.

ALAN R. RAUCHER

HOFFMANN, Banesh (6 Sept. 1906–5 Aug. 1986), mathematical physicist, was born in Richmond, England, the son of Polish immigrants Maurice Hoffmann, a tailor, and Leah Brozel. Hoffmann attended

St. Paul's School near Richmond before entering Oxford University. He received a B.A. in 1929 with first class honors in mathematics from Merton College and while an undergraduate met Princeton professor Oswald Veblen, who was lecturing at Oxford (as an exchange professor for G. H. Hardy). At the time Veblen was interested in generalized projective geometry and projective relativity, and, being much impressed by Hoffmann's abilities, he invited Hoffmann to do doctoral work at Princeton. Hoffmann accepted and was an associate at Princeton from 1929 until he received his Ph.D. in 1932. His dissertation, "On the Spherically Symmetric Field in Relativity," written under Veblen's supervision, was a notable, if little-known, contribution. He then went to the University of Rochester, as a research associate in 1932, before returning to Princeton in 1935 as a member of the Institute for Advanced Study, where he collaborated with Albert Einstein and Leopold Infeld on the problem of motion in general relativity.

In 1937 Hoffmann began a lifelong association with Queen's College of the City University of New York, as an instructor (1937–1940), assistant professor (1940–1949), associate professor (1949–1953), and finally professor of mathematics (1953–1977). He became a naturalized U.S. citizen in 1940 and during World War II was a civilian consultant with the U.S. Navy and an electrical engineer at the Federal Telegraph and Telephone Laboratory in New York (1944–1945). He returned to the Institute for Advanced Study in 1947–1948, and also served as a consultant for the Westinghouse Science Talent Search (1944–1970), an honorary research associate in physics and education for the Harvard Physics Project (1966–1967), and a consultant for the National Consortium of Testing (1977–1984). In 1959 he was a visiting professor of mathematics at King's College of the University of London. He was a fellow of the American Physical Society, an editor (1958–1966) of the *Journal of Mathematics and Mechanics* (Indiana University), and an editor of the journal *Tensor* and honorary patron of the Tensor Society (Japan). In 1938 he married Doris Goodday; they had one son and one daughter.

Virtually all of Hoffmann's mathematical research was concerned with relativity theory. His earliest work, on projective relativity with Veblen (1930), gave a four-dimensional projective geometric interpretation of the five-dimensional Kaluza-Klein unified field theory (the latter is still of interest). Hoffmann later produced a variant of this theory that involved vector mesons (1947), and this led to a study of a similarity theory of geometry and relativity (1948, 1953). His dissertation resulted in several noteworthy papers on spherically symmetric fields (1932, 1933, 1935), and a useful exposition of the geometric / physical foundations of general relativity (1932).

Hoffmann's most famous and influential paper, written with Einstein and Infeld (1938), contained the so-called "EIH-approximation scheme" for studying the theory of motion of particles in general relativity. While this was not the first such analysis of the prob-

lem of motion, it has become the standard one, and all subsequent schemes are essentially modifications of it. This work is commonly regarded as Einstein's last great contribution to general relativity. Hoffmann's final work dealt with the red-shift phenomena, which is concerned with one of the crucial tests of Einstein's theory. Although he wrote several dozen papers on relativity theory, Hoffmann's research, apart from the EIH-approximation, was low key and seldom in the mainstream of contemporary work. Nevertheless, his contributions were solid and thoughtful. In 1964 he received first prize from the Gravity Research Foundation for his essay "Negative Mass as a Gravitational Source of Energy in the Quasi-Stellar Radio Sources."

Hoffmann was a gifted writer and produced several popular books: *The Strange Story of the Quantum* (1947); *About Vectors* (1960); and, with Helen Dukas (Einstein's former secretary), *Albert Einstein, Creator and Rebel* (1972) and *Albert Einstein, the Human Side: New Glimpses from His Archives* (1979). All of these are insightful and contain much more than is usually found in "popular" accounts. Although there are more substantial works dealing with Einstein and his life, the latter two books are unique in their perspective and sensitivity. In 1973 Hoffmann won the Science Writing Award of the American Institute of Physics and the U.S. Steel Foundation.

Despite the success of his scientific research and writing, Hoffmann was best known to the general public for his 25-year crusade against the inequities and inappropriateness of standardized scholastic aptitude tests. His campaign was primarily directed at the College Entrance Examination Board tests as prepared by the Educational Testing Service of Princeton, New Jersey. He began this assault with "Tyranny of Multiple-Choice Testing," which first appeared in *Harper's* magazine (Mar. 1961) and was later expanded into a bestselling book, *The Tyranny of Testing* (1962). This criticism was sharpened in an article, "The College Boards Fail the Test," in the *New York Times Magazine* (17 Oct. 1964), which was reprinted in the *U.S. Congressional Record* (111, pt. 21 [22 Oct. 1964]). Hoffmann's contention was that the reliance on multiple-choice questions was inadequate and that the questions themselves were often ambiguous and superficial. He maintained that when such tests are employed to exclusively assess the academic potential of a candidate, they are no more than a cheap and unreliable expediency for colleges. These charges were controversial, and although Hoffmann hoped for a more balanced approach with a reform of testing procedures, he also enjoyed the furor that his views generated.

In person, Hoffmann was a quiet, modest man who possessed a delightful wit and great personal charm. As his books show, he was a bit of a maverick and enjoyed being provocative and entertaining. The popular literature on Einstein and relativity is notably enriched by his contributions. He was an amateur pianist, and, on occasion, he and Einstein (with his violin) played duets. As Hoffmann's wife later recalled, both seemed to enjoy themselves, but the result was not something for anyone to hear. Hoffmann died peacefully in his home in Flushing, New York.

• Most of Hoffmann's popular books remain in print in paperback editions and continue to inform and delight succeeding generations of readers. An obituary (with a picture) is in the *New York Times*, 6 Aug. 1986.

JOSEPH D. ZUND

HOFFMANN, Francis Arnold (5 June 1822–23 Jan. 1903), German-American political leader, businessman, and agricultural writer, was born in Herford, Westphalia, Prussia, the son of Frederick William Hoffmann, a bookbinder, and Wilhelmina Groppe. Educated at the Gymnasium in Herford, he left home in 1840 to emigrate to the United States. He traveled first to Chicago, where he worked briefly as a hotel porter then took a position as teacher for a German congregation in Addison township, Du Page County, Illinois, west of Chicago. He also led hymns and read sermons in the church services. In 1841 he went to Michigan to study under clergy of the Lutheran Michigan Synod and was ordained. He returned to Addison to serve as pastor and also served other congregations in northeastern Illinois. In 1844 he married Cynthia Gilbert, a native of Ohio. The exact number of their children is unknown; four survived Hoffmann. He acquired citizenship by naturalization in 1846.

Although the German church at Addison was a "united" or "free" congregation, combining elements of both Lutheran and Reformed practice, Hoffmann was among those attending the organizational meeting of the Lutheran Missouri Synod in Chicago in May 1847. The same year he moved to Schaumburg township, twenty miles northwest of Chicago, to be its full-time Lutheran minister. He became postmaster of the community and in 1851 was elected town clerk.

Hoffmann's evolution from small-town community leader to a major German-American spokesman began in 1851, when ill health caused him to resign his ministry and move to Chicago. He read law for a year and was admitted to the bar in 1852. A Democrat, he was elected alderman of the largely German Eighth Ward in 1853, but he resigned the next year to enter the banking and real estate business, developing close ties with Chicago's rapidly growing German community by providing banking services, selling land, and promoting Chicago as a destination for new arrivals from Germany. He also helped organize many social and cultural institutions for the city's German population and headed the committee that built the Deutsches Haus, which opened in 1856 as a community center for Chicago's Germans.

Hoffmann's greatest influence as a political leader was in leading many German-Americans into the nascent Republican party during the 1850s. Like most German-Americans at the time, Hoffmann was a Democrat, but he broke with that party when Illinois senator Stephen A. Douglas in January 1854 sponsored the Kansas-Nebraska Bill. The bill potentially allowed the expansion of slavery into the western territories, which had been prohibited for thirty-four years by the Missouri Compromise. On 8 February 1854 Hoffmann was among the earliest German leaders to speak out against it, and at a mass rally of Chicago Germans against the bill in March, he declared that his longstanding loyalty to Douglas and the Democrats was at an end: "Justice is paramount to party, and the dictates of conscience and humanity are superior to those of my party leaders." The passage of the Kansas-Nebraska Act in May 1854 set in motion a sweeping party realignment in the North over the next two years. Hoffmann continued his efforts to bring Germans into the anti-Nebraska coalition, despite the antiforeign elements within it. When the Republican party in Illinois achieved formal organization out of the anti-Nebraska movement in 1856, the state party convention adopted a platform repudiating nativist legislation and placed Hoffmann on the state ticket as candidate for lieutenant governor. Hoffmann accepted but two months later resigned from the ticket, when he discovered that he did not fulfill state constitutional requirements that the lieutenant governor be at least thirty-five years of age and a citizen for at least fourteen years. Hoffmann nevertheless continued to campaign for the party, which won the state election (but not the national one) in 1856. During the next four years, Hoffmann continued his efforts both to encourage the adherence of Germans to the party and to discourage any nativist influences on party policy. In 1860 Illinois Republicans once again nominated him for lieutenant governor, a post for which he now qualified. He was elected in the same Republican victory that brought Abraham Lincoln to the presidency. Hoffmann served as lieutenant governor from January 1861 to January 1865 and in the turbulent politics of the Civil War won praise for his impartiality and skill in presiding over the state senate, even when the Democratic opposition party took control of the legislature in 1863.

Hoffmann's banking house was forced into insolvency in 1861, when southern state bonds that it held became irredeemable after secession. In 1862 he entered into a contract with the Illinois Central Railroad to act as its German land agent. Over the next four years he sold over 80,000 acres of railroad land and settled 1,500 German families on the prairies of central Illinois. His commissions helped him regain his wealth, and he reentered the banking business in 1866, joining with other investors to form a bank that became the International Bank of Chicago. After the Great Chicago Fire of 1871, he chaired a committee of bankers working to restore order and stability to Chicago's banking system.

In 1873 Hoffmann, suffering from a nervous condition, retired from business and in 1875 relocated to a farm he had bought in the Rock River valley of southern Wisconsin. Scientific farming and horticulture, lifetime interests of Hoffmann, now became the basis of a new career for the last three decades of his life. He undertook the editing of the *Haus und Bauern-*

freund (Household and Farm Friend), a weekly agricultural supplement circulated with three German newspapers in Milwaukee, Chicago, and Buffalo. Under the name "Hans Buschbauer," he became widely known among German-Americans for his counsel on horticulture, animal husbandry, and household management (writing on the latter subject as "Grete Buschbauer"). He declined all efforts to involve him in politics, preferring the peace and calm of rural life. He died at his home near Jefferson, Wisconsin.

Hoffmann's leadership among German Americans was characterized by an ability developed in his preaching days to speak to them directly, simply, and unpretentiously. He strongly defended German-American cultural preservation, while believing at the same time that Germans should become full participants in American society and politics.

• Manuscripts and scrapbooks about Hoffmann are in the Illinois State Historical Library, Springfield, and in the Concordia Historical Institute, St. Louis. He wrote a number of books in German on agricultural matters, including *Amerikanische Bienenzucht* (1886) and *Die Familienschatz* (1888), a collection of his magazine articles. Articles about Hoffmann include J. H. A. Lacher, "Francis A. Hoffmann of Illinois and Hans Buschbauer of Wisconsin," *Wisconsin Magazine of History* 13 (1930): 327–55; Karl Kretzmann, "Francis Arnold Hoffmann," *Concordia Historical Institute Quarterly* 18 (1945): 37–54; and Emil Mannhardt, "Franz Arnold Hoffmann: Ein Führer seines Volkes," *Deutsch-amerikanische Geschichtsblätter* 3 (1903): 56–62. A sketch of Hoffmann as an immigrant leader is in Victor Greene, *American Immigrant Leaders, 1800–1910* (1987). Hoffmann's granddaughter, Minna Frances Nehrling, wrote "Memoirs of Riverside Farm," *Wisconsin Magazine of History* 13 (1930): 356–64.

JAMES M. BERGQUIST

HOFHEINZ, Roy Mark (10 Apr. 1912–21 Nov. 1982), sports executive, was born in Beaumont, Texas, the son of Frederick Joseph Hofheinz, a laundry-truck driver, and Nonie Planchard. He attended Rice Institute and the University of Houston, from which he received an LL.B. degree in 1933. That same year he married Irene Cafcalas; they had three children. Because he was a Democratic representative in the Texas legislature (1934–1936) and a Harris County magistrate (1936–1944), he was given the lifelong nickname "Judge," used by both friends and enemies.

After leaving office Hofheinz vowed to become a millionaire before he reentered politics. He accomplished this before he was forty and often confirmed his business agreements with a mere handshake. In partnership with George Mattison, Jr., of Birmingham, Alabama, he formed Houston Slag Materials Company, which utilized waste materials from steel mills in road construction. With W. N. "Dick" Hooper, Hofheinz established radio station KTHT in 1941 and in 1979 became part owner of KTRK-TV. Both stations served the Houston area. With Hugh Roy Cullen, Hofheinz invested in various real estate ventures. He was also mayor of Houston, Texas, from 1953 to 1955.

Hofheinz is best known for the building of the Astrodome, the first covered, air-conditioned baseball stadium in the world. Led by Hofheinz, a group of investors formed the Houston Sports Association, bought the minor-league Houston Buffaloes baseball team, and acquired a National League baseball franchise in 1960. The expansion team, the Colt 45's, began its first season in 1962. The owners had promised the league a new stadium, and Hofheinz, noting Houston's hot, humid climate, proposed an air-conditioned facility. The idea was not original, but no one had yet built one. Engineers, including Buckminster Fuller, assured Hofheinz that it was theoretically possible, and Hofheinz hired Houston architects Harmon Lloyd and S. I. Morris to assemble a model with a rigid dome. Hofheinz then sold the idea to the Chamber of Commerce and the voters of Harris County.

He won approval of $31.6 million in Harris County bonds and obtained an additional $3.75 million from the city and state, rights-of-way worth $4 million from property owners, and $6 million from the Houston Sports Association for restaurants, skyboxes, and an elaborate scoreboard. The county gave the association control of the $45 million facility for forty years in exchange for a yearly rent of $750,000. The principals of the group then initiated construction on South Main Street, Houston's major thoroughfare, not by turning the sod with a shiny shovel but with Colt 45 pistols fired into the ground.

Hofheinz changed the name of the baseball team to the Astros and named the new stadium the Astrodome. It opened on 9 April 1965 with a 642-foot elongated dome that encompassed six colorful tiers of unencumbered seats topped by blue skyboxes available for long-term rental. The playing field was Bermuda grass, and the scoreboard was 474 feet long. The only major problem was that players were unable to track high-flying baseballs against the latticework of small beams that held the plastic roof in place. The solution was to paint the outside of the dome, but then the grass died for lack of light. Hofheinz, however, replaced the grass with an artificial surface being tested by Chemstrand, which he named "Astro Turf."

He also built for himself a private apartment overlooking center field. It contained a shooting gallery, a putting green, a puppet theater, and a bowling lane, as well as a tavern with a tilted floor and a trick elevator that shook but did not move, both of which served as practical jokes played on visitors. In keeping with Hofheinz's eccentric personality, the apartment was decorated and furnished in bizarre fashion, but he lived there much of the time, especially after his wife's death in 1966. He married, for a second time in 1969. His new wife was Mary Francis Gougenheim, his long-time secretary.

Following the opening of the Astrodome for baseball, Hofheinz worked to attract other activities, including football games, circuses, bullfights, and conventions, to the facility. He was initially successful and expanded the "Astrodomain" to include a convention center, motels, and an amusement park. He even indulged a lifelong fascination by purchasing Ringling Brothers, Barnum and Bailey Circus, which he later sold to the Mattel toy company in exchange for stock. Although the Astrodome itself remained profitable, the Astrodomain fell into default. Compounding Hofheinz's difficulties was a stroke in 1970 that left him weak and confined to a wheelchair. In addition, Mattel stock dropped in value and the Astros played losing seasons. The result was that Hofheinz lost control of the Astrodomain and the team in 1975.

Hofheinz died of heart failure in Houston in 1982, and his apartment was dismantled during a renovation of the Astrodome in 1988. Hofheinz, nonetheless, left as his legacy a sports stadium with such innovation as air-conditioning, multiple-use facilities, skyboxes, artificial playing surfaces, and large scoreboards. Since his time other cities have included an enclosed stadium in their skylines.

• The most complete biography is Edgar W. Ray, *The Grand Huckster: Houston's Judge Roy Hofheinz, Genius of the Astrodome* (1980). It was written before Hofheinz's death, but after his stroke. The best summary of his impact on sports is Steve Rushin, "1954–1994: How We Got Here," *Sports Illustrated* (16 Aug. 1994, pp. 42–49. An obituary is in the *Houston Chronicle*, 23 Nov. 1982.

DAVID G. McCOMB

HOFMANN, Hans (21 Mar. 1880–17 Feb. 1966), artist and teacher, was born Johann Georg Albert Hofmann in Weissenberg, Germany, the son of Theodor Hofmann, a government official, and Franciska Manger. The Hofmann family moved to Munich when he was six years of age. He left home at the age of sixteen to take a position with the State of Bavaria (secured for him by his father). For two years Hofmann worked on engineering and architectural projects for the state, and during this period he invented a number of devices. He was rewarded by his father, who hoped he would study science, with a gift of 1,000 Deutsch Marks meant to encourage him in his technical education. Despite his father's wishes Hofmann used the money to leave his job and enroll at Moritz Heymann's Munich art school. Through his teacher, Willi Schwartz, Hofmann became familiar with the post-impressionist style. By 1908 he was exhibiting in Berlin alongside many of the well-known pioneers of modern art.

In 1904 a wealthy Berlin collector became Hofmann's patron, providing him the financing necessary to live and work in Paris. Hofmann moved to Paris with his lifelong companion Maria "Miz" Wolfegg, whom he had met in 1900 and eventually married in 1929. Until 1914 he studied alongside Henri Matisse and associated with Pablo Picasso and Georges Braque, the originators of cubism. He was close to Robert Delaunay, whose philosophy of color as form and subject was one of the basic elements of Hofmann's teaching throughout his life. He drew from the new artistic movements blossoming across Europe: fauvism, cubism, futurism, and expressionism. Hof-

mann's exact role in the development of early modernism is difficult to determine, however, because none of his painting from this period has survived.

Hofmann remained aware of developments in Germany, where he often spent his summers. He was especially interested in the 1911 formation of the expressionist movement led by Wassily Kandinsky and Gabriele Münter in Munich. Münter and Miz Hofmann were close friends, and during World War I, when Kandinsky fled Germany, Hofmann stored many of his canvases. Kandinsky's belief in the spiritual nature of art had a lasting effect on Hofmann's teaching and artistic philosophy.

During a 1914 visit to Munich Hofmann was trapped by the war. Exempted from military service because of a lung affliction, and having lost the financial support of his Berlin patron due to the war, Hofmann turned to teaching. In 1915 he opened the Hans Hofmann School for Modern Art in Munich, beginning a teaching career that lasted more than four decades. At first his teacher's role so dominated his life that he nearly gave up painting. Throughout his career Hofmann had difficulty reconciling his roles as teacher and painter.

Hofmann's instruction attempted to combine and synthesize a number of sources including the ideas of cubism and fauvism and the concepts of Kandinsky and earlier philosophers of art, especially Goethe's quasi-mystical, quasi-rational philosophies of color. The basics of Hofmann's teaching philosophy remained consistent throughout his lifetime. He taught that the painter had to deal with three interacting factors: nature and natural laws; the medium and its possibilities; and the spiritual, intuitive feeling of the artist. The interaction between nature and the medium Hofmann saw as creating a higher, spiritual realm.

The only shift in Hofmann's ideas seems to have been a move from his early emphasis on drawing and line to a later emphasis on color to create volume and depth. Hofmann referred to the ongoing struggle between the two-dimensional nature of the canvas and the creation of illusionary depth as the "plastic" nature of art. Creation of this plasticity could not be simulated by the arrangement of objects towards a vanishing point. Instead, depth must be created without violating the integrity of the picture plane, solely through the arrangement of colored and toned points, lines, and planes. Hofmann described this creation of depth that acknowledges the basic flatness of the picture plane as "push-pull."

Hofmann soon gained an international reputation for his teaching. In 1930 he was invited to teach a summer session at the University of California at Berkeley. He welcomed the opportunity to come to the United States and escape the rising political turmoil in Europe. He taught in Los Angeles in the spring of 1931 and again at Berkeley the following summer. In 1932 he joined the faculty at the Art Students' League in New York, and in 1933 he founded the New York School; he operated it until 1958, when he closed it in order to concentrate on painting.

Hofmann returned to painting in the 1930s. His images became increasingly more abstracted and experimental in technique as he attempted to synthesize cubist composition and fauve color in Kandinsky-like landscapes. In the 1940s he began splattering and pouring paints directly onto the canvas and experimented with the surrealist technique of automatism. He showed an increased interest in the mythological subjects that fascinated the early abstract expressionists.

In 1944, the same year he became a U.S. citizen, Hofmann was given his first solo exhibition at the Art of This Century Gallery, where the majority of the New York art world first saw his work. His inclusion in the circle of this gallery led to an increasing identification with the emerging New York School. It was in a review of a Hofmann exhibition of 1946 that a critic first coined the term abstract expressionism. By the mid-1950s rectangles began to appear in his work; from the late 1950s until his death in New York City, these rectangles became more prominent, gradually increasing in size and simplicity. Simultaneous with this development, he created a separate series of paintings by spilling or hurling paint at the surface of the canvas. In 1961 Hofmann's wife died, and in 1964 he married Renate Schmidt.

Hofmann's life is a lesson in the development of modern art. The extent to which his painting influenced, or was influenced by, American abstraction is unclear. His effect as a teacher is better understood. Hofmann's teaching directly influenced the geometric abstractionists of the 1930s. By 1937 nearly half of the charter members of the Abstract Artists of America were former Hofmann students, and among his later students were important second-generation abstract expressionists. His ideas had a major effect on critical thought as well. More enduringly, Hofmann taught generations of artists, who in turn became the teachers of thousands more American art students, applying the lessons and principles he had developed early in the century.

• Hofmann's own writings include *Creation in Form and Color: A Textbook for Instruction in Art* (1931), and a collection of five essays in Sam Hunter, *Hans Hofmann* (1963). In typescript, in the library of the Museum of Modern Art, New York, are two works by Hofmann: *The Painter and His Problems: A Manual Dedicated to Painting* (1963), and *Selected Writings on Art* (1963). An excellent description of his teaching methods, along with statements from former students, can be found in Irving Sandler, "Hans Hofmann: The Pedagogical Master," *Art in America* 61 (1973): 48–57. Sandler also contributed a valuable essay on Hofmann's push-pull theory to one of the most recent and most complete assessments of Hofmann's contributions, Cynthia Goodman, *Hans Hofmann* (1990). Much information, as well as a number of Hofmann's own statements on art, can be found in exhibition catalogs. Among the best are Frederick S. Wight, *Hans Hofmann* (1957); William C. Seitz, *Hans Hofmann* (1963); and Walter Darby Bannard, *Hans Hofmann: A Retrospective Exhibition* (1976).

STEPHEN K. SMITH

HOFMANN, Josef Casimir (20 Jan. 1876–16 Feb. 1957), pianist, was born in Podgorze, near Cracow, Poland, the son of Casimir Hofmann, a pianist, teacher, and conductor of light opera, and Matylda Wysocka, a singer of light opera. His father began instructing him in piano and composition when he was about four years of age. He played his first public recital when he was five, thus beginning one of the most amazing careers as a child prodigy since that of the young Wolfgang Mozart. He toured throughout Europe during the next six years, creating a public furor and winning praise from such famous musicians as Franz Liszt, Camille Saint-Saëns, and Anton Rubinstein.

Hofmann made his American debut on 29 November 1887 at the Metropolitan Opera House in New York. He won rave reviews from even the toughest New York newspaper critics. This was the beginning of a tour that ran to more than fifty concerts, during which he became a popular sensation. Even more concerts had been booked by his American management, but the triumphal progression came to a sudden end in February 1888, following charges in the press by the Society for the Prevention of Cruelty to Children that young Hofmann was being exploited to the endangerment of his health. A New York banker and philanthropist, Alfred Corning Clark, offered his family $50,000 on the condition that he withdraw from the concert stage to study until he reached the age of eighteen. His father accepted the offer, and the Hofmanns sailed for Europe in March 1888. Josef Hofmann in later years asserted repeatedly that his health had been in no danger and that his forced retirement had been both unnecessary and unwise.

Hofmann and his family settled in Berlin, where he studied piano for a time with Moritz Moszkowski and composition with Heinrich Urban. From 1892 to 1894 he studied with Anton Rubinstein, being the only private pupil Rubinstein ever accepted. He considered Rubinstein to be his most important musical influence, and he later wrote an interesting description of the great Russian pianist's pedagogical methods (*Piano Playing*, pp. 57–69). Hofmann began performing in public again in 1894 and was soon appearing all over Europe. He toured the United States in 1898 and annually thereafter for many years. He settled permanently in the United States around 1900 and became an American citizen in 1926. In 1905 he married Marie Clarisse Eustis, a divorced New Orleans socialite who was ten years his senior. They had one daughter. They were divorced in 1927, and that same year he married a piano student, Betty Short, who was nearly thirty years his junior. They had three sons.

In the years of his prime from around 1910 to the mid-1930s, Hofmann was generally considered by music lovers, critics, and other musicians to be one of the best, if not the best, pianists of his era and perhaps of all time. He was believed to have all of the qualities, in perfect proportion, needed to make a great pianist, including musical intelligence, the power to produce every gradation of dynamics from the softest to the loudest (despite the fact that he was a small, rather delicate-looking man), firm but flexible rhythm, the ability to impart an infinite variety of coloration to the music, and an incredible mastery of the sheer technique of piano playing that enabled him to make even the most difficult works seem easy. He had an enormous repertoire at that time; though he was a poor sight reader, he had the ability to memorize a composition after hearing it two or three times. He also composed a number of musical works, some of them under the pseudonym of Michel Dvorsky. He frequently performed his own compositions, but they have been forgotten since his death. He was also gifted in mathematics, science, and mechanics, and he received patents for a number of inventions.

Hofmann participated in the original planning for the Curtis Institute of Music in Philadelphia, founded in 1924 by Mary Louise Curtis Bok, the daughter of Cyrus H. K. Curtis (founder of the Curtis Publishing Company) and her husband Edward William Bok. The institute, ultimately endowed with $12.5 million of Curtis family money, was intended to provide the finest training for talented composers and performing musicians, completely tuition-free. Hofmann became the head of the school's piano department in 1924 and served as the director of the entire institution from 1926 to 1938. His great prestige made him a fine figurehead for the institute and he attracted many eminent musicians to teach there. He appears to have given the various department heads free rein to run their areas as they wished. The conductor Fritz Reiner, for example, who came to the institute in 1931, had full control of the student orchestra and of his own class of student conductors. Hofmann took a similarly active role in his own piano department. He taught a number of talented students who went on to notable careers, including Abram Chasins, Shura Cherkassky, and Nadia Reisenberg. Chasins later wrote a brief memoir of Hofmann, which included a splendid example of Hofmann's ability to analyze a young pianist's problems and prospects upon first hearing him play.

Most commentators on Hofmann's career agree that, from sometime in the mid- to late 1930s onward, his piano playing underwent first a gradual, and later a catastrophic, decline. Chasins, for example, felt that even in the famous concert at the Metropolitan Opera House on 28 November 1937, celebrating the fifty-year anniversary of his American debut, Hofmann did not perform up to his best standards of previous years and, after hearing Hofmann play poorly in a 1939 radio broadcast, "resolved never to hear him again." The wife of the conductor Artur Rodzinski recalled a sad day in 1945 when Hofmann played so wretchedly that Rodzinski and a friend had to persuade him to cancel scheduled rehearsals and concerts with the New York Philharmonic. To some degree, this decline may have been due to advancing age. However, Rodzinski and many others have stated that the primary cause was alcoholism. Hofmann's last recital in New York took place on 19 January 1946, and soon thereafter he ceased public performance entirely. He had made his home in Los Angeles since 1939; he died there in a nursing home.

• Hofmann from 1901 to 1917 wrote brief articles on, and answered readers' questions about, piano playing in an occasional feature page of the *Ladies' Home Journal*, edited by his friend Edward William Bok. A selection of the articles, questions, and answers were printed in two brief books: *Piano Playing: A Little Book of Simple Suggestions* (1908) and *Piano Questions Answered* (1909). He made only a very few recordings, many of which are no longer extant and none of which adequately represent his playing at the peak of his powers. Informed discussions of his career and musical characteristics are included in Abram Chasins, *Speaking of Pianists*, 2d ed. (1961), and Harold C. Schonberg, *The Great Pianists*, rev. ed. (1987). On Hofmann's years at the Curtis Institute of Music, see Carl Flesch, *The Memoirs of Carl Flesch* (1957), Boris Goldovsky, *My Road to Opera* (1979), and Philip Hart, *Fritz Reiner: A Biography* (1994). Goldovsky's book, together with Nell S. Graydon and Margaret D. Sizemore, *The Amazing Marriage of Marie Eustis & Josef Hofmann* (1965), allow the careful reader to straighten out the often incorrectly given dates of Hofmann's two marriages and his divorce. See also Halina Rodzinski, *Our Two Lives* (1976), and the *New York Times*, 31 May 1927, 3 Apr. 1928, 29 Nov. 1937, 20 Jan. 1946, and 18, 19, and 24 Feb. 1957.

JOHN E. LITTLE